The HUTCHINSON

ALMANAC

1999

The HUTCHINSON
ALMANAC
1999

Helicon

Copyright © Helicon Publishing Ltd 1998 (unless otherwise credited)
© Crown copyright information is reproduced under licence
from the Controller of Her Majesty's Stationery Office

First published 1998

Helicon Publishing Ltd
42 Hythe Bridge Street
Oxford OX1 2EP

e-mail: admin@helicon.co.uk
Web site: http://www.helicon.co.uk

Printed and bound in Italy by
Tipografica San Paolo

ISBN 1–85986–259–4

British Cataloguing in Publication Data

A catalogue record of this book is available
from the British Library

CONTENTS

SPECIAL FEATURES

ERRATA

Page 49

The item <u>Largest 30 Islands in the UK</u> contains inaccuracies.

The largest islands in Scotland are in fact as follows:

Name	Location	Area sq km	Area sq mi
Lewis with Harris	Outer Hebrides	2,225	859
Skye	Inner Hebrides	1,666	643
Mainland, Shetland	Shetland Islands	967	373
Mull	Inner Hebrides	899	347
Islay	Inner Hebrides	614	237
Mainland, Orkney	Orkney Islands	536	207
Arran	Firth of Clyde	435	168
Jura	Inner Hebrides	370	143
North Uist	Outer Hebrides	351	136
South Uist	Outer Hebrides	332	128
Yell	Shetland Islands	214	83
Hoy	Orkney Islands	137	53

The largest islands in Wales are:

Name	Location	Area sq km	Area sq mi
Anglesey	northwest coast of Wales	714	276
Holy Island	west of the Isle of Anglesey	39	15
Skomer	Pembrokeshire	3	1

The largest islands in England are:

Name	Location	Area sq km	Area sq mi
Isle of Wight	south coast of England	381	147
Sheppey	north coast of Kent	94	36
Hayling	Hampshire	27	10

Page 149

A map of Albania has inadvertently been placed in the <u>Algeria</u> article. A map showing the location of Algeria is included opposite.

PREFACE

Welcome to the first edition of *The Hutchinson Almanac*. This 1999 edition takes a fresh look at the needs of information seekers by presenting thousands of facts, figures, and statistics about today's world, as well as helpful practical information, in one accessible and clearly-organized volume.

The almanac is divided into 20 chapters covering all aspects of modern life. The Contents list summarizes the main topics covered in each chapter (for reasons of space, these summaries do not always exactly reflect the subheadings contained within the body of the book).

Within each chapter, the items have been carefully grouped, and are presented mostly in table, list, or graph form, for ease of reference. Throughout the almanac, special features examine some of the year's key developments and news stories in more depth than is possible elsewhere in the book. Where relevant, a Review of the Year is included at the beginning of each chapter, and a list of useful Web site addresses is included at the end. The full index quickly guides readers to specific pieces of information.

The information in the almanac has been derived from the most accurate and up-to-date sources available at the time of compilation. Comments and suggestions from readers are welcome, whether to suggest new or additional information for future editions, or to correct existing information. Your feedback is invaluable for the continual improvement of the almanac, which the editors hope you will enjoy now and for many editions to come.

July 1998

CONTRIBUTORS AND STAFF

QUOTATIONS OF THE YEAR

Joy and woe are woven fine, / A clothing for the soul divine.

QUEEN ELIZABETH II. Quoting the English poet William Blake in her Christmas Day broadcast. British TV and radio, 25 December 1997.

The whole point about being a minister without portfolio is that you don't have a portfolio.

BENJAMIN WIGG-PROSSER Spokesman for Peter Mandelson MP, the minister responsible for the Millennium Dome. On his employer's refusal to answer Parliamentary Questions. *Independent* 27 December 1997.

Parents are responsible for their children. That is the key belief and assertion.

JACK STRAW Home Secretary. Outlining his government's 'family policy' after escorting his 17-year-old son to a police station, where he was charged with selling £10's worth of cannabis to a *Daily Mirror* journalist; reporting restrictions were lifted the following week. *Daily Telegraph* 27 December 1997.

There was a mood of civilized defiance.

DAVID ACKERMAN Oxfordshire hunt follower. Describing possibly the last Boxing day meet of the Hesthorp Hunt at Chipping Norton. *Daily Telegraph* 27 December 1997.

The problem with the Maze is that we are not allowed to run it as a prison.

ANONYMOUS Northern Ireland prison officer. After Loyalist prisoner Billy Wright was shot dead by Republican fellow-inmates. *Daily Telegraph* 29 December 1997.

People outside California think we're nuts. What will be next – sausages?

PHIL ELWELL Owner of Ye Olde King's Head, California's largest British pub. As smoking in all the state's bars and casinos is banned from midnight on 31 December 1997. *Daily Telegraph* 30 December 1997.

. . . — — — . . .

MORSE CODE SOS in Morse Code, which was abolished on 1 January 1998.

Not going to the moon and banging on it with my own hammer has been my biggest disappointment in life.

EUGENE SHOEMAKER US planetary geologist, who died in July 1997. On 7 January 1998 an ounce of his ashes travelled to the moon in a memorial capsule aboard Lunar Prospector. *Daily Telegraph* 7 January 1998.

It was inevitable that the Titanic *would set sail, but that does not mean it was a good idea to be on it.*

WILLIAM HAGUE Leader of the Conservative party. Illustrating his attitude to Britain joining the Single European Currency. Interviewed in the *Daily Telegraph* 7 January 1998.

God made man in His own image...Cloning and the reprogramming of DNA is the first serious step to becoming one with God.

RICHARD SEED US physicist. On his plan to establish a clinic to clone human beings. *Daily Telegraph* 8 January 1998.

I thought, 'Hang on, that's my wallpaper'.

DONNA WEARN Inhabitant of Selsey, West Sussex. On her reaction to watching a TV news broadcast of tornado damage to her town on the night of 7–8 January while she was away from home. The wall of the room in which her husband had been sleeping was one casualty. *Daily Telegraph* 9 January 1998.

Daily avoidance of assorted professional beggars, alcoholics and deranged individuals in the streets of Cambridge.

GEORGE SALMOND Professor of Molecular Microbiology at Cambridge University. Listing his recreations in *Who's Who*. *Times* 10 January 1998.

Putting my case face-to-face, arguing it through with them, I thought was the best way of doing it so I'm here.

MO MOWLAM Secretary of state for Northern Ireland. On her meeting with Loyalist terrorist prisoners in the Maze Prison on 9 January 1998, in an effort to sustain the 'peace process'. *Independent* 10 January 1998.

You have less to do, but then you have fewer people to help you do it.

MICHAEL HOWARD Former home secretary and shadow foreign secretary. On life in opposition. *Independent* 10 January 1998.

We are not having any more newspapers stolen than before.

DAVID MACREDMOND Travel retail manager, W H Smith. On the success of his firm's 'honesty box' for newspaper purchases at Heathrow Airport. *Independent on Sunday* 11 January 1998.

It is not an event that has very much to do with Christianity. It is to do with time.

TERENCE CONRAN Creative consultant to the Greenwich Millennium Dome. Advising against 'turning the Dome Project over to happy-clappy evangelists'. *Daily Telegraph* 12 January 1998.

Games are not about winning beauty prizes, how many corners you had or how much possession, but goals. So, ipso facto, we lost.

ROY HODGSON Manager of Blackburn Rovers. Explaining how his team won the argument but lost the match, 3-1, to Derby County on 11 January 1998. *Daily Telegraph* 12 January 1998.

Like a lot of figures we give, it doesn't reflect real life.

ANONYMOUS Spokesman for the Department of Social Security. On his boss Harriet Harman's claim that women earning £1 million a year were entitled to claim £18,000 a week in Maternity Benefit. *Daily Telegraph* 13 January 1998.

Another day, another billion dollar program.

PHIL GRAMM Republican senator. On the public spending plans of President Clinton, widely seen as a boost to the ambitions of Vice President Gore. *The Washington Post* 14 January 1998.

....

The Welfare State starts with work. I want a Welfare State that is built around the work ethic.

GORDON BROWN Chancellor of the Exchequer. On the 'modernization of the Welfare State' being undertaken by the Government. Interview in the *Daily Telegraph* 15 January 1998.

....

It was not planned, but at the same time we did not do anything to stop it happening.

LIZ BUTTLE Carmarthenshire farmer and grandmother. On giving birth to a son at the age of 60; her previous child was born 35 years earlier. She later became Britain's oldest single parent when the baby's father returned to his wife and children. A few days after that it was revealed that Ms Buttle had received fertility treatment, claiming to be 49. *Daily Telegraph* 15 January 1998.

....

Fashion today is a total disaster. It means nothing. It is not wearable.

HUBERT JAMES MARCEL TAFFIN DE GIVENCHY French fashion designer. On the couture of his successors. Interview in the *Daily Telegraph* 15 January 1998.

....

The idea for the article came from The Sun *'s political editor in a discussion with me about Japan's desire to improve its United Kingdom media relations.*

ALASTAIR CAMPBELL Press secretary to Tony Blair. Explains how Japanese prime minister, Ryutewo Hashimoto, came to apologize, in an article in the *The Sun*, for his country's war record. Letter to the *Daily Telegraph* 16 January 1998.

....

The idea that we are going to go around tipping people out of wheelchairs is ridiculous.

ANONYMOUS Government spokesman. On planned welfare reforms. *Daily Telegraph* 16 January 1998.

....

It's not like we're creating any dangerous precedent here that any senator can fly upon retirement. There's only one John Glenn.

JOHN PIKE Spokesman for the US Federation of Scientists. On the announcement that Senator Glenn, the first American in space in 1962, is to make a return trip at the age of 78. *Daily Telegraph* 16 January 1998.

....

Tamworths are very spirited pigs, even without wild boar blood.

GRENVILLE WELSH Chief Executive of the British Pig Association. On the two Tamworth boars who escaped from an abattoir in Malmesbury, Wiltshire, swam across the River Avon, and eluded capture for over a week. *Daily Telegraph* 16 January 1998.

....

It looks like everything is contamination.

JEFF BADA Member of the Scripps Institution of Oceanography, California. Announcing that the Martian meteorite that fell on Antarctica 13,000 years ago does not, after all, contain extra-terrestrial fossils. *Science* 16 January 1998.

....

My heart will be warm just taking part.

PHILIP BOIT Kenyan cross-country skier. Preparing to take part in the Winter Olympics, just two years after first seeing snow. *Daily Telegraph* 16 January 1998.

....

Alas, in a culture that encourages feeble-minded political correctness, great monuments and great works of art are not to be expected.

STEPHEN BAYLEY Ex-creative director of the Millennium Dome. On the influence of 'focus groups' on the project. *Independent* 17 January 1998.

....

I've done something with my life. I've made kids happy around the world.

WALTER DIENER Inventor of bubble-gum. Speaking shortly before his death. *Independent* 17 January 1998.

....

Housing the mentally ill in these havens isn't Dickensian. Sending them out to beg on the streets is.

MARJORIE WALLACE Chief executive of the mental health charity SANE. Welcoming the reported plans of Health Secretary Frank Dobson MP to scrap 'care in the community'. *Daily Telegraph* 17 January 1998.

....

The BBC has televised the Cup Final from pre-war years. Only Hitler stopped them.

DESMOND LYNHAM BBC football commentator. After Sky and ITV jointly outbid the BBC, paying £15 million for the right to screen the match live from 1998 to 2001. *Daily Telegraph Sport on Saturday* 17 January 1998.

....

I'm not going to tell you what I think, and I don't know if I should think what I do think.

GARLAND BURELL JR Jr Judge presiding over the trial of alleged 'Unabomber', Theodore Kaczynski. On the legal arguments surrounding Mr Kaczynski's refusal to be examined by psychologists or plead insanity in his defence. *Time* 19 January 1998.

....

I trained six hours a day for ten years of my life and if I was beaten by a cheat, then I want that known.

SHARRON DAVIES Silver swimming medallist in the 1980 Olympic Games. After revelations of widespread hormone and steroid doping among athletes and swimmers of the former East Germany. *Time* 19 January 1998.

....

His physical condition is not so good, but Leeds paid £4.5 million for him two years ago and we got him for nowt.

STEVE COPPELL Manager of Crystal Palace FC. On signing Thomas Brolin. *Daily Telegraph* 19 January 1998.

....

Instead of seeing a meeting between an angel and the devil, couldn't one think of a meeting between two angels?

FIDEL CASTRO Cuban president. Giving a six-hour television address on the forthcoming visit of Pope John Paul II. *Daily Telegraph* 20 January 1998.

....

If you hang on to things long enough they come back into style – like me.

BURT REYNOLDS US film actor. On winning a Golden Globe Award for his performance in *Boogie Nights. Daily Telegraph* 20 January 1998.

....

He looked at us, why can't we look at him?

SLOGAN Chanted by women demanding admission to a chapel containing 11 Goya frescoes in an enclosed monastery in Spain; a corridor, segregating visiting women from the monks, is to be built. Radio 5 Live, 21 January 1998.

....

I was worried you were going to ask me that. I think it is 54.

STEPHEN BYERS Education minister responsible for school standards. Answering interviewer Eleanor Oldroyd, who asked him, 'What are eight sevens?'. Radio 5 Live, 21 January 1998.

....

I am still fond of the old monster, but even if he buries us in lawyers the only thing I couldn't bring myself to do is take him seriously.

MAX HASTINGS Editor of the *Evening Standard*. After Alan Clark MP won a High Court judgement preventing the paper from publishing a spoof 'Alan Clark's Secret Political Diary'. Henceforward the word 'not' was to be inserted. Radio 5 Live, 21 January 1998.

....

You don't see that Hillary Clinton runnin' down my song now.

TAMMY WYNETTE Country-and-western singer-songwriter. Recalling how the First Lady, at the time of her husband's difficulties with Gennifer Flowers during the 1992 election campaign, disparaged Wynette's song, *Stand By Your Man*. *Daily Telegraph* 23 January 1998.

....

Their goalscorer cost £15 million. Ours cost three packets of crisps and a Mars Bar.

PAUL FAIRCLOUGH Manager of Stevenage Borough of the Vauxhall Conference. On the difference between Alan Shearer, of Newcastle United and England, and his team's Giuliano Grazioli as Stevenage hold the Premier League club to a 1-1 draw in the FA Cup. Radio 5 Live, 24 January 1998.

....

I'm not here to apologize.

PW BOTHA South African politician, prime minister from 1978 to 1989. In court answering charges of refusing to appear before the Truth and Reconciliation Commission; he described apartheid as 'good neighbourliness'. *Daily Telegraph* 24 January 1998.

....

Once we realized what we were holding, it was obvious who was going to win.

HAZEL RUFFLES Whist player of Bucklesham, near Ipswich. On dealing four hands each of one complete suit from a well shuffled pack. In 1939 the mathematician Horace Norton of University College, London, calculated the odds against this (or any other specified four-hand combination) as 2,235,197,406,895,366,368,301,600,000 – 1. *Daily Telegraph* 27 January 1998.

....

The great story here…is this vast right-wing conspiracy that has been conspiring against my husband since the day he announced for president.

HILLARY CLINTON US lawyer and First Lady. Defending her husband against charges of adultery and perjury, and accusing his attackers of 'scratching for dirt and intimidating witnesses'. NBC *Today* 27 January 1998.

....

How far into the speech will we forget the trousers?

JON SNOW Television journalist and news presenter. Introducing coverage of President Clinton's State of the Union Address. Channel Four *News Special* 28 January 1998.

....

A horrible shock…a mess of clashing flavours…swiftly thrown into the bin.

GORDON RAMSAY Cookery writer and two-star Michelin restaurateur. Samples a recipe from the Duchess of York's cookery book, *Dining with the Duchess* (Simon & Schuster, New York). *Daily Telegraph* 28 January 1998.

....

It is in the interests of everyone to establish the truth and close this painful chapter once and for all.

TONY BLAIR Prime minister. Announcing a Judicial Tribunal of Inquiry into the Bloody Sunday killing by British troops of 14 people in Londonderry in 1972. *Daily Telegraph* 30 January 1998.

....

Even the candidate does not know. He may dream about it, but he does not know.

BORIS YELTSIN Russian president. Refusing to divulge the name of his chosen successor in 2000. Tass news agency, 30 January 1998.

....

He's had enough of being the one who's arrested.

ANONYMOUS Friend of Swampy (Daniel Hooper). On the roads protestor's retirement from campaigning. *Daily Telegraph* 31 January 1998.

....

New Labour's most irritating characteristic is the belief that its spokesman can ignore the facts of history and deny the rules of logic without anybody noticing.

ROY HATTERSLEY British Labour politician and author. On the modernizing ideology of his successors. *Independent* 31 January 1998.

....

Management…wouldn't know how to broadcast if it was put up against a wall and you said you were going to shoot them.

KATE ADIE Chief News Correspondent for BBC TV. On the 'suits' at the BBC. *Press Gazette*, February 1998.

....

I kept hearing these Oohs and Aahs from the boys watching on the dressing room telly. It became such a lottery I stopped caring.

ANGUS FRASER England cricketer. On waiting to bat in the first Test against the West Indies at Sabina Park, Jamaica, on 29 January 1998. An unplayable pitch forced the abandonment of the match after 50 minutes and 61 balls, with England on 17-3; the physiotherapist had attended injured batsmen seven times. *Independent on Sunday* 1 February 1998.

....

I guess I saved the Navy £25 million.

ANONYMOUS Royal Navy pilot. After managing to land his Harrier safely after the cockpit canopy blew out at 40,000 feet. *Independent on Sunday* 1 February 1998.

....

It'll go away. It'll pass. The president will remain in office, he'll do a good job, we'll all, hopefully, have a sound economy, keep our jobs, and I think everything's going to be fine.

WILLIAM GINSBURG Monica Lewinsky's attorney. Appears to puncture the 'sex and perjury' scandal surrounding his client and President Clinton. NBC, *Meet the Press* 1 February 1998.

The stories in the press with regard to the Foreign Secretary are trivial and should be laid to rest so that he can get on with his job which he does well.

MARGARET COOK Haematologist and former wife of Foreign Secretary Robin Cook MP. On allegations that her estranged husband had attempted to install his mistress, Gaynor Regan, in the publicly-funded post of diary secretary. *Daily Telegraph* 2 February.

....

If diplomacy runs out we have reserved the right to use force and if we do so it will be substantial.

MADELEINE ALBRIGHT US secretary of state. On the pressure being put on Saddam Hussein to allow UN inspectors free access to suspected stockpiles of chemical and biological weapons in Iraq. UPI, 2 February 1998.

....

My veracity was not questioned in the court. I'm going to continue to do the job that's given to me by the Lottery Act.

PETER DAVIS National Lottery regulator. Following Richard Branson's libel victory against Guy Snowden, who resigned as a director of Camelot plc. After meeting Heritage Secretary Chris Smith MP a few hours later, Mr Davis also resigned. Radio 5 Live, 3 February 1998.

....

Ever since my daughter was born I feel the fleetingness of time, and I don't want to waste it in getting the perfect lip colour.

MADONNA US singer and actress. Interview in the *Daily Telegraph* 3 February 1998.

Here she comes, baby doll, she's all yours.

RICHARD THORNTON Husband of murder victim Ruth Thornton. Watches as his wife's murderer, Karla Faye Tucker, is executed by lethal injection in Huntsville, Texas, despite a worldwide campaign to have her sentence commuted to life imprisonment. *Daily Telegraph* 5 February 1998.

....

We wish them well in the FA Trophy. I hope they get beat in the next round.

KENNY DALGLISH Manager of Newcastle United FC. Pays ungracious tribute to non-league Stevenage Borough, beaten 2-1 by Newcastle in an FA Cup fourth round replay. BBC Radio Newcastle, 5 February 1998.

....

Everyone said, 'Oh how sweet. We just love your accent.' So far, it's been fun.

HELEN BAXENDALE Actress. On being chosen to join the cast of *Friends*. Interview in the *Daily Telegraph* 5 February 1998.

....

He's said some kind things about me. Now let me say some kind things about him.

TONY BLAIR Prime minister. At a joint press conference with President Clinton at the White House. *Daily Telegraph* 6 February 1998.

....

A downmarket, dumbed-down, over-staffed, over-bureaucratic, ridiculous organization.

ANONYMOUS Official spokesman for the prime minister. Berates the BBC after its chief political correspondent, John Sergeant, asked if Tony Blair was worried about the sex scandal surrounding President Clinton during the Prime minister's visit to the USA. *Daily Telegraph* 6 February 1998.

....

Then there's the Stepford Wives – that's those female New Labour MPs who've had the chip inserted in their brains to keep them on message.

BRIAN SEDGEMORE Labour MP for Hackney South and Shoreditch. Speech at the Tate Gallery on 6 February 1998

....

It fills the page so I don't have to do a background.

BERYL COOK Artist. On why she likes painting fat people. *Independent on Sunday* 8 February 1998.

....

Before we all become too gung-ho, let us all remind ourselves that this is not going to be a rerun of February 1991.

PETER DE LA BILLIÈRE Commander of the British forces in the Gulf War. On US and UK threats to bomb Iraq. *Independent on Sunday* 8 February 1998.

....

This is what is called res ipsa loquitur, *the thing speaks for itself.*

WILLIAM COHEN US defense secretary. On aircraft surveillance photographs showing 17 vans being loaded and driven away from an Iraqi weapons site while UN inspectors were kept waiting for 3 hours to inspect it. *Daily Telegraph* 9 February 1998.

....

All political lives, unless they are cut off in midstream at a happy juncture, end in failure, because that is the nature of politics and human affairs.

ENOCH POWELL Conservative politician. In his biography of Joseph Chamberlain, published in 1977. Obituary in the *Daily Telegraph* 9 February 1998.

....

They'll want planning permission for building a snowman next.

ANONYMOUS Father of a 14-year-old boy who was given an absolute discharge by magistrates in Selby, Yorkshire, after police had arrested him for making an ice slide on the road outside his house. *Daily Telegraph* 11 February 1998.

There was a conspiracy and I will not rest until I have established exactly what happened.

MOHAMMED FAYED Proprietor of Harrods and father of Dodi Fayed, boyfriend of Diana, Princess of Wales. Claiming that the couple's death was arranged by British secret agents. Interview in the *Daily Mirror* 11 February 1998.

....

Save us from the time of trial.

ANONYMOUS Part of the Lord's Prayer as revised by the General Synod of the Church of England. It replaces 'Lead us not into temptation'. *Daily Telegraph* 12 February 1998.

....

Kids and dog for hire. Long term contract. Sad gits need not apply.

LAUREN AND ASHTON MILLS Advertisement by two 10-year-olds in the *Oxford Mail* for replacement parents after their lone parent mother died of cancer. *Daily Telegraph* 12 February 1998.

....

I don't think this will evaporate, but I anticipate it will slowly dissipate over time, reaching insubstantiality.

HILLARY CLINTON US lawyer and First Lady. On the agglomeration of allegations against her husband. *Washington Post* 12 February 1998

....

I do not know the real reason why I was sacked. I may never find the answer to it in my life.

RUUD GULLIT Dutch international footballer and ex-player-manager of Chelsea FC. Speaking at a press conference on 13 February 1998 following his dismissal.

....

It's better to send middle-aged men abroad to bore each other than send young men abroad to kill each other.

ROBIN COOK Foreign secretary from 1997. On UN negotiations with Saddam Hussein. *Independent* 14 February 1998.

....

This director said, 'You have everything wrong with your face.' I have never got over it.

JUDI DENCH English actress. Explaining why she has made so few films. *Independent on Sunday* 15 February 1998.

....

Our own Armed Forces are endangered by irresponsible exports.

GENERALS SIR HUGH BEACH and **SIR MICHAEL ROSE**, and **ADMIRAL SIR JAMES EBERLE** Members of the British American Security Information Council. Calling for a tough code to regulate arms sales, after it was revealed that the means to make biological weapons were exported to Iraq from Britain, with government approval, as recently as 1996. Letter to the *Daily Telegraph* 16 February 1998.

Maybe there'll be a simple, innocent explanation. I don't think so, because I think we would have offered that up already…I don't think it's going to be entirely easy to explain maybe.

MICHAEL MCCURRY White House press secretary. On the Monica Lewinsky scandal; afterwards he said, 'I goofed'. *Chicago Tribune* 17 February 1998.

....

She is amazing.

PRINCE CHARLES. On his 97-year-old grandmother, Queen Elizabeth the Queen Mother, as she left hospital on her own two feet, 23 days after an emergency hip replacement. *Daily Telegraph* 18 February 1998.

....

I accept that it's news to have a black member of the Prince of Wales's Household, but I think that's where the news starts and where it ends.

COLLEEN HARRIS Deputy press secretary to HRH The Prince of Wales. On her appointment. *Daily Telegraph* 19 February 1998.

....

I have a broken heart. But I don't have a discouraged heart. I have a heart that is filled with hope.

BILL MCCARTNEY Chief executive of the Promise Keepers. Speech addressing employees of the organization on 19 February 1998. He then sacked them all.

....

There is better quality control if you are buying a lawnmower.

PAUL FLYNN Campaigner on behalf of hip replacement patients. After 3M Health Care was ordered to pay for repeat operations for about 4,700 people fitted with its faulty 'Capital' joint. *Daily Telegraph* 20 February 1998.

....

There was an old person of Dean, / Who dined on a pea and a bean. / He said, 'More than that / Would make me grow fat!' / That bombilious old person of Dean.

EDWARD LEAR English artist and humorist. Limerick found among papers belonging to the Baring banking family by archivist Stuart Bridges. *Daily Telegraph* 21 February 1998.

....

I am in the departure lounge of life; my only hope is that my plane will be delayed.

ROBIN DAY British journalist. Addressing the Oxford Union. *Daily Telegraph* 21 February 1998.

....

The House views with incredulity the failure of the referee to award a penalty kick.

THREE BARNSLEY MPS Early Day Motion after Barnsley FC drew 1-1 away to Manchester United in the FA Cup. They won the replay 3-2. *Independent on Sunday* 22 February 1998.

....

You can do a lot with diplomacy, but of course you can do a lot more with diplomacy backed up by fairness and force.

Kofi Annan Secretary general of the United Nations. Addressing a press conference after negotiating a settlement with Iraq over inspections of 'weapons of mass destruction'. CNN, 23 February 1998

Everyone tells about how terrible it is to be famous. I love being famous. You get to meet some really interesting people, I tell you.

Bob Hoskins English actor. Interviewed at the release of *The Secret Agent*, his production of the Joseph Conrad novel. *Daily Telegraph* interview 23 February 1998.

We will say to ourselves with pride: this is our Dome. Britain's Dome. And, believe me, it will be the envy of the world.

Tony Blair Prime minister. Unveiling some of the contents of the £758 million Millennium Dome. Radio 5 Live, 24 February 1998.

Fortunately, the MCC is a private club whose views are not representative of the game as a whole.

Tim Lamb Chief executive of the English Cricket Board. After members of the MCC voted by 6,969 to 5,528 to admit women as members – 11 percent short of the two-thirds majority required. *Daily Telegraph* 25 February 1998.

It is not perhaps a prudent culmination for a criminal justice system which is human and therefore fallible.

Lord Justice Rose Appeal Court judge. On the death penalty, after he and two colleagues posthumously acquitted Mahmood Hussein Mattan, hanged for murder in 1952. *Daily Telegraph* 25 February 1998.

This photo, which meant more to Dr Ngor than life itself, is the reason why he died.

Craig Hum Prosecutor in Los Angeles Superior Court. On the murder of gynaecologist Dr Haing Ngor, Oscar-winning actor in *The Killing Fields* and survivor of Khmer Rouge persecution in which his pregnant wife was murdered; he was killed by muggers after refusing to part with a gold locket containing her photograph. *Los Angeles Times* 25 February 1998.

Only tigers.

Nigel Wesson Chipperfield Circus worker. Having been admitted to Oxford's John Radcliffe Hospital after his arm was bitten off by a tiger, Nigel Wesson was asked if he was allergic to anything. *Daily Telegraph* 26 February 1998

Urban society has to realize how easily alienation from the natural world can develop in the plastic-wrapped supermarket culture.

Jim Thompson Bishop of Bath and Wells (and former Bishop of Stepney). Lending his support to the Countryside March, called to protest at threats to English rural life. *Daily Telegraph* 26 February 1998.

KRM has outlined the negative aspects of publication.

Eddie Bell Chairman of HarperCollins UK. Memo to Anthea Disney, Chairman of News America Publishing. KRM – Rupert Murdoch, owner of News International and HarperCollins – ordered that publication of the memoirs of Chris Patten, last governor of Hong Kong, be scrapped lest they cause offence to the government of China, where he has extensive business interests. After refusing to pretend that the book was not of a publishable standard, Stuart Proffitt, publisher of HarperCollins' main books division, was suspended from duty; he then resigned. Mr Patten's book was taken on by MacMillan. *Daily Telegraph* 27 February 1998.

Listen to us.

Slogan of the Countryside March of 1 March 1998, in which at least 250,000 people demonstrated in London against threats to farming and the rural way of life.

They just want to blame somebody. I try to cheer them up. Sometimes if they're rude I tell them I'll make it keep raining.

Al Nino Retired US navy pilot of Nipomo, California. On being telephoned by people complaining about the effects of the El Niño weather system. *Los Angeles Times* 3 March 1998.

You are not talking about something from the DIY store which may collapse after a year or two.

Lord Irvine UK Lord chancellor. Defending the spending of £59,000 on new wallpaper for his official residence in the Palace of Westminster. Radio 5 Live, 3 March 1998.

They screwed up. They put me in a completely inexcusable position.

Rupert Murdoch Chairman of News International. On senior HarperCollins executives who commissioned Chris Patten's memoirs. Two days later, he expressed his 'full confidence' in them, publicly apologized to Mr Patten for untrue allegations made against his book, and settled his Court action against the publisher with an undisclosed six-figure payment. *Daily Telegraph* 5 March 1998.

The principle is familiar: it's the same as if the vendors did not declare faulty central heating.

Stephen Savage Solicitor. Acting for Andrew and Josie Smith of Derbyshire, who planned to sue the previous owners of their house for failing to declare that it was haunted. *Daily Telegraph* 5 March 1998.

It was extraordinary to watch them create an Eddie Grundy in front of our eyes.

Vanessa Whitburn Editor of *The Archers*. On *Tembea na Majire*, the Kenyan equivalent of *The Archers*. *Daily Telegraph* 5 March 1998.

Are you scared that there are other Damiens and Philips all over Northern Ireland?

Brian Hackett Parish priest of Poyntzpass, Co. Armagh. At the funeral of Damien Trainor, a Roman Catholic who, with his Protestant friend Philip Allen – who was to have been best man at his wedding – was murdered by gunmen while drinking in the Railway Bar. The village was targeted for its reputation for easygoing integration. *Daily Telegraph* 7 March 1998.

The words to describe what I had seen refused to come out.

Elisabetta Carnabuci Archaeologist. On fainting after her discovery, in an ancient Roman passageway, of a fresco appearing to show a bird's-eye view of the city before the great fire of 64 AD. *Daily Telegraph* 7 March 1998.

I want to say thank you very much to David. It was very fair racing and excellent teamwork.

Mika Hakkinen Formula One driver and winner of the Australian Grand Prix. On second-placed David Coulthard, who pulled over at the last moment to allow his Maclaren team-mate to finish first. *Daily Telegraph* 9 March 1998.

The great thing about Graham was that he adored bad taste.

John Cleese English actor and comedian. As the surviving members of Monty Python's Flying Circus prepare to perform at Aspen, Colorado, with an urn purportedly containing the ashes of the late Graham Chapman. *Daily Telegraph* 9 March 1998.

For the last few months, people have been trying to blacken my name, and it is time to say something about it. It is a vendetta.

John Prescott Deputy prime minister. On anonymous allegations concerning the dealings in his Hull constituency of a property company of which his son is a director. *Times* 10 March 1998.

We're looking for an acquittal. Nothing else will satisfy us. If there's a retrial, there will be no conviction.

ANDREW GOOD Attorney for Louise Woodward. As the Massachusetts Supreme Court begins its deliberations on appeals from the former nanny and her prosecutors against a manslaughter conviction. *The Times* 10 March 1998.

....

The idea of a baby laughing in the sun projects a false image of the world.

JILL McCURDY Member of Warner Brothers USA. Describing *The Teletubbies* at a world summit on children's television. *Times* 10 March 1998.

....

I conspired to damage you and your presidency ... I wanted to pop you right between the eyes.

DAVID BROCK Journalist and author of the December 1993 story in the *American Spectator* that first alleged a sexual encounter between President Clinton and Paula Jones. Repenting and withdrawing his allegations in an open letter to the President. *Esquire* 10 March 1998.

....

I'm falling apart.

PRINCE CHARLES. Talking to patients at a South Wales hospital the day after undergoing keyhole surgery on a torn cartilage. *Daily Telegraph* 11 March 1998.

....

Now you can use your title, isn't that nice.

QUEEN ELIZABETH II. Dubs Sir Paul Getty, US-born billionaire and new British Citizen, 12 years after the honorific award of his knighthood. *Daily Telegraph* 11 March 1998.

....

The more popular a work you make today, the more derided you are likely to be.

PETER BENNETT-JONES Chairman of Tiger Aspect. On the film *Bean*, which was described by one critic as 'insulting to the intelligence of blue-green algae' and passed over for Oscar and BAFTA nomination. *Daily Telegraph* 11 March 1998.

....

This is big.

BRIAN MARSDEN Member of the International Astronomical Association. On reports that the mile-wide asteroid XF11 may – or may not – collide with Earth at 7.30 a.m. on Thursday 26 October 2028. *Daily Telegraph* 12 March 1998.

....

All popular radio is based on repetition and familiarity. It's almost that the listener knows what you're going to say before you say it ... If you did it for long enough, you wouldn't have to say anything at all. You could sit there and pick your nose.

TERRY WOGAN Broadcaster. *Independent on Sunday* 15 March 1998.

....

It's a very difficult prison to manage. It's not like managing an estate agent's office.

ADAM INGRAM Northern Ireland security minister. On the 'self-regulated' Maze prison where David Keys, on remand as a suspect in the Poyntzpass killings, was murdered by fellow-inmates. *Daily Telegraph* 17 March 1998.

....

Many firm believers have not-so-firm bodies.

KENNETH FERRARO Member of Purdue University, Indiana. On research suggesting that Christians have a tendency to be overweight. *Daily Telegraph* 17 March 1998.

....

Respect children, because they're human beings and they deserve respect.

BENJAMIN SPOCK Author of *Baby and Child Care* (1946). Expounding his basic philosophy in one of the last interviews before his death on 16 March. *Daily Telegraph* 17 March 1998.

....

Can a handshake be so difficult for the Israeli government?

ANONYMOUS British spokesman. During the foreign secretary Robin Cook's visit to the Middle East. He had shaken hands with a Palestinian representative during a visit to an Israeli settlement in occupied Jerusalem. Israel's Prime minister, Benjamin Netanyahu, cancelled a dinner in his honour. *Daily Telegraph* 18 March 1998.

....

Apparently in the Prime Minister's case it should be called the Unread Book.

WILLIAM HAGUE Leader of the Conservative Party. On the Red Book, the Treasury's post-Budget document, during the Commons debate on the Budget; the prime minister had queried some data Mr Hague quoted from it. *Hansard*, 18 March 1998.

....

We knew it couldn't bomb Exeter or Okehampton, but short of that it doesn't get any worse than this.

STEVE BENNETT Rocket scientist of Salford University. On Starchaser 3, which should have reached 15,000 feet before descending in three stages by parachute, but instead reached 300 feet before diving to Earth and exploding. *Daily Telegraph* 21 March 1998.

....

If I am given the privilege of becoming the first democratically elected Lord Mayor I'll never write another book.

JEFFREY ARCHER English writer and politician. *Independent* 21 March 1998.

....

Yeltsin always wants to show that he is in charge. To the West it might seem slightly irrational to do that by sacking the whole government, but in a Russian context it can work.

ANONYMOUS NATO spokesman. On President Yeltsin's dismissal of the Russian government. *Daily Telegraph* 24 March 1998.

....

I say be proud of our diversity and let subsidiarity rule. We don't want a Europe of conformity.

TONY BLAIR Prime minister. Addressing the French National Assembly on 24 March 1998.

....

I'm the king of the world!

JAMES CAMERON US film director. Receiving the Best Film Oscar for *Titanic*, which won 10 other Oscars in the 1998 awards. *Daily Telegraph* 26 March 1998.

....

I have been asked many times what it is like to be in a depth-charge attack. Two words: bloody awful.

JOE BRIGHTON Submarine torpedo gunner. On serving throughout World War II. *Daily Telegraph* 26 March 1998.

....

My life is over.

MITCHELL JOHNSON 14-year-old schoolboy of Jonesboro, Arkansas, accused of shooting to death four pupils and a teacher at his school. Speaking to a Baptist minister as he awaits trial. *Daily Telegraph* 27 March 1998.

....

It is, put quite simply, too late. The outcome will range from inconvenience to disaster.

ROBIN GUERNIER Former head of Taskforce 2000. On the threat of the 'Millennium Bug' to computer systems. *Daily Telegraph* 27 March 1998.

....

The US, as leader of the world, should ... call on its enemies and say, let's sit down and talk peace. I've no doubt that the role of the US as a world leader would be tremendously advanced.

NELSON MANDELA President of South Africa. Addressing US President Bill Clinton in Cape Town. CNN, 27 March 1998.

....

The captaincy has never been a burden. I've enjoyed every minute of it.

MIKE ATHERTON English cricketer. On resigning as captain of England after 52 tests. *Independent on Sunday* 29 March 1998.

....

Free The Weatherfield One.

SLOGAN On tee-shirts worn by aficionados of *Coronation Street* after Deirdre Rachid (formerly Barlow, née Hunt) received an 18 month prison sentence, in the episode of 29 March, for a crime she did not commit.

....

We invited 90 fashion journalists to have a fitting with a Gossard corsetière, and only three of them knew their size.

JUDY BENNETT Public relations executive. At the launch of the Gossard Ultrabra Smooth. *Daily Telegraph* 30 March 1998.

....

Obviously his knowledge of ballet is considerably further along than it was before Saturday night.

ANONYMOUS Spokesman for the Royal Opera House. After the accountant Pelham Allen, its acting head, had attended his first production of the Royal Ballet. *Daily Telegraph* 31 March 1998.

....

Is this an April Fool joke?

BILL CLINTON President of the USA. On being told that the sexual harassment case brought against him by Paula Jones had been thrown out of Court. CNN, 1 April 1998.

....

The chap next to me said, 'Be lucky,' and I said, 'You too.'

KEITH HARVEY Commercial director of Leeds United FC. On the crash-landing at Stansted Airport of a British Aerospace 748 carrying the football team home from an away match at West Ham United. *Daily Telegraph* 1 April 1998.

....

It makes them more rounded and less self-conscious.

BRYAN JONES Animal behaviourist of the Roslin Institute. On the benefits of television for battery chickens. *Daily Telegraph* 2 April 1998.

....

France wants an administration and police who have consciences and souls.

SERGE KLARSFELD Nazi-hunter. On the sentence of 10 years' imprisonment passed on former bureaucrat Maurice Papon, 87, for his role in the deportation of Jews from Vichy, France. *Daily Telegraph* 3 April 1998.

....

The offence was a revolting one and an affront to every reasonable and decent concept of human behaviour.

GEOFFREY RIVLIN Judge. Passing sentence of nine months' imprisonment on Anthiny-Noel Kelly, who stole human body parts from the Royal College of Surgeons in order to turn them into art exhibits. *Daily Telegraph* 4 April 1998.

....

The whole thing has made me closer to the tree. We've made it through a difficult time and now we have a better relationship.

DANIELE MALPELI New York delicatessen owner. In lieu of a $1,000 fine for chaining his bicycle to a honey locust tree, Daniele Malpeli apologized to it, gave it a hug, and promised to keep it watered. *Daily Telegraph* 4 April 1998.

....

It is the sacrifice of history and tradition to the great god Mammon. We are being closed to save money for the Lord Chancellor's curtains.

MARTIN BENTLEY Prosecutor. On the closing of Marlborough Street Magistrates' Court, which passed its first sentence in 1795. *Daily Telegraph* 4 April 1998.

....

We are leading the world in BSE research, which is quite right because we did, after all, give the world BSE in the first place.

ANONYMOUS Whitehall spokesman. On plans for a 7-year research programme into mad cow disease. *Independent* 4 April 1998.

....

They ain't gaffes. They are ideas.

TONY BANKS Minister for sport. Defending his habit of making controversial remarks. *Independent* 4 April 1998.

....

Suppose Tony Blair came to your house, tripped over a piece of loose stair carpet, and ended up in hospital. We would be liable. The risk is too great.

ADRIAN WEBB Spokesman for Direct Line Insurance. On his company's refusal to insure anyone who 'has contact with famous people'. *Independent* 4 April 1998.

....

I'm a jammy git.

CARL LLEWELLYN Jockey. On riding Earth Summit to victory in the Grand National. BBC TV, 4 April 1998.

....

Can we play you every year?

CHELSEA FC FANS. After their club repeated the FA Cup Final result of 1997 by beating Middlesborough FC 2–0 in the Coca-Cola Cup Final of 1998. Radio 5 Live, 4 April 1998.

....

The rape of British industry by BMW is systematically going ahead.

DONALD LONGMORE Secretary of the Rolls Royce Acquisition Consortium. On BMW's intention to buy Rolls Royce. *Independent on Sunday* 5 April 1998.

....

This is not the time for soundbites. I feel the hand of history upon our shoulders.

TONY BLAIR Prime minister. Addressing a press conference on his arrival in Belfast, as the Northern Ireland talks appear to be on the brink of collapse. Radio 5 Live, 7 April 1998.

....

I wouldn't touch it with a forty-foot pole.

JOHN TAYLOR Chief negotiator for the Ulster Unionist Party. On the 65-page draft of the Northern Ireland constitutional settlement prepared by former US Senator George Mitchell, calling it 'a Sinn Féin wish-list'. *Daily Telegraph* 8 April 1998.

....

I won't. I don't even know you. And besides, I'm going out and I'm busy getting ready.

VIOLET HOOK Inhabitant of Rolvenden, Kent. Refusing to surrender her toy cap gun to some 30 armed policemen outside her terraced home. A telephone engineer had reported seeing Ms Hook firing the gun from her bedroom window; she had been using it to scare rooks off her roof. *Daily Telegraph* 8 April 1998.

....

The trouble with this situation is that words matter; every word matters. So it is very hard.

TONY BLAIR Prime minister. As the Northern Ireland talks appear set to overrun the deadline of midnight on 9 April 1998. *Daily Telegraph* 9 April 1998.

....

If goofy ideas ever go up to $40 a barrel I'd like to have drilling rights to Dick Armey's head.

PAUL BEGALA Political adviser to President Clinton. On Congressman Richard Armey, who had called the President 'a shameless person' and called on him to resign. *Daily Telegraph* 9 April 1998.

....

In some countries, genocide is not really important.

FRANÇOIS MITTERAND The late President of France. Speaking to his staff in 1994, and reported as details emerge of French complicity in the massacre of some 800,000 Tutsis by Hutu forces in the former French colony of Rwanda. *Daily Telegraph* 10 April 1998.

....

You almost don't dare to hope too much.

GEORGE MITCHELL Former US Senator and, for 22 months, chairman of the Northern Ireland talks. As agreement is finally reached shortly before 5pm on Good Friday, 10 April 1998. *Daily Telegraph* 11 April 1998.

....

She was a privileged woman who found charity work gave her the adulation she wanted.

GALLUP POLL STATEMENT On the subject of Diana, Princess of Wales, 61 percent of 985 adult respondents agreed with this statement in a telephone survey; 29 percent thought she 'bordered on saintliness'. *Daily Telegraph* 11 April 1998.

....

I think every man would like a few years at the end of his life to prepare his soul for death.

BASIL HUME Archbishop of Westminster from 1976. After his request for retirement at the age of 75 was turned down by the Pope. *Independent on Sunday* 12 April 1998.

....

We had 15 varieties of lettuce and they ate every one. But we were fair. Once, I put cabbage out with a sign saying, 'For my darling rabbits'. The next day, everything was gone. So we shot them.

RAYMOND BLANC Chef and restaurateur. On pest control at the Manoir aux Quat' Saisons, Oxfordshire. *Daily Telegraph* 13 April 1998.

....

I did not vote Labour because they've heard of Oasis and nobody is going to vote Tory because William Hague has got a baseball cap. It's sad, it really is.

BEN ELTON Comedian and author. On New Labour's 'rebranding' of Britain as 'Cool Britannia'. *Radio Times* 14 April 1998.

....

If he had said, 'Bomb the White House tomorrow', there would have been 10,000 people who would have done it. It was in the best interests of the United States to have my dad killed. Definitely.

SEAN LENNON Musician and son of the late ex-Beatle John Lennon. Blaming the US government for his father's murder in 1980. *New Yorker* 14 April 1998.

....

How long will it be before the water companies tell us that we have had 'the wrong kind of floods'?

ROBERT WARNER After widespread storms over Easter. Letter to the *Daily Telegraph* 14 April 1998.

....

I call for a travelling shot, and then I grab my heart, contort in pain, drop to the sidewalk, and expire very tragically.

WOODY ALLEN US film writer, director, and actor. Imagining the ideal way to make his final exit. *Daily Telegraph* 15 April 1998.

....

This agreement is as good and as fair as it gets. If you think otherwise, then what is your alternative?

DAVID TRIMBLE Northern Ireland politician, leader of the Ulster Unionist party from 1995. Attacking Rev Ian Paisley's Democratic Unionist Party. *Daily Telegraph* 17 April 1998.

....

I'm not saying he hasn't got any principles, it's just that I don't know what they are.

PD JAMES English detective novelist. On the prime minister, Tony Blair. *Daily Telegraph* 17 April 1998.

....

Diana's personal canonization was at the same time a canonization of what she stood for – the elevation of feeling, image and spontaneity over reason, reality and restraint ... In the Diana story, duty is a notion which is entirely absent.

ANTHONY O'HEAR Professor of Philosophy at the University of Bradford. Discussing a doctrine of 'emotional correctness' in the public perception of Diana, Princess of Wales. *Faking It – The Sentimentalisation of Modern Society*, published by the Social Affairs Unit on 17 April 1998.

....

I cannot think of many toadies that have prospered or many toadies who have become household names and who have gone down here terribly well.

BETTY BOOTHROYD British Labour politician, speaker of the House of Commons from 1992. On the sycophancy of the new intake of Labour MPs. *Daily Telegraph* 18 April 1998.

....

Well done, David.

GERRY ADAMS Northern Ireland politician, president of Sinn Féin (the political wing of the Irish Republican Army) from 1978. Congratulating Ulster Unionist leader David Trimble, whose party's ruling council voted 72%–28% in favour of the Northern Ireland Agreement. Radio 5 Live, 18 April 1998.

....

He's got this unbelievable belief.

PAUL MERSON Middlesbrough FC footballer. On his former manager, Arsène Wenger, whose Arsenal team won the double of the Premier League Championship and the FA Cup. *Independent on Sunday* (remark orginally made on BBC TV, *Match of the Day*) 19 April 1998.

....

I joined the project for patriotic reasons. I thought at the time we were involved in a war for survival.

DANIEL GOOSEN South African veterinarian and pathologist. On a 1980s project of the apartheid government to develop an anti-fertility drug for clandestine use on black people. *Sunday Independent*, Johannesburg, 19 April 1998.

....

The buck stops at the top and I believe that Dr Oliver should pack his bags and go.

DONALD DEWAR Secretary of state for Scotland. Calling for the resignation of Dr Ian Oliver, chief constable of Grampian Police, after a report found 'serious corporate failure' in his force's handling of the murder of a young boy by a known paedophile. Radio 5 Live, 19 April 1998.

....

We cannot defend ourselves to the general public, to our owners, our horses, or live with our consciences if we ever allow our horses to race in such conditions again.

JENNY PITMAN Racehorse trainer. In a memo to the Chairman of Aintree Racecourse dated 6 April, the day after three horses died in the Grand National. *Daily Telegraph* 20 April 1998.

....

I'm not an African. The Africans know I'm not an African. I'm an American. This is my country. My people helped to build it and we've been here for centuries. Just call me black if you want to call me anything.

WHOOPI GOLDBERG US actress and comedienne. Refusing to be known as an 'African-American'. Interview in the *Daily Telegraph* 20 April 1998.

....

Britain must know she still has friends on the other side of the Atlantic.

NEWT GINGRICH US Republican politician, speaker of the House of Representatives from 1995. Lending his support to calls for Britain to be offered associate membership of the North American Free Trade Agreement, as an alternative to the Single European Currency. *Chicago Sun Times* 20 April 1998.

....

He did the wrong thing for the right reasons.

ALEX FERGUSON Manager of Manchester United FC. On his player Ole Gunnar Solskjaer, who deliberately tripped Newcastle United's Robert Lee just outside the penalty area to deny him an almost certain opportunity to put his relegation-threatened team ahead and end Manchester United's chances of winning the Premier League Championship. Solskjaer was sent off to a standing ovation from Manchester United fans. *Daily Telegraph* 20 April 1998.

....

It is a professional thing – the guy's got to do what he's got to do.

KENNY DALGLISH Manager of Newcastle United FC. On the tripping of Robert Lee by Ole Gunnar Solskjaer. *Daily Telegraph* 20 April 1998.

....

There is no nuclear button, nothing but sandwiches and clean socks.

ALASTAIR CAMPBELL Press secretary to Tony Blair. On the contents of two red suitcases that accompanied him everywhere on his visit to the Middle East. *Daily Telegraph* 21 April 1998.

....

They would host a meeting and by doing so perhaps gain some prestige, which would not cost us anything.

TSAHI HANEGBI Israel's Justice Minister. Speaking on Israeli Army Radio, on the British plan to chair a meeting between Israel and the Palestine Authority in London. *Daily Telegraph* 21 April 1998.

We've been having a lot of challenges here with us fitting in the chair.

JIM PAWELCZYK NASA astronaut. On the experimental chair on board the shuttle *Columbia*, which is too small for people over 6ft, especially as humans expand by about 5 cm/2 in in zero gravity. *Daily Telegraph* 22 April 1998.

The god in whom I believe doesn't care if I have breasts or not.

DANA INTERNATIONAL Transsexual singer. Chosen to represent Israel in the Eurovision Song Contest and condemned by Orthodox Jews as 'an abomination'. *Daily Telegraph* 22 April 1998.

Hello and welcome to the World Cup France Reservations and Information Service.

RECORDED MESSAGE Heard by very few of the 20 million people, 15 million of them in Britain, who telephoned the French ticket 'hotline' on 22 April 1998; there was a 1 in 2,000,000 chance of getting through. Radio 5 Live, 22 April 1998.

More than half a century has passed and we can still hear the last cries, the final prayers, the gasps of our brothers and sisters.

BINJAMIN NETANYAHU Israeli politician and diplomat, leader of the Likud (Consolidation Party) from 1993 and prime minister from 1996. Leading 'March of the Living' on the former death camps of Auschwitz and Birkenau to mark Israel's 50th anniversary. *Daily Telegraph* 23 April 1998.

To set a torch under the middle-market.

ROSIE BOYCOTT Ex-editor of the *Independent on Sunday* and editor of *The Express*. Defining her new mission as editor of *The Express*. *Daily Telegraph* 25 April 1998.

Here we have an attempt to bend the whole country to the will of a single man. Russia has become a hostage to someone who has only his own interest at heart.

MIKHAIL GORBACHEV Former president of the USSR. On Russian President Boris Yeltsin, who persuaded the Duma to accept Sergei Kiriyenko as prime minister at the third time of asking. *Daily Telegraph* 25 April 1998.

I have a one-to-one relationship with God. I am God's instrument. No-one chooses this work. You have to be chosen by God.

EILEEN DREWERY 'Spiritual healer'. Hired by England football manager Glen Hoddle to help his team prepare for the World Cup. *Independent* 25 April 1998.

Why can't this century end right now? Why can't we call it quits? You know, push a button and agree to go on to the next century? I'm tired of this one.

DOUGLAS COUPLAND Author of *Generation X*. On the Millennium. *Independent* 25 April 1998.

They always used to come to me going 'pow, pow'. He probably went up to Carlos and did the same thing.

TABATHA WHITE 12-year-old neighbour of Carlos Gilmer. On the shooting of 6-year-old Carlos Gilmer by his 4-year-old friend with a loaded .38 calibre pistol he found in a handbag at his grandmother's house in Greensboro, North Carolina. *Daily Telegraph* 27 April 1998.

Like the British when they lost India.

NORMAN MAILER US writer and journalist. Describing how he felt about the Women's Liberation Movement. *Time* 27 April 1998.

Andrew and I believe in co-parenting. … It is very good for the children. That is why we are an example to young people who get divorced with children.

SARAH FERGUSON The Duchess of York. On the arrangement whereby she and her ex-husband share their former marital home, and 'play away matches' when they need company. *The Jay Leno Show* (NBC), 28 April 1998.

It doesn't make you 21 again, but it does solve the problem.

ROBERT SHAY 70-year-old resident of Los Angeles, California. On Viagra, the 'magic bullet' remedy for male impotence. *Daily Telegraph* 28 April 1998.

The police are merely doing their duty by saying they are keeping the murder file open but they know as well as the rest of us that my husband died 25 years ago.

LADY LUCAN Wife of Lord Lucan. On her husband, who disappeared in November 1974 and is suspected of murdering his children's nanny in mistake for his wife. *Daily Telegraph* 28 April 1998.

Satire died the day they gave Henry Kissinger the Nobel Peace Prize. There were no jokes left after that.

TOM LEHRER US humorist and mathematician. On his retirement from showbusiness. *Daily Telegraph* 29 April 1998.

I can't wait to see my dad, although I know he will stink. Normally he has a bath before I see him.

ALICIA HEMPLEMAN-ADAMS 8-year-old daughter of mountaineer David Hempleman-Adams. After her father walked to the geographic North Pole to complete the 'Adventurers' Grand Slam' of climbing the highest peak in each continent and walking to the geographic and magnetic North and South Poles. *Daily Telegraph* 30 April 1998.

There appears to be yet another attempt to raise the decommissioning issue as an obstacle to progress. Let us make it clear there will be no decommissioning by the IRA.

IRISH REPUBLICAN ARMY Statement issued by the IRA in Dublin at the start of the Referendum campaign, on both sides of the Irish border, on the 'Good Friday proposals'. *Daily Telegraph* 1 May 1998.

Clearly, because we are in a dynamic environment, minor bounces like this are not unusual.

ANONYMOUS Spokesman for the Royal Navy. After Lt Susan Moore's ship, *HMS Dasher*, damaged her sister ship, *Puncher*, while docking in Guernsey. *Daily Telegraph* 1 May

I might well use 'newt' in my slogan, but I certainly wouldn't use 'New'.

KEN LIVINGSTONE Labour politician and amphibian aficionado. On his campaign to become Mayor of London. *Independent* 2 May 1998.

I'm just so excited – it's wonderful – and a very good quality wine here.

WENDY RICHARD Actress. On her first meeting with the Queen. *Independent* 2 May 1998.

Boring, boring Arsenal!

ARSENAL FC SUPPORTERS Chant as Arsenal beats Everton 4–0 to win the Premier League title. Radio 5 Live, 2 May 1998.

I don't care whether he's Alan Shearer or the Pope, you do not do that.

MARTIN O'NEILL Manager of Leicester City FC. On the Newcastle United and England football captain Alan Shearer, who allegedly aimed a kick at the head of Leicester player Neil Lennon. *Independent on Sunday* 3 May 1998.

These officials in departments are sometimes called teenyboppers, do you know what I mean? You put your money on me.

JOHN PRESCOTT Deputy prime minister. On suggestions that officials at the prime minister's Policy Unit were trying to tone down his White Paper on transport policy because it was 'anti-car'. *Daily Telegraph* 4 May 1998.

Talking with colleagues is not the same as going home and talking to someone in shorthand, and screaming with laughter without having to over-explain.

CAROLINE QUENTIN Actress. On her separation from comedian Paul Merton. Interview with Elizabeth Grice in the *Daily Telegraph* 4 May 1998.

....

I guess some people would rather live in the past.

JOHN TELNACK Vice-president of Ford. On the popularity in the USA of the re-launched Volkswagen Beetle. *Daily Telegraph* 5 May 1998.

....

Judah is going to cure cancer in two years.

JAMES DEWEY WATSON US biologist. On Dr Judah Folkman, developer of a 'drug cocktail' to fight cancerous tumours by disconnecting them from blood vessels. *Daily Telegraph* 6 May 1998.

....

Many, many discoveries that look fine in mice don't work in humans.

JUDAH FOLKMAN Oncologist. Warning against euphoria as human tests begin on his 'drug cocktail' cancer treatment. *Daily Telegraph* 6 May 1998.

....

We thought Arthur Scargill had been put to bed.

KEN JACKSON General Secretary of the Amalgamated Engineering and Electrical Union. On the election of Dave Rix, a member of Mr Scargill's Socialist Labour Party, as leader of the train drivers' union ASLEF. *Daily Telegraph* 7 May 1998.

....

One drunken person recording another bunch of drunks does not constitute a business deal.

GEORGE HARRISON Ex-member of the English pop group the Beatles. Giving evidence in the Beatles' successful court action to prevent Lingasong Music from selling a 'bootleg' CD, recorded in a Hamburg bar, of the group performing in 1962. *Daily Telegraph* 7 May 1998.

....

I got a bit miffed because he was pinching my pension money and I couldn't afford that.

ARTHUR WILLEY Former wrestler. On grappling an armed robber to the floor during an attempted hold-up of the Bristol and West Building Society in Bristol. *Daily Telegraph* 7 May 1998.

....

Pregnant women are not walking wombs but individuals who have the same rights as anyone else to refuse medical treatment and reject doctors' advice.

ANN FUREDI Director of the Birth Control Trust. On a High Court ruling that a Health Authority acted illegally by forcing a woman suffering from pre-eclampsia to give birth by Caesarean section instead of in a barn in Wales, as she wished. *Daily Telegraph* 8 May 1998.

....

It's an anthem of life, innit? A reflection of life in England today.

DAMIEN HIRST English artist. On his World Cup song, *Vindaloo*, inspired by a crowd chant he heard at a Bristol Rovers v Fulham football match. *Daily Telegraph* 8 May 1998.

....

He's Gallic. I think I am probably very English. I'm rather bad at all this self-analysis. Actually, I've given it up. I'm not exactly stiff upper lip or Princess Diana. Just English.

JOHN MAJOR British prime minister 1990–97. Comparing and contrasting himself with Tony Blair after sharing a platform with him to campaign for a Yes vote in the referendum on the Northern Irish settlement. Interview by Rachel Sylvester and Alice Thompson in the *Daily Telegraph* 9 May 1998.

....

It would be outrageous if only civil servants resigned while Ministers responsible for the policy were able to abdicate their responsibilities

ROBIN COOK Foreign secretary. Speaking in 1996 on the 'Arms to Iraq' affair; his words were quoted against him as he and his junior minister Tony Lloyd became embroiled in allegations that Britain, acting through 'military consultancy' Sandline International and with support from the Royal Navy, gave assistance to the counter-coup that reinstated the elected government of Sierra Leone, in apparent defiance of a UN arms embargo. *Daily Telegraph* 9 May 1998.

....

It's funny these people like Ben Elton suddenly criticizing New Labour. I think it is the first-ever recorded case of rats leaving a floating ship.

ALEXEI SAYLE Comedian. On criticisms of 'Cool Britannia'. *Independent* 9 May 1998.

....

I'm sorry, but our writers don't like your government.

ROY HUDD Comedian and compère of *The News Huddlines*. Explaining to Downing Street press officer Alastair Campbell why his team will not be supplying any more gags for Tony Blair's speeches. *Independent on Sunday* 10 May 1998.

....

I don't see there's any ceasefire on while I'm lying here like this.

JOHN BROWNE Resident of Northern Ireland. Speaking after being 'knee-capped' by Republican gunmen. *Independent on Sunday* 10 May 1998.

....

It isn't all gloom. I've got a huge amount of faith in myself and you can be so scared of dying you don't spend the day living.

IAN DURY Rock star. On living with colon cancer. *Independent on Sunday* 10 May 1998.

....

The single European currency is a bad idea whose time has come.

ANONYMOUS German civil servant. On the Euro. Quoted by Dominic Lawson in the *Sunday Telegraph* 10 May 1998.

....

I'm glad when I don't have to go any more.

ANONYMOUS Supporter of Everton FC. On the anguish of supporting his team, which ended the season with a 1-1 home draw against Coventry City and avoided relegation from the Premier League on goal difference. *Daily Telegraph* 11 May 1998.

....

Don't let us forget that what was happening was that the UN and the UK were both trying to help the democratic regime restore its position from an illegal military coup. They were quite right in trying to do it.

TONY BLAIR Prime minister. Dismissing allegations that his government connived to breach the UN embargo on arms supplies to Sierra Leone, which his government had drafted. *Daily Telegraph* 12 May 1998.

....

I like the angel but there are probably 20,000 people up here who feel they'd like to do something to it.

KEVIN WAUGH Newcastle United fan. On the 65-foot 'Angel of the North' statue near the A1 south of Gateshead, which he and some friends decorated with a 29-foot x 17-foot replica of the team shirt worn by Newcastle striker Alan Shearer. *Daily Telegraph* 13 May 1998.

....

This was the intelligence failure of the decade.

JOHN PIKE Technical intelligence expert at the Federation of America Scientists. On the failure of CIA spy satellites to spot preparations in India for three underground nuclear tests on 11 May; two more followed, amid global condemnation of India's action, which made it the world's sixth nuclear state, and fears that Pakistan would follow suit and instigate an Asian arms race. *Daily Telegraph* 13 May 1998.

....

All weekend I never slept a wink. I was scared that I wouldn't wake up if he started crying.

DAVID LOW 17-year-old schoolboy. Volunteer for a programme aimed at putting young people off the idea of teenage parenthood by making them responsible for the welfare of 'virtual baby' Tobi, a computerized doll. *Daily Telegraph* 14 May 1998.

....

Robin Cook would gain more sympathy from his predecessors if he did not set himself up as our moral superior. We all did our bit to make a British contribution to a more decent world and it is mildly irritating to be dismissed as immoral rogues.

DOUGLAS HURD Home secretary 1985–89 and foreign secretary 1989–95. On his Labour successor. Article in the *Daily Telegraph* 14 May 1998.

....

I agreed to have my photograph taken because they were nice blokes but I never thought it would lead to this.

MARGE POTTER Birmingham housewife. Whose face adorned posters all over Birmingham, venue for the G8 Summit, above the slogan, 'Get Your Hair Done, Marge – Bill Clinton's Coming To Town'. *Daily Telegraph* 15 May 1998.

....

Frank walks like America. Cocksure.

SONNY BONO Singer and politician. On Frank Sinatra, who died on 15 May 1998. *Independent* 16 May 1998.

....

For the last seven years I've had the odd fag now and again when I'm relaxed – which is never.

PAUL GASCOIGNE ('GAZZA') Middlesborough FC and England footballer. On allegations of a nicotine habit. *Independent* 16 May 1998.

....

We want to show that normal, sexy, boy-interested girls play hockey and you don't have to look like a horse.

MONICA PICKERSGILL President of the English Hockey Association. On the English Hockey Association's poster promoting the two England v Australia women's matches. The poster showed Lucilla Wright, 18-year-old England player, reclining in a small black dress alongside the slogan: '8.30 p.m. – My Place'. *Daily Telegraph* 16 May 1998.

....

If I am no longer trusted I will become a sage and endeavour to get close to God.

THOJIB I SUHARTO Indonesian politician and general, president 1967–98. After anti-government riots in Jakarta, in which hundreds of people died. *Independent on Sunday* 17 May 1998.

....

Either he is an unbelievable athlete or I have a career as a golf instructor.

BILL CLINTON President of the USA. On his pupil Tony Blair, who showed unsuspected aptitude on the golf course during a break from the G8 Summit in Birmingham. *Daily Telegraph* 19 May 1998.

....

One could find oneself trapped in the economic equivalent of a burning building with no exits.

WILLIAM HAGUE Leader of the Conservative party. Addressing students at a business school in Fontainbleu on the single European currency. *Daily Telegraph* 20 May 1998.

....

Life goes on. Criminals will get their dues. Cases come and go, but relations between countries are based on very solid interests.

GHAZI ALGOSAIBI Saudi Arabian Ambassador to Great Britain. On the return to Britain from Saudi Arabia of Lucille McLauchlan and Deborah Parry, two nurses jailed in 1997 for murder. *Daily Telegraph* 21 May 1998.

....

I see Northern Ireland as a Grand National without a finishing post; there are just high fences which you have to go on jumping.

DOUGLAS HURD Home secretary 1985–89 and foreign secretary 1989–95. On the road to a political settlement. Radio 5 Live, 21 May 1998.

....

If I am prepared to sit down with Sinn Féin, why can't Mr Paisley? He has never fought for his country, although he has made sure that a lot of other people did by what he said. The fact is they talk about not wanting to talk to republicans when what they mean is they don't want to talk to Catholics.

DEL WILLIAMS Formerly a soldier with the Royal Regiment of Wales, who lost a leg after being shot by the IRA in 1971, and now an official of the Ulster Democratic Party. Speaking on his way to vote in the Referendum on 22 May. *Independent* 23 May 1998.

....

The little games and pantomimes in which I once enthusiastically took part now appear completely irrelevant. What appeared from within so significant seems pointless and infantile when observed from without.

NEIL HAMILTON Former Conservative MP. Looking back on parliamentary procedures. *Manifesto* 23 May 1998.

....

A BBC executive came onto the set and said, 'What are you cluttering up Broadcasting House for?' 'I'm sorry,' I replied, 'we're making a programme.' 'I'm just going to a meeting to stamp out this sort of nuisance,' he said. He had clipboards under his arm, and I daresay a few flow-charts, too.

STEPHEN FRY Actor. On filming Mark Tavener's novel about the BBC, *In The Red*. *Independent* 23 May 1998.

....

In Northern Ireland, at last, the future has defeated the past.

JOHN MAJOR Prime minister 1990–97. On the 71 percent 'Yes' vote in the Referendum on the 'Good Friday proposals'; in the Irish Republic, 94 percent voted in favour of abolishing the Republic's constitutional claim to the province. *Independent on Sunday* 24 May 1998.

....

Certainly, we have never asked people to vote Ulster Unionist before, nor have they asked people to back us, but I think we are in a new type of electoral context.

SEAMUS MALLON Deputy Leader of the SDLP. On the campaign for the new Northern Ireland Assembly, to be elected on a system of proportional representation in which 'excess' votes can be transferred to other candidates. *Daily Telegraph* 25 May 1998.

....

Exploit an idiot: rent a room to a football fan.

SLOGAN Poster slogan in Montpelier, France, as the French hospitality industry braces itself for the 1998 World Cup. *The Times* 26 May 1998.

....

We're already run by the Scots. It feels a little like living under the Raj.

JEREMY PAXMAN Journalist and author. Foreseeing the rise of English Nationalism on Australian television. *Daily Telegraph* 26 May 1998.

....

The Empress and I can never forget the many kinds of suffering so many people have undergone because of that war. At the thought of the scars they bear, our hearts are filled with deep sorrow and pain.

AKIHITO Emperor of Japan from 1989. Speaking at a Buckingham Palace banquet after being invested in the Order of the Garter. Earlier, survivors of Japanese POW labour camps had turned their backs, booed, and whistled *Colonel Bogey* as his carriage passed along the Mall. *Independent* 27 May 1998.

....

Please don't take me off. I want to carry on.

MICHAEL OWEN Liverpool FC and England footballer. Speaking to manager Glen Hoddle after being knocked out in a friendly match against Morocco; later, he became the youngest player to score for England this century. *Daily Telegraph* 28 May 1998.

....

The Church of England is asking more of teachers than they do of their own clergy.

LIZ PAVER Retiring president of the National Association of Head Teachers and a member of the Church of England Synod. As the NAHT voted to lobby the Government to end the requirement for schools in England and Wales to hold a daily act of religious worship. *Daily Telegraph* 29 May 1998.

....

They should be liable for something like this. It's like giving a loaded gun to someone who had not been trained to shoot.

ROBERTA BURKE Partner of Frank Bernado, who left her after taking the anti-impotency drug Viagra. Contemplating suing Pfizer, the manufacturer of Viagra. *Daily Telegraph* 30 May 1998.

Earing up the Apprentice Boys' march in Derry would be the ultimate. Just imagine ears on all those bowler hats.

ANTHONY SAMUELSON Millionaire. On giving commuters the chance to enter for the Turner Prize by wearing cardboard ears proclaiming 'Art Iz Us' as they walked over London Bridge. *Daily Telegraph* 30 May 1998.

The impression that emerges is of an enclosed culture run by people who had known and worked with each other for 20 years. I think what we are looking at is the pathology of an institution.

RUDOLF KLEIN Professor of Social Policy at Bath University. On the censuring by the General Medical Council of two heart surgeons and an NHS manager at Bristol Royal Infirmary, where 29 children died and 4 suffered brain damage following surgery. *Independent* 30 May 1998.

The Pakistani people will be very proud that in the sub-continent they now have the upper edge, and that the military balance ... is now in favour of Pakistan.

GOHAR AYUB KHAN Foreign Minister of Pakistan. After the Pakistani government carried out six nuclear warhead tests in response to the five tests conducted by India. *Independent on Sunday* 31 May 1998.

A few years ago he couldn't have done that. The mobsters would have stopped him at the fish market.

RUDOLF W GIULIANI American Republican politician, mayor of New York from 1993. After attending the premiere of *Godzilla*, on the monster's trail of destruction through the city. *Time* 1 June 1998.

I'll be back.

GERI HALLIWELL Former member of the Spice Girls. On leaving the group. *Daily Telegraph* 1 June 1998.

Paul's getting injuries because he's not physically fit. It's not misfortune. We could throw him in for a one-off game but this is a tournament against the best in the world.

GLEN HODDLE Manager of the England football team. On the non-inclusion of Paul Gascoigne in his 22-man squad for the World Cup Finals. *Daily Telegraph* 2 June 1998.

Does the Prime Minister recall how we used to groan at the fawning, obsequious, softball, well-rehearsed, planted questions which were put by Conservative MPs to the former Prime Minister? Will he distinguish his period of office by discouraging such a practice?

ANDREW MACKINLAY Labour MP for Thurrock. Ignores the 'suggestions' of party whips and asks his own question of the prime minister. Radio 5 Live, 3 June 1998.

I fully respect my Honourable Friend's independence of mind and will do my best to ensure that he retains it.

TONY BLAIR Prime minister. Replying to Andrew MacKinlay, who ignored the 'suggestions' of party whips and asked his own question of the prime minister. Radio 5 Live, 3 June 1998.

Does the Prime Minister agree that Labour Governments are always good news for the Health Service?

JOHN HUTTON Labour MP. Asking the next question after Andrew MacKinlay. Radio 5 Live, 3 June 1998.

How much further do waiting lists have to rise before the secretary of state considers it appropriate to sack himself?

ANNE WIDDECOMBE Opposition spokeswoman on health. Questioning Frank Dobson MP, secretary of state for health, on his party's election promise to cut hospital waiting lists. *Daily Telegraph* 3 June 1998.

I think we may be, in a sense, matching accessories, as neither of us would count as being at the fashionable end of politics.

FRANK DOBSON Secretary of state for health. Replying to Anne Widdecombe. *Daily Telegraph* 3 June 1998.

His views on Europe are extreme. The Conservative Party is a broad church but Norman is up in the belfry.

EDWARD MCMILLAN-SCOTT Leader of the British Conservative group in the European Parliament. On former Chancellor Norman Lamont, who announced his intention of standing in the European Election. *Daily Telegraph* 3 June 1998.

There was a loud boom, a dust cloud, and then silence.

HANNELORE DOMKEWITZ German housewife. On the rail disaster of 3 June 1998 in which a high-speed train derailed and smashed into a road bridge, destroying it; 98 people died. *Daily Telegraph* 4 June 1998.

People like her are on another planet. She's a snob. I'm just a working-class guy.

MOHAMMED FAYED Proprietor of Harrods and father of Dodi Fayed, boyfriend of Diana, Princess of Wales. On Frances Shand-Kydd, Diana's mother, who, he alleged, did not wish to speak to him when they met at an examination called by the Paris judge leading the investigation into the fatal car crash. *Independent* 6 June 1998.

Soundbite and slogan, strapline and headline: at every turn we meet hyperbole. The soaring inflation of the English language is more urgently in need of control than the economic variety.

TREVOR NUNN Artistic director of the National Theatre. On the standard of public discourse. *Independent* 6 June 1998.

What a week. First Gazza, then Geri, then me.

STUART HIGGINS Editor of the *Sun*. On announcing his resignation with effect from Monday 8 June 1998. *Independent on Sunday* 7 June 1998.

There are, we believe, three places that guarantee a turnover: airports, railway stations, and hospitals. They provide a recession-free environment with no competition.

NICK ELKINS Development manager for HealthGate, a company developing shopping malls in NHS hospitals. *Independent on Sunday* 7 June 1998.

They hate the term 'tax exile'. It sounds like someone sitting by a pool in Marbella sipping a piña colada. We're talking about a hardworking band.

BERNARD DOCHERTY Spokesman for the pop group, the Rolling Stones. On the band's decision to abandon until after 5 April 1999 the four British concerts of its world tour, following tax law changes which would have landed its members with a £12 million demand from the Inland Revenue. *Daily Telegraph* 9 June 1998.

I keep wondering what they've spiked my beer with. You couldn't make it up, it's too daft.

GRANT GRAHAM Scottish football supporter from Dundee. Passing comment on the surreal display put on by the Paris authorities to celebrate the start of the World Cup Finals. *Daily Telegraph* 10 June 1998.

If any future Nigerian leader acts in any manner that can be held remotely parallel to Abacha's depravity, I swear to you, that is the end of Nigeria. The nation will not hold.

WOLE SOYINKA Nigerian author and dramatist. On the death of his country's military dictator, Sani Abacha, and the appointment of his successor, General Abdusalam Abubakar, who promised to resign, following elections, no later than 1 October. *Nigerian News Du Jour* 10 June 1998.

....

Books are nothing but timber with squiggles on them.

HAMMOND INNES English novelist. Obituary in the *Daily Telegraph* 12 June 1998.

....

I will go on writing until I die.

CATHERINE COOKSON Author of 101 books, 8 of which have yet to be published. Obituary in the *Daily Telegraph* 12 June 1998.

....

I always thought I would get out some time. Somehow or other I still retained a little faith in the system.

PATRICK NICHOLLS 69-year-old ex-prisoner. On being freed by the Appeal Court after serving 23 years for a 'crime' that never happened. *Daily Telegraph* 13 June 1998.

....

The intention, I understood, was to reduce his level of intellectuality and effectiveness by inducing brain damage.

SCHALK VAN RENSBURG Former director of a South African chemical company. Giving evidence to the Truth and Reconciliation Commission on a plan to poison Nelson Mandela with thallium as part of the former regime's policy of waging chemical warfare against black people. *Independent* 13 June 1998.

....

It was imperative we defended the system of free education. If we dump that, who's to say that we won't dump the NHS?

LLEW SMITH Labour MP for Blaenau Gwent. One of 31 Labour MPs to vote against their government's education reforms abolishing the student maintenance grant. *Independent on Sunday* 14 June 1998.

....

The extreme right will doom our party to election defeat.

GERALD FORD 38th president of the USA 1974–77. On Republican chances in the 2000 election. *Time* 15 June 1998.

....

That was great. We scored two goals and I had permission from my wife to be here.

HARRY ENFIELD Comedian. On England's 2-0 victory over Tunisia in their first World Cup group match. *Daily Telegraph* 16 June 1998.

....

We're not much into football, but we support Scotland now.

MUSTAFA AOLAD Bournemouth restaurateur. On receiving a £1,400 take-away order from 10 Scottish fans in Bordeaux. *Daily Telegraph* 16 June 1998.

....

Brainless, senseless, sacks of beer. The only thing they represent is brutish stupidity in its purest form, with gratuitous violence and a desire to destroy other people as their only means of expression.

LIBERATION French daily newspaper. On rioting England football fans in Marseilles. Quoted in the *Daily Telegraph* 17 June 1998.

....

I'll sing for you – if you sing for me.

NELSON MANDELA South African president. Talking to primary schoolchildren in Cardiff before leading them in a rendition of *Twinkle, Twinkle, Little Star*. *Daily Telegraph* 17 June 1998.

....

I am very pleased. It was a Solomonic judgement.

ALAN DERSHOWITZ Harvard Professor of Law. On the verdict of the Massachusetts Court of Appeal, upholding both the verdict of involuntary manslaughter against former au pair Louise Woodward, and her sentence of 'time served', and restoring her passport. *Daily Telegraph* 17 June 1998.

....

I want to say to you that I am truly sorry that we have let you down.

IAN JOHNSTON Assistant Commissioner of the Metropolitan Police. Offering a belated apology to the parents of Stephen Lawrence, a black London teenager stabbed to death at a bus stop in 1993, for the systematic bungling of the murder investigation. *Daily Telegraph* 18 June 1998.

....

You poor wee mite, you'll still be paying for this when you're my age.

ANDREW BONAR LAW British Conservative politician and prime minister 1922–1923. Addressing his baby godson, Bonar Sykes, while calculating Britain's War Debt in 1922. Obituary of Bonar Sykes in the *Daily Telegraph* 18 June 1998.

....

The system has not worked perfectly.

SEPP BLATTER President of FIFA, the world governing body of Association Football. On ticketing arrangements for the World Cup. *Daily Telegraph* 19 June 1998.

....

What is needed is a new offence of bringing the country into disrepute.

RONALD THWAITES QC. Suggesting a cure for football hooliganism. Letter to the *Daily Telegraph* 19 June 1998.

....

It is good to get a chance to do the right thing.

NICHOLAS WINTON British banker. On his rescue of over 600 Jewish children in Czechoslovakia in 1938, finding them homes in Britain. *Independent* 20 June 1998.

....

I love tackling, love it. It's better than sex. I love hearing the noise of a crunching tackle, the 'arrgh!' from the other player.

PAUL INCE Liverpool FC and England footballer. *Daily Telegraph* 20 June 1998.

....

If this was a big, unattractive woman with no teeth and tattoos, would the public have had a different opinion?

WILLIAM BYRNE Boston police officer who arrested Louise Woodward. E-mails the BBC as Miss Woodward, still convicted of the manslaughter of baby Matthew Eappen, is interviewed on *Panorama*. *Daily Telegraph* 23 June 1998.

....

Is THIS the most dangerous man in Britain?

HEADLINE On the front page of *The Sun*. Suspecting that Tony Blair favours Britain's membership of the Single European Currency. *The Sun* 24 June 1998.

....

The worst-prepared popinjay of a reporter that I have ever encountered.

CAMILLE PAGLIA US writer and academic. On Jonathan Dimbleby, after storming out of a recorded interview on 'the death of classic liberal feminism'. *Daily Telegraph* 25 June 1998.

....

Talk of early release for terrorists is madness. The bomb that killed my brother was planned during a ceasefire.

IHSAN BASHIR Brother of Inam, a newsagent, who was killed by the IRA's Docklands bomb in February 1996. On the sentencing of James McArdle to 25 years' imprisonment for making the Docklands bomb; under the terms of the 'Good Friday agreement' he will probably be free after two years. *Daily Telegraph* 26 June 1998.

....

We have to continue to drag behind us this dead weight of people who have difficulty moving into the future.

DAVID TRIMBLE Northern Ireland politician, leader of the Ulster Unionist party from 1995. On the Ulster Unionist Party, which, despite winning a majority of seats in the new Northern Ireland Assembly, remained deeply split. *Daily Telegraph* 27 June 1998.

....

Dublin is sick, Tony Blair is sick, and the sickest man of all is David Trimble. He is sickened unto death because today the people of Northern Ireland wrote the obituary notice of Trimbleism.

IAN PAISLEY Northern Ireland politician, cleric, and leader of the Democratic Unionist Party from 1971. On the Northern Ireland Assembly elections, in which 28 percent of voters supported anti-agreement candidates. *Independent* 27 June 1998.

....

The rudderless, bickering, embarrassing emotional wreck that the US team represented slinks back home today with its head bowed in disgrace.

THE NEW YORK POST On the US soccer team, eliminated from the group stage of the World Cup with no points and one goal. Quoted in the *Independent* 27 June 1998.

....

I ain't shocked. It's nothing to do with me.

JAMIE ACOURT One of five men widely suspected of murdering black teenager Stephen Lawrence in 1994. On the transcript of a video recording in which his brother is heard to support threats of violence against black people. He was giving evidence at the enquiry into the police handling of the case. *Daily Telegraph* 30 June 1998.

....

Yet again I have had to sit here and listen to people peddle lies and there was nothing I could do. Then I had to sit here and watch these people walk away.

NEVILLE LAWRENCE Father of murdered teenager Stephen Lawrence. Speaking after the five men suspected of killing his son had left the enquiry. *Daily Telegraph* 1 July 1998.

....

CALENDARS AND TIME

Time Zones and Relative Times in Cities Throughout the World

The surface of the Earth is divided into 24 time zones. Each zone represents 15° of longitude or 1 hour of time. Countries to the east of London and the Greenwich meridian are ahead of Greenwich Mean Time (GMT) and countries to the west are behind. The time indicated in the table below is fixed by law and is called standard time. Use of daylight saving time (such as British Summer Time) varies widely. At 12.00 noon, GMT, the standard time elsewhere around the world is as follows:

City	Time	City	Time	City	Time
Abu Dhabi, United Arab Emirates	16:00	Denver (CO), USA	05:00	Nairobi, Kenya	15:00
Accra, Ghana	12:00	Dhaka, Bangladesh	18:00	New Orleans (LA), USA	06:00
Addis Ababa, Ethiopia	15:00	Dubai, United Arab Emirates	16:00	New York (NY), USA	07:00
Adelaide, Australia	21:30	Dublin, Republic of Ireland	12:00	Nicosia, Cyprus	14:00
Alexandria, Egypt	14:00	Florence, Italy	13:00	Oslo, Norway	13:00
Algiers, Algeria	13:00	Frankfurt, Germany	13:00	Ottawa, Canada	07:00
Al Manamah (also called Bahrain), Bahrain	15:00	Gdansk, Poland	13:00	Panama City, Panama	07:00
		Geneva, Switzerland	13:00	Paris, France	13:00
Amman, Jordan	14:00	Gibraltar	13:00	Perth, Australia	20:00
Amsterdam, The Netherlands	13:00	Hague, The, The Netherlands	13:00	Port Said, Egypt	14:00
Anchorage (AK), USA	02:00	Harare, Zimbabwe	14:00	Prague, Czech Republic	13:00
Ankara, Turkey	14:00	Havana, Cuba	07:00	Rangoon, Myanmar	18:30
Athens, Greece	14:00	Helsinki, Finland	14:00	Rawalpindi, Pakistan	17:00
Auckland, New Zealand	24:00	Hobart, Australia	22:00	Reykjavik, Iceland	12:00
Baghdad, Iraq	21:00	Ho Chi Minh City, Vietnam	19:00	Rio de Janeiro, Brazil	09:00
Bahrain	15:00	Hong Kong, China	20:00	Riyadh, Saudi Arabia	15:00
Bangkok, Thailand	19:00	Istanbul, Turkey	14:00	Rome, Italy	13:00
Barcelona, Spain	13:00	Jakarta, Indonesia	19:00	San Francisco (CA), USA	04:00
Beijing, China	20:00	Jerusalem, Israel	14:00	Santiago, Chile	08:00
Beirut, Lebanon	14:00	Johannesburg, South Africa	14:00	Seoul, South Korea	21:00
Belgrade, Yugoslavia	13:00	Karachi, Pakistan	17:00	Shanghai, China	20:00
Berlin, Germany	13:00	Kiev, Ukraine	15:00	Singapore City, Singapore	20:00
Berne, Switzerland	13:00	Kuala Lumpur, Malaysia	01:00	Sofia, Bulgaria	14:00
Bogota, Colombia	07:00	Kuwait City, Kuwait	15:00	St Petersburg, Russia	15:00
Bombay, India	17:30	Kyoto, Japan	21:00	Stockholm, Sweden	13:00
Bonn, Switzerland	13:00	Lagos, Nigeria	13:00	Sydney, Australia	22:00
Brazzaville, Republic of the Congo	13:00	Le Havre, France	13:00	Taipei, China	20:00
Brisbane, Australia	22:00	Lima, Peru	07:00	Tashkent, Uzbekistan	18:00
Brussels, Belgium	13:00	Lisbon, Portugal	12:00	Tehran, Iran	15:30
Bucharest, Romania	19:00	London, England	12:00	Tel Aviv, Israel	14:00
Budapest, Hungary	13:00	Luanda, Angola	13:00	Tenerife, Canary Islands	12:00
Buenos Aires, Argentina	14:00	Luxembourg, Luxembourg	13:00	Tokyo, Japan	21:00
Cairo, Egypt	14:00	Lyon, France	13:00	Toronto, Canada	07:00
Calcutta, India	17:30	Madras, India	17:30	Tripoli, Libya	13:00
Canberra, Australia	22:00	Madrid, Spain	13:00	Tunis, Tunisia	13:00
Cape Town, South Africa	14:00	Manila, Philippines	20:00	Valparaiso, Chile	08:00
Caracas, Venezuela	08:00	Marseilles, France	13:00	Vancouver, Canada	04:00
Casablanca, Morocco	12:00	Mecca, Saudi Arabia	15:00	Vatican City	13:00
Chicago (IL), USA	06:00	Melbourne, Australia	22:00	Venice, Italy	13:00
Cologne, Germany	13:00	Mexico City, Mexico	06:00	Vienna, Austria	13:00
Colombo, Sri Lanka	17:30	Milan, Italy	13:00	Vladivostok, Russia	22:00
Copenhagen, Denmark	13:00	Minsk, Belarus	15:00	Volgograd, Russia	16:00
Damascus, Syria	14:00	Monrovia, Liberia	11:00	Warsaw, Poland	13:00
Dar es Salaam, Tanzania	15:00	Montevideo, Uruguay	09:00	Wellington, New Zealand	24:00
Darwin, Australia	21:30	Montreal, Canada	07:00	Yokohama, Japan	06:00
Delhi, India	17:30	Moscow, Russia	15:00	Zagreb, Yugoslavia	13:00
		Munich, Germany	13:00	Zürich, Switzerland	13:00

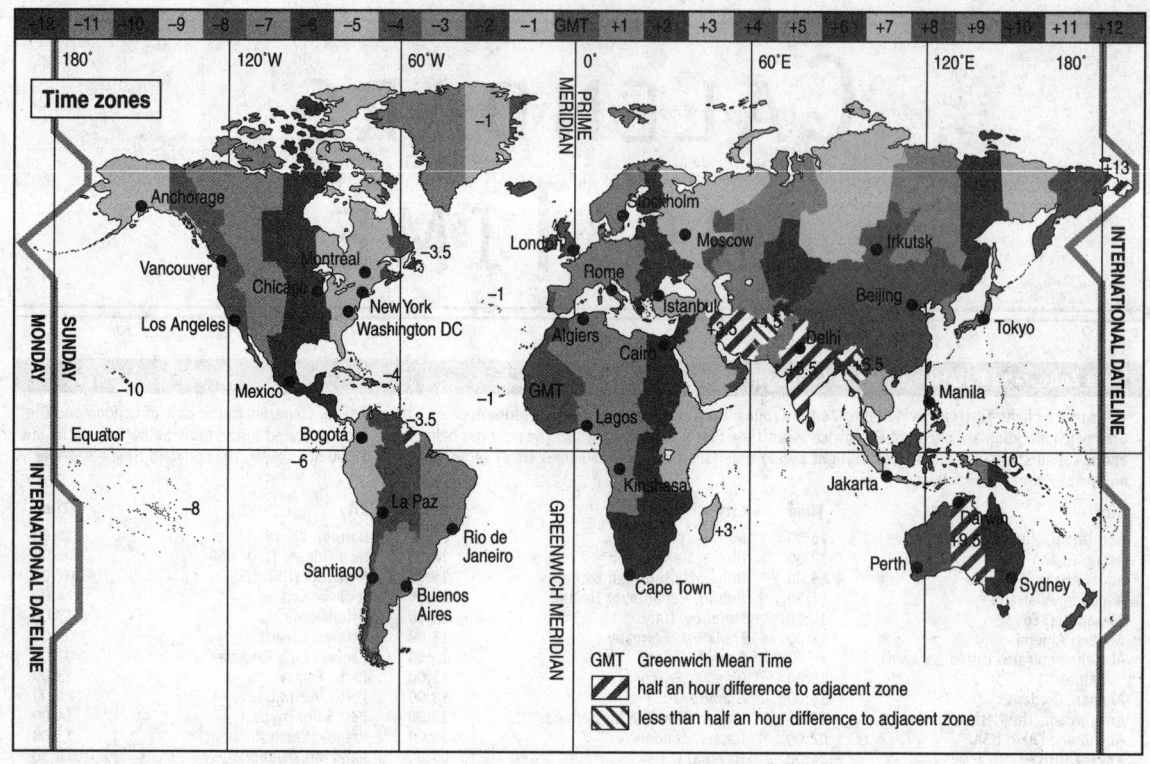

| -12 | -11 | -10 | -9 | -8 | -7 | -6 | -5 | -4 | -3 | -2 | -1 | GMT | +1 | +2 | +3 | +4 | +5 | +6 | +7 | +8 | +9 | +10 | +11 | +12 |

Time zones

180°   120°W   60°W   0°   60°E   120°E   180°

PRIME MERIDIAN

SUNDAY / MONDAY   INTERNATIONAL DATELINE

GREENWICH MERIDIAN

INTERNATIONAL DATELINE

Anchorage, Vancouver, Los Angeles, Mexico, Chicago, Montreal, New York, Washington DC, Bogotá, La Paz, Santiago, Rio de Janeiro, Buenos Aires, Equator, London, Rome, Algiers, GMT, Lagos, Cairo, Istanbul, Kinshasa, Cape Town, Stockholm, Moscow, Irkutsk, Beijing, Delhi, Tokyo, Manila, Jakarta, Perth, Darwin, Sydney

−1, −3.5, −4, −6, −8, −10, +3, +10, +13

GMT   Greenwich Mean Time

half an hour difference to adjacent zone

less than half an hour difference to adjacent zone

Chief Public or Legal Holidays in the UK

(– = not applicable.)

Public holidays[1]	England and Wales	Scotland	Northern Ireland	Public holidays[1]	England and Wales	Scotland	Northern Ireland
1999				*2000*			
New Year	1 January	1, 4 January	1 January	New Year	3 January	3, 4 January	3 January
St Patrick's Day	–	–	17 March	St Patrick's Day	–	–	17 March
Good Friday[2]	2 April	2 April	2 April	Good Friday[2]	21 April	21 April	21 April
Easter Monday	5 April	–	5 April	Easter Monday	24 April	–	24 April
May Day	3 May	3 May	3 May	May Day	1 May	1 May	1 May
Spring	31 May	31 May	31 May	Spring	29 May	29 May	29 May
Battle of the Boyne	–	–	12 July	Battle of the Boyne	–	–	12 July
Summer	30 August	2 August	30 August	Summer	28 August	7 August	28 August
Christmas[2]	27, 28 December	27, 28 December	27, 28 December	Christmas[2]	25, 26 December	25, 26 December	25, 26 December

[1] In the Channel Islands, Liberation Day (9 May) is a bank and public holiday.
[2] In England, Wales, and Northern Ireland, Christmas Day and Good Friday are common law holidays.

Perpetual Calendar

The number shown for each year indicates which Gregorian calendar to use.

1821 .. 2	1847 .. 6	1873 .. 4	1899 .. 1	1925 .. 5	1951 .. 2	1977 .. 7	2003 .. 4	2029 .. 2	2055 .. 6
1822 .. 3	1848 .. 14	1874 .. 5	1900 .. 2	1926 .. 6	1952 .. 10	1978 .. 1	2004 .. 12	2030 .. 3	2056 .. 14
1823 .. 4	1849 .. 2	1875 .. 6	1901 .. 3	1927 .. 7	1953 .. 5	1979 .. 2	2005 .. 7	2031 .. 4	2057 .. 2
1824 .. 12	1850 .. 3	1876 .. 14	1902 .. 4	1928 .. 8	1954 .. 6	1980 .. 10	2006 .. 1	2032 .. 12	2058 .. 3
1825 .. 7	1851 .. 4	1877 .. 2	1903 .. 5	1929 .. 3	1955 .. 7	1981 .. 5	2007 .. 2	2033 .. 7	2059 .. 4
1826 .. 1	1852 .. 12	1878 .. 3	1904 .. 13	1930 .. 4	1956 .. 8	1982 .. 6	2008 .. 10	2034 .. 1	2060 .. 12
1827 .. 2	1853 .. 7	1879 .. 4	1905 .. 1	1931 .. 5	1957 .. 3	1983 .. 7	2009 .. 5	2035 .. 2	2061 .. 7
1828 .. 10	1854 .. 1	1880 .. 12	1906 .. 2	1932 .. 13	1958 .. 4	1984 .. 8	2010 .. 6	2036 .. 10	2062 .. 1
1829 .. 5	1855 .. 2	1881 .. 7	1907 .. 3	1933 .. 1	1959 .. 5	1985 .. 3	2011 .. 7	2037 .. 5	2063 .. 2
1830 .. 6	1856 .. 10	1882 .. 1	1908 .. 11	1934 .. 2	1960 .. 13	1986 .. 4	2012 .. 8	2038 .. 6	2064 .. 10
1831 .. 7	1857 .. 5	1883 .. 2	1909 .. 6	1935 .. 3	1961 .. 1	1987 .. 5	2013 .. 3	2039 .. 7	2065 .. 5
1832 .. 8	1858 .. 6	1884 .. 10	1910 .. 7	1936 .. 11	1962 .. 2	1988 .. 13	2014 .. 4	2040 .. 8	2066 .. 6
1833 .. 3	1859 .. 7	1885 .. 5	1911 .. 1	1937 .. 6	1963 .. 3	1989 .. 1	2015 .. 5	2041 .. 3	2067 .. 7
1834 .. 4	1860 .. 8	1886 .. 6	1912 .. 9	1938 .. 7	1964 .. 11	1990 .. 2	2016 .. 13	2042 .. 4	2068 .. 8
1835 .. 5	1861 .. 3	1887 .. 7	1913 .. 4	1939 .. 1	1965 .. 6	1991 .. 3	2017 .. 1	2043 .. 5	2069 .. 4
1836 .. 13	1862 .. 4	1888 .. 8	1914 .. 5	1940 .. 9	1966 .. 7	1992 .. 11	2018 .. 2	2044 .. 13	2070 .. 4
1837 .. 1	1863 .. 5	1889 .. 3	1915 .. 6	1941 .. 4	1967 .. 1	1993 .. 6	2019 .. 3	2045 .. 1	2071 .. 5
1838 .. 2	1864 .. 13	1890 .. 4	1916 .. 14	1942 .. 5	1968 .. 9	1994 .. 7	2020 .. 11	2046 .. 2	2072 .. 13
1839 .. 3	1865 .. 1	1891 .. 5	1917 .. 3	1943 .. 6	1969 .. 4	1995 .. 1	2021 .. 6	2047 .. 3	2073 .. 1
1840 .. 11	1866 .. 2	1892 .. 13	1918 .. 3	1944 .. 14	1970 .. 5	1996 .. 9	2022 .. 7	2048 .. 11	2074 .. 2
1841 .. 6	1867 .. 3	1893 .. 1	1919 .. 4	1945 .. 2	1971 .. 6	1997 .. 4	2023 .. 1	2049 .. 6	2075 .. 3
1842 .. 7	1868 .. 11	1894 .. 2	1920 .. 12	1946 .. 3	1972 .. 14	1998 .. 5	2024 .. 9	2050 .. 7	2076 .. 11
1843 .. 1	1869 .. 6	1895 .. 3	1921 .. 7	1947 .. 4	1973 .. 2	1999 .. 6	2025 .. 4	2051 .. 1	2077 .. 6
1844 .. 9	1870 .. 7	1896 .. 11	1922 .. 1	1948 .. 12	1974 .. 3	2000 .. 14	2026 .. 5	2052 .. 9	2078 .. 7
1845 .. 4	1871 .. 1	1897 .. 6	1923 .. 2	1949 .. 7	1975 .. 4	2001 .. 2	2027 .. 6	2053 .. 4	2079 .. 1
1846 .. 5	1872 .. 9	1898 .. 7	1924 .. 10	1950 .. 1	1976 .. 12	2002 .. 3	2028 .. 14	2054 .. 5	2080 .. 9

1

```
JANUARY              MAY                  SEPTEMBER
S  M  T  W  T  F  S   S  M  T  W  T  F  S   S  M  T  W  T  F  S
 1  2  3  4  5  6  7      1  2  3  4  5  6                  1  2
 8  9 10 11 12 13 14   7  8  9 10 11 12 13   3  4  5  6  7  8  9
15 16 17 18 19 20 21  14 15 16 17 18 19 20  10 11 12 13 14 15 16
22 23 24 25 26 27 28  21 22 23 24 25 26 27  17 18 19 20 21 22 23
29 30 31              28 29 30 31           24 25 26 27 28 29 30

FEBRUARY             JUNE                 OCTOBER
S  M  T  W  T  F  S   S  M  T  W  T  F  S   S  M  T  W  T  F  S
          1  2  3  4            1  2  3   1  2  3  4  5  6  7
 5  6  7  8  9 10 11   4  5  6  7  8  9 10   8  9 10 11 12 13 14
12 13 14 15 16 17 18  11 12 13 14 15 16 17  15 16 17 18 19 20 21
19 20 21 22 23 24 25  18 19 20 21 22 23 24  22 23 24 25 26 27 28
26 27 28              25 26 27 28 29 30     29 30 31

MARCH                JULY                 NOVEMBER
S  M  T  W  T  F  S   S  M  T  W  T  F  S   S  M  T  W  T  F  S
          1  2  3  4                  1            1  2  3  4
 5  6  7  8  9 10 11   2  3  4  5  6  7  8   5  6  7  8  9 10 11
12 13 14 15 16 17 18   9 10 11 12 13 14 15  12 13 14 15 16 17 18
19 20 21 22 23 24 25  16 17 18 19 20 21 22  19 20 21 22 23 24 25
26 27 28 29 30 31     23 24 25 26 27 28 29  26 27 28 29 30
                      30 31

APRIL                AUGUST               DECEMBER
S  M  T  W  T  F  S   S  M  T  W  T  F  S   S  M  T  W  T  F  S
                  1      1  2  3  4  5  6                  1  2
 2  3  4  5  6  7  8   7  8  9 10 11 12 13   3  4  5  6  7  8  9
 9 10 11 12 13 14 15  14 15 16 17 18 19 20  10 11 12 13 14 15 16
16 17 18 19 20 21 22  21 22 23 24 25 26 27  17 18 19 20 21 22 23
23 24 25 26 27 28 29  28 29 30 31           24 25 26 27 28 29 30
30                                          31
```

2

```
JANUARY              MAY                  SEPTEMBER
S  M  T  W  T  F  S   S  M  T  W  T  F  S   S  M  T  W  T  F  S
    1  2  3  4  5  6      1  2  3  4  5                     1
 7  8  9 10 11 12 13   6  7  8  9 10 11 12   2  3  4  5  6  7  8
14 15 16 17 18 19 20  13 14 15 16 17 18 19   9 10 11 12 13 14 15
21 22 23 24 25 26 27  20 21 22 23 24 25 26  16 17 18 19 20 21 22
28 29 30 31           27 28 29 30 31        23 24 25 26 27 28 29
                                            30

FEBRUARY             JUNE                 OCTOBER
S  M  T  W  T  F  S   S  M  T  W  T  F  S   S  M  T  W  T  F  S
             1  2  3               1  2         1  2  3  4  5  6
 4  5  6  7  8  9 10   3  4  5  6  7  8  9   7  8  9 10 11 12 13
11 12 13 14 15 16 17  10 11 12 13 14 15 16  14 15 16 17 18 19 20
18 19 20 21 22 23 24  17 18 19 20 21 22 23  21 22 23 24 25 26 27
25 26 27 28           24 25 26 27 28 29 30  28 29 30 31

MARCH                JULY                 NOVEMBER
S  M  T  W  T  F  S   S  M  T  W  T  F  S   S  M  T  W  T  F  S
             1  2  3   1  2  3  4  5  6  7               1  2  3
 4  5  6  7  8  9 10   8  9 10 11 12 13 14   4  5  6  7  8  9 10
11 12 13 14 15 16 17  15 16 17 18 19 20 21  11 12 13 14 15 16 17
18 19 20 21 22 23 24  22 23 24 25 26 27 28  18 19 20 21 22 23 24
25 26 27 28 29 30 31  29 30 31              25 26 27 28 29 30

APRIL                AUGUST               DECEMBER
S  M  T  W  T  F  S   S  M  T  W  T  F  S   S  M  T  W  T  F  S
 1  2  3  4  5  6  7            1  2  3  4                     1
 8  9 10 11 12 13 14   5  6  7  8  9 10 11   2  3  4  5  6  7  8
15 16 17 18 19 20 21  12 13 14 15 16 17 18   9 10 11 12 13 14 15
22 23 24 25 26 27 28  19 20 21 22 23 24 25  16 17 18 19 20 21 22
29 30                 26 27 28 29 30 31     23 24 25 26 27 28 29
                                            30 31
```

3

JANUARY
S	M	T	W	T	F	S
		1	2	3	4	5
6	7	8	9	10	11	12
13	14	15	16	17	18	19
20	21	22	23	24	25	26
27	28	29	30	31		

FEBRUARY
S	M	T	W	T	F	S
					1	2
3	4	5	6	7	8	9
10	11	12	13	14	15	16
17	18	19	20	21	22	23
24	25	26	27	28		

MARCH
S	M	T	W	T	F	S
					1	2
3	4	5	6	7	8	9
10	11	12	13	14	15	16
17	18	19	20	21	22	23
24	25	26	27	28	29	30
31						

APRIL
S	M	T	W	T	F	S
	1	2	3	4	5	6
7	8	9	10	11	12	13
14	15	16	17	18	19	20
21	22	23	24	25	26	27
28	29	30				

MAY
S	M	T	W	T	F	S
			1	2	3	4
5	6	7	8	9	10	11
12	13	14	15	16	17	18
19	20	21	22	23	24	25
26	27	28	29	30	31	

JUNE
S	M	T	W	T	F	S
						1
2	3	4	5	6	7	8
9	10	11	12	13	14	15
16	17	18	19	20	21	22
23	24	25	26	27	28	29
30						

JULY
S	M	T	W	T	F	S
	1	2	3	4	5	6
7	8	9	10	11	12	13
14	15	16	17	18	19	20
21	22	23	24	25	26	27
28	29	30	31			

AUGUST
S	M	T	W	T	F	S
				1	2	3
4	5	6	7	8	9	10
11	12	13	14	15	16	17
18	19	20	21	22	23	24
25	26	27	28	29	30	31

SEPTEMBER
S	M	T	W	T	F	S
1	2	3	4	5	6	7
8	9	10	11	12	13	14
15	16	17	18	19	20	21
22	23	24	25	26	27	28
29	30					

OCTOBER
S	M	T	W	T	F	S
		1	2	3	4	5
6	7	8	9	10	11	12
13	14	15	16	17	18	19
20	21	22	23	24	25	26
27	28	29	30	31		

NOVEMBER
S	M	T	W	T	F	S
					1	2
3	4	5	6	7	8	9
10	11	12	13	14	15	16
17	18	19	20	21	22	23
24	25	26	27	28	29	30

DECEMBER
S	M	T	W	T	F	S
1	2	3	4	5	6	7
8	9	10	11	12	13	14
15	16	17	18	19	20	21
22	23	24	25	26	27	28
29	30	31				

4

JANUARY
S	M	T	W	T	F	S
			1	2	3	4
5	6	7	8	9	10	11
12	13	14	15	16	17	18
19	20	21	22	23	24	25
26	27	28	29	30	31	

FEBRUARY
S	M	T	W	T	F	S
						1
2	3	4	5	6	7	8
9	10	11	12	13	14	15
16	17	18	19	20	21	22
23	24	25	26	27	28	

MARCH
S	M	T	W	T	F	S
						1
2	3	4	5	6	7	8
9	10	11	12	13	14	15
16	17	18	19	20	21	22
23	24	25	26	27	28	29
30	31					

APRIL
S	M	T	W	T	F	S
		1	2	3	4	5
6	7	8	9	10	11	12
13	14	15	16	17	18	19
20	21	22	23	24	25	26
27	28	29	30			

MAY
S	M	T	W	T	F	S
				1	2	3
4	5	6	7	8	9	10
11	12	13	14	15	16	17
18	19	20	21	22	23	24
25	26	27	28	29	30	31

JUNE
S	M	T	W	T	F	S
1	2	3	4	5	6	7
8	9	10	11	12	13	14
15	16	17	18	19	20	21
22	23	24	25	26	27	28
29	30					

JULY
S	M	T	W	T	F	S
		1	2	3	4	5
6	7	8	9	10	11	12
13	14	15	16	17	18	19
20	21	22	23	24	25	26
27	28	29	30	31		

AUGUST
S	M	T	W	T	F	S
					1	2
3	4	5	6	7	8	9
10	11	12	13	14	15	16
17	18	19	20	21	22	23
24	25	26	27	28	29	30
31						

SEPTEMBER
S	M	T	W	T	F	S
	1	2	3	4	5	6
7	8	9	10	11	12	13
14	15	16	17	18	19	20
21	22	23	24	25	26	27
28	29	30				

OCTOBER
S	M	T	W	T	F	S
			1	2	3	4
5	6	7	8	9	10	11
12	13	14	15	16	17	18
19	20	21	22	23	24	25
26	27	28	29	30	31	

NOVEMBER
S	M	T	W	T	F	S
						1
2	3	4	5	6	7	8
9	10	11	12	13	14	15
16	17	18	19	20	21	22
23	24	25	26	27	28	29
30						

DECEMBER
S	M	T	W	T	F	S
	1	2	3	4	5	6
7	8	9	10	11	12	13
14	15	16	17	18	19	20
21	22	23	24	25	26	27
28	29	30	31			

5

JANUARY
S	M	T	W	T	F	S
				1	2	3
4	5	6	7	8	9	10
11	12	13	14	15	16	17
18	19	20	21	22	23	24
25	26	27	28	29	30	31

FEBRUARY
S	M	T	W	T	F	S
1	2	3	4	5	6	7
8	9	10	11	12	13	14
15	16	17	18	19	20	21
22	23	24	25	26	27	28

MARCH
S	M	T	W	T	F	S
1	2	3	4	5	6	7
8	9	10	11	12	13	14
15	16	17	18	19	20	21
22	23	24	25	26	27	28
29	30	31				

APRIL
S	M	T	W	T	F	S
			1	2	3	4
5	6	7	8	9	10	11
12	13	14	15	16	17	18
19	20	21	22	23	24	25
26	27	28	29	30		

MAY
S	M	T	W	T	F	S
					1	2
3	4	5	6	7	8	9
10	11	12	13	14	15	16
17	18	19	20	21	22	23
24	25	26	27	28	29	30
31						

JUNE
S	M	T	W	T	F	S
	1	2	3	4	5	6
7	8	9	10	11	12	13
14	15	16	17	18	19	20
21	22	23	24	25	26	27
28	29	30				

JULY
S	M	T	W	T	F	S
			1	2	3	4
5	6	7	8	9	10	11
12	13	14	15	16	17	18
19	20	21	22	23	24	25
26	27	28	29	30	31	

AUGUST
S	M	T	W	T	F	S
						1
2	3	4	5	6	7	8
9	10	11	12	13	14	15
16	17	18	19	20	21	22
23	24	25	26	27	28	29
30	31					

SEPTEMBER
S	M	T	W	T	F	S
		1	2	3	4	5
6	7	8	9	10	11	12
13	14	15	16	17	18	19
20	21	22	23	24	25	26
27	28	29	30			

OCTOBER
S	M	T	W	T	F	S
				1	2	3
4	5	6	7	8	9	10
11	12	13	14	15	16	17
18	19	20	21	22	23	24
25	26	27	28	29	30	31

NOVEMBER
S	M	T	W	T	F	S
1	2	3	4	5	6	7
8	9	10	11	12	13	14
15	16	17	18	19	20	21
22	23	24	25	26	27	28
29	30					

DECEMBER
S	M	T	W	T	F	S
		1	2	3	4	5
6	7	8	9	10	11	12
13	14	15	16	17	18	19
20	21	22	23	24	25	26
27	28	29	30	31		

6

JANUARY
S	M	T	W	T	F	S
					1	2
3	4	5	6	7	8	9
10	11	12	13	14	15	16
17	18	19	20	21	22	23
24	25	26	27	28	29	30
31						

FEBRUARY
S	M	T	W	T	F	S
	1	2	3	4	5	6
7	8	9	10	11	12	13
14	15	16	17	18	19	20
21	22	23	24	25	26	27
28						

MARCH
S	M	T	W	T	F	S
	1	2	3	4	5	6
7	8	9	10	11	12	13
14	15	16	17	18	19	20
21	22	23	24	25	26	27
28	29	30	31			

APRIL
S	M	T	W	T	F	S
				1	2	3
4	5	6	7	8	9	10
11	12	13	14	15	16	17
18	19	20	21	22	23	24
25	26	27	28	29	30	

MAY
S	M	T	W	T	F	S
						1
2	3	4	5	6	7	8
9	10	11	12	13	14	15
16	17	18	19	20	21	22
23	24	25	26	27	28	29
30	31					

JUNE
S	M	T	W	T	F	S
	1	2	3	4	5	
6	7	8	9	10	11	12
13	14	15	16	17	18	19
20	21	22	23	24	25	26
27	28	29	30			

JULY
S	M	T	W	T	F	S
				1	2	3
4	5	6	7	8	9	10
11	12	13	14	15	16	17
18	19	20	21	22	23	24
25	26	27	28	29	30	31

AUGUST
S	M	T	W	T	F	S
1	2	3	4	5	6	7
8	9	10	11	12	13	14
15	16	17	18	19	20	21
22	23	24	25	26	27	28
29	30	31				

SEPTEMBER
S	M	T	W	T	F	S
			1	2	3	4
5	6	7	8	9	10	11
12	13	14	15	16	17	18
19	20	21	22	23	24	25
26	27	28	29	30		

OCTOBER
S	M	T	W	T	F	S
					1	2
3	4	5	6	7	8	9
10	11	12	13	14	15	16
17	18	19	20	21	22	23
24	25	26	27	28	29	30
31						

NOVEMBER
S	M	T	W	T	F	S
	1	2	3	4	5	
6	7	8	9	10	11	12
13	14	15	16	17	18	19
20	21	22	23	24	25	26
27	28	29	30			

DECEMBER
S	M	T	W	T	F	S
			1	2	3	4
5	6	7	8	9	10	11
12	13	14	15	16	17	18
19	20	21	22	23	24	25
26	27	28	29	30	31	

7

JANUARY
S	M	T	W	T	F	S
						1
2	3	4	5	6	7	8
9	10	11	12	13	14	15
16	17	18	19	20	21	22
23	24	25	26	27	28	29
30	31					

MAY
S	M	T	W	T	F	S
1	2	3	4	5	6	7
8	9	10	11	12	13	14
15	16	17	18	19	20	21
22	23	24	25	26	27	28
29	30	31				

SEPTEMBER
S	M	T	W	T	F	S
					1	2	3
4	5	6	7	8	9	10
11	12	13	14	15	16	17
18	19	20	21	22	23	24
25	26	27	28	29	30	

FEBRUARY
S	M	T	W	T	F	S
		1	2	3	4	5
6	7	8	9	10	11	12
13	14	15	16	17	18	19
20	21	22	23	24	25	26
27	28					

JUNE
S	M	T	W	T	F	S
			1	2	3	4
5	6	7	8	9	10	11
12	13	14	15	16	17	18
19	20	21	22	23	24	25
26	27	28	29	30		

OCTOBER
S	M	T	W	T	F	S
						1
2	3	4	5	6	7	8
9	10	11	12	13	14	15
16	17	18	19	20	21	22
23	24	25	26	27	28	29
30	31					

MARCH
S	M	T	W	T	F	S
		1	2	3	4	5
6	7	8	9	10	11	12
13	14	15	16	17	18	19
20	21	22	23	24	25	26
27	28	29	30	31		

JULY
S	M	T	W	T	F	S
					1	2
3	4	5	6	7	8	9
10	11	12	13	14	15	16
17	18	19	20	21	22	23
24	25	26	27	28	29	30
31						

NOVEMBER
S	M	T	W	T	F	S
		1	2	3	4	5
6	7	8	9	10	11	12
13	14	15	16	17	18	19
20	21	22	23	24	25	26
27	28	29	30			

APRIL
S	M	T	W	T	F	S
					1	2
3	4	5	6	7	8	9
10	11	12	13	14	15	16
17	18	19	20	21	22	23
24	25	26	27	28	29	30

AUGUST
S	M	T	W	T	F	S
	1	2	3	4	5	6
7	8	9	10	11	12	13
14	15	16	17	18	19	20
21	22	23	24	25	26	27
28	29	30	31			

DECEMBER
S	M	T	W	T	F	S
				1	2	3
4	5	6	7	8	9	10
11	12	13	14	15	16	17
18	19	20	21	22	23	24
25	26	27	28	29	30	31

8

JANUARY
S	M	T	W	T	F	S
1	2	3	4	5	6	7
8	9	10	11	12	13	14
15	16	17	18	19	20	21
22	23	24	25	26	27	28
29	30	31				

MAY
S	M	T	W	T	F	S
		1	2	3	4	5
6	7	8	9	10	11	12
13	14	15	16	17	18	19
20	21	22	23	24	25	26
27	28	29	30	31		

SEPTEMBER
S	M	T	W	T	F	S
						1
2	3	4	5	6	7	8
9	10	11	12	13	14	15
16	17	18	19	20	21	22
23	24	25	26	27	28	29
30						

FEBRUARY
S	M	T	W	T	F	S
			1	2	3	4
5	6	7	8	9	10	11
12	13	14	15	16	17	18
19	20	21	22	23	24	25
26	27	28	29			

JUNE
S	M	T	W	T	F	S
					1	2
3	4	5	6	7	8	9
10	11	12	13	14	15	16
17	18	19	20	21	22	23
24	25	26	27	28	29	30

OCTOBER
S	M	T	W	T	F	S
	1	2	3	4	5	6
7	8	9	10	11	12	13
14	15	16	17	18	19	20
21	22	23	24	25	26	27
28	29	30	31			

MARCH
S	M	T	W	T	F	S
				1	2	3
4	5	6	7	8	9	10
11	12	13	14	15	16	17
18	19	20	21	22	23	24
25	26	27	28	29	30	31

JULY
S	M	T	W	T	F	S
1	2	3	4	5	6	7
8	9	10	11	12	13	14
15	16	17	18	19	20	21
22	23	24	25	26	27	28
29	30	31				

NOVEMBER
S	M	T	W	T	F	S
				1	2	3
4	5	6	7	8	9	10
11	12	13	14	15	16	17
18	19	20	21	22	23	24
25	26	27	28	29	30	

APRIL
S	M	T	W	T	F	S
1	2	3	4	5	6	7
8	9	10	11	12	13	14
15	16	17	18	19	20	21
22	23	24	25	26	27	28
29	30					

AUGUST
S	M	T	W	T	F	S
			1	2	3	4
5	6	7	8	9	10	11
12	13	14	15	16	17	18
19	20	21	22	23	24	25
26	27	28	29	30	31	

DECEMBER
S	M	T	W	T	F	S
						1
2	3	4	5	6	7	8
9	10	11	12	13	14	15
16	17	18	19	20	21	22
23	24	25	26	27	28	29
30	31					

9

JANUARY
S	M	T	W	T	F	S
	1	2	3	4	5	6
7	8	9	10	11	12	13
14	15	16	17	18	19	20
21	22	23	24	25	26	27
28	29	30	31			

MAY
S	M	T	W	T	F	S
			1	2	3	4
5	6	7	8	9	10	11
12	13	14	15	16	17	18
19	20	21	22	23	24	25
26	27	28	29	30	31	

SEPTEMBER
S	M	T	W	T	F	S
1	2	3	4	5	6	7
8	9	10	11	12	13	14
15	16	17	18	19	20	21
22	23	24	25	26	27	28
29	30					

FEBRUARY
S	M	T	W	T	F	S
				1	2	3
4	5	6	7	8	9	10
11	12	13	14	15	16	17
18	19	20	21	22	23	24
25	26	27	28	29		

JUNE
S	M	T	W	T	F	S
						1
2	3	4	5	6	7	8
9	10	11	12	13	14	15
16	17	18	19	20	21	22
23	24	25	26	27	28	29
30						

OCTOBER
S	M	T	W	T	F	S
		1	2	3	4	5
6	7	8	9	10	11	12
13	14	15	16	17	18	19
20	21	22	23	24	25	26
27	28	29	30	31		

MARCH
S	M	T	W	T	F	S
					1	2
3	4	5	6	7	8	9
10	11	12	13	14	15	16
17	18	19	20	21	22	23
24	25	26	27	28	29	30
31						

JULY
S	M	T	W	T	F	S
	1	2	3	4	5	6
7	8	9	10	11	12	13
14	15	16	17	18	19	20
21	22	23	24	25	26	27
28	29	30	31			

NOVEMBER
S	M	T	W	T	F	S
					1	2
3	4	5	6	7	8	9
10	11	12	13	14	15	16
17	18	19	20	21	22	23
24	25	26	27	28	29	30

APRIL
S	M	T	W	T	F	S
	1	2	3	4	5	6
7	8	9	10	11	12	13
14	15	16	17	18	19	20
21	22	23	24	25	26	27
28	29	30				

AUGUST
S	M	T	W	T	F	S
				1	2	3
4	5	6	7	8	9	10
11	12	13	14	15	16	17
18	19	20	21	22	23	24
25	26	27	28	29	30	31

DECEMBER
S	M	T	W	T	F	S
1	2	3	4	5	6	7
8	9	10	11	12	13	14
15	16	17	18	19	20	21
22	23	24	25	26	27	28
29	30	31				

10

JANUARY
S	M	T	W	T	F	S
		1	2	3	4	5
6	7	8	9	10	11	12
13	14	15	16	17	18	19
20	21	22	23	24	25	26
27	28	29	30	31		

MAY
S	M	T	W	T	F	S
				1	2	3
4	5	6	7	8	9	10
11	12	13	14	15	16	17
18	19	20	21	22	23	24
25	26	27	28	29	30	31

SEPTEMBER
S	M	T	W	T	F	S
				1	2	3
4	5	6	7	8	9	10
11	12	13	14	15	16	17
18	19	20	21	22	23	24
25	26	27	28	29	30	

FEBRUARY
S	M	T	W	T	F	S
					1	2
3	4	5	6	7	8	9
10	11	12	13	14	15	16
17	18	19	20	21	22	23
24	25	26	27	28		

JUNE
S	M	T	W	T	F	S
1	2	3	4	5	6	7
8	9	10	11	12	13	14
15	16	17	18	19	20	21
22	23	24	25	26	27	28
29	30					

OCTOBER
S	M	T	W	T	F	S
			1	2	3	4
5	6	7	8	9	10	11
12	13	14	15	16	17	18
19	20	21	22	23	24	25
26	27	28	29	30	31	

MARCH
S	M	T	W	T	F	S
						1
2	3	4	5	6	7	8
9	10	11	12	13	14	15
16	17	18	19	20	21	22
23	24	25	26	27	28	29
30	31					

JULY
S	M	T	W	T	F	S
		1	2	3	4	5
6	7	8	9	10	11	12
13	14	15	16	17	18	19
20	21	22	23	24	25	26
27	28	29	30	31		

NOVEMBER
S	M	T	W	T	F	S
						1
2	3	4	5	6	7	8
9	10	11	12	13	14	15
16	17	18	19	20	21	22
23	24	25	26	27	28	29
30						

APRIL
S	M	T	W	T	F	S
		1	2	3	4	5
6	7	8	9	10	11	12
13	14	15	16	17	18	19
20	21	22	23	24	25	26
27	28	29	30			

AUGUST
S	M	T	W	T	F	S
					1	2
3	4	5	6	7	8	9
10	11	12	13	14	15	16
17	18	19	20	21	22	23
24	25	26	27	28	29	30
31						

DECEMBER
S	M	T	W	T	F	S
	1	2	3	4	5	6
7	8	9	10	11	12	13
14	15	16	17	18	19	20
21	22	23	24	25	26	27
28	29	30	31			

11

JANUARY

S	M	T	W	T	F	S
			1	2	3	4
5	6	7	8	9	10	11
12	13	14	15	16	17	18
19	20	21	22	23	24	25
26	27	28	29	30	31	

FEBRUARY

S	M	T	W	T	F	S
						1
2	3	4	5	6	7	8
9	10	11	12	13	14	15
16	17	18	19	20	21	22
23	24	25	26	27	28	29

MARCH

S	M	T	W	T	F	S
1	2	3	4	5	6	7
8	9	10	11	12	13	14
15	16	17	18	19	20	21
22	23	24	25	26	27	28
29	30	31				

APRIL

S	M	T	W	T	F	S
			1	2	3	4
5	6	7	8	9	10	11
12	13	14	15	16	17	18
19	20	21	22	23	24	25
26	27	28	29	30		

MAY

S	M	T	W	T	F	S
					1	2
3	4	5	6	7	8	9
10	11	12	13	14	15	16
17	18	19	20	21	22	23
24	25	26	27	28	29	30
31						

JUNE

S	M	T	W	T	F	S
	1	2	3	4	5	6
7	8	9	10	11	12	13
14	15	16	17	18	19	20
21	22	23	24	25	26	27
28	29	30				

JULY

S	M	T	W	T	F	S
			1	2	3	4
5	6	7	8	9	10	11
12	13	14	15	16	17	18
19	20	21	22	23	24	25
26	27	28	29	30	31	

AUGUST

S	M	T	W	T	F	S
						1
2	3	4	5	6	7	8
9	10	11	12	13	14	15
16	17	18	19	20	21	22
23	24	25	26	27	28	29
30	31					

SEPTEMBER

S	M	T	W	T	F	S
		1	2	3	4	5
6	7	8	9	10	11	12
13	14	15	16	17	18	19
20	21	22	23	24	25	26
27	28	29	30			

OCTOBER

S	M	T	W	T	F	S
				1	2	3
4	5	6	7	8	9	10
11	12	13	14	15	16	17
18	19	20	21	22	23	24
25	26	27	28	29	30	31

NOVEMBER

S	M	T	W	T	F	S
1	2	3	4	5	6	7
8	9	10	11	12	13	14
15	16	17	18	19	20	21
22	23	24	25	26	27	28
29	30					

DECEMBER

S	M	T	W	T	F	S
		1	2	3	4	5
6	7	8	9	10	11	12
13	14	15	16	17	18	19
20	21	22	23	24	25	26
27	28	29	30	31		

12

JANUARY

S	M	T	W	T	F	S
				1	2	3
4	5	6	7	8	9	10
11	12	13	14	15	16	17
18	19	20	21	22	23	24
25	26	27	28	29	30	31

FEBRUARY

S	M	T	W	T	F	S
1	2	3	4	5	6	7
8	9	10	11	12	13	14
15	16	17	18	19	20	21
22	23	24	25	26	27	28
29						

MARCH

S	M	T	W	T	F	S
	1	2	3	4	5	6
7	8	9	10	11	12	13
14	15	16	17	18	19	20
21	22	23	24	25	26	27
28	29	30	31			

APRIL

S	M	T	W	T	F	S
				1	2	3
4	5	6	7	8	9	10
11	12	13	14	15	16	17
18	19	20	21	22	23	24
25	26	27	28	29	30	

MAY

S	M	T	W	T	F	S
						1
2	3	4	5	6	7	8
9	10	11	12	13	14	15
16	17	18	19	20	21	22
23	24	25	26	27	28	29
30	31					

JUNE

S	M	T	W	T	F	S
		1	2	3	4	5
6	7	8	9	10	11	12
13	14	15	16	17	18	19
20	21	22	23	24	25	26
27	28	29	30			

JULY

S	M	T	W	T	F	S
				1	2	3
4	5	6	7	8	9	10
11	12	13	14	15	16	17
18	19	20	21	22	23	24
25	26	27	28	29	30	31

AUGUST

S	M	T	W	T	F	S
1	2	3	4	5	6	7
8	9	10	11	12	13	14
15	16	17	18	19	20	21
22	23	24	25	26	27	28
29	30	31				

SEPTEMBER

S	M	T	W	T	F	S
			1	2	3	4
5	6	7	8	9	10	11
12	13	14	15	16	17	18
19	20	21	22	23	24	25
26	27	28	29	30		

OCTOBER

S	M	T	W	T	F	S
					1	2
3	4	5	6	7	8	9
10	11	12	13	14	15	16
17	18	19	20	21	22	23
24	25	26	27	28	29	30
31						

NOVEMBER

S	M	T	W	T	F	S
	1	2	3	4	5	6
7	8	9	10	11	12	13
14	15	16	17	18	19	20
21	22	23	24	25	26	27
28	29	30				

DECEMBER

S	M	T	W	T	F	S
			1	2	3	4
5	6	7	8	9	10	11
12	13	14	15	16	17	18
19	20	21	22	23	24	25
26	27	28	29	30	31	

13

JANUARY

S	M	T	W	T	F	S
					1	2
34	5	6	7	8	9	10
11	12	13	14	15	16	17
18	19	20	21	22	23	24
25	26	27	28	29	30	31

FEBRUARY

S	M	T	W	T	F	S
	1	2	3	4	5	6
7	8	9	10	11	12	13
14	15	16	17	18	19	20
21	22	23	24	25	26	27
28	29					

MARCH

S	M	T	W	T	F	S
		1	2	3	4	5
6	7	8	9	10	11	12
13	14	15	16	17	18	19
20	21	22	23	24	25	26
27	28	29	30	31		

APRIL

S	M	T	W	T	F	S
					1	2
3	4	5	6	7	8	9
10	11	12	13	14	15	16
17	18	19	20	21	22	23
24	25	26	27	28	29	30

MAY

S	M	T	W	T	F	S
1	2	3	4	5	6	7
8	9	10	11	12	13	14
15	16	17	18	19	20	21
22	23	24	25	26	27	28
29	30	31				

JUNE

S	M	T	W	T	F	S
			1	2	3	4
56	7	8	9	10	11	12
13	14	15	16	17	18	19
20	21	22	23	24	25	26
27	28	29	30			

JULY

S	M	T	W	T	F	S
					1	2
3	4	5	6	7	8	9
10	11	12	13	14	15	16
17	18	19	20	21	22	23
24	25	26	27	28	29	30
31						

AUGUST

S	M	T	W	T	F	S
	1	2	3	4	5	6
7	8	9	10	11	12	13
14	15	16	17	18	19	20
21	22	23	24	25	26	27
28	29	30	31			

SEPTEMBER

S	M	T	W	T	F	S
				1	2	3
4	5	6	7	8	9	10
11	12	13	14	15	16	17
18	19	20	21	22	23	24
25	26	27	28	29	30	

OCTOBER

S	M	T	W	T	F	S
						1
2	3	4	5	6	7	8
9	10	11	12	13	14	15
16	17	18	19	20	21	22
23	24	25	26	27	28	29
30	31					

NOVEMBER

S	M	T	W	T	F	S
		1	2	3	4	5
6	7	8	9	10	11	12
13	14	15	16	17	18	19
20	21	22	23	24	25	26
27	28	29	30			

DECEMBER

S	M	T	W	T	F	S
				1	2	3
4	5	6	7	8	9	10
11	12	13	14	15	16	17
18	19	20	21	22	23	24
25	26	27	28	29	30	31

14

JANUARY

S	M	T	W	T	F	S
						1
2	3	4	5	6	7	8
9	10	11	12	13	14	15
16	17	18	19	20	21	22
23	24	25	26	27	28	29
30	31					

FEBRUARY

S	M	T	W	T	F	S
		1	2	3	4	5
6	7	8	9	10	11	12
13	14	15	16	17	18	19
20	21	22	23	24	25	26
27	28	29				

MARCH

S	M	T	W	T	F	S
			1	2	3	4
5	6	7	8	9	10	11
12	13	14	15	16	17	18
19	20	21	22	23	24	25
26	27	28	29	30	31	

APRIL

S	M	T	W	T	F	S
						1
2	3	4	5	6	7	8
9	10	11	12	13	14	15
16	17	18	19	20	21	22
23	24	25	26	27	28	29
30						

MAY

S	M	T	W	T	F	S
	1	2	3	4	5	6
7	8	9	10	11	12	13
14	15	16	17	18	19	20
21	22	23	24	25	26	27
28	29	30	31			

JUNE

S	M	T	W	T	F	S
				1	2	3
4	5	6	7	8	9	10
11	12	13	14	15	16	17
18	19	20	21	22	23	24
25	26	27	28	29	30	

JULY

S	M	T	W	T	F	S
						1
2	3	4	5	6	7	8
9	10	11	12	13	14	15
16	17	18	19	20	21	22
23	24	25	26	27	28	29
30	31					

AUGUST

S	M	T	W	T	F	S
		1	2	3	4	5
6	7	8	9	10	11	12
13	14	15	16	17	18	19
20	21	22	23	24	25	26
27	28	29	30	31		

SEPTEMBER

S	M	T	W	T	F	S
					1	2
3	4	5	6	7	8	9
10	11	12	13	14	15	16
17	18	19	20	21	22	23
24	25	26	27	28	29	30

OCTOBER

S	M	T	W	T	F	S
1	2	3	4	5	6	7
8	9	10	11	12	13	14
15	16	17	18	19	20	21
22	23	24	25	26	27	28
29	30	31				

NOVEMBER

S	M	T	W	T	F	S
			1	2	3	4
5	6	7	8	9	10	11
12	13	14	15	16	17	18
19	20	21	22	23	24	25
26	27	28	29	30		

DECEMBER

S	M	T	W	T	F	S
					1	2
3	4	5	6	7	8	9
10	11	12	13	14	15	16
17	18	19	20	21	22	23
24	25	26	27	28	29	30
31						

The Western Calendar

The calendar is the division of the year into months, weeks, and days, and the method of ordering the years. All early calendars except the ancient Egyptian calendar were lunar. The word 'calendar' comes from the Latin kalendae or calendae, the first day of the month on which, in ancient Rome, solemn proclamation was made of the appearance of the new moon.

The Western or Gregorian calendar derives from the Julian calendar instituted by Julius Caesar in 46 BC. The Julian calendar was adjusted in 1582 by Pope Gregory XIII, who eliminated error caused by the faulty calculation of the length of a year. The 'New Style' Gregorian calendar was only gradually adopted: Britain and its colonies, including America, adopted it in 1752, when the error amounted to 11 days, so that 3 September 1752 became 14 September 1752, and at the same time the beginning of the year was put back from 25 March to 1 January. Russia did not adopt the Gregorian calendar until after the October Revolution of 1917, so that the event (then 25 October) is currently celebrated on 7 November.

Leap years

From year one in the Western calendar, the assumed date of the birth of Jesus, dates are calculated backwards (BC 'before Christ' or BCE 'before the common era') and forwards (AD Latin Anno Domini, 'in the year of the Lord', or CE 'common era'). The lunar month (the period between one new moon and the next) naturally averages 29.5 days, but the Western calendar uses for convenience a calendar month with a complete number of days, 30 or 31 (February has 28). Since this method leaves six extra hours per year, they are normally added to February as a 29th day every fourth year – a leap year. Leap year numbers are divisible by 4, with the exception of century years, which are leap years only if they are divisible by 400.

Millennia

A millennium is a period of 1000 years. The question of which year is the first year of the millennium hinges on the date of the first year AD. The sequence of years going from BC to AD does not include the year 0. The sequence of years runs 3 BC, 2 BC, 1 BC, AD 1, AD 2, AD 3, etc. This means that the first year of the first millennium was AD 1. The one thousandth year was AD 1000 and the first day of the second millennium was in AD 1001. It is thus clear that that start of the new millennium will be 1 January 2001. Year AD 2000 will certainly be celebrated, as is natural for a year with such a round number, but accurately speaking we will be celebrating the last year of the millennium, not the start of the new millennium.

Year Equivalents for Gregorian, Jewish, Islamic, and Hindu Calendars

Gregorian equivalents are given and are AD (Anno Domini).

Jewish[1] (AM)		Islamic[2] (AH)		Hindu[3] (SE)	
5750	30 September 1989–19 September 1990	1410	4 August 1989–23 July 1990	1911	22 March 1989–21 March 1990
5751	20 September 1990–8 September 1991	1411	24 July 1990–12 July 1991	1912	22 March 1990–21 March 1991
5752	9 September 1991–27 September 1992	1412	13 July 1991–1 July 1992	1913	22 March 1991–20 March 1992
5753	28 September 1992–15 September 1993	1413	2 July 1992–20 June 1993	1914	21 March 1992–21 March 1993
5754	16 September 1993–5 September 1994	1414	21 June 1993–9 June 1994	1915	22 March 1993–21 March 1994
5755	6 September 1994–24 September 1995	1415	10 June 1994–30 May 1995	1916	22 March 1994–21 March 1995
5756	25 September 1995–13 September 1996	1416	31 May 1995–18 May 1996	1917	22 March 1995–20 March 1996
5757	14 September 1996–1 October 1997	1417	19 May 1996–8 May 1997	1918	21 March 1996–21 March 1997
5758	2 October 1997–20 September 1998	1418	8 May 1997–27 April 1998	1919	22 March 1997–21 March 1998
5759	21 September 1998–10 September 1999	1419	27 April 1998–16 April 1999	1920	22 March 1998–21 March 1999
5760	11 September 1999–29 September 2000	1420	17 April 1999–5 April 2000	1921	22 March 1999–21 March 2000

[1] Calculated from 3761 BC, said to be the year after the creation of the world. AM = Anno Mundi. Some say that the Jewish calendar as used today was formulated in AD 358 by Rabbi Hillel II; others that this formulation occurred later. A Jewish year may have 12 or 13 months, each of which normally alternates between 29 and 30 days, and may be one of the following six types: Minimal Common 353 days; Regular Common 354 days; Full Common 355 days; Minimal Leap 383 days; Regular Leap 384 days; Full Leap 385 days.

[2] Calculated from AD 622, the year in which the prophet Mohammed went from Mecca to Medina. AH = Anno Hegirae. The years are purely lunar, and consist of 12 months with alternately 29 or 30 days, plus one extra day at the end of the 12th month in each leap year, of which there are 11 in each cycle of 30 years. The Islamic calendar being lunar, each month begins on the day immediately following the first observation of the new moon in the night sky. Owing to the Earth's axial rotation, the time of this observation varies from place to place. New Year's Day, and the first days of all the months, are therefore also subject to variation.

[3] Calculated from AD 78, the beginning of the Saka Era (SE), used alongside Gregorian dates in Government of India publications since 22 March 1957. Other important Hindu eras include: Vikrama Era (58 BC); Kalacuri Era (AD 248); Gupta Era (AD 320); and Harsa Era (AD 606).

MILLENNIUM BUG: PREPARING COMPUTERS FOR THE YEAR 2000

BY SCOTT KIRSNER

Digital Disarray

It sounds like a bad riddle: how will two missing digits create a $600 billion industry when the calendar flips from 1999 to 2000?

Unfortunately, it's not a riddle; it's reality. As the 20th century draws to a close, an expensive computer problem dubbed 'the millennium bug' has emerged. In brief, most computers handle dates using a two-digit shorthand: 98 instead of the four-digit 1998. When presented with a date like 00, they become hopelessly confused. Since they're missing the two digits that indicate what millennium and century the date is in (19 or 20), computers tend to assume that 00 is actually 1900. So they'll either begin making errors of calculation or they'll stop working altogether. Reprogramming them to be capable of comprehending dates in the new millennium is expected to cost as much as $600 billion worldwide.

The origins of the problem are simple. First, the programmers who wrote software in the 1960s for the first generation of commercial mainframe computers were shortsighted. They didn't imagine that the programs they were creating – or the machines they were creating them for – would still be in service in the far-off year of 2000. So they conserved the computers' memory by using a two-digit shorthand for the year. Every byte of memory was precious in those days, and lopping off 19 from dates was an obvious way to save a few bytes here and there.

Banks were among the first institutions to notice the downside to that approach. When they began writing long-term mortgages and approving loans that lasted past 1999, they were forced to confront the millennium bug. But the problem received little widespread attention until the mid-1990s. Technology consultants began writing articles and giving speeches about 'the year 2000 problem'. Business executives began to take notice, and even consumers couldn't ignore the problem when credit card issuers and driver's licence organizations began to renew cards and licences for shorter periods of time, because their systems couldn't handle an expiration date past 1999.

How might businesses and consumers be affected by the millennium bug? Computers, both new and old, in every industry are vulnerable. They might shut down as a result of being asked to process the date 00. Some say that is the best-case scenario, because at least businesses will know something is wrong. Worse would be if computers continued to operate, making numerous date-related errors that would be difficult to identify and fix.

The areas of greatest concern are defence, health care, transportation, telecommunications, financial services, and national and local governments. Technology experts warn of the hazards of air travel if the airline computers can't manage data properly, the danger of hospital stays if the computers that monitor patients go awry, and the possibility of social unrest if the government can't provide services in 2000.

Date Expansion or Windowing?

Fixing the millennium bug is a labour-intensive endeavour. An organization can opt to replace its systems entirely with new ones that can function in the 21st century, or it may pursue one of two basic repair strategies – 'date expansion' or 'windowing'.

Date expansion involves changing the two-digit dates to four. That entails converting all of the data an organization has stored from one format to the other, and reprogramming systems to handle four-digit dates like 2001.

Windowing is considered a simpler, less expensive solution, but it's only a temporary patch. Rather than converting all of a company's data, the windowing approach merely adds logic to a program to help it determine whether a two-digit date belongs in the 20th century or the 21st. Programmers might create a 'window' of time – from 00 to 30, for example – and then instruct the computer to assume that those dates should all be preceded by 20, whereas dates between 31 and 99 should be preceded by 19. But when 2031 rolls around, that hypothetical company would have a new problem on its hands. Windowing assumes that an organization will either replace its older systems before the window of time closes, or reprogram them yet again.

Eradicating the millennium bug is a multi-stage process. An organization must first assess which of its systems will be unable to handle dates in the 21st century. Then, it must convert those systems, either through expansion or windowing. Finally, it has to test the systems to ensure that they will work after the clock ticks past midnight on 31 December, 1999.

Ripple Effects

But even if companies successfully repair their own systems, they're still vulnerable to what has been dubbed 'the ripple effect'. One of their suppliers or customers, or a government regulator, could send them unconverted data and contaminate their systems. Or even worse, a key supplier might be unable to provide services or raw materials as a result of the bug, hamstringing its customers. For those reasons, organizations must make sure that everyone else with whom they do business is solving their own year 2000 problems. Certain sectors of the economy, like the financial services arena, are even coordinating massive, interorganizational tests to make sure that stock exchanges, banks, regulators, and clearing houses will be able to work together in the new millennium.

And waiting in the wings are the lawyers. If software or hardware fails, they'll be scrutinizing contracts to see who is liable. If a conversion project turns out to have been defective, they may bring litigation against the service provider that was contracted to perform the fix. And if a company's stock takes a dive as a result of year 2000-related failures, lawyers may file negligence lawsuits against the Board of Directors. Once litigation and damages are figured into the cost of the millennium bug, some analysts believe the total worldwide cost could skyrocket to as much as $3.6 trillion.

The sudden emergence of the year 2000 problem has created an entire mini-economy. Programmers and technology managers are finding that they can demand and receive higher salaries, computer consultants have more work than they can handle, and software companies have begun to market tools aimed at making assessment, conversion, and testing more efficient. There are dozens of Web sites and books devoted to the problem. The American Stock Exchange has even created an options index that enables investors to speculate on the fortunes of 18 companies selling software or services intended to solve the year 2000 problem.

Few participants in this mini-economy are willing to speculate about the extent to which the world will be affected by the millennium bug. Will 1 January, 2000 arrive without a hitch, or will, as some technology experts predict, the front pages of every major newspaper be filled with stories about date-related computer crises? All that's certain is that programmers and their technology managers won't be among the celebrants on New Year's Eve, 1999; they'll be huddled over their mainframes, fingers crossed.

The Chinese Year

The Chinese year is traditionally divided into 12 lunar months, beginning at the second new moon after the winter solstice. As there is a shortfall of approximately 11 days between the lunar and the solar year, an intercalary month is added every two and a half years. The year is also divided into 24 periods of 15–16 days, according to the movement of the Sun. Both the traditional and, from 1911, the Western calendars are in use in China.

Chinese period	English translation	Chinese period	English translation	Chinese period	English translation
Li Chun	Spring Begins	Mang Zhong	Grain in Ear	Han Lu	Cold Dew
Yu Shui	Rain Water	Xia Zhi	Summer Solstice	Shuang Jiang	Frost Descends
Jing Zhe	Insects Waken	Xiao Shu	Slight Heat	Li Dong	Winter Begins
Chun Fen	Vernal Equinox	Da Shu	Great Heat	Xiao Xue	Little Snow
Qing Ming	Clear and Bright	Li Qiu	Autumn Begins	Da Xue	Heavy Snow
Gu Yu	Grain Rains	Chu Shu	Heat Ends	Dong Zhi	Winter Solstice
Li Xia	Summer Begins	Bai Lu	White Dew	Xiao Han	Little Cold
Xiao Man	Grain Fills	Qui Fen	Autumn Equinox	Da Han	Severe Cold

Months of the Year

Month	Derivation of name	Number of days
January	Janus, Roman god of doorways and beginnings	31
February	Februa, Roman festival of purification	28 (29 in a leap year)
March	Mars, Roman god of war	31
April	Latin *aperire*, 'to open'	30
May	Maia, Roman goddess of spring	31
June	Juno, Roman goddess of marriage	30
July	Julius Caesar, Roman general and dictator	31
August	Augustus, Roman emperor	31
September	Latin *septem*, 'seven'; September was the seventh month of the earliest Roman calendar	30
October	Latin *octo*, 'eight'; October was the eighth month of the earliest Roman calendar	31
November	Latin *novem*, 'nine'; November was the ninth month of the earliest Roman calendar	30
December	Latin *decem*, 'ten'; December was the tenth month of the earliest Roman calendar	31

Month Equivalents for Gregorian, Jewish, Islamic, and Hindu Calendars

Gregorian equivalents to other calendars are given in parentheses; the figures refer to the number of solar days in each month.
(– = not applicable.)

Gregorian (Basis: sun)	Jewish (Basis: combination of solar and lunar cycles)	Islamic[1] (Basis: visibility of the new moon)	Hindu (Basis: moon)
January (31)	Tishri (September–October) (30)	Muharram (30)	Caitra (March–April) (29 or 30)
February (28 or 29)	Heshvan (October–November) (29 or 30)	Safar (29)	Vaisakha (April–May) (29 or 30)
March (31)	Kislev (November–December) (29 or 30)	Rabi I (30)	Jaistha (May–June) (29 or 30)
April (30)	Tebet (December–January) (29)	Rabi II (29)	Asadha (June–July) (29 or 30)
May (31)	Shebat (January–February) (30)	Jumada I (30)	Dvitiya Asadha (certain leap years)
June (30)	Adar (February–March) (29 or 30)	Jumada II (29)	Sravana (July–August) (29 or 30)
July (31)	Adar Sheni (leap years only)	Rajab (30)	Dvitiya Sravana (certain leap years)
August (31)	Nisan (March–April) (29)	Shaban (29)	Bhadrapada (August–September) (29 or 30)
September (30)	Iyar (April–May) (30)	Ramadan (30)	Aswin (September–October) (29 or 30)
October (31)	Sivan (May–June) (30)	Shawwal (29)	Kartik (October–November) (29 or 30)
November (30)	Tammuz (June–July) (29)	Dhu al-Qadah (30)	Agra Hayana (November–December) (29 or 30)
December (31)	Av (July–August) (30)	Dhu al-Hijjah (29 or 30)	Paus (December–January) (29 or 30)
–	Elul (August–September) (29)	–	Magh (January–February) (29 or 30)
–	–	–	Phalgun (February–March) (29 or 30)

[1] These are the months of the Islamic calendar. Their equivalents with the Gregorian calendar vary each year.

National Days of Countries Around the World

This list includes the chief days of national celebration for each nation given; it is not exhaustive.

Country	National day	Country	National day	Country	National day
Afghanistan	19 August	Grenada	7 February	Pakistan	23 March, 14 August
Albania	28 November	Guatemala	15 September	Palau	1 October
Algeria	1 November	Guinea	2 October	Panama	3 November
Andorra	8 September	Guinea-Bissau	24 September	Papua New Guinea	16 September
Angola	11 November	Guyana	23 February, 26 May	Paraguay	14–15 May
Antigua and Barbuda	1 November	Haiti	1 January	Peru	28–29 July
Argentina	25 May	Honduras	15 September	Philippines	12 June
Armenia	21 September	Hungary	15 March, 20 August,	Poland	3 May
Australia	26 January		23 October	Portugal	10 June
Austria	26 October	Iceland	17 June	Qatar	3 September
Azerbaijan	28 May	India	26 January	Romania	1 December
Bahamas	10 July	Indonesia	17 August	Russia	12 June
Bahrain	16 December	Iran	11 February	Rwanda	1 July
Bangladesh	26 March, 16 December	Iraq	8 February, 14 July,	St Kitts and Nevis	19 September
Barbados	30 November		17 July, 8 August	St Lucia	22 February
Belarus	3 July, 27 July	Ireland, Republic of	17 March	St Vincent and	27 October
Belgium	21 July	Israel	–	the Grenadines	
Belize	21 September	Italy	2 June	Samoa	1–3 June
Benin	1 August, 30 November	Jamaica	first Monday in August	San Marino	3 September
Bhutan	17 December	Japan	23 December	São Tomé e Príncipe	12 July
Bolivia	6 August	Jordan	25 May	Saudi Arabia	23 September
Bosnia-Herzegovina	1 March	Kazakhstan	25 October	Senegal	4 April
Botswana	30 September	Kenya	12 December	Seychelles	5 June, 18 June, 29 June
Brazil	7 September	Kiribati	12 July	Sierra Leone	27 April
Brunei	23 February	Korea, North	16 February, 9 September	Singapore	9 August
Bulgaria	3 March	Korea, South	1 March, 15 August	Slovak Republic	1 January, 5 July,
Burkina Faso	4 August, 11 December	Kuwait	25 February		29 August, 1 September
Burundi	1 July	Kyrgyzstan	31 August	Slovenia	25 June, 26 December
Cambodia	9 November	Laos	2 December	Solomon Islands	7 July
Cameroon	20 May	Latvia	18 November	Somalia	1 July
Canada	1 July	Lebanon	22 November	South Africa	27 April
Cape Verde	5 July	Lesotho	4 October	Spain	12 October
Central African	1 December	Liberia	26 July	Sri Lanka	4 February
Republic		Libya	1 September	Sudan	1 January
Chad	13 April, 11 August	Liechtenstein	15 August	Suriname	25 November
Chile	18 September	Lithuania	16 February	Swaziland	6 September
China	1–2 October	Luxembourg	23 June	Sweden	6 June
Colombia	20 July	Macedonia, Former	2 August, 8 September	Switzerland	1 August
Comoros	6 July	Yugoslav Republic of		Syria	17 April
Congo, Democratic	24 November	Madagascar	26 June	Taiwan	10 October
Republic of		Malawi	6 July	Tajikistan	9 September
Congo, Republic	15 August	Malaysia	31 August	Tanzania	26 April
of the		Maldives	26 July	Thailand	5 December
Costa Rica	15 September	Mali	22 September	Togo	13 January
Côte d'Ivoire	7 August, 7 December	Malta	31 March, 7 June,	Tonga	4 June
Croatia	30 May		8 September, 21	Trinidad and	31 August, 24 September
Cuba	1 January		September, 13 December	Tobago	
Cyprus	1 October	Marshall Islands	1 May, 21 October	Tunisia	20 March
Czech Republic	8 May, 6 July, 28 October	Mauritania	28 November	Turkey	29 October
Denmark	16 April, 5 June	Mauritius	12 March	Turkmenistan	27–28 October
Djibouti	27 June	Mexico	16 September	Tuvalu	1 October
Dominica	3 November	Micronesia	–	Uganda	9 October
Dominican Republic	27 February	Moldova	27 August	UK	1 March, 17 March,
Ecuador	10 August	Monaco	19 November		23 April, 30 November
Egypt	23 July	Mongolia	11 July	Ukraine	24 August
El Salvador	15 September	Morocco	3 March	United Arab	2 December
Equatorial Guinea	12 October	Mozambique	25 June	Emirates	
Eritrea	24 May	Myanmar	4 January	Uruguay	25 August
Estonia	24 February	Namibia	21 March	USA	4 July
Ethiopia	2 March, 6 April	Nauru	31 January	Uzbekistan	1 September, 8 December
Fiji	10 October	Nepal	18 February, 28 December	Vanuatu	30 July
Finland	6 December	Netherlands	30 April	Vatican City State[1]	22 October
France	14 July	New Zealand	6 February	Venezuela	5 July
Gabon	17 August	Nicaragua	15 September	Vietnam	1–2 September
Gambia	18 February	Niger	18 December	Yemen	22 May
Georgia	26 May	Nigeria	1 October	Yugoslavia (Serbia	27 April,
Germany	3 October	Norway	17 May	and Montenegro)	29–30 November
Ghana	6 March	Oman	18 November	Zambia	24 October
Greece	25 March			Zimbabwe	18 April

[1] The Vatican City State has as its national holiday the date of the current pope's installation; this date is therefore subject to change.

Saints' Days

January
1 Fulgentius
2 Basil and Gregory of Nazianzus, Macarius of Alexandria, Seraphim of Sarov
3 Geneviève
4 Elizabeth Seton
5 Simeon Stylites
6 Balthasar, Caspar and Melchior
7 Lucian of Antioch, Raymond of Peñafort
8 Gudule, Severinus
9 Hadrian the African, Basilissa
10 Agatho, Marcian
11 Theodosius the Cenobiarch
12 Ailred, Benedict Biscop, Arcadius
13 Hilary of Poitiers
14 Kentigern, Sava, Felix
15 Macarius of Egypt, Maurus, Paul of Thebes
16 Honoratus, Priscilla, Juliana
17 Antony of Egypt
18 Prisca
19 Wulfstan
20 Euthymius, Fabian, Sebastian
21 Agnes, Fructuosus, Meinrad
22 Vincent
23 Ildefonsus
24 Babylas, Francis de Sales
25 Paul, Praejectus
26 Paula, Timothy and Titus
27 Angela Merici
28 Thomas Aquinas
29 Gildas
30 Martina, Bathildis
31 John Bosco

February
1 Bridget (or Bride)
2 Joan de Lestonnac
3 Anskar, Blaise, Werburga
4 Gilbert of Sempringham, Isidore of Pelusium, Phileas, Andrew Corsini
5 Agatha, Avitus
6 Dorothy, Paul Miki and companions, Vedast
7 Theodore the General
8 Jerome Emiliani
9 Teilo, Apollonia
10 Scholastica
11 Benedict of Aniane, Caedmon, Gregory II
12 Meletius, Julian the Hospitaler
13 Agabus, Catherine dei Ricci
14 Cyril and Methodius, Valentine
15 Sigfrid (patron of Sweden)
16 Juliana
17 Fintan
18 Bernadette (in France), Colman, Flavian, Simeon
19 Conrad
20 Wulfric
21 Peter Damian
22 Margaret of Cortona
23 Polycarp
24 Ethelbert
25 Tarasius, Walburga
26 Alexander, Porphyrius
27 Leander
28 Oswald of York and Worcester

March
1 David
2 Chad, Simplicius
3 Ailred, Cunegund
4 Casimir, Adrian
5 Eusebius of Cremona
6 Chrodegang
7 Perpetua and Felicity
8 Felix, John of God, Pontius
9 Frances of Rome, Gregory of Nyssa, Pacian
10 John Ogilvie, Macarius of Jerusalem, Simplicius
11 Constantine, Oengus, Sophronius
12 Gregory (the Great), Maximilian
13 Nicephorus
14 Matilda
15 Clement Hofbauer, Louise de Marillac
16 Heribert
17 Gertrude, Joseph of Arimathea, Patrick
18 Anselm of Lucca, Cyril of Jerusalem, Edward
19 Joseph
20 Cuthbert, Martin of Braga
21 Serapion of Thmuis, Nicholas of Fluë
22 Basil
23 Turibius de Mongrovejo, Gwinear
24 Catherine of Vadstena
25 Dismas, Alfwold
26 Ludger
27 Rupert of Salzburg
28 Gontran
29 Jonah and Berikjesus
30 John Climacus
31 Acacius

April
1 Hugh of Grenoble, Melito
2 Francis of Paola, Mary of Egypt
3 Richard of Chichester
4 Isidore of Seville
5 Vincent Ferrer
6 William of Eskill
7 Hegesippus, John Baptist de la Salle
8 Perpetuus
9 Madrun
10 Fulbert, Hedda
11 Gemma Galgani, Guthlac, Stanislaus
12 Julius I, Zeno
13 Martin I
14 Caradoc, Tiburtius and Valerian
15 Paternus of Wales, Ruadhan
16 Bernadette, Magnus
17 Stephen Harding
18 Apollonius
19 Alphege, Leo IX
20 Agnes of Montepulciano
21 Anastasius, Anselm, Beuno
22 Alexander and Epipodius
23 George
24 Egbert, Fidelis of Sigmaringen, Mellitus
25 Mark
26 Anacletus, Stephen of Perm
27 Zita
28 Peter Chanel, Vitalis and Valeria
29 Catherine of Siena, Hugh of Cluny, Peter Martyr, Robert
30 Pius V

May
1 Asaph, Joseph the Worker
2 Athanasius
3 Philip and James (the Less)
4 Gotthard, Pelagia, Florian
5 Hilary of Arles
6 Edbert
7 John of Beverley
8 Peter of Tarantaise
9 Pachomius
10 Antoninus, John of Avila
11 Mamertus
12 Epiphanius, Nereus and Achilleus, Pancras
13 Andrew Hubert Fournet
14 Matthias
15 Isidore
16 Brendan, John of Nepomuk, Simon Stock
17 Paschal Baylon
18 John I
19 Dunstan, Ivo, Pudens, Pudentiana
20 Bernadino of Siena
21 Andrew Bobola, Collen, Godric
22 Rita of Cascia
23 Ivo of Chartres, Desiderius
24 Vincent of Lérins, David I of Scotland
25 Bede, Gregory VII, Mary Magdalene de Pazzi
26 Philip Neri, Quadratus
27 Augustine of Canterbury
28 Germain of Paris
29 Theodosia
30 Joan of Arc
31 Petronilla

June
1 Justin Martyr, Pamphilus
2 Erasmus, Marcellinus and Peter, Pothinus
3 Charles Lwanga and companions, Clotilde, Kevin
4 Optatus, Petrock
5 Boniface
6 Norbert
7 Paul of Constantinople, Willibald, Meriadoc
8 William of York
9 Columba, Ephraem
10 Landry of Paris
11 Barnabas
12 Leo III
13 Anthony of Padua
14 Methodius, Dogmael
15 Orsisius, Vitus
16 Cyricus and Julitta
17 Alban, Botulph, Rainerius
18 Gregory Barbarigo
19 Gervasius and Protasius, Romuald
20 Alban
21 Albinus of Mainz, Aloysius Gonzaga
22 John Fisher and Thomas More, Nicetas, Paulinus of Nola
23 Etheldreda
24 Birth of John the Baptist
25 Prosper of Aquitaine, Prosper of Reggio
26 John and Paul
27 Cyril of Alexandria, Ladislaus
28 Irenaeus
29 Peter and Paul
30 First Martyrs of the Church of Rome, Martial, Theobald of Provins

July
1 Oliver Plunket
2 Processus and Martinian
3 Anatolius, Thomas
4 Andrew of Crete, Elizabeth of Portugal, Ulrich
5 Anthony Zaccaria   *(continued)*

Saints' Days (*continued*)

6 Maria Goretti
7 Palladius, Pantaenus
8 Kilian, Aquila and Prisca (or Priscilla), Procopius
9 Veronica Giuliani
10 Rufina and Secunda, Seven Brothers
11 Benedict
12 John Gualbert, Veronica
13 Mildred, Silas, Henry the Emperor
14 Camillus of Lellis, Deusdedit
15 Bonaventure, Swithin, Vladimir
16 Eustathius, Helier
17 Ennodius, Leo IV, Marcellina, Alexis
18 Arnulf
19 Macrina, Symmachus, Arsenius
20 Aurelius, Margaret
21 Lawrence of Brindisi, Praxedes
22 Mary Magdalene
23 Apollinaris, Bridget of Sweden
24 Christina the Astonishing
25 Christopher, James (the Great)
26 Anne and Joachim
27 Pantaleon
28 Samson
29 Martha, Lupus, Olaf
30 Peter Chrysologus
31 Germanus, Joseph of Arimathea, Ignatius of Loyola

August
1 Alphonsus Liguori, Ethelwold
2 Eusebius of Vercelli, Stephen I
3 Waldef (or Waltheof)
4 Jean-Baptiste Vianney
5 Afra
6 Justus and Pastor
7 Cajetan, Sixtus II and companions
8 Dominic
9 Romanus
10 Laurence
11 Clare, Susanna
12 Euplius
13 Maximus, Pontian and Hippolytus, Radegunde
14 Maximilian Kolbe
15 Arnulf, Tarsicius
16 Roch, Stephen of Hungary
17 Hyacinth
18 Helena, Agapitus
19 John Eudes, Sebaldus
20 Bernard, Oswin, Philibert
21 Pius X
22 Symphorianus
23 Rose of Lima
24 Bartholomew, Ouen
25 Joseph Calasanctius, Louis IX, Menas of Constantinople
26 Zephyrinus
27 Caesarius, Monica
28 Augustine of Hippo
29 Sabina
30 Pammachius
31 Aidan, Paulinus of Trier

September
1 Giles
2 William of Roskilde
3 Gregory (the Great)
4 Boniface I, Rosalia
5 Bertin, Laurence Giustiniani

6 Cagnoald
7 Sozon
8 Adrian and Natalia
9 Peter Claver
10 Nicholas of Tolentino
11 Deiniol, Paphnutius
12 Ailbe, Eanswida
13 John Chrysostom
14 Notburga
15 Catherine of Genoa
16 Cornelius, Cyprian of Carthage, Euphemia, Ninian
17 Robert Bellarmine, Hildegard, Lambert, Satyrus
18 Joseph of Copertino
19 Januarius, Theodore of Tarsus
20 Agapetus and Eustace
21 Matthew
22 Maurice and his legion
23 Adamnan
24 Pacificus, Gerard
25 Sergius of Rostov
26 Cosmas and Damian, Cyprian of Carthage, John of Meda
27 Vincent de Paul
28 Exuperius, Wenceslaus
29 Michael (Michaelmas Day), Gabriel and Raphael
30 Jerome

October
1 Remigius, Romanus, Teresa of Lisieux
2 Leodegar (or Leger)
3 Thomas de Cantilupe
4 Ammon, Francis of Assisi, Petronius
5 Placid and Maurus
6 Bruno, Faith
7 Justina
8 Triduana
9 Demetrius of Alexandria, Denis and companions, Dionysius of Paris, John Leonardi
10 Francis Borgia, Paulinus of York
11 Bruno (Bishop of Cologne), Nectarius
12 Wilfrid, Ethelburga of Barking
13 Edward the Confessor
14 Callistus I
15 Teresa of Avila
16 Gall, Hedwig, Lullus, Margaret Mary Alacoque
17 Ignatius of Antioch
18 Luke
19 John de Bréboeuf, Isaac Jogues and companions, Paul of the Cross, Peter of Alcántara
20 Acca
21 Hilarion, Ursula
22 Abercius
23 John of Capistrano
24 Anthony Claret
25 Crispin and Crispinian, Forty Martyrs of England and Wales, Gaudentius
26 Bean, Eata, Cedd
27 Frumentius
28 Simon and Jude
29 Narcissus of Jerusalem
30 Serapion of Antioch
31 Wolfgang

November
1 All Saints, Marcel of Paris, Benignus

2 Victorinus
3 Hubert, Malachy, Martin de Porres, Pirminus, Winifred
4 Charles Borromeo, Vitalis and Agricola, Emeric (or Americus)
5 Elizabeth
6 Illtyd, Leonard
7 Willibrord
8 Willehad
9 Theodore the Recruit
10 Justus, Leo I
11 Martin of Tours, Menas of Egypt, Theodore of Studios
12 Josaphat, Nilus the Ascetic
13 Abbo, Nicholas I
14 Dubricius, Gregory Palamas, Laurence O'Toole
15 Albert the Great, Machutus (or Malo)
16 Edmund of Abingdon, Eucherius, Gertrude (the Great), Margaret of Scotland
17 Elizabeth of Hungary, Gregory Thaumaturgus (the Wonderworker), Gregory of Tours, Hugh of Lincoln
18 Odo, Romanus
19 Nerses
20 Edmund the Martyr
21 Gelasius
22 Cecilia
23 Amphilochius, Clement I, Columban, Felicity, Gregory of Agrigentum
24 Chrysogonus
25 Mercurius, Catherine of Alexandria
26 Siricius, John Berchmans
27 Barlam and Josaphat
28 Simeon Metaphrastes, Catherine Labouré
29 Brendan of Birr
30 Andrew

December
1 Eligius (or Eloi)
2 Chromatius
3 Francis Xavier
4 Barbara, John Damascene, Osmund
5 Sabas
6 Nicholas
7 Ambrose
8 Romaric
9 Leocadia, Peter Fourier
10 Miltiades, Eulalia
11 Damasus, Daniel
12 Jane Frances de Chantal, Vicelin
13 Lucy, Odilia
14 John of the Cross, Spyridon
15 Mary di Rosa, Nino, Valerian
16 Adelaide
17 Begga, Lazarus
18 Winebald, Flannan
20 Dominic of Silos
21 Peter Canisius, Thomas
22 Chaeremon
23 John of Kanty
24 Charbel Makhlouf
25 Anastasia
26 Stephen
27 John the Divine, Fabiola
28 The Holy Innocents
29 Thomas à Becket, Trophimus of Arles (or San Tropez)
30 Anysia
31 Sylvester I

Major Religious Festivals

Festival	Normally held	1998	1999	2000	2001
Buddhism					
Theravada (Southern Buddhism) Predominant mainly in Sri Lanka and Southeast Asia.					
New Year Festival Images of the Buddha are bathed in scented water and stupas of sand are built on river banks or in temple grounds to be washed away at New Year, symbolizing the clearing away of negative deeds	beginning of Citta	Apr. 1998	Apr. 1999[1]	Apr. 2000[1]	Apr. 2001[1]
Vesakha Celebrates the Buddha's birth, enlightenment, and passing into nirvana; processions take place in the temple, bodhi trees are sprinkled with scented water, lanterns are lit, and street stalls are erected	full moon of Vesakha	10 May 1998	30 Apr. 1999	18 May 2000	7 May 2001
Asalha Commemorates the Buddha's first sermon and marks the beginning of the three-month rainy season, a period of temple retreat known as Vassa	full moon of Asalha	9 Jul. 1998	28 Jul. 1999	16 Jul. 2000	5 Jul. 2001
Assayuja Celebrates the return of the Buddha from heaven after passing on the teachings to his mother; Assayuja marks the end of Vassa	third full moon of Vassa	Oct. 1998[1]	Oct. 1999[1]	Oct. 2000[1]	Oct. 2001[1]
Kattika Commemorates the first Buddhist missionaries who went out to spread the Buddha's teachings; this is also the date for the end of Vassa if the rains continue longer than usual	full moon of Kattika	Nov. 1998[1]	Nov. 1999[1]	Nov. 2000[1]	Nov. 2001[1]
Kathina Offerings, especially robes, are presented to the monasteries in elaborate ceremonies	end of Vassa	Oct./Nov. 1998[1]	Oct./Nov. 1999[1]	Oct./Nov. 2000[1]	Oct./Nov. 2001[1]
Mahayana/East (Eastern Buddhism) (Predominant mainly in China, Taiwan, Korea, and Japan.)					
Birth of the Buddha Images of the Buddha as a child are bathed in scented water or tea, and offerings are made at temples and shrines	eighth day of the fourth lunar month	8 Apr. 1998 (Japan)	8 Apr. 1999 (Japan)	8 Apr. 2000 (Japan)	8 Apr. 2001 (Japan)
Birth of Kuan Yin The Bodhisattva of Mercy; offerings and prayers are made to her by those who seek help in times of need	19th day of second lunar month	Feb./Mar. 1998	Feb./Mar. 1999[1]	Feb./Mar. 2000[1]	Feb./Mar. 2001[1]
Enlightenment of Kuan Yin	19th day of sixth lunar month	Jun./Jul. 1998	Jun./Jul. 1999[1]	Jun./Jul. 2000[1]	Jun./Jul. 2001[1]
Death of Kuan Yin	19th day of ninth lunar month	Sept./Oct. 1998	Sept./Oct. 1999[1]	Sept./Oct. 2000[1]	Sept./Oct. 2001[1]
Hungry Ghost Festival Unsettled spirits of the dead are calmed with chanting and offerings to enable them to pass peacefully into the next world	8–15th days of the Chinese seventh lunar month	Jul./Aug. 1998	Jul./Aug. 1999[1]	Jul./Aug. 2000[1]	Jul./Aug. 2001[1]
O-Bon Families reunite to remember and honour their ancestors; offerings are made to the Buddha and monks visit home shrines to read Buddhist scriptures	13–15 Jul. (Japan)	13–15 Jul. 1998 (Japan)	13–15 Jul. 1999 (Japan)	13–15 Jul. 2000 (Japan)	13–15 Jul. 2001 (Japan)
Mahayana/North (Northern Buddhism) (Predominant mainly in Tibet, Nepal, Bhutan, Mongolia, parts of western China, southern Siberia, and northern India.)					
Tibetan New Year Houses are cleaned to sweep away any negative aspects from the last year; costumed monks perform new year rituals and chants; people light firecrackers or torches to chase away the spirits	new moon of Feb.	27 Feb. 1998	17 Feb. 1999	6 Feb. 2000	25 Jan. 2001
Modlam Chenmo The Great Prayer Festival is celebrated with traditional stories, puppet shows, and butter sculptures in the monasteries	8–15th of the first lunar month	Feb. 1998	Feb. 1999[1]	Feb. 2000[1]	Feb. 2001[1]
The Buddha's Enlightenment and Passing into Nirvana Pilgrims visit monasteries to make offerings; traditional Chan dancing is performed	15th day of the fourth lunar month	May 1998	May 1999[1]	May 2000[1]	May 2001[1]
Guru Rinpoche's Birthday Commemorates the Indian teacher who helped establish Buddhist teachings in Tibet towards the end of the 8th century AD	tenth day of the sixth lunar month	Jul. 1998	Jul. 1999[1]	Jul. 2000[1]	Jul. 2001[1]
Chokhor Duchen Celebrates the Buddha's first sermon after his enlightenment	fourth day of the sixth lunar month	Jul. 1998	Jul. 1999[1]	Jul. 2000[1]	Jul. 2001[1]

(continued)

Major Religious Festivals (*continued*)

Festival	Normally held	1998	1999	2000	2001
Lhabab Duchen Commemorates the descent of the Buddha from heaven after giving the teachings to his mother	22nd day of the ninth lunar month	Oct. 1998[1]	Oct. 1999[1]	Oct. 2000[1]	Oct. 2001[1]
Christianity [2]					
Christmas Day Celebration of the birth of Jesus in Bethlehem; Christians meet for worship, often at midnight, when the events are retold through words, music, drama, and pictures		25 Dec. 1998	25 Dec. 1999	25 Dec. 2000	25 Dec. 2001
Epiphany Celebrates the arrival of the three wise men from the east who came looking for a newborn king and were led by a bright star to Bethlehem; they brought Jesus gifts of gold, frankincense, and myrrh		6 Jan. 1998	6 Jan. 1999	6 Jan. 2000	6 Jan. 2001
Ash Wednesday In many churches, people come forward to be marked with ashes, an ancient symbol of sorrow and repentance; Lent is a time of reflection and fasting which recalls the 40 days Jesus spent fasting and praying in the desert	start of Lent (six weeks before Easter)	25 Feb. 1998	17 Feb. 1999	8 Mar. 2000	28 Feb. 2001
Palm Sunday Christians recall Jesus's entry into Jerusalem during the last week of his life, when he was welcomed by people waving palm fronds; other important days of Holy Week are Maundy Thursday, when Jesus shared the last supper with his disciples, and Good Friday, when he was crucified	start of Holy Week (one week before Easter)	5 Apr. 1998	28 Mar. 1999	16 Apr. 2000	8 Apr. 2001
Easter Sunday Time of rejoicing that recalls the disciples' discovery that Jesus was alive, and that he had been resurrected; many churches keep a vigil throughout Saturday night so that they can greet Easter Day with services, family meals, and the exchange of flowers and eggs	between 23 Mar. and 24 Apr. in the Roman Catholic and Protestant churches	12 Apr. 1998	4 Apr. 1999	23 Apr. 2000	15 Apr. 2001
Ascension Day This day commemorates the disciples witnessing Jesus being lifted up to heaven 40 days after Easter Day	40 days after Easter	21 May 1998	13 May 1999	1 Jun. 2000	24 May 2001
Pentecost or Whitsun When Jesus left his disciples for the last time after his resurrection, he promised them a 'comforter' who would be with them forever; Pentecost celebrates the coming of the Holy Spirit upon the disciples	seventh Sunday after Easter	31 May 1998	23 May 1999	11 Jun. 2000	3 Jun. 2001
Hinduism					
Mahashivaratri 'Great Night of Shiva' when Shiva, his wife Parvati, and their child Ganesh are honoured; offerings are made to Shiva between midnight and sunrise and the 24-hour fast is broken at dawn	13th or 14th day of dark half of Magh	25 Feb. 1998	15 Feb. 1999	4 Mar. 2000	21 Feb. 2001
Sarasvati Puja Sarasvati, the patron of the arts and learning, is celebrated with music and by wearing yellow clothes, symbolizing the warmth of spring	first day of spring season (Phalgun)	Feb./Mar. 1998	Feb./Mar. 1999[1]	Feb./Mar. 2000[1]	Feb./Mar. 2001[1]
Holi The pranks that Krishna played as a child are celebrated, and the story of Prahalad, a prince who was willing to sacrifice himself for Vishnu, is remembered; offerings are made around bonfires and coloured water or powder is sprayed in high-spirited games	full moon day of Phalgun	14 Mar. 1998	3 Mar. 1999	21 Mar. 2000	10 Mar. 2001
Rama Naumi Celebrates the birthday of the god Rama, hero of the epic Ramayana that is recited during the festival; offerings are also made in temples to a statue of the baby Rama	ninth day of the bright half of Caitra	5 Apr. 1998[3]	25 Mar. 1999[3]	12 Apr. 2000[3]	2 Apr. 2001[3]
Ratha Yatra A statue of Vishnu, also called Jagganath, Lord of the Universe, is placed on a large wooden chariot and pulled through the streets where lamps, flowers, and other offerings are laid in his path	16th day of Asadha	7 Jul. 1998	Jun./Jul. 1999[1]	Jun./Jul. 2000[1]	Jun./Jul. 2001[1]
Raksha Bandhan Sisters tie rakhis, silk threads decorated with flowers, onto their brothers' wrists as a symbol of protection	full moon day of Sravana	8 Aug. 1998	26 Aug. 1999	15 Aug. 2000	4 Aug. 2001

Major Religious Festivals (*continued*)

Festival	Normally held	1998	1999	2000	2001
Janmashtarni The birth of Krishna is celebrated as an image of the child Krishna is washed with yoghurt, ghee, honey, and milk, and then placed on a swing	eighth day of Bhadrapada	14 Aug. 1998	2 Sept. 1999	22 Aug. 2000	12 Aug. 2001
Navaratri Dusshera The festival of Dusshera follows immediately after Navaratri; over nine nights different manifestations of the goddess Durga are honoured; in the form of Durga she is the destroyer of evil, as Kali she is the destroyer of time, and as Parvati she is the faithful wife of Shiva; at Dusshera, an effigy of the demon Ravana is burnt to celebrate Durga's power over demons	first ten days of the bright half of Aswin	1 Oct. 1998	19 Oct. 1999	7 Oct. 2000	26 Oct. 2001
Divali Accounts are settled at this time and worship is given to Lakshmi, goddess of wealth and good fortune; coloured patterns are made on the ground; windows are illuminated with lamps and candles; this festival also celebrates the return of Rama and Sita from exile, a story told in the Ramayana	13th day of the dark half of Aswin	19 Oct. 1998	7 Nov. 1999	26 Oct. 2000	14 Nov. 2001
Islam *Islamic years* (AH) AH = Anno Hegirae, the Muslim era. The Islamic calendar is entirely lunar, and unlike most other lunar calendars, is not adjusted to keep in step with the solar year.[4]		*1419*	*1420*	*1421*	*1422*
Festival of Ashura Festival commemorating both the escape of the Israelites from Egypt, and also the day Noah's ark touched ground after the flood; in Shi'a Islam, Ashura also celebrates the martyrdom of Ali	10 Muharram	7 May 1998	26 Apr. 1999	15 Apr. 2000	4 Apr. 2001[3]
Ramadan This month of fasting is one of the Five Pillars of Islam, when adult Muslims refrain from drinking, eating, smoking, and conjugal relations from dawn until dusk	ninth month of the year	20 Dec. 1998	9 Dec. 1999	27 Nov. 2000	17 Nov. 2001[3]
The Night of Power–Lailat ul Qadr During the last ten days of Ramadan many Muslims spend time praying in the mosque since prayers made on the Night of Power are said to be 'better than a thousand months'	around 27 Ramadan	25 Jan. 1998	14 Jan. 1999	3 Jan. 2000	3 Dec. 2001[3]
Eid ul-Fitr Important time of communal prayer and celebration when families and friends gather to share special foods and exchange gifts	end of Ramadan, heralded by the sight of a new moon	30 Jan. 1998	19 Jan. 1999	8 Jan. 2000	16 Dec. 2001[3]
Pilgrimage to Mecca In the Five Pillars of Islam, this is the most important time, but only those who have sufficient finances and are physically able are expected to make the journey	8–13 Dhu al-Hijjah	6–11 Apr. 1998	26–31 Mar. 1999	14–19 Mar. 2000	Apr. 2001[1]
Eid-ul-Adha The willingness of the prophet Ibrahim to sacrifice his son Ishmael is remembered; at God's command a lamb was sacrificed instead, an act commemorated at this time in the sacrifice of a lamb or goat	10 Dhu al-Hijjah	7 Apr. 1998	28 Mar. 1999	16 Mar. 2000[3]	6 Mar. 2001[3]
Birthday of the Prophet Mohammed (Milad-un-Nabi) The scale of celebrations varies according to country; for example, thousands of pilgrims gather on Lamu island off the coast of Kenya for processions, speeches, and prayers	month of Rabi I	7 Jul. 1998	26 Jun. 1999	15 Jun. 2000	4 Jun. 2001
Judaism *Jewish years* (AM) Jewish year AM = Anno Mundi; runs from September to August		*5759*	*5760*	*5761*	*5762*
Rosh Hashanah Jewish New Year, a ten-day period of repentance leading up to Yom Kippur	1 Tishri	21–22 Sept. 1998	11–12 Sept. 1999	30 Sept.–1 Oct. 2000	18–19 Sept. 2001
Yom Kippur Day of Atonement, a time when Jews seek forgiveness of those who have been wronged; also the major fast of the year	10 Tishri	30 Sept. 1998	20 Sept. 1999	9 Oct. 2000	27 Sept. 2001
Succoth Feast of Tabernacles, a time when families build and eat in open-air shelters in commemoration of the temporary desert shelters built by the Israelites during their journey to the Promised Land	15–23 Tishri	5–13 Oct. 1998	25 Sept.–3 Oct. 1999	14–22 Oct. 2000	2–10 Oct. 2001

(continued)

Major Religious Festivals (*continued*)

Festival	Normally held	1998	1999	2000	2001
Simhat Torah End of Succoth and the end of the annual reading of the Torah, which is processed around the synagogue on this day	24 Tishri	13 Oct. 1998	3 Oct. 1999	22 Oct. 2000	10 Oct. 2001
Hanukkah Dedication of the Temple, a time when the eight-branched Hanukkah candle is lit commemorating the rededication of the Temple in Jerusalem in the 2nd century BC, when the Temple lamp miraculously stayed alight for ten days, even though there was only enough oil to last one day	25 Kislev–3 Tebet	14 Dec. 1998	4 Dec. 1999	22 Dec. 2000	30 Nov. 2001
Purim Celebration of the story of Esther who saved her people from destruction at the hands of Haman; the congregation dress in unusual clothes for the synagogue service and boo when Haman's name is read out from the scrolls of Esther	14 Adar	12 Mar. 1998	2 Mar. 1999	21 Mar. 2000	9 Mar. 2001
Pesach Passover, celebrating God's deliverance of the Israelites from captivity in Egypt; families gather for the first evening of the festival to share the Seder meal, which recalls in words and symbols the departure of the Israelites from Egypt	15–22 Nisan	11–18 Apr. 1998	1–8 Apr. 1999	20–27 Apr. 2000	8–15 Apr. 2001
Shavuot Also known as the Pentecost or the Feast of Weeks, this is both a harvest festival and a thanksgiving for the gift of Torah to Moses on Mount Sinai	6–7 Sivan	31 May–1 Jun. 1998	21–22 May 1999	9–10 Jun. 2000	28–29 May 2001
Tishah B'Av This date recalls the disasters that have befallen the Jewish people, including the destruction of the first and second temples in Jerusalem; it is also a time to mourn the events of the Holocaust	9 Av	2 Aug. 1998	22 Jul. 1999	10 Aug. 2000	29 Jul. 2001
Sikhism					
Baisakhi Commemorates the founding of the Order of the Khalsa in 1699, the community of committed Sikhs who undertake to uphold their faith and defend the weak; it is the usual time for Sikhs to join the Khalsa	13 Apr. (occasionally on the 14 Apr.), first day of the solar month of Baisākh (Sanskrit Vaiśakha)	13 Apr. 1998	14 Apr. 1999	13 Apr. 2000	Apr. 2001[1]
Martyrdom of the Guru Arjan Dev Time of celebration and sorrow when Sikhs remember those who have suffered for their faith; there is a continuous reading of the Guru Granth Sahib in the gurdwara	fourth Jaistha	29 May 1998	17 Jun. 1999	5 Jun. 2000	Jun. 2001[1]
Divali Divali lamps are lit at home, and the release from prison of Guru Hargobind is commemorated	second day of Kartik	19 Oct. 1998	7 Nov. 1999	26 Oct. 2000	Oct. 2001[1]
Guru Nanak's Birthday Colourful street processions are held and hymns honouring Guru Gobind Singh (1469–1539), the founder of the Khalsa, are sung in the gurdwara	full moon day of Kartik	4 Nov. 1998[5]	23 Nov. 1999[5]	11 Nov. 2000[5]	Nov. 2001[1][5]
Hola Mohalla Falls at the same time as the Hindu festival of Holi; celebrated with games and pranks; sporting contests take place as well as religious congregations, political conferences, pilgrimages, and administration of baptism	starting a day earlier and finishing a day later than Holi; full moon day of Phalgun	13–15 Mar. 1998	2–4 Mar. 1999	20–22 Mar. 2000	9–11 Mar. 2001

[1] Date unknown.

[2] The calendar reform by pope Gregory XIII in 1582 was rejected by the Orthodox Church. Since 1923, the Orthodox Church has been divided over the calendar. The Greek Church adopted the new calendar except the days that depend on Easter. Others (mostly Slavic) have retained the Julian calendar and therefore remain 13 days behind in their dating (Christmas: 7 Jan., New Year: 14 Jan.).

[3] Unconfirmed.

[4] Some dates are approximate and some are not yet known by the relevant authorities; this applies particularly to movable feasts, based on lunar reckonings.

[5] Date AD varies from year to year in accordance with traditional dates of the Indian Calendar (Bikrami Sambat); often falls in November.

Signs of the Zodiac

The dates for the Sun moving into each constellation are based on Greenwich Mean Time (GMT).

Sign	Symbol	1999	Sign	Symbol	1999	Sign	Symbol	1999
Aries		21 March–20 April	Leo		23 July–23 August	Sagittarius		22 November–22 December
Taurus		20 April–21 May	Virgo		23 August–23 September	Capricorn		22 December–20 January
Gemini		21 May–21 June	Libra		23 September–23 October	Aquarius		20 January–19 February
Cancer		21 June–23 July	Scorpio		23 October–22 November	Pisces		19 February–21 March

The Chinese Zodiac Characteristics

 **Rat** charming, quick-witted, loves company, spendthrift

 **Buffalo/ox** calm, dependable, self-contained, a leader, but stubborn and inclined to shift blame onto others

 **Tiger** thoughtful, strong, brave, dynamic, and imaginative, but inclined to be rash and touchy

 **Cat/rabbit/hare** methodical, cautious, comfort-loving, tactful and lucky, but also gossipy and moody

 **Dragon** eccentric, self-confident, dynamic, perfectionist, highly sexd and loyal, but proud and incapable of routine

 **Dog** honest, loyal, idealistic, but a fault-finder who needs to be led

 **Snake** attractive and wise, but can be possessive and conceited

 **Horse** sociable and likeable, sporty, practical and logical, but can be prejudiced and intolerant

 **Goat/sheep** harmony-loving, humorous, easy to get on with, but impressionable and easily lead

 **Monkey** intelligent, fast-talking and good with figures, but insecure and sometimes superficial

 **Rooster** hard-working, great organizers, punctual, competitive but either very thrifty or very wasteful

 **Pig** well-mannered, industrious, domesticated, but obstinate, egocentric, and bad at planning

Wedding Anniversaries

In many Western countries, wedding anniversaries have become associated with gifts of different materials. There is variation between countries.

Anniversary	Material	Anniversary	Material	Anniversary	Material
1st	cotton	10th	tin	35th	coral
2nd	paper	11th	steel	40th	ruby
3rd	leather	12th	silk, fine linen	45th	sapphire
4th	fruit, flowers	13th	lace	50th	gold
5th	wood	14th	ivory	55th	emerald
6th	sugar, iron	15th	crystal	60th	diamond
7th	wool	20th	china	70th	platinum
8th	bronze, electrical appliances	25th	silver		
9th	copper, pottery	30th	pearl		

Days of the Week

The names of the days are based on the seven heavenly bodies used in traditional astrology (the Sun, the Moon, Mars, Mercury, Jupiter, Venus, and Saturn). These bodies were believed at the time (between 1100–1500) to revolve around the Earth and influence its events. The seven-day week became part of the Roman calendar in AD 321.

English	Latin	Saxon	German	French	Italian	Spanish
Sunday	Dies Solis	Sunnandaeg – Sun's Day	Sonntag	dimanche	domenica	domingo
Monday	Dies Lunae	Mōnandaeg – Moon's Day	Montag	lundi	lunedì	lunes
Tuesday	Dies Martis	Tiwesdaeg – Tiw's Day[1]	Dienstag	mardi	martedì	martes
Wednesday	Dies Mercurii	Wōdnesdaeg – Woden's[2] Day	Mittwoch	mercredi	mercoledì	miércoles
Thursday	Dies Jovis	Thunresdaeg – Thor's Day[3]	Donnerstag	jeudi	giovedì	jueves
Friday	Dies Veneris	Frigedaeg – Frigg's Day[4]	Freitag	vendredi	venerdì	viernes
Saturday	Dies Saturni	Saetern-daeg – Saturn's Day	Samstag	samedi	sabato	sábado

[1] Tiw: Anglo-Saxon name for Nordic Tyr, son of Odin and god of war, closest to Mars (Greek Ares), son of Roman god Jupiter (Greek Zeus).
[2] Woden: Anglo-Saxon name for Odin, Nordic dispenser of victory, closest to Mercury (Greek Hermes), Roman messenger of victory.
[3] Thor: Nordic god of thunder, eldest son of Odin, closest to Roman Jupiter (Greek Zeus).
[4] Frigg (or Freyja): wife of Odin, the Nordic goddess of love, equivalent to Venus (Greek Aphrodite).

Birth Flowers

Month	Flower
January	carnation, snowdrop
February	primrose, violet
March	jonquil, violet
April	daisy, sweet pea
May	hawthorn, lily of the valley
June	honeysuckle, rose
July	larkspur, water lily
August	gladiolus, poppy
September	aster, morning glory
October	calendula, cosmos
November	chrysanthemum
December	holly, narcissus, poinsettia

Birthstones

Month	Stone	Quality
January	garnet	constancy
February	amethyst	sincerity
March	aquamarine, bloodstone	courage
April	diamond	innocence
May	emerald	love
June	alexandrite, pearl	health and purity
July	ruby	contentment
August	peridot, sardonyx	married happiness
September	sapphire	clear thinking
October	opal, tourmaline	hope
November	topaz	fidelity
December	turquoise, zircon	wealth

WEIGHTS, MEASURES, AND NUMBERS

Weights and Measures

Units in the Metric System

Length

1 centimetre	= 10 millimetres	
1 decimetre	= 10 centimetres	= 100 millimetres
1 metre	= 10 decimetres	= 1,000 millimetres
1 decametre	= 10 metres	
1 hectometre	= 10 decametres	= 100 metres
1 kilometre	= 10 hectometres	= 1,000 metres

Area

1 square centimetre	= 100 square millimetres	
1 square metre	= 10,000 square centimetres	= 1,000,000 square millimetres
1 are	= 100 square metres	
1 hectare	= 100 ares	= 10,000 square metres
1 square kilometre	= 100 hectares	= 1,000,000 square metres

Mass (avoirdupois)

1 centigram	= 10 milligrams	
1 decigram	= 10 centigrams	= 100 milligrams
1 gram	= 10 decigrams	= 1,000 milligrams
1 decagram	= 10 grams	
1 hectogram	= 10 decagrams	= 100 grams
1 kilogram	= 10 hectograms	= 1,000 grams
1 metric ton	= 1,000 kilograms	

Volume

1 cubic centimetre	= 1,000 cubic millimetres	
1 cubic decimetre	= 1,000 cubic centimetres	= 1,000,000 cubic millimetres
1 cubic metre	= 1,000 cubic decimetres	= 1,000,000,000 cubic millimetres

Capacity

1 centilitre	= 10 millilitres	
1 decilitre	= 10 centilitres	= 100 millilitres
1 litre	= 10 decilitres	= 1,000 millilitres
1 decalitre	= 10 litres	
1 hectolitre	= 10 decalitres	= 100 litres
1 kilolitre	= 10 hectolitres	= 1,000 litres

Units in the Imperial System

Length

1 foot	= 12 inches
1 yard	= 3 feet
1 rod	= $5\frac{1}{2}$ yards (= $16\frac{1}{2}$ feet)
1 chain	= 4 rods (= 22 yards)
1 furlong	= 10 chains (= 220 yards)
1 mile	= 5,280 feet
1 mile	= 1,760 yards
1 mile	= 8 furlongs

Nautical

1 fathom	= 6 feet
1 cable length	= 120 fathoms
1 nautical mile	= 6,076 feet

Area

1 square foot	= 144 square inches
1 square yard	= 9 square feet
1 square rod	= $30\frac{1}{4}$ square yards
1 acre	= 4 roods
1 acre	= 4,840 square yards
1 square mile	= 640 acres

Volume

1 cubic foot	= 1,728 cubic inches
1 cubic yard	= 27 cubic feet
1 bulk barrel	= 5.8 cubic feet

Shipping

| 1 register ton | = 100 cubic feet |

Capacity

1 fluid ounce	= 8 fluid drams
1 gill	= 5 fluid ounces
1 pint	= 4 gills
1 quart	= 2 pints
1 gallon	= 4 quarts
1 peck	= 2 gallons
1 bushel	= 4 pecks
1 quarter	= 8 bushels
1 bulk barrel	= 36 gallons

Weight (avoirdupois)

1 ounce	= $437\frac{1}{2}$ grains
1 ounce	= 16 drams
1 pound	= 16 ounces
1 stone	= 14 pounds
1 quarter	= 28 pounds
1 hundredweight	= 4 quarters
1 ton	= 20 hundredweight

Imperial and Metric Conversion Factors

To convert from imperial to metric	Multiply by	To convert from metric to imperial	Multiply by
Length			
inches	25.4	millimetres	0.0393701
feet	0.3048	metres	3.28084
yards	0.9144	metres	1.09361
furlongs	0.201168	kilometres	4.97097
miles	1.609344	kilometres	0.621371
Area			
square inches	6.4516	square centimetres	0.1550
square feet	0.092903	square metres	10.7639
square yards	0.836127	square metres	1.19599
square miles	2.589988	square kilometres	0.386102
acres	4046.856422	square metres	0.000247
acres	0.404866	hectares	2.469955
Volume/capacity			
cubic inches	16.387064	cubic centimetres	0.061024
cubic feet	0.028317	cubic metres	35.3147
cubic yards	0.764555	cubic metres	1.30795
cubic miles	4.1682	cubic kilometres	0.239912
fluid ounces (imperial)	28.413063	millilitres	0.035195
fluid ounces (US)	29.5735	millilitres	0.033814
pints (imperial)	0.568261	litres	1.759754
pints (US)	0.473176	litres	2.113377
quarts (imperial)	1.136523	litres	0.879877
quarts (US)	0.946353	litres	1.056688
gallons (imperial)	4.54609	litres	0.219969
gallons (US)	3.785412	litres	0.364172
Mass/weight			
ounces	28.349523	grams	0.035274
pounds	0.453592	kilograms	2.20462
stone (14 lb)	6.350293	kilograms	0.157473
tons (imperial)	1016.046909	kilograms	0.000984
tons (US)	907.18474	kilograms	0.001102
tons (imperial)	1.016047	metric tonnes	0.984207
tons (US)	0.907185	metric tonnes	1.10231
Speed			
miles per hour	1.609344	kilometres per hour	0.621371
feet per second	0.3048	metres per second	3.28084
Force			
pound-force	4.44822	newton	0.224809
kilogram-force	9.80665	newton	0.101972
Pressure			
pound-force per square inch	6.89476	kilopascals	0.145038
tons-force per square inch (imperial)	15.4443	megapascals	0.064779
atmospheres	10.1325	newtons per square centimetre	0.098692
atmospheres	14.695942	pound-force per square inch	0.068948
Energy			
calorie	4.1868	joule	0.238846
watt hour	3,600	joule	0.000278
Power			
horsepower	0.7457	kilowatts	1.34102
Fuel consumption			
miles per gallon (imperial)	0.3540	kilometres per litre	2.824859
miles per gallon (US)	0.4251	kilometres per litre	2.3521
gallons per mile (imperial)	2.824859	litres per kilometre	0.3540
gallons per mile (US)	2.3521	litres per kilometre	0.4251

SI Units

(French *Système International d'Unités*) A standard system of scientific units used by scientists worldwide.

Originally proposed in 1960, it replaces the m.k.s. (metre, kilogram, second), c.g.s. (centimetre, gram, second), and f.p.s. (foot, pound, second) systems. It is based on seven basic units: the metre (m) for length, kilogram (kg) for mass, second (s) for time, ampere (A) for electrical current, kelvin (K) for temperature, mole (mol) for amount of substance, and candela (cd) for luminosity.

Quantity	SI unit	Symbol
absorbed radiation dose	gray	Gy
amount of substance	mole*	mol
electric capacitance	farad	F
electric charge	coulomb	C
electric conductance	siemens	S
electric current	ampere*	A
energy or work	joule	J
force	newton	N
frequency	hertz	Hz
illuminance	lux	lx
inductance	henry	H
length	metre*	m
luminous flux	lumen	lm
luminous intensity	candela*	cd
magnetic flux	weber	Wb
magnetic flux density	tesla	T
mass	kilogram*	kg
plane angle	radian	rad
potential difference	volt	V
power	watt	W
pressure	pascal	Pa
radiation dose equivalent	sievert	Sv
radiation exposure	roentgen	R
radioactivity	becquerel	Bq
resistance	ohm	Ω
solid angle	steradian	sr
sound intensity	decibel	dB
temperature	°Celsius	°C
temperature, thermodynamic	kelvin*	K
time	second*	s

* SI base unit.

SI Prefixes

Multiple	Prefix	Symbol	Example
1,000,000,000,000,000,000 (10^{18})	exa-	E	Eg (exagram)
1,000,000,000,000,000 (10^{15})	peta-	P	PJ (petajoule)
1,000,000,000,000 (10^{12})	tera-	T	TV (teravolt)
1,000,000,000 (10^{9})	giga-	G	GW (gigawatt)
1,000,000 (10^{6})	mega-	M	MHz (megahertz)
1,000 (10^{3})	kilo-	k	kg (kilogram)
100 (10^{2})	hecto-	h	hm (hectometre)
10 (10^{1})	deca-	da	daN (decanewton)
1/10 (10^{-1})	deci-	d	dC (decicoulomb)
1/100 (10^{-2})	centi-	c	cm (centimetre)
1/1,000 (10^{-3})	milli-	m	mm (millimetre)
1/1,000,000 (10^{-6})	micro-	μ	μF (microfarad)
1/1,000,000,000 (10^{-9})	nano-	n	nm (nanometre)
1/1,000,000,000,000 (10^{-12})	pico-	p	ps (picosecond)
1/1,000,000,000,000,000 (10^{-15})	femto-	f	frad (femtoradian)
1/1,000,000,000,000,000,000 (10^{-18})	atto-	a	aT (attotesla)

Physical Constants

Physical constants, or fundamental constants, are standardized values whose parameters do not change.

Constant	Symbol	Value in SI units	Constant	Symbol	Value in SI units
acceleration of free fall	**g**	9.80665 m s^{-2}	Loschmidt's number	**NL**	2.686763×10^{25} m^{-3}
Avogadro's constant	**NA**	6.0221367×10^{23} mol^{-1}	neutron rest mass	**mn**	$1.6749286 \times 10^{-27}$ kg
Boltzmann's constant	**k**	1.380658×10^{-23} J K^{-1}	Planck's constant	**h**	$6.6260755 \times 10^{-34}$ J s
elementary charge	**e**	$1.60217733 \times 10^{-19}$ C	proton rest mass	**mp**	$1.6726231 \times 10^{-27}$ kg
electronic rest mass	**me**	$9.1093897 \times 10^{-31}$ kg	speed of light in a vacuum	**c**	2.99792458×10^{8} m s^{-1}
Faraday's constant	**F**	9.6485309×10^{4} C mol^{-1}	standard atmosphere	**atm**	1.01325×10^{5} Pa
gas constant	**R**	8.314510 J K^{-1} mol^{-1}	Stefan–Boltzmann constant	θ	5.67051×10^{-8} W m^{-2} K^{-4}
gravitational constant	**G**	6.672×10^{-11} N m^{2} kg^{-2}			

Table of Equivalent Temperatures

Celsius and Fahrenheit temperatures can be interconverted as follows:
$C = (F - 32) \times 100/180$; $F = (C \times 180/100) + 32$.

°C	°F	°C	°F	°C	°F	°C	°F
100	212.0	70	158.0	40	104.0	10	50.0
99	210.2	69	156.2	39	102.2	9	48.2
98	208.4	68	154.4	38	100.4	8	46.4
97	206.6	67	152.6	37	98.6	7	44.6
96	204.8	66	150.8	36	96.8	6	42.8
95	203.0	65	149.0	35	95.0	5	41.0
94	201.2	64	147.2	34	93.2	4	39.2
93	199.4	63	145.4	33	91.4	3	37.4
92	197.6	62	143.6	32	89.6	2	35.6
91	195.8	61	141.8	31	87.8	1	33.8
90	194.0	60	140.0	30	86.0	0	32.0
89	192.2	59	138.2	29	84.2	-1	30.2
88	190.4	58	136.4	28	82.4	-2	28.4
87	188.6	57	134.6	27	80.6	-3	26.6
86	186.8	56	132.8	26	78.8	-4	24.8
85	185.0	55	131.0	25	77.0	-5	23.0
84	183.2	54	129.2	24	75.2	-6	21.2
83	181.4	53	127.4	23	73.4	-7	19.4
82	179.6	52	125.6	22	71.6	-8	17.6
81	177.8	51	123.8	21	69.8	-9	15.8
80	176.0	50	122.0	20	68.0	-10	14.0
79	174.2	49	120.2	19	66.2	-11	12.2
78	172.4	48	118.4	18	64.4	-12	10.4
77	170.6	47	116.6	17	62.6	-13	8.6
76	168.8	46	114.8	16	60.8	-14	6.8
75	167.0	45	113.0	15	59.0	-15	5.0
74	165.2	44	111.2	14	57.2	-16	3.2
73	163.4	43	109.4	13	55.4	-17	1.4
72	161.6	42	107.6	12	53.6	-18	-0.4
71	159.8	41	105.8	11	51.8	-19	-2.2

Richter Scale

The Richter scale is based on measurement of seismic waves, used to determine the magnitude of an earthquake at its epicenter. The magnitude of an earthquake differs from its intensity, measured by the Mercalli scale, which is subjective and varies from place to place for the same earthquake. The Richter scale was named after US seismologist Charles Richter (1900–1985). The relative amount of energy released indicates the ratio of energy between earthquakes of different magnitude.

Magnitude	Relative amount of energy released	Examples	Year
1	1		
2	31		
3	960		
4	30,000	Carlisle, England (4.7)	1979
5	920,000	Wrexham, Wales (5.1)	1990
6	29,000,000	San Fernando (CA) (6.5)	1971
		northern Armenia (6.8)	1988
7	890,000,000	Loma Prieta (CA) (7.1)	1989
		Kobe, Japan (7.2)	1995
		Rasht, Iran (7.7)	1990
		San Francisco (CA) (7.7–7.9)[1]	1906
8	28,000,000,000	Tangshan, China (8.0)	1976
		Gansu, China (8.6)	1920
		Lisbon, Portugal (8.7)	1755
9	850,000,000,000	Prince William Sound (AK) (9.2)	1964

[1] Richter's original estimate of a magnitude of 8.3 has been revised by two recent studies carried out by the California Institute of Technology and the US Geological Survey.

Decibel Scale

The decibel scale is used primarily to compare sound intensities although it can be used to compare voltages.

Decibels	Typical sound
0	threshold of hearing
10	rustle of leaves in gentle breeze
10	quiet whisper
20	average whisper
20–50	quiet conversation
40–45	hotel; theatre (between performances)
50–65	loud conversation
65–70	traffic on busy street
65–90	train
75–80	factory (light/medium work)
90	heavy traffic
90–100	thunder
110–140	jet aircraft at take-off
130	threshold of pain
140–190	space rocket at take-off

International Paper Sizes

Name	Dimensions	Classic series
Classic series		
large post	419 × 533 mm	$16\frac{1}{2} \times 21$ in
demy	444 × 572 mm	$17\frac{1}{2} \times 22\frac{1}{2}$ in
medium	457 × 584 mm	18×23 in
royal	508 × 635 mm	20×25 in
double crown	508 × 762 mm	20×30 in
A Series (Books, Magazines, Stationery)		
A0	841 × 1189 mm	$33\frac{1}{8} \times 46\frac{3}{4}$ in
A1	594 × 841 mm	$23\frac{3}{8} \times 33\frac{1}{8}$ in
A2	420 × 594 mm	$16\frac{1}{2} \times 23\frac{3}{8}$ in
A3	297 × 420 mm	$11\frac{3}{4} \times 16\frac{1}{2}$ in
A4	210 × 297 mm	$8\frac{1}{4} \times 11\frac{3}{4}$ in
A5	148 × 210 mm	$5\frac{7}{8} \times 8\frac{1}{4}$ in
B Series (Posters etc.)		
B0	1414 × 1000 mm	$55\frac{5}{8} \times 39\frac{3}{8}$ in
B1	1000 × 707 mm	$39\frac{3}{8} \times 27\frac{7}{8}$ in
B2	707 × 500 mm	$27\frac{7}{8} \times 19\frac{5}{8}$ in
B3	500 × 353 mm	$19\frac{5}{8} \times 13\frac{7}{8}$ in
B4	353 × 250 mm	$13\frac{7}{8} \times 9\frac{7}{8}$ in
B5	250 × 176 mm	$9\frac{7}{8} \times 7$ in
C Series (Envelopes)		
C4	324 × 229 mm	$12\frac{3}{4} \times 9$ in
C5	229 × 162 mm	$9 \times 6\frac{3}{8}$ in
C6	162 × 114 mm	$6\frac{3}{8} \times 4\frac{1}{2}$ in
DL	220 × 110 mm	$8\frac{5}{8} \times 4\frac{3}{8}$ in

Metric Book Publishing Paper Sizes

Name	Trimmed page	Untrimmed page	Quad sheet	Pages to view	Pages from sheet
metric crown 8vo	186 × 123 mm	192 × 126 mm	768 × 1,008 mm	32	64
metric crown 4to	246 × 189 mm	252 × 192 mm	768 × 1,008 mm	16	32
metric large crown 8vo	198 × 129 mm	204 × 132 mm	816 × 1,056 mm	32	64
metric large crown 4to	258 × 201 mm	264 × 204 mm	816 × 1,056 mm	16	32
metric demy 8vo	216 × 138 mm	222 × 141 mm	888 × 1,128 mm	32	64
metric demy 4to	276 × 219 mm	282 × 222 mm	888 × 1,128 mm	16	32
metric royal 8vo	234 × 156 mm	240 × 159 mm	960 × 1,272 mm	32	64
metric royal 4to	312 × 237 mm	318 × 240 mm	960 × 1,272 mm	16	32

International Clothing Sizes

	USA	UK	Europe		USA	UK	Europe		USA	UK	Europe
Women's dresses	6	8	36	**Men's shoes**	$5\frac{1}{2}$	5	38	**Women's shoes** (continued)	8	$6\frac{1}{2}$	39–40
	8	10	38		6	$5\frac{1}{2}$	38–39		$8\frac{1}{2}$	7	40
	10	12	40		$6\frac{1}{2}$	6	39		9	$7\frac{1}{2}$	40–41
	12	14	42		7	$6\frac{1}{2}$	40		$9\frac{1}{2}$	8	41
	14	16	44		$7\frac{1}{2}$	7	40–41		10	$8\frac{1}{2}$	41–42
	16	18	46		8	$7\frac{1}{2}$	41		$10\frac{1}{2}$	9	42
	18	20	48		$8\frac{1}{2}$	8	41–42		11	$9\frac{1}{2}$	42–43
	20	22	50		9	$8\frac{1}{2}$	42–43				
	22	24	52		$9\frac{1}{2}$	9	43	**Children's shoes**	0	0	15
					10	$9\frac{1}{2}$	43–44		1	1	16–17
Men's suits	36	36	46		$10\frac{1}{2}$	10	44		2	2	18
	38	38	48		11	$10\frac{1}{2}$	45		3	3	19
	40	40	50		$11\frac{1}{2}$	11	45–46		4	4	20–21
	42	42	52		12	$11\frac{1}{2}$	46		5	5	22
	44	44	54						6	6	23
	46	46	56						7	7	24
				Women's shoes	$4\frac{1}{2}$	3	36		8	8	25–26
Men's shirts	14	14	36		5	$3\frac{1}{2}$	36–37		9	9	27
	$14\frac{1}{2}$	$14\frac{1}{2}$	37		$5\frac{1}{2}$	4	37		10	10	28
	15	15	38		6	$4\frac{1}{2}$	37–38		11	11	29
	$15\frac{1}{2}$	$15\frac{1}{2}$	39		$6\frac{1}{2}$	5	38		12	12	30–31
	16	16	40		7	$5\frac{1}{2}$	38–39		13	13	32
	$16\frac{1}{2}$	$16\frac{1}{2}$	41		$7\frac{1}{2}$	6	39				
	17	17	42								
	$17\frac{1}{2}$	$17\frac{1}{2}$	43								

Cooking Conversions

Liquid measures

Imperial		Metric
UK	US	
$\frac{1}{6}$ fluid ounce	1 teaspoon	5 millilitres
$\frac{1}{2}$ fluid ounce	1 tablespoon	15 millilitres
1 fluid ounce	2 tablespoons	30 millilitres
8 fluid ounces	1 cup	240 millilitres
$\frac{1}{2}$ pint (10 fluid ounces)	$1\frac{1}{4}$ cups	300 millilitres
16 fluid ounces	1 pint (2 cups)	470 millilitres
1 pint (20 fluid ounces)	$2\frac{1}{2}$ cups	600 millilitres
34 fluid ounces	$4\frac{1}{3}$ cups	1 litre
$1\frac{3}{4}$ pints	$4\frac{1}{3}$ cups	1 litre

Dry measures

Imperial (UK and US)	Metric
1 ounce	28 grams
$3\frac{1}{2}$ ounces	100 grams
4 ounces	113 grams
8 ounces	225 grams
1 pound	450 grams
35 ounces (2.2 pounds)	1 kilogram

Oven temperatures

Gas mark	Electric		Rating
	°C	°F	
$\frac{1}{2}$	130	250	very cool
1	140	275	
2	150	300	cool
3	170	325	warm
4	180	350	moderate
5	190	375	fairly hot
6	200	400	
7	220	425	hot
8	230	450	very hot
9	240	475	

Mercalli Scale

The Mercalli scale is a measure of the intensity of an earthquake. It differs from the Richter scale, which measures magnitude. It is named after the Italian seismologist Giuseppe Mercalli (1850–1914). The scale shown here is the Modified Mercalli Intensity Scale, developed in 1931 by US seismologists Harry Wood and Frank Neumann.

Intensity value	Description
I	not felt except by a very few under especially favourable conditions
II	felt only by a few persons at rest, especially on upper floors of buildings
III	felt quite noticeably by persons indoors, especially on upper floors of buildings; many people do not recognize it as an earthquake; standing motor cars may rock slightly; vibrations similar to the passing of a truck; duration estimated
IV	felt indoors by many, outdoors by few during the day; at night, some awakened; dishes, windows, doors disturbed; walls make cracking sound; sensation like heavy truck striking building; standing motor cars rock noticeably
V	felt by nearly everyone; many awakened; some dishes, windows broken; unstable objects overturned; pendulum clocks may stop
VI	felt by all, many frightened; some heavy furniture moved; a few instances of fallen plaster; damage slight
VII	damage negligible in buildings of good design and construction; slight to moderate in well-built ordinary structures; considerable damage in poorly-built or badly-designed structures; some chimneys broken
VIII	damage slight in specially-designed structures; considerable damage in ordinary substantial buildings with partial collapse; damage great in poorly-built structures; fall of chimneys, factory stacks, columns, monuments, walls; heavy furniture overturned
IX	damage considerable in specially-designed structures; well-designed frame structures thrown out of plumb; damage great in substantial buildings, with partial collapse; buildings shifted off foundations
X	some well-built wooden structures destroyed; most masonry and frame structures destroyed with foundations; rails bent
XI	few, if any (masonry) structures remain standing; bridges destroyed; rails bent greatly
XII	damage total; lines of sight and level are distorted; objects thrown into the air

Beaufort Scale

The Beaufort scale is a system of recording wind velocity (speed) devised in 1806 by Francis Beaufort (1774–1857). It is a numerical scale ranging from 0 for calm to 12 for a hurricane.

Number and description	Features	Air speed	
		kph	mph
0 calm	smoke rises vertically; water smooth	0–2	0–1
1 light air	smoke shows wind direction; water ruffled	2–5	1–3
2 light breeze	leaves rustle; wind felt on face	6–11	4–7
3 gentle breeze	loose paper blows around	12–19	8–12
4 moderate breeze	branches sway	20–29	13–18
5 fresh breeze	small trees sway, leaves blown off	30–39	19–24
6 strong breeze	whistling in telephone wires; sea spray from waves	40–50	25–31
7 near gale	large trees sway	51–61	32–38
8 gale	twigs break from trees	62–74	39–46
9 strong gale	branches break from trees	75–87	47–54
10 storm	trees uprooted; weak buildings collapse	88–101	55–63
11 violent storm	widespread damage	102–117	64–73
12 hurricane	widespread structural damage	above 118	above 74

Miscellaneous Units

Unit	Definition
acoustic ohm	c.g.s. unit of acoustic impedance (the ratio of sound pressure on a surface to sound flux through the surface)
acre	traditional English land measure; 1 acre = 4,480 sq yd (4,047 sq m or 0.4047 ha)
acre-foot	unit sometimes used to measure large volumes of water such as reservoirs; 1 acre-foot = 1,233.5 cu m/43,560 cu ft
astronomical unit	unit (symbol AU) equal to the mean distance of the Earth from the Sun: 149,597,870 km/ 92,955,808 mi
atmosphere	unit of pressure (abbreviation atm); 1 standard atmosphere = 101,325 Pa
barn	unit of area, especially the cross-sectional area of an atomic nucleus; 1 barn = 10^{-28} sq m
barrel	unit of liquid capacity; the volume of a barrel depends on the liquid being measured and the country and state laws. In the USA, 1 barrel of oil = 42 gal (159 l/34.97 imperial gal), but for federal taxing of fermented liquor (such as beer), 1 barrel = 31 gal (117.35 l/25.81 imperial gal). Many states fix a 36-gallon barrel for cistern measurement and federal law uses a 40-gallon barrel to measure 'proof spirits'. 1 barrel of beer in the UK = 163.66 l (43.23 US gal/36 imperial gal)
base box	imperial unit of area used in metal plating; 1 base box = 20.232 sq m/31,360 sq in
baud	unit of electrical signalling speed equal to 1 pulse per second
brewster	unit (symbol B) for measuring reaction of optical materials to stress
British thermal unit	imperial unit of heat (symbol Btu); 1 Btu = approximately 1,055 J
bushel	measure of dry and (in the UK) liquid volume. 1 bushel (struck measure) = 8 dry US gallons (64 dry US pt/35.239 l/2,150.42 cu in). 1 heaped US bushel = 1,278 bushels, struck measure (81.78 dry pt/45.027 l/2,747.715 cu in), often referred to a $1\frac{1}{4}$ bushels, struck measure. In the UK, 1 bushel = 8 imperial gallons (64 imperial pt); 1 UK bushel = 1.03 US bushels

Unit	Definition
cable	unit of length used on ships, taken as $\frac{1}{10}$ of a nautical mile (185.2 m/607.6 ft)
calorie	c.g.s. unit of heat, now replaced by the joule; 1 calorie = 4.1868 J
carat	unit for measuring mass of precious stones; 1 carat = 0.2 g/0.00705 oz
carat	unit of purity in gold; pure gold is 24-carat
carcel	obsolete unit of luminous intensity
cental	name for the short hundredweight; 1 cental = 45.36 kg/100 lb
chaldron	obsolete unit measuring capacity; 1 chaldron = 1.309 cu m/46.237 cu ft
clausius	in engineering, a unit of entropy; defined as the ratio of energy to temperature above absolute zero
cleanliness unit	unit for measuring air pollution; equal to the number of particles greater than 0.5 μm in diameter per cu ft of air
clo	unit of thermal insulation of clothing; standard clothes have insulation of about 1 clo, the warmest have about 4 clo per 2.5 cm/1 in of thickness
clusec	unit for measuring the power of a vacuum pump
condensation number	in physics, the ratio of the number of molecules condensing on a surface to the number of molecules touching that surface
cord	unit for measuring the volume of wood cut for fuel; 1 cord = 3.62 cu m/128 cu ft, or a stack 2.4 m/8 ft long, 1.2 m/4 ft wide and 1.2 m/4 ft high
crith	unit of mass for weighing gases; 1 crith = the mass of 1 litre of hydrogen gas at standard temperature and pressure
cubit	earliest known unit of length; 1 cubit = approximately 45.7 cm/18 in, the length of the human forearm from the tip of the middle finger to the elbow
curie	former unit of radioactivity (symbol Ci); 1 curie = 3.7×10^{10} becquerels
dalton	international atomic mass unit, equivalent to $\frac{1}{12}$ of the mass of a neutral carbon-12 atom
darcy	c.g.s. unit (symbol D) of permeability, used mainly in geology to describe the permeability of rock
darwin	unit of measurement of evolutionary rate of change

(continued)

Miscellaneous Units (*continued*)

Unit	Definition
decontamination factor	unit measuring the effectiveness of radiological decontamination; the ratio of original contamination to the radiation remaining
demal	unit measuring concentration; 1 demal = 1 gram-equivalent of solute in 1 cu dm of solvent
denier	unit used to measure the fineness of yarns; 9,000 m of 15 denier nylon weighs 15 g/0.5 oz
dioptre	optical unit measuring the power of a lens; the reciprocal of the focal length in metres
dram	unit of apothecaries' measure; 1 dram = 60 grains/3.888 g
dyne	c.g.s. unit of force; 10^5 dynes = 1 N
einstein unit	unit for measuring photoenergy in atomic physics
eotvos unit	unit (symbol E) for measuring small changes in the intensity of the Earth's gravity with horizontal distance
erg	c.g.s. unit of work; equal to the work done by a force of 1 dyne moving through 1 cm
erlang	unit for measuring telephone traffic intensity; for example, 90 minutes of carried traffic measured over 60 minutes = 1.5 erlangs ('carried traffic' refers to the total duration of completed calls made within a specified period)
fathom	unit of depth measurement in mining and seafaring; 1 fathom = 1.83 m/6 ft
finsen unit	unit (symbol FU) for measuring intensity of ultraviolet light
fluid ounce	measure of capacity; equivalent in the USA to $\frac{1}{16}$ of a pint ($\frac{1}{20}$ of a pint in the UK and Canada)
foot	imperial unit of length (symbol ft), equivalent to 0.3048 m
foot-candle	unit of illuminance, replaced by the lux; 1 foot-candle = 10.76391 lux
foot-pound	imperial unit of energy (symbol ft-lb); 1 ft-lb = 1.356 joule
frigorie	unit (symbol fg) used in refrigeration engineering to measure heat energy, equal to a rate of heat extraction of 1 kilocalorie per hour
furlong	unit of measurement, originating in Anglo-Saxon England, equivalent to 201.168 m/220 yd
galileo	unit (symbol Gal) of acceleration; 1 galileo = 10^{-2} m s^{-2}
gallon	imperial liquid or dry measure subdivided into 4 quarts or 8 pints; 1 US gal = 3.785 l; 1 imperial gal = 4.546 l
gauss	c.g.s. unit (symbol) of magnetic flux density, replaced by the tesla; 1 gauss = 1×10^{-4} tesla
gill	imperial unit of volume for liquid measure; equal to $\frac{1}{4}$ of a pint (in the USA, 4 fl oz/0.118 l; in the UK, 5 fl oz/0.142 l)
grain	smallest unit of mass in the three English systems of measurement (avoirdupois, troy, apothecaries' weights) used in the UK and USA; 1 grain = 0.0648 g
hand	unit used in measuring the height of a horse from front hoof to shoulder (withers); 1 hand = 10.2 cm/4 in
hardness number	unit measuring hardness of materials. There are many different hardness scales: Brinell, Rockwell, and Vickers scales measure the degree of indentation or impression of materials; Mohs' scale measures resistance to scratching against a standard set of minerals
hartree	atomic unit of energy, equivalent to atomic unit of charge divided by atomic unit of length; 1 hartree = 4.850×10^{-18} J

Unit	Definition
haze factor	unit of visibility in mist or fog; the ratio of brightness of mist compared with that of the object
Hehner number	unit measuring concentration of fatty acids in oils; a Hehner number of 1 = 1 kg of fatty acid in 100 kg of oil or fat
hide	unit of measurement used in the 12th century to measure land; 1 hide = 60–120 acres/25–50 ha
horsepower	imperial unit (abbreviation hp) of power; 1 horsepower = 746 W
hundredweight	imperial unit (abbreviation cwt) of mass; 1 cwt = 45.36 kg/100 lb in the USA and 50.80 kg/112 lb in the UK
inch	imperial unit (abbreviation in) of linear measure, $\frac{1}{12}$ of a ft; 1 in = 2.54 cm
inferno	unit used in astrophysics for describing the temperature inside a star; 1 inferno = 1 billion K (degrees Kelvin)
iodine number	unit measuring the percentage of iodine absorbed in a substance, expressed as grams of iodine absorbed by 100 grams of material
jansky	unit used in radio astronomy to measure radio emissions or flux densities from space; 1 jansky = 10^{-26} W m^{-2} Hz^{-1}. Flux density is the energy in a beam of radiation which passes through an area normal to the beam in a single unit of time. A jansky is a measure-ment of the energy received from a cosmic radio source per unit area of detector in a single time unit
kayser	unit used in spectroscopy to measure wave number (number of waves in a unit length); a wavelength of 1.0 cm has a wave number of 1 kayser
knot	unit used in navigation to measure a ship's speed; 1 knot = 1 nautical mile per hour, or about 1.15 miles per hour
league	obsolete imperial unit of length; 1 league = 3 nautical mi/5.56 km or 3 statute mi/4.83 km
light year	unit used in astronomy to measure distance; the distance travelled by light in one year, approximately 9.46×10^{12} km/5.88×10^{12} mi
mache	obsolete unit of radioactive concentration; 1 mache = 3.7×10^{-7} curies of radioactive material per cu m of a medium
maxwell	c.g.s. unit (symbol Mx) of magnetic flux, the strength of a magnetic field in an area multiplied by the area; 1 maxwell = 10^{-8} weber
megaton	measurement of the explosive power of a nuclear weapon; 1 megaton = 1 million tons of trinitrotoluene (TNT)
mil	(a) one-thousandth of a litre; contraction of the word millilitre; (b) imperial measure of length, equal to one-thousandth of an inch; also known as the thou
mile	imperial unit of linear measure; 1 statute mile = 1.60934 km/5,280 ft; 1 international nautical mile = 1.852 km/6,076 ft
millimetre of mercury	unit of pressure (symbol mmHg) used in medicine for measuring blood pressure
morgan	arbitrary unit used in genetics; 1 morgan is the distance along the chromosome in a gene that gives a recombination frequency of 1%
nautical mile	unit of distance used in navigation, equal to the average length of 1 minute of arc on a great circle of the Earth; 1 international nautical mile = 1.852 km/6,076 ft

Miscellaneous Units (*continued*)

Unit	Definition
neper	unit used in telecommunications; gives the attenuation of amplitudes of currents or powers as the natural logarithm of the ratio of the voltage between two points or the current between two points
oersted	c.g.s. unit (symbol Oe) of magnetic field strength, now replaced by amperes per metre (1 Oe = 79.58 amp per m)
ounce	unit of mass, $\frac{1}{16}$ of a pound avoirdupois, equal to 437.5 grains/28.35 g; or 14.6 pound troy, equal to 480 grains/31.10 g
parsec	unit (symbol pc) used in astronomy for distances to stars and galaxies; 1 pc = 3.262 light years, 2.063 × 10^5 astronomical units, or 3.086 × 10^{13} km
peck	obsolete unit of dry measure, equal to 8 imperial quarts or 1 quarter bushel (8.1 l in the USA or 9.1 l in the UK)
pennyweight	imperial unit of mass; 1 pennyweight = 24 grains = 1.555 × 10^{-3} kg
perch	obsolete imperial unit of length; 1 perch = $5\frac{1}{2}$ yards = 5.029 m, also called the rod or pole
pint	imperial unit of liquid or dry measure; in the USA, 1 liquid pint = 16 fl oz/0.473 l, while 1 dry pint = 0.551 l; in the UK, 1 pt = 20 fl oz, $\frac{1}{2}$ quart, $\frac{1}{8}$ gal, or 0.568 l
point	metric unit of mass used in relation to gemstones; 1 point = 0.01 metric carat = 2 × 10^{-3} g
poise	c.g.s. unit of dynamic viscosity; 1 poise = 1 dyne-second per sq cm
pound	imperial unit (abbreviation lb) of mass; the avoirdupois pound or imperial standard pound = 0.45 kg/7,000 grains, while the pound troy (used for weighing precious metals) = 0.37 kg/5,760 grains
poundal	imperial unit (abbreviation pdl) of force; 1 poundal = 0.1383 newton
quart	imperial liquid or dry measure; in the USA, 1 liquid quart = 0.946 l, while 1 dry quart = 1.101 l; in the UK, 1 quart = 2 pt/1.137 l
rad	unit of absorbed radiation dose, replaced in the SI system by the gray; 1 rad = 0.01 joule of radiation absorbed by 1 kg of matter
relative biological effectiveness	relative damage caused to living tissue by different types of radiation
rood	imperial unit of area; 1 rood = $\frac{1}{4}$ acre = 1,011.7 sq m
roentgen	unit (symbol R) of radiation exposure, used for X- and gamma rays
rydberg	atomic unit of energy; 1 rydberg = 2.425 × 10^{-18} J
sabin	unit of sound absorption, used in acoustical engineering; 1 sabin = absorption of 1 sq ft (0.093 sq m) of a perfectly absorbing surface
scruple	imperial unit of apothecaries' measure; 1 scruple = 20 grains = 1.3 × 10^{-3} kg
shackle	unit of length used at sea for measuring cable or chain; 1 shackle = 15 fathoms (90 ft/27 m)
slug	obsolete imperial unit of mass; 1 slug = 14.59 kg/ 32.17 lb
snellen	unit expressing the visual power of the eye
sone	unit of subjective loudness
standard volume	in physics, the volume occupied by 1 kilogram molecule (molecular mass in kilograms) of any gas at standard temperature and pressure; approximately 22.414 cu m
stokes	c.g.s. unit (symbol St) of kinematic viscosity; 1 stokes = 10^{-4} m² s⁻¹
stone	imperial unit (abbreviation st) of mass; 1 stone = 6.35 kg/14 lb
strontium unit	measures concentration of strontium-90 in an organic medium relative to the concentration of calcium
tex	metric unit of line density; 1 tex is the line density of a thread with a mass of 1 gram and a length of 1 kilometre
tog	measure of thermal insulation of a fabric, garment, or quilt; the tog value is equivalent to 10 times the temperature difference (in °C) between the two faces of the article, when the flow of heat across it is equal to 1 W per sq m
ton	1 unit of mass; the long ton (UK) = 1,016 kg/2,240 lb; 1 short ton (USA) = 907 kg/2,000 lb; 1 metric ton = 1000 kg/2205 lb
yard	imperial unit (symbol yd) of length, equivalent to 0.9144 m/3 ft

Numbers

Large Numbers

USA and France

Nomenclature for large numbers varies in different countries. In the USA and France, numbers advance by increments of a thousand:

billion	1,000,000,000	1×10^9
trillion	1,000,000,000,000	1×10^{12}
quadrillion	1,000,000,000,000,000	1×10^{15}

UK and Germany

However, in the UK and Germany numbers have traditionally advanced by increments of a million:

million	1,000,000	1×10^6
billion	1,000,000,000,000	1×10^{12}
trillion	1,000,000,000,000,000,000	1×10^{18}
quadrillion	1,000,000,000,000,000,000,000,000	1×10^{24}

This has a certain amount of logic on its side, particularly for classical scholars:

billion = million²	(bi-)
trillion = million³	(tri-)
quadrillion = million⁴	(quadr-)

Higher numbers

The US usage is becoming prevalent in the UK and Germany, particularly as it is now universally used by economists and statisticians. The higher numbers, in both styles, are as follows:

Number	USA	UK
quintillion	1×10^{18}	1×10^{30}
sextillion	1×10^{21}	1×10^{36}
septillion	1×10^{24}	1×10^{42}
octillion	1×10^{27}	1×10^{48}
nonillion	1×10^{30}	1×10^{54}
decillion	1×10^{33}	1×10^{60}
vigintillion	1×10^{63}	1×10^{120}
centillion	1×10^{303}	1×10^{600}

Roman Numerals

Roman	Arabic	Roman	Arabic	Roman	Arabic
I	1	XI	11	CD	400
II	2	XIX	19	D	500
III	3	XX	20	CM	900
IV	4	XXX	30	M	1,000
V	5	XL	40	X̄	5,000
VI	6	L	50	X̄	10,000
VII	7	LX	60	L̄	50,000
VIII	8	XC	90	C̄	100,000
IX	9	C	100	D̄	500,000
X	10	CC	200	M̄	1,000,000

Number Systems

Binary (Base 2)	Octal (Base 8)	Decimal (Base 10)	Hexadecimal (Base 16)
0	0	0	0
1	1	1	1
10	2	2	2
11	3	3	3
100	4	4	4
101	5	5	5
110	6	6	6
111	7	7	7
1000	10	8	8
1001	11	9	9
1010	12	10	A
1011	13	11	B
1100	14	12	C
1101	15	13	D
1110	16	14	E
1111	17	15	F
10000	20	16	10
11111111	377	255	FF
11111010001	3721	2001	7D1

Prime Numbers

All the prime numbers between 1 and 1,000.

2	97	227	367	509	661	829
3	101	229	373	521	673	839
5	103	233	379	523	677	853
7	107	239	383	541	683	857
11	109	241	389	547	691	859
13	113	251	397	557	701	863
17	127	257	401	563	709	877
19	131	263	409	569	719	881
23	137	269	419	571	727	883
29	139	271	421	577	733	887
31	149	277	431	587	739	907
37	151	281	433	593	743	911
41	157	283	439	599	751	919
43	163	293	443	601	757	929
47	167	307	449	607	761	937
53	173	311	457	613	769	941
59	179	313	461	617	773	947
61	181	317	463	619	787	953
67	191	331	467	631	797	967
71	193	337	479	641	809	971
73	197	347	487	643	811	977
79	199	349	491	647	821	983
83	211	353	499	653	823	991
89	223	359	503	659	827	997

Multiplication Table

	2	3	4	5	6	7	8	9	10	11	12	13	14	15	16	17	18	19	20	21	22	23	24	25
2	4	6	8	10	12	14	16	18	20	22	24	26	28	30	32	34	36	38	40	42	44	46	48	50
3	6	9	12	15	18	21	24	27	30	33	36	39	42	45	48	51	54	57	60	63	66	69	72	75
4	8	12	16	20	24	28	32	36	40	44	48	52	56	60	64	68	72	76	80	84	88	92	96	100
5	10	15	20	25	30	35	40	45	50	55	60	65	70	75	80	85	90	95	100	105	110	115	120	125
6	12	18	24	30	36	42	48	54	60	66	72	78	84	90	96	102	108	114	120	126	132	138	144	150
7	14	21	28	35	42	49	56	63	70	77	84	91	98	105	112	119	126	133	140	147	154	161	168	175
8	16	24	32	40	48	56	64	72	80	88	96	104	112	120	128	136	144	152	160	168	176	184	192	200
9	18	27	36	45	54	63	72	81	90	99	108	117	126	135	144	153	162	171	180	189	198	207	216	225
10	20	30	40	50	60	70	80	90	100	110	120	130	140	150	160	170	180	190	200	210	220	230	240	250
11	22	33	44	55	66	77	88	99	110	121	132	143	154	165	176	187	198	209	220	231	241	253	264	275
12	24	36	48	60	72	84	96	108	120	132	144	156	168	180	192	204	216	228	240	252	264	276	288	300
13	26	39	52	65	78	91	104	117	130	143	156	169	182	195	208	221	234	247	260	273	286	299	312	325
14	28	42	56	70	84	98	112	126	140	154	168	182	196	210	224	238	252	266	280	294	308	322	336	350
15	30	45	60	75	90	105	120	135	150	165	180	195	210	225	240	255	270	285	300	315	330	345	360	375
16	32	48	64	80	96	112	128	144	160	176	192	208	224	240	256	272	288	304	320	336	352	368	384	400
17	34	51	68	85	102	119	136	153	170	187	204	221	238	255	272	289	306	323	340	357	374	391	408	425
18	36	54	72	90	108	126	144	162	180	198	216	234	252	270	288	306	324	342	360	378	396	414	432	450
19	38	57	76	95	114	133	152	171	190	209	228	247	266	285	304	323	342	361	380	399	418	437	456	475
20	40	60	80	100	120	140	160	180	200	220	240	260	280	300	320	340	360	380	400	420	440	460	480	500
21	42	63	84	105	126	147	168	189	210	231	252	273	294	315	336	357	378	399	420	441	462	483	504	525
22	44	66	88	110	132	154	176	198	220	242	264	286	308	330	352	374	396	418	440	462	484	506	528	550
23	46	69	92	115	138	161	184	207	230	253	276	299	322	345	368	391	414	437	460	483	506	529	552	575
24	48	72	96	120	144	168	192	216	240	264	288	312	336	360	384	408	432	456	480	504	528	552	576	600
25	50	75	100	125	150	175	200	225	250	275	300	325	350	375	400	425	450	475	500	525	550	575	600	625

Fractions as Decimals

Fraction	Decimal	Fraction	Decimal	Fraction	Decimal	Fraction	Decimal	Fraction	Decimal	Fraction	Decimal
$\frac{1}{2}$	0.5000	$\frac{3}{7}$	0.4286	$\frac{8}{9}$	0.8889	$\frac{9}{11}$	0.8182	$\frac{15}{16}$	0.9375	$\frac{9}{32}$	0.2812
$\frac{1}{3}$	0.3333	$\frac{4}{7}$	0.5714	$\frac{1}{10}$	0.1000	$\frac{10}{11}$	0.9091	$\frac{1}{20}$	0.0500	$\frac{11}{32}$	0.3438
$\frac{2}{3}$	0.6667	$\frac{5}{7}$	0.7143	$\frac{3}{10}$	0.3000	$\frac{1}{12}$	0.0833	$\frac{3}{20}$	0.1500	$\frac{13}{32}$	0.4062
$\frac{1}{4}$	0.2500	$\frac{6}{7}$	0.8571	$\frac{7}{10}$	0.7000	$\frac{5}{12}$	0.4167	$\frac{7}{20}$	0.3500	$\frac{15}{32}$	0.4688
$\frac{3}{4}$	0.7500	$\frac{1}{8}$	0.1250	$\frac{9}{10}$	0.9000	$\frac{7}{12}$	0.5833	$\frac{9}{20}$	0.4500	$\frac{17}{32}$	0.5312
$\frac{1}{5}$	0.2000	$\frac{3}{8}$	0.3750	$\frac{1}{11}$	0.0909	$\frac{11}{12}$	0.9167	$\frac{11}{20}$	0.5500	$\frac{19}{32}$	0.5938
$\frac{2}{5}$	0.4000	$\frac{5}{8}$	0.6250	$\frac{2}{11}$	0.1818	$\frac{1}{16}$	0.0625	$\frac{13}{20}$	0.6500	$\frac{21}{32}$	0.6562
$\frac{3}{5}$	0.6000	$\frac{7}{8}$	0.8750	$\frac{3}{11}$	0.2727	$\frac{3}{16}$	0.1875	$\frac{17}{20}$	0.8500	$\frac{23}{32}$	0.7188
$\frac{4}{5}$	0.8000	$\frac{1}{9}$	0.1111	$\frac{4}{11}$	0.3636	$\frac{5}{16}$	0.3125	$\frac{19}{20}$	0.9500	$\frac{25}{32}$	0.7812
$\frac{1}{6}$	0.1667	$\frac{2}{9}$	0.2222	$\frac{5}{11}$	0.4545	$\frac{7}{16}$	0.4375	$\frac{1}{32}$	0.0312	$\frac{27}{32}$	0.8438
$\frac{5}{6}$	0.8333	$\frac{4}{9}$	0.4444	$\frac{6}{11}$	0.5455	$\frac{9}{16}$	0.5625	$\frac{3}{32}$	0.9038	$\frac{29}{32}$	0.9062
$\frac{1}{7}$	0.1429	$\frac{5}{9}$	0.5556	$\frac{7}{11}$	0.6364	$\frac{11}{16}$	0.6875	$\frac{5}{32}$	0.1562	$\frac{31}{32}$	0.9688
$\frac{2}{7}$	0.2857	$\frac{7}{9}$	0.7778	$\frac{8}{11}$	0.7273	$\frac{13}{16}$	0.8125	$\frac{7}{32}$	0.2188		

Percentages as Fractions or Decimals

%	Decimal	Fraction	%	Decimal	Fraction	%	Decimal	Fraction	%	Decimal	Fraction
1	0.01	$\frac{1}{100}$	16	0.16	$\frac{4}{25}$	32	0.32	$\frac{8}{25}$	48	0.48	$\frac{12}{25}$
2	0.02	$\frac{1}{50}$	$16\frac{2}{3}$	0.167	$\frac{1}{6}$	33	0.33	$\frac{33}{100}$	49	0.49	$\frac{49}{100}$
3	0.03	$\frac{3}{100}$	17	0.17	$\frac{17}{100}$	$33\frac{1}{3}$	0.333	$\frac{1}{3}$	50	0.50	$\frac{1}{2}$
4	0.04	$\frac{1}{25}$	18	0.18	$\frac{9}{50}$	34	0.34	$\frac{17}{50}$	55	0.55	$\frac{11}{20}$
5	0.05	$\frac{1}{20}$	19	0.19	$\frac{19}{100}$	35	0.35	$\frac{7}{20}$	60	0.60	$\frac{3}{5}$
6	0.06	$\frac{3}{50}$	20	0.20	$\frac{1}{5}$	36	0.36	$\frac{9}{25}$	65	0.65	$\frac{13}{20}$
7	0.07	$\frac{7}{100}$	21	0.21	$\frac{21}{100}$	37	0.37	$\frac{37}{100}$	66	0.66	$\frac{66}{100}$
8	0.08	$\frac{2}{25}$	22	0.22	$\frac{11}{50}$	38	0.38	$\frac{19}{50}$	$66\frac{2}{3}$	0.667	$\frac{2}{3}$
$8\frac{1}{3}$	0.083	$\frac{1}{12}$	23	0.23	$\frac{23}{100}$	39	0.39	$\frac{39}{100}$	70	0.70	$\frac{7}{10}$
9	0.09	$\frac{9}{100}$	24	0.24	$\frac{6}{25}$	40	0.40	$\frac{2}{5}$	75	0.75	$\frac{3}{4}$
10	0.10	$\frac{1}{10}$	25	0.25	$\frac{1}{4}$	41	0.41	$\frac{41}{100}$	80	0.80	$\frac{4}{5}$
11	0.11	$\frac{11}{100}$	26	0.26	$\frac{13}{50}$	42	0.42	$\frac{21}{50}$	85	0.85	$\frac{17}{20}$
12	0.12	$\frac{3}{25}$	27	0.27	$\frac{27}{100}$	43	0.43	$\frac{43}{100}$	90	0.90	$\frac{9}{10}$
$12\frac{1}{2}$	0.125	$\frac{1}{8}$	28	0.28	$\frac{7}{25}$	44	0.44	$\frac{11}{25}$	95	0.95	$\frac{19}{20}$
13	0.13	$\frac{13}{100}$	29	0.29	$\frac{29}{100}$	45	0.45	$\frac{9}{20}$	100	1.00	1
14	0.14	$\frac{7}{50}$	30	0.30	$\frac{3}{10}$	46	0.46	$\frac{23}{50}$			
15	0.15	$\frac{3}{20}$	31	0.31	$\frac{31}{100}$	47	0.47	$\frac{47}{100}$			

Playing Cards and Dice Chances

Poker

Hand	Number possible	Odds against
royal flush	4	649,739 to 1
straight flush	36	72,192 to 1
four of a kind	624	4,164 to 1
full house	3,744	693 to 1
flush	5,108	508 to 1
straight	10,200	254 to 1
three of a kind	54,912	46 to 1
two pairs	123,552	20 to 1
one pair	1,098,240	1.37 to 1
high card	1,302,540	1 to 1
total	2,598,960	

Dice (Chances with two dice and a single throw)

Total count	Odds against
2	35 to 1
3	17 to 1
4	11 to 1
5	8 to 1
6	31 to 5
7	5 to 1
8	31 to 5
9	8 to 1
10	11 to 1
11	17 to 1
12	35 to 1

Bridge

Suit distribution in a hand	Odds against
4–4–3–2	4 to 1
5–4–2–2	8 to 1
6–4–2–1	20 to 1
7–4–1–1	254 to 1
8–4–1–0	2,211 to 1
13–0–0–0	158,753,389,899 to 1

THE UNITED KINGDOM

The Year in Review

2 July 1997 The first budget of the new Labour government stays within the previous administration's spending levels but with increased assistance for health and education.

6 July 1997 Violence flares at an Orange Order march in Drumcree, Northern Ireland; the Order subsequently agrees (11 July) to cancel or re-route marches in Londonderry, Belfast, Newry, and Armagh.

10 July 1997 Around 100,000 people participate in a pro-hunting rally in Hyde Park, London, in protest of a proposed bill that would ban hunting with dogs.

20 July 1997 The Irish Republican Army (IRA) restores its cease-fire (broken on 9 February 1996) in order to participate in talks on the future of Northern Ireland.

22 July 1997 The government announces plans for partial home rule in Wales, whereby an elected assembly would have some power to govern local affairs. Wales voted against devolution in 1979.

24 July 1997 The government announces a proposal for Scottish home rule, whereby a Scottish parliament of 129 seats would have the power to tax and legislate on local issues. Scotland voted against devolution in 1979.

28 July 1997 British government officials and Sinn Féin (the political wing of the IRA) members meet for the first time since the IRA called a cease-fire, in Belfast, Northern Ireland. The participants discuss plans for a meeting with Sinn Fein and Northern Ireland Secretary Mo Mowlam.

28 July 1997 The Labour MP Gordon McMaster kills himself, leaving a suicide note accusing fellow MP Tommy Graham of instigating a whispering campaign against him and his alleged homosexuality; Graham is subsequently suspended by the Labour Party (19 August).

29 July 1997 The government announces a proposal to create a Greater London Authority (GLA), a city government for London comprising a mayor and an elected assembly of 24–32 members. The Tory party abolished the most recent London government in 1986.

7 August 1997 The management of South Crofty mine in Cornwall, announces that the mine will close permanently. The closing of the mine, the last active tin mine in England, would result in 270 job losses.

24 August 1997 Britain's Development Secretary Clare Short dismisses demands by the inhabitants of Montserrat in the Leeward Islands, West Indies, for compensation following the volcanic explosion on the island, saying they will want 'golden elephants' next; the following day the foreign secretary Robin Cook announces the establishment of a special committee to deal with the problem.

29 August 1997 The Northern Ireland Secretary Mo Mowlam invites Sinn Féin, the political arm of the Irish Republican Army (IRA), to all-party talks on Northern Ireland.

31 August 1997 Diana, Princess of Wales, her companion Dodi Fayed, and their driver are killed in a car crash in the Place de l'Alma underpass in Paris, France. Blame for the crash is initially laid with photographers chasing the car but it is revealed on 1 September that the driver, Henri Paul, had been drinking and was taking prescription drugs.

2 September 1997 A court in Denmark sentences three neo-Nazis to jail terms for sending letter bombs to mixed-race couples and other targets in Britain.

6 September 1997 The funeral service for Diana, Princess of Wales, is held in Westminster Abbey, London: her body is subsequently taken to Althorp, the Spencer family estate in Northamptonshire, for burial. An estimated 2 billion people worldwide watch the service on television.

11 September 1997 In a referendum, 74.3% of Scottish voters approve the creation of their own parliament, with 63.5% voting in favour of giving it tax-raising powers.

15 September 1997 The Queen issues a public statement denying claims that she and her son, Charles, Prince of Wales, disagreed over the possibility of a state funeral for Charles's ex-wife, Diana, Princess of Wales. The statement was in part a reaction to general public criticism of the Queen for seeming to remain aloof as the country mourned the princess.

18 September 1997 Welsh voters narrowly approve the establishment of a representative assembly for Wales (50.3% in favour).

22 September 1997–25 September 1997 The Liberal Democrat party holds its annual conference, in Eastbourne. The conference is dominated by party leader Paddy Ashdown's recent suggestions that the Liberal Democrats should ally themselves with the Labour government.

29 September 1997–3 October 1997 The ruling Labour Party holds its annual conference, in Brighton. The conference focuses on plans to reform both the party and the government, with emphasis on the 'New Labour' image that moves away from socialism, as well as on national issues such as education, the National Heath System, and the economy.

September 1997 There is an unprecedented massive outpouring of public grief at the death of Diana, Princess of Wales. Thousands of floral tributes are laid in her memory at Kensington Palace in London, and at other locations worldwide.

1 October 1997 Fiji formally rejoins the British Commonwealth, having repealed legislation discriminating against Fijian Indians which had led to its expulsion in 1987.

7 October 1997 The High Court rules that the general election result in the constituency of Winchester is void due to procedural errors, and must be recontested.

7–10 October 1997 The Conservative Party holds its annual conference, in Blackpool. The conference focuses on rebuilding the party's popularity after its landslide defeat in the May elections. William Hague, John Major's replacement as leader of the party, emphasizes in his keynote speech his opposition to Britain's early participation in a single European currency.

13 October 1997 Tony Blair meets Gerry Adams at Stormont Castle, Belfast, the first meeting between a British prime minister and a Sinn Féin leader since 1921.

14 October 1997 The Conservative MP Piers Merchant resigns over his relationship with the former nightclub hostess Anna Cox.

William Hague (with Ffion Jenkins), has declared his opposition to Britain's early participation in a single European currency.
Sean Aidan

25 October 1997 A bomb explodes under a car in Bangor, County Down, Northern Ireland, killing driver Glen Greer. No one claims responsibility, but authorities say that Greer might have been targeted in a dispute between rival Protestant militant groups.

27 October 1997 In a speech before Parliament, Chancellor of the Exchequer Gordon Brown says the government will not join the European Monetary Union (EMU), scheduled for 1999, until 2002 at the earliest.

30 October 1997 A bomb explodes in a British government office in Londonderry, Northern Ireland. The masked deliverer of the bomb shouted a warning in time to evacuate the building, and no one was injured. The Continuity Army Council, an extremist military offshoot of the IRA, claims responsibility.

6 November 1997 A report by the House of Commons committee on standards and privileges strongly criticizes the former MP Neil Hamilton for taking payments to ask parliamentary questions.

10 November 1997 The government says that it will return a campaign donation of £1,000,000 made by Formula One Association president Bernie Ecclestone. The disclosure of the large donation fuelled the scandal created when the Labour government confirmed that Formula One automobile racing was exempt from a ban on sponsorship by tobacco companies.

20 November 1997 The Winchester by-election is won by the Liberal Democrat candidate Mark Oaten with a majority of 21,536; he took the seat by a margin of 2 votes at the general election on 1 May but the result was successfully challenged in the High Court by the Conservative candidate Gerry Malone.

25 November 1997 The Chancellor of the Exchequer Gordon Brown announces in a pre-Budget report that the British welfare system is to be radically revised; he also allocates extra money for out-of-school work clubs and pensioners' heating bills.

28 November 1997 The House of Commons approves a bill that bans hunting with dogs, with a vote of 411–151. The bill, however, is not expected to become law in the near future.

30 November 1997 Demonstrators in northwestern Wales dump 40 metric tons of mince imported from Ireland into the harbour at the port of Holyhead, protesting against the importation of cheap Irish beef.

1 December 1997 The government establishes an independent commission to recommend alternative voting systems, promising a referendum on the issue before the next election.

2 December 1997 Social Security Secretary Harriet Harman announces that the government is freezing the amount of benefit to be paid to single parents, sparking the first significant public opposition by Labour supporters to the Labour government.

2 December 1997 The Heritage Lottery fund announces details of funding for upgrading and restoring urban parks, representing a growing trend in the development of parks and the pedestrianization of inner city areas. Since January 1996 102 parks in the UK have been restored at a cost of £67.2 million.

3 December 1997 Agriculture Secretary Jack Cunningham announces that the government will ban the sale of beef on the bone to help prevent the transmission of bovine spongiform encephalopathy, 'mad cow disease', to humans.

11 December 1997 Irish Republican Army (IRA) leader Gerry Adams meets Prime Minister Tony Blair at 10 Downing Street, marking the first time in 76 years an Irish republican leader has visited the prime minister at his residence.

11 December 1997 The royal yacht, *Britannia*, is formally retired at a decommissioning ceremony in Portsmouth, England.

11 December 1997 The government unveils proposed legislation that would guarantee public access to most government information and documents.

17 December 1997 Labour MP for Scotland's Glasgow Govan constituency Mohammad Sarwar is charged with electoral fraud and obstruction of justice. Sarwar, Britain's first Muslim MP, denies the charges and is released on bail.

18 December 1997 The Scottish Secretary Donald Dewar announces plans to create a Scottish parliament in Edinburgh, in accordance with the referendum passed in September on Scottish devolution. The Scotland Bill states that the new parliament would have lawmaking powers in the areas of education, the environment, health, law enforcement, and transport.

19 December 1997 Leader of the Opposition William Hague marries Ffion Jenkins.

24 December 1997 The *Mirror* newspaper publishes a story in which journalist Dawn Alford reports that she bought marijuana from the 17-year-old son of an unnamed British cabinet minister. She is arrested four days later for possession when she goes to a police station to turn it in.

24 –26 December 1997 A fierce storm with winds up to 130 kph/80 mph hits southern England, killing 13 people and leaving thousands of homes without electricity.

27 December 1997 Billy Wright, a leading member of the Loyalist Volunteer Force (LVF), is shot and killed by two members of the Irish National Liberation Army (INLA) at the Maze Prison, near Belfast, Northern Ireland. The incident escalates concerns for the future of the Northern Ireland peace process.

27 December 1997 Former Irish Republican Army (IRA) member Seamus Dillon is shot and killed at the Dungannon Hotel in County Tyrone, where he worked as a doorman. The Loyalist Volunteer Force claim responsibility, saying it was revenge for the death of Protestant military leader Billy Wright in the Maze Prison.

30 December 1997 British singer and composer Elton John is among 976 recipients of knighthood and other honours awarded by the British government.

1997 The local council in Swansea, Wales, allows the Monty Python film *The Life of Brian* to be shown, after a 17-year ban.

2 January 1998 Home Secretary Jack Straw reveals that it was his son, William, who was the previously unnamed 17-year-old son of a cabinet minister who sold marijuana to undercover *Daily Mirror* reporter Dawn Alford. A court injunction had prevented the press and Straw himself from revealing the name of the seller until now. The incident was particularly embarrassing for Straw, who had adopted a tough anti-drugs policy.

5 January 1998 The government lauches a pilot programme to help combat unemployment in the 18–25 age group, guaranteeing a job or job training to those young people who have been out of work for at least six months.

5 January 1998 Tickets go on sale for the grave site of Diana, Princess of Wales. The site is at Althorp House, Northamptonshire, Diana's family home, and is only open to the public in July and August. Within 24 hours, 40,000 of the 152,500 available tickets are sold.

8 January 1998 Scottish Secretary Donald Dewar announces that he will run for a seat in the new Scottish parliament, created by the referendum in September 1997. He is seen as the leading candidate to become the 'first minister', the Scottish prime minister.

11 January 1998 Foreign Secretary Robin Cook makes public his rumoured affair with his former secretary, Gaynor Regan. He announces that he plans to marry her after he divorces his wife.

12 January 1998 During a five-day meeting in Tokyo, Japan, Japanese premier Ryutaro Hashimoto apologizes on behalf of his country to British prime minister Tony Blair for the Japanese treatment of British prisoners of war during World War II.

14 January 1998 Agriculture Minister Jack Cunningham announces that the government will create the Food Standards Agency, an independent body to monitor the safety of food.

14 January 1998 The British government reports that the unemployment rate fell to 5% in December, the lowest since 1980.

20 January 1998 The British Conservative party faces an election donations scandal when news breaks that a Hong Kong businessman demands the return of a £1 million campaign gift after certain conditions were not met. The businessman, Oriental Press Group executive director Ma Ching-kwan, is alleged to have demanded that his father, the founder of the company, be cleared of drug trafficking charges filed in Hong Kong 20 years ago. Conservative Party leader William Hague denies that the party accepted any campaign gifts with strings attached.

23 January 1998 The High Court rules in favour of six former miners, who sued formerly government owned British Coal for failing to take sufficient health precautions, resulting in the miners' chronic respiratory problems.

26 January 1998 A ban on the possession of all handguns goes into effect in Britain.

26 January 1998 The Queen Mother, 97,

has hip replacement surgery in London the day after she fractured her hip from a fall at the royal family home at Sandringham.

29 January 1998 Chairman of the London and Continental Railways consortium Derek Hornby announces that the group is withdrawing from a project to build a high-speed rail link between London and Folkestone, where trains enter the Channel Tunnel in England, due to lack of funds.

29 January 1998 Prime Minister Tony Blair announces that the government will launch a new investigation into 'Bloody Sunday', the 1972 killing of 14 unarmed Catholic protesters by British troops in Londonderry, Northern Ireland.

3 February 1998 Postage stamps commemorating the life of Diana, Princess of Wales, go on sale in Britain.

4–7 February 1998 Prime Minister Tony Blair makes his first official visit to the USA as leader of the British government. Many comparisons are made between Blair and the American president Bill Clinton.

9 February 1998 An unidentified gunman shoots and kills Brendan Campbell, a suspected drug dealer, outside a restaurant in Belfast. Although Campbell was Catholic, the Irish Republican Army (IRA) is suspected because of their hard-line anti-drugs laws.

10 February 1998 An unidentified gunman shoots and kills Robert Dougan, a Protestant linked to the Ulster Defense Association, a militant unionist group, near Belfast. The Irish Republican Army (IRA) is suspected, although the group does not claim responsibility.

14 February 1998 Prime Minister Tony Blair criticizes what he deems tacky souvenirs, including T-shirts, dishes, and videos, commemorating the life of Diana, Princess of Wales.

20 February 1998 The British and Irish governments suspend Sinn Féin from peace talks as a result of the murders on 9 and 10 February in which the governments hold the Irish Republican Army (IRA) responsible.

23 February 1998 Princess Margaret suffers a mild stroke while on holiday in Mustique, an island in the Caribbean.

27 February 1998 A junior minister in the Home Office, Lord Williams of Mostyn, announces that Queen Elizabeth II supports plans to remove the gender bias from British succession rules which currently states that succession goes to the first born son.

1 March 1998 The biggest political demonstrations in the UK for over a decade take place when 250,000 protestors march through London for a stronger voice for rural communities in the cabinet.

2 March 1998 The will of Diana, Princess of Wales is made public. Of the total £22 million, £9 million is paid in taxes, and most of the remaining £13 million is divided into trust funds for her sons, William and Harry. Her former butler and friend, Paul Burrell, and her 17 godchildren are also beneficiaries.

3 March 1998 In an unusual terrorist attack, unidentified gunmen open fire in a pub in Poyntzpass, Northern Ireland, killing close friends Philip Allen, a Protestant, and Damien Trainor, a Catholic. No one claims responsibility, but the Loyalist Volunteer Force (LVF), a militant Protestant group opposed to the peace talks, is suspected.

8 March 1998 Press reports reveal that Deputy Prime Minister John Prescott failed to register a £27,750 campaign donation made in 1996. In a separate development, Prescott's son Jonathan is accused of participating in a property deal in which 20 government-owned houses were sold to his property company at an average of £5,300 each, when they were actually valued by independent developers at an average of £20,000 each.

11 March 1998 The Lord Chancellor, Lord Irvine of Lairg, appears before a panel of Labour members of parliament to explain his purchase of £650,000 worth of renovations to his private residence using government money.

12 March 1998 After a meeting with Prime Minister Tony Blair in London, England, Sinn Féin leader Gerry Adams says that his party will soon rejoin the peace talks. Blair announces that a framework for a peace agreement in Northern Ireland is nearly in place.

12 March 1998 The UK Office for National Statistics indicates the highest level of teenage pregnancies – 9.4 per 1,000 – for more than a decade.

13 March 1998 A bill that bans hunting with dogs fails to be enacted when it does not receive the necessary support in Parliament. Prime Minister Tony Blair, while supporting the bill, does not include it as a top legislative priority.

14 March 1998 The Oblivion ride opens at Alton Towers theme park in Staffordshire. The world's first vertical drop ride, thrill seekers are plunged face first into pitch black at 112 kph/70 mph.

16 March 1998 David Keys, an alleged member of the Protestant militant Loyalist Volunteer Force (LVF) who was arrested in connection with the 3 March murder of a Catholic and a Protestant in Poyntzpass, Northern Ireland, is found dead in his cell in the Maze prison, beaten, cut, and hanged by a sheet by fellow inmates.

23 March 1998 Sinn Féin re-enters Northern Ireland peace negotiations after being suspended on February 20 for two execution-style murders in mid-February that were blamed on the Irish Republican Army (IRA).

27 March 1998 Two unidentified gunmen shoot and kill Cyril Stewart, a retired police officer, in Armagh, Northern Ireland. A hardline offshoot of the Irish Republican Army (IRA), the Irish National Liberation Army (INLA), claims responsibility.

10 April 1998 Ireland, Britain, and the political parties in Northern Ireland reach a historic peace agreement over Northern Ireland (known as The Good Friday Agreement), involving the devolution of a wide range of executive and legislative powers to a Northern Ireland Assembly.

18 April 1998 The predominantly protestant Ulster Unionist Party in Northern Ireland formally backs the peace agreement passed 10 April. Of the party council, 72% vote to endorse the plan and 28% vote against it.

30 April 1998 The Irish Republican Army (IRA) releases a statement endorsing the Northern Ireland peace agreement, but refuses to follow one of the agreement's stipulations: its surrender of arms.

April 1998 According to a report from the BBC, Britain recycles only 6% of its domestic waste, compared with 25% for the USA and up to 70% in parts of Canada. Britain recycles only 27% of its glass compared with 80% for the Netherlands; and 16% of steel packaging compared with 67% for Germany.

10 May 1998 Sinn Féin endorses the Northern Ireland peace agreement reached 10 April at a party conference in Dublin, Ireland.

25 May 1998 Amid protests by British World War II veterans, Japanese Emperor Akihito arrives in London, England, on a five-day visit to Britain.

7 June 1998 The British rock group The Rolling Stones cancel their concert dates in the UK, claiming that changes in the tax law would have cost the band £12 million in tax.

8 June 1998 Social Security Secretary Harriet Harman announces new legislation that will enable women to claim a fair share of their husband's pension on divorce. The plan, which will benefit an estimated 50,000 women a year, will enable divorce courts to treat pension rights like any other assets, such as a house, when dividing property between couples.

14 June 1998 A Home Office report finds that half of rapes in Britain are 'date rapes', which is thought to explain the drop in conviction rates, as rapists who know their victims are more difficult to prove guilty.

22 June 1998 The House of Commons votes 336–129 to lower the homosexual age of consent from 18 to 16, bringing it in line with the age of consent for heterosexuals.

General Information

Countries of the UK

Country	Area		Population (1995)	Population density (persons per sq km)	Capital	Parliamentary constituencies[1]	
	sq km	sq mi				UK (number of MPs)	Europe (number of MEPs)
England	130,423	50,356	48,903,000	375	London	529	71
Wales	20,779	8,023	2,917,000	140	Cardiff	40	5
Scotland	78,133	30,167	5,137,000	66	Edinburgh	72	8
Northern Ireland	13,576	5,242	1,649,000	121	Belfast	18	3

[1] As of 12 May 1998.

Highest Points in the UK by Region

Region	Highest point	Height m	Height ft
England			
Avon	East Harptree	264	867
Bedfordshire	Dunstable Down	243	798
Berkshire	Walbury Hill	279	974
Buckinghamshire	Wendover Woods	267	876
Cambridgeshire	Great Chishill	146	478
Cheshire	Shining Tor	559	1,834
Cleveland	Gisborough Moor	329	1,078
Cornwall	Brown Willy	420	1,377
Cumbria	Scafell Pike[1]	978	3,210
Derbyshire	Kinder Scout	636	2,088
Devon	High Willhays	621	2,038
Dorset	Pilsdon Pen	277	908
Durham	Mickle Fell	790	2,591
East Sussex	Ditchling Beacon	248	813
Essex	Oldfield Grove, Langley	147	482
Gloucestershire	Cleeve Cloud	330	1,083
Hampshire	Pilot Hill	286	937
Hereford and Worcester	Black Mountains	703	2,306
Hertfordshire	Hastoe	244	802
Humberside	Cot Nab	246	807
Kent	Westerham Hill	251	824
Lancashire	Gragareth	627	2,057
Leicestershire	Bardon Hill	279	916
Lincolnshire	Normanby-le-Wold	168	551
London, Greater	Westerham Heights	247	809
Manchester, Greater	Featherbed Moss	541	1,774
Merseyside	Billinge Hill	180	589
Norfolk	Roman Camp Beacon, Sheringham	105	344
Northamptonshire	Arbury Hill	224	734
Northumberland	The Cheviot	815	2,674
North Yorkshire	Whernside	736	2,415
Nottinghamshire	Herrod's Hill	202	663
Oxfordshire	Whitehorse Hill	261	856
Salop	Brown Clee Hill	540	1,772
Scilly, Isles of	St Mary's	51	166
Somerset	Dunkery Beacon	520	1,705
South Yorkshire	Magarey Hill	546	1,791
Staffordshire	Oliver Hill	513	1,684
Suffolk	Rede	128	419
Surrey	Leith Hill	294	965
Tyne and Wear	near Chopwell	259	851
Warwickshire	Ilmington Downs	260	854
West Midlands	Turner's Hill	269	882
West Sussex	Black Down Hill	280	919
West Yorkshire	Black Hill	582	1,908
Wight, Isle of	St Boniface's Down	239	785
Wiltshire	Milk Hill and Tan Hill	294	964
Wales			
Clwyd	Moel Sych	827	2,713
Dyfed	near Fan Foel	773	2,537
Gwent	Chwarel-y-Fan	679	2,228
Gwynedd	Snowdon[2]	1,085	3,559
Mid Glamorgan	Carn Foesen	584	1,917
Powys	Pen-y-Fan	886	2,907
South Glamorgan	Pant-glas	264	867
West Glamorgan	Cefnffordd	600	1,969
Scotland			
Borders	Broad Law	840	2,756
Central Scotland	Ben More	1,174	2,852
Dumfries and Galloway	Merrick	844	2,770
Fife	West Lomond	522	1,714
Grampian	Ben Macdui	1,309	4,269
Highland	Ben Nevis[3]	1,344	4,406
Lothian	Blackhope Scar	651	2,137
Orkney	Ward Hill, Hoy	479	1,570
Shetland	Ronas Hill, Mainland	450	1,475
Strathclyde	Bidean Nam Bian	1,150	3,773
Tayside	Ben Lawers	1,214	3,984
Western Isles	Clisham, Harris	799	2,622
Northern Ireland			
Antrim	Trostan	551	1,808
Armagh	Slieve Gullion	575	1,885
Down	Slieve Donard[4]	850	2,789
Fermanagh/Cavan Border	Cuilcagh	664	2,179
Londonderry	Sawel	680	2,231
Tyrone	Mullaghclogha	634	2,080

[1] Scafell Pike is the highest point in England.
[2] Snowdon is the highest point in Wales.
[3] Ben Nevis is the highest point in Scotland and the highest point in the UK.
[4] Slieve Donard is the highest point in Northern Ireland.

Largest 30 Islands in the UK

Name	Location	Area sq km	Area sq mi	Name	Location	Area sq km	Area sq mi
Benbecula	Outer Hebrides	9,200	3,552	Holy Island	west of the Isle of Anglesey, northwest Wales	78	32
Lewis	Outer Hebrides	2,220	857				
Skye	Inner Hebrides	1,740	672	Tiree	Inner Hebrides	77	48
Mull	Inner Hebrides	950	367	Raasay	Inner Hebrides	60	24
Anglesey	northwest coast of Wales	720	278	Shapinsay	Orkney Islands	56	20
Islay	Inner Hebrides	610	235	Fetlar	Shetland Islands	50	19
Arran	Firth of Clyde	427	165	Westray	Orkney Islands	48	19
Jura	Inner Hebrides	380	147	South Ronaldsay	Orkney Islands	46	18
Wight, Isle of	south coast of England	380	147	Bressay	Shetland Islands	40	15
Yell	Shetland Islands	208	80	Eigg	Inner Hebrides	40	15
Bute	Firth of Clyde	120	46	Sanday	Orkney Islands	40	15
Unst	Shetland Islands	120	46	Whalsay	Shetland Islands	32	12
Rum	Inner Hebrides	110	42	Lismore	west coast of Argyll and Bute at the mouth of Loch Linnhe	30	9
Barra	Outer Hebrides	90	35				
Sheppey	north coast of Kent	80	31	Eday	Orkney Islands	22	8
Stronsay	Orkney Islands	80	30	St Kilda	Outer Hebrides	20	8

Longest Rivers in the UK

Name	Source	Outlet	Length km	Length mi
Thames	Oxfordshire	North Sea	338	210
Severn	Ceredigion	Bristol Channel	336	208
Trent	Staffordshire/Cheshire border	Humber Estuary, North Sea	275	170
Great Ouse	Northamptonshire	The Wash	250	160
Wye	Ceredigion	River Severn	208	130
Tay	Highland	North Sea	193	120
Spey	Highland	Moray Firth	172	107
Clyde	South Lanarkshire	Firth of Clyde	171	106
Tweed	Dumfries and Galloway	North Sea	156	97
Avon (also known as Upper Avon or Warwickshire Avon)	Northamptonshire	River Severn	154	96
Nene	Northamptonshire	The Wash, North Sea	145	90
Dee (Scotland)	Highland	North Sea (by an artificial channel)	137	85
Usk	Carmarthenshire	Bristol Channel	137	85
Don	Aberdeenshire	North Sea	133	83
Tees	Cumbria	North Sea	130	80
Witham	Rutland	The Wash, North Sea	129	80
Ribble	North Yorkshire	Irish Sea	120	75
Teifi	Ceredigion	Cardigan Bay	118	73
Dee (Wales)	Bala Lake, Gywnedd	Irish Sea	112	70
Mersey	confluence of the Goyt and Tame rivers at Stockport, Greater Manchester	Irish Sea	112	70
Nith	East Ayrshire	Solway Firth	112	70
Towy	Ceredigion	Carmarthen Bay	111	69
Welland	Leicestershire	The Wash, North Sea	110	68
Aire	North Yorkshire	River Ouse (Yorkshire)	110	68
Tywi	Carmarthenshire	Carmarthen Bay	108	68
Wear	County Durham	North Sea	107	67
Eden	Cumbria	Solway Firth	104	65
Deveron	Aberdeenshire	North Sea	100	63
Tamar	Cornwall	Plymouth Sound	97	60
Swale	Cumbria/North Yorkshire border	River Ure	97	60

England: Administrative Divisions

Beginning in 1995, far-reaching local government changes took effect in England, based on recommendations of a government commission set up under the Local Government Act of 1992. The changes were implemented in stages, and resulted in a combination of the existing two-tier structure, with new single-tier (unitary) authorities. In 1995 and 1996, unitary authorities were introduced for the Isle of Wight, Avon, Cleveland, and Humberside (the latter three being abolished as counties) and the unitary authorities which replaced them are listed on page 55. More counties underwent changes in 1997, with their main urban centres becoming unitary authorities and the rest of the county keeping the existing two-tier system. The changes were completed in April 1998.

For counties, population figures are for the entire county, rather than the area administered by the county council. The land areas include the newly-separated unitary authorities, which still remain part of the county geographically. Unitary authorities created since the 1995–96 changes are not listed separately in this section.

Statistics for unemployment rate, average gross weekly full-time earnings, percentage of live births outside marriage, and deaths per 1,000 population are from *Office for National Statistics: Regional Trends 32, 1997 Edition* © Crown copyright 1997.

England: Counties

Bedfordshire

County of southern central England.

Area 1,192 sq km/460 sq mi; **Towns and cities** Bedford (administrative headquarters); Dunstable; **Geographical features** Chiltern Hills; **Rivers** Ouse; Cam; **Unemployment rate** 8.3% (May 1996); Population 373,000 (1995); **Average gross weekly full-time earnings** £368.60 (April 1996); **Percentage of live births outside marriage** 28%; **Deaths per 1,000 population** 8.6 (1995); **Industries and products** Cereals; vegetables; agricultural machinery; electrical goods; cement; clay; chalk; sand; gravel; bricks; packaging; motor vehicles and parts.

Berkshire

County of southern central England. The county of Berkshire was abolished in April 1998, and split into six unitary authorities: Bracknell Forest; West Berkshire; Reading; Windsor and Maidenhead; Slough, and Woking.

Area 1,260 sq km/486 sq mi; **Towns and cities** Reading (administrative headquarters); Eton; Slough; Maidenhead; Ascot; Bracknell; Newbury; Windsor; Wokingham; **Geographical features** Inkpen Beacon; Bagshot Heath; Ridgeway Path; **Rivers** Thames; Kennet; **Population** 769,200 (1994); **Unemployment rate** 4.5% (May 1996); **Average gross weekly full-time earnings** £420.90 (April 1996, highest in the UK); **Percentage of live births outside marriage** 26% (1995); **Deaths per 1,000 population** 8.4 (1995); **Industries and products** Agricultural and horticultural goods; electronics; plastics; pharmaceuticals; engineering; paints; biscuits; pigs; poultry; barley; dairy products.

Buckinghamshire

County of southeast central England.

Area 1,565 sq km/604 sq mi; **Towns and cities** Aylesbury (administrative headquarters); Buckingham; High Wycombe; Beaconsfield; Olney; **Geographical features** Chiltern Hills; Burnham Beeches; **Rivers** Great Ouse; Ray; Thames; **Population** 468,700 (1997 estimate); **Unemployment rate** 6.0% (May 1996); **Average gross weekly full-time earnings** £391.20 (April 1996); **Percentage of live births outside marriage** 26% (1995); **Deaths per 1,000 population** 8.3 (1995); **Industries and products** Furniture; agricultural goods (including barley, wheat, oats, sheep, cattle, poultry, pigs).

Cambridgeshire

County of eastern England. Peterborough became a unitary authority in April 1998.

Area 3,410 sq km/1,316 sq mi; **Towns and cities** Cambridge (administrative headquarters); Ely; Huntingdon; Peterborough; **Geographical features** Fens; flat with very fertile fenland soil; Isle of Ely; **Rivers** Ouse; Cam; Nene; **Population** 686,900 (1994); **Unemployment rate** 6.7% (May 1996); **Average gross weekly full-time earnings** £342.60 (April 1996); **Percentage of live births outside marriage** 26% (1995); **Deaths per 1,000 population** 9.1 (1995); **Industries and products** Agriculture (including cereals, fruit, and vegetables); electronics; food processing; mechanical engineering; scientific and pharmaceutical research.

Cheshire

County of northwest England. Halton and Warrington became unitary authorities in April 1998.

Area 2,320 sq km/896 sq mi; **Towns and cities** Chester (administrative headquarters); Warrington; Crewe; Widnes; Macclesfield; Congleton; **Geographical features** Chiefly a fertile plain, the Pennines, salt mines; **Rivers** Mersey; Dee; Weaver; **Population** 975,600 (1994); **Unemployment rate** 7.7% (May 1996); **Average gross weekly full-time earnings** £354.30 (April 1996); **Percentage of live births outside marriage** 32% (1995); **Deaths per 1,000 population** 10.4 (1995); **Industries and products** Textiles; chemicals; dairy products; aerospace industry; salt; pharmaceuticals; vehicles.

Cornwall

County of southwest England including the Isles of Scilly (Scillies).

Area (excluding Scillies) 3,550 sq km/1,370 sq mi; **Towns and cities** Truro (administrative headquarters); Camborne; Launceston; Bude; Falmouth; Newquay; Penzance; St Ives; **Geographical features** Bodmin Moor (including Brown Willy, 419 m/1,375 ft); Land's End peninsula; Lizard peninsula; St Michael's Mount; **Rivers** Tamar; Fowey; Fal; Camel; Poldhu; **Population** 479,600 (1994); **Unemployment rate** 8.6% (May 1996); **Average gross weekly full-time earnings** £272.20 (April 1996, lowest average wage in England); **Percentage of live births outside marriage** 33% (1995); **Deaths per 1,000 population** 12.8 (1995); **Industries and products** Tourism; electronics; spring flowers; dairy farming; market gardening.

Cumbria

County of northwest England, created in 1974 from Cumberland, Westmorland, and parts of northwest Lancashire and northwest Yorkshire.

Railway viaduct, Tamar River, Calstock, Cornwall Corel

Area 6,810 sq km/2,629 sq mi; **Towns and cities** Carlisle (administrative headquarters); Barrow; Kendal; Whitehaven; Workington; Penrith; **Geographical features** Lake District National Park: Scafell Pike, 978 m/3,210 ft (highest mountain in England); Helvellyn, 950 m/3,118 ft; Lake Windermere (largest lake in England), 17 km/10.5 mi long, 1.6 km/1 mi wide; other lakes (Derwent Water; Ullswater; Coniston Water; Ennerdale Water; Hawes Water); Grizedale Forest sculpture project; Furness peninsula; **Rivers** Calder; Derwent; Eden; Esk; Lune; Ure; **Population** 490,200 (1994); **Unemployment rate** 7.0% (May 1996); **Average gross weekly full-time earnings** £323.60 (April 1996); **Percentage of live births outside marriage** 32% (1995); **Deaths per 1,000 population** 12.2 (1995); **Industries and products** Tourism; agriculture; chemicals; plastics; marine engineering; shipbuilding.

Derbyshire

County of northern central England.

Area 2,550 sq km/984 sq mi; **Towns and cities** Matlock (administrative headquarters); Chesterfield; Ilkeston; **Geographical features** Peak District National Park, including Kinder Scout, 636 m/2,088 ft; **Rivers** Derwent; Dove; Rother; Trent; **Population** 726,000 (1995 estimate); **Unemployment rate** 8.2% (May 1996); **Average gross weekly full-time earnings** £325.60 (April 1996); **Percentage of live births outside marriage** 34% (1995); **Deaths per 1,000 population** 11.3 (1995); **Industries and products** Cereals; dairy and sheep farming; textiles; motor vehicles; quarrying; heavy engineering.

Devon

County of southwest England; Plymouth and Torbay are now unitary authorities and are administered separately.

Area 6,720 sq km/2,594 sq mi; **Towns and cities** Exeter (administrative headquarters); Plymouth; Paignton; Torquay; Teignmouth; Ilfracombe; Barnstaple; Crediton; Okehampton; Newton Abbot; Tiverton; **Geographical features** National Parks: Dartmoor; Exmoor; Lundy Island; **Rivers** Dart; Exe; Tamar; Teign; Torridge; Otter; **Population** 1,053,400 (1994); **Unemployment rate** 8.3% (May 1996); **Average gross weekly full-time earnings** £297.30 (April 1996); **Percentage of live births outside marriage** 33% (1995); **Deaths per 1,000 population** 12.7 (1995); **Industries and products** Tourism; sheep and dairy farming; beef cattle; cider; clotted cream; kaolin; Honiton lace; Dartington glass; carpets (Axminster); quarrying; fishing.

Dorset

County of southwest England.

Area 2,541 sq km/981 sq mi; **Towns and cities** Dorchester (administrative headquarters); Shaftesbury; Sherborne; Lyme Regis; Weymouth; Swanage; **Geographical features** Chesil Bank (a shingle bank along the coast 19 km/11 mi long); Isle of Purbeck (peninsula); Cranborne Chase; Canford Heath; **Rivers** Frome; Stour; **Population** 374,800 (1994 estimate); **Unemployment rate** 6.7% (May 1996); **Average gross weekly full-time earnings** £328.60 (April 1996); **Percentage of live births outside marriage** 32% (1995); **Deaths per 1,000 population** 13.6 (1995); **Industries and products** Tourism; agriculture; onshore oilfields (Wytch Farm; Wareham).

Durham

County of northeast England.

Area 2,232 sq km/862 sq mi; **Towns and cities** Durham (administrative headquarters); Peterlee; Newton Aycliffe; **Geographical features** Pennine Hills; **Rivers** Wear; Tees; **Population** 492,900 (1995 estimate); **Unemployment rate** 9.1% (May 1996); **Average gross weekly full-time earnings** £305.90 (April 1996); **Percentage of live births outside marriage** 38% (1995); **Deaths per 1,000 population** 11.9 (1995); **Industries and products** Sheep and dairy produce; clothing; chemicals; iron and steel processing; light engineering.

East Sussex

County of southeast England, created in 1974, formerly part of Sussex.

Area 1,725 sq mi sq km/666 sq mi; **Towns and cities** Lewes (administrative headquarters); Newhaven; Eastbourne; Hastings; Bexhill; Winchelsea; Rye; **Geographical features** Beachy Head (highest headland on the south coast at 180 m/590 ft, South Downs); the Weald (including Ashdown Forest); Friston Forest; Romney Marsh; **Rivers** Ouse; Cuckmere; Rother; **Population** 482,800 (1995); **Unemployment rate** 9.4% (May 1996); **Average gross weekly full-time earnings** £322.50 (April 1996); **Percentage of live births outside marriage** 36% (1995); **Deaths per 1,000 population** 14.6 (1995); **Industries and products** Tourism; electronics; gypsum; timber; light engineering; agriculture.

Essex

County of southeast England; Southend and Thurrock became separate unitary authorities in April 1998.

Area 3,670 sq km/1,417 sq mi; **Towns and cities** Chelmsford (administrative headquarters); Colchester; Harwich; Tilbury; Harlow; Braintree; Clacton; **Geographical features** former royal hunting ground of Epping Forest (controlled from 1882 by the City of London); marshy coastal headland of the Naze; **Rivers** Blackwater; Colne; Crouch; **Population** 1,528,600 (1991); **Unemployment rate** 7.2% (May 1996); **Average gross weekly full-time earnings** £346.00 (April 1996); **Percentage of live births outside marriage** 31% (1995); **Deaths per 1,000 population** 10.7 (1995); **Industries and products** Dairy products; cereals; fruit; sugar beet; oysters; cars.

Gloucestershire

County of southwest England.

Area 2,640 sq km/1,019 sq mi; **Towns and cities** Gloucester (administrative headquarters); Stroud; Cheltenham; Tewkesbury; Cirencester; **Geographical features** Cotswold Hills; **Rivers** Severn; Windrush; **Population** 549,500 (1994); **Unemployment rate** 6.6% (May 1996); **Average gross weekly full-time earnings** £344.60 (April 1996); **Percentage of live births outside marriage** 30% (1995); **Deaths per 1,000 population** 11.0 (1995); **Industries and products** Cereals; fruit; dairy products; engineering; timber; aerospace industry.

Hampshire

County of south England. Portsmouth and Southampton became unitary authorities in April 1997.

Area 3,679 sq km/1,420 sq mi; **Towns and cities** Winchester (administrative headquarters); Southampton; Portsmouth; Gosport; **Geographical features** New Forest (area 373 sq km/144 sq mi); Hampshire Basin (onshore and offshore oil); **Rivers** Test; Itchen; **Population** 1,213,600 (1995); **Unemployment rate** 6.6% (May 1996); **Average gross weekly full-time earnings** £349.50 (April 1996); **Percentage of live births outside marriage** 30% (1995); **Deaths per 1,000 population** 10.2 (1995); **Industries and products** Agricultural products (including watercress); oil refining; chemicals; pharmaceuticals; brewing; aeronautics; perfume; electronics; shipbuilding

Hereford and Worcester

County of western central England, created in 1974 from the counties of Herefordshire and Worcestershire. The county was abolished in April 1998 and split into the unitary authority of Herefordshire (with pre-1974 boundaries) and the two-tier county of Worcestershire.

Area 3,930 sq km/1,517 sq mi; **Towns and cities** Worcester; Hereford; Kidderminster; Evesham; Ross-on-Wye; Ledbury; **Geographical features** Malvern Hills (high point Worcester Beacon, 425 m/1,395 ft); Black Mountains; Vale of Evesham; subterranean brine reservoir; **Rivers** Wye; Severn; **Population** 699,900 (1994); **Unemployment rate** 7.1% (May 1996); **Average gross weekly full-time earnings** £311.20 (April 1996); **Percentage of live births outside marriage** 30% (1995); **Deaths per 1,000 population** 11.0 (1995); **Industries and products** Apples; pears; cider; hops; vegetables; Hereford cattle; carpets; porcelain; chemicals; salt; food processing; engineering; car accessories; tourism.

Hertfordshire

County of southeast England.

Area 1,630 sq km/629 sq mi; **Towns and cities** Hertford (administrative headquarters); St Albans; Watford; Hatfield; Hemel Hempstead; Bishop's Stortford; Letchworth (the first 'garden city', followed by Welwyn in 1919 and Stevenage in 1947); **Geographical features** Part of the Chiltern Hills; **Rivers** Lea; Stort; Colne; **Population** 975,800 (1991); **Unemployment rate** 6.4% (May 1996); **Average gross weekly full-time earnings** £374.00 (April 1996); **Percentage of live births outside marriage** 26% (1995); **Deaths per 1,000 population** 9.4 (1995); **Industries and products** Engineering; aircraft; electrical goods; paper and printing; agriculture; horticulture; tanning; computer electronics; plastics; pharmaceuticals.

Kent

County of southeast England, known as the 'garden of England'; Rochester and Gillingham joined in 1998 to become the new unitary authority of the Medway Towns.

Area 3,730 sq km/1,440 sq mi; **Towns and cities** Maidstone (administrative headquarters); Canterbury; Dover; Chatham; Rochester; Tunbridge Wells; Folkestone; Margate; Ramsgate; Sheerness; **Geographical features** North Downs; Romney Marsh; Isles of Grain, Sheppey, and Thanet; Weald (agricultural area); **Rivers** Thames; Darent; Medway; Stour; **Population** 1,546,300 (1994); **Unemployment rate** 7.5% (May 1996); **Average gross weekly full-time earnings** £339.10 (April 1996); **Percentage of live births outside marriage** 34% (1995); **Deaths per 1,000 population** 11.2 (1995); **Industries and products** Hops; apples; soft fruit; cement; paper; oil refining; shipbuilding.

Lancashire

County of northwest England; Blackburn and Blackpool became unitary authorities in April 1998.

Area 3,040 sq km/1,173 sq mi; **Towns and cities** Preston (administrative headquarters); Lancaster; Accrington; Burnley; Fleetwood; Heysham; Morecambe; Southport; **Geographical features** the Pennines; the Forest of Bowland (moors and farming valleys); Pendle Hill; **Rivers** Ribble; Wyre; Hodder; **Population** 1,424,000 (1994); **Unemployment rate** 6.4% (May 1996); **Average gross weekly full-time earnings** £315.60 (April 1996); **Percentage of live births outside marriage** 37% (1995); **Deaths per 1,000 population** 12.2 (1995); **Industries and products** Aerospace; electronics; dairy farming; market gardening.

Leicestershire

County of central England. The city of Leicester and the county of Rutland became unitary authorities in April 1997.

Area 2,084 sq km/804 sq mi; **Towns and cities** Leicester (administrative headquarters); Loughborough; Melton Mowbray; Market Harborough; **Geographical features** Charnwood Forest; Vale of Belvoir; **Rivers** Soar; **Population** 592,700 (1995); **Unemployment rate** 6.5% (May 1996); **Average gross weekly full-time earnings** £321.10 (April 1996); **Percentage of live births outside marriage** (1995) 30%; **Deaths per 1,000 population** 9.6 (1995); **Industries and products** Horses; cattle; sheep; dairy products; coal; Stilton cheese; hosiery; footwear; bell founding.

Lincolnshire

County of eastern England.

Area 5,890 sq km/2,274 sq mi; **Towns and cities** Lincoln (administrative headquarters); Skegness; **Geographical features** Lincoln Wolds; marshy coastline; the Fens in the southeast; Gibraltar Point National Nature Reserve; **Rivers** Witham; Welland; **Population** 605,600 (1994); **Unemployment rate** 7.1% (May 1996); **Average gross weekly full-time earnings** £303.70 (April 1996); **Percentage of live births outside marriage** 32% (1995); **Deaths per 1,000 population** 11.9 (1995); **Industries and products** Cattle; sheep; horses; cereals; flower bulbs; oil; vegetables.

Manchester, Greater

Metropolitan county of northwest England, created in 1974; in 1986, most of the functions of the former county council were transferred to metropolitan district councils.

Area 1,290 sq km/498 sq mi; **Towns and cities** Manchester; Bolton; Oldham; Rochdale; Salford; Stockport; Wigan; **Geographical features** Manchester Ship Canal; **Rivers** Irwell; Roch; **Population** 2,758,000 (1995); **Unemployment rate** 8.9% (May 1996); **Average gross weekly full-time earnings** £329.50 (April 1996); **Percentage of live births outside marriage** 41% (1995); **Deaths per 1,000 population** 11.3 (1995); **Industries and products** Engineering; textiles; textile machinery; chemicals; plastics; electrical goods; electronic equipment; paper; printing; rubber; asbestos.

Merseyside

Metropolitan county of northwest England, created in 1974; in 1986, most of the functions of the former county council were transferred to metropolitan district councils.

Area 650 sq km/251 sq mi; **Towns and cities** Liverpool; Bootle; Birkenhead; St Helens; Wallasey; Southport; **Rivers** Mersey; **Population** 1,403,600 (1991); **Unemployment rate** 13.0% (May 1996); **Average gross weekly full-time earnings** £325.40 (April 1996); **Percentage of live births outside marriage** 47% (1995); **Deaths per 1,000 population** 12.2 (1995); **Industries and products** Chemicals; electrical goods; vehicles; glass making.

Norfolk

County of east England.

Area 5,360 sq km/2,069 sq mi; **Towns and cities** Norwich (administrative headquarters); King's Lynn; Great Yarmouth; Cromer; Hunstanton; **Geographical features** Lowlying; Norfolk Broads; Halvergate Marshes wildlife area; Grime's Graves (Neolithic flint mines); **Rivers** Ouse; Yare; Bure; Waveney; **Population** 768,500 (1994); **Unemployment rate** 7.8% (May 1996); **Average gross weekly full-time earnings** £310.00 (April 1996); **Percentage of live births outside marriage** (1995) 32%; **Deaths per 1,000 population** 12.1 (1995); **Industries and products** Cereals; turnips; sugar beets; turkeys; geese; offshore natural gas; fishing; traditional reed thatching; tourism.

Northamptonshire

County of central England.

Area 2,370 sq km/915 sq mi; **Towns and cities** Northampton (administrative headquarters); Kettering; Wellingborough; Corby; Daventry; **Geographical features** Site of Battle of Naseby (1645); **Rivers** Welland; Nene; **Population** 594,800 (1994); **Unemployment rate** 5.1% (May 1996); **Average gross weekly full-time earnings** £331.70 (April 1996); **Percentage of live births outside marriage** 34% (1995); **Deaths per 1,000 population** 9.7 (1995); **Industries and products** Cereals; cattle; sugar beet; shoemaking; food processing; printing; engineering.

Northumberland

County of northern England.

Area 5,030 sq km/1,942 sq mi; **Towns and cities** Morpeth (administrative headquarters); Berwick-upon-Tweed; Hexham; **Geographical features** Cheviot Hills; Northumberland National Park in the west; Holy Island; the Farne island group; moorland; Kielder Water (largest artificial lake in northern Europe, 1982); **Rivers** Tweed; upper Tyne; **Population** 307,700 (1994); **Unemployment rate** 7.9% (May 1996); **Average gross weekly full-time earnings** £290.80 (April 1996); **Percentage of live births outside marriage** 32% (1995); **Deaths per 1,000 population** 12.1 (1995); **Industries and products** Sheep; fishing; tourism.

North Yorkshire

County of northeast England, created in 1974 from most of the North Riding and parts of the East and West Ridings of Yorkshire.

Area 8,037 sq km/3,102 sq mi; **Towns and cities** Northallerton (administrative headquarters); Harrogate; Scarborough; Whitby; **Geographical features** Pennines; Vale of York; Cleveland Hills and North Yorkshire Moors, which form a national park; Yorkshire Dales National Park (including Swaledale, Wensleydale, and Bolton Abbey in Wharfedale); **Rivers** Derwent; Ouse; **Population** 556,200 (1995); **Unemployment rate** 6.6% (May 1996); **Average gross weekly full-time earnings** £302.30; **Percentage of live births outside marriage** 25% (1995); **Deaths per 1,000 population** 11.6 (1995); **Industries and products** Cereals; wool and meat from sheep; dairy products; coal; electrical goods; footwear; clothing; vehicles; plastics; foodstuffs; high technology industries; light industry.

Nottinghamshire

County of central England; Nottingham City became a unitary authority in April 1998.

Area 2,160 sq km/834 sq mi; **Towns and cities** Nottingham (administrative headquarters); Mansfield; Worksop; Newark; **Geographical features** Sherwood Forest (home of Robin Hood); Cresswell Crags (remains of prehistoric humans); **Rivers** Trent; **Population** 1,030,900 (1994); **Unemployment rate** 8.3% (May 1996); **Average gross weekly full-time earnings** £306.80 (April 1996); **Percentage of live births outside marriage** 39% (1995); **Deaths per 1,000 population** 10.7 (1995); **Industries and products** Cereals; cattle; sheep; light engineering; footwear; limestone; coal mining; ironstone; oil; cigarettes; tanning; furniture; pharmaceuticals; typewriters; gypsum; gravel; market gardening.

Oxfordshire

County of southern central England.

Area 2,610 sq km/1,007 sq mi; **Towns and cities** Oxford (administrative headquarters); Abingdon; Banbury; Henley-on-Thames; Witney; Woodstock; **Geographical features** Cotswolds; Chiltern Hills; **Rivers** Thames and tributaries; Cherwell; Windrush; Evenlode; **Population** 590,200 (1994); **Unemployment rate** 4.2% (May 1996); **Average gross weekly full-time earnings** £357.60 (April 1996); **Percentage of live births outside marriage** 24% (1995); **Deaths per 1,000 population** 8.6 (1995); **Industries and products** Cereals; cars; paper; bricks; cement; medical electronic equipment; dairy farming; high-technology industries; aluminium; sheep; publishing; nuclear research; scientific services; tourism.

Shropshire

County of west England. Sometimes abbreviated to 'Salop', it was officially known by this name from 1974 until local protest reversed the decision in 1980. The Wrekin, an area including the towns of Telford, Wellington, Ironbridge, Newport, Coalport, Coalbrookdale, Madeley, Hadley, and Dawley, became a unitary authority in April 1998.

Area 3,490 sq km/1,347 sq mi; **Towns and cities** Shrewsbury (administrative headquarters); Oswestry; Ludlow; **Geographical features** Lake Ellesmere; Clee Hills; Clun Forest; **Rivers** Severn; **Population** 416,500 (1994); **Unemployment rate** 6.8% (May 1996); **Average gross weekly full-time earnings** £302.40 (April 1996); **Percentage**

of live births outside marriage 33% (1995); **Deaths per 1,000 population** 10.4 (1995); **Industries and products** Sheep and cattle; cereals; sugar beet; iron (main iron-producing county in England); engineering.

Somerset

County of southwest England.

Area 3,460 sq km/1,336 sq mi; **Towns and cities** Taunton (administrative headquarters); Wells; Bridgwater; Glastonbury; Yeovil; Minehead; **Geographical features** marshy coastline on the Bristol Channel; Mendip Hills (including Cheddar Gorge and Wookey Hole, limestone caves where Stone Age remains have been found); Quantock Hills; Exmoor; Blackdown Hills; **Rivers** Avon; Parret; Exe; Brue; **Population** 477,900 (1994); **Unemployment rate** 6.8% (May 1996); **Average gross weekly full-time earnings** £317.90 (April 1996); **Percentage of live births outside marriage** 29% (1995); **Deaths per 1,000 population** 11.9 (1995); **Industries and products** Tourism; agriculture; engineering; dairy products; cider; food processing; textiles; helicopters; stone quarrying; leather.

South Yorkshire

Metropolitan county of northeast England, created in 1974; in 1986, most of the functions of the former county council were transferred to the metropolitan district councils.

Area 1,560 sq km/602 sq mi; **Towns and cities** Barnsley; Sheffield; Doncaster; Rotherham; **Geographical features** Part of Peak District National Park; the 1995 Millennium Commission award will enable the Earth Centre for environmental research to be built near Doncaster; **Rivers** Don; **Population** 1,262,600 (1991); **Unemployment rate** 10.7% (May 1996); **Average gross weekly full-time earnings** £308.08 (April 1996); **Percentage of live births outside marriage** 40% (1995); **Deaths per 1,000 population** 11.4 (1995); **Industries and products** Metalwork; coal; dairy; sheep; arable farming.

Staffordshire

County of western central England.

Area 2,623 sq km/1,012 sq mi; **Towns and cities** Stafford (administrative headquarters); Newcastle-under-Lyme; **Geographical features** Cannock Chase; North Staffordshire Moors; **Rivers** Trent; **Population** 802,100 (1995); **Unemployment rate** 6.1% (May 1996); **Average gross weekly full-time earnings** £308.90 (April 1996); **Percentage of live births outside marriage** 34% (1995); **Deaths per 1,000 population** 10.7 (1995); **Industries and products** China and earthenware; tractors and agricultural equipment; dairy farming; electrical engineering.

Suffolk

County of east England.

Area 3,800 sq km/1,467 sq mi; **Towns and**

cities Ipswich (administrative headquarters); Bury St Edmunds; Lowestoft; Felixstowe; **Geographical features** undulating lowlands and flat coastline; part of the Norfolk Broads; Minsmere marshland bird reserve, near Aldeburgh; the Sandlings (heathlands and birds); **Rivers** Waveney; Alde; Deben; Orwell; Stour; Little Ouse; **Population** 649,500 (1994); **Unemployment rate** 5.9% (May 1996); **Average gross weekly full-time earnings** £318.90 (April 1996); **Percentage of live births outside marriage** 30% (1995); **Deaths per 1,000 population** 11.2 (1995); **Industries and products** Cereals; sugar beet; timber; working horses (Suffolk punches); fertilizers; agricultural machinery; fishing; electronics; telecommunications research; printing; motor vehicle components; food processing; North Sea oil and gas exploration.

Surrey

County of south England.

Area 1,660 sq km/641 sq mi; **Towns and cities** Kingston upon Thames (administrative headquarters); Guildford; Woking; Reigate; Leatherhead; **Geographical features** Box Hill; Leith Hill; North Downs; **Rivers** Thames; Mole; Wey; **Population** 1,041,200 (1994); **Unemployment rate** 4.7% (May 1996); **Average gross weekly full-time earnings** £405.50 (April 1996, highest in UK); **Percentage of live births outside marriage** 22% (1995); **Deaths per 1,000 population** 10.3 (1995); **Industries and products** Vegetables; agricultural products; service industries; horticulture; gravel.

Tyne and Wear

Metropolitan county of northeast England, created in 1974; in 1986, most of the functions of the former county council were transferred to the metropolitan district councils.

Area 540 sq km/208 sq mi; **Towns and cities** Newcastle upon Tyne; South Shields; North Shields; Gateshead; Sunderland; **Rivers** Tyne; Wear; **Population** 1,131,000 (1995); **Unemployment rate** 12.1% (May 1996); **Average gross weekly full-time earnings** £316.20 (April 1996); **Percentage of live births outside marriage** 43% (1995); **Deaths per 1,000 population** 11.8 (1995); **Industries and products** Car manufacturing; electronics; offshore technology (floating production vessels); automobile components; pharmaceuticals; computer science.

Warwickshire

Area 1,980 sq km/764 sq mi; **Towns and cities** Warwick (administrative headquarters); Royal Leamington Spa; Nuneaton; Rugby; Stratford-upon-Avon; **Geographical features** Forest of Arden; **Rivers** Avon; **Population** 496,300 (1994); **Unemployment rate** 5.9% (May 1996); **Average gross weekly full-time earnings** £329.10 (April 1996); **Percentage of live births outside marriage** 29% (1995); **Deaths per 1,000**

The Royal Shakespeare Theatre,
Stratford-upon-Avon, Warwickshire Corel

population 10.7 (1995); **Industries and products** Mainly agricultural; tourism; engineering; textiles; motor industry.

West Midlands

Metropolitan county of central England, created in 1974; in 1986, most of the functions of the former county council were transferred to the metropolitan district councils.

Area 900 sq km/347 sq mi; **Towns and cities** Birmingham; Wolverhampton; Coventry; Walsall; Dudley; Solihull; **Geographical features** Forest of Arden; **Rivers** Stour; **Population** 2,551,700 (1991); **Unemployment rate** 11.3% (May 1996); **Average gross weekly full-time earnings** £334.40 (April 1996); **Percentage of live births outside marriage** 37% (1995); **Deaths per 1,000 population** 11.0 (1995);

Industries and products Industrial goods; coal mining; chemicals; machine tools; engineering; motor vehicles; aircraft components; electrical equipment; motor components; glass.

West Sussex

County of south England, created in 1974, formerly part of Sussex.

Area 2,020 sq km/780 sq mi; **Towns and cities** Chichester (administrative headquarters); Crawley; Horsham; Haywards Heath; Shoreham; Worthing; Littlehampton; Bognor Regis; **Geographical features** The Weald; South Downs; **Rivers** Arun; West Rother; Adur; **Population** 722,100 (1994); **Unemployment rate** 6.3% (May 1996); **Average gross weekly full-time earnings** £365.10 (April 1996); **Percentage of live births outside marriage** 26% (1995); **Deaths per 1,000 population** 13.2 (1995); **Industries and products** Cereals; root crops; dairy produce; electronics; light engineering.

West Yorkshire

Metropolitan county of northeast England, created in 1974; in 1986, most of the functions of the former county council were transferred to the metropolitan district councils.

Area 2,040 sq km/787 sq mi; **Towns and cities** Wakefield; Leeds; Bradford; Halifax;

Huddersfield; **Geographical features** Ilkley Moor; Haworth Moor; part of the Peak District National Park; **Rivers** Caulder; Aire; **Population** 2,013,700 (1991); **Unemployment rate** 7.6% (May 1996); **Average gross weekly full-time earnings** £320.08 (April 1996); **Percentage of live births outside marriage** 35% (1995); **Deaths per 1,000 population** 10.6 (1995); **Industries and products** Woollen textiles; plastics: paper; leather goods; engineering; chemicals; financial services.

Wiltshire

County of southwest England.

Area 3,255 sq km/1,256 sq mi; **Towns and cities** Trowbridge (administrative headquarters); Salisbury; Wilton; **Geographical features** Marlborough Downs; Savernake Forest; Salisbury Plain (military training area used since Napoleonic times); **Rivers** Kennet; Wylye; Avon; **Population** 424,600 (1997 estimate); **Unemployment rate** 5.0% (May 1996); **Average gross weekly full-time earnings** £354.00 (April 1996); **Percentage of live births outside marriage** 27% (1995); **Deaths per 1,000 population** 9.9 (1995); **Industries and products** Wheat; cattle; pig and sheep farming; rubber; engineering; clothing; brewing; electronics; computing; pharmaceuticals; plastics.

England: Unitary Authorities

N/A = not available.

Bath and North East Somerset

Unitary authority in southwest England created in 1996 from part of the former county of Avon.

Area 351 sq km/136 sq mi; **Towns and cities** Bath (administrative headquarters); **Geographical features** Hot springs; Chew Valley Lake; **Rivers** Avon; **Population** 158,700 (1996); **Unemployment rate** N/A; **Average gross weekly full-time earnings** £334.70 (April 1996); **Percentage of live births outside marriage** 28% (1995); **Deaths per 1,000 population** 11.3 (1995); **Industries and products** Printing; plastics; engineering; tourism.

East Riding of Yorkshire

Unitary authority in north England created in 1996 from part of the former county of Humberside.

Area 2,416 sq km/933 sq mi; **Towns and cities** Beverley (administrative headquarters); Driffield; Goole; Hornsea; Bridlington; **Geographical features** Holderness Peninsula; The Wolds; Hornsea Mere; **Rivers** Humber; Hull; Ouse; **Population** 310,000 (1996);

Unemployment rate 4.7% (May 1996); **Average gross weekly full-time earnings** £319.70; **Percentage of live births outside marriage** 30% (1995); **Deaths per 1,000 population** 11.8 (1995); **Industries and products** Agriculture; leather tanning; car accessories.

Hartlepool

Unitary authority in northeast England created in 1996 from part of the former county of Cleveland.

Area 94 sq km/36 sq mi; **Population** 90,400 (1996); **Unemployment rate** 17.3% (May 1996); **Average gross weekly full-time earnings** N/A; **Percentage of live births outside marriage** 50% (1995); **Deaths per 1,000 population** 11.1 (1995); **Industries and products** Metal industries; engineering.

Middlesbrough

Industrial town, port, and unitary authority, on the river Tees, northeast England.

Area 54 sq km/21 sq mi; **Population** 146,000 (1996); **Unemployment rate** 19.8% (May 1996); **Average gross weekly full-time earnings** £327.50; **Percentage of live births outside marriage** 50% (1995);

Deaths per 1,000 population 10.5 (1995); **Industries and products** Construction; electronics; engineering; shipbuilding; iron; steel; chemicals (including petrochemicals).

North East Lincolnshire

Unitary authority in east England created in 1996 from part of the former county of Humberside.

Area 192 sq km/74 sq mi; **Towns and cities** Grimsby (administrative headquarters); Immingham; Cleethorpes; **Rivers** Freshney; Humber; **Population** 164,000 (1996 estimate); **Unemployment rate** 10.9% (May 1996); **Average gross weekly full-time earnings** £327.00; **Percentage of live births outside marriage** 47% (1995); **Deaths per 1,000 population** 11.2 (1995); **Industries and products** Fishing; fish processing; tourism; chemicals.

North Lincolnshire

Unitary authority in east England created in 1996 from part of the former county of Humberside.

Area 850 sq km/328 sq mi; **Towns and cities** Scunthorpe (administrative headquarters); Epworth; **Geographical features** Isle of

Axholme; Wetland nature reserves; **Rivers** Humber; Trent; **Population** 153,000 (1996); **Unemployment rate** 10.4% (May 1996); **Average gross weekly full-time earnings** £336.90; **Percentage of live births outside marriage** 37% (1995); **Deaths per 1,000 population** 11.0 (1995); **Industries and products** Oil refining; steel; other metals.

North Somerset

Unitary authority in southwest England created in 1996 from part of the former county of Avon.

Area 372 sq km/144 sq mi; **Towns and cities** Weston-super-Mare (administrative headquarters); Clevedon; Portishead; Nailsea; **Geographical features** Mendip Hills; **Rivers** Avon; Severn; Yea; **Population** 177,000 (1996); **Unemployment rate** N/A; **Average gross weekly full-time earnings** £321.00; **Percentage of live births outside marriage** 31% (1995); **Deaths per 1,000 population** 12.5 (1995); **Industries and products** Tourism; agriculture; plastics; engineering.

Redcar and Cleveland

Unitary authority in northeast England created in 1996 from part of the former county of Cleveland; administrative headquarters South Bank, Middlesbrough.

Area 240 sq km/93 sq mi; **Towns and cities** Redcar; Skelton; Guisborough; **Geographical features** Boulby Cliffs; Cleveland Way; North Yorkshire Moors; **Rivers** Tees; **Population** 144,000 (1996); **Unemployment rate** 12% (May 1996); **Average gross weekly full-time earnings** £370.00; **Percentage of live births outside marriage** 45% (1995); **Deaths per 1,000 population** 11.3 (1995); **Industries and products** Steel; fabrics; chemicals.

South Gloucestershire

Unitary authority in southwest England created in 1996 from part of the former county of Avon.

Area 497 sq km/192 sq mi; **Towns and cities** Thornbury (administrative headquarters); Chipping Sodbury; Wick; **Population** 220,000 (1996); **Geographical features** Vale of Berkeley; **Rivers** Severn; **Unemployment rate** 4.6% (May 1996); **Average gross weekly full-time earnings** £358.60; **Percentage of live births outside marriage** 24% (1995); **Deaths per 1,000 population** 8.0 (1995); **Industries and products** Agriculture.

Stockton-on-Tees

Unitary authority in northeast England created in 1996 from part of the former county of Cleveland; administrative headquarters Stockton-on-Tees.

Area 200 sq km/77 sq mi; **Population** 176,600 (1996); **Unemployment rate** 14.1% (May 1996); **Average gross weekly full-time earnings** £329.80; **Percentage of live births outside marriage** 40% (1995); **Deaths per 1,000 population** 9.9 (1995); **Industries and products** Electronics; chemicals; plastics; heavy engineering.

The Isle of Wight

Island and unitary authority of south England.

Area 380 sq km/147 sq mi; **Towns and cities** Newport (administrative headquarters); Ryde; Sandown; Shanklin; Ventnor; Cowes; **Geographical features** The Needles (group of pointed chalk rocks up to 30 m/100 ft high in the sea to the west); the Solent; **Rivers** Medina; **Population** 130,000 (1996); **Unemployment rate** 11.9% (May 1996); **Average gross weekly full-time earnings** £296.80 (April 1996); **Percentage of live births outside marriage** 42% (1995); **Deaths per 1,000 population** 14.9 (1995); **Industries and products** Agriculture; shipbuilding; tourism; aircraft components; electronics; plastics; marine engineering.

Wales: Unitary Authorities

N/A = not available.

In April 1996 the eight counties of Wales – Clwyd, Dyfed, Gwent, Gwynedd, Mid Glamorgan, Powys, South Glamorgan, and West Glamorgan – were replaced with 22 counties and county borough unitary authorities.

Statistics for unemployment rate, average gross weekly full-time earnings, percentage of live births outside marriage, and deaths per 1,000 population are from *Office for National Statistics: Regional Trends 32, 1997 Edition*. © Crown copyright 1997.

Anglesey

Island and unitary authority off the northwest coast of Wales.

Area 720 sq km/278 sq mi.; **Towns and cities** Llangefni (administrative headquarters); Holyhead; Menai Bridge; Amlwch; Beaumaris; **Geographical features** Menai Strait; **Population** 71,100 (1996); **Unemployment rate** N/A; **Average gross weekly full-time earnings** N/A; **Percentage of live births outside marriage** 36% (1995); **Deaths per 1,000 population** 12.9 (1995); **Industries and products** Tourism; agriculture; toy-making; electrical goods; bromine extraction from the sea.

Blaenau Gwent

Unitary authority in South Wales created in 1996 from part of the former county of Gwent; administrative headquarters Ebbw Vale.

Area 109 sq km/42 sq mi; **Geographical features** Brecon Beacons National Park; **Population** 73,000 (1996); **Unemployment rate** N/A; **Average gross weekly full-time earnings** £255.10; **Percentage of live births outside marriage** 47% (1995); **Deaths per 1,000 population** 12.8 (1995); **Industries** Tourism; tin-plate manufacture; engineering.

Bridgend

Unitary authority in South Wales created in 1996 from part of the former county of Mid Glamorgan.

Area 40 sq km/15 sq mi; **Towns and cities** Bridgend (administrative headquarters); Maesteg; Porthcawl; Llanilltyd Fawr; **Population** 128,300 (1996); **Unemployment rate** 10.9% (May 1996); **Average gross weekly full-time earnings** N/A; **Percentage of live births outside marriage** 41% (1995); **Deaths per 1,000 population** 12.0 (1995); **Industries and products** Civil engineering; chocolate manufacture.

Caerphilly

Unitary authority in South Wales created in 1996 from parts of the former counties of Mid Glamorgan and Gwent.

Area 270 sq km/104 sq mi; **Towns and cities** Hengoed (administrative headquarters); Rhymney; Risca; Caerphilly; **Rivers** Taff; Rhymney; **Population** 172,000 (1996); **Unemployment rate** N/A (May 1996); **Average gross weekly full-time earnings** £296.20; **Percentage of live births outside marriage** 44% (1995); **Deaths per 1,000 population** 11.4 (1995); **Industries and products** Agriculture; tourism; light industry.

Cardiff

City, seaport, unitary authority, and capital of Wales (since 1955).

Area 139 sq km/54 sq mi (unitary authority); **Population** 306,500 (1996); **Unemployment rate** 8.8% (May 1996); **Average gross weekly full-time earnings** £332.90; **Percentage of live births outside marriage** 39% (1995); **Deaths per 1,000 population** 10.1 (1995); **Universities** University of Wales; University of Wales College of Medicine; University of Wales Institute; **Airports** Cardiff Airport; **Mainline railway stations** Cardiff Central Station; Queen Street Station; **Main bus station** Penarth Road Bus Station; **Industries and products** Car components; flour milling; ship repairs; electrical goods; paper; cigars; high-tech industries; **Places of interest** Cathays Park: Law Courts, City Hall, National Museum of Wales, the Welsh Office (established 1964), Temple of Peace and Health; Llandaff cathedral; Cardiff Castle; Welsh Industrial and Maritime Museum; Welsh Folk Museum; Cardiff International Arena; **Cultural organizations** Cardiff Bay

Chamber Orchestra; BBC National Orchestra of Wales; Welsh National Opera; Sherman Theatre; **Newspapers** *Western Mail and Echo*; **Tourist Information Centre** Central Station, Cardiff CF1 1QY; phone: (01222) 227281; **Chamber of Commerce** 1st Floor, Corys' Buildings, 57 Bute Street, Cardiff CF1 6AJ; Phone: (01222) 481648; Fax: (01222) 489785; e-mail Info@walescci.-celtic.co.uk.

Carmarthenshire

Unitary authority in South Wales. A former county, it was part of Dyfed 1975–1996.

Area 2,390 sq km/923 sq mi; **Towns and cities** Carmarthen (administrative headquarters); Llanelli; Ammanford; Burry Port; Llandovery; Kidwelly; **Geographical features** Black Mountains; **Rivers** Towy; Loughor; Taff; **Population** 68,900 (1996); **Unemployment rate** 9.3% (May 1996); **Average gross weekly full-time earnings** £303.70; **Percentage of live births outside marriage** 34% (1995); **Deaths per 1,000 population** 13.9 (1995); **Industries and products** Dairy cattle; sheep; tourism; tin plate; copper smelting; chemicals; bricks.

Ceredigion

Unitary authority in southwest Wales created in 1996 from part of the former county of Dyfed.

Area 1,793 sq km/ 692 sq mi; **Towns and cities** Aberaeron (administrative headquarters); Cardigan; Aberystwyth; Lampeter; **Geographical features** Cambrian Mountains, including Plynlimon Fawr, 752 m/2,468 ft; **Rivers** Rheidol; Ystwyth; Teifi; **Population** 68,900 (1996); **Unemployment rate** N/A; **Average gross weekly full-time earnings** N/A; **Percentage of live births outside marriage** 33% (1995); **Deaths per 1,000 population** 12.6 (1995); **Industries and products** Dairy cattle; sheep; tourism.

Conwy

Unitary authority in North Wales created in 1996 from parts of the former counties of Clwyd and Gwynedd.

Area 1,107 sq km/427 sq mi; **Towns and cities** Conwy (administrative headquarters); Llanrwst; Colwyn Bay; Llanfairfechan; Abergele; Penmaenmawr; **Geographical features** Snowdonia National Park; **Rivers** Conwy; **Population** 113,000 (1996); **Unemployment rate** N/A; **Average gross weekly full-time earnings** N/A; **Percentage of live births outside marriage** 37% (1995); **Deaths per 1,000 population** 15.3 (1995); **Industries and products** Dairy cattle; sheep; tourism.

Denbighshire

Unitary authority in North Wales. A former county, it was part of Clwyd and Gwynedd 1974–96.

Area 844 sq km/326 sq mi; **Towns and cities** Ruthin (administrative headquarters); Denbigh; Llangollen; St Asaph; Rhyl; Prestatyn; **Geographical features** Snowdonia National Park; Llyn Brenig; Alwen Reservoir; **Rivers** Dee; Clwyd; **Population** 91,000 (1996); **Unemployment rate** N/A; **Average gross weekly full-time earnings** N/A; **Percentage of live births outside marriage** 40% (1995); **Deaths per 1,000 population** 13.0 (1995); **Industries and products** Dairy cattle; sheep; tourism; furniture.

Flintshire

Unitary authority in North Wales. A former county, it was part of Clwyd 1974–1996.

Area 437 sq km/167 sq mi; **Towns and cities** Mold (administrative headquarters); Flint; Shotton; **Geographical features** Clwydian Hills; **Rivers** Dee; Clwyd; **Population** 144,000 (1996); **Unemployment rate** N/A; **Average gross weekly full-time earnings** £334.10; **Percentage of live births outside marriage** 31% (1995); **Deaths per 1,000 population** 10.4 (1995); **Industries and products** Agriculture; dairy cattle; sheep; tourism; steel plate and strip-milled steel products.

Gwynedd

Unitary authority in northwest Wales, created in 1996 from part of the former county of Gwynedd.

Area 2,546 sq km/983 sq mi; **Towns and cities** Caernarfon (administrative headquarters); Dolgellau; Harlech; Bangor; Bala; Bethesda; Blaenau Ffestiniog; Barmouth; Porthmadog; **Geographical features** Snowdonia National Park with Snowdon, 1,085 m/3,561 ft; Cader Idris, 892 m/2,928 ft; and the largest Welsh lake, Llyn Tegid (Bala Lake); Lleyn Peninsula; Bardsey Island; **Population** 116,000 (1996); **Unemployment rate** 10.9% (May 1996); **Average gross weekly full-time earnings** £275.50; **Percentage of live births outside marriage** 36% (1995); **Deaths per 1,000 population** 12.2 (1995); **Industries and products** Agriculture; dairy cattle; sheep; tourism; gold (at Dolgellau); textiles; electronics; slate.

Caernarfon Castle, Gwynedd Corel

Merthyr Tydfil

Unitary authority in South Wales created in 1996 from part of the former county of Mid Glamorgan.

Area 111 sq km/43 sq mi; **Towns and cities** Merthyr Tydfil (administrative headquarters); **Geographical features** Largest land reclamation scheme in Europe; part of the Brecon Beacons National Park; **Rivers** Taff; **Population** 60,000 (1996); **Unemployment rate** N/A (May 1996); **Average gross weekly full-time earnings** N/A; **Percentage of live births outside marriage** 47% (1995); **Deaths per 1,000 population** 12.4 (1995); **Industries and products** Light engineering; electrical goods.

Monmouthshire

Unitary authority in southeast Wales. A former county, it was part of Gwent 1974–96.

Area 851 sq km/328 sq mi; **Towns and cities** Cwmbran (administrative headquarters); Monmouth; Abergavenny; Usk; Raglan; **Geographical features** Wye Valley; Mynydd Pen-y-fal, 596 m/1,955 ft, the 'Sugar Loaf' mountain; **Rivers** Wye; Usk; Gavenny; Monnow; **Population** 80,400 (1996); **Unemployment rate** N/A; **Average gross weekly full-time earnings** N/A; **Percentage of live births outside marriage** 27% (1995); **Deaths per 1,000 population** 11.2 (1995); **Industries and products** Tourism; agriculture; scientific instruments; car components; nylon; biscuits.

Neath Port Talbot

Unitary authority in South Wales created in 1996 from part of the former county of West Glamorgan

Area 442 sq km/171 sq mi; **Towns and cities** Port Talbot (administrative headquarters); Neath; **Geographical features** Wye Valley; Mynydd Pen-y-fal, 596 m/1,955 ft, the 'Sugar Loaf'; **rivers** Wye; Usk; Gavenny; Monnow; **Population** 139,400 (1996); **Unemployment rate** 12.4% (May 1996); **Average gross weekly full-time earnings** £338.90; **Percentage of live births outside marriage** 38% (1995); **Deaths per 1,000 population** 12.9 (1995); **Industries and products** Tinplate; chemicals; steel strip mill.

Newport

Unitary authority in South Wales created in 1996 from part of the former county of Gwent

Area 190 sq km/73 sq mi; **Towns and cities** Newport (administrative headquarters); Caerleon; Llanwern; **Rivers** Wye; Usk; **Population** 133,300 (1996); **Unemployment rate** N/A; **Average gross weekly full-time earnings** £331.20; **Percentage of live births outside marriage** 44% (1995); **Deaths per 1,000 population** 11.2 (1995); **Industries and products** Steelworks; telephone systems; engineering; chemicals; fertilizers; aluminium; electronics.

Pembrokeshire

Unitary authority in southwest Wales. A former county, it was part of the new county of Dyfed from 1974–1996.

Area 1,588 sq km/613 sq mi; **Towns and cities** Haverfordwest (administrative headquarters); Milford Haven; Fishguard; Pembroke; Tenby; **Geographical features** Pembrokeshire Coast National Park; **Rivers** West Cleddau; **Population** 117,700 (1996); **Unemployment rate** 14.0% (May 1996); **Average gross weekly full-time earnings** N/A; **Percentage of live births outside marriage** 34% (1995); **Deaths per 1,000 population** 12.0 (1995); **Industries and products** Tourism; agriculture; oil refining.

Powys

Unitary authority in central Wales, created in 1996 from the former county of Powys.

Area 5,179 sq km/1,999 sq mi; **Towns and cities** Llandrindod Wells (administrative headquarters); Machynlleth; Newtown; Presteigne; Builth Wells; Rhayader; Welshpool; **Geographical features** Brecon Beacons National Park; the Black Mountains; Gilfach Nature Reserve; Lake Vyrnwy; **Rivers** Wye; Severn; Dovey; Lugg; **Population** 123,600 (1996); **Unemployment rate** N/A; **Average gross weekly full-time earnings** £275.80; **Percentage of live births outside marriage** 29% (1995); **Deaths per 1,000 population** 12.8 (1995); **Industries and products** Agriculture; dairy cattle; sheep; tourism; light industry; textiles.

Rhondda Cynon Taff

Unitary authority in South Wales created in 1996 from part of the former county of Mid Glamorgan.

Area 440 sq km/170 sq mi; **Towns and cities** Clydach Vale (administrative headquarters);

Rhondda; Llantrisant; Abercynon; Mountain Ash; Aberdare; **Rivers** Taff; Rhondda; **Population** 232,600 (1996); **Unemployment rate** 9.6% (May 1996); **Average gross weekly full-time earnings** £306.70; **Percentage of live births outside marriage** 42% (1995); **Deaths per 1,000 population** 12.5 (1995); **Industries and products** Former coal mining centre, Rhondda Heritage Park recreates a 1920s-style mining village; light engineering; Royal Mint; electrical cables.

Swansea

Unitary authority in South Wales created in 1996 from part of the former county of West Glamorgan.

Area 377 sq km/156 sq mi; **Towns and cities** Swansea (administrative headquarters); **Geographical features** Gower Peninsula; **Rivers** Tawe; **Population** 232,600 (1996); **Unemployment rate** 12.4 % (May 1996); **Average gross weekly full-time earnings** £298.60; **Percentage of live births outside marriage** 38% (1995); **Deaths per 1,000 population** 12.5 (1995); **Industries and products** Tourism; agriculture; tinplate manufacturing; chemicals; oil refining; vehicle licensing centre for the UK.

Torfaen

Unitary authority in South Wales created in 1996 from part of the former county of Gwent.

Area 98 sq km/38 sq mi; **Towns and cities** Pontypool (administrative headquarters), Blaenavon; **Geographical features** Ogof Draenen, one of Britain's largest cave systems; **Rivers** Afon Llwyd; **Population** 90,700 (1996); **Unemployment rate** N/A; **Average**

gross weekly full-time earnings £323.00; **Percentage of live births outside marriage** 40% (1995); **Deaths per 1,000 population** 11.6 (1995); **Industries and products** Electronics; engineering; synthetic textiles; scientific instruments; former coal mining and steel manufacturing area with industrial museums.

Vale of Glamorgan

Unitary authority in South Wales created in 1996 from parts of the former counties of Mid Glamorgan and South Glamorgan.

Area 337 sq km/130 sq mi; **Towns and cities** Barry (administrative headquarters); Cowbridge; Llantwit Major; **Rivers** Rhondda; **Population** 119,500 (1996); **Unemployment rate** N/A; **Average gross weekly full-time earnings** £326.50; **Percentage of live births outside marriage** 34% (1995); **Deaths per 1,000 population** 11.5 (1995); **Industries and products** Agriculture; sheep; tourism.

Wrexham

Unitary authority in northeast Wales created in 1996 from part of the former county of Clywd.

Area 500 sq km/193 sq mi; **Towns and cities** Wrexham (administrative headquarters); Ruabon; **Geographical features** Clywedog Valley, Chirk Aqueduct; **Population** 123,500 (1996); **Unemployment rate** N/A (May 1996); **Average gross weekly full-time earnings** N/A; **Percentage of live births outside marriage** 39% (1995); **Deaths per 1,000 population** 11.7 (1995); **Industries and products** Agriculture; sheep; food manufacture; plastics; pharmaceuticals; high-technology industries.

Scotland: Unitary Authorities and Islands

N/A = not available.

The Local Government (Scotland) Bill of 1994 abolished the two-tier system of local government that had been established for the nine Scottish regions in 1975. Since April 1996 there have been 29 mainland unitary authorities; the three island areas (the Orkney Islands, Shetland Islands, and Western Isles) have retained their existing single-tier administrative divisions.

Statistics for unemployment rate, average gross weekly full-time earnings, percentage of live births outside marriage, and deaths per 1,000 population are from *Office for National Statistics: Regional Trends 32, 1997 Edition.* © Crown copyright1997.

Aberdeen City

Unitary authority in eastern Scotland created in 1996 from part of the former Grampian Region.

Area 184 sq km/71 sq mi; **Population** 219,100 (1996); **Unemployment total** 4,900

(January 1997); **Average gross weekly full-time earnings** £397.60; **Percentage of live births outside marriage** 33% (1995); **Deaths per 1,000 population** 10.9 (1995); **Industries and products** Oil; gas; fishing; textiles; papermaking.

Aberdeenshire

Unitary authority in northeast Scotland. A former county of the same name, it was created in 1996 from three districts within the former Grampian Region.

Area 6,289 sq km/2,428 sq mi; **Towns and cities** Aberdeen (administrative headquarters only); Ballater; Banchory; Ellon; Fraserburgh; Huntly; Inverurie; Kintore; Oldmeldrum; Banff; Cruden Bay; Cullen; Inverbervie; Macduff; Stonehaven; **Geographical features** Grampian Mountains; Aviemore Ski resort; **Rivers** Dee; Spey; Deveron; Bogie; Don; **Population** 226,500 (1996); **Unemployment total** 4,500 (January 1997); **Average gross weekly full-time**

earnings £307.20; **Percentage of live births outside marriage** 22% (1995); **Deaths per 1,000 population** 9.4 (1995); **Industries and products** Oil; gas; paper making; whisky distilling; farming; beef; fishing; seafood; tourism.

Angus

Unitary authority on the east coast of Scotland. A former county, it was part of Tayside Region 1975–96.

Area 2,184 sq km/843 sq mi; **Towns and cities** Forfar (administrative headquarters); Brechin; Kirriemuir; Arbroath; Carnoustie; Montrose; **Rivers** Tay; Esk; **Population** 111,300 (1996); **Unemployment total** 3,600 (January 1997); **Average gross weekly full-time earnings** £292.60; **Percentage of live births outside marriage** 30% (1995); **Deaths per 1,000 population** 12.9 (1995); **Industries and products** Agriculture; tourism; timber; fishing; distilling; light engineering; textiles; agricultural engineering.

Argyll and Bute

Unitary authority in western Scotland created in 1996 from part of the former Strathclyde Region.

Area 4,001 sq km/1,545 sq mi; **Towns and cities** Lochgilphead (administrative headquarters); Campbeltown; Inveraray; Dunoon; Helensburgh; Oban; **Geographical features** Loch Lomond; Loch Fyne; Gare Loch; Loch Linnhe; Loch Gilp; Inner Hebrides Islands (Coll; Colonsay; Islay; Mull; Tiree); Lismore; Great Cumbrae; **Rivers** Clyde; **Population** 89,300 (1996); **Unemployment total** 3,400 (January 1997); **Average gross weekly full-time earnings** £287.60; **Percentage of live births outside marriage** 29% (1995); **Deaths per 1,000 population** 13.8 (1995); **Industries and products** Agriculture; tourism; fishing; distilling; boat building.

Clackmannanshire

Unitary authority in central Scotland, bordering the Firth of Forth. A former county, it was a district of the Central Region 1975–96.

Area 161 sq km/62 sq mi; **Towns and cities** Alloa (administrative headquarters); Alva; Clackmannan; **Geographical features** Ochil Hills; **Rivers** Forth; **Population** 47,700 (1996); **Unemployment total** 1,900 (Jan 1997); **Average gross weekly full-time earnings** N/A; **Percentage of live births outside marriage** 38% (1995); **Deaths per 1,000 population** 10.6 (1995); **Industries and products** Brewing and distilling; bottle manufacture; knitwear; textiles; printing; canning.

Dumfries and Galloway

Unitary authority in southern Scotland, former region 1975–96.

Area 6,394 sq km/2,468 sq mi; **Towns and cities** Dumfries (administrative headquarters); Annan; Dalbeattie; Lockerbie; Stranraer; **Geographical features** Solway Firth; Galloway Hills; Glen Trool National Park; Carlingwark Loch; Eskdalemuir Forest; **Rivers** Annan; **Population** 147,900 (1996); **Unemployment total** 5,200 (January 1997); **Average gross weekly full-time earnings** £282.90; **Percentage of live births outside marriage** 30% (1995); **Deaths per 1,000 population** 11.9 (1995); **Industries and products** Horses; cattle; sheep; timber; agriculture; granite.

Dundee City

City and unitary authority in eastern Scotland, on the north side of the Firth of Tay.

Area 65 sq km/25 sq mi; **Rivers** Tay; **Population** 155,000 (1996); **Unemployment total** 7,700 (January 1997); **Average gross weekly full-time earnings** £307.30; **Percentage of live births outside marriage** 47% (1995); **Deaths per 1,000 population** 12.4 (1995); **Industries and products** Engineering; textiles; electronics; printing; fishing; food processing; marmalade.

East Ayrshire

Unitary authority in southwest Scotland created in 1996 from part of the former Strathclyde Region.

Area 1,271 sq km/491 sq mi; **Towns and cities** Kilmarnock (administrative headquarters); Auchinleck; Hurlford; Cumnock Stewarton; **Rivers** Irvine; **Population** 124,000 (1996); **Unemployment total** 5,700 (January 1997); **Average gross weekly full-time earnings** £287.50; **Percentage of live births outside marriage** 38% (1995); **Deaths per 1,000 population** 11.9 (1995); **Industries and products** Agriculture; textiles; engineering; printing.

East Dunbartonshire

Unitary authority in central Scotland created in 1996 from part of the former Strathclyde Region.

Area 202 sq km/78 sq mi; **Towns and cities** Kirkintilloch (administrative headquarters); Lennoxtown; **Geographical features** Campsie Fells; **Rivers** Clyde; **Population** 110,000 (1996); **Unemployment total** 2,500 (January 1997); **Average gross weekly full-time earnings** N/A; **Percentage of live births outside marriage** 17% (1995); **Deaths per 1,000 population** 8.6 (1995); **Industries and products** Iron and steel; hosiery; waterproof materials.

East Lothian

Unitary authority in southeast Scotland; a former county, that merged with West Lothian and Midlothian 1975–96 in Lothian Region.

Area 681 sq km/263 sq mi; **Towns and cities** Haddington (administrative headquarters); Cockenzie; Prestonpans; Musselburgh; Tranent; North Berwick; **Geographical features** Lammermuir Hills; Bass Rock in the Firth of Forth; noted for seabirds; **Rivers** Tyne; Esk; **Population** 85,500 (1996); **Unemployment total** 2,300 (January 1997); **Average gross weekly full-time earnings** N/A; **Percentage of live births outside marriage** 27% (1995); **Deaths per 1,000 population** 12.3 (1995); **Industries and products** Agriculture; fishing; market gardening; net, twine, and wire manufacture.

East Renfrewshire

Unitary authority in central Scotland created in 1996 from part of the former Strathclyde Region.

Area 172 sq km/66 sq mi; **Towns and cities** Giffnock (administrative headquarters); North Berwick; **Rivers** Clyde; **Population** 86,800 (1996); **Unemployment total** 1,800 (January 1997); **Average gross weekly full-time earnings** N/A; **Percentage of live births outside marriage** 27% (1995); **Deaths per 1,000 population** 9.5 (1995); **Industries and products** Agriculture; light industry; textiles.

Edinburgh City

Capital of Scotland and unitary authority;.

Area 261 sq km/101 sq mi (unitary authority); **Population** 447,550 (1996); **Unemployment total** 14,900 (Jan 1997); **Average gross weekly full-time earnings** £344.30; **Percentage of live births outside marriage** 32% (1995); **Deaths per 1,000 population** 11.4 (1995); **Universities** Edinburgh University; Heriot-Watt University; Napier University; **Airports** Edinburgh Airport; **Mainline railway stations** Waverley Station; **Main bus station** St Andrew Square; **Industries and products** Printing; publishing; banking; insurance; chemical manufactures; electronics; distilling; brewing; **Places of interest** Edinburgh Castle (contains 12th-century St Margaret's chapel); Holyrood House (15th–16th centuries); Parliament House (begun 1632); Royal Scottish Academy; National Gallery of Scotland; cathedral of St Mary; St Giles parish church (mostly 15th century); Royal Observatory (1896); Edinburgh International Festival of Music and Drama (begun 1947, the largest in the world); **Cultural organizations** Royal Lyceum Theatre Company; BBC Scottish Symphony Orchestra; Scottish Opera; Scottish Chamber Orchestra; **Tourist Information Centre** Edinburgh and Lothians Tourist Board, 3 Princes Street, Edinburgh EH2 2QP; phone: (0131) 557 1700; **Chamber of Commerce** Chamber of Commerce and Manufacturers, 3 Randolph Crescent, Edinburgh EH3 7U.

Falkirk

Unitary authority in central Scotland created in 1996 from part of the former Central Region.

Area 294 sq km/114 sq mi; **Towns and cities** Falkirk (administrative headquarters); Grangemouth; Bo'ness; Larbert; **Rivers** Carron; Kelvin; **Population** 142,500 (1996); **Unemployment total** 5,100 (January 1997); **Average gross weekly full-time earnings** £318.70; **Percentage of live births outside marriage** 33% (1995); **Deaths per 1,000 population** 11.5 (1995); **Industries and products** Chemical and petroleum industries; brewing; distilling; manufacture of buses; bookbinding; papermaking; soft drinks; toffees; castings.

Fife

Unitary authority in eastern Scotland; former region 1975–96.

Area 1,340 sq km/517 sq mi; **Towns and cities** Glenrothes (administrative headquarters); Dunfermline; St Andrews; Kirkcaldy; Cupar; **Geographical features** Lomond Hills; **Rivers** Eden; Leven; **Population** 351,200 (1996); **Unemployment total** 13,500 (January 1997); **Average gross weekly full-time earnings** £307.10; **Percentage of live births outside marriage** 33% (1995); **Deaths per 1,000 population** 11.3 (1995); **Industries and products** Agri-

The Forth Railway Bridge, Inverkeithing, Fife
Corel

culture; light engineering; aluminium refining; coal mining; fishing.

Glasgow City

City and unitary authority in Central Scotland.

Area 176 sq km/68 sq mi; **Population** 618,400 (1996); **Unemployment total** 31,600 (January 1997); **Average gross weekly full-time earnings** £323.40; **Percentage of live births outside marriage** 48% (1995); **Deaths per 1,000 population** 14.3 (1995); **Education** 83 nursery schools; 206 primary schools; 39 secondary schools; 40 special schools; **Universities** Glasgow University; Strathclyde University; Glasgow Meridian University; **Airports** Glasgow International Airport; **Mainline railway stations** Central Station; Queen Street Station; Glasgow subway; **Main bus station** Buchanan Bus Station; **Industries and products** Engineering; chemicals; printing; whisky distilling and blending; brewing; electronics; textiles; shipbuilding (Kvaerner-Govan and Yarrow shipyards); **Places of interest** Cathedral of St Mungo; the Cross Steeple (part of the historic Tolbooth); the Royal Exchange; the Stock Exchange; Kelvingrove Art Gallery; the Glasgow School of Art, designed by C R Mackintosh; the Burrell Collection at Pollock Park, bequeathed by shipping magnate William Burrell; Mitchell Library; 19th-century Greek Revival buildings designed by Alexander Thomson; Gallery of Modern Art; **Cultural Organizations** Scottish Opera, Scottish Ballet, and the Royal Scottish Orchestra; **Newspapers** *Daily Record*; *Sunday Mail*; *The Glasgow Herald*; *Glasgow Evening Times*; **Tourist Information Centre** Glasgow City Centre Tourist Information Centre, 35 St Vincent Place, Glasgow G1 2ER; phone: (0141) 204 4400; **Chamber of Commerce** Glasgow Chamber of Commerce and Manufacturers, 30 George Street, Glasgow G2 1EQ; phone: (0141) 204 2121; fax: (0141) 221 2336.

Highland

Unitary authority in northern Scotland; former region 1975–96.

Area 25,304 sq km/9,767 sq mi (almost half the country of Scotland); **Towns and cities** Inverness (administrative headquarters); Thurso; Wick; Alness; Dingwall; Fort William; Nairn; **Geographical features** Grampian Mountains; Ben Nevis (highest

peak in the UK); Great Glen; Loch Ness; Loch Linnhe; Loch Gairloch; Loch Broom; Caledonian Canal; Inner Hebrides; Eigg; Raasay; **Rivers** Leven Ness; Spey; Attric; Inver; Beauly; Brora; Ericht; Ective; Garry; Roy; Thurso; Lochy; Ewe Oich; Shin; Oykel; Moriston; **Population** 207,500 (1996); **Unemployment total** 9,600 (January 1997); **Average gross weekly full-time earnings** £285.80; **Percentage of live births outside marriage** 30% (1995); **Deaths per 1,000 population** 11.7 (1995); **Industries and products** Tourism; oil services; winter sports; timber; livestock; grouse, and deer hunting; salmon fishing; sheep farming; aluminium smelting; pulp and paper production; distilling.

Inverclyde

Unitary authority in western Scotland created in 1996 from part of the former Strathclyde Region.

Area 157 sq km/60 sq mi; **Towns and cities** Greenock (administrative headquarters); Port Glasgow; Gourock; **Rivers** Clyde; **Population** 90,000 (1996); **Unemployment total** 2,900 (January 1997); **Average gross weekly full-time earnings** £324.10; **Percentage of live births outside marriage** 40% (1995); **Deaths per 1,000 population** 13.9 (1995); **Industries and products** Tourism; shipbuilding; clothing; textiles; outdoor equipment.

Midlothian

Unitary authority in southeast Scotland, south of the Firth of Forth. A former county, it was included in Lothian Region 1975–96.

Area 355 sq km/137 sq mi; **Towns and cities** Dalkeith (administrative headquarters); Bonnyrigg and Lasswade; Loanhead; Newtongrange; **Geographical features** Moorfoot Hills; **Rivers** North Esk; South Esk; **Population** 79,900 (1996); **Unemployment total** 1,900 (January 1997); **Average gross weekly full-time earnings** N/A; **Percentage of live births outside marriage** 32% (1995); **Deaths per 1,000 population** 10.7 (1995); **Industries and products** Coal; iron moulding; carpet weaving; brush making; brewing; electronics.

Moray

Unitary authority in northeast Scotland created in 1996 from part of the former Grampian Region.

Area 2,217 sq km/856 sq mi; **Towns and cities** Elgin (administrative headquarters); Buckie; Forres; Keith; Lossiemouth; **Rivers** Spey; **Population** 85,000 (1996); **Unemployment total** 2,700 (January 1997); **Average gross weekly full-time earnings** £284.70; **Percentage of live births outside marriage** 23% (1995); **Deaths per 1,000 population** 11.3 (1995); **Industries and products** Fishing; boat-building; distilling (notably malt whiskey); food processing/canning; agriculture.

North Ayrshire

Unitary authority in western Scotland created in 1996 from part of the former Strathclyde Region.

Area 878 sq km/339 sq mi; **Towns and cities** Irvine (administrative headquarters); Dalry; Ardrossan; Beith; Kilbirnie; Kilwinning; Stevenston; Largs; Saltcoats; **Geographical features** Islands: Arran; Great Cumbrae; Little Cumbrae; **Rivers** Clyde; Garnock; **Population** 139,200 (1996); **Unemployment total** 6,100 (January 1997); **Average gross weekly full-time earnings** £320.80; **Percentage of live births outside marriage** 37% (1995); **Deaths per 1,000 population** 11.8 (1995); **Industries and products** Tweeds; hosiery; bricks; pharmaceuticals; shipbuilding; oil refining; tourism.

North Lanarkshire

Unitary authority in central Scotland created in 1996 from part of the former Strathclyde Region.

Area 466 sq km/180 sq mi; **Towns and cities** Motherwell (administrative headquarters); Airdrie; Bellshill; Mossend; Kilsyth; Newmains; Shotts; Coatbridge; Cumbernauld; **Geographical features** Grotto at Cartin; **Rivers** Clyde; **Population** 326,750 (1996); **Unemployment total** 12,600 (January 1997); **Average gross weekly full-time earnings** £331.10; **Percentage of live births outside marriage** 35% (1995); **Deaths per 1,000 population** 11.1 (1995); **Industries and products** Paper manufacture; pharmaceuticals; iron and steel; hosiery.

Orkney Islands

Island group off the northeast coast of Scotland.

Area 970 sq km/375 sq mi; **Towns and cities** Kirkwall (administrative headquarters); Stromness; **Geographical features** Comprises about 90 islands – the main ones being: South Ronaldsay; Mainland; Burray; Eday; Flotta; Hoy; North Ronaldsay; Sanday; Shapinsay; Stronsay; Westray – and islets, low-lying and treeless; **Population** 19,600 (1996); **Unemployment total** N/A; **Average gross weekly full-time earnings** N/A; **Percentage of live births outside marriage** 29% (1995); **Deaths per 1,000 population** 11.9 (1995); **Industries and products** Fishing; farming; beef cattle; poultry; fish curing; woollen weaving; wind power; distilling; boat-building.

Perth and Kinross

Unitary authority in central Scotland created in 1996 from part of the former Tayside Region.

Area 5,328 sq km/2,058 sq mi; **Towns and cities** Perth (administrative headquarters); New Scone; Blairgowrie and Rattray; Crieff; Kinross; **Geographical features** Sidlaw Hills; Loch Tay; Loch Rannoch; Loch Faskally; **Rivers** Tay; Isla; **Population**

131,800 (1996); **Unemployment total** 3,500 (January 1997); **Average gross weekly full-time earnings** N/A; **Percentage of live births outside marriage** 30% (1995); **Deaths per 1,000 population** 12.9 (1995); **Industries and products** Tourism; agriculture; distilling; textiles; carpets.

Renfrewshire

Unitary authority in west central Scotland, bordering the Firth of Clyde, formed from the northern and western parts of Renfrew district in the former Strathclyde region (1975–96), which in turn was formed from the former county of Renfrewshire (until 1974).

Area 260 sq km/100 sq mi; **Towns and cities** Paisley (administrative headquarters), Renfrew, Johnstone, Erskine; **Geographical features** Mainly low lying, but hilly in the west, rising to Hill of Stake (525 m/1,723 ft); sculptural stones at Inchinnan, near Erskine **Rivers** Clyde, Gryfe, White Cart, Black Cart; **Population** 178,000 (1995); **Unemployment total** 6,600 (January 1997); **Average gross weekly full-time earnings** £334.80 (April 1996); **Percentage of live births outside marriage** 37% (1995); **Deaths per 1,000 population** 11.2 (1995); **Industries and products** Engineering, computers, electronics, chemicals.

Scottish Borders

Unitary authority in southeast Scotland created in 1996 to replace the former Borders region.

Area 4,712 sq km/1,819 sq mi; **Towns and cities** Melrose (administrative headquarters); Coldstream; Duns; Eyemouth; Galashiels; Hawick; Kelso; Peebles; Selkirk; Jedburgh; **Geographical features** Lammermuir; Pentland; Moorfoot Hills; Gala Water; Jed Water; **Rivers** Tweed; **Population** 105,300 (1996); **Unemployment total** 2,200 (January 1997); **Average gross weekly full-time earnings** N/A; **Percentage of live births outside marriage** 28% (1995); **Deaths per 1,000 population** 13.2 (1995); **Industries and products** Agriculture; tourism; electronics; timber; textiles; fishing.

Shetland Islands

Islands off the north coast of Scotland, beyond the Orkney Islands. The Islands are an important centre of the North Sea oil industry.

Area 1,400 sq km/541 sq mi; **Towns and cities** Lerwick (administrative headquarters); **Geographical features** 100 islands, 19 inhabited. The main islands are: Bressay; Fair Isle; Fetlar; Unst (contains the most northerly point of the British Isles); Whalsay; and Yell; **Population** 22,500 (1996); **Unemployment total** N/A; **Average gross weekly full-time earnings** N/A; **Percentage of live births outside marriage** 30% (1995);

Deaths per 1,000 population 10.1 (1995); **Industries and products** Oil and gas; processed fish; handknits; Shetland ponies; fishing; agriculture.

South Ayrshire

Unitary authority in southwest Scotland, created in 1996 from part of the former Strathclyde Region.

Area 1,202 sq km/464 sq mi; **Towns and cities** Ayr (administrative headquarters); Maybole; Prestwick; Girvan; Troon; **Geographical features** Fenwick Moors; **Rivers** Clyde; Ayr; **Population** 114,000 (1996); **Unemployment total** 4,500 (January 1997); **Average gross weekly full-time earnings** £339.10; **Percentage of live births outside marriage** 32 % (1995); **Deaths per 1,000 population** 13.5 (1995); **Industries and products** Tourism; agriculture; aerospace and high-technology industries.

South Lanarkshire

Unitary authority in south central Scotland created in 1996 from part of the former Strathclyde Region.

Area 1,776 sq km/686 sq mi; **Towns and cities** Hamilton (administrative headquarters); Blantyre; Bothwell; Carluke; Larkhall; Stonehouse; Strathaven; East Kilbride; Lanark; **Geographical features** Douglas Water; **Rivers** Clyde; **Population** 307,100 (1996); **Unemployment total** 10,300 (January 1997); **Average gross weekly full-time earnings** £321.10; **Percentage of live births outside marriage** 30 % (1995); **Deaths per 1,000 population** 11.2 (1995); **Industries and products** Engineering; clothing; printing; electrical equipment; electronics; textiles.

Stirling

Unitary authority in central Scotland created in 1996 from part of the former Central Region.

Area 2,195 sq km/848 sq mi; **Towns and cities** Stirling (administrative headquarters); Bannockburn; Bridge of Allan; Dunblane; **Geographical features** The Trossachs; Ochil Hills; Airthrey mineral springs; Loch Lomond; Loch Tay; **Rivers** Forth; Bannock; Teith; **Population** 82,000 (1996); **Unemploy-ment total** 2,500 (January 1997); **Average gross weekly full-time earnings** £304.70; **Percentage of live births outside marriage** 32% (1995); **Deaths per 1,000 population** 10.8 (1995); **Industries and products** Tourism; agriculture; textiles; agricultural machinery; chemicals; carpets.

West Dunbartonshire

Unitary authority in west central Scotland created in 1996 from part of the former

Strathclyde Region.

Area 155 sq km/60 sq mi; **Towns and cities** Dunbarton (administrative headquarters); Alexandria; **Geographical features** Loch Long; **Rivers** Leven; **Population** 97,800 (1996); **Unemployment total** 4,900 (January 1997); **Average gross weekly full-time earnings** N/A; **Percentage of live births outside marriage** 40% (1995); **Deaths per 1,000 population** 11.9 (1995); **Industries and products** Light manufacturing; service industries; marine engineering; distilling; electronics.

Western Isles

Island area of Scotland, comprising the Outer Hebrides.

Area 2,900 sq km/1,120 sq mi; **Towns and cities** Stornoway (administrative headquarters); **Geographical features** Islands: Lewis; Harris; North Uist; South Uist; Barra; Benbecula; Eriskay; **Population** 27,800 (1996); **Unemployment total** 1,400 (January 1997); **Average gross weekly full-time earnings** N/A; **Percentage of live births outside marriage** 20% (1995); **Deaths per 1,000 population** 14.8 (1995); **Industries and products** Tourism; Harris tweed; sheep; fish; cattle.

Megalithic standing stones, Callanish, Isle of Lewis, Western Isles Corel

West Lothian

Unitary authority in central Scotland, bordering the southern shore of the Firth of Forth. A former county, it was part of Lothian Region 1975–1996.

Area 475 sq km/183 sq mi; **Towns and cities** Livingston (administrative headquarters); Linlithgow; Armadale; Bathgate; Broxburn; Whitburn; **Geographical features** Lammermuir Hills; Bass Rock; Firth of Forth; **Rivers** Forth; **Population** 147,900 (1996); **Unemployment total** 4,400 (January 1997); **Average gross weekly full-time earnings** £318.10; **Percentage of live births outside marriage** 32% (1995); **Deaths per 1,000 population** 9.1 (1995); **Industries and products** Tourism; iron and steel; motor industry.

Northern Ireland: Administrative Divisions

Northern Ireland has a single-tier system of 26 district councils. Historically there are six counties but these perform no administrative function. Health and Social Services, and Education and Library Services are organized by regional boards.

Statistics for unemployment rate, average gross weekly full-time earnings, percentage of live births outside marriage, and deaths per 1,000 population are from *Office for National Statistics: Regional Trends 32, 1997 Edition* © Crown copyright 1997.

Northern Ireland: Counties

Antrim

Area 2,830 sq km/1,092 sq mi; **Towns and cities** Belfast; Larne; Antrim; **Geographical features** Giant's Causeway, a World Heritage site of natural hexagonal basalt columns on the North coast; Lough Neagh; **Industries and products** Potatoes; oats; linen; synthetic textiles; flax; shipbuilding.

Northern Ireland Parliament Buildings, Stormont, Belfast Corel

Armagh

Area 1,250 sq km/483 sq mi; **Towns and cities:** Armagh; Lurgan; Portadown; Keady; **Geographical features** Flat in the north, with many bogs; low hills in the south; Lough Neagh; **Rivers** Bann; Blackwater; Callan; **Industries and products** Agriculture; apples; potatoes; flax; linen manufacture; milling; light engineering; concrete; potato crisps.

Down

Area 2,470 sq km/953 sq mi; **Towns and cities** Downpatrick; Bangor; Strangford; **Geographical features** Mourne Mountains; Strangford sea lough; **Industries and products** Agriculture; linen; potatoes; oats; light manufacturing; plastics; high technology and computers.

Fermanagh

Area 1,680 sq km/648 sq mi; **Towns and cities** Enniskillen; Lisnaskea; Irvinestown; **Geographical features** flat land; Loch Erne; **Industries and products** Agriculture; livestock; potatoes; tweeds; clothing; cotton thread; food processing; light engineering; china; tourism; electronics.

Londonderry

Area 2,070 sq km/799 sq mi; **Towns and cities** Londonderry; Coleraine; Portstewart; **Geographical features** Lough Neagh; **Rivers** Bann; Foyle; Roe; **Industries and products** Agriculture; flax; cattle; sheep; food processing; textiles; light engineering; salmon and eel fisheries; stone and lime quarrying; shirt manufacturing.

Tyrone

Area 3,160 sq km/1,220 sq mi; **Towns and cities** Omagh; Dungannon; Strabane; Cookstown; **Geographical features** Lough Neagh; Sperrin Mountains; **Rivers** Derg; Blackwater; Foyle; **Industries and products** Agriculture; barley; flax; potatoes; turnips; cattle; sheep; brick making; linen; hosiery; shirts.

Northern Ireland: Regional Board Statistics

Area and Population by Board and District of Northern Ireland

1995

Board[1] and district	Area		Population per:		Total population
	sq km	sq mi	sq km	sq mi	
Eastern					
Ards	380	147	175	68	67,000
Belfast	110	42	2,707	1,045	297,000
Castlereagh	85	33	746	288	63,000
Down	649	251	94	36	61,000
Lisburn	447	173	237	92	106,000
North Down	81	31	915	353	74,000
Total	1,751	676	381	147	668,000
Northern					
Antrim	421	163	115	44	49,000
Ballymena	630	243	91	35	58,000
					(continued)

Area and Population by Board and District of Northern Ireland (*continued*)

1995

Board[1] and district	Area		Population per		Total population
	sq km	sq mi	sq km	sq mi	
Ballymoney	416	161	59	23	25,000
Carrickfergus	81	31	432	167	35,000
Coleraine	486	188	111	43	54,000
Cookstown	514	198	61	24	31,000
Larne	336	130	89	34	30,000
Magherafelt	564	218	66	25	37,000
Moyle	494	191	30	12	15,000
Newtownabbey	151	58	522	202	79,000
Total	4,093	1,580	100	39	411,000
Southern					
Armagh	671	259	78	30	53,000
Banbridge	451	174	83	32	37,000
Craigavon	282	109	277	107	78,000
Dungannon	772	298	61	24	47,000
Newry and Mourne	898	347	94	36	84,000
Total	3,075	1,187	97	37	299,000
Western					
Derry	1,699	656	32	12	55,000
Fermanagh	586	226	53	20	31,000
Limavady	381	147	270	104	103,000
Omagh	1,130	436	42	16	47,000
Strabane	862	333	42	16	36,000
Total	4,658	1,798	58	22	271,000
Northern Ireland total	13,576	5,242	121	47	1,649,000
UK total	242,910	93,788	241	93	58,606,000

[1] Health and Social Services Board areas.

Source: Office for National Statistics; *Regional Trends 32,* 1997 Edition. © Crown copyright 1997

Social Statistics by Board in Northern Ireland

1995

Board[1]	Deaths per 1,000 population	Percentage of live births outside marriage
Eastern	10.2	28
Northern	8.8	21
Southern	8.6	15
Western	8.5	24
Northern Ireland average	9.3	23
UK average	10.9	34

[1] Health and Social Services Board areas.

Source: Office for National Statistics; *Regional Trends 32,* 1997 Edition. © Crown copyright 1997

Unemployment Rates in Northern Ireland

Statistics are by 'Travel to Work' areas. (As of January 1997.)

Region	Total claimants unemployed	Region	Total claimants unemployed
Antrim	1,400	Larne	1,100
Ards	2,100	Limavady	1,700
Armagh	2,100	Lisburn	3,300
Ballymena	1,900	Magherafelt	1,500
Ballymoney	1,100	Moyle	900
Banbridge	900	Newry and Mourne	4,500
Belfast	16,300	Newtownabbey	2,300
Carrickfergus	1,200	North Down	2,200
Castlereagh	1,800	Omagh	2,400
Coleraine	2,500	Strabane	2,100
Cookstown	1,500		
Craigavon	2,500	**Northern Ireland**	
Derry	6,200	**total**	70,800
Down	2,500		
Dungannon	2,200	**UK total**	1,907,800
Fermanagh	2,800		

Source: Office for National Statistics; *Regional Trends 32,* 1997 Edition. © Crown copyright 1997

Local Government of England

County	Council offices	Chief executive
Bedfordshire	County Hall, Cauldwell Street, Bedford MK42 9AP; phone: (01234) 363222; fax: (01234) 272982; e-mail: bcclgis@bcclgis.gov.uk	Mr Denis Cleggett
Buckinghamshire	County Hall, Walton Street, Aylesbury, Bucks HP20 1UA; phone: (01296) 395000; fax: (01296) 382481	Mr I Crookhall
Cambridgeshire	Shire Hall, Castle Hill, Cambridge CB3 0AP; phone: (01223) 717111; fax: (01223) 717201	Mr Alan Barnish
Cheshire	County Hall, Chester CH1 1SF; phone: (01244) 602424; fax: (01244) 602100	Mr Colin Cheeseman (acting)
Cornwall	New County Hall, Truro, Cornwall TR1 3AY; phone: (01872) 322000; fax: (01872) 270340	Mr John Mills
Cumbria	The Courts, Carlisle CA3 8NA; phone: (01228) 606060; fax: (01228) 606302; e-mail: policy@cumbria/policy.demon.co.uk	Mr Bill Swarbrick
Derbyshire	County Hall, Matlock, Derbyshire DE4 3AG; phone: (01629) 580000; fax: (01629) 585220	Mr Nick Hodgson
Devon	County Hall, Topsham Road, Exeter EX2 4QD; phone: (01392) 382000; fax: (01392) 382286	Mr Philip Jenkinson
Dorset	County Hall, Colliton Park, Dorchester, Dorset DT1 1XJ; phone: (01305) 251000; fax: (01305) 224839	Mr Peter Harvey
Durham	County Hall, Durham DH1 5UL; phone: (0191) 386 4411; fax: (0191) 383 3243	Mr K Smith
East Sussex	Pelham House, St Andrew's Lane, Lewes, East Sussex BN7 1UN; phone: (01273) 481000; fax: (01273) 473321	Mrs Cheryl Miller
Essex	County Hall, Chelmsford CM1 1LX; phone: (01245) 492211; fax: (01245) 352710	Mr Stuart Ashurst
Gloucestershire	Shire Hall, Westgate Street, Gloucester GL1 2TG; phone: (01452) 425000; fax: (01452) 425850	Mr Richard Cockcroft (Director of Corporate Services)
Hampshire	The Castle, Winchester SO23 8UJ; phone: (01962) 841841; fax: (01962) 867273	Mr Peter Robertson
Hertfordshire	County Hall, Heggs Lane, Hertford, Hertfordshire SG13 8DE; phone: (01992) 555555; fax: (01992) 555505	Mr Bill Ogley
Kent	Session House, County Hall, Maidstone, Kent ME14 1XQ; phone: (01622) 671411; fax: (01622) 694060; e-mail: mick.pitt@kent.gov.uk	Mr Michael Pitt
Lancashire	County Hall, PO Box 78, Preston PR1 8XJ; phone: (01772) 254868; fax: (01772) 263506	Mr G A Johnson
Leicestershire	County Hall, Leicester Road, Glenfield, Leicester LE3 8RA; phone: (0116) 232 3232; fax: (0116) 265 6260	Mr J B Sinnott
Lincolnshire	County Offices, Newland, Lincoln LN1 1YL; phone: (01522) 552000; fax: (01522) 552004	Mr M J Spink (acting)
Norfolk	County Hall, Martineau Lane, Norwich NR1 2DH; phone: (01603) 222222; fax: (01603) 222959	Mr Tim Byles
Northamptonshire	George Row, Northampton NN1 1AN; phone: (01604) 236236; fax: (01604) 236223	Mr John Picking
Northumberland	County Hall, Morpeth NE61 2EF; phone: (01670) 533000; fax: (01670) 533124	Mr Ken Morris
North Yorkshire	County Hall, Race Course Lane, Northallerton, North Yorkshire DL7 8AD; phone: (01609) 780780; fax: (01609) 780447	Mr John Ransford
Nottinghamshire	County Hall, West Bridgford NG2 7QP; phone: (0115) 982 3823; fax: (0115) 977 2419	Mr Peter Housden
Oxfordshire	County Hall, New Road, Oxford OX1 1ND; phone: (01865) 792422; fax: (01865) 815199; e-mail: oxcis@dial.pipex.com	Mr John Harwood
Shropshire	The Shire Hall, Abbey Foregate, Shrewsbury, Shropshire SY2 6ND; phone: (01743) 251000; fax: (01743) 360315	Mr N Pursey
Somerset	County Hall, Taunton, Somerset TA1 4DY; phone: (01823) 355455; fax: (01823) 355887	Dr David Radford
Staffordshire	Walton Building, PO Box 11, Martin Street, Stafford ST16 2LH; phone: (01785) 223121; fax: (01785) 215153	Mr Bernard Price (Clerk and Chief Executive)
Suffolk	County Hall, St Helen Court, Ipswich IP4 2JS; phone: (01473) 230000	P F Bye
Surrey	County Hall, Penrhyn Road, Kingston upon Thames KT1 2DN; phone: (0181) 541 8800; fax: (0181) 541 9005	Mr Paul Coen
Warwickshire	PO Box 9, Shire Hall, Warwick CV34 4RR; phone: (01926) 412003; fax: (01926) 412479	Mr Ian Caulfield
West Sussex	County Hall, West Street, Chichester PO19 1RQ; phone: (01243) 777100; fax: (01243) 777697	Mr Paul Rigg
Wiltshire	County Hall, Bythesea Road, Trowbridge, Wiltshire BA14 8JG; phone: (01225) 713000; fax: (01225) 713092	Mr Keith Robinson
Worcestershire	County Hall, Spetchley Road, Worcester WR5 2NP; phone: (01905) 766333	Mr Rob Sykes

The Political Composition of English County Councils

(– = not applicable.)

County	Conservative	Labour	Liberal Democrat	Independent/ other	Controlling party	Total councillors
Bedfordshire	25	14	10	0	Conservative	49
Buckinghamshire	38	5	10	1	Conservative	54
Cambridgeshire	33	10	16	0	Conservative	59
Cheshire	19	20	9	0	no overall control	48
Cornwall	8	8	38	25	no overall control	79
Cumbria	23	44	12	4	Labour	83
Derbyshire	12	45	6	1	Labour	64
Devon	14	4	31	5	Liberal Democrats	54
Dorset	15	5	21	1	no overall control	42
Durham	2	53	2	4	Labour	61
East Sussex	21	7	16	0	no overall control	44
Essex	39	24	15	1	no overall control	79
Gloucestershire	21	18	22	2	no overall control	63
Hampshire	42	8	22	2	Conservative	74
Hertfordshire	38	30	9	0	no overall control	77
Kent	46	23	15	0	Conservative	84
Lancashire	23	47	7	1	Labour	78
Leicestershire	25	17	11	1	no overall control	54
Lincolnshire	43	19	11	3	Conservative	76
Norfolk	36	34	13	1	no overall control	84
North Yorkshire	35	12	21	6	no overall control	74
Northamptonshire	27	37	4	0	Labour	68
Northumberland	13	43	8	2	Labour	66
Nottinghamshire	18	41	4	0	Labour	63
Oxfordshire	27	22	19	2	no overall control	70
Shropshire	17	8	13	6	no overall control	44
Somerset	17	3	37	0	Liberal Democrats	57
Staffordshire	20	40	2	0	Labour	62
Suffolk	31	33	15	1	no overall control	80
Surrey	47	6	17	6	Conservative	76
Warwickshire	22	31	8	1	no overall control	62
West Sussex	37	9	24	1	Conservative	71
Wiltshire	23	4	19	1	no overall control	47
Worcestershire	25	22	8	2	no overall control	57
Total	882	746	495	80	–	2,203

Source: Local Government Chronicle Elections Centre, University of Plymouth

The Addresses of London Borough Councils

Borough	Council offices	Chief executive
Barking and Dagenham	Civic Centre, Dagenham RM10 7BN; phone: (0181) 592 4500; fax: (0181) 252 8045	Mr W C Smith
Barnet	The Town Hall, The Burroughs, London NW4 4BG; phone: (0181) 359 2000	Mr Max Caller
Bexley	Bexley Civic Offices, Broadway, Bexleyheath, London DA6 7LB; phone: (0181) 303 7777	Mr Chris Duffield (Chief Executive and Director of Finance)
Brent	Brent Town Hall, Forty Lane, Wembley HA9 9HD; phone: (0181) 937 1234	Mr Gareth Daniel (acting)
Bromley	Bromley Civic Centre, Stockwell Close, Kentish Way, Bromley BR1 3UH; phone: (0181) 464 3333	Mr Michael Blanch
Camden	Town Hall, Argyle Street, London WC1H 8NL; phone: (0171) 278 4444	Mr Steve Bundred
Croydon	Taberner House, Park Lane, Croydon CR9 3JS; phone: (0181) 686 4433	Mr David Wechsler
Ealing	Town Hall, New Broadway, London W5 2BY; phone: (0181) 579 2424	Ms Gillian Guy
Enfield	Civic Centre, Silver Street, Enfield, London EN1 3XA; phone: (0181) 366 6565; fax: (0181) 379 4453	Mr David Plank
Greenwich	Town Hall, Wellington Street, London SE18 6PW; phone: (0181) 854 8888	Mr David Brooks
Hackney	Town Hall, Mare Street, London E8 1EA; phone: (0181) 989 9511	Mr T Elliston
Hammersmith and Fulham	Town Hall, King Street, Hammersmith, London W6 9JU; phone: (0181) 748 3020	Mr Neil Newton (Managing Director)
Haringey	Civic Centre, PO Box 264, High Road, London N22 8LE; phone: (0181) 975 9700	Mr Gurbux Singh
Harrow	Civic Centre, Station Road, Harrow HA1 2XF; phone: (0181) 863 5611; Web site: www.harrowlb.demon.co.uk	Mr Anthony Redmond (Chief Executive and Director of Finance)
Havering	Havering Town Hall, Main Road, Romford RM1 3BD; phone: (01708) 772222	Mr Harold Tinworth
Hillingdon	Civic Centre, Uxbridge UB8 1UW; phone: (01895) 250111; fax: (01895) 273636	Mr Dorian Leatham

The Addresses of London Borough Councils (*continued*)

Borough	Council offices	Chief executive
Hounslow	Civic Centre, Lampton Road, London TW3 4DN; phone: (0181) 570 7728; fax: (0181) 572 4819	Mr Derek Myers
Islington	Town Hall, Upper Street, London N1 2UD; phone: (0171) 226 1234	Ms Leisha Fullick
Kensington and Chelsea	Town Hall, Hornton Street, London W8 7NX; phone: (0171) 937 5464; fax: (0171) 938 1445	Mr Alan Taylor
Kingston upon Thames	Guildhall, Kingston upon Thames KT1 1EU; phone: (0181) 546 2121	Mr Bernard Quorroll
Lambeth	Town Hall, Brixton Hill, London SW2 1RW; phone: (0171) 926 1000; fax: (0171) 926 2255	Ms Heather Rabbatts
Lewisham	Town Hall, Catford Road, Catford, London SE6 4IU; phone: (0181) 695 6000	Mr Barry Quirk
Merton	Merton Civic Centre, London Road, Morden SM4 5DX; phone: (0181) 543 2222; fax: (0181) 545 4054 (press office)	Mr Richard Paine (acting)
Newham	Town Hall, East Ham, London E6 2RP; phone: (0181) 472 1430; fax: (0171) 557 8777	Dr Wendy Thomson
Redbridge	Town Hall, 128–142 High Road, Ilford, Essex IG1 1DD; phone: (0181) 478 3020	Mr Michael Frater
Richmond upon Thames	Civic Centre, 44 York Street, Twickenham TW1 3BZ; phone: (0181) 891 1411; e-mail: press-prrichmond.gov.uk	Mr Richard Harbord (Chief Executive and Director of Finance)
Southwark	Town Hall, Peckham Road, London SE5 8UB; phone: (0171) 525 7171	Mr Robert Coomber
Sutton	Civic Offices, St Nicholas Way, Sutton SM1 1EA; phone: (0181) 770 5000; Web site: www.sutton.gov.uk	Ms Patricia Hughes
Tower Hamlets	Mulberry Place, 5 Clove Crescent, London E14 2BG; phone: (0171) 364 5000; fax: (0171) 364 4296	Ms Sylvie Pierce
Waltham Forest	Town Hall, Forest Road, London E17 4JF; phone: (0181) 527 5544	Mr Alan Tobias
Wandsworth	Town Hall, Wandsworth High Street, London SW18 2PU; phone: (0181) 871 6000; fax: (0181) 871 7560	Mr Gerald Jones
Westminster	City Hall, 64 Victoria Street, London SW1E 6QP; phone: (0171) 641 6000	Mr William Roots

The Political Composition of London Borough Councils

(– = not applicable.)

Borough	Conservative	Labour	Liberal Democrat	Independent/ other	Controlling party	Total councillors
Barking and Dagenham	0	47	1	3	Labour	51
Barnet	28	26	6	0	no overall control	60
Bexley	32	24	6	0	Conservative	62
Brent	19	43	4	0	Labour	66
Bromley	28	7	25	0	no overall control	60
Camden	10	43	6	0	Labour	59
Croydon	31	38	1	0	Labour	70
Ealing	15	53	3	0	Labour	71
Enfield	23	43	0	0	Labour	66
Greenwich	8	52	2	0	Labour	62
Hackney	12	29	17	2	no overall control	60
Hammersmith and Fulham	14	36	0	0	Labour	50
Haringey	2	54	3	0	Labour	59
Harrow	20	32	9	2	Labour	63
Havering	14	29	3	17	no overall control	63
Hillingdon	34	31	4	0	no overall control	69
Hounslow	11	44	4	1	Labour	60
Islington	0	26	26	0	no overall control	52
Kensington and Chelsea	39	15	0	0	Conservative	54
Kingston upon Thames	21	10	19	0	no overall control	50
Lambeth	5	41	18	0	Labour	64
Lewisham	2	61	4	0	Labour	67
Merton	12	39	3	3	Labour	57
Newham	0	60	0	0	Labour	60
Redbridge	23	30	9	0	no overall control	62
Richmond upon Thames	14	4	34	0	Liberal Democrats	52
Southwark	4	33	27	0	Labour	64
Sutton	5	5	46	0	Liberal Democrats	56
Tower Hamlets	0	41	9	0	Labour	50
Waltham Forest	15	30	12	0	Labour	57
Wandsworth	50	11	0	0	Conservative	61
Westminster	47	13	0	0	Conservative	60
Total	538	1,050	301	28	–	1,917

Source: Local Government Chronicle Elections Centre, University of Plymouth

The Addresses of English Metropolitan Boroughs

Borough	Council offices	Chief executive
Barnsley	Town Hall, Church Street, Barnsley S70 2TA; phone: (01226) 770770	Mr John Edwards
Birmingham	The Council House, Victoria Square, Birmingham B1 1BB; phone: (0121) 303 2000	Mr Michael Lyons
Bolton	Town Hall, Civic Centre, Bolton B21 1RU; phone: (01204) 522311	Mr Bernard Knight
Bradford	City Hall, Channing Way, Bradford BD1 1HY; phone: (01274) 752111	Mr Richard Penn
Bury	Town Hall, Knowsley Street, Bury BL9 0SW; phone: (0161) 253 5000; Web site: www.bury.gov.uk	Mr Dennis Taylor
Calderdale	Town Hall, Crossley Street, Halifax HX1 1UJ; phone: (01422) 357257	Mr Paul Sheehan
Coventry	Council House, Earl Street, Coventry CV1 5RR; phone: (01203) 833333	Mr Ian Roxburgh
Doncaster	2 Priory Place, Doncaster DN1 1BN; phone: (01302) 734000; fax: (01302) 734040	Mr Alf Taylor
Dudley	The Council House, Priory Road, Dudley DY1 1HF; phone: (01384) 818181	Mr A V Astling
Gateshead	Civic Centre, Regent Street, Gateshead NE8 1HH; phone: (0191) 477 1011; fax: (0191) 478 3495	Mr Leslie Elton
Kirklees	Crown Court Building, Princess Street, Huddersfield HD1 2TT; phone: (01484) 221801; fax: (01484) 221803	Mr Tony Elson
Knowsley	Municipal Buildings, Archway Road, Huyton L36 9UX; phone: (0151) 489 6000	Mr David Henshaw
Leeds	Civic Hall, Leeds LS1 1UR; phone: (0113) 234 8080; fax: (0113) 247 4338	Mr Philip Smith
Liverpool	Municipal Buildings, Dale Street, Liverpool L69 2DH; phone: (0151) 227 3911	Mr Peter Bounds
Manchester	Town Hall, Manchester M60 2LA; phone: (0161) 234 5000; fax: (0161) 236 5909	Mr Arthur Sandford
Newcastle upon Tyne	Civic Centre, Newcastle upon Tyne NE99 2BN; phone: (0191) 232 8520	Mr Kevin Lavery
North Tyneside	Town Hall, High Street East, Wallsend NE28 7RR; phone: (0191) 200 6565; fax: (0191) 200 7273	Mr Gallant, Mr Roberts, Mr Walton, Mr Wright, Mr Jackson (Directors), Mr Doughty (acting)
Oldham	PO Box 160, Civic Centre, West Street, Oldham OL1 1UG; phone: (0161) 911 3000; fax: (0161) 911 4684	Mr Colin Smith
Rochdale	Municipal Offices, Smith Street, Rochdale OL16 1XG; phone: (01706) 647474	Ms Frances Done
Rotherham	Civic Building, Walker Place, Rotherham S65 1UF; phone: (01709) 382121; fax: (01709) 823251	Mr Alan Carruthers
St Helens	Town Hall, Victoria Square, Corporation Street, St Helens WA10 1HP; phone: (01744) 456000; fax: (01744) 733337	Ms Carol Hudson
Salford	Salford Civic Centre, Chorley Road, Swinton, Salford M27 5FJ; phone: (0161) 794 4711	Mr John Willis
Sandwell	The Sandwell Council House, Oldbury, Warley B69 3DE; phone: (0121) 569 2200; Web site: www.sandwell.gov.uk	Mr Nigel Summers
Sefton	Town Hall, Lord Street, Southport PR8 1DA; phone: (01704) 533133; fax: (0151) 934 2256	Mr Graham Haywood
Sheffield	Town Hall, Pinstone Street, Sheffield S1 2HH; phone: (0114) 272 6444	Mr Bob Kerslake
Solihull	PO Box 18, Council House, Solihull B91 3QS; phone: (0121) 704 6000; fax: (0121) 704 6884	Mr Norman Perry
South Tyneside	Town Hall and Civic Offices, Westoe Road, South Shields NE33 2RL; phone: (0191) 427 1717	Mr Peter Haigh (Director of Corporate Services)
Stockport	Town Hall, Edward Street, Stockport SK1 3XE; phone: (0161) 480 4949; fax: (0161) 474 3009	Mr John Schultz
Sunderland	Civic Centre, Burdon Road, Sunderland SR2 7DN; phone: (0191) 553 1000; fax: (0191) 553 1020	Mr Colin Sinclair
Tameside	Wellington Road, Ashton-under-Lyne, Lancashire OL6 6DL; phone: (0161) 342 8355; fax: (0161) 342 3070	Mr Michael Greenwood
Trafford	Trafford Town Hall, Talbot Road, Trafford M32 0YT; phone: (0161) 912 1212; fax: (0161) 912 4184	Mr Alan Lewis
Wakefield	Town Hall, Wood Street, Wakefield WF1 2HQ; phone: (01924) 306090	Mr Roger Mather
Walsall	Civic Centre, Darwall Street, Walsall WS1 1TP; phone: (01922) 650000	Mr David Winchurch
Wigan	New Town Hall, Library Street, Greater Manchester WN1 1YN; phone: (01942) 244991; fax: (01942) 827415	Mr Stephen Jones
Wirral	Town Hall, Brighton Street, Wallasey L44 8ED; phone: (0151) 638 7070	Mr Stephen Maddox
Wolverhampton	Civic Centre, St Peter's Square, Wolverhampton WV1 1SH; phone: (01902) 556556	Mr Derek Anderson

The Political Composition of English Metropolitan Boroughs

(– = not applicable.)

Borough	Conservative	Labour	Liberal Democrat	Independent/ other	Controlling party	Total councillors
Barnsley	1	63	0	2	Labour	66
Birmingham	17	83	16	1	Labour	117
Bolton	8	47	5	0	Labour	60
Bradford	18	65	7	0	Labour	90
Bury	6	39	3	0	Labour	48
Calderdale	13	28	12	1	Labour	54
Coventry	7	45	0	2	Labour	54
Doncaster	3	47	6	7	Labour	63
Dudley	7	58	7	0	Labour	72
Gateshead	0	51	15	0	Labour	66
Kirklees	7	43	20	2	Labour	72
Knowsley	0	65	1	0	Labour	66
Leeds	9	80	9	1	Labour	99
Liverpool	0	39	52	8	Liberal Democrats	99
Manchester	0	84	15	0	Labour	99
Newcastle upon Tyne	0	65	13	0	Labour	78
North Tyneside	8	43	7	2	Labour	60
Oldham	0	36	23	1	Labour	60
Rochdale	6	36	18	0	Labour	60
Rotherham	1	65	0	0	Labour	66
St Helens	2	42	10	0	Labour	54
Salford	0	57	3	0	Labour	60
Sandwell	2	60	9	1	Labour	72
Sefton	14	31	23	1	no overall control	69
Sheffield	1	50	36	0	Labour	87
Solihull	20	17	11	3	no overall control	51
South Tyneside	0	51	6	3	Labour	60
Stockport	3	27	30	3	no overall control	63
Sunderland	4	68	2	1	Labour	75
Tameside	2	49	2	4	Labour	57
Trafford	23	36	4	0	Labour	63
Wakefield	2	60	0	1	Labour	63
Walsall	16	30	6	8	no overall control	60
Wigan	0	70	1	1	Labour	72
Wirral	16	41	8	1	Labour	66
Wolverhampton	14	44	2	0	Labour	60
Total	230	1,815	382	54	–	2,481

Source: Local Government Chronicle Elections Centre, University of Plymouth

The Addresses of English Unitary Authorities

Authority	Council offices	Chief executive
Bath and North East Somerset	The Guildhall, High Street, Bath BA1 5AW; phone: (01225) 477793; fax: (01225) 477442	Mr John Everitt
Blackburn/Blackburn with Darwen	Town Hall, King William Street, Blackburn BB1 7DY; phone: (01254) 585585; fax: (01254) 680870	Mr Philip Watson
Blackpool	Municipal Buildings, PO Box 77, Town Hall, Blackpool FY1 1NA; phone: (01253) 477477; fax: (01253) 477101	Mr G Essex-Crosby
Bournemouth	Town Hall, Bourne Avenue, Bournemouth BH2 6DY; phone: (01202) 451451; fax: (01202) 451001	Mr David Newell
Bracknell	Civic Offices, Easthampstead House, Town Square, Bracknell RG12 1AQ; phone: (01344) 424642; fax: (01344) 352810	Mr Gordon Mitchell
Brighton and Hove	Kings House, Grand Avenue, Hove BN3 2LS; phone: (01273) 290000	Mr Glynn Jones
Bristol	The Council House, College Green, Bristol BS1 5TR; phone: (0117) 922 2000	Ms Lucy de Groot
Darlington	Town Hall, Darlington DL1 5QT; phone: (01325) 380651; fax: (01325) 382032	Mr Barry Keel
Derby	The Council House, Corporation Street, Derby DE1 2FS; phone: (01332) 293111	Mr Ray Cowlishaw
East Riding of Yorkshire	County Hall, Beverley, East Riding of Yorkshire HU17 9BA; phone: (01482) 887100; fax: (01482) 884150	Mr Darryl Stephenson
Halton	Municipal Building, Kingsway, Widnes WA8 7QF; phone: (0151) 424 2061	Mr Mike Cuff
Hartlepool	Civic Centre, Victoria Road, Hartlepool TS24 8AY; phone: (01429) 266522; fax: (01429) 523005	Mr Brian Dinsdale

(continued)

The Addresses of English Unitary Authorities (continued)

Authority	Council offices	Chief executive
Herefordshire	PO Box 239, Hereford HR1 1ZU; phone: (01432) 260000; fax: (01432) 340189	Mr Neil Pringle
Isle of Wight	County Hall, Newport, Isle of Wight PO30 1UD; phone: (01983) 823000	Mr Felix Hetherington (Clerk to the Council)
Kingston upon Hull	Guildhall, Alfred Gelder Street, Kingston upon Hull HU1 2AA; phone: (01482) 610610; fax: (01482) 615135	Mr Ian Crookham
Leicester	New Walk Centre, Welford Place, Leicester LE1 6ZG; phone: (0116) 254 9922	Mr Rodney Green
Luton	Town Hall, George Street, Luton LU1 2BQ; phone: (01582) 746000	Ms K Jones
Medway Towns	Civic Centre, Strood, Rochester ME2 4AU; phone: (01634) 727777; fax: (01634) 732756	Ms Judith Armitt
Middlesbrough	PO Box 99A, Municipal Buildings, Middlesbrough TS1 2QQ; phone: (01642) 245432; fax: (01642) 263827	Mr John Foster (Managing Director)
Milton Keynes	Civic Office, 1 Saxon Gate East, Milton Keynes MK9 3EJ; phone: (01908) 691691; fax: (01908) 252456	Mr Howard Miller
Newbury/West Berkshire	Council Offices, Market Street, Newbury RG14 5LD; phone: (01635) 42400; fax: (01635) 519431	Ms Stella Manzie
North East Lincolnshire	Municipal Offices, Town Hall Square, Grimsby DN31 1HU; phone: (01472) 313131	Mr Roy Benson
North Lincolnshire	Pittwood House, Ashby Road, Scunthorpe DN16 1AB; phone: (01724) 296296; fax: (01724) 281705	Dr Michael Garnett
North Somerset	Town Hall, Walliscote Grove Road, Weston-super-Mare, BS23 1UJ; phone: (01934) 888888; fax: (01934) 418194	Mr Paul May
Nottingham	The Guildhall, Nottingham NG1 4DE; phone: (0115) 915 5555	Mr Edward Cantle
Peterborough	Town Hall, Bridge Street, Peterborough PE1 1HG; phone: (01733) 563141; fax: (01733) 452537	Mr W E Samuels
Plymouth	Civic Centre, Armada Way, Plymouth PL1 2EW; phone: (01752) 668000; fax: (01752) 304880	Ms Alison Stone
Poole	Civic Centre, Poole BH15 2RU; phone: (01202) 633633; fax: (01202) 633706	Mr Jim Brooks
Portsmouth	Civic Offices, Guildhall Square, Portsmouth PO1 2AL; phone: (01705) 822251	Mr Nick Gurney
Reading	Civic Centre, Reading RG1 7TD; phone: (0118) 939 0900; fax: (0118) 958 9770	Ms Joyce Markham
Redcar and Cleveland	Town Hall, PO Box 8, Fabian Road, South Bank TS6 9AR; phone: (01642) 444000; fax: (01642) 444599	Mr Andrew Kilburn
Rutland	Council Offices, Catmose, Oakham, Rutland LE15 6HP; phone: (01572) 722577; fax: (01572) 758307	Dr Janice Morphet
Slough	Town Hall, Bath Road, Slough SL1 3UQ; phone: (01753) 552288; fax: (01753) 692499	Ms Cheryl Coppell
Southampton	Civic Centre, Southampton SO14 7LY; phone: (01703) 223855	Mr John Cairns
Southend on Sea	Civic Centre, Victoria Avenue, Southend on Sea SS2 6ER; phone: (01702) 215000	Mr George Krawiec
South Gloucestershire	The Council Office, Castle Street, Thornbury BS35 1HF; phone: (01454) 868686	Mr Mike Robinson
Stockton-on-Tees	PO Box 11, Municipal Buildings, Church Road, Stockton-on-Tees TS18 1LD; phone: (01642) 393939; fax: (01642) 393092	Mr George Garlick
Stoke on Trent City	PO Box 636, Civic Centre, Glebe Street, Stoke on Trent ST4 1RN; phone: (01782) 234567	Mr Brian Smith
Swindon	Civic Offices, Swindon, Wilts SN1 2JH; phone: (01793) 463000	Mr Paul Doherty
Thurrock	Civic Offices, New Road, Grays RM17 6SL; phone: (01375) 390000; fax: (01375) 652359	Mr Keith Barnes
Torbay	Civic Offices, Castle Circus, Torquay TQ1 3DR; phone: (01803) 201201	Mr Anthony Hodgkiss
Warrington	Town Hall, Warrington WA1 1UH; phone: (01925) 442140; fax: (01925) 442024	Mr Steven Broomhead
Windsor and Maidenhead	Town Hall, St Ives Road, Maidenhead, Berks SL6 1RF; phone: (01628) 798888; fax: (01628) 796408	Mr David Lunn
Wokingham	PO Box 150, Shute End, Wokingham RG40 1WQ; phone: (0118) 978 6833	Ms Gillian Norton
Wrekin, The	Civic Office, Telford TF3 4LD; phone: (01952) 202100; fax: (01952) 291692	Mr David Hutchison
York	Library Square, Museum Street, York YO1 7ZW; phone: (01904) 613161; fax: (01904) 551190	Mr David Clark

The Political Composition of English Unitary Authorities

(– = not applicable.)

Authority	Conservative	Labour	Liberal Democrat	Independent/ other	Controlling party	Total councillors
Bath & North East Somerset	16	21	28	0	no overall control	65
Blackburn/Blackburn with Darwen	12	46	4	0	Labour	62
Blackpool	8	33	3	0	Labour	44
Bournemouth	19	6	28	4	no overall control	57
Bracknell	23	17	0	0	Conservative	40
Brighton & Hove	23	54	0	1	Labour	78
Bristol	7	44	17	0	Labour	68
Darlington	13	36	2	1	Labour	52
Derby	4	37	3	0	Labour	44
East Riding Of Yorkshire	19	22	20	6	no overall control	67
Halton	1	47	8	0	Labour	56
Hartlepool	5	33	8	1	Labour	47
Herefordshire	8	2	32	18	Liberal Democrats	60
Isle of Wight	15	4	16	13	no overall control	48
Kingston upon Hull	1	53	4	2	Labour	60
Leicester	7	39	10	0	Labour	56
Luton	3	36	9	0	Labour	48
Medway Towns	20	39	21	0	no overall control	80
Middlesbrough	2	45	4	2	Labour	53
Milton Keynes	4	27	19	1	Labour	51
Newbury/West Berkshire	15	0	38	1	Liberal Democrats	54
North East Lincolnshire	2	32	7	1	Labour	42
North Lincolnshire	7	35	0	0	Labour	42
North Somerset	17	6	30	6	Liberal Democrats	59
Nottingham	3	50	2	0	Labour	55
Peterborough	24	27	2	4	no overall control	57
Plymouth	13	47	0	0	Labour	60
Poole	13	3	23	0	Liberal Democrats	39
Portsmouth	8	21	10	0	Labour	39
Reading	3	36	6	0	Labour	45
Redcar and Cleveland	1	49	7	2	Labour	59
Rutland	2	2	7	9	no overall control	20
Slough	4	34	3	0	Labour	41
Southampton	3	28	14	0	Labour	45
Southend on Sea	19	7	13	0	no overall control	39
South Gloucestershire	8	31	30	1	no overall control	70
Stockton-on-Tees	7	44	4	0	Labour	55
Stoke on Trent	1	54	3	2	Labour	60
Swindon	5	40	9	0	Labour	54
Thurrock	3	36	0	0	Labour	39
Torbay	12	2	22	0	Liberal Democrats	36
Warrington	4	45	11	0	Labour	60
Windsor and Maidenhead	22	0	29	7	no overall control	58
Wokingham	31	0	23	0	Conservative	54
Wrekin, The	9	38	4	3	Labour	54
York	3	30	18	2	Labour	53
Total	449	1,338	551	87	–	2,425

Source: Local Government Chronicle Elections Centre, University of Plymouth

Local Government of Wales

The Addresses of Welsh Unitary Authorities

Authority	Council offices	Chief executive
Aberconwy and Colwyn/Conwy	Bodlondeb, Bangor Road, Conwy LL32 8DU; phone: (01492) 574000; fax: (01492) 592114	Mr Derek Barker
Anglesey	Council Offices, Llangefni, Anglesey Ll77 7TW; phone: (01248) 752480; fax: (01248) 752192; Web site: www.anglesey.gov.uk/	Mr Leon Gibson
Blaenau Gwent	Municipal Offices, Civic Centre, Ebbw Vale NP3 6XB; phone: (01495) 350555; fax: (01495) 301255	Mr Roger Leadbeter
Bridgend	Civic Offices, Angel Street, Bridgend CF31 1LX; phone: (01656) 643643; fax: (01656) 668126	Mr Kerry Lewis
Caerphilly	Nelson Road, Tredomen, Ystrad Mynach, Hengoed CF82 7WF; phone: (01443) 815588; fax: (01443) 864211; Web site: www.caerphilly.gov.uk/	Mr Malgwyn Davies
Cardiff	County Hall, Atlantic Wharf, Cardiff CF1 5UW; phone: (01222) 873208/ 873206; fax: (01222) 873201; e-mail: O.Jenkins@cardiff.gov.uk; Web site: www.cardiff.gov.uk/	Mr Byron Davies
Cardiganshire/Ceredigion	Penmorfa, Aberaeron SA46 0PA; phone: (01545) 572000; fax: (01545) 572009;Web site: www.ceredigion.gov.uk/	Mr R Owen Watkin
Carmarthenshire	County Hall, Carmarthen SA31 1JP; phone: (01267) 234567; fax: (01267) 222097; Web site: www.carmarthenshire.gov.uk/	Mr Bradley Roynon
Caernarfonshire and Merionethshire/Gwynedd	Swyddfa'r Cyngor, Caernarfon LL55 1SH; phone: (01286) 672255; fax: (01286) 673993; e-mail: enquiries@gwynedd.gov.uk; Web site: www.gwynedd.gov.uk/	Mr Geraint R Jones
Denbighshire	Council Offices, Wynnstay Road, Ruthin LL15 1YN; phone: (01824) 706000; fax: (01824) 707446; Web site: www.denbighshire.gov.uk/	Mr Huw Vaughan Thomas
Flintshire	County Hall, Mold CH7 6NB; phone: (01352) 702100; fax: (01352) 755910	Mr Philip McGreevy
Merthyr Tydfil	Civic Centre, Castle Street, Merthyr Tydfil CF47 8AN; phone: (01685) 725000; fax: (01685) 722146; Web site: www.merthyr.gov.uk/	Mr Gary Meredith
Monmouthshire	County Hall, Cwmbran NP44 2XH; phone: (01633) 644644; fax: (01633) 644666	Ms Joyce Redfearn
Neath and Port Talbot	Civic Centre, Port Talbot SA13 1PJ; phone: (01639) 763333; fax: (01639) 763444	Mr Ken Sawyers
Newport	Civic Centre, Newport NP9 4UR; phone: (01633) 244491; fax: (01633) 244721; Web site: www.newport.gov.uk/	Mr R D Sandy Blair
Pembrokeshire	Cambria House, Haverfordwest, Pembrokeshire SA61 1TP; phone: (01437) 764551; fax: (01437) 760703; Web site: www.pembrokeshire.gov.uk/	Mr Bryn Parry-Jones
Powys	County Hall, Spa Road, Llandrindod Wells LD1 5LG; phone: (01597) 826368; fax: (01597) 826220; Web site: www.powys.gov.uk/	Mr Neil Pringle
Rhondda/Cynon/Taff	The Pavilions, Cambrian Park, Clydach Vale CF40 2XX; phone: (01443) 424000; fax: (01443) 424024; Web site: www.rhondda-cynon-taff.gov.uk/	Mr Geoffrey Thomas
Swansea	County Hall, Swansea SA1 3SN; phone: (01792) 636000; fax: (01792) 636340; Web site: www.swansea.gov.uk/	Ms Vivienne Sugar
Torfaen	Civic Centre, Pontypool, Gwent NP4 6YB; phone: (01495) 762200; fax: (01495) 755513	Dr Clive Grace
Vale of Glamorgan	Civic Offices, Holton Road, Barry CF63 4RU; phone: (01446) 700111; fax: 01446 745566; Web site: www.valeofglamorgan.gov.uk/	Mr David Foster
Wrexham County Borough	Guildhall, Wrexham LL11 1WF; phone: (01978) 292000; fax: (01978) 292106	Mr Derek Griffin

The Political Composition of Welsh Unitary Authorities

(– = not applicable.)

Authority	Conservative	Labour	Liberal Democrat	Independent/ other	Plaid Cymru	Controlling party	Total councillors
Aberconwy and Colwyn/Conwy	10	18	16	13	3	no overall control	60
Anglesey	1	6	0	26	7	Independent	40
Blaenau Gwent	1	33	0	7	1	Labour	42
Bridgend	2	40	2	3	1	Labour	48
Caernarfonshire And Merionethshire/Gwynedd	0	9	3	26	45	Plaid Cymru	83
Caerphilly	0	56	0	3	9	Labour	68
Cardiff	1	56	9	0	1	Labour	67
Cardiganshire/Ceredigion	0	1	12	25	7	Independent	45
Carmarthenshire	1	37	3	32	7	no overall control	80
Denbighshire	0	20	3	20	7	no overall control	50
Flintshire	3	45	6	16	1	Labour	71
Merthyr Tydfll	0	29	0	4	0	Labour	33
Monmouthshire	11	26	1	4	0	Labour	42
Neath and Port Talbot	0	52	1	9	3	Labour	65
Newport	1	46	0	0	0	Labour	47
Pembrokeshire	0	11	3	42	4	Independent	60
Powys	4	10	9	59	1	Independent	83
Rhondda/Cynon/Taff	0	57	0	4	14	Labour	75
Swansea	1	55	8	8	1	Labour	73
Torfaen	1	41	1	1	0	Labour	44
Vale of Glamorgan	6	35	0	0	5	Labour	46
Wrexham	3	33	4	11	0	Labour	51
Total	46	716	81	313	117	–	1,273

Source: Local Government Chronicle Elections Centre, University of Plymouth

Local Government of Scotland

The Addresses of Scottish Unitary Authorities

Authority	Council offices	Chief executive
Aberdeen	Town House, Broad Street, Aberdeen AB10 1FY; phone: (01224) 522000; fax: (01224) 644346	Mr Douglas Paterson
Aberdeenshire	Woodhill House, Westburn Road, Aberdeen AB16 5GB; phone: (01467) 620981; fax: (01224) 665444; Web site: www.aberdeenshire.gov.uk/	Mr Alan G Campbell
Angus	Angus Council, 7 The Cross, Forfar, Angus DD8 1BX; phone: (01307) 461460; fax: (01307) 461874; e-mail: chiefexec@angus.gov.uk; Web site: www.angus.gov.uk/	Mr Andy Watson
Argyll and Bute	Kilmory, Lochgilphead, Argyll PA31 8RT; phone: (01546) 604263; fax: (01546) 604349; Web site: www.argyll-bute.gov.uk/	Mr James McLellan
Borders	Council Headquarters, Newtown Street, Boswells, Melrose TD6 0SA; phone: (01835) 824000; fax: (01835) 825059	Mr Alastair M Croall
Clackmannanshire	Greenfield, Alloa, Clackmannanshire FK10 2AD; phone: (01259) 452000; fax: (01259) 452010	Mr Bob Allan
Dumfries and Galloway	Council Offices, English Street, Dumfries DG1 2DD; phone: (01387) 260000; fax: (01387) 260034; e-mail: CIS@dumgal.gov.uk; Web site: www.dumgal.gov.uk/	Mr Ian Smith
Dundee	21 City Square, Dundee DD1 3BY; phone: (01382) 434000; fax: (01382) 434996; Web site: www.dundeecity.gov.uk/	Mr Alex Stephen
East Ayrshire	Council Headquarters, London Road, Kilmarnock KA3 7BU; phone: (01563) 576000; fax: (01563) 576500; Web site: www.east-ayrshire.gov.uk/	Mr David Montgomery
East Dunbartonshire	PO Box 4, Tom Johnston House, Civic Way, Kirkintilloch G66 4TJ; phone: (0141) 578 8000; fax: (0141) 777 8576	Mr Con Mallon
East Lothian	Council Buildings, 25 Court Street, Haddington EH41 3HA; phone: (01620) 824161; fax: (01620) 827888	Mr John Lindsay
East Renfrewshire	Council Headquarters, Eastwood Park, Rouken Glen Road, Giffnock G46 6UG; phone: (0141) 577 3000; fax: (0141) 577 3100; Web site: www.eastrenfrewshire.gov.uk/	Mr Peter Daniels
Edinburgh	City Chambers, High Street, Edinburgh EH1 1YJ; phone: (0131) 200 2000; fax: (0131) 529 7607	Mr Tom Aitchison

(continued)

The Addresses of Scottish Unitary Authorities (continued)

Authority	Council offices	Chief executive
Falkirk	Municipal Buildings, West Bridge Street, Falkirk FK1 5RS; phone: (01324) 506070; fax: (01324) 506061; Web site: www.falkirk.electricscotland.com/	Ms Mary Pitcaithly
Fife	Fife House, North Street, Glenrothes KY7 5LT; phone: (01592) 414141; fax: (01592) 414142	Dr John Markland
Glasgow	City Chambers, Glasgow G2 1DU; phone: (0141) 287 2000; fax: (0141) 287 5666	Mr James Andrews (acting)
Highlands	Regional Buildings, Glenurquhart Road, Inverness IV3 5NX; phone: (01463) 702000; fax: (01463) 702830	Mr Arthur McCourt
Inverclyde	Municipal Buildings, Greenock PA15 1LY; phone: (01475) 724400; fax: (01475) 712010	Mr Gerry Douglas
Midlothian	Midlothian House, Buccleuch Street, Dalkeith EH22 1DJ; phone: (0131) 663 2881; fax: (0131) 271 3050; e-mail: info@midlothian.gov.uk; Web site: www.midlothian.gov.uk/	Mr Trevor Muir
Moray	Council Office, High Street, Elgin IV30 1BX; phone: (01343) 543451; fax: (01343) 540183; Web site: www.moray.org/	vacant
North Ayrshire	Cunninghame House, Irvine KA12 8EE; phone: (01294) 324100; fax: (01294) 324144	Mr Bernard Devine
North Lanarkshire	PO Box 14, Civic Centre, Motherwell ML1 1TW; phone: (01698) 302222; fax: (01698) 275125	Mr Andrew Cowe
Orkney	Council Offices, School Place, Kirkwall, Orkney KW15 1NY; phone: (01856) 873535; fax: (01856) 874615	Mr Alastair Buchan
Perth and Kinross	PO Box 77, 2 High Street, Perth, PH1 5PH; phone: (01738) 475000; fax: (01738) 475710; e-mail: enquiries@pkc.gov.uk; Web site: www.pkc.gov.uk/	Mr Harry Robertson
Renfrewshire	North Building, Cotton Street, Paisley PA1 1WB; phone: (0141) 842 5000; fax: (0141) 840 3212	Mr Thomas Scholes
Shetland	Town Hall, Hillhead, Lerwick, Shetland ZE1 0HB; phone: (01595) 693535; fax: (01595) 695590; e-mail: sic@shetland.gov.uk; Web site: www.shetland.gov.uk/	Mr Nicholas Reiter
South Ayrshire	County Buildings, Wellington Square, Ayr KA7 1DR; phone: (01292) 612000; fax: (01292) 612143; Web site: www.south-ayrshire.gov.uk/	Mr George Thorley
South Lanarkshire	Council Offices, Almada Street, Hamilton ML3 0AA; phone: (01698) 454444; fax: (01698) 454275	Mr Alastair MacNish
Stirling	Council Headquarters, Viewforth, Stirling FK8 2ET; phone: (01786) 443322; fax: (01786) 443078; Web site: www.stirling.gov.uk/	Mr Keith Yates
West Dunbartonshire/ Dumbarton and Clydebank	Council Offices, Garshake Road, Dumbarton G82 3PU; phone: (01389) 737000; fax: (01389) 737582; e-mail: wdcmgr1@post.almac.co.uk; Web site: www.west-dunbarton.gov.uk/	Mr Michael Watters
Western Isles (Comhairle nan Eilean Siar)	Council Offices, Balivanich, Benbecula HS7 5LA; phone: (01870) 602425; fax: (01870) 602332; Web site: www.w-isles.gov.uk/	Mr Brian Stewart
West Lothian	West Lothian House, Almondvale Boulevard, Livingston EH54 6QG; phone: (01506) 777000; fax: (01506) 777249	Mr Alex Linkston

The Political Composition of Scottish Unitary Authorities

(– = not applicable.)

Authority	Conservative	Labour	Liberal Democrat	Scottish Party National	Independent/ other	Controlling party	Total councillors
Aberdeen	9	29	11	1	0	Labour	50
Aberdeenshire	5	0	16	15	11	no overall control	47
Angus	2	0	2	21	1	Scottish National Party	26
Argyll and Bute	3	2	4	4	20	Independent	33
Borders	3	2	14	8	31	Independent	58
Clackmannanshire	1	8	0	3	0	Labour	12
Dumbarton and Clydebank/ West Dunbartonshire	0	14	0	8	0	Labour	22
Dumfries and Galloway	2	21	10	9	28	no overall control	70
Dundee	4	28	0	3	1	Labour	36
East Ayrshire	0	21	0	9	0	Labour	30
East Dunbartonshire	2	15	9	0	0	Labour	26
East Lothian	3	15	0	0	0	Labour	18
East Renfrewshire	9	8	2	0	1	no overall control	20
Edinburgh	14	33	10	1	0	Labour	58
Falkirk	2	23	0	8	3	Labour	36
Fife	0	53	25	11	3	Labour	92
Glasgow	3	76	1	2	2	Labour	84
Highlands	1	6	5	8	52	Independent	72
Inverclyde	1	13	6	0	0	Labour	20
Midlothian	0	13	0	2	0	Labour	15

The Political Composition of Scottish Unitary Authorities (*continued*)

Authority	Conservative	Labour	Liberal Democrat	Scottish Party National	Independent/ other	Controlling party	Total councillors
Moray	0	3	0	13	2	Scottish National Party	18
North Ayrshire	1	26	0	1	1	Labour	29
North Lanarkshire	0	59	0	8	2	Labour	69
Orkney	0	0	0	0	28	Independent	28
Perthshire and Kinross	2	5	6	18	1	Scottish National Party	32
Renfrewshire	2	22	3	13	0	Labour	40
Shetland	0	1	2	0	23	Independent	26
South Ayrshire	5	20	0	0	0	Labour	25
South Lanarkshire	2	61	2	8	0	Labour	73
Stirling	7	13	0	2	0	Labour	22
Western Isles	0	4	0	0	26	Independent	30
West Lothian	1	15	0	11	0	Labour	27
Total	84	609	128	187	236	–	1,244

Source: Local Government Chronicle Elections Centre, University of Plymouth

Local Government of Northern Ireland

The Addresses of Northern Ireland District Councils

Council	Council offices	Chief executive
Antrim	Council Offices, The Steeple, Antrim BT41 1BJ; phone: (01849) 463113; e-mail: contact@antrim.gov.uk; Web site: www.antrim.gov.uk/	S J Magee
Ards	2 Church Street, Newtownards, Co Down BT23 4AP; phone: (01247) 824000; fax: (01247) 819628; e-mail: ards@ards-council.gov.uk; Web site: www.ards-council.gov.uk/	David Fallows
Armagh	The Palace Demesne, Armagh BT60 4EL; phone: (01861) 529600; fax: (01861) 529601; e-mail: info@armagh.gov.uk; Web site: www.armagh.gov.uk/	D R D Mitchell
Ballymena	'Ardeevin', 80 Galgorm Road, Ballymena, BT42 1AB; phone: (01266) 660300; e-mail: townclerk@ballymena.gov.uk; Web site: www.ballymena.gov.uk/	M Rankin
Ballymoney	Riada House, 14 Charles Street, Ballymoney BT53 6DZ; phone: (012656) 62280; fax: (012656) 65150	John Dempsey
Banbridge	Civic Building, Downshire Road, Banbridge BT32 3JY; phone: (01820) 662991; fax: (01820) 62595/24791	Robert Gilmore
Belfast	City Hall, Belfast, BT1 5GS; phone: (01232) 320202; e-mail: webmaster@belfastcity.gov.uk; Web site: www.belfastcity.gov.uk/	Brian Hanna
Carrickfergus	Town Hall, Carrickfergus BT38 7DL; phone: (01960) 351604; fax: (01960) 366676; e-mail: info@carrickfergus.org; Web site: www.carrickfergus.org/	R Boyd
Castlereagh	Borough Offices, 368 Cregagh Road, Belfast BT6 9EZ; phone: (01232) 799021; fax: (01232) 704158; e-mail: chief@castlereagh.gov.uk; Web site: www.castlereagh.gov.uk/	Adrian Donaldson
Coleraine	Cloonavin, 41 Portstewart Road, Coleraine BT52 1EY; phone: (01265) 52181; fax: (01265) 53489	H W T Moore
Cookstown	Council Offices, Burn Road, Cookstown BT80 8DT; phone: (016487) 62205; fax: (016487) 64360	Michael McGuckin
Craigavon	Civic Centre, PO Box 66, Lakeview Road, Craigavon, BT64 1AL; phone: (01762) 341199; fax: (01762) 345514; e-mail: info@craigavon.gov.uk; Web site: www.craigavon.gov.uk/	T E Reaney
Derry	Council Offices, 98 Strand Road, Derry BT48 7NN; phone: (01504) 365151; fax: (01504) 368536	John Keanie
Down	24 Strangford Road, Downpatrick, County Down BT30 6SR; phone: (01396) 610800; fax: (01396) 610801; Web site: www.downdc.gov.uk/	Owen P O'Connor
Dungannon	Council Offices, Circular Road, Dungannon BT71 6DT; phone: (01868) 725311; e-mail: general@dungannon.gov.uk; Web site: www.dungannon.gov.uk/	William Beattie
Fermanagh	Townhall, Enniskillen BT74 4BA; phone: (01365) 325050; Web site: www.fermanagh.gov.uk/	Aideen McGinley
Larne	Smiley Buildings, Victoria Road, Larne BT40 1RU; phone: (01574) 272313; fax: (01574) 260660; e-mail: mail@larne-bc.com; Web site: www.larne.com/borough_council/	Colm McGarry
Limavady	7 Connell Street, Limavady, Co Londonderry BT49 0HA; phone: (015047) 22226; fax: (015047) 22010	John Stevenson
Lisburn	Borough Offices, The Square, Hillsborough BT26 6AH; phone: (01846) 682477; fax: (01846) 689016; e-mail: lisburnbc@compuserve.com; Web site: www.lisburn.gov.uk/	Norman Davidson

(continued)

The Addresses of Northern Ireland District Councils (continued)

Council	Council offices	Chief executive
Magherafelt	Council Offices, 50 Ballyronan Road, Magherafelt BT45 6EN; phone: (01648) 32151; (01648) 31240	John McLaughlin
Moyle	Sheskburn House, 7 Mary Street, Ballycastle BT54 6QH; phone: (012657) 62225; fax: (012657) 62515; e-mail: info@moyle-council.org.uk; Web site: www.moyle-council.org/	R G Lewis
Newry and Mourne	O'Hagan House, District Council Offices, Monaghan Row, Newry BT35 8DL; phone: (01693) 65411; fax: (01693) 65313	Kevin O'Neill
Newtownabbey	Headquarters, 1 The Square, Ballyclare BT39 9BA; phone: (01960) 352681; fax: (01960) 340417	Norman Dunn
North Down	Town Hall, The Castle, Bangor BT20 4BT; phone: (01247) 270371; fax: (01247) 271370; e-mail: edo@north-down.gov.uk; Web site: www.north-down.gov.uk/	Adrian McDowell
Omagh	Council Offices, The Grange, Mountjoy Road, Omagh BT79 7BL; phone: (01662) 245321; fax: (01662) 243888; Web site: www.omagh.gov.uk/	J P McKinney
Strabane	District Council Offices, 47 Derry Road, Strabane BT82 8DY; phone: (01504) 382204; fax: (01504) 382264; e-mail: strabanedc@nics.gov.uk; Web site: www.strabanedc.org.uk/	Victor Eakin

The Political Composition of Northern Ireland District Councils

Council	Ulster Unionist	Social Democratic and Labour Party	Democratic Unionist Party	Sinn Féin	Alliance	Independent	Independent Unionist	Progressive Unionist	Ulster Democratic Party	Other	Total
Antrim	9	4	3	1	2	0	0	0	0	0	19
Ards	10	1	5	0	5	0	2	0	0	0	23
Armagh	10	7	2	3	0	0	0	0	0	0	22
Ballymena	11	3	8	0	1	1	0	0	0	0	24
Ballymoney	4	3	6	1	0	2	0	0	0	0	16
Banbridge	9	3	3	0	0	2	0	0	0	0	17
Belfast City	13	7	7	13	6	0	1	3	1	0	51
Carrickfergus	4	0	3	0	5	3	1	0	0	1	17
Castlereagh	5	2	10	0	4	0	1	0	0	1	23
Coleraine	10	3	5	0	3	1	0	0	0	0	22
Cookstown	4	4	2	5	0	0	1	0	0	0	16
Craigavon	11	7	3	2	1	0	0	0	0	2	26
Derry City	3	14	4	8	0	0	1	0	0	0	30
Down	6	12	2	2	0	0	0	0	0	1	23
Dungannon	8	4	3	5	0	0	0	0	0	2	22
Fermanagh	9	4	2	5	0	1	0	0	0	2	23
Larne	0	6	1	3	0	1	1	0	0	3	15
Limavady	7	7	0	1	0	0	0	0	0	0	15
Lisburn	13	2	2	4	3	0	0	0	2	4	30
Magherafelt	2	5	4	5	0	0	0	0	0	0	16
Moyle	3	3	3	1	0	4	0	0	0	1	15
Newry and Mourne	5	12	1	8	0	4	0	0	0	0	30
Newtonabbey	10	1	2	0	3	0	3	1	0	4	24
North Down	6	0	2	0	6	2	1	2	0	6	25
Omagh	3	5	3	6	1	0	0	0	0	3	21
Strabane	3	5	3	4	0	1	0	0	0	0	16
Total	183	119	91	74	41	25	11	6	3	27	580

British Dependent Territories

Anguilla

Flag Blue with the flag of the UK in the upper left quadrant and the Anguillan coat of arms (three orange dolphins on a white background arranged in a circular design with blue wavy water below) centred in the outer half of the flag; **Topography** Anguilla is the most northerly of the Leeward Islands in the eastern Caribbean, a flat and low-lying island of coral and limestone; **Area** 96 sq km/36 sq mi; **Major towns and cities** The Valley (capital); **Total population** 8,960 (1992); **Climate** Tropical, moderated by northeast trade winds; average temperature 27°C/80°F; average annual rainfall 89 cm/35 in; **Time** Greenwich Mean Time less 4 hours; **Currency** East Caribbean dollar; **Languages** English; **Religion** Christianity; **Head of state** Queen Elizabeth II, represented by Governor Alan N Poole; **Head of government** Chief Minister Hubert Hughes; **Major industries** Finance; tourism; boat building; salt; fishing; **Agriculture** Pigeon peas; corn; sweet potatoes; sheep; goats; pigs; cattle; poultry; **Chamber of Commerce** Chamber of Commerce, PO Box 321, The Valley, Anguilla; phone: (001809) 497 2701; **Tourist department** Anguilla Tourist Board, Factory Plaza, The Valley, Anguilla, BWI; phone: (001809) 497 2759; fax: (001809) 497 3091; e-mail: abtour@candw.com.ai; Web site: www.candw.com.ai; **UK office** Anguilla Tourist Board, 3 Epirus Road, London SW6 7UJ; phone: (0171) 937 7725; fax: (0171) 938 4793.

Bermuda

Flag Red with the flag of the UK in the upper left quadrant and the Bermudian coat of arms (white and blue shield with a red lion holding a scrolled shield showing the sinking of the *Sea Venture* off Bermuda in 1609) centred on the outer half of the flag; **Topography** Consists of some 150 islands and islets situated at latitude 32°N and longitude 65°W in western Atlantic Ocean, off the US (North Carolina) coast. About 20 islands are inhabited. Ten main islands linked by causeways and bridges form a distinctive fishhook-shaped chain. The landscape consists mainly of rolling hills. The coast is dotted with sandy bays, coves, and craggy cliffs. There are no rivers or lakes; **Area** 52 sq km/20 sq mi; **Highest point** 78.9 m/849 ft; **Major towns and cities** Hamilton (capital); St George; **Total population** 60,500 (1994); **Climate** Sub-tropical, mainly humid; average temperature 21°C/70°F; average annual rainfall 146 cm/57 in; **Time** Greenwich Mean Time less 4 hours; **Currency** Bermudan dollar; **Languages** English; **Religion** Christianity; **Head of state** Queen Elizabeth II, represented by Governor John Thorold Masefield; **Head of**

government Premier Pamela Gordon; **Major industries** Tourism (70% of gross domestic product); offshore insurance; pharmaceutical and paint manufacturing; construction; ship-repairing and boat-building; **Agriculture** Bananas; potatoes; tomatoes; carrots; cabbage; citrus fruits; **Chamber of Commerce** Bermuda Chamber of Commerce, 1 Point Pleasant Road, PO Box HM 655, Hamilton HM CX, Bermuda; phone: (001441) 295 4201; fax: (001441) 292 5779; e-mail: bcc@ibl.bm; **Tourist department** Bermuda Department of Tourism, Global House, 43 Church Street, Hamilton HM, Bermuda; phone: (001441) 292 0023; Web site: www.bermudatourism.org; UK office: Bermuda Tourism, 1 Battersea Church Road, London SW11 3LY, phone: (0171) 777 7001; fax: (0171) 771 7037.

British Virgin Islands

Flag Blue with the flag of the UK in the upper left quadrant and the Virgin Islander coat of arms (a woman flanked on either side by a vertical column of six oil lamps above a scroll bearing the inscription *vigilate* (be watchful)) centred in the outer half of the flag; **Topography** A chain of about 60 islands, islets, and cays, 16 inhabited, lying at east end of the Greater Antilles chain, with the Lesser Antilles chain to east and south, in the Caribbean on latitude 18°N and longitude 64°W. The main islands are Tortola, Anegada, Virgin Gorda, and Jost Van Dyke. The landscape consists mainly of steep, thickly wooded hills, with coral reefs, coves, and beaches. There are no rivers; **Area** 150 sq km/58 sq mi; **Highest point** Sage Mountain, 540 m/1,772 ft, on Tortola; **Major towns and cities** Road Town (capital), Tortola Island; East End; Long Look; **Total population** 16,100 (1991); **Climate** Sub-tropical, temperatures moderated by trade winds, occasional droughts; temperature ranges: winter 22–28°C/71–82°F; summer 26–31°C/79–88°F; erratic rainfall averaging 127 cm/50 in annually; **Time** Greenwich Mean Time less 4 hours; **Currency** US dollar; **Languages** English; **Religion** Christianity; **Head of state** Queen Elizabeth II, represented by Governor David MacKilligin; **Head of government** Chief Minister and Minister of Finance Ralph T O'Neal; **Major industries** Tourism (75% of gross domestic product); financial services; fishing; rum distilling; construction; **Agriculture** Livestock (including poultry); fish; fruit; vegetables; **Tourist department**, British Virgin Islands Tourist Board, PO Box 134, Road Town, Tortola, BVI; phone: (001284) 494 3134; fax: (001284) 494 3866; UK office British Virgin Islands Tourist Board, 110 St Martin's Lane, London WC2N 4DY; phone: (0171) 240 4259; fax: (0171) 240 4270.

Cayman Islands

Flag Blue with the flag of the UK in the upper left quadrant and the Caymanian coat of arms (a pineapple and turtle above a shield with three stars (representing the three islands) and a scroll at the bottom bearing the motto 'he hath founded it upon the seas'; on a white disk) centred on the outer half of the flag; the coat of arms; **Topography** Three islands of Grand Cayman, Little Cayman, and Cayman Brac lie in Caribbean Sea northwest of Jamaica latitude 19°N and longitude 79–82°W. Low-lying, 18 m/59 ft above sea level, except in Cayman Brac where the eastern end rises to 42 m/138 ft; rock-bound coasts protected by coral reefs enclosing a few fair anchorages; no rivers; **Area** 260 sq km/100 sq mi; **Highest point** 42 m/138 ft; **Major towns and cities** George Town (capital); West Bay; **Total population** 31,150 (1993); **Climate** Tropical tempered by trade winds, warm rainy summers (May–October) and cool, relatively dry winters (November–April); average temperature N/A; average annual rainfall 142 cm/56 in; **Time** Greenwich Mean Time less 5 hours; **Currency** Cayman Islands dollars; **Languages** English; **Religion** Christianity; **Head of state** Queen Elizabeth II, represented by Governor John Wynn Owen; **Head of government** Governor and President of the Executive Council John Wynn Owen; **Major industries** Tourism (70% of gross domestic product); banking; insurance and finance; real estate and construction; **Agriculture** Minor production of vegetables and fruit; livestock; turtle farming; **Chamber of Commerce** Cayman Islands Chamber of Commerce, PO Box 1000 GT, Grand Cayman; phone: (001345) 949-8090; fax: (001345) 949-0220; e-mail: chamber@candw.ky; **Tourist department** PO Box 67, George Town, Grand Cayman; phone: (001345) 949 0623; fax: (001345) 949 4053; UK office: 6 Arlington Street, London SW1A 1RE; phone: (0171) 491 7771; fax: (0171) 409 7773.

Falkland Islands

Flag Blue with the flag of the UK in the upper left quadrant and the Falkland Island coat of arms (a white ram above the *Desire* with a scroll at the bottom bearing the motto 'desire the right' in a white disk) centred on the outer half of the flag; **Topography** The Falkland Islands comprise two large islands, East Falkland and West Falkland, and some 200 smaller islands between latitudes 51–53°S and longitudes 57–61°W in the south Atlantic, approximately 770 km/478 mi northeast of Cape Horn, South America. On the main islands deeply indented coastlines afford good anchorages. Generally hilly, the landscape is mainly stony, treeless grassland with no large inland waters; **Area** 12,170 sq km/4,680 sq mi; **Highest point** Mt Usborne on East Falkland, 705 m/2,313 ft; **Major towns and cities** Stanley, on East Falkland (capital); Goose Green; **Total population** 2,120 (March 1991); **Climate** Gales in spring, and generally windy, low rainfall evenly distributed throughout the year, with frequent cloud cover, frequent snow which quickly melts; average temperature 5.6°C/42°F; average annual rainfall 62.5 cm/24.6 in; **Time** Greenwich Mean Time less 4 hours; **Currency** Falkland Islands pound; **Languages** English; **Religion** Christianity; **Head of state** Queen Elizabeth II; **Head of government** David Everard Tatham; **Major industries** Wool processing; **Agriculture** Sheep farming; small dairy herds; fodder crops; **Chamber of Commerce** Falkland Islands Development Corporation, PO Box 580, Stanley, Falkland Islands; phone: (010500) 27211; Fax: (001500) 27210; **Tourist department** Falkland Islands Tourist Board, Stanley, Falkland Islands, PO Box 580, Stanley, Falkland Islands; UK office: Falkland House, 14 Broadway, London SW1H 0BH; phone: (0171) 222 2542; fax: (0171) 222 2375.

Gibraltar

Flag Two horizontal bands of white (top, double width) and red with a three-towered red castle in the centre of the white band; hanging from the castle gate is a gold key centred in the red band; **Topography** Narrow rocky peninsula latitude 36°N longitude 5°W. Juts out steeply from the adjoining low-lying coast of southwest Spain, at the east end of Strait of Gibraltar, overlooking the west entrance to Mediterranean. The Rock of Gibraltar is a long, high mountain with a sandy plain to the north. It has a 2.4 km/1.5 mi knife edge running from a steep north escarpment, then a 1.6 km/1 mi slope to the south, ending in vertical cliffs 30.5 m/100 ft high. The Spanish port of Algeciras lies 8 km/5 mi across the bay to the west, while the coast of Morocco is 21 km/13 mi across the Strait of Gibraltar to the south; **Area** 6.5 sq km/2.5 sq mi; **Highest point** 423 m/1,388 ft; **Major towns and cities** Gibraltar (capital); **Total population** 29,000 (1993); **Climate** Mild and temperate, snow or frost extremely rare; rainy season September to May; average temperature 17°C/63°F; average annual rainfall 77 cm/30 in; **Time** Greenwich Mean Time plus 1 hour; **Currency** Gibraltar pound; **Languages** English; Spanish; **Religion** Christianity; Islam; **Head of state** Queen Elizabeth II, represented by Governor and Commander-in-Chief Sir John Chapple; **Head of government** Chief Minister Joe Bossano; **Major industries** Tourism; banking and finance; construction; commerce; support to large UK naval and air bases; transit trade and supply depot in the port; light manufacturing of tobacco, roasted coffee, ice, mineral waters, candy, beer, and canned fish; **Chamber of Commerce** Gibraltar Information Bureau Ltd (Administration),

Engineer Battery, 32 B Rosia Road, Gibraltar; phone: (001350) 42542; fax: (001350); 70029 e-mail: gib2@gibnet.gi; **Tourist department** Gibraltar Tourist Board, Duke of Kent House, Cathedral Square, Gibraltar; phone: (001350) 74950; fax: (001350) 74943; e-mail: giblondon@-aol.com; UK office: Gibraltar Tourist Board, Arundel Great Court, 179 Strand, London WC2R 1EH; phone: (0171) 836 0777; fax: (0171) 240 6612.

Guernsey

Flag White with the red cross of Saint George extending to the edges of the flag; **Topography** The second largest of the Channel Islands. Lies at 50°N latitude and 2°W longitude. 130 km/81 mi south of England, 48 km/30 mi west of Normandy, France, and roughly triangular in shape. In the south, Guernsey rises in a plateau to about 90 m/295 ft, with ragged coastal cliffs. It descends in steps and is drained mainly by streams flowing northward in deeply incised valleys. Northern Guernsey is low-lying, although small outcrops of resistant rock form hills (hougues). The soil on lower ground is of blown sand, raised beach deposits, and the fills of old lagoons. The jurisdiction also covers the smaller islands of Alderney, Herm, and Sark; **Area** 194 sq km/75 sq mi (includes Alderney, Guernsey, Herm, Sark, and some other smaller islands); **Highest point** 90 m/295 ft; **Major towns and cities** St Peter Port (capital); St Sampson; **Total population** 60,000 (1993); **Climate** Temperate with mild winters and cool summers; about 50% of days are overcast; average temperature 11°C/51.8°F; average annual rainfall 75–90 cm/29.5–35.4 in; **Time** Greenwich Mean Time in summer; Greenwich Mean Time plus 1 hour in winter; **Currency** Guernsey pound; **Languages** English, French; Norman-French dialect spoken in country districts; **Religion** Christianity; **Head of state** Queen Elizabeth II; **Head of government** Lieutenant Governor John Cavard; Bailiff Graham Dorey; **Major industries** Tourism; banking; **Agriculture** Tomatoes; flowers (mostly grown in greenhouses); sweet peppers; aubergines; other vegetables and fruit; Guernsey cattle; **Chamber of Commerce** Chamber of Commerce, States Arcade, St Peter Port; phone: (001481) 727483; fax: (001481) 710755; **Tourist department** States Tourist Board, PO Box 23, Guernsey, CI; phone: (001481) 23552.

The Isle of Man

Flag Red with the Three Legs of Man emblem (Trinacria) in the centre; **Topography** An island in the Irish Sea, located 51 km/32 mi east of Ireland, 48 km/30 mi west of England, and 24 km/15 mi south of Scotland. It has a rocky, indented coastline and is about 53 km/33 mi long by 10–19 km/6–12 mi wide. The island is well watered, the principal rivers being the Santon, the Silver Burn, the Neb-Rhenass, the Sulby (near Ramsey), and the

Dhoo and Glass rivers which form the River Douglas. Mountains extend nearly the length of the island. Some of the valleys have rich pastures, and livestock is raised extensively; **Area** 588 sq km/227 sq mi; **Highest point** Snaefell, 620 m/2,034 ft; **Major towns and cities** Douglas (capital); Peel; Castletown; Ramsey; **Total population** 69,800 (1991); **Climate** Cool summers and mild winters, humid, overcast about half the time; average temperature 8.1°C/46.6°F; average annual rainfall 114.6 cm/45 in; **Time** Greenwich Mean Time summer; Greenwich Mean Time plus 1 hour winter; **Currency** Manx pound; **Languages** English; Manx Gaelic; **Religion** Christianity; **Head of state** Queen Elizabeth II, represented by Sir Timothy Daunt; **Head of government** President of the Legislative Council Sir Charles Kerrvish. (The parliament of the Isle, The Tynwald, is the oldest surviving parliamentary body in the world.) **Major industries** Financial services; light manufacturing; tourism; **Agriculture** Oats; barley; wheat; turnips; potatoes; cattle; sheep; pigs; poultry; **Chamber of Commerce** Chamber of Commerce, 17 Drinkwater Street, Douglas; phone: (001624) 674941; fax: (001624) 663367; **Tourist department** Department of Tourism and Leisure Headquarters, Sea Terminal, Douglas, Isle of Man IM1 2RG; phone (001624) 686801.

Jersey

Flag White with the diagonal red cross of Saint Patrick extending to the corners of the flag; **Topography** The largest and southernmost of the Channel Islands, 19 km/12 mi west of the Cotentin peninsula of France. Situated at 49 °N longitude, 2 °W longitude, Jersey is about 16 km/10 mi across and 8 km/5 mi from north to south and has an area of 115 sq km/44 sq mi. The island is largely a plateau mantled with loess, with deeply incised valleys sloping from north to south. Picturesque cliffs reaching 148 m/486 ft in height line the northern coast; elsewhere, rocky headlands enclose sandy bays bordered by infilled lagoons. Coasts are reef-strewn, but a breakwater in St Aubin's Bay protects St Helier harbour from southwest gales. Blown sand forms dunes at the northern and southern ends of St Ouen's Bay on the western coast.; **Area** 117 sq km/45 sq mi; **Highest point** (unnamed) 143 m/496 ft; **Major towns and cities** St Helier (capital); St Saviour; Gorey; St Aubin; **Total population** 84,000 (1993); **Climate** Temperate, mild winters and cool summers; average temperature 11°C/51.8°F; average annual rainfall 75–90 cm/29.5–35.4 in; **Time** Greenwich Mean Time in summer; Greenwich Mean Time plus 1 hour in winter; **Currency** Jersey pound; **Languages** English; French; Norman-French dialect; **Religion** Christianity; **Head of state** Queen Elizabeth II; **Head of government** Lieutenant Governor General Sir Michael Wilkes; Bailiff Sir Phillip Bailhache; **Major industries** Tourism; banking and finance; granite quarrying; fishing; electrical goods; textiles; clothing; **Agriculture** Potatoes; cauliflowers; tomatoes;

flowers; dairy and cattle farming; **Chamber of Commerce** Chamber of Commerce, 19 Royal Square, St Helier; phone: (001534) 24536; fax: (001534) 34942; **Tourist department** Jersey Tourism, Liberation Square, St Helier, Jersey JE1 1BB; phone: (001534) 500700; fax: (001534) 500899; e-mail: jtourism@itl.net; Web site: www.jersey.gov.uk/tourism/; UK office: Jersey Tourism; 38 Dover Street, London W1X 3RB; phone: (0171) 493 5278; fax: (0171) 491 1565; e-mail: jersey@jerlonwo.demon.co.uk.

Montserrat

Flag Blue with the flag of the UK in the upper left quadrant and the Montserratian coat of arms (depicting a woman standing beside a yellow harp with her arm around a black cross) centred in the outer half of the flag; **Topography** One of the Leeward islands in the eastern Caribbean, latitude 17°N longitude 62°W. Volcanic in origin, very mountainous. Comprises three main mountain ranges in the north, centre, and south. Soufriere Hills Volcano erupted on 18 July 1995 and eruptions have been continuing since, causing major devastation to the south and central island destroying the capital of Plymouth and many other small towns; **Area** 100 sq km/39 sq mi; **Highest point** Chances Peak 910 m/2,986 ft; **Major towns and cities** Plymouth Olde Towne (capital); **Total population** 12,000 (1991); **Climate** Tropical but windy, lies in hurricane zone, September–November rainy, March–June dry; average temperature 28°C/82°F; average annual rainfall 148 cm/58 in; **Time** Greenwich Mean Time less 4 hours; **Currency** Eastern Caribbean dollar; **Languages** English; **Religion** Christianity; **Head of state** Queen Elizabeth II, represented by Governor Frank J Savage; **Head of government** Chief Minister Bertrand Osborne.

Pitcairn Islands

Flag Blue with the flag of the UK in the upper left quadrant and the Pitcairn Islander coat of arms (yellow, green, and light blue with a shield featuring a yellow anchor) centred on the outer half of the flag; **Topography** Rugged volcanic formation; rocky coastline with cliffs; Pitcairn is the main island with smaller Henderson, Ducie, Sandy, and Oeno islands; **Area** 47 sq km/18 sq mi; **Major towns and cities** Adamstown (capital); **Total population** 56 (1994); **Climate** Tropical, hot, humid, modified by southeast trade winds, subject to typhoons, especially in the rainy season (November–March); average temperature 21 °C/70°F; average annual rainfall 203 cm/80 in; **Time** Greenwich Mean Time less 9 hours; **Currency** New Zealand dollar; **Languages** English; Tahitian-English dialect; **Religion** Christianity; **Head of state** Queen Elizabeth II, represented by Governor and UK High Commissioner to New Zealand (non-resident) David Joseph Moss; **Head of government** Island Magistrate and Chairman of the Island Council Jay Warren; **Major industries** Postage stamp sales; handicrafts; **Agriculture** Subsistence fishing and farming; wide variety of fruits and vegetables.

St Helena

Flag Blue with the flag of the UK in the upper left quadrant and the St Helenian shield (depicting rocky coastline and three-masted sailing ship) centred on the outer half of the flag; **Topography** Incorporates the islands of St Helena, latitude 16°S longitude 6°W, Ascension, 8°S 14°W, and Tristan da Cunha, 37°S 12°W. St Helena is 1,131 km/703 mi southeast of Ascension, and 1,932 km/1,200 mi from the southwest coast of Africa; Tristan da Cunha is 2,415 km/1,501 mi southwest of St Helena. The islands are volcanic, mountainous, and barren. Tristan da Cunha rises to a volcanic peak, which last erupted in 1961; **Area** St Helena: 122 sq km/47 sq mi; Ascension Island: 88 sq km/34 sq mi; Tristan da Cunha: 110 sq km/42 sq mi; **Highest point** St Helena: Diana's Peak, 810 km/2.657 ft; Tristan da Cunha: 2,060 m/6,758 ft; **Major towns and cities** Jamestown, St Helena (capital); Georgetown, Ascension Island (capital); **Total population** 5,640 (1997); **Climate** Mild and varies little; average temperature 21°C/70°F; average annual rainfall 32–92 cm/13–36 in; **Time** Greenwich Mean Time; **Currency** St Helena pound; **Languages** English; **Religion** Christianity; **Head of state** Queen Elizabeth II; **Head of government** Governor and Commander in Chief David Smallman; **Major industries** Tristan da Cunha: fishing and fish-freezing; sale of postage stamps; handicrafts; **Agriculture** St Helena: maize; potatoes; sweet potatoes, vegetables. Ascension: fresh meat; vegetables; fruit. Tristan da Cunha: potatoes; apples; peaches.

Turks and Caicos Islands

Flag Blue with the flag of the UK in the upper left quadrant and the colonial shield (yellow and depicting a conch shell, lobster, and cactus) centred on the outer half of the flag; **Topography** Two island groups, latitude 20–22°N, longitude 70–73°W, southeast of the Bahamas in the North Atlantic Ocean. The Turks group consists of two inhabited islands, Grand Turk and Salt Cay, and uninhabited islets, rocks, and reef. The Caicos group comprises the main islands of South Caicos, East Caicos, Middle (or Grand) Caicos, North Caicos, Providenciales, and West Caicos, and other islets. The terrain is flat, arid, and stony; **Area** 430 sq km/166 sq mi; **Major towns and cities** Cockburn Town, Grand Turk (capital); Cockburn Harbour, South Caicos; **Total population** 12,400 (1990); **Climate** Tropical, marine, moderated by trade winds, sunny and relatively dry; average temperature 30°C/84°F; average annual rainfall 53.5 cm/21 in; **Time** Greenwich Mean Time less 5 hours; **Currency** US dollar in use; **Languages** English; **Religion** Christianity; **Head of state** Queen Elizabeth II, represented by Governor John P Kells; **Head of government** Chief Minister Derek Taylor; **Major industries** Tourism; offshore financial services; fishing; crawfish and conch processing; **Agriculture** Subsistence farming, based on corn and beans; **Chamber of Commerce** Turks and Caicos Chamber of Commerce, PO Box 148, Grand Turk, Turks and Caicos Islands, British West Indies; phone: (001649) 946 2324; fax: (001649) 946 2714; **Tourist department** Tourist Information, Pond Street, Cockburn Town, Grand Turk; phone: (001649) 946 2321.

Cities and Major Towns

Barnsley

Town in South Yorkshire, England; **Population** 220,900 (1991); **Local Authority maintained schools** 2 nursery schools; 48 nursery units attached to infant and primary schools; 90 primary schools; 14 secondary schools; 3 special schools; **Mainline railway stations** Barnsley Station; **Industries** Iron; steel; glass; paper; carpets; cakes (Lyons); sports equipment (Dunlop-Slazenger); clothing; **Places of interest** Civic theatre; Cooper Gallery; Monk Bretton Priory (12th century); Cannon Hall museum (17th century); **Newspapers** *Barnsley Chronicle* **Tourist Information Centre** Barnsley Tourist Information Centre, 56 Eldon Street, Barnsley, South Yorkshire S70 2JL; phone: (01226) 206757; **Chamber of Commerce** Chamber of Commerce and Industry, Commerce House, Westgate, Barnsley S70 2DX.

Belfast

City and industrial port in County Antrim and County Down, Northern Ireland, and the capital of Northern Ireland. Protestants form the majority in east Belfast, Catholics in the west; **Population** 290,000 (1994 estimate); **Universities** Queen's University; **Airports** Belfast City Airport; Belfast International Airport; **Mainline railway stations** Central Station; Great Victoria Street Station; **Main bus sta-**

tions Laganside Bus Centre; Europa Bus Centre; **Ferries** to Scotland (Cairnryan or Stranraer), Liverpool, and the Isle of Man; **Industries** Shipbuilding; engineering; electronics; aircraft; textiles; tobacco; linen; rope; aircraft components; fertilizers; **Places of interest** City Hall (19th century); Stormont (site of Northern Ireland parliament, 1932, until suspended, 1972); Waterfront Hall (1997); Ulster Museum Linen Hall Library; Crown Liquor Saloon; Belfast Zoo; Belfast Castle; St Anne's Cathedral; Grand Opera House; **Cultural organizations** Lyric Theatre; **Newspapers** *Belfast Telegraph*; *Sunday Life*; *Irish News*; *News Letter*; **Tourist Information Centre** Northern Ireland Tourist Board, St Anne's Court, 59 North Street, Belfast BT1 1NB; phone: (01849) 246609; **Chamber of Commerce** Northern Ireland Chamber of Commerce and Industry, Chamber of Commerce House, 22 Great Victoria Street, Belfast BT2 7BJ.

Birmingham

Industrial city in the West Midlands and the second largest city of the UK; **Population** 1,220,000; metropolitan area 2,632,000 (1994 estimate); **Local Authority maintained schools** 164 nursery schools; 327 primary schools; 61 secondary schools; 31 special schools; **Universities** Birmingham University; Aston University; University of Central England; **Airports** Birmingham International Airport; **Mainline railway stations** Birmingham New Street; Birmingham International; **Industries** Engineering; motor vehicles; machine tools; aerospace control systems; plastics; chemicals; food; chocolates; jewellery; tyres; glass; cars; guns; **Places of interest** The National Exhibition Centre and National Indoor Arena; Barber Institute of Fine Arts; Birmingham Conservatoire (now part of the University of Central England); the City Art Gallery; Symphony Hall; International Convention Centre; **Cultural organizations** City of Birmingham Symphony Orchestra; Birmingham Royal Ballet; **Newspapers** *Birmingham Evening Mail*; *Birmingham Post*; *Sunday Mercury*; *Birmingham Metronews*; **Tourist Information Centre** Birmingham Tourist Information Centre, Birmingham Convention/Visitor Bureau, 2 City Arcade, Birmingham B2 4TX; phone: (0121) 643 2514; fax: (0121) 616 1038; **Chamber of Commerce** Birmingham Chamber of Commerce and Industry, Chamber of Commerce House, 75 Harborne Road, Birmingham B15 3DH; phone: (0121) 454 6171; fax: (0121) 455 8670.

Bradford

Industrial city in South Yorkshire; **Population** 357,000 (1994 estimate); **Local Authority maintained schools** 6 nursery schools; 113 primary schools; 60 secondary schools; **Universities** Bradford University; **Airports** Leeds and Bradford International Airport; **Mainline railway stations** Bradford Travel Interchange (bus and train); Forster Square Train Station; **Main bus station** Bradford Travel Interchange (bus and train); **Industries** Engineering; chemicals; machine tools; elec-

tronics; printing; financial services; wool textiles; **Places of interest** cathedral (15th century); Cartwright Hall art gallery; National Museum of Photography, Film, and Television (1983, with Britain's largest cinema screen, 14 m × 20 m/46 ft × 66 ft); 1853 Gallery (David Hockney); **Cultural organizations** Priestley Arts Centre; **Newspapers** *Bradford Telegraph*; *Argus*; **Tourist Information Centre** Bradford Tourist Information Centre, Central Library, Prince's Way, Bradford BD1 1NN; phone: (01274) 753678; **Chamber of Commerce** Bradford Chamber of Commerce Phoenix House, Rushton Avenue, Bradford, BD3 7BH; phone: (01274) 722777; fax: (01274) 771081.

Bristol

Industrial port in southwest England; unitary authority created in 1996 from part of the former county of Avon; **Area** 109 sq km/42 sq mi; **Population** 374,300 (1996); **Unemployment rate** 9.8% (May 1996); **Average gross weekly full-time earnings** £339.10; **Percentage of live births outside marriage** 40% (1995); **Deaths per 1,000 population** 10.6 (1995); **Local Authority maintained schools** 16 nursery schools; 132 primary schools; 22 secondary schools; 12 special schools; **Universities** Bristol University; University of the West of England; **Airports** Bristol Airport; **Mainline railway stations** Bristol Temple Meads, Bristol Parkway; **Main bus station** Marlborough Street Bus Station; **Industries** Aircraft engines; engineering; micro-electronics; tobacco; chemicals; paper; printing; soap; metal refining; chocolate; banking; insurance; **Places of interest** National Lifeboat Museum; cathedral (12th century); church of St Mary Redcliffe (14th century); Acton Court (16th century); Clifton Suspension Bridge; *SS Great Britain*; Bristol Zoo; **Cultural organizations** Bristol Old Vic Theatre School; Bristol Community Dance Centre; Arnolfini; **Newspapers**; *Bristol Evening Post*; *Western Daily Press*; **Tourist Information Centre** Bristol Tourist Information Centre, St Nicholas Church, Bristol BS1 1UE; phone: (0117) 926 0767; e-mail: Bristol@Tourism. Bristol.Gov.uk; **Chamber of Commerce** Bristol Chamber of Commerce and Industry, 16 Clifton Park, Bristol BS8 3BY; phone: (0117) 973 7373; fax: (0117) 974 5365.

Cardiff See Cardiff (Wales: Unitary Authorities).

Coventry

Industrial city in the West Midlands, England; **Population** 303,000 (1994); **Local Authority maintained schools** 1 nursery school; 96 primary schools; 19 secondary schools; **Universities** University of Warwick; Coventry University; **Mainline railway stations** Coventry Train Station; **Main bus station** Pool Meadow Bus and Coach Station; **Industries** Cars; electronic equipment; machine tools; agricultural machinery; man-made fibres; aerospace components; telecommunications equipment; engineering; coal mining;

Places of interest Coventry Cathedral; St Mary's Hall; two gates of the old city walls (1356); Belgrade Theatre (1958); Coventry Art Gallery and Museum; Museum of British Road Transport; **Newspapers** *Coventry Evening Telegraph*; **Tourist Information Centre** Bayley Lane, Coventry, West Midlands CV1 5RN; phone: (01203) 832303; fax: (01203) 832370.

Edinburgh See Edinburgh City (Scotland: Unitary Authorities and Islands).

Glasgow See Glasgow City (Scotland: Unitary Authorities and Islands).

Kingston-upon-Hull

City, port, and unitary authority on the north bank of the Humber estuary, eastern England, where the river Hull flows into it; **Area** 71 sq km/27 sq mi; **Population** 265,000 (1996); **Unemployment rate** 9.9% (May 1996); **Average gross weekly full-time earnings** £314.10; **Percentage of live births outside marriage** 53% (1995); **Deaths per 1,000 population** 10.9 (1995); **Local Authority maintained schools** 3 nursery schools; 81 primary schools; 16 secondary schools; special schools; **Universities** Hull University; University of Humberside; **Mainline railway stations** Hull Station; **Main bus station** Hull Coach Station; **Ferries** North Sea Ferries to Rotterdam and Zeebrugge; **Industries** fish processing; vegetable oils; flour milling; electrical goods; textiles; paint, pharmaceuticals; chemicals; caravans; aircraft; sawmilling; paper; marine engineering; food processing; **Places of interest** Holy Trinity Church (13th century); Guildhall; Ferens Art Gallery; Humber Bridge (world's longest single-span suspension bridge); **Cultural organizations** Hull Truck Theatre Company; **Newspapers** *Hull Daily Mail*; **Tourist Information Centre** 1 Paragon Street, Hull HU1 3NA; phone: (01482) 223559; fax: (01482) 613959; **Chamber of Commerce** Incorporated Chamber of Commerce and Shipping, Samman House, Bowlalley Lane, Hull HU1 1XT.

Leeds

Industrial city in West Yorkshire, England, on the river Aire.; **Population** 529,000 (1994); **Local Authority maintained schools** 1 nursery school; 244 primary schools; 43 secondary schools; 13 special schools; **Universities** Leeds University; Leeds Metropolitan University; **Airports** Leeds and Bradford International Airport; **Mainline railway stations** Leeds City Station; **Main bus station** Kirkgate Market bus and coach station; **Industries** Engineering; printing; chemicals; glass; woollens; clothing; plastics; paper; metal goods; leather goods; **Places of interest** Town Hall (designed by Cuthbert Brodrick); Art Gallery (1844); Temple Newsam museum (early 16th century, altered about 1630); Cistercian Abbey of Kirkstall (1147); **Cultural organizations** Opera North; West Yorkshire Playhouse; Yorkshire Dance Centre; Northern School of Contemporary Dance; **Newspapers** *Yorkshire Post*; **Tourist Information Centre** Gateway

Yorkshire, Regional Travel and Tourism Centre, The Arcade, Leeds City Station, Leeds LS1 1PL; phone: (0113) 242 5242; **Chamber of Commerce** Chamber of Commerce and Industry, Commerce House, 2 St Albans Place, Wade Lane, Leeds LS2 8HZ.

Leicester

Industrial city and unitary authority in central England, on the river Soar; **Population** 270,500 (1996); **Local Authority maintained schools** 85 primary schools; 21 secondary schools; **Universities** Leicester University; De Montfort University; **Airports** East Midlands Airport; **Mainline railway stations** Leicester Station; **Main bus station** St Margaret's Bus Station; **Industries** Food processing; hosiery; footwear; knitwear; engineering; electronics; printing; plastics; **Places of interest** Guildhall (13th century); Newarke House Museum; Jain Temple; **Cultural organizations** Leicester Haymarket Theatre; **Newspapers** *Leicester Mercury*; **Tourist Information Centre** 7–9 Every Street, Leicester LE1 6AG; phone: (0116) 265 0555; fax: (0116) 255 5726; **Chamber of Commerce** Leicestershire Chamber of Commerce and Industry (inc), 4th Floor, York House, 91 Granby Street, Leicester LE1 6EA.

Liverpool

Unitary authority and the UK's chief Atlantic port. The Mersey Tunnel (1886), rail tunnel, and Queensway Tunnel (1934) link Liverpool with Birkenhead. The Kingsway Tunnel (1971) links Liverpool with Wallasey; **Population** 664,000 (1994); **Universities** Liverpool Hope University; Liverpool John Moores University; University of Liverpool; **Airports** Liverpool Airport; **Mainline railway stations** Liverpool Lime Street; **Main bus station** Islington Street bus station; **Underground** Merseyrail network; **Ferries** Isle of Man Steam Packet Company Ltd; Norse Irish Ferries; **Industries** Flour-milling; sugar refining; electrical engineering; food processing; chemicals; soap; margarine; tanning; motor vehicles; **Places of interest** Bluecoat Chambers (1717); Town Hall (1754); St George's Hall (1838–54); Anglican Cathedral (begun 1904, completed 1980); Roman Catholic Metropolitan Cathedral of Christ; King Tate Gallery (1987); Walker Art Gallery (1877); Speke Hall (16th century); St George's Hall; Liverpool Institute for the Performing Arts (1995); **Cultural organizations** Royal Liverpool Philharmonic Orchestra; Liverpool Playhouse; **Newspapers** *Liverpool Daily Post*; *Liverpool Echo*; **Tourist Information Centre** Merseyside Tourism and Conference Bureau, Atlantic Pavilion, Liverpool L3 4AE; phone: (0151) 709 2444; fax: (0151) 709 8129; e-mail: tourism@mail. cybase. co.uk; **Chamber of Commerce** Liverpool Chamber of Commerce, Number One, Old Hall Street, Liverpool L3 9HG; phone (0151) 227 1234: fax: (0151) 236 0121.

London

Capital of England and the United Kingdom, on the river Thames; Greater London, from

Canary Wharf, Docklands, London Corel

1965, comprises the City of London and 32 boroughs. London is the only major European capital without a strategic authority covering the whole area. In a referendum held on 7 May 1998, Londoners voted in favour of the instigation of office of elected mayor. **Area** 1,580 sq km/610 sq mi (Greater London); **Population** 7,007,000 (1995); **Unemployment rate** 11.6% (May 1996); **Average gross weekly full-time earnings** £454.30; **Percentage of live births outside marriage** 33% (1995); **Deaths per 1,000 population** 9.5 (1995); **Universities** University of London (Birkbeck College; Goldsmiths College; University College; King's

London Royal Parks

Managed by the Royal Parks Agency, London's royal parks are official public open spaces belonging to the crown.

Name	Park office	Notes
Brompton Cemetery	The Chapel Office, Brompton Cemetery, Fulham Road, London SW10 9UG; phone: (0171) 352 1201	laid out in 1840 by Benjamin Baud; has a central avenue leading to an octagonal chapel with flanking colonnades; catacombs run under the colonnades and along the west wall; around 205,000 burials have been recorded with an estimated 35,000 headstones; burial record search (small fee includes map and location of grave)
Bushy Park and Longford River	Stockyard Education Centre, Bushy Park, Hampton Court Road, Hampton Hill, Middlesex TW12 2EJ; phone: (0181) 979 1586	enclosed by Cardinal Wolsey and Henry VIII between 1500 and 1537; Longford River is an artificial waterway created by Charles I in 1639 and running from the River Colne, beyond Heathrow Airport, to the River Thames at Hampton
Greenwich Park	Park Manager, Blackheath Gate, Greenwich Park, London SE10 8QY; phone: (0181) 858 2608	created in 1433, the first Royal Park to be enclosed; the Old Royal observatory; observatory planetarium (by appointment)
Hyde Park	Park Manager, Rangers Lodge, Hyde Park, London W2 2UH; phone: (0171) 298 2100	came into existence in 1536; has a tradition of events and public spectacles; gun salutes are fired from the Parade Ground of Knightsbridge barracks on its boundary
Kensington Gardens	Park Manager, Magazine Storeyard, Magazine Gate, Kensington Gardens, London W2 2UH	formed from land taken from Hyde Park in 1689; Serpentine Gallery
Regent's Park and Primrose Hill	Park Manager, The Store Yard, Inner Circle, Regent's Park, London NW1 4NR; phone: (0171) 486 7905	evolved from the 1811 plans of John Nash, Crown Architect; also contains the London Zoo; open air theatre
Richmond Park	Superintendent's Office, Holly Lodge, Bog Lodge Yard, Richmond Park, Surrey TW10 5HS; phone: (0181) 948 3209	enclosed as a hunting park by Charles I in 1637; herds of fallow and red deer roam the park; in 1992 the park was notified as a Site of Special Scientific Interest by English Nature; Pen Ponds
St James's Park and Green Park	Park Manager, The Storeyard, St James's Park, Horse Guards Parade, London SW1A 2BJ; phone (0171) 930 1793	these two parks lying to the east of Buckingham Palace were acquired by Henry VIII in 1536; provide the backdrop for British ceremonial life with The Mall, the processional route between the Palace and Whitehall and Horse Guards Parade, the venue for major ceremonial occasions

College; Imperial College; Queen Mary & Westfield College; Royal Holloway & Bedford College); City University; Greenwich University; Kingston University; London Guildhall University; London School of Economics and Political Science; Middlesex University; University of East London; University of North London; South Bank University; Thames Valley University; Westminster University; **Airports** Gatwick; Heathrow; Stansted; **Rail** London has an extensive rail network which is linked to the London Underground (tube) at all mainline and several branch railway lines; the Eurostar service to the continent runs from Waterloo Station; **Major railway stations** Euston; Charing Cross; King's Cross; St Pancras; Paddington; Waterloo; Victoria; **Main bus station** Victoria Coach Station; **Industries and products** Finance (major international centre); newspapers; broadcasting; film; recording; tourism; government; the world's largest office development project is at Canary Wharf; **Places of interest** The Tower of London (houses the crown jewels and the royal armouries); Westminster Abbey; The Palace of Westminster (containing the houses of Parliament); Lambeth Palace; Southwark Cathedral; St James's Palace; Buckingham Palace; Horse Guards Parade; St Paul's Cathedral; Mansion House (residence of the lord mayor); Guildhall (15th century); Trafalgar Square; Nelson's Column; Criminal Court (Old Bailey) and the Inner and Middle Temples; The Royal Parks; **Shopping** Oxford Street; Bond Street; Knightsbridge; Covent Garden; markets at Portobello Road, Greenwich, and Camden Lock; **Cultural organizations** The National Gallery; The National Portrait Gallery; The British Museum; The Science Museum; The Natural History Museum; The Tate Gallery; The Victoria and Albert Museum; Wallace Collection; Courtauld Institute; The South Bank Complex (Royal Festival Hall; Hayward Gallery; National Theatre; Barbican arts and conference centre); Royal Opera House with the Royal Ballet and Opera Companies; The Royal Albert Hall; many other theatres in the West End; Royal Philharmonic and London Symphony Orchestras; **Tourist Information Centre** London Tourist Board, 26 Grosvenor Gardens, London SW1W 0DU; phone: (UK) (0171) 730 3450; fax: (UK) (0171) 730 9367; **Chamber of Commerce** London Chamber of Commerce & Industry (LCCI) 33 Queen Street, London EC4R 1AP; phone: (0171) 248 4444.

Manchester

City in northwest England, on the river Irwell. It is linked by the Manchester Ship Canal (opened 1894) to the river Mersey and the sea; **Population** 404,900 (1991); **Universities** Manchester University; Salford University; University of Manchester Institute of Science and Technology (UMIST); Manchester Metropolitan University; Manchester Business School; **Airports** Manchester Airport; **Mainline railway stations** Victoria; Piccadilly; **Main bus station** Chorlton Street Coach Station; **Trams** Metrolink tram

system; **Industries** Textile machinery; chemicals; rubber; engineering; electrical equipment; paper; printing; processed foods; financial centre; **Places of interest** Royal Exchange (built 1869, now a theatre); Free Trade Hall (1843), Liverpool Road station (the world's oldest surviving passenger station); Whitworth Art Gallery; Cotton Exchange (now a leisure centre); Castlefield Urban Heritage Park (includes the Granada television studios and the set of the soap opera *Coronation Street*); Museum of Science and Industry; Manchester Cathedral (15th century); Bridgewater Hall; **Cultural organizations** Hallé Orchestra; BBC Philharmonic; Royal Northern College of Music; Chetham's School of Music; Corner House Theatre; **Newspapers** *Manchester Evening News*; *Stretford and Urmstrong Messenger*; **Tourist Information Centre** Manchester Tourist Information Centre, Town Hall Extension, St Peter's Square, Manchester M60 2LA; phone: (0161) 234 3157/234 3158; **Chamber of Commerce** Chamber of Commerce and Industry, 56 Oxford Street, Manchester M60 7HJ.

Newcastle-upon-Tyne

City in northeast England on the River Tyne opposite Gateshead; **Population** 274,000 (1994); **Local Authority maintained schools** 8 nursery schools; 79 primary schools; 21 secondary schools; **Universities** Newcastle University; University of Northumbria; **Airports** Newcastle Airport; **Mainline railway stations** Central Station; **Main bus station** Gallowgate Bus station; **Underground** Metro; **Industries** Engineering (including offshore technology); food processing; brewing; electronics; **Places of interest** castle (12th century); cathedral (14th century); church (12th century); Guildhall (1658); Laing Art Gallery; Hancock Museum; **Cultural organizations** Northern Sinfonia; Theatre Royal; Tyne Theatre and Opera House; Newcastle Playhouse; **Newspapers** *Newcastle Journal*; *Newcastle Evening Chronicle*; **Tourist Information Centre** Central Library, Princess Square, Newcastle-upon-Tyne NE99 1DX; phone: (0191) 261 0610; fax: (0191) 261 0115; **Chamber of Commerce** Tyne and Wear Chamber of Commerce, 65 Quayside, Newcastle-upon-Tyne NE1 3DS.

Nottingham

City and unitary authority on the River Trent in the East Midlands; **Population** 285,000 (1994); **Local Authority maintained schools** 260 primary schools; 46 secondary schools; **Universities** Nottingham University; Nottingham Trent University; **Airports** East Midlands Airport; **Mainline railway stations** Nottingham Station; **Main bus station** Digbeth Coach Station; **Industries** Engineering; coal mining; bicycles; textiles; knitwear; pharmaceuticals; tobacco; lace; electronics; **Places of interest** Church of St Mary (15th century); Nottingham Castle; Trip to Jerusalem (oldest pub in England); **Cultural organizations**

Playhouse; Theatre Royal; **Newspapers** *Nottingham Evening Post*; **Tourist Information Centre** 1–4 Smithy Row, Nottingham NG1 2BY; phone: (0115) 947 0661; fax: (0115) 935 0883; **Chamber of Commerce** Nottinghamshire Chamber of Commerce and Industry, 395 Mansfield Road, Nottingham NG5 2DL.

Plymouth

City, seaport, and unitary authority (April 1998) at the mouth of the river Plym; **Population** 257,000 (1994); **Local Authority maintained schools** 2 nursery schools; 90 primary schools; 18 secondary schools; **Universities** Plymouth University; **Airports** Plymouth Airport; **Mainline railway stations** Plymouth Train Station; **Main bus station** Exeter Street Bus Station; **Ferries** to Santander and Roscoff; **Industries** Clothing; radio equipment; processed foods; refitting of nuclear submarines; **Places of interest** Plymouth Hoe; Smeaton's Tower; harbourside Elizabethan House; St Andrew's bombed-out Gothic church; Museum and Art Gallery; **Cultural organizations** Theatre Royal; Drum Theatre; **Newspapers** *The Evening Herald*; *Western Morning News*; **Tourist Information Centre** Island House, 9 The Barbican, Plymouth, Devon PL1 2LS; phone: (01752) 264849; fax: (01752) 257955; **Chamber of Commerce** Chamber of Commerce and Industry, 29 Looe Street, Plymouth PL4 0EA.

Sheffield

Industrial city on the river Don, South Yorkshire, England; **Population** 429,000 (1994); **Local Authority maintained schools** 5 nursery schools; 142 primary schools; 31 secondary schools; 16 special schools; **Universities** Sheffield University; Sheffield Hallam University; **Airports** Sheffield City Airport; **Mainline railway stations** Sheffield Station; **Trams** Supertram (Britain's most modern light rail system); **Industries** Steel; electroplating; type-founding; optical glass; **Places of interest** Cathedral parish church of St Peter and St Paul (14th–15th century); Sheffield Arena; Meadowhall shopping complex; Ponds Forge Olympic standard swimming pool; Abbeydale Industrial Hamlet; Don Valley Stadium; **Cultural organizations** Sheffield Crucible Theatre; Lyceum Theatre; **Newspapers** *The Star*; **Tourist Information Centre** Peace Gardens, Sheffield S1 2HH; phone: (0114) 273 4671; fax: (0114) 273 4672; **Chamber of Commerce** Chamber of Commerce, Commerce House, Earl Street, Sheffield S1 3FX.

Stoke-on-Trent

City and unitary authority in central England, on the river Trent; **Population** 254,200 (1996); **Local Authority maintained schools** 14 nursery schools; 88 primary schools; 17 secondary schools; 5 special schools; **Universities** Stafford University; Keele University; **Mainline rail-**

way stations Stoke-on-Trent Railway Station; **Main bus station** Hanley Bus and Coach Station; **Industries** Ceramics; clay ware; steel; chemicals; engineering machinery; paper; rubber; **Places of interest** Gladstone Pottery Museum; Wedgwood, Spode, and Royal Doulton ceramics factories; Stoke-on-Trent Museum and Art Gallery; **Cultural organizations** Victoria Theatre; **Newspapers** *The Sentinel*; **Tourist Information Centre** 1 Glebe Street, Stoke-on-Trent ST4 1HP; phone: (01782) 411000; **Chamber of Commerce** North Staffordshire Chamber of Commerce and Industry, Commerce House, Festival Park, Stoke-on-Trent ST1 5BE.

Wakefield

Cathedral city and administrative headquarters of West Yorkshire, England, on the river Calder, south of Leeds; **Population** 306,300 (1991); **Local Authority maintained schools** 3 nursery schools; 52 primary schools; 7 secondary schools; 5 special schools; **Industries** Chemicals; machine tools; wool textiles; **Places of interest** The National Coal Mining Museum for England; **Tourist Information Centre** Town Hall, Wood Street, Wakefield WF1 2HQ; phone: (01924) 295000; fax: (01924) 295283; **Chamber of Commerce** Kirklees and Wakefield Chamber of Commerce and Industry Ltd, Commerce House, Wakefield Road, Aspley, Huddersfield HD5 9AA.

Wolverhampton

Industrial town in the West Midlands, England; **Population** 245,000 (1994); **Local Authority maintained schools** 18 primary schools; 16 secondary schools; **Universities** University of Wolverhampton; **Mainline railway stations** Wolverhampton; **Main bus station** Pipers Row bus station; **Industries** Metalworking; chemicals; tyres; aircraft; bicycles; locks and keys; engineering; commercial vehicles; **Places of interest** Wolverhampton Art Gallery and Museum; **Cultural organizations** D'Oyly Carte Opera Company; Grand Theatre; **Newspapers** *Wolverhampton Express and Star*; **Tourist Information Centre** 18 Queen Square, Wolverhampton, West Midlands WV1 1TQ; phone: (01902) 312051; fax: (01902) 716091; **Chamber of Commerce** Wolverhampton Chamber of Commerce and Industry, 93 Tettenhall Road, Wolverhampton WV3 9PE.

Towns and Cities over 20,000 Population in England

City/town	Population	City/town	Population	City/town	Population
Bath and northeast Somerset		***Cumbria***		***Gloucestershire***	
Bath	78,700 (1991)	Barrow in Furness	73,100 (1991)	Cheltenham	91,300 (1991)
		Carlisle	99,800 (1991)	Gloucester	102,000 (1994 est)
Bedfordshire		Kendal	25,500 (1991)	Stroud	38,230 (1981)
Bedford	73,900 (1991)	Whitehaven	26,500 (1991)	Tewkesbury	67,700 (1991)
Dunstable	49,700 (1991)	Workington	26,000 (1991)		
				Greater Manchester	
Bracknell Forest		***Darlington***		Ashton under Lyne	177,000 (1994 est)
Bracknell	93,800 (1991 est)	Darlington	100,600 (1996)	Bolton	210,000 (1994 est)
				Bury	62,600 (1991)
Bournemouth		***Derby***		Chadderton	31,200 (1991)
Bournemouth	160,900 (1995 est)	Derby	218,800 (1996)	Eccles	36,000 (1991)
				Manchester	404,900 (1991)
Brighton and Hove		***Derbyshire***		Marple	23,000 (1991)
Brighton	155,000 (1994 est)	Chesterfield	71,900 (1991)	Oldham	176,000 (1994 est)
Hove	67,600 (1991)	Ilkeston	35,100 (1991)	Radcliffe	32,500 (1991)
				Rochdale	138,000 (1994 est)
Bristol		***Devon***		Salford	198,000 (1994 est)
Bristol	374,300 (1996)	Barnstaple	24, 878 (1981)	Stockport	120,000 (1994 est)
		Exeter	107,000 (1994 est)	Stretford	44,000 (1991)
Buckinghamshire		Exmouth	28,400 (1991)	Swinton	24,500 (1991)
Amersham	21,490 (1981)				
Aylesbury	50,000 (1991)	***Dorset***		***Hampshire***	
High Wycombe	71,700 (1991)	Christchurch	36,400 (1991)	Aldershot	51,400 (1991)
		Weymouth	46,100 (1991)	Andover	30,900 (1981)
Cambridgeshire		Yeovil	27,200 (1991)	Basingstoke	77,800 (1991)
Cambridge	117,000 (1994 est)			Fareham	102,000 (1994 est)
		East Riding Yorkshire		Farnborough	52,500 (1991)
Cheshire		Bridlington	31,000 (1991)	Gosport	75,000 (1991)
Chester	115,000 (1991)			Winchester	36,100 (1991)
Crewe	63,400 (1991)	***East Sussex***			
Ellesmere Port	64,500 (1991)	Bexhill on Sea	38,900 (1991)	***Hereford***	
Macclesfield	69,000 (1990 est)	Eastbourne	81,400 (1991)	Hereford	50,200 (1991)
Nantwich	36,100 (1991)	Hastings	80,800 (1991)		
Runcorn	64,200 (1991)			***Hertfordshire***	
Widnes	56,000 (1991)	***Essex***		Bishop's Stortford	26,700 (1991)
Wilmslow	48,100 (1991)	Basildon	101,000 (1994 est)	Hatfield	31,100 (1991)
		Chelmsford	97,500 (1991)	Hemel Hempstead	79,200 (1991)
County Durham		Clacton on Sea	45,100 (1991)	Hertford	25,000 (1989 est)
Durham	80,700 (1991)	Colchester	87,500 (1991 est)	Hitchin	32,200 (1991)
Newton Aycliffe	25,100 (1991)	Rochford	72,900 (1991)	Letchworth	31,400 (1991)
Peterlee	31,100 (1991)	Witham	26,100 (1991)	St Albans	80,400 (1991)
Sedgefield	88,400 (1991)			Stevenage	76,100 (1991)

(continued)

Towns and Cities over 20,000 Population in England (*continued*)

City/town	Population
Watford	74,600 (1991)
Welwyn Garden City	42,100 (1991)
Kent	
Ashford	52,000 (1991)
Broadstairs	24,000 (1991)
Dartford	28,400(1991)
Deal	27,000 (1989 est)
Dover	34,200 (1991)
Folkestone	45,600 (1991)
Gravesend	51,400 (1991)
Herne Bay	27,800 (1985 est)
Maidstone	90,900 (1991)
Margate	56,700 (1991)
Ramsgate	37,900 (1991)
Royal Tunbridge Wells	60,300 (1991)
Sevenoaks	24,500 (1991)
Sittingbourne	56,300 (1991)
Tonbridge	99,100 (1991)
Whitstable	28,900 (1991)
Kingston-upon-Hull	
Kingston-upon-Hull	265,000 (1996)
Lancashire	
Accrington	36,500 (1991)
Blackburn	106,000 (1991)
Blackpool	156,000 (1994 est)
Burnley	85,400 (1989 est)
Chorley	33,500 (1991)
Fleetwood	24,500 (1981)
Lancaster	125,600 (1991)
Leyland	37,300 (1991)
Lytham St Annes	40,900 (1991)
Morecambe	46,700 (1991)
Preston	126,100 (1991)
Skelmersdale	42,100 (1991)
Wigan	100,000 (1994 est)
Leicester	
Leicester	270,500 (1996 est)
Leicestershire	
Hinckley	40,600 (1991)
Loughborough	46,900 (1991)
Melton Mowbray	24,350 (1991)
Lincolnshire	
Boston	34,600 (1991)
Grantham	33,200 (1991)
Lincoln	82,000 (1991)
Liverpool	664,000 (1994 est)
London	
London	6,967,000 (1994 est)
Luton	
Luton	181,400 (1997)
Medway	
Chatham	71,700 (1991)
Gillingham	92,100 (1991)
Rochester-upon-Medway	24,000 (1991)
Merseyside	
Bebington	60,100 (1991)
Birkenhead	218,000 (1994 est)

City/town	Population
Bootle	65,500 (1991)
Southport	98,000 (1981)
St Helens	175,300 (1991)
Middlesbrough	
Middlesbrough	146,000 (1996)
Milton Keynes	
Milton Keynes	198,600 (1996)
Norfolk	
Great Yarmouth	56,200 (1991)
King's Lynn	41,300 (1991)
Norwich	130,000 (1994 est)
Northeast Lincolnshire	
Cleethorpes	35,500 (1987 est)
Grimsby	90,500 (1991)
Scunthorpe	76,000 (1991)
North Somerset	
Weston-super-Mare	69,400 (1991)
North Yorkshire	
Harrogate	66,200 (1991)
Scarborough	38,800 (1991)
Northamptonshire	
Corby	49,100 (1991)
Northampton	175,000 (1994 est)
Wellingborough	65,600 (1991)
Northumberland	
Blyth	77,236 (1991)
Nottingham	
Nottingham	285,000 (1994 est)
Nottinghamshire	
Beeston Stapleford	35,900 (1991)
Mansfield	71,900 (1991)
Newark	35,100 (1991)
Sutton in Ashfield	40,200 (1990 est)
Worksop	37,200 (1991)
Oxfordshire	
Abingdon	35,200 (1991)
Banbury	39,900 (1991)
Oxford	121,000 (1994 est)
Peterborough	
Peterborough	139,000 (1994 est)
Plymouth	
Plympton	26,900 (1991)
Plymouth	257,000 (1994 est)
Poole	
Poole	138,100 (1996)
Portsmouth	
Portsmouth	189,300 (1996)
Reading	
Reading	131,000 (1994 est)

City/town	Population
Shropshire	
Shrewsbury	90,900 (1991)
Slough	
Slough	105,000 (1994 est)
Somerset	
Bridgwater	34,600 (1991)
Taunton	55,900 (1991)
Southend	
Southend-on-Sea	171,000 (1994 est)
South Yorkshire	
Doncaster	71,600 (1991)
Rotherham	154,000 (1994 est)
Sheffield	429,000 (1994 est)
Southampton	
Southampton	207,100 (1997 est)
Staffordshire	
Burton-upon-Trent	60,500 (1991)
Lichfield	28,300 (1987 est)
Newcastle-under-Lyme	73,700 (1991)
Rugeley	40,000 (1991)
Tamworth	70,100 (1991)
Stockton-on-Tees	
Stockton-on-Tees	157,000 (1994 est)
Stoke-on-Trent	
Stoke-on-Trent	254,200 (1996)
Suffolk	
Bury St Edmunds	31,200 (1991)
Felixstowe	21,000 (1981)
Ipswich	115,000 (1994 est)
Lowestoft	58,000 (1990 est)
Surrey	
Camberley	45,700 (1981)
Epsom	64,400 (1991) with Ewell
Farnham	20,900 (1985 est)
Guildford	66,000 (1991)
Leatherhead	42,900 (1991)
Reigate	47,600 (1991 with Redhill)
Sunbury-on-Thames	27,400 (1991)
Woking	82,300 (1991)
Torbay	
Torquay	59,600 (1991)
Tyne and Wear	
Jarrow	29,300 (1991)
Newcastle-upon-Tyne	274,000 (1994 est)
North Shields	41,600 (1981)
South Shields	83,700 (1991)
Sunderland	176,000 (1994 est)
Wallsend	45,300 (1991)
Washington	56,800 (1991)
Warwickshire	
Kenilworth	21,400 (1986 est)
Nuneaton	66,700 (1991)

Towns and Cities over 20,000 Population in England (*continued*)

City/town	Population	City/town	Population	City/town	Population
Rugby	61,100 (1991)	Chichester	26,600 (1991)	Swindon	170,000 (1996)
Stratford-upon-Avon	22,200 (1991)	Crawley	73,000 (1981)	Trowbridge	29,300 (1991)
Warwick	22,500 (1991)	Horsham	45,600 (1991)		
		Worthing	96,200 (1991)	***Windsor and Maidenhead***	
West Berkshire				Maidenhead	59,600 (1991)
Newbury	33,300 (1991)	***West Yorkshire***		Windsor	30,100 (1991)
		Barnsley	220,900 (1991)		
West Midlands		Batley	34,600 (1991)	***Wokingham***	
Bilston	25,100 (1991)	Bradford	357,000 (1994 est)	Wokingham	31,900 (1991)
Birmingham	1,220,000 (1994 est)	Castleford	36,000 (1991)		
Coventry	303,000 (1994 est)	Halifax	91,100 (1991)	***Worcester***	
Dudley	141,000 (1994 est)	Huddersfield	139,000 (1994 est)	Bromsgrove	88,500 (1991)
Kidderminster	54,600 (1991)	Keighley	49,600 (1991)	Malvern	31,500 (1991)
Royal Leamington Spa	55,400 (1991)	Leeds	529,000 (1994 est)	Redditch	73,400 (1991)
Solihull	192,200 (1991)	Morley	46,100 (1991)	Worcester	81,700 (1991)
Stourbridge	55,600 (1991)	Pontefract	28,400 (1991)		
Walsall	115,000 (1994 est)	Shipley	28,700 (1991)	***Wrekin, The***	
Wednesbury	24,300 (1991)	Wakefield	306,300 (1991)	Telford	100,000 (1991)
West Bromwich	146,400 (1991)	Wetherby	23,300 (1991)		
Willenhall	26,200 (1991)			***York***	
Wolverhampton	245,000 (1994 est)	***Warrington***		York	107,000 (1994 est)
		Warrington	151,000 (1994 est)		
West Sussex					
Bognor Regis	56,700 (1991)	***Wiltshire***			
Burgess Hill	24,400 (1991)	Salisbury	39,300 (1991)		

Towns and Cities over 20,000 Population in Wales

City/town	Population	City/town	Population
Caerphilly		***Neath Port Talbot***	
Caerphilly	35,900 (1991)	Neath	46,000 (1991)
		Port Talbot	37,600 (1991)
Cardiff			
Cardiff	290,000 (1994 est)	***Newport***	
		Newport	111,000 (1994 est)
Carmarthenshire			
Llanelli	45,000 (1991)	***Rhondda Cynon Taff***	
		Aberdare	38,000 (1982 est)
Conwy		Pontypridd	33,600 (1990 est)
Colwyn Bay	29,000 (1991)	Rhondda	59,900 (1991)
Denbighshire		***Swansea***	
Rhyl	24,900 (1991)	Swansea	172,000 (1994 est)
Merthyr Tydfil		***Torfaen***	
Merthyr Tydfil	39,500 (1991)	Pontypool	35,600 (1991)
Monmouthshire		***Vale of Glamorgan***	
Cwmbran	46,000 (1991)	Barry	49,900 (1991)
Monmouth	75,000 (1991)		
		Wrexham	
		Wrexham	40,600 (1991)

Towns and Cities over 20,000 Population in Scotland

City/town	Population	City/town	Population
Angus		*Highland*	
Arbroath	23,500 (1991)	Inverness	41,200 (1991)
Clydebank		*Inverclyde*	
Clydebank	29,200 (1991)	Greenock	50,000 (1991)
Dumfries and Galloway		*North Ayrshire*	
Dumfries	32,100 (1991)	Irvine	33,000 (1991)
Dundee		*North Lanarkshire*	
Dundee	155,000 (1996)	Airdrie	37,000 (1991)
Dunfermline		Coatbridge	43,600 (1991)
Dunfermline	55,100 (1991)	Cumbernauld	48,800 (1991)
		Motherwell	60,500 (1991)
East Ayrshire		*Perth and Kinross*	
Kilmarnock	44,300 (1991)	Perth	41,500 (1991)
East Dunbartonshire		*Renfrewshire*	
Kirkintilloch	31,000 (1991)	Paisley	75,500 (1991)
Edinburgh		*South Ayrshire*	
Edinburgh	447,550 (1996)	Ayr	48,000 (1991)
Falkirk		*South Lanarkshire*	
Falkirk	35,600 (1991)	East Kilbride	70,400 (1991)
		Hamilton	50,000 (1991)
Fife		*Stirling*	
Glenrothes	38,650 (1991)	Stirling	30,500 (1991)
Kirkcaldy	47,200 (1991)		
Glasgow		*West Dunbartonshire*	
Glasgow	618,400 (1996)	Dumbarton	22,000 (1991)
		West Lothian	
		Livingston	41,600 (1991)

Towns and Cities over 20,000 Population in Northern Ireland

City/town	Population
County Antrim	
Antrim	23,500 (1991)
Ballymena	28,300 (1991)
Belfast	290,000 (1994 est)
Carrickfergus	32,750 (1991)
Lisburn	42,100 (1991)
County Armagh	
Craigavon	62,000 (1990 est)
County Down	
Bangor	52,400 (1991)
County Londonderry	
Londonderry	95,400 (1991)

Roman Names of English and Welsh Cities and Towns

City/town	Roman settlement	City/town	Roman settlement	City/town	Roman settlement
England		Cirencester	Corinium Dobunnorum	Salisbury	Sorbiodonum
Ancaster	Causennae	Colchester	Camulodunum	Shrewsbury	Viroconium
Bath	Aquae Sulis	Dorchester	Durnovaria	Tadcaster	Calcaria
Buxton	Aquae Arnemetiae	Dover	Dubris	Towcester	Lactodorum
Canterbury	Durovernum Cantiacorum	Exeter	Isca Dumnoniorum	Winchester	Venta Belgarum
		Gloucester	Glevum	York	Eboracum
Carlisle	Luguvalium	Leicester	Ratae Coritanorum		
Castleford	Lagentium	Lincoln	Lindum	*Wales*	
Catterick	Cataractonium	London	Londinium	Abergavenny	Gobannium
Chelmsford	Caesaromagus	Manchester	Mancunium	Caerwent	Venta Silurum
Chester	Deva	Newcastle-upon-Tyne	Pons Aelius	Carmarthen	Maridunum
Chichester	Noviomagus Regnensium	Rochester-upon-Medway	Durobrivae		

UK Population and Demography

Death Rates per 1,000 Population in the UK

(N/A = not available.)

Year	0–4	5–9	10–14	15–19	20–24	25–34	35–44	45–54	55–64	65–74	75–84	85 and over	All ages
Male													
1900–02	57.0	4.1	2.4	3.7	5.0	6.6	11.0	18.6	35.0	69.9	143.6	289.6	18.4
1910–12	40.5	3.3	2.0	3.0	3.9	5.0	8.0	14.9	29.8	62.1	133.8	261.5	14.9
1920–22	33.4	2.9	1.8	2.9	3.9	4.5	6.9	11.9	25.3	57.8	131.8	259.1	13.5
1930–32	22.3	2.3	1.5	2.6	3.3	3.5	5.7	11.3	23.7	57.9	134.2	277.0	12.9
1940–42	N/A	N/A	N/A	N/A	N/A	N/A	N/A	N/A	N/A	N/A	N/A	N/A	N/A
1950–52	7.7	0.7	0.5	0.9	1.4	1.6	3.0	8.5	23.2	55.2	127.6	272.0	12.6
1960–62	6.4	0.5	0.4	0.9	1.1	1.1	2.5	7.4	22.2	54.4	123.4	251.0	12.5
1970–72	4.6	0.4	0.4	0.9	1.0	1.0	2.4	7.3	20.9	52.9	116.3	246.1	12.4
1980–82	3.2	0.3	0.3	0.8	0.9	0.9	1.9	6.3	18.2	46.7	107.1	224.9	12.1
1990–92	2.0	0.2	0.2	0.7	0.9	0.9	1.8	4.6	14.3	38.7	92.9	195.7	11.1
1996	1.6	0.1	0.2	0.6	0.9	1.0	1.7	4.2	12.4	35.4	86.5	195.5	10.6
Female													
1900–02	47.9	4.3	2.6	3.5	4.3	5.8	9.0	14.4	27.9	59.3	127.0	262.6	16.3
1910–12	34.0	3.3	2.1	2.9	3.4	4.4	6.7	11.5	23.1	50.7	113.7	234.0	13.3
1920–22	26.9	2.8	1.9	2.8	3.4	4.1	5.6	9.3	19.2	45.6	111.5	232.4	11.9
1930–32	17.7	2.1	1.5	2.4	2.9	3.3	4.6	8.3	17.6	43.7	110.1	246.3	11.5
1940–42	N/A	N/A	N/A	N/A	N/A	N/A	N/A	N/A	N/A	N/A	N/A	N/A	N/A
1950–52	6.0	0.5	0.4	0.7	1.0	1.4	2.3	5.3	12.9	35.5	98.4	228.8	11.2
1960–62	4.9	0.3	0.3	0.4	0.5	0.8	1.8	4.5	11.0	30.8	87.3	218.5	11.2
1970–72	3.6	0.3	0.2	0.4	0.4	0.6	1.6	4.5	10.5	27.5	76.7	196.1	11.3
1980–82	2.3	0.2	0.2	0.3	0.4	0.5	1.3	3.9	9.9	24.8	67.2	179.5	11.4
1990–92	1.6	0.1	0.2	0.3	0.3	0.4	1.1	2.9	8.4	22.2	58.5	154.6	11.1
1996	1.2	0.1	0.1	0.3	0.3	0.5	1.1	2.7	7.3	21.2	56.8	153.7	11.1

Source: *Annual Abstract of Statistics, 1998*, Office for National Statistics © Crown copyright 1998

Average Weekly Earnings and Hours of Full-Time Employees on Adult Rates in Great Britain

Earnings and hours are calculated in April for each year.

Worker category	Average weekly earnings[1]		Average hours	
	1994	1997	1994	1997
All men	362.1	408.7	41.6	41.8
manual	280.7	314.3	44.7	45.1
non-manual	428.2	483.5	38.9	39.1
All women	261.5	297.2	37.6	37.6
manual	181.9	201.1	40.1	40.2
non-manual	278.4	317.8	37.0	37.1
Total	325.7	367.6	40.1	40.3

[1] Figures exclude those whose pay was affected by absence.

Source: *Annual Abstract of Statistics, 1998*, Office for National Statistics © Crown copyright 1998

Households by Type of Occupancy in Great Britain

A household is defined as a person or group of persons residing at the same address. Figures are expressed as percentages of the total.

Household	1961	1971	1981	1991	1996–97
One person					
under pensionable age	4	6	8	11	12
over pensionable age	7	12	14	16	15
Two or more unrelated adults	5	4	5	3	2
Single family households[1]					
couple, no children	26	27	26	28	28
couple, one or two dependent children[2]	30	26	25	20	21
couple, three or more dependent children[2]	8	9	6	5	5
couple, non-dependent children only	10	8	8	8	6
lone parent, dependent children[2]	2	3	5	6	7
lone parent, non-dependent children only	4	4	4	4	3
Multi-family households	3	1	1	1	1

[1] Other individuals who were not family members may be included.
[2] May also include non-dependent children.

Source: *Annual Abstract of Statistics, 1998,* Office for National Statistics © Crown copyright 1998

Individuals Below Various Percentiles of the Equivalized Income Distribution in the UK

Equivalized income is calculated, using the McClements equivalence scales, to reflect the size of household and excludes housing costs. Figures are expressed as percentages of the total and are for combined years 1994–95 and 1995–96.

Status	Bottom 10%	Bottom 20%	Bottom 30%	Bottom 40%	Bottom 50%	All individuals
Self-employed	15	10	8	8	8	10
Single or couple, all in full-time work	2	2	3	5	7	23
One in full-time, one in part-time work	1	2	4	7	9	13
One in full-time, one not working	5	9	10	11	12	13
One or more in part-time work	11	10	10	10	10	7
Head or spouse age 60 or over	17	23	26	27	25	17
Head or spouse unemployed	26	20	15	13	11	6
Other[1]	24	24	22	19	17	10

[1] Includes long-term sick and disabled people and non-working single parents.

Source: *Annual Abstract of Statistics, 1998,* Office for National Statistics © Crown copyright 1998

Individual Distribution of Wealth in the UK

Marketable wealth owned by sectors of the population. Figures are expressed as percentages of the total.

Sector[1]	1976	1981	1986	1991	1994
Most wealthy 1%	21	18	18	17	19
Most wealthy 5%	38	36	36	35	38
Most wealthy 10%	50	50	50	47	51
Most wealthy 25%	71	73	73	71	73
Most wealthy 50%	92	92	90	92	93

[1] Adults aged 18 and over.

Source: *Annual Abstract of Statistics, 1998,* Office for National Statistics © Crown copyright 1998

Legal Abortions in Great Britain

1996

Age	England and Wales	Scotland
Under 15	1,098	87
15	2,547	236
16–19	28,790	2,355
20–24	46,356	3,566
25–29	39,311	2,599
30–34	28,228	1,801
35–39	16,118	959
40–44	5,027	331
45 and over	428	27
All ages	167,916	11,961

Source: *Annual Abstract of Statistics, 1998,* Office for National Statistics © Crown copyright 1998.

Life Expectancy in the UK

(Data give interim life tables, 1994–96. In years.)

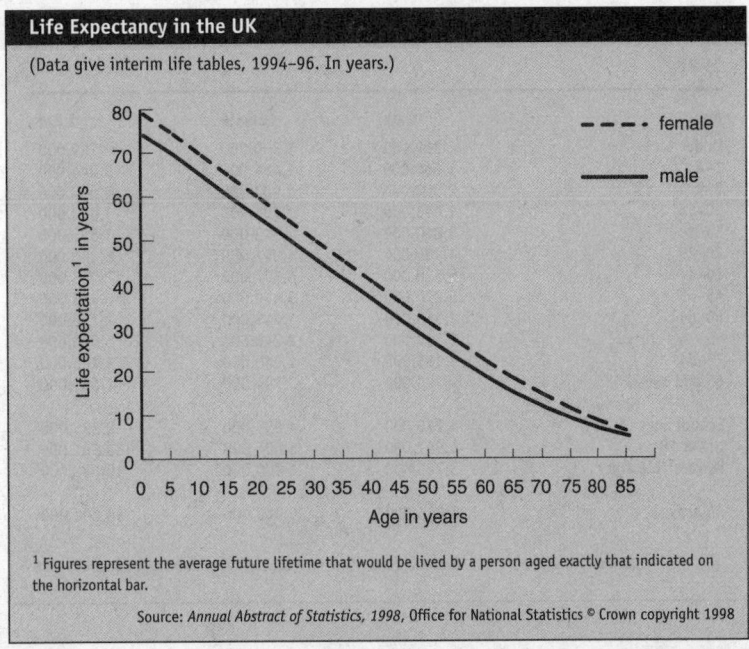

[1] Figures represent the average future lifetime that would be lived by a person aged exactly that indicated on the horizontal bar.

Source: *Annual Abstract of Statistics, 1998,* Office for National Statistics © Crown copyright 1998

Migration into and out of the UK

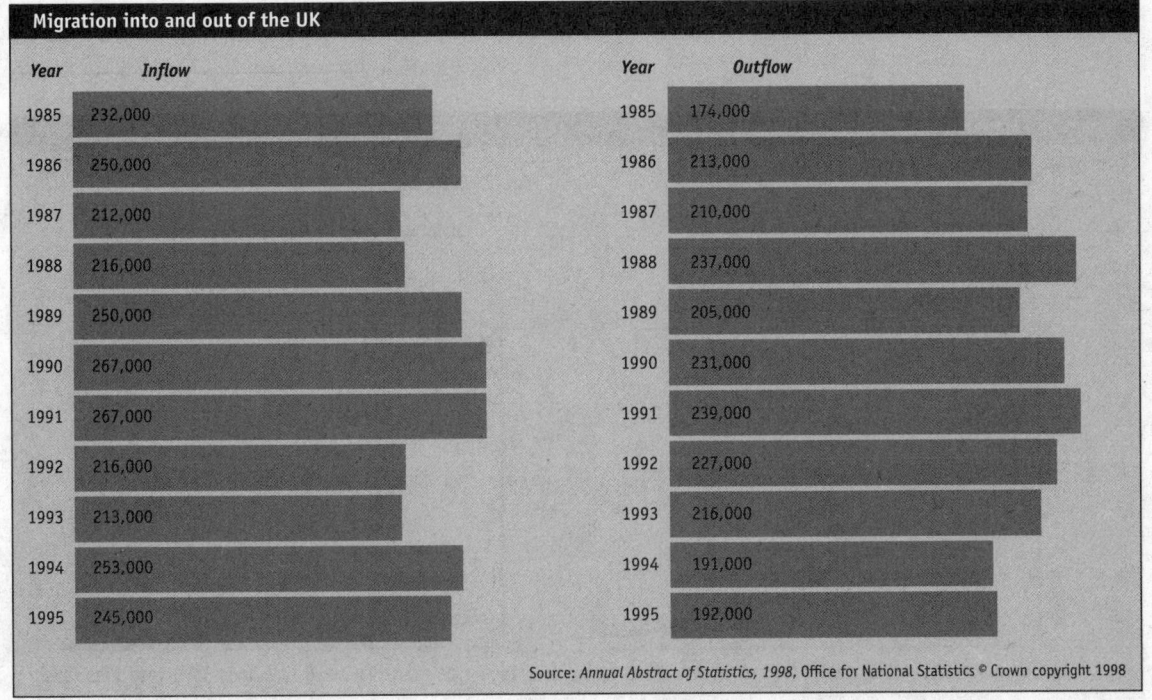

Year	Inflow
1985	232,000
1986	250,000
1987	212,000
1988	216,000
1989	250,000
1990	267,000
1991	267,000
1992	216,000
1993	213,000
1994	253,000
1995	245,000

Year	Outflow
1985	174,000
1986	213,000
1987	210,000
1988	237,000
1989	205,000
1990	231,000
1991	239,000
1992	227,000
1993	216,000
1994	191,000
1995	192,000

Source: *Annual Abstract of Statistics, 1998,* Office for National Statistics © Crown copyright 1998

Age Distribution in the UK

1996

Age	Male	Female	Total
Under 1	369,000	350,000	719,000
1–4	1,560,000	1,484,000	3,044,000
5–9	2,002,000	1,903,000	3,905,000
10–14	1,895,000	1,795,000	3,690,000
15–19	1,810,000	1,713,000	3,522,000
20–29	4,289,000	4,091,000	8,380,000
30–44	6,538,000	6,397,000	12,935,000
45–59	5,270,000	5,312,000	10,582,000
60–64	1,355,000	1,418,000	2,772,000
65–74	2,310,000	2,748,000	5,058,000
75–84	1,185,000	1,940,000	3,125,000
85 and over	273,000	794,000	1,067,000
School ages (5–15)	4,276,000	4,059,000	8,335,000
Under 18	6,957,000	6,604,000	13,561,000
Pensionable age	3,768,000	6,900,000	10,668,000
All ages	28,856,000	29,946,000	58,801,000

Source: *Annual Abstract of Statistics, 1998,* Office for National Statistics © Crown copyright 1998

Population by Ethnic Group in Great Britain

(Average over the period Spring 1993 to Spring 1996.)

Ethnic group	Number
Black	
Caribbean	503,000
African	273,000
other (non-mixed)	85,000
mixed	131,000
Indian	872,000
Pakistani	547,000
Bangladeshi	181,000
Chinese	137,000
Other	
Asian (non-mixed)	169,000
other (non-mixed)	131,000
mixed	190,000
All ethnic minority groups	3,220,000
White	52,747,000
All ethnic groups[1]	55,981,000

[1] Figure includes ethnic groups not stated.

Source: *Annual Abstract of Statistics, 1998,* Office for National Statistics © Crown copyright 1998

Infant and Maternal Mortality in the UK

(Per 1,000 live births.)

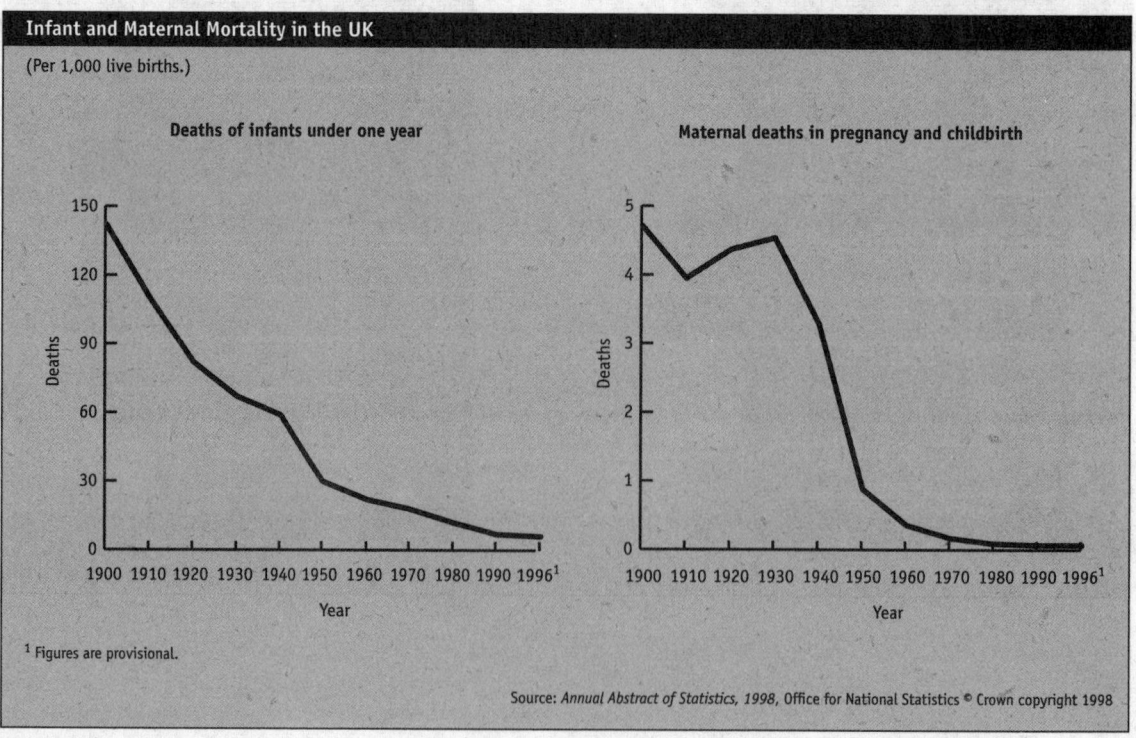

Deaths of infants under one year

Maternal deaths in pregnancy and childbirth

[1] Figures are provisional.

Source: *Annual Abstract of Statistics, 1998,* Office for National Statistics © Crown copyright 1998

Population by Marital Status in the UK

Marital status	Male			Female		
	1971	1981	1991[1]	1971	1981	1991[1]
Single	12,120,000	12,168,000	12,874,000	11,131,000	10,860,000	11,231,000
Married	14,067,000	13,791,000	13,237,000	14,130,000	13,856,000	13,364,000
Widowed	779,000	793,000	828,000	3,178,000	3,331,000	3,370,000
Divorced	201,000	657,000	1,306,000	321,000	897,000	1,598,000

[1] Mid-1991 population estimates by marital status are still provisional.

Source: *Annual Abstract of Statistics, 1998;* Office for National Statistics, © Crown copyright 1998

Distribution of the Workforce in the UK

(Figures are taken at mid-June of each year.)

Category	1990	1991	1992	1993	1994	1995	1996	1997
Workforce[1]	28,813,000	28,614,000	28,483,000	28,279,000	28,160,000	28,113,000	28,184,000	28,107,000
Unemployed[2]	1,615,000	2,301,000	2,734,000	2,919,000	2,644,000	2,313,000	2,150,000	1,600,000
Workforce in employment[3]	27,198,000	26,313,000	25,749,000	25,360,000	25,517,000	25,800,000	26,034,000	26,507,000
HM forces[4]	303,000	297,000	290,000	271,000	250,000	230,000	221,000	210,000
Self-employed persons[5]	3,562,000	3,413,000	3,230,000	3,190,000	3,302,000	3,357,000	3,291,000	3,338,000
Employees in employment[6]	22,909,000	22,250,000	21,904,000	21,588,000	21,663,000	21,987,000	22,340,000	22,792,000
Work-related government-supported training programmes[7]	423,000	353,000	325,000	311,000	302,000	225,000	181,000	167,000

[1] Data are for workforce in employment plus the claimant unemployed.
[2] Claimant unemployed: those people who were claiming unemployment benefits (Unemployment Benefit, Income Support, or National Insurance Credits) at Employment Service local offices on the day of the monthly count.
[3] Figures include employees in employment, the self-employed, HM forces, and work-related government-supported training programmes.
[4] Data give total number of UK service personnel in HM Regular Forces, wherever serving, and include those on release leave (MoD figures).
[5] Figures include self-employed persons with and without employees and are based on results of the Labour Force Survey. Northern Ireland estimates are not seasonally adjusted.
[6] For all dates, individuals with two jobs as employees of different employers are counted twice.
[7] Figures include all participants on work-related government-supported training programmes who are receiving some work experience on their placement but do not have a contract of employment. The numbers are not subject to seasonal adjustment.

Source: *Annual Abstract of Statistics, 1998,* Office for National Statistics © Crown copyright 1998

Population Changes in the UK

Year	Population at start of period[1]	Average annual change				
		Overall annual change (increase)	Births	Deaths[2]	Excess of births over deaths	Net migration and other adjustments[3]
1901–11	38,237,000	385,000	1,091,000	624,000	467,000	−82,000
1911–21	42,082,000	195,000	975,000	689,000	286,000	−92,000
1921–31	44,027,000	201,000	824,000	555,000	268,000	−67,000
1931–51	46,038,000	213,000	793,000	603,000	190,000	22,000
1951–61	50,225,000	258,000	839,000	593,000	246,000	12,000
1961–71	52,807,000	230,000	962,000	638,000	324,000	−14,000
1971–81	55,928,000	42,000	736,000	666,000	69,000	−27,000
1981–91	56,352,000	146,000	757,000	655,000	103,000	43,000
1991–96	57,808,000	199,000	756,000	640,000	116,000	83,000
1996–2001[4]	58,801,000	163,000	723,000	634,000	89,000	74,000
2001–11	59,618,000	131,000	690,000	624,000	66,000	65,000
2011–21	60,929,000	131,000	694,000	628,000	66,000	65,000

[1] Figures give census-enumerated population up to 1951; mid-year estimates of resident population from 1961 to 1996 and mid-1996-based projections of resident population thereafter.
[2] Figures include deaths of non-civilians and merchant seamen who died outside the country. These deaths numbered 577,000 in 1911–21 and 240,000 in 1931–51 for England and Wales; 74,000 in 1911–21, and 34,000 in 1931–51 for Scotland; and 10,000 in 1911–26 for Northern Ireland.
[3] Other adjustments include changes in census visitor balance, in Armed Forces, asylum seekers, etc.
[4] Figures are 1996-based national population projections.

Source: *Annual Abstract of Statistics, 1998,* Office for National Statistics © Crown copyright 1998

Population Summary of the UK

Year	Male	Female	Total	Year	Male	Female	Total
Enumerated Population: Census Figures				1979	28,867,000	27,373,000	56,240,000
1851	11,404,000	10,855,000	22,259,000	1980	28,919,000	27,411,000	56,330,000
1901	19,745,000	18,492,000	38,237,000	1981	28,943,000	27,409,000	56,352,000
1911	21,725,000	20,357,000	42,082,000	1982	28,927,000	27,391,000	56,318,000
1921	22,994,000	21,033,000	44,027,000	1983	28,948,000	27,429,000	56,377,000
1931	23,978,000	22,060,000	46,038,000	1984	28,995,000	27,511,000	56,506,000
1951	26,107,000	24,118,000	50,225,000	1985	29,074,000	27,611,000	56,685,000
1961	27,228,000	25,481,000	52,709,000	1986	29,153,000	27,698,000	56,852,000
				1987	29,220,000	27,789,000	57,009,000
Resident Population: Mid-Year Estimates				1988	29,282,000	27,876,000	57,158,000
1964	27,800,000	26,191,000	53,991,000	1989	29,368,000	27,989,000	57,358,000
1965	27,982,000	26,368,000	54,350,000	1990	29,443,000	28,118,000	57,561,000
1966	28,132,000	26,511,000	54,643,000	1991	29,562,000	28,246,000	57,808,000
1967	28,286,000	26,673,000	54,214,000	1992	29,645,000	28,362,000	58,006,000
1968	28,429,000	26,784,000	55,214,000	1993	29,718,000	28,474,000	58,191,000
1969	28,553,000	26,908,000	55,461,000	1994	29,803,000	28,592,000	58,395,000
1970	28,641,000	26,992,000	55,632,000	1995	29,878,000	28,727,000	58,606,000
1971	28,761,000	27,167,000	55,928,000	1996	29,946,000	28,856,000	58,801,000
1972	28,837,000	27,259,000	56,709,000				
1973	28,891,000	27,332,000	56,223,000	*Resident Population: Projections (Mid-Year)*[1]			
1974	28,887,000	27,349,000	56,236,000	2001	30,241,000	29,377,000	59,618,000
1975	28,865,000	27,361,000	56,226,000	2006	30,477,000	29,809,000	60,287,000
1976	28,856,000	27,360,000	56,216,000	2011	30,723,000	30,206,000	60,929,000
1977	28,845,000	27,345,000	56,190,000	2021	31,328,000	30,916,000	62,244,000
1978	28,849,000	27,330,000	56,178,000				

[1] These projections are 1996 -based.

Source: *Annual Abstract of Statistics, 1998,* Office for National Statistics © Crown copyright 1998

Unemployment Benefit Claimant Count Rates in the UK

The number of unemployment-related benefit claimants is given as a percentage of the estimated total workforce (the sum of claimants, employees in employment, self-employed, participants on work-related government training programmes, and armed forces) at mid-year. Figures are seasonally adjusted and exclude claimants under 18.

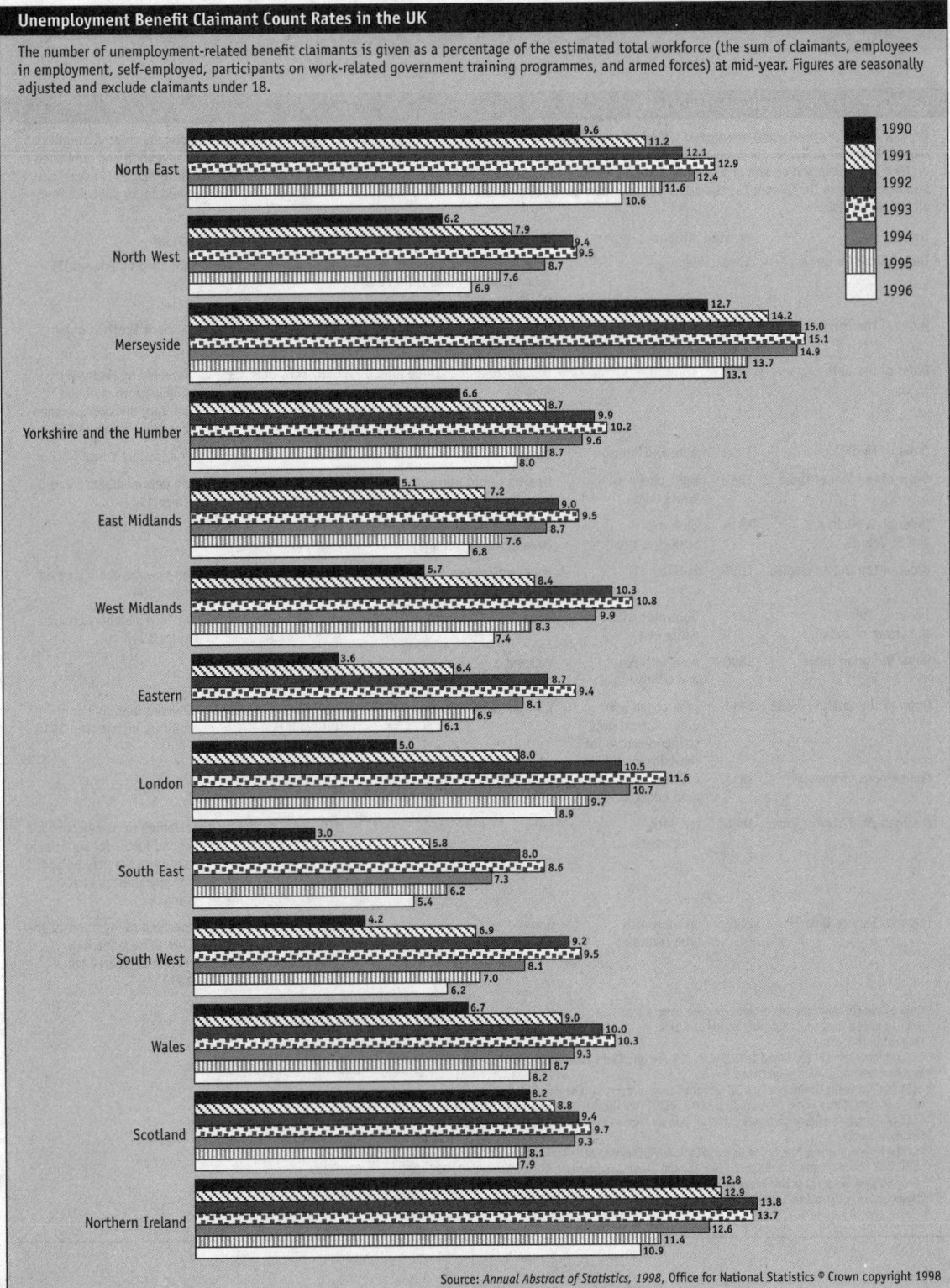

Legend:
- 1990
- 1991
- 1992
- 1993
- 1994
- 1995
- 1996

North East
- 9.6
- 11.2
- 12.1
- 12.9
- 12.4
- 11.6
- 10.6

North West
- 6.2
- 7.9
- 9.4
- 9.5
- 8.7
- 7.6
- 6.9

Merseyside
- 12.7
- 14.2
- 15.0
- 15.1
- 14.9
- 13.7
- 13.1

Yorkshire and the Humber
- 6.6
- 8.7
- 9.9
- 10.2
- 9.6
- 8.7
- 8.0

East Midlands
- 5.1
- 7.2
- 9.0
- 9.5
- 8.7
- 7.6
- 6.8

West Midlands
- 5.7
- 8.4
- 10.3
- 10.8
- 9.9
- 8.3
- 7.4

Eastern
- 3.6
- 6.4
- 8.7
- 9.4
- 8.1
- 6.9
- 6.1

London
- 5.0
- 8.0
- 10.5
- 11.6
- 10.7
- 9.7
- 8.9

South East
- 3.0
- 5.8
- 8.0
- 8.6
- 7.3
- 6.2
- 5.4

South West
- 4.2
- 6.9
- 9.2
- 9.5
- 8.1
- 7.0
- 6.2

Wales
- 6.7
- 9.0
- 10.0
- 10.3
- 9.3
- 8.7
- 8.2

Scotland
- 8.2
- 8.8
- 9.4
- 9.7
- 9.3
- 8.1
- 7.9

Northern Ireland
- 12.8
- 12.9
- 13.8
- 13.7
- 12.6
- 11.4
- 10.9

Source: *Annual Abstract of Statistics, 1998*, Office for National Statistics © Crown copyright 1998

See Also   Public Spending (Economy and Business)

The Honours System

Orders of Chivalry and the Honours List

Modern orders of chivalry are awarded as a mark of royal favour or as a reward for public services. Members of orders are normally created Knights or Dames, titled Sir or Dame; some orders are graded, with the lower grades not being knighted. Honours are awarded by the sovereign and published on New Year's Day, and on the official royal birthday in June. Suggestions for awards are provided by: (1) senior government officials; (2) personal nominations from the Queen; (3) the major political parties, through the Chief Whip; and (4) the prime minister, who can add to, or subtract from, all the above lists.

Order	Created	Ribbon	Motto	Initials	Other
Order of the Garter[1]	1348	blue	*honi soit qui mal y pense* (shame on him who thinks evil of it)	KG	founded by Edward III
Order of the Thistle[2]	1687[3]	green	*nemo me impune lacessit* (no one provokes me with impunity)	KT	ancient Scottish order
Order of the Bath	1725	crimson	*tria juncta in ino* (three joined in one)	GCB, KCB, DCB, CB[4]	founded by Henry IV; divided into civil and military divisions; women became eligible in 1971
Order of Merit[1][5]	1902	blue and crimson	none	OM	founded by Edward VII
Order of the Star of India	1861	light blue with white edges	Heaven's light our guide	GCSI, KCSI, CSI[6]	no new members created since 1947
Order of St Michael and St George	1818	blue with scarlet centre	*auspicium melioris aevi* (token of a better age)	GCMG, KCMG, DCMG, CMG[7]	
Order of the Indian Empire	1868	purple	*imperatricis auspiciis* (under the auspices of the Empress)	GCIE, KCIE, CIE[8]	no new members created since 1947
Imperial Order of the Crown of India[9]	1877	light blue with white edge	none	CI	no new members created since 1947
Royal Victorian Order	1896	blue with red and white edges	Victoria	GCVO, KCVO, DCVO, CVO, LVO, MVO[10]	
Order of the British Empire	1917	pink edged with grey; vertical grey stripe in centre for the military division	for God and the Empire	GBE, KBE, DBE, CBE, OBE, MBE[11]	divided into civil and military divisions in 1918
Companions of Honour[5][12]	1917	carmine with gold edges	none	CH	
Distinguished Service Order	1886	red with blue edges	none	DSO	awarded to members of the armed forces for services in action; a bar may be added for any additional act of service
Imperial Service Order[13]	1902	crimson with blue centre	none	ISO	awarded to members of the Civil Service; no new members created since 1993

[1] Only 24 people may hold this order at any one time.
[2] Only 16 people may hold this order at any one time.
[3] Revived in this year.
[4] GCB (Knight/Dame of the Grand Cross); KCB, DCB (Knight/Dame Commander); CB (Companion).
[5] Members are not given a knighthood.
[6] GCSI (Knight Grand Commander); KCSI (Knight Commander); CSI (Companion).
[7] GCMG (Knight/Dame Grand Commander); KCMG, DCMG (Knight/Dame Commander); CMG (Companion).
[8] GCIE (Knight/Dame Grand Commander); KCIE (Knight/Dame Commander); CIE (Companion).
[9] For women only.
[10] GCVO (Knight/Dame of The Grand Cross); KCVO, DCVO (Knight/Dame Commander); LVO (Lieutenant); MVO (Member).
[11] GBE/KBE (Knight/Dame Grand Cross); DBE (Knight/Dame Commander); CBE (Commander); OBE (Officer); MBE (Member).
[12] Only 65 people may hold this order at any one time.
[13] Membership is limited to 1,900 people.

The Peerage

The Peerage

The peerage comprises holders, in descending order, of the titles of duke, marquess, earl, viscount, and baron. Most hereditary peerages pass on death to the nearest male relative, but some of these titles may be held by a woman in default of a male heir; no title can be passed on to the untitled husband of a woman peer. In the late 19th century, the peerage was augmented by the Lords of Appeal in Ordinary (the nonhereditary life peers) and, from 1958, by a number of specially created life peers of either sex (usually long-standing members of the House of Commons). Since 1963 peers have been able to disclaim their titles, usually to enable them to take a seat in the Commons (where peers are disqualified from membership).

Duke
The title originated in England in 1337, when Edward III created his son Edward, Duke of Cornwall; **Coronet:** eight strawberry leaves; **Title:** His Grace, The Duke of; **Wife's title:** Her Grace, The Duchess of; **Eldest son's title:** takes his father's second title (Marquess, Earl, or Viscount) as a courtesy title; **Younger sons' title:** 'Lord' before forename and family name; **Daughters' title:** 'Lady' before forename and family name.

Marquess
The first English marquess was created in 1385, but the lords of the Scottish and Welsh Marches were known as marchiones before this date; **Coronet:** four strawberry leaves alternating with four silver balls; **Title:** The Most Honourable, The Marquess of; **Wife's title:** The Most Honourable, The Marchioness of; **Eldest son's title:** takes his father's second title (Earl or Viscount) as a courtesy title; **Younger sons' title:** 'Lord' before forename and family name; **Daughters' title:** 'Lady' before forename and family name.

Earl
Earldoms first became hereditary during the Norman period, and the title of earl was the highest hereditary dignity until 1337; **Coronet:** eight silver balls on stalks alternating with eight gold strawberry leaves; **Title:** The Right Honourable, The Earl of; **Wife's title:** The Right Honourable, The Countess of; **Eldest son's title:** takes his father's second title as a courtesy title; **Younger sons' title:** 'The Honourable' before forename and family name; **Daughters' title:** 'Lady' before forename and family name.

Viscount
The title was first granted in England in 1440 to John, Lord Beaumont. Originally the title was given to the deputy sheriff, who acted on behalf of an earl within his estate;

Coronet: sixteen silver balls; **Title:** The Right Honourable, The Viscount of; **Wife's title:** The Right Honourable, The Viscountess of; **Eldest son's title:** takes his father's second title as a courtesy title; **Younger sons' title:** 'The Honourable' before forename and family name; **Daughters' title:** 'The Honourable' before forename and family name.

Baron
Historically, a baron is any member of the higher nobility, a direct vassal (feudal servant) of the king, not bearing other titles such as duke or count. Life peers, created under the Act of 1958, are always of this rank; **Coronet:** six silver balls; **Title:** The Right Honourable, The Lord; **Wife's title:** The Right Honourable, The Lady; **Eldest son's title:** 'The Honourable' before forename and family name; **Younger sons' title:** 'The Honourable' before forename and family name; **Daughters' title:** 'The Honourable' before forename and family name.

Notes
For Royal Dukes, His Royal Highness and Her Royal Highness are used instead of His or Her Grace. In Scotland, Marquis is used for peers created before the union with England. In Scotland, 'The Master of' followed by the Viscount's title can be used. The title Baron does not exist in Scotland.

The Royal Family

The Civil List

Under the Civil List Acts, The Queen Mother and The Duke of Edinburgh receive annual parliamentary allowances to enable them to carry out their public duties. Since 1993, The Queen has repaid to the Treasury the annual parliamentary allowances received by other members of the Royal family.

The amounts payable in 1996–97 to members of the Royal Family were as follows: **Parliamentary annuities (not repaid by The Queen)** Her Majesty Queen Elizabeth The Queen Mother £643,000; His Royal Highness The Duke of Edinburgh £359,000; **Parliamentary annuities (repaid by The Queen)** His Royal Highness The Duke of York £249,000; His Royal Highness The Prince Edward £96,000; Her Royal Highness The Princess Royal £228,000; Her Royal Highness The Princess Margaret £219,000; Her Royal Highness Princess Alice, Duchess of Gloucester £87,000; Their Royal Highnesses The Duke and Duchess of Gloucester £175,000; Their Royal Highnesses The Duke and Duchess of Kent £236,000; Her Royal Highness Princess Alexandra, Hon Lady Ogilvy £225,000.

Her Majesty Queen Elizabeth the Queen Mother on a visit to St Mary's Hospital, Paddington, June 1998, to open a new Accident and Emergency department.   Richard Watt

Sources of Income

The Queen
The Queen (or officials of the Royal Household acting on her behalf) has four sources of funding:

The Civil List
Set by Parliament as a fixed annual amount of £7.9 million for a period of up to ten years; it is not taxed.

Grants-in-Aid
Paid by the appropriate government departments for expenses incurred.

Property Paid annually by the Department of Culture, Media, and Sport and used for the upkeep of the palaces occupied by members of the Royal Family. These are Buckingham Palace, St James's Palace and Clarence House, Marlborough House Mews, parts of Kensington Palace, Windsor Castle and related buildings, and Hampton Court Mews and Paddocks. Accounts are published and presented to Parliament each year. In 1996–97 the Grant-in-Aid amounted to £19,609,000.

Travel From April 1997, the Royal Household received a Grant-in-Aid from Parliament, through the Department of the Environment, Transport, and the Regions to pay for Royal travel. The Grant-in-Aid amounts to £19.5 million, including £16.5 million for flying on official engagements by 32 (The Royal) Squadron.

The Privy Purse

The Privy Purse Office manages the Sovereign's private income from the Duchy of Lancaster. This amounted to £5.32 million before tax for the year to 31 March 1997. The Duchy is a landed estate held in trust for the Sovereign since 1399. The Queen uses the larger part of the Privy Purse to meet official expenses incurred by other Members of the Royal Family. Only the Queen Mother and the Duke of Edinburgh receive payments from Parliament which are not reimbursed by the Queen.

The Queen's Personal Wealth and Income

The Queen's personal income, derived from her personal investment portfolio, is used to meet private expenditure. The Queen owns Balmoral and Sandringham, both inherited from her father. She also owns the stud at Sandringham (with a small amount of land in Hampshire), West Ilsley Stables, and Sunninghill Park, home of the Duke of York. Income derived from public access to Balmoral and Sandringham goes to charity and towards meeting the costs of managing the properties. The Queen owns no property outside the UK.

The Prince of Wales

The Prince of Wales does not receive any money from the state. Instead, he receives the

---

Members of The Royal Family

Senior members of the Royal Family are all related to the three middle sons of King George V: King George VI (1895–1952); Henry, Duke of Gloucester (1900–1974); George, Duke of Kent (1902–1942); the eldest son, the Duke of Windsor (1894–1972), who abdicated from the throne as King Edward VIII in 1936 and died childless. (– = not applicable.)

Name and titles	Married	Date of birth	Office	Official residence(s)	Issue
Family of George VI					
The Sovereign: Her Majesty Queen Elizabeth II, Of the United Kingdom of Great Britain and Northern Ireland and of her other Realms and Territories, Queen, Head of the Commonwealth, Defender of the Faith	His Royal Highness The Duke of Edinburgh, 20 November 1947	21 April 1926	Buckingham Palace, London SW1A 1AA; phone: (0171) 930 4832	Buckingham Palace, Windsor Castle, Palace of Holyrood House	Prince Charles, Princess Anne, Prince Andrew, Prince Edward
Husband of The Queen: His Royal Highness, The Prince Phillip, Duke of Edinburgh, KG, KT, OM, GBE, AC, QSO, PC, Ranger of Windsor Great Park	Her Majesty The Queen, 20 November 1947	10 June 1921			
Mother of The Queen: Her Majesty Queen Elizabeth The Queen Mother, Lady of The Garter, Lady of The Thistle, CI, GCVO, GBE, Dame Grand Cross of the Order of St John, Royal Victorian Chain, Lord Warden and Admiral of the Cinque Ports, Constable of Dover Castle	Prince Albert, Duke of York (later King George VI; died 1952), 26 April 1923	4 August 1900	Clarence House, St James' Palace, London SW1A 1BA; phone: (0171) 930 3141	Clarence House; Royal Lodge, Windsor; Castle of Mey	Queen Elizabeth II, Princess Margaret
Children of The Queen					
His Royal Highness The Prince of Wales (Prince Charles), KG, KT, GCB and Great Master of the Order of the Bath, AK, QSO, PC, ADP (P)	Lady Diana Spencer (later Diana, Princess of Wales; died 1997), 29 July 1981, marriage dissolved 1996	14 November 1948	St James' Palace, London SW1A 1BA; phone: (0171) 930 4832	St James' Palace, Highgrove, Tetbury	His Royal Highness Prince William of Wales (born 21 June 1982), His Royal Highness Prince Henry of Wales (born 15 September 1984)
Her Royal Highness The Princess Royal (Princess Anne), KG, GCVO	Captain Mark Phillips, 14 November 1973, marriage dissolved 1992; Captain Timothy Laurence, 12 December 1992	15 August 1950	Buckingham Palace, London SW1A 1AA; phone: (0171) 930 4832	Gatcombe Park, Minchinhampton	Peter Phillips (born 15 November 1977), Zara Phillips (born 15 May 1981)
His Royal Highness The Duke of York (Prince Andrew), CVO, ADC(P)	Sarah Ferguson (now Sarah, Duchess of York), 23 July 1986, marriage dissolved 1996	19 February 1960		Buckingham Palace; Sunninghill Park, Ascot	Princess Beatrice (born 8 August 1988), Princess Eugenie (born 23 March 1990)
His Royal Highness The Prince Edward, CVO	–	10 March 1964		Buckingham Palace	none

Members of The Royal Family (continued)

Name and titles	Married	Date of birth	Office	Official residence(s)	Issue
Sister of The Queen					
Her Royal Highness The Princess Margaret, Countess of Snowdon, CI, GCVO, Royal Victorian Chain, Dame Grand Cross of the Order of St John of Jerusalem	Antony Armstrong-Jones (later Earl of Snowdon), 6 May 1960, marriage dissolved 1978	21 August 1930	Kensington Palace, London W8 4PU; phone: (0171) 930 3141	Kensington Palace	David, Viscount Linley (born 3 November 1961), Lady Sarah Chatto[1] (born 1 May 1964)
Family of Henry, Duke of Gloucester **Aunt of The Queen**					
Her Royal Highness Princess Alice, Duchess of Gloucester, GCB, CI, GCVO, GBE	Prince Henry, Duke of Gloucester (died 1974), 6 November 1935	25 December 1901	Kensington Palace, London W8 4PU; phone: (0171) 930 6374	Kensington Palace	Prince William (1941–72), Richard, Duke of Gloucester
Cousins of The Queen					
His Royal Highness The Duke of Gloucester (Prince Richard), KG, GCV, Grand Prior of the Order of St John of Jerusalem	Birgitte Eva van Deurs (now HRH The Duchess of Gloucester), 8 July 1972	26 August 1944	Kensington Palace, London W8 4PU; phone: (0171) 930 6374	Kensington Palace	Alexander, Earl of Ulster (born 24 October 1974), Lady Davina Windsor (born 19 November 1977), Lady Rose Windsor (born 1 March 1980)
Family of George, Duke of Kent					
His Royal Highness The Duke of Kent (Prince Edward), KG, GCMG, GCVO, ADC (P)	Katherine Worsley (now HRH The Duchess of Kent), 8 June 1961	9 October 1935	York House, St James' Palace, London SW1 1BQ; phone: (0171) 930 4872	Wren House, London	George, Earl of St Andrews[2] (born 26 June 1962), Lady Helen Taylor[3] (born 28 April 1964), Lord Nicholas Windsor (born 25 July 1970)
Her Royal Highness Princess Alexandra, The Honourable Lady Ogilvy, GCVO	The Right Honourable Sir Angus Ogilvy, 24 April 1963	25 December 1936	Buckingham Palace, London SW1A 1AA; phone: (0171) 930 1860	Thatched House Lodge, Richmond Park, Surrey	James Ogilvy[4] (born 29 February 1964), Marina Mowatt[5] (born 31 July 1966)
His Royal Highness Prince Michael of Kent, KCVO	Baroness Marie-Christine von Reibnitz (now HRH Princess Michael of Kent), 30 June 1978	4 July 1942	Kensington Palace, London W8 4PU; phone: (0171) 930 3519	Kensington Palace; Nether Lypiatt Manor, Stroud	Lord Frederick Windsor (born 6 April 1979), Lady Gabriella Windsor (born 23 April 1981)

[1] Has one son: Daniel Chatto (born 28 July 1996).
[2] Has three children: Lady Marina Windsor (born 30 September 1982), Edward, Baron Downpatrick (born 2 December 1988), Lady Amelia Windsor (born 24 August 1995).
[3] Has two children: Columbus Taylor (born 6 August 1994), Cassius Taylor (born 26 December 1996).
[4] Has two children: Flora Ogilvy (born 15 December 1994), Alexander Ogilvy (born 12 November 1996).
[5] Has two children: Zenouska Mowatt (born 26 May 1990), Christian Mowatt (born 4 June 1993).

annual net revenues of the Duchy of Cornwall and uses them to meet the costs of all aspects of his public and private commitments and those of his children.

The Duchy of Cornwall
From 1 January 1996 to 31 March 1997 (the 15-month account period is due to a change in the Duchy's accounting year), the Prince of Wales received £6.8 million before tax. On an annualized basis, this represents an income of approximately £5.4 million before tax.

The Succession to the Throne

The current succession was determined following the end of the Commonwealth in the 17th century, by the Bill of Rights of 1689. This was amended by the Act of Settlement which also laid down that only Protestant descendants of Princess Sophia – the Electress of Hanover, granddaughter of James I – can succeed. In February 1998 the government announced that The Queen has agreed that the law should be changed to give females equal rights to succeed to the throne.

The Bill which should result from this decision will negate the rule of male primogeniture written into the 1701 Act of Settlement on which royal succession is currently based.

National Anthems and Patriotic Songs

The National Anthem: 'God Save The Queen'

The melody resembles a composition by John Bull and similar words are found from the 16th century. In its present form it was arranged by Dr Thomas Arne, under the title 'Song for Two Voices'. This version was first performed at Drury Lane Theatre in London on 28 September 1745, following the news of the defeat of the army of King George II by the 'Young Pretender' to the British Throne, Prince Charles Edward Stuart, at the battle of Prestonpans. The song immediately became popular as an anti-Jacobite Party song during the 1745 Jacobite Rebellion.

The words below are those sung in 1745, substituting 'Queen' for 'King' where appropriate. On official occasions, only the first verse is usually sung.

> God save our gracious Queen, Long live
> our noble Queen
> God save the Queen!
> Send her victorious, Happy and Glorious
> Long to reign over us
> God save the Queen!
>
> O Lord our God arise, Scatter her
> enemies
> And make them fall,
> Confound their politics,
> Frustrate their knavish tricks
> On Thee our hopes we fix
> Oh, save us all!
>
> Thy choicest gifts in store
> On her be pleased to pour
> Long may she reign
> May she defend our laws,
> And ever give us cause
> To sing with heart and voice
> God save the Queen!
>
> Not in this land alone,
> But be God's mercies known
> From shore to shore!
> Lord, make the nations see,
> That men should brothers be,
> And form one family
> The wide world over.
>
> From every latent foe,
> From the assassins blow
> God save the Queen!
> O'er her thine arm extend,
> For Britain's sake defend
> Our mother, prince, and friend
> God save the Queen!

Rule Britannia

Words by James Thomson.

> When Britain first, at heaven's command
> Arose from out the azure main
> This was the charter the charter of the
> land
> And guardian Angels sung this strain:
>
> Rule, Britannia, rule the waves
> Britons never will be slaves.
>
> The nations, not so blest as thee
> Must, in their turns, to tyrants fall
> While thou shalt flourish great and free
> The dread and envy of them all.
>
> Still more majestic shalt thou rise
> More dreadful, from each foreign stroke
> As the loud blast that tears the skies
> Serves but to root thy native oak.
>
> Thee haughty tyrants ne'er shall tame
> All their attempts to bend thee down
> Will but arouse thy generous flame
> But work their woe, and thy renown.
>
> To thee belongs the rural reign
> Thy cities shall with commerce shine
> All thine shall be the subject main
> And every shore it circles thine.
>
> The Muses, still with freedom found
> Shall to thy happy coast repair
> Blest isle! with matchless beauty crowned
> And manly hearts to guard the fair.

The Unofficial English National Anthem: 'Land of Hope and Glory'

Although this anthem can identify with the whole of the UK by references to the empire 'wider and still wider, shall thy bounds be set', it is also the unofficial national anthem of England, and is used for the English teams at the Commonwealth Games, although the English national football and rugby teams use God Save the Queen.

Words by A C Benson, music by Sir Edward Elgar from 'Pomp & Circumstance March No 1'.

> Dear Land of Hope, thy hope is
> crowned.
> God make thee mightier yet!
> On Sov'ran brows, beloved, renowned,
> Once more thy crown is set.
> Thine equal laws, by Freedom gained,
> Have ruled thee well and long
> By Freedom gained, by Truth
> maintained,
> Thine Empire shall be strong.

> Land of Hope and Glory, Mother of the
> Free
> How shall we extol thee, who are born
> of thee?
> Wider still and wider shall thy bounds
> be set
> God, who made thee mighty, make thee
> mightier yet,
> God, who made thee mighty, make thee
> mightier yet.
>
> Thy fame is ancient as the days,
> As Ocean large and wide
> A pride that dares, and heeds not praise,
> A stern and silent pride
> Not that false joy that dreams content
> With what our sires have won
> The blood a hero sire hath spent,
> Still nerves a hero son.

The Scottish National Anthem: 'Flower of Scotland'

Although modern, this anthem commemorates the Battle of Bannockburn in 1314 when the Scottish Army under Robert I (the Bruce) King of Scots defeated Edward II, King of England.

> O Flower of Scotland,
> When will we see Your like again
> That fought and died for,
> Your wee bit Hill and Glen
> And stood against him, Proud Edward's
> Army
> And sent him homeward, Tae think again.
>
> The Hills are bare now, and
> Autumn leaves lie thick and still
> O'er land that is lost now,
> Which those so dearly held
> That stood against him,
> Proud Edward's Army
> And sent him homeward, Tae think again.
>
> Those days are past now,
> And in the past they must remain
> But we can still rise now,
> And be the nation again
> That stood against him, Proud Edward's
> Army
> And sent him homeward, Tae think again.
>
> Flower of Scotland, When will we see
> Your like again
> That fought and died for,
> Your wee bit Hill and Glen
> And stood against him,
> Proud Edward's Army And sent him
> homeward, Tae think again.

Scotland the Brave

Hark where the night is falling
Hark hear the pipes a calling
Loudly and proudly calling down thru the glen
There where the hills are sleeping
Now feel the blood a leaping
High as the spirits of the old highland men

Towering in gallant fame
Scotland my mountain hame
High may your proud standards gloriously wave
Land of my high endeavour
Land of the shining river
Land of my heart forever,
Scotland the Brave

High in the misty mountains
Out by the purple highlands
Brave are the hearts that beat beneath Scottish skies
Wild are the winds to meet you
Staunch are the friends that greet you
Kind as the love that shines from fair maidens eyes.

The Welsh National Anthem: 'Wlad Fy Nhadau/Land of my Fathers'

The words are given in Welsh and English.

Wlad Fy Nhadau

Mae hen wlad fy nhadau yn annwyl i mi
Gwlad beirdd a chantorion, enwogion o fri
Ei gwrol ryfelwyr, gwladgarwyr tra mad
Tros ryddid collasant eu gwaed.

Gwlad, gwlad, pleidiol wyf i'm gwlad
Tra mor yn fur i'r bur hoffbau
O bydded i'r heniaith barhau.

Hen Gymru fynyddig, paradwys y bardd
Pob dyffryn, pob clogwyn i'm golwg sydd hardd
Trwy deimlad gwladgarol, mor swynol yw si
Ei nentydd, afonydd, i mi.

Os treisiodd y gelyn fy ngwlad tan ei droed
Mae hen iaith y Cymry mor fyw ag erioed
Ni luddiwyd yr awen gan erchyll law brad
Na thelyn berseiniol fy ngwlad.

Land of my Fathers

The land of my fathers is dear unto me
Old land where the minstrels are honoured and free
Its warring defenders so gallant and brave
For freedom their life's blood they gave.

Home, home, true am I to home
While seas secure the land so pure
O may the old language endure.

Old land of the mountains, the Eden of bards
Each gorge and each valley a loveliness guards
Through love of my country, charmed voices will be
Its streams, and its rivers, to me.

Though foemen have trampled my land 'neath their feet
The language of Cambria still knows no retreat
The muse is not vanquished by traitor's fell hand.

Constitution and Important Legislation

Constitution of the UK: Introduction

The UK is one of the few countries not to adopt a written constitution; instead it has an accumulation of customs and precedents, together with a body of laws defining certain of its aspects. The most important laws affecting constitutional matters, both current and historic, are described in this section.

Act of Settlement, 1701

A law passed during the reign of King William III to ensure a Protestant succession to the throne by allowing only descendants of Princess Sophia the Electress of Hanover (granddaughter of James I) to succeed. The act excluded the Roman Catholic descendants of James II. Elizabeth II still reigns under this act.

English Bill of Rights Act, 1689

The Bill of Rights embodied the Declaration of Rights (the statement issued by the Convention Parliament which contained the conditions on which William and Mary were offered the throne). The act made illegal the suspension of laws by royal authority without Parliament's consent; the power to dispense with laws; the establishment of special courts of law; levying money by royal prerogative without Parliament's consent; and the maintenance of a standing army in peacetime without Parliament's consent. It also

asserted a right to petition the sovereign, freedom of parliamentary elections, freedom of speech in parliamentary debates, and the necessity of frequent Parliaments.

The Bill of Rights is the nearest approach to a written constitution that the UK possesses. Its provisions, where applicable, were incorporated in the US constitution ratified in 1788.

Habeas Corpus, 1679

Writ directed to someone who has custody of a person, ordering them to bring the person before the court issuing the writ, and to justify why the person is detained in custody. Embodied in the English Habeas Corpus Act 1679 by Anthony Ashley Cooper, 1st Earl of Shaftesbury. The main principles were adopted in the US Constitution. The Scottish equivalent is the Wrongous Imprisonment Act, 1701.

Magna Carta, 1215

Essentially a historic document of feudal times, this charter was granted by King John at Runnymede on 15 June 1215. It was originally proposed to the English barons in 1213 by the Archbishop of Canterbury, Stephen Langton, as a reply to the King's demands for excessive feudal dues and attacks on the privileges of the church. The charter defined the barons' obligations to the monarch, confirmed the liberties of the English church, and opposed the arbitrary application of justice. The charter was reissued with changes

in 1216, 1217, and 1225. As feudalism declined, the Magna Carta lost its significance, and under the Tudors was almost forgotten. During the 17th century it was rediscovered and reinterpreted by the Parliamentary party as a democratic document. Four original copies exist: one each in Salisbury and Lincoln cathedrals and two in the British Library in London.

Parliament Acts

The Parliament Act of 1911 A statute which prohibited the House of Lords from interfering with financial legislation passed by the House of Commons and abolished the power of the Lords to reject other types of legislation passed by the Commons, restricting them to delaying it for up to two years. The law also reduced the maximum life of a parliament from seven years to five. The act was introduced after the Lords rejected Lloyd George's radical People's Budget of 1909. It was fiercely resisted by the Lords and only received their assent when George V agreed to create sufficient Liberal peers to force it through.

The Parliament Act of 1949 This act further limited the period the Lords could delay legislation to one year.

Petition of Right, 1628

In British law, the procedure whereby, before the passing of the Crown Proceedings Act,

1947, a subject petitioned for legal relief against the crown, for example for money due under a contract, or for property of which the crown had taken possession. The most important example is that drawn up by Edward Coke (former Lord Chief Justice of England) and accepted by Charles I in 1628, declaring illegal: taxation without parliamentary consent, imprisonment without trial, billeting of soldiers on private persons, and use of martial law. When parliament challenged Charles over military funding in 1629 he dissolved parliament, imprisoned its leaders, and ruled without parliament until his execution in 1640.

Reform Acts

UK acts of Parliament that extended voting rights and redistributed parliamentary seats, also known as Representation of the People Acts.

1832 Reform Act abolished pocket and rotten boroughs (English parliamentary constituencies that returned members to Parliament in spite of having a small numbers of electors, thus leading to an unrepresentative House), redistributed seats on a more equitable basis in the counties, and formed some new boroughs. The franchise was extended to male householders in property worth £10 a year or more in the boroughs and to owners of freehold property worth £2 a year, £10 copyholders, or £50 leaseholders in the counties.

1867 (Second) Reform Act redistributed seats from corrupt and small boroughs to the counties and large urban areas. It also extended the franchise in boroughs to adult male heads of households, and in counties to males who owned, or held on long leases, land worth £5 a year, or who occupied land worth £12 on which they paid poor rates.

1884 (Third) Reform Act extended the franchise to male agricultural labourers

1918 Representation of The People Act gave the vote to men over the age of 21 and women over the age of 30; **1928 Representation of The People Act** extended the vote to women to over the age of 21; **1948 Representation of The People Act** abolished the right, held by certain individuals, to have more than one vote; **1969 Representation of The People Act** reduced the minimum age of voting to 18.

Triennial and Septennial Acts

Acts affecting the length of Parliament and the frequency of its meetings.

1641 Triennial Act required that Parliament should meet every three years, for at least 50 days; **1664 Triennial Act** reinstated the act of 1641 which had fallen into abeyance; **1694 Triennial Act** stipulated that Parliament should meet at least once every three years and not last more than three years; **1716 Septennial Act** extended the term of a Parliament from three to seven years.

Acts of Union

Several statutes that accomplished the joining of England with Wales (1536), England and Wales with Scotland (1707), and Great Britain with Ireland (1800).

Act of Union of 1536

The Act of Union passed in 1536, during the reign of King Henry VIII, the second English monarch descended from the Welsh House of Tudor. The Act formally united England and Wales. By its terms, the Welsh Marches, estates held for centuries by semi-independent Marcher lords, became several new counties or were added to older counties. Counties and boroughs in Wales were granted representation in the English Parliament.

Act of Union of 1707

The Act of Union passed in 1707 by the parliaments of England and Scotland created the Kingdom of Great Britain. Although Scotland retained its judicial system and its Presbyterian church, its parliament was joined with that of England. The crowns of the two countries had been united in 1603 when James Stuart (James VI of Scotland) succeeded Elizabeth I as James I of England, but the kingdoms otherwise remained separate.

Act of Union of 1800

The Act of Union, which was passed in 1800 and went into effect on January 1, 1801, joined the Kingdom of Great Britain and all of Ireland into the United Kingdom of Great Britain and Ireland. The act was revoked when the Irish Free State was constituted in 1922.

National Government

Prime Ministers of Great Britain and the UK

Term	Name	Party	Term	Name	Party
1721–42	Robert Walpole[1]	Whig	1852–55	George Hamilton-Gordon, 4th Earl of Aberdeen	Peelite
1742–43	Spencer Compton, Earl of Wilmington	Whig	1855–58	Henry John Temple, 3rd Viscount Palmerston	Liberal
1743–54	Henry Pelham	Whig			
1754–56	Thomas Pelham-Holles, 1st Duke of Newcastle	Whig	1858–59	Edward Geoffrey Stanley, 14th Earl of Derby	Conservative
1756–57	William Cavendish, 4th Duke of Devonshire	Whig	1859–65	Henry John Temple, 3rd Viscount Palmerston	Liberal
1757–62	Thomas Pelham-Holles, 1st Duke of Newcastle	Whig	1865–66	John Russell, 1st Earl Russell	Liberal
1762–63	John Stuart, 3rd Earl of Bute	Tory	1866–68	Edward Geoffrey Stanley, 14th Earl of Derby	Conservative
1763–65	George Grenville	Whig			
1765–66	Charles Watson Wentworth, 2nd Marquess of Rockingham	Whig	1868	Benjamin Disraeli	Conservative
1766–68	William Pitt, 1st Earl of Chatham	Tory	1868–74	William Ewart Gladstone	Liberal
1768–70	Augustus Henry Fitzroy, 3rd Duke of Grafton	Whig	1874–80	Benjamin Disraeli[4]	Conservative
			1880–85	William Ewart Gladstone	Liberal
1770–82	Frederick North, Lord North[2]	Tory	1885–86	Robert Cecil, 3rd Marquess of Salisbury	Conservative
1782	Charles Watson Wentworth, 2nd Marquess of Rockingham	Whig	1886	William Ewart Gladstone	Liberal
			1886–92	Robert Cecil, 3rd Marquess of Salisbury	Conservative
1782–83	William Petty-Fitzmaurice, 2nd Earl of Shelburne[3]	Whig	1892–94	William Ewart Gladstone	Liberal
1783	William Henry Cavendish-Bentinck, 3rd Duke of Portland	Whig	1894–95	Archibald Philip Primrose, 5th Earl of Rosebery	Liberal
1783–1801	William Pitt, The Younger	Tory	1895–1902	Robert Cecil, 3rd Marquess of Salisbury	Conservative
1801–04	Henry Addington	Tory	1902–05	Arthur James Balfour	Conservative
1804–06	William Pitt, The Younger	Tory	1905–08	Sir Henry Campbell-Bannerman	Liberal
1806–07	William Wyndham Grenville, 1st Baron Grenville	Whig	1908–16	H H Asquith	Liberal
1807–09	William Henry Cavendish-Bentinck, 3rd Duke of Portland	Whig	1916–22	David Lloyd George	Liberal
			1922–23	Bonar Law	Conservative
1809–12	Spencer Perceval	Tory	1923–24	Stanley Baldwin	Conservative
1812–27	Robert Banks Jenkinson, 2nd Earl of Liverpool	Tory	1924	Ramsay Macdonald	Labour
			1924–29	Stanley Baldwin	Conservative
1827	George Canning	Tory	1929–35	Ramsay Macdonald	Labour
1827–28	Frederick John Robinson, 1st Viscount Goderich	Tory	1935–37	Stanley Baldwin	Conservative
1828–30	Arthur Wellesley, 1st Duke of Wellington	Tory	1937–40	Neville Chamberlain	Conservative
1830–34	Charles Grey, 2nd Earl Grey	Whig	1940–45	Winston Churchill	Conservative
1834	William Lamb, 2nd Viscount Melbourne	Whig	1945–51	Clement Attlee	Labour
1834	Arthur Wellesley, 1st Duke of Wellington	Tory	1951–55	Winston Churchill[5]	Conservative
1834–35	Sir Robert Peel, 2nd Baronet	Tory	1955–57	Sir Anthony Eden	Conservative
1835–41	William Lamb, 2nd Viscount Melbourne	Whig	1957–63	Harold Macmillan	Conservative
1841–46	Sir Robert Peel, 2nd Baronet	Conservative	1963–64	Sir Alec Douglas-Home	Conservative
1846–52	John Russell, Lord Russell	Whig-Liberal	1964–70	Harold Wilson	Labour
1852	Edward Geoffrey Stanley, 14th Earl of Derby	Conservative	1970–74	Edward Heath	Conservative
			1974–76	Harold Wilson	Labour
			1976–79	James Callaghan	Labour
			1979–90	Margaret Thatcher	Conservative
			1990–97	John Major	Conservative
			1997–	Tony Blair	Labour

[1] From 1725, Sir Robert Walpole.
[2] From 1790, 2nd Earl of Guilford.
[3] From 1784, 1st Marquess of Lansdowne.
[4] From 1876, Earl of Beaconsfield.
[5] From 1953, Sir Winston Churchill.

Robert Peel *was the founder of the modern Conservative Party. He later split the party over the Corn Laws.* Philip Sauvain Picture Collection

UK Chancellors of the Exchequer

Date appointed	Name
July 1945	Hugh Dalton
November 1947	Sir Stafford Cripps
October 1950	Hugh Gaitskell
October 1951	'Rab' Butler
December 1955	Harold Macmillan
January 1957	Peter Thorneycroft
January 1958	Derick Heathcoat Amory
July 1960	Selwyn Lloyd
July 1962	Reginald Maudling
October 1964	James Callaghan
November 1967	Roy Jenkins
June 1970	Iain Macleod
July 1970	Anthony Barber
March 1974	Denis Healey
May 1979	Sir Geoffrey Howe
June 1983	Nigel Lawson
October 1989	John Major
November 1990	Norman Lamont
May 1993	Kenneth Clarke
May 1997	Gordon Brown

UK Leaders of the House of Commons

Date appointed	Name
July 1945	Herbert Morrison
March 1951	Chuter Ede
October 1951	Harry Crookshank
April 1955	'Rab' Butler
October 1961	Iain Macleod
October 1963	Selwyn Lloyd
October 1964	Herbert Bowden
August 1966	Richard Crossman
April 1968	Fred Peart
June 1970	William Whitelaw
April 1972	Robert Carr
November 1972	James Prior
March 1974	Edward Short
April 1976	Michael Foot
May 1979	Norman St John Stevas
January 1981	Francis Pym
April 1982	John Biffen
June 1987	John Wakeham
July 1989	Sir Geoffrey Howe
November 1990	John MacGregor
April 1992	Tony Newton
May 1997	Ann Taylor

UK Secretaries of State for Foreign and Commonwealth Affairs

Known as Secretary of State for Foreign Affairs before 1968.

Date appointed	Name
July 1945	Ernest Bevin
March 1951	Herbert Morrison
October 1951	Sir Anthony Eden
December 1955	Selwyn Lloyd
July 1960	Earl of Home
October 1963	'Rab' Butler
October 1964	Patrick Gordon-Walker
January 1965	Michael Stewart
August 1966	George Brown
March 1968	Michael Stewart
June 1970	Sir Alec Douglas-Home
March 1974	James Callaghan
April 1976	Anthony Crosland
Feb 1977	David Owen
May 1979	Lord Carrington
April 1982	Francis Pym
June 1983	Sir Geoffrey Howe
June 1989	John Major
October 1989	Douglas Hurd
July 1995	Malcolm Rifkind
May 1997	Robin Cook

UK Secretaries of State for Defence

Known as Minister of Defence before 1964.

Date appointed	Name
July 1945	Clement Attlee
December 1946	Alan Alexander
Feb 1950	Emanuel Shinwell
October 1951	Sir Winston Churchill
March 1952	Earl Alexander of Tunis
October 1954	Harold Macmillan
April 1955	Selwyn Lloyd
December 1955	Sir Walter Monckton
October 1956	Anthony Head
January 1957	Duncan Sandys
October 1959	Harold Watkinson
July 1962	Peter Thorneycroft
October 1964	Denis Healey
June 1970	Lord Carrington
January 1974	Ian Gilmour
March 1974	Roy Mason
September 1976	Fred Mulley
May 1979	Francis Pym
January 1981	John Nott
January 1983	Michael Heseltine
January 1986	George Younger
July 1989	Tom King
April 1992	Malcolm Rifkind
July 1995	Michael Portillo
May 1997	George Robertson

Robin Cook Sean Aidan

UK POLITICAL REVIEW

BY I D AND J D DERBYSHIRE

Since the September 1992 withdrawal of sterling from the European Exchange Rate Mechanism (ERM), John Major's Conservative government had consistently trailed far behind the opposition Labour Party in national opinion polls. Despite strong growth in the economy from the mid-1990s, Conservative Party splits over policy concerning Europe and allegations of 'sleaze' further reduced the poll ratings, while, from January 1997, following a string of by-election defeats, the Conservatives lost their overall parliamentary majority. Prime Minister Major delayed calling a new election until the last possible moment, announcing, on 17 March 1997, that Parliament would be dissolved on 8 April and a general election held on 1 May.

With 44% of the vote, Labour returned to power with its greatest ever number of seats, 419 – of which 101 were won by women – and achieved a parliamentary majority of 179, a 20th-century record. The 10% swing from Conservative to Labour was remarkable. The Liberal Democrats, with 17% of the vote, also performed well, increasing their House of Commons representation from 16 to 46 seats: their best result since 1929. The Scottish Nationalist Party (SNP) also made advances. However, the Conservatives, accruing 31% of the vote, their lowest share since 1832, saw their representation slumping to just 165 seats. Support fell particularly sharply in southern England and among women and middle-class voters. The Referendum Party, which promoted an anti-European Union platform, also polled poorly, its candidates attracting, on average, only 3% of the vote. During the early hours of 2 May, John Major conceded defeat, with great dignity. He also announced his resignation as Conservative Party leader, reflecting: 'When the curtain comes down it is time to leave the stage.'

Labour in Power: The First 100 Days

Tony Blair, at 43 the century's youngest prime minister, made the presence of New Labour swiftly felt. His first cabinet of 22 members, which included five women, contained few real surprises. Its three key members were: Gordon Brown, the new Chancellor; Robin Cook, the Foreign Secretary; and John Prescott, the Deputy Prime Minister, with overarching responsibility for the environment, transport, and the regions. Blair also brought in, as Lord Chancellor, his old mentor and employer, Derry Irvine, now Lord Irvine of Lairg. This meant that, with north-of-the border politicians, including the Edinburgh-born Blair, occupying the four senior offices, it was the most Scottish government in British history. Meanwhile, Peter Mandelson became a minister without portfolio, with a brief 'to assist in the strategic implementation of government policies and their effective presentation to the public'.

There was immediate evidence of a changing style in the conduct of government work, involving a mix of greater outward informality with tighter central control. The party spin doctors carefully managed government information and projected Blair in a presidential manner. Key early initiatives included the announcements that: Britain would sign the European Social Chapter; pursue a 'more ethical' foreign policy; give the Bank of England sole responsibility for setting interest rates; and, in the National Health Service, transfer £100 million from red tape and bureaucracy to patient care and treatment. The Queen's Speech, unveiled on day 13, listed 26 bills, including measures to raise school standards and to use funds freed by phasing out the 'assisted places scheme' to reduce class sizes; Scottish and Welsh devolution; the introduction of a minimum wage; a crackdown on juvenile crime; provision for an elected mayor of London; and incorporation into UK law of the main elements of the European Convention on Human Rights.

On 2 July 1997, in a special budget, Chancellor Brown introduced a £5 billion windfall-profits tax on privatized utilities to generate funds for a £3.5 billion 'welfare to work' programme, under which firms would be given subsidies for hiring the young unemployed; a cut in the rate of value added tax (VAT) on domestic fuel; and the imposition of new tax burdens on pension funds. Brown described it as a 'people's budget for Britain's future'. However, most significant was its adherence to Labour's manifesto pledge to keep to the Conservative's expenditure limits during its first two years in office and not to raise personal taxes. Brown consequently became dubbed the 'Iron Chancellor' and experienced frictions with spending ministers, as hospital waiting lists rose by 100,000 by February 1998, and with 'Old' Labour backbenchers.

Progress on the Constitutional Front

In August 1997, at the end of its 'first 100 days', the government showed little sign of running out of steam and pressed on with further initiatives. In September devolution referenda were successfully held in Scotland and Wales. In Scotland, 74% of voters approved the creation in the year 2000 of a Scottish assembly, and 63% also supported giving it tax-varying powers. In Wales, where there had been a 4:1 vote against devolution in 1979, the margin in favour was much closer. Only 50.3% voted in favour of an assembly: the turnout recorded as 51%. A further referendum, on creating a directly elected London mayor, was promised for May 1998.

Northern Ireland: Peace at Last?

In October 1997 multiparty talks on Northern Ireland's future commenced. The participants included the republican Sinn Féin, which had been admitted following the announcement of the Irish Republican Army (IRA) of a second cease-fire in July 1997 and whose leader, Gerry Adams, had had a face-to-face meeting with Tony Blair. This angered more militant loyalists and the Reverend Ian Paisley's Democratic Unionists boycotted the talks. However, to keep the peace process on track, the Northern Ireland Secretary, Marjorie Mowlam, entered the Maze prison in January 1998 for discussions with loyalist inmates. Following a number of shootings in Belfast in which a breakaway faction of the IRA was implicated, Sinn Féin was temporarily suspended

(continued)

(continued)

from the talks; however, it subsequently returned. Weeks of negotiations, brokered by the former US senator George Mitchell, culminated on Good Friday, 10 April 1998, with the unveiling of an agreement designed to bring an end to 30 years of 'Troubles' which had claimed more than 3,600 lives.

The deal involved the creation of: an elected 108-member Northern Ireland assembly, in which decisions would require the support of a majority of deputies from both the Protestant and Catholic communities; a 12-member executive committee; a North–South ministerial council, responsible to the assembly and the Irish parliament; a British–Irish Council, representing the parliaments at Westminister and Dublin, and the new Scottish and Welsh assemblies; and the staged release of paramilitary prisoners. Additionally, the Irish government committed itself to rescind its constitutional claim to the territory of Northern Ireland and the British government agreed to redraw the Government of Ireland Act, so as to incorporate the principle of consent by the population of Northern Ireland about its future. The agreement was to be put to the Northern Ireland electorate in a referendum on 22 May 1998.

The Conservatives under New Leadership

John Major's resignation had forced the Conservatives, demoralized and humbled by their crushing electoral defeat, to hold a snap leadership contest in June 1997. Five candidates contested, but only one, the former chancellor Kenneth Clarke, was a figure with a high national profile. Defeat at the election had robbed the party of its right-wing standard bearer, Michael Portillo, while heart problems had persuaded the popular Michael Heseltine not to stand for the leadership.

Voting was confined to Conservative Members of Parliament and while Clarke, a centre-left pro-European, finished top in the first ballot, on 10 June he attracted only a third of the vote. In second position was William Hague, the representative of the party's centre-right, while the remaining votes were split between three candidates from the party's right wing: John Redwood, with 27 votes; Peter Lilley, 24 votes; and Michael Howard, 23 votes. In the third and final run-off ballot, held a week later, Hague defeated Clarke and, at the age of 36, became the party's youngest leader since the 24-year-old Pitt the Younger in 1783.

Applying the lessons learned from Labour's years in opposition, Hague's initial focus has been on reforming the party's organization, with the aim of reversing the recent sharp fall in membership, establishing greater central control, and giving the rank-and-file a say in the election of future leaders. Aware also of how John Major's standing had been damaged by policy 'fudging' on European Monetary Union (EMU), Hague also sought to draw a clear 'line in the sand' by ruling out UK membership of EMU within the next 10 years. This satisfied the party's Eurosceptic majority, but meant that the centre-left was effectively excluded from the shadow cabinet.

An End-of-First-Year Report

In November 1997 the first charges of sleaze were laid against New Labour when, following the announcement that Formula One motor racing would be exempted from the government's ban on tobacco advertising, the press revealed that the Formula One head, Bernie Ecclestone, had donated £1 million to Labour before the election. In the wake of the resulting outcry, the party agreed to repay this donation. In the following month the government endured its first serious backbench revolt, when 47 Old Labour Members of Parliament voted against its decision to cut benefits paid to lone parents. Fourteen abstained and one junior minister resigned.

Although, by adhering to Conservative Party public spending limits, the government had disillusioned some of its traditional supporters, as it approached the close of its first year in office, it had retained the support of a remarkable number of its newer converts. In a March 1998 opinion poll, Labour registered a national support rating of 52%, 25 points ahead of the Conservatives, and a record for a governing party at this stage of a parliament. Prime Minister Blair's personal rating, at 60%, was even higher.

The public supported the government's pragmatic building on the achievements of its predecessor, in areas such as Northern Ireland and on its financial management. However, the New Labour government's longer-term agenda was more ambitious. Its aim was to create a modernized, more secure, and better educated New Britain.

The constitutional reforms introduced during 1997–98 were key elements. Further measures, covering freedom of information and reform of the House of Lords, are planned for 1998–99. Electoral reform is also on the agenda. Proportional representation (PR) will form the basis for the Scottish and Welsh assemblies, to be elected in May 1999, and for the June 1999 European Parliament elections, while a small commission, established in December 1997 under the chairmanship of the Liberal Democrat peer Lord Jenkins, is to recommend, in October 1998, an appropriate form of PR for Westminster elections. New Labour's modernization programme extends even to a rebranding of British identity, as 'Cool Britannia'.

However, the most difficult changes are still to come: in the area of welfare reform. Influenced by the thinking of New Democrats in the United States, Prime Minister Blair has the vision of establishing a 'third way' in which the state has an enabling role, intermediate between socialist interventionism and free-market *laissez-faire*, to equip its citizens for a changing world. Central to this is a recasting of the welfare state away from the inherited Beveridge model, with its 'welfare dependency' and 'social exclusion', to one which, through a mixture of incentives and penalties, encourages work and self-support. Examples of this 'New Deal' approach were the 'welfare to work' and working families tax credit initiatives in Chancellor Brown's first two budgets. The broader blueprint was unveiled in the March 1998 green paper, 'A New Contract for Welfare'. This will be the field of key parliamentary battles ahead.

UK Secretaries of State for Home Affairs

Date appointed	Name	Date appointed	Name
August 1945	Chuter Ede	March 1974	Roy Jenkins
October 1951	Sir David Maxwell Fyfe	September 1976	Merlyn Rees
October 1954	Gwilym Lloyd-George	May 1979	William Whitelaw
January 1957	'Rab' Butler	June 1983	Leon Brittan
July 1962	Henry Brooke	September 1985	Douglas Hurd
October 1964	Sir Frank Soskice	October 1989	David Waddington
December 1965	Roy Jenkins	November 1990	Kenneth Baker
November 1967	James Callaghan	April 1992	Kenneth Clarke
June 1970	Reginald Maudling	May 1993	Michael Howard
July 1972	Robert Carr	May 1997	Jack Straw

The Northern Ireland Peace Process since 1993: Chronology

15 December 1993
The prime ministers of the UK and the Republic of Ireland, John Major and Albert Reynolds, make the 'Downing Street Declaration', stating the basis for talks on peace in Northern Ireland; constitutional change will require the majority agreement of the population of Northern Ireland and the Republic of Ireland.

31 January 1994
Gerry Adams, the president of the Irish republican party Sinn Féin, is granted a visa to visit the USA.

31 August 1994
The Irish Republican Army (IRA) in Northern Ireland announces its complete cessation of violence (the British government lifts it broadcasting ban on representatives of Sinn Féin on 16 September).

22 February 1995
At a press conference in Belfast, the prime ministers of the Republic of Ireland and the UK, John Bruton and John Major, present a framework document for all-party peace negotiations over the future of Northern Ireland.

16 March 1995
The US President Bill Clinton meets Gerry Adams at the White House, Washington, DC, and permits him to raise funds in the USA.

10 May 1995
The British government minister Michael Ancram meets representatives of Sinn Féin, led by Martin McGuiness, in Belfast, the first meeting of a government minister and Sinn Féin since 1973.

24 May 1995
Patrick Mayhew, secretary of state for Northern Ireland, meets Gerry Adams in Washington, DC.

28 November 1995
On the eve of President Bill Clinton's visit to the British Isles, the prime ministers of the UK and the Republic of Ireland, John Major and John Bruton, announce the establishment of a three-person commission to examine the decommissioning of terrorist arms and the aim of holding all-party talks on Northern Ireland by the end of February 1996.

30 November 1995– 1 December 1995
President Clinton visits Northern Ireland and Dublin.

9 February 1996
The bombing of South Quay, Canary Wharf, London, breaks the IRA's 17-month cease-fire.

10 June 1996
All-party talks on the future of Northern Ireland begin at Stormont Castle, Belfast; Sinn Féin is not admitted because of the IRA's cease-fire violations.

7–13 July 1996
The Royal Ulster Constabulary (RUC) bans a controversial Loyalist apprentice boys' march in Londonderry; the decision is reversed on 11 July and the march takes place; violence continues until 13 July.

21 December 1996
Loyalist terrorists in Northern Ireland break their cease-fire, in force since August 1994, with a car-bomb attack in Belfast.

5 April 1997
The Grand National at Aintree is postponed less than an hour before it is due to start after a coded IRA bomb warning is received. Two days later Lord Gyllene, ridden by Northern Ireland's Tony Dobbin, wins the rescheduled race.

6 July 1997
Violence flares at an Orange Order march in Drumcree; the Order subsequently agrees (11 July) to cancel or re-route marches in Londonderry, Belfast, Newry, and Armagh.

20 July 1997
The IRA restores its cease-fire (broken on 9 February 1996) in order to participate in talks on the future of Northern Ireland.

29 August 1997
Britain's Northern Ireland Secretary Mo Mowlam invites Sinn Féin to all-party talks.

13 October 1997
Tony Blair meets Gerry Adams at Stormont Castle, Belfast, the first meeting between a British prime minister and a Sinn Féin leader since 1921.

27 December 1997
Billy Wright, a leading member of the Loyalist Volunteer Force (LVF), is shot and killed by two members of the Irish Liberation Army (INLA) at the Maze Prison, near Belfast. The incident escalates concerns for the future of the Northern Ireland peace process.

10 April 1998
Ireland, Britain, and the political parties in Northern Ireland reach a historic peace agreement over Northern Ireland (known as the Good Friday Agreement) involving the devolution of a wide range of executive and legislative powers to a Northern Ireland Assembly.

13 July 1998
Orangemen throughout Northern Ireland march to celebrate the 308th anniversary of the Battle of the Boyne – despite pressure to abandon the march following the deaths of three Catholic brothers in an arson attack.

UK Government Agencies

Agency	Address	Key responsibilities
ECGD (Export Credits Guarantee Department)	PO Box 2200, 2 Exchange Tower, Harbour Exchange Square, London E14 9GS; phone: (0171) 512 7000	supporting the export of capital and project-related goods and services from the UK; provides insurance to British project and capital goods exporters against not being paid for goods and services; insures new British investment overseas
Her Majesty's Customs and Excise	New King's Beam House, 22 Upper Ground, London SE1 9PJ; phone: (0171) 620 1313	collecting and accounting for Customs and Excise revenues; controlling imports and exports, compiling trade statistics; policing prohibited goods
Her Majesty's Procurator General and Treasury Solicitor	Queen Anne's Chambers, 28 Broadway, London SW1H 9JS; phone: (0171) 210 3000	providing legal services to many government departments, agencies, and public bodies, including litigation, general legal advice, and instructing Parliamentary Counsel on drafting legislation
Her Majesty's Stationery Office	St Clements House, 2–16 Colegate, Norwich NR3 1BQ; phone: (01603) 621000	body within the Office of Public Service with responsibilities for printing legislation and government publications; controls and administers Crown copyright and administers parliamentary copyright
Inland Revenue	Somerset House, London WC2R 1LB; phone: (0171) 438 6622	collection and administration of direct taxes in Britain
Legal Secretariat to the Law Officers	Attorney General's Chambers, 9 Buckingham Gate, London SW1E 6JP; phone: (0171) 828 7155	supports Law Officers of the Crown in their activities as the Government's main legal advisers
Lord Chancellor's Office	Selborne House, 54–60 Victoria Street, London SW1E 6QW; phone: (0171) 210 8500	administers, through the Court Service, the Supreme Court, county and crown courts; responsible for civil and criminal legal aid, the Law Commission
Office for National Statistics	Great George Street, London SW1P 3AQ; phone: (0171) 270 3000	agency created by merger of the Central Statistical Office and the Office of Population, Censuses and Surveys; responsibilities include collection and interpretation of key national economic and population statistics; administration of marriage laws; local registration of births, deaths, and marriages
Office of the Data Protection Registrar	Wycliffe House, Water Lane, Wilmslow, Cheshire SK9 5AF; phone: (01625) 545745	reporting directly to Parliament, maintains public register of data users and computer bureaux, enforces data protection legislation and investigates complaints about breaches of the Data Protection Act
Office of the Paymaster General	Sutherland House, Russell Way, Crawley, West Sussex RH10 1UH; phone: (01293) 560999	provides banking services for government departments and administers and pays public service pensions
Ordnance Survey	Romsey Road, Southampton SO16 4GU; phone: (01703) 792000	reporting to the Secretary of State for the Environment, provides official surveying, mapping, and related scientific work in Britain and some foreign countries
Parliamentary Counsel	36 Whitehall, London SW1A 2AY; phone: (0171) 210 6633	responsible for the drafting of government Bills (except those that relate only to Scotland) and advising department on parliamentary procedure in England, Wales, and Northern Ireland
Royal Mint	Llantrisant, Pontyclun, Mid Glamorgan CF72 8YT; phone: (01443) 222111	produces and issues coinage for Britain, including circulation coins and commemorative coins and medals

UK Cabinet Ministers

Cabinet ministers	Position
Beckett; The Right Honourable Margaret Beckett MP	Leader of the House of Commons
Blair; The Right Honourable Tony Blair MP	Prime Minister, First Lord of the Treasury and Minister for the Civil Service
Blunkett; The Right Honourable David Blunkett MP	Secretary of State for Education and Employment
Brown; The Right Honourable Gordon Brown MP	Chancellor of the Exchequer
Brown; The Right Honourable Nick Brown MP	Secretary of State for Agriculture, Fisheries, and Food
Byers; The Right Honourable Stephen Byers MP	Chief Secretary to the Treasury
Cook; The Right Honourable Robin Cook MP	Secretary of State for Foreign and Commonwealth Affairs
Cunningham; The Right Honourable Dr Jack Cunningham MP	Minister for the Cabinet Office and Chancellor of the Duchy of Lancaster
Darling; The Right Honourable Alistair Darling MP	Secretary of State for Social Security
Davies; The Right Honourable Ron Davies MP	Secretary of State for Wales
Dewar; The Right Honourable Donald Dewar MP	Secretary of State for Scotland
Dobson; The Right Honourable Frank Dobson MP	Secretary of State for Health
Irvine; The Right Honourable The Lord Irvine of Lairg QC	Lord Chancellor
Jay: The Right Honourable The Baroness Jay	Leader of the House of Lords and Minister for Women
Mandelson: The Right Honourable Peter Mandelson MP	Secretary of State for Trade and Industry
Mowlam: The Right Honourable Dr Marjorie Mowlam MP	Secretary of State for Northern Ireland
Prescott; The Right Honourable John Prescott MP	Deputy Prime Minister and Secretary of State for the Environment, Transport, and the Regions

UK Cabinet Ministers (*continued*)

Cabinet ministers	Position
Reid: The Right Honourable John Reid MP	Minister for Transport
Robertson; The Right Honourable George Robertson MP	Secretary of State for Defence
Short; The Right Honourable Clare Short MP	Secretary of State for International Development
Smith; The Right Honourable Chris Smith MP	Secretary of State for Culture, Media, and Sport
Straw; The Right Honourable Jack Straw MP	Secretary of State for the Home Department
Taylor; The Right Honourable Ann Taylor MP	Chief Whip

The Shadow Cabinet

(As of 3 June 1998).

Position	Name
Leader of the Opposition	William Hague
Shadow Minister for Agriculture, Fisheries, and Food	Michael Jack
Spokesman on Constitutional Affairs	Liam Fox
Shadow Minister for Defence	John Maples
Shadow Minister for Education and Employment	David Willetts
Shadow Minister for the Environment, Transport, and the Regions	Gillian Shephard
Shadow Minister for Foreign and Commonwealth Affairs	Michael Howard
Shadow Minister for Health	Ann Widdecombe
Shadow Minister for Home Affairs	Sir Norman Fowler
Shadow Leader of the House of Commons	Sir George Young
Shadow Leader of the House of Lords	Viscount Cranborne
Shadow Minister for Culture, Media, and Sport	Peter Ainsworth
Shadow Minister for Northern Ireland	Andrew Mackay
Shadow Minister for Social Security	Iain Duncan-Smith
Shadow Minister for Trade and Industry	John Redwood
Shadow Chancellor	Francis Maude
Opposition Chief Whip	James Arbuthnot
Opposition Chief Whip (House of Lords)	Lord Strathclyde
Party Chairman	Lord Parkinson
Shadow Chief Secretary to the Treasury	David Heathcoat-Amory
Deputy Party Chairman	Peter Lilley
Shadow Minister for International Development	Gary Streeter

UK Government Departments

(– = not applicable.)

Department	Address	Responsibilities	Title	Ministers	Executive agencies
Agriculture, Fisheries, and Food (Ministry of)	3–8 Whitehall Place, London SW1A 2HH; phone: (0171) 270 3000	agriculture, horticulture, fisheries, and food; related environmental and rural issues	Minister	Nick Brown	ADAS (Food, Farming, Land, and Leisure); Central Science Laboratory; Intervention Board; Meat Hygiene Service; Pesticides Safety Directorate; Laboratories Agency; Veterinary Medicines Directorate
			Minister of State for Food Safety and Animal Health	Jeff Rooker	
			Minister for Fisheries and Countryside	Elliot Morley	
			Minister for Farming and Food Industry	Lord Donoughue	
Cabinet Office (Office of Public Service)	70 Whitehall, London SW1A 2AS; phone: (0171) 270 1234	key policy areas and issues include: Citizen's Charter; freedom of information; improving the effectiveness and efficiency of Central Government; machinery of Government and Standards; Her Majesty's Stationery Office; historical government records and official histories; public bodies and public appointments; quangos; MPs' and MEPs' pay; management of the Civil Service; Central Office of Information	Minister for the Cabinet Office and Chancellor of the Duchy of Lancaster	Jack Cunningham	The Buying Agency; Central Computer and Telecommunications Agency; Chessington Computer Centre; Civil Service College; Occupational Health and Safety Agency; Property Advisers to the Civil Estate; Security Facilities Executive; Central Office of Information
			Chancellor of the Duchy of Lancaster	David Clark	
			Under Secretary of State, Office of Public Service	Peter Kilfoyle	
Culture, Media, and Sport	2–4 Cockspur Street, London SW1Y 5DH; phone: (0171) 211 6000	the arts; public libraries; national museums; tourism; sport; film industry; press regulation; the National Lottery	Secretary of State	Chris Smith	Historic Royal Palaces Agency; Royal Parks Agency
			Minister of State for Film and Tourism	Tom Clarke	
			Minister for Sport	Tony Banks	
			Minister for the Arts	Mark Fisher	
Defence	Main Building, Whitehall, London SW1A 2HB; phone: (0171) 218 9000	defence policy; control and administration of the armed services	Secretary of State	George Robertson	Army Base Repair Organization; Army Base Storage and Distribution Agency; Army Individual Training Organization; Army Technical Support Agency; Defence Analytical Services Agency; Defence Animal Centre; Defence Bills Agency; Defence Clothing and Textiles Agency; Defence Dental Agency; Defence Evaluation and Research Agency; Defence Postal and Courier Services Agency; Defence Transport and Movements Executive; Disposal Sales Agency; Duke of York's Royal Military School; Hydrographic Office; Joint Air Reconnaissance Intelligence Centre Agency; Logistic Information Systems Agency; Medical Supplies Agency; Meteorological Office; Military Survey; Ministry of Defence Police; Naval Aircraft Repair Organization; Naval Recruiting and Training Agency; Pay and Personnel Agency; Queen Victoria School; RAF Maintenance Group; RAF Signals Engineering Establishment; RAF Training Group; Service Children's Education
			Minister for Defence Procurement	Lord Gilbert	
			Minister for Armed Forces	Doug Henderson	
			Under Secretary of State	John Spellar	

UK Government Departments (*continued*)

Department	Address	Responsibilities	Title	Ministers	Executive agencies
Education and Employment	Sanctuary Buildings, Great Smith Street, London SW1P 3BT; phone: (0171) 925 5000	school, college, and university education; the Careers Service, Employment Service; youth and adult training policy and programmes; equal opportunities in employment, social policy, and programmes in Europe	Secretary of State	David Blunkett	Employment Service; Teacher's Pensions Agency
			Minister for Employment and Disability Rights	Andrew Smith	
			Minister for School Standards	Stephen Byers	
			Minister for Higher Education	Baroness Blackstone	
			Minister for Schools Standards	Estelle Morris	
			Minister for Lifelong Learning	Kim Howells	
			Minister for Employment and Equal Opportunities	Alan Howarth	
Environment	2 Marsham Street, London SW1P 3EB; phone: (0171) 276 0900	land use planning; housing; construction industry; environmental protection; water industry; urban and rural regeneration; countryside and wildlife protection; local government finance and structure	Deputy Prime Minister and Secretary of State for the Environment, Transport, and the Regions	John Prescott	Building Research Establishment; Planning Inspectorate; Queen Elizabeth II Conference Centre
			Minister for the Environment	Michael Meacher	
			Minister for Local Government and Housing	Hilary Armstrong	
			Minister for the Regions, Regeneration, and Planning	Richard Caborn	
			Minister for London and Construction	Nick Raynsford	
			Junior Minister for Environment and Regions	Angela Eagle	
Foreign and Commonwealth Affairs	Downing Street, London SW1A 2AL; phone: (0171) 270 1500	Britain's overseas relations, including relations with overseas governments and international organizations; administration of British Dependent Territories, promoting British trade and exports; protecting British interests, and the welfare of Britons abroad	Secretary of State	Robin Cook	Wilton Park Conference Centre
			Minister for Europe	Doug Henderson	
			Minister for the Far East, South East Asia, Pacific, and Middle East	Derek Fatchett	
			Minister for Latin America and Africa	Tony Lloyd	
			Under Secretary of State for North America and the Caribbean	Baroness Symons of Vernham Dean	
Health	Richmond House, 79 Whitehall, London SW1A 2NS; phone: (0171) 210 3000	National Health Service; local authority social services; public health issues	Secretary of State	Frank Dobson	Medical Devices Agency; Medicines Control Agency; NHS Estates; NHS Pensions Agency
			Minister of State	Alan Milburn	
			Ministers for Public Health	Tessa Jowell and Baroness Jay of Paddington, Deputy Leader of the House of Lords	

(*continued*)

UK Government Departments (*continued*)

Department	Address	Responsibilities	Title	Ministers	Executive agencies
Home Office	50 Queen Anne's Gate, London SW1H 9AT; phone: (0171) 273 3000	criminal law, probation and prison services; the police; crime prevention; licensing laws; passports, immigration, and nationality; race relations; administration of justice	Secretary of State	Jack Straw	Fire Service College; Forensic Science Service; HM Prison Service; UK Passport Agency
			Minister of State for Crime and Police	Alun Michael	
			Minister of State for Prisons and Immigration	Joyce Quin	
			Under Secretaries of State	George Howarth, Mike O'Brien, and Lord Williams of Mostyn	
International Development (formerly the Overseas Development Agency – ODA)	94 Victoria Street, London SW1E 5JL; phone: (0171) 917 7000	Britain's overseas aid to developing countries; global environmental assistance; overseas superannuation	Secretary of State	Clare Short	Natural Resources Institute
			Under Secretary of State	George Foulkes	

Clare Short, Secretary of State for International Development Sean Aidan

Department	Address	Responsibilities	Title	Ministers	Executive agencies
Northern Ireland Office	Stormont Castle, Belfast BT4 3ST; phone: (01232) 520 700; Whitehall, London SW1A 2AZ; phone: (0171) 210 3000	constitutional developments; law and order; security and electoral issues	Secretary of State	Marjorie (Mo) Mowlam	The Compensation Agency; Forensic Science Agency of Northern Ireland; Northern Ireland Prison Service
			Minister of State for Security and Economic Development:	Adam Ingram	
			Minister for Stormont Talks, Finance and Personnel	Paul Murphy	
			Under Secretary of State: Minister for Education, Employment and Health	Tony Worthington	
			Minister for Environment, and Agriculture	Lord Dubs	
Scottish Office	St Andrew's House, Edinburgh EH1 3TG; phone: (0131) 556 8400; Dover House, Whitehall, London SW1A 2AU; phone: (0171) 270 3000	planning and development of Scottish economy; agriculture; law and order; environmental protection and conservation; local government; housing; health; education; legal services	Secretary of State	Donald Dewar	
			Minister for Home Affairs and Devolution	Henry McLeish	
			Minister for Education and Industry	Brian Wilson	
			Minister for Local Government and Transport	Malcolm Chisholm	
			Minister for Health and the Arts	Sam Galbraith	
			Minister for Agriculture, Fisheries, and Food	Lord Sewel	
Social Security	Richmond House, 79 Whitehall, London SW1A 2NS; phone: (0171) 210 3000	the British social security system	Secretary of State for Social Security	Alistair Darling	Benefits Agency; Child Support Agency; Contributions Agency; Information Technology Services Agency; War Pensions Agency
			Minister of State for Welfare Reform	John Denham	
			Under Secretaries of State	Keith Bradley, John Denham, Baroness Hollis of Heigham	

UK Government Departments (*continued*)

Department	Address	Responsibilities	Title	Ministers	Executive agencies
Trade and Industry	1–19 Victoria Street, London SW1H 0ET; phone: (0171) 215 5000	industrial and commercial affairs; innovation policy; regional industrial policy; international trade policy; competition policy; small businesses; business and education; industrial relations; employment legislation	Secretary of State for Trade and Industry	Peter Mandelson	Companies House; Insolvency Service; National Weights and Measures Laboratory; Patent Office; Radiocommunications Agency
			Minister for Trade and Competitiveness in Europe	Lord Simon of Highbury	
			Minister for Trade and Exports	Lord Clinton-Davis	
			Minister for Labour Market, Company Law, and Corporate Affairs	Ian McCartney	
			Minister for Manufacturing and Services, Energy, Science, and Technology	John Battle	
			Minister for Consumer Affairs	Nigel Griffiths	
			Minister for Small Firms	Barbara Roche	
Transport	Great Minster House, 76 Marsham Street, London SW1P 4DR; phone: (0171) 271 5000	land, sea, and air transport; domestic and international civil aviation; shipping and ports; marine pollution; regulation of the road haulage industry; motorways and trunk roads; London Transport; British Rail; Railtrack; Civil Aviation Authority	Minister for Transport	John Reid	Coastguard Agency; Driver and Vehicle Licensing Agency; Driving Standards Agency; Highways Agency; Marine Safety Agency; Transport Research Laboratory; Certification Agency; Vehicle Inspectorate
HM Treasury	Parliament Street, London SW1P 3AG; phone: (0171) 270 3000	overseeing of Britain's tax and monetary policy; planning and control of public spending; international financial relations; Civil Service management	Prime Minister, First Lord of the Treasury and Minister for the Civil Service	Tony Blair	–
			Chancellor of the Exchequer	Gordon Brown	
			Chief Secretary	Alistair Darling	
			Financial Secretary	Dawn Primarolo	
			Paymaster General	Geoffrey Robinson	
			Economic Secretary	Helen Liddell	
Welsh Office	Cathays Park, Cardiff CF1 3NQ; phone: (01222) 825111; Gwydyr House, Whitehall, London SW1A 2ER; phone: (0171) 270 3000	health; social services; education; Welsh language and culture; agriculture and fisheries; forestry; local government; housing; environmental protection; sport; town and country planning; arts; museums and libraries; roads; tourism	Secretary of State	Ron Davies	CADW – Welsh Historic Monuments
			Under Secretaries of State	Peter Hain, Win Griffiths	

Devolution for Scotland and Wales: Chronology

31 October 1973 The Kilbrandon Commission on the British constitution recommends devolved parliaments for Scotland and Wales.

27 November 1975 The British government White Paper, Our Changing Democracy, proposes devolution for Scotland and Wales.

18 January 1976 The British Labour members of Parliament Jim Sillars and John Robertson launch the Scottish Labour Party (SLP) to campaign for greater devolution for Scotland.

30 November 1976 The British government publishes a devolution bill for Scotland and Wales.

22 February 1977 The British government is defeated in a motion to stifle debate on the devolution bill for Scotland and Wales; 22 Labour members of Parliament vote 'no' and 20 others abstain.

25 January 1978 The British government passes an amendment to the Scottish and Welsh devolution bill requiring the approval of 40% of the electorate in a referendum for the devolution to take effect.

31 July 1978 Queen Elizabeth II of Britain gives the royal assent to the devolution bill for Scotland and Wales.

1 March 1979 Referendums are held in Britain on devolution in Scotland and Wales. Devolution is approved in Scotland by 51.6% of the voters, but this falls short of the required 40% of the electorate. Devolution is rejected in Wales by 79.8% of the voters.

11 September 1997 In a referendum, 74.3% of Scottish voters approve the creation of their own parliament, with 63.5% voting in favour of giving it tax-raising powers.

18 September 1997 Welsh voters narrowly approve the establishment of a representative assembly for Wales (50.3% in favour).

The Northern Ireland Assembly

Elections for the new Northern Ireland Assembly took place at the end of June 1998.

The Assembly – held at Castle Buildings, Stormont – is made up of 108 members, six from each of the 18 Westminster constituencies in Northern Ireland. The members were elected by proportional representation, a system of single transferable votes having been applied.

The Assembly has legislative powers and is specifically charged with setting up interconnecting bodies between Northern Ireland and the Republic of Ireland. Important decisions of the Assembly are made by a weighted majority system, which is designed to ensure that minority interests in the Assembly can influence legislation.

The First Minister of the Assembly is David Trimble of the Ulster Unionist Party. His Deputy is Seamus Mallon of the Social Democratic and Labour Party (SDLP).

The Assembly consists of members of the following parties:

Ulster Unionists	28
SDLP	24
Democratic Unionists	20
Sinn Féin	18
Alliance	6
United Kingdom Unionists	5
Independent Unionists	3
Progressive Unionists	2
Women's Coalition	2

Parliament

UK Parliamentary Glossary

Term	Description
Abstention	refusal by an MP to vote for or against a motion
Act of Parliament	bill passed by the Houses of Parliament (Commons and Lords) and signed by the Queen
Address	formal message to the Crown, presented to the Monarch by a Commons whip when the House of Commons wishes to make a point to the Monarch; the message is answered by the Monarch and returned to the Commons by a whip or to the Lords by the Lord Chamberlain
Adjournment of the House	request by an MP in the House of Commons to terminate the day's proceedings
Admonition	reprimand to an MP who has done something wrong, made by the Speaker of the House of Commons
Amendment	alteration proposed in a motion or a bill; amendments can be voted on in order to change what is written in a bill
Back bencher	MP who does not hold office in the Government, or any senior position on the leading opposition party
Ballot	paper on which an MP registers his/her vote in matters requiring the use of ballots to decide issues in Parliament
Bar of the House	marked by a leather strip, the Bar of the House is the line at the entrance to the House of Commons which non-MPs must not cross
Bill	draft of an Act of Parliament, presented to either the House of Commons or the House of Lords to vote on. If successful, the bill is forwarded for Royal Assent; if granted, it becomes an Act
Black Rod	officer of the Royal Household who looks after the doorkeepers and messengers of the House of Lords; Black Rod also issues the orders for entry into the Stranger's Gallery

UK Parliamentary Glossary (*continued*)

Term	Description
Budget	annual financial statement of the Chancellor of the Exchequer
By-Election	election to fill a vacancy in a constituency that arises during the course of a Parliament, usually as a result of the death or resignation of an MP
Catching the speaker's eye	any MP who wishes to speak in the Houses of Commons must stand and wait for the Speaker to see him/her and give him/her permission to speak
Clause	subdivision of an Act or Bill
Count	if there are less that 40 MPs present in the House of Commons, the Speaker can close the House
Crossing the floor	changing allegiance from one political party to another is signified by 'crossing the floor' of the House and taking a seat with an opposing party
Dissolution	bringing to an end the Parliament of the Houses of Commons and Lords by the Monarch; it is followed by a general election
Father of the House	longest serving MP in the House of Commons, currently Sir Edward Heath
Front benches	benches where members of the Government and senior opposition members sit in the House of Commons; nearest to the centre of the Table of the Commons
Galleries	areas in the House of Commons set aside for the public and press to attend sittings
General election	election of a new government by all eligible voters in the country following the dissolution of Parliament
Government bill	bill introduced by a Government Minister
Hansard	House of Commons' written reports
Houses of Parliament	Palace housing the House of Commons and the House of Lords
Independent member	elected MP who is not a member of any recognized political party. MPs can also leave or be expelled by a political party during a Parliament and sit as independents
Maiden speech	first speech in the House of Commons by a new member; traditionally, a new MP standing will be given preference over others by the Speaker
Majority government	government formed by the party with the majority of seats in the House of Commons
Minority government	government formed by a party that does not hold a majority of seats; it must maintain the confidence of the House in order to remain in government
Oath of allegiance	oath of loyalty to the Sovereign that must be made by an MP before he/she can take his/her seat in the House of Commons
Order paper	daily timetable of events in the House of Commons and the House of Lords
Pairs	if an MP does not wish to vote in the Chamber, he/she has to come to an arrangement with an opposition MP who will not vote either. The overall vote is then reduced by one on each side
Parliamentary procedure	rules by which the House of Commons and the House of Lords conduct their business
Passage of a bill	process by which a bill obtains Parliamentary approval and becomes law. Once Parliamentary approval has been granted, the bill is forwarded to the Monarch for Royal assent
Point of order	a technical or procedural breach of order can be brought to the attention of the Speaker by an MP at any time during a debate or as House business is being conducted; the Speaker decides on the validity of the matter raised and his/her decision is final
Portfolio	responsibilities of a Cabinet minister
Question time	time when government ministers have to answer questions put by members of the House of Commons and the House of Lords. Prime Ministers' questions are on Wednesdays; other days are rotated among other government departments
Recess	period between the end of one Parliament and the start of another
Royal assent	approval by the Monarch of a bill passed by the House of Commons and the House of Lords, making it an Act of Parliament
Teller	appointed by the Speaker to count the number of ayes and noes in a vote
Ten-minute rule	MPs are given ten minutes in which to make their comments or statements. The Speaker keeps time and ends the session at the end of the ten minutes
Whip	Member who makes sure that fellow party members vote according to party wishes; they are paid a higher salary than normal back-bench MPs

Members of the House of Commons

Christian names given are the preferred form of address as stated by Member's parliamentary office.

Member	Date of birth	Party[1]	Constituency	Majority at 1997 election	Opponents[1]
Abbott, Diane	27/9/53	Lab	Hackney North and Stoke Newington	15,627	Michael Lavender: Con; Douglas Taylor: LD
Adams, Gerry[2]	6/10/48	SF	Belfast West	7,909	Joe Hendron: SDLP; Fred Parkinson: UUP
Adams, Irene	27/12/47	Lab	Paisley North	12,814	Ian Mackay: SNP; Kenneth Brookes: Con; Alan Jalfs: Lib Dem
Ainger, Nick	24/10/49	Lab	Carmarthen West and Pembrokeshire South	9,621	Owen Williams: Con; Daniel Llewellyn: PC
Ainsworth, Bob	19/6/52	Lab	Coventry North East	22,569	Michael Burnett: Con; Geoffrey Sewards: LD
Ainsworth, Peter	16/11/56	Con	Surrey East	15,093	Belinda Ford: LD; David Ross: Lab
Alexander, Douglas	26/10/67	Lab	Paisley South	2731[3]	Ian Blackford: SNP; Eilen McCartin: LD; Sheila Lawson: Con ; John Deighan: PLA; Frances Curran: SSA; Chris Herriot: SL; Charles McLauchlan: SIL; Kenneth Blair: RA

(*continued*)

Members of the House of Commons (*continued*)

Member	Date of birth	Party[1]	Constituency	Majority at 1997 election	Opponents[1]
Allan, Richard	11/2/66	LD	Sheffield Hallam	8,271	Irvine Patnick: Con; Steven Conquest: Lab
Allen, Graham	11/1/53	Lab	Nottingham North	18,801	Gillian Shaw: Con; Rachel Oliver: LD
Amess, David	26/3/52	Con	Southend West	2,615	Nina Stimson: LD; Alan Harley: Lab
Ancram, Michael	7/7/45	Con	Devizes	9,782	Anthony Vickers: LD Frank Jeffrey: Lab
Anderson, Donald	17/6/39	Lab	Swansea East	25,569	Catherine Dibble: Con; Elwyn Jones: LD
Anderson, Janet	6/12/49	Lab	Rossendale and Darwen	10,949	Patricia Buzzard: Con; Brian Denning LD
Arbuthnot, James	4/8/52	Con	Hampshire North East	14,398	Ian Mann: LD; Peter Dare: Lab
Armstrong, Hilary	30/11/45	Lab	Durham North West	24,754	Louise St John Howe: Con; Anthony Gillings: LD
Ashdown, Paddy	27/2/41	LD	Yeovil	11,403	Nicholas Cambrook: Con; Patrick Conway: Lab
Ashton, Joe	9/10/33	Lab	Bassetlaw	17,348	Martin Cleasby: Con; Mike Kerrigan: LD
Atherton, Candy	17/4/60	Lab	Falmouth and Cambourne	2,688	Sebastian Coe: Con; Terrye Jones: LD
Atkins, Charlotte	24/9/50	Lab	Staffordshire Moorlands	10,049	Andrew Ashworth: Con; Christina Jebb: LD
Atkinson, David	24/3/40	Con	Bournemouth East	4,342	Douglas Eyre: LD; Jessica Stevens: Lab
Atkinson, Peter	19/1/43	Con	Hexham	222	Ian McMinn: Lab; Philip Carr: LD
Austin, John	21/8/44	Lab	Erith and Thamesmead	17,424	Nadhim Zahawi: Con; Alexander Grigg: LD
Baker, Norman	26/7/57	LD	Lewes	1,300	Tim Rathbone: Con; Mark Patton: Lab
Baldry, Antony	10/7/50	Con	Benbury	4,737	Hazel Peperell: Lab; Catherine Bearder: LD
Ballard, Jackie	4/1/53	LD	Taunton	2,452	David Nicholson: Con; Elizabeth Lisgo: Lab
Banks, Tony	8/4/45	Lab	West Ham	19,494	Mark MacGregor: Con; Samantha McDonough: LD
Barnes, Harry	22/7/36	Lab	Derbyshire North East	18,321	Simon Elliott: Con; Stephen Hardy: LD
Barron, Kevin	26/10/46	Lab	Rother Valley	23,485	Steven George Stanbury: Con; Stan Burgess: LD
Battle, John	26/4/51	Lab	Leeds West	19,771	John Whelan: Con; Nigel Amor: LD
Bayley, Hugh	9/1/52	Lab	York, City of	20,523	Simon Mallett: Con; Andrew Waller: LD
Beard, Nigel	10/10/36	Lab	Bexleyheath and Crayford	3,415	David Evennett: Con; Francoise Montford: LD
Beckett, Margaret	15/1/43	Lab	Derby South	16,106	Javed Arain: Con; Jeremy Beckett: LD
Begg, Anne	16/12/55	Lab	Aberdeen South	3,365	Nicol Stephen: LD; Raymond Robertson: Con
Beggs, Roy	20/2/36	UUP	Antrim East	6,389	Sean Neeson: APNI; Jack McKee: DUP
Beith, Alan	20/4/43	LD	Berwick-upon-Tweed	8,042	Paul Brannen: Lab; Nick Herbert: Con
Bell, Martin	31/8/38	Ind	Tatton	11,077	Neil Hamilton: Con; Sam Hill: Ind
Bell, Stuart	16/5/38	Lab	Middlesborough	25,018	Liam Benham: Con; Alison Charlesworth: LD
Benn, Tony	3/4/25	Lab	Chesterfield	5,775	Tony Rogers: LD; Martin Potter: Con
Bennett, Andrew	9/3/39	Lab	Denton and Reddish	20,311	Barbara Nutt: Con; Iain Donaldson: LD
Benton, Joe	28/9/33	Lab	Bootle	28,421	Rupert Matthews: Con; Kiron Reid: LD
Bercow, John	19/1/63	Con	Buckingham	12,386	Robert Lehmann: Lab; Neil Stuart: LD
Beresford, Paul	6/4/46	Con	Mole Valley	10,221	Stephen Cooksey: LD; Christopher Payne: Lab
Bermingham, Gerry	20/8/40	Lab	St Helens South	23,739	Mary Russell: Con; Brian Spencer: LD
Berry, Roger	4/7/48	Lab	Kingswood	14,253	Jonathan Howard: Con; Jeanne Pinkerton: LD
Best, Harold	18/12/37	Lab	Leeds North	3,844	Keith Hampson: Con; Barbara Pearce: LD
Betts, Clive	13/1/50	Lab	Sheffield Attercliffe	21,818	Brendan Peter Doyle: Con; Alice Gail Smith: LD
Blackman, Liz	26/9/49	Lab	Erewash	9,135	Angela Knight: Con; Martin Garnett: LD
Blair, Tony	6/5/53	Lab	Sedgefield	25,143	Elizabeth Pitman: Con; Ronald Beadle: LD
Blears, Hazel	14/5/56	Lab	Salford	17,069	Elliot Bishop: Con; Norman Owen: LD
Blizzard, Bob	31/5/50	Lab	Waveney	12,093	David Porter: Con; Christopher Thomas: LD
Blunkett, David	6/6/47	Lab	Sheffield Brightside	19,954	Francis Butler: LD; Christopher Buckwell: Con
Blunt, Crispin	15/6/60	Con	Reigate	7,741	Andrew Howard: Lab; Peter Samuel: LD
Boateng, Paul	14/6/51	Lab	Brent South	19,691	Stewart Jackson: Con; Julian Brazil: LD
Body, Richard	18/5/27	Con	Boston and Skegness	647	Phil McCauley: Lab; James Dodsworth: LD
Boothroyd, Betty	8/10/29	Speaker	West Broomwich West	15,423	Richard Silvester: Ind Lab; Steve Edwards: Nat Dem
Borrow, David	2/8/52	Lab	Ribble South	5,084	Robert Atkins: Con; Tim Farron: LD
Boswell, Tim	2/12/42	Con	Daventry	7,378	Ken Ritchie: Lab; John Gordon: LD
Bottomley, Peter	30/7/44	Con	Worthing West	7,713	Christopher Hare: LD; John Adams: Lab
Bottomley, Virginia	12/3/48	Con	Surrey South West	2,694	Neil Sherlock: LD; Margaret Leicester: Lab
Bradley, Keith	17/5/50	Lab	Manchester Withington	18,581	Jonathan Smith: Con; Yasmen Zalzala: LD
Bradley, Peter	12/4/53	Lab	Wrekin, The	3,025	Peter Bruinvels: Con; Ian Jenkins: LD
Bradshaw, Ben	30/8/60	Lab	Exeter	11,705	Adrian Rogers: Con; Dennis Brewer: LD
Brady, Graham	20/5/67	Con	Altrincham and Sale West	1,505	Jane Baugh: Lab; Marc Ramsbottom: LD
Brake, Thomas	6/5/62	LD	Carshalton and Wallington	2,267	Nigel Forman: Con; Andrew Theobald: Lab
Brand, Peter	16/5/47	LD	Isle of Wight	6,406	Andrew Turner: Con; Deborah Gardiner: Lab
Brazier, Julian	24/7/53	Con	Canterbury	3,964	Cheryl Hall: Lab; Martin Vye: LD
Breed, Colin	4/5/47	LD	Cornwall South East	6,480	Warwick Lightfoot: Con; Dorothy Kirk: Lab
Brinton, Helen	23/12/54	Lab	Peterborough	7,323	Jacqueline Foster: Con; David Howarth: LD
Brooke, Peter	3/3/34	Con	London and Westminster	4,881	Kate Green: Lab; Michael Dumigan: LD
Brown, Gordon	20/2/51	Lab	Dunfermline East	18,741	John Ramage: SNP; Iain Mitchell QC: Con
Brown, Nick	13/6/50	Lab	Newcastle upon Tyne East and Wallsend	23,811	Jeremy Middleton: Con; Graham Morgan: LD
Brown, Russell	17/9/51	Lab	Dumfries	9,643	Struan Stevenson: Con; Robert Higgins: SNP
Browne, Desmond	22/3/52	Lab	Kilmarnock and Loudoun	7,256	Alex Neil: SNP; Douglas Taylor: Con
Browning, Angela	4/12/46	Con	Tiverton and Honiton	1,653	Jim Barnard: LD; John King: Lab

Members of the House of Commons (*continued*)

Member	Date of birth	Party[1]	Constituency	Majority at 1997 election	Opponents[1]
Bruce, Ian	14/3/47	Con	Dorset South	77	Jim Knight: Lab; Michael Plummer: LD
Bruce, Malcolm	17/11/44	LD	Gordon	6,997	John Porter: Con; Richard Lochhead: SNP
Buck, Karen	30/8/58	Lab	Regent's Park and Kensington North	14,657	Paul McGuinness: Con; Emily Gasson: LD
Burden, Richard	1/9/54	Lab	Birmingham Northfield	11,443	Alan Blumenthal: Con; Michael Ashall: LD
Burgon, Colin	22/4/48	Lab	Elmet	8,779	Spencer Batiste: Con; Brian Jennings: LD
Burnett, John	19/9/45	LD	Devon West and Torridge	1,957	Ian Liddell-Grainger: Con; David Brenton: Lab
Burns, Simon	6/9/52	Con	Chelmsford West	6,691	Martin Bracken: LD; Roy Chad: Lab
Burstow, Paul	13/5/62	LD	Sutton and Cheam	2,097	Olga Maitland: Con; Mark Allison: Lab
Butler, Christine	14/12/43	Lab	Castle Point	1,116	Robert Spink: Con; Michael Baker: LD
Butterfill, John	14/2/41	Con	Bournemouth West	5,710	Janet Dover: LD; Dennis Gritt: Lab
Byers, Stephen	13/4/53	Lab	Tyneside North	26,643	Michael McIntyre: Con; Thomas Malvenna: LD
Cable, Vincent	9/5/43	LD	Twickenham	4,281	Toby Jessel: Con; Eva Tutchell: Lab
Caborn, Richard	6/10/43	Lab	Sheffield Central	16,906	Ali Qadar: LD; Martin Hess: Con
Campbell, Alan	8/7/57	Lab	Tynemouth	11,273	Martin Callanan: Con; Andrew Duffield: LD
Campbell, Anne	6/4/40	Lab	Cambridge	14,137	David Platt: Con; Geoffrey Heathcock: LD
Campbell, Menzies	22/5/41	LD	Fife North East	10,356	Adam Robert Bruce: Con; Colin Welsh: SNP
Campbell, Ronnie	14/8/43	Lab	Blyth Valley	17,736	Andrew Lamb: LD; Barbara Musgrave: Con
Campbell-Savours, Dale	23/8/43	Lab	Workington	19,656	Robert Blunden: Con; Philip Roberts: LD
Canavan, Dennis	8/8/42	Lab	Falkirk West	13,761	David Alexander: SNP; Carol Buchanan: Con
Cann, Jamie	28/6/46	Lab	Ipswich	10,439	Stephen Castle: Con; Nigel Roberts: LD
Caplin, Ivor	8/11/58	Lab	Hove	3,959	Robert Guy: Con; Thomas Pearce: LD
Casale, Roger	22/5/60	Lab	Wimbledon	2,990	Charles Goodson-Wickes: Con; Alison Willott: LD
Cash, William	10/5/40	Con	Stone	3,818	John Wakefield: Lab; Barry Stamp: LD
Caton, Martin	16/6/51	Lab	Gower	13,007	Alan Hugh Cairns: Con; Howard Evans: LD
Cawsey, Ian	14/4/60	Lab	Brigg and Goole	6,389	Donald Stewart: Con; Mary-Rose Hardy: LD
Chapman, Ben	8/7/40	Lab	Wirral South	7,004	Leslie Byrom: Con; Phillip Gilchrist: LD
Chapman, Sydney	17/10/35	Con	Chipping Barnet	1,035	Geoffrey Cooke: Lab; Sean Hooker: LD
Chaytor, David	3/8/49	Lab	Bury North	7,866	Alistair Burt: Con; Neville Kenyon: LD
Chidgey, David	9/7/42	LD	Eastleigh	754	Stephen Reid: Con; Alan Lloyd: Lab
Chisholm, Malcolm	7/3/49	Lab	Edinburgh North and Leith	10,978	Anne Dana: SNP; Ewen Stewart: Con
Chope, Christopher	19/5/47	Con	Christchurch	2,165	Diana Maddock: LD; Charles Mannan: Lab
Church, Judith	19/9/53	Lab	Dagenham	17,054	James Fairrie: Con; Thomas Dobrashian: LD
Clapham, Michael	15/5/43	Lab	Barnsley West and Penistone	17,267	Paul Watkins: Con; Winifred Knight: LD
Clappison, James	14/9/56	Con	Hertsmere	3,075	Beth Kelly: Lab; Ann Gray: LD
Clark, Alan	13/4/28	Con	Kensington and Chelsea	9,519	John Atkinson: Lab; Robert Woodthorpe Brown: LD
Clark, David	19/10/39	Lab	South Shields	22,153	Mark Hoban: Con; David Ord: LD
Clark, Lynda	26/2/49	Lab	Edinburgh Pentlands	4,862	Malcolm Rifkind: Con; Stewart Gibb: SNP
Clark, Michael	8/8/35	Con	Rayleigh	10,684	Raymond Ellis: Lab; Sidney Cumberland: LD
Clark, Paul	29/4/57	Lab	Gillingham	1,980	James Couchman: Con; Robert Sayer: LD
Clark, Tony	6/9/63	Lab	Northampton South	744	Michael Morris: Con; Anthony Worgan: LD
Clarke, Charles	21/9/50	Lab	Norwich South	14,239	Bashir Khanbhai: Con; Andrew Aalders-Dunthorne: LD
Clarke, Eric	9/4/33	Lab	Midlothian	9,870	Lawrence Millar: SNP; Anne Harper: Con
Clarke, Kenneth	2/7/40	Con	Rushcliffe	5,055	Jocelyn Pettitt: Lab; Samuel Boote: LD
Clarke, Tom	10/1/41	Lab	Coatbridge and Chryston	19,295	Brian Nugent: SNP; Piers Wauchope: Con
Clelland, David	27/6/43	Lab	Tyne Bridge	22,906	Adrian Lee: Con; Mary Wallace: LD
Clifton-Brown, Geoffrey	23/3/53	Con	Cotswold	11,965	David Gayler: LD; David Elwell: Lab
Clwyd, Ann	21/3/37	Lab	Cynon Valley	19,755	Alun Davies: PC; Huw Price: LD
Coaker, Vernon	17/6/53	Lab	Gedling	3,802	Andrew Mitchell: Con; Raymond Poynter: LD
Coffey, Ann	31/8/46	Lab	Stockport	18,912	Stephen Fitzsimmons: Con; Sylvia Roberts: LD
Cohen, Harry	10/12/49	Lab	Leyton and Wanstead	15,186	Robert Vaudry: Con; Charles Anglin: LD
Coleman, Iain	18/1/58	Lab	Hammersmith and Fulham	3,842	Matthew Carrington: Con; Alexi Sugden: LD
Collins, Tim	7/5/64	Con	Westmorland and Lonsdale	4,521	Stan Collins: LD; John Harding: Lab
Colman, Anthony	24/7/43	Lab	Putney	2,976	David Mellor: Con; Russell Pyne: LD
Colvin, Michael	27/9/32	Con	Romsey	8,585	Mark Cooper: LD; Joanne Ford: Lab
Connarty, Michael	3/9/47	Lab	Falkirk East	13,385	Keith Brown: SNP; Malcolm Nicol: Con
Cook, Frank	3/11/35	Lab	Stockton North	21,365	Bryan Johnston: Con; Suzanne Fletcher: LD
Cook, Robin	28/2/46	Lab	Livingston	11,747	Peter Johnston: SNP; Hugh Craigie Halkett: Con
Cooper, Yvette	20/3/69	Lab	Pontefract and Castleford	25,725	Adrian Flook: Con; Wesley Paxton: LD
Corbett, Robin	22/12/33	Lab	Birmingham Erdington	12,657	Anthony Tomkins: Con; Ian Garrett: LD
Corbyn, Jeremy	26/5/49	Lab	Islington North	19,955	James Kempton: LD; Simon Fawthrop: Con
Cormack, Patrick	18/5/39	Con	Staffordshire South	7,821	Judith LeMaistre: Lab; Jamie Calder: LD
Corston, Jean	5/5/42	Lab	Bristol East	16,159	Edward Vaizey: Con; Peter Tyzack: LD
Cotter, Brian	24/8/38	LD	Weston-super-Mare	1,274	Margaret Daly: Con; Derek Kraft: Lab

(*continued*)

Members of the House of Commons (*continued*)

Member	Date of birth	Party[1]	Constituency	Majority at 1997 election	Opponents[1]
Cousins, Jim	23/2/44	Lab	Newcastle-upon-Tyne Central	16,480	Newmark Brooks: Con; Ruth Berry: LD
Cox, Tom	19/1/30	Lab	Tooting	15,011	James Hutchings: Con; Simon James: LD
Cran, James	28/1/44	Con	Beverley and Holderness	811	Norman O'Neill: Lab; John Melling: LD
Cranston, Ross	23/7/48	Lab	Dudley North	9,457	Charles MacNamara: Con; Gerry Lewis: LD
Crausby, David	17/6/46	Lab	Bolton North East	12,669	Robert Wilson: Con; Edmund Critchley: LD
Cryer, Ann	14/12/39	Lab	Keighley	7,132	Gary Waller: Con; Michael Doyle: LD
Cryer, John	11/4/64	Lab	Hornchurch	5,680	Robin Squire: Con; Rabinda Martins: LD
Cummings, John	6/7/43	Lab	Easington	30,012	Jason Hollands: Con; James Heppell: LD
Cunliffe, Lawrence	25/3/29	Lab	Leigh	24,496	Edward Young: Con; Peter Hough: LD
Cunningham, Jack	4/8/39	Lab	Copeland	11,944	Andrew Cumpsty: Con; Roger Putnam: LD
Cunningham, Jim	4/12/41	Lab	Coventry South	10,953	Paul Ivey: Con; Gordon Macdonald: LD
Cunningham, Roseanna	27/7/51	SNP	Perth	3,141	John Godfrey: Con; Douglas Alexander: Lab
Curry, David	13/6/44	Con	Skipton and Ripon	11,620	Thomas Mould: LD; Robert Marchant: Lab
Curtis-Thomas, Clare	30/4/58	Lab	Crosby	7,182	Malcolm Thornton: Con; Paul McVey: LD
Dafis, Cynog	1/4/38	PC	Ceredigion	6,961	Robert Harris: Lab; David Davies: LD
Dalyell, Tam	9/8/32	Lab	Linlithgow	10,838	Kenny MacAskill: SNP; Tom Kerr: Con
Darling, Alistair	28/11/53	Lab	Edinburgh Central	11,070	Michael Scott-Hayward: Con; Fiona Hyslop: SNP
Darvill, Keith	28/5/48	Lab	Upminster	2,770	Nicholas Bonsor: Con; Pamela Peskett: LD
Davey, Edward	25/12/65	LD	Kingston and Surbiton	56	Richard Tracey: Con; Sheila Griffin: Lab
Davey, Valerie	16/4/40	Lab	Bristol West	1,493	William Waldegrave: Con; Charles Boney: LD
Davidson, Ian	8/9/50	Lab Coop	Glasgow Pollock	13,791	David Logan: SNP; Tommy Sheridan: Scot Soc
Davies, Denzil	9/10/38	Lab	Llanelli	16,039	Marc Phillips: PC; Andrew Hayes: Con
Davies, Geraint	3/5/60	Lab	Croydon Central	3,897	David Congdon: Con; George Schlich: LD
Davies, Quentin	29/5/44	Con	Grantham and Stamford	2,692	Peter Denning: Lab; John Sellick: LD
Davies, Ron	6/8/46	Lab	Caerphilly	25,839	Hugh Harris: Con; Lindsay Whittle: PC
Davis, David	23/12/48	Con	Haltemprice and Howden	7,514	Diana Wallis: LD; George McManus: Lab
Davis, Terry	5/1/38	Lab	Birmingham Hodge Hill	14,200	Edward Grant: Con; Haydn Thomas: LD
Dawson, Hilton	30/9/53	Lab	Lancaster and Wyre	1,295	Keith Mans: Con; John Humberstone: LD
Day, Stephen	30/10/48	Con	Cheadle	3,189	Patsy Calton: LD; Paul Diggett: Lab
Dean, Janet	28/1/49	Lab	Burton	6,330	Ivan Lawrence: Con; David Fletcher: LD
Denham, John	15/7/53	Lab	Southampton Itchen	14,229	Peter Fleet: Con; David Harrison: LD
Dewar, Donald	21/8/37	Lab	Glasgow Anniesland	15,154	William Wilson: SNP; Robert Andrew Palles Brocklehurst: Con
Dismore, Andrew	2/9/54	Lab	Hendon	6,155	John Gorst: Con; Wayne Casey: LD
Dobbin, Jim	26/5/41	Lab Coop	Heywood and Middleton	17,542	Edward Sebastian Grigg: Con; David Clayton: LD
Dobson, Frank	15/3/40	Lab	Holborn and St Pancras	17,903	Julian Smith: Con; Justine McGuinness: LD
Donaldson, Jeffrey	7/12/62	UUP	Lagan Valley	16,925	Seamus Close: APNI; Edwin Poots: DUP
Donohoe, Brian	10/9/48	Lab	Cunninghame South	14,869	Margaret Burgess: SNP; Pamela Paterson: Con
Doran, Frank	13/4/49	Lab	Aberdeen Central	10,801	Jill Wisely: Con; Brian Topping: SNP
Dorrell, Stephen	25/3/52	Con	Charnwood	5,900	David Knaggs: Lab; Roger Wilson: LD
Dowd, Jim	5/3/51	Lab	Lewisham West	14,317	Clare Whelan: Con; Kathy McGrath: LD
Drew, David	13/4/52	Lab Coop	Stroud	2,910	Roger Knapman: Con; Paul Hodgkinson: LD
Drown, Julia	23/8/62	Lab	Swindon South	5,645	Simon Coombs: Con; Stanley Pajak: LD
Duncan, Alan	31/3/57	Con	Rutland and Melton	8,836	John Meads: Lab; Kim Lee: LD
Duncan Smith, Iain	9/4/54	Con	Chingford and Woodford Green	5,714	Thomas Hutchinson: Lab; Geoffrey Seeff: LD
Dunwoody, Gwyneth	12/12/30	Lab	Crewe and Nantwich	15,798	Michael Loveridge: Con; David Cannon: LD
Eagle, Angela	19/1/61	Lab	Wallasey	19,074	Madeleine Wilcock: Con; Peter Reisdorf: LD
Eagle, Maria	17/2/61	Lab	Liverpool Garston	18,387	Flo Clucas: LD; Nigel Gordon-Johnson: Con
Edwards, Huw	12/4/53	Lab	Monmouth	4,178	Roger Evans: Con; Mark Williams: LD
Efford, Clive	10/7/58	Lab	Eltham	10,182	Clive Blackwood: Con; Amanda Taylor: LD
Ellman, Louise	14/11/45	Lab Coop	Liverpool Riverside	21,799	Beatrice Fraenkel: LD; David Sparrow: Con
Emery, Peter	27/2/26	Con	Devon East	7,489	Rachel Trethewey: LD; Andrew Siantonas: Lab
Ennis, Jeff	13/11/52	Lab	Barnsley East and Mexborough	26,763	Jane Ellison: Con; David Willis: LD
Etherington, William	17/7/41	Lab	Sunderland North	19,697	Andrew Selous: Con; Geoffrey Pryke: LD
Evans, Nigel	10/11/57	Con	Ribble Valley	6,640	Michael Carr: LD; Marcus Johnstone: Lab
Ewing, Margaret	1/9/45	SNP	Moray	5,566	Andrew Findlay: Con; Lewis Macdonald: Lab
Faber, David	7/7/61	Con	Westbury	6,068	John Miller: LD; Kevin Small: Lab
Fabricant, Michael	12/6/50	Con	Lichfield	238	Susan Woodward: Lab; Roger Bennion: LD
Fallon, Michael	14/5/52	Con	Sevenoaks	10,461	John Hayes: Lab; Roger Waslhe: LD
Fatchett, Derek	22/8/45	Lab	Leeds Central	20,689	William Wild: Con; David Freeman: LD
Fearn, Ronnie	6/2/31	LD	Southport	6,170	Matthew Banks: Con; Sarah Norman: Lab
Field, Frank	16/7/42	Lab	Birkenhead	21,845	Albert John Crosby: Con; Roy Wood: LD
Fisher, Mark	29/10/44	Lab	Stoke-on-Trent Central	19,924	David Neil Jones: Con; Edward Fordham: LD

Members of the House of Commons (*continued*)

Member	Date of birth	Party[1]	Constituency	Majority at 1997 election	Opponents[1]
Fitzpatrick, Jim	4/4/52	Lab	Poplar and Canning Town	18,915	Benet Steinberg: Con; Janet Ludlow: LD
Fitzsimons, Lorna	6/8/67	Lab	Rochdale	4,545	Liz Lynne: LD; Mervyn Turnberg: Con
Flight, Howard	16/6/48	Con	Arundel and South Downs	14,035	John Goss: LD; Richard Black: Lab
Flint, Caroline	20/9/61	Lab	Don Valley	14,659	Clare Gledhill: Con; Paul Johnston: LD
Flynn, Paul	9/2/35	Lab	Newport West	14,537	Peter Clarke: Con; Stan Wilson: LD
Follett, Barbara	25/12/42	Lab	Stevenage	11,582	Tim Wood: Con; Alex Wilcock: LD
Forsythe, Clifford	24/8/29	UUP	Antrim South	16,611	Donovan McClelland: SDLP; David Ford: APNI
Forth, Eric	9/9/44	Con	Bromley and Chislehurst	11,118	Rob Yeldham: Lab; Paul Booth: LD
Foster, Derek	25/6/37	Lab	Bishop Auckland	21,064	Josephine Fergus: Con; Les Ashworth: LD
Foster, Don	31/3/47	LD	Bath	9,319	Alison McNair: Con; Tim Bush: Lab
Foster, Michael	1/2/46	Lab	Hastings and Rye	2,560	Jacqui Mait: Con; Monroe Palmer: LD
Foster, Michael	14/1/63	Lab	Worcester	7,425	Nicholas Bourne: Con; Paul Chandler: LD
Foulkes, George	21/1/42	Lab Coop	Carrick, Cumnock and Doon Valley	21,062	Alasdair Marshall: Con; Christine Hutchison: SNP
Fowler, Norman	2/2/38	Con	Sutton Coldfield	14,885	Alan York: Lab; James Whorwood: LD
Fox, Liam	22/9/61	Con	Woodspring	7,734	Nanette Kirsen: LD; Debbie Sander: Lab
Fraser, Christopher	19/1/62	Con	Dorset Mid and Poole North	681	Alan Leaman: LD; David Collis: Lab
Fyfe, Maria	25/11/38	Lab	Glasgow Maryhill	14,264	John Wailes: SNP; Elspeth Attwooll: LD
Galbraith, Sam	18/10/45	Lab	Strathkelvin and Bearsden	16,292	David Sharpe: Con; Graeme McCormick: SNP
Gale, Roger	20/8/43	Con	Thanet North	2,766	Iris Johnson: Lab; Paul Kendrick: LD
Galloway, George	16/8/54	Lab	Glasgow Kelvin	9,665	Sandra White: SNP; Elspeth Buchanan: LD
Gapes, Mike	4/9/52	Lab Coop	Ilford South	14,200	Neil Thorne: Con; Aina Khan: LD
Gardiner, Barry	10/3/57	Lab	Brent North	4,019	Rhodes Boyson: Con; Paul Lorber: LD
Garnier, Edward	26/10/52	Con	Harborough	6,524	Mark Cox: LD; Nicholas Holden: Lab
George, Andrew	2/12/58	LD	St Ives	7,170	William Rogers: Con; Christopher Fegan: Lab
George, Bruce	1/6/42	Lab	Walsall	11,312	Leslie Leek: Con; Harry Harris: LD
Gerrard, Neil	3/7/42	Lab	Walthamstow	17,149	Jill Andrew: Con; Jane Jackson: LD
Gibb, Nick	3/9/60	Con	Bognor Regis and Littlehampton	7,321	Roger Nash: Lab; James Walsh: LD
Gibson, Ian	26/9/38	Lab	Norwich North	9,470	Robert Kinghorn: Con; Paul Young: LD
Gill, Christopher	28/10/36	Con	Ludlow	5,909	Ian Huffer: LD; Nuala O'Kane: Lab
Gillan, Cheryl	21/4/52	Con	Chesham and Amersham	13,859	Michael Brand: LD; Christopher Farrelly: Lab
Gilroy, Linda	19/7/49	Lab Coop	Plymouth Sutton	9,440	Andrew Crisp: Con; Steven Melia: LD
Godman, Norman	19/4/38	Lab	Greenock and Inverclyde	13,040	Brian Goodall: SNP; Rodney Ackland: LD
Godsiff, Roger	7/11/46	Lab	Birmingham Sparkbrook and Small Heath	19,526	Kenneth Haredman: Con; Roger Harmer: LD
Goggins, Paul	16/10/53	Lab	Wythenshawe and Sale East	15,019	Paul Fleming: Con; Vanessa Tucker: LD
Golding, Llin	21/3/33	Lab	Newcastle-under-Lyme	17,206	Marcus Hayes: Con; Robin Studd: LD
Goodlad, Alastair	4/7/43	Con	Eddisbury	1,185	Margaret Hanson: Lab; David Reaper: LD
Gordon, Eileen	22/10/46	Lab	Romford	649	Michael Neubert: Con; Nigel Meyer: LD
Gorman, Teresa	30/9/31	Con	Billericay	1,356	Paul Richards: Lab; Geoff Williams: LD
Gorrie, Donald	2/4/33	LD	Edinburgh West	7,253	James Douglas-Hamilton: Con; Lesley Hinds: Lab
Graham, Thomas	5/12/43	Lab	Renfrewshire West	7,979	Colin Campbell: SNP; Charles Cormack: Con
Grant, Bernie	17/2/44	Lab	Tottenham	20,200	Andrew Scantlebury: Con; Neil Hughes: LD
Gray, James	7/11/54	Con	Wiltshire North	3,475	Simon Cordon: LD; Nigel Knowles: Lab
Green, Damian	17/1/56	Con	Ashford	5,345	John Richard Ennals: Lab; John Williams: LD
Greenway, John	19/2/46	Con	Ryedale	5,058	John Keith Orrell: LD; Alison Hiles: Lab
Grieve, Dominic	24/5/56	Con	Beaconsfield	13,987	Peter Mapp: LD; Alastair Hudson: Lab
Griffiths, Jane	17/4/54	Lab	Reading East	3,795	John Watts: Con; Robert Samuel: LD
Griffiths, Nigel	20/5/55	Lab	Edinburgh South	11,452	Elizabeth Smith: Con; Michael Pringle: LD
Griffiths, Win	11/2/43	Lab	Bridgend	15,248	David Davies: Con; Andrew McKinlay: LD
Grocott, Bruce	1/11/40	Lab	Telford	11,290	Bernard Gentry: Con; Nathaniel Green: LD
Grogan, John	24/2/61	Lab	Selby	3,836	Kenneth Hind: Con; Ted Batty: LD
Gummer, John	26/11/39	Con	Suffolk Coastal	3,254	Mark Campbell: Lab; Alexandra Jones: LD
Gunnell, John	1/10/33	Lab	Morley and Rothwell	14,750	Alan Barraclough: Con; Mitchell Galdas: LD
Hague, William	26/3/61	Con	Richmond (Yorks)	10,051	Stephen Merritt: Lab; Jane Harvey: LD
Hain, Peter	16/2/50	Lab	Neath	26,741	David Evans: Con; Trefor Jones: PC
Hall, Mike	20/9/52	Lab	Weaver Vale	13,448	James Byrne: Con; Trevor Griffiths: LD
Hall, Patrick	20/10/51	Lab	Bedford	8,300	Robert John Blackman: Con; Christopher Noyce: LD
Hamilton, Archie	30/12/41	Con	Epsom and Ewell	11,525	Philip Woodford: Lab; John Vincent: LD
Hamilton, Fabian	12/4/55	Lab	Leeds North East	6,959	Tim Kirkhope: Con; Bill Winlow: LD
Hammond, Philip	4/12/55	Con	Runnymede and Weybridge	9,875	Ian Peacock: Lab; Geoffrey Taylor: LD
Hancock, Mike	9/4/46	LD	Portsmouth South	4,327	David Martin: Con; Alan Burnett: Lab
Hanson, David	5/7/57	Lab	Delyn	12,693	Karen Lumley: Con; David Lloyd: LD
Harman, Harriet	30/7/50	Lab	Camberwell and Peckham	16,451	Mark Humphreys: Con; Nigel Williams: LD
Harris, Evan	21/10/65	LD	Oxford West and Abingdon	6,285	Laurence Harris: Con; Susan Brown: Lab

(*continued*)

Members of the House of Commons (*continued*)

Member	Date of birth	Party[1]	Constituency	Majority at 1997 election	Opponents[1]
Harvey, Nick	3/8/61	LD	Devon North	6,181	Richard Ashworth: Con; Eithne Brenton: Lab
Haselhurst, Alan	23/6/37	Con	Saffron Walden	10,573	Mervin Caton: LD; Malcolm Fincken: Lab
Hawkins, Nick	27/3/57	Con	Surrey Heath	16,287	David Newman: LD; Susan Jones: Lab
Hayes, John	23/6/58	Con	South Holland and The Deepings	7,991	John Lewis: Lab; Peter Millen: LD
Heal, Sylvia	20/7/42	Lab	Halesowen and Rowley Regis	10,337	John Kennedy: Con; Elaine Todd: LD
Heald, Oliver	15/12/54	Con	Hertfordshire North East	3,088	Ivan Gibbons: Lab; Stephen Jarvis: LD
Healey, John	13/2/60	Lab	Wentworth	23,959	Karl Hamer: Con; James Charters: LD
Heath, David	16/3/54	LD	Somerton and Frome	130	Mark Robinson: Con; Robert Ashford: Lab
Heath, Edward	9/7/16	Con	Old Bexley and Sidcup	3,569	Richard Justham: Lab; Iain King: LD
Heathcoat-Amory, David	21/3/49	Con	Wells	528	Peter Gold: LD; Michael Eavis: Lab
Henderson, Doug	9/6/49	Lab	Newcastle-upon-Tyne North	19,332	Gregory White: Con; Peter Allen: LD
Henderson, Ivan	7/6/58	Lab	Harwich	1,216	Iain Sproat: Con; Ann Elvin: LD
Hepburn, Stephen	6/12/59	Lab	Jarrow	21,933	Mark Allatt: Con; Tim Stone: LD
Heppell, John	3/11/48	Lab	Nottingham East	15,419	Andrew Raca: Con; Kevin Mulloy: LD
Heseltine, Michael	21/3/33	Con	Henley	11,167	Timothy Horton: LD; Duncan Enright: Lab
Hesford, Stephen	27/5/57	Lab	Wirral West	2,738	David Hunt: Con; John Thornton: LD
Hewitt, Patricia	2/12/48	Lab	Leicester West	12,864	Richard Thomas: Con; Mark Jones: LD
Hill, Keith	28/7/43	Lab	Streatham	18,423	Ernest Noad: Con; Roger O'Brien: LD
Hinchliffe, David	14/10/48	Lab	Wakefield	14,604	Jonathan Peacock: Con; Douglas Dale: LD
Hodge, Margaret	8/9/44	Lab	Barking	15,896	Keith Langford: Con; Mark Marsh: LD
Hoey, Kate	21/6/46	Lab	Vauxhall	18,660	Keith Kerr: LD; Richard Bacon: Con
Hogg, Douglas	5/2/45	Con	Sleaford and North Hykeham	5,123	Sean Harriss: Lab; John Marriott: LD
Home Robertson, John	5/12/48	Lab	East Lothian	14,221	Murdo Fraser: Con; David McCarthy: SNP
Hood, Jimmy	16/5/48	Lab	Clydesdale	13,809	Andrew Doig: SNP; Mark Andrew Izatt: Con
Hoon, Geoffrey	6/12/53	Lab	Ashfield	22,728	Mark Simmonds: Con; William Smith: LD
Hope, Phil	19/4/55	Lab Coop	Corby	11,860	William Powell: Con; Ian Hankinson: LD
Hopkins, Kelvin	22/8/41	Lab	Luton North	9,626	David Senior: Con; Kathryn Newbound: LD
Horam, John	7/3/39	Con	Orpington	2,952	Christopher Maines: LD; Susan Polydorou: Lab
Howard, Michael	7/7/41	Con	Folkestone and Hythe	6,332	David Laws: LD; Peter Doherty: Lab
Howarth, Alan	11/6/44	Lab	Newport	13,523	David Evans: Con; Alastair Cameron: LD
Howarth, George	29/6/49	Lab	Knowsley North and Sefton East	26,147	Carl Doran: Con; David Bamber: LD
Howarth, Gerald	12/9/47	Con	Aldershot	6,621	Adrian Collett: LD; Terrence Bridgeman: Lab
Howells, Kim	19/1/46	Lab	Pontypridd	23,129	Jonathan Cowen: Con; Gareth Llywelyn: PC
Hoyle, Lindsay	10/6/57	Lab	Chorley	9,870	Den Dover: Con; Simon Jones: LD
Hughes, Beverley	30/3/50	Lab	Stretford and Urmston	13,640	John Gregory: Con; John Bridges: LD
Hughes, Kevin	15/12/52	Lab	Doncaster North	21,937	Peter Kennerley: Con; Michael Cook: LD
Hughes, Simon	17/5/51	LD	Southwark North and Bermondsey	3,387	Jeremy Fraser: Lab; Grant Shapps: Con
Humble, Joan	3/3/51	Lab	Blackpool North and Fleetwood	8,946	Harold Elletson: Con; Beverley Hill: LD
Hume, John	18/1/37	SDLP	Foyle	13,664	Mitchell McLaughlin: SF; William Hay: DUP
Hunter, Andrew	8/1/43	Con	Basingstoke	2,397	Nigel Lickley: Lab; Martin Rimmer: LD
Hurst, Alan	2/9/45	Lab	Braintree	1,451	Tony Newton: Con; Trevor Ellis: LD
Hutton, John	6/5/55	Lab	Barrow and Furness	14,497	Richard Hunt: Con; Aileen Metcalfe: LD
Iddon, Brian	5/7/40	Lab	Bolton South East	21,311	Paul Carter: Con; Frank Harasiwka: LD
Illsley, Eric	9/4/55	Lab	Barnsley Central	24,501	Simon Gutteridge: Con; Darren Finlay: LD
Ingram, Adam	1/2/47	Lab	East Kilbride	17,384	George Gebbie: SNP; Clifford Herbertson: Con
Jack, Michael	17/9/46	Con	Fylde	8,963	John Garrett: Lab; William Greene: LD
Jackson, Glenda	9/5/36	Lab	Hampstead and Highgate	13,289	Elizabeth Gibson: Con; Bridget Fox: LD
Jackson, Helen	19/5/39	Lab	Sheffield Hillsborough	16,451	Arthur Dunworth: LD; David Nuttall: Con
Jackson, Robert	24/9/46	Con	Wantage	6,089	Celia Wilson: Lab; Jenny Riley: LD
Jamieson, David	18/5/47	Lab	Plymouth Devonport	19,127	Anthony Johnson: Con; Richard Cpous: LD
Jenkin, Bernard	9/4/59	Con	Essex North	5,476	Timothy Young: Lab; Andrew Phillips: LD
Jenkins, Brian	19/9/42	Lab	Tamworth	7,496	Ann Lightbown: Con; Jennifer Pinkett: LD
Johnson, Alan	5/9/34	Lab	Hull West and Hessle	15,525	Robert Tress: LD; Cormach Moore: Con
Johnson, Melanie	5/2/55	Lab	Welwyn Hatfield	5,595	David Evans: Con; Rodney Schwartz: LD
Johnson Smith, Geoffrey	16/4/24	Con	Wealden	14,204	Michael Skinner: LD; Nicholas Levine: Lab
Jones, Barry	26/6/38	Lab	Alyn and Deeside	16,403	Timothy Peter Roberts: Con; Eleanor Burnham: LD
Jones, Fiona	27/2/57	Lab	Newark	3,016	Richard Alexander: Con; Peter Harris: LD
Jones, Helen	24/12/54	Lab	Warrington North	19,527	Ray Lacey: Con; Ian Greenhalgh: LD

Members of the House of Commons (*continued*)

Member	Date of birth	Party[1]	Constituency	Majority at 1997 election	Opponents[1]
Jones, Ieuan Wyn	22/5/49	PC	Ynys Mon	2,481	Owen Edwards: Lab; Gwilym Owen: Con
Jones, Jenny	8/2/48	Lab	Wolverhampton South West	5,118	Nicholas Budgen: Con; Matthew Green: LD
Jones, Jon Owen	19/4/54	Lab Coop	Cardiff Central	7,923	Jennifer Randerson: LD; David Melding: Con
Jones, Lynne	26/4/51	Lab	Birmingham Selly Oak	14,088	Graham Green: Con; David Osborne: LD
Jones, Martin	1/3/47	Lab	Clwyd South	13,810	Brosi Johnson: Con; Andrew Chadwick: LD
Jones, Nigel	30/3/48	LD	Cheltenham	6,645	William John Todman: Con; Barry Leach: Lab
Jowell, Tessa	17/9/47	Lab	Dulwich and West Norwood	16,769	Roger Gough: Con; Susan Kramer: LD
Kaufman, Gerald	21/6/30	Lab	Manchester Gorton	17,342	Jackie Pearcey: LD; Guy Senior: Con
Keeble, Sally	13/10/51	Lab	Northampton North	10,000	Tony Marlow: Con; Lesley Dunbar: LD
Keen, Alan	25/11/37	Lab Coop	Feltham and Heston	15,473	Reginald Ground: Con; Colin Penning: LD
Keen, Ann	26/11/48	Lab	Brentford and Isleworth	14,424	Nirj Deva: Con; Gareth Hartwell: LD
Keetch, Paul	21/5/61	LD	Hereford	6,648	Colin Shepherd: Con; Arthur Chappell: Lab
Kelly, Ruth	9/5/68	Lab	Bolton West	7,072	Tom Sackville: Con; Barbara Ronson: LD
Kemp, Fraser	1/9/58	Lab	Houghton and Washington East	26,555	Philip Booth: Con; Keith Miller: LD
Kennedy, Charles	25/11/59	LD	Ross, Skye and Inverness West	4,019	Donnie Munro: Lab; Margaret Paterson: SNP
Kennedy, Jane	19/1/58	Lab	Liverpool Wavertree	19,701	Richard Kemp: LD; Christopher Malthouse: Con
Key, Robert	22/4/45	Con	Salisbury	6,276	Yvonne Emmerson-Pierce: LD; Richard Rogers: Lab
Khabra, Piara	20/11/24	Lab	Ealing Southall	21,423	John Penrose: Con; Nicola Thomson: LD
Kidney, David	21/3/55	Lab	Stafford	4,314	David Cameron: Con; Pamela Hornby: LD
Kilfoyle, Peter	9/6/46	Lab	Liverpool Walton	27,038	Richard Roberts: LD; Mark Kotecha: Con
King, Andrew	14/9/48	Lab	Rugby and Kenilworth	495	James Powsey: Con; Jeremy Roodhouse: LD
King, Oona	22/10/67	Lab	Bethnal Green and Bow	11,285	Kabir Choudhury: Con; Syed Islam: LD
King, Tom	13/6/33	Con	Bridgwater	1,796	Michael Hoban: LD; Roger Lavers: Lab
Kingham, Tess	4/5/63	Lab	Gloucester	8,259	Douglas French: Con; Peter Munisamy: LD
Kirkbride, Julie	5/6/60	Con	Bromsgrove	4,895	Peter McDonald: Lab; Jennette Davy: LD
Kirkwood, Archy	22/4/46	LD	Roxburgh and Berwickshire	7,906	Douglas Younger: Con; Helen Eadie: Lab
Kumar, Ashok	28/5/56	Lab	Middlesbrough South and Cleveland East	10,607	Michael Bates: Con; Hamish Garrett: KD
Ladyman, Stephen	6/11/52	Lab	Thanet South	2,878	Jonathan Aitken: Con; Barbara Hewitt-Silk: LD
Laing, Eleanor	1/2/58	Con	Epping Forest	5,252	Stephen Murray: Lab; Stephen Robinson: LD
Lait, Jackie	16/12/47	Con	Beckenham	1227[4]	Robert Hughes: Lab; Rosemary Vetterlein: LD; Philip Rimmer: Lib; John McAuley: NF; Leonard Mead: NBR; Terence Campion: SFP; John Small: NL
Lansley, Andrew	11/12/56	Con	Cambridgeshire South	8,712	James Quinlan: LD; Tony Gray: Lab
Lawrence, Jackie	9/8/48	Lab	Preseli Pembrokeshire	8,736	Robert Buckland: Con; Jeffrey Clarke: LD
Laxton, Bob	7/9/44	Lab	Derby North	10,615	Greg Knight: Con; Robert Charlesworth: LD
Leigh, Edward	20/7/50	Con	Gainsborough	6,826	Paul Taylor: Lab; Neil Taylor: LD
Lepper, David	15/9/45	Lab Coop	Brighton Pavilion	13,181	Derek Spencer: Con; Ken Blanshard: LD
Leslie, Christopher	28/6/72	Lab	Shipley	2,996	Marcus Fox: Con; John Cole: LD
Letwin, Oliver	19/5/56	Con	Dorset West	1,840	Robin Legg: LD; Robert Bygraves: Lab
Levitt, Tom	10/4/54	Lab	High Peak	8,791	Charles Hendry: Con; Susan Barber: LD
Lewis, Ivan	4/3/67	Lab	Bury South	12,387	David Sumberg: Con; Victor D'Albert: LD
Lewis, Julian	26/9/51	Con	New Forest East	5,215	George Dawson: LD; Alan Goodfellow: Lab
Lewis, Terry	29/12/35	Lab	Worsley	17,741	Damien Garrido: Con; Robert Bleakley: LD
Liddell, Helen	6/12/50	Lab	Airdrie and Shotts	15,412	Keith Robertson: SNP; Nicholas Brook: Con
Lidington, David	30/6/56	Con	Aylesbury	8,419	Sharon Bowles: LD; Robert Langridge: Lab
Lilley, Peter	23/8/43	Con	Hitchen and Harpenden	6,671	Rosemary Sanderson: Lab; Christopher White: LD
Linton, Martin	11/8/44	Lab	Battersea	5,360	John Bowis: Con; Paula Keaveney: LD
Livingstone, Ken	17/6/45	Lab	Brent East	15,882	Mark Gino Francois: Con; Ian Hunter: LD
Livsey, Richard	2/5/35	LD	Brecon and Radnorshire	5,097	Jonathan Evans: Con; Christopher Mann: Lab
Lloyd, Peter	12/11/37	Con	Fareham	10,358	Michael Prior: Lab; Grace Hill: LD
Lloyd, Tony	25/2/50	Lab	Manchester Central	19,682	Alison Firth: LD; Simon McIlwaine: Con
Llwyd, Elfyn	26/9/51	PC	Meirionnydd Nant Conwy	6,805	Hefin Rees: Lab; Jeremy Quin: Con
Lock, David	2/5/60	Lab	Wyre Forest	6,946	Anthony Coombs: Con; David Cropp: LD
Lord, Michael	17/10/38	Con	Suffolk Central and Ipswich North	3,538	Carole Jones: Lab; Madeline Goldspink: LD
Loughton, Tim	30/5/62	Con	Worthing East and Shoreham	5,098	Martin Ling: LD; Mark Williams: Lab
Love, Andrew	21/3/49	Lab Coop	Edmonton	13,472	Ian Twinn: Con; Andrew Wiseman: LD
Luff, Peter	18/2/55	Con	Worcestershire Mid	9,412	Diane Smith: Lab; David Barwick: LD
Lyell, Nicholas	6/12/38	Con	Bedfordshire North East	5,883	John Lehall: Lab; Philip Bristow: LD
McAllion, John	13/2/48	Lab	Dundee East	9,961	Shona Robison: SNP; Bruce Mackie: Con
McAvoy, Thomas	14/12/43	Lab Coop	Glasgow Rutherglen	15,007	Ian Gray: SNP; Robert Brown: LD
McCabe, Steve	4/8/55	Lab	Birmingham Hall Green	8,420	Andrew Hargeaves: Con; Charles Dow: LD
McCafferty, Chris	14/10/45	Lab	Calder Valley	6,255	Donald Thompson: Con; Stephen Pearson: LD
McCartney, Ian	25/4/51	Lab	Makerfield	26,177	Michael Winstanley: Con; Bruce Hubbard: LD

(*continued*)

Members of the House of Commons (*continued*)

Member	Date of birth	Party[1]	Constituency	Majority at 1997 election	Opponents[1]
McCartney, Robert	24/4/36	UKU	North Down	1,449	Alan McFarland: UUP; Oliver Napier: APNI
McDonagh, Siobhain	20/2/60	Lab	Mitcham and Morden	13,741	Angela Rumbold: Con; Nicholas Harris: LD
MacDonald, Calum	7/5/56	Lab	Western Isles	3,576	Anne Lorne Gillies: SNP; James McGrigor: Con
McDonnell, John	8/9/51	Lab	Hayes and Harlington	14,289	Andrew Retter: Con; Anthony Little: LD
McFall, John	14/10/44	Lab Coop	Dumbarton	10,883	Bill Mackechnie: SNP; Peter Ramsey: Con
McGrady, Eddie	3/6/35	SDLP	Down South	9,933	Dermott Nesbitt: UUP; Mick Murphy: SF
MacGregor, John	14/2/37	Con	Norfolk South	7,378	Barbara Hacker: LD; Jane Ross: Lab
McGuinness, Martin[2]	23/5/50	SF	Ulster Mid	1,883	William McCrea: DUP; Denis Haughey: SDLP
McGuire, Anne	26/5/49	Lab	Stirling	6,411	Michael Forsyth: Con; Ewan Dow: SNP
McIntosh, Anne	20/9/54	Con	Vale of York	9,721	Matthew Carter: Lab; Charles Hall: LD
McIsaac, Shona	3/4/60	Lab	Cleethorpes	9,176	Michael Brown: Con; Keith Melton: LD
MacKay, Andrew	27/8/49	Con	Bracknell	10,387	Anne Snelgrove: Lab; Alan Hilliar: LD
McKenna, Rosemary	8/5/41	Lab	Cumbernauld and Kilsyth	11,128	Colin Barrie: SNP; Ian Sewell: Con
Mackinlay, Andrew	24/4/49	Lab	Thurrock	17,256	Andrew Rosindell: Con; Joe White: LD
MacLean, David	16/5/53	Con	Penrith and The Border	10,233	Kenneth Walker: LD; Margaret Melling: Lab
McLeish, Henry	15/6/48	Lab	Fife Central	13,713	Tricia Marwick: SNP; Jacob Rees-Mogg: Con
MacLennan, Robert	26/6/36	LD	Caithness, Sutherland and Easter Ross	2,259	James Hendry: Lab; Evan Harper: SNP
McLoughlin, Patrick	30/11/57	Con	Derbyshire West	4,885	Stephen Clamp: Lab; Christopher Seeley: LD
McNamara, Kevin	5/9/34	Lab	Hull North	19,705	David Lee: Con; David Nolan: LD
McNulty, Tony	3/11/58	Lab	Harrow East	9,737	Hugh Dykes: Con; Baldev Kumar Sharma: LD
MacShane, Denis	21/5/48	Lab	Rotheram	21,469	Simon Gordon: Con; David Wildgoose: LD
MacTaggart, Fiona	12/9/53	Lab	Slough	13,071	Peta Jane Buscombe: Con; Chris Bushill: LD
McWalter, Tony	20/3/45	Lab Coop	Hemel Hempstead	3,636	Rob Jones: Con; Patricia Lindsley: LD
McWilliam, John	16/5/41	Lab	Blaydon	16,605	Peter Maughan: LD; Mark Watson: Con
Madel, David	6/8/38	Con	Bedforshire South West	132	Andrew Date: Lab; Stephen Owen: LD
Maginnis, Ken	21/1/38	UUP	Fermanagh and South Tyrone	13,688	Gerry McHugh: SF; Tommy Gallagher: SDLP
Mahon, Alice	28/9/37	Lab	Halifax	11,212	Robert Light: Con; Edgar Waller: LD
Major, John	29/3/43	Con	Huntingdon	18,140	Jason Reece: Lab; Matthew Owen: LD
Malins, Humfrey	31/7/45	Con	Woking	5,678	Philip Goldenberg: LD; Katie Hanson: Lab
Mallaber, Judy	10/7/51	Lab	Amber Valley	11,613	Phillip Oppenheim: Con; Roger Shelley: LD
Mallon, Seamus	17/8/36	SDLP	Newry and Armagh	4,889	Danny Kennedy: UUP; Pat McNamee: SF
Mandelson, Peter	21/10/53	Lab	Hartlepool	17,508	Michael Horsley: Con; Reginald Clark: LD
Maples, John	22/4/43	Con	Stratford-on-Avon	14,106	Susan Juned: LD; Stewart Stacey: Lab
Marek, John	24/12/40	Lab	Wrexham	11,762	Stuart Andrew: Con; Andrew Thomas: LD
Marsden, Gordon	18/3/68	Lab	Blackpool South	11,616	Richard Booth: Con; Doreen Holt: LD
Marsden, Paul	18/3/68	Lab	Shrewsbury and Atcham	1,670	Derek Conway: Con; Anne Woodland: LD
Marshall, David	7/5/41	Lab	Glasgow Shettleston	15,868	Humayan Hanif: SNP; Colin Simpson: Con
Marshall, Jim	13/3/41	Lab	Leicester South	16,493	Christopher Heaton-Harris: Con; Barry Coles: LD
Marshall-Andrews, Robert	10/4/44	Lab	Medway	5,354	Peggy Fenner: Con; Roger Roberts: LD
Martin, Michael	3/7/45	Lab	Glasgow Springburn	17,326	John Brady: SNP; Mark Holdsworth: Con
Martlew, Eric	3/1/49	Lab	Carlisle	12,390	Richard Lawrence: Con; Christopher Mayho: LD
Mates, Michael	9/6/34	Con	Hampshire East	11,590	Robert Booker: LD; Robert Hoyle: Lab
Maude, Francis	4/7/53	Con	Horsham	14,862	Morwen Millson: LD; Maureen Walsh: Lab
Mawhinney, Brian	26/7/40	Con	Cambridgeshire North West	7,754	Lee Steptoe: Lab; Barbara McCoy: LD
Maxton, John	5/5/36	Lab	Glasgow Cathcart	12,965	Maire Whitehead: SNP; Alistair Muir: Con
May, Theresa	1/10/56	Con	Maidenhead	11,981	Andrew Ketteringham: LD; Denise Robson: Lab
Meacher, Michael	4/11/39	Lab	Oldham West and Royton	16,201	Jonathan Lord: Con; Howard Cohen: LD
Meale, Alan	31/7/49	Lab	Mansfield	20,518	Tim Frost: Con; Philip Smith: LD
Merron, Gillian	12/4/59	Lab	Lincoln	11,130	Anthony Brown: Con; Lisa Gabriel: LD
Michael, Alun	22/8/43	Lab Coop	Cardiff South and Penarth	13,881	Caroline Roberts: Con; Simon Wakefield: LD
Michie, Bill	24/11/35	Lab	Sheffield Heeley	17,078	Roger Davison: Con; John Harthman: Con
Michie, Ray	4/2/34	LD	Argyll and Bute	6,081	Neil MacCormick: SNP; Ralph McIlroy Leishman: Con
Milburn, Alan	27/1/58	Lab	Darlington	16,025	Peter Scrope: Con; Les Boxell: LD
Miller, Andrew	23/3/49	Lab	Ellesmere Port and Neston	16,036	Lynn Turnbull: Con; Joanna Pemberton: LD
Mitchell, Austin	19/9/34	Lab	Great Grimsby	16,244	Dean Godson: Con; Andrew De Freitas: LD
Moffatt, Laura	9/4/54	Lab	Crawley	11,707	Jospehine Crabb: Con; Harold De Souza: LD
Moonie, Lewis	25/2/47	Lab Coop	Kirkcaldy	10,710	Stewart Hosie: SNP; Charlotte Black: Con
Moore, Michael	3/6/65	LD	Tweeddale, Ettrick and Lauderdale	2,290	Keith Gedder: Lab; Alister Jack: Con
Moran, Margaret	19/1/55	Lab	Luton South	11,319	Graham Bright: Con; Keith Fitchett: LD
Morgan, Alasdair	21/4/45	SNP	Galloway and Upper Nithsdale	5,624	Ian Lang: Con; Katy Clark: Lab
Morgan, Julie	2/11/44	Lab	Cardiff North	8,126	Gwilym Jones: Con; Robyn Rowland: LD
Morgan, Rhodri	29/9/39	Lab	Cardiff West	15,628	Simon Hoare: Con; Jacqui Gasson: LD
Morley, Elliott	6/7/52	Lab	Scunthorpe	14,173	Martyn Fisher: Con; Gordon Smith: LD
Morris, Estelle	17/6/52	Lab	Birmingham Yardley	5,315	John Hemming: LD; Anne Jobson: Con

Members of the House of Commons (*continued*)

Member	Date of birth	Party[1]	Constituency	Majority at 1997 election	Opponents[1]
Morris, John	5/11/31	Lab	Aberavon	21,571	Ron McConville: LD; Peter Harper: Con
Moss, Malcolm	6/3/43	Con	Cambridgeshire North East	5,101	Virginia Bucknor: Lab; Andrew Nash: LD
Mountford, Kali	12/1/54	Lab	Colne Valley	4,840	Graham Riddick: Con; Nigel Priestley: LD
Mowlam, Marjorie	18/9/49	Lab	Redcar	21,664	Andrew Isaacs: Con; Joyce Benbow: LD
Mudie, George	6/2/45	Lab	Leeds East	17,466	John Emsley: Con; Madeleine Kirk: LD
Mullin, Chris	12/12/47	Lab	Sunderland South	19,638	Timothy Schofield: Con; John Lennox: LD
Murphy, Denis	2/11/48	Lab	Wansbeck	32,367	Alan Thompson: LD; Paul Green: Con
Murphy, Jim	23/8/67	Lab	Eastwood	3,236	Paul Cullen: Con; Douglas Yates: SNP
Murphy, Paul	25/11/48	Lab	Torfaen	24,536	Neil Parish: Con; Jean Gray: LD
Naysmith, Douglas	1/4/41	Lab Coop	Bristol North West	11,382	Michael Stern: Con; Ian Parry: LD
Nicholls, Patrick	14/11/48	Con	Teignbridge	281	Richard Younger-Ross: LD; Sue Dann: Lab
Norman, Archie	1/5/54	Con	Tunbridge Wells	7,506	Anthony Clayton: LD; Peter Warner: Lab
Norris, Dan	28/1/60	Lab	Wansdyke	4,799	Michael Mark Prisk: Con; Jeff Manning: LD
O'Brien, Brill	25/1/29	Lab	Normanton	15,893	Fiona Bulmer: Con; David Ridgway: LD
O'Brien, Mike	19/1/54	Lab	Warwickshire North	14,767	Stephen Hammond: Con; William Powell: LD
O'Hara, Eddie	1/10/37	Lab	Knowsley South	30,708	Gary Robertson: Con; Clifford Mainey: LD
O'Neill, Martin	6/1/45	Lab	Ochil	4,652	George Reid: SNP; Allan Hogarth: Con
Oaten, Mark	8/3/64	LD	Winchester	21 556[5]	Gerald Malone: Con; Patrick Davies: Lab; Robin Page: Ref; Richard Huggett: Lit.Dem. ; Rosemary Barry: NL; Roger Everest: EC
Olner, Bill	9/5/42	Lab	Nuneaton	13,540	Richard Blunt: Con; Ron Cockings: LD
Opik, Lembit	2/3/65	LD	Montgomeryshire	6,303	Glyn Davies: Con; Angharad Davies: Lab
Organ, Diana	21/2/52	Lab	Forest of Dean	6,343	Paul Marland: Con; Anthony Lynch: LD
Osborne, Sandra	23/2/56	Lab	Ayr	6,543	Phil Gallie: Con; Ian Blackford: SNP
Ottaway, Richard	24/5/45	Con	Croydon South	11,930	Charles Burling: Lab; Steven Gauge: LD
Page, Richard	22/2/41	Con	Hertfordshire South West	10,021	Mark Wilson: Lab; Ann Shaw: LD
Paice, James	24/4/49	Con	Cambridgeshire South East	9,349	Rex Collinson: Lab; Sarah Brinton: LD
Paisley, Ian	6/4/26	DUP	Antrim North	10,574	James Leslie: UUP; Sean Farren: SDLP
Palmer, Nick	5/2/50	Lab	Broxtowe	5,575	Jim Lester: Con; Terrence Miller: LD
Paterson, Owen	24/6/56	Con	Shropshire North	2,195	Ian Lucas: Lab; John Stevens: LD
Pearson, Ian	5/4/59	Lab	Dudley South	13,027	George Simpson: Con; Richard Burt: LD
Pendry, Tom	10/6/34	Lab	Stalybridge and Hyde	14,806	Nicholas de Bois: Con; Martin Cross: LD
Perham, Linda	29/6/47	Lab	Ilford North	3,224	Vivian Bendall: Con; Alan Dean: LD
Pickles, Eric	20/4/52	Con	Brentwood and Ongar	9,690	Elizabeth Bottomley: LD; Marc Young: Lab
Pickthall, Colin	13/9/44	Lab	Lancashire West	17,119	Christopher Varley: Con; Arthur Wood: LD
Pike, Peter	26/6/37	Lab	Burnley	17,062	William Wiggin: Con; Gordon Birtwhistle: LD
Plaskitt, James	23/6/54	Lab	Warwick and Leamington	3,398	Dudley Smith: Con; Nigel Hicks: LD
Pollard, Kerry	27/4/44	Lab	St Albans	4,459	David Rutley: Con; Anthony Rowlands: LD
Pond, Chris	25/9/52	Lab	Gravesham	5,779	Jacques Arnold: Con; Jean Canet: LD
Pope, Greg	29/8/60	Lab	Hyndburn	11,448	Peter Britcliffe: Con; Les Jones: LD
Pound, Stephen	3/7/48	Lab	Ealing North	7,010	Harry Greenway: Con; Anjan Gupta: LD
Powell, Raymond	19/6/28	Lab	Ogmore	24,447	David Unwin: Con; Kirsty Williams: LD
Prentice, Bridget	28/12/52	Lab	Lewisham East	12,127	Philip Hollobone: Con; David Buxton: LD
Prentice, Gordon	28/1/51	Lab	Pendle	10,824	John Midgley: Con; Tony Greaves: LD
Prescott, John	31/5/38	Lab	Hull East	23,318	Angus West: Con; Jim Wastling: LD
Primarolo, Dawn	2/5/54	Lab	Bristol South	19,328	Michael Roe: Con; Stephen Williams: LD
Prior, David	2/12/54	Con	Norfolk North	1,084	Norman Lamb: LD; Michael Cullingham: Lab
Prosser, Gwyn	27/4/43	Lab	Dover	11,739	David Shaw: Con; Mark Corney: LD
Purchase, Ken	8/1/39	Lab Coop	Wolverhampton North East	12,987	David Harvey: Con; Brian Niblett: LD
Quin, Joyce	26/11/44	Lab	Gateshead East and Washington West	24,950	Jacqui Burns: Con; Alan Ord: LD
Quinn, Lawrie	25/12/56	Lab	Scarborough and Whitby	5,124	John Sykes: Con; Martin Allinson: LD
Radice, Giles	4/10/36	Lab	Durham North	26,299	Mark Hardy: Con; Brian Moore: LD
Rammell, Bill	10/10/59	Lab	Harlow	10,514	Jerry Hayes: Con; Lorna Spenceley: LD
Randall, John	5/8/55	Con	Uxbridge	3,766[6]	Andrew Slaughter: Lab; Keith Kerr: LD; Lord Sutch: RA; Julia Leonard: SP; Francis Taylor: BNP; John McCauly: NF; Ian Anderson: NP; James Feisenburger: UIP; Ronnie Carroll: RA
Rapson, Syd	17/4/42	Lab	Portsmouth North	4,323	Peter Griffiths: Con; Steve Sollitt: LD
Raynsford, Nick	28/1/45	Lab	Greenwich and Woolwich	18,128	Michael Mitchell: Con; Cherry Luxton: LD
Redwood, John	15/6/51	Con	Wokingham	9,365	Royce Longton: LD; Patricia Colling: Lab
Reed, Andrew	17/9/64	Lab Coop	Loughborough	5,712	Kenneth Andrew: Con; Diana Brass: LD
Reid, John	8/5/47	Lab	Hamilton North and Bellshill	17,067	Michael Matheson: SNP; Gordon McIntosh: Con
Rendel, David	15/4/49	LD	Newbury	8,617	Richard Benyon: Con; Paul Hannon: LD
Robathan, Andrew	17/7/51	Con	Blaby	6,474	Ross Willmott: Lab; Geoffrey Welsh: LD
Robertson, George	12/4/46	Lab	Hamilton South	15,878	Ian Black: SNP; Robert Dow Kilgour: Con
Robertson, Lawrence	29/3/58	Con	Tewkesbury	9,234	John Sewell: LD; Kelvin Tustin: Lab
Robinson, Geoffrey	25/5/39	Lab	Coventry North West	16,601	Paul Bartlett: Con; Napier Penlington: LD

(continued)

Members of the House of Commons (continued)

Member	Date of birth	Party[1]	Constituency	Majority at 1997 election	Opponents[1]
Robinson, Peter	29/12/48	DUP	Belfast East	6,754	Reg Empey: UUP; Jim Hendron: APNI
Roche, Barbara	13/4/54	Lab	Hornsey and Wood Green	20,499	Helena Hart: Con; Lynne Featherstone: LD
Roe, Marion	15/7/36	Con	Broxbourne	6,653	Ben Coleman: Lab; Julia Davies: LD
Rogers, Allan	24/10/32	Lab	Rhondda	24,931	Leanne Wood: PC; Rodney Berman: LD
Rooker, Jeff	5/6/41	Lab	Birmingham Perry Barr	18,957	Andrew Dunnett: Con; Ray Hassall: LD
Rooney, Terry	11/11/50	Lab	Bradford North	12,770	Rasjid Skinner: Con; Terry Browne: LD
Ross, Ernie	27/7/42	Lab	Dundee West	11,859	John Dorward: SNP; Neil Powrie: Con
Ross, William	4/2/36	UUP	Londonderry East	3,794	Gregory Campbell: DUP; Arthur Docherty: SDLP
Rowe, Andrew	11/99/35	Con	Faversham and Kent Mid	4,173	Alan Stewart: Lab; Bruce Parmenter: LD
Rowlands, Ted	23/1/40	Lab	Merthyr Tydfil and Rhymney	27,086	Duncan Ansty: LD; Jonathan Morgan: Con
Roy, Frank	29/8/58	Lab	Motherwell and Wishaw	12,791	James McGuigan: SNP; Scott Dickson: Con
Ruane, Chris	8/7/58	Lab	Vale of Clwyd	8,955	David Edwards: Con; Daniel Munford: LD
Ruddock, Joan	28/12/43	Lab	Lewisham Deptford	18,878	Irene Kimm: Con; Kofi Appiah: LD
Ruffley, David	18/4/62	Con	Bury St Edmunds	368	Mark Ereira: Lab; David Cooper: LD
Russell, Bob	31/3/46	LD	Colchester	1,551	Stephan Shakespeare: Con; Roderick Green: Lab
Russell, Christine	25/3/45	Lab	Chester, City of	10,553	Gyles Brandreth: Con; David Simpson: LD
Ryan, Joan	8/9/55	Lab	Enfield North	6,812	Mark Field: Con; Michael Hopkins: LD
St Aubyn, Nick	19/11/55	Con	Guildford	4,791	Margaret Sharp: LD; Joseph Burns: Lab
Salmond, Alex	31/12/54	SNP	Banff and Buchan	12,845	William Bell-Frain: Con; Megan Harris: Lab
Salter, Martin	19/4/54	Lab	Reading West	2,997	Nicholas Bennett: Con; Dierdre Tomlin: LD
Sanders, Adrian	25/4/59	LD	Torbay	12	Rupert Allason: Con; Michael Morey: Lab
Sarwar, Mohammad	18/8/52	Lab	Glasgow Govan (suspended)	2,914	Nicola Sturgeon: SNP; William Thomas: Con
Savidge, Malcolm	9/5/46	Lab	Aberdeen North	10,010	Brian Adam: SNP; James Gifford: Con
Sawford, Phil	26/6/50	Lab	Kettering	189	Roger Freeman: Con; Roger Aron: LD
Sayeed, Jonathan	20/3/48	Con	Bedfordshire Mid	7,090	Neil Mallett: Lab; Timothy Hill: LD
Sedgemore, Brian	17/3/37	Lab	Hackney South and Shoreditch	14,990	Martin Pantling: LD; Christopher O'Leary: Con
Shaw, Jonathon	3/6/66	Lab	Chatham and Aylesford	2,790	Richard Knox-Johnston: Con; Robin Murray: LD
Sheerman, Barry	17/8/40	Lab Coop	Huddersfield	15,848	Bill Forrow: Con; Gordon Beever: LD
Sheldon, Robert	13/9/23	Lab	Ashton-under-Lyne	22,965	Richard Mayson: Con; Timothy Pickstone: LD
Shephard, Gillian	22/1/40	Con	Norfolk South West	2,434	Adrian Heffernan: Lab; David Buckton: LD
Shepherd, Richard	6/12/42	Con	Aldridge-Brownhills	2,526	Janos Toth: Lab; Celia Downie: LD
Shipley, Debra	22/6/57	Lab	Stourbridge	5,645	Warren Hawksley: Con; Chris Bramau: LD
Short, Clare	15/2/46	Lab	Birmingham Ladywood	23,082	Shailesh Vara: Con; Sardul Singh Marwa: LD
Simpson, Alan	20/9/48	Lab	Nottingham South	13,364	Brian Kirsch: Con; Gareth Long: LD
Simpson, Keith	29/3/49	Con	Norfolk Mid	1,336	Daniel Zeichner: Lab; Susan Frary: LD
Singh, Marsha	11/10/54	Lab	Bradford West	3,877	Mohammed Riaz: Con; Helen Wright: LD
Skinner, Dennis	11/2/32	Lab	Bolsover	27,149	Richard Harwood: Con; Ian Cox: LD
Smith, Andrew	1/2/51	Lab	Oxford East	16,665	Jonathan Djanogly: Con; George Kershaw: LD
Smith, Angela	7/1/59	Lab Coop	Basildon	13,280	John Baron: Con; Lindsay Granshaw: LD
Smith, Chris	24/7/51	Lab	Islington South and Finsbury	14,563	Sarah Ludford: LD; David Berens: Con
Smith, Geraldine	29/8/61	Lab	Morecambe and Lunesdale	5,965	Mark Lennox-Boyd: Con; June Greenwell: LD
Smith, Jacqui	3/11/62	Lab	Redditch	6,125	Anthea McIntyre: Con; Malcolm Hall: LD
Smith, John	17/3/51	Lab	Vale of Glamorgan	10,532	Walter Sweeney: Con; Suzanne Campbell: LD
Smith, Llew	16/4/44	Lab	Blaenau Gwent	28,032	Geraldine Layton: LD; Margrit Williams: Con
Smith, Robert	15/4/58	LD	Aberdeenshire West and Kincardine	2,662	George Kynoch: Con; Joy Mowatt: SNP
Smyth, Martin	15/6/31	UUP	Belfast South	4,600	Alasdair McDonald: SDLP; David Ervine: PUP
Snape, Peter	12/2/42	Lab	West Bromwich East	13,584	Brian Matsell: Con; Martyn Smith: LD
Soames, Nicholas	12/2/48	Con	Sussex Mid	6,854	Margaret Collins: LD; Mervyn Hamilton: Lab
Soley, Clive	7/5/39	Lab	Ealing Acton and Shepherd's Bush	15,650	Barabara Yerolemou: Con; Andrew Mitchell: LD
Southworth, Helen	13/11/56	Lab	Warrington South	10,807	Christopher Grayling: Con; Peter Walker: LD
Spellar, John	5/8/47	Lab	Warley	15,451	Christopher Pincher: Con; Jeremy Pursehouse: LD
Spelman, Caroline	4/5/58	Con	Meriden	582	Brian Seymour-Smith: Lab; Anthony Dupont: LD
Spicer, Michael	22/1/43	Con	Worcestershire West	3,846	Michael Hadley: LD; Meil Stone: Lab
Spring, Richard	24/9/46	Con	Suffolk West	1,867	Michael Jeffreys: Lab; Adrian Graves: LD
Squire, Rachel	13/7/54	Lab	Dunfermline West	12,354	John Lloyd: SNP; Elizabeth Harris: LD
Stanley, John	19/1/42	Con	Tonbridge and Malling	10,230	Barbara Withstandley: Lab; Keith Brown: LD
Starkey, Phyllis	4/1/47	Lab	Milton Keynes South West	10,092	Barry Legg: Con; Peter Jones: LD
Steen, Anthony	22/7/39	Con	Totnes	877	Rob Chave: LD; Victor Ellery: Lab
Steinberg, Gerry	20/4/45	Lab	Durham, City of	22,504	Richard Chalk: Con; Nigel Martin: LD
Stevenson, George	30/8/38	Lab	Stoke-on-Trent South	18,303	Sheila Scott: Con; Peter Barnett: LD
Stewart, David	5/5/56	Lab	Inverness East, Nairn and Lochaber	2,339	Fergus Ewing: SNP; Stephen Gallagher: LD
Stewart, Ian	28/8/50	Lab	Eccles	21,916	Gregory Barker: Con; Robert Boyd: LD
Stinchcombe, Paul	25/4/62	Lab	Wellingborough	187	Peter Fry: Con; Peter Smith: LD

Members of the House of Commons (*continued*)

Member	Date of birth	Party[1]	Constituency	Majority at 1997 election	Opponents[1]
Stoate, Howard	14/4/54	Lab	Dartford	4,328	Bob Dunn: Con; Dorothy Webb: LD
Stott, Roger	7/8/43	Lab	Wigan	22,643	Mark Loveday: Con; Trevor Beswick: LD
Strang, Gavin	10/7/43	Lab	Edinburgh East and Mussleburgh	14,530	Derrick White: SNP; Kenneth Ward: Con
Straw, Jack	3/8/46	Lab	Blackburn	14,445	Sangeeta Kaur Sidhu: Con; Stephen Fenn: LD

Jack Straw, home secretary and MP for Blackburn Sean Aidan

Streeter, Gary	19/1/55	Con	Devon South West	7,433	Chris Mavin: Lab; Keith Baldry: LD
Stringer, Graham	17/2/50	Lab	Manchester Blackley	19,588	Stephen Barclay: Con; Simon Wheale: LD
Stuart, Gisela	26/11/55	Lab	Birmingham Edgbaston	4,842	Andrew Marshall: Con; James Gallagher: LD
Stunnell, Andrew	24/11/42	LD	Hazel Grove	11,814	Brendan Murphy: Con; Jeffrey Lewis: Lab
Sutcliffe, Gerry	13/5/53	Lab	Bradford South	12,936	Anne Hawkesworth: Con; Alexander Wilson-Fletcher: LD
Swayne, Desmond	20/8/56	Con	New Forest West	11,332	Robert Hale: LD; David Griffiths: Lab
Swinney, John	13/4/64	SNP	Tayside North	4,160	Bill Walker: Con; Ian McFatridge: Lab
Syms, Robert	15/8/56	Con	Poole	5,298	Alan Tetlow: LD; Hadyn White: Lab
Tapsell, Peter	1/2/30	Con	Louth and Horncastle	6,900	John Hough: Lab; Fiona Martin: LD
Taylor, Ann	2/7/47	Lab	Dewsbury	8,323	Paul McCormick: Con; Kingsley Hill: LD
Taylor, Dari	13/12/44	Lab	Stockton South	11,585	Tim Devlin: Con; Peter Monck: LD
Taylor, David	22/8/46	Lab Coop	Leicestershire North West	13,219	Robert Goodwill: Con; Stanley Heptinstall: LD
Taylor, Ian	18/4/45	Con	Esher and Walton	14,528	Julie Reay: Lab; Gary Miles: LD
Taylor, John D	24/12/37	UUP	Strangford	5,852	Iris Robinson: DUP; Kieran McCarthy: APNI
Taylor, John M	19/8/41	Con	Solihull	11,397	Michael Southcombe: LD; Rachel Harris: Lab
Taylor, Matthew	3/1/63	LD	Truro and St Austell	12,501	Neil Badcock: Con; Michael Dooley: Lab
Taylor, Teddy	18/4/37	Con	Rochford and Southend East	4,225	Nigel Smith: Lab; Paula Smith: LD
Temple-Morris, Peter	12/2/38	Con	Leominster	8,835	Terence James: LD; Richard Westwood: Lab
Thomas, Gareth	25/9/54	Lab	Clwyd West	1,848	Rod Richards: Con; Eryl Williams: PC
Thomas, Gareth R	15/7/67	Lab	Harrow West	1,240	Robert Hughes: Con; Pash Nandhra: LD
Thompson, William	26/10/39	UUP	Tyrone West	1,161	Jo Byrne: SDLP; Pat Doherty: SF
Timms, Stephen	29/7/55	Lab	East Ham	19,358	Angela Bray: Con; Imran Khan: SLP
Tipping, Paddy	24/10/49	Lab	Sherwood	16,812	Roland Spencer: Con; Bruce Moult: LD
Todd, Mark	29/12/54	Lab	Derbyshire South	13,967	Edwina Currie: Con Robert Reynold: LD
Tonge, Jenny	19/2/41	LD	Richmond Park	2,951	Jeremy Hanley: Con; Sue Jenkins: Lab
Touhig, Don	5/12/47	Lab Coop	Islwyn	23,931	Chris Worker: LD; David Walters: Con
Townend, John	12/6/34	Con	Yorkshire East	3,337	Ian Male: Lab; David Leadley: LD
Tredinnick, David	19/1/50	Con	Bosworth	1,027	Andrew Furlong: Lab; Jonathan Ellis: LD
Trend, Michael	19/4/52	Con	Windsor	9,917	Christopher Fox: LD; Amanda Williams: Lab
Trickett, Jon	2/7/50	Lab	Hemsworth	23,992	Norman Hazell: Con; Jacqueline Kirby: LD
Trimble, David	15/10/44	UUP	Upper Bann	9,252	Brid Rodgers: SDLP; Bernadette O'Hagan: SF
Truswell, Paul	17/11/55	Lab	Pudsey	6,207	Peter Bone: Con; Jonathan Brown: LD
Turner, Dennis	26/8/42	Lab Coop	Wolverhampton South East	15,182	William Hanbury: Con; Richard Whitehouse: LD
Turner, Desmond	17/7/39	Lab	Brighton Kemptown	3,234	Andrew Bowden: Con; Clive Gray: LD
Turner, George	9/8/40	Lab	Norfolk North West	1,339	Henry Bellingham: Con; Evelyn Knowles: LD
Twigg, Derek	9/7/59	Lab	Halton	23,650	Philip Balmer: Con; Janet Jones: LD
Twigg, Stephen	25/12/66	Lab	Enfield Southgate	1,433	Michael Portillo: Con; Jeremy Browne: LD
Tyler, Paul	29/10/41	LD	Cornwall North	13,847	Nigel Linacre: Con; Anne Lindo: Lab
Tyrie, Andrew	15/1/57	Con	Chichester	9,734	Peter Gardiner: LD; Charlie Smith: Lab
Vaz, Keith	26/11/56	Lab	Leicester East	18,422	Simon Milton: Con; Jay Matabudul: LD
Viggers, Peter	13/3/38	Con	Gosport	6,258	Ivan Gray: Lab; Stephen Hogg: LD
Vis, Rudi	4/4/41	Lab	Finchley and Golders Green	3,189	John Marshall: Con; Jonathan Davies: LD
Walker, Cecil	17/12/24	UUP	Belfast North	13,024	Alban Maginness: SDLP; Gerry Kelly: SF

(*continued*)

Members of the House of Commons (continued)

Member	Date of birth	Party[1]	Constituency	Majority at 1997 election	Opponents[1]
Wallace, Jim	25/8/54	LD	Orkney and Shetland	6,968	James Paton: Lab; Willie Ross: SNP
Walley, Joan	23/1/49	Lab	Stoke-on-Trent North	17,392	Christopher Day: Con; Henry Jebb: LD
Walter, Robert	3/5/48	Con	Dorset North	2,746	Paula Yates: LD; John Fitzmaurice: Lab
Ward, Claire	9/5/72	Lab	Watford	5,792	Robert Gordon: Con; Andrew Canning: LD
Wardle, Charles	23/8/39	Con	Bexhill and Battle	11,100	Kathryn Field: LD; Robert Beckwith: Lab
Wareing, Robret	20/8/30	Lab	Liverpool West Derby	25,965	Steve Radford: Lib; Anne Hines: LD
Waterson, Nigel	12/10/50	Con	Eastbourne	1,994	Christopher Berry: LD; David Lines: Lab
Watts, Dave	26/8/51	Lab	St Helens North	23,417	Pelham Walker: Con; John Beirne: LD
Webb, Steven	18/7/65	LD	Northavon	2,137	John Cope: Con; Ron Stone: Lab
Wells, Bowen	4/8/35	Con	Hertford and Stortford	6,885	Simon Speller: Lab; Michael Wood: LD
Welsh, Andrew	19/4/44	SNP	Angus	10,189	Sebastian Leslie: Con; Catherine Taylor: Lab
White, Brian	5/5/57	Lab	Milton Keynes North East	240	Peter Butler: Con; Graham Mabbutt: LD
Whitehead, Alan	15/9/50	Lab	Southampton Test	13,684	James Hill: Con; Alan Dowden: LD
Whitney, Raymond	28/11/30	Con	Wycombe	2,370	Christopher Bryant: Lab; Paul Bensilum: LD
Whittingdale, John	16/10/59	Con	Maldon and Chelmsford	10,039	Kevin Freeman: Lab; Graham Pooley: LD
Wicks, Malcolm	1/7/47	Lab	Croydon North	18,398	Ian Martin: Con; Martin Morris: LD
Widdecombe, Ann	4/10/47	Con	Maidstone and The Weald	9,603	John Morgan: Lab; Jane Nelson: LD
Wigley, Dafydd	1/4/43	PC	Caernarfon	7,949	Elwyn Williams: Con; Joan MacQueen: LD
Wilkinson, John	23/9/40	Con	Ruislip Northwood	7,794	Paul Barker: Lab; Chris Edwards: LD
Willetts, David	9/3/56	Con	Havant	3,729	Lynne Armstrong: Lab; Michael Kooner: LD
Williams, Alan	14/10/30	Lab	Swansea West	14,459	Andrew Baker: Con; John Newbury: LD
Williams, Alan Wynne	21/12/45	Lab	Carmarthen East and Dinefwr	3,450	Rhodri Thomas: PC; Edmund Hayward: Con
Williams, Betty	31/7/44	Lab	Conwy	1,596	Roger Roberts: LD; David Jones: Con
Willis, Phil	30/11/41	LD	Harrogate and Knaresborough	6,236	Norman Lamont: Con; Barbara Boyce: Lab
Wills, Michael	20/5/52	Lab	Swindon North	7,688	Guy Opperman: Con; Mike Evemy: LD
Wilshire, David	16/9/43	Con	Spelthorne	3,473	Keith Dibble: Lab; Edward Glynn: LD
Wilson, Brian	13/12/48	Lab	Cunninghame North	11,039	Margaret Mitchell: Con; Kim Nicoll: SNP
Winnick, David	26/6/33	Lab	Walsall North	12,588	Michael Bird: Con; Tracy O'Brien: LD
Winterton, Ann	6/3/41	Con	Congleton	6,130	Joan Walmsley: LD; Freda Scholey: Lab
Winterton, Nicholas	31/3/38	Con	Macclesfield	8,654	Janet Jackson: Lab; Mike Flynn: LD
Winterton, Rosie	10/8/58	Lab	Doncaster Central	17,856	David Turtle: Con; Simon Tarry: LD
Wise, Audrey	4/1/35	Lab	Preston	18,680	Paul Gray: Con; William Chadwick: LD
Wood, Mike	3/3/46	Lab	Batley and Spen	6,141	Elizabeth Peacock: Con; Kath Pinnock: LD
Woodward, Shaun	26/10/58	Con	Witney	7,028	Alexander Hollingsworth: Lab; Angela Lawrence: LD
Woolas, Phil	11/12/59	Lab	Oldham East and Saddleworth	3,389	Chris Davies: LD; John Hudson: Con
Worthington, Tony	11/10/41	Lab	Clydebank and Milngavie	13,320	James Yuill: SNP; Nancy Morgan: Con
Wray, James	28/4/38	Lab	Glasgow Bailliestown	14,840	Patsy Thomson: SNP; Malcolm Gordon Kelly: Con
Wright, Tony	11/3/48	Lab	Cannock Chase	14,478	John Backhouse: Con; Richard Kirby: LD
Wright, Tony	12/8/54	Lab	Great Yarmouth	8,668	Michael Carttiss: Con; Derek Wood: LD
Wyatt, Derek	4/12/49	Lab	Sittingbourne and Sheppey	1,929	Roger Moate: Con; Roger Truelove: LD
Yeo, Tim	20/3/45	Con	Suffolk South	4,175	Paul Bishop: Lab; Anne Pollard: LD
Young, George	16/7/41	Con	Hampshire North West	11,551	Charles Fleming: LD; Michael Mumford: Lab

[1] BNP, British National Party; Con, Conservative; DUP, Democratic Unionist Party; EC, Euro Conservative; Ind, Independent; Lab, Labour; Lab Coop, Labour Cooperative; LD, Liberal Democrats; Lit.Dem., Literal Democrats; NBR, New British Referendum; NF, National Front; NL, Natural Law; NP, National Party; PC, Plaid Cymru; PLA, Pro Life Alliance; Ref, Referendum; RA, Rainbow Alliance; SDLP, Social Democratic Labour Party; SF, Sinn Fein; SFP, Social Foundation Party; Scot Soc, Scottish Socialists; SIL, Scottish Independent Labour Party; SNP, Scottish National Party; SP, Socialist Party; SSA, Scottish Socialist Alliance; UIP, UK Independence Party; UUP, Ulster Unionist Party.

[2] Do not take their seats.

[3] After a by election on 6, November, 1997 following the death of Mr Gordon McMaster (Lab; majority at the 1997 General Election 12,750) on 28, July, 1997.

[4] After a by election on 20, November, 1997 following the resignation of Mr Piers Merchant (Con; majority at the 1997 General Election 4,953) on 21, October, 1997.

[5] After a by election on 20, November, 1997 following a successful election petition against the general election result where the majority over the conservative candidate was 2.

[6] After a by election on 31, July, 1997 following the death of Sir Michael Shersby (Con; majority at the 1997 General Election 724) on 8 May, 1997.

House of Commons Select Committees

These were intended to restore parliamentary control of the executive, improve the quality of legislation, and scrutinize public spending and the work of government departments. Select committees represent the major parliamentary reform of the 20th century, and a possible means – through their all-party membership – of avoiding the repeal of one government's measures by its successor.

Name	Number of members	Chair
Accommodation and Works Committee	9	Sydney Chapman
Agriculture Committee	11	Peter Luff
Culture, Media, and Sport Select Committee	11	Gerald Kaufman
Defence Select Committee	11	Bruce George
Deregulation Select Committee	18	Peter L Pike
Education and Employment Committee		
Education Sub-Committee	10	Margaret Hodge
Employment Sub-Committee	9	Derek Foster
Environment, Transport, and Regional Affairs Select Committee		
Environment Sub-Committee	11	Andrew F Bennett
Transport Sub-Committee	11	Gwyneth Dunwoody
Environmental Audit Select Committee	15	John Horam
European Legislation Select Committee	16	Jimmy Hood
Foreign Affairs Select Committee	12	Donald Anderson
Health Committee	11	David Hinchliffe
Home Affairs Committee	11	Chris Mullin
Information Committee	9	Richard Allan
International Development Committee	11	Bowen Wells
Liaison Committee	31	Robert Sheldon
Select Committee on the Modernization of the House of Commons	15	Ann Taylor
Northern Ireland Affairs Select Committee	13	Peter Brooke
Joint Committee on Parliamentary Privilege	12	Lord Nicholls of Birkenhead
Procedure Committee	14	Nicholas Winterton
Committee of Public Accounts	15	David Davis
Select Committee on Public Administration	11	Rhodri Morgan
Science and Technology Select Committee	11	Michael Clark
Scottish Affairs Select Committee	11	David Marshall
Social Security Select Committee	11	Archy Kirkwood
Standards and Privileges Select Committee	11	Robert Sheldon
Trade and Industry Select Committee	11	Martin O'Neill
Treasury Select Committee	12	Giles Radice
Welsh Affairs Select Committee	11	Martyn Jones

Members of Parliament Returned with a Majority Less Than 1,000

At the election of 1 May 1997.

Rank	Member	Party	Constituency	Majority
1	Oaten, M J	Liberal Democrat	Hampshire, Winchester[1]	2
2	Sanders, A M	Liberal Democrat	Torbay	12
3	Davey, E	Liberal Democrat	Kingston-upon-Thames, Kingston, and Surbiton	56
4	Bruce, I C	Conservative	South Dorset	77
5	Heath, D	Liberal Democrat	Somerset, Somerton and Frome	130
6	Madel, W D	Conservative	Bedfordshire, South West Bedfordshire	132
7	Stinchcombe, P D	Labour	Northamptonshire, Wellingborough	187
8	Sawford, P A	Labour	Northamptonshire, Kettering	189
9	Atkinson, P L	Conservative	Northumberland, Hexham	222
10	Fabricant, M L D	Conservative	Staffordshire, Lichfield	238
11	White, B	Labour	Buckinghamshire, North East Milton Keynes	240
12	Nicholls, P C M	Conservative	Devon, Teignbridge	281
13	Ruffley, D	Conservative	Suffolk, Bury St Edmunds	368
14	King, A	Labour	Warwickshire, Rugby, and Kenilworth	495
15	Heathcoat-Amory, D P	Conservative	Somerset, Wells	528
16	Spelman, C A	Conservative	West Midlands, Meriden	582
17	Body, R B F S	Conservative	Lincolnshire, Boston, and Skegness	647
18	Gordon, E	Labour	Havering, Romford	649
19	Fraser, C J	Conservative	Mid Dorset, Poole North	681
20	Shersby, J M	Conservative	Hillingdon, Uxbridge	724
21	Clark, T	Labour	Northampton, South	744
22	Chidgey, D W G	Liberal Democrat	Eastleigh	754
23	Cran, J D	Conservative	Humberside, Beverley, and Holderness	811
24	Steen, A D	Conservative	Devon, Totnes	877

[1] The Conservative candidate, Gerald Malone, won a petition to have the election reheld. At the by-election of 20 November 1997, Michael Oaten won with a majority of 21,556 (an increase of 21,554), the largest Liberal Democrat majority in Parliament.

Members of Parliament: Pay

Year	Salary (£)	Year	Salary (£)
1911	400	1983	15,308
1931	360	1984	16,106
1934	380	1985	16,904
1935	400	1986	17,702
1937	600	1987	18,500
1946	1,000	1988	22,548
1954[1]	1,250	1989	24,107
1957	1,750	1990	26,701
1964	3,250	1991	28,970
1972	4,500	1992	30,854
1975	5,750	1993	30,854
1976	6,062	1994	31,687
1977	6,270	1995	33,189
1978	6,897	1996	34,085
1979	9,450	1996	43,000
1980	11,750	1997	43,860
1981	13,950	1998	45,066
1982	14,510		

[1] Includes Sessional Allowance.

Source: Fact Sheet No. 17 – *Members' Pay, Pensions and Allowances*; House of Commons Information Office

Members of Parliament: Office Cost Allowances

These allowances were first introduced in 1969. These figures represent the maximum that can be claimed.

Year	Allowance (£)	Year	Allowance (£)
1969	500	1986	20,140
1972	1,000	1987	21,302
1974	1,750	1988	22,588
1975	3,200	1989	24,903
1976	3,512	1990	27,166
1977	3,687	1991	28,986
1978	4,200	1992	39,960
1979	4,600	1993	40,380
1980	6,750	1994	41,308
1980	8,000	1995	42,754
1981	8,480	1996 (paid at first)[1]	43,908
1982	8,820	1996 (from July 1996)	46,364
1983	11,364	1997	47,568
1984	12,437	1998	49,232
1985	13,211		

[1] In July 1996 the House decided by resolution that allowances in any one quarter in the year should not exceed £11,591. Increases in subsequent years are to be linked to the Retail Prices Index for March and will apply from April.

Source: Fact Sheet No. 17 – *Members' Pay, Pensions and Allowances*; House of Commons Information Office

Members of Parliament: Non-Office Cost Allowances

1998–99 figures. These allowances were first introduced in 1969.

Allowance	Provisions	Amount
Supplementary London allowance	Members whose constituency is within Inner London can claim a London Supplement payment	£1,406
Additional costs allowance	Members with constituencies outside Inner London can claim additional expenses incurred in staying overnight away from home while on Parliamentary duties	annual maximum of £12,717
Motor mileage	for journeys made on Parliamentary business between home, constituency, and Westminster	50.1 pence per mile up to 20,000 miles per annum; 23.1 pence per mile after 20,000 miles per annum
Bicycle allowance	for journeys undertaken by bicycle while on Parliamentary duties in the UK	6.4 pence per mile
Travel warrants	Members receive travel warrants which can be exchanged for tickets to travel by rail, sea, or air on Parliamentary business; journeys cover home, constituency, and Westminster. For journeys outside this triangle, on Parliamentary business, costs can be reimbursed if the Fees Office is notified at least three days in advance (three day rule can be waived in exceptional circumstances)	cost of journey
Parking	Members can use the Parliamentary car park	free
Travel for spouses and children	travel warrants are available for Members' spouses and children under the age of 18, between London and the constituency and/or London and home by rail, sea, or air. Children and spouses can make 15 return journeys per calendar year	cost of journey
Travel to European Community institutions	Members can reclaim their travel costs on Parliamentary business between the UK and the European Community Institutions in Brussels, Luxembourg, or Strasbourg. Members are allowed one visit per calendar year	cost of a business class air fare from a London airport and a maximum of two days subsistence at the Civil Service Class A rate
Postage and telephone costs	Members receive free stationery, and free inland telephone and postal services on Parliamentary business	free
Winding-up allowance	up to a third of the annual office costs allowance can be paid to reimburse the cost of any work done on Parliamentary business undertaken on behalf of a retiring, defeated, or deceased Member, after the date of cessation.	annual limit £16,411
Resettlement grant	to assist with the costs of adjusting to 'non-parliamentary life', a Member receives this grant if he loses his seat at a General Election	amount varies between 50% and 100% of the Member's annual salary at the time of the Dissolution of Parliament, prior to the General Election; amount is based on age

Source: Fact Sheet No. 17 – *Members' Pay, Pensions and Allowances*; House of Commons Information Office

UK Ministers' Pay

Full ministerial salary entitlement for Ministers in Commons (excluding Parliamentary salary). (In pounds.)

Year	Prime minister	Cabinet minister Commons	Cabinet minister Lords	Minister of state Commons[1]	Minister of state Lords	Parliamentary under secretary Commons	Parliamentary under secretary Lords
1965	14,000	8,500	8,500	5,625	5,625	3,750	3,750
1972	20,000	13,000	13,000	7,500	7,500	5,500	5,500
1976	20,000	13,000	13,000	7,500	7,500	5,500	5,500
1977	20,000	13,000	13,000	7,500	7,500	5,500	6,020
1978	22,000	14,300	14,300	8,250	8,822	6,050	6,622
1979	33,000	19,650	19,650	12,625	12,911	9,525	9,811
1980	34,650	23,500	23,500	16,250	16,400	12,350	12,500
1981	36,725	27,825	27,825	19,775	23,275	15,100	18,600
1982	38,200	28,950	28,950	20,575	24,200	15,700	19,350
1983	38,987	29,367	30,110	20,867	25,350	15,917	20,390
1984	40,424	30,304	31,680	21,364	26,670	16,154	21,450
1985	41,891	31,271	33,260	21,881	28,000	16,411	22,520
1986	43,328	32,208	34,820	22,378	29,320	16,648	23,580
1987	44,775	33,145	36,390	22,875	30,640	16,885	24,640
1988	45,787	34,157	40,438	23,887	34,688	17,897	28,688
1989	46,109	34,479	41,997	24,209	37,047	18,219	30,647
1990	46,750	35,120	44,591	24,850	39,641	18,860	33,241
1991	50,724	38,105	48,381	26,962	43,010	20,463	36,066
1992	53,007	39,820	50,558	28,175	44,945	21,384	37,689
1994	54,438	40,895	52,260	28,936	46,333	21,961	38,894
1995	57,018	42,834	55,329	30,307	48,835	23,002	41,065
1996	58,557	43,991	57,161	31,125	50,328	23,623	42,361
1996	58,557	43,991	58,876	31,125	51,838	23,623	43,632
1997[2]	100,000	60,000	77,963	31,125	51,838	23,623	43,632
1998	102,750	61,650	80,107	31,981	53,264	24,273	44,832

[1] Until 1980 some Ministers of State received salaries higher than those shown here
[2] In 1997, the Prime Minister and Cabinet Ministers decided to accept the pre-election salaries of £58,557 (Prime Minister), £43,991 (Cabinet Commons), and £58,876 (Cabinet Lords).

Source: *Fact Sheet No. 31 Ministerial Salaries,* House of Commons Information Office

Women MPs in the House of Commons by Political Party

(As of 22 June 1998.)

Political party	Number of members	Number of women members	(%) women members	Political party	Number of members	Number of women members	(%) women members
Labour	418	101	24	Sinn Féin (have not taken their seats)	2	0	0
Conservative	162	14	9	United Kingdom Unionist	1	0	0
Liberal Democrats	46	3	7	Independent	1	0	0
Ulster Unionists	10	0	0	The Speaker and three Deputies (do not normally vote)	4	1	25
Scottish National Party	6	2	33	Vacant seats	0	0	0
Plaid Cymru	4	0	0				
Social Democratic and Labour Party	3	0	0	*Total*	659	121	18
Ulster Democratic Unionist Party	2	0	0				

Parliamentary Standards: Chronology

20 July 1994
Prime Minister John Major suspends two members of Parliament, David Tredinnick and Graham Riddick, as parliamentary private secretaries following allegations that they accepted money for asking questions in the House of Commons.

11 May 1995
The Nolan Report on standards in British public life (commissioned in 1994) recommends the appointment of a Parliamentary Commissioner for Standards, the disclosure of MPs' Parliament-related consultancy work and remuneration, that ministers who wish to accept business appointments within two years of leaving office should obtain permission from an advisory committee, and the appointment of an independent commissioner to scrutinize appointments to 'quangos' (quasi-autonomous nongovernmental organizations).

30 September 1996
Neil Hamilton, MP for Tatton, Cheshire and Ian Greer, a parliamentary lobbyist, drop legal action against *The Guardian* newspaper, which had alleged that Mr Hamilton had received payments to ask questions on behalf of Mohamed Fayed, the owner of Harrods department store.

11 December 1996
Britain's paymaster-general David Willetts resigns over allegations that he 'dissembled' during the 'cash for questions' scandal (in which members of Parliament allegedly took payments for asking parliamentary questions) in order to protect fellow MP Neil Hamilton.

21 March 1997
The decision of Conservative prime minister John Major to prorogue (discontinue) Parliament early means that Sir Gordon Downey's report on parliametary standards in Britain will not be available until after the 1 May 1997 general election.

26 March 1997
Tim Smith, a Conservative MP implicated with Neil Hamilton in the 'cash for questions' scandal, announces that he is to stand down as a candidate in the forthcoming general election.

June 1997
Jack Straw, the home secretary, proposes plans by which MPs who offer or accept a bribe will face a prison sentence.

3 July 1997
The Downey report concludes that two Conservative members of Parliament did take money for asking questions in the House of Commons.

6 November 1997
A report by the House of Commons committee on standards and privileges strongly criticizes the former member of Parliament Neil Hamilton for taking payments to ask parliamentary questions.

Political Parties

Political Parties Represented in Parliament

This table includes parties represented in Parliament. Other political parties which stood in the general election of 1997 were: Albion Party; Alliance Party of Northern Ireland; British National Party; Green Party; Monster Raving Loony Party; National Democrats; Natural Law Party; New Communist Party; Prolife Alliance; Progressive Unionist Party; Referendum Party; Revolutionary Platform of the Socialist Labour Party; Socialist Party; Third Way; UK Independence Party; UK Virtual Party; Ulster Democratic Party.

Party	Headquarters	Leader	Chairperson	Brief history	Political position
Labour	Millbank Tower, Millbank, London SW1P 4GT; phone: (0171) 802 1000; fax: (0171) 802 1234; e-mail: labour-partygeo2.poptel.org.uk; Web site: www.labour.org.uk	Tony Blair	Tom Sawyer (general secretary)	founded in 1900 as the Labour Representation Committee, the party simplified its name to the Labour Party in 1906. It first became the official opposition in 1922. The party's first government (minority) was in 1924, with its first elected majority government in 1945. It is traditionally associated with the Trade Union Movement, who provided much of its funding.	traditionally a party of the left, its policies include: devolution of power to the regions, reform of the second chamber, and social and educational reform. The party has moved from an ethos of government control (nationalization of industry, strong employment legislation) towards a more free-market ideology, with a subsequent backing from the world of finance and the management of industry.
Conservative and Unionist Party	32 Smith Square, Westminster, London SW1P 3HH; phone: (0171) 222 9000; fax: (0171) 222 1135; e-mail: www.conservative-party.org.uk/email; Web site: www.conservative-party.org.uk	William Hague	Lord Cecil Parkinson	historically one of the two great parties. Originally known as the Tory Party, the name Conservative was first used in 1830. The current name results from a merger with the Irish Liberal Unionist Party in 1912. The main party in British politics together with the Whigs (Liberal Democrats) until the 20th century, when the Labour party usurped the latter. Produced the first British woman Prime Minister, Margaret Thatcher.	traditionally a party of the right, with commitment to maintaining the unity of the Nation, low levels of taxation, and low inflation. The present Conservative Party's free-market capitalism is supported by the world of finance and the management of industry.
Liberal Democrats	4 Cowley Street, London SW1P 3NB; phone: (0171) 222 7999; fax: (0171) 799 2170; Web site: www.libdems.org.uk	Paddy Ashdown	Charles Kennedy (UK party president)	historically one of the two great parties. Originally known as the Whigs, the modern Liberal Party began in 1859 and formed its first government in 1868, It last held power in 1919, although the party did forge a 'Lib-Lab' pact with the minority Labour government in 1977. It merged with the breakaway Labour party group, the Social Democratic Party (SDP), in 1988 to become the Social Liberal Democrats (SDP). Became Liberal Democrats in 1989.	centrist, openly pro-European party, committed to electoral reform and the devolution of power. Advocates increase in taxation to raise money for health and education. Organized on a regional basis with separate headquarters for Welsh and Scottish Parties.

Paddy Ashdown, *Liberal Democrat leader*
Sean Aidan (Eye Ubiquitous)

Party	Headquarters	Leader	Chairperson	Brief history	Political position
Plaid Cymru	18 Park Grove, Caerdydd CF1 3BN; phone: (01222) 646000; Web site: www.plaid-cymru.wales.com	Dafydd Wigley	Marc Phillips	formed in 1925, and won its first parliamentary seat in 1966. Now the second party in Wales, with four members of parliament.	Welsh Nationalist Party, committed to a separate socialist Welsh nation, including the promotion of the Welsh language and culture. Forms a joint parliamentary group with the SNP.
Scottish National Party (SNP)	6 North Charlotte Street, Edinburgh EH2 4JH; phone: (0131) 226 3661; fax: (0131) 226 7373; Web site: www.snp.org.uk	Winnie Ewing (President); Alex Salmond (national convener)	Alasdair Morgan (national secretary)	formed in 1934 by the amalgamation of several early nationalist parties. Won its first parliamentary seat in 1945. SNP support was essential to the minority Labour government of 1977. It is the second party in Scotland, with six MPs.	Scottish nationalist party, advocating the separation of Scotland from the UK as an independent state within the European Union. Forms a joint parliamentary group with Plaid Cymru.

(continued)

Political Parties Represented in Parliament (*continued*)

Party	Headquarters	Leader	Chairperson	Brief history	Political position
Ulster Unionist Party (UUP)	3 Glengall Street, Belfast BT12 5AE; phone: (01232) 324601; fax: (01232) 246738; e-mail: uup@uup. org; Web site: www.uup.org	David Trimble	John D Taylor (deputy leader)	formed in 1905. Formally known as the Ulster Unionist Council, it governed the province from 1921–72. Following the suspension of Home Rule in 1972, the party split in 1973, and other Unionist parties were formed. The Ulster Unionists rejected the Anglo-Irish Agreement of 1985, and joined forces with the DUP to campaign against it. All its MPs resigned their seats. The UUP is in favour of the 1998 Northern Ireland Peace Deal. Currently the largest political party in Northern Ireland, with ten MPs. Its leader David Trimble was elected first minister of the new Northern Ireland Assembly in June 1998.	Protestant party of Northern Ireland. Right-of-centre in orientation, it advocates equality for Northern Ireland within the UK, and opposes union with the Republic of Ireland. The party favours hard-line policies on law and order (advocates the death penalty). Has traditionally voted with the Conservative Party in parliament.
Democratic Unionist Party (DUP)	91 Dundela Avenue, Belfast BT4 3BU; phone: (01232) 471155; e-mail: info@dup.org.uk; Web site: www.dup.org.uk	Dr Ian R K Paisley	James McClure	formed in 1973 as a breakaway group from the Ulster Unionist Council.	Protestant party, dedicated to maintaining the Constitution of Northern Ireland as an integral part of the UK. Usually supports the Conservative Party.
Social Democratic and Labour Party (SDLP)	611c Lisburn Road, Belfast BT9 7GT; phone: (01232) 247700; Web site: www.indigo.ie/sdlp	John Hume	Jonathan Stephenson	formed in 1970. It was responsible for setting up the New Ireland Forum in 1983. In 1993 it initiated talks with the leader of Sinn Féin, which prompted a joint UK-Irish peace initiative, and set in motion a Northern Ireland cease-fire (1994–96). Currently has three MPs.	largely Catholic, left-of-centre party. Aims ultimately at Irish unification, but has distanced itself from violent tactics, adopting a constitutional, conciliatory role. Has traditionally voted with the Labour Party.
Sinn Féin	Sinn Féin, 51/55 Falls Road, Belfast; phone: (01232) 624421; fax: (01232) 622112; Web site: www.sinnfein.ie	Gerry Adams	Martin McGuinness	Irish party founded in 1905. The driving political force behind Irish nationalism between 1916 and 1921. It returned to prominence with the outbreak of 'the Troubles' in Northern Ireland in the late 1960s, when it split into Provisional and Official wings at the same time as the Irish Republican Army (IRA), with which it is closely associated. Currently has two MPs in the UK parliament, and one in the Irish parliament.	Nationalist party. Aims to create a united republican Ireland. The current members do not take their seats, and take no part in the parliamentary process.

The City of London

The City Guilds (Livery Companies)

The City of London companies, collectively known as the Livery, are surviving members of medieval trade and craft associations, known as guilds. Each livery company is governed by an annually elected court, typically composed as follows: The Master (elected from the Wardens); Upper Warden; Middle Warden; Lower Warden (elected from the Court assistant); between 10 and 20 Court Assistants (elected from the Livery); a Clerk (to keep the records); a Beadle (to keep order).

After years of dispute, an order of precedence for livery companies was settled in 1515, starting with Mercers at number 1 and so on down to number 48. Merchant Taylors and Skinners, however, continued to alternate between numbers 6 and 7 in alternate years, following a compromise reached some 30 years earlier. Numbers 1 to 12 inclusive are known as the Great Twelve. Through choice, the companies of Parish Clerks and Watermen and Lightermen remain City Guilds without grant of livery.

Livery companies in order of precedence
Mercers (general merchants); Grocers; Drapers; Fishmongers; Goldsmiths; Merchant Taylors (tailors); Skinners (fur trade); Haberdashers; Salters; Ironmongers; Vintners; Clothworkers; Dyers; Brewers; Leathersellers; Pewterers; Barbers (also surgeons and dentists); Cutlers; Bakers; Waxchandlers; Tallowchandlers; Armourers and Brasiers (armour-makers and workers in brass); Girdlers (girdles and belts as clothing); Butchers; Saddlers; Carpenters; Cordwainers (workers in fine leather); Painter Stainers; Curriers (dressers of tanned leather); Masons; Plumbers; Innholders; Founders; Poulters; Cooks; Coopers (barrel makers); Tylers and Bricklayers; Bowyers (longbow makers); Fletchers (arrow makers); Blacksmiths; Joiners; Weavers; Woolmen (winders and packers of wool); Scriveners (writers of court letters and legal documents); Fruiterers; Plaisterers (plasterers); Stationers and Newspaper Makers; Broderers (embroiderers); Upholders (upholsterers); Musicians; Turners; Basketmakers; Glaziers; Horners; Farriers (shoers of horses/veterinary surgeons); Paviors (paving, highways); Loriners (stirrups and other harness for horses); Apothecaries (medicine); Shipwrights; Spectaclemakers; Clock-makers; Glovers; Feltmakers (hats); Framework Knit-

ters; Needlemakers; Gardeners; Tinplate Workers; Wheelwrights; Distillers; Pattenmakers (makers of wooden clog-style footwear); Glass Sellers; Coachmakers and Coach Harness Makers; Gunmakers; Gold and Silver Wyre Drawers (gold and silver braid for uniforms); Makers of Playing Cards; Fan Makers; Carmen; Master Mariners; Solicitors; Farmers; Air Pilots and Air Navigators; Tobacco Pipe Makers and Tobacco Blenders; Furniture Makers; Scientific Instrument Makers; Chartered Surveyors; Chartered Accountants; Chartered Secretaries and Administrators; Builders Merchants; Launderers; Marketors; Actuaries; Insurers; Arbitrators; Engineers; Fuellers; Lightmongers; Environmental Cleaners; Chartered Architects; Constructors; Information Technologists.

The Corporation of London

The Corporation of London is the local authority for the City of London, known as the 'square mile'. Its responsibilities extend beyond the City boundaries, and it provides a number of additional facilities. The Corporation of London is unique in operating on a non-party political basis. It is currently engaged in a major review of its electoral arrangements. In response to the Government's Green paper, New Leadership for London, the Corporation is examining ways in which it can improve the City's franchise and work alongside the proposed strategic authority for London. Further information about the review is available from the City Secretary, Corporation of London, PO Box 270, Guildhall, London EC2P 2EJ.

Committees

Twenty-three committees of elected Members set Corporation policy and oversee the work of departments. These committees are: Barbican Centre; Barbican Residential; Billingsgate and Leadenhall Markets; Board of Governors, City of London Freemen's School; Board of Governors, City of London School; Board of Governors, City of London School for Girls; Board of Governors of the Museum of London; Central Markets; City Lands and Bridge House Estates; City of London Police; Committee of Managers of West Ham Park; Education; Epping Forest and Open Spaces; Establishment; Finance; Hampstead Heath Management; Housing and Sports Development; Libraries, Art Galleries, and Records; Music and Drama; Planning and Transportation; Policy and Resources; Port and City of London Health and Social Services; Spitalfields Market.

Departments

Barbican Centre; Barbican Estate; Billingsgate Market; City of London Cemetery and Crematorium; City of London Freemen's School; City of London Police; City of London School; City of London School for Girls; City Secretary's; City Surveyor's; Cleansing; Comptroller and City Solicitor; Education; Environmental Health and Consumer Protection; Epping Forest; Guildhall School of Music and Drama; Hampstead Heath; Housing and Sports Development; Keeper of Guildhall; Libraries and Art Galleries; London Central Markets; Mansion House; Museum of London; Parks and Gardens; Planning; Remembrancer's; Secondary's; Social Services; Spitalfields; Technical Services; Town Clerk and Chamberlain; West Wickham and Coulsdon Commons, Ashtead Common and Burnham Beeches.

The Wards

Within the geographical area covered by the Corporation of London there are 25 wards or voting districts. Each ward elects an Alderman and between four and twelve Commoners to represent them in the Court of Common Council, the City of London's 'town council'. All Members of the following wards can be contacted via the Corporation of London, PO Box 270, Guildhall, London EC2P 2EJ.

Aldersgate Nicholas Anstee (Alderman), Clifford Green, Neville Littlestone, Jeremy Mayhew, Joyce Nash (Deputy), Barbara Newman, Arthur Simpson; **Aldgate** John Bowman, Bruce Farthing, Dr Peter Hardwick, John Holland (Deputy), Clive Martin (Sheriff Alderman), Patrick O'Ferrall; **Bassishaw** Kenneth Ayers, Nigel Branson, David Brewer (Alderman), John Brewster, Peter Martinelli (Deputy); **Billingsgate** William Baverstock Brooks, John Hughesdon (Alderman), Douglas Mobsby (Deputy), Clive Thorp, John Trotter; **Bishopsgate** William Dove, Graham Forbes, Stanley Ginsburg, Anthony Graves, Bernard Morgan, James Oliver (Alderman), Dorothy Robinson, Esmond Roney (Deputy), Philip Willoughby; **Bread Street** Christopher Davis, Rodney FitzGerald (Deputy), Tom Jackson, Michael Savory (Alderman), John Taylor; **Bridge and Bridge Without** John Bird, Daniel Caspi, Maurice Hart (Deputy), John Owen-Ward, Sir David Rowe-Ham (Alderman); **Broad Street** Sir Christopher Collett (Alderman), Fergus Falk, Archibald Galloway, Brian Harris, David Mizen (Deputy), John Spanner; **Candlewick** Kevin Everett, Stanley Knowles (Sheriff), the Rt Hon the Lord Mayor Richard Nichols (Alderman), Richard Saunders (Deputy), Richard Scriven; **Castle Baynard** Richard Agutter (Alderman), Henry Balls, Sir Colin Cole, Catherine McGuinness, Christopher Mitchell (Deputy); **Cheap** Simon Block,

Peter Bull (Alderman), Joseph Byllam-Barnes, Robin Eve, Ann Pembroke (Deputy); **Coleman Street** Hugh Barnes-Yallowley, Michael Cassidy (Deputy), Robert Finch (Alderman), Stuart Fraser, Michael Henderson-Begg, Derek Kemp, Gordon Wixley; **Cordwainer** George Gillon, Sir Brian Jenkins (Alderman), Stephen Sellon, Michael Snyder (Deputy), Reginald Wilmot; **Cornhill** Wilfred Archibald (Deputy), John Haynes, David Howard (Alderman), Keith Sargant, Dr James White; **Cripplegate Within** Gavyn Arthur (Alderman), Lionel Altman, John Barker (Deputy), David Bradshaw, Christopher Punter, Francis Stevenson, Douglas Warner; **Cripplegate Without** Gavyn Arthur (Alderman), Ernest Angell, Jeffrey Bailey, Stephanie Currie (Deputy), Roger Daily-Hunt, Rosemary Griffiths, Raymond Harries; **Dowgate** Peter Biroum-Smith, Edwina Coven (Deputy), Alison Gowman, Sir Christopher Leaver (Alderman), Michael Sherlock; **Farringdon Within North Side**: Sir Christopher Walford (Alderman), Benson Catt, Henry Horlock (Deputy), Peter Rigby, David Shalit; South Side: Sir Christopher Walford (Alderman), Anthony Eskenzi, Benjamin Hall, Joseph Reed (Deputy), Frank Wooldridge; **Farringdon Without North Side**: Sir Peter Gadsden (Alderman), George Darwin, Michael Farrow, John Platts-Mills, Lady Ponsonby (Deputy), Edward Price, Simon Walsh; South Side: Sir Peter Gadsden (Alderman), John Absalom, Jonathan Charkham, Gregory Lawrence, Julian Malins (Deputy), Wendy Mead, Marguerite Smith; **Langbourn** Frederick Bramwell, George Challis, John Henderson (Deputy), Janet Owen, Sir Alan Traill (Alderman); **Lime Street** Michael Beale (Deputy), Christine Cohen, Dennis Cotgrove, Frederick Everard (Alderman), Ian McNeil; **Portsoken** Roger Brighton, Alfred Dunitz, Geoffrey Lawson, Lord Peter Levene (Alderman), Iris Samuel (Deputy); **Queenhithe** John Fell, Sir Alexander Graham (Alderman), Richard Martin, Judith Mayhew, Ivy Sharp (Deputy); **Tower** Roger Chadwick, Sir Roger Cork (Alderman), Maureen Kellett, Anthony Moss, Gerald Pulman (Deputy); **Vintry** Sir John Chalstrey (Alderman), William Fraser, Elizabeth Holliday, Andrew Parmley, Peter Revell-Smith (Deputy), Walbrook David Brown (Deputy), Pauline Halliday, Andrew MacLellan, Sir Paul Newall (Alderman), Peter Northall-Laurie.

The Lord Mayor

Richard Everard Nichols Born: 29 April 1938 Elected Member of the Common Council for the Ward of Candlewick (1983), Elected to the Court of Aldermen (1984), Elected Sheriff of the City of London (1994).

The Legal System and the Judiciary

Acts of Parliament and How a Bill Becomes Law

Statutory law in Britain is provided by Acts of Parliament. Before an act receives the royal assent it is known as a bill; bills are normally proposed by the government. Individual MPs may also propose bills (known as **Private Members Bills**). The right to propose these is selected by ballot. Government departments normally detail proposed legislation in a **Green Paper** which sets out various aspects of a matter on which legislation is contemplated, and invites public discussion and suggestions. This will be followed by a **White Paper** which is the introduction to a bill.

How a Bill Becomes an Act of Parliament

1. First reading of the bill The title is read out in the House of Commons and a minister names a day for the second reading.

2. The bill is officially printed.

3. Second reading A debate on the whole bill in the House of Commons followed by a vote on whether or not the bill should go on to the next stage.

4. Committee stage A committee of MPs considers the bill in detail and makes amendments.

5. Report stage The bill is referred back to the House of Commons which may make further amendments.

6. Third reading The House of Commons votes whether the bill should be sent on to the House of Lords.

7. House of Lords The bill passes through much the same stages in the Lords as in the House of Commons. (Bills may be introduced in the Lords, in which case the House of Commons considers them at this stage.)

8. Last amendments The House of Commons considers any Lords' amendments, and may make further amendments which must usually be agreed by the Lords.

House of Commons Corel

9. Royal assent The Queen gives her formal assent.

10. The bill becomes an act of parliament at royal assent. However, it may not come into force until a day appointed in the act.

The Law in Britain: Useful Addresses

The Law Society 113 Chancery Lane, London WC2A 1PL; phone: (0171) 242 1222; **The Council of Legal Education** 9 Gray's Inn Place, London WC1R 5DX; phone: (0171) 404 5787; **The British Institute of International and Comparative Law** Charles Clore House, 17 Russell Square, London WC1B 5DR; phone: (0171) 636 5802; **The British Council** Bridgewater House, 58 Whitworth Street, Manchester M1 6BB; phone: (0161) 957 7000; **Institute of Advanced Legal Studies** University of London, Charles Clore House, 17 Russell Square, London WC1B 5DR; phone: (0171) 637 1731.

The Law in Britain: The Courts

In England and Wales the court system was reorganized under the Courts Act 1971. The higher courts are:

House of Lords The highest court for the whole of Britain, deals with both civil and criminal appeals.

Court of Appeal This court is divided between criminal and civil appeal courts; it sits in London at the Royal Courts of Justice. The criminal division deals with appeals from the Crown Court and is presided over by the Lord Chief Justice who is the most senior judge in England and Wales. The 25 Lord Justices of Appeal are assisted by High Court judges when required.

High Court of Justice This court deals with important civil cases, it sits at the Royal Courts of Justice and at County Courts around the country: land, patent issues, industrial disputes, property and inheritance matters are dealt with by its Chancery Division. The Queen's Bench Division deals with common law business such as tort and contractual disputes. There is also a Family Division. Appeal is to the Court of Appeal (Civil Division), which also hears appeals from the County Courts and from tribunals.

Crown Courts These courts sit in over 90 permanent centres throughout England and Wales, each centre being designated as first, second, or third tier, reflecting the seriousness of the offences tried. Trial of cases is by a jury of twelve people selected at random from the electoral register. They are directed on matters of law by a judge, who may be any one of the 84 High Court Judges, 478 Circuit Judges, 787 Recorders and 454 Assistant Recorders

(Recorders and Assistant Recorders are part-time appointments), which handle criminal cases.

County Courts There are 250 county courts which deal with civil matters. Cases are heard before District Judges, who hear uncontested and smaller value claims; higher value claims being dealt with by Circuit Judges. Each court is assigned at least one District and one Circuit Judge.

Magistrates' Courts The lowest tier of criminal court in England and Wales, dealing with about 98 percent of all criminal cases. The 450 courts are funded jointly by local and central government and deal with minor criminal cases and are served by Justices of the Peace or stipendiary (paid) magistrates.

Juvenile Courts These courts are presided over by specially qualified justices. There are also special courts, such as the Restrictive Practices Court and the Employment Appeal Tribunal.

The Courts in Scotland The supreme civil court is the House of Lords, below which comes the Court of Session, and then the Sheriff's Court (in some respects similar to the English county court, but with criminal as well as civil jurisdiction). More serious criminal cases are heard by the High Court of Justiciary which also sits as a Court of Criminal Appeal (with no appeal to the Lords). Juries have 15 members, and a verdict of 'not proven' can be given. There is no coroner, inquiries into deaths being undertaken by the procurator fiscal.

Judiciary System: The Lords of Appeal

The House of Lords, Westminster, London SW1A 0PW; phone: (0171) 219 3000.

The Lord High Chancellor of Great Britain
The Right Honourable The Lord Irvine of Lairg.

The Lords of Appeal in Ordinary
The Right Honourable The Lord Goff of Chievely, The Right Honourable The Lord Browne-Wilkinson, The Right Honourable The Lord Slynn of Hadley, The Right Honourable The Lord Lloyd of Berwick, The Right Honourable The Lord Nolan, The Right Honourable The Lord Nicholls of Birkenhead, The Right Honourable The Lord Steyn, The Right Honourable The Lord Hoffmann, The Right Honourable The Lord Hope of Craighead, The Right Honourable The Lord Clyde, The Right Honourable The Lord Hutton, The Right Honourable The Lord Saville.

Registrar, The Clerk of the Parliaments
J M Davies, Esquire.

A Glossary of the Law in Britain: Courts, Professionals, and Important Bodies

(– = not applicable.)

Term	Definition	Notes
Admiralty court	English court that tries and gives judgement in maritime causes	the court is now incorporated within the Queen's Bench Division of the High Court and deals with such matters as salvage and damages arising from collisions between ships
Attorney General	principal law officer of the crown and head of the English Bar	the post is one of great political importance
Barrister	a lawyer qualified by study at the Inns of Court to plead for a client in court	barristers also undertake the writing of opinions on the prospects of a case before trial; they act for clients through the intermediary of solicitors
Central criminal court	crown court in the City of London, able to try all treasons and serious offences committed in the City or Greater London	–
Chambers	in the UK, rented offices used by a group of barristers	chambers in London are usually within the precincts of one of the four law courts
Chancery	a division of the High Court that deals with such matters as the administration of the estates of deceased persons, the execution of trusts, the enforcement of sales of land, and foreclosure of mortgages	–
Circuit	the geographic district that constitutes a particular area of jurisdiction	in England and Wales the six different centres to which High Court and circuit judges travel to try civil and criminal cases are: Midland and Oxford, Northeastern, Northern, Southeastern, Wales and Chester, and Western
Circuit judge	full-time judicial officer; sits as court judge in civil cases and presiding judge in the crown court	circuit judges must have been barristers for ten years or recorders for three years
Commissioner for oaths	a person appointed by the Lord Chancellor with power to administer oaths or take affidavits	all practising solicitors have these powers but must not use them in proceedings in which they are acting for any of the parties or in which they have an interest
Common law	that part of the English law not embodied in legislation. Consists of rules of law based on common custom and usage and on judicial decisions	English common law became the basis of law in the USA and many other English-speaking countries
Coroner	official who investigates the deaths of persons who have died suddenly by acts of violence or under suspicious circumstances, by holding an inquest or ordering a postmortem examination (autopsy)	–
County court	English court of law; exists to try civil cases; presided over by one or more circuit judges	–
Court of Appeal	UK law court comprising a Civil Division and a Criminal Division, set up under the Criminal Appeals Act 1968	the Criminal Division of the Court of Appeal has the power to revise sentences or quash a conviction on the grounds that in all the circumstances of the case the verdict is unsafe or unsatisfactory, or that the judgement of the original trial judge was wrong in law, or that there was a material irregularity during the course of the trial
Court of Arches	in the UK, ecclesiastical court of the archbishop of Canterbury; the presiding judge is the dean of the Arches	–
Court of Protection	in English law, a department of the High Court that deals with the estates of people who are incapable, by reason of mental disorder, of managing their own property and affairs	–
Court of Session	supreme civil court in Scotland, established 1532	the court sits in Edinburgh
Criminal Injuries Compensation Board	UK board established in 1964 to administer financial compensation by the state for victims of crimes of violence	–
Crown court	in England and Wales, any of several courts that hear serious criminal cases referred from magistrates' courts after committal proceedings	–
Crown Prosecution Service	body established by the Prosecution of Offences Act 1985, responsible for prosecuting all criminal offences in England and Wales; headed by the Director of Public Prosecutions (DPP)	–
Director of Public Prosecutions	the head of the Crown Prosecution Service (established 1985), responsible for the conduct of all criminal prosecutions in England and Wales	–

(continued)

A Glossary of the Law in Britain: Courts, Professionals, and Important Bodies (*continued*)

Term	Definition	Notes
Ecclesiastical law	in England, the Church of England has special ecclesiastical courts to administer church law	–
European Court of Human Rights	court that hears cases referred from the European Commission of Human Rights, if the Commission has failed to negotiate a friendly settlement in a case where individuals' rights have been violated by a member state, as defined in the 1950 European Convention on Human Rights; the court sits in Strasbourg and comprises one judge for every state that is a party to the 1950 convention	Britain has never incorporated the Human Rights Convention into its laws, which means that a statute that directly contradicts the convention will always prevail over a Strasbourg decision in a British court; in practice, however, the UK has always passed the necessary legislation to make its laws comply with the court's decisions
European Court of Justice	the court of the European Union (EU); it sits in Luxembourg with judges from the member states	–
Faculty of Professional Advocates	organization for Scottish advocates	incorporated in 1532
Inns of Court	four private legal societies in London, England: Lincoln's Inn, Gray's Inn, Inner Temple, and Middle Temple; all barristers (advocates in the English legal system) must belong to one of the Inns of Court	the main function of each Inn is the education, government, and protection of its members; each is under the administration of a body of Benchers (judges and senior barristers)
Judge	person invested with power to hear and determine legal disputes	in the UK, judges are chosen from barristers of long standing, but solicitors can be appointed circuit judges; the independence of the higher judiciary is ensured by the principle that they hold their office during good behaviour and not at the pleasure of the crown; they can be removed from office only by a resolution of both houses of Parliament
Jury	body of 12 (15 in Scotland) lay people sworn to decide the facts of a case and reach a verdict in a court of law	in England, jurors are selected at random from the electoral roll; certain people are ineligible for jury service (such as lawyers and clerics), and others can be excused (such as members of Parliament and doctors) if the jury cannot reach a unanimous verdict it can give a majority verdict (at least 10 of the 12)
Justice of the peace	an unpaid magistrate	–
Land Registry, HM	official body set up in 1925 to register legal rights to land in England and Wales	the records are open to public inspection (since December 1990)
Law Commission	either of two statutory bodies established in 1965 (one for England and Wales and one for Scotland) which consider proposals for law reform and publish their findings	they also keep British law under constant review, systematically developing and reforming it by, for example, the repeal of obsolete and unnecessary enactments
Law lords	in England, the ten Lords of Appeal who, together with the Lord Chancellor and other peers, make up the House of Lords in its judicial capacity	the House of Lords is the final court of appeal in both criminal and civil cases; law lords rank as life peers
Law Society	professional governing body of solicitors in England and Wales	it also functions as a trade union for its members; the society, incorporated in 1831, regulates training, discipline, and standards of professional conduct
Lord Advocate	chief law officer of the crown in Scotland who has ultimate responsibility for criminal prosecutions in Scotland	–
Lord Chancellor	head of the judiciary	a political appointment, the Lord Chancellor is also a member of the cabinet and holds the office of Keeper of the Great Seal
Lord Chief Justice of England	head of the Queen's Bench	ranks second only to the Lord Chancellor
Lord Justice of Appeal	in England and Wales, one of 14 lords justices who form, together with the Lord Chancellor, the Lord Chief Justice of England, the Master of the Rolls, and the president of the Family Division as ex officio members, the penultimate court of appeal (the Court of Appeal) for England and Wales.	–
Lord Lieutenant	the sovereign's representative in a county, who recommends magistrates for appointment	it is an unpaid position and the retirement age is 75
Magistrate	a person who presides in a magistrates' court: either a justice of the peace or a stipendiary magistrate	–

A Glossary of the Law in Britain: Courts, Professionals, and Important Bodies (*continued*)

Term	Definition	Other
Magistrates' court	in England and Wales, a local law court that mainly deals with minor criminal cases	a magistrates' court consists of between two and seven lay justices of the peace (who are advised on the law by a clerk to the justices), or a single paid lawyer called a stipendiary magistrate
Master of the Rolls	English judge who is the president of the civil division of the Court of Appeal, besides being responsible for Chancery records and for the admission of solicitors	–
Notary public	legal practitioner who attests or certifies deeds and other documents. British diplomatic and consular officials may exercise notarial functions outside the UK	–
Old Bailey	popular term for the Central Criminal Court	–
Police Complaints Authority	an independent group of people set up under the Police and Criminal Evidence Act 1984 to supervise the investigation of complaints against the police by members of the public	–
Probate	formal proof of a will	–
Procurator fiscal	officer of a Scottish sheriff's court who (combining the role of public prosecutor and coroner) inquires into suspicious deaths and carries out the preliminary questioning of witnesses to crime	–
Queen's counsel (QC)	in England, a barrister of senior rank	the title QC is awarded by the Queen on the recommendation of the Lord Chancellor; a QC wears a silk gown, and takes precedence over a junior member of the Bar. When the monarch is a king, the title is King's Council
Recorder	in the English legal system, a part-time judge who usually sits in the crown courts in less serious cases but may also sit in the county courts or the High Court	–
Royal assent	formal consent given by a British sovereign to the passage of a bill through Parliament	last instance of a royal refusal was the rejection of the Scottish Militia Bill of 1702 by Queen Anne
Royal prerogative	powers, immunities, and privileges recognized in common law as belonging to the crown	most prerogative acts in the UK are now performed by the government on behalf of the crown
Serious Fraud Office	set up in 1987 to investigate and prosecute serious or complex criminal fraud cases	–
Sheriff	in England and Wales, the crown's chief executive officer in a county for ceremonial purposes; in Scotland, the equivalent of the English county-court judge, but also dealing with criminal cases	–
Silk	in UK law, a Queen's Counsel, a senior barrister entitled to wear a silk gown in court	–
Slander	spoken defamatory statement	if written, or broadcast on radio or television, it constitutes libel
Solicitor	member of one of the two branches of the English legal profession who provides all-round legal services (making wills, winding up estates, conveyancing, divorce, and litigation)	a solicitor cannot appear at High Court level, but must brief a barrister on behalf of his or her client; solicitors may become circuit judges and recorders
Solicitor General	a law officer of the Crown, deputy to the Attorney General, a political appointee with ministerial rank	–
Stipendiary magistrate	paid, qualified lawyers, working mainly in London and major cities	–
The Bar	the profession of barristers collectively; to be 'called to the Bar' is to become a barrister	–
Treasury counsel	in the UK, a group of barristers who receive briefs from the DPP to appear for the prosecution in criminal trials at the Central Criminal Court	–
Treasury solicitor	the official representing the crown in matrimonial, probate, and admiralty cases	Queen's Proctor is an obsolete term for treasury solicitor
Tribunal	in English law for a body appointed by the government to arbitrate in disputes, or investigate certain matters	tribunals usually consist of a lawyer as chair, sitting with two lay assessors
Writers to the Signet	society of Scottish solicitors	–

Legal System of England and Wales

The Supreme Court of Judicature, Court of Appeal

Royal Courts of Justice, The Strand, London WC2A 2LL; phone: (0171) 936 6000; **Civil Appeals Office** Registrar: J D R Adams; phone: (0171) 936 6409; **Criminal Appeal and Courts Martial Appeal Office** Registrar: Master McKenzie (Michael McKenzie); phone: (0171) 936 6190.

Ex-officio Judges

The Lord High Chancellor of Great Britain The Right Honourable The Lord Irvine of Lairg (President); **The Lord Chief Justice of England** The Right Honourable The Lord Bingham of Cornwall; **The Right Honourable The Master of the Rolls** The Right Honourable The Lord Woolf; **The Right Honourable The President of the Family Division** The Right Honourable Sir Stephen Brown; **The Right Honourable The Vice-Chancellor** The Right Honourable Sir Richard Scott.

Lords Justices

Years of appointment are given in brackets. The Right Honourable Sir Martin Nourse (1985), The Right Honourable Dame Elizabeth Butler-Sloss (1988), The Right Honourable Sir Murray Stuart-Smith (1988), The Right Honourable Sir Christopher Staughton (1988), The Right Honourable Sir Roy Beldam (1989), The Right Honourable Sir Paul Kennedy (1992), The Right Honourable Sir David Hirst (1992), The Right Honourable Sir Simon Brown (1992), The Right Honourable Sir Anthony Evans (1992), The Right Honourable Sir Christopher Rose (1992), The Right Honourable Sir John Roch (1993), The Right Honourable Sir Peter Gibson (1993), The Right Honourable Sir John Hobhouse (1993), The Right Honourable Sir Denis Henry (1993), The Right Honourable Sir Peter Millett (1994), The Right Honourable Sir Swinton Thomas (1994), The Right Honourable Sir Andrew Morritt (1994), The Right Honourable Sir Philip Otton (1994), The Right Honourable Sir Robin Auld (1995), The Right Honourable Sir Malcolm Pill (1995), The Right Honourable Sir William Aldous (1995), The Right Honourable Sir Alan Ward (1995), The Right Honourable Sir Michael Hutchison (1995), The Right Honourable Sir Konrad Schiemann (1995), The Right Honourable Sir Nicholas Phillips (1995), The Right Honourable Sir Mathew Thorpe (1995), The Right Honourable Sir Mark Potter (1996), The Right Honourable Sir Henry Brooke (1996), The Right Honourable Sir Igor Judge (1996), The Right Honourable Sir Mark Waller (1996), The Right Honourable Sir John Mummery (1996), The Right Honourable Sir Charles Mantell (1997), The

Right Honourable Sir John Chadwick (1997), The Right Honourable Sir Richard Buxton (1997).

The High Court of Justice

Chancery Division

Royal Courts of Justice, The Strand, London WC2A 2LL; phone (0171) 936 6000.

Chancery Chambers Chief Master: J M Dyson; Court Manager: G C Robinson; phone: (0171) 936 6075; **Bankruptcy and Companies Courts** Chief Registrar: M C B Buckley; Court Manager: M A Brown; phone: (0171) 936 7343; **Restrictive Practices Court** Clerk to the Court: M C B Buckley; Court Manager: M A Brown; phone: (0171) 936 7343.

Chancery Division: Judges

The Lord High Chancellor of Great Britain The Right Honourable The Lord Irvine of Lairg (President); **The Right Honourable The Vice-Chancellor** The Right Honourable Sir Richard Scott.
Years of appointment are given in brackets. The Honourable Sir Jeremiah Harman (1982), The Honourable Sir Donald Rattee (1989), The Honourable Sir Francis Ferris (1990), The Honourable Sir Jonathan Parker (1991), The Honourable Sir John Lindsay (1992), The Honourable Dame Mary Arden (Chairman of The Law Commission) (1993), The Honourable Sir Edward Evans-Lombe (1993), The Honourable Sir Robin Jacob (1993), The Honourable Sir William Blackburne (1993), The Honourable Sir Gavin Lightman (1994), The Honourable Sir Robert Carnwath (1994), The Honourable Sir Colin Rimer (1994), The Honourable Sir Hugh Laddie (1995), The Honourable Sir Timothy Lloyd (1996), The Honourable Sir David Neuberger (1996).

Queen's Bench Division

Royal Courts of Justice, London WC2A 2LL; phone: (0171) 936 6000; Senior Master and Queen's Rememberance: R L Turner; phone: (0171) 936 6105; **Crown Office** Master of the Crown Office, Queen's Coroner and Attorney: Master McKenzie (Michael McKenzie); phone: (0171) 936 6108.

Queens' Bench Division: Judges

The Lord Chief Justice of England The Right Honourable The Lord Bingham of Cornwall (President). Years of appointment are given in brackets. The Honourable Sir Charles McCullough (1981), The Honourable Sir Oliver Popplewell (1983), The Honourable Sir Richard Tucker (1985), The Honourable Sir Patrick Garland (1985), The Honourable Sir Michael Turner (1985), The Honourable Sir John Alliott (1986), The Honourable Sir Harry Ognall (1986),

The Honourable Sir John Owen (1986), The Honourable Sir Humphrey Potts (1986), The Honourable Sir Richard Rougier (1986), The Honourable Sir Ian Kennedy (1986), The Honourable Sir Stuart McKinnon (1988), The Honourable Sir Edwin Jowitt (1988), The Honourable Sir Scott Baker (1988), The Honourable Sir Douglas Brown (1989), The Honourable Sir Michael Morland (1989), The Honourable Sir Roger Buckley(1989), The Honourable Sir Anthony Hidden (1989), The Honourable Sir Michael W (1990), The Honourable Sir John Blofeld (1990), The Honourable Sir Peter Cresswell (1990), The Honourable Sir Anthony May (1991), The Honourable Sir John Laws (1992), The Honourable Dame Ann Ebsworth (1992), The Honourable Sir Simon Tuckey (Judge in charge of the Commerical List) (1992), The Honourable Sir David Latham (1992), The Honourable Sir Christopher Holland (1992), The Honourable Sir John Kay (1992), The Honourable Sir Richard Curtis (1992), The Honourable Sir Stephen Sedley (1992), The Honourable Dame Janet Smith (1992), The Honourable Sir Anthony Colman (1992), The Honourable Sir Anthony Clarke (1992), The Honourable Sir John Dyson (1993), The Honourable Sir Thayne Forbes (1993), The Honourable Sir Michael Sachs (1993), The Honourable Sir Stephen Mitchell (1993), The Honourable Sir Roger Bell (1993), The Honourable Sir Michael Harrison (1993), The Honourable Sir Bernard Rix (1993), The Honourable Dame Heather Steele (1993), The Honourable Sir William Gage (1993), The Honourable Sir Jonathan Mance (1993), The Honourable Sir Andrew Longmore (1993), The Honourable Sir Thomas Morison (1993), The Honourable Sir David Keene (1994), The Honourable Sir Andrew Collins (1994), The Honourable Sir Maurice Kay (1994), The Honourable Sir Brian Smedley (1995), The Honourable Sir Anthony Hooper (1995), The Honourable Sir Neil Butterfield (1995), The Honourable Sir George Newman (1995), The Honourable Sir David Poole (1995), The Honourable Sir Martin Moore-Bick (1995), The Honourable Sir Gordon Langley (1995), The Honourable Sir John Thomas (1995), The Honourable Sir Roger Toulson (1996), The Honourable Sir Robert Nelson (1996), The Honourable Sir Michael Astill (1996), The Honourable Sir Alan Moses (1996), The Honourable Sir Timothy Walker (1996), The Honourable Sir David Eady (1996).

Family Division

Royal Courts of Justice, The Strand, London WC2A 2LL; phone (0171) 936 6000.

Family Division: Judges

The President of the Family Division The Right Honourable Sir Stephen Brown; **Senior District Judge of the Family**

Division G B N A Aspel; phone: (0171) 936 6934. Years of appointment are given in brackets; The Honourable Sir Edward Cazalet (1988), The Honourable Sir Robert Johnson (1989), The Honourable Dame Joyanne Bracewell (1990), The Honourable Sir Michael Connell (1991), The Honourable Sir Peter Singer (1993), The Honourable Sir Nicholas Wilson (1993), The Honourable Sir Nicholas Wall(1993), The Honourable Sir Andrew Kirkwood (1993), The Honourable Sir Christopher Stuart-White (1993), The Honourable Dame Brenda Hale (1994), The Honourable Sir Hugh Bennett (1995), The Honourable Sir James Homan (1995), The Honourable Dame Mary Claire Hogg (1995), The Honourable Sir Christopher Summer (1996).

The Midland and Oxford Circuit

Courts

First Tier Centres Birmingham; Lincoln (Combined Court Centre); Nottingham (Combined Court Centre); Oxford (Combined Court Centre); Stafford (Combined Court Centre); Warwick (Combined Court Centre); **Second Tier Centres** Leicester; Northampton (Combined Court Centre); Shrewsbury; Worcester; **Third Tier Centres** Coventry (Combined Court Centre); Derby (Combined Court Centre); Grimsby (Combined Court Centre); Hereford; Peterborough (Combined Court Centre); Stoke-on-Trent (Combined Court Centre); Wolverhampton (Combined Court Centre).

Offices

Circuit Office The Priory Courts, 33 Bull Street, Birmingham B4 6DW; phone:(0121) 681 3203; fax: (0121) 681 3210; **Circuit Administrator** Peter Handcock; **Birmingham Group** The Priory Courts, 33 Bull Street, Birmingham B4 6DW; phone:(0121) 681 3451; **Group Manager** Keith Dickerson; **Coventry Group** The Priory Courts, 33 Bull Street, Birmingham B4 6DW; phone: (0121) 681 3221; **Group Manager** Donna Ponsonby; **Lincoln Group** Lincoln Combined Courts Centre, 360 High Street, Lincoln LN5 7RL; phone: (01522) 883000; **Group Manager** Alan Phillips; **Northampton Group** 2nd Floor, St Katharine's House, St Katherine's Street, Northampton NN1 2TD; phone: (01604) 601636 **Group Manager:** Steven Smith; **Nottingham Group** Chaddesden House, 77 Talbot Street, Nottingham NG1 5GN; phone: (0115) 911 1666; **Group Manager** Elizabeth Folman; **Stafford Group** 4th Floor, Kemley House, 2 Victoria Road, Stafford ST16 2AE; phone: (01785) 255219; **Group Manager** David Bennett; **Presiding Judges** The Honourable Sir David Latham; The Honourable Sir Edwin Jowitt.

The Northeastern Circuit

Courts

First Tier Centres Leeds; Newcastle-upon-Tyne; Sheffield; Teesside; **Second Tier Centres** York; Bradford; **Third Tier Centres** Doncaster; Durham; Kingston-upon-Hull.

Offices

Circuit Office 17th Floor, West Riding House, Albion Street, Leeds LS1 5AA; phone: (0113) 251 1200; fax: (0113) 251 1247; **Circuit Administrator** P J Farmer; **Bradford Group** The Law Courts, Exchange Square, Drake Street, Bradford BD1 1JA; phone: (01274) 843553; **Group Manager** F Taylor; **Leeds Group** 1st Floor, Symons House, Belgrave Street, Leeds LS2 8DD; phone: (0113) 245 9611; **Group Manager** P M Norris; **Newcastle-upon-Tyne Group** 4th Foor, Westgate House, Westgate Road, Newcastle-upon-Tyne; phone: (0191) 232 7102; **Group Manager** K Budgen; **Sheffield Group** 10th Floor, Pennine Centre, 20–22 Hawley Street, Sheffield S1 2EA; phone: (0114) 275 5866 **Group Manager** G Bingham; **Teesside Group** The Law Courts, Russell Street, Middlesbrough, Cleveland TS1 2EA; phone: (01642) 340000; **Group Manager** Miss E Yates; **Presiding Judges** The Honourable Dame Janet Smith (1992); The Honourable Sir Anthony Hooper (1995).

The Northern Circuit

Courts

First Tier Centres Carlisle; Liverpool; Manchester (Crown Square); Preston; **Third Tier Centres** Barrow-in-Furness; Bolton; Burnley; Lancaster; Manchester (Minshull Street).

Offices

Circuit Office 15 Quay Street, Manchester M60 9FD; phone: (0161) 833 1004; fax: (0161) 832 8596; **Circuit Administrator** R A Vincent; **Liverpool Group** Group Manager's Office, The Queen Elizabeth II Law Courts, Derby Square, Liverpool L2 1XA; phone: (0151) 236 5211; **Group Manager** Julie Roche; **Manchester Central Group** Group Manager's Office, 3rd Floor, 15 Quay Street, Manchester M60 9FD; phone: (0161) 833 1004; **Group Manager** C A Mayer; **Outer Manchester Group** Group Manager's Office, 3rd Floor, 15 Quay Street, Manchester M60 9FD; phone: (0161) 833 1004; **Group Manager** Beverley Handcock; **Preston Group** Sessions House, Lancaster Road, Preston PR1 3JJ; phone: (01772) 821451; **Group Manager** Barry Wilson; **Presiding Judges** The Honourable Sir John Kay (1992); The Honourable Sir Thayne Forbes (1993); **Vice Chancellor of the County Palatine of Lancaster** The Honourable Sir Jonathan Parker (1991).

The Southeastern Circuit

Courts

First Tier Centres Chelmsford; Croydon (Combined Court Centre); Lewes (Combined Court Centre); Norwich (Combined Court Centre); **Second Tier Centres** Central Criminal Court; Ipswich; Luton; Maidstone; Reading; St Albans; **Third Tier Centres** Aylesbury; Basildon (Combined Court Centre); Bury St Edmonds; Cambridge; Canterbury (Combined Court Centre); Chichester (Combined Court Centre); Guildford; King's Lynn; and other Greater London Courts (Croydon, Harrow, Inner London Sessions House, Isleworth, Kingston-upon-Thames, Knightsbridge, Middlesex Guildhall, Snaresbrook, Southwark, Wood Green, Woolwich.

Offices

Circuit Office – London Courts New Cavendish House, 18 Maltravers Street, London WC2R 3EU; phone: (0171) 936 7234; fax: (0171) 936 7230; **Circuit Administrator** R J Clark; **Circuit Office – Provincial Courts** 1st Floor, Steeple House, Chelmsford, Essex CM1 1NH; phone: (01245) 257425; fax: (01245) 493216; **Circuit Administrator** J L Powell; **Chelmsford Group** 1st Floor, Steeple House, Chelmsford, Essex CM1 1NH; phone: (01245) 287974; **Group Manager** M Littlewood; **Kingston-upon-Thames Group** Group Manager's Office, 6–8 Penryhn Rd, Kingston-upon-Thames, Surrey KT1 2BB; phone: (0181) 240 2599; **Group Manager** Sheila Proudcock; **Lewes Group** The Law Courts, 182 High Street, Lewes BN7 1YB; phone: (01273) 485284; **Group Manager** B MacBeth; **Luton Group** 7 George Street, Luton, Bedfordshire LU1 2AA; phone: (01582) 485331; **Group Manager** M McIver; **Maidstone Group** Group Manager's Office, Concorde House, 10–12 London Road, Maidstone, Kent ME16 8QA; phone: (01622) 200120; **Group Manager** Helen Hartwell; **Presiding Judges** The Right Honourable Sir Michael Wright (1990); The Right Honourable Sir William Gage (1993).

The Wales and Chester Circuit

Courts

First Tier Centres Caernarfon; Cardiff; Chester; Mold; Swansea; **Second Tier Centres** Carmarthen; Newport; Welshpool; Merthyr Tydfil; Warrington; **Third Tier Centres** Dolgellau; Haverfordwest; Knutsford.

Offices

Circuit Office 2nd Floor, Churchill House, Churchill Way, Cardiff CF1 4HH; phone: (01222) 396925; fax: (01222) 345786; **Circuit Administrator** Peter Risk; **Cardiff Group** Group Manager's Office, 2nd Floor, Churchill House, Churchill Way, Cardiff CF1 4HH; phone: (01222) 341545; **Group Manager** Mr Graham Pickett; **Mold Group** The Law Courts, County Civic Centre, Mold CH7 1AE; phone: (01352) 754562; **Group Manager** George Kenney; **Swansea Group** 1st Floor, Carvella House, Quay West, Quay Parade, Swansea SA1 1SP; phone: (01792) 510351; **Group Manager** Diane Thomas;

Presiding Judges The Honourable Sir Richard Curtis, QB (1992);The Right Honourable Sir Maurice Kay, QB (1995).

The Western Circuit

Courts

First Tier Centres Bristol; Exeter (Combined Court Centre); Truro (Combined Court Centre); Winchester (Combined Court Centre); **Second Tier Centres** Gloucester (Combined Court Centre); Plymouth (Combined Court Centre); Weymouth and Dorchester (Combined Court Centre); **Third Tier Centres** Barnstaple; Bournemouth (Combined Court Centre); Newport (Isle of Wight) (Combined Court Centre); Portsmouth (Combined Court Centre); Salisbury (Combined Court Centre); Southampton (Combined Court Centre); Swindon (Combined Court Centre); Taunton (Combined Court Centre)

Offices

Circuit Office Bridge House, Sion Place, Clifton, Bristol BS8 4BN; phone: (0117) 974 3763; fax: (0117) 974 4133; **Circuit Administrator** D Ryan; **Bristol Group** Whitefriars, Southgate, Lewins Mead, Bristol BS1 2NT; phone: (0117) 925 0296; **Group Manager** N Jeffery; **Exeter Group** The Castle, Exeter, Devon EX4 3TH; phone: (01392) 748767; **Group Manager** D E Gentry; **Winchester Group** South Side Offices, The Law Courts, The Castle, Winchester, Hants SO23 9EL; phone: (01962) 876004; **Group Manager** A Davison; **Presiding Judges** The Honourable Sir Neil Butterfield, QB (1995);The Honourable Sir Roger Toulson, QB (1996).

The Crown Prosecution Service

The Crown Prosecution Service (CPS) is responsible for the independent review and conduct of criminal proceedings instituted by police forces in England and Wales.

Headquarters 50 Ludgate Hill, London EC4M 7EX; phone: (0171) 273 8000; fax: (0171) 329 8002; public enquiry point: (0171) 273 8152; **Director of Public Prosecutions (Grade 1)** Dame Barbara Mills, QC (resigned May 1998); **Director of Corporate Services (Grade 3)** D Nooney; **Director of Casework Services (Grade 3)** G Duff; **Director of Casework Evaluation (Grade 3)** C W P Newell; **Head of Casework Services Division I (Grade 5)** P Lewis; **Head of Casework Services Division II (Grade 5)** D Sharpling; **Head of Casework Performance and Resources Division (Grade 5)** B Spear; **Head of Management Services Division (Grade 5)** A Butler; **Head of Personnel, Training, and Development Division (Grade 5)** G Harvey; **Head of Planning and Finance Division (Grade 5)** J Graham; **Head of Strategic and Change Management (Grade 5)** D Ingham.

North Northumbria, Durham, Cumbria, and Cleveland police forces, 1st Floor, Benton House, 136 Sandyford Road, Newcastle-upon-Tyne NE2 1QE; phone: (0191) 201 2390; **Chief Crown Prosecutor** M Graham; **Assistant Chief Crown Prosecutor** D Farmer; **Area Administrator** A Storey.

Yorkshire North Yorkshire and West Yorkshire police forces, Area HQ, 6th Floor, Ryedale Building, 60 Piccadilly, York, North Yorkshire YO1 1NS; phone: (01904) 610726; fax: (01904) 644518; **Chief Crown Prosecutor** D Dickenson **Assistant Chief Crown Prosecutor** D Magson; **Area Administrator** J A Jones.

Mersey/Lancashire Merseyside and Lancashire police forces, Area HQ, 7th Floor (South), Royal Liver Building, Pier Head, Liverpool L3 1HN; phone: (0151) 236 7575; fax: (0151) 255 0642; **Chief Crown Prosecutor** G Brown; **Assistant Chief Crown Prosecutor** G Saul; **Area Administrator** K Fox.

Humber South Yorkshire, Humberside, and Lincolnshire police forces, Area HQ, Greenfield House, Scotland Street, Sheffield S3 7OQ; phone: (0114)291 2164; fax: (0114) 291 2169; **Chief Crown Prosecutor** D Adams; **Assistant Chief Crown Prosecutor** J Bermingham; **Area Administrator** A Burgess

North West Greater Manchester and Cheshire police forces, Area HQ, Ashburner House, Seymour Grove, Old Trafford, Manchester M16 0LD; phone: (0161) 869 7402; fax: (0161) 872 3628; **Chief Crown Prosecutor** A R Taylor; **Assistant Chief Crown Prosecutor** C Barker; **Area Administrator** K Fox.

East Midlands Derbyshire, Leicestershire, Northamptonshire, and Nottinghamshire police forces, Area HQ, 2 King Edward Court, King Edward Street, Nottingham NG1 1EL; phone: (0115) 948 0480; fax: (0115) 941 8397; **Chief Crown Prosecutor** B T McArdle; **Assistant Chief Crown Prosecutor** D Adams; **Area Administrator** N Bulbeck.

Wales North Wales, Dyfed, Powys, South Wales, and Gwent police forces, Area HQ, Tudor house, 16 Cathedral Road, Cardiff CF1 9LJ; phone: (01222) 783000; fax: (01222) 783098; **Chief Crown Prosecutor** R A Prickett; **Assistant Chief Crown Prosecutor** N Reasbeck; **Area Administrator** M Grist.

Midlands West Midlands, Staffordshire, and Warwickshire police forces, Area HQ, 14th Floor, Colmore Gate, 2 Colmore Row, Birmingham B3 2QA; phone: (0121) 629 7200; fax: (0121) 629 7314; **Chief Crown Prosecutor** D Blundell; **Assistant Chief Crown Prosecutor** D Scott; **Area Administrator** J Gilmore.

Anglia Essex, Norfolk, Suffolk, Hertfordshire, Bedfordshire, and Cambridgeshire police forces, Area HQ, Queen's House, 588 Victoria Street, St Albans AL1 3HZ; phone: (01727) 818107; fax: (01727) 344076; **Chief Crown Prosecutor** R J Chronnell; **Assistant Chief Crown Prosecutor** C Ingham; **Area Administrator** A Machray.

Severn/Thames West Mercia, Gloucestershire, Wiltshire, and Thames police forces, Area HQ, Artillery House, Heritage Way, Droitwich, Worcester WR9 8YB; phone: (01905) 795477; fax: (01905) 795896; **Chief Crown Prosecutor** N Franklin; **Assistant Chief Crown Prosecutor** J Wilcox; **Area Administrator** G Choldcroft.

South West Avon and Somerset, Devon and Cornwall, and Dorset police forces, Area HQ, Hawkins House, Pynes Hill, Rydon Lane, Exeter, Devon EX2 5SS; phone: (01392) 445422; fax: (01392) 45352; **Chief Crown Prosecutor** P Boeuf; **Assistant Chief Crown Prosecutor** A Cresswell; **Area Administrator** J Chambers.

London Metropolitan and City of London police forces, Area HQ, Portland House, Stag Place, London SW1E 5BH; phone: (0171) 915 5700; fax: (0171) 915 5994; **Chief Crown Prosecutor** G D Etherington; **Assistant Chief Crown Prosecutor** B Hughes, S O'Doherty, J Bell; **Area Administrator** R Jones.

South East Kent, Sussex, Surrey, and Hampshire police forces, Area HQ, One Onslow Street, Guildford, Surrey GU1 4YA; phone: (01483) 882600; fax: (01483) 882601; **Chief Crown Prosecutor** C Nicholls; **Assistant Chief Crown Prosecutor** R Drybrough-Smith; **Area Administrator** vacant; **CPS Central Casework** 50 Ludgate Hill, London EC4M 7EX; phone: (0171) 273 8000; fax: (0171) 329 8002; **Chief Crown Prosecutor** D Kyle; **Assistant Chief Crown Prosecutor** R Booth (Fraud and Central Confiscation); G Martin (Prosecutions, International and Legal Services).

Legal System of Northern Ireland

The Courts of Northern Ireland

The Supreme Court

Royal Courts of Justice, Chichester Street, Belfast BT1 3JF; phone: (01232) 235111.

Offices

Queen's Bench, Appeals', and Clerk of the Crown in Northen Ireland Master: J W Wilson, QC; High Court Master: Mrs D M Kennedy; **Office of Care and Protection** Master: F B Hall; **Bankruptcy and Companies Office** Master: J B C Glass; **Chancery Office** Master: R A Ellison; **Probate and Matrimonial Office** Master: vacant; **Taxing Office** Master: J C Napier; **Court Funds**

Office Accountant General: H G Thompson; **Official Solicitor** C W G Redpath; **Recorders** His Honour Judge Hart, QC; His Honour Judge Burgess; His Honour Judge Martin, QC.

Judges

The Lord Chief Justice The Right Honourable Sir Robert Douglas Carswell; Principal Secretary: G W Johnston; The Right Honourable Sir John Clarke MacDermott; The Right Honourable Sir William Paschal McCollum; The Right Honourable Sir James Michael Anthony Nicholson; The Honourable Sir William Anthony Campbell; The Honourable Sir John Joseph Sheil; The Honourable Sir Brian Francis Kerr; The Honourable Sir John Kenneth Pringle; The

Honourable Sir Malachy Joseph Higgins; The Honourable Sir Frederick Paul Girvan; The Honourable Sir Patrick Coghlin; **Northern Ireland Court Service** Headquarters: Windsor House, Bedford Street, Belfast BT1 3JF; phone: (01232) 328594; **District Judges; Division of Belfast** District Judge Wells; **Division of Londonderry and Antrim** District Judge Keegan; **Division of Armagh and South Down, and Fermanagh and Tyrone** District Judge (vacant); **Division of Craigavon and Ards** District Judge Wheeler; **Director of Public Prosecutions** A M Fraser, QC Royal Courts of Justice, Chichester Street, Belfast BT1 3JF; phone: (01232) 235111; **Crown Solicitor** N P Roberts, Royal Courts of Justice, Belfast; phone: (01232) 235111.

Legal System of Scotland

The Supreme Court of Scotland

The Supreme Courts in Scotland comprise the Court of Session and the High Court of Justiciary.

Court of Session

The Civil Court, comprising the Inner House with its two divisions, and the Outer House.

Address Parliament House, Parliament Square, Edinburgh EH1 1RQ; phone: (0131) 225 2595.

The Inner House

First Division; The Lord President The Right Honourable The Lord Rodger of Earlsferry (1995); **Judges** The Honourable Lord Sutherland (1985); The Honourable Lord Prosser (1986); The Honourable Lord Caplan (1989); **Second Division; The Lord Justice Clerk** The Right Honourable Lord Cullen (1986); **Judges** The Right Honourable The Lord McCluskey of Churchill (1985); The Honourable Lord Kirkwood (1987); The Honourable Lord Coulsfield (1987).

The Outer House

Judges: The Honourable Lord Milligan (1988); The Right Honourable The Lord Cameron of Lochbroom (1989); The Honourable Lord Marnoch (1990); The Honourable Lord MacLean (1990); The Honourable Lord Penrose (1990); The Honourable Lord Osborne (1990); The Honourable Lord Abernethy (1992); The Honourable Lord Johnston (1994); The Honourable Lord Gill (1994); The Honourable Lord Hamilton (1995); The Honourable Lord Dawson (1995); The Honourable Lord

Macfadyen (1995); The Honourable Lady Cosgrove (1996); The Honourable Lord Nimmo Smith (1996); The Honourable Lord Philip (1996); The Honourable Lord Kingarth (1997); The Honourable Lord Bonomy (1997); The Honourable Lord Eassie (1997); **Principal Clerk of Session** J L Anderson; **Deputy Principal Clerk of Session and Principal Extractor** G McKeand; **Deputy Principal Clerk and Keeper of The Rolls** T M Thomson.

Addresses

High Court of Justiciary Parliament House, Edinburgh EH1 1RQ; phone: (0131) 225 2595; **Council on Tribunals** Scottish Committee, 44 Palmerstone Place, Edinburgh EH12 5BJ; phone: (0131) 220 1236; **Crown Office** 25 Chambers Street, Edinburgh EH1 1LA; phone: (0131) 226 2626; **Faculty of Advocates** Parliament House, Edinburgh EH1 1RF; phone: (0131) 225 5071; **Industrial Tribunals For Scotland** 3rd Floor, Eagle Building, 215 Bothwell Street, Glasgow G2 7TS; phone: (0141) 204 0730; **Lands Tribunal For Scotland** 1 Grosvenor Crescent, Edinburgh EH12 5ER; phone: (0131) 225 7996; **The Law Society of Scotland** Law Society's Hall, 26 Drumsheugh Gardens, Edinburgh EH3 7YR; phone: (0131) 225 7411; **Secretary of Commissions For Scotland** Saughton House, Broomhouse Drive, Edinburgh EH11 3XD; phone: (0131) 244 2691; **Scottish Courts Administration** Hayweight House, 23 Lauriston Street, Edinburgh EH3 9DQ; phone: (0131) 221 9200; **Scottish Land Court:** Grosvenor Crescent, Edinburgh EH12 5ER; phone: (0131) 225 3595; **Sheriff Court of Chancery** 27 Chambers Street, Edinburgh EH1 1LB; phone (0131) 225 2525; **Trans-**

port Tribunal Parliament House, Edinburgh EH1 1RQ; phone: (0131) 225 2595.

The Sheriff Courts of Scotland

Central Scotland

Sheriff Principal J J Maguire, QC; **Alloa** Sheriff Court House, Alloa FK10 1HR; phone: (01259) 722734; **Sheriff** W M Reid; **Sheriff Clerk** R G McKeand; **Falkirk** Sheriff Court House, Falkirk FK1 4AR; phone: (01324) 620822; **Sheriffs** A V Sheehan; A J Murphy; **Sheriff Clerk** D F Forrester; **Stirling** Sheriff Court House, PO Box 10, Viewfield Place, Stirling FK8 1NH; phone: (01786) 462191; **Sheriff** The Honourable R E G Younger; **Sheriff Clerk** J M Clark.

Dumfries and Galloway

Sheriff Principal G L Cox, QC; **Dumfries** Sheriff Court House, Dumfries DG1 2AN; phone: (01387) 262334; **Sheriffs** K G Barr; J M Fletcher; **Sheriff Clerk** P McGonigle; **Kirkudbright** Sheriff Court House, DG6 4JW; phone: (01557) 330574; **Sheriff** J R Smith; **Sheriff Clerk** B J Lindsay; **Stranraer** Sheriff Court House, Stranraer DG9 7AA; phone: (01776) 702138; **Sheriff** J R Smith; **Sheriff Clerk** W McIntosh.

Fife

Sheriff Principal J J Maguire, QC; **Cupar** Sheriff Court House, Cupar KY15 4LX; phone: (01334) 652121; **Sheriff** vacant; **Sheriff Clerk** R M Hughes; **Dunfermline** Sheriff Court House, Dunfermline KY12 7HJ; phone: (01383) 724666; **Sheriffs** J S Forbes; C W Palmer; **Sheriff Clerk** W

McCulloch; **Kirkcaldy** Sheriff Court House, Kirkcaldy KY1 1XQ; phone: (01592) 260171; **Sheriffs:** W J Christie; Mrs L G Patrick; **Sheriff Clerk** I Hay.

Grampian

Sheriff Principal D J Risk, QC; **Aberdeen** Sheriff Court House, Aberdeen AB9 1AP; phone: (01224) 648316; **Sheriffs** G Wartner; A Pollock; D W Bogie; D Kelbie; **Floating Sheriff** A M Cowan; **Sheriff Clerk** E Laing; **Banff** Sheriff Court House, Banff AB4 1AU; phone: (01261) 812140; **Sheriff** K A McLernan; **Sheriff Clerk** F MacPherson; **Elgin** Sheriff Court House, Elgin IV30 1BU; phone: (01343) 542505; **Sheriff** N McPartlin; **Sheriff Clerk** M McBey; **Peterhead** Sheriff Court House, Peterhead AB4 6TP; phone: (01779) 476676; **Sheriff** K A McLernan; **Sheriff Clerk** A H Hempseed; **Stonehaven** Sheriff Court House, Stonehaven AB3 2JH; phone: (01569) 762758; **Sheriff** A S Jessop; **Sheriff Clerk** I P Smith.

Lothian and Borders

Sheriff Principal C G B Nicholson, QC; **Edinburgh** Sheriff Court House, Edinburgh EH1 2NS; phone: (0131) 225 2525; **Sheriffs** R G Craik, QC; G I W Shiach; I A Poole; R J D Scott; A M Bell; J M S Horsburgh; J A Farrell; I D McPhail; C N Stoddart; A B Wilkinson, QC; D J Robertson; N M P Morrison, QC; M L E Jarvie, QC; **Floating Sheriffs** A Lothian; F J Keane; M M Stephen; **Sheriff Clerk** J Ross; **Haddington** Sheriff Court House, Haddington EH41 3HN; phone: (0162) 082 2325; **Sheriff** G W S Presslie; **Sheriff Clerk** J O'Donnell; **Jedburgh** Sheriff Court House, Jedburgh TD8 6AP; phone: (01835) 863231; **Sheriff** J V Paterson; **Sheriff Clerk** I W Williamson; **Linlithgow** Sheriff Court House, Linlithgow EH49 7EQ; phone: (01506) 842922; **Sheriffs** G Fleming, QC; H R Maclean; **Floating Sheriff** K A Ross; **Sheriff Clerk** R D Sinclair; **Peebles** Sheriff Court House, Peebles EH45 8SW; phone: (01721) 720204; **Sheriffs** Richard Scott, Roger Craik; **Sheriff Clerk** R McArthur; **Selkirk** Sheriff Court House, Selkirk TD7 4LE; phone: (01750) 21269; **Sheriff** J V Paterson; **Sheriff Clerk** L McFarlane.

Northern

Sheriff Principal D J Risk, QC; **Dingwall** Sheriff Court House, Dingwall IV15 9QX; phone: (01349) 863153; **Sheriff** J O A Fraser; **Sheriff Clerk** W M Cochrane; **Dornoch** Sheriff Court House, Dornoch IV25 3FD; phone: (01862) 810224; **Sheriff** I A Cameron; **Sheriff Clerk** K Kerr; **Fort William** Sheriff Court House, Fort William PH33 6EE; phone: (01397) 702087; **Sheriff** C G McKay; **Sheriff Clerk** G D Hood; **Inverness** Sheriff Court House, Inverness IV2 3EG; phone: (01463) 230782; **Sheriffs** G D Booker-Millburn; W J Fulton; J O A Fraser; **Sheriff Clerk** J Robertson; **Kirkwall** Sheriff Court House, Kirkwall KW15 1PD; phone: (01856) 872110; **Sheriff** C S Mackenzie; **Sheriff Clerk** P Cushen; **Lerwick** Sheriff Court House, Lerwick, Shetland ZE1 0HD; phone: (01595) 693914; **Sheriff** C S Mackenzie; **Sheriff Clerk** A C Norris; **Lochmaddy** Sheriff Court House, Lochmaddy PA82 5AE; phone: (01876) 500340; **Sheriff** J O A Fraser; **Sheriff Clerk** M Campbell; **Portree** Sheriff Court House, Portree IV51 9EH; phone: (01478) 612191; **Sheriff** W J Fulton; **Sheriff Clerk** M Campbell; **Stornoway** Sheriff Court House, Stornoway PA87 2JF; phone: (01851) 702231; **Sheriff** I A Cameron; **Sheriff Clerk** M MacDonald; **Tain** Sheriff Court House, Tain IV19 1AB; phone: (01862) 892518; **Sheriff** D Booker-Millburn; **Sheriff Clerk** L MacLachlan; **Wick** Sheriff Court House, Wick KW1 4AJ; phone: (01955) 602846; **Sheriff** I A Cameron; **Sheriff Clerk** J McEwan.

Strathclyde

Sheriffs Principal vacant (Glasgow and Strathkelvin); R C Hay, QC, CBE, WS (North Strathclyde); G L Cox (South Strathclyde, Dumfries, and Galloway); **Airdree** Sheriff Court House, Airdree ML6 6EE; phone: (01236) 751121; **Sheriff** I C Simpson; R H Dickson; **Sheriff Clerk** M Bonar; **Ayr** Sheriff Court House, Ayr KA7 1DR; phone: (01292) 268474; **Sheriffs** N Gow, QC; R G McEwan, QC; **Floating Sheriff** C B Miller; **Sheriff Clerk** G Waddell; **Campbeltown** Sheriff Court House, Campbeltown PA28 6AN; phone: (01586) 552503; **Sheriff** W Dunlop; **Sheriff Clerk** P Hay; **Dumbarton** Sheriff Court House, Dumbarton G82 1QR; phone: (01389) 763266; **Sheriffs** J T Fitzsimmons; T Scott; S W H Fraser; **Sheriff Clerk** P G Corcoran; **Dunoon** Sheriff Court House, Dunoon PA23 8BQ; phone: (01369) 704166; **Sheriff** A W Noble; **Sheriff Clerk** C Carson; **Glasgow** Sheriff Court House, PO Box 23, 1 Carlton Place, Glasgow G5 9DA; phone: (0141) 429 8888; **Sheriffs** B A Kerr, QC; B Kearney; G H Gordon, CBE, QC; B A Lockhart; I G Pirie; A L A Duncan; G J Evans; E H Galt; A C Henry; J K Mitchell; A G Johnston; J P Murphy; D Convery; J McGowan; S Raeburn, QC; M A F Gimblett; I A S Peebles, QC; C W MacFarlane; K M MacIver; H Matthews, QC; J D Lowe; **Floating Sheriff** J A Baird; **Sheriff Clerk** I Scott; **Greenock** Sheriff Court House, Greenock PA15 1TR; phone: (01475) 787073; **Sheriffs** J P Herald; Sir Stephen Young, Bt; **Sheriff Clerk** J T Tannahill; **Hamilton** Sheriff Court House, Hamilton ML3 6AA; phone: (01698) 282957; **Sheriffs** L Cameron; A C Macpherson; D C Russell; H Stirling; W F Lunny; V J Canavan; W E Gibson; J H Stewart; **Floating Sheriff** H S Neilson; **Sheriff Clerk** P Feeney; **Kilmarnock** Sheriff Court House, Kilmarnock KA1 1ED; phone: (01563) 520211; **Sheriffs** T M Croan; D B Smith; T F Russell; **Sheriff Clerk** N Weir; **Lanark** Sheriff Court House, Lanark ML11 7NQ; phone: (01555) 661531; **Sheriff** J Douglas Allan; **Sheriff Clerk** A Whyte; **Oban** Sheriff Court House, Oban PA34 4AL; phone: (01631) 62414; **Sheriff** C G McKay; **Sheriff Clerk** J G Whitelaw; **Paisley** Sheriff Court House, St James Street, Paisley PA23 2HW; phone: (0141) 887 5291; **Sheriffs** R G Smith; N Douglas; J Spy; C K Higgins; **Floating Sheriffs** W Dunlop; D J Pender; **Sheriff Clerk** R MacMillan; **Rothesay** Sheriff Court House, Rothesay PA20 9HA; phone: (01700) 502982; **Sheriff** J P Herald; **Sheriff Clerk** C K McCormick

Tayside

Sheriff Principal J J Maguire, QC; **Arbroath** Sheriff Court House, Arbroath DD11 1HL; phone: (01241) 876600; **Sheriff** C N R Stein; **Sheriff Clerk** M Herbertson; **Dundee** Sheriff Court House, Dundee DD1 9AD; phone: (01382) 229961; **Sheriffs** R A Davidson; A L Stewart, QC; **Floating Sheriff** J N Young; **Sheriff Clerk** J S Doig; **Perth** Sheriff Court House, Perth PH2 8NL; phone: (01738) 620546; **Sheriff** J F Wheatley, QC; J C McInnes, QC; **Floating Sheriff** P M M Bowman; **Sheriff Clerk** W Jones.

Foreign Embassies

Foreign Embassies and Ambassadors in the UK

Source: *The London Diplomatic List,* December 1997 © Crown Copyright 1997.

Afghanistan 31 Prince's Gate, London SW7 1QQ; phone: (0171) 589 8891; fax: (0171) 581 3452; *Ambassador* (vacant); **Albania** 4th Floor, 38 Grosvenor Gardens, London SW1W 0EB; phone: (0171) 730 5709; fax: (0171) 730 5747; *Ambassador* Agim Besim Fagu; **Algeria** 54 Holland Park, London W11 3RS; phone: (0171) 221 7800; fax: (0171) 221 0448; *Ambassador* Ahmed Benyamina; **Angola** 98 Park Lane, London W1Y 3TA; phone: (0171) 495 1752; fax: (0171) 495 1635; *Ambassador* Antonio da Costa Fernandes; **Antigua and Barbuda** 15 Thayer Street, London W1M 5LD; phone: (0171) 486 7073; fax: (0171) 486 9970; *High Commissioner* Ronald M Sanders; **Argentina** 65 Brook Street, London W1Y 1YE; phone: (0171) 318 1300; fax: (0171) 318 1301; *Ambassador* Rogelio Pfirter; **Armenia** 25A Cheniston Gardens, London W8 6TG; phone: (0171) 938 5435; fax: (0171) 938 2595; *Ambassador* (vacant); **Australia** Australia House, Strand, London WC2B 4LA; phone: (0171) 379 4334; fax: (0171) 240 5333; *High Commissioner* Neal Blewett; **Austria** 18 Belgrave Mews West, London SW1X 8HU; phone: (0171) 235 3731; fax: (0171) 344 0292; *Ambassador* Eva Nowotny; **Azerbaijan** 4 Kensington Court, London W8 5DL; phone: (0171) 938 5482/3412; fax: (0171) 937 1783; *Ambassador* Mahmud Mamed-Kuliyev; **Bahamas** 10 Chesterfield Street, London W1X 8AH; phone: (0171) 408 4488; fax: (0171) 499 9937; *High Commissioner* Arthur Foulkes; **Bahrain** 98 Gloucester Road, London SW7 4AU; phone: (0171) 370 5132/3; fax: (0171) 370 7773; *Ambassador* Shaikh Abdul Aziz Bin Mubarak Al Khalifa; **Bangladesh** 28 Queen's Gate, London SW7 5JA; phone: (0171) 584 0081; fax: (0171) 225 2130; *High Commissioner* A H Mahmood Ali; **Barbados** 1 Great Russell Street, London WC1B 3JY; phone: (0171) 631 4975; fax: (0171) 323 6872; *High Commissioner* Peter Patrick Simmons; **Belarus** 6 Kensington Court, London W8 5DL; phone: (0171) 937 3288 (Chancery) (0171) 938 1633 (Economic and Trade Section) (0171) 938 3677/(0171) 937 3288 (Consular and Visa Section); fax: (0171) 361 0005; *Ambassador* Uladzimir Shchasny; **Belgium** 103–105 Eaton Square, London SW1W 9AB; phone: (0171) 470 3700; fax: (0171) 259 6213; *Ambassador* Lode Willems; **Belize** 22 Harcourt House, 19 Cavendish Square, London W1M 9AD; phone: (0171) 499 9728; fax: (0171) 491 4139; *High Commissioner* Ursula H Barrow; **Bolivia** 106 Eaton Square, London SW1W 9AD; phone: (0171) 235 4248/2257; fax:

(0171) 235 1286; *Ambassador* (vacant); **Bosnia-Herzegovina** 4th Floor, Morley House, 320 Regent Street, London W1R 5AB; phone: (0171) 255 3758; fax: (0171) 255 3760; *Ambassador* (vacant); **Botswana** 6 Stratford Place, London W1N 9AE; phone: (0171) 499 0031; fax: (0171) 495 8595; *High Commissioner* Tuelonyana Ditlhabi-Oliphant; **Brazil** 32 Green Street, Mayfair, London W1Y 4AT; phone: (0171) 499 0877; *Ambassador* Rubens Antonio Barbosa; **Brunei** 19/20 Belgrave Square, London SW1X 8PG; phone: (0171) 581 0521; fax: (0171) 235 9717; *High Commissioner* Pehin Dato Jaya Abdul Latif; **Bulgaria** 186–188 Queen's Gate, London SW7 5HL; phone: (0171) 584 9400/9433; fax: (0171) 584 4948; *Ambassador* (vacant); **Cameroon** 84 Holland Park, London W11 3SB; phone: (0171) 727 0771; fax: (0171) 792 9353; *High Commissioner* Samuel Libock Mbei; **Canada** Macdonald House, 1 Grosvenor Square, London W1X 0AB; phone: (0171) 258 6000; fax: (0171) 258 6333; *High Commissioner* Roy McLaren; **Chile** 12 Devonshire Street, London W1N 2DS; phone: (0171) 580 6392; fax: (0171) 436 5204; *Ambassador* Mario Artaza; **China** 49–51 Portland Place, London W1N 4JL; phone: (0171) 636 9375/5726; *Ambassador* Ma Zhengang; **Colombia** Flat 3A, 3 Hans Crescent, London SW1X 0LN; phone: (0171) 589 9177/(0171) 589 5037; fax: (0171) 581 1829; *Ambassador* Carlos A Lemos-Simmonds; **Congo, Democratic Republic of** 26 Chesham Place, London SW1X 8HH; phone: (0171) 235 6137; fax: (0171) 235 9048; *Ambassador* (vacant); **Costa Rica** Flat 1, 14 Lancaster Gate, London W2 3LH; phone: (0171) 706 8844; fax: (0171) 706 8655; *Ambassador* Jorge Borbón; **Côte d'Ivoire** 2 Upper Belgrave Street, London SW1X 8BJ; phone: (0171) 235 6991; fax: (0171) 259 5320; *Ambassador* Kouadio Adjoumani; **Croatia** 21 Conway Street, London W1P 5HL; phone: (0171) 387 2022; fax: (0171) 387 0310; *Ambassador* Andrija Kojakovic; **Cuba** 167 High Holborn, London WC1 6PA; phone: (0171) 240 2488; fax: (0171) 836 2602; *Ambassador* Rodney Alejandro Lopez Clemente; **Cyprus** 93 Park Street, London W1Y 4ET; phone: (0171) 499 8272; fax: (0171) 491 0691; *High Commissioner* Vanias Markides; **Czech Republic** 26–30 Kensington Palace Gardens, London W8 4QY; phone: (0171) 243 1115; fax: (0171) 727 9654; *Ambassador* Pavel Seifter; **Denmark** 55 Sloane Street, London SW1X 9SR; phone: (0171) 333 0200; fax: (0171) 333 0270; *Ambassador* Ole Lønsmann Poulsen; **Dominica** 1 Collingham Gardens, South Kensington, London SW5 0HW; phone: (0171) 370 5194/5; fax: (0171) 373 8743; *Ambassador* George E Williams; **Dominican Republic** 139 Inverness Terrace, Bayswater, London W2; phone: (0171) 727 6285; fax: (0171) 727 3693; *Ambassador* Pedro L Padilla Tonos; **Eastern Caribbean States**

(St Kitts and Nevis; St Lucia; St Vincent and the Grenadines) 10 Kensington Court, London W8 5DL; phone: (0171) 937 9522; fax: (0171) 937 5514; *High Commissioner* Aubrey E Hart; **Ecuador** Flat 3B, 3 Hans Crescent, Knightsbridge, London SW1X 0LS; phone: (0171) 584 2648/1367/8084; fax: (0171) 823 9701; *Ambassador* Patricio Maldonado; **Egypt** 12 Curzon Street, London W1Y 7FJ; phone: (0171) 499 2401/3304; fax: (0171) 355 3568; *Ambassador* Adel El-Gazzar; **El Salvador** Tennyson House, 159 Great Portland Street, London W1N 5FD; phone: (0171) 436 8282; fax: (0171) 436 8181; *Ambassador* Manual Gutierrez Ruiz; **Estonia** 16 Hyde Park Gate, London SW7 5DG; phone: (0171) 589 3428; fax: (0171) 589 3430; *Ambassador* Raul Mälk; **Ethiopia** 17 Prince's Gate, London SW7 1PZ; phone: (0171) 589 7212-5; fax: (0171) 584 7054; *Ambassador* Solomon Gidada; **Fiji** 34 Hyde Park Gate, London SW7 5DN; phone: (0171) 584 3661; fax: (0171) 584 2838; *High Commissioner* Filimone Jitoko; **Finland** 38 Chesham Place, London SW1X 8HW; phone: (0171) 838 6200; fax: (0171) 235 3680; *Ambassador* Pertti Salolainen; **France** 58 Knightsbridge, London SW1X 7JT; phone: (0171) 201 1000; fax: (0171) 201 1004; *Ambassador* Jean Gueguinou; **Gabon** 27 Elvaston Place, London SW7 5NL; phone: (0171) 823 9986; fax: (0171) 584 0047; *Ambassador* Honorine Dossou-Naki; **Gambia** 57 Kensington Court, London W8 5DG; phone: (0171) 937 6316/7/8; fax: (0171) 937 9095; *High Commissioner* John P Bojang; **Georgia** 3 Hornton Place, Kensington, London W8 4LZ; phone: (0171) 937 8233; fax: (0171) 938 4108; *Ambassador* Teimuraz Mamatsashvili; **Germany** 23 Belgrave Square, 1 Chesham Place, London SW1X 8PZ; phone: (0171) 824 1300; fax: (0171) 824 1435; *Ambassador* Gebhardt von Moltke; **Ghana** 13 Belgrave Square, London SW1X 8PN; phone: (0171) 235 4142; fax: (0171) 245 9552; *High Commissioner* James E K Aggrey-Orleans; **Greece** 1A Holland Park, London W11 3TP; phone: (0171) 229 3850; fax: (0171) 229 7221; *Ambassador* Vassilis S Zafiropoulos; **Grenada** 1 Collingham Gardens, Earl's Court, London SW5 0HW; phone: (0171) 373 7809; fax: (0171) 379 7040; *High Commissioner* F Marcelle Gairy; **Guatemala** 13 Fawcett Street, London SW10 9HN; phone: (0171) 351 3042; fax: (0171) 376 5708; *Ambassador* Fernando Andrade Diaz-Duran; **Guinea-Bissau** 8 Palace Gate, London W8 4RP; phone: (0171) 589 5253; fax: (0171) 589 9590; **Guyana** 3 Palace Court, Bayswater Road, London W2 4LP; phone: (0171) 229 7684–8; fax: (0171) 727 9809; *Ambassador* Laleshwar K N Singh; **Haiti:** the Embassy of the Republic of Haiti closed on 30 March 1987; **Honduras** 115 Gloucester Place, London W1H 3PJ; phone: (0171) 486 4880; fax: (0171) 486 4550; *Ambassador* Iván Romero Martinez; **Hungary** 35 Eaton

Place, London SW1X 8BY; phone: (0171) 235 5218; fax: (0171) 823 1348; *Ambassador* Gábor Szentiványi; **Iceland** 1 Eaton Terrace, London; phone: (0171) 590 1100; fax: (0171) 730 1683; *Ambassador* Benedikt Ásgeirsson; **India** India House, Aldwych, London WC2B 4NA; phone: (0171) 836 8484; fax: (0171) 836 4331; *High Commissioner* L M Singhvi; **Indonesia** 38 Grosvenor Square, London W1X 9AD; phone: (0171) 499 7661; fax: (0171) 491 4993; *Ambassador* Rahardjo Jamtomo; **Iran** 16 Prince's Gate, London SW7 1PT; phone: (0171) 225 3000; fax: (0171) 589 4440; *Ambassador* G Ansari; **Iraq:** Following the break of diplomatic relations with Iraq on 6 February 1991, the Embassy of the Hashemite Kingdom of Jordan has undertaken the task of protecting Iraqi interests in the UK. An Iraqi Interests Section has therefore been established at the Embassy of the Hashemite Kingdom of Jordan. See Jordan; **Ireland, Republic of** 17 Grosvenor Place, London SW1X 7HR; phone: (0171) 235 2171; fax: (0171) 245 6961; *Ambassador* Edward Barrington; **Israel** 2 Palace Green, Kensington, London W8 4QB; phone: (0171) 957 9500; fax: (0171) 957 9555; *Ambassador* Moshe Raviv; **Italy** 14 Three Kings Yard, Davies Street, London W1Y 2EH; phone: (0171) 312 2200; fax: (0171) 499 2283; *Ambassador* Paolo Galli; **Jamaica** 1–2 Prince Consort Road, London SW7 2BZ; phone: (0171) 823 9911; fax: (0171) 589 5154; *Ambassador* Derick R Heaven; **Japan** 101–104 Piccadilly, London W1V 9FN; phone: (0171) 465 6500; fax: (0171) 491 9348; *Ambassador* Sadayuki Hayashi; **Jordan** 6 Upper Phillimore Gardens, Kensington, London W8 7HB; phone: (0171) 937 3685; fax: (0171) 937 8795; *Ambassador* Fouad Ayoub; **Iraqi Interests Section** 21 Queen's Gate, London SW7 5JG; phone: (0171) 584 7141/6; fax: 584 7716; **Minister/Head of Interests Section:** Zuhair M Ibrahim; **Kazakhstan** 33 Thurlowe Square, London SW7 2DS; phone: (0171) 581 4646; *Ambassador* Kanat B Saudabaev; **Kenya** 45 Portland Place, London W1N 4AS; phone: (0171) 636 2371/5; fax: (0171) 323 6717; *Ambassador* Mwanyengela Ngali; **Korea** 60 Buckingham Gate, London SW1E 6AJ; phone: (0171) 227 5500; fax: (0171) 227 5503; *Ambassador* Dong-Jin Choi; **Kuwait** 2 Albert Gate, Knightsbridge, London SW1X 7JU; phone: (0171) 590 3400; fax: (0171) 823 1712; *Ambassador* Khaled Al-Duwaisan; **Kyrgyzstan** phone: (0171) 431 5611; *Ambassador* Roza Otunbayeva; **Latvia** 45 Nottingham Place, London W1M 3FE; phone: (0171) 312 0040; fax: (0171) 312 0042; *Ambassador* Normans Penke; **Lebanon** 21 Kensington Palace Gardens, London W8 4QM; phone: (0171) 229 7265/6; fax: (0171) 243 1699; *Ambassador* Mahmoud Hammoud; **Lesotho** 7 Chesham Place, Belgravia, London SW1 8HN; phone: (0171) 235 5686; fax: (0171) 235 5023; *Ambassador* Benjamin M Masilo; **Liberia** 2 Pembridge Place, London W2 4XB; phone: (0171) 221 1036; *Ambassador* (vacant); **Libya** Following the break of diplomatic relations with the Socialist People's Libyan Arab Jamahiriya on 22 April 1984 the Royal

Embassy of Saudi Arabia has undertaken the task of protecting Libyan interests in the UK. A Libyan Interests Section has therefore been established in the Royal Embassy of Saudi Arabia. See Saudi Arabia; **Lithuania** 84 Gloucester Place, London W1H 3HN; phone: (0171) 486 6401/2; fax: (0171) 486 6403; *Ambassador* Justas V Paleckis; **Luxembourg** 27 Wilton Crescent, London SW1X 8SD; phone: (0171) 235 6961; fax: (0171) 235 9734; *Ambassador* Josehp Weyland; **Macedonia, Former Yugoslav Republic of** 10 Harcourt House, 19A Cavendish Square, London W1M 9AD; phone: (0171) 499 5152/1854; fax: (0171) 499 2864; *Ambassador* Stevo Crvenkovski; **Malawi** 33 Grosvenoer Street, London W1X 0DE; phone: (0171) 491 4172/7; fax: (0171) 491 9916; *High Commissioner* T Jake Muwamba; **Malaysia** 45 Belgrave Square, London SW1X 8QT; phone: (0171) 235 8033; fax: (0171) 235 5161; *High Commissioner* Dato Kamarudin Abu; **Maldives** 22 Nottingham Place, London W1M 3FB; phone: (0171) 224 2135; fax: (0171) 224 2157; *High Commissioner* (vacant); **Malta** Malta House, 36–38 Piccadilly, London W1V 0PQ; phone: (0171) 292 4800; fax: (0171) 734 1831; *High Commissioner* Richard A Matrenza; **Mauritius** 32–33 Elvaston Place, London SW7 5NW; phone: (0171) 581 0294/5; fax: (0171) 823 8437; *High Commissioner* Satcam Boolell; **Mexico** 42 Hertford Street, Mayfair, London W1Y 7TF; phone: (0171) 499 8586; fax: (0171) 495 4035; *Ambassador* Santiago Oñate; **Mongolia** 7 Kensington Court, London W8 5DL; phone: (0171) 937 0150; *Ambassador* Tsedenjavyn Suhbaatar; **Morocco** 49 Queen's Gate Gardens, London SW7 5NE; phone: (0171) 581 5001/4; fax: (0171) 225 3862; *Ambassador* Khalil Haddaoui; **Mozambique** 21 Fitzroy Square, London W1P 5HJ; phone: (0171) 383 3800; fax: (0171) 383 3801; *High Commissioner* Jose Baciao Koloma; **Myanmar** 19A Charles Street, Berkeley Square, London W1X 8ER; phone: (0171) 499 8841; fax: (0171) 629 4169; *Ambassador* U Win Aung; **Namibia** 6 Chandos Street, London W1M 0LQ; phone: (0171) 636 6244; fax: (0171) 637 5694; *High Commissioner* Ben Ulenga; **Nepal** 12A Kensington Palace Gardens, London W8 4QU; phone: (0171) 229 1594/6231; fax: (0171) 792 9861; *Ambassador* Singha B Basnyat; **Netherlands** 38 Hyde Park Gate, London SW7 5DP; phone: (0171) 590 3200; *Ambassador* Jan Herman R D van Rouen; **New Zealand** New Zealand House, Haymarket, London SW1Y 4TQ; phone: (0171) 930 8422; fax: (0171) 839 4580; *High Commissioner* Richard Grant; **Nicaragua** The Embassy of Nicaragua closed on 31 May 1997.; **Nigeria** Nigeria House, 9 Northumberland Avenue, London WC2N 5BX; phone: (0171) 839 1244; fax: (0171) 839 8746; *High Commissioner* (vacant); **Norway** 25 Belgrave Square, London SW1X 8QD; phone: (0171) 591 5500; fax: (0171) 245 6993; *Ambassador* Kjell Colding; **Oman** 167 Queen's Gate, London SW7 5HE; phone: (0171) 225 0001; fax: (0171) 589 2505; *Ambassador* Hussain Ali Abdullatif; **Pak-**

istan 35–36 Lowndes Square, London SW1X 9JN; phone: (0171) 664 9200; fax: (0171) 664 9200; *High Commissioner* Mian Riaz Samee; **Panama** Ground Floor and Basement, 48 Park Street, London W1Y 3PD; phone: (0171) 493 4646; fax: (0171) 493 4333; *Ambassador* (vacant); **Papua New Guinea** 3rd Floor, 14 Waterloo Place, London SW1R 4AR; phone: (0171) 930 0922/7; fax: (0171) 930 0828; *High Commissioner* Kina Bona; **Paraguay** Braemar Lodge, Cornwall Gardens, London SW7 4AQ; phone: (0171) 937 1253/6629; fax: (0171) 937 5687; *Ambassador* (vacant); **Peru** 52 Sloane Street, London SW1X 9SP; phone: (0171) 235 1917/2545/3802; fax: (0171) 235 4463; **Philippines** 9A Palace Green, London W8 4QE; phone: (0171) 937 1600; fax: (0171) 937 2925; *Ambassador* Jesus P Tambunting; **Poland** 47 Portland Place, London W1N 3AG; phone: (0171) 580 4324/9; fax: (0171) 323 4018; *Ambassador* Ryszard Stemplowski; **Portugal** 11 Belgrave Square, London SW1X 8PP; phone: (0171) 235 5331; fax: (0171) 245 1287; *Ambassador* José Gregório Faria; **Qatar** 1 South Audley Street, London W1Y 5DQ; phone: (0171) 493 2200; fax: (0171) 493 2661; *Ambassador* Ali M Jaidah; **Romania** 4 Palace Green, London W8 4QD; phone: (0171) 937 9666; fax: (0171) 937 8069; *Ambassador* Radu Onofrei; **Russia** 13 Kensington Palace Gardens, London W8 4QX; phone: (0171) 229 2666/3628/6412; fax: (0171) 727 8625; *Ambassador* Yuri E Fokine; **Rwanda** Uganda House, 58–59 Trafalgar Square, London WC2N 5DX; phone: (0171) 930 2570; fax: (0171) 930 2572; *Ambassador* Zac Nsenga; **St Kitts and Nevis** See Eastern Caribbean States; **St Lucia** See Eastern Caribbean States; **St Vincent and the Grenadines** See Eastern Caribbean States; **Saudi Arabia** 30 Charles Street, Mayfair, London W1X 7PM; phone: (0171) 917 3000; *Ambassador* Ghazi A Algosaibi; **Libyan Interests Section** c/o 119 Harley Street, London W1; phone: (0171) 486 8387; **Head of Interests Section:** Isa Baruni Edaeki; **Senegal** 39 Marloes Road, London W8 6LA; phone: (0171) 937 7237/938 4048; fax: (0171) 938 2546; **Seychelles** Box 4PE, 2nd Floor, Eros House, 111 Baker Street, London W1M 1FE; phone: (0171) 224 1660; fax: (0171); *High Commissioner* (vacant); **Sierra Leone** 33 Portland Place, London W1N 3AG; phone: (0171) 636 6483–6; fax: (0171) 927 8130; *Ambassador* Cyril Patrick Foray; **Singapore** 9 Wilton Crescent, London SW1X 8RW; phone: (0171) 235 8315; fax: (0171) 245 6583; *High Commissioner* J Y Pillay; **Slovak Republic** 25 Kensington Palace Gardens, London W8 4QY; phone: (0171) 243 0803; fax: (0171) 727 5824; *Ambassador* Igor Slobodnik; **Slovenia** Suite 1, Cavendish Court, 11–15 Wigmore Street, London W1H 9LA; phone: (0171) 495 7775; fax: (0171) 495 7776; *Ambassador* (vacant); **Somalia** The Embassy of the Somali Democratic Republic closed on 2 January 1992; **South Africa** South Africa House, Trafalgar Square, London WC2N 5DP; phone: (0171) 451 7299; fax: (0171) 451 7284; *High Commis-*

sioner Mendi M T B Msimang; **Spain** 39 Chesham Place, London SW1X 8SB; phone: (0171) 235 5555; fax: (0171) 235 9905; *Ambassador* Alberto Aza Arias; **Sri Lanka** 13 Hyde Park Gardens, London W2 2LU; phone: (0171) 262 1841–7; fax: (0171) 262 7970; *High Commissioner* Sarath Kusum Wickremesinghe; **Sudan** 3 Cleveland Row, St James's, London SW1A 1DD; phone: (0171) 839 8080; fax: (0171) 839 7560; *Ambassador* Omer Yousif Bireedo; **Swaziland** 20 Buckingham Gate, London SW1E 6LB; phone: (0171) 630 6611; fax: (0171) 630 6564; *High Commissioner* Percy S Mngomezulu; **Sweden** 11 Montagu Place, London W1H 2AL; phone: (0171) 917 6400; fax: (0171) 724 4174; *Ambassador* Mats Bergquist; **Switzerland** 16/18 Montagu Place, London W1H 2BQ; phone: (0171) 616 6000; fax: (0171) 724 7001; *Ambassador* François Nordmann; **Syria** 8 Belgrave Square, London SW1X 8PH; phone: (0171) 245 9012; fax: (0171) 235 4621; *Ambassador* (vacant); **Tanzania** 43 Hertford Street, London W1Y 8DB; phone: (0171) 499 8951–4; fax: (0171) 491 9321; *High Commissioner* Abdul-Kader A Shareef; **Thailand** 29–30 Queen's Gate, London SW7 5JP; phone: (0171) 589 0173/9244; fax: (0171) 823 9695; *Ambassador* Vidhya Rayananonda; **Tonga** 36 Molyneux Street, London W1H 6AB; phone: (0171) 724 5828; *High Commissioner* Akosita Fineanganofo; **Trinidad and Tobago** 42 Belgrave Square, London SW1X 8NT; phone: (0171) 245 9351; fax: (0171) 823 1065; *High Commissioner* Mrs Sheelagh M De Osuna; **Tunisia** 29 Prince's Gate, London SW7 1QG; phone: (0171) 584 8117; fax: (0171) 225 2884; *Ambassador* Mohammed Ben Ahmed; **Turkey** 43 Belgrave Square, London SW1X 8PA; phone: (0171) 393 0202; *Ambassador* Ôzdem Sanberk; **Turkmenistan** 2nd Floor South, St George's House, 14/17 Wells Street, London W1P 3FP; phone: (0171) 255 1071; fax: (0171) 323 9184; *Ambassador* Murad Chariev; **Uganda** Uganda House, 58–59 Trafalgar Square, London WC2N 5DX; phone: (0171) 839 5783; fax: (0171) 839 8925; *High Commissioner* George Kirya; **Ukraine** 78 Kensington Park Road, London W11 2PL; phone: (0171) 727 6312; fax: (0171) 792 1708; *Ambassador* Sergui Komissarenko; **United Arab Emirates** 30 Princes Gate, London SW7 1PT; phone: (0171) 581 1281; fax: (0171) 581 9616; *Ambassador* Easa Saleh Al Gurg; **USA** Grosvenor Square, London W1A 1AE; phone: (0171) 499 9000; fax: (0171) 499 9000; *Ambassador* Philip Lader; **Uruguay** 2nd Floor, 140 Brompton Road, London SW3 1HY; phone: (0171) 584 8192; fax: (0171) 581 9585; *Ambassador* Juan Enrique Fischer; **Uzbekistan** 41 Holland Park, London W11 2RP; phone: (0171) 229 7679; fax: (0171) 229 7029; **Vatican City State** 54 Parkside, London SW19 5NF; phone: (0181) 946 1410/7971; fax: (0181) 947 2494; *Apostolic Nuncio* Archbishop Pablo Puente; **Venezuela** 1 Cromwell Road, London SW7; phone: (0171) 584 4206/7; fax: (0171) 589 8887; *Ambassador* Roy Chaderton-Matos; **Vietnam** 12–14 Victoria Road, London W8 5RD; phone: (0171) 937 1912; fax: (0171) 937 6108; *Ambassador* Huynh Ngoc An; **Yemen** 57 Cromwell Road, London SW7 2ED; phone: (0171) 584 6607; fax: (0171) 589 3350; *Ambassador* Hussein Abdullah Al-Amri; **Yugoslavia** 5 Lexham Gardens, London W8 5JJ; phone: (0171) 370 6105; fax: (0171) 370 3838; *Ambassador* Milos Radulovic; **Zambia** 2 Palace Gate, Kensington, London W8; phone: (0171) 589 6655; fax: (0171) 581 1353; *High Commissioner* Moses Musonda; **Zimbabwe** Zimbabwe House, 429 Strand, London WC2R 0SA; phone: (0171) 836 7755; *High Commissioner* Ngoni Togarepi Chideya.

Foreign Honorary Consuls in the UK

Source: *The London Diplomatic List,* December 1997 © Crown copyright 1997.

Benin Dolphin House, 16 The Broadway, Stanmore, Middlesex HA7 4DW; phone: (0181) 954 8800; fax: (0181) 954 8844; *Honorary Consul* Lawrence L Landau; **Burkina** 5 Cinnamon Row, Plantation Wharf, London SW11 3TW; phone: (0171) 738 1800; fax: (0171) 738 2820; *Honorary Consul* Stuart G Singer; **Cape Verde** 43 Upper Grosvenor Street, London W1X 9PG; phone: (0171) 493 4840; fax: (0171) 493 4299; *Honorary Consul* Stephen Gray; **Congo** Alliance House, 12 Caxton Street, London SW1H 0QS; phone: (0171) 222 7575; fax: (0171) 233 2087; *Honorary Consul* Louis Muzzo; **Guinea** 20 Upper Grosvenor Street, London W1X 9PB; phone: (0171) 333 0044; fax: (0171) 333 8312; *Honorary Consul* Alexander J C Harper; **Mauritania** 140 Bow Common Lane, London E3 4BH; phone: (0181) 980 4382; fax: (0181) 980 2232; *Honorary Consul* Jonathan Fryer; **Nauru** Romshed, Underriver, Near Sevenoaks, Kent TN15 0SD; phone: (01732) 746061; fax: (01732) 454136; *Honorary Consul* Martin W L Weston; **Samoa** 18 Northumberland Avenue, London WC2N 5BJ; phone: (0171) 930 6733; fax: (0171) 930 9705; *Honorary Consul* Prunella Scarlett; **São Tomé and Principe** 42 North Audley Street, London W1A 4PY; phone: (0171) 499 1995; fax: (0171) 629 6460; *Honorary Consul* William S Wilder; **Solomon Islands** 19 Springfield Road, Wimbledon, London SW19 7AL; phone: (0181) 296 0232; fax: (0181) 946 1744; *Honorary Consul* E E Edward Nielson; **Tajikistan** 33 Ovington Square, London SW3 1LJ; phone: (0171) 584 5111; fax: (0171) 581 2669; *Honorary Consul* Benjamin Brahms.

Web Sites

Argyll and Bute Council

URL: 'http://www.argyll-bute.gov.uk/'

Official guide to Argyll and Bute with details of accommodation for visitors, a 'what's on' guide to local events, and a bibliography of publications concerning Argyll and Bute.

Birmingham (UK)

URL: 'http://www.birmingham.gov.uk/'

Full details on the city of Birmingham, for both visitors and residents. .

Brief History of Wales

URL: 'http://www.britannia.com/wales/whist.html'

From the Britannia Internet Magazine, a history of Wales in 21 chapters, written by Welsh historian, Peter N Williams.

Bristol City Council

URL: 'http://www.bristol-city.gov.uk/'

Huge official source of information on the city of Bristol. In addition to details of services offered by the city's council, there is a comprehensive visitor's guide to the city and its attractions.

Cardiff, Capital City of Wales

URL: 'http://www.cardiff.gov.uk/'

Official guide to the Welsh capital. Local government functions are fully explained and investment opportunities outlined.

City of Bradford

URL: 'http://www.bradford.gov.uk/'

Official guide to Bradford, with an account of the history of the former wool capital of the world and its evolution into a modern multicultural city.

City of Leeds

URL: 'http://www.leeds.gov.uk/'

Colourful presentation of the main aspects of life in Leeds. Community and benefit services information is offered. The city's history is superbly covered with vast numbers of photos which can also be sent as 'postcards' across the Web.

Dartmoor National Park Authority

URL: 'http://www.dartmoor-npa.gov.uk/'

Official guide to the moors and valleys of Dartmoor. There are sections on geology, history, and conservation activities and additional educational materials for those wishing to learn more.

Derby Tourist Information Web Site

URL: "http://www.derby-city-
council.gov.uk/"

Official guide to Derby.

Destination England

URL: "http://www.lonelyplanet.com/
dest/eur/eng.htm"

History and tourist attractions of England
according to 'Lonely Planet'. The history of
England is briefly described here, starting
from the Stone Age and running right
through to Tony Blair's election success.

Destination Wales

URL: "http://www.lonelyplanet.com/
dest/eur/wal.htm"

History and tourist attractions of Wales
according to 'Lonely Planet'.

Dundee City Council

URL: "http://www.dundeecity.gov.uk/"

Official guide to Dundee. The home page
clearly sets out details of the site's material on
local government services, business opportunities, and education.

Edinburgh

URL: "http://www.city.net/countries/
united_kingdom/scotland/edinburgh/"

Comprehensive guide to the Scottish capital.

Gateway to Scotland

URL: "http://www.geo.ed.ac.uk/
home/scotland/scotland.html"

Guide to all things Scottish, including an
'active map', a guide to the major cities, and
information on the language, as well as sections on famous residents and history.

Glasgow

URL: "http://www.city.net/countries/
united_kingdom/scotland/glasgow/"

Concise guide to the city.

Harrogate Borough Council

URL: "http://www.harrogate.gov.uk/
frames.htm"

Profiles of all the communities in the area and
a wealth of practical information for visitors
and residents.

HighPeakNet

URL: "http://www.highpeaknet.com/"

Excellent unofficial guide to Britain's
longest-established national park. Click on
'OPEAK' on the home page for a comprehensive guide to the geology, geography, and
history of the Peaks.

Historical Cornwall

URL: "http://www.cranstar.co.uk/
History.htm"

Collection of pages devoted to Cornwall, its
history, culture, and industry.

Historic Lancaster

URL: "http://theboard.newsquest.co.uk/
llt/lancaster/lancaster.html"

Locally-prepared guide to the heritage of
Lancaster. Text accompanying J M W Turner
landscapes provides further information on
Lancaster's long history.

It's Better in Bournemouth

URL: "http://www.bournemouth.gov.uk/"

Official information from the local council
on business opportunities, convention facilities, and tourist amenities.

Lake District National Park Authority

URL: "http://www.lake-
district.gov.uk/index.htm"

Official guide to the attractions of Britain's
largest National Park. There are sections on
geology, history, conservation activities, and
exhibitions in the Park's visitor's centre.
There is also a daily weather report.

London Street Maps

URL: "http://www.multimap.com/london/"

Simple but effective site allowing you to
search for any street in the Greater London
area. You can see the street and its surroundings at a variety of scales from 1:200,000
down to 1:5,000.

Pembrokeshire Coast National Park

URL: "http://www.PembrokeshireCoast.org/"

Official guide to Britain's only coastal national
park. There is information on the coastline,
beaches, and the area's Celtic and Norman heritage.

States of Jersey

URL: "http://www.jersey.gov.uk/"

Coverage of the history and cultural heritage
of Jersey.

Virtual Brighton and Hove

URL: "http://www.brighton.co.uk/"

Searchable guide to the attractions of
Brighton. The needs of convention organizers, holiday-makers, day-trippers, shoppers,
and students are all catered for. There is also
a section on the gay scene in the town.

Welcome to the Yorkshire Dales

URL: "http://www.yorkshirenet.co.uk/
ydales/index.html"

Well organized guide to the Dales. There is
easily accessible information on the habitat,
landscape, and history of the area.

Welcome to York

URL: "http://www.britain.co.uk/
wel2york.html"

Complete guide to the English city of York.

THE WORLD

The Year in Review

1 July 1997 The British crown colony of Hong Kong reverts to Chinese control, ending 156 years of colonial rule. Hong Kong becomes a Special Administrative Region within China.

5 July 1997 Second Prime Minister Hun Sen of the Cambodian People's Party overthrows First Prime Minister Norodom Ranariddh of the royalist United Front for an Independent, Neutral, Peaceful, and Cooperative Cambodia (FUNCINPEC) in a coup in Cambodia.

6 July 1997 The ruling Institutional Revolutionary Party, suffering its worst electoral defeats in 70 years, loses control of the lower house in legislative elections in Mexico.

10 July 1997 The US Senate confirms the appointment of George J Tenet as director of the Central Intelligence Agency. His nomination was approved unanimously after the Justice Department decided not to investigate Tenet's personal finances.

12 July 1997 A crowd of 500,000 people demonstrate in Bilbao, Spain, for the release of Miguel Angel Blanco, a government official held hostage by ETA (*Euskadi ta Askatasuna*, 'Basque Nation and Liberty') Basque separatist terrorists demanding the relocation of ETA prisoners to the Basque country; Blanco is found dead the following day.

12 July 1997 The recently discovered remains of the Latin American revolutionary activist Che Guevara are returned to Cuba from Bolivia, where he was killed in 1967.

14 July 1997 Kocheril Raman Narayanan is elected president of India. He is the first president to be from India's lowest, 'untouchable' caste.

15 July 1997 Italian fashion designer Gianni Versace is shot and killed outside his Miami Beach, Florida home. Police later identify Andrew Cunanan, who is wanted in connection with four other murders, as the killer.

19 July 1997 The warlord Charles Taylor is elected president of Liberia; his National People's Party wins legislative elections.

20 July 1997 The anti-Talibaan United Islamic Front for the Salvation of Afghanistan captures the town of Charikar, and subsequently advances to within 32 km/20 mi of the Afghan capital, Kabul.

23 July 1997 Sadi Berisha resigns as president of Albania following months of unrest over the collapse of pyramid investment schemes.

23 July 1997 Slobodan Milosevic is sworn in as president of Yugoslavia, a federation of Serbia and Montenegro. He was nearing the end of his second five-year term as president of Serbia, and ran unopposed for the new position.

25 July 1997 The socialist Fatos Nano becomes prime minister of Albania, following elections.

30 July 1997 Two suicide bombers set off explosives in a crowded market in West Jerusalem, killing at least 13 people and injuring at least 150 others. The extremist Palestinian Islamic organization Hamas claims responsibility.

3 August 1997–8 August 1997 Soufrière Hills volcano on the Caribbean island of Montserrat, after nearly two years of constant eruption, enters a phase of violent eruption and major pyroclastic flow which, over the next few months, virtually destroys the capital city of Plymouth. The British government considers permanently relocating all of Montserrat's citizens off the island.

5 August 1997 Hugo Bánzer Suárez is elected president by the Bolivian Congress.

13 August 1997 The Russian Deputy Prime Minister Alfred Kokh resigns following allegations of corruption in his handling of the privatization of the state nickel mining group.

25 August 1997 The former Cambodian prime minister and Khmer Rouge leader Pol Pot is found guilty by a Khmer Rouge court in Cambodia of ordering the murder of his rival Son Sen and given a life sentence.

25 August 1997 The government of Andris Skele in Latvia resigns; Guntar Krasts forms a coalition three days later.

27 August 1997 The governments of Sweden and Norway admit to sterilizing thousands of people deemed 'substandard' (including those of low intelligence and the mentally or physically disabled) between 1934 and 1976.

27 August 1997 The voluntary evacuation of Montserrat begins because of the threat of further volcanic activity.

4 September 1997 Three suicide bombers from an offshoot of the Palestinian Hamas organization kill three Israelis and injure 190 others in attacks on west Jerusalem.

10 September 1997 The US secretary of state Madeleine Albright visits the Middle East; on 11 September she calls on Israel to stop its settlement building programme.

12 September 1997 The 15th Congress of the Chinese Communist Party confirms Jiang Zemin as general secretary and endorses the continuation of the late Deng Xiaoping's liberal economic policies.

14 September 1997 After discussions in Calgary, Alberta, the premiers of nine out of Canada's ten provinces and the commissioners of its two territories agree to recognize the unique character of Quebec's culture and society. Quebec's separatist premier, Lucien Bouchard, boycotts the meeting.

15 September 1997 William Weld, US President Bill Clinton's nominee for ambassador to Mexico, withdraws his candidacy after the refusal by Jesse Helms, chairman of the US Senate foreign-relations committee, to schedule a hearing for his nomination.

18 September 1997 A ruling Socialist Party member of the Albanian parliament shoots and wounds an opposition delegate in the People's Assembly in Tirana, triggering widespread riots.

19 September 1997 Ted Turner, billionaire founder of the television news network Cable News Network (CNN), announces that he will donate $100 million to the United Nations (UN) every year for ten years.

21 September 1997 The right-wing Solidarity Electoral Alliance wins the legislative elections in Poland.

23 September 1997 Turkish troops conduct large-scale attacks on bases of the Workers' Party of Kurdistan (PKK, a Kurdish guerrilla organization) in northern Iraq.

3 October 1997 The US attorney general Janet Reno orders the Justice Department to investigate allegations of illegal campaign financing involving Vice President Al Gore; the investigation is extended to President Bill Clinton on 15 October.

10 October 1997 French Prime Minister Lionel Jospin pledges to introduce legislation to cut the maximum length of the working week from 39 to 35 hours by 2000.

12 October 1997 Forty thousand Zapatista National Liberation Army guerrillas and their supporters march through Mexico City, Mexico, demanding greater rights for Native Americans.

13 October 1997 Kjell Magne Bondevik of the Christian People's Party becomes prime minister of a minority coalition government in Norway following elections.

13 October 1997 The legislators of Nevis vote to secede from the federation of St

Kitts and Nevis. The initiative was to be decided by a referendum.

17 October 1997 France opens official archives relating to the killing of Algerian demonstrators by police in 1961; the number of dead, previously put at two, is now estimated at over 90.

23 October 1997 The rebel 'Cobra' militia leader Denis Sassau-Nguesso arrives in Brazzaville, the capital of the Republic of Congo, following victory in his war with President Pascal Lissouba.

25 October 1997 An estimated 1.5 million black women participate in the Million Woman March in Philadelphia, Pennsylvania, to protest against the notion of blacks as victims.

31 October 1997 Jerzy Buzek of the right-wing Solidarity Electoral Alliance (AWS) forms a coalition government with the pro-business Freedom Union (UW) in Poland.

17 November 1997 Up to 68 people are killed when Islamic terrorists attack two tourist buses near Luxor, Egypt.

19 November 1997 The first septuplets to be successfully delivered alive are born in Des Moines, Iowa, to Kenny and Bobbi McCaughey, who had been taking fertility drugs.

24 November 1997 The Truth and Reconciliation Committee in South Africa begins hearing allegations of involvement in political murder against Winnie Mandela, former wife of President Nelson Mandela.

25 November 1997 The Federal Energy Regulatory Commission orders the US company Edwards Manufacturing to demolish the 160-year-old Edwards Dam on the Kennebec River, Maine, to give sturgeon and salmon a chance to reach their spawning grounds. It is the first time a working hydroelectric dam has been ordered to be removed.

28 November 1997 In India, I K Gujral's minority United Front government collapses when Congress (I) withdraws support. An early general election is called 4 December.

30 November 1997 Carlos Roberto Flores Facussé is re-elected president of Honduras; his Liberal Party wins legislative elections.

2 December 1997 Attorney General Janet Reno announces that she will not recommend the appointment of a special prosecutor into possible violations of campaign finance law by President Bill Clinton and Vice President Al Gore.

8 December 1997 Jenny Shipley of the National Party becomes New Zealand's first woman prime minister, replacing Jim Bolger, who announced 3 November that he would resign the leadership of the National Party and the premiership.

9 December 1997 North Korea, South Korea, the USA, and China meet in Geneva, Switzerland, to start talks about a permanent peace agreement in place of the armistice that ended the Korean War in 1953.

12 December 1997 Mouaouia Ould Sidi Mohammed Taya is reelected president of Mauritania. The election is boycotted by the main opposition parties.

13 December 1997 At a meeting in Luxembourg, European Union (EU) heads of government invite Cyprus, the Czech Republic, Estonia, Hungary, Poland, and Slovenia to start talks in March 1998 on joining the EU.

17 December 1997 Thabo Mbeki becomes president of the ruling African National Congress (ANC) during the party's 50th national conference at Mafikeng, South Africa. Mbeki replaces Nelson Mandela, who steps down as party leader while remaining president of South Africa.

18 December 1997 Kim Dae Jung of the opposition National Congress for New Politics wins presidential elections in South Korea.

29 December 1997 Presidential and legislative elections in Kenya are disrupted by violence (in which at least ten people are killed), allegations of polling irregularities, and floods. Because of these disruptions, polling is extended by an extra day. President Daniel arap Moi, already in power for 19 years, is sworn in for a further five-year term on 5 January 1998.

1 January 1998 Mohammed Rafiq Tarar is elected president of Pakistan in a landslide.

1 January 1998 The Pakistani government's anticorruption commission brings corruption charges against former Prime Minister Benazir Bhutto, her husband, and her mother, for allegedly accumulating wealth through kickbacks while she had been prime minister.

1 January 1998–14 January 1998 At least 1,700 men, women, and children are massacred in Algeria by Islamic fundamentalists.

2 January 1998 A new caretaker government takes office in the Czech Republic, headed by Josef Tosovsky, a former governor of the Czech National Bank.

3 January 1998 Swedish police arrest 314 youths at a rock concert outside Stockholm organized by a white supremacist group linked to the neo-Nazi organization Nordland.

5 January 1998 Daniel arap Moi, who was reelected president of Kenya in December, 1997, is sworn in for a fifth term. Moi has been president since 1978.

5 January 1998 Lituhanian-American Valdus Adamkus is elected president of Lithuania. He pledges to develop Lithuania's integration with Western Europe and to deepen its links with the USA.

6 January 1998 The United Nations World Food Program launches an appeal for $378 million to provide food for North Korea. It is the largest such appeal in the programme's history.

11 January 1998 Sonia Gandhi, the wife of the former Indian Prime Minister Rajiv Gandhi who was assassinated in 1991, begins a campaign to restore support for the Congress (I), the party founded by her husband's former family.

12 January 1998 The Australian deputy Prime Minister Tim Fischer sends military troops to assist rescue efforts in Queensland, which suffered severe four-day flooding.

13 January 1998 Iraq prevents a team of United Nations inspectors, led by the

USA, from continuing their search for weapons depots. Iraq banned US members of an inspection team the previous November. The USA warns that it is likely to take military action against Iraq.

18 January 1998 Moderate Serb Milorad Dodik of the Independent Social Democrat party is elected premier of Bosnia-Herzegovina.

20 January 1998 Vaclav Havel is reelected president of the Czech Republic, to serve another five-year term.

21 January 1998 An investigation is launched into whether US President Bill Clinton urged Monica Lewinsky, a 24 year old trainee, to lie under oath and deny that she had an affair with him. Investigations continue until the end March amid further accusations and denials.

21 January 1998 The Pope begins an historic week-long visit to Cuba. He presses Cuban Prime Minister Fidel Castro over human rights and the rights of the family over the state.

26 January 1998 US and British naval forces begin to assemble in the Persian Gulf and to draw up plans for a bombing campaign against Iraq because Iraqi president Saddam Hussein continues to hinder the work of UN weapons inspectors.

28 January 1998 The Turkish government releases a report confirming that some government officials did participate in mid-1990s death-squad attacks, mostly aimed at Kurdish rebels.

1 February 1998 Businessman and economist Miguel Rodriguez of the Social Christian Unity Party is elected president of Costa Rica, replacing President Jose Figueres Olsen of the National Liberation Party.

4 February 1998 Nearly 4,000 are killed and 30,000 people lose their homes when an earthquake measuring 6.1 on the Richter scale hits the mountainous province of Takhar in northern Afghanistan.

6 February 1998 South African President Nelson Mandela opens the 1998 session of parliament in Pretoria, South Africa. He stresses employment and anti-corruption measures in his state-of-the-nation speech.

8 February 1998–11 February 1998 A European Union delegation visits Algeria on a four-day peace mission amid ongoing bloodshed in the country's civil war, instigated by militant Islamic rebels.

9 February 1998 Around 24 gunmen open fire on Georgian President Eduard Shevardnadze's motorcade in Tbilisi, Georgia, in the second assassination attempt on the president. Shevardnadze is unharmed, but three people die and four people suffer injuries in the attack.

9 February 1998–23 April 1998 Nigeria launches an artillery attack against Sierra Leone's military junta in Freetown, Sierra Leone. Fighting continues for several weeks until ousted President Ahmad Tejan Kabbah returns.

13 February 1998 Nigerian-led troops under an alliance of West African countries ousts Johnny Paul Koromah's military government of Sierra Leone. Koromah seized power from democratically-elected President Ahmad Kabbah in May 1997.

13 February 1998 The Australian Constitutional Convention votes to replace the Queen as head of state with a president chosen by a bipartisan parliamentary majority. A public referendum in 1999 will decide whether the country should become a republic.

15 February 1998 Glafkos John Clerides is reelected president of Cyprus and in March begins talks with the European Union on the country's possible accession.

19 February 1998 An armed gang demanding the release of seven suspects being held for an assassination attempt on Georgian President Eduard Shevardnadze attack a United Nations office in western Georgia, taking 10 hostages. One of the hostages is released on 22 February and the rest are released three days later.

24 February 1998 Cuba's National Assembly reelects Fidel Castro and his brother Raul Castro as president and first vice president of Cuba. Castro has ruled the country as a communist, one-party state since 1959.

25 February 1998 National Congress for New Politics leader Kim Dae Jung is inaugurated president of South Korea. A dissident under the country's past military governments, he was elected in December 1997.

25 February 1998 Switzerland's first legal brothel opens in Zurich.

26 February 1998 US chat-show host Oprah Winfrey is cleared of slander charges by a federal grand jury in Amarillo, Texas. A group of cattle ranchers had sued her for $12 million, claiming that her negative comments about beef, in reference to 'mad cow' disease during an April 1996 broadcast of *The Oprah Winfrey Show*, caused US beef prices to plummet.

February 1998–March 1998 Hundreds of fires in Sumatra and Kalimantan, the Indonesian portion of Borneo, blanket the islands in smoke. Singapore asks for international aid.

1 March 1998 Serbia sends troops into the southern province of Kosovo to flush out ethnic Albanian secessionist paramilitaries. Hundreds of men, women, and children are killed over the next few weeks. It is the worst bloodshed to date in Kosovo's nine-year campaign by its Albanian majority to regain their autonomy.

6 March 1998 The Ontario government agrees to pay four million Canadian dollars to the Dionne sisters, the three living siblings of the world's first surviving quintuplets. The government had taken custody of the girls soon after their birth and put them on display for more than nine years at a theme park called 'Quintland', which generated more than 500 million Canadian dollars.

9 March 1998 Britain, France, Germany, Italy, Russia, and the USA announce that they will impose sanctions on Yugoslavia in an effort to stem Serbian violence against ethnic Albanians in the southern province of Kosovo. The Yugoslav

President Slobodan Milosevic is given ten days to withdraw troops from Kosovo.

10 March 1998 President Ahmad Kabbah returns to power as Sierra Leone's president, after Nigerian-led West African peacekeeping forces ousted Johnny Paul Koromah's military government in February. Koromah had seized power from Kabbah in May 1997.

10 March 1998 Thojib Suharto is 'reelected' president of Indonesia despite his deteriorating health and an economy weakened by a sharp decline in value of Indonesian currency. He remains opposed to economic reforms demanded by the International Monetary Fund (IMF) which has arranged a $43 billion/£27 billion economic bail-out programme.

11 March 1998 Ten police officers who were accused of torturing and sexually abusing 14 teenagers in December 1995 are acquitted by a court in Manisa, Turkey. The judges in the case claim that the prosecution has not produced indisputable evidence.

11 March 1998 The centre-left coalition leader Poul Rasmussen is reelected premier of Denmark by a narrow margin.

15 March 1998 Kathleen Willey, a former campaign volunteer and part-time White House staffer, appears on the Central Broadcasting Service (CBS) programme *60 Minutes* to discuss an incident in 1993 in which US President Bill Clinton allegedly kissed and fondled her. Her testimony is a key part of the lawsuit of Paula Jones, who is suing the president for sexual harassment while he was governor of Arkansas in 1991.

17 March 1998 Zhu Rongli is elected prime minister of China. He quickly announces that he is axing half of its eight million civil servant jobs to combat budget deficits. Many believe his reforms will mark a new era in Chinese politics.

19 March 1998 Atal Behari Vajpayee, Nationalist BJP party leader, is elected prime minister of India. He calls for national 'reconciliation and accord', but also threatens that India might install and deploy nuclear weapons.

23 March 1998 Russian President Boris Yeltsin dismisses all 29 of his ministers including two of its pivotal figures – Viktor Chernomyrdin, the prime minister, and his most aggressive free-marketeer, Anatoly Chubais, the first deputy prime minister. The government crisis lasts until 24 April when the state Duma bows to President Yeltsin's will and endorses Sergei Kiriyenko as prime minister.

23 March 1998–1 April 1998 Forest fires in Brazil destroy 51,800 sq km/20,000 sq mi of highland savannah and rainforest. Heavy rains finally quench the fires.

25 March 1998 Britain, France, Germany, Italy, Russia, and the USA agree to delay imposing economic sanctions on Yugoslavia for one month. The countries threatened sanctions on Yugoslavia earlier in the month in an effort to stem Serbian violence against ethnic Albanians in the southern province of Kosovo. The countries still, however, plan to seek a United Nations arms embargo against Yugoslavia.

29 March 1998 The Vasco da Gama bridge across the Tagus River north of Lisbon, Portugal, is officially opened. It is the longest bridge in Europe: 18 km/11.25 mi long with 12 km/7.5 mi of bridges and viaducts.

30 March 1998 Premier Robert Kocharyan is elected president of Armenia.

31 March 1998 The United Nations Security Council votes unanimously to impose an arms embargo on Yugoslavia in an effort to stem Serbian violence against ethnic Albanians in the southern province of Kosovo.

1 April 1998 US federal judge Susan Wright dismisses the four-year-old civil lawsuit of Paula Jones against US President Bill Clinton in which Jones charged Clinton with sexual harassment in 1991 when he was governor of Arkansas.

5 April 1998 The world's largest suspension bridge, linking Kobe and Awaji Island in Japan, opens to traffic. It cost £2.2. billion and is 3.9 km/2.4 mi long.

12 April 1998 The US Census Bureau reports that 26 million Americans, nearly one in ten, is an immigrant. Most come from Central or south America.

15 April 1998 Cambodian Khmer Rouge leader Pol Pot, who was responsible for the deaths of 1.7 million Cambodians, dies, reportedly of heart failure, near the border of Cambodia and Thailand.

19 April 1998 Austrian President Thomas Klestil is reelected to a second six-year term.

19 April 1998 Wang Dan, a leader of the 1989 Tiananmen Square demonstrations in Beijing, China, who has been imprisoned for almost nine years, is released on medical parole and sent to Detroit, Michigan for treatment.

20 April 1998 British Prime Minister Tony Blair announces that the USA will invite Israeli Prime Minister Benjamin Netanyahu and Palestine Liberation Organization (PLO) leader Yasir Arafat to Middle East peace talks in London.

22 April 1998 Animal Kingdom, one of the world's largest live-animal theme parks, opens in Disneyland, California.

23 April 1998 Belgian Interior Minister Johan Lanotte and Justice Minister Stefaan De Clerck resign over the brief escape of suspected child killer Marc Dutroux, who was charged with five murders and the rape of several young girls. Dutroux was captured after four hours.

23 April 1998 The Mongolia parliament elects former journalist Tsakhiagiin Elbegdorj premier of the country. Elbegdorj, the 35-year-old leader of the National Democratic Party, becomes the youngest-ever premier of Mongolia.

24 April 1998 The largest public execution in recent history takes place in a football field in Kigali, Rwanda, when 22 people are shot for their part in the massacre of 500,000 Hutus in 1994.

29 April 1998 Britain, France, Germany, Italy, Russia, and the USA declare an international freeze on all of the Yugoslav government's foreign assets, in a move to try to stem Serbian violence against ethnic Albanians in the southern province of Kosovo.

1 May 1998   Jean Kambanda, the former premier of Rwanda, pleads guilty to six counts of genocide during the country's civil war in 1994, before the International Criminal Tribunal for Rwanda, in Arusha, Tanzania.

13 May 1998   The European parliament approves a ban on all tobacco advertising and sponsorship.

18 May 1998   The USA and the European Union (EU) reach a compromise in their dispute over US sanctions against foreign companies doing business with Cuba, Iran, and Libya. The US agrees to relax sanctions against energy companies, and the EU agrees to tighten controls over the export of weapons to Iran.

21 May 1998   Indonesian President Suharto resigns after a week of riots in Jakarta in which much of the city is burned. He is replaced by his Vice President Bucharuddin Jusuf Habibie.

24 May 1998   In Hong Kong's first legislative elections since it reverted to Chinese sovereignty, pro-democracy parties win more than 60% of the popular vote.

15 June 1998   Australian politician Pauline Hanson, One Nation party candidate who is opposed to immigration and seeks welfare cuts for Aborigines, wins 30% of votes in Queensland state elections.

25 June 1998   US President Bill Clinton arrives in China for a nine-day visit, the first by a US president since the Tiananmen Square massacre in 1989.

June 1998   Hundreds of thousands of refugees flee the capital city of Bissau in Guinea-Bissau after a coup attempt. Senegal and Guinea send troops to support loyalist forces.

June 1998   The human rights group Amnesty International reports that as many as 141 countries are not adhering to the Universal Declaration of Human Rights, which is 50 years old, citing cases of executions without trial, torture, prisoners of conscience, and poverty.

Countries of the World

Countries of the World: Selected Definitions

Gross domestic product (GDP) The total output of goods and services for final use produced by an economy, by both residents and non-residents, regardless of the allocation to domestic and foreign claims. It does not include deductions for depreciation of physical capital or depletion and degradation of natural resources.

Real GDP per capita (PPP) The GDP per capita of a country converted into US dollars on the basis of the purchasing power parity (PPP) of the country's currency. The system of purchasing power parities was developed by the United Nations International Comparison Programme (ICP) to make more accurate international comparisons of GDP and its components than those based on official exchange rates, which can be subject to considerable fluctuation.

Gross national product (GNP) Comprises GDP plus net factor income from abroad, which is the income residents receive from abroad for factor services (labour and capital), minus similar payments made to non-residents who contribute to the domestic economy.

Foreign debt The sum of public, publicly guaranteed, and private non-guaranteed long-term debt, use of IMF credit, and short-term debt. It includes interest arrears on long-term debt outstanding and disbursed that are due but not paid on a cumulative basis. Available data permit no distinction between public and private non-guaranteed short-term debt.

THE MIDDLE EAST PEACE PROCESS

BY DENIS DERBYSHIRE

In 1991, the US government embarked on a fresh initiative for peace in the Middle East. After strenuous rounds of shuttle diplomacy, US Secretary of State James Baker persuaded the main parties to an agreement – Israel, Jordan, Syria, and the Palestinians – to attend a regional conference, and at the end of the year the Israeli government entered bilateral talks with Palestinian representatives. In 1993 it agreed to meet the Palestine Liberation Organization (PLO).

The arrival of a Democratic administration in Washington, under Bill Clinton, furthered the drive for achieving peace and by late 1995 it seemed to be broadly on track. After months of hard bargaining between the PLO leader, Yassir Arafat, and the Israeli Foreign Minister, Shimon Peres, which had begun in Oslo and continued in various locations, an interim agreement on the expansion of Palestinian self-rule in the occupied West Bank was reached.

The 'Oslo B' Agreement

The provisions of the agreement were: an Israeli withdrawal from part of the West Bank within six months; elections for an 82-member Palestinian Council and its executive president; a three-stage release of Palestinian prisoners in Israel; an Israeli phased withdrawal from more West Bank territory, to be completed by May 1999; and the revocation by the PLO of those articles in its charter which called for the destruction of Israel. The agreement, known as 'Oslo B', although welcomed by the West and moderate Palestinians and Israelis, was criticized by Syria, Iraq, Iran, Libya, the Lebanese government, the Palestinian fundamentalist groups, Hamas and Islamic Jihad, as well as right-wing politicians in Israel. The new leader of Israel's right-wing Likud party, Binyamin Netanyahu, was one of its critics but, significantly, he did not say he would repudiate it if Likud returned to power.

In October 1995 the Israeli parliament (Knesset) endorsed 'Oslo B' and its implementation began. Some Israeli withdrawals from occupied areas were made and preparations for the Palestinian Council elections started. At the same time, the PLO sought a rapprochement with Hamas by inviting it to talks on self-rule and to engage in the January 1996 Palestinian Council elections. The Hamas response was not encouraging.

The Assassination of Rabin

Meanwhile, other opponents of the peace process were on the move. On 4 November 1995, the Israeli Prime Minister, Yitzhak Rabin, was assassinated by a young Israeli extremist opposed to the Israeli government's dealings with the Palestinians, and the peace process seemed to be mortally threatened. However, Shimon Peres, who immediately assumed his country's leadership, pledged himself to continue the search for a lasting peace and was supported by moderates in both the Israeli and Arab camps, including Yassir Arafat. By December 1995 Israel had withdrawn from six towns on the West Bank, as had been agreed. The Palestinian Council elections duly took place, overseen by a large international group of observers, and Arafat and his supporters won an overwhelming victory. The PLO leader was elected president with more than 88 percent of the vote.

The Election of Netanyahu

The prospects of achieving a lasting settlement received another potentially fatal blow in May 1996 when Peres, needing a renewal of his mandate to govern, called a general election, and the Likud leader, Binjamin Netanyahu, became Israel's first directly-elected prime minister. However, his party did not secure a majority in the Knesset and he was forced to rely on the support of small, mainly religious, parties, some of them clearly opposed to the peace process. He also had to placate hardline members of his own cabinet, who were totally opposed to the creation of a Palestinian state.

Peace Process Threatened

In September 1996, Netanyahu met face-to-face with Yassir Arafat, but a genuine agreement still seemed to be threatened by Israeli actions. These included the Israeli reopening of the tunnel to the Jewish quarter of Jerusalem, the continued expansion of Jewish settlements in East Jerusalem, and delays in the withdrawal of Israeli forces from the key West Bank town of Hebron. As 1996 drew to a close, tension between Arabs and Jews remained high and in January 1997 an Israeli soldier fired shots into Hebron's open market, again threatening the process. However, Netanyahu said that this action made him even more determined to reach agreement and, by the middle of the month,

an Israeli withdrawal was announced (but only 9 percent of the West Bank was to be released, despite the promise of a 30 percent withdrawal). Meanwhile, new Israeli settlements were started in Arab East Jerusalem. In response to these acts, Palestinian suicide bombers caused havoc and civilian casualties in Tel Aviv in March and in Jerusalem in July and September.

Attempts To Regenerate the Negotiations

Despite these setbacks, and the failure of Netanyahu to respond to international calls to halt the new settlements, the USA, through the new secretary of state, Madeleine Albright, made strenuous efforts to restart Israeli-Palestinian negotiations. In October 1997 Netanyahu and Arafat met, and in November formal talks were reopened in Washington. Progress was slow but there were signs of more flexibility on the Israeli side, Netanyahu having survived a crucial confidence vote in the Knesset in January 1998.

The expansion of Jewish settlements remained the chief obstacle, prompting the European Union (EU) to announce, in March 1998, an intensive effort to accelerate progress; in May 1998 the British Prime Minister, Tony Blair, bolstered by success in peace negotiations in Northern Ireland, used his six-month presidency of the European Commission to host a series of bilateral meetings in London, with the strong cooperation of Madeleine Albright. President Clinton threw his full political weight behind the operation, using Israel's dependence on US economic and diplomatic support as his lever, and proposed an Israeli withdrawal from 13 percent of West Bank territory within three months. Prime Minister Netanyahu was asked to come to Washington with his government's agreement to the proposal on 11 May 1998. Failure to do so would, according to secretary Albright, force the USA 'to re-examine [its] approach to the peace process.'

Netanyahu thus found himself squeezed between American pressure for a speedy settlement and the intransigence of those Knesset deputies on whose support his political future depended. In the event, after meeting Clinton's special envoy, Dennis Ross, he decided that declining the invitation was preferable to facing up to his critics in Israel. For his part, President Clinton seemed determined to continue to apply pressure, even if his deadline was ignored. 1998 still promised to be a decisive year for peace in the Middle East.

Afghanistan Republic of

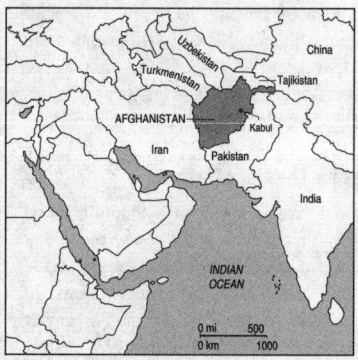

National name: *Islamic Emirate of Afghanistan* **Area:** 652,090 sq km/251,771 sq mi **Capital:** Kabul **Major towns/cities:** Kandahar, Herat, Mazar-i-Sharif, Jalalabad **Physical features:** mountainous in centre and NE (Hindu Kush mountain range; Khyber and Salang passes, Wakhan salient, and Panjshir Valley), plains in N and SW, Amu Darya (Oxus) River, Helmand River, Lake Saberi

Government

Head of state and government: Mohammad Rabbani from 1996 **Political system:** transitional **Administrative divisions:** 32 provinces **Political parties:** Hezb-i-Islami, Islamic fundamentalist Mujaheddin, anti-Western; Jamiat-i-Islami, Islamic fundamentalist Mujaheddin; National Liberation Front, moderate Mujaheddin **Armed forces:** approximately 429,000 (1996) **Conscription:** compulsory for four years, with break of three years after second year (since 1992 conscription has been difficult to enforce and desertion is common) **Death penalty:** retains and uses the death penalty for ordinary crimes **Defence spend:** (% GDP) 15.4 (1996) **Education spend:** (% GNP) 2.0 (1992) **Health spend:** (% GDP) 1.6 (1990)

Economy and resources

Currency: afgháni **GDP:** ($ US) 12.8 billion (1995 est) **Real GDP per capita (PPP):** ($ US) 600 (1995 est) **GDP growth rate:** N/A **Average annual inflation:** 56.7% (1991) **Foreign debt:** ($ US) 9.58 billion (1993) **Major trading partners:** former USSR countries, Japan, Singapore, Germany **Resources:** natural gas, coal, iron ore, barytes, lapis lazuli, salt, talc, copper, chrome, gold, silver, asbestos, small petroleum reserves **Industries:** food products, cotton textiles, cement, coalmining, chemical fertilizers, small vehicle assembly plants, processed hides and skins, carpetmaking, sugar manufacture, leather and plastic goods **Exports:** fruit and nuts, carpets, wool, karakul skins, cotton, natural gas. Principal market: Kyrgyzstan 37.3% (1995) **Imports:** basic manufactured goods and foodstuffs (notably wheat), petroleum products, textiles, fertilizers, vehicles and spare parts. Principal source: Japan 25.6% (1995) **Arable land:** 12.1% (1995) **Agricultural products:** wheat, barley, maize, rice; livestock rearing (sheep, goats, cattle, and camels); world's leading opium producer (1995)

Population and society

Population: 20,883,000 (1996 est) **Population growth rate:** 5.8% (1990–95); 2.7% (2000–05) **Population density:** (per sq km) 32 (1996 est) **Urban population:** (% of total) 20 (1995) **Age distribution:** (% of total population) <15 40.8%, 15–65 56.4%, >65 2.8% (1995) **Ethnic groups:** Pathans, or Pushtuns, comprise the largest ethnic group, 54% of the population, followed by the Tajiks (concentrated in the N, 27%), the Uzbeks (8%), and Hazaras (7%) **Language:** Pushtu, Dari (Persian), Uzbek, Turkoman, Kirgiz **Religion:** Muslim (85% Sunni, 15% Shi'ite) **Education:** (compulsory years) 6 **Literacy rate:** 44% (men); 14% (women) (1995 est) **Labour force:** 41% of population: 61% agriculture, 14% industry, 25% services (1992) **Life expectancy:** 45 (men); 46 (women) (1995–2000) **Child mortality rate:** (under 5, per 1,000 live births) 248 (1996) **Physicians:** 1 per 6,730 people (1990 est)

Practical information

Visa requirements: UK: visa required. USA: visa required **Embassy in the UK:** 31 Prince's Gate, London SW7 1QQ. Tel: (0171) 589 8891; fax: (0171) 581 3452 **British embassy:** Karte Parwan, Kabul. Tel: (93) 30511 (the embassy is closed at present) **Chamber of commerce:** Afghan Chamber of Commerce and Industry, Mohd Jah Khan Wat, Kabul. Tel: (93) 26796; telex: 245 **Airports:** two international airports: Kabul (Khwaja Rawash) and Kandahar; 18 domestic airports; total passenger km: 197 million (1994) **Major holidays:** 27 April, 1 May, 19 August; variable: Eid-ul-Adha, Arafa, Ashora, end of Ramadan, New Year (Hindu), Prophet's Birthday, first day of Ramadan

Chronology

6th century BC: Part of Persian Empire under Cyrus II and Darius I. **329 BC:** Conquered by Alexander the Great. **323 BC:** Fell to the Seleucids, who ruled from Babylon. **304 BC:** Ruled by Mauryan dynasty in S and independent Bactria in N. **135 BC:** Central Asian tribes established Kusana dynasty. **3rd–7th centuries AD:** Decline of Kusana dynasty. Emergence of Sassanids as ruling power with Hepthalites (central Asian nomads) and western Turks also fighting for control. **642–11th century:** First Muslim invasion followed by a succession of Muslim dynasties, including Mahmud of Ghazni 998. **1219–14th century:** Mongol invasions led by Genghis Khan and Tamerlane. **16th–18th centuries:** Much of Afghanistan came under the rule of the Mogul Empire under Babur (Zahir) and Nadir Shah. **1747:** Afghanistan became an independent emirate under Dost Muhammad. **1838–42:** First Afghan War, instigated by Britain to counter the threat to British India from expanding Russian influence in Afghanistan. **1878–80:** Second Afghan War. **1919:** Afghanistan recovered full independence following Third Afghan War. **1953:** Lt-Gen Daud Khan became prime minister and introduced social and economic reform programme. **1963:** Daud Khan forced to resign and constitutional monarchy established. **1973:** Monarchy overthrown in coup by Daud Khan. **1978:** Daud Khan assassinated in coup; Muhammad Taraki and the communist People's Democratic Party of Afghanistan (PDPA) took over. Start of Muslim guerrilla (Mujaheddin) resistance. **1979:** Taraki ousted and murdered; replaced by Hafizullah Amin. USSR entered country to prop up government, installing Babrak Karmal in power. Amin executed. **1986:** Replacement of Karmal as PDPA leader by Dr Najibullah Ahmadzai. Partial Soviet troop withdrawal. **1988:** New non-Marxist constitution adopted. **1989:** Withdrawal of Soviet troops; state of emergency imposed as Mujaheddin continued resistance to PDPA regime and civil war intensified. **1991:** US and Soviet military aid withdrawn. Mujaheddin began talks with Russians and Kabul government. **1992:** Najibullah government overthrown. Mujaheddin leader Burhanuddin Rabbani elected president. Hezb-i-Islami barred from government. **1993:** Intensive fighting around Kabul. Peace agreement between Rabbani and dissident Hezb-i-Islami leader Gulbuddin Hekmatyar made Hekmatyar prime minister. **1994:** Continuing rebel attacks on Kabul finally quelled. Hekmatyar dismissed from office. **1995:** Talibaan Islamic fundamentalist army claimed town of Herat and advanced on Kabul. **1996:** Talibaan controlled two-thirds of country, including Kabul; country split between Talibaan-controlled fundamentalist S and more liberal N; interim council of clerics installed, headed by Mohamad Rabbani; strict Islamic law imposed; new regime not recognized by international community. **1997:** Talibaan controlled majority of provinces, and were recognized as legitimate government of Afghanistan by Pakistan and Saudi Arabia. New country name adopted: The Islamic Emirate of Afghanistan. **1998:** Feb: earthquake in northern province of Takhar killed more than 3,800 people. June: another earthquake in same area killed up to 5,000 people.

Albania Republic of

National name: *Republika e Shqipërisë*
Area: 28,748 sq km/11,099 sq mi **Capital:** Tiranê (Tirana) **Major towns/cities:** Durrês, Shkodêr, Elbasan, Vlorê, Korçê **Major ports:** Durrês **Physical features:** mainly mountainous, with rivers flowing E–W, and a narrow coastal plain

Government

Head of state: Rexhep Mejdani from 1997 **Head of government:** Fatos Nano from 1997 **Political system:** emergent democracy **Administrative divisions:** 12 prefectures **Political parties:**

Democratic Party of Albania (PDS; formerly the Democratic Party: DP), moderate, market-oriented; Socialist Party of Albania (PSS), ex-communist; Human Rights Union (HMU), Greek minority party **Armed forces:** 54,000 (1996) **Conscription:** compulsory for 15 months **Death penalty:** retains the death penalty for ordinary crimes, but considered abolitionist in practice; committed 1996 to put into place a moratorium on executions until total abolition **Defence spend:** (% GDP) 6.7 (1996) **Education spend:** (% GDP) 3.0 (1993–94) **Health spend:** (% GDP) 2.7 (1990–95)

Economy and resources
Currency: lek **GDP:** ($ US) 2 billion (1994) **Real GDP per capita (PPP):** ($ US) 2,788 (1994) **GDP growth rate:** 7.4% (1994); 1.4% (1990–95) **Average annual inflation:** 11.5% (1996) **Foreign debt:** ($ US) 709 million (1995) **Major trading partners:** Italy, Greece, USA, Germany, Bulgaria **Resources:** chromite (one of world's largest producers), copper, coal, nickel, petroleum and natural gas **Industries:** food processing, mining, textiles, oil products, cement, energy generation **Exports:** chromium and chrome products, processed foodstuffs, plant and animal products, bitumen, electricity, tobacco. Principal market: Italy 52% (1994) **Imports:** machinery, fuels and minerals, plant and animal raw materials, chemical products. Principal source: Italy 34% (1994) **Arable land:** 21% (1995) **Agricultural products:** wheat, sugar beet, maize, potatoes, barley, sorghum, cotton, tobacco

Population and society
Population: 3,401,000 (1996 est) **Population growth rate:** 0.9% (1990–95); 1.1% (2000–05) **Population density:** (per sq km) 118 (1996) **Urban population:** (% of total) 37 (1995) **Age distribution:** (% of total population) <15 31.4%, 15–65 63.1%, >65 5.5% (1995) **Ethnic groups:** 90% of Albanian, non-Slavic, descent; 8% ethnic Greek (concentrated in the S) **Language:** Albanian, Greek **Religion:** Muslim, Orthodox, Roman Catholic **Education:** (compulsory years) 8 **Literacy rate:** 85% (men); 85% (women) (1994) **Labour force:** 48% of population: 55% agriculture, 23% industry, 22% services (1990) **Unemployment:** 19.8% (1994) **Life expectancy:** 70 (men); 76 (women) (1995–2000) **Child mortality rate:** (under 5, per 1,000 live births) 38 (1996) **Physicians:** 1 per 530 people (1993 est)

Practical information
Visa requirements: UK: visa not required. USA: visa not required **Embassy in the UK:** 4th Floor, 38 Grosvenor Gardens, London SW1W 0EB. Tel: (0171) 730 5709; fax: (0171) 730 5747 **British embassy:** Office of the British Chargé d'Affaires, c/o French Embassy, Rruga Skënderben 14, Tiranê. Tel: (42) 34250; telex: 2150 **Chamber of commerce:** Chamber of Commerce of the Republic of Albania, Rruga Kavajes 6, Tiranê. Tel/fax: (42) 27997 **Airports:** international airport: Tiranê (Rinas); no regular domestic air service; total passenger km: 2 million (1994) **Major holidays:** 1–2, 11 January, 8 March, 1 May, 28 November, 25 December; variable: end of Ramadan, Easter Monday, Good Friday, Eid-ul-Adha, Orthodox Easter

Chronology
2000 BC: Part of Illyria. **168 BC:** Illyria conquered by Romans. **AD**

395: Became part of Byzantine Empire. **6th–14th centuries:** Byzantine decline exploited by Serbs, Normans, Slavs, Bulgarians, and Venetians. **1381:** Ottoman invasion of Albania followed by years of resistance to Turkish rule. **1468:** Resistance led by national hero Skanderbeg (George Kastrioti) largely collapsed, and Albania passed to Ottoman Empire. **15th–16th centuries:** Thousands fled to S Italy to escape Ottoman rule; over half of the rest of the population converted to Islam. **1878:** Foundation of Albanian League promoted emergence of nationalism. **1912:** Achieved independence from Turkey as a result of First Balkan War and end of Ottoman Empire in Europe. **1914–20:** Occupied by Italy. **1925:** Declared itself a republic. **1928–39:** Monarchy of King Zog. **1939:** Italian occupation led by Benito Mussolini. **1943–44:** Under German rule following Italian surrender. **1946:** Proclaimed Communist People's Republic of Albania, with Enver Hoxha as premier. **1949:** Developed close links with Joseph Stalin in USSR and entered Comecon (Council for Mutual Economic Assistance). **1961:** Broke with USSR in wake of Nikita Khrushchev's denunciation of Stalin, and withdrew from Comecon. **1978:** Severed diplomatic links with China, choosing isolationism and neutrality. **1982:** Hoxha made Ramiz Alia head of state. **1985:** Death of Hoxha. Alia became head of the Party of Labour of Albania (PLA). **1987:** Normal diplomatic relations restored with Canada, Greece, and West Germany. **1988:** Albania attended conference of Balkan states for the first time since the 1930s. **1990:** One-party system abandoned in face of popular protest; first opposition party formed. **1991:** Communist PLA won first multiparty elections; Alia re-elected president. PLA renamed PSS. **1992:** Presidential elections won by Sali Berisha of the Democratic Party (DP). Alia and other former communist officials charged with corruption and abuse of power. Totalitarian and communist parties banned. **1993:** Open conflict began between ethnic Greeks and Albanians, followed by a purge of ethnic Greeks from senior positions in the civil service and army. Alia sentenced to eight years' imprisonment. DP renamed PDS. **1995:** Alia released from prison following appeal-court ruling. Communist-era MPs and Communist Party officials banned from national and local elections until 2002. **1996:** Ruling PDS accused of ballot-rigging following overwhelming victory in elections. **1997:** Anti-government riots followed collapse of bogus 'investment' schemes; police killed demonstrators in southern port of Vlorê. Southern Albania fell under rebel control. General election won by PSS; Rexhep Mejdani elected president; ex-communist Fatos Nano became prime minister at head of broad coalition. Convictions of communist-era leaders overturned. Government signed World Bank and IMF rescue package to salvage economy.

Algeria Democratic and Popular Republic of

National name: al-Jumhuriya al-Jazairiya ad-Dimuqratiya ash-Shabiya **Area:** 2,381,741 sq km/919,590 sq mi **Capital:** Algiers (al-Jaza'ir) **Major towns/cities:** Oran, Annaba, Blida, Sétif, Constantine (Qacentina) **Major ports:** Oran (Ouahran), Annaba (Bône) **Physical features:** coastal plains backed by mountains in N, Sahara desert in S; Atlas mountains, Barbary Coast, Chott Melrhir depression, Hoggar mountains

Government

Head of state: Liamine Zeroual from 1994 **Head of government:** Ahmed Ouyahia from 1995 **Political system:** military rule **Administrative divisions:** 48 departments **Political parties:** National Liberation Front (FLN), nationalist, socialist; Socialist Forces Front (FSS), Berber-based, left of centre; Islamic Front for Salvation (FIS), Islamic fundamentalist (banned from 1992); National Democratic Rally (RND), left of centre **Armed forces:** 123,700 (1996) **Conscription:** compulsory for 18 months **Death penalty:** retained and used for ordinary crimes **Defence spend:** (% GDP) 4.0 (1996) **Education spend:** (% GNP) 5.6 (1993–94) **Health spend:** (% GDP) 3.3 (1990–95)

Economy and resources

Currency: Algerian dinar **GDP:** ($ US) 41.9 billion (1994) **Real GDP per capita (PPP):** ($ US) 5,442 (1994) **GDP growth rate:** 0.1% (1990–95) **Average annual inflation:** 20% (1996) **Foreign debt:** ($ US) 33.4 billion (1996) **Major trading partners:** France, Italy, Germany, USA, the Netherlands **Resources:** natural gas and petroleum, iron ore, phosphates, lead, zinc, mercury, silver, salt, antimony, copper **Industries:** food processing, machinery and transport equipment, textiles, cement, tobacco **Exports:** crude oil, gas, vegetables, tobacco, hides, dates. Principal market: Italy 18.8% (1995) **Imports:** machinery and transportation equipment, food and basic manufactures. Principal source: France 29.6% (1995) **Arable land:** 3.2% (1995) **Agricultural products:** wheat, barley, potatoes, citrus fruits, olives, grapes; livestock rearing (sheep and cattle)

Population and society

Population: 28,784,000 (1996 est) **Population growth rate:** 2.3% (1990–95); 2% (2000–05) **Population density:** (per sq km) 12 (1996) **Urban population:** (% of total) 56 (1995) **Age distribution:** (% of total population) <15 38.7%, 15–65 57.7%, >65 3.6% (1995) **Ethnic groups:** 99% of Arab Berber origin, the remainder of European descent, mainly French **Language:** Arabic (official); Berber, French **Religion:** Sunni Muslim (state religion) **Education:** (compulsory years) 9 **Literacy rate:** 64% (men); 45% (women) (1995 est) **Labour force:** 28% of population: 26% agriculture, 31% industry, 43% services (1990) **Unemployment:** 25% (1995) **Life expectancy:** 67 (men); 70 (women) (1995–2000) **Child mortality rate:** (under 5, per 1,000 live births) 54 (1996) **Physicians:** 1 per 1,062 people (1993 est)

Practical information

Visa requirements: UK: visa required. USA visa required **Embassy in the UK:** 54 Holland Park, London W11 3RS. Tel: (0171) 221 7800; fax: (0171) 221 0448 **British embassy:** BP 43, Résidence Cassiopée, Bâtiment B, 7 chemin des Glycines, 16000 Alger-Gare, Algiers. Tel: (2) 622 411; fax: (2) 692 410 **Chamber of commerce:** Chambre Nationale de Commerce (CNC), BP100, Palais Consulaire, rue Amilcar Cabral, Algiers. Tel: (2) 575 555; fax: (2) 629 991 **Airports:** international airports: Algiers (Houari Boumédienne), Annaba (El Mellah), Oran (Es Senia), Constantine (Ain El Bey); ten domestic airports; total passenger km: 2,706 million (1994) **Major holidays:** 1 January, 1 May, 19 June, 5 July, 1 November; variable: Eid-ul-Adha, Ashora, end of Ramadan, New Year (Muslim), Prophet's Birthday

Chronology

9th century BC: Part of Carthaginian Empire, centred on Tunisia to the E, with Annaba, Algiers, and Skikda emerging as important trading posts en route to Spain. **146 BC:** Conquered by Romans, who called the area Numidia. **AD 396:** St Augustine, one of the great early Christian leaders, became Bishop of Hippo, modern Annaba. **6th century:** Part of the Byzantine Empire. **late 7th century:** Conquered by Muslim Arabs, who spread Islam as the basis of a new Berberized Arab-Islamic civilization. **1516:** Ottoman Turks expelled recent Christian Spanish invaders. Under Ottoman rule much influence was left to local Arab tribes, Berbers, Barbary pirates, and deys, administrative officers who were elected for life. **1816:** Anglo-Dutch forces bombarded Algiers as a reprisal against the Barbary pirates' attacks on Mediterranean shipping. **1830–47:** French occupation of

Algiers, followed by extension of control to the N, overcoming fierce resistance from Amir Abd al-Qadir, a champion of Arab Algerian nationalism, and from Morocco. **1850–70:** Mountainous inland region, inhabited by the Kabyles, occupied by French. **1871:** Major rebellion against French rule as French settlers began to immigrate and take over the best agricultural land. **1900–09:** Sahara region subdued by France, who kept it under military rule. **1937:** Algerian People's Party (PPA) formed by the charismatic separatist Messali Hadj. **1940:** Following France's defeat by Nazi Germany, Algeria became allied to the pro-Nazi Vichy regime during World War II. **1945:** 8,000 died following the ruthless suppression of an abortive PPA-supported uprising against French rule. **1954–62:** Battle of Algiers: bitter war of independence fought between the National Liberation Front (FLN) and the French colonial army. **1958:** French inability to resolve the escalating civil war in Algeria, where French settlers had risen in favour of integration with France, toppled the Fourth Republic and brought to power, in Paris, Gen Charles de Gaulle, who accepted the principle of national self-determination. **1962:** Independence achieved from France. Republic declared. Ahmed Ben Bella of the FLN elected prime minister; many French settlers fled. **1963:** Ben Bella elected Algeria's first president and one-party state established. **1965:** Ben Bella deposed by military, led by Col Houari Boumédienne (FLN). **1971:** Oil and gas industry nationalized. **1976:** New Islamic-socialist constitution approved. **1978:** Death of Boumédienne. **1979:** Benjedid Chadli (FLN) elected president. Ben Bella freed after 14 years of house arrest. **1981:** Algeria helped secure release of US hostages in Iran. **1988:** Riots in protest at austerity policies; 170 killed. Reform programme introduced. Diplomatic relations restored with Morocco after a 12-year break. **1989:** Constitutional changes introduced limited political pluralism. **1991:** Elections cancelled after Islamic fundamentalist Islamic Salvation Front (FIS) won first round of multiparty elections. **1992:** Chadli resigned; military took control of government; Muhammad Boudiaf became president. State of emergency declared and FIS ordered to disband. Boudiaf assassinated, allegedly by fundamentalists; replaced by Ali Kafi. **1993:** Worsening civil strife; assassinations of politicians and other public figures; foreigners murdered. **1994:** Gen Lamine Zeroual replaced Kafi as president. Fundamentalists' campaign of violence intensified. **1995:** Zeroual won presidential elections. **1996:** Constitution amended to increase president's powers and counter religious fundamentalism. Arabic declared official public language. **1997:** Widespread killing of civilians by Armed Islamic Group (GIA). Ahmed Ouyuahia reappointed prime minister. Campaign of terror intensified; FIS urged 'national conference of reconciliation'. **1998:** Massacres continued, with over 1,700 people killed by Islamic fundamentalists in the first two weeks of January.

Andorra Principality of

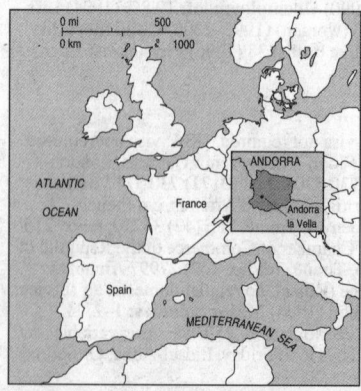

National name: *Principat d'Andorra* **Area:** 468 sq km/181 sq mi **Capital:** Andorra-la-Vella **Major towns/cities:** Les Escaldes, Escaldes-Engordany (suburb of capital) **Physical features:** mountainous, with narrow valleys; the E Pyrenees, Valira River

Government

Heads of state: Joan Marti i Alanis (bishop of Urgel, Spain) and Jacques Chirac (president of France) **Head of government:** Marc Forne from 1994 **Political system:**

co-principality **Administrative divisions:** seven parishes **Political parties:** National Democratic Grouping (AND; formerly the Democratic Party of Andorra: PDA) moderate, centrist; National Democratic Initiative (IND), left of centre; New Democracy Party (ND), centrist; National Andorran Coalition (CNA), centrist; Liberal Union (UL), right of centre **Armed forces:** no standing army **Death penalty:** abolished 1990 (last execution 1943)

Economy and resources
Currency: French franc and Spanish peseta **GDP:** ($ US) 1 billion (1993 est) **Real GDP per capita (PPP):** ($ US) 16,200 (1993 est) **GDP growth rate:** N/A **Major trading partners:** France, Spain **Resources:** iron, lead, alum, hydro power **Industries:** cigar and cigarette manufacturing, textiles, leather goods, wood products, processed foodstuffs, furniture, tourism, banking and financial services **Exports:** cigars and cigarettes, furniture, electricity. Principal market: France 46.7% (1994) **Imports:** foodstuffs, electricity, mineral fuels. Principal source: Spain 38.9% (1994) **Arable land:** 2.2% (1995) **Agricultural products:** tobacco, potatoes, rye, barley, oats, vegetables; livestock rearing (mainly sheep) and timber production

Population and society
Population: 71,000 (1996 est) **Population growth rate:** 5.5% (1990–95) **Population density:** (per sq km) 157 (1996) **Urban population:** (% of toal) 63 (1995) **Age distribution:** (% of total population) <15 18%, 15–65 72.1%, >65 9.9% (1989) **Ethnic groups:** 25% Andorrans, 75% immigrant Spanish workers **Language:** Catalan (official); Spanish, French **Religion:** Roman Catholic **Education:** (compulsory years) 10 **Literacy rate:** 99% (men); 99% (women) (1995 est) **Labour force:** 4% agriculture, 23% industry, 73% services (1992) **Unemployment:** 0% (1994) **Life expectancy:** 70 (men); 73 (women) (1994 est) **Physicians:** 1 per 8 people (1994 est)

Practical information
Visa requirements: UK: visa not required. USA: visa not required **Embassy in the UK:** none; Andorran Trade Delegation, 63 Westover Road, London SW18 2RF. Tel: (0181) 874 4806 **British embassy:** British Consulate (Barcelona), 13th Floor, Edificio Torre de Barcelona, Avenida Diagonal 477, 08036 Barcelona. Tel: (3) 419 9044; fax: (3) 405 2411 **Chamber of commerce:** Sindicat d'Initiativa de las Valls d'Andorra, Carrer Dr Vilanova, Andorra la Vella. Tel: 820 214; fax: 825 823 **Airports:** international airports: none; closest airport for Andorran traffic 20 km/12.5 mi from Andorra at Seo de Urgel, Spain **Major holidays:** 1, 6, January, 19 March, 1 May, 24 June, 15 August, 8 September, 1, 4, November, 8, 25–26 December; variable: Ascension Thursday, Carnival, Corpus Christi, Good Friday, Easter Monday, Whit Monday

Chronology
AD 803: Holy Roman Emperor Charlemagne liberated Andorra from Muslim control. **819:** Louis I, 'the Pious', the son of Charlemagne, granted control over the area to the Spanish bishop of Urgel. **1278:** Treaty signed making Spanish bishop and French count joint rulers of Andorra (through marriage the king of France later inherited the count's right). **1806:** After temporary suspension during the French Revolution, from 1789 the feudal arrangement of dual allegiance to the co-princes (French and Spanish rulers) was re-established by the French emperor Napoleon Bonaparte. **1970:** Extension of franchise to third-generation female and second-generation male Andorrans. **1976:** First political organization, Democratic Party of Andorra, formed. **1977:** Franchise extended to first-generation Andorrans. **1981:** First prime minister appointed by General Council. **1991:** Links with European Community formalized. **1993:** New constitution legalized political parties and introduced first direct elections, leading to coalition government being formed under acting prime minister, Oscar Ribas Reig. Became member of United Nations. **1994:** Reig resigned after coalition lost support and was succeeded by Marc Forne; joined Council of Europe. **1997:** Liberal Union (UL) won assembly majority in general election.

Angola People's Republic of

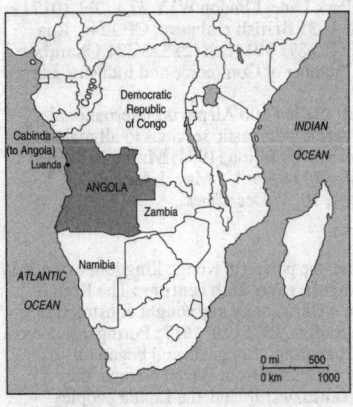

National name: *República Popular de Angola* **Area:** 1,246,700 sq km/481,350 sq mi **Capital:** Luanda (and chief port) **Major towns/cities:** Lobito, Benguela, Huambo, Lubango, Malange, Namibe (formerly Moçâmedes) **Major ports:** Huambo, Lubango, Malange **Physical features:** narrow coastal plain rises to vast interior plateau with rainforest in NW; desert in S; Cuanza, Cuito, Cubango, and Cunene rivers

Government
Head of state: José Eduardo dos Santos from 1979 **Head of government:** Fernando Franca van Dunem from 1996 **Political system:** emergent democracy **Administrative divisions:** 18 provinces **Political parties:** People's Movement for the Liberation of Angola–Workers' Party (MPLA–PT), Marxist-Leninist; National Union for the Total Independence of Angola (UNITA); National Front for the Liberation of Angola (FNLA) **Armed forces:** 97,000 (1996); plus a paramilitary force of approximately 40,000 **Conscription:** military service is compulsory for two years **Death penalty:** abolished 1992 **Defence spend:** (% GDP) 6.4 (1996) **Education spend:** (% GNP) 2.8 (1992); N/A (1993–94) **Health spend:** (% GDP) 4.0 (1990–95)

Economy and resources
Currency: kwanza **GDP:** ($ US) 3.72 billion (1995) **Real GDP per capita (PPP):** ($ US) 1,600 (1994 est) **GDP growth rate:** 8.6% (1994); –4.1% (1990–95) **Average annual inflation:** 972% (1994) **Foreign debt:** ($ US) 12.3 billion (1996) **Major trading partners:** Portugal, USA, Germany, France, Japan, Brazil, the Netherlands **Resources:** petroleum, diamonds, granite, iron ore, marble, salt, phosphates, manganese, copper **Industries:** mining, petroleum refining, food processing, textiles, construction materials **Exports:** petroleum and petroleum products, diamonds, gas. Principal market: USA 65.4% (1995) **Imports:** foodstuffs, transport equipment, base metals, electrical equipment. Principal source: France 23.4% (1995) **Arable land:** 2.4% (1995) **Agricultural products:** coffee, sugar cane, bananas, cassava, maize, sweet potatoes

Population and society
Population: 11,185,000 (1996 est) **Population growth rate:** 3.7% (1990–95); 3.1% (2000–05) **Population density:** (per sq km) 9 (1996) **Urban population:** (% of total) 32 (1995) **Age distribution:** (% of total population) <15 47.1%, 15–65 50%, >65 2.9% (1995) **Ethnic groups:** eight main ethnic groups (Bakonga, Mbunda, Ovimbundu, Lunda-Tchokwe, Nganguela, Nyaneka-Humbe, Hiriro, and Ambo), and about 100 subgroups. A major exodus of Europeans in the 1970s left around 30,000, mainly Portuguese **Language:** Portuguese (official); Bantu dialects **Religion:** Roman Catholic 68%, Protestant 20%, animist 12% **Education:** (compulsory years) 8 **Literacy rate:** 56%(men); 28% (women) (1995 est) **Labour force:** 68.2% agriculture, 10.5% industry, 21.3% services (1991) **Unemployment:** 15% (1993) **Life expectancy:** 47 (men); 51 (women) (1995–2000) **Child mortality rate:** (under 5, per 1,000 live births) 179 (1996) **Physicians:** 1 per 23,725 people (1993 est)

Practical information

Visa requirements: UK: visa required. USA: visa required **Embassy in the UK:** 98 Park Lane, London W1Y 3TA. Tel: (0171) 495 1752; fax: (0171) 495 1635 **British embassy:** CP 1244, Rua Diogo Cão 4, Luanda. Tel: (2) 392 991; fax: (2) 333 331 **Chamber of commerce:** Angolan Chamber of Commerce and Industry, Largo do Kinaxixi 14, 1 °
 andar, CP 92, Luanda. Tel: (2) 344 506 **Airports:** international airports: Luanda (4 de Fevereio); domestic services to all major towns; total passenger km: 1,396 million (1994) **Major holidays:** 1 January, 4 February, 27 March, 14 April, 1 May, 1 August, 17 September, 11 November, 1, 10, 25 December

Chronology

14th century: Under Wene, the powerful Kongo kingdom extended control over much of N Angola. **early 16th century:** The Kongo ruler King Afonso I adopted Christianity and sought constructive relations with Portuguese traders. **1575 and 1617:** Portugal secured control over the ports of Luanda and Benguela and began to pentetrate inland, meeting resistance from Queen Nzinga, the Ndonga ruler. **17th–18th centuries:** Inland, the Lunda peoples established powerful kingdoms which stretched into S Congo; the Portuguese made Angola a key centre for the export of slaves; over one million were shipped to Brazil 1580–1680. **1836:** Slave trade officially abolished. **1885–1915:** Military campaigns waged by Portugal to conquer the interior. **1926:** Modern borders delineated. **1951:** Angola became an overseas territory of Portugal. **1956:** Formation of People's Movement for the Liberation of Angola (MPLA), a socialist guerrilla independence movement based in the Congo to the N. **1961:** 50,000 massacred in rebellion on coffee plantations; forced labour abolished, but armed struggle for independence now waged. **1962:** Second nationalist guerrilla movement formed, the National Front for the Liberation of Angola (FNLA), based in N. **1966:** National Union for the Total Independence of Angola (UNITA) formed in SE Angola as a breakaway from the FNLA. **1975:** Independence achieved from Portugal. MPLA (backed mainly by Cuba) proclaimed People's Republic of Angola under the presidency of Dr Agostinho Neto. FNLA and UNITA (backed by South Africa and the USA) proclaimed People's Democratic Republic of Angola. **1976:** MPLA gained control of most of the country. South African troops withdrew, but Cuban units remained as civil war continued. **1979:** Neto died and was succeeded by José Eduardo dos Santos. **1980:** UNITA guerrillas, aided by South Africa, continued raids against the Luanda government and bases of the Namibian South West Africa People's Organization (SWAPO) in Angola. **1988:** Peace treaty, providing for the withdrawal of all foreign troops, signed with South Africa and Cuba. **1989:** Cease-fire agreed with UNITA broke down and guerrilla activity resumed. **1991:** Peace agreement ended civil war. Amnesty for all political prisoners. New multiparty constitution. **1992:** MPLA general election victory, led by dos Santos, was fiercely disputed by UNITA, and plunged the country into renewed civil war. **1993:** MPLA government recognized by USA. United Nations (UN) sanctions imposed against UNITA. **1994:** Peace treaty signed by government and UNITA representatives. **1995:** UN peacekeepers drafted in. **1996:** UNITA leader Jonas Savimbi rejected offer of vice presidency. **1997:** Delay in formation of national unity government. Unity government eventually sworn in but boycotted by Savimbi.

Antigua and Barbuda State of

Area: Antigua 280 sq km/108 sq mi, Barbuda 161 sq km/62 sq mi, plus Redonda 1 sq km/0.4 sq mi (440 sq km/169 sq mi altogether) **Capital:** St John's (on Antigua) (and chief port) **Major towns/cities:** Codrington (on Barbuda) **Physical features:** low-lying tropical islands of limestone and coral with some higher volcanic outcrops; no rivers and low rainfall result in frequent droughts and deforestation. Antigua is the largest of the Leeward Islands; Redonda is an uninhabited island of volcanic rock rising to 305 m/1,000 ft

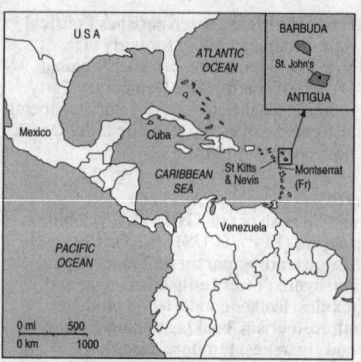

Government

Head of state: Elizabeth II from 1981, represented by governor general James B Carlisle from 1993 **Head of government:** Lester Bird from 1994 **Political system:** liberal democracy **Administrative divisions:** six parishes **Political parties:** Antigua Labour Party (ALP), moderate left of centre; United Progressive Party (UPP), centrist; Barbuda People's Movement (BPM), left of centre **Armed forces:** 200 (1996); US government leases two military bases on Antigua **Conscription:** military service is voluntary **Death penalty:** retained and used for ordinary crimes **Defence spend:** (% GDP) 0.8% (1996) **Education spend:** (% GNP) 3.7% (1988); N/A (1993–94)

Economy and resources

Currency: Eastern Caribbean dollar **GDP:** ($ US) 494 million (1994) **Real GDP per capita (PPP):** ($ US) 8,977 (1994) **GDP growth rate:** 5.3% (1994) **Average annual inflation:** 4% (1996) **Foreign debt:** ($ US) 435 million (1996) **Major trading partners:** USA, UK, Canada, Trinidad and Tobago, Barbados **Industries:** oil refining, food and beverage products, paint, bedding, furniture, electrical components. Tourism is the main economic activity. **Exports:** petroleum products, food, manufactures, machinery and transport equipment. Principal market: USA (mainly re-exports) **Imports:** petroleum, food and live animals, machinery and transport equipment, manufactures, chemicals. Principal source: USA 27% (1994 est) **Arable land:** 18.2% (1995) **Agricultural products:** cucumbers, pumpkins, mangoes, coconuts, limes, melons, pineapples, cotton; fishing

Population and society

Population: 66,000 (1996 est) **Population growth rate:** 0.6% (1990–95) **Population density:** (per sq km) 150 (1996) **Urban population:** (% of total) 31 (1992) **Age distribution:** (% of total population) <15 38%, 15–65 56.9%, >65 5.1% (1992) **Ethnic groups:** population almost entirely of black African descent **Language:** English **Religion:** Christian (mostly Anglican) **Education:** (compulsory years) 11 **Literacy rate:** 92% (men); 88% (women) (1992) **Labour force:** 11% agriculture, 19.7% industry, 69.3% services (1991) **Unemployment:** 3.2% (1990) **Life expectancy:** 70 (men); 74 (women) (1994 est) **Child mortality rate:** (under 5, per 1,000 live births) 22 (1995) **Physicians:** 1 per 3,750 people (1990)

Practical information

Visa requirements: UK: visa not required. USA: visa not required **Embassy in the UK:** 15 Thayer Street, London W1M 5LD. Tel: (0171) 486 7073/4/5; fax: (0171) 486 9970 **British embassy:** British High Commission, PO Box 483, Price Waterhouse Centre, 11 Old Parham Road, St John's. Tel: 462 0008/9; fax: 462 2806 **Chamber of commerce:** Antigua and Barbuda Chamber of Commerce and Industry Ltd, Redcliffe Street, POB 774, St John's. Tel: 462 0743; fax: 462 4575 **Airports:** international airports: St John's (V C Bird International); one airstrip on Barbuda; total passenger km: 240 million (1994) **Major holidays:** 1 January, 1 July, 1 November, 25–26 December; variable: Good Friday, Easter Monday, Whit Monday, Labour Day (May), CARICOM (July), Carnival (August)

Chronology

1493: Antigua, then peopled by Native American Caribs, visited by Christopher Columbus; he named it after a painting in the Church of

Sante Maria la Antigua, in Seville. **1632:** Antigua colonized by British settlers from St Kitts. **1667:** Treaty of Breda formally ceded Antigua to Britain, ending French claim. **1674:** Christopher Codrington, a sugar planter from Barbados, established sugar plantations and acquired Barbuda island on lease from the British monarch in 1685; Africans brought in as slaves. **1834:** Antigua's slaves were freed. **1860:** Annexation of Barbuda. **1871–1956:** Antigua and Barbuda administered as part of the Leeward Islands federation. **1946:** Antigua Labour Party (ALP) formed by Vere Bird. **1958–62:** Part of the West Indies Federation. **1967:** Antigua and Barbuda became an associated state within the Commonwealth, with full internal independence, but Britain responsible for defence and foreign affairs. **1969:** Separatist movement developed on Barbuda. **1971:** Progressive Labour Movement (PLM) won the general election, defeating ALP, and George Walter replaced Bird as prime minister. **1976:** PLM called for early independence, but ALP urged caution. ALP, led by Bird, won the general election. **1981:** Independence from Britain achieved. **1983:** Assisted US invasion of Grenada, despite policy on nonalignment. **1991:** Bird remained in power despite calls for his resignation. **1993:** Lester Bird succeeded his father as ALP leader.

Argentina Republic of

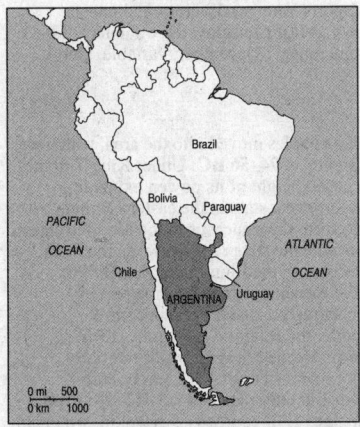

National name:
República Argentina
Area: 2,780,092 sq km/1,073,393 sq mi
Capital: Buenos Aires **Major towns/cities:** Rosario, Córdoba, San Miguel de Tucumán, Mendoza, Santa Fé, La Plata **Major ports:** La Plata and Bahía Blanca **Physical features:** mountains in W, forest and savanna in N, pampas (treeless plains) in E central area, Patagonian plateau in S; rivers Colorado, Salado, Paraná, Uruguay, Río de La Plata estuary; Andes mountains, with Aconcagua the highest peak in the W hemisphere; Iguaçu Falls **Territories:** claims Falkland Islands (*Islas Malvinas*), South Georgia, the South Sandwich Islands, and part of Antarctica

Government
Head of state: Carlos Menem from 1989 **Head of government:** Carlos Menem from 1989 **Political system:** democratic federal republic **Administrative divisions:** 23 provinces and one federal district (Buenos Aires) **Political parties:** Radical Civic Union Party (UCR), moderate centrist; Justicialist Party (PJ), right-wing Perónist; Movement for Dignity and Independence (Modin), right-wing; Front for a Country in Solidarity (Frepaso), centre left **Armed forces:** 72,500 plus paramilitary gendarmerie of 31,200 (1996) **Conscription:** abolished 1995 **Death penalty:** reintroduced 1976 **Defence spend:** (% GDP) 1.5 (1996) **Education spend:** (% GNP) 3.6 (1993–94) **Health spend:** (% GDP) 4.3 (1990–95)

Economy and resources
Currency: peso = 10,000 australs (which it replaced 1992) **GDP:** ($ US) 281.9 billion (1994) **Real GDP per capita (PPP):** ($ US) 8,937 (1994) **GDP growth rate:** 7.4% (1994); 5.7% (1990–95) **Average annual inflation:** 0.4% (1996); 255.4% (1985–95) **Foreign debt:** ($ US) 91.2 billion (1996) **Major trading partners:** USA, Brazil, the Netherlands, Germany, Italy, Uruguay, Chile **Resources:** coal,

crude oil, natural gas, iron ore, lead ore, zinc ore, tin, gold, silver, uranium ore, marble, borates, granite **Industries:** petroleum and petroleum products, primary iron, crude steel, sulphuric acid, synthetic rubber, paper and paper products, crude oil, cement, cigarettes, motor vehicles **Exports:** meat and meat products, prepared animal fodder, cereals, petroleum and petroleum products, soya beans, vegetable oils and fats. Principal market: Brazil 20.8% (1995) **Imports:** machinery and transport equipment, chemicals and mineral products. Principal sources: USA 26.2% (1995) **Arable land:** 9.1% (1995) **Agricultural products:** wheat, maize, soya beans, sugar cane, rice, sorghum, potatoes, tobacco, sunflowers, cotton, vine fruits, citrus fruit; livestock production (chiefly cattle)

Population and society
Population: 35,219,000 (1996 est) **Population growth rate:** 1.2% (1990–95); 1.1% (2000–05) **Population density:** (per sq km) 13 (1996) **Urban population:** (% of total) 88 (1995) **Age distribution:** (% of total population) <15 28.7%; 15–65 61.8%; >65 9.5% (1995) **Ethnic groups:** 85% of European descent, mainly Spanish; 15% mestizo (offspring of Spanish–American and Native American parents) **Language:** Spanish 95% (official); Italian 3% **Religion:** Roman Catholic (state-supported) **Education:** (compulsory years) 7; age limits 7–16 **Literacy rate:** 95% (men); 95% (women) (1995 est) **Labour force:** 38% of population: 12% agriculture, 32% industry, 55% services **Unemployment:** 18.8% (1995) **Life expectancy:** 70 (men); 77 (women) (1995–2000) **Child mortality rate:** (under 5, per 1,000 live births) 25 (1996) **Physicians:** 1 per 330 people (1993 est)

Practical information
Visa requirements: UK: visa not required for tourist visits; visa required for business purposes. USA: visa not required for tourist visits; visa required for business purposes **Embassy in the UK:** 53 Hans Place, London SW1X 0LA. Tel: (0171) 584 6494; fax: (0171) 589 3106 **British embassy:** Casilla de Correo 2050, Dr Luis Agote 2412/52, 1425 Buenos Aires. Tel: (1) 803 7070/1; fax: (1) 803 1731 **Chamber of commerce:** Cámara Argentina de Comercio, Avda Leandro N Alem 36, 1003 Buenos Aires. Tel: (1) 331 8051; fax: (1) 331 8055 **Airports:** international airports: Buenos Aires, Aeroparque Jorge Newbery, Córdoba, Corrientes, El Plumerillo, Ezeiza, Jujuy, Resistencia, Río Gallegos, Salta, San Carlos de Bariloche; domestic services to all major towns; total passenger km: 11,250 million (1994) **Major holidays:** 1 January, 1, 25 May, 10, 20 June, 9 July, 17 August, 12 October, 8, 25, 31 December; variable: Good Friday, Holy Thursday

Chronology
1516: Spanish navigator Juan Diaz de Solis discovered Río de La Plata. **1536:** Buenos Aires founded, but soon abandoned because of attacks by Native Americans. **1580:** Buenos Aires re-established as part of Spanish province of Asunción. **1617:** Buenos Aires became a separate province within Spanish viceroyalty of Lima. **1776:** Spanish South American Empire reorganized: Atlantic regions became viceroyalty of La Plata, with Buenos Aires as capital. **1810:** After French conquest of Spain, Buenos Aires junta took over government of viceroyalty. **1816:** Independence proclaimed as United Provinces of Río de La Plata, but Bolivia and Uruguay soon seceded; civil war followed between federalists and those who wanted a unitary state. **1835–52:** Dictatorship of General Juan Manuel Rosas. **1853:** Adoption of federal constitution based on US model; Buenos Aires refused to join confederation. **1861:** Buenos Aires incorporated into Argentine confederation by force. **1865–70:** Argentina took part in War of Triple Alliance against Paraguay. **late 19th century:** Large-scale European immigration and rapid economic development; Argentina became a major world supplier of meat and grain. **1880:** Buenos Aires became a special federal district and national capital. **1880–1916:** Government dominated by oligarchy of conservative landowners; each president effectively chose his own successor. **1916:** Following introduction of secret ballot, Radical Party of Hipólito Irigoyen won election victory, beginning a period of 14 years in government. **1930:** Military coup ushered in a series of conservative governments sustained by

violence and fraud. **1943:** Group of pro-German army officers seized power; Colonel Juan Perón emerged as a leading figure. **1946:** Perón won free presidential election; he secured working-class support through welfare measures, trade unionism, and the popularity of his wife, Eva Perón (Evita). **1949:** New constitution abolished federalism and increased powers of president. **1952:** Death of Evita. Support for Perón began to decline. **1955:** Perón overthrown; constitution of 1853 restored. **1966–70:** Dictatorship of General Juan Carlos Ongania. **1973:** Perónist Party won free elections; Perón returned from exile in Spain to become president. **1974:** Perón died; succeeded by his third wife, Isabel Perón. **1976:** Coup resulted in rule by military junta headed by Lt-Gen Jorge Videla (until 1978; succeeded by General Roberto Viola 1978–81 and General Leopoldo Galtieri 1981–82). **1976–83:** Military regime conducted murderous campaign ('Dirty War') against left-wing elements. **1982:** Invasion of Falkland Islands by Argentina. Intervention and defeat by UK; Galtieri replaced by Gen Reynaldo Bignone. **1983:** Return to civilian rule under President Raúl Alfonsín; investigation launched into 'disappearance' of more than 8,000 people during 'Dirty War'. **1985:** Economic austerity programme failed to halt hyperinflation. **1989:** Perónist candidate Carlos Menem won presidential election. Annual inflation reached 12,000%. **1990:** Full diplomatic relations with UK restored. **1995:** President Menem re-elected. **1997:** PJ lost its assembly majority.

Armenia Republic of

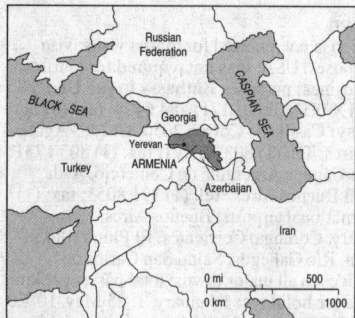

National name:
Haikakan Hanrapetoutioun
Area: 29,800 sq km/11,505 sq mi
Capital: Yerevan
Major towns/cities: Gyumri (formerly Leninakan), Vanadzor (formerly Kirovakan) **Physical features:** mainly mountainous (including Mount Ararat), wooded

Government

Head of state: Levon Ter-Petrossian from 1990 **Head of government:** Robert Kocharyan from 1997 **Political system:** authoritarian nationalist **Administrative divisions:** 10 regions **Political parties:** Armenian Pan-National Movement (APM), nationalist, left of centre; Armenian Revolutionary Federation (ARF), centrist (banned 1994); Communist Party of Armenia (banned 1991–92); National Unity, opposition coalition **Armed forces:** 57,400 (1996) **Conscription:** compulsory for 18 months **Death penalty:** retained and used for ordinary crimes **Defence spend:** (% GDP) 6.2 (1996) **Education spend:** (% GNP) 3.5 (1993) **Health spend:** (% GDP) 3.1 (1990–95)

Economy and resources

Currency: dram (replaced Russian rouble 1993) **GDP:** ($ US) 3 billion (1994) **Real GDP per capita (PPP):** ($ US) 1,737 (1994) **GDP growth rate:** 5.4% (1994); –21.2% (1990–95) **Average annual inflation:** 28.7% (1996); 179.4% (1985–95) **Foreign debt:** ($ US) 374 million (1995) **Major trading partners:** Russia, Ukraine, Belarus, Georgia, Kazakhstan, Turkmenistan, USA **Resources:** copper, zinc, molybdenum, iron, silver, marble, granite **Industries:** food processing and beverages, fertilizers, synthetic rubber, machinery and metal products, textiles, garments **Exports:** machinery and metalworking products, chemical and petroleum products. Principal market: Russia 20% (1995) **Imports:** light industrial products, petroleum and derivatives, industrial raw materials. Principal source: Russia 32.3% (1995) **Arable land:**

21.2% (1995) **Agricultural products:** potatoes, vegetables, fruits, cotton, almonds, olives, figs, cereals; livestock rearing (sheep and cattle)

Population and society

Population: 3,638,000 (1996 est) **Population growth rate:** 1.4% (1990–95); 1% (2000–05) **Population density:** (per sq km) 122 (1996) **Urban population:** (% of total) 69 (1995) **Age distribution:** (% of total population) <15 29.6 %, 15–65 63%, >65 7.4% (1995) **Ethnic groups:** 91% of Armenian ethnic descent, 5% Azeri, 2% Russian, and 2% Kurdish **Language:** Armenian **Religion:** Armenian Christian **Education:** (compulsory years) 9 **Literacy rate:** 99% (men); 99% (women) (1995) **Labour force:** 32.2% agriculture, 32.8% industry, 35% services (1993) **Unemployment:** 9.1% (1996) **Life expectancy:** 76 (men); 70 (women) (1995–2000) **Child mortality rate:** (under 5, per 1,000 live births) 23 (1996) **Physicians:** 1 per 250 people (1994 est)

Practical information

Visa requirements: UK: visa required. USA: visa required **Embassy in the UK:** 25A Cheniston Gardens, London W8 6TG. Tel: (0171) 938 5435; fax: (0171) 938 2595 **British embassy:** Armenia Hotel, 1 Vramshapouh Arka Street, Yerevan 375010. Tel: (2) 151 807; fax: (2) 151 803 **Chamber of commerce:** Chamber of Commerce and Industry of the Republic of Armenia, ulitsa Alevardyan 39, Yerevan. Tel: (2) 565 438; fax: (2) 565 071 **Airports:** international airports Yerevan (Zvarnots); domestic services to most major towns **Major holidays:** 1, 6 January, 28–31 March, 24, 28 May, 21 September, 7 December; variable: Good Friday, Easter Monday

Chronology

6th century BC: Armenian peoples moved into the area, which was then part of the Persian Empire. **c. 94–56 BC:** Under King Tigranes II 'the Great', Armenia reached height of its power, expanding southwards to become the strongest state in the eastern Roman empire, controlling an area from the Caucasus to the Mediterranean. **c. AD 300:** Christianity became the state religion when the local ruler was converted by St Gregory the Illuminator. **c. AD 390:** Divided between Byzantine Armenia, which became part of Byzantine Empire, and Persarmenia, under Persian control. **886–1045:** Independent under the Bagratid monarchy. **13th century:** After being overrun by the Mongols, a substantially independent Little Armenia survived until 1375. **early 16th century:** Conquered by Muslim Ottoman Turks. **1813–28:** Russia took control of E Armenia. **late 19th century:** Revival in Armenian culture and national spirit, provoking Ottoman backlash in W Armenia and international concern at Armenian maltreatment: the 'Armenian Question'. **1894–96:** Massacre of Armenians by Turkish soldiers to suppress unrest. **1915:** Suspected of pro-Russian sympathies, two-thirds of Armenia's population of 2 million were deported to Syria and Palestine. Around 600,000–1 million died en route: the survivors contributed towards an Armenian diaspora in Europe and North America. **1916:** Conquered by tsarist Russia and became part of a brief 'Transcaucasian Alliance' with Georgia and Azerbaijan. **1918:** Became an independent republic. **1920:** Occupied by Red Army of Soviet Union (USSR), but W Armenia remained part of Turkey and NW Iran. **1936:** Became constituent republic of USSR; rapid industrial development. **late 1980s:** Armenian 'national reawakening', encouraged by *glasnost* (openness) initiative of Soviet leader Mikhail Gorbachev. **1988:** Earthquake – around 20,000 people died. **1989:** Strife-torn Nagorno-Karabakh placed under direct rule from Moscow; civil war erupted with Azerbaijan over Nagorno-Karabakh and Nakhichevan, an Azerbaijani-peopled enclave in Armenia. **1990:** Nationalists secured control of Armenian parliament in elections in May; former dissident Ter-Petrossian indirectly elected president; independence declared, but ignored by Moscow and international community. **1991:** After collapse of USSR, Armenia joined new Commonwealth of Independent States. Ter-Petrossian directly elected president. Nagorno-Karabakh declared its independence. **1992:** Armenia recognized as independent state by USA and admitted into United

Nations. **1993:** Armenian forces gained control of more than one-fifth of Azerbaijan, including much of Nagorno-Karabakh. **1994:** Nagorno-Karabakh cease-fire ended conflict. **1995:** Privatization and price-liberalization programme launched. Ruling APM re-elected, amid reports of intimidation of opposition candidates. **1996:** Ter-Petrossian re-elected president. Hrand Bagratian replaced as prime minister by Armen Sarkissian. **1997:** Sarkissian resigned for health reasons; replaced by Robert Kocharyan. Border fighting with Azerbaijan. Arkady Gukasyan elected president of Nagorno-Karabakh.

Australia Commonwealth of

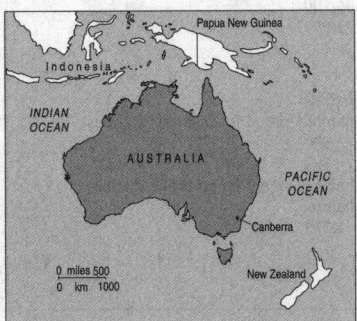

Area: 7,682,300 sq km/2,966,136 sq mi **Capital:** Canberra **Major towns/cities:** Adelaide, Alice Springs, Brisbane, Darwin, Melbourne, Perth, Sydney, Hobart, Geelong, Newcastle, Townsville, Wollongong **Physical features:** Ayers Rock; Arnhem Land; Gulf of Carpentaria; Cape York Peninsula; Great Australian Bight; Great Sandy Desert; Gibson Desert; Great Victoria Desert; Simpson Desert; the Great Barrier Reef; Great Dividing Range and Australian Alps in the E (Mount Kosciusko, 2,229 m/7,136 ft, Australia's highest peak). The fertile SE region is watered by the Darling, Lachlan, Murrumbridgee, and Murray rivers. Lake Eyre basin and Nullarbor Plain in the S **Territories:** Norfolk Island, Christmas Island, Cocos (Keeling) Islands, Ashmore and Cartier Islands, Coral Sea Islands, Heard Island and McDonald Islands, Australian Antarctic Territory

Government
Head of state: Elizabeth II from 1952, represented by governor general William George Hayden from 1989 **Head of government:** John Howard from 1996 **Political system:** federal constitutional monarchy **Administrative divisions:** six states and two territories **Political parties:** Australian Labor Party, moderate left of centre; Liberal Party of Australia, moderate, liberal, free enterprise; National Party of Australia (formerly Country Party), centrist non-metropolitan **Armed forces:** 57,800 (1996) **Conscription:** military service is voluntary **Death penalty:** abolished 1985 **Defence spend:** (%GDP) 2.2 (1996) **Education spend:** (% GDP) 2.5% (1995) **Health spend:** (%GNP) 4.6 (1995)

Economy and resources
Currency: Australian dollar **GDP:** ($ US) 392.6 billion (1996) **Real GDP per capita (PPP):** ($ US) 20,368 (1996) **GDP growth rate:** 3% (1996); 3.5% (1990–95) **Average annual inflation:** 2.9% (1996); 3.7% (1985–95) **Major trading partners:** USA, Japan, UK, New Zealand, Republic of Korea, China, Taiwan, Singapore **Resources:** coal, iron ore (world's third-largest producer), bauxite, copper, zinc (world's second-largest producer), nickel (world's fifth-largest producer), uranium, gold, diamonds **Industries:** mining, metal products, textiles, wood and paper products, chemical products, electrical machinery, transport equipment, printing, publishing and recording media, tourism, electronic communications **Exports:** major world producer of raw materials: iron ore, aluminium, coal, nickel, zinc, lead, gold, tin, tungsten, uranium, crude oil; wool, meat, cereals, fruit, sugar, wine. Principal markets: Japan 22% (1996) **Imports:** processed industrial supplies,

transport equipment and parts, road vehicles, petroleum and petroleum products, medicinal and pharmaceutical products, organic chemicals, consumer goods. Principal source: USA 23% (1996) **Arable land:** 6.3% (1995) **Agricultural products:** wheat, barley, oats, rice, sugar cane, fruit, grapes; livestock (cattle and sheep) and dairy products

Population and society
Population: 18,057,000 (1996 est) **Population growth rate:** 1.4% (1990–95); 1.1% (2000–05) **Population density:** (per sq km) 2 (1996) **Urban population:** (% of total) 85 (1995) **Age distribution:** (% of total population) <15 21.6%, 15–65 66.8%, >65 11.6% (1995) **Ethnic groups:** 99% of European descent; remaining 1% Aborigine or Asian **Language:** English, Aboriginal languages **Religion:** Anglican 26%, other Protestant 17%, Roman Catholic 26% **Education:** (compulsory years) 10 or 11 (states vary) **Literacy rate:** 99% (men); 99% (women) (1995 est) **Labour force:** 50.2% of total population: 5.1% agriculture, 22.5% industry, 72.4% services (1996) **Unemployment:** 8.6% (1996) **Life expectancy:** 75 (men); 81 (women) (1995–2000) **Child mortality rate:** (under 5, per 1,000 live births) 8 (1996) **Physicians:** 1 per 438 people (1991)

Practical information
Visa requirements: UK: visa required. USA: visa required **Embassy in the UK:** High Commission, Australia House, The Strand, London WC2B 4LA. Tel: (0171) 379 4334; fax: (0171) 240 5333 **British embassy:** British High Commission, Commonwealth Avenue, Yarralumla, Canberra, ACT 2600. Tel: (6) 270 6666; fax: (6)273 3236 **Chamber of commerce:** International Chamber of Commerce, POB E118, Queen Victoria Terrace, Canberra, ACT 2600. Tel: (6) 295 1961; fax: (6) 295 0170. Australian Chamber of Commerce and Industry, POB E14, Queen Victoria Terrace, Canberra ACT 2600. Tel: (6) 273 2311; fax: (6) 273 3196 **Airports:** international airports: Sydney (NSW), Melbourne (Victoria), Canberra, Brisbane, Cairns (Queensland), Perth (Western Australia), Adelaide (South Australia), Hobart (Tasmania), Townsville (Quensland), Darwin (Northern Territory); domestic services to all major resorts and cities; total passenger km: 61,124 million (1994) **Major holidays:** 1 January, 25 April, 25–26 December (except South Australia); variable: Good Friday, Easter Monday, Holy Saturday; additional days vary between states

Chronology
c. 40,000 BC: Aboriginal immigration from S India, Sri Lanka, and SE Asia. **AD 1606:** First recorded sightings of Australia by Europeans including discovery of Cape York by Dutch explorer Willem Jansz in *Duyfken*. **1770:** Captain James Cook claimed New South Wales for Britain. **1788:** Sydney founded as British penal colony. **late 18th–19th centuries:** Great age of exploration: coastal surveys by George Bass and Matthew Flinders; interior by Charles Sturt, Edward Eyre, Robert Burke and William Wills, John McDouall Stuart, and John Forrest. Overlanders and squatters also opened up new territory, as did bushrangers, including Ned Kelly. **1804:** Castle Hill Rising by Irish convicts in New South Wales. **1813:** Crossing of Blue Mountains removed major barrier to exploration of interior. **1825:** Tasmania seceded from New South Wales. **1829:** Western Australia colonized. **1836:** South Australia colonized. **1840–68:** End of convict transportation. **1850:** British Act of Parliament permitted Australian colonies to draft their own constitutions and achieve virtual self-government. **1851–61:** Gold rushes contributed to exploration and economic growth. **1851:** Victoria seceded from New South Wales. **1855:** Victoria achieved self-government. **1856:** New South Wales, South Australia, and Tasmania achieved self-government. **1859:** Queensland formed from New South Wales and achieved self-government. **1860:** (National) Country Party founded. **1890:** Western Australia achieved self-government. **1891:** Depression gave rise to Australian Labor Party. **1899–1900:** South African War – forces offered by individual colonies. **1901:** Creation of Commonwealth of Australia. **1902:** Immigration Restriction Act introduced language tests for potential settlers; women gained right to vote. **1914–18:** World War I: over 300,000 Australian volunteers fought in Middle East and on western front. **1919:** Australia given mandates over Papua

Australia: States and Territories

(– = not applicable.)

State	Capital	Area sq km	Area sq mi	Population (1994)
New South Wales	Sydney	801,600	309,500	5,997,400
Queensland	Brisbane	1,727,200	666,872	3,196,900
South Australia	Adelaide	984,377	380,070	1,463,200
Tasmania	Hobart	67,800	26,177	472,400
Victoria	Melbourne	227,620	87,884	4,475,500
Western Australia	Perth	2,525,500	975,095	1,715,300
Territory				
Australian Capital Territory	Canberra	2,400	926	304,100
Northern Territory	Darwin	1,346,200	519,767	173,900
External Territory				
Ashmore and Cartier Islands	–	5	2	uninhabited
Australian Antarctic Territory	–	6,044,000	2,333,590	uninhabited except for scientific stations
Christmas Island	–	135	52	2,500
Cocos (Keeling) Islands	–	14	5.5	593
Coral Sea Islands	–	1[1]	1[1]	uninhabited except for scientific stations
Heard Island and McDonald Islands	–	410	158	uninhabited
Norfolk Island	–	40	15.5	1,770

[1] Sea area of Coral Sea Islands is 780,000 sq km/301,158 sq mi; land area of the islands is aproximately 2.6 sq km/1 sq mi.

New Guinea and Solomon Islands. **1927:** Seat of federal government moved to Canberra. **1931:** Statute of Westminster confirmed Australian independence. **1933:** Western Australia's vote to secede was overruled. **1939–45:** World War II: Australian troops fought in Greece, N Africa, and SW Pacific. **1941:** Curtin's appeal to USA for military help marked shift away from exclusive relationship with Britain. **1944:** Liberal Party founded by Menzies. **1948–75:** Influx of around 2 million new immigrants, chiefly from continental Europe. **1950–53:** Australia contributed troops to United Nations (UN) forces in Korean War. **1951:** Australia joined USA and New Zealand in ANZUS Pacific security alliance. **1965–72:** Australian troops participated in Vietnam War. **1967:** Referendum gave Australian Aborigines full citizenship rights. Australia became a member of the Association of South East Asian Nations (ASEAN). **1973:** Britain entered European Economic Community (EEC), and in 1970s Japan became Australia's chief trading partner. **1974:** 'White Australia' immigration restrictions abolished. **1975:** Constitutional crisis: Governor General John Kerr dismissed Prime Minister Gough Whitlam after senate blocked financial legislation. Papua New Guinea became independent. **1978:** Northern Territory achieved self-government. **1983:** Labor Party returned to power under Bob Hawke. **1986:** Australia Act passed by British Parliament eliminating last vestiges of British legal authority in Australia. **1988:** Free Trade Agreement signed with New Zealand. **1992:** Citizenship Act removed oath of allegiance to British crown. **1993:** Labor Party won record fifth election victory. **1996:** Liberal-National coalition, headed by John Howard, won general election. **1997:** Democrat Party leader switched to Labor Party.

Austria Republic of

National name: *Republik Österreich* **Area:** 83,500 sq km/32,239 sq mi **Capital:** Vienna **Major towns/cities:** Graz, Linz, Salzburg, Innsbruck, Klagenfurt **Physical features:** landlocked mountainous state, with Alps in W and S (Austrian Alps, including Grossglockner and Brenner and Semmering passes, Lechtaler and Allgauer Alps N of River Inn, Carnic Alps on Italian border) and low relief in E where most of the population is concentrated; River Danube

Government
Head of state: Thomas Klestil from 1992 **Head of government:** Franz Vranitzky from 1986 **Political system:** democratic federal republic **Administrative divisions:** nine provinces **Political parties:** Social Democratic Party of Austria (SPÔ), democratic socialist; Austrian People's Party (ÔVP), progressive centrist; Freedom (formerly Freedom Party of Austria: FPÔ), right wing; United Green Party of Austria (VGÔ), conservative ecological; Green Alternative Party (ALV), radical ecological **Armed forces:** 55,800 (1996) **Conscription:** 6 months **Death penalty:** abolished 1968 **Defence spend:** (% GDP) 0.9 (1996) **Education spend:** (% GNP) 5.5 (1993–94) **Health spend:** (% GDP) 6.2 (1994)

Economy and resources
Currency: schilling **GDP:** ($ US) 226.1 billion (1996) **Real GDP per capita (PPP):** ($ US) 21,120 (1996) **GDP growth rate:** 0.3% (1996); 1.9% (1990–95) **Average annual inflation:** 1.8% (1996); 3.2% (1985–95) **Major trading partners:** EU, Switzerland, USA, Japan **Resources:** lignite, iron, kaolin, gypsum, talcum, magnesite, lead, zinc, forests **Industries:** raw and rolled steel, machinery, cellulose, paper, cardboard, cement, fertilizers, viscose staple yarn, sawn timber, flat glass, salt, sugar, milk, margarine **Exports:** dairy products, food products, wood and paper products, machinery and transport equipment, metal and metal products, chemical products. Principal market for exports: EU countries 63.6% (1993) **Imports:** petroleum and petroleum products, food and live animals, chemicals and related products, textiles, clothing. Principal source: EU countries 67% (1993) **Arable land:** 17.2% (1995) **Agricultural**

Austria: Provinces

Province	Capital	Area		Population (1995)	Province	Capital	Area		Population (1995)
		sq km	sq mi				sq km	sq mi	
Burgenland	Eisenstadt	3,965	1,531	274,334	Tirol	Innsbruck	12,648	4,883	658,312
Carinthia	Klagenfurt	9,533	3,681	560,994	Upper Austria	Linz	11,980	4,625	1,385,769
Lower Austria	St Pölten	19,174	7,403	1,518,254	Vienna	Vienna	415	160	1,592,596
Salzburg	Salzburg	7,154	2,762	506,850	Vorarlberg	Bregenz	2,601	1,004	343,109
Styria	Graz	16,388	6,327	1,206,317					

products: wheat, barley, rye, oats, potatoes, maize, sugar beet; dairy products

Population and society
Population: 8,106,000 (1996 est) **Population growth rate:** 0.7% (1990–95); 0.2% (2000–05) **Population density:** (per sq km) 97 (1996) **Urban population:** (% of total) 56 (1995) **Age distribution:** (% of total population) <15 17.8%, 15–65 67.3%, >65 14.9% (1995) **Ethnic groups:** 98% German, 0.7% Croatian, 0.3% Slovene **Language:** German **Religion:** Roman Catholic 78%, Protestant 5% **Education:** (compulsory years) 9 **Literacy rate:** 99% (men); 99% (women) (1995) **Labour force:** 48.3% of population: 7.2% agriculture, 33.2% industry, 59.6% services (1994) **Unemployment:** 4.4% (1996) **Life expectancy:** 74 (men); 80 (women) (1995–2000) **Child mortality rate:** (under 5, per 1,000 live births) 8 (1996) **Physicians:** 1 per 253 people (1996)

Practical information
Visa requirements: UK: visa not required. USA: visa not required **Embassy in the UK:** 18 Belgrave Mews West, London SW1X 8HV. Tel: (0171) 235 3731; fax: (0171) 235 8025 **British embassy:** Juarèsgasse 12, 1030 Vienna. Tel: (1) 713 1575; fax: (1) 714 7824 **Chamber of commerce:** Wirtschaftskammer Österreich (Austrian Economic Chamber), Wiedner Haupstrasse 63, 1045 Vienna. Tel: (1) 50105; fax: (1) 50206 **Airports:** international airports: Vienna (Wien-Schwechat), Graz (Thalerhof), Innsbruck (Kranebitten), Klagenfurt (Wörthersee), Linz (Hörsching), Salzburg (Maxglam); domestic services between the above; total passenger km: 5,933 million (1994) **Major holidays:** 1, 6 January, 1 May, 15 August, 26 October, 1 November, 8, 24–26 December; variable: Ascension Thursday, Corpus Christi, Easter Monday, Whit Monday

Chronology
14 BC: Country S of River Danube conquered by Romans. **5th century AD:** Region occupied by Vandals, Huns, Goths, Lombards, and Avars. **791:** Charlemagne conquered Avars and established East Mark, nucleus of future Austrian Empire. **976:** Holy Roman Emperor Otto II granted East Mark to House of Babenburg, which ruled until 1246. **1156:** Margrave of Austria raised to duke. **1282:** Holy Roman Emperor Rudolf of Habsburg seized Austria and invested his son as its duke; for over 500 years most rulers of Austria were elected Holy Roman emperor. **1453:** Austria became an archduchy. **1519–56:** Emperor Charles V was both archduke of Austria and king of Spain; Habsburgs dominant in Europe. **1526:** Bohemia came under Habsburg rule. **1529:** Vienna besieged by the Ottoman Turks. **1618–48:** Thirty Years' War: Habsburgs weakened by failure to secure control over Germany. **1683:** Polish-Austrian force led by Jan Sobieski defeated the Turks at Vienna. **1699:** Treaty of Karlowitz: Austrians expelled the Turks from Hungary, which came under Habsburg rule. **1713:** By the Treaty of Utrecht, Austria obtained the Spanish Netherlands (Belgium) and political control over most of Italy. **1740–48:** War of Austrian Succession: Prussia (supported by France and Spain) attacked Austria (supported by Holland and England) on the pretext of disputing rights of Maria Theresa; Austria lost Silesia to Prussia. **1772:** Austria joined in partition of Poland, annexing Galicia. **1780–90:** 'Enlightened despotism': Joseph II tried to impose radical reforms. **1792:** Austria went to war with revolutionary France. **1804:** Francis II took the title

Emperor of Austria. **1806:** Holy Roman Empire abolished. **1809–48:** Guided by foreign minister Prince Klemens von Metternich, Austria took a leading role in resisting liberalism and nationalism throughout Europe. **1815:** After the Napoleonic Wars, Austria lost its Netherlands but received Lombardy and Venetia. **1848:** Outbreak of liberal-nationalist revolts throughout the Austrian Empire; Ferdinand I abdicated in favour of Franz Joseph; revolutions suppressed with difficulty. **1859:** France and Sardinia expelled Austrians from Lombardy by force. **1866:** Seven Weeks' War: Prussia defeated Austria, which ceded Venetia to Italy. **1867:** Austria conceded equality to Hungary within the dual monarchy of Austria-Hungary. **1878:** Treaty of Berlin: Austria-Hungary occupied Bosnia-Herzegovina; annexed 1908. **1914:** Archduke Franz Ferdinand, the heir to the throne, assassinated by a Serbian nationalist; Austria-Hungary invaded Serbia, precipitating World War I. **1916:** Death of Franz Joseph; succeeded by Karl I. **1918:** Austria-Hungary collapsed in military defeat; empire dissolved; republic proclaimed. **1919:** Treaty of St Germain reduced Austria to its present boundaries and prohibited union with Germany. **1934:** Political instability culminated in brief civil war; right-wingers defeated socialists. **1938:** The *Anschluss* : Nazi Germany incorporated Austria into the Third Reich. **1945:** Following World War II, the victorious Allies divided Austria into four zones of occupation (US, British, French, and Soviet); Second Republic established under Karl Renner. **1955:** Austrian State Treaty ended occupation; Austria regained independence on condition of neutrality. **1960–70s:** Austria experienced rapid industrialization and prosperity under governments dominated by moderate socialists and centrists. **1986:** Election of Kurt Waldheim as president, despite allegations of war crimes during World War II, led to a measure of diplomatic isolation until Waldheim's replacement 1992. **1995:** Became a full member of the European Union (EU).

Azerbaijan Republic of

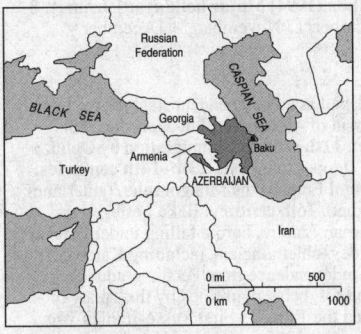

National name: *Azerbaijchan Respublikasy* **Area:** 86,600 sq km/33,436 sq mi **Capital:** Baku **Major towns/cities:** Gyandzha (formerly Kirovabad), Sumgait, Nakhichevan, Stepanakert **Physical features:** Caspian Sea with rich oil reserves; the country ranges from semidesert to the Caucasus Mountains

Government
Head of state: Geidar Aliyev from 1993 **Head of government:** Artur Rasizade from 1996 **Political system:** authoritarian nationalist **Administrative divisions:** 54 regions, 11 cities, and one autonomous republic (Nakhchyuan) **Political parties:** Popular

Front of Azerbaijan (FPA), democratic nationalist; New Azerbaijan, ex-communist; Communist Party of Azerbaijan (banned 1991–93); Muslim Democratic Party (Musavat), Islamic, pro-Turkic unity **Armed forces:** 70,700 (1996) **Conscription:** military service is for 17 months **Death penalty:** retained and used for ordinary crimes **Defence spend:** (% GDP) 5.8 (1996) **Education spend:** (% GNP) 5.5 (1993–94) **Health spend:** (% GDP) 1.4 (1990–95)

Economy and resources

Currency: manat (left rouble zone 1993) **GDP:** ($ US) 4 billion (1994) **Real GDP per capita (PPP):** ($ US) 1,670 (1994) **GDP growth rate:** –21.9% (1994); –20.2 (1990–95) **Average annual inflation:** 21% (1996) **Foreign debt:** ($ US) 321 million (1995) **Major trading partners:** Iran, Turkey, former USSR (principally Russia, Ukraine, and Turkmenistan), Greece **Resources:** petroleum, natural gas, iron ore, aluminium, copper, barytes, cobalt, precious metals, limestone, salt **Industries:** petroleum extraction and refining, chemicals, petrochemicals, construction, machinery, food processing, textiles, timber **Exports:** refined petroleum products, machinery, food products, textiles. Principal market: Iran 30% (1995) **Imports:** industrial raw materials, processed food, machinery. Principal source: Turkey 21.2% (1995) **Arable land:** 56.7% (1995) **Agricultural products:** grain, grapes and other fruit, vegetables, cotton, silk, tobacco; livestock rearing (cattle, sheep, and goats); fisheries (about 10 tonnes of caviar are produced annually); silkworm breeding

Population and society

Population: 7,594,000 (1996 est) **Population growth rate:** 1.2% (1990–95); 1% (2000–05) **Population density:** (per sq km) 88 (1996) **Urban population:** (% of total) 56 (1995) **Age distribution:** (% of total population) <15 31.8%, 15–65 62.3%, >65 5.9% (1995) **Ethnic groups:** 83% of Azeri descent, 6% Russian, 6% Armenian **Language:** Azeri **Religion:** Shi'ite Muslim 62%, Sunni Muslim 26%, Orthodox Christian 12% **Education:** (compulsory years) 11 **Literacy rate:** 96% (men); 96% (women) (1995 est) **Labour force:** 33.7% agriculture, 24.3% industry, 42% services (1991) **Unemployment:** 1% (1996) **Life expectancy:** 68 (men); 75 (women) (1995–2000) **Child mortality rate:** (under 5, per 1,000 live births) 37 (1996) **Physicians:** 1 per 278 people (1994 est)

Practical information

Visa requirements: UK: visa required. USA: visa required **Embassy in the UK:** 4 Kensington Court, London W8 5DL. Tel: (0171) 938 5482; fax: (0171) 937 1783 **British embassy:** c/o Old Intourist Hotel, Room 214, Baku. Tel: (12) 924 813; fax: (12) (873) 144 6456 **Chamber of commerce:** Chamber of Commerce and Industry, Istiglaliyat Street 31/33, 370001 Baku. Tel: (12) 928 912; fax: (12) 989 324 **Airports:** international airports: Baku; total passenger km: 1,731 million (1994) **Major holidays:** 1 January, 8 March, 28 May, 9, 18 October, 17 November, 31 December

Chronology

4th century BC: Established as an independent state for the first time by Atrophates, a vassal of Alexander III of Macedon. **7th century:** Spread of Islam. **11th century:** Immigration by Oghuz Seljuk peoples, from the steppes to the NE. **13th–14th centuries:** Incorporated within Mongol Empire; the Mongol ruler Tamerlane had his capital at Samarkand. **16th century:** Baku besieged and incorporated within Ottoman Empire, before falling under Persian dominance. **1805:** Khanates (chieftaincies), including Karabakh and Shirvan, which had won independence from Persia, gradually became Russian protectorates, being confirmed by the Treaty of Gulistan, which concluded the 1804–13 First Russo-Iranian War. **1828:** Under Treaty of Turkmenchai, which concluded the Second Russo-Iranian War begun in 1826, Persia was granted control over the S and Russia over N Azerbaijan. **late 19th century:** Petroleum industry developed, resulting in large influx of Slav immigrants to Baku, which supplied half of Russia's oil needs by 1901. **1906:** Himmat ('Effort') Party, linked to the Russian Social-Democrat Labour Party (Bolshevik), founded in Baku. **1912:** Himmat Party

banned; Islamic nationalist Musavat ('Equality') Party formed in Baku. **1917–18:** Member of anti-Bolshevik Transcaucasian Federation. **1918:** Became an independent republic. **1920:** Occupied by Red Army and subsequently forcibly secularized. **1922–36:** Became part of the Transcaucasian Federal Republic with Georgia and Armenia. **early 1930s:** Peasant uprisings against agricultural collectivization and Stalinist purges of the local Communist Party. **1936:** Became a constituent republic of the USSR. **late 1980s:** Growth in nationalist sentiment, taking advantage of the *glasnost* initiative of the reformist Soviet leader Mikhail Gorbachev. **1988:** Riots followed the request of Nagorno-Karabakh, an Armenian-peopled enclave within Azerbaijan, for transfer to Armenia. **1989:** Nagorno-Karabakh placed under direct rule from Moscow; civil war broke out with Armenia over Nagorno-Karabakh. **1990:** Soviet troops dispatched to Baku to restore order, amid Azeri calls for secession from USSR. **1991:** Independence declared after collapse of anti-Gorbachev coup in Moscow, which had been supported by Azeri communist leadership. Joined new Commonwealth of Independent States (CIS); Nagorno-Karabakh declared independence. **1992:** Admitted into United Nations and accorded diplomatic recognition by the USA; Albulfaz Elchibey, leader of the nationalist Popular Front, elected president; renewed campaign to capture Nagorno-Karabakh. **1993:** Elchibey fled military revolt, replaced in a coup by former Communist Party leader Geidar Aliyev, later elected president. Rebel military leader Surat Huseynov appointed prime minister. Nagorno-Karabakh overtaken by Armenian forces. **1994:** Nagorno-Karabakh cease-fire agreed. After coup attempt, Huseynov replaced as premier by Fuad Kuliyev. State of emergency imposed. **1995:** Attempted coup foiled. Pro-Aliyev legislature elected and market-centred economic reform programme introduced. **1996:** Kuliyev replaced by Artur Rasizade. **1997:** Border fighting with Armenia. Arkady Gukasyan elected president of Nagorno-Karabakh. Sharp rise in Caspian Sea oil extraction. Former president Elchibey returned from exile to lead opposition coalition.

Bahamas Commonwealth of the

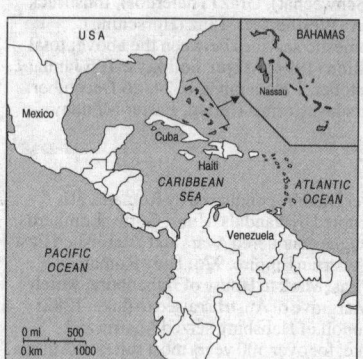

Area: 13,864 sq km/5,352 sq mi **Capital:** Nassau (on New Providence Island) **Major towns/cities:** Freeport (on Grand Bahama) **Physical features:** comprises 700 tropical coral islands and about 1,000 cays; the Exumas are a narrow spine of 365 islands; only 30 of the desert islands are inhabited; Blue Holes of Andros, the world's longest and deepest submarine caves **Principal islands:** Andros, Grand Bahama, Abaco, Eleuthera, New Providence, Berry Islands, Bimini Islands, Great Inagua, Acklins Island, Exuma Islands, Mayguana, Crooked Island, Long Island, Cat Islands, Rum Cay, Watling (San Salvador) Island, Inagua Islands

Government

Head of state: Elizabeth II from 1973, represented by governor general Orville Turnquest from 1995 **Head of government:** Hubert Ingraham from 1992 **Political system:** constitutional monarchy **Administrative divisions:** 21 districts **Political parties:** Progressive Liberal Party (PLP), centrist; Free National Movement (FNM), centre left **Armed forces:** a paramilitary coastguard numbering 900 (1996) **Conscription:** military service is voluntary **Death penalty:** retained and used for ordinary crimes **Defence**

spend: (% GDP) 0.6 (1996) **Education spend:** (% GNP) 3.9 (1993–94) **Health spend:** (% GDP) 2.5 (1994)

Economy and resources
Currency: Bahamian dollar **GDP:** ($ US) 3.4 billion (1994) **Real GDP per capita (PPP):** ($ US) 15,875 (1994) **GDP growth rate:** 0.3% (1994) **Average annual inflation:** 2% (1996) **Foreign debt:** ($ US) 380 million (1996) **Major trading partners:** USA, Aruba, UK, France, Canada **Resources:** aragonite (extracted from seabed), chalk, salt **Industries:** pharmaceutical chemicals, salt, rum, beer, cement, shipping, financial services, tourism **Exports:** foodstuffs (fish), oil products and transhipments, chemicals, rum, salt. Principal market: USA 23.7% (1995) **Imports:** machinery and transport equipment, basic manufactures, petroleum and products, chemicals. Principal source: USA 29.4% (1995) **Arable land:** 1% (1995) **Agricultural products:** sugar cane, cucumbers, tomatoes, pineapples, papayas, mangoes, avocados, limes and other citrus fruit; commercial fishing (conches and crustaceans)

Population and society
Population: 284,000 (1996 est) **Population growth rate:** 1.5% (1990–95) **Population density:** (per sq km) 20 (1996) **Urban population:** (% of total) 66 (1995) **Age distribution:** (% of total population) <15 30%, 15–65 65%, >65 5% (1994) **Ethnic groups:** about 85% of the population is of African origin, remainder mainly British, American, and Canadian **Language:** English and some Creole **Religion:** Christian 94% (Roman Catholic 26%, Anglican 21%, other Protestant 48%) **Education:** (compulsory years) 10 **Literacy rate:** 98% (men); 95% (women) (1995 est) **Labour force:** 50% of population: 6.5% agriculture, 12.1% industry, 81.4% services (1993) **Unemployment:** 13% (1994) **Life expectancy:** 70 (men); 79 (women) (1995–2000) **Child mortality rate:** (under 5, per 1,000 live births) 24 (1996) **Physicians:** 1 per 800 people (1994 est)

Practical information
Visa requirements: UK: visa not required. USA: visa not required **Embassy in the UK:** 10 Chesterfield St, London W1X 8AH. Tel: (0171) 408 4488; fax: (0171) 499 9937 **British embassy:** British High Commission, PO Box N-7516, 3rd Floor, Bitco Building, East St, Nassau. Tel: 325 7471/2/3; fax: 323 3871 **Chamber of commerce:** Bahamas Chamber of Commerce, Shirley St, POB N-665, Nassau. Tel: 322 2145; fax: 322 4649 **Airports:** international airports: Nassau, Freeport, Moss Town; four domestic airports serve internal chartered flights; total passenger km: 191 million (1994) **Major holidays:** 1 January, 10 July, 25–26 December; variable: Good Friday, Easter Monday, Whit Monday, Labour Day (June), Emancipation (August), Discovery (October)

Chronology
8th–9th centuries AD: Arawak Indians driven northwards to the islands by the Caribs. **1492:** First visited by Christopher Columbus; Arawaks deported to provide cheap labour for the gold and silver mines of Cuba and Hispaniola (Haiti). **1629:** The English king Charles I granted the islands to Robert Heath. **1666:** Colonization of New Providence island began. **1783:** Recovered after brief Spanish occupation and became a British colony, being settled during the American War of Independence by American loyalists, who brought with them black slaves. **1838:** Slaves were emancipated. **1940–45:** The Duke of Windsor, the former King Edward VIII, was governor of Bahamas. **from 1950s:** Major development of the tourist trade, especially from the USA. **1964:** Became internally self-governing. **1967:** First national assembly elections; Lynden Pindling, of the centrist Progressive Liberal Party (PLP), became prime minister. **1973:** Full independence achieved, within the British Commonwealth. **1983:** Allegations of drug trafficking by government ministers. **1984:** Deputy prime minister and two cabinet ministers resigned. Pindling denied any personal involvement and was endorsed as party leader. **1992:** Centre-left Free National Movement (FNM) led by Hubert Ingraham won absolute majority in assembly elections, ending 25 years of rule by Pindling.

Bahrain State of

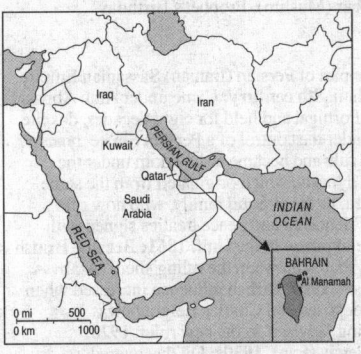

National name: *Dawlat al Bahrayn* **Area:** 688 sq km/266 sq mi **Capital:** Al Manamah on the largest island (also called Bahrain) **Major towns/cities:** Muharraq, Jiddhafs, Isa Town, Hidd, Rifa'a, Sitra **Major ports:** Mina Sulman **Physical features:** archipelago of 35 islands in Arabian Gulf, composed largely of sand-covered limestone; generally poor and infertile soil; flat and hot; causeway linking Bahrain to mainland Saudi Arabia

Government
Head of state: Sheik Isa bin Sulman al-Khalifa from 1961 **Head of government:** Sheik Khalifa bin Sulman al-Khalifa from 1970 **Political system:** absolute emirate **Administrative divisions:** 12 districts **Political parties:** none **Armed forces:** 11,000 (1996) **Conscription:** military service is voluntary **Death penalty:** retained and used for ordinary crimes **Defence spend:** (% GDP) 5.5 (1996) **Education spend:** (% GNP) 4.7 (1993–94) **Health spend:** (% GDP) 3.1 (1994)

Economy and resources
Currency: Bahraini dinar **GDP:** ($ US) 7.3 billion (1995 est) **Real GDP per capita (PPP):** ($ US) 12,000 (1994) **GDP growth rate:** 2.7% (1995 est) **Average annual inflation:** –1% (1996) **Foreign debt:** ($ US) 2.96 billion (1996) **Major trading partners:** USA, UK, Saudi Arabia, Japan, South Korea, Australia **Resources:** petroleum and natural gas **Industries:** petroleum refining, aluminium smelting, petrochemicals, shipbuilding and repairs, electronics assembly (banking) **Exports:** petroleum and petroleum products, aluminium. Principal market: India 21.5% (1994) **Imports:** crude petroleum, machinery and transport equipment, chemicals, basic manufactures. Principal source: Saudi Arabia 40% (1994) **Arable land:** 1.4% (1995) **Agricultural products:** dates, tomatoes, melons, vegetables; poultry products and fishing

Population and society
Population: 570,000 (1996 est) **Population growth rate:** 2.8% (1990–95) **Population density:** (per sq km) 840 (1996) **Urban population:** (% of total) 84 (1995) **Age distribution:** (% of total population) <15 32%, 15–65 65%, >65 3% (1994) **Ethnic groups:** about 73% Arab and 9% Iranian; Pakistani and Indian minorities **Language:** Arabic (official); Farsi, English, Urdu **Religion:** 85% Muslim (Shi'ite 60%, Sunni 40%), Christian; Islam is the state religion **Education:** (compulsory years) 12 **Literacy rate:** 89% (men); 79% (women) (1995 est) **Labour force:** 45% of population: 2% agriculture, 30% industry, 68% services (1990) **Unemployment:** 1.8% (1995 official rate; Western diplomats estimate 25–30%) **Life expectancy:** 71 (men); 75 (women) (1995–2000) **Child mortality rate:** (under 5, per 1,000 live births) 23 (1996) **Physicians:** 1 per 775 people (1991)

Practical information
Visa requirements: UK: visa not required. USA: visa required **Embassy in the UK:** 98 Gloucester Road, London SW7 4AV. Tel: (0171) 370 5132/3; fax: (0171) 370 7773 **British embassy:** PO Box 114, 21 Government Avenue, Manama, 306. Tel: (973) 534 404; fax: (973) 531 273 **Chamber of commerce:** Bahrain Chamber of Commerce and Industry, PO Box 248, Manama. Tel: (973) 233 913; fax: (973) 241 294 **Airports:** international airports: Muharraq

(Bahrain); total passenger km: 2,439 million (1994) **Major holidays:** 1 January, 16 December; variable: Eid-ul-Adha, Ashora, end of Ramadan, New Year (Muslim), Prophet's Birthday

Chronology

4th century AD: Became part of Persian (Iranian) Sassanian Empire. **7th century:** Adopted Islam. **8th century:** Came under Arab Abbasid control. **1521:** Seized by Portugal and held for eight decades, despite local unrest. **1602:** Fell under the control of a Persian Shi'ite dynasty. **1783:** Overthrew Persian rule and became a sheikdom under the Sunni Muslim al-Khalifa dynasty, which originated from the same tribal federation, the Anaza, as the al-Saud family, who now rule Saudi Arabia. **1816–20:** Friendship and peace treaties signed with Britain, which sought to end piracy in the Gulf. **1861:** Became British protectorate, government shared between the ruling sheik (Arab leader) and a British adviser. **1923:** British influence increased when Sheik Isa al-Khalifa was deposed and Charles Belgrave was appointed as the dominating 'adviser' to the new ruler. **1928:** Sovereignty claimed by Persia (Iran). **1930s:** Oil discovered, providing backbone for country's wealth. **1953–56:** Council for National Unity was formed by Arab nationalists, but suppressed after large demonstrations against British participation in the Suez War. **1968:** Britain announced its intention to withdraw its forces. Bahrain formed, with Qatar and the Trucial States of the United Arab Emirates, the Federation of Arab Emirates. **1970:** Iran accepted a United Nations (UN) report showing that Bahrain's inhabitants preferred independence to Iranian control. **1971:** Qatar and the Trucial States withdrew from the federation; Bahrain became an independent state under Sheik Sulman al-Khalifa. **1973:** New constitution adopted, with an elected national assembly dominated by left-nationalist Bahrain National Liberation Front (BNLF). **1975:** Prime minister Sheik al-Khalifa resigned; national assembly dissolved and political activists driven underground. Emir and his family assumed virtually absolute power. **early 1980s:** Tensions between the Sunni and Shi'ite Muslim communities heightened by Iranian Shi'ite Revolution of 1979. **1986:** Gulf University established in Bahrain. Causeway opened linking the island with Saudi Arabia. **1991:** Bahrain joined UN coalition that ousted Iraq from its occupation of Kuwait; signed defence cooperation agreement with USA. **1994:** Antimonarchy protests by Shi'ite Muslim majority community. **1995:** Sheik al-Khalifa reappointed prime minister. Prodemocracy demonstrations violently suppressed, with 11 deaths. **1996:** Emir proposed an expanded consultative assembly in move towards democracy.

Bangladesh People's Republic of (formerly East Pakistan)

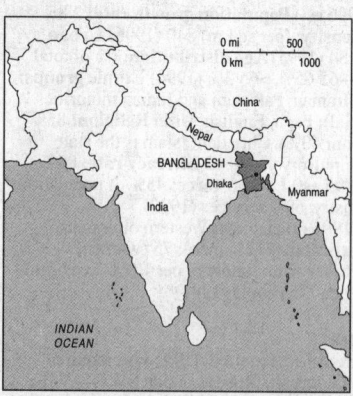

National name: *Gana Prajatantri Bangladesh* **Area:** 144,000 sq km/55,598 sq mi **Capital:** Dhaka (formerly Dacca) **Major towns/cities:** Rajshahi, Khulna, Chittagong, Comilla, Barisal, Sylhet **Major ports:** Chittagong, Khulna **Physical features:** flat delta of rivers Ganges (Padma) and Brahmaputra (Jamuna), the largest estuarine delta in the world; annual rainfall of 2,540 mm/100 in; some 75% of the land is less than 3 m/10 ft above sea level; hilly in extreme SE and NE

Government

Head of state: Abdur Rahman Biswas from 1991 **Head of government:** Sheikha Hasina Wazed from 1996 **Political system:** emergent democracy **Administrative divisions:** 64 districts within five divisions **Political parties:** Bangladesh Nationalist Party (BNP), Islamic, right of centre; Awami League (AL), secular, moderate socialist; Jatiya Dal (National Party), Islamic nationalist **Armed forces:** 117,500 (1996) **Conscription:** military service is voluntary **Death penalty:** retained and used for ordinary crimes **Defence spend:** (% GDP) 1.7 (1996) **Education spend:** (% GNP) 2.3 (1993–94) **Health spend:** (% GDP) 1.2 (1990–95)

Economy and resources

Currency: taka **GDP:** ($ US) 26.2 billion (1994) **Real GDP per capita (PPP):** ($ US) 1,330 (1994) **GDP growth rate:** 4.6% (1994); 4.1% (1990–95) **Average annual inflation:** 6.5% (1996) **Foreign debt:** ($ US) 18.2 billion (1996) **Major trading partners:** USA, Hong Kong, Japan, Singapore, UK **Resources:** natural gas, coal, limestone, china clay, glass sand **Industries:** textiles, food processing, industrial chemicals, petroleum refineries, cement **Exports:** raw jute and jute goods, tea, clothing, leather and leather products, shrimps and frogs' legs. Principal market: USA 31.5% (1995) **Imports:** wheat, crude petroleum and petroleum products, pharmaceuticals, cement, raw cotton, machinery and transport equipment. Principal source: India 15.3% (1995) **Arable land:** 65% (1995) **Agricultural products:** rice, jute, wheat, tobacco, tea; fishing and fish products

Population and society

Population: 120,073,000 (1996 est) **Population growth rate:** 2.2% (1990–95); 2% (2000–05) **Population density:** (per sq km) 834 (1996) **Urban population:** (% of total) 18 (1995) **Age distribution:** (% of total population) <15 39.5%, 15–65 57.5%, >65 3.1% (1995) **Ethnic groups:** 98% of Bengali descent, half a million Bihari, and around 1 million belonging to 'tribal' communities **Language:** Bengali (official); English **Religion:** Sunni Muslim 85%, Hindu 12%; Islam is the state religion **Education:** (compulsory years) 5 **Literacy rate:** 57% (men); 22% (women) (1995 est) **Labour force:** 49% of population: 56.5% agriculture, 9.8% industry, 33.7% services (1993) **Unemployment:** 30% (1991 est) **Life expectancy:** 58 (men); 58 (women) (1995–2000) **Child mortality rate:** (under 5, per 1,000 live births) 144 (1996) **Physicians:** 1 per 12,884 people (1993 est)

Practical information

Visa requirements: UK: visa required. USA: visa not required for a tourist visit of up to 15 days **Embassy in the UK:** 28 Queen's Gate, London SW7 5JA. Tel: (0171) 584 0081; fax: (0171) 255 2130 **British embassy:** British High Commission, PO Box 6079, United Nations Road, Baridhara, Dhaka 12. Tel: (2) 882 705; fax: (2) 883 437 **Chamber of commerce:** Federation of Bangladesh Chambers of Commerce and Industry, Federation Bhaban, 60 Motijheel C/A, 4th Floor, POB 2079, Dhaka 1000. Tel: (2) 250 566 **Airports:** international airports: Dhaka (Zia), Chittagong, Sylhet; seven domestic airports; total passenger km: 2,936 million (1994) **Major holidays:** 21 February, 26 March, 1 May, 1 July, 7 November, 16, 25, 31 December; variable: Eid-ul-Adha, end of Ramadan, New Year (Bengali), New Year (Muslim), Prophet's Birthday, Jumat-ul-Wida (May), Shab-e-Barat (April), Buddah Purnima (April/May), Shab-I-Qadr (May), Durga-Puza (October)

Chronology

c. 1000 BC: Arrival of Bang tribe in lower Ganges valley, establishing the kingdom of Banga (Bengal). **8th–12th centuries AD:** Bengal ruled successively by the Buddhist Pala and Hindu Senha dynasties. **1199:** Bengal was invaded and briefly ruled by the Muslim Khiljis from Central Asia. **1517:** Portuguese merchants arrived in Chittagong. **1576:** Bengal conquered by Muslim Mogul emperor Akbar. **1651:** British East India Company established a commercial factory in Bengal. **1757:** Bengal came under de facto British rule after Robert Clive defeated the nawab (ruler) of Bengal at Battle of Plassey. **1905–12:** Bengal briefly partitioned by the

British Raj between a Muslim-dominated E and Hindu-dominated W. **1906:** Muslim League (ML) founded in Dhaka. **1947:** Bengal formed into E province of Pakistan on partition of British India, with ML administration in power. **1952:** 12 students killed by troops in anti-Urdu and pro-Bengali language riots in Dhaka. **1954:** The opposition United Front, dominated by the Awami League (AL) and campaigning for East Bengal's autonomy, trounced ML in elections. **1955:** East Bengal renamed East Pakistan. **1966:** Sheik Mujibur Rahman of AL announced a Six-Point Programme of autonomy for East Pakistan. **1970:** 500,000 people killed in cyclone. Pro-autonomy AL secured crushing electoral victory in East Pakistan. **1971:** Bangladesh ('land of the Bangla speakers') emerged as independent nation, under leadership of Sheik Mujibur Rahman, after bloody civil war with Indian military intervention on the side of East Pakistan; 10 million refugees fled to India. **1974:** Hundreds of thousands died in famine; state of emergency declared. **1975:** Mujibur Rahman assassinated. Martial law imposed. **1976–77:** Maj-Gen Zia ur-Rahman assumed power as president. **1978–79:** Elections held and civilian rule restored with clear victory for Zia's BNP. **1981:** Maj-Gen Zia assassinated during attempted military coup. Abdul Sattar (BNP) elected president. **1982:** Lt-Gen Hussain Mohammed Ershad assumed power in army coup. Martial law reimposed; market-oriented economic programme adopted. **1986:** Elections held but disputed and boycotted by BNP. Martial law ended. **1987:** State of emergency declared in response to opposition demonstrations and violent strikes. **1988:** Assembly elections boycotted by main opposition parties. State of emergency lifted. Islam made state religion. Monsoon floods left 30 million homeless and thousands dead. **1989:** Power devolved to Chittagong Hill Tracts to end 14-year conflict between local people and army-protected settlers. **1990:** Following mass anti-government protests, President Ershad resigned; chief justice Shahabuddin Ahmad became interim president. **1991:** Former president Ershad jailed for corruption and illegal possession of arms. Cyclone killed around 139,000 and left up to 10 million homeless. Elections resulted in coalition government with BNP dominant. Parliamentary government restored, with Abdur Rahman Biswas as president and Begum Khaleda Zia prime minister. **1994–95:** Opposition boycotted parliament, charging government with fraud. **1996:** Zia handed over power to neutral caretaker government. General election won by AL, led by Sheika Hasina Wazed, daughter of Sheik Mujibur Rahman. BNP boycotted parliament. Agreement with India on sharing of River Ganges water. **1997:** Former president Ershad released from prison. BNP boycotted parliament and called a one-day strike in protest against government 'repression'.

Barbados

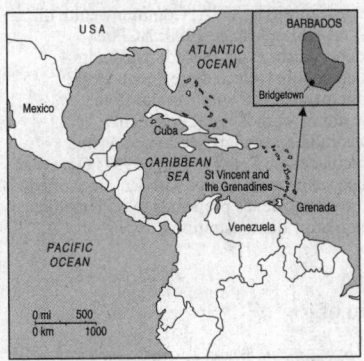

Area: 430 sq km/166 sq mi **Capital:** Bridgetown **Major towns/cities:** Speightstown, Holetown, Oistins **Physical features:** most easterly island of the West Indies; surrounded by coral reefs; subject to hurricanes June–November; highest point Mount Hillaby 340 m/1,115 ft

Government
Head of state: Elizabeth II from 1966, represented by Denys Williams from 1995 **Head of government:** Owen Arthur from 1994 **Political system:** constitutional monarchy **Administrative divisions:** 11 parishes **Political parties:** Barbados Labour Party (BLP), moderate left of centre; Democratic Labour Party (DLP), moderate left of centre; National Democratic Party (NDP), centrist **Armed forces:** 600 (1996) **Conscription:** military service is voluntary **Death penalty:** retained and used for ordinary crimes **Defence spend:** (% GDP) 0.7 (1996) **Education spend:** (% GNP) 7.5 (1993–94) **Health spend:** (% GDP) 10 (1990)

Economy and resources
Currency: Barbados dollar **GDP:** ($ US) 1.7 billion (1994) **Real GDP per capita (PPP):** ($ US) 11,051 (1994) **GDP growth rate:** 4.1% (1994) **Average annual inflation:** 3.3% (1996) **Foreign debt:** ($ US) 590 million (1996) **Major trading partners:** USA, Trinidad and Tobago, Canada, Jamaica, St Lucia **Resources:** petroleum and natural gas **Industries:** sugar refining, food processing, industrial chemicals, beverages, tobacco, household applicances, electrical components, plastic products, electronic parts, tourism **Exports:** sugar, molasses, syrup-rum, chemicals, electrical components. Principal market: USA 20% (1995) **Imports:** machinery, foodstuffs, motor cars, construction materials, basic manufactures. Principal source: USA 30% (1995) **Arable land:** 37.2% (1995) **Agricultural products:** sugar cane, cotton, sweet potatoes, yams, carrots and other vegetables; fishing (740 fishing vessels employed in 1994)

Population and society
Population: 261,000 (1996 est) **Population growth rate:** 0.3% (1990–95) **Population density:** (per sq km) 608 (1996) **Urban population:** (% of total) 48% (1995) **Age distribution:** (% of total population) <15 24%, 15–65 64%, >65 12% (1994) **Ethnic groups:** about 80% of African descent, about 16% mixed ethnicity, and 4% of European origin (mostly British) **Language:** English and Bajan (Barbadian English dialect) **Religion:** 33% Anglican, 13% Pentecostalist, 6% Methodist, 4% Roman Catholic **Education:** (compulsory years) 12 **Literacy rate:** 98% (men); 97% (women) (1995 est) **Labour force:** 5.9% agriculture, 18.7% industry, 65% services (1994) **Unemployment:** 15.6% (1996) **Life expectancy:** 74 (men); 79 (women) (1995–2000) **Child mortality rate:** (under 5, per 1,000 live births) 15 (1996) **Physicians:** 1 per 1,100 people (1993)

Practical information
Visa requirements: UK: visa not required (some visitors will require a business visa). USA: visa not required (some visitors will require a business visa) **Embassy in the UK:** High Commission, 1 Great Russell Street, London WCN 22B 3JY. Tel: (0171) 631 4975; fax: (0171) 323 6872 **British embassy:** British High Commission, PO Box 676, Lower Collymore Rock, St Michael. Tel: 436 6694; fax: 436 5398 **Chamber of commerce:** Barbados Chamber of Commerce Inc, Nemwil House, 1st Floor, Lower Collymore Rock, PO Box 189, St Michael. Tel: 426 2056; fax: 429 2907 **Airports:** international airports: Bridgetown (Grantley Adams) **Major holidays:** 1 January, 30 November, 25–26 December; variable: Good Friday, Easter Monday, Whit Monday, Kadooment (August), May Holiday, United Nations (October)

Chronology
1536: Visited by Portuguese explorer Pedro a Campos and the name Los Barbados ('The Bearded Ones') given in reference to its 'bearded' fig trees. Indigineous Arawak people was virtually wiped out, via epidemics, after contact with Europeans. **1627:** British colony established; developed as a sugar-plantation economy, initially on basis of black slaves brought in from W Africa. **1639:** Island's first parliament, the House of Assembly, established. **1816:** Last and largest-ever revolt by slaves led by Bussa. **1834:** Slaves freed. **1937:** Outbreak of riots, followed by the establishment of the Barbados Labour Party (BLP) by Grantley Adams, and moves towards a more independent political system. **1951:** Universal adult suffrage introduced. BLP won general election. **1954:** Ministerial government established, with BLP leader Adams as first prime minister. **1955:** A group broke away from the BLP and formed the Democratic Labour Party (DLP). **1961:** Independence achieved from Britain. DLP, led by Errol Barrow, in power. **1966:** Barbados achieved full independence within Commonwealth, with Barrow as prime minister. **1967:** Became a member of the United Nations.

1972: Diplomatic relations with Cuba established. **1976:** BLP, led by Tom Adams, the son of Grantley Adams, returned to power. **1983:** Barbados supported US invasion of Grenada. **1985:** Adams died; Bernard St John became prime minister. **1986:** DLP, led by Barrow, returned to power. **1987:** Barrow died; Erskine Lloyd Sandiford became prime minister. **1994:** BLP, led by Owen Arthur, won decisive election victory.

Belarus Republic of

National name: *Respublika Belarus* **Area:** 207,600 sq km/80,154 sq mi **Capital:** Minsk (Mensk) **Major towns/cities:** Gomel, Vitebsk, Mogilev, Bobruisk, Hrodna, Brest **Physical features:** more than 25% forested; rivers Dvina, Dnieper and its tributaries, including the Pripet and Beresina; the Pripet Marshes in the E; mild and damp climate

Government

Head of state: Alexandr Lukashenko from 1994 **Head of government:** Syargey Ling from 1996 **Political system:** emergent democracy **Administrative divisions:** six regions (oblasts) **Political parties:** Belarus Communist Party (BCP, banned 1991–92); Belarus Patriotic Movement (BPM), populist; Belarusian Popular Front (BPF; Adradzhenne), moderate nationalist; Christian Democratic Union of Belarus, centrist; Socialist Party of Belarus, left of centre **Armed forces:** 85,500 (1996) **Conscription:** compulsory for 18 months **Death penalty:** retained and used for ordinary crimes **Defence spend:** (% GDP) 4.2 (1996) **Education spend:** (% GNP) 4.5 (1995 est) **Health spend:** (% GDP) 3.4 (1995)

Economy and resources

Currency: rouble and zaichik **GDP:** ($ US) 20 billion (1994) **Real GDP per capita (PPP):** ($ US) 4,713 (1994) **GDP growth rate:** –10.1% (1995); –9.3% (1990–95) **Average annual inflation:** 50% (1996) **Foreign debt:** ($ US) 1.65 billion (1995) **Major trading partners:** former USSR (principally Russia, Ukraine, and Kazakhstan), Germany, Poland, USA **Resources:** petroleum, natural gas, peat, salt, coal, lignite **Industries:** machine building, metalworking, electronics, chemicals, construction materials, food processing, textiles **Exports:** machinery, chemicals and petrochemicals, iron and steel, light industrial goods. Principal market: Russia 41.6% (1996) **Imports:** petroleum, natural gas, chemicals, machinery, processed foods. Principal source: Russia 50.5% (1996) **Arable land:** 29.3% (1995) **Agricultural products:** potatoes, grain, sugar beet; livestock rearing (cattle and pigs) and dairy products. Livestock sector accounts for approximately 60% of agricultural output

Population and society

Population: 10,138,000 (1996 est) **Population growth rate:** –0.1% (1990–95); –0.1% (2000–05) **Population density:** (per sq km) 88 (1996 est) **Urban population:** (% of total) 71 (1995) **Age distribution:** (% of total population) <15 21.6%, 15–65 65.8%, >65 12.6% (1995) **Ethnic groups:** 75% of Belarusian ('eastern Slav') descent, 13% ethnic Russian, 4% Polish, 3% Ukranian, 1% Jewish **Language:** Belarusian (official); Russian, Polish **Religion:** Russian Orthodox, Roman Catholic; Baptist, Muslim, and Jewish minorities **Education:** (compulsory years) 11 **Literacy rate:** 98% (men); 98%

(women) (1995 est) **Labour force:** 21.2% agriculture, 34.9% industry, 43.9% services (1994) **Unemployment:** 3.8% (1996) **Life expectancy:** 68 (men); 75 (women) (1995–2000) **Child mortality rate:** (under 5, per 1,000 live births) 19 (1996) **Physicians:** 1 per 243 people (1995)

Practical information

Visa requirements: UK: visa required. USA: visa required **Embassy in the UK:** 6 Kensington Court, London W8 5DL. Tel: (0171) 937 3288; fax: (0171) 3361 0005 **British embassy:** Zakharova 26, 220034 Minsk. Tel: (172) 368 687; fax: (172) 144 7226 **Chamber of commerce:** Chamber of Commerce and Industry, Masherava 14, 220600 Minsk. Tel: (172) 269 172; fax: (172) 269 860 **Airports:** international airports: Minsk; total passenger km: 2,604 million (1994) **Major holidays:** 1, 7 January, 8 March, 1, 9 May, 3, 27 July, 2 November, 25 December; variable: Good Friday, Easter Monday

Chronology

5th–8th centuries: Settled by East Slavic tribes, ancestors of present-day Belarusians. **11th century:** Minsk founded. **12th century:** Part of Kievan Russia, to the S, with independent Belarus state developing around Polotsk, on River Dvina. **14th century:** Incorporated within Slavonic Grand Duchy of Lithuania, to the W. **1569:** Union with Poland. **late 18th century:** Came under control of tsarist Russia as Belarussia ('White Russia'), following three partitions of Poland in 1772, 1793, and 1795. **1812:** Minsk destroyed by French emperor Napoleon Bonaparte during his military campaign against Russia. **1839:** Belarusian Catholic Church forcibly abolished. **1914–18:** Belarus was the site of fierce fighting between Germany and Russia during World War I. **1918–19:** Briefly independent from Russia. **1919–20:** Wars between Poland and Soviet Russia over control of Belarus. **1921:** West Belarus ruled by Poland; East Belarus became a Soviet republic. **1930s:** Agriculture collectivized despite peasant resistance; more than 100,000 people, chiefly writers and intellectuals, shot in mass executions ordered by Soviet dictator Joseph Stalin. **1939:** West Belarus occupied by Soviet troops. **1941–44:** Nazi occupation resulted in the death of 1.3 million people, including many Jews; Minsk destroyed. **1945:** Became founding member of the United Nations; much of West Belarus incorporated into the Soviet republic. **1950s–60s:** Large-scale immigration of ethnic Russians and 'Russification'. **1986:** Fallout from the nearby Chernobyl nuclear reactor in Ukraine rendered a fifth of agricultural land unusable. **1989:** Belarusian Popular Front established as national identity revived under *glasnost* initiative of Soviet leader Mikhail Gorbachev. **1990:** Belarusian established as state language and republican sovereignty declared. **1991:** Strikes and unrest in Minsk; BCP suspended following attempted coup against Gorbachev in Moscow; moderate nationalist Stanislav Shushkevich elected president. Independence recognized by USA; Commonwealth of Independent States (CIS) formed in Minsk. **1993:** BCP re-established. **1994:** President Shushkevich ousted; Alexandre Lukashenko, a pro-Russian populist, elected president. **1995:** Friendship and cooperation pact signed with Russia. **1996:** Agreement on 'economic union' with Russia. President's referendum for a new constitution popularly endorsed. Prime Minister Mikhas Chygir replaced by Syargey Ling. **1997:** Observer status in Council of Europe suspended. Treaty with Russia ratified. Council of Republic rejected President's proposals to curb media. Anti-government pro-democracy demonstrations.

Belgium Kingdom of

National name: French *Royaume de Belgique* , Flemish *Koninkrijk België* **Area:** 30,510 sq km/11,779 sq mi **Capital:** Brussels **Major towns/cities:** Antwerp, Ghent, Liège, Charleroi, Bruges, Mons, Namur, Leuven **Major ports:** Antwerp, Ostend, Zeebrugge **Physical features:** fertile coastal plain in NW, central rolling hills rise eastwards, hills and forest in SE; Ardennes Forest; rivers Schelde and Meuse

Government

Head of state: King Albert from 1993 **Head of government:** Jean-Luc Dehaene from 1992 **Political system:** federal constitutional monarchy **Administrative divisions:** ten provinces within three regions **Political parties:** Flemish Christian Social Party (CVP), centre left; French Social Christian Party (PSC), centre left; Flemish Socialist Party (SP), left of centre; French Socialist Party (PS), left of centre; Flemish Liberal Party (PVV), moderate centrist; French Liberal Reform Party (PRL), moderate centrist; Flemish People's Party (VU), federalist; Flemish Vlaams Blok, right wing; Flemish Green Party (Agalev); French Green Party (Ecolo) **Armed forces:** 46,300 (1996) **Conscription:** abolished 1995 **Death penalty:** abolished 1996 **Defence spend:** (% GDP) 1.6 (1996) **Education spend:** (% GNP) 5.6 (1993–94) **Health spend:** (% GDP) 7.2 (1994)

Economy and resources

Currency: Belgian franc **GDP:** ($ US) 264.4 billion (1996) **Real GDP per capita (PPP):** ($ US) 21,454 (1996) **GDP growth rate:** 2.4% (1996); 1.1% (1990–95) **Average annual inflation:** 1.9% (1996); 3.1% (1985–95) **Major trading partners:** Germany, the Netherlands, Belgium, Luxembourg, France, UK, USA **Resources:** coal, coke, natural gas, iron **Industries:** wrought and finished steel, cast iron, sugar refining, glassware, chemicals and related products, beer, textiles, rubber and plastic products **Exports:** food, livestock and livestock products, gem diamonds, iron and steel manufacturers, machinery and transport equipment, chemicals and related products. Principal market: Germany 20.6% (1996) **Imports:** food and live animals, machinery and transport equipment, precious metals and stones, mineral fuels and lubricants, chemicals and related products. Principal source: Germany 19.9% (1996) **Arable land:** 22% (1995) **Agricultural products:** wheat, barley, potatoes, beet (sugar and fodder), fruit, tobacco; livestock (pigs and cattle) and dairy products

Population and society

Population: 10,159,000 (1996 est) **Population growth rate:** 0.3% (1990–95); 0.1% (2000–05) **Population density:** (per sq km) 333 (1996 est) **Urban population:** (% of total) 97 (1995) **Age distribution:** (% of total population) <15 17.8%, 15–65 66.4%, >65 15.8% **Ethnic groups:** mainly Flemings in N, Walloons in S **Language:** in the N (Flanders) Flemish (a Dutch dialect, known as *Vlaams*) 55%; in the S (Wallonia) Walloon (a French dialect) 32%; bilingual 11%; German (E border) 0.6%. Dutch is official in the N, French in the S; Brussels is officially bilingual **Religion:** Roman Catholic 75%, various Protestant denominations **Education:** (compulsory years) 12 **Literacy rate:** 99% (men); 99% (women) (1995 est) **Labour force:** 42.2% of population: 2.6% agriculture, 27.7% industry, 69.7% services (1992) **Unemployment:** 9.8% (1996) **Life expectancy:** 74 (men); 81 (women) (1995–2000) **Child mortality rate:** (under 5, per 1,000 live births) 7 (1996) **Physicians:** 1 per 267 people (1995)

Practical information

Visa requirements: UK: visa not required. USA: visa not required **Embassy in the UK:** 103–105 Eaton Square, London SW1W 9AB. Tel: (0171) 470 3700; fax: (0171) 259 6213 **British embassy:** 85 rue d'Arlon, B-1040 Brussels. Tel: (2) 287 6211; fax: (2) 287 6355 **Chamber of commerce:** Kamer van Koophandel en Nijverheid van Antwerpen, 12 Markgravestraat, B-2000 Antwerp. Tel: (3) 232 2219; fax: (3) 233 6442. Chambre de Commerce et d'Industrie de Bruxelles, 500 ave Louise, 1050 Brussels. Tel: (2) 648 5002; fax: (2) 640 9228 **Airports:** international airports: Brussels (Zaventem), Antwerp (Deurne), Ostend, Liège, Charleroi; total passenger km: 7,496 million (1994) **Major holidays:** 1 January, 30 November, 25–26 December; variable: Ascension Thursday, Easter Monday, Whit Monday, May, August, and November holidays

Chronology

57 BC: Romans conquered the Belgae (the indigenous Celtic people), and formed province of Belgica. **3rd–4th centuries AD:** Region overrun by Franks and Saxons. **8th–9th centuries:** Part of Frankish Empire; peace and order fostered growth of Ghent, Bruges, and Brussels. **843:** Division of Holy Roman Empire; became part of Lotharingia, but frequent repartitioning followed. **10th–11th centuries:** Seven feudal states emerged: Flanders, Hainaut, Namur, Brabant, Limburg, and Luxembourg, all nominally subject to French king or Holy Roman emperor, but in practice independent. **12th century:** Economy began to flourish: textiles in Bruges, Ghent, and Ypres; copper and tin in Dinant and Liège. **15th century:** One by one, states came under rule of dukes of Burgundy. **1477:** Passed into Habsburg dominions through marriage of Mary of Burgundy to Maximilian, archduke of Austria. **1555:** Division of Habsburg dominions; Low Countries allotted to Spain. **1648:** Independence of Dutch Republic recognized; S retained by Spain. **1713:** Treaty of Utrecht transferred Spanish Netherlands to Austrian rule. **1792–97:** Austrian Netherlands invaded by revolutionary France and finally annexed. **1815:** Congress of Vienna reunited N and S Netherlands as one kingdom under House of Orange. **1830:** Largely French-speaking people in S rebelled against union with Holland and declared Belgian independence. **1831:** Leopold of Saxe-Coburg-Gotha became first king of Belgium. **1839:** Treaty of London recognized independence of Belgium and guaranteed its neutrality. **1847–70:** Government dominated by Liberals; growth of heavy industry. **1870–1914:** Catholic Party predominant. **1914–18:** Invaded and occupied by Germany. Belgian forces under King Albert I fought in conjunction with Allies. **1919:** Acquired Eupen-Malmédy region from Germany. **1940:** Second invasion by Germany; King Leopold III ordered Belgian army to capitulate. **1944–45:** Belgium liberated. **1948:** Belgium formed Benelux customs union with Luxembourg and the Netherlands. **1949:** Belgium was a founding member of North Atlantic Treaty Organization (NATO). **1951:** Leopold III abdicated in favour of his son Baudouin. **1958:** Belgium was a founding member of European Economic Community (EEC), which made Brussels its headquarters. **1967:** NATO made Brussels its headquarters. **1971:** Constitution amended to safeguard cultural rights of Flemish- (in Flanders in N) and French-speaking communities (Walloons in SE) in an effort to ease linguistic dispute. **1974:** Separate regional councils and ministerial committees established for Flemings and Walloons. **1980:** Open violence over language divisions; regional assemblies for Flanders and Wallonia and three-member executive for Brussels created. **1993:** Federal system adopted, based on Flanders, Wallonia, and Brussels. King Baudouin died, succeeded by his brother Albert. **1995:** Dehaene-led coalition re-elected.

Belize (formerly British Honduras)

Area: 22,963 sq km/8,866 sq mi **Capital:** Belmopan **Major towns/cities:** Belize City, Dangriga, Orange Walk, Corozal **Major ports:** Belize City, Dangriga, Punta Gorda **Physical features:** tropical swampy coastal plain, Maya Mountains in S; over 90% forested

Government

Head of state: Elizabeth II from 1981, represented by governor general Dr Norbert Colville Young from 1993 **Head of government:** Manuel Esquivel from 1993 **Political system:** constitutional monarchy **Administrative divisions:** six districts

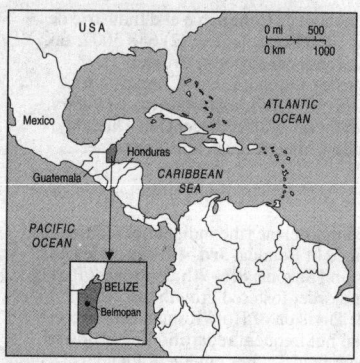

Political parties:
People's United
Party (PUP), left of
centre; United
Democratic Party
(UDP), moderate
conservative
Armed forces:
1,100 (1996); plus
700 militia reserves
Conscription:
military service is
voluntary **Death
penalty:** retained
and used for
ordinary crimes
Defence spend: (%
GDP) 2.5 (1996)
Education spend: (% GNP) 5.9 (1995) **Health spend:** (% GDP)
5.7 (1995)

Economy and resources

Currency: Belize dollar **GDP:** ($ US) 552 million (1994) **Real GDP
per capita (PPP):** ($ US) 5,590 (1994) **GDP growth rate:** 1.6%
(1994) **Average annual inflation:** 40% (1996); 3.5% (1985–95)
Foreign debt: ($ US) 185 million (1996) **Major trading partners:**
USA, UK, Mexico, Canada **Industries:** clothing, agricultural
products (particularly sugar cane for sugar and rum), timber, tobacco
Exports: sugar, clothes, citrus products, forestry and fish products,
bananas. Principal market: UK 40.2% (1994) **Imports:** foodstuffs,
machinery and transport equipment, mineral fuels, chemicals, basic
manufactures. Principal source: USA 53.1% (1994) **Arable land:**
2.6% (1995) **Agricultural products:** sugar cane, citrus fruits,
bananas, maize, red kidney beans, rice; livestock rearing (cattle, pigs,
and poultry); fishing; timber reserves

Population and society

Population: 219,000 (1996 est) **Population growth rate:** 2.6%
(1990–95); 2.3% (2000–05) **Population density:** (per sq km) 10
(1996 est) **Urban population:** (% of total) 47 (1995) **Age
distribution:** (% of total population) <15 42.3%, 15–65 53.5%, >65
4.2% (1995) **Ethnic groups:** Creoles, Mestizos, Caribs, East Indians,
Mennonites, Canadians and Europeans, including Spanish and British
Language: English (official); Spanish (widely spoken), Creole
dialects **Religion:** Roman Catholic 60%, Protestant 35% **Education:**
(compulsory years) 10 **Literacy rate:** 93% (men); 93% (women)
(1994) **Labour force:** 31% of population: 34% agriculture, 19%
industry, 48% services (1990) **Unemployment:** 13.1% (1994) **Life
expectancy:** 73 (men); 76 (women) (1995–2000) **Child mortality
rate:** (under 5, per 1,000 live births) 37 (1996) **Physicians:** 1 per
2,127 people (1993)

Practical information

Visa requirements: UK: visa not required. USA: visa not required
Embassy in the UK: 22 Harcourt House, 19 Cavendish Square,
London W1M 9AD. Tel: (0171) 499 9728; fax: (0171) 491 4139
British embassy: British High Commission, PO Box 91, Embassy
Square, Belmopan. Tel: (8) 22146/7; fax: (8) 22761 **Chamber of
commerce:** Belize Chamber of Commerce and Industry, 63 Regent
Street, POB 291, Belize City. Tel: (2) 75924; fax: (2) 74984
Airports: international airports: Belize City (Philip S W Goldson);
domestic air services provide connections to major towns and
offshore islands **Major holidays:** 1 January, 9 March, 1, 24 May,
10, 24 September, 12 October, 19 November, 25–26 December;
variable: Good Friday, Easter Monday, Holy Saturday

Chronology

325–925 AD: Part of the Native American Maya civilization. **1600s:**
Colonized by British buccaneers and log-cutters **1862:** Formally
declared a British colony, known as British Honduras. **1893:**
Mexico renounced its long-standing claim to the territory. **1954:**
Constitution adopted, providing for limited internal self-
government. General election won by PUP led by George Price.

1964: Self-government achieved from the UK. Universal adult
suffrage and a two-chamber legislature introduced. **1970:** Capital
moved from Belize City to new town of Belmopan. **1973:** Name
changed to Belize. **1975:** British troops sent to defend the long-
disputed frontier with Guatemala. **1980:** United Nations called for
full independence. **1981:** Full independence achieved, with Price as
prime minister. **1984:** Price defeated in general election. Manuel
Esquivel of the right-of-centre United Democratic Party (UDP)
formed government. The UK reaffirmed its undertaking to defend
the frontier. **1989:** Price and PUP won general election. **1991:**
Diplomatic relations re-established with Guatemala, which finally
recognized Belize's sovereignty. **1993:** UDP defeated PUP in
general election; Esquivel returned as prime minister. UK
announced intention to withdraw troops following resolution of the
border dispute with Guatemala.

Benin People's Republic of (formerly known as Dahomey 1904–75)

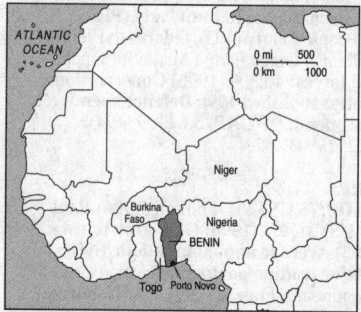

National name:
*République
Populaire du Bénin*
Area: 112,622 sq
km/43,483 sq mi
Capital: Porto-
Novo (official),
Cotonou (de facto)
Major towns/cities:
Abomey, Natitin-
gou, Parakou, Kandi,
Ouidah, Djougou,
Bohicou **Major
ports:** Cotonou
Physical features:
flat to undulating terrain; hot and humid in S; semiarid in N; coastal
lagoons with fishing villages on stilts; Niger River in NE

Government

Head of state and government: Mathieu Kerekou from 1996
Political system: socialist pluralist republic **Administrative
divisions:** six provinces **Political parties:** Union for the Triumph of
Democratic Renewal (UTDR); National Party for Democracy and
Development (PNDD); Party for Democratic Renewal (PRD); Social
Democratic Party (PSD); National Union for Solidarity and Progress
(UNSP); National Democratic Rally (RND). The general orientation
of most parties is left of centre **Armed forces:** 4,800 (1996)
Conscription: by selective conscription for 18 months **Death
penalty:** retained and used for ordinary crimes **Defence spend:** (%
GDP) 1.4 (1996) **Education spend:** (% GNP) 5.6 (1990) **Health
spend:** (% GDP) 1.7 (1993)

Economy and resources

Currency: franc CFA **GDP:** ($ US) 1.5 billion (1994) **Real GDP
per capita (PPP):** ($ US) 1,696 (1994) **GDP growth rate:** 4.8%
(1994) **Average annual inflation:** 9% (1996) **Foreign debt:** ($ US)
1.7 billion (1995) **Major trading partners:** Morocco, France,
USA, Portugal, China, Ghana, Nigeria, Thailand, Côte d'Ivoire,
Italy **Resources:** petroleum, limestone, marble **Industries:** palm-oil
processing, brewing, cement, cotton ginning, sugar refining, textiles
Exports: cotton, crude petroleum, palm oil and other palm
products. Principal market: Morocco 37.6% (1994) **Imports:**
foodstuffs (particularly cereals), miscellaneous manufactured
articles (notably cotton yarn and fabrics), fuels, machinery and
transport equipment, chemicals, beverages, tobacco. Principal
source: France 24.3% (1994) **Arable land:** 12% (1995)
Agricultural products: cotton, maize, yarns, cassava, sorghum,
millet; fishing

Population and society

Population: 5,563,000 (1996 est) **Population growth rate:** 3.1%
(1990–95); 2.8% (2000–05) **Population density:** (per sq km) 49

(1996 est) **Urban population:** (% of total) 31 (1995) **Age distribution:** (% of total population) <15 47.4%, 15–65 49.7%, >65 2.8% (1995) **Ethnic groups:** 98% indigenous African, distributed among 42 ethnic groups, the largest being the Fon, Adja, Yoruba, and Braiba; small European (mainly French) community **Language:** French (official); Fon 47% and Yoruba 9% in S; six major tribal languages in N **Religion:** animist 60%, Muslim, Roman Catholic **Education:** (compulsory years) 6 **Literacy rate:** 32% (men); 16% (women) (1995 est) **Labour force:** 46% of population: 64% agriculture, 8% industry, 28% services (1990) **Life expectancy:** 47 (men); 51 (women) (1995–2000) **Child mortality rate:** (under 5, per 1,000 live births) 158 (1996) **Physicians:** 1 per 16,000 people (1994 est)

Practical information
Visa requirements: UK: visa required. USA: visa required **Embassy in the UK:** Dolphin House, 16 The Broadway, Stanmore, Middlesex HA7 4DW. Tel: (0181) 954 8800; fax: (0181) 954 8844 **British embassy:** British Consulate, Lot 24, Patte d'oie, Cotonou. (All staff based in Nigeria.) Tel: 301120 **Chamber of commerce:** Chambre de Commerce, d'Agriculture et d'Industrie de la République du Bénin, ave du Général de Gaulle, BP31, Cotonou. Tel: 313 299 **Airports:** international airports: Cotonou (Cootonou-Cadjehoun); four domestic airports; total passenger km: 215 million (1994) **Major holidays:** 1, 16 January, 1 April, 1 May, 26 October, 30 November, 25, 31 December; variable: Eid-ul-Adha, end of Ramadan, Good Friday, Easter Monday, Whit Monday

Chronology
12th–13th centuries: Settled by Ewe-speaking people, called the Aja, who mixed with local peoples and gradually formed the Fon ethnic group. **16th century:** Aja kingdom, called Great Ardha, at its peak. **early 17th century:** Kingdom of Dahomey established in S by Fon peoples, who defeated the neighbouring Dan; following contact with European traders, the kingdom became became an intermediary in the slave trade, which was particularly active along the Bight (Bay) of Benin, between Ghana and Nigeria, during the 16th–19th centuries. **1800–50:** King Dezo of Dahomey raised regiments of female soldiers to attack the Yoruba ('land of the big cities') kingdom of E Benin and SW Nigeria to obtain slaves; palm-oil trade developed. **1857:** French base established at Grand-Popo. **1892–94:** War between the French and Dahomey, after which the victorious French established a protectorate. **1899:** Incorporated in federation of French West Africa as Dahomey. **1914:** French troops from Dahomey participated in conquest of German-ruled Togoland to W, during World War I. **1940–44:** Along with the rest of French West Africa, supported the 'Free French' anti-Nazi resistance cause during World War II. **1960:** Independence achieved from France. **1960–72:** Acute political instability, with frequent switches from civilian to military rule, and regional ethnic disputes. **1972:** Military regime established by Major Mathieu Kerekou. **1974:** Kerekou announced that country would follow a path of 'scientific socialism'. **1975:** Name of country changed from Dahomey to Benin. **1977:** Return to civilian rule under new constitution, but with Kerekou as president. **1989:** Army deployed against antigovernment strikers and protesters, inspired by E European revolutions; Marxist-Leninism dropped as official ideology and market-centred economic reform programme adopted. **1990:** Referendum backed establishment of multiparty politics. **1991:** In multiparty elections, President Kerekou was replaced by the leader of the new Benin Renaissance Party (PRB), Nicéphore Soglo, who formed a ten-party coalition government. **1996:** Kerekou defeated Soglo in presidential election run-off despite opposition claims of fraud.

Bhutan Kingdom of

National name: *Druk-yul* **Area:** 46,500 sq km/17,953 sq mi **Capital:** Thimphu (Thimbu) **Major towns/cities:** Paro, Punakha, Mongar, P'sholing, W'phodrang, Bumthang **Physical features:** occupies southern slopes of the Himalayas; Gangkar Punsum (7,529

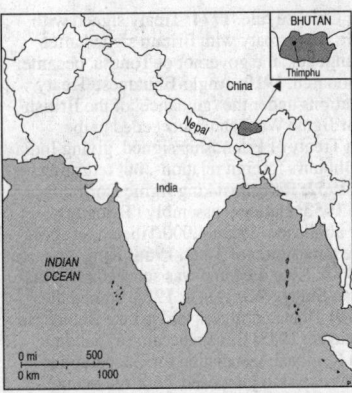

m/24,700 ft) is one of the world's highest unclimbed peaks; cut by valleys formed by tributaries of the Brahmaputra; thick forests in the S

Government
Head of state and government: Jigme Singye Wangchuk from 1972 **Political system:** absolute monarchy **Administrative divisions:** 20 districts **Political parties:** none officially; illegal Bhutan People's Party (BPP) and Bhutan National Democratic Party (BNDP), both ethnic Nepali **Armed forces:** 6,000 (1996) **Conscription:** military service is voluntary **Death penalty:** retains the death penalty for ordinary crimes but can be considered abolitionist in practice (date of last known execution 1964) **Education spend:** (% GNP) 4.2 (1995) **Health spend:** (% GDP) 4.1 (1995)

Economy and resources
Currency: ngultrum; also Indian currency **GDP:** ($ US) 1.3 billion (1995 est) **Real GDP per capita (PPP):** ($ US) 730 (1995 est) **GDP growth rate:** 6% (1995 est) **Average annual inflation:** 8.6% (1995 est) **Foreign debt:** ($ US) 85 million (1991–93) **Major trading partners:** India, Middle East, Singapore, Europe **Resources:** limestone, gypsum, coal, slate, dolomite, lead, talc, copper **Industries:** food processing, cement, calcium carbide, textiles, tourism, cardamon, gypsum, timber, handicrafts, cement, fruit, electricity (to India), precious stones, spices **Exports:** cardamon, cement, timber, fruit, electricity (to India), precious stones, spices. Principal market: India 94% (1994) **Imports:** aircraft, mineral fuels, machinery and transport equipment, rice. Principal source: India 77% (1994) **Arable land:** 2.8% (1995) **Agricultural products:** potatoes, rice, apples, oranges, cardamoms; timber production

Population and society
Population: 1,812,000 (1996 est) **Population growth rate:** 1.2% (1990–95); 2.3% (2000–05) **Population density:** (per sq km) 39 (1996 est) **Urban population:** (% of total) 6 (1995) **Age distribution:** (% of total population) <15 41.1%, 15–65 55.5%, >65 3.5% (1995) **Ethnic groups:** 54% Bhotia, living principally in the N and E; 32% of Tibetan descent; a substantial Nepali minority lives in the S – they are prohibited from moving into the Bhotia-dominated N **Language:** Dzongkha (official, a Tibetan dialect), Sharchop, Bumthap, Nepali, and English **Religion:** 70% Mahayana Buddhist (state religion), 25% Hindu **Education:** not compulsory **Literacy rate:** 51% (men); 25% (women) (1995 est) **Labour force:** 51% of population: 94% agriculture, 1% industry, 5% services (1990) **Life expectancy:** 52 (men); 55 (women) (1995–2000) **Child mortality rate:** (under 5, per 1,000 live births) 145 (1996) **Physicians:** 1 per 6,000 people (1996)

Practical information
Visa requirements: UK: visa required. USA: visa required **Embassy in the UK:** no diplomatic representation **British embassy:** no diplomatic representation **Chamber of commerce:** Bhutan Chamber of Commerce and Industry, POB 147, Thimphu. Tel: (2) 23140; fax: (2) 23936 **Airports:** international airports: Paro; total passenger km: 5 million (1994) **Major holidays:** 2 May, 2 June, 21 July, 11–13 November, 17 December

Chronology
to 8th century: Under effective Indian control. **16th century:** Came under Tibetan rule. **1616–51:** Unified by Ngawang Namgyal, leader of the Drukpa Kagyu (Thunder Dragon) Tibetan Buddhist

branch. **1720:** Came under Chinese rule. **1774:** Treaty signed with East India Company. **1865:** Trade treaty with Britain signed after invasion. **1907:** Ugyen Wangchuk, the governor of Tongsa, became Bhutan's first hereditary monarch. **1910:** Anglo-Bhutanese Treaty signed, placing foreign relations under the 'guidance' of the British government in India. **1926:** Jigme Wangchuk succeeded to the throne. **1949:** Indo-Bhutan Treaty of Friendship signed, giving India continued influence over Bhutan's foreign relations, but returning territory annexed in 1865. **1952:** Reformist king Jigme Dorji Wangchuk came to power. **1953:** National assembly (Tshogdu) established. **1958:** Slavery abolished. **1959:** 4,000 Tibetan refugees given asylum after Chinese annexation of Tibet. **1968:** King established first cabinet. **1972:** King died and was succeeded by his Western-educated son Jigme Singye Wangchuk. **1973:** Joined the nonaligned movement. **1979:** Tibetan refugees told to take Bhutanese citizenship or leave; most stayed. **1983:** Bhutan became a founding member of the South Asian Regional Association for Cooperation. **1988:** Buddhist Dzongkha/Drukpa king imposed 'code of conduct' suppressing the customs of the large Hindu-Nepali community in the S. **1990:** Hundreds of people allegedly killed during prodemocracy demonstrations. **1993:** Leader of banned Bhutan People's Party (BPP) sentenced to life imprisonment for 'antinational activities'.

Bolivia Republic of

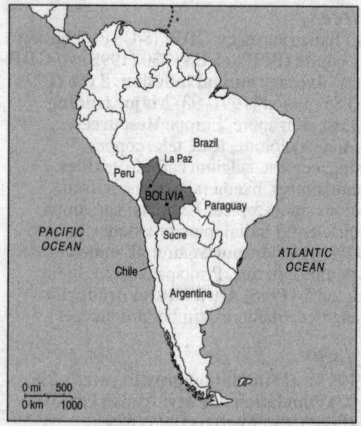

National name: *República de Bolivia* **Area:** 1,098,581 sq km/424,162 sq mi **Capital:** La Paz (seat of government), Sucre (legal capital and seat of judiciary) **Major towns/cities:** Santa Cruz, Cochabamba, Oruro, El Alto, Potosí **Physical features:** high plateau (Altiplano) between mountain ridges (cordilleras); forest and lowlands (llano) in the E; Andes; lakes Titicaca (the world's highest navigable lake, 3,800 m/12,500 ft) and Poopó

Government
Head of state and government: Hugo Banzer Suarez from 1997 **Political system:** emergent democracy **Administrative divisions:** nine departments **Political parties:** National Revolutionary Movement (MNR), centre right; Movement of the Revolutionary Left (MIR), left of centre; Nationalist Democratic Action Party (ADN), right wing; Solidarity and Civic Union (UCS), populist, free market **Armed forces:** 33,500 (1996) **Conscription:** selective conscription for 12 months at the age of 18 **Death penalty:** retained and used for ordinary crimes but can be considered abolitionist in practice (last execution 1974) **Defence spend:** (% GDP) 2.6 (1995) **Education spend:** (% GNP) 5.4 (1993–94) **Health spend:** (% GDP) 1.9 (1993)

Economy and resources
Currency: boliviano **GDP:** ($ US) 5.5 billion (1994) **Real GDP per capita (PPP):** ($ US) 2,598 (1994) **GDP growth rate:** 4.2% (1994); 3.8% (1990–95) **Average annual inflation:** 12.6 (1996) **Foreign debt:** ($ US) 5.4 billion (1996) **Major trading partners:** USA, Argentina, UK, Brazil, Japan, Belgium **Resources:** petroleum, natural gas, tin (world's fifth-largest producer), zinc, silver, gold, lead, antimony, tungsten, copper **Industries:** mining,

food products, petroleum refining, tobacco, textiles **Exports:** metallic minerals, natural gas, jewellery, soya beans, wood. Principal market: USA 24.1% (1995). Illegal trade in coca and its derivatives (mainly cocaine) was worth approximately $600 million in 1990 – almost equal to annual earnings from official exports **Imports:** industrial materials, machinery and transport equipment, consumer goods. Principal source: USA 19.4% (1995) **Arable land:** 2% (1995) **Agricultural products:** coffee, coca, soya beans, sugar cane, rice, chestnuts, maize, potatoes; livestock products (beef and hides); forest resources

Population and society
Population: 7,593,000 (1996 est) **Population growth rate:** 2.4% (1990–95); 2.2% (2000–05) **Population density:** (per sq km) 7 (1996 est) **Urban population:** (% of total) 61 (1995) **Age distribution:** (% of total population) <15 40.6%, 15–65 55.6%, >65 3.8% (1995) **Ethnic groups:** 30% Quechua Indians, 25% Aymara Indians, 25–30% mixed, 5–15% of European descent **Language:** Spanish (official); Aymara, Quechua **Religion:** Roman Catholic 95% (state-recognized) **Education:** (compulsory years) 8 **Literacy rate:** 85% (men); 71% (women) (1995 est) **Labour force:** 40% of population: 47% agriculture, 19% industry, 34% services (1993) **Unemployment:** 3.6% (1995) **Life expectancy:** 60 (men); 63 (women) (1995–2000) **Child mortality rate:** (under 5, per 1,000 live births) 88 (1996) **Physicians:** 1 per 2,348 people (1993 est)

Practical information
Visa requirements: UK: visa not required for a stay of up to 90 days. USA: visa not required for a stay of up to 90 days **Embassy in the UK:** Embassy and Consulate, 106 Eaton Square, London SW1W 9AD. Tel: (0171) 235 4248; fax: (0171) 235 1286 **British embassy:** Avenida Arce 2732, Casilla 694, La Paz. Tel: (2) 357 424; fax: (2) 391 063 **Chamber of commerce:** Cámara Nacional de Comercio, Edificio Cámara Nacional de Comercio, Avda Mariscal Santa Cruz 1392, 1°, Casilla 7, La Paz. Tel: (2) 350 042; fax: (2) 391 004 **Airports:** international airports: La Paz (El Alto), Santa Cruz (Viru-Viru); 28 domestic airports; total passenger km: 1,139 million (1994) **Major holidays:** 1 January, 1 May, 6 August, 1 November, 25 December; variable: Carnival, Corpus Christi, Good Friday

Chronology
c. AD 600: Development of sophisticated civilization at Tiahuanaco, S of Lake Titicaca. **c. 1200:** Tiahuanaco culture was succeeded by smaller Aymara-speaking kingdoms. **16th century:** Became incorporated within westerly Quechua-speaking Inca civilization, centred in Peru. **1538:** Conquered by Spanish and, known as 'Upper Peru', became part of the Viceroyalty of Peru, whose capital was at Lima (Peru); Charcas (now Sucre) became the local capital. **1545:** Silver discovered at Potosí in the SW, which developed into chief silver-mining town and most important city in South America in the 17th and 18th centuries. **1776:** Transferred to the Viceroyalty of La Plata, with its capital in Buenos Aires. **late 18th century:** Increasing resistance of Native Americans and Mestizos to Spanish rule; silver production slumped. **1825:** Liberated from Spanish rule by the Venezuelan freedom fighter Simón Bolívar, after whom the country was named, and his general, Antonio José de Sucre, after battle of Tumulsa; Sucre became Bolivia's first president. **1836–39:** Part of a federation with Peru, headed by Bolivian president Andres Santa Cruz, but it dissolved following defeat in war with Chile. **1879–84:** Lost coastal territory in the Atacama, containing valuable minerals, after defeat in war with Chile. **1880:** Start of a period of civilian rule which lasted until 1936. **1903:** Lost territory to Brazil. **1932–35:** Lost further territory after defeated by Paraguay in the Chaco War, fought over control of the Chaco Boreal. **1952:** After military regime overthrown by peasants and mineworkers in the Bolivian National Revolution, the formerly exiled Dr Victor Paz Estenssoro of the centrist National Revolutionary Movement (MNR) became president and introduced social and economic reforms, including universal suffrage, nationalization of tin mines, and land redistribution. **1956:** Dr Hernán Siles Zuazo (MNR) became president, defeating Paz. **1960:** Paz returned to power. **1964:** Army coup led by Vice President Gen René Barrientos. **1967:** Peasant uprising, led by Ernesto 'Che' Guevara, put down with US help; Guevara was killed. **1969:** Barrientos killed in plane crash, replaced by Vice President Siles Salinas, who was soon

deposed in army coup. **1971:** Col Hugo Banzer Suárez came to power after further military coup. **1974:** Attempted coup prompted Banzer to postpone promised elections and ban political and trade-union activity. **1980:** Inconclusive elections were followed by the country's 189th coup, led by Gen Luis García. Allegations of corruption and drug trafficking led to cancellation of US and European Community (EC) aid. **1981:** García forced to resign. Replaced by Gen Celso Torrelio Villa. **1982:** Torrelio resigned and, with economy worsening, junta handed power over to civilian administration headed by Siles Zuazo. **1983:** US and EC economic aid resumed as austerity measures introduced. **1985:** President Siles resigned after general strike and attempted coup. Election result inconclusive; veteran Dr Paz Estenssoro (MNR) chosen by congress as president. Inflation rate 23,000%. **1989:** Jaime Paz Zamora, of the left-wing Movement of Revolutionary Left (MIR) chosen as president in power-sharing arrangement with Banzer. **1993:** Gonzalo Sanchez de Lozada (MNR) elected president after Banzer withdrew his candidacy. Foreign investment encouraged as inflation fell to single figures. **1997:** Banzer elected president.

Bosnia-Herzegovina Republic of

National name: *Republika Bosna i Hercegovina* **Area:** 51,129 sq km/19,740 sq mi **Capital:** Sarajevo **Major towns/cities:** Banja Luka, Mostar, Prijedor, Tuzla, Zenica **Physical features:** barren, mountainous country, part of the Dinaric Alps; limestone gorges; 20 km/12 mi of coastline with no harbour

Government

Heads of state: Alija Izetbegović from 1990, Momcilo Krajisnik and Kerismir Zubak from 1996 **Heads of government:** Haris Silajdzic and Boro Bosnic from 1997 **Political system:** emergent democracy **Political parties:** Party of Democratic Action (PDA), Muslim-oriented; Serbian Renaissance Movement (SPO), Serbian nationalist; Croatian Christian Democratic Union of Bosnia-Herzegovina (CDU), Croatian nationalist; League of Communists (LC) and Socialist Alliance (SA), left wing **Armed forces:** 92,000 (1996) **Death penalty:** retained and used for ordinary crimes **Defence spend:** (% GDP) 6.3 (1996)

Economy and resources

Currency: dinar **GDP:** ($ US) 1 billion (1995 est) **Real GDP per capita (PPP):** ($ US) 300 (1995 est) **GDP growth rate:** N/A **Average annual inflation:** 120% (1992) **Foreign debt:** ($ US) 3.4 billion (1995 est) **Resources:** copper, lead, zinc, iron ore, coal, bauxite, manganese **Industries:** iron and crude steel, armaments, cement, textiles, vehicle assembly, wood products, oil refining, electrical appliances, cigarettes; industrial infrastructure virtually destroyed by war **Exports:** coal, domestic appliances (industrial production and mining remain low). Principal market: Italy 29.4% (1995) **Imports:** foodstuffs, basic manufactured goods, processed and semiprocessed goods. Principal source: Croatia 44% (1995) **Arable land:** 9.8% (1995) **Agricultural products:** before the war, these were maize, wheat, potatoes, rice, tobacco, fruit, olives, grapes; livestock rearing (sheep and cattle); timber reserves

Population and society

Population: 3,628,000 (1996 est) **Population growth rate:** –4.4%

(1990–95); 0.2% (2000–05) **Population density:** (per sq km) 71 (1996 est) **Urban population:** (% of total) 49 (1995) **Age distribution:** (% of total population) <15 22.2%, 15–65 70%, >65 7.8% (1995) **Ethnic groups:** 44% ethnic Muslim, 31% Serb, 17% Croat, 6% 'Yugoslav'. Croats are most thickly settled in SW Bosnia and W Herzegovina, Serbs in eastern and western Bosnia. Since the start of the civil war in 1992 many Croats and Muslims have fled as refugees to neighbouring states **Language:** Serbian variant of Serbo-Croatian **Religion:** Sunni Muslim, Serbian Orthodox, Roman Catholic **Education:** (compulsory years) 8 **Literacy rate:** 90% (men); 90% (women) (1992) **Labour force:** 2% agriculture, 45% industry, 53% services (1990 est) **Unemployment:** 28% (1992 est) **Life expectancy:** 70 (men); 76 (women) (1995–2000) **Child mortality rate:** (per 1,000 live births) 20 (1996)

Practical information

Visa requirements: UK: visa not required. USA: visa not required **Embassy in the UK:** 40–41 Conduit Street, London W1R 9FB. Tel: (0171) 734 3758; fax: (0171) 734 3760 **British embassy:** 8 Mustafe Golubica, 71000 Sarajevo. Tel: (71) 444 429; fax: (71) 444 429 **Chamber of commerce:** Chamber of Economy of Bosnia and Herzegovina, Mis. Irbina 13, 71000 Sarajevo. Tel: (71) 211777 **Airports:** international airport: Sarajevo; two smaller civil airports (civil aviation was severely disrupted by fighting in early 1990s; no air services to Sarajevo since 1992); **Major holidays:** 1–2 January, 1 March, 1–2 May, 27 July, 25 November

Chronology

1st century AD: Part of Roman province of Illyricum. **395:** On division of Roman Empire, stayed in W, along with Croatia and Slovenia, whereas Serbia to E became part of the Byzantine Empire. **7th century:** Settled by Slav tribes. **12–15th centuries:** Independent state. **1463 and 1482:** Bosnia and Herzegovina, in S, successively conquered by Ottoman Turks; many Slavs were converted to Sunni Islam. **1878:** Became an Austrian protectorate, following Bosnian revolt against Turkish rule in 1875–76. **1908:** Annexed by Austrian Habsburgs in wake of Turkish Revolution. **1914:** Archduke Franz Ferdinand, the Habsburg heir, assassinated in Sarajevo by a Bosnian-Serb extremist, precipitating World War I. **1918:** On collapse of Habsburg Empire, became part of Serb-dominated 'Kingdom of Serbs, Croats, and Slovenes', known as Yugoslavia from 1929. **1941:** Occupied by Nazi Germany and became 'Greater Croatia' fascist puppet state and scene of fierce fighting. **1943–44:** Liberated by the communist Partisans, led by Marshal Tito. **1945:** Became republic within Yugoslav Socialist Federation. **1980:** Upsurge in Islamic nationalism. **1990:** Ethnic violence erupted between Muslims and Serbs. Communists defeated in multiparty elections; coalition formed by Serb, Muslim, and Croatian parties, with a nationalist Muslim, Alija Izetbegovic, as president. **1991:** Serb-Croat civil war in Croatia spread disorder into Bosnia. Fears that Serbia aimed to annex Serb-dominated parts of the republic led to 'sovereignty' declaration by parliament. Serbs within Bosnia established own autonomous enclaves. **1992:** In a Serb-boycotted referendum, Bosnian Muslims and Croats voted overwhelmingly for independence, which was recognized by USA and European Community (EC); admitted into United Nations (UN). Violent civil war broke out, as independent 'Serbian Republic of Bosnia-Herzegovina', comprising parts of E and W, proclaimed by Bosnian-Serb militia leader Radovan Karadzic, with Serbian backing. UN forces drafted into Sarajevo to break Serb siege of city; accusations of 'ethnic cleansing', particularly of Muslims, by Bosnian Serbs. **1993:** UN–EC peace plan failed. USA began airdrops of food and medical supplies. Six UN 'safe areas' created (Srebrenica, Tuzla, Zepa, Gorazde, Bihac, Sarajevo), intended as havens for Muslim civilians. Croat-Serb partition plan rejected by Muslims. **1994:** Serb siege of Sarajevo lifted after UN–NATO ultimatum and Russian diplomatic intervention. Croat-Muslim federation formed after cease-fire in N. Cease-fire negotiated by former US president Jimmy Carter. **1995:** Hostilities resumed; 'safe areas' of Srebrenica (where more than 4,000 Muslims were massacred) and Zepa were overrun before the Serbs were halted by Croatians near Bihac. US-sponsored peace accord, providing for two sovereign states (one Muslim–Croat, one Serb) and cease-fire agreed at Dayton, Ohio, USA; peace accord reached; 60,000-strong NATO peacekeeping force deployed. **1996:** International Criminal Tribunal for Former Yugoslavia began in the Hague. Arms-control accord signed. Three-person presidency elected, consisting of Alija Izetbegovic (incumbent Muslim president), Momcilo Krajisnik (Serb), and Kresimir Zubak (Croat). Biljana Plavisic elected president of Serb-controlled Bosnia. Bosnian Serb prime minister Rajko Kasagic dismissed. Full diplomatic relations established with Yugoslavia. New government formed, with Gojko Klickovic as prime minister. NATO-led Stabilization Force replaced Implementation Force. Herceg-Bosna para-state and the Bosnian Republic replaced by Muslim-Croat Federation, with Edhem Bicakcic as prime minister. **1997:** A Muslim, Haris Silajdzic, and a Serb, Boro Bosic, appointed co-chairs of the all-Bosnian Council of Ministers. Serb-dominated part of Bosnia signed customs agreement with Yugoslavia. Croat Vladimir Soljic elected president of Muslim-Croat Federation, with Muslim Ejup Ganic as his deputy. Slow progress on implementation of Dayton Peace Accord. Municipal elections held after 12-month delay; nationalist parties successful. Three-man presidency agreed common passport and citizenship law.

Botswana Republic of

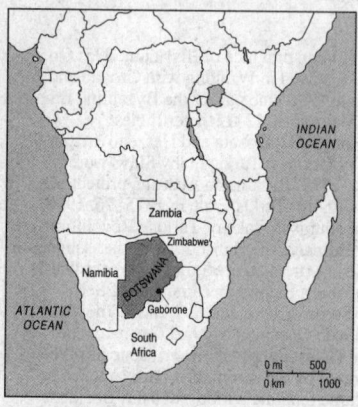

Area: 582,000 sq km/224,710 sq mi **Capital:** Gaborone **Major towns/cities:** Mahalapye, Serowe, Tutume, Bobonong Francistown, Selebi-Phikwe, Lobatse, Molepolol, Kange **Physical features:** Kalahari Desert in SW (70–80% of national territory is desert), plains (Makgadikgadi salt pans) in E, fertile lands and Okavango Delta in N

Government
Head of state and government: Festus Mogae from 1998 **Political system:** democracy **Administrative divisions:** ten districts and four town councils **Political parties:** Botswana Democratic Party (BDP), moderate centrist; Botswana National Front (BNF), moderate left of centre **Armed forces:** 7,500 (1996) **Conscription:** military service is voluntary **Death penalty:** retained and used for ordinary crimes **Defence spend:** (% GDP) 6.4 (1996) **Education spend:** (% GNP) 8.3 (1995) **Health spend:** (% GDP) 2.2 (1995)

Economy and resources
Currency: franc CFA **GDP:** ($ US) 4 billion (1994) **Real GDP per capita (PPP):** ($ US) 5,367 (1994) **GDP growth rate:** 4.1% (1994); 4.2% (1990–95) **Average annual inflation:** 10.4% (1996) **Foreign debt:** ($ US) 720 million (1996) **Major trading partners:** Lesotho, Namibia, South Africa, Swaziland – all fellow SACU (Southern African Customs Union) members; UK and other European countries, USA **Resources:** diamonds (world's third-largest producer), copper-nickel ore, coal, soda ash, gold, cobalt, salt, plutonium, asbestos, chromite, iron, silver, manganese, talc, uranium **Industries:** mining, food processing, textiles and clothing, beverages, soap, chemicals, paper, plastics, electrical goods **Exports:** diamonds, copper and nickel, beef. Principal market: Europe 86.7% (1994) **Imports:** machinery and transport equipment, food, beverages, tobacco, chemicals and rubber products, textiles and footwear, fuels, wood and paper products. Principal source: SACU 79.6% (1994) **Arable land:** 0.6% (1995)

Agricultural products: sorghum, vegetables, pulses; cattle raising (principally for beef production) is main agricultural activity

Population and society
Population: 1,484,000 (1996 est) **Population growth rate:** 3.1% (1990–95); 2.7% (2000–05) **Population density:** (per sq km) 3 (1996 est) **Urban population:** (% of total) 28% (1995) **Age distribution:** (% of total population) <15 43.2%, 15–65 54.3%, >65 2.4% (1995) **Ethnic groups:** about 90% Tswana and 5% Kung and other hunter-gatherer groups; the remainder is European **Language:** English (official), Setswana (national) **Religion:** Christian 50%, animist, Baha'i, Muslim, Hindu **Education:** not compulsory **Literacy rate:** 84% (men); 65% (women) (1995 est) **Labour force:** 44% of population: 46% agriculture, 20% industry, 33% services (1990) **Unemployment:** approximately 20% (1995) **Life expectancy:** 65 (men); 69 (women) (1995–2000) **Child mortality rate:** (under 5, per 1,000 live births) 57 (1996) **Physicians:** 1 per 4,130 people (1994)

Practical information
Visa requirements: UK: visa not required. USA: visa not required **Embassy in the UK:** High Commission, 6 Stratford Place, London W1N 9AE. Tel: (0171) 499 0031; fax: (0171) 495 8595 **British embassy:** British High Commission, Private Bag 0023, Gaborone. Tel: 352 841/2/3; fax: (0171) 356 105 **Chamber of commerce:** Botswana National Chamber of Commerce and Industry, PO Box 20344, Gaborone. Tel: 52677 **Airports:** international airports: Gaborone (Sir Seretse Khama), Kasane; six domestic airports; total passenger km: 58 million (1994) **Major holidays:** 1–2 January, 30 September, 25–26 December; variable: Ascension Thursday, Good Friday, Easter Monday, Holy Saturday, President's Day (July), July Holiday, October Holiday

Chronology
18th century: Formerly inhabited by nomadic hunter-gatherer groups, including the Kung, the area was settled by the Tswana people, from whose eight branches the majority of the people are descended. **1872:** Khama III the Great, a converted Christian, became chief of the Bamangwato, the largest Tswana group. He developed a strong army and greater unity among the Botswana peoples. **1885:** Became the British protectorate of Bechuanaland at the request of Chief Khama, who feared invasion by Boers from the Transvaal (South Africa) following the discovery of gold. **1895:** The southern part of the Bechuanaland Protectorate was annexed by Cape Colony (South Africa). **1960:** New constitution created a legislative council controlled (until 1963) by a British High Commissioner. **1965:** Capital transferred from Mafeking to Gaborone. Internal self-government achieved, with Seretse Khama, the grandson of Khama III and leader of the centrist Democratic Party (BDP), elected head of government. **1966:** Independence achieved from Britain. Name changed to Botswana; Seretse Khama elected president under new presidentialist constitution. **mid-1970s:** The economy grew rapidly as diamond mining expanded. **1980:** Seretse Khama died, and was succeeded by Vice President Quett Masire (BDP). **1985:** South African raid on Gaborone, allegedly in search of African National Congress (ANC) guerrillas. **1993:** Relations with South Africa fully normalized following ending of apartheid and establishment of a multiracial government. **1997:** Major constitutional changes reduced voting age to 18.

Brazil Federal Republic of

National name: *República Federativa do Brasil* **Area:** 8,511,965 sq km/3,286,469 sq mi **Capital:** Brasília **Major towns/cities:** São Paulo, Belo Horizonte, Nova Iguaçu, Rio de Janeiro, Belém, Recife, Pôrto Alegre, Salvador, Curitiba, Manaus, Fortaleza **Major ports:** Rio de Janeiro, Belém, Recife, Pôrto Alegre, Salvador **Physical features:** the densely forested Amazon basin covers the northern half of the country with a network of rivers; the S is fertile; enormous energy resources, both hydroelectric (Itaipú Reservoir on the Paraná, and Tucuruí on the Tocantins) and nuclear

(uranium ores); mostly tropical climate

Government

Head of state and government: Fernando Henrique Cardoso from 1994 **Political system:** democratic federal republic **Administrative divisions:** 26 states and one federal district **Political parties:** Workers' Party (PT), left of centre; Social Democratic Party (PSDB), moderate, left of centre; Brazilian Democratic Movement Party (PMDB), centre left; Liberal Front Party (PFL), right wing; National Reconstruction Party (PRN), centre right **Armed forces:** 295,000; public security forces under army control 385,600 (1996) **Conscription:** 12 months **Death penalty:** for exceptional crimes only; last execution 1855 **Defence spend:** (% GDP) 2.1 (1996) **Education spend:** (% GNP) 1.3 (1995 est) **Health spend:** (% GDP) 2.2 (1995 est)

Economy and resources

Currency: real **GDP:** ($ US) 554.6 billion (1994) **Real GDP per capita (PPP):** ($ US) 5,362 (1994) **GDP growth rate:** 5.8% (1994); 2.7% (1990–95) **Average annual inflation:** 18.7% (1996); 873.8% (1985–95) **Foreign debt:** ($ US) 177.8 billion (1996) **Major trading partners:** USA, Germany, Japan, Iran, the Netherlands, France, Argentina, UK **Resources:** iron ore (world's second-largest producer), tin (world's fourth-largest producer), aluminium (world's fourth-largest producer), gold, phosphates, platinum, bauxite, uranium, manganese, coal, copper, petroleum, natural gas, hydroelectric power, forests **Industries:** mining, steel, machinery and transport equipment, food processing, textiles and clothing, chemicals, petrochemicals, cement, lumber **Exports:** steel products, transport equipment, coffee, iron ore and concentrates, aluminium, iron, tin, soya beans, orange juice (85% of world's concentrates), tobacco, leather footwear, sugar, beef, textiles. Principal market: USA 18.9% (1995) **Imports:** mineral fuels, machinery and mechanical appliances, chemical products, foodstuffs, coal, wheat, fertilizers, cast iron and steel. Principal source: USA 23.9% (1995) **Arable land:** 6.3% (1995) **Agricultural products:** soya beans, coffee (world's largest producer), tobacco, sugar cane (world's third-largest producer), cocoa beans (world's second-largest producer), maize, rice, cassava, oranges; livestock (beef and poultry)

Population and society

Population: 161,087,000 (1996 est) **Population growth rate:** 1.7% (1990–95); 1.4% (2000–05) **Population density:** (per sq km) 19 (1996 est) **Urban population:** (% of total) 78 (1995) **Age distribution:** (% of total population) <15 32.3%, 15–65 62.5%, >65 5.2% (1995) **Ethnic groups:** wide range of ethnic groups, including 55% of European origin (mainly Portuguese, Italian, and German), 38% of mixed parentage, 6% of African origin, as well as Native Americans and Japanese **Language:** Portuguese (official); 120 Indian languages **Religion:** Roman Catholic 89%; Indian faiths **Education:** (compulsory years) 8 **Literacy rate:** 82% (men); 80% (women) (1995 est) **Labour force:** 44% of population: 23% agriculture, 23% industry, 54% services (1990) **Unemployment:** 4.6% (1995) **Life expectancy:** 65 (men); 70 (women) (1995–2000) **Child mortality rate:** (under 5, per 1,000 live births) 69 (1996) **Physicians:** 1 per 844 people (1993 est)

Practical information

Visa requirements: UK: visa not required for tourist visits. USA: visa required **Embassy in the UK:** 32 Green Street, London W1Y 4AT. Tel: (0171) 499 0877; fax: (0171) 493 5105 **British embassy:** Caixa Postal 07-0586, Setor de Embaixadas Sul, Quadra 801, Conjunto K, 70408-900 Brasília, Distrito Federal. Tel: (61) 225 2710; fax: (61) 225 1777 **Chamber of commerce:** Confederaçao Nacional do Comércio, SCS, Edif. Presidente Dutra, 4 º andar, Quadra 11, 70327 Brasília, Distrito Federal. Tel: (61) 223 0578 **Airports:** principal international airports: Rio de Janeiro (Brasília and Guarulhos), São Paulo (Guarulhos, Viracopos, and Congonhas), Manaus (Eduardo Gomes), Salvador (Dois de Julho); 27 domestic airports; total passenger km: 32,139 million (1994) **Major holidays:** 1 January, 21 April, 1 May, 7 September, 12 October, 2, 15 November, 25 December; variable: Carnival (2 days), Corpus Christi, Good Friday, Holy Saturday, Holy Thursday

Chronology

1500: Originally inhabited by South American Indians. Portuguese explorer Pedro Alvares Cabral sighted and claimed Brazil for Portugal. **1530:** Start of Portuguese colonization; Portugal monopolized trade but colonial government was decentralized. **1580–1640:** Brazil, with Portugal, came under Spanish rule. **17th century:** Huge sugar-cane plantations established with slave labour in coastal regions, making Brazil world's largest supplier of sugar; cattle ranching developed inland. **1695:** Discovery of gold in central highlands. **1763:** Colonial capital moved from Bahia to Rio de Janeiro. **1770:** Brazil's first coffee plantations established in Rio de Janeiro. **18th century:** Population 1798 totalled 3.3 million, of which around 1.9 million were slaves, mainly of African origin; significant growth of gold-mining industry. **19th century:** Rapid expansion in coffee growing. **1808:** Following Napoleon's invasion of Portugal, the Portuguese regent, Prince John, arrived in Brazil and established his court at Rio de Janeiro; Brazilian trade opened to foreign merchants. **1815:** United Kingdom of Portugal, Brazil, and Algarve made Brazil co-equal with Portugal and Rio de Janeiro as capital. **1821:** Political disorder in Portugal forced King John VI to return to Europe, leaving government of Brazil to his son, Crown Prince Pedro. **1822:** Pedro defied orders from Portuguese parliament to return to Portugal; he declared Brazil's independence to avoid reversion to colonial status. **1825:** King John VI recognized his son as Emperor Pedro I of Brazil. **1831:** Pedro I abdicated in favour of his infant son, Pedro II; regency (to 1840) dominated by Brazilian politicians. **1847:** First prime minister appointed, but emperor retained wide-ranging powers. **1865–70:** Brazilian efforts to control Uruguay led to War of the Triple Alliance with Paraguay. **1888:** Abolition of slavery in Brazil. **1889:** Monarch overthrown by liberal revolt; federal republic established with central government controlled by coffee planters; by 1902 Brazil produced 65% of world's coffee. **1915–19:** Lack of European imports during World War I led to rapid industrialization, especially in state of São Paulo. **1930:** Revolution against planter oligarchy placed Getúlio Vargas in power; he introduced social reforms and economic planning. **1937:** Vargas established authoritarian corporate state. **1942:** Brazil entered World War II as ally of USA; small fighting force sent to Italy 1944. **1945:** Vargas ousted by military coup, but Gen Eurico Gaspar Dutra soon forced to abandon free-market policies. **1951:** Vargas elected president; continued to extend state control of economy. **1954:** Vargas committed suicide. **1956–61:** Juscelino Kubitschek became president, pursuing measures geared towards rapid economic growth. **1960:** Capital moved to Brasília. **1961:** Janio Quadros elected president, introducing controversial programme for radical reform; resigned after seven months; succeeded by Vice President João Goulart. **1964:** Bloodless coup established technocratic military regime; free political parties abolished; intense concentration on industrial growth aided by foreign investment and loans. **1970s:** Economic recession and inflation undermined public support for military regime. **1985:** After gradual democratization from 1979, Tancredo Neves became first civilian president in 21 years; on Neves's death, Vice President José Sarney took office.

1988: New constitution reduced powers of president. **1989:** Fernando Collor (PRN) elected president, promising economic deregulation; Brazil suspended foreign debt payments. **1992:** Collor charged with corruption and replaced by Vice President Itamar Franco. **1994:** New currency introduced (third in eight years). Fernando Henrique Cardoso (PSDB) elected president. Collor cleared of corruption charges. **1997:** Constitution amended to allow president to seek second term of office.

Brunei State of

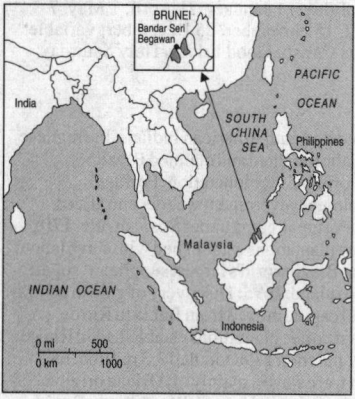

National name: *Negara Brunei Darussalam* **Area:** 5,765 sq km/2,225 sq mi **Capital:** Bandar Seri Begawan **Major towns/cities:** Seria, Kuala Belait, Bangar **Physical features:** flat coastal plain with hilly lowland in W and mountains in E (Mount Pagon 1,850 m/6,070 ft); 75% of the area is forested; the Limbang valley splits Brunei in two, and its cession to Sarawak 1890 is disputed by Brunei; tropical climate; Temburong, Tutong, and Belait rivers

Government

Head of state and government: HM Muda Hassanal Bolkiah Mu'izzaddin Waddaulah, Sultan of Brunei, from 1967 **Political system:** absolute monarchy **Administrative divisions:** four districts **Political parties:** Brunei National Democratic Party (BNDP) and Brunei National United Party (BNUP) (both banned since 1988); Brunei People's Party (BPP) (banned since 1962) **Armed forces:** 5,000 (1996); plus paramilitary forces of 4,100 **Conscription:** military service is voluntary **Death penalty:** retains the death penalty for ordinary crimes but can be considered abolitionist in practice (last execution 1957) **Defence spend:** (% GDP) 6.5 (1996) **Education spend:** (% GNP) 4.5 (1994) **Health spend:** (% GDP) 2.2 (1994)

Economy and resources

Currency: Brunei dollar (ringgit) **GDP:** ($ US) 6.47 billion (1994) **Real GDP per capita (PPP):** ($ US) 30,447 (1994) **GDP growth rate:** 2% (1995 est) **Average annual inflation:** 0.3% (1985–95) **Major trading partners:** Singapore, Japan, USA, EU countries, Malaysia, South Korea, Thailand **Resources:** petroleum, natural gas **Industries:** petroleum refining, textiles, cement, mineral water, canned foods, rubber **Exports:** crude petroleum and natural gas (accounting for 91.7% of total export earnings 1993). Principal market: Japan 50% (1994) **Imports:** machinery and transport equipment, basic manufactures, food and live animals, chemicals. Principal source: Singapore 29% (1994) **Arable land:** 0.6% (1995) **Agricultural products:** rice, cassava, bananas, pineapples, vegetables; fishing; forest resources

Population and society

Population: 300,000 (1996 est) **Population growth rate:** 2.1% (1990–95) **Population density:** (per sq km) 52 (1996 est) **Urban population:** (% of total) 58 (1995) **Age distribution:** (% of total population) <15 34%, 15–65 63%, >65 3% (1994) **Ethnic groups:** 68% indigenous Malays, predominating in government service and agriculture; more than 20% Chinese, predominating in the commercial sphere **Language:** Malay (official), Chinese (Hokkien), English **Religion:** Muslim 66%, Buddhist 14%, Christian 10% **Education:**

(compulsory years) 12 **Literacy rate:** 93% (men); 83% (women) (1995 est) **Labour force:** 41% of population: 2% agriculture, 24% industry, 74% services (1990) **Unemployment:** 4.8% (1992) **Life expectancy:** 73 (men); 77 (women) (1995–2000) **Child mortality rate:** (under 5, per 1,000 live births) 13 (1996) **Physicians:** 1 per 1,522 people (1994 est)

Practical information

Visa requirements: UK: visa not required for visits of up to 30 days. USA: visa not required **Embassy in the UK:** 19/20 Belgrave Square, London SW1X 8PG. Tel: (0171) 581 0521; fax: (0171) 235 9717 **British embassy:** British High Commission, PO Box 2197, 3rd Floor, Hong Kong Bank Chambers, Jalan Pemancha, Bandar Seri Begawan 2085. Tel: (2) 222 231; fax: (2) 226 002 **Chamber of commerce:** Brunei Darussalem International Chamber of Commerce and Industry, POB 2246, Bandar Seri Begawan 1922. Tel: (2) 236 601; fax: (2) 228 389 **Airports:** international airports: Bandar Seri Begawan (Brunei International); total passenger km: 2,029 million (1994) **Major holidays:** 1 January, 23 February, 31 May, 15 July, 25 December; variable: Eid-ul-Adha, end of Ramadan, Good Friday, New Year (Chinese), New Year (Muslim), Prophet's Birthday, first day of Ramadan, Meraj (March/April), Revelation of the Koran (May)

Chronology

15th century: Islamic monarchy established, ruling Brunei and north Borneo, including Sabah and Sarawak states of Malaysia. **1841:** Lost control of Sarawak. **1888:** Brunei became a British protectorate. **1906:** Became a dependency when British resident was appointed adviser to the sultan. **1929:** Oil was discovered. **1941–45:** Occupied by Japan. **1950:** Sir Omar became the 28th sultan. **1959:** Written constitution made Britain responsible for defence and external affairs. **1962:** Sultan began rule by decree after plan to join Federation of Malaysia was opposed by a week-long rebellion organized by the Brunei People's Party (BPP). **1967:** Sultan Omar abdicated in favour of his son Hassanal Bolkiah, but remained chief adviser. **1971:** Brunei given full internal self-government. **1975:** United Nations resolution called for independence for Brunei. **1984:** Independence achieved from Britain, with Britain maintaining a small force to protect the oil and gas fields. **1985:** A 'loyal and reliable' political party, the Brunei National Democratic Party (BNDP), legalized. **1986:** Death of former sultan, Omar. Formation of multiethnic Brunei National United Party (BNUP); nonroyals given key cabinet posts for the first time. **1988:** BNDP and BNUP banned. **1991:** Joined nonaligned movement.

Bulgaria Republic of

National name: *Republika Bulgaria* **Area:** 110,912 sq km/42,823 sq mi **Capital:** Sofia **Major towns/cities:** Plovdiv, Varna, Ruse, Burgas, Stara Zagora **Major ports:** Black Sea ports Burgas and Varna **Physical features:** lowland plains in N and SE separated by mountains (Balkan and Rhodope) that cover three-quarters of the country; River Danube in N

Government

Head of state: Petar Stoyanov from 1997 **Head of government:** Ivan Kostov from 1997 **Political system:** emergent democracy **Administrative divisions:** nine regions **Political parties:** Union of

Democratic Forces (UDF), right of centre; Bulgarian Socialist Party (BSP), left wing, ex-communist; Movement for Rights and Freedoms (MRF), Turkish-oriented, centrist; Civic Alliances for the Republic (CAR), left of centre; Real Reform Movement (DESIR) **Armed forces:** 103,500 (1996) **Conscription:** compulsory for 12 months **Death penalty:** retained and used for ordinary crimes **Defence spend:** (% GDP) 3.3 (1996) **Education spend:** (% GNP) 4.5 (1993–94) **Health spend:** (% GDP) 1.2 (1994)

Economy and resources

Currency: lev **GDP:** ($ US) 10 billion (1994) **Real GDP per capita (PPP):** ($ US) 4,533 (1994) **GDP growth rate:** 2.6% (1995); –4.3 (1990–95) **Average annual inflation:** 125% (1996); 45.3% (1985–95) **Foreign debt:** ($ US) 10.9 billion (1995) **Major trading partners:** EU countries (principally Germany, Greece, Italy), former USSR (principally Russia), Macedonia, USA **Resources:** coal, iron ore, manganese, lead, zinc, petroleum **Industries:** food products, petroleum and coal products, metals, mining, paper, beverages and tobacco, electrical machinery, textiles **Exports:** base metals, chemical and rubber products, processed food, beverages, tobacco, textiles, footwear. Principal market: EU 38.9% (1995) **Imports:** mineral products and fuels, chemical and rubber products, textiles, footwear, machinery and transport equipment, medicines. Principal source: EU 45.2% (1995) **Arable land:** 36.2% (1995) **Agricultural products:** wheat, maize, barley, sunflower seeds, grapes, potatoes, tobacco, roses; viticulture (world's fourth-largest exporter of wine 1989); forest resources

Population and society

Population: 8,468,000 (1996 est) **Population growth rate:** 2.8% (1990–95); 2.5% (2000–05) **Population density:** (per sq km) 76 (1996 est) **Urban population:** (% of total) 71 (1995) **Age distribution:** (% of total population) <15 18.3%, 15–65 67.1%, >65 14.5% (1995) **Ethnic groups:** Southern Slavic Bulgarians constitute around 90% of the population; 9% are ethnic Turks, who during the later 1980s were subjected to government pressure to adopt Slavic names and to resettle elsewhere **Language:** Bulgarian, Turkish **Religion:** Eastern Orthodox Christian, Muslim, Roman Catholic, Protestant **Education:** (compulsory years) 8 **Literacy rate:** 93% (men); 93% (women) (1995 est) **Labour force:** 22.1% agriculture, 36.6% industry, 41.3% services (1993) **Unemployment:** 12.5% (1996) **Life expectancy:** 68 (men); 75 (women) (1995–2000) **Child mortality rate:** (under 5, per 1,000 live births) 18 (1996) **Physicians:** 1 per 298 people (1995)

Practical information

Visa requirements: UK: visa required. USA: visa not required for tourist visits of up to 30 days **Embassy in the UK:** 186–188 Queen's Gate, London SW7 5HL. Tel: (0171) 584 9400; fax: (0171) 584 4948 **British embassy:** Boulevard Vassil Levski 65–67, Sofia 1000. Tel: (2) 885 361/2; fax: (2) 656 022 **Chamber of commerce:** Bulgarian Chamber of Commerce and Industry, 1040 Sofia, Suborna ST 11A. Tel: (2) 872 631; fax: (2) 873 209 **Airports:** international airports: Sofia, Varna, Burgas; seven domestic airports; total passenger km: 2,241 million (1994) **Major holidays:** 1 January, 3 March, 1, 24 May, 24–25 December; variable: Easter Monday

Chronology

c. 3500 BC onwards: Settlement of semi-nomadic pastoralists from central Asian steppes, who formed the Thracian community. **mid-5th century BC:** Thracian state formed, which was to extend over Bulgaria, N Greece, and N Turkey. **4th century BC:** Phillip II and Alexander the Great of Macedonia, to the SW, waged largely unsuccessful campaigns against the Thracian Empire. **AD 50:** Thracians subdued and incorporated within Roman Empire as the province of Moesia Inferior. **3rd–6th centuries:** Successively invaded from the N and devastated by the Goths, Huns, Bulgars, and Avars. **681:** The Bulgars, an originally Turkic group that had merged with earlier Slav settlers, revolted against the Avars and established, S of the River Danube, the first Bulgarian kingdom, with its capital at Pliska, in the Balkans. **864:** Orthodox Christianity adopted by Boris I. **1018:** Subjugated by the Byzantines, whose empire had its capital at Constantinople; led to Bulgarian Church breaking with Rome in

1054. **1185:** Second independent Bulgarian Kingdom formed. **mid-13th century:** Bulgarian state destroyed by Mongol incursions. **1396:** Bulgaria became the first European state to be absorbed into the Turkish Ottoman Empire; the imposition of a harsh feudal system and the sacking of monasteries followed. **1859:** Bulgarian Catholic Church re-established links with Rome. **1876:** Bulgarian nationalist revolt against Ottoman rule crushed brutally by Ottomans, with 15,000 massacred at Plovdiv ('Bulgarian Atrocities'). **1878:** At the Congress of Berlin, concluding a Russo-Turkish war in which Bulgarian volunteers had fought alongside the Russians, the area S of the Balkans, Eastern Rumelia, remained an Ottoman province, but the area to the N became the autonomous Principality of Bulgaria, with a liberal constitution and Alexander Battenberg as prince. **1885:** Eastern Rumelia annexed by the Principality; Serbia defeated in war. **1908:** Full independence proclaimed from Turkish rule, with Ferdinand I as tsar. **1913:** Following defeat in the Second Balkan War, King Ferdinand I abdicated and was replaced by his son Boris III. **1919:** Bulgarian Agrarian Union government, led by Alexander Stamboliiski, came to power and redistributed land to poor peasants. **1923:** Agrarian government overthrown in right-wing coup and Stamboliiski murdered. **1934:** Semifascist dictatorship established by King Boris III, who sided with Germany during World War II, but died mysteriously in 1943 after a visit to Adolf Hitler. **1944:** Soviet invasion of German-occupied Bulgaria. **1946:** Monarchy abolished and communist-dominated people's republic proclaimed following plebiscite. **1947:** Gained South Dobruja in the NE, along the Black Sea, from Romania; Soviet-style constitution established a one-party state; industries and financial institutions nationalized and cooperative farming introduced. **1949:** Death of Georgi Dimitrov, the communist government leader; replaced by Vulko Chervenkov. **1954:** Election of Todor Zhivkov as Bulgarian Communist Party (BCP) general secretary; Bulgaria became a loyal and cautious satellite of the USSR. **1968:** Participated in the Soviet-led invasion of Czechoslovakia. **1971:** Zhivkov became president, under new constitution. **1985–89:** Haphazard administrative and economic reforms, known as *preustroistvo* ('restructuring'), introduced under stimulus of reformist Soviet leader Mikhail Gorbachev. **1989:** Programme of enforced 'Bulgarianization' resulted in mass exodus of ethnic Turks to Turkey. Zhivkov ousted by foreign minister Petar Mladenov. Opposition parties tolerated. **1990:** BCP reformed under new name Bulgarian Socialist Party (BSP). Zhelyu Zhelev of the centre-right Union of Democratic Forces (UDF) indirectly elected president. Following mass demonstrations and general strike, BSP government replaced by coalition. **1991:** New liberal-democratic constitution adopted. UDF beat BSP in general election by narrow margin; formation of first noncommunist, UDF-minority government. **1992:** Zhelev became Bulgaria's first directly elected president. Following industrial unrest, Lyuben Berov became head of a non-party government. Zhivkov sentenced to seven years' imprisonment for corruption while in government. **1993:** Voucher-based 'mass privatization' programme launched. **1994:** Berov resigned; general election won by BSP. **1995:** Zhan Videnov (BSP) became prime minister. **1996:** Radical economic and industrial reforms imposed. Petar Stoyanov replaced Zhelev as president. Mounting inflation and public protest at the state of the economy. **1997:** General strike. Interim government led by Stefan Sofiyanski. UDF leader Ivan Kostov became prime minister. Former communist leader Todor Zhivkov released from house arrest. Bulgarian currency pegged to German Mark in return for support from International Monetary Fund. New political group, the Real Reform Movement (DESIR), formed.

Burkina Faso The People's Democratic Republic of (formerly Upper Volta)

National name: *République Démocratique Populaire de Burkina Faso* **Area:** 274,122 sq km/105,838 sq mi **Capital:** Ouagadougou **Major towns/cities:** Bobo-Dioulasso, Koudougou **Physical features:** landlocked plateau with hills in W and SE; headwaters of the river Volta; semiarid in N, forest and farmland in S; linked by rail to Abidjan in Côte d'Ivoire, Burkina Faso's only outlet to the sea

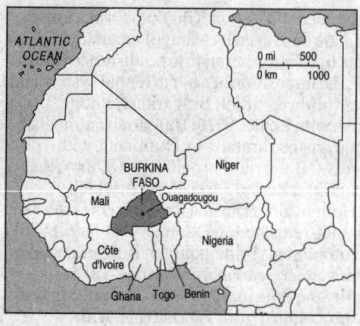

Government

Head of state:
Blaise Compaoré
from 1987 **Head of
government:** Kadre
Desire Ouedraogo
from 1996 **Political
system:** emergent
democracy
**Administrative
divisions:** 30
provinces **Political
parties:** Popular
Front (FP), centre-
left coalition
grouping; National
Convention of Progressive Patriots–Democratic Socialist Party
(CNPP–PSD), left of centre **Armed forces:** 5,800 (1996); includes
gendarmerie of 4,500 **Conscription:** military service is voluntary
Death penalty: retained and used for ordinary crimes **Defence
spend:** (% GDP) 2.4 (1996) **Education spend:** (% GNP) 3.6
(1993–94) **Health spend:** (% GDP) 2.3 (1990–95)

Economy and resources

Currency: franc CFA **GDP:** ($ US) 1.9 billion (1994) **Real GDP
per capita (PPP):** ($ US) 796 (1994) **GDP growth rate:** 1%
(1994); 2.6% (1990–95) **Average annual inflation:** 4% (1996)
Foreign debt: ($ US) 1.26 billion (1995) **Major trading
partners:** France, Côte d'Ivoire, Thailand, Italy, Taiwan, Niger,
Nigeria **Resources:** manganese, zinc, limestone, phosphates,
diamonds, gold, antimony, marble, silver, lead **Industries:** food
processing, textiles, cotton ginning, brewing, processing of hides
and skins **Exports:** cotton, gold, livestock and livestock products.
Principal market: France 13.2% (1994) **Imports:** machinery and
transport equipment, miscellaneous manufactured articles, food
products (notably cereals), refined petroleum products, chemicals.
Principal source: Côte d'Ivoire 25.6% (1994) **Arable land:** 12.5%
(1995) **Agricultural products:** cotton, sesame seeds, sheanuts
(karité nuts), millet, sorghum, maize, sugar cane, rice, groundnuts;
livestock rearing (cattle, sheep, and goats)

Population and society

Population: 10,780,000 (1996 est) **Population growth rate:**
–0.5% (1990–95); –0.4% (2000–05) **Population density:** (per sq
km) 39 (1996 est) **Urban population:** (% of total) 27% (1995)
Age distribution: (% of total population) <15 44.9%, 15–65 52%,
>65 3.1% (1995) **Ethnic groups:** over 50 ethnic groups, including
the nomadic Mossi (48%), Fulani (10%), and Gourma (5%).
Settled tribes include: in the N the Lobi-Dagari (7%) and the
Mande (7%); in the SE the Bobo (7%); and in the SW the Senoufu
(6%) and Gourounsi (5%) **Language:** French (official); about 50
Sudanic languages spoken by 90% of population **Religion:** animist
53%, Sunni Muslim 36%, Roman Catholic 11% **Education:**
(compulsory years) 6 **Literacy rate:** 28% (men); 9% (women)
(1995 est) **Labour force:** 54% of population: 92% agriculture, 2%
industry, 6% services (1990) **Unemployment:** 8.1% (1994 est)
Life expectancy: 45 (men); 48 (women) (1995–2000) **Child
mortality rate:** (under 5, per 1,000 live births) 186 (1996)
Physicians: 1 per 34,804 people (1993 est)

Practical information

Visa requirements: UK: visa required. USA: visa required
Embassy in the UK: Honorary Consulate, 5 Cinnamon Row,
Plantation Wharf, London SW11 3TW. Tel: (0171) 738 1800; fax:
(0171) 738 2820 **British embassy:** British Consulate, BP 1918
Ouagadougou. (All staff based in Abidjan, Côte d'Ivoire.) Tel:
(226) 336 363 **Chamber of commerce:** Chambre de Commerce,
d'Industrie et d'Artisanat du Burkina, ave Nelson Mandela, 01 BP
502, Ouagadougou 01. Tel: (226) 306 114; fax: (226) 306 116
Airports: international airports: Ouagadougou, Bobo-Dioulasso;
total passenger km: 239 million (1994) **Major holidays:** 1, 3
January, 1 May, 4, 15 August, 1 November, 25 December;

variable: Ascension Thursday, Eid-ul-Adha, Easter Monday, end
of Ramadan, Prophet's Birthday, Whit Monday

Chronology

13th–14th centuries: Formerly settled by Bobo, Lobi, and Gurunsi
peoples, E and centre were conquered by Mossi and Gurma peoples,
who established powerful warrior kingdoms, some of which survived
until late 19th century. **1895–1903:** France secured protectorates over
the Mossi kingdom of Yatenga and the Gurma region, and annexed the
Bobo and Lobi lands, meeting armed resistance. **1904:** The French-
controlled region, known as Upper Volta, was attached
administratively to French Sudan; tribal chiefs were maintained in
their traditional seats and the region was to serve as a labour reservoir
for more developed colonies to S. **1919:** Made a separate French
colony. **1932:** Partitioned between French Sudan, Ivory Coast, and
Niger. **1947:** Became a French overseas territory. **1960:** Independence
achieved, with Maurice Yaméogo as the first president. **1966:** Military
coup led by Lt-Col Sangoulé Lamizana, and a supreme council of the
armed forces established. **1977:** Ban on political activities removed.
Referendum approved a new constitution based on civilian rule.
1978: Lamizana elected president. **1980:** Lamizana overthrown in
bloodless coup led by Col Saye Zerbo as economy deteriorated. **1982:**
Zerbo ousted in a coup by junior officers: Maj Jean-Baptiste
Ouedraogo became president and Capt Thomas Sankara prime
minister. **1983:** Sankara seized complete power. **1984:** Upper Volta
renamed Burkina Faso ('land of upright men') to signify break with
colonial past; literacy and afforestation campaigns by radical
Sankara, who established links with Libya, Benin, and Ghana. **1987:**
Sankara killed in coup led by Capt Blaise Compaoré. **1991:** New
constitution approved. Compaoré re-elected president. **1992:**
Multiparty elections won by pro-Compaoré Popular Front (FP),
despite opposition claims of ballot-rigging. **1996:** Kadre Desire
Ouedraogo appointed prime minister. **1997:** CDP assembly election
victory. Ouedraogo reappointed prime minister.

Burundi Republic of

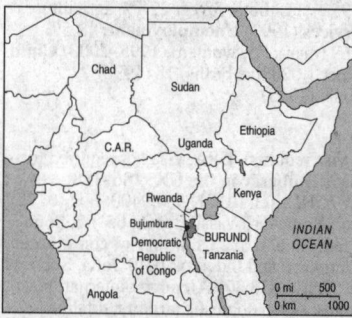

National name:
Republika y'Uburundi
Area: 27,834 sq
km/10,746 sq mi
Capital: Bujumbura
Major towns/cities:
Kitega, Bururi, Ngozi,
Muhinga, Muramuya
Physical features:
landlocked grassy
highland straddling
watershed of Nile and
Congo; Lake
Tanganyika, Great
Rift Valley

Government

Head of state: Pierre Buyoya from 1996 **Head of government:**
Pascal-Firmin Ndimira from 1996 **Political system:** authoritarian
nationalist **Administrative divisions:** 15 provinces **Political
parties:** Front for Democracy in Burundi (FRODEBU), left of
centre; Union for National Progress (UPRONA), nationalist
socialist **Armed forces:** 18,500 (1996); plus paramilitary forces of
3,500 **Conscription:** military service is voluntary **Death penalty:**
retained and used for ordinary crimes but can be considered
abolitionist in practice (last execution 1982) **Defence spend:** (%
GDP) 4.1 (1996) **Education spend:** (% GNP) 3.8 (1993–94)
Health spend: (% GDP) 0.9 (1990–95)

Economy and resources

Currency: Burundi franc **GDP:** ($ US) 1 billion (1994) **Real GDP
per capita (PPP):** ($ US) 698 (1994) **GDP growth rate:** –18%
(1994); –3.1% (1990–95) **Average annual inflation:** 14.9% (1994);
6.1% (1985–95) **Foreign debt:** ($ US) 1.1 billion (1995) **Major**

trading partners: Belgium, Germany, France, Tanzania, Japan, USA **Resources:** nickel, gold, tungsten, phosphates, vanadium, uranium, peat, petroleum deposits have been detected **Industries:** textiles, leather, food and agricultural products **Exports:** coffee, tea, glass products, hides and skins. Principal market: UK 28.3% (1995) **Imports:** machinery and transport equipment, petroleum and petroleum products, cement, malt (and malt flour). Principal source: Belgium and Luxembourg 15.4% (1995) **Arable land:** 36.2% **Agricultural products:** coffee, tea, cassava, sweet potatoes, bananas, beans; cattle rearing

Population and society
Population: 6,221,000 (1996 est) **Population growth rate:** 3% (1990–95); 2.6% (2000–05) **Population density:** (per sq km) 224 (1996 est) **Urban population:** (% of total) 8% (1995) **Age distribution:** (% of total population) <15 46.3%, 15–65 50.8%, >65 3% (1995) **Ethnic groups:** two main groups: the agriculturalist Hutu, comprising about 85% of the population, and the predominantly pastoralist Tutsi, about 14%. There is a small Pygmy minority, comprising about 1% of the population, and a few Europeans and Asians **Language:** Kirundi (a Bantu language) and French (both official), Kiswahili **Religion:** Roman Catholic 62%, Pentecostalist 5%, Anglican 1%, Muslim 1%, animist **Education:** (compulsory years) 6 **Literacy rate:** 61% (men); 40% (women) (1995 est) **Labour force:** 54% of population: 92% agriculture, 3% industry, 6% services (1990) **Unemployment:** 7.3% (1992) **Life expectancy:** 50 (men); 53 (women) (1995–2000) **Child mortality rate:** (under 5, per 1,000 live births) 143 (1996) **Physicians:** 1 per 17,153 people (1993 est)

Practical information
Visa requirements: UK: visa required. USA: visa required **Embassy for the UK:** Square Marie Louise 46, 1040 Brussels, Belgium. Tel: (2) 230 4535; fax: (2) 230 7883 **British embassy:** British Consulate, 43 Avenue Bubanza, BP 1344, Bujumbura. (All staff based in Kampala, Uganda.) Tel: (2) 23711 **Chamber of commerce:** Chambre de Commerce et de l'Industrie du Burundi, BP 313, Bujumbura. Tel: (2) 22280 **Airports:** international airports: Bujumbura; total passenger km: 2 million (1994) **Major holidays:** 1 January, 1 May, 1 July, 15 August, 18 September, 1 November, 25 December; variable: Ascension Thursday

Chronology
10th century: Originally inhabited by the hunter-gatherer Twa Pygmies. Hutu peoples settled in the region and became peasant farmers. **13th century:** Taken over by Banu Hutus. **15th–17th centuries:** The majority Hutu community came under the dominance of the cattle-owning Tutsi peoples, immigrants from the E, who became a semi-aristocracy; the minority Tutsis developed a feudalistic political system, organized around a nominal king, with royal princes in control of local areas. **1890:** Known as Urundi, the Tutsi kingdom, along with neighbouring Rwanda, came under nominal German control as Ruanda-Urundi. **1916:** Occupied by Belgium during World War I. **1923:** Belgium was granted a League of Nations mandate to administer Ruanda-Urundi; it was to rule 'indirectly' through the Tutsi chiefs. **1962:** Separated from Ruanda-Urundi, as Burundi, and given independence as a monarchy under Tutsi King Mwambutsa IV. **1965:** King refused to appoint a Hutu prime minister after an election in which Hutu candidates were victorious; attempted coup by Hutus brutally suppressed. **1966:** King deposed by his teenage son Charles, who became Ntare V; he was in turn deposed by his Tutsi prime minister Col Michel Micombero, who declared Burundi a republic; the Tutsi-dominated Union for National Progress (UPRONA) declared only legal political party. **1972:** Ntare V killed, allegedly by Hutus, provoking a massacre of 150,000 Hutus by Tutsi soldiers; 100,000 Hutus fled to Tanzania. **1976:** Army coup deposed Micombero and appointed the Tutsi Col Jean-Baptiste Bagaza as president, who launched a drive against corruption and a programme of land reforms and economic development. **1987:** Bagaza deposed in coup by the Tutsi Maj Pierre Buyoya. **1988:** About 24,000 Hutus killed by Tutsis and 60,000 fled as refugees to Rwanda. **1992:** New multiparty constitution adopted following referendum. **1993:** Melchior Ndadaye, a Hutu, elected

president in first-ever democratic contest but later killed in coup by Tutsi-dominated army; massacres followed, claiming 100,000 lives. **1994:** Cyprien Ntaryamira, a Hutu, became president but later killed in air crash along with Rwandan president Juvenal Habyarimana. Ethnic violence; 750,000 Hutus fled to Rwanda. Hutu Sylvestre Ntibantunganya became head of state, serving with a Tutsi prime minister, as part of a four-year power-sharing agreement between main political parties. **1995:** Renewed ethnic violence in the capital, Bujumbura, following massacre of Hutu refugees. **1996:** Former Tutsi president Pierre Buyoya seized power amid renewed ethnic violence; coup provoked economic sanctions by other African countries. 'Government of national unity' appointed, with Pascal-Firmin Ndimira as premier. Bujumbura shelled by Hutu rebels.

Cambodia State of (formerly **Khmer Republic** 1970–76, **Democratic Kampuchea** 1976–79, **People's Republic of Kampuchea** 1979–89)

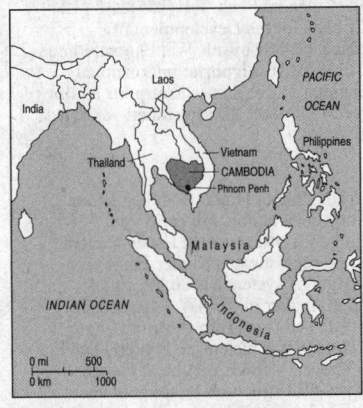

National name: *Roat Kampuchea* **Area:** 181,035 sq km/69,897 sq mi **Capital:** Phnom Penh **Major towns/cities:** Battambang, Kompong Cham **Major ports:** Kompong Cham **Physical features:** mostly flat, forested plains with mountains in SW and N; Mekong River runs N–S; Lake Tonle Sap

Government
Head of state: Prince Norodom Sihanouk from 1991 **Head of government:** joint prime ministers Ung Huot and Hun Sen from 1997 **Political system:** limited constitutional monarchy **Administrative divisions:** 22 provinces **Political parties:** United Front for an Independent, Neutral, Peaceful, and Cooperative Cambodia (FUNCINPEC), nationalist, monarchist; Liberal Democratic Party (BLDP), republican, anticommunist (formerly the Khmer People's National Liberation Front (KPNLF)); Cambodian People's Party (CPP), reform socialist (formerly the communist Kampuchean People's Revolutionary Party (KPRP)); Cambodian National Unity Party (CNUP) (political wing of the Khmer Rouge), ultranationalist communist **Armed forces:** 87,700 (1996) **Conscription:** military service is compulsory for five years between ages 18 and 35 **Death penalty:** abolished 1989 **Defence spend:** (% GDP) 5.7 (1996) **Education spend:** (% GNP) 1 (1994) **Health spend:** (% GDP) 0.5 (1994)

Economy and resources
Currency: Cambodian riel **GDP:** ($ US) 2.77 billion (1995) **Real GDP per capita (PPP):** ($ US) 660 (1995 est) **GDP growth rate:** 7.6% (1995); 6.4% (1990–95) **Average annual inflation:** 7% (1996); 70.3% (1985–95) **Foreign debt:** ($ US) 2.03 billion (1995) **Major trading partners:** Singapore, Thailand, Vietnam, Japan, Hong Kong, Indonesia, Taiwan **Resources:** phosphates, iron ore, gemstones, bauxite, silicon, manganese **Industries:** rubber processing, seafood processing, rice milling, textiles and garments, pharmaceutical products, cigarettes **Exports:** timber, rubber, fishery products. Principal market: Thailand 41.7% (1995) **Imports:** cigarettes, construction materials, petroleum products, motor vehicles, alcoholic beverages, consumer electronics. Principal source: Singapore 35.2% (1995) **Arable land:** 21.6% (1995) **Agricultural products:** rice, maize, sugar cane, cassava,

bananas; timber and rubber (the two principal export commodities); fishing

Population and society

Population: 10,273,000 (1996 est) **Population growth rate:** 3% (1990–95); 2.3% (2000–05) **Population density:** (per sq km) 57 (1996 est) **Urban population:** (% of total) 21% **Age distribution:** (% of total population) <15 44.9%, 15–65 52.4%, >65 2.6% (1995) **Ethnic groups:** 91% Khmer, 4% Vietnamese, 3% Chinese **Language:** Khmer (official), French **Religion:** Theravāda Buddhist 95%, Muslim, Roman Catholic **Education:** (compulsory years) 6 **Literacy rate:** 48% (men); 65% (women) (1995 est) **Labour force:** 50% of population: 74% agriculture, 8% industry, 19% services (1990) **Life expectancy:** 53 (men); 55 (women) (1995–2000) **Child mortality rate:** (under 5, per 1,000 live births) 137 (1996) **Physicians:** 1 per 9,374 people (1993 est)

Practical information

Visa requirements: UK: visa required. USA: visa required **Embassy in the UK:** no diplomatic representation in the UK **British embassy:** 29 Street 75, Phnom Penh. Tel: (855) 232 7124 **Chamber of commerce:** Council for the Development of Cambodia, Government Palace, quai Sisowath, Wat Phnom, Phnom Penh. Tel: (23) 50428; fax: (23) 61616 **Airports:** international airports: Phnom Penh (Pochentong); five domestic airports **Major holidays:** 9 January, 17 April, 1, 20 May, 22 September; variable: New Year (April)

Chronology

1st century AD: Part of the kingdom of Hindu-Buddhist Funan (Fou Nan), centred on Mekong delta region. **6th century:** Conquered by the Chenla kingdom. **9th century:** Establishment by Jayavarman II of extensive and sophisticated Khmer Empire, supported by an advanced irrigation system and architectural achievements, with a capital at Angkor in the NW. **14th century:** Theravāda Buddhism replaced Hinduism. **15th century:** Came under the control of Siam (Thailand), which made Phnom Penh the capital and, later, Champa (Vietnam). **1863:** Became a French protectorate, but traditional political structures left largely intact. **1887:** Became part of French Indo-China Union, which included Laos and Vietnam. **1941:** Prince Norodom Sihanouk was elected king. **1941–45:** Occupied by Japan during World War II. **1946:** Recaptured by France; parliamentary constitution adopted. **1949:** Guerrilla war for independence secured semi-autonomy within the French Union. **1953:** Independence achieved from France as the Kingdom of Cambodia. **1955:** Norodom Sihanouk abdicated as king and became prime minister, representing the Popular Socialist Community mass movement. **1960:** On the death of his father, Norodom Sihanouk became head of state. **later 1960s:** Mounting guerrilla insurgency, led by the communist Khmer Rouge, and civil war in neighbouring Vietnam. **1970:** Sihanouk overthrown by US-backed Lt-Gen Lon Nol in a right-wing coup; name of Khmer Republic adopted; Sihanouk, exiled in China, formed own guerrilla movement. **1975:** Lon Nol overthrown by Khmer Rouge, which was backed by North Vietnam and China; name Kampuchea adopted, with Sihanouk as head of state. **1976–78:** Khmer Rouge, led by Pol Pot, introduced an extreme Maoist communist programme, forcing urban groups into rural areas and resulting in over 2.5 million deaths from famine, disease, and maltreatment; Sihanouk removed from power. **1978–79:** Vietnamese invasion and installation of government headed by Heng Samrin, an anti-Pol Pot communist. **1980–82:** Faced by guerrilla resistance from Pol Pot's Chinese-backed Khmer Rouge and Sihanouk's ASEAN and US-backed nationalists, more than 300,000 Cambodians fled to refugee camps in Thailand and thousands of soldiers were killed. **1985:** Reformist Hun Sen appointed prime minister and more moderate economic and cultural policies pursued. **1987–89:** Vietnamese troop withdrawal. **1989:** Renamed State of Cambodia and Buddhism was re-established as state religion. **1991:** Peace agreement signed in Paris provided for a cease-fire and a United Nations Transitional Authority in Cambodia (UNTAC) to administer country in conjunction with all-party Supreme National Council; communism abandoned. Sihanouk returned as head of state. **1992:** Political

prisoners released; refugees resettled; freedom of speech and party formation restored. Khmer Rouge refused to disarm in accordance with peace process. **1993:** Free general elections (boycotted by Khmer Rouge) resulted in surprise win by FUNCINPEC; new constitution adopted. Sihanouk reinstated as constitutional monarch; Prince Norodom Ranariddh, FUNCINPEC leader, appointed executive prime minister, with reform-socialist CPP leader Hun Sen deputy premier. Khmer Rouge continued fighting. **1994:** Antigovernment coup foiled. Surrender of 7,000 guerrillas of outlawed Khmer Rouge in response to government amnesty. **1995:** Prince Norodom Sirivudh, FUNCINPEC leader and half-brother of King Sihanouk, exiled for allegedly plotting to assassinate Hun Sen and topple government. **1996:** Opposition leader Sam Rainsy assassinated. Serious split in Khmer Rouge when deputy leader Ieng Sary formed new Democratic National United Movement (DNUM) and granted amnesty by Sihanouk. Kov Samuth assassinated. Heightened tensions between Hun Sen's CPP and the royalist FUNCINPEC. **1997:** 16 killed in street demonstration; opposition blamed supporters of Hun Sen. Relations between joint prime ministers deteriorated. Divisions within Khmer Rouge. Pol Pot sentenced to life imprisonment after trial by Khmer Rouge. FUNCINPEC troops routed by CPP, led by Hun Sen. First prime minister Prince Norodom Ranariddh deposed and replaced by Ung Huot. Peace restored in Phnom Penh. Fighting resumed between supporters of Hun Sen and Prince Norodom Ranariddh.

Cameroon Republic of

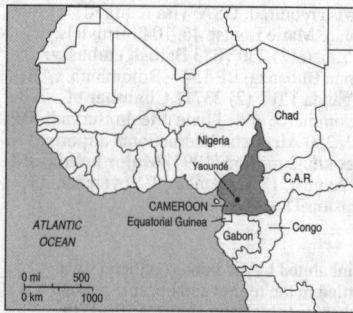

National name: *République du Cameroun* **Area:** 475,440 sq km/183,567 sq mi **Capital:** Yaoundé **Major towns/cities:** Garoua, Douala, Nkongsamba, Maroua, Bamenda, Bafoussam **Major ports:** Douala **Physical features:** desert in far N in the Lake Chad basin, mountains in W, dry savanna plateau in the intermediate area, and dense tropical rainforest in S; Mount Cameroon 4,070 m/13,358 ft, an active volcano on the coast, W of the Adamawa Mountains

Government

Head of state: Paul Biya from 1982 **Head of government:** Simon Achidi Achu from 1992 **Political system:** emergent democracy **Administrative divisions:** ten provinces **Political parties:** Cameroon People's Democratic Movement (RDPC), nationalist, left of centre; Front of Allies for Change (FAC), centre left **Armed forces:** 13,100 (1996); plus 9,000 paramilitary forces **Conscription:** military service is voluntary; paramilitary compulsory training programme in force **Death penalty:** retained and used for ordinary crimes **Defence spend:** (% GDP) 2.4 (1996) **Education spend:** (% GNP) 3.1 (1993–94) **Health spend:** (% GDP) 1 (1990–95)

Economy and resources

Currency: franc CFA **GDP:** ($ US) 7.5 billion (1994) **Real GDP per capita (PPP):** ($ US) 2,120 (1994) **GDP growth rate:** 3.2% (1994); –1.8% (1990–95) **Average annual inflation:** 6% (1996); 2% (1985–95) **Foreign debt:** ($ US) 9.3 billion (1996) **Major trading partners:** France, Spain, Italy, Germany, the Netherlands, Belgium, USA **Resources:** petroleum, natural gas, tin ore, limestone, bauxite, iron ore, uranium, gold **Industries:** petroleum refining, aluminium smelting, cement, food processing, footwear, beer, cigarettes **Exports:** crude petroleum and petroleum products, timber and timber products, coffee, aluminium, cotton, bananas.

Principal market: France 22.8% (1995) **Imports:** machinery and transport equipment, basic manufactures, chemicals, fuel. Principal source: France 38.3% (1995) **Arable land:** 12.8% (1995) **Agricultural products:** coffee, cocoa, cotton, cassava, sorghum, millet, maize, plantains, palm (oil and kernels), rubber, bananas; livestock rearing (cattle and sheep); forestry and fishing

Population and society
Population: 13,560,000 (1996 est) **Population growth rate:** 2.8% (1990–95); 2.8% (2000–05) **Population density:** (per sq km) 29 (1996 est) **Urban population:** (% of total) 45 (1995) **Age distribution:** (% of total population) <15 44%, 15–65 52.4%, >65 3.6% (1995) **Ethnic groups:** main groups include the Cameroon Highlanders (31%), Equatorial Bantu (19%), Kirdi (11%), Fulani (10%), Northwestern Bantu (8%), and Eastern Nigritic (7%) **Language:** French and English in pidgin variations (official); there has been some discontent with the emphasis on French – there are 163 indigenous peoples with their own African languages (Sudanic languages in N, Bantu languages elsewhere) **Religion:** Roman Catholic 35%, animist 25%, Muslim 22%, Protestant 18% **Education:** (compulsory years) 6 in Eastern Cameroon; 7 in Western Cameroon **Literacy rate:** 66% (men); 43% (women) (1995 est) **Labour force:** 40% of population: 70% agriculture, 9% industry, 21% services (1990) **Unemployment:** 25% (1990) **Life expectancy:** 57 (men); 60 (women) (1995–2000) **Child mortality rate:** (under 5, per 1,000 live births) 109 (1996) **Physicians:** 1 per 11,996 people (1993 est)

Practical information
Visa requirements: UK: visa not required. USA: visa not required **Embassy in the UK:** 84 Holland Park, London W11 3SB. Tel: (0171) 727 0771/3; fax: (0171) 792 9353 **British embassy:** BP 547, Avenue Winston Churchill, Yaoundé. Tel: (237) 220 545/796; fax: (237) 220 148 **Chamber of commerce:** Chambre de Commerce, d'Industrie et des Mines du Cameroun, BP 4011, Place de Gouvernement, Douala. Tel: (237) 423 690; fax: (237) 425 596 **Airports:** international airports: Douala, Garoua, Yaoundé; eight domestic airports; total passenger km: 436 million (1994) **Major holidays:** 1 January, 11 February, 1, 20 May, 15 August, 25 December; variable: Ascension Thursday, Eid-ul-Adha, end of Ramadan, Good Friday

Chronology
1472: First visited by the Portuguese, who named it the Rio dos Camaroes ('River of Prawns') after the giant shrimps they found in the Wouri River estuary, and later introduced slave trading. **early 17th century:** The Douala people migrated to the coastal region from the E and came to serve as intermediaries between Portuguese, Dutch, and English traders and interior tribes. **1809–48:** Northern savannas conquered by the Fulani, Muslim pastoral nomads from S Sahara, forcing forest and upland peoples southwards. **1856:** Douala chiefs signed a commercial treaty with Britain and invited British protection. **1884:** Treaty signed establishing German rule as the protectorate of Kamerun; cocoa, coffee, and banana plantations developed. **1916:** Captured by Allied forces in World War I. **1919:** Divided under League of Nations' mandates between Britain, which administered the SW and N, adjoining Nigeria, and France, which administered the E and S (comprising four-fifths of the area), and developed palm oil and cocoa plantations. **1946:** French Cameroon and British Cameroons made UN trust territories. **1955:** French crushed a revolt by the Union of the Cameroon Peoples (UPC), southern-based radical nationalists. **1960:** French Cameroon became the independent Republic of Cameroon, with Ahmadou Ahidjo, a Muslim from the N, elected president; UPC rebellion in SW crushed, and a state of emergency declared. **1961:** Following a UN plebiscite, northern part of British Cameroons merged with Nigeria and southern part joined the Republic of Cameroon to become the Federal Republic of Cameroon, with French and English as official languages. **1966:** Autocratic one-party regime introduced; government and opposition parties merged to form Cameroon National Union (UNC). **1970s:** Petroleum exports made possible successful investment in education and agriculture. **1972:** New constitution made Cameroon a unitary state. **1982:** President

Ahidjo resigned; succeeded by his prime minister Paul Biya, a Christian from the S. **1983:** Biya began to remove the northern Muslim political 'barons' close to Ahidjo, who went into exile in France. **1984:** Biya defeated a plot by Muslim officers from the N to overthrow him. **1985:** UNC adopted the name RDPC. **1990:** Widespread public disorder as living standards declined; Biya granted amnesty to political prisoners. **1992:** Ruling RDPC won first multiparty elections in 28 years. Biya's presidential victory challenged by opposition, who claimed ballot-rigging. **1995:** Cameroon admitted to Commonwealth. **1997:** RDPC assembly election victory; President Biya re-elected.

Canada

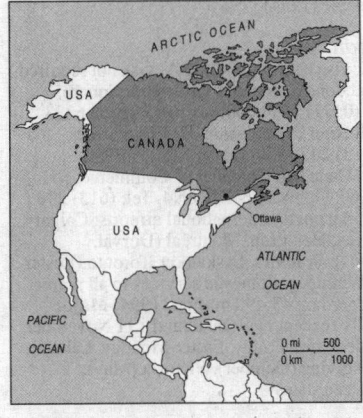

Area: 9,970,610 sq km/3,849,652 sq mi **Capital:** Ottawa **Major towns/cities:** Toronto, Montréal, Vancouver, Edmonton, Calgary, Winnipeg, Québec, Hamilton, Saskatoon, Halifax, Regina, Windsor, Oshawa, London, Kitchener **Physical features:** mountains in W, with low-lying plains in interior and rolling hills in E; St Lawrence Seaway, Mackenzie River; Great Lakes; Arctic Archipelago; Rocky Mountains; Great Plains or Prairies; Canadian Shield; Niagara Falls; climate varies from temperate in S to arctic in N; 45% of country forested

Government
Head of state: Elizabeth II from 1952, represented by governor general Roméo A LeBlanc from 1995 **Head of government:** Jean Chrétien from 1993 **Political system:** federal constitutional monarchy **Administrative divisions:** ten provinces and two territories **Political parties:** Liberal Party, nationalist, centrist; Bloc Québécois, Québec-based, separatist; Reform Party, populist, right wing; New Democratic Party (NDP), moderate left of centre; Progressive Conservative Party (PCP), free enterprise, right of centre **Armed forces:** 70,500 (1996) **Conscription:** military service is voluntary **Death penalty:** for exceptional crimes only; last execution 1962 **Defence spend:** (% GDP) 1.5 (1996) **Education spend:** (% GNP) 7.6 (1993–94) **Health spend:** (% GDP) 7 (1994)

Economy and resources
Currency: Canadian dollar **GDP:** ($ US) 579.3 billion (1996) **Real GDP per capita (PPP):** ($ US) 21,465 (1996) **GDP growth rate:** 2.8% (1996); 1.8% (1990–95) **Average annual inflation:** 1.6% (1996); 2.9% (1985–95) **Major trading partners:** USA, EU countries, Japan, China, Mexico, South Korea **Resources:** petroleum, natural gas, coal, copper (world's third-largest producer), nickel (world's second-largest producer), lead (world's fifth-largest producer), zinc (world's largest producer), iron, gold, uranium, timber **Industries:** transport equipment, food products, paper and related products, wood industries, chemical products, machinery **Exports:** motor vehicles and parts, lumber, wood pulp, paper and newsprint, crude petroleum, natural gas, aluminium and alloys, petroleum and coal products. Principal market: USA 81.4% (1996) **Imports:** motor vehicle parts, passenger vehicles, computers, foodstuffs, telecommunications equipment. Principal source: USA 75.7% (1996) **Arable land:** 4.9% (1995) **Agricultural products:** wheat, barley, maize, oats, rapeseed, linseed; livestock production (cattle and pigs)

Population and society

Population: 29,680,000 (1996 est) **Population growth rate:** 1.2% (1990–95); 0.9% (2000–05) **Population density:** (per sq km) 3 (1996 est) **Urban population:** (% of total) 77% (1995) **Age distribution:** (% of total population) <15 20.8%, 15–65 67.3%, >65 11.8% (1995) **Ethnic groups:** about 45% of British origin, 29% French, 23% of other European descent, and about 3% Native Americans and Inuit **Language:** English, French (both official; 60% English mother tongue, 24% French mother tongue); there are also Native American languages and the Inuit Inuktitut **Religion:** Roman Catholic, various Protestant denominations **Education:** (compulsory years) 10 **Literacy rate:** 99% (men); 99% (women) (1995 est) **Labour force:** 50.8% of population: 4.1% agriculture, 22.8% industry, 73.1% services (1996) **Unemployment:** 9.7% (1996) **Life expectancy:** 75 (men); 81 (women) (1995–2000) **Child mortality rate:** (under 5, per 1,000 live births) 8 (1996) **Physicians:** 1 per 454 people (1994)

Practical information

Visa requirements: UK: visa not required. USA: visa not required **Embassy in the UK:** Macdonald House, 1 Grosvenor Square, London W1X 0AB. Tel: (0171) 258 6600; fax: (0171) 258 6333 **British embassy:** British High Commission, 80 Elgin Street, Ottawa KIP 5K7. Tel: (613) 237 1530; fax: (613) 237 7980 **Chamber of commerce:** Canadian Chamber of Commerce, 55 Metcalfe Street, Suite 1160, Ottawa ON KIP 6N4. Tel: (613) 238 400; fax: (613) 238 7643 **Airports:** international airports: Calgary, Edmonton, Gander, Halifax, Hamilton, Montréal (Dorval, Mirabel), Ottawa (Uplands), St John's, Saskatoon, Toronto (Lester B Pearson), Vancouver, Winnipeg; domestic services to all major cities/towns; total passenger km: 43,490 million (1994) **Major holidays:** 1 January, 1 July (except Newfoundland), 11 November, 25–26 December; variable: Good Friday, Easter Monday, Labour Day (September), Thanksgiving (October), Victoria (May), additional days vary between states

Chronology

35,000 BC: First evidence of people reaching North America from Asia by way of Beringia. **c. 2000 BC:** Inuit (Eskimos) began settling Arctic coast from Siberia eastwards to Greenland. **c. 1000 AD:** Vikings, including Leif Ericsson, established Vinland, a settlement in NE America that did not survive. **1497:** John Cabot, an Italian navigator in the service of English king Henry VII, landed on Cape Breton Island and claimed the area for England. **1534:** French navigator Jacques Cartier reached the Gulf of St Lawrence and claimed the region for France. **1608:** Samuel de Champlain, a French explorer, founded Québec; French settlers developed fur trade and fisheries. **1663:** French settlements in Canada formed the colony of New France, which expanded southwards. **1670:** Hudson's Bay Company established trading posts N of New France, leading to Anglo-French rivalry. **1689–97:** King William's War: Anglo-French conflict in North America arising from the 'Glorious Revolution' in Europe. **1702–13:** Queen Anne's War: Anglo-French conflict in North America arising from the War of the Spanish Succession in Europe; Britain gained Newfoundland. **1744–48:** King George's War: Anglo-French conflict in North America arising from the War of Austrian Succession in Europe. **1756–63:** Seven Years' War: James Wolfe captured Québec 1759; France ceded Canada to Britain by the Treaty of Paris. **1775–83:** American Revolution caused influx of 40,000 United Empire Loyalists, who formed New Brunswick 1784. **1791:** Canada divided into Upper Canada (much of modern Ontario) and Lower Canada (much of modern Québec). **1793:** British explorer Alexander Mackenzie crossed the Rocky Mountains to reach the Pacific coast. **1812–14:** War of 1812 between Britain and USA; US invasions repelled by both provinces. **1820s:** Start of large-scale immigration from British Isles caused resentment among French Canadians. **1837:** Rebellions led by Louis Joseph Papineau in Lower Canada and William Lyon Mackenzie in Upper Canada. **1841:** Upper and Lower Canada united as Province of Canada; achieved internal self-government 1848. **1867:** British North America Act united Ontario, Québec, Nova Scotia, and New Brunswick in Dominion of

Canada: Provinces and Territories

Province	Capital	Area sq km	Area sq mi	Population (1995 est)
Alberta	Edmonton	661,190	255,285	2,656,000
British Columbia	Victoria	947,800	365,946	3,529,000
Manitoba	Winnipeg	649,950	250,946	1,105,000
New Brunswick	Fredericton	73,440	28,355	738,000
Newfoundland	St John's	405,720	156,648	570,000
Nova Scotia	Halifax	55,490	21,425	918,000
Ontario	Toronto	1,068,580	412,579	10,768,000
Prince Edward Island	Charlottetown	5,660	2,185	131,000
Québec	Québec	1,540,680	594,857	7,134,000
Saskatchewan	Regina	652,330	251,865	978,000
Territory				
Northwest Territories	Yellowknife	3,426,320	1,322,902	62,000
Yukon Territory	Whitehorse	483,450	186,660	31,000

Canada. **1869:** Red River Rebellion of Métis (people of mixed French and Native American descent), led by Louis Riel, against British settlers in Rupert's Land. **1870:** Manitoba (part of Rupert's Land) formed the fifth province of Canada; British Columbia became the sixth in 1871, and Prince Edward Island became the seventh in 1873. **late 19th century:** Growth of large-scale wheat farming, mining, and railways. **1885:** Northwest Rebellion crushed and Riel hanged; Canadian Pacific Railway completed. **1896:** Wilfred Laurier was the first French Canadian to become prime minister. **1905:** Alberta and Saskatchewan formed from Northwest Territories and became provinces of Canada. **1914–18:** Half a million Canadian troops fought for the British Empire on the western front in World War I. **1931:** Statute of Westminster affirmed equality of status between Britain and Dominions. **1939–45:** World War II: Canadian participation in all theatres. **1949:** Newfoundland became the tenth province of Canada; Canada was a founding member of the North Atlantic Treaty Organization (NATO). **1950s:** Postwar boom caused rapid expansion of industry. **1957:** Progressive Conservatives returned to power after 22 years in opposition. **1960:** Québec Liberal Party of Jean Lesage launched 'Quiet Revolution' to re-assert French–Canadian identity. **1970:** Pierre Trudeau invoked War Measures Act to suppress separatist terrorists of the Front de Libération du Québec. **1976:** Parti Québécois won control of Québec provincial government; referendum rejected independence 1980. **1982:** 'Patriation' of constitution removed Britain's last legal control over Canada. **1987:** Meech Lake Accord: constitutional amendment proposed to increase provincial powers (to satisfy Québec); failed to be ratified 1990. **1989:** Canada and USA agreed to establish free trade by 1999. **1992:** Self-governing homeland for Inuit approved; constitutional reform package, the Charlottetown Accord, rejected in national referendum. **1993:** Progressive Conservatives reduced to two seats in crushing election defeat. **1994:** Canada formed the North American Free Trade Area with USA and Mexico. **1995:** Québec referendum narrowly rejected sovereignty proposal. **1997:** Liberals re-elected by narrow margin.

Cape Verde Republic of

National name: *República de Cabo Verde* **Area:** 4,033 sq km/1,557 sq mi **Capital:** Praia **Major towns/cities:** Mindelo **Major ports:** Mindelo **Physical features:** archipelago of ten volcanic islands 565 km/350 mi W of Senegal; the windward (Barlavento) group includes Santo Antão, São Vicente, Santa Luzia, São Nicolau, Sal, and Boa Vista; the leeward (Sotovento) group comprises Maio, São Tiago, Fogo, and Brava; all but Santa Luzia are inhabited

Government

Head of state: Monteiro Mascarenhas from 1991 **Head of government:** Carlos Viega from 1991 **Political system:** emergent democracy **Administrative divisions:** 14 districts **Political parties:** African Party for the Independence of Cape Verde (PAICV), African nationalist; Movement for Democracy (MPD), moderate, centrist **Armed forces:** 1,100 (1996) **Conscription:** selective conscription **Death penalty:** abolished 1981 **Defence spend:** (% GDP) 1.7 (1996) **Education spend:** (% GNP) 4.4 (1993–94) **Health spend:** (% GDP) 2 (1993)

Economy and resources

Currency: Cape Verde escudo **GDP:** ($ US) 309.5 million (1994) **Real GDP per capita (PPP):** ($ US) 1,862 (1994) **GDP growth rate:** 4% (1994) **Average annual inflation:** 8.5% (1996); 7.2 % (1985–95) **Foreign debt:** ($ US) 210 million (1996) **Major trading partners:** Portugal, the Netherlands, Algeria, Italy, Côte d'Ivoire, Spain, USA, Brazil, Japan **Resources:** salt, pozzolana (volcanic rock), limestone, basalt, kaolin **Industries:** fish processing, machinery and electrical equipment, transport equipment, textiles, chemicals, rum **Exports:** fish, shellfish and fish products, salt, bananas. Principal market: Portugal 50% (1995) **Imports:** food and live animals, machinery and electrical equipment, transport equipment, mineral products, metals. Principal source: Portugal 45% (1995) **Arable land:** 9.7% (1995) **Agricultural products:** maize, beans, potatoes, cassava, coconuts, sugar cane, bananas, coffee, groundnuts; fishing (mainly tuna, lobster, shellfish)

Population and society

Population: 396,000 (1996 est) **Population growth rate:** 2.8% (1990–95) **Population density:** (per sq km) 98 (1996 est) **Urban population:** (% of total) 53 (1994) **Age distribution:** (% of total population) <15 42%, 15–65 54%, >65 4% (1994) **Ethnic groups:** about 60% of mixed descent (Portuguese and African), known as *mestiços* or creoles; the remainder is mainly African. The European population is very small **Language:** Portuguese (official), Creole **Religion:** Roman Catholic 93%, Protestant (Nazarene Church) **Education:** (compulsory years) 6 **Literacy rate:** 80% (men); 60% (women) (1995 est) **Labour force:** 37% of population: 31% agriculture, 30% industry, 40% services (1990) **Unemployment:** 25.8% (1990 est) **Life expectancy:** 65 (men); 67 (women) (1995–2000) **Child mortality rate:** (under 5, per 1,000 live births) 60 (1996) **Physicians:** 1 per 5,280 people (1990 est)

Practical information

Visa requirements: UK: visa required. USA: visa required **Embassy for the UK:** 44 Konninginnegracht, 2514 AD, The Hague, the Netherlands. Tel: (70) 346 9623; fax: (70) 346 7702 **British embassy:** British Consulate, c/o Shell Cabo Verde, Sarl Ave, Amílcar Cabral CP4, Sarl Vincente. (All staff based in Dakar, Senegal.) Tel: (238) 314 470; fax: (238) 314 755 **Chamber of commerce:** Associaçao Comercial, Industrial e Agricola de Barlavento, CP 62 Mindelo, São Vicente. Tel: (238) 313 281; fax: (238) 317 110 **Airports:** international airports: Sal Island (Amílcar Cabral), São Tiago; eight domestic airports; total passenger km: 173 million (1994) **Major holidays:** 1, 20 January, 8 March, 1 May, 1 June, 12 September, 24–25 December; variable: Good Friday

Chronology

1462: Originally uninhabited; settled by Portuguese, who brought in slave labour from W Africa. **later 19th century:** Decline in prosperity as slave trade ended. **1950s:** Liberation movement developed on the islands and the Portuguese African mainland colony of Guinea-Bissau. **1951:** Became an overseas territory of Portugal. **1975:** Independence achieved. National people's assembly elected, with Aristides of the PAICV as the first executive president; a policy of nonalignment followed. **1981:** Goal of union with Guinea-Bissau abandoned; became one-party state. **1988:** Rising unrest and demand for political reforms. **1991:** In first multiparty elections, new MPD won majority and Monteiro Mascarenhas became president; market-centred economic reforms introduced.

Central African Republic

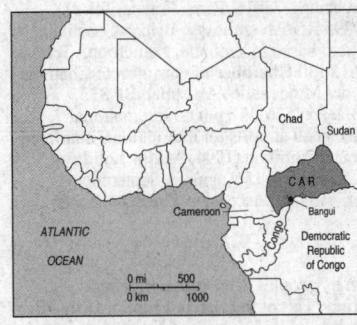

National name: *République Centrafricaine* **Area:** 622,436 sq km/240,322 sq mi **Capital:** Bangui **Major towns/cities:** Berbérati, Bouar, Bambari, Bossangoa, Carnot **Physical features:** landlocked flat plateau, with rivers flowing north and south, and hills in NE and SW; dry in N, rainforest in SW; mostly wooded; Kotto and Mbali river falls; the Oubangui River rises 6 m/20 ft at Bangui during the wet season (June–November)

Chronology

Head of state: Ange-Felix Patasse from 1993 **Head of government:** Gabriel Koyambounou from 1995 **Political system:** emergent democracy **Administrative divisions:** 16 prefectures **Political parties:** Central African People's Liberation Party (MPLC), left of centre; Central African Democratic Rally (RDC), nationalist, right of centre **Armed forces:** 2,700 (1996); plus 2,300 in paramilitary forces **Conscription:** selective national service for two-year period **Death penalty:** retains the death penalty for ordinary crimes but can be considered abolitionist in practice (last execution 1981) **Defence spend:** (% GDP) 2.4 (1996) **Education spend:** (% GNP) 2.8 (1993–94) **Health spend:** (% GDP) 1.7 (1990–95)

Economy and resources

Currency: franc CFA **GDP:** ($ US) 9 million (1994) **Real GDP per capita (PPP):** ($ US) 1,130 (1994) **GDP growth rate:** 5.8% (1994); 1% (1990–95) **Average annual inflation:** 7% (1996); 3.7% (1985–95) **Foreign debt:** ($ US) 871 million (1996) **Major trading partners:** France, Belgium, Luxembourg, Cameroon, Germany, Japan, Switzerland, Democratic Republic of Congo **Resources:** gem diamonds and industrial diamonds, gold, uranium, iron ore, manganese, copper **Industries:** food processing, beverages, tobacco, furniture, textiles, paper, soap **Exports:** diamonds, coffee, timber, cotton. Principal market: France 40.1% (1995) **Imports:** machinery, road vehicles and parts, basic manufactures, food and chemical products. Principal source: France 37% (1995) **Arable land:** 3.1% (1995) **Agricultural products:** cassava, coffee, yams, maize, bananas, groundnuts; forestry

Population and society

Population: 3,344,000 (1996 est) **Population growth rate:** 2.5% (1990–95); 2.3% (2000–05) **Population density:** (per sq km) 5 (1996 est) **Urban population:** (% of total) 39 (1995) **Age distribution:** (% of total population) <15 42.7%, 15–65 53.4%, >65 4% (1995) **Ethnic groups:** over 80 ethnic groups, but 66% of the population falls into one of three: the Banda (30%), the Baya-Mandjia (29%), and the Mbaka (7%). There are clearly defined ethnic zones: the forest region, inhabited by Bantu groups, the Mbaka, Lissongo, Mbimu, and Babinga; the river banks, populated by the Sango, Yakoma, Baniri, and Buraka; and the savanna region, where the Banda, Sande, Sara, Ndle, and Bizao live. Europeans number fewer than 7,000, the majority being French **Language:** French (official), Sangho (national), Arabic, Hunsa, and Swahili **Religion:** Protestant, Roman Catholic, Muslim, animist **Education:** (compulsory years) 8 **Literacy rate:** 52% (men); 25% (women) (1995 est) **Labour force:** 49% of population: 80% agriculture, 4% industry, 16% services (1990) **Unemployment:** 5.6% (1993) **Life expectancy:** 48 (men); 53 (women) (1995–2000) **Child mortality rate:** (under 5, per 1,000 live births) 149 (1996) **Physicians:** 1 per 25,920 people (1993 est)

Practical information

Visa requirements: UK: visa required. USA: visa required **Embassy for the UK:** 30 rue des Perchamps, 75016, Paris, France. Tel: (1) 4224 4256; fax: (1) 4288 9895 **British embassy:** British Consulate, PO Box 728, Bangui. (All staff based in Yaoundé, Cameroon.) Tel: (236) 610 300; fax: (236) 615 130 **Chamber of commerce:** Chambre de Commerce, d'Industrie, des Mines et de l'Artisanat, BP 813, Bangui. Tel: (236) 614 255; telex: 5261 **Airports:** international airports: Bangui-M'Poko; 37 small airports for international chartered services; total passenger km: 227 million (1994) **Major holidays:** 1 January, 29 March, 1 May, 1 June, 13, 15 August, 1 September, 1 November, 1, 25 December; variable: Ascension Thursday, Easter Monday, Whit Monday

Chronology

10th century: Immigration by peoples from Sudan to E and Cameroon to W. **16th century:** Part of the Gaoga Empire. **16th–18th centuries:** Population reduced greatly by slave raids both by coastal traders and Arab empires in Sudan and Chad. **19th century:** The Zande nation of the Bandia peoples became powerful in E. Bantu speakers immigrated from Zaire and the Baya from N Cameroon. **1889–1903:** The French established control over the area, quelling insurrections; a French colony known as Oubangi-Chari was formed and partitioned among commercial concessionaries. **1920–30:** Series of rebellions against forced labour on coffee and cotton plantations savagely repressed by French. **1946:** Given a territorial assembly and representation in French parliament. **1958:** Achieved self-government within French Equatorial Africa, with Barthélémy Boganda, founder of the pro-independence Movement for the Social Evolution of Black Africa (MESAN) prime minister. **1960:** Achieved independence as Central African Republic; David Dacko, nephew of the late Boganda, elected president. **1962:** The republic made a one-party state, dominated by MESAN and loyal to the French interest. **1965:** Dacko ousted in military coup led by Col Jean-Bedel Bokassa as the economy deteriorated. **1972:** Bokassa, a violent and eccentric autocrat, declared himself president for life. **1977:** Bokassa made himself emperor of the 'Central African Empire'. **1979:** Bokassa deposed by Dacko in French-backed bloodless coup, following violent repressive measures including the massacre of 100 children by the emperor, who went into exile. **1981:** Dacko deposed in a bloodless coup, led by Gen André Kolingba, and military government established. **1983:** Clandestine opposition movement formed. **1984:** Amnesty for all political party leaders announced. President Mitterrand of France paid a state visit. **1988:** Bokassa, who had returned from exile, found guilty of murder and embezzlement; he received death sentence, later commuted to life imprisonment. **1991:** Opposition parties allowed to form. **1992:** Multiparty elections promised, but cancelled with Kolingba in last place. **1993:** Kolingba released several thousand prisoners, including Bokassa. Ange-Felix Patasse of the leftist African People's Labour Party (MLPC) elected president, ending 12 years of military dictatorship. **1996:** Army revolt over pay; Patasse forced into hiding.

Chad Republic of

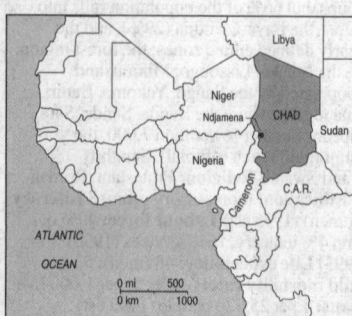

National name: *République du Tchad* **Area:** 1,284,000 sq km/495,752 sq mi **Capital:** N'djaména (formerly Fort Lamy) **Major towns/cities:** Sarh, Moundou, Abéché, Bongor, Doba **Physical features:** landlocked state with mountains (Tibetsi) and part of Sahara Desert in N; moist

savanna in S; rivers in S flow NW to Lake Chad

Government

Head of state: Idriss Deby from 1990 **Head of government:** Nassour Ouaidou Guelendouksia from 1997 **Political system:** emergent democracy **Administrative divisions:** 14 prefectures **Political parties:** Patriotic Salvation Movement (MPS), centre left; Alliance for Democracy and Progress (RDP), centre left; Union for Democracy and Progress (UPDT), centre left; Action for Unity and Socialism (ACTUS), centre left; Union for Democracy and the Republic (UDR), centre left **Armed forces:** 25,400 (1996); plus 9,500 in paramilitary forces **Conscription:** conscription is for three years **Death penalty:** retained and used for ordinary crimes **Defence spend:** (% GDP) 2.7 (1996) **Education spend:** (% GNP) 2.2 (1993–94) **Health spend:** (% GDP) 1.8 (1990–95)

Economy and resources

Currency: franc CFA **GDP:** ($ US) 9 million (1994) **Real GDP per capita (PPP):** ($ US) 700 (1994) **GDP growth rate:** 4% (1994 est); 1.9% (1990–95) **Average annual inflation:** 9% (1995); 3.1% (1985–95) **Foreign debt:** ($ US) 868 million (1996) **Major trading partners:** France, Portugal, Nigeria, Cameroon, USA, Belgium, Luxembourg, Italy, Germany **Resources:** petroleum, tungsten, tin ore, bauxite, iron ore, gold, uranium, limestone, kaolin, titanium **Industries:** cotton processing, sugar refinery, beer, cigarettes, soap, bicycles **Exports:** cotton, live cattle, meat, hides and skins. Principal market: Portugal 16.3% (1995) **Imports:** petroleum and petroleum products, cereals, pharmaceuticals, chemicals, machinery and transport equipment, electrical equipment. Principal source: France 39% (1995) **Arable land:** 2.6% (1995) **Agricultural products:** cotton, millet, sugar cane, sorghum, groundnuts; livestock rearing (cattle, sheep, and goats)

Population and society

Population: 6,515,000 (1996 est) **Population growth rate:** 2.7% (1990–95); 2.5% (2000–05) **Population density:** (per sq km) 5 (1996 est) **Urban population:** (% of total) 21 (1995) **Age distribution:** (% of total population) <15 43.4%, 15–65 53%, >65 3.6% (1995) **Ethnic groups:** mainly Arabs in the N, and Pagan, or Kirdi, groups in the S. There is no single dominant group in any region, the largest are the Sara, who comprise about a quarter of the total population. Europeans, mainly French, constitute a very small minority **Language:** French, Arabic (both official), over 100 African languages spoken **Religion:** Muslim, Christian, animist **Education:** (compulsory years) 8 **Literacy rate:** 42% (men); 18% (women) (1995 est) **Labour force:** 49% of population: 83% agriculture, 4% industry, 13% services (1990) **Life expectancy:** 48 (men); 51 (women) (1995–2000) **Child mortality rate:** (under 5, per 1,000 live births) 172 (1996) **Physicians:** 1 per 28,570 people (1994 est)

Practical information

Visa requirements: UK: visa required. USA: visa required **Embassy for the UK:** 65 rue des Belles Feuilles, 75116 Paris, France. Tel: (1) 4553 3675; fax: (1) 4553 1609 **British embassy:** British Consulate, BP 877, avenue Charles de Gaulle, N'djaména. (All staff based in Abuja, Nigeria.) Tel: (235) 513 064; telex: 5234 **Chamber of commerce:** Chambre de Commerce, Chambre Consulaire, BP 458, N'djaména. Tel: (235) 515 264 **Airports:** international airports: N'djaména; 12 small airports for domestic services; total passenger km: 222 million (1994) **Major holidays:** 1 January, 1, 25 May, 7 June, 11 August, 1, 28 November, 25 December; variable: Eid-ul-Adha, Easter Monday, end of Ramadan, Prophet's Birthday

Chronology

7th–9th centuries: Berber pastoral nomads, the Zaghawa, immigrated from north and became ruling aristocracy, dominating the Sao people, sedentary black farmers, and established Kanem state. **9th–19th centuries:** The Zaghawa's Saifi dynasty formed the kingdom of Bornu, which stretched to the W and S of Lake Chad, and converted to Islam in the 11th century. At its height between the 15th and 18th centuries, it raided the S for slaves, and faced rivalry from the 16th century from the Baguirmi and Ouadai Arab kingdoms. **1820s:** Visited by British explorers. **1890s–1901:** Conquered by France, who ended slave raiding by Arab kingdoms. **1910:** Became a colony in French Equatorial Africa and cotton production expanded in the S. **1944:** The pro-Nazi Vichy government signed agreement giving Libya rights to the Aouzou Strip in N Chad. **1946:** Became overseas territory of French Republic, with its own territorial assembly and representation in the French parliament. **1960:** Independence achieved, with François Tombalbaye of the Chadian Progressive Party (CPT), dominated by Sara Christians from the S, as president. **1963:** Violent opposition in the Muslim N, led by the Chadian National Liberation Front (Frolinat), backed by Libya following the banning of opposition parties. **1968:** Revolt of northern militias quelled with France's help. **1973:** Africanization campaign launched by Tombalbaye, who changed his first name to Ngarta. **1975:** Tombalbaye killed in military coup led by southerner Gen Félix Malloum. Frolinat continued its resistance. **1978:** Malloum tried to find a political solution by forming a coalition government with former Frolinat leader Hissène Habré, but it soon broke down. **1979:** Malloum forced to leave the country; interim government set up under Gen Goukouni Oueddei (Frolinat). Habré continued his opposition with his Army of the North (FAN), and Libya provided support for Goukouni. **1981–82:** Habré gained control of half the country. Goukouni fled and set up a 'government in exile'. **1983:** Habré's regime recognized by the Organization of African Unity (OAU) and France, but in the N, Goukouni's supporters, with Libya's help, fought on. Eventually a cease-fire was agreed, with latitude 16°N dividing the country. **1987:** Chad, France, and Libya agreed on OAU cease-fire to end the civil war between the Muslim Arab N and Christian and animist black African S. **1988:** Libya relinquished its claims to the Aouzou Strip. **1990:** President Habré ousted after army defeated by Libyan-backed Patriotic Salvation Movement (MPS) rebel troops based in the Sudan and led by Habré's former ally Idriss Deby. **1991–92:** Several antigovernment coups foiled. **1993:** Transitional charter adopted, as prelude to full democracy at a later date. **1997:** Nassour Ouaidou Guelendouksia appointed prime minister. Reconciliation agreement with rebel forces signed.

Chile Republic of

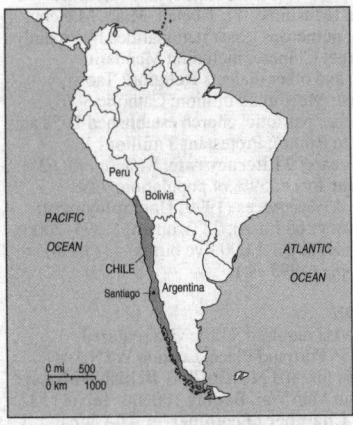

National name: *República de Chile* **Area:** 756,950 sq km/292,258 sq mi **Capital:** Santiago **Major towns/cities:** Concepción, Viña del Mar, Valparaiso, Talcahuano, San Bernardo, Puente Alto, Chillán, Rancagua, Talca, Temuco **Major ports:** Valparaíso, Antofagasta, Arica, Iquique, Punta Arenas **Physical features:** Andes mountains along E border, Atacama Desert in N, fertile central valley, grazing land and forest in S
Territories: Easter Island, Juan Fernández Islands, part of Tierra del Fuego, claim to part of Antarctica

Government
Head of state: Eduardo Frei from 1993 **Head of government:** Dante Cordova from 1995 **Political system:** emergent democracy **Administrative divisions:** 12 regions and one metropolitan area **Political parties:** Christian Democratic Party (PDC), moderate centrist; National Renewal Party (RN), right wing; Socialist Party of Chile (PS), left wing; Independent Democratic Union (UDI), right

wing; Party for Democracy (PPD), left of centre; Union of the Centre-Centre (UCC), right wing; Radical Party (PR), left of centre **Armed forces:** 89,700 (1996) **Conscription:** one year (army) or two years (navy and air force) **Death penalty:** retained and used for ordinary crimes **Defence spend:** (% GDP) 3.5 (1996) **Education spend:** (% GNP) 2.9 (1993–94) **Health spend:** (% GDP) 4.5 (1994)

Economy and resources
Currency: Chilean peso **GDP:** ($ US) 52 billion (1994) **Real GDP per capita (PPP):** ($ US) 9,129 (1994) **GDP growth rate:** 4.2% (1994); 7.3% (1990–95) **Average annual inflation:** 7.4% (1996); 17.9% (1985–95) **Foreign debt:** ($ US) 24.2 billion (1996) **Major trading partners:** USA, Japan, Brazil, Germany, Argentina, UK **Resources:** copper (world's largest producer), gold, silver, iron ore, molybdenum, cobalt, iodine, saltpetre, coal, natural gas, petroleum, hydroelectric power **Industries:** nonferrous metals, food processing, petroleum refining, chemicals, paper products (cellulose, newsprint, paper and cardboard), motor tyres, beer, glass sheets, motor vehicles **Exports:** copper, fruits, timber products, fishmeal, vegetables, manufactured foodstuffs and beverages. Principal market: USA 16.6% (1996) **Imports:** machinery and transport equipment, wheat, chemical and mineral products, consumer goods, raw materials. Principal source: USA 23.7% (1996) **Arable land:** 5.3% (1995) **Agricultural products:** wheat, sugar beet, potatoes, maize, fruit and vegetables; livestock

Population and society
Population: 14,421,000 (1996 est) **Population growth rate:** 1.6% (1990–95); 1.2% (2000–05) **Population density:** (per sq km) 19 (1996 est) **Urban population:** (% of total) 84 (1995) **Age distribution:** (% of total population) <15 29.5%, 15–65 63.8%, >65 6.6% (1995) **Ethnic groups:** 65% mestizo (mixed Native American and Spanish descent), 30% European, remainder mainly Native American **Language:** Spanish **Religion:** Roman Catholic **Education:** (compulsory years) 8 **Literacy rate:** 93% (men); 93% (women) (1995 est) **Labour force:** 38% of population: 19% agriculture, 25% industry, 56% services (1990) **Unemployment:** 6.4% (1996) **Life expectancy:** 71 (men); 78 (women) (1995–2000) **Child mortality rate:** (under 5, per 1,000 live births) 17 (1996) **Physicians:** 1 per 942 people (1993 est)

Practical information
Visa requirements: UK: visa not required. USA: visa not required **Embassy in the UK:** 12 Devonshire Street, London W1N 2DS. Tel: (0171) 580 6392; fax: (0171) 436 5204 **British embassy:** Avenida El Bosque Norte (Casilla 16552), Santiago 9. Tel: (2) 231 3737; fax: (2) 231 9771 **Chamber of commerce:** Cámara de Comercio de Santiago de Chile, AG, Santa Lucía 302, 3 º. Casilla 1297, Santiago. Tel: (2) 632 1232; fax: (2) 633 0962 **Airports:** international airports: Santiago (Arturo Merino Benítez), Arica (Chacalluta); domestic services to main towns; total passenger km: 5,398 million (1994) **Major holidays:** 1 January, 1, 21 May, 29 June, 15 August, 11, 18–19 September, 12 October, 1 November, 8, 25, 31, December; variable: Good Friday, Holy Saturday

Chronology
1535: First Spanish invasion of Chile abandoned in face of fierce resistance from indigenous Araucanian Indians. **1541:** Pedro de Valdivia began Spanish conquest and founded Santiago. **1553:** Valdivia captured and killed by Araucanian Indians led by Chief Lautaro. **17th century:** Spanish developed small agricultural settlements ruled by government subordinate to viceroy in Lima, Peru. **1778:** King of Spain appointed a separate captain-general to govern Chile. **1810:** Santiago junta proclaimed Chilean autonomy after Napoleon dethroned King of Spain. **1814:** Spanish viceroy regained control of Chile. **1817:** Army of the Andes, led by José de San Martín and Bernardo O'Higgins, defeated the Spanish. **1818:** Achieved independence from Spain with O'Higgins as supreme director. **1823–30:** O'Higgins forced to resign; civil war between conservative centralists and liberal federalists ended with conservative victory. **1833:** Autocratic republican constitution created unitary Roman Catholic state with strong president and limited franchise. **1851–61:** President Manuel Montt bowed to pressure to

liberalize constitution and reduce privileges of landowners and church. **1879–84:** Chile defeated Peru and Bolivia in War of the Pacific and increased its territory by a third. **late 19th century:** Mining of nitrate and copper became major industry; large-scale European immigration followed 'pacification' of Araucanian Indians. **1891:** Constitutional dispute between president and congress led to civil war; congressional victory reduced president to figurehead status. **1920:** Election of liberal president Arturo Alessandri Palma; congress blocked his social reform programme. **1925:** New constitution increased presidential powers, separated church and state, and made primary education compulsory. **1927:** Military coup led to dictatorship of Gen Carlos Ibáñez del Campo. **1931:** Sharp fall in price of copper and nitrate caused dramatic economic and political collapse. **1932:** Re-election of President Alessandri, who restored order by harsh measures. **1938:** Popular Front of Radicals, Socialists, and Communists took power under Pedro Aguirre Cedra, who introduced economic policies based on US New Deal. **1947:** Communists organized violent strikes to exploit discontent over high inflation. **1948–58:** Communist Party banned. **1952:** General Ibáñez elected president on law-and-order platform; austerity policies reduced inflation to 20%. **1958:** Jorge Alessandri (son of former president) succeeded Ibáñez as head of Liberal-Conservative coalition. **1964:** Christian Democrat Eduardo Frei Montalva became president; he introduced cautious 'communitarian' social reforms, but failed to combat inflation. **1970:** Salvador Allende, leader of Popular Unity coalition, became world's first democratically elected Marxist president; he embarked on an extensive programme of nationalization and radical social reform. **1973:** Allende killed in CIA-backed military coup; Gen Augusto Pinochet established dictatorship combining severe political repression with free-market economics. **1981:** Pinochet began eight-year term as president under new constitution described as 'transition to democracy'. **1983:** Economic recession provoked growing opposition to regime from all sides. **1988:** Referendum on whether Pinochet should serve a further term resulted in a clear 'No' vote; he agreed to hold elections in following year. **1990:** End of military regime; Christian Democrat Patricio Aylwin became president, with Pinochet as commander in chief of army; investigation into over 2,000 political executions during military regime. **1994:** Eduardo Frei (son of former president) succeeded Aylwin as president. **1995:** Frei introduced measures to reduce military influence in government. **1997:** Pinochet's attempt to become senator for life thwarted.

China People's Republic of

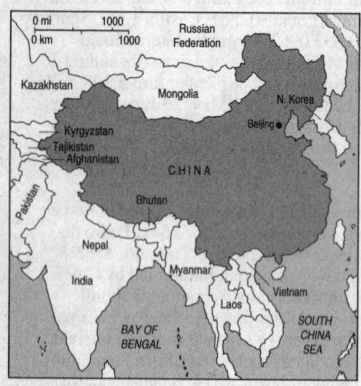

National name: *Zhonghua Renmin Gonghe Guo* **Area:** 9,572,900 sq km/3,696,000 sq mi **Capital:** Beijing (Peking) **Major towns/cities:** Shanghai, Hong Kong, Chongqing (Chungking), Tianjin, Guangzhou (Canton), Shenyang (Mukden), Wuhan, Nanjing (Nanking), Harbin, Chengdu, Xiang, Zibo **Major ports:** Tianjin (Tientsin), Shanghai, Hong Kong, Qingdao (Tsingtao), Guangzhou (Canton) **Physical features:** two-thirds of China is mountains or desert (N and W); the low-lying E is irrigated by rivers Huang He (Yellow River), Chang Jiang (Yangtze-Kiang), Xi Jiang (Si Kiang)

Government

Head of state: Jiang Zemin from 1993 **Head of government:** Zhu Rongli from 1998 **Political system:** communist republic **Administrative divisions:** 22 provinces, five autonomous regions, and three municipalities **Political party:** Chinese Communist Party (CCP), Marxist-Leninist-Maoist **Armed forces:** 2,935,000; reserves approximately 1.2 million (1996) **Conscription:** selective: 3 years (army and marines), 4 years (air force and navy) **Death penalty:** retained and used for ordinary crimes **Defence spend:** (% GDP) 5.7 (1996) **Education spend:** (% GNP) 2.6 (1993–94) **Health spend:** (% GDP) 1.8 (1990–95)

Economy and resources

Currency: yuan **GDP:** ($ US) 522.2 billion (1994) **GDP per capita:** ($ US) 2,604 (1994) **GDP growth rate:** 10.2% (1995); 12.8% (1990–95) **Average annual inflation:** 10% (1996); 9.5% (1985–95) **Foreign debt:** ($ US) 107.3 billion (1996) **Major trading partners:** Japan, USA, Taiwan **Resources:** coal, graphite, tungsten, molybdenum, antimony, tin (world's largest producer), lead (world's fifth-largest producer), mercury, bauxite, phosphate rock, iron ore (world's largest producer), diamonds, gold, manganese, zinc (world's third-largest producer), petroleum, natural gas, fish **Industries:** raw cotton and cotton cloth, cement, paper, sugar, salt, plastics, aluminium ware, steel, rolled steel, chemical fertilizers, silk, woollen fabrics, bicycles, cameras, electrical appliances; tourism is growing **Exports:** basic manufactures, miscellaneous manufactured articles (particularly clothing and toys), crude petroleum, machinery and transport equipment, fishery products, cereals, canned food, tea, raw silk, cotton cloth. Principal market: Japan 20.9% (1996) **Imports:** machinery and transport equipment, basic manufactures, chemicals, wheat, rolled steel, fertilizers. Principal source: Japan 22.1% (1996) **Arable land:** 9.9% (1995) **Agricultural products:** sweet potatoes, wheat, maize, soya beans, rice, sugar cane, tobacco, cotton, jute; world's largest fish catch (over 17 tonnes in 1993)

Population and society

Population: 1,232,083,000 (1996 est) **Population growth rate:** 1.1% (1990–95); 0.8% (2000–05) **Population density:** (per sq km) 128 (1996 est) **Urban population:** (% of total) 30 (1995) **Age distribution:** (% of total population) <15 26.4%, 15–65 67.5%, >65 6.1% (1995) **Ethnic groups:** 94% Han Chinese, the remainder being Zhuang, Uygur, Hui (Muslims), Yi, Tibetan, Miao, Manchu, Mongol, Buyi, or Korean; numerous lesser nationalities live mainly in border regions **Language:** Chinese, including Mandarin (official), Cantonese, Wu, and other dialects **Religion:** Taoist, Confucianist, and Buddhist; Muslim 20 million; Catholic 3–6 million (divided between the 'patriotic' church established 1958 and the 'loyal' church subject to Rome); Protestant 3 million **Education:** (compulsory years) 9 **Literacy rate:** 84% (men); 62% (women) (1995 est) **Labour force:** 59% of population: 72% agriculture, 15% industry, 13% services (1990) **Unemployment:** 2.8% (1994) **Life expectancy:** 68 (men); 72 (women) (1995–2000) **Child mortality rate:** (under 5, per 1,000 live births) 43 (1996) **Physicians:** 1 per 636 people (1995 est)

Practical information

Visa requirements: UK: visa required. USA: visa required **Embassy in the UK:** 49–51 Portland Place, London W1N 3AH. Tel: (0171) 636 9375/5726; fax: (0171) 636 2981 **British embassy:** 11 Guang Hua Lu, Jian Guo Men Wai, Beijing 100600. Tel: (1) 532 1961/5; fax: (1) 532 1937 **Chamber of commerce:** All-China Federation of Industry and Commerce, 93 Beiheyan Dajie, Beijing 100006. Tel: (1) 513 6677; fax: (1) 512 2631 **Airports:** international airports: Beijing (Capital International Central), Guangzhou (Baiyun), Shanghai (Hongqiao), Hong Kong (Kai Tak); 59 domestic airports; total passenger km: 51,395 million (1994) **Major holidays:** 1 January, 8 March, 1 May, 1 August, 9 September, 1–2 October; variable: Spring Festival (January/February, 4 days),

Chronology

c. 3000 BC: Yangshao culture reached its peak in the Huang He Valley; displaced by Longshan culture in E China. **c. 1766–c. 1122**

China: Provinces

(– = not applicable.)

Province	Alternative transliteration	Capital	Area		Population (1990)
			sq km	sq mi	
Anhui	Anhwei	Hefei	139,900	54,015	56,181,000
Fujian	Fukien	Fuzhou	123,100	47,528	30,048,000
Gansu	Kansu	Lanzhou	530,000	204,633	22,371,000
Guangdong	Kwantung	Guangzhou	231,400	89,343	62,829,000
Guizhou	Kweichow	Guiyang	174,000	67,181	32,392,000
Hainan	–	Haikou	34,000	13,127	6,420,000
Hebei	Hopei	Shijiazhuang	202,700	78,262	61,082,000
Heilongjiang	Heilungkiang	Harbin	463,600	178,996	35,215,000
Henan	Honan	Zhengzhou	167,000	64,479	85,510,000
Hubei	Hupei	Wuhan	187,500	72,394	53,969,000
Hunan	–	Changsha	210,500	81,274	60,660,000
Jiangsu	Kiangsu	Nanjing	102,200	39,459	67,057,000
Jiangxi	Kiangsi	Nanchang	164,800	63,629	37,710,000
Jilin	Kirin	Changchun	187,000	72,201	24,659,000
Liaoning	–	Shenyang	151,000	58,301	39,460,000
Qinghai	Tsinghai	Xining	721,000	278,378	4,457,000
Shaanxi	Shensi	Xian	195,800	75,598	32,882,000
Shandong	Shantung	Jinan	153,300	59,189	84,393,000
Shanxi	Shansi	Taiyuan	157,100	60,656	28,759,000
Sichuan	Szechwan	Chengdu	569,000	219,691	107,218,000
Yunnan	–	Kunming	436,200	168,417	36,973,000
Zhejiang	Chekiang	Hangzhou	101,800	39,305	41,446,000

Autonomous Region

Guangxi Zhuang	Kwangsi Chuang	Nanning	220,400	85,096	42,246,000
Nei Mongol	Inner Mongolia	Hohhot	450,000	173,745	21,457,000
Ningxia Hui	Ninghsia-Hui	Yinchuan	170,000	65,637	4,655,000
Xinjiang Uygur	Sinkiang Uighur	Urumqi	1,646,800	635,829	15,156,000
Xizang	Tibet	Lhasa	1,221,600	471,660	2,196,000

Municipality

Beijing	Peking	–	17,800	6,873	10,870,000
Shanghai	–	–	5,800	2,239	13,510,000
Tianjin	Tientsin	–	4,000	1,544	8,830,000

BC: First major dynasty, the Shang, arose from Longshan culture; writing and calendar developed. **c. 1122–256 BC:** Zhou people of W China overthrew Shang and set up new dynasty; development of money and written laws. **c. 500 BC:** Confucius expounded philosophy which guided Chinese government and society for the next 2,000 years. **403–221 BC:** 'Warring States Period': Zhou Empire broke up into small kingdoms. **221–206 BC:** Qin kingdom defeated all rivals and established first empire with strong central government; emperor Shi Huangdi built Great Wall of China. **202 BC–AD 220:** Han dynasty expanded empire into central Asia; first overland trade with Europe; art and literature flourished; Buddhism introduced from India. **220–581:** Large-scale rebellion destroyed Han dynasty; empire split into three competing kingdoms; several short-lived dynasties ruled parts of China. **581–618:** Sui dynasty reunified China and repelled Tatar invaders. **618–907:** Tang dynasty enlarged and strengthened the empire; great revival of culture; major rebellion 875–84. **907–60:** 'Five Dynasties and Ten Kingdoms': disintegration of empire amid war and economic decline; development of printing. **960–1279:** Song dynasty reunified China and restored order; civil service examinations introduced; population reached 100 million; Manchurians occupied northern China 1127. **1279:** Mongols conquered all China, which became part of the vast empire of Kublai Khan, founder of the Yuan dynasty; Venetian traveller Marco Polo visited China 1275–92. **1368:** Rebellions drove out the Mongols; Ming dynasty expanded empire; architecture flourished in new capital of Beijing; dislike of Mongols led to contempt for all things foreign. **1516:** Portuguese explorers reached Macau; other European traders followed; first Chinese porcelain arrived in Europe 1580. **1644:** Manchurian invasion established the Qing (or Manchu) dynasty; Manchurians assimilated and Chinese

trade and culture continued to thrive. **1796–1804:** Anti-Manchu revolt weakened Qing dynasty; population increase in excess of food supplies led to falling living standards and cultural decline. **1839–42:** First Opium War; Britain forced China to cede Hong Kong and open five ports to European trade; Second Opium War extracted further trade concessions 1856–60. **1850–64:** Millions died in Taiping Rebellion; Taipings combined Christian and Chinese beliefs and demanded land reform. **1894–95:** Sino-Japanese War: Chinese driven out of Korea. **1897–98:** Germany, Russia, France, and Britain leased ports in China; conquest by European empires seemed likely. **1898:** Hong Kong was secured by Britain on a 99-year lease. **1900:** Anti-Western Boxer Rebellion crushed by foreign intervention; jealousy between Great Powers prevented partition. **1911:** Revolution broke out; Republic of China proclaimed by Sun Yat-sen of Guomindang (National People's Party). **1912:** Abdication of infant emperor Pu-i; General Yuan Shih-K'ai became dictator. **1916:** Power of central government collapsed on death of Yuan Shih-K'ai; N China dominated by local warlords. **1919:** Beijing students formed 4th May movement to protest at transfer of German possessions in China to Japan. **1921:** Sun Yat-sen elected president of nominal national government; Chinese Communist Party founded; communists worked with Guomindang to reunite China from 1923. **1925:** Death of Sun Yat-sen; leadership of Guomindang gradually passed to military commander Chiang Kai-shek. **1926–28:** Revolutionary Army of Chiang Kai-shek reunified China; Guomindang broke with communists and tried to suppress them in civil war. **1932:** Japan invaded Manchuria and established puppet state of Manchukuo. **1934–35:** Communists undertook Long March from Jiangxi and Fujian in S to Yan'an in N to escape encirclement by Guomindang.

1937–45: Japan renewed invasion of China; Chiang Kai-shek received help from USA and Britain from 1941. **1946:** Civil war resumed between Guomindang and communists led by Mao Zedong. **1949:** Victorious communists proclaimed People's Republic of China under Chairman Mao; Guomindang fled to Taiwan. **1950–53:** China intervened heavily in Korean War. **1958:** 'Great Leap Forward': extremist five-year plan to accelerate output severely weakened economy. **1960:** Sino-Soviet split: China accused USSR of betraying communism; USSR withdrew technical advisers; border clashes on Ussuri River 1969. **1962:** Economic recovery programme under Liu Shaoqi caused divisions between 'rightists' and 'leftists'; brief border war with India. **1966–69:** 'Great Proletarian Cultural Revolution'; leftists overthrew Liu Shaoqi with support of Mao; Red Guards disrupted education, government, and daily life in attempt to enforce revolutionary principles. **1970:** Mao supported efforts of Prime Minister Zhou Enlai to restore order. **1971:** People's Republic of China admitted to United Nations; full diplomatic relations with USA established in 1979. **1976:** Deaths of Zhou Enlai and Mao Zedong led to power struggle between rightists and leftists; Hua Guofeng became leader and arrested leftist 'Gang of Four'. **1977–81:** Rightist Deng Xiaoping emerged as supreme leader; pragmatic economic policies introduced market incentives and encouraged foreign trade. **1987:** Deng Ziaoping retired from Politburo but remained a dominant figure. **1989:** Over 2,000 killed when army crushed prodemocracy student demonstrations in Tiananmen Square, Beijing; international sanctions imposed. **1991:** China and USSR reached agreement on disputed border. **1996:** Reunification with Taiwan declared a priority. **1997:** Deng Xiaoping died aged 92. China and Russia signed border agreement. Reductions in armed forces. Government reported strong growth in economy. Hong Kong returned to Chinese sovereignty. President Jiang Zemin promised widespread privatization. Relations with USA improved; Jiang visited USA. Pro-democracy dissident Wei Jingsheng released from prison. **1998** Zhu Rongli was voted in as new prime minister.

Colombia Republic of

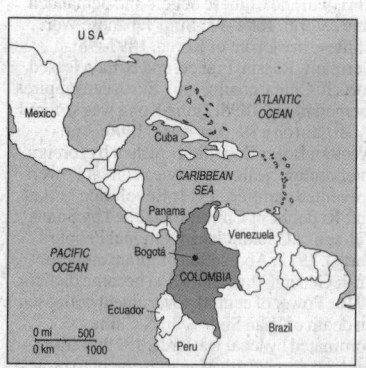

National name: *República de Colombia* **Area:** 1,141,748 sq km/440,828 sq mi **Capital:** Bogotá **Major towns/cities:** Medellín, Cali, Barranquilla, Cartagena, Bucaramanga, Buenaventura **Major ports:** Barranquilla, Cartagena, Buenaventura **Physical features:** the Andes mountains run N–S; flat coastland in W and plains (llanos) in E; Magdalena River runs N to Caribbean Sea; includes islands of Providencia, San Andrés, and Mapelo; almost half the country is forested

Government

Head of state and government: Andres Pastrana from 1998 **Political system:** democracy **Administrative divisions:** 32 departments and one capital district **Political parties:** Liberal Party (PL), centrist; Conservative Party (PSC), right of centre; M-19 Democratic Alliance (ADM-19), left of centre; National Salvation Movement (MSN), right-of-centre coalition grouping **Armed forces:** 146,300 (1996); plus a paramilitary police force of 87,000 **Conscription:** selective conscription for 1–2 years **Death penalty:** abolished 1910 **Defence spend:** (% GDP) 2.6 (1996) **Education spend:** (% GNP) 3.7 (1993–94) **Health spend:** (% GDP) 1 (1995)

Economy and resources

Currency: Colombian peso **GDP:** ($ US) 67.3 billion (1994) **Real GDP per capita (PPP):** ($ US) 6,107 (1994) **GDP growth rate:** 5.7% (1994); 4.6% (1990–95) **Average annual inflation:** 20.4% (1996); 25.2% (1985–95) **Foreign debt:** ($ US) 24.7 billion (1996) **Major trading partners:** USA, EU countries, Argentina, Brazil, Chile, Mexico, Venezuela, Japan **Resources:** petroleum, natural gas, coal, nickel, emeralds (accounts for about half of world production), gold, manganese, copper, lead, mercury, platinum, limestone, phosphates **Industries:** food processing, chemical products, textiles, beverages, transport equipment, cement **Exports:** coffee, petroleum and petroleum products, coal, gold, bananas, cut flowers, cotton, chemicals, textiles, paper. Principal market: USA 33.6% (1995). Illegal trade in cocaine in 1995 it was estimated that approximately $3.5 billion (equivalent to about 4% of GDP) was entering Colombia as the proceeds of drug-trafficking **Imports:** machinery and transport equipment, chemicals, minerals, food, metals. Principal source: USA 39% (1995) **Arable land:** 2.3% (1995) **Agricultural products:** coffee (world's second-largest producer), cocoa, sugar cane, bananas, tobacco, cotton, cut flowers, rice, potatoes, maize; timber; beef production

Population and society

Population: 36,444,000 (1996 est) **Population growth rate:** 1.7% (1990–95); 1.3% (2000–05) **Population density:** (per sq km) 32 (1996 est) **Urban population:** (% of total) 73 (1995) **Age distribution:** (% of total population) <15 32.9%, 15–65 62.6%, >65

4.5% (1995) **Ethnic groups:** main ethnic groups are of mixed Spanish, Native American, and African descent; Spanish customs and values predominate **Language:** Spanish **Religion:** Roman Catholic **Education:** (compulsory years) 5 **Literacy rate:** 87% (men); 86% (women) (1995 est) **Labour force:** 40% of population: 27% agriculture, 23% industry, 50% services (1990) **Unemployment:** 11.9% (1996) **Life expectancy:** 67 (men); 73 (women) (1995–2000) **Child mortality rate:** (under 5, per 1,000 live births) 40 (1996) **Physicians:** 1 per 1,105 people (1993 est)

Practical information

Visa requirements: UK: visa not required for a stay of up to 90 days. USA: visa not required for a stay of up to 90 days **Embassy in the UK:** Flat 3A, 3 Hans Crescent, London SW1X 0LN. Tel: (0171) 589 9177; fax: (0171) 581 1829 **British embassy:** Apartado Aéreo 4508, Torre Propaganda Sancho, Calle 98, No. 9–03, Piso 4, Santa Fe de Bogotá DC. Tel: (1) 218 5111; fax: (1) 218 2460 **Chamber of commerce:** Instituto Colombiano de Comercio Exterior, Apartado Aéreo 240193, Calle 28, No. 13-A-15, 5 º Santa Fe de Bogotá DC. Tel: (1) 283 3284; fax: (1) 281 2560, 283 1953 **Airports:** international airports: Santa Fe de Bogotá, DC (El Dorado International), Medellín, Cali, Barranguilla, Bucaramanga, Cartagena, Cúcuta, Leticia, Pereira, San Andrés, Santa Maria; over 80 smaller airports serving domestic flights; total passenger km: 5,675 million **Major holidays:** 1, 6 January, 29 June, 20 July, 7, 15 August, 12 October, 1, 15 November, 8, 25, 30–31 December; variable: Ascension Thursday, Corpus Christi, Good Friday, Holy Thursday, St Joseph (March), Sacred Heart (June)

Chronology

late 15th century: S Colombia became part of Inca Empire, whose core lay in Peru. **1522:** Spanish conquistador Pascual de Andagoya reached San Juan River. **1536–38:** Spanish conquest by Jimenez de Quesada overcame powerful Chibcha Indian chiefdom, which had its capital in the uplands at Bogotá and was renowned for its gold crafts; became part of Spanish Viceroyalty of Peru, which covered much of South America. **1717:** Bogotá became capital of new Spanish Viceroyalty of Nueva (New) Granada, which also ruled Ecuador and Venezuela. **1809:** Struggle for independence from Spain began. **1819:** Venezuelan freedom fighter Simón Bolívar, 'The Liberator', who had withdrawn to Colombia 1814, raised a force of 5,000 British mercenaries and defeated Spanish at the battle of Boyaca, establishing Colombia's independence; Gran Colombia formed, also comprising Ecuador, Panama, and Venezuela. **1830:** Became separate state, which included Panama, on dissolution of Republic of Gran Colombia. **1863:** Became major coffee exporter. Federalizing, anti-clerical Liberals came to power, with country divided into nine largely autonomous 'sovereign' states; church disestablished. **1885:** Conservatives came to power, beginning 45 years of political dominance; power was recentralized and church restored to influence. **1899–1903:** Civil war between Liberals and Conservatives, ended with Panama's separation as an independent state. **1930:** Liberals returned to power at the time of the economic depression; social legislation introduced and labour movement encouraged. **1946:** Conservatives returned to power after Liberal vote divided between rival candidates. **1948:** Left-wing mayor of Bogotá assassinated; widespread outcry. **1949:** Start of civil war, 'La Violencia', during which over 250,000 people died. **1957:** Hoping to halt violence, Conservatives and Liberals agreed to form National Front, sharing the presidency. **1970:** National Popular Alliance (ANAPO) formed as left-wing opposition to National Front. **1974:** National Front accord temporarily ended. **1975:** Civil unrest due to disillusionment with government. **1978:** Liberals, under Julio Turbay, revived the accord and began an intensive fight against drug dealers. **1982:** Liberals maintained their control of congress but lost the presidency. Conservative president Belisario Betancur granted guerrillas an amnesty and freed political prisoners. **1984:** Minister of justice assassinated by drug dealers; campaign against them stepped up. **1986:** Virgilio Barco Vargas, Liberal, elected president by record margin. **1989:** Drug cartel assassinated leading presidential candidate; Vargas declared antidrug war; bombing campaign by drug traffickers killed hundreds; police killed José Rodríguez Gacha, one of the most wanted cartel leaders. **1990:**

Cesar Gaviria Trujillo elected president. Liberals maintained control of congress. **1991:** New constitution prohibited extradition of Colombians wanted for trial in other countries; several leading drug traffickers arrested. Many guerrillas abandoned the armed struggle, but the Colombian Revolutionary Armed Forces (Farc) and National Liberation Army remained active. Liberals won general election. **1992:** Medellín drug-cartel leader Pablo Escobar escaped from prison. State of emergency declared. **1993:** Escobar shot while attempting to avoid arrest. **1994:** Liberals returned to power, with reduced majority. Ernesto Samper Pizano, Liberal, elected president. **1995:** Samper under pressure to resign over corruption allegations; state of emergency declared. Leaders of Cali drug-cartel imprisoned. **1998:** Andres Pastrana elected president, ending the Liberal Party's 12-year lock on the presidency.

Comoros Federal Islamic Republic of

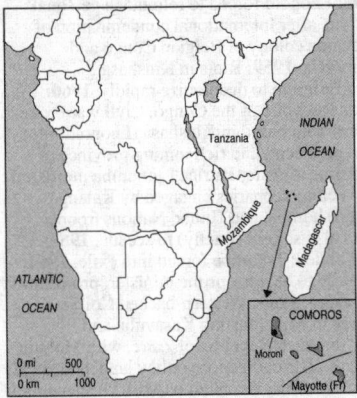

National name: *Jumhurīyat al-Qumur al-Itthādīyah al-Islāmīyah* or *République Fédérale Islamique des Comoros* **Area:** 1,862 sq km/718 sq mi **Capital:** Moroni **Major towns/cities:** Mutsamudu, Domoni, Fomboni, Dzaoudzi **Physical features:** comprises the volcanic islands of Njazídja, Nzwani, and Mwali (formerly Grande Comore, Anjouan, Moheli); at N end of Mozambique Channel in Indian Ocean between Madagascar and coast of Africa

Government
Head of state: Muhammad Taki Abdoulkarim from 1996 **Head of government:** Ahmed Abdou from 1996 **Political system:** emergent democracy **Administrative divisions:** three prefectures (each of the three main islands is a prefecture) **Political parties:** National Union for Democracy in the Comoros (UNDC), Islamic, nationalist; Rally for Democracy and Renewal (RDR), left of centre **Armed forces:** 800 (1995) **Conscription:** military service is voluntary **Death penalty:** retained and used for ordinary crimes but can be considered abolitionist in practice (no executions since independence) **Education spend:** (% GNP) 3.7 (1994) **Health spend:** (% GDP) 3.3 (1990)

Economy and resources
Currency: Comorian franc **GDP:** ($ US) 370 million (1994 est) **Real GDP per capita (PPP):** ($ US) 700 (1994 est) **GDP growth rate:** 0.9% (1994) **Average annual inflation:** 7.5% (1996); 4% (1985–95) **Foreign debt:** ($ US) 190 million (1994) **Major trading partners:** France, USA, Bahrain, Kenya, Botswana, Brazil, South Africa **Industries:** sawmilling, processing of vanilla and copra, printing, soft drinks, plastics **Exports:** vanilla, cloves, ylang-ylang, essences, copra, coffee. Principal market: France 54.6% (1995) **Imports:** rice, petroleum products, transport equipment, meat and dairy products, cement, iron and steel, clothing and footwear. Principal source: France 60.1% (1995) **Arable land:** 35% (1995) **Agricultural products:** vanilla, ylang-ylang, cloves, basil, cassava, sweet potatoes, rice, maize, pulses, coconuts, bananas

Population and society
Population: 632,000 (1996 est) **Population growth rate:** 3.7% (1990–95) **Population density:** (per sq km) 283 (1996 est) **Urban**

population: (% of total) 30 (1994) **Age distribution:** (% of total population) <15 49%, 15–65 49%, >65 2% (1994) **Ethnic groups:** population of mixed origin, with Africans, Arabs, and Malaysians predominating; the principal ethnic group is the Antalaotra **Language:** Arabic (official), Comorian (Swahili and Arabic dialect), Makua, French **Religion:** Muslim; Islam is the state religion **Education:** (compulsory years) 9 **Literacy rate:** 64% (men); 50% (women) (1995 est) **Labour force:** 44% of population: 77% agriculture, 9% industry, 13% services (1990) **Unemployment:** 16% (1990) **Life expectancy:** 58 (men); 59 (women) (1995–2000) **Child mortality rate:** (under 5, per 1,000 live births) 111 (1996) **Physicians:** 1 per 7,500 people (1990)

Practical information
Visa requirements: UK: visa required. USA: visa required **Embassy for the UK:** 20 rue Marbeau, 75016 Paris, France. Tel: (1) 4067 9054; fax: (1) 4067 7296 **British embassy:** British Consulate, Henri Fraise et Fils 38, Co Océan Indien, PO Box 986, Moroni. Tel: (269) 733 182; fax: (269) 733 182. (All staff based in Madagascar.) **Chamber of commerce:** Chambre de Commerce, d'Industrie et d'Agriculture, BP 763, Moroni. Tel: (269) 610 426 **Airports:** international airport: Moroni-Hahaya, on Njazídja; each of the three other islands has a small airfield; total passenger km: 3 million (1994) **Major holidays:** 6 July, 27 November; variable: Eid-ul-Adha, Arafa, Ashora, first day of Ramadan, end of Ramadan, New Year (Muslim), Prophet's Birthday

Chronology
5th century AD: First settled by Malay-Polynesian immigrants. **7th century:** Converted to Islam by Arab seafarers and fell under the rule of local sultans. **late 16th century:** First visited by European navigators. **1886:** Moheli island in S became a French protectorate. **1904:** Slave trade abolished, ending influx of Africans. **1912:** Grande Comore and Anjouan, the main islands, joined Moheli to become a French colony, which was attached to Madagascar from 1914. **1947:** Became a French Overseas Territory separate from Madagascar. **1961:** Internal self-government achieved. **1975:** Independence achieved from France, but island of Mayotte to the SE voted to remain part of France. Joined the United Nations. **1976:** President Ahmed Abdallah overthrown in a coup by Ali Soilih; relations deteriorated with France as a Maoist-Islamic socialist programme was pursued. **1978:** Soilih killed by French mercenaries led by Bob Denard. Federal Islamic republic proclaimed, with exiled Abdallah restored as president; diplomatic relations re-established with France. **1979:** The Comoros became a one-party state; powers of the federal government increased. **1989:** Abdallah killed by French mercenaries who, under French and South African pressure, turned authority over to French administration; Said Muhammad Djohar became president in a multiparty democracy. **1990–92:** Antigovernment coups foiled. **1993:** Djohar's supporters won overall majority in assembly elections. **1995:** Djohar overthrown in coup led by Col Denard, who was persuaded to withdraw by French troops. **1996:** Djohar allowed to return from exile in a nonpolitical capacity and Muhammad Taki Abdoulkarim elected president. National Rally for Development (RND) virtually unopposed in assembly elections. Ahmed Abdou appointed prime minister. **1997:** Secessionist rebels took control of the island of Anjouan.

Congo Democratic Republic of (formerly Zaire)

National name: *République Démocratique du Congo* **Area:** 2,344,900 sq km/905,366 sq mi **Capital:** Kinshasa **Major towns/cities:** Lubumbashi, Kananga, Mbuji-Mayi, Kisangani, Bukavu, Kikwit, Matadi **Major ports:** Matadi, Kalemie **Physical features:** Zaïre/Congo River basin has tropical rainforest (second-largest remaining in world) and savanna; mountains in E and W; lakes Tanganyika, Albert, Edward; Ruwenzori Range; Victoria Falls

Government
Head of state and government: Laurent Kabila from 1997 **Political system:** transitional **Administrative divisions:** ten regions **Political**

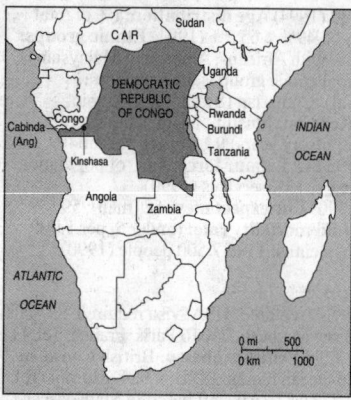

parties: Popular Movement of the Revolution (MPR), African socialist; Democratic Forces of Congo–Kinshasa (formerly Sacred Union, an alliance of some 130 opposition groups), moderate, centrist; Union for Democracy and Social Progress (UPDS), left of centre; Congolese National Movement–Lumumba (MNC), left of centre **Armed forces:** 28,100 (1996); plus paramilitary forces of 37,000 **Conscription:** military service is compulsory **Death penalty:** retained and used for ordinary crimes **Defence spend:** (% GDP) 2.8 (1996) **Education spend:** (% GNP) 0.9 (1990) **Health spend:** (% GDP) 0.8 (1990)

Economy and resources
Currency: zaïre **GDP:** ($ US) 7.2 billion (1994 est) **Real GDP per capita (PPP):** ($ US) 429 (1994) **GDP growth rate:** –0.6% (1995) **Average annual inflation:** 542% (1995) **Foreign debt:** ($ US) 13.96 billion (1996) **Major trading partners:** Belgium/Luxembourg, USA, France, UK, Germany, South Africa **Resources:** petroleum, copper, cobalt (65% of world's reserves), manganese, zinc, tin, uranium, silver, gold, diamonds (one of the world's largest producers of industrial diamonds) **Industries:** textiles, cement, food processing, tobacco, rubber, engineering, wood products, leather, metallurgy and metal extraction, electrical equipment, transport vehicles **Exports:** mineral products (mainly copper, cobalt, industrial diamonds, and petroleum), agricultural products (chiefly coffee). Principal market: Belgium/Luxembourg 37% (1995) **Imports:** manufactured goods, food and live animals, machinery and transport equipment, chemicals, mineral fuels and lubricants. Principal source: Belgium/Luxembourg 15% (1995) **Arable land:** 3.2% (1995) **Agricultural products:** coffee, palm oil, palm kernels, sugar cane, cassava, plantains, maize, groundnuts, bananas, yams, rice, rubber, seed cotton; forest resources

Population and society
Population: 46,812,000 (1996 est) **Population growth rate:** 3.2% (1990–95); 3% (2000–05) **Population density:** (per sq km) 20 (1996 est) **Urban population:** (% of total) 29 (1995) **Age distribution:** (% of total population) <15 48%, 15–65 49.1%, >65 2.9% (1995) **Ethnic groups:** almost entirely of African descent, distributed among over 200 ethnic groups, the most numerous being the Kongo, Luba, Lunda, Mongo, and Zande **Language:** French (official); Swahili, Lingala, Kikongo, and Tshiluba are recognized as national languages; over 200 other languages **Religion:** Roman Catholic, Protestant, Kimbanguist; also half a million Muslims **Education:** (compulsory years) 6 **Literacy rate:** 84% (men); 61% (women) (1995 est) **Labour force:** 43% of population: 68% agriculture, 13% industry, 19% services (1990) **Unemployment:** 35% (1993 est) **Life expectancy:** 50 (men); 53 (women) (1995–2000) **Child mortality rate:** (under 5, per 1,000 live births) 131 (1996) **Physicians:** 1 per 15,150 people (1993 est)

Practical information
Visa requirements: UK: visa required. USA: visa required **Embassy in the UK:** 26 Chesham Place, London SW1X 8HH. Tel: (0171) 235 6137; fax: (0171) 235 9048 **British embassy:** BP 8049, avenue des Trois Z, Kinshasa-Gombe. Tel: (12) 34775/8 **Chamber of commerce:** Chambre de Commerce, d'Industrie et d'Agriculture, BP 7247, 10 avenue des Aviateurs, Kinshasa. Tel: (12) 22286; telex: 21071 **Airports:** international airports: Kinshasa (N'djili), Luano (near Lubumbashi), Bukava, Goma, Kisangani; over 40 domestic airports and 150 landing strips; total passenger km: 480 million (1994) **Major holidays:** 1, 4 January, 1, 20 May, 24, 30 June, 1 August, 14, 27 October, 17, 24 November, 25 December

Chronology
13th century: Rise of Kongo Empire, centred on banks of Zaïre/Congo river. **1483:** First visited by Portuguese, who named the area Zaire (from Zadi, 'big water') and converted local rulers to Christianity. **16th–17th centuries:** Great development of slave trade by Portuguese, Dutch, British, and French merchants, initially supplied by Kongo intermediaries. **18th century:** Rise of Luba state, in southern copper belt of N Katanga, and Lunda, in Kasai region in central S. **mid-19th century:** Eastern Zaire invaded by Arab slave traders from E Africa. **1874–77:** British explorer Henry Morton Stanley navigated Congo River to Atlantic Ocean. **1879–87:** Stanley engaged by King Leopold II of Belgium to sign protection treaties with local chiefs and 'Congo Free State' awarded to Leopold by 1884–85 Berlin Conference; great expansion in rubber export, using forced labour. **1908:** Leopold forced to relinquish personal control of Congo Free State, after international condemnation of human-rights abuses. Became colony of Belgian Congo and important exporter of minerals. **1959:** Riots in Kinshasa (Leopoldville) persuaded Belgium to decolonize rapidly. **1960:** Independence achieved as Republic of the Congo. Civil war broke out between central government based in Kinshasa (Leopoldville) with Joseph Kasavubu as president, and rich mining province of Katanga. **1961:** Former prime minister Patrice Lumumba murdered in Katanga; fighting between mercenaries engaged by Katanga secessionist leader Moise Tshombe, and United Nations troops; Kasai and Kivu provinces also sought (briefly) to secede. **1963:** Katanga secessionist war ended; Tshombe forced into exile. **1964:** Tshombe returned from exile to become prime minister; pro-Marxist groups took control of E Zaire. **1965:** Western-backed Col Sese Seko Mobutu seized power in coup, ousting Kasavubu and Tshombe. **1971:** Country renamed Republic of Zaire, with Mobutu as president as *authenticité* (Africanization) policy launched. **1972:** Mobutu's Popular Movement of the Revolution (MPR) became only legal political party. Katanga province renamed Shaba. **1974:** Foreign-owned businesses and plantations seized by Mobutu and given to his political allies. **1977:** Original owners of confiscated properties invited back. Zairean guerrillas, chiefly Lundas, invaded Shaba province from Angola, but were repulsed by Moroccan, French, and Belgian paratroopers. **1980s:** International creditors forced launch of series of austerity programmes, after level of foreign indebtedness had mounted with collapse in world copper prices. **1991:** After antigovernment riots, Mobutu agreed to end ban on multiparty politics and share power with opposition; Etienne Tshisekedi appointed premier, but soon dismissed. **1992:** Tshisekedi reinstated against Mobutu's wishes after renewed rioting. **1993:** Rival pro- and anti-Mobutu governments created. **1994:** Kengo Wa Dondo elected prime minister by interim parliament, with Mobutu's agreement. Mass influx of Rwandan refugees. **1995:** Continuing secessionist activity in Shaba and Kasai provinces and interethnic warfare in Kivu, adjoining Rwanda in E. **1996:** Zaire on brink of war with Rwanda after Rwandan support of Hutu killings by Tutsis in Zaire. Massive Hutu refugee crisis narrowly averted as thousands allowed to return to Rwanda. **1997:** Mobutu ousted by rebel forces of Laurent Kabila, who declared himself president and renamed Zaire the Democratic Republic of Congo. Fighting between rival army factions.

Congo Republic of the

National name: *République du Congo* **Area:** 342,000 sq km/132,046 sq mi **Capital:** Brazzaville **Major towns/cities:** Pool, Pointe-Noire, Nkayi, Loubomo, Bouenza, Cuvette, Niari, Plateaux **Major ports:** Pointe-Noire **Physical features:** narrow coastal plain rises to central plateau, then falls into northern basin; Congo River on the border with the Democratic Republic of Congo; half the country is rainforest

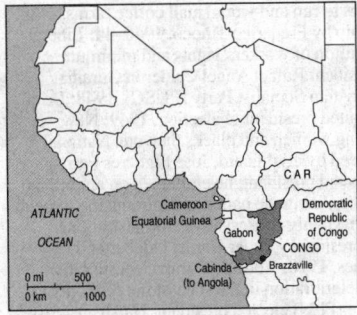

Government

Head of state: Denis Sassou-Nguessou from 1997 **Head of government:** Charles David Ganao from 1996 **Political system:** emergent democracy **Administrative divisions:** nine regions and one capital district **Political parties:** Pan-African Union for Social Democracy (UPADS), moderate, left of centre; Congolese Movement for Democracy and Integral Development (MCDDI), moderate, left of centre; Congolese Labour Party (PCT), left wing **Armed forces:** 10,000 (1996); plus a paramilitary force of 5,000 **Conscription:** national service is voluntary **Death penalty:** retains the death penalty for ordinary crimes but can be considered abolitionist in practice (last execution 1982) **Defence spend:** (% GDP) 1.9 (1996) **Education spend:** (% GNP) 8.3 (1993–94) **Health spend:** (% GDP) 3.6 (1990–95)

Economy and resources

Currency: franc CFA **GDP:** ($ US) 1.6 billion (1994) **Real GDP per capita (PPP):** ($ US) 2,410 (1994) **GDP growth rate:** –4.9% (1994); –0.6% (1990–95) **Average annual inflation:** 7% (1996); 2.2% (1985–95) **Foreign debt:** ($ US) 6.03 billion (1995) **Major trading partners:** France, Belgium, Luxembourg, USA, Italy, Spain, China **Resources:** petroleum, natural gas, lead, zinc, gold, copper, phosphate, iron ore, potash, bauxite **Industries:** mining, food processing, textiles, cement, metal goods, chemicals, forest products **Exports:** petroleum and petroleum products, saw logs and veneer logs, veneer sheets. Principal market: Belgium and Luxembourg 24.3% (1995) **Imports:** machinery, chemical products, iron and steel, transport equipment, foodstuffs. Principal source: France 31.2% (1995) **Arable land:** 0.4% (1995) **Agricultural products:** cassava, plantains, sugar cane, oil palm, maize, coffee, cocoa; forestry

Population and society

Population: 2,668,000 (1996 est) **Population growth rate:** 3% (1990–95); 2.6% (2000–05) **Population density:** (per sq km) 8 (1996 est) **Urban population:** (% of total) 59 (1995) **Age distribution:** (% of total population) <15 45.6%, 15–65 51%, >65 3.4% (1995) **Ethnic groups:** predominantly Bantu; population comprises 15 main ethnic groups and 75 tribes. The Kongo, or Bakongo, account for about 45% of the population, then come the Bateke, or Teke, at about 20%, and then the Mboshi, or Boubangui, about 16% **Language:** French (official); Kongo languages; local patois Monokutuba and Lingala **Religion:** animist, Christian, Muslim **Education:** (compulsory years) 10 **Literacy rate:** 70% (men); 44% (women) (1995 est) **Labour force:** 42% of population: 49% agriculture, 15% industry, 37% services (1990) **Life expectancy:** 48 (men); 52 (women) (1995–2000) **Child mortality rate:** (under 5, per 1,000 live births) 133 (1996) **Physicians:** 1 per 3,713 people (1993 est)

Practical information

Visa requirements: UK: visa required. USA: visa required **Embassy in the UK:** Honorary Consulate of the Republic of the Congo, Alliance House, 12 Caxton Street, London SW1H 0QS. Tel: (0171) 222 7575; fax: (0171) 233 2087 **British embassy:** British Consulate, Côte de l'Hotel Méridien, rue Lyantey 26, Brazzaville. Tel: (242) 838 527; fax: (242) 837 257 (The embassy closed 26 July 1991; diplomatic accreditation has been transferred to the British embassy in Kinshasa on a nonresident basis.) **Chamber of commerce:** Chambre Nationale de Commerce, BP 1438, Brazzaville. Tel: (242) 832 956 **Airports:** international airports: Brazzaville (Maya-Maya), Pointe-Noire; six domestic airports; total passenger km: 264 million (1994) **Major

holidays: 1 January, 18 March, 1 May, 31 July, 13–15 August, 1 November, 25, 31 December; variable: Good Friday, Easter Monday

Chronology

late 15th century: First visited by Portuguese explorers, at which time the Bakongo (a six-state confederation centred S of the Congo River in Angola) and Bateke, both Bantu groups, were the chief kingdoms. **16th century:** Portuguese, in collaboration with coastal peoples, exported slaves from the interior to plantations in Brazil and São Tomé; missionaries spread Roman Catholicism. **1880:** French explorer Pierre Savorgnan de Brazza established French claims to coastal region, with the makoko (king) of the Bateke accepting French protection. **1905:** International outrage at revelations of the brutalities of forced labour, which decimated the population, as ivory and rubber resources were ruthlessly exploited by private concessionaries. **1910:** As Moyen-Congo, became part of French Equatorial Africa, which also comprised Gabon and the Central African Republic, with the capital at Brazzaville. **1920s:** More than 17,000 were killed as forced labour used to build the Congo-Ocean railroad; first Bakongo political organization founded. **1940–44:** Supported the 'Free French' anti-Nazi resistance cause during World War II, Brazzaville serving as capital for Gen Charles de Gaulle's forces. **1946:** Became autonomous, with a territorial assembly and representation in French parliament. **1960:** Achieved independence from France, with Abbé Fulbert Youlou, a moderate Catholic Bakongo priest, as the first president. **1963:** Youlou forced to resign after labour unrest. Alphonse Massamba-Débat became president with Pascal Lissouba as prime minister, and a single-party state was established under the socialist National Revolutionary Movement (MNR). **1968:** Military coup, led by Capt Marien Ngouabi, ousted Massamba-Débat. **1970:** A Marxist People's Republic declared, with Ngouabi's PCT the only legal party. **1977:** Ngouabi assassinated in a plot by Massamba-Débat, who was executed; Col Joachim Yhombi-Opango became president. **1979:** Yhombi-Opango handed over the presidency to the PCT, who chose Col Denis Sassou-Nguessou as his successor. **early 1980s:** Petroleum production increased fivefold. **1990:** With the collapse of Eastern European communism, the PCT abandoned Marxist-Leninism and promised multiparty politics and market-centred reforms in an economy crippled by foreign debt. **1992:** Multiparty elections gave the coalition dominated by the Pan-African Union for Social Democracy (UPADS) an assembly majority, with Pascal Lissouba elected president. **1993:** Yhombi-Opango appointed prime minister; violent strikes and unrest after opposition disputed election results. **1994:** International panel appointed to investigate results; UPADS-dominated coalition declared winner. **1995:** New broad-based government formed, including opposition groups; market-centred economic reforms, including privatization. **1996:** Charles David Ganao appointed prime minister. **1997:** Violence between factions continued despite unity government. Sassou-Nguesso took over presidency.

Costa Rica Republic of

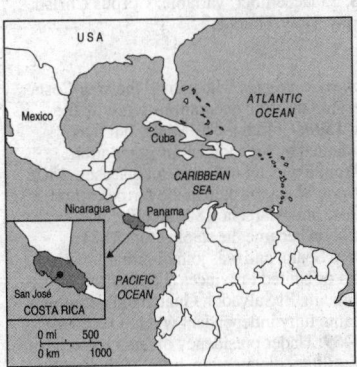

National name: *República de Costa Rica* **Area:** 51,100 sq km/19,729 sq mi **Capital:** San José **Major towns/cities:** Alajuela, Cartago, Limón, Puntarenas **Major ports:** Limón, Puntarenas **Physical features:** high central plateau and tropical coasts; Costa Rica was once entirely forested, containing an estimated 5% of the Earth's flora and fauna

Government

Head of state and government: Miguel Rodrigues from 1998
Political system: liberal democracy **Administrative divisions:**
seven provinces **Political parties:** National Liberation Party (PLN),
left of centre; Christian Socialist Unity Party (PUSC), centrist
coalition; ten minor parties **Armed forces:** army abolished 1948;
4,300 civil guards and 3,200 rural guards **Death penalty:** abolished
1887 **Defence spend:** (% GDP) 0.6 (1996) **Education spend:** (%
GNP) 4.7 (1993–94) **Health spend:** (% GDP) 6.3 (1994)

Economy and resources

Currency: colón **GDP:** ($ US) 8.3 billion (1994) **Real GDP per
capita (PPP):** ($ US) 5,919 (1994) **GDP growth rate:** 4.5% (1994);
5.1% (1990–95) **Average annual inflation:** 17.5% (1996); 18.5%
(1985–95) **Foreign debt:** ($ US) 3.8 billion (1996) **Major trading
partners:** USA, Japan, Venezuela, Germany, Italy, Guatemala
Resources: gold, salt, hydro power **Industries:** food processing,
chemical products, beverages, paper and paper products, textiles and
clothing, plastic goods, electrical equipment **Exports:** bananas,
coffee, sugar, cocoa, textiles, seafood, meat, tropical fruit. Principal
market: USA 38.6% (1995) **Imports:** raw materials for industry and
agriculture, consumer goods, machinery and transport equipment,
construction materials. Principal source: USA 36.4% (1995) **Arable
land:** 5.6% (1995) **Agricultural products:** bananas, coffee, sugar
cane, maize, potatoes, tobacco, tropical fruit; livestock rearing (cattle
and pigs); fishing

Population and society

Population: 3,500 ,000 (1996 est) **Population growth rate:** 2.4%
(1990–95); 1.8% (2000–05) **Population density:** (per sq km) 68
(1996 est) **Urban population:** (% of total) 50 (1995) **Age
distribution:** (% of total population) <15 35%, 15–65 60.4%, >65
4.7% (1995) **Ethnic groups:** about 97% of the population is of
European descent, mostly Spanish, and about 2% is of African origin
Language: Spanish (official) **Religion:** Roman Catholic 90%
Education: (compulsory years) 9 **Literacy rate:** 93% (men); 93%
(women) (1995 est) **Labour force:** 38% of population: 26%
agriculture, 27% industry, 47% services (1990) **Unemployment:**
5.2% (1995) **Life expectancy:** 76 (men); 79 (women) (1995–2000)
Child mortality rate: (under 5, per 1,000 live births) 14 (1996)
Physicians: 1 per 979 people (1995)

Practical information

Visa requirements: UK: visa not required. USA: visa not required
Embassy in the UK: Embassy and Consulate, Flat 1, 14 Lancaster
Gate, London W2 3LH. Tel: (0171) 706 8844; fax: (0171) 706 8655
British embassy: Apartado 815, 11th Floor, Edificio Centro Colón,
1007 San José. Tel (506) 221 5566; fax: (506) 233 9938 **Chamber
of commerce:** Cámara de Comercio de Costa Rica, Apartado 1114,
Urbanización Tournón, 1000 San José. Tel: (506) 221 0005; fax:
(506) 233 7091 **Airports:** international airports: San José (Juan
Santamaría), Liberia (Daniel Oduber Quirós); 11 domestic airports
as well as charter services to provincial towns and villages); total
passenger km: 1,611 million (1994) **Major holidays:** 1 January, 19
March, 11 April, 1 May, 29 June, 25 July, 2, 15 August, 15
September, 12 October, 8, 25 December; variable: Corpus Christi,
Good Friday, Holy Saturday, Holy Thursday

Chronology

1502: Visited by Christopher Columbus, who named the area Costa
Rica (the rich coast), observing the gold decorations worn by the
Native American Guaymi. **1506:** Colonized by Spain, but fierce
guerrilla resistance was mounted by the indigenous population,
although many later died from exposure to European diseases. **18th
century:** Settlements began to be established in the fertile central
highlands, including San José and Alajuela. **1808:** Coffee was
introduced from Cuba and soon became the staple crop. **1821:**
Independence achieved from Spain, and was joined initially with
Mexico. **1824:** Became part of United Provinces (Federation) of
Central America, also embracing El Salvador, Guatemala, Honduras,
and Nicaragua. **1838:** Became fully independent when it seceded
from the Federation. **1849–59:** Under presidency of Juan Rafael
Mora. **1870–82:** Period of military dictatorship. **later 19th century:**

Immigration by Europeans to run and work small coffee farms.
1917–19: Brief dictatorship by Frederico Tinoco. **1940–44:** Liberal
reforms, including recognition of workers' rights and minimum
wages, introduced by President Rafael Angel Calderón Guradia,
founder of the United Christian Socialist Party (PUSC). **1948:** Brief
civil war following a disputed presidential election. **1949:** New
constitution adopted, giving women and blacks the vote. National
army abolished and replaced by civil guard. José Figueres Ferrer,
cofounder of the PLN, elected president; he embarked on ambitious
socialist programme, nationalizing the banks and introducing a social
security system. **1958–73:** Mainly conservative administrations.
1974: PLN regained the presidency under Daniel Oduber and
returned to socialist policies. **1978:** Rodrigo Carazo, conservative,
elected president. Sharp deterioration in the state of the economy.
1982: Luis Alberto Monge (PLN) elected president. Harsh austerity
programme introduced. Pressure from the USA to abandon neutral
stance and condemn Sandinista regime in Nicaragua. **1985:**
Following border clashes with Nicaraguan Sandinista forces, a US-
trained antiguerrilla guard formed. **1986:** Oscar Arias Sanchez (PLN)
won the presidency on a neutralist platform. **1987:** Arias won Nobel
Prize for Peace for devising a Central American peace plan signed by
leaders of Nicaragua, El Salvador, Guatemala, and Honduras. **1990:**
Rafael Calderón of the centrist PUSC elected president as economy
deteriorated. **1994:** José Maria Figueres Olsen (PLN), son of José
Figueres Ferrer elected president. **1998:** Conservative economist
Miguel Rodriguez elected president.

Côte d'Ivoire Republic of

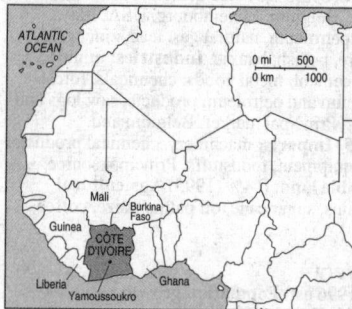

National name:
*République de la
Côte d'Ivoire* **Area:**
322,463 sq
km/124,502 sq mi
Capital:
Yamoussoukro
Major towns/cities:
Abidjan, Bouaké,
Daloa, Man, Korhogo
Major ports:
Abidjan, San Pedro
Physical features:
tropical rainforest
(diminishing as
exploited) in S; savanna and low mountains in N; coastal plain;
Vridi canal, Kossou dam, Monts du Toura

Government

Head of state: Henri Konan Bedie from 1993 **Head of
government:** Kablan Daniel Duncan from 1993 **Political system:**
emergent democracy **Administrative divisions:** 10 regions,
comprising 50 departments **Political parties:** Democratic Party of
Côte d'Ivoire (PDCI), nationalist, free enterprise; Rally of
Republicans (RDR), nationalist; Ivorian Popular Front (FPI), left of
centre; Ivorian Labour Party (PIT), left of centre **Armed forces:**
8,400 (1996); plus paramilitary forces numbering 7,800
Conscription: selective conscription for six months **Death penalty:**
retains the death penalty for ordinary crimes but can be considered
abolitionist in practice **Defence spend:** (% GDP) 0.9 (1996)
Education spend: (% GNP) 5.6 (1994) **Health spend:** (% GDP)
1.3 (1994)

Economy and resources

Currency: franc CFA **GDP:** ($ US) 6.7 billion (1994) **Real GDP
per capita (PPP):** ($ US) 1,668 (1994) **GDP growth rate:** 1.7%
(1994); 0.7% (1990–95) **Average annual inflation:** 4.5% (1996);
2.1% (1985–95) **Foreign debt:** ($ US) 19.45 billion (1996) **Major
trading partners:** France, Nigeria, Germany, the Netherlands, Italy,
USA **Resources:** petroleum, natural gas, diamonds, gold, nickel,
reserves of manganese, iron ore, bauxite **Industries:** agro-
processing (dominated by cocoa, coffee, cotton, palm kernels,

pineapples, fish), petroleum refining, tobacco **Exports:** cocoa beans and products, petroleum products, timber, coffee, cotton, tinned tuna. Principal market: France 16% (1994) **Imports:** crude petroleum, machinery and vehicles, pharmaceuticals, fresh fish, plastics, cereals. Principal source: France 28% (1994) **Arable land:** 9.1% (1995) **Agricultural products:** cocoa (world's largest producer), coffee (world's fifth-largest producer), cotton, rubber, palm kernels, bananas, pineapples, yams, cassava, plantains; fishing; forestry

Population and society

Population: 14,015,000 (1996 est) **Population growth rate:** 3.5% (1990–95); 3.2% (2000–05) **Population density:** (per sq km) 43 (1996 est) **Urban population:** (% of total) 44 (1995) **Age distribution:** (% of total population) <15 49.1%, 15–65 48.2%, >65 2.6% (1995) **Ethnic groups:** no single dominant ethnic group; main groups include the Agni, Baoule, Krou, Senoufou, and Mandingo. There are about 2 million Africans who have settled from neighbouring countries, particularly Burkina Faso. Europeans number about 70,000 **Language:** French (official); over 60 local languages **Religion:** animist, Muslim (mainly in N), Christian (mainly Roman Catholic in S) **Education:** (compulsory years) 6 **Literacy rate:** 67% (men); 40% (women) (1995 est) **Labour force:** 37% of population: 60% agriculture, 10% industry, 30% services (1990) **Unemployment:** 20% (1992 est) **Life expectancy:** 49 (men); 51 (women) (1995–2000) **Child mortality rate:** (under 5, per 1,000 live births) 137 (1996) **Physicians:** 1 per 18,000 people (1994 est)

Practical information

Visa requirements: UK: visa required. USA: visa not required for a stay of less than 90 days **Embassy in the UK:** 2 Upper Belgrave Street, London SW1X 8BJ. Tel: (0171) 235 6991; fax: (0171) 259 5439 **British embassy:** 3rd Floor, Immeuble 'Les Harmonies', Angle boulevard Carde et avenue Dr Jamot, Plateau, Abidjan. Tel: (225) 226850/1/2; fax: (225) 223 221 **Chamber of commerce:** Chambre de Commerce et d'Industrie de Côte d'Ivoire, 01 BP 1399, 6 avenue Joseph Anoma, Abidjan 01. Tel: (225) 331 600; fax: (225) 323 946 **Airports:** international airports: Abidjan (Port Bouet), Bouaké, Yamoussoukro (San Pedro); domestic services to all major towns; total passenger km: 282 million (1994) **Major holidays:** 1 January, 1 May, 15 August, 1 November, 7, 24–25, 31 December; variable: Ascension Thursday, Eid-ul-Adha, Good Friday, Easter Monday, Whit Monday, end of Ramadan

Chronology

1460s: Portuguese navigators arrived. **16th century:** Ivory export trade developed by Europeans and slave trade, though to a lesser extent than neighbouring areas; Krou people migrated from Liberia to the W and Senoufo and Lobi from the N. **late 17th century:** French coastal trading posts established at Assini and Grand Bassam. **18th–19th centuries:** Akan peoples, including the Baoulé, immigrated from the E and Malinke from the NW. **1840s:** French began to conclude commercial treaties with local rulers. **1893:** Colony of Côte d'Ivoire created by French, after war with Mandinkas; Baoulé resistance continued until 1917. **1904:** Became part of French West Africa; cocoa production encouraged. **1940–42:** Under pro-Nazi French Vichy regime. **1946:** Became overseas territory in French Union, with own territorial assembly and representation in French parliament: Felix Houphouët-Boigny, a Western-educated Baoulé chief who had formed the Democratic Party (PDCI) to campaign for autonomy, was elected to the French assembly. **1947:** A French-controlled area to the N, which had been added to Côte d'Ivoire in 1932, separated to create new state of Upper Volta (now Burkina Faso). **1950–54:** Port of Abidjan constructed. **1958:** Achieved internal self-government. **1960:** Independence secured, with Houphouët-Boigny as president of a one-party state. **1960s–1980s:** Political stability, close links maintained with France and economic expansion of 10% per annum, as the country became one of the world's largest coffee producers. **1986:** Name changed officially from Ivory Coast to Côte d'Ivoire. **1987–93:** Per capita incomes fell by 25% owing to an austerity programme promoted by the International Monetary Fund.

1990: Strikes and student unrest, but Houphouët-Boigny re-elected in a contested presidential election, as multiparty politics re-established. **1993:** Houphouêt-Boigny died and was succeeded by parliamentary speaker and Baoulé Henri Konan Bedie. **1995:** Bedie and PDCI re-elected in contest boycotted by opposition.

Croatia Republic of

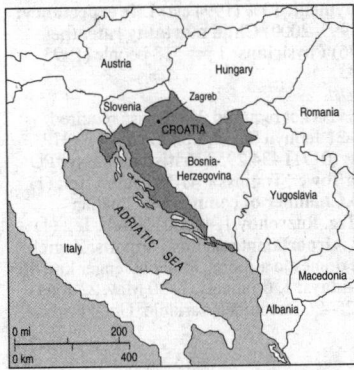

National name: *Republika Hrvatska* **Area:** 56,538 sq km/21,829 sq mi **Capital:** Zagreb **Major towns/cities:** Osijek, Split, Dubrovnik, Rijeka, Zadar, Pula **Major ports:** chief port: Rijeka (Fiume); other ports: Zadar, Sibenik, Split, Dubrovnik **Physical features:** Adriatic coastline with large islands; very mountainous, with part of the Karst region and the Julian and Styrian Alps; some marshland

Government

Head of state: Franjo Tudjman from 1990 **Head of government:** Zlatko Matesa from 1995 **Political system:** emergent democracy **Administrative divisions:** 21 counties **Political parties:** Croatian Democratic Union (CDU), Christian Democrat, right of centre, nationalist; Croatian Social-Liberal Party (CSLP), centrist; Social Democratic Party of Change (SDP), reform socialist; Croatian Party of Rights (HSP), Croat-oriented, ultranationalist; Croatian Peasant Party (HSS), rural-based; Serbian National Party (SNS), Serb-oriented **Armed forces:** 64,700 (1996); plus 40,000 in paramilitary forces **Conscription:** compulsory for ten months **Death penalty:** abolished 1990 **Defence spend:** (% GDP) 6.8 (1996) **Education spend:** (% GDP) 3.2 (1994) **Health spend:** (% GDP) 0.6 (1994)

Economy and resources

Currency: kuna **GDP:** (\$ US) 14 billion (1994) **Real GDP per capita (PPP):** (\$ US) 3,960 (1994) **GDP growth rate:** 0.8% (1994) **Average annual inflation:** 3.5% (1996) **Foreign debt:** (\$ US) 4.7 billion (1996) **Major trading partners:** Germany, Italy, Slovenia, Austria, Iran, former USSR, Bosnia-Herzegovina **Resources:** petroleum, natural gas, coal, lignite, bauxite, iron ore, salt **Industries:** food processing, textiles, chemicals, ship-building, metal processing, construction materials, Tourism was virtually eliminated during hostilities, but a revival began 1992 **Exports:** machinery and transport equipment, chemicals, foodstuffs, miscellaneous manufactured items (mainly clothing). Principal market: Germany 22.1% (1994) **Imports:** machinery and transport equipment, basic manufactures, mineral fuels, miscellaneous manufactured articles. Principal source: Germany 21.2% (1994) **Arable land:** 20% (1995) **Agricultural products:** wheat, maize, potatoes, plums, sugar beet; livestock rearing (cattle and pigs); dairy products

Population and society

Population: 4,501,000 (1996 est) **Population growth rate:** –0.1% (1990–95); –0.1% (2000–05) **Population density:** (per sq km) 80 (1996 est) **Urban population:** (% of total) 64 (1995) **Age distribution:** (% of total population) <15 19.1%, 15–65 68.2%, >65 12.8% (1995) **Ethnic groups:** in 1991, 77% of the population were ethnic Croats, 12% were ethnic Serbs, and 1% were Slovenes. Since the civil war began 1992, more than 300,000 Croats have been displaced from Serbian enclaves within the republic, and there are an estimated 500,000 refugees from Bosnia in the republic. Serbs are most thickly settled in areas bordering Bosnia-Herzegovina, and in Slavonia, although more than 150,000 fled from Krajina to Bosnia-Herzegovina and Serbia following the region's recapture by the Croatian army in August 1995 **Language:** Croatian variant of Serbo-Croatian (official); Serbian variant of Serbo-Croatian also widely spoken, particularly in border areas in E **Religion:** Roman Catholic (Croats); Orthodox Christian (Serbs) **Education:** (compulsory years) 8 **Literacy rate:** 97% (men); 97% (women) (1995 est) **Labour force:** 5.3% agriculture, 59.4% industry, 35.3% services (1992) **Unemployment:** 13% (1994 est) **Life expectancy:** 68 (men); 77 (women) (1995–2000) **Child mortality rate:** (per 1,000 live births) 16 (1996) **Physicians:** 1 per 518 people (1993 est)

Practical information

Visa requirements: UK: visa not required. USA: visa required **Embassy in the UK:** 18–21 Jermyn Street, London SW1Y 6HP. Tel: (0171) 434 2946; fax: (0171) 434 2953 **British embassy:** PO Box 454, 2nd Floor, Astra Tower, Tratinska, 4100 Zagreb. Tel: (1) 334 245; fax: (1) 338 893 **Chamber of commerce:** Croatian Chamber of Commerce, Trg. Ruzveltov 1, 41000 Zagreb. Tel: (1) 453 422; fax: (1) 448 618 **Airports:** international airports: Zagreb (Pleso), Dubrovnik; three domestic airports; total passenger km: 405 million (1994) **Major holidays:** 1, 6 January, 1, 30 May, 22 June, 15 August, 1 November, 25–26 December; variable: Good Friday, Easter Monday

Chronology

early centuries AD: Part of Roman region of Pannonia. **AD 395:** On division of Roman Empire, stayed in W half, along with Slovenia and Bosnia. **7th century:** Settled by Carpathian Croats, from NE; Christianity adopted. **924:** Formed by Tomislav into independent kingdom, which incorporated Bosnia from 10th century. **12th–19th centuries:** Enjoyed autonomy under Hungarian crown, following dynastic union in 1102. **1526–1699:** Slavonia, in E, held by Ottoman Turks, while Serbs were invited by Austria to settle along the border with Ottoman-ruled Bosnia, in Vojna Krajina (military frontier). **1797–1815:** Dalmatia, in W, ruled by France. **19th century:** Part of Austro-Hungarian Habsburg Empire. **1918:** On dissolution of Habsburg Empire, joined Serbia, Slovenia, and Montenegro in 'Kingdom of Serbs, Croats, and Slovenes', under Serbian Karageorgevic dynasty. **1929:** The Kingdom became Yugoslavia. Croatia continued its campaign for autonomy. **1930s:** Ustasa, a Croat terrorist organization, began a campaign against dominance of Yugoslavia by the non-Catholic Serbs. **1941–44:** Following German invasion, a 'Greater Croatia' Nazi puppet state, including most of Bosnia and W Serbia, formed under Ustasa leader, Ante Pavelic; more than half a million Serbs, Jews, and members of the Romany community were massacred in extermination camps. **1945:** Became constituent republic of Yugoslavia Socialist Federation after communist partisans, led by Croat Marshal Tito, overthrew Pavelic. **1970s:** Separatist demands resurfaced, provoking a crackdown. **late 1980s:** Spiralling inflation and a deterioration in living standards sparked industrial unrest and a rise in nationalist sentiment, which affected the local communist party. **1989:** Formation of opposition parties permitted. **1990:** Communists defeated by conservative nationalist CDU led by ex-Partisan Franjo Tudjman in first free election since 1938. 'Sovereignty' declared. **1991:** Serb-dominated region of Krajina in SW announced secession from Croatia. Croatia declared independence, leading to military conflict with Serbia, and internal civil war ensued. **1992:** United Nations (UN) peace accord accepted; independence recognized by European Community and USA; Croatia entered UN. UN peacekeeping force stationed in Croatia. Tudjman directly elected president. **1993:** Government offensive launched to retake parts of Serb-held Krajina, violating 1992 UN peace accord. **1994:** Accord with Muslims and ethnic Croats within Bosnia, to the E, to link recently formed Muslim–Croat federation with Croatia. **1995:** Serb-held W Slavonia and Krajina captured by government forces; mass exodus of Croatian Serbs. Offensive extended into Bosnia-Herzegovina to halt Bosnian Serb assault on Bihac in W Bosnia. Serbia agreed to cede control of E Slavonia to Croatia over a two-year period. **1996:**

Diplomatic relations between Croatia and Yugoslavia restored. Croatia entered Council of Europe. **1997:** Opposition successes in local elections. Tudjman re-elected despite failing health. Last Serb enclave in E Slavonia reintegrated into Croatia. Constitution amended to prevent weakening of Croatia's national sovereignty.

Cuba Republic of

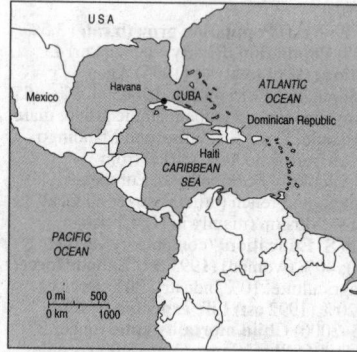

National name: *República de Cuba* **Area:** 110,860 sq km/42,803 sq mi **Capital:** Havana **Major towns/cities:** Santiago de Cuba, Camagüey, Holguín, Guantánamo, Santa Clara, Bayamo, Cienfuegos **Physical features:** comprises Cuba and smaller islands including Isle of Youth; low hills; Sierra Maestra mountains in SE; Cuba has 3,380 km/2,100 mi of coastline, with deep bays, sandy beaches, coral islands and reefs

Government

Head of state and government: Fidel Castro Ruz from 1959 **Political system:** communist republic **Administrative divisions:** 14 provinces and the special municipality of the Isle of Youth (Isla de la Juventud) **Political party:** Communist Party of Cuba (PCC), Marxist-Leninist **Armed forces:** 100,000 (1996) **Conscription:** compulsory for two years **Death penalty:** retained and used for ordinary crimes **Defence spend:** (% GDP) 5.4 (1996) **Education spend:** (% GNP) 6.6 (1993–94) **Health spend:** (% GDP) 7.9 (1990–95)

Economy and resources

Currency: Cuban peso **GDP:** ($ US) 11.9 billion (1994) **Real GDP per capita (PPP):** ($ US) 3,000 (1994) **GDP growth rate:** 0.7% (1994) **Average annual inflation:** 50% (1994 est) **Foreign debt:** ($ US) 13.6 billion (1996) **Major trading partners:** Canada, Spain, Russia, China, Mexico, Bulgaria **Resources:** iron ore, copper, chromite, gold, manganese, nickel, cobalt, silver, salt **Industries:** mining, textiles and footwear, cigarettes, cement, food processing (sugar and its by-products), fertilizers **Exports:** sugar, minerals, tobacco, citrus fruits, fish products. Principal market: Canada 15.8% (1995 est) **Imports:** mineral fuels, machinery and transport equipment, foodstuffs, beverages. Principal source: Spain 17.3% (1995 est) **Arable land:** 34.2% (1995) **Agricultural products:** sugar cane (world's fourth-largest producer of sugar), tobacco, rice, citrus fruits, plantains, bananas; forestry; fishing

Population and society

Population: 11,018,000 (1996 est) **Population growth rate:** 0.8% (1990–95); 0.5% (2000–05) **Population density:** (per sq km) 99 (1996 est) **Urban population:** (% of total) 76 (1995) **Age distribution:** (% of total population) <15 22.9%, 15–65 68.2%, >65 8.9% (1995) **Ethnic groups:** predominantly of mixed Spanish and African or Spanish and Native American origin **Language:** Spanish **Religion:** Roman Catholic; also Episcopalians and Methodists **Education:** (compulsory years) 6 **Literacy rate:** 95% (men); 93% (women) (1995 est) **Labour force:** 45% of population: 18% agriculture, 30% industry, 51% services (1990) **Unemployment:** 17.3% (1994) **Life expectancy:** 74 (men); 78 (women) (1995–2000) **Child mortality rate:** (under 5, per 1,000 live births) 13 (1996) **Physicians:** 1 per 212 people (1993 est)

Practical information

Visa requirements: UK: visa required. USA: visa required
Embassy in the UK: 167 High Holborn, London WC1V 6PA. Tel:
(0171) 240 2488; fax: (0171) 836 2602 **British embassy:** Calle 34,
708 Miramar, Havana. Tel: (7) 331 771; fax: (7) 338 104 **Chamber
of commerce:** Cámara de Comercio de la República de Cuba, Calle
21, No. 661/701, esq Calle A, Apartado 4237, Vedado, Havana. Tel:
(7) 303 356; fax: (7) 333 042 **Airports:** international airports:
Havana, Santiago de Cuba, Holguín, Camagüey, Varadero; 11
domestic airports; total passenger km: 1,556 million (1994) **Major
holidays:** 1 January, 1 May, 25–26 July, 10 October

Chronology

3rd century AD: The Ciboney, Cuba's earliest known inhabitants,
were dislodged by the immigration of Taino, Arawak Indians from
Venezuela. **1492:** Christopher Columbus landed in Cuba and
claimed it for Spain. **1511:** Spanish settlement established at
Baracoa by Diego Velazquez. **1523:** Decline of Native American
population and rise of sugar plantations led to import of slaves
from Africa. **mid-19th century:** Cuba produced one-third of the
world's sugar. **1868–78:** Unsuccessful first war for independence
from Spain. **1886:** Slavery was abolished. **1895–98:** Further
uprising against Spanish rule, led by José Martí, who died in
combat; 200,000 soldiers deployed by Spain. **1898:** USA defeated
Spain in Spanish-American War; Spain gave up all claims to Cuba,
which was ceded to the USA. **1901:** Cuba achieved independence;
Tomás Estrada Palma became first president of the Republic of
Cuba. **1906–09:** Brief period of US administration after Estrada
resigned in the face of an armed rebellion by political opponents.
1909: The liberal, José Miguel Gomez became president, but soon
became tarred by corruption. **1924:** Gerado Machado, an admirer
of the Italian fascist leader Benito Mussolini, established a brutal
dictatorship which lasted nine years. **1925:** Socialist Party
founded, from which the Communist Party later developed. **1933:**
Army sergeant Fulgencio Batista seized power. **1934:** USA
abandoned its right to intervene in Cuba's internal affairs. **1944:**
Batista retired and was succeeded by the civilian Ramon Gray San
Martin. **1952:** Batista seized power again to begin an oppressive
and corrupt regime. **1953:** Fidel Castro Ruz led an unsuccessful
coup against Batista on the 100th anniversary of the birth of Martí.
1956: Second unsuccessful coup by Castro. **1959:** Batista
overthrown by Castro and his 9,000-strong guerrilla army.
Constitution of 1940 replaced by a 'Fundamental Law', making
Castro prime minister, his brother Raúl Castro his deputy, and
Argentinian-born Ernesto 'Che' Guevara third in command. **1960:**
All US businesses in Cuba appropriated without compensation;
USA broke off diplomatic relations. **1961:** USA sponsored an
unsuccessful invasion by Cuban exiles at the Bay of Pigs. Castro
announced that Cuba had become a communist state, with a
Marxist-Leninist programme of economic development, and
became allied with the USSR. **1962:** Cuban missile crisis: Cuba
was expelled from the Organization of American States. Castro
responded by tightening relations with the USSR, which installed
nuclear missiles in Cuba (subsequently removed at US insistence).
US trade embargo imposed. **1965:** Cuba's sole political party
renamed Cuban Communist Party (PCC). With Soviet help, Cuba
began to make considerable economic and social progress. **1972:**
Cuba became a full member of the Moscow-based Council for
Mutual Economic Assistance (COMECON). **1976:** New socialist
constitution approved; Castro elected president. **1976–81:** Castro
became involved in extensive international commitments, sending
troops as Soviet surrogates, particularly to Africa. **1982:** Cuba
joined other Latin American countries in giving moral support to
Argentina in its dispute with Britain over the Falklands. **1984:**
Castro tried to improve US-Cuban relations by discussing
exchange of US prisoners in Cuba for Cuban 'undesirables' in the
USA. **1988:** Peace accord with South Africa signed, agreeing to
withdrawal of Cuban troops from Angola, as part of a reduction in
Cuba's overseas military activities. **1991:** Soviet troops withdrawn
with the collapse of the USSR. **1993:** US trade embargo tightened;
market-oriented reforms introduced in face of deteriorating
economy. **1994:** Mass refugee exodus; US policy on Cuban
asylum seekers revised.

Cyprus Greek Republic of Cyprus in south, and Turkish Republic of Northern Cyprus in north

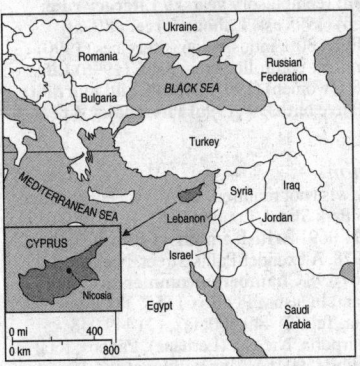

National name:
*Kypriakí
Dimokratía* (S), and
Kibris Cumhuriyeti
(N) **Area:** 9,251 sq
km/3,571 sq mi
(3,335 sq km/1,287
sq mi is Turkish-
occupied) **Capital:**
Nicosia (divided
between Greek and
Turkish Cypriots)
Major towns/cities:
Morphou, Limassol,
Larnaca,
Famagusta, Paphos
Major ports:
Limassol, Larnaca,
and Paphos (Greek); Kyrenia and Famagusta (Turkish) **Physical
features:** central plain between two E–W mountain ranges

Government

Head of state and government: Glafkos Clerides (Greek) from
1993, Rauf Denktas (Turkish) from 1976 **Political system:**
democratic divided republic **Administrative divisions:** six districts
Political parties: *Greek zone* : Democratic Party (DEKO),
federalist, centre left; Progressive Party of the Working People
(AKEL), socialist; Democratic Rally (DISY), centrist; Socialist
Party–National Democratic Union of Cyprus (SK–EDEK), socialist;
Turkish zone : National Unity Party (NUP), Communal Liberation
Party (CLP), Republican Turkish Party (RTP), New British Party
(NBP) **Armed forces:** National Guard of 10,000 (1996); Turkish
Republic of Northern Cyprus (TRNC) 4,000, plus 26,000 reserves
(1995) **Conscription:** is for 26 months **Death penalty:** laws
provide for the death penalty only for exceptional crimes such as
under military law or crimes committed in exceptional
circumstances such as wartime **Defence spend:** (% GDP) 5.2
(1996) **Education spend:** (% GNP) 4 (1992); N/A (1993–94)
Health spend: (% GDP) 2.1 (1994)

Economy and resources

Currency: Cyprus pound and Turkish lira **GDP:** ($ US) 7.19 billion
(1994) **Real GDP per capita (PPP):** ($ US) 13,071 (1994) **GDP
growth rate:** 5.1% (1994) **Average annual inflation:** 3% (1996)
Foreign debt: ($ US) 2.1 billion (1993) **Major trading partners:**
government-controlled area: UK, USA, Arab countries, France,
Germany, Greece, Japan, Italy; TRNC area: Turkey, UK, other EU
countries **Resources:** copper precipitates, beutonite, umber and
other ochres **Industries:** food processing, beverages, textiles,
clothing and leather, chemicals and chemical petroleum, metal
products, wood and wood products, tourism, financial services (24
offshore banking units in December 1994) **Exports:** government-
controlled area: clothing, potatoes, pharmaceutical products.
Principal market: UK 27.1% (1994); TRNC area: citrus fruits,
industrial products. Principal market: UK 46.3% (1994) **Imports:**
government-controlled area: mineral fuels, textiles, vehicles, metals,
foodstuffs, tobacco. Principal source: UK 11.4% (1994); TRNC
area: basic manufactures, machinery and transport equipment, food
and live animals. Principal source: Turkey 45.1% (1994) **Arable
land:** 10.8% (1995) **Agricultural products:** government-controlled
area: barley, potatoes, grapes, citrus fruit, olives; TRNC area: wheat,
barley, potatoes, citrus fruit, olives; livestock rearing (sheep and
goats)

Population and society

Population: 756,800 (1996 est) **Population growth rate:** 1.1%
(1990–95) **Population density:** (per sq km) 82 (1996 est) **Urban
population:** (% of total) 56 (1994) **Age distribution:** (% of total
population) <15 26%, 15–65 64%, >65 10% (1994) **Ethnic groups:**
about 80% of the population is of Greek origin, while about 18% are

of Turkish descent, and live in the northern part of the island within the self-styled Turkish Republic of Northern Cyprus **Language:** Greek and Turkish (official), English **Religion:** Greek Orthodox, Sunni Muslim **Education:** (compulsory years) 9 **Literacy rate:** 94% (men); 94% (women) (1995 est) **Labour force:** 48% of population: 14% agriculture, 30% industry, 56% services (1990) **Unemployment:** government-controlled area: 9.4% (1996) **Life expectancy:** 76 (men); 80 (women) (1995–2000) **Child mortality rate:** (under 5, per 1,000 live births) 9 (1996) **Physicians:** 1 per 1,000 people (1994 est)

Practical information

Visa requirements: UK: visa not required. USA: visa not required **Embassy in the UK:** 93 Park Street, London W1Y 4ET. Tel: (0171) 499 8272; fax: (0171) 491 0691 **British embassy:** British High Commission, PO Box 1978, Alexander Pallis Street, Nicosia. Tel: (2) 473 131/7; fax: (2) 367 198 **Chamber of commerce:** Cyprus Chamber of Commerce and Industry, PO Box 1455, 38 Grivas Dhigenis Avenue, Nicosia. Tel: (2) 449 500; fax: (2) 449 048 **Airports:** international airports: Nicosia (Larnaca), Paphos; total passenger km: 2,810 million (1994) **Major holidays:** 1, 6 January, 25 March, 1 May, 28–29 October, 25–26 December; variable: Eid-ul-Adha, Good Friday, Easter Monday, end of Ramadan, Holy Saturday, Prophet's Birthday

Chronology

14th–11th centuries BC: Colonized by Myceneans and Achaeans from Greece. **9th century BC:** Phoenicans settled in Cyprus. **7th century BC:** Several Cypriot kingdoms flourished under Assyrian influence. **414–374 BC:** Under Evagoras of Salamis (in eastern Cyprus) the island's ten city kingdoms were united into one state and Greek culture, including the Greek alphabet, was promoted. **333–58 BC:** Became part of the Greek Hellenistic and then, from 294 BC, the Egypt-based Ptolemaic empire. **58 BC:** Cyprus was annexed by the Roman Empire. **AD 45:** Christianity introduced. **AD 395:** When the Roman Empire divided, Cyprus was allotted to the Byzantine Empire. **7th–10th centuries:** Byzantines and Muslim Arabs fought for control of Cyprus. **1191:** Richard I of England, 'the Lionheart', conquered Cyprus as a base for Crusades; he later sold it to a French noble, Guy de Lusignan, who established a feudal monarchy which ruled for three centuries. **1498:** Venetian Republic took control of Cyprus. **1571:** Conquered by Ottoman Turks, who introduced Turkish Muslim settlers, but permitted Christianity to continue in rural areas. **1821–33:** Period of unrest, following execution of popular Greek Orthodox Archbishop Kyprianos. **1878:** Anglo-Turkish Convention: Turkey ceded Cyprus to British administration in return for defensive alliance. **1914:** Formally annexed by Britain after Turkey entered World War I as a Central Power. **1915:** Greece rejected an offer of Cyprus in return for entry into World War I on Allied side. **1925:** Cyprus became a crown colony. **1931:** Greek Cypriots rioted in support of demand for union with Greece (*enosis*); legislative council suspended. **1948:** Greek Cypriots rejected new constitution because it did not offer links with Greece. **1951:** Britain rejected Greek proposals for *enosis* . **1955:** National Organization of Cypriot Fighters (EOKA), led by George Grivas, began terrorist campaign for *enosis* . **1956:** British authorities deported Archbishop Makarios, head of the Cypriot Orthodox Church, for encouraging EOKA. **1958:** Britain proposed autonomy for Greek and Turkish Cypriot communities under British sovereignty; plan accepted by Turks, rejected by Greeks; violence increased. **1959:** Britain, Greece, and Turkey agreed to Cypriot independence, with partition and *enosis* both ruled out. **1960:** Cyprus became an independent republic with Archbishop Makarios as president; Britain retained two military bases. **1963:** Makarios proposed major constitutional reforms; Turkish Cypriots withdrew from government and formed separate enclaves; communal fighting broke out. **1964:** United Nations (UN) peacekeeping force installed. **1968:** Intercommunal talks made no progress; Turkish Cypriots demanded federalism; Greek Cypriots insisted on unitary state. **1974:** Coup by Greek officers in Cypriot National Guard installed Nikos Sampson as president; Turkey, fearing *enosis* , invaded northern Cyprus; Greek Cypriot military regime collapsed; President Makarios restored. **1975:** Northern Cyprus declared itself

the Turkish Federated State of Cyprus, with Rauf Denktas as president. **1977:** Makarios died; succeeded by Spyros Kyprianou. **1983:** Denktas proclaimed independent Turkish Republic of Cyprus; recognized only by Turkey. **1985:** Summit meeting between Kyprianou and Denktas failed to reach agreement; further peace talks failed 1989 and 1992. **1988:** Kyprianou succeeded as Greek Cypriot president by Georgios Vassiliou. **1993:** Glafkos Clerides (DISY) replaced Vassiliou. **1994:** European Court of Justice declared trade with northern Cyprus illegal. **1996:** Further peace talks jeopardized by boundary killing of Turkish Cypriot soldier; mounting tension between N and S. **1997:** Decision to purchase Russian anti-aircraft missiles created tension. UN-mediated peace talks between Clerides and Denktascollapsed.

Czech Republic

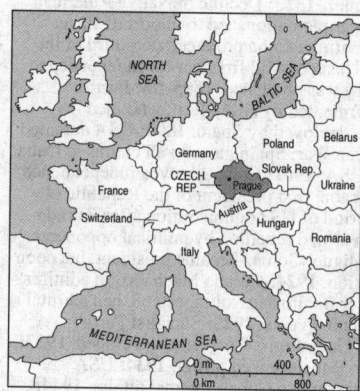

National name: *Česká Republika* **Area:** 78,864 sq km/30,449 sq mi **Capital:** Prague **Major towns/cities:** Brno, Ostrava, Olomouc, Liberec, Plzeň, Ustí nad Labem, Hradec Králové **Physical features:** mountainous; rivers: Morava, Labe (Elbe), Vltava (Moldau)

Government

Head of state: Václav Havel from 1993 **Head of government:** Josef Tosovsky from 1997 **Political system:** emergent democracy **Administrative divisions:** eight regions **Political parties:** Civic Democratic Party (CDP), right of centre, free-market; Civic Democratic Alliance (CDA), right of centre, free-market; Civic Movement (CM), liberal, left of centre; Communist Party of Bohemia and Moravia (KSCM), reform socialist; Agrarian Party, centrist, rural-based; Liberal National Social Party (LNSP; formerly the Czech Socialist Party (SP)), reform socialist; Czech Social Democratic Party (CSDP), moderate left of centre; Christian Democratic Union–Czech People's Party (CDU–CPP), centre right; Movement for Autonomous Democracy of Moravia and Silesia (MADMS), Moravian and Silesian-based, separatist; Czech Republican Party, far right **Armed forces:** 70,000 (1996) **Conscription:** compulsory for 12 months **Death penalty:** abolished 1990 **Defence spend:** (% GDP) 2.4 (1996) **Education spend:** (% GNP) 5.9 (1993–94) **Health spend:** (% GDP) 7.8 (1990–95)

Economy and resources

Currency: koruna (based on Czechoslovak koruna) **GDP:** ($ US) 36 billion (1994) **Real GDP per capita (PPP):** ($ US) 9,201 (1994) **GDP growth rate:** 4.8% (1995); –2.6% (1990–95) **Average annual inflation:** 8.9% (1996); 12.2% (1985–95 est) **Foreign debt:** ($ US) 18.6 billion (1996) **Major trading partners:** EU countries, Slovak Republic, Poland, Russia, USA **Resources:** coal, lignite **Industries:** steel, cement, motor cars, textiles, bicycles, beer, trucks and tractors **Exports:** basic manufactures, machinery and transport equipment, miscellaneous manufactured articles, beer. Principal market: EU 37.4% (1995) **Imports:** machinery and transport equipment, basic manufactures, chemicals and chemical products, mineral fuels. Principal source: EU 34.7% (1995) **Arable land:** 40.7% (1995) **Agricultural products:** wheat, barley, sugar beet, potatoes, hops; livestock rearing (cattle, pigs, and poultry); dairy farming

Population and society

Population: 10,251,000 (1996 est) **Population growth rate:** 0% (1990–95); –0.1% (2000–05) **Population density:** (per sq km) 130 (1996 est) **Urban population:** (% of total) 65 (1995) **Age distribution:** (% of total population) <15 19.4%, 15–65 68.1%, >65 12.5% (1995) **Ethnic groups:** predominantly Western Slav Czechs; there is also a sizeable Slovak minority and small Polish, German, and Hungarian minorities **Language:** Czech (official) **Religion:** Roman Catholic, Hussite, Presbyterian Evangelical Church of Czech Brethren, Orthodox **Education:** (compulsory years) 9 **Literacy rate:** 99% (men); 99% (women) (1995 est) **Labour force:** 50.2% of population; 6.3% agriculture, 42% industry, 51.7% services (1996) **Unemployment:** 3.1% (1996) **Life expectancy:** 68 (men); 75 (women) (1995–2000) **Child mortality rate:** (under 5, per 1,000 live births) 10 (1996) **Physicians:** 1 per 273 people (1993 est)

Practical information

Visa requirements: UK: visa not required. USA: visa not required **Embassy in the UK:** 26–30 Kensington Palace Gardens, London W8 4QY. Tel: (0171) 243 1115; fax: (0171) 727 9654 **British embassy:** Thunovská 14, 11 800 Prague 7. Tel: (2) 2451 0439; fax: (2) 539 927 **Chamber of commerce:** Czech Chamber of Commerce and Industry, Argentinská 38, 170 05 Prague 7. Tel: (2) 6679 4880; fax: (2) 875 348 **Airports:** international airports: Prague (Ruzyň), Brno (Cernovice), Ostrava (International and Mosnov – domestic), Karlovy Vary; total passenger km: 1,976 million (1994) **Major holidays:** 1 January, 1 May, 5–6, July, 28 October, 24–26 December; variable: Easter Monday

Chronology

5th century: Settled by West Slavs. **8th century:** Part of Charlemagne's Holy Roman Empire. **9th century:** Kingdom of Greater Moravia, centred around the eastern part of what is now the Czech Republic, founded by the Slavic prince Sviatopluk; Christianity adopted. **906:** Moravia conquered by the Magyars (Hungarians). **995:** Independent state of Bohemia in the NW, centred around Prague, formed under the Premysl rulers, who had broken away from Moravia; became kingdom in 12th century. **1029:** Moravia became a fief of Bohemia. **1355:** King Charles IV of Bohemia became Holy Roman Emperor. **early 15th century:** Nationalistic Hussite religion, opposed to German and papal influence, founded in Bohemia by John Huss. **1526:** Bohemia came under the control of the Austrian Catholic Habsburgs. **1618:** Hussite revolt precipitated the Thirty Years' War, which resulted in the Bohemians' defeat, more direct rule by the Habsburgs, and re-Catholicization. **1867:** With creation of dual Austro-Hungarian monarchy, Bohemia was reduced to a province of Austria, leading to a growth in national consciousness. **1918:** Austro-Hungarian Empire dismembered; Czechs joined Slovaks in forming Czechoslovakia as independent democratic nation, with Tomas Masaryk president. **1938:** Under the Munich Agreement, Czechoslovakia was forced to surrender the Sudeten German districts in the N to Germany. **1939:** The remainder of Czechoslovakia annexed by Germany, Bohemia-Moravia being administered as a 'protectorate'; President Eduard Beneš set up a government-in-exile in London; liquidation campaigns against intelligentsia. **1945:** Liberated by Soviet and American troops; communist-dominated government of national unity formed under Beneš; 2 million Sudeten Germans expelled. **1948:** Beneš ousted; communists assumed full control under a Soviet-style single-party constitution. **1950s:** Political opponents purged; nationalization of industries. **1968:** 'Prague Spring' political liberalization programme, instituted by Communist Party leader Alexander Dubček, crushed by invasion of Warsaw Pact forces to restore the 'orthodox line'. **1969:** New federal constitution, creating a separate Czech Socialist Republic; Gustáv Husák became Communist Party leader. **1977:** Formation of the 'Charter '77' human-rights group by intellectuals, including the playwright Václav Havel, encouraged a crackdown against dissidents. **1987:** Reformist Miloš Jakeš replaced Husák as communist leader, and introduced a *prestvaba* ('restructuring') reform programme on the Soviet leader Mikhail Gorbachev's *perestroika* model. **1989:** Major prodemocracy demonstrations in Prague; new political parties formed and legalized, including Czech-based Civic Forum under Havel; Communist Party stripped of powers. New 'grand coalition' government formed; Havel appointed state president. Amnesty granted to 22,000 prisoners. **1990:** Multiparty elections won by Civic Forum. **1991:** Civic Forum split into centre-right Civic Democratic Party (CDP) and centre-left Civic Movement (CM); evidence of increasing Czech and Slovak separatism. **1992:** Václav Klaus, leader of the Czech-based CDP, became prime minister; Havel resigned following nationalist Slovak gains in assembly elections. Creation of separate Czech and Slovak states and a customs union agreed. Market-centred economic-reform programme launched, including mass privatizations. **1993:** Czech Republic became sovereign state within the United Nations, with Klaus as prime minister. Havel elected president. **1994:** Joined NATO's 'partnership for peace' programme. Strong economic growth registered. **1996:** Applied for EU membership. Klaus-led coalition lost its parliamentary majority after elections but remained in power. Ruling coalition successful in upper-house elections. **1997:** Former communist leader Miloš Jakeš charged with treason. Ruling coalition survived a currency crisis and criticism by President Havel. Czech Republic invited to join NATO and to begin EU membership negotiations. Klaus resigned after allegations of misconduct; Josef Tosovsky, governor of central bank, appointed as interim, non-party, successor.

Denmark Kingdom of

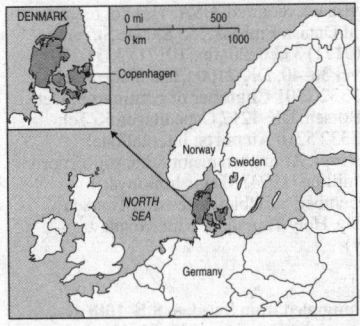

National name: *Kongeriget Danmark* **Area:** 43,075 sq km/16,631 sq mi **Capital:** Copenhagen **Major towns/cities:** Århus, Odense, Ålborg, Esbjerg, Randers **Major ports:** Århus, Odense, Ålborg, Esbjerg **Physical features:** comprises the Jutland peninsula and about 500 islands (100 inhabited) including Bornholm in the Baltic Sea; the land is flat and cultivated; sand dunes and lagoons on the W coast and long inlets on the E; the main island is Sjæland (Zealand), where most of Copenhagen is located (the rest is on the island of Amager) **Territories:** the dependencies of Faroe Islands and Greenland

Government

Head of state: Queen Margrethe II from 1972 **Head of government:** Poul Nyrup Rasmussen from 1993 **Political system:** liberal democracy **Administrative divisions:** 14 counties, one city and one borough **Political parties:** Social Democrats (SD), left of centre; Conservative People's Party (KF), moderate centre right; Liberal Party (V), centre left; Socialist People's Party (SF), moderate left wing; Radical Liberals (RV), radical internationalist, left of centre; Centre Democrats (CD), moderate centrist; Progress Party (FP), radical antibureaucratic; Christian People's Party (KrF), interdenominational, family values **Armed forces:** 32,900; 70,400 reservists and volunteer Home Guard of 65,200 (1996) **Conscription:** 9–12 months (27 months for some ranks) **Death penalty:** abolished 1978 **Defence spend:** (% GDP) 1.7 (1996) **Education spend:** (% GNP) 8.5 (1993–94) **Health spend:** (% GDP) 5.4 (1994)

Economy and resources

Currency: Danish krone **GDP:** ($ US) 174.2 billion (1996) **Real GDP per capita (PPP):** ($ US) 22,314 (1996) **GDP growth rate:** 2.5% (1996); 2% (1990–95) **Average annual inflation:** 2.3%

(1996); 2.8% (1985–95) **Major trading partners:** EU (principally Germany, Sweden, and UK), Norway, USA **Resources:** crude petroleum, natural gas, salt, limestone **Industries:** mining, food processing, fisheries, machinery, textiles, furniture, electronic goods and transport equipment, chemicals and pharmaceuticals, printing and publishing **Exports:** pig meat and pork products, other food products, fish, industrial machinery, chemicals, transport equipment. Principal market: Germany 35.8% (1995) **Imports:** food and live animals, machinery, transport equipment, iron, steel, electronics, petroleum, cereals, paper. Principal source: Germany 32.4% (1995) **Arable land:** 54.8% (1995) **Agricultural products:** wheat, rye, barley, oats, potatoes, sugar beet, dairy products; livestock production (pigs) and dairy products; fishing

Population and society
Population: 5,237,000 (1996 est) **Population growth rate:** 0.2% (1990–95); 0% (2000–05) **Population density:** (per sq km) 122 (1996 est) **Urban population:** (% of total) 85 (1995) **Age distribution:** (% of total population) <17.2%, 15–65 67.6%, >65 15.2% (1995) **Ethnic groups:** all Danes are part of the Scandinavian ethnic group **Language:** Danish (official); there is a German-speaking minority **Religion:** Lutheran 97% **Education:** (compulsory years) 9 **Literacy rate:** 99% (men); 99% (women) (1995 est) **Labour force:** 53.6% of population: 4% agriculture, 27% industry, 69% services (1996) **Unemployment:** 6.9% (1996) **Life expectancy:** 73 (men); 79 (women) (1995–2000) **Child mortality rate:** (under 5, per 1,000 live births) 8 (1996) **Physicians:** 1 per 357 people (1993)

Practical information
Visa requirements: UK: visa not required. USA: visa not required **Embassy in the UK:** Royal Danish Embassy, 55 Sloane Street, London SW1X 9SR. Tel: (0171) 333 0200; fax: (0171) 333 0270 **British embassy:** Kastelsvej 36–40, DK-2100 Copenhagen. Tel: (45) 3526 4600; fax: (45) 3332 1501 **Chamber of commerce:** Det Danske Handelskammer, Børsen, DK-1217 Copenhagen K. Tel: (45) 3395 0500; fax: (45) 3332 5216 **Airports:** international airports: Copenhagen (Kastrup), Århus; ten major domestic airports; total passenger km: 5,112 million (1994) **Major holidays:** 1 January, 5 June, 24–26 December; variable: Ascension Thursday, Good Friday, Easter Monday, Holy Thursday, Whit Monday, General Prayer (April/May)

Chronology
5th–6th centuries: Danes migrated from Sweden. **8th–10th centuries:** Viking raids throughout Europe. **c. 940–85:** Harald Bluetooth unified Kingdom of Denmark and established Christianity. **1014–35:** King Canute I created empire embracing Denmark, Norway, and England; empire collapsed after his death. **12th century:** Denmark re-emerged as dominant Baltic power. **1340–75:** Valdemar IV restored order after period of civil war and anarchy. **1397:** Union of Kalmar: Denmark, Sweden, and Norway (with Iceland) united under a single monarch. **1449:** Sweden broke away from union. **1460:** Christian I secured duchies of Schleswig and Holstein. **1523:** Denmark recognized Sweden's independence. **1536:** Lutheranism established as official religion of Denmark. **1563–70:** Unsuccessful war to recover Sweden. **1625–29:** Denmark sided with Protestants in Thirty Years' War. **1643–45:** Second attempt to reclaim Sweden ended in failure. **1657–60:** Further failed attempt to reclaim Sweden. **1665:** Frederick III made himself absolute monarch. **1729:** Greenland became Danish province. **1780–81:** Denmark, Russia, and Sweden formed 'Armed Neutrality' coalition to protect neutral shipping during War of American Independence. **1788:** Serfdom abolished. **1800:** France persuaded Denmark to revive Armed Neutrality against British blockade. **1801:** First Battle of Copenhagen: much of Danish fleet destroyed by British navy. **1807:** Second Battle of Copenhagen: British seized rebuilt fleet to pre-empt Danish entry into Napoleonic War on French side. **1814:** Treaty of Kiel: Denmark ceded Norway to Sweden as penalty for supporting France in Napoleonic War; Denmark retained Iceland. **1848–50:** Germans of Schleswig-Holstein revolted with Prussian support. **1849:** Liberal pressure compelled Frederick VII to grant democratic constitution. **1864:**

Prussia seized Schleswig-Holstein after short war. **1914–1919:** Denmark neutral during World War I. **1918:** Iceland achieved full self-government. **1919:** Denmark recovered northern Schleswig under peace settlement after World War I. **1929–40:** Welfare state established under left-wing coalition government dominated by Social Democrat Party. **1940–45:** German occupation. **1944:** Iceland declared independence. **1949:** Denmark became a founding member of North Atlantic Treaty Organization (NATO). **1960:** Denmark joined European Free Trade Association (EFTA). **1973:** Withdrew from EFTA and joined European Economic Community (EEC). **1981:** Greenland achieved full self-government. **1992:** Referendum rejected Maastricht Treaty on European union. **1993:** Second referendum approved Maastricht Treaty after government negotiated a series of 'opt-out' clauses. **1996:** Centre Democrats withdrew from governing coalition.

Djibouti Republic of

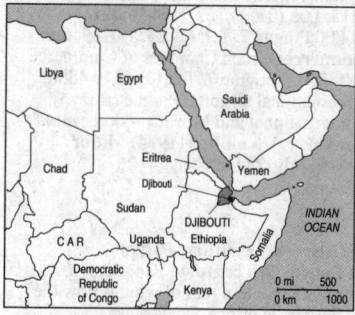

National name: *Jumhouriyya Djibouti* **Area:** 23,200 sq km/8,957 sq mi **Capital:** Djibouti (and chief port) **Major towns/cities:** Tadjoura, Obock, Dikhil, Ali-Sabieh **Physical features:** mountains divide an inland plateau from a coastal plain; hot and arid

Government
Head of state: Hassan Gouled Aptidon from 1977 **Head of government:** Barkat Gourad from 1981 **Political system:** emergent democracy **Administrative divisions:** five districts **Political parties:** People's Progress Assembly (RPP), nationalist; Democratic Renewal Party (PRD), moderate left of centre **Armed forces:** 8,400 (1996); plus 3,900 French troops **Conscription:** military service is voluntary **Death penalty:** retains the death penalty for ordinary crimes but can be considered abolitionist in practice (no executions since independence) **Defence spend:** (% GDP) 5.2 (1996) **Education spend:** (% GNP) 3.8 (1993–94) **Health spend:** (% GDP) 2.1 (1994)

Economy and resources
Currency: Djibouti franc **GDP:** ($ US) 500 million (1994 est) **Real GDP per capita (PPP):** ($ US) 1,200 (1994 est) **GDP growth rate:** −2.9% (1994) **Average annual inflation:** 3% (1993) **Foreign debt:** ($ US) 247 million (1994) **Major trading partners:** Kenya, Thailand, France, Ethiopia, Somalia **Industries:** mineral water bottling, dairy products and other small-scale enterprises; an important port serving the regional hinterland **Exports:** hides, cattle, coffee (exports are largely re-exports). Principal market: Kenya 42% (1995) **Imports:** vegetable products, foodstuffs, beverages, vinegar, tobacco, machinery and transport equipment, mineral products. Principal source: Thailand 15.4% (1995) **Arable land:** 10% (1995) **Agricultural products:** mainly market gardening (for example, tomatoes); livestock rearing (over 50% of the population are pastoral nomads, herding goats, sheep, and camels); fishing

Population and society
Population: 617,000 (1996 est) **Population growth rate:** 2.2% (1990–95) **Population density:** (per sq km) 27 (1996 est) **Urban population:** (% of total) 83 (1994) **Age distribution:** (% of total population) <15 42%, 15–65 55%, >65 3% (1994) **Ethnic groups:** population divided mainly into two Hamitic groups; the Issas

(Somalis) in the S, and the minority Afars (or Danakil) in the N and W. There are also minorities of Europeans (mostly French), as well as Arabs, Sudanese, and Indians **Language:** French (official), Somali, Afar, Arabic **Religion:** Sunni Muslim **Education:** (compulsory years) 6 **Literacy rate:** 60% (men); 33% (women) (1995 est) **Unemployment:** 40% (1995 est) **Life expectancy:** 49 (men); 52 (women) (1995–2000) **Child mortality rate:** (under 5, per 1,000 live births) 164 (1996) **Physicians:** 1 per 6,590 people (1993 est)

Practical information
Visa requirements: UK: visa required. USA: visa required **Embassy for the UK:** 26 rue Emile Ménier, 75116 Paris, France. Tel: (1) 4727 4922; fax: (1) 4553 5053 **British embassy:** British Consulate, BP 81 Gellatly Hankey et Cie, Djibouti. Tel: (253) 351 940; fax: (253) 353 294 **Chamber of commerce:** Chambre Internationale de Commerce et d'Industrie, BP 84, Place de Lagarde, Djibouti. Tel: (253) 351 070; fax: (253) 350 096 **Airports:** international airport: Djibouti (Ambouli); six domestic airports **Major holidays:** 1 January, 1 May, 27 June (2 days), 25 December; variable: Eid-ul-Adha (2 days), end of Ramadan (2 days), New Year (Muslim), Prophet's Birthday, Al-Isra Wal-Mira'age (March–April)

Chronology
3rd century BC: The N settled by Able immigrants from Arabia, whose descendants are the Afars (Danakil). **early Christian era:** Somali Issas settled in coastal areas and S, ousting Afars. **825:** Islam introduced by missionaries. **16th century:** Portuguese arrived to challenge trading monopoly of Arabs. **1862:** French acquired a port at Obock. **1888:** Annexed by France as part of French Somaliland. **1900s:** Railroad linked Djibouti port with the Ethiopian hinterland. **1946:** Became overseas territory within French Union, with own assembly and representation in French parliament. **1958:** Voted to become overseas territorial member of French Community. **1967:** French Somaliland renamed the French Territory of the Afars and the Issas. **early 1970s:** Issas (Somali) peoples campaigned for independence, but the minority Afars, of Ethiopian descent, and Europeans sought to remain French. **1977:** Independence achieved as Djibouti, with Hassan Gouled Aptidon, the leader of the independence movement, elected president. **1981:** New constitution made the People's Progress Assembly (RPP) the only legal party. Treaties of friendship signed with Ethiopia, Somalia, Kenya, and Sudan. **1984:** Policy of neutrality reaffirmed. Economy undermined by severe drought. **1992:** New multiparty constitution adopted; fighting erupted between government forces and Afar Front for Restoration of Unity and Democracy (FRUD) guerrilla movement in the NE. **1993:** Opposition parties allowed to operate, but Gouled re-elected president. **1994:** Peace agreement reached with Afar FRUD militants, ending civil war.

Dominica Commonwealth of

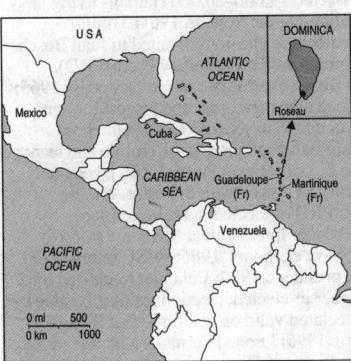

Area: 751 sq km/290 sq mi **Capital:** Roseau, with a deepwater port **Major towns/cities:** Portsmouth, Berekua, Marigot, Rosalie **Major ports:** Roseau, Portsmouth, Berekua, Marigot, Rosalie **Physical features:** second largest of the Windward Islands, mountainous central ridge with tropical rainforest

Government
Head of state: Clarence Seignoret from 1983 **Head of government:** Edison James from 1995 **Political system:** liberal democracy **Administrative divisions:** ten parishes **Political parties:** Dominica Freedom Party (DFP), centrist; Labour Party of Dominica (LPD), left-of-centre coalition; Dominica United Workers' Party (DUWP), left of centre **Armed forces:** defence force disbanded 1981; police force of approximately 300 **Death penalty:** retained and used for ordinary crimes **Education spend:** (% GNP) 5.8 (1992); N/A (1993–94)

Economy and resources
Currency: Eastern Caribbean dollar; pound sterling; French franc **GDP:** ($ US) 207 million (1994) **Real GDP per capita (PPP):** ($ US) 6,118 (1994) **GDP growth rate:** 1% (1994) **Average annual inflation:** 1.2% (1996); 4.4% (1985–95) **Foreign debt:** ($ US) 110 million (1996) **Major trading partners:** USA, UK, the Netherlands, South Korea, Belgium, Japan, Trinidad and Tobago **Resources:** pumice, limestone, clay **Industries:** banana packaging, vegetable oils, soap, canned juice, cigarettes, rum, beer, furniture, paint, cardboard boxes, candles, tourism **Exports:** bananas, soap, coconuts, grapefruit, galvanized sheets. Principal market: UK 25.3% (1995) **Imports:** food and live animals, basic manufactures, machinery and transport equipment, mineral fuels. Principal source: USA 13% (1995) **Arable land:** 4% (1995) **Agricultural products:** bananas, coconuts, mangoes, avocados, papayas, ginger, citrus fruits, vegetables; livestock rearing; fishing

Population and society
Population: 71,000 (1996 est) **Population growth rate:** –0.1 (1990–95) **Population density:** (per sq km) 94 (1996 est) **Urban population:** (% of total) 41 (1993) **Age distribution:** (% of total population) <15 37.5%, 15–65 54.2%, >65 8.3% (1993) **Ethnic groups:** majority descended from African slaves; a small number of the indigenous Arawaks remain **Language:** English (official), but the Dominican patois reflects earlier periods of French rule **Religion:** Roman Catholic 80% **Education:** (compulsory years) 10 **Literacy rate:** 94% (men); 94% (women) (1994 est) **Labour force:** 25.8% agriculture, 21.2% industry, 53% services (1990) **Unemployment:** 23% (1994) **Life expectancy:** 72 (men); 76 (women) (1994 est) **Child mortality rate:** (under 5, per 1,000 live births) 21 (1995) **Physicians:** 1 per 2,952 people (1993)

Practical information
Visa requirements: UK: visa not required for stays of up to six months. USA: visa not required for stays of up to six months **Embassy in the UK:** High Commisssion, 1 Collingham Gardens, London SW5 0HW. Tel: (0171) 370 5194/5; fax: (0171) 373 8743 **British embassy:** British High Commission, British Consulate, Office of the Honorary British Consul, PO Box 6, Roseau. (All staff based in Bridgetown, Barbados.) Tel: (809) 448 1000; fax: (809) 448 1110 **Chamber of commerce:** Dominica Association of Industry and Commerce, PO Box 85, 111 Bath Road, Roseau. Tel: (809) 448 2874; fax: (809) 448 6868 **Airports:** international airports: Roseau (Canefield), Portsmouth/Marigot (Melville Hall); aircraft arrivals and departures: 16,678 (1993) **Major holidays:** 1 January, 1 May, 3–4 November, 25–26 December; variable: Carnival (2 days), Good Friday, Easter Monday, Whit Monday, August Monday

Chronology
1493: Visited by the explorer Christopher Columbus, who named the island Dominica ('Sunday Island'). **1627:** Presented by the English King Charles I to the Earl of Carlisle, but initial European attempts at colonization were fiercely resisted by the indigenous Carib community. **later 18th century:** Succession of local British and French conflicts over control of the fertile island. **1763:** British given possession of the island by the Treaty of Paris (ending the Seven Years' War), but France continued to challenge this militarily until 1805, when there was formal cession in return for the sum of £12,000. **1834:** Slaves, who had been brought in from Africa, were emancipated. **1870:** Became part of the British Leeward Islands federation. **1940:** Transferred to British Windward Islands

federation. **1951:** Universal adult suffrage established. **1958–62:** Part of the West Indies Federation. **1960:** Granted separate, semi-independent status, with a legislative council and chief minister. **1961:** Edward leBlanc, leader of newly formed DLP, became chief minister. **1974:** LeBlanc retired; replaced as chief minister by Patrick John (DLP). **1978:** Independence achieved as a republic within the Commonwealth, with John as prime minister. **1980:** DFP won convincing victory in general election, and Eugenia Charles became Caribbean's first woman prime minister. **1981:** John implicated in plot to overthrow government, but subsequently acquitted. **1983:** Small force participated in US-backed invasion of Grenada. **1985:** John retried, found guilty, and sentenced to 12 years' imprisonment. Regrouping of left-of-centre parties resulted in new Labour Party of Dominica (LPD). **1991:** Windward Islands confederation comprising St Lucia, St Vincent, Grenada, and Dominica proposed. **1993:** Charles resigned DFP leadership, but continued as prime minister. **1995:** DUWP won general election; Edison James appointed prime minister and Eugenia Charles retired from politics.

Dominican Republic

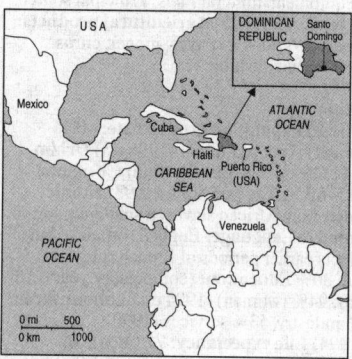

National name: *República Dominicana* **Area:** 48,442 sq km/18,703 sq mi **Capital:** Santo Domingo **Major towns/cities:** Santiago de los Caballeros, La Romana, San Pedro de Macoris, San Francisco de Macoris, Concepcion de la Vega, San Juan **Physical features:** comprises eastern two-thirds of island of Hispaniola; central mountain range with fertile valleys; Pico Duarte 3,174 m/10,417 ft, highest point in Caribbean islands

Government

Head of state and government: Leoned Fernandez from 1996 **Political system:** democracy **Administrative divisions:** 29 provinces and a national district (Santo Domingo) **Political parties:** Dominican Revolutionary Party (PRD), moderate, left of centre; Christian Social Reform Party (PRSC), independent socialist; Dominican Liberation Party (PLD), nationalist **Armed forces:** 24,500 (1996); plus a paramilitary force of 15,000 **Conscription:** military service is voluntary **Death penalty:** abolished 1966 **Defence spend:** (% GDP) 1.1 (1996) **Education spend:** (% GNP) 1.9 (1993–94) **Health spend:** (% GDP) 3 (1994)

Economy and resources

Currency: Dominican Republic peso **GDP:** ($ US) 10.4 billion (1994) **Real GDP per capita (PPP):** ($ US) 3,933 (1994) **GDP growth rate:** 4.3% (1994); 3.9% (1990–95) **Average annual inflation:** 5.8% (1996); 26.3% (1985–95) **Foreign debt:** ($ US) 4.26 billion (1996) **Major trading partners:** USA, Venezuela, Mexico, Japan, South Korea, the Netherlands, Belgium **Resources:** ferro-nickel, gold, silver **Industries:** food processing (including sugar refining), petroleum refining, beverages, chemicals, cement **Exports:** raw sugar, molasses, coffee, cocoa, tobacco, ferro-nickel, gold, silver. Principal market: USA 45.1% (1995) **Imports:** petroleum and petroleum products, coal, foodstuffs, wheat, machinery. Principal source: USA 44.1% (1995) **Arable land:** 27.8% (1995) **Agricultural products:** sugar cane, cocoa, coffee, bananas, tobacco, rice, tomatoes

Population and society

Population: 7,961,000 (1996 est) **Population growth rate:** 1.9% (1990–95); 1.4% (2000–05) **Population density:** (per sq km) 163 (1996 est) **Urban population:** (% of total) 65 (1995) **Age distribution:** (% of total population) <15 35.1%, 15–65 60.9%, >65 4% (1995) **Ethnic groups:** about 73% of the population are mulattos, of mixed European and African descent; about 16% are European; 11% African **Language:** Spanish (official) **Religion:** Roman Catholic **Education:** (compulsory years) 8 **Literacy rate:** 85% (men); 82% (women) (1995 est) **Labour force:** 44% of population: 12.9% agriculture, 23% industry, 64.1% services (1995) **Unemployment:** 30% (1990 est) **Life expectancy:** 69 (men); 73 (women) (1995–2000) **Child mortality rate:** (under 5, per 1,000 live births) 46 (1996) **Physicians:** 1 per 949 people (1993)

Practical information

Visa requirements: UK: visa not required for stays of up to 90 days. USA: visa not required for stays of up to 60 days **Embassy in the UK:** Honorary Consulate of the Dominican Republic, 6 Queen's Mansions, Brook Green, London W6 7EB. Tel: (0171) 602 1885 **British embassy:** Edificio Corominas Pepin, Ave 27 Febrero No. 233, Santo Domingo. Tel: (809) 472 7111; fax: (809) 472 7574 **Chamber of commerce:** Cámara de Comercio y Produccíon del Distrito Nacional, Apartado Postal 815, Arz. Nouel 206, Santo Domingo. Tel: (809) 682 7206; fax: (809) 685 2228 **Airports:** international airports: Santo Domingo (Internacional de las Americas), Puerto Plata (La Union), Punta Cana, La Romana; most main cities have domestic airports; total passenger km: 234 million (1994) **Major holidays:** 1, 6, 21, 26 January, 27 February, 1 May, 16 August, 24 September, 25 December; variable: Corpus Christi, Good Friday

Chronology

14th century: Settled by Carib Indians, who followed an earlier wave of Arawak Indian immigration. **1492:** Visited by Christopher Columbus, who named it Hispaniola ('Little Spain'). **1496:** At Santo Domingo, the Spanish established the first European settlement in the western hemisphere, which became capital of all Spanish colonies in America. **first half of 16th century:** One-third of a million Arawaks and Caribs died, as a result of enslavement and exposure to European diseases; black African slaves were consequently brought in to work the island's gold and silver mines, which were swiftly exhausted. **1697:** Divided between France, which held the western third (Haiti), and Spain, which held the E (Dominican Republic, or Santo Domingo). **1795:** Santo Domingo was ceded to France. **1808:** Following a revolt by Spanish Creoles, with British support, Santo Domingo was retaken by Spain. **1821:** Became briefly independent after uprising against Spanish rule, and then fell under the control of Haiti. **1844:** Separated from Haiti to form Dominican Republic. **1861–65:** Under Spanish protection. **1904:** The USA took over the near-bankrupt republic's debts. **1916–24:** Temporarily occupied by US forces. **1930:** Military coup established personal dictatorship of General Rafael Trujillo Molina after overthrow of president Horacio Vázquez. **1937:** Army massacred 19,000–20,000 Haitians living in the Dominican provinces adjoining the frontier. **1961:** Trujillo assassinated. **1962:** First democratic elections resulted in Juan Bosch, founder of the left-wing Dominican Revolutionary Party (PRD), becoming president. **1963:** Bosch overthrown in military coup. **1965:** 30,000 US marines intervened to restore order and protect foreign nationals after Bosch had attempted to seize power. **1966:** New constitution adopted. Joaquín Balaguer, protégé of Trujillo and leader of the centre-right Christian Social Reform Party (PRSC), became president. **1978:** PRD returned to power, with Silvestre Antonio Guzmán as president. **1982:** PRD re-elected, with Jorge Blanco as president. **1985:** Blanco forced by International Monetary Fund to adopt austerity measures to save economy. **1986:** PRSC returned to power; Balaguer re-elected president. **1990:** Balaguer re-elected by a small majority. **1994:** Balaguer re-elected; election results disputed by opposition but eventually declared valid on condition that Balaguer serve reduced two-year term. **1996:** Leoned Fernandez of the left-wing Dominican Liberation Party (PLD) was elected president.

Ecuador Republic of

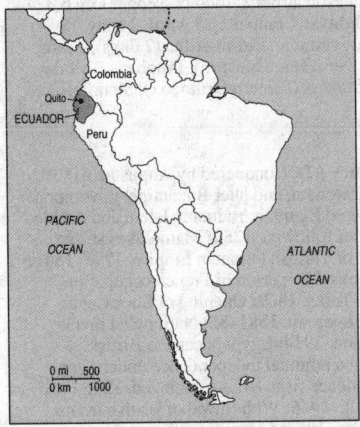

National name: *República del Ecuador* **Area:** 270,670 sq km/104,505 sq mi **Capital:** Quito **Major towns/cities:** Guayaquil, Cuenca, Machala, Portoviejo, Manta, Ambeto, Esmeraldas **Major ports:** Guayaquil **Physical features:** coastal plain rises sharply to Andes Mountains, which are divided into a series of cultivated valleys; flat, low-lying rainforest in the E; Galápagos Islands; Cotopaxi, the world's highest active volcano. Ecuador is crossed by the equator, from which it derives its name

Government
Head of state and government: (interim) Fabian Alarcon from 1997 **Political system:** emergent democracy **Administrative divisions:** 21 provinces **Political parties:** Social Christian Party (PSC), right wing; Ecuadorean Roldosist Party (PRE), populist, centre left; United Republican Party (PUR), right-of-centre coalition; Democratic Left (ID), moderate socialist; Conservative Party (PC), right wing **Armed forces:** 57,100 (1996) **Conscription:** military service is selective for one year **Death penalty:** abolished 1906 **Defence spend:** (% GDP) 3.4 (1996) **Education spend:** (% GNP) 3 (1993–94) **Health spend:** (% GDP) 2 (1990–95)

Economy and resources
Currency: sucre **GDP:** ($ US) 16.6 billion (1994) **Real GDP per capita (PPP):** ($ US) 4,626 (1994) **GDP growth rate:** 4% (1994); 3.4% (1990–95) **Average annual inflation:** 26.3% (1996); 45.5% (1985–95) **Foreign debt:** ($ US) 19.2 billion (1996) **Major trading partners:** USA, Colombia, Germany, Chile, Peru, Japan, Italy, Spain **Resources:** petroleum, natural gas, gold, silver, copper, zinc, antimony, iron, uranium, lead, coal **Industries:** food processing, petroleum refining, cement, chemicals, textiles **Exports:** petroleum and petroleum products, bananas, shrimps (a major exporter), coffee, seafood products, cocoa beans and products, cut flowers. Principal market: USA 42.4% (1994) **Imports:** machinery and transport equipment, basic manufactures, chemicals, consumer goods. Principal source: USA 25.3% (1994) **Arable land:** 5.7% (1995) **Agricultural products:** bananas, coffee, cocoa, rice, potatoes, maize, barley, sugar cane; fishing (especially shrimp industry); forestry

Population and society
Population: 11,699,000 (1996 est) **Population growth rate:** 2.2% (1990–95); 1.7% (2000–05) **Population density:** (per sq km) 41 (1996 est) **Urban population:** (% of total) 58 (1995) **Age distribution:** (% of total population) <15 36.4%, 15–65 59.2%, >65 4.4% (1995) **Ethnic groups:** about 55% mestizo (of Spanish-American and Native American parentage), 25% Native American, 10% Spanish, 10% African **Language:** Spanish (official), Quechua, Jivaro, and other indigenous languages **Religion:** Roman Catholic **Education:** (compulsory years) 6 **Literacy rate:** 88% (men); 84% (women) (1995 est) **Labour force:** 35% of population: 33% agriculture, 19% industry, 48% services (1990) **Unemployment:** 8.9% (1993) **Life expectancy:** 67 (men); 73 (women) (1995–2000) **Child mortality rate:** (under 5, per 1,000 live births) 57 (1996) **Physicians:** 1 per 918 people (1993)

Practical information
Visa requirements: UK: visa not required (except for business visits of three–six months). USA: visa not required (except for business visits of three–six months) **Embassy in the UK:** Flat 3B, 3 Hans Crescent, London SW1X 0LS. Tel: (0171) 584 1367; fax: (0171) 823 9701 **British embassy:** Casilla 314, Calle González Suárez 111, Quito. Tel: (2) 560 669; fax: (2) 560 730 **Chamber of commerce:** Federación Nacional de Cámaras de Comercio del Ecuador, Avenida Olmedo 414, Casila y Boyacá, Guayaquil. Tel: (4) 323 130; fax: (4) 323 478 **Airports:** international airports: Quito (Mariscal Sucre), Guayaquil (Simón Bolívar); six domestic airports; total passenger km: 1,410 million (1994) **Major holidays:** 1 January, 1, 24 May, 30 June, 24 July, 10 August, 9, 12 October, 2–3 November, 6, 25, 31 December; variable: Carnival (2 days), Good Friday, Holy Thursday

Chronology
1450s: The Caras people, whose kingdom had its capital at Quito, conquered by Incas of Peru. **1531:** Spanish conquistador Francisco Pizarro landed on Ecuadorian coast, en route to Peru, where Incas were defeated. **1534:** Conquered by Spanish. Quito, which had been destroyed by Native Americans, was refounded by Sebastian de Belalcazar; the area became part of Spanish Viceroyalty of Peru, which covered much of South America, with its capital at Lima (Peru). **later 16th century:** Spanish established large agrarian estates, owned by Europeans and worked by Native American peons. **1739:** Became part of new Spanish Viceroyalty of Nueva Granada, which included Colombia and Venezuela, with its capital in Bogotá (Colombia). **1809:** With the Spanish monarchy having been overthrown by Napoleon Bonaparte, creole middle class began to press for independence. **1822:** Spanish Royalists defeated by Field Marshal Antonio José de Sucre, fighting for Simón Bolívar, 'The Liberator', at battle of Pichincha, near Quito; became part of independent Gran Colombia, which also comprised Colombia, Panama, and Venezuela. **1830:** Became fully independent state, after leaving Gran Colombia. **1845–60:** Political instability, with five presidents holding power, increasing tension between conservative Quito and liberal Guayaquil on the coast, and minor wars with Peru and Colombia. **1860–75:** Power held by Gabriel García Moreno, an autocratic theocrat-Conservative who launched education and public-works programmes. **1895–1912:** Dominated by Gen Eloy Alfaro, a radical, anticlerical Liberal from the coastal region, who reduced the power of the church. **1925–48:** Great political instability; no president completed his term of office. **1941:** Lost territory in Amazonia after defeat in war with Peru. **1948–55:** Liberals in power. **1956:** Camilo Ponce became first conservative president in 60 years. **1960:** Liberals in power, with José María Velasco Ibarra returning as president. **1961:** Velasco deposed and replaced by the vice president. **1962:** Military junta installed. **1968:** Velasco returned as president. **1970s:** Ecuador emerged as a significant oil producer. **1972:** A coup put the military back in power. **1979:** New democratic constitution; Liberals in power but opposed by right- and left-wing parties. **1981:** Border dispute with Peru flared up again. **1982:** Deteriorating economy and austerity measures provoked strikes, demonstrations, and a state of emergency. **1984–85:** No party with a clear majority in the national congress; León Febres Cordero narrowly won the presidency for the Conservatives. **1988:** Rodrigo Borja Cevallos elected president for moderate left-wing coalition and introduced unpopular austerity measures. **1992:** PUR leader Sixto Duran Ballen elected president; PSC became largest party in congress. Ecuador withdrew from OPEC to enable it to increase its oil exports. **1994:** Mounting opposition to Duran's economic liberalization and privatization programme. **1995:** Parliament dismissed three key ministers, including the finance minister for corruption; long-standing border dispute with Peru resolved. **1996:** Abdala Bucaram elected president. **1997:** Bucaram removed from office and replaced by vice-president Rosalia Arteaga, but a national referendum later ratified Fabian Alarcon as interim president.

Egypt Arab Republic of

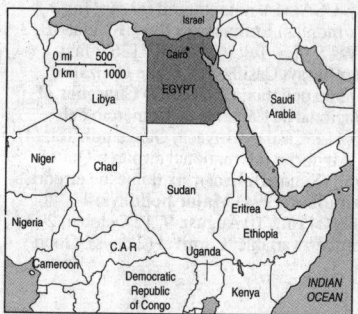

National name: *Jumhuriyat Misr al-Arabiya* **Area:** 1,001,450 sq km/386,659 sq mi **Capital:** Cairo **Major towns/cities:** El Gîza, Shubra Al Khayma, Alexandria, Port Said, El-Mahalla el-Koubra, Tauta, El-Mansoura **Major ports:** Alexandria, Port Said, Suez, Damietta, Shubra Al Khayma **Physical features:** mostly desert; hills in E; fertile land along Nile valley and delta; cultivated and settled area is about 35,500 sq km/13,700 sq mi; Aswan High Dam and Lake Nasser; Sinai

Government
Head of state: Hosni Mubarak from 1981 **Head of government:** Kamal Ahmed Ganzouri from 1996 **Political system:** democracy **Administrative divisions:** 26 governates **Political parties:** National Democratic Party (NDP), moderate, left of centre; Socialist Labour Party (SLP), right of centre; Liberal Socialist Party, free enterprise; New Wafd Party, nationalist; National Progressive Unionist Party, left wing **Armed forces:** 440,000 (1996) **Conscription:** 3 years (selective) **Death penalty:** retained and used for ordinary crimes **Defence spend:** (% GDP) 4.5 (1996) **Education spend:** (% GNP) 5 (1993–94) **Health spend:** (% GDP) 1 (1990)

Economy and resources
Currency: Egyptian pound **GDP:** ($ US) 42.9 billion (1994) **Real GDP per capita (PPP):** ($ US) 3,846 (1994) **GDP growth rate:** 2% (1994); 1.3% (1990–95) **Average annual inflation:** 7.5% (1996); 15.7% (1985–95) **Foreign debt:** ($ US) 33.1 billion (1996) **Major trading partners:** USA, Italy, Germany, France **Resources:** petroleum, natural gas, phosphates, manganese, uranium, coal, iron ore, gold **Industries:** petroleum and petroleum products, food processing, petroleum refining, textiles, metals, cement, tobacco, sugar crystal and refined sugar, electrical appliances, fertilizers **Exports:** petroleum and petroleum products, textiles, clothing, food, live animals. Principal market: Italy 18.6% (1995) **Imports:** wheat, maize, dairy products, machinery and transport equipment, wood and wood products, consumer goods. Principal source: USA 18.9% (1995) **Arable land:** 2.8% (1995) **Agricultural products:** wheat, cotton, rice, corn, beans

Population and society
Population: 63,271,000 (1996 est) **Population growth rate:** 2.2% (1990–95); 1.7% (2000–05) **Population density:** (per sq km) 63 (1996 est) **Urban population:** (% of total) 45 (1995) **Age distribution:** (% of total population) <15 38%, 15–65 57.8%, >65 4.2% (1995) **Ethnic groups:** 93% indigenous **Language:** Arabic (official); ancient Egyptian survives to some extent in Coptic; English; French **Religion:** Sunni Muslim 90%, Coptic Christian 7% **Education:** (compulsory years) 5 **Literacy rate:** 63% (men); 34% (women) (1995 est) **Labour force:** 35% of population: 34% agriculture, 21% industry, 45% services (1995) **Unemployment:** 13% (1993) **Life expectancy:** 65 (men); 67 (women) (1995–2000) **Child mortality rate:** (under 5, per 1,000 live births) 70 (1996) **Physicians:** 1 per 1,316 people (1993 est)

Practical information
Visa requirements: UK: visa required. USA: visa required **Embassy in the UK:** 26 South Street, London W1Y 8EL. Tel: (0171) 499 2401; fax: (0171) 355 3568 **British embassy:** 7 Sharia Ahmad Raghab, Garden City, Cairo. Tel: (2) 354 0850; fax: (2) 354 0859 **Chamber of commerce:** Federation of Chambers of Commerce, 4 el-Falaki Square, Cairo. Tel: (2) 355 1164; telex: 92645 **Airports:** international airports: Cairo (two), Alexandria (El Nouzha), Luxor; eight domestic airports; total passenger km: 6,324 million (1994) **Major holidays:** 7 January, 25 April, 1 May, 18 June, 1, 23 July, 6 October; variable: Eid-ul-Adha (2 days), Arafa, end of Ramadan (2 days), New Year (Muslim), Prophet's Birthday, Palm Sunday and Easter Sunday (Eastern Orthodox), Sham-el-Nessim (April/May)

Chronology
1st century BC–7th century AD: Conquered by Augustus AD 30, Egypt passed under rule of Roman, and later Byzantine, governors. **AD 639–42:** Arabs conquered Egypt, introducing Islam and Arabic; succession of Arab dynasties followed. **1250:** Mamelukes seized power. **1517:** Became part of Turkish Ottoman Empire. **1798–1801:** Invasion by Napoleon followed by period of French occupation. **1801:** Control regained by Turks. **1869:** Opening of Suez Canal made Egypt strategically important. **1881–82:** Nationalist revolt resulted in British occupation. **1914:** Egypt became a British protectorate. **1922:** Achieved nominal independence under King Fuad I. **1936:** Full independence from Britain achieved. King Fuad succeeded by his son Farouk. **1946:** Withdrawal of British troops except from Suez Canal zone. **1952:** Farouk overthrown by army in bloodless coup. **1953:** Egypt declared a republic, with Gen Neguib as president. **1956:** Neguib replaced by Col Gamal Nasser. Nasser announced nationalization of Suez Canal; Egypt attacked by Britain, France, and Israel. Cease-fire agreed following US intervention. **1958:** Short-lived merger of Egypt and Syria as United Arab Republic (UAR). **1967:** Six-Day War with Israel ended in Egypt's defeat and Israeli occupation of Sinai and Gaza Strip. **1970:** Nasser died suddenly; succeeded by Anwar Sadat. **1973:** Attempt to regain territory lost to Israel led to Yom Kippur War; cease-fire arranged by US secretary of state Henry Kissinger. **1978–79:** Camp David talks in USA resulted in a peace treaty between Egypt and Israel. Egypt expelled from Arab League. **1981:** Sadat assassinated by Muslim fundamentalists, succeeded by Hosni Mubarak. **1983:** Improved relations between Egypt and Arab world; only Libya and Syria maintained trade boycott. **1987:** Egypt readmitted to Arab League. **1989:** Improved relations with Libya; diplomatic relations with Syria restored. **1991:** Participation in Gulf War on US-led side. Major force in convening Middle East peace conference in Spain. **1992:** Violence between Muslims and Christians. **1994:** Government crackdown on Islamic militants. **1995:** Abortive attempt to assassinate Mubarak. **1996:** Kamal Ahmed Ganzouri appointed prime minister. **1997:** Islamic extremists killed and injured tourists at Luxor.

El Salvador Republic of

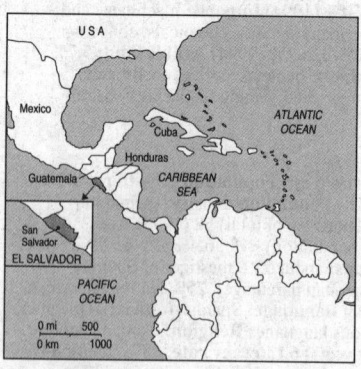

National name: *República de El Salvador* **Area:** 21,393 sq km/8,259 sq mi **Capital:** San Salvador **Major towns/cities:** Soyapango, Santa Ana, San Miguel, Nueva San Salvador, Mejicanos **Physical features:** narrow coastal plain, rising to mountains in N with central plateau

Government
Head of state and government: Armando Calderón Sol from 1994 **Political system:** emergent democracy **Administrative divisions:** 14 departments **Political parties:** Christian Democrats (PDC), anti-imperialist; Farabundo Martí Liberation Front (FMLN), left wing;

National Republican Alliance (ARENA), extreme right wing;
National Conciliation Party (PCN), right wing **Armed forces:**
28,400 (1996); plus 12,000 in paramilitary forces **Conscription:**
selective conscription for two years **Death penalty:** laws provide
for the death penalty only for exceptional crimes such as crimes
under military law or crimes committed in exceptional
circumstances such as wartime (last known execution 1973)
Defence spend: (% GDP) 1.5 (1996) **Education spend:** (% GNP)
1.6 (1993–94) **Health spend:** (% GDP) 1.2 (1990–95)

Economy and resources

Currency: Salvadorean colón **GDP:** ($ US) 8.1 billion (1994) **Real
GDP per capita (PPP):** ($ US) 2,417 (1994) **GDP growth rate:**
6% (1994); 6.3% (1990–95) **Average annual inflation:** 10.3%
(1996); 14.7% (1985–95) **Foreign debt:** ($ US) 2.7 billion (1996)
Major trading partners: USA, Guatemala, Costa Rica, Honduras,
Mexico, Japan, Germany, Venezuela **Resources:** salt, limestone,
gypsum **Industries:** food processing, beverages, petroleum
products, textiles, tobacco, paper products, chemical products
Exports: coffee, textiles and garments, sugar, shrimp, footwear,
pharmaceuticals. Principal market: USA 53.4% (1996) **Imports:**
petroleum and other minerals, cereals, chemicals, iron and steel,
machinery and transport equipment, consumer goods. Principal
source: USA 49.9% (1996) **Arable land:** 26.3% (1995)
Agricultural products: coffee, sugar cane, cotton, maize, beans,
rice, sorghum; fishing (shrimp)

Population and society

Population: 5,796,000 (1996 est) **Population growth rate:** 2.2%
(1990–95); 2% (2000–05) **Population density:** (per sq km) 275
(1996 est) **Urban population:** (% of total) 45 (1995) **Age
distribution:** (% of total population) <15 40.7%, 15–65 55.2%, >65
4.1% (1995) **Ethnic groups:** about 92% of the population are
mestizos, 6% Indians, and 2% of European origin **Language:**
Spanish, Nahuatl **Religion:** Roman Catholic, Protestant **Education:**
(compulsory years) 9 **Literacy rate:** 76% (men); 70% (women)
(1995 est) **Labour force:** 36% of population: 36% agriculture, 21%
industry, 43% services (1990) **Unemployment:** 7.7% (1993) **Life
expectancy:** 66 (men); 71 (women) (1995–2000) **Child mortality
rate:** (under 5, per 1,000 live births) 64 (1996) **Physicians:** 1 per
1,515 people (1993 est)

Practical information

Visa requirements: UK: visa not required for a stay of up to 90
days. USA: visa required (Tourist Card) **Embassy in the UK:**
Tennyson House, 159 Great Portland Street, London W1N 5FD. Tel:
(0171) 436 8282; fax: (0171) 436 8181 **British embassy:** PO Box
1591, Paeso General Escalón 4828, San Salvador. Tel: (503) 298
1768/9; fax: (503) 298 3328 **Chamber of commerce:** Cámara de
Comercio e Industria de El Salvador, Apartado 1640, 9a Avenida
Norte y 5a Calle Poniente, San Salvador. Tel: (503) 771 2055; fax:
(503) 771 4461 **Airports:** international airport: San Salvador (El
Salvador International); three domestic airports; total passenger km:
1,573 million (1994) **Major holidays:** 1 January, 1 May, 29–30
June, 15 September, 12 October, 2, 5 November, 24–25, 30–31
December; variable: Good Friday, Holy Thursday, Ash Wednesday,
San Salvador (4 days)

Chronology

11th century: Pipils, descendants of the Nahuatl-speaking Toltec
and Aztec peoples of Mexico, settled in the country and came to
dominate El Salvador until the Spanish conquest. **1524:** Conquered
by the Spanish adventurer Pedro de Alvarado and made a Spanish
colony, with resistance being crushed by 1540. **1821:** Independence
achieved from Spain; briefly joined with Mexico. **1823:** Became
part of United Provinces (Federation) of Central America, also
embracing Costa Rica, Guatemala, Honduras, and Nicaragua. **1833:**
Unsuccessful rebellion against Spanish control of land led by
Anastasio Aquino. **1840:** Became fully independent when
Federation dissolved. **1859–63:** Coffee growing introduced by
president Gerardo Barrios. **1932:** Peasant uprising, led by Augustín
Farabundo Martí, suppressed by military at a cost of the lives of
30,000, virtually eliminating Native American Salvadoreans. **1961:**

Following a coup, the right-wing National Conciliation Party (PCN)
established and in power. **1969:** Brief 'Football War' with
Honduras, which El Salvador attacked, at the time of a football
competition between the two states, following evictions of
thousands of Salvadoran illegal immigrants from Honduras. **1977:**
Allegations of human-rights violations; growth of left-wing
Farabundo Martí National Liberation Front (FMLN) guerrilla
activities. Gen Carlos Romero elected president. **1979:** A coup
replaced Romero with a military-civilian junta. **1980:** The
archbishop of San Salvador and human-rights champion, Oscar
Romero, assassinated; country on verge of civil war. José Napoleón
Duarte (PDC) became first civilian president since 1931. **1981:**
Mexico and France recognized the FMLN guerrillas as a legitimate
political force, but the USA actively assisted the government in its
battle against them; 30,000 were killed 1979–81 by right-wing death
squads. **1982:** Assembly elections boycotted by left-wing parties.
Held amid considerable violence, they were won by far-right
National Republican Alliance (ARENA). **1984:** Duarte won
presidential election. **1986:** Duarte sought a negotiated settlement
with the guerrillas. **1989:** Alfredo Cristiani (ARENA) became
president in rigged elections; rebel attacks intensified. **1991:** United
Nations-sponsored peace accord signed by representatives of the
government and the socialist guerrilla group, the FMLN, which now
became a political party. **1993:** UN-sponsored commission
published report on war atrocities; government amnesty for those
implicated; top military leaders officially retired. **1994:** Armando
Calderón Sol (ARENA) elected president.

Equatorial Guinea Republic of

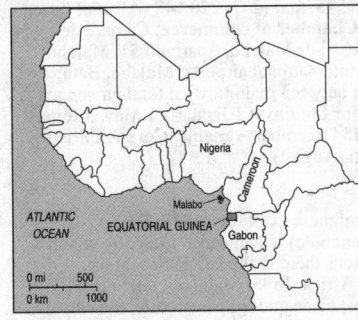

National name:
*República de
Guinea Ecuatorial*
Area: 28,051 sq
km/10,830 sq mi
Capital: Malabo
Major towns/cities:
Bata, Evinayong,
Ebebiyin, Mongomo
Physical features:
comprises mainland
Río Muni, plus the
small islands of
Corisco, Elobey
Grande and Elobey
Chico, and Bioko
(formerly Fernando Po) together with Annobón (formerly Pagalu);
nearly half the land is forested; volcanic mountains on Bioko

Government

Head of state: Teodoro Obiang Nguema Mbasogo from 1979 **Head
of government:** Silvestre Siale Bileka from 1993 **Political system:**
emergent democracy **Administrative divisions:** seven provinces
Political parties: Democratic Party of Equatorial Guinea (PDGE),
nationalist, right of centre, militarily controlled; People's Social
Democratic Convention (CSDP), left of centre; Democratic
Socialist Union of Equatorial Guinea (UDSGE), left of centre
Armed forces: 1,320 (1996) **Conscription:** military service is
voluntary **Death penalty:** retained and used for ordinary crimes
Defence spend: (% GDP) 1 (1996) **Education spend:** (% GNP) 1.8
(1993–94)

Economy and resources

Currency: franc CFA **GDP:** ($ US) 142 million (1994) **Real GDP
per capita (PPP):** ($ US) 1,673 (1994) **GDP growth rate:** 8.9%
(1994) **Average annual inflation:** 7% (1996); 4.1% (1985–95)
Foreign debt: ($ US) 291 million (1994) **Major trading partners:**
USA, Spain, Italy, the Netherlands, Liberia, France, Nigeria,
Cameroon **Resources:** petroleum, natural gas, gold, uranium, iron
ore, tantalum, manganese **Industries:** wood processing, food
processing **Exports:** timber, re-exported ships and boats, textile

fibres and waste, cocoa, coffee. Principal market: USA 34% (1995) **Imports:** ships and boats, petroleum and related products, food and live animals, machinery and transport equipment, beverages and tobacco, basic manufactures. Principal source: Spain 51% (1995) **Arable land:** 4.6% (1995) **Agricultural products:** cocoa, coffee, cassava, sweet potatoes, bananas, palm oil, palm kernels; exploitation of forest resources (principally of *okoumé* and *akoga* timber)

Population and society

Population: 410,000 (1995 est) **Population growth rate:** 2.6% (1990–95); 2.4% (2000–05) **Population density:** (per sq km) 15 (1996 est) **Urban population:** (% of total) 42 (1995) **Age distribution:** (% of total population) <15 43.3%, 15–65 52.8%, >65 4% (1995) **Ethnic groups:** 80–90% of the Fang ethnic group, of Bantu origin; most other groups have been pushed to the coast by Fang expansion **Language:** Spanish (official); pidgin English is widely spoken, and on Annobón (whose people were formerly slaves of the Portuguese) a Portuguese patois; Fang and other African patois spoken on Río Muni **Religion:** Roman Catholic, Protestant, animist **Education:** (compulsory years) 8 **Literacy rate:** 89% (men); 67% (women) (1995 est) **Labour force:** 77% agriculture, 2% industry, 21% services (1990) **Life expectancy:** 48 (men); 52 (women) (1995–2000) **Child mortality rate:** (under 5, per 1,000 live births) 167 (1996) **Physicians:** 1 per 3,520 people (1991)

Practical information

Visa requirements: UK: visa required. USA: visa required **Embassy for the UK:** 6 rue Alfred de Vigny, 75008 Paris, France. Tel: (1) 4766 4433; fax: (1) 4764 9452 **British embassy:** British Consulate, Winston Churchill Avenue, BP 547, Yaoundé, Cameroon. Tel: (237) 220 545; fax: (237) 220 148 (All staff based in Yaoundé, Cameroon.) **Chamber of commerce:** Cámara de Comercio Agrícola y Forestal de Malabo, Apartado 51, Malabo. Tel: (240) 151 **Airports:** international airports: Malabo, Bata; domestic services operate between major towns; total passenger km: 7 million (1994) **Major holidays:** 1 January, 1 May, 5 June, 3 August, 12 October, 10, 25 December; variable: Corpus Christi, Good Friday, Constitution (August)

Chronology

1472: First visited by Portuguese explorers. **1778:** Bioko (formerly known as Fernando Po) Island ceded to Spain, which established cocoa plantations there in the late 19th century, importing labour from W Africa. **1885:** Mainland territory of Mbini (formerly Rio Muni) came under Spanish rule, the whole colony being known as Spanish Guinea, with the capital at Malabu on Bioko Island. **1920s:** League of Nations special mission sent to investigate the forced, quasi-slave labour conditions on the Bioko cocoa plantations, then the largest in the world. **1959:** Became a Spanish Overseas Province; African population finally granted full citizenship. **early 1960s:** On the mainland, the Fang people spearheaded a nationalist movement directed against Spanish favouritism towards Bioko Island and its controlling Bubi tribe. **1963:** Achieved internal autonomy. **1968:** Independence achieved from Spain. Macias Nguema, a nationalist Fang, became first president, discriminating against the Bubi community. **1970s:** Economy collapsed as Spanish settlers and other minorities fled in the face of intimidation by Nguema's brutal, dictatorial regime, which was marked by the murder, torture, and imprisonment of tens of thousands of political opponents and rivals, as well as the closing of churches. **1979:** Nguema overthrown, tried, and executed. He was replaced by his nephew, Teodoro Obiang Nguema Mbasogo, who established a military regime, but released political prisoners and imposed restrictions on the Catholic church. **1992:** New pluralist constitution approved by referendum. **1993:** Obiang's PDGE won first multiparty elections on low turnout. **1996:** Obiang re-elected amid claims of fraud by opponents.

Eritrea State of

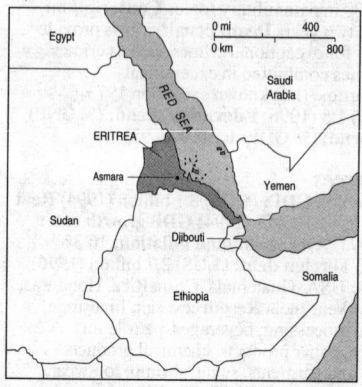

Area: 125,000 sq km/48,262 sq mi
Capital: Asmara
Major towns/ cities: Asab, Keren, Massawa, Adigrat **Major ports:** Asab, Massawa
Physical features: coastline along the Red Sea 1,000 km/620 mi; narrow coastal plain that rises to an inland plateau; Dahlak Islands

Government

Head of state and government: Issaias Afwerki from 1993 **Political system:** emergent democracy **Administrative divisions:** ten provinces **Political parties:** People's Front for Democracy and Justice (PFDJ) (formerly Eritrean People's Liberation Front: EPLF), left of centre; Eritrean National Pact Alliance (ENPA), moderate, centrist **Armed forces:** 55,000 (1996) **Conscription:** compulsory for 18 months **Death penalty:** retained and used for ordinary crimes **Defence spend:** (% GDP) 7.5 (1996) **Education spend:** (% GDP) 3.2 (1993) **Health spend:** (% GDP) 1.1 (1990–95)

Economy and resources

Currency: Ethiopian birr **GDP:** ($ US) 558 million (1994 est) **Real GDP per capita (PPP):** ($ US) 960 (1994) **GDP growth rate:** 9.4% (1994) **Average annual inflation:** 10% (1995 est) **Major trading partners:** Ethiopia, Saudi Arabia, Italy, Sudan, United Arab Emirates **Resources:** gold, silver, copper, zinc, sulphur, nickel, chrome, potash, basalt, limestone, marble, sand, silicates **Industries:** food processing, textiles, leatherwear, building materials, glassware, petroleum products **Exports:** textiles, leather and leather products, beverages, petroleum products, basic household goods. Principal market: Ethiopia 68.7% (1993) **Imports:** machinery and transport equipment, petroleum, food and live animals, basic manufactures. Principal source: Saudi Arabia 31% (1993) **Arable land:** 4.4% (1995) **Agricultural products:** sorghum, teff (an indigenous grain), maize, wheat, millet; livestock rearing (goats and camels); fisheries

Population and society

Population: 3,280,000 (1996 est) **Population growth rate:** 2.7% (1990–95); 2.5% (2000–05) **Population density:** (per sq km) 28 (1996 est) **Urban population:** (% of total) 17 (1995) **Age distribution:** (% of total population) <15 44%, 15–65 53.1%, >65 2.9% (1995) **Ethnic groups:** several ethnic groups, including the Amhara and the Tigrais **Language:** Amharic (official), Tigrinya (official), Arabic, Afar, Bilen, Hidareb, Kunama, Nara, Rashaida, Saho, and Tigre **Religion:** Sunni Muslim, Coptic Christian **Education:** (compulsory years) 7 **Literacy rate:** 20–25% (men); 5–10% (women) (1995 est) **Unemployment:** 50% (1994 est) **Life expectancy:** 51 (men); 55 (women) (1995–2000) **Child mortality rate:** (under 5, per 1,000 live births) 146 (1996) **Physicians:** 1 per 45,588 people (1993 est)

Practical information

Visa requirements: UK: visa required. USA: visa required **Embassy in the UK:** Eritrean Consulate, 96 White Lion Street, London N1 9PF. Tel: (0171) 713 0096; fax: (0171) 713 0161 **British embassy:** British Consulate, PO Box 5584, c/o Mitchell Gotts Building, Emperor Yohannes Avenue 5, Asmara. Tel: (1) 120 145; fax: (1) 120 104 **Chamber of commerce:** Asmara Chamber of Commerce, PO Box 856, Asmara. Tel: (1) 21388; fax: (1) 20138 **Airports:** international airport: Asmara (Yohannes IV); two domestic airports **Major holidays:** 1, 6 January, 24 May, 20 June, 1 September, 25 December; variable: Eid-ul-Adha, Arafa, end of Ramadan

Chronology

4th–7th centuries AD: Part of Ethiopian Aksum kingdom. **8th century:** Islam introduced to coastal areas by Arabs. **12th–16th centuries:** Under the influence of Ethiopian Abyssinian kingdoms. **mid-16th century:** Came under the control of the Turkish Ottoman Empire. **1882:** Occupied by Italy. **1889:** Italian colony of Eritrea created out of Ottoman areas and coastal districts of Ethiopia. **1920s:** Massawa developed into largest port in E Africa. **1935–36:** Used as base for Italy's conquest of Ethiopia and became part of Italian East Africa. **1941:** Became British protectorate after Italy removed from N Africa. **1952:** Federation formed with Ethiopia by United Nations (UN). **1958:** Eritrean People's Liberation Front (EPLF) formed to fight for independence after general strike brutally suppressed by Ethiopian rulers. **1962:** Annexed by Ethiopia, sparking a secessionist rebellion which was to last 30 years and claim 150,000 lives. **1974:** Ethiopian emperor Haile Selassie deposed by military; EPLF continued struggle for independence. **1977–78:** EPLF cleared the territory of Ethiopian forces, but position was soon reversed by Marxist Ethiopian government of Col Mengistu Haile Mariam, which had Soviet backing. **mid-1980s:** Severe famine in Eritrea and refugee crisis as Ethiopian government sought forcible resettlement. **1990:** Strategic port of Massawa captured by Eritrean rebel forces. **1991:** Ethiopian president Mengistu overthrown. EPLF secured whole of Eritrea and provisional government formed under Issaias Afwerki. **1993:** Independence approved in regional referendum and recognized by Ethiopia. Transitional government established for four-year period, with Afwerki elected president; 500,000 refugees outside Eritrea began to return. **1994:** EPLF renamed PFDJ. **1997:** New constitution adopted. **1998:** Border dispute with Ethiopia escalated into an undeclared war, with bombing raids from both sides.

Estonia Republic of

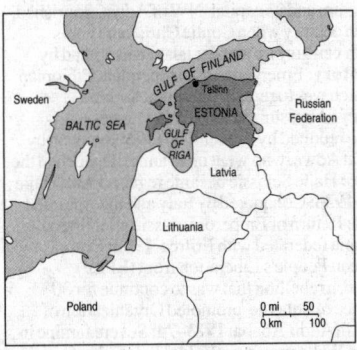

National name: *Eesti Vabariik* **Area:** 45,000 sq km/17,374 sq mi **Capital:** Tallinn **Major towns/cities:** Tartu, Narva, Kohtla-Järve, Pärnu **Physical features:** lakes and marshes in a partly forested plain; 774 km/481 mi of coastline; mild climate; Lake Peipus and Narva River forming boundary with Russian Federation; Baltic islands, the largest of which is Saaremaa

Government

Head of state: Lennart Meri from 1992 **Head of government:** Mart Siimann from 1997 **Political system:** emergent democracy **Administrative divisions:** 15 counties and six towns **Political parties:** Coalition Party (KMU), ex-communist, left of centre, 'social market'; Isamaa (National Fatherland Party, or Pro Patria), right wing, nationalist, free market; Estonian Reform Party (ERP), freemarket; Centre Party (CP), moderate nationalist (formerly the Estonian Popular Front (EPF; Rahvarinne); Estonian National Independence Party (ENIP), radical nationalist; Communist Party of Estonia (CPE); Our Home is Estonia; Estonian Social Democratic Party (ESDP) (last three draw much of their support from ethnic Russian community) **Armed forces:** 3,500 (1996); plus a reserve

militia of 6,000 and a paramilitary border guard of 2,000 **Conscription:** compulsory for 12 months (men and women) **Death penalty:** retained and used for ordinary crimes **Defence spend:** (% GDP) 2.4 (1996) **Education spend:** (% GNP) 5.8 (1993–94) **Health spend:** (% GDP) 5.9% (1990–95)

Economy and resources

Currency: kroon **GDP:** ($ US) 5 billion (1994) **Real GDP per capita (PPP):** ($ US) 4,294 (1994) **GDP growth rate:** 4.7% (1994); –9.2% (1990–95) **Average annual inflation:** 23% (1996); 76.2% (1985–95) **Foreign debt:** ($ US) 309 million (1995) **Major trading partners:** Finland, Russia, Sweden, Germany, Latvia, the Netherlands, Lithuania, UK, Japan **Resources:** oilshale, peat, phosphorite ore, superphosphates **Industries:** machine building, electronics, electrical engineering, textiles, fish and food processing, consumer goods **Exports:** foodstuffs, animal products, textiles, timber products, base metals, mineral products, machinery. Principal market: Finland 19.8% (1996) **Imports:** machinery and transport equipment, food products, textiles, mineral products. Principal source: Finland 36.7 (1996) **Arable land:** 26.7% (1995) **Agricultural products:** wheat, rye, barley, potatoes, other vegetables; livestock rearing (cattle and pigs); dairy farming

Population and society

Population: 1,471,000 (1996 est) **Population growth rate:** –0.6% (1990–95); –0.3 (2000–05) **Population density:** (per sq km) 33 (1996 est) **Urban population:** (% of total) 73 (1995) **Age distribution:** (% of total population) <15 20.6%, 15–65 66.6%, >65 12.8% (1995) **Ethnic groups:** 62% Finno-Ugric ethnic Estonians, 30% Russian, 3% Ukrainian, 2% Belarussian, 1% Finnish **Language:** Estonian (official), Russian **Religion:** Lutheran, Russian Orthodox **Education:** (compulsory years) 9 **Literacy rate:** 99% (men); 99% (women) (1995 est) **Labour force:** 8.7% agriculture, 35.7% industry, 55.6% services (1994) **Unemployment:** 2.2% (1996) **Life expectancy:** 64 (men); 75 (women) (1995–2000) **Child mortality rate:** (under 5, per 1,000 live births) 19 (1996) **Physicians:** 1 per 312 people (1993)

Practical information

Visa requirements: UK: visa not required. USA: visa not required **Embassy in the UK:** 16 Hyde Park Gate, London SW7 5DG. Tel: (0171) 589 3428; fax: (0171) 589 3430 **British embassy:** Kentmanni 20, EE-0100 Tallinn. Tel: (2) 313 353; fax: (2) 313 354 **Chamber of commerce:** Chamber of Commerce and Industry of the Republic of Estonia, Toom-Kooli Street 17, EE-0001 Tallinn. Tel: (2) 444 929; fax: (2) 443 656 **Airports:** international airports: Tallinn; three domestic airports; total passenger km: 92 million (1994) **Major holidays:** 1 January, 24 February, 1 May, 23–24 June, 25–26 December; variable: Good Friday

Chronology

1st century AD: First independent state formed. **9th century:** Invaded by Vikings. **13th century:** Tallinn, in the Danish-controlled N, joined Hanseatic League, a N European union of commercial towns; Livonia, comprising S Estonia and Latvia, came under control of German Teutonic Knights and was converted to Christianity. **1561:** Sweden took control of N Estonia. **1629:** Sweden took control of S Estonia from Poland. **1721:** Sweden ceded the country to tsarist Russia. **late 19th century:** Estonian nationalist movement developed in opposition to Russian political and cultural repression and German economic control. **1914:** Occupied by German troops. **1918–19:** Estonian nationalists, led by Konstantin Pats, proclaimed and achieved independence, despite efforts by the Russian Red Army to regain control. **1920s:** Land reforms and cultural advances under democratic regime. **1934:** Pats overthrew parliamentary democracy in a quasi-fascist coup at a time of economic depression; Baltic Entente mutual defence pact signed with Latvia and Lithuania. **1940:** Estonia incorporated into Soviet Union (USSR); 100,000 Estonians deported to Siberia or killed. **1941–44:** German occupation during World War II. **1944:** USSR regained control; 'Sovietization' followed, including agricultural collectivization and immigration of ethnic Russians. **late 1980s:** Beginnings of nationalist dissent, encouraged by *glasnost* initiative of reformist Soviet leader Mikhail Gorbachev. **1988:** Popular Front (EPF) established to campaign for democracy. Sovereignty declaration issued by state assembly rejected by USSR as unconstitutional. **1989:** Estonian replaced Russian as main language. **1990:** CPE monopoly of power abolished; pro-independence candidates secured majority after multiparty elections; coalition government formed with EPF leader Edgar Savisaar as prime minister; Arnold Rüütel became president. Prewar constitution partially restored. **1991:** Independence achieved after attempted anti-Gorbachev coup in Moscow; CPE outlawed. Estonia joined United Nations. **1992:** Savisaar resigned over food and energy shortages; Isamaa leader Lennart Meri became president and free-marketer Mart Laar prime minister. **1993:** Joined Council of Europe; free-trade agreement with Latvia and Lithuania. **1994:** Last Russian troops withdrawn. Radical economic-reform programme introduced; controversial law on 'aliens' passed, requiring non-ethnic Estonians to apply for residency. Laar resigned. **1995:** Former communists won largest number of seats in general election; left-of-centre coalition formed under Tiit Vahi. **1996:** President Meri re-elected. Ruling coalition collapsed; Prime Minister Tiit Vahi continued with a minority government. **1997:** Vahi, accused of corruption, resigned and was replaced by Mart Siimann. Estonia invited to begin European Union membership negotiations.

Ethiopia Federal Democratic Republic of (formerly known as Abyssinia)

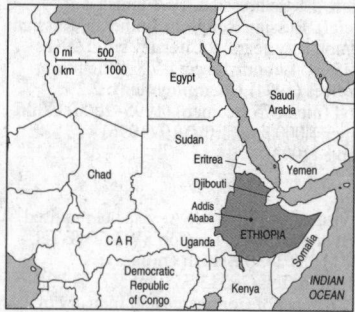

National name: *Hebretesebawit Ityopia* **Area:** 1,096,900 sq km/423,513 sq mi **Capital:** Addis Ababa **Major towns/cities:** Jimma, Dire Dawa, Harar, Nazret, Dessie, Gonder, Mek'elē **Physical features:** a high plateau with central mountain range divided by Rift Valley; plains in E; source of Blue Nile River; Danakil and Ogaden deserts

Government
Head of state: Negasso Ghidada from 1995 **Head of government:** Meles Zenawi from 1995 **Political system:** transition to democratic federal republic **Administrative divisions:** nine states and one metropolitan area **Political parties:** Ethiopian People's Revolutionary Democratic Front (EPRDF), nationalist, left of centre; Tigré People's Liberation Front (TPLF); Ethiopian People's Democratic Movement (EPDM); United Oromo Liberation Front, Islamic nationalist **Armed forces:** 120,000 (1996) **Conscription:** mlitary service is voluntary **Death penalty:** retained and used for ordinary crimes **Defence spend:** (% GDP) 2 (1996) **Education spend:** (% GNP) 5.1 (1992) **Health spend:** (% GDP) 1.1 (1990–95)

Economy and resources
Currency: Ethiopian birr **GDP:** ($ US) 4.7 billion (1994) **Real GDP per capita (PPP):** ($ US) 427 (1994) **GDP growth rate:** 4.8% (1994) **Average annual inflation:** 1% (1996); 5.9% (1985–95 est) **Foreign debt:** ($ US) 5.22 billion (1995) **Major trading partners:** Germany, Saudi Arabia, USA, Japan, UK, Italy, France **Resources:** gold, salt, platinum, copper, potash. Reserves of petroleum have not been exploited **Industries:** food processing, petroleum refining, beverages, textiles **Exports:** coffee, hides and skins, petroleum products, fruit and vegetables. Principal market: Germany 31.7% (1994) **Imports:** machinery, aircraft and other vehicles, petroleum and petroleum products, basic manufactures, chemicals and related products. Principal source: Saudi Arabia 15%

(1994) **Arable land:** 11.3% (1995) **Agricultural products:** coffee, teff (an indigenous grain), barley, maize, sorghum, sugar cane; livestock rearing (cattle and sheep) and livestock products (hides, skins, butter and ghee)

Population and society
Population: 58,243,000 (1996 est) **Population growth rate:** 3% (1990–95); 2.9% (2000–05) **Population density:** (per sq km) 53 (1996 est) **Urban population:** (% of total) 13 (1995) **Age distribution:** (% of total population) <15 46.4%, 15–65 50.8%, >65 2.9% (1995) **Ethnic groups:** over 70 different ethnic groups, the two main ones are the Galla (mainly in the E and S of the central plateau), who comprise about 40% of the population, and the Amhara and Tigré (largely in the central plateau itself), who constitute about 35% **Language:** Amharic (official), Tigrinya, Orominga, Arabic **Religion:** Sunni Muslim, Christian (Ethiopian Orthodox Church, which has had its own patriarch since 1976) 40%, animist **Education:** (compulsory years) 6 **Literacy rate:** 45% (men); 25% (women) (1995 est) **Labour force:** 88.6% agriculture, 2% industry, 9.4% services (1995) **Unemployment:** 40.5% (1992 est) **Life expectancy:** 48 (men); 52 (women) (1995–2000) **Child mortality rate:** (under 5, per 1,000 live births) 170 (1996) **Physicians:** 1 per 32,499 people (1993 est)

Practical information
Visa requirements: UK: visa required. USA: visa required **Embassy in the UK:** 17 Prince's Gate, London SW7 1PZ. Tel: (0171) 589 7212; fax: (0171) 584 7054 **British embassy:** PO Box 858, Fikre Mariam Abatechan Street, Addis Ababa. Tel: (1) 612 354; fax: (1) 610 588 **Chamber of commerce:** Ethiopian Chamber of Commerce, PO Box 517, Mexico Square, Addis Ababa. Tel: (1) 518 240; telex: 21213 **Airports:** international airports: Addis Ababa (Bole), Dire Dawa; over 40 small domestic airports or airfields; total passenger km: 1,607 million (1994) **Major holidays:** 7, 19 January, 2 March, 6 April, 1 May, 12, 27 September; variable: Eid-ul-Adha, end of Ramadan, Ethiopian New Year (September), Prophet's Birthday, Ethiopian Good Friday and Easter

Chronology
1st–7th centuries AD: Founded by Semitic immigrants from Saudi Arabia, the kingdom of Aksum and its capital, NW of Adwa, flourished. It reached its peak in the 4th century when Coptic Christianity was introduced from Egypt. **7th century onwards:** Islam was spread by Arab conquerors. **11th century:** Emergence of independent Ethiopian kingdom of Abyssinia, which was to remain dominant for nine centuries. **late 15th century:** Abyssinia visited by Portuguese explorers. **1889:** Abyssinia reunited by Menelik II. **1896:** Invasion by Italy defeated by Menelik at Adwa, who went on to annex Ogaden in the SE and areas to the W. **1916:** Haile Selassie became regent. **1930:** Haile Selassie became emperor. **1936:** Conquered by Italy and incorporated in Italian East Africa. **1941:** Return of Emperor Selassie after liberation by the British. **1952:** Ethiopia federated with Eritrea. **1962:** Eritrea annexed by Selassie; Eritrean People's Liberation front (EPLF) resistance movement began, a rebellion that was to continue for 30 years. **1963:** First conference of Selassie-promoted Organization of African Unity (OAU) held in Addis Ababa. **1973–74:** Severe famine in N Ethiopia; 200,000 died in Wallo province. **1974:** Haile Selassie deposed and replaced by a military government led by Gen Teferi Benti. **1977:** Teferi Benti killed and replaced by Col Mengistu Haile Mariam. Somali forces ejected from the Somali-peopled Ogaden in the SE. **1977–79:** 'Red Terror' period in which Mengistu's single-party Marxist regime killed thousands of people and promoted collective farming; Tigré People's Liberation Front guerrillas began fighting for regional autonomy in the northern highlands. **1984:** Workers' Party of Ethiopia (WPE) declared the only legal political party. **1985:** Worst famine in more than a decade; Western aid sent and forcible internal resettlement programmes undertaken in Eritrea and Tigré in the N. **1987:** Mengistu Mariam elected president under new constitution. New famine; food aid hindered by guerrillas. **1989:** Coup attempt against Mengistu foiled. Peace talks with Eritrean rebels mediated by former US president Jimmy Carter. **1991:** Mengistu overthrown; transitional government set up by opposing Ethiopian People's Revolutionary Democratic Front (EPRDF), headed by Meles Zenawi. EPLF took control over Eritrea.

Famine gripped the country. **1993:** Eritrean independence recognized after referendum; private farming and market sector encouraged by EPRDF government. **1994:** New federal constitution adopted. **1995:** Ruling EPRDF won majority of seats in first multiparty elections to a interim parliament. Negasso Ghidada chosen as president; Zenawi appointed premier. **1998:** Border dispute with Eritrea escalated into an undeclared war, with bombing raids from both sides.

Fiji Republic of

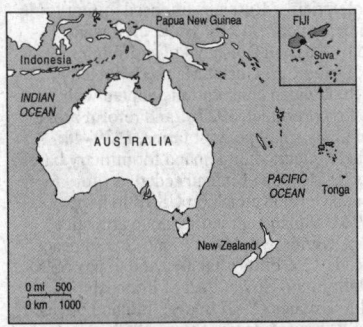

Area: 18,333 sq km/7,078 sq mi **Capital:** Suva **Major towns/cities:** Lautoka, Nadi, Ba, Labasa **Major ports:** Lautoka and Levuka **Physical features:** comprises about 844 Melanesian and Polynesian islands and islets (about 100 inhabited), the largest being Viti Levu (10,429 sq km/4,028 sq mi) and Vanua Levu (5,556 sq km/2,146 sq mi); mountainous, volcanic, with tropical rainforest and grasslands; almost all islands surrounded by coral reefs; high volcanic peaks

Government
Head of state: Ratu Sir Kamisese Mara from 1994 **Head of government:** Col Sitiveni Rabuka from 1992 **Political system:** democracy **Administrative divisions:** 14 provinces **Political parties:** National Federation Party (NFP), moderate left of centre, Indian; Fijian Labour Party (FLP), left of centre, Indian; United Front, Fijian; Fijian Political Party (FPP), Fijian centrist **Armed forces:** 3,600 (1996) **Conscription:** military service is voluntary **Death penalty:** laws provide for the death penalty only for exceptional crimes such as crimes under military law or crimes committed in exceptional cricumstances such as wartime (last execution 1964) **Defence spend:** (% GDP) 2.6 (1996) **Education spend:** (% GNP) 5.4 (1993–94) **Health spend:** (% GDP) 1.3 (1994)

Economy and resources
Currency: Fiji dollar **GDP:** ($ US) 1.84 billion (1994) **Real GDP per capita (PPP):** ($ US) 5,763 (1994) **GDP growth rate:** 5.2% (1994) **Average annual inflation:** 2.5% (1996); 4.9% (1985–95) **Foreign debt:** ($ US) 298.8 million (1994) **Major trading partners:** Australia, New Zealand, Japan, UK, USA **Resources:** gold, silver, copper **Industries:** food processing (sugar, molasses, and copra), ready-made garments, animal feed, cigarettes, cement, tourism **Exports:** sugar, gold, fish and fish products, clothing, re-exported petroleum products, timber, ginger, molasses. Principal market: Australia 22.4% (1995) **Imports:** basic manufactured goods, machinery and transport equipment, food, mineral fuels. Principal source: Australia 39.2% (1995) **Arable land:** 10.9% (1995) **Agricultural products:** sugar cane, coconuts, ginger, rice, tobacco, cocoa; forestry (for timber)

Population and society
Population: 797,000 (1996 est) **Population growth rate:** 1.5% (1990–95); 1.5% (2000–05) **Population density:** (per sq km) 44 (1996 est) **Urban population:** (% of total) 41 (1995) **Age distribution:** (% of total population) <15 34.6%, 15–65 61.5%, >65 3.8% (1995) **Ethnic groups:** 48% Fijians (of Melanesian and Polynesian descent), 51% Asians **Language:** English (official), Fijian, Hindi **Religion:** Methodist, Hindu, Muslim, Sikh **Education:** not compulsory **Literacy rate:** 94% (men); 89% (women) (1995 est) **Labour force:** 34% of population: 46% agriculture, 15% industry,

39% services (1990) **Unemployment:** 5.4% (1995) **Life expectancy:** 71 (men); 75 (women) (1995–2000) **Child mortality rate:** (under 5, per 1,000 live births) 23 (1996) **Physicians:** 1 per 2,011 people (1992)

Practical information
Visa requirements: UK: visa not required. USA: visa not required **Embassy in the UK:** 34 Hyde Park Gate, London SW7 5DN. Tel: (0171) 839 2200; fax: (0171) 839 9050 **British embassy:** PO Box 1355, Victoria House, 47 Gladstone Road, Suva. Tel: (679) 311 033; fax: (679) 301 406 **Chamber of commerce:** Suva Chamber of Commerce, PO Box 337, 2nd Floor, GB Hari Building, 12 Pier Street, Suva. Tel: (679) 303 854; fax: (679) 300 475 **Airports:** international airports: Nadi; 16 domestic airports and airfields; total passenger km: 1,101 million (1994) **Major holidays:** 1 January, 12 October, 25–26 December; variable: Diwali, Good Friday, Easter Monday, Holy Saturday, Prophet's Birthday, August Bank Holiday, Queen's Birthday (June), Prince Charles's Birthday (November)

Chronology
c. 1500 BC: Peopled by Polynesian and, later, by Melanesian settlers. **1643:** The islands were visited for the first time by a European, the Dutch navigator Abel Tasman. **1830s:** Arrival of Western Christian missionaries. **1840s–50s:** Western Fiji came under dominance of a Christian convert prince, Cakobau, ruler of Bau islet, who proclaimed himself Tui Viti (King of Fiji), while the E was controlled by Ma'afu, a Christian prince from Tonga. **1857:** British consul appointed, encouraging settlers from Australia and New Zealand to set up cotton farms in Fiji. **1874:** Fiji became a British crown colony after deed of cession signed by King Cakobau. **1875–76:** A third of the Fijian population wiped out by a measles epidemic; rebellion against British suppressed with the assitance of Fijian chiefs. **1877:** Fiji became headquarters of the British Western Pacific High Commission (WPHC), which controlled other British protectorates in the Pacific region. **1879–1916:** Indian labourers brought in, on ten-year indentured contracts, to work sugar plantations. **1904:** Legislative Council formed, with elected Europeans and nominated Fijians, to advise the British governor. **1963:** Legislative Council enlarged; women and Fijians were enfranchised. The predominantly Fijian Alliance Party (AP) formed. **1970:** Independence achieved from Britain; Ratu Sir Kamisese Mara of the AP elected as first prime minister. **1973:** Ratu Sir George Cakobau, great-grandson of the chief who had sworn allegiance to the British in 1874, became governor general. **1985:** FLP formed by Timoci Bavadra, with trade-union backing. **1987:** After general election had brought to power an Indian-dominated coalition led by Bavadra, Lt-Col Sitiveni Rabuka seized power after a military coup, and proclaimed a Fijian-dominated republic outside the Commonwealth. **1990:** New constitution, favouring indigenous (Melanese) Fijians, introduced. Civilian rule re-established, with resignations from cabinet of military officers, but Rabuka remained as home affairs minister, with Mara as prime minister. **1992:** General election produced coalition government with Rabuka of the FPP as prime minister. **1993:** President Ganilau died and was replaced by Ratu Sir Kamisese Mara. **1994:** Rabuka and FPP re-elected. **1997:** Fiji re-admitted to the Commonwealth.

Finland Republic of

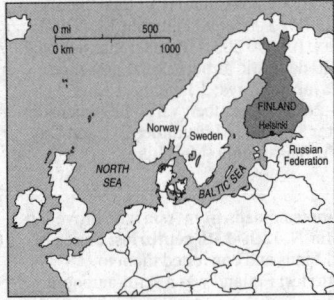

National name: *Suomen Tasavalta* **Area:** 338,145 sq km/130,557 sq mi **Capital:** Helsinki (Helsingfors) **Major towns/cities:** Tampere, Turku, Espoo, Vantaa **Major ports:** Turku, Oulu **Physical features:** most of the country is forest, with low hills and about 60,000 lakes; one-third

is within the Arctic Circle; archipelago in S includes Åland Islands; Helsinki is the most northerly national capital on the European continent. At the 70th parallel there is constant daylight for 73 days in summer and 51 days of uninterrupted night in winter.

Government

Head of state: Martti Ahtisaari from 1994 **Head of government:** Paavo Lipponen from 1995 **Political system:** democracy **Administrative divisions:** 12 provinces **Political parties:** Finnish Social Democratic Party (SSDP), moderate left of centre; National Coalition Party (KOK), moderate right of centre; Finnish Centre Party (KESK), radical centrist, rural-oriented; Swedish People's Party (SFP), independent Swedish-oriented; Finnish Rural Party (SMP), farmers and small businesses; Left-Wing Alliance (VL), left wing **Armed forces:** 32,500 (1996) **Conscription:** up to 11 months, followed by refresher training of 40–100 days (before age 50) **Death penalty:** abolished 1972 **Defence spend:** (% GDP) 2.0 (1996) **Education spend:** (% GNP) 8.4 (1993–94) **Health spend:** (% GDP) 6.2 (1994)

Economy and resources

Currency: markka **GDP:** ($ US) 124 billion (1996) **Real GDP per capita (PPP):** ($ US) 18,657 (1996) **GDP growth rate:** 3.9% (1996); –0.5% (1990–95) **Average annual inflation:** 1.2% (1996); 3.8% (1985–95) **Major trading partners:** Germany, Sweden, UK, USA, Russia, Denmark, Norway, the Netherlands **Resources:** copper ore, lead ore, gold, zinc ore, silver, peat, hydro power, forests **Industries:** food processing, paper and paper products, machinery, printing and publishing, wood products, metal products, shipbuilding, chemicals, clothing and footwear **Exports:** metal and engineering products, gold, paper and paper products, machinery, ships, wood and pulp, clothing and footwear, chemicals. Principal market: Germany 12.1% (1996) **Imports:** mineral fuels, machinery and transport equipment, food and live animals, chemical and related products, textiles, iron and steel. Principal source: Germany 15.1% (1996) **Arable land:** 8.3% (1995) **Agricultural products:** oats, sugar beet, potatoes, barley, hay; forestry and animal husbandry

Population and society

Population: 5,126,000 (1996 est) **Population growth rate:** 0.5% (1990–95); 0.3% (2000–05) **Population density:** (per sq km) 15 (1996 est) **Urban population:** (% of total) 63 (1995) **Age distribution:** (% of total population) <15 19.1%, 15–65 66.8%, >65 14.1% (1995) **Ethnic groups:** majority descended from Russian inhabitants **Language:** Finnish 93%, Swedish 6% (both official); small Saami- and Russian-speaking minorities **Religion:** Lutheran 90%, Orthodox 1% **Education:** (compulsory years) 9 **Literacy rate:** 100% (men); 100% (women) (1995 est) **Labour force:** 49.4% of population: 7.1% agriculture, 27.6% industry, 65.3% services (1996) **Unemployment:** 15.8% (1996) **Life expectancy:** 73 (men); 80 (women) (1995–2000) **Child mortality rate:** (under 5, per 1,000 live births) 6 (1996) **Physicians:** 1 per 345 people (1994)

Practical information

Visa requirements: UK: visa not required. USA: visa not required **Embassy in the UK:** 38 Chesham Place, London SW1X 8HW. Tel: (0171) 235 9531; fax: (0171) 235 3680 **British embassy:** Itäinen Puistotie 17, 00140 Helsinki. Tel: (0) 661 293; fax: (0) 661 342 **Chamber of commerce:** Keskuskauppakamari (Central Chamber of Commerce of Finland), PO Box 1000, Fabianinkatu 14, 00101 Helsinki. Tel: (0) 650 133; fax: (0) 650 303 **Airports:** international airports: Helsinki (Vantaa); 20 domestic airports; total passenger km: 6,720 million (1994) **Major holidays:** 1 January, 1 May, 31 October, 1 November, 1, 24–26, 31 December; variable: Ascension Thursday, Good Friday, Easter Monday, Midsummer Eve and Day (June), Twelfthtide (January), Whitsuntide (May/June)

Chronology

1st century: Occupied by Finnic nomads from Asia who drove out native Saami (Lapps) to the far N. **12th–13th centuries:** Series of Swedish crusades conquered Finns and converted them to Christianity. **16th–17th centuries:** Finland was a semi-autonomous Swedish duchy with Swedish landowners ruling Finnish peasants; Finland allowed relative autonomy, becoming a grand duchy 1581. **1634:** Finland fully incorporated into Swedish kingdom. **1700–21:** Great Northern War between Sweden and Russia; half of Finnish population died in famine and epidemics. **1741–43 and 1788–90:** Further Russo–Swedish wars; much of the fighting took place in Finland. **1808:** Russia invaded Sweden (with support of Napoleon). **1809:** Finland ceded to Russia as grand duchy with Russian tsar as grand duke; Finns retained their own legal system and Lutheran religion and were exempt from Russian military service. **1812:** Helsinki became capital of grand duchy. **19th century:** Growing prosperity was followed by rise of national feeling among new Finnish middle class. **1904–05:** Policies promoting Russification of Finland provoked national uprising; Russians imposed military rule. **1917:** Finland declared independence. **1918:** Bitter civil war between Reds (supported by Russian Bolsheviks) and Whites (supported by Germany); Baron Carl Gustaf Mannerheim led Whites to victory. **1919:** Republican constitution adopted with Kaarlo Juho Ståhlberg as first president. **1927:** Land reform broke up big estates and created many small peasant farms. **1939–40:** Winter War: USSR invaded Finland after demand for military bases was refused. **1940:** Treaty of Moscow: Finland ceded territory to USSR. **1941:** Finland joined German attack on USSR in hope of regaining lost territory. **1944:** Finland agreed separate armistice with USSR; German troops withdrawn. **1947:** Finno-Soviet peace treaty: Finland forced to cede 12% of its total area and to pay $300 million in reparations. **1948:** Finno-Soviet Pact of Friendship, Cooperation, and Mutual Assistance (YYA treaty): Finland pledged to repel any attack on USSR through its territories. **1950s:** Unstable centre-left coalitions excluded communists from government and adopted strict neutrality in foreign affairs. **1955:** Finland joined United Nations (UN) and Nordic Council. **1956:** Urho Kekkonen elected president. General strike as a result of unemployment and inflation. **1973:** Trade agreements signed with European Economic Community (EEC) and Comecon. **1982:** Mauno Koivisto elected president. **1987:** New coalition of Social Democrats and conservatives formed. **1991:** Big swing to Centre Party in general election. **1994:** Martti Ahtisaari (SSDP) elected president. **1995:** Finland joined European Union (EU); Social Democrats won general election.

France French Republic

National name: *République Française* **Area:** (including Corsica) 543,965 sq km/210,024 sq mi **Capital:** Paris **Major towns/cities:** Lyon, Lille, Bordeaux, Toulouse, Nantes, Strasbourg, Montpellier, Saint-Etienne, Rennes, Reims, Grenoble **Major ports:** Marseille, Nice, Le Havre **Physical features:** rivers Seine, Loire, Garonne, Rhône; mountain ranges Alps, Massif Central, Pyrenees, Jura, Vosges, Cévennes; Auvergne mountain region; Mont Blanc (4,810 m/15,781 ft); Ardennes forest; Riviera; caves of Dordogne with relics of early humans; the island of Corsica **Territories:** Guadeloupe, French Guiana, Martinique, Réunion, St Pierre and Miquelon, Southern and Antarctic Territories, New Caledonia, French Polynesia, Wallis and Futuna, Mayotte

Government

Head of state: Jacques Chirac from 1995 **Head of government:** Lionel Jospin from 1997 **Political system:** liberal democracy **Administrative divisions:** 22 regions containing 96 departments, four overseas departments, two territorial collectivities, and four overseas territories **Political parties:** Rally for the Republic (RPR), neo-Gaullist conservative; Union for French Democracy (UDF), centre right; Socialist Party (PS), left of centre; Left Radical Movement (MRG), centre left; French Communist Party (PCF), Marxist-Leninist; National Front, far right; Greens, fundamentalist-ecologist; Génération Ecologie, pragmatic ecologist; Movement for France, right wing, anti-Maastricht **Armed forces:** 398,900; paramilitary gendarmerie 92,400 (1996) **Conscription:** compulsory for 10 months **Death penalty:** abolished 1981 **Defence spend:** (% GDP) 3.1 (1996) **Education spend:** (% GNP) 5.8 (1993–94) **Health spend:** (% GDP) 7.6 (1994)

Economy and resources

Currency: franc **GDP:** ($ US) 1,540.1 billion (1996) **Real GDP per capita (PPP):** ($ US) 20,534 (1996) **GDP growth rate:** 1.1% (1996); 1% (1990–95) **Average annual inflation:** 1% (1996); 2.8% (1985–95) **Major trading partners:** EU (principally Germany, Italy, Benelux, UK); USA **Resources:** coal, petroleum, natural gas, iron ore, copper, zinc, bauxite **Industries:** mining, quarrying, food products, transport equipment, non-electrical machinery, electrical machinery, weapons, metals and metal products, yarn and fabrics, wine, tourism, aircraft, weapons **Exports:** machinery and transport equipment, food and live animals, beverages and tobacco, textile yarn, fabrics and other basic manufactures, clothing and accessories, perfumery and cosmetics. Principal market: Germany 17.1% (1996) **Imports:** food and live animals, mineral fuels, machinery and transport equipment, chemicals and chemical products, basic manufactures. Principal source: Germany 17.4% (1996) **Arable land:** 33.3% (1995) **Agricultural products:** wheat, sugar beet, maize, barley, vine fruits, potatoes, fruit, vegetables; livestock and dairy products

Population and society

Population: 58,333,000 (1996 est) **Population growth rate:** 0.4% (1990–95); 0.2% (2000–05) **Population density:** (per sq km) 106 (1996 est) **Urban population:** (% of total) 73 (1995) **Age distribution:** (% of total population) <15 19.6%, 15–65 65.5%, >65 14.9% (1995) **Ethnic groups:** predominantly French ethnic, of Celtic and Latin descent; Basque minority in the SW; 7% of the population are immigrants – a third of these are from Algeria and Morocco and live mainly in the Marseille Midi region and in northern cities, 20% originate from Portugal, and 10% each from Italy and Spain **Language:** French (regional languages include Basque, Breton, Catalan, and Provençal) **Religion:** Roman Catholic; also Muslim, Protestant, and Jewish minorities **Education:** (compulsory years) 10 **Literacy rate:** 100% (men); 100% (women) (1995 est) **Labour force:** 44% of population: 5.1% agriculture, 27.7% industry, 67.2% services (1993) **Unemployment:** 12.6% (1997) **Life expectancy:** 74 (men); 81 (women) (1995–2000) **Child mortality rate:** (under 5, per 1,000 live births) 9 (1996) **Physicians:** 1 per 345 people (1994)

Practical information

Visa requirements: UK: visa not required. USA: visa not required **Embassy in the UK:** 58 Knightsbridge, London SW1X 7JT. Tel: (0171) 201 1000; fax: (0171) 201 1004 **British embassy:** 35 rue du Faubourg St Honoré, 75383 Paris. Tel: (1) 4266 9142; fax: (1) 4266 9590 **Chamber of commerce:** Chambre de Commerce et d'Industrie de Paris, 27 avenue de Friedland, 75382 Paris. Tel: (1) 4289 7000; fax: (1) 4289 7286 **Airports:** international airports: Paris (Orly, Roissy-Charles de Gaulle, Le Bourget), Bordeaux (Merignac), Lille (Lesquin), Lyon, Marseille, Nice, Strasbourg, Toulouse (Blagnac); 45 domestic airports; total passenger km: 68,019 million (1994) **Major holidays:** 1 January, 1, 8 May, 14 July, 14, 15 August, 31 October, 1, 11 November, 24–25, 31 December; variable: Ascension Eve, Ascension Thusday, Good Friday, Easter Monday, Holy Saturday, Whit Holiday Eve, Whit Monday, Law of 20 December 1906, Law of 23 December 1904

Chronology

5th century BC: Celtic peoples invaded the region. **58–51 BC:** Romans conquered Celts and formed province of Gaul. **5th century AD:** Gaul overrun by Franks and other Germanic tribes. **481–511:** Frankish chief Clovis accepted Christianity and formed a kingdom based at Paris; under his successors, the Merovingian dynasty, the kingdom disintegrated. **751–68:** Pepin the Short usurped the Frankish throne, reunified the kingdom, and founded the Carolingian dynasty. **768–814:** Charlemagne conquered much of W Europe and created the Holy Roman Empire. **843:** Treaty of Verdun divided the Holy Roman Empire into three, with the western portion corresponding to modern France. **9th–10th centuries:** Weak central government allowed the great nobles to become virtually independent. **987:** Frankish crown passed to House of Capet; the Capets ruled the district around Paris, but were surrounded by vassals more powerful than themselves. **1180–1223:** Philip II doubled the royal domain and tightened control over the nobles; the power of the Capets gradually extended with support of church and towns. **1328:** When Charles IV died without an heir, Philip VI established the House of Valois. **1337:** Start of the Hundred Years' War: Edward III of England disputed the Valois succession and claimed the throne. English won victories at Crécy 1346 and Agincourt 1415. **1429:** Joan of Arc raised the siege of Orléans; Hundred Years' War ended with Charles VII expelling the English 1453. **1483:** France annexed Burgundy and Brittany after Louis XI had restored royal power. **16th–17th centuries:** French kings fought the Habsburgs (of Holy Roman Empire and Spain) for supremacy in W Europe. **1562–98:** Civil wars between nobles were fought under religious slogans, Catholic versus Protestant (or Huguenot). **1589–1610:** Henry IV, first king of Bourbon dynasty, established peace, religious tolerance, and absolute monarchy. **1634–48:** The ministers Richelieu and Mazarin, by intervening in the Thirty Years' War, secured Alsace and made France the leading power

France: Regions

Region	Capital	Area sq km	Area sq mi	Population (1990)
Alsace	Strasbourg	8,280	3,197	1,624,400
Aquitaine	Bordeaux	41,308	15,949	2,795,800
Auvergne	Clermont-Ferrand	26,013	10,044	1,321,200
Basse-Normandie	Caen	17,589	6,791	1,391,300
Brittany (Bretagne)	Rennes	27,208	10,505	2,795,600
Burgundy (Bourgogne)	Dijon	31,582	12,194	1,609,700
Centre	Orléans	39,151	15,116	2,371,000
Champagne-Ardenne	Châlons-sur-Marne	25,606	9,886	1,347,900
Corsica	Ajaccio	8,680	3,351	250,400
Franche-Comté	Besançon	16,202	6,256	1,097,400
Haute-Normandie	Rouen	12,317	4,756	1,737,200
Ile de France	Paris	12,012	4,638	10,660,600
Languedoc-Roussillon	Montpellier	27,376	10,570	2,114,900
Limousin	Limoges	16,942	6,541	722,800
Lorraine	Metz	23,547	9,091	2,305,700
Midi-Pyrénées	Toulouse	45,348	17,509	2,430,700
Nord-Pas-de-Calais	Lille	12,414	4,793	3,965,100
Pays de la Loire	Nantes	32,082	12,387	3,059,200
Picardie	Amiens	19,399	7,490	1,810,700
Poitou-Charentes	Poitiers	25,809	9,965	1,595,100
Provence-Alpes-Côte d'Azur	Marseille	31,400	12,123	4,257,900
Rhône-Alpes	Lyon	43,698	16,872	5,350,800

in Europe. **1701–14:** War of the Spanish Succession: England, Austria, and allies checked expansionism of France under Louis XIV. **1756–63:** Seven Years' War: France lost most of its colonies in India and Canada to Britain. **1789:** French Revolution abolished absolute monarchy and feudalism; First Republic proclaimed and revolutionary wars began 1792. **1799:** Napoleon Bonaparte seized power in coup; crowned himself emperor 1804; France conquered much of Europe. **1814:** Defeat of France; restoration of Bourbon monarchy; comeback by Napoleon defeated at Waterloo 1815. **1830:** Liberal revolution deposed Charles X in favour of his cousin Louis Philippe, the 'Citizen King'. **1848:** Revolution established Second Republic; conflict between liberals and socialists; Louis Napoleon, nephew of Napoleon I, elected president. **1852:** Louis Napoleon proclaimed Second Empire, taking title Napoleon III. **1870–71:** Franco-Prussian War: France lost Alsace-Lorraine; Second Empire abolished; Paris Commune crushed; Third Republic founded. **late 19th century:** France colonized Indochina, much of N Africa, and S Pacific. **1914–18:** France resisted German invasion in World War I; Alsace-Lorraine recovered 1919. **1936–37:** Left-wing 'Popular Front' government of Léon Blum introduced many social reforms. **1939:** France entered World War II. **1940:** Germany invaded and occupied N France; Marshal Pétain formed right-wing puppet regime at Vichy; resistance maintained by Maquis and Free French; Germans occupied all France 1942. **1944:** Allies liberated France; provisional government formed by Gen Charles de Gaulle, leader of Free French. **1946:** Fourth Republic proclaimed. **1949:** Became a member of NATO; withdrew from military command structure 1966. **1954:** French withdrew from Indochina after eight years of war; start of guerrilla war against French rule in Algeria. **1957:** France was a founder member of the European Economic Community. **1958:** Algerian crisis caused collapse of Fourth Republic; de Gaulle took power, becoming president of the Fifth Republic 1959. **1962:** Algeria achieved independence. **1968:** 'May events': revolutionary students rioted in Paris; general strike throughout France. **1981:** François Mitterrand elected Fifth Republic's first socialist president. **1986–88:** 'Cohabitation' of socialist president with conservative prime minister; again 1993–95. **1995:** Conservative Jacques Chirac elected president. Widespread condemnation of government's decision to resume nuclear tests in Pacific region. **1996:** End to nuclear testing in S Pacific. Spending cuts agreed to meet European Monetary Union entry criteria. Unemployment at post-war high. Leader of Corsican separatist wing of outlawed National Liberation Front captured by police. **1997:** General election called by President Chirac. Victory for Socialists; Lionel Jospin appointed prime minister.

Gabon Gabonese Republic

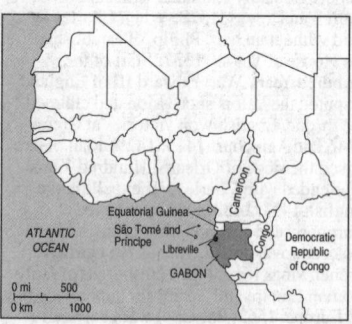

National name: *République Gabonaise* **Area:** 267,667 sq km/103,346 sq mi **Capital:** Libreville **Major towns/cities:** Port-Gentil, Masuku (Franceville), Lambaréné, Mouanda **Major ports:** Port-Gentil and Owendo **Physical features:** virtually the whole country is tropical rainforest; narrow coastal plain rising to hilly interior with savanna in E and S; Ogooué River flows N–W

Government
Head of state: Omar Bongo from 1964 **Head of government:** Paulin Obame-Nguema from 1994 **Political system:** emergent democracy **Administrative divisions:** nine provinces **Political**

parties: Gabonese Democratic Party (PDG), nationalist; Gabone Progress Party (PGP), left of centre; National Rally of Woodcutters (RNB), left of centre **Armed forces:** 4,700; plus a paramilitary force of 4,800 (1996) **Conscription:** military service is voluntary **Death penalty:** retained and used for ordinary crimes **Defence spend:** (% GDP) 2 (1996) **Education spend:** (% GNP) 3.2 (1993–94) **Health spend:** (% GDP) 0.5 (1990–95)

Economy and resources
Currency: franc CFA **GDP:** (\$ US) 3.9 billion (1994) **Real GDP per capita (PPP):** (\$ US) 3,641 (1994) **GDP growth rate:** 1.3% (1994); –2.5% (1990–95) **Average annual inflation:** 5% (1996); 4.8% (1985–95) **Foreign debt:** (\$ US) 4.06 billion (1996) **Major trading partners:** France, USA, Germany, Spain, Japan, the Netherlands **Resources:** petroleum, natural gas, manganese (one of world's foremost producers and exporters), iron ore, uranium, gold, niobium, talc, phosphates **Industries:** mining, food processing (particularly sugar), petroleum refining, processing of other minerals, timber preparation, chemicals **Exports:** petroleum and petroleum products, manganese, timber and wood products, uranium. Principal market: USA 49.9% (1994) **Imports:** machinery and apparatus, transport equipment, food products, metals and metal products. Principal source: France 39.8% (1994) **Arable land:** 1.3% (1995) **Agricultural products:** cassava, sugar cane, cocoa, coffee, plantains, maize, groundnuts, bananas, palm oil; forestry (forests cover approximately 75% of the land)

Population and society
Population: 1,106,000 (1996 est) **Population growth rate:** 2.8% (1990–95); 2.5% (2000–05) **Population density:** (per sq km) 4 (1996 est) **Urban population:** (% of total) 50 (1995) **Age distribution:** (% of total population) <15 39.2%, 15–65 55.1%, >65 5.8% (1995) **Ethnic groups:** 40 Bantu peoples in four main groupings: the Fang, Eshira, Mbede, and Okande; there are also Pygmies and about 10% Europeans (mainly French) **Language:** French (official), Bantu **Religion:** Roman Catholic, also Muslim, animist **Education:** (compulsory years) 10 **Literacy rate:** 73% (men); 48% (women) (1995 est) **Labour force:** 64.2% agriculture, 10.8% industry, 25% services (1994) **Life expectancy:** 54 (men); 57 (women) (1995–2000) **Child mortality rate:** (under 5, per 1,000 live births) 130 (1996) **Physicians:** 1 per 1,987 people (1993 est)

Practical information
Visa requirements: UK: visa required. USA: visa required **Embassy in the UK:** 27 Elvaston Place, London SW7 5NL. Tel: (0171) 823 9986; fax: (0171) 584 0047 **British embassy:** the British Embassy in Gabon closed in July 1991; all staff based in Yaoundé, Cameroon. The West African Department of the Foreign and Commonwealth Office is currently handling consular and commercial enquiries for Gabon; tel: (0171) 270 2516; fax: (0171) 270 3739 **Chamber of commerce:** Chambre de Commerce, d'Agriculture, d'Industrie et de Mines du Gabon, BP 2234, Libreville. Tel: (241) 722 064; fax: (241) 746 477 **Airports:** international airports: Port-Gentil, Masuku, Libreville; 65 public domestic-services airfields; total passenger km: 719 million (1994) **Major holidays:** 1 January, 12 March, 1 May, 17 August, 1 November, 25 December; variable: Eid-ul-Adha, Easter Monday, end of Ramadan, Whit Monday

Chronology
12th century: Immigration of Bantu speakers into an area previously peopled by Pygmies. **1472:** Gabon Estuary first visited by Portuguese navigators, who named it Gabao ('hooded cloak'), after the shape of the coastal area. **17th–18th centuries:** Fang, from Cameroon in N, and Omiene peoples colonized the area, attracted by presence in coastal areas of European traders, who developed the ivory and slave trades, which lasted until the mid-19th century. **1839–42:** Mpongwe coastal chiefs agreed to transfer sovereignty to France; Catholic and Protestant missionaries attracted to the area. **1849:** Libreville ('Free Town') formed by slaves from a slave ship liberated by the French. **1889:** Became part of French Congo, with Congo. **1910:** Became part of French Equatorial Africa, which also comprised Congo, Chad, and Central African Republic.

1890s–1920s: Human and natural resources exploited by private concessionary companies. **1940–44:** Supported the 'Free French' anti-Nazi cause during World War II. **1946:** Became overseas territory within the French Community, with its own assembly. **1960:** Independence achieved; Léon M'ba, a Fang of the pro-French Gabonese Democratic Block (BDG) became the first president. **1964:** Attempted military coup by supporters of rival party foiled with French help. **1967:** M'ba died and was succeeded by his protégé Albert Bernard Bongo, drawn from the Teke community. **1968:** One-party state established, with BDG dissolved and replaced by Gabonese Democratic Party (PDG). **1973:** Bongo converted to Islam and changed his first name to Omar, but continued to follow pro-Western policy course and exploit rich mineral resources to increase prosperity. **1989:** Coup attempt against Bongo defeated as economy deteriorated. **1990:** PDG won first multiparty elections since 1964 amid allegations of ballot-rigging. French troops sent in to maintain order following antigovernment riots. **1993:** National unity government formed, including some opposition members. **1997:** Paulin Obame-Nguema was reappointed prime minister after ruling Gabonese Democratic Party (PDG) won large assembly majority.

Gambia Republic of

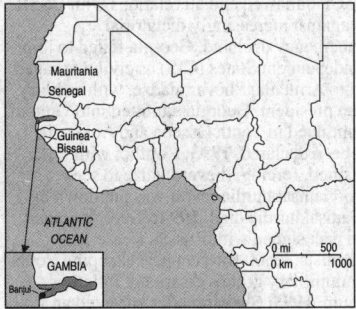

Area: 10,402 sq km/4,016 sq mi
Capital: Banjul
Major towns/cities: Serekunda, Birkama, Bakau, Farafenni, Sukuta, Gunjur, Georgetown
Physical features: consists of narrow strip of land along the River Gambia; river flanked by low hills

Government
Head of state and government: (interim) Yahya Jameh from 1994 **Political system:** transitional **Administrative divisions:** 35 districts, grouped into six Area Councils **Political parties:** Progressive People's Party (PPP), moderate centrist; National Convention Party (NCP), left of centre **Armed forces:** 800 (1996) **Conscription:** military service is mainly voluntary **Death penalty:** retains the death penalty for ordinary crimes but can be considered abolitionist in practice (last execution 1981) **Defence spend:** (% GDP) 3.9 (1996) **Education spend:** (% GNP) 2.7 (1993–94) **Health spend:** (% GDP) 1.8 (1990–95)

Economy and resources
Currency: dalasi **GDP:** ($ US) 4 million (1994) **Real GDP per capita (PPP):** ($ US) 939 (1994) **GDP growth rate:** 6.2% (1994); 1.6% (1990–95) **Average annual inflation:** 5% (1996); 10.3% (1985–95 est) **Foreign debt:** ($ US) 426 million (1995) **Major trading partners:** UK, Belgium, Italy, Hong Kong, China, Japan **Resources:** ilmenite, zircon, rutile, petroleum (well discovered, but not exploited) **Industries:** food processing (fish, fish products, and vegetable oils), beverages, construction materials **Exports:** groundnuts and related products, cotton lint, fish and fish preparations, hides and skins. Principal market: UK 25% (1995) **Imports:** food and live animals, basic manufactures, machinery and transport equipment, mineral fuels and lubrications, miscellaneous manufactured articles, chemicals. Principal source: UK 14.3% (1995) **Arable land:** 17.5% (1995) **Agricultural products:** groundnuts, cotton, rice, citrus fruits, avocados, sesame seed, millet, sorghum, maize; livestock rearing (cattle); fishing

Population and society
Population: 1,141,000 (1996 est) **Population growth rate:** 3.8% (1990–95); 2.4% (2000–05) **Population density:** (per sq km) 101 (1996 est) **Urban population:** (% of total) 26 (1995) **Age distribution:** (% of total population) <15 41.3%, 15–65 55.8%, >65 2.9% **Ethnic groups:** wide mix of ethnic groups, the largest is the Mandingo (about 40%); other main groups are the Fula, Wolof, Jola, and Serahuli **Language:** English (official), Mandinka, Fula, and other indigenous tongues **Religion:** Muslim 90%, with animist and Christian minorities **Education:** free, but not compulsory **Literacy rate:** 53% (men); 25% (women) (1995 est) **Labour force:** 50% of population: 79.6% agriculture, 4.2% industry, 16.2% services (1994) **Unemployment:** 26% (1994 est) **Life expectancy:** 45 (men); 47 (women) (1995–2000) **Child mortality rate:** (under 5, per 1,000 live births) 190 (1996) **Physicians:** 1 per 14,530 people (1991)

Practical information
Visa requirements: UK: visa not required for visits of up to 90 days. USA: visa required **Embassy in the UK:** 57 Kensington Court, London W8 5DG. Tel: (0171) 937 6316/7/8; fax: (0171) 937 9095 **British embassy:** British High Commission, PO Box 507, 48 Atlantic Road, Fajara, Banjul. Tel: (220) 495 133/4; fax: (220) 496 134 **Chamber of commerce:** Gambia Chamber of Commerce and Industry, PO Box 33, 78 Wellington Street, Banjul. Tel: (220) 227 765 **Airports:** international airport: Banjul (Yundum); total passenger km: 50 million (1994) **Major holidays:** 1 January, 1, 18 February, 1 May, 15 August, 25 December; variable: Eid-ul-Adha, Ashora, end of Ramadan (2 days), Good Friday, Prophet's Birthday

Chronology
13th century: Wolof, Malinke (Mandingo), and Fulani tribes settled in the region from E and N. **14th century:** Became part of the great Muslim Mali Empire, which, centred to NE, also extended across Senegal, Mali, and S Mauritania. **1455:** Gambia River first sighted by the Portuguese. **1663 and 1681:** British and French established small settlements on the river at Fort James and Albreda. **1843:** The Gambia became a British crown colony, administered with Sierra Leone until 1888. **1965:** Independence achieved as a constitutional monarchy within the Commonwealth, with Dawda K Jawara of the People's Progressive Party (PPP) as prime minister at the head of a multiparty democracy. **1970:** Became a republic, with Jawara as president. **1981:** Attempted coup foiled with the help of Senegal. **1982:** Formed with Senegal the Confederation of Senegambia, which involved integration of military forces, economic and monetary union, and coordinated foreign policy. **1994:** Jawara ousted in military coup, and fled to Senegal; Yahya Jameh named acting head of state. **1995:** Counter-coup attempt failed. **1996:** Civilian constitution adopted.

Georgia Republic of

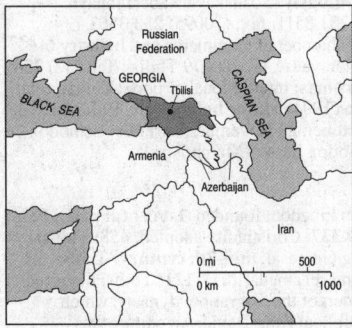

Area: 69,700 sq km/26,911 sq mi
Capital: Tbilisi
Major towns/cities: Kutaisi, Rustavi, Batumi, Sukhumi
Physical features: largely mountainous with a variety of landscape from the subtropical Black Sea shores to the ice and snow of the crest line of the Caucasus; chief rivers are Kura and Rioni

Government

Head of state: Eduard Shevardnadze from 1992 **Head of government:** Otar Patsatsia from 1993 **Political system:** transitional **Political parties:** Citizens' Union of Georgia (CUG), nationalist, pro-Shevardnadze; National Democratic Party of Georgia (NDPG), nationalist; Round Table/Free Georgia Bloc, nationalist; Georgian Popular Front (GPF), moderate nationalist, prodemocratization; Georgian Communist Party (GCP); National Independence Party (NIP), ultranationalist; Front for the Reinstatement of Legitimate Power in Georgia, strong nationalist **Armed forces:** 10,000 (1996); 9,000 (1995); approximately 22,000 Russian troops were stationed in three military bases in1996 **Conscription:** compulsory for two years **Death penalty:** retained and used for ordinary crimes **Defence spend:** (% GDP) 3.4 (1996) **Education spend:** (% GDP) 1.9% (1993–94) **Health spend:** (% GDP) 0.3 (1990–95)

Economy and resources

Currency: lari **GDP:** ($ US) 2 billion (1994) **Real GDP per capita (PPP):** ($ US) 1,585 (1994) **GDP growth rate:** 8% (1996); –26.9% (1990–95) **Average annual inflation:** 44.1% (1996); 310% (1985–95) **Foreign debt:** ($ US) 1.64 billion (1996) **Major trading partners:** Russia, Turkey, Turkmenistan, Azerbaijan **Resources:** coal, manganese, barytes, clay, petroleum and natural gas deposits, iron and other ores, gold, agate, marble, alabaster, arsenic, tungsten, mercury **Industries:** metalworking, light industrial goods, motor cars, food processing, textiles (including silk), chemicals, construction materials **Exports:** metal products, machinery, tea, beverages. Principal market: Russia 29% (1996) **Imports:** mineral fuels, chemical and petroleum products, food products (mainly wheat and flour), light industrial products, beverages. Principal source: Russia 21% (1996) **Arable land:** 11.1% (1995) **Agricultural products:** grain, tea, citrus fruits, wine grapes, flowers, tobacco, almonds, sugar beet; sheep and goat farming; forest resources

Population and society

Population: 5,442,000 (1996 est) **Population growth rate:** 0.1% (1990–95); 0.4% (2000–05) **Population density:** (per sq km) 78 (1996 est) **Urban population:** (% of total) 58 (1995) **Age distribution:** (% of total population) <15 23.7%, 15–65 64.8%, >65 11.4% (1995) **Ethnic groups:** 70% ethnic Georgian, 8% Armenian, 7% ethnic Russian, 5% Azeri, 3% Ossetian, 2% Abkhazian, and 2% Greek **Language:** Georgian **Religion:** Georgian Orthodox, also Muslim **Education:** (compulsory years) 9 **Literacy rate:** 99% (men); 99% (women) (1995 est) **Labour force:** 27.1% agriculture, 19.4% industry, 53.5% services (1991) **Unemployment:** 2% (1993) **Life expectancy:** 70 (men); 78 (women) (1995–2000) **Child mortality rate:** (under 5, per 1,000 live births) 21 (1996) **Physicians:** 1 per 200 people (1994)

Practical information

Visa requirements: UK: visa required. USA: visa required **Embassy in the UK:** 45 Avanmore Road, London W14. Tel/fax: (0171) 603 5325 **British embassy:** Sosiiskaya Naberzehnaya, Moscow 72. Tel: (70095) 231 8511; fax: (70095) 233 3563 **Chamber of commerce:** Chamber of Commerce and Industry of Georgia, Prospekt I, Chavchavadze 11, 380079 Tbilisi. Tel: (32) 230 045; fax: (32) 235 760 **Airports:** international airports: Tbilisi; total passenger km: 283 million (1994) **Major holidays:** 1, 19 January, 3, 26 May, 28 August, 14 October, 23 November; variable: Orthodox Christmas (January), Orthodox Easter (March/April)

Chronology

4th century BC: Georgian kingdom founded. **1st century BC:** Part of the Roman Empire. **AD 337:** Christianity adopted. **458:** Tbilisi founded by King Vakhtang Gorgasal. **mid-7th century:** Tbilisi brought under Arab rule and renamed Tiflis. **1121:** Tbilisi liberated by King David II the Builder, of the Gagrationi dynasty, which traced its ancestry to the biblical King David. An empire was established across the Caucasus region, remaining powerful until Mongol onslaughts in the 13th and 14th centuries. **1555:** W Georgia fell to Turkey and E Georgia to Persia (Iran). **1783:** Treaty of

Georgievsk established Russian dominance over Georgia. **1804–13:** First Russo-Iranian war fought largely over Georgia. **late 19th century:** Abolition of serfdom and beginnings of industrialization, but Georgian church suppressed. **1918:** Independence established after Russian Revolution. **1921:** Invaded by Red Army; Soviet republic established. **1922–36:** Linked with Armenia and Azerbaijan as the Transcaucasian Federation. **1930s:** Rapid industrial development, but resistance to agricultural collectivization and violent political purges instituted by the Georgian Soviet dictator Joseph Stalin. **1936:** Became separate republic within the USSR. **early 1940s:** 200,000 Meskhetians deported from S Georgia to Central Asia on Stalin's orders. **1972:** Drive against endemic corruption launched by new Georgian Communist Party (GCP) leader Eduard Shevardnadze. **1977:** Initiative Group for the Defence of Human Rights formed by Zviad Gamsakhurdia, a nationalist intellectual. **1978:** Violent demonstrations by nationalists in Tbilisi. **1981–88:** Increasing demands for autonomy encouraged from 1986 by the *glasnost* initiative of the reformist Soviet leader Mikhail Gorbachev. **1989:** Formation of nationalist Georgian Popular Front led the minority Abkhazian and Ossetian communities in NW and central N Georgia to demand secession, provoking interethnic clashes. State of emergency imposed in Abkhazia; 20 pro-independence demonstrators massacred in Tbilisi by Soviet troops; Georgian sovereignty declared by parliament. **1990:** Nationalist coalition triumphed in elections and Gamsakhurdia became president. GCP seceded from Communist Party of USSR. **1991:** Independence declared. GCP outlawed and all relations with USSR severed. Demonstrations against increasingly dictatorial Gamsakhurdia; state of emergency declared. Georgia failed to join new Commonwealth of Independent States (CIS) as civil war raged. **1992:** Gamsakhurdia fled to Armenia; Shevardnadze, with military backing, appointed interim president. Georgia admitted into United Nations (UN). Clashes continued in South Ossetia and Abkhazia, where independence had been declared. **1993:** Conflict with Abkhazi separatists intensified, forcing Shevardnadze to seek Russian military help. Pro-Gamsakhurdia revolt was put down by government forces and Gamsakhurdia died. **1994:** Georgia joined CIS. Military cooperation pact signed with Russia. Cease-fire agreed with Abkhazi separatists; 2,500 Russian peacekeeping troops deployed in region and paramilitary groups disarmed. Inflation exceeded 5,000% per annum. **1995:** Shevardnadze survived an assassination attempt and was re-elected; mass privatization programme launched. **1996:** Cooperation pact with European Union signed as economic growth resumed and monthly inflation fell to below 3%. Elections to secessionist Abkhazi parliament declared illegal by Georgian government. **1997:** New opposition party formed, Front for the Reinstatement of Legitimate Power in Georgia. Talks between government and breakaway Abkhazi government.

Germany Federal Republic of

National name: *Bundesrepublik Deutschland* **Area:** 357,041 sq km/137,853 sq mi **Capital:** Berlin (government offices moving in phases from Bonn back to Berlin) **Major towns/cities:** Cologne, Hamburg, Munich, Essen, Frankfurt am Main, Dortmund, Stuttgart, Düsseldorf, Leipzig, Dresden, Bremen, Duisburg, Hannover

Major ports: Hamburg, Kiel, Bremerhaven, Rostock **Physical features:** flat in N, mountainous in S with Alps; rivers Rhine, Weser, Elbe flow N, Danube flows SE, Oder, Neisse flow N along Polish frontier; many lakes, including Müritz; Black Forest, Harz Mountains, Erzgebirge (Ore Mountains), Bavarian Alps, Fichtelgebirge, Thüringer Forest

Government

Head of state: Roman Herzog from 1994 **Head of government:** Helmut Kohl from 1982 **Political system:** liberal democratic federal republic **Administrative divisions:** 16 states **Political parties:** Christian Democratic Union (CDU), right of centre, 'social market'; Christian Social Union (CSU), right of centre; Social Democratic Party (SPD), left of centre; Free Democratic Party (FDP), liberal; Greens, environmentalist; Party of Democratic Socialism (PDS), reform-socialist (formerly Socialist Unity Party: SED) **Armed forces:** 358,400 (1996) **Conscription:** 10 months **Death penalty:** abolished in the Federal Republic of Germany 1949 and in the German Democratic Republic 1987 **Defence spend:** (% GDP) 1.7 (1996) **Education spend:** (% GNP) 4.8 (1993–94) **Health spend:** (% GDP) 7 (1995)

Economy and resources

Currency: Deutschmark **GDP:** ($ US) 2,353.2 billion (1996) **Real GDP per capita (PPP):** ($ US) 21,116 (1996) **GDP growth rate:** 2.8% (1996); 1.9% (1994–95) **Average annual inflation:** 1.9% (1996) **Major trading partners:** EU (particularly France, the Netherlands, and Ireland), USA, Japan, Switzerland **Resources:** lignite, hard coal, potash salts, crude oil, natural gas, iron ore, copper, timber, nickel, uranium **Industries:** mining, road vehicles, chemical products, transport equipment, nonelectrical machinery, metals and metal products, electrical machinery, electronic goods, cement, food and beverages **Exports:** road vehicles, electrical machinery, metals and metal products, textiles, chemicals. Principal market: France 10.9% (1996) **Imports:** road vehicles, electrical machinery, food and live animals, clothing and accessories, crude petroleum and petroleum products. Principal source: France 10.6% (1996) **Arable land:** 33.9% (1995) **Agricultural products:** potatoes, sugar beet, barley, wheat, maize, rapeseed, vine fruits; livestock (cattle, pigs, and poultry) and fishing

Population and society

Population: 81,992,000 (1996 est) **Population growth rate:** 0.6% (1990–95); –0.1% (2000–05) **Population density:** (per sq km) 230 (1996 est) **Urban population:** (% of total) 87 (1995) **Age distribution:** (% of total population) <15 16.1%, 15–65 68.7%, >65 15.2% (1995) **Ethnic groups:** predominantly Germanic; notable Danish and Slavonic ethnic minorities in the N; significant population of foreigners, including 1.9 million officially recognized *Gastarbeiter* ('guest workers'), predominantly Turks, Greeks,

Italians, and Yugoslavs; by 1993 Germany had received more than 200,000 refugees fleeing the Yugoslav civil war **Language:** German **Religion:** Protestant (mainly Lutheran) 43%, Roman Catholic 36% **Education:** (compulsory years) 12 **Literacy rate:** 100% (men); 100% (women) (1995 est) **Labour force:** 48.2% of population: 3.3% agriculture, 37.5% industry, 59.1% services (1996) **Unemployment:** 11% (1997) **Life expectancy:** 74 (men); 80 (women) (1995–2000) **Child mortality rate:** (under 5, per 1,000 live births) 7 (1996) **Physicians:** 1 per 303 people (1994)

Practical information

Visa requirements: UK: visa not required. USA: visa not required **Embassy in the UK:** 23 Belgrave Square, London SW1X 8PZ. Tel: (0171) 824 1300; fax: (0171) 824 1435 **British embassy:** Friedrich-Ebert-Allée 77, 53113 Bonn. Tel: (228) 91670; fax: (228) 9167 331 **Chamber of commerce:** Deutscher Industrie- und Handelstag (Association of German Chambers of Industry and Commerce), Adenauerallée 148, 53113 Bonn. Tel: (228) 1040; fax: (228) 104 158 **Airports:** international airports: Berlin-Tegel (Otto Lilienthal), Berlin-Schönefeld, Berlin-Tempelhof, Leipzig/Halle, Dresden (Klotsche), Bremen (Neuenland), Cologne, Düsseldorf (Lohausen), Frankfurt, Hamburg, Hannover (Langenhagen), Munich (Franz Joseph Strauss), Münster-Osnabrück, Nuremberg, Saarbrucken (Ensheim), Stuttgart (Echterdingen); several domestic airports; total passenger km: 56,903 million (1994) **Major holidays:** 1, 6 January, 1 May, 3 October, 1 November, 25–26 December; variable: Good Friday, Easter Monday, Ascension Thursday, Whit Monday, Corpus Christi, Assumption

Chronology

c. 1000 BC: Germanic tribes from Scandinavia began to settle the region between the rivers Rhine, Elbe, and Danube. **AD 9:** Romans tried and failed to conquer Germanic tribes. **5th century:** Germanic tribes plundered Rome, overran W Europe, and divided it into tribal kingdoms. **496:** Clovis, King of the Franks, conquered the Alemanni tribe of western Germany. **772–804:** After series of fierce wars, Charlemagne extended Frankish authority over Germany, subjugated Saxons, imposed Christianity, and took title of Holy Roman emperor. **843:** Treaty of Verdun divided the Holy Roman Empire into three, with E portion corresponding to modern Germany; local princes became virtually independent. **919:** Henry the Fowler restored central authority and founded Saxon dynasty. **962:** Otto the Great enlarged the kingdom and revived title of Holy Roman emperor. **1024–1254:** Emperors of Salian and Hohenstaufen dynasties came into conflict with popes; frequent civil wars allowed German princes to regain independence. **12th century:** German expansion eastwards into lands between rivers Elbe and Oder. **13th–14th centuries:** Hanseatic League of Allied German cities became a great commercial and naval power. **1438:** Title of Holy Roman emperor became virtually hereditary in the Habsburg family of Austria. **1517:** Martin Luther began the Reformation; Emperor Charles V tried to suppress Protestantism; civil war ensued. **1555:** Peace of Augsburg: Charles V forced to accept that each German prince could choose religion of his own lands. **1618–48:** Thirty Years' War: bitter conflict, partly religious, between certain German princes and emperor, with foreign intervention; the war wrecked the German economy and reduced the Holy Roman Empire to a name. **1701:** Frederick I, Elector of Brandenburg, promoted to King of Prussia. **1740:** Frederick the Great of Prussia seized Silesia from Austria and retained it through war of Austrian Succession (1740–48) and Seven Years' War (1756–63). **1772–95:** Prussia joined Russia and Austria in the partition of Poland. **1792:** Start of French Revolutionary Wars, involving many German states, with much fighting on German soil. **1806:** Holy Roman Empire abolished; France formed puppet Confederation of the Rhine in western

Germany: States

State	Capital	Area		Population
		sq km	sq mi	(1995)
Baden-Württemberg	Stuttgart	35,752	13,804	10,319,400
Bavaria	Munich	70,551	27,240	11,993,500
Berlin	Berlin	889	343	3,471,400
Brandenburg	Potsdam	29,479	11,382	2,542,000
Bremen	Bremen	404	156	679,800
Hamburg	Hamburg	755	292	1,705,900
Hessen	Wiesbaden	21,114	8,152	6,009,900
Lower Saxony	Hannover	47,606	18,381	7,780,400
Mecklenburg-West Pomerania	Schwerin	23,170	8,946	1,823,100
North Rhine-Westphalia	Düsseldorf	34,077	13,157	17,893,000
Rhineland-Palatinate	Mainz	19,852	7,665	3,983,300
Saarland	Saarbrücken	2,570	992	1,084,400
Saxony	Dresden	18,412	7,109	4,566,600
Saxony-Anhalt	Magdeburg	20,446	7,894	2,738,900
Schleswig-Holstein	Kiel	15,770	6,089	2,725,500
Thuringia	Erfurt	16,171	6,244	2,503,800

Germany and defeated Prussia at Battle of Jena. **1813–15:** National revival enabled Prussia to take part in defeat of Napoleon at Battles of Leipzig and Waterloo. **1814–15:** Congress of Vienna rewarded Prussia with Rhineland, Westphalia, and much of Saxony; loose German Confederation formed by 39 independent states. **1848–49:** Liberal revolutions in many German states; Frankfurt Assembly sought German unity; revolutions suppressed. **1862:** Otto von Bismarck became prime minister of Prussia. **1866:** Seven Weeks' War: Prussia defeated Austria, dissolved German Confederation, and established North German Confederation under Prussian leadership. **1870–71:** Franco-Prussian War; S German states agreed to German unification; German Empire proclaimed, with King of Prussia as emperor and Bismarck as chancellor. **1890:** Wilhelm II dismissed Bismarck and sought to make Germany a leading power in world politics. **1914:** Germany encouraged Austrian attack on Serbia that started World War I; Germany invaded Belgium and France. **1918:** Germany defeated; revolution overthrew monarchy. **1919:** Treaty of Versailles: Germany lost land to France, Denmark, and Poland; demilitarization and reparations imposed; Weimar Republic proclaimed. **1922–23:** Hyperinflation: in 1922, one dollar was worth 50 marks; in 1923, one dollar was worth 2.5 trillion marks. **1929:** Start of economic slump caused mass unemployment and brought Germany close to revolution. **1933:** Adolf Hitler, leader of Nazi Party, became chancellor. **1934:** Hitler took title of *Führer* (leader), murdered rivals, and created one-party state with militaristic and racist ideology; rearmament reduced unemployment. **1938:** Germany annexed Austria and Sudeten; occupied remainder of Czechoslovakia 1939. **1939:** German invasion of Poland started World War II; Germany defeated France 1940, attacked USSR 1941, and pursued extermination of Jews. **1945:** Germany defeated and deprived of its conquests; eastern lands transferred to Poland; USA, USSR, UK, and France established zones of occupation. **1948–49:** Disputes between Western allies and USSR led to Soviet blockade of West Berlin. **1949:** Partition of Germany: US, French, and British zones in West Germany became Federal Republic of Germany with Konrad Adenauer as chancellor; Soviet zone in East Germany became communist German Democratic Republic led by Walter Ulbricht. **1953:** Uprising in East Berlin suppressed by Soviet troops. **1955:** West Germany became a member of NATO; East Germany joined the Warsaw Pact. **1957:** West Germany was a founder member of the European Economic Community. **1960s:** 'Economic miracle': West Germany achieved rapid growth and great prosperity. **1961:** East Germany constructed Berlin Wall to prevent emigration to West Berlin (part of West Germany). **1969:** Willy Brandt, Social Democratic Party chancellor of West Germany, sought better relations with USSR and East Germany. **1971:** Erich Honecker succeeded Ulbricht as Communist Party leader, and became head of state 1976. **1972:** Basic Treaty established relations between West Germany and East Germany as between foreign states. **1982:** Helmut Kohl (Christian Democratic Union) became West German chancellor. **1989:** Mass exodus of East Germans to West Germany via Hungary; Honecker replaced; East Germany opened frontiers, including Berlin Wall. **1990:** Collapse of communist regime in East Germany; reunification of Germany with Kohl as chancellor. **1991:** Maastricht Treaty: Germany took the lead in pressing for closer European integration. **1995:** Unemployment reached postwar high of 3.8 million. **1996:** Public-sector labour dispute over welfare reform plans and the worsening economy. Spending cuts agreed to meet European Monetary Union entry criteria. **1997:** Unemployment reached highest postwar levels. Former East German leader Egon Krenz and two colleagues convicted of manslaughter. SPD polled badly in local elections.

Ghana Republic of (formerly the Gold Coast)

Area: 238,305 sq km/92,009 sq mi **Capital:** Accra **Major towns/cities:** Kumasi, Tamale, Tema, Sekondi-Takoradi, Cape Coast, Sunyani, Koforidua, Ho, Yendi, Tarkwa, Wa, Bolgatanga **Major ports:** Sekondi, Tema **Physical features:** mostly tropical lowland plains; bisected by River Volta

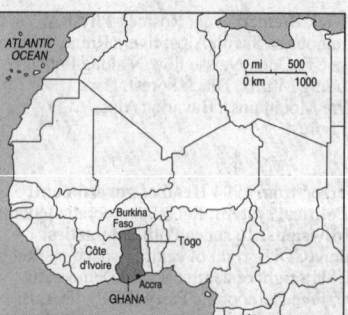

Government

Head of state and government: Jerry Rawlings from 1981 **Political system:** emergent democracy **Administrative divisions:** ten regions **Political parties:** National Democratic Congress (NDC), centrist, progovernment; New Patriotic Party (NPP), left of centre **Armed forces:** 7,000; plus a paramilitary force of 7,500 (1996) **Conscription:** military service is voluntary **Death penalty:** retained and used for ordinary crimes **Defence spend:** (% GDP) 1.4 (1996) **Education spend:** (% GNP) 3.1 (1993–94) **Health spend:** (% GDP) 1 (1990–95)

Economy and resources

Currency: cedi **GDP:** ($ US) 5.4 billion (1994) **Real GDP per capita (PPP):** ($ US) 1,960 (1994) **GDP growth rate:** 3.8% (1994); 4.3% (1990–95) **Average annual inflation:** 55% (1996); 28.4% (1985–95) **Foreign debt:** ($ US) 5.88 billion (1995) **Major trading partners:** UK, USA, Germany, Nigeria, Japan, France **Resources:** diamonds, gold, manganese, bauxite **Industries:** food processing, textiles, vehicles, aluminium, cement, paper, chemicals, petroleum products, tourism **Exports:** gold, cocoa and related products, timber. Principal market: USA 14.6% (1995) **Imports:** raw materials, machinery and transport equipment, petroleum, food, basic manufactures. Principal source: UK 16.2% (1995) **Arable land:** 12.3% (1995) **Agricultural products:** cocoa (world's third-largest producer), coffee, bananas, oil palm, maize, rice, cassava, plantain, yams, coconuts, kola nuts, limes, shea nuts; forestry (timber production)

Population and society

Population: 17,832,000 (1996 est) **Population growth rate:** 3% (1990–95); 2.8% (2000–05) **Population density:** (per sq km) 75 (1996 est) **Urban population:** (% of total) 36 (1995) **Age distribution:** (% of total population) <15 45.3%, 15–65 51.8%, >65 2.9% (1995) **Ethnic groups:** over 75 ethnic groups; most significant are the Akan in the S and W (44%), the Mole-Dagbani in the N, the Ewe in the S, the Ga in the region of the capital city, and the Fanti in the coastal area **Language:** English (official) and African languages **Religion:** Christian 62%, Muslim 16%, animist **Education:** (compulsory years) 9 **Literacy rate:** 70% (men); 51% (women) (1995 est) **Labour force:** 47% of population: 47.5% agriculture, 12.8% industry, 39.7% services (1994) **Unemployment:** 10% (1991) **Life expectancy:** 57 (men); 60 (women) (1995–2000) **Child mortality rate:** (under 5, per 1,000 live births) 111 (1996) **Physicians:** 1 per 22,970 people (1993 est)

Practical information

Visa requirements: UK: visa required. USA: visa required **Embassy in the UK:** (education and visas) 104 Highgate Hill, London N6 5HE. Tel: (0181) 342 8686; fax: (0181) 342 8566; (tourist information) 102 Park Street, London W1Y 3RJ. Tel: (0171) 493 4901; fax: (0171) 629 1730 **British embassy:** British High Commission, PO Box 296, Osu Link, off Gamel Abdul Nasser Avenue, Accra. Tel: (21) 221 665; fax: (21) 664 652 **Chamber of commerce:** Ghana National Chamber of Commerce, PO Box 2325, Accra. Tel: (21) 662 427; fax: (21) 662 210 **Airports:** international airport: Accra (Koteka); four domestic airports; total passenger km: 478 million (1994) **Major holidays:** 1 January, 6 March, 1 May, 4 June, 1 July, 25–26, 31 December; variable: Good Friday, Easter Monday, Holy Saturday

Chronology

5th–12th century: Ghana Empire (from which present-day country's name derives) flourished, with its centre 500 mi/800 km to the NW, in Mali. **13th century:** In coastal and forest areas Akan peoples founded first states. **15th century:** Gold-seeking Mande traders entered N Ghana from the NE, founding Dagomba and Mamprussi states; Portuguese navigators visited coastal region, naming it the 'Gold Coast', building a fort at Elmina, and slave trading began. **17th century:** Gonja kingdom founded in N by Mande speakers; Ga and Ewe states founded in the SE by immigrants from Nigeria; in central Ghana, controlling gold reserves around Kumasi, the Ashanti, a branch of the Akans, founded what became the most powerful state in precolonial Ghana. **1618:** British trading settlement established on Gold Coast. **18th–19th centuries:** Centralized Ashanti kingdom at its height, dominating between Komoe River in the W and Togo Mountains in the E and active in slave trade; Fante state powerful along coast in the S. **1874:** Britain, after ousting the Danes and Dutch and defeating the Ashanti, made the Gold Coast (the southern provinces) a crown colony. **1898–1901:** After three further military campaigns, Britain finally subdued and established protectorates over Ashanti and the northern territories. **early 20th century:** The colony developed into a major cocoa-exporting region. **1917:** West Togoland, formerly German-ruled, was administered with the Gold Coast as British Togoland. **1949:** Campaign for independence launched by Kwame Nkrumah, who formed Convention People's Party (CPP) and became prime minister in 1952. **1957:** Independence achieved, within the Commonwealth, as Ghana, which included British Togoland; Nkrumah became prime minister. Policy of 'African socialism' and nonalignment pursued. **1960:** Became a republic, with Nkrumah as president. **1964:** Ghana became a one-party state, dominated by the CCP, and developed links with communist bloc. **1966:** Nkrumah deposed in military coup and replaced by Gen Joseph Ankrah; political prisoners released. **1969:** Ankrah replaced by Gen Akwasi Afrifa, who initiated a return to civilian government. **1970:** Edward Akufo-Addo elected president. **1972:** Another coup placed Col Ignatius Acheampong at the head of a military government as economy deteriorated. **1978:** Acheampong deposed in a bloodless coup led by Frederick Akuffo; another coup put Flight-Lt Jerry Rawlings, a populist soldier who launched a drive against corruption, in power. **1979:** Return to civilian rule under Hilla Limann. **1981:** Rawlings seized power again. All political parties banned. **1992:** Pluralist constitution approved in referendum, lifting the ban on political parties. Rawlings won presidential elections. **1996:** Rawlings re-elected. New Democratic Congress (NDC) won assembly majority.

Greece Hellenic Republic

National name: *Elliniki Dimokratia* **Area:** 131,957 sq km/50,948 sq mi **Capital:** Athens **Major towns/cities:** Thessaloníki, Piraeus, Patras, Irákleion, Larissa, Volos **Major ports:** Piraeus, Thessaloníki, Patras, Irákleion **Physical features:** mountainous (Mount Olympus); a large number of islands, notably Crete, Corfu, and Rhodes, and Cyclades and Ionian Islands

Government

Head of state: Costis Stephanopoulos from 1995 **Head of government:** Costis Simitis from 1996 **Political system:** democracy **Administrative divisions:** 13 regions divided into 51 departments **Political parties:** Panhellenic Socialist Movement (PASOK), nationalist, democratic socialist; New Democracy Party (ND), centre right; Democratic Renewal (DIANA), centrist; Communist Party (KJKE), left wing; Political Spring, moderate, left of centre **Armed forces:** 168,300 (1996) **Conscription:** 19–24 months **Death penalty:** abolished 1993 **Defence spend:** (% GDP) 4.8 (1996) **Education spend:** (% GNP) 3 (1993–94) **Health spend:** (% GDP) 2.8 (1995)

Economy and resources

Currency: drachma **GDP:** ($ US) 122.8 billion (1996) **Real GDP per capita (PPP):** ($ US) 12,694 (1996) **GDP growth rate:** 2.2% (1996); 1.1% (1990–95) **Average annual inflation:** 5.4% (1996); 15.1% (1985–95) **Major trading partners:** Germany, Italy, France, the Netherlands, USA, UK **Resources:** bauxite, nickel, iron pyrites, magnetite, asbestos, marble, salt, chromite, lignite **Industries:** food products, metals and metal products, textiles, petroleum refining, machinery and transport equipment, tourism, wine **Exports:** fruit and vegetables, clothing, mineral fuels and lubricants, textiles, iron and steel, aluminium and aluminium alloys. Principal market: Germany 27.7% (1995) **Imports:** petroleum and petroleum products, machinery and transport equipment, food and live animals, chemicals and chemical products. Principal source: Germany 17.9% (1995) **Arable land:** 18.6% (1995) **Agricultural products:** fruit and vegetables, cereals, sugar beet, tobacco, olives; livestock and dairy products

Population and society

Population: 10,490,000 (1996 est) **Population growth rate:** 0.4% (1990–95); 0% (2000–05) **Population density:** (per sq km) 79 (1996 est) **Urban population:** (% of total) 65 (1995) **Age distribution:** (% of total population) <15 16.7%, 15–65 67.4%, >65 15.9% (1995) **Ethnic groups:** predominantly Greek; main minorities are Turks, Slavs, and Albanians **Language:** Greek (official), Macedonian (100,000–200,000 est) **Religion:** Greek Orthodox; also Roman Catholic **Education:** (compulsory years) 9 **Literacy rate:** 98% (men); 89% (women) (1995 est) **Labour force:** 40.6% of population: 20.4% agriculture, 23.2% industry, 56.4% services (1995) **Unemployment:** 8.8% (1995) **Life expectancy:** 76 (men); 81 (women) (1995–2000) **Child mortality rate:** (under 5, per 1,000 live births) 10 (1996) **Physicians:** 1 per 312 people (1993)

Practical information

Visa requirements: UK: visa not required. USA: visa not required **Embassy in the UK:** Embassy of the Hellenic Republic, 1A Holland Park, London W11 3TP. Tel: (0171) 221 6467; fax: (0171) 243 3202 **British embassy:** Odos Ploutarchon 1, 106 75 Athens. Tel: (1) 723 6211/9; fax: (1) 724 1872 **Chamber of commerce:** Athens Chamber of Commerce, Odos Akademias 7, 106 71 Athens. Tel: (1) 360 2411; fax: (1) 360 7897 **Airports:** international airports: Athens (Athinai), Iráklion/Crete, Thessaloníki (Micra), Corfu (Kerkira), Rhodes (Paradisi); 25 domestic airports, of which 14 are also international; total passenger km: 8,429 million (1994) **Major holidays:** 1, 6 January, 25 March, 1 May, 15 August, 28 October, 25–26 December; variable: Monday in Lent, Good Friday, Easter Monday, Whit Monday

Chronology

c. 2000–1200 BC: Mycenaean civilization flourished. **c. 1500–1100 BC:** Central Greece and Peloponnese invaded by tribes of Achaeans, Aeolians, Ionians, and Dorians. **c. 1000–500 BC:** Rise of the Greek city states; Greek colonies established around the shores of the Mediterranean. **c. 490–404 BC:** Ancient Greek culture reached its zenith in the democratic city state of Athens. **357–338 BC:** Philip II of Macedon won supremacy over Greece; cities fought to regain and preserve independence. **146 BC:** Roman Empire defeated Macedon and annexed Greece. **476 AD:** Western Roman Empire ended; Eastern Empire continued as Byzantine Empire, based at Constantinople, with essentially Greek culture. **1204:** Crusaders partitioned Byzantine Empire; Athens, Achaea, and Thessaloniki came under Frankish rulers. **late 14th century–1461:** Ottoman Turks conquered mainland Greece and captured Constantinople 1453; Greek language and culture preserved by Orthodox Church. **1685:** Venetians captured Peloponnese; regained by Turks 1715. **late 18th century:** Beginnings of Greek nationalism among émigrés and merchant class. **1814:** *Philike Hetairia* ('Friendly Society') formed by revolutionary Greek nationalists in Odessa. **1821:** *Philike Hetairia* raised Peloponnese brigands in revolt against Turks; War of Independence ensued. **1827:** Battle of Navarino: Britain, France, and Russia intervened to destroy Turkish fleet; Count Ioannis Kapodistrias elected president of Greece. **1829:** Treaty of Adrianople: under Russian pressure, Turkey recognized independence of small Greek state. **1832:** Great Powers elected Otto of Bavaria as king of Greece. **1843:** Coup forced King Otto to grant a constitution. **1862:** Mutiny and rebellion led King Otto to abdicate. **1863:** George of Denmark became king of the Hellenes. **1864:** Britain transferred Ionian islands to Greece. **1881:** Following Treaty of Berlin 1878, Greece was allowed to annex Thessaly and part of Epirus. **late 19th century:** Politics dominated by Kharilaos Trikoupis, who emphasized economic development, and Theodoros Deliyiannis, who emphasized territorial expansion. **1897:** Greco-Turkish War ended in Greek defeat. **1908:** Cretan Assembly led by Eleutherios Venizelos proclaimed union with Greece. **1910:** Venizelos became prime minister and introduced financial, military, and constitutional reforms. **1912–13:** Balkan Wars: Greece annexed a large area of Epirus and Macedonia. **1916:** 'National Schism': Venizelos formed rebel pro-Allied government while royalists remained neutral. **1917–18:** Greek forces fought on Allied side in World War I. **1919–22:** Greek invasion of Asia Minor; after Turkish victory, a million refugees came to Greece. **1924:** Republic declared amid great political instability. **1935:** Greek monarchy restored with George II. **1936:** Gen Ioannia Metaxas established right-wing dictatorship. **1940:** Greece successfully repelled Italian invasion. **1941–44:** German occupation of Greece; rival monarchist and communist resistance groups operated from 1942. **1946–49:** Civil war: communists defeated by monarchists with military aid from Britain and USA. **1952:** Became a member of NATO. **1967:** 'Greek Colonels' seized power under George Papadopoulos; political activity banned; King Constantine II exiled. **1973:** Republic proclaimed with Papadopoulos as president. **1974:** Cyprus crisis caused downfall of military regime; Constantine Karamanlis returned from exile to form Government of National Salvation and restore democracy. **1981:** Andreas Papandreou elected Greece's first socialist prime minister; Greece entered the European Community. **1989–93:** Election defeat of Panhellenic Socialist Movement (PASOK) followed by unstable coalition governments. **1993:** PASOK returned to power. **1996:** Costis Simitis succeeded Papandreou as prime minister. PASOK retained its majority in the general election. **1997:** Direct talks with Turkey resulted in agreement to settle all future disputes peacefully.

Grenada

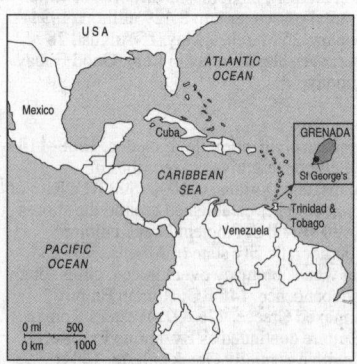

Area: (including the southern Grenadine Islands, notably Carriacou and Petit Martinique) 344 sq km/133 sq mi **Capital:** St George's **Major towns/cities:** Grenville, Sauteurs, Victoria, Hillsborough (Carriacou) **Physical features:** southernmost of the Windward Islands; mountainous; Grand-Anse beach; Annandale Falls; the Great Pool volcanic crater

Government

Head of state: Elizabeth II from 1974, represented by governor general Reginald Palmer from 1992 **Head of government:** Keith Mitchell from 1995 **Political system:** emergent democracy **Administrative divisions:** six parishes **Political parties:** Grenada United Labour Party (GULP), nationalist, left of centre; National Democratic Congress (NDC), centrist; National Party (TNP), centrist **Armed forces:** no standing army; 730-strong regional security unit (1995) **Death penalty:** retained and used for ordinary crimes but can be considered abolitionist in practice (last execution 1978)

Economy and resources

Currency: Eastern Caribbean dollar **GDP:** ($ US) 172 million (1994) **Real GDP per capita (PPP):** ($ US) 5,137 (1994) **GDP growth rate:** 0.9% (1994) **Average annual inflation:** 2.6% (1996); 5.3% (1985–95) **Foreign debt:** ($ US) 97 million (1996) **Major trading partners:** USA, UK, Trinidad and Tobago, the Netherlands, Germany **Industries:** agricultural products (nutmeg oil distillation), rum, beer, soft drinks, cigarettes, clothing, tourism **Exports:** cocoa, bananas, cocoa, mace, fresh fruit. Principal market: UK, USA, France 18.5% each (1995) **Imports:** foodstuffs, mineral fuels, machinery and transport equipment, basic manufactures, beverages, tobacco. Principal source: USA 30% (1995) **Arable land:** 11.8% (1995) **Agricultural products:** cocoa, bananas, nutmeg (world's second-largest producer), and mace, sugar cane, fresh fruit and vegetables; livestock productions (for domestic use); fishing

Population and society

Population: 92,000 (1996 est) **Population growth rate:** 0.3% (1990–95) **Population density:** (per sq km) 269 (1996 est) **Urban population:** (% of total) 25 (1992) **Age distribution:** (% of total population) <15 35.2%, 15–65 58.2%, >65 6.6% (1993) **Ethnic groups:** majority is of black African descent **Language:** English (official); some French-African patois spoken **Religion:** Roman Catholic 53%, Anglican, Seventh Day Adventist, Pentecostal **Education:** (compulsory years) 11 **Literacy rate:** 85% (1994 est) **Labour force:** 19.8% agriculture, 24.5% industry, 55.7% services (1989) **Unemployment:** 40% (1995 est) **Life expectancy:** 68 (men); 73 (women) (1996 est) **Child mortality rate:** (under 5, per 1,000 live births) 33 (1995) **Physicians:** 1 per 1,428 people (1991)

Practical information

Visa requirements: UK: visa not required. USA: visa not required **Embassy in the UK:** 1 Collingham Gardens, London SW5 0HW. Tel: (0171) 373 7809; fax: (0171) 370 7040 **British embassy:** British High Commission, 14 Church Street, St George's. Tel: 440 3222; fax: 440 4939 **Chamber of commerce:** Grenada Chamber of Industry and Commerce, PO Box 129, Decaul Building, Mount Gay, St George's. Tel: 440 2937; fax: 440 6627 **Airports:** international airports: St George's (Point Salines); total passengers landed: 82,320 (1993) **Major holidays:** 1–2 January, 7 February, 1 May, 3–4 August, 25 October, 25–26 December; variable: Corpus Christi, Good Friday, Easter Monday, Whit Monday

Chronology

1498: Sighted by the explorer Christopher Columbus; Spanish named it Grenada since its hills were reminiscent of the Andalusian city. **1650:** Colonized by French settlers from Martinique, who faced resistance from the local Carib Indian community armed with poison arrows, before the defeated Caribs performed a mass suicide. **1783:** Ceded to Britain as a colony by the Treaty of Versailles; black African slaves imported to work cotton, sugar, and tobacco plantations. **1795:** Abortive rebellion against British rule led by Julien Fedon, a black planter inspired by the ideas of the French Revolution. **1834:** Slavery abolished. **1950:** Left-wing Grenada United Labour Party (GULP) founded by trade union leader Eric Gairy. **1951:** Universal adult suffrage granted and GULP elected to power in a nonautonomous local assembly. **1958–62:** Part of the Federation of the West Indies. **1967:** Internal self-government achieved. **1974:** Independence achieved within the Commonwealth, with Gairy as prime minister. **1979:** Autocratic Gairy removed in bloodless coup led by left-wing Maurice Bishop of the New Jewel Movement; constitution suspended and a People's Revolutionary

Government established. **1982:** Relations with the USA and Britain deteriorated as ties with Cuba and the USSR strengthened. **1983:** After attempts to improve relations with the USA, Bishop was overthrown by left-wing opponents, precipitating military coup by Gen Hudson Austin. Bishop and three colleagues executed. USA invaded, accompanied by troops from other E Caribbean countries; there were 250 fatalities. Austin arrested and 1974 constitution reinstated. **1984:** Newly formed centre-left New National Party (NNP) won general election and its leader, Herbert Blaize, became prime minister. **1989:** Blaize replaced as leader of NNP, but remained as head of government; on his death, he was succeeded by Ben Jones. **1991:** Inconclusive general election; Nicholas Braithwaite of the centrist National Democratic Congress (NDC) became prime minister. Windward Islands confederation proposed. **1995:** Braithwaite retired and was succeeded as prime minister by the new NDC leader, George Brizan. General election won by NNP, led by Keith Mitchell. A plague of pink mealy bugs caused damage to crops estimated at $60 million, depriving 15,000 farmers of an income.

Guatemala Republic of

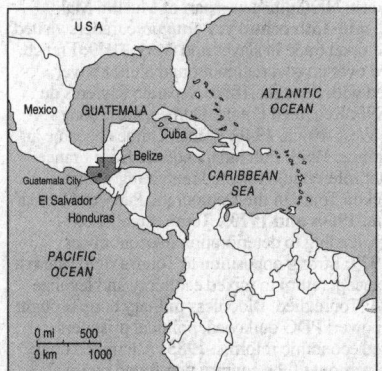

National name: *República de Guatemala* **Area:** 108,889 sq km/42,042 sq mi **Capital:** Guatemala City **Major towns/cities:** Quezaltenango, Escuintla, Puerto Barrios (naval base), Retalhuleu, Chiquimula **Physical features:** mountainous; narrow coastal plains; limestone tropical plateau in N; frequent earthquakes

Government

Head of state and government: Alvaro Arzú from 1996 **Political system:** democracy **Administrative divisions:** 22 departments **Political parties:** Guatemalan Christian Democratic Party (PDCG), Christian, centre left; Centre Party (UCN), centrist; Revolutionary Party (PR), radical; Movement of National Liberation (MLN), extreme right wing; Democratic Institutional Party (PID), moderate conservative; Solidarity and Action Movement (MAS), right of centre; Guatemalan Republican Front (FRG), right wing; National Advancement Party (PAN), right of centre; Social Democratic Party (PSD), right of centre **Armed forces:** 44,200; plus paramilitary forces of 12,300 (1996) **Conscription:** selective conscription for 30 months **Death penalty:** retained and used for ordinary crimes **Defence spend:** (% GDP) 1.4 (1996) **Education spend:** (% GNP) 1.6 (1993–94) **Health spend:** (% GDP) 0.9 (1990–95)

Economy and resources

Currency: quetzal **GDP:** ($ US) 12.9 billion (1994) **Real GDP per capita (PPP):** ($ US) 3,208 (1994) **GDP growth rate:** 4% (1994); 4.0% (1990–95) **Average annual inflation:** 11.3% (1996); 18.6% (1985–95) **Foreign debt:** ($ US) 3 billion (1996) **Major trading partners:** USA, El Salvador, Mexico, Costa Rica, Venezuela, Germany, Japan, Honduras **Resources:** petroleum, antimony, gold, silver, nickel, lead, iron, tungsten **Industries:** food processing, textiles, pharmaceuticals, chemicals, tobacco, non-metallic minerals, sugar, electrical goods, tourism **Exports:** coffee, bananas, sugar, cardamoms, shellfish, tobacco. Principal market: USA 36.6% (1996) **Imports:** raw materials and intermediate goods for industry,

consumer goods, mineral fuels and lubricants. Principal source: USA 43.9% (1996) **Arable land:** 12.5% (1995) **Agricultural products:** coffee, sugar cane, bananas, cardamoms, cotton; one of the largest sources of essential oils (citronella and lemon grass); livestock rearing; fishing (chiefly shrimp); forestry (mahogany and cedar)

Population and society

Population: 10,928,000 (1996 est) **Population growth rate:** 2.9% (1990–95); 2.7% (2000–05) **Population density:** (per sq km) 100 (1996 est) **Urban population:** (% of total) 41 (1995) **Age distribution:** (% of total population) <15 44.3%, 15–65 52.2%, >65 3.5% (1995) **Ethnic groups:** two main ethnic groups: Native Americans and ladinos (others, including Europeans, black Africans, and mestizos). Native Americans are descended from the highland Mayas **Language:** Spanish (official); 45% speak Mayan languages **Religion:** Roman Catholic 70%, Protestant 30% **Education:** (compulsory years) 6 **Literacy rate:** 63% (men); 47% (women) (1995 est) **Labour force:** 35% of population (1990): 48% agriculture, 23% industry, 29% services (1993) **Unemployment:** 6.1% (1993) **Life expectancy:** 65 (men); 70 (women) (1995–2000) **Child mortality rate:** (under 5, per 1,000 live births) 67 (1996) **Physicians:** 1 per 3,999 people (1993 est)

Practical information

Visa requirements: UK: visa required for business visits and tourist visits of over 90 days. USA: visa not required for a stay of up to 90 days **Embassy in the UK:** 13 Fawcett Street, London SW10 9HN. Tel: (0171) 351 3042; fax: (0171) 376 5708 **British embassy:** British Embassy, 7th Floor, Edificio Centro Financiero, Tower Two, 7a Avenida 5–10, Zona 4, Guatemala City. Tel: (2) 321 601/2/4; fax: (2) 341 904 **Chamber of commerce:** Cámara de Comercio de Guatemala, 10a Calle 3–80, Zona 1, Guatemala City. Tel: (2) 82681; fax: (2) 514 197 **Airports:** international airport: Guatemala City (La Aurora); over 380 airstrips serving internal travel; total passenger km: 411 million (1994) **Major holidays:** 1 January, 1 May, 30 June, 1 July, 15 September, 12, 20 October, 1 November, 24–25, 31 December; variable: Good Friday, Holy Thursday, Holy Saturday

Chronology

c. AD 250–900: Part of culturally advanced Maya civilization. **1524:** Conquered by the Spanish adventurer Pedro de Alvarado and became a Spanish colony. **1821:** Independence achieved from Spain, joining Mexico initially. **1823:** Became part of United Provinces (Federation) of Central America, also embracing Costa Rica, El Salvador, Honduras, and Nicaragua. **1839:** Achieved full independence. **1844–65:** Rafael Carrera held power as president. **1873–85:** The country was modernized on liberal lines by President Justo Rufino Barrios, the army was built up, and coffee growing introduced. **1944:** Juan José Arevalo became president, ending a period of rule by dictators. Socialist programme of reform instituted by Arevalo and his successor, from 1951, Col Jacobo Arbenz Guzman, including establishing a social security system and redistributing land expropriated from large estates to landless peasants. **1954:** Col Carlos Castillo Armas became president in US-backed coup, after United Fruit Company plantations had been nationalized by Arbenz. Land reform halted. **1963:** Castillo assassinated and military coup made Col Enrique Peralta president. **1966:** Cesar Méndez elected president as civilian rule restored. **1970s:** More than 50,000 died in a spate of political violence as the military regime sought to liquidate left-wing dissidents. **1970:** Carlos Araña elected president, with military back in power. **1976:** Earthquake killed 27,000 and left more than 1 million homeless. **1981:** Growth of antigovernment guerrilla movement. Death squads and soldiers killed an estimated 11,000 civilians during the year. **1982:** Right-wing army coup installed Gen Ríos Montt as head of junta and then as president, determined to fight corruption and end violence. **1983:** Montt removed in coup led by Gen Mejía Victores, who declared amnesty for the guerrillas. **1985:** New constitution adopted; PDCG won congressional elections; Marco Vinicio Cerezo Arevalo became civilian president. **1989:** Coup attempt against Cerezo foiled. Over 100,000 people killed and 40,000 reported missing since 1980. **1991:** Jorge Serrano Elías of MAS elected president. Diplomatic relations established with Belize, which Guatemala had long claimed. **1993:** President Serrano deposed after attempting to impose authoritarian regime; Ramiro de Leon Carpio, a human-rights ombudsman, elected president by assembly. **1994:** Peace talks held with Guatemalan Revolutionary National Unity (URNG) rebels. Right-wing parties secured a majority in congress after elections. **1995:** Government criticized by USA and United Nations for widespread human-rights abuses. First cease-fire by rebels in 30 years. **1996:** Alvaro Arzú elected president. Peace agreement ended 36-year war.

Guinea Republic of

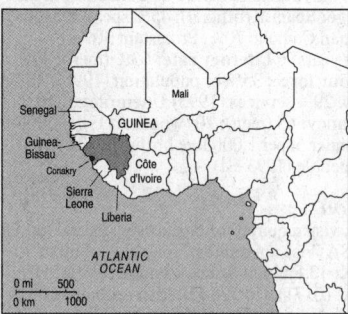

National name: *République de Guinée* **Area:** 245,857 sq km/94,925 sq mi **Capital:** Conakry **Major towns/cities:** Labé, Nzérékoré, Kankan, Kindia **Physical features:** flat coastal plain with mountainous interior; sources of rivers Niger, Gambia, and Senegal; forest in SE; Fouta Djallon, area of sandstone plateaux, cut by deep valleys

Government

Head of state and government: Lansana Conté from 1984 **Political system:** emergent democracy **Administrative divisions:** 34 provinces (including Conakry) **Political parties:** Party of Unity and Progress (PUP), centrist; Rally of the Guinean People (RPG), left of centre; Union of the New Republic (UNR), left of centre; Party for Renewal and Progress (PRP), left of centre **Armed forces:** 9,700; plus paramilitary forces of 9,600 (1996) **Conscription:** military service is compulsory for two years **Death penalty:** retained and used for ordinary crimes **Defence spend:** (% GDP) 1.9 (1996) **Education spend:** (% GNP) 2.2 (1993) **Health spend:** (% GDP) 0.9 (1990–95)

Economy and resources

Currency: Guinean franc **GDP:** ($ US) 3.4 billion (1994) **Real GDP per capita (PPP):** ($ US) 1,103 (1994) **GDP growth rate:** 4% (1994); 3.8% (1990–95) **Average annual inflation:** 10% (1996); 16.8% (1985–95 est) **Foreign debt:** ($ US) 3.24 billion (1995) **Major trading partners:** France, USA, Belgium, Hong Kong, Spain, Ireland, Côte d'Ivoire **Resources:** bauxite (world's top exporter of bauxite and second-largest producer of bauxite ore), alumina, diamonds, gold, granite, iron ore, uranium, nickel, cobalt, platinum **Industries:** processing of agricultural products, cement, beer, soft drinks, cigarettes **Exports:** bauxite, alumina, diamonds, coffee. Principal market: USA 16.1% (1995) **Imports:** foodstuffs, mineral fuels, semi-manufactured goods, consumer goods, textiles and clothing, machinery and transport equipment. Principal source: France 23.3% (1995) **Arable land:** 2.8% (1995) **Agricultural products:** cassava, millet, rice, fruits, oil palm, groundnuts, coffee, vegetables, sweet potatoes, yams, maize; livestock rearing (cattle); fishing; forestry

Population and society

Population: 7,518,000 (1996 est) **Population growth rate:** 3% (1990–95); 2.9% (2000–05) **Population density:** (per sq km) 31 (1996 est) **Urban population:** (% of total) 30 (1995) **Age distribution:** (% of total population) <15 47.1%, 15–65 50.3%, >65 2.6% (1995) **Ethnic groups:** 24 ethnic groups, including the Malinke, Peul, and Soussou **Language:** French (official), African languages (of which eight are official) **Religion:** Muslim 95%,

Christian **Education:** (compulsory years) 6 **Literacy rate:** 35% (men); 13% (women) (1995 est) **Labour force:** 49% of population: 87% agriculture, 2% industry, 11% services (1990) **Life expectancy:** 46 (men); 47 (women) (1995–2000) **Child mortality rate:** (under 5, per 1,000 live births) 196 (1996) **Physicians:** 1 per 7,445 people (1993 est)

Practical information

Visa requirements: UK: visa required. USA: visa required **Embassy for the UK:** 51 rue de la Faisanderie, 75016 Paris, France. Tel: (1) 4704 8148; fax: (1) 4704 5765 **British embassy:** British Consulate, BP 834, Conakry. (All staff based in Dakar, Senegal.) Tel: (224) 442 959; fax: (224) 414 215 **Chamber of commerce:** Chambre de Commerce, d'Industrie et d'Agriculture de Guinée, BP 545, Conakry. Tel: (224) 444 495; telex: 609 **Airports:** international airport: Conakry; eight domestic airports; total passenger km: 33 million (1994) **Major holidays:** 1 January, 3 April, 1 May, 15 August, 2 October, 1 November, 25 December; variable: Eid-ul-Adha, Easter Monday, end of Ramadan, Prophet's Birthday

Chronology

c. AD 900: The Susi people, a community related to the Malinke, immigrated from NE, pushing the indigenous Baga towards the Atlantic coast. **13th century:** Susi kingdoms established, extending their influence to the coast; NE Guinea was part of Muslim Mali Empire, centred to NE. **mid-15th century:** Portuguese traders visited the coast and later developed trade in slaves and ivory. **1849:** French protectorate established over coastal region around Nunez River, which was administered with Senegal. **1890:** Separate Rivières du Sud colony formed. **1895:** Renamed French Guinea, the colony became part of French West Africa. **1946:** French Guinea became an overseas territory of France. **1958:** Full independence from France achieved as Guinea after referendum rejected remaining within French Community; Sékou Touré of the Democratic Party of Guinea (PDG) elected president. **1960s and 1970s:** Touré established socialist one-party state, leading to deterioration in economy as 200,000 fled abroad. **1979:** Strong opposition to Touré's rigid Marxist policies forced him to accept return to mixed economy and legalize private enterprise. **1984:** Touré died. Bloodless military coup brought Col Lansana Conté to power; PDG outlawed, political prisoners released; market-centred economic reforms. **1985:** Attempted coup against Conté while he was out of the country was foiled by loyal troops. **1991:** Antigovernment general strike and mass protests. **1992:** Constitution amended to allow for multiparty politics. **1993:** Conté narrowly re-elected in first direct presidential election. **1995:** Assembly elections won by Conté's supporters. **1996:** Attempted military coup thwarted.

Guinea-Bissau Republic of (formerly Portuguese Guinea)

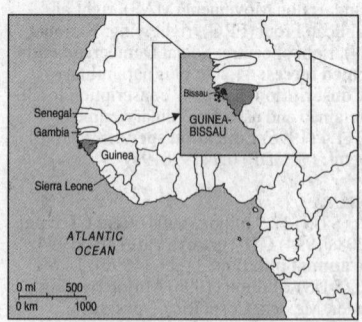

National name: *República da Guiné-Bissau* **Area:** 36,125 sq km/13,947 sq mi **Capital:** Bissau (main port) **Major towns/cities:** Mansôa, São Domingos, Bolama/Bijagós, Catio, Buba, Butata, Farim, Cacine **Physical features:** flat coastal plain rising to savanna in E

Government

Head of state: João Bernardo Vieira from 1980 **Head of government:** Carlos Correia from 1997 **Political system:** emergent democracy **Administrative divisions:** eight regions **Political parties:**

African Party for the Independence of Portuguese Guinea and Cape Verde (PAIGC), nationalist socialist; Party for Social Renovation (PRS), left of centre; Guinea-Bissau Resistance–Bafata Movement (PRGB-MB), centrist **Armed forces:** 7,300; plus paramilitary gendarmerie of 2,000 (1996) **Conscription:** selective conscription **Death penalty:** abolished 1993 **Defence spend:** (% GDP) 2.9 (1996) **Education spend:** (% GNP) 2.8 (1990) **Health spend:** (% GDP) 1.1 (1990–95)

Economy and resources

Currency: Guinean peso **GDP:** ($ US) 0.2 billion (1994) **Real GDP per capita (PPP):** ($ US) 793 (1994) **GDP growth rate:** 6.9% (1994); 3.5% (1990–95) **Average annual inflation:** 40% (1996); 62.8% (1985–95) **Foreign debt:** ($ US) 894 million (1995) **Major trading partners:** Spain, Thailand, India, Portugal, Côte d'Ivoire, the Netherlands, Japan **Resources:** bauxite, phosphate, petroleum (largely unexploited) **Industries:** food processing, brewing, cotton processing, fish and timber processing **Exports:** cashew nuts, palm kernels, groundnuts, fish and shrimp, timber. Principal market: Spain 38% (1995) **Imports:** foodstuffs, machinery and transport equipment, fuels, construction materials. Principal source: Thailand 26.6% (1995) **Arable land:** 10.7% (1995) **Agricultural products:** groundnuts, sugar cane, plantains, palm kernels, rice, coconuts, millet, sorghum, maize, cashew nuts; fishing; forest resources

Population and society

Population: 1,091,000 (1996 est) **Population growth rate:** 2.1% (1990–95); 2.1% (2000–05) **Population density:** (per sq km) 30 (1996 est) **Urban population:** (% of total) 22 (1995) **Age distribution:** (% of total population) <15 41.7%, 15–65 54.2%, >65 4.1% (1995) **Ethnic groups:** majority originated in Africa, and comprises five main ethnic groups: the Balante in the central region, the Fulani in the N, the Malinke in the northern central area, and the Mandyako and Pepel near the coast **Language:** Portuguese (official); Crioulo (Cape Verdean dialect of Portuguese), African languages **Religion:** animist 65%, Muslim 38%, Christian 5% (mainly Roman Catholic) **Education:** (compulsory years) 6 **Literacy rate:** 50% (men); 24% (women) (1995 est) **Labour force:** 48% of population: 85% agriculture, 2% industry, 13% services (1990) **Unemployment:** 5.1% (1992) **Life expectancy:** 44 (men); 47 (women) (1995–2000) **Child mortality rate:** (under 5, per 1,000 live births) 203 (1996) **Physicians:** 1 per 7,473 person (1991)

Practical information

Visa requirements: UK: visa required. USA: visa required **Embassy in the UK:** Consulate General of the Republic of Guinea-Bissau, 8 Palace Gate, London W8 4RP. Tel: (0171) 589 5253; fax: (0171) 589 9590 **British embassy:** British Consulate, Maregro Int., CP 100, Bissau. (All staff reside at Dakar, Senegal.) Tel: (245) 201 224; fax: (245) 201 265 **Chamber of commerce:** Associacão Comercial e Industrial e Agricola da Guiné-Bissau, Bissau. Tel/fax: (245) 201 602 **Airports:** international airport: Bissau (Bissalanca); ten domestic airports; total passenger km: 10 million (1994) **Major holidays:** 1, 20 January, 8 February, 8 March, 1 May, 3 August, 12, 24 September, 14 November, 25 December

Chronology

10th century: Known as Gabu, became a tributary kingdom of the Mali Empire to NE. **1446:** Portuguese arrived, establishing nominal control over coastal areas and capturing slaves to send to Cape Verde. **1546:** Gabu kingdom became independent of Mali and survived until 1867. **1879:** Portugal, which had formerly administered the area with Cape Verde islands, created the separate colony of Portuguese Guinea. **by 1915:** The interior had been subjugated by the Portuguese. **1956:** African Party for the Independence of Portuguese Guinea and Cape Verde (PAIGC) formed to campaign for independence from Portugal. **1961:** The PAIGC began to wage a guerrilla campaign against Portuguese rule. **1973:** Independence was declared in the two-thirds of the country that had fallen under the control of the PAIGC; heavy losses sustained by Portuguese troops who tried to put down the uprising. **1974:** Independence separately from Cape Verde accepted by

Portugal, with Luiz Cabral (PAIGC) president. **1980:** Cabral deposed, and João Vieira became chair of a council of revolution. **1981:** PAIGC confirmed as the only legal party, with Vieira as its secretary general; Cape Verde decided not to form a union. **1984:** New constitution made Vieira head of both government and state. **1991:** Other parties legalized in response to public pressure. **1994:** PAIGC secured a clear assembly majority and Vieira narrowly won first multiparty presidential elections. **1997:** Carlos Correia appointed prime minister.

Guyana Cooperative Republic of

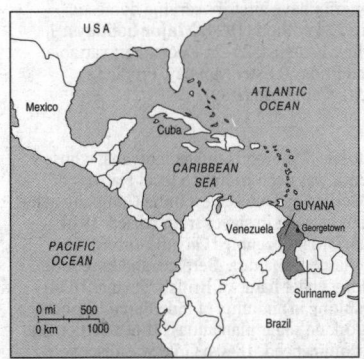

Area: 214,969 sq km/82,999 sq mi **Capital:** Georgetown (and port) **Major towns/cities:** Linden, New Amsterdam, Rose Hall, Corriverton **Major ports:** New Amsterdam **Physical features:** coastal plain rises into rolling highlands with savanna in S; mostly tropical rainforest; Mount Roraima; Kaietur National Park, including Kaietur Falls on the Potaro (tributary of Essequibo) 250 m/821 ft

Government

Head of state: Janet Jagan from 1997 **Head of government:** Samuel Hinds from 1992 **Political system:** democracy **Administrative divisions:** ten regions **Political parties:** People's National Congress (PNC), Afro-Guyanan, nationalist socialist; People's Progressive Party (PPP), Indian-based, left wing **Armed forces:** 1,600; plus a paramilitary force of 1,500 (1996) **Conscription:** military service is voluntary **Death penalty:** retained and used for ordinary crimes **Defence spend:** (% GDP) 1 (1996) **Education spend:** (% GNP) 5.0 (1993–94)

Economy and resources

Currency: Guyana dollar **GDP:** ($ US) 540 million (1994 est) **Real GDP per capita (PPP):** ($ US) 2,730 (1994) **GDP growth rate:** 8.5% (1994) **Average annual inflation:** 6.5% (1996); 51.1% (1985–95) **Foreign debt:** ($ US) 1.73 billion (1996) **Major trading partners:** USA, Canada, UK, Trinidad and Tobago, Italy, France, Japan **Resources:** gold, diamonds, bauxite, copper, tungsten, iron, nickel, quartz, molybdenum **Industries:** agro-processing (sugar, rice, coconuts, and timber), mining, rum, pharmaceuticals, textiles **Exports:** sugar, bauxite, alumina, rice, gold, rum, timber, molasses, shrimp. Principal market: Canada 24.9% (1995) **Imports:** mineral fuels and lubricants, machinery, capital goods, consumer goods. Principal source: USA 30.8% (1995) **Arable land:** 2.4% (1995) **Agricultural products:** sugar cane, rice, coffee, cocoa, coconuts, copra, tobacco, fruit and vegetables; forestry (timber production; approximately 76% of total land area was forested 1993)

Population and society

Population: 838,000 (1996 est) **Population growth rate:** 0.9% (1990–95); 1.1% (2000–05) **Population density:** (per sq km) 4 (1996 est) **Urban population:** (% of total) 36 (1995) **Age distribution:** (% of total population) <15 32.2%, 15–65 63.7%, >65 4% (1995) **Ethnic groups:** about 51% descended from settlers from the subcontinent of India; about 43% Afro-Indian; small minorities of Native Americans, Chinese, and Europeans **Language:** English (official), Hindi, Native American languages **Religion:** Hindu 54%, Christian 27%, Sunni Muslim 15% **Education:** (compulsory years) 10 **Literacy rate:** 98% (men); 97% (women) (1995 est) **Labour force:** 40% of population

(1990): 27% agriculture, 26% industry, 47% services (1993)
Unemployment: 13.5% (1991) **Life expectancy:** 65 (men); 70
(women) (1995–2000) **Child mortality rate:** (under 5, per 1,000 live
births) 60 (1996) **Physicians:** 1 per 3,360 people (1991)

Practical information
Visa requirements: UK: visa not required. USA: visa not required
Embassy in the UK: 3 Palace Court, Bayswater Road, London W2
4LP. Tel: (0171) 229 7684; fax: (0171) 727 9809 **British embassy:**
British High Commission, PO Box 10849, 44 Main Street,
Georgetown. Tel: (2) 65881–4; fax: (2) 53555 **Chamber of
commerce:** Georgetown Chamber of Commerce and Industry, PO
Box 10110, 156 Waterloo Street, Cumminsburg, Georgetown. Tel: (2)
63519 **Airports:** international airport: Georgetown (Timehri); the
larger settlements in the interior have airstrips serving domestic
flights; total passenger km: 224 million (1994) **Major holidays:** 1
January, 23 February, 1 May, 1 August, 25–26 December; variable:
Eid-ul-Adha, Diwali, Good Friday, Easter Monday, Prophet's
Birthday, Phagwah (March), Caribbean (July)

Chronology
1498: The explorer Christopher Columbus sighted Guyana, whose
name, 'land of many waters', was derived from a local Native
American word. **c. 1620:** Settled by Dutch West India Company, who
established armed bases and brought in slaves from Africa. **1814:**
After period of French rule, Britain occupied Guyana during the
Napoleonic Wars and purchased Demerara, Berbice, and Essequibo.
1831: Became British colony under name of British Guiana. **1834:**
Slavery was abolished, resulting in an influx of indentured labourers
from India and China to work on sugar plantations. **1860:** Settlement
of the Rupununi Savanna commenced. **1860s:** Gold was discovered.
1899: International arbitration tribunal found in favour of British
Guiana in a long-running dispute with Venezuela over lands W of
Essequibo River. **1953:** Assembly elections won by left-wing People's
Progressive Party (PPP), drawing most support from the Indian
community; Britain suspended constitution and installed interim
administration, fearing communist takeover. **1961:** Internal self-
government granted; Cheddi Jagan (PPP) became prime minister.
1964: PNC leader Forbes Burnham led PPP–PNC coalition; racial
violence between the Asian- and African-descended communities.
1966: Independence achieved from Britain as Guyana, with Burnham
as prime minister. **1970:** Guyana became a republic within the
Commonwealth, with Raymond Arthur Chung as president; Burnham
remained as prime minister. **1980:** Burnham became first executive
president under new constitution, which ended the three-year boycott
of parliament by the PPP. **1985:** Burnham died; succeeded by
Desmond Hoyte (PNC), as economy deteriorated. **1992:** PPP had
decisive victory in first completely free assembly elections for 20
years; Cheddi Jagan became president; privatization programme
launched. **1997:** Samuel Hinds became interim president on the death
of Cheddi Jagan. Cheddi Jagan's wife Janet Jagan elected president.

Haiti Republic of

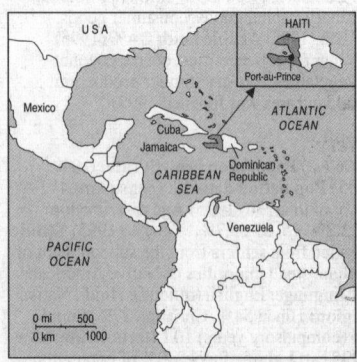

National name:
République d'Haïti
Area: 27,750 sq
km/10,714 sq mi
Capital: Port-au-
Prince **Major
towns/cities:** Cap-
Haïtien, Gonaïves,
Les Cayes, Port-de-
Paix, Jérémie,
Jacmée, St Marc
Physical features:
mainly mountainous
and tropical; occupies
western third of
Hispaniola Island in
Caribbean Sea

Government
Head of state: René Preval from 1995 **Head of government:** Herve
Denis from 1997 **Political system:** transitional **Administrative
divisions:** nine departments **Political parties:** National Front for
Change and Democracy (FNCD), left of centre; Lavalas Political
Organization, populist **Armed forces:** 7,300 (1994); armed forces
effectively dissolved 1995 following restoration of civilian rule
1994; a 4,000-strong civilian police force has been formed
Conscription: military service is voluntary **Death penalty:**
abolished 1987 **Defence spend:** (% GDP) 3.5 (1996) **Education
spend:** (% GNP) 1.4 (1993–94) **Health spend:** (% GDP) 1.3
(1990–95)

Economy and resources
Currency: gourde **GDP:** ($ US) 1.6 billion (1994) **Real GDP per
capita (PPP):** ($ US) 896 (1994) **GDP growth rate:** –13.2%
(1994); –6.5% (1990–95) **Average annual inflation:** 22% (1996);
14.7% (1985–95) **Foreign debt:** ($ US) 807 million (1995) **Major
trading partners:** USA, the Netherlands, Antilles, France, Italy,
Germany, Japan, UK **Resources:** marble, limestone, calcareous
clay, unexploited copper and gold deposits **Industries:** food
processing, metal products, machinery, textiles, chemicals, clothing,
toys, electronic and electrical equipment, tourism; much of industry
closed down during the international embargo imposed by the UN
after Aristide was deposed 1991 **Exports:** manufactured articles,
coffee, essential oils, sisal. Principal market: USA 73.5% (1995)
Imports: food and live animals, mineral fuels and lubricants,
textiles, machinery, chemicals, pharmaceuticals, raw materials,
vehicles. Principal source: USA 65% (1995) **Arable land:** 20.3%
(1995) **Agricultural products:** coffee, sugar cane, rice, maize,
sorghum, cocoa, sisal, sweet potatoes, bananas, cotton

Population and society
Population: 7,259,000 (1996 est) **Population growth rate:** 2%
(1990–95); 2.1% (2000–05) **Population density:** (per sq km) 262
(1996 est) **Urban population:** (% of total) 32 (1995) **Age
distribution:** (% of total population) <15 40.2%, 15–65 55.9%, >65
3.9% (1995) **Ethnic groups:** about 95% black African descent, the
remainder are mulattos or Europeans **Language:** French (official,
spoken by literate 10% minority), Creole (official) **Religion:**
Christian 95% (of which 80% are Roman Catholic), voodoo 4%
Education: (compulsory years) 6 **Literacy rate:** 59% (men); 47%
(women) (1995 est) **Labour force:** 45% of population: 68%
agriculture, 9% industry, 23% services (1990) **Unemployment:**
12.7% (1994) **Life expectancy:** 57 (men); 60 (women)
(1995–2000) **Child mortality rate:** (under 5, per 1,000 live births)
104 (1996) **Physicians:** 1 per 10,855 people (1993)

Practical information
Visa requirements: UK: visa not required. USA: visa not required
Embassy for the UK: BP 25, 160A avenue Louise, B-1050
Brussels, Belgium. Tel: (2) 649 7381; fax: (2) 640 6080 **British
embassy:** British Consulate, PO Box 1302, Hotel Montana, rue F
Cardoza, Bourchon, Port-au-Prince. (All staff reside at Kingston,
Jamaica.) Tel: (509) 573 969; fax: (509) 574 048 **Chamber of
commerce:** Chambre de Commerce et de l'Industrie de Haiti, BP
982, Harry Truman Boulevard, Port-au-Prince. Tel: (509) 222 475;
fax: (509) 220 281 **Airports:** international airport: Port-au-Prince
(Mais Gaté); one domestic airport (Cap-Haïtien) and four smaller
airfields **Major holidays:** 1–2 January, 14 April, 1 May, 15 August,
17, 24 October, 1–2, 18 November, 5, 25 December; variable:
Ascension Thursday, Carnival, Corpus Christi, Good Friday

Chronology
14th century: Settled by Carib Indians, who followed an earlier
wave of Arawak Indian immigration. **1492:** The first landing place
of the explorer Christopher Columbus in the New World, who
named the island Hispaniola ('Little Spain'). **1496:** At Santo
Domingo, now in the Dominican Republic to the E, the Spanish
established the first European settlement in the Western hemisphere,
which became capital of all Spanish colonies in America. **first half
of 16th century:** A third of a million Arawaks and Caribs died, as a
result of enslavement and exposure to European diseases; black

African slaves were consequently brought in to work the island's gold and silver mines, which were swiftly exhausted. **1697:** Spain ceded western third of Hispaniola to France, which became known as Haiti, but kept the E, which was known as Santo Domingo (the Dominican Republic). **1804:** Independence achieved after uprising against French colonial rule led by the former slave Toussaint l'Ouverture, who died in prison 1803, and Jean-Jacques Dessalines. **1818–43:** Ruled by Jean-Pierre Boyer, who excluded the blacks from power. **1821:** Santo Domingo fell under the control of Haiti until 1844. **1847–59:** Blacks reasserted themselves under President Faustin Soulouque. **1915:** Haiti invaded by USA as a result of political instability caused by black-mulatto friction; remained under US control until 1934. **1956:** Dr François Duvalier (Papa Doc), a voodoo physician, seized power in military coup and was elected president one year later. **1964:** Duvalier pronounced himself president for life, establishing a dictatorship based around a personal militia, the Tonton Macoutes. **1971:** Duvalier died, succeeded by his son Jean-Claude (Baby Doc); thousands murdered during Duvalier era. **1986:** Duvalier deposed and fled the country; replaced by Lt-Gen Henri Namphy as head of a governing council. **1988:** Leslie Manigat became president, but was ousted in military coup by Brig-Gen Prosper Avril, who installed a civilian government under military control. **1989:** Coup attempt against Avril foiled; US aid resumed. **1990:** Left-wing Catholic priest Jean-Bertrand Aristide elected president. **1991:** Aristide overthrown in military coup led by Brig-Gen Raoul Cedras. Sanctions imposed by Organization of American States (OAS) and USA. **1993:** United Nations (UN) embargo imposed. Aristide's return blocked by military. **1994:** Threat of US invasion led to regime recognizing Aristide as president, under agreement brokered by former US president Jimmy Carter. US troops landed peacefully; Cedras relinquished power and withdrew to Panama; Aristide returned. **1995:** UN peacekeepers drafted in to replace US troops. Assembly elections won by Aristide's supporters. René Preval elected to replace Aristide as president. **1996:** Peaceful handover of power to Preval. **1997:** Prime Minister Smarth resigned, following a series of strikes and protests; he was replaced by Herve Denis.

Honduras Republic of

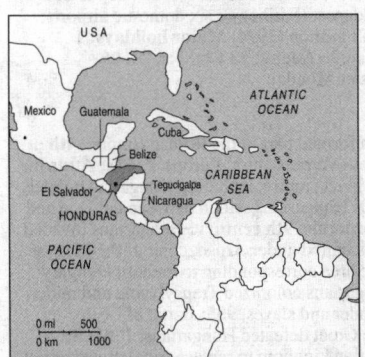

National name: *República de Honduras* **Area:** 112,100 sq km/43,281 sq mi **Capital:** Tegucigalpa **Major towns/cities:** San Pedro Sula, La Ceiba, El Progreso, Choluteca, Juticalpa, Danlí **Major ports:** La Ceiba, Puerto Cortés **Physical features:** narrow tropical coastal plain with mountainous interior, Bay Islands, Caribbean reefs

Government

Head of state and government: Carlos Flores from 1997 **Political system:** democracy **Administrative divisions:** 18 departments **Political parties:** Liberal Party of Honduras (PLH), centre left; National Party of Honduras (PNH), right wing **Armed forces:** 18,800; plus paramilitary forces numbering 5,500 (1996) **Conscription:** military service is voluntary (conscription abolished 1995) **Death penalty:** abolished 1956 **Defence spend:** (% GDP) 1.3 (1996) **Education spend:** (% GNP) 4 (1994) **Health spend:** (% GDP) 2.8 (1990–95)

Economy and resources

Currency: lempira **GDP:** ($ US) 3.3 billion (1994) **Real GDP per capita (PPP):** ($ US) 2,050 (1994) **GDP growth rate:** –1.4% (1994); 3.5% (1990–95) **Average annual inflation:** 26% (1996); 14.2% (1985–95) **Foreign debt:** ($ US) 4.7 billion (1996) **Major trading partners:** USA, Guatemala, Japan, El Salvador, Germany, Belgium, UK **Resources:** lead, zinc, silver, gold, tin, iron, copper, antimony **Industries:** food processing, petroleum refining, cement, beverages, wood products, chemical products, textiles, beer, rum **Exports:** bananas, lobsters and prawns, zinc, meat. Principal market: USA 68.5% (1995) **Imports:** machinery, appliances and electrical equipment, mineral fuels and lubricants, chemical products, consumer goods. Principal source: USA 55.5% (1995) **Arable land:** 15.1% (1995) **Agricultural products:** coffee, bananas, maize, sorghum, plantains, beans, rice, sugar cane, citrus fruits; fishing (notably shellfish); livestock rearing (cattle); timber production

Population and society

Population: 5,816,000 (1996 est) **Population growth rate:** 3% (1990–95); 2.5% (2000–05) **Population density:** (per sq km) 52 (1996 est) **Urban population:** (% of total) 44 (1995) **Age distribution:** (% of total population) <15 43.8%, 15–65 53.1%, >65 3.1% (1995) **Ethnic groups:** about 90% of mixed Native American and Spanish descent (known as ladinos or mestizos); there are also Salvadorean, Guatemalan, American, and European minorities **Language:** Spanish (official); English, Native American languages **Religion:** Roman Catholic **Education:** (compulsory years) 6 **Literacy rate:** 75% (men); 71% (women) (1995 est) **Labour force:** 34% of population: 43.5% agriculture, 19.2% industry, 37.3% services (1994) **Unemployment:** 40% (1994 est) **Life expectancy:** 68 (men); 72 (women) (1995–2000) **Child mortality rate:** (under 5, per 1,000 live births) 50 (1996) **Physicians:** 1 per 1,266 people (1993 est)

Practical information

Visa requirements: UK: visa not required with full British passport. USA: visa not required **Embassy in the UK:** 115 Gloucester Place, London W1H 3PJ. Tel: (0171) 486 4880; fax: (0171) 486 4550 **British embassy:** Apartado Postal 290, Edificio Palmira, 3 º Piso, Colonia Palmira, Tegucigalpa. Tel: (504) 325 429; fax: (504) 325 480 **Chamber of commerce:** Federación de Cámaras de Comercio e Industrias de Honduras, Apartado Postal 3393, Edificio Castañito 2 º Nivel, 6a Avenida, Colonia Los Castaños, Tegucigalpa. Tel: (504) 326 083; fax: (504) 321 870 **Airports:** international airports: Tegucigalpa (Toncontín), San Pedro Sula, Roatún, La Ceiba; over 30 smaller airports serving domestic flights; total passenger km: 323 million (1994) **Major holidays:** 1 January, 14 April, 1 May, 15 September, 3, 12, 21 October, 25, 31 December; variable: Good Friday, Holy Thursday

Chronology

c. AD 250–900: Part of culturally advanced Maya civilization. **1502:** Visited by Christopher Columbus, who named the country Honduras ('depths') after the deep waters off the N coast. **1525:** Colonized by Spain, who founded the town of Trujillo, but met with fierce resistance from the Native American population. **17th century onwards:** The northern 'Mosquito Coast' fell under the control of British buccaneers, as the Spanish concentrated on the inland area, with a British protectorate being established over the coast until 1860. **1821:** Achieved independence from Spain and became part of Mexico. **1823:** Became part of United Provinces (Federation) of Central America, also embracing Costa Rica, El Salvador, Guatemala, and Nicaragua, with the Honduran liberal Gen Francisco Morazan, president of the Federation from 1830. **1838:** Achieved full independence when the federation dissolved. **1880:** Capital transferred from Comayagua to Tegucigalpa. **later 19th–early 20th centuries:** The USA's economic involvement significant, with banana production, which provided two-thirds of exports in 1913, being controlled by the United Fruit Company; political instability, with frequent changes of constitution and military coups. **1925:** Brief civil war. **1932–49:** Under a right-wing National Party (PNH) dictatorship, led by Gen Tiburcio Carias Andino. **1963–74:** Following a series of military coups, Gen Oswaldo López Arelano held power, before resigning after allegedly accepting bribes from a US company. **1969:** Brief 'Football War' with El Salvador, which attacked Honduras at the time of a football competition between the two states, following evictions of thousands of Salvadoran illegal immigrants from Honduras. **1980:** First civilian government in more than a century elected, with Dr Roberto Suazo of the centrist Liberal Party (PLH) as president, but the commander in chief of the army, Gen Gustavo Alvárez, retained considerable power. **1983:** Close involvement with the USA in providing naval and air bases and allowing Nicaraguan counter-revolutionaries ('Contras') to operate from Honduras. **1984:** Alvarez ousted in coup led by junior officers led by Gen Walter López Reyes, resulting in policy review towards USA and Nicaragua. **1986:** José Azcona del Hoyo (PLH) elected president after electoral law changed, making Suazo ineligible for presidency, and despite receiving fewer votes than his opponent. **1989:** Government and opposition declared support for Central American peace plan to demobilize Nicaraguan Contras (thought to number 55,000 with their dependents) based in Honduras. PNH won assembly elections; its leader, Rafael Leonardo Callejas Romero, elected president. **1992:** Border dispute with El Salvador dating from 1861 finally resolved. **1993:** PLH, under Carlos Roberto Reina Idiaquez, won assembly and presidential elections. **1997:** Carlos Flores (PLH) elected president.

Hungary Republic of

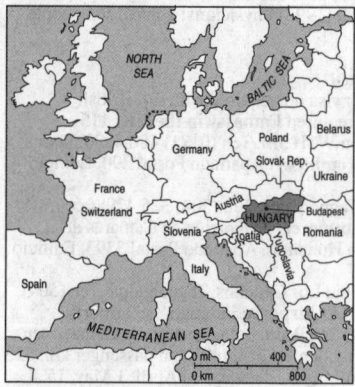

National name: *Magyar Köztársaság* **Area:** 93,032 sq km/35,919 sq mi **Capital:** Budapest **Major towns/cities:** Miskolc, Debrecen, Szeged, Pécs, Gyor, Nyiregyháza, Székesfehérvár, Kecskemét **Physical features:** Great Hungarian Plain covers eastern half of country; Bakony Forest, Lake Balaton, and Transdanubian Highlands in the W; rivers Danube, Tisza, and Raba; more than 500 thermal springs

Government

Head of state: Arpád Göncz from 1990 **Head of government:** Gyula Horn from 1994 **Political system:** emergent democracy **Administrative divisions:** 19 counties and the capital city (with 22 districts) **Political parties:** over 50, including Hungarian Socialist Party (HSP), reform-socialist; Alliance of Free Democrats (AFD), centrist, radical free market; Hungarian Democratic Forum (MDF), nationalist, centre right; Independent Smallholders Party (ISP), right of centre, agrarian; Christian Democratic People's Party (KDNP), right of centre; Federation of Young Democrats, liberal, anticommunist **Armed forces:** 64,300 (1996) **Conscription:** 12 months (men aged 18–23) **Death penalty:** abolished 1990 **Defence spend:** (% GDP) 1.7 (1996) **Education spend:** (% GNP) 6.3 (1994) **Health spend:** (% GDP) 6.8 (1990–95)

Economy and resources

Currency: forint **GDP:** ($ US) 41.4 billion (1994) **Real GDP per capita (PPP):** ($ US) 6,437 (1994) **GDP growth rate:** 1% (1996);

−1% (1990–95) **Average annual inflation:** 24% (1996); 19.9% (1985–95) **Foreign debt:** ($ US) 29.4 billion (1996) **Major trading partners:** Germany, CIS countries, Italy, Austria, USA **Resources:** lignite, brown coal, natural gas, petroleum, bauxite, hard coal **Industries:** food and beverages, tobacco, steel, chemicals, petroleum and plastics, engineering, transport equipment, pharmaceuticals, textiles, cement **Exports:** raw materials, semi-finished products, industrial consumer goods, food and agricultural products, transport equipment. Principal market: Germany 29% (1996) **Imports:** mineral fuels, raw materials, semi-finished products, transport equipment, food products, consumer goods. Principal source: Germany 23.6% (1996) **Arable land:** 52% (1995) **Agricultural products:** wheat, maize, sugar beet, barley, potatoes, sunflowers, grapes; livestock and dairy products

Population and society

Population: 10,049,000 (1996 est) **Population growth rate:** −0.5% (1990–95); −0.3% (2000–05) **Population density:** (per sq km) 108 (1996 est) **Urban population:** (% of total) 65 (1995) **Age distribution:** (% of total population) <15 18.1%, 15–65 67.9%, >65 14% (1995) **Ethnic groups:** 93% indigenous, or Magyar; there is a large Romany community of around 600,000; other ethnic minorities include Germans, Croats, Romanians, Slovaks, Serbs, and Slovenes **Language:** Hungarian (or Magyar), one of the few languages of Europe with non-Indo-European origins; it is grouped with Finnish, Estonian, and others in the Finno-Ugric family **Religion:** Roman Catholic 67%, Calvinist 20%, other Christian denominations, Jewish **Education:** (compulsory years) 10 **Literacy rate:** 99% (men); 99% (women) (1995 est) **Labour force:** 39.7% of population: 8.4% agriculture, 33% industry, 58.6% services (1996) **Unemployment:** 11% (1996) **Life expectancy:** 65 (men); 74 (women) (1995–2000) **Child mortality rate:** (under 5, per 1,000 live births) 17 (1996) **Physicians:** 1 per 241 people (1994)

Practical information

Visa requirements: UK: visa not required. USA: visa not required **Embassy in the UK:** 35 Eaton Place, London SW1X 8BY. Tel: (0171) 235 4048; fax: (0171) 823 1348 **British embassy:** Harmincad Utca 6, 1051 Budapest. Tel: (1) 266 2888; fax: (1) 266 0907 **Chamber of commerce:** Magyar Kereskedelmi és Iparkamara (Hungarian Chamber of Commerce and Industry), PO Box 106, H-1389 Budapest. Tel: (1) 153 3333; fax: (1) 153 1285 **Airports:** international airport: Budapest (Ferihegy); six domestic airports; total passenger km: 1,653 million (1994) **Major holidays:** 1 January, 15 March, 1 May, 20 August, 23 October, 25–26 December; variable: Easter Monday

Chronology

1st century AD: Region formed part of the Roman Empire. **4th century:** Germanic tribes overran central Europe. **c. 445:** Attila the Hun established a short-lived empire, including Hungarian nomads living far to the E. **c. 680:** Hungarians settled between the Don and Dniepr rivers under Khazar rule. **9th century:** Hungarians invaded central Europe; ten tribes united under Árpád, chief of the Magyar tribe, who conquered the area corresponding to modern Hungary 896. **10th century:** Hungarians colonized Transylvania and raided their neighbours for plunder and slaves. **955:** Battle of Lech: Germans led by Otto the Great defeated Hungarians. **1001:** St Stephen founded Hungarian kingdom to replace tribal organization and converted Hungarians to Christianity. **12th century:** Hungary became a major power when King Béla III won temporary supremacy over the Balkans. **1308–86:** Angevin dynasty ruled after Arpádian line died out. **1456:** Battle of Belgrade: János Hunyadi defeated Ottoman Turks and saved Hungary from invasion. **1458–90:** Under Mátyás I Corvinus, Hungary enjoyed military success and cultural renaissance. **1526:** Battle of Mohács: Turks under Suleiman the Magnificent decisively defeated Hungarians. **16th century:** Partition of Hungary between Turkey, Austria, and semi-autonomous Transylvania. **1699:** Treaty of Karlowitz: Austrians expelled the Turks from Hungary, which was reunified under Habsburg rule. **1707:** Prince Ferenc Rákóczi II led uprising against Austrians, who promised to respect Hungarian constitution 1711. **1780–90:** Joseph II's attempts to impose uniform administration throughout Austrian Empire provoked nationalist reaction among Hungarian nobility. **early 19th century:** 'National Revival' movement led by Count Stephen Széchenyi and Lajos Kossuth. **1848:** Hungarian Revolution: nationalists proclaimed self-government; Croat minority resisted Hungarian rule. **1849:** Kossuth repudiated Habsburg monarchy; Austrians crushed revolution with Russian support. **1867:** Austria conceded equality to Hungary within the dual monarchy of Austria-Hungary. **1918:** Austria-Hungary collapsed in military defeat; Count Mihály Károlyi proclaimed Hungarian Republic. **1919:** Communists took power under Béla Kun; Romanians invaded; Admiral Miklós Horthy overthrew Béla Kun. **1920:** Treaty of Trianon: Hungary lost 72% of its territory to Czechoslovakia, Romania, and Yugoslavia; Horthy restored Kingdom of Hungary with himself as regent. **1921:** Count István Bethlen became prime minister of authoritarian aristocratic regime. **1938–41:** Diplomatic collaboration with Germany allowed Hungary to regain territories lost 1920; Hungary declared war on USSR in alliance with Germany 1941. **1944:** Germany occupied Hungary and installed Nazi regime. **1945:** USSR 'liberated' Hungary; Smallholders' Party won free elections, but communists led by Mátyás Rákosi took over by stages 1946–49. **1947:** Peace treaty restored 1920 frontiers. **1949:** Hungary became a Soviet-style dictatorship; Rákosi pursued Stalinist policies of collectivization and police terror. **1956:** Hungarian uprising: anti-Soviet demonstrations led prime minister Imre Nagy to propose democratic reforms and neutrality; USSR invaded, crushed dissent, and installed János Kádár as communist leader. **1961:** Kádár began to introduce pragmatic liberal reforms of a limited kind. **1988:** Károly Grosz replaced Kádár and accelerated reform; Hungarian Democratic Forum formed by opposition groups. **1989:** Communist dictatorship dismantled; transitional constitution restored multiparty democracy; opening of border with Austria destroyed the 'Iron Curtain'. **1990:** Elections won by centre-right coalition led by József Antall, who pursued radical free-market reforms. **1991:** Withdrawal of Soviet forces completed. **1994:** Gyula Horn, the leader of the ex-communist Hungarian Socialist Party, became prime minister, pledging to continue reform policies. **1996:** Friendship treaty with Slovak Republic signed. Cooperation treaty with Romania. **1997:** Hungary invited to join NATO and to begin negotiations for membership of the European Union. Referendum gave clear vote in favour of joining NATO.

Iceland Republic of

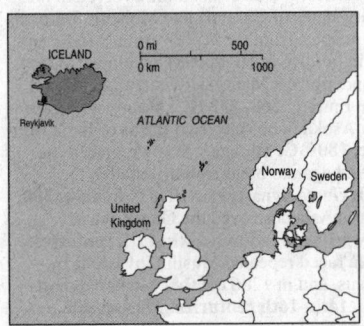

National name: *Lýveldi Ísland* **Area:** 103,000 sq km/39,768 sq mi **Capital:** Reykjavík **Major towns/cities:** Akureyri, Akranes, Kópavogur, Hafnerfjördur, Vestmannaeyjar **Physical features:** warmed by the Gulf Stream; glaciers and lava fields cover 75% of the country; active volcanoes (Hekla was once thought the gateway to Hell), geysers, hot springs, and new islands created offshore (Surtsey in 1963); subterranean hot water heats 85% of Iceland's homes; Sidujokull glacier moving at 100 metres a day

Government

Head of state: Olafur Raguar Grimson from 1996 **Head of government:** Davíd Oddsson from 1991 **Political system:** democracy **Administrative divisions:** 23 counties within eight districts **Political parties:** Independence Party (IP), right of centre; Progressive Party (PP), radical socialist; People's Alliance (PA), socialist; Social Democratic Party (SDP), moderate, left of centre; Citizens' Party, centrist; Women's Alliance, women- and family-oriented **Armed forces:** no defence forces of its own; US forces under NATO are stationed there: 2,500 military personnel and a 130-strong coastguard (1995) **Death penalty:** abolished 1928 **Education spend:** (% GNP) 5.4 (1993–94) **Health spend:** (% GDP) 6.8 (1994)

Economy and resources

Currency: krona **GDP:** ($ US) 7.3 billion (1996) **Real GDP per capita (PPP):** ($ US) 23,434 (1996) **GDP growth rate:** 4.2% (1996); 2% (1994–95) **Average annual inflation:** 2.5% (1996); 11.8% (1985–95) **Major trading partners:** EU (principally Germany, UK, and Denmark), Norway, USA, Japan **Resources:** aluminium, diatomite, hydroelectric and thermal power, fish **Industries:** mining, fish processing, processed aluminium, fertilizer, construction, cement **Exports:** fish products, aluminium, ferrosilicon, diatomite, fertilizer, animal products. Principal market: UK 19.3% (1995) **Imports:** machinery and transport equipment, motor vehicles, petroleum and petroleum products, foodstuffs, textiles. Principal source: Germany 11.4% (1995) **Arable land:** 0.1% (1995) **Agricultural products:** hay, potatoes, turnips; fishing industry, dairy products and livestock (lamb)

Population and society

Population: 271,000 (1996 est) **Population growth rate:** 1.1% (1990–95); 0.9% (2000–05) **Population density:** (per sq km) 3 (1996 est) **Urban population:** (% of total) 92 (1995) **Age distribution:** (% of total population) <15 24.5%, 15–65 64.3%, >65 11.2% (1995) **Ethnic groups:** most of the population is descended from Norwegians and Celts **Language:** Icelandic, the most archaic Scandinavian language **Religion:** Evangelical Lutheran **Education:** (compulsory years) 9 **Literacy rate:** 99% (men); 99% (women) (1995 est) **Labour force:** 54.6% of population: 9.5% agriculture, 24.2% industry, 66.3% services (1996) **Unemployment:** 4.4% (1996) **Life expectancy:** 76 (men); 81 (women) (1995–2000) **Child mortality rate:** (under 5, per 1,000 live births) 4 (1996) **Physicians:** 1 per 334 people (1993)

Practical information

Visa requirements: UK: visa not required. USA: visa not required **Embassy in the UK:** 1 Eaton Terrace, London SW1W 8EY. Tel: (0171) 730 5131/2; fax: (0171) 730 1683 **British embassy:** PO Box 460, Laufásvegur 49, 101 Reykjavík. Tel: (354) 551 5883/4; fax: (354) 552 7940 **Chamber of commerce:** Verzlunarráð Islands (Chamber of Commerce), Hús verslunarinnar, 103 Reykjavík. Tel: (354) 588 6666; fax: (354) 568 6564 **Airports:** international airport: Keflavik (45 km/28 mi southwest of Reykjavík); ten major domestic airports, 12 local airports; total passenger km: 2,297 million (1994) **Major holidays:** 1 January, 1 May, 17 June, 25–26 December; variable: Ascension Thursday, Good Friday, Easter Monday, Holy Thursday, First Day of Summer, August Holiday Monday

Chronology

7th century: Iceland discovered by Irish seafarers. **874:** First Norse settler, Ingólfr Arnarson, founded a small colony at Reykjavík. **c. 900:** Norse settlers came in larger numbers, mainly from Norway. **930:** Settlers established an annual parliament, the Althing, to make laws and resolve disputes. **985:** Eric the Red left Iceland to found a settlement in Greenland. **1000:** Icelanders adopted Christianity. **1263:** Icelanders recognized authority of the king of Norway after brief civil war. **1397:** Norway and Iceland united with Denmark and Sweden under a single monarch. **15th century:** Norway and Iceland were increasingly treated as appendages of Denmark, especially after Sweden seceded in 1449. **1602:** Denmark introduced a monopoly on Icelandic trade. **1783:** Poisonous volcanic eruption caused great loss of life. **1814:** Norway passed to the Swedish crown; Iceland remained under Danish rule. **1845:** Althing re-established in modernized form. **1854:** Danish monopoly on trade abolished. **1874:** New constitution gave Iceland limited autonomy. **1918:** Iceland achieved full self-government under the Danish crown. **1940:** British forces occupied Iceland after Germany invaded Denmark; US troops took over 1941. **1944:** Iceland became an independent republic under President Sveinn Björnsson. **1949:** Became a member of NATO. **1953:** Joined the Nordic Council. **1958:** Introduction of exclusive 19-km/12-mi fishing limit led to first 'Cod War', when Icelandic patrol boats clashed with British fishing boats. **1972–73:** Iceland extended its fishing limit 80 km/50 mi; renewed confrontation with Britain. **1975–76:** Further extension of fishing limit to 341 km/200 mi caused third 'Cod War' with the UK. **1980:** Vigdis Finnbogadóttir became the first woman president of Iceland. **1985:** Iceland declared itself a nuclear-free zone. **1992:** Iceland defied world ban to resume whaling industry.

India Republic of

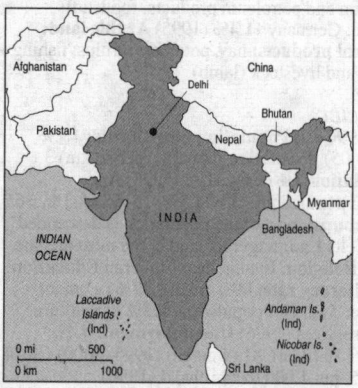

National name: Hindi *Bharat* **Area:** 3,166,829 sq km/1,222,713 sq mi **Capital:** Delhi **Major towns/cities:** Bombay, Calcutta, Chennai (Madras), Bangalore, Hyderabad, Ahmadabad, Kanpur, Pune, Nagpur, Bhopal, Jaipur, Lucknow, Surat **Major ports:** Calcutta, Bombay, Chennai (Madras) **Physical features:** Himalaya mountains on N border; plains around rivers Ganges, Indus, Brahmaputra; Deccan peninsula S of the Narmada River forms plateau between Western and Eastern Ghats mountain ranges; desert in W; Andaman and Nicobar Islands, Lakshadweep (Laccadive Islands)

Government

Head of state: Kocheril Raman Narayanan from 1997 **Head of government:** Atal Behari Vajpayee from 1998 **Political system:** liberal democratic federal republic **Administrative divisions:** 25 states and seven centrally administered union territories **Political parties:** All India Congress Committee, or Congress, cross-caste and cross-religion coalition, left of centre; Janata Dal (People's Party), secular, left of centre; Bharatiya Janata Party (BJP), radical right wing, Hindu-chauvinist; Communist Party of India (CPI), Marxist-Leninist; Communist Party of India–Marxist (CPI–M), West Bengal–based moderate socialist **Armed forces:** 1,450,000 (1996) **Conscription:** none, although all citizens are constitutionally obliged to perform national service when called upon **Death penalty:** limited to exceptional circumstances, such as political assassinations. Method: hanging **Defence spend:** (% GDP) 2.8 (1996) **Education spend:** (% GNP) 3.8 (1993–94) **Health spend:** (% GDP) 0.7 (1990–95)

Economy and resources

Currency: rupee **GDP:** ($ US) 293.6 billion (1994) **Real GDP per capita (PPP):** ($ US) 1,348 (1994) **GDP growth rate:** 6.3% (1994); 4.6% (1990–95) **Average annual inflation:** 9.7% (1996); 9.8% (1985–95) **Foreign debt:** ($ US) 101.1 billion (1996) **Major trading partners:** USA, CIS, UK, Germany **Resources:** coal, iron ore, copper ore, bauxite, chromite, gold, manganese ore, zinc, lead, limestone, crude oil, natural gas, diamonds **Industries:** mining (including coal, iron and manganese ores, diamonds, and gold), manufacturing (iron and steel, mineral oils, shipbuilding, chemical products, road transport, cotton cloth, sugar, petroleum

refining products) **Exports:** tea (world's largest producer), coffee, fish, iron and steel, leather, textiles, clothing, polished diamonds, handmade carpets, engineering goods, chemicals. Principal market: USA 17.4% (1995–96) **Imports:** nonelectrical machinery, mineral fuels and lubricants, pearls, precious and semiprecious stones, chemicals, transport equipment. Principal source: USA 10.5% (1995–96) **Arable land:** 55.9% (1995) **Agricultural products:** cotton, tea, wheat, rice, coffee, cashew nuts, jute, spices, sugar cane, oil seeds;

Population and society

Population: 994,580,000 (1996 est) **Population growth rate:** 1.9% (1990–95); 1.6% (2000–05) **Population density:** (per sq km) 287 (1996 est) **Urban population:** (% of total) 27 (1995) **Age distribution:** (% of total population) <15 35.2%, 15–65 60.2%, >65 4.6% (1995) **Ethnic groups:** 72% of Indo-Aryan descent; 25% (predominantly in the S) Dravidian; 3% Mongoloid **Language:** Hindi, English, and 17 other official languages: Assamese, Bengali, Gujarati, Kannada, Kashmiri, Konkani, Malayalam, Manipur, Marathi, Nepali, Oriya, Punjabi, Sanskrit, Sindhi, Tamil, Telugu, Urdu; more than 1,650 dialects **Religion:** Hindu 83%, Sunni Muslim 11%, Christian 2.5%, Sikh 2% **Education:** (compulsory years) 8 **Literacy rate:** 62% (men); 34% (women) (1995 est) **Labour force:** 43% of population: 64% agriculture, 16% industry, 20% services (1990) **Unemployment:** 9.1% **Life expectancy:** 63 (men); 63 (women) (1995–2000) **Child mortality rate:** (under 5, per 1,000 live births) 99 (1996) **Physicians:** 1 per 2,459 people (1993 est)

Practical information

Visa requirements: UK: visa required. USA: visa required **Embassy in the UK:** Office of the High Commissioner for India, India House, Aldwych, London WC2B 4NA. Tel: (0171) 836 8484; fax: (0171) 836 4331 **British embassy:** British High Commission, Shanti Path, Chanakyapuri, New Delhi 110021. Tel: (11) 687 2161; fax: (11) 687 2882 **Chamber of commerce:** India Exchange, 4 India Exchange Place, Calcutta 700001. Tel: (33) 220 3243; fax: (33) 220 4495 **Airports:** international airports: Ahmadabad, Bombay, Calcutta, Delhi (Indira Gandhi), Goa, Hyderabad, Madras, Thiruvanathapuram; over 70 domestic airports; total passenger km: 17,581 million (1994) **Major holidays:** 1 (some states), 26 January, 1 May (some states), 30 June, 15 August, 2 October, 25, 31 December; variable: New Year (Parsi, some states)

Chronology

c. 2500–1500 BC: The earliest Indian civilization evolved in the Indus Valley with the city states of Harappa and Mohenjo Daro. **c. 1500–1200 BC:** Aryan peoples from the NW overran N India and the Deccan; Brahmanism (a form of Hinduism) developed. **321 BC:** Chandragupta, founder of the Mauryan dynasty, began to unite N India in a Hindu Empire. **268–232 BC:** Mauryan Empire reached its height under Asoka, who ruled two-thirds of India from his capital Pataliputra. **c. 180 BC:** Shunga dynasty replaced the Mauryans; Hindu Empire began to break up into smaller kingdoms. **AD 320–480:** Gupta dynasty reunified N India. **c. 500:** Raiding Huns from central Asia destroyed the Gupta dynasty; India reverted to many warring kingdoms. **11th–12th centuries:** Rajput princes of N India faced repeated Muslim invasions by Arabs, Turks, and Afghans, and in 1206 the first Muslim dynasty was established at Delhi. **14th–16th centuries:** Muslim rule extended over N India and the Deccan; S remained independent under the Hindu Vijayanagar dynasty. **1498:** Explorer Vasco da Gama reached India, followed by Portuguese, Dutch, French, and English traders. **1526:** Last Muslim invasion: Zahir ud-din Muhammad (Babur) defeated the Sultan of Delhi at Battle of Panipat and established the Mogul Empire, which was consolidated by Akbar the Great (1556–1605). **1600:** East India Company founded by English merchants, who settled in Madras, Bombay, and Calcutta. **1632:** The Mogul emperor Shah Jahan began the building of the Taj Mahal as a mausoleum for his favourite wife Mumtaz Mahal (who died in 1631). **17th century:** Mogul Empire reached its zenith under Jahangir (1605–27), Shah

India: States and Union Territories

State	Capital	Area		Population (1994 est.)
		sq km	sq mi	
Andhra Pradesh	Hyderabad	275,045	106,195	71,800,000
Arunachal Pradesh	Itanagar	83,743	32,333	965,000
Assam	Dispur	78,438	30,285	24,200,000
Bihar	Patna	173,877	67,134	93,080,000
Goa	Panaji	3,702	1,429	1,235,000
Gujarat	Gandhinagar	196,024	75,685	44,235,000
Haryana	Chandigarh	44,212	17,070	17,925,000
Himachal Pradesh	Shimla	55,673	21,495	5,530,000
Jammu and Kashmir[1]	Srinagar	222,236	85,805	8,435,000
Karnataka	Bangalore	191,791	74,051	48,150,000
Kerala	Trivandrum	38,863	15,005	30,555,000
Madhya Pradesh	Bhopal	443,446	171,215	71,950,000
Maharashtra	Bombay	307,713	118,808	85,565,000
Manipur	Imphal	22,327	8,620	2,010,000
Meghalaya	Shillong	22,429	8,660	1,960,000
Mizoram	Aizawl	21,081	8,139	775,000
Nagaland	Kohima	16,579	6,401	1,410,000
Orissa	Bhubaneshwar	155,707	60,118	33,795,000
Punjab	Chandigarh	5,362	2,070	21,695,000
Rajasthan	Jaipur	342,239	132,138	48,040,000
Sikkim	Gangtok	7096	2,740	444,000
Tamil Nadu	Madras	130,058	50,215	58,840,000
Tripura	Agartala	10,486	4,049	3,055,000
Uttar Pradesh	Lucknow	294,411	113,672	150,695,000
West Bengal	Calcutta	88,752	34,267	73,600,000
Union Territory				
Andaman and Nicobar Islands	Port Blair	8,249	3,185	322,000
Chandigarh	Chandigarh	114	44	725,000
Dadra and Nagar Haveli	Silvassa	491	190	153,000
Daman and Diu	Daman	112	43	111,000
Delhi	Delhi	1,483	573	10,865,000
Lakshadweep	Kavaratti	32	12	56,000
Pondicherry	Pondicherry	492	190	894,000

[1] Includes area occupied by Pakistan and China.

Jehan (1628–58), and Aurangzeb (1658–1707). **1739:** Persian king Nadir Shah invaded India and destroyed Mogul prestige; British and French supported rival Indian princes in subsequent internal wars. **1757:** Battle of Plassey: Robert Clive defeated Siraj al-Daulah, nawab of Bengal; Bengal came under control of British East India Company. **1772–85:** Warren Hastings, British governor general of Bengal, raised Indian army and pursued expansionist policies. **early 19th century:** British took control (directly or indirectly) throughout India by defeating powerful Indian states in a series of regional wars. **1858:** 'Indian Mutiny': mutiny in Bengal army erupted into widespread anti-British revolt; rebels sought to restore powers of Mogul emperor. **1858:** British defeated the rebels; East India Company dissolved; India came under the British crown. **1885:** Indian National Congress founded in Bombay as focus for nationalism. **1909:** Morley–Minto Reforms: Indians received right to elect members of Legislative Councils; Hindus and Muslims formed separate electorates. **1919:** British forces killed 379 Indian demonstrators at Amritsar; India Act (Montagu–Chelmsford Reforms) conceded a measure of provincial self-government. **1920–22:** Mohandas Gandhi won control of the Indian National Congress, which launched campaign of civil disobedience in support of demand for complete self-rule. **1935:** India Act provided for Indian control of federal legislature, with defence and external affairs remaining the viceroy's responsibility. **1940:** Muslim League called for India to be partitioned along religious lines. **1947:** British India partitioned into two independent dominions of India (mainly Hindu) and Pakistan (mainly Muslim) amid bloody riots; Jawaharlal Nehru of Congress Party became prime minister. **1950:** India became a republic within the Commonwealth. **1962:** India lost brief border war with China; retained Kashmir in war with Pakistan 1965. **1966:** Indira Gandhi, daughter of Nehru, became prime minister. **1971:** India defeated Pakistan in war and helped East Pakistan become independent as Bangladesh. **1975:** Found guilty of electoral corruption, Mrs Gandhi declared state of emergency and arrested opponents. **1977–79:** Janata Party formed government under Morarji Desai. **1980:** Mrs Gandhi, heading Congress Party splinter group, Congress (I) ('I' for Indira), returned to power. **1984:** Troops cleared Sikh separatists from the Golden Temple, Amritsar; Mrs Gandhi assassinated by Sikh bodyguards; her son Rajiv Gandhi became prime minister. **1989:** After financial scandals, Congress ('I' was removed after Mrs Gandhi's assassination) lost elections; V P Singh formed Janata Dal minority government. **1990:** Direct rule imposed on Jammu and Kashmir after upsurge in Muslim separatist violence; rising interethnic and religious conflict in Punjab and elsewhere. **1991:** Rajiv Gandhi assassinated during election campaign; P V Narasimha Rao formed minority Congress government. **1992:** Destruction of mosque at Ayodhya, N India, by Hindu extremists resulted in widespread violence. **1996:** H D Deve Gowda became prime minister of a coalition government. Madras renamed Chennai. Rao resigned as Congress Party president and was replaced by Sitaram Kesri. Direct central rule imposed on Uttar Pradesh after inconclusive assembly elections. **1997:** Deve Gowda's government defeated in confidence vote. United Front government reformed and led by Inder Kumar Gujral. Kocheril Raman Narayanan became first 'untouchable' to be elected president. It was announced that former prime minister Rao would face corruption charges. Discussions began to normalize relations with Pakistan. Prime Minister Inder Gujral resigned, but agreed to stay on until 1998 election. **1998:** Atal Behari Vajpayee, leader of Bharatiya Janata party, elected prime minister. May: India carried out five underground nuclear explosions, meeting with international condemnation and the imposition of sanctions by the USA.

Indonesia Republic of

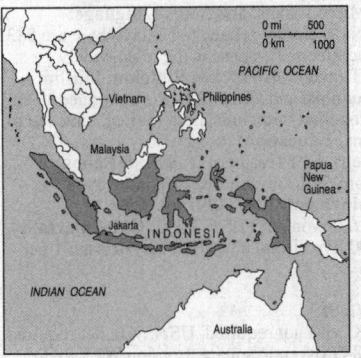

National name: *Republik Indonesia* **Area:** 1,904,569 sq km/735,354 sq mi **Capital:** Jakarta **Major towns/cities:** Surabaya, Bandung, Yogyakarta (Java), Medan, Semarang (Java), Banda Aceh, Palembang (Sumatra), Ujung Pandang (Sulawesi), Denpasar (Bali), Kupang (Timor), Padang, Malang **Major ports:** Tanjung Priok, Surabaya, Semarang (Java), Ujung Pandang (Sulawesi) **Physical features:** comprises 13,677 tropical islands (over 6,000 of them are inhabited): the Greater Sundas (including Java, Madura,

Sumatra, Sulawesi, and Kalimantan [part of Borneo]), the Lesser Sunda Islands/Nusa Tenggara (including Bali, Lombok, Sumbawa, Flores, Sumba, Alor, Lomblen, Timor, Roti, and Savu), Maluku/Moluccas (over 1,000 islands including Ambon, Ternate, Tidore, Tanimbar, and Halmahera), and Irian Jaya (part of New Guinea); over half the country is tropical rainforest; it has the largest expanse of peatlands in the tropics

Government

Head of state and government: Bacharuddin Jusuf Habibie from 1998 **Political system:** authoritarian nationalist republic **Administrative divisions:** 27 provinces **Political parties:** Sekber Golkar, ruling military-bureaucrat-farmers' party; United Development Party (PPP), moderate Islamic; Indonesian Democratic Party (PDI), nationalist Christian **Armed forces:** 299,200; paramilitary forces 186,000 (1996) **Conscription:** 2 years (selective) **Death penalty:** retained and used for ordinary crimes **Defence spend:** (% GDP) 2.1 (1996) **Education spend:** (% GNP) 1.3 (1993–94) **Health spend:** (% GDP) 0.7 (1990–95)

Economy and resources

Currency: rupiah **GDP:** ($ US) 174.6 billion (1994) **Real GDP per capita (PPP):** ($ US) 3,740 (1994) **GDP growth rate:** 7.3% (1994); 7.6% (1990–95) **Average annual inflation:** 7.1% (1996); 8.8% (1985–95) **Foreign debt:** ($ US) 101.9 billion (1996) **Major trading partners:** Japan, Singapore, USA, Hong Kong, Australia, Germany, the Netherlands **Resources:** petroleum (principal producer of petroleum in the Far East), natural gas, bauxite, nickel (world's third-largest producer), copper, tin (world's second-largest producer), gold, coal, forests **Industries:** petroleum refining, food processing, textiles, wood products, tobacco, chemicals, fertilizers, rubber, cement **Exports:** petroleum and petroleum products, natural and manufactured gas, textiles, rubber, palm oil, wood and wood products, electrical and electronic products, coffee, fishery products, coal, copper, tin, pepper, tea. Principal market: Japan 27.1% (1995) **Imports:** machinery, transport and electrical equipment, manufactured goods, chemical and mineral products. Principal source: Japan 22.7% (1995) **Arable land:** 9.5% (1995) **Agricultural products:** rice, cassava, maize, coffee, spices, tea, cocoa, tobacco, sugar cane, sweet potatoes, palm, rubber, coconuts, nutmeg; fishing

Population and society

Population: 200,453,000 (1996 est) **Population growth rate:** 1.6% (1990–95); 1.3% (2000–05) **Population density:** (per sq km) 105 (1996 est) **Urban population:** (% of total) 35% (1995) **Age distribution:** (% of total population) <15 33%, 15–65 62.7%, >65 4.3% (1995) **Ethnic groups:** comprises more than 300 ethnic groups, the majority of which are of Malay descent; important Malay communities include Javanese (about one-third of the population), Sundanese (7%), and Madurese (3%); the largest non-Malay community is the Chinese (2%); substantial numbers of Indians, Melanesians, Micronesians, and Arabs **Language:** Bahasa Indonesia (official), closely related to Malay; there are 583 regional languages and dialects; Javanese is the most widely spoken local language. Dutch is also spoken **Religion:** Muslim 88%, Christian 10%, Buddhist and Hindu 2% (the continued spread of Christianity, together with an Islamic revival, have led to greater religious tensions) **Education:** (compulsory years) 6 **Literacy rate:** 84% (men); 68% (women) (1995 est) **Labour force:** 44% of population: 55% agriculture, 14% industry, 31% services (1990) **Unemployment:** 10% (1997 est) **Life expectancy:** 63 (men); 67 (women) (1995–2000) **Child mortality rate:** (under 5, per 1,000 live births) 63 (1996) **Physicians:** 1 per 7,028 people (1993 est)

Practical information

Visa requirements: UK: visa not required. USA: visa not required **Embassy in the UK:** 38 Grosvenor Square, London W1X 9AD. Tel: (0171) 499 7661; fax: (0171) 491 4993 **British embassy:** Jalan M H Thamrin 75, Jakarta 10310. Tel: (21) 330 904; fax: (21) 314 1824 **Chamber of commerce:** Indonesian Chamber of Commerce and Industry, 3rd–5th Floors, Chandra Building, Jalan

M H Thamrin 20, Jakarta 10350. Tel: (21) 324 000; fax: (21) 310 6098 **Airports:** international airports: Jakarta (Sukarno-Hatta), Irian Jaya (Frans Kaisepo), Bali (Ngurah Rai), Surabaya, Manado (Sam Ratulangi); over 60 domestic airports; total passenger km: 21,166 million (1994) **Major holidays:** 1 January, 17 August, 25 December; variable: Ascension Thursday, Eid-ul-Adha, end of Ramadan (2 days), Good Friday, New Year (Icaka, March), New Year (Muslim), Prophet's Birthday, Ascension of the Prophet (March/April), Waisak (May)

Chronology

3000–500 BC: Immigrants from S China displaced original Melanesian population. **6th century AD:** Start of Indian cultural influence; small Hindu and Buddhist kingdoms developed. **8th century:** Buddhist maritime empire of Srivijaya expanded to include all Sumatra and Malay peninsula. **13th century:** Islam introduced to Sumatra by Arab merchants; spread throughout archipelago over next 300 years. **14th century:** Eastern Javanese kingdom of Majapahit destroyed Srivijaya and dominated the region. **c. 1520:** Empire of Majapahit disintegrated; Javanese nobles fled to Bali. **16th century:** Portuguese merchants broke Muslim monopoly of spice trade. **1602:** Dutch East India Company founded; it displaced the Portuguese and monopolized trade with the Spice Islands. **1619:** Dutch East India Company captured port of Jakarta in Java and renamed it Batavia. **17th century:** Dutch introduced coffee plants and established informal control over central Java through divide-and-rule policy among local potentates. **1749:** After frequent military intervention, the Dutch East India Company obtained formal sovereignty over Mataram. **1799:** The Netherlands took over interests of bankrupt Dutch East India Company. **1808:** French forces occupied Java; British expelled them 1811 and returned Java to the Netherlands 1816. **1824:** Anglo-Dutch Treaty: Britain recognized entire Indonesian archipelago as Dutch sphere of influence. **1825–30:** Java War: Prince Dipo Negoro led unsuccessful revolt against Dutch rule; further revolt 1894–96. **19th century:** Dutch formalized control over Java and conquered other islands; cultivation of coffee and sugar under tight official control made the Netherlands Indies one of the richest colonies in the world. **1901:** Dutch introduced 'Ethical Policy' supposed to advance local interests. **1908:** Dutch completed conquest of Bali. **1927:** Communist revolts suppressed; Achmed Sukarno founded Indonesian Nationalist Party (PNI) to unite diverse anti-Dutch elements. **1929:** Dutch imprisoned Sukarno and tried to suppress PNI. **1942–45:** Japanese occupation; PNI installed as anti-Western puppet government. **1945:** When Japan surrendered, President Sukarno declared an independent republic, but Dutch set about restoring colonial rule by force. **1947:** Dutch 'police action': all-out attack on Java and Sumatra conquered two-thirds of the republic. **1949:** Under US pressure, Dutch agreed to transfer sovereignty of the Netherlands Indies (except Dutch New Guinea or Irian Jaya) to the Republic of the United States of Indonesia. **1950:** President Sukarno abolished federalism and proclaimed unitary Republic of Indonesia dominated by Java; revolts in Sumatra and South Moluccas. **1959:** To combat severe political instability, Sukarno imposed authoritarian 'guided democracy'. **1963:** The Netherlands ceded Irian Jaya to Indonesia. **1963–66:** Indonesia tried to break up Malaysia by means of blockade and guerrilla attacks. **1965–66:** Clashes between communists and army; Gen Raden Suharto imposed emergency administration and massacred up to 700,000 alleged communists. **1968:** Suharto formally replaced Sukarno as president and proclaimed 'New Order' under strict military rule. **1970s:** Rising oil exports brought significant agricultural and industrial growth. **1975:** Indonesia invaded East Timor when Portuguese rule collapsed; 200,000 died in ensuing war. **1986:** After suppressing revolt on Irian Jaya, Suharto introduced a transmigration programme to settle 65,000 Javanese there and on outer islands. **1991:** Democracy Forum launched to promote political dialogue. **1993:** President Suharto re-elected for sixth consecutive term. **1994:** Sukarno's daughter Megawati Sukarnoputri elected head of opposition party PDI. **1996:** Megawati ousted by rival faction within PDI (aided by Suharto); government crackdown on opponents, including PDI supporters. **1997:** Hundreds killed in ethnic riots in west Kalimantan province. Drought and famine in Irian Jaya. **1998** forest fires continued to burn out of control in Borneo and Sumatra. May: Following civil unrest and mass riots provoked by breakdown of the economy, Suharto stepped down and handed presidency to vice-president B J Habibie.

Iran Islamic Republic of (formerly Persia)

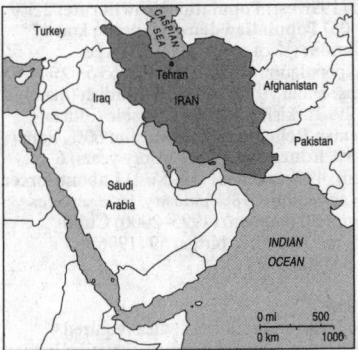

National name: *Jomhori-e-Islami-e-Irân* **Area:** 1,648,000 sq km/636,292 sq mi **Capital:** Tehran **Major towns/cities:** Esfahan, Mashhad, Tabriz, Shiraz, Ahvaz, Bakhtaran, Qom, Kara **Major ports:** Abadan **Physical features:** plateau surrounded by mountains, including Elburz and Zagros; Lake Rezayeh; Dasht-e-Kavir desert; occupies islands of Abu Musa, Greater Tunb and Lesser Tunb in the Gulf

Government

Head of state and government: Seyyed Mohammad Khatami from 1997 **Leader of the Islamic Revolution:** Seyed Ali Khamenei from 1989 **Political system:** authoritarian Islamic republic **Administrative divisions:** 25 provinces **Political parties:** none officially recognized **Armed forces:** 513,000; plus 350,000 army reserves and 350,000 paramilitary forces (1996) **Conscription:** military service is compulsory for two years **Death penalty:** retained and used for ordinary crimes **Defence spend:** (% GDP) 5 (1996) **Education spend:** (% GNP) 5.9 (1993–94) **Health spend:** (% GDP) 2.8 (1990–95)

Economy and resources

Currency: rial **GDP:** ($ US) 63.7 billion (1994) **Real GDP per capita (PPP):** ($ US) 5,766 (1994) **GDP growth rate:** –1% (1994); 4.2% (1990–95) **Average annual inflation:** 40% (1996); 24.2% (1985–95) **Foreign debt:** ($ US) 24.9 billion (1996) **Major trading partners:** Germany, Japan, UK, Italy, United Arab Emirates, Turkey **Resources:** petroleum, natural gas, coal, magnetite, gypsum, iron ore, copper, chromite, salt, bauxite, decorative stone **Industries:** mining, petroleum refining, textiles, food processing, transport equipment **Exports:** crude petroleum and petroleum products, agricultural goods, metal ores. Principal market: Japan 13.8% (1995) **Imports:** machinery and motor vehicles, paper, textiles, iron and steel and mineral products, chemicals and chemical products. Principal source: Germany 14.7% (1995) **Arable land:** 10.5% (1995) **Agricultural products:** wheat, barley, sugar beet, sugar cane, rice, fruit, tobacco, livestock (cattle, sheep, and chickens) for meat and wool production

Population and society

Population: 69,975,000 (1996 est) **Population growth rate:** 2.7% (1990–95); 2.5% (2000–05) **Population density:** (per sq km) 42 (1996 est) **Urban population:** (% of total) 59 (1995) **Age distribution:** (% of total population) <15 43.5%, 15–65 52.6%, >65 3.9% (1995) **Ethnic groups:** about 63% of Persian origin, 18% Turkic, 13% other Iranian, 3% Kurdish, and 3% Arabic **Language:** Farsi (official), Kurdish, Turkish, Arabic, English, French **Religion:** Shi'ite Muslim (official) 94%, Sunni Muslim,

Zoroastrian, Christian, Jewish, Baha'i **Education:** (compulsory years) 5 **Literacy rate:** 89% (men); 43% (women) (1995 est) **Labour force:** 29% of population: 39% agriculture, 23% industry, 39% services (1990) **Unemployment:** 10% (1993 est) **Life expectancy:** 69 (men); 70 (women) (1995–2000) **Child mortality rate:** (under 5, per 1,000 live births) 59 (1996) **Physicians:** 1 per 3,142 people (1993 est)

Practical information

Visa requirements: UK: visa required. USA: visa required **Embassy in the UK:** 16 Prince's Gate, London SW7 1PT. Tel: (0171) 584 8101; fax: (0171) 589 4440 **British embassy:** PO Box 11365–4474, 143 Ferdowsi Avenue, Tehran 11344. Tel: (21) 675 011; fax: (21) 678 021 **Chamber of commerce:** Iran Chamber of Commerce, Industries and Mines, 254 Taleghani Avenue, Tehran. Tel: (21) 836 0319; fax: (21) 882 5111 **Airports:** international airports: Tehran (Mehrabad), Abadan, Esfahan; over 20 domestic airports; total passenger km: 5,238 million (1994) **Major holidays:** 11 February, 20–25 March, 1–2 April, 5 June; variable: Eid-ul-Adha, Ashora, end of Ramadan, Prophet's Birthday, Prophet's Mission (April), Birth of the Twelfth Imam (April/May), Martyrdom of Imam Ali (May), Death of Imam Jaffar Sadegh (June/July), Birth of Imam Reza (July), Id-E-Gihadir (August), Death of the Prophet and Martyrdom of Imam Hassan (October/November)

Chronology

c. 2000 BC: Migration from southern Russia of Aryans, from whom Persians claim descent. **612 BC:** The Medes, from NW Iran, destroyed Iraq-based Assyrian Empire to the W and established their own empire which extended into central Anatolia (Turkey-in-Asia). **550 BC:** Cyrus the Great overthrew Medes' empire and founded First Persian Empire, the Achaemenid, conquering much of Asia Minor, including Babylonia (Palestine and Syria) in 539 BC. Expansion continued into Afghanistan under Darius I, who ruled 521–486 BC. **499–449 BC:** The Persian Wars with Greece ended Persian domination of the ancient world. **330 BC:** Collapse of Achaemenid Empire following defeat by Alexander the Great of Macedon. **AD 224:** Sassanian Persian Empire founded by Ardashir, with its capital at Ctesiphon, in the NE. **637:** Sassanian Empire destroyed by Muslim Arabs at battle of Qadisiya; Islam replaced Zoroastrianism. **750–1258:** Dominated by the Persianized Abbasid dynasty, who reigned as caliphs (Islamic civil and religious leaders), with a capital in Baghdad (Iraq). **1380s:** Conquered by the Mongol leader, Tamerlane. **1501:** Emergence of Safavids; the arts and architecture flourished, particularly under Abbas I, 'the Great', who ruled 1588–1629. **1736:** The Safavids were deposed by the warrior Nadir Shah Afshar, who ruled until 1747. **1790:** Rise of the Qajars, who transferred the capital from Esfahan in central Iran to Tehran, further N. **19th century:** Increasing influence in the N of tsarist Russia, which took Georgia and much of Armenia 1801–28. Britain exercised influence in the S and E, and fought Iran 1856–57 over claims to Herat (W Afghanistan). **1906:** Parliamentary constitution adopted after a brief revolution. **1925:** Weak and corrupt Qajar dynasty overthrown, with some British official help, in a coup by Col Reza Khan, a nationalist Iranian Cossack military officer, who was crowned shah ('king of kings'), with the title Reza Shah Pahlavi. **1920s onwards:** Economic modernization, Westernization, and secularization programme launched, which proved unpoular with traditionalist elements. **1935:** Name changed from Persia to Iran. **1941:** Owing to his pro-German sentiments, Pahlavi Shah was forced to abdicate during World War II by Allied occupation forces and was succeeded by his son Mohammad Reza Pahlavi, who continued the modernization programme. **1946:** British, US, and Soviet occupation forces left Iran. **1951:** Oilfields nationalized by radical prime minister Muhammad Mossadeq as anti-British and US sentiment increased. **1953:** Mossadeq deposed, the nationalization plan changed, and the US-backed shah, Muhammad Reza Shah Pahlavi, took full control of the government. **1963:** Hundreds of protesters, who demanded the release of the arrested fundamentalist Shi'ite Muslim leader Ayatollah Ruhollah

Khomeini, were killed by troops. **1970s:** Spiralling world oil prices brought rapid economic expansion. **1975:** Shah introduced single-party system. **1977:** Mysterious death in An Najaf of Mustafa, eldest son of the exiled Ayatollah Ruhollah Khomeini, sparked demonstrations by theology students, which were suppressed with the loss of six lives. **1978:** Opposition to the Shah organized from France by Ayatollah Ruhollah Khomeini, who demanded a return to the principles of Islam. Hundreds of demonstrators were killed by troops in Jaleh Square, Tehran. **1979:** Amid mounting demonstrations by students and clerics, the shah left the country; Khomeini returned to create a nonparty theocratic Islamic state. Revolutionaries seized 66 US hostages at embassy in Tehran; US economic boycott. **1980:** Iraq invaded Iran, provoking a bitter war; death of exiled shah. **1981:** US hostages released. **1985–87:** Fighting intensified in Iran–Iraq War, with heavy loss of life. **1988:** Cease-fire in the war; talks with Iraq began. **1989:** Khomeini issued a fatwa (public order) for the death of British writer Salman Rushdie for blasphemy against Islam. On Khomeini's death, Ayatollah Ali Khamenei was elected interim Leader of the Revolution; the speaker of Iranian parliament Hashemi Rafsanjani was elected president. **1990:** Generous peace terms with Iraq accepted to close Iran–Iraq war. **1991:** Nearly one million Kurds arrived from NW Iraq, fleeing persecution by Saddam Hussein after the Gulf War between Iraq and UN forces. **1993:** President Rafsanjani re-elected, but with a smaller margin; free-market economic reforms introduced. **1996:** Rafsanjani supporters won assembly elections. **1997:** Moderate politician Seyyed Mohammad Khatami elected president.

Iraq Republic of

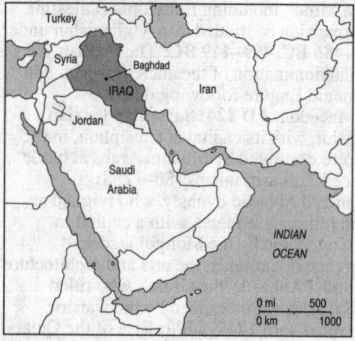

National name: *al Jumhouriya al `Iraqia* **Area:** 434,924 sq km/167,924 sq mi **Capital:** Baghdad **Major towns/cities:** Mosul, Basra, Kirkuk, Hilla, Najaf, Nasiriya **Major ports:** Basra and Um Qass closed from 1980 **Physical features:** mountains in N, desert in W; wide valley of rivers Tigris and Euphrates running NW–SE; canal linking Baghdad and Persian Gulf opened 1992

Government

Head of state and government: Saddam Hussein al-Tikriti from 1979 **Political system:** one-party socialist republic **Administrative divisions:** 18 governates **Political party:** Arab Ba'ath Socialist Party, nationalist socialist **Armed forces:** 382,500 (1996) **Conscription:** military service is compulsory for 18–24 months; it is waived on the payment of the equivalent of $800 **Death penalty:** retained and used for ordinary crimes **Defence spend:** (% GDP) 8.3 (1996) **Education spend:** (% GNP) 4.6 (1988)

Economy and resources

Currency: Iraqi dinar **GDP:** ($ US) 57.7 billion (1994 est) **Real GDP per capita (PPP):** ($ US) 3,159 (1994) **GDP growth rate:** 0% (1994) **Average annual inflation:** 225% (1996) **Foreign debt:** ($ US) 100.4 billion (1996) **Major trading partners:** Jordan, Brazil, Turkey, Japan, the Netherlands, Spain, UK, France **Resources:** petroleum, natural gas, sulphur, phosphates **Industries:** chemical, petroleum, coal, rubber and plastic products, food processing, nonmetallic minerals, textiles, mining

Exports: crude petroleum (accounting for more than 98% of total export earnings (1980–89), dates and other dried fruits. Principal market: Jordan 95% (1995) **Imports:** machinery and transport equipment, basic manufactured articles, cereals and other foodstuffs, iron and steel, military goods. Principal source: Jordan 48.7% (1995) **Arable land:** 12.6% (1995) **Agricultural products:** dates, wheat, barley, maize, sugar beet, sugar cane, melons, rice; livestock rearing (notably production of eggs and poultry meat)

Population and society

Population: 20,607,000 (1996 est) **Population growth rate:** 2.5% (1990–95); 2.8% (2000–05) **Population density:** (per sq km) 47 (1996 est) **Urban population:** (% of total) 75 (1995) **Age distribution:** (% of total population) <15 43.6%, 15–65 53.2%, >65 3% (1995) **Ethnic groups:** about 79% Arab, 16% Kurdish (mainly in the NE), 3% Persian, 2% Turkish **Language:** Arabic (official); Kurdish, Assyrian, Armenian **Religion:** Shi'ite Muslim 60%, Sunni Muslim 37%, Christian 3% **Education:** (compulsory years) 6 **Literacy rate:** 77% (men); 49% (women) (1995 est) **Labour force:** 26% of population: 16% agriculture, 18% industry, 66% services **Life expectancy:** 67 (men); 70 (women) (1995–2000) **Child mortality rate:** (under 5, per 1,000 live births) 59 (1996) **Physicians:** 1 per 1,659 people (1993 est)

Practical information

Visa requirements: UK: visa required. USA: visa required **Embassy in the UK:** Iraq has no diplomatic representation in the UK. The Embassy of the Hashemite Kingdom of Jordan deals with enquiries relating to Iraq: Iraq Interests Section, 21 Queen's Gate, London SW7 5JG. Tel: (0171) 584 7141/6; fax: (0171) 584 7716 **British embassy:** the UK has no diplomatic representation in Iraq **Chamber of commerce:** Federation of Iraqi Chambers of Commerce, Mustansir Street, Baghdad. Tel: (1) 888 6111 **Airports:** international airports: Baghdad (Saddam), Basra, Bamerui; at least three domestic airports (many civilian airports sustained heavy damage during the 1991 Gulf War); total passenger km: 35 million (1992) **Major holidays:** 1, 6 January, 8 February, 21 March, 1 May, 14, 17 July; variable: Eid-ul-Adha (4 days), Ashora, end of Ramadan (3 days), New Year (Muslim), Prophet's Birthday

Chronology

c. 3400 BC: The world's oldest civilization, the Sumerian, arose in the land between the rivers Euphrates and Tigris, known as lower Mesopotamia, which lies in the heart of modern Iraq. Its cities included Lagash, Eridu, Uruk, Kish, and Ur. **c. 2350 BC:** The confederation of Sumerian city-states was forged into an empire by the Akkadian leader Sargon. **7th century BC:** In northern Mesopotamia, the Assyrian Empire, based around the River Tigris and formerly dominated by Sumeria and Euphrates-centred Babylonia, created a vast empire covering much of the Middle East. **612 BC:** The Assyrian capital of Nineveh was destroyed by Babylon and Mede (in NW Iran). **c. 550 BC:** Mesopotamia came under Persian control. **AD 114:** Conquered by the Romans. **266:** Came under the rule of the Persian-based Sassanians. **637:** Sassanian Empire destroyed by Muslim Arabs at battle of Qadisiya, in southern Iraq; Islam spread. **750–1258:** Dominated by Abbasid dynasty, who reigned as caliphs (Islamic civil and religious leaders) in Baghdad. **1258:** Baghdad invaded and burned by Tatars. **1401:** Baghdad destroyed by Mongol ruler Tamerlane. **1533:** Annexed by Suleiman the Magnificent, becoming part of the Ottoman Empire until the 20th century, despite recurrent anti-Ottoman insurrections. **1916:** Occupied by Britain during World War I. **1920:** Iraq became a British League of Nations protectorate. **1921:** Hashemite dynasty established, with Faisal I installed by Britain as king. **1932:** Independence achieved from British protectorate status, with Gen Nuri-el Said as prime minister. **1941–45:** Occupied by Britain during World War II. **1955:** Signed the Baghdad Pact collective security treaty with the UK, Iran, Pakistan, and Turkey. **1958:** Monarchy overthrown in military-led revolution, in which King Faisal was assassinated; Iraq became a republic; joined Jordan in an Arab Federation; withdrew from

Baghdad Pact as left-wing military regime assumed power. **1963:** Joint socialist-nationalist Ba'athist-military coup headed by Col Salem Aref and backed by US Central Intelligence Agency; reign of terror launched against the left. **1968:** Ba'athist military coup put Maj-Gen Ahmed Hassan al-Bakr in power. **1979:** Al-Bakr replaced by Saddam Hussein of the Arab Ba'ath Socialist Party. **1980:** War between Iraq and Iran broke out. **1985–87:** Fighting intensified, with heavy loss of life. **1988:** Cease-fire; talks began with Iran. Iraq used chemical weapons against Kurdish rebels seeking greater autonomy in the NW. **1989:** Unsuccessful coup against President Hussein; Iraq successfully launched ballistic test missile. **1990:** Peace treaty favouring Iran agreed. Iraq invaded and annexed Kuwait in Aug. US forces massed in Saudi Arabia at request of King Fahd. UN ordered Iraqi withdrawal and imposed total trade ban; further UN resolution sanctioned force. All foreign hostages released. **1991:** US-led Allied forces launched aerial assault on Iraq and destroyed country's infrastructure; land–sea–air offensive to free Kuwait successful. Uprisings of Kurds and Shi'ites brutally suppressed by surviving Iraqi troops. Allied troops established 'safe havens' for Kurds in N prior to withdrawal, and left rapid-reaction force near Turkish border. **1992:** UN imposed 'no-fly zone' over S Iraq to protect Shi'ites. **1993:** Iraqi incursions into 'no-fly zone' prompted US-led alliance aircraft to bomb 'strategic' targets in Iraq. Continued persecution of Shi'ites in the S. **1995:** UN sanctions extended. **1996:** Iraqi-backed attacks on Kurds prompted US retaliation; air strikes destroyed Iraqi military bases in S. **1997:** Iraq continued to resist US and Allied pressure to allow UN weapons inspections. **1998:** Iraq expelled UN weapons inspectors, leading to build-up of US military strength in the Gulf; military conflict was averted by agreement secured by UN Secretary-General Kofi Annan. April: UN inspectors' report showed that Iraq had failed to meet UN requirements on the destruction of chemical and biological weapons.

Ireland Republic of

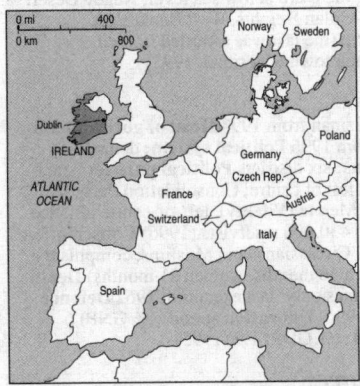

National name: *Eire* **Area:** 70,282 sq km/27,135 sq mi **Capital:** Dublin **Major towns/cities:** Cork, Limerick, Galway, Waterford, Wexford **Major ports:** Cork, Dun Laoghaire, Limerick, Waterford, Galway **Physical features:** central plateau surrounded by hills; rivers Shannon, Liffey, Boyne; Bog of Allen; Macgillicuddy's Reeks, Wicklow Mountains; Lough Corrib, lakes of Killarney; Galway Bay and Aran Islands

Government

Head of state: Mary McAleese from 1997 **Head of government:** Bertie Ahern from 1997 **Political system:** democracy **Administrative divisions:** 26 counties within four provinces **Political parties:** Fianna Fáil (Soldiers of Destiny), moderate centre right; Fine Gael (Irish Tribe or United Ireland Party), moderate centre left; Labour Party, moderate left of centre; Progressive Democrats, radical free-enterprise **Armed forces:** 12,700 (1996) **Conscription:** military service is voluntary **Death penalty:** abolished 1990 **Defence spend:** (% GDP) 1.1 (1996) **Education spend:** (% GNP) 6.4 (1993–94) **Health spend:** (% GDP) 5.1 (1993)

Economy and resources

Currency: Irish pound (punt Eireannach) **GDP:** ($ US) 69.6 billion (1996) **Real GDP per capita (PPP):** ($ US) 18,784 (1996) **GDP growth rate:** 6.5% (1996); 4.7% (1990–95) **Average annual inflation:** 1.8% (1996); 2.5% (1985–95) **Major trading partners:** UK, USA, Germany, France **Resources:** lead, zinc, peat, limestone, gypsum, petroleum, natural gas, copper, silver **Industries:** textiles, machinery, chemicals, electronics, motor vehicle manufacturing and assembly, food processing, beer, tourism **Exports:** beef and dairy products, live animals, machinery and transport equipment, electronic goods, chemicals. Principal market: UK 25.4% (1995) **Imports:** petroleum products, machinery and transport equipment, chemicals, foodstuffs, animal feed, textiles and clothing. Principal source: UK 35.6% (1995) **Arable land:** 19.3% (1995) **Agricultural products:** barley, potatoes, sugar beet, wheat, oats; livestock (cattle) and dairy products

Population and society

Population: 3,554,000 (1996 est) **Population growth rate:** 0.3% (1990–95); 0.4% (2000–05) **Population density:** (per sq km) 51 (1996 est) **Urban population:** (% of total) 58 (1995) **Age distribution:** (% of total population) <15 24.4%, 15–65 64.3%, >65 11.2% (1995) **Ethnic groups:** most of the population has Celtic origins **Language:** Irish Gaelic and English (both official) **Religion:** Roman Catholic 95%, Church of Ireland, other Protestant denominations **Education:** (compulsory years) 9 **Literacy rate:** 99% (men); 99% (women) (1995 est) **Labour force:** 41.3% of population: 10.4% agriculture, 27.2% industry, 62.3% services (1996) **Unemployment:** 11.8% (1996) **Life expectancy:** 73 (men); 79 (women) (1995–2000) **Child mortality rate:** (under 5, per 1,000 live births) 7 (1996) **Physicians:** 1 per 431 people (1995)

Practical information

Visa requirements: UK: visa not required. USA: visa not required **Embassy in the UK:** 17 Grosvenor Place, London SW1X 7HR. Tel: (0171) 235 2171; fax: (0171) 245 6961 **British embassy:** 31–33 Merrion Road, Dublin 4. Tel: (1) 269 5211; fax: (1) 283 8423 **Chamber of commerce:** Chambers of Commerce of Ireland, 22 Merrion Square, Dublin 2. Tel: (1) 661 2888; fax: (1) 661 2811 **Airports:** international airports: Dublin, Shannon, Cork, Knock (Horan), Galway; five domestic airports; total passenger km: 4,920 million (1994) **Major holidays:** 1 January, 17 March, 25–26 December; variable: Good Friday, Easter Monday, June Holiday, August Holiday, October Holiday, Christmas Holiday

Chronology

3rd century BC: The Gaels, a Celtic people, invaded Ireland and formed about 150 small kingdoms. **AD c. 432:** St Patrick introduced Christianity. **5th–9th centuries:** Irish Church remained a centre of culture and scholarship. **9th–11th centuries:** The Vikings raided Ireland until defeated by High King Brian Boru at Clontarf 1014. **12th–13th centuries:** Anglo-Norman adventurers conquered much of Ireland, but no central government was formed and many became assimilated. **14th–15th centuries:** Irish chieftains recovered their lands, restricting English rule to the Pale around Dublin. **1536:** Henry VIII of England made ineffectual efforts to impose the Protestant Reformation on Ireland. **1541:** Irish Parliament recognized Henry VIII as king of Ireland; Henry gave peerages to Irish chieftains. **1579:** English suppressed Desmond rebellion, confiscated rebel lands, and tried to 'plant' them with English settlers. **1610:** James I established plantation of Ulster with Protestant settlers from England and Scotland. **1641:** Catholic Irish rebelled against English rule; Oliver Cromwell brutally reasserted English control 1649–50; Irish landowners evicted and replaced with English landowners. **1689–91:** Williamite War: following the 'Glorious Revolution', the Catholic Irish unsuccessfully supported James II against Protestant William III in civil war. Penal laws barred Catholics from obtaining wealth and power. **1720:** Act passed declaring British Parliament's right to legislate for Ireland. **1739–41:** Famine killed one-third of population of 1.5 million. **1782:** Protestant landlords led by Henry

Republic of Ireland: Provinces and Counties

Province/county	Administrative headquarters	Area sq km	Area sq mi	Population (1996 est.)
Ulster Province				
Cavan	Cavan	1,890	729	52,900
Donegal	Lifford	4,830	1,864	129,400
Monaghan	Monaghan	1,290	498	51,300
Munster Province				
Clare	Ennis	3,190	1,231	93,900
Cork	Cork	7,460	2,880	420,300
Kerry	Tralee	4,700	1,814	125,900
Limerick	Limerick	2,690	1,038	177,900
Tipperary (North)	Nenagh	2,000	772	57,900
Tipperary (South)	Clonmel	2,260	872	75,400
Waterford	Waterford	1,840	710	94,600
Leinster Province				
Carlow	Carlow	900	347	41,600
Dublin	Dublin	920	355	1,056,700
Kildare	Naas	1,690	652	134,900
Kilkenny	Kilkenny	2,060	795	75,200
Laois (or Laoighis)	Port Laoise	1,720	664	52,800
Longford	Longford	1,040	401	30,100
Louth	Dundalk	820	316	92,200
Meath	Navan	2,340	903	109,400
Offaly	Tullamore	2,000	772	59,100
Westmeath	Mullingar	1,760	679	63,200
Wexford	Wexford	2,350	907	104,300
Wicklow	Wicklow	2,030	783	102,400
Connacht (or Connaught) Province				
Galway	Galway	5,940	2,293	188,600
Leitrim	Carrick-on-Shannon	1,530	590	25,000
Mayo	Castlebar	5,400	2,084	111,400
Roscommon	Roscommon	2,460	949	51,900
Sligo	Sligo	1,800	694	55,600

Grattan secured end of restrictions on Irish trade and parliament. **1798:** British suppressed revolt by Society of United Irishmen (with French support) led by Wolfe Tone. **1800:** Act of Union abolished Irish parliament and created United Kingdom of Great Britain and Ireland, effective 1801. **1829:** Daniel O'Connell secured Catholic Emancipation Act, which permitted Catholics to enter parliament. **1846–51:** Potato famine reduced population by 20% through starvation and emigration. **1870:** Land Act increased security for tenants but failed to halt agrarian disorder; Isaac Butt formed political party to campaign for Irish Home Rule (devolution). **1885:** Home Rulers, led by Charles Stewart Parnell, held balance of power in parliament; first Home Rule Bill rejected 1886; second Home Rule Bill defeated 1893. **1905:** Arthur Griffith founded the nationalist movement Sinn Féin ('Ourselves Alone'). **1914:** Ireland came close to civil war as Ulster prepared to resist implementation of Home Rule Act (postponed because of World War I). **1916:** Easter Rising: nationalists proclaimed a republic in Dublin; British crushed revolt and executed 15 leaders. **1919:** Sinn Féin MPs formed Irish parliament in Dublin in defiance of British government. **1919–21:** Irish Republican Army (IRA) waged guerrilla war against British forces. **1921:** Anglo-Irish Treaty partitioned Ireland; N Ireland (Ulster) remained part of the United Kingdom; S Ireland won full internal self-government with dominion status. **1922:** Irish Free State proclaimed; IRA split over Anglo-Irish Treaty led to civil war 1922–23. **1932:** Anti-Treaty party, Fianna Fáil, came to power under Éamonn de Valéra. **1937:** New constitution established Eire (Gaelic name for Ireland) as a sovereign state and refused to acknowledge partition. **1949:** After remaining neutral in World War II, Eire left the Commonwealth

and became the Republic of Ireland. **1973:** Ireland joined European Economic Community. **1985:** Anglo-Irish Agreement gave the Republic of Ireland a consultative role, but no powers, in the government of Northern Ireland. **1993:** Downing Street Declaration: joint Anglo-Irish peace proposal for Northern Ireland issued. **1994:** Cease-fires announced by Catholic and Protestant paramilitaries in Northern Ireland. **1995:** Ulster framework peace document issued. **1998:** Following multi-party talks, a historic agreement (known as the Good Friday Agreement) was reached on the future of Northern Ireland; in the May referendum, 94% of votes were cast for dropping Ireland's claim to the North.

Israel State of

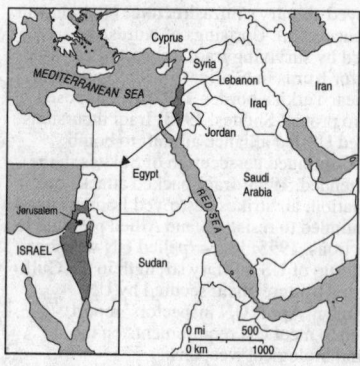

National name: *Medinat Israel* **Area:** 20,800 sq km/8,030 sq mi (as at 1949 armistice) **Capital:** Jerusalem (not recognized by United Nations) **Major towns/cities:** Tel Aviv-Yafo, Haifa, Bat-Yam, Holon, Ramat Gan, Petach Tikva, Rishon Leziyyon, Beersheba **Major ports:** Tel Aviv-Yafo, Haifa, 'Akko (formerly Acre), Eilat **Physical features:** coastal plain of Sharon between Haifa and Tel Aviv noted since ancient times for its fertility; central mountains of Galilee, Samaria, and Judea; Dead Sea, Lake Tiberias, and River Jordan Rift Valley along the E are below sea level; Negev Desert in the S; Israel occupies Golan Heights, West Bank, East Jerusalem, and Gaza Strip (the last was awarded limited autonomy, with West Bank town of Jericho, 1993)

Government

Head of state: Ezer Weizman from 1993 **Head of government:** Binyamin Netanyahu from 1996 **Political system:** democracy **Administrative divisions:** six districts **Political parties:** Israel Labour Party, moderate, left of centre; Consolidation Party (Likud), right of centre; Meretz (Vitality), left-of-centre alliance **Armed forces:** 175,000; 430,000 reservists (1996) **Conscription:** voluntary for Christians, Circassians, and Muslims; compulsory for Jews and Druzes (men 36 months, women 21 months) **Death penalty:** exceptional crimes only; last execution 1962 **Defence spend:** (% GDP) 12.1 (1996) **Education spend:** (% GNP) 6 (1993–94) **Health spend:** (% GDP) 1.9 (1993)

Economy and resources

Currency: shekel **GDP:** ($ US) 78 billion (1994) **Real GDP per capita (PPP):** ($ US) 16,023 (1994) **GDP growth rate:** 7.1% (1995); 6.4% (1990–95) **Average annual inflation:** 12% (1996); 17.1% (1985–95) **Foreign debt:** 30.4 billion (1996) **Major trading partners:** USA, UK, Germany, Belgium, Italy, Japan, Switzerland **Resources:** potash, bromides, magnesium, sulphur, copper ore, gold, salt, petroleum, natural gas **Industries:** food processing, beverages, tobacco, electrical machinery, chemicals, petroleum and coal products, metal products, diamond polishing, transport equipment, tourism **Exports:** citrus fruits, worked diamonds, machinery and parts, military hardware, food products, chemical products, textiles and clothing. Principal market: USA 30.1% (1995) **Imports:** machinery and parts, rough diamonds, chemicals and related products, crude petroleum and petroleum products, motor vehicles. Principal source: USA 18.6% (1995) **Arable land:** 17% (1995) **Agricultural products:** citrus fruits, vegetables, potatoes, wheat, melons, pumpkins, avocados; poultry and fish production

Population and society

Population: 5,664,000 (1996 est) **Population growth rate:** 3.8% (1990–95); 1.3% (2000–05) **Population density:** (per sq km) 269 (1996 est) **Urban population:** (% of total) 91 (1995) **Age distribution:** (% of total population) <15 29.1%, 15–65 61.4%, >65 9.5% (1995) **Ethnic groups:** around 85% of the population is Jewish, the majority of the remainder Arab. Under the Law of Return 1950, 'every Jew shall be entitled to come to Israel as an immigrant'; those from the East and Eastern Europe are Ashkenazim, and those from Mediterranean Europe (Spain, Portugal, Italy, France, Greece) and Arab Africa are Sephardim (over 50% of the population is now of Sephardic descent); an Israeli-born Jew is a Sabra **Language:** Hebrew and Arabic (official); English, Yiddish, European and W Asian languages **Religion:** Israel is a secular state, but the predominant faith is Judaism 85%; also Sunni Muslim, Christian, and Druse **Education:** (compulsory years) 11 **Literacy rate:** 97% (men); 93% (women) (1995 est) **Labour force:** 39% of population: 4% agriculture, 29% industry, 67% services (1990) **Unemployment:** 6.7% (1996) **Life expectancy:** 75 (men); 79 (women) (1995–2000) **Child mortality rate:** (under 5, per 1,000 live births) 9 (1996) **Physicians:** 1 per 350 people (1991)

Practical information

Visa requirements: UK: visa not required. USA: visa not required **Embassy in the UK:** 2 Palace Green, London W8 4QB. Tel: (0171) 957 9500; fax: (0171) 957 9555 **British embassy:** 192 Rehov Hayarkon, Tel Aviv 63405. Tel: (3) 524 9171/8; fax: (3) 524 3313 **Chamber of commerce:** Federation of Israeli Chambers of Commerce, PO Box 20027, 84 Hahashmonaim Street, Tel Aviv 67011. Tel: (3) 563 1010; fax: (3) 561 9025 **Airports:** international airports: Tel Aviv (Ben Gurion), Eilat; domestic airports in all major cities; total passenger km: 9,662 million (1994) **Major holidays:** 1 January, 14 May; variable: New Year (Jewish, September/October), Purim (March), first day of Passover (April), last day of Passover (April), Pentecost (June), Fast of Av (August), Yom Kippur (October), Feast of Tabernacles (October, 2 days)

Chronology

c. 2000 BC: Abraham, father of the Jewish people, is believed to have come to Palestine from Mesopotamia. **c. 1225 BC:** Moses led the Jews out of slavery in Egypt towards the promised land of Palestine. **11th century BC:** Saul established a Jewish kingdom in Palestine; developed by kings David and Solomon. **586 BC:** Jews defeated by Babylon and deported; many returned to Palestine 539 BC. **333 BC:** Alexander the Great of Macedonia conquered the entire region. **3rd century BC:** Control of Palestine contested by Ptolemies of Egypt and Seleucids of Syria. **142 BC:** Jewish independence restored after Maccabean revolt. **63 BC:** Palestine fell to the Roman Empire. **70 AD:** Romans crushed the Zealot rebellion and destroyed Jerusalem; start of dispersion of Jews (diaspora). **614:** Persians took Jerusalem from Byzantine Empire. **637:** Muslim Arabs conquered Palestine. **1099:** First Crusade captured Jerusalem; Christian kingdom lasted a century before falling to sultans of Egypt. **1517:** Palestine conquered by the Ottoman Turks. **1897:** Theodor Herzl organized the First Zionist Congress at Basel to publicize Jewish claims to Palestine. **1917:** The Balfour Declaration: Britain expressed support for the creation of a Jewish National Home in Palestine. **1918:** British forces expelled the Turks from Palestine, which became a British League of Nations mandate 1920. **1929:** Severe communal violence around Jerusalem caused by Arab alarm at doubling of Jewish population in ten years. **1933:** Jewish riots in protest at British attempts to restrict Jewish immigration. **1937:** The Peel Report, recommending partition, accepted by most Jews but rejected by Arabs; open warfare ensued 1937–38. **1939:** Britain postponed independence plans on account of World War II, and increased military presence. **1946:** Resumption of terrorist violence; Jewish extremists blew up British headquarters in Jerusalem. **1947:** United Nations (UN) voted for partition of Palestine. **1948:** Britain withdrew; Independent State of Israel proclaimed with David Ben-Gurion as prime minister; Israel repulsed invasion by Arab nations; many Palestinian Arabs settled in refugee camps in the Gaza Strip and West Bank. **1952:** Col Gamal Nasser of Egypt stepped up blockade of Israeli ports and support of Arab guerrillas in Gaza. **1956:** War between Israel and Egypt; Israeli invasion of Gaza and Sinai followed by withdrawal 1957. **1963:** Levi Eshkol succeeded Ben-Gurion as prime minister. **1964:** Palestine Liberation Organization (PLO) founded to unite Palestinian Arabs with the aim of overthrowing the state of Israel. **1967:** Israel defeated Egypt, Syria, and Jordan in the Six-Day War; Gaza, West Bank, E Jerusalem, Sinai, and Golan Heights captured. **1969:** Golda Meir (Labour) elected prime minister; Yassir Arafat became chair of the PLO; escalation of terrorism and border raids. **1973:** Yom Kippur War: Israel repulsed surprise attack by Egypt and Syria. **1974:** Golda Meir succeeded by Yitzhak Rabin. **1977:** Right-wing Likud bloc took office under Menachem Begin; President Anwar Sadat of Egypt began peace initiative. **1979:** Camp David talks ended with signing of peace treaty between Israel and Egypt; Israel withdrew from Sinai. **1980:** United Jerusalem declared capital of Israel. **1982:** Israeli forces invaded S Lebanon to drive out PLO guerrillas; occupation continued until 1985. **1985:** Labour and Likud formed coalition government led by Shimon Peres 1985–86 and Yitzhak Shamir 1986–90. **1988:** Israeli handling of Palestinian uprising (Intifada) in occupied territories provoked international criticism. **1990:** Shamir headed Likud government following the breakup of the coalition; PLO formally recognized the state of Israel. **1991:** Iraq launched missile attacks on Israel during Gulf War; Middle East peace talks began in Madrid. **1992:** Labour government elected under Yitzhak Rabin. **1993:** Rabin and Arafat signed peace accord; Israel granted limited autonomy to Gaza Strip and Jericho. **1994:** Arafat became head of autonomous Palestinian authority in Gaza and Jericho; peace agreement between Israel and Jordan. **1995:** Rabin assassinated by Jewish opponent of peace accord; Peres became prime minister. **1996:** Likud government elected under Binyamin Netanyahu, critic of peace accord. Revival of communal violence; peace process threatened. The opening of a 2,000-year-old tunnel near the Al-Aqsa mosque in Jerusalem in Sept provoked renewed Palestinian–Israeli conflict. **1997:** Jewish settlement in E Jerusalem widely condemned. Suicide bombs by Hamas in Jerusalem. Partial and limited West Bank withdrawal. **1998** May: violence flared on West Bank between Palestinian and Israeli troops. Netanyahu demanded guarantees of security from the Palestinian authorities.

Italy Republic of

National name: *Repubblica Italiana* **Area:** 301,300 sq km/116,331 sq mi **Capital:** Rome **Major towns/cities:** Milan, Naples, Turin, Palermo, Genoa, Bologna **Major ports:** Naples, Genoa, Palermo, Bari, Catania, Trieste **Physical features:** mountainous (Maritime Alps, Dolomites, Apennines) with narrow coastal lowlands; continental Europe's only active volcanoes: Vesuvius, Etna, Stromboli; rivers Po, Adige, Arno, Tiber, Rubicon; islands of Sicily, Sardinia, Elba, Capri, Ischia, Lipari, Pantelleria; lakes Como, Maggiore, Garda

Italy: Regions

Region	Capital	Area		Population
		sq km	sq mi	(1995)
Abruzzi	L'Aquila	10,794	4,168	1,267,700
Basilicata	Potenza	9,992	3,858	610,700
Calabria	Catanzaro	15,080	5,822	2,076,100
Campania	Naples	13,595	5,249	5,745,800
Emilia-Romagna	Bologna	22,123	8,542	3,922,600
Friuli-Venezia Giulia[1]	Trieste	7,846	3,029	1,191,200
Lazio	Rome	17,203	6,642	5,193,200
Liguria	Genoa	5,416	2,091	1,663,700
Lombardy	Milan	23,856	9,211	8,910,500
Marche	Ancona	9,694	3,743	1,441,000
Molise	Campobasso	4,438	1,714	332,200
Piedmont	Turin	25,399	9,807	4,298,000
Puglia	Bari	19,347	7,470	4,075,800
Sardinia[1]	Cagliari	24,090	9,301	1,659,500
Sicily[1]	Palermo	25,708	9,926	5,082,700
Trentino-Alto Adige[1]	Trento	13,613	5,256	908,700
Tuscany	Florence	22,992	8,877	3,526,000
Umbria	Perugia	8,456	3,265	822,500
Valle d'Aosta[1]	Aosta	3,262	1,259	118,500
Veneto	Venice	18,364	7,090	1,122,300

[1] Special autonomous region.

Government

Head of state: Oscar Luigi Scalfaro from 1992 **Head of government:** Romano Prodi from 1996 **Political system:** democracy **Administrative divisions:** 94 provinces within 20 regions (of which five have a greater degree of autonomy) **Political parties:** Forza Italia (Go Italy!), free market, right of centre; Northern League (LN), Milan-based, federalist, right of centre; National Alliance (AN), neofascist; Italian Popular Party (PPI), Catholic, centrist; Italian Renewal Party, centrist; Democratic Party of the Left (PDS), pro-European, moderate left wing (ex-communist); Italian Socialist Party (PSI), moderate socialist; Italian Republican Party (PRI), social democratic, left of centre; Democratic Alliance (AD), moderate left of centre; Christian Democratic Centre (CCD), Christian, centrist; Olive Tree alliance, centre left; Panella List, radical liberal; Union of the Democratic Centre (UDC), right of centre; Pact for Italy, reformist; Communist Refoundation (RC), Marxist; Verdi, environmentalist; La Rete (the Network), anti-Mafia **Armed forces:** 325,500 (1996) **Conscription:** 12 months **Death penalty:** abolished 1994 **Defence spend:** (% GDP) 2.2 (1996) **Education spend:** (% GNP) 5.2 (1993–94) **Health spend:** (% GDP) 6.2 (1993)

Economy and resources

Currency: lira **GDP:** ($ US) 1,207.7 billion (1996) **Real GDP per capita (PPP):** ($ US) 19,950 (1996) **GDP growth rate:** –0.4% (1996); 1% (1990–95) **Average annual inflation:** 3.9% (1996); 6% (1985–95) **Major trading partners:** EU (principally Germany, France, and UK), USA **Resources:** lignite, lead, zinc, mercury, potash, sulphur, fluorspar, bauxite, marble, petroleum, natural gas, fish **Industries:** machinery and machine tools, textiles, leather, footwear, food and beverages, steel, motor vehicles, chemical products, wine, tourism **Exports:** machinery and transport equipment, textiles, clothing, footwear, wine (leading producer and exporter), metals and metal products, chemicals, wood, paper and rubber goods. Principal market: Germany 18.7% (1995) **Imports:** mineral fuels and lubricants, machinery and transport equipment, chemical products, foodstuffs, metal products. Principal source: Germany 19.1% (1995) **Arable land:** 27.6% (1995) **Agricultural products:** sugar beet, grapes, wheat, maize, tomatoes, olives, citrus fruits, vegetables; fishing

Population and society

Population: 57,226,000 (1996 est) **Population growth rate:** 0.1%

(1990–95); –0.2% (2000–05) **Population density:** (per sq km) 190 (1996 est) **Urban population:** (% of total) 67% (1995) **Age distribution:** (% of total population) <15 15.1%, 15–65 68.9%, >65 16% (1995) **Ethnic groups:** mainly Italian; some minorities of German origin **Language:** Italian; German, French, Slovene, and Albanian minorities **Religion:** Roman Catholic 100% (state religion) **Education:** (compulsory years) 8 **Literacy rate:** 98% (men); 96% (women) (1995 est) **Labour force:** 44.6% of the population: 7% agriculture, 32.1% industry, 60.9% services (1996) **Unemployment:** 12% (1996) **Life expectancy:** 75 (men); 81 (women) (1995–2000) **Child mortality rate:** (under 5, per 1,000 live births) 9 (1996) **Physicians:** 1 per 192 people (1993)

Practical information

Visa requirements: UK: visa not required. USA: visa not required **Embassy in the UK:** 14 Three Kings Yard, Davies Street, London W1Y 2EH. Tel: (0171) 312 2200; fax: (0171) 312 2230 **British embassy:** Via XX Settembre 80A, 00187 Rome. Tel: (6) 482 5551; fax: (6) 487 3324 **Chamber of commerce:** Unione Italiana delle Camere di Commercio, Industria, Artigianato e Agricoltura, Piazza Sallustio 21, 00187 Rome. Tel: (6) 47041; telex: 622 327 **Airports:** international airports: Bologna (G Marconi), Genoa (Cristoforo Colombo), Milan (Linate and Malpensa), Naples (Capodichino), Palermo (Punta Rais), Pisa (Galileo Galilei), Rome (Leonardo da Vinci and Ciampino), Turin, Venice (Marco Polo); over 30 domestic airports; total passenger km: 31,738 million (1994) **Major holidays:** 1, 6 January, 25 April, 1 May, 14 August (mid-August holiday, 2 days), 1 November, 8, 25–26 December; variable: Easter Monday

Chronology

4th and 3rd centuries BC: Italian peninsula united under Roman rule. **AD 476:** End of Western Roman Empire. **568:** Invaded by Lombards. **756:** Papal States created in central Italy. **800:** Charlemagne united Italy and Germany in Holy Roman Empire. **12th and 13th centuries:** Papacy and Holy Roman Empire contended for political supremacy; papal power reached its peak under Innocent III (1198–1216). **1183:** Cities of Lombard League (founded 1164) became independent. **14th century:** Beginnings of Renaissance in N Italy. **15th century:** Most of Italy ruled by five rival states: the city-states of Milan, Florence, and Venice; the Papal States; and the Kingdom of Naples. **1494:** Charles VIII of France invaded Italy. **1529–59:** Spanish Habsburgs secured dominance in Italy. **17th century:** Italy effectively part of Spanish Empire; economic and cultural decline. **1713:** Treaty of Utrecht gave political control of most of Italy to Austrian Habsburgs. **1796–1814:** France conquered Italy, setting up satellite states and introducing principles of French Revolution. **1815:** Old regimes largely restored; Italy divided between Austria, Papal States, Naples, Sardinia, and four duchies. **1831:** Giuseppe Mazzini

The dome of Florence Cathedral, designed by the 15th century architect Filippo Brunelleschi
© Linda Proud

founded 'Young Italy' movement with aim of creating unified republic. **1848–49:** Liberal revolutions occurred throughout Italy; reversed everywhere except Sardinia, which became centre of nationalism under leadership of Count Camillo di Cavour. **1859:** France and Sardinia forcibly expelled Austrians from Lombardy. **1860:** Sardinia annexed duchies and Papal States (except Rome); Giuseppe Garibaldi overthrew Neapolitan monarchy. **1861:** Victor Emmanuel II of Sardinia proclaimed King of Italy in Turin. **1866:** Italy gained Venetia after defeat of Austria by Prussia. **1870:** Italian forces occupied Rome in defiance of Pope, completing unification of Italy. **1882:** Italy joined Germany and Austria-Hungary in Triple Alliance. **1896:** Attempt to conquer Ethiopia defeated at Battle of Adowa. **1900:** King Umberto I assassinated by an anarchist. **1912:** Annexation of Libya and Dodecanese after Italo-Turkish War. **1915:** Italy entered World War I on side of Allies. **1919:** Peace treaties awarded Trentino, South Tyrol, and Trieste to Italy. **1922:** Mussolini established fascist dictatorship following period of strikes and agrarian revolts. **1935–36:** Conquest of Ethiopia. **1939:** Invasion of Albania. **1940:** Italy entered World War II as ally of Germany. **1943:** Allies invaded southern Italy; Mussolini removed from power; Germans occupied northern and central Italy. **1945:** Allies completed liberation. **1946:** Monarchy replaced by republic. **1947:** Peace treaty stripped Italy of its colonies. **1948:** New constitution adopted; Christian Democrats emerged as main party of government in political system marked by ministerial instability. **1957:** Italy became a founder member of European Economic Community (EEC). **1963:** Creation of first of long series of fragile centre-left coalition governments. **1976:** Communists attempt to join coalition, the 'historic compromise', rejected by Christian Democrats. **1978:** Christian Democrat Aldo Moro, architect of historic compromise, murdered by Red Brigade guerrillas infiltrated by Western intelligence agents. **1983–87:** Bettino Craxi, Italy's first Socialist prime minister, led coalition; economy improved. **1993:** Major political crisis triggered by exposure of government corruption and Mafia links; governing parties discredited; new electoral system replaced proportional representation with 75% majority voting. **1994:** Media tycoon Silvio Berlusconi created new party, Forza Italia, and formed right-wing coalition. **1995:** Lamberto Dini headed non-party government of 'experts'. **1996:** Olive Tree Alliance won general election; Romano Prodi became prime minister. **1997:** Prodi resigned, 'grand coalition' sought; Communist support persuaded Prodi to continue. Berlusconi sentenced but sentence immediately quashed; Prodi cleared of corruption charges.

Jamaica

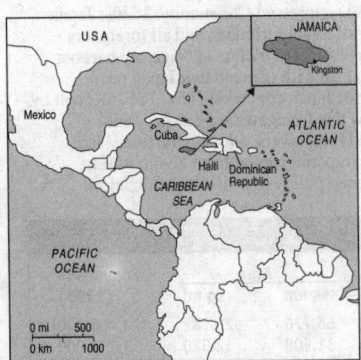

Area: 10,957 sq km/4,230 sq mi **Capital:** Kingston **Major towns/cities:** Montego Bay, Spanish Town, St Andrew, Portmore, May Pen **Physical features:** mountainous tropical island; Blue Mountains (so called because of the haze over them)

Government

Head of state: Elizabeth II from 1962, represented by governor general Howard Felix Hanlan Cooke from 1991 **Head of government:** Percival Patterson from 1992 **Political system:** constitutional monarchy **Administrative divisions:** 13 parishes **Political parties:** Jamaica Labour Party (JLP), moderate, centrist; People's National Party (PNP), left of centre; National Democratic Union (NDM), centrist **Armed forces:** 3,320 (1996) **Conscription:** military service is voluntary **Death penalty:** retained and used for ordinary crimes **Defence spend:** (% GDP) 0.6 (1996) **Education spend:** (% GNP) 4.2 (1994) **Health spend:** (% GDP) 3 (1990–95)

Economy and resources

Currency: Jamaican dollar **GDP:** ($ US) 4.2 billion (1994) **Real GDP per capita (PPP):** ($ US) 3,816 (1994) **GDP growth rate:** 0.8% (1994); 2.9% (1990–95) **Average annual inflation:** 26.5% (1996); 28.3% (1985–95) **Foreign debt:** ($ US) 4.4 billion (1996) **Major trading partners:** USA, UK, Mexico, Venezuela, Germany, Canada, Norway **Resources:** bauxite (one of world's major producers), marble, gypsum, silica, clay **Industries:** mining and quarrying, bauxite processing, food processing, petroleum refining, clothing, cement, glass, tourism **Exports:** bauxite, alumina, gypsum, sugar, bananas, garments, rum. Principal market: USA 45.4% (1995) **Imports:** mineral fuels, machinery and transport equipment, basic manufactures, chemicals, food and live animals, miscellaneous manufactured articles. Principal source: USA 58% (1995) **Arable land:** 16.3% (1995) **Agricultural products:** sugar cane, bananas, citrus fruit, coffee, cocoa, coconuts; livestock rearing (goats, cattle, and pigs)

Population and society

Population: 2,491,000 (1996 est) **Population growth rate:** 0.7% (1990–95); 1% (2000–05) **Population density:** (per sq km) 227 (1996 est) **Urban population:** (% of total) 54 (1995) **Age distribution:** (% of total population) <15 30.8%, 15–65 62.6%, >65 6.6% (1995) **Ethnic groups:** nearly 80% of African descent; about 15% of mixed African-European origin. There are also Chinese, Indian, and European minorities **Language:** English, Jamaican creole **Religion:** Protestant 70%, Rastafarian **Education:** (compulsory years) 6 **Literacy rate:** 98% (men); 99% (women) (1995 est) **Labour force:** 49% of population: 25% agriculture, 23% industry, 52% services (1990) **Unemployment:** 15.7% (1992) **Life expectancy:** 72 (men); 77 (women) (1995–2000) **Child mortality rate:** (under 5, per 1,000 live births) 20 (1996) **Physicians:** 1 per 6,420 people (1993)

Practical information

Visa requirements: UK: visa not required. USA: visa not required **Embassy in the UK:** 1–2 Prince Consort Road, London SW7 2BZ. Tel: (0171) 823 9911; fax: (0171) 589 5154 **British embassy:** British High Commission, PO Box 575, Trafalgar Road, Kingston 10. Tel: (809) 926 9050; fax: (809) 929 7869 **Chamber of commerce:** PO Box 172, 7–8 East Parade, Kingston. Tel: (809) 922 0150; fax: (809) 924 9056 **Airports:** international airports: Kingston (Norman Manley), Montego Bay (Donald Sangster); four domestic airports; total passenger km: 1,430 million (1994) **Major holidays:** 1 January, 23 May, 5 August, 20 October, 25–26 December; variable: Ash Wednesday, Good Friday, Easter Monday

Chronology

c. AD 900: Settled by Arawak Indians, who gave the island the name Jamaica ('well watered'). **1494:** The explorer Christopher Columbus reached Jamaica. **1509:** Occupied by Spanish; much of the Arawak community died from exposure to European diseases; black African slaves were brought in to work the sugar plantations. **1655:** Captured by Britain and became its most valuable Caribbean colony. **1838:** Slavery abolished. **1870:** Banana plantations established as sugar cane industry declined in face of competition from European beet sugar. **1938:** Serious riots during the economic depression and, as a sign of growing political awareness, the People's National Party (PNP) was formed by Norman Manley. **1944:** First constitution adopted. **1958–62:** Part of West Indies Federation. **1959:** Internal self-government granted. **1962:** Independence achieved within the Commonwealth, with Alexander Bustamante of the centre-right Jamaica Labour Party (JLP) as prime minister. **1967:** JLP re-elected under Hugh Shearer. **1972:** Michael Manley of the PNP became prime minister and pursued a policy of economic self-reliance. **1980:** JLP elected, with Edward Seaga as prime minister, following violent election campaign. **1981:** Diplomatic links with Cuba severed; free-market economic programme pursued. **1983:** JLP won all 60 seats in the general election. **1988:** Island badly damaged by Hurricane Gilbert. **1989:** PNP won a landslide victory with a newly moderate Manley returning as prime minister. **1992:** Manley retired; succeeded by Percival Patterson. **1993:** PNP increased its majority in general election.

Japan

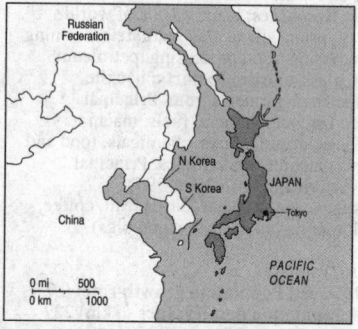

National name: *Nippon* **Area:** 377,535 sq km/145,766 sq mi **Capital:** Tokyo **Major towns/cities:** Yokohama, Osaka, Nagoya, Fukuoka, Kitakyushu, Kyoto, Sapporo, Kobe, Kawasaki, Hiroshima **Major ports:** Osaka, Nagoya, Yokohama, Kobe

Physical features: mountainous, volcanic (Mount Fuji, volcanic Mount Aso, Japan Alps); comprises over 1,000 islands, the largest of which are Hokkaido, Honshu, Kyushu, and Shikoku

Government

Head of state: (figurehead) Emperor Akihito (Heisei) from 1989 **Head of government:** Ryutaro Hashimoto from 1996 **Political system:** liberal democracy **Administrative divisions:** 47 prefectures **Political parties:** Liberal Democratic Party (LDP), right of centre; Shinshinto (New Frontier Party) opposition coalition, centrist reformist; Social Democratic Party of Japan (SDPJ, former Socialist Party), left of centre but moving towards centre; Shinto Sakigake (New Party Harbinger), right of centre; Japanese Communist Party (JCP), socialist; Democratic Party of Japan (DPJ), Sakigake and SDPJ dissidents **Armed forces:** self-defence forces: 235,500; US forces stationed there: 44,800 (1996) **Conscription:** military service is voluntary **Death penalty:** retained and used for ordinary crimes **Defence spend:** (% GDP) 1 (1996) **Education spend:** (% GNP) 4.7 (1993–94) **Health spend:** (% GDP) 5.2 (1993)

Economy and resources

Currency: yen **GDP:** ($ US) 4,599.7 billion (1996) **Real GDP per capita (PPP):** ($ US) 22,863 (1996) **GDP growth rate:** 2.6% (1996); 1% (1990–95) **Average annual inflation:** 0.3% (1996); 1.4% (1985–95) **Major trading partners:** USA, China, Australia, South Korea, Indonesia, Germany, Taiwan, Hong Kong **Resources:** coal, iron, zinc, copper, natural gas, fish **Industries:** motor vehicles, steel, machinery, electrical and electronic equipment, chemicals, textiles **Exports:** motor vehicles, electronic goods and components, chemicals, iron and steel products, scientific and optical equipment. Principal market: USA 27.2% (1996) **Imports:** mineral fuels, foodstuffs, live animals, bauxite, iron ore, copper ore, coking coal, chemicals, textiles, wood. Principal source: USA 22.7% (1996) **Arable land:** 10.5% (1995) **Agricultural products:** rice, potatoes, cabbages, sugar cane, sugar beet, citrus fruit; one of the world's leading fishing nations

Population and society

Population: 125,351,000 (1996 est) **Population growth rate:** 0.3% (1990–95); 0.1% (2000–05) **Population density:** (per sq km) 332 (1996 est) **Urban population:** (% of total) 78 (1995) **Age distribution:** (% of total population) <15 16.2%, 15–65 69.6%, >65 14.1% (1995) **Ethnic groups:** more than 99% of Japanese descent; Ainu (aboriginal people of Japan) in N Japan (Hokkaido, Kuril Islands) **Language:** Japanese; also Ainu **Religion:** Shinto, Buddhist (often combined), Christian **Education:** (compulsory years) 9

Literacy rate: 99% (men); 99% (women) (1995 est) **Labour force:** 53.8% of population: 5.5% agriculture, 33.3% industry, 61.2% services (1996) **Unemployment:** 3.4% (1996) **Life expectancy:** 77 (men); 83 (women) (1995–2000) **Child mortality rate:** (under 5, per 1,000 live births) 6 (1996) **Physicians:** 1 per 542 people (1994)

Practical information

Visa requirements: UK: visa not required. USA: visa not required for a stay of up to 90 days **Embassy in the UK:** 101–104 Piccadilly, London W1V 9FN. Tel: (0171) 465 6500; fax: (0171) 491 9348 **British embassy:** No. 1 Ichiban-cho, Chiyoda-ku, Tokyo 102. Tel: (3) 3265 5511; fax: (3) 5275 3164 **Chamber of commerce:** 2nd Floor, Salisbury House, 29 Finsbury Circus, London EC2M 5QQ. Tel: (0171) 628 0069; fax: (0171) 628 0248. Nippon Shoko Kaigi-sho, 3-2-2, Marunouchi, Chiyoda-ku, Tokyo 10. Tel: (3) 3283 7851 **Airports:** international airports: Tokyo (Narita), Fukuoka, Kagoshima, Kansai, Nagoya, Osaka; one principal domestic services airport (Haneda), smaller airports cover connections between major towns and islands; total passenger km: 118,011 million (1994) **Major holidays:** 1–3, 15 January, 11 February, 21 March, 29 April, 3, 5 May, 15, 23 September, 10 October, 3, 23 November

Chronology

660 BC: According to legend, Jimmu Tenno, descendent of the Sun goddess, became the first emperor of Japan. **c. 400 AD:** The Yamato, one of many warring clans, unified central Japan; Yamato chiefs are the likely ancestors of the imperial family. **5th–6th centuries:** Writing, Confucianism, and Buddhism spread to Japan from China and Korea. **646:** Start of the Taika Reform: Emperor Kotoku organized central government on the Chinese model. **794:** Heian became imperial capital; later called Kyoto. **858:** Imperial court fell under control of the Fujiwara clan, who reduced the emperor to a figurehead. **11th century:** Central government grew ineffectual; real power exercised by great landowners (daimyo) with private armies of samurai. **1185:** Minamoto clan seized power under Yoritomo, who established military rule. **1192:** Emperor gave Yoritomo the title of shogun (general); the shogun ruled in the name of the emperor. **1274:** Mongol conqueror Kublai Khan attempted to invade Japan, making a second attempt 1281; each time Japan was saved by a typhoon. **1336:** Warlord Takauji Ashikaga overthrew the Minamoto shogunate; emperor recognized Ashikaga shogunate 1338. **16th century:** Power of Ashikagas declined; constant civil war. **1543:** Portuguese sailors were the first Europeans to reach Japan; followed by Spanish, Dutch, and English traders. **1549:** Spanish missionary St Francis Xavier began to preach Roman Catholic faith in Japan. **1585–98:** Warlord Hideyoshi took power and attempted to conquer Korea 1592 and 1597. **1603:** Ieyasu Tokugawa founded new shogunate at Edo, reformed administration, and suppressed Christianity. **1630s:** Japan adopted policy of isolation: all travel forbidden and all foreigners expelled except small colony of Dutch traders in Nagasaki harbour. **1853:** USA sent warships to Edo with demand that Japan open diplomatic and trade relations; Japan conceded 1854. **1867:** Revolt by isolationist nobles overthrew the Tokugawa shogunate. **1868:** Emperor Mutsuhito assumed full powers, adopted the title *Meiji* ('enlightened rule'), moved imperial capital from Kyoto to Edo (renamed Tokyo), and launched policy of swift Westernization.

Japan: Regions				
Region	**Chief city**	**Area**		**Population**
		sq km	**sq mi**	**(1995)**
Chubu	Nagoya	66,776	25,782	21,400,000
Chugoku	Hiroshima	31,908	12,320	7,775,000
Hokkaido	Sapporo	83,451	32,220	5,692,000
Kanto	Tokyo	32,418	12,517	39,518,000
Kinki	Osaka	33,094	12,778	22,468,000
Kyushu	Fukuoka	42,154	16,276	13,424,000
Okinawa	Naha	2,265	875	1,274,000
Shikoku	Matsuyama	18,798	7,258	4,183,000
Tohoku	Sendai	66,883	25,824	9,834,000

1894–95: Sino-Japanese War: Japan expelled Chinese from Korea. **1902:** Japan entered a defensive alliance with Britain; ended 1921. **1904–05:** Russo-Japanese War: Japan drove Russians from Manchuria and Korea; Korea annexed 1910. **1914:** Japan entered World War I and occupied German possessions in Far East. **1923:** Earthquake destroyed much of Tokyo and Yokohama. **1931:** Japan invaded Chinese province of Manchuria and created puppet state of Manchukuo; Japanese government came under control of military and extreme nationalists. **1937:** Japan resumed invasion of China. **1940:** After Germany defeated France, Japan occupied French Indo-China. **1941:** Japan attacked US fleet at Pearl Harbor; USA and Britain declared war on Japan. **1942:** Japanese conquered Thailand, Burma, Malaya, Dutch East Indies, Philippines, and northern New Guinea. **1945:** USA dropped atomic bombs on Hiroshima and Nagasaki; Japan surrendered; US general Douglas MacArthur headed Allied occupation administration. **1947:** MacArthur supervised introduction of democratic 'Peace Constitution', accompanied by demilitarization and land reform. **1952:** Occupation ended. **1955:** Liberal Democratic Party (LDP) founded with support of leading business people. **1956:** Japan admitted to United Nations. **1950s–70s:** Rapid economic development; growth of manufacturing exports led to great prosperity. **1993:** Economic recession and financial scandals brought downfall of LDP government in general election. Coalition government formed. **1995:** Earthquake devastated Kobe. **1996:** General election produced inconclusive result; minority LDP government subsequently formed. New party, the Taiyoto (Sun Party) formed by former prime minister Tsutomu Hata. **1997:** Ryutaro Hashimoto's new government pledged itself to different economic policies. Strong growth in economy. Hashimoto reelected LDP president. Financial crash after bank failures. **1998:** Prime Minister Hashimoto resigned after his Liberal Democratic Party suffered major defeat in elections.

Jordan Hashemite Kingdom of

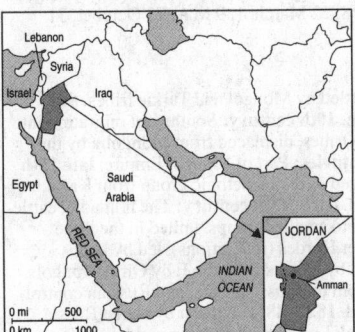

National name: *Al Mamlaka al Urduniya al Hashemiyah* **Area:** 89,206 sq km/34,442 sq mi (West Bank 5,879 sq km/2,269 sq mi) **Capital:** Amman **Major towns/cities:** Zarqa, Irbid, Saet, Ma'an **Major ports:** Aqaba **Physical features:** desert plateau in E; Rift Valley separates E and W banks of the River Jordan

Government
Head of state: King Hussein ibn Tal Abdulla el Hashim from 1952 **Head of government:** Abdul-Karim Kabariti from 1996 **Political system:** constitutional monarchy **Administrative divisions:** eight governates **Political parties:** independent groups loyal to the king predominate; of the 21 parties registered since 1992, the most significant is the Islamic Action Front (IAF), Islamic fundamentalist **Armed forces:** 98,700; plus paramilitary forces of approximately 30,000 (1996) **Conscription:** selective **Death penalty:** retained and used for ordinary crimes **Defence spend:** (% GDP) 6.7 (1995) **Education spend:** (% GNP) 3.8 (1993–94) **Health spend:** (% GDP) 1.8 (1990)

Economy and resources
Currency: Jordanian dinar **GDP:** ($ US) 6.1 billion (1994) **Real GDP per capita (PPP):** ($ US) 4,187 (1994) **GDP growth rate:** 5.7% (1994); 8.2% (1990–95) **Average annual inflation:** 6.4%

(1996); 7.1% (1985–95 est) **Foreign debt:** ($ US) 7 billion (1996) **Major trading partners:** Iraq, India, Saudi Arabia, Germany, Italy, UK, USA, Japan **Resources:** phosphates, potash, shale **Industries:** mining and quarrying, petroleum refining, chemical products, alcoholic drinks, food products, phosphate, cement, potash, tourism **Exports:** phosphate, potash, fertilizers, foodstuffs, pharmaceuticals, fruit and vegetables, cement. Principal market: Iraq 18.9% (1995) **Imports:** food and live animals, basic manufactures, mineral fuels, machinery and transport equipment. Principal source: Iraq 12.2% (1995) **Arable land:** 3.6% (1995) **Agricultural products:** wheat, barley, maize, tobacco, vegetables, fruits, nuts; livestock rearing (sheep and goats)

Population and society
Population: 5,581,000 (1996 est) **Population growth rate:** 4.9% (1990–95); 3% (2000–05) **Population density:** (per sq km) 57 (1996 est) **Urban population:** (% of total) 71 (1995) **Age distribution:** (% of total population) <15 43.3%, 15–65 54%, >65 2.7% (1995) **Ethnic groups:** majority of Arab descent; small Circassian, Armenian, and Kurdish minorities **Language:** Arabic (official), English **Religion:** Sunni Muslim 80%, Christian 8% **Education:** (compulsory years) 10 **Literacy rate:** 75% (men); 70% (women) (1995 est) **Labour force:** 27% of population: 15% agriculture, 23% industry, 61% services (1990) **Unemployment:** 25% (1992 est) **Life expectancy:** 68 (men); 72 (women) (1995–2000) **Child mortality rate:** (under 5, per 1,000 live births) 39 (1996) **Physicians:** 1 per 825 people (1994)

Practical information
Visa requirements: UK: visa required. USA: visa required **Embassy in the UK:** 6 Upper Phillimore Gardens, London W8 7HB. Tel: (0171) 937 3685; fax: (0171) 937 8795 **British embassy:** PO Box 87, Abdoun, Amman. Tel: (6) 823 100; fax: (6) 813 759 **Chamber of commerce:** Amman Chamber of Commerce, PO Box 287, Amman. Tel: (6) 666 151; telex: 21543 **Airports:** international airports: Amman (charter flights only), Zizya (Queen Alia, 30 km south of Amman), Aqaba; internal flights operate between Amman and Aqaba; total passenger km: 4,155 million (1994) **Major holidays:** 1 January, 1, 25 May, 10 June, 11 August, 14 November, 25 December; variable: Eid-ul-Adha (4 days), first day of Ramadan, end of Ramadan (4 days), New Year (Muslim), Prophet's Birthday

Chronology
13th century BC: Oldest known 'states' of Jordan, including Gideon, Ammon, Moab, and Edom, established. **c. 1000 BC:** East Jordan was part of kingdom of Israel, under David and Solomon. **4th century BC:** SE Jordan occupied by the independent Arabic-speaking Nabataeans. **64 BC:** Conquered by Romans and became part of province of Arabia. **AD 636:** Became largely Muslim after the Byzantine forces of Emperor Heraclius were defeated by Arab armies at battle of Yarmuk, in N Jordan. **1099–1187:** Part of the Latin Kingdom established by the Crusaders in Jerusalem. **from early 16th century:** Part of Turkish Ottoman Empire, administered from Damascus. **1920:** Trans-Jordan (the area E of the River Jordan) and Palestine (which includes the West Bank) were placed under British administration by a League of Nations mandate. **1923:** Trans-Jordan was separated from Palestine and recognized by Britain as a substantially independent state under the rule of Emir Abdullah ibn Hussein, a member of the Hashemite dynasty of Arabia. **1946:** Trans-Jordan achieved independence from Britain, with Abd Allah as king; name changed to Jordan. **1948:** British mandate for Palestine expired, leading to fighting between Arabs and Jews, who each claimed the area. **1950:** Jordan annexed West Bank; 400,000 Palestinian refugees flooded into Jordan, putting pressure on the economy. **1951:** King Abdullah assassinated in Jerusalem; succeeded by his son King Talal. **1952:** Partially democratic constitution introduced. **1953:** Hussein ibn Tal Abdulla el Hashim officially became king of Jordan, after his father, King Talal, stepped down. **1958:** Jordan and Iraq formed Arab Federation that ended when the Iraqi monarchy was deposed. **1967:** Israel defeated Egypt, Syria, and Jordan in the Arab–Israeli Six-Day War, and captured and occupied the West Bank, including Arab Jerusalem. Martial law imposed. **1970–71:** Jordanians moved

against the increasingly radicalized Palestine Liberation Organization (PLO), which had launched guerrilla raids on Israel from Jordanian territory, resulting in bloody civil war, before PLO leadership fled abroad. **1976:** Lower house dissolved, political parties banned, elections postponed until further notice. **1980:** Jordan emerged as important ally of Iraq in its war against Iran, an ally of Syria, with whom Jordan's relations were tense. **1982:** Hussein tried to mediate in Arab–Israeli conflict, following the Israeli invasion of Lebanon. **1984:** Women voted for the first time; parliament recalled. **1985:** Hussein and PLO leader Yassir Arafat put forward framework for Middle East peace settlement. Secret meeting between Hussein and Israeli prime minister. **1988:** Hussein announced willingness to cease administering the West Bank as part of Jordan, passing responsibility to the PLO, and the suspension of parliament. **1989:** Prime Minister Zaid al-Rifai resigned; Hussein promised new parliamentary elections. Riots over price increases of up to 50% following fall in oil revenues. First parliamentary elections for 22 years; Muslim Brotherhood won 25 of 80 seats but exiled from government; martial law lifted. **1990:** Hussein unsuccessfully tried to mediate after Iraq's invasion of Kuwait. Huge refugee problems as thousands fled to Jordan from Kuwait and Iraq. **1991:** 24 years of martial law ended; ban on political parties lifted; remained neutral during the Gulf War involving Saddam Hussein's Iraq. **1993:** Candidates loyal to Hussein won majority in parliamentary elections; several leading Islamic fundamentalists lost their seats. **1994:** Economic cooperation pact singed with PLO. Peace treaty signed with Israel, ending 46-year-old 'state of war'. **1996:** Abdul-Karim Kabariti appointed prime minister. **1997:** Success for government supporters in assembly elections.

Kazakhstan Republic of

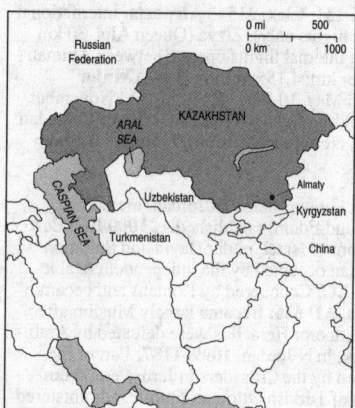

National name: *Kazak Respublikasy* **Area:** 2,717,300 sq km/1,049,150 sq mi **Capital:** Akmola **Major towns/cities:** Karaganda, Pavlodar, Semipalatinsk, Petropavlovsk, Chimkent **Physical features:** Caspian and Aral seas, Lake Balkhash; Steppe region; natural gas and oil deposits in the Caspian Sea

Government

Head of state: Nursultan Nazarbayev from 1990 **Head of government:** Nurlan Balgimbayev from 1997 **Political system:** authoritarian nationalist **Administrative divisions:** 19 provinces **Political parties:** Congress of People's Unity of Kazakhstan, moderate, centrist; People's Congress of Kazakhstan, moderate, ethnic; Socialist Party of Kazakhstan (SPK), left wing; Republican Party, right-of-centre coalition **Armed forces:** 40,000 (1996) **Death penalty:** retained and used for ordinary crimes **Defence spend:** (% GDP) 2.6 (1996) **Education spend:** (% GNP) 5.4 (1993–94) **Health spend:** (% GDP) 2.2 (1990–95)

Economy and resources

Currency: tenge **GDP:** ($ US) 18 billion (1994) **Real GDP per capita (PPP):** ($ US) 3,284 (1994) **GDP growth rate:** −8.9% (1995); −11.9% (1990–95) **Average annual inflation:** 39.1% (1996); 307.3% (1985–95 est) **Foreign debt:** ($ US) 3.7 billion (1995) **Major trading partners:** Russia and other CIS nations, Germany, the Netherlands, Switzerland,

Czech Republic, Italy **Resources:** petroleum, natural gas, coal, bauxite, chromium, copper, iron ore, lead, titanium, magnesium, tungsten, molybdenum, gold, silver, manganese **Industries:** metal processing, heavy engineering, mining and quarrying, chemicals, fuel, power, machine-building, textiles, food processing, household appliances **Exports:** ferrous and non-ferrous metals, mineral products (including petroleum and petroleum products), chemicals. Principal market: Russia 42.1% (1995) **Imports:** energy products and electricity, machinery and transport equipment, chemicals. Principal source: Russia 46.2% (1995) **Arable land:** 11.9% (1995) **Agricultural products:** fruits, sugar beet, vegetables, potatoes, cotton, cereals; livestock rearing (particularly sheep); karakul and astrakhan wool

Population and society

Population: 16,820,000 (1996 est) **Population growth rate:** 0.5% (1990–95); 0.8% (2000–05) **Population density:** (per sq km) 6 (1996 est) **Urban population:** (% of total) 60 (1995) **Age distribution:** (% of total population) <15 29.8%, 15–65 63.2%, >65 7% (1995) **Ethnic groups:** 40% of Kazakh descent, 38% ethnic Russian, 6% German, 5% Ukrainian, 2% Uzbek, and 2% Tatar **Language:** Kazakh (official), related to Turkish; Russian **Religion:** Sunni Muslim **Education:** (compulsory years) 11 **Literacy rate:** 97.5% (men); 97.5% (women) (1995 est) **Labour force:** 24% agriculture, 20.4% industry, 55.6% services (1992) **Unemployment:** 3.5% (1996) **Life expectancy:** 67 (men); 75 (women) (1995–2000) **Child mortality rate:** (under 5, per 1,000 live births) 31 (1996) **Physicians:** 1 per 254 people (1994)

Practical information

Visa requirements: UK: visa required. USA: visa required **Embassy in the UK:** 3 Warren Mews, London W1P 5DJ. Tel/fax: (0171) 387 1047 **British embassy:** 173 Furmanova Street, Almaty. Tel: (3272) 506 191; fax: (3272) 506 260 **Chamber of commerce:** Chamber of Commerce and Industry of Kazakhstan, pr. Ablaikhana 93/95, 480091 Almaty. Tel: (3272) 621 446; fax: (3272) 620 594 **Airports:** international airports: Almaty, Aktau, Atyrau; 18 domestic airports; total passenger km: 1,787 million (1994) **Major holidays:** 1, 28 January, 8, 22 March, 1, 9 May, 25 October, 31 December

Chronology

early Christian era: Settled by Mongol and Turkic tribes. **8th century:** Spread of Islam. **10th century:** Southward migration into E Kazakhstan of Kazakh tribes, displaced from Mongolia by the Mongols. **13th–14th centuries:** Part of Mongol Empire. **late 15th century:** Kazakhs emerged as distinct ethnic group from Kazakh Orda tribal confederation. **early 17th century:** The nomadic, cattle-breeding Kazakhs split into smaller groups, united in the three Large, Middle, and Lesser Hordes (federations), led by khans (chiefs). **1731–42:** Faced by attacks from the E by Oirot Mongols, protection was sought from the Russian tsars, and Russian control was gradually established. **1822–48:** Conquest by tsarist Russia completed; khans deposed. Large-scale Russian and Ukrainian peasant settlement of the steppes after the abolition of serfdom in Russia in 1861. **1887:** Alma-Alta (now Almaty), established 1854 as a fortified trading centre and captured by the Russians 1865, destroyed by earthquake. **1916:** 150,000 killed as anti-Russian rebellion brutally repressed. **1917:** Bolshevik coup in Russia followed by outbreak of civil war in Kazakhstan. **1920:** Autonomous republic in USSR. **early 1930s:** More than 1 million died of starvation during campaign to collectivize agriculture. **1936:** Joined USSR and became a full union republic. **early 1940s:** Volga Germans deported to the republic by Soviet dictator Joseph Stalin. **1954–56:** Part of Soviet leader Nikita Khrushchev's ambitious 'Virgin Lands' agricultural extension programme; large influx of Russian settlers made Kazakhs a minority in their own republic. **1986:** Nationalist riots in Alma-Alta (now Almaty) after reformist Soviet leader Mikhail Gorbachev ousted local communist leader and installed an ethnic Russian. **1989:** Nursultan Nazarbayev, a reformist and mild nationalist, became leader of Kazakh Communist Party (KCP) and instituted economic and cultural reform programmes, encouraging foreign inward investment. **1990:** Nazarbayev became head of state; economic sovereignty declared.

1991: Nazarbayev condemned attempted anti-Gorbachev coup in Moscow; KCP abolished. Joined new Commonwealth of Independent States, formed at Almaty; independence recognized by USA. **1992:** Admitted into United Nations and Conference on Security and Cooperation in Europe (CSCE; now the Organization on Security and Cooperation in Europe, OSCE). **1993:** Presidential power increased by new constitution. Privatization programme launched; Kazakhstan ratified START-1 (disarmament treaty) and the Nuclear Non-Proliferation Treaty. **1994:** Economic, social, and military union with Kyrgyzstan and Uzbekistan. **1995:** Economic and military cooperation pact with Russia. Achieved nuclear-free status. Nazarbayev's popular mandate reratified in national referendum. **1996:** Agreement signed with Kyrgyzstan and Uzbekistan to form single economic market. **1997:** Nurlan Balgimbayev appointed prime minister. Major oil agreements with China. Akmola designated as new capital.

Kenya Republic of

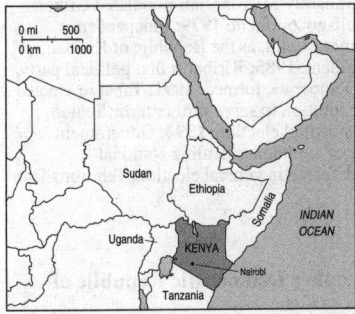

National name:
Jamhuri ya Kenya
Area: 582,600 sq km/224,941 sq mi
Capital: Nairobi
Major towns/cities: Mombasa, Kisumu, Nakuru, Eldoret, Nyeri **Major ports:** Mombasa **Physical features:** mountains and highlands in W and centre; coastal plain in S; arid interior and tropical coast; semi-desert in N; Great Rift Valley, Mount Kenya, Lake Nakuru (salt lake with world's largest colony of flamingos), Lake Turkana (Rudolf)

Government
Head of state and government: Daniel arap Moi from 1978 **Political system:** authoritarian nationalist **Administrative divisions:** seven provinces and the Nairobi municipality **Political parties:** Kenya African National Union (KANU), nationalist, centrist; Forum for the Restoration of Democracy–Kenya (FORD–Kenya), left of centre; Forum for the Restoration of Democracy–Asili (FORD–Asili), left of centre; Democratic Party (DP), centrist; Safina, centrist **Armed forces:** 24,200; paramilitary force 5,000 (1996) **Conscription:** military service is voluntary **Death penalty:** retained and used for ordinary crimes **Defence spend:** (% GDP) 2.2 (1996) **Education spend:** (% GNP) 6.8 (1993–94) **Health spend:** (% GDP) 1.9 (1990–95)

Economy and resources
Currency: Kenya shilling **GDP:** ($ US) 6.9 billion (1994) **Real GDP per capita (PPP):** ($ US) 1,404 (1994) **GDP growth rate:** 3% (1994); 1.4% (1990–95) **Average annual inflation:** 10% (1996); 13% (1985–95) **Foreign debt:** ($ US) 7.42 billion (1996) **Major trading partners:** Uganda, UK, Tanzania, Germany, Japan, United Arab Emirates **Resources:** soda ash, fluorspar, salt, limestone, rubies, gold, vermiculite, diatonite, garnets **Industries:** food processing, petroleum refining and petroleum products, textiles and clothing, leather products, chemicals, cement, paper and paper products, beverages, tobacco, ceramics, rubber and metal products, vehicle assembly, tourism **Exports:** coffee, tea, petroleum products, soda ash, horticultural products. Principal market: Uganda 15.8% (1995) **Imports:** crude petroleum, motor vehicles, industrial machinery, iron and steel, chemicals, basic manufactures. Principal source: UK 12.6% (1995) **Arable land:** 7% (1995) **Agricultural products:** coffee, tea, maize, wheat, sisal, sugar cane, pineapples, cotton, horticulture; dairy products

Population and society
Population: 27,799,000 (1996 est) **Population growth rate:** 3.6% (1990–95); 3% (2000–05) **Population density:** (per sq km) 48 (1996 est) **Urban population:** (% of total) 28 (1995) **Age distribution:** (% of total population) <15 47.7%, 15–65 49.4%, >65 2.9% (1995) **Ethnic groups:** main ethnic groups are the Kikuyu (about 21%), the Luhya (14%), the Luo (13%), the Kalenjin (11%), the Kamba (11%), the Kisii (6%), and the Meru (5%); there are also Asian, Arab, and European minorities **Language:** Kiswahili (official), English; there are many local dialects **Religion:** Roman Catholic, Protestant, Muslim, traditional tribal religions **Education:** (years) 8 (not compulsory, but free) **Literacy rate:** 86% (men); 70% (women) (1995 est) **Labour force:** 48% of population: 80% agriculture, 7% industry, 13% services (1990) **Unemployment:** 16% (1992 est) **Life expectancy:** 57 (men); 61 (women) (1995–2000) **Child mortality rate:** (under 5, per 1,000 live births) 106 (1996) **Physicians:** 1 per 6,430 people (1994)

Practical information
Visa requirements: UK: visa not required. USA: visa required **Embassy in the UK:** 45 Portland Place, London W1N 4AS. Tel: (0171) 636 2371/5; fax: (0171) 323 6717 **British embassy:** British High Commission, PO Box 30465, Bruce House, Standard Street, Nairobi. Tel: (2) 335 944; fax: (2) 333 196 **Chamber of commerce:** Kenya National Chamber of Commerce and Industry, PO Box 47024, Ufanisi House, Hailé Sélassie Avenue, Nairobi. Tel: (2) 334 413 **Airports:** international airports: Mombasa (Moi), Nairobi (Jomo Kenyatta), Eldoret (opening date of 1997 delayed); three domestic airports; total passenger km: 1,737 million (1994) **Major holidays:** 1 January, 1 May, 1 June, 10, 20 October, 12, 25–26 December; variable: Good Friday, Easter Monday, end of Ramadan

Chronology
8th century: Arab traders began to settle along coast of E Africa. **16th century:** Portuguese defeated coastal states and exerted spasmodic control over them. **18th century:** Sultan of Oman reasserted Arab overlordship of E African coast, making it subordinate to Zanzibar. **19th century:** Europeans, closely followed by Christian missionaries, began to explore inland. **1887:** British East African Company leased area of coastal territory from sultan of Zanzibar. **1895:** Britain claimed large inland region as East African Protectorate. **1903:** Railway from Mombasa to Uganda built using Indian labourers, many of whom settled in the area; British and South African settlers began to farm highlands. **1920:** East African Protectorate became crown colony of Kenya, with legislative council elected by white settlers (and by Indians and Arabs soon afterwards). **1923:** Britain rejected demand for internal self-government by white settlers. **1944:** First African appointment to legislative council; Kenyan African Union (KAU) founded to campaign for African rights. **1947:** Jomo Kenyatta became leader of KAU, which was dominated by Kikuyu tribe. **1952:** Mau Mau (Kikuyu secret society) began terrorist campaign to drive white settlers from tribal lands; Mau Mau largely suppressed by 1954 but state of emergency lasted for eight years. **1953:** Kenyatta charged with management of Mau Mau activities and imprisoned by the British. **1956:** Africans allowed to elect members of legislative council on restricted franchise. **1959:** Kenyatta released from prison, but exiled to N Kenya. **1960:** Britain announced plans to prepare Kenya for majority African rule. **1961:** Kenyatta allowed to return to help negotiate Kenya's independence. **1963:** Kenya achieved independence with Kenyatta as prime minister. **1964:** Kenya became a republic with Kenyatta as president. **1967:** East African Community (EAC) formed by Kenya, Tanzania, and Uganda to retain customs union inherited from colonial period. **1969:** Kenya became one-party state under Kenyan African National Union (KANU). **1977:** Political and economic disputes led to collapse of EAC. **1978:** Death of President Kenyatta; succeeded by Daniel arap Moi. **1984:** Violent clashes between government troops and ethnic Somali population at Wajir. **1989:** Moi announced release of political prisoners. **1991:** Multiparty system conceded after Oginga Odinga launched opposition group. **1992:** Moi re-elected in multiparty elections amid allegations of fraud. **1995:** New Centrist party, Safina,

formed by palaeoanthropologist Richard Leakey. **1997:**
Demonstrations calling for democratic reform. Constitutional refoms
adopted.

Kiribati Republic of (formerly part of the Gilbert and Ellice Islands)

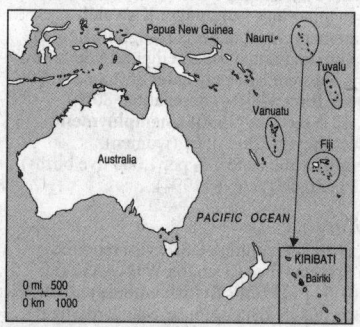

National name:
*Ribaberikin
Kiribati* **Area:** 717
sq km/277 sq mi
Capital: Bairiki
(on Tarawa Atoll)
(and port) **Towns:**
pricipal atolls:
North Tarawa,
Gilbert group,
Abaiang, Tabiteuea
Major ports: Betio
(on Tarawa)
Physical features:
comprises 33
Pacific coral
islands: the Kiribati (Gilbert), Rawaki (Phoenix), Banaba (Ocean
Island), and three of the Line Islands including Kiritimati
(Christmas Island); island groups crossed by Equator and
International Date Line

Government
Head of state and government: Teburoro Tito from 1994 **Political
system:** liberal democracy **Political parties:** Maneaban Te Mauri
(MTM), dominant faction; National Progressive Party (NPP),
former governing faction 1979–94 **Armed forces:** no standing army
Death penalty: abolished 1979 **Education spend:** (% GNP) 6.5
(1991)

Economy and resources
Currency: Australian dollar **GDP:** ($ US) 68 million (1995 est)
Real GDP per capita (PPP): ($ US) 860 (1995 est) **GDP growth
rate:** 2.6% (1995 est) **Average annual inflation:** 2.9% (1994);
3.8% (1985–95) **Foreign debt:** ($ US) 21 million (1993) **Major
trading partners:** Australia, Bangladesh, Japan, Fiji, USA, France,
New Zealand, China **Resources:** phosphate, salt **Industries:**
handicrafts, coconut-based products, soap, foods, furniture, leather
goods, garments, tourism **Exports:** copra, fish, seaweed, bananas,
breadfruit, taro. Principal market: Bangladesh 67% (1993) **Imports:**
foodstuffs, machinery and transport equipment, mineral fuels, basic
manufactures. Principal source: Australia (1993) **Arable land:**
50.7% (1995) **Agricultural products:** copra, coconuts, bananas,
screw-pine, papaya, breadfruit; livestock rearing (pigs and
chickens); fishing and seaweed cultivation

Population and society
Population: 80,000 (1996 est) **Population growth rate:** 1.7%
(1990–95) **Population density:** (per sq km) 110 (1996 est) **Urban
population:** (% of total) 35.7 (1995) **Age distribution:** (% of total
population) <15 38.1%, 15–65 55.9%, >65 6% (1992) **Ethnic
groups:** predominantly Micronesian, with a Polynesian minority;
also European and Chinese minorities **Language:** English (official),
Gilbertese **Religion:** Roman Catholic, Protestant
(Congregationalist) **Education:** (compulsory years) 9 **Literacy
rate:** 90% (men); 90%(women) (1993 est) **Unemployment:** 2.8%
(1990) **Life expectancy:** 51 (men); 56 (women) (1992) **Child
mortality rate:** (per 1,000 live births) 98.4 (1994) **Physicians:** 1
per 4,685 people (1991)

Practical information
Visa requirements: UK: visa not required for a stay of up to 28
days. USA: visa required **Embassy in the UK:** Consulate of
Kiribati, Faith House, 7 Tufton Street, London SW1P 3QN. Tel:
(0171) 222 6952; fax: (0171) 976 7180 **British embassy:** the British

High Commission in Suva (see Fiji) deals with enquiries relating to
Kiribati **Chamber of commerce:** none **Airports:** international
airports: South Tarawa (Bonikri), Kiritimati Island (Cassidy),
Butaritari Island (Antekana), Kanton Island, Tabuaeran Island; 15
domestic airports; total passenger km: 10 million (1994) **Major
holidays:** 1 January, 12 June (3 days), 25–26 December; variable:
Good Friday, Easter Monday, Holy Saturday, Youth (August)

Chronology
1st millenium BC: Settled by Austronesian-speaking peoples.
1606: Visited by Spanish explorers. **late 18th century:** Visited by
British naval officers. **1857:** Christian mission established. **1892:**
Gilbert (Kiribati) and Ellice (Tuvalu) Islands proclaimed a British
protectorate. **1916–39:** Uninhabited Phoenix Islands, Christmas
Island, Ocean Island, and Line Island (Banaba) added to colony.
1942–43: Occupied by Japanese, it was the scene of fierce fighting
with US troops. **late 1950s:** UK tested nuclear weapons on
Christmas Island (Kiritimati). **1958:** Christmas Island transferred to
Australia. **1963:** Legislative council established. **1974:** Legislative
council replaced by an elected House of Assembly. **1975:** The
mainly Melanesian-populated Ellice Islands separated to become
Tuvalu. **1977:** The predominantly Micronesian-populated Gilbert
Islands granted internal self-government. **1979:** Independence
achieved within the Commonwealth, as the Republic of Kiribati,
with Ieremia Tabai as president. **1985:** Kiribati's first political party,
the opposition Christian Democrats, formed. **1991:** Tabai re-elected
but not allowed under constitution to serve further term; Teatao
Teannaki won run-off presidential election. **1994:** Government
resigned, after losing vote of confidence. Ruling National
Progressive Party (NPP) defeated in general election. Teburoro Tito
elected president.

Korea, North People's Democratic Republic of

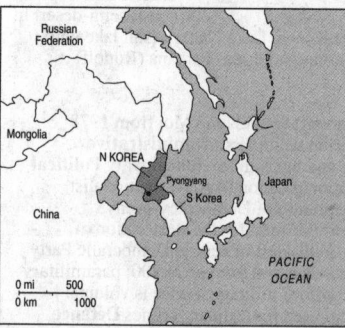

National name:
*Chosun Minchu-chui
Inmin Konghwa-guk*
Area: 120,538 sq
km/46,539 sq mi
Capital: Pyongyang
Major towns/cities:
Hamhung, Chongjin,
Nampo, Wonsan,
Sinuiji **Physical
features:** wide coastal
plain in W rising to
mountains cut by deep
valleys in interior

Government
Head of state: Kim Jong Il from 1994 **Head of government:** Hong
Song Nam from 1997 **Political system:** communism
Administrative divisions: three cities and nine provinces **Political
parties:** Korean Workers' Party (KWP), Marxist-Leninist (leads
Democratic Front for the Reunification of the Fatherland, including
Korean Social Democratic Party and Chondoist Chongu Party)
Armed forces: 1,054,000 (1996) **Conscription:** conscription is
selective for 3–10 years **Death penalty:** retained and used for
ordinary crimes **Defence spend:** (% GDP) 27.2% (1996)

Economy and resources
Currency: won **GDP:** ($ US) 21.5 billion (1995 est) **Real GDP per
capita (PPP):** ($ US) 920 (1995 est) **GDP growth rate:** –5% (1995
est) **Average annual inflation:** N/A **Foreign debt:** ($ US) 9.8
billion (1994 est) **Major trading partners:** China, Japan, CIS,
South Korea, Germany, Italy, Hong Kong, Iran **Resources:** coal,
iron, lead, copper, zinc, tin, silver, gold, magnesite (has 40–50% of
world's deposits of magnesite) **Industries:** mining, metallurgy,
electricity, machine-building, textiles, cement, chemicals, cotton,

silk and rayon weaving, foods **Exports:** base metals, textiles, vegetable products, machinery and equipment. Principal market: Japan 27.9% (1995 est) **Imports:** petroleum and petroleum products, machinery and equipment, grain, coal, foodstuffs. Principal source: China 32.6% (1995 est) **Arable land:** 14.1% (1995) **Agricultural products:** rice, maize, sweet potatoes, soya beans; livestock rearing (cattle and pigs); forestry; fishing

Population and society

Population: 22,466,000 (1996 est) **Population growth rate:** 1.9% (1990–95); 1.3% (2000–05) **Population density:** (per sq km) 186 (1996 est) **Urban population:** (% of total) 61 (1995) **Age distribution:** (% of total population) <15 29.1%, 15–65 66.3%, >65 4.6% (1995) **Ethnic groups:** entirely Korean, with the exception of a 50,000 Chinese minority **Language:** Korean **Religion:** Chondoist, Buddhist, Christian, traditional beliefs **Education:** (compulsory years) 10 **Literacy rate:** 99% (men); 99%(women) (1995 est) **Labour force:** 50% of population: 38% agriculture, 31% industry, 31% services (1990) **Life expectancy:** 69 (men); 75 (women) (1995–2000) **Child mortality rate:** (under 5, per 1,000 live births) 26 (1996) **Physicians:** 1 per 370 people (1993)

Practical information

Visa requirements: UK: visa required. USA: visa required **Embassy for the UK:** General Delegation of the DPRK, 104 boulevard Bineau, 92200 Neuilly-sur-Seine, France. Tel: (1) 4745 1797; fax: (1) 4738 1250 **British embassy:** the UK has no diplomatic representation in North Korea **Chamber of commerce:** DPRK Committee for the Promotion of External Economic Cooperation, Jungsongdong, Central District, Pyongyang. Tel: (2) 33974; fax: (2) 814 498 **Airports:** international airport: Pyongyang (Sunan); two domestic airports (which foreigners are not allowed to use); total passenger km: 197 million (1994) **Major holidays:** 1 January, 16 February, 8 March, 15 April, 9 September, 10 October, 27 December

Chronology

2333 BC: Legendary founding of Korean state by Tangun dynasty. **1122 BC–4th century AD:** Period of Chinese Kija dynasty. **668–1000:** Peninsula unified by Buddhist Shilla kingdom, with capital at Kyongju. **1392–1910:** Period of Chosun, or Yi, dynasty, during which Korea became a vassal of China and Confucianism became dominant intellectual force. **1910:** Korea formally annexed by Japan. **1920s and 1930s:** Heavy industries developed in the coal-rich N, with Koreans forcibly conscripted as low-paid labourers; suppression of Korean culture led to development of resistance movement. **1945:** Russian and US troops entered Korea at the end of World War II, forced surrender of Japanese, and divided the country in two at the 38th parallel. Soviet troops occupied North Korea. **1946:** Soviet-backed provisional government installed, dominated by Moscow-trained Korean communists, including Kim Il Sung; radical programme of land reform and nationalization launched. **1948:** Democratic People's Republic of Korea declared after pro-USA Republic of Korea founded in the S; Soviet troops withdrew. **1950:** North Korea invaded South Korea to unite the nation, beginning the Korean War. **1953:** Armistice agreed to end Korean War, which had involved US participation on the side of South Korea, and Chinese on that of North Korea. The war ended in stalemate, at a cost of 2 million lives. **1961:** Friendship and mutual assistance treaty signed with China. **1972:** New constitution, with executive president, adopted. Talks with South Korea about possible reunification. **1983:** Four South Korean cabinet ministers assassinated in Rangoon, Burma (Myanmar), by North Korean army officers. **1985:** Improved relations with the Soviet Union (USSR). **1990:** Diplomatic contacts with South Korea and Japan suggested a thaw in North Korea's relations with rest of world. **1991:** Became a member of the United Nations. Signed nonaggression agreement with South Korea. **1992:** Signed Nuclear Safeguards Agreement, allowing international inspection of nuclear facilities. Also signed pact with South Korea for mutual inspection of nuclear facilities. **1994:** Kim Il Sung died; succeeded by his son, Kim Jong Il. Agreement to halt nuclear-development programme in return for US aid, resulting in easing of 44-year-old US trade embargo. **1996:** US

aid sought in the face of severe famine; rice imported from South Korea. Floods caused near-famine conditions; food aid provided by UN. **1997:** Kang Song San replaced as prime minister by Hong Song Nam. Grave food shortages revealed.

Korea, South Republic of Korea

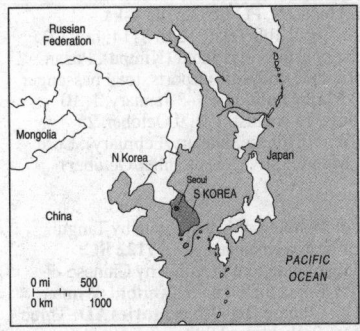

National name: *Daehan Min-kuk* **Area:** 98,799 sq km/38,146 sq mi **Capital:** Seoul **Major towns/cities:** Pusan, Taegu, Inchon, Kwangju, Taejon **Major ports:** Pusan, Inchon **Physical features:** southern end of a mountainous peninsula separating the Sea of Japan from the Yellow Sea

Government

Head of state: Kim Young Sam from 1993 **Head of government:** Kim Dae Jung from 1998 **Political system:** emergent democracy **Administrative divisions:** nine provinces and six cities with provincial status **Political parties:** New Korea Party (NKP, formerly Democratic Liberal Party (DLP)), right of centre; National Congress for New Politics (NCNP), centre left; Democratic Party (DP), left of centre; New Democratic Party (NDP), centrist, pro-private enterprise; United Liberal Democratic Party (ULD), ultra-conservative, pro-private enterprise **Armed forces:** 660,000 (1996) **Conscription:** 26 months (army); 30 months (navy and air force) **Death penalty:** retained and used for ordinary crimes **Defence spend:** (% GDP) 3.3 (1996) **Education spend:** (% GNP) 4.5 (1993–94) **Health spend:** (% GDP) 1.8 (1990–95)

Economy and resources

Currency: won **GDP:** ($ US) 376.5 billion (1994) **Real GDP per capita (PPP):** ($ US) 10,656 (1994) **GDP growth rate:** 8.4% (1994); 7.2% (1990–95) **Average annual inflation:** 4.5% (1996); 6.8% (1985–95) **Foreign debt:** ($ US) 95.5 billion (1996) **Major trading partners:** USA, Japan, Germany, Saudi Arabia, Australia, Hong Kong, Singapore, China **Resources:** coal, iron ore, tungsten, gold, molybdenum, graphite, fluorite, natural gas, hydroelectric power, fish **Industries:** electrical machinery, transport equipment (principally motor vehicles and shipbuilding), chemical products, textiles and clothing, iron and steel, electronics equipment, food processing, tourism **Exports:** electrical machinery, textiles, clothing, footwear, telecommunications and sound equipment, chemical products, ships ('invisible export' – overseas construction work). Principal market: USA 16.7% (1996) **Imports:** machinery and transport equipment (especially electrical machinery), petroleum and petroleum products, grain and foodstuffs, steel, chemical products, basic manufactures. Principal source: USA 22.2% (1996) **Arable land:** 18.1% (1995) **Agricultural products:** rice, maize, barley, potatoes, sweet potatoes, fruit; livestock (pigs and cattle)

Population and society

Population: 45,314,000 (1996 est) **Population growth rate:** 1% (1990–95); 0.8% (2000–05) **Population density:** (per sq km) 458 (1996 est) **Urban population:** (% of total) 81 (1995) **Age distribution:** (% of total population) <15 37.1%, 15–65 57.1%, >65 5.8% (1995) **Ethnic groups:** with the exception of a small Nationalist Chinese minority, the population is almost entirely of Korean descent **Language:** Korean **Religion:** Shamanist, Buddhist, Confucian, Protestant, Roman Catholic **Education:** (compulsory years) 9 **Literacy rate:** 99% (men); 93% (women) (1995 est) **Labour force:** 46.5% of population: 11.6% agriculture, 32.5% industry, 55.9% services (1996) **Unemployment:** 2% (1996) **Life expectancy:** 69

(men); 76 (women) (1995–2000) **Child mortality rate:** (under 5, per 1,000 live births) 13 (1996) **Physicians:** 1 per 888 people (1993)

Practical information

Visa requirements: UK: visa not required for a stay of up to 90 days. USA: visa not required **Embassy in the UK:** 4 Palace Gate, London W8 5NF. Tel: (0171) 581 0247; fax: (0171) 581 8076 **British embassy:** 4 Chung-dong, Chung-ku, Seoul 100. Tel: (2) 735 7341/3; fax: (2) 733 8368 **Chamber of commerce:** Korean Chamber of Commerce and Industry, PO Box 25, 45 4-ka, Namdaemun-no, Chung-ku, Seoul 100.Tel: (2) 316 3114; fax: (2) 757 9475 **Airports:** international airports: Seoul (Kimpo), Pusan (Kim Hae), Cheju; three principal domestic airports; total passenger km: 39,579 million (1994) **Major holidays:** 1–3 January, 1, 10 March, 5 May, 6 June, 17 July, 15 August, 1, 3, 9 October, 25 December; variable: New Year (Chinese, January/February), Lord Buddha's Birthday (May), Moon Festival (September/October)

Chronology

2333 BC: Traditional date of founding of Korean state by Tangun (mythical son from union of bear-woman and god). **1122 BC:** Ancient texts record founding of kingdom in Korea by Chinese nobleman Kija. **194 BC:** NW Korea united under warlord, Wiman. **108 BC:** Korea conquered by Chinese. **1st–7th centuries AD:** Three Korean kingdoms – Koguryo, Paekche, and Silla – competed for supremacy. **668:** Korean peninsula unified by Buddhist Silla kingdom; culture combining Chinese and Korean elements flourished. **935:** Silla dynasty overthrown by Wang Kon of Koguryo, who founded Koryo dynasty in its place. **1258:** Korea accepted overlordship of Mongol Yüan Empire. **1392:** Yi dynasty founded by Gen Yi Song-gye, vassal of Chinese Ming Empire; Confucianism replaced Buddhism as official creed; extreme conservatism characterized Korean society. **1592 and 1597:** Japanese invasions repulsed by Korea. **1636:** Manchu invasion forced Korea to sever ties with Ming dynasty. **18th–19th centuries:** Korea resisted change in political and economic life and rejected contact with Europeans. **1864:** Attempts to reform government and strengthen army by Taewongun (who ruled in name of his son, King Kojong); converts to Christianity persecuted. **1873:** Taewongun forced to cede power to Queen Min; reforms reversed; government authority collapsed. **1882:** Chinese occupied Seoul and installed governor. **1894–95:** Sino-Japanese War: Japan forced China to recognize independence of Korea; Korea fell to Japanese influence. **1896:** Fearing for his life, King Kojong sought protection of Russian legation. **1904–05:** Russo-Japanese War: Japan ended Russian influence in Korea. **1910:** Korea formally annexed by Japan; Japanese settlers introduced modern industry and agriculture; Korean language banned. **1919:** 'Samil' nationalist movement suppressed by Japanese. **1945:** After defeat of Japan in World War II, Russia occupied regions of Korea N of 38th parallel (demarcation line agreed at Yalta Conference) and US occupied regions S of it. **1948:** USSR refused to permit United Nations (UN) supervision of elections in N zone; S zone became independent as Republic of Korea, with Syngman Rhee as president. **1950:** North Korea invaded South Korea; UN forces (mainly from USA) intervened to defend South Korea; China intervened in support of North Korea. **1953:** Korean War ended with armistice which restored 38th parallel; no peace treaty agreed and US troops remained in South Korea. **1960:** President Syngman Rhee forced to resign by student-led protests against corruption and fraudulent elections. **1961:** Military coup placed Gen Park Chung Hee in power; major programme of industrial development began. **1972:** Martial law imposed; presidential powers increased. **1979:** President Park assassinated; interim government of President Choi Kyu-Hah introduced liberalizing reforms. **1979:** Gen Chun Doo Hwan assumed power after anti-government riots; Korea emerged as leading shipbuilding nation and exporter of electronic goods. **1987:** Constitution made more democratic as a result of Liberal pressure; ruling Democratic Justice Party (DJP) candidate Roh Tae Woo elected president amid allegations of fraud. **1988:** Olympic Games held in Seoul. **1991:** Large-scale anti-government protests forcibly suppressed; South Korea joined UN. **1992:** South Korea established diplomatic relations with China; Kim Young Sam elected president. **1994:** US military presence stepped up in response to perceived

threat from North Korea. **1996:** Roh Tae Woo and Chun Doo Hwan charged with treason for alleged role in massacre of demonstrators 1980. **1997:** South Korea admitted to OECD. **1998:** Kim Dae Jung, former dissident and political prisoner, inaugurated as president, becoming first opposition politician to lead South Korea.

Kuwait State of

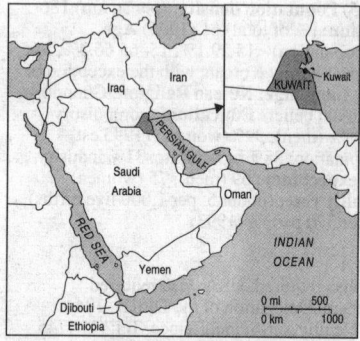

National name: *Dowlat al Kuwait* **Area:** 17,819 sq km/6,879 sq mi **Capital:** Kuwait (also chief port) **Major towns/cities:** as-Salimiya, Hawalli, Faranawiya, Abraq Kheetan, Jahra, Ahmadi, Fahaheel **Physical features:** hot desert; islands of Failaka, Bubiyan, and Warba at NE corner of Arabian Peninsula

Government

Head of state: Sheikh Jabir al-Ahmad al-Jabir as-Sabah from 1977 **Head of government:** Crown Prince Sheikh Saad al-Abdullah as-Salinas as-Sabah from 1978 **Political system:** absolute monarchy **Administrative divisions:** five governates **Political parties:** none **Armed forces:** 15,300 (1996) **Conscription:** compulsory for two years **Death penalty:** retained and used for ordinary crimes **Defence spend:** (% GDP) 12.9 (1996) **Education spend:** (% GNP) 5.6 (1993–94) **Health spend:** (% GDP) 3.5 (1994)

Economy and resources

Currency: Kuwaiti dinar **GDP:** ($ US) 26.7 billion (1995) **Real GDP per capita (PPP):** ($ US) 21,630 (1995) **GDP growth rate:** –4% (1994); 12.2% (1990–95) **Average annual inflation:** 3% (1996 est); –0.5 (1985–95) **Foreign debt:** ($ US) 5.8 billion (1996) **Major trading partners:** USA, Japan, Germany, France, Saudi Arabia, United Arab Emirates, India, UK, Italy **Resources:** petroleum, natural gas, mineral water **Industries:** petroleum refining, petrochemicals, food processing, gases, construction **Exports:** petroleum and petroleum products (accounted for more than 93% of export revenue 1994), chemical fertilizer, gas (natural and manufactured), basic manufactures. Principal market: Japan 23.5% (1996) **Imports:** machinery and transport equipment, basic manufactures (especially iron, steel, and textiles) and other manufactured goods, live animals and food. Principal source: USA 16.3% (1996) **Arable land:** 0.3% (1995) **Agricultural products:** melons, tomatoes, cucumbers, onions; livestock rearing (poultry); fishing

Population and society

Population: 1,687,000 (1996 est) **Population growth rate:** –6.5% (1990–95); 2.5% (2000–05) **Population density:** (per sq km) 95 (1996 est) **Urban population:** (% of total) 97 (1995) **Age distribution:** (% of total population) <15 39.8%, 15–65 58.5%, >65 1.7% (1995) **Ethnic groups:** about 42% Kuwaiti, 40% non-Kuwaiti Arab, 5% Indian and Pakistani, 4% Iranian **Language:** Arabic (official) 78%, Kurdish 10%, Farsi 4%, English **Religion:** Sunni Muslim, Shi'ite Muslim, Christian **Education:** (compulsory years) 8 **Literacy rate:** 61% (men); 67% (women) (1995 est) **Labour force:** 42% of population: 1% agriculture, 25% industry, 74% services (1990) **Unemployment:** 0.5% (1995 est) **Life expectancy:** 74 (men); 78 (women) (1995–2000) **Child mortality rate:** (under 5, per 1,000 live births) 16 (1996) **Physicians:** 1 per 581 people (1993)

Practical information

Visa requirements: UK: visa required. USA: visa required **Embassy in the UK:** 45–46 Queen's Gate, London SW7 5HR. Tel:

(0171) 589 4533; fax: (0171) 589 7183 **British embassy:** PO Box 2, Arabian Gulf Street, 13001 Safat, Kuwait City. Tel: (965) 240 3324/5/6; fax: (965) 240 7395 **Chamber of commerce:** Kuwait Chamber of Commerce and Industry, PO Box 775, Chamber's Building, Ali as-Salem Street, 13008 Safat, Kuwait City. Tel: (965) 243 3864; fax: (965) 240 4110 **Airports:** international airports: Kuwait City; total passenger km: 4,509 million (1994) **Major holidays:** 1 January, 25 February (3 days); variable: Eid-ul-Adha (3 days), end of Ramadan (3 days), New Year (Muslim), Prophet's Birthday, Ascension of the Prophet (March/April), Standing on Mount Arafat (August)

Chronology

c. 3000 BC: Archaeological evidence suggests that coastal parts of Kuwait may have been part of a commercial civilization contemporary with the Sumerian, based in Mesopotamia (the Tigris and Euphrates valley area of Iraq). **c. 323 BC:** Visited by Greek colonists at time of Alexander the Great. **7th century AD:** Islam introduced. **late 16th century:** Fell under nominal control of the Turkish Ottoman Empire. **1710:** Control was assumed by the Utab, a member of the Anaza tribal confederation in N Arabia, and Kuwait city was founded, soon developing from a fishing village into an important port. **1756:** Autonomous sheikdom of Kuwait founded by Abd Rahman of the al-Sabah family, a branch of the Utab. **1776:** British East India Company set up a base in the Gulf. **1899:** Concerned at the potential threat of growing Ottoman and German influence, Britain signed a treaty with Kuwait, establishing a self-governing protectorate in which the Emir received an annual subsidy from Britain in return for agreeing not to alienate any territory to a foreign power. **1914:** Britain recognized Kuwait as an 'independent government under British protection'. **1922–33:** Agreement on frontiers with Iraq, to the N, and Nejd (later Saudi Arabia) to the SW. **1938:** Oil discovered; large-scale exploitation after World War II transformed the economy. **1961:** Full independence achieved from Britain, with Sheik Abdullah al-Salem al-Sabah as emir. Attempted Iraqi invasion discouraged by dispatch of British troops to the Gulf. **1962:** Constitution introduced, with franchise restricted to 10% of the population. **1965:** Sheik Abdullah died; succeeded by his brother, Sheik Sabah al-Salem al-Sabah. **1977:** Sheik Sabah died; succeeded by Crown Prince Jabir. National Assembly dissolved. **1981:** National Assembly was reconstituted. **1983:** Shi'ite guerrillas bombed targets in Kuwait; 17 arrested. **1986:** National assembly dissolved. **1987:** Kuwaiti oil tankers reflagged, received US Navy protection; missile attacks by Iran. **1988:** Aircraft hijacked by pro-Iranian Shi'ites demanding release of convicted guerrillas; Kuwait refused. **1989:** Two of the convicted guerrillas released. **1990:** Prodemocracy demonstrations suppressed. Kuwait annexed by Iraq in Aug, causing extensive damage to property and environment. Emir set up government in exile in Saudi Arabia. **1991:** US-led coalition forces defeated Iraqi forces in Kuwait during the Gulf War. New government omitted any opposition representatives. **1992:** Reconstituted national assembly elected, with opposition nominees, including Islamic candidates, winning majority of seats. **1993:** Incursions by Iraq into Kuwait repelled by US-led air strikes on Iraqi military sites. **1994:** Massing of Iraqi troops on Kuwait border prompted US-led response. Iraqi president Saddam Hussein publicly renounced claim to Kuwait.

Kyrgyzstan Republic of

National name: *Kyrgyz Respublikasy* **Area:** 198,500 sq km/76,640 sq mi **Capital:** Bishkek (formerly Frunze) **Major towns/cities:** Osh, Przhevalsk, Kyzyl-Kiya, Tokmak, Djalal-Abad **Physical features:** mountainous, an extension of the Tian Shan range

Government

Head of state: Askar Akayev from 1990 **Head of government:** Apas Jumagulov from 1993 **Political system:** emergent democracy **Administrative divisions:** six provinces **Political parties:** Party of Communists of Kyrgyzstan (banned 1991–92); Ata Meken, Kyrgyz-nationalist; Erkin Kyrgyzstan, Kyrgyz-nationalist; Social

Democratic Party, nationalist, pro-Akayev; Democratic Movement of Kyrgyzstan, nationalist reformist **Armed forces:** 7,000 (1996) **Conscription:** compulsory for 12–18 months **Death penalty:** retained and used for ordinary crimes **Defence spend:** (% GDP) 2.6 (1996) **Education spend:** (% GNP) 6.5 (1994) **Health spend:** (% GDP) 3.2 (1994 est)

Economy and resources

Currency: som **GDP:** ($ US) 3 billion (1994) **Real GDP per capita (PPP):** ($ US) 1,930 (1994) **GDP growth rate:** –6.7% (1995) **Average annual inflation:** 32% (1996); 172.3% (1985–95 est) **Foreign debt:** ($ US) 610 million (1995) **Major trading partners:** Russia, Kazakhstan, Uzbekistan, Turkey, China, UK, Cuba, Ukraine **Resources:** petroleum, natural gas, coal, gold, tin, mercury, antimony, zinc, tungsten, uranium **Industries:** metallurgy, machinery, electronics and instruments, textiles, food processing (particularly sugar refining), mining **Exports:** wool, cotton yarn, tobacco, electric power, electronic and engineering products, non-ferrous metallurgy, food and beverages. Principal market: Kazakhstan 28% (1994) **Imports:** petroleum, natural gas, engineering products, food products. Principal source: Russia 22% (1994) **Arable land:** 4.3% (1995) **Agricultural products:** grain, potatoes, cotton, tobacco, sugar beet, hemp, kenat, kendyr, medicinal plants; livestock rearing (sheep, cattle, goats, yaks, and horses) is the mainstay of agricultural activity

Population and society

Population: 4,469,000 (1996 est) **Population growth rate:** 1.7% (1990–95); 1.5% (2000–05) **Population density:** (per sq km) 23 (1996 est) **Urban population:** (% of total) 39 (1995) **Age distribution:** (% of total population) <15 37.1%, 15–65 57.1%, >65 5.8% (1995) **Ethnic groups:** 53% ethnic Kyrgyz, 22% Russian, 13% Uzbek, 3% Ukrainian, and 2% German **Language:** Kyrgyz, a Turkic language **Religion:** Sunni Muslim **Education:** (compulsory years) 9 **Literacy rate:** 97% (men); 97% (women) (1995 est) **Labour force:** 43% agriculture, 21% industry, 36% services (1994) **Unemployment:** 4.4% (1996) **Life expectancy:** 67 (men); 74 (women) (1995–2000) **Child mortality rate:** (under 5, per 1,000 live births) 39 (1996) **Physicians:** 1 per 337 people (1994)

Practical information

Visa requirements: UK: visa not required. USA: visa not required **Embassy for the UK:** 32 rue de Châtelain, 1050 Brussels, Belgium. Tel: (2) 627 1916; fax: (2) 627 1900 **British embassy:** the British Embassy in Almaty (see Kazakhstan) deals with enquiries relating to Kyrgyzstan **Chamber of commerce:** Kyrgyz Chamber of Commerce and Industry, Kievskaya 107, 720001 Bishkek. Tel: (3312) 210 574; fax: (3312) 210 575 **Airports:** international airports: Bishkek (Bishkek Manas), Osh; three domestic airports; total passenger km: 568 million (1994) **Major holidays:** 1, 7 January, 8, 21 March, 1, 9 May, 31 August

Chronology

8th century: Spread of Islam. **10th century onwards:** Southward migration of Kyrgyz people from upper Yenisey River region to Tian-Shan region; accelerated following rise of Mongol Empire in 13th century. **13th–14th centuries:** Part of Mongol Empire. **1685:** Came under control of Mongol Oirots following centuries of Turkic rule. **1758:** Kyrgyz people became nominal subjects of Chinese Empire, following Oirots' defeat by Chinese rulers, the Manchus. **early 19th**

century: Came under suzerainty of Khanate (chieftaincy) of Kokand, to the W. **1864–76:** Incorporated into tsarist Russian Empire. **1916–17:** Many Kyrgyz migrated to China after Russian suppression of rebellion in Central Asia and outbreak of civil war following 1917 October Revolution in Russia, with local armed guerrillas (*basmachi*) resisting Bolshevik Red Army. **1917–1924:** Part of independent Turkestan republic. **1920s:** Land reforms resulted in settlement of many formerly nomadic Kyrgyz; literacy and education improved. **1924:** Became autonomous republic within USSR. **1930s:** Agricultural collectivization programme provoked *basmachi* resistance and local 'nationalist communists' were purged from Kyrgyz Communist Party (KCP). **1936:** Became full union republic within USSR. **1990:** State of emergency imposed in Bishkek after ethnic clashes. Askar Akayev, a reform communist, chosen as president. **1991:** Akayev condemned attempted coup in Moscow against the reformist Mikhail Gorbachev; Kyrgyzstan joined new Commonwealth of Independent States (CIS); independence recognized by USA. **1992:** Joined the United Nations and Conference on Security and Cooperation in Europe (CSCE; now the Organization on Security and Cooperation in Europe, OSCE). Market-centred economic reform programme instituted. **1994:** National referenda overwhelmingly supported Akayev's presidency. Joined Central Asian Union, with Kazakhstan and Uzbekistan. **1995:** Pro-Akayev independents successful in elections to a new bicameral legislature. **1996:** Constitutional amendment increased powers of president. Agreement with Kazakhstan and Uzbekistan to create single economic market. **1997:** Private ownership of land legalized but privatization programme suspended. Agreement on border controls with Russia.

Laos Lao People's Democratic Republic

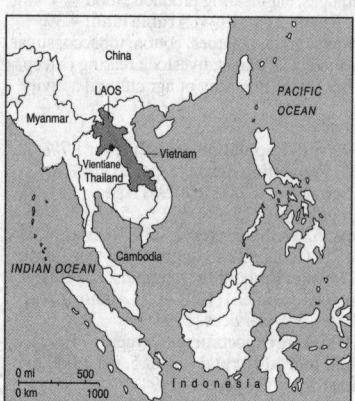

National name: *Saathiaranagroat Prachhathippatay Prachhachhon Lao* **Area:** 236,790 sq km/91,424 sq mi **Capital:** Vientiane **Major towns/cities:** Louangphrabang (the former royal capital), Pakse, Savannakhet **Physical features:** landlocked state with high mountains in E; Mekong River in W; rainforest covers nearly 60% of land

Government

Head of state: Nouhak Phoumsavan from 1992 **Head of government:** General Khamtay Siphandon from 1991 **Political system:** communist, one-party state **Administrative divisions:** 17 provinces **Political party:** Lao People's Revolutionary Party (LPRP, the only legal party) **Armed forces:** 37,000 (1996) **Conscription:** military service is compulsory for a minimum of 18 months **Death penalty:** retained and used for ordinary crimes **Defence spend:** (% GDP) 4.1 (1996) **Education spend:** (% GNP) 2.3 (1993–94) **Health spend:** (% GDP) 0.8 (1990–95)

Economy and resources

Currency: new kip **GDP:** ($ US) 1.5 billion (1994) **Real GDP per capita (PPP):** ($ US) 2,484 (1994) **GDP growth rate:** 8.4% (1994) **Average annual inflation:** 25% (1996); 22.6 (1985–95 est) **Foreign debt:** ($ US) 2.16 billion (1995) **Major trading partners:** Thailand, Japan, Germany, France, China, Italy **Resources:** coal, tin, gypsum, baryte, lead, zinc, nickel, potash, iron ore; small

quantities of gold, silver, and precious stones **Industries:** processing of agricultural produce, sawmilling, textiles and garments, handicrafts, basic consumer goods **Exports:** timber, textiles and garments, motorcycles, electricity, coffee, tin, gypsum. Principal market: Thailand 20.8% (1994) **Imports:** food (particularly rice and sugar), mineral fuels, machinery and transport equipment, cement, cotton yarn. Principal source: Thailand 48.5% (1994) **Arable land:** 3.8% (1995) **Agricultural products:** rice, maize, tobacco, cotton, coffee, sugar cane, cassava, potatoes; sweet potatoes; livestock rearing (pigs, poultry, and cattle); fishing; forest resources including valuable wood such as Teruk (logging suspended 1991 to preserve the forest area); opium is produced but its manufacture is controlled by the state

Population and society

Population: 5,035,000 (1996 est) **Population growth rate:** 3% (1990–95); 2.6% (2000–05) **Population density:** (per sq km) 21 (1996 est) **Urban population:** (% of total) 22 (1995) **Age distribution:** (% of total population) <15 44.8%, 15–65 52.2%, >65 3% (1995) **Ethnic groups:** 60% Laotian, predominantly Lao Lum, 35% hill dwellers, and 5% Vietnamese and Chinese **Language:** Lao (official), French, English **Religion:** Theravāda Buddhist 85%, animist beliefs among mountain dwellers **Education:** (compulsory years) 5 **Literacy rate:** 92% (men); 76% (women) (1995 est) **Labour force:** 50% of population: 78% agriculture, 6% industry, 16% services (1990) **Unemployment:** 3% (1993) **Life expectancy:** 52 (men); 55 (women) (1995–2000) **Child mortality rate:** (under 5, per 1,000 live births) 143 (1996) **Physicians:** 1 per 4,446 person (1993 est)

Practical information

Visa requirements: UK: visa required. USA: visa required **Embassy for the UK:** 74 avenue Raymond Poincaré, 75116 Paris, France. Tel: (1) 4553 0298; fax: (1) 4727 5789 **British embassy:** Laos has no diplomatic representation in the UK; the British Embassy in Bangkok (see Thailand) deals with enquiries relating to Laos **Chamber of commerce:** Lao National Chamber of Commerce and Industry, BP 4596, rue Phonsay, Vientiane. Tel: (21) 412 392; fax: (21) 414 383 **Airports:** international airports: Vientiane (Wattai); three domestic airports; total passenger km: 209 million (1994) **Major holidays:** 24 January, 13–15 April, 1 May, 2 December

Chronology

c. 2000–500 BC: Early Bronze Age civilizations in central Mekong River and Plain of Jars regions. **5th–8th centuries:** Occupied by immigrants from S China. **8th century onwards:** Theravāda Buddhism spread by Mon monks. **9th–13th centuries:** Part of the sophisticated Khmer Empire, centred on Angkor in Cambodia. **12th century:** Small independent principalities, notably Louangphrabang, established by Lao invaders from Thailand and Yunnan, S China; they adopted Buddhism. **14th century:** United by King Fa Ngum; the first independent Laotian state, Lan Xang, formed. It was to dominate for four centuries, broken only by a period of Burmese rule 1574–1637. **17th century:** First visited by Europeans. **1713:** The Lan Xang kingdom split into three separate kingdoms, Louangphrabang, Vientiane, and Champassac, which became tributaries of Siam (Thailand) from the late 18th century. **1893–1945:** Laos was a French protectorate, comprising the three principalities of Louangphrabang, Vientiane, and Champassac. **1945:** Temporarily occupied by Japan. **1946:** Retaken by France, despite opposition by the Chinese-backed Lao Issara (Free Laos) nationalist movement. **1950:** Granted semi-autonomy in French Union, as an associated state under the constitutional monarchy of the king of Louangphrabang. **1954:** Independence achieved from France under the Geneva Agreements, but civil war broke out between a moderate royalist faction of the Lao Issara, led by Prince Souvanna Phouma, and the communist Chinese-backed Pathet Lao (Land of the Lao) led by Prince Souphanouvong (Souvanna's half-brother). **1957:** Coalition government, headed by Souvanna Phouma, established by Vientiane Agreement. **1959:** Savang Vatthana became king. **1960:** Right-wing pro-Western government seized power, headed by Prince Boun Gum. **1962:** Geneva

Agreement established new coalition government, led by Souvanna Phouma, but civil war continued, the Pathet Lao receiving backing from the North Vietnamese, and Souvanna Phouma from the USA. **1973:** Vientiane cease-fire agreement divided the country between the communists and the Souvanna Phouma regime and brought the withdrawal of US, Thai, and North Vietnamese forces. **1975:** Communists seized power; republic proclaimed, with Prince Souphanouvong as head of state and the Communist Party leader Kaysone Phomvihane as the controlling prime minister. **1979:** Food shortages and the flight of 250,000 refugees to Thailand led to an easing of the drive towards nationalization and agricultural collectivization. **1985:** Greater economic liberalization received encouragement from the Soviet Union's reformist leader Mikhail Gorbachev. **1989:** First assembly elections since communist takeover; Vietnamese troops withdrawn from the country. **1991:** Kaysone Phomvihane was elected president and the army commander General Khamtay Siphandon became prime minister. Security and cooperation pact signed with Thailand, and agreement reached on phased repatriation of Laotian refugees. **1992:** Phomvihane died; replaced as president by Nouhak Phoumsavan. **1995:** The US lifted its 20-year aid embargo. **1996:** Military tightened its grip on political affairs; but inward investment and private enterprise continued to be encouraged, fuelling economic expansion. **1997:** Membership of Association of South East Asian Nations (ASEAN) announced.

Latvia Republic of

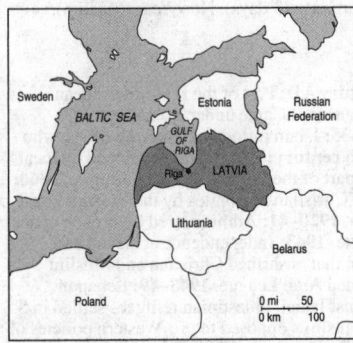

National name: *Latvijas Republika* **Area:** 63,700 sq km/24,594 sq mi **Capital:** Riga **Major towns/cities:** Daugavpils, Leipāja, Jurmala, Jelgava, Ventspils **Major ports:** Ventspils, Leipāja **Physical features:** wooded lowland (highest point 312 m/1,024 ft), marshes, lakes; 472 km/293 mi of coastline; mild climate

Government

Head of state: Guntis Ulmanis from 1993 **Head of government:** Guntar Krasts from 1997 **Political system:** emergent democracy **Administrative divisions:** 26 districts and seven municipalities **Political parties:** Latvian Way, right of centre; Latvian National and Conservative Party (LNNK), right wing, nationalist; Economic-Political Union (formerly known as Harmony for Latvia and Rebirth of the National Economy), centrist; Ravnopravie (Equal Rights), centrist; For the Fatherland and Freedom (FFF), extreme nationalist; Latvian Peasants' Union (LZS), rural based, centre left; Union of Christian Democrats, centre right; Democratic Centre Party, centrist; Movement for Latvia, pro-Russian, populist; Master in Your Own Home (Saimnieks), ex-communist, populist; Latvian National Party of Reforms, right of centre nationalist coalition **Armed forces:** 8,000 (1996) **Conscription:** compulsory for 18 months **Death penalty:** retained and used for ordinary crimes **Defence spend:** (% GDP) 3.5 (1996) **Education spend:** (% GNP) 6.4 (1994) **Health spend:** (% GDP) 3.7 (1990–95)

Economy and resources

Currency: lat **GDP:** ($ US) 6 billion (1994) **Real GDP per capita (PPP):** ($ US) 3,332 (1994) **GDP growth rate:** 1.5% (1996); –13.7% (1990–95) **Average annual inflation:** 18% (1996); 73.2% (1985–95) **Foreign debt:** ($ US) 462 million (1995) **Major trading partners:** Russia, Germany, Lithuania, Finland, Sweden, Estonia **Resources:**

peat, gypsum, dolomite, limestone, amber, gravel, sand **Industries:** food processing, machinery and equipment (major producer of electric railway passenger cars and long-distance telephone exchanges), chemicals and chemical products, sawn timber, paper and woollen goods **Exports:** timber and timber products, textiles, food and agricultural products, machinery and electrical equipment, metal industry products. Principal market: Russia 22.8% (1996) **Imports:** mineral fuels and products, machinery and electrical equipment, chemical industry products. Principal source: Russia 20.2% (1996) **Arable land:** 27.6% (1995) **Agricultural products:** oats, barley, rye, potatoes, flax; cattle and dairy farming and pig breeding are the chief agricultural occupations

Population and society

Population: 2,504,000 (1996 est) **Population growth rate:** –0.9% (1990–95); –0.5% (2000–05) **Population density:** (per sq km) 39 (1996 est) **Urban population:** (% of total) 73 (1995) **Age distribution:** (% of total population) <15 20.6%, 15–65 66.1%, >65 13.3% (1995) **Ethnic groups:** 53% of Latvian ethnic descent, 34% ethnic Russian, 4% Belarusian, 3% Ukrainian, 2% Polish, 1% Lithuanian **Language:** Latvian **Religion:** Lutheran, Roman Catholic, Russian Orthodox **Education:** (compulsory years) 9 **Literacy rate:** 99% (men); 99% (women) (1995 est) **Labour force:** 19.5% agriculture, 28.5% industry, 52% services (1993) **Unemployment:** 7% (1996) **Life expectancy:** 63 (men); 75 (women) (1995–2000) **Child mortality rate:** (under 5, per 1,000 live births) 20 (1996) **Physicians:** 1 per 293 people (1994)

Practical information

Visa requirements: UK: visa not required. USA: visa required **Embassy in the UK:** 45 Nottingham Place, London W1M 3FE. Tel: (0171) 312 0040; fax: (0171) 312 0042 **British embassy:** Alunana iela 5, LV-1010 Riga. Tel: (371) 782 8126; fax: (371) 733 8132 **Chamber of commerce:** Latvian Chamber of Commerce and Industry, Brivibas bulvaris 21, LV-1849 Riga. Tel: (371) 722 5595; fax: (371) 782 0092 **Airports:** international airport: Riga (Spilva), Jelgava; total passenger km: 145 million (1994) **Major holidays:** 1 January, 1 May, 23–24 June, 18 November, 25–26 December; variable: Good Friday

Chronology

9th–10th centuries: Invaded by Vikings and Russians. **13th century:** Conquered by crusading German Teutonic Knights, who named the area Livonia and converted population to Christianity; Riga joined Hanseatic League, a N European union of commercial towns. **1520s:** Lutheranism established as a result of the Reformation. **16th–17th centuries:** Successively under Polish, Lithuanian, and Swedish rule. **1721:** Tsarist Russia took control. **1819:** Serfdom abolished. **1900s:** Emergence of independence movement. **1914–18:** Under partial German occupation during World War I. **1918–19:** Independence proclaimed and achieved after Russian Red Army troops expelled by German, Polish, and Latvian forces. **1920s:** Land reforms introduced by Farmers' Union government of Karlis Ulmanis. **1934:** Democracy overthrown and, at time of economic depression, Ulmanis established autocratic regime; Baltic Entente mutual defence pact with Estonia and Lithuania. **1940:** Incorporated into Soviet Union (USSR) as constituent republic, following secret German–Soviet agreement. **1941–44:** Occupied by Germany. **1944:** USSR regained control; mass deportations of Latvians to Central Asia, followed by immigration of ethnic Russians; agricultural collectivization. **1960s and 1970s:** Extreme repression of Latvian cultural and literary life. **1980s:** Nationalist dissent began to grow, influenced by the Polish Solidarity movement and Mikhail Gorbachev's *glasnost* ('openness') initiative in the USSR. **1988:** Latvian Popular Front established to campaign for independence. Prewar flag readopted; official status given to Latvian language. **1989:** Latvian parliament passed sovereignty declaration. **1990:** Popular Front secured majority in local elections and its leader, Ivan Godmanir, became prime minister. Latvian Communist Party split into pro-independence and pro-Moscow wings. Entered 'transitional period of independence'; Baltic Council reformed. **1991:** Soviet troops briefly seized key installations in Riga. Overwhelming vote for independence in referendum. Full independence achieved following failure of anti-Gorbachev coup attempt in Moscow; CP outlawed. Joined United Nations (UN); market-centred economic reform programme instituted. **1992:** Curbing of rights of noncitizens prompted Russia to request minority protection by UN. **1993:** Right-of-centre Latvian Way won most seats in general election, and Valdis Birkavs became premier; free-trade agreement with Estonia and Lithuania. **1994:** Last Russian troops departed. Birkavs replaced by Maris Gailis; economic growth resumed. **1995:** Trade and cooperation agreement signed with European Union (EU). General election produced 'hung parliament', in which extremist parties received most support. Latvia applied officially for EU membership. Independent Andris Skele became prime minister. **1996:** Guntis Ulmanis re-elected president. Finance minister and deputy prime minister resigned from eight-party coalition. **1997:** New political party formed, Latvian National Party of Reforms. Prime Minister Skele replaced by Guntar Krasts. Former Communist leader Alfred Rubiks released from prison.

Lebanon Republic of

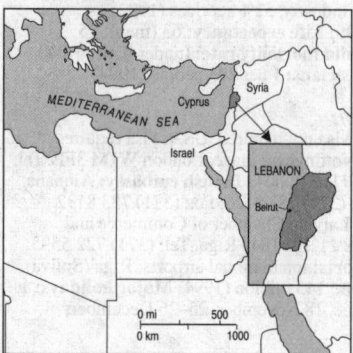

National name: *Jumhouria al-Lubnaniya* **Area:** 10,452 sq km/4,035 sq mi **Capital:** Beirut (and port) **Major towns/cities:** Tripoli, Zahlé, Baabda, Baalbek, Jezzine **Major ports:** Tripoli, Tyre, Sidon, Jounie **Physical features:** narrow coastal plain; fertile Bekka valley running N–S between Lebanon and Anti-Lebanon mountain ranges

Government

Head of state: Elias Hrawi from 1989 **Head of government:** Rafik al-Hariri from 1992 **Political system:** emergent democracy **Administrative divisions:** six governates **Political parties:** Phalangist Party, Christian, radical, nationalist; Progressive Socialist Party (PSP), Druse, moderate, socialist; National Liberal Party (NLP), Maronite, centre left; National Bloc, Maronite, moderate; Lebanese Communist Party (PCL), nationalist, communist; Parliamentary Democratic Front, Sunni Muslim, centrist **Armed forces:** 48,900 (1996); in 1995 there were 30,000 Syrian troops and the pro-Israeli South Lebanese army numbered 2,500 **Conscription:** compulsory for 12 months **Death penalty:** retained and used for ordinary crimes **Defence spend:** (% GDP) 4.4 (1996) **Education spend:** (% GNP) 1.5 (1994) **Health spend:** (% GDP) 2.1 (1990–95)

Economy and resources

Currency: Lebanese pound **GDP:** ($ US) 10.31 billion (1994) **Real GDP per capita (PPP):** ($ US) 4,863 (1994) **GDP growth rate:** 8.5% (1994) **Average annual inflation:** 12% (1996); 45.8% (1985–95 est) **Foreign debt:** ($ US) 3 billion (1996) **Major trading partners:** United Arab Emirates, Italy, Saudi Arabia, Syria, Germany, USA, France, Kuwait, Jordan **Resources:** there are no commercially viable mineral deposits; small reserves of lignite and iron ore **Industries:** food processing, petroleum refining, textiles, furniture and woodworking, paper and paper products **Exports:** paper products, textiles, fruit and vegetables, jewellery. Principal market: UAE 28.7% (1995) **Imports:** electrical equipment, vehicles, petroleum, metals, machinery, consumer goods. Principal source: Italy 13% (1995) **Arable land:** 20.7% (1995) **Agricultural products:** citrus fruits, potatoes, melons, apples, grapes (viticulture is significant), wheat, sugar beet, olives, bananas; livestock rearing (goats and sheep); although illegal, hashish is an important export crop

Population and society

Population: 3,084,000 (1996 est) **Population growth rate:** 3.3% (1990–95); 1.5% (2000–05) **Population density:** (per sq km) 297 (1996 est) **Urban population:** (% of total) 87 (1995) **Age distribution:** (% of total population) <15 34.1%, 15–65 60.4%, >65 5.5% (1995) **Ethnic groups:** about 90% Arab, with Armenian, Assyrian, Jewish, Turkish, and Greek minorities **Language:** Arabic (official), French, Armenian, English **Religion:** Muslim 58% (Shiite 35%, Sunni 23%), Christian 27% (mainly Maronite), Druse 3%; other Christian denominations including Orthodox, Armenian, and Roman Catholic **Education:** not compulsory **Literacy rate:** 88% (men); 73% (women) (1995 est) **Labour force:** 31% of population: 7% agriculture, 31% industry, 62% services (1990) **Unemployment:** 35% (1993 est) **Life expectancy:** 68 (men); 72 (women) (1995–2000) **Child mortality rate:** (under 5, per 1,000 live births) 36 (1996) **Physicians:** 1 per 537 people (1993 est)

Practical information

Visa requirements: UK: visa required. USA: visa required **Embassy in the UK:** 21 Kensington Palace Gardens, London W8 4QH. (0171) 229 7265; fax: (0171) 243 1699 **British embassy:** British Embassy in West Beirut, Shamma Building, Raoucheh, Ras Beirut. Tel: (1) 812 849; telex: 20465 **Chamber of commerce:** Beirut Chamber of Commerce and Industry, PO Box 11-1801, Sanayeh, Beirut. Tel: (1) 349 530; fax: (1) 865 802 **Airports:** international airports: Beirut (Khaldeh); most major cities have domestic airports; total passenger km: 1,588 million (1994) **Major holidays:** 1 January, 9 February, 1 May, 15 August, 1, 22 November, 25 December; variable: Eid-ul-Adha (3 days), Ashora, Good Friday, Easter Monday, end of Ramadan (3 days), New Year (Muslim), Prophet's Birthday

Chronology

5th century BC–1st century AD: Part of the E Mediterranean Phoenician Empire. **1st century:** Came under Roman rule; Christianity introduced. **635:** Islam introduced by Arab tribes, who settled in S Lebanon. **11th century:** Druse faith developed by local Muslims. **1516:** Became part of the Turkish Ottoman Empire. **1860:** Massacre of thousands of Christian Maronites by the Muslim Druse led to French intervention. **1920–41:** Administered by French under League of Nations mandate. **1943:** Independence achieved as a republic, with constitution that enshrined Christian and Muslim power-sharing. **1945:** Joined Arab League. **1948–49:** Lebanon joined first Arab war against Israel; Palestinian refugees settled in S. **1958:** Revolt by radical Muslims opposed to pro-Western policies of Christian president, Camille Chamoun. **1964:** Palestine Liberation Organization (PLO) founded in Beirut. **1967:** More Palestinian refugees settled in Lebanon following Arab–Israeli war. **1971:** PLO expelled from Jordan; established headquarters in Lebanon. **1975:** Outbreak of civil war between conservative Christians and leftist Muslims backed by PLO. **1976:** Cease-fire agreed; Syrian-dominated Arab deterrent force formed to keep the peace, but considered by Christians as an occupying force. **1978:** Israel launched limited invasion of S Lebanon in search of PLO guerrillas. International United Nations peacekeeping force unable to prevent further fighting. **1979:** Part of S Lebanon declared an 'independent free Lebanon' by right-wing army officer. **1982:** Bachir Gemayel, a Maronite Christian, elected president but assassinated; he was succeeded by his brother Amin Gemayel. Israel again invaded Lebanon. Palestinians withdrew from Beirut under supervision of international peacekeeping force; PLO moved its headquarters to Tunis. **1983:** Agreement reached for withdrawal of Syrian and Israeli troops but abrogated under Syrian pressure; intense fighting between Christian Phalangists and Muslim Druse militias. **1984:** Most of international peacekeeping force withdrawn. Radical Muslim militia took control of W Beirut. **1985:** Lebanon in chaos; many foreigners taken hostage and Israeli troops withdrawn. **1987:** Syrian troops sent into Beirut. **1988:** Agreement on Christian successor to Gemayel failed and Gen Michel Aoun appointed to head caretaker military government; Premier Selim el-Hoss set up rival government; threat of partition hung over country. **1989:** Gen Aoun declared 'war of liberation' against Syrian occupation; Arab

League-sponsored talks resulted in cease-fire and revised constitution recognizing Muslim majority; René Mouhawad assassinated after 17 days as president; Maronite Christian Elias Hrawi named as successor; Aoun occupied presidential palace, rejecting constitution. **1990:** Release of Western hostages began. Gen Aoun, crushed by Syrians, surrendered and legitimate government was restored. **1991:** Government extended control to the whole country. Treaty of cooperation with Syria signed. **1992:** Remaining Western hostages released. Pro-Syrian administration re-elected with Rafik al-Hariri as prime minister after many Christians boycotted general election. **1993:** Israel launched attacks against Shia fundamentalist Hezbollah strongholds in S Lebanon before USA and Syria brokered agreement to avoid use of force. **1996:** Israel launched a rocket attack on S Lebanon, in response to Hezbollah activity. USA, Israel, Syria, and Lebanon attempted to broker new cease-fire.

Lesotho Kingdom of

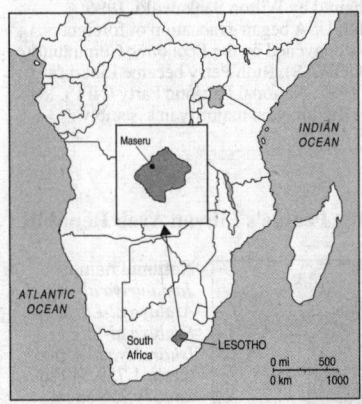

Area: 30,355 sq km/11,720 sq mi **Capital:** Maseru **Major towns/cities:** Qacha's Nek, Teyateyaneng, Mafeteng, Hlotse, Roma, Quthing **Physical features:** mountainous with plateaux, forming part of South Africa's chief watershed

Government
Head of state: King Letsie III from 1996 **Head of government:** Ntsu Mokhehle from 1993 **Political system:** constitutional monarchy **Administrative divisions:** ten districts **Political parties:** Basotho National Party (BNP), traditionalist, nationalist, right of centre; Basutoland Congress Party (BCP), left of centre **Armed forces:** 2,000 (1996) **Conscription:** military service is voluntary **Death penalty:** retained and used for ordinary crimes **Defence spend:** (% GDP) 5.0 (1996) **Education spend:** (% GNP) 4.8 (1993–94) **Health spend:** (% GDP) 3.5 (1990–95)

Economy and resources
Currency: loti **GDP:** ($ US) 0.9 billion (1994) **Real GDP per capita (PPP):** ($ US) 1,109 (1994) **GDP growth rate:** 11.9% (1994); 7.5% (1990–95) **Average annual inflation:** 10% (1996); 13.6% (1985–95) **Foreign debt:** ($ US) 659 million (1995) **Major trading partners:** SACU (South African Customs Union) members: Lesotho, Botswana, Swaziland, Namibia, and South Africa); Taiwan, Hong Kong, USA, Canada, Italy, and other EU countries **Resources:** diamonds, uranium, lead, iron ore; believed to have petroleum deposits **Industries:** food products and beverages, textiles and clothing, mining, baskets, furniture; approximately 35% of Lesotho's adult male labour force was employed in South African mines 1995 **Exports:** clothing, footwear, furniture, food and live animals (cattle), hides, wool and mohair, baskets. Principal market: SACU 51.4% (1994) **Imports:** food and live animals, machinery and transport equipment, electricity, petroleum products. Principal source: SACU 81.8% (1994) **Arable land:** 10.5% (1995) **Agricultural products:** maize, wheat, sorghum, asparagus, peas, and other vegetables; livestock rearing (sheep, goats, and cattle)

Population and society
Population: 2,078,000 (1996 est) **Population growth rate:** 2.7%

(1990–95); 2.6% (2000–05) **Population density:** (per sq km) 68 (1996 est) **Urban population:** (% of total) 23 (1995) **Age distribution:** (% of total population) <15 42.1%, 15–65 53.9%, >65 4% (1995) **Ethnic groups:** almost entirely Bantus (of Southern Sotho) or Basotho **Language:** Sesotho, English (official), Zulu, Xhosa **Religion:** Protestant 42%, Roman Catholic 38%, indigenous beliefs **Education:** (compulsory years) 7 **Literacy rate:** 62% (men); 84% (women) (1995 est) **Labour force:** 76.3% agriculture, 11.1% industry, 12.6% services (1994 est) **Unemployment:** 50% (1993 est) **Life expectancy:** 61 (men); 66 (women) (1995–2000) **Child mortality rate:** (under 5, per 1,000 live births) 81 (1996) **Physicians:** 1 per 14,306 people (1993)

Practical information
Visa requirements: UK: visa not required for visits of up to 30 days. USA: visa required **Embassy in the UK:** 7 Chesham Place, Belgravia, London SW1 8HN. Tel: (0171) 235 5686; fax: (0171) 235 5023 **British embassy:** British High Commission, PO Box Ms 521, Maseru 100. Tel: (266) 313 961; fax: (266) 310 120 **Chamber of commerce:** Lesotho Chamber of Commerce and Industry, PO Box 79, Maseru 100. Tel: (266) 323 482 **Airports:** international airports: Maseru (Moshoeshoe I); 40 airstrips, of which 14 receive charter and regular scheduled air services; total passenger km: 9 million (1994) **Major holidays:** 1 January, 12, 21 March, 2 May, 4 October, 25–26 December; variable: Ascension Thursday, Good Friday, Easter Monday, Family (July), National Sports (October)

Chronology
18th century: Formerly inhabited by nomadic hunter-gatherer San, Zulu-speaking Ngunis, and Sotho-speaking peoples settled in the region. **1820s:** Under the name of Basutoland, Sotho nation founded by Moshoeshoe I, who united the people to repulse Zulu attacks from S. **1843:** Moshoeshoe I negotiated British protection as tension with South African Boers increased. **1868:** Became British territory, administered by Cape Colony (in South Africa) from 1871. **1884:** Became British crown colony, after revolt against Cape Colony control; Basuto chiefs allowed to govern according to custom and tradition, but rich agricultural land W of the Caledon river was lost to South Africa. **1900s:** Served as a migrant labour reserve for South Africa's mines and farms. **1952:** Left-of-centre Basutoland African Congress, later Congress Party (BCP), founded by Ntsu Mokhehle to campaign for self rule. **1966:** Independence achieved within Commonwealth, as Kingdom of Lesotho, with Moshoeshoe II as king and Chief Leabua Jonathan of conservative Basotho National Party (BNP) as prime minister. **1970:** State of emergency declared; king briefly forced into exile after attempting to increase his authority. **1973:** State of emergency lifted; BNP won majority of seats in general election. **1975:** Members of ruling party attacked by South African-backed guerrillas, who opposed African National Congress (ANC) guerrillas using Lesotho as a base. **1986:** South Africa imposed border blockade, forcing deportation of 60 ANC members. Gen Lekhanya ousted Chief Jonathan in a coup. **1990:** Lekhanya replaced in coup by Col Elias Ramaema; Moshoeshoe II dethroned and replaced by son, as King Letsie III. **1993:** Free multiparty elections ended military rule; Ntsu Mokhehle (BCP) became prime minister. **1994:** Fighting between rival army factions ended by peace deal, brokered by Organization of African Unity. **1995:** Letsie abdicated to restore King Moshoeshoe II to the throne. **1996:** King Moshoeshoe II killed in car accident; King Letsie III restored to throne.

Liberia Republic of

Area: 111,370 sq km/42,999 sq mi **Capital:** Monrovia (and port) **Major towns/cities:** Bensonville, Saniquillie, Gbarnga, Voinjama, Buchanan **Major ports:** Buchanan, Greenville **Physical features:** forested highlands; swampy tropical coast where six rivers enter the sea

Government
Head of state and government: Ruth Perry from 1996 **Political system:** emergent democracy **Administrative divisions:** 13

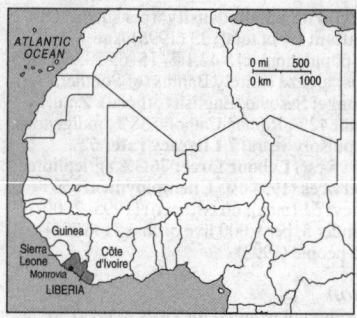

counties **Political parties:** National Democratic Party of Liberia (NDPL), nationalist, left of centre; National Patriotic Front of Liberia (NPFL), left of centre; United Democratic Movement of Liberia for Democracy (Ulimo), left of centre; National Patriotic Party (NPP) **Armed forces:** 22,000 (1996) **Conscription:** military service is voluntary **Death penalty:** retained and used for ordinary crimes **Defence spend:** (% GDP) 3.3 (1996) **Education spend:** (% GNP) 2.7 (1988) **Health spend:** (% GDP) 3.5 (1990)

Economy and resources

Currency: Liberian dollar **GDP:** ($ US) 2.3 billion (1994 est) **Real GDP per capita (PPP):** ($ US) 800 (1994 est) **GDP growth rate:** 0% (1994 est) **Average annual inflation:** 10% (1995); 4.6% (1980–89) **Foreign debt:** ($ US) 2.06 billion (1994) **Major trading partners:** Belgium/Luxembourg, Japan, USA, Germany, the Netherlands, Italy, France **Resources:** iron ore, diamonds, gold, barytes, kyanite **Industries:** beverages (soft drinks and beer), mineral products, chemicals, tobacco and other agricultural products, cement, mining, rubber, furniture, bricks, plastics **Exports:** iron ore, rubber, timber, coffee, cocoa, palm-kernel oil, diamonds, gold. Principal market: Belgium/Luxembourg 56.3% (1994 est) **Imports:** machinery and transport equipment, mineral fuels, rice, basic manufactures, food and live animals. Principal source: Japan 37.2% (1994 est) **Arable land:** 1.3% (1995) **Agricultural products:** rice, cassava, coffee, citrus fruits, cocoa, palm kernels, sugar cane; timber production; rubber plantation

Population and society

Population: 2,245,000 (1996 est) **Population growth rate:** 3.3% (1990–95); 3.1% (2000–05) **Population density:** (per sq km) 20 (1996 est) **Urban population:** (% of total) 45 (1995) **Age distribution:** (% of total population) <15 46%, 15–65 50.4%, >65 3.7% (1995) **Ethnic groups:** 95% indigenous peoples, including the Kpelle, Bassa, Gio, Kru, Grebo, Mano, Krahn, Gola, Ghandi, Loma, Kissi, Vai, and Bella; 5% descended from repatriated US slaves **Language:** English (official), over 20 Niger-Congo languages **Religion:** animist, Sunni Muslim, Christian **Education:** (compulsory years) 9 **Literacy rate:** 50% (men); 29% (women) (1995 est) **Labour force:** 41% of population: 72% agriculture, 6% industry, 22% services (1990) **Unemployment:** 80% (1995 est) **Life expectancy:** 56 (men); 59 (women) (1995–2000) **Child mortality rate:** (under 5, per 1,000 live births) 151 (1996)

Practical information

Visa requirements: UK: visa required. USA: visa required **Embassy in the UK:** 2 Pembridge Place, London W2 4XB. Tel: (0171) 221 1036 **British embassy:** the British High Commission in Abidjan (see Ivory Coast) deals with enquiries relating to Liberia **Chamber of commerce:** PO Box 92, Monrovia. Tel: (231) 223 738; telex: 44211 **Airports:** international airports: Monrovia (Robertsfield and Spriggs Payne); regular services operate from Monrovia to major towns (most air services have been suspended since 1992); total passenger km: 7 million (1992) **Major holidays:** 1 January, 11 February, 15 March, 12 April, 14 May, 26 July, 24 August, 29 November, 25 December; variable: Decoration (March), National Fast and Prayer (April), Thanksgiving (November)

Chronology

1821: Purchased by philanthropic American Colonization Society and turned into settlement for liberated black slaves from southern USA. **1847:** Recognized as an independent republic. **1869:** The True Whig Party founded, which was to dominate politics for more than a century, providing all presidents. **1926:** Large concession sold to Firestone Rubber Company as foreign indebtedness increased. **1944:** William Tubman, descendant of US slaves, elected president. **1971:** Tubman died; succeeded by William Tolbert. **1980:** Tolbert assassinated in military coup led by Sgt Samuel Doe, who banned political parties and launched anticorruption drive. **1984:** New constitution approved in referendum. National Democratic Party (NDPL) founded by Doe as political parties relegalized. **1985:** Doe and the NDPL won decisive victories in allegedly rigged elections. **1990:** Doe killed as bloody civil war broke out, involving Charles Taylor and Gen Hezekiah Bowen, who led rival rebel armies, the National Patriotic Front (NPFL) and the Armed Forces of Liberia (AFL). War left 150,000 dead and 2 million homeless. West African peacekeeping force drafted in. Amos Sawyer, with NPFL backing, became interim head of government. **1992:** Monrovia under siege by Taylor's rebel forces as fighting continued. **1993:** Peace agreement signed under OAU–UN auspices, but soon collapsed. **1995:** Ghanaian-backed peace proposals accepted by rebel factions; interim Council of State established, comprising leaders of three main rebel factions and chaired by Wilton Sankawulo. **1996:** Renewed fighting in capital; USA began evacuation of foreigners. Peace plan reached in talks convened by the Economic Community of West African States (ECOWAS); Ruth Perry became Liberia's first female head of state. **1997:** National Patriotic Party (NPP), led by former warlord Charles Taylor, won majority in assembly elections.

Libya Great Socialist People's Libyan Arab Republic

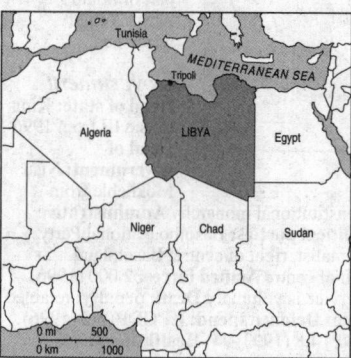

National name: *Jamahiriya al-Arabiya al-Libya al-Shabiya al-Ishtirakiya al-Uzma* **Area:** 1,759,540 sq km/679,358 sq mi **Capital:** Tripoli **Towns and cities:** Benghazi, Misurata, Az-Zaiwa, Tobruk, Ajdabiya, Derna **Major ports:** Benghazi, Misurata, Az-Zaiwa, Tobruk, Ajdabiya, Derna **Physical features:** flat to undulating plains with plateaux and depressions stretch S from the Mediterranean coast to an extremely dry desert interior

Government

Head of state and government: Moamer al-Khaddhafi from 1969 **Political system:** one-party socialist state **Administrative divisions:** 25 municipalities **Political party:** Arab Socialist Union (ASU), radical, left wing **Armed forces:** 65,000 (1996) **Conscription:** conscription is selective for two years **Death penalty:** retained and used for ordinary crimes **Defence spend:** (% GDP) 5.1 (1996) **Education spend:** (% GNP) 9.6 (1986); N/A (1993–94)

Economy and resources

Currency: Libyan dinar **GDP:** ($ US) 32.8 billion (1994 est) **Real GDP per capita (PPP):** ($ US) 6,125 (1994) **GDP growth rate:** –4.5% (1994) **Average annual inflation:** 35% (1996) **Foreign debt:** ($ US) 4.2 billion (1996 est) **Major trading partners:** Italy, Germany, Greece, Spain, UK, France, Turkey, Morocco, the Netherlands **Resources:** petroleum, natural gas, iron ore, potassium, magnesium, sulphur, gypsum **Industries:** petroleum refining, processing of agricultural products, cement and other building materials, fish processing and canning, textiles, clothing and footwear **Exports:** crude petroleum (accounted for 94% of 1991 export earnings), chemicals and related products. Principal market: Italy 39.8% (1995) **Imports:** machinery and transport equipment, basic manufactures, food and live animals, miscellaneous manufactured articles. Principal source: Italy 21.7% (1995) **Arable land:** 1% (1995) **Agricultural products:** barley, wheat, grapes, olives, dates; livestock rearing (sheep, goats, and camels); fishing

Population and society
Population: 5,593,000 (1996 est) **Population growth rate:** 3.5% (1990–95); 3.2% (2000–05) **Population density:** (per sq km) 3 (1996 est) **Urban population:** (% of total) 86 (1995) **Age distribution:** (% of total population) <15 45.4%, 15–65 52%, >65 2.6% (1995) **Ethnic groups:** majority are of Berber and Arab origin, with a small number of Tebou and Touareg nomads and semi-nomads, mainly in S **Language:** Arabic **Religion:** Sunni Muslim **Education:** (compulsory years) 9 **Literacy rate:** 75% (men); 50% (women) (1995 est) **Labour force:** 29% of population: 18% agriculture, 31% industry, 51% services (1990) **Unemployment:** 30% (1995 est) **Life expectancy:** 64 (men); 68 (women) (1995–2000) **Child mortality rate:** (under 5, per 1,000 live births) 80 (1996) **Physicians:** 1 per 957 people (1993 est)

Practical information
Visa requirements: UK: visa required. USA: visa required **Embassy for the UK:** British Interests Section, c/o Embassy of the Italian Republic, PO Box 4206, Sharia Uahran 1, Tripoli. Tel: (21) 333 1191; telex: 20296 (a/b BRITEMB LY) **British embassy:** c/o Permanent Mission of the Socialist People's Libyan Arab Jamahiriya to the United Nations, 309–315 East 48th Street, New York, NY 10017, USA. Tel: (212) 752 5775; fax: (212) 593 4787. Paris Libyan People's Bureau. Tel: (1) 4720 1970 **Chamber of commerce:** Tripoli Chamber of Commerce, Industry and Agriculture, PO Box 2321, Sharia al-Fatah September, Tripoli. Tel: (21) 333 3755; telex: 20181 **Airports:** international airports: Tripoli, Benghazi (Benina), Sebhah (international civilian links with Libya have been suspended since April 1992, in accordance with a UN Security Council Resolution of March 1992); seven domestic airports; total passenger km: 425 million (1994) **Major holidays:** 2, 8, 28 March, 11 June, 23 July, 1 September, 7 October; variable: Eid-ul-Adha (4 days), end of Ramadan (3 days), Prophet's Birthday

Chronology
7th century BC: Tripolitania, in western Libya, was settled by Phoenicians, who founded Tripoli; it became an eastern province of Carthaginian kingdom, which was centred on Tunis to the W. **4th century BC:** Cyrenaica, in eastern Libya, colonized by Greeks, who called it Libya. **74 BC:** Became a Roman province, with Tripolitania part of Africa Nova province and Cyrenaica combined with Crete as a province. **19 BC:** The desert region of Fezzan (Phazzania), inhabited by Garmante people, was conquered by Rome. **6th century AD:** Came under control of Byzantine Empire. **7th century:** Conquered by Arabs, who spread Islam: Egypt ruled Cyrenaica and Morrocan Berber Almohads controlled Tripolitania. **mid-16th century:** Became part of Turkish Ottoman Empire, who combined the three ancient regions into one regency in Tripoli. **1711:** Karamanli (Qaramanli) dynasty established virtual independence from Ottomans. **1835:** Ottoman control reasserted. **1911–12:** Conquered by Italy. **1920s:** Resistance to Italian rule by Sanusi order and Umar al-Mukhtar. **1934:** Colony named Libya. **1942:** Italians ousted, and area divided into three provinces: Fezzan (under French control), Cyrenaica, and Tripolitania (under British control). **1951:** Achieved independence as United Kingdom of Libya, under King Idris, former Amir of Cyrenaica and leader of Sanusi order. **1959:** Discovery of oil transformed economy, but also led to unsettling social changes. **1969:** King deposed in military coup led by Col Moamer al-Khaddhafi. Revolution Command Council set up and Arab Socialist Union (ASU) proclaimed the only legal party in a new puritanical Islamic-socialist republic which sought Pan-Arab unity. **1970s:** Economic activity collectivized, oil industry nationalized, opposition suppressed by Khaddhafi's revolutionary regime. **1972:** Proposed federation of

Libya, Syria, and Egypt abandoned. **1980:** Proposed merger with Syria abandoned. Libyan troops began fighting in northern Chad. **1986:** US bombed Khaddhafi's headquarters, following allegations of his complicity in terrorist activities. **1988:** Diplomatic relations with Chad restored; political prisoners freed; economy liberalized. **1989:** US navy shot down two Libyan planes; reconciliation with Egypt. **1992:** Khaddhafi under international pressure to extradite suspected Lockerbie and UTA (Union de Transports Aérians) bombers for trial outside Libya. United Nations sanctions imposed; several countries severed diplomatic and air links with Libya. **1995:** Antigovernment campaign of violence by Islamicists. Hundreds of Palestinians and thousands of foreign workers expelled.

Liechtenstein Principality of

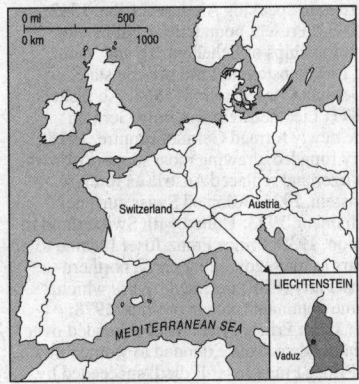

National name: *Fürstentum Liechtenstein* **Area:** 160 sq km/62 sq mi **Capital:** Vaduz **Major towns/cities:** Balzers, Schaan, Ruggell, Triesen, Eschen **Physical features:** landlocked Alpine; includes part of Rhine Valley in W

Government
Head of state: Prince Hans Adam II from 1989 **Head of government:** Mario Frick from 1993 **Political system:** constitutional monarchy **Administrative divisions:** 11 communes **Political parties:** Patriotic Union (VU), conservative; Progressive Citizens' Party (FBP), conservative **Armed forces:** no standing army since 1868; there is a police force of 59 men and 19 auxiliaries **Conscription:** in an emergency Liechtensteiners under the age of 60 are liable to military service **Death penalty:** abolished 1987 (last execution 1785)

Economy and resources
Currency: Swiss franc **GDP:** ($US) 1.52 billion (1994) **Real GDP per capita (PPP):** ($US) 23,200 (1992) **GDP growth rate:** –0.1% (1994) **Average annual inflation:** 0.9% (1994) **Major trading partners:** Switzerland and other EFTA countries, EU countries **Resources:** hydro power **Industries:** small machinery, textiles, ceramics, chemicals, furniture, precision instruments, pharmaceutical products, heating appliances, financial services, tourism **Exports:** small machinery, artificial teeth and other material for dentistry, stamps, precision instruments, ceramics. Principal market: Switzerland 14% (1994) **Imports:** machinery and transport equipment, foodstuffs, textiles, metal goods. Principal source: Switzerland **Arable land:** 25% (1995) **Agricultural products:** maize, potatoes; cattle rearing and dairy farming

Population and society
Population: 31,000 (1996 est) **Population growth rate:** 1.4% (1990–95) **Population density:** (per sq km) 195 (1996 est) **Urban population:** (% of total) 21 (1995) **Age distribution:** (% of total population) <15 19.8%, 15–65 69.4%, >65 10.8% (1990) **Ethnic groups:** indigenous population of Alemannic origin; one-third of the population are foreign-born resident workers **Language:** German (official); an Alemannic dialect is also spoken **Religion:** Roman Catholic (87%), Protestant **Education:** (compulsory years) 8 **Literacy rate:** 99% (men); 99% (women) (1995 est) **Labour force:** 1.7% agriculture, 47.6% industry, 50.7% services (1994) **Unemployment:** 1% (1994) **Life expectancy:** 78 (men); 83 (women) (1995–2000) **Child mortality rate:** (per 1,000 live births) 0.03 (1993)

Practical information

Visa requirements: UK: visa not required. USA: visa not required **Embassy in the UK:** Liechtenstein is generally represented overseas by Switzerland **British embassy:** enquiries relating to Liechtenstein are dealt with by the British Consulate General, Dufourstrasse 56, CH-8008 Zürich, Switzerland. Tel: (1) 261 1520–6; fax: (1) 252 8351 **Chamber of commerce:** Liechtenstein Industrie-und Handeslkammer (Chamber of Industry and Commerce), Postfach 232, Josef Rheinberger-Strasse 11, FL-9490 Vaduz. Tel: (4175) 232 2744; fax: (4175) 233 1503 **Airports:** international airports: none, the nearest is at Zürich, Switzerland **Major holidays:** 1, 6 January, 2 February, 19 March, 1 May, 15 August, 1 November, 8, 24–26, 31 December; variable: Ascension Thursday, Carnival, Corpus Christi, Good Friday, Easter Monday, Whit Monday

Chronology

c. AD 500: Settled by Germanic-speaking Alemanni tribe. **1342:** Became sovereign state. **1434:** Present boundaries established. **1719:** Former independent lordships of Schellenberg and Vaduz were united by Princes of Liechtenstein to form present state. **1815–66:** A member of German Confederation. **1868:** Abolished standing armed forces. **1871:** Liechtenstein was only German principality to stay outside newly formed German Empire. **1918:** Patriotic Union (VU) party founded, drawing most support from the mountainous S. **1919:** Switzerland replaced Austria as foreign representative of Liechtenstein. **1921:** Adopted Swiss currency; constitution created a parliament. **1923:** United with Switzerland in customs and monetary union. **1938:** Prince Franz Josef II came to power. **1970:** After 42 years as main governing party, northern-based Progressive Citizens' Party (FBP) defeated by VU which, except for 1974–78, became dominant force in politics. **1978:** Joined Council of Europe. **1984:** Prince Franz Josef II handed over power to Crown Prince Hans Adam. Vote extended to women in national elections. **1989:** Prince Franz Josef II died; succeeded by Hans Adam II. **1990:** Became a member of United Nations. **1991:** Became seventh member of European Free Trade Association. **1993:** Mario Frick of VU became Europe's youngest head of government, aged 28, after two general elections. **1997:** Mario Frick and ruling VU-FBP government retained power after general election. FBP withdrew from coalition.

Lithuania Republic of

National name: *Lietuvos Respublika* **Area:** 65,200 sq km/25,173 sq mi **Capital:** Vilnius **Major towns/cities:** Kaunas, Klaipeda, Siauliai, Panevezys **Physical features:** central lowlands with gentle hills in W and higher terrain in SE; 25% forested; some 3,000 small lakes, marshes, and complex sandy coastline; river Nemen

Government

Head of state: Algirdas Brazauskas from 1993 **Head of government:** Gediminas Vagnorius from 1996 **Political system:** emergent democracy **Administrative divisions:** 12 regions **Political parties:** Lithuanian Democratic Labour Party (LDLP), reform-socialist (ex-communist); Homeland Union–Lithuanian Conservatives (Tevynes Santara), right of centre, nationalist; Christian Democratic Party of Lithuania, centre right; Lithuanian Social Democratic Party, left of centre **Armed forces:** 5,100 (1996)

Conscription: military service is compulsory for 12 months **Death penalty:** retained and used for ordinary crimes **Defence spend:** (% GDP) 4.3 (1996) **Education spend:** (% GNP) 4.2 (1994) **Health spend:** (% GDP) 3.2 (1994)

Economy and resources

Currency: litas **GDP:** ($ US) 5 billion (1994) **Real GDP per capita (PPP):** ($ US) 4,011 (1994) **GDP growth rate:** 1% (1996); –9.7% (1990–95) **Average annual inflation:** 24.2% (1996); 151% (1985–95 est) **Foreign debt:** ($ US) 802 million (1995) **Major trading partners:** Russia, Germany, Belarus, Latvia, Ukraine, Poland, Italy, the Netherlands **Resources:** small deposits of petroleum, natural gas, peat, limestone, gravel, clay, sand **Industries:** petroleum refining and petroleum products, cast iron and steel, textiles, mineral fertilizers, fur coats, refrigerators, TV sets, bicycles, paper **Exports:** textiles, machinery and equipment, non-precious metals, animal products, timber. Principal market: Russia 23.8 (1996) **Imports:** petroleum and natural gas products, machinery and transport equipment, chemicals, fertilizers, consumer goods. Principal source: Russia 29.1% (1996) **Arable land:** 45.5% (1995) **Agricultural products:** cereals, sugar beet, potatoes, vegetables; livestock rearing and dairy farming (animal husbandry accounted for more than 50% of the value of total agricultural production 1992)

Population and society

Population: 3,728,000 (1996 est) **Population growth rate:** –0.1% (1990–95); 0.1% (2000–05) **Population density:** (per sq km) 57 (1996 est) **Urban population:** (% of total) 72 (1995) **Age distribution:** (% of total population) <15 21.9%, 15–65 66%, >65 12.2% (1995) **Ethnic groups:** 80% Lithuanian ethnic descent, 9% ethnic Russian, 7% Polish, 2% Belarussian, 1% Ukrainian **Language:** Lithuanian (official) **Religion:** predominantly Roman Catholic; Lithuanian Lutheran Church **Education:** (compulsory years) 9 **Literacy rate:** 98% (men); 98% (women) (1995 est) **Labour force:** 19.6% agriculture, 38% industry, 42.4% services (1992) **Unemployment:** 7.1% (1996) **Life expectancy:** 65 (men); 76 (women) (1995–2000) **Child mortality rate:** (under 5, per 1,000 live births) 17 (1996) **Physicians:** 1 per 247 people (1994)

Practical information

Visa requirements: UK: visa not required for a stay of up to 90 days. USA: visa not required for a stay of up to 90 days **Embassy in the UK:** 17 Essex Villas, London W8 7BP. Tel: (0171) 938 2481; fax: (0171) 938 3329 **British embassy:** PO Box 863, Anta Kalnio 2, 2055 Vilnius. Tel: (2) 222 070; fax: (2) 357 579 **Chamber of commerce:** Association of Lithuanian Chambers of Commerce and Industry, Kudirkos 18, 2600 Vilnius. Tel: (2) 222 630; fax: (2) 222 621 **Airports:** international airports: Vilnius, Kaunas, Siauliai; few domestic flights; total passenger km: 241 million (1994) **Major holidays:** 1 January, 16 February, 5 May, 6 July, 1 November, 25–26 December; variable: Easter Monday

Chronology

late 12th century: Became a separate nation. **1230:** Mindaugas united Lithuanian tribes to resist attempted invasions by German and Livonian Teutonic Knights, and adopted Christianity. **14th century:** Strong Grand Duchy formed by Gediminas, founder of Vilnius and Jogaila dynasty, and his son, Algirdas; absorbing Ruthenian territories to E and S, it stretched from the Baltic to the Black Sea and E, nearly reaching Moscow. **1410:** Led by Duke Vytautas, and in alliance with Poland, the Teutonic Knights were defeated decisively at Battle of Tannenberg. **1569:** Joined Poland in a confederation, under the Union of Lublin, in which Poland had the upper hand and Lithuanian upper classes were Polonized. **1795:** Came under control of Tsarist Russia, following partition of Poland; 'Lithuania Minor' (Kaliningrad) fell to Germany. **1831 and 1863:** Failed revolts for independence. **1880s:** Development of organized nationalist movement. **1914–18:** Occupied by German troops during World War I. **1918–19:** Independence declared and, after uprising against attempted imposition of Soviet Union (USSR) control, was achieved as a democracy. **1920–39:** Province and city of Vilnius occupied by Poles. **1926:** Democracy overthrown in authoritarian coup by Antanas Smetona, who became president. **1934:** Baltic Entente mutual-defence pact signed with Estonia and Latvia. **1939–40:** Secret German–Soviet agreement brought most of Lithuania under Soviet influence as a constituent republic. **1941:** Lithuania revolted and established own government, but during World War II Germany again occupied the country and 210,000, mainly Jews, were killed. **1944:** USSR resumed rule. **1944–52:** Lithuanian guerrillas fought USSR, which persecuted the Catholic Church, collectivized agriculture, and deported half a million Balts to Siberia. **1972:** Demonstrations against Soviet government. **1980s:** Growth in nationalist dissent, influenced by Polish Solidarity movement and glasnost ('openness') initiative of reformist Soviet leader Mikhail Gorbachev. **1988:** Popular Front, the Sajudis, formed to campaign for increased autonomy; parliament declared Lithuanian the state language and readopted the flag of interwar republic. **1989:** Communist Party (CP) split into pro-Moscow and nationalist wings, and lost local monopoly of power; over 1 million took part in nationalist demonstrations. **1990:** Nationalist Sajudis won elections; their leader, Vytautas Landsbergis, became president; unilateral declaration of independence rejected by USSR, who imposed an economic blockade. **1991:** Soviet paratroopers briefly occupied key buildings in Vilnius, killing 13; CP outlawed; independence recognized by USSR and Western nations and admitted into United Nations. **1992:** Ex-communist Democratic Labour Party (LDLP) won majority in parliamentary elections as economic restructuring caused contraction in GDP. **1993:** LDLP leader Algirdas Brazauskas elected president, and Adolfas Slezevicius became prime minister. Free-trade agreement with other Baltic states. Last Russian troops departed. **1994:** Friendship and cooperation treaty with Poland. **1994:** Trade and cooperation agreement with European Union. **1996:** Slezevicius resigned over banking scandal; replaced by Laurynas Stankevicius. New conservative coalition formed, led by Gediminas Vagnorius. **1997:** Border treaty signed with Russia.

Luxembourg Grand Duchy of

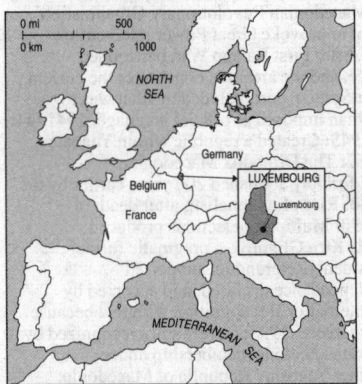

National name: *Grand-Duché de Luxembourg* **Area:** 2,586 sq km/998 sq mi **Capital:** Luxembourg **Major towns/cities:** Esch-Alzette, Differdange, Dudelange, Petange **Physical features:** on the river Moselle; part of the Ardennes (Oesling) forest in N

Government

Head of state: Grand Duke Jean from 1964 **Head of government:** Jean-Claude Juncker from 1995 **Political system:** liberal democracy **Administrative divisions:** 12 cantons **Political parties:** Christian Social Party (PCS), moderate, left of centre; Luxembourg Socialist Workers' Party (POSL), moderate, socialist; Democratic Party (PD), centre left; Communist Party of Luxembourg, pro-European left wing **Armed forces:** 800; gendarmerie 600 (1996) **Conscription:** military service is voluntary **Death penalty:** abolished 1979 **Defence spend:** (% GDP) 0.7 (1996) **Education spend:** (% GNP) 3.1 (1993–94) **Health spend:** (% GDP) 6.3 (1993)

Economy and resources

Currency: Luxembourg franc **GDP:** ($ US) 17.5 billion (1996) **Real GDP per capita (PPP):** ($ US) 32,665 (1996) **GDP growth**

rate: 2.1% (1996); 3.7% (1994–95) **Average annual inflation:** 1.4% (1996); 4.7% (1985–95) **Major trading partners:** EU (principally Belgium, Germany, and France) **Resources:** iron ore **Industries:** steel and rolled steel products, chemicals, rubber and plastic products, metal and machinery products, paper and printing products, food products, financial services **Exports:** base metals and manufactures, mechanical and electrical equipment, rubber and related products, plastics, textiles and clothing. Principal market: Germany 28.2% (1993) **Imports:** machinery and electrical apparatus, transport equipment, mineral products. Principal source: Belgium 38.1% (1993) **Arable land:** 22% **Agricultural products:** maize, roots and tubers, wheat, forage crops, grapes; livestock rearing and dairy farming

Population and society

Population: 412,000 (1996 est) **Population growth rate:** 1.3% (1990–95) **Population density:** (per sq km) 160 (1996 est) **Urban population:** (% of total) 89.1 (1995) **Age distribution:** (% of total population) <15 17%, 15–65 69%, >65 14% (1994) **Ethnic groups:** majority descended from the Moselle Franks **Language:** French, German, local Letzeburgesch (all official) **Religion:** Roman Catholic **Education:** (compulsory years) 9 **Literacy rate:** 99% (1995 est) **Labour force:** 51.2% of population: 2.6% agriculture, 27.7% industry, 69.7% services (1992) **Unemployment:** 3.4% (1995) **Life expectancy:** 73 (men); 80 (women) (1995–2000) **Child mortality rate:** (under 5, per 1,000 live births) 8 (1996) **Physicians:** 1 per 469 people (1994)

Practical information

Visa requirements: UK: visa not required. USA: visa not required for a stay of up to 90 days **Embassy in the UK:** 27 Wilton Crescent, London SW1X 8SD. Tel: (0171) 235 6961; fax: (0171) 235 9734 **British embassy:** 14 boulevard Roosevelt, L-2450 Luxembourg-Ville. Tel: (352) 229 864/5/6; fax: (352) 229 867 **Chamber of commerce:** 7 rue Alcide de Gasperi, L-2981 Luxembourg-Kirchberg. Tel: (352) 435 853; fax: (352) 438 326 **Airports:** international airports: Luxembourg (Findel); no domestic airports; total passenger km: 361 million (1994) **Major holidays:** 1 January, 1 May, 23 June, 15 August, 1–2 November, 25–26, 31 December; variable: Ascension Thursday, Easter Monday, Whit Monday, Shrove Monday

Chronology

963: Luxembourg became autonomous within Holy Roman Empire under Siegfried, Count of Ardennes. **1060:** Conrad, descendent of Siegfried, took the title Count of Luxembourg. **1354:** Emperor Charles IV promoted Luxembourg to status of duchy. **1441:** Luxembourg ceded to dukes of Burgundy. **1482:** Luxembourg came under Habsburg control. **1555:** Luxembourg became part of Spanish Netherlands on division of Habsburg domains. **1684–97:** Much of Luxembourg occupied by France. **1713:** Treaty of Utrecht transferred Spanish Netherlands to Austria. **1797:** Conquered by revolutionary France. **1815:** Congress of Vienna made Luxembourg a grand duchy, under King William of the Netherlands. **1830:** Most of Luxembourg supported Belgian revolt against the Netherlands. **1839:** Western part of Luxembourg assigned to Belgium. **1842:** Luxembourg entered the Zollverein (German customs union). **1867:** Treaty of London confirmed independence and neutrality of Luxembourg to allay French fears about possible inclusion in a unified Germany. **1870s:** Development of iron and steel industry. **1890:** Link with Dutch crown ended on accession of Queen Wilhelmina, since Luxembourg's law of succession did not permit a woman to rule; Adolphe of Nassau-Weilburg became grand duke. **1912:** Revised law of succession allowed Marie-Adelaide to become grand duchess. **1914–18:** Occupied by Germany. **1919:** Plebiscite overwhelmingly favoured continued independence; Marie-Adelaide abdicated after allegations of collaboration with Germany; succeeded by Grand Duchess Charlotte. **1921:** Entered into close economic links with Belgium. **1940:** Invaded by Germany. **1942–44:** Annexed by Germany. **1948:** Luxembourg formed Benelux customs union with Belgium and the Netherlands. **1949:** Luxembourg became founding member of North Atlantic Treaty Organization (NATO). **1958:** Luxembourg became founding member of European Economic Community (EEC). **1964:** Grand Duchess Charlotte abdicated in favour of her son Jean. **1974–79:** Christian Social Party outside governing coalition for first time since 1919. **1994:** Former premier Jacques Santer became president of European Commission (EC). **1995:** Jean-Claude Juncker became prime minister.

Macedonia Former Yugoslav Republic of (official international name); Republic of Macedon (official internal name)

National name: *Republika Makedonija* **Area:** 25,700 sq km/9,922 sq mi **Capital:** Skopje **Major towns/cities:** Bitolj, Prilep, Kumanovo, Tetovo **Physical features:** mountainous; rivers: Struma, Vardar; lakes: Ohrid, Prespa, Scutari; partly Mediterranean climate with hot summers

Government
Head of state: (acting) Stojan Andov from 1995 **Head of government:** Branko Crvenkovski from 1992 **Political system:** emergent democracy **Administrative divisions:** 34 communes **Political parties:** Socialist Party (SP); Social Democratic Alliance of Macedonia (SM) bloc, left of centre; Party for Democratic Prosperity (PDP), ethnic Albanian, left of centre; Internal Macedonian Revolutionary Organization–Democratic Party for Macedonian National Unity (VMRO–DPMNE), radical nationalist; Democratic Party of Macedonia (DPM), nationalist, free market **Armed forces:** 10,450; plus paramilitary force of 7,500 (1996) **Conscription:** military service is compulsory for nine months **Death penalty:** laws do not provide for the death penalty for any crime **Defence spend:** (% GDP) 9.2 (1996) **Education spend:** (% GNP) 5.6 (1993–94) **Health spend:** (% GDP) 6.8 (1990–95)

Economy and resources
Currency: Macedonian denar **GDP:** ($ US) 2 billion (1994) **Real GDP per capita (PPP):** ($ US) 3,965 (1994) **GDP growth rate:** 3% (1996); –40% (1989–93) **Average annual inflation:** 4% (1996) **Foreign debt:** ($ US) 1.4 billion (1996) **Major trading partners:** Bulgaria, Yugoslavia, Germany, Russia, Italy, Slovenia, Croatia, USA, Turkey, the Netherlands **Resources:** coal, iron, zinc, chromium, manganese, lead, copper, nickel, silver, gold **Industries:** metallurgy, chemicals, textiles, buses, refrigerators, detergents, medicines, wood pulp, wine **Exports:** manufactured goods, machinery and transport equipment, miscellaneous manufactured articles, sugar beet, vegetables, cheese, lamb, tobacco. Principal market: Bulgaria 20% (1994) **Imports:** mineral fuels and lubricants, manufactured goods, machinery and transport equipment, food and live animals, chemicals. Principal source: Yugoslavia 23% (1994) **Arable land:** 23.8% (1995) **Agricultural products:** rice, wheat, barley, sugar beet, fruit and vegetables, tobacco, sunflowers, potatoes, grapes (wine industry is important); livestock rearing and dairy farming

Population and society
Population: 2,174,000 (1996 est) **Population growth rate:** 1.1% (1990–95); 0.7% (2000–05) **Population density:** (per sq km) 85 (1996 est) **Urban population:** (% of total) 60 (1995) **Age

distribution: (% of total population) <15 24.4%, 15–65 67.5%, >65 8.2% (1995) **Ethnic groups:** 66% Macedonian ethnic descent, 22% ethnic Albanian, 5% Turkish, 3% Romanian, 2% Serb, and 2% Muslim, comprising Macedonian Slavs who converted to Islam during the Ottoman era, and are known as Pomaks. This ethnic breakdown is disputed by Macedonia's ethnic Albanian population, who claim that they form 40% of the population, and seek autonomy and by ethnic Serbs, who claim that they form 11.5% **Language:** Macedonian, closely allied to Bulgarian and written in Cyrillic **Religion:** Christian, mainly Orthodox; Muslim 2.5% **Education:** (compulsory years) 8 **Literacy rate:** 94% (1995 est) **Labour force:** 8.6% agriculture, 48.7% industry, 42.7% services (1994) **Unemployment:** 35.6% (1995) **Life expectancy:** 70 (men); 76 (women) (1995–2000) **Child mortality rate:** (per 1,000 live births) 37 (1996) **Physicians:** 1 per 479 people (1994)

Practical information
Visa requirements: UK: visa not required. USA: visa required **Embassy in the UK:** 10 Harcourt House, 19A Cavendish Square, London W1M 9AD. Tel: (0171) 499 5152; fax (0171) 499 2864 **British embassy:** Office of the British Government Representative, Ul VeljkoVlahovic 26, 91000 Skopje. Tel: (91) 116 772; fax: (91) 117 005 **Chamber of commerce:** Economic Chamber of Macedonia, PO Box 324, Dimitrie Cupovski 13, 91000 Skopje. Tel: (91) 233 215; fax: (91) 116 210 **Airports:** international airports: Skopje, Ohrid; domestic services between Skopje and Ohrid; total passenger km: 319 million (1994) **Major holidays:** 1–2 January, 1–2 May, 2 August, 11 October

Chronology
4th century BC: Part of ancient great kingdom of Macedonia, which included N Greece and SW Bulgaria and, under Alexander the Great, conquered a vast empire; Thessaloniki founded. **146 BC:** Macedonia became a province of the Roman Empire. **395 AD:** On the division of the Roman Empire, came under the control of Byzantine Empire, with its capital at Constantinople. **6th century:** Settled by Slavs, who later converted to Christianity. **9th–14th centuries:** Under successive rule by Bulgars, Byzantium, and Serbia. **1371:** Became part of Islamic Ottoman Empire. **late 19th century:** The 'Internal Macedonian Revolutionary Organization', through terrorism, sought to provoke Great Power intervention against Turks. **1912–13:** After First Balkan War, partitioned between Bulgaria, Greece, and the area that constitutes the current republic of Serbia. **1918:** Serbian part included in what was to become Yugoslavia; Serbian imposed as official language. **1941–44:** Occupied by Bulgaria. **1945:** Created a republic within Yugoslav Socialist Federation. **1967:** The Orthodox Macedonian archbishopric of Skopje, forcibly abolished 200 years earlier by the Turks, was restored. **1980:** Rise of nationalism after death of Yugoslav leader Tito. **1990:** Multiparty elections produced inconclusive result. **1991:** Kiro Gligorov, a pragmatic former communist, became president. Referendum supported independence. **1992:** Independence declared, and accepted by Serbia/Yugoslavia, but international recognition withheld because of objections to name by Greece. **1993:** Sovereignty recognized by UK and Albania; won United Nations membership under provisional name of Former Yugoslav Republic of Macedonia; Greece blocked full European Union (EU) recognition. **1994:** Independence recognized by USA; trade embargo imposed by Greece, causing severe economic damage. **1995:** Independence recognized by Greece; trade embargo lifted. President Gligorov survived assassination attempt. **1997:** Plans to reduce strength of UN Preventive Deployment Force (UNPREDEP) were abandoned. Government announced compensation for public's losses in failed investment schemes.

Madagascar Democratic Republic of

National name: *Repoblika Demokratika n`i Madagaskar* **Area:** 587,041 sq km/226,656 sq mi **Capital:** Antananarivo **Major towns/cities:** Antsirabe, Mahajanga, Fianarantsoa, Toamasina,

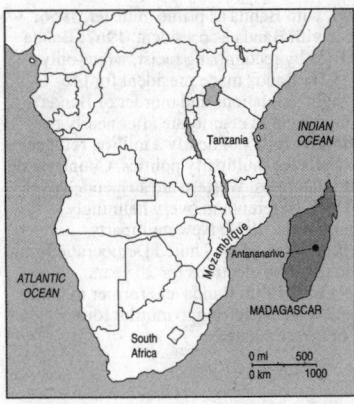

Ambatondrazaka **Major ports:** Toamasina, Antsiranana, Toliary, Mahajanga **Physical features:** temperate central highlands; humid valleys and tropical coastal plains; arid in S

Government

Head of state: Didier Ratsiraka from 1996 **Head of government:** Pascal Rakotomavo from 1997 **Political system:** emergent democracy **Administrative divisions:** six provinces **Political parties:** National Front for the Defence of the Malagasy Socialist Revolution (FNDR), left-of-centre coalition; Comité des Forces Vives, pro-Zafy, left-of-centre coalition **Armed forces:** 21,000; plus paramilitary gendarmerie of 7,500 **Conscription:** military service is compulsory for 18 months **Death penalty:** retains the death penalty for ordinary crimes but can be considered abolitionist in practice (last known execution 1958) **Defence spend:** (% GDP) 0.8 (1996) **Education spend:** (% GDP) 1.9 (1993–94) **Health spend:** (% GDP) 1 (1990–95)

Economy and resources

Currency: Malagasy franc **GDP:** ($ US) 1.9 billion (1994) **Real GDP per capita (PPP):** ($ US) 694 (1994) **GDP growth rate:** 0% (1994); 2.5% (1990–95) **Average annual inflation:** 22% (1996); 17.9% (1985–95) **Foreign debt:** ($ US) 4.3 billion (1995) **Major trading partners:** France, Japan, Germany, USA **Resources:** graphite, chromite, mica, titanium ore, small quantities of precious stones, bauxite and coal deposits, petroleum reserves **Industries:** food products, textiles and clothing, beverages, chemical products, cement, fertilizers, pharmaceuticals **Exports:** coffee, shrimps, cloves, vanilla, petroleum products, chromium, cotton fabrics. Principal market: France 29.2% (1995) **Imports:** minerals (crude petroleum), chemicals, machinery, vehicles and parts, metal products, electrical equipment. Principal source: France 31.8% (1995) **Arable land:** 4.4% (1995) **Agricultural products:** rice, cassava, mangoes, bananas, potatoes, sugar cane, seed cotton, sisal, vanilla, cloves, coconuts, tropical fruits; cattle-farming; sea-fishing

Population and society

Population: 15,353,000 (1996 est) **Population growth rate:** 3.2% (1990–95); 3.1% (2000–05) **Population density:** (per sq km) 26 (1996 est) **Urban population:** (% of total) 27 (1995) **Age distribution:** (% of total population) <15 46.1%, 15–65 51.1%, >65 2.8% (1995) **Ethnic groups:** 18 main Malagasy tribes of Malaysian–Polynesian origin; also French, Chinese, Indians, Pakistanis, and Comorans **Language:** Malagasy (official); French, English **Religion:** traditional beliefs, Roman Catholic, Protestant **Education:** (compulsory years) 5 **Literacy rate:** 88% (men); 73% (women) (1995 est) **Labour force:** 48% of population: 78% agriculture, 7% industry, 15% services (1990) **Life expectancy:** 58 (men); 61 (women) (1995–2000) **Child mortality rate:** (under 5, per 1,000 live births) 121 (1996) **Physicians:** 1 per 8,385 people (1993 est)

Practical information

Visa requirements: UK: visa required. USA: visa required **Embassy in the UK:** Consulate of the Republic of Madagascar, 16 Lanark Mansions, Pennard Road, London W12 8DT. Tel: (0181) 746 0133; fax: (0181) 746 0134 **British embassy:** BP 167, 1er Etage, Immeuble 'Ny Havana', Cité de 67 Ha, 101 Antananarivo. Tel: (2) 27749; fax: (2) 26690 **Chamber of commerce:** Fédération des Chambres de Commerce, d'Industrie et d'Agriculture de Madagascar, BP 166, 20 rue Colbert, 101 Antananarivo. Tel: (2)

21567 **Airports:** international airports: Antananarivo (Ivato), Mahajunga (Amborovi); two domestic airports and 57 airfields open to public air traffic; total passenger km: 567 million (1994) **Major holidays:** 1 January, 29 March, 1 May, 26 June, 15 August, 1 November, 25, 30 December; variable: Ascension Thursday, Good Friday, Easter Monday, Whit Monday

Chronology

c. 6th–10th centuries AD: Settled by migrant Indonesians. **1500:** First visited by European navigators. **17th century:** Development of Merina and Sakalava kingdoms in the central highlands and W coast. **1642–74:** France established a coastal settlement at Fort-Dauphin, which they abandoned after a massacre by local inhabitants. **late 18th–early 19th century:** Merinas, united by their ruler Andrianampoinimerina, became dominant kingdom; court converted to Christianity. **1861:** Ban on Christianity (imposed 1828) and entry of Europeans lifted by Merina king, Radama II. **1885:** Became French protectorate. **1895:** Merina army defeated by French and became a colony; slavery abolished. **1942–43:** British troops invaded to overthrow French administration allied to the pro-Nazi Germany Vichy regime and install anti-Nazi Free French government. **1947–48:** Nationalist uprising brutally suppressed by French. **1960:** Independence achieved from France, with Philibert Tsiranana, the leader of the Social Democratic Party (PSD), as president. **1972:** Merina-dominated army overthrew Tsiranana's government, dominated by the cotier (coastal tribes), as economy deteriorated. **1975:** Martial law imposed; new one-party state Marxist constitution adopted, with Lt-Commander Didier Ratsiraka as president. **1978:** More than 1,000 people killed in race riots in Majunga city in NW. **1980:** Ratsiraka abandoned Marxist experiment, which had involved nationalization and severing ties with France. **1983:** Ratsiraka re-elected, despite strong opposition from radical socialist movement under Monja Jaona. **1990:** Political opposition legalized; 36 new parties created. **1991:** Antigovernment demonstrations. Ratsiraka formed new unity government, which included opposition members. **1992:** Constitutional reform approved by referendum. **1993:** Albert Zafy elected president and pro-Zafy left-of-centre coalition won majority in multiparty assembly elections. **1995:** Referendum backed appointment of prime minister by president, rather than assembly. **1996:** Norbert Ratsirahonana became prime minister and then interim president upon parliament's removal of Zafy. Didier Ratsiraka elected president. **1997:** Pascal Rakotomavo appointed prime minister.

Malawi Republic of (formerly Nyasaland)

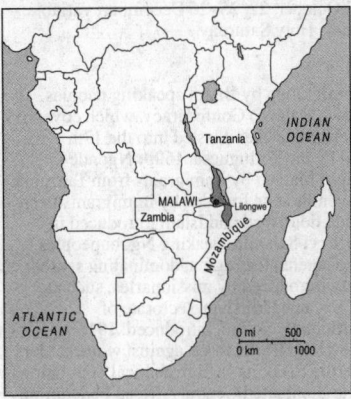

National name: *Malawi* **Area:** 118,000 sq km/45,559 sq mi **Capital:** Lilongwe **Major towns/cities:** Blantyre, Lilongwe, Mzuzu, Zomba **Physical features:** landlocked narrow plateau with rolling plains; mountainous W of Lake Nyasa

Government

Head of state and government: Bakili Muluzi from 1994 **Political system:** emergent democracy

Administrative divisions: three regions, subdivided into 24 districts **Political parties:** Malawi Congress Party (MCP), multiracial, right wing; United Democratic Front (UDF), left of centre; Alliance for Democracy (AFORD), left of centre **Armed forces:** 9,800 (1996) **Conscription:** military service is voluntary

Death penalty: retained and used for ordinary crimes **Defence spend:** (% GDP) 1.2 (1996) **Education spend:** (% GNP) 3.3 (1992); N/A (1993–94) **Health spend:** (% GDP) 2.3 (1990–95)

Economy and resources
Currency: Malawi kwacha **GDP:** ($ US) 1.3 million (1994) **Real GDP per capita (PPP):** ($ US) 694 (1994) **GDP growth rate:** –12% (1994); 0.7% (1990–95) **Average annual inflation:** 30% (1996); 22% (1985–95) **Foreign debt:** ($ US) 2.33 billion (1996) **Major trading partners:** South Africa, UK, Japan, Germany, the Netherlands **Resources:** marble, coal, gemstones, bauxite and graphite deposits, reserves of phosphates, uranium, glass sands, asbestos, vermiculite **Industries:** food products, chemical products, textiles, beverages, cement **Exports:** tobacco, tea, sugar, cotton, groundnuts. Principal market: South Africa 13.8% (1995) **Imports:** petroleum products, fertilizers, coal, machinery and transport equipment, miscellaneous manufactured articles. Principal source: South Africa 34.4% (1995) **Arable land:** 17.8% (1995) **Agricultural products:** maize, cassava, groundnuts, pulses, tobacco, tea, sugar cane

Population and society
Population: 9,845,000 (1996 est) **Population growth rate:** 3.5% (1990–95); 2% (2000–05) **Population density:** (per sq km) 83 (1996 est) **Urban population:** (% of total) 14 (1995) **Age distribution:** (% of total population) <15 46.7%, 15–65 50.5%, >65 2.7% (1995) **Ethnic groups:** almost all indigenous Africans, divided into numerous ethnic groups, such as the Chewa, Nyanja, Tumbuka, Yao, Lomwe, Sena, Tonga, and Ngoni. There are also Asian and European minorities **Language:** English, Chichewa (both official) **Religion:** Christian 75%, Muslim 20% **Education:** (compulsory years) 8 **Literacy rate:** 52% (men); 31% (women) (1995 est) **Labour force:** 87% agriculture, 5% industry, 8% services (1990) **Unemployment:** 1.3% (1989) **Life expectancy:** 44 (men); 45 (women) (1995–2000) **Child mortality rate:** (under 5, per 1,000 live births) 212 (1996) **Physicians:** 1 per 44,205 people (1993 est)

Practical information
Visa requirements: UK: visa not required. USA: visa not required **Embassy in the UK:** 33 Grosvenor Street, London W1X 0DE. Tel: (0171) 491 4172/7; fax: (0171) 491 9916 **British embassy:** British High Commission, PO Box 30042, Lingadzi House, Lilongwe 3. Tel: (265) 782 400; fax: (265) 782 657 **Chamber of commerce:** Associated Chambers of Commerce and Industry of Malawi, PO Box 258, Chichiri Trade Fair Grounds, Blantyre. Tel: (265) 671 988; fax: (265) 671 147 **Airports:** international airports: Lilongwe (Kamuzu), Blantyre (Chileka); three domestic airports; total passenger km: 289 million (1994) **Major holidays:** 1 January, 3 March, 14 May, 6 July, 17 October, 22, 25–26 December; variable: Good Friday, Easter Monday, Holy Saturday

Chronology
1st–4th centuries AD: Immigration by Bantu-speaking peoples. **1480:** Foundation of Maravi (Malawi) Confederacy, which covered much of central and southern Malawi and lasted into the 17th century. **1530:** First visited by the Portuguese. **1600:** Ngonde kingdom founded in northern Malawi by immigrants from Tanzania. **18th century:** Chikulamayembe state founded by immigrants from E of Lake Nyasa; slave trade flourished and Islam introduced in some areas. **mid-19th century:** Swahili-speaking Ngoni peoples, from South Africa, and Yao entered the region, dominating settled agriculturalists; Christianity introduced by missionaries, such as David Livingstone. **1891:** Became British protectorate of Nyasaland; cash crops, particularly coffee, introduced. **1915:** Violent uprising, led by Rev John Chilembwe, against white settlers who had moved into the fertile S, taking land from local population. **1953:** Became part of white-dominated Central African Federation, which included South Rhodesia (Zimbabwe) and North Rhodesia (Zambia). **1958:** Dr Hastings Kamuzu Banda returned to the country after working abroad for 40 years and became head of conservative-nationalist Nyasaland/Malawi Congress Party (MCP), which spearheaded campaign for independence. **1963:** Central African Federation dissolved. **1964:** Independence achieved, within

Commonwealth, as Malawi, with Banda as prime minister. **1966:** Became one-party republic, with Banda as president. **1967:** Banda became pariah of Black Africa by recognizing racist, white-only republic of South Africa. **1971:** Banda made president for life. **1970s:** Reports of human-rights violations and murder of Banda's opponents. **1980s:** Economy began to deteriorate after nearly two decades of expansion. **1986–89:** Influx of nearly a million refugees from Mozambique. **1992:** Calls for multiparty politics. Countrywide industrial riots caused many fatalities. Western aid suspended over human-rights violations. **1993:** Referendum overwhelmingly supported ending of one-party rule. **1994:** New multiparty constitution adopted. Bakili Muluzi, of the United Democratic Front (UDF), elected president in first free elections for 30 years. Inconclusive assembly elections. **1995:** Banda and former minister of state John Tembo charged with conspiring to murder four political opponents 1983, but were cleared.

Malaysia Federation of

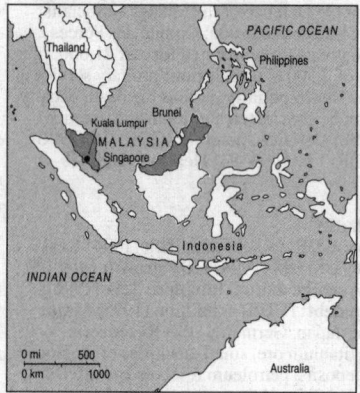

National name: *Persekutuan Tanah Malaysia* **Area:** 329,759 sq km/127,319 sq mi **Capital:** Kuala Lumpur **Major towns/cities:** Johor Baharu, Ipoh, George Town (Penang), Kuala Trengganu, Kuala Baharu, Petalong Jaya, Kelang, Kuching in Sarawak, Kota Kinabalu in Sabah **Major ports:** Kelang **Physical features:** comprises peninsular Malaysia (the nine Malay states – Johore, Kedah, Kelantan, Negri Sembilan, Pahang, Perak, Perlis, Selangor, Trengganu – plus Malacca and Penang); states of Sabah and Sarawak and federal territory of Kuala Lumpur; 75% tropical rainforest; central mountain range (Mount Kinabalu, the highest peak in SE Asia); swamps in E; Niah caves (Sarawak)

Government
Head of state: Jaafar bin Abd al-Rahman from 1994 **Head of government:** Mahathir bin Mohamed from 1981 **Political system:** liberal democracy **Administrative divisions:** 13 states **Political parties:** New United Malays' National Organization (UMNO Baru), Malay-oriented nationalist; Malaysian Chinese Association (MCA), Chinese-oriented, conservative; Gerakan Party, Chinese-oriented, socialist; Malaysian Indian Congress (MIC), Indian-oriented; Democratic Action Party (DAP), multiracial but Chinese-dominated, left of centre; Pan-Malayan Islamic Party (PAS), Islamic; Semangat '46 (Spirit of 1946), moderate, multiracial **Armed forces:** 114,500; reserve force 58,300; paramilitary force 25,800 (1996) **Conscription:** military service is voluntary **Death penalty:** retained and used for ordinary crimes **Defence spend:** (% GDP) 4.2 (1996) **Education spend:** (% GNP) 4.4 (1994) **Health spend:** (% GDP) 1.4 (1990–95)

Economy and resources
Currency: ringgit **GDP:** ($ US) 70.6 billion (1994) **Real GDP per capita (PPP):** ($ US) 8,865 (1994) **GDP growth rate:** 9.2% (1994); 8.7% (1990–95) **Average annual inflation:** 3.8% (1996); 3.3% (1985–95) **Foreign debt:** ($ US) 33.7 billion (1996) **Major trading partners:** Japan, USA, Singapore, Taiwan, UK and other EU countries **Resources:** tin, bauxite, copper, iron ore, petroleum, natural gas, forests **Industries:** electrical and electronic appliances (particularly radio and TV receivers), food processing, rubber products, industrial chemicals, wood products, petroleum refinery,

motor vehicles, tourism **Exports:** palm oil, rubber, crude petroleum, machinery and transport equipment, timber, tin, textiles, electronic goods. Principal market: USA 20.7% (1995) **Imports:** machinery and transport equipment, chemicals, foodstuffs, crude petroleum, consumer goods. Principal source: Japan 27.3% (1995) **Arable land:** 5.5% (1995) **Agricultural products:** rice, cocoa, palm, rubber, pepper, coconuts, tea, pineapples

Population and society
Population: 20,581,000 (1996 est) **Population growth rate:** 2.4% (1990–95); 1.7% (2000–05) **Population density:** (per sq km) 62 (1996 est) **Urban population:** (% of total) 54 (1995) **Age distribution:** (% of total population) <15 38%, 15–65 58.1%, >65 3.9% (1995) **Ethnic groups:** 58% of the population is Malay, four-fifths of whom live in rural areas; 32% is Chinese, four-fifths of whom are in towns; 9% is Indian, mainly Tamil **Language:** Malay (official), English, Chinese, Tamil, Iban **Religion:** Muslim (official), Buddhist, Hindu, local beliefs **Education:** (compulsory years) 11 **Literacy rate:** 86% (men); 70% (women) (1995 est) **Labour force:** 39% of population: 27% agriculture, 23% industry, 50% services (1990) **Unemployment:** 2.8% (1995) **Life expectancy:** 70 (men); 74 (women) (1995–2000) **Child mortality rate:** (under 5, per 1,000 live births) 22 (1996) **Physicians:** 1 per 2,441 people (1993 est)

Practical information
Visa requirements: UK: visa not required. USA: visa not required **Embassy in the UK:** 45 Belgrave Square, London SW1X 8QT. Tel: (0171) 235 8033; fax: (0171) 235 5161 **British embassy:** British High Commission, PO Box 11030, 185 Jalan Ampang, 50450 Kuala Lumpur. Tel: (3) 248 2122; fax: (3) 248 0880 **Chamber of commerce:** Malaysian International Chamber of Commerce and Industry, PO Box 12921, Wisma Damansara, 10th Floor, Jalah Semantan, 50792 Kuala Lumpur. Tel: (3) 254 2677; fax: (3) 255 4946 **Airports:** international airports: Kuala Lumpur (Subang), Penang (Bayan Lepas), Kota Kinabalu, Kuching; 15 domestic airports; total passenger km: 20,335 million (1994) **Major holidays:** 1 January (in some states), 1 May, 3 June, 31 August, 25 December; variable: Eid-ul Adha, Diwali (in most states), end of Ramadan (2 days), New Year (Chinese, January/February, most states), New Year (Muslim), Prophet's Birthday, Wesak (most states), several local festivals

Chronology
1st century AD: Peoples of Malay peninsula influenced by Indian culture and Buddhism. **8th–13th centuries:** Malay peninsula formed part of Buddhist Srivijaya Empire based in Sumatra. **14th century:** Siam (Thailand) expanded to included most of Malay peninsula. **1403:** Muslim traders founded port of Malacca, which became a great commercial centre, encouraging spread of Islam. **1511:** Portuguese attacked and captured Malacca. **1641:** Portuguese ousted from Malacca by Dutch after seven-year blockade. **1786:** British East India Company established a trading post on island of Penang. **1795–1815:** Britain occupied Dutch colonies after France conquered the Netherlands. **1819:** Stamford Raffles of East India Company obtained Singapore from Sultan of Johore. **1824:** Anglo-Dutch Treaty ceded Malacca to Britain in return for territory in Sumatra. **1826:** British possessions of Singapore, Penang, and Malacca formed Straits Settlements, ruled by governor of Bengal; ports prospered and expanded. **1840:** Sultan of Brunei gave Sarawak to James Brooke, whose family ruled it as an independent state until 1946. **1851:** Responsibility for Straits Settlements assumed by governor general of India. **1858:** British government, through India Office, took over administration of Straits Settlements. **1867:** Straits Settlements became crown colony of British Empire. **1874:** British protectorates established over four Malay states of Perak, Salangor, Pahang, and Negri Sembilan, which federated 1896. **1888:** Britain declared protectorate over N Borneo (Sabah). **late 19th century:** Millions of Chinese and thousands of Indians migrated to Malaya to work in tin mines and on rubber plantations. **1909–14:** Britain assumed indirect rule over five northern Malay states after agreement with Siam (Thailand). **1941–45:** Japanese occupation. **1946:** United Malay National Organization (UMNO) founded to oppose British plans for centralized Union of Malaya. **1948:** Britain federated nine Malay states with Penang and Malacca to form single colony of Federation of Malaya. **1948–60:** Malayan emergency: British forces suppressed insurrection by communist guerrillas. **1957:** Federation of Malaya became independent with Prince Abdul Rahman (leader of UMNO) as prime minister. **1963:** Federation of Malaya combined with Singapore, Sarawak, and Sabah to form Federation of Malaysia. **1963–66:** 'The Confrontation' – guerrillas supported by Indonesia opposed federation with intermittent warfare. **1965:** Singapore withdrew from Federation of Malaysia. **1968:** Philippines claimed sovereignty over Sabah. **1969:** Malay resentment of Chinese economic dominance resulted in race riots in Kuala Lumpur. **1971:** *Bumiputra* policies which favoured ethnic Malays in education and employment introduced by Tun Abul Razak of UMNO. **1981:** Mahathir bin Muhammad (UMNO) became prime minister; government increasingly dominated by Muslim Malays. **1987:** Malay–Chinese relations deteriorated; over 100 opposition activists arrested. **1988:** UMNO split over Mahathir's leadership style; his supporters formed UMNO Baru (New UMNO); his critics formed Semangat '46, a new multiracial party 1989. **1991:** Launch of economic development policy aimed at 7% annual growth. **1996:** Semangat '46 rejoined UMNO Baru, which remained under Mahathir's leadership. **1997:** Currency allowed to float. Parts of Borneo and Sumatra covered by thick smoke as forest-clearing fires burned out of control.

Maldives Republic of the

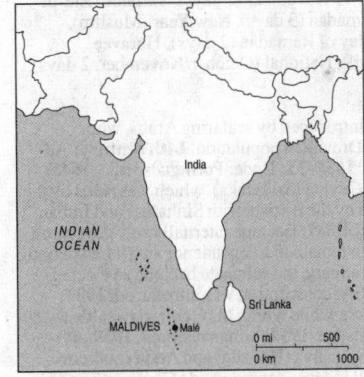

National name: *Divehi Raajjeyge Jumhooriyaa* **Area:** 298 sq km/115 sq mi **Capital:** Malé **Major towns/cities:** Seenu, Kurehdhu, Kunfunadhoo, Dhiggiri, Anthimatha **Physical features:** comprises 1,196 coral islands, grouped into 12 clusters of atolls, largely flat, none bigger than 13 sq km/5 sq mi, average elevation 1.8 m/6 ft; 203 are inhabited

Government
Head of state and government: Maumoon Abd al-Gayoom from 1978 **Political system:** authoritarian nationalist **Administrative divisions:** 20 districts **Political parties:** none; candidates elected on basis of personal influence and clan loyalties **Armed forces:** no standing army **Death penalty:** retains the death penalty for ordinary crimes but can be considered abolitionist in practice (last known execution 1952) **Education spend:** (% GNP) 8.1 (1993–94) **Health spend:** (% GDP) 5 (1990)

Economy and resources
Currency: rufiya **GDP:** ($ US) 390 million (1994 est) **Real GDP per capita (PPP):** ($ US) 1,560 (1994 est) **GDP growth rate:** 6.6% (1994) **Average annual inflation:** 16.5% (1994); 9.2% (1985–95 est) **Foreign debt:** ($ US) 162 million (1994) **Major trading partners:** UK, Singapore, USA, India, Sri Lanka, Thailand, Germany, Japan **Resources:** coral (mining was banned as a measure against the encroachment of the sea) **Industries:** fish canning, clothing, soft-drink bottling, shipping, lacquer work, shell craft, tourism **Exports:** marine products (tuna bonito ('Maldive Fish'), clothing. Principal market: UK 26% (1995) **Imports:** consumer manufactured goods, petroleum products, food, intermediate and capital goods. Principal source: Singapore 27.4% (1995) **Arable land:** 10% (1995) **Agricultural products:** coconuts, maize,

cassava, sweet potatoes, chillies; fishing (the Maldives' second largest source of foreign exchange after tourism 1995)

Population and society

Population: 263,000 (1996 est) **Population growth rate:** 3.3% (1990–95) **Population density:** (per sq km) 884 (1996 est) **Urban population:** (% of total) 33 (1995) **Age distribution:** (% of total population) <15 47%, 15–65 50%, >65 3% (1994) **Ethnic groups:** four main groups: Dravidian in the northern islands, Arab in the middle islands, Sinhalese in the southern islands, and African **Language:** Divehi (Sinhalese dialect), English **Religion:** Sunni Muslim **Education:** not compulsory **Literacy rate:** 93% (men); 93% (women) (1995 est) **Labour force:** 41% of population: 32% agriculture, 31% industry, 37% services (1990) **Unemployment:** 1.6% (1985) **Life expectancy:** 66 (men); 63 (women) (1995–2000) **Child mortality rate:** (under 5, per 1,000 live births) 68 (1996) **Physicians:** 1 per 6,057 people (1992)

Practical information

Visa requirements: UK: visa required. USA: visa required **Embassy in the UK:** Honorary Tourism Representative for the Maldives Republic in the UK, Toni the Maldive Lady, 3 Esher House, 11 Edith Terrace, London SW10 0TH. Tel: (0171) 352 2246; fax: (0171) 351 3382 **British embassy:** the British High Commission in Colombo (see Sri Lanka) deals with enquiries relating to the Maldives **Chamber of commerce:** State Trading Organisation, STO Building, 7 Haveeree Higun, Malé 20-02. Tel: (960) 323 279; fax: (960) 325 218 **Airports:** international airports: Malé, Gan; total passenger km: 7 million (1994) **Major holidays:** 1 January, 26 July (2 days), 11 November (2 days); variable: Eid-ul-Adha (4 days), end of Ramadan (3 days), New Year (Muslim), Prophet's Birthday, first day of Ramadan (2 days), Huravee (February), Martyrs (April), National (October/November, 2 days)

Chronology

12th century AD: Islam introduced by seafaring Arabs, who displaced the indigenous Dravidian population. **14th century:** Ad-Din sultanate established. **1558–73:** Under Portuguese rule. **1645:** Became a dependency of Ceylon (Sri Lanka), which was ruled by the Dutch until 1796 and then by the British, with Sinhalese and Indian colonies being established. **1887:** Became internally self-governing British protectorate, which remained a dependency of Sri Lanka until 1948. **1932:** Formerly hereditary, the sultanate became an elected position when Maldives' first constitution was introduced. **1953:** Maldive Islands became a republic within the Commonwealth, as the ad-Din sultanate was abolished. **1954:** Sultan restored. **1959–60:** Secessionist rebellion in Suvadiva (Huvadu) and Addu southern atolls. **1965:** Achieved full independence outside Commonwealth. **1968:** Sultan deposed after referendum; republic reinstated with Ibrahim Nasir as president. **1975:** Closure of British airforce staging post on southern island of Gan led to substantial loss in income. **1978:** The autocratic Nasir retired; replaced by Maumoon Abd al-Gayoom. **1980s:** Economic growth boosted by rapid development of tourist industry. **1982:** Rejoined Commonwealth. **1985:** Became founder member of South Asian Association for Regional Cooperation. **1986:** The High Court sentenced exiled Nasir in absentia to 25 years' banishment on charges of embezzlement of public funds, but pardon was granted two years later. **1988:** Coup attempt by Sri Lankan mercenaries, thought to have the backing of former president Nasir, foiled by Indian paratroops.

Mali Republic of

National name: *République du Mali* **Area:** 1,240,142 sq km/478,818 sq mi **Capital:** Bamako **Major towns/cities:** Mopti, Kayes, Ségou, Timbuktu, Sikasso **Physical features:** landlocked state with river Niger and savanna in S; part of the Sahara in N; hills in NE; Senegal River and its branches irrigate the SW

Government

Head of state: Alpha Oumar Konare from 1992 **Head of government:** Ibrahim Boubaker Keita from 1994 **Political system:**

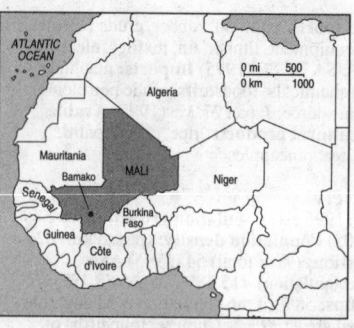

emergent democracy **Administrative divisions:** capital district of Bamako and eight regions **Political parties:** Alliance for Democracy in Mali (ADEMA), left of centre; National Committee for Democratic Initiative (CNID), centre left; Assembly for Democracy and Progress (RDP), left of centre; Civic Society and the Democracy and Progress Party (PDP), left of centre; Malian People's Democratic Union (UDPM), nationalist socialist **Armed forces:** 7,400; plus paramilitary forces of 7,800 (1996) **Conscription:** selective conscription for two years **Death penalty:** retains the death penalty for ordinary crimes but can be considered abolitionist in practice (last execution 1980) **Defence spend:** (% GDP) 1.8 (1995) **Education spend:** (% GNP) 2.1 (1993–94) **Health spend:** (% GDP) 1.3 (1990–95)

Economy and resources

Currency: franc CFA **GDP:** ($ US) 1.9 billion (1994) **Real GDP per capita (PPP):** ($ US) 543 (1994) **GDP growth rate:** 2.4% (1994); 2.5% (1990–95) **Average annual inflation:** 9.5% (1996); 151.9% (1985–95) **Foreign debt:** ($ US) 2.85 billion (1996) **Major trading partners:** Côte d'Ivoire, Thailand, CIS countries, Belgium, France, China, Ireland, Senegal **Resources:** iron ore, uranium, diamonds, bauxite, manganese, copper, lithium, gold **Industries:** food processing, cotton processing, textiles, clothes, cement, pharmaceuticals **Exports:** cotton, livestock, gold, miscellaneous manufactured articles. Principal market: Thailand 18.5% (1995) **Imports:** machinery and transport equipment, food products, petroleum products, other raw materials, chemicals, miscellaneous manufactured articles. Principal source: Côte d'Ivoire 22% (1995) **Arable land:** 2.8% (1995) **Agricultural products:** seed cotton, cotton lint, groundnuts, millet, sugar cane, rice, sorghum, sweet potatoes, mangoes, vegetables; livestock rearing (cattle, sheep, and goats); fishing

Population and society

Population: 11,134,000 (1996 est) **Population growth rate:** 3.2% (1990–95); 2.9% (2000–05) **Population density:** (per sq km) 9 (1996 est) **Urban population:** (% of total) 27 (1995) **Age distribution:** (% of total population) <15 47.4%, 15–65 50%, >65 2.5% (1995) **Ethnic groups:** around 50% belong to the Mande group, including the Bambara, Malinke, and Sarakole; other significant groups include the Fulani, Minianka, Senutu, Songhai, and the nomadic Tuareg in the N **Language:** French (official), Bambara **Religion:** Sunni Muslim 90%, animist, Christian **Literacy rate:** 41% (men); 24% (women) (1995 est) **Labour force:** 50% of population: 86% agriculture, 2% industry, 12% services (1990) **Life expectancy:** 46 (men); 50 (women) (1995–2000) **Child mortality rate:** (under 5, per 1,000 live births) 184 (1996) **Physicians:** 1 per 18,376 people (1993 est)

Practical information

Visa requirements: UK: visa required. USA: visa required **Embassy for the UK:** 487 avenue Molière, B-1060 Brussels, Belgium. Tel: (2) 345 7432; fax: (2) 344 5700 **British embassy:** British Consulate, BP 1598, Plan International, Bamako. Tel: (223) 230 583; fax: (223) 228 143 **Chamber of commerce:** Chambre de Commerce et d'Industrie de Mali, BP 46, place de la Liberté, Bamako. Tel: (223) 225 036; fax: (223) 222 120 **Airports:** international airports: Bamako (Senou), Mopti; ten domestic airports; total passenger km: 215 million (1994) **Major holidays:** 1, 20 January, 1, 25 May, 22 September, 19 November, 25 December; variable: Eid-ul-Adha, end of Ramadan, Prophet's Birthday, Prophet's Baptism (November)

Chronology

5th–13th centuries: Ghana Empire founded by agriculturist Soninke people, based on the Saharan gold trade for which Timbuktu became an important centre. At its height in the 11th century it covered much of the western Sahel, comprising parts of present-day Mali, Senegal, and Mauritania. Wars with Muslim Berber tribes from the N led to its downfall. Its capital was at Kumbi, 125 mi/200 km N of Bamako, in SE Mauritania. **13th–15th centuries:** Ghana Empire superseded by Muslim Mali Empire of Malinke (Mandingo) people of SW, from which Mali derives its name. At its peak, under Mansa Musa in the 14th century, it covered parts of Mali, Senegal, Gambia, and S Mauritania. **15th–16th centuries:** Muslim Songhai Empire, centred around Timbuktu and Gao, superseded Mali Empire. Under Sonni Ali Ber, who ruled 1464–92, it covered Mali, Senegal, Gambia, and parts of Mauritania, Niger, and Nigeria, and included a professional army and civil service. **1591:** Songhai Empire destroyed by Moroccan Berbers, under Ahmad al-Mansur, who launched an invasion to take over western Sudanese gold trade and took control over Timbuktu. **18th–19th centuries:** Niger valley region was divided between the nomadic Tuareg, in the area around Gao in the NE, and the Fulani and Bambara kingdoms, around Macina and Bambara in the centre and SW. **late 18th century:** Western Mali visited by Scottish explorer Mungo Park. **mid-19th century:** The Islamic Tukolor, as part of a jihad (holy war) conquered much of western Mali, including Fulani and Bambara kingdoms, while in the S, Samori Ture, a Muslim Malinke (Mandingo) warrior, created a small empire. **1880–95:** Region conquered by French, who overcame Tukolor and Samori resistance to establish colony of French Sudan. **1904:** Became part of federation of French West Africa. **1946:** French Sudan became an overseas territory within the French Union, with its own territorial assembly and representation in the French parliament; the pro-autonomy Sudanese Union and Sudanese Progressive Parties founded in Bamako. **1959:** With Senegal, formed the Federation of Mali. **1960:** Separated from Senegal and became independent Republic of Mali, with Modibo Keita, an authoritarian socialist of the Sudanese Union party, as president. **1968:** Keita replaced in army coup by Lt Moussa Traoré, as economy deteriorated: constitution suspended and political activity banned. **1974:** New constitution made Mali a one-party state, dominated by Traoré's nationalistic socialist Malian People's Democratic Union (UDPM), formed 1976. **1979:** More than a dozen killed after a student strike was crushed. **1985:** Five-day conflict with Burkina Faso over long-standing border dispute; mediated by International Court of Justice. **late 1980s:** Closer ties developed with the West and free-market economic policies pursued, including privatization, as Soviet influence waned. **1991:** Violent demonstrations and strikes against one-party rule led to 150 deaths; Traoré ousted in a coup led by Lt-Col Amadou Toumani Toure. **1992:** Referendum endorsed new democratic constitution. The opposition Alliance for Democracy in Mali (ADEMA) won multiparty elections; Alpha Oumar Konare elected president. Coalition government formed. Peace pact signed with Tuareg rebels fighting in N Mali for greater autonomy. **1993–94:** Student unrest forced two changes of prime minister. Ex-president Traoré sentenced to death for his role in suppressing the 1991 riots. **1997:** President Konare re-elected.

Malta Republic of

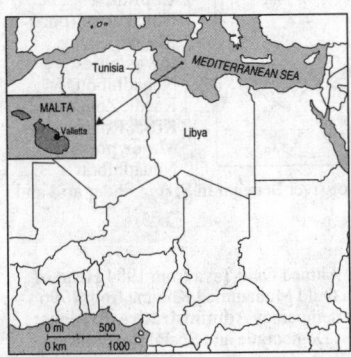

National name: *Repubblika Ta'Malta* **Area:** 320 sq km/124 sq mi **Capital:** Valletta (and port) **Major towns/cities:** Rabat, Birkirkara, Qormi, Sliema, Zetjun, Zabor **Major ports:** Marsaxlokk, Valletta **Physical features:** includes islands of Gozo 67 sq km/26 sq mi and Comino 3 sq km/1 sq mi

Government

Head of state: Mifsud Bonnici from 1994 **Head of government:** Edward Fenech Adami from 1987 **Political system:** liberal democracy **Administrative divisions:** 67 local councils **Political parties:** Malta Labour Party (MLP), moderate, left of centre; Nationalist Party (PN), Christian, centrist, pro-European **Armed forces:** 2,000 (1996) **Conscription:** military service is voluntary **Death penalty:** laws provide for the death penalty only for exceptional crimes such as crimes under military law or crimes committed in exceptional circumstances such as wartime (last execution 1943) **Defence spend:** (% GDP) 1.1 (1996) **Education spend:** (% GNP) 5.1 (1993–94)

Economy and resources

Currency: Maltese lira **GDP:** ($ US) 2.6 billion (1994) **Real GDP per capita (PPP):** ($ US) 13,009 (1994) **GDP growth rate:** 5.1% (1994) **Average annual inflation:** 5% (1996); 2.9% (1985–95 est) **Foreign debt:** ($ US) 806.6 million (1994) **Major trading partners:** Italy, Germany, UK, USA, France, Libya, the Netherlands **Resources:** stone, sand; offshore petroleum reserves were under exploration 1988–95 **Industries:** transport equipment and machinery, food and beverages, textiles and clothing, chemicals, ship repair and shipbuilding, tourism **Exports:** machinery and transport equipment, manufactured articles (including clothing), beverages, chemicals, tobacco. Principal market: Italy 37.5% 1994 **Imports:** machinery and transport equipment, basic manufactures (including textile yarn and fabrics), food and live animals, mineral fuels. Principal source: Italy 26.5% (1994) **Arable land:** 31.3% (1995) **Agricultural products:** potatoes, tomatoes, peaches, plums, nectarines, apricots, melons, strawberries, wheat, barley; livestock rearing (cattle, pigs, and poultry) and livestock products (chicken eggs, pork, and dairy products)

Population and society

Population: 369,000 (1996 est) **Population growth rate:** 0.7% (1990–95) **Population density:** (per sq km) 1,168 (1996 est) **Urban population:** (% of total) 89 (1995) **Age distribution:** (% of total population) <15 22%, 15–65 67%, >65 11% (1994) **Ethnic groups:** essentially European, supposedly originated from ancient North African kingdom of Carthage **Language:** Maltese, English (both official) **Religion:** Roman Catholic 98% **Education:** (compulsory years) 10 **Literacy rate:** 86% (men); 86% (women) (1995 est) **Labour force:** 2.5% agriculture, 34% industry, 63.5% services (1992) **Unemployment:** 3.5% (1995) **Life expectancy:** 75 (men); 79 (women) (1995–2000) **Child mortality rate:** (per 1,000 live births) 11 (1996) **Physicians:** 1 per 406 people (1995)

Practical information

Visa requirements: UK: visa not required. USA: visa not required **Embassy in the UK:** Malta House, 36–38 Piccadilly, London W1V 0PP. Tel: (0171) 292 4800; fax: (0171) 734 1832 **British embassy:** British High Commission, PO Box 506, 7 St Anne Street, Floriana, Valetta. Tel: (356) 233 134; fax: (356) 242 001 **Chamber of commerce:** Exchange Building, Republic Street, Valetta VLT 05. Tel: (356) 247 233; fax: (356) 245 223 **Airports:** international airports: Luga (Malta, 8 km/5 mi from Valetta); helicopter service between Malta and Gozo; total passenger km: 1,821 million (1994) **Major holidays:** 1 January, 31 March, 1 May, 15 August, 13, 25 December; variable: Good Friday

Chronology

7th century BC: Invaded and subjugated by Carthaginians from North Africa. **218 BC:** Came under Roman control. **AD 60:** Converted to Christianity by the apostle Paul, who was shipwrecked. **395:** On division of Roman Empire, became part of Eastern (Byzantine) portion, dominated by Constantinople. **870:** Came under Arab rule. **1091:** Arabs defeated by Norman Count Roger I of Sicily; Roman Catholic Church re-established. **1530:** Handed over by Holy Roman Emperor Charles V to religious military order, the Hospitallers (Knights of St John of Jerusalem). **1798–1802:** Briefly occupied by French. **1814:** Annexed to Britain by Treaty of Paris on condition that Roman Catholic Church was maintained and Maltese Declaration of Rights honoured. **later 19th century– early 20th century:** Became vital British naval base, with famous dockyard that developed as island's economic mainstay. **1942:** Awarded George Cross for valour in resisting severe Italian aerial attacks during World War II. **1947:** Achieved self-government. **1955:** Dom Mintoff of left-of-centre Malta Labour Party (MLP) became prime minister. **1956:** Referendum approved MLP's proposal for integration with UK. Plebiscite opposed and boycotted by right-of-centre Nationalist Party (PN). **1958:** MLP rejected final British integration proposal. **1962:** PN elected, with Dr Giorgio Borg Olivier as prime minister. **1964:** Independence achieved from Britain, within Commonwealth. Ten-year defence and economic-aid treaty with UK signed. **1971:** Mintoff adopted policy of nonalignment and declared 1964 treaty invalid; negotiations began for leasing NATO base in Malta. **1972:** Seven-year NATO agreement signed. **1974:** Became a republic. **1979:** British military base closed; closer links established with communist and Arab states, including Libya. **1984:** Mintoff retired; replaced by Karmenu Mifsud Bonnici as prime minister and MLP leader. **1987:** Edward Fenech Adami (PN) narrowly elected prime minister; he adopted a more pro-European and pro-American policy stance than preceding administration. **1990:** Formal application made for European Community membership. **1994:** Mifsud Bonnici elected president.

Marshall Islands Republic of the

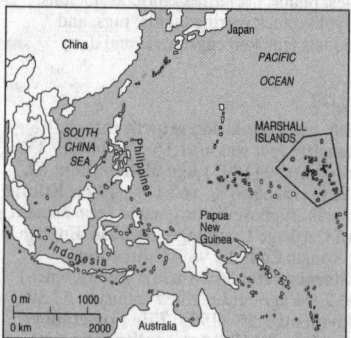

Area: 181 sq km/70 sq mi **Capital:** Dalap-Uliga-Darrit (on Majuro atoll) **Major towns/cities:** Ebeye (the only other town) **Physical features:** comprises the Ratak and Ralik island chains in the W Pacific, which together form an archipelago of 31 coral atolls, 5 islands, and 1,152 islets

Government
Head of state and government: Imata Kabua from 1997 **Political system:** liberal democracy **Political parties:** no organized party system, but in 1991 an opposition grouping, the Ralik Ratak Democratic Party, was founded to oppose the ruling group **Armed forces:** the USA maintains a military presence on the Kwajalein Atoll (the Compact of Free Association gave the USA responsibility for defence in return for US assistance) **Death penalty:** abolished 1991 **Education spend:** (% GDP) 6 (1994)

Economy and resources
Currency: US dollar **GDP:** ($ US) 94 million (1995 est) **Real GDP per capita (PPP):** ($ US) 1,680 (1995 est) **GDP growth rate:** 1.5% (1995 est) **Average annual inflation:** 4% (1995 est); 5.4% (1985–95 est) **Foreign debt:** ($ US) 170 million (1994) **Major trading partners:** USA, Japan, Australia **Resources:** phosphates **Industries:** processing of agricultural products, handicrafts, fish products and canning, tourism **Exports:** coconut products, trochus shells, copra, handicrafts, fish, live animals. Principal market: USA **Imports:** foodstuffs, beverages and tobacco, building materials, machinery and transport equipment, mineral fuels, chemicals. Principal source: USA **Agricultural products:** coconuts, tomatoes, melons, breadfruit, cassava, sweet potatoes, copra; fishing; seaweed and pearl oyster cultivation developed during first half of 1990s

Population and society

Population: 57,000 (1996 est) **Population growth rate:** 2.9% (1990–95) **Population density:** (per sq km) 313 (1996 est) **Urban population:** (% of total) 69.1 (1995) **Ethnic groups:** 97% Marshallese, of predominantly Micronesian descent **Language:** Marshallese, English (both official) **Religion:** Christian (mainly Protestant) and Baha'i **Education:** (compulsory years) 8 **Literacy rate:** 91% (men); 90% (women) (1994 est) **Labour force:** 26.1% agriculture, 9.5% industry, 64.4% services (1989) **Unemployment:** 16% (1991 est) **Life expectancy:** 62 (men); 65 (women) (1995) **Child mortality rate:** (per 1,000 live births) 48 (1994) **Physicians:** 1 per 2,631 people (1990)

Practical information
Visa requirements: UK: visa required. USA: visa required **Embassy in the UK:** none; enquiries relating to the Marshall Islands are dealt with by the Marshall Islands Visitors Authority, PO Box 1727, Ministry of Resources and Development, Majuro 96960. Tel: (692) 625 3206; fax: (692) 625 3218 **British embassy:** none **Chamber of commerce:** Majuro Chamber of Commerce, Majuro 96960. Tel: (692) 625 3051; fax: (692) 625 3343 **Airports:** international airports: Majuro; ten domestic airports; total passenger km: 41 million (1994) **Major holidays:** 1 January, 1 March, 1 May, 1 July, 21 October, 17 November, 4, 25 December

Chronology
after c. 1000 BC: Micronesians first settled the islands. **1529:** Visited by Spanish navigator Miguel de Saavedra and thereafter came under Spanish influence. **1875:** Spanish rule formally declared in face of increasing encroachment by German traders. **1885:** German protectorate established. **1914:** Seized by Japan on the outbreak of World War I. **1920–44:** Administered under League of Nations mandate by Japan and vigorously colonized. **1944:** Japanese removed after heavy fighting with US troops during World War II. **1946–63:** Eniwetok and Bikini atolls used for US atom-bomb tests; islanders later demanded rehabilitation and compensation for the damage. **1947:** Became part of United Nations (UN) Pacific Islands Trust Territory, administered by USA. **1979:** Amata Kabua elected president as internal self-government established. **1986:** Compact of Free Association with USA granted islands self-government, with USA retaining responsibility for defence and security until 2001. **1990:** UN trust status terminated. **1991:** Independence agreed with Kabua as president; UN membership granted. **1996:** Death of President Amata Kabua. **1997:** Imata Kabua elected president.

Mauritania Islamic Republic of

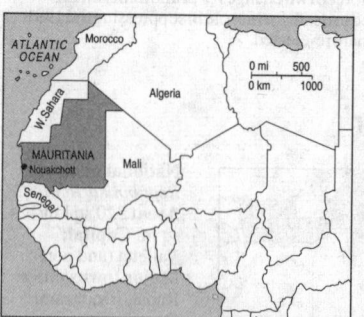

National name: *République Islamique Arabe et Africaine de Mauritanie* **Area:** 1,030,700 sq km/397,953 sq mi **Capital:** Nouakchott (port) **Major towns/cities:** Nouâdhibou, Kaédi, Zouerate, Kiffa, Rosso, Atar **Major ports:** Nouâdhibou

Physical features: valley of river Senegal in S; remainder arid and flat

Government
Head of state: Maaoya Sid'Ahmed Ould Taya from 1984 **Head of government:** Cheik el Avia Ould Muhammad Khouna from 1996 **Political system:** emergent democracy **Administrative divisions:** 12 regions **Political parties:** Democratic and Social Republican

Party (PRDS), centre left, militarist; Rally for Democracy and National Unity (RDNU), centrist; Mauritian Renewal Party (MPR), centrist; Umma, Islamic fundamentalist **Armed forces:** 15,700 (1995); plus paramilitary force of around 5,000 **Conscription:** military service is by authorized conscription for two years **Death penalty:** retained and used for ordinary crimes **Defence spend:** (% GDP) 1.9 (1995) **Education spend:** (% GNP) 4.0 (1994) **Health spend:** (% GDP) 1.5 (1990–95)

Economy and resources
Currency: ouguiya **GDP:** ($ US) 1 billion (1994) **Real GDP per capita (PPP):** ($ US) 1,593 (1994) **GDP growth rate:** 4.6% (1994); 4% (1990–95) **Average annual inflation:** 4% (1996); 6.9% (1985–95) **Foreign debt:** ($ US) 2.5 billion (1995) **Major trading partners:** Japan, France, Spain, Italy, Belgium, Germany **Resources:** copper, gold, iron ore, gypsum, phosphates, sulphur, peat **Industries:** fish products, cheese and butter, processing of minerals (including imported petroleum), mining **Exports:** fish and fish products, iron ore. Principal market: Japan 27.2% (1995) **Imports:** machinery and transport equipment, foodstuffs, consumer goods, building materials, mineral fuels. Principal source: France 23.9% (1995) **Arable land:** 0.2% (1995) **Agricultural products:** millet, sorghum, dates, maize, rice, pulses, groundnuts, sweet potatoes; livestock rearing (the principal occupation of rural population); fishing (providing 56% of export earnings 1993). Only 1% of Mauritania receives enough rain to grow crops

Population and society
Population: 2,333,000 (1996 est) **Population growth rate:** 2.5% (1990–95); 2.5% (2000–05) **Population density:** (per sq km) 2 (1996 est) **Urban population:** (% of total) 54 (1995) **Age distribution:** (% of total population) <15 43.1%, 15–65 53.7%, >65 3.2% (1995) **Ethnic groups:** over 80% of the population is of Moorish or Moorish-black origin; about 18% is black African (concentrated in the S); there is a small European minority **Language:** French and Hasaniya Arabic (both official), African languages including Pulaar, Soninke, and Wolof **Religion:** Sunni Muslim **Education:** not compulsory **Literacy rate:** 47% (men); 21% (women) (1995 est) **Labour force:** 46% of population: 55% agriculture, 10% industry, 34% services (1990) **Unemployment:** 20% (1991 est) **Life expectancy:** 52 (men); 55 (women) (1995–2000) **Child mortality rate:** (under 5, per 1,000 live births) 142 (1996) **Physicians:** 1 per 11,316 people (1994)

Practical information
Visa requirements: UK: visa required. USA: visa required **Embassy in the UK:** Honorary Consulate of the Islamic Republic of Mauritania, 140 Bow Common Lane, London E3 4BH. Tel: (0181) 980 4382; fax: (0181) 980 2232 **British embassy:** the British Embassy in Rabat (see Morocco) deals with enquiries relating to Mauritania **Chamber of commerce:** Chambre de Commerce, d'Agriculture, d'Elevage, d'Industrie et des Mines de Mauritanie, BP 215 Nouakchott. Tel: (222) 52214; telex: 581 **Airports:** international airports: Nouakchott, Nouâdhibou; six domestic airports; total passenger km: 289 million (1994) **Major holidays:** 1 January, 1, 25 May, 10 July, 28 November; variable: Eid-ul-Adha, end of Ramadan, New Year (Muslim), Prophet's Birthday

Chronology
early Christian era: A Roman province with the name Mauritania, after the Mauri, its Berber inhabitants who became active in the long-distance salt trade. **7th–11th centuries:** Eastern Mauritania was incorporated in the larger Ghana Empire, centred on Mali to the E, but with its capital at Kumbi in SE Mauritania. The Berbers were reduced to vassals and converted to Islam in the 8th century. **11th–12th centuries:** The area's Sanhadja Berber inhabitants, linked to the Morocco-based Almoravid Empire, destroyed the Ghana Empire and spread Islam among neighbouring peoples. **13th–15th centuries:** SE Mauritania formed part of Muslim Mali Empire, which extended to E and S. **1441:** Coast visited by Portuguese, who founded port of Arguin and captured Africans to sell as slaves. **15th–16th centuries:** Eastern Mauritania formed part of Muslim Songhai Empire, which spread across western Sahel, and

Arab tribes migrated into the area. **1817:** Senegal Treaty recognized coastal region (formerly disputed by European nations) as French sphere of influence. **1903:** Formally became French protectorate. **1920:** Became French colony, within French West Africa. **1960:** Independence achieved, with Moktar Ould Daddah, leader of Mauritanian People's Party (PPM), as president. New capital built at Nouakchott. **1968:** Underlying tensions between agriculturalist black population of S and economically dominant semi-nomadic Arabo-Berber peoples, or Moors, of desert N became more acute after Arabic was made an official language (with French). **1976:** Western Sahara, to the NW, ceded by Spain to Mauritania and Morocco. Mauritania occupied the southern area and Morocco the mineral-rich N. Polisario Front formed in Sahara to resist this occupation and guerrilla war broke out, with the Polisario receiving backing from Algeria and Libya. **1978:** Daddah deposed in bloodless coup; replaced by Col Mohamed Khouna Ould Haidalla in military government. **1979:** Peace accord signed with Polisario Front in Algiers, in which Mauritania, crippled by cost of military struggle over a largely uninhabited area, renounced claims to southern Western Sahara (Tiris el Gharbia region) and recognized Polisario regime; diplomatic relations restored with Algeria. **1981:** Diplomatic relations with Morocco broken after it annexed southern Western Sahara. **1984:** Haidalla overthrown by Col Maaoya Sid'Ahmed Ould Taya. **1985:** Relations with Morocco restored. **1989:** Violent clashes in Mauritania and Senegal between Moors and black Africans, chiefly of Senegalese origins; over 50,000 Senegalese expelled. **1991:** Amnesty for political prisoners. Calls for resignation of President Taya. Political parties legalized and new multiparty constitution approved in referendum. **1992:** First multiparty elections largely boycotted by opposition; Taya and his Social Democratic Republican Party (DSRP) re-elected. Diplomatic relations with Senegal resumed. **1996:** Cheikh el Avia Ould Muhammad Khouna appointed prime minister.

Mauritius Republic of

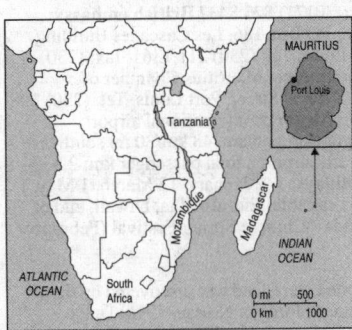

Area: 1,865 sq km/720 sq mi; the island of Rodrigues is part of Mauritius; there are several small island dependencies **Capital:** Port Louis (port) **Major towns/cities:** Beau Bassin-Rose Hill, Curepipe, Quatre Bornes, Vacoas-Phoenix **Physical features:** mountainous, volcanic island surrounded by coral reefs

Government
Head of state: Cassam Uteem from 1992 **Head of government:** Navim Ramgoolam from 1995 **Political system:** liberal democracy **Administrative divisions:** five municipalities and four district councils **Political parties:** Mauritius Socialist Movement (MSM), moderate socialist-republican; Mauritius Labour Party (MLP), democratic socialist, Hindu-oriented; Mauritius Social Democratic Party (PMSD), conservative, Francophile; Mauritius Militant Movement (MMM), Marxist-republican; Organization of Rodriguan People (OPR), left of centre **Armed forces:** no standing defence forces; 1,300-strong police mobile unit (1996) **Death penalty:** abolished 1995 **Defence spend:** (% GDP) 2.3 (1996) **Education spend:** (% GNP) 3.6 (1993) **Health spend:** (% GDP) 2.2 (1990–95)

Economy and resources

Currency: Mauritian rupee **GDP:** ($ US) 3.4 billion (1994) **Real GDP per capita (PPP):** ($ US) 13,172 (1994) **GDP growth rate:** 5.1% (1994); 4.9% (1990–95) **Average annual inflation:** 8.5% (1996); 8.8% (1985–95) **Foreign debt:** ($ US) 1.8 billion (1995) **Major trading partners:** UK, France, South Africa, India, Australia, Germany **Industries:** textiles and clothing, footwear and other leather products, food products, diamond cutting, jewellery, electrical components, chemical products, furniture, tourism **Exports:** raw sugar, clothing, tea, molasses, jewellery. Principal market: UK 34% (1995) **Imports:** textile yarn and fabrics, petroleum products, industrial machinery, motor vehicles, manufactured goods. Principal source: France 19.9% (1995) **Arable land:** 49.3% (1995) **Agricultural products:** sugar cane, tea, tobacco, potatoes, maize; poultry farming; fishing; forest resources

Population and society

Population: 1,129,000 (1996 est) **Population growth rate:** 1.1% (1990–95); 1.1% (2000–05) **Population density:** (per sq km) 553 (1996 est) **Urban population:** (% of total) 41 (1995) **Age distribution:** (% of total population) <15 27.7%, 15–65 66.4%, >65 5.8% (1995) **Ethnic groups:** five principal ethnic groups: French, black Africans, Indians, Chinese, and Mulattos (or Creoles). Indo-Mauritians predominate, constituting 67% of the population, followed by Creoles (29%), Sino-Mauritians (3.5%), and Europeans (0.5%) **Language:** English (official), French, Creole, Indian languages **Religion:** Hindu, Christian (mainly Roman Catholic), Muslim **Education:** (compulsory years) 7 **Literacy rate:** 87% (men); 78% (women) (1995 est) **Labour force:** 15.7% agriculture, 43.7% industry, 40.6% services (1992) **Unemployment:** 7.1% (1994) **Life expectancy:** 68 (men); 75 (women) (1995–2000) **Child mortality rate:** (under 5, per 1,000 live births) 17 (1996) **Physicians:** 1 per 1,000 people (1993)

Practical information

Visa requirements: UK: visa not required. USA: visa not required **Embassy in the UK:** 32/33 Elvaston Place, London SW7 5NW. Tel: (0171) 581 0294; fax: (0171) 823 8437 **British embassy:** British High Commission, PO Box 186, Les Cascades Building, Edith Cavell Street, Port Louis. Tel: (230) 211 1361; fax: (230) 211 1369 **Chamber of commerce:** Mauritius Chamber of Commerce and Industry, 3 Royal Street, Port Louis. Tel: (230) 208 3301; fax: (230) 208 0076 **Airports:** international airport: Plaisance (Sir Seewoosagur Ramgoolam, 48 km/30 mi southeast of Port Louis); two domestic airports; total passenger km: 2,972 million (1994) **Major holidays:** 1–2 January, 12 March, 1 May, 1 November, 25 December; variable: Eid-ul-Adha, Diwali, end of Ramadan, Prophet's Birthday, Chinese Spring Festival (February)

Chronology

1598: Previously uninhabited, the island was discovered by the Dutch and named after Prince Morris of Nassau. **1710:** Dutch colonists withdrew. **1721:** Reoccupied by French East India Company, who renamed it Île de France, and established sugar cane and tobacco plantations worked by imported African slaves. **1814:** Ceded to Britain by Treaty of Paris. **1835:** Slavery abolished; indentured Indian and Chinese labourers imported to work the sugar-cane plantations, which were later hit by competition from beet sugar. **1903:** Formerly administered with Seychelles, it became a single colony. **1936:** Mauritius Labour Party (MLP) founded, drawing strong support from sugar workers. **1957:** Internal self-government granted. **1968:** Independence achieved from Britain within Commonwealth, with Seewoosagur Ramgoolam of centrist Indian-dominated MLP as prime minister. **1971:** State of emergency temporarily imposed as a result of industrial unrest. **1982:** Aneerood Jugnauth, of the moderate socialist Mauritius Socialist Movement (MSM) became prime minister, pledging a programme of nonalignment, nationalization, and the creation of a republic. **1992:** Mauritius became a republic, within the Commonwealth, with Cassam Uteem elected president. **1995:** MLP and cross-community Mauritian Militant Movement (MMM) coalition won landslide election victory; Navim Ramgoolam (MLP) became prime minister.

Mexico United States of

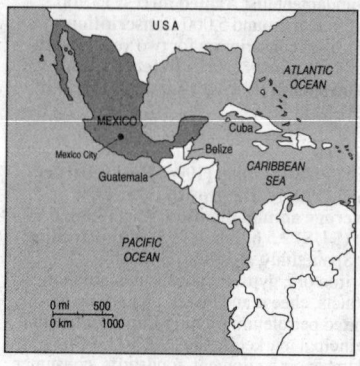

National name: *Estados Unidos Mexicanos* **Area:** 1,958,201 sq km/756,061 sq mi **Capital:** Mexico City **Major towns/cities:** Guadalajara, Monterrey, Puebla, Netzahualcóyotl, Ciudad Juárez, Tijuana **Major ports:** 49 ocean ports **Physical features:** partly arid central highlands; Sierra Madre mountain ranges E and W; tropical coastal plains; volcanoes, including Popocatepetl; Rio Grande

Government

Head of state and government: Ernesto Zedillo Ponce de Leon from 1994 **Political system:** federal democracy **Administrative divisions:** 31 states and a Federal District **Political parties:** Institutional Revolutionary Party (PRI), moderate, left wing; National Action Party (PAN), moderate, Christian, centre right; Party of the Democratic Revolution (PRD), centre left **Armed forces:** 175,000; rural defence militia of 15,000 (1996) **Conscription:** one year, part-time (conscripts selected by lottery) **Death penalty:** only for exceptional crimes; last execution 1937 **Defence spend:** (% GDP) 0.8 (1996) **Education spend:** (% GNP) 5.8 (1993–94) **Health spend:** (% GDP) 3.1 (1994)

Economy and resources

Currency: Mexican peso **GDP:** ($ US) 334.2 billion (1996) **Real GDP per capita (PPP):** ($ US) 7,744 (1996) **GDP growth rate:** 5% (1996); 1.1% (1990–95) **Average annual inflation:** 34.2% (1996); 36.7% (1985–95) **Foreign debt:** ($ US) 170.5 billion (1996) **Major trading partners:** USA, Japan, Spain, France, Germany, Brazil, Canada **Resources:** petroleum, natural gas, zinc, salt, silver, copper, coal, mercury, manganese, phosphates, uranium, strontium sulphide **Industries:** motor vehicles, food processing, iron and steel, chemicals, beverages, electrical machinery, electronic goods, petroleum refining, cement, metals and metal products, tourism **Exports:** petroleum and petroleum products, engines and spare parts for motor vehicles, motor vehicles, electrical and electronic goods, fresh and preserved vegetables, coffee, cotton. Principal market: USA 83.9% (1996) **Imports:** motor vehicle chassis, industrial machinery and equipment, iron and steel, telecommunications apparatus, organic chemicals, cereals and cereal preparations, petroleum and petroleum products. Principal source: USA 75.5% (1996) **Arable land:** 7.5% (1995) **Agricultural products:** maize, wheat, sorghum, barley, rice, beans, potatoes, coffee, cotton, sugar cane, fruit and vegetables; livestock raising and fisheries

Population and society

Population: 92,718,000 (1996 est) **Population growth rate:** 2.1% (1990–95); 1.5% (2000–05) **Population density:** (per sq km) 47 (1996 est) **Urban population:** (% of total) 75 (1995) **Age distribution:** (% of total population) <15 35.9%, 15–65 59.9%, >65 4.2% (1995) **Ethnic groups:** around 60% mestizo (mixed Native American and Spanish descent), 30% Native Americans, remainder mainly of European origin **Language:** Spanish (official); Nahuatl, Maya, Zapoteco, Mixteco, Otomi **Religion:** Roman Catholic **Education:** (compulsory years) 6 **Literacy rate:** 89% (men); 85% (women) (1995 est) **Labour force:** 64.4% of population: 23.5% agriculture, 21.7% industry, 54.8% services (1995) **Unemployment:** 5.5% (1996) **Life expectancy:** 69 (men); 75 (women) (1995–2000) **Child mortality rate:** (under 5, per 1,000 live births) 40 (1996) **Physicians:** 1 per 889 people (1994)

Mexico: States

State	Capital	Area		Population
		sq km	sq mi	(1995 est)
Aguascalientes	Aguascalientes	5,589	2,157	862,300
Baja California Norte	Mexicali	70,113	27,071	2,108,100
Baja California Sur	La Paz	73,677	28,447	375,450
Campeche	Campeche	51,833	20,013	642,100
Chiapas	Tuxtla Gutiérrez	73,887	28,528	3,606,800
Chihuahua	Chihuahua	247,087	95,400	2,793,000
Coahuila	Saltillo	151,571	58,522	2,172,100
Colima	Colima	5,455	2,106	487,300
Durango	Victoria de Durango	119,648	46,196	1,431,000
Guanajuato	Guanajuato	30,589	11,810	4,393,200
Guerrero	Chilpancingo	63,794	24,631	2,915,500
Hidalgo	Pachuca de Soto	20,987	8,103	2,111,800
Jalisco	Guadalajara	80,137	30,941	5,990,100
México	Toluca de Lerdo	21,461	8,286	11,704,900
Michoacán	Morelia	59,864	23,113	3,869,100
Morelos	Cuernavaca	4,941	1,908	1,442,600
Nayarit	Tepic	27,621	10,664	896,000
Nuevo León	Monterrey	64,555	24,925	3,549,300
Oaxaca	Oaxaca de Juárez	95,364	36,820	3,224,300
Puebla	Puebla de Zaragoza	33,919	13,096	4,624,200
Querétaro	Querétaro	11,769	4,544	1,248,800
Quintana Roo	Chetumal	50,350	19,440	703,400
San Luis Potosí	San Luis Potosí	62,848	24,266	2,191,700
Sinaloa	Culiacán Rosales	58,092	22,429	2,424,700
Sonora	Hermosillo	184,934	71,403	2,083,600
Tabasco	Villahermosa	24,661	9,522	1,748,700
Tamaulipas	Ciudad Victoria	79,829	30,821	2,526,400
Tlaxcala	Tlaxcala	3,914	1,511	883,600
Veracruz	Jalapa Enríquez	72,815	28,114	6,734,500
Yucatán	Mérida	39,340	15,189	1,555,700
Zacatecas	Zacatecas	75,040	28,973	1,336,300

Practical information

Visa requirements: UK: visa (tourist card) required. USA: visa (tourist card) required **Embassy in the UK:** 42 Hertford Street, London W1Y 7TF. Tel: (0171) 499 8586; fax: (0171) 495 4053 **British embassy:** Apartado 96 bis, Rió Lerma 71, Colonia Cuauhtémoc, 06500 Mexico Distrito Federal. Tel: (5) 207 2089; fax: (5) 207 7672 **Chamber of commerce:** Confederacíon de Cámaras Nacionales de Comercio, Servicios y Turismo, Apartado 113 bis, 2 ° y 3 °, Balderas 144, Centro Curuhtémoc, 06079 Mexico Distrito Federal. Tel: (5) 709 1559; fax: (5) 709 1152 **Airports:** international airports: Mexico City (Benito Juárez), Guadalajara (Miguel Hidalgo), Acapulco (General Juan N Alvarez), Monterrey (General Mariano Escobeno), and 40 others; 39 domestic airports; total passenger km: 23,521 million (1994) **Major holidays:** 1 January, 5 February, 21 March, 1, 5 May, 1, 16 September, 12 October, 2, 20 November, 12, 25, 31 December; variable: Holy Thursday, Good Friday

Chronology

c. 2600 BC: Mayan civilization originated in Yucatán peninsula. **1000–500 BC:** Zapotec civilization developed around Monte Albán in S Mexico. **4th–10th centuries AD:** Mayan Empire at its height. **10th–12th centuries:** Toltecs ruled much of Mexico from their capital at Tula. **12th century:** Aztecs migrated south into valley of Mexico. **c. 1325:** Aztecs began building their capital Tenochtitlán on site of present-day Mexico City. **15th century:** Montezuma I built up Aztec Empire in central Mexico. **1519–21:** Hernán Cortes conquered Aztec Empire and secured Mexico for Spain. **1520:** Montezuma II, last king of the Aztecs, killed. **1535:** Mexico became Spanish viceroyalty of New Spain; plantations and mining developed with Indian labour. **1519–1607:** Indigenous population reduced from 21 million to 1 million, due mainly to lack of resistance to diseases transported from Old World. **1810:** Father Miguel Hidalgo led unsuccessful revolt against Spanish. **1821:**

Independence proclaimed by Augustín de Iturbide with support of Church and landowners. **1822:** Iturbide overthrew provisional government and proclaimed himself Emperor Augustín I. **1824:** Federal republic established amid continuing public disorder. **1824–55:** Military rule of Antonio López de Santa Anna, who imposed stability (he became president 1833). **1846–48:** Mexican War: Mexico lost California and New Mexico to USA. **1848:** Revolt of Mayan Indians suppressed. **1855:** Benito Juárez aided overthrow of Santa Anna's dictatorship. **1857–60:** Sweeping liberal reforms and anti-clerical legislation introduced by Juárez led to civil war with conservatives. **1861:** Mexico suspended payment on foreign debt leading to French military intervention; Juárez resisted with US support. **1864:** Supported by conservatives, France installed Archduke Maximilian of Austria as emperor of Mexico. **1867:** Maximilian shot by republicans as French troops withdrew; Juárez resumed presidency. **1872:** Death of Juárez. **1876:** Gen Porfirio Diaz established dictatorship; Mexican economy modernized through foreign investment. **1911:** Revolution overthrew Diaz; liberal president Francisco Madero introduced radical land reform and labour legislation but political disorder increased. **1914 and 1916–17:** US military intervened to quell disorder. **1917:** New constitution, designed to ensure permanent democracy, adopted with US encouragement. **1924–35:** Government dominated by anti-clerical Gen Plutarco Calles, who introduced further social reforms. **1929:** Foundation of National Revolutionary Party (PRFN). **1938:** President Lázaro Cárdenas nationalized all foreign-owned oil wells in face of US opposition.

1942: Mexico declared war on Germany and Japan (and so regained US favour). **1946:** PRFN renamed PRI. **1946–52:** Miguel Alemán first of succession of authoritarian PRI presidents to seek moderation and stability rather than further radical reform. **1960s:** Rapid industrial growth partly financed by borrowing. **1976:** Discovery of huge oil reserves in SE state of Chiapas; oil production tripled in six years. **1982:** Falling oil prices caused grave financial crisis; Mexico defaulted on debt. **1985:** Earthquake in Mexico City killed thousands. **1994:** Uprising in Chiapas by Zapatista National Liberation Army (EZLN), seeking rights for Mayan Indian population; Mexico formed North American Free Trade Area with USA and Canada. **1995:** Government agreed to offer greater autonomy to Mayan Indians in Chiapas. **1996:** Short-lived peace talks with EZLN; violent attacks against government by new leftist Popular Revolutionary Army (EPR) increased. **1997:** PRI lost its assembly majority. Civilian counterpart to the Zapatista rebels formed, the Zapatista National Liberation Front (FZLN).

Micronesia Federated States of

Area: 700 sq km/270 sq mi **Capital:** Kolonia, in Pohnpei state **Major towns/cities:** Weno, in Chuuk state; Lelu, in Kosrae state **Major ports:** Teketik, Lepukos, Okak **Physical features:** an archipelago of 607 equatorial, volcanic islands in the W Pacific

Government

Head of state and government: Bailey Olter from 1991 **Political system:** democratic federal state **Administrative divisions:** four states **Political parties:** no formally organized political parties **Armed forces:** USA is responsible for country's defence **Death**

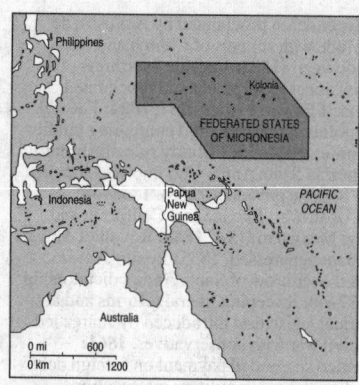

penalty: laws do not provide for the death penalty for any crime

Economy and resources

Currency: US dollar **GDP:** ($ US) 205 million (1994 est) **Real GDP per capita (PPP):** ($ US) 1,700 (1994 est) **GDP growth rate:** 1.4% (1994 est) **Average annual inflation:** 4% (1994 est); 4.5% (1985–95 est) **Major trading partners:** USA, Japan **Industries:** food processing (coconut products), tourism **Exports:** copra, pepper, fish **Imports:** manufactured goods, machinery and transport equipment, mineral fuels **Agricultural products:** mainly subsistence farming; coconuts, cassava, sweet potatoes, breadfruit, bananas, copra, citrus fruits, taro, peppers; fishing

Population and society

Population: 126,000 (1996 est) **Population growth rate:** 2.8% (1990–95) **Population density:** (per sq km) 180 (1996 est) **Urban population:** (% of total) 27.6 (1995) **Ethnic groups:** main ethnic groups are the Trukese (41%) and Pohnpeian (26%), both Micronesian **Language:** English (official) and eight local languages **Religion:** Christianity (mainly Roman Catholic in Yap state, Protestant elsewhere) **Education:** (compulsory years) 8 **Literacy rate:** 91% (men); 88% (women) (1980 est) **Labour force:** 48% agriculture, 6% industry, 46% services (1990) **Unemployment:** 13.5% (1990) **Life expectancy:** 68 (men); 72 (women) (1995–2000) **Child mortality rate:** (per 1,000 live births) 37 (1994) **Physicians:** 1 per 2,380 people (1993)

Practical information

Visa requirements: UK: visa not required for a stay of up to 30 days. USA: visa not required **Embassy in the UK:** Micronesia has no diplomatic representation in the UK; the Department of Trade and Industry has a Pacific Islands Desk. Tel: (0171) 215 4760; fax: (0171) 215 4398 **British embassy:** the UK has no diplomatic representation in Micronesia **Chamber of commerce:** Resources and Development Department, Pohnpei 96941. Tel: (691) 320 5133. Resources and Development Department, Chuuk 96942. Tel: (691) 330 2552; fax: (691) 330 4194 **Airports:** international airports: Pohnpei (5 km/3 mi from Kolonia), Chuuk, Yap, Kosrae; domestic services also operate between these airports **Major holidays:** 1 January, 10 May, 24 October, 3 November, 25 December (some variations from island to island)

Chronology

c. 1000 BC: Micronesians first settled the islands. **1525:** Portuguese navigators first visited Yap and Ulithi islands in the Carolines (Micronesia). **later 16th century:** Fell under Spanish influence. **1874:** Spanish rule formally declared in face of increasing encroachment by German traders. **1885:** Yap seized by German naval forces, but restored to Spain after arbitration by Pope Leo XIII on condition that Germany was allowed freedom of trade. **1899:** Purchased for $4.5 million by Germany from Spain, after the latter's defeat in the Spanish–American War. **1914:** Occupied by Japan on outbreak of World War I. **1919:** Administered under League of Nations mandate by Japan, and vigorously colonized. **1944:** Occupied by USA after Japanese forces defeated in World War II. **1947:** Administered by USA as part of the United Nations (UN) Trust Territory of the Pacific Islands, under the name of the Federated States of Micronesia (FSM). **1979:** Constitution adopted, establishing a federal system for its four constituent states (Yap, Chuuk, Pohnpei, and Kosrae) and internal self-government. **1986:**

Compact of Free Association entered into with USA, granting the islands self-government with USA retaining responsibility for defence and security until 2001. **1990:** UN trust status terminated. **1991:** Independence agreed, with Bailey Olter as president. Entered into UN membership.

Moldova Republic of

National name: *Republica Moldoveneasca* **Area:** 33,700 sq km/13,011 sq mi **Capital:** Chisinău (Kishinev) **Major towns/cities:** Tiraspol, Beltsy, Bendery **Physical features:** hilly land lying largely between the rivers Prut and Dniester; N Moldova comprises the level plain of the Beltsy Steppe and uplands; the climate is warm and moderately continental

Government

Head of state: Petru Lucinschi from 1997 **Head of government:** Ion Cebuc from 1997 **Political system:** emergent democracy **Administrative divisions:** 38 districts, four municipalities, and two autonomous territorial units – Gauguz (Gagauzi Yeri) and Transdniestr (status of latter was under dispute 1996) **Political parties:** Agrarian Democratic Party (ADP), nationalist, centrist; Socialist Party and Yedinstvo/Unity Movement, reform-socialist; Peasants and Intellectuals, Romanian nationalist; Christian Democratic Popular Front (CDPF), Romanian nationalist; Gagauz-Khalky (GKPM; Gagauz People's Movement), Gagauz separatist **Armed forces:** 11,900 (1996) **Conscription:** military service is compulsory for up to 18 months **Death penalty:** abolished 1995 **Defence spend:** (% GDP) 4.2 (1996) **Education spend:** (% GNP) 5.2 (1994) **Health spend:** (% GDP) 6.4 (1995 est)

Economy and resources

Currency: leu **GDP:** ($ US) 4 billion (1994) **Real GDP per capita (PPP):** ($ US) 1,576 (1994) **GDP growth rate:** 1.5% (1996) **Average annual inflation:** 21% (1996); 32.4% (1980–93) **Foreign debt:** ($ US) 600 million (1996) **Major trading partners:** CIS countries (Russia and Ukraine), Romania, Germany, Bulgaria, USA **Resources:** lignite, phosphorites, gypsum, building materials; petroleum and natural gas deposits discovered early 1990s were not yet exploited 1996 **Industries:** food processing, wine, tobacco, metalworking, light industry, machine building, cement, textiles, footwear **Exports:** food and agricultural products, machinery and equipment, textiles, clothing. Principal market: Russia 59.9% (1996) **Imports:** mineral fuels, energy and mineral products, mechanical engineering products, foodstuffs, chemicals, textiles, clothing. Principal source: Russia 28% (1996) **Arable land:** 53.8% (1995) **Agricultural products:** grain, sugar beet, potatoes, vegetables, wine grapes and other fruit, tobacco; livestock products (milk, pork, and beef)

Population and society

Population: 4,444,000 (1996 est) **Population growth rate:** 0.3% (1990–95); 0.5% (2000–05) **Population density:** (per sq km) 132 (1996 est) **Urban population:** (% of total) 52 (1995) **Age distribution:** (% of total population) <15 26.4%, 15–65 64.4%, >65 9.3% (1995) **Ethnic groups:** 65% ethnic Moldovan (Romanian), 14% Ukrainian, 13% ethnic Russian, 4% Gagauzi, 2% Bulgarian, 2% Jewish **Language:** Moldovan **Religion:** Russian Orthodox

Education: (compulsory years) 11 **Literacy rate:** 98.9% (men); 98.9% (women) (1995 est) **Labour force:** 43.3% agriculture, 26% industry, 30.7% services (1992) **Unemployment:** 1.5% (1996); 'hidden unemployment' is considerably higher **Life expectancy:** 64 (men); 72 (women) (1995–2000) **Child mortality rate:** (under 5, per 1,000 live births) 28 (1996) **Physicians:** 1 per 258 people (1994)

Practical information

Visa requirements: UK: visa required. USA: visa required
Embassy in the UK: 219 Marsh Wall, Isle of Dogs, London E14 9PD. Tel: (0171) 538 8600; fax: (0171) 538 5967 **British embassy:** the British Embassy in Moscow (see Russian Federation) deals with enquiries relating to Moldova **Chamber of commerce:** Chamber of Commerce and Industry of the Republic of Moldova, 28 Emineskou, 277012 Chisināu. Tel: (2) 221 552; fax: (2) 233 810 **Airports:** international airports: Chisināu; no domestic services; total passenger km: 1,078 million (1994) **Major holidays:** 1, 7–8 January, 8 March, 9 May, 27, 31 August; variable: Mertsishor (Spring Festival, first week in March), Good Friday, Easter Monday

Chronology

AD 106: The current area covered by Moldova, which lies chiefly between the Prut river, bordering Romania in the W, and the Dniestr river, with Ukraine in the E, was conquered by the Roman Emperor Trajan and became part of the Roman province of Dacia. It was known in earlier times as Bessarabia. **mid-14th century:** Formed part of an independent Moldovan principality, which included areas, such as Bukovina to the W, that are now part of Romania. **late 15th century:** Under Stephen IV 'the Great' the principality reached the height of its power. **16th century:** Became a tributary of the Ottoman Turks. **1774–75:** Moldovan principality, though continuing to recognize Turkish overlordship, was placed under Russian protectorship; Bukovina was lost to Austria. **1812:** Bessarabia ceded to tsarist Russia. **1856:** Remainder of Moldovan principality became largely independent of Turkish control. **1859:** Moldovan Assembly voted to unite with Wallachia, to the SW, to form state of Romania, ruled by Prince Alexandru Ion Cuza. State became fully independent 1878. **1918:** Following Russian Revolution, Bessarabia was seized and incorporated within Romania. **1924:** Moldovan autonomous Soviet Socialist Republic (SSR) created, as part of Soviet Union, comprising territory E of Dniestr river. **1940:** Romania returned Bessarabia, E of Prut River, to Soviet Union, which divided it between Moldovan SSR and Ukraine, with Trans-Dniestr region transferred from Ukraine to Moldova. **1941:** Moldovan SSR occupied by Romania and its wartime ally Germany. **1944:** Red Army reconquered Bessarabia. **1946–47:** Widespread famine as agriculture was collectivized; rich farmers and intellectuals liquidated. **1950:** Immigration by settlers from Russia and Ukraine as industries were developed. **late 1980s:** Upsurge in Moldovan nationalism, encouraged by *glasnost* initiative of reformist Soviet leader Mikhail Gorbachev. **1988:** Moldovan Movement in Support of Perestroika (economic restructuring) campaigned for accelerated political reform. **1989:** Nationalist demonstrations in Kishinev (now Chisināu). Moldovan Popular Front (MPF) founded; Moldovan made state language. Campaigns for autonomy among ethnic Russians, strongest in industrialized Trans-Dniestr region, and Turkish-speaking but Orthodox Christian Gagauz minority in SW. **1990:** MPF polled strongly in parliamentary elections and Mircea Snegur, a reform-nationalist communist, became president. Economic and political sovereignty declared. **1991:** Independence declared and Communist Party outlawed after conservative coup in Moscow against Gorbachev; joined Commonwealth of Independent States (CIS). Insurrection in Trans-Dniestr region. **1992:** Admitted into United Nations and the Conference on Security and Cooperation in Europe; peace agreement signed with Russia to end civil war in Trans-Dniestr, giving special status to the region. MPF-dominated government fell; 'Government of national accord' formed, headed by Andrei Sangheli and dominated by ADP. **1993:** New currency, the leu, introduced. Privatization programme launched and closer ties established with Russia. **1994:** Parliamentary elections won by ADP. Plebiscite rejected nationalist demands for merger with Romania. Russia agreed to withdraw Trans-Dniestr troops by 1997. **1995:**

Joined Council of Europe; economic growth resumed. **1996:** Petru Lucinschi elected president. Dnestr region president Igor Smirnov re-elected. **1997:** Ion Cebuc appointed prime minister. New centrist party formed, supporting President Lusinschi. Major party realignments. Cooperation agreement signed with Dnestr region. Law passed providing for elections to paliament using proportional representation.

Monaco Principality of

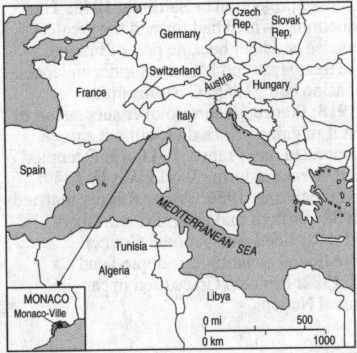

National name: *Principauté de Monaco* **Area:** 1.95 sq km/0.75 sq mi **Capital:** Monaco-Ville **Major towns/cities:** Monte Carlo, La Condamine; heliport Fontvieille **Physical features:** steep and rugged; surrounded landwards by French territory; being expanded by filling in the sea

Government

Head of state: Prince Rainier III from 1949 **Head of government:** Paul Dijoud from 1994 **Political system:** constitutional monarchy under French protectorate **Administrative divisions:** four districts **Political parties:** no formal parties, but lists of candidates: Liste Campora, moderate, centrist; Liste Medecin, moderate, centrist **Armed forces:** no standing defence forces; defence is the responsibility of France **Death penalty:** abolished 1962 **Education spend:** (% GNP) 5.6 (1992)

Economy and resources

Currency: French franc **GDP:** ($ US) 788 million (1994 est) **Real GDP per capita (PPP):** ($ US) 25,000 (1994 est) **GDP growth rate:** N/A **Major trading partners:** full customs integration with France (for external trade figures, see France) **Industries:** chemicals, pharmaceuticals, plastics, microelectronics, electrical goods, paper, textiles and clothing, gambling, banking and finance, real estate, tourism (which provided an estimated 25% of total government revenue 1991) **Imports:** largely dependent on imports from France **Agricultural products:** no agricultural land; some fish farming

Population and society

Population: 32,000 (1996 est) **Population growth rate:** 1.2% (1990–95) **Population density:** (per sq km) 32,097 (1996 est) **Urban population:** (% of total) 100 (1995) **Age distribution:** (% of total population) <15 11.9%, 15–65 65.6%, >65 22.5% (1990) **Ethnic groups:** 58% French; 19% Monegasque **Language:** French (official); English, Italian **Religion:** Roman Catholic **Education:** (compulsory years) 10 **Literacy rate:** 99% (men); 99% (women) (1995 est) **Unemployment:** 2.2% (1994 est) **Life expectancy:** 74 (men); 83 (women) (1995) **Child mortality rate:** (per 1,000 live births) 7 (1994) **Physicians:** 1 per 254 people (1994)

Practical information

Visa requirements: UK: visa not required. USA: visa not required **Embassy in the UK:** Embassy and Consulate General, 4 Cromwell Place, London SW7 2JE. Tel: (0171) 225 2679; fax: (0171) 581 8161 **British embassy:** British Consulate, BP 265, 33 boulevard Princesse Charlotte, MC-98005, Monaco, Cedex. Tel: 9350 9966; fax: 9350 1447 **Chamber of commerce:** Conseil Economique, 8 rue Louis Notari, MC-98000, Monaco, Cedex. Tel: 9330 2082; fax: 9350 0596 **Airports:** international airports: none – helicopter services link the principality with the nearest airport, Nice (Nice-Côte d'Azur); total passenger km: 1 million (1994) **Major holidays:** 1, 27 January, 1, 8 May, 14 July, 15 August, 3 September, 1, 11, 19 November, 8, 25 December; variable: Easter Monday, Whit Monday

Chronology

1191: The Genoese took control of Monaco, which had formerly been part of the Holy Roman Empire. **1297:** Came under the rule of the Grimaldi dynasty, the current ruling family, who initially allied themselves to the French. **1524–1641:** Came under Spanish protection. **1793:** Annexed by France during French Revolutionary Wars. One member of ruling family was guillotined; the rest imprisoned. **1815:** Placed under protection of Sardinia. **1848:** The towns of Menton and Roquebrune, which had formed the greater part of the principality, seceded and later became part of France. **1861:** Franco-Monagesque treaty restored Monaco's independence under French protection; casino built. **1865:** Customs union established with France. **1918:** France given veto over succession to throne and established that if reigning prince dies without a male heir, Monaco is to be incorporated into France. **1941–45:** Occupied successively by Italians and Germans during World War II. **1949:** Prince Rainier III ascended the throne. **1956:** Prince Rainier married US actress Grace Kelly. **1958:** Birth of male heir, Prince Albert. **1959:** Constitution of 1911 suspended and National Council dissolved. **1962:** New, more liberal constitution adopted and National Council restored. **1982:** Princess Grace died in car accident. **1993:** Joined United Nations.

Mongolia State of (Outer Mongolia until 1924; People's Republic of Mongolia until 1991)

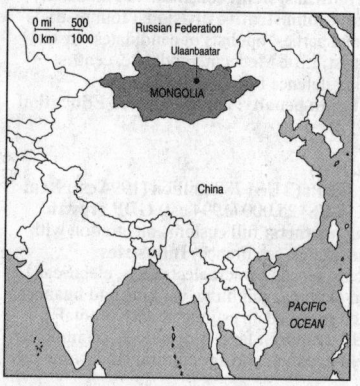

National name: *Mongol Uls* **Area:** 1,565,000 sq km/604,246 sq mi **Capital:** Ulaanbaatar (Ulan Bator) **Major towns/cities:** Darhan, Choybalsan, Erdenet **Physical features:** high plateau with desert and steppe (grasslands); Altai Mountains in SW; salt lakes; part of Gobi desert in SE; contains both the world's southernmost permafrost and northernmost desert

Government

Head of state: Natsagiyn Bagabandi from 1997 **Head of government:** Tsakhiagiin Elbegdorj from 1998 **Political system:** emergent democracy **Administrative divisions:** 18 provinces and three municipalities **Political parties:** Mongolian People's Revolutionary Party (MPRP), reform-socialist (ex-communist); Mongolian National Democratic Party (MNDP), traditionalist, promarket economy; Union Coalition (UC, comprising the MNPD and the Social Democratic Party (SDP)), democratic, promarket economy **Armed forces:** 21,000; plus a paramilitary force of around 12,500 (1996) **Conscription:** military service is compulsory for 12 months **Death penalty:** retained and used for ordinary crimes **Defence spend:** (% GDP) 1.7 (1996) **Education spend:** (% GNP) 5.2 (1994) **Health spend:** (% GDP) 1.6 (1995 est)

Economy and resources

Currency: tugrik **GDP:** ($ US) 700 million (1994) **Real GDP per capita (PPP):** ($ US) 3,766 (1994) **GDP growth rate:** 2.1%

(1994); –3.3% (1990–95) **Average annual inflation:** 100% (1006); 51.6% (1985–95) **Foreign debt:** ($ US) 512 million (1995) **Major trading partners:** Russia, China, Japan, Kazakhstan, South Korea, Germany, USA **Resources:** copper, nickel, zinc, molybdenum, phosphorites, tungsten, tin, fluorospar, gold, lead; reserves of petroleum discovered 1994 **Industries:** mostly small-scale; food products, copper and molybdenum concentrates, cement, lime, wood and metal-worked products, beverages, leather articles **Exports:** minerals and metals (primarily copper concentrate), consumer goods, foodstuffs, agricultural products. Principal market: Japan 18.7% (1995) **Imports:** engineering goods, mineral fuels and products, industrial consumer goods, foodstuffs. Principal source: Russia 52% (1995) **Arable land:** 0.8% (1995) **Agricultural products:** wheat, oats, barley, potatoes, vegetables; animal herding (particularly cattle rearing) is country's main economic activity (there were 28.6 million cattle, sheep, goats, horses, and camels 1995)

Population and society

Population: 2,515,000 (1996 est) **Population growth rate:** 2% (1990–95); 1.9% (2000–05) **Population density:** (per sq km) 2 (1996 est) **Urban population:** (% of total) 61 (1995) **Age distribution:** (% of total population) <15 38%, 15–65 58.5%, >65 3.4% (1995) **Ethnic groups:** 90% Mongol, 4% Kazakh, 2% Chinese, and 2% Russian **Language:** Khalkha Mongolian (official); Chinese, Russian, and Turkic languages **Religion:** officially none (Tibetan Buddhist Lamaism suppressed in 1930s) **Education:** (compulsory years) 8 **Literacy rate:** 88% (men); 76% (women) (1995 est) **Labour force:** 43% agriculture, 16% industry, 41% services (1995) **Unemployment:** 8.5% (1994) **Life expectancy:** 64 (men); 67 (women) (1995–2000) **Child mortality rate:** (under 5, per 1,000 live births) 68 (1996) **Physicians:** 1 per 371 people (1993 est)

Practical information

Visa requirements: UK: visa required. USA: visa required **Embassy in the UK:** 7 Kensington Court, London W8 5DL. Tel: (0171) 937 0150; fax: (0171) 937 1117 **British embassy:** PO Box 703, 30 Enkh Taivny Gudammzh, Ulaanbaatar 13. Tel: (1) 358 133; fax: (1) 358 036 **Chamber of commerce:** Mongolian Chamber of Commerce and Industry, Sambuugiyn Gudamj 11, Ulaanbaatar 38. Tel: (1) 324 620; telex: 79336 **Airports:** international airports: Ulaanbaatar (Buyant Ukha); six domestic airports; total passenger km: 491 million (1994) **Major holidays:** 1–2 January, 8 March, 1 May, 1 June, 10 July (3 days), 7 November; variable: Tsagaan (Lunar New Year, January/February, 2 days)

Chronology

AD 1206: Nomadic Mongol tribes united by Genghis Khan to form nucleus of vast Mongol Empire which, stretching across central Asia, reached its zenith under Genghis Khan's grandson, Kublai Khan. **late 17th century:** Conquered by China to become province of Outer Mongolia. **1911:** Independence proclaimed by Mongolian nationalists after Chinese 'republican revolution'; Tsarist Russia helped Mongolia to secure autonomy, under a traditionalist Buddhist monarchy in the form of a reincarnated lama. **1915:** Chinese sovereignty reasserted. **1921:** Chinese rule overthrown with Soviet help. **1924:** People's Republic proclaimed on death of king, when the monarchy was abolished; defeudalization programme launched, entailing collectivization of agriculture and suppression of Lama Buddhism. **1932:** Armed antigovernment uprising suppressed with Soviet assistance; 100,000 killed in political purges. **1946:** China recognized Mongolia's independence. **1952:** Death of Marshal Horloogiyn Choybalsan, the dominant force in the ruling communist Mongolian People's Revolutionary Party (MPRP) since 1939. **1958:** Yumjaagiyn Tsedenbal became dominant figure in MPRP and country. **1962:** Joined Comecon. **1966:** 20-year friendship, cooperation, and mutual-assistance pact signed with Soviet Union (USSR). Relations with China deteriorated. **1984:** Tsedenbal, the effective leader, retired; replaced by Jambyn Batmunkh. **1987:** Reduction in number of Soviet troops; Mongolia's external contacts broadened. Tolerance of traditional social customs encouraged nationalist revival. **1989:** Further Soviet troop reductions. **1990:** Demonstrations and democratization campaign launched, influenced by events in E Europe; Batmunkh resigned and charged with corruption. Ex-communist MPRP elected in first free multiparty elections; Punsalmaagiyn Ochirbat indirectly elected president. Mongolian script readopted. **1991:** Massive privatization programme launched. GDP declined by 10%. Ochirbat resigned from MPRP in wake of anti-Gorbachev attempted coup in USSR. **1992:** MPRP returned to power in assembly elections held under new, non-communist constitution. Economic situation worsened; GDP again declined by 10%. **1993:** Ochirbat won first direct presidential elections. **1996:** Economy showed signs of revival. Union Coalition won assembly elections, defeating MPRP and ending 75 years of communist rule. Defence cooperation agreement signed with USA. Mendsayhany Enhsayhan became prime minister. **1997:** Ex-communist Natsagiyn Bagabandi elected MPRP chairman. Economic 'shock therapy' programme, supervised by IMF and World Bank, created unemployment and made government unpopular. Bagabandi elected president. Mongolia first country to abolish all taxes and tariffs on trade.

Morocco Kingdom of

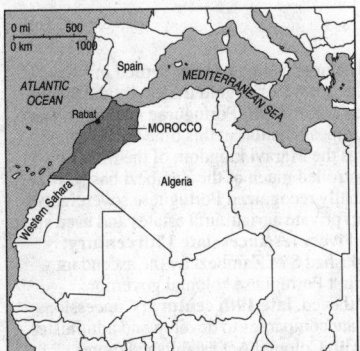

National name: *al-Mamlaka al-Maghrebia* **Area:** 458,730 sq km/177,115 sq mi (excluding Western Sahara) **Capital:** Rabat **Major towns/cities:** Casablanca, Marrakesh, Fez, Oujda, Kenitra, Tetouan, Meknès **Major ports:** Casablanca, Tangier, Agadir **Physical features:** mountain ranges, including the Atlas Mountains NE–SW; fertile coastal plains in W

Government

Head of state: Hassan II from 1961 **Head of government:** Abd al-Latif Filali from 1994 **Political system:** constitutional monarchy **Administrative divisions:** 49 provinces and prefectures with seven economic regions **Political parties:** Constitutional Union (UC), right wing; National Rally of Independents (RNI), royalist; Popular Movement (MP), moderate, centrist; Istiqlal, nationalist, centrist; Socialist Union of Popular Forces (USFP), progressive socialist; National Democratic Party (PND), moderate, nationalist **Armed forces:** 194,000; paramilitary forces of 42,000 (1996) **Conscription:** 18 months **Death penalty:** retained and used for ordinary crimes **Defence spend:** (% GDP) 4.3 (1996) **Education spend:** (% GNP) 4.8 (1994) **Health spend:** (% GDP) 1.6 (1990–95)

Economy and resources

Currency: dirham (DH) **GDP:** ($ US) 30.8 billion (1994) **Real GDP per capita (PPP):** ($ US) 3,681 (1994) **GDP growth rate:** 11.8% (1994); 1.2% (1990–95) **Average annual inflation:** 4.2 % (1996); 4.8% (1985–95) **Foreign debt:** ($ US) 23.2 billion (1996) **Major trading partners:** France, Spain, USA, Japan, UK, Italy, Iran **Resources:** phosphate rock and phosphoric acid, coal, iron ore, barytes, lead, copper, manganese, zinc, petroleum, natural gas, fish **Industries:** phosphate products (chiefly fertilizers), petroleum refining, food processing, textiles, clothing, leather goods, paper and paper products, tourism **Exports:** phosphates and phosphoric acid, mineral products, seafoods and seafood products, citrus fruit, tobacco, clothing, hosiery. Principal market: France 29.7% (1995) **Imports:** crude petroleum, raw materials, wheat, chemicals, sawn wood, consumer goods. Principal source: France 21.8% (1995)

Arable land: 19.3% (1995) **Agricultural products:** wheat, barley, sugar beet, citrus fruits, tomatoes, potatoes; fishing (seafoods)

Population and society

Population: 27,021,000 (1996 est) **Population growth rate:** 2.1% (1990–95); 1.6% (2000–05) **Population density:** (per sq km) 61 (1996 est) **Urban population:** (% of total) 48 (1995) **Age distribution:** (% of total population) <15 36.1%, 15–65 59.8%, >65 4.1% (1995) **Ethnic groups:** majority indigenous Berbers; sizeable Jewish minority **Language:** Arabic (official) 75%; Berber 25%, French, Spanish **Religion:** Sunni Muslim **Education:** (compulsory years) 6 **Literacy rate:** 61% (men); 38% (women) (1995 est) **Labour force:** 38% of population: 45% agriculture, 25% industry, 31% services (1990) **Unemployment:** 16% (1994) **Life expectancy:** 64 (men); 68 (women) (1995–2000) **Child mortality rate:** (under 5, per 1,000 live births) 76 (1996) **Physicians:** 1 per 3,790 people (1994)

Practical information

Visa requirements: UK: visa not required. USA: visa not required **Embassy in the UK:** 49 Queen's Gate Gardens, London SW7 5NE. Tel: (0171) 581 5001–4; fax: (0171) 225 3862 **British embassy:** BP 45, 17 boulevard de la Tour Hassan, Rabat. Tel: (7) 720 905/6; fax: (7) 704 531 **Chamber of commerce:** La Fédération des Chambres de Commerce et de l'Industrie du Maroc, 6 rue d'Erfoud, Rabat-Agdal. Tel: (7) 767 078; fax: (7) 767 076 **Airports:** international airports: Casablanca (Mohammed V), Rabat (Salé), Tangier (Boukhalef Sohahel), Agadir (Al Massira), Fez (Sais), Marrakesh, Oujda, Al-Hocina el-Aaiun, Ouarzazate; domestic services operate between these; total passenger km: 4,573 million (1994) **Major holidays:** 1 January, 3 March, 1, 23 May, 9 July, 14 August, 6, 18 November; variable: Eid-ul-Adha (2 days), end of Ramadan (2 days), New Year (Muslim), Prophet's Birthday

Chronology

10th–3rd centuries BC: Phoenicians from Tyre settled along N coast. **1st century AD:** NW Africa became Roman province of Mauritania. **5th–6th centuries:** Invaded by Vandals and Visigoths. **682:** Start of Arab conquest, followed by spread of Islam. **8th century:** King Idris I established small Arab kingdom. **1056–1146:** The Almoravids, a Berber dynasty based at Marrakesh, built an empire embracing Morocco and parts of Algeria and Spain. **1122–1268:** After a civil war, the Almohads, a rival Berber dynasty, overthrew the Almoravids; Almohads extended empire but later lost most of Spain. **1258–1358:** Beni Merin dynasty supplanted Almohads. **14th century:** Moroccan Empire fragmented into separate kingdoms, based in Fez and Marrakesh. **15th century:** Spain and Portugal occupied Moroccan ports; expulsion of Muslims from Spain 1492. **16th century:** Saadian dynasty restored unity of Morocco and resisted Turkish invasion. **1649:** Foundation of current Alaouite dynasty of sultans; Morocco remained independent and isolated kingdom. **1856:** Under British pressure, sultan opened Morocco to European commerce. **1860:** Spain invaded Morocco, which was forced to cede the SW region of Ifni. **1905:** Major international crisis caused by German objections to increasing French influence in Morocco. **1911:** Agadir Crisis: further German objections to French imperialism in Morocco overcome by territorial compensation in central Africa. **1912:** Morocco divided into French and Spanish protectorates; sultan reduced to puppet ruler. **1921:** Moroccan rebels, the Riffs, led by Abd el-Krim, defeated large Spanish force at Anual. **1923:** City of Tangier separated from Spanish Morocco and made a neutral international zone. **1926:** French forces crushed Riff revolt. **1944:** Nationalist party, Istiqlal, founded to campaign for full independence. **1948:** Consultative assemblies introduced. **1953–55:** Serious anti-French riots. **1956:** French and Spanish forces withdrew; Morocco regained effective independence under Sultan Muhammad V, who took title of king 1957. **1961:** Muhammad V succeeded by Hassan II. **1962:** First constitution adopted; replaced 1970 and 1972. **1965–77:** King Hassan suspended constitution and ruled by decree. **1969:** Spanish overseas province of Ifni returned to Morocco. **1975:** Spain withdrew from Western Sahara, leaving Morocco and Mauritania to divide it between themselves. **1976:** Polisario Front, supported by

Algeria, began guerrilla war in Western Sahara with aim of securing its independence as Sahrahwi Arab Democratic Republic. **1979:** Mauritania withdrew from its portion of Western Sahara, which Morocco annexed after major battles with Polisario. **1984:** Morocco signed mutual defence with Libya, which had previously supported Polisario. **1991:** UN-sponsored cease-fire came into effect in Western Sahara. **1992:** Constitution amended in attempt to increase influence of parliament. **1994:** Abd-al Latif Filali became prime minister. **1996:** New two-chamber assembly approved. **1997:** Assembly elections proved inconclusive.

Mozambique People's Republic of

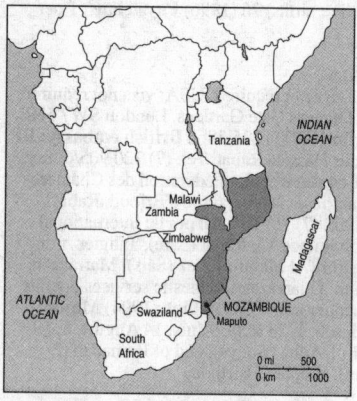

National name: *República Popular de Moçambique* **Area:** 799,380 sq km/308,640 sq mi **Capital:** Maputo (and chief port) **Major towns/cities:** Beira, Nampula, Nacala, Chimoio **Major ports:** Beira, Nacala, Quelimane **Physical features:** mostly flat tropical lowland; mountains in W; rivers Zambezi and Limpopo

Government

Head of state: Joaquim Alberto Chissano from 1986 **Head of government:** Pascoal Mocumbi from 1994 **Political system:** emergent democracy **Administrative divisions:** 10 provinces **Political parties:** National Front for the Liberation of Mozambique (Frelimo), free market; Renamo, or Mozambique National Resistance (MNR), former rebel movement, right of centre **Armed forces:** 11,000 (1996) **Conscription:** early 1996 government was seeking to reintroduce compulsory military service, which had been suspended under the General Peace Accord **Death penalty:** abolished 1990 **Defence spend:** (% GDP) 3.7 (1996) **Education spend:** (% GNP) 6.2 (1992) **Health spend:** (% GDP) 4.6 (1990–95)

Economy and resources

Currency: metical **GDP:** ($ US) 1.5 billion (1994) **Real GDP per capita (PPP):** ($ US) 986 (1994) **GDP growth rate:** 5% (1994); 7.1% (1990–95) **Average annual inflation:** 27% (1996); 52.2% (1985–95) **Foreign debt:** ($ US) 5.8 billion (1995) **Major trading partners:** Spain, South Africa, USA, Japan, Italy, India, Zimbabwe, Portugal, France **Resources:** coal, salt, bauxite, graphite; reserves of iron ore, gold, precious and semi-precious stones, marble, natural gas (all largely unexploited 1996) **Industries:** food products, steel, engineering, textiles and clothing, beverages, tobacco, chemical products **Exports:** shrimps and other crustaceans, cashew nuts, raw cotton, sugar, copra, lobsters. Principal market: Spain 16.1% (1995) **Imports:** foodstuffs, capital goods, crude petroleum and petroleum products, machinery and spare parts, chemicals. Principal source: South African 51.7% (1995) **Arable land:** 3.8% (1995) **Agricultural products:** cassava, maize, bananas, rice, groundnuts, copra, cashew nuts, cotton, sugar cane; fishing (shrimps, prawns, and lobsters) is principal export activity (42% of export earnings 1994); forest resources (eucalyptus, pine, and rare hardwoods)

Population and society

Population: 17,796,000 (1996 est) **Population growth rate:** 2.4% (1990–95); 2.8% (2000–05) **Population density:** (per sq km) 22 (1996 est) **Urban population:** (% of total) 34 (1995) **Age

distribution: (% of total population) <15 44.7%, 15–65 52%, >65 3.2% (1995) **Ethnic groups:** the majority belong to local groups, the largest being the Makua-Lomue, who comprise about 38% of the population; the other significant group is the Tsonga (24%) **Language:** Portuguese (official); 16 African languages **Religion:** animist, Roman Catholic, Muslim **Education:** (compulsory years) 7 **Literacy rate:** 64% (men); 37% (women) (1995 est) **Labour force:** 53% of population: 83% agriculture, 8% industry, 9% services (1990) **Unemployment:** 50% (1990 est) **Life expectancy:** 45 (men); 48 (women) (1995–2000) **Child mortality rate:** (under 5, per 1,000 live births) 176 (1996) **Physicians:** 1 per 36,225 people (1993 est)

Practical information

Visa requirements: UK: visa required. USA: visa required **Embassy in the UK:** 21 Fitzroy Square, London W1P 5HJ. Tel: (0171) 383 3800; fax: (0171) 383 3801 **British embassy:** Caixa Postal 55, Avenida Vladimir I Léuine 310, Maputo. Tel: (1) 420 111/2/5/6/7; fax: (1) 421 666 **Chamber of commerce:** Câmara de Comercio de Mozambique, CP 1836, Rua Mateus Sansão Mutemba 452, Maputo. Tel: (1) 491 970; telex: 6498 **Airports:** international airports: Maputo (Mavalane), Beira, Nampula; five domestic airports; total passenger km: 443 million (1994) **Major holidays:** 1 January, 3 February, 7 April, 1 May, 25 June, 7, 25 September, 25 December

Chronology

1st–4th centuries AD: Bantu-speaking peoples settled in Mozambique. **8th–15th century:** Arab gold traders established independent city-states on coast. **1498:** Portuguese navigator Vasco da Gama was the first European visitor; at this time the most important local power was the Maravi kingdom of the Mwene Matapa peoples, who controlled much of the Zambezi basin. **1626:** The Mwene Matapa formally recognized Portuguese sovereignty. Portuguese soldiers set up private agricultural estates and used slave labour to exploit gold and ivory resources. **late 17th century:** Portuguese temporarily pushed S of Zambezi by the ascendant Rozwi kingdom. **1752:** First Portuguese colonial governor appointed; slave trade outlawed. **late 19th century:** Concessions given by Portugal to private companies to develop and administer parts of Mozambique. **1930:** Colonial Act established more centralized Portuguese rule, ending concessions to monopolistic companies and forging closer integration with Lisbon. **1951:** Became an overseas province of Portugal and, economically, a cheap labour reserve for South Africa's mines. **1962:** Frelimo (National Front for the Liberation of Mozambique) established in exile in Tanzania by Marxist guerrillas, including Samora Machel, to fight for independence. **1964:** Fighting broke out between Frelimo forces and Portuguese troops, starting a ten-year liberation war; Portugal despatched 70,000 troops to Mozambique. **1969:** Eduardo Mondlane, leader of Frelimo, was assassinated. **1975:** Following revolution in Portugal, independence achieved as a socialist republic, with Machel as president, Joaquim Chissano as prime minister, and Frelimo as sole legal party; Portuguese settlers left the country. Lourenço Marques renamed Maputo. Key enterprises nationalized. **1977:** Renamo resistance group formed, with covert backing of South Africa. **1979:** Machel encouraged Patriotic Front guerrillas in Rhodesia to accept Lancaster House Agreement, creating Zimbabwe. **1983:** Good relations restored with Western powers. **1984:** Nkomati Accord of nonaggression signed with South Africa. **1986:** Machel killed in air crash near South African border; succeeded by Chissano. **1988:** Tanzanian troops withdrawn from Mozambique. **1989:** Renamo continued attacks on government facilities and civilians. **1990:** One-party rule officially ended, and Frelimo abandoned Marxist–Leninism and embraced market economy. **1992:** Peace accord signed with Renamo. **1993:** Price riots in Maputo as IMF-promoted reforms to restructure the economy devastated by war and drought were implemented. **1994:** Demobilization of contending armies completed. Chissano and Frelimo re-elected in first multiparty elections; Renamo (now a political party) agreed to cooperate with government. **1995:** Mozambique admitted to Commonwealth.

Myanmar Union of (formerly Burma)

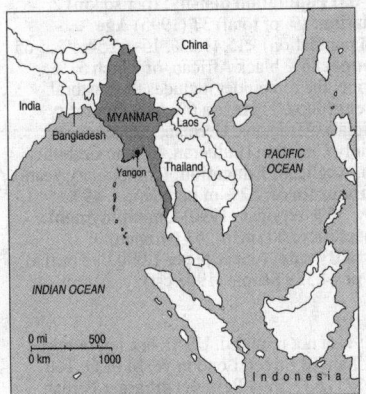

National name: *Thammada Myanmar Naingngandaw* **Area:** 676,577 sq km/261,226 sq mi **Capital:** Yangon (formerly Rangoon) (and chief port) **Major towns/cities:** Mandalay, Mawlamyine, Bago, Bassein, Taunggyi, Sittwe, Manywa **Physical features:** over half is rainforest; rivers Irrawaddy and Chindwin in central lowlands ringed by mountains in N, W, and E

Government

Head of state and government: Than Shwe from 1992 **Political system:** military republic **Administrative divisions:** seven states and seven divisions **Political parties:** National Unity Party (NUP), military-socialist ruling party; National League for Democracy (NLD), pluralist opposition grouping **Armed forces:** 321,000; plus two paramilitary units totalling 85,300 (1996) **Conscription:** military service is voluntary **Death penalty:** retained and used for ordinary crimes **Defence spend:** (% GDP) 7.6 (1996) **Education spend:** (% GNP) 2.4 (1992); N/A (1993–94) **Health spend:** (% GDP) 0.5 (1990–95)

Economy and resources

Currency: kyat **GDP:** ($ US) 79.2 billion (1994) **Real GDP per capita (PPP):** ($ US) 600 (1994) **GDP growth rate:** 6.8% (1994); 5.7% (1990–95) **Average annual inflation:** 29% (1996) **Foreign debt:** ($ US) 6.5 billion (1994) **Major trading partners:** China, Singapore, India, Japan, Malaysia, Hong Kong **Resources:** natural gas, petroleum, zinc, tin, copper, tungsten, coal, lead, gems, silver, gold **Industries:** food processing, beverages, cement, fertilizers, plywood, petroleum refining, textiles, paper, motor cars, tractors, bicycles **Exports:** teak, rice, pulses and beans, rubber, hardwood, base metals, gems, cement. Principal market: Singapore 12.9% (1995) **Imports:** raw materials, machinery and transport equipment, tools and spares, construction materials, chemicals, consumer goods. Principal source: China 31.3% (1995) **Arable land:** 14.5 (1995) **Agricultural products:** rice, sugar cane, maize, groundnuts, pulses, rubber, tobacco; fishing; forest resources (teak and hardwood) – teak is frequently felled illegally and smuggled into Thailand; cultured pearls and oyster shells are part of aquacultural fish production

Population and society

Population: 45,922,000 (1996 est) **Population growth rate:** 2.1% (1990–95); 1.9% (2000–05) **Population density:** (per sq km) 68 (1996 est) **Urban population:** (% of total) 26 (1995) **Age distribution:** (% of total population) <15 37.4%, 15–65 58.5%, >65 4.1% (1995) **Ethnic groups:** Burmans, who predominate in the fertile central river valley and southern coastal and delta regions, constitute the ethnic majority, comprising 72% of the total population. Out of more than 100 minority communities, the most important are the Karen (7%), Shan (6%), Indians (6%), Chinese (3%), Kachin (2%), and Chin (2%). The indigenous minority communities, who predominate in mountainous border regions, show considerable hostility towards the culturally and politically dominant Burmans, undermining national unity **Language:** Burmese (official), English **Religion:** Hinayāna Buddhist 85%, animist, Christian, Muslim **Education:** (compulsory years) 5

Literacy rate: 89% (men); 72% (women) (1995 est) **Labour force:** 68.7% agriculture, 9.8% industry, 21.5% services (1994) **Unemployment:** 2.1% (1994 est) **Life expectancy:** 59 (men); 62 (women) (1995–2000) **Child mortality rate:** (under 5, per 1,000 live births) 95 (1996) **Physicians:** 1 per 3,554 people (1994)

Practical information

Visa requirements: UK: visa required. USA: visa required **Embassy in the UK:** 19a Charles Street, Berkeley Square, London W1X 8ER. Tel: (0171) 629 6966; fax: (0171) 629 4169 **British embassy:** PO Box 638, 80 Strand Road, Yangon. Tel: (1) 95300; fax: (1) 89566 **Chamber of commerce:** Myanmar Foreign Trade Bank, PO Box 203, 80–86 Maha Bandoola Garden Street, Yangon. Tel: (1) 83129; fax: (1) 89585 **Airports:** international airports: Yangon (Mingaladon); 21 domestic airports; total passenger km: 140 million (1994) **Major holidays:** 4 January, 12 February, 2, 27 March, 1 April, 1 May, 19 July, 1 October, 25 December; variable: New Year (Burmese), Thingyan (April, 4 days), end of Buddhist Lent (Oct), Full Moon days

Chronology

3rd century BC: Sittoung valley settled by Mons; Buddhism introduced by missionaries from India. **3rd century AD:** Arrival of Burmans from Tibet. **1057:** First Burmese Empire established by King Anawrahta, who conquered Thaton, established a capital inland at Pagan, and adopted Theravāda Buddhism. **1287:** Pagan sacked by Mongols. **1531:** Founding of Toungoo dynasty, which survived until the mid-18th century. **1755:** Nation reunited by Alaungpaya, with port of Rangoon as capital. **1824–26:** First Anglo-Burmese war resulted in Arakan coastal strip, between Chittagong and Cape Negrais, being ceded to British India. **1852:** Following defeat in second Anglo-Burmese war, Lower Burma, including Rangoon, was annexed by British. **1886:** Upper Burma ceded to British after defeat of Thibaw in third Anglo-Burmese war; British united Burma, which was administered as a province of British India. **1886–96:** Guerrilla warfare waged against British in northern Burma. **early 20th century:** Burma developed as major rice, teak and, later, oil exporter, drawing in immigrant labourers and traders from India and China. **1937:** Became British crown colony in Commonwealth, with a degree of internal self-government. **1942:** Invaded and occupied by Japan, who installed anti-British nationalist puppet government headed by Ba Maw. **1945:** Liberated from Japanese control by British, assisted by nationalists Aung San and U Nu, formerly ministers in puppet government, who had formed the socialist Anti Fascist People's Freedom League (AFPFL). **1947:** Assassination of Aung San and six members of interim government by political opponents. **1948:** Independence achieved from Britain as Burma, with U Nu as prime minister. Left Commonwealth. Quasi-federal state established. **1958–60:** Administered by emergency government, formed by army chief of staff Gen Ne Win. **1962:** Gen Ne Win reassumed power in left-wing army coup; he proceeded to abolish federal system and follow 'Burmese Way to Socialism', involving sweeping nationalization and international isolation, which crippled the economy. **1973–74:** Adopted presidential-style 'civilian' constitution. **1975:** Opposition National Democratic Front formed by regionally-based minority groups, who mounted guerrilla insurgencies. **1987:** Student demonstrations in Rangoon as food shortages worsened. **1988:** Government resigned after violent student demonstrations and workers' riots. Gen Saw Maung seized power in military coup believed to have been organized by the ousted Ne Win; over 2,000 killed. **1989:** Martial law declared; thousands arrested including advocates of democracy and human rights. Country renamed Myanmar and capital Yangon. **1990:** Landslide victory for opposition National League for Democracy (NLD) in general election ignored by military junta; NLD leaders U Nu and Suu Kyi, the daughter of Aung San, placed under house arrest. Breakaway opposition group formed 'parallel government'. **1991:** Martial law and human-rights abuses continued. Government crackdown on Karen ethnic rebels in SE. Suu Kyi, still imprisoned, awarded Nobel Peace Prize. Pogrom against Muslim community in Arakan province in SW Myanmar. Western countries imposed sanctions. **1992:** Saw Maung replaced by Than Shwe. Several political prisoners liberated. Martial law lifted, but restrictions on political freedom remained. **1993:** Cease-fire agreed with Kachin rebels in NE. **1995:** Karen rebels forced to flee to Thailand after further military crackdown. Suu Kyi released from house arrest, but her appointment as NLD leader declared illegal. NLD boycotted constitutional convention. **1996:** Karen rebels agreed to peace talks. Suu Kyi held first party congress since her release; 200 supporters detained by government. Major demonstrations in support of Suu Kyi. **1997:** Admission to Association of South East Asian Nations (ASEAN) granted, despite US sanctions for human-rights abuses. Currency under threat from speculators. Major realigmnents within ruling military junta.

Namibia Republic of (formerly South West Africa)

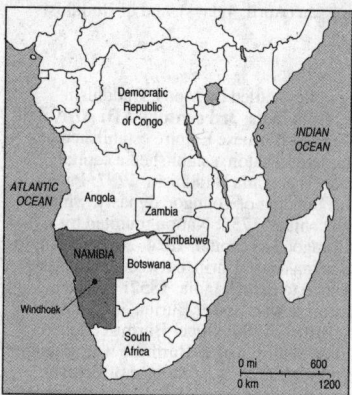

Area: 824,300 sq km/318,262 sq mi
Capital: Windhoek
Major towns/cities: Swakopmund, Rehoboth, Rundu
Major ports: Walvis Bay
Physical features: mainly desert (Namib and Kalahari); Orange River; Caprivi Strip links Namibia to Zambezi River; includes the enclave of Walvis Bay (area 1,120 sq km/432 sq mi)

Government

Head of state: Sam Nujoma from 1990 **Head of government:** Hage Geingob from 1990 **Political system:** democracy **Administrative divisions:** 13 regions **Political parties:** South West Africa People's Organization (SWAPO), socialist Ovambo-oriented; Democratic Turnhalle Alliance (DTA), moderate, multiracial coalition; United Democratic Front (UDF), disaffected ex-SWAPO members; National Christian Action (ACN), white conservative **Armed forces:** 8,100 (1996) **Conscription:** military service is voluntary **Death penalty:** abolished 1990 **Defence spend:** (% GDP) 3.0 (1996) **Education spend:** (% GNP) 8.7 (1993/94) **Health spend:** (% GDP) 3.9 (1990–95)

Economy and resources

Currency: Namibia dollar **GDP:** ($ US) 2.9 billion (1994) **Real GDP per capita (PPP):** ($ US) 4,027 (1994) **GDP growth rate:** 5.4% (1994); 3.8% (1990–95) **Average annual inflation:** 8.5% (1996); 10.5% (1985–95) **Foreign debt:** ($ US) 4.7 billion (1993) **Major trading partners:** South Africa, UK, Japan, Germany, France, USA **Resources:** uranium, copper, lead, zinc, silver, tin, gold, salt, semi-precious stones, diamonds (one of the world's leading producers of gem diamonds), hydrocarbons, lithium, manganese, tungsten, cadmium, vanadium **Industries:** food processing (fish), mining and quarrying, metal and wooden products, brewing, meat processing, chemicals, textiles, cement, leather shoes **Exports:** diamonds, fish and fish products, live animals and meat, uranium, karakul pelts. Principal market: UK 37% (1994) **Imports:** food and live animals, beverages, tobacco, transport equipment, mineral fuels, chemicals, electrical and other machinery. Principal source: South Africa 85% (1994) **Arable land:** 1% (1995) **Agricultural products:** wheat, maize, sunflower seed, sorghum, vegetables (crop farming is greatly limited by scarcity of water and poor rainfall); fishing; principal agricultural activity is livestock rearing (cattle, sheep, and goats); beef and karakul sheepskin are also produced

Population and society

Population: 1,575,000 (1996 est) **Population growth rate:** 2.7% (1990–95); 2.5% (2000–05) **Population density:** (per sq km) 2 (1996 est) **Urban population:** (% of total) 37 (1995) **Age distribution:** (% of total population) <15 41.9%, 15–65 54.4%, >65 3.7% (1995) **Ethnic groups:** 85% black African, of which 51% belong to the Ovambo tribe; the remainder includes the pastoral Nama and hunter-gatherer groups. There is a 6% white minority **Language:** English (official), Afrikaans, German, indigenous languages **Religion:** mainly Christian (Lutheran, Roman Catholic, Dutch Reformed Church, Anglican) **Education:** (compulsory years) 7 **Literacy rate:** N/A **Labour force:** 42% of population: 49% agriculture, 15% industry, 36% services (1990) **Unemployment:** 38% (1995 est) **Life expectancy:** 60 (men); 63 (women) (1995–2000) **Child mortality rate:** (under 5, per 1,000 live births) 91 (1996) **Physicians:** 1 per 4,328 people (1993 est)

Practical information

Visa requirements: UK: visa not required. USA: visa not required **Embassy in the UK:** 6 Chandos Street, London W1M 0LQ. Tel: (0171) 636 6244; fax: (0171) 637 5694 **British embassy:** British High Commission, PO Box 22202, 116 Robert Mugabe Avenue, Windhoek. Tel: (61) 223 022; fax: (61) 228 895 **Chamber of commerce:** Namibia National Chamber of Commerce and Industry, PO Box 9355, Windhoek. Tel: (61) 228 809; fax: (61) 228 009 **Airports:** international airports: Windhoek; all major towns have domestic airports or landing strips; total passenger km: 751 million (1994) **Major holidays:** 1 January, 21 March, 1, 4, 16, 25 May, 26 August, 10, 25–26 December; variable: Good Friday, Easter Monday

Chronology

1480s: Coast visited by European explorers. **16th century:** Bantu-speaking Herero migrated into NW and Ovambo settled in northernmost areas. **1840s:** Rhenish Missionary Society began to spread German influence; Jonkar Afrikaner conquest state dominant in southern Namibia. **1884:** Germany annexed most of the area, calling it South West Africa, with Britain incorporating a small enclave around Walvis Bay in the Cape Colony of South Africa. **1892:** German farmers arrived to settle in the region. **1903–04:** Uprisings by the long-settled Nama (Khoikhoi) and Herero peoples brutally repressed by Germans, with over half the local communities slaughtered. **1908:** Discovery of diamonds led to a larger influx of Europeans. **1915:** German colony invaded and seized by South Africa during World War I and the Ovambo, in the N, were conquered. **1920:** Administered by South Africa, under League of Nations mandate. **1946:** Full incorporation in South Africa refused by United Nations (UN). **1949:** White voters in South West Africa given representation in the South African parliament. **1958:** South West Africa People's Organization (SWAPO) formed to campaign for racial equality and full independence. **1960:** Radical wing of SWAPO, led by Sam Nujoma, forced into exile. **1964:** UN voted to end South Africa's mandate, but South Africa refused to relinquish control or soften its policies towards the economically disenfranchised black majority. **1966:** South Africa's apartheid laws extended to the country; 60% of land was allocated to whites, who formed 10% of the population. **1968:** South West Africa redesignated Namibia by UN; SWAPO, drawing strong support from the Ovambo people of the N, began armed guerrilla struggle against South African rule, establishing People's Liberation Army of Namibia (PLAN). **1971:** Prolonged general strike by black Namibian contract workers. **1973:** UN

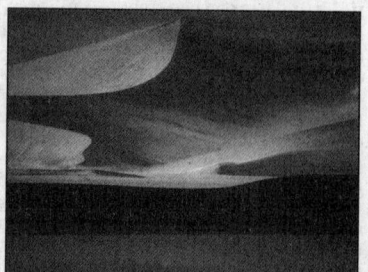

***Namib Desert,** Namibia* Premaphoto Wildlife

recognized SWAPO as the 'authentic representative of the Namibian people'. **1975–76:** Establishment of new Marxist regime in independent Angola strengthened position of SWAPO guerrilla movement, but also led to increased military involvement of South Africa in the region. **1978:** UN Security Council Resolution 435 for the granting of full independence accepted by South Africa and then rescinded. **1983:** Direct rule reimposed by Pretoria after the resignation of the Democratic Turnhalle Alliance (DTA), a conservative administration dominated by whites. **1985:** South Africa installed new puppet administration, the Transitional Government of National Unity (TGNU), which tried to reform apartheid system, but was not recognized by UN. **1988:** Peace talks between South Africa, Angola, and Cuba led to agreement on troop withdrawals and full independence for Namibia. **1989:** UN peacekeeping force stationed to oversee free elections to assembly to draft new constitution; SWAPO won the elections. **1990:** Liberal multiparty constitution adopted; independence achieved. Sam Nujoma, SWAPO's former guerrilla leader, elected president. Joined Commonwealth. **1993:** South Africa, with its new multiracial government, relinquished claim to Walvis Bay sovereignty. Namibia dollar launched with South African rand parity. **1994:** SWAPO won assembly elections; Nujoma re-elected president.

Nauru Republic of

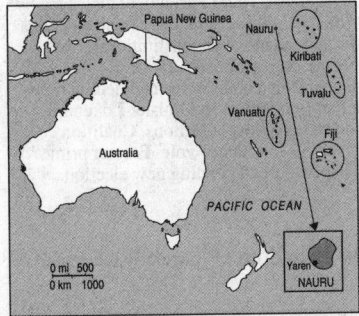

National name: *Naoero* **Area:** 21 sq km/8.1 sq mi **Capital:** (seat of government) Yaren District **Physical features:** tropical coral island in SW Pacific; plateau encircled by coral cliffs and sandy beaches

Government
Head of state and government: Kinza Klodimar from 1997 **Political system:** liberal democracy **Administrative divisions:** 14 districts **Political parties:** candidates are traditionally elected as independents, grouped into pro- and antigovernment factions; Democratic Party of Nauru (DPN), only formal political party, antigovernment **Armed forces:** no standing army; Australia is responsible for Nauru's defence **Death penalty:** retains the death penalty for ordinary crimes but can be considered abolitionist in practice (no executions since independence)

Economy and resources
Currency: Australian dollar **GDP:** ($ US) 100 million (1993 est) **Real GDP per capita (PPP):** ($ US) 10,000 (1993 est) **Average annual inflation:** –3.6% (1993) **Major trading partners:** Australia, New Zealand, Philippines, Japan **Resources:** phosphates **Industries:** phosphate mining, financial services **Exports:** phosphates. Principal market: Australia **Imports:** food and live animals, building construction materials, petroleum, machinery, medical supplies. Principal source: Australia **Agricultural products:** small-scale production; coconuts, bananas, pineapples, screw-pines, livestock rearing (pigs and chickens); almost all the country's requirements (including most of its drinking water) are imported

Population and society
Population: 11,000 (1996 est) **Population growth rate:** 2.6% (1990–95) **Population density:** (per sq km) 510 (1996 est) **Urban population:** (% of total) 100 (1995) **Ethnic groups:** about 87% of European origin (mostly British), about 9% Maori, and about 2% Pacific Islander **Language:** Nauruan (official), English **Religion:** Protestant, Roman Catholic **Education:** (compulsory years) 10

Literacy rate: 99% (men); 99% (women) (1994 est) **Life expectancy:** 64 (men); 69 (women) (1996 est) **Child mortality rate:** (per 1,000 live births) 40 (1994) **Physicians:** 1 per 700 people (1990)

Practical information
Visa requirements: UK: visa required. USA: visa required **Embassy in the UK:** Nauru Government Office, 3 Chesham Street, London SW1X 8ND. Tel: (0171) 235 6911; fax: (0171) 235 7423 **British embassy:** the British Embassy in Suva (see Fiji) deals with enquiries relating to Nauru **Chamber of commerce:** Central Bank of Nauru, PO Box 289, Nauru. Tel: 444 3238; fax: 444 3203 **Airports:** international airports: Nauru Island; total passenger km: 206 million (1994) **Major holidays:** 1, 31 January, 17 May, 1 July, 27 October, 25–26 December; variable: Good Friday, Easter Monday, Easter Tuesday

Chronology
1798: British whaler Capt John Fearn first visited Nauru and named it 'Pleasant Island'. **1830s–80s:** The island was a haven for white runaway convicts and deserters. **1888:** Annexed by Germany at the request of German settlers who sought protection from local clan unrest. **1899:** Phosphate deposits discovered; mining began eight years later, with indentured Chinese labourers brought in to work British Australian-owned mines. **1914:** Occupied by Australia on outbreak of World War I. **1920:** Administered by Australia on behalf of itself, New Zealand, and the UK until independence, except 1942–43, when occupied by Japan, and two-thirds of the population were deported briefly to Micronesia. **1951:** Local Government Council set up to replace Council of Chiefs. **1956:** Hammer DeRoburt became head chief of Nauru. **1968:** Independence achieved, with 'special member' British Commonwealth status. Hammer DeRoburt elected president. **1976:** Bernard Dowiyogo elected president as criticism of DeRoburt's personal style of government mounted. **1978:** DeRoburt re-elected. **1986:** DeRoburt briefly replaced as president by opposition leader Kennan Adeang. **1987:** Adeang established Democratic Party of Nauru. **1989:** DeRoburt replaced by Kenas Aroi, who was later succeeded by Dowiyogo. **1992:** DeRoburt died. **1994:** Australia agreed to out-of-court settlement of A$107 million, payable over 20 years, for environmental damage caused by phosphate mining which had left 80% of land agriculturally barren. **1995:** Lagumot Harris replaced Dowiyogo as president. **1996:** President Harris replaced by Bernard Dowiyogo, following general election. **1997:** President Dowiyogo defeated in confidence motion. Kinza Klodimar became president after new general election; new cabinet included former presidents Dowiyogo and Kennan Adeang.

Nepal Kingdom of

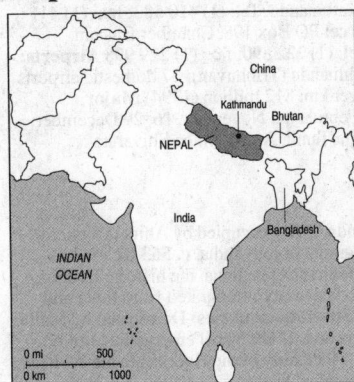

National name: *Nepal Adhirajya* **Area:** 147,181 sq km/56,826 sq mi **Capital:** Kathmandu **Major towns/cities:** Pátan, Moráng, Bhádgáon, Biratnagar, Lalitpur, Bhaktapur, Pokhara **Physical features:** descends from the Himalayan mountain range in N through foothills to the river Ganges plain in S; Mount Everest, Mount Kanchenjunga

Government
Head of state: King Birendra Bir Bikram Shah Dev from 1972 **Head of government:** Surya Bahadur Thapa from 1997 **Political**

system: constitutional monarchy **Administrative divisions:** 14 zones **Political parties:** Nepali Congress Party (NCP), left of centre; United Nepal Communist Party (UNCP; Unified Marxist–Leninist), left wing; Rashtriya Prajatantra Party (RPP), monarchist **Armed forces:** 43,000 (1996) **Conscription:** military service is voluntary **Death penalty:** laws provide for the death penalty only for exceptional crimes such as crimes under military law or crimes committed in exceptional circumstances such as wartime (last execution 1979) **Defence spend:** (% GDP) 0.9 (1996) **Education spend:** (% GNP) 2.9 (1993/94) **Health spend:** (% GDP) 1.2 (1990–95)

Economy and resources
Currency: Nepalese rupee **GDP:** ($ US) 4 billion (1994) **Real GDP per capita (PPP):** ($ US) 1,137 (1994) **GDP growth rate:** 11.1% (1994); 5.1% (1990–95) **Average annual inflation:** 6.8% (1996); 11.6% (1985–95) **Foreign debt:** ($ US) 2.4 billion (1995) **Major trading partners:** Germany, Thailand, India, Japan, Singapore, USA, Switzerland **Resources:** lignite, talcum, magnesite, limestone, copper, cobalt **Industries:** bricks and tiles, carpets, clothing, paper, cotton fabrics, cement, leather, jute goods, electrical cable, soap, edible oils, sugar, tourism **Exports:** woollen carpets, clothing, hides and skins, food grains, jute, timber, oil seeds, ghee, potatoes, medicinal herbs, cattle. Principal market: Germany 38.7% (1995) **Imports:** basic manufactures, machinery and transport equipment, chemicals, pharmaceuticals. Principal source: Thailand 10.3% (1995) **Arable land:** 20.4% (1995) **Agricultural products:** rice, maize, wheat, sugar cane, millet, potatoes, barley, tobacco, cardamoms, fruits, oil seeds; livestock rearing (cattle and pigs)

Population and society
Population: 22,021,000 (1996 est) **Population growth rate:** 2.6% (1990–95); 2.4% (2000–05) **Population density:** (per sq km) 156 (1996 est) **Urban population:** (% of total) 14 (1995) **Age distribution:** (% of total population) <15 42.4%, 15–65 54.2%, >65 3.4% (1995) **Ethnic groups:** 80% of Indo-Nepalese origin, including the Gurkhas, Paharis, Newars, and Tharus; 20% of Tibeto-Nepalese descent (concentrated in the N and E) **Language:** Nepali (official); 20 dialects spoken **Religion:** Hindu 90%; Buddhist, Muslim, Christian **Education:** (compulsory years) 5 **Literacy rate:** 38% (men); 13% (women) (1995 est) **Labour force:** 47% of population: 93% agriculture, 1% industry, 6% services (1991) **Unemployment:** 4.9% (1990) **Life expectancy:** 57 (men); 57 (women) (1995–2000) **Child mortality rate:** (under 5, per 1,000 live births) 122 (1996) **Physicians:** 1 per 13,634 people (1993)

Practical information
Visa requirements: UK: visa required. USA: visa required **Embassy in the UK:** 12a Kensington Palace Gardens, London W8 4QV. Tel: (0171) 229 1594; fax: (0171) 792 9861 **British embassy:** PO Box 106, Lainchaur, Kathmandu. Tel: (1) 410 583; fax: (1) 411 789 **Chamber of commerce:** PO Box 198, Chamber Bhavan, Kantipath, Kathmandu. Tel: (1) 222 890; fax: (1) 229 998 **Airports:** international airports: Kathmandu (Tribhuvan); 37 domestic airports and airfields; total passenger km: 812 million (1994) **Major holidays:** 11 January, 19 February, 8 November, 16, 29 December; variable: New Year (Sinhala/Tamil, April), Maha Shivarata (February/March)

Chronology
8th century BC: Kathmandu Valley occupied by Ahirs (shepherd kings), Tibeto-Burman migrants from N India. **c. 563 BC:** In Lumbini in far S, Prince Siddhartha Gautama, the historic Buddha, was born. **AD 300:** Licchavis dynasty immigrated from India and introduced caste system. **13th–16th centuries:** Dominated by Malla dynasty, great patrons of the arts. **1768:** Nepal emerged as unified kingdom after ruler of the principality of the Gurkhas in the W, King Prithwi Narayan Shah, conquered Kathmandu Valley. **1792:** Nepal's expansion halted by defeat at the hands of Chinese in Tibet; commercial treaty signed with Britain. **1815–16:** Anglo-Nepali 'Gurkha War'; Nepal became British-dependent buffer state with British resident stationed in Kathmandu. **1846:** Fell under sway of

Rana family, who became hereditary chief ministers, dominating powerless monarchy and isolating Nepal from outside world. **1923:** Full independence formally recognized by Britain. **1951:** Monarchy restored to power and Ranas overthrown in 'palace revolution' supported by Nepali Congress Party (NCP). **1959:** Constitution created elected legislature. **1960–61:** Parliament dissolved by King Mahendra; political parties banned after NCP's pro-India socialist leader B P Koirala became prime minister. **1962:** New constitution provided for tiered, traditional system of indirectly elected local councils (*panchayats*) and an appointed prime minister. **1972:** King Mahendra died; succeeded by his son, King Birendra Bikram Shah Dev. **1980:** Constitutional referendum held following popular agitation led by B P Koirala resulted in introduction of direct, but nonparty, elections to National Assembly. **1983:** Overthrow of monarch-supported prime minister by directly elected deputies to National Assembly. **1986:** New assembly elections returned majority opposed to *panchayat* system of partyless government. **1988:** Strict curbs placed on opposition activity; over 100 supporters of banned NCP arrested; censorship imposed. **1989:** Border blockade imposed by India during treaty dispute. **1990:** *Panchayat* system collapsed after mass NCP-led violent prodemocracy demonstrations; new democratic constitution introduced, and ban on political parties lifted. **1991:** Nepali Congress Party, led by Girija Prasad Koirala, won general election. **1992:** Communists led antigovernment demonstrations in Kathmandu and Pátan. **1994:** Koirala's government defeated on confidence motion; parliament dissolved. After new elections, minority communist government formed under Man Mohan Adhikari. **1995:** Parliament dissolved by King Birendra at Prime Minister Adhikari's request; fresh elections called but Supreme Court ruled the move unconstitutional. Sher Bahadur Deuba (NCP) became prime minister. **1997:** Deuba defeated in vote of confidence. New coalition formed, led by right-wing Rastriya Prajatantra Party under Prime Minister Lokendra Bahadur Chand. UCPN successes in local elections. Coalition divided; government defeated on confidence vote. Former prime minister Surya Bahadur Thapa returned pending new election.

Netherlands, the Kingdom of (popularly referred to as Holland)

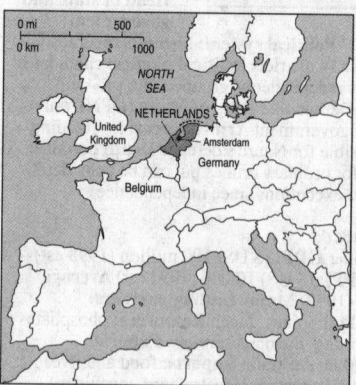

National name: *Koninkrijk der Nederlanden* **Area:** 41,863 sq km/16,163 sq mi **Capital:** Amsterdam **Major towns/cities:** Rotterdam, The Hague (seat of government), Utrecht, Eindhoven, Groningen, Tilburg, Maastricht, Haarlem, Apeldoorn, Nijmegen, Enschede **Major ports:** Rotterdam **Physical features:** flat coastal lowland; rivers Rhine, Schelde, Maas; Frisian Islands **Territories:** Aruba, Netherlands Antilles (Caribbean)

Government
Head of state: Queen Beatrix Wilhelmina Armgard from 1980 **Head of government:** Wim Kok from 1994 **Political system:** constitutional monarchy **Administrative divisions:** 12 provinces **Political parties:** Christian Democratic Appeal (CDA), Christian, right of centre; Labour Party (PvdA), democratic socialist, left of centre; People's Party for Freedom and Democracy (VVD), liberal, free enterprise; Democrats 66 (D66), ecologist, centrist; Political Reformed Party (SGP), moderate Calvinist; Evangelical Political

Federation (RPF), radical Calvinist; Reformed Political Association (GPV), fundamentalist Calvinist; Green Left, ecologist; General League of the Elderly (AOV), pensioner-oriented **Armed forces:** 63,100 (1996) **Conscription:** military service is voluntary **Death penalty:** abolished 1982 **Defence spend:** (% GDP) 2.1 (1996) **Education spend:** (% GNP) 5.5 (1993/94) **Health spend:** (% GDP) 6.9 (1994)

Economy and resources

Currency: guilder **GDP:** ($ US) 392.4 billion (1996) **Real GDP per capita (PPP):** ($ US) 20,626 (1996) **GDP growth rate:** 2.1% (1996); 1.8% (1990–95) **Average annual inflation:** 2.3% (1996); 1.7% (1985–95) **Major trading partners:** EU (principally Germany, Benelux, UK, France, and Italy), USA **Resources:** petroleum, natural gas **Industries:** electrical machinery, metal products, food processing, electronic equipment, chemicals, rubber and plastic products, petroleum refining, dairy farming, horticulture, diamond cutting **Exports:** machinery and transport equipment, foodstuffs, live animals, petroleum and petroleum products, natural gas, chemicals, plants and cut flowers, plant-derived products. Principal market: Germany 28.6% (1995) **Imports:** electrical machinery, cars and other vehicles, mineral fuels, metals and metal products, plastics, paper and cardboard, clothing and accessories. Principal source: Germany 23.4% (1995) **Arable land:** 26% (1995) **Agricultural products:** sugar beet, potatoes, wheat, barley, flax, fruit, vegetables, flowers; dairy farming

Population and society

Population: 15,575,000 (1996 est) **Population growth rate:** 0.7% (1990–95); 0.3% (2000–05) **Population density:** (per sq km) 381 (1996 est) **Urban population:** (% of total) 89 (1995) **Age distribution:** (% of total population) <15 18.4%, 15–65 68.4%, >65 13.2% (1995) **Ethnic groups:** primarily Germanic, with some Gallo-Celtic mixtures; sizeable Indonesian and Surinamese minorities **Language:** Dutch **Religion:** Roman Catholic, Dutch Reformed Church **Education:** (compulsory years) 11 **Literacy rate:** 99% (men); 99% (women) (1995 est) **Labour force:** 48.5% of population: 3.9% agriculture, 22.4% industry, 73.8% services (1996) **Unemployment:** 6.3% (1996) **Life expectancy:** 75 (men); 81 (women) (1995–2000) **Child mortality rate:** (under 5, per 1,000 live births) 8 (1996) **Physicians:** 1 per 394 people (1994)

Practical information

Visa requirements: UK: visa not required. USA: visa not required **Embassy in the UK:** 38 Hyde Park Gate, London SW7 5DP. Tel: (0171) 584 5040; fax: (0171) 581 3458 **British embassy:** Lange Voorhout 10, 2514 ED The Hague. Tel: (70) 364 5800; fax: (70) 427 0345 **Chamber of commerce:** The Hague Chamber of Commerce and Industry, Konigskade 30, 2596 AA The Hague. Tel: (70) 328 7100; fax: (70) 324 0684 **Airports:** international airports: Amsterdam (Schipol), Rotterdam (Zestienhoven), Eindhoven (Welschap), Maastricht (Beck), Groningen (Eelde), Enschede (Twente); domestic services operate between these; total passenger km: 42,435 million (1994) **Major holidays:** 1 January, 30 April, 5 May, 25–26 December; variable: Ascension Thursday, Good Friday, Easter Monday, Whit Monday

Chronology

55 BC: Julius Caesar brought lands S of Rhine under Roman rule. **4th century AD:** Region overrun by Franks and Saxons. **7th–8th centuries:** Franks subdued Saxons N of Rhine and imposed Christianity. **843–12th centuries:** Division of Holy Roman Empire: the Netherlands repeatedly partitioned, not falling clearly into either French or German kingdoms. **12th–14th centuries:** Local feudal lords, led by count of Holland and bishop of Utrecht, became practically independent; Dutch towns became prosperous trading centres, usually ruled by small groups of merchants. **15th century:** Low Countries (Holland, Belgium, and Flanders) came under rule of dukes of Burgundy. **1477:** Low Countries passed by marriage to Habsburgs. **1555:** The Netherlands passed to Spain upon division of Habsburg domains. **1568:** Dutch rebelled under leadership of William the Silent, Prince of Orange, and fought a long war of independence. **1579:** Union of Utrecht: seven northern rebel

provinces formed United Provinces. **17th century:** 'Golden Age': Dutch led world in trade, art, and science, and founded colonies in East and West Indies, primarily through Dutch East India Company, founded 1602. **1648:** Treaty of Westphalia: United Provinces finally recognized as independent Dutch Republic. **1652–54:** Commercial and colonial rivalries led to naval war with England. **1652–72:** Johann de Witt ruled Dutch Republic as premier after conflict between republicans and House of Orange. **1665–67:** Second Anglo-Dutch war. **1672–74:** Third Anglo-Dutch war. **1672:** William of Orange became stadholder (ruling as chief magistrate) of the Dutch Republic, an office which became hereditary in the Orange family. **1672–78:** The Netherlands fought to prevent domination by King Louis XIV of France. **1688–97 and 1701–13:** War with France resumed. **18th century:** Exhausted by war, the Netherlands ceased to be a Great Power. **1795:** Revolutionary France conquered the Netherlands and established Batavian Republic. **1806:** Napoleon made his brother Louis king of Holland. **1810:** France annexed the Netherlands. **1815:** Northern and southern Netherlands (Holland and Belgium) unified as Kingdom of the Netherlands under King William I of Orange, who also became grand duke of Luxembourg. **1830:** Southern Netherlands rebelled and declared independence as Belgium. **1848:** Liberal constitution adopted. **1890:** Queen Wilhelmina succeeded to throne; dynastic link with Luxembourg broken. **1894–96:** Dutch suppressed colonial revolt in Java. **1914–18:** The Netherlands neutral during World War I. **1940–45:** Occupied by Germany during World War II. **1948:** The Netherlands formed Benelux customs union with Belgium and Luxembourg; Queen Wilhelmina abdicated in favour of her daughter Juliana. **1949:** Became founding member of North Atlantic Treaty Organization (NATO); most of Dutch East Indies became independent as Indonesia after four years of war. **1953:** Dykes breached by storm; nearly two thousand people and tens of thousands of cattle died in flood. **1954:** Remaining Dutch colonies achieved internal self-government. **1958:** The Netherlands became founding member of European Economic Community (EEC). **1963:** Dutch colony of Western New Guinea ceded to Indonesia. **1975:** Dutch Guiana became independent as Suriname. **1980:** Queen Juliana abdicated in favour of her daughter Beatrix. **1994:** Following inconclusive general election, three-party coalition formed under PvdA leader Wim Kok.

New Zealand Dominion of

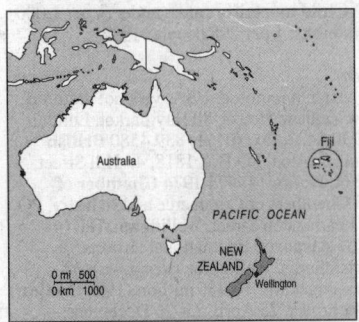

Area: 268,680 sq km/103,737 sq mi **Capital:** Wellington (and port) **Major towns/cities:** Auckland, Hamilton, Palmerston North, Christchurch, Dunedin, Napier-Hastings **Major ports:** Auckland **Physical features:** comprises North Island, South Island, Stewart Island, Chatham Islands, and minor islands; mainly mountainous; Ruapehu in North Island, 2,797 m/9,180 ft, highest of three active volcanoes; geysers and hot springs of Rotorua district; Lake Taupo (616 sq km/238 sq mi), source of Waikato River; Kaingaroa state forest. In South Island are Southern Alps and Canterbury Plains **Territories:** Tokelau (three atolls transferred 1926 from former Gilbert and Ellice Islands colony); Niue Island (one of the Cook Islands, separately administered from 1903: chief town Alafi); Cook Islands are internally self-governing but share common citizenship with New Zealand; Ross Dependency in Antarctica

Government

Head of state: Queen Elizabeth II from 1952, represented by governor general Catherine Tizard from 1990 **Head of government:** Jenny Shipley from 1997 **Political system:** constitutional monarchy **Administrative divisions:** 93 counties, 12 regions, and 6 territorial authorities **Political parties:** Labour Party, moderate, left of centre; New Zealand National Party, free enterprise, centre right; Alliance Party bloc, left of centre, ecologists; New Zealand First Party (NZFP), centrist; United New Zealand Party (UNZ), centrist **Armed forces:** 9,900; around 6,700 reserves (1996) **Conscription:** military service is voluntary **Death penalty:** abolished 1989 **Defence spend:** (% GDP) 1.3 (1996) **Education spend:** (% GNP) 7.3 (1993/94) **Health spend:** (% GDP) 5.9 (1993)

Economy and resources

Currency: New Zealand dollar **GDP:** ($ US) 65.1 billion (1996) **Real GDP per capita (PPP):** ($ US) 17,264 (1996) **GDP growth rate:** 1.2% (1996); 3.6% (1990–95) **Average annual inflation:** 1.1% (1996); 3.9% (1985–95) **Major trading partners:** Australia, USA, Japan, UK **Resources:** coal, clay, limestone, dolomite, natural gas, hydroelectric power, pumice, iron ore, gold, forests **Industries:** food processing, machinery, textiles and clothing, fishery, wood and wood products, paper and paper products, metal products; farming, particularly livestock and dairying, cropping, fruit growing, horticulture **Exports:** meat, dairy products, wool, fish, timber and wood products, fruit and vegetables, aluminium, machinery. Principal market: Australia 20.3% (1995) **Imports:** machinery and mechanical appliances, vehicles and aircraft, petroleum, fertilizer, consumer goods. Principal source: Australia 23.5% (1995) **Arable land:** 5.9% (1995) **Agricultural products:** barley, wheat, maize, fodder crops, exotic timber, fruit (kiwi fruit and apples); livestock and dairy farming

Population and society

Population: 3,602,000 (1996 est) **Population growth rate:** 1.2% (1990–95); 0.8% (2000–05) **Population density:** (per sq km) 13 (1996 est) **Urban population:** (% of total) 86 (1995) **Age distribution:** (% of total population) <15 23.4%, 15–65 65.3%, >65 11.3% (1995) **Ethnic groups:** around 87% of European origin, 9% Maori, 2% Pacific Islander **Language:** English (official), Maori **Religion:** Christian **Education:** (compulsory years) 11 **Literacy rate:** 99% (men); 99% (women) (1995 est) **Labour force:** 49.6% of population: 9.5% agriculture, 24.6% industry, 65.9% services (1996) **Unemployment:** 6.1% (1996) **Life expectancy:** 73 (men); 79 (women) (1995–2000) **Child mortality rate:** (under 5, per 1,000 live births) 10 (1996) **Physicians:** 1 per 298 people (1994)

Practical information

Visa requirements: UK: visa not required. USA: visa not required **Embassy in the UK:** New Zealand House, 80 Haymarket, London SW1Y 4TQ. Tel: (0171) 930 8422; fax: (0171) 839 4580 **British embassy:** British High Commission, PO Box 1818, 44 Hill Street, Wellington 1. Tel: (4) 472 6049; fax: (4) 471 1974 **Chamber of commerce:** New Zealand Chambers of Commerce and Industry, PO Box 1590, 9th Floor, 109 Featherston Street, Wellington. Tel: (4) 472 2725; fax: (4) 471 1767 **Airports:** international airports: Auckland (Mangere), Christchurch, Wellington (Rongotai); 32 domestic airports; total passenger km: 16,946 million (1994) **Major holidays:** 1, 2 January, 6 February, 25 April, 25–26 December; variable: Good Friday, Easter Monday, Queen's Birthday (June), Labour (October)

Chronology

1642: Dutch explorer Abel Tasman reached New Zealand but indigenous Maoris prevented him from going ashore. **1769:** English explorer James Cook surveyed coastline of islands. **1773 and 1777:** Cook again explored coast. **1815:** First British missionaries arrived in New Zealand. **1826:** New Zealand Company founded in London to establish settlement. **1839:** New Zealand Company relaunched, after initial failure, by Edward Gibbon Wakefield. **1840:** Treaty of Waitangi: Maoris accepted British sovereignty; colonization began and large-scale sheep farming developed. **1845–47:** Maori revolt against loss of

land. **1851:** Became separate colony (was originally part of Australian colony of New South Wales). **1852:** Colony procured constitution after dissolution of New Zealand Company; self-government fully implemented 1856. **1860–72:** Second Maori revolt led to concessions, including representation in parliament. **1891:** New

Auckland, New Zealand New Zealand Tourist Board

Zealand took part in Australasian Federal Convention in Sydney but rejected idea of joining Australian Commonwealth. **1893:** Became first country to give women the right to vote in parliamentary elections. **1898:** Liberal government under Richard Seddon introduced pioneering old-age pension scheme. **1899–1902:** Volunteers from New Zealand fought alongside imperial forces in Boer War. **1907:** New Zealand achieved dominion status within British Empire. **1912–25:** Government of Reform Party, led by William Massey, reflected interests of North Island farmers and strongly supported imperial unity. **1914–18:** 130,000 New Zealanders fought for British Empire in World War I. **1916:** Labour Party of New Zealand established. **1931:** Statute of Westminster affirmed equality of status between Britain and dominions, effectively granting independence to New Zealand. **1935–49:** Labour governments of Michael Savage and Peter Fraser introduced social reforms and encouraged state intervention in industry. **1936:** Liberal Party merged with Reform Party to create National Party. **1939–45:** New Zealand troops fought in World War II, notably in Crete, N Africa, and Italy. **1947:** Parliament confirmed independence of New Zealand within British Commonwealth. **1951:** New Zealand joined Australia and USA in ANZUS Pacific security treaty. **1965–72:** New Zealand contingent took part in Vietnam War. **1973:** British entry into European Economic Community (EEC) forced New Zealand to seek closer trading relations with Australia. **1985:** Non-nuclear military policy led to disagreements with France and USA. **1986:** USA suspended defence obligations to New Zealand after it banned entry of US warships. **1988:** Free-trade agreement signed with Australia. **1992:** Ban on entry of US warships lifted. **1996:** Inconclusive general election result; coalition formed, led by Jim Bolger. **1997:** Bolger replaced as National Party leader and prime minister by Jenny Shipley. **1998:** In an unprecedented move, the government was ordered to return over NZ $6.1 million/£2 million worth of land to its original Maori owners.

Nicaragua Republic of

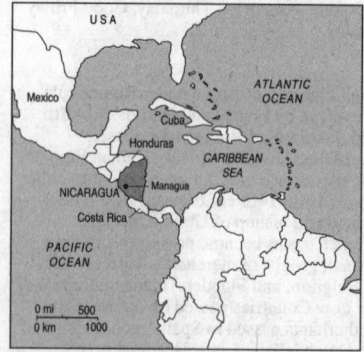

National name: *República de Nicaragua* **Area:** 127,849 sq km/49,362 sq mi **Capital:** Managua **Major towns/cities:** León, Chinandega, Masaya, Granada **Major ports:** Corinto, Puerto Cabezas, El Bluff **Physical features:** narrow Pacific coastal plain separated from broad Atlantic coastal plain by volcanic mountains and lakes Managua and Nicaragua; one of world's most active earthquake regions

Government

Head of state and government: Arnoldo Aleman from 1996
Political system: emergent democracy **Administrative divisions:**
16 departments **Political parties:** Sandinista National Liberation
Front (FSLN), Marxist–Leninist; Opposition Political Alliance
(APO, formerly National Opposition Union: UNO), loose US-
backed coalition **Armed forces:** 17,000 (1996) **Conscription:**
military service is voluntary (since 1990) **Death penalty:** abolished
1979 **Defence spend:** (% GDP) 1.5 (1996) **Education spend:** (%
GNP) 3.7 (1994) **Health spend:** (% GDP) 4.3 (1990–95)

Economy and resources

Currency: cordoba **GDP:** ($ US) 1.8 billion (1994) **Real GDP per
capita (PPP):** ($ US) 1,580 (1994) **GDP growth rate:** 2.5%
(1994); 1.1% (1990–95) **Average annual inflation:** 11.7% (1996);
963.7% (1985–95) **Foreign debt:** ($ US) 4.4 billion (1996) **Major
trading partners:** USA, Germany, Japan, Canada, Cuba, Costa
Rica, Venezuela **Resources:** gold, silver, copper, lead, antimony,
zinc, iron, limestone, gypsum, marble, bentonite **Industries:** food
products, beverages, petroleum refining, chemicals, metallic
products, processed leather, cement **Exports:** coffee, meat, cotton,
sugar, seafood, bananas, chemical products. Principal market: USA
46.7% (1995) **Imports:** machinery and transport equipment, food
and live animals, consumer goods, mineral fuels and lubricants,
basic manufactures, chemicals and related products. Principal
source: USA 26.3% (1995) **Arable land:** 20.2% (1995)
Agricultural products: coffee, cotton, sugar cane, bananas, maize,
rice, beans, green tobacco; livestock rearing (cattle and pigs);
fishing; forest resources

Population and society

Population: 4,238,000 (1996 est) **Population growth rate:** 3.7%
(1990–95); 2.8% (2000–05) **Population density:** (per sq km) 33
(1996 est) **Urban population:** (% of total) 63 (1995) **Age
distribution:** (% of total population) <15 46%, 15–65 50.9%, >65
3.1% (1995) **Ethnic groups:** over 70% of mixed Indian, Spanish,
and African origin; about 9% African; 5% Indian **Language:**
Spanish (official), Indian, English **Religion:** Roman Catholic 95%
Education: (compulsory years) 6 **Literacy rate:** 64% (men); 66%
(women) (1995 est) **Labour force:** 34% of population: 28%
agriculture, 26% industry, 46% services (1990) **Unemployment:**
15% (1992) **Life expectancy:** 67 (men); 70 (women) (1995–2000)
Child mortality rate: (under 5, per 1,000 live births) 66 (1996)
Physicians: 1 per 1,566 people (1993)

Practical information

Visa requirements: UK: visa not required for a stay of up to 90
days. USA: visa not required for a stay of up to 90 days **Embassy in
the UK:** 2nd Floor, 36 Upper Brook Street, London W1Y 1PE. Tel:
(0171) 409 2536; fax: (0171) 409 2593 **British embassy:** Apartado
A-169, El Reparto 'Los Robles', Primera Etapa, Entrada principal
de la Carretera a Massaya, 4a Casa a Mano Derecha, Managua. Tel:
(2) 780 014; fax: (2) 784 085 **Chamber of commerce:** Cámara de
Comercio de Nicaragua, Apartado 135, Frente a Lotería Popular, C
C Managua JR. Tel: (2) 670 718 **Airports:** international airports:
Managua (Augusto Cesar Sandino); total passenger km: 72 million
(1994) **Major holidays:** 1 January, 1 May, 19 July, 14–15
September, 8, 25 December; variable: Good Friday, Holy Thursday

Chronology

10th century AD: Indians from Mexico and Mesoamerica migrated
to Nicaragua's Pacific lowlands. **1522:** Visited by Spanish explorer
Gil Gonzalez de Avila, who named the area Nicaragua after local
Indian chief, Nicarao. **1523–24:** Colonized by the Spanish, under
Francisco Hernandez de Cordoba, who was attracted by local gold
deposits and founded cities of Granada and León. **17th–18th
centuries:** British were dominant force on Caribbean side of
Nicaragua, while Spain controlled Pacific lowlands. **1821:**
Independence achieved from Spain; Nicaragua was initially part of
Mexican Empire. **1823:** Became part of United Provinces
(Federation) of Central America, also embracing Costa Rica, El
Salvador, Guatemala, and Honduras. **1838:** Became fully independent
when it seceded from the Federation. **1857–93:** Ruled by succession

of Conservative Party governments. **1860:** The British ceded control
over Caribbean ('Mosquito') Coast to Nicaragua. **1893:** Liberal Party
leader, José Santos Zelaya, deposed Conservative president and
established dictatorship which lasted until overthrown by US marines
in 1909. **1912–25:** At Nicaraguan government's request, with political
situation deteriorating, USA established military bases and stationed
marines. **1927–33:** Re-stationed US marines faced opposition from
anti-American guerrilla group led by Augusto César Sandino, who
was assassinated 1934 on the orders of the commander of the US-
trained National Guard, Gen Anastasio Somoza Garcia. **1937:** Gen
Somoza elected president; start of near-dictatorial rule by Somoza
family, which amassed huge personal fortune. **1956:** Gen Somoza
assassinated and succeeded as president by his elder son, Luis
Somoza Debayle. **1961:** Left-wing Sandinista National Liberation
Front (FSLN) formed to fight Somoza regime. **1967:** Luis Somoza
died and was succeeded as president by his brother Anastasio Somoza
Debayle, who headed an even more oppressive regime. **1978:**
Nicaraguan Revolution: Pedro Joaquin Chamorro, a popular publisher
and leader of anti-Somoza Democratic Liberation Union (UDEL),
was assassinated, sparking general strike and mass movement in
which moderates joined with FSLN to overthrow Somoza regime.
1979: Somoza government ousted by FSLN after military offensive.
1980: Anastasio Somoza assassinated in Paraguay; FSLN junta took
power in Managua, headed by Daniel Ortega Saavedra; lands held by
Somozas were nationalized and farming cooperatives established.
1982: Subversive activity against government by right-wing Contra
guerrillas promoted by USA and attacking from bases in Honduras.
State of emergency declared. **1984:** US troops mined Nicaraguan
harbours. Action condemned by World Court 1986 and $17 billion in
reparations ordered. FSLN won assembly elections. **1985:**
Denunciation of Sandinista government by US president Ronald
Reagan, who vowed to 'remove it' and imposed US trade embargo.
1987: Central American peace agreement cosigned by Nicaraguan
leaders. **1988:** Peace agreement failed. Nicaragua held talks with
Contra rebel leaders. Hurricane left 180,000 people homeless. **1989:**
Demobilization of rebels and release of former Somozan supporters;
cease-fire ended but economy in ruins after Contra war; 60%
unemployment. **1990:** FSLN defeated by right-of-centre National
Opposition Union (UNO), a US-backed coalition; Violeta Barrios de
Chamorro, widow of the murdered Pedro Joaquin Chamorro, elected
president. Antigovernment riots. **1992:** Around 16,000 made
homeless by earthquake. **1994:** Peace accord with remaining Contra
rebels. **1996:** Right-wing candidate Arnoldo Aleman won presidential
elections.

Niger Republic of

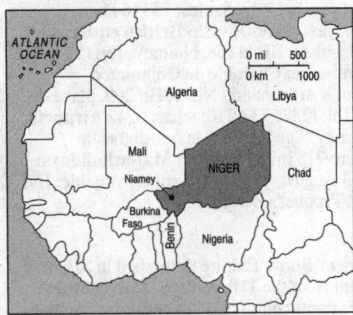

National name:
République du Niger
Area: 1,186,408 sq
km/458,072 sq mi
Capital: Niamey
Major towns/cities:
Zinder, Maradi,
Tahoua, Agadez, Birui
N'Konui **Physical
features:** desert plains
between hills in N and
savanna in S; river
Niger in SW, Lake
Chad in SE

Government

Head of state: Ibrahim Barre Mainassara from 1996 **Head of
government:** Amadou Boubacar Cisse from 1997 **Political system:**
transitional **Administrative divisions:** seven regions and the
municipality of Niamey **Political parties:** National Movement for a
Development Society (MNSD–Nassara), left of centre; Alliance of
the Forces for Change (AFC), left-of-centre coalition; Party for

Democracy and Socialism–Tarayya (PNDS–Tarayya), left of centre **Armed forces:** 5,300; plus paramilitary forces of 5,400 (1996) **Conscription:** conscription is selective for two years **Death penalty:** retains the death penalty for ordinary crimes but can be considered abolitionist in practice (last known execution 1976) **Defence spend:** (% GDP) 0.9 (1996) **Education spend:** (% GNP) 3.1 (1993/94) **Health spend:** (% GDP) 2.2 (1990–95)

Economy and resources

Currency: franc CFA **GDP:** ($ US) 1.5 billion (1994) **Real GDP per capita (PPP):** ($ US) 787 (1994) **GDP growth rate:** 2.6% (1994); 0.5% (1990–95) **Average annual inflation:** 7.5% (1996); 1.3% (1985–95) **Foreign debt:** ($ US) 1.63 billion (1995) **Major trading partners:** France, Nigeria, Japan, USA, Côte d'Ivoire, Spain **Resources:** uranium (one of world's leading producers), phosphates, gypsum, coal, cassiterite, tin, salt, gold; deposits of other minerals (including petroleum, iron ore, copper, lead, diamonds, and tungsten) have been confirmed **Industries:** processing of agricultural products, textiles, furniture, chemicals, brewing, cement **Exports:** uranium ore, live animals, hides and skins, cow-peas, cotton. Principal market: EU 75.2% (1994) **Imports:** machinery and transport equipment, miscellaneous manufactured articles, cereals, chemicals, refined petroleum products. Principal source: EU 33% (1994) **Arable land:** 3.9% (1995) **Agricultural products:** millet, maize, sorghum, groundnuts, cassava, sugar cane, sweet potatoes, cotton; livestock rearing (cattle and sheep) is especially important among the nomadic population; agricultural production is dependent upon adequate rainfall

Population and society

Population: 9,465,000 (1996 est) **Population growth rate:** 3.4% (1990–95); 3.2% (2000–05) **Population density:** (per sq km) 7 (1996 est) **Urban population:** (% of total) 17 (1995) **Age distribution:** (% of total population) <15 48.4%, 15–65 49.2%, >65 2.4% (1995) **Ethnic groups:** three ethnic groups make up over 75% of the population: the Hausa (mainly in central areas and the S), Djerma-Songhai (SW), and Beriberi-Manga (E); there is also a significant number of the mainly nomadic Fulani people, and the Tuareg in the N **Language:** French (official), Hausa, Djerma, and other minority languages **Religion:** Sunni Muslim; also Christian, and traditional animist beliefs **Education:** (compulsory years) 8 **Literacy rate:** 40% (men); 17% (women) (1995 est) **Labour force:** 49% of population: 90% agriculture, 4% industry, 6% services **Unemployment:** 20.9% (1991) **Life expectancy:** 47 (men); 50 (women) (1995–2000) **Child mortality rate:** (under 5, per 1,000 live births) 182 (1996) **Physicians:** 1 per 53,986 people (1993 est)

Practical information

Visa requirements: UK: visa required. USA: visa required **Embassy for the UK:** 154 rue du Longchamps, 75116 Paris, France. Tel: (1) 4504 8060; fax: (1) 4504 6226 **British embassy:** Honorary British Vice-Consulate, BP 11168, Niamey. Tel: (227) 732 015/539 **Chamber of commerce:** Chambre de Commerce, d'Agriculture, d'Industrie et d'Artisanat du Niger, BP 209, place de la Concertation, Niamey. Tel: (227) 732 210; telex: 5242 **Airports:** international airports: Niamey, Agadez; four major domestic airports; total passenger km: 215 million (1994) **Major holidays:** 1 January, 15 April, 1 May, 3 August, 18, 25 December; variable: Eid-ul-Adha, end of Ramadan, Prophet's Birthday

Chronology

10th–13th centuries: Kanem-Bornu Empire flourished in SE, near Lake Chad, spreading Islam from the 11th century. **15th century:** Tuareg sultanate of Agades dominant in N. **17th century:** Songhai-speaking Djerma established an empire on Niger river. **18th century:** Powerful Gobir kingdom founded by Hausa people, who had migrated from S in 14th century. **late 18th–early 19th centuries:** Visited by European explorers, including the Scottish explorer, Mungo Park; Sultanate of Sokoto formed by Islamic revivalist Fulani, who had defeated the Hausa in a jihad (holy war). **1890s:** French conquered region and ended local slave trade. **1904:** Became part of French West Africa, although Tuareg resistance continued until 1922. **1946:** Became French overseas territory, with

its own territorial assembly and representation in French Parliament. **1958:** Became autonomous republic within French community. **1960:** Achieved full independence; Hamani Diori of Niger Progressive Party (NPP) elected president, but maintained close ties with France. **1971:** Uranium production commenced. **1974:** Diori ousted in army coup led by Lt-Col Seyni Kountché after long Sahel drought had led to civil disorder; military government launched drive against corruption. **1977:** Cooperation agreement signed with France. **1984:** Partial privatization of state firms as a result of further drought and increased government indebtedness as world uranium prices slumped. **1987:** Kountché died; replaced by Gen Ali Saibu. **1989:** Ali Saibu elected president without opposition. **1991:** Saibu stripped of executive powers, and transitional government formed amid student and industrial unrest. **1992:** Transitional government collapsed amid economic problems and ethnic unrest among secessionist-minded Tuareg in N. Referendum approved of new multiparty constitution. **1993:** Alliance of the Forces for Change (AFC) left-of-centre coalition won absolute majority in assembly elections. Mahamane Ousmane, a Muslim Hausa, elected president in first free presidential election. **1994:** Peace agreement with northern Tuareg. **1995:** AFC coalition won general election with reduced majority. **1996:** President Ousmane ousted in military coup led by Ibrahim Barre Mainassara. Civilian government restored with Boukary Adji as premier; Mainassara formally elected president amidst claims of electoral fraud. **1997:** Amadou Boubacar Cisse appointed prime minister.

Nigeria Federal Republic of

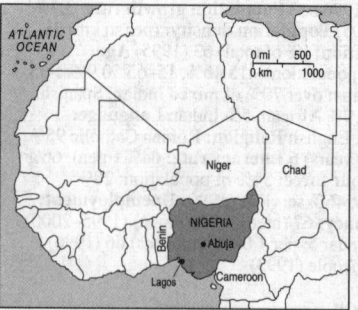

Area: 923,773 sq km/356,668 sq mi **Capital:** Abuja **Major towns/cities:** Ibadan, Lagos, Ogbomosho, Kano, Oshogbo, Ilorin, Abeokuta, Zaria, Ouitsha, Iwo, Kaduna **Major ports:** Lagos, Port Harcourt, Warri, Calabar **Physical features:** arid savanna in N; tropical rainforest in S, with mangrove swamps along coast; river Niger forms wide delta; mountains in SE

Government

Head of state and government: General Abdulsalam Abubakar from 1998 **Political system:** military republic **Administrative divisions:** 30 states and a Federal Capital Territory **Political parties:** Social Democratic Party (SDP), left of centre; National Republican Convention (NRC), right of centre (all parties dissolved on resumption of military rule 1992) **Armed forces:** 77,100 (1996) **Conscription:** military service is voluntary **Death penalty:** retained and used for ordinary crimes **Defence spend:** (% GDP) 3.5 (1996) **Education spend:** (% GNP) 1.3 (1993/94) **Health spend:** (% GDP) 1.2 (1990)

Economy and resources

Currency: naira **GDP:** ($ US) 35.2 billion (1994) **Real GDP per capita (PPP):** ($ US) 1,351 (1994) **GDP growth rate:** 1.3% (1994); 1.6% (1990–95) **Average annual inflation:** 35% (1996); 33% (1985–95) **Foreign debt:** ($ US) 38.5 billion (1996) **Major trading partners:** USA, UK, Germany, France, Spain, the Netherlands, Italy **Resources:** petroleum, natural gas, coal, tin, iron ore, uranium, limestone, marble, forest **Industries:** food processing, brewing, petroleum refinery, iron and steel, motor vehicles (using imported components), textiles, cigarettes, footwear, pharmaceuticals, pulp and paper, cement **Exports:** petroleum, cocoa beans, rubber, palm products, urea and ammonia, fish. Principal market: USA 39.4% (1995) **Imports:** machinery and transport equipment, basic manufactures, cereals, chemicals, foodstuffs. Principal source: UK 13.4% (1995) **Arable land:** 33.3% (1995) **Agricultural products:** cocoa, groundnuts, oil palm, rubber, rice, maize, taro, yams, cassava, sorghum, millet, plantains; livestock (principally goats, sheep, cattle, and poultry) and fisheries

Population and society
Population: 115,020,000 (1996 est) **Population growth rate:** 3% (1990–95); 2.7% (2000–05) **Population density:** (per sq km) 125 (1996 est) **Urban population:** (% of total) 39 (1995) **Age distribution:** (% of total population) <15 46.5%, 15–65 51.7%, >65 2.8% (1995) **Ethnic groups:** over 250 tribal groups; major tribes include the Hausa and Fulani in N, Yoruba in S, and Ibo in E **Language:** English (official), Hausa, Ibo, Yoruba **Religion:** Sunni Muslim 50% (in N), Christian 40% (in S), local religions 10% **Education:** (compulsory years) 6 **Literacy rate:** 62% (men); 39% (women) (1995 est) **Labour force:** 40% of population: 43% agriculture, 7% industry, 50% services (1990) **Unemployment:** 3.4% (1992) **Life expectancy:** 51 (men); 54 (women) (1995–2000) **Child mortality rate:** (under 5, per 1,000 live births) 146 (1996) **Physicians:** 1 per 5,208 people (1993 est)

Practical information
Visa requirements: UK: visa required. USA: visa required **Embassy in the UK:** Nigeria House, 9 Northumberland Avenue, London WC2N 5BX. Tel: (0171) 839 1244; fax: (0171) 839 8746 **British embassy:** British High Commission, Private Mail Bag 12136, 11 Eleke Crescent, Victoria Island, Lagos. Tel: (1) 619 531; fax: (1) 666 909 **Chamber of commerce:** The Nigerian Association of Chambers of Commerce, Industry, Mines and Agriculture; Private Mail Bag 12816; 15a Ikorodu Road, Maryland, Lagos. Tel: (1) 496 4737; telex 21368 **Airports:** international airports: Lagos (Murtala Mohammed), Kano, Abuja, Port Harcourt, Calabar; 14 domestic airports; total passenger km: 985 million (1994) **Major holidays:** 1 January, 1 May, 1 October, 25–26 December; variable: Eid-ul-Adha (2 days), end of Ramadan (2 days), Good Friday, Easter Monday, Prophet's Birthday

Chronology
4th century BC–2nd century AD: Highly organized Nok culture flourished in N Nigeria. **9th century:** NE Nigeria became part of empire of Kanem-Bornu, based around Lake Chad. **11th century:** Creation of Hausa states, including Kano and Katsina. **13th century:** Arab merchants introduced Islam in N. **15th century:** Empire of Benin at its height in S; first contact with European traders. **17th century:** Oyo Empire dominant in SW; development of slave trade in Niger delta. **1804–17:** Islamic Fulani (or Sokoto) Empire established in N. **1861:** British traders procured Lagos; spread of Christian missionary activity in S. **1884–1904:** Britain occupied most of Nigeria by stages. **1914:** N and S protectorates united; growth of railway network and trade. **1946:** Nigerians allowed a limited role in decision-making in three regional councils (N, W, and E). **1951:** Introduction of elected representation led to formation of three regional political parties. **1954:** New constitution increased powers of regions. **1958:** Oil discovered in SE. **1960:** Achieved independence from Britain, within Commonwealth; breakdown of law and order amid growing ethnic and regional conflict. **1963:** Became a republic, with Nnamdi Azikiwe as president. **1966:** Gen Aguiyi-Ironsi of Ibo tribe seized power and imposed unitary government; massacre of Ibo by Hausa in N; Gen Gowon seized power and restored federalism. **1967:** Conflict over oil revenues led to secession of eastern region as independent Ibo state of Biafra; ensuing civil war claimed up to a million lives. **1970:** Surrender of Biafra and end of civil war; development of oil industry financed more effective central government. **1975:** Gowon ousted in military coup; second coup put Gen Olusegun Obasanjo in power. **1979:** Civilian rule restored under President Shehu Shagari. **1983:** Bloodless coup staged by Maj-Gen Muhammadu Buhari; economy suffered as a result of falling oil prices. **1985:** Buhari replaced by Maj-Gen Ibrahim Babangida; Islamic northerners dominant in regime. **1989:** Ban on political activity lifted; two official non-regional political parties created. **1992:** Multiparty elections won by Babangida's SDP. **1993:** Moshood Abiola (SDP) won first free

presidential election; results suspended. Gen Sani Abacha restored military rule and dissolved political parties. **1995:** Commonwealth membership suspended in protest at human-rights abuses by military regime. **1998:** Gen Abdulsalam Abubakar took over as president following the death of Gen Abacha. July: Nigeria's most prominent political prisoner, Moshood Abiola, died of a heart attack, sparking riots in Lagos and other cities.

Norway Kingdom of

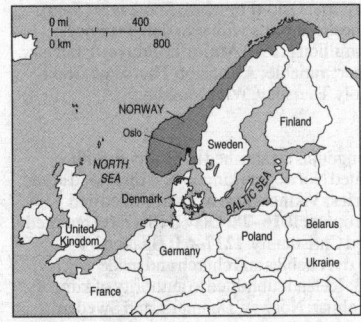

National name: *Kongeriket Norge* **Area:** 387,000 sq km/149,420 sq mi (includes Svalbard and Jan Mayen) **Capital:** Oslo **Major towns/cities:** Bergen, Trondheim, Stavanger, Kristiansand, Drammen **Physical features:** mountainous with fertile valleys and deeply indented coast; forests cover 25%; extends N of Arctic Circle **Territories:** dependencies in the Arctic (Svalbard and Jan Mayen) and in Antarctica (Bouvet and Peter I Island, and Queen Maud Land)

Government
Head of state: Harald V from 1991 **Head of government:** Kjell Magne Bondevik from 1997 **Political system:** constitutional monarchy **Administrative divisions:** 19 counties **Political parties:** Norwegian Labour Party (DNA), moderate left of centre; Conservative Party, progressive, right of centre; Christian People's Party (KrF), Christian, centre left; Centre Party (Sp), left of centre, rural-oriented; Progress Party (FrP), right wing, populist **Armed forces:** 30,000 (1996); 255,000 reservists (1996) **Conscription:** 12 months, with 4–5 refresher training periods **Death penalty:** abolished 1979 **Defence spend:** (% GDP) 2.4 (1996) **Education spend:** (% GNP) 9.2 (1993/94) **Health spend:** (% GDP) 7.6 (1993)

Economy and resources
Currency: Norwegian krone **GDP:** ($ US) 156.2 billion (1996) **Real GDP per capita (PPP):** ($ US) 24,169 (1996) **GDP growth rate:** 0.4% (1996); 3.5% (1990–95) **Average annual inflation:** 2.2% (1996); 3.1% (1985–95) **Major trading partners:** EU (principally UK and Sweden), USA, Japan **Resources:** petroleum, natural gas, iron ore, iron pyrites, copper, lead, zinc, forests **Industries:** mining, fishery, food processing, non-electrical machinery, metals and metal products, paper products, printing and publishing, shipbuilding, chemicals **Exports:** petroleum, natural gas, fish products, non-ferrous metals, wood pulp and paper. Principal market: UK 19.8% (1995) **Imports:** machinery and transport equipment, chemicals, clothing, fuels and lubricants, iron and steel, office machines and computers, telecommunications and sound apparatus and equipment. Principal source: Sweden 15.4% (1995) **Arable land:** 3.2% (1995) **Agricultural products:** wheat, barley, oats, potatoes, fruit; fishing industry, including fish farming

Population and society
Population: 4,348,000 (1996 est) **Population growth rate:** 0.5% (1990–95); 0.3% (2000–05) **Population density:** (per sq km) 13 (1996 est) **Urban population:** (% of total) 73 (1995) **Age distribution:** (% of total population) <15 19.5%, 15–65 64.7%, >65 15.9% (1995) **Ethnic groups:** majority of Nordic descent; Saami minority in far N **Language:** Norwegian (official); there are Saami-(Lapp) and Finnish-speaking minorities **Religion:** Evangelical Lutheran (endowed by state) **Education:** (compulsory years) 9 **Literacy rate:** 99% (men); 99% (women) (1995 est) **Labour force:** 50.3% of population: 5.2% agriculture, 23.4% industry, 71.5%

services (1995) **Unemployment:** 4.9% (1996) **Life expectancy:** 74 (men); 81 (women) (1995–2000) **Child mortality rate:** (under 5, per 1,000 live births) 9 (1996) **Physicians:** 1 per 300 people (1994)

Practical information

Visa requirements: UK: visa not required. USA: visa not required **Embassy in the UK:** 25 Belgrave Square, London SW1X 8QD. Tel: (0171) 235 7151; fax: (0171)245 6993 **British embassy:** Thomas Heftyesgate 8, 0244 Oslo 2. Tel: (22) 552 400; fax: (22) 434 005 **Chamber of commerce:** Norwegian Trade Council, Drammensveien 40, 0243 Oslo. Tel: (22) 926 300; fax: (22) 926 400 **Airports:** international airports: Oslo (Fornebu), Stavanger (Sola), Bergen (Flesland); 54 domestic airports with scheduled services; total passenger km: 7,663 million (1994) **Major holidays:** 1 January, 1, 17 May, 25–26 December; variable: Ascension Thursday, Good Friday, Easter Monday, Holy Thursday, Whit Monday

Chronology

5th century: First small kingdoms established by Goths. **c. 900:** Harald Fairhair created united Norwegian kingdom; it dissolved after his death. **8th–11th centuries:** Vikings from Norway raided and settled in many parts of Europe. **c. 1016–28:** Olav II (St Olav) reunited the kingdom and introduced Christianity. **1217–63:** Haakon VI established royal authority over nobles and church and made monarchy hereditary. **1263:** Iceland submitted to authority of king of Norway. **1397:** Union of Kalmar: Norway, Denmark, and Sweden united under a single monarch. **15th century:** Norway, the weakest of the three kingdoms, was increasingly treated as an appendage of Denmark. **1523:** Secession of Sweden further undermined Norway's status. **16th century:** Introduction of sawmill precipitated development of timber industry and growth of export trade. **1661:** Denmark restored formal equality of status to Norway as a twin kingdom. **18th century:** Norwegian merchants profited from foreign wars which increased demand for naval supplies. **1814:** Treaty of Kiel: Denmark ceded Norway (minus Iceland) to Sweden; Norway retained its own parliament but cabinet appointed by king of Sweden. **19th century:** Economic decline followed slump in timber trade due to Canadian competition; expansion of merchant navy and whaling industry. **1837:** Democratic local government introduced. **1884:** Achieved internal self-government when king of Sweden made Norwegian cabinet accountable to Norwegian parliament. **1895:** Start of constitutional dispute over control of foreign policy: Norway's demand for a separate consular service refused by Sweden. **1905:** Union with Sweden dissolved; Norway achieved independence under King Haakon VII. **1907:** Norway became first European country to grant women the right to vote in parliamentary elections. **early 20th century:** Development of industry based on hydroelectric power; long period of Liberal government committed to neutrality and moderate social reform. **1935:** First Labour government took office. **1940–45:** German occupation with Vidkun Quisling as puppet leader. **1945–65:** Labour governments introduced economic planning and permanent price controls. **1949:** Became a founding member of North Atlantic Treaty Organization (NATO). **1952:** Joined Nordic Council. **1957:** Olaf V succeeded his father King Haakon VII. **1960:** Joined European Free Trade Association (EFTA). **1972:** National referendum rejected membership of European Economic Community (EEC). **1975:** Export of North Sea oil began. **1981:** Gro Harlem Brundtland (Labour) became Norway's first woman prime minister. **1982:** Kare Willoch formed first Conservative government since 1928. **1986:** Falling oil prices caused recession; Labour re-elected under Brundtland. **1991:** Olaf V succeeded by his son Harald V. **1994:** National referendum rejected membership of European Union (formerly EC). **1996:** Brundtland resigned; succeeded by Thorbjoern Jagland. **1997:** Jagland failed to win decisive majority in general election. Kjell Magne Bondevik (KrF) became prime minister.

Oman Sultanate of

National name: *Saltanat `Uman* **Area:** 272,000 sq km/105,019 sq mi **Capital:** Muscat **Major towns/cities:** Salalah, Ibri, Sohar, Al-Buraimi, Nizwa **Major ports:** Mina Qaboos, Mina Raysut **Physical features:**

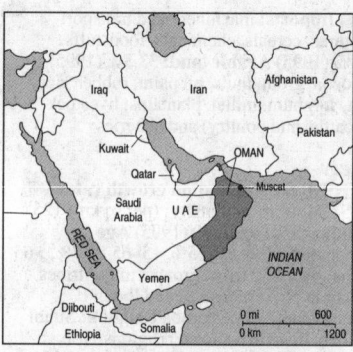

mountains to N and S of a high arid plateau; fertile coastal strip; Jebel Akhdar highlands; Kuria Muria Islands

Government

Head of state and government: Qaboos bin Said from 1970 **Political system:** absolute monarchy **Administrative divisions:** eight regional governates and 59 districts **Political parties:** none **Armed forces:** 43,500 (1996) **Conscription:** military service is voluntary **Death penalty:** retained and used for ordinary crimes **Defence spend:** (% GDP) 15.6 (1996) **Education spend:** (% GNP) 4.0 (1994) **Health spend:** (% GDP) 2.5 (1990–95)

Economy and resources

Currency: Omani rial **GDP:** ($ US) 11.6 billion (1994) **Real GDP per capita (PPP):** ($ US) 10,078 (1994) **GDP growth rate:** 3.5% (1994); 6% (1990–95) **Average annual inflation:** 0.5% (1996); –0.2 (1985–95) **Foreign debt:** ($ US) 2.9 billion (1996) **Major trading partners:** United Arab Emirates, Japan, South Korea, China **Resources:** petroleum, natural gas, copper, chromite, gold, salt, marble, gypsum, limestone **Industries:** mining, petroleum refining, cement, construction materials, copper smelting, food processing, chemicals, textiles **Exports:** petroleum, metals and metal goods, textiles, animals and products. Principal market: Japan 32.2% (1995) **Imports:** machinery and transport equipment, basic manufactures, food and live animals, beverages, tobacco. Principal source: UAE 24.8% (1995) **Arable land:** 0.1% (1995 **Agricultural products:** dates, tomatoes, limes, alfalfa, mangoes, melons, bananas, coconuts, cucumbers, onions, peppers, frankincense (agricultural production is mainly at subsistence level); livestock; fishing

Population and society

Population: 2,302,000 (1996 est) **Population growth rate:** 4.2% (1990–95); 3.7% (2000–05) **Population density:** (per sq km) 11 (1996 est) **Urban population:** (% of total) 13 (1995) **Age distribution:** (% of total population) <15 47.5%, 15–65 49.9%, >65 2.6% (1995) **Ethnic groups:** predominantly Arab, with substantial Iranian, Baluchi, Indo-Pakistani, and East African minorities **Language:** Arabic (official); English, Urdu, other Indian languages **Religion:** Ibadhi Muslim 75%, Sunni Muslim, Shi'ite Muslim, Hindu **Education:** not compulsory **Literacy rate:** 52% (men); 34% (women) (1994 est) **Labour force:** 9.4% agriculture, 27.8% industry, 62.8% services (1993) **Unemployment:** 11.9% (1993) **Life expectancy:** 69 (men); 73 (women) (1995–2000) **Child mortality rate:** (under 5, per 1,000 live births) 32 (1996) **Physicians:** 1 per 1,265 people (1994)

Practical information

Visa requirements: UK: visa required. USA: visa required **Embassy in the UK:** 167 Queen's Gate, London SW7 5HE. Tel: (0171) 225 0001; fax: (0171) 589 2505 **British embassy:** PO Box 300, 113 Muscat. Tel: (968) 693 077; fax: (968) 693 087 **Chamber of commerce:** Oman Chamber of Commerce and Industry, PO Box 1400, 112 Ruwi. Tel: (968) 707 684; fax: (968) 708 497 **Airports:** international airports: Muscat (Seeb), Salalah; domestic services operate between these; total passenger km: 2,439 million (1994) **Major holidays:** 18 November (2 days), 31 December; variable: Eid-ul-Adha (5 days), end of Ramadan (4 days), New Year (Muslim), Prophet's Birthday, Lailat al-Miraj (March/April)

Chronology

c. 3000 BC: Archaeological evidence suggests Oman may have been the semilegendary Magan, a thriving seafaring state at the time of the Sumerian Civilization of Mesopotamia (the Tigris and

Euphrates region of Iraq). **9th century BC:** Migration of Arab clans to Oman, notably the Qahtan family from SW Arabia and the Nizar from NW Arabia, between whom rivalry has continued. **4th century BC–AD 800:** North Oman under Persian control. **AD 630:** Converted to Islam. **751:** Julanda ibn Masud was elected imam (spiritual leader); Oman remained under imam rule until 1154. **1151:** Dynasty established by Banu Nabhan. **1428:** Dynastic rule came under challenge from the imams. **1507:** Coastal area, including port city of Muscat, fell under Portuguese control. **1650:** Portuguese ousted by Sultan ibn Sayf, a powerful Ya'ariba leader. **early 18th century:** Civil war between the Hinawis (descendents of the Qahtan) and the Ghafiris (descendents of the Nizar). **1749:** Independent Sultanate of Muscat and Oman established by Ahmad ibn Said, founder of the Al Bu Said dynasty that still rules Oman. **first half of 19th century:** Muscat and Oman was most powerful state in Arabia, ruling Zanzibar until 1861, and coastal parts of Persia, Kenya, and Pakistan; came under British protection. **1951:** The Sultanate of Muscat and Oman achieved full independence from Britain. Treaty of Friendship with Britain signed. **1964:** Discovery of oil led to transformation of undeveloped kingdom into modern state. **1970:** After 38 years' rule, Sultan Said bin Taimur replaced in bloodless coup by his son Qaboos bin Said. Name changed to Sultanate of Oman and modernization programme launched. **1975:** Left-wing rebels in Dhofar in the S, who had been supported by South Yemen, defeated with UK military assistance, ending a ten-year insurrection. **1981:** Consultative Council set up; Oman played key role in establishment of six-member Gulf Cooperation Council. **1982:** Memorandum of Understanding with UK signed, providing for regular consultation on international issues. **1991:** Joined US-led coalition opposing Iraq's occupation of Kuwait. **1994:** Proposal to allow women members of parliament.

Pakistan Islamic Republic of

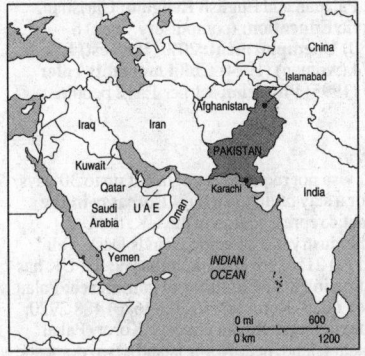

National name: *Islami Jamhuriya e Pakistan* **Area:** 796,100 sq km/307,374 sq mi; one-third of Kashmir under Pakistani control **Capital:** Islamabad **Major towns/cities:** Lahore, Rawalpindi, Faisalabad, Karachi, Hyderabad, Multan, Peshawar, Gujranwala, Sialkot, Sargodha, Quetta, Islamabad **Major ports:** Karachi, Port Qasim **Physical features:** fertile Indus plain in E, Baluchistan plateau in W, mountains in N and NW; the 'five rivers' (Indus, Jhelum, Chenab, Ravi, and Sutlej) feed the world's largest irrigation system; K2 mountain; Khyber Pass

Government

Head of state: Rafiq Tarar from 1997 **Head of government:** Nawaz Sharif from 1997 **Political system:** emergent democracy **Administrative divisions:** four provinces, the Federal Capital Territory, and the federally administered tribal areas **Political parties:** Islamic Democratic Alliance (IDA), conservative; Pakistan People's Party (PPP), moderate, Islamic, socialist; Pakistan Muslim League (PML), Islamic conservative (contains pro- and anti-government factions); Pakistan Islamic Front (PIF), Islamic fundamentalist, right wing; Awami National Party (ANP), left wing; National Democratic Alliance (NDA) bloc, left of centre; Mohajir National Movement (MQM), Sind-based *mohajir* settlers (Muslims previously living in India); Movement for Justice,

reformative, anti-corruption **Armed forces:** 587,000; paramilitary forces 248,000 (1996) **Conscription:** military service is voluntary **Death penalty:** retained and used for ordinary crimes **Defence spend:** (% GDP) 5.7 (1996) **Education spend:** (% GNP) 2.7 (1993/94) **Health spend:** (% GDP) 0.8 (1990–95)

Economy and resources

Currency: Pakistan rupee **GDP:** ($ US) 52 billion (1994) **Real GDP per capita (PPP):** ($ US) 2,154 (1994) **GDP growth rate:** 3.1% (1994); 4.6% (1990–95) **Average annual inflation:** 12.3% (1996); 9.3% (1985–95) **Foreign debt:** ($ US) 34.2 billion (1996) **Major trading partners:** Japan, USA, Germany, UK, Saudi Arabia **Resources:** iron ore, natural gas, limestone, rock salt, gypsum, silica, coal, petroleum, graphite, copper, manganese, chromite **Industries:** textiles (principally cotton), food processing, petroleum refining, leather production, soda ash, sulphuric acid, bicycles **Exports:** cotton, textiles, petroleum and petroleum products, clothing and accessories, leather, rice, food and live animals. Principal market: USA 15% (1995) **Imports:** machinery and transport equipment, mineral fuels and lubricants, chemicals and related products, edible oil. Principal source: Japan 10.7% (1995) **Arable land:** 27.3% (1995) **Agricultural products:** cotton, rice, wheat, maize, sugar cane

Population and society

Population: 139,973,000 (1996 est) **Population growth rate:** 2.8% (1990–95); 2.7% (2000–05) **Population density:** (per sq km) 156 (1996 est) **Urban population:** (% of total) 35 (1995) **Age distribution:** (% of total population) <15 44.3%, 15–65 52.7%, >65 3% (1995) **Ethnic groups:** four principal, regionally based, antagonistic communities: Punjabis in the Punjab; Sindhis in Sind; Baluchis in Baluchistan; and the Pathans (Pushtans) in the Northwest Frontier Province **Language:** Urdu (official); English, Punjabi, Sindhi, Pashto, Baluchi, other local dialects **Religion:** Sunni Muslim 75%, Shi'ite Muslim 20%; also Hindu, Christian, Parsee, Buddhist **Education:** (years) 5–12 (not compulsory, but free) **Literacy rate:** 47% (men); 21% (women) (1995 est) **Labour force:** 35% of population: 52% agriculture, 19% industry, 30% services (1990) **Unemployment:** 10% (1991 est) **Life expectancy:** 63 (men); 65 (women) (1995–2000) **Child mortality rate:** (under 5, per 1,000 live births) 104 (1996) **Physicians:** 1 per 1,929 people (1993)

Practical information

Visa requirements: UK: visa required. USA: visa required **Embassy in the UK:** 40 Lowndes Square, London SW1X 9JN. Tel: (0171) 235 2044 **British embassy:** British High Commission, PO Box 1122, Diplomatic Enclave, Ramna 5, Islamabad. Tel: (51) 822 131/5; fax: (51) 823 439 **Chamber of commerce:** Chamber of Commerce and Industry, PO Box 4833, Talpur Road, Karachi. Tel: (21) 241 0814; fax: (21) 242 7315 **Airports:** international airports: Karachi (Civil), Lahore, Islamabad, Peshawar, Quetta, Rawalpindi; 30 domestic airports; total passenger km: 1,400 million (1994) **Major holidays:** 23 March, 1 May, 1 July, 14 August, 6, 11 September, 9 November, 25, 31 December; variable: Eid-ul-Adha (3 days), Ashora (2 days), end of Ramadan (3 days), Prophet's Birthday, first day of Ramadan

Chronology

2500–1600 BC: The area was the site of the Indus Valley civilization, a sophisticated, city-based ancient culture. **327 BC:** Invaded by Alexander the Great of Macedonia. **1st–2nd centuries:** North Pakistan was the heartland of the Kusana Empire, formed by invaders from Central Asia. **8th century:** First Muslim conquests, in Baluchistan and Sind, followed by increasing immigration by Muslims from the W, from the 10th century. **1206:** Establishment of Delhi Sultanate, stretching from NW Pakistan and across northern India. **16th century:** Sikh religion developed in Punjab. **16th–17th centuries:** Lahore served intermittently as a capital city for the Mogul Empire, which stretched across the northern half of the Indian subcontinent. **1843–49:** Sind and Punjab annexed by British and incorporated within empire of 'British India'. **late 19th century:** Major canal irrigation projects in West Punjab and the northern Indus Valley drew in settlers from the E, as wheat and cotton production expanded. **1933:** The name 'Pakistan' (Urdu for 'Pure Nation') invented by Choudhary Rahmat Ali, as Muslims within British India began to campaign for the establishment of an independent Muslim territory that would embrace the four provinces of Sind, Baluchistan, Punjab, and the Northwest Frontier. **1940:** The All-India Muslim League (established 1906), led by Karachi-born Muhammad Ali Jinnah, endorsed the concept of a separate nation for Muslims in the Lahore Resolution. **1947:** Independence achieved from Britain, as dominion within the Commonwealth. Pakistan, which included East Bengal, a Muslim-dominated province more than 1,600 km/1,000 mi from Punjab, was formed following the partition of British India. Large-scale and violent cross-border migrations of Muslims, Hindus, and Sikhs followed, and a brief border war with India over disputed Kashmir. **1948:** Jinnah, the country's first governor general, died. **1956:** Proclaimed a republic. **1958:** Military rule imposed by Gen Ayub Khan. **1965:** Border war with India over disputed territory of Kashmir. **1969:** Power transferred to Gen Yahya Khan following strikes and riots. **1970:** General election produced clear majority in East Pakistan for pro-autonomy Awami League, led by Sheikh Mujibur Rahman, and in West Pakistan for Islamic socialist Pakistan People's Party (PPP), led by Zulfiqar Ali Bhutto. **1971:** East Pakistan secured independence, as Bangladesh, following a civil war in which it received decisive military support from India. Power was transferred from the military to the populist Bhutto in Pakistan. **1977:** Bhutto overthrown in military coup by Gen Zia ul-Haq following months of civil unrest; martial law imposed. **1979:** Bhutto executed for alleged murder; tight political restrictions imposed by Zia regime. **1980:** 3 million refugees fled to Northwest Frontier Province and Baluchistan as a result of Soviet invasion of Afghanistan. **1981:** Broad-based Opposition Movement for the Restoration of Democracy formed. Islamization process pushed forward by government. **1985:** Martial law and ban on political parties lifted. **1986:** Agitation for free elections launched by Benazir Bhutto, the daughter of Zulfiqar Ali Bhutto. **1988:** Islamic legal code, the Shari'a, introduced; Zia killed in military plane crash. Benazir Bhutto became prime minister after the now centrist PPP won the general election. **1989:** Tension with India increased by outbreaks of civil war in Kashmir. Pakistan rejoined the Commonwealth, which it had left in 1972. **1990:** Bhutto dismissed as prime minister by President Ghulam Ishaq Khan on charges of incompetence and corruption. The conservative Islamic Democratic Alliance (IDA), led by Nawaz Sharif, won general election and launched a privatization and economic deregulation programme. **1993:** Khan and Sharif resigned, ending months of political stalemate and unrest; Benazir Bhutto and PPP re-elected. Farooq Leghari (PPP) elected president. **1994:** Escalation in regional sectarian violence between Shiah and Sunni Muslims, centred in Karachi. **1996:** Justice Movement formed by former cricket captain Imran Khan. Benazir Bhutto dismissed by Leghari amid allegations of corruption and mismanagement. Meraj Khalid appointed interim prime minister. **1997:** Landslide victory for right-of-centre Pakistan Muslim League in general election, returning Nawaz Sharif to power as prime minister. President Leghari resigned after clashes with judiciary; Rafiq Tarar elected president. **1998** May: In response to nuclear tests carried out by India, Pakistan conducted six nuclear tests, its first ever, provoking international condemnation and the imposition of sanctions by the USA.

Palau **Republic of** (also known as **Belau**)

Area: 508 sq km/196 sq mi **Capital:** Koror (on Koror Island) **Major towns/cities:** Melekeiok, Garusuun, Malakal **Physical features:** more than 350 (mostly uninhabited) islands, islets, and atolls in the W Pacific; warm, humid climate, susceptible to typhoons

Government

Head of state and government: Kuniwo Nakamura from 1992 **Political system:** liberal democracy **Administrative divisions:** 16

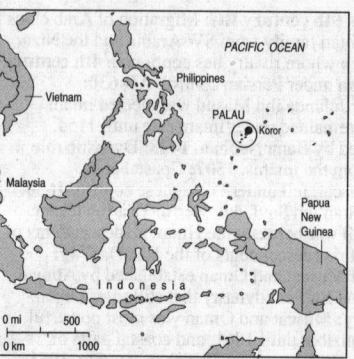

states **Political parties:** there are no formally organized political parties **Armed forces:** no defence forces of its own; under the Compact of Free Association, the USA is responsible for the defence of Palau; two US military bases operate on the islands **Death penalty:** laws do not provide for the death penalty for any crime

Economy and resources

Currency: US dollar **GDP:** ($ US) 81.8 million (1994 est) **Real GDP per capita (PPP):** ($ US) 5,000 (1994 est) **Average annual inflation:** N/A **Foreign debt:** ($ US) 100 million (1990) **Major trading partners:** USA, UK, Japan **Industries:** processing of agricultural products, fish products, handicrafts, tourism **Exports:** copra, coconut oil, handicrafts, trochus, tuna **Imports:** food and live animals, crude materials, mineral fuels, beverages, tobacco, chemicals, basic manufactures, machinery and transport equipment **Agricultural products:** coconuts, cassava, bananas, sweet potatoes; farming and fishing are mainly on a subsistence level; fishing licences are sold to foreign fleets including those of the USA, Taiwan, Japan, and the Philippines

Population and society

Population: 17,000 (1996 est) **Population growth rate:** 2.3% (1990–95) **Population density:** (per sq km) 37 (1996 est) **Urban population:** (% of total) 70.6 (1995) **Ethnic groups:** predominantly Micronesian **Language:** Palauan and English **Religion:** Christian, principally Roman Catholic **Education:** (compulsory years) 8 **Literacy rate:** 92% (1980) **Unemployment:** 20% (1988 est) **Life expectancy:** 68 (men); 74 (women) (1994) **Child mortality rate:** (per 1,000 live births) 35 (1995) **Physicians:** 1 per 1,512 people (1990)

Practical information

Visa requirements: UK: visa not required for a stay of up to 30 days. USA: visa not required for a stay of up to 30 days **Embassy in the UK:** Palau has no diplomatic representation in the UK; the UK Department of Trade and Industry has a Pacific Islands Desk. Tel: (0171) 215 4760; fax: (0171) 215 4398 **British embassy:** the UK has no diplomatic representation in Palau **Chamber of commerce:** Palau Visitors Authority, PO Box 6028, Koror 96940. Tel: (680) 488 2920; fax: (680) 488 2911 **Airports:** international airports: Koror (Palau International, on Babelthaup Island, near Koror Island); two domestic airfields **Major holidays:** 1 January, 15 March, 5 May, 1 June, 9 July, 5 September, 24 October, 24 November, 25 December

Chronology

c. 1000 BC: Micronesians first settled the islands. **1543:** First visited by Spanish navigator Ruy Lopez de Villalobos. **16th century:** Colonized by Spain. **later 16th century:** Fell under Spanish influence. **1899:** Purchased from Spain by Germany. **1914:** Occupied by Japan at the outbreak of World War I. **1920:** Administered by Japan under League of Nations mandate. **1944:** Occupied by USA after Japanese removed during World War II. **1947:** Became part of United Nations (UN) Pacific Islands Trust Territory, administered by USA. **1981:** Acquired autonomy as the Republic of Belau (Palau) under a constitution which prohibited the entry, storage, or disposal of nuclear or biological weapons. **1982:** Compact of Free Association signed with USA, providing for the right to maintain US military facilities in return for economic aid. However, the compact could not come into force since it contradicted the constitution, which could only be amended by a 75% vote in favour. **1985:** President Haruo Remeliik assassinated; succeeded by Lazarus Salii. **1988:** President

Salii committed suicide and was succeeded by Ngiratkel Etpison. **1992:** Kuniwo Nakamura elected president. **1993:** Referendum approved constitutional amendment allowing implementation of Compact of Free Association with USA. **1994:** Independence achieved; UN membership granted.

Panama Republic of

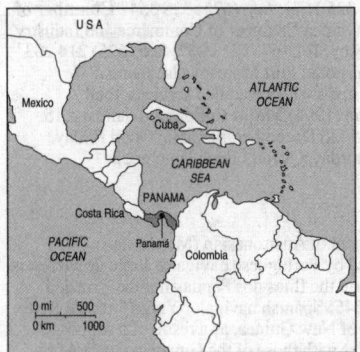

National name: *República de Panamá* **Area:** 77,100 sq km/29,768 sq mi **Capital:** Panamá (Panama City) **Major towns/cities:** San Miguelito, Colón, David, La Chorrera, Santiago, Chitré **Major ports:** Colón, Cristóbal, Balboa **Physical features:** coastal plains and mountainous interior; tropical rainforest in E and NW; Archipelago de las Perlas in Gulf of Panama; Panama Canal

Government
Head of state and government: Ernesto Pérez Balladares from 1994 **Political system:** emergent democracy **Administrative divisions:** nine provinces and one special territory (San Blas) **Political parties:** Democratic Revolutionary Party (PRD), right wing; Arnulfista Party (PA), left of centre; Authentic Liberal Party (PLA), left of centre; Nationalist Liberal Republican Movement (MOLIRENA), right of centre; Papa Ego Movement (MPE), moderate, centre left **Armed forces:** army abolished by National Assembly (1994); paramilitary forces numbered 11,800 (1996); National Maritime and National Air Services each numbered 400 (1995) **Conscription:** military service is voluntary **Death penalty:** laws do not provide for the death penalty for any crime (last known execution 1903) **Defence spend:** (% GDP) 1.4 (1996) **Education spend:** (% GNP) 5.0 (1994)

Economy and resources
Currency: balboa **GDP:** ($ US) 7 billion (1994) **Real GDP per capita (PPP):** ($ US) 6,104 (1994) **GDP growth rate:** 4.7% (1994); 6.3% (1990–95) **Average annual inflation:** 0.7% (1996); 1.7% (1985–95) **Foreign debt:** ($ US) 7.1 billion (1996) **Major trading partners:** USA, Japan, Costa Rica, Ecuador, Germany, Venezuela, Italy **Resources:** limestone, clay, salt; deposits of coal, copper, and molybdenum have been discovered **Industries:** food processing, petroleum refining and petroleum products, chemicals, paper and paper products, beverages, textiles and clothing, plastic products, light assembly, tourism **Exports:** bananas, shrimps and lobsters, sugar, clothing, coffee. Principal market: USA 41.9% (1995) **Imports:** machinery and transport equipment, petroleum and mineral products, chemicals and chemical products, electrical and electronic equipment, foodstuffs. Principal source: USA 39.1% (1995) **Arable land:** 6.7% (1995) **Agricultural products:** rice, maize, dry beans, bananas, sugar cane, coffee, oranges, mangoes, cocoa; cattle rearing; tropical timber; fishing (particularly shrimps for export)

Population and society
Population: 2,677,000 (1996 est) **Population growth rate:** 1.9% (1990–95); 1.4% (2000–05) **Population density:** (per sq km) 35 (1996 est) **Urban population:** (% of total) 53 (1995) **Age distribution:** (% of total population) <15 33.4%, 15–65 61.4%, >65

5.2% (1995) **Ethnic groups:** about 70% mestizos (of Spanish–American and American–Indian descent), 14% West Indian, 10% white American or European, and 6% Indian **Language:** Spanish (official), English **Religion:** Roman Catholic **Education:** (compulsory years) 8 **Literacy rate:** 88% (men); 88% (women) (1995 est) **Labour force:** 39% of population: 26% agriculture, 16% industry, 58% services (1990) **Unemployment:** 13.7% (1995) **Life expectancy:** 72 (men); 76 (women) (1995–2000) **Child mortality rate:** (under 5, per 1,000 live births) 28 (1996) **Physicians:** 1 per 562 people (1993 est)

Practical information
Visa requirements: UK: visa not required (business visitors need a business visa). USA: visa required **Embassy in the UK:** 48 Park Street, London W1Y 3PD. Tel: (0171) 493 4646; fax: (0171) 493 4333 **British embassy:** Apartado 889, Zona 1, 4th and 5th Floors, Torre Banco Sur, Calle 53 Este, Panama 1. Tel: (2) 690 866; fax: (2) 230 730 **Chamber of commerce:** Cámara de Comercio, Industrias y Agricultura de Panamá, Apartado 74, Edificio Comosa, Avenida Samuel Lewis, Planta Baja, Panamá 1. Tel: (2) 271 233; fax: (2) 274 186 **Airports:** international airports: Panama City (Tocumen); two domestic airports; total passenger km: 405 million (1994) **Major holidays:** 1, 9 January, 1 May, 11–12 October, 3–4, 28 November, 8, 25 December; variable: Carnival (2 days), Good Friday

Chronology
1502: Visited by Spanish explorer Rodrigo de Bastidas, at which time it was inhabited by Cuna, Choco, Guaymi, and other Indian groups. **1513:** Spanish conquistador Vasco Núñez de Balboa explored Pacific Ocean from Darien isthmus; he was made governor of Panama (meaning 'abundance of fish'), but was later executed as a result of Spanish court intrigue. **1519:** Spanish city established at Panama, which became part of the Spanish viceroyalty of New Andalucia (later New Granada). **1572–95 and 1668–71:** Spanish settlements sacked by British buccaneers Francis Drake and Henry Morgan. **1821:** Achieved independence from Spain; joined confederacy of Gran Colombia, which included Colombia, Venezuela, Ecuador, Peru, and Bolivia. **1830:** Gran Colombia split up and Panama became part of Colombia. **1846:** Treaty signed with USA, allowing it to construct a railway across the isthmus. **1880s:** French attempt to build a Panama canal connecting the Atlantic and Pacific Oceans failed as a result of financial difficulties and the death of 22,000 workers from yellow fever and malaria. **1903:** Full independence achieved with US help on separation from Colombia; USA bought rights to build Panama Canal, and were given control of a 10-mile strip, the Canal Zone, in perpetuity. **1914:** Panama Canal opened. **1939:** Panama's status as a US protectorate was terminated by mutual agreement. **1968–81:** Military rule of Gen Omar Torrijos Herrera, leader of the National Guard, who deposed the elected president and launched a costly programme of economic modernization. **1977:** USA–Panama treaties transferred the canal to Panama (effective from 2000), with the USA guaranteeing protection and annual payment. **1984:** Nicolás Ardito Barletta of the right-wing Democratic Revolutionary Party (PRD) elected president by narrow margin. **1985:** Barletta resigned; replaced by Eric Arturo del Valle, to the dissatisfaction of the USA. **1987:** Gen Manuel Noriega (head of the National Guard and effective ruler since 1983) resisted calls for his removal, despite suspension of US military and economic aid. **1988:** Del Valle replaced by Manuel Solis Palma after trying to oust Noriega. Noriega, charged with drug smuggling by the USA, declared a state of emergency after the coup against him failed. **1989:** Assembly elections declared invalid when won by opposition. 'State of war' with USA announced, and US invasion (codenamed 'Operation Just Cause') deposed Noriega; 4,000 Panamanians died in the fighting. Guillermo Endara, who had won earlier elections, was installed as president in Dec. **1991:** Attempted antigovernment coup foiled. Constitutional reforms approved by assembly, including abolition of standing army; privatization programme introduced. **1992:** Noriega found guilty of drug offences and given 40-year prison sentence in USA. Referendum rejected proposed constitutional reforms. **1994:** Ernesto Pérez Balladares (PRD) elected president. Constitution amended by assembly; army formally abolished.

Papua New Guinea

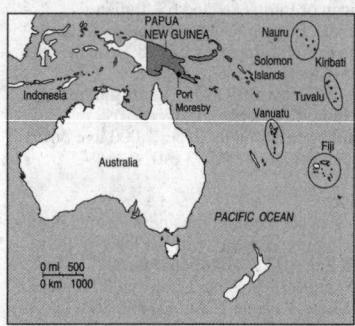

Area: 462,840 sq km/178,702 sq mi
Capital: Port Moresby (on E New Guinea) (also port)
Major towns/cities: Lae, Madang, Arawa, Wewak, Goroka, Rabaul, Mount Hagen
Major ports: Rabaul **Physical features:** mountainous; swamps and plains; monsoon climate; tropical islands of New Ireland, New Britain, and Bougainville; Admiralty Islands, D'Entrecasteaux Islands, and Louisiade Archipelago; active volcanoes Vulcan and Tavurvur

Government

Head of state: Queen Elizabeth II, represented by governor general Silas Atopare from 1997 **Head of government:** Bill Skate from 1997 **Political system:** liberal democracy **Administrative divisions:** 19 provinces and the National Capital District **Political parties:** Papua New Guinea Party (Pangu Pati: PP), urban- and coastal-oriented nationalist; People's Democratic Movement (PDM), 1985 breakaway from the PP; National Party (NP), highlands-based, conservative; Melanesian Alliance (MA), Bougainville-based, pro-autonomy, left of centre; People's Progress Party (PPP), conservative; People's Action Party (PAP), right of centre **Armed forces:** 3,700 (1996) **Conscription:** military service is voluntary **Death penalty:** retains the death penalty for ordinary crimes but can be considered abolitionist in practice (last execution 1950) **Defence spend:** (% GDP) 1.5 (1996) **Education spend:** (% GNP) 6.3 (1993 est) **Health spend:** (% GDP) 2.8 (1990–95)

Economy and resources

Currency: kina **GDP:** ($ US) 5.4 billion (1994) **Real GDP per capita (PPP):** ($ US) 2,821 (1994) **GDP growth rate:** 3.5% (1994); 9.3% (1990–95) **Average annual inflation:** 13% (1996); 4.6% (1985–95) **Foreign debt:** ($ US) 2.77 billion (1996) **Major trading partners:** Australia, Japan, USA, Singapore, Germany, South Korea, UK **Resources:** copper, gold, silver; deposits of chromite, cobalt, nickel, quartz; substantial reserves of petroleum and natural gas (petroleum production began 1992) **Industries:** food processing, beverages, tobacco, timber products, metal products, machinery and transport equipment, fish canning **Exports:** gold, copper ore and concentrates, crude petroleum, timber, coffee beans, coconut and copra products. Principal market: Australia 32.5% (1995) **Imports:** machinery and transport equipment, manufactured goods, food and live animals, miscellaneous manufactured articles, chemicals, mineral fuels. Principal source: Australia 51.6% (1995) **Arable land:** 0.1% (1995) **Agricultural products:** coffee, cocoa, coconuts, pineapples, palm oil, rubber, tea, pyrethrum, peanuts, spices, potatoes, maize, taro, bananas, rice, sago, sweet potatoes; livestock; poultry; fishing; timber production

Population and society

Population: 4,400,000 (1996 est) **Population growth rate:** 2.3% (1990–95); 2.1% (2000–05) **Population density:** (per sq km) 10 (1996 est) **Urban population:** (% of total) 16% (1995) **Age distribution:** (% of total population) <15 39.5%, 15–65 57.5%, >65 2.9% (1995) **Ethnic groups:** mainly Melanesian, particularly in coastal areas; inland (on New Guinea and larger islands), Papuans predominate. On the outer archipelagos and islands, mixed Micronese-Melanesians are found. A small Chinese minority also exists **Language:** English (official); pidgin English, 715 local languages **Religion:** Protestant, Roman Catholic, local faiths **Education:** not compulsory **Literacy rate:** 65% (men); 38% (women) (1995 est) **Labour force:** 49% of population: 79%

agriculture, 7% industry, 14% services (1990) **Life expectancy:** 57 (men); 59 (women) (1995–2000) **Child mortality rate:** (under 5, per 1,000 live births) 82 (1996) **Physicians:** 1 per 12,754 people (1993 est)

Practical information

Visa requirements: UK: visa required. USA: visa required **Embassy in the UK:** 14 Waterloo Place, London SW1Y 4AR. Tel: (0171) 930 0922/7; fax: (0171) 930 0828 **British embassy:** British High Commission, PO Box 4778, Kiroki Street, Waigani, Boroko, Port Moresby. Tel: (675) 325 1677; fax: (675) 325 3547 **Chamber of commerce:** Papua New Guinea Chamber of Commerce and Industry, PO Box 1621, Port Moresby. Tel: (675) 213 057; fax: (675) 214 203 **Airports:** international airports: Port Moresby (Jackson); 177 domestic airports and airstrips with scheduled services; total passenger km: 837 million (1994) **Major holidays:** 1 January, 15 August, 16 September, 25–26 December; variable: Good Friday, Easter Monday, Holy Saturday, Queen's Birthday (June), Remembrance (July)

Chronology

c. 3000 BC: New settlement of Austronesian (Melanesian) immigrants. **1526:** Visited by Portuguese navigator Jorge de Menezes, who named the main island the Ilhos dos Papua after the 'frizzled' hair of the inhabitants. **1545:** Spanish navigator Ynigo Ortis de Retez gave the island the name of New Guinea, as a result of a supposed resemblance of the peoples with those of the Guinea coast of Africa. **17th century:** Regularly visited by Dutch merchants. **1828:** Dutch East India Company incorporated western part of New Guinea into Netherlands East Indies (becoming Irian Jaya, in Indonesia). **1884:** NE New Guinea annexed by Germany; SE claimed by Britain. **1870s:** Visits by Western missionaries and traders increased. **1890s:** Copra plantations developed in German New Guinea. **1906:** Britain transferred its rights to Australia, which renamed the lands Papua. **1914:** German New Guinea occupied by Australia at outbreak of World War I; from the merged territories Papua New Guinea was formed. **1920–42:** Held as League of Nations mandate by Australia. **1942–45:** Occupied by Japan, who lost 150,000 troops resisting Allied counterattack. **1947:** Held as United Nations Trust Territory by Australia. **1951:** Legislative Council established. **1964:** Elected House of Assembly formed. **1967:** Pangu Party (Pangu Pati; PP) formed to campaign for home rule. **1975:** Independence achieved from Australia, within Commonwealth, with Michael Somare (PP) as prime minister. **1980:** Sir Julius Chan of People's Progress Party (PPP) became prime minister. **1982:** Somare returned to power. **1985:** Somare challenged by deputy prime minister Paias Wingti, who later left the PP and formed the People's Democratic Movement (PDM); he became head of a five-party coalition government. **1988:** Wingti defeated on no-confidence vote; replaced by Rabbie Namaliu (PP), heading coalition government. Joined Solomon Islands and Vanuatu to form Spearhead Group, aiming to preserve Melanesian cultural traditions. **1989:** State of emergency imposed on copper-rich Bougainville in response to separatist violence. **1990:** Bougainville Revolutionary Army (BRA) issued unilateral declaration of independence. **1991:** Economic boom as gold production doubled. **1992:** Wingti appointed premier, heading a three-party coalition. **1994:** Wingti replaced as premier by Sir Julius Chan. Short-lived peace agreement with BRA. **1996:** Prime minister of Bougainville murdered, jeopardizing peace process. Gerard Sinato elected president of the transitional Bougainville government. **1997:** Army and police mutinied following government's use of mercenaries against secessionist rebels. Prime Minister Chan forced to resign but returned after being cleared of corruption charges. Chan's coalition polled badly in general election; Bill Skate (PDM) appointed prime minister. Silas Atopare appointed governor general. Skate resisted calls for his resignation.

Paraguay Republic of

National name: *República del Paraguay* **Area:** 406,752 sq km/157,046 sq mi **Capital:** Asunción (and port) **Major towns/cities:**

Ciudad del Este, Pedro Juan Caballero, San Lorenzo, Fernando de la Mora, Lambare, Concepción, Villartica, Encaración **Major ports:** Concepción **Physical features:** low marshy plain and marshlands; divided by Paraguay River; Paraná River forms SE boundary

Government

Head of state and government: Juan Carlos Wasmosy from 1993 **Political system:** emergent democracy **Administrative divisions:** 17 departments **Political parties:** National Republican Association (Colorado Party), right of centre; Authentic Radical Liberal Party (PLRA), centrist; National Encounter, right of centre; Radical Liberal Party (PLR), centrist; Liberal Party (PL), centrist **Armed forces:** 20,200 (1996) **Conscription:** 12 months (army); 24 months (navy) **Death penalty:** retains the death penalty only for exceptional crimes such as crimes under military law or crimes committed in exceptional circumstances such as wartime (last execution 1928) **Defence spend:** (% GDP) 1.3 (1996) **Education spend:** (% GNP) 2.7 (1994) **Health spend:** (% GDP) 1.0 (1990–95)

Economy and resources

Currency: guaraní **GDP:** ($ US) 7.8 billion (1994) **Real GDP per capita (PPP):** ($ US) 3,531 (1994) **GDP growth rate:** 3.5% (1994); 3.1% (1990–95) **Average annual inflation:** 10.9% (1996); 24.9 (1985–95) **Foreign debt:** ($ US) 2 billion (1996) **Major trading partners:** Brazil, Argentina, the Netherlands, Japan, USA, France, UK **Resources:** gypsum, kaolin, limestone, salt; deposits (not commercially exploited) of bauxite, iron ore, copper, manganese, uranium; deposits of natural gas discovered 1994; exploration for petroleum deposits ongoing mid-1990s **Industries:** food processing, beverages, tobacco, wood and wood products, textiles (cotton), clothing, leather, chemicals, metal products, machinery **Exports:** soya beans (and other oil seeds), cotton, timber and wood manufactures, hides and skins, meat. Principal market: Brazil 46.5% (1996) **Imports:** machinery, vehicles and parts, mineral fuels and lubricants, beverages, tobacco, chemicals, foodstuffs. Principal source: Brazil 23.7% (1996) **Arable land:** 5.5 % (1995) **Agricultural products:** cassava, soya beans, maize, cotton, wheat, rice, tobacco, sugar cane, 'yerba maté' (strongly flavoured tea); livestock rearing; forest resources

Population and society

Population: 4,957,000 (1996 est) **Population growth rate:** 2.8% (1990–95); 2.3% (2000–05) **Population density:** (per sq km) 12 (1996 est) **Urban population:** (% of total) 53 (1995) **Age distribution:** (% of total population) <15 40.3%, 15–65 55.9%, >65 3.8% (1995) **Ethnic groups:** predominantly mixed-race mestizos; less than 5% Spanish or Indian **Language:** Spanish 6% (official), Guaraní 90% **Religion:** Roman Catholic (official religion); Mennonite, Anglican **Education:** (compulsory years) 6 **Literacy rate:** 92% (men); 88% (women) (1995 est) **Labour force:** 45.2% agriculture, 22.5% industry, 32.3% services (1994) **Unemployment:** 9% (1993) **Life expectancy:** 69 (men); 73 (women) (1995–2000) **Child mortality rate:** (under 5, per 1,000 live births) 47(1996) **Physicians:** 1 per 1,231 people (1993 est)

Practical information

Visa requirements: UK: visa not required. USA: visa not required **Embassy in the UK:** Braemar Lodge, Cornwall Gardens, London

SW7 4AQ. Tel: (0171) 937 1253; fax: (0171) 937 5687 **British embassy:** Casilla 404, Calle Presidente Franco 706, Asunción. Tel: (21) 444 472; fax: (21) 446 385 **Chamber of commerce:** Cámara y Bolsa de Comercio, Estrella 540, Asunción. Tel: (21) 493 321; fax: (21) 440 817 **Airports:** international airports: Asunción (Silvio Pettirossi), Ciudad del Este (Guaraní); three domestic airports; total passenger km: 1,235 million (1994) **Major holidays:** 1 January, 3 February, 1 March, 1, 14–15 May, 12 June, 15, 25 August, 29 September, 12 October, 1 November, 8, 25, 31 December; variable: Corpus Christi, Good Friday, Holy Thursday

Chronology

1526: Visited by Italian navigator Sebastian Cabot, who travelled up Paraná river; at this time the E of the country had long been inhabited by Guaraní-speaking Amerindians, who gave the country its name, which means 'land with an important river'. **1537:** Spanish made an alliance with Guaraní Indians against hostile Chaco Indians, enabling them to colonize interior plains; Asunción founded by Spanish. **1609:** Jesuits arrived from Spain to convert local population to Roman Catholicism and administer the country. **1767:** Jesuit missionaries expelled. **1776:** Formerly part of Spanish Viceroyalty of Peru, which covered much of South America, became part of Viceroyalty of La Plata, with capital at Buenos Aires (Argentina). **1808:** With Spanish monarchy overthrown by Napoleon Bonaparte, La Plata Viceroyalty became autonomous, but Paraguayans revolted against rule from Buenos Aires. **1811:** Independence achieved from Spain. **1814:** Under dictator Gen José Gaspar Rodriguez Francia ('El Supremo'), Paraguay became an isolated state. **1840:** Francia was succeeded by his nephew, Carlos Antonio Lopez, who opened country to foreign trade and whose son, Francisco Solano Lopez, as president from 1862, built up powerful army. **1865–70:** War with Argentina, Brazil, and Uruguay over access to sea; more than half the population died and 150,000 sq km/58,000 sq mi of territory lost; President Lopez killed. **later 1880s:** Conservative Colorado Party and Liberal Party founded. **1912:** Liberal leader Edvard Schaerer came to power, ending decades of political instability. **1932–35:** Territory in W won from Bolivia during Chaco War (settled by arbitration 1938). **1940–48:** Presidency of autocratic Gen Higinio Morínigo. **1948–54:** Political instability; six different presidents. **1954:** Gen Alfredo Stroessner seized power in coup. He ruled as a ruthless autocrat, suppressing civil liberties; received initial US backing as economy expanded. **1989:** Stroessner ousted in coup led by Gen Andrés Rodríguez. Rodríguez elected president; right-of-centre military-backed Colorado Party won assembly elections. **1992:** New democratic constitution adopted. **1993:** Colorado Party won most seats in first free multiparty elections, but no overall majority; its candidate, Juan Carlos Wasmosy, won first free presidential elections.

Peru Republic of

National name: *República del Perú* **Area:** 1,285,200 sq km/496,216 sq mi **Capital:** Lima **Major towns/cities:** Arequipa, Iquitos, Chiclayo, Trujillo, Cuzco, Piura, Chimbote **Major ports:** Callao, Chimbote, Salaverry **Physical features:** Andes mountains NW–SE cover 27% of Peru, separating Amazon river-basin jungle in NE from coastal plain in W; desert along coast N–S (Atacama Desert); Lake Titicaca

Government

Head of state: Alberto Fujimori from 1990 **Head of government:** to be announced **Political system:** democracy **Administrative divisions:** 24 departments and the constitutional province of Callao **Political parties:** American Popular Revolutionary Alliance (APRA), moderate, left wing; United Left (IU), left wing; Change 90 (Cambio 90), centrist; New Majority (Nueva Mayoria), centrist; Popular Christian Party (PPC), right of centre; Liberal Party (PL), right wing **Armed forces:** 125,000 (1995); plus paramilitary forces numbering 68,600 (1996) **Conscription:** conscription is selective for two years **Death penalty:** retains the death penalty only for exceptional crimes such as crimes under military law or crimes committed in exceptional circumstances such as wartime (last execution 1979) **Defence spend:** (% GDP) 1.9 (1996) **Education spend:** (% GNP) 3.5 (1992); N/A (1993/94) **Health spend:** (% GDP) 2.6 (1990–95)

Economy and resources

Currency: nuevo sol **GDP:** ($ US) 50.1 billion (1994) **Real GDP per capita (PPP):** ($ US) 3,645 (1994) **GDP growth rate:** 12.9% (1994) **Average annual inflation:** 21.2% (1996); 398.5% (1985–95) **Foreign debt:** ($ US) 30.8 billion (1995) **Major trading partners:** USA, Japan, UK, Germany, Italy, China, Argentina, Brazil, Colombia **Resources:** lead, copper, iron, silver, zinc (world's fourth-largest producer), petroleum **Industries:** food processing, textiles and clothing, petroleum refining, metals and metal products, chemicals, machinery and transport equipment, beverages, tourism **Exports:** copper, fishmeal, zinc, gold, refined petroleum products. Principal market: USA 20.9% (1995) **Imports:** machinery and transport equipment, basic foodstuffs, basic manufactures, chemicals, mineral fuels, consumer goods. Principal source: USA 27.6% (1995) **Arable land:** 3% (1995) **Agricultural products:** potatoes, wheat, seed cotton, coffee, rice, maize, beans, sugar cane; fishing (particularly for South American pilchard and the anchovetta)

Population and society

Population: 23,944,000 (1996 est) **Population growth rate:** 1.9% (1990–95); 1.7% (2000–05) **Population density:** (per sq km) 19 (1996 est) **Urban population:** (% of total) 72 (1995) **Age distribution:** (% of total population) <15 35.1%, 15–65 60.8%, >65 4.1% (1995) **Ethnic groups:** about 45% South American Indian, 37% mestizo, 15% European, and 3% African **Language:** Spanish, Quechua (both official), Aymara **Religion:** Roman Catholic (state religion) **Education:** (compulsory years) 11 **Literacy rate:** 92% (men); 88% (women) (1995 est) **Labour force:** 33% agriculture, 16.9% industry, 53.1% services (1992) **Unemployment:** 9.4% (1994 est) **Life expectancy:** 66 (men); 69 (women) (1995–2000) **Child mortality rate:** (under 5, per 1,000 live births) 71 (1996) **Physicians:** 1 per 939 people (1993 est)

Practical information

Visa requirements: UK: visa not required for a stay of up to 90 days. USA: visa not required for a stay of up to 90 days **Embassy in the UK:** 52 Sloane Street, London SW1X 9SP. Tel: (0171) 235 1917; fax: (0171) 235 4463 **British embassy:** PO Box 854, Natalio Sanchez 125, Edificio El Pacifico, Pisos 11/12, Plaza Washington, Lima 100. Tel: (1) 433 5032; fax: (1) 433 4738 **Chamber of commerce:** Confederación de Cámaras de Comercio y Producción del Perú, Avenida Gregorio Escobedo 398, Lima 11. Tel: (1) 463 3434; fax: (1) 463 2820 **Airports:** international airports: Lima (Jorge Chávez), Iquitos (Colonel Francisco Secada Vignetta), Cuzco (Velasco Astete), Arequipa (Rodríguez Ballón); 27 domestic airports; total passenger km: 2,601 million (1994) **Major holidays:** 1 January, 1 May, 29–30 June, 28 July (2 days), 30 August, 8 October, 1 November, 8, 25, 31 December; variable: Good Friday, Holy Thursday

Chronology

4000 BC: Evidence of early settled agriculture in Chicama Valley. **AD 700–1100:** Period of Wari Empire, first expansionist militarized empire in Andes. **1200:** Manco Capac became first emperor of South American Indian Quechua-speaking Incas, who established a growing and sophisticated empire centred on the Andean city of Cuzco, and believed their ruler was descended from the Sun. **late 15th century:** At its zenith, Inca Empire stretched from Quito in Ecuador to beyond Santiago in S Chile. It superseded Chimu civilization, which had flourished in Peru 1250–1470. **1532–33:** Incas defeated by Spanish conquistadores, led by Francisco Pizarro. King Atahualpa killed. Empire came under Spanish rule, as part of Viceroyalty of Peru, with capital in Lima, founded 1535. **1541:** Pizarro assassinated as rivalries broke out among conquistadores. **1780:** Tupac Amaru, who claimed to be descended from last Inca chieftain, led failed native revolt against Spanish. **1810:** Peru became headquarters for Spanish government as European settlers rebelled elsewhere in Spanish America. **1820–22:** Fight for liberation from Spanish rule led by Gen José de San Martín and Army of Andes which, after freeing Argentina and Chile, invaded S Peru. **1824:** Became last colony in Central and South America to achieve independence from Spain after attacks from N by Field Marshal Sucre, acting for freedom fighter Simón Bolívar. **1836–39:** Failed attempts at union with Bolivia. **1845–62:** Economic progress under rule of Gen Ramón Castilla. **1849–74:** Around 80,000–100,000 Chinese labourers arrived in Peru to fill menial jobs such as collecting guano. **1866:** Victorious naval war fought with Spain. **1879–83:** Pacific War fought in alliance with Bolivia and Chile over nitrate fields of the Atacama Desert in the S; three provinces along coastal S lost to Chile. **1902:** Boundary dispute with Bolivia settled. **mid-1920s:** After several decades of civilian government, series of right-wing dictatorships held power. **1927:** Boundary dispute with Colombia settled. **1929:** Tacna province, lost to Chile 1880, was returned. **1941:** Brief war with Ecuador secured Amazonian territory. **1945:** Civilian government, dominated by left-of-centre American Popular Revolutionary Alliance (APRA, formed 1924), came to power after free elections. **1948:** Army coup installed military government led by Gen Manuel Odría, who remained in power until 1956. **1963:** Return to civilian rule, with centrist Fernando Belaúnde Terry as president. **1968:** Return of military government in bloodless coup by Gen Juan Velasco Alvarado, following industrial unrest. Populist land reform programme introduced. **1975:** Velasco replaced, in a bloodless coup, by Gen Morales Bermúdez. **1980:** Return to civilian rule, with Fernando Belaúnde as president; agrarian and industrial reforms pursued. Sendero Luminoso ('Shining Path') Maoist guerrilla group active. **1981:** Boundary dispute with Ecuador renewed. **1985:** Belaúnde succeeded by Social Democrat Alan García Pérez, who launched campaign to remove military and police 'old guard'. **1987:** President García delayed nationalization of Peru's banks after vigorous campaign against the proposal. **1988:** García pressured to seek help from International Monetary Fund (IMF) as economy deteriorated. Sendero Luminoso increased campaign of violence. **1990:** Right-of-centre Alberto Fujimori, the son of Japanese immigrants, defeated ex-communist writer Vargas Llosa in presidential elections. Assassination attempt on president failed. Inflation 400%; privatization programme launched. **1992:** Fujimori allied himself with the army and suspended constitution, provoking international criticism. Sendero Luminoso leader arrested and sentenced to life imprisonment after 'show trial'. New single-chamber legislature elected. **1993:** New constitution adopted, enabling Fujimori to seek re-election. **1994:** Fujimori removed his wife as First Lady on the grounds of disloyalty; 6,000 Sendero Luminoso guerrillas surrendered to the authorities. **1995:** Border dispute with Ecuador resolved after armed clashes. Fujimori re-elected to second term. Controversial amnesty granted to those previously convicted of human-rights abuses. **1996:** Prime Minister Dante Cordova resigned in protest against rapid pace of market reform. Hostages held in Japanese embassy by Marxist Tupac Amaru Revolutionary Movement (MRTA) guerrillas. **1997:** Hostage siege successfully ended.

Philippines Republic of the

National name: *Republika ng Pilipinas* **Area:** 300,000 sq km/115,830 sq mi **Capital:** Manila (on Luzon) (and chief port)

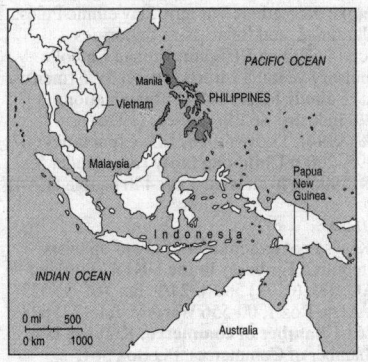

Major towns/cities: Quezon City (on Luzon), Davao, Caloocan, Cebu, Zamboanga **Major ports:** Cebu, Davao (on Mindanao), Iloilo, Zamboanga (on Mindanao) **Physical features:** comprises over 7,000 islands; volcanic mountain ranges traverse main chain N–S; 50% still forested. The largest islands are Luzon 108,172 sq km/41,754 sq mi and Mindanao 94,227 sq km/36,372 sq mi; others include Samar, Negros, Palawan, Panay, Mindoro, Leyte, Cebu, and the Sulu group; Pinatubo volcano (1,759 m/5,770 ft); Mindanao has active volcano Apo (2,954 m/9,690 ft) and mountainous rainforest

Government

Head of state and government: Fidel Ramos from 1992 **Political system:** emergent democracy **Administrative divisions:** 15 regions (two of which are autonomous) **Political parties:** Laban ng Demokratikong Pilipino (Democratic Filipino Struggle Party; LDP–DFSP), centrist, liberal-democrat coalition; Lakas ng Edsa (National Union of Christian Democrats; LNE–NUCD), centrist; Liberal Party, centrist; Nationalist Party (Nacionalista), right wing; New Society Movement (NSM; Kilusan Bagong Lipunan), conservative, pro-Marcos; National Democratic Front, left-wing umbrella grouping, including the Communist Party of the Philippines (CPP); Mindanao Alliance, island-based decentralist body **Armed forces:** 107,500 (1995); reserve forces 131,000; paramilitary forces around 42,500 (1996) **Conscription:** university/college students must complete 2 years' military training **Death penalty:** retained in law, but considered abolitionist in practice; last execution 1976 **Defence spend:** (% GDP) 2.0 (1996) **Education spend:** (% GNP) 2.4 (1993/94) **Health spend:** (% GDP) 1.3 (1990–95)

Economy and resources

Currency: peso **GDP:** ($ US) 64.2 billion (1994) **Real GDP per capita (PPP):** ($ US) 2,681 (1994) **GDP growth rate:** 4.3% (1994); 1% (1990–95) **Average annual inflation:** 9.1% (1996); 9.8% (1985–95) **Foreign debt:** ($ US) 47.2 billion (1996) **Major trading partners:** Japan, USA, Singapore, Taiwan, South Korea, Hong Kong **Resources:** copper ore, gold, silver, chromium, nickel, coal, crude petroleum, natural gas, forests **Industries:** food processing, petroleum refining, textiles, chemical products, pharmaceuticals, electrical machinery (mainly telecommunications equipment), metals and metal products, tourism **Exports:** electronic products (notably semiconductors and microcircuits), garments, agricultural products (particularly fruit and seafood), woodcraft and furniture, lumber, chemicals, coconut oil. Principal market: USA 35.3% (1995) **Imports:** machinery and transport equipment, mineral fuels, basic manufactures, food and live animals, textile yarns, base metals, cereals and cereal preparations. Principal source: Japan 22.4% (1995) **Arable land:** 18.5% (1995) **Agricultural products:** rice, maize, cassava, coconuts, sugar cane, bananas, pineapples; livestock (chiefly pigs, buffaloes, goats, and poultry) and fisheries

Population and society

Population: 69,282,000 (1996 est) **Population growth rate:** 2.1% (1990–95); 1.8% (2000–05) **Population density:** (per sq km) 231 (1996 est) **Urban population:** (% of total) 54 (1995) **Age distribution:** (% of total population) <15 38.3%, 15–65 58.3%, >65 3.4% (1995) **Ethnic groups:** comprises more than 50 ethnic communities, although 95% of the population is designated 'Filipino', an Indo-Polynesian ethnic grouping **Language:** Tagalog (Filipino, official); English and Spanish; Cebuano, Ilocano, and more than 70 other indigenous languages **Religion:** mainly Roman Catholic; Protestant, Muslim, local religions **Education:** (compulsory years) 6 **Literacy rate:** 90% (men); 89% (women) (1995 est) **Labour force:** 40% of population: 46% agriculture, 15% industry, 39% services (1990) **Unemployment:** 8.4% (1995) **Life expectancy:** 67 (men); 70 (women) (1995–2000) **Child mortality rate:** (under 5, per 1,000 live births) 45 (1996) **Physicians:** 1 per 853 people (1993)

Practical information

Visa requirements: UK: visa not required for a stay of up to 21 days. USA: visa not required for a stay of up to 21 days **Embassy in the UK:** 9a Palace Green, London W8 4QE. Tel: (0171) 937 1600; fax: (0171) 937 2925 **British embassy:** 15th–17th Floors, LV Locsin Building, 6752 Ayala Avenue, Makati, Metro Manila 1226. Tel: (2) 816 7116; fax: (2) 819 7206 **Chamber of commerce:** Philippine Chamber of Commerce and Industry, Ground Floor, CCP Complex, Roxas Boulevard, Makati, Metro Manila 2801. Tel: (2) 833 8591; fax: (2) 816 1946 **Airports:** international airports: Manila (Ninoy Aquino), Cebu (Mactan), Laoag City, Davao, Zamboanga, Puerto Princesa City, Subic Bay, Freeport; comprehensive internal services; total passenger km: 13,977 million (1994) **Major holidays:** 1 January, 1 May, 12 June, 4 July, 1, 30 November, 25, 30–31 December; variable: Good Friday, Holy Thursday

Chronology

14th century: Traders from Malay peninsula introduced Islam and created Muslim principalities of Manila and Jolo. **1521:** Portuguese navigator Ferdinand Magellan reached the islands, but was killed in battle with islanders. **1536:** Philippines named after Charles V's son (later Philip II of Spain) by Spanish navigator Ruy López de Villalobos. **1565:** Philippines conquered by Spanish army led by Miguel López de Lagazpi. **1571:** Manila was made capital of the colony, which was part of the viceroyalty of Mexico. **17th century:** Spanish missionaries converted much of lowland population to Roman Catholicism. **1762–63:** British occupied Manila. **1834:** End of Spanish monopoly on trade; British and American merchants bought sugar and tobacco. **1896–97:** Emilio Aguinaldo led revolt against Spanish rule. **1898:** Spanish-American War: US navy destroyed Spanish fleet in Manila Bay; Aguinaldo declared independence, but Spain ceded Philippines to USA. **1898–1901:** Nationalist uprising suppressed by US troops; 200,000 Filipinos killed. **1907:** Americans set up elected legislative assembly. **1916:** Bicameral legislature introduced on US model. **1935:** Philippines gained internal self-government with Manuel Quezon as president. **1942–45:** Occupied by Japan. **1946:** Philippines achieved independence from USA under President Manuel Roxas; USA retained military bases and supplied economic aid. **1957–61:** 'Filipino First' policy introduced by President Carlos García to reduce economic power of Americans and Chinese; official corruption increased. **1965:** Ferdinand Marcos elected president. **1972:** Marcos declared martial law and ended freedom of press; economic development financed by foreign loans, of which large sums were diverted by Marcos for personal use. **1981:** Martial law officially ended but Marcos retained sweeping emergency powers, ostensibly needed to combat long-running Muslim and communist insurgencies. **1983:** Opposition leader Benigno Aquino murdered at Manila airport while surrounded by government troops. **1986:** Marcos falsified election results. Corazon Aquino (widow of Benigno Aquino) used 'people's power' to force Marcos to flee country. **1987:** 'Freedom constitution' adopted; Aquino's People's Power won congressional elections. **1989:** State of emergency declared after sixth coup attempt suppressed with US aid. **1991:** Philippine senate called for withdrawal of US forces; US renewal of Subic Bay naval base lease rejected. **1992:** Fidel Ramos elected to succeed Aquino; 'Rainbow Coalition' government formed. **1995:** Imelda Marcos (widow of Ferdinand Marcos) elected to House of Representatives while on bail from prison. **1996:** LDP withdrew from coalition. Peace agreement between government and Moro National Liberation Front (MNLF) after 25 years of civil unrest on Mindanao. **1997:** Preliminary peace talks between government and

Muslim secessionist Moro Islamic Liberation Front (MILF). Major changes in political parties. Supreme Court rejected proposal to allow second presidential term.

Poland Republic of

National name: *Rzeczpospolita Polska* **Area:** 312,683 sq km/120,726 sq mi **Capital:** Warsaw **Major towns/cities:** Lódź, Kraków (Cracow), Wrocław (Breslau), Poznań (Posen), Gdańsk (Danzig), Szczecin (Stettin), Katowice (Kattowitz), Bydgoszcz (Bromberg), Lublin **Major ports:** Gdańsk (Danzig), Szczecin (Stettin), Gdynia (Gdingen) **Physical features:** part of the great plain of Europe; Vistula, Oder, and Neisse rivers; Sudeten, Tatra, and Carpathian mountains on S frontier

Government

Head of state: Aleksander Kwasniewski from 1995 **Head of government:** Jerzy Buzek from 1997 **Political system:** emergent democracy **Administrative divisions:** 49 voivodships (or provinces) **Political parties:** Democratic Left Alliance (SLD), reform socialist (ex-communist); Polish Peasant Party (PSL), moderate, agrarian; Freedom Union (UW), moderate, centrist; Labour Union (UP), left wing; Non-Party Bloc in Support of Reforms (BBWR), Christian Democrat, right of centre, pro-Wałcsa; Confederation for an Independent Poland (KPN), right wing; Solidarity Electoral Action (AWS), Christian, right wing **Armed forces:** 248,500 (1996) **Conscription:** military service is compulsory **Death penalty:** abolished 1997 **Defence spend:** (% GDP) 2.8 (1996) **Education spend:** (% GNP) 5.5 (1993/94) **Health spend:** (% GDP) 4.5 (1994)

Economy and resources

Currency: złoty **GDP:** ($ US) 93 billion (1994) **Real GDP per capita (PPP):** ($ US) 5,002 (1994) **GDP growth rate:** 6% (1996); 2.4% (1990–95) **Average annual inflation:** 19.9% (1996); 91.8% (1985–95) **Foreign debt:** ($ US) 42.3 billion (1995) **Major trading partners:** Germany, the Netherlands, Russia, Italy, UK, France, USA **Resources:** coal (world's fifth-largest producer), copper, sulphur, silver, petroleum and natural gas reserves **Industries:** machinery and transport equipment, food products, metals, chemicals, beverages, tobacco, textiles and clothing, petroleum refining, wood and paper products, tourism **Exports:** machinery and transport equipment, textiles, chemicals, coal, coke, copper, sulphur, steel, food and agricultural products, clothing and leather products, wood and paper products. Principal market: Germany 38.3% (1995) **Imports:** electro-engineering products, fuels and power (notably crude petroleum and natural gas), textiles, food products, iron ore, fertilizers. Principal source: Germany 26.6% (1995) **Arable land:** 46.7% (1995) **Agricultural products:** wheat, rye, barley, oats, maize, potatoes, sugar beet; livestock rearing; forest resources

Population and society

Population: 38,601,000 (1996 est) **Population growth rate:** 0.1% (1990–95); 0.3% (2000–05) **Population density:** (per sq km) 119 (1996 est) **Urban population:** (% of total) 65 (1995) **Age distribution:** (% of total population) <15 22.9%, 15–65 66.1%, >65

11% (1995) **Ethnic groups:** 98% ethnic Western-Slav ethnic Poles; small ethnic German, Ukrainian, and Belarussian minorities **Language:** Polish (official), German **Religion:** Roman Catholic 95% **Education:** (compulsory years) 8 **Literacy rate:** 99% (men); 99% (women) (1995 est) **Labour force:** 44.5% of population: 22.1% agriculture, 31.7% industry, 46.2% services (1996) **Unemployment:** 16.4% (1994); 13.5% (1996) **Life expectancy:** 67 (men); 76 (women) (1995–2000) **Child mortality rate:** (under 5, per 1,000 live births) 18 (1996) **Physicians:** 1 per 440 people (1994)

Practical information

Visa requirements: UK: visa not required for a stay of up to six months. USA: visa not required **Embassy in the UK:** 47 Portland Place, London W1N 3AG. Tel: (0171) 580 4324/9; fax: (0171) 323 4018 **British embassy:** Aleje Róz 1, 00-556 Warsaw. Tel: (22) 628 1001–5; fax: (22) 217 161 **Chamber of commerce:** Krajowa Izba Gospodarcza (Polish Chamber of Commerce), PO Box 361, Tr[ecedil]backa 4, 00-077 Warsaw. Tel: (22) 260 221; fax: (22) 274 673 **Airports:** international airports: Warsaw (Okecie), Kraków (Balice), Wrocław (Strachowice), Gdańsk; four domestic airports; total passenger km: 3,690 million (1994) **Major holidays:** 1 January, 1, 3, 9 May, 15 August, 1, 11 November, 25–26 December; variable: Corpus Christi, Easter Monday

Chronology

966: Polish Slavic tribes under Mieszko I, leader of Piast dynasty, adopted Christianity and united region around Poznań to form first Polish state. **1241:** Devastated by Mongols. **13th–14th centuries:** German and Jewish refugees settled among Slav population. **1386:** Jagellion dynasty came to power: golden age for Polish culture. **1569:** Poland united with Lithuania to become largest state in Europe. **1572:** Jagellion dynasty became extinct; future kings were elected by nobility and gentry, who formed 10% of the population. **mid-17th century:** Defeat in war against Russia, Sweden, and Brandenburg (in Germany) set in a process of irreversible decline. **1772–95:** Partitioned between Russia, which ruled the NE; Prussia, the W, including Pomerania; and Austria in the south-centre, including Galicia, where there was greatest autonomy. **1815:** After Congress of Vienna, Russian eastern portion of Poland re-established as kingdom within Russian Empire. **1830 and 1863:** Uprisings against repressive Russian rule. **1892:** Nationalist Polish Socialist Party (PPS) founded. **1918:** Independent Polish republic established after World War I, with Marshal Józef Piłsudski, founder of the PPS, elected president. **1919–21:** Abortive advance into Lithuania and Ukraine. **1926:** Piłsudski seized full power in coup and established autocratic regime. **1935:** On Piłsudski's death, military regime held power under Marshal Smigły-Rydz. **1939:** Invaded by Germany; W Poland incorporated into Nazi Reich (state) and the rest became a German colony; 6 million Poles – half of them Jews – were slaughtered in the next five years. **1944–45:** Liberated from Nazi rule by Soviet Union's Red Army; boundaries redrawn westwards at Potsdam Conference. One half of 'old Poland', 180,000 sq km/70,000 sq mi in the E, was lost to the Soviet Union; 100,000 sq km/40,000 sq mi of ex-German territory in Silesia, along the Oder and Neisse rivers, was added, shifting the state 240 km/150 mi westwards; millions of Germans were expelled. **1947:** Communist people's republic proclaimed after manipulated election. **1949:** Joined Comecon. **early 1950s:** Harsh Stalinist rule under communist leader Bolesław Bierut: nationalization; rural collectivization; persecution of Catholic Church members. **1955:** Joined Warsaw Pact defence organization. **1956:** Poznań strikes and riots. The moderate Władysław Gomułka installed as Polish United Workers' Party (PUWP) leader. **1960s:** Private farming reintroduced and Catholicism tolerated. **1970:** GomuLka replaced by Edward Gierek after Gdańsk riots against food price rises. **1970s:** Poland heavily indebted to foreign creditors after failed attempt to boost economic growth. **1980:** Solidarity, led by Lech Wałesa, emerged as free trade union following Gdańsk disturbances. **1981:** Martial law imposed by Gen Wojciech Jaruzelski, trade-union activity banned and Solidarity leaders and supporters arrested. **1983:** Martial law ended. **1984:** Amnesty for 35,000 political prisoners. **1988:** Solidarity-led strikes and demonstrations for pay increases. Reform-communist Mieczysław

Rakowski became prime minister. **1989:** Agreement to relegalize Solidarity, allow opposition parties, and adopt a more democratic constitution, after round-table talks involving Solidarity, the Communist Party, and the Catholic Church. Widespread success for Solidarity in first open elections for 40 years; noncommunist 'grand coalition' government formed, headed by Tadeusz Mazowiecki of Solidarity; economic austerity and free-market restructuring programme began. **1990:** PUWP dissolved and re-formed as Democratic Left Alliance (SLD). Wałesa was elected president and Jan Bielecki became prime minister. **1991:** Shock-therapy economic restructuring programme, including large-scale privatization, produced sharp fall in living standards and rise in unemployment rate to 11%. Unpopular Bielecki resigned and, after inconclusive elections, Jan Olszewski formed fragile centre-right coalition government. **1992:** Political instability continued, with Waldemar Pawlak, of centre-left Polish Peasant Party (PSL), and Hanna Suchocka, of centrist Democratic Union, successively replacing Olszewski as prime minister. **1993:** Economy became first in Central Europe to grow since collapse of communism. After new elections, Pawlak formed coalition government with ex-communist SLD, which pledged to continue to build market-based economy and seek early entry into European Union. **1994:** Joined NATO 'partnership for peace' programme; last Russian troops left Poland. **1995:** Ex-communist Józef Oleksy replaced Pawlak as prime minister. Wałesa narrowly defeated by Aleksander Kwasniewski, leader of the SLD, in presidential election. **1996:** Oleksy resigned as prime minister amid allegations of spying for Russia's secret service; replaced by Włodzimierz Cimoszewicz. **1997:** Speeding-up of structural reform and privatization. Gdańsk shipyard closed. New constitution approved. Poland invited to join NATO and begin negotiations to join European Union. General election won by Solidarity Electoral Action (AWS). Coalition government formed, led by Jerzy Buzek.

Portugal Republic of

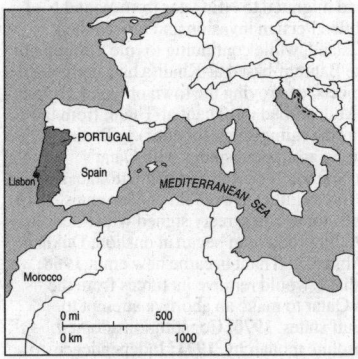

National name: *República Portuguesa* **Area:** 92,000 sq km/35,521 sq mi (including the Azores and Madeira) **Capital:** Lisbon **Major towns/cities:** Porto, Coimbra, Amadora, Setúbal, Guarde, Portalegre **Major ports:** Porto, Setúbal **Physical features:** mountainous in the N (Serra da Estrêla mountains); plains in the S; rivers Minho, Douro, Tagus (Tejo), Guadiana

Government
Head of state: Jorge Sampaio from 1996 **Head of government:** Antonio Guterres from 1995 **Political system:** democracy **Administrative divisions:** 18 districts and two autonomous regions **Political parties:** Social Democratic Party (PSD), moderate left of centre; Socialist Party (PS), centre left; People's Party (PP), right wing, anti-European integration **Armed forces:** 54,200 (1996) **Conscription:** 4–18 months **Death penalty:** abolished 1976 **Defence spend:** (% GDP) 2.8 (1996) **Education spend:** (% GNP) 5.4 (1993/94) **Health spend:** (% GDP) 4.1 (1993)

Economy and resources
Currency: escudo **GDP:** ($ US) 104 billion (1996) **Real GDP per capita (PPP):** ($ US) 13,059 (1996) **GDP growth rate:** 2.8% (1996); 0.8%(1990–95) **Average annual inflation:** 3.1% (1996);

11.2% (1985–95) **Major trading partners:** EU (principally Spain, Germany, and France) **Resources:** limestone, granite, marble, iron, tungsten, copper, pyrites, gold, uranium, coal, forests **Industries:** textiles and clothing, footwear, paper pulp, cork items (world's largest producer of cork), chemicals, petroleum refining, fish processing, viticulture, electrical appliances, ceramics, tourism **Exports:** textiles, clothing, footwear, pulp and waste paper, wood and cork manufactures, tinned fish, electrical equipment, wine, refined petroleum. Principal market: Germany 21.6% (1995) **Imports:** foodstuffs, machinery and transport equipment, crude petroleum, natural gas, textile yarn, coal, rubber, plastics, tobacco. Principal source: Spain 20.8% (1995) **Arable land:** 25.2% (1995) **Agricultural products:** wheat, maize, rice, potatoes, tomatoes, grapes, olives, fruit; fishing (1993 sardine catch was the world's largest at 89,914 tonnes)

Population and society
Population: 9,808,000 (1996 est) **Population growth rate:** –0.1% (1990–95); 0% (2000–05) **Population density:** (per sq km) 106 (1996 est) **Urban population:** (% of total) 36 (1995) **Age distribution:** (% of total population) <15 18.8%, 15–65 67%, >65 14.1% (1995) **Ethnic groups:** most of the population is descended from Caucasoid peoples who inhabited the whole of the Iberian peninsula in classical and pre-classical times; there are a number of minorities from Portugal's overseas possessions and former possessions **Language:** Portuguese **Religion:** Roman Catholic 97% **Education:** (compulsory years) 9 **Literacy rate:** 89% (men); 81% (women) (1995 est) **Labour force:** 49.2% of population: 12.2% agriculture, 31.4% industry, 56.4% services (1996) **Unemployment:** 7.3% (1996) **Life expectancy:** 72 (men); 79 (women) (1995–2000) **Child mortality rate:** (under 5, per 1,000 live births) 11 (1996) **Physicians:** 1 per 345 people (1994)

Practical information
Visa requirements: UK: visa not required for a stay of up to three months. USA: visa not required for a stay of up to two months **Embassy in the UK:** 11 Belgrave Square, London SW1X 8PP. Tel: (0171) 235 5331/4; fax: (0171) 245 1287 **British embassy:** Rua de São Bernardo 33, 1200 Lisbon. Tel: (1) 396 1191; fax: (1) 397 6768 **Chamber of commerce:** Confederação do Comércio Português, Rua dos Correeiros 79, 1 ° Andar, 1100 Lisbon. Tel: (1) 301 0192; fax: (1) 301 0626 **Airports:** international airports: Lisbon (Portela de Sacavem), Faro, Oporto (Oporto Sá Carneiro), Madeira (Funchal), Azores (Santa Maria), São Miguel; domestic services operate between these; total passenger km: 7,880 million (1994) **Major holidays:** 1 January, 25 April, 10 June, 15 August, 5 October, 1 November, 1, 8, 24–25 December; variable: Carnival, Corpus Christi, Good Friday

Chronology
2nd century BC: Romans conquered Iberian peninsula. **5th century AD:** Iberia overrun by Vandals and Visigoths after fall of Roman Empire. **711:** Visigoth kingdom overthrown by Muslims invading from N Africa. **997–1064:** Christians resettled northern area, which came under rule of Léon and Castile. **1139:** Afonso I, son of Henry of Burgundy, defeated Muslims; the area became an independent kingdom. **1340:** Final Muslim invasion defeated. **1373:** Anglo-Portuguese alliance signed. **15th century:** Age of exploration: Portuguese mariners surveyed coast of Africa, opened sea route to India (Vasco da Gama), and reached Brazil (Pedro Cabral). **16th century:** 'Golden Age': Portugal flourished as commercial and colonial power. **1580:** Philip II of Spain took throne of Portugal. **1640:** Spanish rule overthrown in bloodless coup; Duke of Braganza proclaimed as King John IV. **1668:** Spain recognized Portuguese independence. **1755:** Lisbon devastated by earthquake. **1755–77:** Politics dominated by chief minister Sebastiao de Carlvalho, Marquis of Pombal, who introduced secular education and promoted trade. **1807:** Napoleonic France invaded Portugal; Portuguese court fled to Brazil. **1807–11:** In the Peninsular War British forces played leading part in liberating Portugal from French. **1820:** Liberal revolution forced King John VI to return from Brazil and accept constitutional government. **1822:** Brazil declared independence; first Portuguese constitution adopted. **1826:** First

constitution replaced by more conservative one. **1828:** Dom Miguel blocked succession of his niece, Queen Maria, and declared himself absolute monarch; civil war ensued between liberals and conservatives. **1834:** Queen Maria regained throne with British, French, and Brazilian help; constitutional government restored. **1840s:** Severe disputes between supporters of radical 1822 constitution and more conservative 1826 constitution. **1851:** 'Regeneration' to promote order and economic growth launched by Duke of Saldanha after coup. **late 19th century:** Government faced severe financial difficulties; rise of socialist, anarchist, and republican parties. **1908:** Assassination of King Carlos I. **1910:** Portugal became republic after three-day insurrection forced King Manuel II to flee. **1911:** New regime adopted liberal constitution, but republic proved unstable, violent, and corrupt. **1916–18:** Portugal fought in World War I on Allied side. **1926–51:** Popular military coup installed Gen António de Fragoso Carmona as president. **1928:** António de Oliveira Salazar became finance minister and introduced successful reforms. **1932:** Salazar became prime minister with dictatorial powers. **1933:** Authoritarian 'Estado Novo' ('New State') constitution adopted; living conditions improved, but Salazar resisted political change at home and in colonies. **1949:** Portugal became founding member of North Atlantic Treaty Organization (NATO). **1968:** Salazar retired; succeeded by Marcello Caetano. **1974:** Army seized power to end stalemate situation in African colonial wars; Gen Antó Ribeiro de Spínola became president; succeeded by Gen Francisco da Costa Gomes. **1975:** Portuguese colonies achieved independence; Gomes narrowly averted communist coup. **1976:** First free elections in 50 years resulted in minority government under socialist leader Mario Soares; Gen António Ramahlo Eanes won presidency. **1980:** Francisco Balsemão (PSD) formed centre-party coalition. **1986:** Soares became first civilian president in 60 years; Portugal joined European Community (EC). **1989:** Social Democrat government started to dismantle socialist economy and privatize major industries. **1996:** Jorge Sampaio (PS) elected president.

Qatar State of

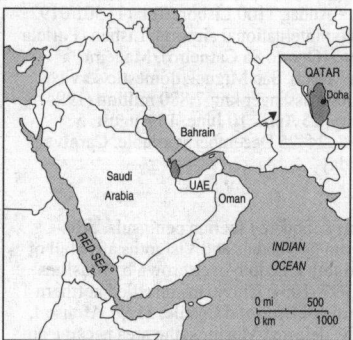

National name:
Dawlat Qatar
Area: 11,400 sq km/4,401 sq mi
Capital: Doha (and chief port) **Major towns/cities:** Dukhan, centre of oil production; Halul, terminal for offshore oilfields; Umm Said, Ruwais, Wakra, Al-Khour **Physical features:** mostly flat desert with salt flats in S

Government
Head of state and government: Sheik Hamad bin Khalifa al-Thani from 1995 **Political system:** absolute monarchy **Administrative divisions:** nine municipalities **Political parties:** none **Armed forces:** 11,800 (1996) **Conscription:** military service is voluntary **Death penalty:** retained and used for ordinary crimes **Defence spend:** (% GDP) 10.2 (1996) **Education spend:** (% GNP) 3.2 (1993) **Health spend:** (% GDP) 3.1 (1990)

Economy and resources
Currency: Qatari riyal **GDP:** ($ US) 7.17 billion (1994) **Real GDP per capita (PPP):** ($ US) 18,403 (1994) **GDP growth rate:** –4.1% (1994) **Average annual inflation:** 2.2% (1996) **Foreign debt:** ($ US) 6.35 billion (1996) **Major trading partners:** Japan, Italy, USA, UK, Germany, France, Saudi Arabia, Spain **Resources:**

petroleum, natural gas, water resources **Industries:** petroleum refining and petroleum products, industrial chemicals, iron and steel, flour, cement, concrete, plastics, paint **Exports:** petroleum. Principal market: Japan 54.3% (1995) **Imports:** machinery and transport equipment, basic manufactures, food and live animals, miscellaneous manufactured articles, chemicals. Principal source: Italy 15.5% (1995) **Arable land:** 0.7% (1995) **Agricultural products:** cereals, vegetables, fruits (especially dates); livestock rearing; fishing

Population and society
Population: 558,000 (1996 est) **Population growth rate:** 2.5% (1990–95) **Population density:** (per sq km) 51 (1996 est) **Urban population:** (% of total) 91 (1995) **Ethnic composition:** only about 25% of the population are indigenous Qataris; 40% are Arabs, and the others Pakistanis, Indians, and Iranians **Language:** Arabic (official); English **Religion:** Sunni Muslim **Education:** not compulsory **Literacy rate:** 78% (men); 78% (women) (1995 est) **Labour force:** 57% of population: 3% agriculture, 32% industry, 65% services (1990) **Unemployment:** dependent on immigrant workers – shortage of indigenous labour **Life expectancy:** 70 (men); 75 (women) (1995–2000) **Child mortality rate:** (under 5, per 1,000 live births) 23 (1996) **Physicians:** 1 per 681 people (1993)

Practical information
Visa requirements: UK: visa not required for a stay of up to 30 days. USA: visa required **Embassy in the UK:** 1 South Audley Street, London W1Y 5DQ. Tel: (0171) 493 2200; fax: (0171) 493 3894 **British embassy:** PO Box 3, Doha. Tel: (974) 421 991; fax: (974) 438 692 **Chamber of commerce:** PO Box 402, Doha. Tel: (974) 425 131; fax: (974) 425 186 **Airports:** international airports: Doha; total passenger km: 2,439 million (1994) **Major holidays:** 3 September, 31 December; variable: Eid-ul-Adha (4 days), end of Ramadan (4 days)

Chronology
7th century AD: Islam introduced. **8th century:** Developed into important trading centre during time of Abbasid Empire. **1783:** The al-Khalifa family, who had migrated to NE Qatar from W and N of the Arabian Peninsula, foiled Persian invasion and moved their headquarters to Bahrain Island, while continuing to rule the area of Qatar. **1867–68:** After the Bahrain-based al-Khalifa had suppressed a revolt by their Qatari subjects, destroying the town of Doha, Britain intervened and installed Muhammad ibn Thani al-Thani, from the leading family of Qatar, as the ruling sheik (or emir). A British Resident was given power to arbitrate disputes with Qatar's neighbours. **1871–1914:** Nominally part of Turkish Ottoman Empire, although in 1893 sheik's forces inflicted a defeat on Ottomans. **1916:** Qatar became British protectorate after treaty signed with Sheik Adbullah al-Thani. **1949:** Oil production began at onshore Dukhan field in W. **1960:** Sheik Ahmad al-Thani became new emir. **1968:** Britain's announcement that it would remove its forces from the Persian Gulf by 1971 led Qatar to make an abortive attempt to arrange a federation of Gulf states. **1970:** Constitution adopted, confirming emirate as absolute monarchy. **1971:** Independence achieved from Britain. **1972:** Emir Sheik Ahmad replaced in bloodless coup by his cousin, the Crown Prince and prime minister Sheik Khalifa ibn Hamad al-Thani. **1991:** Forces joined United Nations coalition in Gulf War against Iraq. **1995:** Sheik Khalifa ousted by his son Crown Prince Sheik Hamad bin Khalifa al-Thani. **1996:** Announcement of plans to introduce democracy were followed by an assassination attempt on Sheik Hamad.

Romania

National name: *România* **Area:** 237,500 sq km/91,698 sq mi **Capital:** Bucharest **Major towns/cities:** Brasov, Timisoara, Cluj-Napoca, IasI, Constanta, Galati, Craiova, Ploiesti **Major ports:** Galati, Constanta, Brăila **Physical features:** mountains surrounding a plateau, with river plains S and E. Carpathian Mountains, Transylvanian Alps; river Danube; Black Sea coast; mineral springs

Government

Head of state: Emil Constantinescu from 1996 **Head of government:** Victor Ciorbea from 1996 **Political system:** emergent democracy **Administrative divisions:** 41 counties **Political parties:** Democratic Convention of Romania (DCR), centre-right coalition; Social Democratic Union (SDU), reformist; Social Democracy Party of Romania (PSDR), social democrat; Romanian National Unity Party (RNUP), Romanian nationalist, right wing, anti-Hungarian; Greater Romania Party (Romania Mare), far right, ultranationalist, anti-Semitic; Democratic Party–National Salvation Front (DP–NSF), promarket; National Salvation Front (NSF), centre left; Hungarian Democratic Union of Romania (HDUR), ethnic Hungarian; Christian Democratic–National Peasants' Party (CD–PNC), centre right, promarket; Socialist Labour Party (SLP), ex-communist **Armed forces:** 228,400 (1996) **Conscription:** military service is compulsory for 12–18 months **Death penalty:** abolished 1989 **Defence spend:** (% GDP) 2.3 (1996) **Education spend:** (% GNP) 3.1 (1994) **Health spend:** (% GDP) 4.8 (1994)

Economy and resources

Currency: leu **GDP:** ($ US) 30 billion (1994) **Real GDP per capita (PPP):** ($ US) 4,037 (1994) **GDP growth rate:** 7.1% (1995); –1.4% (1990–95) **Average annual inflation:** 37% (1996); 69.1% (1985–95) **Foreign debt:** ($ US) 7.8 billion (1996) **Major trading partners:** Germany, Russia, Italy, USA, France, Iran, China, Turkey **Resources:** brown coal, hard coal, iron ore, salt, bauxite, copper, lead, zinc, methane gas, petroleum (reserves expected to be exhausted by mid to late 1990s) **Industries:** metallurgy, mechanical engineering, chemical products, timber and wood products, textiles and clothing, food processing **Exports:** base metals and metallic articles, textiles and clothing, machinery and equipment, mineral products, foodstuffs. Principal market: Germany 17.9% (1996) **Imports:** mineral products, machinery and mechanical appliances, textiles, motor cars. Principal source: Germany 17.1% (1996) **Arable land:** 40.5% (1995) **Agricultural products:** wheat, maize, potatoes, sugar beet, barley, apples, grapes, sunflower seeds; wine production; forestry; fish breeding

Population and society

Population: 22,655,000 (1996 est) **Population growth rate:** –0.3% (1990–95); –0.2% (2000–05) **Population density:** (per sq km) 95 (1996 est) **Urban population:** (% of total) 55 (1995) **Age distribution:** (% of total population) <15 20.4%, 15–65 67.7%, >65 11.8% (1995) **Ethnic groups:** 89% non-Slavic ethnic Romanian; substantial Hungarian, German, and Serbian minorities **Language:** Romanian (official), Hungarian, German **Religion:** mainly Romanian Orthodox **Education:** (compulsory years) 8 **Literacy rate:** 97% (men); 97% (women) (1995 est) **Labour force:** 35.9% agriculture, 35.8% industry, 28.3% services (1993) **Unemployment:** 7.8% (1996) **Life expectancy:** 67 (men); 73 (women) (1995–2000) **Child mortality rate:** (under 5, per 1,000 live births) 30 (1996) **Physicians:** 1 per 561 people (1995)

Practical information

Visa requirements: UK: visa required. USA: visa not required for a stay of up to 30 days **Embassy in the UK:** Arundel House, 4 Palace Green, London W8 4QD. Tel: (0171) 937 9666/8; fax: (0171) 937 8069 **British embassy:** Strada Jules Michelet 24, 70154 Bucharest. Tel: (1) 312 0305; fax: (1) 312 0229 **Chamber of commerce:** Chamber of Commerce and Industry of Romania, Boulevard Nicolae Balcescu 22, 79502 Bucharest. Tel: (1) 615 4703; fax: (1) 312 2091 **Airports:** international airports: Bucharest (Otopeni), Constanta (Mihail Kogăiniceanu), Timisoara, Arad; 12 domestic airports; total passenger km: 2,584 million (1994) **Major holidays:** 1–2 January, 15 April, 1 May, 1, 25–26 December

Chronology

106: Formed heartland of ancient region of Dacia, which was conquered by Roman Emperor Trajan and became a province of Roman Empire; Christianity introduced. **275:** Taken from Rome by invading Goths, a Germanic people. **4th–10th centuries:** Invaded by successive waves of Huns, Avars, Bulgars, Magyars, and Mongols. **c. 1000:** Transylvania, in N, became an autonomous province under Hungarian crown. **mid-14th century:** Two Romanian principalities emerged, Wallachia in S, around Bucharest, and Moldova in NE. **15th–16th centuries:** The formerly autonomous principalities of Wallachia, Moldova, and Transylvania became tributaries to Ottoman Turks, despite peasant uprisings and resistance from Vlad Tepes ('the Impaler'), ruling prince of Wallachia. **late 17th century:** Transylvania conquered under Austrian Habsburgs. **1829:** Wallachia and Moldova brought under tsarist Russian suzerainty. **1859:** Under Prince Alexandru Ion Cuza, Moldova and Wallachia united to form Romanian state. **1878:** Romania's independence recognized by Great Powers in Congress of Berlin. **1881:** Became kingdom under Carol I. **1916–18:** Fought on Triple Entente side (Britain, France, and Russia) during World War I; acquired Transylvania and Bukovina, in N, from dismembered Austro-Hungarian Empire, and Bessarabia, in E, from Russia. This made it largest state in Balkans. **1930:** To counter growing popularity of fascist and antisemitic 'Iron Guard' mass movement, King Carol II abolished democratic institutions and established dictatorship. **1940:** Forced to surrender Bessarabia and N Bukovina, adjoining Black Sea, to Soviet Union, and N Transylvania to Hungary; King Carol II abdicated, handing over effective power to Gen Ion Antonescu, who signed Axis Pact with Germany. **1941–44:** Fought on Germany's side against Soviet Union; thousands of Jews massacred. **1944:** Antonescu ousted; Romania joined war against Germany. **1945:** Occupied by Soviet Union; communist-dominated government installed. **1947:** Paris Peace Treaty reclaimed Transylvania for Romania, but lost S Dobruja to Bulgaria and N Bukovina and Bessarabia to Soviet Union; King Michael, son of Carol II, abdicated and People's Republic proclaimed. **1948–49:** New Soviet-style constitution; joined Comecon; nationalization and agricultural collectivization. **1955:** Romania joined Warsaw Pact. **1958:** Soviet occupation forces removed. **1965:** Nicolae Ceausescu replaced Gheorghe Gheorghiu-Dej as Romanian Communist Party leader, and pursued foreign policy autonomous of Moscow, refusing to participate in Warsaw Pact manoeuvres. **1975:** Ceausescu made president. **1985–86:** Winters of austerity and power cuts as Ceausescu refused to liberalize the economy. **1987:** Workers' demonstrations against austerity programme brutally crushed at Brasov. **1988–89:** Relations with Hungary deteriorated over 'systematization programme', designed to forcibly resettle ethnic Hungarians in Transylvania. **1989:** Bloody overthrow of Ceausescu regime in 'Christmas Revolution'; Ceausescu and wife tried and executed; estimated 10,000 dead in civil war. Power assumed by NSF, headed by Ion Iliescu. **1990:** Securitate secret police replaced by new Romanian Intelligence Service; Eastern Orthodox Church and private farming re-legalized; systematization programme abandoned. **1991:** Privatization law passed. Prime minister Petre Roman resigned following riots by striking miners; succeeded by Theodor Stolojan heading a new cross-party coalition government. **1992:** NSF split; Iliescu re-elected president; Nicolai Vacaroiu appointed prime minister of minority coalition government. **1994:** Military cooperation pact with Bulgaria. Far-right parties brought into governing coalition. **1996:** Signs of economic growth; parliamentary elections won by DCR who formed coalition government with SDU; Emil Constantinescu of Democratic Convention elected president; Victor Ciorbea appointed prime minister. **1997:** Economic 'shock therapy' reform programme and drive against corruption announced. Sharp increase in inflation.

Former King Michael returned from exile. Finance minister dismissed in shake-up of economic ministries.

Russian Federation (formerly to 1991 Russian Soviet Federal Socialist Republic (RSFSR))

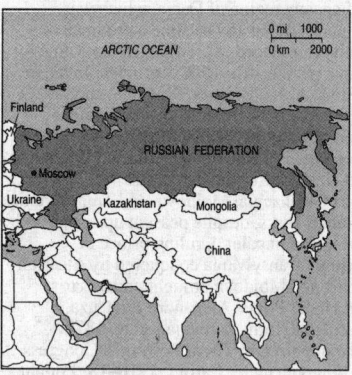

National name: *Rossiskaya Federatsiya* **Area:** 17,075,400 sq km/6,592,811 sq mi **Capital:** Moscow **Major towns/cities:** St Petersburg (Leningrad), Nizhniy Novgorod (Gorky), Rostov-na-Donu, Samara (Kuibyshev), Tver (Kalinin), Volgograd, Vyatka (Kirov), Ekaterinburg (Sverdlovsk), Novosibirsk,
Chelyabinsk, Kazan, Omsk, Perm, Ufa **Physical features:** fertile Black Earth district; extensive forests; the Ural Mountains with large mineral resources; Lake Baikal, world's deepest lake

Government
Head of state: Boris Yeltsin from 1991 **Head of government:** Sergei Kiriyenko from 1998 **Political system:** emergent democracy **Administrative divisions:** 21 republics, 6 territories, 49 provinces, 10 autonomous areas, two cities with federal status, and one autonomous region **Political parties:** Russia is Our Home, centrist; Party of Unity and Accord (PRUA), moderate reformist; Communist Party of the Russian Federation (CPRF), left wing, conservative (ex-communist); Agrarian Party, rural-based, centrist; Liberal Democratic Party, far right, ultranationalist; Congress of Russian Communities, populist, nationalist; Russia's Choice, reformist, centre right; Yabloko, gradualist free market; Russian Social Democratic People's Party (Derzhava), communist-nationalist; Patriotic Popular Union of Russia (PPUR), communist-led; Russian People's Republican Party (RPRP) **Armed forces:** 1,270,000; paramilitary forces of 352,000 (1996) **Conscription:** two years **Death penalty:** retained and used for ordinary crimes **Defence spend:** (% GDP) 7.4 (1995) **Education spend:** (% GNP) 4.4 (1993–94) **Health spend:** (% GDP) 4.1 (1990–95)

Economy and resources
Currency: rouble **GDP:** ($ US) 377 billion (1994) **Real GDP per capita (PPP):** ($ US) 4,828 (1994) **GDP growth rate:** –4% (1995); –9.8% (1990–95) **Average annual inflation:** 47.6% (1996); 148.9% (1985–95) **Foreign debt:** ($ US) 120.4 billion (1995) **Major trading partners:** CIS republics, Germany, UK, China, USA, Japan, Italy **Resources:** petroleum, natural gas, coal, peat, copper (world's fourth-largest producer), iron ore, lead, aluminium, phosphate rock, nickel, manganese, gold, diamonds, platinum, zinc, tin **Industries:** cast iron, steel, rolled iron, synthetic fibres, soap, cellulose, paper, cement, machinery and transport equipment, glass, bricks, food processing, confectionery **Exports:** mineral fuels, ferrous and non-ferrous metals and derivatives, precious stones, chemical products, machinery and transport equipment, weapons, timber and paper products. Principal market: Ukraine 9% (1996) **Imports:** machinery and transport equipment, grain and foodstuffs, chemical products, textiles, clothing, footwear, pharmaceuticals, metals. Principal source: Ukraine 14% (1996) **Arable land:** 7.8% (1995) **Agricultural products:** grain, potatoes, flax, sunflower seed, vegetables, fruit and berries, tea; livestock and dairy farming

Population and society
Population: 148,146,000 (1996 est) **Population growth rate:** –0.1% (1990–95); –0.2% (2000–05) **Population density:** (per sq km) 9 (1996 est) **Urban population:** (% of total) 76 (1995) **Age distribution:** (% of total population) <15 21.1%, 15–65 66.9%, >65 12.1% (1995) **Ethnic groups:** predominantly ethnic Russian (eastern Slav); significant Tatar, Ukranian, Chuvash, Belarussian, Bashkir, and Chechen minorities **Language:** Russian **Religion:** traditionally Russian Orthodox **Education:** (compulsory years) 9 **Literacy rate:** 99% (men); 99% (women) (1995 est) **Labour force:** 52% of population: 14% agriculture, 42% industry, 45% services (1990) **Unemployment:** 3.5% (1996) **Life expectancy:** 62 (men); 74 (women) (1995–2000) **Child mortality rate:** (under 5, per 1,000 live births) 27 (1996) **Physicians:** 1 per 222 people (1994)

Practical information
Visa requirements: UK: visa required. USA: visa required **Embassy in the UK:** 13 Kensington Palace Gardens, London W8 4QX. Tel: (0171) 229 3628; fax: (0171) 727 8625 **British embassy:** Sofiyskaya Naberezhnaya 14, Moscow 72. Tel: (095) 956 7200; fax: (095) 956 7420 **Chamber of commerce:** Chamber of Commerce and Industry of the Russian Federation, Ulitsa Ilynka 6, 103684 Moscow. Tel: (095) 925 3581 **Airports:** international airports: Moscow (Sheremetyevo), St Petersburg (Pulkovo); six principal domestic airports operate services to all major cities; total passenger km: 65,144 million (1994) **Major holidays:** 1, 7 January, 8 March, 15 April, 1–2, 9 May, 12 June, 22 August, 7 November

Chronology
9th–10th centuries: Viking chieftains established own rule in Novgorod, Kiev, and other cities. **10th–12th centuries:** Kiev temporarily united Russian peoples into its empire. Christianity introduced from Constantinople 988. **13th century:** Mongols (Golden Horde) overran the southern steppes 1223, compelling Russian princes to pay tribute. **14th century:** Byelorussia and Ukraine came under Polish rule. **1462–1505:** Ivan the Great, grand duke of Muscovy, threw off Mongol yoke and united lands in NW. **1547–84:** Ivan the Terrible assumed title of tsar and conquered Kazan and Astrakhan; colonization of Siberia began. **1613:** First Romanov tsar, Michael, elected after period of chaos. **1667:** Following Cossack revolt, E Ukraine reunited with Russia. **1682–1725:** Peter the Great modernized the bureaucracy and army; he founded a navy and a new capital, St Petersburg, introduced Western education, and wrested the Baltic seaboard from Sweden. By 1700 colonization of Siberia had reached the Pacific. **1762–96:** Catherine the Great annexed the Crimea and part of Poland and recovered W Ukraine and Byelorussia. **1798–1814:** Russia intervened in Revolutionary and Napoleonic Wars (1798–1801, 1805–07); repelled Napoleon, and took part in his overthrow (1812–14). **1827–29:** Russian attempts to dominate Balkans led to war with Turkey. **1853–56:** Crimean War. **1856–64:** Caucasian War of conquest completed annexation of N Caucasus, causing more than a million people to emigrate. **1858–60:** Treaties of Aigun 1858 and Peking 1860 imposed on China, annexing territories N of the Amur and E of the Ussuri rivers; Vladivostok founded on Pacific coast. **1861:** Serfdom abolished (on terms unfavourable to peasants). Rapid growth of industry followed, a working-class movement developed, and revolutionary ideas spread, culminating in assassination of Alexander II 1881. **1877–78:** Russo-Turkish War **1898:** Social Democratic Party founded by Russian Marxists; split into Bolshevik and Menshevik factions 1903. **1904–05:** Russo-Japanese War caused by Russian expansion in Manchuria. **1905:** A revolution, though suppressed, forced tsar to accept parliament (Duma) with limited powers. **1914:** Russo-Austrian rivalry in Balkans was a major cause of outbreak of World War I; Russia fought in alliance with France and Britain. **1917:** Russian Revolution: tsar abdicated, provisional government established; Bolsheviks seized power under Vladimir Lenin. **1918:** Treaty of Brest-Litovsk ended war with Germany; murder of former tsar; Russian Empire collapsed; Finland, Poland, and Baltic States seceded. **1918–22:** Civil War between Red Army, led by Leon Trotsky, and White Russian forces with foreign support; Red Army ultimately victorious; control regained over Ukraine, Caucasus, and

Central Asia. **1922:** Former Russian Empire renamed Union of Soviet Socialist Republics. **1924:** Death of Lenin. **1928:** Joseph Stalin emerged as absolute ruler after ousting Trotsky. **1928–33:** First Five-Year Plan collectivized agriculture by force; millions died in famine. **1936–38:** The Great Terror: Stalin executed his critics and imprisoned millions of people on false charges of treason and sabotage. **1939:** Nazi-Soviet nonaggression pact; USSR invaded eastern Poland and attacked Finland. **1940:** USSR annexed Baltic States. **1941–45:** 'Great Patriotic War' against Germany ended with Soviet domination of eastern Europe and led to 'Cold War' with USA and its allies. **1949:** Council for Mutual Economic Assistance (Comecon) created to supervise trade in Soviet bloc. **1953:** Stalin died; 'collective leadership' in power. **1955:** Warsaw Pact created. **1956:** Nikita Khrushchev made 'secret speech' criticizing Stalin; USSR invaded Hungary. **1957–58:** Khrushchev ousted his rivals and became effective leader, introducing limited reforms. **1960:** Rift between USSR and Communist China. **1962:** Cuban missile crisis: Soviet nuclear missiles installed in Cuba but removed after ultimatum from USA. **1964:** Khrushchev ousted by new 'collective leadership' headed by Leonid Brezhnev and Alexei Kosygin. **1968:** USSR and allies invaded Czechoslovakia. **1970s:** 'Détente' with USA and western Europe. **1979:** USSR invaded Afghanistan; fighting continued until Soviet withdrawal ten years later. **1982:** Brezhnev died; Uri Andropov became leader. **1984:** Andropov died; Konstantin Chernenko became leader. **1985:** Chernenko died; Mikhail Gorbachev became leader and announced wide-ranging reform programme (*perestroika*). **1986:** Chernobyl nuclear disaster. **1988:** Special All-Union Party Congress approved radical constitutional changes and market reforms; start of open nationalist unrest in Caucasus and Baltic republics. **1989:** Multi-candidate elections held in move towards 'socialist democracy'; collapse of Soviet satellite regimes in eastern Europe; end of Cold War. **1990:** Anti-communists and nationalists polled strongly in multi-party local elections; Baltic and Caucasian republics defied central government; Boris Yeltsin became president of Russian Federation and left Communist Party. **1991:** Unsuccessful coup by hardline communists; republics declared independence; dissolution of communist rule in Russian Federation; USSR replaced by loose Commonwealth of Independent States (CIS). **1992:** Russia assumed former USSR seat on United Nations (UN) Security Council; new constitution devised; end of price controls. **1993:** Power struggle between Yeltsin and Congress of People's Deputies; congress dissolved; attempted coup foiled; new parliament elected. **1994:** Russia joined North Atlantic Treaty Organization (NATO) 'Partnership for Peace'; Russian forces invaded breakaway republic of Chechnya. **1995:** Bloody civil war in Chechnya continued. **1996:** Re-election of President Yeltsin. Peace plan and final withdrawal of Russian troops from Chechnya. **1997:** Peace treaty with Chechnya signed. Yeltsin agreed to expansion of NATO into central Europe, and signed agreement on cooperation with NATO. Russia gained effective admission to G-7 group. World Bank loan and International Monetary Fund (IMF) credit agreed in return for continuing economic reforms. Convention outlawing production and use of chemical weapons ratified by lower house of parliament.**1998:** Following Yeltsin's sacking of his entire government, parliamentary elections confirmed Sergei Kiriyenko as prime minister, heading a younger, more market-oriented cabinet committed to economic reform.

Rwanda Republic of

National name: *Republika y'u Rwanda* **Area:** 26,338 sq km/10,169 sq mi **Capital:** Kigali **Major towns/cities:** Butare, Ruhengeri, Gisenyi **Physical features:** high savanna and hills, with volcanic mountains in NW; part of lake Kivu; highest peak Mount Karisimbi 4,507 m/14,792 ft; Kagera River (whose headwaters are the source of the Nile)

Government
Head of state: Pasteur Bizimungu from 1994 **Head of government:** Pierre Celestin Rwigema from 1995 **Political system:** transitional **Administrative divisions:** 10 prefectures **Political parties:** National Revolutionary Development Movement (MRND),

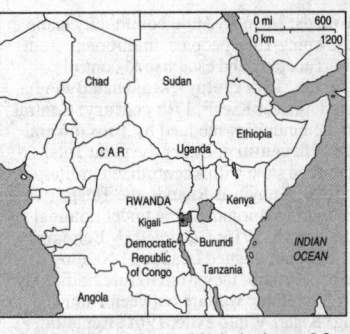

nationalist-socialist, Hutu-oriented; Social Democratic Party (PSD), left of centre; Christian Democratic Party (PDC), Christian, centrist; Republican Democratic Movement (MDR), Hutu nationalist; Liberal Party (PL), moderate centrist; Rwanda Patriotic Front (FPR), Tutsi-led but claims to be multiethnic **Armed forces:** 33,000 (1996) **Conscription:** military service is voluntary **Death penalty:** retains the death penalty for ordinary crimes but can be considered abolitionist in practice (last execution 1982) **Defence spend:** (% GDP) 6.3 (1996) **Education spend:** (% GNP) 3.8 (1992); N/A (1993/94) **Health spend:** (% GDP) 1.9 (1990–95)

Economy and resources
Currency: Rwanda franc **GDP:** ($ US) 0.6 billion (1994) **Real GDP per capita (PPP):** ($ US) 352 (1994) **GDP growth rate:** 25% (1995 est); –12.8% (1990–95) **Average annual inflation:** 25% (1996); 10.4% (1985–95) **Foreign debt:** ($ US) 1 billion (1995) **Major trading partners:** Brazil, Kenya, Belgium, Germany, the Netherlands, South Africa, France, UK **Resources:** cassiterite (a tin-bearing ore), wolframite (a tungsten-bearing ore), natural gas, gold, columbo-tantalite, beryl **Industries:** food processing, beverages, tobacco, mining, chemicals, rubber and plastic products, metals and metal products, machinery **Exports:** coffee, tea, tin ores and concentrates, pyrethrum, quinquina. Principal market: Brazil 45.5% (1995) **Imports:** food, clothing, mineral fuels and lubricants, construction materials, transport equipment, machinery, tools, consumer goods. Principal source: Kenya 19.3% (1995) **Arable land:** 34.5% (1995) **Agricultural products:** sweet potatoes, cassava, dry beans, sorghum, plantains, coffee, tea, pyrethrum; livestock rearing (long-horned Ankole cattle and goats)

Population and society
Population: 5,397,000 (1996 est) **Population growth rate:** 2.6% (1990–95); 2.5% (2000–05) **Population density:** (per sq km) 205 (1996 est) **Urban population:** (% of total) 6 (1995) **Age distribution:** (% of total population) <15 46%, 15–65 51.5%, >65 2.5% (1995) **Ethnic groups:** about 84% belong to the Hutu tribe, most of the remainder being Tutsis; there are also Twa and Pygmy minorities **Language:** Kinyarwanda, French (official); Kiswahili **Religion:** Roman Catholic 54%, animist 23%, Protestant 12%, Muslim 9% **Education:** (compulsory years) 7 **Literacy rate:** 64% (men); 37% (women) (1995 est) **Labour force:** 52% of population: 92% agriculture, 3% industry, 5% services (1990) **Life expectancy:** 45 (men); 48 (women) (1995–2000) **Child mortality rate:** (under 5, per 1,000 live births) 161 (1996) **Physicians:** 1 per 24,967 people (1993 est)

Practical information
Visa requirements: UK: visa required. USA: visa required **Embassy in the UK:** 42 Aylmer Road, London N2. Tel/fax: (0171) 347 6967 **British embassy:** the British Embassy in Kampala (see Uganda) deals with enquiries relating to Rwanda; British Consulate, BP 356, Avenue Paul VI, Kigali. Tel: 75219 or 75905; telex: 509 (a/b 09 RWANDEX RW) **Chamber of commerce:** Chambre de Commerce et de l'Industrie du Rwanda, BP 319, Kigali. **Airports:** international airports: Kigali (Kanombe), Kamembe; four domestic airfields; total passenger km: 2 million (1994) **Major holidays:** 1, 28 January, 1 May, 1, 5 July, 1, 15 August, 25 September, 26 October, 1 November, 1, 8, 24–25 December; variable: Carnival, Corpus Christi, Good Friday

Chronology
10th century onwards: Hutu peoples settled in region formerly inhabited by hunter-gatherer Twa Pygmies, becoming peasant

farmers. **14th century onwards:** Majority Hutu community came under dominance of cattle-owning Tutsi peoples, immigrants from the E, who became a semi-aristocracy and established control through land and cattle contracts. **15th century:** Ruganzu Bwimba, a Tutsi leader, founded kingdom near Kigali. **17th century:** Central Rwanda and outlying Hutu communities subdued by Tutsi mwami (king) Ruganzu Ndori. **late 19th century:** Under the great Tutsi king, Kigeri Rwabugiri, a unified state with a centralized military structure was established. **1890:** Known as Ruandi, the Tutsi kingdom, along with neighbouring Burundi, came under nominal German control, as Ruanda-Urundi. **1916:** Occupied by Belgium, during World War I. **1923:** Belgium granted League of Nations mandate to administer Ruanda-Urundi; they were to rule 'indirectly' through Tutsi chiefs. **1959:** Interethnic warfare between Hutu and Tutsi, forcing mwami (king) Kigeri V into exile. **1961:** Republic proclaimed after mwami deposed. **1962:** Independence from Belgium achieved as Rwanda, with Hutu Grégoire Kayibanda as president; many Tutsis left the country. **1963:** 20,000 killed in interethnic clashes, after Tutsis exiled in Burundi had launched a raid. **1973:** Kayibanda ousted in military coup led by Hutu Maj-Gen Juvenal Habyarimana; this was caused by resentment of Tutsis, who held some key government posts. **1981:** Elections created civilian legislation, but dominated by Hutu socialist National Revolutionary Development Movement (MRND), in a one-party state. **1988:** Hutu refugees from Burundi massacres streamed into Rwanda. **1990:** Government attacked by Rwanda Patriotic Front (FPR), a Tutsi refugee military-political organization based in Uganda, which controlled parts of N Rwanda. **1992:** Peace accord with FPR. **1993:** United Nations mission sent to monitor peace agreement. **1994:** President Habyarimana and Burundian Hutu president Ntaryamira killed in air crash; involvement of FPR suspected. Half a million killed in ensuing civil war, with many Tutsi massacred by Hutu death squads and exodus of 2 million refugees to neighbouring countries. Government fled as FPR forces closed in. French peacekeeping troops established 'safe zone' in SW. Interim coalition government installed, with moderate Hutu and FPR leader, Pasteur Bizimungu, as president. **1995:** War-crimes tribunal opened. Government human-rights abuses reported. **1996:** Rwanda and Zaire (Democratic Republic of Congo) on brink of war after Tutsi killings of Hutu in Zaire. Massive Hutu refugee crisis narrowly averted as thousands allowed to return to Rwanda. **1997:** Tutsi killings by Hutus.

St Kitts and Nevis (or St Christopher and Nevis)
Federation of

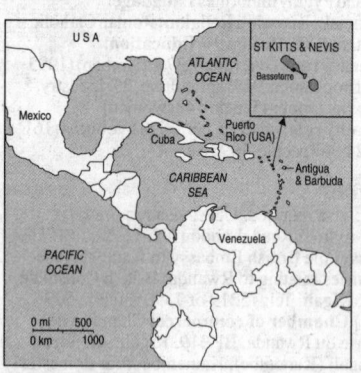

Area: 262 sq km/101 sq mi (St Kitts 168 sq km/65 sq mi, Nevis 93 sq km/36 sq mi) **Capital:** Basseterre (on St Kitts) (and chief port) **Major towns/cities:** Charlestown (largest on Nevis), Newcastle, Sandy Point Town, Dieppe Bay Town **Physical features:** both islands are volcanic; fertile plains on coast; black beaches

Government
Head of state: Queen Elizabeth II from 1983, represented by governor general Clement Arrindell from 1983 **Head of government:** Denzil Douglas from 1995 **Political system:** federal constitutional monarchy **Administrative divisions:** 14 parishes **Political parties:** People's Action Movement (PAM), centre right;

Nevis Reformation Party (NRP), Nevis-separatist, centrist; Labour Party (SKLP), moderate left of centre **Armed forces:** army disbanded 1981 and absorbed by Volunteer Defence Force; participates in US-sponsored Regional Security System established 1982 **Death penalty:** retained and used for ordinary crimes **Education spend:** (% GNP) 2.7 (1993) **Health spend:** (% GDP) 3.4 (1990)

Economy and resources
Currency: East Caribbean dollar **GDP:** ($ US) 220 million (1995 est) **Real GDP per capita (PPP):** ($ US) 9,380 (1995 est) **GDP growth rate:** 3.4% (1995) **Average annual inflation:** 3% (1996); 5.5% (1985–95) **Foreign debt:** ($ US) 50 million (1996) **Major trading partners:** USA, UK, Trinidad and Tobago, St Vincent and the Grenadines, Canada, Barbados **Industries:** electronic equipment, food and beverage processing (principally sugar and cane spirit), clothing, footwear, tourism **Exports:** sugar, manufactures, postage stamps; sugar and sugar products accounted for approximately 40% of export earnings 1992. Principal market: UK 48.7% (1992) **Imports:** foodstuffs, basic manufactures, machinery, mineral fuels. Principal source: USA 38.7% (1992) **Arable land:** 22.2% (1995) **Agricultural products:** sugar cane, coconuts, yams, sweet potatoes, groundnuts, sweet peppers, carrots, cabbages, bananas, cotton; fishing

Population and society
Population: 41,000 (1996 est) **Population growth rate:** –0.3 (1990–95) **Population density:** (per sq km) 158 (1996 est) **Urban population:** (% of total) 42.4 (1995) **Age distribution:** (% of total population) <15 30%, 15–65 55%, >65 15% (1992) **Ethnic groups:** almost entirely of African descent **Language:** English (official) **Religion:** Anglican 36%, Methodist 32%, other Protestant 8%, Roman Catholic 10% **Education:** (compulsory years) 12 **Literacy rate:** 98% (men); 86% (women) (1993 est) **Labour force:** 29.6% agriculture, 24.3% industry, 48.8% services (1985) **Unemployment:** 4.3% (1995 est) **Life expectancy:** 66 (men); 72 (women) (1995 est) **Child mortality rate:** (under 5, per 1,000 live births) 40 (1995) **Physicians:** 1 per 2,200 people (1991)

Practical information
Visa requirements: UK: visa not required. USA: visa not required **Embassy in the UK:** High Commission for Eastern Caribbean States, 10 Kensington Court, London W8 5DL. Tel: (0171) 937 9522; fax: (0171) 937 5514 **British embassy:** the British High Commission in St John's (see Antigua and Barbuda) deals with enquiries relating to St Kitts and Nevis **Chamber of commerce:** St Kitts and Nevis Chamber of Industry and Commerce, PO Box 332, South Square Street, Basseterre. Tel: (809) 465 2980; fax: (809) 465 4490 **Airports:** international airports: Basseterre (Golden Rock), Charlestown on Nevis (Newcastle Airfield); domestic services operate between these **Major holidays:** 1 January, 19 September, 25–26, 31 December; variable: Good Friday, Easter Monday, Whit Monday, Labour (May), Queen's Birthday (June), August Monday

Chronology
1493: Visited by the explorer Christopher Columbus, after whom the main island is named, but for next two centuries the islands were left in the possession of the indigenous Caribs. **1623 and 1628:** St Kitts and Nevis islands successively settled by British as their first Caribbean colony, with 2,000 Caribs brutally massacred in 1626. **1783:** In the Treaty of Versailles France, which had long disputed British possession, rescinded its claims to the islands, on which sugar cane plantations developed, worked by imported African slaves. **1816:** Anguilla was joined politically to the two islands. **1834:** Abolition of slavery. **1871–1956:** Part of the Leeward Islands Federation. **1932:** Centre-left Labour Party founded to campaign for independence. **1937:** Internal self-government granted. **1952:** Universal adult suffrage granted. **1958–62:** Part of the Federation of the West Indies. **1967:** St Kitts, Nevis, and Anguilla achieved internal self-government, within the British Commonwealth, with Robert Bradshaw, Labour Party leader, as prime minister. **1970:** NRP formed, calling for separation for Nevis. **1971:** Anguilla returned to being a British dependency after rebelling against

domination by St Kitts. **1978:** Bradshaw died; succeeded by Paul Southwell. **1979:** Southwell died; succeeded by Lee L Moore. **1980:** People's Action Movement (PAM) and NRP centrist coalition government, led by Kennedy Simmonds, formed after inconclusive general election. **1983:** Full independence achieved within the Commonwealth. **1993:** Simmonds continued in office despite strong criticism of his leadership. Antigovernment demonstrations followed inconclusive general election. **1994:** Three-week state of emergency imposed after violent antigovernment riots by Labour Party supporters in Basseterre. **1995:** Labour Party won general election; Denzil Douglas became prime minister. **1997:** Nevis withdrew from the federation.

St Lucia

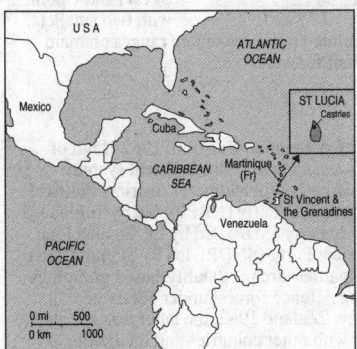

Area: 617 sq km/238 sq mi
Capital: Castries
Major towns/cities: Soufrière, Vieux-Fort, Laborie
Major ports: Vieux-Fort
Physical features: mountainous island with fertile valleys; mainly tropical forest; volcanic peaks; Gros and Petit Pitons

Government
Head of state: Queen Elizabeth II from 1979, represented by governor general Stanislaus A James from 1992 **Head of government:** Kenny Anthony from 1997 **Political system:** constitutional monarchy **Administrative divisions:** eight regions **Political parties:** United Workers' Party (UWP), moderate left of centre; St Lucia Labour Party (SLP), moderate left of centre; Progressive Labour Party (PLP), moderate left of centre **Armed forces:** none; participates in the US-sponsored Regional Security System established 1982; police force numbers around 300 **Death penalty:** retained and used for ordinary crimes **Education spend:** (% GNP) 5.2 (1992); N/A (1993/94)

Economy and resources
Currency: East Caribbean dollar **GDP:** ($ US) 513 million (1994) **Real GDP per capita (PPP):** ($ US) 6,182 (1994) **GDP growth rate:** 2.2% (1994) **Average annual inflation:** 3% (1996); 3.2% (1985–95 est) **Foreign debt:** ($ US) 115 million (1996) **Major trading partners:** USA, UK, Trinidad and Tobago (and other CARICOM member states), Japan, Canada, Italy **Resources:** geothermal energy **Industries:** processing of agricultural products (principally coconut oil, meal, and copra), clothing, rum, beer, and other beverages, plastics, paper and packaging, electronic assembly, tourism **Exports:** bananas, coconut oil, cocoa beans, copra, beverages, tobacco, miscellaneous articles. Principal market: USA 26.3% (1993) **Imports:** machinery and transport equipment, foodstuffs, basic manufactures, mineral fuels. Principal source: USA 36.2% (1993) **Arable land:** 8.2% (1995) **Agricultural products:** bananas, cocoa, coconuts, mangoes, citrus fruits, spices, breadfruit

Population and society
Population: 144,000 (1996 est) **Population growth rate:** 1.4% (1990–95) **Population density:** (per sq km) 232 (1996 est) **Urban population:** (% of total) 48.1 (1995) **Age distribution:** (% of total population) <15 41.3%, 15–65 52.7%, >65 6% (1992) **Ethnic groups:** great majority of African descent **Language:** English; French patois **Religion:** Roman Catholic 90% **Education:**

(compulsory years) 10 **Literacy rate:** 82% (men); 79%(women) (1993 est) **Labour force:** 24% agriculture, 13.6% industry, 62.4% services (1991) **Unemployment:** 20% (1993 est) **Life expectancy:** 68 (men); 75 (women) (1995 est) **Child mortality rate:** (under 5, per 1,000 live births) 22 (1995) **Physicians:** 1 per 2,125 people (1993)

Practical information
Visa requirements: UK: visa not required. USA: visa not required **Embassy in the UK:** High Commission for Eastern Caribbean States, 10 Kensington Court, London W8 5DL. Tel: (0171) 937 9522; fax: (0171) 937 5514 **British embassy:** British High Commission, PO Box 227, Derek Walcott Square, Castries. Tel: (809) 452 2484; fax: (809) 453 1543 **Chamber of commerce:** St Lucia Chamber of Commerce, Industry and Agriculture, PO Box 482, Micond Street, Castries. Tel: (809) 452 3165; fax: (809) 453 6907 **Airports:** international airports: Castries (Vigie), Vieux Fort (Hewanorra); domestic flights operate between these; aircraft arrivals: 42,436 (1993) **Major holidays:** 1–2 January, 22 February, 1 May, 13, 25–26 December; variable: Carnival, Corpus Christi, Good Friday, Easter Monday, Whit Monday, Emancipation (August), Thanksgiving (October)

Chronology
1502: Sighted by the explorer Christopher Columbus on St Lucia's day but not settled for more than a century due to hostility of the island's Carib Indian inhabitants. **1635:** Settled by French, who brought in slaves to work sugar cane plantations as Carib community was annihilated. **1814:** Ceded to Britain as a crown colony, following Treaty of Paris; black African slaves brought in to work sugar cane plantations. **1834:** Slavery abolished. **1860s:** A major coal warehousing centre until the switch to oil and diesel fuels in 1930s. **1871–1956:** Part of Leeward Islands Federation. **1951:** Universal adult suffrage granted. **1967:** Acquired internal self-government as a West Indies associated state. **1979:** Independence achieved within Commonwealth with John Compton, leader of United Workers' Party (UWP), as prime minister; Compton was replaced by Allan Louisy, leader of the St Lucia Labour Party (SLP), following elections. **1981:** Louisy resigned; replaced by Winston Cenac. **1982:** Compton returned to power at head of UWP government. **1991:** Integration with other Windward Islands (Dominica, Grenada, and St Vincent) proposed. **1993:** Unrest and strikes by farmers and agricultural workers as a result of depressed prices for the chief cash crop, bananas. **1997:** SLP won general election; Kenny Anthony appointed prime minister.

St Vincent and the Grenadines

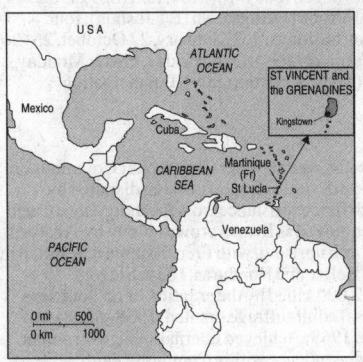

Area: 388 sq km/150 sq mi, including islets of the Northern Grenadines 43 sq km/17 sq mi
Capital: Kingstown **Major towns/cities:** Georgetown, Châteaubelair, Layon, Baronallie
Physical features: volcanic mountains, thickly forested; La Soufrière volcano

Government
Head of state: Queen Elizabeth II from 1979, represented by governor general David Jack from 1989 **Head of government:** James Mitchell from 1984 **Political system:** constitutional

monarchy **Administrative divisions:** six parishes **Political parties:** New Democratic Party (NDP), right of centre; St Vincent Labour Party (SVLP), moderate left of centre **Armed forces:** none – police force only; participates in the US-sponsored Regional Security System established 1982 **Death penalty:** retained and used for ordinary crimes **Education spend:** (% GNP) 6.7 (1993/94) **Health spend:** (% GDP) 4.4 (1990)

Economy and resources

Currency: East Caribbean dollar **GDP:** ($ US) 256.6 million (1994) **Real GDP per capita (PPP):** ($ US) 5,650 (1994) **GDP growth rate:** 3.8% (1995) **Average annual inflation:** 3% (1996); 3.6% (1985–95) **Foreign debt:** ($ US) 93 million (1996) **Major trading partners:** USA, UK, Trinidad and Tobago, Antigua and Barbuda, Barbados, Canada, Japan, St Lucia **Industries:** clothing, assembly of electronic equipment, processing of agricultural products (including brewing, flour milling, rum distillation, dairy products), industrial gases, plastics, tourism **Exports:** bananas, eddoes, dasheen, sweet potatoes, flour, ginger, tannias, plantains. Principal market: UK 32% (1994) **Imports:** basic manufactures, machinery and transport equipment, food and live animals, mineral fuels, chemicals, miscellaneous manufactured articles. Principal source: USA 36.1% (1994) **Arable land:** 10.3% (1995) **Agricultural products:** bananas, cocoa, citrus fruits, mangoes, avocado pears, guavas, sugar cane, vegetables, spices; world's leading producer of arrowroot starch; fishing

Population and society

Population: 113,000 (1996 est) **Population growth rate:** 0.9% (1990–95) **Population density:** (per sq km) 290 (1996 est) **Urban population:** (% of total) 47 (1995) **Age distribution:** (% of total population) <15 34.6%, 15–65 59.8%, >65 5.6% (1992) **Ethnic groups:** largely of African origin; most of the original indigenous Caribs have disappeared **Language:** English; French patois **Religion:** Anglican, Methodist, Roman Catholic **Education:** not compulsory **Literacy rate:** 92% (men); 86% (women) (1993 est) **Labour force:** 25.1% agriculture, 21.1% industry, 53.8% services (1991) **Unemployment:** 20% (1991) **Life expectancy:** 70 (men); 75 (women) (1995 est) **Child mortality rate:** (under 5, per 1,000 live births) 23 (1995) **Physicians:** 1 per 4,037 people (1992)

Practical information

Visa requirements: UK: visa not required. USA: visa not required **Embassy in the UK:** High Commission for East Caribbean States, 10 Kensington Court, London W8 5DL. Tel: (0171) 937 9522; fax: (0171) 937 5514 **British embassy:** British High Commission, PO Box 132, Granby Street, Kingstown. Tel: (809) 457 1701/2; fax: (809) 456 2720 **Chamber of commerce:** St Vincent and the Grenadines Chamber of Industry and Commerce, PO Box 134, Halifax Street, Kingstown. Tel: (809) 457 1464; fax: (809) 456 2944 **Airports:** international airports: Kingstown (E T Joshua); four domestic airports **Major holidays:** 1, 22 January, 27 October, 25–26 December; variable: Carnival (July), Good Friday, Easter Monday, Whit Monday, Labour (May), Caricom (July), Emancipation (August)

Chronology

1498: Main island visited by the explorer Christopher Columbus on St Vincent's day. **17th–18th centuries:** Possession disputed by France and Britain, with fierce resistance from the indigenous Carib community. **1783:** Recognized as British crown colony by Treaty of Versailles. **1795–97:** Carib uprising, with French support, resulted in deportation of 5,000 to Belize and Honduras. **1834:** Slavery abolished. **1902:** Over 2,000 killed by the eruption of La Soufrière volcano. **1951:** Universal adult suffrage granted. **1958–62:** Part of West Indies Federation. **1969:** Achieved internal self-government. **1979:** Achieved full independence within Commonwealth, with Milton Cato of centre-left St Vincent Labour Party (SVLP) as prime minister. **1981:** General strike against new industrial-relations legislation at a time of economic recession. **1984:** James Mitchell, of the centre-right New Democratic Party (NDP), replaced Cato as prime minister. **1991:** Integration with other Windward Islands (Dominica, Grenada, and St Lucia) proposed.

Samoa Independent State of

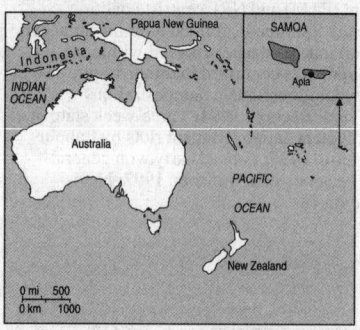

National name: *Malotutu'atasi o Samoa i Sisifo* **Area:** 2,830 sq km/1,092 sq mi **Capital:** Apia (on Upolu island) (and chief port) **Major towns/cities:** Lalomanu, Falevai, Tuasivi, Falealupo **Physical features:** comprises South Pacific islands of Savai'i and Upolu, with two smaller tropical islands and uninhabited islets; mountain ranges on main islands; coral reefs; over half forested

Government

Head of state: King Malietoa Tanumafili II from 1962 **Head of government:** Tofilau Eti Alesana from 1988 **Political system:** liberal democracy **Administrative divisions:** 11 districts **Political parties:** Human Rights Protection Party (HRPP), led by Tofilau Eti Alesana; Samoa Democratic Party (SDP), led by Le Tagaloa Pita; Samoa National Development Party (SNDP), led by Tupuola Taisi Efi and Va'ai Kolone. All 'parties' are personality-based groupings **Armed forces:** no standing defence forces; under Treaty of Friendship signed with New Zealand 1962, the latter acts as sole agent in Samoa's dealings with other countries and international organizations **Death penalty:** retains the death penalty for ordinary crimes, but can be considered abolitionist in practice **Education spend:** (% GNP) 4.2 (1993/94) **Health spend:** (% GDP) 5.6 (1990)

Economy and resources

Currency: tala, or Samoa dollar **GDP:** ($ US) 415 million (1995 est) **Real GDP per capita (PPP):** ($ US) 1,900 (1995 est) **GDP growth rate:** 9.6% (1995 est) **Average annual inflation:** 3.8% (1996); 10.6% (1985–95 est) **Foreign debt:** ($ US) 154.8 million (1994) **Major trading partners:** New Zealand, Australia, Fiji, American Samoa, Japan, USA **Industries:** coconut-based products, timber, light engineering, construction materials, beer, cigarettes, clothing, leather goods, wire, tourism **Exports:** coconut cream, beer, cigarettes, taro, copra, cocoa, bananas, timber. Principal market: New Zealand 45.5% (1994) **Imports:** food and live animals, machinery and transport equipment, mineral fuel, clothing and other manufactured goods. Principal source: New Zealand 37.3% (1994) **Arable land:** 19.4% (1995) **Agricultural products:** coconuts, taro, copra, bananas, papayas, mangoes, pineapples, cocoa, taamu, breadfruit, maize, yams, passion fruit; livestock rearing (pigs, cattle, poultry, and goats) is important for local consumption; forest resources provide an important export commodity (47% of land was forest and woodland early 1990s)

Population and society

Population: 166,000 (1996 est) **Population growth rate:** 1.1% (1990–95) **Population density:** (per sq km) 59 (1996 est) **Urban population:** (% of total) 21 (1995) **Age distribution:** (% of total population) <15 47%, 15–65 50%, >65 3% (1994) **Ethnic groups:** 90% of Samoan (Polynesian) origin; 10% Euronesian (mixed European and Polynesian) **Language:** English, Samoan (official) **Religion:** Congregationalist; also Roman Catholic, Methodist **Education:** not compulsory **Literacy rate:** 92% (men); 88% (women) (1994 est) **Labour force:** 58% agriculture (1990) **Life expectancy:** 68 (men); 71 (women) (1995–2000) **Child mortality rate:** (under 5, per 1,000 live births) 71 (1996) **Physicians:** 1 per 3,665 people (1992)

Practical information
Visa requirements: UK: visa not required. USA: visa not required **Embassy for the UK:** avenue Franklin D Roosevelt 123, B-1050 Brussels, Belgium. Tel: (2) 660 8454; fax: (2) 675 0336 **British embassy:** Office of the Honorary British Representative, c/o Kruse Va'ai and Barlow, PO Box 2029, Apia. Tel: (685) 21895, fax: (685) 21407 **Chamber of commerce:** c/o Pacific Forum Line, Matantutai, PO Box 655, Apia. Tel: (685) 20345 **Airports:** international airports: Apia (Faleolo); two domestic airstrips **Major holidays:** 1–2 January, 25 April, 1 June (3 days), 12 October, 25–26 December; variable: Good Friday, Easter Monday, Holy Saturday

Chronology
c. 1000 BC: Settled by Polynesians from Tonga. **AD 950–1250:** Ruled by Tongan invaders; the Matai (chiefly) system was developed. **15th century:** United under the Samoan Queen Salamasina. **1722:** Visited by Dutch traders. **1768:** Visted by the French navigator Louis Antoine de Bougainville. **1830:** Christian mission established and islanders were soon converted to Christianity. **1887–89:** Samoan rebellion against German attempt to depose paramount ruler and install its own puppet regime. **1889:** Under the terms of the Act of Berlin, Germany took control of the nine islands of Western Samoa, while the USA was granted American Samoa, and Britain Tonga and the Solomon Islands. **1900s:** More than 2,000 Chinese brought in to work coconut plantations. **1914:** Occupied by New Zealand on the outbreak of World War I. **1918:** Nearly a quarter of the population died in an influenza epidemic. **1920s:** Development of nationalist movement, the Mau, which resorted to civil disobedience. **1920–61:** Administered by New Zealand under League of Nations and, later, United Nations mandate. **1959:** Local government established, headed by chief minister Fiame Mata'afa Mulinu'u. **1961:** Referendum favoured independence. **1962:** Independence achieved within Commonwealth, with Mata'afa as prime minister, a position he retained (apart from a short break 1970–73) until his death in 1975. **1976:** Tupuola Taisi Efi became first nonroyal prime minister. **1982:** Va'ai Kolone, the head of the opposition Human Rights Protection Party (HRPP), became prime minister, but was forced to resign over charges of electoral malpractice. The new HRPP leader, Tofilau Eti Alesana, became prime minister. **1985:** Tofilau Eti Alesana resigned after opposition to budget; head of state invited Va'ai Kolone to lead the government. **1988:** Elections produced hung parliament, with first Tupuola Efi as prime minister and then Tofilau Eti Alesana. **1990:** Universal adult suffrage introduced and power of Matai (elected clan leaders) reduced. **1991:** Fiame Naome became first woman in cabinet; major damage caused by 'Cyclone Val'.

San Marino Most Serene Republic of

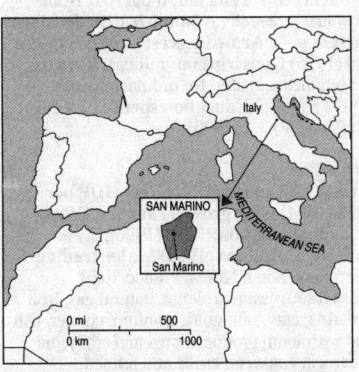

National name: *Serenissima Repubblica di San Marino* **Area:** 61 sq km/24 sq mi **Capital:** San Marino **Major towns/cities:** Serravalle (industrial centre), Faetano, Fiorentino, Monte Giardino **Physical features:** the slope of Mount Titano

Government
Head of state and government: two captains regent, elected for a six-month period **Political system:** direct democracy

Administrative divisions: nine districts **Political parties:** San Marino Christian Democrat Party (PDCS), Christian centrist; Progressive Democratic Party (PDP) (formerly the Communist Party: PCS), moderate left wing; Socialist Party (PS), left of centre **Armed forces:** voluntary military forces and a paramilitary gendarmerie **Conscription:** military service is not compulsory, but all citizens between the ages of 15 and 55 may be enlisted in certain circumstances to defend the state **Death penalty:** abolished 1865

Economy and resources
Currency: Italian lira **GDP:** ($ US) 480 million (1993 est) **Real GDP per capita (PPP):** ($ US) 20,100 (1993 est) **GDP growth rate:** 2.4% (1993 est) **Average annual inflation:** 5.5% (1993) **Major trading partners:** maintains customs union with Italy (for trade data see Italy) **Resources:** limestone and other building stone **Industries:** cement, synthetic rubber, leather, textiles, ceramics, tiles, wine, chemicals, olive oil, tourism, postage stamps **Exports:** wood machinery, chemicals, wine, olive oil, textiles, tiles, ceramics, varnishes, building stone, lime, chestnuts, hides. Principal market: Italy **Imports:** consumer goods, raw materials, energy supply. Principal source: Italy **Arable land:** 16.7% (1995) **Agricultural products:** wheat, barley, maize, grapes, olives, fruit, vegetables; viticulture; dairy farming

Population and society
Population: 25,000 (1996 est) **Population growth rate:** 1.5% (1990–95) **Population density:** (per sq km) 415 (1996 est) **Urban population:** (% of total) 94.2 (1995) **Age distribution:** (% of total population) <15 17.7%, 15–65 69.5%, >65 12.8% (1990) **Ethnic groups:** predominantly Italian **Language:** Italian **Religion:** Roman Catholic 95% **Education:** (compulsory years) 8 **Literacy rate:** 98% (men); 98% (women) (1995 est) **Labour force:** 1.6% agriculture, 43% industry, 55.1% services (1995) **Unemployment:** 4.4% (1996) **Life expectancy:** 75 (men); 81 (women) (1995 est) **Child mortality rate:** (per 1,000 live births) 6 (1994) **Physicians:** 1 per 405 people (1990)

Practical information
Visa requirements: UK: visa not required. USA: visa not required **Embassy in the UK:** San Marino has no diplomatic representation in the UK; the UK Department of Trade and Industry has an Italy desk. Tel: (0171) 215 4385; fax (0171) 215 4711 **British embassy:** British Consulate, Lungarno Corsini 2, 50123 Florence, Italy. Tel: (55) 284 133; fax: (55) 219 112 **Airports:** international airports: none (the closest are at Rimini and Bologna, in Italy; a bus service connects San Marino with Rimini) **Major holidays:** 1, 6 January, 5 February, 25 March, 1 May, 28 July, 1 August, 3 September, 1 October, 1–2 November, 8, 25–26 December; variable: Corpus Christi, Easter Monday

Chronology
c. AD 301: Founded as a republic (the world's oldest surviving) by St Marinus and a group of Christians who settled there to escape persecution. **12th century:** Self-governing commune. **1600:** Statutes (constitution) provided for a parliamentary form of government, based around the Great and General Council. **1815:** Independent status of the republic recognized by the Congress of Vienna. **1862:** Treaty with Italy signed; independence recognized under Italy's protection. **1945–57:** Communist–Socialist administration in power, eventually ousted in a bloodless 'revolution'. **1957–86:** Governed by a series of left-wing and centre-left coalitions. **1971:** Treaty with Italy renewed. **1986:** Formation of Communist and centre-right Christian Democrat (PDCS) 'grand coalition'. **1992:** Joined the United Nations. PDCS withdrew from 'grand coalition' to form alliance with Socialist Party.

São Tomé and Príncipe Democratic Republic of

National name: *República Democrática de São Tomé e Príncipe* **Area:** 1,000 sq km/386 sq mi **Capital:** São Tomé **Major towns/cities:** São António, Santana, Porto-Alegre **Physical**

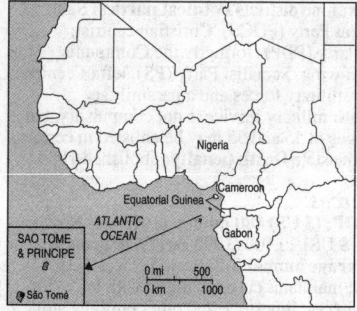

features: comprises two main islands and several smaller ones, all volcanic; thickly forested and fertile

Government
Head of state: Miguel Trovoada from 1991 **Head of government:** Carlos da Graca from 1994 **Political system:** emergent democracy

Administrative divisions: two provinces **Political parties:** Movement for the Liberation of São Tomé e Príncipe–Social Democratic Party (MLSTP–PSD), nationalist socialist; Democratic Convergence Party–Reflection Group (PCD–GR), moderate left of centre; Independent Democratic Action (ADI), centrist **Armed forces:** no proper army; reorganization of island's armed forces (estimated at 900) and police into two separate police forces (one for public order, the other for criminal investigations) was initiated 1992 **Death penalty:** abolished 1990 **Education spend:** (% GNP) 4.3 (1986); N/A (1993/94)

Economy and resources
Currency: dobra **GDP:** ($ US) 138 million (1994 est) **Real GDP per capita (PPP):** ($ US) 980 (1994 est) **GDP growth rate:** 1.5% (1994 est) **Average annual inflation:** 38% (1994 est); 40.1% (1985–95) **Foreign debt:** ($ US) 165 million (1995) **Major trading partners:** Portugal, the Netherlands, Germany, Spain, Belgium, France, Japan, Angola **Industries:** agricultural and timber processing, soft drinks, soap, textiles, beer, bricks, ceramics, shirts **Exports:** cocoa, copra, coffee, bananas, palm oil. Principal market: the Netherlands 75.7% (1995) **Imports:** capital goods, food and live animals (of which 60.7% were donations 1994), petroleum and petroleum products. Principal source: Portugal 32.2% (1995) **Arable land:** 2.1% (1995) **Agricultural products:** cocoa, coconuts, copra, bananas, palm oil, cassava, sweet potatoes, yams, coffee; fishing; forest resources (75% of land area was forest and woodland early 1990s)

Population and society
Population: 135,100 (1996 est) **Population growth rate:** 2.2% (1990–95) **Population density:** (per sq km) 140 (1996 est) **Urban population:** (% of total) 46.7 (1995) **Age distribution:** (% of total population) <15 46.4%, 15–65 38.8%, >65 4.8% (1992) **Ethnic groups:** predominantly African **Language:** Portuguese (official); Fang (a Bantu language) **Religion:** Roman Catholic 80%, animist **Education:** (compulsory years) 4 **Literacy rate:** 85% (men); 62% women (1991 est) **Labour force:** 39.9% agriculture, 13.6% industry, 46.5% services (1991) **Unemployment:** 38% (1995) **Life expectancy:** 67 (men); 73 (women) (1994 est) **Child mortality rate:** (under 5, per 1,000 live births) 81 (1995) **Physicians:** 1 per 1,780 people (1992)

Practical information
Visa requirements: UK: visa required. USA: visa required **Embassy in the UK:** 42 avenue Brugmann, 1060 Brussels, Belgium. Tel: (2) 347 5375; fax: (2) 347 5408; Honorary Consulate of the Democratic Republic of São Tomé e Príncipe, 42 North Audley Street, London W1A 4PY. Tel: (0171) 499 1995; fax: (0171) 629 6460 **British embassy:** British Consulate, c/o Hull Blythe (Angola) Ltd, BP 15, São Tomé. Telex: 220 (a/b HBALTD ST) (the British Embassy in Luanda, Angola deals with enquiries relating to São Tomé e Príncipe) **Chamber of commerce:** the British Embassy in Luanda (see Angola) deals with queries relating to São Tomé and Príncipe **Airports:** international airports: São Tomé; one domestic airport (Príncipe); total passenger km: 8 million (1994) **Major holidays:** 1 January, 3 February, 1 May, 12 July, 6, 30 September, 21, 25 December; variable: Corpus Christi, Good Friday, Easter Monday

Chronology
1471: First visited by the Portuguese, who imported convicts and slaves to work on sugar plantations in the formerly uninhabited islands. **1522:** Became a province of Portugal. **1530:** Slaves successfully revolted, forcing plantation owners to flee to Brazil; thereafter became a key staging post for Congo-Americas slave trade. **19th century:** Forced contract labour used to work coffee and cocoa plantations. **1953:** More than 1,000 striking plantation workers gunned down by Portuguese troops. **1960:** First political party formed, the forerunner of the socialist-nationalist Movement for the Liberation of São Tomé e Príncipe (MLSTP). **1974:** Military coup in Portugal led to strikes, demonstrations, and army mutiny in São Tomé; thousands of Portuguese settlers fled the country. **1975:** Independence achieved, with Manuel Pinto da Costa (MLSTP) as president; close links developed with communist bloc, and plantations nationalized. **1984:** Formally declared a nonaligned state as economy deteriorated. **1988:** Coup attempt against da Costa foiled by Angolan and East European troops. **1990:** Influenced by collapse of communism in Eastern Europe, MLSTP abandoned Marxism; new pluralist constitution approved in referendum. **1991:** In first multiparty elections, the ruling MLSTP lost its majority and the independent Miguel Trovoada, MLSTP prime minister before 1978, was elected president. **1994:** MLSTP returned to power with Carlos da Graca as prime minister. **1995:** Abortive coup by junior army officers; unemployment at 38% and foreign indebtedness $165 million.

Saudi Arabia Kingdom of

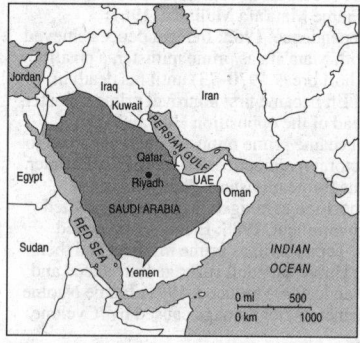

National name: *Mamlaka al-'Arabiya as-Sa'udiya* **Area:** 2,200,518 sq km/849,620 sq mi **Capital:** Riyadh **Major towns/cities:** Jiddah, Mecca, Medina, Taif, Dammam, Hufuf **Major ports:** Jiddah, Dammam, Jubail, Jizan, Yanbu **Physical features:** desert, sloping to the Persian Gulf from a height of 2,750 m/9,000 ft in the W

Government
Head of state and government: King Fahd Ibn Abdul Aziz from 1996 **Political system:** absolute monarchy **Administrative divisions:** 13 provinces **Political parties:** none **Armed forces:** 162,500 (1995); paramilitary forces 16,000 (1996) **Conscription:** military service is voluntary **Death penalty:** retained and used for ordinary crimes **Defence spend:** (% GDP) 12.8 (1996) **Education spend:** (% GNP) 6.4 (1992) **Health spend:** (% GDP) 3.1 (1990)

Economy and resources
Currency: rial **GDP:** ($ US) 117.2 billion (1994) **Real GDP per capita (PPP):** ($ US) 9,338 (1994) **GDP growth rate:** 0% (1994); 1.7% (1990–95) **Average annual inflation:** 1.7% (1996); 2.7% (1985–95) **Foreign debt:** US $ 17.8 billion (1996) **Major trading partners:** USA, Japan, Germany, South Korea, France, Italy, Singapore, the Netherlands **Resources:** petroleum, natural gas, iron ore, limestone, gypsum, marble, clay, salt, gold, uranium, copper, fish **Industries:** petroleum and petroleum products, urea and ammonia fertilizers, steel, plastics, cement **Exports:** crude and refined petroleum, petrochemicals, wheat. Principal market: Japan 17.6% (1995) **Imports:** machinery and transport equipment, foodstuffs, beverages, tobacco, chemicals and chemical products, base metals and metal manufactures, textiles and clothing. Principal source: USA

21.4% (1995) **Arable land:** 1.7% (1995) **Agricultural products:** wheat, barley, sorghum, millet, tomatoes, dates, watermelons, grapes; livestock (chiefly poultry) and dairy products

Population and society
Population: 18,836,000 (1996 est) **Population growth rate:** 2.2% (1990–95); 3.1% (2000–05) **Population density:** (per sq km) 9 (1996 est) **Urban population:** (% of total) 80 (1995) **Age distribution:** (% of total population) <15 41.9%, 15–65 55.4%, >65 2.7% (1995) **Ethnic groups:** around 90% Arab; 10% Afro-Asian **Language:** Arabic **Religion:** Sunni Muslim; there is a Shi'ite minority **Literacy rate:** 73% (men); 48% (women) (1995 est) **Labour force:** 34% of population: 19% agriculture, 20% industry, 61% services (1990) **Life expectancy:** 70 (men); 73 (women) (1995–2000) **Child mortality rate:** (under 5, per 1,000 live births) 30 (1996) **Physicians:** 1 per 636 people (1994)

Practical information
Visa requirements: UK: visa required. USA: visa required **Embassy in the UK:** 30 Charles Street, London W1X 7PH. Tel: (0171) 917 3000; fax: (0171) 917 3330 **British embassy:** PO Box 94351, Riyadh 11693. Tel: (1) 488 0077; fax: (1) 488 2373 **Chamber of commerce:** Riyadh Chamber of Commerce and Industry, PO Box 596, Riyadh 11421. Tel: (1) 404 0044; fax: (1) 402 1103 **Airports:** international airports: Riyadh (King Khaled), Dhahran (Al Khobar), Jiddah (King Abdul Aziz); 20 domestic airports; total passenger km: 18,250 million (1994) **Major holidays:** 23 September; variable: Eid-ul-Adha (7 days), end of Ramadan (4 days)

Chronology
622: Muhammad began to unite Arabs in Muslim faith. **7th–8th centuries:** Muslim Empire expanded, ultimately stretching from India to Spain, with Arabia itself being relegated to a subordinate part. **12th century:** Decline of Muslim Empire; Arabia grew isolated and internal divisions multiplied. **13th century:** Mameluke sultans of Egypt became nominal overlords of Hejaz in W Arabia. **1517:** Hejaz became a nominal part of Ottoman Empire after Turks conquered Egypt. **18th century:** Al Saud family united tribes of Nejd in central Arabia in support of the Wahhabi religious movement. **c.1830:** The Al Saud established Riyadh as the Wahhabi capital. **c.1870:** Turks took effective control of Hejaz and also Hasa on Persian Gulf. **late 19th century:** Rival Wahhabi dynasty of Ibn Rashid became leaders of Nejd. **1902:** Ibn Saud organized Bedouin revolt and regained Riyadh. **1913:** Ibn Saud completed the reconquest of Hasa from Turks. **1915:** Britain recognized Ibn Saud as emir of Nejd and Hasa. **1916–18:** British-backed revolt, under aegis of Sharif Hussein of Mecca, expelled Turks from Arabia. **1919–25:** Ibn Saud fought and defeated Sharif Hussein and took control of Hejaz. **1926:** Proclamation of Ibn Saud as king of Hejaz and Nejd. **1932:** Hejaz and Nejd renamed the United Kingdom of Saudi Arabia. **1933:** Saudi Arabia allowed American-owned Standard Oil Company to prospect for oil, which was discovered in Hasa 1938. **1939–45:** Although officially neutral in World War II, Saudi Arabia received subsidies from USA and Britain. **1940s:** Commercial exploitation of oil began, bringing great prosperity. **1953:** Ibn Saud died; succeeded by his eldest son, Saud. **1964:** King Saud forced to abdicate; succeeded by his brother, Faisal. **1975:** King Faisal assassinated; succeeded by his half-brother, Khalid. **1982:** King Khalid died; succeeded by his brother, Fahd. **1987:** Rioting by Iranian pilgrims caused 400 deaths in Mecca and breach in diplomatic relations with Iran. **1990:** Iraqi troops invaded Kuwait and massed on Saudi Arabian border, prompting King Fahd to call for assistance from US and UK forces. **1991:** Saudi Arabia fought on Allied side against Iraq in Gulf War. **1992:** Under international pressure to move towards democracy, King Fahd formed a 'consultative council' to assist in government of kingdom. **1995:** King Fahd suffered a stroke and transferred power to Crown Prince Abdullah. **1996:** King Fahd resumed power.

Senegal Republic of

National name: *République du Sénégal* **Area:** 196,200 sq km/75,752 sq mi **Capital:** Dakar (and chief port) **Major towns/cities:** Thiès,

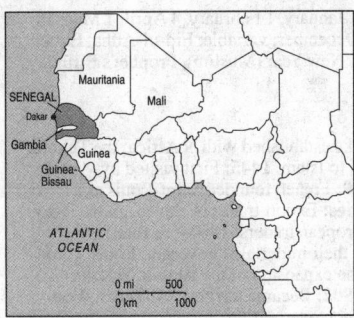

Kaolack, Saint-Louis, Ziguinchor, Diourbel **Physical features:** plains rising to hills in SE; swamp and tropical forest in SW; river Senegal; The Gambia forms an enclave within Senegal

Government
Head of state: Abdou Diouf from 1981 **Head of government:** Habib Thiam from 1993 **Political system:** emergent socialist democracy **Administrative divisions:** ten regions **Political parties:** Senegalese Socialist Party (PS), democratic socialist; Senegalese Democratic Party (PDS), centrist **Armed forces:** 13,400 (1996) **Conscription:** military services is by selective conscription for two years **Death penalty:** retains the death penalty for ordinary crimes but can be considered abolitionist in practice (last execution 1967) **Defence spend:** (% GDP) 1.7 (1996) **Education spend:** (% GNP) 4.4 (1993) **Health spend:** (% GDP) 2.3 (1990)

Economy and resources
Currency: franc CFA **GDP:** ($ US) 3.9 billion (1994) **Real GDP per capita (PPP):** ($ US) 1,596 (1994) **GDP growth rate:** 2% (1994); 1.9% (1990–95) **Average annual inflation:** 3.5% (1996); 3.7% (1985–95) **Foreign debt:** ($ US) 3.89 billion (1996) **Major trading partners:** France, India, Italy, USA, Mali, Côte d'Ivoire, Nigeria, Thailand **Resources:** calcium phosphates, aluminium phosphates, salt, natural gas; offshore deposits of petroleum to be developed **Industries:** food processing (principally fish, groundnuts, palm oil, and sugar), mining, cement, artificial fertilizer, chemicals, textiles, petroleum refining (imported petroleum), tourism **Exports:** fresh and processed fish, refined petroleum products, chemicals, groundnuts and related products, calcium phosphates and related products. Principal market: France 30% (1995) **Imports:** food and live animals, machinery and transport equipment, mineral fuels and lubricants (mainly crude petroleum), basic manufactures, chemicals. Principal source: France 37.8% (1995) **Arable land:** 11.7% (1995) **Agricultural products:** groundnuts, cotton, millet, sorghum, rice, maize, cassava, vegetables; fishing

Population and society
Population: 8,532,000 (1996 est) **Population growth rate:** 2.5% (1990–95); 2.6% (2000–05) **Population density:** (per sq km) 43 (1996 est) **Urban population:** (% of total) 42 (1995) **Age distribution:** (% of total population) <15 44.6%, 15–65 52.5%, >65 2.9% (1995) **Ethnic groups:** the Wolof group are the most numerous, comprising about 36% of the population; the Fulani comprise about 21%; the Serer 19%; the Diola 7%; and the Mandingo 6% **Language:** French (official); Wolof **Religion:** mainly Sunni Muslim **Education:** (compulsory years) 6 **Literacy rate:** 52% (men); 25% (women) (1995 est) **Labour force:** 45% of population: 77% agriculture, 8% industry, 16% services (1990) **Unemployment:** 10.2% (1993) **Life expectancy:** 50 (men); 52 (women) (1995–2000) **Child mortality rate:** (under 5, per 1,000 live births) 157 (1996) **Physicians:** 1 per 18,192 people (1993 est)

Practical information
Visa requirements: UK: visa not required. USA: visa not required **Embassy in the UK:** 11 Phillimore Gardens, London W8 7QG. Tel: (0171) 937 0925/6; fax: (0171) 937 8130 **British embassy:** BP 6025, 20 rue du Docteur Guillet, Dakar. Tel: (221) 237 392; fax: (221) 232 766 **Chamber of commerce:** Chambre de Commerce et d'Industrie et d'Agriculture de la Région de Dakar, BP 118, 1 place de l'Indépendance, Dakar. Tel: (221) 237 189; telex: 61112 **Airports:** international airports: Dakar (Dakar-Yoff); three domestic airports and 12 smaller airfields; total passenger km: 224 million

(1994) **Major holidays:** 1 January, 1 February, 4 April, 1 May, 15 August, 1 November, 25 December; variable: Eid-ul-Adha, Easter Monday, end of Ramadan, New Year (Muslim), Prophet's Birthday, Whit Monday

Chronology
10th–11th centuries: Links established with N Africa; the Tukolor community was converted to Islam. **1445:** First visited by Portuguese explorers. **1659:** French founded Saint-Louis as a colony. **17th–18th centuries:** Export trades in slaves, gums, ivory, and gold developed by European traders. **1854–65:** Interior occupied by French under their imperialist governor, Louis Faidherbe, who checked the expansion of the Islamic Tukolor Empire; Dakar founded. **1902:** Became territory of French West Africa. **1946:** Became French overseas territory, with own territorial assembly and representation in French parliament. **1948:** Leopold Sedar Senghor founded Senegalese Democratic Bloc to campaign for independence. **1959:** Formed Federation of Mali with French Sudan. **1960:** Achieved independence and withdrew from federation. Senghor, leader of socialist Senegalese Progressive Union (UPS), became president. **1966:** UPS declared only legal party. **1974:** Pluralist system re-established. **1976:** UPS reconstituted as Socialist Party (PS). Prime Minister Abdou Diouf nominated as Senghor's successor. **1980:** Senghor resigned; succeeded by Diouf. Troops sent to defend The Gambia against suspected Libyan invasion. **1981:** Military help again sent to The Gambia to thwart coup attempt. **1982:** Confederation of Senegambia came into effect. **1983:** Diouf re-elected. Post of prime minister abolished. **1989:** Diplomatic links with Mauritania severed after 450 died in violent clashes; over 50,000 people repatriated from both countries. Senegambia federation abandoned. **1992:** Post of prime minister reinstated. Diplomatic links with Mauritania re-established. **1993:** Assembly and presidential elections won by ruling PS.

Seychelles Republic of

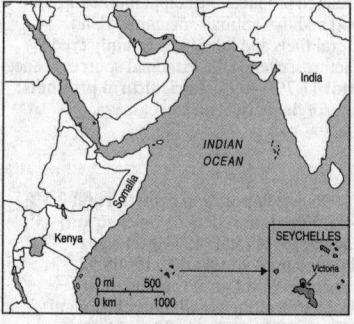

Area: 453 sq km/174 sq mi
Capital: Victoria (on Mahé island) (and chief port)
Major towns/cities: Cascade, Port Glaud, Misere
Physical features: comprises two distinct island groups: one, the Granitic group, concentrated, the other, the Outer or Coralline group, widely scattered; totals over 100 islands and islets

Government
Head of state and government: France-Albert René from 1977
Political system: emergent democracy **Administrative divisions:** 23 districts **Political parties:** Seychelles People's Progressive Front (SPPF), nationalist socialist; Democratic Party (DP), left of centre **Armed forces:** 300 (1996); plus a coastguard numbering 500 (1995); plus 1,000-strong national guard (1996) **Conscription:** military service is voluntary **Death penalty:** retains death penalty only for exceptional crimes such as crimes under military law or crimes committed in exceptional circumstances such as wartime **Defence spend:** (% GDP) 3.9 (1995) **Education spend:** (% GNP) 7.4 (1993/94) **Health spend:** (% GDP) 3.8 (1994 est)

Economy and resources
Currency: Seychelles rupee **GDP:** ($ US) 474.6 million (1994 est) **Real GDP per capita (PPP):** ($ US) 7,891 (1994) **GDP**

growth rate: –3% (1994) **Average annual inflation:** 0.5% (1996); 3.3% (1985–95) **Foreign debt:** ($ US) 170.1 million (1994) **Major trading partners:** UK, Singapore, Bahrain, South Africa, France, USA, Réunion, Japan **Resources:** guano; natural gas and metal deposits were being explored mid-1990s **Industries:** food processing (including cinnamon, coconuts, and tuna canning), beer and soft drinks, petroleum refining, cigarettes, paper, metals, chemicals, wood products, paints, tourism **Exports:** fresh and frozen fish, canned tuna, shark fins, cinnamon bark, refined petroleum products. Principal market: UK 16.6% (1995) **Imports:** machinery and transport equipment, food and live animals, petroleum and petroleum products, chemicals, basic manufactures. Principal source: Singapore 24.7% (1995) **Arable land:** 2.2% (1995) **Agricultural products:** coconuts, copra, cinnamon bark, tea, patchouli, vanilla, limes, sweet potatoes, cassava, yams, sugar cane, bananas; poultry meat and egg production are important for local consumption; fishing

Population and society
Population: 74,000 (1996 est) **Population growth rate:** 1.1% (1990–95) **Population density:** (per sq km) 163 (1996 est) **Urban population:** (% of total) 54.5 (1994) **Age distribution:** (% of total population) <15 36.8%, 15–65 56.8%, >65 6.4% (1992) **Ethnic groups:** predominantly Creole (of mixed African and European descent); small European minority (mostly French and British) **Language:** creole (Asian, African, European mixture) 95%, English, French (all official) **Religion:** Roman Catholic **Education:** (compulsory years) 9 **Literacy rate:** 86% (men); 82% (women) (1994 est) **Labour force:** 9.9% agriculture, 18.8% industry, 71.3% services (1989) **Unemployment:** 8.3% (1993) **Life expectancy:** 69 (men); 78 (women) (1994 est) **Child mortality rate:** (under 5, per 1,000 live births) 20 (1995) **Physicians:** 1 per 1,032 people (1993)

Practical information
Visa requirements: UK: visa not required. USA: visa not required **Embassy in the UK:** 2nd Floor, Eros House, 111 Baker Street, London W1M 1FE. Tel: (0171) 224 1660; fax: (0171) 487 5756 **British embassy:** British High Commission, PO Box 161, 3rd Floor, Victoria House, Victoria, Mahé. Tel: (248) 225 225; fax: (248) 225 127 **Chamber of commerce:** Seychelles Chamber of Commerce and Industry, PO Box 443, 38 Premier Building, Victoria, Mahé. Tel: (248) 223 812 **Airports:** international airports: Mahé Island (Seychelles); five domestic airports; total passenger km: 685 million (1994) **Major holidays:** 1–2 January, 1 May, 5, 29 June, 15 August, 1 November, 8, 25 December; variable: Corpus Christi, Good Friday, Holy Saturday

Chronology
early 16th century: First sighted by European navigators. **1744:** Became French colony. **1756:** Claimed as French possession and named after an influential French family. **1770s:** French colonists brought African slaves to settle the previously uninhabited islands; plantations established. **1794:** Captured by British during French Revolutionary Wars. **1814:** Ceded by France to Britain; incorporated as dependency of Mauritius. **1835:** Slavery abolished by British, leading to influx of liberated slaves from Mauritius and Chinese and Indian immigrants. **1903:** Became British crown colony, separate from Mauritius. **1963–64:** First political parties formed. **1976:** Independence achieved from Britain as republic within Commonwealth, with a moderate, James Mancham, of the centre-right Seychelles Democratic Party (SDP) as president. **1977:** More radical France-Albert René ousted Mancham in armed bloodless coup and took over presidency; white settlers emigrated. **1979:** Nationalistic socialist Seychelles People's Progressive Front (SPPF) became sole legal party under new constitution; became nonaligned state. **1981:** Attempted coup by South African mercenaries thwarted. **1991:** Multiparty politics promised. **1993:** New multiparty constitution adopted. René defeated Mancham, who had returned from exile, in competitive presidential elections; the SPPF won parliamentary elections.

Sierra Leone Republic of

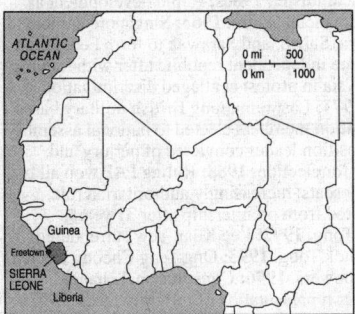

Area: 71,740 sq km/27,698 sq mi
Capital: Freetown
Major towns/cities: Koidu, Bo, Kenema, Makeni
Major ports: Bonthe-Sherbro
Physical features: mountains in E; hills and forest; coastal mangrove swamps

Government

Head of state and government: Ahmad Tejan Kabbah from 1996
Political system: transitional **Administrative divisions:** four provinces **Political parties:** All People's Congress (APC), moderate socialist; United Front of Political Movements (UNIFORM), centre left. Party political activity suspended from 1992 **Armed forces:** 14,200 (1996) **Conscription:** military service is voluntary **Death penalty:** retained and used for ordinary crimes **Defence spend:** (% GDP) 5.7 (1995) **Education spend:** (% GNP) 1.4 (1992) **Health spend:** (% GDP) 1.6 (1990–95)

Economy and resources

Currency: leone **GDP:** ($ US) 800 million (1994) **Real GDP per capita (PPP):** ($ US) 643 (1994) **GDP growth rate:** –4% (1994) **Average annual inflation:** 20% (1996); 61.5% (1985–95) **Foreign debt:** ($ US) 1.2 billion (1995) **Major trading partners:** Belgium/Luxembourg, UK, USA, the Netherlands, Nigeria, Germany **Resources:** gold, diamonds, bauxite, rutile (titanium dioxide) **Industries:** palm oil and other agro-based industries, rice mills, textiles, mining, sawn timber, furniture making **Exports:** rutile, diamonds, bauxite, gold, coffee, cocoa beans. Principal market: Belgium/Luxembourg 42% (1995) **Imports:** machinery and transport equipment, food and live animals, basic manufactures, chemicals, miscellaneous manufactured articles. Principal source: UK 18.7% (1995) **Arable land:** 6.8% (1995) **Agricultural products:** rice, cassava, palm oil, coffee, cocoa, bananas; cattle production

Population and society

Population: 4,297,000 (1996 est) **Population growth rate:** 2.4% (1990–95); 2.3% (2000–05) **Population density:** (per sq km) 60 (1996 est) **Urban population:** (% of total) 36 (1995) **Age distribution:** (% of total population) <15 44.2%, 15–65 52.8%, >65 3% (1995) **Ethnic groups:** 18 ethnic groups, 3 of which (the Mende, Tenne, and Limbe) comprise almost 70% of the population **Language:** English (official), Krio (a creole language) **Religion:** animist 52%, Muslim 39%, Protestant 6%, Roman Catholic 2% (1980 est) **Education:** not compulsory **Literacy rate:** 31% (men); 11% (women) (1995 est) **Labour force:** 37% of population: 67% agriculture, 15% industry, 17% services (1990) **Unemployment:** 12% (1990) **Life expectancy:** 40 (men); 43 (women) (1995–2000) **Child mortality rate:** (under 5, per 1,000 live births) 242 (1996) **Physicians:** 1 per 11,619 people (1990)

Practical information

Visa requirements: UK: visa required. USA: visa required **Embassy in the UK:** 33 Portland Place, London W1N 3AG. Tel: (0171) 636 6483/6; fax: (0171) 323 3159 **British embassy:** British High Commission, Standard Chartered Bank Building, Lightfoot-Boston Street, Freetown. Tel: (232) 223 961/5; telex: 3235 (a/b 3235 UKREP SL) **Chamber of commerce:** Sierra Leone Chamber of Commerce, Industry and Agriculture, PO Box 502, 5th Floor, Guma Building, Lamina, Sankoh Street, Freetown. Tel: (232) 226 305; fax: (232) 228 005 **Airports:** international airports: Freetown (Lungi); six domestic airports; total passenger km: 66 million (1994) **Major holidays:** 1 January, 19 April, 25–26 December; variable: Eid-ul-Adha, end of Ramadan, Good Friday, Easter Monday, Prophet's Birthday

Chronology

15th century: Mende, Temne, and Fulani peoples moved from Senegal into region formerly populated by Bulom, Krim, and Gola peoples. The Portuguese, who named the area Serra Lyoa, established a coastal fort, trading manufactured goods for slaves and ivory. **17th century:** English trading posts established on Bund and York islands. **1787–92:** English abolitionists and philanthropists bought land to establish settlement for liberated and runaway African slaves (including 1,000 rescued from Canada), known as Freetown. **1808:** Became a British colony and Freetown a base for British naval operations against slave trade, after parliament declared it illegal. **1896:** Hinterland conquered and declared British protectorate. **1951:** First political party, Sierra Leone People's Party (SLPP), formed by Dr Milton Margai, who became 'leader of government business', in 1953. **1961:** Independence achieved within Commonwealth, with Margai as prime minister. **1964:** Margai died; succeeded by his half-brother, Albert Margai. **1965:** Free-trade area pact signed with Guinea, Liberia, and Ivory Coast. **1967:** Election won by All People's Congress (APC), led by Siaka Stevens, but disputed by army, who set up National Reformation Council and forced governor general to leave the country. **1968:** Army revolt brought back Stevens as prime minister. **1971:** New constitution made Sierra Leone a republic, with Stevens as president. **1978:** New constitution made APC the only legal party. **1985:** Stevens retired; succeeded as president and APC leader by Maj-Gen Joseph Momoh. **1989:** Attempted coup against President Momoh foiled. **1991:** Referendum endorsed multiparty politics and new constitution. Liberian-based rebel group began guerrilla activities. **1992:** President Momoh overthrown by military and party politics suspended as National Provisional Ruling Council established under Capt Valentine Strasser; 500,000 Liberians fled to Sierra Leone as a result of civil war. **1995:** Ban on political parties lifted. Coup attempt foiled. **1996:** Strasser overthrown by deputy, Julius Maada Bio, who was replaced as president by Ahmad Tejan Kabbah after multiparty elections. **1997:** President Kabbah's civilian government ousted by mutinous troops in bloody coup. Major Johnny Paul Koroma seized presidency; UN Security Council voted to impose sanctions in an effort to condemn military junta. **1998:** Nigerian-led peacekeeping force drove out Major Koroma's junta; President Kabbah returned from exile.

Singapore Republic of

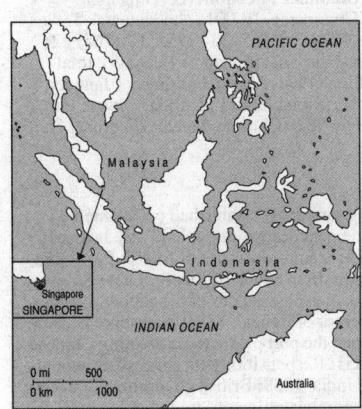

Area: 622 sq km/240 sq mi **Capital:** Singapore City
Major towns/cities: Jurong, Changi
Physical features: comprises Singapore Island, low and flat, and 57 small islands; Singapore Island is joined to the mainland by causeway across Strait of Johore

Government

Head of state: Ong Teng Cheong from 1993 **Head of government:** Goh Chok Tong from 1990 **Political system:** liberal democracy with strict limits on dissent **Administrative divisions:** five districts **Political parties:** People's Action Party (PAP), conservative, free market, multi-ethnic; Workers' Party (WP), socialist; Singapore Democratic Party (SDP), liberal pluralist **Armed forces:** 53,900; 221,000 reserves (1996) **Conscription:** two years **Death penalty:** retained and used for ordinary crimes **Defence spend:** (% GDP) 5.5 (1996) **Education spend:** (% GNP) 2.4 (1994) **Health spend:** (% GDP) 1.1 (1990–95)

Economy and resources
Currency: Singapore dollar **GDP:** ($ US) 68.9 billion (1994) **Real GDP per capita (PPP):** ($ US) 20,987 (1994) **GDP growth rate:** 10.1% (1994); 8.7% (1990–95) **Average annual inflation:** 1.3 (1996); 3.9% (1985–95) **Foreign debt:** ($ US) 7.2 billion (1996) **Major trading partners:** Japan, USA, Malaysia, Hong Kong, Thailand **Resources:** granite **Industries:** electrical machinery (particularly radios and televisions), petroleum refining and petroleum products, transport equipment (especially shipbuilding), chemicals, metal products, machinery, food processing, clothing, finance and business services **Exports:** electrical and nonelectrical machinery, transport equipment, petroleum products, chemicals, rubber, foodstuffs, clothing, metal products, iron and steel, orchids and other plants, aquarium fish. Principal market: USA 18.4% (1996) **Imports:** electrical and nonelectrical equipment, crude petroleum, transport equipment, chemicals, food and live animals, textiles, scientific and optical instruments, paper and paper products. Principal source: Japan 18.2% (1996) **Arable land:** 1.6% (1995) **Agricultural products:** vegetables, plants, orchids; poultry and fish production

Population and society
Population: 3,384,000 (1996 est) **Population growth rate:** 1% (1990–95); 0.6% (2000–05) **Population density:** (per sq km) 5,476 (1996 est) **Urban population:** (% of total) 100 (1995) **Age distribution:** (% of total population) <15 22.7%, 15–65 70.5%, >65 6.7% (1995) **Ethnic groups:** 77% of Chinese ethnic descent, predominantly Hokkien, Teochew, and Cantonese; 15% Malay; 7% Indian, chiefly Tamil **Language:** Malay (national tongue), Chinese, Tamil, English (all official) **Religion:** Buddhist, Taoist, Muslim, Hindu, Christian **Education:** (compulsory years) 6 **Literacy rate:** 93% (men); 79% (women) (1995 est) **Labour force:** 49% of population: 0% agriculture, 36% industry, 64% services (1990) **Unemployment:** 2.7% (1995) **Life expectancy:** 74 (men); 79 (women) (1995–2000) **Child mortality rate:** (under 5, per 1,000 live births) 9 (1996) **Physicians:** 1 per 709 people (1994)

Practical information
Visa requirements: UK: visa not required. USA: visa not required **Embassy in the UK:** 9 Wilton Cresscent, London SW1X 8SA. Tel: (0171) 235 8315; fax: (0171) 245 6583 **British embassy:** British High Commission, Tanglin Road, Singapore 1024. Tel: (65) 473 9333; fax: (65) 475 2320 **Chamber of commerce:** Singapore International Chamber of Commerce, 10-001 John Hancock Tower, 6 Raffles Quay, Singapore 0104. Tel: (65) 224 1255; fax: (65) 224 2785 **Airports:** international airports: Singapore (Changi); total passenger km: 44,947 million (1994) **Major holidays:** 1 January, 1 May, 9 August, 25 December; variable: Eid-ul-Adha, Diwali, end of Ramadan, Good Friday, New Year (Chinese, January/February, 2 days), Vesak

Chronology
12th century: First trading settlement established on Singapore Island. **14th century:** Settlement destroyed, probably by Javanese Empire of Mahapahit. **1819:** Stamford Raffles of British East India Company obtained Singapore from sultan of Johore. **1826:** Straits Settlements formed from British possessions of Singapore, Penang, and Malacca ruled by governor of Bengal. **1832:** Singapore became capital of Straits Settlements; the port prospered, attracting Chinese and Indian immigrants. **1851:** Responsibility for Straits Settlements fell to governor general of India. **1858:** British government, through the India Office, took over administration of Straits Settlements. **1867:** Straits Settlements became crown colony of British Empire. **1922:** Singapore chosen as principal British military base in Far East. **1942:** Japan captured Singapore, taking 70,000 British and Australian prisoners. **1945:** British rule restored after defeat of

Japan. **1946:** Singapore became separate crown colony. **1959:** Internal self-government achieved as State of Singapore with Lee Kuan Yew (PAP) as prime minister. **1960s:** Rapid development as leading commercial and financial centre. **1963:** Singapore combined with Federation of Malaya, Sabah, and Sarawak to form Federation of Malaysia. **1965:** Became independent republic after withdrawing from Federation of Malaysia in protest at alleged discrimination against ethnic Chinese. **1971:** Last remaining British military bases closed. **1984:** Two opposition members elected to national assembly for first time. **1986:** Opposition leader convicted of perjury and prohibited from standing for election. **1988:** Ruling PAP won all but one of available assembly seats; increasingly authoritarian rule. **1990:** Lee Kuan Yew retired from premiership after 31 years; succeeded by Goh Chok Tong. **1992:** Lee Kuan Yew surrendered PAP leadership to Goh Chok Tong. **1993:** Ong Teng Cheong elected president with increased powers. **1996:** Constitutional change introduced, allowing better representation of minority races. **1997:** PAP, led by Prime Minister Goh Chok Tong, won general election.

Slovak Republic

National name: *Slovenská Republika* **Area:** 49,035 sq km/18,932 sq mi **Capital:** Bratislava **Major towns/cities:** Košice, Nitra, Prešov, Banská Bystrica, Zilina, Trnava **Physical features:** Western range of Carpathian Mountains, including Tatra and Beskids in N; Danube plain in S; numerous lakes and mineral springs

Government
Head of state: Michal Kovak from 1993 **Head of government:** Vladimir Meciar from 1994 **Political system:** emergent democracy **Administrative divisions:** four regions **Political parties:** Movement for a Democratic Slovakia (MDS), centre left, nationalist-populist; Democratic Union of Slovakia (DUS), centrist; Christian Democratic Movement (KSDH), right of centre; Slovak National Party (SNP), nationalist; Party of the Democratic Left (PDL), reform socialist, (ex-communist); Association of Workers of Slovakia, left wing; Hungarian Coalition, ethnic Hungarian **Armed forces:** 42,600 (1996) **Conscription:** military service is compulsory for 18 months **Death penalty:** abolished 1990 **Defence spend:** (% GDP) 2.6 (1996) **Education spend:** (% GNP) 4.3 (1994) **Health spend:** (% GDP) 6.3 (1990–95)

Economy and resources
Currency: Slovak koruna (based on Czechoslovak koruna) **GDP:** ($ US) 12 billion (1994) **Real GDP per capita (PPP):** ($ US) 6,389 (1994) **GDP growth rate:** 6.9% (1996); –2.8% (1990–95) **Average annual inflation:** 5.8% (1996); 10.4% (1985–95 est) **Foreign debt:** ($ US) 5.7 billion (1995) **Major trading partners:** Czech Republic, Germany, Russia, Austria, Hungary, Italy **Resources:** brown coal, lignite, copper, zinc, lead, iron ore, magnesite **Industries:** chemicals, pharmaceuticals, heavy engineering, munitions, mining, textiles, clothing, glass, leather, footwear, construction materials, televisions, transport equipment (cars, lorries, and motorcycles) **Exports:** basic manufactures, machinery and transport equipment, miscellaneous manufactured articles. Principal market: Czech Republic 35.2% (1995) **Imports:** machinery and transport equipment, mineral fuels and lubricants, basic manufactures, chemicals and related products. Principal source: Czech Republic

27.5% (1995) **Arable land:** 30.8% (1995) **Agricultural products:** wheat and other grains, sugar beet, potatoes and other vegetables; livestock rearing (cattle, pigs, and poultry)

Population and society

Population: 5,347,000 (1996 est) **Population growth rate:** 0.4% (1990–95); 0.4% (2000–05) **Population density:** (per sq km) 109 (1996 est) **Urban population:** (% of total) 59 (1995) **Age distribution:** (% of total population) <15 22.9%, 15–65 66.3%, >65 10.8% (1995) **Ethnic groups:** 87% ethnic Slovak, 11% ethnic Hungarian (Magyar); small Czech, Moravian, Silesian, and Romany communities **Language:** Slovak (official) **Religion:** Roman Catholic (over 50%), Lutheran, Reformist, Orthodox **Education:** (compulsory years) 9 **Literacy rate:** 99% (men); 99% (women) (1995 est) **Labour force:** 12.1% agriculture, 39.8% industry, 48.1% services (1993) **Unemployment:** 13.1% (1995); 12.6% (1996) **Life expectancy:** 67 (men); 75 (women) (1995–2000) **Child mortality rate:** (under 5, per 1,000 live births) 14 (1996) **Physicians:** 1 per 287 people (1993)

Practical information

Visa requirements: UK: visa not required. USA: visa not required **Embassy in the UK:** 25 Kensington Palace Gardens, London W8 4QY. Tel: (0171) 243 0803; fax: (0171) 727 5824 **British embassy:** Grösslingova 35, 811 09 Bratislava. Tel: (7) 364 420; fax: (7) 364 396 **Chamber of commerce:** Slovak Chamber of Commerce and Industry, Gorkéno 9, 816 03 Bratislava. Tel: (7) 362 787; fax: (7) 362 222 **Airports:** international airports: Bratislava (M R Stefanik), Poprad-Tatry, Košice, Piešt'any, Sliaš; domestic services to most major cities; total passenger km: 12 million (1994) **Major holidays:** 1, 6 January, 1 May, 5 July, 29 August, 1, 15 September, 1 November, 24–26 December; variable: Good Friday, Easter Monday

Chronology

9th century: Part of kingdom of Greater Moravia, in Czech lands to W, founded by Slavic Prince Sviatopluk; Christianity adopted. **906:** Came under Magyar (Hungarian) domination and adopted Roman Catholicism. **1526:** Came under Austrian Habsburg rule. **1867:** With creation of dual Austro-Hungarian monarchy, came under separate Hungarian rule; policy of forced Magyarization stimulated a revival of Slovak national consciousness. **1918:** Austro-Hungarian Empire dismembered; Slovaks joined Czechs to form independent state of Czechoslovakia. Slovak-born Tomas Masaryk remained president until 1935, but political and economic power became concentrated in Czech lands. **1939:** Germany annexed Czechoslovakia, which became Axis puppet state under the Slovak autonomist leader Monsignor Jozef Tiso; Jews persecuted. **1944:** Popular revolt against German rule ('Slovak Uprising'). **1945:** Liberated from German rule by Soviet troops; Czechoslovakia re-established. **1948:** Communists assumed power in Czechoslovakia. **1950s:** Heavy industry introduced into previously rural Slovakia; Slovak nationalism and Catholic Church forcibly suppressed. **1968–69:** 'Prague Spring' political reforms introduced by Slovak-born Communist Party leader Alexander Dubček; Warsaw Pact forces invaded Czechoslovakia to stamp out reforms; Slovak Socialist Republic, with autonomy over local affairs, created under new federal constitution; Slovak-born Gustáv Husák became Communist Party leader in Czechoslovakia. **1989:** Prodemocracy demonstrations in Bratislava; new political parties, including centre-left People Against Violence (PAV), formed and later legalized; Communist Party stripped of powers; new government formed, with ex-dissident playwright Václav Havel as president. **1990:** Slovak nationalists polled strongly in multiparty elections, with Vladimir Meciar (PAV) becoming prime minister. **1991:** Increasing Slovak separatism, as economy deteriorated with exposure to market forces. Meciar formed PAV splinter group, Movement for a Democratic Slovakia (HZDS), pledging greater autonomy for Slovakia. Pro-Meciar rallies in Bratislava followed his dismissal. **1992:** Meciar returned to power following electoral victory for HZDS. Slovak parliament's declaration of sovereignty led to Havel's resignation; 'velvet divorce' agreement on separate Czech and Slovak states established a free-trade customs union. **1993:** Slovak Republic entered United Nations and Council of Europe as sovereign state,

with Meciar as prime minister and Michal Kovac, formerly of HZDS, as president. **1994:** Joined NATO's 'Partnership for Peace' programme. Meciar ousted on no-confidence vote, but later returned after new elections, heading 'red-brown' coalition government that included ultranationalists and socialists. **1995:** Second wave of mass privatization postponed; Slovak made sole official language; Treaty of Friendship and Cooperation signed with Hungary, easing tensions among Hungarian minority community. **1996:** Anti-Meciar coalition formed, the Slovak Democratic Coalition, comprising five opposition parties. **1997:** Referendum on NATO membership and direct presidential elections declared invalid after government caused confusion over voting papers.

Slovenia Republic of

National name: *Republika Slovenija* **Area:** 20,251 sq km/7,818 sq mi **Capital:** Ljubljana **Major towns/cities:** Maribor, Kranj, Celji, Velenje, Koper (Capodistria) **Major ports:** Koper **Physical features:** mountainous; Sava and Drava rivers

Government

Head of state: Milan Kučan from 1990 **Head of government:** Janez Drnovšek from 1992 **Political system:** emergent democracy **Administrative divisions:** 62 districts **Political parties:** Slovenian Christian Democrats (SKD), right of centre; Slovenian People's Party (SPP), conservative; Liberal Democratic Party of Slovenia (LDS), centrist; Slovenian Nationalist Party (SNS), right-wing nationalist; Democratic Party of Slovenia (LDP), left of centre; United List of Social Democrats (ZLSD) left of centre, ex-communist **Armed forces:** 9,600; plus reserve forces of 53,000 and a paramilitary police force of 4,500 (1996) **Conscription:** military service is compulsory for seven months **Death penalty:** abolished 1989 **Defence spend:** (% GDP) 1.5% (1995) **Education spend:** (% GNP) 5.6% (1994)

Economy and resources

Currency: tolar **GDP:** ($ US) 14 billion (1994) **Real GDP per capita (PPP):** ($ US) 10,404 (1994) **GDP growth rate:** 3.1% (1996) **Average annual inflation:** 10.7% (1996) **Foreign debt:** ($ US) 3.5 million (1995) **Major trading partners:** Germany, Italy, Croatia, France, Austria, former USSR, USA **Resources:** coal, lead, zinc; small reserves/deposits of natural gas, petroleum, salt, uranium **Industries:** metallurgy, furniture making, sports equipment, electrical equipment, food processing, textiles, paper and paper products, chemicals, wood and wood products **Exports:** raw materials, semi-finished goods, machinery, electric motors, transport equipment, foodstuffs, clothing, pharmaceuticals, cosmetics. Principal market: Germany 30.7% (1996) **Imports:** machinery and transport equipment, raw materials, semi-finished goods, foodstuffs, chemicals, miscellaneous manufactured articles, mineral fuels and lubricants. Principal source: Germany 21.7% (1996) **Arable land:** 11.6% (1995) **Agricultural products:** wheat, maize, sugar beet, potatoes, cabbage, fruits (especially grapes); forest resources (approximately 45% of total land area was forest 1994)

Population and society

Population: 1,924,000 (1996 est) **Population growth rate:** 0.3% (1990–95); –0.1% (2000–05) **Population density:** (per sq km) 95 (1996 est) **Urban population:** (% of total) 64 (1995) **Age distribution:** (% of total population) <15 18.3%, 15–65 69.2%, >65

12.4% (1995) **Ethnic groups:** 98% of Slovene origin, 3% ethnic Croat, 2% Serb **Language:** Slovene, resembling Serbo-Croat, written in Roman characters **Religion:** Roman Catholic **Education:** (compulsory years) 8 **Literacy rate:** 96% (men); 96% (women) (1995 est) **Labour force:** 11.5% agriculture, 42.3% industry, 46.2% services (1994) **Unemployment:** 14% (1997) **Life expectancy:** 69 (men); 78 (women) (1995–2000) **Child mortality rate:** (per 1,000 live births) 12 (1996) **Physicians:** 1 per 481 people (1995)

Practical information
Visa requirements: UK: visa not required. USA: visa not required **Embassy in the UK:** Suite 1, Cavendish Court, 11–15 Wigmore Street, London W1H 9LA. Tel: (0171) 495 7775; fax: (0171) 495 7776 **British embassy:** 4th Floor, Trg Republike 3, 61000 Ljubljana. Tel: (61) 125 7191; fax: (61) 125 0174 **Chamber of commerce:** Chamber of Economy of Slovenia, Slovenska 41, 61000 Ljubljana. Tel: (61) 125 0122; fax: (61) 219 536 **Airports:** international airports: Ljubljana (Brnik), Maribor, Portoroz; two domestic airports; total passenger km: 329 million (1994) **Major holidays:** 1–2 January, 8 February, 27 April, 1–2 May, 25 June, 15 August, 31 October, 1 November, 25–26 December; variable: Good Friday, Easter Monday

Chronology
1st century BC: Came under Roman rule. **AD 395:** In division of Roman Empire, stayed in W, along with Croatia and Bosnia. **6th century:** Settled by the Slovene South Slavs. **7th century:** Adopted Christianity as Roman Catholics. **8th–9th centuries:** Under successive rule of Franks and dukes of Bavaria. **907–55:** Came under Hungarian domination. **1335:** Absorbed in Austro-Hungarian Habsburg Empire, as part of Austrian crownlands of Carniola, Styria, and Carinthia. **1848:** Slovene struggle for independence began. **1918:** On collapse of Habsburg Empire, Slovenia united with Serbia, Croatia, and Montenegro to form the 'Kingdom of Serbs, Croats and Slovenes', under Serbian Karageorgevic dynasty. **1929:** Kingdom became known as Yugoslavia. **1941–45:** Occupied by Nazi Germany and Italy during World War II; anti-Nazi Slovene Liberation Front formed and became allies of Marshal Tito's communist-led Partisans. **1945:** Became constituent republic of Yugoslav Socialist Federal Republic. **mid-1980s:** Slovenian Communist Party liberalized itself and agreed to free elections. Yugoslav counterintelligence (KOV) began repression. **1989:** Constitution changed to allow secession from federation. **1990:** Nationalist Democratic Opposition of Slovenia (DEMOS) coalition secured victory in first multiparty parliamentary elections; Milan Kučan, a reform communist, became president. Sovereignty declared. Independence overwhelmingly approved in referendum. **1991:** Seceded from Yugoslav federation, along with Croatia; 100 killed after Yugoslav federal army intervened; cease-fire brokered by European Community (EC) brought withdrawal of Yugoslav army. **1992:** Janez Drnovšek, a centrist Liberal Democrat, appointed prime minister; independence recognized by EC and USA. Admitted into United Nations. Liberal Democrats and Christian Democrats won assembly elections. **1996:** Governing coalition weakened by withdrawal of ZLSD. LDS failed to win overall majority in assembly elections. **1997:** New government formed by ruling LDS, led by Prime Minister Janez Drnovsek. President Kucan re-elected. European Union agreed to open membership talks with Slovenia.

Solomon Islands

Area: 27,600 sq km/10,656 sq mi **Capital:** Honiara (on Guadalcanal) (and chief port) **Major towns/cities:** Gizo, Kieta, Auki **Major ports:** Yandina **Physical features:** comprises all but the northernmost islands (which belong to Papua New Guinea) of a Melanesian archipelago stretching nearly 1,500 km/900 mi. The largest is Guadalcanal (area 6,500 sq km/2,510 sq mi); others are Malaita, San Cristobal, New Georgia, Santa Isabel, Choiseul; mainly mountainous and forested

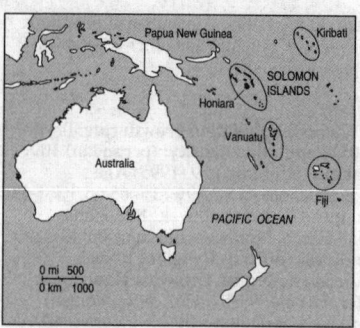

Government
Head of state: Queen Elizabeth II, represented by governor general Moses Pitakaka from 1994 **Head of government:** Bartholomew Ulufa'alu from 1997 **Political system:** constitutional monarchy **Administrative divisions:** seven provinces and a capital territory **Political parties:** Group for National Unity and Reconciliation (GNUR), centrist coalition; National Coalition Partners (NCP), broad-based coalition; People's Progressive Party (PPP); People's Alliance Party (PAP) **Armed forces:** no standing army; 80-strong marine wing of police force (1995) **Death penalty:** laws do not provide for the death penalty for any crime **Education spend:** (% GNP) 4.2 (1993/94) **Health spend:** (% GDP) 5 (1990)

Economy and resources
Currency: Solomon Island dollar **GDP:** ($ US) 218 million (1994 est) **Real GDP per capita (PPP):** ($ US) 2,310 (1994 est) **GDP growth rate:** 5.2% (1994) **Average annual inflation:** 11.3% (1996); 11.7% (1985–95) **Foreign debt:** ($ US) 165.1 million (1994) **Major trading partners:** Australia, Japan, UK, New Zealand, Singapore, South Korea **Resources:** bauxite, phosphates, gold, silver, copper, lead, zinc, cobalt, asbestos, nickel **Industries:** food processing (mainly palm oil and rice milling, fish, and coconut-based products), saw milling, logging, tobacco, furniture, handicrafts, boats, clothing, tourism **Exports:** timber, fish products, oil palm products, copra, cocoa, coconut oil. Principal market: Japan 41.1% (1994) **Imports:** rice, machinery and transport equipment, meat preparations, refined sugar, mineral fuels, basic manufactures, construction materials. Principal source: Australia 37.2% (1994) **Arable land:** 1.5% (1995) **Agricultural products:** coconuts, cocoa, rice, cassava, sweet potatoes, yam, taro, banana, palm oil; livestock rearing (pigs and cattle); fishing, sea shells, and seaweed farming; forestry

Population and society
Population: 391,000 (1996 est) **Population growth rate:** 3.3% (1990–95); 3.1% (2000–05) **Population density:** (per sq km) 14 (1996 est) **Urban population:** (% of total) 17 (1995) **Age distribution:** (% of total population) <15 44.2%, 15–65 52.9%, >65 2.9% (1995) **Ethnic groups:** 93% Melanesian, 4% Polynesian, 1.5% Micronesian, 0.7% European, 0.2% Chinese **Language:** English (official); there are some 120 Melanesian dialects spoken by 85% of the population, and Papuan and Polynesian languages **Religion:** Anglican, Roman Catholic, South Sea Evangelical, other Protestant **Education:** not compulsory **Literacy rate:** 60% (men); 60% (women) (1994 est) **Labour force:** 27.4% agriculture, 13.7% industry, 58.9% services (1993) **Life expectancy:** 70 (men); 74 (women) (1995–2000) **Child mortality rate:** (under 5, per 1,000 live births) 29 (1996) **Physicians:** 1 per 5,190 people (1991)

Practical information
Visa requirements: UK: visa not required. USA: visa not required **Embassy for the UK:** BP 3, avenue de l'Yser 13, B-1040 Brussels, Belgium. Tel: (2) 732 7082; fax: (2) 732 6885; Solomon Islands Honorary Consulate, 19 Springfield Road, London SW19 7AL. Tel: (0181) 296 6232; fax: (0181) 946 1744 **British embassy:** British High Commission, PO Box 676, Telekom House, Mendana Avenue, Honiara. Tel: 21705/6; fax: 20765 **Chamber of commerce:** PO Box 64, Honiara. Tel: 22960 **Airports:** international airport: Honiara (Henderson); 26 domestic airports; total passenger km: 5 million (1994) **Major holidays:** 1 January, 7 July, 25–26 December; variable: Good Friday, Easter Monday, Holy Saturday, Whit Monday, Queen's Birthday (June)

Chronology

1568: The islands, rumoured in South America to be the legendary gold-rich 'Islands of Solomon', were first sighted by Spanish navigator Alvaro de Mendana, journeying from Peru. **1595 and 1606:** Unsuccessful Spanish efforts to settle the islands, which had long been peopled by Melanesians. **later 18th century:** Visited again by Europeans. **1840s:** Christian missions established. **1870s:** Development of copra export trade and shipment of islanders to work on sugar cane plantations in Australia and Fiji. **1886:** Northern Solomon Islands became German protectorate. **1893:** Southern Solomon Islands placed under British protection. **1899:** Germany ceded Solomon Islands possessions to Britain in return for British recognition of its claims to Western Samoa. **1900:** Unified British Solomon Islands Protectorate formed and placed under jurisdiction of Western Pacific High Commission (WPHC), with its headquarters in Fiji. **1942–43:** Occupied by Japan. Site of fierce fighting, especially on Guadalcanal, which was recaptured by US forces, with the loss of 21,000 Japanese and 5,000 US troops. **1943–50:** Development of Marching Rule (Ma'asina Ruru) cargo cult populist movement on Malaita island, campaigning for self-rule. **1945:** Headquarters of WPHC moved to Honiara. **1960:** Legislative and executive councils established by constitution. **1974:** Became substantially self-governing, with Solomon Mamaloni of centre-left People's Progressive Party (PPP) as chief minister. **1976:** Became fully self-governing, with Peter Kenilorea of right-of-centre Solomon Islands United Party (SIUPA) as chief minister. **1978:** Independence achieved from Britain within Commonwealth, with Kenilorea as prime minister. **1981:** Mamaloni (PPP) became prime minister, pledging to decentralize power. **1984:** Kenilorea returned to power, heading coalition government. **1986:** Kenilorea resigned after allegations of corruption; replaced by his deputy, Ezekiel Alebua. **1988:** Kenilorea elected deputy prime minister. Joined Vanuatu and Papua New Guinea to form Spearhead Group, aiming to preserve Melanesian cultural traditions. **1989:** Mamaloni, now leader of People's Alliance Party (PAP), appointed prime minister. **1990:** Mamaloni resigned as PAP party leader, but continued as head of a government of national unity, which included Keniloea as foreign minister. **1993:** New Mamaloni-led coalition won largest number of seats in general election, but Francis Billy Hilly, an independent politician, appointed prime minister. **1994:** Billy Hilly resigned; Mamaloni returned to power. **1997:** Bartholomew Ulufa'alu elected prime minister.

Somalia Somali Democratic Republic

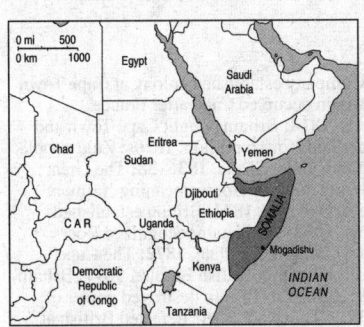

National name: *Jamhuriyadda Dimugradiga ee Soomaliya* **Area:** 637,700 sq km/246,215 sq mi **Capital:** Mogadishu (and port) **Major towns/cities:** Hargeysa, Berbera, Kismayo, Marka **Major ports:** Berbera, Marka, Kismayo **Physical features:** mainly flat, with hills in N

Government

Head of state and government (interim): Hussein Aidid from 1996 **Political system:** transitional **Administrative divisions:** 18 regions **Political parties:** parties are mainly clan-based and include the United Somali Congress (USC), Hawiye clan; Somali Patriotic Movement (SPM), Darod clan; Somali Southern Democratic Front (SSDF), Majertein clan; Somali Democratic Alliance (SDA), Gadabursi clan; United Somali Front (USF), Issa clan; Somali National Movement (SNM) based in self-proclaimed Somaliland Republic **Armed forces:** 225,000 (1996) **Death penalty:** retained

and used for ordinary crimes **Defence spent:** (% GDP) 4.8 (1996) **Education spend:** (% GNP) 0.5 (1985); N/A (1993/94) **Health spend:** (% GDP) 0.9 (1990)

Economy and resources

Currency: Somali shilling **GDP:** ($ US) 3.6 billion (1995 est) **Real GDP per capita (PPP):** ($ US) 650 (1995 est) **GDP growth rate:** 2% (1995 est) **Average annual inflation:** N/A **Foreign debt:** ($ US) 2.61 billion (1994) **Major trading partners:** Saudi Arabia, Kenya, Italy, USA, UK, Germany, Ethiopia **Resources:** chromium, coal, salt, tin, zinc, copper, gypsum, manganese, iron ore, uranium, gold, silver; deposits of petroleum and natural gas have been discovered but remain unexploited **Industries:** food processing (especially sugar refining), textiles, petroleum refining, processing of hides and skins **Exports:** livestock, skins and hides, bananas, fish and fish products, myrrh. Principal market: Saudi Arabia 47.6% (1992) **Imports:** petroleum, fertilizers, foodstuffs, machinery and parts, manufacturing raw materials. Principal source: Italy 30% (1991) **Arable land:** 1.6% (1995) **Agricultural products:** bananas, sugar cane, maize, sorghum, grapefruit, seed cotton; agriculture is based on livestock rearing (cattle, sheep, goats, and camels) – 80% of the population depend on this activity

Population and society

Population: 9,822,000 (1996 est) **Population growth rate:** 1.3% (1990–95); 3% (2000–05) **Population density:** (per sq km) 15 (1996 est) **Urban population:** (% of total) 26 (1995) **Age distribution:** (% of total population) <15 47.5%, 15–65 49.8%, >65 2.7% (1995) **Ethnic groups:** 98% indigenous Somali (about 84% Hamitic and 14% Bantu); population is divided into around 100 clans **Language:** Somali, Arabic (both official), Italian, English **Religion:** Sunni Muslim **Education:** (compulsory years) 8 **Literacy rate:** 36% (men); 14% (women) (1995 est) **Labour force:** 44% of population: 75% agriculture, 8% industry, 16% services (1990) **Life expectancy:** 47 (men); 51 (women) (1995–2000) **Child mortality rate:** (under 5, per 1,000 live births) 176 (1996) **Physicians:** 1 per 5,691 people (1990)

Practical information

Visa requirements: UK: visa required. USA: visa required **Embassy in the UK:** no diplomatic representation at present **British embassy:** all staff have been withdrawn for the present; the British Embassy in Addis Ababa (see Ethiopia) deals with enquiries relating to Somalia **Airports:** international airports: Mogadishu, Berbera; seven domestic airports and airfields; passengers carried: 46,000 (1991) **Major holidays:** 1 January, 1 May, 26 June, 1 July, 21 October (2 days); variable: Eid-ul-Adha (2 days), end of Ramadan (2 days), Prophet's Birthday

Chronology

8th–10th centuries: Arab ancestors of Somali clan families migrated to the region and introduced Sunni Islam; coastal trading cities, including Mogadishu, were formed by Arabian immigrants and developed into sultanates. **11th–14th century:** Southward and westward movement of Somalis and Islamization of Christian Ethiopian interior. **early 16th century:** Portuguese contacts with coastal region. **1820s:** First British contacts with N Somalia. **1884–87:** British protectorate of Somaliland established in N. **1889:** Italian protectorate of Somalia established in S. **1927:** Italian Somalia became a colony and part of Italian East Africa from 1936. **1941:** Italian Somalia occupied by Britain during World War II. **1943:** Somali Youth League (SYL) formed as nationalist party. **1950:** Italy resumed control over Italian Somalia under UN trusteeship. **1960:** Independence achieved from Italy and Britain as Somalia, with Aden Abdullah Osman as president. **1963:** Border dispute with Kenya; diplomatic relations broken with Britain for five years. **1967:** Dr Abdirashid Ali Shermarke (SYL) became president. **1969:** President Ibrahim Egal assassinated in army coup led by Maj-Gen Muhammad Siad Barre; constitution suspended, political parties banned, Supreme Revolutionary Council set up, and socialist-Islamic state formed. **1972:** 20,000 died in severe drought. **1978:** Defeated in eight-month war with Ethiopia fought on behalf of Somali guerrillas in Ogaden to the SW. Armed insurrection began in N and hundreds of thousands became refugees. **1979:** New constitution for socialist one-party state dominated by Somali Revolutionary Socialist Party (SRSP). **1982:** Antigovernment Ethiopian-backed Somali National Movement (SNM) formed in N. Oppressive countermeasures by government. **late 1980s:** Guerrilla activity increased in N as civil war intensified. **1991:** Mogadishu captured by rebels; Barre fled; Ali Mahdi Muhammad named president; free elections promised. Secession of NE Somalia, as Somaliland Republic, announced but not recognized internationally. **1992:** Widespread famine. Western food-aid convoys hijacked by 'warlords'. United Nations peacekeeping troops, led by US Marines, sent in to protect relief operations. **1993:** Leaders of armed factions (excepting Somaliland-based faction) agreed to federal system of government. US-led UN forces destroyed headquarters of warlord Gen Muhammad Farah Aidid after killing of Pakistani peacekeepers. **1994:** Ali Mahdi Muhammad and Aidid signed truce. Majority of Western peacekeeping troops withdrawn, but clan-based fighting continued. **1995:** Last UN peacekeepers withdrawn. **1996:** Aidid killed in renewed faction fighting; his son Hussein Aidid succeeded him, as interim president. **1997:** Peace agreement signed between USC and breakaway USC-SNA.

South Africa Republic of

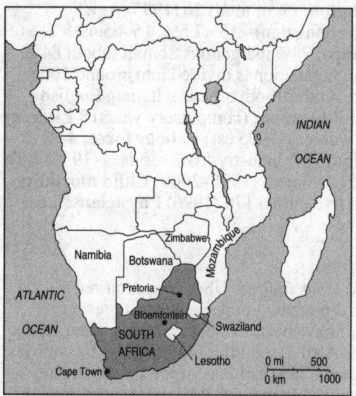

National name: *Republiek van Suid-Afrika* **Area:** 1,222,081 sq km/471,845 sq mi **Capital:** Cape Town (legislative) (and port), Pretoria (administrative), Bloemfontein (judicial) **Major towns/cities:** Johannesburg, Durban, Port Elizabeth, Vereeniging, East London, Pietermaritzburg, Kimberley **Major ports:** Durban, Port Elizabeth, East London **Physical features:** southern end of large plateau, fringed by mountains and lowland coastal margin; Drakensberg Mountains, Table Mountain; Limpopo and Orange rivers **Territories:** Marion Island and Prince Edward Island in the Antarctic

Government

Head of state and government: Nelson Mandela from 1994 **Political system:** liberal democracy **Administrative divisions:** nine provinces **Political parties:** African National Congress (ANC), left of centre; National Party (NP), right of centre; Inkatha Freedom Party (IFP), centrist, multiracial (formerly Zulu nationalist); Freedom Front (FF), right wing; Democratic Party (DP), moderate, centre left, multiracial; Pan-Africanist Congress (PAC), black, left wing; African Christian Democratic Party (ACDP), Christian, right of centre **Armed forces:** 137,900 (1996) **Conscription:** none **Death penalty:** for exceptional crimes only (from 1995) **Defence spend:** (% GDP) 1.8 (1996) **Education spend:** (% GNP) 7.1 (1993/94) **Health spend:** (% GDP) 3.6 (1990–95)

Economy and resources

Currency: rand **GDP:** ($ US) 121.9 billion (1994) **Real GDP per capita:** ($ US) 4,291 (1994) **GDP growth rate:** 2.3% (1994); 0.6% (1990–95) **Average annual inflation:** 7.7% (1996); 13.7% (1985–95) **Foreign debt:** ($ US) 34.3 billion (1996) **Major trading partners:** Germany, Italy, UK, USA, Japan, Switzerland **Resources:** gold (world's largest producer), coal, platinum, iron ore,

diamonds, chromium, manganese, limestone, asbestos, fluorspar, uranium, copper, lead, zinc, petroleum, natural gas **Industries:** chemicals, petroleum and coal products, gold, diamonds, food processing, transport equipment, iron and steel, metal products, machinery, fertilizers, textiles, paper and paper products, clothing, wood and cork products **Exports:** metals and metal products, gold, precious and semiprecious stones, mineral products and chemicals, natural cultured pearls, machinery and mechanical appliances, wool, maize, fruit, sugar. Principal market: Italy 7.8% (1995) **Imports:** machinery and electrical equipment, transport equipment, chemical products, mechanical appliances, textiles and clothing, vegetable products, wood, pulp, paper and paper products. Principal source: Germany 15.9% (1995) **Arable land:** 12.3% (1995) **Agricultural products:** maize, sugar cane, sorghum, fruits, wheat, groundnuts, grapes, vegetables; livestock rearing, wool production

Population and society

Population: 38,000,000 (1996 est) **Population growth rate:** 2.2% (1990–95); 2.1% (2000–05) **Population density:** (per sq km) 35 (1996 est) **Urban population:** (% of total) 51 (1995) **Age distribution:** (% of total population) <15 37.3%, 15–65 58.3%, >65 4.4% (1995) **Ethnic groups:** 77% of the population is black African, 12% white (of European descent), 9% of mixed African–European descent, and 2% Asian. **Language:** English and Afrikaans (both official); main African languages: Xhosa, Zulu, and Sesotho (all official) **Religion:** Dutch Reformed Church and other Christian denominations, Hindu, Muslim **Education:** (compulsory years) 10 **Literacy rate:** 81% (men); 81% (women) (1995 est) **Labour force:** 39% of population: 14% agriculture, 32% industry, 55% services (1990) **Unemployment:** 29% (early 1995) **Life expectancy:** 62 (men); 68 (women) (1995–2000) **Child mortality rate:** (under 5, per 1,000 live births) 73 (1996) **Physicians:** 1 per 1,528 people (1994)

Practical information

Visa requirements: UK: visa not required. USA: visa not required **Embassy in the UK:** South Africa House, Trafalgar Square, London WC2N 5DP. Tel: (0171) 930 4488; fax: (0171) 451 7284 **British embassy:** British High Commission, 255 Hill Street, Arcadia, Pretoria 0002. Tel: (12) 433 121; fax: (12) 433 207 **Chamber of commerce:** South African Chamber of Business, PO Box 91267, Auckland Park 20006. Tel: (11) 482 2524; fax: (11) 726 1344 **Airports:** international airports: Cape Town (D F Malan), Durban (Louis Botha), Johannesburg (Jan Smuts); six domestic airports, 212 public aerodromes; total passenger km: 12,352 million (1994) **Major holidays:** 1 January, 21 March, 27 April, 1 May, 16 June, 9 August , 24 September, 16, 25–26 December; variable: Good Friday

Chronology

1652: Dutch East India Company established colony at Cape Town as a port of call. **1795:** Britain occupied Cape after France conquered the Netherlands. **1814:** Britain bought Cape Town and hinterland from the Netherlands for £6 million. **1820s:** Zulu people established military kingdom under Shaka. **1836–38:** The Great Trek: 10,000 Dutch settlers (known as Boers, meaning 'farmers') migrated north to escape British rule. **1843:** Britain established colony of Natal on E coast. **1852–54:** Britain recognized Boer republics of Transvaal and Orange Free State. **1872:** The Cape became self-governing colony within British Empire. **1877:** Britain annexed Transvaal. **1879:** Zulu War: Britain destroyed power of Zulus. **1881:** First Boer War: Transvaal Boers defeated British at Majuba Hill and regained independence. **1886:** Disovery of gold on Witwatersrand attracted many migrant miners (uitlanders) to Transvaal, which denied them full citizenship. **1895:** Jameson Raid: uitlanders, backed by Cecil Rhodes, tried to overthrow President Paul Kruger of Transvaal. **1899–1902:** Second South African War (also known as Boer War): dispute over rights of uitlanders led to conflict which ended with British annexation of Boer republics. **1907:** Britain granted internal self-government to Transvaal and Orange Free State on whites-only franchise. **1910:** Cape Colony, Natal, Transvaal, and Orange Free State formed Union of South Africa, with Louis Botha as prime minister. **1912:** Gen Barry

Hertzog founded (Boer) Nationalist Party; ANC formed to campaign for rights of black majority. **1914:** Boer revolt in Orange Free State suppressed; South African troops fought for British Empire in World War I. **1919:** Jan Smuts succeeded Botha as premier; South West Africa (Namibia) became South African mandate. **1924:** Hertzog became prime minister, aiming to sharpen racial segregation and loosen ties with British Empire. **1939–45:** Smuts led South Africa into World War II despite neutralism of Hertzog; South African troops fought with Allies in Middle East, East Africa, and Italy. **1948:** Policy of apartheid ('separateness') adopted when National Party (NP) took power under Daniel Malan; continued by his successors Johannes Strijdom 1954–58, Hendrik Verwoerd 1958–66, B J Vorster 1966–78, and P J Botha 1978–89. **1950:** Entire population classified by race; Group Areas Act segregated blacks and whites; ANC responded with campaign of civil disobedience. **1960:** 70 black demonstrators killed at Sharpville; ANC banned. **1961:** South Africa left Commonwealth and became republic. **1964:** ANC leader Nelson Mandela sentenced to life imprisonment. **1967:** Terrorism Act introduced indefinite detention without trial. **1970s:** Over 3 million people forcibly resettled in black 'homelands'. **1976:** Over 600 killed in clashes between black protesters and security forces in Soweto. **1984:** New constitution gave segregated representation to coloureds and Asians, but continued to exclude blacks. **1985:** Growth of violence in black townships led to proclamation of state of emergency. **1986:** USA and Commonwealth imposed limited economic sanctions against South Africa. **1989:** F W de Klerk succeeded P W Botha as president; public facilities desegregated; many ANC activists released. **1990:** Ban on ANC lifted; Mandela released; talks began between government and ANC; daily average of 35 murders; Namibia became independent. **1991:** De Klerk repealed remaining apartheid laws; sanctions lifted; severe fighting between ANC and Zulu Inkatha movement. **1993:** Interim majority rule constitution adopted; de Klerk and Mandela agreed to form government of national unity after free elections. **1994:** ANC victory in first nonracial elections; Mandela became president; Commonwealth membership restored. **1996:** De Klerk withdrew NP from coalition after new constitution failed to provide for power-sharing after 1999. **1997:** New constitution signed by President Mandela. F W de Klerk announced his retirement from politics. Thabo Mbeki succeeded Mandela as ANC president.

Spain Kingdom of

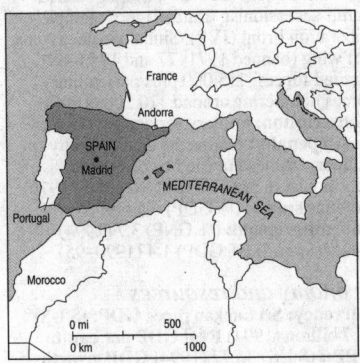

National name: *Reino de España* **Area:** 504,750 sq km/194,883 sq mi **Capital:** Madrid **Major towns/cities:** Barcelona, Valencia, Zaragoza, Seville, Málaga, Bilbao, Las Palmas de Gran Canarias, Murcia, Córdoba, Palma de Mallorca, Granada **Major ports:** Barcelona, Valencia, Cartagena, Málaga, Cádiz, Vigo, Santander, Bilbao

Physical features: central plateau with mountain ranges, lowlands in S; rivers Ebro, Douro, Tagus, Guadiana, Guadalquivir; Iberian Plateau (Meseta); Pyrenees, Cantabrian Mountains, Andalusian Mountains, Sierra Nevada **Territories:** Balearic and Canary Islands; in N Africa: Ceuta, Melilla, Alhucemas, Chafarinas Is, Peñón de Vélez

Government
Head of state: King Juan Carlos I from 1975 **Head of government:**

José Maria Aznar from 1996 **Political system:** constitutional monarchy **Administrative divisions:** 17 autonomous regions (contain 50 provinces) **Political parties:** Socialist Workers' Party (PSOE), democratic socialist; Popular Party (PP), centre right **Armed forces:** 206,800 (1996) **Conscription:** nine months **Death penalty:** abolished 1995 **Defence spend:** (% GDP) 1.5 (1996) **Education spend:** (% GNP) 4.7 (1993/94) **Health spend:** (% GDP) 5.7 (1993)

Economy and resources
Currency: peseta **GDP:** ($ US) 581.6 billion (1996) **Real GDP per capita (PPP):** ($ US) 14,794 (1996) **GDP growth rate:** 2.9% (1996); 1.1% (1990–95) **Average annual inflation:** 3.6% (1996); 6.3% (1985–95) **Major trading partners:** EU (principally France, Germany, Italy, and UK), USA, Japan **Resources:** coal, lignite, anthracite, copper, iron, zinc, uranium, potassium salts **Industries:** machinery, motor vehicles, textiles, footwear, chemicals, electrical appliances, wine, olive oil, fishery products, steel, cement, tourism **Exports:** motor vehicles, machinery and electrical equipment, vegetable products, metals and their manufactures, foodstuffs. Principal market: France 20.5% (1995) **Imports:** machinery and transport equipment, electrical equipment, petroleum and petroleum products, chemicals, consumer goods. Principal source: France 17.1% (1995) **Arable land:** 30.5% (1995) **Agricultural products:** barley, wheat, sugar beet, vegetables, citrus fruit, grapes, olives; fishing (one of world's largest fishing fleets)

Population and society
Population: 39,674,000 (1996 est) **Population growth rate:** 0.2% (1990–95); 0% (2000–05) **Population density:** (per sq km) 79 (1996 est) **Urban population:** (% of total) 76 (1995) **Age distribution:** (% of total population) <15 16.5%, 15–65 68.6%, >65 14.9% (1995) **Ethnic groups:** mostly of Moorish, Roman, and Carthaginian descent **Language:** Spanish (Castilian, official), Basque, Catalan, Galician **Religion:** Roman Catholic **Education:** (compulsory years) 10 **Literacy rate:** 97% (men); 93% (women) (1995 est) **Labour force:** 41.1% of population: 8.7% agriculture, 29.7% industry, 61.6% services (1996) **Unemployment:** 22.1% (1996) **Life expectancy:** 75 (men); 81 (women) (1995–2000) **Child mortality rate:** (under 5, per 1,000 live births) 8 (1996) **Physicians:** 1 per 246 people (1994)

Practical information
Visa requirements: UK: visa not required. USA: visa not required **Embassy in the UK:** 24 Belgrave Square, London SW1X 8SB. Tel: (0171) 235 5555/6/7; fax: (0171) 235 9905 **British embassy:** Calle de Fernando el Santo 16, 28010 Madrid. Tel: (1) 319 0200, fax: (1) 319 0423 **Chamber of commerce:** Consejo Superior de Cámaras Officiales de Comercio, Industria y Navigación de España, Calle Claudio Coello 19, 1 º, 28001 Madrid. Tel: (1) 575 3400; fax: (1) 435 2392 **Airports:** international airports: Alicante (Altet), Barcelona (del Prat), Bilbao, Tenerife (2), Madrid (Barajas), Málaga, Santiago de Compostela, Gerona, Gran Canaria, Lanzarote, Palma de Mallorca, Mahon, Valladolid, Seville, Valencia, Zarragoza; domestic services to all major towns; total passenger km: 26,654 million (1994) **Major holidays:** 1, 6 January, 19 March (most areas), 1 May, 25 July, 15 August, 12 October, 1 November, 8, 25 December; variable: Corpus Christi, Good Friday, Holy Saturday, Holy Thursday

Chronology
2nd century BC: Roman conquest of the Iberian peninsula, which became the province of Hispania. **5th century AD:** After the fall of the Roman Empire, Iberia was overrun by Vandals and Visigoths. **711:** Muslims invaded from N Africa and overthrew Visigoth kingdom. **9th century:** Christians in northern Spain formed kingdoms of Asturias, Aragón, Navarre, and Léon, and county of Castile. **10th century:** Abd-al-Rahman III established caliphate of Córdoba; Muslim culture at its height in Spain. **1230:** Léon and Castile united under Ferdinand III, who drove the Muslims from most of southern Spain. **14th century:** Spain consisted of Christian kingdoms of Castile, Aragón, and Navarre, and the Muslim emirate of Granada. **1469:** Marriage of Ferdinand of Aragón and Isabella of

Castile; kingdoms united on their accession 1479. **1492:** Conquest of Granada ended Muslim rule in Spain. **1494:** Treaty of Tordesillas; Spain and Portugal divided newly discovered America; Spain became a world power. **1519–56:** Emperor Charles V was both King of Spain and Archduke of Austria; he also ruled Naples, Sicily, and the Low Countries; Habsburgs dominant in Europe. **1555:** Charles V divided his domains between Spain and Austria before retiring; Spain retained the Low Countries and southern Italy as well as South American colonies. **1568:** Dutch rebelled against Spanish rule; Spain recognized independence of Dutch Republic 1648. **1580:** Philip II of Spain inherited the throne of Portugal, where Spanish rule lasted until 1640. **1588:** The Spanish Armada: attempt to invade England defeated. **17th century:** Spanish power declined amid wars, corruption, inflation, and loss of civil and religious freedom. **1701–14:** War of the Spanish Succession: allied powers fought France to prevent Philip of Bourbon inheriting throne of Spain. **1713–14:** Treaties of Utrecht and Rastat: Bourbon dynasty recognized, but Spain lost Gibraltar, southern Italy, and Spanish Netherlands. **1793:** Spain declared war on revolutionary France; reduced to a French client state 1795. **1808:** Napoleon installed his brother Joseph as King of Spain. **1808–14:** Peninsular War: British forces played a large part in liberating Spain and restoring Bourbon dynasty. **1810–30:** Spain lost control of its South American colonies. **1833–39:** Carlist civil war: Don Carlos (backed by conservatives) unsuccessfully contested the succession of his niece Isabella II (backed by liberals). **1870:** Offer of Spanish throne to Leopold of Hohenzollern-Sigmaringen sparked Franco-Prussian War. **1873–74:** First republic ended by military coup which restored Bourbon dynasty with Alfonso XII. **1898:** Spanish-Amercian War: Spain lost Cuba and Philippines. **1923–30:** Dictatorship of General Primo de Rivera with support of Alfonso XIII. **1931:** Proclamation of Second Republic, initially dominated by anticlerical radicals and socialists. **1933:** Moderates and Catholics won elections; insurrection by socialists and Catalans 1934. **1936:** Left-wing Popular Front narrowly won fresh elections; General Francisco Franco launched military rebellion. **1936–39:** Spanish Civil War: Nationalists (with significant Italian and German support) defeated Republicans (with limited Soviet support); Franco became dictator of nationalist-fascist regime. **1941:** Though officially neutral in World War II, Spain sent 40,000 troops to fight USSR. **1955:** Spain admitted to the United Nations (UN). **1975:** Death of Franco; succeeded by King Juan Carlos I. **1978:** Referendum endorsed democratic constitution. **1982:** Socialists took office under Felipe González; Spain joined the North Atlantic Treaty Organization (NATO); Basque separatist organization (ETA) stepped up terrorist campaign. **1986:** Spain joined the European Economic Community (EEC). **1996:** José Maria Aznar formed a minority PP government. **1997:** Political leaders of ETA went on trial in Madrid.

Sri Lanka Democratic Socialist Republic of (formerly to 1972 **Ceylon**)

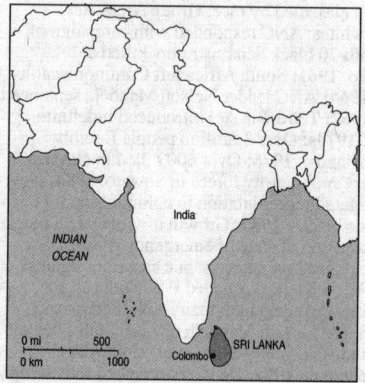

National name: *Sri Lanka Prajathanthrika Samajawadi Janarajaya* **Area:** 65,610 sq km/25,332 sq mi **Capital:** Colombo (and chief port) **Major towns/cities:** Kandy, Dehiwala-Mount Lavinia, Moratuwa, Jaffna, Kotte, Kandy **Major ports:** Jaffna, Galle, Negombo, Trincomalee **Physical features:** flat in N and around coast; hills and mountains in S and central interior

Government

Head of state: Chandrika Bandaranaike Kumaratunga from 1994 **Head of government:** Sirimavo Bandaranaike from 1994 **Political system:** liberal democracy **Administrative divisions:** nine provinces, 25 districts **Political parties:** United National Party (UNP), right of centre; Sri Lanka Freedom Party (SLFP), left of centre; Democratic United National Front (DUNF), centre left; Tamil United Liberation Front (TULF), Tamil autonomy (banned from 1983); Eelam People's Revolutionary Liberation Front (EPRLF), Indian-backed Tamil-secessionist 'Tamil Tigers'; People's Liberation Front (JVP), Sinhalese-chauvinist, left wing (banned 1971–77 and 1983–88). **Armed forces:** 115,000 plus paramilitary forces numbering around 110,200 (1996) **Conscription:** military service is voluntary **Death penalty:** retains the death penalty for ordinary crimes but can be considered abolitionist in practice (last execution 1976) **Defence spend:** (% GDP) 6.5 (1996) **Education spend:** (% GNP) 3.7 (1994) **Health spend:** (% GDP) 1.4 (1990–95)

Economy and resources

Currency: Sri Lankan rupee **GDP:** ($ US) 11.7 billion (1994) **Real GDP per capita (PPP):** ($ US) 3,277 (1994) **GDP growth rate:** 5.6% (1994); 4.8% (1990–95) **Average annual inflation:** 14% (1996); 11.1% (1985–95) **Foreign debt:** ($ US) 8.23 million (1995) **Major trading partners:** Japan, USA, Germany, UK, India, Malaysia, Singapore, Hong Kong, Taiwan, China, Iran **Resources:** gemstones, graphite, iron ore, monazite, rutile, uranium, iemenite sands, limestone, salt, clay **Industries:** food processing, textiles, clothing, petroleum

Spain: Regions

(– = not applicable.)

Region	Capital	Area		Population
		sq km	sq mi	(1995 est)
Andalusia	Seville	87,268	33,694	7,314,600
Aragon	Zaragoza	47,669	18,405	1,205,700
Asturias	Oviedo	10,565	4,079	1,117,400
Balearic Islands	Palma de Mallorca	5,014	1,935	788,000
Basque Country	Vitoria	7,261	2,803	2,130,800
Canary Islands	Las Palmas and Santa Cruz de Tenerife	7,273	2,808	1,631,500
Cantabria	Santander	5,289	2,042	541,900
Castilla–La Mancha	Toledo	79,226	30,589	1,730,700
Castilla–León	Valladolid	94,147	36,350	2,584,400
Catalonia	Barcelona	31,930	12,328	6,226,900
Extremadura	Mérida	41,602	16,063	1,100,500
Galicia	Santiago de Compostela	29,434	11,364	2,825,000
La Rioja	Longroño	5,034	1,944	268,200
Madrid	Madrid	7,995	3,087	5,181,700
Murcia	Murcia[1]	11,317	4,369	1,110,000
Navarra	Pamplona	10,421	4,024	536,200
Valencia	Valencia	23,305	8,998	4,028,800
Ceuta[2]	–	18	7	73,100
Melilla[2]	–	14	5	64,700

[1] Regional parliament is in Cartagena.
[2] Spanish enclave on the north coast of Morocco.

refining, leather goods, chemicals, rubber, plastics, tourism
Exports: clothing and textiles, tea (world's largest exporter and
third-largest producer), precious and semi-precious stones, coconuts
and coconut products, rubber. Principal market: USA 34% (1996)
Imports: machinery and transport equipment, petroleum, food and
live animals, beverages, construction materials. Principal source:
India 10.4% (1996) **Arable land:** 14.1% (1995) **Agricultural
products:** rice, tea, rubber, coconuts; livestock rearing (cattle,
buffaloes, pigs, and poultry); fishing

Population and society
Population: 18,100,000 (1996 est) **Population growth rate:** 1.3%
(1990–95); 1.1% (2000–05) **Population density:** (per sq km) 276
(1996 est) **Urban population:** (% of total) 22 (1995) **Age
distribution:** (% of total population) <15 30.7%, 15–65 63.5%, >65
5.8% (1995) **Ethnic groups:** 73% Sinhalese, 19% Tamil, and 7%
Moors or Muslims (concentrated in E); the Tamil community is
divided between the long-settled 'Sri Lankan Tamils' (11% of the
population), who reside in northern and eastern coastal areas, and
the more recent immigrant 'Indian Tamils' (8%), who settled in the
Kandyan highlands during the 19th and 20th centuries **Language:**
Sinhala, Tamil, English **Religion:** Buddhist 69%, Hindu 15%,
Muslim 8%, Christian 7% **Education:** (compulsory years) 10
Literacy rate: 93% (men); 83% (women) (1995 est) **Labour force:**
42.6% agriculture, 11.7% industry, 45.7% services (1993)
Unemployment: 12.5% (1995) **Life expectancy:** 71 (men); 75
(women) (1995–2000) **Child mortality rate:** (under 5, per 1,000
live births) 19 (1996) **Physicians:** 1 per 6,843 people (1993 est)

Practical information
Visa requirements: UK: visa only required by business visitors.
USA: visa only required by business visitors **Embassy in the UK:**
13 Hyde Park Gardens, London W2 2LU. Tel: (0171) 262 1841; fax:
(0171) 262 7970 **British embassy:** PO Box 1433, 190 Galle Road,
Kollupitiya, Colombo 3. Tel: (1) 437 336; fax: (1) 430 308
Chamber of commerce: Federation of Chambers of Commerce and
Industry of Sri Lanka, 29 Gregory's Road, Colombo 7. Tel: (1) 698
225; fax: (1) 699 530 **Airports:** international airports: Colombo
(Katunayake); five domestic airports; total passenger km: 3,683
million (1994) **Major holidays:** 14 January, 4 February, 1, 22 May,
30 June, 25, 31 December; variable: Eid-ul-Adha, Diwali, end of
Ramadan, Good Friday, New Year (Sinhala/Tamil, April), Prophet's
Birthday, Maha Sivarathri (February/March), Full Moon (monthly)

Chronology
c. 550 BC: Arrival of the Sinhalese, led by Vijaya, from N India,
displacing long-settled Veddas. **5th century BC:** Sinhalese
kingdom of Anuradhapura founded by King Pandukabaya. **c.
250–210 BC:** Buddhism, brought from India, became established in
Sri Lanka. **AD 992:** Downfall of Anuradhapura kingdom, defeated
by South Indian Colas. **1070:** Overthrow of Colas by Vijayabahu I
and establishment of the Sinhalese kingdom of Polonnaruva, which
survived for more than two centuries before a number of regional
states arose. **late 15th century:** Kingdom of Kandy established in
central highlands. **1505:** Arrival of Portuguese navigator Lorenço de
Almeida, attracted by spice trade developed by Arab merchants who
had called the island Serendip. **1597–1618:** Portuguese controlled
most of Sri Lanka, with the exception of Kandy. **1658:** Dutch
conquest of Portuguese territories. **1795–98:** British conquest of
Dutch territories. **1802:** Treaty of Amiens recognized island as
British colony of Ceylon. **1815:** British won control of Kandy,
becoming first European power to rule whole island. **1830s:**
Immigration of S Indian Hindu Tamil labourers to work central
coffee plantations. **1880s:** Tea and rubber become chief cash crops
after blight ended production of coffee. **1919:** Formation of the
Ceylon National Congress to campaign for self rule; increasing
conflicts between Sinhalese majority community and Tamil
minority. **1931:** Universal adult suffrage introduced for elected
legislature and executive council in which power was shared with
British. **1948:** Ceylon achieved independence from Britain within
Commonwealth, with Don Senanayake of conservative United
National Party (UNP) as prime minister. **1949:** Indian Tamils
disenfranchised. **1952:** Death of Don Senanayake, who was

succeeded as prime minister by his son, Dudley. **1956:** Sinhala
established as official language; Solomon Bandaranaike became
prime minister. **1959:** Bandaranaike assassinated. **1960:** Sirimavo
Bandaranaike, the widow of Solomon, won general election and
formed SLFP government, which nationalized oil industry. **1965:**
General election won by UNP; Dudley Senanayake became prime
minister. **1970:** Sirimavo Bandaranaike returned to power as prime
minister, leading United Front government. **1971:** Sinhalese Marxist
uprising, led by students and People's Liberation Army (JVP). **1972:**
Socialist Republic of Sri Lanka proclaimed; Buddhism given
'foremost place' in new state, antagonizing Tamils. **1976:** Tamil
United Liberation Front formed to fight for independent Tamil state
('Eelam') in N and E Sri Lanka. **1978:** Presidential constitution
adopted by new free-market government headed by Junius
Jayawardene of UNP. **1983:** Ethnic riots as Tamil guerrilla violence
escalated; state of emergency imposed; more than 1,000 Tamils
killed by Sinhalese mobs. **1987:** President Jayawardene and Indian
prime minister Rajiv Gandhi signed Colombo Accord aimed at
creating new provincial councils, disarming Tamil militants ('Tamil
Tigers'), and stationing 7,000-strong Indian Peace Keeping Force.
Violence continued despite cease-fire policed by Indian troops.
1988: Left-wing JVP guerrillas campaigned against Indo-Sri
Lankan peace pact. Prime Minister Ranasinghe Premadasa elected
president. **1989:** Dingiri Banda Wijetunga became prime minister.
Leaders of Tamil Tigers and banned Sinhala extremist JVP
assassinated. **1990:** Indian peacekeeping force withdrawn. Violence
continued, with death toll exceeding 1,000 per month. **1991:**
Defence minister Ranjan Wijeratne assassinated; Sri Lankan army
killed 2,552 Tamil Tigers at Elephant Pass in northern Jaffna region.
Impeachment motion against President Premadasa failed. A new
party, Democratic National United Front (DUNF), formed by
former members of UNP. **1992:** Several hundred Tamil Tiger rebels
killed in army offensive, code-named 'Strike Force Two'. **1993:**
DUNF leader and President Premadasa assassinated by Tamil Tiger
terrorists; succeeded by Dingiri Banda Wijetunge. **1994:** UNP
narrowly defeated in general election; Chandrika Kumaratunga
became prime minister of SLFP-led left-of-centre coalition. Peace
talks opened with Tamil Tigers. Kumaratunga elected first female
president; her mother, Sirimavo Bandaranaike, became prime
minister. **1995:** Renewed bombing campaign by Tamil Tigers.
Major offensive drove out Tamil Tigers from Jaffna city. **1996:** State
of emergency extended nationwide after Tamils bombed capital.
Government forces launched new major offensive against Tamil
Tigers. **1997:** Major offensive launched against Tamil separatists.
Bomb attack and clashes with Tamil separatists threatened to derail
government's peace initiative.

Sudan Democratic Republic of

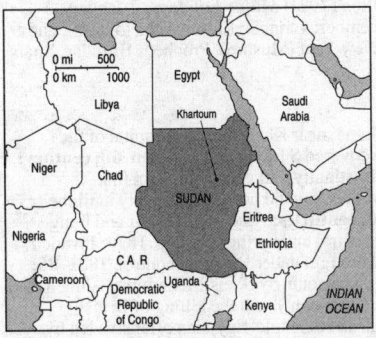

National name:
*Jamhuryat es-
Sudan* **Area:**
2,505,800 sq
km/967,489 sq mi
Capital:
Khartoum **Major
towns/cities:**
Omdurman, Port
Sudan, Juba, Wadi
Medani, al-Obeid,
Kassala, Atbara,
al-Qadarif, Kosti
Major ports: Port
Sudan **Physical
features:** fertile
Nile valley
separates Libyan Desert in W from high rocky Nubian Desert in E

Government
Head of state and government: General Omar Hassan Ahmed al-
Bashir from 1989 **Political system:** military republic

Administrative divisions: 26 states **Political parties:** officially banned from 1989, but an influential grouping is the fundamentalist National Islamic Front **Armed forces:** 89,000 (1996) **Conscription:** military service is compulsory for three years **Death penalty:** retained and used for ordinary crimes **Defence spend:** (% GDP) 4.3 (1996) **Education spend:** (% GNP) 4 (1985); N/A (1993/94) **Health spend:** (% GDP) 0.5 (1990)

Economy and resources

Currency: Sudanese dinar **GDP:** ($ US) 17.2 billion (1994) **Real GDP per capita (PPP):** ($ US) 1,084 (1994) **GDP growth rate:** 2% (1994) **Average annual inflation:** 130% (1996); 63.2% (1985–95 est) **Foreign debt:** ($ US) 18.2 billion (1996) **Major trading partners:** Saudi Arabia, Libya, Thailand, Italy, Germany, UK, China, Japan **Resources:** petroleum, marble, mica, chromite, gypsum, gold, graphite, sulphur, iron, manganese, zinc, fluorspar, talc, limestone, dolomite, pumice **Industries:** food processing (especially sugar refining), textiles, cement, petroleum refining, hides and skins **Exports:** cotton, sesame seed, gum arabic, sorghum, livestock, hides and skins. Principal market: Saudi Arabia 16.6% (1995) **Imports:** basic manufacture, crude materials (mainly petroleum and petroleum products), foodstuffs, machinery and equipment. Principal source: Libya 17.6% (1995) **Arable land:** 5.4% (1995) **Agricultural products:** sorghum, sugar cane, groundnuts, cotton, millet, wheat, sesame, fruits; livestock rearing (cattle, sheep, goats, and poultry)

Population and society

Population: 27,291,000 (1996 est) **Population growth rate:** 2.7% (1990–95); 2.6% (2000–05) **Population density:** (per sq km) 11 (1996 est) **Urban population:** (% of total) 25 (1995) **Age distribution:** (% of total population) <15 43.8%, 15–65 53.3%, >65 2.9% (1995) **Ethnic groups:** over 50 ethnic groups and almost 600 subgroups; the population is broadly distributed between Arabs in the N and black Africans in the S **Language:** Arabic 51% (official), local languages **Religion:** Sunni Muslim; also animist and Christian **Education:** (compulsory years) 6 **Literacy rate:** 43% (men); 12% (women) (1995 est) **Labour force:** 36% of population: 69% agriculture, 8% industry, 22% services (1990) **Unemployment:** 30% (1993 est) **Life expectancy:** 54 (men); 56 (women) (1995–2000) **Child mortality rate:** (under 5, per 1,000 live births) 112 (1996) **Physicians:** 1 per 8,979 people (1990)

Practical information

Visa requirements: UK: visa required. USA: visa required **Embassy in the UK:** 3 Cleveland Row, St James Street, London SW1A 1DD. Tel: (0171) 839 8080; fax: (0171) 839 7560 **British embassy:** PO Box 801, Street 10, off Sharia Al Baladiya, Khartoum East. Tel: (11) 770 769; telex: 22189 (a/b PRDRM SD) **Chamber of commerce:** PO Box 81, Khartoum. Tel: (11) 72346 **Airports:** international airports: Khartoum (civil); 20 domestic airports; total passenger km: 615 million (1994) **Major holidays:** 1 January, 3 March, 6 April, 25 December; variable: Eid-ul-Adha (5 days), end of Ramadan (5 days), New Year (Muslim), Prophet's Birthday, Sham al-Naseem (April/May)

Chronology

c. 600 BC–AD 350: Meroê, near Khartoum, was capital of the Nubian Empire, which covered S Egypt and N Sudan. **6th century:** Converted to Coptic Christianity. **7th century:** Islam first introduced by Arab invaders, but did not spread widely until the 15th century. **16th–18th centuries:** Arab-African Fur and Fung Empires established in central and northern Sudan. **1820:** Invaded by Muhammad Ali and brought under Egyptian control. **1881–85:** Revolt led to capture of Khartoum by Sheik Muhammad Ahmed, a self-proclaimed Mahdi ('messiah'), and the killing of British general Charles Gordon. **1898:** Anglo-Egyptian offensive led by Lord Kitchener subdued Mahdi revolt at Battle of Omdurman in which 20,000 Sudanese died. **1899:** Sudan administered as Anglo-Egyptian condominium. **1923:** White Flag League formed by Sudanese nationalists in N; British instituted policy of reducing contact between northern and southern Sudan, with the aim that S would eventually become part of federation of eastern African

states. **1955:** Civil war between the dominant Arab Muslim N and black African Christian and animist S broke out. **1956:** Sudan achieved independence from Britain and Egypt as a republic. **1958:** Military coup replaced civilian government with Supreme Council of the Armed Forces. **1964:** Civilian rule reinstated after October Revolution of student demonstrations. **1969:** Coup led by Col Gaafar Mohammed al-Nimeri abolished political institutions and concentrated power in a leftist Revolutionary Command Council. **1971:** Nimeri confirmed as president and the Sudanese Socialist Union (SSU) declared the only legal party by a new constitution. **1972:** Plans to form Federation of Arab Republics, comprising Sudan, Egypt, and Syria, abandoned due to internal opposition. To end 17-year-long civil war, Nimeri agreed to give S greater autonomy. **1974:** National assembly established. **1980:** Country reorganized into six regions, each with own assembly and effective autonomy. **1983:** Shari'a (Islamic law) imposed. Sudan People's Liberation Movement (SPLM) formed in S as civil war broke out again. **1985:** Nimeri deposed in a bloodless coup led by Gen Swar al-Dahab following industrial unrest in N. State of emergency declared. **1986:** Coalition government formed after general election, with Sadiq al-Mahdi, great-grandson of the Mahdi, as prime minister. **1987:** Virtual civil war with Sudan People's Liberation Army (SPLA), military wing of SPLM; drought and famine in S and refugee influx from Ethiopa and Chad. **1988:** Peace pact signed with SPLA, but fighting continued. **1989:** Al-Mahdi overthrown in coup led by Islamic fundamentalist Gen Omar Hassan Ahmed el-Bashir. All political activity suspended. **1991:** Federal system introduced, with division of country into nine states as civil war continued. **1995:** SPLA faction leaders agreed to cease-fire, but fighting continued. **1996:** First presidential and parliamentary elections held since coup of 1989. **1997:** Treaty signed between Sudan's Islamic government and four southern rebel groups. Peace talks between government and rebels.

Suriname Republic of (formerly Dutch Guiana)

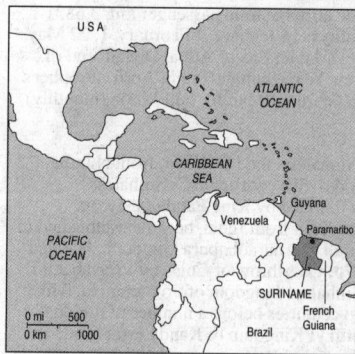

National name: *Republiek Suriname* **Area:** 163,820 sq km/63,250 sq mi **Capital:** Paramaribo **Major towns/cities:** Nieuw Nickerie, Moengo, Pontoetoe, Brokopondo, Nieuw Amsterdam **Physical features:** hilly and forested, with flat and narrow coastal plain; Suriname River

Government

Head of state: Jules Wijdenbosch from 1996 **Head of government:** to be announced **Political system:** emergent democracy **Administrative divisions:** ten districts **Political parties:** New Front (NF), alliance of four left-of-centre parties: Party for National Unity and Solidarity (KTPI), Suriname National Party (NPS), Progressive Reform Party (VHP), Suriname Labour Party (SPA); National Democratic Party (NDP), left of centre; Democratic Alternative 1991 (DA '91), alliance of three left-of-centre parties **Armed forces:** 1,800 (1996) **Conscription:** military service is voluntary **Death penalty:** retains the death penalty for ordinary crimes but can be considered abolitionist in practice (last execution 1982) **Defence spend:** (% GDP) 3.5 (1996) **Education spend:** (% GNP) 3.6 (1993/94) **Health spend:** (% GDP) 5.7 (1990)

Economy and resources

Currency: Suriname guilder **GDP:** ($ US) 1.3 billion (1995 est) **Real GDP per capita (PPP):** ($ US) 2,950 (1995 est) **GDP growth rate:** 4% (1995 est) **Average annual inflation:** 9% (1996); 48.5%

(1985–95) **Foreign debt:** ($ US) 68.2 million (1995) **Major trading partners:** USA, Norway, Trinidad and Tobago, the Netherlands, Netherlands Antilles, Brazil, Japan **Resources:** petroleum, bauxite (one of the world's leading producers), iron ore, copper, manganese, nickel, platinum, gold, kaolin **Industries:** bauxite refining and smelting, food processing, beverages, cigarettes, wood products, chemical products, cement **Exports:** alumina, aluminium, shrimps, bananas, plantains, rice, wood and wood products. Principal market: Norway 26% (1996) **Imports:** raw materials and semi-manufactured goods, mineral fuels and lubricants, investment goods, foodstuffs, cars and motorcycles, textiles. Principal source: USA 42.4% (1996) **Arable land:** 0.4% (1995) **Agricultural products:** rice, citrus fruits, bananas, plantains, vegetables, coconuts, cassava, root crops, sugar cane; forest resources; commercial fishing

Population and society
Population: 432,900 (1996 est) **Population growth rate:** 1.1% (1990–95) **Population density:** (per sq km) 3 (1996 est) **Urban population:** (% of total) 50 (1995) **Age distribution:** (% of total population) <15 35%, 15–65 60%, >65 5% (1995) **Ethnic groups:** a wide ethnic composition, including Creoles, East Indians, Indonesians, Africans, Native Americans, Europeans, and Chinese **Language:** Dutch (official), Sranan (creole), English, Hindi, Javanese, Chinese. Spanish is the main working language **Religion:** Christian, Hindu, Muslim **Education:** (compulsory years) 11 **Literacy rate:** 95% (men); 95% (women) (1994 est) **Labour force:** 20% agriculture, 20% industry, 60% services (1992) **Unemployment:** 16.3% (1993) **Life expectancy:** 69 (men); 74 (women) (1995–2000) **Child mortality rate:** (under 5, per 1,000 live births) 26 (1996) **Physicians:** 1 per 1,605 people (1994)

Practical information
Visa requirements: UK: visa not required. USA: visa required **Embassy for the UK:** Alexander Gogelweg 2, 2517 JH The Hague, The Netherlands. Tel: (70) 365 0844; fax: (70) 361 7445 **British embassy:** British Honorary Consulate, c/o VSH United Buildings, PO Box 1860, Van't Hogerhuysstraat 9–11, Paramaribo. Tel: (597) 472 870; fax: (597) 475 515 **Chamber of commerce:** Suriname Chamber of Commerce and Industry, PO Box 149, Dr J C de Mirandasstraat 10, Paramaribo. Tel: (597) 473 527; fax: (597) 474 779 **Airports:** international airport: Paramaribo (Johan A Pengel); one domestic airport and 35 airstrips; total passenger km: 541 million (1994) **Major holidays:** 1 January, 25 February, 1 May, 1 July, 25 November, 25–26 December; variable: Good Friday, Easter Monday, end of Ramadan, Holi (March)

Chronology
AD 1593: Visited and claimed by Spanish explorers; the name Suriname derived from the country's earliest inhabitants, the Surinen, who were driven out by other Amerindians in the 16th century. **1602:** Dutch settlements established. **1651:** British colony founded by settlers sent from Barbados. **1667:** Became a Dutch colony, received in exchange for New Amsterdam (New York) by Treaty of Breda. **1682:** Coffee and sugar cane plantations introduced, worked by imported African slaves. **1795–1802 and 1804–16:** Under British rule. **1863:** Slavery abolished and indentured labourers brought in from China, India, and Java. **1915:** Bauxite discovered and gradually became main export. **1954:** Achieved internal self-government as Dutch Guiana. **1958–69:** Politics dominated by Johan Pengel, charismatic leader of the mainly Creole Suriname National Party (NPS). **1975:** Independence achieved, with Dr Johan Ferrier as president and Henck Arron (NPS) as prime minister; 40% of population emigrated to the Netherlands. **1980:** Arron's government overthrown in army coup; Ferrier refused to recognize military regime; appointed Dr Henk Chin A Sen of the Nationalist Republican Party (PNR) to lead civilian administration. Army replaced Ferrier with Dr Chin A Sen. **1982:** Army, led by Lt Col Desi Bouterse, seized power, setting up a Revolutionary People's Front; economic aid from the Netherlands and US cut off after opposition leaders, charged with plotting a coup, were executed. **1985:** Ban on political activities lifted. **1986:** Antigovernment rebels brought economic chaos to Suriname. **1988:**

Ramsewak Shankar of the combined opposition parties elected president under new constitution. **1989:** Bouterse rejected peace accord reached by President Shankar with guerrilla insurgents, the Bush Negro (descendents of escaped slaves) maroons, and vowed to continue fighting. **1990:** Shankar deposed in army coup engineered by Bouterse. **1991:** Johan Kraag (NPS) became interim president. New Front opposition alliance won assembly majority. Ronald Venetiaan elected civilian president. **1992:** Peace accord reached with guerrilla groups. **1996:** General election result inconclusive.

Swaziland Kingdom of

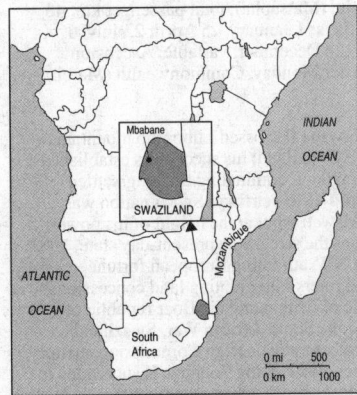

National name: *Umbuso we Swatini* **Area:** 17,400 sq km/6,718 sq mi **Capital:** Mbabane **Major towns/cities:** Manzini, Big Bend, Mhlume, Havelock Mine, Nhlangano **Physical features:** central valley; mountains in W (Highveld); plateau in E (Lowveld and Lubombo plateau)

Government
Head of state: King Mswati III from 1986 **Head of government:** Barnabas Sibusiso Dlamini from 1997 **Political system:** transitional absolute monarchy **Administrative divisions:** four regions **Political parties:** Imbokodvo National Movement (INM), nationalist monarchist; Swaziland United Front (SUF), left of centre; Swaziland Progressive Party (SPP), left of centre; People's United Democratic Movement, left of centre **Armed forces:** 127,280 (1995) **Conscription:** military service is compulsory for two years **Death penalty:** retained and used for ordinary crimes **Defence spend:** (% GDP) 2.5 (1993 est) **Education spend:** (% GNP) 6.8 (1993/94) **Health spend:** (% GDP) 1.1 (1990)

Economy and resources
Currency: lilangeni **GDP:** ($ US) 98.8 billion (1994 est) **Real GDP per capita (PPP):** ($ US) 2,841 (1994 est) **GDP growth rate:** –3% (1994) **Average annual inflation:** 14.7% (1995); 11.7% (1985–95) **Foreign debt:** ($ US) 23.7 billion (1994) **Major trading partners:** South Africa, UK, the Netherlands, Switzerland, France **Resources:** coal, asbestos, diamonds, gold, tin, kaolin, iron ore, talc, pyrophyllite, silica **Industries:** food processing, paper, textiles, wood products, beverages, metal products **Exports:** sugar, wood pulp, cotton yarn, canned fruits, asbestos, coal, diamonds, gold. Principal market: South Africa 32% (1994) **Imports:** machinery and transport equipment, minerals, fuels and lubricants, manufactured items, food and live animals. Principal source: South Africa 83.3% (1994) **Arable land:** 10.9% (1995) **Agricultural products:** sugar cane, cotton, citrus fruits, pineapples, maize, sorghum, tobacco, tomatoes, rice; livestock rearing (cattle and goats); commercial forestry

Population and society
Population: 881,000 (1996 est) **Population growth rate:** 2.8% (1990–95); 2.6% (2000–05) **Population density:** (per sq km) 51 (1996 est) **Urban population:** (% of total) 31 (1995) **Age distribution:** (% of total population) <15 43%, 15–65 54.4%, >65 2.7% (1995) **Ethnic groups:** about 90% indigenous African, comprising the Swazi, Zulu, Tonga, and Shangaan peoples; there are European and Afro-European (Eurafrican) minorities numbering around 22,000 **Language:** Swazi, English (both official) **Religion:** Christian, animist **Education:** (compulsory years) 7 **Literacy rate:**

76% (men); 73% (women) (1995 est) **Labour force:** 34% of population: 39% agriculture, 22% industry, 38% services (1990) **Unemployment:** 30% (1994 est) **Life expectancy:** 58 (men); 62 (women) (1995–2000) **Child mortality rate:** (under 5, per 1,000 live births) 99 (1996) **Physicians:** 1 per 9,091 people (1991)

Practical information

Visa requirements: UK: visa not required. USA: visa not required **Embassy in the UK:** 20 Buckingham Street, London SW1E 6LB. Tel: (0171) 630 6611; fax: (0171) 630 6564 **British embassy:** British High Commission, Allister Miller Street, Private Bag, Mbabane. Tel: (268) 42581; fax: (268) 42585 **Chamber of commerce:** Swaziland Chamber of Commerce and Industry, PO Box 72, Mbabane. Tel: (268) 44408; fax: (268) 45442 **Airports:** international airport: Manzini (Matsapha); total passenger km: 48 million (1994) **Major holidays:** 1 January, 25 April, 22 July, 6 September, 24 October, 25–26 December; variable: Ascension Thursday, Good Friday, Easter Monday, Commonwealth (March)

Chronology

late 16th century: King Ngwane II crossed Lubombo mountains from the E and settled in SE Swaziland; his successors established a strong centralized Swazi kingdom, dominating the long-settled Nguni and Sothi peoples. **mid-19th century:** Swazi nation was ruled by the warrior King Mswati who, at the height of his power, controlled an area three times the size of the present-day state. **1882:** Gold was discovered in the NW, attracting European fortune hunters, who coerced Swazi rulers into granting land concessions. **1894:** Came under joint rule of Britain and the Boer republic of Transvaal. **1903:** Following the South African War, Swaziland became a special British protectorate, or High Commission territory, against South Africa's wishes. **1922:** King Sobhuza II succeeded to the Swazi throne. **1968:** Independence achieved within the Commonwealth, as the Kingdom of Swaziland, with King (or Ngwenyama) Sobhuza II as head of state. **1973:** The king suspended the constitution, banned political activity, and assumed absolute powers after the opposition deputies had been elected to parliament. **1977:** King announced substitution of traditional tribal communities (*tinkhundla*) for the parliamentary system, arguing it was more suited to Swazi values. **1982:** King Sobhuza died; his place was taken by one of his wives, Queen Dzeliwe, until his son, Prince Makhosetive, reached the age of 21. **1983:** Queen Dzeliwe ousted by a younger wife, Queen Ntombi, as real power passed to the prime minister, Prince Bhekimpi Dlamini. **1984:** After royal power struggle, it was announced that the crown prince would become king at 18. **1986:** Crown prince formally invested as King Mswati III. **1993:** Direct elections of *tinkhundla* candidates held for the first time; Prince Jameson Mbilini Dlamini appointed premier. **1996:** Prince Dlamini dismissed without a successor being named.

Sweden Kingdom of

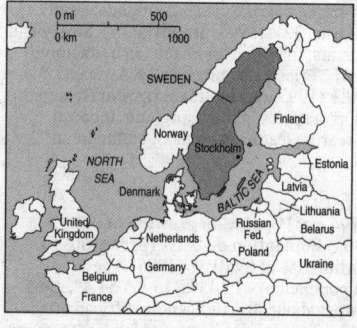

National name: *Konungariket Sverige* **Area:** 450,000 sq km/173,745 sq mi **Capital:** Stockholm (and chief port) **Major towns/cities:** Göteborg, Malmö, Uppsala, Norrköping, Västerås, Linköping, Orebro, Jönköping, Helsingborg, Borås **Major ports:** Helsingborg, Malmö, Göteborg **Physical features:** mountains in W; plains in S; thickly forested; more than 20,000 islands off the Stockholm coast; lakes, including Vänern, Vättern, Mälaren, and Hjälmaren

Government

Head of state: King Carl XVI Gustaf from 1973 **Head of government:** Goran Persson from 1996 **Political system:** constitutional monarchy **Administrative divisions:** 24 counties **Political parties:** Christian Democratic Community Party (KdS), Christian, centrist; Left Party (Vp), European, Marxist; Social Democratic Labour Party (SAP), moderate, left of centre; Moderate Party (M), right of centre; Liberal Party (Fp), centre left; Centre Party (C), centrist; Ecology Party (MpG), ecological; New Democracy (NG), right wing, populist **Armed forces:** 62,600 (1996) **Conscription:** 7–15 months (army and navy); 8–12 months (air force) **Death penalty:** abolished 1972 **Defence spend:** (% GDP) 2.9 (1996) **Education spend:** (% GNP) 8.4 (1993/94) **Health spend:** (% GDP) 6.4 (1994)

Economy and resources

Currency: Swedish krona **GDP:** ($ US) 250.3 billion (1996) **Real GDP per capita (PPP):** ($ US) 19,117 (1996) **GDP growth rate:** 1.7% (1996); –0.1% (1990–95) **Average annual inflation:** 0.6% (1996); 5.5% (1985–95) **Major trading partners:** Germany, UK, Norway, USA, Denmark, France **Resources:** iron ore, uranium, copper, lead, zinc, silver, hydroelectric power, forests **Industries:** motor vehicles, foodstuffs, machinery, precision equipment, iron and steel, metal products, wood products, chemicals, shipbuilding, electrical goods **Exports:** forestry products (wood, pulp, and paper), machinery, motor vehicles, power-generating non-electrical machinery, chemicals, iron and steel. Principal market: Germany 11.7% (1996) **Imports:** machinery and transport equipment, chemicals, mineral fuels and lubricants, textiles, clothing, footwear, food and live animals. Principal source: Germany 18.7% (1996) **Arable land:** 6.7% (1995) **Agricultural products:** barley, wheat, oats, potatoes, sugar beet, tame hay, oil seed; livestock and dairy products

Population and society

Population: 8,819,000 (1996 est) **Population growth rate:** 0.5% (1990–95); 0.3% (2000–05) **Population density:** (per sq km) 20 (1996 est) **Urban population:** (% of total) 83 (1995) **Age distribution:** (% of total population) <15 19%, 15–65 63.7%, >65 17.3% (1995) **Ethnic groups:** predominantly of Teutonic descent, with small Saami (Lapp), Finnish, and German minorities **Language:** Swedish; there are Finnish- and Saami-speaking minorities **Religion:** Evangelical Lutheran (established national church) **Education:** (compulsory years) 9 **Literacy rate:** 99% (men); 99% (women) (1995 est) **Labour force:** 48..4% of population: 2.9% agriculture, 26.1% industry, 71% services (1996) **Unemployment:** 10% (1996) **Life expectancy:** 76 (men); 82 (women) (1995–2000) **Child mortality rate:** (under 5, per 1,000 live births) 6 (1996) **Physicians:** 1 per 393 people (1994)

Practical information

Visa requirements: UK: visa not required. USA: visa not required **Embassy in the UK:** 11 Montagu Place, London W1H 2AL. Tel: (0171) 917 6400; fax: (0171) 724 4174 **British embassy:** PO Box 27819, Skarpögatan 6–8, 115 93 Stockholm. Tel: (8) 671 9000; fax: (8) 662 9989 **Chamber of commerce:** Federation of Swedish Commerce and Trade, PO Box 5512, Grevgatan 34, 114 85 Stockholm. Tel: (8) 666 1100; fax: (8) 662 7457 **Airports:** international airports: Stockholm (Arlanda), Göteborg (Landvetter), Malmö (Sturup); over 30 domestic airports; total passenger km: 1,064 million (1994) **Major holidays:** 1, 6 January, 1 May, 1 November, 24–26, 31 December; variable: Ascension Thursday, Good Friday, Easter Monday, Whit Monday, Midsummer Eve and Day (June)

Chronology

8th century: Kingdom of the Svear, based near Uppsala, extended its rule across much of southern Sweden. **9th–11th centuries:** Swedish Vikings raided and settled along the rivers of Russia. **c. 1000:** Olaf Skötkonung, king of the Svear, adopted Christianity and united much of Sweden (except S and W coasts, which remained Danish until 17th century). **11th–13th centuries:** Sweden existed as isolated kingdom under the Stenkil, Sverker, and Folkung dynasties; series of crusades incorporated Finland. **1397:** Union of Kalmar: Sweden, Denmark, and Norway united under a single monarch; Sweden effectively ruled by succession of regents. **1448:** Breach with Denmark: Sweden alone elected Charles VIII as king. **1523:** Gustavus Vasa, leader of insurgents, became king of fully independent Sweden. **1527:** Swedish Reformation: Gustavus confiscated Church property and encouraged Lutherans. **1544:** Swedish crown became hereditary in House of Vasa. **1592–1604:** Sigismund Vasa, a Catholic, was king of both Sweden and Poland until ousted from Swedish throne by his Lutheran uncle Charles IX. **17th century:** Sweden, a great military power under Gustavus Adolphus 1611–32, Charles X 1654–60, and Charles XI 1660–97, fought lengthy wars with Denmark, Russia, Poland, and Holy Roman Empire. **1709:** Battle of Poltava: Russians inflicted major defeat on Swedes under Charles XII. **1720:** Limited monarchy established; political power passed to *Riksdag* (parliament) dominated by nobles. **1721:** Great Northern War ended with Sweden losing nearly all its conquests of the previous century. **1741–43:** Sweden defeated in disastrous war with Russia; further conflict 1788–90. **1771–92:** Gustavus III increased royal power and introduced wide-ranging reforms; assassinated at a masked ball. **1809:** Russian invaders annexed Finland; Swedish nobles staged coup and restored powers of Riksdag. **1810:** Napoleonic marshal, Jean-Baptiste Bernadotte, elected crown prince of Sweden, as Charles XIII had no heir. **1812:** Bernadotte allied Sweden with Russia against France. **1814:** Treaty of Kiel: Sweden obtained Norway from Denmark. **1818–44:** Bernadotte reigned in Sweden as Charles XIV John. **1846:** Free enterprise established by abolition of trade guilds and monopolies. **1866:** Series of liberal reforms culminated in new two-chambered *Riksdag* dominated by bureaucrats and farmers. **late 19th century:** Development of large-scale forestry and iron-ore industry; neutrality adopted in foreign affairs. **1905:** Union with Norway dissolved. **1907:** Adoption of proportional representation and universal suffrage. **1920s:** Economic boom transformed Sweden from an agricultural to an industrial economy. **1932:** Social Democrat government of Per Halbin Hansson introduced radical public-works programme to combat trade slump. **1940–43:** Under duress, neutral Sweden permitted limited transit of German forces through its territory. **1946–69:** Social Democrat government of Tage Erlander developed comprehensive welfare state. **1959:** Sweden joined European Free Trade Association. **1969–76:** Social Democratic Party in power, under Prime Minister Olaf Palme. **1971:** Constitution amended to create single-chamber Riksdag. **1975:** Remaining constitutional powers of monarch removed. **1976–82:** Centre-right government of Thorbjörn Fälldin ended 44 years of Social Democrat dominance. **1982:** Palme regained premiership; assassinated 1986. **1995:** Sweden became a member of European Union.

Switzerland Swiss Confederation

National name: German *Schweiz*, French *Suisse*, Romansch *Svizra* **Area:** 41,300 sq km/15,945 sq mi **Capital:** Bern (Berne) **Major towns/cities:** Zürich, Geneva, Basel, Lausanne, Luzern, St Gallen, Winterthur **Major ports:** river port Basel (on the Rhine) **Physical features:** most mountainous country in Europe (Alps and Jura mountains); highest peak Dufourspitze 4,634 m/15,203 ft in Apennines

Government

Head of state and government: Arnold Koller from 1997 **Government:** federal democracy **Administrative divisions:** 20 cantons and six demi-cantons **Political parties:** Radical Democratic Party (FDP/PRD), radical, centre left; Social Democratic Party (SP/PS), moderate, left of centre; Christian Democratic People's Party (CVP/PDC), Christian, moderate, centrist; Swiss People's Party (SVP/UDC), centre left; Liberal Party (LPS/PLS), federalist, right of centre; Green Party (GPS/PES), ecological **Armed forces:** 27,300 (1996) **Conscription:** 17 weeks' recruit training, followed by refresher training of varying length according to age **Death penalty:** abolished 1992 **Defence spend:** (% GDP) 1.6 (1996) **Education spend:** (% GNP) 5.6 (1993/94) **Health spend:** (% GDP) 6.8 (1993)

Economy and resources

Currency: Swiss franc **GDP:** ($ US) 293.4 billion (1996) **Real GDP per capita (PPP):** ($ US) 25,141 (1996) **GDP growth rate:** –0.7% (1996); 0.1% (1990–95) **Average annual inflation:** 0.5% (1996); 3.4% (1985–95) **Major trading partners:** EU (principally Germany, France, Italy, and UK), USA, Japan **Resources:** salt, hydroelectric power, forest **Industries:** heavy engineering, machinery, precision engineering (clocks and watches), jewellery, textiles, chocolate, dairy products, cigarettes, footwear, wine, international finance and insurance services, tourism **Exports:** machinery and equipment, pharmaceutical and chemical products, foodstuffs, precision instruments, clocks and watches, metal products. Principal market: Germany 23.3% (1996) **Imports:** machinery, motor vehicles, agricultural and forestry products, construction material, fuels and lubricants, chemicals, textiles and clothing. Principal source: Germany 32.8% (1996) **Arable land:** 10.1% (1995) **Agricultural products:** sugar beet, potatoes, wheat, apples, pears, tobacco, grapes; livestock and dairy products, notably cheese

Population and society

Population: 7,224,000 (1996 est) **Population growth rate:** 1.1% (1990–95); 0.5% (2000–05) **Population density:** (per sq km) 175 (1996 est) **Urban population:** (% of total) 61 (1995) **Age distribution:** (% of total population) <15 17.7%, 15–65 68.1%, >65 14.2% (1995) **Ethnic groups:** majority of Alpine descent; sizeable Nordic element **Language:** German 64%, French 19%, Italian 8%, Romansch 0.6% (all official) **Religion:** Roman Catholic 50%, Protestant 48% **Education:** (compulsory years) 8–9 (depending on canton) **Literacy rate:** 99% (men); 99% (women) (1995 est) **Labour force:** 53.8% of population: 4.5% agriculture, 27.8% industry, 67.7% services (1996) **Unemployment:** 3.3% (1996) **Life expectancy:** 75 (men); 82 (women) (1995–2000) **Child mortality rate:** (under 5, per 1,000 live births) 7 (1996) **Physicians:** 1 per 322 people (1994)

Practical information

Visa requirements: UK: visa not required. USA: visa not required **Embassy in the UK:** 16–18 Montagu Place, London W1H 2BQ. Tel: (0171) 616 6000; fax: (0171) 724 7001 **British embassy:** Thunstrasse 50, CH-3005 Bern 15. Tel: (31) 352 5021/6; fax: (31) 352 0583 **Chamber of commerce:** Schweizerischer Handels- und Industrie-Verein (Swiss Federation of Commerce and Industry), PO Box 690, Mainaustrasse 49, CH-8034 Zürich. Tel: (1) 382 2323; fax: (1) 382 2332 **Airports:** international airports: Zürich (Kloten), Geneva, Bern (Belp), Basel (Basel-Mulhouse); domestic services operate between these; total passenger km: 18,858 million (1994) **Major holidays:** 1 January, 1, 15 August (many cantons), 1 November (many cantons), 24–26 December; variable: Ascension Thursday, Corpus Christi (many cantons), Good Friday, Easter Monday, Whit Monday; many local holidays

Chronology

58 BC: Celtic Helvetii tribe submitted to Roman authority after defeat by Julius Caesar. **4th century AD:** Region overrun by Germanic tribes, Burgundians, and Alemannians. **7th century:**

Formed part of Frankish kingdom and embraced Christianity. **9th century:** Included in Charlemagne's Holy Roman Empire. **12th century:** Many autonomous feudal holdings developed as power of Holy Roman Empire declined. **13th century:** Habsburgs became dominant as overlords of eastern Switzerland. **1291:** Cantons of Schwyz, Uri, and Lower Unterwalden formed Everlasting League, a loose confederation to resist Habsburg control. **1315:** Battle of Morgarten: Swiss Confederation defeated Habsburgs. **14th century:** Luzern, Zürich, Basel, and other cantons joined Swiss Confederation, which became independent of Habsburgs. **1523–29:** Zürich, Bern, and Basel accepted Reformation but rural cantons remained Roman Catholic. **1648:** Treaty of Westphalia recognized Swiss independence from Holy Roman Empire. **1798:** French invasion established Helvetic Republic, a puppet state with centralized government. **1803:** Napoleon's Act of Mediation restored considerable autonomy to cantons. **1814:** End of French domination; Switzerland reverted to loose confederation of sovereign cantons with a weak federal parliament. **1815:** Great Powers recognized 'Perpetual Neutrality' of Switzerland. **1845:** Seven Catholic cantons founded Sonderbund league to resist any strengthening of central government by Liberals. **1847:** Federal troops defeated Sonderbund in brief civil war. **1848:** New constitution introduced greater centralization; Bern chosen as capital. **1874:** Powers of federal government increased; principle of referendum introduced. **late 19th century:** Development of industry, railways, and tourism led to growing prosperity. **1920:** League of Nations selected Geneva as its headquarters. **1923:** Switzerland formed customs union with Liechtenstein. **1960:** Joined European Free Trade Association (EFTA). **1971:** Women gained right to vote in federal elections. **1986:** Referendum rejected proposal for membership of United Nations (UN). **1992:** Closer ties with European Community (EC) rejected in national referendum. **1996:** Jean-Paul Delamuraz became president. **1997:** Arnold Koller elected president.

Syria Syrian Arab Republic

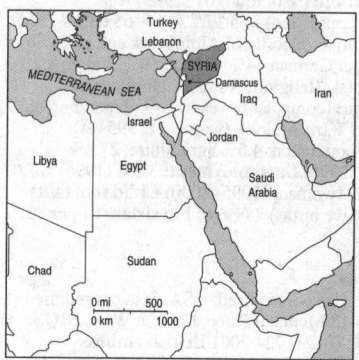

National name: *al-Jamhuriya al-Arabya as-Suriya* **Area:** 185,200 sq km/71,505 sq mi **Capital:** Damascus **Major towns/cities:** Aleppo, Homs, Latakia, Hama **Major ports:** Latakia **Physical features:** mountains alternate with fertile plains and desert areas; Euphrates River

Government

Head of state and government: Hafez al-Assad from 1971 **Political system:** socialist republic **Administrative divisions:** 14 administrative districts **Political parties:** National Progressive Front (NPF), pro-Arab, socialist coalition, including the Communist Party of Syria, the Arab Socialist Party, the Arab Socialist Unionist Party, the Syrian Arab Socialist Union Party, the Ba'ath Arab Socialist Party **Armed forces:** 421,000; reserve forces 500,000; paramiltary forces 8,000 (1996) **Conscription:** 30 months **Death penalty:** retained and used for ordinary crimes **Defence spend:** (% GDP) 6.8 (1995) **Education spend:** (% GNP) 4.2 (1992); N/A (1993/94) **Health spend:** (% GDP) 0.4 (1990)

Economy and resources

Currency: Syrian pound **GDP:** ($ US) 16.8 billion (1995) **Real GDP per capita (PPP):** ($ US) 5,397 (1994) **GDP growth rate:**

5.8% (1995 est); –0.6% (1990–95) **Average annual inflation:** 20% (1996); 15.8% (1985–95) **Foreign debt:** ($ US) 23 billion (1996) **Major trading partners:** Germany, Italy, France, Lebanon, Japan, UK, Romania, Belgium **Resources:** petroleum, natural gas, iron ore, phosphates, salt, gypsum, sodium chloride, bitumen **Industries:** petroleum and petroleum products, coal, rubber and plastic products, textiles, clothing, leather products, tobacco, processed food **Exports:** crude petroleum, textiles, vegetables, fruit, raw cotton, natural phosphate. Principal market: Germany 16.7% (1995) **Imports:** crude petroleum, wheat, base metals, metal products, foodstuffs, machinery, motor vehicles. Principal source: Italy 8.6% (1995) **Arable land:** 27.3% (1995) **Agricultural products:** cotton, wheat, barley, maize, olives, lentils, sugar beet, fruit, vegetables; livestock (principally sheep and goats)

Population and society

Population: 14,574,000 (1996 est) **Population growth rate:** 3.4% (1990–95); 3.2% (2000–05) **Population density:** (per sq km) 79 (1996 est) **Urban population:** (% of total) 52 (1995) **Age distribution:** (% of total population) <15 47.3%, 15–65 49.9%, >65 2.8% (1995) **Ethnic groups:** predominantly Arab, with many differences in language and regional affiliations **Language:** Arabic 89% (official); Kurdish 6%, Armenian 3% **Religion:** Sunni Muslim 90%; other Islamic sects, Christian **Education:** (compulsory years) 6 **Literacy rate:** 53% (men); 51% (women) (1995 est) **Labour force:** 28% of population: 33% agriculture, 24% industry, 43% services (1990) **Life expectancy:** 67 (men); 71 (women) (1995–2000) **Child mortality rate:** (under 5, per 1,000 live births) 43 (1996) **Physicians:** 1 per 969 people (1994)

Practical information

Visa requirements: UK: visa required. USA: visa required **Embassy in the UK:** 8 Belgrave Square, London SW1X 8PH. Tel: (0171) 245 9012; fax: (0171) 235 4621 **British embassy:** PO Box 37, Quarter Malki, 11 rue Mohammed Kurd Ali, Immeuble Kotob, Damascus. Tel: (11) 712 561/2/3; fax: (11) 713 592 **Chamber of commerce:** Federation of Syrian Chambers of Commerce, PO Box 5909, rue Mousa Ben Nousair, Damascus. Tel: (11) 333 7344; fax: (11) 333127 **Airports:** international airports: Damascus, Aleppo (Nejrab), Latakia (chartered flights); four domestic airports; total passenger km: 820 million (1994) **Major holidays:** 1 January, 8 March, 17 April, 1, 6 May, 23 July, 1 September, 6 October, 25 December; variable: Eid-ul-Adha (3 days), end of Ramadan (4 days), Easter Sunday, New Year (Muslim), Prophet's Birthday

Chronology

c.1750 BC: Syria became part of Babylonian Empire; during the next millennium it was successively conquered by Hittites, Assyrians, Chaldeans, and Persians. **333 BC:** Alexander the Great of Macedonia conquered Persia and Syria. **301 BC:** Seleucus I, one of the generals of Alexander the Great, founded kingdom of Syria, which the Seleucid dynasty ruled for over 200 years. **64 BC:** Syria became part of Roman Empire. **4th century AD:** After division of Roman Empire, Syria came under Byzantine rule. **634:** Arabs conquered most of Syria and introduced Islam. **661–750:** Damascus was capital of Muslim Empire. **1055:** Seljuk Turks overran Syria. **1095–99:** First Crusade established Latin states on Syrian coast. **13th century:** Mameluke sultans of Egypt took control. **1516:** Ottoman Turks conquered Syria. **1831:** Egyptians led by Mehemet Ali drove out Turks. **1840:** Turkish rule restored; Syria opened up to European trade. **late 19th century:** French firms built ports, roads, and railways in Syria. **1916:** Sykes-Picot Agreement: secret Anglo-French deal to partition Turkish Empire allotted Syria to France. **1918:** British expelled Turks with help of Arab revolt. **1919:** Syrian national congress called for independence under Emir Faisal and opposed transfer to French rule. **1920:** Syria became League of Nations protectorate, administered by France. **1925:** People's Party founded to campaign for independence and national unity; insurrection by Druse religious sect against French control. **1936:** France promised independence within three years, but martial law imposed 1939. **1941:** British forces ousted Vichy French regime in Damascus and occupied Syria in conjunction with Free French. **1944:** Syrian independence proclaimed but French military resisted transfer of power. **1946:** Syria achieved effective independence when French forces withdrew. **1948–49:** Arab–Israeli War: Syria joined unsuccessful invasion of newly independent Israel. **1958:** Syria and Egypt merged to form United Arab Republic (UAR). **1959:** USSR agreed to give financial and technical aid to Syria. **1961:** Syria seceded from UAR. **1964:** Ba'ath Socialist Party established military dictatorship. **1967:** Six-Day War: Syria lost Golan Heights to Israel. **1970–71:** Syria invaded Jordan in support of Palestinian guerrillas. **1970:** Hafez al-Assad staged coup; elected president 1971. **1973:** Yom Kippur War: Syrian attack on Israel repulsed. **1976:** Start of Syrian military intervention in Lebanese civil war. **1978:** Syria opposed peace deal between Egypt and Israel. **1986:** Britain broke off diplomatic relations, accusing Syria of involvement in international terrorism. **1990:** Diplomatic links with Britain restored. **1991:** Syria contributed troops to US-led coalition in Gulf War against Iraq. US Middle East peace plan approved by Assad. **1994:** Israel offered partial withdrawal from Golan Heights in return for peace, but Syria remained sceptical. **1995:** Security framework agreement with Israel.

Taiwan Republic of China

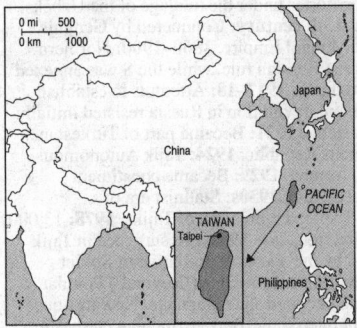

National name: *Chung Hua Min Kuo* **Area:** 36,179 sq km/13,968 sq mi **Capital:** Taipei **Major towns/cities:** Kaohsiung, Taichung, Tainan, Panchiao, Yunlin **Major ports:** Kaohsiung, Keelung **Physical features:** island (formerly Formosa) off People's Republic of China; mountainous, with lowlands in W; Penghu (Pescadores), Jinmen (Quemoy), Mazu (Matsu) islands

Government

Head of state: Lee Teng-hui from 1988 **Head of government:** Vincent Siew from 1997 **Political system:** emergent democracy **Administrative divisions:** 16 counties, five municipalities, and two special municipalities (Taipei and Kaohsiung) **Political parties:** Nationalist Party of China (Kuomintang: KMT), anticommunist, Chinese nationalist; Democratic Progressive Party (DPP), centrist-pluralist, proself-determination grouping; Workers' Party (Kuntang), left of centre **Armed forces:** 376,000; plus paramilitary forces numbering 26,700 and reserves totalling 1,657,500 (1996) **Conscription:** military service is compulsory for two years **Death penalty:** retained and used for ordinary crimes **Defence spend:** (% GDP) 4.9 (1996) **Education spend:** (% GDP) 2.5 (1994)

Economy and resources

Currency: New Taiwan dollar **GDP:** ($ US) 241.9 billion (1994) **Real GDP per capita (PPP):** ($ US) 11,900 (1994) **GDP growth rate:** 6% (1995) **Average annual inflation:** 3.3% (1996) **Foreign debt:** ($ US) 29.8 billion (1996) **Major trading partners:** USA, Japan, Hong Kong, Germany, Singapore, South Korea, Australia, China **Resources:** coal, copper, marble, dolomite; small reserves of petroleum and natural gas **Industries:** electronics, plastic and rubber goods, textiles and clothing, base metals, vehicles, aircraft, ships, footwear, cement, fertilizers, paper **Exports:** electronic products, base metals and metal articles, textiles and clothing, machinery, information and communication products, plastic and rubber products, vehicles and transport equipment, footwear, headwear, umbrellas, toys, games, sports equipment. Principal market: USA 23.3% (1996) **Imports:** machinery and transport

equipment, basic manufactures, chemicals, base metals and metal articles, minerals, textile products, crude petroleum, plastics, precision instruments, clocks and watches, musical instruments. Principal source: Japan 27.2% (1996) **Arable land:** 24% (1993) **Agricultural products:** rice, tea, bananas, pineapples, sugar cane, maize, sweet potatoes, soya beans, peanuts; fishing; forest resources

Population and society

Population: 21,465,900 (1996 est) **Population growth rate:** 0.9% (1994) **Population density:** (per sq km) 589 (1994) **Urban population:** (% of total) 75 (1994) **Age distribution:** (% of total population) <15 29.6%, 15–65 62.2%, >65 8.2% (1992) **Ethnic groups:** 98% Han Chinese and 2% aboriginal by descent; around 87% are Taiwan-born and 13% are 'mainlanders' **Language:** Mandarin Chinese (official); Taiwan, Hakka dialects **Religion:** officially atheist; Taoist, Confucian, Buddhist, Christian **Education:** (compulsory years) 9 **Literacy rate:** 95% (men); 93% (women) (1995 est) **Labour force:** 10.9% agriculture, 39.2% industry, 49.9% services (1994) **Unemployment:** 2.1% (1995) **Life expectancy:** 72 (men); 78 (women) (1995) **Child mortality rate:** (per 1,000 live births) 6 (1994) **Physicians:** 1 per 878 people (1995); 3,030 doctors of traditional Chinese medicine (1995)

Practical information

Visa requirements: UK: visa not required for a stay of up to 14 days. USA: visa not required for a stay of up to 14 days **Embassy in the UK:** Taipei Representative Office in the UK, 50 Grosvenor Gardens, London SW1W 0EB. Tel: (0171) 396 9152; fax: (0171) 396 9151 **British embassy:** the UK has no diplomatic representation in Taiwan **Chamber of commerce:** General Chamber of Commerce, 6th Floor, 390 Flushing South Road, Section 1, Taipei. Tel: (2) 701 2671; fax: (2) 755 5493 **Airports:** international airports: Taipei (Chaing Kai-shek), Kaohsiung; 14 domestic airports; total passenger km: 38,247 million (1995) **Major holidays:** 1–3 January, 29 March, 5 April, 1 July, 28 September, 10, 25, 31 October, 12 November, 25 December; variable: New Year (Chinese, January/February, 3 days), Dragon Boat Festival (June), Mid-Autumn Festival (September/October)

Chronology

7th century AD: Island occupied by aboriginal community of Malayan descent; immigration of Chinese from mainland began, but remained limited before 15th century. **1517:** Sighted by Portuguese vessels en route to Japan and named Ilha Formosa ('beautiful island'). **1624:** Occupied and controlled by Dutch. **1662:** Dutch defeated by Chinese Ming general, Cheng Ch'eng-kung (Koxinga), whose family came to rule Formosa for a short period. **1683:** Annexed by China's rulers, the Manchu Qing. **1786:** Major rebellion against Chinese rule. **1860:** Ports opened to Western trade. **1895:** Ceded 'in perpetuity' to Japan under Treaty of Shominoseki at end of Sino-Japanese war. **1945:** Recovered by China's Nationalist Kuomintang (Guomindang) government at end of World War II. **1947:** Rebellion against Chinese rule brutally suppressed. **1949:** Flight of Nationalist government, led by Generalissimo Chiang Kai-shek, to Taiwan after Chinese communist revolution. They retained the designation of Republic of China (ROC), claiming to be the legitimate government for all China, and were recognized by USA and United Nations (UN). **1950s onwards:** Rapid economic growth as Taiwan became successful export-orientated Newly Industrializing Country (NIC) and land was redistributed from the gentry 'to-the-tiller'. **1954:** US–Taiwanese mutual defence treaty. **1971:** Expulsion from UN as USA adopted new policy of détente towards communist China. **1972:** Commencement of legislature elections as programme of gradual democratization and Taiwanization launched by mainlander-dominated Kuomintang. **1975:** President Chiang Kai-shek died; replaced as Kuomintang leader by his son, Chiang Ching-kuo. **1979:** USA severed diplomatic relations and annulled 1954 security pact. **1986:** Centrist Democratic Progressive Party (DPP) formed as opposition to nationalist Kuomintang. **1987:** Martial law lifted; opposition parties legalized; press restrictions lifted. **1988:** President Chiang Ching-kuo died; replaced by Taiwanese-born Lee Teng-hui. **1990:** Chinese-born Kuomintang members became minority in parliament.

1991: President Lee Teng-hui declared end to civil war with China. Constitution amended. Kuomintang won landslide victory in elections to new National Assembly, the 'superparliament'. **1993:** Cooperation pact with China signed. **1995:** Ruling Kuomintang retained majority in working assembly (Legislative Yuan) by slim margin. **1996:** Lee Teng-hui elected president in first-ever Chinese democratic election. **1997:** Government narrowly survived no-confidence motion. Vincent Siew became prime minister.

Tajikistan Republic of

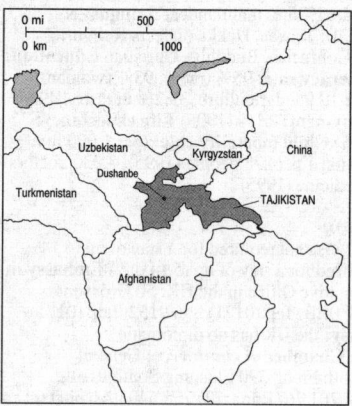

National name: *Respublika i Tojikiston* **Area:** 143,100 sq km/55,250 sq mi **Capital:** Dushanbe **Major towns/cities:** Khodzhent (formerly Leninabad), Kurgan-Tyube, Kulyab **Physical features:** mountainous, more than half of its territory lying above 3,000 m/10,000 ft; huge mountain glaciers, which are the source of many rapid rivers

Government
Head of state: Imamali Rakhmanov from 1994 **Head of government:** Yahya Azimov from 1996 **Political system:** authoritarian nationalist **Administrative divisions:** two provinces and one autonomous region (Gornyi Badakhstan) **Political parties:** Communist Party of Tajikistan (CPT), pro-Rakhmanov; Democratic Party of Tajikistan (DP), anticommunist (banned from 1993); Party of Popular Unity and Justice, anticommunist **Armed forces:** 7,000; paramilitary forces around 16,500 (1996) **Death penalty:** retained and used for ordinary crimes **Defence spend:** (% GDP) 11 (1996) **Education spend:** (% GNP) 9.5 (1993/94)

Economy and resources
Currencies: Tajik and Russian rouble **GDP:** ($ US) 2 billion (1994) **Real GDP per capita (PPP):** ($ US) 1,117 (1994) **GDP growth rate:** 16.7% (1996); –18.1% (1990–95) **Average annual inflation:** 65% (1996); 146.6% (1985–95) **Foreign debt:** ($ US) 730 million (1995) **Major trading partners:** Uzbekistan, the Netherlands, Switzerland, Russia, UK **Resources:** coal, aluminium, lead, zinc, iron, tin, uranium, radium, arsenic, bismuth, gold, mica, asbestos, lapis lazuli; small reserves of petroleum and natural gas **Industries:** mining, aluminium production, engineering, food processing, textiles (including silk), carpet making, clothing, footwear, fertilizers **Exports:** aluminium, cotton lint. Principal market: the Netherlands 34.1% (1995) **Imports:** industrial products and machinery (principally for aluminium plants), unprocessed agricultural products, food and beverages, petroleum and chemical products, consumer goods. Principal source: Uzbekistan 31.5% (1995) **Arable land:** 5.8% (1995) **Agricultural products:** cotton, jute, rice, millet, fruit, vegetables; livestock rearing (cattle, sheep, goats, and pigs)

Population and society
Population: 5,935,000 (1996 est) **Population growth rate:** 2.9% (1990–95); 2.5% (2000–05) **Population density:** (per sq km) 41 (1996 est) **Urban population:** (% of total) 32 (1995) **Age distribution:** (% of total population) <15 43.1%, 15–65 52.6%, >65 4.3% (1995) **Ethnic groups:** 62% ethnic Tajik, 24% Uzbek, 8%

ethnic Russian, 1% Tatar, 1% Kyrgyz, and 1% Ukrainian **Language:** Tajik (official), similar to Farsi (Persian) **Religion:** Sunni Muslim **Education:** (compulsory years) 9 **Literacy rate:** 97% (men); 97% (women) (1995 est) **Labour force:** 51.2% agriculture, 18.1% industry, 30.7% services (1993) **Unemployment:** 2.5% (1996) **Life expectancy:** 69 (men); 74 (women) (1995–2000) **Child mortality rate:** (under 5, per 1,000 live births) 56 (1996) **Physicians:** 1 per 442 people (1994)

Practical information
Visa requirements: UK: visa required. USA: visa required **Embassy in the UK:** Tajikistan has no diplomatic representation in the UK **British embassy:** the British Embassy in Tashkent (see Uzbekistan) deals with all enquiries relating to Tajikistan **Chamber of commerce:** Chamber of Commerce and Industry, Ulitsa Mazayeva 21, Dushanbe 7340012. Tel: (3772) 279 519 **Airports:** international airport: Dushanbe; three domestic airports; total passenger km: 2,231 million (1994) **Major holidays:** 1 January, 8, 21 March, 9 May, 9 September, 14 October; variable: end of Ramadan

Chronology
c. 330: Formed an eastern part of empire of Alexander the Great of Macedonia. **8th century:** Tajiks established as distinct ethnic group, with semi-independent territories under the tutelage of the Uzbeks, to the W; spread of Islam. **13th century:** Conquered by Genghis Khan and became part of Mongol Empire. **1860–1900:** Northern Tajikistan came under tsarist Russian rule, while the S was annexed by Emirate of Bukhara, to the W. **1917–18:** Attempts to establish Soviet control after Bolshevik revolution in Russia resisted initially by armed guerrillas (basmachi). **1921:** Became part of Turkestan Soviet Socialist Autonomous Republic. **1924:** Tajik Autonomous Soviet Socialist Republic formed. **1929:** Became constituent republic of Soviet Union (USSR). **1930s:** Stalinist era of collectivization led to widespread repression of Tajiks. **1978:** 13,000 participated in anti-Russian riots. **late 1980s:** Resurgence in Tajik consciousness, stimulated by the *glasnost* initiative of Soviet leader Mikhail Gorbachev. **1989:** Rastokhez ('Revival') Popular Front established and Tajik declared state language. New mosques constructed. **1990:** Violent interethnic Tajik–Armenian clashes in Dushanbe; state of emergency imposed. **1991:** President Kakhar Makhkamov, local communist leader since 1985, forced to resign after supporting failed anti-Gorbachev coup in Moscow. Independence declared. Rakhman Nabiyev, communist leader 1982–85, elected president. Joined new Commonwealth of Independent States (CIS). **1992:** Joined Muslim Economic Cooperation Organization, the Conference on Security and Cooperation in Europe (CSCE; now the Organization on Security and Cooperation in Europe, OSCE), and United Nations. Violent demonstrations by Islamic and prodemocracy groups forced Nabiyev to resign. Civil war between pro- and anti-Nabiyev forces claimed 20,000 lives, made 600,000 refugees, and wrecked the economy. Imamali Rakhmanov, a communist sympathetic to Nabiyev, took over as head of state. **1993:** Nabiyev and his militia ally, Sangak Safarov, died. Government forces regained control of most of the country. CIS peacekeeping forces drafted in to patrol border with Afghanistan, the base of pro-Islamic rebels. **1994:** Cease-fire agreed. Rakhmanov popularly elected president under new constitution. **1995:** Parliamentary elections won by Rakhmanov's supporters. Renewed fighting on Afghan border. **1996:** Pro-Islamic rebels captured towns in SW. UN-sponsored cease-fire between government and pro-Islamic rebels. **1997:** Four-stage peace plan signed. President Rakhmanov seriously injured by grenade. Peace accord with Islamic rebel group, the United Tajik Opposition (UTO).

Tanzania United Republic of

National name: *Jamhuri ya Muungano wa Tanzania* **Area:** 945,000 sq km/364,864 sq mi **Capital:** Dodoma (since 1983) **Major towns/cities:** Zanzibar Town, Mwanza, Tabora, Mbeya, Tanga

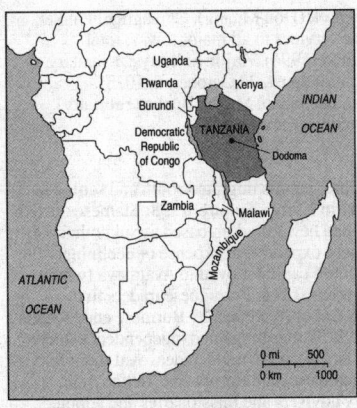

Major ports: (former capital) Dar es Salaam **Physical features:** central plateau; lakes in N and W; coastal plains; lakes Victoria, Tanganyika, and Nyasa; half the country is forested; comprises islands of Zanzibar and Pemba; Mount Kilimanjaro, 5,895 m/19,340 ft, the highest peak in Africa; Olduvai Gorge; Ngorongoro Crater, 14.5 km/9 mi across, 762 m/2,500 ft deep

Government
Head of state: Benjamin Mkapa from 1995 **Head of government:** Cleoopa Msuya from 1994 **Political system:** emergent democracy **Administrative divisions:** 25 administrative regions **Political parties:** Revolutionary Party of Tanzania (CCM), African, socialist; Civic Party (Chama Cha Wananchi), left of centre; Tanzania People's Party (TPP), left of centre; Democratic Party (DP), left of centre; Zanzibar United Front (Kamahuru), Zanzibar-based, centrist **Armed forces:** 34,600; citizen's militia of 80,000 (1996) **Conscription:** two years **Death penalty:** retained and used for ordinary crimes **Defence spend:** (% GDP) 2.5 (1996) **Education spend:** (% GNP) 5.0 (1993/94) **Health spend:** (% GDP) 2.8 (1990–95)

Economy and resources
Currency: Tanzanian shilling **GDP:** ($ US) 3.4 billion (1994) **Real GDP per capita (PPP):** ($ US) 656 (1994) **GDP growth rate:** 3.5% (1994); 3.2% (1990–95) **Average annual inflation:** 21.5% (1996); 32.3% (1985–95) **Foreign debt:** ($ US) 7.9 billion (1996) **Major trading partners:** UK, Germany, Japan, India, the Netherlands, Belgium, Italy, Oman **Resources:** diamonds, other gemstones, gold, salt, phosphates, coal, gypsum, tin, kaolin (exploration for petroleum in progress) **Industries:** food processing, textiles, cigarette production, pulp and paper, petroleum refining, diamonds, cement, brewing, fertilizers, clothing, footwear, pharmaceuticals, electrical goods, metalworking, vehicle assembly **Exports:** coffee beans, raw cotton, tobacco, tea, cloves, cashew nuts, minerals, petroleum products. Principal market: Germany 9.2% (1995) **Imports:** machinery and transport equipment, crude petroleum and petroleum products, construction materials, foodstuffs, consumer goods. Principal source: UK 9.6% (1995) **Arable land:** 3.5% (1995) **Agricultural products:** coffee, cotton, tobacco, cloves, tea, cashew nuts, sisal, pyrethrum, sugar cane, coconuts, cardamoms

Population and society
Population: 30,799,000 (1996 est) **Population growth rate:** 3% (1990–95); 2.6% (2000–05) **Population density:** (per sq km) 33 (1996 est) **Urban population:** (% of total) 24% (1995) **Age distribution:** (% of total population) <15 45.9%, 15–65 51.6%, >65 2.6% (1995) **Ethnic groups:** 99% of the population are Africans, ethnically classified as Bantus, and distributed among over 130 tribes; main tribes are Bantu, Vilotic, Nilo-Hamitic, Khoisan, and Iraqwi **Language:** Kiswahili, English (both official) **Religion:** Muslim, Christian, traditional religions **Education:** (compulsory years) 7 **Literacy rate:** 79% (men); 54% (women) (1995 est) **Labour force:** 52% of population: 84% agriculture, 5% industry, 11% services (1990) **Life expectancy:** 50 (men); 53 (women) (1995–2000) **Child mortality rate:** (under 5, per 1,000 live births) 126 (1996) **Physicians:** 1 per 23,053 people (1991)

Practical information
Visa requirements: UK: visa required. USA: visa required **Embassy in the UK:** 43 Hertford Street, London W1Y 8D8. Tel: (0171) 499 8951; fax: (0171) 499 8954 **British embassy:** British High Commission, PO Box 9200, Hifadhi House, Samora Avenue, Dar es Salaam. Tel: (51) 46300/4; fax: (51) 46301 **Chamber of commerce:** Dar es Salaam Chamber of Commerce, PO Box 41, Kelvin House, Samora Machel Avenue, Dar es Salaam. Tel: (51) 21893 **Airports:** international airports: Dar es Salaam, Kilimanjaro, Zanzibar; 50 domestic airports and landing strips; total passenger km: 165 million (1994) **Major holidays:** 1, 12 January, 5 February, 1 May, 7 July, 9, 25 December; variable: Eid-ul-Adha, Good Friday, Easter Monday, end of Ramadan (2 days), Prophet's Birthday

Chronology
8th century: Growth of city states along coast after settlement by Arabs from Oman. **1499:** Portuguese navigator Vasco da Gama visited island of Zanzibar. **16th century:** Portuguese occupied Zanzibar, defeated coastal states, and exerted spasmodic control over them. **1699:** Portuguese ousted from Zanzibar by Arabs of Oman. **18th century:** Sultan of Oman reasserted Arab overlordship of E African coast, which became subordinate to Zanzibar. **1744–1837:** Revolt of ruler of Mombasa against Oman spanned 93 years until final victory of Oman. **1822:** Moresby Treaty: Britain recognized regional dominance of Zanzibar, but protested against slave trade. **1840:** Sultan Seyyid bin Sultan moved his capital from Oman to Zanzibar; trade in slaves and ivory flourished. **1861:** Sultanates of Zanzibar and Oman separated on death of Seyyid. **19th century:** Europeans started to explore inland, closely followed by Christian missionaries. **1884:** German Colonization Society began to acquire territory on mainland in defiance of Zanzibar. **1890:** Britain obtained protectorate over Zanzibar, abolished slave trade, and recognized German claims to mainland. **1897:** German East Africa formally established as colony. **1905–06:** Maji Maji revolt suppressed by German troops. **1916:** Conquest of German East Africa by British and South African forces, led by Gen Jan Smuts. **1919:** Most of German East Africa became British League of Nations mandate of Tanganyika. **1946:** Britain continued to govern Tanganyika as United Nations (UN) trusteeship. **1954:** Julius Nyerere organized the Tanganyikan African National Union (TANU) to campaign for independence. **1961:** Tanganyika achieved independence from Britain with Nyerere as prime minister. **1962:** Tanganyika became republic under President Nyerere. **1963:** Zanzibar achieved independence. **1964:** Arab-dominated sultanate of Zanzibar overthrown by Afro-Shirazi Party in violent revolution; Zanzibar merged with Tanganyika to form United Republic of Tanzania. **1967:** East African Community (EAC) formed by Tanzania, Kenya, and Uganda to retain customs union formed in colonial period; Arusha Declaration by Nyerere pledged to build socialist state. **1977:** Revolutionary Party of Tanzania (CCM) proclaimed as only legal party; EAC dissolved. **1979:** Tanzanian troops intervened in Uganda to help overthrow President Idi Amin. **1985:** Nyerere retired as president; succeeded by Ali Hassan Mwinyi. **1990:** Nyerere surrendered leadership of CCM to Mwinyi. **1992:** Multiparty politics permitted. **1995:** Benjamin Mkapa of CCM elected president.

Thailand Kingdom of

National name: *Prathet Thai* or *Muang Thai* **Area:** 513,115 sq km/198,113 sq mi **Capital:** Bangkok (and chief port) **Major towns/cities:** Chiangmai, Hat Yai, Khon Kaen, Songkhla, Chon Buri, Nakhon Si Thammarat, Lampang, Phitsannlok, Ratchasima **Major ports:** Nakhon Sawan **Physical features:** mountainous, semi-arid plateau in NE, fertile central region, tropical isthmus in S; rivers Chao Phraya, Mekong, and Salween

Government
Head of state: King Bhumibol Adulyadej from 1946 **Head of government:** Chavalit Yongchaiyudh from 1996 **Political system:**

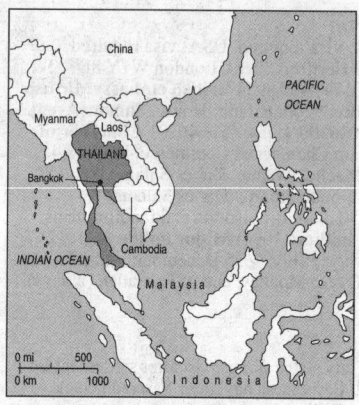

military-controlled emergent democracy **Administrative divisions:** 76 provinces **Political parties:** Democrat Party (DP), centre left; Thai Nation (Chart Thai), right wing, pro-private enterprise; New Aspiration Party (NAP), centrist; Palang Dharma Party (PDP), anti-corruption, Buddhist; Social Action Party (SAP), moderate, conservative; Chart Pattana (National Development), conservative **Armed forces:** 254,000 (1996) **Conscription:** two years **Death penalty:** retained and used for ordinary crimes **Defence spend:** (% GDP) 2.5 (1996) **Education spend:** (% GNP) 3.8 (1993/94) **Health spend:** (% GDP) 1.4 (1990–95)

Economy and resources
Currency: baht **GDP:** ($ US) 143.2 billion (1994) **Real GDP per capita (PPP):** ($ US) 7,104 (1994) **GDP growth rate:** 8.6% (1995); 8.4% (1990–95) **Average annual inflation:** 5.8% (1996); 5% (1985–95) **Foreign debt:** ($ US) 82.1 billion (1996) **Major trading partners:** Japan, USA, Singapore, Germany, Taiwan, Hong Kong **Resources:** tin ore, lignite, gypsum, antimony, manganese, copper, tungsten, lead, gold, zinc, silver, rubies, sapphires, natural gas, petroleum, fish **Industries:** textiles and clothing, electronics, electrical goods, cement, petroleum refining, sugar refining, motor vehicles, agricultural products, beverages, tobacco, metals and metal products, plastics, furniture, tourism **Exports:** textiles and clothing, electronic goods, rice, rubber, gemstones, sugar, cassava (tapioca), fish (especially prawns), machinery and manufactures, chemicals. Principal market: USA 17.8% (1995) **Imports:** petroleum and petroleum products, machinery, chemicals, iron and steel, consumer goods. Principal source: Japan 30.6% (1995) **Arable land:** 33.4% (1995) **Agricultural products:** rice, cassava, rubber, sugar cane, maize, kenat (a jute-like fibre), tobacco, coconuts; fishing (especially prawns) and livestock (mainly buffaloes, cattle, pigs, and poultry)

Population and society
Population: 58,703,000 (1996 est) **Population growth rate:** 1.1% (1990–95); 0.9% (2000–05) **Population density:** (per sq km) 114 (1996 est) **Urban population:** (% of total) 20% (1995) **Age distribution:** (% of total population) <15 28.3%, 15–65 66.7%, >65 5% (1995) **Ethnic groups:** 75% of the population is of Thai descent; 14% ethnic Chinese, one-third of whom live in Bangkok; Thai Malays constitute the next largest minority, followed by hill tribes; a substantial Kampuchean (Khmer) refugee community resides in border camps **Language:** Thai and Chinese (both official); Lao, Chinese, Malay, Khmer **Religion:** Buddhist **Education:** (compulsory years) 6 **Literacy rate:** 96% (men); 90% (women) (1995 est) **Labour force:** 57% of population: 64% agriculture, 14% industry, 22% services (1990) **Unemployment:** 3.2% (1993) **Life expectancy:** 65 (men), 72 (women) (1995–2000) **Child mortality rate:** (under 5, per 1,000 live births) 43 (1996) **Physicians:** 1 per 4,416 people (1993 est)

Practical information
Visa requirements: UK: visa not required. USA: visa not required **Embassy in the UK:** 1/3 Yorkshire House, Grosvenor Crescent, London SW1X 7ET. Tel: (0171) 371 7621; fax: (0171) 235 9808 **British embassy:** Wireless Road, Bangkok 10200. Tel: (2) 253 0191; fax: (2) 255 8619 **Chamber of commerce:** 150 Thanon Rajbopit, Bangkok 10200. Tel: (2) 225 0086; fax: (2) 225 3372 **Airports:** international airports: Bangkok (Don Muang), Chiangmai, Phuket, Hat Yai, U-tapao; domestic services to all major towns; total passenger km: 25,242 million (1994) **Major holidays:** 1 January, 6, 13 April, 1, 5 May, 1 July, 12 August, 23 October, 5, 10, 31 December; variable: end of Ramadan, Makha Bucha (February), Visakha Bucha (May), Buddhist Lent (July)

Chronology
13th century: Siamese (Thai) people migrated south and settled in valley of Chao Phraya river in Khmer Empire. **1238:** Siamese ousted Khmer governors and formed new kingdom based at Sukhothai. **14th and 15th centuries:** Siamese expanded at expense of declining Khmer Empire. **1350:** Siamese capital moved to Ayatthaya (which also became name of kingdom). **1511:** Portuguese traders first reached Siam. **1569:** Conquest of Ayatthaya by Burmese ended years of rivalry and conflict. **1589:** Siamese regained independence under King Naresuan. **17th century:** Foreign trade under royal monopoly developed with Chinese, Japanese, and Europeans. **1690s:** Siam expelled European military advisers and missionaries and adopted policy of isolation. **1767:** Burmese invaders destroyed city of Ayatthaya, massacred ruling families, and withdrew, leaving Siam in a state of anarchy. **1782:** Reunification of Siam after civil war under Gen Phraya Chakri, who founded new capital at Bangkok and proclaimed himself King Rama I. **1824–51:** King Rama III reopened Siam to European diplomats and missionaries. **1851–68:** King Mongkut employed European advisers to help modernize government, legal system, and army. **1856:** Royal monopoly on foreign trade ended. **1868–1910:** King Chulalongkorn continued modernization and developed railway network using Chinese immigrant labour; Siam became major exporter of rice. **1896:** Anglo-French agreement recognized Siam as independent buffer state between British Burma and French Indo-China. **1932:** Bloodless coup forced King Rama VII to grant a constitution with mixed civilian-military government. **1939:** Siam changed its name to Thailand (briefly reverting to Siam 1945–49). **1941:** Japanese invaded; Thailand became puppet ally of Japan under Field Marshal Phibun Songkhram. **1945:** Japanese withdrawal; Thailand compelled to return territory taken from Laos, Cambodia, and Malaya. **1946:** King Ananda Mahidol assassinated. **1947:** Phibun regained power in military coup, reducing monarch to figurehead; Thailand adopted strongly pro-American foreign policy. **1955:** Political parties and free speech introduced. **1957:** State of emergency declared; Phibun deposed in bloodless coup; military dictatorship continued under Gen Sarit Thanarat (1957–63) and Gen Thanom Kittikachorn (1963–73). **1967–72:** Thai troops fought in alliance with USA in Vietnam War. **1973:** Military government overthrown by student riots. **1974:** Adoption of democratic constitution, followed by civilian coalition government. **1976:** Military reassumed control in response to mounting strikes and political violence. **1978:** Gen Kriangsak Chomanan introduced constitution with mixed civilian–military government. **1980:** Gen Prem Tinsulanonda assumed power. **1983:** Prem relinquished army office to head civilian government; martial law maintained. **1988:** Chatichai Choonhavan succeeded Prem as prime minister. **1991:** Military coup imposed new military-oriented constitution despite mass protests. **1992:** General election produced five-party coalition; riots forced Prime Minister Suchinda Kraprayoon to flee; Chuan Leekpai formed new coalition government. **1995:** Ruling coalition collapsed; Banharn Silpa-archa appointed premier. **1996:** Banharn resigned; general election resulted in new six-party coalition led by Chavalit Yongchaiyudh. **1997:** Major financial crisis led to floating of currency. Austerity rescue plan agreed with International Monetary Fund (IMF).

Togo Republic of (formerly Togoland)

National name: *République Togolaise* **Area:** 56,800 sq km/21,930 sq mi **Capital:** Lomé **Major towns/cities:** Sokodé, Kpalimé, Kara, Atakpamé, Bassar, Tsévié **Physical features:** two savanna plains, divided by range of hills NE–SW; coastal lagoons and marsh; Mono Tableland, Oti Plateau, Oti River

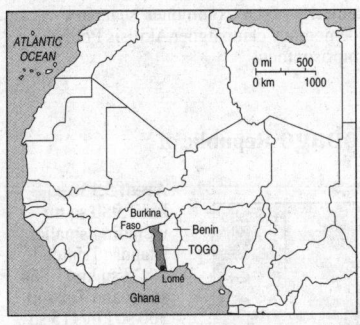

Government

Head of state: Etienne Gnassingbé Eyadéma from 1967 **Head of government:** Kwasi Klutse from 1996 **Political system:** emergent democracy **Administrative divisions:** five regions **Political parties:** Rally of the Togolese People (RPT), nationalist, centrist; Action Committee for Renewal (CAR), left of centre; Togolese Union for Democracy (UTD), left of centre **Armed forces:** 7,000 (1996) **Conscription:** military service is by selective conscription for two years **Death penalty:** retains the death penalty for ordinary crimes, but can be considered abolitionist in practice **Defence spend:** (% GDP) 2.5 (1996) **Education spend:** (% GNP) 6.1 (1993/94) **Health spend:** (% GDP) 1.7 (1990–95)

Economy and resources

Currency: franc CFA **GDP:** ($ US) 1 billion (1994) **Real GDP per capita (PPP):** ($ US) 1,109 (1994) **GDP growth rate:** 16.3% (1994); –3.4% (1990–95) **Average annual inflation:** 6% (1996); 3% (1985–95 est) **Foreign debt:** ($ US) 1.5 billion (1996) **Major trading partners:** Canada, Ghana, France, Nigeria, Mexico, the Netherlands, Japan, USA, Spain **Resources:** phosphates, limestone, marble, deposits of iron ore, manganese, chromite, peat; exploration for petroleum and uranium was under way in the early 1990s **Industries:** processing of phosphates, steel rolling, cement, textiles, processing of agricultural products, beer, soft drinks **Exports:** phosphates (mainly calcium phosphates), ginned cotton, green coffee, cocoa beans. Principal market: Canada 9.2% (1995) **Imports:** machinery and transport equipment, cotton yarn and fabrics, cigarettes, antibiotics, food (especially cereals) and live animals, chemicals, refined petroleum products, beverages. Principal source: Ghana 17.3% (1995) **Arable land:** 38% (1995) **Agricultural products:** cotton, cocoa, coffee, oil palm, yams, cassava, maize, millet, sorghum

Population and society

Population: 4,201,000 (1996 est) **Population growth rate:** 3.2% (1990–95); 2.9% (2000–05) **Population density:** (per sq km) 74 (1996 est) **Urban population:** (% of total) 31 (1995) **Age distribution:** (% of total population) <15 45.7%, 15–65 51.1%, >65 3.2% (1995) **Ethnic groups:** predominantly of Sudanese Hamitic origin in the N, and black African in the S; they are distributed among 37 different ethnic groups. There are also European, Syrian, and Lebanese minorities **Language:** French (official), Ewe, Kabre, Gurma **Religion:** animist, Catholic, Muslim, Protestant **Education:** (compulsory years) 6 **Literacy rate:** 56% (men); 31% (women) (1995 est) **Labour force:** 42% of population: 66% agriculture, 10% industry, 24% services (1990) **Unemployment:** 2.5% (1989 est) **Life expectancy:** 55 (men); 59 (women) (1995–2000) **Child mortality rate:** (under 5, per 1,000 live births) 118 (1996) **Physicians:** 1 per 11,385 people (1993 est)

Practical information

Visa requirements: UK: visa not required. USA: visa not required **Embassy in the UK:** 8 rue Alfred Roll, 75017 Paris, France. Tel: (1) 4380 1213; fax: (1) 4380 9071 **British embassy:** British Honorary Consulate, BP 20050, British School of Lomé, Lomé. Tel: (228) 264 606; fax: (228) 214 989 **Chamber of commerce:** Chambre de Commerce, d'Agriculture et d'Industrie du Togo, BP 360, angle avenue de la Présidence, Lomé. Tel: (228) 217 065; fax: (228) 214 730 **Airports:** international airports: Lomé, Niamtougou; four domestic airports and several smaller airfields; total passenger km: 215 million (1994) **Major holidays:** 1, 13, 24 January, 24, 27 April, 1 May, 15 August, 1 November, 25 December; variable: Ascension Thursday, Eid-ul-Adha, end of Ramadan

Chronology

15th–17th centuries: Formerly dominated by Kwa peoples in SW and Gur-speaking Votaic peoples in N, Ewe clans immigrated from Nigeria and the Ane (Mina) from Ghana and Ivory Coast. **18th century:** Coastal area held by Danes. **1847:** Arrival of German missionaries. **1884–1914:** Togoland was a German protectorate until captured by Anglo-French forces; cocoa and cotton plantations developed, using forced labour. **1922:** Divided between Britain and France under League of Nations mandate. **1946:** Continued under United Nations trusteeship. **1957:** British Togoland, comprising one-third of the area and situated in the W, integrated with Ghana, following a plebiscite. **1960:** French Togoland, situated in the E, achieved independence from France as Republic of Togo with Sylvanus Olympio, leader of United Togolese (UP) party, as head of state. **1963:** Olympio killed in a military coup. His brother-in-law, Nicolas Grunitzky, became president. **1967:** Grunitzky replaced by Lt-Gen Etienne Gnassingbé Eyadéma in bloodless coup; political parties banned. **1969:** Assembly of the Togolese People (RPT) formed by Eyadéma as sole legal political party. **1975:** EEC Lomé convention signed in Lomé, establishing trade links with developing countries. **1977:** Assassination plot against Eyadéma, allegedly involving Olympio family, thwarted. **1979:** Eyadéma returned in election. Further EEC Lomé convention signed. **1986:** Attempted coup failed and situation stabilized with help of French troops. **1990:** Violent antigovernment demonstrations in Lomé suppressed with casualties; Eyadéma relegalized political parties. **1991:** Gilchrist Olympio returned from exile. Eyadéma was forced to call a national conference which limited the president's powers, and elected Joseph Kokou Koffigoh head of interim government. Three attempts by Eyadéma's troops to unseat government failed. **1992:** Strikes in S Togo; Olympio was attacked by soldiers and fled to France. Overwhelming referendum support for multiparty politics. New constitution adopted. **1993:** Eyadéma won first multiparty presidential elections amid widespread opposition. **1994:** Antigovernment coup foiled. Opposition CAR polled strongly in assembly elections. Eyadéma appointed Edem Kodjo of the minority UTD as prime minister. **1996:** Kwasi Klutse appointed prime minister.

Tonga Kingdom of (or Friendly Islands)

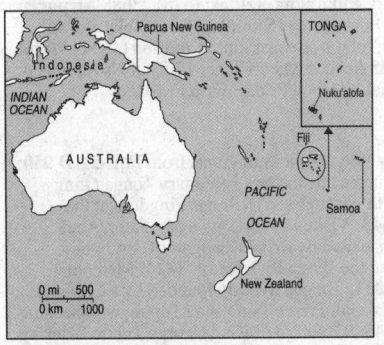

National name: *Pule'anga Fakatu'i 'o Tonga* **Area:** 750 sq km/290 sq mi **Capital:** Nuku'alofa (on Tongatapu Island) **Major towns/cities:** Pangai, Neiafu **Physical features:** three groups of islands in SW Pacific, mostly coral formations, but actively volcanic in W; of the 170 islands in the Tonga group, 36 are inhabited

Government

Head of state: King Taufa'ahau Tupou IV from 1965 **Head of government:** Baron Vaea from 1991 **Political system:** constitutional monarchy **Administrative divisions:** five divisions comprising 23 districts **Political parties:** legally none, but one prodemocracy grouping, the People's Party **Armed forces:** 125-strong naval force (1995) **Conscription:** military service is voluntary **Death penalty:** retains the death penalty for ordinary crimes, but can be considered abolitionist in practice (last execution 1982) **Education spend:** (% GNP) 4.8 (1992) **Health spend:** (% GDP) 4.1 (1991 est)

Economy and resources

Currency: Tongan dollar or pa'anga **GDP:** ($ US) 228 million (1995 est) **Real GDP per capita (PPP):** ($ US) 2,160 (1995 est) **GDP growth rate:** –1.6% (1995) **Average annual inflation:** 1.2% (1996); 7.9% (1985–95 est) **Foreign debt:** ($ US) 64.4 million (1994) **Major trading partners:** New Zealand, Japan, Australia, Fiji, USA, UK **Industries:** concrete blocks, small excavators, clothing, coconut oil, furniture, handicrafts, sports equipment (including small boats), brewing, sandalwood processing, tourism **Exports:** vanilla beans, pumpkins, coconut oil and other coconut products, watermelons, knitted clothes, cassava, yams, sweet potatoes, footwear. Principal market: Japan 48% (1995) **Imports:** foodstuffs, basic manufactures, machinery and transport equipment, mineral fuels. Principal source: New Zealand 38% (1995) **Arable land:** 23.6% (1995) **Agricultural products:** coconuts, copra, cassava, vanilla, pumpkins, yams, taro, sweet potatoes, watermelons, tomatoes, lemons and limes, oranges, groundnuts, breadfruit; livestock rearing (pigs, goats, poultry, and cattle); fishing

Population and society

Population: 98,000 (1996 est) **Population growth rate:** 0.4% (1990–95) **Population density:** (per sq km) 132 (1996 est) **Urban population:** (% of total) 41.1 (1995) **Age distribution:** (% of total population) <15 39.6%, 15–65 54.7%, >65 5.7% (1992) **Ethnic groups:** 98% of Tongan ethnic origin, a Polynesian group with a small mixture of Melanesian; the remainder is European and part-European **Language:** Tongan (official); English **Religion:** Free Wesleyan Church **Education:** (compulsory years) 8 **Literacy rate:** 95% (men); 89% (women) (1994 est) **Labour force:** 38.1% agriculture, 20.6% industry, 41.3% (1990) **Unemployment:** 4.2% (1990) **Life expectancy:** 67 (men); 71 (women) (1996 est) **Child mortality rate:** (per 1,000 live births) 20 (1994) **Physicians:** 1 per 2,325 people (1991)

Practical information

Visa requirements: UK: visa required (issued on arrival). USA: visa required (issued on arrival) **Embassy in the UK:** 36 Molyneux Street, London W1H 6AB. Tel: (0171) 724 5828; fax: (0171) 723 9074 **British embassy:** British High Commission, PO Box 56, Vuna Road, Nuku'alofa. Tel: (676) 21020/1; fax: (676) 24109 **Chamber of commerce:** Office of the Minister of Labour, Commerce and Industries, PO Box 110, Nuku'alofa. Tel/fax: (676) 23688 **Airports:** international airports: Fua'amotu (15 km/9 mi from Nuku'alofa); five domestic airstrips; total passenger km: 11 million (1994) **Major holidays:** 1 January, 25 April, 5 May, 4 June, 4 July, 4 November, 4, 25–26 December; variable: Good Friday, Easter Monday

Chronology

c. 1000 BC: Settled by Polynesian immigrants from Fiji. **c. AD 950:** The legendary Aho'eitu became the first hereditary Tongan king (Tu'i Tonga). **13th–14th centuries:** Tu'i Tonga kingdom at the height of its power. **1643:** Visited by the Dutch navigator, Abel Tasman. **1773:** Islands visited by British navigator Capt James Cook, who named them the 'Friendly Islands'. **1826:** Methodist mission established. **1831:** Tongan dynasty founded by a Christian convert and chief of Ha'apai, Prince Taufa'ahau Tupou, who became king 14 years later. **1845–93:** Reign of King George Tupou I, during which the country was reunited after half a century of civil war; Christianity was spread and a modern constitution adopted 1875. **1900:** Friendship ('Protectorate') treaty signed between King George Tupou II and Britain, establishing British control over defence and foreign affairs, but leaving internal political affairs under Tongan control. **1918:** Queen Salote Tupou III ascended the throne. **1965:** Queen Salote died; succeeded by her son, King Taufa'ahau Tupou IV, who had been prime minister since 1949. **1970:** Independence from Britain, but remained within Commonwealth. **1993:** Six prodemocracy candidates elected. Calls for reform of absolutist power. **1996:** Prodemocracy movement led

by People's Party won a majority of the 'commoner' seats in legislative assembly. Prodemocracy campaigner Akilisis Pohiva released after a month's imprisonment.

Trinidad and Tobago Republic of

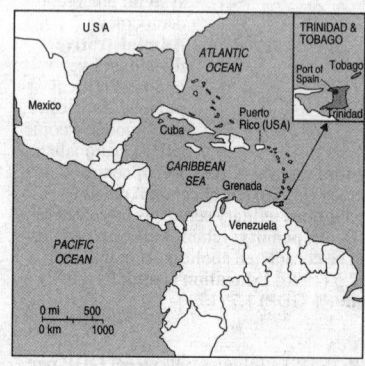

Area: 5,130 sq km/1,980 sq mi including smaller islands (Trinidad 4,828 sq km/1,864 sq mi and Tobago 300 sq km/115 sq mi) **Capital:** Port-of-Spain (and port) **Major towns/cities:** San Fernando, Arima, Point Fortin **Major ports:** Scarborough, Point Lisas **Physical features:** comprises two main islands and some smaller ones in Caribbean Sea; coastal swamps and hills E–W

Government

Head of state: Noor Hassanali from 1987 **Head of government:** Basdeo Panday from 1995 **Political system:** democracy **Administrative divisions:** nine counties, two municipalities, and three borough corporations, plus the island of Tobago **Political parties:** National Alliance for Reconstruction (NAR), nationalist, left of centre; People's National Movement (PNM), nationalist, moderate, centrist; United National Congress (UNC), left of centre; Movement for Social Transformation (Motion), left of centre **Armed forces:** 2,100; plus a paramlitary force of 4,800 (1996) **Conscription:** military service is voluntary **Death penalty:** retained and used for ordinary crimes **Defence spend:** (% GDP) 1.1 (1996) **Education spend:** (% GNP) 4.1 (1994) **Health spend:** (% GDP) 2.6 (1990–95)

Economy and resources

Currency: Trinidad and Tobago dollar **GDP:** ($ US) 4.8 billion (1994) **Real GDP per capita (PPP):** ($ US) 9,124 (1994) **GDP growth rate:** 4.7% (1994); 1% (1990–95) **Average annual inflation:** 3.2% (1996); 6.8% (1985–95) **Foreign debt:** ($ US) 2.5 million (1995) **Major trading partners:** USA, Venezuela, UK, Germany, Canada, Barbados, Jamaica, Guyana, Netherlands Antilles **Resources:** petroleum, natural gas, asphalt (world's largest deposits of natural asphalt) **Industries:** petroleum refining, food processing, iron and steel, beverages, chemicals, cement, beer, cigarettes, motor vehicles, paper, printing and publishing, tourism (third-largest source of foreign exchange) **Exports:** mineral fuels and lubricants, chemicals, basic manufactures, food. Principal market: USA 42.9% (1995) **Imports:** machinery and transport equipment, manufactured goods, mineral fuel products, food and live animals, chemicals. Principal source: USA 49.9% (1995) **Arable land:** 14.6% (1995) **Agricultural products:** sugar cane, coffee, cocoa, citrus fruits; fishing

Population and society

Population: 1,297,000 (1996 est) **Population growth rate:** 1.1% (1990–95); 1.1% (2000–05) **Population density:** (per sq km) 253 (1996 est) **Urban population:** (% of total) 72 (1995) **Age distribution:** (% of total population) <15 32.3%, 15–65 62%, >65 5.7% (1995) **Ethnic groups:** the two main ethnic groups are Africans and East Indians; there are also European, Afro-European, and Chinese minorities. The original Carib population has largely disappeared **Language:** English (official); Hindi, French, Spanish **Religion:** Roman Catholic, Anglican, Hindu, Muslim **Education:**

(compulsory years) 7 **Literacy rate:** 97% (men); 95% (women)
(1995 est) **Labour force:** 12.4% agriculture, 25.4% industry, 62.2%
services (1994) **Unemployment:** 16.2 (1996 est) **Life expectancy:** 71
(men); 75 (women) (1995–2000) **Child mortality rate:** (under 5, per
1,000 live births) 17 (1996) **Physicians:** 1 per 1,113 people (1994)

Practical information

Visa requirements: UK: visa not required for a stay of up to three
months. USA: visa not required for a stay of up to three months
Embassy in the UK: 42 Belgrave Square, London SW1X 8NT. Tel:
(0171) 245 9351; fax: (0171) 823 1065 **British embassy:** British
High Commission, PO Box 778, 19 Clair Avenue, St Clair, Port of
Spain. Tel: (809) 622 2748; fax: (809) 622 4555 **Chamber of
commerce:** Trinidad and Tobago Chamber of Industry and
Commerce, PO Box 499, Room 950–952, Hilton Hotel, Port of Spain.
Tel: (809) 627 4461; fax: (809) 627 4376 **Airports:** international
airports: Port of Spain, Trinidad (Piarco), Crown Point (near
Scarborough, Tobago); domestic services between these; total
passenger km: 4,112 million (1994) **Major holidays:** 1 January, 19
June, 1, 31 August, 24 September, 25–26 December; variable: Corpus
Christi, Good Friday, Easter Monday, Whit Monday

Chronology

1498: Visited by the explorer Christopher Columbus, who named
Trinidad after the three peaks at its SE tip and Tobago after the local
form of tobacco pipe. Carib and Arawak Indians comprised the
indigenous community. **1532:** Trinidad colonized by Spain. **1630s:**
Tobago settled by Dutch, who introduced sugar-cane growing. **1797:**
Trinidad captured by Britain and ceded by Spain five years later under
Treaty of Amiens. **1814:** Tobago ceded to Britain by France. **1834:**
Abolition of slavery resulted in indentured labourers being brought in
from India, rather than Africa, to work sugar plantations. **1889:**
Trinidad and Tobago amalgamated as British colony. **1956:** The
People's National Movement (PNM) founded by Eric Williams, a
moderate nationalist. **1958–62:** Part of West Indies Federation. **1959:**
Achieved internal self-government, with Williams as chief minister.
1962: Independence achieved within Commonwealth, with Williams
as prime minister. **1970:** Army mutiny and violent Black Power riots
directed against minority East Indian population; state of emergency
imposed for two years. **1976:** Became a republic, with former
governor general Ellis Clarke as president and Williams as prime
minister. **1981:** Williams died; succeeded by George Chambers.
1986: Tobago-based National Alliance for Reconstruction (NAR),
headed by Arthur Robinson, won general election. **1987:** Noor
Hassanali became president. **1990:** Attempted antigovernment coup
by Islamic fundamentalists foiled. **1991:** General election victory for
PNM, with Patrick Manning as prime minister. **1995:** United National
Congress (UNC), a breakaway from the NAR rooted in the Indian
community, and PNM tied in general election; UNC–NAR coalition
formed, led by Basdeo Panday.

Tunisia Tunisian Republic

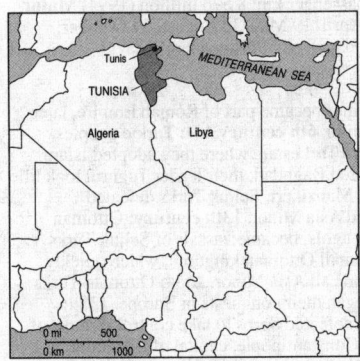

National name: *al-
Jumhuriya at-
Tunisiya* **Area:**
164,150 sq
km/63,378 sq mi
Capital: Tunis (and
chief port) **Major
towns/cities:** Sfax,
Ariana, Bizerte,
Djerba, Gabès,
Sousse, Kairouan,
Bardo, La Goulette
Major ports: Sfax,
Sousse, Bizerte
Physical features:
arable and forested
land in N graduates
towards desert in S;
fertile island of Jerba, linked to mainland by causeway (identified
with island of lotus-eaters); Shott el Jerid salt lakes

Government

Head of state: Zine el-Abidine Ben Ali from 1987 **Head of
government:** Hamed Karoui from 1989 **Political system:** emergent
democracy **Administrative divisions:** 23 governates **Political
parties:** Constitutional Democratic Rally (RCD), nationalist,
moderate, socialist; Popular Unity Movement (MUP), radical, left
of centre; Democratic Socialists Movement (MDS), left of centre;
Renovation Movement (MR), reformed communists **Armed forces:**
35,500; plus paramilitary forces numbering 23,000 (1996)
Conscription: military service is by selective conscription for 12
months **Death penalty:** retained and used for ordinary crimes
Defence spend: (% GDP) 2 (1996) **Education spend:** (% GNP) 6.3
(1993/94) **Health spend:** (% GDP) 3.0 (1990–95)

Economy and resources

Currency: Tunisian dinar **GDP:** ($ US) 15.8 billion (1994) **Real
GDP per capita (PPP):** ($ US) 5,319 (1994) **GDP growth rate:**
2.4% (1995); 3.9% (1990–95) **Average annual inflation:** 5.4%
(1996); 6% (1985–95) **Foreign debt:** ($ US) 10.3 billion (1996)
Major trading partners: France, Italy, Germany, Belgium, USA,
Spain, the Netherlands, UK, Libya, Japan **Resources:** petroleum,
natural gas, phosphates, iron, zinc, lead, aluminium fluoride,
fluorspar, sea salt **Industries:** processing of agricultural and mineral
products (including superphosphate and phosphoric acid), textiles
and clothing, machinery, chemicals, paper, wood, motor vehicles,
radio and television sets, tourism **Exports:** textiles and clothing,
crude petroleum, phosphates and fertilizers, olive oil, fruit, leather
and shoes, fishery products, machinery and electrical appliances.
Principal market: France 28% (1995) **Imports:** machinery, textiles,
food (mainly cereals, dairy produce, meat, and sugar) and live
animals, petroleum and petroleum products. Principal source:
France: 25.6% (1995) **Arable land:** 18.3 (1995) **Agricultural
products:** wheat, barley, olives, citrus fruits, dates, almonds, grapes,
melons, apples, apricots and other fruits, chickpeas, sugar beet,
tobacco; fishing

Population and society

Population: 9,156,000 (1996 est) **Population growth rate:** 1.9%
(1990–95); 1.5% (2000–05) **Population density:** (per sq km) 56
(1996 est) **Urban population:** (% of total) 57 (1995) **Age
distribution:** (% of total population) <15 34.9%, 15–65 60.7%, >65
4.4% (1995) **Ethnic groups:** about 10% of the population is Arab;
the remainder are of Berber-Arab descent. There are small Jewish
and French communities **Language:** Arabic (official); French
Religion: Sunni Muslim; Jewish, Christian **Education:**
(compulsory years) 9 **Literacy rate:** 74% (men); 56% (women)
(1995 est) **Labour force:** 21.6% agriculture, 34.4% industry, 44%
services (1994) **Unemployment:** 15% (1995 est) **Life expectancy:**
68 (men); 71 (women) (1995–2000) **Child mortality rate:** (under
5, per 1,000 live births) 49 (1996) **Physicians:** 1 per 1,549 people
(1993 est)

Practical information

Visa requirements: UK: visa not required. USA: visa not required
Embassy in the UK: 29 Prince's Gate, London SW7 1QG. Tel:
(0171) 584 8117; fax: (0171) 225 2884 **British embassy:** 5 place de
la Victoire, Tunis. Tel: (1) 341 444; fax: (1) 354 877 **Chamber of
commerce:** Chambre de Commerce et d'Industrie de Tunis, 1 rue
des Entrepreneurs, 1000 Tunis. Tel: (1) 242 872; fax: (1) 354 744
Airports: international airports: Tunis (Carthage), Monastir
(Skanes), Djerba (Melita), Sfax, Tozeur (Nefta), Tabarka; domestic
services operate between these; total passenger km: 1,977 million
(1994) **Major holidays:** 1, 18 January, 20 March, 9 April, 1 May,
1–2 June, 25 July, 3, 13 August, 3 September, 15 October; variable:
Eid-ul-Adha (2 days), end of Ramadan (2 days), New Year
(Muslim), Prophet's Birthday

Chronology

814 BC: Phoenician emigrants from Tyre, in Lebanon, founded
Carthage, near modern Tunis, as a trading post. By 6th century BC

Carthaginian kingdom dominated western Mediterranean. **146 BC:** Carthage destroyed by Punic Wars with Rome, which began 264 BC; Carthage became part of Rome's African province. **AD 533:** Came under control of Byzantine Empire. **7th century:** Invaded by Arabs, who introduced Islam. Succession of Islamic dynasties followed, including Aghlabids (9th century), Fatimids (10th century), and Almohads (12th century). **1574:** Became part of Islamic Turkish Ottoman Empire and a base for 'Barbary Pirates' who operated against European shipping until 19th century. **1705:** Husayn Bey founded local dynasty, which held power under rule of Ottomans. **early 19th century:** Ahmad Bey launched programme of economic modernization, which was to nearly bankrupt the country. **1881:** Became French protectorate, with bey retaining local power. **1920:** Destour (Constitution) Party, named after original Tunisian constitution of 1861, founded to campaign for equal Tunisian participation in French-dominated government. **1934:** Habib Bourguiba founded radical splinter party, the Neo-Destour Party, to spearhead nationalist movement. **1942–43:** Brief German occupation during World War II. **1956:** Independence achieved as monarchy under bey, with Bourguiba as prime minister. **1957:** Bey deposed; Tunisia became one-party republic with Bourguiba as president. **1975:** Bourguiba made president for life. **1979:** Headquarters for Arab League moved to Tunis after Egypt signed Camp David Accords with Israel. **1981:** Multiparty elections held, as a sign of political liberalization, but were won by Bourguiba's Destourian Socialist Party (DSP). **1982:** Allowed Palestine Liberation Organization (PLO) to use Tunis for its headquarters. **1985:** Diplomatic relations with Libya severed; Israel attacked PLO headquarters. **1987:** Zine el-Abidine Ben Ali, new prime minister, declared Bourguiba (now aged 84) incompetent for government and seized power as president. **1988:** 2,000 political prisoners freed; privatization initiative. Diplomatic relations with Libya restored. DSP renamed RCD. **1990:** Arab League's headquarters returned to Cairo, Egypt. **1991:** Opposition to US actions during Gulf War. Crackdown on religious fundamentalists; Renaissance Party banned. **1992:** Western criticism of human-rights transgressions. **1994:** Ben Ali and RCD re-elected. PLO transferred headquarters to Gaza City in Palestine.

Turkey Republic of

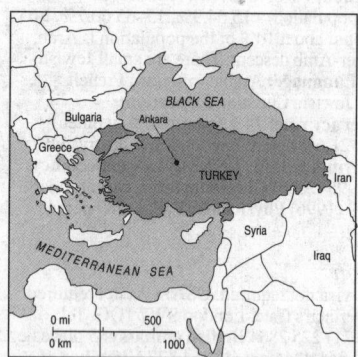

National name: *Türkiye Cumhuriyeti* **Area:** 779,500 sq km/300,964 sq mi **Capital:** Ankara **Major towns/cities:** Istanbul, Izmir, Adana, Bursa, Antakya, Gaziantep, Konya, Mersin, Kayseri, Edirne, Antalya **Major ports:** Istanbul and Izmir **Physical features:** central plateau surrounded by mountains, partly in Europe (Thrace) and partly in Asia (Anatolia); Bosporus and Dardanelles; Mount Ararat (highest peak Great Ararat, 5,137 m/16,854 ft); Taurus Mountains in SW (highest peak Kaldi Dag, 3,734 m/12,255 ft); sources of rivers Euphrates and Tigris in E

Government

Head of state: Suleiman Demirel from 1993 **Head of government:** Mesut Yilmaz from 1997 **Political system:** democracy **Administrative divisions:** 73 provinces **Political parties:** Motherland Party (ANAP), Islamic, nationalist, right of centre; Republican People's Party (CHP), centre left; True Path Party (DYP), centre right, pro-Western; Welfare Party (Refah), Islamic

fundamentalist **Armed forces:** 525,000 (1996) **Conscription:** 18 months **Death penalty:** retained for ordinary crimes, but considered abolitionist in practice; last execution 1984 **Defence spend:** (% GDP) 3.9 (1996) **Education spend:** (% GNP) 2.9 (1994) **Health spend:** (% GDP) 1.4 (1993)

Economy and resources

Currency: Turkish lira **GDP:** ($ US) 182.6 billion (1996) **Real GDP per capita (PPP):** ($ US) 6,103 (1996) **GDP growth rate:** 7.4% (1996); 3.2% (1990–95) **Average annual inflation:** 85.2% (1996); 64.6% (1985–95) **Foreign debt:** ($ US) 76.4 billion (1996) **Major trading partners:** Germany, USA, Italy, France, Saudi Arabia, UK **Resources:** chromium, copper, mercury, antimony, borax, coal, petroleum, natural gas, iron ore, salt **Industries:** textiles, food processing, petroleum refining, coal, iron and steel, industrial chemicals, tourism **Exports:** textiles and clothing, agricultural products and foodstuffs (including figs, nuts, and dried fruit), tobacco, leather, glass, refined petroleum and petroleum products. Principal market: Germany 23.3% (1995) **Imports:** machinery, construction material, motor vehicles, consumer goods, crude petroleum, iron and steel, chemical products, fertilizer, livestock. Principal source: Germany 15.5% (1995) **Arable land:** 32% (1995) **Agricultural products:** barley, wheat, maize, sunflower and other oilseeds, sugar beet, potatoes, tea (world's fifth-largest producer), olives, fruits, tobacco

Population and society

Population: 61,797,000 (1996 est) **Population growth rate:** 2% (1990–95); 1.5% (2000–05) **Population density:** (per sq km) 79 (1996 est) **Urban population:** (% of total) 69 (1995) **Age distribution:** (% of total population) <15 33.9%, 15–65 61.1%, >65 5% (1995) **Ethnic groups:** over 90% of the population are Turks, although only about 5% are of Turkic or Western Mongoloid descent; most are descended from earlier conquerors, such as the Greeks **Language:** Turkish (official); Kurdish, Arabic **Religion:** Sunni Muslim; Orthodox, Armenian churches **Education:** (compulsory years) 5 **Literacy rate:** 90% (men); 71% (women) (1995 est) **Labour force:** 36.3% of population: 44.9% agriculture, 22% industry, 33.1% services (1996) **Unemployment:** 6.9% (1996) **Life expectancy:** 67 (men); 71 (women) (1995–2000) **Child mortality rate:** (under 5, per 1,000 live births) 65 (1996) **Physicians:** 1 per 909 people (1994)

Practical information

Visa requirements: UK: visa not required for a stay of up to three months. USA: visa not required for a stay of up to three months **Embassy in the UK:** 43 Belgrave Square, London SW1X 8PA. Tel: (0171) 393 0202; fax: (0171) 393 0066 **British embassy:** Senit Ersan Caddesi 46/A, Cankaya, Ankara. Tel: (312) 468 6230; fax: (312) 468 3214 **Chamber of commerce:** Union of Chambers of Commerce, Industry, Maritime Commerce and Commodity Exchanges of Turkey, Atatürk Bul 149, Bakanhliklar, 06640, Ankara. Tel: (312) 417 7700; fax: (312) 418 3568 **Airports:** international airports: Ankara (Esenboga), Istanbul (Atatürk), Izmir (Adnan Menderes), Adana, Trabzon, Dalaman, Antalya; 15 domestic airports; total passenger km: 8,576 million (1994) **Major holidays:** 1 January, 23 April, 19 May, 30 August, 29 October; variable: Eid-ul-Adha (4 days), end of Ramadan (3 days)

Chronology

1st century BC: Asia Minor became part of Roman Empire, later passing to Byzantine Empire. **6th century AD:** Turkic peoples spread from Mongolia into Turkestan, where they adopted Islam. **1055:** Seljuk Turks captured Baghdad; their leader Tughrul took title of sultan. **1071:** Battle of Manzikert: Seljuk Turks defeated Byzantines and conquered Asia Minor. **13th century:** Ottoman Turks, driven west by Mongols, became vassals of Seljuk Turks. **c. 1299:** Osman I founded small Ottoman kingdom, which quickly displaced Seljuks to include all Asia Minor. **1354:** Ottoman Turks captured Gallipoli and began their conquests in Europe. **1389:** Battle of Kossovo: Turks defeated Serbs to take control of most of Balkan peninsula. **1453:** Constantinople, capital of Byzantine Empire, fell to the Turks; became capital of Ottoman Empire as

Istanbul. **16th century:** Ottoman Empire reached its zenith under Suleiman the Magnificent 1520–66; Turks conquered Egypt, Syria, Arabia, Mesopotamia, Tripoli, Cyprus, and most of Hungary. **1683:** Failure of Siege of Vienna marked start of decline of Ottoman Empire. **1699:** Treaty of Karlowitz: Turks forced out of Hungary by Austrians. **1774:** Treaty of Kuchuk Kainarji: Russia drove Turks from Crimea and won the right to intervene on behalf of Christian subjects of the sultan. **19th century:** 'The Eastern Question': Ottoman weakness caused intense rivalry between great Powers to shape future of Near East. **1821–29:** Greek war of independence: Greeks defeated Turks with help of Russia, Britain, and France. **1854–56:** Crimean War: Britain and France fought to defend Ottoman Empire from further pressure by Russians. **1877–78:** Russo-Turkish War ended with Treaty of Berlin and withdrawal of Turks from Bulgaria. **1908:** Young Turk revolution forced sultan to grant constitution; start of political modernization. **1911–12:** Italo-Turkish War: Turkey lost Tripoli (Libya). **1912–13:** Balkan War: Greece, Serbia, and Bulgaria expelled Turks from Macedonia and Albania. **1914:** Ottoman Empire entered World War I on German side. **1919:** Following Turkish defeat, Mustapha Kemal launched nationalist revolt to resist foreign encroachments. **1920:** Treaty of Sèvres partitioned Ottoman Empire, leaving no part of Turkey fully independent. **1922:** Kemal, having defied Allies, expelled Greeks, French, and Italians from Asia Minor; sultanate abolished. **1923:** Treaty of Lausanne recognized Turkish independence; secular republic established by Kemal, who imposed rapid Westernization. **1935:** Kemal adopted surname Atatürk ('Father of the Turks'). **1938:** Death of Kemal Atatürk; succeeded as president by Ismet Inönü. **1950:** First free elections won by opposition Democratic Party; Adnan Menderes became prime minister. **1952:** Turkey became a member of NATO. **1960:** Military coup led by Gen Cemal Gürsel deposed Menderes, who was executed 1961. **1961:** Inönü returned as prime minister; politics dominated by the issue of Cyprus. **1965:** Justice Party came to power under Suleyman Demirel. **1971–73:** Prompted by strikes and student unrest, army imposed military rule. **1974:** Turkey invaded northern Cyprus. **1980–83:** Political violence led to further military rule. **1984:** Kurds began guerrilla war in quest for greater autonomy. **1989:** Application to join European Community rejected. **1990–91:** Turkey joined UN coalition against Iraq in Gulf War. **1995:** Turkish offensives against Kurdish bases in N Iraq; Islamicist Welfare Party won largest number of seats in general election. **1997:** Plans agreed for curbing of Muslim fundamentalism. Mesut Yilmaz appointed prime minister. Agreement with Greece on peaceful resolution of disputes.

Turkmenistan Republic of

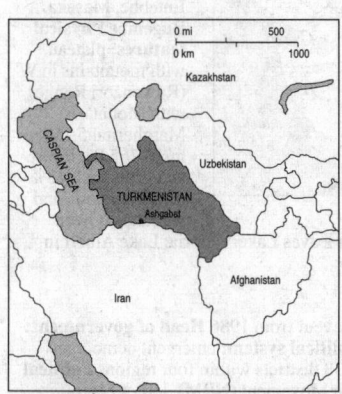

Area: 488,100 sq km/188,455 sq mi
Capital: Ashgabat
Major towns/cities: Chardzhov, Mary (Merv), Nebit-Dag, Krasnovodsk **Major ports:** Turkmenbashi
Physical: about 90% of land is desert including the Kara Kum 'Black Sands' desert (area 310,800 sq km/120,000 sq mi)

Government
Head of state and government: Saparmurad Niyazov from 1991 **Political system:** authoritarian nationalist **Administrative divisions:** five regions **Political parties:** Democratic Party of Turkmenistan, ex-communist, pro-Niyazov; Turkmen Popular Front (Agzybirlik), nationalist **Armed forces:**

18,000 (1996) **Conscription:** military service is compulsory for 18 months **Death penalty:** retained and used for ordinary crimes **Defence spend:** (% GDP) 2.8 (1994) **Education spend:** (% GNP) 7.9 (1993/94) **Health spend:** (% GDP) 2.8 (1990–95)

Economy and resources
Currency: manat **GDP:** ($ US) 5 billion (1994) **Real GDP per capita (PPP):** ($ US) 3,469 (1994) **GDP growth rate:** –3% (1996); –10.6% (1990–95) **Average annual inflation:** 992% (1996); 381.4% (1985–95) **Foreign debt:** ($ US) 418 million (1994) **Major trading partners:** Germany, Ukraine, Russia, Armenia, Azerbaijan, Turkey, Switzerland, Italy **Resources:** petroleum, natural gas, coal, sulphur, magnesium, iodine-bromine, sodium sulphate and different types of salt **Industries:** mining, petroleum refining, energy generation, textiles, chemicals, cement, mineral fertilizer, footwear **Exports:** natural gas, cotton yarn, electric energy, petroleum and petroleum products. Principal market: Germany 11.4% (1995) **Imports:** machinery and metalwork, light industrial products, processed food, agricultural products. Principal source: Germany 25.4% (1995) **Arable land:** 3% (1995)

Population and society
Population: 4,155,000 (1996 est) **Population growth rate:** 2.3% (1990–95); 1.9% (2000–05) **Population density:** (per sq km) 9 (1996 est) **Urban population:** (% of total) 45 (1995) **Age distribution:** (% of total population) <15 39.5%, 15–65 56.4%, >65 4.2% (1995) **Ethnic groups:** 72% ethnic Turkmen, 10% ethnic Russian, 9% Uzbek, 3% Kazakh, 1% Ukrainian **Language:** West Turkic, closely related to Turkish **Religion:** Sunni Muslim **Education:** (compulsory years) 9 **Literacy rate:** 98% (1995 est) **Labour force:** 43.4% agriculture, 20.8% industry, 35.8% services (1993) **Unemployment:** 2.5% (1992 est) **Life expectancy:** 64 (men); 70 (women) (1995–2000) **Child mortality rate:** (under 5, per 1,000 live births) 66 (1996) **Physicians:** 1 per 311 people (1994)

Practical information
Visa requirements: UK: visa required. USA: visa required **Embassy in the UK:** Turkmenistan has no diplomatic representation in the UK; the Department of Trade and Industry has a desk which deals with enquiries relating to Turkmenistan. Tel: (0171) 215 8427; fax: (0171) 215 4817 **British embassy:** the UK has no diplomatic representation in Turkmenistan **Chamber of commerce:** Commission for International Economic Affairs of the Office of the President of Turkmenistan, Ulitsa Kemine 92, Ashgabat 744000. Tel: (3632) 298 770; fax: (3632) 297 524 **Airports:** international airports: Ashgabat; three domestic airports; total passenger km: 1,562 million (1994) **Major holidays:** 1, 12 January, 19, 22 February, 8 March, 29 April, 9, 18 May, 27–28 October

Chronology
6th century BC: Part of Persian Empire of Cyrus the Great. **4th century BC:** Part of empire of Alexander the Great of Macedonia. **7th century:** Spread of Islam into Transcaspian region, followed by Arab rule from 8th century. **10th–13th centuries:** Immigration from NE by nomadic Oghuz Seljuk and Mongol tribes, whose Turkic-speaking descendants now dominate the country; conquest by Genghis Khan. **16th century:** Came under dominance of Persia, to the S. **1869–81:** Fell under control of tsarist Russia after 150,000 Turkmen were killed in Battle of Gok Tepe 1881; became part of Russia's Turkestan Governor-Generalship. **1916:** Turkmen revolted violently against Russian rule; autonomous Transcaspian government formed after Russian Revolution of 1917. **1919:** Brought back under Russian control following invasion by the Soviet Red Army. **1921:** Part of Turkestan Soviet Socialist Autonomous Republic. **1925:** Became constituent republic of USSR. **1920s–30s:** Soviet programme of agricultural collectivization and secularization provoked sporadic guerrilla resistance and popular uprisings. **1960–67:** Lenin Kara-Kum Canal built, leading to dramatic expansion in cotton production in previously semidesert region. **1985:** Saparmurad Niyazov replaced Muhammad Gapusov, local communist leader since 1971, whose regime had been viewed as corrupt. **1989:** Stimulated by *glasnost*

initiative of reformist Soviet leader Mikhail Gorbachev, Agzybirlik 'popular front' formed by Turkmen intellectuals. **1990:** Economic and political sovereignty declared. Niyazov elected state president. **1991:** Niyazov initially supported attempted anti-Gorbachev coup in Moscow. Independence was later declared; joined new Commonwealth of Independent States (CIS). **1992:** Joined Muslim Economic Cooperation Organization and United Nations; new constitution adopted. **1993:** New currency, manat, introduced and programme of cautious economic reform introduced, with foreign investment in country's huge oil and gas reserves encouraged; but economy contracted to 1995. **1994:** Nationwide referendum overwhelmingly backed Niyazov's presidency. Ex-communists won most seats in parliamentary elections. **1997:** Private land ownership legalized.

Tuvalu South West Pacific State of (formerly Ellice Islands)

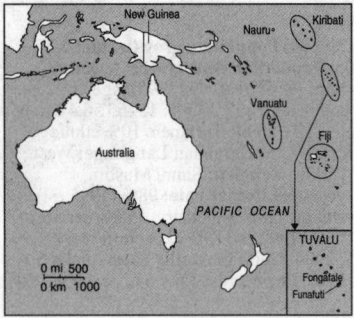

Area: 25 sq km/9.6 sq mi **Capital:** Fongafale (on Funafuti atoll) **Major towns/cities:** Vaitupu, Niutao, Nanumea **Physical features:** nine low coral atolls forming a chain of 579 km/650 mi in the SW Pacific

Government

Head of state: Queen Elizabeth II from 1978, represented by governor general Tulaga Manuella from 1994 **Head of government:** Bikenibeu Paeniu from 1996 **Political system:** liberal democracy **Administrative divisions:** one town council and seven island councils **Political parties:** none; members are elected to parliament as independents **Armed forces:** no standing defence force **Death penalty:** laws do not provide for the death penalty for any crime

Economy and resources

Currency: Australian dollar **GDP:** ($ US) 8 million (1995 est) **Real GDP per capita (PPP):** ($ US) 800 (1995 est) **GDP growth rate:** N/A **Average annual inflation:** 3.9 (1985–93) **Foreign debt:** ($ US) 6 million (1993) **Major trading partners:** Australia, Fiji, New Zealand, UK **Industries:** processing of agricultural products (principally coconuts), soap, handicrafts, tourism; a large source of income is from Tuvaluans working abroad, especially in the phosphate industry on Nauru **Exports:** copra. Principal market: Australia **Imports:** food and live animals, beverages, tobacco, consumer goods, machinery and transport equipment, mineral fuels. Principal source: Australia **Agricultural products:** coconuts, pulaka, taro, papayas, screw-pine (pandanus), bananas; livestock rearing (pigs, poultry, and goats); honey production and fishing supplement basic subsistence; fishing is largely unexploited, although Japan, Taiwan, and South Korea have been granted licences to fish since the late 1980s

Population and society

Population: 10,000 (1996 est) **Population growth rate:** 1.4% (1990–95) **Population density:** (per sq km) 372 (1996 est) **Urban population:** (% of total) 46.2 (1995) **Ethnic groups:** almost entirely of Polynesian origin, maintaining close ties with Samoans and Tokelauans to the S and E **Language:** Tuvaluan, English **Religion:** Christian (mainly Protestant) **Education:** (compulsory years) 9 **Literacy rate:** N/A **Life expectancy:** 63 (men); 65 (women) (1995) **Child mortality rate:** (per 1,000 live births) 28 (1994) **Physicians:** 1 per 2,743 people (1990)

Practical information

Visa requirements: UK: visa not required. USA: visa required **Embassy for the UK:** Honorary Consulate General of Tuvalu, Klövensteenweg 115A, 22559 Hamburg, Germany. Tel: (40) 810 580; fax: (40) 811 016 **British embassy:** the British Embassy in Suva (see Fiji) deals with enquiries relating to Tuvalu **Chamber of commerce:** Development Bank of Tuvalu, PO Box 9, Vaiaku, Funafuti. Tel: (688) 20198; telex: 4800 **Airports:** international airport: Funafuti; no internal air service **Major holidays:** 1 January, 4 March, 15 June, 5 August, 1–2 October, 14 November, 25–26 December; variable: Good Friday, Easter Monday

Chronology

c. 300 BC: First settled by Polynesian peoples. **16th century:** Invaded and occupied by Samoans. **1765:** Islands first reached by Europeans. **1850–75:** Population decimated by European slave traders capturing Tuvaluans to work in South America and by exposure to European diseases. **1856:** The four southern islands, including Funafuti, claimed by USA. **1865:** Christian mission established. **1877:** Came under control of British Western Pacific High Commission (WPHC), with its headquarters in Fiji. **1892:** Known as the Ellice Islands, they were joined with Gilbert Islands (now Kiribati) to form British protectorate. **1916:** Gilbert and Ellice Islands colony formed. **1942–43:** Became base for US airforce operations when Japan occupied Gilbert Islands during World War II. **1975:** Following referendum, the predominantly Melanesian-peopled Ellice Islands, fearing domination by Micronesian-peopled Gilbert Islands in an independent state, were granted separate status. **1978:** Independence achieved within Commonwealth, with Toaripi Lauti as prime minister; reverted to former name Tuvalu ('eight standing together'). **1979:** The USA signed friendship treaty, relinquishing its claim to the four southern atolls in return for continued access to military bases. **1981:** Dr Tomasi Puapua became premier after Louti implicated in alleged investment scandal. **1986:** Islanders rejected proposal for republican status. **1989:** Bikenibeu Paeniu became prime minister. **1993:** Kamuta Laatasi became prime minister. **1995:** Union flag removed from national flag, presaging move towards republican status. **1996:** Bikenibeu Paeniu appointed prime minister.

Uganda Republic of

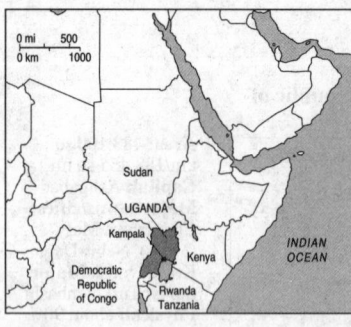

Area: 236,600 sq km/91,351 sq mi **Capital:** Kampala **Major towns/cities:** Jinja, Mbale, Entebbe, Masaka, Bugembe **Physical features:** plateau with mountains in W (Ruwenzori Range, with Mount Margherita, 5,110 m/16,765 ft); forest and grassland; 18% is lakes, rivers, and wetlands (Owen Falls on White Nile where it leaves Lake Victoria; Lake Albert in W); arid in NE

Government

Head of state: Yoweri Museveni from 1986 **Head of government:** Kinti Musoke from 1994 **Political system:** emergent democracy **Administrative divisions:** 38 districts within four regions **Political parties:** National Resistance Movement (NRM), left of centre; Democratic Party (DP), centre left; Conservative Party (CP), centre right; Uganda People's Congress (UPC), left of centre; Uganda Freedom Movement (UFM), left of centre. From 1986, political parties were forced to suspend activities **Armed forces:** 50,000 (1996) **Conscription:** military service is voluntary **Death penalty:**

retained and used for ordinary crimes **Defence spend:** (% GDP) 2.4 (1996) **Education spend:** (% GNP) 1.9 (1993/94) **Health spend:** (% GDP) 1.8 (1990–95)

Economy and resources
Currency: Uganda new shilling **GDP:** ($ US) 4 billion (1994) **Real GDP per capita (PPP):** ($ US) 1,370 (1994) **GDP growth rate:** 8.5% (1995); 6.6% (1990–95) **Average annual inflation:** 8% (1996); 65.5% (1985–95 est) **Foreign debt:** ($ US) 3.5 billion (1995) **Major trading partners:** Kenya, Spain, UK, Germany, the Netherlands, USA, France **Resources:** copper, apatite, limestone; believed to possess the world's second-largest deposit of gold (hitherto unexploited); also reserves of magnetite, tin, tungsten, beryllium, bismuth, asbestos, graphite **Industries:** processing of agricultural products, brewing, vehicle assembly, textiles, cement, soap, fertilizers, footwear, metal products, paints, batteries, matches **Exports:** coffee, cotton, tea, tobacco, oil seeds and oleaginous fruit; hides and skins, textiles. Principal market: Spain 22.8% (1995) **Imports:** machinery and transport equipment, basic manufactures, petroleum and petroleum products, chemicals, miscellaneous manufactured articles, iron and steel. Principal source: Kenya 26.2% (1995) **Arable land:** 28.3% (1995) **Agricultural products:** coffee, cotton, tea, maize, tobacco, sugar cane, cocoa, horticulture, plantains, cassava, sweet potatoes, millet, sorghum, beans, groundnuts, rice; livestock rearing (cattle, goats, sheep, and poultry); freshwater fishing

Population and society
Population: 20,256,000 (1996 est) **Population growth rate:** 3.4% (1990–95); 2.7% (2000–05) **Population density:** (per sq km) 86 (1996 est) **Urban population:** (% of total) 13 (1995) **Age distribution:** (% of total population) <15 48.8%, 15–65 48.8%, >65 2.4% (1995) **Ethnic groups:** about 40 different peoples concentrated into four main groups; the Bantu (the most numerous), Eastern Nilotic, Western Nilotic, and Central Sudanic; there are also Rwandan, Sudanese, Zairean, and Kenyan minorities **Language:** English (official), Kiswahili, Bantu and Nilotic languages **Religion:** Christian 50%, animist 40%, Muslim 10% **Education:** not compulsory **Literacy rate:** 62% (men); 45% (women) (1995 est) **Labour force:** 51% of population; 85% agriculture, 5% industry, 11% services (1990) **Life expectancy:** 42 (men); 44 (women) (1995–2000) **Child mortality rate:** (under 5, per 1,000 live births) 172 (1996) **Physicians:** 1 per 22,399 people (1993 est)

Practical information
Visa requirements: UK: visa not required. USA: visa not required **Embassy in the UK:** Uganda House, 58–59 Trafalgar Square, London WC2N 5DX. Tel: (0171) 839 5783; fax: (0171) 839 8925 **British embassy:** British High Commission, PO Box 7070, 101–12 Parliament Avenue, Kampala. Tel: (41) 257 301/4; telex: 61202 (a/b UKREP KAMPALA) **Chamber of commerce:** Uganda Investment Authority, PO Box 7418, Investment Center, Kampala Road, Kampala. Tel: (41) 234 105; fax: (41) 242 903 **Airports:** international airports: Entebbe; domestic services operate to all major towns; total passenger km: 52 million (1994) **Major holidays:** 1 January, 1 April, 1 May, 9 October, 25–26 December; variable: Good Friday, Easter Monday, Holy Saturday, end of Ramadan

Chronology
16th century: Bunyoro kingdom founded by immigrants from SE Sudan. **17th century:** Rise of kingdom of Buganda people, which became particularly powerful from 17th century. **mid-19th century:** Arabs, trading ivory and slaves, reached Uganda; first visits by European explorers and Christian missionaries. **1885–87:** Uganda Martyrs: Christians persecuted by Buganda ruler, Mwanga. **1890:** Royal Charter granted to British East African Company, a trading company whose agent, Frederick Lugard, concluded treaties with local rulers, including the Buganda and the western states of Ankole and Toro. **1894:** British protectorate established, with Buganda retaining some autonomy under its traditional prince (Kabaka) and other resistance being crushed. **1904:** Cotton growing introduced by Buganda peasants. **1958:** Internal self-government granted. **1962:**

Independence achieved from Britain, within Commonwealth, with Milton Obote of Uganda People's Congress (UPC) as prime minister. **1963:** Proclaimed federal republic with King Mutesa II (of Buganda) as president and Obote as prime minister. **1966:** King Mutesa, who opposed creation of one-party state, ousted in coup led by Obote, who ended federal status and became executive president. **1969:** All opposition parties banned after assassination attempt on Obote; key enterprises nationalized. **1971:** Obote overthrown in army coup led by Maj-Gen Idi Amin Dada; constitution suspended and ruthlessly dictatorial regime established; nearly 49,000 Ugandan Asians expelled; over 300,000 opponents of regime killed. **1976:** Relations with Kenya strained by Amin's claims to parts of Kenya. **1979:** After annexing part of Tanzania, Amin forced to leave country by opponents backed by Tanzanian troops. Provisional government set up with Yusuf Lule as initial president and then Godfrey Binaisa. **1978–79:** Fighting broke out against Tanzanian troops. **1980:** Binaisa overthrown by army. Elections held and Milton Obote returned to power. **1985:** After opposition by pro-Lule National Resistance Army (NRA), and indiscipline in army, Obote ousted by Gen Tito Okello; constitution suspended; power-sharing agreement entered into with NRA leader Yoweri Museveni. **1986:** Museveni became president, heading broad-based coalition government. **1993:** King of Buganda reinstated as formal monarch, in the person of Ronald Muwenda Mutebi II. **1996:** Landslide victory won by Museveni in first direct presidential elections. **1997:** Allied Democratic Forces (ADF) led uprisings by rebels.

Ukraine

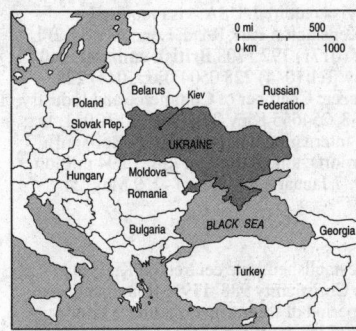

Area: 603,700 sq km/233,088 sq mi **Capital:** Kiev **Major towns/cities:** Kharkov, Donetsk, Dnepropetrovsk, Lugansk (Voroshilovgrad), Lviv (Lvov), Mariupol (Zhdanov), Krivoy Rog, Zaporozhye, Odessa **Physical features:** Russian plain; Carpathian and Crimean Mountains; rivers: Dnieper (with the Dnieper dam 1932), Donetz, Bug

Government
Head of state: Leonid Kuchma from 1994 **Head of government:** Valery Pustovoitenko from 1997 **Political system:** emergent democracy **Administrative divisions:** 24 provinces and one semi-autonomous region (Crimea) **Political parties:** Ukrainian Communist Party (UCP), left wing, anti-nationalist (banned 1991–93); Peasants' Party of the Ukraine (PPU), conservative agrarian; Ukrainian Socialist Party (SPU), left wing, anti-nationalist; Ukrainian People's Movement (Rukh), Ukrainian Republican Party (URP), Congress of Ukrainian Nationalists (CUN), and Democratic Party of Ukraine (DPU) – all moderate nationalist; Social Democratic Party of Ukraine (SDPU), federalist **Armed forces:** 400,800 (1996) **Conscription:** 18 months (males over 18) **Death penalty:** moratorium placed on executions since 1991 as condition for application to join Council of Europe (joined 1995). Despite continued demands by Council to uphold moratorium, executions have continued **Defence spend:** (% GDP) 3 (1996) **Education spend:** (% GNP) 6.8 (1994) **Health spend:** (% GDP) 5.4 (1990–95)

Economy and resources
Currency: hryvna **GDP:** ($ US) 91 billion (1994) **Real GDP per capita (PPP):** ($ US) 2,718 (1994) **GDP growth rate:** –10% (1996); –14.3% (1990–95) **Average annual inflation:** 80% (1996);

362.5% (1985–95 est) **Foreign debt:** ($ US) 8.4 billion (1995)
Major trading partners: Russia, Belarus, China, Moldova,
Turkmenistan, USA, Switzerland, Germany **Resources:** coal, iron
ore (world's fifth-largest producer), crude oil, natural gas, salt,
chemicals, brown coal, alabaster, gypsum **Industries:** metallurgy,
mechanical engineering, chemicals, machinery products **Exports:**
grain, coal, oil, various minerals. Principal market: Russia 38.7%
(1996) **Imports:** mineral fuels, machine-building components,
chemicals and chemical products. Principal source: Russia 48%
(1996) **Arable land:** 55.2% (1993) **Agricultural products:** wheat,
buckwheat, sugar beet, potatoes, fruit and vegetables, sunflowers,
cotton, flax, tobacco, hops; animal husbandry accounts for more
than 50% of agricultural activity

Population and society
Population: 51,608,000 (1996 est) **Population growth rate:** –0.1%
(1990–95); –0.2% (1993–2000) **Population density:** (per sq km) 85
(1996 est) **Urban population:** (% of total) 70 (1995) **Age
distribution:** (% of total population) <15 20.1%, 15–65 65.9%, >65
14% (1995) **Ethnic groups:** 73% of the population is of Ukrainian
descent; 22% ethnic Russian; 1% Jewish; 1% Belarussian
Language: Ukrainian (a Slavonic language) **Religion:** traditionally
Ukrainian Orthodox; also Ukrainian Catholic **Education:**
(compulsory years) 8 (7–15 age limit) **Literacy rate:** 99% (men);
99% (women) (1995 est) **Labour force:** 50% of population: 20%
agriculture, 40% industry, 40% services (1990) **Unemployment:**
0.6% (1995) **Life expectancy:** 64 (men); 74 (women) (1995–2000)
Child mortality rate: (under 5, per 1,000 live births) 21 (1996)
Physicians: 1 per 226 people (1994)

Practical information
Visa requirements: UK: visa required. USA: visa required
Embassy in the UK: 78 Kensington Park Road, London W11 2PL.
Tel: (0171) 727 6312; fax: (0171) 792 1708 **British embassy:** vul
Desyatinna 9, 252025 Kiev. Tel: (044) 228 0504; fax: (044) 228
3972 **Chamber of commerce:** Chamber of Commerce and Industry,
vul Velyka Zhytomyrska 33, 254655 Kiev. Tel: (044) 212 2911; fax:
(044) 212 3353 **Airports:** international airports: Kiev (Borispol);
four principal domestic airports; total passenger km: 1,294 million
(1994) **Major holidays:** 1, 7 January, 8 March, 1–2, 9 May, 24
August

Chronology
9th century: Rus' people established state centred on Kiev and
adopted Eastern Orthodox Christianity 988. **1199:** Reunification of
southern Rus' lands, after period of fragmentation, under Prince
Daniel of Galicia-Volhynia. **13th century:** Mongol-Tatar Golden
Horde sacked Kiev and destroyed Rus' state. **14th century:** Poland
annexed Galicia; Lithuania absorbed Volhynia and expelled Tatars;
Ukraine peasants became serfs of Polish and Lithuanian nobles.
1569: Poland and Lithuania formed single state; clergy of Ukraine
formed Uniate Church, which recognized papal authority but
retained Orthodox rites, to avoid Catholic persecution. **16th and
17th centuries:** Runaway serfs known as Cossacks ('outlaws')
formed autonomous community in eastern borderlands. **1648:**
Cossack revolt led by Gen Bogdan Khmelnitsky drove out Poles
from central Ukraine; Khmelnitsky accepted Russian protectorate
1654. **1660–90:** 'Epoch of Ruins': Ukraine devastated by civil war
and invasions by Russians, Poles, and Turks; Poland regained W
Ukraine. **1687:** Gen Ivan Mazepa entered into alliance with Sweden
in effort to regain Cossack autonomy from Russia. **1709:** Battle of
Poltava: Russian victory over Swedes ended hopes of Cossack
independence. **1772–95:** Partition of Poland: Austria annexed
Galicia, Russian annexations included Volhynia. **1846–47:** Attempt
to promote Ukrainian national culture through formation of Cyril
and Methodius Society. **1899:** Revolutionary Ukrainian Party
founded. **1917:** Revolutionary parliament (Rada), proclaimed
Ukrainian autonomy within a federal Russia. **1918:** Ukraine
declared full independence; civil war ensued between Rada (backed
by Germans) and Reds (backed by Russian Bolsheviks). **1919:**
Galicia united with Ukraine; conflict escalated between Ukrainian
nationalists, Bolsheviks, anarchists, White Russians, and Poles.

1921: Treaty of Riga: Russia and Poland partitioned Ukraine.
1921–22: Several million people perished in famine. **1922:**
Ukrainian Soviet Socialist Republic (Ukrainian SSR) became part
of Union of Soviet Socialist Republics (USSR). **1932–33:** Enforced
collectivization of agriculture caused another catastrophic famine
with more than 7.5 million deaths. **1939:** USSR annexed E Poland
and added Galicia-Volhynia to Ukrainian SSR. **1940:** USSR seized
N Bukhovina from Romania and added it to Ukrainian SSR.
1941–44: Germany occupied Ukraine; many Ukrainians
collaborated; millions of Ukrainians and Ukrainian Jews enslaved
and exterminated by Nazis. **1945:** USSR annexed Ruthenia from
Czechoslovakia and added it to Ukrainian SSR, which became a
nominal member of United Nations (UN). **1946:** Uniate Church
forcibly merged with Russian Orthodox Church. **1954:** Crimea
transferred from Russian Federation to Ukrainian SSR. **1986:** Major
environmental disaster caused by explosion of nuclear reactor at
Chernobyl, N of Kiev. **1989:** Rukh (nationalist movement)
established as political party; ban on Uniate Church lifted. **1990:**
Ukraine declared sovereignty under President Leonid Kravchuk,
leader of the CP. **1991:** Ukraine declared independence from USSR;
President Kravchuk left CP; Ukraine joined newly formed
Commonwealth of Independent States (CIS). **1992:** Crimean
sovereignty declared but then rescinded. **1994:** Election gains for
radical nationalists in W Ukraine and Russian unionists in E
Ukraine; Leonid Kuchma succeeded Kravchuk as president. **1996:**
New constitution replaced Soviet system, making presidency
stronger; remaining nuclear warheads returned to Russia for
destruction; new currency introduced. **1997:** New government
appointments made to speed economic reform. Treaty of friendship
with Russia signed, solving issue of Russian Black Sea fleet. Prime
Minister Lazarenko replaced by Valery Pustovoitenko. Loan of $750
million from International Monetary Fund (IMF) approved.
Disagreements between president and Supreme Council.

United Arab Emirates (UAE) federation of the
emirates of Abu Dhabi, Ajman, Dubai, Fujairah, Ras al Khaimah,
Sharjah, Umm al Qaiwain

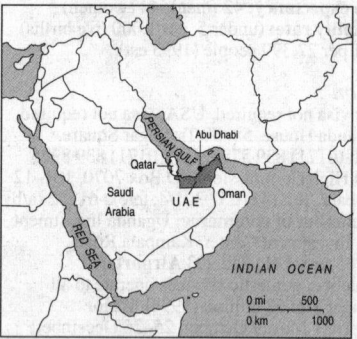

National name:
*Ittihad al-Imarat al-
Arabiyah* **Area:**
83,657 sq
km/32,299 sq mi
Capital: Abu Dhabi
Major towns/cities:
Dubai, Sharjah, Ras
al-Khaimah, Ajman,
Fujairah **Major
ports:** Dubai
Physical features:
desert and flat
coastal plain;
mountains in E

Government
Head of state and government: Sheik Zayed bin Sultan al-
Nahayan of Abu Dhabi from 1971 **Supreme council of rulers:** *Abu
Dhabi* Sheik Zayed bin Sultan al-Nahayan, president (1966);
Ajman Sheik Humaid bin Rashid al-Nuami (1981); *Dubai* Sheik
Maktoum bin Rashid al-Maktoum (1990); *Fujairah* Sheik Hamad
bin Muhammad al-Sharqi (1974); *Ras al Khaimah* Sheik Saqr bin
Muhammad al-Quasimi (1948); *Sharjah* Sheik Sultan bin
Muhammad al-Quasimi (1972); *Umm al Qaiwain* Sheik Rashid bin
Ahmad al-Mu'alla (1981) **Political system:** absolutism
Administrative divisions: seven emirates **Political parties:** none
Armed forces: 64,500 (1996) **Conscription:** military service is
voluntary **Death penalty:** retained and used for ordinary crimes
Defence spend: (% GDP) 5.2 (1996) **Education spend:** (% GNP)
1.8 (1993) **Health spend:** (% GDP) 1.8 (1994)

Economy and resources
Currency: UAE dirham **GDP:** ($ US) 35.4 billion (1994) **Real GDP per capita (PPP):** ($ US) 16,000 (1994) **GDP growth rate:** 1.8% (1995) **Average annual inflation:** 4.5% (1996) **Foreign debt:** ($ US) 16.06 billion (1996) **Major trading partners:** Japan, USA, UK, Germany, South Korea, France, Thailand, Italy, India **Resources:** petroleum and natural gas **Industries:** petroleum production and refining, gas handling, petrochemicals and other petroleum products, aluminium products, cable, cement, chemicals, fertilizers, rolled steel, plastics, tools, clothing **Exports:** crude petroleum, natural gas, re-exports (mainly machinery and transport equipment). Principal market: Japan 38% (1995) **Imports:** machinery and transport equipment, food and live animals, fuels and lubricants, chemicals, basic manufactures. Principal source: Japan 8.6% (1995) **Arable land:** 0.4% (1995) **Agricultural products:** dates, tomatoes, aubergines, other vegetables and fruits; livestock rearing; fishing

Population and society
Population: 2,260,000 (1996 est) **Population growth rate:** 2.6% (1990–95); 1.8% (2000–05) **Population density:** (per sq km) 27 (1996 est) **Urban population:** (% of total) 84 (1995) **Age distribution:** (% of total population) <15 31.3%, 15–65 67%, >65 1.7% (1995) **Ethnic groups:** 75% Iranians, Indians, and Pakistanis; about 25% Arabs **Language:** Arabic (official), Farsi, Hindi, Urdu, English **Religion:** Muslim 96%; Christian, Hindu **Education:** (compulsory years) 6 **Literacy rate:** 78% (men); 78% (women) (1995 est) **Labour force:** 51% of population: 8% agriculture, 27% industry, 65% services (1990); 93% of workforce were non-UAE nationals (1992 est) **Life expectancy:** 74 (men); 77 (women) (1995–2000) **Child mortality rate:** (under 5, per 1,000 live births) 19 (1996) **Physicians:** 1 per 715 people (1993)

Practical information
Visa requirements: UK: visa not required for a stay of up to 30 days. USA: visa required **Embassy in the UK:** 30 Prince's Gate, London SW7 1PT. Tel: (0171) 581 1281; fax: (0171) 581 9616 **British embassy:** PO Box 248, Abu Dhabi. Tel: (2) 326 600; fax: (2) 341 744 **Chamber of commerce:** Dubai Chamber of Commerce and Industry, PO Box 1457, Diera, Dubai. Tel: (4) 221 181; fax: (4) 211 646 **Airports:** international airports: Abu Dhabi (Nadia), Dubai, Ras al-Khaimah, Sharjah, Fujairah; domestic services operate between Abu Dhabi and Dubai; total passenger km: 1,225 million (1994) **Major holidays:** 1 January, 6 August, 2 December (2 days); variable: Eid-ul-Adha (3 days), end of Ramadan (4 days), New Year (Muslim), Prophet's Birthday, Lailat al-Miraj (March/April)

Chronology
7th century AD: Islam introduced. **early 16th century:** Portuguese established trading contacts with Persian Gulf states. **18th century:** Rise of trade and seafaring among Qawasim and Bani Yas, respectively in Ras al-Khaimah and Sharjah in N and Abu Dhabi and Dubai in desert of S. Emirates' current ruling families are descended from these peoples. **early 19th century:** Britain signed treaties ('truces') with local rulers, ensuring that British shipping through the Gulf was free from 'pirate' attacks and bringing Emirates under British protection. **1892:** Trucial Sheiks signed Exclusive Agreements with Britain, agreeing not to cede, sell, or mortgage territory to another power. **1952:** Trucial Council established by seven sheikdoms of Abu Dhabi, Ajman, Dubai, Fujairah, Ras al Khaimah, Sharjah, and Umm al Qawain, with a view to later forming a federation. **1958:** Large-scale exploitation of oil reserves led to rapid economic progress. **1968:** Britain's announcement that it would remove its forces from the Persian Gulf by 1971 led to abortive attempt to arrange federation between seven Trucial States and Bahrain and Qatar. **1971:** Bahrain and Qatar ceded from Federation of Arab Emirates, which was dissolved. Six Trucial States formed United Arab Emirates, with ruler of Abu Dhabi, Sheik Zayed, as president. Provisional constitution adopted. **1972:** Seventh state, Ras al Khaimah, joined federation. **1976:** Sheik Zayed threatened to relinquish presidency unless progress towards centralization became more rapid. **1985:** Diplomatic and economic links with Soviet Union and China established. **1987:** Diplomatic relations with Egypt restored. **1990–91:** Iraqi invasion of Kuwait opposed; UAE troops fought as part of United Nations coalition. **1991:** Bank of Commerce and Credit International (BCCI), controlled by Abu Dhabi's ruler, collapsed at cost to the UAE of $10 billion. **1992:** Border dispute with Iran. **1994:** Abu Dhabi agreed to pay BCCI creditors $1.8 billion.

United Kingdom of Great Britain and Northern Ireland

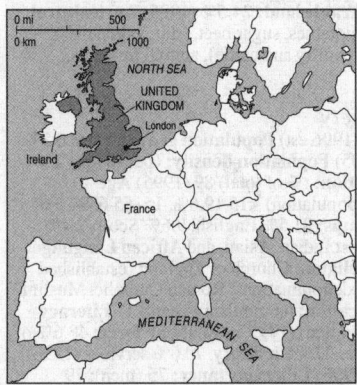

Area: 244,100 sq km/94,247 sq mi **Capital:** London **Major towns/cities:** Birmingham, Glasgow, Leeds, Sheffield, Liverpool, Manchester, Edinburgh, Bradford, Bristol, Coventry, Belfast, Newcastle upon Tyne, Cardiff **Major ports:** London, Grimsby, Southampton, Liverpool **Physical features:** became separated from European continent about 6000 BC; rolling landscape, increasingly mountainous towards the N, with Grampian Mountains in Scotland, Pennines in N England, Cambrian Mountains in Wales; rivers include Thames, Severn, and Spey **Territories:** Anguilla, Bermuda, British Antarctic Territory, British Indian Ocean Territory, British Virgin Islands, Cayman Islands, Falkland Islands, Gibraltar, Montserrat, Pitcairn Islands, St Helena and Dependencies (Ascension, Tristan da Cunha), Turks and Caicos Islands; the Channel Islands and the Isle of Man are not part of the UK but are direct dependencies of the crown

Government
Head of state: Queen Elizabeth II from 1952 **Head of government:** Tony Blair from 1997 **Political system:** liberal democracy **Administrative divisions:** England: 34 non-metropolitan counties, 46 unitary authorities, 6 metropolitan counties, (with 36 metropolitan boroughs), 32 London boroughs, and the Corporation of London; Scotland: 9 regions, 29 unitary authorities, and 3 island authorities (from 1996); Wales: 9 counties and 22 unitary authorities/county boroughs (from 1996); Northern Ireland: 26 districts within 6 geographical counties **Political parties:** Conservative and Unionist Party, right of centre; Labour Party, moderate left of centre; Social and Liberal Democrats, centre left; Scottish National Party (SNP), Scottish nationalist; Plaid Cymru (Welsh Nationalist Party), Welsh nationalist; Official Ulster Unionist Party (OUP), Democratic Unionist Party (DUP), Ulster People's Unionist Party (UPUP), all Northern Ireland right of centre, in favour of remaining part of United Kingdom; Social Democratic Labour Party (SDLP), Northern Ireland, moderate left of centre; Green Party, ecological **Armed forces:** 226,000 (1996) **Conscription:** military service is voluntary **Death penalty:** abolished for ordinary crimes 1973; laws provide for the death penalty for exceptional crimes only; last execution 1964 **Defence spend:** (% GDP) 3.0 (1996) **Education spend:** (% GNP) 5.4 (1993–94) **Health spend:** (% GDP) 5.8 (1994)

Economy and resources
Currency: pound sterling (£) **GDP:** ($ US) 1,145.8 billion (1996) **Real GDP per capita (PPP):** ($ US) 18,616 (1996) **GDP growth rate:** 2.3% (1996); 1.4% (1990–95) **Average annual inflation:** 3.3% (1996); 5.1% (1985–95) **Major trading partners:** Germany, USA, France, the Netherlands, Japan **Resources:** coal, limestone,

crude petroleum, natural gas, tin, iron, salt, sand and gravel
Industries: machinery and transport equipment, steel, metals and
metal products, food processing, shipbuilding, aircraft, petroleum
and gas extraction, electronics and communications, chemicals and
chemical products, business and financial services, tourism
Exports: industrial and electrical machinery, automatic data-
processing equipment, motor vehicles, petroleum, chemicals,
finished and semi-finished manufactured products, agricultural
products and foodstuffs. Principal market: Germany 12% (1996)
Imports: industrial and electrical machinery, motor vehicles, food
and live animals, petroleum, automatic data processing equipment,
consumer goods, textiles, paper, paper board. Principal source:
Germany 14.1% (1996) **Arable land:** 24.5% (1995) **Agricultural
products:** wheat, barley, potatoes, sugar beet, fruit, vegetables;
livestock rearing (chiefly poultry and cattle), animal products,
fishing

Population and society

Population: 58,144,000 (1996 est) **Population growth rate:** 0.3%
(1990–95); 0.2% (2000–05) **Population density:** (per sq km) 238
(1996 est) **Urban population:** (% of total) 89 (1995) **Age
distribution:** (% of total population) <15 19.6%, 15–65 65%, >65
15.5% (1995) **Ethnic groups:** 81.5% English; 9.6% Scots; 2.4%
Irish; 1.9% Welsh; 2% West Indian, Asian, and African **Language:**
English, Welsh, Gaelic **Religion:** Church of England (established
Church); other Protestant denominations, Roman Catholic, Muslim,
Jewish, Hindu, Sikh **Education:** (compulsory years) 11 **Literacy
rate:** 99% (men); 99% (women) (1995 est) **Labour force:** 48.6% of
population: 2% agriculture, 27.4% industry, 70.6% services (1996)
Unemployment: 8.2% (1996) **Life expectancy:** 75 (men); 79
(women) (1995–2000) **Child mortality rate:** (under 5, per 1,000
live births) 8 (1996) **Physicians:** 1 per 629 people (1993)

Practical information

Visa requirements: USA: visa not required **Chamber of
commerce:** Association of British Chambers of Commerce, 9
Tufton Street, London SW1P 3QB. Tel: (0171) 222 1555; fax:
(0171) 799 2202 **Airports:** international airports: London
(Heathrow, Gatwick, London City, Stansted, Luton), Birmingham,
Manchester, Newcastle, Bristol, Cardiff, Norwich, Derby,
Edinburgh, Glasgow, Leeds/Bradford, Liverpool, Southampton; 22
domestic airports; total passenger km: 139,088 million (1994)
Major holidays: 1 January, 25–26 December; variable: Good
Friday, Easter Monday (not Scotland), Early May, Late May and
Summer (August) Bank Holidays; Northern Ireland also has 17
March, 29 December; Scotland has 2 January

Chronology

c. 400–200 BC: British Isles conquered by Celts. **55–54 BC:**
Romans led by Julius Caesar raided Britain. **AD 43–60:** Romans
conquered England and Wales, which formed the province of
Britannia; Picts stopped them penetrating further N. **5th–7th
centuries:** After Romans withdrew, Anglo-Saxons overran most of
England and formed kingdoms, including Wessex, Northumbria,
and Mercia; Wales was stronghold of Celts. **500:** The Scots, a
Gaelic-speaking tribe from Ireland, settled in the kingdom of
Dalriada (Argyll). **5th–6th centuries:** British Isles converted to
Christianity. **829:** King Egbert of Wessex accepted as overlord of
all England. **c. 843:** Kenneth McAlpin unified Scots and Picts to
become first king of Scotland. **9th–11th centuries:** Vikings raided
British Isles, conquering N and E England and N Scotland. **1066:**
Normans led by William I defeated Anglo-Saxons at Battle of
Hastings and conquered England. **12th–13th centuries:** Anglo-
Norman adventurers conquered much of Ireland, but effective
English rule remained limited to area around Dublin. **1215:** King
John of England forced to sign Magna Carta, which placed limits
on royal powers. **1265:** Simon de Montfort summoned the first
English parliament in which the towns were represented. **1284:**
Edward I of England invaded Scotland; Scots defeated English at
Battle of Stirling Bridge 1297. **1314:** Robert the Bruce led Scots to
victory over English at Battle of Bannockburn; England
recognized Scottish independence 1328. **1455–85:** Wars of the
Roses: House of York and House of Lancaster disputed English

throne. **1513:** Battle of Flodden: Scots defeated by English; James
IV of Scotland killed. **1529:** Henry VIII founded Church of
England after break with Rome; Reformation effective in England
and Wales, but not in Ireland. **1536–43:** Acts of Union united
Wales with England, with one law, one parliament, and one official
language. **1541:** Irish parliament recognized Henry VIII of
England as king of Ireland. **1557:** First Covenant established
Protestant faith in Scotland. **1603:** Union of crowns: James VI of
Scotland became James I of England also. **1607:** First successful
English colony in Virginia marked start of three centuries of
overseas expansion. **1610:** James I established plantation of Ulster
in Northern Ireland with Protestant settlers from England and
Scotland. **1642–52:** English Civil War between king and
Parliament, with Scottish intervention and Irish rebellion, resulted
in victory for Parliament. **1649:** Execution of Charles I; Oliver
Cromwell appointed Lord Protector 1653; monarchy restored
1660. **1689:** 'Glorious Revolution' confirmed power of Parliament;
replacement of James II by William III resisted by Scottish
Highlanders and Catholic Irish. **1707:** Act of Union between
England and Scotland created United Kingdom of Great Britain,
governed by a single parliament. **1721–42:** Cabinet government
developed under Robert Walpole, in effect the first prime minister.
1745: 'The Forty-Five': rebellion of Scottish Highlanders in
support of Jacobite pretender to throne; defeated 1746. **c.
1760–1850:** Industrial Revolution: Britain became the first
industrial nation in the world. **1775–83:** American Revolution:
Britain lost 13 American colonies; empire continued to expand in
Canada, India, and Australia. **1793–1815:** Britain at war with
revolutionary France, except for 1802–03. **1800:** Act of Union
created United Kingdom of Great Britain and Ireland, governed by
a single parliament; effective 1801. **1832:** Great Reform Act
extended franchise; further extensions 1867, 1884, 1918, and 1928.
1846: Repeal of Corn Laws reflected shift of power from
landowners to industrialists. **1870:** Home Rule Party formed to
campaign for restoration of separate Irish parliament. **1880–90s:**
Rapid expansion of British Empire in Africa. **1906–14:** Liberal
governments introduced social reforms and curbed power of House
of Lords. **1914–18:** United Kingdom played leading part in World
War I; British Empire expanded in Middle East. **1919–21:** Anglo-
Irish war ended with secession of S Ireland as Irish Free State;
Ulster remained within United Kingdom of Great Britain and
Northern Ireland with some powers devolved to Northern Irish
parliament. **1924:** First Labour government led by Ramsay
MacDonald. **1926:** General Strike arose from coal dispute.
Equality of status recognized between United Kingdom and
Dominions of British Commonwealth. **1931:** National Government
coalition formed to face economic crisis; unemployment reached 3
million. **1939–45:** United Kingdom played a leading part in World
War II. **1945:** First Scottish Nationalist MP elected; first Welsh
Nationalist MP 1966. **1945–51:** Labour government of Clement
Attlee created welfare state and nationalized major industries.
1947–71: Decolonization brought about end of British Empire.
1969: Start of Troubles in Northern Ireland; Northern Irish
Parliament suspended 1972. **1973:** UK joined European Economic
Community. **1979:** Referenda failed to approve devolution of
power to Scottish and Welsh assemblies. **1979–90:** Conservative
government of Margaret Thatcher pursued radical free-market
economic policies. **1982:** Unemployment over 3 million. Falklands
War. **1991:** British troops took part in US-led war against Iraq
under United Nations umbrella. Severe economic recession and
unemployment. **1993:** Peace proposal for Northern Ireland, the
Downing Street Declaration, issued jointly with Irish government.
1994: Irish Republican Army and Protestant paramilitary declared
cease-fire in Northern Ireland. **1996:** IRA renewed bombing
campaign in London. **1997:** Labour Party won landslide victory in
general election; Tony Blair became prime minister. Blair launched
new Anglo-Irish peace initiative; IRA declared a cease-fire.
Princess Diana killed in car crash. **1998:** Following multi-party
peace talks in Northern Ireland, a historic agreement (known as the
Good Friday Agreement) was reached on the future of Northern
Ireland; in the May referendum, 71% of voters in Northern
Ireland backed the agreement. **1998:** Gordon Brown, Chancellor of the
Exchequer, announced a £110 billion boost to public spending.

United States of America

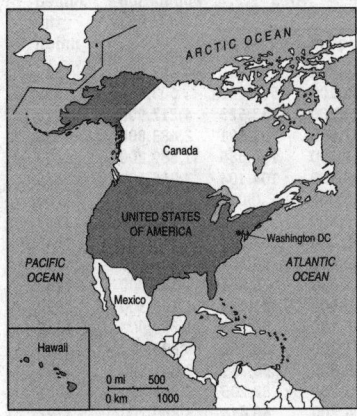

Area: 9,372,615 sq km/3,618,766 sq mi
Capital: Washington DC
Major towns/cities: New York, Los Angeles, Chicago, Philadelphia, Detroit, San Francisco, Washington, Dallas, San Diego, San Antonio, Houston, Boston, Baltimore, Phoenix, Indianapolis, Memphis, Honolulu, San José
Physical features: topography and vegetation from tropical (Hawaii) to arctic (Alaska); mountain ranges parallel with E and W coasts; the Rocky Mountains separate rivers emptying into the Pacific from those flowing into the Gulf of Mexico; Great Lakes in N; rivers include Hudson, Mississippi, Missouri, Colorado, Columbia, Snake, Rio Grande, Ohio **Territories:** the commonwealths of Puerto Rico and Northern Marianas; Guam, the US Virgin Islands, American Samoa, Wake Island, Midway Islands, and Johnston and Sand Islands

Government
Head of state and government: Bill Clinton from 1993 **Political system:** liberal democracy **Administrative divisions:** 50 states **Political parties:** Democratic Party, liberal centre; Republican Party, centre right **Armed forces:** 1,483,800 (1996) **Conscription:** military service is voluntary **Death penalty:** retained and used for ordinary crimes **Defence spend:** (% GDP) 3.6 (1996) **Education spend:** (% GNP) 5.5 (1993–94) **Health spend:** (% GDP) 6.7 (1994)

Economy and resources
Currency: US dollar **GDP:** ($ US) 7,341.9 billion (1996) **Real GDP per capita (PPP):** ($ US) 27,655 (1996) **GDP growth rate:** 2.8% (1996); 2.6% (1990–95) **Average annual inflation:** 2.9% (1996); 3.2% (1985–95) **Major trading partners:** Canada, Japan, Mexico, EU (principally UK and Germany) **Resources:** coal, copper (world's second-largest producer), iron, bauxite, mercury, silver, gold, nickel, zinc (world's fifth-largest producer), tungsten, uranium, phosphate, petroleum, natural gas, timber **Industries:** machinery, petroleum refining and products, food processing, motor vehicles, pig iron and steel, chemical products, electrical goods, metal products, printing and publishing, fertilizers, cement **Exports:** machinery, motor vehicles, agricultural products and foodstuffs, aircraft, weapons, chemicals, electronics. Principal market: Canada 22% (1996) **Imports:** machinery and transport equipment, crude and partly refined petroleum, office machinery, textiles and clothing. Principal source: Canada 19.8% (1996) **Arable land:** 20.3% (1995) **Agricultural products:** hay, potatoes, maize, wheat, barley, oats, sugar beet, soya beans, citrus and other fruit, cotton, tobacco; livestock (principally cattle, pigs, and poultry)

Population and society
Population: 269,444,000 (1996 est) **Population growth rate:** 1% (1990–95); 0.8% (2000–05) **Population density:** (per sq km) 29 (1996 est) **Urban population:** (% of total) 76 (1995) **Age distribution:** (% of total population) <15 22%, 15–65 65.3%, >65 12.6% (1995) **Ethnic groups:** approximately three-quarters of the population are of European origin, including 29% who trace their descent from Britain and Ireland, 8% from Germany, 5% from Italy, and 3% each from Scandinavia and Poland; 12% are African-Americans, 8% Hispanic, and 3% Asian and Pacific islander;

African-Americans form 30% of the population of the states of the 'Deep South', namely Alabama, Georgia, Louisiana, Mississippi, and South Carolina; Asians are most concentrated in California **Language:** English, Spanish **Religion:** Christian 86.5% (Roman Catholic 26%, Baptist 19%, Methodist 8%, Lutheran 5%); Jewish 1.8%; Muslim 0.5%; Buddhist and Hindu less than 0.5% **Education:** (compulsory years) 10 **Literacy rate:** 99% (men); 99% (women) (1995 est) **Labour force:** 51% of population: 2.8% agriculture, 23.8% industry, 73.3% services (1996) **Unemployment:** 5.4% (1996) **Life expectancy:** 73 (men); 80 (women) (1995–2000) **Child mortality rate:** (under 5, per 1,000 live births) 9 (1996) **Physicians:** 1 per 398 people (1994)

Practical information
Visa requirements: UK: visa not required for a stay of up to 90 days **Embassy in the UK:** 24 Grosvenor Square, London W1A 1AE, Tel: (0171) 499 9000; fax: (0171) 629 9124 **British embassy:** 3100 Massachusetts Avenue, NW, Washington DC 20008. Tel: (202) 462 1340; fax: (202) 898 4255 **Chamber of commerce:** 1615 H Street, NW, Washington DC 20062–0001. Tel: (202) 659 6000; fax: (202) 463 5836 **Airports:** international airports: Anchorage, Atlanta (Hartsfield), Baltimore (Baltimore/Washington), Boston (Logan), Chicago (O'Hare), Cincinnati (Northern Kentucky), Cleveland (Hopkins), Dallas/Fort Worth, Denver (Stapleton), Detroit Metropolitan, Honolulu, Houston Intercontinental, Kansas City, Las Vegas (McCarran), Los Angeles, Miami, Minneapolis/St Paul, New Orleans, New York (John F Kennedy, La Guardia, Newark), Orlando, Philadelphia, Phoenix (Sky Harbor), Pittsburgh, Portland, St Louis (Lambert), Salt Lake City, San Diego (Lindbergh Field), San Francisco, Seattle-Tacoma, Tampa, Washington DC (Dulles, National); about 800 domestic airports; total passenger km: 822,152 million (1994) **Major holidays:** 1 January, 4 July, 12 October (not all states), 11 November, 25 December; variable: Martin Luther King's birthday (January, not all states), George Washington's birthday (February), Memorial (May), Labor (first Mon in September), Columbus (October), Thanksgiving (last Thu in November); much local variation

Chronology
c.15,000 BC: First evidence of human occupation in North America. **1513:** Ponce de Léon of Spain explored Florida in search of the Fountain of Youth; Francisco Coronado explored SW region of North America 1540–42. **1565:** Spanish founded St Augustine (Florida), the first permanent European settlement in N America. **1585:** Sir Walter Raleigh tried to establish English colony on Roanoke Island in what he called Virginia. **1607:** English colonists founded Jamestown, Virginia, and began growing tobacco. **1620:** The Pilgrim Fathers founded Plymouth Colony (near Cape Cod); other English Puritans followed them to New England. **1624:** Dutch formed colony of New Netherlands; Swedes formed New Sweden 1638; both taken by England 1664. **17th–18th centuries:** Millions of Africans were sold into slavery on American cotton and tobacco plantations. **1733:** Georgia became thirteenth British colony on E coast. **1763:** British victory over France in Seven Years' War secured territory as far W as Mississippi River. **1765:** British first attempted to levy tax in American colonies with Stamp Act; protest forced repeal in 1767. **1773:** 'Boston Tea Party': colonists boarded ships and threw cargoes of tea into sea in protest at import duty. **1774:** British closed Boston harbour and billeted troops in Massachusetts; colonists formed First Continental Congress. **1775:** American Revolution: colonies raised Continental Army led by George Washington to fight against British rule. **1776:** American colonies declared independence; France and Spain supported them in war with Britain. **1781:** Americans defeated British at Battle of Yorktown; rebel states formed loose confederation, codified in Articles of Confederation. **1783:** Treaty of Paris: Britain accepted loss of colonies. **1787:** 'Founding Fathers' devised new constitution for United States of America. **1789:** Washington elected first president of USA. **1791:** Bill of Rights guaranteed individual freedom. **1803:** Louisiana Purchase: France sold former Spanish lands between Mississippi River and Rocky Mountains to USA. **1812–14:** War with Britain arose from dispute over blockade rights during Napoleonic Wars.

United States of America: States

State	Nickname(s)	Abbreviation	Capital	Area sq km	Area sq mi	Population (1995)	Joined the union
Alabama	Heart of Dixie/Camellia State	AL	Montgomery	134,700	51,994	4,253,000	1819
Alaska	Mainland State/The Last Frontier	AK	Juneau	1,531,100	591,005	603,600	1959
Arizona	Grand Canyon State/Apache State	AZ	Phoenix	294,100	113,523	4,217,900	1912
Arkansas	Bear State/Land of Opportunity	AR	Little Rock	137,800	53,191	2,483,800	1836
California	Golden State	CA	Sacramento	411,100	158,685	31,589,200	1850
Colorado	Centennial State	CO	Denver	269,700	104,104	3,746,600	1876
Connecticut	Constitution State/Nutmeg State	CT	Hartford	13,000	5018	3,274,700	1788
Delaware	First State/Diamond State	DE	Dover	5,300	2,046	717,200	1787
Florida	Sunshine State/Everglade State	FL	Tallahassee	152,000	58,672	14,165,600	1845
Georgia	Empire State of the South/Peach State	GA	Atlanta	152,600	58,904	7,200,900	1788
Hawaii	Aloha State	HI	Honolulu	16,800	6,485	1,186,800	1959
Idaho	Gem State	ID	Boise	216,500	83,569	1,163,300	1890
Illinois	Inland Empire/Prairie State/Land of Lincoln	IL	Springfield	146,100	56,395	11,829,900	1818
Indiana	Hoosier State	IN	Indianapolis	93,700	36,168	5,803,500	1816
Iowa	Hawkeye State/Corn State	IA	Des Moines	145,800	56,279	2,841,800	1846
Kansas	Sunflower State/Jayhawker State	KS	Topeka	213,200	82,295	2,565,300	1861
Kentucky	Bluegrass State	KY	Frankfort	104,700	40,414	3,860,200	1792
Louisiana	Pelican State/Sugar State/Creole State	LA,	Baton Rouge	135,900	52,457	4,342,300	1792
Maine	Pine Tree State	ME	Augusta	86,200	33,273	1,241,400	1820
Maryland	Old Line State/Free State	MD	Annapolis	31,600	12,198	5,042,400	1788
Massachusetts	Bay State/Old Colony	MA	Boston	21,500	8,299	6,073,550	1788
Michigan	Great Lakes State/Wolverine State	MI	Lansing	151,600	58,518	9,549,400	1837
Minnesota	North Star State/Gopher State	MN	St Paul	218,700	84,418	4,609,500	1858
Mississippi	Magnolia State	MS	Jackson	123,600	47,710	2,697,200	1817
Missouri	Show Me State/Bullion State	MO	Jefferson City	180,600	69,712	5,323,500	1821
Montana	Treasure State/Big Sky Country	MT	Helena	381,200	147,143	870,300	1889
Nebraska	Cornhusker State/Beef State	NE	Lincoln	200,400	77,354	1,637,100	1867
Nevada	Sagebrush State/Silver State/Battleborn State	NV	Carson City	286,400	110,550	1,530,100	1864
New Hampshire	Granite State	NH	Concord	24,000	9,264	1,148,300	1788
New Jersey	Garden State	NJ	Trenton	20,200	7,797	7,945,300	1787
New Mexico	Land of Enchantment/Sunshine State	NM	Santa Fé	315,000	121,590	1,685,400	1912
New York	Empire State	NY	Albany	127,200	49,099	18,136,100	1788
North Carolina	Tar Heel State/Old North State	NC	Raleigh	136,400	52,650	7,195,100	1789
North Dakota	Peace Garden State	ND	Bismarck	183,100	70,677	641,400	1889
Ohio	Buckeye State	OH	Columbus	107,100	41,341	11,150,500	1803
Oklahoma	Sooner State	OK	Oklahoma City	181,100	69,905	3,277,700	1907
Oregon	Beaver State/Sunset State	OR	Salem	251,500	97,079	3,140,600	1859
Pennsylvania	Keystone State	PA	Harrisburg	117,400	45,316	12,071,800	1787
Rhode Island	Little Rhody/Ocean State	RI	Providence	3,100	1,197	989,800	1790
South Carolina	Palmetto State	SC	Columbia	80,600	31,112	3,673,300	1788
South Dakota	Coyote State/Mount Rushmore State	SD	Pierre	199,800	77,123	729,000	1889
Tennessee	Volunteer State	TN	Nashville	109,200	42,151	5,256,100	1796
Texas	Lone Star State	TX	Austin	691,200	266,803	18,724,000	1845
Utah	Beehive State/Mormon State	UT	Salt Lake City	219,900	84,881	1,951,400	1896
Vermont	Green Mountain State	VT	Montpelier	24,900	9,611	584,800	1791
Virginia	Old Dominion State/Mother of Presidents	VA	Richmond	105,600	40,762	6,618,400	1788
Washington	Evergreen State/Chinook State	WA	Olympia	176,700	68,206	5,430,900	1889
West Virginia	Mountain State/Panhandle State	WV	Charleston	62,900	24,279	1,828,100	1863
Wisconsin	Badger State/America's Dairyland	WI	Madison	145,500	56,163	5,122,900	1848
Wyoming	Equality State	WY	Cheyenne	253,400	97,812	480,200	1890
District of Columbia (Federal	–	DC	Washington	180	69	554,300	est. by Act of Congress

1819: USA bought Florida from Spain. **19th centuries:** Mass immigration from Europe; settlers moved westwards, crushing Indian resistance and claiming 'manifest destiny' of USA to control North America. By end of century, number of states in the Union had increased from 17 to 45. **1846–48:** Mexican War: Mexico ceded vast territory to USA. **1854:** Kansas–Nebraska Act heightened controversy over slavery in southern states; abolitionists formed Republican Party. **1860:** Abraham Lincoln (Republican) elected president. **1861:** Civil war broke out after 11 southern states, wishing to retain slavery, seceded from USA and formed Confederate States of America under Jefferson Davis.

1865: USA defeated Confederacy; slavery abolished; President Lincoln assassinated. **1867:** Alaska bought from Russia. **1869:** Railway linked E and W coasts; rapid growth of industry and agriculture 1870–1920 made USA very rich. **1876:** Sioux Indians defeated US troops at Little Big Horn; Indians finally defeated at Wounded Knee 1890. **1898:** Spanish–American War: USA gained Puerto Rico and Guam; also Philippines (until 1946) and Cuba (until 1901); USA annexed Hawaii. **1913:** 16th amendment to constitution gave federal government power to levy income tax. **1917–18:** USA intervened in World War I; President Woodrow Wilson took leading part in peace negotiations 1919, but USA rejected membership of League of Nations. **1920:** Women received right to vote; sale of alcohol prohibited, until 1933. **1924:** Native Americans made citizens of USA by Congress. **1929:** 'Wall Street Crash': stock market collapse led to Great Depression with 13 million unemployed by 1933. **1933:** President Franklin Roosevelt launched 'New Deal' with public works to alleviate Depression. **1941:** Japanese attacked US fleet at Pearl Harbor, Hawaii; USA declared war on Japan; Germany declared war on USA, which henceforth played a leading part in World War II. **1945:** USA ended war in Pacific by dropping two atomic bombs on Hiroshima and Nagasaki, Japan. **1947:** 'Truman Doctrine' pledged US aid for nations threatened by communism; start of Cold War between USA and USSR. **1950–53:** US forces engaged in Korean War. **1954:** Racial segregation in schools deemed unconstitutional; start of campaign to secure civil rights for black Americans. **1962:** Cuban missile crisis: USA forced USSR to withdraw nuclear weapons from Cuba. **1963:** President John F Kennedy assassinated. **1964–68:** President Lyndon Johnson introduced 'Great Society' programme of civil-rights and welfare measures. **1961–75:** USA involved in Vietnam War. **1969:** US astronaut Neil Armstrong was first person on Moon. **1974:** 'Watergate' scandal: evidence of domestic political espionage compelled President Richard Nixon to resign. **1979–80:** Iran held US diplomats hostage, humiliating President Jimmy Carter. **1981–89:** Tax-cutting policies of President Ronald Reagan led to large federal budget deficit. **1986:** 'Irangate' scandal: secret US arms sales to Iran illegally funded Contra guerrillas in Nicaragua. **1990:** President George Bush declared end to Cold War. **1991:** Gulf War: USA played leading part in expelling Iraqi forces from Kuwait. **1992:** Democrat Bill Clinton won presidential elections; his running mate Al Gore became vice president. **1996:** Clinton re-elected. US missile attacks on Iraq in response to Hussein's incursions into Kurdish safe havens. Public criticism brought about tightening of Democratic Party funding. **1997:** Budget deal agreed between President and Congress. Reform in welfare law brought substantial drop in number of welfare recipients. President used increased veto powers to block military construction projects. Democratic Party's 1996 election fund-raising investigated. Republicans polled well in Virginia and New Jersey governorship elections; New York City mayor re-elected.

Uruguay Oriental Republic of

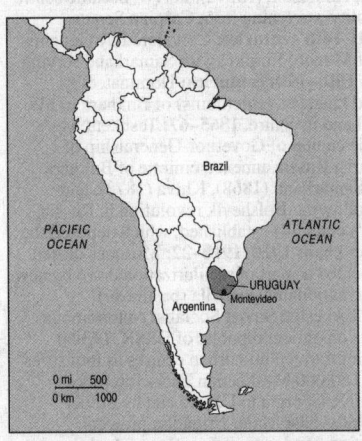

National name: *República Oriental del Uruguay* **Area:** 176,200 sq km/68,030 sq mi **Capital:** Montevideo **Major towns/cities:** Salto, Paysandú, Las Piedras **Physical features:** grassy plains (pampas) and low hills; rivers Negro, Uruguay, Río de la Plata

Government

Head of state and government: Julio Maria Sanguinetti from 1994 **Political system:** democracy **Administrative divisions:** 19 departments **Political parties:** Colorado Party (PC), progressive, centre left; National (Blanco) Party (PN), traditionalist, right of centre; New Space (NE), moderate, left wing; Progressive Encounter (EP), left wing **Armed forces:** 25,600; plus paramilitary forces of 2,500 (1996) **Conscription:** military service is voluntary **Death penalty:** abolished 1907

Defence spend: (% GDP) 2.3 (1996) **Education spend:** (% GNP) 2.5 (1994) **Health spend:** (% GDP) 2.0 (1990–95)

Economy and resources
Currency: Uruguayan peso **GDP:** ($ US) 15.5 billion (1994) **Real GDP per capita (PPP):** ($ US) 6,752 (1994) **GDP growth rate:** –2.4% (1995); 4% (1990–95) **Average annual inflation:** 28.5% (1996); 70.5% (1985–95) **Foreign debt:** ($ US) 5.4 billion (1996) **Major trading partners:** Brazil, Argentina, USA, Italy, Germany, Spain, China **Resources:** small-scale extraction of building materials, industrial minerals, semi-precious stones; gold deposits are being developed **Industries:** food processing, textiles and clothing, beverages, cement, chemicals, light engineering and transport equipment, leather products **Exports:** textiles, meat (chiefly beef), live animals and by-products (mainly hides and leather products), cereals, footwear. Principal market: Brazil 34.6% (1996) **Imports:** machinery and appliances, transport equipment, chemical products, petroleum and petroleum products, agricultural products. Principal source: Brazil 26.1% (1996) **Arable land:** 7.2% (1995) **Agricultural products:** rice, sugar cane, sugar beet, wheat, potatoes, barley, maize, sorghum; livestock rearing (sheep and cattle) is traditionally country's major economic activity – exports of animals, meat, skins, and hides accounted for 36.6% of total export revenue (1994)

Population and society
Population: 3,204,000 (1996 est) **Population growth rate:** 0.6% (1990–95); 0.6% (2000–05) **Population density:** (per sq km) 18 (1996 est) **Urban population:** (% of total) 90 (1995) **Age distribution:** (% of total population) <15 24.4%, 15–65 63.3%, >65 12.3% (1995) **Ethnic groups:** predominantly of European descent: about 54% Spanish, 22% Italian, with minorities from other European countries **Language:** Spanish (official) **Religion:** mainly Roman Catholic **Education:** (compulsory years) 6 **Literacy rate:** 97% (men); 96% (women) (1995 est) **Labour force:** 15% agriculture, 18% industry, 67% services (1993) **Unemployment:** 10.2% (1995) **Life expectancy:** 70 (men); 76 (women) (1995–2000) **Child mortality rate:** (under 5, per 1,000 live births) 20 (1996) **Physicians:** 1 per 515 people (1990)

Practical information
Visa requirements: UK: visa not required. USA: visa not required **Embassy in the UK:** 2nd Floor, 140 Brompton Road, London SW3 1HY. Tel: (0171) 584 8192; fax: (0171) 581 9585 **British embassy:** PO Box 16024, Calle Marco Bruto 1073, 1130 Montevideo. Tel: (2) 623 630; fax: (2) 627 815 **Chamber of commerce:** Cámara Nacional de Comercio, Edificio de la Bolsa de Comercio, Misiones 1400, Casilla 1000, 11000 Montevideo. Tel: (2) 961 277; fax: (2) 961 243 **Airports:** international airport: Montevideo (Carrasco); seven domestic airports; total passenger km: 645 million (1994) **Major holidays:** 1 January, 19 April, 1, 18 May, 19 June, 18 July, 25 August, 12 October, 2 November, 25 December; variable: Carnival (2 days), Good Friday, Holy Thursday, Mon–Wed of Holy Week

Chronology
1516: Río de la Plata visited by Spanish navigator Juan Diaz de Solis, who was killed by native Charrua Amerindians. This discouraged European settlement for more than a century. **1680:** Portuguese from Brazil founded Nova Colonia do Sacramento on Río de la Plata estuary. **1726:** Spanish established fortress at Montevideo and wrested control over Uruguay from Portugal, with much of the Amerindian population being killed. **1776:** Became part of Viceroyalty of La Plata, with capital at Buenos Aires. **1808:** With Spanish monarchy overthrown by Napoleon Bonaparte, La Plata Viceroyalty became autonomous, but Montevideo remained loyal to Spanish Crown and rebelled against Buenos Aires control. **1815:** Dictator José Gervasio Artigas overthrew Spanish and Buenos Aires control. **1820:** Artigas ousted by Brazil, which disputed control of Uruguay with Argentina. **1825:** Independence declared after fight led by Juan Antonio Lavalleja. **1828:** Independence recognized by country's neighbours. **1836:** Civil war between Reds and Whites, after which Colorado and Blanco parties were named. **1840:** Merino

sheep introduced by British traders, who later established meat processing factories for export trade. **1865–70:** Fought successfully alongside Argentina and Brazil in war against Paraguay. **1903:** After period of military rule, José Battle y Ordonez, a progressive from centre-left Colorado Party, became president. As president 1903–07 and 1911–15, he gave women the franchise and created an advanced welfare state as a successful ranching economy developed. **1930:** First constitution adopted, but period of military dictatorship followed during Depression period. **1958:** After 93 years out of power, right-of-centre Blanco Party returned to power. **1967:** Colorado Party in power, with Jorge Pacheco Areco as president. Period of labour unrest and urban guerrilla activity by left-wing Tupamaros. **1972:** Juan María Bordaberry Arocena of Colorado Party became president. **1973:** Parliament dissolved and Bordaberry shared power with military dictatorship, which crushed Tupamaros and banned left-wing groups. **1976:** Bordaberry deposed by army; Dr Aparicio Méndez Manfredini became president. **1981:** Gen Grigorio Alvárez Armellino became new military ruler. **1984:** Violent antigovernment protests after ten years of repressive rule and deteriorating economy. **1985:** Agreement reached between army and political leaders for return to constitutional government and freeing of political prisoners. Colorado Party won general election; Dr Julio María Sanguinetti became president. **1986:** Government of national accord established under President Sanguinetti. **1989:** Luis Alberto Lacalle Herrera of Blanco Party elected president. **1992:** Public voted against privatization in national referendum. **1994:** Colorado candidate Julio Maria Sanguinetti elected president.

Uzbekistan Republic of

National name: *Ozbekistan Respublikasy* **Area:** 447,400 sq km/172,741 sq mi **Capital:** Tashkent **Major towns/cities:** Samarkand, Bukhara, Namangan, Andizhan **Physical features:** oases in deserts; rivers: Amu Darya, Syr Darya; Ferghana Valley; rich in mineral deposits

Government

Head of state: Islam Karimov from 1990 **Head of government:** Otkir Sultonov from 1995 **Political system:** authoritarian nationalist **Administrative divisions:** 12 regions and one autonomous republic (Karakalpakstan) **Political parties:** People's Democratic Party of Uzbekistan (PDP), reform socialist (ex-communist); Fatherland Progress Party (FP; Vatan Taraqioti), pro-private enterprise; Erk (Freedom Democratic Party), mixed economy; Social Democratic Party of Uzbekistan, pro-Islamic; National Revival Democratic Party, centrist, intelligentsia-led **Armed forces:** 30,000 (1996) **Conscription:** military service is compulsory for 18 months **Death penalty:** retained and used for ordinary crimes **Defence spend:** (% GDP) 3.8 (1996) **Education spend:** (% GNP) 11 (1993/94) **Health spend:** (% GDP) 3.5 (1990–95)

Economy and resources

Currency: som **GDP:** (\$ US) 22 billion (1994) **Real GDP per capita (PPP):** (\$ US) 2,438 (1994) **GDP growth rate:** 1.6% (1996); –4.4% (1990–95) **Average annual inflation:** 64% (1996); 239% (1985–95 est) **Foreign debt:** (\$ US) 1.6 billion (1995) **Major trading partners:** CIS nations (principally Russia, Tajikistan, and Kazakhstan),

Switzerland, Czech Republic, the Netherlands **Resources:** petroleum, natural gas, coal, gold (world's seventh-largest producer), silver, uranium (world's fourth-largest producer), copper, lead, zinc, tungsten **Industries:** processing of agricultural and mineral raw materials, agricultural machinery, chemical products, metallurgy, cement, mineral fertilizer, paper, textiles, footwear, electrical appliances **Exports:** cotton fibre, textiles, machinery, food and energy products, gold. Principal market: Russia 22.3% (1996) **Imports:** machinery, light industrial goods, food and raw materials. Principal source: Russia 24.9% (1996) **Arable land:** 9.9% (1995) **Agricultural products:** cotton (among the world's five largest producers), grain, potatoes, vegetables, fruit and berries; livestock rearing; silkworm breeding

Population and society

Population: 23,209,000 (1996 est) **Population growth rate:** 2.2% (1990–95); 1.9% (2000–05) **Population density:** (per sq km) 50 (1994) **Urban population:** (% of total) 41 (1995) **Age distribution:** (% of total population) <15 39.9%, 15–65 55.6%, >65 4.4% (1995) **Ethnic groups:** 71% Uzbek, 8% ethnic Russian, 4% Tajik, 3% Kazakh, 2% Tatar **Language:** Uzbek, a Turkic language **Religion:** Sunni Muslim **Education:** (compulsory years) 9 **Literacy rate:** 97% (men); 96% (women) (1995 est) **Labour force:** 43.4% agriculture, 21.3% industry, 35.3% services (1992) **Unemployment:** 0.4% (1996) **Life expectancy:** 68 (men); 73 (women) (1995–2000) **Child mortality rate:** (under 5, per 1,000 live births) 47 (1996) **Physicians:** 1 per 284 people (1994)

Practical information

Visa requirements: UK: visa required. USA: visa required **Embassy in the UK:** 72 Wigmore Street, London W1H 9DL. Tel: (0171) 935 1899; fax: (0171) 935 9554 **British embassy:** 6 Murtazayeva Street, Tashkent 700084. Tel: (3712) 345 652; fax: (873) 340 465 **Chamber of commerce:** Tashkent International Business Centre, Ulitsa Pushkina 17, Tashkent. Tel: (3712) 323 231; fax: (3712) 334 414 **Airports:** international airport: Tashkent; eight domestic airports; total passenger km: 4,855 million (1994) **Major holidays:** 1–2 January, 8, 21 March, 1 September, 8 December

Chronology

6th century BC: Part of Persian Empire of Cyrus the Great. **4th century BC:** Part of empire of Alexander the Great of Macedonia. **1st century BC:** Samarkand (Maracanda) developed as transit point on strategic Silk Road trading route between China and Europe. **7th century:** City of Tashkent founded; spread of Islam. **12th century:** Tashkent taken by Turks; Khorezem (Khiva), in NW, became centre of large Central Asian polity, stretching from Caspian Sea to Samarkand in the E. **13th–14th centuries:** Conquered by Genghis Khan and became part of Mongol Empire, with Samarkand serving as capital for Tamerlane. **18th–19th centuries:** Dominated by independent emirates and khanates (chiefdoms) of Bukhara in SW, Kokand in E, and Samarkand in centre. **1865–67:** Tashkent was taken by Russia and made capital of Governor-Generalship of Turkestan. **1868–76:** Tsarist Russia annexed emirate of Bukhara (1868); and khanates of Samarkand (1868), Khiva (1873), and Kokand (1876). **1917:** Following Bolshevik revolution in Russia, Tashkent soviet ('people's council') established, which deposed the emir of Bukhara and other khans 1920. **1918–22:** Mosques closed and Muslim clergy persecuted as part of secularization drive by new communist rulers, despite nationalist guerrilla (basmachi) resistance. **1921:** Part of Turkestan Soviet Socialist Autonomous Republic. **1925:** Became constituent republic of USSR. **1930s:** Skilled ethnic Russians immigrated into urban centres as industries developed. **1944:** About 160,000 Meskhetian Turks forcibly transported from their native Georgia to Uzbekistan by Soviet dictator Joseph Stalin. **1950s–80s:** Major irrigation projects stimulated cotton production, but led to desiccation of Aral Sea. **late 1980s:** Upsurge in Islamic consciousness stimulated by *glasnost* initiative of Soviet Union's reformist leader Mikhail Gorbachev. **1989:** Birlik ('Unity'), nationalist movement, formed. Violent attacks on Meskhetian and other minority communities in Ferghana Valley. **1990:** Economic and political sovereignty declared by increasingly nationalist UCP, led by Islam Karimov, who became president. **1991:** Attempted anti-Gorbachev coup by conservatives in Moscow initially supported by President Karimov. Independence declared. Joined new Commonwealth of Independent States (CIS); Karimov directly elected president. **1992:** Violent food riots in Tashkent. Joined Economic Cooperation Organization and United Nations. New constitution adopted. **1993:** Crackdown on Islamic fundamentalists as economy deteriorated. **1994:** Economic, military, and social union formed with Kazakhstan and Kyrgyzstan. Economic integration treaty signed with Russia. Links with Turkey strengthened and foreign inward investment encouraged. **1995:** Ruling PDP (formerly UCP) won general election, from which opposition was banned from participating. Karimov's tenure extended for further five-year term by national plebiscite. **1996:** Agreement with Kazakhstan and Kyrgyzstan to create single economic market. **1997:** New law governing political parties.

Vanuatu Republic of

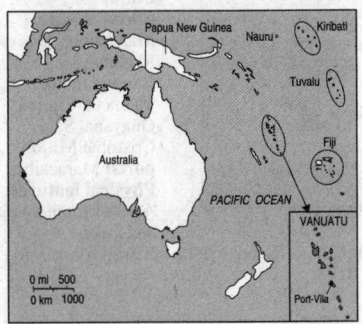

National name: *Ripablik blong Vanuatu* **Area:** 14,800 sq km/5,714 sq mi **Capital:** Port-Vila (on Efate) (and chief port) **Major towns/cities:** Luganville (on Espíritu Santo) **Major ports:** Santo **Physical features:** comprises around 70 inhabited islands, including Espíritu Santo, Malekula, and Efate; densely forested, mountainous; three active volcanoes; cyclones on average twice a year

Government
Head of state: Jean Marie Leye from 1994 **Head of government:** Serge Vohor from 1996 **Political system:** democracy **Administrative divisions:** six provincial authorities **Political parties:** Union of Moderate Parties (UMP), Francophone centrist; National United Party (NUP), formed by Walter Lini; Vanua'aku Pati (VP), Anglophone centrist; Melanesian Progressive Party (MPP), Melanesian centrist; Fren Melanesian Party **Armed forces:** no standing defence force; paramilitary force of around 300; police naval service of around 50 (1995) **Death penalty:** laws do not provide for the death penalty for any crime **Education spend:** (% GNP) 4.8 (1993/94) **Health spend:** (% GDP) 2.9 (1990)

Economy and resources
Currency: vatu **GDP:** ($ US) 198.9 million (1994 est) **Real GDP per capita (PPP):** ($ US) 2,276 (1994) **GDP growth rate:** 3.2% (1995) **Average annual inflation:** 2% (1996); 5.5% (1985–95) **Foreign debt:** ($ US) 237 million (1994) **Major trading partners:** Japan, Australia, the Netherlands, New Zealand, New Caledonia, France **Resources:** manganese; gold, copper, and large deposits of petroleum have been discovered but have hitherto remained unexploited **Industries:** processing of agricultural products (chiefly copra, meat canning, fish freezing, saw milling), soft drinks, building materials, furniture, aluminium, tourism, offshore banking, shipping registry **Exports:** copra, beef, timber, cocoa, shells. Principal market: Japan 24.1% (1995) **Imports:** machinery and transport equipment, food and live animals, basic manufactures, miscellaneous manufactured articles, mineral fuels, chemicals, beverages, tobacco. Principal source: Japan 35.4% (1995) **Arable land:** 1.6% (1995) **Agricultural products:** coconuts and copra, cocoa, coffee, yams, taro, cassava, breadfruit, squash and other vegetables, bananas; livestock rearing (cattle, pigs, goats, and poultry); forest resources

Population and society
Population: 174,000 (1996 est) **Population growth rate:** 2.5% (1990–95) **Population density:** (per sq km) 14 (1996 est) **Urban population:** (% of total) 19.3 (1995) **Age distribution:** (% of total population) <15 45.6%, 15–65 50.4%, >65 4% (1990) **Ethnic groups:** 95% Melanesian, 3% European or mixed European, 2% Vietnamese, Chinese, or other Pacific islanders **Language:** Bislama 82%, English, French (all official) **Religion:** Christian 80%, animist **Education:** (compulsory years) 6 **Literacy rate:** 54% (men); 23% (women) (1995 est) **Labour force:** 68% agriculture, 8% industry, 24% services (1990) **Life expectancy:** 66 (men); 70 (women) (1995–2000) **Child mortality rate:** (under 5, per 1,000 live births) 48 (1996) **Physicians:** 1 per 7,147 people (1990)

Practical information
Visa requirements: UK: visa not required. USA: visa not required **Embassy in the UK:** Vanuatu has no diplomatic representation in the UK; the UK Department of Trade and Industry has a Pacific Islands Desk. Tel: (0171) 215 4985; fax: (0171) 215 4398 **British embassy:** British High Commission, PO Box 567, KPMG House, rue Pasteur, Port-Vila. Tel: (678) 23100; fax: (678) 23651 **Chamber of commerce:** PO Box 189, Port-Vila. Tel/fax: (678) 23255 **Airports:** international airports: Port-Vila (Banerfield); 28 domestic airports and airstrips; total passenger km: 143 million (1994) **Major holidays:** 1 January, 5 March, 1 May, 30 July 15 August, 25–26 December; variable: Ascension, Good Friday, Easter Monday, Constitution (October), Unity (November)

Chronology
1606: First visited by Portuguese navigator Pedro Fernandez de Queiras, who named the islands Espíritu Santo. **1774:** Visited by British navigator Capt James Cook, who named them the New Hebrides, after the Scottish islands. **1830s:** European merchants attracted to islands by sandalwood trade. Christian missionaries arrived, but many were attacked by the indigenous Melanesians who, in turn, were ravaged by exposure to European diseases. **later 19th century:** Britain and France disputed control; islanders were shipped to Australia, Fiji, Samoa, and New Caledonia to work as plantation labourers. **1906:** Islands jointly administered by France and Britain as the Condominium of the New Hebrides. **1963:** Indigenous Na-Griamel (NG) political grouping formed on Espíritu Santo to campaign against European acquisition of more than a third of the land area. **1975:** Representative assembly established following pressure from the VP, formed 1972 by English-speaking Melanesian Protestants. **1978:** Government of national unity formed, with Father Gerard Leymang as chief minister. **1980:** Revolt on the island of Espíritu Santo by French settlers and pro-NG plantation workers delayed independence but it was achieved within the Commonwealth, with George Kalkoa (adopted name Sokomanu) as president and left-of-centre Father Walter Lini (VP) as prime minister. **1988:** Dismissal of Lini by Sokomanu led to Sokomanu's arrest for treason. Lini reinstated. **1989:** Sokomanu succeeded as president by Fred Timakata. **1991:** Lini voted out by party members; replaced by Donald Kalpokas. General election produced coalition government of the Francophone Union of Moderate Parties (UMP) and Lini's new National United Party (NUP) under Maxime Carlot Korman. **1993:** Cyclone caused extensive damage. **1994:** Timakata succeeded as president by Jean Marie Leye. **1995:** Governing UMP–NUP coalition won general election, but Serge Vohor, of VP-dominated Unity Front, became prime minister. **1996:** Vohor briefly replaced by Maxime Carlot Korman, but Vohor returned to power leading new coalition after Carlot government implicated in financial scandal. MFT expelled from governing coalition and replaced by Vanua'aku Party, led by Donald Kalpokas. **1997:** Prime Minister Vohor formed new coalition. Legislature dissolved and new elections called after no-confidence motion against Vohor.

Vatican City State

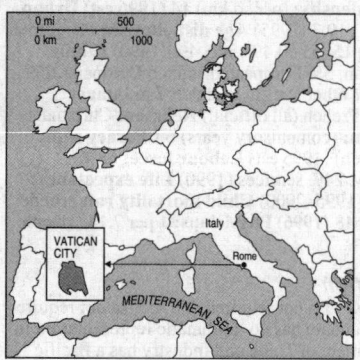

National name:
Stato della Città del Vaticano **Area:** 0.4 sq km/0.2 sq mi
Physical features: forms an enclave in the heart of Rome, Italy

Government
Head of state: John Paul II from 1978
Head of government: Cardinal Sebastiano Baggio **Political system:** absolute

Catholicism **Death penalty:** abolished 1969

Economy and resources
Currency: Vatican City lira; Italian lira **GDP:** see Italy **Real GDP per capita (PPP):** see Italy **GDP growth rate:** see Italy **Industries:** the Vatican has three main sources of income: the Istituto per le Opere di Religione, 'Peter's pence' (voluntary contributions), and interest on investments managed by the Administration of the Patrimony of the Holy See

Population and society
Population: 1,000 (1996 est) **Population density:** (per sq km) 2,273 (1996 est) **Urban population:** (% of total) 100 (1995) **Language:** Latin (official), Italian **Religion:** Roman Catholic **Literacy rate:** see Italy **Life expectancy:** see Italy

Practical information
Visa requirements: see Italy. There is free access to certain areas, including St Peter's Church and Square, the Vatican Museum, and Vatican Gardens; special permission is required to visit all other areas **Embassy in the UK:** Apostolic Nunciature, 54 Parkside, London SW19 5NE. Tel: (0181) 946 1410; fax: (0181) 947 2494 **British embassy:** Via Condotti 91, 00187 Rome. Tel: (6) 678 9462; fax: (6) 994 0684 **Chamber of commerce:** Prefecture of the Economic Affairs of the Holy See, Palazzo delle Congregazioni, Largo del Colonnato 3, 00193 Rome. Tel: (6) 6988 4263; fax: (6) 6988 5011 **Airports:** international airports: one heliport serves visiting heads of state and Vatican officials; the closest international airport is Rome (see Italy) **Major holidays:** see Italy

Chronology
AD 64: Death of St Peter, a Christian martyr who, by legend, was killed in Rome and became regarded as the first bishop of Rome. The Pope, as head of the Roman Catholic Church, is viewed as the spiritual descendent of St Peter. **756:** The Pope became temporal ruler of the Papal States, which stretched across central Italy, centred around Rome. **11th–13th centuries:** Under Gregory VII and Innocent III the papacy enjoyed its greatest temporal power. **1377:** After seven decades in which the papacy was based in Avignon (France), Rome once again became the headquarters for the Pope, with the Vatican Palace becoming the official residence. **1860:** Umbria, Marche, and much of Emilia Romagna which, along with Lazio formed the Papal States, were annexed by the new unified Italian state. **1870:** First Vatican Council defined as a matter of faith the absolute primacy of the Pope and the infallibility of his pronouncements on 'matters of faith and morals'. **1870–71:** French forces, which had been protecting the Pope, were withdrawn, allowing Italian nationalist forces to capture Rome, which became the capital of Italy; Pope Pius IX retreated into the Vatican Palace, from which no Pope was to emerge until 1929. **1929:** Lateran Agreement, signed by the Italian fascist leader Benito Mussolini and Pope Pius XI, restored full sovereign jurisdiction over the Vatican City State to the bishopric of Rome (Holy See) and declared the new

state to be a neutral and inviolable territory. **1947:** New Italian constitution confirmed the sovereignty of the Vatican City State. **1962:** Second Vatican Council called by Pope John XXIII. **1978:** John Paul II became the first non-Italian pope for more than 400 years. **1985:** New concordat signed under which Roman Catholicism ceased to be Italy's state religion. **1992:** Relations with East European states restored.

Venezuela Republic of

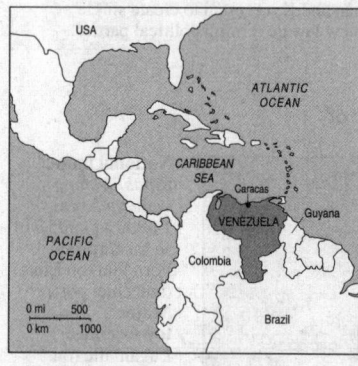

National name:
República de Venezuela **Area:** 912,100 sq km/352,161 sq mi
Capital: Caracas
Major towns/cities: Maracaibo, Maracay, Barquisimeto, Valencia, Ciudad Guayana, San Cristobál **Major ports:** Maracaibo **Physical features:** Andes Mountains and Lake Maracaibo in NW; central plains (llanos); delta of river Orinoco in E; Guiana Highlands in SE

Government
Head of state and government: Rafael Caldera Rodriguez from 1993 **Political system:** federal democracy **Administrative divisions:** 20 states, two federal territories, one federal district, and 72 federal dependencies **Political parties:** Democratic Action Party (AD), moderate left of centre; Christian Social Party (COPEI), Christian, centre right; National Convergence (CN), broad coalition grouping; Movement towards Socialism (MAS), left of centre; Radical Cause (LCR), left wing **Armed forces:** 46,000 (1996) **Conscription:** military service is by selective conscription for 30 months **Death penalty:** abolished 1863 **Defence spend:** (% GDP) 1.2 (1996) **Education spend:** (% GNP) 5.1 (1993/94) **Health spend:** (% GDP) 2.3 (1990–95)

Economy and resources
Currency: bolívar **GDP:** ($ US) 58.3 billion (1994) **Real GDP per capita (PPP):** ($ US) 8,120 (1994) **GDP growth rate:** 3.4% (1995); 2.4% (1990–95) **Average annual inflation:** 100% (1996); 37.6% (1985–95) **Foreign debt:** ($ US) 39.1 billion (1996) **Major trading partners:** USA, Japan, Germany, Italy, the Netherlands, Antilles, Colombia, Brazil **Resources:** petroleum, natural gas, aluminium, iron ore, coal, diamonds, gold, zinc, copper, silver, lead, phosphates, manganese, titanium **Industries:** refined petroleum products, metals (mainly aluminium, steel and pig-iron), food products, chemicals, fertilizers, cement, paper, vehicles **Exports:** petroleum and petroleum products, metals (mainly aluminium and iron ore), natural gas, chemicals, basic manufactures, motor vehicles and parts. Principal market: USA 49.2% (1995) **Imports:** machinery and transport equipment, chemicals, food and live animals, basic manufactures, crude materials. Principal source: USA 42.1% (1995) **Arable land:** 3% (1995) **Agricultural products:** coffee, cocoa, sugar cane, bananas, maize, rice, plantains, oranges, sorghum, cassava, wheat, tobacco, cotton, beans, sisal; livestock rearing (cattle)

Population and society
Population: 22,311,000 (1996 est) **Population growth rate:** 2.3% (1990–95); 1.8% (2000–05) **Population density:** (per sq km) 24 (1996 est) **Urban population:** (% of total) 93 (1995) **Age distribution:** (% of total population) <15 36.2%, 15–65 59.7%, >65

4.1% (1995) **Ethnic groups:** 67% mestizos (of Spanish-American and American-Indian descent), 21% Europeans, 10% Africans, 2% Indians **Language:** Spanish (official), Indian languages 2% **Religion:** Roman Catholic **Education:** (compulsory years) 10 **Literacy rate:** 87% (men); 86% (women) (1995 est) **Labour force:** 9.7% agriculture, 26.3% industry, 64% services (1993) **Unemployment:** 10.7% (1995) **Life expectancy:** 70 (men); 76 (women) (1995–2000) **Child mortality rate:** (under 5, per 1,000 live births) 25 (1996) **Physicians:** 1 per 633 people (1993 est)

Practical information

Visa requirements: UK: visa not required. USA: visa not required **Embassy in the UK:** 1 Cromwell Road, London SW7 2HW. Tel: (0171) 584 4206/7; fax: (0171) 589 8887 **British embassy:** Apartado 1246, Edificio Torre Las Mercedes, 3 °, Avenida la Estancia, Chuao, Caracas 1060. Tel: (2) 993 4111; fax: (2) 993 9989 **Chamber of commerce:** Federación Venezolana de Cámaras y Associaciones de Comercio y Producción, Apartado 2568, Edificio Fedecámaras, 5 °, Avenida El Empalme, Urb El Bosque, Caracas. Tel: (2) 731 1711; fax: (2) 731 0220 **Airports:** international airports: Caracas (Simón Bolívar), Cabello, Maracaibo; domestic services operate to most large towns; total passenger km: 6,426 million (1994) **Major holidays:** 1, 6 January, 19 March, 19 April, 1 May, 24, 29 June, 5, 24 July, 15 August, 12 October, 1 November, 8, 25 December; variable: Ascension Thursday, Carnival (2 days), Corpus Christi, Good Friday, Holy Thursday

Chronology

1st millenium BC: Beginnings of settled agriculture. **AD 1498–99:** Visited by Christopher Columbus and Alonso de Ojeda, at which time the principal indigenous Indian communities were the Caribs, Arawaks, and Chibchas; it was named Venezuela ('little Venice') since the coastal Indians lived in stilted thatched houses. **1521:** Spanish settlement established on the NE coast and was ruled by Spain from Santo Domingo (Dominican Republic). **1567:** Caracas founded by Diego de Losada. **1739:** Became part of newly created Spanish Viceroyalty of New Granada, with capital at Bogotá (Colombia), but, lacking gold mines, retained great autonomy. **1749:** First rebellion against Spanish colonial rule. **1806:** Rebellion against Spain, led by Francisco Miranda. **1811–12:** First Venezuelan Republic declared by patriots, taking advantage of Napoleon Bonaparte's invasion of Spain, but Spanish Royalist forces re-established their authority. **1813–14:** The Venezuelan, Simón Bolívar, 'El Libertador' (the Liberator), created another briefly independent republic, before being forced to withdraw to Colombia. **1821:** After battle of Carabobo, Venezuelan independence achieved within Republic of Gran Colombia (which also comprised Colombia, Ecuador, and Panama). **1829:** Became separate state of Venezuela after leaving Republic of Gran Colombia. **1830–48:** Gen José Antonio Páez, the first of a series of caudillos (military leaders), established political stability. **1870–88:** Antonio Guzmán Blanco ruled as benevolent liberal–conservative dictator, modernizing infrastructure and developing agriculture (notably coffee) and education. **1899:** International arbitration tribunal found in favour of British Guiana (Guyana) in long-running dispute over border with Venezuela. **1902:** Ports blockaded by British, Italian, and German navies as a result of Venezuela's failure to repay loans. **1908–35:** Harsh rule of dictator Juan Vicente Gómez, during which period Venezuela became world's largest exporter of oil, which had been discovered in 1910. **1947:** First truly democratic elections held, but the new president, Rómulo Gallegos, was removed within eight months by the military in the person of Col Marcos Pérez Jimenez. **1958:** Overthrow of Perez and establishment of an enduring civilian democracy, headed by left-wing Romulo Betancourt of Democratic Action Party (AD). **1964:** Dr Raúl Leoni (AD) became president in first-ever constitutional handover of civilian power. **1969:** Dr Rafael Caldera Rodríguez, of centre-right Christian Social Party (COPEI), became president. **1974:** Carlos Andrés Pérez (AD) became president, with economy remaining buoyant through oil revenues. Oil and iron industries nationalized. **1979:** Dr Luis Herrera (COPEI) became president. **1984:** Dr Jaime Lusinchi (AD) became president; social pact established between government, trade unions, and business; national debt rescheduled as oil revenues plummetted.

1987: Widespread social unrest triggered by inflation; student demonstrators shot by police. **1989:** Carlos Andrés Pérez (AD) elected president. Economic austerity programme enforced by a loan of $4.3 billion from International Monetary Fund. Price increases triggered riots known as 'Caracazo'; 300 people killed. Martial law declared. General strike followed. Elections boycotted by opposition groups. **1992:** Attempted antigovernment coups failed, at a cost of 120 lives. **1993:** Pérez resigned, accused of corruption; Ramon José Velasquez succeeded him as interim head of state. Former president Dr Rafael Caldera (COMEI) re-elected. **1996:** Pérez found guilty on corruption charges and imprisoned.

Vietnam Socialist Republic of

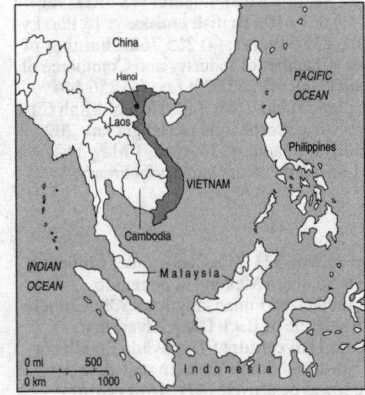

National name: *Công Hòa Xã Hôi Chu Nghĩa Viêt Nam* **Area:** 329,600 sq km/127,258 sq mi **Capital:** Hanoi **Major towns/cities:** Ho Chi Minh City (formerly Saigon), Haiphong, Da Nang, Can Tho, Nha Trang, Nam Dinh **Major ports:** Ho Chi Minh City (formerly Saigon), Da Nang, Haiphong **Physical features:** Red River and Mekong deltas, centre of cultivation and population; tropical rainforest; mountainous in N and NW

Government

Head of state: Tran Duc Luong from 1997 **Head of government:** Phan Van Khai from 1997 **Political system:** communism **Administrative divisions:** 53 provinces within seven regions **Political party:** Communist Party **Armed forces:** 572,000; plus paramilitary forces numbering 50,000 and around 3 million reserves (1996) **Conscription:** military service is compulsory for two years **Death penalty:** retained and used for ordinary crimes **Defence spend:** (% GDP) 4.0 (1996) **Education spend:** (% GNP) 2.7 (1994) **Health spend:** (% GDP) 1.1 (1990–95)

Economy and resources

Currency: dong **GDP:** ($ US) 15.6 billion (1994) **Real GDP per capita (PPP):** ($ US) 1,208 (1994) **GDP growth rate:** 9.5% (1995); 8.3% (1990–95) **Average annual inflation:** 6.5% (1996); 88.3% (1985–95) **Foreign debt:** ($ US) 26.5 billion (1995) **Major trading partners:** Singapore, Japan, Hong Kong, France, Germany, South Korea **Resources:** petroleum, coal, tin, zinc, iron, antimony, chromium, phosphate, apatite, bauxite **Industries:** food processing, chemicals, machinery, textiles, beer, glass and glassware, cigarettes, crude steel, cement, fertilizers, tourism (steady growth in early 1990s) **Exports:** rice (leading exporter), crude petroleum, coal, coffee, marine products, handicrafts, light industrial goods, rubber, nuts, tea, garments, tin. Principal market: Japan 28.5% (1995) **Imports:** petroleum products, machinery and spare parts, steel, artificial fertilizers, basic manufactures, consumer goods. Principal source: Singapore 17% (1995) **Arable land:** 16.9% (1995) **Agricultural products:** rice (world's fifth-largest producer), coffee, tea, rubber, cotton, groundnuts, sugar cane, coconuts; livestock rearing; fishing

Population and society

Population: 75,181,000 (1996 est) **Population growth rate:** 2.2% (1990–95); 1.9% (2000–05) **Population density:** (per sq km) 227

(1996 est) **Urban population:** (% of total) 21 (1995) **Age distribution:** (% of total population) <15 37.5%, 15–65 57.7%, >65 4.9% (1995) **Ethnic groups:** 88% Viet (also known as Kinh), 2% Chinese, 2% Khmer, 8% consists of more than 50 minority nationalities, including the Hmong, Meo, Muong, Nung, Tay, Thai, and Tho tribal groups **Language:** Vietnamese (official); French, English, Khmer, Chinese, local languages **Religion:** Taoist, Buddhist, Roman Catholic **Education:** (compulsory years) 5 **Literacy rate:** 92% (men); 84% (women) (1995 est) **Labour force:** 73% agriculture, 13.3% industry, 13.7% services (1994) **Unemployment:** 7% (1994 est) **Life expectancy:** 65 (men); 70 (women) (1995–2000) **Child mortality rate:** (under 5, per 1,000 live births) 56 (1996) **Physicians:** 1 per 2,279 people (1993 est)

Practical information

Visa requirements: UK: visa required. USA: visa required **Embassy in the UK:** 12–14 Victoria Road, London W8 5RD. Tel: (0171) 937 1912; fax: (0171) 937 6108 **British embassy:** 16 Pho Ly Thuong Kiet, Hanoi. Tel: (4) 252 349; fax: (4) 265 762 **Chamber of commerce:** Vietcochamber (Chamber of Industry and Commerce of Vietnam), 33 Ba Trieu, Hanoi. Tel: (4) 253 023; fax: (4) 256 446 **Airports:** international airports: Hanoi (Noi Bai), Ho Chi Minh City (Tan Son Nhat); seven domestic airports; total passenger km: 209 million (1994) **Major holidays:** 1 January, 30 April, 1 May, 1–2 September; variable: Têt, Lunar New Year (January/February, 3 days)

Chronology

300 BC: Rise of Dong Son culture. **111 BC:** Came under Chinese rule. **1st–6th centuries AD:** Southern Mekong delta region controlled by independent Indianized Funan kingdom. **939:** Chinese overthrown by Ngo Quyen at battle of Bach Dang River; first Vietnamese dynasty founded. **11th century:** Theravāda Buddhism promoted. **15th century:** North and South Vietnam united, as kingdom of Champa in the S was destroyed 1471. **16th century:** Contacts with French missionaries and European traders as political power became decentralized. **early 19th century:** Under Emperor Nguyen Anh authority was briefly recentralized. **1858–84:** Conquered by France and divided into protectorates of Tonkin (North Vietnam) and Annam (South Vietnam). **1887:** Became part of French Indo-China Union, which included Cambodia and Laos. **late 19th–early 20th century:** Development of colonial economy based in S on rubber and rice, drawing migrant labourers from N. **1930:** Indochinese Communist Party (ICP) formed by Ho Chi Minh to fight for independence. **1941:** Occupied by Japanese during World War II; ICP formed Vietminh as guerrilla resistance force designed to overthrow Japanese-installed puppet regime headed by Bao Dai, Emperor of Annam. **1945:** Japanese removed from Vietnam at end of World War II; Vietminh, led by Ho Chi Minh, in control of much of the country, declared independence. **1946:** Vietminh war began against French, who tried to reassert colonial control and set up noncommunist state in S 1949. **1954:** France decisively defeated at Dien Bien Phu. Vietnam divided along 17th parallel between communist-controlled N and US-backed S. **1963:** Ngo Dinh Diem, leader of South Vietnam, overthrown in military coup by Lt-Gen Nguyen Van Thieu. **1964:** US combat troops entered Vietnam War as N Vietnamese army began to attack S and allegedly attacked US destroyers in the Tonkin Gulf. **1969:** Death of Ho Chi Minh, who was succeeded as Communist Party leader by Le Duan. US forces, which numbered 545,000 at their peak, gradually began to be withdrawn from Vietnam as a result of domestic opposition to the rising casualty toll. **1973:** Paris cease-fire agreement provided for withdrawal of US troops and release of US prisoners of war. **1975:** Saigon captured by North Vietnam, violating Paris Agreements. **1976:** Socialist Republic of Vietnam proclaimed. Hundreds of thousands of southerners became political prisoners; many more fled abroad. Collectivization extended to S. **1978:** Diplomatic relations severed with China. Admission into Comecon. Vietnamese invasion of Cambodia. **1979:** Sino-Vietnamese 17-day border war; 700,000 Chinese and middle-class Vietnamese fled abroad as refugee 'boat people'. **1986:** Death of Le Duan and retirement of 'old guard' leaders; pragmatic Nguyen Van Linh became Communist Party leader and encouraged the private

sector through *doi moi* ('renovation') initiative. **1987–88:** Over 10,000 political prisoners released. **1989:** Troops fully withdrawn from Cambodia. **1991:** Economic reformer Vo Van Kiet replaced Do Muoi as prime minister. Cambodia peace agreement signed. Relations with China normalized. **1992:** New constitution adopted, guaranteeing economic freedoms. Conservative Le Duc Anh elected president. Relations with South Korea normalized. **1994:** US 30-year-old trade embargo removed. **1995:** Full diplomatic relations re-established with USA. Became full member of ASEAN. **1996:** Economic upturn gained pace. **1997:** Diplomatic relations with USA restored. Tran Duc Luong and Phan Van Khai elected president and prime minister respectively. Reduction in size of standing army.

Yemen Republic of

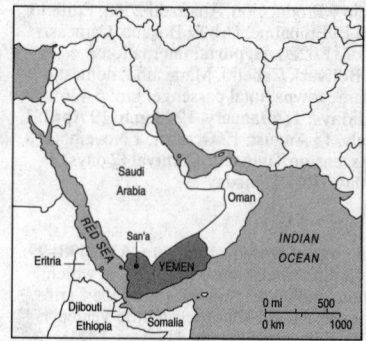

National name: *Jamhuriya al Yamaniya* **Area:** 531,900 sq km/205,366 sq mi **Capital:** San'a **Major towns/cities:** Aden, Ta'izz, Al Mukalla, Hodeida, Ibb, Dhamar **Major ports:** Aden **Physical features:** hot, moist coastal plain, rising to plateau and desert

Government

Head of state: Ali Abdullah Saleh from 1990 **Head of government:** Farag Said Ben Ghanem from 1997 **Political system:** emergent democracy **Administrative divisions:** 17 governates **Political parties:** General People's Congress (GPC), left of centre; Yemen Socialist Party (YSP), left wing; Yemen Reform Group (al-Islah), Islamic, right of centre; National Opposition Front, left of centre **Armed forces:** 42,000; plus paramilitary forces numbering at least 70,000 (1996) **Conscription:** military service is compulsory for two years **Death penalty:** retained and used for ordinary crimes **Defence spend:** (% GDP) 3.9 (1995) **Education spend:** (% GNP) 5.8 (1990) **Health spend:** (% GDP) 1.1 (1990–95)

Economy and resources

Currency: riyal (North); dinar (South), both legal currency throughout the country **GDP:** ($ US) 18.17 billion (1994 est) **Real GDP per capita (PPP):** ($ US) 805 (1994) **GDP growth rate:** 1% (1995) **Average annual inflation:** 85% (1996) **Foreign debt:** ($ US) 6.2 billion (1995) **Major trading partners:** China, United Arab Emirates, USA, Saudi Arabia, Japan, UK, Germany **Resources:** petroleum, natural gas, gypsum, salt; deposits of copper, gold, lead, zinc, molybdenum **Industries:** petroleum refining and petroleum products, building materials, food processing, beverages, tobacco, chemical products, textiles, leather goods, metal goods **Exports:** petroleum and petroleum products, cotton, basic manufactures, clothing, live animals, hides and skins, fish, rice, coffee. Principal market: China 23.4% (1995) **Imports:** textiles and other manufactured consumer goods, petroleum products, sugar, grain, flour, other foodstuffs, cement, machinery, chemicals. Principal source: UAE 14.2% (1995) **Arable land:** 2.7% (1995) **Agricultural products:** sorghum, sesame, millet, potatoes, tomatoes, cotton, wheat, grapes, watermelons, coffee, alfalfa, dates, bananas; livestock rearing; fishing

Population and society

Population: 15,678,000 (1996 est) **Population growth rate:** 5% (1990–95); 3.1% (2000–05) **Population density:** (per sq km) 30 (1996 est) **Urban population:** (% of total) 34 (1995) **Age distribution:** (% of total population) <15 46.7%, 15–65 50.9%, >65

2.4% (1995) **Ethnic groups:** predominantly Arab **Language:** Arabic **Religion:** Sunni Muslim 63%, Shi'ite Muslim 37% **Education:** (compulsory years): 6 (North); 8 (South) **Literacy rate:** 53% (men); 26% (women) (1995 est) **Labour force:** 30% of population: 61% agriculture, 17% industry, 22% services (1990) **Unemployment:** 36% (1993) **Life expectancy:** 52 (men); 52 (women) (1995–2000) **Child mortality rate:** (under 5, per 1,000 live births) 155 (1996) **Physicians:** 1 per 4,498 people (1993 est)

Practical information

Visa requirements: UK: visa required. USA: visa required **Embassy in the UK:** 57 Cromwell Road, London SW7 2ED. Tel: (0171) 584 6607; fax: (0171) 589 3350 **British embassy:** PO Box 1287, 129 Haddah Road, Sana'a. Tel: (1) 215 630; fax: (1) 263 059 **Chamber of commerce:** Federation of Chambers of Commerce, PO Box 16992, Sana'a. Tel: (1) 221 765; telex: 2229 **Airports:** international airports: Sana'a (El-Rahaba), Ta'izz (al-Jahad), Hodeida, Aden (Khormaksar), Mukalla (Riyan), Seybun; domestic services operate between these; total passenger km: 1,183 million (1994) **Major holidays:** 1 May, 26 September; variable: Eid-ul-Adha (5 days), end of Ramadan (4 days), New Year (Muslim), Prophet's Birthday

Chronology

1st millenium BC: South Yemen (Aden) divided between economically advanced Qataban and Hadramawt kingdoms. **c. 5th century BC:** Qataban fell to the Sabaeans (Shebans) of North Yemen (Sana). **c. 100 BC–AD 525:** All of Yemen became part of Himyarite kingdom. **AD 628:** Islam introduced. **1174–1229:** Under control of Egyptian Ayyubids. **1229–1451:** 'Golden age' for arts and sciences under the Rasulids, who had served as governors of Yemen under the Ayyubids. **1538:** North Yemen came under control of Turkish Ottoman Empire. **1636:** Ottomans left North Yemen and power fell into hands of Yemeni Imams, based on local Zaydi tribes, who also held South Yemen until 1735. **1839:** Aden became a British territory. Port developed into important ship refuelling station after opening of Suez Canal 1869; protectorate was gradually established over 23 Sultanates inland. **1870s:** The Ottomans re-established control over North Yemen. **1918:** North Yemen became independent, with Imam Yahya from Hamid al-Din family as king. **1937:** Aden became British crown colony. **1948:** Imam Yahya assassinated by exiled Free Yemenis nationalist movement, but uprising was crushed by his son, Imam Ahmad. **1959:** Federation of South Arabia formed by Britain between city of Aden and feudal Sultanates (Aden Protectorate). **1962:** Military coup on death of Imam Ahmad; North Yemen declared Yemen Arab Republic (YAR), with Abdullah al-Sallal as president. Civil war broke out between royalists (supported by Saudi Arabia) and republicans (supported by Egypt). **1963:** Armed rebellion by National Liberation Front (NLF) began against British rule in Aden. **1967:** Civil war ended with republicans victorious. Sallal deposed and replaced by Republican Council. The Independent People's Republic of South Yemen formed after British withdrawal from Aden. Many fled to N as repressive communist NLF regime took over in S. **1970:** People's Republic of South Yemen renamed People's Democratic Republic of Yemen. **1971–72:** War between South Yemen and YAR; union agreement brokered by Arab League signed but not kept. **1974:** The pro-Saudi Col Ibrahim al-Hamadi seized power in North Yemen; Military Command Council set up. **1977:** Hamadi assassinated; replaced by Col Ahmed ibn Hussein al-Ghashmi. **1978:** Constituent people's assembly appointed in North Yemen and Military Command Council dissolved. Ghashmi killed by envoy from South Yemen; succeeded by Ali Abdullah Saleh. War broke out again between two Yemens. South Yemen president deposed and executed; Yemen Socialist Party (YSP) formed in S by communists. **1979:** Cease-fire agreed with commitment to future union. **1980:** YSP leader Ali Nasser Muhammad became head of state in South Yemen. **1986:** Civil war in South Yemen; autocratic Ali Nasser dismissed. New administration formed under more moderate Haydar Abu Bakr al-Attas, who was committed to negotiating union with N as a result of deteriorating economy in S. **1989:** Draft multiparty constitution for single Yemen state published. **1990:** Border between two Yemens opened; countries formally united 22

May as Republic of Yemen. **1991:** New constitution approved; Yemen opposed US-led operations against Iraq in Gulf War. **1992:** Anti-government riots. **1993:** Saleh's General People's Congress (GPC) won most seats in general election but no overall majority; five-member presidential council elected, including Saleh as president, YSP leader Ali Salim al-Baidh as vice president, and Bakr al-Attas as prime minister. **1994:** Fighting erupted between northern forces, led by President Saleh, and southern forces, led by Vice President al-Baidh, as southern Yemen announced its secession. Saleh inflicted crushing defeat on al-Baidh and new GPC coalition appointed. **1997:** GPC election victory. Farag Said Ben Ghanem appointed prime minister.

Yugoslavia Federal Republic of

National name: *Federativna Republika Jugoslavija* **Area:** 58,300 sq km/22,509 sq mi **Capital:** Belgrade **Major towns/cities:** Priština, Novi Sad, Niš, Rijeka, Kragujevac, Podgorica (formerly Titograd), Subotica **Physical features:** federation of republics of Serbia and Montenegro and two former autonomous provinces, Kosovo and Vojvodina

Government

Head of state: Slobodan Milošević from 1997 **Head of government:** Radoje Kontic from 1993 **Political system:** socialist pluralist republic **Administrative divisions:** 29 districts **Political parties:** Socialist Party of Serbia (SPS), Serb nationalist, reform socialist (ex-communist); Montenegrin Social Democratic Party (SDPCG), federalist, reform socialist (ex-communist); Serbian Radical Party (SRS), Serb nationalist, extreme right wing; People's Assembly Party, Christian democrat, centrist; Democratic Party (DS), moderate nationalist; Democratic Party of Serbia (DSS), moderate nationalist; Democratic Community of Vojvodina Hungarians (DZVM), ethnic Hungarian; Democratic Party of Albanians/Party of Democratic Action (DPA/PDA), ethnic Albanian; New Socialist Party of Montenegro (NSPM), left of centre **Armed forces:** 113,900 (1996) **Conscription:** military service is compulsory for 12–15 months; voluntary military service for women introduced 1983 **Death penalty:** retained and used for ordinary crimes **Defence spend:** (% GDP) 8.7 (1996) **Education spend:** (% GNP) 6.1 (1992; former Yugoslavia)

Economy and resources

Currency: new Yugoslav dinar **GDP:** (\$ US) 15.9 billion (1995 est) **Real GDP per capita (PPP):** (\$ US) 4,400 (1995 est) **GDP growth rate:** 4% (1995 est) **Average annual inflation:** 95% (1996) **Foreign debt:** (\$ US) 11.6 billion (1996 est) **Major trading partners:** Germany, CIS nations, Italy, USA, Macedonia **Resources:** petroleum, natural gas, coal, copper ore, bauxite, iron ore, lead, zinc **Industries:** crude steel, pig-iron, steel castings, cement, machines, passenger cars, electrical appliances, artificial fertilizers, plastics, bicycles, textiles and clothing **Exports:** basic manufactures, machinery and transport equipment, clothing, miscellaneous manufactured articles, food and live animals. Principal market: developed countries 40.2% (1996) **Imports:** machinery and transport equipment, electrical goods, agricultural produce, mineral fuels and lubricants, basic manufactures, foodstuffs, chemicals. Principal source: developed countries 51.7% (1996) **Arable land:** 36.6% (1995) **Agricultural products:** maize, sugar beet, wheat, potatoes, grapes, plums, soya beans, vegetables; livestock production declined 1991–95

Population and society

Population: 10,294,000 (1996 est) **Population growth rate:** 1.3% (1990–95); 0.4% (2000–05) **Population density:** (per sq km) 101 (1996 est) **Urban population:** (% of total) 57 (1995) **Age distribution:** (% of total population) <15 22%, 15–65 66.6%, >65 11.4% (1995) **Ethnic groups:** according to the 1991 census, 62% of the population of the rump federal republic is ethnic Serb, 17% Albanian, 5% Montenegrin, 3% 'Yugoslav', and 3% Muslim. Serbs predominate in the republic of Serbia, where they form (excluding the autonomous areas of Kosovo and Vojvodina) 85% of the population; in Vojvodina they comprise 55% of the population. Albanians constitute 77% of the population of Kosovo; Montenegrins comprise 69% of the population of the republic of Montenegro; and Muslims predominate in the Sandzak region, which straddles the Serbian and Montenegrin borders. Since 1992 an influx of Serb refugees from Bosnia and Kosovo has increased the proportion of Serbs in Serbia, while many ethnic Hungarians have left Vojvodina, and an estimated 500,000 Albanians have left Kosovo **Language:** Serbo-Croatian; Albanian (in Kosovo) **Religion:** Serbian and Montenegrin Orthodox; Muslim in S Serbia **Education:** (compulsory years) 8 **Literacy rate:** 97% (men); 88% (women) (1995 est) **Labour force:** 6% agriculture, 41% industry, 53% services (1993 est) **Unemployment:** 23.8% (1994) **Life expectancy:** 70 (men); 75 (women) (1995–2000) **Child mortality rate:** (per 1,000 live births) 23 (1995) **Physicians:** 1 per 506 people (1993)

Practical information

Visa requirements: UK: visa required. USA: visa required **Embassy in the UK:** 5–7 Lexham Gardens, London W8 5JJ. Tel: (0171) 370 6105; fax: (0171) 370 3838 **British embassy:** Ulica Generala Zdanova 46, 11000 Belgrade. Tel: (1) 645 055; fax: (1) 659 651 **Chamber of commerce:** Chamber of Economy of Serbia, Ulica Generala Zdanova 13–15, 11000 Belgrade. Tel: (1) 340 611; fax: (1) 330 949. Chamber of Economy of Montenegro, Novaka Miloseva 29/II, 81000 Podgorica. Tel: (81) 31071; fax: (81) 34926 **Airports:** international airports: Belgrade (Surcin), Podgorica; three domestic airports; total passenger km: 3,443 million (1991) **Major holidays:** 1–2 January, 1–2 May, 4, 7 (Serbia only), 13 (Montenegro only) July, 29–30 November; Orthodox Christian holidays may also be celebrated throughout much of the region

Chronology

3rd century BC: Serbia (then known as Moesia Superior) conquered by Romans; empire was extended to Belgrade centuries later by Emperor Augustus. **6th century AD:** Slavic tribes, including Serbs, Croats, and Slovenes, crossed river Danube and settled in Balkan Peninsula. **879:** Serbs converted to Orthodox Church by Sts Cyril and Methodius. **mid-10th–11th centuries:** Serbia broke free briefly from Byzantine Empire to establish independent state. **1217:** Independent Serbian kingdom re-established, reaching its height in mid-14th century under Stefan Dushan, when it controlled much of Albania and northern Greece. **1389:** Serbian army defeated by Ottoman Turks at Battle of Kosovo; area became Turkish *pashalik* (province). Montenegro in SW survived as sovereign principality. Croatia and Slovenia in NW became part of Habsburg Empire. **18th century:** Vojvodina enjoyed protection from the Austrian Habsburgs. **1815:** Uprisings against Turkish rule secured autonomy for Serbia. **1878:** Independence achieved as Kingdom of Serbia, after Turks defeated by Russians in war over Bulgaria. **1912–13:** During Balkan Wars, Serbia expanded its territory at expense of Turkey and Bulgaria. **1918:** Joined Croatia and Slovenia, formerly under Austrian Habsburg control, to form Kingdom of Serbs, Croats, and Slovenes under Serbian Peter Karageorgevic (Peter I); Montenegro's citizens voted to depose their ruler, King Nicholas, and join the union. **1929:** New name of Yugoslavia ('Land of the Southern Slavs') adopted; Serbian-dominated military dictatorship established by King Alexander I as opposition mounted from Croatian

federalists. **1934:** Alexander I assassinated by a Macedonian with Croatian terrorist links; his young son Peter II succeeded, with Paul, his uncle, as regent; Nazi Germany and fascist Italy increased their influence. **1941:** Following coup by pro-Allied air-force officers, Nazi Germany invaded. Peter II fled to England. Armed resistance to German rule began, spearheaded by pro-royalist, Serbian-based Chetniks ('Army of the Fatherland'), led by Gen Draza Mihailović, and communist Partisans ('National Liberation Army'), led by Marshal Tito. An estimated 900,000 Yugoslavs died in the war, including more than 400,000 Serbs and 200,000 Croats. **1943:** Provisional government formed by Tito at liberated Jajce in Bosnia. **1945:** Yugoslav Federal People's Republic formed under leadership of Tito; communist constitution introduced. **1948:** Split with Soviet Union after Tito objected to Soviet 'hegemonism'; expelled from Cominform. **1953:** Workers' self-management principle enshrined in constitution and private farming supported; Tito became president. **1961:** Nonaligned movement formed under Yugoslavia's leadership. **1971:** In response to mounting separatist demands in Croatia, new system of collective and rotating leadership introduced. **1980:** Tito died; collective leadership assumed power. **1981–82:** Armed forces suppressed demonstrations in Kosovo province, S Serbia, by Albanians demanding full republic status. **1986:** Slobodan Milošević, a populist-nationalist hardliner who had the ambition of creating a 'Greater Serbia', became leader of communist party in the Serbian republic. **1988:** Economic difficulties: 1,800 strikes, 250% inflation, 20% unemployment. Ethnic unrest in Montenegro and Vojvodina, and separatist demands in rich NW republics of Croatia and Slovenia; 'market socialist' reform package, encouraging private sector, inward investment, and liberalizing prices combined with austerity wage freeze. **1989:** Reformist Croatian Ante Marković became prime minister. Ethnic riots in Kosovo province against Serbian attempt to end autonomous status of Kosovo and Vojvodina; at least 30 were killed and a state of emergency imposed. **1990:** Multiparty systems established in republics; Kosovo and Vojvodina stripped of autonomy. In Croatia, Slovenia, Bosnia, and Macedonia elections bought to power new non-communist governments seeking a looser confederation. **1991:** Demonstrations against Serbian president Slobodan Milošević in Belgrade crushed violently by riot police and tanks. Slovenia and Croatia declared independence, resulting in clashes between federal and republican armies; Slovenia accepted peace pact sponsored by European Community, but fighting intensified in Croatia, where Serb militias controlled over one-third of the republic; Federal President Stipe Mesic and Prime Minister Markovic resigned. **1992:** EC-brokered cease-fire in Croatia; EC and USA recognized Slovenia's and Croatia's independence. Bosnia-Herzegovina and Macedonia declared independence. Bosnia-Herzegovina recognized as independent by EC and USA. New Federal Republic of Yugoslavia (FRY) proclaimed by Serbia and Montenegro but not recognized externally. International sanctions imposed. UN membership suspended. Ethnic Albanians proclaimed new 'Republic of Kosovo', but it was not recognized. **1993:** Pro-Milošević Zoran Lilic became Yugoslav president. Antigovernment rioting in Belgrade. Macedonia recognized as independent under name of Former Yugoslav Republic of Macedonia. Economy severely damaged by international sanctions. **1994:** Border blockade imposed by Yugoslavia against Bosnian Serbs; sanctions eased as a result. **1995:** Serbia played key role in US-brokered Dayton peace accord for Bosnia-Herzegovina and accepted separate existence of Bosnia and Croatia. US economic sanctions against Serbia lifted. **1996:** Diplomatic relations restored between Serbia and Croatia. UN sanctions against Serbia lifted. Allies of Milošević successful in parliamentary elections. Full diplomatic relations established with Bosnia-Herzegovina. Ruling party won assembly elections. Mounting opposition to Milošević's government, following its refusal to accept opposition victories in municipal elections. **1997:** Serbian parliament passed legislation recognizing the elections, thus ending opposition demonstrations. Slobodan Milošević elected president. Anti-Milošević candidate elected president of Montenegro. **1998:** Serbian offensive against ethnic-Albanian separatists in the province of Kosovo. June: EU and USA imposed sanctions, and NATO forces were sent to the region with the threat of military intervention.

Zambia Republic of (formerly Northern Rhodesia)

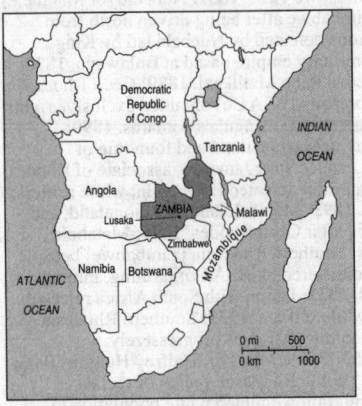

Area: 752,600 sq km/290,578 sq mi
Capital: Lusaka
Major towns/cities: Kitwe, Ndola, Kabwe, Mufulira, Chingola, Luanshya, Livingstone
Physical features: forested plateau cut through by rivers; Zambezi River, Victoria Falls, Kariba Dam

Government

Head of state and government: Frederick Chiluba from 1991 **Political system:** emergent democracy **Administrative divisions:** nine provinces **Political parties:** United National Independence Party (UNIP), African socialist; Movement for Multiparty Democracy (MMD), moderate, left of centre; Multiracial Party (MRP), moderate, left of centre, multiracial; National Democratic Alliance (NADA), left of centre; Democratic Party (DP), left of centre **Armed forces:** 21,600; plus paramilitary forces of 1,400 (1996) **Conscription:** military service is voluntary **Death penalty:** retained and used for ordinary crimes **Defence spend:** (% GDP) 1.8 (1996) **Education spend:** (% GNP) 2.6 (1993/94) **Health spend:** (% GDP) 2.6 (1990–95)

Economy and resources

Currency: Zambian kwacha **GDP:** ($ US) 3.5 billion (1994) **Real GDP per capita (PPP):** ($ US) 962 (1994) **GDP growth rate:** –3.9% (1995); –0.2% (1990–95) **Average annual inflation:** 31.7% (1995); 91.6% (1985–95) **Foreign debt:** ($ US) 6.3 billion (1995) **Major trading partners:** South Africa, Japan, UK, Germany, France, Thailand, India **Resources:** copper (world's fourth-largest producer), cobalt, zinc, lead, coal, gold, emeralds, amethysts and other gemstones, limestone, selenium **Industries:** metallurgy (smelting and refining of copper and other metals), food canning, fertilizers, explosives, textiles, bottles, bricks, copper wire, batteries **Exports:** copper, zinc, lead, cobalt, tobacco. Principal market: Japan 16% (1995) **Imports:** machinery and transport equipment, mineral fuels, lubricants, electricity, basic manufactures, chemicals, food and live animals. Principal source: South Africa 33.1% (1995) **Arable land:** 7.1% (1995) **Agricultural products:** maize, sugar cane, seed cotton, tobacco, groundnuts, wheat, rice, beans, cassava, millet, sorghum, sunflower seeds, horticulture; cattle rearing

Population and society

Population: 8,275,000 (1996 est) **Population growth rate:** 3% (1990–95); 2.4% (2000–05) **Population density:** (per sq km) 11 (1996 est) **Urban population:** (% of total) 43 (1995) **Age distribution:** (% of total population) <15 47.4%, 15–65 50.2%, >65 2.4% (1995) **Ethnic groups:** over 95% indigenous Africans, belonging to more than 70 different ethnic groups, including the Bantu-Botatwe and the Bemba **Language:** English (official); Bantu languages **Religion:** Christian, animist, Hindu, Muslim **Education:** (compulsory years) 7 **Literacy rate:** 81% (men); 65% (women) (1995 est) **Labour force:** 42% of population: 75% agriculture, 8% industry, 17% services (1990) **Life expectancy:** 45 (men); 47 (women) (1995–2000) **Child mortality rate:** (under 5, per 1,000 live births) 140 (1996) **Physicians:** 1 per 10,917 people (1993 est)

Practical information

Visa requirements: UK: visa not required. USA: visa required **Embassy in the UK:** 2 Palace Gate, London W8 5NG. Tel: (0171) 589 6655; fax: (0171) 581 1353 **British embassy:** British High Commission, PO Box 50050, Independence Avenue, 15101 Ridgeway, Lusaka. Tel: (1) 251 133; fax: (1) 253 798 **Chamber of commerce:** Ministry of Commerce, Trade and Industry, PO Box 31968, Kwacha Annex, Cairo Road, Lusaka. Tel: (1) 228 301; fax: (1) 226 727 **Airports:** international airports: Lusaka; over 127 domestic airports, aerodromes, and airstrips; total passenger km: 428 million (1994) **Major holidays:** 1 January, 1, 25 May, 24 October, 25 December; variable: Good Friday, Holy Saturday, Youth (March), Heroes (July), Unity (July), Farmers (August)

Chronology

16th century: Immigration of peoples from Luba and Lunda Empires of Zaire, to the NW, who set up small kingdoms. **late 18th century:** Visited by Portuguese explorers. **19th century:** Instability with immigration of Ngoni from E, Kololo from W, establishment of Bemba kingdom in N, and slave-trading activities of Portuguese and Arabs from E Africa. **1851:** Visited by British missionary and explorer David Livingstone. **1889:** As Northern Rhodesia, came under administration of British South Africa Company of Cecil Rhodes, and became involved in copper mining, especially from 1920s. **1924:** Became a British protectorate. **1948:** Northern Rhodesia African Congress (NRAC) formed by black Africans to campaign for self-rule. **1953:** Became part of Central African Federation, which included South Rhodesia (Zimbabwe) and Nyasaland (Malawi). **1960:** UNIP formed by Kenneth Kaunda as breakaway from NRAC, as African socialist body to campaign for independence and dissolution of Federation dominated by South Rhodesia's white minority. **1963:** Federation dissolved; internal self-government achieved. **1964:** Independence achieved within Commonwealth as Republic of Zambia with Kaunda of the UNIP as president. **later 1960s:** Key enterprises brought under state control. **1972:** UNIP declared only legal party. **1975:** Opening of Tan-Zam railway from Zambian copperbelt, 322 mi/200 km N of Lusaka, to port of Dar es Salaam in Tanzania. This reduced Zambia's dependence on rail route via Rhodesia for its exports. **1976:** Zambia declared support for Patriotic Front (PF) guerrillas fighting to topple white-dominated regime in Rhodesia (Zimbabwe). **1980:** Unsuccessful South African-promoted coup against President Kaunda; relations with Zimbabwe improved when PF came to power. **1985:** Kaunda elected chair of African Front Line States. **1991:** New multiparty constitution adopted. MMD won landslide election victory, and its leader Frederick Chiluba became president in what was the first democratic change of government in English-speaking black Africa. **1993:** State of emergency declared after rumours of planned anti-government coup, privatization programme launched. **1996:** Kaunda barred from future elections; President Chiluba re-elected. **1997:** Abortive anti-government coup.

Zimbabwe Republic of (formerly Southern Rhodesia)

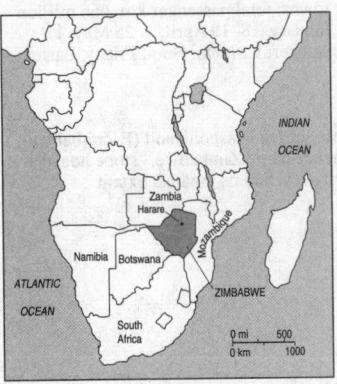

Area: 390,300 sq km/150,694 sq mi
Capital: Harare
Major towns/cities: Bulawayo, Gweru, Kwekwe, Mutare, Hwange, Chitungwiza
Physical features: high plateau with central high veld and mountains in E; rivers Zambezi, Limpopo; Victoria Falls

Government

Head of state and government: Robert Mugabe from 1987 **Political system:** effectively one-party socialist republic **Administrative divisions:** eight provinces and two cities with provincial status **Political**

parties: Zimbabwe African National Union–Patriotic Front (ZANU–PF), African socialist; opposition parties exist but none have mounted serious challenge to ruling party **Armed forces:** 43,000; 21,800 paramilitary forces (1996) **Conscription:** military service is voluntary **Death penalty:** retained and used for ordinary crimes **Defence spend:** (% GDP) 3.9 (1996) **Education spend:** (% GNP) 8.3 (1993/94) **Health spend:** (% GDP) 2.1 (1990–95)

Economy and resources
Currency: Zimbabwe dollar **GDP:** ($ US) 5.4 billion (1994) **Real GDP per capita (PPP):** ($ US) 2,196 (1994) **GDP growth rate:** 7.4% (1994); 1.0% (1990–95) **Average annual inflation:** 21.5% (1996); 20.9% (1985–95) **Foreign debt:** ($ US) 4.9 billion (1995) **Major trading partners:** South Africa, UK, Germany, Japan, USA **Resources:** gold, nickel, asbestos, coal, chromium, copper, silver, emeralds, lithium, tin, iron ore, cobalt **Industries:** metal products, food processing, textiles, furniture and other wood products, chemicals, fertilizers **Exports:** tobacco, metals and metal alloys, textiles and clothing, cotton lint. Principal market: South Africa 13.5% (1995) **Imports:** machinery and transport equipment, basic manufactures, mineral fuels, chemicals, foodstuffs. Principal source: South Africa 40.9% (1995) **Arable land:** 8% (1995) **Agricultural products:** tobacco, maize, cotton, coffee, sugar cane, wheat, soya beans, groundnuts, horticulture; livestock (cattle)

Population and society
Population: 11,439,000 (1996 est) **Population growth rate:** 2.6% (1990–95); 2% (2000–05) **Population density:** (per sq km) 29 (1996 est) **Urban population:** (% of total) 32 (1995) **Age distribution:** (% of total population) <15 44.1%, 15–65 53.1%, >65 2.8% (1995) **Ethnic groups:** four distinct ethnic groups: indigenous Africans, who account for about 95% of the population, Europeans (mainly British), who account for about 3.5%, and Afro-Europeans and Asians, who each comprise about 0.5% **Language:** English (official), Shona, Sindebele **Religion:** Christian, Muslim, Hindu, animist **Education:** (compulsory years) 8 **Literacy rate:** 74% (men); 60% (women) (1995 est) **Labour force:** 46% of population: 68% agriculture, 8% industry, 24% services (1990) **Unemployment:** 44% (1993) **Life expectancy:** 50 (men); 52 (women) (1995–2000) **Child mortality rate:** (under 5, per 1,000 live births) 103 (1996) **Physicians:** 1 per 7,384 people (1993 est)

Practical information
Visa requirements: UK: visa not required. USA: visa not required **Embassy in the UK:** Zimbabwe House, 429 Strand, London WC2R 0SA. Tel: (0171) 836 7755; (0171) 379 1167 **British embassy:** British High Commission, PO Box 4490, Stanley House, Jason Moyo Avenue, Harare. Tel: (4) 793 781; fax: (4) 728 380 **Chamber of commerce:** Zimbabwe National Chambers of Commerce, PO Box 1934, Equity House, Rezende Street, Harare. Tel: (4) 753 444; fax: (4) 753 450 **Airports:** international airports: Harare, Bulowayo, Victoria Falls; domestic air services operate between most of the larger towns; total passenger km: 666 million (1994) **Major holidays:** 1 January, 18–19 April, 1, 25 May, 11 August (2 days), 25–26 December; variable: Good Friday, Easter Monday

Chronology
13th century: Shona people settled Mashonaland (E Zimbabwe), erecting stone buildings (hence name Zimbabwe, 'stone house'). **15th century:** Shona Empire reached its greatest extent.

16th–17th centuries: Portuguese settlers developed trade with Shona states and achieved influence over kingdom of Mwanamutapa in N Zimbabwe 1629. **1837:** Ndebele (or Matabele) people settled in SW Zimbabwe after being driven north from Transvaal by Boers; Shona defeated by Ndebele led by King Mzilikazi who formed military empire based at Bulawayo. **1870:** King Lobengula succeeded King Mzilikazi. **1889:** Cecil Rhodes' British South Africa Company (BSA Co) obtained exclusive rights to exploit mineral resources in Lobengula's domains. **1890:** Creation of white colony in Mashonaland and founding of Salisbury (Harare) by Leander Starr Jameson, associate of Rhodes. **1893:** Matabele War: Jameson defeated Lobengula; white settlers took control of country. **1895:** Matabeleland, Mashonaland, and Zambia named Rhodesia after Cecil Rhodes. **1896:** Matabele revolt suppressed. **1898:** Southern Rhodesia (Zimbabwe) became British protectorate administered by BSA Co; farming, mining, and railways developed. **1922:** Union with South Africa rejected by referendum among white settlers. **1923:** Southern Rhodesia became self-governing colony; Africans progressively disenfranchised. **1933–53:** Prime Minister Godfrey Huggins (later Lord Malvern) pursued 'White Rhodesia' policy of racial segregation. **1950s:** Immigration doubled white population to around 250,000, while indigenous African population stood at around 6 million. **1953:** Southern Rhodesia formed part of Federation of Rhodesia and Nyasaland. **1961:** Zimbabwe African People's Union (ZAPU) formed with Joshua Nkomo as leader; declared illegal a year later. **1962:** Rhodesia Front party of Winston Field took power in Southern Rhodesia, pledging to preserve white rule. **1963:** Federation of Rhodesia and Nyasaland dissolved as Zambia and Malawi moved towards independence; Zimbabwe African National Union (ZANU) formed, with Robert Mugabe as secretary; declared illegal a year later. **1964:** Ian Smith became prime minister; he rejected British terms for independence which required moves towards black majority rule; Nkomo and Mugabe imprisoned. **1965:** Smith made unilateral declaration of independence (UDI); Britain broke off all relations. **1966–68:** United Nations (UN) imposed economic sanctions on Rhodesia, which still received help from South Africa and Portugal. **1969:** Rhodesia declared itself a republic. **1972:** Britain rejected draft independence agreement as unacceptable to African population. **1974:** Nkomo and Mugabe released and jointly formed Patriotic Front to fight Smith regime in mounting civil war. **1975:** Geneva Conference between British, Smith regime, and African nationalists failed to reach agreement. **1978:** At height of civil war, whites were leaving Rhodesia at rate of 1,000 per month. **1979:** Rhodesia became Zimbabwe-Rhodesia with new 'majority' constitution which nevertheless retained special rights for whites; Bishop Abel Muzorewa became premier; Mugabe and Nkomo rejected settlement; Lancaster House Agreement temporarily restored Rhodesia to British rule. **1980:** Zimbabwe achieved independence from Britain with full transition to African majority rule; Mugabe became prime minister with Rev Canaan Banana as president. **1981:** Rift between Mugabe (ZANU-PF) and Nkomo (ZAPU); Nkomo dismissed from cabinet 1982. **1984:** ZANU-PF party congress agreed to principle of one-party state. **1987:** Mugabe combined posts of head of state and prime minister as executive president; Nkomo became vice president. **1989:** ZANU-PF and ZAPU formally merged; Zimbabwe Unity Movement founded by Edgar Tekere to oppose one-party state. **1992:** United Party formed to oppose ZANU-PF. Mugabe declared drought and famine a national disaster. **1996:** Mugabe re-elected president.

World Population

Largest Countries by Area

Rank	Country	Area	
		sq km	sq mi
1	Russia	17,075,400	6,592,811
2	Canada	9,970,610	3,849,652
3	China	9,572,900	3,695,942
4	USA	9,372,615	3,618,766
5	Brazil	8,511,965	3,286,469
6	Australia	7,682,300	2,966,136
7	India	3,166,829	1,222,713
8	Argentina	2,780,092	1,073,393
9	Kazakhstan	2,717,300	1,049,150
10	Sudan	2,505,800	967,489
11	Algeria	2,381,741	919,590
12	Congo, Democratic Republic of	2,344,900	905,366
13	Saudi Arabia	2,200,518	849,620
14	Mexico	1,958,201	756,061
15	Indonesia	1,904,569	735,354
16	Libya	1,759,540	679,358
17	Iran	1,648,000	636,292
18	Mongolia	1,565,000	604,246
19	Peru	1,285,200	496,216
20	Chad	1,284,000	495,752

Smallest Countries by Area

Rank	Country	Area	
		sq km	sq mi
1	Vatican City State	0.4	0.2
2	San Marino	61	24
3	Liechtenstein	160	62
4	Marshall Islands	181	70
5	St Kitts and Nevis	262	101
6	Maldives	298	115
7	Malta	320	124
8	Grenada	344	133
9	St Vincent and the Grenadines	388	150
10	Barbados	430	166
11	Antigua and Barbuda	440	169
12	Seychelles	453	175
13	Andorra	468	181
14	St Lucia	617	238
15	Singapore	622	240
16	Bahrain	688	266
17	Micronesia	700	270
18	Kiribati	717	277
19	Tonga	750	290
20	Dominica	751	290

Largest Cities in the World

(Urban agglomerations with populations of over 6 million.)

1996

Rank	City	Population (millions)	Rank	City	Population (millions)
1	Tokyo, Japan	27.2	18=	Tianjin, China	9.6
2	Mexico City, Mexico	16.9	18=	Paris, France	9.6
3	São Paulo, Brazil	16.8	18=	Manila, Philippines	9.6
4	New York (NY), USA	16.4	21	Moscow, Russia	9.3
5	Bombay, India	15.7	22	Dhaka, Bangladesh	9.0
6	Shanghai, China	13.7	23	Jakarta, Indonesia	8.8
7	Los Angeles (CA), USA	12.6	24	Istanbul, Turkey	8.2
8	Calcutta, India	12.1	25	London, UK	7.6
9	Buenos Aires, Argentina	11.9	26=	Chicago (IL), USA	6.9
10	Seoul, South Korea	11.8	26=	Tehran, Iran	6.9
11	Beijing, China	11.4	28	Lima, Peru	6.8
12	Lagos, Nigeria	10.9	29	Bangkok, Thailand	6.7
13	Osaka, Japan	10.6	30	Essen, Germany	6.5
14=	Delhi, India	10.3	31	Bogotá, Columbia	6.2
14=	Rio de Janeiro, Brazil	10.3	32	Madras, India	6.1
16	Karachi, Pakistan	10.1			
17	Cairo, Egypt	9.9			

Source: UN Population Division

Largest Cities in the World 1950–2015

Rank	City	Population (millions)	Rank	City	Population (millions)	Rank	City	Population (millions)
1950			**1980**			**1995**		
1	New York (NY), USA	12.30	1	Tokyo, Japan	21.90	1	Tokyo, Japan	26.84
2	London, UK	8.70	2	New York (NY), USA	15.60	2	São Paulo, Brazil	16.42
3	Tokyo, Japan	6.90	3	Mexico City, Mexico	13.90	3	New York (NY), USA	16.33
4=	Paris, France	5.40	4	São Paulo, Brazil	12.10	4	Mexico City, Mexico	15.64
4=	Moscow, Russia	5.40	5	Shanghai, China	11.70	5	Bombay, India	15.09
6=	Shanghai, China	5.30	6	Osaka, Japan	10.00	6	Shanghai, China	15.08
6=	Essen, Germany	5.30	7	Buenos Aires, Argentina	9.90	7	Los Angeles (CA), USA	12.41
8	Buenos Aires, Argentina	5.00	8	Los Angeles (CA), USA	9.50	8	Beijing, China	12.36
9	Chicago (IL), USA	4.90	9=	Calcutta, India	9.00	9	Calcutta, India	11.67
10	Calcutta, India	4.40	9=	Beijing, China	9.00	10	Seoul, South Korea	11.64
2000			**2010**			**2015**		
1	Tokyo, Japan	27.90	1	Tokyo, Japan	28.70	1	Tokyo, Japan	28.70
2	Bombay, India	18.10	2	Bombay, India	24.30	2	Bombay, India	27.40
3	São Paulo, Brazil	17.80	3	Shanghai, China	21.50	3	Lagos, Nigeria	24.40
4	Shanghai, China	17.20	4	Lagos, Nigeria	20.80	4	Shanghai, China	23.40
5	New York (NY), USA	16.60	5	São Paulo, Brazil	20.10	5	Jakarta, Indonesia	21.20
6	Mexico City, Mexico	16.40	6	Jakarta, Indonesia	19.20	6	São Paulo, Brazil	20.80
7	Beijing, China	14.20	7	Mexico City, Mexico	18.20	7	Karachi, Pakistan	20.60
8	Jakarta, Indonesia	14.10	8	Beijing, China	17.80	8	Beijing, China	19.40
9	Lagos, Nigeria	13.50	9	Karachi, Pakistan	17.60	9	Dhaka, Bangladesh	19.00
10	Los Angeles (CA), USA	13.10	10	New York (NY), USA	17.30	10	Mexico City, Mexico	18.80

Source: UN Population Division

Largest Countries by Population Size

Rank	Country	Population (millions)	% of world population	Rank	Country	Population (millions)	% of world population	Rank	Country	Population (millions)	% of world population
1996				**2015**				**2050**			
1	China	1,232	21.4	1	China	1,409	19.3	1	India	1,533	16.4
2	India	945	16.4	2	India	1,212	16.6	2	China	1,516	16.2
3	USA	269	4.7	3	USA	311	4.2	3	Pakistan	357	3.8
4	Indonesia	200	3.5	4	Indonesia	252	3.5	4	USA	348	3.7
5	Brazil	161	2.8	5	Pakistan	224	3.1	5	Nigeria	338	3.6
6	Russia	148	2.6	6	Brazil	200	2.7	6	Indonesia	318	3.4
7	Pakistan	140	2.4	7	Nigeria	191	2.6	7	Brazil	243	2.6
8	Japan	125	2.2	8	Bangladesh	163	2.2	8	Bangladesh	218	2.3
9	Bangladesh	120	2.1	9	Russia	138	1.9	9	Ethiopia	213	2.3
10	Nigeria	115	2.0	10	Japan	126	1.7	10	Iran	170	1.8

Source: UN Department for Economic and Social Information

Countries with the Fastest and Slowest Growing Populations

1995–2000

Rank	Country	Average population growth rate (%)	Rank	Country	Average population growth rate (%)	Rank	Country	Average population growth rate (%)
Fastest Growing Populations			15=	Madagascar	3.1	6=	Russia	–0.2
1	Afghanistan	5.6	15=	Nicaragua	3.1	6=	Ukraine	–0.2
2	Bosnia-Herzegovina	4.5	15=	Somalia	3.1	9=	Belarus	–0.1
3	Oman	3.9	18=	Iraq	3.0	9=	Denmark	–0.1
4	Saudi Arabia	3.5	18=	Mali	3.0	11=	Germany	0.0
5	Mozambique	3.4	18=	Togo	3.0	11=	Italy	0.0
6=	Angola	3.3				11=	Lithuania	0.0
6=	Jordan	3.3	*Slowest Growing Populations*			11=	Portugal	0.0
6=	Libya	3.3	1	Latvia	–0.7	11=	Slovenia	0.0
6=	Niger	3.3	2	Estonia	–0.5	16=	Czech Republic	0.1
6=	Syria	3.3	3=	Croatia	–0.3	16=	Spain	0.1
11=	Côte d'Ivoire	3.2	3=	Hungary	–0.3	18=	Greece	0.2
11=	Kuwait	3.2	3=	Yugoslavia	–0.3	18=	Japan	0.2
11=	Liberia	3.2	6=	Romania	–0.2	18=	Poland	0.2
11=	Yemen	3.2						

Source: UN Population Fund

World Population Growth by Major Area

(Percentage of world population by area, and total number of population.)

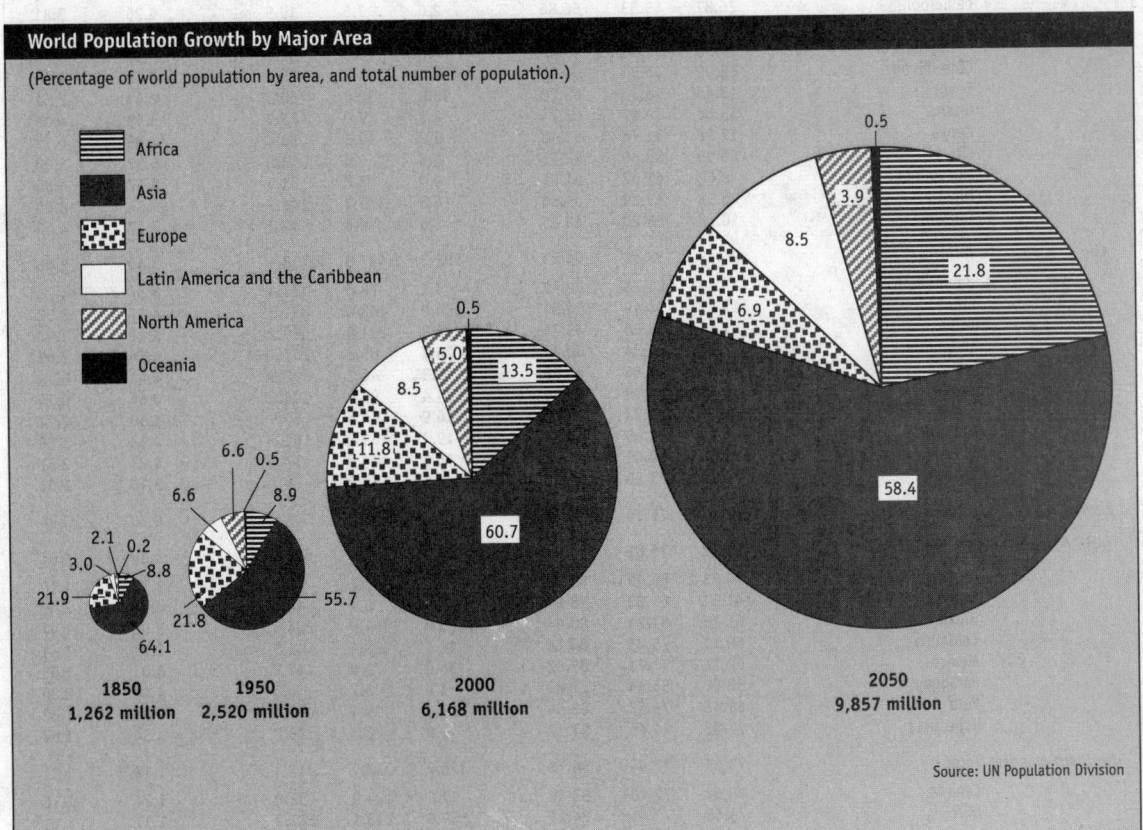

Source: UN Population Division

World Population Growth Rates and Percentage Increases

Region	Average annual growth rate 1950–94 (%)	% increase		
		1950–94	1994–2050	1950–2050
Africa	2.62	217	202	858
Asia	2.01	143	69	311
Europe	0.64	32	–7	24
Latin America and the Caribbean	2.38	186	77	406
North America	1.27	75	34	134
Oceania	1.74	123	64	265

Source: UN Population Division

Urban Population Growth

Region/country		Level of urbanization % of total population in urban settlements			Urban population				
					Total number in millions			% annual growth rate	
		1975	2000	2025	1975	2000	2025	1975–2000	2000–25
Africa	Total	25.15	37.30	53.77	104.1	310.1	804.2	4.37	3.81
	Algeria	40.33	59.65	74.05	6.4	18.5	33.6	4.23	2.38
	Angola	17.79	36.17	55.59	1.1	4.7	14.8	5.88	4.56
	Cameroon	26.87	49.33	66.86	2.0	7.5	19.5	5.25	3.81
	Congo, Democratic Republic of	29.50	31.03	49.82	6.8	15.8	52.1	3.35	4.76
	Côte d'Ivoire	32.09	46.95	64.13	2.1	7.8	23.6	5.16	4.40
	Egypt	43.45	46.36	62.20	16.8	32.0	60.5	2.57	2.54
	Ghana	30.06	39.17	57.74	2.9	7.9	21.9	3.93	4.08
	Kenya	12.92	31.76	51.48	1.7	10.3	32.6	7.05	4.59
	Libya	60.95	88.35	92.75	1.5	5.6	11.9	5.32	3.00
	Mozambique	8.62	41.07	61.09	0.9	7.8	21.5	8.62	4.05
	Nigeria	23.38	43.29	61.64	14.6	55.7	146.9	5.34	3.88
	Tanzania	10.08	28.20	48.25	1.6	9.6	30.3	7.17	4.60
Asia	Total	24.62	37.68	54.81	592.3	1,407.8	2,718.4	3.46	2.63
	Bangladesh	9.28	21.28	39.99	7.1	28.6	78.4	5.57	4.03
	China	17.25	34.49	54.51	106.0	443.0	831.8	4.07	2.52
	India	21.31	28.56	45.24	132.3	291.9	629.7	3.17	3.08
	Indonesia	19.36	40.34	60.74	26.2	85.8	167.4	4.74	2.67
	Iran	45.82	61.86	74.86	15.3	46.2	92.5	4.42	2.78
	Japan	75.69	78.39	84.86	84.4	99.1	103.2	0.64	0.16
	Korea, South	48.04	86.22	93.70	16.9	40.6	50.9	3.50	0.91
	Pakistan	26.40	37.85	56.73	19.7	61.2	161.6	4.53	3.88
	Philippines	35.56	59.01	74.26	15.3	44.0	77.6	4.23	2.27
	Thailand	15.10	21.90	39.08	6.2	13.5	28.7	3.10	3.01
Europe	Total	67.07	75.14	83.22	453.4	548.4	597.6	0.76	0.34
Latin America	Total	61.32	76.61	84.67	196.2	401.1	600.9	2.86	1.61
	Argentina	80.73	89.40	93.39	21.0	32.7	43.0	1.77	1.10
	Bolivia	41.51	65.23	78.97	1.9	5.4	10.4	4.05	2.59
	Brazil	61.15	81.21	88.94	66.0	141.9	204.8	3.06	1.47
	Colombia	60.71	75.21	84.14	14.4	28.4	41.5	2.71	1.51
	Mexico	62.76	77.71	85.82	36.9	79.6	117.2	3.07	1.55
	Paraguay	38.98	56.44	71.82	1.0	3.2	6.5	4.44	2.86
	Peru	61.46	74.52	83.54	9.3	19.4	30.6	9.94	1.82
	Venezuela	77.83	94.45	97.17	9.9	22.8	33.8	3.34	1.57
Northern America	Total	73.85	77.44	84.78	176.7	237.2	313.3	1.18	1.11
	Canada	75.61	77.16	83.67	17.5	23.9	32.0	1.24	1.16
	USA	73.65	77.46	84.91	159.0	213.1	281.2	1.17	1.11
Oceania	Total	71.78	70.25	74.86	15.4	21.5	30.7	1.34	1.42
	Australia	85.92	84.69	88.59	11.9	16.3	21.8	1.24	1.18
	New Zealand	82.78	87.20	91.64	2.5	3.3	4.0	1.00	0.81
World	Total	37.73	47.52	61.07	1,538.3	2,926.4	5,065.3	2.57	2.19
	More developed regions	69.84	76.52	83.98	729.3	904.2	1,040.0	0.86	0.56
	Less developed regions	26.68	40.52	57.05	809.0	2,022.1	4,025.3	3.66	2.75

Source: UN Population Division

Highest and Lowest Urban Populations

1996

Rank	Country	Population living in urban areas (%)	Rank	Country	Population living in urban areas (%)
Highest Urban Population			*Lowest Urban Population*		
1=	Kuwait	100	1=	Bhutan	6
1=	Monaco	100	1=	Rwanda	6
1=	Nauru	100	3	Burundi	8
1=	Singapore	100	4	Nepal	11
5	Belgium	97	5	Uganda	13
6	San Marino	96	6	Malawi	14
7=	Iceland	92	7=	Burkina Faso	16
7=	Qatar	92	7=	Ethiopia	16
9	Bahrain	91	7=	Papua New Guinea	16
10=	Israel	90	10=	Eritrea	18
10=	Luxembourg	90	10=	Solomon Islands	18
10=	Uruguay	90	12=	Bangladesh	19
13=	Malta	89	12=	Niger	19
13=	Netherlands	89	12=	Vanuatu	19
13=	UK	89	12=	Vietnam	19

Source: UNICEF

Highest and Lowest Population Densities

1996

Country	Population per sq km	Country	Population per sq km
Highest Density		*Lowest Density*	
Monaco	32,097	Namibia	2
Singapore	5,476	Mongolia	2
Vatican City State	2,273	Mauritania	2
Malta	1,168	Australia	2
Maldives	884	Suriname	3
Bahrain	840	Libya	3
Bangladesh	834	Iceland	3
Barbados	608	Canada	3
Taiwan	589	Botswana	3
Mauritius	553	Guyana	4
		Gabon	4

Source: UN Population Division

Youngest and Oldest Populations

1995

Rank	Country	% of population	Rank	Country	% of population
Youngest Populations (aged under 15)			*Oldest Populations (aged over 60)*		
1	Côte d'Ivoire	49.1	1	Sweden	17.3
2	Uganda	48.8	2	Italy	16.0
3	Congo, Democratic Republic of	48.0	3=	Greece	15.9
4	Kenya	47.7	3=	Norway	15.9
5=	Oman	47.5	5	Belgium	15.8
5=	Somalia	47.5	6	UK	15.5
7=	Benin	47.4	7=	Denmark	15.2
7=	Mali	47.4	7=	Germany	15.2
7=	Zambia	47.4	9=	Austria	14.9
10	Syria	47.3	9=	France	14.9
11=	Angola	47.1	9=	Spain	14.9
11=	Guinea	47.1	12	Bulgaria	14.5
13=	Malawi	46.7	13	Switzerland	14.2
13=	Yemen	46.7	14=	Finland	14.1
15	Ethiopia	46.4	14=	Japan	14.1
16	Burundi	46.3	14=	Portugal	14.1
17	Madagascar	46.1	17	Ukraine	14.0
18=	Liberia	46.0	18	Latvia	13.3
18=	Nicaragua	46.0	19	Netherlands	13.2
18=	Rwanda	46.0	20=	Croatia	12.8
			20=	Estonia	12.8

Source: UNICEF

Birth and Death Rates Worldwide

(Birth rate data are for live births; selected countries.)

1996

Region/country	Birth rate (per thousand)	Death rate (per thousand)	Region/country	Birth rate (per thousand)	Death rate (per thousand)	Region/country	Birth rate (per thousand)	Death rate (per thousand)
Africa			Indonesia	24	8	Bolivia	34	9
Average	40	15	Iran	35	6	Brazil	20	7
Algeria	30	6	Iraq	37	9	Colombia	24	6
Angola	49	19	Japan	10	8	Cuba	14	7
Burundi	44	18	Korea, North	21	6	Mexico	25	5
Congo, Democratic			Korea, South	15	6	Venezuela	26	5
Republic of	46	14	Pakistan	37	8			
Côte d'Ivoire	38	14	Philippines	29	6	**North America**		
Ethiopia	48	17				*Average*	14	8
Ghana	39	11	**Europe**			Canada	13	7
Kenya	37	11	*Average*	11	12	USA	14	9
Lesotho	36	11	France	12	9			
Nigeria	43	14	Germany	9	11	**Oceania**		
Sudan	34	12	Greece	10	10	*Average*	27	7
			Hungary	11	15	Australia	14	7
Asia			Russia	10	14	New Zealand	16	8
Average	28	7	Sweden	12	11	Papua New Guinea	33	10
Afghanistan	52	21	UK	12	11			
Bangladesh	27	10				**World**		
China	17	7	**Latin America**			*Average*	23	9
India	26	9	*Average*	23	6	More developed regions	12	9
			Argentina	20	8	Less developed regions	26	9

Source: UNICEF

Highest and Lowest Fertility Rates Worldwide

(Fertility rate is average number of children per woman.)

1995–2000

Rank	Country	Fertility rate	Rank	Country	Fertility rate
Highest Fertility Rates			**Lowest Fertility Rates**		
1	Yemen	7.60	1	Italy	1.19
2	Oman	7.20	2	Spain	1.22
3=	Niger	7.10	3=	Estonia	1.30
3=	Uganda	7.10	3=	Germany	1.30
5=	Ethiopia	7.00	3=	Slovenia	1.30
5=	Somalia	7.00	6	Russia	1.35
7	Afghanistan	6.90	7=	Greece	1.38
8	Maldives	6.80	7=	Ukraine	1.38
9=	Angola	6.69	9=	Belarus	1.40
9=	Laos	6.69	9=	Bosnia-Herzegovina	1.40
9=	Malawi	6.69	9=	Czech Republic	1.40
12	Mali	6.60	9=	Hungary	1.40
13	Guinea	6.61	9=	Latvia	1.40
14	Burkina Faso	6.57	9=	Romania	1.40
15	Liberia	6.33	15	Austria	1.42
16	Burundi	6.28	16	Bulgaria	1.45
17	Congo, Democratic Republic of	6.24	17	Switzerland	1.46
18	Togo	6.08	18=	Japan	1.48
19=	Mozambique	6.06	18=	Portugal	1.48
19=	Sierra Leone	6.06	20	Lithuania	1.50

Source: UN Population Fund

Maternal Deaths Worldwide

(Numbers of maternal deaths per year in pregnancy and childbirth. By continent.)

1996

Rank	Region/country	Maternal deaths per year
1	Asia and Pacific	291,000
2	Sub-Saharan Africa	219,000
3	Middle East and North Africa	35,000
4	Americas	23,000
5	Central Asia	14,000
6	Europe	3,000
	World	585,000

Source: UNICEF

Maternal Death Rates per 100,000 Live Births

(Numbers of maternal deaths per year in pregnancy and childbirth; regional averages, and countries with highest rates. By country.)

Rank	Region/country	Maternal deaths per year	Rank	Region/country	Maternal deaths per year
Sub-Saharan Africa			**Asia and Pacific**		
Average		980	*Average*		390
1	Sierra Leone	1,800	1	Bhutan	1,600
2=	Somalia	1,600	2	Nepal	1,500
2=	Guinea	1,600	3	Papua New Guinea	930
4=	Mozambique	1,500	4	Cambodia	900
4=	Chad	1,500	5	Bangladesh	850
Middle East and North Africa			**Americas**		
Average		300	*Average*		140
1	Yemen	1,400	1	Haiti	1,000
2	Sudan	660	2	Bolivia	650
3	Morocco	610	3	El Salvador	300
4	Iraq	310	4	Peru	280
5	Lebanon	300	5	Honduras	220
Central Asia			**Europe**		
Average		560	*Average*		36
1	Afghanistan	1,700	1	Romania	130
2	Tajikistan	130	2	Russia	75
3	Kyrgyzstan	110	3	Albania	65
4	Kazakhstan	80	4	Moldova	60
5	Uzbekistan	55	5	Ukraine	50

Source: UNICEF

Infant Mortality and Female Fertility Rates

(Fertility rate is average number of children per woman; ranked by highest infant mortality rate by region.)

1995–2000

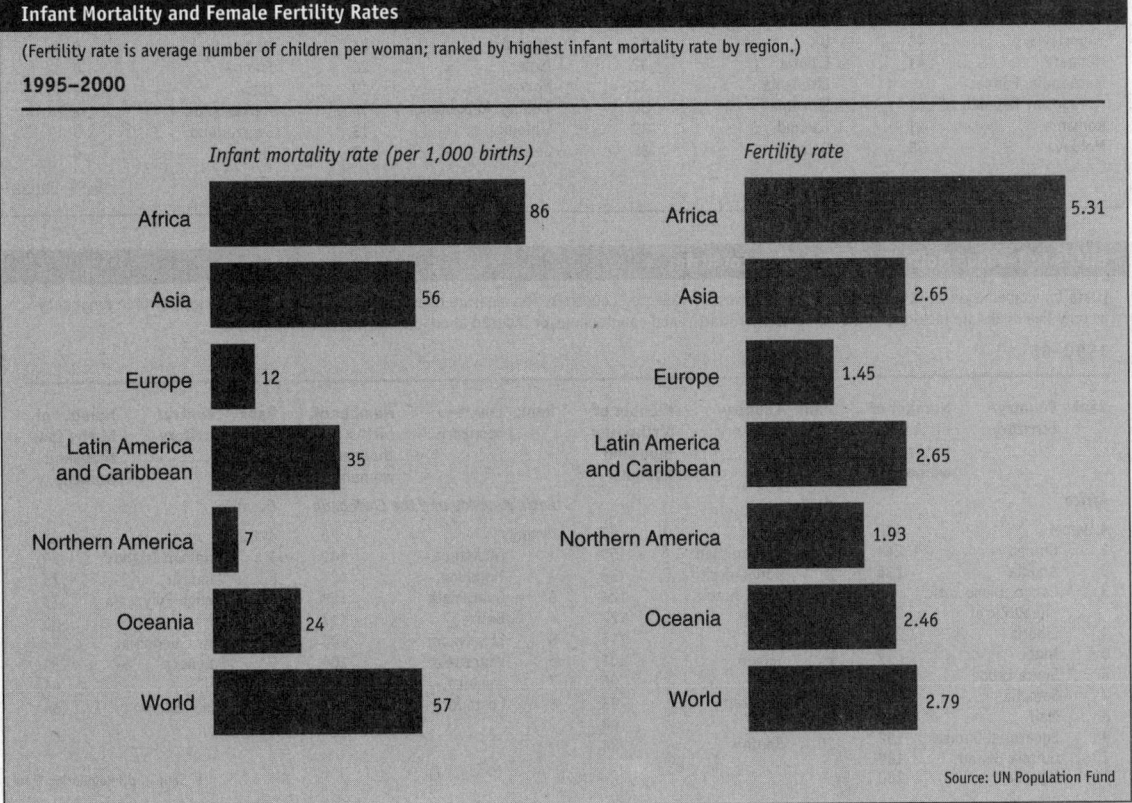

Infant mortality rate (per 1,000 births)

Africa	86
Asia	56
Europe	12
Latin America and Caribbean	35
Northern America	7
Oceania	24
World	57

Fertility rate

Africa	5.31
Asia	2.65
Europe	1.45
Latin America and Caribbean	2.65
Northern America	1.93
Oceania	2.46
World	2.79

Source: UN Population Fund

Numbers and Rates of Abortions Worldwide

(Numbers and rates of legally-induced abortions; ranked highest to lowest rate for selected countries.)

1994

Country	Number	Rate (per hundred live births)	Country	Number	Rate (per hundred live births)	Country	Number	Rate (per hundred live births)
Romania	530,191	214.88	Croatia	19,673	40.49	USA	1,267,415	21.00
Russia	2,481,493	176.21	Singapore	15,690	31.66	Finland	10,013	15.35
Latvia	26,795	110.46	Japan	364,350	29.42	Germany	103,586	13.45
Lithuania	30,326	70.80	Sweden	32,293	28.76	Netherlands	20,811	10.64
Hungary	74,491	64.43	Kyrgyzstan	31,389	28.50	Mexico	28,734	0.98
Slovenia	11,324	58.18	Denmark	17,598	25.25	Poland	874	0.84
Slovak Republic	34,883	52.55	Italy	124,334	23.57			
Czech Republic	54,836	51.45	UK	169,964	22.64			

Source: UN Department for Economic and Social Information; US Department of Health and Human Services

Births to Teenage Mothers in Developed Countries

(Data for women aged 15–19; ranked highest to lowest for selected countries. The measure does not indicate the full dimensions of teen pregnancy as only live births are included in the numerator; stillbirths and spontaneous or induced abortions are not reflected.)

1990–95

Country/ territory	Number of births (per thousand women)	Country/ territory	Number of births (per thousand women)	Country/ territory	Number of births (per thousand women)	Country/ territory	Number of births (per thousand women)
USA	64	Russia	37	Poland	28	Luxembourg	13
Bulgaria	59	Latvia	35	Canada	27	Sweden	13
Czech Republic	46	New Zealand	35	Portugal	25	Malta	12
Slovak Republic	44	Estonia	34	Austria	23	Spain	12
Ukraine	43	Bosnia-Herzegovina	33	Greece	22	Belgium	10
Yugoslavia	43	UK	33	Australia	21	Denmark	10
Hungary	41	Croatia	32	Israel	20	France	9
Macedonia, Former Yugoslav Republic of	41	Lithuania	32	Norway	19	Italy	9
Romania	41	Slovenia	30	Ireland, Republic of	16	Netherlands	7
Moldova	38	Iceland	29	Finland	13	Switzerland	5
		Belarus	28	Germany	13	Japan	4

Source: UNICEF

Births to Teenage Mothers in Developing Countries

(Data for women aged 15–19; ranked highest to lowest for selected countries. The measure does not indicate the full dimensions of teen pregnancy as only live births are included in the numerator; stillbirths and spontaneous or induced abortions are not reflected.)

1990–95

Rank	Country/ territory	Number of births (per thousand women)	Rank	Country/ territory	Number of births (per thousand women)	Rank	Country/ territory	Number of births (per thousand women)	Rank	Country/ territory	Number of births (per thousand women)
Africa			**Asia**			**Latin America and the Caribbean**			**Oceania**		
Average		130	*Average*		57	*Average*		78	*Average*		28
1	Guinea	241	1	Afghanistan	153	1	Nicaragua	149	1	Solomon Islands	99
2	Angola	236	2	Bangladesh	138	2	Honduras	127	2	Vanuatu	75
3	Congo, Democratic Republic of	231	3	Saudi Arabia	124	3	Guatemala	123	3	French Polynesia	73
4	Liberia	230	4	Oman	122	4	Belize	117	4	Micronesia	65
5	Niger	219	5	India	116	5	El Salvador	105	5	New Caledonia	53
6	Sierra Leone	212	6	Yemen	102	6	Venezuela	101	6	Polynesia	50
7	Somalia	208	7	Iran	96	7	Jamaica	95	7	Fiji	46
8	Mali	199	8	Pakistan	93	8	Costa Rica	93	8	Melanesia	34
9	Equatorial Guinea	192	9	Nepal	92						
10	Guinea-Bissau	189	10	Bhutan	86						
11	Uganda	180									

Source: UN Population Fund

Marriage and Divorce Rates

(– = not applicable.)

Country	Marriages (per thousand people)		Divorces (per thousand people)		Country	Marriages (per thousand people)		Divorces (per thousand people)	
	1985	1995	1985	1995		1985	1995	1985	1995
Austria	5.9	5.3	2.0	2.3	Italy	5.3	4.9	0.3	0.5[2]
Belgium	5.8	5.1	1.9	3.5	Japan	6.1	6.3[2]	1.4	1.6[2]
Canada	7.1	5.5[1]	2.4	2.7[1]	Luxembourg	5.4	5.1	1.8	1.8
Denmark	5.7	6.7	2.8	2.5	Netherlands	5.7	5.2	2.3	2.2
Finland	5.3	4.6	1.8	2.7	Norway	4.9	4.8[2]	2.0	2.5[2]
France	4.9	4.4	1.9	2.0[2]	Portugal	6.8	6.7[2]	0.9	1.4[2]
Germany	6.4	5.3	2.3	2.0[2]	Spain	5.2	5.0	0.5	2.0[2]
Greece	6.4	6.2	0.8	0.7	Sweden	4.6	3.8	2.4	2.5
Iceland	5.2	4.5	2.2	1.9	Switzerland	6.0	5.8	1.8	2.2
Ireland,					UK	6.9	5.9[1]	3.1	3.0[2]
Republic of	5.3	4.6[2]	–[3]	–[3]	USA	10.1	9.1[2]	5.0	4.6[2]

[1] 1993.
[2] 1994.
[3] Divorce was not allowed in the Republic of Ireland until 1997.

Source: Office for Official Publications of the European Communities, Luxembourg

Dependency Ratios

(Dependency ratio is the ratio of the population under 15 and over 65 to the population aged 15–64.)

Region	Age	Dependency ratio (per hundred people)			Region	Age	Dependency ratio (per hundred people)		
		1995	2025	2050			1995	2025	2050
Africa					**Europe**				
Eastern Africa	0–14	91.2	64.5	36.5	Eastern Europe	0–14	31.4	26.7	30.2
	>65	5.5	5.5	9.9		>65	18.5	26.8	35.3
	Total	96.6	70.0	46.4		Total	49.9	53.5	65.5
Northern Africa	0–14	67.9	40.8	32.6	Northern Europe	0–14	30.2	29.3	30.7
	>65	6.7	10.1	18.9		>65	23.3	30.8	37.2
	Total	74.6	50.9	51.5		Total	53.5	60.0	67.9
Southern Africa	0–14	65.6	43.7	33.4	Southern Europe	0–14	25.3	21.6	27.0
	>65	7.4	10.0	17.5		>65	21.3	34.5	54.5
	Total	73.0	53.7	50.8		Total	46.6	56.1	81.5
Western Africa	0–14	89.6	65.7	36.7	Western Europe	0–14	26.2	24.4	28.4
	>65	5.4	6.1	9.5		>65	22.1	35.4	47.1
	Total	95.1	71.8	46.1		Total	48.3	59.8	75.5
Total	0–14	83.4	59.5	36.0	Total	0–14	28.7	25.5	29.3
	>65	6.0	6.9	11.4		>65	20.6	30.9	41.7
	Total	89.4	66.4	47.4		Total	49.3	56.4	71.0
Asia					**Latin America and the Caribbean**				
Eastern Asia	0–14	37.6	29.6	30.7	Caribbean	0–14	48.3	38.5	32.9
	>65	10.0	19.2	30.7		>65	10.2	16.3	25.0
	Total	47.6	48.8	61.4		Total	58.8	54.9	57.9
South-central Asia	0–14	63.3	36.8	30.7	Central America	0–14	64.1	37.3	31.8
	>65	7.3	10.8	20.6		>65	7.0	12.1	24.6
	Total	70.6	47.6	51.3		Total	71.1	49.4	56.3
Southeast Asia	0–14	57.1	35.1	31.4	South America	0–14	53.0	34.4	31.3
	>65	7.0	11.5	22.6		>65	8.9	15.5	27.2
	Total	64.1	46.6	53.9		Total	61.8	49.9	58.5
Western Asia	0–14	65.9	46.2	32.7	Total	0–14	55.4	35.5	31.6
	>65	7.6	10.8	17.2		>65	8.5	14.6	26.3
	Total	73.5	57.0	49.9		Total	63.9	50.1	57.8
Total	0–14	51.1	34.6	30.9	**North America**	0–14	33.5	31.6	31.1
	>65	8.5	13.9	23.7		>65	19.2	29.2	34.6
	Total	59.6	48.4	54.7	Total		52.7	60.7	65.7

(continued)

Dependency Ratios (continued)

Region	Age	Dependency ratio (per hundred people)			Region	Age	Dependency ratio (per hundred people)		
		1995	2025	2050			1995	2025	2050
Oceania					*World*				
Australia and New Zealand	0–14	32.8	30.7	30.9	More developed regions[1]	0–14	29.4	27.2	29.9
	>65	17.4	27.0	37.2		>65	20.1	31.4	40.4
	Total	50.2	57.7	68.0		Total	49.5	58.6	70.3
Total	0–14	40.4	34.6	31.6	Less developed regions[2]	0–14	57.0	39.7	32.3
	>65	14.8	21.3	29.6		>65	7.7	12.1	20.4
	Total	55.2	55.9	61.2		Total	64.7	51.8	52.8
					Least developed countries[3]	0–14	81.9	57.0	35.4
						>65	5.6	6.5	11.5
						Total	87.5	63.5	46.9
					Total	0–14	50.9	37.9	32.1
						>65	10.5	14.9	22.7
						Total	61.4	52.8	54.7

[1] More developed regions comprise Northern America, Japan, Europe, and Australia and New Zealand.
[2] Less developed regions comprise all regions of Africa, Asia (excluding Japan), Latin America and the Caribbean, Melanesia, Micronesia, and Polynesia.
[3] Least developed countries according to standard UN designation.

Source: UN Population Division

Life Expectancy Worldwide

1995–2000

Region	Country	Life expectancy at birth (years)		Region	Country	Life expectancy at birth (years)	
		Male	Female			Male	Female
Africa	*Average*	52.3	55.3	**Europe**	*Average*	68.3	77.0
	Algeria	67.5	70.3		Austria	73.7	80.1
	Angola	44.9	48.1		Croatia	68.1	76.5
	Ethiopia	48.4	51.6		Czech Republic	69.8	76.0
	Ghana	56.2	59.9		Estonia	63.9	75.0
	Kenya	52.3	55.7		Finland	73.0	80.1
	Madagascar	57.0	60.0		France	74.6	82.9
	Mauritius	68.3	75.0		Germany	73.4	79.9
	Nigeria	50.8	54.0		Greece	75.5	80.6
	Rwanda	40.8	43.4		Hungary	64.5	73.8
	Sierra Leone	36.0	39.1		Ireland, Republic of	74.0	79.4
	South Africa	62.3	68.3		Italy	75.1	81.4
	Sudan	53.6	56.4		Norway	74.8	80.6
	Tunisia	68.4	70.7		Romania	66.0	73.2
	Uganda	40.4	42.3		Sweden	76.2	80.8
					Switzerland	75.3	81.8
Asia	*Average*	64.8	67.7		UK	74.5	79.8
	Afghanistan	45.0	46.0	***Latin America and Caribbean***	*Average*	66.4	72.9
	Bhutan	51.6	54.9		Argentina	69.6	76.8
	Cambodia	52.6	55.4		Bolivia	59.8	63.2
	China	68.2	71.7		Brazil	63.4	71.2
	India	62.1	62.7		Chile	72.3	78.3
	Iraq	66.9	63.9		Colombia	68.2	73.7
	Israel	75.7	79.5		Costa Rica	74.5	79.2
	Japan	76.9	82.9		Cuba	74.2	78.0
	Korea, North	68.9	75.1		Dominican Republic	68.9	73.1
	Korea, South	68.8	76.0		Guatemala	64.7	69.8
	Laos	52.0	55.0		Haiti	52.8	56.0
	Philippines	66.6	70.2		Jamaica	72.4	76.8
	Singapore	75.1	79.5		Mexico	69.5	75.5
	Syria	66.7	71.2		Nicaragua	65.8	70.6
	Yemen	57.4	58.4		Peru	65.9	70.9

Life Expectancy Worldwide (*continued*)

1995–2000

Region	Country	Life expectancy at birth (years)	
		Male	**Female**
North America	Average	73.6	80.3
	Canada	76.1	81.8
	USA	73.4	80.1
Oceania	Average	71.5	76.4
	Australia	75.4	81.2
	Micronesia	67.2	70.9
	New Zealand	74.7	79.7
	Papua New Guinea	57.2	58.7
	Vanuatu	65.5	69.5

Region	Country	Life expectancy at birth (years)	
		Male	**Female**
Selected Countries of the Former USSR			
	Armenia	67.2	74.0
	Belarus	64.4	74.8
	Georgia	68.5	76.7
	Kazakhstan	62.8	72.4
	Russia	58.0	71.5
	Turkmenistan	61.2	68.0
	Ukraine	63.6	74.0
World	More developed regions[1]	70.6	78.4
	Less developed regions[2]	62.1	65.2
	Least developed countries[3]	50.9	53.0
	Total	63.4	67.7

[1] More developed regions comprise Northern America, Japan, Europe, and Australia and New Zealand.
[2] Less developed regions comprise all regions of Africa, Asia (excluding Japan), Latin America and the Caribbean, Melanesia, Micronesia, and Polynesia.
[3] Least developed countries according to standard UN designation.

Source: UN Population Fund

Estimated Populations of Indigenous Peoples

(Data from early–mid 1990s for selected countries.)

Country	Indigenous peoples	Estimated numbers	% of total population
Australia	Aborigines	250,000	1.40
	Torres Strait Islanders	26,000	0.14
Bhutan	various	170,000	10.00
Bolivia	Aymara, Quechua, Chiquitano, Guaraní, Moxeño, and others	4,100,000	65.00
Cambodia	Cham and indigenous hill peoples	510,000	5.00
Canada	First Nations (including Huétis and Inuit)	1,000,000–1,200,000	3–4.10
Chile	Mapuche, Aymara, Rapanui, and others	990,000	7.00
Colombia	Arhuaco, Embera, Guambiano, Wayúu, Nukak, Kuna, Kogi, Paez, Zenu, and others	620,000	1.70
Costa Rica	various	25,000	0.78
El Salvador	Pipil, Pocoman, and Lenca	324,000–1,080,000	6–20.00
Guatemala	Maya	5,782,000	59.00
India	Adivasis (scheduled tribes)	69,000,000	7.50
	(including Nagas)	700,000	0.10
Indonesia	Batak	3,300,000	1.60
	Dayak	4,100,000	2.00
	Achnese	3,700,000	1.80
	Minangkabau	3,700,000	1.80
	Sundanese	30,500,000	15.00
	West Irians	1,200,000	0.60
Malaysia	Orang Asli	86,000	0.50
	Kadazan-Dusun	400,000	2.10
	Bajau	240,000	1.26
	Murut	64,000	0.34
	Dayak-Iban	570,000	3.00
	Bidayuh	171,000	0.90
Mexico	56 indigenous peoples	10,000,000–20,000,000	10.8–23.80
Papua New Guinea	Bougainvilleans	159,000	4.00
Paraguay	Guaraní, Ayoreo, Toba-Maskoy, Aché, Sanapan, and others	95,000	2.30
Peru	Aguaruna, Ashaninka, Huambisa, Quechua, Aymara, and others	8,800,000	39.20
Philippines	various	2,050,000	3.00
Russia	Nenets	34,000	0.02
	Evenk	30,000	0.02
	Chukchi	15,000	0.01
	Koriaks	9,000	<0.01
Taiwan	Atayal, Bunun, Tsou, Paiwan, Rukai, Puyuma, Ami, Yami, Saisiyat, and others	423,000	2.00
USA	Native Americans (including 240,000 Native Hawaiians and 80,000 Inuit and Alaska Natives)	1,960,000	0.79

Source: *World Directory of Minorities* © Minority Rights Group (edited and published by Minority Rights Group International, 1997, London, UK)

Refugees Worldwide

The number of uprooted people around the world approached 50 million in 1997, including all those estimated displaced within their own countries. One out of every 120 people in the world has been forced into flight. The UN High Commissioner for Refugees (UNHCR) protects and assists more than 22 million people who have fled war or persecution.
(– = not applicable. As of January 1997.)

Region	Refugees	Returnees	Others of concern	Internally displaced people	Total of concern to UNHCR
Africa	4,341,000	1,693,000	–	2,058,000	8,091,000
Asia	4,809,000	1,241,000	156,000	1,719,000	7,925,000
Europe	3,166,000	308,000	1,209,000	1,066,000	5,749,000
Latin America	88,000	70,000	–	11,000	169,000
North America	720,000	–	–	–	720,000
Oceania	750,000	–	–	–	75,000
Total	13,200,000	3,311,000	1,365,000	4,854,000	22,729,000

Source: UN High Commissioner for Refugees

Famine: Chronology

1982–1984 Civil war and drought cause a major famine in Ethiopia; at least 800,000 people die and 1.5 million flee the country before foreign grain is received the following year.

1984 The Band Aid single 'Do They Know It's Christmas?' raises £8 million for famine relief in Africa. It is the best-selling record ever in Britain.

4 November 1984 The Royal Air Force begins an airlift of food supplies to the famine-stricken Tigre province of Ethiopia; however, civil war and poor roads prevent much of it from reaching the starving.

13 July 1985 Live Aid, organized by Band Aid to raise funds for famine-relief in Africa, is a day-long concert held simultaneously at Wembley Stadium in London, England, and JFK Stadium in Philadelphia, Pennsylvania. Over $70 million is raised worldwide.

1990 The USA, China, and the USSR all have bumper wheat crops, forcing prices down from $3.72 per bushel to $2.20. However, political and economic wrangles in the USSR cause Moscow and Leningrad stores to run out of bread, and food supplies to fall so low as to threaten famine.

1992 A famine in Somalia kills more than 300,000 people.

5 August 1993 The government of Sudan launches a major offensive against the Sudan People's Liberation Army (SPLA), displacing 100,000 people and threatening famine.

1 February 1996 The USA announces that it will assist the United Nations (UN) food assistance programme for North Korea, established to prevent famine following floods in 1995.

January 1998 The German Red Cross estimates that 10,000 children a month are dying from malnutrition in North Korea and that two million died in 1997. The famine has been caused by poor agricultural practices that have brought environmental catastrophe.

May 1998 Aid agencies report that 800,000 people in southern Sudan are threatened with famine due to civil war in that country.

International Political Organizations

NATO Expansion

BY DAVID SHUKMAN

Some call the plan a dangerous mistake. Others claim it is the best hope for guaranteeing stability in a turbulent Europe. And everyone is worried about the risk of the bill running into billions of dollars. The plan in question: the expansion of the North Atlantic Treaty Organization from its current 16 members, led by the USA, to a new total of 19 with the forthcoming admission of the former communist countries of Poland, Hungary, and the Czech Republic during 1999.

History

With its headquarters in Brussels, Belgium, NATO is without question the largest and most successful international military organization in history. Also known as the 'Atlantic alliance' or simply the 'alliance', it was founded in the aftermath of World War II. Stalin's USSR was cementing its grip on Eastern Europe and threatening to strike into Western Europe. In 1948 West Berlin had come within a whisker of being occupied by Soviet troops. So amid an atmosphere of nervousness and insecurity, 12 countries gathered in Washington on 4 April 1949, to sign the treaty establishing NATO. The original members were Belgium, Canada, Denmark, France, Iceland, Italy, Luxembourg, the Netherlands, Norway, Portugal, the UK, and the USA.

The organization's founding principle was that an attack on any one member would be regarded as an attack on them all. In practical terms that meant that the countries taking part had to promise to commit their forces to a communal defence. Common systems for communication were established, along with NATO-wide standards for military procedure and preparedness to fight. In the dark days of the Cold War, with East and West engaged in a tense stand-off and both sides amassing huge arsenals, the organization had a real and vital purpose. Other countries eagerly swelled the NATO ranks: Greece, Turkey, West Germany, and Spain.

Rethinking NATO's Role

Yet the war that NATO stood ready to fight never came. There were scares – such as the Cuban missile crisis of 1962 – but no conflict. Instead, the opposite happened and, to many, the impact was just as shocking. In November 1989 the discredited regime of East Germany allowed its citizens to pour over the Berlin Wall into the West. The Cold War fault line suddenly collapsed. Within two years the USSR abandoned communism and itself broke apart. The entire Eastern bloc, including its military alliance the Warsaw Pact, simply vanished. In the West, there was jubilation but also uncertainty: NATO had lost its enemy.

An immediate round of soul-searching began. Critics of the alliance wondered whether the organization was still needed. Budgetary officials demanded that NATO be scaled back to save money. But just as insiders were questioning NATO's value, outsiders were clamouring to join up. The new democracies of eastern Europe, liberated from the communist grip but nervous of the Kremlin's reaction, quickly applied for membership. The unpredictability of Russia was cited by all of them as the chief reason. A cover design for a Hungarian news magazine in 1991 summed up the fear: it depicted the shadow of a Russian bear looming over a map of eastern Europe, with Hungary and the other former communist countries scurrying for the shelter of a giant umbrella marked 'NATO'.

But it has proved easier to talk about admitting new members than to do so in practice. The first obstacle was Russia, as expected. During 1996 and 1997 the Russian president Boris Yeltsin warned repeatedly that he would not tolerate Moscow's old adversary expanding towards his borders. And this view was supported by some in the West, worried about the risks of antagonizing a weakened but still nuclear-armed Russia. The former US diplomat George Kennan, who in the Cold War had played a pivotal role in shaping the West's 'containment' of the USSR, argued that the expansion of NATO would be a disaster, 'the most fateful error in American policy in the entire post-Cold War era'.

Green Light for Expansion

After prolonged negotiations, Moscow's concerns were satisfied by a diplomatic deal. In exchange for accepting NATO's expansion into eastern Europe, Russia was granted a unique status in the alliance, and was even allowed to set up a permanent mission at NATO headquarters and to attend many meetings. This trade-off cleared the way for President Clinton and other alliance leaders to announce formally, at a special summit in Madrid in July 1997, that Poland, Hungary, and the Czech Republic would become members. And the door would remain open for others to follow.

The admission process is far from simple, however. The move needs to be ratified by each existing member state – and in the US Senate approval has been long delayed. One objection is to the cost of updating the Soviet-designed military systems of the candidate countries. The US Congressional Budget Office puts the bill at between $60 billion and $125 billion over the next ten years. The US government gives a cheaper estimate of $27 billion–$35 billion. NATO officials say the figures have been deliberately exaggerated to fuel opposition to expansion and that the cost will be far lower. Still unsettled is the question of how much of the extra financial burden will be carried by the USA and how much by Europe.

Those pushing for expansion believe it will encourage stability inside the alliance – and beyond it. NATO forces keeping the peace in Bosnia is one example. As President Clinton stated in a letter to senators, the goal of the USA is to see 'a Europe that is peaceful, democratic, and united', and taking in new members will help that aim. But left unresolved and untested are some highly sensitive questions. Will NATO expansion eventually include the Baltic states, anxious to join, yet once part of the USSR? Will Russia use its new influence at NATO to undermine policies that it objects to? And, in an alliance that is already large, unwieldly, and slow-moving, will the arrival of yet more members lead to paralysis? Having outlived the Cold War, NATO is on the brink of undreamed-of change and no one can predict the outcome.

Amazon Pact

(Amazon Cooperation Treaty) Agreement to protect and control the industrial or commercial development of the Amazon River region. The pact provides for technical and scientific cooperation in exploiting the natural resources of this ecologically important area.

Date established 1978

Founding members Bolivia, Brazil, Colombia, Ecuador, Guyana, Peru, Suriname, Venezuela

Current members same

Address Tratado de Cooperación Amazónica, Avda Prolongación Primavera 654, Chacarilla, Surco, Lima 33, Peru; phone: (51 14) 499 084; fax: (51 14) 499 718

Andean Community

(Communidad Andino; full name: Junta del Acuerdo di Cartagena [JUNAC]) South American organization aimed at economic and social cooperation between member states. Its ultimate aim is to create a free-trade area.

Date established 1969

Founding members Bolivia, Chile, Colombia, Ecuador, Peru

Current members Bolivia, Colombia, Ecuador, Peru, Venezuela. Observer: 1

Address Av Paseo de la Republica 3895, Lima 21, Peru; phone: (511) 221 3329; fax: (511) 221 2222

Arab League

(League of Arab States) Organization of Arab states established to promote Arab unity, primarily in opposition to Israel.

Date established 1945

Founding members Egypt, Iraq, Lebanon, Saudi Arabia, Syria, Transjordan, Yemen

Current members Algeria, Bahrain, Comoros, Djibouti, Egypt, Iraq, Jordan, Kuwait, Lebanon, Libya, Mauritania, Morocco, Oman, Palestine, Qatar, Saudi Arabia, Somalia, Sudan, Syria, Tunisia, United Arab Emirates, Yemen

Address Arab League Building, Tahrir Square, Cairo, Egypt; phone: (20 2) 575 0511; fax: (20 2) 577 5626

Arab Maghreb Union (AMU)

Association formed to promote cooperation among the Arab states in North Africa. It aims to formulate common policies on military, economic, international, and cultural issues.

Date established 1989

Founding members Algeria, Libya, Mauritania, Morocco, Tunisia

Current members same

Address 26–27 Rue Ogba, Rabat-Agdal, Morocco; phone: (212 7) 777 2668; fax: (212 7) 777 2693

Association of Caribbean States (ACS)

Organization sponsored by the Caribbean Community and Common Market (CARICOM) formed to promote social, political, and economic cooperation in the region, and eventual integration.

Date established 1994

Founding members Antigua and Barbuda, Bahamas, Barbados, Belize, Colombia, Costa Rica, Cuba, Dominica, Dominican Republic, El Salvador, Grenada, Guatemala, Guyana, Haiti, Honduras, Jamaica, Mexico, Nicaragua, Panama, St Kitts and Nevis, St Lucia, St Vincent and the Grenadines, Suriname, Trinidad and Tobago, Venezuela

Current members same. Associate members: 11 dependent territories in the region

Address 11–13 Victoria Avenue, Port of Spain, Trinidad and Tobago; phone: (809) 623 2783; fax: (809) 623 2679

Web site www.acs-aec.org/

Association of South East Asian Nations (ASEAN)

Regional alliance formed to promote peace and economic, social, and cultural development. It took over the nonmilitary role of the Southeast Asia Treaty Organization in 1975.

Date established 1967

Founding members Indonesia, Malaysia, Philippines, Singapore, Thailand

Current members Brunei, Indonesia, Laos, Malaysia, Myanmar, Philippines, Singapore, Thailand, Vietnam

Address ASEAN Secretariat, PO Box 2072, 7-A Jl. Sisingamangaraja, Jakarta, Indonesia; phone: (62 21) 726 2410; fax: (62 21) 739 8234

Web site www.asean.or.id/

Caribbean Community and Common Market (CARICOM)

Organization for economic and foreign policy coordination, and political and cultural unity in the Caribbean region. It replaced the Caribbean Integrated Free Trade Area.

Date established 1973

Founding members Barbados, Guyana, Jamaica, Trinidad and Tobago

Current members Antigua and Barbuda, Bahamas (a member of the Community but not of the Common Market), Barbados, Belize, Dominica, Grenada, Guyana, Haiti, Jamaica, Montserrat, St Kitts and Nevis, St Lucia, St Vincent and the Grenadines, Suriname, and Trinidad and Tobago. Associate members: British Virgin Islands, Turks and Caicos Islands. Observers: 11

Address Bank of Guyana Building, PO Box 10827, Georgetown, Guyana; phone: (592 2) 69281; fax: (592 2) 67816

Web site www.caricom.org/expframe.htm

British Commonwealth

Association of 53 countries and their dependencies, the majority of which once formed part of the British Empire. The Commonwealth has no charter or constitution, and is founded more on tradition and sentiment than on political or economic factors.

Date established 1931

Founding members Anguilla, Australia, Bermuda, British Antarctic Territory, British Virgin Islands, Canada, Cayman Islands, Channel Islands, Cook Islands, Falkland Islands, Falkland Islands Dependency, Gibraltar, Isle of Man, Montserrat, New Zealand, Niue, Norfolk Island, Pitcairn Islands, Tokelau, Turks and Caicos Islands, St Helena, UK

Current members Antigua and Barbuda, Australia, Bahamas, Bangladesh, Barbados, Belize, Botswana, Brunei, Cameroon, Canada, Cyprus, Dominica, Fiji, Gambia, Ghana, Grenada, Guyana, India, Jamaica, Kenya, Kiribati, Lesotho, Malawi, Malaysia, Maldives, Malta, Mauritius, Mozambique, Namibia, Nauru (not a full participant), New Zealand, Pakistan, Papua New Guinea, St Kitts and Nevis, St Lucia, St Vincent and the Grenadines, Samoa, Seychelles, Sierra Leone, Singapore, Solomon Islands, South Africa, Sri Lanka, Swaziland, Tanzania, Tonga, Trinidad and Tobago, Tuvalu (not a full participant), Uganda, UK, Vanuatu, Zambia, Zimbabwe

Address Commonwealth Secretariat, Marlborough House, Pall Mall, London SW1 5HX, UK; phone: (0171) 839 3411; fax: (0171) 930 0827

Web site www.thecommonwealth.org/

Commonwealth of Independent States (CIS)

Successor body to the Union of Soviet Socialist Republics, formed to ensure continued cooperation in trade and military policy, and recognition of borders. It has no formal political institutions, and its role is uncertain.

Date established 1991

Founding members Belarus, Russia, Ukraine

Current members Armenia, Azerbaijan, Belarus, Georgia, Kazakhstan, Kyrgyzstan, Moldova, Russia, Tajikistan, Turkmenistan, Ukraine, Uzbekistan

Address 220000 Minsk, Kirava 17, Belarus; phone: (375 172) 293 517; fax: (375 172) 272 339

Council of Europe

Intergovernmental body set up to achieve greater unity between European countries, to facilitate their economic and social progress, and to uphold the principles of parliamentary democracy and respect for human rights.

Date established 1949

Founding members Belgium, Denmark, France, Greece, Republic of Ireland, Italy, Luxembourg, Netherlands, Norway, Sweden, Turkey, UK

Current members Albania, Andorra, Austria, Belgium, Bulgaria, Croatia, Cyprus, Czech Republic, Denmark, Estonia, Finland, France, Germany, Greece, Hungary, Iceland, Republic of Ireland, Italy, Latvia, Liechtenstein, Lithuania, Luxembourg, Former Yugoslav Republic of Macedonia, Malta, Moldova, Netherlands, Norway, Poland, Portugal, Romania, Russia, San Marino, Slovenia, Slovak Republic, Spain, Sweden, Switzerland, Turkey, UK, Ukraine

Address Palais de l'Europe, F-67075 Strasbourg, CEDEX, France; phone: (33 3) 88 41 20 00; fax: (33 3) 88 41 27 81

Web site www.coe.fr/

Council of the Baltic Sea States

Organization founded to foster closer economic and political cooperation between states in the Baltic region.

Date established 1992

Founding members Denmark, Estonia, Finland, Iceland, Germany, Latvia, Lithuania, Norway, Poland, Russia, Sweden, the European Union (EU)

Current members same

Address 2 Asiatisk Plads, DK-1448 Copenhagen K, Denmark; phone: (45 3) 392 2000; fax: (45 3) 154 0533

Council of the Entente (CE)

(Conseil de l'Entente) Organization of West African states for strengthening economic links and promoting industrial development.

Date established 1959

Founding members Benin, Burkina Faso, Côte d'Ivoire, Niger

Current members Benin, Burkina Faso, Côte d'Ivoire, Niger, Togo

Address Mutual Aid and Loan Guarantee Fund, 01 B.P. 3734, Abidjan 01, Côte d'Ivoire; phone: (225 33) 2835; fax: (225 33) 1149

Group of Seven (G7)

The seven leading industrial nations of the world. The aim of their meetings was initially to coordinate international management of exchange rates. They now meet annually to discuss topical issues rather than to formulate policy. From 1991 Russia participated increasingly in G7 summits; the 1997 and 1998 summits were termed 'The Summit of the Eight', with full Russian participation.

US President Bill Clinton at the 1998 G7 meeting in Birmingham © Richard Watt

Date established 1975

Founding members Canada, France, West Germany, Italy, Japan, UK, USA

Current members Canada, France, Germany, Italy, Japan, UK, USA

Address no permanent secretariat

Gulf Cooperation Council (GCC)

Organization for promoting peace in the Persian Gulf area. It aims to bring about integration, coordination, and cooperation in economic, social, military, and political affairs among Arab Gulf states.

Date established 1981

Founding members Bahrain, Kuwait, Oman, Qatar, Saudi Arabia, United Arab Emirates

Current members same

Address PO Box 7153, Riyadh 11462, Saudi Arabia; phone: (966 482) 7777; fax (966 482) 9089

International Organization for Migration (IOM)

Intergovernmental body set up to help resettle refugees and displaced persons, and encourage social and economic development through migration. It also aims to advance understanding of migration issues. IOM works closely with the United Nations and the International Catholic Migration Commission.

Date established founded in 1951 as the Intergovernmental Committee for European Migration; became the IOM in 1989

Founding members Australia, Austria, Belgium, Bolivia, Brazil, Canada, West Germany, Greece, Italy, Luxembourg, Netherlands, Switzerland, Turkey, USA

Current members Albania, Angola, Argentina, Armenia, Australia, Austria, Bangladesh, Belgium, Bolivia, Canada, Chile, Colombia, Costa Rica, Croatia, Cyprus, Czech Republic, Denmark, Dominican Republic, Ecuador, Egypt, El Salvador, Finland, France, Germany, Greece, Guatemala, Haiti, Honduras, Hungary, Israel, Italy, Japan, Kenya, South Korea, Luxembourg, Netherlands, Nicaragua, Norway, Pakistan, Panama, Paraguay, Peru, Philippines, Poland, Portugal, Senegal, Slovak Republic, Sri Lanka, Sweden, Switzerland, Tajikistan, Thailand, Uganda, Uruguay, USA, Venezuela, Zambia. Observers: 49

Address 17 Route de Morillons, CP 71, CH-1211 Geneva 19, Switzerland

Web site www.iom.ch/iom/

Nordic Council

Consultative body founded to discuss mutual interests and increase cooperation in the Nordic region.

Date established 1952

Founding members Denmark, Iceland, Norway, Sweden

Current members Denmark, Finland, Iceland, Norway, Sweden

Address Tyrgatan 7, Box 19506, 10432 Stockholm, Sweden; phone: (46 8) 453 4700; fax: (46 8) 411 7536

North Atlantic Treaty Organization (NATO)

Military and political association set up to provide for the collective defence of the main western European and North American states against the perceived threat from the USSR. It maintains troops and weapons, including nuclear weapons, in Europe. In 1994 NATO launched a 'Partnership for Peace' programme, inviting ex-Soviet republics and ex-Warsaw Pact countries to take part in a range of military cooperation agreements; by October 1997, 28 countries had joined the Partnership. As of mid-1997 Poland, Hungary, and the Czech Republic were the prime candidates for full membership in NATO.

Date established 1949

Founding members Belgium, Canada, Denmark, France, Iceland, Italy, Luxembourg, Netherlands, Norway, Portugal, UK, USA

Current members Belgium, Canada, Denmark, France, Germany, Greece, Iceland, Italy, Luxembourg, Netherlands, Norway, Portugal, Spain, Turkey, UK, USA

Address NATO, 1110 Brussels, Belgium; phone: (32 2) 707 4111; fax: (32 2) 707 4117

Web site www.nato.int/

Organization for Security and Cooperation in Europe (OSCE)

International forum set up to reach agreement in security, economics, science, technology, and human rights. It was originally known (until 1994) as the Conference on Security and Cooperation in Europe (CSCE).

Date established 1972

Founding members Albania, Austria, Belgium, Bulgaria, Canada, Cyprus, Czechoslovakia, Denmark, Finland, France, East Germany, West Germany, Greece, Hungary, Iceland, Republic of Ireland, Italy, Liechtenstein, Luxembourg, Malta, Monaco, Netherlands, Norway, Poland, Portugal, Romania, San Marino, Spain, Sweden, Switzerland, Turkey, UK, USA, USSR, Yugoslavia

Current members Albania, Andorra, Armenia, Austria, Azerbaijan, Belarus, Belgium, Bosnia-Herzegovina, Bulgaria, Canada, Croatia, Cyprus, Czech Republic, Denmark, Estonia, Finland, France, Georgia, Germany, Greece, Hungary, Iceland, Republic of Ireland, Italy, Kazakhstan, Kyrgyzstan, Latvia, Liechtenstein, Lithuania, Luxembourg, Former Yugoslav Republic of Macedonia, Malta, Moldova, Monaco, Netherlands, Norway, Poland, Portugal, Romania, Russia, San Marino, Slovakia, Slovenia, Spain, Sweden, Switzerland, Tajikistan, Turkey, UK, Ukraine, USA, Uzbekistan, Yugoslavia

Address Kärntnerring 5–7, A-1010, Vienna, Austria; phone: (43 1) 514 360; fax: (43 1) 514 3699

Web site www.osceprag.cz/

Organization of African Unity (OAU)

Association formed to eradicate colonialism and improve economic, cultural, and political cooperation in Africa. It also aims to coordinate military, scientific, and health policies.

Date established 1963

Founding members Cameroon, Central African Republic, Chad, Republic of the Congo, Côte d'Ivoire, Dahomey, Ethiopia, Gabon, Liberia, Madagascar, Mauritania, Niger, Nigeria, Senegal, Sierra Leone, Somalia, Togo, Tunisia, Upper Volta

Current members Algeria, Angola, Benin, Botswana, Burkina Faso, Burundi, Cameroon, Cape Verde, Central African Republic, Chad, Comoros, Democratic Republic of Congo, Republic of the Congo, Côte d'Ivoire, Djibouti, Egypt, Equatorial Guinea, Eritrea, Ethiopia, Gabon, Gambia, Ghana, Guinea, Guinea-Bissau, Kenya, Lesotho, Liberia, Libya, Madagascar, Malawi, Mali, Mauritania, Mauritius, Mozambique, Namibia, Niger, Nigeria, Rwanda, São Tomé and Príncipe, Senegal, Seychelles, Sierra Leone, Somalia, South Africa, Sudan, Swaziland, Tanzania, Togo, Tunisia, Uganda, Zambia, Zimbabwe

Address PO Box 3243, Addis Ababa, Ethiopia; phone: (251 1) 517 7000; fax: (251 1) 513 036

Organization of American States (OAS)

Association founded to maintain peace and solidarity within the western hemisphere, also concerned with the social, cultural, and economic development of Latin America.

Date established 1948

Founding members Antigua and Barbuda, Argentina, Bahamas, Barbados, Bolivia, Brazil, Chile, Colombia, Costa Rica, Cuba, Dominica, Dominican Republic, Ecuador, El Salvador, Grenada, Guatemala, Guyana, Haiti, Honduras, Jamaica, Mexico, Nicaragua, Panama, Paraguay, Peru, St Kitts and Nevis, St Lucia, St Vincent and the Grenadines, Suriname, Trinidad and Tobago, Uruguay, USA, Venezuela

Current members Antigua and Barbuda, Argentina, Bahamas, Barbados, Belize, Bolivia, Brazil, Canada, Chile, Colombia, Costa Rica, Dominica, Dominican Republic, Ecuador, El Salvador, Grenada, Guatemala, Guyana, Haiti, Honduras, Jamaica, Mexico, Nicaragua, Panama, Paraguay, Peru, St Kitts and Nevis, St Lucia, St Vincent and the Grenadines, Suriname, Trinidad and Tobago, Uruguay, USA, Venezuela. Observers: 40

Address 17th Street and Constitution Avenue NW, Washington DC 20006, USA; phone: (202) 458-3000; fax: (202) 458-3967; e-mail: info@oas.org

Web site www.oas.org/

Organization of the Islamic Conference (OIC)

Association of states in the Middle East, Africa, and Asia, formed to promote Islamic solidarity between member countries, to consolidate economic, social, cultural, and scientific cooperation, and to eliminate racial discrimination.

Date established 1971

Founding members Afghanistan, Algeria, Bahrain, Bangladesh, Benin, Brunei, Burkina Faso, Cameroon, Chad, Comoros, Djibouti, Egypt, Gabon, Gambia, Guinea, Guinea-Bissau, Indonesia, Iran, Iraq, Jordan, Kuwait, Lebanon, Libya, Malaysia, Maldives, Mali, Mauritania, Morocco, Niger, Nigeria, Oman, Pakistan, Palestine, Qatar, Saudi Arabia, Senegal, Sierra Leone, Somalia, Sudan, Syria, Tunisia, Uganda, United Arab Emirates, Zanzibar

Current members Afghanistan, Albania, Algeria, Azerbaijan, Bahrain, Bangladesh, Benin, Brunei, Burkina Faso, Cameroon, Chad, Comoros, Djibouti, Egypt, Gabon, Gambia, Guinea, Guinea-Bissau, Indonesia, Iran, Iraq, Jordan, Kazakhstan, Kuwait, Kyrgyzstan, Lebanon, Libya, Malaysia, Maldives, Mali, Mauritania, Morocco, Mozambique, Niger, Nigeria, Oman, Pakistan, Palestine, Qatar, Saudi Arabia, Senegal, Sierra Leone, Somalia, Sudan, Suriname, Syria, Tajikistan, Tunisia, Turkey, Turkmenistan, Uganda, United Arab Emirates, Yemen. Observers: 2

Address Kilo 6, Mecca Road, PO Box 178, Jeddah 21411, Saudi Arabia; phone: (966 2) 680 0800; fax: (966 2) 687 3568

Schengen Group

Association of states within the European Union that in theory adhere to the ideals of the Schengen Convention, notably the abolition of passport controls at common internal borders and the strengthening of external borders.

Date established 1995

Founding members Belgium, France, Germany, Luxembourg, Netherlands

Current members Austria, Belgium, Germany, Greece, Italy, Luxembourg, Netherlands, Portugal, Spain. Observers: 5

Address c/o Benelux Union Economique, Rue de la Régence 39, B-1000 Brussels, Belgium; phone: (32 2) 519 3811; fax: (32 2) 513 4206

Secretariat of the Pacific Community (SPC)

Organization (known until 1998 as the South Pacific Commission) formed to promote economic and social cooperation between Pacific countries and those with dependencies in the region. A nuclear-free zone in the Pacific is another aim.

Date established 1947

Founding members Australia, France, Netherlands, New Zealand, UK, USA

Current members American Samoa, Australia, Cook Islands, Fiji, France, French Polynesia, Guam, Kiribati, Marshall Islands, Federated States of Micronesia, Nauru, New Caledonia, New Zealand, Niue, Northern Marianas, Palau, Papua New Guinea, Pitcairn Islands, Samoa, Solomon Islands, Tokelau, Tonga, Tuvalu, USA, Vanuatu, Wallis and Futuna

Address B.P. D5, 98848 Noumea Cedex, New Caledonia; phone: (687) 262 000; fax: (687) 263 818; e-mail: spc@spc.org.nc

Web site www.spc.org.nc/

South Asian Association for Regional Cooperation (SAARC)

Organization aiming to promote the welfare and economic, social, and cultural development of the region.

Date established 1985

Founding members Bangladesh, Bhutan, India, Maldives, Nepal, Pakistan, Sri Lanka

Current members same

Address PO Box 4222, Kathmandu, Nepal

Unrepresented Nations' and Peoples' Organization (UNPO)

International association founded to represent ethnic and minority groups unrecognized by the United Nations and to defend the right to self-determination of oppressed peoples around the world.

Date established 1991

Founding members representatives of Native Americans, Armenia, Australian Aborigines, the Crimea, Estonia, Georgia, the Greek minority in Albania, the Kurds, the minorities of the Cordillera in the Philippines, the non-Chinese in Taiwan, Tibet, Turkestan, the Volga region, West Irians, West Papuans

Current members 47 ethnic and minority groups, including the above

Address 40A Javastraat, NL-2585 The Hague, The Netherlands; phone: (31 70) 360 3318; fax: (31 70) 360 3346; e-mail: unponl@antenna.nl

Web site www.unpo.org/

Visegrad Group

Association formed to promote cooperation and free trade between the neighbouring member states.

Date established 1991

Founding members Czechoslovakia, Hungary, Poland

Current members Czech Republic, Hungary, Poland, Slovak Republic

Address (no permanent headquarters) c/o Secretary of State, Aleje Ujazdowskie 9, 00-583 Warsaw, Poland

Western European Union (WEU)

Organization set up as a consultative forum for military issues, in close cooperation with NATO. The WEU is the defence component of the European Union and the potential basis of a common European defence policy.

Date established 1954

Founding members Belgium, France, West Germany, Italy, Luxembourg, Netherlands, UK

Current members Belgium, France, Germany, Greece, Italy, Luxembourg, Netherlands, Portugal, Spain, UK

Address Secretariat-General, 4 Rue de la Régence, B-1000 Brussels, Belgium; phone: (32 2) 513 4365; fax: (32 2) 511 3519

World Trade Organization (WTO)

Permanent body replacing the General Agreement on Tariffs and Trade (GATT). The WTO monitors agreements to reduce barriers to trade, such as tariffs, subsidies, quotas, and regulations that discriminate against imported products. It is also a forum for trade negotiations between countries.

Date established 1995

Founding members GATT had 128 members, all of whom could join the WTO and most of whom subsequently did so

Current members 132 countries; 29 observers; 8 observers to the General Council

Address Centre William Rappard, 154 Rue de Lausanne, CH-1211 Geneva 21, Switzerland

Web site www.wto.org/

European Union

THE EUROPEAN UNION: HEADING EAST

BY DAVID SHUKMAN

On 12 March 1998 the leaders of the member countries of the European Union committed themselves to an irrevocable step which will affect the lives of every EU citizen for years to come. It was on this day that the prosperous club of Western European nations first formally opened its doors to the poorer, former communist countries to the east. To mark what will be the EU's largest and most controversial expansion, 26 presidents and prime ministers gathered in London – 15 from current members of the Union, 11 from applicant countries.

Nine years after the fall of the Berlin Wall, this glittering event was meant to symbolize the final burying of the Cold War. The Queen hosted a lunch for the leaders at Buckingham Palace. The conference chairman, the British prime minister Tony Blair, described the day as historic. One EU diplomat said it was a milestone towards reuniting Europe.

A Difficult Road Ahead

Yet opening up the EU to the former communist states is easier said than done. As one senior official put it, 'now comes the hard part'. Over the years, the Union has built up a highly complex set of rules to govern both the running of its free market and its growing political role on the international stage. So the process of negotiating membership is always difficult – and, in this case, is likely to last at least five years, maybe far longer. And, as in the past, it could become a bruising experience. Existing members, mindful of the impact of a new arrival on their own industries or farmers, will push to safeguard their interests. The applicant countries too will fight for the best possible deal.

Until now, the Union has expanded in more modest stages. It was founded back in the 1950s, as the European Economic Community or 'Common Market', with France, Germany, Italy, and the three Benelux countries (Belgium, the Netherlands, and Luxembourg). Twenty years later, this cosy group of just six members was joined by Britain, Ireland, and Denmark. Then came the so-called 'Club Med' countries of Greece (1981), Portugal (1986), and Spain (1986). Most recently, the European Union has taken in Austria, Finland, and Sweden, bringing the total membership to 15.

Some European politicians and officials say the EU is already too cumbersome and slow to make decisions, even before the next stage of expansion. All too often a handful of countries – or even just one – will hold up developments which most of the rest regard as important. For example, in 1996 Britain blocked all EU business for several weeks in protest at the ban on British beef exports. The following year, Greece vetoed an aid package for a dozen developing nations because of its dispute with Turkey. So the question is whether an even larger Union of up to 26 members could ever run smoothly – or would it descend into paralysis?

Smaller Shares in a Bigger Pie?

Just as sensitive is the likely cost of expansion. All of the applicant countries are poorer than current EU members. Even the six which have been selected for fast-track membership – Cyprus, the Czech Republic, Estonia, Hungary, Poland, and Slovenia – are relatively underdeveloped. Some of the others, including Bulgaria and Romania, are even further behind. Yet if their hope is that joining the EU will bring an instant and massive flow of funds, they are sure to be disappointed.

Despite talking warmly about the merits of expansion, none of the EU's current members wants to hand over any more money to the central pot. Germany, the largest donor, has signalled that it will not increase its contributions. And countries such as Spain and Portugal which are on the receiving end of huge EU grants are resisting any attempt to divert their share of funding to future members from the east. Britain, as a net contributor, is bound to lose out, with less EU money available for the poorer regions of Merseyside and Scotland. The squabbling and bad blood over this will intensify.

Most difficult of all is the level of future support for agriculture – and the protests have already started. Early signs of trouble came in February 1998 when French farmers stormed the headquarters of the European Commission in Brussels to demand that EU expansion should not mean a reduction in their incomes. The problem is that eastern European farms are backward and require massive investment. Yet the EU's Common Agricultural Policy is already under strain and the EU simply cannot afford to extend its benefits eastwards. It is no surprise therefore that in March 1998 in Poland, hundreds of farmers marched through the capital, Warsaw, calling for their 'fair share' of European money.

Ironically, it is the most prosperous of the candidate countries, Cyprus, which may cause the biggest headache of all. Cyprus, the majority of whose population is Greek-speaking, was promised membership on the insistence of Greece. Yet the island has been divided by a heavily armed ceasefire line ever since the northern part of Cyprus was occupied by Turkey in a lightning invasion in 1974. Cyprus remains a flashpoint, with tension mounting over the question of EU membership. The Turkish Cypriots say their Greek counterparts have no right to join. But, unless Cyprus is admitted, Greece threatens to block the membership of all other applicants. This represents the most explosive and potentially dangerous dispute facing the EU.

The gathering in London on 12 March 1998 showed how, in an optimistic future, the Union could stretch from the shores of the Atlantic to the territories of the former USSR, from the Arctic Circle to the edge of the Middle East. The advocates of such an expansion foresee a vast zone of peace and prosperity in which the communist legacy is finally shaken off – and in which Europe's age-old ethnic and national rivalries give way to fruitful cooperation and lasting political stability.

The critics, however, warn that the EU itself will see worsening internal strife over its financing and power-sharing and that, by expanding, the Union will needlessly involve itself in the myriad disputes of the more turbulent corners of eastern Europe. Either way, the EU is on the brink of momentous change.

European Union (EU)

Organization working towards political and monetary union, a common foreign and security policy, and cooperation on justice and home affairs. The Maastricht Treaty established a single market with free movement of goods and capital in 1993, and a Charter of Social Rights.

Date established 1957 (as the European Economic Community)

Founding members Belgium, France, West Germany, Italy, Luxembourg, Netherlands

Current members Austria, Belgium, Denmark, Finland, France, Germany, Greece, Republic of Ireland, Italy, Luxembourg, Netherlands, Portugal, Spain, Sweden, UK

Address c/o European Commission, Rue de la Loi 200, B-1049 Brussels, Belgium. In the USA: European Union, Delegation of the European Commission to the United States, 2300 M Street N-, Washington, DC 20037; phone: (202) 862 9500; fax: (202) 429 1766

Web site www.europ.eu.int and www.eurunion.org/

European Union: Central Organs

European Commission initiates EU action. Its 20 members (two each from France, Germany, Italy, Spain, and UK; and one each from Austria, Belgium, Denmark, Finland, Greece, Republic of Ireland, Luxembourg, Netherlands, Portugal, and Sweden) are pledged to independence of national interests. Headquarters: Rue de la Loi 200, B-1049 Brussels, Belgium.

Council of Ministers of the European Union makes decisions on the Commission's proposals. Headquarters: Rue de la Loi 200, B-1049 Brussels, Belgium.

Committee of the Regions represents the regions within the EU, with 222 members serving a four-year term. Headquarters: Rue Belliard 79, B-1040 Brussels, Belgium.

Committee of Permanent Representatives (COREPER) consists of permanent officials (one group comprising ambassadors to the EU and one comprising deputy permanent representatives of member states) temporarily seconded by member states to work for the European Commission.

Economic and Social Committee established 1957, a consultative body with 222 members drawn from employers, workers, consumers, and other interest groups within member states. Headquarters: Rue Ravenstein 2, B-1000 Brussels, Belgium.

European Parliament assembly of the EU, directly elected from 1979, which comments on the legislative proposals of the European Commission. Members are elected for a five-year term. The European Parliament has 626 seats, apportioned on the basis of population. It can dismiss the whole Commission and reject the EU budget in its entirety. Full sittings are in Strasbourg, most committees meet in Brussels, and the seat of the secretariat is in Luxembourg. Headquarters: Palais de l'Europe, Avenue Robert Schuman, BP 1024, F-67070 Strasbourg, CEDEX, France.

European Court of Justice established 1957 to safeguard interpretation of the Rome Treaties that form the basis of the EU. It consists of 15 judges and 9 advocates-general drawn from member states for six-year terms. Headquarters: Court of Justice of the European Commission, L-2925 Luxembourg, Luxembourg.

European Union: Selected Specialized Organizations

European Atomic Energy Community (EURATOM) established 1957 to promote cooperation of EU member states in nuclear research and the rapid and large-scale development of nonmilitary nuclear energy. Headquarters: c/o European Commission, Rue de la Loi 200, B-1049 Brussels, Belgium.

European Coal and Steel Community (EDSC) established 1952 to coordinate the coal and steel industries of member countries and eliminate tariffs and other restrictions. Headquarters: Bâtiment Jean Monnet, Rue Alcide de Gasperi, Plateau du Kirchberg, L-3424 Luxembourg, Luxembourg.

European Investment Bank (EIB) established 1957 to provide interest-free, long-term financing of approved capital projects. Headquarters: 100 Boulevard Konrad Adenauer, L-2950 Luxembourg, Luxembourg.

European Monetary System (EMS) established 1979 to promote financial cooperation and monetary stability. Central to the EMS is the Exchange Rate Mechanism (ERM), a voluntary system of semi-fixed exchange rates based on the European currency unit (ECU), planned as a stepping stone towards the introduction of a common currency, the euro. Headquarters: D-2-ecu, Rue de la Loi 200, B-1049 Brussels, Belgium.

European Commission: Division of Portfolios 1995–99

Jacques Santer, President (Luxembourg)
Secretariat-General
Legal Service
Security Office
Forward Studies Unit
Inspectorate General
Joint Interpreting and Conference Service (SCIC)
Spokesman's Service
Monetary matters (with Mr de Silguy)
Common foreign and security policy (with Mr van den Broek)
Institutional questions and intergovernmental conference (with Mr Oreja)

Manuel Marin, Vice President (Spain)
External relations with the Mediterranean (South), Middle and Near East, Latin America, Asia (except Japan, China, South Korea, Hong Kong, Macao, Taiwan), including development aid

Sir Leon Brittan, Vice President (UK)
External relations with North America, Australia, New Zealand, Japan, China, South Korea, Hong Kong, Macao, Taiwan
Common commercial policy
Relations with OECD and WTO

Martin Bangemann (Germany)
Industrial affairs
Information and telecommunications technologies

Karel Van Miert (Belgium)
Competition

Hans van den Broek (Netherlands)
External relations with the countries of Central and Eastern Europe, the former USSR, Turkey, Cyprus, Malta, and other European countries
Common foreign and security policy (in agreement with the President)
External missions

João de Deus Pinheiro (Portugal)
External relations with the countries of Africa, the Caribbean, and the Pacific, and South Africa
Lomé Convention

Padraig Flynn (Republic of Ireland)
Employment and social affairs
Relations with the Economic and Social Committee

Marcelio Oreja (Spain)
Relations with the European Parliament
Relations with the member states on openness, communication, and information
Culture and audiovisual policy
Office for official publications
Institutional questions

Edith Cresson (France)
Science, research, and development
Joint Research Centre
Human resources, education, training, and youth

Ritt Bjerregaard (Denmark)
Environment
Nuclear safety

Monika Wulf-Mathies (Germany)
Regional policies
Relations with the Committee of the Regions
Cohesion Fund (in agreement with Mr Kinnock and Mrs Bjerregaard)

Neil Kinnock: *European Transport Minister*
© Sean Aidan

Neil Kinnock (UK)
Transport (including trans-European networks)

Mario Monti (Italy)
Internal market
Financial services and financial integration
Customs
Taxation

Emma Bonino (Italy)
Fisheries
Consumer policy
European Community Humanitarian Office (ECHO)

Yves-Thibault de Silguy (France)
Economic and financial affairs
Monetary matters (in agreement with the President)

Credit and investments
Statistical office

Christos Papoutsis (Greece)
Energy and Euratom Supply Agency
Small and medium enterprises
Tourism

Anita Gradin (Sweden)
Immigration, home affairs, and justice
Relations with the Ombudsman
Financial control
Anti-fraud measures

Franz Fischler (Austria)
Agriculture and rural development

Erkki Liikanen (Finland)
Budget
Personnel and administration
Translation and in-house computer services

Voting Procedure in the EU Council of Ministers

The Council of Ministers adopts legislation either by simple majority, qualified majority, or unanimity. In most cases, however, either unanimity or qualified majority is stipulated (by the EC and Euratom Treaties), in order to facilitate Community decision-making and protect the interests of the smaller member states. It eliminates the risk of two of the larger member states constituting a blocking minority. A qualified majority is 62 votes out of a total of 87. A blocking minority is 26 votes.

Qualified Majority Voting System
A weighted voting system gives each member state a vote roughly proportional to its population and economic strength.

Country	Population (1996 est)	Number of votes	Country	Population (1996 est)	Number of votes
France	58,333,000	10	Portugal	9,808,000	5
Germany	81,992,000	10	Austria	8,106,000	4
Italy	57,226,000	10	Sweden	8,819,000	4
UK	58,144,000	10	Denmark	5,237,000	3
Spain	39,674,000	8	Finland	5,126,000	3
Belgium	10,159,000	5	Ireland,		
Greece	10,490,000	5	Republic of	3,554,000	3
Netherlands	15,575,000	5	Luxembourg	412,000	2

European Parliament: Composition by Seats

Although the number of seats allocated to each country takes account of population size, representation is not strictly proportional and favours the smaller countries.

Member state	Number of seats
Austria	21
Belgium	25
Denmark	16
Finland	16
France	87
Germany	99
Greece	25
Ireland, Republic of	15
Italy	87
Luxembourg	6
Netherlands	31
Portugal	25
Spain	64
Sweden	22
UK	87
Total	626

Political Groups in the European Parliament

Abbreviation	Full party name	Number of seats (1994–99)
PES	Party of European Socialists Group	217
EPP	European People's Party Group (Christian-Democratic Group)	173
UFE	Union for Europe Group	54
ELDR	European Liberal, Democratic and Reform Party Group	52
EUL/NGL	European United Left/Nordic Green Left Group	33
Green	Green Group	27
ERA	European Radical Alliance Group	20
I-EDN	Independents for a Europe of Nations Group (coordination group)	19
NA	Non-attached Group	31

Presidency of the Council of Ministers

Year	1 January–30 June	1 July–31 December
1998	UK	Austria
1999	Germany	Finland
2000	Portugal	France
2001	Sweden	Belgium
2002	Spain	Denmark
2003	Greece	

UK Members of the European Parliament

1994–99

MEP	Political party	Constituency	MEP	Political party	Constituency
Gordon Adam[1]	Labour Party	Northumbria	Graham Mather	Conservative and Unionist Party	Hampshire North and Oxford
Richard Balfe[1]	Labour Party	London South Inner			
Roger Barton[1]	Labour Party	Sheffield	Tom Megahy[1]	Labour Party	Yorkshire South West
Angela Billingham	Labour Party	Northamptonshire and Blaby	Bill Miller	Labour Party	Glasgow
			James Moorhouse[1]	Conservative and Unionist Party	London South and Surrey East
David Bowe[1]	Labour Party	Cleveland and Richmond			
Bryan Cassidy[1]	Conservative and Unionist Party	Dorset and Devon East	Eluned Morgan	Labour Party	Wales Mid and West
			David Morris[1]	Labour Party	South Wales West
Giles Chichester	Conservative and Unionist Party	Devon and Plymouth East	Simon Murphy	Labour Party	Midlands West
			Clive Needle	Labour Party	Norfolk
Ken Coates[1]	Labour Party	Nottinghamshire North and Chesterfield	Stan Newens[1]	Labour Party	London Central
			Edward Newman[1]	Labour Party	Greater Manchester Central
Kenneth Collins[1]	Labour Party	Strathclyde East			
Richard Corbett[1]	Labour Party	Merseyside West	James Nicholson[1]	Ulster Unionist Party	Northern Ireland
John Corrie	Conservative and Unionist Party	Worcestershire and Warwickshire South	Christine Oddy[1]	Labour Party	Coventry and Warwickshire North
Peter Crampton[1]	Labour Party	Humberside			
Christine Crawley[1]	Labour Party	Birmingham East	Ian Paisley[1]	Democratic Unionist Party	Northern Ireland
Tony Cunningham	Labour Party	Cumbria and Lancashire North	Roy Perry	Conservative and Unionist Party	Wight and Hampshire South
Wayne David[1]	Labour Party	South Wales Central			
Alan Donnelly[1]	Labour Party	Tyne and Wear	Henry Plumb[1]	Conservative and Unionist Party	Cotswolds
Brendan Donnelly	Conservative and Unionist Party	Sussex South and Crawley			
			Anita Pollack[1]	Labour Party	London South West
James Elles[1]	Conservative and Unionist Party	Buckinghamshire and Oxfordshire East	James Provan	Conservative and Unionist Party	South Downs West
Michael Elliott[1]	Labour Party	London West	Mel Read[1]	Labour Party	Nottingham and Leicestershire North West
Robert Evans	Labour Party	London North West			
Winnie Ewing[1]	Scottish National Party	Highlands and Islands	Barry Seal[1]	Labour Party	Yorkshire West
Alex Falconer[1]	Labour Party	Scotland Mid and Fife	Brian Simpson[1]	Labour Party	Cheshire East
Glyn Ford[1]	Labour Party	Greater Manchester East	Peter Skinner	Labour Party	Kent West
Pauline Green[1]	Labour Party	London North	Alex Smith[1]	Labour Party	Scotland South
David Hallam	Labour Party	Herefordshire and Shropshire	Tom Spencer[1]	Conservative and Unionist Party	Surrey
Veronica Hardstaff	Labour Party	Lincolnshire and Humberside South	Shaun Spiers	Labour Party	London South East
			John Stevens[1]	Conservative and Unionist Party	Thames Valley
Lyndon Harrison[1]	Labour Party	Cheshire West and Wirral			
Mark Hendrick	Labour Party	Lancashire Central	Jack Stewart-Clark[1]	Conservative and Unionist Party	Sussex East and Kent South
Michael Hindley[1]	Labour Party	Lancashire South			
Richard Howitt	Labour Party	Essex South	Robert Sturdy	Conservative and Unionist Party	Cambridgeshire
Stephen Hughes[1]	Labour Party	Durham			
John Hume[1]	Social Democratic and Labour Party	Northern Ireland	Micahel Tappin	Labour Party	Staffordshire West and Congleton
Caroline Jackson[1]	Conservative and Unionist Party	Wiltshire North and Bath	Robin Teverson	Liberal Democrats	Cornwall and Plymouth West
Edward Kellett-Bowman[1]	Conservative and Unionist Party	Itchen, Test and Avon	David Thomas	Labour Party	Suffolk and Norfolk South West
Hugh Kerr	Labour Party	Essex West and Hertfordshire East	Gary Titley[1]	Labour Party	Greater Manchester West
			John Tomlinson[1]	Labour Party	Birmingham West
Glenys Kinnock	Labour Party	South Wales East	Carole Tongue[1]	Labour Party	London East
Alf Lomas[1]	Labour Party	London North East	Peter Truscott	Labour Party	Hertfordshire
Allan Macartney	Scottish National Party	Scotland North East	Sue Waddington	Labour Party	Leicester
			Graham Watson	Liberal Democrats	Somerset and Devon North
Arlene McCarthy	Labour Party	Peak District			
Michael McGowan[1]	Labour Party	Leeds	Mark Watts	Labour Party	Kent East
Anne McIntosh[1]	Conservative and Unionist Party	Essex North and Suffolk South	Norman West[1]	Labour Party	Yorkshire South
			Ian White[1]	Labour Party	Bristol
Hugh McMahon[1]	Labour Party	Strathclyde West	Phillip Whitehead	Labour Party	Staffordshire East and Derby
Edward McMillan-Scott[1]	Conservative and Unionist Party	Yorkshire North			
			Joe Wilson[1]	Labour Party	Wales North
Eryl McNally	Labour Party	Bedfordshire and Milton Keynes	Terence Wynn[1]	Labour Party	Merseyside East and Wigan
David Martin[1]	Labour Party	Lothians			

[1] Member of the previous European Parliament.

United Nations

United Nations (UN)

Association of states for international peace, security, and cooperation. The UN was established as a successor to the League of Nations, and has played a role in many areas, such as refugees, development assistance, disaster relief, cultural cooperation, and peacekeeping.

Date established 1945

Founding members 51 states: Argentina, Australia, Belgium, Bolivia, Brazil, Byelorussian Soviet Socialist Republic, Canada, Chile, China, Colombia, Costa Rica, Cuba, Czechoslovakia, Denmark, Dominican Republic, Ecuador, Egypt, El Salvador, Ethiopia, France, Greece, Guatemala, Haiti, Honduras, India, Iran, Iraq, Lebanon, Liberia, Luxembourg, Mexico, Netherlands, New Zealand, Nicaragua, Norway, Panama, Paraguay, Peru, Philippines, Poland, Saudi Arabia, South Africa, Syria, Turkey, UK, Ukrainian Soviet Socialist Republic, Uruguay, USA, USSR, Venezuela, Yugoslavia

Current members 185 states in 1998

Budget The UN had a two-year zero-growth budget of US $2.6 billion for 1996–97. The proposed budget for 1998–99 is US $2.48 billion. Initiatives to make the UN leaner and more effective were launched by the Secretary General in July 1997.

The total operating expenses for the entire UN system – including the World Bank, the International Monetary Fund, and all the UN funds, programmes, and specialized agencies – come to US $18.2 billion a year.

The top seven contributors to the UN are: the USA (25.0%); Japan (15.7%); Germany (9.1%); France (6.4%); the UK (5.3%); Italy (5.2%); and Russia (4.3%). Collectively, they account for 71% of the regular UN budget.

The USA owes more in unpaid assessments than any other member state: over $1.4 billion.

Address United Nations, 1 United Nations Plaza, New York, NY 10017, USA; phone: (212) 963-4475

Web site www.un.org/

United Nations Charter: Preamble

The Charter of the United Nations (UN) was signed on 26 June 1945 in San Francisco, at the conclusion of the UN Conference on International Organization, and came into force on 24 October 1945. The Statute of the International Court of Justice is an integral part of the charter.

Preamble

We the peoples of the UN determined to save succeeding generations from the scourge of war, which twice in our lifetime has brought untold sorrow to mankind, and to reaffirm faith in fundamental human rights, in the dignity and worth of the human person, in the equal rights of men and women and of nations large and small, and to establish conditions under which justice and respect for the obligations arising from treaties and other sources of international law can be maintained, and to promote social progress and better standards of life in larger freedom, and for these ends to practise tolerance and live together in peace with one another as good neighbours, and to unite our strength to maintain international peace and security, and to ensure, by the acceptance of principles and the institution of methods, that armed force shall not be used, save in the common interest, and to employ international machinery for the promotion of the economic and social advancement of all peoples, have resolved to combine our efforts to accomplish these aims.

Accordingly, our respective governments, through representatives assembled in the city of San Francisco, who have exhibited their full powers found to be in good and due form, have agreed to the present Charter of the United Nations and do hereby establish an international organization to be known as the United Nations.

United Nations: Members and Contributions

Country	Year of admission	Scale of assessments 1998 (%)	Gross contributions for 1998 (US $)	Country	Year of admission	Scale of assessments 1998 (%)	Gross contributions for 1998 (US $)
Afghanistan	1946	0.004	47,636	Burundi	1962	0.001	11,909
Albania	1955	0.003	35,727	Cambodia	1955	0.001	11,909
Algeria	1962	0.116	1,381,455	Cameroon	1960	0.014	166,727
Andorra	1993	0.004	47,636	Canada[1]	1945	2.825	33,643,180
Angola	1976	0.010	119,091	Cape Verde	1975	0.001	11,909
Antigua and Barbuda	1981	0.002	23,818	Central African Republic	1960	0.002	23,818
Argentina[1]	1945	0.768	9,146,181	Chad	1960	0.001	11,909
Armenia	1992	0.027	321,545	Chile[1]	1945	0.113	1,345,727
Australia[1]	1945	1.471	17,518,272	China[1]	1945	0.901	10,730,090
Austria	1955	0.935	11,134,999	Colombia[1]	1945	0.108	1,286,182
Azerbaijan	1992	0.060	714,545	Comoros	1975	0.001	11,909
Bahamas	1973	0.015	178,636	Congo, Democratic Republic of	1960	0.008	95,273
Bahrain	1971	0.018	214,364	Congo, Republic of the	1960	0.003	35,727
Bangladesh	1974	0.010	119,091	Costa Rica[1]	1945	0.017	202,455
Barbados	1966	0.008	95,273	Côte d'Ivoire	1960	0.012	142,909
Belarus[1]	1945	0.164	1,953,091	Croatia	1992	0.056	666,909
Belgium[1]	1945	1.096	13,052,363	Cuba[1]	1945	0.039	464,455
Belize	1981	0.001	11,909	Cyprus	1960	0.034	404,909
Benin	1960	0.002	23,818	Czech Republic	1993	0.169	2,012,636
Bhutan	1971	0.001	11,909	Denmark[1]	1945	0.687	8,181,545
Bolivia[1]	1945	0.008	95,273	Djibouti	1977	0.001	11,909
Bosnia-Herzegovina	1992	0.005	59,546	Dominica	1978	0.001	11,909
Botswana	1966	0.010	119,091	Dominican Republic[1]	1945	0.016	190,546
Brazil[1]	1945	1.514	18,030,363	Ecuador[1]	1945	0.022	262,000
Brunei	1984	0.020	238,182	Egypt[1]	1945	0.069	821,727
Bulgaria	1955	0.045	535,909				
Burkina Faso	1960	0.002	23,818				

United Nations: Members and Contributions (*continued*)

Country	Year of admission	Scale of assessments 1998 (%)	Gross contributions for 1998 (US $)	Country	Year of admission	Scale of assessments 1998 (%)	Gross contributions for 1998 (US $)
El Salvador[1]	1945	0.012	142,909	Nepal	1955	0.004	47,636
Equatorial Guinea	1968	0.001	11,909	Netherlands[1]	1945	1.619	19,280,817
Eritrea	1993	0.001	11,909	New Zealand[1]	1945	0.221	2,631,909
Estonia	1991	0.023	273,909	Nicaragua[1]	1945	0.002	23,818
Ethiopia[1]	1945	0.007	83,364	Niger	1960	0.002	23,818
Fiji	1970	0.004	47,636	Nigeria	1960	0.070	833,636
Finland	1955	0.538	6,407,091	Norway[1]	1945	0.605	7,205,000
France[1]	1945	6.494	77,337,632	Oman	1971	0.050	595,455
Gabon	1960	0.018	214,364	Pakistan	1947	0.060	714,545
Gambia	1965	0.001	11,909	Palau	1994	0.001	11,909
Georgia	1992	0.058	690,727	Panama[1]	1945	0.016	190,546
Germany[2]	1973/1990	9.630	114,684,539	Papua New Guinea	1975	0.007	83,364
Ghana	1957	0.007	83,364	Paraguay[1]	1945	0.014	166,727
Greece[1]	1945	0.368	4,382,545	Peru[1]	1945	0.085	1,012,273
Grenada	1974	0.001	11,909	Philippines[1]	1945	0.077	917,000
Guatemala[1]	1945	0.019	226,273	Poland[1]	1945	0.251	2,989,182
Guinea	1958	0.003	35,727	Portugal	1955	0.368	4,382,545
Guinea-Bissau	1974	0.001	11,909	Qatar	1971	0.033	393,000
Guyana	1966	0.001	11,909	Romania	1955	0.102	1,214,727
Haiti[1]	1945	0.002	23,818	Russia[3]	1945	2.873	34,214,816
Honduras[1]	1945	0.004	47,636	Rwanda	1962	0.002	23,818
Hungary	1955	0.119	1,417,182	St Kitts and Nevis	1983	0.001	11,909
Iceland	1946	0.032	381,091	St Lucia	1979	0.001	11,909
India[1]	1945	0.305	3,632,273	St Vincent and the			
Indonesia	1950	0.173	2,060,273	Grenadines	1980	0.001	11,909
Iran[1]	1945	0.303	3,608,454	Samoa	1976	0.001	11,909
Iraq[1]	1945	0.087	1,036,091	San Marino	1992	0.002	23,818
Ireland, Republic of	1955	0.223	2,655,727	São Tomé and Príncipe	1975	0.001	11,909
Israel	1949	0.329	3,918,091	Saudi Arabia[1]	1945	0.594	7,074,000
Italy	1955	5.394	64,237,633	Senegal	1960	0.006	71,455
Jamaica	1962	0.006	71,455	Seychelles	1976	0.002	23,818
Japan	1956	17.981	214,137,351	Sierra Leone	1961	0.001	11,909
Jordan	1955	0.008	95,273	Singapore	1965	0.167	1,988,818
Kazakhstan	1992	0.124	1,476,727	Slovak Republic	1993	0.053	631,182
Kenya	1963	0.007	83,364	Slovenia	1992	0.060	714,545
Korea, North	1991	0.031	369,182	Solomon Islands	1978	0.001	11,909
Korea, South	1991	0.955	11,373,181	Somalia	1960	0.001	11,909
Kuwait	1963	0.154	1,834,000	South Africa[1]	1945	0.365	4,346,818
Kyrgyzstan	1992	0.015	178,636	Spain	1955	2.571	30,618,271
Laos	1955	0.001	11,909	Sri Lanka	1955	0.013	154,818
Latvia	1991	0.046	547,818	Sudan	1956	0.009	107,182
Lebanon[1]	1945	0.016	190,546	Suriname	1975	0.004	47,636
Lesotho	1966	0.002	23,818	Swaziland	1968	0.002	23,818
Liberia[1]	1945	0.002	23,818	Sweden	1946	1.099	13,088,090
Libya	1955	0.160	1,905,454	Syria[1]	1945	0.062	738,364
Liechtenstein	1990	0.005	59,546	Tajikistan	1992	0.008	95,273
Lithuania	1991	0.045	535,909	Tanzania	1961	0.004	47,636
Luxembourg[1]	1945	0.066	786,000	Thailand	1946	0.158	1,881,636
Macedonia, Former				Togo	1960	0.002	23,818
Yugoslav Republic of	1993	0.005	59,546	Trinidad and Tobago	1962	0.018	214,364
Madagascar	1960	0.003	35,727	Tunisia	1956	0.028	333,455
Malawi	1964	0.002	23,818	Turkey[1]	1945	0.440	5,240,000
Malaysia	1957	0.168	2,000,727	Turkmenistan	1992	0.015	178,636
Maldives	1965	0.001	11,909	Uganda	1962	0.004	47,636
Mali	1960	0.003	35,727	UK[1]	1945	5.076	60,450,542
Malta	1964	0.014	166,727	Ukraine[1]	1945	0.678	8,074,363
Marshall Islands	1991	0.001	11,909	United Arab Emirates	1971	0.177	2,107,909
Mauritania	1961	0.001	11,909	Uruguay[1]	1945	0.049	583,545
Mauritius	1968	0.009	107,182	USA[1]	1945	25.000	297,727,256
Mexico[1]	1945	0.941	11,206,454	Uzbekistan	1992	0.077	917,000
Micronesia	1991	0.001	11,909	Vanuatu	1981	0.001	11,909
Moldova	1992	0.043	512,091	Venezuela[1]	1945	0.235	2,798,636
Monaco	1993	0.003	35,727	Vietnam	1977	0.010	119,091
Mongolia	1961	0.002	23,818	Yemen[2]	1947	0.010	119,091
Morocco	1956	0.041	488,273	Yugoslavia[4]	1945	0.060	714,545
Mozambique	1975	0.002	23,818	Zambia	1964	0.003	35,727
Myanmar	1948	0.009	107,182	Zimbabwe	1980	0.009	107,182
Namibia	1990	0.007	83,364	*Total*		100.00	1,190,909,022

[1] Founder member.
[2] Represented by two countries until unification in 1990.
[3] Became a separate member upon the demise of the USSR, which was a founder member in 1945.
[4] Founder member, but suspended from membership in 1993.

Source: UN Secretariat

United Nations: Economic and Social Council (ECOSOC)

Organ of the UN that guides and coordinates the General Assembly's economic programme. It initiates studies of international economic, social, cultural, educational, health, and related matters. It also coordinates the activities of the Food and Agriculture Organization.

Date established 1945

Founding members Belgium, Canada, Chile, China, Colombia, Cuba, Czechoslovakia, France, Greece, India, Lebanon, Norway, Peru, UK, Ukrainian Soviet Socialist Republic, USA, USSR, Yugoslavia

Current members 54 members elected for three years, one-third retiring in rotation

Address United Nations, 1 United Nations Plaza, New York, NY 10017, USA
    The council includes five regional commissions:

Economic Commission for Africa (ECA) established 1958 to promote and facilitate concerted action for the economic and social development of Africa through research and the coordination of national policies. Headquarters: Africa Hall, PO Box 3001, Addis Ababa, Ethiopia.

Economic and Social Commission for Asia and the Pacific (ESCAP) established 1947 (present name from 1974) to promote regional economic cooperation, poverty alleviation through economic growth and social development, and environmentally sustainable development. Headquarters: UN Building, Rajadamnern Avenue, Bangkok 10200, Thailand.

Economic Commission for Europe (UN/ECE) established 1947 to generate and improve economic relations between member and other countries and to strengthen cooperation between governments, particularly in environment, transport, statistics, trade facilitation, and economic analysis. Headquarters: Palais des Nations, 8–14 Avenue de la Paix, CH-1211 Geneva 10, Switzerland.

Economic Commission for Latin America and the Caribbean (ECLAC) established 1948 to raise the level of economic activity in the region and strengthen the economic relations of member countries with one another and with other countries. Headquarters: Avenida Vitacura 3030, PO Box 179-D, Santiago, Chile.

Economic and Social Commission for Western Asia (ESCWA) established 1973 to raise the level of economic activity in the Middle East and northern Africa, and strengthen the economic relations of member countries with one another and with other countries. Headquarters: PO Box 927115, Amman, Jordan.

United Nations: General Assembly

The largest decisionmaking body of the UN, consisting of one representative from each of the member states. The General Assembly meets annually. It controls UN finances and approves the budget. Other decisions are not binding; it merely makes recommendations to the Security Council or a member state. It elects the nonpermanent members of the Security Council.

Date established 1945

Current members 185 states

Address United Nations, 1 United Nations Plaza, New York, NY 10017, USA

United Nations: International Court of Justice

The main judicial organ of the UN. Only states, not individuals, can be parties to cases before the court. There is no appeal. Decisions of the court are binding, but states are not obliged to submit cases to it. The court gives advisory opinions at the request of UN bodies.

Date established 1945

Members 15 independent judges, elected by the Security Council and the General Assembly on the basis of their competence in international law and irrespective of their nationalities, except that no two judges can be nationals of the same state

Address Peace Palace, NL-2517 KJ The Hague, The Netherlands

United Nations: Secretariat

Secretary-General
Kofi Annan (Ghana)

Economic and Social Affairs

Undersecretaries-General
Policy Coordination and Sustainable Development: Nitin Desai (India)
Development Support and Management Services: Jongjian Jin (China)

Assistant Secretary-General
Advancement of Women: Angela King (Jamaica)

Political, Security, and Humanitarian Affairs

Undersecretaries-General
Humanitarian Affairs: Yasushi Akashi (Japan)
Peacekeeping Operations: Bernard Miyet (France)
Political Affairs: Kieran Prendergast (UK)

United Nations Secretaries-General		
Term	Secretary-General	Nationality
1946–53	Trygve Lie	Norwegian
1953–61	Dag Hammarskjöld	Swedish
1961–71	U Thant	Burmese
1972–81	Kurt Waldheim	Austrian
1982–92	Javier Pérez de Cuéllar	Peruvian
1992–96	Boutros Boutros-Ghali	Egyptian
1997–	Kofi Annan	Ghanaian

Assistant Secretaries-General
Peacekeeping Operations: Hedi Annabi (Tunisia), Manfred Eisele (Germany)
Political Affairs: Alvar de Soto (Peru), Ibrahima Fall (Senegal)

Legal, Administrative Affairs, and Public Information

Undersecretaries-General
Administration and Management: Joseph Connor (USA)
UN Legal Counsel: Hans Corell (Sweden)

Assistant Secretaries-General
UN Controller: Jean-Pierre Halbwachs (Mauritius)
Human Resources: Rafiah Salim (Malaysia)
Public Information: Samir Sanbar (Lebanon)
Conference and Support Services: Benon Sevan (Cyprus)
UN Compensation Commission in connection with Iraq: Jean-Claude Aimé (Haiti)

Secretary-General's Executive Office
Chef de Cabinet and Undersecretary-General: S Iqbal Riza (Pakistan)
External Relations and Assistant Secretary-General: Gillian Sorensen (USA)
Spokesman for the Secretary-General: Fred Eckhard (USA)

United Nations: Security Council

The most powerful body of the UN, responsible for maintaining international peace and security. UN member states undertake to accept and carry out its decisions. Any permanent member of the council can veto a decision. The council may investigate disputes, make recommendations, and call on members to take economic or military measures to enforce its decisions, and if these measures are deemed inadequate it may take military action.

Date established 1945

Founding members China, France, UK, USA, USSR

Current members permanent members: China, France, Russia, UK, USA; rotating

United Nations Peacekeeping Operations

United Nations peacekeeping operations come within the jurisdiction of the Security Council. This table gives operations current as of March 1998. Strength figures include military and civilian police personnel; fatality figures include military, civilian police, civilian international, and local staff. The number of fatalities from 1948 to March 1998 was 1,546. The estimated total cost of operations from 1948 to 30 June 1996 was about US $16.0 billion.

Operation	Date of establishment	Area of operation	Fatalities (as of March 1998)	Strength (as of March 1998)	Budget estimate ($ million)[1]
UNTSO United Nations Truce Supervision Organization	1948	Middle East	38	155	23.7[2]
UNMOGIP United Nations Military Observer Group in India and Pakistan	1949	India and Pakistan	9	45	6.4[2]
UNFICYP United Nations Peacekeeping Force in Cyprus	1964	Cyprus	168	1,200	50.3
UNDOF United Nations Disengagement Observer Force	1974	Syria	37	1,045	32.4
UNIFIL United Nations Interim Force in Lebanon	1978	Lebanon	215	4,564	122.2
UNIKOM United Nations Iraq–Kuwait Observation Mission	1991	Iraq/Kuwait	9	1,082	50.7
MINURSO United Nations Mission for the Referendum in Western Sahara	1991	Western Sahara	7	238	29.1
UNOMIG United Nations Observer Mission in Georgia	1993	Georgia	2	116	19.9
UNMOT United Nations Mission of Observers in Tajikistan	1994	Tajikistan	1	23	8.0
UNPREDEP United Nations Preventive Deployment Force	1995	Former Yugoslav Republic of Macedonia	4	1,147	44.3
UNMIBH United Nations Mission in Bosnia-Herzegovina	1995	Bosnia-Herzegovina	4	1,698	165.6
UNMOP United Nations Mission of Observers in Prevlaka	1996	Croatia	0	28	[6]
MONUA United Nations Observer Mission in Angola	1997	Angola	5	1,558	155
MIPONUH United Nations Civilian Police Mission in Haiti	1997	Haiti	0	300	14 [4]
United Nations Civilian Police Support Group	1998	Croatia	0	396	17.6[5]

[1] 1 July 1997–30 June 1998.
[2] Data for 1997.
[3] 15 February–31 May 1997. This estimate includes the military observer component only.
[4] Six-month estimate.
[5] Nine-month estimate.
[6] included in UNMIBH estimate

Source: UN Department of Public Information

members (1996–97): Chile, Egypt, Guinea-Bissau, South Korea, Poland; (1997–98): Costa Rica, Japan, Kenya, Portugal, Sweden

Address United Nations, Room S-3380A, New York, NY 10017, USA

United Nations: Selected Programmes and Organs

International Atomic Energy Agency (IAEA) established 1957 to advise and assist member countries in the development and peaceful application of nuclear power, and to guard against its misuse. It is an independent intergovernmental organization under the aegis of the UN. Headquarters: Wagramerstrasse 5, PO Box 100, A-1400 Vienna, Austria.

United Nations Centre for Human Settlements (UNCHS, Habitat) established 1978 to service the intergovernmental Commission on Human Settlements by providing planning, construction, land development, and finance. It is a standing committee under the Economic and Social Council and the General Assembly. Headquarters: 2 United Nations Plaza, Room DC-2-0943, New York, NY 10017, USA.

United Nations Children's Fund (UNICEF) established 1946 to improve the lives of children throughout the world. It carries out programmes in health, nutrition, education, water and sanitation, the environment, women in development, and other areas of importance to children. Headquarters: 3 United Nations Plaza, New York, NY 10017, USA.

United Nations Conference on Trade and Development (UNCTAD) established 1964 to promote international trade, particularly in developing countries. Headquarters: Palais des Nations, 8–14 Avenue de la Paix, CH-1211 Geneva 10, Switzerland.

United Nations Development Fund for Women (UNIFEM) established 1976 to help women achieve equality through economic and social development. It provides direct technical and financial support to women's initiatives. Headquarters: 304 East 45th Street, 6th Floor, New York, NY 10017, USA.

United Nations Development Programme (UNDP) established 1965 to eradicate poverty, especially in the least developed countries, and to achieve sustainable human development, the empowerment of women, and the protection and regeneration of the environment. Headquarters: 1 United Nations Plaza, New York, NY 10017, USA.

United Nations Environment Programme (UNEP) established 1972 to monitor the state of the environment and promote environmentally sound developments throughout the world. Headquarters: PO Box 30552, Nairobi, Kenya.

United Nations High Commissioner for Refugees (UNHCR) established 1951 to help refugees and displaced people worldwide, to give them international protection, and to find solutions to their problems. Headquarters: Centre William Rappard, 154 Rue de Lausanne, CH-1202 Geneva, Switzerland.

United Nations Institute for Training and Research (UNITAR) established 1965 to improve the effectiveness of the UN through training and research. It is a standing committee under the Economic and Social Council and the General Assembly. Headquarters: Palais des Nations, Bureau 1070, 8–14 Avenue de la Paix, CH-1211 Geneva 10, Switzerland.

United Nations Population Fund (UNFPA) established 1972 under the umbrella of UNDP to help countries, at their request, to address issues of reproductive health and population, and to raise awareness of this in all countries. Headquarters: 220 East 42nd Street, New York, NY 10017, USA.

United Nations Research Institute for Social Development (UNRISD) established 1964 to conduct research into problems and policies of social and economic development. It is a standing committee under the Economic and Social Council and the General Assembly. Headquarters: Palais des Nations, Bureau 1070, 8–14 Avenue de la Paix, CH-1211 Geneva 10, Switzerland.

World Food Programme (WFP) established 1963 to improve economic and social development through food aid and to provide emergency relief. It is a standing committee under the Economic and Social Council and the General Assembly. Headquarters: Via Cristoforo Colombo 426, I-00145 Rome, Italy.

United Nations: Specialized Agencies

Food and Agriculture Organization (FAO) established 1945 to coordinate activities to improve food and timber production and levels of nutrition throughout the world. It is also concerned with investment in agriculture and dispersal of emergency food supplies. Headquarters: Viale delle Terme di Caracalla, I-00100 Rome, Italy.

International Civil Aviation Organization (ICAO) established 1947 to promote safety and efficiency in aviation, international facilities, and air law. Headquarters: 999 University Street, Montréal, H3C 5H7, Canada.

International Fund for Agricultural Development (IFAD) established 1977 to provide additional funds for benefiting the poorest in developing countries. Headquarters: Via del Serafico 107, I-00142 Rome, Italy.

International Labour Organization (ILO) established 1919 to formulate standards for labour and social conditions. Headquarters: 4 Route des Morillons, CH-1211 Geneva, Switzerland.

International Maritime Organization (IMO) established 1958 to promote safety at sea, pollution control, and the abolition of restrictive practices. Headquarters: 4 Albert Embankment, London SE1 7SR, UK.

International Monetary Fund (IMF) established 1944 to promote world trade and to smooth loan repayments among member states; the IMF also makes loans to members in balance-of-payments difficulties, on certain conditions. Headquarters: 700 19th Street NW, Washington, DC 20431, USA.

International Telecommunication Union (ITU) established 1934 to promote international regulations for telephone, radio, and telegraph communications, and to allocate radio frequencies. Headquarters: Palais des Nations, 8–14 Avenue de la Paix, CH-1211 Geneva 10, Switzerland.

United Nations Educational, Scientific, and Cultural Organization (UNESCO) established 1946 to promote cooperation among nations through education, science,

and culture, and to further respect for justice, the rule of law, and human rights and fundamental freedoms. It pays special attention to women's issues and youth development. Headquarters: 7 Place de Fontenoy, F-75352 Paris 075P, France.

United Nations Industrial Development Organization (UNIDO) established 1966 to promote industrial development and coordination. It acts as the chief coordinating body for industrial activities within the UN system. Headquarters: Vienna International Centre, PO Box 300, A-1400 Vienna, Austria.

Universal Postal Union (UPU) established 1875 to coordinate international collaboration of postal services. It became an agency of the UN in 1947. Headquarters: Bureau International de l'UPU, Weltpoststrasse 4, CH-3000 Bern 15, Switzerland.

World Health Organization (WHO) established 1946 to assist all peoples in attaining the highest possible levels of health, to prevent the spread of diseases, and to eradicate them. It is creating a worldwide early-warning system for infectious diseases. Headquarters: 20 Avenue Appia, CH-1211 Geneva 27, Switzerland.

World Intellectual Property Organization (WIPO) established 1974 to protect copyright, patents, and trademarks in the arts, science, and industry. Headquarters: 34 Chemin des Colombettes, Case Postale 18, CH-1211 Geneva 20, Switzerland.

World Meteorological Organization (WMO) established 1951 to facilitate worldwide cooperation in the creation and maintenance of a network of stations for making meteorological observations and to ensure the rapid exchange of information. Headquarters: Case Postale 2300, 41 Avenue Giuseppe-Motta, CH-1211 Geneva 2, Switzerland.

United Nations: World Bank Group

International Bank for Reconstruction and Development (IBRD, World Bank) established 1945 to promote economic development by lending money to countries in need. The loans are on commercial terms and guaranteed by member states. Headquarters: 1818 H Street NW, Washington, DC 20433, USA.

International Development Association (IDA) established 1960 to meet the need for lending to poor countries on easy terms; administered by the World Bank. Headquarters: 1818 H Street NW, Washington, DC 20433, USA.

International Finance Corporation (IFC) established 1956 to encourage private enterprise in developing countries. It is affiliated to the World Bank. Headquarters: 1850 I Street NW, Washington, DC 20433, USA.

Multilateral Investment Guarantee Agency (MIGA) established 1988 to encourage the flow of private investment to developing member countries. Headquarters: 1818 H Street NW, Washington, DC 20433, USA.

Universal Declaration of Human Rights: Preamble

On 10 December 1948 the General Assembly of the United Nations adopted and proclaimed the Universal Declaration of Human Rights. Following this historic act, the Assembly called upon all member countries to publicize the text of the declaration and 'to cause it to be disseminated, displayed, read, and expounded principally in schools and other educational institutions, without distinction based on the political status of countries or territories'.

Preamble
Whereas recognition of the inherent dignity and of the equal and inalienable rights of all members of the human family is the foundation of freedom, justice and peace in the world,

Whereas disregard and contempt for human rights have resulted in barbarous acts which have outraged the conscience of mankind, and the advent of a world in which human beings shall enjoy freedom of speech and belief and freedom from fear and want has been proclaimed as the highest aspiration of the common people,

Whereas it is essential, if man is not to be compelled to have recourse, as a last resort, to rebellion against tyranny and oppression, that human rights should be protected by the rule of law,

Whereas it is essential to promote the development of friendly relations between nations,

Whereas the peoples of the United Nations have in the Charter reaffirmed their faith in fundamental human rights, in the dignity and worth of the human person and in the equal rights of men and women and have determined to promote social progress and better standards of life in larger freedom,

Whereas member states have pledged themselves to achieve, in cooperation with the United Nations, the promotion of universal respect for and observance of human rights and fundamental freedoms,

Whereas a common understanding of these rights and freedoms is of the greatest importance for the full realization of this pledge,

Now, therefore, the General Assembly proclaims this Universal Declaration of Human Rights as a common standard of achievement for all peoples and all nations, to the end that every individual and every organ of society, keeping this Declaration constantly in mind, shall strive by teaching and education to promote respect for these rights and freedoms and by progressive measures, national and international, to secure their universal and effective recognition and observance, both among the peoples of member states themselves and among the peoples of territories under their jurisdiction.

Universal Declaration of Human Rights: Articles

Article 1
All human beings are born free and equal in dignity and rights. They are endowed with reason and conscience and should act towards one another in a spirit of brotherhood.

Article 2
Everyone is entitled to all the rights and freedoms set forth in this Declaration, without distinction of any kind, such as race, colour, sex, language, religion, political or other opinion, national or social origin, property, birth, or other status. Furthermore, no distinction shall be made on the basis of the political, jurisdictional, or international status of the country or territory to which a person belongs, whether it be independent, trust, non-self-governing, or under any other limitation of sovereignty.

Article 3
Everyone has the right to life, liberty, and security of person.

Article 4
No one shall be held in slavery or servitude; slavery and the slave trade shall be prohibited in all their forms.

Article 5
No one shall be subjected to torture or to cruel, inhuman or degrading treatment or punishment.

Article 6
Everyone has the right to recognition everywhere as a person before the law.

Article 7
All are equal before the law and are entitled without any discrimination to equal protection of the law. All are entitled to equal protection against any discrimination in violation of this Declaration and against any incitement to such discrimination.

Article 8
Everyone has the right to an effective remedy by the competent national tribunals for acts violating the fundamental rights granted him by the constitution or by law.

Article 9
No one shall be subjected to arbitrary arrest, detention, or exile.

Article 10
Everyone is entitled in full equality to a fair and public hearing by an independent and impartial tribunal, in the determination of his rights and obligations and of any criminal charge against him.

Article 11
1. Everyone charged with a penal offence has the right to be presumed innocent until proved guilty according to law in a public trial at which he has had all the guarantees necessary for his defence.
2. No one shall be held guilty of any penal offence on account of any act or omission which did not constitute a penal offence, under national or international law, at the time when it was committed. Nor shall a heavier penalty be imposed than the one that was applicable at the time the penal offence was committed.

Article 12
No one shall be subjected to arbitrary interference with his privacy, family, home, or correspondence, nor to attacks upon his honour and reputation. Everyone has the right to the protection of the law against such interference or attacks.

Article 13
1. Everyone has the right to freedom of movement and residence within the borders of each state.
2. Everyone has the right to leave any country, including his own, and to return to his country.

Article 14
1. Everyone has the right to seek and to enjoy in other countries asylum from persecution.
2. This right may not be invoked in the case of prosecutions genuinely arising from nonpolitical crimes or from acts contrary to the purposes and principles of the United Nations (UN).

Article 15
1. Everyone has the right to a nationality.
2. No one shall be arbitrarily deprived of his nationality nor denied the right to change his nationality.

Article 16
1. Men and women of full age, without any limitation due to race, nationality, or religion, have the right to marry and to found a family. They are entitled to equal rights as to marriage, during marriage, and at its dissolution.
2. Marriage shall be entered into only with the free and full consent of the intending spouses.
3. The family is the natural and fundamental group unit of society and is entitled to protection by society and the state.

Article 17
1. Everyone has the right to own property alone as well as in association with others.
2. No one shall be arbitrarily deprived of his property.

Article 18
Everyone has the right to freedom of thought, conscience, and religion; this right includes freedom to change his religion or belief, and freedom, either alone or in community with others and in public or private, to manifest his religion or belief in teaching, practice, worship, and observance.

Article 19
Everyone has the right to freedom of opinion and expression; this right includes freedom to hold opinions without interference and to seek, receive and impart information and ideas through any media and regardless of frontiers.

Article 20
1. Everyone has the right to freedom of peaceful assembly and association.
2. No one may be compelled to belong to an association.

Article 21
1. Everyone has the right to take part in the government of his country, directly or through freely chosen representatives.
2. Everyone has the right of equal access to public service in his country.
3. The will of the people shall be the basis of the authority of government; this will shall be expressed in periodic and genuine elections which shall be by universal and equal suffrage and shall be held by secret vote or by equivalent free voting procedures.

Article 22
Everyone, as a member of society, has the right to social security and is entitled to realization, through national effort and international cooperation and in accordance with the organization and resources of each state, of the economic, social, and cultural rights indispensable for his dignity and the free development of his personality.

Article 23
1. Everyone has the right to work, to free choice of employment, to just and favourable conditions of work, and to protection against unemployment.
2. Everyone, without any discrimination, has the right to equal pay for equal work.
3. Everyone who works has the right to just and favourable remuneration ensuring for himself and his family an existence worthy of human dignity, and supplemented, if necessary, by other means of social protection.
4. Everyone has the right to form and to join trade unions for the protection of his interests.

Article 24
Everyone has the right to rest and leisure, including reasonable limitation of working hours and periodic holidays with pay.

Article 25
1. Everyone has the right to a standard of living adequate for the health and well-being of himself and of his family, including food, clothing, housing, and medical care and necessary social services, and the right to security in the event of unemployment, sickness, disability, widowhood, old age, or other lack of livelihood in circumstances beyond his control.
2. Motherhood and childhood are entitled to special care and assistance. All children, whether born in or out of wedlock, shall enjoy the same social protection.

Article 26

1. Everyone has the right to education. Education shall be free, at least in the elementary and fundamental stages. Elementary education shall be compulsory. Technical and professional education shall be made generally available and higher education shall be equally accessible to all on the basis of merit.
2. Education shall be directed to the full development of the human personality and to the strengthening of respect for human rights and fundamental freedoms. It shall promote understanding, tolerance, and friendship among all nations, racial or religious groups, and shall further the activities of the UN for the maintenance of peace.
3. Parents have a prior right to choose the kind of education that shall be given to their children.

Article 27

1. Everyone has the right freely to participate in the cultural life of the community, to enjoy the arts, and to share in scientific advancement and its benefits.
2. Everyone has the right to the protection of the moral and material interests resulting from any scientific, literary, or artistic production of which he is the author.

Article 28

Everyone is entitled to a social and international order in which the rights and freedoms set forth in this Declaration can be fully realized.

Article 29

1. Everyone has duties to the community in which alone the free and full development of his personality is possible.

2. In the exercise of his rights and freedoms, everyone shall be subject only to such limitations as are determined by law solely for the purpose of securing due recognition and respect for the rights and freedoms of others and of meeting the just requirements of morality, public order, and the general welfare in a democratic society.
3. These rights and freedoms may in no case be exercised contrary to the purposes and principles of the UN.

Article 30

Nothing in this Declaration may be interpreted as implying for any state, group or person any right to engage in any activity or to perform any act aimed at the destruction of any of the rights and freedoms set forth herein.

International Human Rights and Relief Organizations

ACTIONAID

International charity focusing on long-term development by working with communities in the developing world to strengthen human resources to alleviate poverty and improve quality of life. ACTIONAID operates in 24 countries.

Date established 1972

Membership over 120,000 active supporters (1998)

Funding private donations, child and community sponsorship, contributions from official bodies such as the British government and the European Union, and income from trading, such as the sale of merchandise

Address: Headquarters ACTIONAID UK, Chataway House, Leach Road, Chard, Somerset TA20 1FA, UK; phone: (01460) 62972; fax: (01460) 67191; e-mail: mail@actionaid.org.uk

Address in Ireland ACTIONAID Ireland, Unity Buildings, 16–17 O'Connell Street, Dublin 1, Republic of Ireland; phone: (01353 1) 878 7911; fax: (01353 1) 878 6245

Web site www.actionaid.org/

Amnesty International

Independent, politically-unaligned organization for the protection of human rights worldwide, as set out in the Universal Declaration of Human Rights. Amnesty campaigns for the release of prisoners of conscience; fair trials for political prisoners; and an end to torture, extrajudicial executions, 'disappearances', and the death penalty. It organizes fact-finding missions and human-rights education. Amnesty operates in more than 100 countries.

Date established 1961

Membership more than 1 million (1997)

Funding private donations and membership fees

Addresses in UK Headquarters: International Secretariat, 1 Easton Street, London WC1X 8DJ, UK; phone: (0171) 413 5500; e-mail: amnestyis@amnesty.org; 99–119 Rosebery Avenue, London EC1R 4RE, UK; phone: (0171) 814 6200; fax: (0171) 833 1510; e-mail: info@amnesty.org.uk

Web site www.amnesty.org/

British Helsinki Human Rights Group

Independent nongovernmental organization dedicated to monitoring the progress of democracy and human rights in the OSCE member states.

Date established 1992

Membership 15

Funding private

Address British Helsinki Human Rights Group, 22 St Margaret's Road, Oxford, UK; phone: (01865) 510 564; fax: (01865) 510 564; e-mail: bhhrg@bhhrg.org

Web site www.bhhrg.org/

CARE International

Nonprofit, nongovernmental organization aiming to relieve human suffering, to provide economic opportunity, and to build sustained capacity for self-help. CARE International operates in 77 countries.

Date established 1946

Membership not a membership organization

Funding corporate and private donations, government grants, contributions in kind, such as agricultural produce donated by governments

Address: Headquarters Boulevard de Régent 58/10, B-1000 Brussels, Belgium; phone: (32 2) 502 4333; fax: (32 2) 502 8202

Address in UK CARE UK, 36–38 Southampton Street, London WC2E 7AF, UK; phone: (0171) 379 5247; fax: (0171) 379 0543

Web site www.care.org/

Caritas Internationalis (International Confederation of Catholic Organizations for Charitable and Social Action)

Confederation of national Catholic organizations that helps coordinate its members' efforts in emergency aid, rehabilitation, and development, with the objective of spreading charity and social justice worldwide.

Date established 1950

Membership 146 member organizations in 194 countries and territories

Funding membership fees

Address: Headquarters Palazzo San Calisto 16, V-00120 Città del Vaticano, Vatican, Italy; phone: (39 6) 6988 7197; fax: (39 6) 6988 7237; e-mail: ci.comm@caritas.va

Children's Aid Direct

A UK-based charity which aims to make an immediate and lasting improvement to the lives of children and their carers who are affected by conflict, poverty, or disaster.

Date established 1990

Membership not a membership organization

Funding EU, US and other governments, corporate sponsorship, private donations

Address 12 Portman Road, Reading, Berkshire RG30 1EA, UK; phone: (0118) 958 4000; fax: (0118) 958 8988; e-mail 100523,3025@compuserve.com

Web site www.cad.org.uk

Concern Worldwide

Nongovernmental organization providing relief, assistance, and advancement to people in need in less developed areas of the world. Concern operates in 13 countries throughout Asia, Africa, and Latin America.

Date established 1968

Membership not a membership organization

Funding private donations and co-funding

Address: Headquarters Camden Street, Dublin 2, Ireland; phone: (01353 1) 475 4162; fax: (01353 1) 475 7362; e-mail: concernd@iol.ie

Address in UK Concern Worldwide UK, 248–250 Lavender Hill, London SW11 1LJ, UK; phone: (0171) 738 1033; fax: (0171) 738 1032; e-mail: concernl.london@btinernet.com

Web site www.irishnet.com/concern.htm

Human Rights Watch

Politically unaligned charity that reports on practices affecting human rights. It documents and publicizes imprisonments, censorship, violation of human-rights laws, and abuses of internationally recognized human rights. It covers more than 70 countries.

Date established 1978 (as Helsinki Watch)

Membership not a membership organization

Funding grants from foundations; private donations

Address: Headquarters 350 Fifth Avenue, New York, NY 10118-3299, USA; phone: (1 212) 290 4700; fax: (212) 736 1300; e-mail: hrwnyc@hrw.org

Address in UK 33 Islington High Street, London N1 9LH, UK; phone: (0171) 713 1995; fax: (0171) 713 1800; e-mail: hrwatchuk@gn.apc.org

Web site www.hrw.org/

Médecins Sans Frontières International (MSF)

Nonprofit humanitarian organization offering assistance to populations in distress and to victims of disasters or armed conflict. MSF volunteers provide primary health care, operate emergency nutrition and sanitation programmes, and train local medical staff. MSF observes strict impartiality and neutrality in the name of universal medical ethics and demands full freedom in exercising its functions. MSF is independent of political, religious, or economic influence, and operates in 80 countries.

Date established 1971

Membership not a membership organization

Funding private donations and grants from international organizations and governments

Address: Headquarters 39 Rue de la Tourelle, B-1040, Brussels, Belgium; phone: (32 3) 280 1881; fax: (32 2) 280 0173

Address in UK 124–132 Clerkenwell Road, London EC1R 5DL, UK; phone: (0171) 713 5600; fax: (0171) 713 5004

Web site www.msf.org/ and www.dwb.org/

Minority Rights Group International (MRG)

Educational trust aiming to secure justice for minority or majority groups suffering discrimination; to alert public opinion to violations of human rights; and to foster international understanding of the factors that cause prejudice. The organization has contacts and groups in 25 countries.

Date established 1970

Membership not a membership organization

Funding private donations and the sale of publications

Address 379 Brixton Road, Brixton, London SW9 7DE, UK; phone: (0171) 978 9498; fax: (0171) 738 6265

Oxfam

Charity aiming to put an end to poverty worldwide. It provides assistance for development and relief by working in partnership with local groups, helping poor people to help themselves. Oxfam campaigns internationally, gives poor people channels to voice their concerns, funds long-term projects such as education and training, and provides emergency aid. The organization operates in over 70 countries. Oxfam UK is a member of Oxfam International.

Date established 1942

Membership not a membership organization

Funding donations from individuals, groups, companies, and trusts; grants from the UK Department for International Development, the European Union, United Nations agencies, and governments

Address: Headquarters 274 Banbury Road, Oxford OX2 7DZ, UK; phone: (01865) 311 311; fax: (01865) 313 770; e-mail: oxfam@oxfam.org.uk

Web site www.oxfam.org.uk/

Panos Institute

Organization aiming to provide access to, and freedom of, information on environmental and social development issues, and to help minority and marginal groups to gain access to a wider public and to government and decisionmaking bodies. Panos operates in southern and southeast Asia, and eastern and southern Africa.

Date established 1986

Membership not a membership organization

Address: Headquarters 10 rue de Mail, 75002 Paris, France; phone: (33 1) 4041 0550; fax: (33 1) 4041 0330; e-mail: panos@worldnet.fr

Address in UK Panos London, 9 White Lion Street, London N1 9PD, UK; phone: (0171) 278 1111; fax: (0171) 278 0345; e-mail: panoslondon@gn.apc.org

Web site www.oneworld.org/panos/

Raoul Wallenberg Institute of Human Rights and Humanitarian Law

Charitable trust promoting research, training, and academic education in the fields of human rights and humanitarian law. It organizes programmes in developing countries, especially in Asia and Africa, for government officials, prison administrators, police, judges, and so on; some courses are also held at the University of Lund, Sweden, where the research library is maintained.

Date established 1984

Membership not a membership organization

Funding supported by grants from the Swedish Ministry for Foreign Affairs and the Swedish International Development Cooperation Agency

Address: Headquarters Stora Gråbrödersgatan 17, PO Box 1155, S-221 05 Lund, Sweden; phone: (46 46) 222 1200; fax: (46 46) 222 1222

Web site www.ldc.lu.se/raoul/

International Committee of the Red Cross (ICRC)

Umbrella body for national Red Cross and Red Crescent societies. It is a neutral, impartial, and independent humanitarian institution. The Red Cross was set up to help all victims of war and internal violence, by providing medical assistance, organizing humanitarian relief, and attempting to ensure implementation of rules restricting armed violence. It also helps victims of natural disasters. The Red Cross operates in more than 50 countries.

Date established 1863

Membership not a membership organization

Funding grants from the states party to the Geneva Convention, and from international organizations such as the European Union, public funds, money from national Red Cross and Red Crescent societies, private donations

Address: Headquarters Public Information Division, 19 Avenue de la Paix, CH 1202 Geneva, Switzerland; phone: (41 22) 734 6001; fax: (41 22) 734 2057; e-mail (press or operational information): press.gva@icrc.org

Web site www.icrc.org/

Save the Children Fund

Charity aiming to achieve lasting benefits for children within the communities in which they live by influencing policy and practice in tackling the underlying causes of poverty. The organization operates in more than 50 countries.

Date established 1919

Membership not a membership organization

Funding government grants, private and corporate donations, shops and trading, donations from sister charities

Address: Headquarters 17 Grove Lane, London SE5 8RD, UK; phone: (0171) 703 5400; fax: (0171) 703 2278; e-mail: info@scflondon.ccmail.compuserve.com

Web site www.oneworld.org/scf/scf_info.html

Survival International

Charity supporting tribal peoples worldwide. It stands for their right to decide their own future and helps them protect their lives, lands, and human rights. It works closely with local indigenous organizations and focuses especially on tribal peoples most recently in contact with the outside world. There were cases in 36 countries worldwide in 1998.

Date established 1969

Membership 18,000 members in 75 countries (1998)

Funding donations from members, private individuals and organizations

Address: Headquarters 11–15 Emerald Street, London WC1N 3QL, UK; phone: (0171) 242 1441; fax: (0171) 242 1771; e-mail: survival@gn.apc.org

Web site www.survival.org.uk/

Voluntary Service Overseas (VSO)

Organization aiming to enable men and women to work alongside people in poorer countries in order to share skills, build capabilities, and promote international understanding and action, in the pursuit of a more equitable world. VSO has recruitment offices in the UK, Canada, and the Netherlands, and operates in 59 countries, with more than 1,950 volunteers overseas in 1997.

Date established 1958

Membership not a membership organization

Funding private donations and foundation grants

Address: Headquarters 317 Putney Bridge Road, London SW15 2PN, UK; phone: (0181) 780 7200; fax: (0181) 780 7300; e-mail: sbernau@vso.org.uk

Web site www.oneworld.org/vso/

World Geography

Deepest Geographical Depressions in the World

Depression	Location	Maximum depth below sea level	
		m	ft
Dead Sea	Israel/Jordan	400	1,312
Turfan Depression	Xinjiang, China	154	505
Lake Assal	Djibouti	153	502
Qattâra Depression	Egypt	133	436
Poloustrov Mangyshlak	Kazakhstan	131	430
Danakil Depression	Ethiopia	120	394
Death Valley	California, USA	86	282
Salton Sink	California, USA	71	233
Zapadnyy Chink Ustyurta	Kazakhstan	70	230
Priaspiyskaya Nizmennost	Russia/Kazakhstan	67	220
Ozera Sarykamysh	Uzbekistan/Kazakhstan	45	148
El Faiyûm	Egypt	44	144
Valdés Peninsula	Argentina	40	131

Largest Deserts in the World

Desert	Location	Area[1]	
		sq km	sq mi
Sahara	northern Africa	9,065,000	3,500,000
Gobi	Mongolia/northeastern China	1,295,000	500,000
Patagonian	Argentina	673,000	260,000
Rub al-Khali	southern Arabian peninsula	647,500	250,000
Kalahari	southwestern Africa	528,800	225,000
Chihuahuan	Mexico/southwestern USA	362,600	140,000
Taklimakan	northern China	362,600	140,000
Great Sandy	northwestern Australia	338,500	130,000
Great Victoria	southwestern Australia	338,500	130,000
Kyzyl Kum	Uzbekistan/Kazakhstan	259,000	100,000
Thar	India/Pakistan	259,000	100,000
Sonoran	Mexico/southwestern USA	181,300	70,000
Simpson	Australia	103,600	40,000
Mojave	southwestern USA	65,000	25,000

[1] Desert areas are very approximate because clear physical boundaries may not occur.

Largest Islands in the World

Island	Location	Area		Island	Location	Area	
		sq km	sq mi			sq km	sq mi
Greenland	northern Atlantic	2,175,600	840,000	Newfoundland	northwestern Atlantic	108,860	42,030
New Guinea	southwestern Pacific	800,000	309,000	Luzon	western Pacific	104,688	40,420
Borneo	southwestern Pacific	744,100	287,300	Iceland	northern Atlantic	103,000	39,768
Madagascar	Indian Ocean	587,041	226,657	Mindanao	western Pacific	94,630	36,537
Baffin	Canadian Arctic	507,450	195,875	Ireland (Northern Ireland and the Republic of Ireland)	northern Atlantic	84,406	32,590
Sumatra	Indian Ocean	424,760	164,000				
Honshu	northwestern Pacific	230,966	89,176				
Great Britain	northern Atlantic	218,078	84,200	Hokkaido	northwestern Pacific	83,515	32,245
Victoria	Canadian Arctic	217,206	83,896	Sakhalin	northwestern Pacific	76,400	29,500
Ellesmere	Canadian Arctic	196,160	75,767	Hispaniola – Dominican Republic and Haiti	Caribbean Sea	76,192	29,418
Sulawesi	Indian Ocean	189,216	73,057				
South Island, New Zealand	southwestern Pacific	149,883	57,870				
				Banks	Canadian Arctic	70,028	27,038
Java	Indian Ocean	126,602	48,900	Tasmania	southwestern Pacific	67,800	26,171
North Island, New Zealand	southwestern Pacific	114,669	44,274	Sri Lanka	Indian Ocean	65,610	25,332
				Devon	Canadian Arctic	55,247	21,331
Cuba	Caribbean Sea	110,860	42,803				

Largest Lakes in the World

Lake	Location	Area		Lake	Location	Area	
		sq km	sq mi			sq km	sq mi
Caspian Sea	Azerbaijan/Russia/Kazakhstan/ Turkmenistan/Iran	370,990	143,239	Great Bear	Canada	31,316	12,091
				Malawi (or Nyasa)	Malawi/Tanzania/Mozambique	28,867	11,146
Superior	USA/Canada	82,071	31,688	Great Slave	Canada	28,560	11,027
Victoria	Tanzania/Kenya/Uganda	69,463	26,820	Erie	USA/Canada	25,657	9,906
Aral Sea	Kazakhstan/Uzbekistan	64,500	24,903	Winnipeg	Canada	25,380	9,799
Huron	USA/Canada	59,547	22,991	Ontario	USA/Canada	19,010	7,340
Michigan	USA	57,735	22,291	Balkhash	Kazakhstan	18,421	7,112
Tanganyika	Tanzania/Democratic Republic of Congo/Zambia/Burundi	32,880	12,695	Ladoga	Russia	17,695	6,832
				Chad	Chad/Cameroon/Nigeria	16,310	6,297
Baikal	Russia	31,499	12,162	Maracaibo	Venezuela	13,507	5,215

Highest Mountains in the World, by Region

Region/mountain	Location	m	ft
Africa			
Kilimanjaro	Tanzania	5,895	19,337
Kenya (Batian)	Kenya	5,199	17,057
Ngaliema (formerly Mt Stanley and Margherita Peak)	Democratic Republic of Congo/Uganda	5,110	16,765
Duwoni (formerly Umberto Peak)	Uganda	4,896	16,063
Baker (Edward Peak)	Uganda	4,843	15,889
Alpine Europe			
Mont Blanc	France/Italy	4,807	15,771
Monte Rosa	Switzerland	4,634	15,203
Dom	Switzerland	4,545	14,911
Liskamm	Switzerland/Italy	4,527	14,852
Weisshorn	Switzerland	4,505	14,780
Antarctica			
Vinson Massif		5,140	16,863
Tyree		4,965	16,289
Shin		4,800	15,748
Gardne		4,690	15,387
Epperle		4,511	14,800
Asia			
Everest	China/Nepal	8,848	29,028
K2	Kashmir/Jammu	8,611	28,251
Kangchenjunga	India/Nepal	8,598	28,208
Lhotse	China/Nepal	8,511	27,923
Yalung Kang	India/Nepal	8,502	27,893
Australia			
Kosciusko	Snowy Mountains, New South Wales	2,230	7,316
Carpathians			
Gerlachvka	Slovak Republic	2,655	8,711
Moldoveanu	Romania	2,544	8,346
Negoiu	Romania	2,535	8,317
Mindra	Romania	2,518	8,261
Peleaga	Romania	2,509	8,232
Caucasia			
Elbrus, West Peak	Russia	5,642	18,510
Dykh Tau	Russia/Georgia	5,203	17,070
Shkhara	Russia/Georgia	5,201	17,063
Kashtan Tau	Russia/Georgia	5,144	16,876
Dzanghi Tau	Russia	5,049	16,565

Region/mountain	Location	m	ft
New Zealand			
Cook (called Aorongi in Maori)	west coast, South Island	3,754	12,316
North and Central America			
McKinley	Alaska, USA	6,194	20,321
Logan, Yukon	Canada	6,050	19,849
Citlaltépetl (Orizaba)	Mexico	5,610	18,405
St Elias	Alaska, USA/Yukon, Canada	5,489	18,008
Popocatépetl	Mexico	5,452	17,887
Oceania[1]			
Jaya	West Irian, Papua New Guinea	5,030	16,502
Daam	West Irian, Papua New Guinea	4,922	16,148
Oost Carstensz (also known as Jayakusumu Timur)	West Irian, Papua New Guinea	4,840	15,879
Trikora	West Irian, Papua New Guinea	4,730	15,518
Enggea	West Irian, Papua New Guinea	4,717	15,476
Polynesia			
Mauna Kea	Hawaii, USA	4,205	13,796
Mauna Loa	Hawaii, USA	4,170	13,681
Pyrenees			
Pico de Aneto	Spain	3,404	11,168
Pico de Posets	Spain	3,371	11,060
Monte Perdido	Spain	3,348	10,984
Pico de la Maladeta	Spain	3,312	10,866
Pic de Vignemale	France/Spain	3,298	10,820
Scandinavia			
Glittertind	Norway	2,472	8,110
Galdhøpiggen	Norway	2,469	8,100
Skagastolstindane	Norway	2,405	7,890
Snohetta	Norway	2,286	7,500
South America			
Cerro Aconcagua	Argentina	6,960	22,834
Ojos del Salado	Argentina/Chile	6,908	22,664
Bonete	Argentina	6,872	22,546
Nevado de Pissis	Argentina/Chile	6,779	22,241
Huascarán Sur	Peru	6,768	22,204

[1] Including all of Papua New Guinea.

Lowest Depressions by Continent

Continent	Location	Depth below sea level	
		m	ft
Africa	Lake Assal, Djibouti	153	502
Antarctica	Lake Vostok[1]	4,000	13,123
Asia	Dead Sea, Israel/Jordan	400	1,312
Europe	Caspian Sea, Azerbaijan/Russia/Kazakhstan/Turkmenistan/Iran	28	92
North America	Death Valley (CA), USA	86	282
Oceania	Lake Eyre, South Australia	16	52
South America	Valdés Peninsula, Argentina	40	131

[1] Discovered by the British Antarctic Survey in 1996, the freshwater Lake Vostok lies beneath the ice sheets and covers an area of 14,000 sq km/5,400 sq mi.

Highest Mountains in the World, with First Ascents

Mountain	Location	Height m	Height ft	Year of first ascent	Expedition nationality (leader)
Everest	China/Nepal	8,848	29,028	1953	British/New Zealander (J Hunt)
K2	Kashmir/Jammu	8,611	28,251	1954	Italian (A Desio)
Kangchenjunga	India/Nepal	8,598	28,208	1955	British (C Evans; by the southwest face)
Lhotse	China/Nepal	8,511	27,923	1956	Swiss (E Reiss)
Yalung Kang (formerly Kangchenjunga West Peak)	India/Nepal	8,502	27,893	1973	Japanese (Y Ageta)
Kangchenjunga South Peak	India/Nepal	8,488	27,847	1978	Polish (W Wróż)
Makalu I	China/Nepal	8,481	27,824	1955	French (J Couzy)
Kangchenjunga Middle Peak	India/Nepal	8,475	27,805	1973	Polish (W Wróż)
Lhotse Shar	China/Nepal	8,383	27,503	1970	Austrian (S Mayerl)
Dhaulagiri	Nepal	8,172	26,811	1960	Swiss/Austrian (K Diemberger)
Manaslu	Nepal	8,156	26,759	1956	Japanese (T Imanishi)
Cho Oyu	China/Nepal	8,153	26,748	1954	Austrian (H Tichy)
Nanga Parbat	Kashmir/Jammu	8,126	26,660	1953	German (K M Herrligkoffer)
Annapurna I	Nepal	8,078	26,502	1950	French (M Herzog)
Gasherbrum I	Kashmir/Jammu	8,068	26,469	1958	US (P K Schoening; by the southwest ridge)
Broad Peak	Kashmir/Jammu	8,047	26,401	1957	Austrian (M Schmuck)
Gasherbrum II	Kashmir/Jammu	8,034	26,358	1956	Austrian (S Larch; by the southwest spur)
Gosainthan	China	8,012	26,286	1964	Chinese (195-strong team; accounts are inconclusive)
Broad Peak (Middle)	Kashmir/Jammu	8,000	26,246	1975	Polish (K Głazek)
Gasherbrum III	Kashmir/Jammu	7,952	26,089	1975	Polish (J Onyszkiewicz)
Annapurna II	Nepal	7,937	26,040	1960	British (C Bonington)
Gasherbrum IV	Kashmir/Jammu	7,923	25,994	1958	Italian (W Bonatti, C Mouri)
Gyachung Kang	Nepal	7,921	25,987	1964	Japanese (Y Kato, K Sakaizqwa)
Disteghil Shar	Kashmir	7,884	25,866	1960	Austrian (G Stärker, D Marchart)
Himalchuli	Nepal	7,864	25,800	1960	Japanese (M Harada, H Tanabe)
Nuptse	Nepal	7,841	25,725	1961	British (D Davis, C Bonington, L Brown)
Manaslu II	Nepal	7,835	25,705	1970	Japanese (H Watanabe, Lhakpa Tsering)
Masherbrum East	Kashmir	7,821	25,659	1960	Pakistani/US (G Bell, W Unsoeld)
Nanda Devi	India	7,817	25,646	1936	British (H W Tilman)
Chomo Lonzo	Nepal	7,815	25,639	1954	French (J Couzy, L Terry)

Major Oceans and Seas in the World

Ocean/sea	Area[1] sq km	Area[1] sq mi	Average depth m	Average depth ft
Pacific Ocean	166,242,000	64,186,000	3,939	12,925
Atlantic Ocean	86,557,000	33,420,000	3,575	11,730
Indian Ocean	73,429,000	28,351,000	3,840	12,598
Arctic Ocean	13,224,000	5,106,000	1,038	3,407
South China Sea	2,975,000	1,149,000	1,464	4,802
Caribbean Sea	2,754,000	1,063,000	2,575	8,448
Mediterranean Sea	2,510,000	969,000	1,501	4,926
Bering Sea	2,261,000	873,000	1,491	4,893
Sea of Okhotsk	1,580,000	610,000	973	3,192
Gulf of Mexico	1,544,000	596,000	1,614	5,297
Sea of Japan	1,013,000	391,000	1,667	5,468
Hudson Bay	730,000	282,000	93	305
East China Sea	665,000	257,000	189	620
Andaman Sea	565,000	218,000	1,118	3,667
Black Sea	461,000	178,000	1,190	3,906
Red Sea	453,000	175,000	538	1,764
North Sea	427,000	165,000	94	308
Baltic Sea	422,000	163,000	55	180
Yellow Sea	294,000	114,000	37	121
Persian Gulf	230,000	89,000	100	328
Gulf of California	153,000	59,000	724	2,375
English Channel	90,000	35,000	54	177
Irish Sea	89,000	34,000	60	197

[1] All figures are approximate, as boundaries of oceans and seas cannot be exactly determined.

Highest Waterfalls in the World

Waterfall	Location	Total drop m	Total drop ft
Angel Falls	Venezuela	979	3,212
Yosemite Falls	USA	739	2,425
Mardalsfossen–South	Norway	655	2,149
Tugela Falls	South Africa	614	2,014
Cuquenan	Venezuela	610	2,000
Sutherland	New Zealand	580	1,903
Ribbon Fall, Yosemite	USA	491	1,612
Great Karamang River Falls	Guyana	488	1,600
Mardalsfossen–North	Norway	468	1,535
Della Falls	Canada	440	1,443
Gavarnie Falls	France	422	1,385
Skjeggedal	Norway	420	1,378
Glass Falls	Brazil	404	1,325
Krimml	Austria	400	1,312
Trummelbach Falls	Switzerland	400	1,312
Takkakaw Falls	Canada	366	1,200
Silver Strand Falls, Yosemite	USA	357	1,170
Wallaman Falls	Australia	346	1,137
Wollomombi	Australia	335	1,100
Cusiana River Falls	Colombia	300	984
Giessbach	Switzerland	300	984
Skykkjedalsfossen	Norway	300	984
Staubbach	Switzerland	300	984

Longest Rivers in the World

River	Location	Approximate length km	Approximate length mi	River	Location	Approximate length km	Approximate length mi
Nile	Africa	6,695	4,160	Yukon	USA/Canada	3,185	1,979
Amazon	South America	6,570	4,083	Rio Grande	USA/Mexico	3,058	1,900
Chang Jiang (Yangtze)	China	6,300	3,915	Indus	Tibet/Pakistan	2,897	1,800
Mississippi–Missouri–Red Rock	USA	6,020	3,741	Danube	central and eastern Europe	2,858	1,776
				Japura	Brazil	2,816	1,750
Huang He (Yellow River)	China	5,464	3,395	Salween	Myanmar/China	2,800	1,740
Ob–Irtysh	China/Kazakhstan/Russia	5,410	3,362	Brahmaputra	Asia	2,736	1,700
Amur–Shilka	Asia	4,416	2,744	Euphrates	Iraq	2,736	1,700
Lena	Russia	4,400	2,734	Tocantins	Brazil	2,699	1,677
Congo–Zaire	Africa	4,374	2,718	Zambezi	Africa	2,650	1,647
Mackenzie–Peace–Finlay	Canada	4,241	2,635	Orinoco	Venezuela	2,559	1,590
Mekong	Asia	4,180	2,597	Paraguay	Paraguay	2,549	1,584
Niger	Africa	4,100	2,548	Amu Darya	Tajikistan/Turkmenistan/Uzbekistan	2,540	1,578
Yenisei	Russia	4,100	2,548	Ural	Russia/Kazakhstan	2,535	1,575
Paraná	Brazil	3,943	2,450	Kolyma	Russia	2,513	1,562
Mississippi	USA	3,779	2,348	Ganges	India/Bangladesh	2,510	1,560
Murray–Darling	Australia	3,751	2,331	Arkansas	USA	2,344	1,459
Missouri	USA	3,726	2,315	Colorado	USA	2,333	1,450
Volga	Russia	3,685	2,290	Dnieper	Russia/Belarus/Ukraine	2,285	1,420
Madeira	Brazil	3,241	2,014	Syr Darya	Asia	2,205	1,370
Purus	Brazil	3,211	1,995	Irrawaddy	Myanmar	2,152	1,337
São Francisco	Brazil	3,199	1,988	Orange	South Africa	2,092	1,300

Major Volcanoes Active in the 20th Century by Region

Volcano	Height m	Height ft	Location	Date of last eruption or activity	Volcano	Height m	Height ft	Location	Date of last eruption or activity
Africa					**Asia (continued)**				
Cameroon	4,096	13,353	isolated mountain, Cameroon	1986	Azuma	2,042	6,700	Honshu, Japan	1977
Nyiragongo	3,470	11,385	Virungu, Democratic Republic of Congo	1994	Sangeang Api	1,935	6,351	Lesser Sunda Island, Indonesia	1988
					Pinatubo	1,759	5,770	Luzon, Philippines	1995
Nyamuragira	3,056	10,028	Democratic Republic of Congo	1994	Kelut	1,730	5,679	Java, Indonesia	1990
					Unzen	1,360	4,462	Japan	1996
Ol Doinyo Lengai	2,886	9,469	Tanzania	1993	Krakatoa	818	2,685	Sumatra, Indonesia	1996
Lake Nyos	918	3,011	Cameroon	1986	Taal	300	984	Philippines	1977
Erta-Ale	503	1,650	Ethiopia	1995					
					Atlantic Ocean				
Antarctica					Pico de Teide	3,716	12,192	Tenerife, Canary Islands, Spain	1909
Erebus	4,023	13,200	Ross Island, McMurdo Sound	1995	Fogo	2,835	9,300	Cape Verde Islands	1995
Deception Island	576	1,890	South Shetland Island	1970	Beerenberg	2,277	7,470	Jan Mayen Island, Norway	1985
					Hekla	1,491	4,920	Iceland	1991
Asia					Krafla	654	2,145	Iceland	1984
Kerinci	3,800	12,467	Sumatra, Indonesia	1987	Helgafell	215	706	Iceland	1973
Rindjani	3,726	12,224	Lombok, Indonesia	1966	Surtsey	174	570	Iceland	1967
Semeru	3,676	12,060	Java, Indonesia	1995					
Slamet	3,428	11,247	Java, Indonesia	1989	**Caribbean**				
Raung	3,322	10,932	Java, Indonesia	1993	La Grande Soufrière	1,467	4,813	Basse-Terre, Guadeloupe	1977
Agung	3,142	10,308	Bali, Indonesia	1964					
On-Taka	3,063	10,049	Honshu, Japan	1991	Pelée	1,397	4,584	Martinique	1932
Merapi	2,911	9,551	Java, Indonesia	1998	La Soufrière St Vincent	1,234	4,048	St Vincent and the Grenadines	1979
Marapi	2,891	9,485	Sumatra, Indonesia	1993					
Asama	2,530	8,300	Honshu, Japan	1990	Soufriere Hills/Chances Peak	968	3,176	Montserrat	1997
Nigata Yake-yama	2,475	8,111	Honshu, Japan	1989					
Mayon	2,462	8,084	Luzon, Philippines	1993	**Central America**				
Canlaon	2,459	8,070	Negros, Philippines	1993	Acatenango	3,960	12,992	Sierra Madre, Guatemala	1972
Chokai	2,225	7,300	Honshu, Japan	1974	Fuego	3,835	12,582	Sierra Madre, Guatemala	1991
Galunggung	2,168	7,113	Java, Indonesia	1984	Tacana	3,780	12,400	Sierra Madre, Guatemala	1988

Major Volcanoes Active in the 20th Century by Region (*continued*)

Volcano	Height m	ft	Location	Date of last eruption or activity	Volcano	Height m	ft	Location	Date of last eruption or activity
Central America (continued)					**North America (continued)**				
Santa Maria	3,768	12,362	Sierra Madre, Guatemala	1993	Shishaldin	2,861	9,387	Aleutian Islands (AK), USA	1997
Irazú	3,452	11,325	Cordillera Central, Costa Rica	1992	St Helens	2,549	8,364	Washington, USA	1995
Turrialba	3,246	10,650	Cordillera Central, Costa Rica	1992	Pavlof	2,517	8,261	Alaska Range (AK), USA	1997
Póas	2,721	8,930	Cordillera Central, Costa Rica	1994	Veniaminof	2,507	8,225	Alaska Range (AK), USA	1995
Pacaya	2,543	8,346	Sierra Madre, Guatemala	1996	Novarupta (Katmai)	2,298	7,540	Alaska Range (AK), USA	1931
San Miguel	2,131	6,994	El Salvador	1986	El Chichon	2,225	7,300	Altiplano de México, Mexico	1982
Arenal	1,552	5,092	Costa Rica	1996	Makushin	2,036	6,680	Aleutian Islands (AK), USA	1987
Europe					**Oceania**				
Kliuchevskoi	4,750	15,584	Kamchatka Peninsula, Russia	1997	Ruapehu	2,796	9,175	New Zealand	1997
Koryakskaya	3,456	11,339	Kamchatka Peninsula, Russia	1957	Ulawun	2,296	7,532	Papua New Guinea	1993
Sheveluch	3,283	10,771	Kamchatka Peninsula, Russia	1997	Ngauruhoe	2,290	7,515	New Zealand	1977
Etna	3,236	10,625	Sicily, Italy	1998	Bagana	1,998	6,558	Papua New Guinea	1993
Bezymianny	2,882	9,455	Kamchatka Peninsula, Russia	1997	Manam	1,829	6,000	Papua New Guinea	1997
Alaid	2,335	7,662	Kurile Islands, Russia	1986	Lamington	1,780	5,844	Papua New Guinea	1956
Tiatia	1,833	6,013	Kurile Islands, Russia	1981	Karkar	1,499	4,920	Papua New Guinea	1979
Sarychev Peak	1,512	4,960	Kurile Islands, Russia	1989	Lopevi	1,450	4,755	Vanuatu	1982
Vesuvius	1,289	4,203	Italy	1944	Ambrym	1,340	4,376	Vanuatu	1991
Stromboli	931	3,055	Lipari Islands, Italy	1996	Tarawera	1,149	3,770	New Zealand	1973
Santorini (Thera)	584	1,960	Cyclades, Greece	1950	Langila	1,093	3,586	Papua New Guinea	1996
					Rabaul	688	2,257	Papua New Guinea	1997
Indian Ocean					Pagan	570	1,870	Mariana Islands	1993
Karthala	2,440	8,000	Comoros	1991	White Island	328	1,075	New Zealand	1995
Piton de la Fournaise (Le Volcan)	1,823	5,981	Réunion Island, France	1998					
					South America				
Mid-Pacific					San Pedro	6,199	20,325	Andes, Chile	1960
					Guallatiri	6,060	19,882	Andes, Chile	1993
Mauna Loa	4,170	13,681	Hawaii, USA	1984	Lascar	5,990	19,652	Andes, Chile	1995
Kilauea	1,247	4,100	Hawaii, USA	1998	San José	5,919	19,405	Andes, Chile	1931
					Cotopaxi	5,897	19,347	Andes, Ecuador	1975
North America					Tutupaca	5,844	19,160	Andes, Ecuador	1902
Popocatépetl	5,452	17,887	Altiplano de México, Mexico	1997	Ubinas	5,710	18,720	Andes, Peru	1969
Colima	4,268	14,003	Altiplano de México, Mexico	1994	Tupungatito	5,640	18,504	Andes, Chile	1986
Spurr	3,374	11,070	Alaska Range (AK), USA	1953	Islunga	5,566	18,250	Andes, Chile	1960
Lassen Peak	3,186	10,453	California, USA	1921	Nevado del Ruiz	5,435	17,820	Andes, Colombia	1992
Redoubt	3,108	10,197	Alaska Range (AK), USA	1991	Tolima	5,249	17,210	Andes, Colombia	1943
Iliamna	3,052	10,016	Alaska Range (AK), USA	1978	Sangay	5,230	17,179	Andes, Ecuador	1996

Latitude, Longitude, and Altitude of the World's Major Cities

City	Latitude °	'	Longitude °	'	Altitude m	ft
Adelaide, Australia	34	55 S	138	36 E	43	140
Algiers, Algeria	36	50 N	03	00 E	59	194
Almaty, Kazakhstan	43	16 N	76	53 E	775	2,543
Amsterdam, Netherlands	52	22 N	04	53 E	3	10
Ankara, Turkey	39	55 N	32	55 E	862	2,825
Asunción, Paraguay	25	15 S	57	40 W	139	456
Athens, Greece	37	58 N	23	43 E	92	300
Bangkok, Thailand	13	45 N	100	31 E	0	0
Barcelona, Spain	41	23 N	02	09 E	93	305
Beijing, China	39	56 N	116	24 E	183	600
Belfast, Northern Ireland	54	37 N	05	56 W	67	217
Belgrade, Yugoslavia	44	52 N	20	32 E	132	433
Berlin, Germany	52	31 N	13	25 E	34	110
Bogotá, Colombia	04	32 N	74	05 W	2,640	8,660
Bombay, India	18	58 N	72	50 E	8	27
Brussels, Belgium	50	52 N	04	22 E	100	328
Bucharest, Romania	44	25 N	26	07 E	92	302
Budapest, Hungary	47	30 N	19	05 E	139	456
Buenos Aires, Argentina	34	36 S	58	28 W	0	0
Cairo, Egypt	30	03 N	31	15 E	116	381
Cape Town, South Africa	33	55 S	18	22 E	17	56
Caracas, Venezuela	10	28 N	67	02 W	1,042	3,418
Copenhagen, Denmark	55	40 N	12	34 E	9	33
Dakar, Senegal	14	40 N	17	28 W	40	131
Delhi, India	28	35 N	77	12 E	218	714
Detroit (MI), USA	42	19 N	83	02 W	178	585
Djibouti, Djibouti	11	30 N	43	03 E	7	23
Dublin, Republic of Ireland	53	20 N	06	15 W	47	154
Edinburgh, Scotland	55	55 N	03	10 W	134	440
Frankfurt, Germany	50	07 N	08	41 E	103	338
Guatemala City, Guatemala	14	37 N	90	31 W	1,480	4,855
Havana, Cuba	23	08 N	82	23 W	24	80
Helsinki, Finland	60	10 N	25	00 E	46	151
Hong Kong, China	22	18 N	114	10 E	33	109
Istanbul, Turkey	41	06 N	29	03 E	114	374
Jakarta, Indonesia	06	10 S	106	48 E	8	26
Jerusalem, Israel	31	46 N	35	14 E	762	2,500
Johannesburg, South Africa	26	12 S	28	05 E	1,750	5,740
Kabul, Afghanistan	34	30 N	69	13 E	1,827	5,955
Karachi, Pakistan	24	48 N	66	59 E	4	13
Katmandu, Nepal	27	43 S	85	19 E	1,372	4,500
Kiev, Ukraine	50	26 N	30	31 E	179	587
Kinshasa, Democratic Republic of Congo	04	18 S	15	17 E	322	1066
Lagos, Nigeria	06	27 N	03	24 E	3	10
La Paz, Bolivia	16	27 S	68	22 W	3,658	12,001
Lhasa, Tibet	29	40 N	91	07 E	3,685	12,090
Lima, Peru	12	00 S	77	02 W	120	394
Lisbon, Portugal	38	44 N	09	09 W	77	253
London, UK	51	32 N	00	05 W	75	245
Los Angeles (CA), USA	34	03 N	118	14 W	104	340
Madrid, Spain	40	26 N	03	42 W	660	2,165
Manila, Philippines	14	35 N	120	57 E	14	47
Mecca, Saudi Arabia	21	27 S	39	49 E	2,000	6,562
Melbourne, Australia	37	47 N	144	58 E	35	115
Mexico City, Mexico	19	24 N	99	09 W	2,239	7,347
Milan, Italy	45	27 S	09	10 E	121	397
Montevideo, Uruguay	34	53 N	56	10 W	22	72
Moscow, Russia	55	45 N	37	35 E	120	394
Nagasaki, Japan	32	48 S	129	57 E	133	436
Nairobi, Kenya	01	25 N	36	55 E	1,820	5,971
New Delhi, India	28	36 N	77	12 E	235	770
New York (NY), USA	40	45 N	73	59 W	17	55
Oslo, Norway	59	57 N	10	42 E	94	308
Ottawa, Canada	45	26 N	75	41 W	56	185
Panama City, Panama	08	58 N	79	32 W	0	0
Paris, France	48	52 N	02	20 E	92	300
Prague, Czech Republic	50	05 N	14	26 E	262	860
Quito, Ecuador	0	13 S	78	30 W	2,811	9,222
Reykjavik, Iceland	64	04 N	21	58 W	18	59
Rio de Janeiro, Brazil	22	43 S	43	13 W	9	30
Rome, Italy	41	53 N	12	30 E	29	95
St Petersburg, Russia	59	56 N	30	18 E	4	13
Santiago, Chile	33	27 S	70	40 W	1,500	4,921
Seoul, South Korea	37	34 N	127	00 E	10	34
Shanghai, China	31	10 N	121	28 E	7	23
Singapore	01	14 N	103	55 E	10	33
Sofia, Bulgaria	42	40 N	23	20 E	550	1,805
Stockholm, Sweden	59	17 N	18	03 E	44	144
Sydney, Australia	33	53 S	151	12 E	8	25
Tehran, Iran	35	40 N	51	26 E	1,110	3,937
Tokyo, Japan	35	42 N	139	46 E	9	30
Toronto, Canada	43	39 N	79	23 W	91	300
Tripoli, Libya	32	54 N	13	11 E	0	0
Vancouver, Canada	49	18 N	123	04 W	43	141
Vienna, Austria	48	14 N	16	20 E	203	666
Warsaw, Poland	52	15 N	21	00 E	110	360
Washington, DC, USA	38	53 N	77	00 W	8	25
Wellington, New Zealand	41	18 S	174	47 E	0	0
Zurich, Switzerland	47	21 N	08	31 E	493	1,618

Major Disasters

Major 20th-Century Earthquakes

(N/A = not available.)

Date	Location	Magnitude (Richter scale)	Estimated number of deaths
18–19 April 1906	San Francisco (CA), USA	7.7-7.9	503
16 August 1906	Valparaiso, Chile	8.6	20,000
28 December 1908	Messina, Italy	7.5	83,000
13 January 1915	Avezzano, Italy	7.5	29,980
16 December 1920	Gansu Province, China	8.6	200,000
1 September 1923	Yokohama, Japan	8.3	143,000
22 May 1927	Nan-Shan, China	8.3	200,000
26 December 1932	Gansu, China	7.6	70,000
31 May 1935	Quetta, India	7.5	60,000
24 January 1939	Chillan, Chile	7.8	30,000
26 December 1939	Erzincan, Turkey	7.9	23,000
21 December 1946	Honshu, Japan	8.4	2,000
28 June 1948	Fukui, Japan	7.3	5,130
6 October 1948	Iran/USSR	7.3	100,000
5 August 1949	Pelileo, Ecuador	6.8	6,000
15 August 1950	Assam, India	8.7	1,530
18 March 1953	northwestern Turkey	7.2	1,200
10–17 June 1956	northern Afghanistan	7.7	2,000
2 July 1957	northern Iran	7.4	2,500
13 December 1957	western Iran	7.1	2,000
29 February 1960	Agadir, Morocco	5.7	12,000
1 September 1962	northwestern Iran	7.1	12,000
26 July 1963	Skopje, Yugoslavia	6.0	1,100
27 March 1964	Anchorage (AL), USA	9.2	131
19 August 1966	eastern Turkey	6.9	2,520
31 August 1968	northeastern Iran	7.4	11,600
5 January 1970	Yunan Province, China	7.7	10,000
31 May 1970	Chimbote, Peru	7.8	67,000
10 April 1972	southern Iran	7.1	5,000
23 December 1972	Managua, Nicaragua	6.2	5,000
28 December 1974	Kashmir, Pakistan	6.3	5,200
4 February 1976	Guatemala City, Guatemala	7.5	22,778
6 May 1976	Friuli, Italy	6.5	939
28 July 1976	Tangshan, China	8.0	255,000[1]
4 March 1977	Romania	7.5	1,541
16 September 1978	northeastern Iran	7.7	25,000
12 December 1979	Colombia/Ecuador	7.9	800
10 October 1980	northern Algeria	7.7	3,000
23 November 1980	southern Italy	7.2	4,800
13 December 1982	northern Yemen	6.0	1,600
30 October 1983	eastern Turkey	6.9	1,300
19, 21 September 1985	Mexico City, Mexico	8.1	5,000[2]
20 August 1988	Nepal/India	6.9	1,000
6 November 1988	southwestern China	7.6	1,000
7 December 1988	Armenia, USSR	6.8	25,000
17 October 1989	San Francisco (CA), USA	7.1	62
20–21 June 1990	northwestern Iran	7.7	37,000
16 July 1990	Luzon, Philippines	7.7	1,660
1 February 1991	Afghanistan/Pakistan	6.8	1,000
April 1991	northern Georgia	7.2	>100
20 October 1991	Uttar Pradesh, India	6.1	1,500
13, 15 March 1992	Erzincan, Turkey	6.7	2,000
12 December 1992	Flores Island, Indonesia	7.5	2,500
12 July 1993	western coast of Hokkaido, Japan	7.8	200
29 September 1993	Maharashtra, India	6.3	9,800
13–16 October 1993	Papua New Guinea	6.8	>60
6 June 1994	Cauca, Colombia	6.8	1,000
19 August 1994	northern Algeria	5.6	200
16 January 1995	Kobe, Japan	7.2	5,500
14 June 1995	Sakhalin Island, Russia	7.6	2,000
2 October 1995	southwestern Turkey	6.0	84
7 October 1995	Sumatra, Indonesia	7.0	>70
9 October 1995	Mexico	7.6	>66
3 February 1996	Yunnan Province, China	7.0	>250
17 February 1996	Irian Jaya, Indonesia	7.5	108
28 March 1996	Ecuador	5.7	21
4, 28 February 1997	Ardabil, Iran	N/A	>1,000
28 February 1997	Baluchistan Province, Pakistan	7.3	>100
10 May 1997	northeastern Iran (Khorasah Province)	7.1	>1,600
22 May 1997	India	6.0	>40
26 September 1997	central Italy	5.8	>11
28 September 1997	Sulawesi, Indonesia	6.0	>20
14 October 1997	north of Santiago, Chile	6.8	>10
21 November 1997	Chittagong, Bangladesh	6.0	17
11 January 1998	northeastern China	6.2	>47
4 February 1998	Takhar province, Afghanistan	6.1	>3,800
30 May 1998	north-east Afghanistan	7.1	>3,000

[1] Early estimates put the death toll as high as 750,000; the figure shown is the official one.
[2] Some estimates put the death toll as high as 20,000.

Most Destructive Earthquakes in the World

(N/A = not available.)

Date	Location	Estimated number of deaths	Magnitude (Richter scale)	Date	Location	Estimated number of deaths	Magnitude (Richter scale)
23 January 1556	Shaanxi, China	830,000	N/A	November 1667	Caucasia, Russia	80,000	N/A
11 October 1737	Calcutta, India	300,000	N/A	18 November 1727	Tabriz, Iran	77,000	N/A
27 July 1976	Tangshan, China[1]	255,000	8.0	28 December 1908	Messina, Italy	70,000–100,000	7.5
9 August 1138	Aleppo, Syria	230,000	N/A	1 November 1755	Lisbon, Portugal	70,000	8.7
22 May 1927	near Xining, China	200,000	8.3	25 December 1932	Gansu, China	70,000	7.6
22 December 856	Damghan, Iran	200,000	N/A	31 May 1970	northern Peru	66,000	7.8
16 December 1920	Gansu, China	200,000	8.6	1268	Cilicia, Asia Minor	60,000	N/A
23 March 893	Ardabil, Iran	150,000	N/A	11 January 1693	Sicily, Italy	60,000	N/A
1 September 1923	Kwanto, Japan	143,000	8.3	4 February 1783	Calabria, Italy	50,000	N/A
30 December 1730	Hokkaido, Japan	137,000	N/A	20 June 1990	Iran	50,000	7.7
September 1290	Chihli, China	100,000	N/A	30 May 1935	Quetta, India	30,000–60,000	7.5

[1] This is the official casualty figure; the estimated death toll is as high as 750,000.

Source: US Geological Survey National Earthquake Information Center

Major Pre-20th Century Volcanic Eruptions

Volcano	Location	Year	Estimated number of deaths
Santorini (Thera)	Greece	c. 1470 BC[1]	
Vesuvius	Italy	AD 79	16,000[2]
Kelut	Java, Indonesia	1586	10,000
Etna	Sicily, Italy	1669	20,000
Vesuvius	Italy	1631	4,000
Papandayan	Java, Indonesia	1772	3,000
Laki	Iceland	1783	9,350
Unzen	Japan	1792	14,500
Tambora	Sumbawa, Indonesia	1815	10,000[3]
Krakatoa	Indonesia	1883	36,000

[1] Number of deaths unknown; the explosion was four times more powerful than Krakatoa.
[2] Estimates vary greatly, from 2,000 (lowest) to 20,000 (highest).
[3] A further 82,000 deaths were caused by starvation and disease brought on by the eruption.

Major Volcanic Eruptions in the 20th Century

Volcano	Location	Year	Estimated number of deaths
Santa María	Guatemala	1902	1,000
Pelée	Martinique	1902	28,000
Taal	Philippines	1911	1,400
Kelut	Java, Indonesia	1919	5,500
Vulcan	Papua New Guinea	1937	500
Lamington	Papua New Guinea	1951	3,000
St Helens	USA	1980	57
El Chichon	Mexico	1982	1,880
Nevado del Ruiz	Colombia	1985	23,000
Lake Nyos	Cameroon	1986	1,700
Pinatubo	Luzon, Philippines	1991	639
Unzen	Japan	1991	39
Mayon	Philippines	1993	70
Loki[1]	Iceland	1996	0
Soufriere	Montserrat	1997	23
Merapi	Java, Indonesia	1998	38

[1] The eruption caused severe flooding, and melted enough ice to create a huge sub-glacial lake.

Major Explosions of the 20th Century

Date	Location	Number of deaths	Date	Location	Number of deaths
10 April 1917	munitions plant, Eddystone (PA), USA	133	11 July 1978	tanker loaded with liquid gas, near Tortosa, Spain	150
6 December 1917	ship collision, Halifax Harbor, Canada	1,654	2 November 1982	Salang Tunnel, Afghanistan	>1,000
18 May 1918	chemical plant, Oakdale (PA), USA	193	25 February 1984	oil pipeline, Cubatao, Brazil	508
11 September 1921	chemicals storage facility, Oppau, Germany	561	19 November 1984	gas storage area, Mexico City, Mexico	334
18 March 1937	schoolhouse, New London (TX), USA	413	3 December 1984	chemical plant, Bhopal, India	3,849
14 April 1944	harbour, Bombay, India	700	6 July 1988	Piper Alpha oil rig, North Sea between UK and Norway	173
6 July 1944	ammunition ships, Port Chicago (CA), USA	322	3 June 1989	petroleum gas pipeline leak, near Ufa, Ural Mountains, Russia	>500
20 October 1944	liquid-gas tanks, Cleveland (OH), USA	130	6 August 1991	oil tanker in harbour, Livorno, Italy	140
16 April 1947	freighter loaded with chemicals, Texas City pier (TX), USA	576	22 April 1992	gas leak in city sewer, Guadalajara, Mexico	210
3 December 1948	ship carrying refugees struck old mine, off Shanghai, China	>3,000	2 February 1995	illegal cache of dynamite, Shaoyang, Hunan Province, China	120
26 May 1954	aircraft carrier, off Quonset Point (RI), USA	103	28 April 1995	gas-main leak at construction site, Taegu, South Korea	>100
7 August 1956	ammunition trucks, Cali, Colombia	1,100	15 February 1996	ammunitions dump, Kabul, Afghanistan	>110
23 July 1964	harbour munitions, Bone, Algeria	100	14 September 1997	oil refinery, Vishakhapatnam, India	>18
14 January 1969	nuclear aircraft carrier, Pearl Harbor (HI), USA	27			

Major Floods and Tsunamis of the 20th Century

A tsunami is an ocean wave generated by vertical movements of the sea floor resulting from earthquakes or volcanic activity.

Year	Event	Location	Number of deaths	Year	Event	Location	Number of deaths
1911	floods	Chang Jiang River, China	100,000		floods	Tanzania	283
1913	floods	Ohio/Indiana, USA	732	1991	floods	Afghanistan	1,367
1915	floods	Galveston (TX), USA	275		floods	Bangladesh	150,450
1918	tsunami	Kuril Islands/Russia/Japan/Hawaii	23		floods	Benin	30
1923	tsunami	Kamchatka/Hawaii	3		floods	Chad	39
1931	floods	Huang He River, China	3,700,000		floods/storm	Chile	199
1939	floods	northern China	200,000		floods	China	6,728
1944	tsunami	Japan	998		floods	India	2,024
1946	tsunami	Japan	1,997		floods	Malawi	1,172
	tsunami	Aleutian Islands/Hawaii/California	159		floods	Peru	40
1949	floods	China	57,000		floods/typhoon	Philippines	8,890
1952	tsunami	Kamchatka/Kuril Islands/Hawaii	many		floods	Romania	138
1953	floods	northwestern Europe	1,794		floods	South Korea	54
1954	floods	China	40,000		floods	Sudan	2,000
	floods	Farhzad, Iran	2,000		floods	Turkey	30
1955	floods	India/Pakistan	1,700		floods	Texas, USA	33
1959	floods	western Mexico	2,000		floods	Vietnam	136
	floods	Fréjus, France	412	1992	floods	Afghanistan	450
1960	tsunami	Chile/Hawaii/Japan	5,000		floods	Argentina	104
	floods	Bangladesh	10,000		floods	Chile	41
1962	floods	North Sea coast, Germany	343		floods	China	197
	floods	Barcelona, Spain	445		floods	India	551
1964	tsunami	Alaska/Aleutian Islands/California	122		floods	Pakistan	1,446
1966	floods	Brazil	200		floods	Vietnam	55
	floods	Florence, Italy	113	1993	floods	Indonesia	18
1967	floods	Brazil	>300		floods	midwestern USA	48
1969	floods	southern California, USA	100	1994	floods	Moldova	47
	floods	South Korea	250		floods	southern China	1,400
	floods	Tunisia	500		floods	India	>600
1970	floods	Romania	160		floods	Vietnam	>175
	floods	Himalayas, India	500		floods	northern Italy	>60
1971	floods	Rio de Janeiro, Brazil	130	1995	floods	Benin	10
1972	floods	West Virginia, USA	118		floods	Bangladesh	>200
	floods	South Dakota, USA	237		floods	Somalia	20
1974	floods	Tubaro, Brazil	1,000		floods	northwestern Europe	40
	floods	Bangladesh	2,500		floods	Hunan Province, China	1,200
1976	tsunami	Philippines	5,000		floods	southwestern Morocco	136
	floods	Colorado, USA	139		floods	Pakistan	>120
1978	floods	northern India	1,200		floods	South Africa	147
1979	tsunami	Indonesia	539		floods	Vietnam	85
	floods	Morvi, India	15,000	1996	floods	southern and western India	>300
1981	floods	northern China	550		floods	Tuscany, Italy	30
1982	floods	Peru	600		floods	North and South Korea	86
	floods	Guangdong, China	430		floods	Pyrenees, France/Spain	84
	floods	El Salvador/Guatemala	>1,300		floods	Yemen	324
1983	tsunami	Japan/South Korea	107		floods	central and southern China	2,300
1984	floods	South Korea	>200	1997	floods	west coast, USA	36
1987	floods	northern Bangladesh	>1,000		floods	Sikkim, India	>50
1988	floods	Brazil	289		floods	Germany/Poland/Czech Republic	>100
	floods	Bangladesh	>1,300		floods	Somalia	>1,700
1990	tsunami	Bangladesh	370		floods	eastern Uganda	>30
	floods	Mexico	85		floods	Spain and Portugal	70
				1998	tsunami	Papua New Guinea	>1,700

Major International Mining Disasters

Date	Location	Cause	Number of deaths	Date	Location	Cause	Number of deaths
12–18 December 1866	The Oaks, Barnsley, Yorkshire, UK	series of underground explosions	361	27 December 1975	Dhanbad, India	explosion and flooding	372
22 October 1877	Blantyre, Scotland, UK	explosion, fire, and firedamp	235	19 December 1984	Huntington (UT), USA	explosion	27
1 May 1900	Scofield (UT), USA	explosion	200	12 December 1990	Tuzla, Yugoslavia	explosion	150
10 March 1906	Courrières, France	explosion	1,060	9 February 1991	Shaanxi Province, China	explosion	147
6 December 1907	Monongah (WV), USA	explosion	361	4 March 1992	near Zonguldak, Turkey	explosion	388
19 December 1907	Jacobs Creek (PA), USA	explosion	239	18 May 1993	Seconda, South Africa	explosion	57
13 November 1909	Cherry (IL), USA	explosion	259	24 January 1994	Nuskenda, near Calcutta, India	fire	>55
14 October 1913	Senghenydd, Wales, UK	fire	440	3 August 1994	Guangxi Province, China	explosion	70
22 October 1923	Dawson (NM), USA	explosion	120	4 September 1994	Slavyavo-Serbskaya, near Lugansk, Ukraine	explosion	39
19 May 1928	Mather (PA), USA	explosion	195	11 May 1995	Vaal Reefs, near Johannesburg, South Africa; gold mine	underground accident	102
5 November 1930	Millfield (OH), USA	explosion	79	31 May, 3 June 1996	Yunan Province, China; gold mine	landslides	238
26 April 1942	Honkeiko, China	explosion	1,572	4 March 1997	Lushan, Henan Province, China	explosion	89
25 March 1947	Centralia (IL), USA	explosion	111	28 May 1997	Fushun, Liaoning Province, China	explosion	68
21 December 1951	West Frankfort (IL), USA	fire	119	2 September 1997	Bobov Dol, Bulgaria	explosion	10
8 August 1956	Marcinelle, Belgium	fire	262	16 November 1997	Huainan, Anhui Province, China	explosion	>87
21 January 1960	Coalbrook, South Africa	explosion	437	2 December 1997	southern Siberia, Russia	explosion	67
7 February 1962	Saarland, Germany	explosion	298	17 January 1998	central Siberia, Russia	explosion	29
9 November 1963	Omuta, Japan	explosion	447				
28 May 1965	Bihar State, India	fire	375				
1 June 1965	near Fukuoka, Japan	explosion	236				
2 May 1972	Kellogg (ID), USA; silver mine	fire	91				
6 June 1972	Wankie, Rhodesia	explosion	427				

Major 20th-Century Hurricanes, Typhoons, Cyclones, and other Storms

Date	Event/name	Location	Estimated number of deaths
27 August–15 September 1900	hurricane	Galveston (TX), USA	6,000
18 September 1906	typhoon	Hong Kong	10,000
19–24 September 1906	hurricane	Louisiana and Mississippi, USA	350
5–23 August 1915	hurricane	eastern Texas and Louisiana, USA	275
2–15 September 1919	hurricane	Louisiana, Florida, and Texas, USA	775
18 March 1925	tornadoes	midwestern USA	800
11–22 September 1926	hurricane	Florida and Alabama, USA	243
20 October 1926	hurricane	Cuba	600
6–20 September 1928	hurricane	southern Florida, USA	1,836
3 September 1930	hurricane	Dominican Republic	2,000
21 March 1932	tornadoes	southern USA	268
29 August–10 September 1935	hurricane	southern Florida, USA	408
5–6 April 1936	tornadoes	southern USA	498
10–22 September 1938	hurricane	east coast, USA	600
11–12 November 1940	blizzard	northeastern and midwestern USA	144
16 October 1942	cyclone	India	40,000
9–16 September 1944	hurricane	east coast, USA	390
4–21 September 1947	hurricane	Florida and mid-Gulf Coast, USA	51
26 December 1947	blizzard	New York and North Atlantic states, USA	55
21–22 March 1952	tornadoes	southern USA	343
22 October 1952	typhoon	Philippines	440
11 May 1953	tornado	Waco (TX), USA	114
8 June 1953	tornado	Flint (MI), USA	116
25–31 August 1954	hurricane, *Carol*	northeastern USA	68
5–18 October 1954	hurricane, *Hazel*	eastern USA/Haiti	347
7–12 August 1955	hurricane, *Diane*	eastern USA	400
12–13 August 1955	hurricane, *Connie*	Carolinas, Virginia, and Maryland, USA	43
19 September 1955	hurricane, *Hilda*	Mexico	200
22–28 September 1955	hurricane, *Janet*	Caribbean	500
1–29 February 1956	blizzard	Europe	1,000
25–30 June 1957	hurricane, *Audrey*	Texas to Alabama, USA	390
5–16 February 1958	blizzard	northeastern USA	171
17–19 September 1959	typhoon, *Sarah*	Japan/South Korea	2,000
26–27 September 1959	typhoon, *Vera*	Japan	4,466
4–12 September 1960	hurricane, *Donna*	Caribbean/eastern USA	148
10 October 1960	cyclone	eastern Pakistan	6,000

(continued)

Nuclear Accidents

Notable accidents since 1957 involving nuclear installations and facilities

29 September 1957 A serious accident occurred when a nuclear waste tank exploded in Kyshtym, USSR, releasing radiation over an area of 300 sq km/116 sq mi. No casualties were disclosed, but 1,150 people were evacuated and 30 small communities were deleted from maps produced in 1958.

7 October 1957 A fire destroyed the core of one of two plutonium-producing reactors at the Windscale (now Sellafield) nuclear power station, Cumbria, UK, releasing radiation and causing 39 deaths to 1977.

3 January 1961 An explosion of the Army Low-Power Reactor resulted in the death of three military personnel at the National Reactor Testing Station in Idaho Falls, Idaho, USA.

5 October 1966 A sodium-cooling system failed at the Enrico Fermi fast breeder reactor near Monroe, Michigan, USA, resulting in a partial core meltdown. Fission products were released from the core but were almost completely contained.

21 January 1969 A coolant malfunction from an experimental underground reactor at Lucens Vad, Switzerland, caused the release of radiation into a cavern, which was then sealed.

17 October 1969 A fuel-loading error sparked a partial meltdown at a gas-cooled power reactor in Saint-Laurent, France.

24 January 1978 A Soviet satellite, Cosmos 954, powered by a nuclear reactor, re-entered the atmosphere over Northwest Territory,

Major 20th-Century Hurricanes, Typhoons, Cyclones, and other Storms (*continued*)

Date	Event/name	Location	Estimated number of deaths
11–14 September 1961	hurricane, *Carla*	Texas, USA	46
31 October 1961	hurricane, *Hattie*	British Honduras	400
28–29 May 1963	cyclone	Bangladesh	22,000
4–8 October 1963	hurricane, *Flora*	Caribbean	6,000
30 June 1964	typhoon, *Winnie*	northern Philippines	107
5 September 1964	typhoon, *Ruby*	Hong Kong/China	735
11 April 1965	tornadoes	midwestern USA	256
11–12 May 1965	cyclone	Bangladesh	17,000
1–2 June 1965	cyclone	Bangladesh	30,000
15 December 1965	cyclone	Karachi, Pakistan	10,000
4–10 June 1966	hurricane, *Alma*	Honduras/eastern USA	51
24–30 September 1966	hurricane, *Inez*	Caribbean/Mexico/southeastern USA	293
9 July 1967	typhoon, *Billie*	southwestern Japan	347
5–23 September 1967	hurricane, *Beulah*	Caribbean/Mexico/Texas, USA	54
12–20 December 1967	blizzard	southwestern USA	51
18–20 November 1968	typhoon, *Nina*	Philippines	63
17–18 August 1969	hurricane, *Camille*	Louisiana and Mississippi, USA	256
30 July–5 August 1970	hurricane, *Celia*	Cuba/Florida and Texas, USA	31
20–21 August 1970	hurricane, *Dorothy*	Martinique	42
15 September 1970	typhoon, *Georgia*	Philippines	300
14 October 1970	typhoon, *Sening*	Philippines	583
15 October 1970	typhoon, *Titang*	Philippines	526
12–13 November 1970	cyclone	Bangladesh	>300,000
1 August 1971	typhoon, *Rose*	Hong Kong	130
29 September 1971	cyclone	Orissa State, India	10,000–25,000
19–29 June 1972	hurricane, *Agnes*	eastern USA	118
3 December 1972	typhoon, *Theresa*	Philippines	169
3–4 April 1974	tornadoes	eastern, southern, and midwestern USA	315
11 June 1974	storm, *Dinah*	Luzon, Philippines	71
11 July 1974	typhoon, *Gilda*	Japan/South Korea	108
19–20 September 1974	hurricane, *Fifi*	Honduras	2,000
25 December 1974	cyclone	Darwin, Australia	50
13–27 September 1975	hurricane, *Eloise*	Caribbean/northeastern USA	71
20 May 1976	typhoon, *Olga*	Philippines	215
25, 31 July 1977	typhoons, *Thelma, Vera*	Taiwan	39
19 November 1977	cyclone	Andhra Pradesh, India	20,000
27 October 1978	typhoon, *Rita*	Philippines	>400
30 August–7 September 1979	hurricane, *David*	Caribbean/eastern USA	1,100
4–11 August 1980	hurricane, *Allen*	Caribbean/Texas, USA	272
25 November 1981	typhoon, *Irma*	Luzon, Philippines	176
18 August 1983	hurricane, *Alicia*	southern Texas, USA	21
2 September 1984	typhoon, *Ike*	southern Philippines	1,363
25 May 1985	cyclone	Bangladesh	10,000
26 October–6 November 1985	hurricane, *Juan*	southeastern USA	63
25 November 1987	typhoon, *Nina*	Philippines	650
10–17 September 1988	hurricane, *Gilbert*	Gulf of Mexico/Caribbean	260
10–22 September 1989	hurricane, *Hugo*	Caribbean/USA	86
12–18 March 1990	storms	Bangladesh	242
6–11 May 1990	cyclone	India	514
June 1990	typhoons	Philippines	156
July–August 1990	typhoons	China	1,802
November 1990	typhoons/storm	Philippines	1,312
30 April 1991	cyclone	Bangladesh	138,866
12 May 1991	storm	Philippines	3,956
10 June 1991	cyclone	Bangladesh	125,720
15 February 1992	cyclone	Vietnam	251
23–26 August 1992	hurricane, *Andrew*	southern Florida and Louisiana, USA	>60
13–14 March 1993	blizzard	eastern USA	270
2 May 1994	cyclone	southeastern Bangladesh	165
22 August 1994	typhoon, *Fred*	Zhejiang Province, China	>710
31 October–3 November 1994	cyclone	India	260
8–18 November 1994	storm	Caribbean/Florida, USA	830
23 January 1995	snowstorms	Kashmir, India	>200
5–7 September 1995	hurricane, *Luis*	Caribbean	14
2–3 November 1995	typhoon, *Angela*	Philippines	722
13 May 1996	tornado	Bangladesh	>600
27–28 July 1996	hurricane, *Cèsar*	Panama/El Salvador/Costa Rica	50
31 July–1 August 1996	typhoon, *Herb*	Taiwan	400
5–6 September 1996	hurricane, *Fran*	North Carolina and Virginia, USA	36
4 November 1996	cyclone	Andhra Pradesh, India	>1,000
4–5 January 1997	storms	Brazil	68
19 May 1997	cyclone	Bangladesh	112
27 September 1997	cyclone	Bangladesh	>47
9 October 1997	hurricane, *Pauline*/floods	Pacific coast of Mexico	128
2–3 November 1997	typhoon, *Linda*	southern Vietnam/Thailand	>358
23 February 1998	tornadoes	central Florida, USA	38
8 April 1998	tornadoes	Alabama, Georgia, Mississippi, USA	>41

Canada, spreading radioactive debris over a 1,000 km/621 mi path. It is estimated that 75 percent of the radioactive isotopes released remained in the upper atmosphere.

28 March 1979 Nuclear-reactor accident at Three Mile Island, near Harrisburg, Pennsylvania, USA. A partial meltdown of one of the reactors caused radioactive gas to be leaked into the atmosphere. However, there was no significant exposure of the public as the containment structures functioned as designed.

11 February 1981 A large amount of radioactive coolant leaked into the containment building of the Tennessee Valley Authority's Sequoyah 1 plant in Tennessee, USA. Eight workers were contaminated.

25 April 1981 Approximately 45 workers were exposed to radioactivity during repairs to a nuclear plant in Tsuruga, Japan.

19 November 1983 Radioactive waste was accidentally discharged into the Irish Sea from the Sellafield nuclear plant in Cumbria, UK.

6 January 1986 One worker died and 100 were injured at a nuclear plant ar Gore, Oklahoma, USA, when a cylinder of nuclear material burst after being improperly treated.

26 April 1986 An explosive leak from a reactor at Chernobyl, Ukraine, resulted in clouds of radioactive material spreading as far as Sweden; 31 people were killed, some 115,000 people were evacuated from a 30 km/19 mi zone around the power plant, and thousands of square kilometers were contaminated. This is the worst nuclear accident on record.

10 February 1991 The Mihama plant near Fukui, Japan, was shut down after the rupture of a pipe in its cooling system. There were no casualties and, according to the Japanese authorities, there was only a slight release of radioactivity into the atmosphere.

8 December 1995 Japan's experimental Monju fast-breeder reactor was closed after an accident involving the leakage of 2–3 tonnes of non-radioactive liquid sodium from the primary cooling system. An emergency session of the Nuclear Safety Commission announced a full investigation into the accident.

4 July 1996 There was a dangerous leak of radioactive material from the Embalse nuclear plant in Argentina. Contamination was contained.

11 March 1997 An explosion occurred at the Tokaimura low-level nuclear reprocessing plant in Ibaraki prefecture, Japan. Nobody was injured in the explosion, but as many as 37 workers were exposed to low levels of radioactivity during a fire that had broken out at the plant earlier in the day.

28 January 1998 Thirteen workers were involved in a radiation scare as they dismantled equipment at the Sellafield plant in Cumbria, UK. The alarm was raised when a bag containing an old air filter from a plutonium finishing split, releasing dust and plutonium oxide into the air. Two of the workers were contaminated, but received very low doses of radiation.

Web Sites

Amnesty International Online

URL: "http://www.amnesty.org/"

Site of the world's foremost human rights organization. It is easy to access information on the structure of AI, its current campaigns, and how to assist them. There is a searchable library of documents, downloadable videos and useful links to other human rights organizations.

Care International

URL: "http://www.care.org/programs/care_international/index.html"

Home page of CARE International, a 'confederation of 10 agencies that delivers relief assistance to people in need and long-term solutions to global poverty'. There are links to all the Care members including those in the UK, and development news, access to related publications and articles, information on regional needs, and regional Care programmes, as well as world development statistics on hunger, poverty, AIDS, environment, children's malnutrition, and illiteracy.

EqIIS – Earthquake Image Information System

URL: "http://www.eerc.berkeley.edu/cgi-bin/eqiis_form?eq=4570 1"

Fully searchable library of almost 8,000 images from more than 80 earthquakes. It is possible to search by earthquake, structure, photographer, and keyword.

European Politics

URL: "http://www.agora.stm.it:80/politic/europe.htm"

As well as giving a country-by-country breakdown of the major political parties in Europe, this network of pages also gives very up-to-date information about election results and political candidates. There is also information on the differing styles of government and country-specific political news.

European Union

URL: "http://europa.eu.int/"

Official, multilingual site for the European Union. It contains information about all areas of the European Union, including policy, the various institutions, up-to-date news, and answers to the most common questions about the Union.

Poverty

URL: "http://www.undp.org/toppages/poverty/povframe.htm"

Analysis of poverty and what to do about it from the United Nations Development Programme. There is news of poverty-eradication programmes around the world. Informative case studies of people struggling to escape the grip of poverty make interesting reading.

Save the Children Fund

URL: "http://www.oneworld.org/scf/"

Well organized home page of Britain's leading children's charity. There is extensive information on the work of SCF in Britain and more than fifty other countries. Key topics in international development are presented in a lively manner.

6 Billion Human Beings

URL: "http://www.popexpo.net/home.htm"

From the 'Musée de l'Homme' in Paris, France, a bilingual site about population growth. It includes pages examining why the number of people has grown so rapidly over the last 250 years and whether the rapid growth rate will change. It also includes a page letting you see how many people were alive when you were born and a continually ticking counter of the current world population.

State of the World Indicators

URL: "http://www.igc.apc.org"

Regularly updated page containing statistics from around the world: from the current population of the globe to the rate at which ozone over the Antarctic is being depleted. There is also a lot of background information, including graphs and diagrams to support the figures.

Treaty on European Union

URL: "http://europa.eu.int/en/record/mt/top.html"

Full text of the treaty of Maastricht in 1992, which brought the European Union into existence in place of the European Community.

UNICEF United Nations Children's Fund

URL: "http://www.weu.int/eng/welcome.html"

UNICEF's well organized site. This is a comprehensive guide to the work of the agency and the tasks it has set itself. Statistical data and narrative information are of a high standard. UNICEF's much-respected annual State of the World's Children can be accessed.

United Nations Development Program

URL: "http://www.undp.org/"

Full account of the work of the UN agency to foster sustainable development in less-developed countries. This is a good source of information on global development issues.

United Nations Documents and Submissions on Fourth World Affairs

URL: "http://www.halcyon.com/FWDP/un.html"

Extensive database of digitized texts maintained by the Fourth World Documentation Project, testifying to the involvement of the United Nations in Fourth World affairs. It includes draft declarations, position papers, session documents, and other statements and submissions dealing with problems that indigenous people all over the world face within their states.

United Nations Educational Scientific and Cultural Organization

URL: "http://www.unesco.org/"

Well organized site detailing UNESCO's work in 186 countries. A fast search engine accesses reports from around the world. The structure of UNESCO and its history are explained. There are also links to UNESCO's 60 field offices and details of internships and employment with the agency.

United Nations High Commissioner for Refugees

URL: "http://www.unicc.org/unhcrcdr/"

Access to databases of the United Nations High Commissioner for Refugees, including an overview of UNHCR's activities and many images.

United Nations Home Page

URL: "http://www.un.org/"

Official site providing a general overview of the United Nations (UN) with news, photographs, key documents, and links to UN departments and information resources.

VolcanoWorld

URL: "http://volcano.und.edu"

Comprehensive, fully searchable site on volcanoes that includes details of the most recent eruptions, the volcanoes that are currently active, a glossary, images and video clips, and even a list of extraterrestrial volcanoes.

Welcome to Oxfam UK and Ireland

URL: "http://www.oxfam.org/"

Web site of Britain's foremost non-governmental development and relief agency. There are comprehensive details of Oxfam's work around the world and updated details of current campaigns for a fairer world.

EDUCATION

The Year in Review

23 July 1997 The British government announces a plan to start charging university students a tuition fee of £1,000 and to scrap grants in favour of student loans. Students and some lawmakers oppose the plan, viewing it as a violation of students' rights to attend university regardless of their ability to pay.

16 August 1997 The Turkish government passes a law that requires children to attend a secular school for at least eight years, three years longer than stipulated in the previous law, in an attempt to limit the influence of Muslim schools.

28 August 1997 A controversial anti-affirmative action measure goes into effect in the state of California. School admissions policies must not include race or gender biases.

5 September 1997 The National University of Samoa opens in Apia, the capital.

30 September 1997 In his keynote speech at the Labour Party conference, British Prime Minister Tony Blair says that Parliament will appropriate £2 billion for school equipment and repairs, £700 million more than was originally promised. He also announces a new initiative in which the government and private business would cooperate to provide all schools with computers and Internet access by 2002.

October 1997 The US Congress votes in favour of legislation requiring young foreign au pairs to be trained in childcare and child safety and to take a minimum number of educational courses during the year they spend in the USA. The vote is prompted by the case of the British au pair Louise Woodward, who was convicted of murdering a baby boy in her care.

10 November 1997 Schools in Ontario, Canada, reopen after unions representing half of Ontario's 126,000 striking teachers decided to end a 10-day walk-out, which kept 2.1 million elementary and high-school students out of class. The strike, the largest of its kind to date in North America, was in protest at major education reforms.

27 November 1997 Tens of thousands of students in Bonn, Germany, protest against declining standards, including overcrowding in classrooms and outdated textbooks, in Germany's university system.

4 December 1997 The British Labour government announces plans to limit the size of infant classes.

19 December 1997 In the first case of its kind in Australia, a primary school principal in Victoria is charged with failing to report a claim by a five-year-old boy that he was being sexually abused by his father.

8 January 1998 The UK charity Childline announces that more than 14,000 children telephoned reports of bullying in 1997, an increase of 40% on the 1996 figure.

9 January 1998 Grant-maintained status is given to two Muslim primary schools in the UK.

12 January 1998 A UK study, conducted on the Atlantic island of St Helena where television was introduced only in 1995, shows that TV violence has had little effect on children.

26 January 1998 The National Education Association and the American Federation of Teachers announce plans to merge, which will create the largest labour union in the USA to date.

January 1998 The British Department of Education publishes its annual league tables of tests in literacy and numeracy of 11-year-olds in state schools. The results show an overall improvement throughout England.

January 1998 The British Education and Employment secretary David Blunkett announces a relaxation of the National Curriculum in order to focus on mathematics and English. Primary schools will now be free to choose what to teach in history, geography, music, art, design and technology, and physical education.

24 February 1998 Scandanavian countries score the highest in an international study of achievement in mathematics and science by the US Department of Education.

25 March 1998 The British House of Commons approves, by a vote of 211–15, a ban on corporal punishment in privately funded schools. Corporal punishment was banned in state schools in 1986.

17 April 1998 A controversial report on Australia's higher education system recommends a more businesslike approach to running universities, whereby they would have to compete for federal funds using a student voucher system.

27 May 1998 Delegates at the National Association of Head Teachers conference in Eastbourne, support a motion to abolish a law requiring schools to hold religious assemblies.

10 June 1998 The British government announces the first national educational scheme using laptops, the Anytime Anywhere Learning pilot project, for introduction in September 1998 at 27 schools. The use of laptops is expected to spread to all schools in the next century.

16 June 1998 British Junior Education Minister Estelle Morris announces the launch of 10 pilot schemes for September 1998 in which gifted children will be offered extra-curricular 'master classes' in languages, maths, sport, and the arts.

23 June 1998 British Education and Employment Secretary David Blunkett announces plans for a joint business and government £75-million initiative for 25 education action zones, some of which are scheduled to begin operating in September 1998. The initiative will experiment with information technology and increased school hours. Each action zone will contain about 20 schools in areas of low educational performance.

World Education

Enrolment Ratios by Level of Education

The data in this table are for the latest year available. Only those countries for which data are available are listed. In some countries a relatively high number of pupils outside the official age range for the respective levels of education attends classes of these levels. Since the enrolment ratio given is for the total enrolment, regardless of age, divided by the population of the official age group, if a country has almost universal education among the school-age population at the first level, the enrolment ratio given will exceed 100. As the school year, in a number of countries, does not coincide with the academic year, the year shown in this table is the one in which the school or academic year starts.
(In percentages. N/A = not available.)

Country/territory	Year	1st level[1]	2nd level[2]	3rd level[3]	Country/territory	Year	1st level[1]	2nd level[2]	3rd level[3]
Afghanistan	1995	49	22	N/A	Georgia	1995	82	73	38.1
Albania	1995	101	35	9.6[4]	Germany	1994	102	103	42.7
Algeria	1995	107	62	10.9	Ghana	1991	76	37	1.4[10]
Angola	1991	88	14	0.7	Greece	1994	98[10]	95	38.1
Argentina	1996	113	77	36.2	Guatemala	1995	84	25	8.1
Armenia	1995	82	79	N/A	Guinea	1995	48	12	N/A
Australia	1995	108	147	71.7	Guinea-Bissau	1994	64	N/A	N/A
Austria	1994	101	104	44.8	Guyana	1994	94	76	8.6
Azerbaijan	1995	104	78	19.8[4]	Haiti	1990	56	22	N/A
Bahamas	1994	94	90	N/A	Honduras	1994	111	32[4]	10.0
Bahrain	1995	108	97	20.2[4]	Hong Kong	1995	96	75	21.9[4]
Bangladesh	1990	69	21	4.4	Hungary	1994	97	81	19.1
Barbados	1991	90	85[5]	28.5	Iceland	1994	97	103	35.2
Belarus	1995	97	94	41.8[4]	India	1995	100	49	6.4
Belgium	1993	103	144	49.1	Indonesia	1994	114	48	11.1
Belize	1994	121	49	N/A	Iran	1994	99	69	14.8
Benin	1995	72	16[6]	2.6	Iraq	1992	90	44	N/A
Bolivia	1990	95	37	22.2	Ireland, Republic of	1994	104	114	37.0
Botswana	1994	115	56	4.1	Israel	1995	99	89	41.1
Brazil	1994	112	45	11.3	Italy	1994	98	88	40.6
Brunei	1994	110	78	6.6[7]	Jamaica	1992	109	66	6.0[9]
Bulgaria	1995	97	78	39.4	Japan	1995	102	99[6]	40.3[6]
Burkina Faso	1994	38	6[4]	1.1	Jordan	1992	94	63[3]	24.5[5]
Burundi	1992	70	7	0.9	Kazakhstan	1995	96	83	32.7
Cambodia	1994	122	27	1.6	Kenya	1995	85	24	N/A
Cameroon	1994	88	27	N/A	Korea, South	1995	101[4]	101	52.0
Canada	1994	102	106	102.9[4]	Kuwait	1995	73	64	25.4
Cape Verde	1993	131	27	N/A	Kyrgyzstan	1995	107	81	12.2
Central African Republic	1991	58	10	1.4	Laos	1993	107	25	1.5
Chad	1994	55	9	0.8	Latvia	1995	89	85	25.7
Chile	1996	100	72	30.3	Lebanon	1995	109	81	27.0
China	1996	120	69	5.7	Lesotho	1994	99	28	2.4
Colombia	1995	114	67	17.2	Libya	1993	110	97[11]	N/A
Comoros	1995	74	22	0.6	Lithuania	1995	96	84	28.2
Congo, Democratic					Luxembourg[12]	1993	104	74	N/A
Republic of	1994	72	26	2.3	Macedonia, Former				
Congo, Republic of the	1995	114	53	N/A	Yugoslav Republic of	1995	89	57	17.5
Costa Rica	1995	107	50	31.9[6]	Madagascar	1993	72	14	3.4[11]
Côte d'Ivoire	1995	69	23	4.4[4]	Malawi	1994	135	6	0.8[4]
Croatia	1995	86	82	28.3	Malaysia	1996	91	58	10.6[6]
Cuba	1995	105	80	12.7	Maldives	1993	134	49	N/A
Cyprus	1995	100	97	20.0	Mali	1995	34	9[6]	N/A
Czech Republic	1994	103	96	20.8	Malta	1994	108	89	21.8
Denmark	1994	99	118	45.0	Mauritania	1995	78	15[6]	4.1[4]
Djibouti	1995	38	13	0.2	Mauritius	1995	107	62	6.3
Dominican Republic	1994	103	41	N/A	Mexico	1994	115	58	14.3
Ecuador[8]	1994	109	50	N/A	Moldova	1995	94	80	25.0
Egypt	1995	100	74	18.1[6]	Mongolia	1995	88	59	15.2
El Salvador	1995	88	32	17.7	Morocco	1995	83	39	11.3[6]
Eritrea	1995	57	19	1.1[6]	Mozambique	1995	60	7	0.5
Estonia	1995	109	86	38.1	Myanmar	1995	100	32	5.4[6]
Ethiopia	1994	31	11	0.7	Namibia	1995	133	62	8.1
Fiji	1992	128	64	11.9[9]	Nepal	1993	110	38	5.2
Finland	1994	100	116	66.9	Netherlands, the	1994	107	139	48.9[4]
France	1994	106	111	49.6[4]	New Zealand	1995	104	117	58.2
Gambia, the	1994	73	22	1.7	Nicaragua	1995	110	47	9.4[11]

Enrolment Ratios by Level of Education (*continued*)

Country/territory	Year	1st level[1]	2nd level[2]	3rd level[3]	Country/territory	Year	1st level[1]	2nd level[2]	3rd level[3]
Niger	1995	29	7	N/A	Swaziland	1994	122	52	5.1[4]
Nigeria	1994	89	30	4.1[4]	Sweden	1994	105	132	42.5
Norway	1994	99	116	54.5	Switzerland[14]	1994	107[4]	91[4]	31.8
Oman	1995	80	66	4.7[4]	Syria	1995	101	44	17.9[7]
Pakistan	1993	74	26[9]	3.0[9]	Tajikistan	1994	89	82	20.3
Panama	1995	106	68	30.0	Tanzania	1995	67	5	0.5
Papua New Guinea	1995	80	14[13]	3.2	Thailand	1995	87	55	20.1
Paraguay	1994	109	38	10.3[4]	Togo	1996	133	27[11]	3.2[6]
Peru	1995	123	70	31.1[6]	Trinidad and Tobago	1995	96	72	7.7[6]
Philippines	1995	116	79	27.4[6]	Tunisia	1995	116	61	12.9
Poland	1994	98	96	27.4[4]	Turkey	1994	105	56	18.2
Portugal	1993	128	102	34.0	Turkmenistan	1990	N/A	N/A	21.8
Qatar	1994	86	82	27.4	Uganda[15]	1995	73	12	1.5[6]
Romania	1995	100	78	18.3	UK	1994	115	134	48.3
Russia	1994	108	87[4]	42.9	Ukraine	1993	87	91	40.6
Rwanda	1991	82	11	0.6[5]	United Arab Emirates	1995	95	78	8.8[11]
Samoa	1995	116	47	N/A	Uruguay	1995	111	82	27.3[11]
Saudi Arabia	1995	78	58	15.3[6]	USA[16]	1994	102	97	81.1
Senegal	1996	69	16[7]	3.4[6]	Uzbekistan	1994	77	93	31.7[9]
Sierra Leone	1990	50	17	1.3	Vanuatu	1992	106	20	N/A
Singapore	1995	104[9]	62[9]	33.7	Venezuela	1993	94	35	28.5[9]
Slovak Republic	1995	100	91	20.2	Vietnam	1995	114	47	4.1
Slovenia	1995	103	91	31.9	Yemen	1993	79	23	4.3[9]
Solomon Islands	1994	97	17	N/A	Yugoslavia	1995	72	65	21.1
South Africa	1995	117	84	17.3	Zaire (see Congo, Democratic Republic of)				
Spain	1994	105	118	46.1					
Sri Lanka	1995	113	75	5.1	Zambia	1995	89	28[6]	2.5[6]
Sudan	1994	54	13	N/A	Zimbabwe	1995	116	47	6.9

[1] These figures are for education at the first level, of which the main function is to provide the basic elements of education (for example, at elementary school and primary school).
[2] These figures are for education at the second level, provided at middle school, secondary school, high school, teacher training school at this level, and schools of a vocational or technical nature. This level of education is based upon at least four years' previous instruction at first level and provides general and/or specialized instruction.
[3] These figures are for education at the third level, which is provided at universities, teachers' colleges, and higher professional schools, and which requires, as a minimum condition of entry, the successful completion of education at the second level, or evidence of the attainment of an equivalent level of knowledge.
[4] Figures for 1993.
[5] Figures for 1989.
[6] Figures for 1994.
[7] Figures for 1992.
[8] Enrolment ratios are for the end of the school year.
[9] Figures for 1991.
[10] Figures for 1990.
[11] Figures for 1995.
[12] Some students study in neighbouring countries.
[13] Education at the second level does not include colleges of distance education.
[14] As the institutional system of education differs from canton to canton, the first six years of enrolment have been taken for the first level, and the following seven years for the second level, throughout the country.
[15] These figures are for government maintained and aided schools only.
[16] Enrolment ratios for first level refer to grades 1 to 6; those for second level to grades 7 to 12.

Source: UNESCO

Countries with the Lowest Percentage of Female Enrolment at First Level of Education

These figures are for education at the first level, of which the main function is to provide the basic elements of education (for example, at elementary school and primary school). Data for each country are for the year in parentheses and are the most recent available.

Rank	Country	Female enrolment (%)	Rank	Country	Female enrolment (%)
1	Pakistan (1993)	31	7	Liberia (1980)	35
2	Afghanistan (1995)	32	8	Benin (1995)	36
3	Chad (1995)	33	9	Ethiopia (1994)	37
4	Bhutan (1985)	34		Guinea-Bissau (1994)	37
	Guinea (1995)	34			
	Somalia (1985)	34			

Source: UNESCO

Participation in Education of 16–18 Year Olds in Selected Countries

The data in this table include apprenticeships in countries such as Austria, Germany, and Switzerland. All figures include full-time and part-time students.
(N/A = not available.)

1994

Country	Minimum leaving age	Age 16 (%)	Age 17 (%)	Age 18 (%)	Country	Minimum leaving age	Age 16 (%)	Age 17 (%)	Age 18 (%)
Australia	15	96	92	65	Korea, South	14	93	85	48
Austria	15	92	86	61	Netherlands	16	98	91	80
Belgium[1]	18	100	100	87	New Zealand[2]	16	94	79	57
Canada	16	94	88	72	Norway	16	94	91	83
Denmark	16	94	81	70	Portugal	14	74	67	55
Finland	16	96	92	83	Spain	16	82	75	63
France	16	96	92	84	Sweden	16	96	95	83
Germany	18	96	93	85	Switzerland	15	87	83	76
Greece	15	82	57	59	Turkey	15	41	24	18
Ireland, Republic of	15	93	83	93	UK[3]	16	87	74	53
Japan	15	96	93	N/A	USA	17	95	86	61

[1] Data include a large number of foreign students in the schools of the French community.
[2] Data include Training Opportunity Programmes.
[3] Data exclude students in private further and higher education, adult education centres, and youth training with employers.

Source: Department for Education and Employment. © Crown copyright 1997

Countries with the Highest Pupil–Teacher Ratios at First Level of Education

These figures are for education at the first level, of which the main function is to provide the basic elements of education (for example, at elementary school and primary school). Data for each country are for the year in parentheses and are the most recent available.

Rank	Country	Number of pupils per teacher	Rank	Country	Number of pupils per teacher
1	Central African Republic (1990)	77	7	Malawi (1994)	62
2	Congo, Republic of the (1995)	70	8	Senegal (1996)	59
2=	Mali (1995)	70	9	Afghanistan (1994)	58
4	Bangladesh (1990)	63	9=	Mozambique (1995)	58
4=	Burundi (1992)	63	9=	Rwanda (1991)	58
4=	Chad (1995)	63			

Source: UNESCO

Countries with the Lowest Pupil–Teacher Ratios at First Level of Education

These figures are for education at the first level, of which the main function is to provide the basic elements of education (for example, at elementary school and primary school). Data for each country are for the year in parentheses and are the most recent available.

Rank	Country	Number of pupils per teacher	Rank	Country	Number of pupils per teacher
1	San Marino (1995)	5	7=	Belgium (1993)	12
2	Qatar (1994)	9	7=	Cuba (1995)	12
3	Denmark (1994)	10	7=	Portugal (1993)	12
4	Italy (1994)	11	7=	Switzerland (1994)	12
4=	Hungary (1994)	11	7=	Libya (1992)	12
4=	Sweden (1994)	11			
7	Austria (1994)	12			

Source: UNESCO

World Illiteracy Rates: Highest 25 Countries

The percentages in this table are all estimates.

1995

Rank	Country	Illiterates (%)	Rank	Country	Illiterates (%)
1	Niger	86.4	14	Bangladesh	61.9
2	Burkina Faso	80.8	15	Liberia	61.7
3	Nepal	72.5	16	Gambia, the	61.4
4	Mali	69.0	17	Côte d'Ivoire	59.9
5	Sierra Leone	68.6	17=	Mozambique	59.9
6	Afghanistan	68.5	19	Angola	59.0[1]
7	Senegal	66.9	20	Bhutan	57.8
8	Burundi	64.7	21	Morocco	56.3
9	Ethiopia	64.5	22	Haiti	55.0
10	Guinea	64.1	23	Madagascar	54.3
11	Benin	63.0	24	Sudan	53.9
12	Mauritania	62.3	25	Chad	51.9
13	Pakistan	62.2			

[1] This is a 1985 estimate.

Source: UNESCO

Public Expenditure on Education by Region of the World

Data for countries of the former USSR are not included in either the world total or regional totals because there is insufficient information to calculate valid estimates for these countries.

Region	Public expenditure on education ($ thousand millions)				Public expenditure on education (% of GNP)				Public expenditure on education per inhabitant ($)			
	1980	1985	1990	1995	1980	1985	1990	1995	1980	1985	1990	1995
Africa	22.9	22.0	25.7	29.1	5.3	5.7	5.6	5.9	48	40	41	41
America	188.6	249.5	374.9	481.7	4.9	4.9	5.2	5.3	307	375	521	623
Asia	93.8	107.6	199.8	302.1	4.0	3.9	3.7	3.6	37	39	66	93
Europe	200.6	165.8	367.5	492.6	5.1	5.1	5.1	5.4	418	340	741	982
Oceania	10.4	10.6	18.6	24.5	5.6	5.6	5.6	6.0	467	439	715	878
World total	516.4	555.6	986.5	1,329.9	4.8	4.8	4.8	4.9	126	124	202	252

Source: UNESCO

Public Expenditure on Education by Region of the World According to Development Status

Data for countries of the former USSR are not included in either the world total or regional totals because there is insufficient information to calculate valid estimates for these countries.

Region	Public expenditure on education ($ thousand millions)				Public expenditure on education (% of GNP)				Public expenditure on education per inhabitant ($)			
	1980	1985	1990	1995	1980	1985	1990	1995	1980	1985	1990	1995
Developing Countries												
Sub-Saharan Africa	15.8	11.3	14.8	18.8	5.1	4.8	5.1	5.6	41	26	29	32
Arab states	18.0	23.7	24.4	27.5	4.1	5.8	5.2	5.2	109	122	110	110
Latin America and the Caribbean	33.5	27.9	44.6	72.8	3.8	3.9	4.1	4.5	93	70	102	153
Eastern Asia and Oceania	16.0	20.1	32.0	59.9	2.8	3.1	3.0	3.0	12	14	20	36
Southern Asia	12.8	14.7	35.8	18.8	4.1	3.3	3.9	3.4	13	14	30	14
Least developed countries	3.1	3.1	4.3	5.3	2.9	3.0	2.7	2.5	9	7	9	9
Total	101.6	100.3	160.9	206.6	3.8	4.0	4.0	3.9	31	28	40	48
Developed Countries												
Total	414.8	455.3	825.6	1,123.3	5.1	5.0	5.0	5.1	487	520	914	1,211
TOTAL	516.4	555.6	986.5	1,329.9	4.8	4.8	4.8	4.9	126	124	202	252

Source: UNESCO

UK Schools and Teachers

An Overview of the School System in the UK

Organization

School education in the UK is a national service locally administered, which means that policies enacted by the national government at Westminster are put into practice by local education authorities (LEAs) in England and Wales, education authorities (EAs) in Scotland, and Education and Library Boards in Northern Ireland. These authorities are part of the democratic system of borough and county councils.

Under the Conservative administration (1979–97) some schools were given greater autonomy, but the Labour government plans to bring these grant-maintained schools back into a more direct relationship with their LEAs. Funding advantages will be phased out.

State schools have boards of governors drawn from parents, the LEA, and the local community. The governors are responsible for school policy and for overseeing the school's budget. The headteacher is responsible for the day-to-day running of the school, and for discipline.

Seven percent of British children attend fee-paying private schools, which range from famous 'public' schools, such as Eton and Harrow, run as non-profitmaking charities, to small private establishments run as businesses. Many private schools have a highly selected intake and are very successful in public examinations.

Growing concern about the performance of schools in some deprived inner-city areas has led the Labour government to set up Education Action Zones. Schools in these areas will be run by partnerships that can involve business and industry as well as the LEA. They will be encouraged to innovate and experiment in an effort to raise standards.

Funding

The main funding for state schools is provided by central government grants to LEAs, with a smaller proportion coming from local taxes. Many schools also raise funds through their parent-teacher associations, and increasingly through sponsorship from business and industry. Individual school budgets are determined by the LEA, but governors have responsibility for allocating funds internally.

Types of School

Schooling in the UK is divided into primary and secondary sectors, with the change of school at age 11 (12 in Scotland). The state system includes a few middle schools taking children from 9 to 13, and private sector secondary schools commonly recruit at 13.

Compulsory schooling begins at five, although an increasing proportion of four-year-olds are being accommodated in primary schools. Nursery education for three- and four-year-olds is not compulsory, but has been expanding in recent years. The Labour government is committed to expanding provision until it is available for all three- to five-year-olds whose parents want it.

The state school system allows some schools to be run in partnership with religious denominations. The majority of these voluntary-aided schools are associated with the Roman Catholic Church and the Church of England. There are a small number of Jewish schools, and approval has recently been given for two Muslim schools to receive government funding.

The vast majority of state secondary schools are comprehensive, which means that they admit children regardless of ability. A few local authorities still maintain selective (grammar) schools, which admit children on the results of an entrance test. The Labour government elected in 1997 is opposed to selection by ability, and plans to allow parents of affected children to ballot on whether local grammar schools should remain selective or become comprehensive.

The Labour government supports some specialization at secondary level, for example in the case of schools specializing in technology, languages, or the performing arts. Additional funding is provided for such schools, and admission is by an assessment of aptitude in the specialist subjects, regardless of general academic ability.

When a school is unable to admit all the children who have applied for places, decisions are usually made on the basis of how close a family lives to the school. There is an appeal system for families who are not satisfied with admissions decisions.

Most children with special needs are given additional help within mainstream classrooms and the most serious are given statements of special needs. However, roughly two percent of such children have serious disabilities or learning difficulties that cannot be catered for in mainstream education, and these children are taught in special day or residential schools.

Compulsory education ends at the age of 16, and although the majority of young people remain in education after that age, they have the option of moving into different institutions. Young people studying for academic qualifications beyond 16 may remain in a school sixth form or move to a sixth form college for the two-year A level course. Those seeking vocational courses may opt to switch to a college of further education. A growing number of tertiary colleges offer 16- to 18-year-olds a range of academic and vocational courses in the same institution.

Curriculum

A National Curriculum was established by the Education Reform Act of 1988 under the Conservative government. This act laid down detailed programmes of study for all the main subjects, together with a system of levels of performance that an average child might be expected to attain between the ages of 5 and 16.

As the National Curriculum was put into practice over a five-year period it became apparent that it was extremely onerous for teachers and pupils, particularly in primary schools. The curriculum was slimmed down after an inquiry conducted by Sir Ron Dearing in 1996, and, shortly after taking office, the new Labour government relaxed the requirements for humanities and arts subjects in primary schools, in order to allow more time to be spent on English, maths, and science. The Labour government has set ambitious targets for achievement in literacy and numeracy. According to these targets, by the year 2002, 75 percent of 11 year olds are to attain level 4 in mathematics and 80 percent are to attain the same level in English.

Public Examinations and Testing

British schoolchildren are subjected to more external assessment than any others in the world. They go through a dual system of school-leaving examination. This system consists of GCSE (Standard Grade in Scotland) taken at 16 and A levels taken at 18 (Highers at 17 in Scotland). There is also a parallel system of vocational qualifications.

It is expected that the majority of children will sit a GCSE examination in all ten National Curriculum subjects. Young people intending to study at university usually go on to take three A levels or five Scottish Higher subjects; entry to a degree course is dependent upon their performance in these examinations.

Since the introduction of the National Curriculum, pupils have also been assessed at the ages of 7, 11, and 14 by means of externally marked standard attainment tests (SATs). Public examination and test results are published on an individual school and an LEA basis, and used by government and the media as a basis for comparison.

Schools are also regularly inspected by the Office for Standards in Education (Ofsted). All inspection reports are published. Schools that are deemed to be 'failing' are expected to improve rapidly, face public humiliation by being 'named and shamed' in the media, and may ultimately be closed.

Education: UK Chronology

12th–15th centuries	First British universities founded: Oxford (12th century), Cambridge (13th century), St Andrews (15th century).
14th–17th centuries	Development of schools, initially by religious orders and urban guilds. Spate of post-Reformation foundations under Edward VI and Elizabeth I.
1780	First Sunday schools established.
1801	Royal Lancastrian Society founded first Nonconformist voluntary schools.
1802	Factory Act provided for the elementary education of apprentices.
1808–11	British and Foreign School Society and National Society for the Education of the Poor formed the first voluntary Church of England schools.
1828	Thomas Arnold became headmaster at Rugby School and began process of public-school reform.
1833	First government grants to education. Factory Act made two hours of schooling for children 9–11 compulsory.
1844	Lord Shaftesbury founded first 'ragged schools'.
1868	Regulatory Public Schools Act.
1870	First Education Act created locally elected school boards to set up dual system of voluntary and local board schools.
1880	Education Act made schooling for all children 5–10 compulsory.
1902	Board schools came under local education authorities' (LEAs) control. They were authorized to develop existing elementary schools and to set up secondary or technical schools.
1918	Education Act raised school-leaving age to 14.
1944	(Butler) Education Act raised school-leaving age to 15 and provided free secondary schooling together with free meals and milk for all. The Board of Education became a Ministry of Education.
1951	General Certificate of Education introduced (Certificate of Secondary Education introduced 1965).

1963	Robbins Committee recommended massive expansion in university sector.
1964	Government supported comprehensive secondary education.
1965	Polytechnics established; public sector assumed responsibility for expansion of higher education.
1969	Open University established.
1973	School-leaving age raised to 16.
1976	All state secondary schools required to become comprehensive.
1979 and 1980	Requirement of the 1976 Education Act repealed and, in theory, increased parental involvement. LEAs were required to publish certain information about schools but were no longer required to provide meals and milk for pupils.
1986	Education Bill introduced changes to the administration of schools, including elected parent-governors.
1987	General Certificate of Secondary Education (GCSE) replaced GCE/CSE system.
1988	Education Reform Act introduced a national curriculum and testing for all schoolchildren, encompassing major subject areas. The powers of school-governing bodies were increased. Schools were empowered to opt out of local-council control.
1993	Education Act extending many previous provisions, notably those on grant maintained schools and education of special needs children.
1994	Revision of National Curriculum published by Sir Ron Dearing of the new Schools Curriculum and Assessment Authority.
1997	A new government is elected and plans to expand nursery education, set up education action zones in deprived areas, and phase out funding advantages of grant-maintained schools.
1998	Compulsory daily hours of literacy and maths introduced in primary schools.

School Meals in England

The data in this table are for grant-maintained schools and those maintained by local education authorities. They do not include boarding pupils. The data are for January 1996 and are percentages of the total number of pupils on roll.

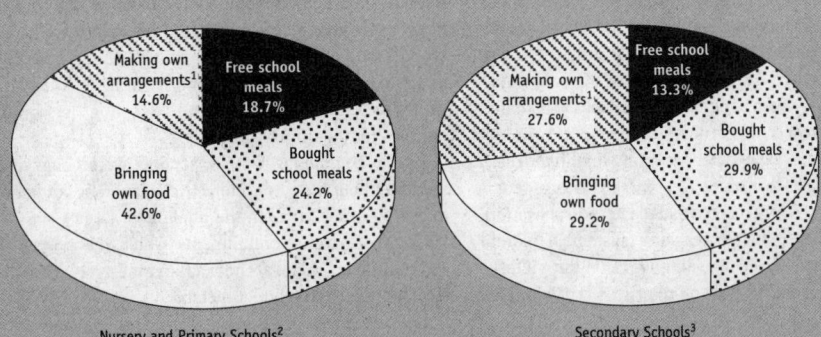

Nursery and Primary Schools[2]

Secondary Schools[3]

[1] Figures include those part-time pupils who were absent on the enumeration date, part-time pupils who do not attend school during the lunch period, and any other day pupils whose arrangements were not known.
[2] Figures include data for middle schools which are deemed primary schools.
[3] Figures include data for middle schools which are deemed secondary schools.

Source: Department for Education and Employment. © Crown copyright 1997

THE NATIONAL CURRICULUM

BY MAUREEN O'CONNOR

The introduction of a National Curriculum in the UK has been a ten-year rollercoaster ride that has not stopped yet. Its introduction was allegedly the result of a chance remark by Prime Minister Margaret Thatcher, to the effect that it should be possible to spell out what children should know in the basic subjects. But by the time it emerged as part of Secretary of State Kenneth Baker's Education Reform Act in 1988, it offered detailed syllabuses in ten subjects for children from the ages of 5 to 16.

Teachers complained from the beginning that a sensible idea had turned into an uncontrollable monster. Civil servants admitted at the time that the full curriculum actually accounted for 120 percent of the school timetable. Schools agonized over how to fit this quart into a pint pot, and teaching unions complained bitterly of work overload and consequent stress. There were also furious debates about what should be included in the new syllabuses.

There were two particular difficulties that have still not been resolved a decade after the Reform Act. The first concerns the priority that needs to be given to reading, writing, and basic maths in primary schools; the second concerns the number and range of subjects secondary pupils can sensibly cope with up to GCSE level.

The Labour government has instructed schools to emphasize and maths ©Richard Watt

A Broad and Compulsory Curriculum

The original National Curriculum was uncompromising. There were to be ten subjects taught: English, maths, science, technology, history, geography, art, music, and PE in all schools; plus a modern language at secondary level. In Wales all children would also study Welsh. And space had to be found for the only other subject that had previously been compulsory: religious education.

In primary schools teachers did not necessarily object to a broad curriculum. Most of them had already been trying to provide that, often in the form of projects that covered aspects of history, geography, and social studies. They accepted that the new dispensation brought method and rigour to the teaching system. Children would no longer find themselves repeating work on the Victorians, or the Wild West, or the Vikings more or less at random as they changed classes or schools.

But primary teachers did complain that the sheer volume of factual knowledge required for teaching the new syllabuses in the humanities, science, and technology was crippling. Most were generalists who were now expected to handle a mountain of specialized knowledge across a wide range of subjects.

At secondary level, difficulties arose at the point at which traditionally pupils had chosen some subjects to take at GCSE and had dropped others. Schools struggled to create timetables that would allow pupils to take all the National Curriculum subjects up

to the age of 16. Extra classes after school and 'half' GCSE courses were some of the solutions canvassed, as schools struggled to balance depth of study with the new broad curriculum. Where pupils had previously had some choice of subject between the ages of 14 and 16, now there would be none. Specialist teachers of non-compulsory subjects – such as drama, home economics, sociology, and classics – lamented the demise of their subjects in British schools.

A Slimmer Curriculum with Greater Choice

Rescue came in the shape of Sir Ron Dearing, a former chairman of the Post Office and an arch-conciliator, who was commissioned to review the whole new curricular edifice. His conclusions, published in 1995, were warmly welcomed by the over-stressed teachers and accepted by the government. He recommended that the primary curriculum should be slimmed down, and that some element of choice should be restored for secondary school pupils at the age of 14.

Ironically, his report immediately met with complaints from specialist teachers' groups for subjects such as history and geography, art, and music; they had watched their subjects changing from optional to compulsory and back to optional again in the upper years of the secondary schools.

Sir Ron Dearing also recommended that the National Curriculum should not be tampered with again until the year 2000, in order to give schools a period of stability. But he and the schools reckoned without the new Labour government that swept to power with a huge majority in 1997. Tony Blair's dedication to 'education, education, education' has brought more changes for the primary schools.

By the beginning of 1998, schools were being instructed to spend an hour a day on literacy teaching and an hour a day on maths, in order to reach the attainment targets set for the year 2002. These were commitments which made even the newly slimmed down National Curriculum for 5- to 11-year-olds impossible to fit into the school timetable.

Before the new government was a year old, teachers' organizations and members of the wider public were campaigning again, this time to make sure that subjects like history and music were not squeezed out of primary schools completely. The orchestral conductor Sir Simon Rattle caused such alarm by his pronouncements on what he saw as the threat to Britain's musical heritage that he was immediately appointed as a creative education adviser to the government. Ten years after the Education Reform Act was supposed to have set the school curriculum in stone for a generation, the argument continues as fiercely as ever.

Pupils Under Five Years of Age in Schools in England

The data in this table are as of January for the year shown.

Maintained Nursery and Primary Schools

Year	Population aged 3 and 4 at previous 31 December	Pupil numbers Ages at previous 31 August				Participation rates (%) Ages at previous 31 August		
		2	3[1]	4[2]	Total	3[1]	4[2]	All pupils under 5[2]
1987	1,182,000	25,000	199,000	293,000	517,000	33	74	44
1989	1,224,000	25,000	214,000	308,000	548,000	35	77	45
1991	1,263,000	28,000	236,000	339,000	604,000	37	81	48
1993	1,295,000	31,000	255,000	370,000	656,000	40	84	51
1995	1,319,000	33,000	279,000	388,000	700,000	42	88	53
1996	1,305,000	32,000	288,000	389,000	708,000	44	88	54

All Schools (Including Independent and Special)

Year	Pupil numbers Ages at previous 31 August				Overall participation rates (%) Ages at previous 31 August		
	2	3[1]	4[3]	Total[3]	3[1]	4[3]	All pupils under 5[2]
1987	31,000	216,000	311,000	558,000	36	79	47
1989	33,000	235,000	327,000	595,000	38	82	49
1991	36,000	258,000	360,000	655,000	41	86	52
1993	40,000	278,000	391,000	709,000	43	89	55
1995	43,000	303,000	409,000	756,000	46	93	57
1996	42,000	314,000	410,000	766,000	48	93	59

[1] Figures include pupils who became 4 years of age by 1 January.
[2] Figures exclude pupils who became 5 years of age by 1 January.
[3] From 1989, figures exclude pupils in all schools who became 5 years of age by 1 January. Up to 1987, such pupils in independent and special schools are included.

Source: Department for Education and Employment. © Crown copyright 1997

Number of School Pupils by Type of School in the UK

(– = not applicable. N/A = not available.)

School	1970/71	1980/81	1990/91	1995/96	1996/97[1]
Public Sector Schools[2]					
Nursery[3]	50,000	89,000	105,000	84,000	83,000
Primary[3]	5,902,000	5,171,000	4,955,000	5,338,000	5,380,000
Secondary					
modern	1,164,000	233,000	94,000	78,000	63,000
grammar	673,000	149,000	156,000	189,000	191,000
comprehensive[4]	1,313,000	3,730,000	2,843,000	3,129,000	3,168,000
other	403,000	434,000	300,000	282,000	288,000
All Public Sector Schools	9,507,000	9,806,000	8,453,000	9,099,000	9,172,000
Non-maintained schools[2]	621,000	619,000	613,000	603,000	610,000
Special schools[5]	103,000	148,000	114,000	115,000	116,000
Pupil referral units	–	–	–	N/A	7,000
All schools	10,230,000	10,572,000	9,180,000	9,816,000	9,905,000

[1] Data for Wales are for 1995/96.
[2] Excludes special schools.
[3] Nursery classes within primary schools are included in primary schools except for Scotland in 1990/91, in which instance they are included in nursery schools.
[4] Excludes sixth form colleges from 1980/81.
[5] Includes maintained and non-maintained sectors.

Source: Department for Education and Employment; Welsh Office; The Scottish Office Education and Industry Department; Department of Education Northern Ireland. © Crown copyright 1998

Numbers of Primary, Secondary, and Special Schools in the UK

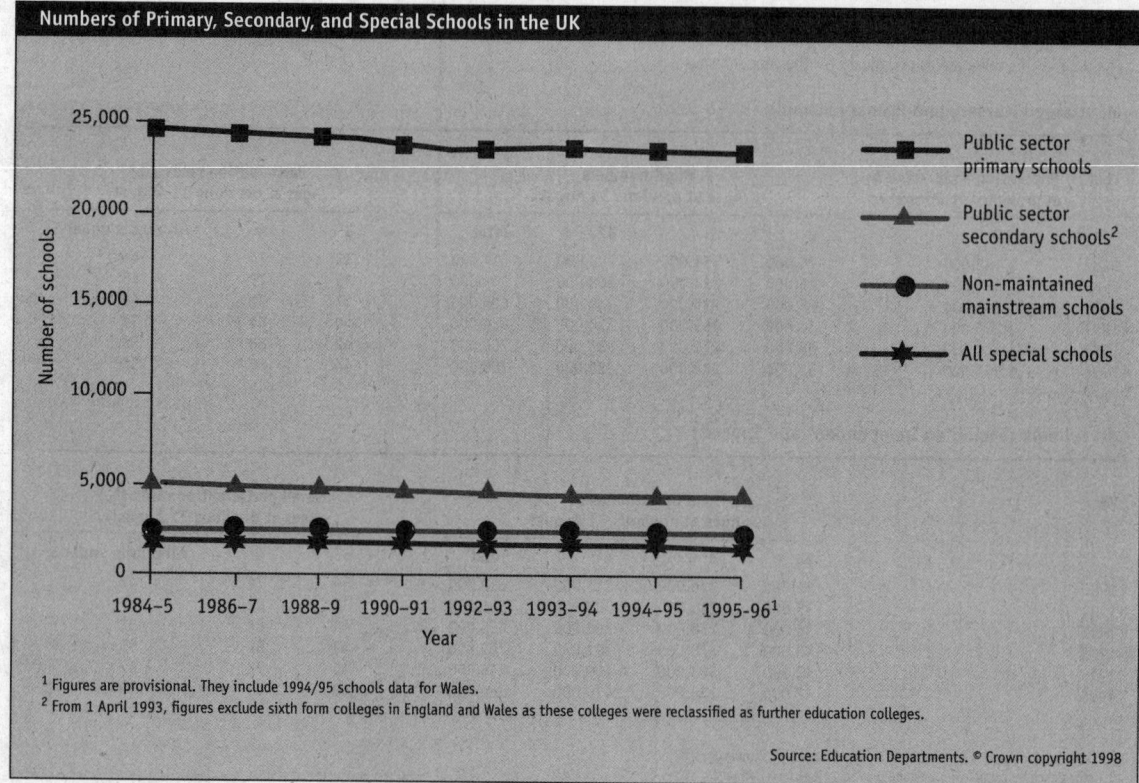

Legend:
- Public sector primary schools
- Public sector secondary schools[2]
- Non-maintained mainstream schools
- All special schools

[1] Figures are provisional. They include 1994/95 schools data for Wales.
[2] From 1 April 1993, figures exclude sixth form colleges in England and Wales as these colleges were reclassified as further education colleges.

Source: Education Departments. © Crown copyright 1998

Full-Time Pupils with Special Needs in Public Sector and Assisted Schools in the UK

The data in this table are as of January for the year shown.
(N/A = not available.)

Category	1986/87	1988/89	1990/91	1991/92	1992/93	1993/94	1994/95	1995/96[1]
Hospital Schools[2]								
Total	3,000	2,600	900	700	500	600	200	200
Other Special Schools or Departments[3]								
Total[3]	120,400	114,100	110,800	111,000	111,700	112,600	112,500	109,900
Pupils with Statements of Special Needs in Other Public Sector Schools[4]								
Public sector primary schools[5][6]	24,000	31,800	40,300	45,300	53,300	61,200	66,400	73,400
Public sector secondary schools[5][7][8]	17,400	25,700	34,800	41,600	49,200	59,000	66,200	75,300
Total	41,300	57,400	75,200	86,900	102,500	120,200	132,500	148,800

[1] Figures are provisional. They include 1994/95 data for Wales.
[2] England and Wales.
[3] From 1987 onwards, figures include schools and pupils that were previously the responsibility of the Northern Ireland Department of Health and Social Security.
[4] For Scotland, pupils with a Record of Needs.
[5] Including estimated primary–secondary split for Wales for 1985/86 and from 1991/92.
[6] For Northern Ireland, figures include preparatory departments of grammar schools.
[7] From 1 April 1993, figures exclude sixth form colleges in England and Wales reclassified as further education colleges.
[8] For Northern Ireland, figures include secondary departments of grammar schools.

Source: Education Departments. © Crown copyright 1998

Numbers of Teachers by Type of School in the UK

Data are for January of each year except in Scotland and Wales, where data are for September.

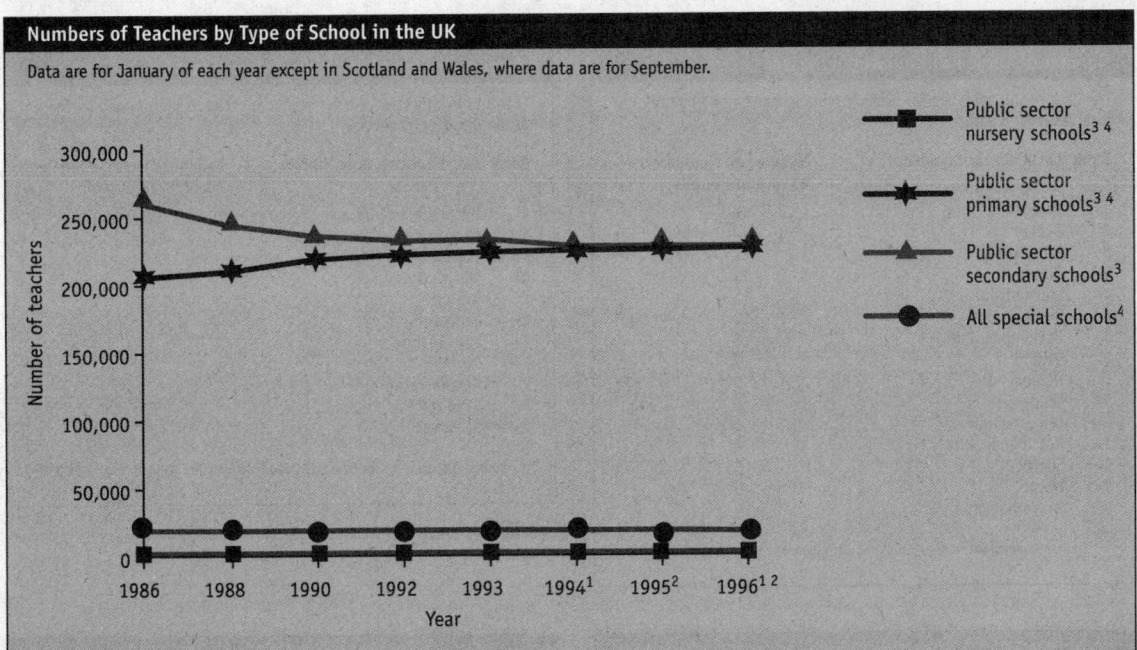

Legend:
- ■ Public sector nursery schools[3] [4]
- ★ Public sector primary schools[3] [4]
- ▲ Public sector secondary schools[3]
- ● All special schools[4]

[1] From 1 April 1993, figures exclude sixth form colleges in England and Wales as these colleges were reclassified as further education colleges.
[2] Figures are provisional. This column includes 1994/95 data for Wales.
[3] Figures of teachers take account of the full-time equivalent of part-time teachers.
[4] Up to 1993/94, figures include unqualified teachers for England and Scotland. From 1994/95, figures include qualified teachers only for all countries.
[5] Figure includes 1984/85 data for Scotland.

Source: Education Departments. © Crown copyright 1998

Pupil/Teacher Ratios by Type of School in the UK

Data are as of January for the year shown, except for Scotland and Wales where they are as of September.

		1986	1988	1990	1992	1993	1994[1]	1995[1]	1996[1] [2]
All Schools or Departments[3] [4]									
UK[5]	England	17.4	17.2	17.0	17.2	17.4	17.7	18.1	18.2
	Wales	18.2	18.0	18.1	18.2	18.2	18.4	18.7	18.7
	Scotland	N/A	15.8	15.3	15.3	15.4	15.5	15.4	15.5
	Northern Ireland	18.5	18.4	18.3	18.3	18.1	17.8	17.3	16.7
Total		17.4[6]	17.1	16.9	17.1	17.3	17.5	17.8	17.9
Public Sector Mainstream Schools or Departments									
Nursery	21.7[6]	21.4	21.8	21.6	21.6	21.6	21.9	21.4	
Primary	22.0	21.9	21.7	21.8	21.9	22.2	22.4	22.6	
Secondary		15.7	15.1	14.8	15.2	15.4	15.7	16.0	16.1
Special Schools[4]									
Total		6.6	6.3	5.8	5.7	5.8	5.9	6.0	6.2

[1] From 1 April 1993, figures exclude sixth form colleges in England and Wales that were reclassified as further education colleges.
[2] Figures are provisional. They include 1994/95 data for Wales.
[3] From 1980 onwards, figures include non-maintained schools or departments, including independent schools in Scotland.
[4] Up to 1993/94, figures include unqualified teachers for England and Scotland. From 1994/95 qualified teachers only for all countries.
[5] Figures take account of the full-time equivalent of part-time teachers.
[6] Includes 1984/85 data for Scotland.

Source: Education Departments. © Crown copyright 1998

Local Education Authorities in England with the Greatest Number of Large Primary School Classes

The data in this table are for primary schools maintained by the local education authority.

Rank	Local education authority	Number of classes with 41 or more pupils
1	Derbyshire	16
2	Dudley	14
3	Manchester	12
4	Bolton	11
4=	Staffordshire	11
6	Bedfordshire	10
7	Buckinghamshire	8
8	Salford	7
9	Humberside	5
9=	Leeds	5
9=	Leicestershire	5
9=	Nottinghamshire	5
9=	Sheffield	5
9=	Walsall	5
9=	Wolverhampton	5

Source: Department for Education and Employment. © Crown copyright 1997

Local Education Authorities in England with the Greatest Number of Large Secondary School Classes

The data in this table are for secondary schools maintained by the local education authority.

Rank	Local education authority	Number of classes with 41 or more pupils
1	Buckinghamshire	2
1=	East Sussex	2
1=	Staffordshire	2
1=	West Sussex	2
2	Bolton	1
2=	Lancashire	1
2=	Lincolnshire	1
2=	Norfolk	1
2=	Northamptonshire	1
2=	Sandwell	1
2=	Somerset	1

Source: Department for Education and Employment. © Crown copyright 1997

Local Education Authorities in England with the Greatest Number of Small Primary School Classes

The data in this table are for primary schools maintained by the local education authority.

Rank	Local education authority	Number of classes with 1–20 pupils
1	Hertfordshire	367
2	Surrey	350
3	Devon	348
4	Kent	333
5	North Yorkshire	332
6	Hereford and Worcester	312
6=	Suffolk	312
8	Norfolk	294
9	Leicestershire	292
10	Hampshire	289
10=	Lancashire	289

Source: Department for Education and Employment. © Crown copyright 1997

Local Education Authorities in England with the Greatest Number of Small Secondary School Classes

The data in this table are for secondary schools maintained by the local education authority.

Rank	Local education authority	Number of classes with 1–20 pupils
1	Kent	1,985
2	Essex	1,581
3	Hertfordshire	1,447
4	Lancashire	1,293
5	Hampshire	1,230
6	Cheshire	1,098
7	Birmingham	1,095
8	Nottinghamshire	1,089
9	Staffordshire	1,075
10	Devon	1,038

Source: Department for Education and Employment. © Crown copyright 1997

See Also **Government Spending on Education in the UK (Economy and Business)**

Pupils Reaching or Exceeding Level 4 at Key Stage 2 in England and Wales

At the end of key stage 2, a typical 11 year old is expected to achieve level 4 on the National Curriculum scale. The government has set targets for 11 year olds. By the year 2002, 75 percent are to attain level 4 in mathematics and 80 percent to attain the same level in English. The National Curriculum only applies to schools in England and Wales.
(In percentages.)

1996

Boys

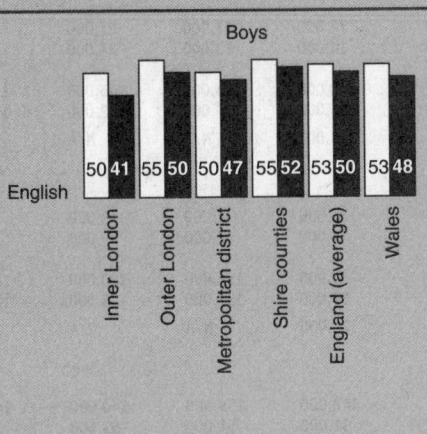

Girls

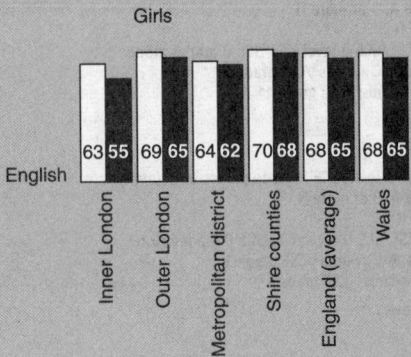

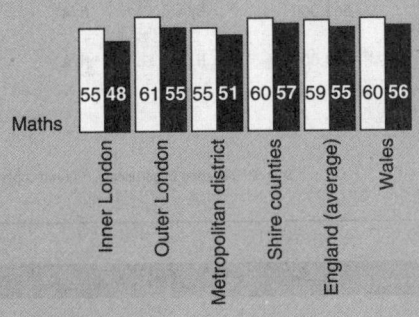

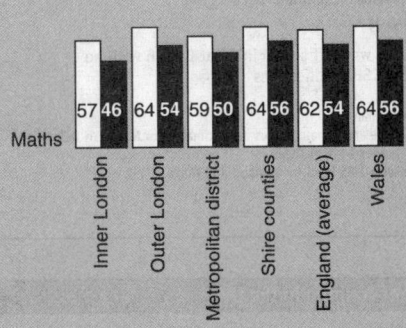

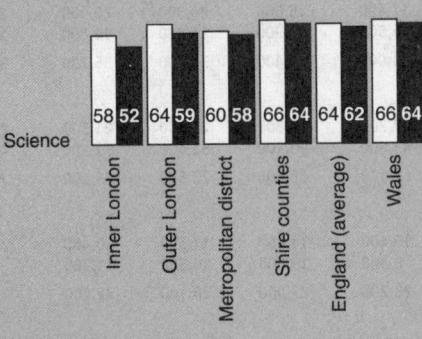

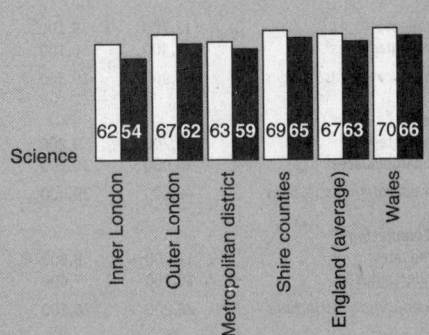

☐ Teacher assessment
■ Test

Source: Department for Education and Employment; Welsh Office. © Crown copyright 1998

GCE, GCSE, CSE, and SCE Qualifications Obtained by School Pupils in the UK

Data up to 1990/91 relate to school leavers. From 1991/92, data relate to pupils of any age for Great Britain and school leavers for Northern Ireland. Figures exclude sixth form colleges in England, which were reclassified as further education colleges from 1 April 1993. (N/A = not available.)

Qualification	1985/86	1990/91	1993/94	1994/95	1995/96[1]
Male[2]					
Pupils with GCE A level/SCE H grade passes or equivalent					
2 or more A, 3 or more H	66,000	72,000	67,000	67,000	70,000
1 A, or 2 H	16,000	14,000	23,000	24,000	16,000
Pupils with GCSE/GCE O level/CSE/SCE O grades alone					
5 or more A–C awards[3]/CSE grade 1	44,000	40,000	133,000	145,000	151,000
1–4 A–C awards[3]/CSE grade 1[4]	108,000	85,000	135,000	132,000	136,000
Total school leavers	444,000	338,000	N/A	N/A	N/A
Female[2]					
Pupils with GCE A level/SCE H grade passes or equivalent					
2 or more A, 3 or more H	61,000	76,000	72,000	73,000	76,000
1 A, or 2 H	18,000	17,000	27,000	29,000	18,000
Pupils with GCSE/GCE O level/CSE/SCE O grades alone					
5 or more A–C awards[3]/CSE grade 1	51,000	51,000	155,000	170,000	180,000
1–4 A–C awards[3]/CSE grade 1[4]	123,000	87,000	137,000	135,000	137,000
Total school leavers	427,000	323,000	N/A	N/A	N/A
All					
Pupils with GCE A level/SCE H grade passes or equivalent					
2 or more A, 3 or more H	127,000	148,000	139,000	140,000	145,000
1 A, or 2 H	34,000	31,000	51,000	53,000	34,000
Pupils with GCSE/GCE O level/CSE/SCE O grades alone					
5 or more A–C awards[3]/CSE grade 1	95,000	91,000	288,000	315,000	331,000
1–4 A–C awards[3]/CSE grade 1[4]	231,000	172,000	272,000	267,000	273,000
Total school leavers	871,000	661,000	N/A	N/A	N/A
Numbers of pupils who left school in Great Britain with no GCSE/GCE/SCE or CSE qualifications	95,000	49,000	N/A	N/A	N/A

[1] Figures are provisional.
[2] From 1993/94, male and female figures are estimated for Northern Ireland.
[3] From 1993/94, grades A*–C at GCSE.
[4] Includes pupils with 1 AS level for England and Wales.

Source: Education Departments. © Crown copyright 1998

Initial Teacher Training in the UK

(N/A = not available.)

Category	1980/81	1985/86	1990/91	1991/92	1992/93	1993/94	1994/95[1]	1995/96[1 2]
New Entrants								
Courses for graduates[3]	12,700	9,100	14,100	17,400	16,500	20,300	20,900	21,000
Courses for undergraduates[4]	9,300	10,100	15,000	15,500	17,900	16,200	14,800	14,300
Total in higher education institutions	21,900	19,300	29,000	33,000	34,400	36,700	35,700	35,200
Total Enrolments								
Courses for graduates[3]	12,700	9,200	14,200	18,200	17,800	21,100	21,300	20,200
Courses for undergraduates[4]	30,000	30,300	41,300	43,800	50,700	51,400	51,800	45,600
Total in higher education institutions	42,800	39,600	55,500	62,100	68,500	72,500	73,100	70,900
Successfully Completing[5 6]								
Courses for graduates	12,000	8,500	12,100	15,400	16,800	17,500	20,400	N/A
Courses for undergraduates	10,200	7,600	7,900	8,300	10,300	10,500	11,700	N/A
Total in higher education institutions	22,200	16,200	20,000	23,700	27,000	28,100	32,200	N/A

[1] Figures are provisional.
[2] Figures include 1994/95 data for Wales.
[3] From 1993/94, England figures include school centred initial teacher training, articled teachers, and Open University.
[4] From 1990/91, figures include licensed/overseas trained teachers for England.
[5] Completers at the end of the academic year.
[6] Figures include students in England and Wales who failed their BEd degree course but have received qualified teacher status on the basis of a non-degree qualification obtained in an earlier year.

Source: Education Departments. © Crown copyright 1998

Adult Literacy Levels by Gender in the UK

The abilities of working people (aged 16 to 65) were measured on three types of literacy: prose literacy (the ability to understand text), document literacy (the ability to locate and use information in charts and timetables), and quantitative literacy (the ability to perform basic arithmetic operations on numbers embedded in text). Performance on each dimension is grouped into five literacy levels, level 1 being the lowest and level 5 the highest. Level 3 is considered by the Organization for Economic Co-operation and Development to be the minimum level required for coping with modern life and work.
(In percentages.)

1996

Dimension	Level 1	Level 2	Level 3	Levels 4/5	All
Male					
Prose	21	30	32	17	100
Document	20	25	31	24	100
Quantitative	18	27	30	25	100
Female					
Prose	22	31	30	16	100
Document	27	29	30	15	100
Quantitative	29	29	30	12	100

Source: Adult Literacy Survey, Office for National Statistics. © Crown copyright 1998

Directory of Local Education Authorities in the UK

Source: Welsh Education Office; Northern Ireland Office Education Department; Scottish Office Education Department; Department for Education and Employment. © Crown copyright 1998

England

Barking and Dagenham A P Larbalestier, England Chief Education Officer, Education Offices, Town Hall, Barking, Essex IG11 7LU; phone: (0181) 592 4500; fax: (0181) 594 9837

Barnet Martyn Kempson, Acting Director of Education Services, LBB Education Services (formerly Friern Barnet Town Hall), Friern Barnet Lane, London N11 3DL; phone: (0181) 359 2000; fax: (0181) 359 3057

Barnsley M E Warrington, Chief Education Officer, Education Offices, Berneslai Close, Barnsley, South Yorkshire S70 2HS; phone: (01226) 770770; fax: (01226) 773599

Bath and North East Somerset Roy Jones, Director of Education, Cultural and Community Service, Bath and North East Somerset Council, PO Box 25, Riverside, Temple Street, Keynsham, Bristol BS18 1DN; phone: (01225) 477000; fax: (01225) 394200

Bedfordshire *(see also Luton)* Paul Brett, Director of Education, Arts and Libraries, County Hall, Bedford MK42 9AP; phone: (01234) 363222; fax: (01234) 228619

Berkshire Keith J Evans, Chief Education Officer, Education Department, Shire Hall, Shinfield Park, Reading RG2 9XE; phone: (0118 987 5444); fax: (0118) 975 0360

Bexley P McGee, Director of Education, Bexley London Borough, Hill View, Hill View Drive, Welling, Kent DA16 3RY; phone: (0181) 303 7777; fax: (0181) 319 4302

Birmingham Tim Brighouse, Chief Education Officer, Education Department, Council House, Margaret Street, Birmingham B3 3BU; phone: (0121) 235 2590; fax: (0121) 235 1318

Bolton Margaret Blenkinsop, Director of Education and Arts, PO Box 53, Paderborn House, Civic Centre, Bolton, Lancashire BL1 1JW; phone: (01204) 522311; fax: (01204) 365492

Bournemouth Kabir Shaikh, Director of Education, Bournemouth Borough Council, Dorset House, 20–22 Christ Church Road, Bournemouth BH1 3NL; phone: (01202) 552151; fax: (01202) 221137

Bradford Diana Cavanagh, Director of Education, Flockton House, Flockton Road, Bradford, West Yorkshire BD4 7RY; phone: (01274) 752111; fax: (01274) 390081

Brent John Simpson, Chief Education Officer, Department of Education, Arts, and Libraries, Brent Council, Chesterfield House, 9 Park Lane, Wembley, Middlesex HA9 7RW; phone: (0181) 937 3190; fax: (0181) 937 3023

Brighton and Hove Ann D Stokoe, Director of Educational Services, Brighton and Hove Council, King's House, Grand Avenue, Hove, East Sussex BN3 2LS; phone: (01273) 290000; fax: (01273) 293456

Bristol Richard Riddell, Director of Education, Bristol City Council, Avon House, The Haymarket, Bristol BS99 7EB; phone: (0117) 922 4401; fax: (0117) 903 7738

Bromley Ken Davis, Director of Education, London Borough of Bromley, Education Department, Bromley Civic Centre, Stockwell Close, Bromley BR1 3UH; phone: (0181) 464 3333; fax: (0181) 313 4049

Buckinghamshire *(see also Milton Keynes)* David McGahey, Chief Education Officer, County Hall, Aylesbury, Buckinghamshire HP20 1UZ; phone: (01296) 395000; fax: (01296) 383367

Bury Harold Williams, Borough Education Officer, Education Department, Athenaeum House, Market Street, Bury, Lancashire BL9 0BN; phone: (0161) 253 5000; fax: (0161) 253 5653

Calderdale Ian Jennings, Director of Education, Education Department, PO Box 33, Northgate House, Nothgate, Halifax, West Yorkshire HX1 1UN; phone: (01422) 357257; fax: (01422) 392515

Cambridgeshire Andrew Baxter, Director of Education, Libraries, and Heritage, Castle Court, Shire Hall, Castle Hill, Cambridge CB3 0AP; phone: (01223) 717111; fax: (01223) 717201

Camden Bob Litchfield, Director of Education, London Borough of Camden, Education Department, Crowndale Centre, 216–220 Eversholt Street, London NW1 1DE; phone: (0171) 911 1525; fax: (0171) 911 1536

Cheshire David Cracknell, Group Director of Educational Services, County Hall, Chester CH1 1SQ; phone: (01244) 602424; fax: (01244) 603800

Cornwall J S Harris, Secretary for Education, Education Offices, County Hall, Truro, Cornwall TR1 3BA; phone: (01872) 322000; fax: (01872) 323835

Corporation of London David Smith, City Education Officer, Corporation of London Education Department, PO Box 270, Guildhall, London EC2P 2EJ; phone: (0171) 332 1750; fax: (0171) 332 1621

Coventry Cathy Goodwin, Chief Education Officer, New Council Offices, Earl Street, Coventry CV1 5RS; phone: (01203) 833333; fax: (01203) 831620

Croydon David Sand, Director of Education, Taberner House, Park Lane, Croydon CR9 1TP; phone: (0181) 686 4433; fax: (0181) 760 0871

Cumbria John Nellist, Director of Education, Education Offices, 5 Portland Square, Carlisle CA1 1PU; phone: (01228) 606060; fax: (01228) 606896

Darlington Geoffrey Pennington, Director of Education, Darlington Borough Council, Town Hall, Darlington DL1 5QT; phone: (01325) 380651; fax: (01325) 382032

Derby Derek D'Hooghe, Director of Education, Derby City Council, 27 St Mary's Gate, Derby DE1 3NN; phone: (01332) 293111; fax: (01332) 292167

Derbyshire *(see also Derby)* Valerie Hannon, Chief Education Officer, County Offices, Matlock, Derbyshire DE4 3AG; phone: (01629) 580000; fax: (01629) 580350

Devon S W G Jenkin, Chief Education Officer, County Hall, Exeter EX2 4QG; phone: (01392) 382000; fax: (01392) 382203; e-mail: education@ched.devon-cc.gov.uk

Doncaster A M Taylor, Director of Education, PO Box 266, The Council House, Doncaster, South Yorkshire DN1 3AD; phone: (01302) 737222; fax: (01302) 737223

Dorset *(see also Bournemouth and Poole)* Richard Ely, County Education Officer, Education Department, County Hall, Colliton Park, Dorchester, Dorset DT1 1XJ; phone: (01305) 251000; fax: (01305) 224499

Dudley R P Colligan, Chief Education Officer, Westox House, 1 Trinity Road, Dudley, West Midlands DY1 1JB; phone: (01384) 818181; fax: (01384) 814216

Durham *(see also Darlington)* Keith Mitchell, Director of Education, Education Department, County Hall, Durham DH1 5UJ; phone: (0191) 386 4411; fax: (0191) 386 0487

Ealing Alan Parker, Director of Education, Perceval House, 14–16 Uxbridge Road, Ealing, London W5 2HL; phone: (0181) 579 2424; fax: (0181) 566 2676

East Riding of Yorkshire John Ginnever, Chief Education Officer, East Riding of Yorkshire Council, County Hall, Beverley, East Riding of Yorkshire HU17 9BA; phone: (01482) 887700; fax: (01482) 871137

East Sussex *(see also Brighton and Hove)* David Mallen, County Education Officer, PO Box 4, County Hall, St Anne's Crescent, Lewes, East Sussex BN7 1SG; phone: (01273) 481000; fax: (01273) 481261

Enfield Liz Graham, Director of Education, Education Department, PO Box 56, Civic Centre, Silver Street, Enfield, Middlesex EN1 3XQ; phone: (0181) 366 6565; fax: (0181) 982 7375

Essex Paul Lincoln, Director of Education, Education Department, PO Box 47, A Block, County Hall, Victoria Road, Chelmsford CM1 1LD; phone: (01245) 492211; fax: (01245) 492759

Gateshead D J Arbon, Director of Education, Education Offices, Civic Centre, Regent Street, Gateshead, Tyne and Wear NE8 1HH; phone: (0191) 477 1011; fax: (0191) 478 3495

Gloucestershire Roger Crouch, Chief Education Officer, Shire Hall, Gloucester GL1 2TP; phone: (01452) 425300; fax: (01452) 425496

Greenwich Julian Kramer, Director of Education, London Borough of Greenwich, 9th Floor, Riverside House, Beresford Street, London SE18 6PW; phone: (0181) 854 8888; fax: (0181) 855 2427

Hackney Acting Director of Education, Hackney Education Directorate, Edith Cavell House, Enfield Road, London N1 5AZ; phone: (0171) 214 8400; fax: (0171) 214 8531

Hammersmith and Fulham Christine Whatford, Director of Education, London Borough of Hammersmith and Fulham, Town Hall, King Street, London W6 9JU; phone: (0181) 748 3020; fax: (0181) 741 0153

Hampshire *(see also Portsmouth and Southampton)* P Coles, County Education Officer, The Castle, Winchester, Hampshire SO23 8UG; phone: (01962) 841841; fax: (01962) 842355

Haringey Sue Allen, Director of Education Services, London Borough of Haringey, Education Offices, 48 Station Road, Wood Green, London N22 4TY; phone: (0181) 975 9700; fax: (0181) 862 3864

Harrow Paul Osburn, Director of Education, PO Box 22, Civic Centre, Harrow, Middlesex HA1 2UW; phone: (0181) 863 5611; fax: (0181) 427 0810

Hartlepool Jeremy Fitt, Director of Education and Community Services, Hartlepool Council, Civic Centre, Victoria Road, Hartlepool, Cleveland TS24 8AY; phone: (01429) 266522; fax: (01429) 869625

Havering Colin Hardy, Director of Education and Community Services, London Borough of Havering, The Broxhill Centre, Broxhill Road, Harold Hill, Romford RM14 1XN; phone: (01708) 772222; fax: (01708) 773850

Hereford and Worcester David Stanley, County Education Officer, PO Box 73, 227 London Road, Worcester WR5 2YA; phone: (01905) 763763; fax: (01905) 763000

Hertfordshire R Shostack, Director of Education, County Hall, Hertford SG13 8DF; phone: (01992) 555827; fax: (01992) 555644; e-mail: HCCEDCH@hertscc.gov.uk

Hillingdon G Moss, Acting Director of Education, London Borough of Hillingdon, Civic Centre, Uxbridge, Middlesex UB8 1UW; phone: (01895) 250111; fax: (01895) 250878

Hounslow J D Trickett, Director of Education, Civic Centre, Lampton Road, Hounslow, Middlesex TW3 4DN; phone: (0181) 570 7728; fax: (0181) 572 4819; e-mail: info@lbhit.parasoft.co.uk

Islington Dr Hilary Nicolle, Director of Education, London Borough of Islington, Laycock Street, London N1 1TH; phone: (0171) 226 1234; fax: (0171) 457 5555

Kensington and Chelsea Roger Wood, Executive Director of Education and Libraries, Royal Borough of Kensington and Chelsea, Town Hall, Hornton Street, London W8 7NX; phone: (0171) 937 5464; fax: (0171) 937 0038

Kent Nick Henwood, Director of Education Services, Education Department, Springfield, Maidstone, Kent ME14 2LJ; phone: (01622) 671411; fax: (01622) 690892

Kingston upon Hull Joan Taylor, Director of Education, Kingston upon Hull City Council, Essex House, Manor Street, Kingston upon Hull HU1 1YD; phone: (01482) 610610; fax: (01482) 613407

Kingston upon Thames John Braithwaite, Director of Education, Royal Borough of Kingston upon Thames, Guildhall, High Street, Kingston upon Thames, Surrey KT1 1EU; phone: (0181) 546 2121; fax: (0181) 547 5296

Kirklees Rob Vincent, Chief Education Officer, Kirklees Metropolitan Council, Oldgate House, 2 Oldgate, Huddersfield HD1 6QW; phone: (01484) 221000; fax: (01484) 225264

Knowsley Peter Wylie, Director of Education, Knowsley Borough Council, Education Office, Huyton Hey Road, Huyton, Merseyside L36 5YH; phone: (0151) 489 6000; fax: (0151) 449 3852

Lambeth Heather du Quesnay, Director of Education, Lambeth Education Department, London Borough of Lambeth, Blue Star House, 234/244 Stockwell Road, London SW9 9SP; phone: (0171) 926 1000; fax: (0171) 926 2633

Lancashire Christopher J Trinick, Chief Education Officer, PO Box 61, County Hall, Preston PR1 8RJ; phone: (01772) 254868; fax: (01772) 261630

Leeds John Rawlinson, Chief Education Officer, Leeds Education Department, Selectapost 17, Merrion House, Merrion Centre, Leeds LS2 8DT; phone: (0113) 234 8080; fax: (0113) 234 1394

Leicester Tom Warren, Director of Education, Leicester City Council, Marlborough House, 38 Welford Road, Leicester LE1 6ZG; phone: (0116) 254 9922; fax: (0116) 285 5096

Leicestershire *(see also Leicester and Rutland)* Jackie Strong, Director of Education, Education Department, County Hall, Glenfield, Leicester LE3 8RF; phone: (0116) 232 3232 fax: (0116) 265 6634

Lewisham Althea Esunshile, Director of Education, London Borough of Lewisham, Laurence House, Town Hall, Catford, London SE6 4RU; phone: (0181) 695 6000; fax: (0181) 690 4392

Lincolnshire Norman Riches, Director of Education, County Offices, Newland, Lincoln LN1 1YQ; phone: (01522) 552222; fax: (01522) 553257

Liverpool M F Cogley, Director of Education, Education Offices, 14 Sir Thomas Street, Liverpool L1 6BJ; phone: (0151) 227 3911; fax: (0151) 225 3029

Inner London see separate entries for the former Inner London Education Authority (ILEA) London Boroughs: Camden, Corporation of London (covering the one square mile of the City of London), Greenwich, Hammersmith and Fulham, Hackney, Islington, Kensington and Chelsea, Lambeth, Lewisham, Southwark, Tower Hamlets, Wandsworth, Westminster

Outer London see separate entries for the following London Boroughs: Barking and Dagenham, Barnet, Bexley, Brent, Bromley, Croydon, Ealing, Enfield, Haringey, Harrow, Havering, Hillingdon, Hounslow, Kingston upon Thames, Merton, Newham, Redbridge, Richmond upon Thames, Sutton, Waltham Forest

Luton Tony Dessent, Director of Education, Luton Borough Council, Unity House, 111 Stuart Street, Luton, Bedfordshire LU1 2NP; phone: (01582) 548001; fax: (01582) 548454

Manchester Roy Jobson, Chief Education Officer, Education Offices, Crown Square, Manchester M60 3BB; phone: (0161) 234 5000; fax: (0161) 234 7073

Merton Jenny Cairns, Director of Education, Leisure and Libraries, London Borough of Merton, Crown House, London Road, Morden, Surrey SM4 5DX; phone: (0181) 543 2222; fax: (0181) 543 7126

Middlesborough Malcolm Shorney, Director of Education, Middlesborough Education Office, PO Box 191, 2nd Floor, Civic Centre, Middlesborough TS1 2XS; phone: (01642) 245432; fax: (01642) 262038

Milton Keynes Jill Stansfield, Director of Learning and Development, Milton Keynes Council, Saxon Court, 502 Avebury Boulevard, Milton Keynes MK9 3HS; phone: (01908) 691691; fax: (01908) 682456

Newcastle upon Tyne David Bell, Chief Education Officer Designate, Education Offices, Civic Centre, Barras Bridge, Newcastle upon Tyne NE1 8PU; phone: (0191) 232 8520; fax: (0191) 211 4983

Newham Ian Harrison, Director of Education, London Borough of Newham, Education Offices, Broadway House, 322 High Street, Stratford, London E15 1EP; phone: (0181) 555 5552; fax: (0181) 503 0014

Norfolk Bryan Slater, County Education Officer, County Hall, Martineau Lane, Norwich NR1 2DL; phone: (01603) 222300; fax: (01603) 222119

North East Lincolnshire Geoff Hill, Head of Professional Service – Education, North East Lincolnshire Council, Eleanor Street, Grimsby DN32 9DU; phone: (01472) 323051; fax: (01472) 323020

North Lincolnshire Trevor Thomas, Director of Education and Personal Development, North Lincolnshire Council, PO Box 35, Hewson House, Station Road, Brigg DN20 8JX; phone: (01724) 297241; fax: (01724) 297242

North Somerset Jane Wreford, Director of Education, North Somerset Council, PO Box 51, Town Hall, Weston-Super-Mare BS23 1ZZ; phone: (01934) 888888; fax: (01934) 888834

North Tyneside Les Walton, Executive Director Education, Wallsend Town Hall, High Street East, Wallsend, Tyne and Wear NE28 7RR; phone: (0191) 200 5151; fax: (0191) 200 6090

North Yorkshire *see also York* Cynthia Welbourn, Director of Education, Libraries, Archives, Museums, and Arts, County Hall, Northallerton, North Yorkshire DL7 8AE; phone: (01609) 780780; fax: (01609) 778611

Northamptonshire J R Atkinson, Director of Education and Libraries, Education Department, PO Box 149, County Hall, Guildhall Road, Northampton NN1 1AU; phone: (01604) 236236; fax: (01604) 236188

Northumberland C C Tipple, Director of Education, Education Department, County Hall, Morpeth, Northumberland NE61 2EF; phone: (01670) 533000; fax: (01670) 533750

Nottinghamshire C R Valentine, Director of Education, County Hall, West Bridgford, Nottingham NG2 7QP; phone: (0115) 982 3823; fax: (0115) 981 2824

Oldham Michael Willis, Director of Education and Leisure, Education Department, Old Town Hall, Middleton Road, Chadderton, Oldham OL9 6PP; phone: (0161) 911 4260; fax: (0161) 628 0433

Oxfordshire Graham Badman, Chief Education Officer, Education Department, Macclesfield House, New Road, Oxford OX1 1NA; phone: (01865) 792422; fax: (01865) 791637

Poole Shirley Goodwin, Policy Director Education, Poole Borough Council, Civic Centre, Poole, Dorset BH15 2RU; phone: (01202) 633633; fax: (01202) 633706

Portsmouth Anna Lawson, City Education Officer, Portsmouth City Council, Civic Offices, Portsmouth PO1 2EA; phone: (01705) 834145; fax: (01705) 834159

Redbridge D Capper, Director of Education, Education Office, London Borough of Redbridge, Lynton House, 255–259 High Road, Ilford, Essex IG1 1NN; phone: (0181) 478 3020; fax: (0181) 553 0895

Redcar and Cleveland Keith Burton, Chief Education Officer, Redcar and Cleveland Borough Council, Redcar Council Offices, PO Box 83, Kirkleatham Street, Redcar TS10 1YA; phone: (01642) 444000; fax: (01642) 444122

Richmond upon Thames G A Alexander, Director of Education, London Borough of Richmond upon Thames, Education Department, Regal House, London Road, Twickenham TW1 3QB; phone: (0181) 891 1411; fax: (0181) 891 7730

Rochdale Brian Atkinson, Director of Education, Education Department, PO Box 70, Municipal Offices, Smith Street, Rochdale OL16 1YD; phone: (01706) 647474; fax: (01706) 659475

Rotherham H C Bower, Director of Education Services, Norfolk House, Walker Place, Rotherham S60 1QT; phone: (01709) 382121; fax: (01709) 372056

Rutland Keith Bartley, Director of Education, Rutland Council, Catmose, Oakham, Rutland LE15 6HP; phone: (01572) 722577; fax: (01572) 758307

Salford David Johnston, Chief Education Officer, Education Office, Chapel Street, Salford M3 5LT; phone: (0161) 832 9751/8; fax: (0161) 835 1561

Sandwell Stuart Gallacher, Director of Education, Sandwell Metropolitan Borough Council, PO Box 41, Shaftesbury House, 402 High Street, West Bromwich, West Midlands B70 9LT; phone: (0121) 525 7366; fax: (0121) 553 1528

Sefton J Marsden, Director of Education, Sefton Borough Council, Education Department, Town Hall, Bootle, Merseyside L20 7AE; phone: (0151) 933 6003; fax: (0151) 934 3349

Sheffield Jonathon Crossley Holland, Director of Education, PO box 67, Leopold Street, Sheffield S1 1RJ; phone: (0114) 272 6341; fax: (0114) 273 6279

Shropshire Carol Adams, Chief Education Officer, The Shirehall, Abbey Foregate, Shrewsbury SY2 6ND; phone: (01743) 251000; fax: (01743) 254415

Solihull David Nixon, Director of Education, PO Box 20, Council House, Solihull, West Midlands B91 3QU; phone: (0121) 704 6000; fax: (0121) 704 6669

Somerset John Rose and John Freeman, Acting Chief Education Officers, County Hall, Taunton, Somerset TA1 4DY; phone: (01823) 355455; fax: (01823) 355332

South Gloucestershire Terese Gillespie, Director of Education, South Gloucestershire Offices, Bowling Hill, Chipping Sodbury BS17 6JX; phone: (01454) 863333; fax: (01454) 863264

South Tyneside I L Reid, Director of Education, Education Department, Town Hall Civic Offices, Westoe Road, South Shields, Tyne and Wear NE33 2RL; phone: (0191) 427 1717; fax: (0191) 427 0584

Southampton Bob Hogg, Director of Education, Southampton City Council, Civic Centre, Southampton SO14 7LL; phone: (01703) 223855; fax: (01703) 833221

Southwark Gordon Mott, Director of Education, London Borough of Southwark, 1 Bradenham Close (off Albany Road), London SE17 2QA; phone: (0171) 525 5000; fax: (0171) 525 5025

St Helens Colin Hilton, Director of Education, Community Education Department, The Rivington Centre, Rivington Road, St Helens, Merseyside WA10 4ND; phone: (01744) 456000; fax: (01744) 455350

Staffordshire *see also Stoke-on-Trent* P J Hunter, Chief Education Officer, County Buildings, Tipping Street, Stafford ST16 2DH; phone: (01785) 223121; fax: (01785) 56727

Stockport Max Hunt, Director of Education, Education Division, Stopford House, Stockport SK1 3XE; phone: (0161) 480 4949; fax: (0161) 477 9530

Stockton-on-Tees Stanley Bradford, Chief Education Officer, Stockton-on-Tees Council, PO Box 228, Municipal Buildings, Church Road, Stockton-on-Tees TS18 1XE; phone: (01642) 393939; fax: (01642) 393479

Stoke-on-Trent Nigel Rigby, Director of Education, City of Stoke-on-Trent Council, Swann House, Boothen Road, Stoke-on-Trent ST4 7TD; phone: (01782) 236100; fax: (01782) 236102

Suffolk David Peachey, Chief Education Officer, Education Department, St Andrew House, County Hall, Ipswich IP4 1LJ; phone: (01473) 584800; fax: (01473) 584624

Sunderland John Williams, Director of Education, Education Department, PO Box 101, Town Hall and Civic Centre, Sunderland SR2 7DN; phone: (0191) 553 1000; fax: (0191) 553 1400

Surrey Paul Gray, County Education Officer, County Hall, Penrhyn Road, Kingston upon Thames KT1 2DJ; phone: (0181) 541 9501; fax: (0181) 541 9503

Sutton Ian Birnbaum, Director of Education, London Borough of Sutton, The Grove, Carshalton SM5 3AL; phone: (0181) 770 5000; fax: (0181) 770 6545

Swindon Mike Lusty, Chief Education Officer, Swindon Borough Council, Sanford House, Sanford Street, Swindon SN1 2QH; phone: (01793) 463000; fax: (01793) 534145

Tameside A M Webster, Director of Education, Tameside Metropolitan Borough Council, Education Department, Council Offices, Wellington Road, Ashton under Lyne, Lancashire OL6 6DL; phone: (0161) 342 8355; fax: (0161) 342 3260

Tower Hamlets Christine Gilbert, Chief Education Officer, London Borough of Tower Hamlets, Education Department, Mulberry Place, 5 Clove Crescent, London E14 2BG; phone: (0171) 364 5000; fax: (0171) 364 4296

Trafford Kathryn August, Director of Education, Trafford Borough Council, PO Box 19, Education Department, Sale Town Hall, Tatton Road, Sale M33 7YR; phone: (0161) 912 1212; fax: (0161) 912 3075

Wakefield John McLeod, Chief Education Officer, Education Department, County Hall, Bond Street, Wakefield, West Yorkshire WF1 2QL; phone: (01924) 306090; fax: (01924) 305632

Walsall Tim Howard, Corporate Director for Education and Culture, The Civic Centre, Darwall Street, Walsall, West Midlands WS1 1DQ; phone: (01922) 650000; fax: (01922) 722322

Waltham Forest Andrew Lockhart, Chief Education Officer, London Borough of Waltham Forest, Municipal Offices, High Road, Leyton, London E10 5QJ; phone: (0181) 527 5544; fax: (0181) 527 5544

Wandsworth Paul Robinson, Director of Education, London Borough of Wandsworth, Town Hall, Wandsworth High Street, London SW18 2PU; phone: (0181) 871 8013; fax: (0181) 871 6609

Warwickshire Eric Wood, County Education Officer, 22 Northgate Street, Warwick CV34 4SR; phone: (01926) 410410; fax: (01926) 412746

West Sussex R D C Bunker, Director of Education, County Hall, West Street, Chichester, West Sussex PO19 1RF; phone: (01243) 777100; fax: (01243) 777229

Westminster Deirdre McGrath, Director of Education and Leisure Department, City of Westminster, PO Box 240, Westminster City Hall, Victoria Street, London SW1E 6QP; phone: (0171) 641 6000; fax: (0171) 641 3404

Wigan R J Clark, Director of Education, Education Offices, Gateway House, Standishgate, Wigan WN1 1XL; phone: (01942) 828891; fax: (01942) 828811

Wiltshire *see also Swindon* Lindsey Davis, Chief Education Officer, County Hall, Bythesea Road, Trowbridge, Wiltshire BA14 8JB; phone: (01225) 713000; fax: (01225) 713982

Wirral D Rigby, Director of Education, Wirral Metropolitan Borough Council, Hamilton Building, Conway Street, Birkenhead L41 4FD; phone: (0151) 666 2121; fax: (0151) 666 4207

Wolverhampton Roy Lockwood, Director of Education, Education Department, Civic Centre, St Peter's Square, Wolverhampton WV1 1RR; phone: (01902) 556556; fax: (01902) 314218

York Mike Peters, Director of Education, City of York Council, 10–12 George Hudson Street, York YO1 1ZG; phone: (01904) 613161; fax: (01904) 554249

The Islands

Guernsey D T Neale, Director of Education, Education Department, Grange Road, St Peter Port, Guernsey, Channel Islands GY1 1RQ; phone: (01481) 710821; fax: (01481) 714475

Jersey B Grady, Director of Education, Education Department, PO Box 142, St Saviour, Jersey JE4 8QJ; phone: (01534) 509500

Isle of Man G A Baker, Director of Education, Education Department, Murray House, Mount Hevelock, Douglas, Isle of Man IM1 2SG; phone: (01624) 685820; fax: (01624) 685834

Isle of Wight Alan Kaye, Director of Education, County Hall, Newport, Isle of Wight PO30 1UD; phone: (01983) 821000; fax: (01983) 521817

Isles of Scilly P S Hygate, Secretary for Education, Education Department, Town Hall, St. Mary's, Isles of Scilly TR21 0LW; phone: (01720) 422537; fax: (01720) 422202

Northern Ireland

Belfast T G J Moag, Chief Executive of the Education and Library Board, 40 Academy Street, Belfast BT1 2NQ; phone (01232) 564000; fax: (01232) 331714

North-Eastern G Topping, Chief Executive of the Education and Library Board, 182 Galgorm Road, Ballymena, Co Antrim BT42 1HN; phone: (01266) 653333; fax: (01266) 46071

South-Eastern J B Fitzsimons, Chief Executive of the Education and Library

Board, Grahamsbridge Road, Dundonald, Belfast BT16 0HS; phone: (01232) 566200; fax: (01232) 566266/7

Southern J G Kelly, Chief Executive of the Education and Library Board, 3 Charlemont Place, The Mall, Armagh BT61 9AX; phone: (01861) 512200; fax: (01861) 512490

Western P J Martin, Chief Executive of the Education and Library Board, 1 Hospital Road, Omagh, Co Tyrone BT79 0AW; phone: (01662) 411411; fax: (01662) 411400

Scotland

Aberdeen J Stodter, Director of Education, Sumerhill Education Centre, Stronsay Drive, Aberdeen AB15 6JA; phone: (01224) 208626; fax: (01224) 208674

Aberdeenshire M White, Director of Education, Woodhill House, Westburn Road, Aberdeen AB16 5GB; phone: (01224) 665420; fax: (01224) 665445

Angus J Anderson, Director of Education, County Buildings, Market Street, Forfar DD8 3WE; phone: (01307) 461460 x 3236; fax: (01307) 461848

Argyll and Bute A Morton, Director of Education, Argyll House, Alexandra Parade, Dunoon, Argyll PA23 8AJ; phone: (01369) 704000; fax: (01369) 702614

Clackmannanshire K Bloomer, Director of Education and Community Services, Lime Tree House, Castle Street, Alloa FK10 1EX; phone: (01259) 450000; fax: (01259) 452440

Comhairle nan Eilann Siar N Galbraith, Director of Education and Leisure Services, Sandwick Road, Stornoway, Isle of Lewis HS1 2BW; phone: (01851) 703773 x 430; fax: (01851) 705796

Dumfries & Galloway K Macleod, Director of Education, 30 Edinburgh Road, Dumfries DG1 1NW; phone: (01387) 260427; fax: (01387) 260453

Dundee A Wilson, Director of Education, Tayside House, Crichton Street, Dundee DD1 3RJ; phone: (01382) 433088; fax: (01382) 433080

East Ayrshire J Mulgrew, Director of Education, Council Headquarters, London Road, Kilmarnock KA3 7BU; phone: (01563) 576000; fax: (01563) 576210

East Dunbartonshire I Mills, Director of Education and Leisure Services, Boclair House, 100 Milngavie Road, Bearsden, Glasgow G61 2TQ; phone: (0141) 942 9000; fax: (0141) 942 6814

East Lothian A Blackie, Director of Education and Community Services, Council Buildings, Haddington EH41 3HA; phone: (01620) 827631; fax: (01620) 827291

East Renfrewshire E Currie, Director of Education, Eastwood Park, Rouken Glen

Road, Giffnock, Glasgow G46 6UG; phone: (0141) 577 3430; fax: (0141) 577 3405

Edinburgh E Reid, Director of Education, George IV Bridge, Edinburgh EH1 1UQ; phone: (0131) 469 3322; fax: (0131) 469 3320

Falkirk G Young, Director of Education, McLaren House, Marchmont Avenue, Polmont FK2 0NZ; phone: (01324) 506600; fax: (01324) 506664

Fife A McKay, Head of Education, Fife House, North Street, Glenrothes, Fife KY7 5LT; phone: (01592) 414141; fax: (01592) 416411

Glasgow K Corsar, Director of Education, House 1, Charing Cross Complex, 20 India Street, Glasgow G2 4PF; phone: (0141) 287 2000; fax: (0141) 287 6892

Highland A Gilchrist, Director of Education, Glenurquhart Road, Inverness IV3 5NX; phone: (01463) 702000; fax: (01463) 702828

Inverclyde B McLeary, Director of Education Services, Department of Education Services, 105 Dalrymple Street, Greenock PA15 1HT; phone: (01475) 882824; fax: (01475) 726412

Midlothian D MacKay, Director of Education, Midlothian House, Buccleugh Street, Dalkeith EH22 1DJ; phone: (0131) 660 7738; fax: (0131) 660 7765

Moray K Gavin, Director of Education, High Street, Elgin IV30 1BX; phone: (01343) 563134; fax: (01343) 563416

North Ayrshire J Travers, Director of Education, Cunninghame House, Friars Croft, Irvine KA12 8EF; phone: (01294) 324411; fax: (01294) 324444

North Lanarkshire M O'Neill, Director of Education, Municipal Building, Kildonan Street, Coatbridge ML5 3BT; phone: (01236) 812336; fax: (01236) 812335

Orkney Islands M Drever, Acting Director of Education, School Place, Kirkwall, Orkney KW15 1NY; phone: (01856) 873535 x 2401; fax: (01856) 870302

Perth & Kinross R McKay, Director of Education, Blackfriars, Perth PH1 5LT; phone: (01738) 476211; fax: (01738) 476210

Renfrewshire S Rae, Director of Education, Cotton Street, Paisley PA1 1LE; phone: (0141) 842 5000; fax: (0141) 842 5655

Scottish Borders J Christie, Director of Education, Council Headquarters, Newtown St Boswells, Melrose TD6 0SA; phone: (01835) 824000 x 451; fax: (01835) 822145

Shetlands Islands J Halcrow, Director of Education, Schlumberger Base, Gremista Industrial Estate, Lerwick, Shetland ZE1 0PX; phone: (01595) 744300; fax: (01595) 692810

South Ayrshire M McCabe, Director of Educational Services, Wellington Square, Ayr KA7 1DR; phone: (01292) 612201; fax: (01292) 612258

South Lanarkshire M Allan, Director of Education, Council Offices, Almada Street, Hamilton ML3 0AA; phone: (01698) 454545; fax: (01698) 454465

Stirling G Jeyes, Director of Education, Viewforth, Stirling FK8 2ET; phone: (01786) 443322; fax: (01786) 442782

West Dunbartonshire I McMurdo, Director of Education, Council Offices, Garshake Road, Dumbarton G82 3PU; phone: (01389) 737000; fax: (01389) 737348

West Lothian R Stewart, Corporate Manager of Education Services, Lindsay House, South Bridge Street, Bathgate EH48 1TS; phone: (01506) 776000; fax: (01506) 776378

Wales

Blaenau Gwent B Mawby, Director of Education, Victoria House, Victoria Business Park, Ebbw Vale NP3 6ER; phone: (01495) 350555; fax: (01495) 355495

Bridgend D Matthews, Director of Education & Leisure Services, Education Department, County Council Offices, Sunnyside, Bridgend CF31 4AR; phone: (01656) 642000; fax: (01656) 642646

Cardiff T Davies, Director of Education, County Hall, Atlantic Wharf, Cardiff CF1 5UW; phone: (01222) 872000; fax: (01222) 872777

Caerphilly J N O Harries, Director of Education & Leisure Services, County Offices, Caerphilly Road, Ystrad Mynach, Hengoed CF82 7EP; phone: (01443) 864948; fax: (01443) 816998

Carmarthenshire K P Davies, Director of Education, Pibwrlwyd, Carmarthen SA31 2NH; phone: (01267) 234567; fax: (01267) 221692

Ceredigion R J Williams, Director of Education, Education Department, County Offices, Marine Terrace, Aberystwyth SY23 2DE; phone: (01970) 617581; fax: (01970) 615348

Conwy R Elwyn Williams, Director of Education, Education Department, Government Buildings, Dinerth Road, Colwyn Bay LL28 4UL; phone: (01492) 544261 x 4561; fax: (01492) 541311

Denbighshire E Lewis, Director of Education, Shire Hall, Mold CH7 6GU; phone: (01824) 706777; fax: (01824) 706780

Flintshire K McDonogh, Director of Education, Libraries, and Information, County Hall, Mold CH7 6ND; phone: (01352) 704010; fax: (01352) 754202

Gwynedd D Whittall, Director of Education, Shire Hall Street, Caernarfon LL55 1SH; phone: (01286) 679162; fax: (01286) 677347

Isle of Anglesey R P Jones, Director of Education, Ffordd Glan Hwfa, Llangefni, Ynys Mon LL77 7HY; phone: (01248) 752920; fax: (01248) 752999/750533

Merthyr Tydfil D Jones, Director of Education, Ty Keir Hardie, Riverside Court, Avenue de Clichy, Mertyr Tydfil CF47 8XD; phone: (01685) 724600

Monmouthshire D Young, Director of Education, County Hall, Cwmbran NP44 2XH; phone: (01633) 644644; fax: (01633) 644488/644525

Neath Port Talbot V Thomas, Director of Education, Civic Centre, Port Talbot SA13 1PJ; phone: (01639) 763333; fax: (01639) 763000

Newport G Bingham, Director of Education, Civic Centre, Newport NP9 4UR; phone: (01633) 232206; fax: (01633) 233376

Pembrokeshire G Davies, Director of Education, Cambria House, PO Box 27, Haverfordwest SA61 1TP; phone: (01437) 764551 x 5860; fax: (01437) 769557

Powys R J Barker, Director of Education, Llandridnod Wells LD1 5LG; phone: (01597) 826433; fax: (01597) 826475

Rhondda Cynon Taff K Ryley, Director of Education, Education Centre, Grawen Street, Porth CF39 0BU; phone: (01443) 687666; fax: (01443) 680286

Swansea R Parry, Acting Director of Education, County Hall, Swansea SA1 3SN; phone: (01792) 636000; fax: (01792) 636333

Torfaen M de Val, Director of Education, County Hall, Cwmbran NP44 2XH; phone: (01633) 648106; fax: (01633) 648164

Vale of Glamorgan A Davies, Director of Education, Civic Offices, Holton Road, Barry CF63 4RU; phone: (01446) 700111; fax: (01446) 745566

Wrexham T Garner, Director of Education and Leisure Services, Roxburgh House, Hill Street, Wrexham LL11 1SN; phone: (01978) 297471; fax: (01978) 297422

UK Further and Higher Education

Numbers and Percentages Continuing Education Aged 16 and over in the UK

The data in this table are provisional. The table includes 1994/95 data for Wales and 1994/95 further education institution data for England. Figures in parentheses are percentages of the total population in that age group.
(– = not applicable. N = nil or negligible.)

1995/96

Sector	All students[1]	Age at 31 August 1995[2]						
		16	17	18	16–18	19–20	21–24	25 and over[3]
Total population	–	729,000	671,000	655,000	2,055,000	1,392,000	3,258,000	N
Full-Time and Sandwich Students								
schools	491,000	278,000 (38.2)	191,000 (28.5)	19,000 (2.9)	488,000 (23.7)	3,000 (0.2)	N	N
further education	764,000	228,000 (31.3)	194,000 (28.9)	104,000 (15.9)	526,000 (25.6)	58,000 (4.2)	48,000 (1.5)	127,000
higher education	1,036,000	1,000 (0.2)	12,000 (1.7)	139,000 (21.3)	152,000 (7.4)	374,000 (26.9)	295,000 (9.1)	213,000
Total	2,291,000	508,000 (69.6)	396,000 (59.0)	262,000 (40.0)	1,166,000 (56.7)	435,000 (31.2)	343,000 (10.5)	340,000
Part-Time Students								
further education	2,803,000	102,000 (14.0)	73,000 (10.9)	73,000 (11.1)	248,000 (12.1)	159,000 (11.4)	424,000 (13.0)	1,955,000
higher education[4]	596,000	1,000 (1.9)	1,000 (2.2)	5,000 (2.5)	7,000 (2.2)	21,000 (2.6)	69,000 (3.2)	486,000
Total	3,398,000	103,000 (14.1)	74,000 (11.1)	78,000 (11.9)	255,000 (12.4)	180,000 (12.9)	493,000 (15.1)	2,441,000
TOTAL[5]	5,690,000	611,000 (83.8)	470,000 (70.1)	339,000 (51.8)	1,421,000 (69.1)	615,000 (44.2)	836,000 (25.7)	2,782,000

[1] At 1 July for Northern Ireland schools and further education, and at 31 December for Northern Ireland higher education and Scotland schools.
[2] Figures include ages unknown for Wales, Scotland, and Northern Ireland.
[3] Figures include ages unknown for Northern Ireland.
[4] Figures exclude 78,900 students enrolled on nursing and paramedical courses at Department of Health establishments.
[5] Figures may not add up to totals due to rounding.

Source: Department for Education and Employment; Welsh Office; The Scottish Office Education and Industry Department; Department of Education Northern Ireland. © Crown copyright 1998

First Destinations of Higher Education Graduates in the UK

(N = nil or negligible.)

1996

Destination	Doctorate degrees	Other postgraduate degrees	Postgraduate certificates in education	First degrees	Undergraduate diplomas/ certificates	Total	%
UK employment[1]	3,500	9,700	13,200	109,700	7,900	144,000	56
UK employment with termination date after 30 September/not fixed term	2,600	7,400	9,200	73,500	5,800	98,400	38
UK employment with termination date before 30 September	500	1,000	2,700	22,800	800	27,700	11
Self-employment in the UK	100	400	N	2,600	200	3,300	1
Overseas employment (UK-domiciled students)	500	600	300	4,400	100	5,900	2
Overseas employment (overseas-domiciled students)	900	3,100	N	2,100	100	6,200	2
Education and training in the UK	200	2,900	200	36,200	8,800	48,300	19
Education and training overseas	N	500	N	1,400	N	2,000	1
Overseas graduates returning overseas (no other information available)	1,300	7,700	200	11,100	600	20,900	8
Not available for employment, study, or training	100	500	300	8,200	400	9,500	4
Assumed to be unemployed	100	800	800	14,400	900	17,000	7
Others[2]	N	100	100	2,800	200	3,200	1
Total of known destination	6,700	25,900	15,100	190,300	19,000	256,900	83
Unknown	1,800	7,100	2,700	35,100	7,200	53,900	17
TOTAL	8,400	33,000	17,800	225,400	26,300	310,800	100

[1] Includes those employed in the UK with unknown employment termination date.
[2] Includes those students whose main activity was given as 'Seeking employment or training', and who had employment, study, or training as a secondary activity.

Source: Higher Education Statistics Agency. © Crown copyright 1998

Degrees and Diplomas Obtained by Full-Time Students in the UK

The data in this table are for calendar years.
(N/A = not available.)

	1985[1][2]	1986[1]	1987[1]	1988[1]	1989[1]	1990[1]	1991[1]	1992[1]	1993[1]	1994/95[3][4]	1995/96[3][4]
Degrees											
First degrees: honours											
men	36,119	35,823	35,845	36,735	37,473	38,342	39,360	41,908	43,624	N/A	N/A
women	26,122	25,988	26,601	27,799	28,578	30,121	31,659	34,423	36,983	N/A	N/A
First degrees: ordinarys[5]											
men	6,057	5,405	5,518	5,520	5,301	4,973	4,879	4,980	4,891	N/A	N/A
women	3,911	3,696	3,853	3,702	3,601	3,745	3,739	3,582	3,591	N/A	N/A
First degree totals											
men	N/A	N/A	N/A	N/A	N/A	N/A	N/A	N/A	N/A	104,977	111,050
women	N/A	N/A	N/A	N/A	N/A	N/A	N/A	N/A	N/A	106,864	115,576
Higher degrees											
men	16,802	17,354	18,559	19,176	20,424	20,905	22,689	24,929	27,568	19,634[6]	23,743
women	6,754	7,219	8,008	8,676	9,794	10,419	11,912	14,034	16,374	20,973[6]	25,283
Total											
Men	58,978	58,582	60,059	61,431	63,198	64,202	66,928	71,817	76,101	124,611	133,793
Women	36,787	36,903	38,475	40,177	41,973	44,285	47,310	52,039	56,948	127,837	140,859
Diplomas and Certificates											
Men	6,447	5,867	6,800	6,659	6,621	6,712	7,914	8,811	9,470	16,606[7]	15,661
Women	5,751	5,706	6,303	6,611	6,599	7,000	8,997	9,881	11,584	17,199[7]	16,975

[1] Figures exclude the Open University and former polytechnics and central institutions that obtained university status in 1992.
[2] Figures include Ulster Polytechnic, which merged with the University of Ulster in 1984.
[3] Figures include students in all publicly funded higher education institutions including the Open University and former polytechnics and colleges.
[4] Data are for the academic year, not the calendar year.
[5] Includes some degrees where the class is not recorded.
[6] Figures include all postgraduate qualifications.
[7] Figures include other undergraduate qualifications.

Source: Higher Education Funding Council for England and Higher Education Statistics Agency. © Crown copyright 1998

Enrolments in Further and Higher Education, by Type of Course and Gender, in the UK

Enrolments include home and overseas students.

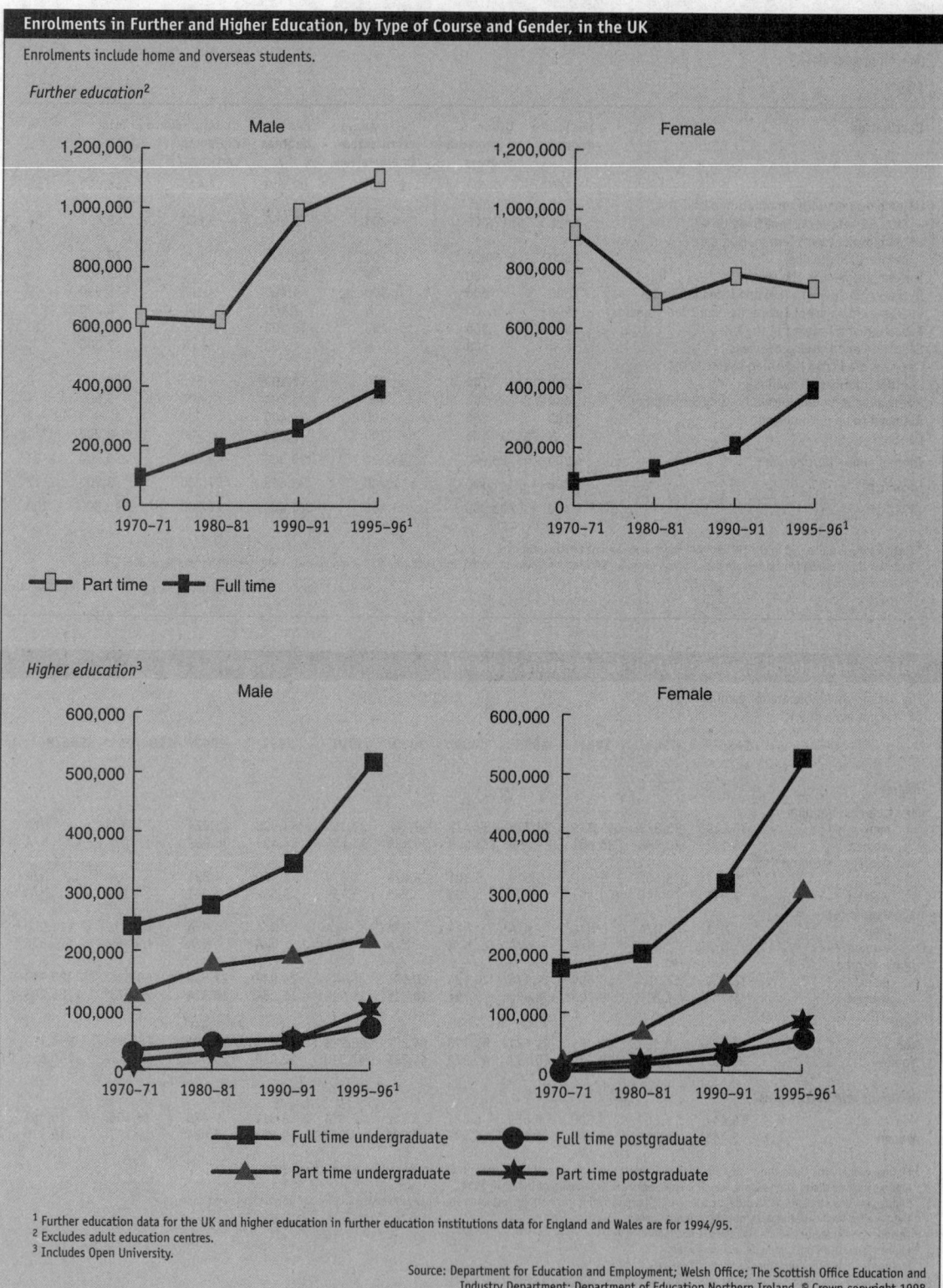

Further education[2]

Male

Female

Part time   Full time

Higher education[3]

Male

Female

Full time undergraduate   Full time postgraduate

Part time undergraduate   Part time postgraduate

[1] Further education data for the UK and higher education in further education institutions data for England and Wales are for 1994/95.
[2] Excludes adult education centres.
[3] Includes Open University.

Source: Department for Education and Employment; Welsh Office; The Scottish Office Education and Industry Department; Department of Education Northern Ireland. © Crown copyright 1998

Loans to Students in the UK

Characteristic	1990/91	1991/92	1992/93	1993/94	1994/95	1995/96	As at 23 July 1997
Take-up for academic year	180,000	261,000	345,000	430,000	517,000	560,000	587,834
Total value of loans	£70 million	£139 million	£227 million	£317 million	£539 million	£701 million	£874.6 million
Estimated number of eligible students	643,000	709,000	786,000	919,000	945,000	948,800	929,500
Take-up percentage	28	37	44	47	55	59	63.2
Size of average loan	£389	£533	£658	£737	£1,043	£1,252	£1,487

Source: Student Loans Company Ltd

Overseas Students in Higher Education in the UK

The data in this table are for the 50 countries with the most students studying in the UK.

1995/96

Country of origin	Postgraduate	First degree	Other undergraduate	Total	Country of origin	Postgraduate	First degree	Other undergraduate	Total
Malaysia	4,778	13,287	467	18,532	Nigeria	855	669	184	1,708
Greece	6,634	9,567	852	17,053	Thailand	1,277	315	61	1,653
Ireland, Republic of	4,233	9,976	2,502	16,711	Denmark	552	616	392	1,560
Germany	3,764	4,677	3,942	12,383	Iran	1,234	131	38	1,403
France	2,803	4,981	3,512	11,296	Korea, South	1,023	257	111	1,391
Hong Kong	5,537	5,464	282	11,283	Australia	907	267	107	1,281
USA	3,750	1,278	3,568	8,596	Saudi Arabia	1,010	149	55	1,214
Spain	1,571	3,085	2,592	7,248	Finland	331	511	324	1,166
Singapore	2,915	3,788	77	6,780	Brazil	948	78	34	1,060
Italy	1,799	1,786	1,261	4,846	South Africa	829	171	46	1,046
Japan	2,131	1,260	844	4,235	Mexico	950	56	38	1,044
Netherlands	1,406	1,313	582	3,301	Sri Lanka	419	523	81	1,023
Canada	2,047	533	311	2,891	Switzerland	439	415	164	1,018
Norway	640	1,877	254	2,771	Austria	349	287	322	958
Taiwan	2,093	529	125	2,747	Mauritius	237	537	167	941
China	2,298	323	125	2,746	Indonesia	703	185	47	935
Cyprus	943	1,600	80	2,623	Brunei	156	640	128	924
Belgium	816	1,236	457	2,509	Zimbabwe	444	303	135	882
Israel	807	1,610	23	2,440	Botswana	347	421	85	853
India	1,561	409	169	2,139	Tanzania	413	263	58	734
Sweden	471	744	644	1,859	United Arab Emirates	397	270	18	685
Pakistan	1,164	524	120	1,808	Muscat and Oman	239	351	53	643
Kenya	606	1,056	128	1,790	Kuwait	332	275	22	629
Turkey	1,371	296	92	1,759	Zambia	300	261	65	626
Portugal	846	643	237	1,726	Libya	580	22	16	618

Source: Higher Education Statistics Agency. © Crown copyright 1998

Grants from Research Councils to Higher Education Institutions in the UK

The data in this table are for the 30 higher education institutions receiving the largest grants from the research councils that come under the Office of Science and Technology. These councils include the Biotechnology and Biological Sciences Research Council, the Natural Environment Research Council, the Engineering and Physical Sciences Research Council, the Economic and Social Sciences Research Councils, the Particle Physics and Astronomy Research Council, and the Medical Research Council. The data also include income from the British Academy.

1995/96

Rank	Institution	Research council grant (£)	Rank	Institution	Research council grant (£)
1	The University of Oxford	41,820,000	16	The University of Newcastle-upon-Tyne	8,728,000
2	The University of Cambridge	38,357,000	17	The University of Warwick	8,647,000
3	University College London	32,423,000	18	The University of Sussex	7,906,000
4	Imperial College of Science, Technology, & Medicine	30,476,000	19	Queen Mary and Westfield College	7,389,000
5	The University of Edinburgh	23,079,000	20	The University of Manchester Institute of Science & Technology	7,134,000
6	The University of Birmingham	18,005,000	21	University of Durham	6,866,000
7	The University of Manchester	17,825,000	22	The University of Reading	6,796,000
8	The University of Southampton	17,298,000	23	The University of York	6,333,000
9	The University of Glasgow	15,774,000	24	The University of Bath	6,301,000
10	The University of Sheffield	14,975,000	25	King's College, London	5,867,000
11	The University of Leeds	14,110,000	26	The University of Strathclyde	5,533,000
12	The University of Nottingham	12,435,000	27	The University of Surrey	5,436,000
13	The University of Leicester	12,351,000	28	The University of Lancaster	5,323,000
14	The University of Bristol	12,330,000	29	The University of Essex	5,119,000
15	The University of Liverpool	12,239,000	30	Loughborough University	5,101,000

Source: Higher Education Statistics Agency. © Crown copyright 1998

New and Current Student Awards in the UK

The figures for current awards include those for new awards.

Awards	1984/85	1986/87	1988/89	1990/91	1991/92[1]	1992/93	1993/94[2]	1994/95
New Awards								
Postgraduate awards: made by education departments and the research councils	9,400	9,300	8,700	11,500	11,300	11,300	11,700[3]	11,700
Local education authorities postgraduate discretionary awards[4]	3,500	4,300	4,900	3,900	3,600	3,200	2,400[3]	1,800
Teacher training awards	18,900	19,500	21,800	26,200	33,300	35,200	37,100	36,500
Full value higher education[5]	174,200	176,900	185,600	232,400	276,000	289,400	310,000	310,400
Full value further education[5]	174,200	176,900	185,600	232,400	276,000	32,800	23,900	19,000
Lesser value further education and higher education[6]	83,500	94,500	88,900	81,200	102,000	97,600	126,700	109,400
All new awards	289,500	304,500	309,900	355,200	426,200	469,400	511,900	488,700
Current Awards								
Postgraduate awards: made by education departments and the research councils	18,200	17,300	17,200	19,500	20,900	21,200	21,200[3]	21,700
Local education authorities postgraduate discretionary awards[4]	4,000	7,000	7,000	4,200	3,900	3,300	2,600[3]	1,900
Teacher training awards	38,100	40,500	43,700	51,500	60,000	66,200	70,200	73,300
Full value higher education[5]	467,700	476,100	501,400	588,800	648,400	730,000	806,700	855,700
Full value further education[5]						50,300	42,300	29,200
Lesser value further education and higher education[6]	127,900	135,200	128,900	114,900	143,900	156,900	177,100	154,000
All current awards	656,000	676,100	698,200	778,900	877,000	1,027,900	1,120,100	1,135,800

[1] Includes 1990/91 data for Northern Ireland.
[2] Includes revised data.
[3] Includes 1992/93 data for Northern Ireland.
[4] Discretionary awards for postgraduate study made under Section 2 of the Education Act, 1962, (excludes initial teacher training) in England and Wales, and discretionary awards for postgraduate study made by the Northern Ireland Education and Library Boards under the Education and Libraries (NI) Order, 1986.
[5] Full value awards are those paid at between 50 and 100% of the mandatory rate.
[6] Lesser value awards are those paid at less than 50% of the mandatory rate.

Source: Education Departments. © Crown copyright 1998

Full-Time Academic Teaching and Research Staff at Higher Education Institutions in the UK

(– = not applicable. N/A = not available.)

Academic years

	Professors	Readers and senior lecturers	Lecturers and assistant lecturers	Researchers	Other	Total	% annual change
1979/80[1]	4,337	8,734	20,518	N/A	661	34,250	1.6
1980/81[1]	4,382	8,809	20,460	N/A	646	34,297	0.1
1981/82[1]	4,351	8,777	20,045	N/A	562	33,735	–1.6
1982/83[1]	4,017	8,284	18,885	N/A	456	31,642	–6.2
1983/84[1]	3,893	8,145	18,595	N/A	463	31,096	–1.7
1984/85[1][2]	3,807	7,942	18,737	N/A	557	31,043	–0.2
1985/86[1]	3,959	8,025	18,850	N/A	578	31,412	1.2
1986/87[1]	4,070	8,074	18,711	N/A	577	31,432	0.1
1987/88[1]	4,160	8,291	18,268	N/A	542	31,261	–0.5
1988/89[1]	4,093	8,266	17,778	N/A	484	30,621	–2.0
1989/90[1]	4,261	8,618	17,903	N/A	558	31,340	2.3
1990/91[1]	4,520	8,842	17,830	N/A	669	31,861	1.7
1991/92[1]	4,872	9,270	17,824	N/A	672	32,638	2.4
1992/93[1]	5,226	9,650	17,854	N/A	717	33,447	2.5
1993/94[1]	5,545	9,890	18,275	N/A	787	34,497	3.1
1994/95[3]	6,762	16,949	39,295	4,662	4,842	72,510	–
1995/96[3]	7,947	17,457	41,503	5,412	5,582	77,901	7.4

[1] Includes full-time teaching and research staff in posts wholly financed from general university funds but excludes the Open University and the former polytechnics and central institutions who obtained university status in 1992.
[2] Includes Ulster Polytechnic, which merged with the University of Ulster in October 1984.
[3] Includes full-time academic staff of at least 25 percent full-time equivalence who are wholly institutionally financed for all publicly funded higher education institutions (including the Open University and the former polytechnics and colleges).

Source: 1974/75–1993/94 Higher Education Funding Council for England; 1994/95–1995/96 Higher Education Statistics Agency. © Crown copyright 1998

Selected Degree Abbreviations in the UK

BA Bachelor of Arts
BAgr Bachelor of Agriculture
BA(Lan) Bachelor of Languages
BAO Bachelor of Obstetrics
BArch Bachelor of Architecture
BChD Bachelor of Dental Surgery
BCL Bachelor of Civil Law
BCom Bachelor of Commerce
BCommunications Bachelor of Communications
BCS Bachelor of Combined Studies
BD Bachelor of Divinity
BDS Bachelor of Dental Surgery
BEd Bachelor of Education
BEng Bachelor of Engineering
BJur Bachelor of Jurisprudence
BLitt Bachelor of Letters
BMedSci Bachelor of Medical Science
BMet Bachelor of Metallurgy
BMus Bachelor of Music
BPharm Bachelor of Pharmacy
BPhil Bachelor of Philosophy
BSc Bachelor of Science

BSc(Econ) Bachelor of Science in Economics
BscEng Bachelor of Science in Engineering
BscTech Bachelor of Technical Science
BSocSc Bachelor of Social Sciences
BTech Bachelor of Technology
BTh Bachelor of Theology
BVSc Bachelor of Veterinary Science
ChB Bachelor of Surgery
ChM Master of Surgery
DCL Doctor of Civil Law
DD Doctor of Divinity
DDS Doctor of Dental Surgery
DDSc Doctor of Dental Science
DLitt Doctor of Letters
DM Doctor of Medicine
DMus Doctor of Music
DPhil Doctor of Philosophy
DSc Doctor of Science
DT Doctor of Theology
LittD Doctor of Letters
LLB Bachelor of Law
LLD Doctor of Law
LLM Master of Law
MA Master of Arts
MArb Master of Arboriculture

MArch Master of Architecture
MB Bachelor of Medicine
MBA Master of Business Administration
MCh Master of Surgery
MChD Master of Dental Surgery
MChemA Master in Chemical Analysis
MCL Master of Civil Law
MCom Master of Commerce
MD Doctor of Medicine
MDS Master of Dental Surgery
MEcon Master of Economics
MEd Master of Education
MEng Master of Engineering
MLing Master of Languages
MLitt Master of Letters
MMus Master of Music
MPharm Master of Pharmacy
MPhil Master of Philosophy
MPhys Master of Physics
MSc Master of Science
MSc(Econ) Master of Science in Economics
MSW Master in Social Work
MTech Master of Technology
MTh Master of Theology
MVSc Master of Veterinary Science
PhD Doctor of Philosophy

Directory of Universities in the UK

Source: Higher Education Statistics Agency.
© Crown copyright 1998

The numbers for students are for undergraduate and postgraduate students, full-time and part-time, for the academic year 1995/6. The numbers for staff are for full-time academic staff in the academic year 1995/6.

Aberdeen University of Aberdeen, University Office, Regent Walk, Aberdeen AB24 3FX; phone: (01224) 272000; fax: (01224) 273717; students: 11,521; staff: 1,132; Chief Officer: Professor C Duncan Rice

Abertay University of Abertay Dundee, Bell Street, Dundee DD1 1HG; phone: (01382) 308000; fax: (01382) 308877; students: 4,127; staff: 265; Chief Officer: Professor B King

Aberystwyth University of Wales at Aberystwyth, Old College, King Street, Aberystwyth, Dyfed SY23 2AX; phone: (01970) 623111; fax: (01970) 611446; students: 8,139; staff: 488; Chief Officer: Professor D L I Morgan

Anglia Anglia Polytechnic University, Rivermead Campus, Bishop Hall Lane, Chelmsford, Essex CM1 1SQ; phone: (01245) 493131; fax: (01245) 495419; students: 19,235; staff: 640; Chief Officer: Mr M C Malone-Lee

Aston Aston University, Aston Triangle, Birmingham B4 7ET; phone: (0121) 359 3611; fax: (0121) 333 6350; students: 5,488; staff: 332; Chief Officer: Professor M T Wright

Bangor University of Wales at Bangor, College Road, Bangor, Gwynedd LL57 2DG; phone: (01248) 351151; fax: (01248) 370451; students: 7,958; staff: 558; Chief Officer: Professor H R Evans

Bath University of Bath, Bath BA2 7AY; phone: (01225) 826826; fax: (01225) 462508; students: 8,044; staff: 806; Chief Officer: Professor V D Vandelinde

Belfast Queen's University of Belfast, University Road, Belfast BT7 1NN; phone: (01232) 245133; fax: (01232) 247895; students: 19,151; staff: 1,165; Chief Officer: Professor George S Bain

Birkbeck College Malet Street, London WC1E 7HX; phone: (0171) 631 6000; fax: (0171) 631 6270; students: 11,213; staff: 375; Chief Officer: Professor Tim O'Shea

Birmingham University of Birmingham, Edgbaston, Birmingham B15 2TT; phone: (0121) 414 3344; fax: (0121) 414 3971; students: 22,567; staff: 2,222; Chief Officer: Professor J M Irvine

Bournemouth Bournemouth University, Talbot Campus, Fern Barrow, Poole, Dorset BH12 5BB; phone: (01202) 524111; fax: (01202) 595069; students: 9,444; staff: 486; Chief Officer: Professor Gillian L Slater

Bradford University of Bradford, Richmond Road, Bradford, West Yorkshire BD7 1DP; phone: (01274) 733466; fax: (01274) 385460; students: 9,123; staff: 669; Chief Officer: Professor D J Johns

Brighton University of Brighton, Mithras House, Lewes Road, Brighton BN2 4AT; phone: (01273) 600900; fax: (01273) 642010; students: 14,192; staff: 722; Chief Officer: Professor D J Watson

Bristol University of Bristol, Senate House, Tyndall Avenue, Bristol BS8 1TH; phone: (0117) 928 9000; fax: (0117) 925 1424; students: 17,566; staff: 1,886; Chief Officer: Sir John F C Kingman

Brunel Brunel University, Uxbridge, Middlesex UB8 3PH; phone: (01895) 274000; fax: (01895) 232806; students: 13,921; staff: 686; Chief Officer: Professor M J Sterling

Cambridge University of Cambridge, University Offices, The Old Schools, Cambridge CB2 1TN; phone: (01223) 337733; fax: (01223) 332332; students: 18,827; staff: 3,581; Chief Officer: Professor Alec Broers

Cardiff University of Wales at Cardiff, PO Box 920, Cardiff CF1 3XP; phone: (01222) 874000; fax: (01222) 874130; students: 17,833; staff: 1,285; Chief Officer: Professor E B Smith

Central England University of Central England in Birmingham, Franchise Street, Perry Barr, Birmingham B42 2SU; phone: (0121) 331 5000; fax: (0121) 331 6317; students: 18,227; staff: 787; Chief Officer: Dr Peter C Knight

Central Lancashire University of Central Lancashire, Preston PR1 2HE; phone: (01772) 201201; fax: (01772) 892936; students: 17,406; staff: 680; Chief Officer: Mr B G Booth

City University The City University, Northampton Square, London EC1V 0HB; phone: (0171) 477 8000; fax: (0171) 477 8561; students: 11,209; staff: 602; Chief Officer: Professor R N Franklin

Coventry Coventry University, Priory Street, Coventry, West Midlands CV1 5FB; phone: (01203) 631313; fax: (01203) 838793; students: 15,022; staff: 762; Chief Officer: Dr M Goldstein

Cranfield Cranfield University, Cranfield, Bedfordshire MK43 0AL; phone: (01234) 750111; fax: (01234) 750972; students: 2,944; staff: 699; Chief Officer: Professor F R Hartley

De Montfort De Montfort University, The Gateway, Leicester LE1 9BH; phone: (0116) 255 1551; fax: (0116) 247 1690; students: 21,242; staff: 1,181; Chief Officer: Professor K Barker

Derby University of Derby, Kedleston Road, Derby DE22 1GB; phone: (01332) 622222; fax: (01332) 294861; students: 11,842; staff: 413; Chief Officer: Professor R Waterhouse

Dundee University of Dundee, Nethergate, Dundee DD1 4HN; phone: (01382) 223181; fax: (01382) 201604; students: 9,080; staff: 929; Chief Officer: Dr Ian J Graham-Bryce

Durham University of Durham, Old Shire Hall, Old Elvet, Durham DH1 3HP; phone: (0191) 374 2000; fax: (0191) 374 7250; students: 11,920; staff: 967; Chief Officer: Professor E A V Ebsworth

East Anglia University of East Anglia, University Plain, Norwich NR4 7TJ; phone: (01603) 456161; fax: (01603) 458553; students: 9,997; staff: 792; Chief Officer: Mr Vincent Watts

East London University of East London, Romford Road, Stratford, London E15 4LZ; phone: (0181) 590 7000; fax: (0181) 519 3740; students: 12,278; staff: 547; Chief Officer: Professor F W Gould

Edinburgh University of Edinburgh, Old College, South Bridge, Edinburgh EH8 9YL; phone: (0131) 650 1000; fax: (0131) 650 2147; students: 17,576; staff: 2,378; Chief Officer: Professor Sir Stewart R Sutherland

Essex University of Essex, Wivenhoe Park, Colchester, Essex CO4 3SQ; phone: (01206) 873333; fax: (01206) 873598; students: 7,345; staff: 482; Chief Officer: Professor I Crewe

Exeter University of Exeter, Northcote House, The Queen's Drive, Exeter, Devon EX4 4QJ; phone: (01392) 263263; fax: (01392) 263108; students: 11,391; staff: 770; Chief Officer: Sir Geoffrey Holland

Glamorgan University of Glamorgan, Pontypridd, Rhondda Cynon Taff CF37 1DL; phone: (01443) 480480; fax: (01443) 480558; students: 14,501; staff: 514; Chief Officer: Professor A L Webb

Glasgow University of Glasgow, The University, University Avenue, Glasgow G12 8QQ; phone: (0141) 339 8855; fax: (0141) 330 4920; students: 18,610; staff: 2,190; Chief Officer: Professor Sir Graeme Davies

Glasgow Caledonian Glasgow Caledonian University, Cowcaddens Road, Glasgow G4 0BA; phone: (0141) 331 3000; fax: (0141) 331 3005; students: 12,165; staff: 654; Chief Officer: Mr W J Laurie

Goldsmiths College University of London, New Cross, London SE14 6NW; phone: (0171) 919 7171; fax: (0171) 919 7113; students: 6,617; staff: 306; Chief Officer: Professor K J Gregory

Greenwich University of Greenwich, Bexley Road, Eltham, London SE9 2PQ; phone: (0181) 331 8000; fax: (0181) 331 8145; students: 16,921; staff: 673; Chief Officer: Dr D Fussey

Heriot-Watt Heriot-Watt University, Riccarton, Edinburgh EH14 4AS; phone: (0131) 449 5111; fax: (0131) 449 5153; students: 8,904; staff: 610; Chief Officer: Professor J S Archer

Hertfordshire University of Hertfordshire, College Lane, Hatfield, Hertfordshire AL10 9AB; phone: (01707) 284000; fax: (01707) 284115; students: 16,605; staff: 755; Chief Officer: Professor N K Buxton

Huddersfield The University of Huddersfield, Queensgate, Huddersfield HD1 3DH; phone: (01484) 422288; fax: (01484) 516151; students: 12,791; staff: 619; Chief Officer: Professor John Tarrant

Hull University of Hull, Cottingham Road, Hull HU6 7RX; phone: (01482) 346311; fax: (01482) 465936; students: 12,084; staff: 781; Chief Officer: Professor D N Dilks

Imperial College of Science, Technology, and Medicine Exhibition Road, South Kensington, London SW7 2AZ; phone: (0171) 589 5111; fax: (0171) 584 7596; students: 8,304; staff: 2,239; Chief Officer: Professor Sir Ronald Oxburgh

Keele Keele University, Keele, Staffordshire ST5 5BG; phone: (01782) 621111; fax: (01782) 632343; students: 10,234; staff: 570; Chief Officer: Professor Janet Finch

Kent University of Kent at Canterbury, The Registry, Canterbury CT2 7NZ; phone: (01227) 764000; fax: (01227) 452196; students: 11,205; staff: 685; Chief Officer: Professor Robin Sibson

King's College London Strand, London WC2R 2LS; phone: (0171) 836 5454; fax: (0171) 836 1799; students: 13,420; staff: 1,361; Chief Officer: Professor A M Lucas

Kingston Kingston University, River House, 53–57 High Street, Kingston upon Thames, Surrey KT1 1LQ; phone: (0181) 547 2000; fax: (0181) 547 7009; students: 13,696; staff: 650; Chief Officer: Dr R C Smith

Lampeter University of Wales at Lampeter, Ceredigion SA48 7ED; phone: (01570) 422351; fax: (01570) 423423; students: 1,757; staff: 105; Chief Officer: Professor Keith G Robbins

Lancaster University of Lancaster, University House, Lancaster LA1 4YW; phone: (01524) 65201; fax: (01524) 594294; students: 11,872; staff: 815; Chief Officer: Professor W Ritchie

Leeds University of Leeds, The University, Leeds LS2 9JT; phone: (0113) 243 1751; fax: (0113) 233 4123; students: 23,125; staff: 2,385; Chief Officer: Professor A G Wilson

Leeds Metropolitan Leeds Metropolitan University, Calverley Street, Leeds LS1 3HE; phone: (0113) 283 2600; fax: (0113) 283 3109; students: 16,986; staff: 651; Chief Officer: Professor L Wagner

Leicester University of Leicester, University Road, Leicester LE1 7RH; phone: (0116) 252 2522; fax: (0116) 252 2200; students: 15,928; staff: 1,276; Chief Officer: Dr K J R Edwards

Liverpool University of Liverpool, PO Box 147, Liverpool L69 3BX; phone: (0151) 794 2000; fax: (0151) 708 6502; students: 16,740;

staff: 1,793; Chief Officer: Professor P N Love

Liverpool John Moores Liverpool John Moores University, Rodney House, 70 Mount Pleasant, Liverpool L3 5UX; phone: (0151) 231 2121; fax: (0151) 709 9864; students: 19,315; staff: 885; Chief Officer: Professor Peter Toyne

London University of London (central institutes and activities), Senate House, Malet Street, London WC1E 7HU; phone: (0171) 636 8000; fax: (0171) 631 0118; Chief Officer: Professor Graham Zellick

London Business School London Business School, Sussex Place, Regent's Park, London NW1 4SA; phone: (0171) 262 5050; fax: (0171) 724 7875; students: 1,002; staff: 110; Chief Officer: Professor George Sayers Bain

London Guildhall London Guildhall University, 31 Jewry Street, London EC3N 2EY; phone: (0171) 320 1000; fax: (0171) 320 1390; students: 10,967; staff: 356; Chief Officer: Professor R C Floud

London School of Economics and Political Science Houghton Street, London WC2A 2AE; phone: (0171) 405 7686; fax: (0171) 242 0392; students: 5,877; staff: 501; Chief Officer: Professor Anthony Giddens

London School of Hygiene and Tropical Medicine Keppel Street, Gower Street, London WC1E 7HT; phone: (0171) 927 2277; fax: (0171) 636 7679; students: 554; staff: 316; Chief Officer: Professor H Spencer

Loughborough Loughborough University of Technology, Ashby Road, Loughborough, Leicestershire LE11 3TU; phone: (01509) 263171; fax: (01509) 223900; students: 10,596; staff: 948; Chief Officer: Professor D J Wallace

Luton University of Luton, Park Square, Luton, Bedfordshire LU1 3JU; phone: (01582) 734111; fax: (01582) 418677; students: 13,063; staff: 625; Chief Officer: Dr A J Wood

Manchester University of Manchester, Oxford Road, Manchester M13 9PL; phone: (0161) 275 2000; fax: (0161) 275 2407; students: 22,282; staff: 2,670; Chief Officer: Professor M B Harris

University of Manchester Institute of Science and Technology (UMIST), PO Box 88, Sackville Street, Manchester M60 1QD; phone: (0161) 236 3311; fax: (0161) 228 7040; students: 6,583; staff: 915; Chief Officer: Professor R F Boucher

Manchester Metropolitan Manchester Metropolitan University, All Saints Building, Manchester M15 6BH; phone: (0161) 247 2000; fax: (0161) 247 6390; students: 28,433; staff: 1,349; Chief Officer: Mrs A V Burslem

Middlesex Middlesex University, Bramley Road, Trent Park, London N14 4YZ; phone: (0181) 362 5000; fax: (0181) 449 0798;

students: 19,978; staff: 684; Chief Officer: Professor Michael Driscoll

Napier Napier University, Craiglockhart Campus, 219 Colinton Road, Edinburgh EH14 1DJ; phone: (0131) 444 2266; fax: (0131) 455 4666; students: 8,788; staff: 610; Chief Officer: Professor J Mavor

Newcastle upon Tyne University of Newcastle upon Tyne, 6 Kensington Terrace, Newcastle upon Tyne NE1 7RU; phone: (0191) 222 6000; fax: (0191) 222 6229; students: 15,501; staff: 1,955; Chief Officer: Mr J R G Wright

Newport University of Wales College Newport, Caerleon Campus, PO Box 179, Newport NP6 1YG; phone: (01633) 430088; fax: (01633) 432006; students: 6,433; staff: 177; Chief Officer: Professor K J Overshott

North London University of North London, 166–220 Holloway Road, London N7 8DB; phone: (0171) 607 2789; fax: (0171) 753 5166; students: 13,233; staff: 64; Chief Officer: Mr B Roper

Northumbria University of Northumbria at Newcastle, Ellison Building, Ellison Place, Newcastle upon Tyne NE1 8ST; phone: (0191) 232 6002; fax: (0191) 227 4017; students: 18,887; staff: 1,019; Chief Officer: Professor G Smith

Nottingham University of Nottingham, University Park, Nottingham NG7 2RD; phone: (0115) 951 5151; fax: (0115) 951 5733; students: 22,143; staff: 1,862; Chief Officer: Professor Sir Colin Campbell

Nottingham Trent Nottingham Trent University, Burton Street, Nottingham NG1 4BU; phone: (0115) 941 8418; fax: (0115) 947 3523; students: 22,542; staff: 896; Chief Officer: Professor R Cowell

Open University The Open University, Walton Hall, Milton Keynes MK7 6AA; phone: (01908) 274066; fax: (01908) 858581; students: 147,951; staff: 980; Chief Officer: Sir John S Daniel

Oxford University of Oxford, University Offices, Wellington Square, Oxford OX1 2JD; phone: (01865) 270000; fax: (01865) 270708; students: 19,957; staff: 3,516; Chief Officer: Dr Colin R Lucas

Oxford Brookes Oxford Brookes University, Gipsy Lane Campus, Gipsy Lane, Headington, Oxford OX3 0BP; phone: (01865) 741111; fax: (01865) 483073; students: 11,392; staff: 572; Chief Officer: Professor G Upton

Paisley University of Paisley, High Street, Paisley, Renfrewshire PA1 2BE; phone: (0141) 848 3000; fax: (0141) 887 0812; students: 7,951; staff: 410; Chief Officer: Professor R W Shaw

Plymouth University of Plymouth, Drake Circus, Plymouth PL4 8AA; phone: (01752) 600600; fax: (01752) 232011; students: 19,464; staff: 878; Chief Officer: Professor R J Bull

Portsmouth University of Portsmouth, University House, Winston Churchill Avenue, Portsmouth PO1 2UP; phone: (01705) 876543; fax: (01705) 843082; students: 14,659; staff: 932; Chief Officer: Professor John Craven

Queen Mary and Westfield College Mile End Road, London E1 4NS; phone: (0171) 975 5555; fax: (0171) 975 5500 ; students: 8,648; staff: 1,260; Chief Officer: Professor G J Zellick

Reading University of Reading, Whiteknights PO Box 217, Reading RG6 6AH; phone: (0118) 987 5123; fax: (0118) 931 4404; students: 13,739; staff: 800; Chief Officer: Professor R Williams

Robert Gordon Robert Gordon University, Schoolhill, Aberdeen AB10 1FR; phone: (01224) 262000; fax: (01224) 263000; students: 7,625; staff: 496; Chief Officer: Professor W Stevely

Royal College of Art Royal College of Art, Kensington Gore, London SW7 2EU; phone: (0171) 590 4444; fax: (0171) 590 4500; students: 791; staff: 43; Chief Officer: Professor Christopher Frayling

Royal College of Music Royal College of Music, Prince Consort Road, London SW7 2BS; phone: (0171) 589 3643; fax: (0171) 589 7740; students: 534; staff: 11; Chief Officer: Dr Janet E Ritterman

Royal Holloway Royal Holloway and Bedford New College, Egham, Surrey TW20 0EX; phone: (01784) 434455; fax: (01784) 437520; students: 5,765; staff: 494; Chief Officer: Professor N W Gowar

St Andrews University of St Andrews, College Gate, North Street, St Andrews KY16 9AJ; phone: (01334) 476161; fax: (01334) 462543; students: 5,890; staff: 669; Chief Officer: Professor S Arnott

Salford University of Salford, Salford M5 4WT; phone: (0161) 745 5000; fax: (0161) 745 5999; students: 8,935; staff: 555; Chief Officer: Professor M Harloe

The School of Oriental and African Studies Thornhaugh Street, Russell Square, London WC1H 0XG; phone: (0171) 637 2388; fax: (0171) 436 3844; students: 3,125; staff: 204; Chief Officer: Sir Tim Lankester

Sheffield University of Sheffield, Firth Court, Western Bank, Sheffield S10 2TN; phone: (0114) 222 2000; fax: (0114) 276 8496; students: 23,625; staff: 1,990; Chief Officer: Professor Sir Gareth Roberts

Sheffield Hallam Sheffield Hallam University, Pond Street, Sheffield S1 1WB; phone: (0114) 272 0911; fax: (0114) 253 2042; students: 20,066; staff: 1,073; Chief Officer: Mr J M Stoddart

Southampton University of Southampton, Highfield, Southampton SO17 1BJ; phone: (01703) 595000; fax: (01703) 593939; students: 15,257; staff: 1,719; Chief Officer: Professor Howard Newby

South Bank South Bank University, 103 Borough Road, London SE1 0AA; phone: (0171) 928 8989; fax: (0171) 815 8155; students: 20,160; staff: 861; Chief Officer: Professor G Bernbaum

Staffordshire Staffordshire University, Beaconside, Stafford ST18 0AD; phone: (01782) 294000; fax: (01782) 745447; students: 15,122; staff: 684; Chief Officer: Professor C E King

Stirling University of Stirling, The University, Stirling FK9 4LA; phone: (01786) 473171; fax: (01786) 463000; students: 7,293; staff: 479; Chief Officer: Professor Andrew Miller

Strathclyde University of Strathclyde, McCance Building, 16 Richmond Street, Glasgow G1 1XQ; phone: (0141) 552 4400; fax: (0141) 552 0775; students: 20,378; staff: 1,433; Chief Officer: Professor J P Arbuthnott

Sunderland University of Sunderland, Langham Tower, Ryhope Road, Sunderland, Tyne and Wear SR2 7EE; phone: (0191) 515 2000; fax: (0191) 515 2435; students: 14,331; staff: 524; Chief Officer: Dr A M Wright

Surrey University of Surrey, Guildford, Surrey GU2 5XH; phone: (01483) 300800; fax: (01483) 300803; students: 11,712; staff: 831; Chief Officer: Professor P J Dowling

Sussex University of Sussex, Sussex House, Falmer, Brighton BN1 9RH; phone: (01273) 606755; fax: (01273) 678335; students: 11,397; staff: 848; Chief Officer: Professor G R Conway

Swansea University of Wales at Swansea, Singleton Park, Swansea SA2 8PP; phone: (01792) 205678; fax: (01792) 295618; students: 11,395; staff: 838; Chief Officer: Professor R H Williams

Teesside University of Teesside, Borough Road, Middlesbrough, Cleveland TS1 3BA; phone: (01642) 218121; fax: (01642) 342067; students: 11,673; staff: 551; Chief Officer: Professor D Fraser

Thames Valley Thames Valley University, St Mary's Road, Ealing, London W5 5RF; phone: (0181) 579 5000; fax: (0181) 566 1353; students: 18,538; staff: 595; Chief Officer: Dr M R Fitzgerald

Ulster University of Ulster, University House, Cromore Road, Coleraine, County Londonderry BT52 1SA; phone: (01265) 44141; fax: (01265) 324927; students: 19,554; staff: 1,211; Chief Officer: Lord Smith

University College London Gower Street, London WC1E 6BT; phone: (0171) 387 7050; fax: (0171) 387 8057; students: 15,341; staff: 2,942; Chief Officer: Sir Derek Roberts

Warwick University of Warwick, Senate House, Coventry CV4 7AL; phone: (01203) 523523; fax: (01203) 461606; students: 19,228; staff: 1,392; Chief Officer: Professor Sir Brian Follett

West of England University of the West of England at Bristol, Coldharbour Lane, Frenchay, Bristol BS16 1QY; phone: (0117) 965 6261; fax: (0117) 976 3972; students: 18,723; staff: 991; Chief Officer: Mr A C Morris

Westminster University of Westminster, 309 Regent Street, London W1R 8AL; phone: (0171) 911 5000; fax: (0171) 911 5103; students: 18,997; staff: 723; Chief Officer: Dr Geoffrey Copland

Wolverhampton University of Wolverhampton, Wulfruna Street, Wolverhampton, West Midlands WV1 1SB; phone: (01902) 321000; fax: (01902) 322680; students: 23,874; staff: 807; Chief Officer: Professor M J Harrison

York University of York, Heslington, York YO1 5DD; phone: (01904) 430000; fax: (01904) 433433; students: 6,770; staff: 868; Chief Officer: Professor R U Cooke

Web Sites

BBC Education Home Page

URL: `"http://www.bbc.co.uk/education/"`

Regularly updated page containing resources for teachers and schoolchildren. As well as Web pages on a variety of issues related to current BBC programmes, the 'learning station' has age and key stage-related online games and exercises for both primary and secondary schoolchildren. This site also contains resources for teachers and parents. There is quite a lot of promotion of the BBC's products here, but there are also plenty of freely available educational resources.

British Council Virtual Education Campus

URL: `"http://www.britcoun.org/
        eis/index.htm"`

Guide to British education provided by the British Council, for those wishing to study in Britain or to learn more about the British educational system.

Global Show-and-Tell

URL: `"http://www.telenaut.com/gst/"`

Gallery of children's art from around the globe.

Independent Schools Information Service

URL: `"http://www.isis.org.uk/"`

Official site of the organization that represents all of the UK's independent schools. As well as a fully searchable list of the schools, there is advice on how to choose a school, information for non-UK residents and recent press releases of the organization.

International Kids Space

URL: `"http://www.kids-space.org/"`

Interactive and colourful space for children's activities. You can pick an image and create a story.

Kids' International Gallery

URL: `"http://www.kids- space.org/
        gallery/gallery.html"`

Fun and interactive gallery for kids to share their artwork and stories and to chat with one another.

Nothing Matters

URL: `"http://www.serve.com/Nowhere/"`

Provocative site that begins with the assumption that teaching and learning are both equally useless pastimes. Through an imaginary conversation, the processes of teaching and learning are examined.

Open University

URL: `"http://www.open.ac.uk/"`

There are examples of the university's distance-learning programmes, an online prospectus, and details of the current crop of BBC weekend programmes.

UCAS Home Page

URL: `"http://www.ucas.ac.uk/"`

Official site for the Universities and Colleges Admissions Service. It is divided into four sections: a comprehensive search facility for all 'universities, colleges, and courses'; an 'advice centre' with information for both prospective students and parents, as well as details of how to apply for university electronically; information for 'for higher education staff'; and 'studentUK' which includes news, views, and advice for students.

UK Sensitive Map – Universities

URL: `"http://www.scit.wlv.ac.uk/
        ukinfo/uk.map.html"`

Clickable map produced by the University of Wolverhampton that allows you to browse around all of the UK's universities and colleges. Click on the town you want to view to be taken straight to the institution's official site. This site also includes a clickable map of many UK research sites.

RELIGION AND BELIEF

The Year in Review

13 July 1997 The General Synod of England, meeting in York, passes a motion calling for renewed debate on homosexuality, focusing on whether practising homosexuals could be ordained as priests.

29 August 1997 An entrance fee for visitors to Westminster Abbey in London, is charged for the first time. Previously, visitors were only charged for viewing certain parts of the Abbey, such as the royal chapels. The fee is set at £4.

29 August 1997 The Roman Catholic church in Rome, issues new guidelines for handling doctrinal differences within the Church.

31 August 1997 A celebration to mark the 100th anniversary of the Zionist movement ends in Basel, Switzerland. Theodor Herzl convened the first Zionist conference there 100 years ago to work towards a Jewish homeland.

3 September 1997 A vote in Newfoundland, Canada, ends church control of state schools. Local Roman Catholic groups are expected to appeal.

13 September 1997 A state funeral is held in Calcutta, India, for Mother Teresa, the Nobel Peace Prize-winning Catholic nun who served the poor in Calcutta for nearly 70 years. Hundreds of thousands of mourners from a range of cultures and religions visited Calcutta to pay their respects since her death on 5 September from heart failure.

26 September 1997 Russian President Boris Yeltsin signs a bill that curbs religious freedom, reversing many freedoms granted in 1990 by the Soviet Union. Activities of religious groups that have not been registered for at least 15 years would be restricted. The Vatican and the USA condemn the bill.

30 September 1997 The Roman Catholic church issues a statement, titled the 'Declaration of Repentance', in which it formally apologizes for its silence when the French government deported Jews to Nazi death camps in Germany and Poland during World War II. The statement is considered the most direct apology for the silence of the Roman Catholic church during the Holocaust.

4 October 1997–5 October 1997 The Promise Keepers, a US right-wing all-male Christian organization with a massive national following, hold an assembly on the Mall in Washington DC. Feminist opponents of the group object to their tenet of unquestioned male authority in the family.

31 October 1997 Pope John Paul II con-

demns the failure of Christians to speak out against the genocide of the Jews at the hands of the Nazis during World War II. Although the pope acknowledges that the church was responsible for anti-semitism in the past, he does not apologize directly to the Jews on behalf of the Roman Catholic church.

1 November 1997 Martin Luther King III, the eldest son of Martin Luther King, Jr, is elected president of the Southern Christian Leadership Conference in the USA.

5 November 1997 English church leader Richard Harries, the Bishop of Oxford, calls for the age of homosexual consent to be lowered from 18 to 16. He is the first current bishop to speak out publicly on the issue.

24 November 1997 The Church of England General Synod begins a five-day conference in London. The agenda includes a review of the church's institutions as well as social issues such as human fertilization.

27 November 1997 Approximately 28,000 couples are married by the Rev. Sun Myung Moon of the Unification Church in Washington DC, in a ceremony broadcast around the world via satellite.

14 December 1997 President Fidel Castro of Cuba, in anticipation of a visit from Pope John Paul II, announces that Christmas will be an official holiday in Cuba for the first time in 30 years.

25 December 1997 In his annual Christmas message, Pope John Paul II calls for action against poverty and freedom from political and ethnic violence.

12 January 1998 The German government announces the establishment of a 200 million mark pension fund that will compensate Jewish Holocaust survivors from Eastern and Central Europe.

16 January 1998 The Constitutional Court in Turkey bans the Islamist Refah (Welfare) Party, the country's largest political party, because it violates a constitutional mandate for a secular government.

21 January 1998–25 January 1998 Pope John Paul II visits Cuba for the first time, where he criticizes the repression of personal and religious freedoms under the communist government of President Fidel Castro.

24 February 1998–27 February 1998 Demonstrations are held in Istanbul, Turkey, to protest against a government ban on religious clothing in state schools and universities that included the traditional Muslim long beards and head scarfs. The government relaxes the ban as a result.

4 March 1998 Roman Catholic priests are outraged when the European Union requires that Communion wafers have a sell-by date.

29 March 1998 Israeli archaeologists announce that they have discovered the oldest ruins ever found of a Jewish synagogue, dating from around 70 BC, near Jericho in the West Bank.

30 March 1998 Thousands of Buddhists gather at Taiwan's Chang Kai-shek airport in Taipei to welcome the arrival from India of a tooth believed to have been from Buddha.

12 April 1998 British gay rights campaigner Peter Tatchell is arrested after climbing the pulpit and disrupting the traditional Easter sermon of the Archbishop of Canterbury, at Canterbury Cathedral. Tatchell, a leader of the gay rights group Outrage!, is protesting against the Archbishop's attitude towards homosexuals.

30 April 1998 The Roman Catholic church apologizes to the victims of Eric Taylor, a priest jailed for seven years for abusing young boys at an orphanage in Coleshill, Warwickshire, in the years 1957–76. Taylor was accused of sexually abusing boys as young as six, then allowing the children to be beaten by nuns when they complained to the nuns of their ordeals.

April 1998 The 1998 John M Templeton Prize for Progress in Religion is awarded to British businessman and philanthropist Sigmund Sternburg.

13 May 1998 A portrait is uncovered on the wall of a chapel in Domremy, France, believed to be the only surviving likeness of the French heroine Joan of Arc.

15 May 1998 The US House of Representatives passes a Religious Persecution Bill by a vote of 375–41. The bill imposes sanctions on nations guilty of extreme acts of persecution such as enslavement and murder.

30 May 1998 The Global March for Jesus, an international Christian movement involving an estimated 10 million people around the world, opens. The focus of the march is religious persecution.

7 June 1998 The Evangelical Alliance in the UK holds a national day of prayer, involving Christians from more than 20 denominations nationwide.

10 June 1998 The Southern Baptist Church, the largest Protestant group in the USA, add an amendment to their basic code of beliefs that says a wife must 'submit graciously' to the leadership of her husband.

World Religions and Beliefs

Major World Faiths

Note: for religions other than Christianity, the abbreviations CE and BCE have been used for dates instead of AD and BC, in accordance with multi-faith practice.

Baha'i

The Baha'i faith originated in the mid-19th century in the area of present-day Iran. It is based on the belief that the man born as Mirza Husayn Ali in 1817 was the prophet sent by God to the present age. He is now known as Baha'u'llah – 'the Glory of God'. Baha'is believe that there have been revelations from God appropriate to each era, including the Torah, the New Testament, the Koran, and the words of the Buddha and the Hindu god Krishna. Baha'is maintain that these revelations have been superseded, although not contradicted, by the writings of Baha'u'llah and his successor Abdul Baha. These writings form the main body of Baha'i scripture. Baha'is believe that humanity is constantly evolving and growing more adult in its understanding and behaviour, and thus gradually becoming capable of forming one world rather than diverse nations, races, and religions. Baha'is also believe in One God, creator of all, and that humanity is a special creation, essentially good. The Baha'i teachings stress economic justice, equal rights, and education for all, and the breaking down of traditional barriers of race, class, and creed. These are seen as flaws that will disappear as the Baha'i faith becomes universal. The Baha'i international headquarters is in Haifa, Israel, and includes an International House of Justice in preparation for the time when there will be one world government, guided by the Baha'i faith. The Baha'i community meet in local spiritual assemblies whose structure is democratic and participatory, intended as a model for universal government. There are 5 million Baha'is worldwide in more than 175 countries, with the largest concentrations in the USA (approximately 300,000) and Africa (approximately 1 million). The claim that the Baha'i sacred texts are the successor to the Koran has led to criticism of Baha'i in many Muslim lands, including Iran, where the faith began. Most Baha'is today are not from Iran.

Buddhism

Buddhists follow the teachings of Siddhartha Gautama, given the title of the Buddha – the 'enlightened' or 'awakened' one. He was born the son of a nobleman in northern India in the 6th century BCE. He grew up in a palace protected from the harsh realities of life, but when he eventually encountered suffering, old age, and death, he left the palace to search for understanding of suffering and the way to end it. When he reached enlightenment, he began to teach the Four Noble Truths: Suffering exists; There is a reason for suffering; There is a way to end suffering; The way to end suffer-ing is through the Eightfold Path. The Eightfold Path consists of Right Views, Right Thoughts, Right Speech, Right Action, Right Livelihood, Right Effort, Right Mindfulness, and Right Concentration. By learning and practising this path one can eventually escape the cycle of birth and death. Buddhists believe that all beings are reborn into many different forms because of the ties of desire. When desire is allowed to cool like a fire going out, the attachment to the cycle of birth and death is loosened. Buddhists try to perfect the qualities of wisdom, compassion, and harmlessness in order to achieve enlightenment, or Buddhahood, leading to the highest peace and freedom, which is nirvana. According to Buddhist tradition, there have been other Buddhas both before and since Siddhartha Gautama. The teachings of the Buddha were handed down orally and eventually written in the first century BCE in a collection of writings called the *Tripitaka* – 'three baskets'. Different versions survive in Chinese, Tibetan, and Pali (an ancient south Indian language), and they are now translated into hundreds of languages worldwide. There are also important Buddhist scriptures written by later sages and scholars, many of them in the ancient Indian language Sanskrit. There are three main branches of Buddhism: Theravada, found mainly in southeast Asia, Sri Lanka, and India; Tibetan Mahayana; and Chinese/Japanese Mahayana. There is also a wide variety of new Buddhist movements. Each branch of Buddhism has its own festivals. The most common is Wesak (May/June), which celebrates the birth, enlightenment, and death of the Buddha, all of which happened on the same day in different years. It is impossible to estimate the number of Buddhists worldwide, as there is no central organization. The majority of Buddhists live in Asia, although Buddhism is growing rapidly beyond Asia, particularly in the USA and UK. More than 85 percent of the population of Myanmar (Burma) and Thailand are Buddhists, and more than 70 percent in Cambodia, Laos, and Japan. Buddhism is the state religion in Thailand and Bhutan. There is no central authority in Buddhism, each school having its own teachers and spiritual guides, although figures such as the Dalai Lama have raised the worldwide profile of Buddhism and voiced a Buddhist viewpoint on world affairs.

Christianity

Christians believe in one God who created the universe, and created human beings to have a special relationship with him. Through human wilfulness, exemplified in the story of Adam and Eve, this relationship was broken. Christians believe that because of his love for humanity, God took on the form of a man, Jesus, in order to bring them back into a relationship with him. The Gospels relate that Jesus was conceived by a virgin, Mary, through the power of God, and was born as a baby in Bethlehem. Modern scholarship now puts his birth around 4 AD. Christians take their name from the title given to Jesus: 'the Christ', meaning the anointed one of God. After three years of teaching, Jesus was crucified and died, but Christians believe that through the power of God he came to life again. This belief was spread by Jesus's closest followers, the Apostles, and Christianity grew rapidly in the first three centuries BC. The Christian Bible consists of the Old Testament, originally written in Hebrew (the same book as the Hebrew Bible read by Jews), and the New Testament, originally written in Greek, which contains accounts of the life and teachings of Jesus, and letters from early Christians. The Bible is translated into many different languages. Major festivals are Christmas (December 25), which celebrates the birth of Jesus, and Easter (March/April), which celebrates his resurrection from death. There are nearly two billion Christians worldwide, especially in Europe, North and South America, southern Africa and Australasia. Christianity has many different branches, referred to as churches or denominations. Catholicism is the largest with 900 million followers under the leadership of the Pope, who is based in Rome. Other major branches are Orthodox and Protestant. The Orthodox churches are self-governing, each led by a Patriarch. There is a large number of Protestant denominations, each with a different organization and authority. The World Council of Churches provides a forum for dialogue amongst the major Protestant Churches.

Hinduism

Hinduism encompasses a wide variety of beliefs originating in India, and is regarded by some as not constituting a formal religion at all. No precise dates can be given for its origins, although the Vedas, the earliest texts of Hinduism, arose from a culture that was probably established in India during the second millennium BCE. Most Hindus believe that God takes many forms and is worshipped by many different names, so the multitude of gods and goddesses in Hindu belief are aspects of the same godhead. God has three main male forms, Brahma the Creator, Vishnu the Preserver, and Shiva the Destroyer. Each of these has a female counterpart: respectively Sarasvati, Lakshmi, and Parvati. God may also come to earth in human form: the best known of these are Krishna and Rama, both incarnations of Vishnu. Each person and each animal embodies a spark (atman) of the universal soul, which is God. After death the atman is reborn in a new body. Therefore God is in every object in the universe, and everything that exists is part of God. Hindus believe that every action, good or bad, has an effect (karma) on this life and on future lives. By accumulating positive karma one can

Hindu Gods

The Hindu pantheon is dominated by the primary gods Shiva and Vishnu, and, to a lesser extent Brahma, the creator, who control the powers of destruction and preservation. Throughout India, Hinduism is organized around the two main sects, Vaishnavism and Shaivism, whose followers regard either Vishnu or Shiva as the pre-eminent deity. Vishnu is also worshipped in up to 22 earthly incarnations. The best-known deities and their aspects or incarnations are listed below.

Agni	god of fire; a three-headed god who rides on a ram	**Mahishasuramardini**	consort of Shiva
Balarama	brother of Krishna	**Matsya**	incarnation of Vishnu as a fish
Bhairava	incarnation of Shiva	**Nandin**	bull vehicle of Shiva
Brahma	god of creation	**Narada**	incarnation of Vishnu
Durga	wife of Shiva, the inaccessible	**Narasimha**	incarnation of Vishnu as a man-lion
Ganesh	elephant-headed son of Shiva	**Nataraja**	aspect of Shiva as the lord of dance and rhythm
Garuda	bird on which Shiva rides	**Parashurama**	incarnation of Vishnu
Hanuman	monkey god	**Parvati**	good wife of Shiva; opposite of Kali
Indra	storm god, bringer of rain	**Pidari**	consort of Shiva
Iswara	collectively represented as Trimurti by Brahma, Vishnu, and Shiva; Iswara corresponds to nature and the human soul	**Pushan**	the enhancer, prosperer, and enlightener
		Radha	consort of Krishna; represents romantic love
		Rama	incarnation of Vishnu
Kali	goddess of destruction; evil wife of Shiva	**Rudra**	the violent, terrifying aspect of Shiva
Kalkin	incarnation of Vishnu as a giant with a horse's head	**Sarasvati**	mother goddess of art, music, and learning; female counterpart of Brahma
Kama	god of desire and sexual lust	**Savitri**	creator of the true and the just
Karaikkal-Ammaiyar	mother goddess and teacher, often shown playing the cymbals	**Shakti**	female symbol of power or energy
		Shani	astral god and bringer of ill-luck
Karrttikeya	six-headed, twelve-armed god who rides on a peacock	**Shiva**	god of creation and destruction; lord of the dance
		Shatrughna	half brother of Rama
Krishna	incarnation of Vishnu which corresponds to the perfect deification of life	**Sita**	wife of Rama
		Skanda	formed from the discarded semen of Shiva
Kurma	incarnation of Vishnu as a tortoise	**Surya**	sun god; the illuminator
Lakshmana	half-brother of Rama	**Uma**	the gracious; ascetic goddess
Lakshmi	(Sri) goddess of wealth and good fortune; wife of Vishnu	**Vamana**	incarnation of Vishnu as a dwarf
		Varaha	incarnation of Vishnu as a boar
Mahadevi Shakti	(Mahasakti) supreme goddess; corresponds to the Absolute (Brahman) and facilitates its self-manifestation	**Virabhadra**	incarnation of Shiva
		Vishnu	god of creation
		Yashoda	foster mother of Krishna

eventually break free from the cycles of birth and death to achieve liberation or moksha, which is complete union with God. There are many sacred books, all written in the ancient Indian language Sanskrit. The oldest are the Vedas, first written in the second millennium BCE, followed by the Upanishads, more philosophical writings. Two great epics, the Mahabharata and the Ramayana, existed in oral form long before they were written around 2,000 years ago. The Mahabharata contains the best-loved Hindu scripture, the Bhagavad Gita, or 'Song of the Lord', about the god Krishna. Festivals vary in different parts of India. Two almost universally celebrated festivals are Holi (March/April), a time of games and pranks with several different associated stories, and Divali (October), a new-year festival that celebrates the story of the god Rama and his wife Sita. There are nearly 750 million Hindus worldwide, almost all living in south Asia. In India there are 650 million Hindus, and other large Hindu communities live in countries where colonial or trading ties encouraged migration from India: the UK, Guyana, Kenya, South Africa, and Indonesia.

Islam

The beliefs of Islam are summed up in the Declaration of Faith: 'There is no god but God, and Muhammad is the Prophet of God'.

Jami Masjid, Delhi, India
the largest Islamic temple in India   Corel

Islam means 'peace' or 'submission', and a Muslim is 'one who submits' (to the will of God). In Islam there is one God (Arabic Allah), who is creator of the universe and the only absolute power. According to Muslim belief, God has sent many prophets, from Adam onwards, to give his message to humanity, but their message was partially lost or misunderstood. The complete message is believed to have been given by the Prophet Muhammad, who lived in Arabia in the 6th century CE. Although this message marked the beginning of a formal religion, Muslims believe that all previous prophets were Muslims, and that Islam is the primordial faith. Muslims regard Muhammad with deep love and respect as God's final prophet, and seek to follow his example, but worship is due only to God. Muslims believe that the Koran was dictated to the Prophet Muhammad by the angel Jibra'il, a messenger from God, and, because it was committed to memory and written down almost immediately, that it is the final and complete revelation from God. The Koran is believed to have been written by God, in Arabic, before time began. Muslims point to the beauty of the language as evidence of its divine origin, and it is always recited in Arabic. Muslim festivals are dated according to the lunar calendar. The main festivals are Eid-Lul-Fitr, celebrating the end of the month of fasting, and Eid-ul-Adha, celebrating the obedience of the prophet Ibrahim (Abraham), and the culmination of the annual pilgrimage to Mecca (Arabic Makkah). There are over a billion Muslims worldwide, especially in the Middle East, North and West Africa, southeastern Europe, Indonesia, and Malaysia. In 19 countries of the Middle East and North Africa, more than 90 percent of the population is Muslim. There are two main branches of Islam: Sunni who make up 80 percent of all Muslims, and Shi'a, who are found mainly in Iran, Iraq, Yemen, and Bahrain. There is no overall world organization is Islam, but several bodies have been set up to promote contact and to give Islam a voice in international affairs. These bodies include the World Muslim Congress, the Muslim World League, and the Organization of the Islamic Conference.

Jainism

The word Jain means follower of the Jinas – 'those who overcome', in the sense of achieving discipline over one's own desires, thoughts, and actions. There were 24 Jinas, also known as Tirthankaras ('bridge-builders'), the last of whom was Mahavira who lived in India in the 5th century BCE. The first is believed to have lived millions of years ago and to have invented human culture. The example of the Jinas helps others to achieve freedom from reincarnation. The belief in non-violence, *ahimsa*, is central to the Jain tradition, and Jains try to avoid violence to life in every form, including animals and plants as well as humans. Jain monks and nuns wear a cloth over the mouth and nose to avoid harming any flying insects, and sweep the ground in front of them to avoid treading on any creature. This central teaching of non-violence has

had a powerful effect on Indian culture and thought and was highlighted by the teachings of Mahatma Gandhi. The main festival is Paryushana (August/September), an eight-day period of confession and fasting. There are 8 million Jains worldwide, over 98 percent of them in India. The two largest Jain communities outside India are in the UK and the USA. The Jain tradition is divided into two groups: Svetambaras, who are concentrated in northeast India, and Digambaras, who mainly live in southern India. There are Jain temples in all the main Indian cities.

Judaism

Jews believe in one God, the Creator and Ruler of the universe. They believe that God made a Covenant, or agreement, with Abraham, who is regarded as the father of the Jewish people, and is believed by some scholars to have lived around 1900 BCE. Keeping the law is the Jewish people's part in this Covenant. Jews look forward to the coming of the Messiah, a leader from God, who will bring peace, fruitfulness, and security to the whole world. At the Messiah's coming, the dead will be brought back to life and judged by God. The Hebrew Bible consists of the Torah (Five Books of Moses), the Prophets, and other writings, including the Psalms. It was originally written in Hebrew, and is still read in Hebrew. The Torah tells the early history of the Jewish people, and contains laws and guidance on one's way of life. Study of the law is an important part of Jewish life. The fifth commandment lays down that no work must be done on the seventh day of the week, the Sabbath, or Shabbat. Since Jewish days are reckoned from nightfall to nightfall, the Sabbath begins as it gets dark on Friday evening, and ends at dusk on Saturday evening. Jewish food laws (called *kashrut*) relate to what is eaten, and how it is slaughtered, prepared, cooked, and eaten. Food is either *kosher* (permitted) or *terefah* (forbidden). Major festivals are Rosh Hashanah (New Year – September/October), Yom Kippur (the Day of Atonement) which is a major fast within the new-year period, and Pesach (Passover – March/April), which celebrates the escape of the Hebrews from slavery in Egypt. Jews have no overall religious authority, but questions of belief and practice are debated by Rabbis who are trained in Jewish law and its interpretation. The most traditional form of Judaism is known as Orthodox. Orthodox Jews use only Hebrew in services, and interpret the laws quite strictly. Conservative Judaism, mainly found in the USA, seeks to interpret the law in the light of changing circumstances, while remaining true to tradition. Reform, or Liberal, Judaism arose in the 19th century and observes fewer dietary laws, as well as holding services in the vernacular rather than in Hebrew. Bodies such as the World Jewish Congress, which represents around 70 percent of all Jews, provide a forum for debate and a Jewish voice in world affairs. There are approximately 12.8 million Jews worldwide, in the sense that a Jew is the child of a Jewish mother, although not all are religious Jews who follow the laws given by God to Moses. Approximately 48 percent live

in North America, 30 percent in Israel, and 20 percent in Europe and Russia.

See Also Judaism: Chronology on page 405

Shintoism

Shinto is the traditional religion of Japan, and means 'the way of the gods'. Shinto religion is closely tied up with the landscape of Japan and with family ancestors. Shinto ceremonies appeal to *kami*, the mysterious powers of nature, for protection and benevolent treatment. *Kami* are associated with natural features such as caves, rocks, streams, trees, and particularly mountains. Communal festivals and personal landmarks are celebrated at Shinto shrines, some of which are linked to particular aspects of life such as a trade, or old age. Major festivals are New Year's Day and the Cherry Blossom Festival in early spring. It is difficult to estimate numbers of Shinto followers, since the majority of Japanese follow Shinto ceremonies and practices for particular occasions or because of a family tradition, but many combine this with another religion, especially Buddhism. Since Shinto worship is so intimately linked with the land of Japan, it is only found there or in émigré communities.

Sikhism

The Sikh faith began in the Punjab in India in the 15th century. Guru Nanak, the founder of Sikhism, taught this new faith that rejected both Hindu and Muslim religious and social practices of the time. The Punjabi word *Sikh* means 'follower' or 'disciple'. Guru Nanak was succeeded by nine further Gurus, or teachers, each of whom was chosen by his predecessor, and each of whom made a distinctive contribution to the development of the Sikh faith. In 1708 the collection of Sikh writings was instituted as the Guru for all time to come. Sikhs revere their scripture, the Guru Granth Sahib, as they would a living teacher. The Guru Granth Sahib contains hymns written by some of the Sikh Gurus. These were collected by Guru Arjan, the fifth Guru, who also added hymns and poems written by devout Muslims and Hindus, saying that God's revelation is not confined to Sikhs. This collection was known as the Adi Granth, or 'first book'. Guru Gobind Singh, the tenth Guru, instituted this collection as the Guru for the Sikhs for all time. It is written in Gurmukhi, a form of written Punjabi. Sikhs believe in one God, described as 'timeless and without form', creator and director of the universe. He cannot be found by religious practices, but makes himself known to those who are ready, as they seek him through prayer and service to others. Sikh teachings emphasize equality, service, and protection of the weak against injustice. Sikhs wear five distinctive marks of their faith, known as the 'five Ks' because their names in Punjabi all begin with K:

Kesh – uncut hair. Devout Sikhs do not cut their hair or beard at any time.
Kanga – a comb to keep the hair in place. The hair is also kept tidy under a turban in imitation of the great Sikh Guru, Gobind Singh.

Kara – a steel bangle, a complete circle symbolizing one God and one truth.

Kirpan – a small sword or dagger, a reminder of the need to fight injustice.

Kacchera – short trousers or breeches, indicating readiness to ride into battle.

The main festivals are Baisakhi (April) which celebrates the founding of the Khalsa, the community of committed Sikhs, and the birthday of Guru Nanak (November). There are approximately 15 million Sikhs worldwide. Most of them (around 13 million) live in India, mainly in the Punjab in northwest India, but Sikhs have migrated to many parts of the world, and there are sizeable communities in the UK (up to half a million), the USA (over 250,000) and Canada (50,000), and smaller ones in East Africa, Europe, Malaysia, Indonesia, Australia, and New Zealand. The Sikh World Council was formed in 1995 to provide a forum and an international voice for Sikhs.

Taoism

Taoism emerged in China around the first century CE, and is named after the Chinese word *Tao* (Way or Path). The Tao is a natural force, the Way of the Universe, which guides all life. Living in harmony with the Tao brings peace and happiness; struggling against it brings suffering. The balance of the universe is created by the forces of yin and yang – opposite forces in continual interaction and change, giving order to all life. Yin is heavy, dark, moist, earthy, and is associated with the feminine. Yang is airy, light, dry, hot, heavenly, and associated with the masculine. All forms of life are either predominantly yin or yang, but never exclusively so. The yin/yang symbol represents the two forces in balance, but each containing a speck of the other. From the 5th to the 3rd century BCE, much was written on the significance of the Tao, most significantly the *Tao Te Ching* of Lao Tzu, the book of the sage Chuang Tzu, and the writings of Kung Fu Tzu (Confucius). They are still influential to this day, but there are also hundreds of other Taoist texts. By the 14th century CE, over 1440 of these had been collected together to form the Taoist Canon. Traditional Taoist practices include the exorcism of evil spirits and ghosts, divination in various forms, and the worship of deities, many of whom have specific roles such as help in childbirth or different illnesses. The art of *feng shui*, or geomancy, is also practised in order to build in accordance with the Tao of the landscape. Major festivals are Chinese New Year (January/February) and the mid-autumn Moon festival. Because of the repression of religion in China, it is impossible to estimate the number of Taoists. However, the number of male and female Taoist priests in China is growing rapidly, and now stands at around 15,000. New temples are being opened and old ones restored. Taoist traditions are followed by members of Chinese communities throughout the world, and Taoist thought, literature, and philosophy is becoming increasingly popular with non-Chinese followers.

The China Taoist Association promotes Taoism in China, although its function is partly political rather than religious.

Important Sites of Pilgrimage in World Religions

Buddhism

Early Buddhist scriptures mention four destinations in Nepal or India that a Buddhist pilgrim might visit – these sites are the Buddha's birthplace at Lumbini in Nepal, Bodh Gaya in India where he found enlightenment, Sarnath where he preached his first sermon, and Kusingara where he died. Relics of the Buddha were housed in specially built structures called stupas. As the traditions of Buddhism have developed and spread, hundreds of sites have become pilgrimage destinations, including temples, stupas, pagodas, mountains, and bodhi-trees (traditionally a religious and spiritual tree).

Important sites include Siripada (Adam's Peak) in Sri Lanka, which attracts not only Buddhists but also Hindu, Muslim, and Christian pilgrims. According to Sri Lankan Buddhist traditions, the Buddha came to Sri Lanka three times during his ministry, and on his third visit he left his footprint on the peak of this mountain. For the Hindu pilgrims the footprint is Krishna's, for the Muslims it is Adam's, and for the Christians it was made by St Thomas. In China there are four main sacred mountains visited by Buddhist pilgrims, and Mount Kailas in Western Tibet is an important destination for Tibetan Buddhist pilgrims.

Christianity

Some pilgrimage sites are specific to a local community, and some are associated with the historic area of Palestine, where Jesus lived. This area is now divided between parts of the modern states of Israel, Jordan, and Syria, and is known in Christianity as the Holy Land. The main focus of a pilgrimage to the Holy Land is Jerusalem, where Jesus died and rose again. Other important sites in the Holy Land are Bethlehem, where Jesus was born, Nazareth where he grew up, and the river Jordan where he was baptized.

Rome is a centre of pilgrimage, particularly for Catholics, as it is the Pope's headquarters, but other Christians visit because of Rome's association with St Peter and St Paul, two of the greatest early Christian leaders.

Santiago de Compostela in northern Spain is believed to be the burial place of St James, one of Jesus' disciples. It was especially popular as a pilgrimage centre in medieval Europe and there are still routes to the shrine from many different countries in Europe. Thousands of pilgrims still walk all or part of the route.

Thousands of people make pilgrimage to Lourdes in France because of a series of visions seen by St Bernadette in 1854, and the healing believed to be associated with the spring of water which arose there.

Hinduism

Pilgrimages are an important part of Hindu devotion, and there are hundreds of pilgrimage sites throughout India. Hindus celebrate many local festivals, often associated with pilgrimage sites or shrines not known outside their own area.

The river Ganges is regarded as holy throughout its length, but particularly at Benares (Varanasi), where pilgrims bathe, and the ashes of the dead are scattered.

Hindus regard the whole range of the Himalayas as sacred, especially Mount Kailas, where it is said that the god Shiva sits in meditation, and where Arjuna (a hero of the Mahabharata) went to visit him.

Vrindavan, on the sacred river Yamuna, is revered as the birthplace of the god Krishna, and attracts pilgrims from all over India and beyond, especially at Janmashtami, the festival celebrating Krishna's birth, when pilgrims travel all round the town to the different temples.

In the town of Puri on the east coast of India, a huge image of the god Vishnu is placed on an enormous wooden chariot called a jagannath and pulled through the streets for the festival of Ratha Yatra. The large, heavy image gave rise to the word 'juggernaut' to describe a large truck.

Islam

All Muslims who can afford it are expected to perform the *hajj*, or pilgrimage, to Mecca (Arabic Makkah) during the month of pilgrimage at least once in a lifetime; however, the Koran specifically states that one must not put one's own or one's family's health or well-being at risk by going.

Muslims believe that the Ka'ba at Mecca was first built by Adam as a house of worship, and subsequently rebuilt by Ibrahim (Abraham) and his son Isma'il. It is a simple cube-shaped stone building, and has been a religious site since very early times. Every year between two and three million Muslims make their pilgrimage there, and no non-Muslim is allowed to enter the city.

Before entering Mecca the pilgrims set aside their normal clothes and wear a simple white garment as a mark of equality with others and humility before God. Each pilgrim performs seven circuits round the Ka'ba, touching or kissing the black stone in the Ka'ba wall if it is possible to do so in the vast throng of pilgrims. Over six days the pilgrims visit several different sites in and around Mecca, performing special ceremonies at each.

The mosque at Medina, Saudi Arabia, which contains Muhammad's tomb, and the Dome of the Rock in Jerusalem, which is built on the place from which Muhammad began his ascent into heaven, are also important sites of pilgrimage.

Judaism

The land of Israel has a special status for Jews. In the Bible, God promised the land of Canaan to Abraham and his descendants. Although there is no injunction to travel to Israel, many Jews like to visit as often as they can.

In ancient times the Temple in Jerusalem

Judaism: Chronology

c. 2000 BCE	Led by Abraham, the ancient Hebrews emigrated from Mesopotamia to Canaan.
18th century–1580 BCE	Some settled on the borders of Egypt and were put to forced labour.
13th century BCE	They were rescued by Moses, who aimed at their establishment in Palestine. Moses received the Ten Commandments from God and brought them to the people. The main invasion of Canaan was led by Joshua in about 1274.
12th–11th centuries BCE	During the period of Judges, ascendancy was established over the Canaanites.
c. 1000 BCE	Complete conquest of Palestine and the union of all Judea was achieved under David, and Jerusalem became the capital.
10th century BCE	Solomon succeeded David and enjoyed a reputation for great wealth and wisdom, but his lack of a constructive policy led, after his death, to the secession of the north of Judea (Israel) under Jeroboam, with only the tribe of Judah remaining under the house of David as the southern kingdom of Judah.
9th–8th centuries BCE	Assyria became the dominant power in the Middle East. Israel purchased safety by tribute, but the basis of the society was corrupt, and prophets such as Amos, Isaiah, and Micah predicted destruction. At the hands of Tiglathpileser and his successor Shalmaneser IV, the northern kingdom (Israel) was made into Assyrian provinces after the fall of Samaria in 721 BC, although the southern kingdom of Judah was spared as an ally.
586–458 BCE	Nebuchadnezzar took Jerusalem and carried off the major part of the population to Babylon. Judaism was retained during exile, and was reconstituted by Ezra on the return to Jerusalem.
520 BCE	The Temple, originally built by Solomon, was restored.
c. 444 BCE	Ezra promulgated the legal code that was to govern the future of the Jewish people.
4th–3rd centuries BCE	After the conquest of the Persian Empire by Alexander the Great, the Syrian Seleucid rulers and the Egyptian Ptolemaic dynasty struggled for control of Palestine, which came under the government of Egypt, although with a large measure of freedom.
2nd century BCE	With the advance of Syrian power, Antiochus IV attempted to intervene in the internal quarrels of the Hebrews, even desecrating the Temple, and a revolt broke out 165 led by the Maccabee family.
63 BCE	Judea's near-independence ended when internal dissension caused the Roman general Pompey to intervene, and Roman suzerainty was established.
1st century CE	A revolt led to the destruction of the Temple (66–70) by the Roman emperor Titus. Judean national sentiment was encouraged by the work of Rabbi Johanan ben Zakkai (*c.* 20–90), and, following him, the president of the Sanhedrin (supreme court) was recognized as the patriarch of Palestinian Jewry.
2nd–3rd centuries	Greatest of the Sanhedrin presidents was Rabbi Judah Ha-Nasi, who codified the traditional law in the *Mishnah*. The Palestinian *Talmud* (*c.* 375) added the *Gemara* to the *Mishnah*.
4th–5th centuries	The intellectual leadership of Judaism passed to the descendants of the 6th century BC exiles in Babylonia, who compiled the Babylonian *Talmud*.
8th–13th centuries	Judaism enjoyed a golden era, producing the philosopher Saadiah, the poet Jehudah Ha-levi (*c.* 1075–1141), the codifier Moses Maimonides, and others.
14th–17th centuries	Where Christianity became the dominant or state religion, the Jews were increasingly segregated from mainstream life and trade by the Inquisition, anti-Semitic legislation, or by expulsion. The Protestant and Islamic states and their colonies allowed for refuge. Persecution led to messianic hopes, strengthened by the 16th century revival of Kabbalism, culminating in the messianic movement of Shabbatai Sevi in the 17th century.
18th–19th centuries	Outbreaks of persecution increased with the rise of European nationalism. Reform Judaism, a rejection of religious orthodoxy and an attempt to interpret it for modern times, began in Germany in 1810 and was soon established in England and the USA. In the late 19th century, large numbers of Jews fleeing persecution (pogroms) in Russia and Eastern Europe emigrated to the USA, leading to the development of large Orthodox, Conservative, and Reform communities there. Many became Americanized and lost interest in religion.
20th century	Zionism, a nationalist movement dedicated to achieving a secure homeland where the Jewish people would be free from persecution, was founded in 1896; this led to the establishment of the state of Israel in 1948. Liberal Judaism (more radical than Reform) developed in the USA. In 1911 the first synagogue in the UK was founded. The Nazi German regime (1933–45) exterminated 6 million European Jews. Hundreds of thousands of survivors took refuge in pre-existing Jewish settlements in what eventually became the new state of Israel. Although most Israeli and American Jews were not affiliated with synagogues after the 1950s, they continued to affirm their Jewish heritage. Both Orthodox and Hasidic Judaism, however, flourished in their new homes and grew rapidly in the 1970s and 1980s.

was the place of worship for all Jews, with the presence of God signified by the Ark of the Covenant in the most sacred place inside. The Western Wall in Jerusalem is all that remains of the last great Temple, destroyed in 70 CE. It is a centre of pilgrimage and prayer for Jews from all over the world, both for private prayer, which is said facing the wall, and for public services and bar mitzvahs.

Many Jews also visit Yad Vashem ('a place and a name') in Jerusalem, a memorial to the Jews who died in the Nazi Holocaust.

Shinto

Mountains are especially important because they are homes of the kami (spirits) and of the dead. Mt Fuji is best known and is venerated throughout Japan as a home of the gods and of the departed.

Shinto shrines can be vast complexes or tiny shrines perched beside a rock or surrounding a venerable tree. The most famous Shinto site is at Ise, the shrine of the Sun goddess Amaterasu, who is believed to be the founder of the Japanese imperial family and thus, in effect, the founder of the Japanese.

Sikhism

Guru Ram Das, the fourth Guru of Sikhism, began building the holy city of Amritsar in the Punjab. Here the House of God (Golden Temple) houses the first copy of the Guru Granth Sahib, the Sikh scripture. The city is the spiritual centre of Sikhism.

Anandpur, the site of the founding of the Khalsa, the community of committed Sikhs, is a popular destination, and many items important to Sikh history can be seen in the Gurdwara there.

Other major pilgrimage sites include places of martyrdom, such as the remains of the building at Sarhind in which the two youngest sons of Guru Gobind Singh were immured and killed.

Taoism

The major pilgrimage sites for Taoism are the five Taoist sacred mountains, Hua Shan,

Heng Shan, Heng Shan, Tai Shan, and Song Shan, although there are countless smaller ones scattered across China. The Tao (Path) that leads the pilgrim up these mountains passes temples, statues of deities and heroes, and commemorations of myths and legends. The sacred mountains are especially associated with sages and those who achieve immortality through rigorous practices.

See Also Major Religious Festivals (Calendars and Time)

Books of the Bible

Name of book	Chapters	Date written
Books of the Old Testament		
Genesis	50	mid-8th century BC
Exodus	40	950–586 BC
Leviticus	27	mid-7th century BC
Numbers	36	850–650 BC
Deuteronomy	34	mid-7th century BC
Joshua	24	c. 550 BC
Judges	21	c. 550 BC
Ruth	4	late 3rd century BC
1 Samuel	31	c. 900 BC
2 Samuel	24	c. 900 BC
1 Kings	22	550–600 BC
2 Kings	25	550–600 BC
1 Chronicles	29	c. 300 BC
2 Chronicles	36	c. 300 BC
Ezra	10	c. 450 BC
Nehemiah	13	c. 450 BC
Esther	10	c. 200 BC
Job	42	600–400 BC
Psalms	150	6th–2nd century BC
Proverbs	31	350–150 BC
Ecclesiastes	12	c. 200 BC
Song of Solomon	8	3rd century BC
Isaiah	66	late 3rd century BC

Name of book	Chapters	Date written
Books of the Old Testament		
Jeremiah	52	604 BC
Lamentations	5	586–536 BC
Ezekiel	48	6th century BC
Daniel	12	c. 166 BC
Hosea	14	c. 732 BC
Joel	3	c. 500 BC
Amos	9	775–750 BC
Obadiah	1	6th–3rd century BC
Jonah	4	600–200 BC
Micah	7	late 3rd century BC
Nahum	3	c. 626 BC
Habakkuk	3	c. 600 BC
Zephaniah	3	3rd century BC
Haggai	2	c. 520 BC
Zechariah	14	c. 520 BC
Malachi	4	c. 430 BC
Books of the New Testament		
Matthew	28	before AD 70
Mark	16	before AD 70
Luke	24	AD 70–80
John	21	AD 90–100
Acts	28	AD 70–80

Name of book	Chapters	Date written
Books of the New Testament		
Romans	16	AD 120
1 Corinthians	16	AD 57
2 Corinthians	13	AD 57
Galatians	6	AD 53
Ephesians	6	AD 140
Philippians	4	AD 63
Colossians	4	AD 140
1 Thessalonians	5	AD 50–54
2 Thessalonians	3	AD 50–54
1 Timothy	6	before AD 64
2 Timothy	4	before AD 64
Titus	3	before AD 64
Philemon	1	AD 60–62
Hebrews	13	AD 80–90
James	5	before AD 52
1 Peter	5	before AD 64
2 Peter	3	before AD 64
1 John	5	AD 90–100
2 John	1	AD 90–100
3 John	1	AD 90–100
Jude	1	AD 75–80
Revelation	22	AD 81–96

Patron Saints

Saint	Occupation
Adam	gardeners
Albert the Great	scientists
Alphonsus Liguori	theologians
Amand	brewers, hotelkeepers
Andrew	fisherfolk
Angelico	artists
Anne	miners
Apollonia	dentists
Augustine	theologians
Barbara	builders, miners
Bernadino (Feltre)	bankers
Bernadino of Siena	advertisers
Camillus de Lellis	nurses
Catherine of Alexandria	librarians, philosophers
Cecilia	musicians, poets, singers
Christopher	motorists, sailors
Cosmas and Damian	barbers, chemists, doctors, surgeons
Crispinian	shoemakers
David	poets
Dismas	undertakers
Dominic	astronomers

Saint	Occupation
Dorothy	florists
Eligius	blacksmiths, jewellers, metalworkers
Erasmus	sailors
Fiacre	gardeners, taxi drivers
Florian	firefighters
Francis de Sales	authors, editors, journalists
Francis of Assisi	merchants
Francis of Paola	sailors
Gabriel	messengers, postal workers, radio workers, television workers
Genesius	actors, secretaries
George	soldiers
Gregory	singers
Gregory the Great	musicians, teachers
Homobonus	tailors
Honoratus	bakers
Isidore	farmers
Ivo	lawyers
James	labourers
Jerome	librarians
Joan of Arc	soldiers

LOUISE WOODWARD FREED

British au pair Louise Woodward appears at the appeal in Boston, USA, against the reduction in November 1997 of the murder conviction against her to one of involuntary manslaughter. Woodward was originally convicted of murder following the death of eight-month-old Matthew Eappen, but was freed following the overturning of the original verdict. She returned to her home in Elton, Cheshire, in June 1998 when the Massachusetts Supreme Court upheld her conviction but refused a retrial requested by the prosecution.

Frank Spooner Pictures (© Jim Bourg / Gamma Liaison)

GOOD FRIDAY AGREEMENT

Above Bono, singer with Irish rock band U2, welcomes Ulster Unionist Party leader David Trimble (*left*) and SDLP leader John Hume (*right*) on to the stage during a concert to support the Northern Ireland peace agreement in May 1998. On 10 April 1998, Ireland, Britain, and the political parties in Northern Ireland reached a peace agreement known as the Good Friday Agreement. Ulster Secretary Mo Mowlam (*left*) said 'I am very happy for the people in Northern Ireland who I believe will now have the opportunity to build a peaceful future for themselves'. Referring to the talks, Sinn Féin president Gerry Adams (*above right,* with Martin McGuinness, Sinn Féin's chief negotiator) said 'Peace cannot be built on exclusion. That has been the price of the last 30 years.'

Bono, Trimble, Hume: *Frank Spooner (© B. Thompson - K. Boyes / FSP / Gamma);* Mowlam: *© Sean Aidan;* Adams, McGuinness: *Frank Spooner (© Karen Davies / FSP / Gamma)*

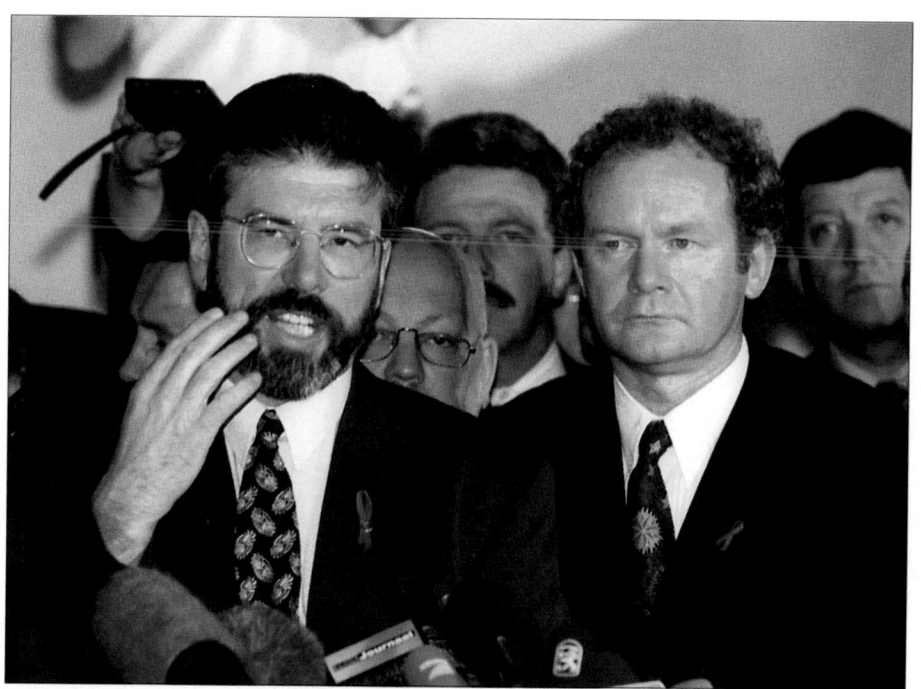

STANDOFF AT DRUMCREE

Above Troops monitor the protest in fields next to Drumcree parish church, Portadown, County Armagh, Northern Ireland, by Orangemen and their supporters in July 1998. The Orangemen were prevented by a huge security presence from taking part in the annual parade down the Nationalist Garvaghy Road in Portadown.
Rex Features, London (© Jim Bennett)

COUNTRYSIDE RALLY
In the biggest demonstration in Britain for more than a decade, at least 250,000 people marched through London in March 1998 to protest against Government policies on farming, the right to roam, and foxhunting.
© *Grosset / Spooner*

STEPHEN LAWRENCE INQUIRY

Doreen and Neville Lawrence (*above*), mother and father of the murdered black teenager, Stephen Lawrence. In June 1998 the inquiry into Stephen's death heard Ian Johnston, a Metropolitan Police Assistant Commissioner, tell the Lawrences that the force had failed them by failing to bring Stephen's killers to justice. He said it had been 'a tragedy' for both the family and the Metropolitan Police.

18-year-old Stephen was stabbed to death in Eltham, southeast London, in 1993. Five men were arrested for the murder, but the case was dropped by the Crown Prosecution Service due to lack of evidence. During the inquiry, Det. Supt. Brian Weeden – the senior detective who led the investigation into the murder – admitted a delay in arresting suspects due to a misunderstanding of the law.

Rex Features, London (© Andre Camara)

PARLIAMENT FOR SCOTLAND

Supporters of a Parliament for Scotland were victorious in a referendum in September 1997. 74.3% of Scottish voters approved the creation of a Scottish assembly. One week later Welsh voters narrowly approved the creation of a Welsh assembly (50.3% in favour).

Rex Features, London (© J. Sutton Hibbert)

BLAIR IN THE CITY
Prime Minister Tony Blair at the London International Financial Futures and Options Exchange (LIFFE). Mr Blair was booed when he visited the LIFFE in October 1997. Commentators suggested that this hostile reception reflected frustration within the City over the Government's confused stance on European monetary union.
© Richard Watt

DIANA MUSEUM
Earl Spencer, at his home, Althorp House, oversees the construction of a museum dedicated to his sister, Diana, Princess of Wales. The museum opened to the public in the summer of 1998.
Rex Features (© Mike Finn-Kelsey)

GERI LEAVES THE SPICE GIRLS
Geri Halliwell performs in Paris with the Spice Girls. Halliwell left the group at the end of May 1998, citing 'differences' with the other members of the group as the reason for her departure.
Frank Spooner Pictures (© Gavin Smith / FSP / Gamma)

WORLD CUP HERO
Michael Owen (pictured in the game against Colombia, which England won 2–0) was the star of the England campaign in the 1998 World Cup tournament. Owen is the youngest player to represent England this century.
Allsport (© Shaun Botterill)

Patron Saints (*continued*)

Saint	Occupation	Saint	Occupation
John Baptist de la Salle	teachers	Martin of Tours	soldiers
John Bosco	labourers	Matthew	accountants, bookkeepers, tax collectors
John of God	book trade, nurses, printers	Michael	grocers, police
Joseph	carpenters	Our Lady of Loreto	aviators
Joseph (Arimathea)	gravediggers, undertakers	Peter	fisherfolk
Joseph (Cupertino)	astronauts	Raymond Nonnatus	midwives
Julian the Hospitaler	hotelkeepers	Sebastian	athletes, soldiers
Lawrence	cooks	Thérèse of Lisieux	florists
Leonard	prisoners	Thomas (Apostle)	architects, builders
Louis	sculptors	Thomas Aquinas	philosophers, scholars, students, theologians
Lucy	glassworkers, writers	Thomas More	lawyers
Luke	artists, butchers, doctors, glassworkers, sculptors, surgeons	Vitus	actors, comedians, dancers
		Wenceslaus	brewers
Martha	cooks, housewives, servants, waiters	Zita	servants

Major Denominations of the Christian Religion

Denomination	Date of origin	Organization	Characteristics	Special rites	Orientation
Baptists	1609	self-governing churches; congregational	only adult Christians, capable of own choice, should be baptized	baptism by total immersion	missionary activities; supports separation of church and state
Calvinists	1566	mostly congregational	belief in predestination; Bible as the only source of authority	simple services	individual faith perceived as the only way to salvation
Lutherans	1517	congregational or episcopal	belief in the symbolic presence of Christ in bread and wine offerings; Bible as the only source of authority; no belief in predestination	simple services; infant baptism	personal faith perceived as the only way to salvation; strong theological and ethical background
Methodists	1738	superintendent system and conferences	scripture, tradition, and experience are at the core of the church's practices	forms of worship vary depending on local tradition; infant or adult baptism	extensive missionary activities and social involvement
Orthodox	1054	independent and autonomous national churches governed by synods of bishops; the Patriarch of Constantinople recognized as 'first among equals'	emphasis on Christ's resurrection; belief that the Holy Spirit descends from God the Father only; tradition as a source of authority; rich traditions of worship; veneration of Mary, the mother of God	elaborate liturgy; seven sacraments; veneration of icons	traditional orientation, usually little social involvement
Pentecostal	1901	a wide range of groups; allows for freedom of organization	emphasis on the personal teachings of the Holy Spirit	spirit baptism; healing; adult baptism; 'speaking in tongues'	charismatic
Presbyterians	16th century (1559 in Scotland)	government by elders (lay people or ordained ministers)	emphasis on self-control and self-discipline; belief in the symbolic presence of Christ in bread and wine offerings	simple services with emphasis on the sermon; infant baptism	strong belief in justice and supremacy of God
Roman Catholics	traditionally founded by Jesus Christ; recognized by the Roman authorities in the 4th century	strict hierarchy with the pope (the Bishop of Rome) as leader	emphasis on teachings of the pope and church authorities; belief in the factual presence of Christ in bread and wine offerings; veneration of Mary, the mother of Jesus Christ	wide range of services focused on the Mass; seven sacraments; rich theological tradition	authority of the church regulates every area of life and belief; controversy over divorce, contraception, and priests' celibacy; since the Second Vatican Council (1962–65) local languages in use

Popes

Name	Date reign began	Name	Date reign began	Name	Date reign began	Name	Date reign began
St Peter	c. 42	St Boniface IV	608	John XIII	965	Urban V	1362
St Linus	c. 67	St Deusdedit (Adeodatus I)	615	Benedict VI	973	Gregory XI	1370
St Anacletus (Cletus)	c. 76	Boniface V	619	Benedict VII	974	Urban VI	1378
St Clement I	c. 88	Honorius I	625	John XIV	983	Boniface IX	1389
St Evaristus	c. 97	Severinus	640	John XV	985	Innocent VII	1404
St Alexander I	c. 105	John IV	640	Gregory V	996	Gregory XII	1406
St Sixtus I	c. 115	Theodore I	642	Sylvester II	999	Martin V	1417
St Telesphorus	c. 125	St Martin I	649	John XVII	1003	Eugene IV	1431
St Hyginus	c. 136	St Eugene I	654	John XVIII	1004	Nicholas V	1447
St Pius I	c. 140	St Vitalian	657	Sergius IV	1009	Callistus III	1455
St Anicetus	c. 155	Adeodatus II	672	Benedict VIII	1012	Pius II	1458
St Soterus	c. 166	Donus	676	John XIX	1024	Paul II	1464
St Eleutherius	175	St Agatho	678	Benedict IX[2]	1032	Sixtus IV	1471
St Victor I	189	St Leo II	682	Gregory VI	1045	Innocent VIII	1484
St Zephyrinus	199	St Benedict II	684	Clement II	1046	Alexander VI	1492
St Callistus I	217	John V	685	Benedict IX[2]	1047	Pius III	1503
St Urban I	222	Conon	686	Damasus II	1048	Julius II	1503
St Pontian	230	St Sergius I	687	St Leo IX	1049	Leo X	1513
St Anterus	235	John VI	701	Victor II	1055	Adrian VI	1522
St Fabius	236	John VII	705	Stephen IX (X)	1057	Clement VII	1523
St Cornelius	251	Sisinnius	708	Nicholas II	1059	Paul III	1534
St Lucius I	253	Constantine	708	Alexander II	1061	Julius III	1550
St Stephen I	254	St Gregory II	715	St Gregory VII	1073	Marcellus II	1555
St Sixtus II	257	St Gregory III	731	Victor III	1086	Paul IV	1555
St Dionysius	259	St Zachary	741	Urban II	1088	Pius IV	1559
St Felix I	269	Stephen II (III)[1]	752	Paschal II	1099	St Pius V	1566
St Eutychian	275	St Paul I	757	Gelasius II	1118	Gregory XIII	1572
St Caius	283	Stephen III (IV)	768	Callistus II	1119	Sixtus V	1585
St Marcellinus	296	Adrian I	772	Hororius II	1124	Urban VII	1590
St Marcellus I	308	St Leo III	795	Innocent II	1130	Gregory XIV	1590
St Eusebius	309	Stephen IV (V)	816	Celestine II	1143	Innocent IX	1591
St Melchiades	311	St Paschal I	817	Lucius II	1144	Clement VIII	1592
St Sylvester I	314	Eugene II	824	Eugene III	1145	Leo XI	1605
St Marcus	336	Valentine	827	Anastasius IV	1153	Paul V	1605
St Julius I	337	Gregory IV	827	Adrian IV	1154	Gregory XV	1621
Liberius	352	Sergius II	844	Alexander III	1159	Urban VIII	1623
St Damasus I	366	St Leo IV	847	Innocent III	1179	Innocent X	1644
St Siricius	384	Benedict III	855	Lucius III	1181	Alexander VII	1655
St Anastasius I	399	St Nicholas (I) the Great	858	Urban III	1185	Clement IX	1667
St Innocent I	402	Adrian II	867	Gregory VIII	1187	Clement X	1670
St Zosimus	417	John VIII	872	Clement III	1187	Innocent XI	1676
St Boniface I	418	Marinus I	882	Celestine III	1191	Alexander VIII	1689
St Celestine I	422	St Adrian III	884	Innocent III	1198	Innocent XII	1691
St Sixtus III	432	Stephen V (VI)	885	Honorius III	1216	Clement XI	1700
St Leo I the Great	440	Formosus	891	Gregory IX	1227	Innocent XIII	1721
St Hilary	461	Boniface VI	896	Celestine IV	1241	Benedict XIII	1724
St Simplicius	468	Stephen VI (VII)	896	Innocent IV	1243	Clement XII	1730
St Felix III	483	Romanus	897	Alexander IV	1254	Benedict XIV	1740
St Gelasius I	492	Theodore II	897	Urban IV	1261	Clement XIII	1758
Anastasius II	496	John IX	898	Clement IV	1265	Clement XIV	1769
St Symmachus	498	Benedict IV	900	Gregory X	1271	Pius VI	1775
St Hormisdas	514	Leo V	903	Innocent V	1276	Pius VII	1800
St John I	523	Sergius III	904	Adrian V	1276	Leo XII	1823
St Felix IV	526	Anastasius III	911	John XXI[3]	1276	Pius VIII	1829
Boniface II	530	Landus	913	Nicholas III	1277	Gregory XVI	1831
John II	533	John X	914	Martin IV	1281	Pius IX	1846
St Agapetus I	535	Leo VI	928	Honorius IV	1285	Leo XIII	1878
St Silverius	536	Stephen VII (VIII)	928	Nicholas IV	1288	St Pius X	1903
Vigilius	537	John XI	931	St Celestine V	1294	Benedict XV	1914
Pelagius I	556	Leo VII	936	Boniface VIII	1294	Pius XI	1922
John III	561	Stephen VII (IX)	939	Benedict XI	1303	Pius XII	1939
Benedict I	575	Marinus II	942	Clement V	1305	John XXIII	1958
Pelagius II	579	Agapetus II	946	John XXII	1316	Paul VI	1963
St Gregory (I) the Great	590	John XII	955	Benedict XII	1334	John Paul I[4]	1978
Sabinianus	604	Leo VIII	963	Clement VI	1342	John Paul II	1978
Boniface III	607	Benedict V	964	Innocent VI	1352		

[1] The original Stephen II died before consecration, and was dropped from the list of popes in 1961; Stephen III became Stephen II and the numbers of the other popes named Stephen were also moved up; [2] Benedict IX was driven from office for scandalous conduct; but returned briefly in 1047; [3] There was no John XX; [4] John Paul I died after only 33 days as Pontiff.

Antipopes

Antipope refers to a claimant to the office of pope set up in opposition to one regularly and canonically appointed.

Name	Term	Name	Term	Name	Term
Hippolytus	217–c. 235	Christopher	903–04	Analectus II	1130–38
Novatian	251–c. 258	Boniface VII	974 and 984–85	Victor IV[1]	1138
Felix II	355–65	John XVI	997–98	Victor IV[1]	1159–64
Eulalius	418–19	Gregory	1012	Paschal III	1164–68
Laurentius	498 and 501–05	Benedict X	1058–59	Calixtus III	1168–78
Dioscorus	530	Honorius II	1061–72	Nicholas V	1328–30
Theodore	687	Clement III	1080 and 1084–100	Clement VII	1378–94
Paschal	687–92	Theodoric	1100–02	Benedict XIII	1394–1423
Constantine II	767–69	Albert	1102	Alexander V	1409–10
Philip	768	Sylvester IV	1105–11	John XXIII	1410–15
John	844	Gregory VIII	1118–21	Clement VIII	1423–29
Anastasius Bibliothecarius	855	Celestine II	1124	Benedict XIV	1425–30
				Felix V	1439–49

[1] The antipopes Victor IV (1138) and Victor IV (1159–64) were different people.

Christianity: Chronology

1st century	The Christian church is traditionally said to have originated at Pentecost, and separated from the parent Jewish religion by the declaration of Saints Barnabas and Paul that the distinctive rites of Judaism were not necessary for entry into the Christian church.
3rd century	Christians were persecuted under the Roman emperors Septimius Severus, Decius, and Diocletian.
312	Emperor Constantine established Christianity as the religion of the Roman Empire.
4th century	A settled doctrine of Christian belief evolved, with deviating beliefs condemned as heresies. Questions of discipline threatened disruption within the Church; to settle these, Constantine called the Council of Arles in 314, followed by the councils of Nicaea (325) and Constantinople (381).
5th century	Councils of Ephesus (431) and Chalcedon (451). Christianity was carried northwards by such figures as Saints Columba and Augustine.
800	Holy Roman Emperor Charlemagne crowned by the pope. The church assisted the growth of the feudal system of which it formed the apex.
1054	The Eastern Orthodox Church split from the Roman Catholic Church.
11th–12th centuries	Secular and ecclesiastical jurisdiction were often in conflict; for example, Emperor Henry IV and Pope Gregory VII, Henry II of England and his archbishop Becket.
1096–1291	The church supported a series of wars in the Middle East, called the Crusades.
1233	The Inquisition was established to suppress heresy.
14th century	Increasing worldliness (against which the foundation of the Dominican and Franciscan monastic orders was a protest) and ecclesiastical abuses led to dissatisfaction and the appearance of the reformers Wycliffe and Huss.
15th–17th centuries	Thousands of women were accused of witchcraft, tortured, and executed.
early 16th century	The Renaissance brought a re-examination of Christianity in northern Europe by the humanists Erasmus, More, and Colet.
1517	The German priest Martin Luther became leader of the Protestant movement and precipitated the Reformation.
1519–64	In Switzerland the Reformation was carried on by Calvin and Zwingli.
1529	Henry VIII renounced papal supremacy and proclaimed himself head of the Church of England.
1545–63	The Counter-Reformation was initiated by the Catholic church at the Council of Trent.
1560	The Church of Scotland was established according to Calvin's Presbyterian system.
17th century	Jesuit missionaries established themselves in China and Japan. Puritans, Quakers, and other sects seeking religious freedom established themselves in North America.
18th century	During the Age of Reason, Christian dogmas were questioned, and intellectuals began to examine society in purely secular terms. In England and America, religious revivals occurred among the working classes in the form of Methodism and the Great Awakening. In England the Church of England suffered the loss of large numbers of Nonconformists.
19th century	The evolutionary theories of Darwin and the historical criticism of the Bible challenged the Book of Genesis. Missionaries converted people in Africa and Asia, suppressing indigenous faiths and cultures.
1948	The World Council of Churches was founded as part of the ecumenical movement to reunite various Protestant sects and, to some extent, the Protestant churches and the Catholic church.
1950s–80s	Protestant evangelicism grew rapidly in the USA, spread by television.
1969	A liberation theology of freeing the poor from oppression emerged in South America, and attracted papal disapproval.
1972	The United Reformed Church was formed by the union of the Presbyterian Church in England and the Congregational Church. In the USA, the 1960s–70s saw the growth of cults, some of them nominally Christian, which were a source of social concern.
1980s	The Roman Catholic Church played a major role in the liberalization of the Polish government; and in the USSR the Orthodox Church and other sects were tolerated and even encouraged under Gorbachev.
1988	The Holy Shroud of Turin, claimed by some to be Christ's mortuary cloth, is shown by carbon dating to date from about 1330.
1990s	The Christian church grappled with the question of its attitude to homosexuality; the policy of most churches was to oppose its public acceptance, declaring that homosexual behaviour conflicted with Christian teachings.
1992	Ater 359 years, the Roman Catholic Church accepted that Galileo was right: the Earth does go round the Sun.

Women Priests: Chronology

May 1955	The US General Assembly of the Presbyterian Church authorized the ordination of female ministers.
November 1971	Two women, Joyce Bennett and Jane Hwang Hsien Yuen, were ordained as priests by the Anglican bishop of Hong Kong.
29 July 1974	Four bishops of the Episcopalian Church in the USA ordained 11 women to the priesthood, defying Church law.
29 July– 17 October 1974	Eleven women were ordained Episcopal ministers in the USA. The ordinates were invalidated by the Episcopal House of Bishops on 15 August, though the body endorsed the principle of ordaining women on 17 October.
16 September 1976	The Episcopian Church in the USA approved the ordination of women to the priesthood.
16 September 1977	Following the 1976 decision of the Episcopalian Church in the USA to ordain women, a breakaway group founded the Anglican Church in North America, claiming to be true heirs to the Anglican tradition.
1978	In Britain, the General Synod of the Church of England rejected the ordination of women to the priesthood and episcopate.
1979	The General Synod of the Church of England refused

	to allow female priests ordained abroad to celebrate holy communion.
12 November 1981	The General Synod of the Church of England voted to recognize the sacraments of the Free Churches and their women ministers and to allow women to be ordained as deacons.
14 June 1984	The Southern Baptist Convention in the USA resolved to oppose the ordination of women.
1985	The General Synod of the Church of England approved by a large majority the ordination of women as deacons.
September 1988	Pope John Paul II reiterated his opposition to women priests in the Catholic Church in his Apostolic Letter 'Mulieris Dignitatem/The Dignity of Women'.
1989	Barbara Harris, the first female Anglican bishop, was ordained in the USA.
1992	The Church of England General Synod and the Anglican church in Australia voted in favour of the ordination of women priests.
5 November 1993	Legislation to allow the Church of England to ordain women priests gained the royal assent in Britain.
June 1998	The Reverend Kathleen Richardson, Moderator of the Free Churches' Council, became a life peer.

Gods of Ancient Egypt

Ammon (Amen, Amun, or Amon; 'the hidden one') king of the gods, a sun god identified by the Greeks with Zeus (Roman Jupiter), portrayed with a ram's head or wearing a headdress bearing two goose plumes

Anubis (Anpu) jackal-headed god of the dead who oversaw the weighing of hearts; son of Osiris

Apis bull god, believed to be the personification of the creator god Ptah

Aton (Aten) sun god, supreme deity, worshipped as the one true god in the monotheistic religion introduced by the pharaoh Akhenaten

Atum a sun god and creator of the universe, the original god of Heliopolis, preceding Ra, shown wearing the double crown of united Egypt, often associated with a serpent

Batet (Bast, Pasht) a goddess identified by the Greeks with Artemis, portrayed originally as a lioness, later as a cat-headed woman, associated with sexual pleasure

Bes god of music and dance, usually shown as a grotesque dwarf

Geb god of earth; son of Shu and Tefnet

Hapi god of the Nile, shown as an overweight man with the breasts of a woman, symbolizing abundance and nourishment

Hathor (temenos [dwelling] of Horus) sky goddess, wife or mother of Horus, also goddess of dance, music, and love, corresponding to the Greek Aphrodite; she is depicted as a cow, or wearing a helmet in the shape of a sun-disc with cow's horns

Horus hawk-headed sun god, son of Isis and Osiris, of whom the pharaohs were declared to be the incarnation

Isis principal goddess of ancient Egypt; daughter of Geb and Nut (Earth and Sky), and sister-wife of Osiris

Khepre (Khepera) god of the rising sun, portrayed as a scarab beetle

Khonsu (Khons) moon god, sometimes portrayed with a falcon's head

Maat (Maut) goddess of order, justice, and truth; wore an ostrich feather on her head against which the hearts of the dead were weighed to estimate their purity

Min an aspect of the god Ammon, one of the oldest Egyptian deities

Montu a god of war and a solar god in Upper Egypt, portrayed as a man with a bull's or a hawk's head

Mut upper Egyptian counterpart of Sekhmet; the vulture was her sacred bird

Neferten son of Ptah and Sekhmet, representing the divine lotus and associated with the sun

Nephthys goddess of the dead; sister and wife of Set

Nu (Nun) personification of the primal waters, the chaos existing before form

Nut creator goddess, the fundamental female principle; portrayed as a cow

Osiris god who ruled the underworld after being killed by Set, the embodiment of goodness

Ptah the divine potter, a personification of the creative force; said to have brought both genders into existence from himself

Ra (Re) ancient sun god, often portrayed with a falcon's head

Sebek a crocodile god

Sekhmet ('the powerful she') goddess of war, portrayed as a lioness

Set god of night, the desert, and of all evils, portrayed as a grotesque animal; Set was the murderer of Osiris

Shu air god, portrayed in human form wearing an ostrich feather on his head

Tefnet (Tefnut) water goddess, portrayed as a lioness or lioness-headed

Thoth (Tehnuti) god of wisdom and learning, represented as a scribe with the head of an ibis, the bird sacred to him

Gods of Ancient Greece

Aeolus god of the winds, who kept them imprisoned in a cave on the Lipari (Aeolian) Islands

Aphrodite goddess of love; unfaithful wife of Hephaestus, and mother of Eros

Apollo god of the sun, music, poetry, prophecy, agriculture, and pastoral life; the twin child (with Artemis) of Zeus and Leto

Ares god of war; the son of Zeus and Hera

Artemis goddess of chastity, the young of all creatures, the Moon, and the hunt; also associated with childbirth; twin sister of Apollo

Asclepius god of medicine whose emblem was the caduceus, a winged staff with two snakes coiled around it; son of Apollo

Athene (Athena, Pallas Athene) goddess of war, wisdom, and the arts and crafts, who was supposed to have sprung fully grown from the head of Zeus; she was the patron of Athens

Boreas god of the north wind

Cronos (Kronus) ancient fertility god who castrated his father and protected himself from a similar fate by eating his children;

son of Gaia and Uranus and husband of Rhea

Demeter goddess of agriculture; daughter of Kronos and Rhea, and mother of Persephone by Zeus

Dione goddess worshipped alongside Zeus at his most ancient shrine at Dodona; said to be the daughter of Okeanos and Tethys and mother of Aphrodite

Dionysus (Bakkhos) god of wine, orgiastic excess, and mystic ecstasy; son of Semele and Zeus

Eos goddess of the dawn; daughter of Hyperion and Thea

Erebos primordial god of darkness who sprang from Chaos; father of Aither (upper air) and Hemera (day)

Eros boy-god of love who fell in love with Psyche, traditionally armed with bow and arrows; the son of Aphrodite

Erinyes (the Furies) goddesses with fearsome faces and serpents twisted in their hair, who visited retribution upon those who had committed crimes, such as filial disobedience, murder, inhospitality and oath-breaking, but who were also associated with fertility; their names were Alecto (relentless), Megara (resentful), and Tisiphone (avenger of murder)

Gaia (Ge) goddess of the Earth; she sprang from primordial Chaos and herself produced Uranus, by whom she was the mother of the Cyclopes and Titans

Graces (Charities) goddesses who personified beauty, grace, and good nature; named Aglaia (splendour), Euphrosyne (rejoicing of the heart), and Thaleia (blossom)

Hades god of the underworld (which bore his name); brother of Zeus and Poseidon

Hebe goddess of youth, who served nectar and ambrosia at Olympian banquets; dutiful daughter of Zeus and Hera

Hecate goddess of the underworld and magic, sometimes identified with Artemis and the Moon

Helios the sun god, thought to make his daily journey across the sky in a chariot; father of Phaethon

Hephaestus god of fire and metalcraft; son of Zeus and Hera, and husband of Aphrodite

Hera goddess of women and marriage; queen of the gods, sister and consort of Zeus, mother of Hephaestus, Hebe, and Ares

Hermes god of merchants, thieves, and travellers, and messenger of the gods who carried a staff around which serpents coiled; son of Zeus and Maia

Hestia goddess of the hearth

Hygieia goddess of health, whose sacred creature was a snake; daughter of Asclepins

Hypnos god of sleep, often depicted carrying a poppy; son of Nyx, brother of Thanatos, and father of Morpheus

Irene goddess of peace and wealth, sometimes regarded as one of the Horae, who presided over the seasons and the order of nature, and were the daughters of Zeus and Themis

Iris virgin rainbow goddess, messenger of the gods, depicted with wings and a staff

Kybele great mother goddess, originally from Phrygia and later identified with Rhea

Metis goddess of wisdom who helped Zeus to overcome his father Cronos; daughter of Okeanos and Tethys

Mnemosyne goddess of memory; the Titan mother, by Zeus, of the nine muses

Moirai (the Fates) the three goddesses who controlled human life: Klotho (spinner) who spun the thread of life, Lachesis (caster of lots) who tended the thread, and Atropos (death's inevitability) who cut the thread

Muses nine daughters of Zeus, who were each associated with a particular art or science: Calliope, epic poetry; Clio, history; Erato, love poetry; Euterpe, lyric poetry; Melpomene, tragedy; Polyhymnia, sacred song; Terpsichore, dance; Thalia, comedy; and Urania, astronomy

Nemesis goddess of justice and retribution

Nike goddess of victory, sometimes represented as winged

Nereus god of water, the sea in particular; older than Poseidon, he was called 'the old man of the sea'; his fifty daughters by the sea nymph Doris were the Nereids (divine sea nymphs)

Okeanos god who embodied the ocean, believed to be a great river encircling the earth

Pan god of flocks and herds, shown as a man with the horns, ears, and hoofed legs of a goat, and playing a shepherd's panpipe

Persephone (Kore) goddess and queen of the underworld: daughter of Zeus and Demeter

Phaethon son of Helios, the sun god, who was allowed to drive his father's chariot of the sun across the sky for one day; he lost control and plunged too close to the Earth, scorching parts of it and blackening the skin of some humans; he was killed by Zeus with a thunderbolt

Plutos (Pluto) a minor god of wealth, sometimes identified with the underworld

Pontos ancient embodiment of the sea

Poseidon chief god of the sea, also worshipped as god of earthquakes; brother of Zeus and Hades

Priapus god of fertility, represented as grotesquely ugly with an exaggerated phallus; son of Dionysus and Aphrodite; he was later a Roman god of gardens

Proteus a sea god with oracular powers; he could assume any shape and would do so to avoid answering questions

Rhea a fertility goddess, one of the Titans; wife of Cronos and mother of several gods, including Zeus

Selene goddess of the Moon; daughter of a Titan, and sister of Helios

Tethys sea goddess; daughter of Uranus and Gaia

Triton a merman sea god; son of Poseidon and the sea goddess Amphitrite

Uranus ('Heaven') the primeval sky god; son and husband of the Earth goddess Gaia, and father of Cronos and the Titans

Zephyrus god of the west wind; husband of Iris

Zeus chief of the gods who dispensed good and evil, he was the father and ruler of all; son of Cronos

Gods of Ancient Rome

Aesculapius god of medicine, equivalent to the Greek Asclepius

Apollo in Greek and Roman mythology, the god of the sun, music, poetry, prophecy, agriculture, and pastoral life; he was the twin of Diana

Aurora goddess of the dawn; her Greek equivalent is Eos

Bacchus god of fertility and of wine; identified with the Greek Dionysus

Bellona goddess of war

Ceres goddess of agriculture; equivalent to the Greek Demeter

Cupid god of love; identified with the Greek Eros

Diana goddess of chastity, hunting, and the Moon; daughter of Jupiter and twin of Apollo; her Greek equivalent is the goddess Artemis

Dis god of the underworld, also known as Orcus, equivalent to the Greek Hades; Dis is also a synonym for the underworld itself

Faunus god of fertility and prophecy, with goat's ears, horns, tail, and hind legs; identified with the Greek Pan

Flora goddess of flowers, youth, and spring

Fortuna goddess of chance and good fortune; identified with the Greek Tyche

Janus god of doorways and passageways, after whom January is named; he is represented as having two faces, one looking forwards and one back; also god of past, present, and future, and considered to be the god who gave agriculture and law to humanity

Juno principal goddess, identified with the Greek Hera; the wife of Jupiter, she was concerned with all aspects of women's lives

Jupiter (Jove) chief god, identified with the Greek Zeus; he was god of the sky, associated with lightning and thunderbolts, the protector in battle, and the bestower of victory

Luna goddess of the moon

Maia earth goddess, sometimes seen as the mother of Mercury

Mars god of war, equivalent to the Greek Ares

Mercury a god, identified with the Greek Hermes, and, like him, represented with winged sandals and a winged staff entwined with snakes; he was the messenger of the gods and was associated particularly with commerce

Minerva goddess of intelligence, and of handicrafts and the arts; equivalent to the Greek Athena

Mithras sun god and god of light

Neptune god of the sea; equivalent to the Greek Poseidon

Ops goddess of harvest and growth of seed; wife of Saturn

Pales goddess of flocks and shepherds

Parcae three goddesses – Decima, Nona, and Morta – equated with the Greek Moirai

Pax goddess of peace; equivalent to the Greek Irene

Pluto god of the underworld

Pomona goddess of fruit trees who is often depicted in art holding a cornucopia, symbolizing the fruits of the earth

Priapus originally a Greek fertility god; later a Roman god of gardens, where his image was frequently used as a scarecrow

Proserpine goddess of the underworld; her Greek equivalent is Persephone

Saturn god of agriculture; identified by the Romans with the Greek god Cronos

Silvanus a woodland god, at times identified with the Greek Pan

Sol sun god

Tellus goddess of the Earth; identified with a number of other agricultural gods and celebrations

Terminus god of land boundaries whose worship was associated with that of Jupiter

Venus goddess of love and beauty, equivalent to the Greek Aphrodite; as mother of Aeneas, she was regarded as guardian of the Roman people, as well as goddess of military victory and patroness of spring

Vertumnus ancient Etruscan god of seasonal change and of fruit; husband of Pomona

Vesta goddess of the hearth; equivalent to the Greek Hestia

Vulcan god of fire and destruction; later identified with the Greek god Hephaestus

Gods of Celtic Mythology

Celtic mythology has three traditions originating from Britain (including Wales), Gaul, and Ireland.

Alisanos god of the rock

Anoniredi (Gaul), **Anna** (Britain), **Anu** (Ireland) goddess of plenty; one aspect of the divine mother

Arianrhod in Welsh mythology, mother of Llew and Dylan

Badhbh war goddess, often portrayed as a crow or raven, also associated with divine metamorphosis

Banbha in Irish mythology, one of the three sisters who – together with Fodla and Eriu – formed the goddess of sovereignty, or the spirit of Ireland

Boann river goddess; mother of Oenghus

Belenus (Gaul), **Bel**, **Beli**, or **Belinus** (Britain), **Bíle** (Ireland) god associated mostly with solar symbolism and light, sometimes compared to the Greek Apollo; his other major aspects were Mabon and Oenghus, perhaps also Merlin. His cult was later replaced with the worship of the Archangel Michael in the Christian church

Blodeuwedd ('the flower maiden') deity associated with love and giving

Borvo, **Bormo**, or **Bormanus** (Gaul) god associated with thermal waters

Brigantu (Gaul), **Brigantia** or **Brighid** (Britain), **Brigit** (Ireland) goddess often associated with the Roman goddess Minerva; she was the patron of livestock and the produce of the earth; also goddess of crafts, therapy, and poetic inspiration. Later worshipped as St Brigit or St Bride in the Christian church

Cernunnos ('the Horned (or Peaked) One') ruler and protector of the animal kingdom, often portrayed in a zoomorphic manner, or accompanied by powerful animals (such as serpents or bulls); also the Lord of the Underworld. Early Christianity targeted him as the Devil; modern paganism endeavours to revive the worship of this deity

Cerridwen Welsh goddess of the Underworld and of dark prophetic powers, represented by a sow

Cliodna goddess of beauty and peace

Condatis god of confluence

Dea Arduinna one of many goddesses associated with wild animals, often portrayed with a wild boar

Dea Artio goddess associated with the bear, often connected to the Irish goddess Flidhais

Daghdha, **Dagda**, **Dana**, or **Donn** (Ireland), **Don** (Britain) the ancestor deity, often perceived to be the lord of the Otherworld, similar to the Roman god of the dead, Dis; sometimes associated with Cernunnos, father of Oenghus (the Irish Maponos); he was the greatest of Irish gods worshipped in Druidism as a god of wisdom and power

Dunatis god of fortified places

Dylan Welsh god associated with the sea; son of Arianrhod

Édain or **Étain** goddess of the Otherworld, maiden of joy and sorrow who was parted from, and then won back by, her divine husband Midhir

Epona (Gaul and Britain) the horse goddess, patroness of cavalry; sometimes associated with the Irish Édain and the Welsh Rhiannon

Flidhais Irish goddess who ruled the wild animals of the forests

Goibhniu (Ireland), **Gofannon** (Britain) god equivalent to the Roman Vulcan, he was thought to be a smith, a patron of crafts, but also of strength; often portrayed as the host of the Otherworld, accompanied by two further aspects, Creidhne (god of metal-working) and Luchtaine (divine wheelwright)

Grannos (Gaul and Britain) god associated primarily with curative powers and healing; similar to the Greek god Apollo

Ialonus god of the clearing of cultivated fields

Llew Welsh god associated with sacred kingship and Threefold Death; son of Arianrhod; sometimes associated with the Irish Lugh (equivalent of the Roman Mercury)

Lugh (Ireland), **Lugos** (Gaul), **Lleu** (Britain) god of skill, arts, crafts, and commerce; in the Gaulish tradition, portrayed like the Roman god Mercury; in the Irish tradition, his images are associated with youth, athleticism, and victory of light over darkness

Macha horse goddess associated with war, battle, and valour; linked also to festivals and ritual games

Maponos or **Maponus** (Gaul), **Mabon** (Britain), **Oenghus** (Ireland) god associated with music, healing, and youth; sometimes portrayed as a hunter; the 'Celtic Apollo'

Manannán (Ireland), **Manawydan** (Britain) deity of patience, wisdom, and counsel; also god of the sea, portrayed riding his chariot across the waves

Matres or **Matronae** (Gaul and Britain) goddesses and divine consorts, usually appearing in groups of three, symbolizing the concept of Earth as a divine mother; also associated with fertility, childbirth, and earthly fecundity

Medhbh of Connacht goddess of sexuality and physical love; a woman-warrior

Merlin one of the aspects of the 'Son of Light', a guardian god of the land; there are certain parallels between his mythical biography and the life of Christ as documented in the New Testament of the Christian church

Modron supreme divine 'Mother'; her divine child was known as Mabon ('Son')

Morríghan ('Phantom Queen') one of the goddesses of war and destruction; often appears in triple form together with Nemhain and Badhbh

Nantosvelta goddess associated with water

Nemhain ('Frenzy') one of the goddesses of war and devastation

Nudd or **Nodons** (Britain), **Nuada** or **Nuadha** (Ireland) god associated with the protection of the kingship and with the sovereignty of the land

Ogmios (Gaul), **Ogmia** (Britain), **Ogma** or **Oghma** (Ireland) a giver of eloquence and strength; often associated with the Roman hero Hercules

Rhiannon Welsh goddess, the 'Great Queen', associated with the horse and totem birds

Silvanus (Gaul and Britain), **Sucellus** (Britain) god associated with the underworld, but also, probably, with the fertility of the earth; he is often portrayed with a mallet, a drinking jar, and, on occasion, with a dog; his companion was the goddess Nantosvelta

Taranis (Gaul), **Taran** (Britain) god of war and of leadership; often portrayed as a fearsome soldier; in Gaulish tradition associated with the Roman gods Mars and Jupiter

Gods of Nordic Mythology

Aegir god of the sea, married to Ran; their nine daughters were waves of the sea

Aesir a race of gods belonging to the sky, warlike in nature, and including most of the more familiar deities

Balder (Beldur) the best, wisest, and most loved of all the gods; son of Odin and Freya and husband of Nanna; he was killed, at Loki's instigation, by a twig of mistletoe shot by the blind god Hoder

Eostre (Ostara) an Anglo-Saxon goddess of spring; identified with the rising sun

Frey (Freyr) fertility god; brother of Freya

Freya (Freyja, Gefn) goddess of married love and the hearth; wife of Odin and mother of Thor

Frigg (Friga) the chief goddess, often confused with Freya; associated with Venus by the Romans

Gefion goddess of virginity and fertility

Heimdall god of light, who was present at the birth of the world, and who watches over the other gods

Hel (Hela) goddess of the underworld

Hoder (Hodur) blind god who killed Balder

Hoenir creator god who, with Odin and Lodur, made the first humans, endowing them with the senses

Idun goddess, keeper of the golden apples of eternal youth

Lodur creator god who, with Odin and Hoenir, made the first humans, endowing them with life and energy

Loki one of the principal gods, but cause of dissension among the gods, and the slayer of Balder; also known as god of mischief

Mimir guardian of the well of knowledge

Nanna wife of Balder; died of grief after his murder

Njord god of sailors and fishermen

Norn any of three goddesses of fate: the goddess of the past (Urd), the goddess of the present (Verdandi), and the goddess of the future (Skuld)

Odin chief god, the **Woden** or **Wotan** of the Germanic peoples; a sky god, he lives in Asgard, at the top of the world-tree, with his wife Freya; together with Hoenir and Lodur, he created the first humans and endowed them with a soul

Ran storm goddess; wife of Aegir

Sif corn goddess; wife of Thor

Sigyn wife of Loki

Skadi mountain goddess; wife of Njord, mother of Frey and Freya

Sol sun goddess who drove her chariot across the sky

Thor god of thunder (his hammer); son of Odin and Freya

Tyr (Tiw, Tiwaz) god of battles

Ull god of justice and fertility; son of Sif

Vali son of Odin, who avenged Balder's death by killing Hoder

Valkyries female warrior spirits who assisted Odin by training and protecting warriors

Vanir a peaceful race of gods associated with the earth and fertility

Ve (Vili) brother of Odin

Vidar son of Odin who avenged his death by killing the wolf Fennir

Religions in the UK

Dioceses of the Church of England

The addresses given are for the Dean or Provost.

Diocese of Bath and Wells Bishop, The Right Reverend J L Thompson; Dean, The Very Reverend Richard Lewis; The Dean's Lodgings, 25 The Liberty, Wells BA5 2SZ; phone: (01749) 670278

Diocese of Birmingham Bishop, The Right Reverend M Santer; Provost, The Very Reverend Peter Berry; Birmingham Cathedral, Colmore Row, Birmingham B5 7SA; phone: (0121) 236 4333/6323; fax: (0121) 212 0868

Diocese of Blackburn Bishop, The Right Reverend A D Chesters; Provost, The Very Reverend David Frayne; Cathedral Close, Blackburn BB2 6SD; phone: (01254) 51491

Diocese of Bradford Bishop, The Right Reverend D J Smith; Provost, The Very Reverend John Richardson; Cathedral Office, 1 Stott Hill, Bradford BD1 4EH; phone: (01274) 777724; fax: (01274) 777730

Wells Cathedral   Corel

Diocese of Bristol Bishop, The Right Reverend B Rogerson; Dean, to be appointed; Cathedral Office, Bristol Cathedral, College Green, Bristol BS1 5TJ; phone: (0117) 926 4879; fax: (0117) 925 3678

Diocese of Canterbury Archbishop, The Most Reverend and Right Honourable George L Carey; Dean, The Very Reverend John Simpson; Cathedral Office, Cathedral House, 11 The Precincts, Canterbury CT1 2EH; phone: (01227) 762862

Diocese of Carlisle Bishop, The Right Reverend I Harland; Dean, The Very Reverend Henry Champneys; Cathedral Office, 7 The Abbey, Carlisle CA3 8TZ; phone: (01228) 48151

Diocese of Chelmsford Bishop, The Right Reverend J F Perry; Provost, The Very Reverend Peter Judd; Cathedral Office, New Street, Chelmsford CM1 1AT; phone: (01245) 263660; fax: (01245) 496802

Diocese of Chester Bishop, The Right Reverend P R Forster; Dean, The Very Reverend Stephen Smalley; Cathedral Office, 12 Abbey Square, Chester CH1 2HU; phone: (01244) 324756; fax: (01244) 341110

Diocese of Chichester Bishop, The Right Reverend E W Kemp; Dean, The Very Reverend John Treadgold; The Deanery, Chichester PO19 1PX; phone: (01243) 787337

Succession List of the Archbishops of Canterbury

Date elected	Name	Date elected	Name	Date elected	Name	Date elected	Name
597	Augustine	1174	Richard (of Dover)	1691	John Tillotson	1868	Archibald Campbell Tait
604	Laurentius	1184	Baldwin	1695	Thomas Tenison	1883	Edward White Benson
619	Mellitus	1193	Hubert Walter	1716	William Wake	1896	Frederick Temple
624	Justus	1207	Stephen Langton	1737	John Potter	1903	Randall Thomas Davidson
627	Honorius	1229	Richard le Grant	1747	Thomas Herring	1928	William Cosmo Gordon
655	Deusdedit	1234	Edmund of Abingdon	1757	Matthew Hutton		Lang
668	Theodore	1245	Boniface of Savoy	1758	Thomas Secker	1942	William Temple
693	Berthwald	1273	Robert Kilwardby	1768	Frederick Cornwallis	1945	Geoffrey Francis Fisher
731	Tatwine	1279	John Peckham	1783	John Moore	1961	Arthur Michael Ramsey
735	Nothelm	1294	Robert Winchelsey	1805	Charles Manners-Sutton	1974	Frederick Donald Coggan
740	Cuthbert	1313	Walter Reynolds	1828	William Howley	1980	Robert Alexander
761	Bregowine	1328	Simon Meopham	1848	John Bird Sumner		Kennedy Runcie
765	Jaenbert	1333	John de Stratford	1862	Charles Thomas Longley	1991–	George Leonard Carey
793	Ethelhard	1349	Thomas Bradwardine				
805	Wulfred	1349	Simon Islip				[1] Restored.
832	Feologeld	1366	Simon Langham				
833	Ceolnoth	1368	William Whittlesey				
870	Ethelred	1375	Simon Sudbury				
890	Plegmund	1381	William Courtenay				
914	Athelm	1396	Thomas Arundel				
923	Wulfhelm	1398	Roger Walden				
942	Oda	1399	Thomas Arundel[1]				
959	Aelfsige	1414	Henry Chichele				
959	Brithelm	1443	John Stafford				
960	Dunstan	1452	John Kempe				
c. 988	Ethelgar	1454	Thomas Bourchier				
990	Sigeric	1486	John Morton				
995	Aelfric	1501	Henry Deane				
1005	Alphege	1503	William Warham				
1013	Lyfing	1533	Thomas Cranmer				
1020	Ethelnoth	1556	Reginald Pole				
1038	Eadsige	1559	Matthew Parker				
1051	Robert of Jumieges	1576	Edmund Grindal				
1052	Stigand	1583	John Whitgift				
1070	Lanfranc	1604	Richard Bancroft				
1093	Anselm	1611	George Abbot				
1114	Ralph d'Escures	1633	William Laud				
1123	William de Corbeil	1660	William Juxon				
1139	Theobald	1663	Gilbert Sheldon				
1162	Thomas à Becket	1678	William Sancroft				

Most Reverend and Rt Hon Dr George Carey, Archbishop of Canterbury
Sean Aidan

Diocese of Coventry Bishop, to be appointed; Provost, The Very Reverend John Fitzmaurice; Pelham Lee House, 7 Priory House, Coventry CV1 5ES; phone: (01203) 227597

Diocese of Derby Bishop, The Right Reverend J S Bailey; Provost, to be appointed; The Provost's House, 9 Highfield Road, Derby DE22 1GX

Diocese of Durham Bishop, The Right Reverend A M A Turnbull; Dean, The Very Reverend John Arnold; The Deanery, Durham DH1 3RS; phone: (0191) 384 7500

Diocese of Ely Bishop, The Right Reverend S W Sykes; Dean, The Very Reverend Michael Higgins; The Deanery, The College, Ely CB7 4DN; phone: (01353) 667735

Diocese of Exeter Bishop, The Right Reverend G H Thompson; Dean, The Very Reverend Keith Jones; Cathedral Office, 1 The Cloisters, Exeter EX1 1HS; phone: (01392) 255573; fax: (01392) 498769

Diocese of Gloucester Bishop, The Right Reverend D E Bentley; Dean, The Very Reverend Nicholas Bury; The Deanery, Miller's Green, Gloucester GL1 2BP; phone: (01452) 524167

Diocese of Guildford Bishop, The Right Reverend J W Gladwin; Dean, The Very Reverend Alexander Wedderspoon; Cathedral Office, Guildford Cathedral, Stag Hill, Guildford GU2 5UP; phone: (01483) 565287; fax: (01483) 303350

Diocese of Hereford Bishop, The Right Reverend J K Oliver; Dean, The Very Reverend Robert Willis; Cathedral Office, 5 College Cloisters, Hereford HR1 2NG; phone: (01432) 359880

Diocese of Leicester Bishop, The Right Reverend T F Butler; Provost, The Very Reverend Derek Hole; Cathedral Office, 1 St Martin's East, Leicester LE1 5FX; phone: (0116) 262 5294

Diocese of Lichfield Bishop, The Right Reverend K N Sutton; Dean, The Very Reverend Tom Wright; Chapter Office, 19a The Close, Lichfield WS13 7LD; phone: (01543) 256120; fax: (01543) 416306

Diocese of Lincoln Bishop, The Right Reverend R M Hardy; Dean, to be appointed; Chapter Office, The Cathedral, Lincoln LN2 1PZ; phone: (01522) 530320

Diocese of Liverpool Bishop, to be appointed; Dean, The Very Reverend Derrick Walters; The Cathedral, St James' Mount, Liverpool L1 7AZ; phone: (0151) 709 6271

Diocese of London Bishop, The Right Reverend R J C Chartres; Dean, The Very Reverend John Moses; Chapter House, St Paul's Churchyard, London EC4M 8AD; phone: (0171) 236 2827; fax: (0171) 332 0298

Frequency of Attending Religious Services in Great Britain

All respondents were asked: 'Apart from such special occasions as weddings, funerals, and baptisms, how often nowadays do you attend services or meetings connected with your religion?'. Those without a religion were not asked the question.
(In percentages. Totals may not add up to 100 due to rounding.)

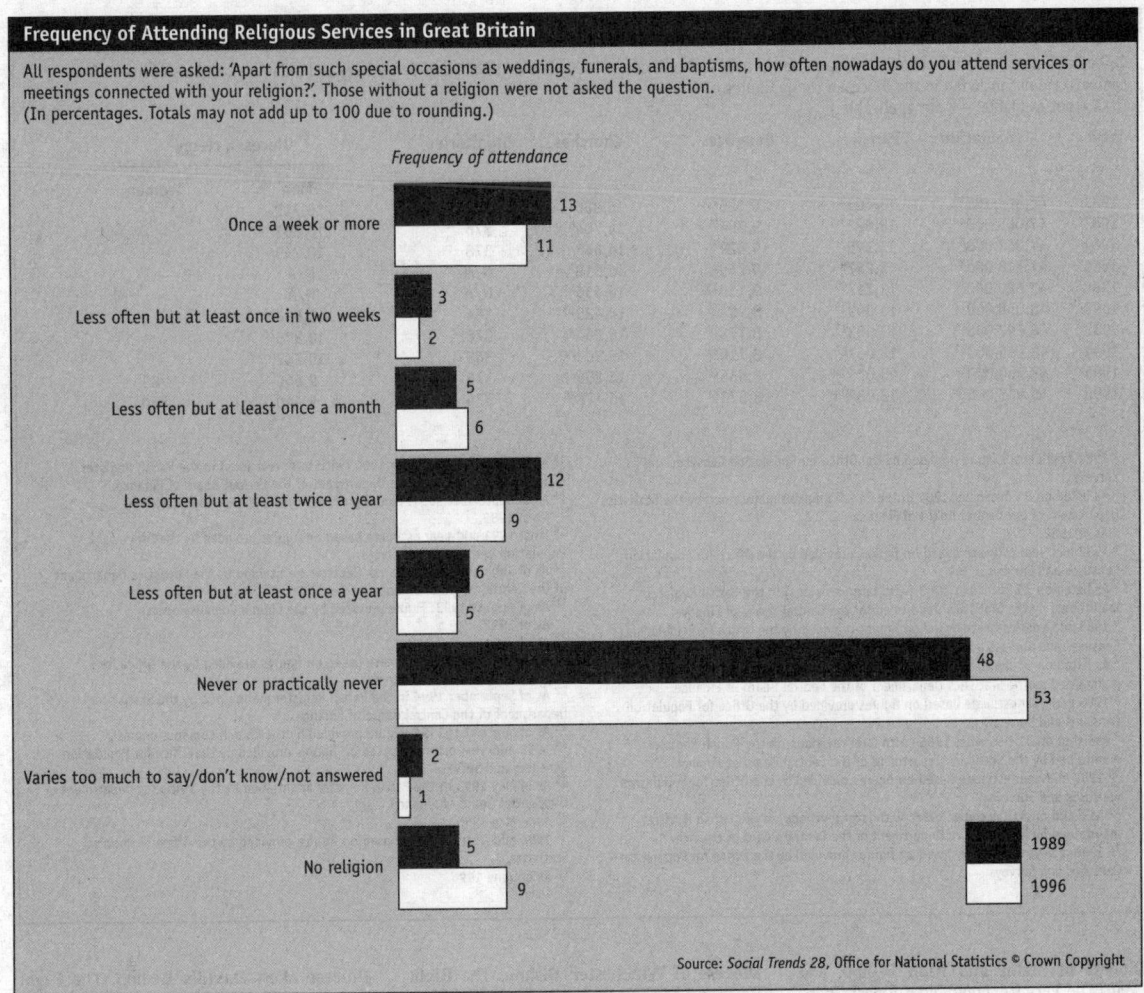

Frequency of attendance

Once a week or more — 13 / 11
Less often but at least once in two weeks — 3 / 2
Less often but at least once a month — 5 / 6
Less often but at least twice a year — 12 / 9
Less often but at least once a year — 6 / 5
Never or practically never — 48 / 53
Varies too much to say/don't know/not answered — 2 / 1
No religion — 5 / 9

1989
1996

Source: *Social Trends 28*, Office for National Statistics © Crown Copyright

Diocese of Manchester Bishop, The Right Reverend C J Mayfield; Dean, The Very Reverend Kenneth Riley; Cathedral Office, The Cathedral, Manchester M3 1SX; phone: (0161) 833 2220; fax: (0161) 839 6226

Diocese of Newcastle Bishop, The Right Reverend J M Wharton; Provost, The Very Reverend Nicholas Coulton; The Cathedral Office, St Nicholas Churchyard, Newcastle upon Tyne, NE1 1PF; phone: (0191) 232 1939; fax: (0191) 230 0735

Diocese of Norwich Bishop, The Right Reverend P J Nott; Dean, The Very Reverend Stephen Platten; Cathedral Office, The Close, Norwich NR1 4DH; phone: (01603) 218483; fax: (01603) 766032

Diocese of Oxford Bishop, The Right Reverend R D Harries; Dean, The Very Reverend John Drury; The Deanery, Christ Church, Oxford OX1 1DP; phone: (01865) 276162; fax: (01865) 276238

Diocese of Peterborough Bishop, The Right Reverend I P M Cundy; Dean, The Very Reverend Michael Bunker; Chapter Office, Minster Precincts, Peterborough PE1 1XX; phone: (01733) 343342; fax: (01733) 52465

Diocese of Portsmouth Bishop, The Right Reverend K W Stevenson; Provost, The Very Reverend Michael Yorke; Cathedral Office, St Thomas's Street, Portsmouth PO1 2HH; phone: (01705) 823300; fax: (01705) 295480

Diocese of Ripon Bishop, The Right Reverend D N de L Young; Dean, The Very Reverend John Methuen; The Chapter House, Ripon Cathedral, Ripon HG4 1QR; phone: (01765) 603615

Diocese of Rochester Bishop, The Right Reverend M J Nazir-Ali; Dean, The Very Reverend Edward Shotter; The Cathedral Office, Garth House, The Precinct, Rochester ME1 1SX; phone: (01634) 843366; fax: (01634) 401410

Diocese of St Albans Bishop, The Right Reverend C W Herbert; Dean, The Very Reverend Christopher Lewis; Cathedral Office, The Chapter House, Sumpter Yard, St Albans AL1 1BY; phone: (01727) 860780; fax: (01727) 850944

Diocese of St Edmundsbury and Ipswich Bishop, The Right Reverend J H R Lewis; Provost, The Very Reverend James Atwell; Cathedral Office, Angel Hill, Bury St Edmunds IP3 1LS; phone: (01284) 754933; fax: (01284) 768655

Diocese of Salisbury Bishop, The Right Reverend D S Stancliffe; Dean, The Very Reverend Derek Watson; The Deanery, 7 The Close, Salisbury SP1 2EF; phone: (01722) 322457

Diocese of Sheffield Bishop, The Right Reverend J Nicholls; Provost, The Very Reverend Michael Sadgrove; Cathedral Office, The Cathedral, Sheffield S1 1HA; phone: (0114) 275 3434

The Church of England: Number of Benifices, Parishes, Churches, Dignitaries, and Diocesan Clergy

Cathedral figures have not been included, except in data for benifices in 1990. The Archbishop of Canterbury and ordained members of his staff at Lambeth are not included in the Diocesan clergy figures.
(N/A = not available. – = not applicable.)

Year	Population	Parishes	Benefices	Churches	Dignitaries	Diocesan clergy	
						Men	Women
1981	46,566,160[1]	13,663[2]	10,125[2]	16,806[2]	370[3]	10,789	–
1983	47,005,000[4]	13,422[5]	9,754[5]	16,704[5]	376	10,807	–
1984	47,052,000[6]	13,395[7]	9,529[7]	16,643[7]	378	10,749	–
1986	47,318,000[8]	13,287[9]	9,259[9]	16,518[9]	N/A	N/A	–
1988	47,620,000[10]	13,213[11]	9,110[11]	16,436[11]	N/A	N/A	–
1990	48,058,000[12]	13,099[13]	8,906[14]	16,425[13]	384	10,530[15]	–
1993	48,297,000[16]	13,083[17]	8,772[18]	16,364[17]	378[19]	10,375[20]	–
1994	48,605,000[21]	13,067[22]	8,710[23]	16,303[22]	369	10,247	–
1995	48,760,000[24]	13,025[25]	8,655[26]	16,255[25]	376	9,666	783
1996	48,935,000[27]	12,982[28]	8,573[28]	16,128[28]	376	9,440	820

[1] 1981 final Census figure provided by the Office for Population Censuses and Surveys.
[2] As listed on 31 December 1981 in the Parish Register maintained by the Statistics Department of the Central Board of Finance.
[3] As of 1982.
[4] 1982 mid-year estimate based on figures provided by the Office for Population Censuses and Surveys.
[5] As listed on 31 December 1983 (with later revisions) in the Parish Register maintained by the Statistics Department of the Central Board of Finance.
[6] 1983 mid-year estimate based on figures provided by the Office for Population Censuses and Surveys.
[7] As listed on 31 December 1984 (with later revisions) in the Parish Register maintained by the Statistics Department of the Central Board of Finance.
[8] 1985 mid-year estimate based on figures provided by the Office for Population Censuses and Surveys.
[9] As listed on 31 December 1986 (with later revisions) in the Parish Register maintained by the Statistics Department of the Central Board of Finance.
[10] 1987 mid-year estimate based on figures provided by the Office for Population Censuses and Surveys.
[11] As listed on 31 December 1988 (with later revisions) in the Parish Register maintained by the Statistics Department of the Central Board of Finance.
[12] 1990 mid-year estimate based on figures provided by the Office for Population Censuses and Surveys.

[13] As listed on 31 December 1990 (with later revisions) in the Parish Register maintained by the Statistics Department of the Central Board of Finance.
[14] As of September 1991. Figure provided by the Church Commissioners.
[15] As of 1989.
[16] Final 1991 mid-year estimate based on figures provided by the Office for Population Censuses and Surveys.
[17] As of June 1993 in the Parish Register maintained by the Statistics Department of the Central Board of Finance.
[18] As of August 1993. Figure provided by the Church Commissioners.
[19] As of 1992.
[20] As of 1991.
[21] Final 1992 mid-year estimate based on figures provided by the Office for Population Censuses and Surveys.
[22] As of September 1994 in the Parish Register maintained by the Statistics Department of the Central Board of Finance.
[23] As of September 1994. Figure provided by the Church Commissioners.
[24] 1993 mid-year estimate based on figures provided by the Office for Population Censuses and Surveys.
[25] As of May 1995 in the Parish Register maintained by the Statistics Department of the Central Board of Finance.
[26] As of May 1995.
[27] 1994 mid-year estimate based on figures provided by the Office of National Statistics.
[28] As of June 1996.

Diocese of Sodor and Man Bishop, and Dean, The Very Reverend Nöel Jones; Chapter Office, 1 Kelly Close, Ramsey IM2 3QN; phone: (01624) 816545; fax: (01624) 816545

Diocese of Southwark Bishop, The Right Reverend R K Williamson; Provost, The Very Reverend Colin Slee; Cathedral Office, Montague Close, London SE1 9DA; phone: (0171) 407 3708; fax: (0171) 357 7389

Diocese of Southwell Bishop, The Right Reverend P B Harris; Provost, The Very Reverend David Leaning; The Minster Office, Trebeck Hall, Bishop's Drive, Southwell NG25 0JP; phone: (01636) 812649; fax: (01636) 815904

Diocese of Truro Bishop, The Right Reverend W Ind; Dean, The Very Reverend David Shearlock; Cathedral Office, 21 Old Bridge Street, Truro TR1 2AH; phone: (01872) 276782; fax: (01872) 277788

Diocese of Wakefield Bishop, The Right Reverend N S McCulloch; Provost, The Very Reverend Canon George Nairn-Briggs; Cathedral Office, Northgate, Wakefield WF1 1HG; phone: (01924) 373923; fax: (01924) 215054

Diocese of Winchester Bishop, The Right Reverend M C Scott-Joynt; Dean, The Very Reverend Peter Marshall; Cathedral Office, 5 The Close, Winchester SO23 9LS; phone: (01962) 853137

Diocese of Worcester Bishop, The Right Reverend P S M Selby; Dean, The Very Reverend Peter Marshall; Cathedral Office, 10a College Green, Worcester WR1 2LH; phone: (01905) 28854; fax: (01905) 611139

Diocese of York Archbishop, The Most Reverend and Right Honourable D M Hope; Dean, The Very Reverend Raymond Furnell; The Deanery, York YO1 2JD; phone: (01904) 623608; fax: (01904) 672002

Dioceses of the Church in Wales

Diocese of St Asaph Archbishop, The Most Reverend Alwyn Rice Jones; Esgobty, St Asaph LL17 0TW; phone: (01745) 583503

Diocese of Bangor Bishop, The Right Reverend Dr Barry C Morgan; Ty'r Esgob, Bangor LL57 2SS; phone: (01248) 362895

Diocese of St David's Bishop, The Right Reverend D Huw Jones; Llys Esgob Abergwili, Carmarthen SA31 2JG; phone: (01267) 236597

Diocese of Llandaff Bishop, The Right Reverend Roy T Davies; Llys Esgob, The Cathedral Green, Llandaff, Cardiff CF5 2JG; phone: (01222) 562400

Diocese of Monmouth Bishop, The Right Reverend Dr Rowan D Williams; Bishopstow, Stow Hill, Newport NP9 4EA; phone: (01633) 263510

Diocese of Swansea and Brecon Bishop, The Right Reverend Dewi M Bridges; Ely Tower, Brecon LD3 9DE; phone: (01874) 622008

Presbyteries of the Church of Scotland

Church Headquarters and Principals
Lord High Commissioner The Lord Macfarlane of Bearsden; **Moderator of the**

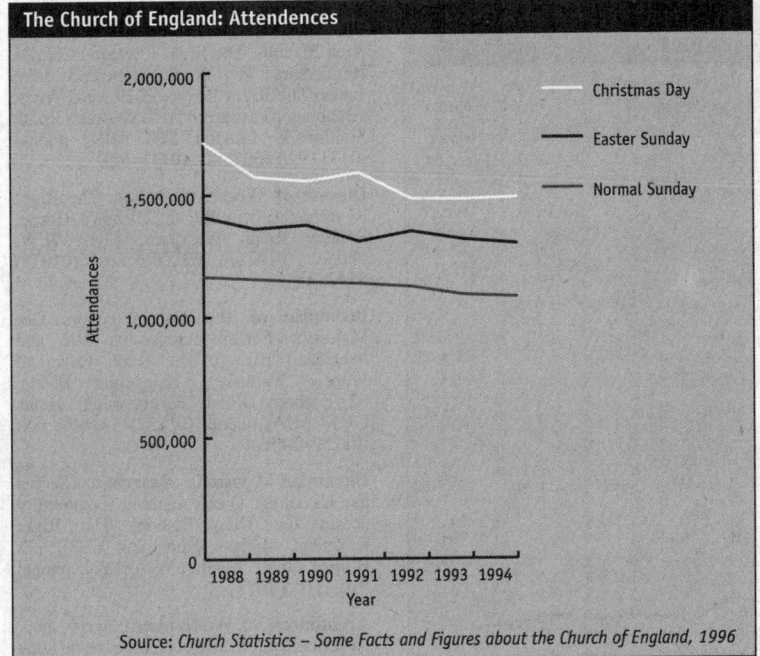

The Church of England: Attendances

- Christmas Day
- Easter Sunday
- Normal Sunday

Source: *Church Statistics – Some Facts and Figures about the Church of England, 1996*

General Assembly The Right Reverend A McDonald; **Principal Clerk** Reverend F A J Macdonald; **Deputy Clerk** Reverend M A MacLean; **Procurator** A Dunlop; **Law Agent and Solicitor of the Church** Mrs J S Wilson; **Parliamentary Agent** I McCulloch (London); **General Treasurer** D F Ross

Church Office
121 George Street, Edinburgh, EH2 4YN; phone: (0131) 225 5722; Fax: (0131) 220 3113

Presbyteries
Edinburgh Reverend W P Graham; **West Lothian** Reverend D Shaw; **Lothian** Reverend J D McCulloch; **Melrose and Peebles** Reverend J H Brown; **Duns** Reverend A C D Cartwright; **Jedburgh** Reverend A D Reid; **Ammandale and Eskdale** Reverend C B Haston; **Dumfries and Kirkcudbright** Reverend G M A Savage; **Wigtown and Stranraer** Reverend D Dutton; **Ayr** Reverend J Crichton; **Irvine and Kilmarnock** Reverend C G F Brodie; **Ardrossan** Reverend D Broster; **Lanark** Reverend I D Cunningham; **Paisley** Reverend D Kay; **Greenock** Reverend D Mill; **Glasgow** Reverend A Cunningham; **Hamilton** Reverend J H Wilson; **Dumbarton** Reverend D P Munro; **South Argyll** Reverend M A J Gossip; **Dunoon** Reverend R Samuel; **Lorn and Mull** Reverend W Hogg; **Falkirk** Reverend D E McClements; **Stirling** Reverend B W Dunsmore; **Dunfermline** Reverend W E Farquhar; **Kirkcaldy** Reverend B L Tomlinson; **St Andrews** Reverend J W Patterson; **Dunkeld and Meigle** Reverend A F Chisholm; **Perth**

Reverend M Ward; **Dundee** Reverend J A Roy; **Angus** Reverend R J Ramsay; **Aberdeen** Reverend A Douglas; **Kincardine and Deeside** Reverend J W S Brown; **Gordon** Reverend I U Thomson; **Buchan** Reverend R Neilson; **Moray** Reverend D J Ferguson; **Abernethy** Reverend J A I MacEwan; **Inverness** Reverend A S Younger; **Lochaber** Reverend A Ramsay; **Ross** Reverend R M MacKinnon; **Sutherland** Reverend R J Goskirk; **Caithness** Reverend M G Mappin; **Lochcarron/Skye** Reverend A I Macarthur; **Uist** Reverend A P J Varwell; **Lewis** Reverend T S Sinclair; **Orkney (Finstown)** Reverend T Hunt; **Shetland (Lerwick)** Reverend N R Whyte; **England (London)** Reverend W A Cairns; **Europe (Portugal)** Reverend J W McLeod

Dioceses of the Church of Ireland

Archbishop of Armagh and Primate of All Ireland
Most Reverend Robert H A Eames

Bishops
Clogher Brian D A Hannon; **Connor** James E Moore; **Derry and Raphoe** James Mehaffey; **Down and Dromore** Harold C Miller; **Kilmore, Elphin, and Ardagh** Michael H G Mayes; **Tuam, Killala, and Achonry** vacant

Archbishop of Dublin, Bishop of Glendalough, and Primate of Ireland
Most Reverend Walton N F Empey

Bishops
Cashel and Ossary John R W Neill; **Cork, Cloyne, and Ross** Robert A Warke; **Limerick and Killaloe** Edward F Darling; **Meath and Kildare** Most Reverend Robert L Clarke

Dioceses of the Roman Catholic Church in England and Wales

The basic administrative unit of the Catholic Church is the diocese – an area presided over by a bishop, sometimes with auxiliary bishops. In England and Wales there are 22 territorial dioceses, plus two dioceses covering the whole country.

Diocese of Arundel and Brighton Bishop, The Right Reverend Cormac Murphy-O'Connor; Bishop's House, The Upper Drive, Hove, East Sussex BN3 6NE; phone: (01273) 506387; fax: (01273) 501527

Archdiocese of Birmingham Bishop, The Most Reverend Maurice Couve de Murville; Auxiliary Bishops, The Right Reverend Philip Pargeter, The Right Reverend Terence Brain; Cathedral House, St Chad's Queensway, Birmingham B4 6EX; phone: (0121) 236 5535; fax: (0121) 233 9266

Diocese of Brentwood Bishop, The Right Reverend Thomas McMahon; Cathedral House, Ingrave Road, Brentwood, Essex CM15 8AT; phone: (01277) 232266; fax: (01277) 261152

Archdiocese of Cardiff Archbishop, The Most Reverend John Aloysius Ward OFMCap.; Archbishop's House, 41–43 Cathedral Road, Cardiff CF1 9HD; phone: (01222) 220411; fax: (01222) 345950

Diocese of Clifton Bishop, The Right Reverend Mervyn Alexander; Egerton Road, Bishopston, Bristol BS7 8HU; phone: (0117) 983 3907

Diocese of East Anglia Bishop, The Right Reverend Peter Smith; The White House, 21 Upgate, Poringland, Norwich NR14 7SH; phone: (01508) 492202; fax: (01508) 495358

Diocese of Hallam Sede vacante; 'Quarters', Carsick Hill Way, Sheffield S10 3LT; phone: (0114) 230 9101; fax: (0114) 230 5722

Diocese of Hexham and Newcastle Bishop, The Right Reverend Dom Ambrose Griffiths OSB; Bishop's House, East Denton Hall, 800 West Road, Newcastle upon Tyne NE5 2BJ; phone: (0191) 228 0003; fax: (0191) 274 0432

Diocese of Lancaster Bishop, The Right Reverend Brian Charles Foley; Bishop's House, Cannon Hill, Lancaster LA1 5NG; phone: (01524) 32231; fax: (01524) 849296

Diocese of Leeds Bishop, The Right Reverend David Konstant; 7 St Marks Avenue, Leeds LS2 9BN; phone: (0113) 244 4788; fax: (0113) 244 8084

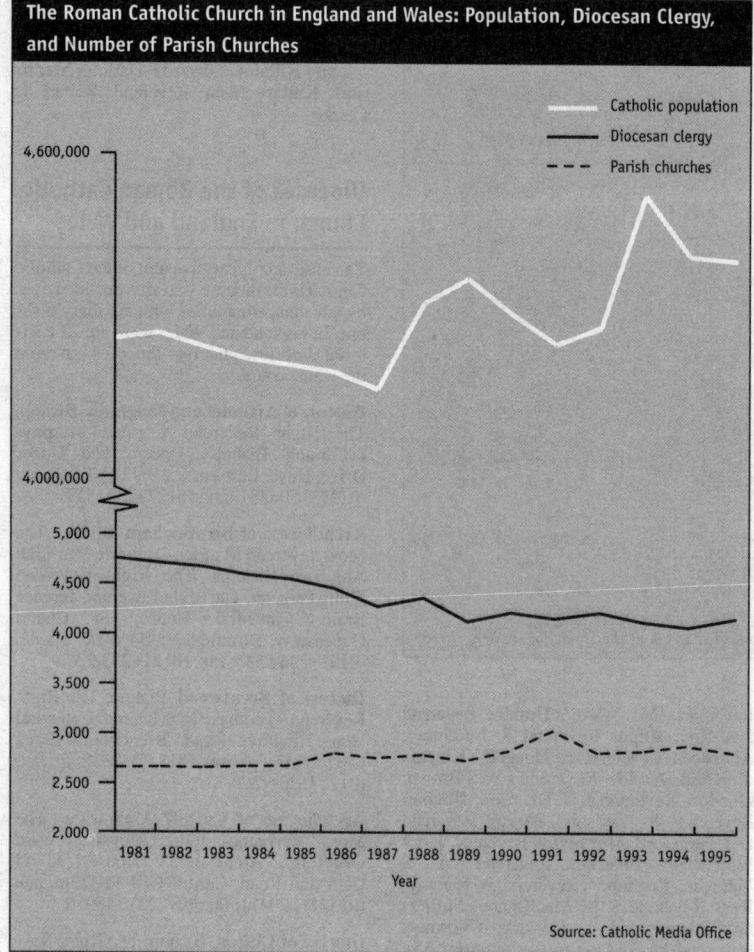

The Roman Catholic Church in England and Wales: Population, Diocesan Clergy, and Number of Parish Churches

- Catholic population
- Diocesan clergy
- - - Parish churches

Source: Catholic Media Office

Archdiocese of Liverpool Bishop, The Most Reverend Patrick Kelly; Auxiliary Bishops, The Right Reverend John Rawsthorne, The Right Reverend Vincent Malone; 152 Brownlow Hill, Liverpool L3 5RQ; phone: (0151) 709 4801; fax: (0151) 708 5167

Diocese of Menevia Bishop, The Right Reverend Daniel Mullins; Curial Office, Convent Street, Swansea SA1 2BX; phone: (01792) 644017; fax: (01792) 458641

Diocese of Middlesbrough Bishop, The Right Reverend John Crowley; Auxiliary Bishop, The Right Reverend Kevin O'Brien; 50a The Avenue, Linthorpe, Middlesbrough, Cleveland TS5 6QT; phone: (01642) 850505; fax: (01642) 851404

Diocese of Northampton Bishop, The Right Reverend Patrick Leo McCartie; Bishop's House, Marriott Street, Northampton NN2 6AW; phone: (01604) 715635; fax: (01604) 792186

Diocese of Nottingham Bishop, The Right Reverend James McGuinness; Willson House, Derby Road, Nottingham NG1 5AW; phone: (0115) 953 9800

Diocese of Plymouth Bishop, The Right Reverend Christopher Budd; Bishop's House, 31 Wyndham Street West, Plymouth, Devon PL1 5RZ; phone: (01752) 224414; fax: (01752) 223750

Diocese of Portsmouth Bishop, The Right Reverend Crispian Hollis; Bishop's House, Edinburgh Road, Portsmouth PO1 3HG; phone: (01705) 820894; fax: (01705) 863086

Diocese of Salford Sede vacante; Cathedral House, 250 Chapel Street, Salford M3 5LL; phone: (0161) 834 9052; fax: (0161) 839 7027

Diocese of Shrewsbury Bishop, The Right Reverend Brian Noble; 2 Park Road South, Birkenhead, Merseyside L43 4UX; phone: (0151) 652 9855; fax: (0151) 653 5172

Archdiocese of Southwark Archbishop, The Most Reverend Michael G Bowen; Area Bishops, The Right Reverend Charles Henderson, The Right Reverend John Jukes, The Right Reverend Howard Tripp; Archbishop's House, 150 St George's Road, Southwark, London SE1 6HX; phone: (0171) 928 5592; fax: (0171) 928 7833

Diocese of Wrexham Bishop, The Right Reverend Edwin Regan; Bishop's House, Sontley Road, Wrexham, LL13 7EW; phone: (01978) 262726; fax: (01978) 354257

Bishopric of the Forces (covers Her Majesty's Forces across the UK and overseas.) Bishop, The Right Reverend Francis Walmsley; Hampshire House, 62 Peabody Road, Farnborough, Hants GU14 6HA; phone: (01252) 543649; fax: (01252) 543649

Ukrainian Apostolic Exarchate (Serves the Ukrainian Greek Catholic community across the UK.) Bishop, The Right Reverend Michael Kuchmiak CSSR; 22 Binney Street, London W1Y 1YN; phone: (0171) 629 1073

Archdiocese of Westminster Archbishop, His Excellency Cardinal George Basil Hume OSB; Auxiliary Bishops, The Right Reverend James O'Brien, The Right Reverend Vincent Nichols, The Right Reverend Patrick O'Donoghue; Archbishop's House, Ambrosden Avenue, London SW1P 1QJ; phone: (0171) 798 9055; fax: (0171) 798 9077

Dioceses of the Roman Catholic Church for Scotland

Diocese of Aberdeen Bishop, The Right Reverend Mario Joseph Conti; Bishop's House, Queen's Cross, Aberdeen AB15 4XU; phone: (01224) 319154

Diocese of Dunkeld Bishop, The Right Reverend Vincent Logan; Bishop's House; 29 Roseangle, Dundee DD1 4LX; phone: (01382) 224327

Diocese of Galloway Bishop, The Right Reverend Maurice Taylor; Candida Casa, 8 Corsehill Road, Ayr KA7 2ST; phone: (01292) 266750

Diocese of Glasgow Archbishop, His Eminence Cardinal Thomas Joseph Winning; 40 Newlands Road, Glasgow G43 2JD

Diocese of Motherwell Bishop, The Right Reverend Joseph Devine; 17 Viewpark Road, Motherwell ML1 3ER; phone: (01698) 263715

Diocese of Paisley Bishop, The Right Reverend Stephen McGill PSS; 13 Newark Street, Greenock, Renfrewshire PA16 7UH; (01475) 783696

Diocese of St Andrews and Edinburgh Archbishop, The Most Reverend Keith Patrick O'Brien; St Bennet's, 42 Greenhill Gardens, Edinburgh EH10 4BJ; phone: (0131) 447 3337

Dioceses of the Roman Catholic Church in Ireland

There is one hierarchy for the whole of Ireland. Several of the dioceses have territory partly in the Republic of Ireland and partly in Northern Ireland.

Apostolic Nuncio to Ireland
The Most Reverend Giovanni Ceirano; 183 Navan Rd, Dublin 7, Republic of Ireland; phone: (00353) 1 380577

The Most Reverend Archbishops
Armagh HE Cardinal Sean Brady; Aracoeli, Armagh BT61 7QY; phone: (01861) 522045

Cashel Dermot Clifford; Archbishop's House, Thurles, County Tipperary, Republic of Ireland; phone: (00353) 504 21512

Dublin Desmond Connell; Archbishop's House, Drumcondra, Dublin 9, Republic of Ireland; phone: (00353) 1 837332

Tuam Michael Neary; Archbishop's House, Tuam, County Galway, Republic of Ireland; phone: (00353) 93 24166

The Most Reverend Bishops
Achonry Thomas Flynn; Bishop's House, Ballaghdaderreen, County Roscommon, Republic of Ireland; phone: (00353) 907 60021

Ardagh and Clonmacnois Colm O'Reilly; Bishop's House, St Michael's Longford, County Longford, Republic of Ireland; phone: (00353) 43 46432

Clogher Joseph Duffy; Bishop's House, Monaghan Republic of Ireland; phone: (00353) 47 81019

Clonfert Joseph Kirby; Bishop's House, St Brendan's, Coorheen, Loughrea, County Galway, Republic of Ireland; phone: (00353) 91 41560

Cloyne John Magee; Diocesan Centre, Cobh, County Cork, Republic of Ireland; phone: (00353) 21 811430

Cork and Ross John Buckley; Bishop's House, Redemption Road, Cork, Republic of Ireland; phone: (00353) 21 301717

Derry Seamus Hegarty; Bishop's House, St Eugene's Cathedral, Derry BT48 9AP; phone: (01504) 262302

Down and Connor Patrick J Walsh; Lisbreen, 73 Somerton Rd, Belfast, County Antrim BT15 4DE; phone: (01232) 776185

Dromore Francis Brooks; Bishop's House, Violet Hill, Newry, County Down BT35 6PN; phone: (01693) 62444

Elphin Christopher Jones; St Mary's Sligo, Republic of Ireland; phone: (00353) 71 62670

Ferns Brendon Comiskey; Bishop's House, Summerhill, Wexford, Republic of Ireland; phone: (00353) 53 22177

Galway and Kilmacduagh James McLoughlin; The Cathedral, Galway, Republic of Ireland; phone: (00353) 91 63566

Kerry William Murphy; Bishop's House, St Brendan's, Killarney, County Kerry, Republic of Ireland; phone: (00353) 64 31168

Kildare and Leighlin Laurence Ryan; Bishop's House, Carlow, Republic of Ireland; phone: (00353) 503 31102

Killaloe William Walsh; Bishop's House, Westbourne, Ennis, County Clare, Republic of Ireland; phone: (00353) 65 28638

Kilmore Francis McKiernan; Bishop's House, Ballina, County Mayo, Republic of Ireland; phone: (00353) 96 21518

Limerick Donal Murray; 66 O'Connoll St, Limerick, Republic of Ireland; phone: (00353) 61 315856

Meath Michael Smith; Bishop's House, Dublin Rd, Mullingar, County Westmeath, Republic of Ireland; phone: (00353) 44 48841

Ossory Laurence Forristal; Sion House, Killkenny, Republic of Ireland; phone: (00353) 56 62448

Raphoe Philip Boyce; Ard Adhamhnain, Letterkenny, County Donegal, Republic of Ireland; phone: (00353) 74 21208

Waterford and Lismore William Lee; Woodleigh, Summerville Avenue, Waterford, Republic of Ireland; phone: (00353) 51 71432

Dioceses of the Orthodox Church in the UK

Ecumenical Patriarchate: Archdiocese of Thyateira and Great Britain
Archdiocese of Thyateira and Great Britain His Eminence Archbishop Gregorios; Thyateira House, 5 Craven Hill, London W2 3EN; phone: (0171) 723 4787

Diocese of Zenoupolis The Right Reverend Bishop Aristarchos; 59 Selborne Gardens, London NW4 4SH; phone: (0181) 202 4821 or 455 7510

Diocese of Kyanea The Right Reverend Bishop Chrysostomos; Greek Cathedral of St Andrew, Kentish Town Road, London NW1 9QA; phone: (0171) 485 6385/0198

Diocese of Telmissos The Right Reverend Bishop Christopher; Greek Cathedral of the Nativity of the Mother of God, 305 Camberwell New Road, London SE5 0TF; phone: (0171) 703 0137

Diocese of Miletoupolis The Right Reverend Bishop Timotheos; Greek Cathedral of St Sophia, Moscow Road, London W2 4LQ; phone: (0171) 229 7260/4643

Diocese of Diokleia The Right Reverend Bishop Kallistos; 15 Staverton Road, Oxford OX2 6XH; phone: (01865) 554023

Ecumenical Patriarchate: Ukrainian Diocese in Britain
Diocese of Parnassos The Right Reverend Bishop Ioan (Derewianka); 2 Azalealaan B2, BUS10, 3600 Genk, Belgium; phone: (89) 382695

Patriarchate of Antioch
Vicariate of Western Europe The Right Reverend Bishop Gabriel (Saliby); 22 Avenue Kleber, 75116 Paris, France; phone: (45) 012115

Russian Orthodox Church (Patriarchate of Moscow) in Great Britain and Ireland
Diocese of Sourozh The Most Reverend Metropolitan Anthony; Russian Orthodox Cathedral of the Dormition of the Mother of God and All Saints, 67 Ennismore Gardens, London SW7 1NH

Diocese of Kerch His Eminence Archbishop Anatoly; 14a Bloom Park Road, Fulham, London SW6 7BG; phone: (0171) 386 7837

Diocese of Sergievo The Right Reverend Bishop Basil; 94a Banbury Road, Oxford OX2 6JT; phone: (01865) 512701

Patriarchate of Serbia
Diocese of Great Britain and Scandinavia The Right Reverend Bishop Dositej; Bägerstavägen 68, S 120 47 Enskede Gård, Sweden; phone: (08 91) 9737

Patriarchate of Romania
Diocese of Central and Western Europe The Most Reverend Metropolitan Serafim of Berlin; Metropolitan and Archbishop for Germany and Western Europe, Ostkirchliches Institut, Ostengstrasse 31, D 93047 Regensburg, Germany; phone: (941) 565742

Patriarchate of Bulgaria
Diocese of Western Europe The Most Reverend Metropolitan Simeon; 1025 Budapest 11, Pajzs u.24–26.faz.13, Hungary; phone: (36) 8648; Leipzigestrasse 24, 10117, Berlin, Germany; phone: (30) 208 6146

Russian Orthodox Church Outside Russia
Diocese of Berlin and Great Britain His Eminence Archbishop Mark; Monastery of St Job of Pochaev, Schirmerweg 78, D-81247, Munich, Germany; phone: (89) 834 8959

Byelosrussian Autocephalous Orthodox Church
The Most Reverend Metropolitan Iziaslav, 66 Cedar Grove, Apt. 10, Somerset, New Jersey 08873-6467, USA

Patriarchate of Serbia
Serbian Orthodox New Gracanica Metropolitanate Episcopal Vicar Very Reverend Protopresbyter Nikola Kotur, 29 Brackley Road, Bedford MK42 9SD; phone: (01234) 273342

Christian Churches and Religious Groups in the UK

American Church in London Whitefield Memorial Church, 79a Tottenham Court Road, London W1P 9HB; phone: (0171) 560 2791; fax: (0171) 580 5013. Founded 1969

Anglican Catholic Church, Missionary Diocese of UK St Mary's House, 13 Byatt's Grove, Longton, Stoke-on-Trent, ST3 2RH; phone: (01782) 330743; fax: (01782) 336361. Founded 1992

Antiochian Orthodox Church 13 Kenwyn Road, Wimbledon, London SW20 8TR; phone: (0181) 879 3046

The Apostolic Church PO Box 389, 24–27 St Helen's Road, Swansea SA1 1ZH; phone: (01792) 473992; fax: (01792) 474087. Founded 1904. 130 churches; 5,500 adherents; 83 ministers

Apostolic Faith Church 95 Fenham Road, Peckham, London SE15 1AE; phone: (0171) 639 9329/8897; fax: (0171) 639 9329. Founded 1906

Armenian Oriental Orthodox Church St Peter's Church, Cranley Gardens, London SW7 3BB; phone: (0171) 373 3565/244 9574

Assemblies of God in Great Britain and Ireland 16 Bridgford Road, West Bridgford, Nottingham NG2 6AF; phone: (0115) 981 1188; fax: (0115) 981 3377. Founded 1924. 653 churches; 75,000 adherents; 880 ministers

Associated Presbyterian Churches PO Box 2, Gairloch IV21 2YA; phone: (01463) 236109. Founded 1989. 20 churches; 1,000 members; 15 ministers

Baptist Union of Great Britain Baptist House, PO Box 44, 129 Broadway, Didcot OX11 8RT; phone: (01235) 512077; fax: (01235) 811537; e-mail: 100442.1750@ compuserve.com. Founded 1812. 2,130 churches; 157,000 members; 1,864 pastors

Baptist Union of Ireland 117 Lisburn Road, Belfast BT9 7AF; phone: (01232) 663108; fax: (01232) 663616; e-mail: buofi@aol.com. Founded 1895. 109 churches; 8,454 members; 83 pastors

Baptist Union of Scotland 14 Aytoun Road, Glasgow G41 5RT; phone: (0141) 423 6169; fax: (0141) 424 1422. Founded 1869. 171 churches; 14,328 members; 140 pastors

Baptist Union of Wales Ty Ilston, 94 Mansel Street, Swansea SA1 5TZ; phone: (01792) 655468/469893; fax: (01792) 469489. Founded 1866. 537 churches; 24,178 members; 118 pastors

Born Again Christ Healing Church 77 Beechwood Road, Hornsey, London N8 7NE; phone: (0181) 340 9962. Founded 1979

British Antiochian Orthodox Deanery Stanfords, 27 Muster Green, Haywards Heath RH16 4AL; phone: (01444) 417007; fax: (01444) 417871; e-mail: 100307.540@ compuserve.com

British Conference of Mennonites London Mennonite Centre, 14 Shepherds Hill, Highgate, London N6 5AQ; phone: (0181) 340 8775; fax: (0181) 341 6807; e-mail: menno@compuserve.com. Founded 1987

The British Orthodox Church (Coptic Orthodox Patriarchate) Church Secretariat, 10 Heathwood Gardens, Charlton, London SE7 8EP; phone: (0181) 854 3090; fax: (0181) 244 7888; e-mail: seraphim@ britorthodox.idiscover.co.uk; Web site: 194.72.60.96/www/orthbrit. Founded 1866

Belorussian Autocephalic Orthodox Church Holy Mother of God of Zyrovicy Church, Chapel Road, Rainsough, Prestwich, Manchester M22 4JW; phone: (0161) 740 8230. Founded 1948

Celtic Orthodox Church 33 Brownlow Street, York YO3 7LW; phone: (01904) 626599. Founded 1866

Chinese Church in London 81 Chiltern Street, London W1M 1HT; phone: (0171) 486 0592/0286; fax: (0171) 935 9113; e-mail: admin@ccil.u-net.com. Founded 1951

Christadelphians 404 Shaftmoor Lane, Hall Green, Birmingham B28 8SZ; phone: (0121) 777 6328; fax: (0121) 778 5024. Founded 1864

Christian Brethren 52 Hornsey Lane, London N6 5LU; phone: (0171) 272 0643. Founded 1828

Church in Wales 39 Cathedral Road, Cardiff CF1 9XF; phone: (01222) 231638; fax: (01222) 387835

Church of Christ 64 Grenville Road, Southcourt, Aylesbury HP21 8EZ; phone: (01296) 482875; e-mail: gfisher888@ aol.com

The Church of Christ, Scientist (Christian Science Church) 2 Elysium Gate, 126 New Kings Road, London SW6 4LZ; phone: (0171) 371 0600; fax: (0171) 371 9204; Web site: www.tfccs.com. Founded 1895. 200 branches in the UK

Church of England General Synod Church House, Great Smith Street, London SW1P 3NZ; phone: (0171) 222 9011; fax: (0171) 233 2660. (For details concerning the history and membership of the Church of England see relevant tables in this section.)

Church of God of Prophecy 6 Beacon Court, Birmingham Road, Great Barr, Birmingham B43 6NN; phone: (0121) 358 2231; fax: (0121) 358 0934. Founded 1953

Church of Ireland Church of Ireland House, Church Avenue, Rathmines, Dublin 6, Ireland; phone: (1) 497 8422; fax: (1) 497 8821

Church of Jesus Christ of Latter-Day Saints (Mormons) Public Affairs, Church Offices, 751 Warwick Road, Solihull B91 3DQ; phone: (0121) 712 1202; fax: (0121) 709 0180; Web site: www.lds.org. Founded 1837. Over 350 congregations; 170,000 members

Church of Scotland 121 George Street, Edinburgh EH2 4YN; phone: (0131) 225 5722; fax: (0131) 220 3113. Founded 1560. 1,600 churches; 700,000 members; 1,200 ministers

Churches of God, UK 23 Walcott Road, Billinghay, Lincoln LN4 4EG; phone: (01526) 860508; e-mail: coguk@aol.com. Founded 1978

Congregational Federation Congregational Centre, 4 Castle Gate, Nottingham NG1 7AS; phone: (0115) 941 3801; fax: (0115) 948 0902. Founded 1972. 313 churches; 11,923 members; 71 ministers

Coptic Orthodox Church Allen Street, Kensington, London W8 6UX; phone: (0171) 603 6701

Coptic Orthodox Church of Scotland Links Street, Kirkcaldy KY1 1QE; phone: (01592) 643333; fax: (01592) 643344; e-mail: vp54@dial.pipex.com. Founded 1977

Cornerstone Central Hall, St Mary Street, Southampton SO14 1NF; phone: (01703) 237700; fax: (01703) 234555; e-mail: cornerstone.communitychurch@dial.pipex. com. Founded 1982

Elim Pentecostal Churches PO Box 38, Cheltenham GL50 3HN; phone: (01242) 519904; fax: (01242) 222279; e-mail: 106000.2410@compuserve.com. Founded 1915. 596 churches; 68,500 adherents; 650 ministers

Evangelical Lutheran Church of England 28 Huntingdon Road, Cambridge; phone: (01223) 355265; fax: (01223) 355265. Founded 1896

Evangelical Presbyterian Church in England and Wales 14 Longshaw Lane, Blackburn BB2 3LU; phone: (01245) 450089; fax: (01245) 260388. Founded 1987

Evangelical Presbyterian Church in Ireland 15 College Square East, Belfast BT1 6DD; phone: (01232) 320529/714820; e-mail: epc@ukonline.co.uk; Web site: web.ukonline.co.uk/epc. Founded 1927

Fellowship of Independent Evangelical Churches (FIEC) 3 Church Road, Croydon CR0 1SG; phone: (0181) 681 7422; fax: (0181) 760 5067. Founded 1922

The Free Church of England St Paul's Rectory, Lowther Road, Fleetwood FY7 7AS; phone: (01253) 873118; fax: (01253) 873118. Founded 1844 (Reformed Episcopal Church of England joined in 1927). 25 churches; 1,500 members; 42 ministers

Free Church of Scotland Free Church Offices, The Mound, Edinburgh EH1 2LS; phone: (0131) 226 5286/4978; fax: (0131) 220 0597; e-mail: freechurch@compuserve.com. Founded 1843. 140 churches; 6,000 members; 110 ministers

Free Presbyterian Church of Scotland 16 Matheson Road, Stornoway HS1 2LA; phone: (01851) 702555. Founded 1893. 50 churches (Scotland); 3,000 members

(Scotland), 7,000 (overseas); 26 ministers (Scotland)

Free Presbyterian Church of Ulster Church House, 356 Ravenhill Road, Belfast BT6 8GL; phone: (01232) 457106; address for correspondence: 40 Lombard Avenue, Lisburn BT28 2UP; phone: (01846) 674664. Founded 1851

General Assembly of Unitarian and Free Christian Churches Essex Hall, 1 Essex Street, Strand, London WC2R 3HY; phone: (0171) 240 2384; fax: (0171) 240 3089; e-mail: ga@unitarian.org.uk; Web site: www.unitarian.org.uk. Founded in 1928. 200 congregations; 7,000 members; 150 ministers

The Greater World Christian Spiritualist Association 3 Conway Street, Fitzrovia,

London W1P 5HA; phone: (0171) 436 7555; fax: (0171) 580 3485. Founded 1921

Greek Orthodox Archdiocese of Thyateira and Great Britain Thyateira House, 5 Craven Hill, London W2 3EN; phone: (0171) 723 4787; fax: (0171) 224 9301. Founded 1922. 101 churches; 102 priests

Independent Methodist Connexion of Churches Office and Resource Centre, Fleet Street, Pemberton, Wigan WN5 0DS; phone: (01942) 223526; fax: (01942) 227768; e-mail: 106570.2444@ compuserve. com. Founded 1805. 100 churches; 3,050 members; 106 ministers

Indian Orthodox (Syrian) Church 44 Newbury Road, Ilford IG2 7HD; phone: (0181) 599 3836. Founded 1975

International Presbyterian Church 53 Drayton Green, Ealing, London W13 0JD; phone: (0181) 997 4706. Founded 1971

Iranian Christian Fellowship 158 Sutton Court Road, Chiswick, London W4 3HR; phone: (0181) 995 4966. Founded 1985

Jehovah's Witnesses Watch Tower House, The Ridgeway, London NW7 1RN; phone: (0181) 906 2211; fax: (0181) 906 3938. Founded 1881. Over 1,400 congregations; 130,000 members

Jesus Fellowship Church (Jesus Army) Nether Heyford, Northampton NN7 3LB; phone: (01327) 349992; fax: (01327) 349997; e-mail: info@jesus.org.uk. Founded 1805. 2,600 members

Kingdom Faith Church Foundry Lane, Horsham RH13 5PX; phone: (01403) 211505; fax: (01403) 211505; e-mail: 106074.700@compuserve.com. Founded 1992

The Liberal Catholic Church 205 Upper Richmond Road, London SW15 6SQ; phone: (0181) 780 5109. Founded 1916

Lutheran Council of Great Britain 5 Kings Croft Road, London NW2 3QE; phone: (0181) 452 9363; fax: (0181) 904 2849. Founded 1948. 100 churches; 27,000 members; 45 ministers

Mar Thoma Syrian Church UK Congregation Mar Thoma Centre, 22 Altmore Avenue, London E6 2BY; phone: (0181) 471 2446. Founded 1957

Methodist Church 25 Marylebone Road, London NW1 5JR; phone: (0171) 486 5502; fax: (0171) 935 1507. Founded 1729; the Wesleyan, Primitive, and United Methodist Churches united in 1932. 6,678 churches; 380,269 members; 3,660 ministers; 12,611 lay preachers

Methodist Church in Ireland 1 Fountainville Avenue, Belfast BT9 6AN; phone: (01232) 324554; fax: (01232) 239467. Founded 1738. 232 churches; 17,636 members; 196 ministers; 316 lay preachers

Moravian Church in Great Britain and Ireland 5 Muswell Hill, London N10 3TH; phone: (0181) 883 3409/1912; fax: (0181) 442 0112. Founded 1737

Mount Zion Pentecostal Apostolic Church 145 Midland Road, Bedford MK40 1DW; phone: (01234) 343609; fax: (01234) 343609. Founded 1965

Multiply Christian Network Jesus Fellowship Central Offices, Nether Heyford, Northampton NN7 3LB; phone: (01327) 349991; fax: (01327) 349997; Web site: www.jesus.org.uk/multiply/. Founded 1992

Musama Disco Christo Church 40 Brailsford Road, Tulse Hill, London SW2 2TE; phone: (0181) 671 5099

New Frontiers International 17 Clarendon Villas, Hove BN3 3RE; phone: (01273)

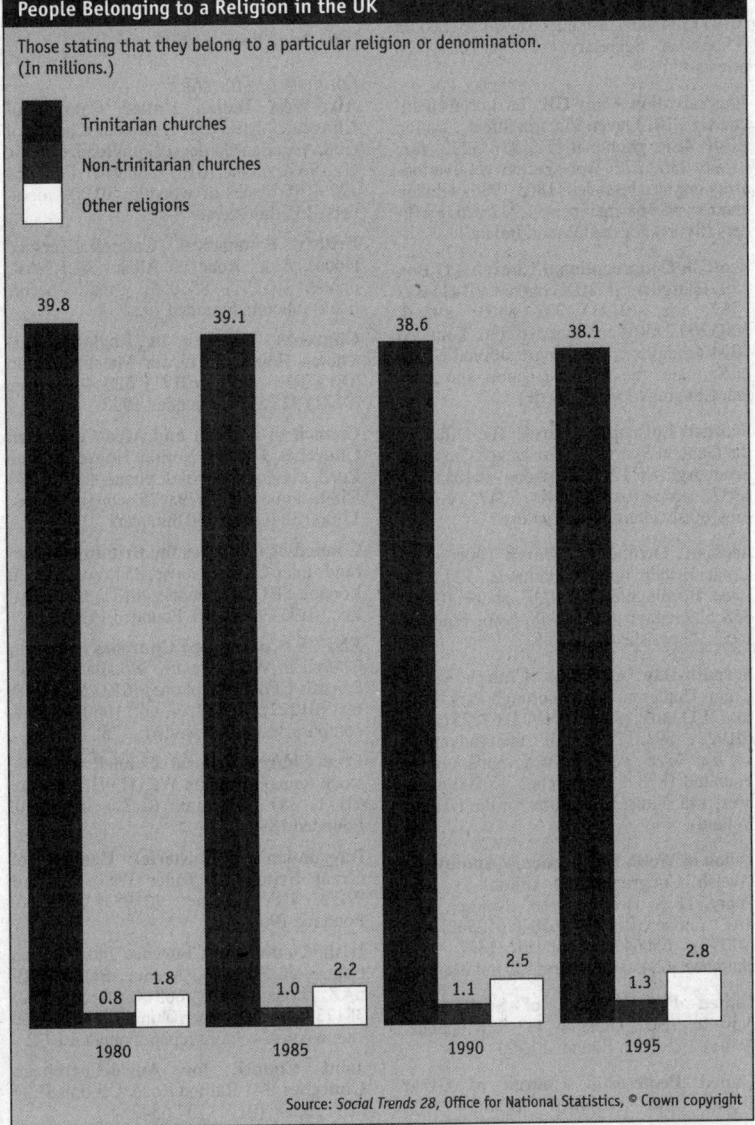

People Belonging to a Religion in the UK

Those stating that they belong to a particular religion or denomination. (In millions.)

■ Trinitarian churches
■ Non-trinitarian churches
□ Other religions

1980	1985	1990	1995
39.8	39.1	38.6	38.1
0.8	1.0	1.1	1.3
1.8	2.2	2.5	2.8

Source: *Social Trends 28*, Office for National Statistics, © Crown copyright

821887; fax: (01273) 770878; e-mail: nfi@compuserve.com; Web site: home.ml. org/nfi. Began in 1980

New Testament Church of God Main House, Overstone Park, Overstone, Northampton NN6 0AD; phone: (01604) 643311/645944; fax: (01604) 790254. Founded 1953. 110 congregations; 20,000 adherents; 7,500 baptized ministers

Old Baptist Union 79 Ainslie Wood Road, Chingford, London E4 9BX; phone: (0181) 529 0783. Founded 1880

Old Roman Catholic Church of Great Britain 11 Calley Close, Tipton DY4 8XY; phone: (0121) 520 0041; fax: (0121) 520 0041. Founded 1908

Orthodox Church in Wales Orthodox Church of the Holy Protection, Blaenau Ffestiniog LL41 4DE; phone: (01766) 831272; fax: (01766) 780932

Pentecostal Revival Church of Christ 220 Ellison Road, Streatham, London SW16 5DJ; phone: (0181) 764 2643. Began in 1973

Pillar of Fire Church 19 Brent Street, Hendon, London NW4 2EU; phone: (0181) 202 3219/7618; fax: (0181) 202 3219. Founded 1915

Pioneer PO Box 79c, Esher KT10 9LP; phone: (01932) 789681; fax: (01932) 789691; e-mail: pioneer_trust@dial. pipex.com. Founded 1982

Plymouth Brethren No 4 c/o 99 Green Lane, Hounslow TW4 6BW; phone: (0181) 577 1603. Founded 1828

The Presbyterian Church in Ireland Church House, Fisherwick Place, Belfast BT1 6DW; phone: (01232) 322284; fax: (01232) 236609; e-mail: clerk@presbyteri-anireland.org; Web site: www.presbyteri-anireland.org. Founded 1662; synods united in 1840. 562 congregations; 297,000 members; 400 ministers (all figures for Ireland)

Presbyterian Church of Wales (or **Calvinic Methodist Church of Wales**) 53 Richmond Road, Cardiff CF2 3UP; phone: (01222) 494913; fax: (01222) 464293. Founded 1811. 939 churches; 51,720 members; 136 ministers

Protestant Episcopal Reformed Church (The Protestant Evangelical Church of England) Provost Office, 23 Limefield Road, Bolton BL1 6LE; phone: (01204) 491977. Founded 1922

Reformed Presbyterian Church of Scotland 4 Burn Brae Avenue, Glasgow G61 3ES; phone: (0141) 942 5056. Founded 1743

Reformed Presbyterian Church of Ireland Cameron House, 98 Lisburn Road, Belfast BT9 6AG; phone: (01232) 660689. Founded 1763

Religious Society of Friends (Quakers) in Britain Quaker Communications Department, Friends House, 173–177 Euston Road,

London NW1 2BJ; phone: (0171) 663 1000; fax: (0171) 663 1001; Web site: www.quaker.org/BYM. Founded 1652. 500 meeting houses; 27,000 members

Reorganized Church of Jesus Christ of Latter Day Saints British Isles Region, Headquarters, 769 Yardley Wood Road, Billesley, Birmingham B123 0PT; phone: (0121) 444 5243; fax: (0121) 444 5243; Web site: www.rlds.org. Founded 1863

Roman Catholic Bishops' Conference Secretariat 39 Eccleston Square, London SW1V 1BX; phone: (0171) 630 8220. (For details concerning the history and membership of the Roman Catholic Church see relevant tables in this section)

Russian Orthodox Diocese of Sourozh All Saints, Ennismore Gardens, London SW7 1NH; phone: (0171) 584 0096; fax: (0171) 584 9864; e-mail: crow@kbnet.co.uk (Diocesan Secretary). 27 parishes; 26 priests

The Salvation Army UK Territorial Headquarters, 101 Queen Victoria Street, London EC4P 4EP; phone: (0171) 236 5222; fax: (0171) 236 6272; Web site: www.salvation-army.org.uk. Founded 1865. 986 worship centres; 65,168 members; 1,732 active officers (figures for the UK and Ireland)

Scottish Congregational Church PO Box 189, Glasgow G1 2BX; phone: (0141) 332 7667; fax: (0141) 332 8463; e-mail: 1005200.2150@compuserve.com. Founded 1994 (comprises the Congregational Union of Scotland, the Women's Union, and Scottish Congregational College)

Scottish Episcopal Church The Office of the General Synod, 21 Grosvenor Crescent, Edinburgh EH12 5EE; phone: (0131) 225 6357; fax: (0131) 346 7247; e-mail: scot_episc_church@ecunet.org

Serbian Orthodox Church Diocese of Great Britain and Scandinavia, 131 Cob Lane, Birmingham B30 1QE; phone: (0121) 458 5273; fax: (0121) 458 4986. Founded 1952. 33 parishes in the UK

Seventh-Day Adventist Church British Union Conference, Stanborough Park, Watford WD2 6JP; phone: (01923) 672251; fax: (01923) 893212; e-mail: buc@adventist. org.uk; Web site: www.adventist.org.uk. Founded 1878. 238 churches; 18,806 members; 145 ministers (figures for the UK and Ireland)

Union of Welsh Independents/ Annibynwr (Welsh Congregational Union) Ty John Penry, 11 St Helen's Road, Swansea SA1 4AL; phone: (01792) 467040/652542; fax: (01792) 650647. Founded 1872. 555 churches; 42,450 members; 150 ministers

United Free Church of Scotland 11 Newton Place, Glasgow G3 7PR; phone: (0141) 332 3435. Founded 1900

United Pentecostal Church of Great Britain and Ireland 41 Bramley Hill,

South Croydon CR2 6NW; phone: (0181) 688 5827; fax: (0181) 688 5827. Founded 1958

United Reformed Church in the United Kingdom 86 Tavistock Place, London WC1H 9RT; phone: (0171) 916 2020; fax: (0171) 916 2021; e-mail: agburnham@ urc.compulink.co.uk; Web site: www.cix.co. uk/_urc. Founded 1972. 1,752 churches; 250,000 members; 1,100 ministers

Wesleyan Reform Union 123 Queen Street, Sheffield S1 2DU; phone: (0114) 272 1938; fax: (0114) 272 1965. Founded 1849. 115 churches; 2,401 members; 20 ministers; 137 lay preachers

The Worldwide Church of God (UK) Elstree House, Elstree Way, Borehamwood WD6 1LU; phone: (0181) 953 1633; fax: (0181) 207 1216; e-mail: wcgeurope@ wcg.org; Web site: www.wcg. org.uk/ index.html. Founded 1957

Councils of Churches

Afro-West Indian United Council of Churches The New Testament Church of God, Arcadian Gardens, High Road, London N22 5AA; phone: (0181) 888 9427. Founded 1979. 65 places of worship; 30,000 members; 135 ministers

British Evangelical Council Evershed House, Alma Road, St Albans AL1 3AR; phone: (01727) 855655; e-mail: becoffice@aol.com. Founded 1952

Churches Together in England Inter-Church House, 35 Lower Marsh, London SE1 7RL; phone: (0171) 620 4444; fax: (0171) 928 5771. Founded 1990

Council of African and Afro-Caribbean Churches UK 31 Norton House, Sidney Road, London SW9 0UJ; phone: (0171) 274 5589. Founded 1979. 75 congregations; 17,000 members; 250 ministers

Council of Churches for Britain and Ireland Inter-Church House, 35 Lower Marsh, London SE1 7RL; phone: (0171) 620 4444; fax: (0171) 928 0010. Founded 1990

ENFYS (Covenanted Churches in Wales) Church in Wales Centre, Woodland Place, Penarth CF6 2EX; phone: (01222)705278; fax: (01222) 712413; e-mail: 106074.133@ compuserve.com. Founded 1975

Free Church Federal Council 27 Tavistock Square, London WC1H 9HH; phone: (0171) 387 8413; fax: (0171) 383 0150. Founded 1896

International Ministerial Council of Great Britain 55 Tudor Walk, Watford WD2 4NY; phone: (01923) 239266. Founded 1968

Irish Council of Churches Inter-Church Centre, 48 Elmwood Avenue, Belfast BT9 6AZ; phone: (01232) 663145; fax: (01232) 381737; e-mail: icpep@unite. co.uk; Web site: www.niweb.org/icpep. Founded 1922

Joint Council for Anglo-Caribbean Churches 141 Railton Road, London SE24 0LT; phone: (0171) 737 6542

Other Faiths Coalition Evangelical Alliance UK Whitefield House, 186 Kennington Park Road, London SE11 4BT; phone: (0171) 207 2100; fax: (0171) 582 6221; e-mail: members@eauk.org; Web site: www.eauk.org

Women's Inter-Church Consultative Committee The Network Office of the Methodist Church, 25 Marylebone Road, London NW1 5JR; phone: (0171) 486 5502

Jewish Religious Organizations in the UK

Office of the Chief Rabbi S Weinberg, Executive Director; 735 High Road, London N12 0US; phone: (0181) 343 6301

Beth Din (Court of the Chief Rabbi) F B Gottlieb, Assistant Registrar; 735 High Road, London N12 0US; phone: (0181) 343 6270

Board of Deputies of British Jews E Tabachnik, President; Commonwealth House, 1–19 New Oxford Street, London WC1A 1NF; phone: (0171) 543 5400

Assembly of Masorti Synagogues H Freedman, Director; 197 Finchley Road, London NW11 0PU; phone: (0181) 201 8772

Federation of Synagogues G Kushner, Administrator; 65 Watford Way, London NW4 3AQ; phone: (0181) 349 4731

Reform Synagogues of Great Britain Rabbi T Bayfield, Chief Executive; The Sternberg Centre for Judaism, 80 East End Road, London N3 2SY; phone: (0181) 349 4731

Spanish and Portuguese Jews' Congregation H Miller, Chief Administrator and Secretary; 2 Ashworth Road, London W9 1JY; phone: (0171) 289 2573

Union of Liberal and Progressive Synagogues R Rosenberg, Director; The Montagu Centre, 21 Maple Street, London W1P 6DS; phone: (0171) 580 1663

Union of Orthodox Hebrew Congregations Rabbi A Klein, Executive Director; 140 Stamford Hill, London N16 6QT; phone: (0181) 802 6226

United Synagogue Head Office J M Lew, Chief Executive; 753 High Road, London N12 0US; phone: (0181) 343 8989

The Chief Rabbinate of Britain

The Chief Rabbinate of Britain has developed from the position of the Rabbi of the Great Synagogue, London. From the early years of the 18th century until recently, he was acknowledged as the spiritual leader of the London Ashkenazi Community and this recognition was also accepted in the provinces and overseas. To conform with constitutional practice, the official designation (1845–1953) was 'Chief Rabbi of the United Hebrew Congregations of the British Commonwealth of Nations' and subsequently 'Chief Rabbi of the United Hebrew Congregations of the Commonwealth'.

The Chief Rabbinate of Britain

Dates of appointement	Name
1709–56	Aaron Hart
1756–64	Hart Lyon
1765–92	David Tevele Schiff
1802–42	Solomon Herschell
1845–90	Nathan Marcus Adler
1891–1911	Hermann Adler
1913–46	Joseph Herman Hertz
1948–65	Israel Brodie
1967–91	Immanuel Jakobovits
1991–	Jonathan Sacks

Other Faiths and Religious Groups in the UK

3HO (Healthy, Happy, Holy) The Lotus Healing Centre, 7 New Court Street, St John's Wood, London NW8 7AA; phone: (0171) 722 5797; fax: (0171) 722 5751. Founded 1975

The Aetherius Society 757 Fulham Road, London SW6 5UU; phone: (0171) 736 4187/731 1094; fax: (0171) 731 1067. Founded 1955

Brahma Kumaris Global Co-operation House, 65 Pound Lane, London NW10 2HH; phone: (0181) 459 1400; fax: (0181) 451 6480. Founded 1937

The Buddhist Society 58 Eccleston Square, London SW1V 1PH; phone: (0171) 834 5858. Founded 1924. 25,000 members; c. 20 temples

Church of Scientology Office of Special Affairs, Saint Hill Manor, East Grinstead RH19 4JY; phone: (01342) 318229; fax: (01342) 325474; Web site: www.scientology.org. Founded 1952

Federation of Jain Organizations in the UK 11 Lindsay Drive, Harrow HA3 0TA; phone: (0181) 204 2871

Friends of the Western Buddhist Order (FWBO) Madhyamaloka, 30 Chantry Road, Moseley, Birmingham B13 8HD; phone: (0121) 700 3077. Founded 1968

Hindu Centre 39 Grafton Terrace, London NW5 4JA; phone: (0171) 485 8200. Founded 1935

Imams and Mosques Council 20–22 Creffield Road, London W5 3RP; phone: (0181) 992 6636. 900 mosques; over 1,000,000 adherents

International Society for Krishna Consciousness Bhaktivedanta Manor, Hilfield Lane, Aldenham, Watford WD2 8EZ; phone: (01923) 857244; fax: (01923) 852896; e-mail: bhaktivedanta.manor@ com.bbt.se. Founded 1969

Islamic Cultural Centre and London Central Mosque 146 Park Road, London NW8 7RG; phone: (0171) 724 3363; fax: (0171) 724 0493. Founded 1944

Islamic Foundation Markfield Conference Centre, Ralby Lane, Markfield, Leicester LE67 9RN; phone: (01530) 244944; fax: (01530) 244946; e-mail: islamicf@islam.demon.co.uk; Web site: www.islamf.demon.co.uk. Founded 1973

Mahikari Sukio Mahikari, Suffolk Road, South Norwood, London SE25 6ES; phone: (0181) 771 7417; fax: (0181) 771 9441. Founded 1983

The Muslim Educational Trust 130 Stroud Green Road, London N4 3RZ; phone: (0171) 272 8502; fax: (0171) 281 3457. Founded 1966

Muslim World League 46 Goodge Street, London W1P 1FJ; phone: (0171) 636 7568

National Council of Hindu Temples c/o Shree Sanatan Mandir, Weymouth Street, Leicester LE4 6FP; phone: (0116) 266 1402. 150 temples; 360,000 adherents

National Spiritual Assembly of the Bahá'is of the United Kingdom 27 Rutland Gate, London SW7 1PD; phone: (0171) 584 2566; fax: (0171) 584 9402

The Pagan Federation BM Box 7097, London WC1N 3XX; phone: (01787) 238257; fax: (01787) 238257; e-mail: secretary@paganfed.demon.co.uk; Web site: www.paganfed.demon.co.uk. Founded 1971

The Raelian Movement BCM Minstrel, London WC1N 3XX; phone: (0117) 923 7447. Founded 1975

Sahaja Yoga Life Eternal Trust, 44 Chelsham Road, Clapham, London SW4 6NP. Founded 1972

Sikh Missionary Society UK 10 Featherstone Road, Southall UB2 5AA; phone: (0181) 574 1902. 250 gurdwaras; 400,000 adherents

Solara, Star-Borne Unlimited Holistic Centre, Unit N&M, Royal Albert Walk, Albert Road, Southsea PO4 0JT; phone: (01705) 293668. Founded 1986

The Spiritualist Association of Great Britain 33 Belgrave Square, London SW1X 8QB; phone: (0171) 235 3351; fax: (0171) 245 9706. Founded 1872

The Theosophical Society in England 50 Gloucester Place, London W1H 4EA; phone: (0171) 935 9261; fax: (0171) 935 9543. Founded 1888

Union of Muslim Organizations in the UK and Eire 109 Campden Hill Road, London W8 7TL; phone: (0171) 229 0538

United Lodge of Theosophists 62

Queen's Gardens, London W2 3AL; phone: (0171) 723 0688/262 8639. Founded 1925

The World Sikh Foundation (Sikh Cultural Society of Great Britain) 88 Molli-

son Way, Edgware HA8 5QW; phone: (0181) 952 1215. Founded 1960

World Zoroastrian Organization 135 Tennyson Road, South Norwood, London

Web Sites

About Islam and Muslims

URL: "http://www.unn.ac.uk/
societies/islamic/"

Site offering extensive information about the Islamic faith and culture. Facts about the *Koran/Quran*, images, links to newspapers and university sites are all included.

Ahimsa – The Hindu Ethic of Non Violence

URL: "http://www.hinduismtoday.kauai.hi.us/
ashram/Resources/Ahimsa/
AhimsaNonViolence.html"

Exposition of the universal values of non-violence and respect for life. The philosophical roots of the practice of non-injury to others is located in Hinduism.

Archbishop of Canterbury

URL: "http://www.church-of-
england.org/main/lambeth/abchome.htm"

Home page of the Archbishop of Canterbury, head of the Anglican church. Alongside a biography of Archbishop George Carey is a description of the role, duties, and history of the post.

Atheist Express

URL: "http://www.hti.net/www/atheism"

Site dedicated to atheism, free thought, humanism, ethics, religious criticism, and state–church separation.

Bahá'í Faith Page

URL: "http://www.bcca.org/~glittle/"

Introduction to this religion, founded in the 19th century. The site also contains access to pages produced by Bahá'í groups around the world.

Bhagavad-Gītā

URL: "http://www.cc.gatech.edu/gvu/
people/Phd/Rakesh.Mullick/gita/
gita.html"

Fully downloadable text of this sacred work.

Bible Gateway

URL: "http://www.gospelcom.net/bible"

Full text of six versions of the Bible, including the New International Version, the Revised Standard Version, and the King James Version. These are fully searchable by passage, phrase, or word, and the text includes hyperlinked footnotes and cross-references. The user can choose from five languages (including Latin).

Brief Introduction to Taoism

URL: "http://www.geocities.com/
HotSprings/2426/Ttaointro.html"

Introduction to Taoism. The evolution of Taoism within Chinese philosophy is described. There are summaries of various types of Taoism including philosophical, devotional, magical, and alchemical.

Buddhist Ethics

URL: "http://jbe.la.psu.edu/"

Includes discursive essays, book reviews, conference reports, and surveys.

Celtic Wheel Of Life

URL: "http://www.radix.net/
~lsspindler/celticwheel.html"

Celtic people measured the solar year on a wheel, circle, or spiral, all of which symbolize creation and the constant movement of the universe. This site details the stages of that cycle as described in Celtic legends.

Church of England

URL: "http://www.church-of-
england.org/"

Web pages of the Church of England. There is information on the structure of the church, the meaning of being an Anglican, and a guide to prayer. There are links to those dioceses that have web pages of their own and a comprehensive listing of Web pages of non-English churches within the Anglican communion.

Classical Mythology Home Page

URL: "http://www.princeton.edu/
~rhwebb/myth.html"

Course materials from the mythology unit of Princeton University's Classics Department. The site contains sections on the Gods, Titans, Monsters, Heroes, Legends, Women, and more.

Confucius

URL: "http://sac.uky.edu/~mdtuck0/
Resources/Confucius.html"

Some background information on Confucius and Confucianism as well as images and versions of most of his famous texts on morality. The texts are available in English translation, or Chinese, if your browser will support the character set.

Development of the Papacy

URL: "http://history.idbsu.edu/
westciv/papacy/"

Part of a larger site on the history of Western civilization maintained by Boise State University, this page provides an introduction to the conflict that existed in the Middle Ages between the church and state.

Dome of the Rock

URL: "http://www.erols.com/ameen/
domerock.htm"

In addition to a history, description, and interior and exterior photographs of Dome of the Rock in Jerusalem, there is an analysis (from a Muslim perspective) of how the structure and dimensions of the Dome of the Rock reflect the Muslim world view.

From Jesus to Christ: The First Christians

URL: "http://www.pbs.org/wgbh/
pages/frontline/shows/religion/"

Companion site to the US Public Broadcasting Service (PBS) television programme *Frontline*, this page includes controversial historical evidence challenging accepted beliefs and opinions about the life of Jesus and the rise of Christianity.

Guide to Early Church Documents

URL: "http://www.iclnet.org/pub/
resources/christian- history.html"

Guide to early church documents including canonical documents, creeds, the writings of the Apostolic Fathers, and other historical texts relevant to church history.

Hinduism Today

URL: "http://www.HinduismToday.
kauai.hi.us/ashram/"

Online magazine produced by Sanatana Dharma's Electronic Ashram. It explores India's ancient spiritual path by providing nine informative sections related to Hinduism.

History of the Orthodox Church

URL: "http://www.goarch.org/access/
Companion_to_Orthodox_Church/
History_of_Orthodox_Church"

Presentation of the history, structures, and crises of the Eastern Orthodox Church.

Islam at a Glance

URL: "http://www.iad.org/books/
WAMY1.html"

Introduction to the key beliefs of Islam. It covers Muhammad, the Koran, prayer, Islam in the modern world, and the Five Pillars of Islam.

Jesus Christ

URL: "http://www.knight.org/advent/
cathen/08374c.htm"

Includes articles on the origin of Jesus' name, a chronology of his life, historical documents mentioning his name, his character, the Incarnation, and Resurrection.

Jewish Culture and History

URL: "http://www.igc.apc.org/
ddickerson/judaica.html"

Wide-ranging collection of information on Judaism. Includes links to online Hebrew texts, and an introduction to Judaism.

Koran

URL: "http://etext.virginia.edu/
koran.html"

Full text of the Koran in searchable SGML form, offered by the Electronic Centre at the University of Virginia, USA.

List of Norse Beings

URL: "http://www.ugcs.caltech.edu/
~cherryne/list.html"

Alphabetical listing of all the main Norse Gods and other beings found in Scandinavian mythology.

Makkah (Mecca)

URL: "http://darkwing.uoregon.edu/
~kbatarfi/makkah.html"

Brief history of the holy city of Mecca, which includes a gallery of several images in and around the Grand Mosque.

Mermaids and Other Mythical Sea Beings

URL: "http://www.eliki.com/realms/
kat/mermaid.html"

Mermaid myths and legends. The mermaid's history from the pre-Christian era to the 20th century.

Mithraism

URL: "http://www.evansville.edu/
~ecoleweb/articles/mithraism.html"

Exploration of the pagan cult dedicated to the worship of the god Mithras with particular emphasis placed on its manifestation in Persia and Ancient Rome.

Muses from Greek Mythology

URL: "http://www.eliki.com/portals/
fantasy/circle/define.html"

Introduction to the nine muses of antiquity. Each muse is accompanied by her main attributes, as well as modern odes and songs inspired by her or dedicated to her.

Mythmedia

URL: "http://www-
lib.haifa.ac.il/www/art/
MYTHOLOGY_WESTART.HTML"

Extensive collection of art images related to classical Greek mythology, created by art historians in Haifa University. It also covers ancient iconography and modern art, including an especially rich section on famous episodes of the Trojan War.

Religious Atheism

URL: "http://www.hypertext.com/
atheisms/"

Compilation of non-traditional sources, including texts according to Christianity, classical atheism, liberation theology, and religious atheists.

Rudolf Steiner Archive

URL: "http://www.elib.com/Steiner/"

Devoted to Austrian spiritual thinker Rudolf Steiner, this site features summaries of his books and articles (plus several full-text translations), a collection of over 6,000 of his lectures, and a gallery of pictures and photographs.

Shi'ite Encyclopedia

URL: "http://www.al-islam.org/encyclo-
pedia/"

Detailed exposition of Shi'ite beliefs and practices. The encyclopedia is compiled by a team seeking to bridge differences between Sunnis and Shi'ites.

Shinto – The Way of the Gods

URL: "http://www.trincoll.edu/~tj/
tj4.4.96/articles/cover.html"

Guide to Shinto beliefs and practices. The link between Shintoism and Japanese mythology is explained prior to a guide to the main Shinto shrines.

Sikhism Home Page

URL: "http://www.sikhs.org/"

The site offers a brief overview of the main principles of Sikhism. It also follows the development of the religion, explores the philosophy and scriptures connected with Sikhism, and describes the main religious problems, role models, ceremonies, and religious dates in the life of a Sikh.

Templenet – The Ultimate Source of Information on Indian Temples

URL: "http://www.indiantemples.com/
encyclo.html"

Information on India's temples. Architectural, archaeological, and historical articles are accompanied by detailed descriptions of thousands of temples. There is also practical information for those planning visits.

Virtual Tour of Jerusalem

URL: "http://virtual.co.il/
communities/jerusalem/pathways/"

Virtual tour of the city of Jerusalem, dealing with the diversity of cultures and faiths which have shaped the city.

What is Theravada Buddhism?

URL: "http://world.std.com/~metta/
theravada.html"

Full introduction to the school of Buddhism drawing its inspiration from the record of Buddha's teachings known as the Pali Canon. There is a guide for those wishing to learn Pali to deepen understanding of the texts.

World Council of Churches

URL: "http://www.wcc-coe.org/"

Large site of the organization, bringing together over 300 Christian churches in 120 countries. It contains information on the ecumenical movement, evangelism, and the role of Christian churches in development.

World Scripture

URL: "http://www.rain.org/
~origin/ws.html"

Comparative anthology of sacred texts containing over 4,000 scriptural passages from 268 sacred texts and 55 oral traditions, organized under 164 different themes. This text is the result of a five-year project involving the collaboration of an international team of 40 recognized scholars representing all the major religious traditions of the world.

Worldwide Study Bible

URL: "http://ccel.wheaton.edu/
wwsb/index.html"

The full text of all the books of the Old and New Testaments, synopses of important sections, explanations of the significance of many of the most important aspects, and a biblical dictionary are all provided.

Zen Buddhism

URL: "http://www.iijnet.or.jp/
iriz/irizhtml/irizhome.htm"

Largest collection of Buddhist primary text materials on the Internet, together with many examples of Zen art, information on Zen centres and masters, Zen dictionary search tools, and bibliographies.

AWARDS AND PRIZES

Nobel Prizes

Nobel Prize: Introduction

The Nobel Prizes were first awarded in 1901 under the will of Alfred B Nobel (1833–1896), a Swedish chemist, who invented dynamite. The interest on the Nobel endowment fund is divided annually among the persons who have made the greatest contributions in the fields of physics, chemistry, medicine, literature, and world peace. The first four are awarded by academic committees based in Sweden, while the peace prize is awarded by a committee of the Norwegian parliament. A sixth prize, for economics, financed by the Swedish National Bank, was first awarded in 1969. The prizes have a large cash award and are given to organizations – such as the United Nations peacekeeping forces, which received the Nobel Peace Prize in 1988– as well as to individuals.

Nobel Prizes

Year	Winner(s)[1]	Awarded for
Nobel Prize for Chemistry		
1988	Johann Deisenhofer (West Germany), Robert Huber (West Germany), and Hartmut Michel (West Germany)	discovery of three-dimensional structure of the reaction centre of photosynthesis
1989	Sidney Altman (USA) and Thomas Cech (USA)	discovery of catalytic function of RNA
1990	Elias James Corey (USA)	new methods of synthesizing chemical compounds
1991	Richard Ernst (Switzerland)	improvements in the technology of nuclear magnetic resonance (NMR) imaging
1992	Rudolph Marcus (USA)	theoretical discoveries relating to reduction and oxidation reactions
1993	Kary Mullis (USA)	invention of the polymerase chain reaction technique for amplifying DNA
	Michael Smith (Canada)	invention of techniques for splicing foreign genetic segments into an organism's DNA in order to modify the proteins produced
1994	George Olah (USA)	development of technique for examining hydrocarbon molecules
1995	F Sherwood Rowland (USA), Mario Molina (USA), and Paul Crutzen (Netherlands)	explaining the chemical process of the ozone layer
1996	Robert Curl, Jr (USA), Harold Kroto (UK), and Richard Smalley (USA)	discovery of fullerenes
1997	John Walker (UK), Paul Boyer (USA), and Jens Skou (Denmark)	study of the enzymes involved in the production of adenosine triphospate (ATP), which acts as a store of energy in bodies called mitochondria inside cells
Nobel Prize for Economics		
1988	Maurice Allais (France)	contributions to the theory of markets and efficient use of resources
1989	Trygve Haavelmo (Norway)	testing fundamental econometric theories
1990	Harry Markowitz (USA), Merton Miller (USA), and William Sharpe (USA)	pioneering theories on managing investment portfolios and corporate finances
1991	Ronald Coase (USA)	work on value and social problems of companies
1992	Gary Becker (USA)	work linking economic theory to aspects of human behaviour, drawing on other social sciences
1993	Robert Fogel (USA) and Douglass North (USA)	creating a new method of studying economic history (cliometrics)
1994	John Nash (USA), John Harsanyi (USA), and Reinhard Selten (Germany)	work on 'game theory', which investigates decision-making in a competitive environment
1995	Robert Lucas (USA)	developing the 'rational expectations' school, which questions a government's ability to steer the economy
1996	James Mirrlees (UK) and William Vickrey (USA)	fundamental contributions to the economic theory of incentives under assymmetric information
1997	Robert Merton (USA) and Myron Scholes (USA)	pioneering contribution to economic sciences by developing a new method of determining the value of derivatives

Nobel Prizes (*continued*)

Year	Winner(s)[1]	Awarded for

Nobel Prize for Peace

Year	Winner(s)	Awarded for
1988	United Nations Peacekeeping Forces	
1989	Dalai Lama (Tibet)	
1990	Mikhail Gorbachev (USSR)	promoting greater openness in the USSR and helping to end the Cold War
1991	Aung San Suu Kyi (Myanmar)	nonviolent campaign for democracy
1992	Rigoberta Menchú (Guatemala)	campaign for indigenous people
1993	Nelson Mandela (South Africa) and Frederik Willem de Klerk (South Africa)	work towards dismantling apartheid and negotiating transition to nonracial democracy
1994	Yassir Arafat (Palestine), Yitzhak Rabin (Israel), and Shimon Perez (Israel)	agreement of an accord on Palestinian self-rule
1995	Joseph Rotblat (UK) and the Pugwash Conferences on Science and World Affairs	campaign against nuclear weapons
1996	Carlos Filipe Ximenes Belo (Timorese) and José Ramos-Horta (Timorese)	work towards a just and peaceful solution to the conflict in East Timor
1997	Jody Williams (USA) and the International to Campaign Ban Landmines (ICBL)	campaign for global ban of anti-personnel mines

Nobel Prize for Physics

Year	Winner(s)	Awarded for
1988	Leon M Lederman (USA), Melvin Schwartz (USA), and Jack Steinberger (USA)	neutrino-beam method, and demonstration of the doublet structure of leptons through discovery of muon neutrino
1989	Norman Ramsey (USA)	measurement techniques leading to discovery of caesium atomic clock
	Hans Dehmelt (USA) and Wolfgang Paul (Germany)	ion-trap method for isolating single atoms
1990	Jerome Friedman (USA), Henry Kendall (USA), and Richard Taylor (Canada)	experiments demonstrating that protons and neutrons are made up of quarks
1991	Pierre-Gilles de Gennes (France)	work on disordered systems including polymers and liquid crystals; development of mathematical methods for studying the behaviour of molecules in a liquid on the verge of solidifying
1992	Georges Charpak (France)	invention and development of detectors used in high-energy physics
1993	Joseph Taylor (USA) and Russell Hulse (USA)	discovery of first binary pulsar (confirming the existence of gravitational waves)
1994	Clifford Shull (USA) and Bertram Brockhouse (Canada)	development of technique known as 'neutron scattering' which led to advances in semiconductor technology
1995	Frederick Reines (USA)	discovery of the neutrino
	Martin Perl (USA)	discovery of the tau lepton
1996	David Lee (USA), Douglas Osheroff (USA), and Robert Richardson (USA)	discovery of superfluidity in helium-3
1997	Claude Cohen-Tannoudji (France), William Phillips (USA), and Steven Chu (USA)	discovery of a way to slow down individual atoms using lasers for study in a near-vacuum

Nobel Prize for Physiology or Medicine

Year	Winner(s)	Awarded for
1988	James Black (UK), Gertrude Elion (USA), and George Hitchings (USA)	work on the principles governing the design of new drug treatment
1989	Michael Bishop (USA) and Harold Varmus (USA)	discovery of oncogenes, genes carried by viruses that can trigger cancerous growth in normal cells
1990	Joseph Murray (USA) and Donnall Thomas (USA)	pioneering work in organ and cell transplants
1991	Erwin Neher (Germany) and Bert Sakmann (Germany)	discovery of how gatelike structures (ion channels) regulate the flow of ions into and out of cells
1992	Edmond Fisher (USA) and Erwin Krebs (USA)	isolating and describing the action of the enzyme responsible for reversible protein phosphorylation, a major biological control mechanism
1993	Phillip Sharp (USA) and Richard Roberts (UK)	discovery of split genes (genes interrupted by nonsense segments of DNA)
1994	Alfred Gilman (USA) and Martin Rodbell (USA)	discovery of a family of proteins (G-proteins) that translate messages – in the form of hormones or other chemical signals – into action inside cells
1995	Edward Lewis (USA), Eric Wieschaus (USA), and Christiane Nüsslein-Volhard (Germany)	discovery of genes which control the early stages of the body's development
1996	Peter Doherty (Australia) and Rolf Zinkernagel (Switzerland)	discovery of how the immune system recognizes virus-infected cells
1997	Stanley Prusiner (USA)	discoveries, including the 'prion' theory, that could lead to new treatments of dementia-related diseases, including Alzheimer's and Parkinson's diseases

Nobel Prize for Literature

Year	Winner(s)
1988	Naguib Mahfouz (Egypt)
1989	Camilo José Cela (Spain)
1990	Octavio Paz (Mexico)
1991	Nadine Gordimer (South Africa)
1992	Derek Walcott (Santa Lucia)
1993	Toni Morrison (USA)
1994	Kenzaburo Oe (Japan)
1995	Seamus Heaney (Ireland)
1996	Wisława Szymborska (Poland)
1997	Dario Fo (Italy)

[1] Nationality given is the citizenship of recipient at the time award was made.

Film

Academy Awards

The Academy Awards ('Oscars') are presented each March for films of the previous year.

Year	Best Picture	Best Director	Best Actor	Best Actress	Best Supporting Actor	Best Supporting Actress
1928	Wings	Frank Borzage Seventh Heaven	Emil Jannings The Way of All Flesh, The Last Command	Janet Gaynor Seventh Heaven, Street Angel, Sunrise	no award	no award
1929	The Broadway Melody	Frank Lloyd The Divine Lady	Warner Baxter In Old Arizona	Mary Pickford Coquette	no award	no award
1930	All Quiet on the Western Front	Lewis Milestone All Quiet on the Western Front	George Arliss Disraeli	Norma Shearer The Divorcee	no award	no award
1931	Cimarron	Norman Taurog Skippy	Lionel Barrymore A Free Soul	Marie Dressler Min and Bill	no award	no award
1932	Grand Hotel	Frank Borzage Bad Girl	Fredric March Dr Jekyll and Mr Hyde Wallace Beery The Champ	Helen Hayes The Sin of Madelon Claudet	no award	no award
1933	Cavalcade	Frank Lloyd Cavalcade	Charles Laughton The Private Life of Henry VIII	Katharine Hepburn Morning Glory	no award	no award
1934	It Happened One Night	Frank Capra It Happened One Night	Clark Gable It Happened One Night	Claudette Colbert It Happened One Night	no award	no award
1935	Mutiny on the Bounty	John Ford The Informer	Victor McLaglen The Informer	Bette Davis Dangerous	no award	no award
1936	The Great Ziegfeld	Frank Capra Mr Deeds Goes to Town	Paul Muni The Story of Louis Pasteur	Luise Rainer The Great Ziegfeld	Walter Brennan Come and Get It	Gale Sondergaard Anthony Adverse
1937	The Life of Emile Zola	Leo McCarey The Awful Truth	Spencer Tracy Captains Courageous	Luise Rainer The Good Earth	Joseph Schildkraut The Life of Emile Zola	Alice Brady In Old Chicago
1938	You Can't Take It With You	Frank Capra You Can't Take It With You	Spencer Tracy Boys' Town	Bette Davis Jezebel	Walter Brennan Kentucky	Fay Bainter Jezebel
1939	Gone With the Wind	Victor Flemming Gone With the Wind	Robert Donat Goodbye, Mr Chips	Vivien Leigh Gone With the Wind	Thomas Mitchell Stagecoach	Hattie McDaniel Gone With the Wind
1940	Rebecca	John Ford The Grapes of Wrath	James Stewart The Philadelphia Story	Ginger Rogers Kitty Foyle	Walter Brennan The Westerner	Jane Darwell The Grapes of Wrath
1941	How Green Was My Valley	John Ford How Green Was My Valley	Gary Cooper Sergeant York	Joan Fontaine Suspicion	Donald Crisp How Green Was My Valley	Mary Astor The Great Lie
1942	Mrs Miniver	William Wyler Mrs Miniver	James Cagney Yankee Doodle Dandy	Greer Garson Mrs Miniver	Van Heflin Johnny Eager	Teresa Wright Mrs Miniver
1943	Casablanca	Michael Curtiz Casablanca	Paul Lukas Watch on the Rhine	Jennifer Jones The Song of Bernadette	Charles Coburn The More the Merrier	Katina Paxinou For Whom the Bell Tolls
1944	Going My Way	Leo McCarey Going My Way	Bing Crosby Going My Way	Ingrid Bergman Gaslight	Barry Fitzgerald Going My Way	Ethel Barrymore None But the Lonely Heart
1945	The Lost Weekend	Billy Wilder The Lost Weekend	Ray Milland The Lost Weekend	Joan Crawford Mildred Pierce	James Dunn A Tree Grows in Brooklyn	Anne Revere National Velvet
1946	The Best Years of Our Lives	William Wyler The Best Years of Our Lives	Fredric March The Best Years of Our Lives	Olivia de Havilland To Each His Own	Harold Russell The Best Years of Our Lives	Anne Baxter The Razor's Edge
1947	Gentleman's Agreement	Elia Kazan Gentleman's Agreement	Ronald Coleman A Double Life	Loretta Young The Farmer's Daughter	Edmund Gwenn Miracle on 34th Street	Celeste Holm Gentleman's Agreement
1948	Hamlet	John Huston Treasure of Sierra Madre	Laurence Olivier Hamlet	Jane Wyman Johnny Belinda	Walter Houston Treasure of Sierra Madre	Claire Trevor Key Largo

Academy Awards (continued)

Year	Best Picture	Best Director	Best Actor	Best Actress	Best Supporting Actor	Best Supporting Actress
1949	All the King's Men	Joseph L Mankiewicz A Letter to Three Wives	Broderick Crawford All the King's Men	Olivia de Havilland The Heiress	Dean Jagger Twelve O'Clock High	Mercedes McCambridge All the King's Men
1950	All About Eve	Joseph L Mankiewicz All About Eve	José Ferrer Cyrano de Bergerac	Judy Holliday Born Yesterday	George Sanders All About Eve	Josephine Hull Harvey
1951	An American in Paris	George Stevens A Place in the Sun	Humphrey Bogart The African Queen	Vivien Leigh A Streetcar Named Desire	Karl Malden A Streetcar Named Desire	Kim Hunter A Streetcar Named Desire
1952	The Greatest Show on Earth	John Ford The Quiet Man	Gary Cooper High Noon	Shirley Booth Come Back Little Sheba	Anthony Quinn Viva Zapata!	Gloria Grahame The Bad and the Beautiful
1953	From Here to Eternity	Fred Zinnemann From Here to Eternity	William Holden Stalag 17	Audrey Hepburn Roman Holiday	Frank Sinatra From Here to Eternity	Donna Reed From Here to Eternity
1954	On the Waterfront	Elia Kazan On the Waterfront	Marlon Brando On the Waterfront	Grace Kelly The Country Girl	Edmond O'Brien The Barefoot Contessa	Eva Marie Saint On the Waterfront
1955	Marty	Delbert Mann Marty	Ernest Borgnine Marty	Anna Magnani The Rose Tattoo	Jack Lemmon Mister Roberts	Jo Van Fleet East of Eden
1956	Around the World in 80 Days	George Stevens Giant	Yul Brynner The King and I	Ingrid Bergman Anastasia	Anthony Quinn Lust for Life	Dorothy Malone Written on the Wind
1957	The Bridge on the River Kwai	David Lean The Bridge on the River Kwai	Alec Guinness The Bridge on the River Kwai	Joanne Woodward The Three Faces of Eve	Red Buttons Sayonara	Miyoshi Umeki Sayonara
1958	Gigi	Vincente Minnelli Gigi	David Niven Separate Tables	Susan Hayward I Want to Live!	Burl Ives The Big Country	Wendy Hiller Separate Tables
1959	Ben Hur	William Wyler Ben Hur	Charlton Heston Ben Hur	Simone Signoret Room at the Top	Hugh Griffith Ben Hur	Shelley Winters The Diary of Anne Frank
1960	The Apartment	Billy Wilder The Apartment	Burt Lancaster Elmer Gantry	Elizabeth Taylor Butterfield 8	Peter Ustinov Spartacus	Shirley Jones Elmer Gantry
1961	West Side Story	Robert Wise and Jerome Robbins West Side Story	Maximillian Schell Judgment at Nuremberg	Sophia Loren Two Women	George Chakiris West Side Story	Rita Moreno West Side Story
1962	Lawrence of Arabia	David Lean Lawrence of Arabia	Gregory Peck To Kill a Mockingbird	Anne Bancroft The Miracle Worker	Ed Begley Sweet Bird of Youth	Patty Duke The Miracle Worker
1963	Tom Jones	Tony Richardson Tom Jones	Sidney Poitier Lilies of the Field	Patricia Neal Hud	Melvyn Douglas Hud	Margaret Rutherford The V.I.P.s
1964	My Fair Lady	George Cukor My Fair Lady	Rex Harrison My Fair Lady	Julie Andrews Mary Poppins	Peter Ustinov Topkapi	Lila Kedrova Zorba the Greek
1965	The Sound of Music	Robert Wise The Sound of Music	Lee Marvin Cat Ballou	Julie Christie Darling	Martin Balsam A Thousand Clowns	Shelley Winters A Patch of Blue
1966	A Man for All Seasons	Fred Zinnemann A Man for All Seasons	Paul Scofield A Man for All Seasons	Elizabeth Taylor Who's Afraid of Virginia Woolf?	Walter Matthau The Fortune Cookie	Sandy Dennis Who's Afraid of Virginia Woolf?
1967	In the Heat of the Night	Mike Nichols The Graduate	Rod Steiger In the Heat of the Night	Katharine Hepburn Guess Who's Coming to Dinner	George Kennedy Cool Hand Luke	Estelle Parsons Bonnie and Clyde
1968	Oliver!	Sir Carol Reed Oliver!	Cliff Robertson Charly	Katharine Hepburn The Lion in Winter Barbra Streisand Funny Girl	Jack Albertson The Subject Was Roses	Ruth Gordon Rosemary's Baby
1969	Midnight Cowboy	John Schlesinger Midnight Cowboy	John Wayne True Grit	Maggie Smith The Prime of Miss Jean Brodie	Gig Young They Shoot Horses, Don't They?	Goldie Hawn Cactus Flower
1970	Patton	Franklin J Schaffner Patton	George C Scott Patton	Glenda Jackson Women in Love	John Mills Ryan's Daughter	Helen Hayes Airport

(continued)

Academy Awards (*continued*)

Year	Best Picture	Best Director	Best Actor	Best Actress	Best Supporting Actor	Best Supporting Actress
1971	The French Connection	William Friedkin *The French Connection*	Gene Hackman *The French Connection*	Jane Fonda *Klute*	Ben Johnson *The Last Picture Show*	Cloris Leachman *The Last Picture Show*
1972	The Godfather	Bob Fosse *Cabaret*	Marlon Brando *The Godfather*	Liza Minnelli *Cabaret*	Joel Grey *Cabaret*	Eileen Heckart *Butterflies Are Free*
1973	The Sting	George Roy Hill *The Sting*	Jack Lemmon *Save the Tiger*	Glenda Jackson *A Touch of Class*	John Houseman *The Paper Chase*	Tatum O'Neal *Paper Moon*
1974	The Godfather Part II	Francis Ford Coppola *The Godfather Part II*	Art Carney *Harry and Tonto*	Ellen Burstyn *Alice Doesn't Live Here Anymore*	Robert De Niro *The Godfather Part II*	Ingrid Bergman *Murder on the Orient Express*
1975	One Flew Over the Cuckoo's Nest	Milos Forman *One Flew Over the Cuckoo's Nest*	Jack Nicholson *One Flew Over the Cuckoo's Nest*	Louise Fletcher *One Flew Over the Cuckoo's Nest*	George Burns *The Sunshine Boys*	Lee Grant *Shampoo*
1976	Rocky	John G Avildsen *Rocky*	Peter Finch *Network*	Faye Dunaway *Network*	Jason Robards *All the President's Men*	Beatrice Straight *Network*
1977	Annie Hall	Woody Allen *Annie Hall*	Richard Dreyfuss *The Goodbye Girl*	Diane Keaton *Annie Hall*	Jason Robards *Julia*	Vanessa Redgrave *Julia*
1978	The Deer Hunter	Michael Cimino *The Deer Hunter*	Jon Voight *Coming Home*	Jane Fonda *Coming Home*	Christopher Walken *The Deer Hunter*	Maggie Smith *California Suite*
1979	Kramer vs Kramer	Robert Benton *Kramer vs Kramer*	Dustin Hoffman *Kramer vs Kramer*	Sally Field *Norma Rae*	Melvyn Douglas *Being There*	Meryl Streep *Kramer vs Kramer*
1980	Ordinary People	Robert Redford *Ordinary People*	Robert De Niro *Raging Bull*	Sissy Spacek *Coal Miner's Daughter*	Timothy Hutton *Ordinary People*	Mary Steenburgen *Melvin and Howard*
1981	Chariots of Fire	Warren Beatty *Reds*	Henry Fonda *On Golden Pond*	Katharine Hepburn *On Golden Pond*	John Gielgud *Arthur*	Maureen Stapleton *Reds*
1982	Gandhi	Richard Attenborough *Gandhi*	Ben Kingsley *Gandhi*	Meryl Streep *Sophie's Choice*	Louis Gossett Jr *An Officer and a Gentleman*	Jessica Lange *Tootsie*
1983	Terms of Endearment	James L Brooks *Terms of Endearment*	Robert Duvall *Tender Mercies*	Shirley Maclaine *Terms of Endearment*	Jack Nicholson *Terms of Endearment*	Linda Hunt *The Year of Living Dangerously*
1984	Amadeus	Milos Forman *Amadeus*	F Murray Abraham *Amadeus*	Sally Field *Places in the Heart*	Haing S Ngor *The Killing Fields*	Dame Peggy Ashcroft *A Passage to India*
1985	Out of Africa	Sydney Pollack *Out of Africa*	William Hurt *Kiss of the Spider Woman*	Geraldine Page *The Trip to Bountiful*	Don Ameche *Cocoon*	Anjelica Huston *Prizzi's Honor*
1986	Platoon	Oliver Stone *Platoon*	Paul Newman *The Color of Money*	Marlee Matlin *Children of a Lesser God*	Michael Caine *Hannah and Her Sisters*	Dianne Wiest *Hannah and Her Sisters*
1987	The Last Emperor	Bernardo Bertolucci *The Last Emperor*	Michael Douglas *Wall Street*	Cher *Moonstruck*	Sean Connery *The Untouchables*	Olympia Dukakis *Moonstruck*
1988	Rain Man	Barry Levington *Rain Man*	Dustin Hoffman *Rain Man*	Jodie Foster *The Accused*	Kevin Kline *A Fish Called Wanda*	Geena Davis *The Accidental Tourist*
1989	Driving Miss Daisy	Oliver Stone *Born on the Fourth of July*	Daniel Day-Lewis *My Left Foot*	Jessica Tandy *Driving Miss Daisy*	Denzel Washington *Glory*	Brenda Fricker *My Left Foot*
1990	Dances With Wolves	Kevin Costner *Dances With Wolves*	Jeremy Irons *Reversal of Fortune*	Kathy Bates *Misery*	Joe Pesci *Goodfellas*	Whoopi Goldberg *Ghost*
1991	The Silence of the Lambs	Jonathan Demme *The Silence of the Lambs*	Anthony Hopkins *The Silence of the Lambs*	Jodie Foster *The Silence of the Lambs*	Jack Palance *City Slickers*	Mercedes Ruehl *The Fisher King*
1992	Unforgiven	Clint Eastwood *Unforgiven*	Al Pacino *Scent of a Woman*	Emma Thompson *Howard's End*	Gene Hackman *Unforgiven*	Marisa Tomei *My Cousin Vinny*
1993	Schindler's List	Steven Spielberg *Schindler's List*	Tom Hanks *Philadelphia*	Holly Hunter *The Piano*	Tommy Lee Jones *The Fugitive*	Anna Paquin *The Piano*
1994	Forrest Gump	Robert Zemeckis *Forrest Gump*	Tom Hanks *Forrest Gump*	Jessica Lange *Blue Sky*	Martin Landau *Ed Wood*	Dianne Wiest *Bullets Over Broadway*

Academy Awards (continued)

Year	Best Picture	Best Director	Best Actor	Best Actress	Best Supporting Actor	Best Supporting Actress
1995	*Braveheart*	Mel Gibson *Braveheart*	Nicolas Cage *Leaving Las Vegas*	Susan Sarandon *Dead Man Walking*	Kevin Spacey *The Usual Suspects*	Mira Sorvino *Mighty Aphrodite*
1996	*The English Patient*	Anthony Minghella *The English Patient*	Geoffrey Rush *Shine*	Frances McDormand *Fargo*	Cuba Gooding Jr *Jerry Maguire*	Juliette Binoche *The English Patient*

1997

Best Picture	*Titanic*
Best Director	James Cameron *Titanic*
Best Actor	Jack Nicholson *As Good As It Gets*
Best Actress	Helen Hunt *As Good As It Gets*
Best Supporting Actor	Robin Williams *Good Will Hunting*
Best Supporting Actress	Kim Basinger *L A Confidential*
Best Original Screenplay	Matt Damon and Ben Affleck *Good Will Hunting*
Best Adapted Screenplay	Brian Helgeland and Curtis Hanson *L A Confidential*
Best Foreign Film	*Character* (Netherlands)
Best Cinematography	Russell Carpenter *Titanic*
Best Film Editing	Conrad Buff, James Cameron, and Richard A Harris *Titanic*
Best Art Direction	Peter Lamont *Titanic*
Best Costume Design	Deborah L Scott *Titanic*
Best Dramatic Score	James Horner *Titanic*
Best Comedy/Musical Score	Anne Dudley *The Full Monty*
Best Original Song	'My Heart Will Go On' (music by James Horner, lyrics by Will Jennings) *Titanic*
Best Makeup	Rick Baker and David Leroy Anderson *Men in Black*
Best Sound	Gary Rydstrom, Tom Johnson, Gary Summers, and Mark Ulano *Titanic*
Best Sound Effects Editing	Tom Bellfort and Christopher Boyes *Titanic*
Best Visual Effects	Robert Legato, Mark Lasoff, Thomas L Fisher, and Michael Kanfer *Titanic*
Best Documentary Feature	*The Long Way Home*
Best Documentary Short Subject	*A Story of Healing*
Best Live-Action Short Film	*Visas and Virtues*
Best Animated Short Film	*Geri's Game*
Honorary Award	Stanley Donen

BAFTA Film Awards

The British Academy of Film and Television Arts (BAFTA) was formed in 1959 as a result of the amalgamation of the British Film Academy (founded in 1948) and the Guild of Television Producers (founded in 1954). Film and television awards are presented for both production and performance categories.

1988–97

Year	Best Film
1988	*Jean de Florette* (France)
1989	*The Last Emperor* (USA)
1990	*Dead Poets Society* (USA)
1991	*Goodfellas* (USA)
1992	*The Commitments* (UK)
1993	*Howard's End* (UK)
1994	*Schindler's List* (USA)
1995	*Four Weddings and a Funeral* (UK)
1996	*Sense and Sensibility* (UK)
1997	*The English Patient* (USA)

1998

Best Film	*The Full Monty* (UK)
The David Lean Award	Baz Luhrmann *William Shakespeare's Romeo + Juliet*
Best Actress	Judi Dench *Mrs Brown*
Best Actor	Robert Carlyle *The Full Monty*
Best Supporting Actress	Sigourney Weaver *The Ice Storm*
Best Supporting Actor	Tom Wilkinson *The Full Monty*
Best Foreign Film	*L'Appartement* (France)
Best Original Screenplay	Gary Oldman *Nil By Mouth*
Best Adapted Screenplay	Craig Pearce/Baz Luhrmann *William Shakespeare's Romeo + Juliet*
The Fellowship	Sean Connery
The Alexander Korda Award for the Outstanding British Film of the Year	*Nil By Mouth*
The Audience Award for the Most Popular Film in association with *The Daily Mail* for the Outstanding British Film of the Year	*The Full Monty*

London Film Critics' Circle Awards

These awards of the London Film Critics' Circle, have been awarded annually since 1980. The Critics' Circle has existed since 1913; its members are the leading critics from Britain's national newspapers and magazines, together with reviewers from television and radio.

1992–96

Year	Best Film
1992	*Unforgiven* (USA)
1993	*The Piano* (New Zealand/Australia)
1994	*Schindler's List* (USA)
1995	*Babe* (Australia)
1996	*Fargo* (USA)

1997

Award	Winner
Director of the Year	Curtis Hanson *L A Confidential*
Actor of the Year	Al Pacino *Donnie Brasco* and *Looking for Richard;* Geoffrey Rush *Shine*
Best Actress	Claire Danes *William Shakespeare's Romeo + Juliet*
Best Screenwriter	Brian Helgeland and Curtis Hanson *L A Confidential*
Film of the Year	*L A Confidential* (USA)
British Film of the Year	*The Full Monty*
Best British Producer	Uberto Pasolini *The Full Monty* and *Palookaville*
British Director of the Year	Anthony Minghella *The English Patient*
Best British Screenwriter	Simon Beaufoy *The Full Monty*
British Actor of the Year	Robert Carlyle *The Full Monty, Carla's Song, Face*
Best British Actress	Judi Dench *Mrs Brown*
Best British Newcomer	Peter Cattaneo *The Full Monty*
Best Foreign Language Film	*Ridicule* (France)
The Dilys Powell Award for Outstanding Achievement	Michael Caine

Berlin Film Festival

This international film festival has been held every year in Berlin since 1950.

1993–97

Year	Golden Bear for Best Film
1993	*Woman from the Lake of Centered Souls* (China); *Wedding Banquet* (Taiwan)
1994	*In the Name of the Father* (USA/Ireland)
1995	*L'Appât* (France)
1996	*Sense and Sensibility* (UK)
1997	*The People vs Larry Flynt* (USA)

1998

Award	Winner
Golden Bear (Grand Prix)	*Central Do Brasil* (Brazil)
Silver Bear (Special Jury Prize)	*Wag the Dog* (USA)
Silver Bear for Best Director	Neil Jordan *The Butcher Boy* (USA/Ireland)
Silver Bear for Best Actress	Fernanda Montenegro *Central Do Brasil* (Brazil)
Silver Bear for Best Actor	Samuel L Jackson *Jackie Brown* (USA)
Silver Bear for Outstanding Single Achievement	Matt Damon *Good Will Hunting* (USA)
Silver Bear for Lifetime Contribution to the Art of Cinema	Alain Resnais
'The Blue Angel' Grand Prize of the European Academy of Film and Television	Jeroen Krabbe *Left Luggage* (Netherlands)

Cannes Film Festival

This international film festival is held every May in Cannes, France. The first festival was held in 1947. The main award is the Palme d'Or (known as the Grand Prix prior to 1955) for best film. Awards for supporting performances were introduced in 1979.

1988–97

Year	Palme d'Or for Best Film
1988	*Pelle the Conqueror* (Denmark)
1989	*Sex, Lies and Videotape* (USA)
1990	*Wild at Heart* (USA)
1991	*Barton Fink* (USA)
1992	*The Best Intentions* (Sweden)
1993	*The Piano* (New Zealand/Australia); *Farewell, My Concubine* (Hong Kong/China)
1994	*Pulp Fiction* (USA)
1995	*Underground* (Bosnia-Herzegovina)
1996	*Secrets and Lies* (UK)
1997	*The Eel/Unagi* Shohei Imamura (Japan)
	The Taste of Cherries Abbas Kiarostami (Iran)

1998

Award	Winner
Palme d'Or for Best Film	*Mia Eoniotita Ke Mia Mera/Eternity and A Day* Theo Angelopoulos (Greece)
Grand Prize	*La Vita é Bella/Life is Beautiful* Roberto Benigni (Italy)
Best Director	John Boorman *The General* (Ireland)
Best Actress	Elodie Bouchez *La Vie Rêvée des Anges/Dreamlife of Angels* (France)
	Natacha Regnier *La Vie Rêvée des Anges/Dreamlife of Angels* (France)
Best Actor	Peter Mullan *My Name is Joe* (UK)
Best Screenplay	Hal Hartley *Henry Fool* (USA)
Special Jury Prize	*Festen/The Celebration* Thomas Vinterberg (Denmark)
	La Classe de Neige Claude Miller (France)
Camera d'Or	*Slam* Marc Levin (from Directors' Fortnight) (USA)
Special Jury Prize for Artistic Contribution	*Velvet Goldmine* Todd Haynes (UK)
Grand Prix Technique	*Tango* Vittorio Storaro (Spain)
Critics' Week Prize (feature)	*Junk Mail* Pal Sletaune (Norway)

Venice Film Festival

International film festival held annually in September, in Venice, Italy.

1985–96

Year	Golden Lion (Grand Prix) for Best Film
1985	*Sans toit ni loi aka Vagabonde* (France)
1986	*Le Rayon Vert* (France)
1987	*Au Revoir les Enfants* (France)
1988	*La Leggenda del Santo Bevitore/The Legend of the Holy Drinker* (Italy)
1989	*Beiqing Chengshi City of Sadness* (Taiwan)
1990	*Rosencrantz and Guildenstern are Dead* (UK)
1991	*Urga* (Russia)
1992	*Story of Qiu Ju* (China)
1993	*Short Cuts* (USA); *Three Colors Blue* (Poland)
1994	*Vive l'Amour* (Taiwan); *Before the Rain* (Macedonia)
1995	*Cyclo* (France)
1996	*Michael Collins* (USA)

1997

Award	Winner
Golden Lion	*Hana-bi* (Japan)
Silver Lion/Special Jury Prize	*Ovosodo* (Italy)
Best Actor	Wesley Snipes *One Night Stand*
Best Actress	Robin Tunney *Niagara, Niagara*
Best Screenplay	Anne Fontaine and Giles Taurand *Nettoyage á Sec/Dry Cleaning* (France)

Golden Globe Awards for Motion Pictures

These US entertainment awards are presented annually in January by the Hollywood Foreign Press Association for motion pictures and television

1997

Award	Winner
Motion Picture (Drama)	*Titanic*
Motion Picture (Musical or Comedy)	*As Good As It Gets*
Actor in a Motion Picture (Drama)	Peter Fonda *Ulee's Gold*
Actress in a Motion Picture (Drama)	Judi Dench *Mrs Brown*
Actor in a Motion Picture (Comedy)	Jack Nicholson *As Good As It Gets*
Actress in a Motion Picture (Comedy)	Helen Hunt *As Good As It Gets*
Supporting Actor in a Motion Picture	Burt Reynolds *Boogie Nights*
Supporting Actress in a Motion Picture	Kim Basinger *L A Confidential*
Director	James Cameron *Titanic*
Foreign Language Film	*Ma vie en rose* (My Life in Pink) (France)
Screenplay	Ben Affleck and Matt Damon *Good Will Hunting*

Television

BAFTA Television Awards

The British Academy of Film and Television Arts (BAFTA) was formed in 1959 as a result of the amalgamation of the British Film Academy (founded in 1948) and the Guild of Television Producers (founded in 1954). Film and television awards are presented for both production and performance categories.

1998

Award	Winner	Award	Winner
The Richard Dimbleby Award	David Dimbleby	The Flaherty Documentary Award	*The Grave (True Stories)*
The Dennis Potter Award	Kay Mellor	Best Actress	Daniela Nardini *This Life*
The Lew Grade Award	*A Touch of Frost*	Best Actor	Simon Russell Beale *A Dance to the Music of Time*
The Alan Clarke Award	Ted Childs		
The Foreign Television Programme	*Friends* (USA)	Best Light Entertainment Performance	Paul Whitehouse *The Fast Show*
Best Single Drama	*No Child of Mine*	Best Comedy Performance	Steve Coogan *I'm Alan Partridge*
Best Drama Series	*Jonathan Creek*	Best News and Current	
Best Drama Serial	*Holding On*	Affairs Journalism	*Panorama: Valentina's Story*
Best Factual Series	*The Nazis – A Warning from History*	Best Sports/Events Coverage in Real Time	Rugby Union (Sky)
Best Light Entertainment	*The Fast Show*		
Best Comedy	*I'm Alan Partridge*		

British Comedy Awards

These awards are presented annually in December with the Writers' Guild of Great Britain, and are for the best comedy on television, radio, film, and stage.

1997

Award	Winner
Top TV Comedy Actor	David Jason
Top TV Comedy Actress	Dawn French
Top BBC1 Personality	Caroline Aherne
Top ITV Personality	Cilla Black
Top Channel 4/BBC2 Entertainment Presenter	Paul Whitehouse
Top Stand-Up Comedian	Jack Dee
Top TV Comedy Newcomer	Graham Norton
Best New TV Comedy	*Harry Hill*
Best Entertainment Programme	*An Evening with Lili Savage*
Best Comedy Show	*The Fast Show*
Best International Comedy	*The Larry Sanders Show*
Best BBC Sitcom	*One Foot in the Grave Christmas Special*
Best ITV Sitcom	*Faith in the Future*
Best Channel 4 Sitcom	*Father Ted Christmas Special*
Best Children's Comedy	*My Dad's a Boring Nerd*
Best BBC Comedy Drama	*The Missing Postman*
Best ITV Comedy Drama	*Cold Feet*
Best Radio Comedy	*People Like Us*
Best Comedy Film	*The Full Monty*
Lifetime Achievement Award	Ray Galton and Alan Simpson
Lifetime Achievement Award for Comedy	Stanley Baxter
Cockburn's Funniest Comedy Moment	*Only Fools and Horses*

Broadcasting Press Guild Television and Radio Awards

These UK media awards were established in 1974 and are presented annually in March for programmes of the previous year.

1997

Award	Winner
Best Entertainment	*I'm Alan Partridge* (BBC 2)
Best Documentary Series	*The Nazis – A Warning from History* (BBC 2)
Best Single Drama	*Breaking the Code* (BBC 1)
Best Actress	Helen Baxendale *Cold Feet, An Unsuitable Job for a Woman*
Best Actor	Simon Russell Beale *A Dance to the Music of Time* (Channel 4)
Best Single Documentary	*Cutting Edge: The Dinner Party* (Channel 4)
Best Performer (Non-Acting)	Jeremy Paxman *University Challenge, Newsnight, Election Night 1997*
Radio Programme of the Year	*I'm Sorry I Haven't A Clue* (BBC Radio 4)
Radio Broadcaster of the Year	Susan Sharpe *Midweek Choice* (BBC Radio 3)
Best Drama Series/Serial	*Holding On* (BBC 2)
Writer's Award	David Renwick *One Foot in the Grave, Jonathan Creek*
Harvey Lee Award for Outstanding Contribution to Broadcasting	Michael Wearing (Head of Drama Serials, BBC TV)

British Press Awards

When first awarded in 1963, these UK press awards were called the Hannen Swaffer National Press Awards; the present name was adopted in 1975. The awards are now sponsored by several major newspaper groups and are widely regarded as the 'Oscars' of the British newspaper industry. The categories of awards vary for each year.

1998

Award	Winner	Award	Winner
National Newspaper of the Year	*Daily Mail*	Feature Writer of the Year	Nick Davies *The Guardian*
Team Reporting Award	*The Guardian* Aitken libel story	Sports Writer of the Year	Michael Parkinson *The Daily Telegraph*
London Press Club Scoop of the Year	Charles Miller (The Press Association)	Columnist of the Year	Ruth Picardie *The Observer*
Reporter of the Year	W F Deedes *The Daily Telegraph*	Critic of the Year	Alexander Walker *The Evening Standard*
Specialist Reporter of the Year	Christine Doyle *The Daily Telegraph*		
Foreign Reporter of the Year	Anton Antonowicz *The Mirror*	Young Journalist of the Year	Libby Brooks *The Guardian*
Sports Reporter of the Year	Harry Harris *The Mirror*	Cartoonist of the Year	Matt Pritchett *The Daily Telegraph*
Interviewer of the Year	Lesley White *The Sunday Times*	Photographer of the Year	Mike Moore *The Mirror*
Business Journalist of the Year	Neil Bennett *The Sunday Telegraph*	Sports Photographer of the Year	David Ashdown *The Independent*

Royal Television Society Awards

These awards began in 1964 (as the Geoffrey Parr Awards, renamed in 1988) and are presented in recognition of excellence in television for the previous year.The Programme and Technology awards are given in February, the Journalism and Sports awards are given in May.

1997

Programme and Technology

Award	Winner
Situation Comedy and Comedy Drama	*Vicar of Dibley* (Tiger Aspect for BBC1)
Entertainment	*Harry Enfield and Chums* (Tiger Aspect for BBC1)
Children's Drama	*Sunny's Ears* (A Film and General Production for Carlton)
Children's Entertainment	*Teletubbies* (Ragdoll Productions for BBC2)
Children's Factual	*Newsround Extra – Bullying* (BBC1)
Actor Male	Simon Russell-Beale *A Dance to the Music of Time* (Table Top Productions for Channel 4)
Actor Female	Sinead Cusack *Have Your Cake and Eat It* (Initial Film and Television for BBC1)
Documentary Series	*Breaking Point* (BBC2)

Award	Winner
Single Documentary	*True Stories – The Grave* (Soul Purpose Productions for Channel 4)
Presenter	Jeremy Clarkson *Top Gear* (BBC2)
Drama Series	*This Life* (World Productions for BBC2)
Single Drama	*The Granton Star Cause* (Picture Palace North for Channel 4)
Drama Serial	*Holding On* (BBC2)
Arts	*The South Bank Show – Gilbert and George* (London Weekend Television)
Television Performance	Chris Morris *Brass Eye* (Talkback Productions for Channel 4)
Team	*Time Team Live* (Videotext Communications for Channel 4)
Cyril Bennett Judges' Award	Michael Wearing

1997

Journalism

Award	Winner
News Award, International	*News at Ten: Plight of Romania's Children* (ITN News on ITV)
News Award, Home	*Channel 4 News: Bloody Sunday* (ITN News for Channel 4 Television)
Regional Daily News Magazine	*BBC Midlands Today* (BBC Birmingham)
News Event Award	*Diana's Death and Funeral* (Sky News) *The Death of Diana* (BBC) *Death of Diana, Princess of Wales* (ITN News on ITV)
Television Technician of the Year	Alan Thompson (ITN News on ITV)
Regional Current Affairs	*Meridian Focus: Murky Waters* (Meridian Broadcasting)
Interview of the Year	*Newsnight: Jeremy Paxman interviews Michael Howard* (BBC)
Journalist of the Year	Denis Murray (BBC)
Young Journalist of the Year	Glenn Campbell (London News Network)
Current Affairs Award, International	*Correspondent: Getting Away With Murder* (BBC) *Panorama: Valentina's Story* (BBC)
Current Affairs Award, Home	*Dispatches: Secrets of the Gaul* (Anglia Television for Channel 4 Television)
Production Award	*Channel 5 News* (ITN News on Channel 5)
Judges' Award	Peter Snow

Sports

Award	Winner
Sports News	*Round the World Yacht Race* (ITN News on ITV)
Live Sports Coverage	*British Grand Prix 1997: Silverstone* (MACH I for ITV Network)
Sports Documentary	*Equinox: Losing It* (A Union Pictures Production for Channel 4 Television)
Regional Sports News	*Kevin Keegan's Resignation* (BBC North East and Cumbria)
Regional Sports Documentary	*24 Hours: Losers Limited* (Central Broadcasting for Carlton Television)
Sports Presenter Award	Jim Rosenthal (MACH I/ISN for ITV Network)
Sports Commentator Award	Ewen Murray and Bruce Critchley (Sky Sports)
Judges' Award	Brian Moore

Sony Radio Awards

These UK awards are given in recognition of excellence in radio broadcasting.

1998

Award	Winner
Gold Award	Chris Evans
The Event Award	*The Funeral of Diana, Princess of Wales* (BBC Network, Regions & Local for BBC Network Radio and BBC World Service)
The Feature Award – Music	*The Club That Scott Built* (BBC Radio 2)
The Feature Award – Talk/News	*The Coroner* (BBC Radio 4)
The Special Interest Music Award	*Songs of the Sufi Mystics* (BBC World Service)
Comedy Award	*Blue Jam* (BBC Radio 1)

(continued)

Sony Radio Awards (continued)

The Sports Award	*Wimbledon* and the *British Lions Test* (BBC Radio 5 Live)
The Drama Award	*The Trick is to Keep Breathing* (BBC Radio Scotland for BBC Radio 4)
The Arts Award	*Designs for Living: Falling Water* (BBC Radio 3)
The Station Branding Award	5 Live Station Branding (BBC Radio 5 Live Productions)
The Magazine Award	*Top of the Pops Radio Show* (BBC Radio 1)
The News Award	*The Death of the Princess of Wales* (BBC Radio 4 and BBC Radio 5 Live)
The Community Award	*The 'Breast Cancer Awareness' Compilation* (BBC Radio Ulster)
The Talk/News Broadcaster Award	Anna Raeburn (Talk Radio)
1998 Station of the Year with up to 1 million listeners	Moray Firth Radio
1998 Station of the Year with between 1 and 12 million listeners	BBC Radio WM
1998 Station of the Year broadcasting primarily to the UK	BBC Radio 5 Live
The DJ Award	Jo Whiley (BBC Radio 1)
Awards to acknowledge continuing commitment and dedication to the radio industry	Roger Bennett (BBC Bristol), Alex Dickson, Piers Plowright, and Cliff Morgan

What the Papers Say Awards

First broadcast in 1956, *What the Papers Say* is the longest running regular weekly programme on British television. Its awards are made in recognition of special achievement in journalism. The awards vary in category from year to year, although most years have included a 'Newspaper of the Year' award.

1998

Award	Winner
Newspaper of the Year	*The Guardian*
Journalist of the Year	John Sweeney *The Observer*
Scoop of the Year	Nate Thayer *The Far Eastern Economic Review*
Political Commentator of the Year	Boris Johnson *The Daily Telegraph*
Royal Reporter of the Year	Richard Kay *Daily Mail*
Columnist of the Year	John Diamond *The Times*
Peter Black Award for Broadcasting Writer of the Year	David Aaronovitch *The Independent on Sunday*
Gerald Barry Lifetime Achievement Award	Ruth Picardie *The Observer*

Emmy Awards: Primetime

These are annual US television awards for primetime programmes. They are announced in September for the previous television season.

1996–97

Award	Winner
Comedy Series	*Frasier*
Drama Series	*Law & Order*
Miniseries	*Prime Suspect 5: Errors of Judgement*
Made for Television Movie	*Miss Evers' Boys*
Lead Actor in a Comedy Series	John Lithgow *3rd Rock From the Sun*
Lead Actress in a Comedy Series	Helen Hunt *Mad About You*
Lead Actor in a Drama Series	Dennis Franz *NYPD Blue*
Lead Actress in a Drama Series	Gillian Anderson *The X-Files*
Supporting Actor in a Comedy Series	Michael Richards *Seinfeld*
Supporting Actress in a Comedy Series	Kristen Johnston *3rd Rock From the Sun*
Supporting Actor in a Drama Series	Hector Elizondo *Chicago Hope*
Supporting Actress in a Drama Series	Kim Delaney *NYPD Blue*
Lead Actor in a Miniseries or Special	Armand Assante *Gotti*
Lead Actress in a Miniseries or Special	Alfre Woodard *Miss Evers' Boys*
Supporting Actor in a Miniseries or Special	Beau Bridges *The Second Civil War*
Supporting Actress in a Miniseries or Special	Diana Rigg *Rebecca*
Guest Actor in a Comedy Series	Mel Brooks *Mad About You*
Guest Actress in a Comedy Series	Carol Burnett *Mad About You*
Guest Actor in a Drama Series	Pruitt Taylor Vince *Murder One*
Guest Actress in a Drama Series	Dianne Wiest *Avonlea*

Literature

Booker Prize

This UK literary prize of £20,000 is awarded annually in October.

Year	Winner	Awarded for
1969	P H Newby	Something to Answer For
1970	Bernice Rubens	The Elected Member
1971	V S Naipaul	In a Free State
1972	John Berger	G
1973	J G Farrell	The Siege of Krishnapur
1974	Nadine Gordimer	The Conservationist
	Stanley Middleton	Holiday
1975	Ruth Prawer Jhabvala	Heat and Dust
1976	David Storey	Saville
1977	Paul Scott	Staying On
1978	Iris Murdoch	The Sea, The Sea
1979	Penelope Fitzgerald	Offshore
1980	William Golding	Rites of Passage
1981	Salman Rushdie	Midnight's Children
1982	Thomas Keneally	Schindler's Ark
1983	J M Coetzee	The Life and Times of Michael K
1984	Anita Brookner	Hotel du Lac
1985	Keri Hulme	The Bone People
1986	Kingsley Amis	The Old Devils
1987	Penelope Lively	Moon Tiger
1988	Peter Carey	Oscar and Lucinda
1989	Kazuo Ishiguro	The Remains of the Day
1990	A S Byatt	Possession
1991	Ben Okri	The Famished Road
1992	Barry Unsworth	Sacred Hunger
	Michael Ondaatje	The English Patient
1993	Roddy Doyle	Paddy Clarke Ha Ha Ha
1994	James Kelman	How Late It Was, How Late
1995	Pat Barker	The Ghost Road
1996	Graham Swift	Last Orders
1997	Arundhati Roy	The God of Small Things

Guardian Fiction Prize

This UK literary prize is chosen by the literary editor and book reviewers of The Guardian newspaper. The award is for a work of fiction by a British or Commonwealth author.

Year	Winner	Awarded for
1997	Anne Michaels	Fugitive Pieces

James Tait Black Memorial Prize

The James Tait Black Memorial Prize was established in 1918. This UK literary award is presented in January or February for the previous year, with a cash prize of £1,500.

1997

Prize	Winner	Awarded for
Fiction	Andrew Miller	Ingenious Pain
Biography	R F Foster	W B Yeats: A Life, Volume 1

Whitbread Literary Award Book of the Year

Whitbread, the UK brewing, food, and leisure company, first endowed this literary award in 1971. Winners of five categories (Novel, Biography, Children's Novel, First Novel, and Poetry) are announced in November each year, and the overall winner (The Book of the Year) is awarded the £21,000 prize the following January.

Year	Winner	Awarded for
1987	Christopher Nolan	Under the Eye of the Clock
1988	Paul Sayer	The Comforts of Madness
1989	Richard Holmes	Coleridge: Early Visions
1990	Nicholas Mosley	Hopeful Monsters
1991	John Richardson	A Life of Picasso
1992	Jeff Torrington	Swing Hammer Swing!
1993	Joan Brady	Theory of War
1994	William Trevor	Felicia's Journey
1995	Kate Atkinson	Behind the Scenes at the Museum
1996	Seamus Heaney	The Spirit Level
1997	Ted Hughes	Tales from Ovid

Betty Trask Award

Awarded annually in June, this UK literary prize was endowed by Betty Trask in 1983 for the first novel of a romantic or traditional nature written by an author under 35. The number of prizes and the values of the prizes varies each year.

Year	Winner	Awarded for
1998	Kiran Desai	Hullabaloo in the Guava Orchard (£10,000)
	Nick Earls	Zigzag Street (£8,000)
	Phil Whitaker	Eclipse of the Sun (£5,000)
	Gail Anderson-Dargatz	The Cure for Death by Lightening (£1,000)
	Tobias Hill	Underground (£1,000)

Duff Cooper Memorial Prize

The Duff Cooper Memorial Prize is a UK literary award for a book of history or biography, in memory of Duff Cooper (1890–1954), statesman, diplomat, and author. It was established in 1956 with a cash prize of £2,000 and is awarded annually in February from a trust fund for a book published the previous year.

Year	Winner	Awarded for
1997	James Buchan	Frozen Desire

Forward Poetry Prizes

The Forward Poetry Prizes were established in 1992 and are awarded annually in October. Awards for the three categories are £10,000 for Best Collection; £5,000 for Best First Collection; and £1,000 for Best Single Poem.

1997

Category	Winner	Awarded for
Best Collection	Jamie McKendrick	Marble Fly
Best First Collection	Robin Robertson	A Painted Field
Best Single Poem	Lavinia Greenlaw	A World Where News Travelled Slowly

Mail on Sunday/John Llewellyn Rhys Prize

A UK literary prize inaugurated in memory of the writer, John Llewellyn Rhys. It is awarded to a citizen of the Commonwealth younger than 35 by the time of publication, for the most promising literary work of the previous year. It has been awarded annually in May since 1942. The winner receives a cash prize of £5,000.

Year	Winner	Awarded for
1997	Phil Whitaker	*Eclipse of the Sun*

Orange Prize

The Orange Prize is a UK literary prize open only to women, of any nationality. It was established in 1996 with a cash award of £30,000.

Year	Winner	Awarded for
1998	Carol Shields	*Larry's Party*

Impac Prize

Founded in 1996, and with a cash award of £103,000, this is the world's most valuable book prize for a single work of fiction. The selection process is unique among literary awards in that the winner is chosen from nominations sent in by municipal libraries around the world. The inaugural ceremony took place in Dublin, Ireland in May 1996.

Year	Winner	Awarded for
1998	Herta Müller, Michael Hofmann (translator)	*The Land of Green Plums*

Prix Goncourt

Founded in 1903, this French literary award is presented annually in November by the Académie Goncourt for the best French novel of the year. The prize is a nominal 50 FF plus a lifelong annuity of 250 FF per year.

Year	Winner	Awarded for
1981	Lucien Bodard	*Anne Marie*
1982	Dominique Fernandez	*Dans la Main de l'ange*
1983	Frederick Tristan	*Les Égarés*
1984	Marguerite Duras	*L'Amant*
1985	Yann Queffelec	*Les Noces Barbares*
1986	Michel Host	*Valet de Nuit*
1987	Tahir Ben Jelloun	*La Nuit Sacrée*
1988	Erik Orsenna	*L'Exposition Coloniale*
1989	Jean Vautrin	*Un Grand Pas vers le Bon Dieu*
1990	Jean Rouault	*Les Champs d'Honneur*
1991	Pierre Combescot	*Les Filles du Calvaire*
1992	Patrick Chamoiseau	*Texaco*
1993	Amin Maalouf	*Le Rocher de Tanios*
1994	Didier van Cauwelaert	*Un Aller Simple*
1995	Andréï Makine	*Le Testament Français*
1996	Pascale Roze	*Le Chasseur Zéro*
1997	Patrick Rambeau	*La Bataille*

W H Smith Literary Award

The W H Smith Literary Award is given to a Commonwealth or UK citizen for a UK-published book. The award was established in 1959 and is presented each March with a cash prize of £10,000.

Year	Winner	Awarded for
1998	Ted Hughes	*Tales from Ovid*

Poets Laureate of the UK

The Poet of the British royal household is so called because of the laurel wreath awarded to eminent poets in the Greco-Roman world. There is a stipend of £70 a year, plus £27 in lieu of the traditional butt of sack (cask of wine).

Appointed	Poet Laureate
1668	John Dryden (1631–1700)
1689	Thomas Shadwell (c 1642–1692)
1692	Nahum Tate (1652–1715)
1715	Nicholas Rowe (1674–1718)
1718	Laurence Eusden (1688–1730)
1730	Colley Cibber (1671–1757)
1757	William Whitehead (1715–1785)
1785	Thomas Warton (1728–1790)
1790	Henry James Pye (1745–1813)
1813	Robert Southey (1774–1843)
1843	William Wordsworth (1770–1850)
1850	Alfred, Lord Tennyson (1809–1892)
1896	Alfred Austin (1835–1913)
1913	Robert Bridges (1844–1930)
1930	John Masefield (1878–1967)
1968	Cecil Day Lewis (1904–1972)
1972	Sir John Betjeman (1906–1984)
1984	Ted Hughes (1930–)

Smarties Book Prize

The Smarties Book Prize aims to encourage British authors to achieve higher standards of writing for children in three age groups. The prize was established in 1985 and is awarded annually in November.

1997

Category	Winner	Awarded for
9–11 years	J K Rowling	*Harry Potter and the Philosopher's Stone*
6–8 years	Jenny Nimmo	*The Owl Tree*
0–5 years	Charlotte Voake	*Ginger*

Somerset Maugham Award

A UK literary award for young British writers to spend on foreign travel; Mr Maugham stressed that originality and promise should be encouraged. The prize (£5,000 to each winner) is awarded annually in June.

1998

Winner	Awarded for
Rachel Cusk	*Country Life*
Jonathan Rendall	*This Bloody Mary Is the Last Thing I Own: A Journey to the End of Boxing*
Kate Summerscale	*The Queen of Whale Cay*
Robert Twigger	*Angry White Pyjamas*

Pulitzer Prize: Introduction

The Pulitzer Prizes were endowed by Joseph Pulitzer (1847–1911), the Hungarian-born US newspaper publisher. The prizes have been awarded since 1917 by Columbia University on the recommendation of the Pulitzer Prize Board. A gold medal is awarded for Meritorious Public Service; all other prizes are $3,000.

Pulitzer Prizes in Letters: Fiction

Year	Winner	Awarded for	Year	Winner	Awarded for
1918	Ernest Poole	*His Family*	1962	Edwin O'Connor	*The Edge of Sadness*
1919	Booth Tarkington	*The Magnificent Ambersons*	1963	William Faulkner	*The Reivers*
1920	no award		1964	no award	
1921	Edith Wharton	*The Age of Innocence*	1965	Shirley Ann Grau	*The Keepers of the House*
1922	Booth Tarkington	*Alice Adams*	1966	Katherine Anne Porter	*The Collected Stories of Katherine Anne Porter*
1923	Willa Cather	*One of Ours*			
1924	Margaret Wilson	*The Able McLaughlins*	1967	Bernard Malamud	*The Fixer*
1925	Edna Ferber	*So Big*	1968	William Styron	*The Confessions of Nat Turner*
1926	Sinclair Lewis	*Arrowsmith*	1969	N Scott Momaday	*House Made of Dawn*
1927	Louis Bromfield	*Early Autumn*	1970	Jean Stafford	*Collected Stories*
1928	Thornton Wilder	*The Bridge of San Luis Rey*	1971	no award	
1929	Julia Peterkin	*Scarlet Sister Mary*	1972	Wallace Stegner	*Angle of Repose*
1930	Oliver La Farge	*Laughing Boy*	1973	Eudora Welty	*The Optimist's Daughter*
1931	Margaret Ayer Barnes	*Years of Grace*	1974	no award	
1932	Pearl S Buck	*The Good Earth*	1975	Michael Shaara	*The Killer Angels*
1933	T S Stribling	*The Store*	1976	Saul Bellow	*Humboldt's Gift*
1934	Caroline Miller	*Lamb in His Bosom*	1977	no award	
1935	Josephine Winslow Johnson	*Now in November*	1978	James Alan McPherson	*Elbow Room*
1936	Harold L Davis	*Honey in the Horn*	1979	John Cheever	*The Stories of John Cheever*
1937	Margaret Mitchell	*Gone With the Wind*	1980	Norman Mailer	*The Executioner's Song*
1938	John Phillips Marquand	*The Late George Apley*	1981	John Kennedy Toole	*A Confederacy of Dunces*
1939	Marjorie Kinnan Rawlings	*The Yearling*	1982	John Updike	*Rabbit is Rich*
1940	John Steinbeck	*The Grapes of Wrath*	1983	Alice Walker	*The Color Purple*
1942	Ellen Glasgow	*In This Our Life*	1984	William Kennedy	*Ironweed*
1943	Upton Sinclair	*Dragon's Teeth*	1985	Alison Lurie	*Foreign Affairs*
1944	Martin Flavin	*Journey in the Dark*	1986	Larry McMurtry	*Lonesome Dove*
1945	John Hersey	*A Bell for Adano*	1987	Peter Taylor	*A Summons to Memphis*
1947	Robert Penn Warren	*All the King's Men*	1988	Toni Morrison	*Beloved*
1948	James A Michener	*Tales of the South Pacific*	1989	Anne Tyler	*Breathing Lessons*
1949	James Gould Cozzens	*Guard of Honor*	1990	Oscar Hijuelos	*The Mambo Kings Play Songs of Love*
1950	A B Guthrie Jr	*The Way West*			
1951	Conrad Richter	*The Town*	1991	John Updike	*Rabbit at Rest*
1952	Herman Wouk	*The Caine Mutiny*	1992	Jane Smiley	*A Thousand Acres*
1953	Ernest Hemingway	*The Old Man and the Sea*	1993	Robert Olen Butler	*A Good Scent From a Strange Mountain*
1955	William Faulkner	*A Fable*			
1956	MacKinley Kantor	*Andersonville*	1994	E Annie Proulx	*The Shipping News*
1957	no award		1995	Carol Shields	*The Stone Diaries*
1958	James Agee	*A Death in the Family*	1996	Richard A Ford	*Independence Day*
1959	Robert Lewis Taylor	*The Travels of Jamie McPheeters*	1997	Steven Millhauser	*Martin Dressler: The Tale of an American Dreamer*
1960	Allen Drury	*Advise and Consent*			
1961	Harper Lee	*To Kill a Mockingbird*	1998	Philip Roth	*American Pastoral*

Pulitzer Prizes in Letters: History

Year	Winner(s)	Awarded for
1989	Taylor Branch	*Parting the Waters*
	James M McPherson	*Battle Cry of Freedom*
1990	Stanley Karnow	*In Our Image: America's Empire in the Philippines*
1991	Laurel Thatcher Ulrich	*A Midwife's Tale: The Life of Martha Ballard, Based on Her Diary, 1785–1812*
1992	Mark E Neely Jr	*The Fate of Liberty: Abraham Lincoln and Civil Liberties*
1993	Gordon S Wood	*The Radicalism of the American Revolution*
1994	no award	
1995	Doris Kearns Goodwin	*No Ordinary Time: Franklin and Eleanor Roosevelt: The Home Front in World War II*
1996	Alan Taylor	*William Cowper's Town: Power and Persuasion on the Frontier of the Early American Republic*
1997	Jack N Rakove	*Original Meetings: Politics and Ideas in the Making of the Constitution*
1998	Edward J Larson	*Summer for the Gods: The Scopes Trial and America's Continuing Debate Over Science and Religion*

Pulitzer Prizes in Letters: Biography or Autobiography

Year	Winner(s)	Awarded for
1989	Richard Ellmann	*Oscar Wilde*
1990	Sebastian de Grazia	*Machiavelli in Hell*
1991	Steven Naifeh and Gregory White Smith	*Jackson Pollock: An American Saga*
1992	Lewis B Puller Jr	*Fortunate Son: The Healing of a Vietnam Vet*
1993	David McCullough	*Truman*
1994	David Levering Lewis	*W E B DuBois: Biography of a Race, 1868–1919*
1995	Jean D Hedrick	*Harriet Beecher Stowe: A Life*
1996	Jack Miles	*God: A Biography*
1997	Frank McCourt	*Angela's Ashes*
1998	Katharine Graham	*Personal History*

Pulitzer Prizes in Letters: General Non-Fiction

Year	Winner(s)	Awarded for
1989	Neil Sheehan	*A Bright Shining Lie*
1990	Dale Maharidge and Michael Williamson	*And Their Children After Them*
1991	Bert Holldobler and Edward O Wilson	*The Ants*
1992	Daniel Yergin	*The Prize: The Epic Quest for Oil, Money and Power*
1993	Garry Wills	*Lincoln at Gettysburg: The Words That Remade America*
1994	David Remick	*Lenin's Tomb: The Last Days of the Soviet Empire*
1995	Jonathan Weiner	*The Beak of the Finch: A Story of Evolution in Our Time*
1996	Tina Rosenberg	*The Haunted Land: Facing Europe's Ghosts After Communism*
1997	Richard Kluger	*Ashes to Ashes: America's Hundred-Year Cigarette War, the Public Health, and the Unabashed Triumph of Philip Morris*
1998	Jared Diamond	*Guns, Germs, and Steel: The Fates of Human Societies*

Pulitzer Prizes in Letters: Poetry

This prize was established in 1922. The awards in 1918 and 1919 were made from gifts provided by the Poetry Society.

Year	Winner(s)	Awarded for
1989	Richard Wilbur	*New and Collected Poems*
1990	Charles Simic	*The World Doesn't End*
1991	Mona Van Duyn	*Near Changes*
1992	James Tate	*Selected Poems*
1993	Louise Gluck	*The Wild Iris*
1994	Yusef Komunyakaa	*Neon Vernacular*
1995	Philip Levine	*Simple Truth*
1996	Jorie Graham	*The Dream of the Unified Field*
1997	Lisel Mueller	*Alive Together: New and Selected Poems*
1998	Charles Wright	*Black Zodiac*

Pulitzer Prizes in Letters: Drama

Year	Winner	Awarded for
1989	Wendy Wasserstein	*The Heidi Chronicles*
1990	August Wilson	*The Piano Lesson*
1991	Neil Simon	*Lost in Yonkers*
1992	Robert Schenkkan	*The Kentucky Cycle*
1993	Tony Kushner	*Angels in America: Millennium Approaches*
1994	Edward Albee	*Three Tall Women*
1995	Horton Foote	*The Young Man from Atlanta*
1996	Jonathan Larson	*Rent*
1997	no award	
1998	Paula Vogel	*How I Learned to Drive*

Music

Brit Awards

These are among the UK's most prestigious and popular music awards. They are run by the British Phonographic Industry; other committee members come from major and independent record companies, publishing and retail sectors, the publicity industry, the media, retailers, promoters, the black music industry, and the Music Publishers' Association.

1993–97

Year	Best Group	Best Newcomer	Best Album	Best Single
1993	Simply Red	Tasmin Archer	Annie Lennox *Diva*	Take That 'Could it be Magic'
1994	Stereo MCs	Gabrielle	Stereo MCs *Connected*	Take That 'Pray'
1995	Blur	Oasis	Blur *Parklife*	Blur 'Parklife'
1996	Oasis	Supergrass	Oasis *(What's the Story) Morning Glory?*	Take That 'Back for Good'
1997	Manic Street Preachers	Kula Shaker	Manic Street Preachers *Everything Must Go*	Spice Girls 'Wannabe'

Brit Awards (*continued*)

1998

Award	Winner
Best Group	The Verve
Best Newcomer	Stereophonics
Best Album	The Verve *Urban Hymns*
Best Single	All Saints 'Never Ever'
Best Male Solo Artist	Finley Quaye
Best Female Solo Artist	Shola Ama
Best International Newcomer	Eels
Best International Group	U2
Best International Male Solo Artist	Jon Bon Jovi
Best International Solo Female Artist	Bjork
Best Dance Act	Prodigy
Best Producer	The Verve, Youth, and Chris Potter (co-producers)
Best Video	All Saints 'Never Ever'
Best Soundtrack/Cast Recording	*The Full Monty*
Outstanding Contribution to the British Music Industry	Fleetwood Mac
Freddie Mercury Award	Elton John 'Candle in the Wind 1997/The Way You Look Tonight'
Top-Selling British Album Act Worldwide 1997 (one-off)	Spice Girls

Eurovision Song Contest

Started in 1956, this European song contest is held annually in May. The 1998 contest was held at the National Indoor Arena, Birmingham, UK.

1998

Winner	Song
Dana International (Israel)	'Diva'

UK entry (2nd place)

Imaani	'Where Are You?'

Mercury Music Prize

This annual music prize is one of the UK's most prestigious arts prizes. Established in 1992, it is sponsored by Mercury Communications and supported by both the BPI (British Phonographic Industry) and BARD (British Association of Record Dealers). All ten shortlisted artists are presented with Shortlist Trophies before the overall winner is announced. The winner receives £25,000.

1997

Winner

Roni Size Reprazent *New Forms*

Shortlist

The Prodigy *The Fat of the Land*
The Spice Girls *Spice*
Beth Orton *Trailer Park*
Roni Size Reprazent *New Forms*
Mark-Anthony Turnage *Your Rockaby*
John Tavener *Svyati*
Suede *Coming Up*
Primal Scream *Vanishing Point*
The Chemical Brothers *Dig Your Own Hole*
Radiohead *OK Computer*

World Music Awards

These awards are presented annually and are chosen by the International Federated Phonograph Industry.

1997

Category	Winner	Category	Winner
International Awards		*National Awards*	
World's Best-Selling Pop Group	Spice Girls	World's Best-Selling African Artist/Group	Wes
World's Best-Selling Rock Group	No Doubt	World's Best-Selling American Artist/Group	LeAnn Rimes
World's Best-Selling R&B Artist	Mariah Carey	World's Best-Selling Australian Artist/Group	Savage Garden
World's Best-Selling Rap Artist	Puff Daddy	World's Best-Selling Benelux Artist/Group	André Rieu
World's Best-Selling Dance Group	Back Street Boys	World's Best-Selling Brazilian Artist/Group	So Pra Contrariar
World's Best-Selling Country Artist	LeAnn Rimes	World's Best-Selling British Artist/Group	Spice Girls
World's Best-Selling Latin Artist	Luis Miguel	World's Best-Selling Canadian Artist/Group	Céline Dion
World's Best-Selling Latin Female Artist	Shakira	World's Best-Selling Eastern European Artist/Group	Golden Ring
World's Best-Selling Classical Artist	Andrea Bocelli	World's Best-Selling French Artist/Group	Pascal Obispo
World's Best-Selling New Artist	Puff Daddy	World's Best-Selling German Artist/Group	Tic Tac Toe
World's Best-Selling New Group	Hanson	World's Best-Selling Greek Artist/Group	Yanni
		World's Best-Selling Irish Artist/Group	U2
Legend Awards		World's Best-Selling Italian Artist/Group	Andrea Bocelli
World's Best-Selling Recording Artist of the 90s	Mariah Carey	World's Best-Selling Japanese Artist/Group	Glay
		World's Best-Selling Middle Eastern Artist/Group	Amr Diab
		World's Best-Selling Scandinavian Artist/Group	Aqua
		World's Best-Selling Spanish Artist/Group	Monica Naranjo
		World's Best-Selling Swiss Artist/Group	DJ Bobo

Gramophone Awards

These UK classical music awards have been given since 1977. The awards have various sponsors each year.
(– = not applicable.)

1997

Award	Composer	Work	Artist(s)	Conductor	Record label
Baroque Vocal	Caldara	*Maddalena ai piedi di Cristo*	Kiehr, Dominguez, Fink, Scholl, Schola Cantorum Basiliensis	Jacobs	Harmonia Mundi
Baroque Non-vocal	Purcell	*Fantazias, In Nomines*	Phantasm	–	Simax
Chamber	Ravel	*Chamber works*	Juillet, Mørk, Rogé	–	Decca
Choral	Haydn	*Die Shöpfung*	McNair, Brown, Schade, Finley, Monteverdi Choir, English Baroque Soloists	Gardiner	Archiv Produktion
Concerto	Szymanowski	*Violin Concertos Nos. 1 and 2; Paganini, Caprices, Romance in D*	Zehetmair, City of Birmingham Symphony Orchestra	Rattle	EMI
Contemporary	Ligeti	*Piano Works*	Aimard	–	Sony Classical
Early Music	Ockeghem	*Requiem etc*	The Clerks' Group	Wickham	ASV Gaudeamus
Early Opera	Rameau	*Hippolyte et Aricie*	Padmore, Panzarella, Hunt, Naouri, Les Arts Florissants	Christie	Erato
Engineering	Dyson	*The Canterbury Pilgrims, etc*	Kenny, Tear, Roberts, London Symphony Chorus, London Symphony Orchestra	Hickox	Chandos
Film Music	Herrmann	*Vertigo*	Royal Scottish National Orchestra	McNeely	Varèse Sarabande
Instrumental	Handel, D Scarlatti	*Keyboard Works*	Perahia	–	Sony Classical
Music Theatre	Lerner and Loewe	*My Fair Lady*	Olafimihan, McCowen, Hoskins, National Symphony Orchestra	Edwards	TER
Opera	Puccini	*La Rondine, Le Villi –* excerpts	Gheorghiu, Alagna, London Voices, London Symphony Orchestra	Pappano	EMI
Orchestral	Sibelius	*Symphonies Nos. 1 and 4*	London Symphony Orchestra	C Davis	RCA Victor Red Seal
Solo Vocal	Schumann	*Complete Lieder*, Volume 1	Schäfer, Johnson	–	Hyperion
Video	Berg	*Lulu*	Schäfer, Schöne, Kuebler, Harries, London Philarmonic Orchestra	A Davis	NVC Arts
Best-Selling Record	various	*Agnus Dei*	New College Choir, Oxford, Capricorn	Higginbottom	Erato
Record of the Year	Puccini	*La Rondine , Le Villi –* excerpts	Gheorghiu, Alagna, London Voices, London Symphony Orchestra	Pappano	EMI

Artist of the Year	Yo-Yo Ma
Young Artist of the Year	Isabelle Faust, for her solo début recording – Bartók *Violin Sonatas* (Harmonia Mundi)
Lifetime Achievement	Mstislav Rostropovich, presented in recognition of his outstanding contribution to classical music
Special Achievement	Luciano Pavarotti, presented in recognition of over £5 million raised via record sales on Decca for the children of Bosnia

MTV Video Music Awards

These awards are announced in September for current year.

1997

Award	Winner	Award	Winner
Best Video	Jamiroquai 'Virtual Insanity'	Best R&B Video	Puff Daddy and the Family 'I'll Be Missing You'
Best Male Video	Beck 'Devil's Haircut'		
Best Female Video	Jewel 'You Were Meant for Me'	Best Rock Video	Aerosmith 'Falling in Love'
Best Group Video	No Doubt 'Don't Speak'	Best Dance Video	Spice Girls 'Wannabe'
Best Rap Video	The Notorious B.I.G. 'Hypnotize'	Best Cinematography	Jamiroquai 'Virtual Insanity'
Breakthrough Video	Jamiroquai 'Virtual Insanity'	Best Editing	Beck 'Devil's Haircut'
Best Direction in a Video	Beck 'The New Pollution'	Best Choreography	Beck 'The New Pollution'
Best Alternative Music Video	Sublime 'What I Got'	Best Special Effects	Jamiroquai 'Virtual Insanity'
Best New Artist in a Video	Fiona Apple 'Sleep to Dream'	Best Art Direction	Beck 'The New Pollution'
Best Video from a Film	Will Smith 'Men in Black'	International Viewers' Choice	Prodigy 'Breathe'

Grammy Awards

US annual music awards which are for outstanding achievement in the record industry for the previous year. The gold-plated disks are presented by the National Academy of Recording Arts and Sciences. The first Grammy Awards were for records released in 1958.

1997

Category	Awarded to	Category	Awarded to
Song of the Year	Shawn Colvin 'Sunny Came Home'	R&B Duo or Group Performance	Blackstreet 'No Diggity'
Album of the Year	Bob Dylan *Time Out of Mind*	R&B Song	R Kelly 'I Believe I Can Fly'
Record of the Year	Shawn Colvin 'Sunny Came Home'	R&B Album	Erykah Badu *Baduizm*
New Artist	Paula Cole	Rap Solo Performance	Will Smith 'Men in Black'
Female Pop Vocal Performance	Sarah McLachlan 'Surfacing'	Rap Duo or Group Performance	Puff Daddy and Faith Evans featuring 112 'I'll Be Missing You'
Male Pop Vocal Performance	Elton John 'Candle in the Wind 1997'	Rap Album	Puff Daddy and The Family *No Way Out*
Pop Duo or Group Performance	Jamiroquai 'Virtual Insanity'	Female Country Vocal Performance	Trisha Yearwood 'How Do I Live'
Rock Song	The Wallflowers 'One Headlight'		
Rock Album	John Fogerty *Blue Moon Swamp*	Male Country Vocal Performance	Vince Gill 'Pretty Little Adriana'
Female Rock Vocal Performance	Fiona Apple 'Criminal'	Country Duo or Group Performance	Alison Kraus and Union Station 'Looking in the Eyes of Love'
Male Rock Vocal Performance	Bob Dylan 'Cold Irons Bound'	Country Song	Bob Carlisle and Randy Thomas 'Butterfly Kisses'
Rock Vocal, Duo or Group Performance	The Wallflowers 'One Headlight'		
Hard Rock Performance	The Smashing Pumpkins 'The End is the Beginning is the End'	Country Album	Johnny Cash *Unchained*
		Jazz Instrumental Solo	Doc Cheatham 'Stardust'
Metal Performance	Tool 'nima'	Individual or Group Jazz Instrumental Performance	Charlie Haden and Pat Metheny 'Beyond the Missouri Sky'
Female R&B Vocal Performance	Erykah Badu 'On and On'		
Male R&B Vocal Performance	R Kelly 'I Believe I Can Fly'		

Grammy Awards: Best Record and Best Album

1958–97

Year	Best Record	Best Album
1958	Domenico Modugno 'Nel Blu Dipinto Di Blu (Volare)'	Henry Mancini *The Music From Peter Gunn*
1959	Bobby Darin 'Mack the Knife'	Frank Sinatra *Come Dance With Me*
1960	Percy Faith 'Theme From a Summer Place'	Bob Newhart *Button Down Mind*
1961	Henry Mancini 'Moon River'	Judy Garland *Judy at Carnegie Hall*
1962	Tony Bennett 'I Left My Heart in San Francisco'	Vaughn Meader *The First Family*
1963	Henry Mancini 'The Days of Wine and Roses'	Barbra Streisand *The Barbra Streisand Album*
1964	Stan Getz, Astrud Gilberto 'The Girl From Ipanema'	Stan Getz, Astrud Gilberto *Getz/Gilberto*
1965	Herb Alpert 'A Taste of Honey'	Frank Sinatra *September of My Years*
1966	Frank Sinatra 'Strangers in the Night'	Frank Sinatra *A Man and His Music*
1967	5th Dimension 'Up, Up and Away'	The Beatles *Sgt Pepper's Lonely Hearts Club Band*
1968	Simon and Garfunkel 'Mrs Robinson'	Glen Campbell *By the Time I Get to Phoenix*
1969	5th Dimension 'Aquarius/Let the Sunshine In'	Blood, Sweat and Tears *Blood, Sweat and Tears*
1970	Simon and Garfunkel 'Bridge Over Troubled Water'	Simon and Garfunkel *Bridge Over Troubled Water*
1971	Carole King 'It's Too Late'	Carole King *Tapestry*
1972	Roberta Flack 'The First Time Ever I Saw Your Face'	various *The Concert for Bangladesh*
1973	Roberta Flack 'Killing Me Softly With His Song'	Stevie Wonder *Innervisions*
1974	Olivia Newton-John 'I Honestly Love You'	Stevie Wonder *Fullingness' First Finale*
1975	Captain and Tennille 'Love Will Keep Us Together'	Paul Simon *Still Crazy After All These Years*
1976	George Benson 'This Masquerade'	Stevie Wonder *Songs in the Key of Life*
1977	Eagles 'Hotel California'	Fleetwood Mac *Rumours*
1978	Billy Joel 'Just the Way You Are'	Bee Gees *Saturday Night Fever*
1979	The Doobie Brothers 'What a Fool Believes'	Billy Joel *52nd Street*
1980	Christopher Cross 'Sailing'	Christopher Cross *Christopher Cross*
1981	Kim Carnes 'Bette Davis Eyes'	John Lennon, Yoko Ono *Double Fantasy*
1982	Toto 'Rosanna'	Toto *Toto IV*
1983	Michael Jackson 'Beat It'	Michael Jackson *Thriller*
1984	Tina Turner 'What's Love Got to Do With It'	Lionel Richie *Can't Slow Down*
1985	USA for Africa 'We Are the World'	Phil Collins *No Jacket Required*
1986	Steve Winwood 'Higher Love'	Paul Simon *Graceland*
1987	Paul Simon 'Graceland'	U2 *The Joshua Tree*
1988	Bobby McFerrin 'Don't Worry, Be Happy'	George Michael *Faith*
1989	Bette Midler 'Wind Beneath My Wings'	Bonnie Raitt *Nick of Time*
1990	Phil Collins 'Another Day in Paradise'	Quincy Jones *Back on the Block*
1991	Natalie Cole, with Nat 'King' Cole 'Unforgettable'	Natalie Cole, with Nat 'King' Cole *Unforgettable*
1992	Eric Clapton 'Tears in Heaven'	Eric Clapton *Unplugged*
1993	Whitney Houston 'I Will Always Love You'	Whitney Houston *The Bodyguard*
1994	Sheryl Crow 'All I Wanna Do'	Tony Bennett *MTV Unplugged*
1995	Seal 'Kiss from a Rose'	Alanis Morissette *Jagged Little Pill*
1996	Eric Clapton 'Change the World'	Celine Dion *Falling into You*
1997	Shawn Colvin 'Sunny Came Home'	Bob Dylan *Time Out of Mind*

Theatre

Evening Standard Drama Awards

These UK annual drama awards are sponsored by the *Evening Standard* newspaper and are awarded in November.

1987–96

Year	Best Play	Best Musical	Best Comedy
1987	*A Small Family Business*	*Follies*	*Serious Money*
1988	*Aristocrats*	no award	*Lettice and Lovage*
1989	*Ghetto*	*Miss Saigon*	*Henceforward*
1990	*Shadowlands*	*Into the Woods*	*Man of the Moment* and *Jeffrey Bernard is Unwell* (joint award)
1991	*Dancing at Lughnasa*	*Carmen Jones*	*Kvetch*
1992	*Angels in America*	*Kiss of the Spider Woman*	*The Rise and Fall of Little Voice*
1993	*Arcadia*	*City of Angels*	*Jamais Vu*
1994	*Three Tall Women*	no award	*My Night With Reg*
1995	*Pentecost*	*Mack and Mabel*	*Dealer's Choice*
1996	*Stanley*	*Passion*	*Art*

1997

Best Play	*The Invention of Love* Tom Stoppard
Best Musical	*Lady in the Dark* Kurt Weill, Ira Gershwin, and Moss Hart
Best Comedy	*Closer* Patrick Marber
Best Actor	Ian Holm *King Lear*
Best Actress	Eileen Atkins *A Delicate Balance*
Best Director	Richard Eyre *King Lear* and *The Invention of Love*

Laurence Olivier Awards

These UK theatre awards are presented annually by the Society of London Theatre.

1998

Award	Winner	Award	Winner
BBC Award for Best New Play	*Closer* Patrick Marber	Special Award	Ed and David Mirrish for their contribution to restoring and operating the Old Vic
Best New Comedy	*Popcorn* Ben Elton		
Best Actor	Ian Holm *King Lear*		
Best Actress	Zoe Wanamaker *Electra*	Outstanding Musical Production	*Chicago* Fred Ebb and John Kander
Best Director	Richard Eyre *King Lear*	Best New Opera Production	The Royal Opera *Paul Bunyan*
Best Actor in a Musical	Philip Quast *The Fix*	Best New Musical	Alan Menken, Howard Ashman, and Tim Rice *Beauty and the Beast*
Best Actress in a Musical	Ute Lemper *Chicago*		
Best Theatre Choreographer	Simon McBurney *The Caucasian Circle*		
Best New Dance Production	Mark Morris Dance Group and English National Opera *L'Allegro, Il Penseroso Ed Il Moderato*		

Obie Awards

These US annual theatre awards are presented in May for the previous off-Broadway season.

1997–98

Performance	Lea DeLaria *On The Town*; Maria Testa *On The Town, From Above*; Tim Hopper *More Stately Mansions*; David Patrick Kelly for Sustained Excellence of Performance; Joseph Wiseman *I Can't Remember Anything*; Heather Gillespie *Mamba's Daughters*; Kate Valk for Sustained Excellence of Performance; Marie Mullen *The Beauty Queen of Leenane*; Matthew Maguire *I Don't Know Who He Was and I Don't Know What He Said*; Yvette Freeman *Dinah Was*; Adriane Lenox *Dinah Was*; Elizabeth Marvel *Therese Raquin, Misalliance*; J Smith Cameron *As Bees in Honey Drown*; Brian Murray for Sustained Excellence of Performance; Joan MacIntosh *More Stately Mansions*
Direction	Ivo van Hove *More Stately Mansions*; David Esbjornson *Therese Raquin*; Jo Bonney for Sustained Excellence of Direction

Obie Awards (continued)

Special Citations	Target Margin Theater *Mamba's Daughters*; David Herskovits, Thomas Cabaniss, Lenore Doxsee, Erika Belsey, David Zinn, Tim Schellenbaum; John Cameron Mitchell *Hedwig and the Angry Inch*; Stephen Trask *Hedwig and the Angry Inch*; Mark Bennett for Sustained Excellence of Sound Design; Alan Johnson for Sustained Excellence of Musical Direction and Pianism; Karen Finley *The American Chestnut*; Philim McDermott, Lee Simpson, Julian Crouch, Guy Dartnell, Ben Park, Steve Tiplady (creators of *70 Hill Lane*); Buzz Cohen for Distinguished Stage Management
Distinguished Design	Darron L West *Bob* (soundscape); Mimi Jordan Sherin *Bob* (lighting design)
Sustained Achievement	Jennifer Tipton
Best Play	Richard Foreman *Pearls for Pigs, Benita Canova*
Ross Wetzsteon Award	Doug Aibel and The Vineyard Theater for sustained support of artists and creativity in the theatre
Grants	$5,000 grant to Victoria McElwaine Housing Works Theater Project; $5,000 grant to Caught in the Act annual one-act festival presented by the Threshold Theater Company

Tony (Antoinette Perry) Awards

These annual US theatre awards are presented on the first Sunday in June for the previous theatre season, ending in April.

1987/88–1996/97

Year	Best Play	Best Musical
1987/88	*M Butterfly*	*The Phantom of the Opera*
1988/89	*The Heidi Chronicles*	*Jerome Robbins' Broadway*
1989/90	*The Grapes of Wrath*	*City of Angels*
1990/91	*Lost in Yonkers*	*The Will Rogers Follies*
1991/92	*Dancing at Lughnasa*	*Crazy for You*
1992/93	*Angels in America: Millennium Approaches*	*Kiss of the Spider Woman*
1993/94	*Angels in America: Perestroika*	*Passion*
1994/95	*Love! Valour! Compassion!*	*Sunset Boulevard*
1995/96	*Master Class*	*Rent*
1996/97	*The Last Night of Ballyhoo*	*Titanic*

1997/98

Best Play	*Art*
Best Musical	*The Lion King*
Best Performance by a Leading Actress in a Play	Marie Mullen *The Beauty Queen of Leenane*
Best Performance by a Leading Actor in a Play	Anthony LaPaglia *A View From The Bridge*
Best Performance by a Leading Actress in a Musical	Natasha Richardson *Cabaret*
Best Performance by a Leading Actor in a Musical	Alan Cumming *Cabaret*
Best Performance by a Featured Actress in a Play	Anna Manahan *The Beauty Queen of Leenane*
Best Performance by a Featured Actor in a Play	Tom Murphy *The Beauty Queen of Leenane*
Best Performance by a Featured Actress in a Musical	Audra McDonald *Ragtime*
Best Performance by a Featured Actor in a Musical	Ron Rifkin *Cabaret*
Best Director of a Play	Gerry Hynes *The Beauty Queen of Leenane*
Best Director of a Musical	Julie Taymor *The Lion King*
Best Revival of a Play	*A View From The Bridge*
Best Revival of a Musical	*Cabaret*
Best Book	Terrence McNally *Ragtime*
Best Score	Lynn Ahrens and Stephen Flaherty *Ragtime*
Best Choreography	Garth Fagan *The Lion King*
Best Costume Design	Julie Taymor *The Lion King*
Best Scenic Design	Richard Hudson *The Lion King*
Best Lighting Design	Donald Holder *The Lion King*
Best Orchestrations	William David Brohn *Ragtime*
Special Tony for Regional Theater	Denver Center Theater Company

Art and Architecture

Turner Prize

Established in 1984 to encourage discussion about new developments in contemporary British art, this prize has often attracted criticism for celebrating what is not traditionally considered to be art. It is open to any British artist under 50 and has a prize of £20,000.

Year	Winner	Year	Winner
1984	Malcolm Morley	1991	Anish Kapoor
1985	Howard Hodgkin	1992	Grenville Davey
1986	Gilbert and George	1993	Rachel Whiteread
1987	Richard Deacon	1994	Antony Gormley
1988	Tony Cragg	1995	Damien Hirst
1989	Richard Long	1996	Douglas Gordon
1990	no award	1997	Gillian Wearing

BP Portrait Award by the National Portrait Gallery

This is an annual art prize of £10,000 and, at the judges' discretion, a commission of £2,000 to paint a well-known person.

Year	Winner	Awarded for
1998	Thomas Watson	*Jude*

Royal Academy Summer Exhibition Awards

UK arts awards held since 1769. Awards vary in amount and are for works in different media.

1998

Award	Amount (£)	Winner
Charles Wollaston Award for the Most Distinguished Work in the Exhibition	25,000	John Hoyland for *Tree Music* (acrylic)
Korn/Ferry International Picture of the Year Award	10,000	Sandra Blow RA for *Sea-Change* (oil)
Diageo Award for First-Time Exhibitor	5,000	Carl Danby for *The Book* (mixed media)
M&G Purchase Prizes		
for a painting by an artist under the age of 35	5,000	Sarah Armstrong-Jones for *South Indian Coast 1* (pastel and gouache)
for a painting by an art student	5,000	Suzanne Cockburn for *Moving into View* (oil)
other	2,500	Andrea McLean for *Tree Map* (oil)
	1,250	Susan-Jayne Hocking for *Off to Market Nepal* (oil)
	1,250	Isabella Easton for *Page E,Q,T out of an Alphabet Book entitled Alf 'n' Betty*
Bovis/*Architects' Journal* Awards for Architecture	7,250 in total	Special Award to Louis Hellman for *The Image of the Architect, Historic Images of the Architect,* and *More Images of the Architect* (hand-coloured photo prints)
Worshipful Company of Chartered Architects (for a measured drawing, or set of drawings, of a work of architecture)	1,000	Terry Pawson for *Church Hall – Wimbledon* (pencil)
Jack Goldhill Award for Sculpture	7,000 commission for a sculpture	Jonathan Froud for *Listening, Learning* (water sculpture)
Nordstern Award (for a print in any medium)	1,000	Sharon Aivaliotis for *Scissors, Paper, Stone* (mezzotint)
House & Garden Award (for a work in any medium depicting an interior)	1,000	Peter Blake RA for *Demonstrations in a Department Store, 2* (silk screen print)
Arts Club Prize	full purchase price	Mary Malenoir for *Hysteria The Sometime Bride* (oil)
Dupree Family Award for a Woman Artist (for a painting or sculpture by a woman artist)	2,500	Kwai Lu for *Canal* (oil)
Royal Watercolour Society Award (for a work in a water-based medium on a paper-based support)	500	Leonard McComb RA for Portrait of *Leonardo Ceragioli* (watercolour)

Royal Gold Medallists of Architecture

Instituted by Queen Victoria, the Royal Gold Medal is an international prize awarded annually in March to a distinguished architect, or group of architects, for work of high merit that has in some way promoted the advancement of architecture.

Year	Winner	Year	Winner	Year	Winner
1848	Charles Robert Cockerell	1899	George Frederick Bodley	1949	Howard Robertson
1849	Luigi Canina	1900	Rodolfo Amadeo Lanciani	1950	Eleil Saarinen
1850	Charles Barry	1901	no award, owing to the death of	1951	Emanuel Vincent Harris
1851	Thomas L Donaldson		Queen Victoria	1952	George Grey Wornum
1852	Leo von Klenze	1902	Thomas Edward Collcutt	1953	Le Corbusier (C E Jeanneret)
1853	Robert Smirke	1903	Charles Follen McKim	1954	Arthur George Stephenson
1854	Philip Hardwick	1904	Auguste Choisy	1955	John Murray Easton
1855	Jacques Ignace Hittorff	1905	Aston Webb	1956	Walter Adolf Georg Gropius
1856	William Tite	1906	L Alma-Tadema	1957	Hugo Alvar Henrik Aalto
1857	Owen Jones	1907	John Belcher	1958	Robert Scholfield Morris
1858	August Stuler	1908	Honore Daumet	1959	Ludwig Mies van der Rohe
1859	G Gilbert Scott	1909	Arthur John Evans	1960	Pier Luigi Nervi
1860	Sydney Smirke	1910	Thomas Graham Jackson	1961	Lewis Mumford
1861	J B Lesueur	1911	Wilhelm Dorpfeld	1962	Sven Gottfrid Markelius
1862	Robert Willis	1912	Basil Champneys	1963	William Holford
1863	Anthony Salvin	1913	Reginald Blomfield	1964	E Maxwell Fry
1864	E Violet leDuc	1914	Jean Louis Pascal	1965	Kenzo Tange
1865	James Pennethorne	1915	Frank Darling	1966	Ove Arup
1866	M Digby Wyatt	1916	Robert Rowland Anderson	1967	Nikolaus Pevsner
1867	Charles Texier	1917	Henri Paul Nenot	1968	Richard Buckminster Fuller
1868	Henry Layard	1918	Ernest Newton	1969	Jack Antonio Coia
1869	C R Lepsius	1919	Leonard Stokes	1970	Robert Matthew
1870	Benjamin Ferrey	1920	Charles Louis Girault	1971	Hubert de Cronin Hastings
1871	James Fergusson	1921	Edwin Landseer Lutyens	1972	Louis I Kahn
1872	Baron von Schmidt	1922	Thomas Hastings	1973	Leslie Martin
1873	Thomas Henry Wyatt	1923	John James Burnet	1974	Powell and Moya
1874	George Edmund Street	1924	no award	1975	Michael Scott
1875	Edmund Sharpe	1925	Giles Gilbert Scott	1976	John Summerson
1876	Joseph Louis Duc	1926	Ragnar Ostberg	1977	Denys Lasdun
1877	Charles Barry	1927	Herbert Baker	1978	Jom Utzon
1878	Alfred Waterhouse	1928	Guy Dawber	1979	The Office of Charles and Ray Earnes
1879	Marquis de Vogue	1929	Victor Alexandre Frederic Laloux	1980	James Stirling
1880	John L Pearson	1930	Percy Scott Worthington	1981	Philip Dowson
1881	George Godwin	1931	Edwin Cooper	1982	Berthold Lubetkin
1882	Baron von Ferstel	1932	Hendrik Petrus Berlage	1983	Norman Foster
1883	Fras Cranmer Penrose	1933	Charles Reed Peers	1984	Charles Corree
1884	William Butterfield	1934	Henry Vaughan Lanchester	1985	Richard Rogers
1885	H Schliemann	1935	Willem Marinus Dudok	1986	Arata Isozaki
1886	Charles Gamier	1936	Charles Henry Holden	1987	Ralph Erskine
1887	Ewan Christian	1937	Raymond Unwin	1988	Richard Meier
1888	Baron von Hansen	1938	Ivar Tengborn	1989	Renzo Piano
1889	Charles T Newton	1939	Percy Thomas	1990	Aldo van Eyck
1890	John Gibson	1940	Charles Francis Annesley Voysey	1991	Colin Stansfield Smith
1891	Arthur Blomfield	1941	Frank Lloyd Wright	1992	Peter Rice
1892	Cesar Daly	1942	William Curtis Green	1993	Giancarlo de Carlo
1893	Richard Morris Hunt	1943	Charles Herbert Reilly	1994	Michael and Patricia Hopkins
1894	Frederic Leighton	1944	Edward Maufe	1995	Colin Rowe
1895	James Brooks	1945	Victor Vessnin	1996	Harry Seilder
1896	Ernest George	1946	Patrick Abercrombie	1997	Tadao Ando
1897	Petrus Josephus Hubertus Cuypers	1947	Albert Edward Richardson	1998	Oscar Neimeyer
1898	George Aitchison	1948	Auguste Perret		

Source: Royal Institute of British Architects

Stirling Prize

This £20,000 prize is awarded each November by the Royal Institute of British Architects, and the winner is chosen from a regional shortlist.

1997

The Music School, Stuttgart by Michael Wilford

Religion

Templeton Foundation Prize for Progress in Religion

The Templeton Prize, an award to encourage progress in religion, was established in 1972 by Sir John Templeton, a Tennessee-born British financier and Presbyterian layman. He established the award to redress the fact that no Nobel Prize is granted for religion. Announced in March, it is awarded at Buckingham Palace in London; its value has increased over the years to more than $1 million.

Year	Winner	Year	Winner
1973	Mother Teresa of Calcutta, founder of the Missionaries of Charity	1986	The Reverend Dr James McCord, Princeton, New Jersey
1974	Brother Roger, founder and prior of the Taize Community in France	1987	The Reverend Professor Stanley L Jaki, Princeton, New Jersey
1975	Dr Sarvepalli Radhakrishnan, former president of India and Oxford professor of eastern religions and ethics	1988	Dr Inamullah Khan, secretary-general of the World Moslem Congress
1976	H E Leon Joseph Cardinal Suenens, archbishop of Malines-Brussels	1989	The Very Reverend Lord MacLeod of the Iona Community, Scotland, and Professor Carl Friedrich von Weizsäcker of Starnberg, West Germany
1977	Chiara Lubich, founder of the Focolare Movement, Italy	1990	Baba Amte, India, and Professor Charles Birch, Sydney, Australia
1978	Professor Thomas F Torrance, president of International Academy of Religion and Sciences, Scotland	1991	The Rt. Hon. Lord Jakobovits, Chief Rabbi of Great Britain and the Commonwealth
1979	Nikkyo Niwano, founder of Rissho Kosel Kai and World Conferences on Religion and Peace, Japan	1992	Dr Kyung-Chik Han, founder of Seoul's Young Nak Presbyterian Church
1980	Professor Ralph Wendell Burhoe, founder and editor of *Zygon*, Chicago	1993	Charles W Colson, founder, Prison Fellowship, Virginia
1981	Dame Cecily Saunders, originator of Modern Hospice Movement, England	1994	Michael Novak, scholar at the American Enterprise Institute, Washington, DC
1982	The Reverend Dr Billy Graham, founder, the Billy Graham Evangelistic Association	1995	Dr Paul Davies, professor, University of Adelaide, Australia
1983	Aleksandr Solzhenitsyn (USA)	1996	Bill Bright, founder of Campus Crusade for Christ, international evangelical ministry
1984	The Reverend Michael Bourdeaux, founder of Keston College, England	1997	Pandurang Shastri Athavale, Indian spiritual leader
1985	Sir Alister Hardy, Oxford, England	1998	Sir Sigmund Sternberg, Chairman of the Executive Committee of the International Council of Christians and Jews (ICCA)

Mathematics and Science

Fields Medal

This international prize for achievement in the field of mathematics is awarded every four years by the International Mathematical Union.

Year	Winner(s)
1936	Lars Ahlfors (Finland); Jesse Douglas (USA)
1950	Atle Selberg (USA); Laurent Schwartz (France)
1954	Kunihiko Kodaira (USA); Jean-Pierre Serre (France)
1958	Klaus Roth (UK); René Thom (France)
1962	Lars Hörmander (Sweden); John Milnor (USA)
1966	Michael Atiyah (UK); Paul J Cohen (USA); Alexander Grothendieck (France); Stephen Smale (USA)
1970	Alan Baker (UK); Heisuke Hironaka (USA); Sergei Novikov (USSR); John G Thompson (USA)
1974	Enrico Bombieri (Italy); David Mumford (USA)
1978	Pierre Deligne (Belgium); Charles Fefferman (USA); G A Margulis (USSR); Daniel Quillen (USA)
1982	Alain Connes (France); William Thurston (USA); S T Yau (USA)
1986	Simon Donaldson (UK); Gerd Faltings (West Germany); Michael Freedman (USA)
1990	Vladimir Drinfeld (USSR); Vaughan F R Jones (USA); Shigefumi Mori (Japan); Edward Witten (USA)
1994	L J Bourgain (USA/France); P-L Lions (France); J-C Yoccoz (France); E I Zelmanov (USA)

Enrico Fermi Award

Named in honor of Enrico Fermi, the atomic pioneer, the $100,000 award is given in recognition of outstanding scientific and technical achievement in the field of nuclear energy. The award is announced by the White House.

Year	Winner	Year	Winner	Year	Winner
1976	William L Russell	1984	Robert R Wilson and Georges Vendryès	1991	no award
1978	Harold M Agnew and Wolfgang K H Panofsky	1985	Norman C Rasmussen and Marshall N Rosenblath	1992	Leon M Lederman, Harold Brown, and John S Foster Jr
1979	no award	1986	Ernest D Courant and M Stanley Livingston	1993	Freeman J Dyson and Liane B Russell
1980	Alvin M Weinberg and Rudolf E Peiris	1987	Luis W Alvarez and Gerald F Tape	1994	no award
1981	W Bennett Lewis	1988	Richard B Setlow and Victor F Weisskopf	1995	Ugo Fano and Martin Kamen
1982	Herbert Anderson and Seth Neddermeyer	1989	no award	1996	Richard Garwin, Mortimer Elkind, and H Rodney Withers
1983	Alexander Hollaender and John Lawrence	1990	George A Cowan and Robley D Evans		

See Also | **Nobel Prizes**

Web Sites

Academy of Motion Picture Arts and Sciences

URL: `"http://www.ampas.org/ampas/"`

Home page of the Academy Awards. This site contains information about the Oscar awards, as well as much useful information on the Academy itself.

BAFTA Awards

URL: `"http://www.bafta.org/"`

Home page of the British Academy of Film and Television Arts. As well as details of the annual awards, this site also includes a history of the organization, recent press releases, and details of various BAFTA events.

Booker Prize Winners and Short-listed Title Page

URL: `"http://www.suntech.com/ brad/booker.htm"`

Chronological listing of Booker Prize winning and shortlisted authors. There are links to selected authors with information about their works, biographical details, reviews, and bibliographies.

Le Festival – Official Selection

URL: `"http://www.festival-cannes.fr/cannes98/va/index.html"`

Official site of the world's foremost international film festival held each May in Cannes, France. There are complete details of films in competition and profiles of the jury.

Nobel Prize Internet Archive

URL: `"http://www.nobelprizes.com/"`

Information on all the Nobel prizewinners with biographies and bibliographies of each laureate.

Pulitzer Prizes

URL: `"http://www.pulitzer.org/ navigation/index.html"`

Brief history of the Pulitzer Prize, along with brief biographies of the winners, and descriptions of their winning pieces of work. An interactive timeline lists all winners since 1917, and an archive of all Pulitzer prizewinning works from the past three years includes photos, editorial cartoons, music clips, and the full text of all winning articles. You can search by year, category, author, or explanatory text.

THE ARTS AND MEDIA

The Year in Review

July 1997 Building begins on the Millennium Dome, a temporary structure to house a millennium exhibition, designed by British architect Richard Rogers, in Greenwich, London.

July 1997 The film *Men in Black,* directed by Barry Sonnenfeld, is released in the USA, starring Tommy Lee Jones and Will Smith.

July 1997 The Japanese firm Panasonic introduces digital video disc (DVD) players into the UK. They can play music and video CDs.

July 1997 The Royal Opera House in London, closes for two years for £214 million of redevelopment work.

30 August 1997 The English rock group Oasis releases the album *Be Here Now.*

13 September 1997 The pop singer Shola Ama releases the album *Much Love.*

20 September 1997 The English pop star Elton John releases the single 'Candle in the Wind 97' as a tribute to Diana, Princess of Wales. It goes immediately to number one and becomes the best-selling single of all time.

26 September 1997 An earthquake in Assisi, Italy, seriously damages frescoes in the St Francis Basilica.

September 1997 The English director Trevor Nunn, formerly of the Royal Shakespeare Company, succeeds Richard Eyre as artistic director of the Royal National Theatre in London.

September 1997 The US writer Don DeLillo publishes his novel *Underworld.*

September 1997 US rock singer Bob Dylan releases the album *Time Out of Mind.*

11 October 1997 The English rock group The Verve releases the album *Urban Hymns.*

19 October 1997 The widely acclaimed futuristic branch of New York's Guggenheim Museum, designed by the US architect Frank Gehry, opens in Bilbao, Spain.

26 October 1997 The Golden Globe awards are held in Beverly Hills, California. The series *X-files* takes best drama, best actress (Gillian Anderson), and best actor (David Duchovny).

October 1997 The Indian writer Arundhati Roy wins the Booker Prize for her novel *The God of Small Things.*

15 November 1997 The English pop group the Spice Girls releases the album *Spice-world.*

November 1997 The British Broadcasting Corporation (BBC) puts its news service online. The address is www.bbc.co.uk/.

November 1997 US writer Charles Frazier wins the National Book Award for his Civil War novel *Cold Mountain.*

10 December 1997 The Italian actor, director, and playwright Dario Fo wins the Nobel Prize for Literature.

December 1997 The 18th James Bond film, *Tomorrow Never Dies,* directed by Roger Spottiswoode, is released in the USA, starring Pierce Brosnan, Jonathan Pryce, Michele Yeoh, and Teri Hatcher.

December 1997 The film *Titanic,* directed by James Cameron, is released in the USA, starring Kate Winslet, Leonardo DiCaprio, Billy Zane, and Gloria Stuart. Costing over $200 million, it is the most expensive movie made to date. In the last two weekends of the year it grosses over $88 million.

December 1997 The Getty Center, a $1-billion arts centre and museum designed by the US architect Richard Meier, opens in Los Angeles, California.

December 1997 The Teletubbies' song 'Teletubbies say Eh-Oh', a novelty record by the stars of the children's television programme, reaches number one in the UK.

December 1997 US country singer Garth Brooks releases the album *Sevens.*

1 January 1998 *The Times* begins serializing a group of previously unpublished poems by British poet Ted Hughes about his late wife, US poet Sylvia Plath, who committed suicide in 1963.

January 1998 US writer Toni Morrison publishes her novel *Paradise.*

24 February 1998 British Prime Minister, Tony Blair, unveils plans for the inside of the Millennium Dome in Greenwich. Organizers expect 12 million visitors to the Dome, which will contain 13 exhibitions, a piazza for live performances, restaurants, and shops.

26 February 1998 US entertainer Oprah Winfrey is cleared of slander charges by a jury in Amarillo, Texas. A group of cattle ranchers had sued her for $12 million, claiming that her negative comments about beef on her talk show caused cattle prices to plummet.

5 March 1998 The world's most expensive sculpture, Antonio Canova's *Three Graces,* is permanently disfigured by a hairline crack thought to have occurred when it was last moved.

March 1998 The US writer Alice Walker publishes her novel *Anything We Love Can Be Saved.*

March 1998 US pop singer Madonna releases a new album, *Ray of Light,* her first album of original songs since *Bedtime stories* in 1994.

14 April 1998 The Pulitzer Special Award goes to the late US composer George Gershwin for his contributions to music in the USA.

23 April 1998 The British publishing and bookselling industries launch World Book Day with events and celebrations; all schoolchildren in the country receive a £1 book token.

April 1998 The play *The Iceman Cometh* by US writer Eugene O'Neill opens at the Almeida Theatre in London, directed by Howard Davies and starring Kevin Spacey.

April 1998 US writer John Irving publishes his novel *A Widow for One Year.*

12 May 1998–12 July 1998 To combat the rise of expensive, technologically sophisticated stages, the Battersea Arts Centre in London, stages all its performances in the dark.

15 May 1998 An estimated 76 million US viewers tune in to the last episode of the US sitcom *Seinfeld,* starring Jerry Seinfeld with Julia Louise-Dreyfus, Michael Richards, and Jason Alexander.

15 May 1998 US singer and actor Frank Sinatra, considered by many critics to be the preeminent singer of this century, dies in Beverly Hills, California. He made

some 1,800 recordings and gathered nine Grammys. An Academy Award-winning actor, he appeared in at least 60 films.

31 May 1998 British singer Geri Halliwell, 'Ginger Spice' of the pop group the Spice Girls, leaves the group. The four other members say they will keep on singing without her.

7 June 1998 British pop musicians Paul McCartney, George Harrison, and Ringo Starr, the three surviving ex-Beatles, make their first public appearance together for 30 years at the memorial service for McCartney's wife, Linda, who died from cancer in May.

Newspapers and Magazines

Top 10 Biggest-Selling Newspapers in Europe

1996

Rank	Newspaper	Country	Circulation
1	*Bild-Zeitung*	Germany	4,644,000
2	*The Sun*	UK	4,007,000
3	*Daily Mirror/Daily Record*	UK	3,168,000
4	*Daily Mail*	UK	2,077,000
5	*Komsomolskaia Pravda*	Russia	1,582,000
6	*Trud*	Russia	1,442,000
7	*Daily Express*	UK	1,221,000
8	*Zeitungsgruppe Waz*	Germany	1,140,000
9	*Daily Telegraph*	UK	1,076,000
10	*Neue Kronen Zeitung*	Austria	965,000

Source: The World Association of Newspapers (FIEJ): *World Press Trends 1997*

Top 10 Biggest-Selling Newspapers in the World

1996

Rank	Newspaper	Country	Circulation
1	*Yomiuri Shimbun*	Japan	14,485,453
2	*Asahi Shimbun*	Japan	12,660,066
3	*Mainichi Shimbun*	Japan	5,867,724
4	*MZ Guangbo Dianshi*	China	5,348,000
5	*Xinmin Wanbao*	China	5,227,000
6	*Bild-Zeitung*	Germany	4,644,000
7	*Nihon Keizai Shimbun*	Japan	4,550,311
8	*Chunichi Shimbun*	Japan	4,394,849
9	*The Sun*	UK	4,007,000
10	*BJ Guangbo Dianshi*	China	3,372,000

Source: The World Association of Newspapers (FIEJ): *World Press Trends 1997*

Newspaper Readership Figures in the UK

Figures are from an unweighted sample of 38,349 adults aged 15 and over. An unweighted sample is 'raw' data which have not been 'weighted' to represent the full population (that is, taking into account age, social grades, and so on). For this survey, the estimated population was 46.15 million and did not include Northern Ireland. Adult coverage is the percentage of the total population aged 15 and over in Great Britain, but not Northern Ireland.

July 1996–June 1997

Newspaper	Adult readers	Adult coverage (%)	Newspaper	Adult readers	Adult coverage (%)
National daily			*The Sunday Telegraph*	2,272,000	4.9
			Sunday Mail	2,066,000	4.5
The Sun	10,074,000	21.8	*The Observer*	1,224,000	2.7
The Mirror	6,153,000	13.3	*Independent on Sunday*	920,000	2.0
Daily Record	1,887,000	4.1	*Sunday Sport*	843,000	1.8
Daily Mail	5,309,000	11.5	*Scotland on Sunday*	326,000	0.7
The Daily Telegraph	2,736,000	5.9	*Any national Sunday*	29,452,000	63.8
The Express	2,671,000	5.8			
Daily Star	2,079,000	4.5	**Regional daily**		
The Times	1,954,000	4.2			
The Guardian	1,270,000	2.8	*The Herald*	308,000	0.7
The Independent	840,000	1.8	*Dundee Courier & Advertiser*	251,000	0.5
Financial Times	660,000	1.4	*Yorkshire Post*	228,000	0.5
The Sporting Life	275,000	0.6	*The Scotsman*	222,000	0.5
Racing Post	260,000	0.6	*London Evening Standard*	1,090,000	2.4
Any national morning	26,360,000	57.1	*Liverpool Echo*	447,000	1.0
			Glasgow Evening Times	354,000	0.8
National Sunday			*Newcastle Evening Chronicle*	317,000	0.7
			Leeds Yorkshire Evening Post	270,000	0.6
News of the World	11,680,000	25.3	*Edinburgh Evening News*	225,000	0.5
Sunday Mirror	6,953,000	15.1	*Dundee Evening Telegraph*	90,000	0.2
The Mail on Sunday	6,167,000	13.4	*Any regional morning/evening*	12,708,000	27.5
The People	5,151,000	11.2	*Any regional evening*	10,579,000	22.9
The Sunday Times	3,784,000	8.2	*Newcastle Sunday Sun*	442,000	1.0
The Express on Sunday	2,962,000	6.4	*Any regional Sunday*	885,000	1.9
The Sunday Post	2,305,000	5.0			

Source: National Readership Survey – Top Line

General Magazine Readership Figures in the UK

Figures are from an unweighted sample of 38,349 adults aged 15 and over. For this survey, the estimated population was 46.15 million and did not include Northern Ireland. Adult coverage is the percentage of the total population aged 15 and over in Great Britain, but not Northern Ireland.

July 1996–June 1997

Periodical	Adult readers	Adult coverage (%)	Periodical	Adult readers	Adult coverage (%)
Weekly			*Motorcycle News*	652,000	1.4
			Shoot	638,000	1.4
Radio Times	4,270,000	9.3	*TES (Times Educational Supplement)*	637,000	1.4
What's on TV	4,048,000	8.8	*Time Out*	616,000	1.3
TV Times	3,665,000	7.9	*Weekly News*	598,000	1.3
TV Quick	2,385,000	5.2	*Match*	597,000	1.3
Auto Trader	2,012,000	4.4	*Angling Times*	554,000	1.2
Exchange & Mart	1,122,000	2.4	*New Scientist*	498,000	1.1
The Big Issue	1,061,000	2.3	*The Economist*	454,000	1.0
TV & Satellite Week	816,000	1.8	*Autocar*	394,000	0.9
NME (New Musical Express)	675,000	1.5			

General Magazine Readership Figures in the UK *(continued)*

Periodical	Adult readers	Adult coverage (%)	Periodical	Adult readers	Adult coverage (%)
Country Life	373,000	0.8	*Men's Health*	479,000	1.0
Auto Express	371,000	0.8	*Classic and Sportscar*	464,000	1.0
Amateur Gardening	312,000	0.7	*The Face*	448,000	1.0
Angler's Mail	298,000	0.6	*Classic Bike*	447,000	1.0
Melody Maker	297,000	0.6	*Maxim*	441,000	1.0
Horse & Hound	286,000	0.6	*Flicks*	434,000	0.9
Autosport	280,000	0.6	*Select*	433,000	0.9
Garden News	277,000	0.6	*Custom Car*	430,000	0.9
Time	269,000	0.6	*Practical Caravan*	430,000	0.9
Kerrang!	189,000	0.4	*Bike*	417,000	0.9
The European	169,000	0.4	*Practical Photography*	415,000	0.9
Amateur Photographer	157,000	0.3	*Total Football*	410,000	0.9
Any general weekly	19,398,000	42.0	*Esquire*	406,000	0.9
			Vox	396,000	0.9
Fortnightly			*The Garden*	359,000	0.8
			Arena	336,000	0.7
Smash Hits	819,000	1.8	*Your Garden*	333,000	0.7
Private Eye	661,000	1.4	*Today's Golfer*	328,000	0.7
Big!	371,000	0.8	*Total Sport*	322,000	0.7
			Practical Classics/Popular Classics	320,000	0.7
Monthly			*Choice*	318,000	0.7
SkyTVguide	5,895,000	12.8	*Fore!*	312,000	0.7
Reader's Digest	5,169,000	11.2	*Trout & Salmon*	302,000	0.7
Cable Guide	2,162,000	4.7	*Practical Boat Owner*	299,000	0.6
BBC Gardener's World	1,850,000	4.0	*Coarse Angling*	275,000	0.6
National Geographic	1,787,000	3.9	*Cars/Car Conversions*	273,000	0.6
BBC Top Gear	1,706,000	3.7	*Sporting Gun*	261,000	0.6
FHM (For Him Magazine)	1,580,000	3.4	*Fiesta*	251,000	0.5
Saga Magazine	1,516,000	3.3	*Moneywise*	246,000	0.5
What Car?	1,437,000	3.1	*Premiere*	244,000	0.5
Loaded	1,364,000	3.0	*Mojo*	240,000	0.5
Max Power	1,359,000	2.9	*The Field*	239,000	0.5
Sky	1,211,000	2.6	*Classic CD*	231,000	0.5
Classic Cars	961,000	2.1	*Yachting Monthly*	231,000	0.5
Practical Gardening	927,000	2.0	*The Scot's Magazine*	230,000	0.5
Golf Monthly	811,000	1.8	*Practical Woodworking*	229,000	0.5
GQ	798,000	1.7	*Focus*	214,000	0.5
Q	796,000	1.7	*Street Machine*	213,000	0.5
Performance Bikes	731,000	1.6	*BBC Music Magazine*	207,000	0.4
Top of the Pops Magazine	706,000	1.5	*Geographical Magazine*	202,000	0.4
Performance Car	694,000	1.5	*Yachting World*	180,000	0.4
What Hi-Fi?	665,000	1.4	*Any general monthly*	23,315,000	50.5
High Life	653,000	1.4			
BBC Wildlife	649,000	1.4	**Bi-monthly**		
FourFourTwo	618,000	1.3	*Viz*	2,102,000	4.6
TV Hits	604,000	1.3	*The Countryman*	206,000	0.4
Car	582,000	1.3			
Empire	576,000	1.2	**Quarterly**		
Golf World	568,000	1.2	*AA Magazine*	4,247,000	9.2
Superbike	532,000	1.2	*The Ford Magazine*	1,045,000	2.3
Goal	522,000	1.1	*Upbeat*	616,000	1.3
Garden Answers	517,000	1.1	*Natural World*	294,000	0.6
Fast Car Magazine	491,000	1.1			
Rugby World	482,000	1.0			

Source: National Readership Survey – Top Line

Women's Magazine Readership Figures in the UK

Figures are from an unweighted sample of 38,349 adults aged 15 and over. For this survey, the estimated population was 46.15 million and did not include Northern Ireland. Adult coverage is the percentage of the total population aged 15 and over in Great Britain, but not Northern Ireland.

July 1996–June 1997

Periodical	Women readers	Women coverage (%)	Periodical	Women readers	Women coverage (%)
Weekly			Company	709,000	3.0
Take a Break	3,792,000	16.0	Mother & Baby	682,000	2.9
Woman's Own	3,092,000	13.0	'19'	634,000	2.7
Bella	2,641,000	11.1	New Woman	627,000	2.6
Woman	2,388,000	10.1	It's Bliss	611,000	2.6
Woman's Weekly	1,930,000	8.1	Country Living	594,000	2.5
Best	1,891,000	8.0	Candis	576,000	2.4
Hello!	1,877,000	7.9	Looks	553,000	2.3
Chat	1,608,000	6.8	Top Santé Health & Beauty	537,000	2.3
My Weekly	1,306,000	5.5	Needlecraft	507,000	2.1
The People's Friend	1,086,000	4.6	Practical Parenting	481,000	2.0
Woman's Realm	1,007,000	4.2	Country Homes and Interiors	466,000	2.0
Eva	792,000	3.3	Slimming	462,000	1.9
That's Life	733,000	3.1	BBC Homes & Antiques	434,000	1.8
Here!	399,000	1.7	Woman's Journal	417,000	1.8
OK!	293,000	1.2	Health & Fitness Magazine	385,000	1.6
The Lady	201,000	0.8	Harpers & Queen	375,000	1.6
Any women's weekly	9,942,000	41.9	Options	334,000	1.4
			Perfect Home	321,000	1.4
Fortnightly			BBC Vegetarian Good Food	311,000	1.3
More!	1,049,000	4.4	Yours	309,000	1.3
Inside Soap	513,000	2.2	Home & Country	304,000	1.3
Mizz	420,000	1.8	Pregnancy & Birth	293,000	1.2
			Vanity Fair	277,000	1.2
Monthly			Tatler	269,000	1.1
Sainsbury's The Magazine	2,127,000	9.0	Our Baby	245,000	1.0
A Taste of Safeway	1,848,000	7.8	Period Living/Traditional Homes	241,000	1.0
Good Houskeeping	1,811,000	7.6	Parents	240,000	1.0
Cosmopolitan	1,690,000	7.1	Inspirations	237,000	1.0
Prima	1,533,000	6.5	Elle Decoration	201,000	0.8
The Somerfield Magazine	1,475,000	6.2	World of Interiors	197,000	0.8
Marie Claire	1,468,000	6.2	Here's Health	127,000	0.5
Vogue	1,375,000	5.8	Any women's monthly	12,331,000	52.0
Ideal Home	1,338,000	5.6			
BBC Good Food	1,144,000	4.8	**Bi-monthly**		
Homes & Gardens	1,140,000	4.8	Weight Watchers	1,092,000	4.6
Homes & Ideas	1,117,000	4.7	Hair	939,000	4.0
Woman & Home	1,082,000	4.6	R Conley Diet/Fitness Magazine	569,000	2.4
Just Seventeen	1,060,000	4.5	Classic Stitches	293,000	1.2
Family Circle	1,039,000	4.4	Slimmer	288,000	1.2
Sugar	1,024,000	4.3	Brides/Set Up Home	219,000	0.9
Elle	935,000	3.9	Wedding & Home	209,000	0.9
She	935,000	3.9	You & Your Wedding	139,000	0.6
Essentials	906,000	3.8			
House & Garden	863,000	3.6	**Quarterly**		
House Beautiful	823,000	3.5	The M&S Magazine	3,332,000	14.0
Clothes Show Magazine	762,000	3.2	Good Idea!	772,000	3.3

Source: National Readership Survey – Top Line

NEGATIVE IMAGES: THE PAPARAZZI AND PRESS INTRUSION

BY GRANVILLE GREENE

The term 'paparazzo' was first introduced to the popular imagination by Italian director Federico Fellini's 1960 film *La Dolce Vita*, which portrayed the comings and goings of the *haute monde* in Rome at the time. A colourful character in the film, Signor Paparazzo, who was allegedly inspired by the real-life Italian photographer John Quinto, set the standard for the contemporary notion of the dogged celebrity photographer, or 'paparazzo', who makes his living by relentlessly following the rich and famous in search of candid pictures to sell to magazines and newspapers.

Decades later, television opened up an even larger outlet for the paparazzi, and as the public's appetite for furtive glimpses into the personal lives of celebrities has grown, so have the fees demanded by the paparazzi for their wares. In the past two decades celebrity photography has become big business, with extraordinary fees paid by tabloid newspapers and television shows for sensational images. As a result, the paparazzi have become outrageously daring in their efforts to get a juicy shot, chasing stars in cars and on motorcycles, camping outside their homes, and even using helicopters.

Celebrities Fight Back

Meanwhile, the subjects of the paparazzi have developed an increasingly uneasy relationship with them. While it is generally accepted that well-known personalities should expect to trade some privacy for their fame and success, there has been a growing trend among the more established celebrities to view the free publicity as an insufficient reward for the nuisance of being constantly stalked by photographers. Having decided that enough is enough, some angry stars have even taken it upon themselves literally to fight back. Actors Sean Penn and Alec Baldwin, for example, have both been charged with assaulting photographers who were stalking them. Others have taken a more diplomatic approach. In the autumn of 1996, *Hard Copy*, a successful US tabloid television show, violated a six-month agreement to refrain from airing stories about rising Hollywood star George Clooney; he vowed to boycott the programme's sister show, *Entertainment Tonight*, until *Hard Copy* backed off. Clooney's stand inspired several other paparazzi-weary stars to follow his lead, including Madonna, Tom Cruise, and Steven Spielberg.

Diana, Princess of Wales

As the paparazzi have progressed from snapping pictures of starlets on the beach at the Cannes film festival to hovering over a celebrity's house in a helicopter and peering through a telephoto lens into the bedroom, a new, more menacing term has been coined, 'the stalkerazzi'. If there is a demand for pictures, it seems that no one can escape their persistence and ingenuity, and no celebrity was hounded by the stalkerazzi more than Diana, Princess of Wales. In the summer of 1996, she won a court injunction forcing a motorcycle-riding paparazzo, Martin Stenning, to stay at least 300 m/9,900 ft away from her at all times. But unfortunately he was only the tip of the iceberg. Relentlessly pursued throughout her marriage to Prince Charles, and perhaps even more so after it ended, her tragic death in a car crash in Paris during the summer of 1997 was blamed by many on the paparazzi who were chasing her car through a tunnel, in pursuit of hot new pictures.

Where Should the Blame Lie?

While Diana was by all accounts a finely tuned publicity machine, who relied as much on the paparazzi to craft her image as they did on her for their bread and butter, her death sparked an international antipaparazzi reaction. Fingers have also been pointed at the purveyors of tabloid media, for providing the forum and the fees for the paparazzi. In their defence, tabloid publishers and television producers have argued that they are only feeding the public's insatiable appetite for celebrity gossip. The so-called 'legitimate' news organizations, the broadcast networks and national dailies, are keen to distance themselves from the sordid antics of the 'tabloid trash', but it would be hard to find any who have not offered frothy servings of 'infotainment' themselves.

Self-Regulation and the Future

In the days following Diana's death, there was a considerable amount of self-criticism among journalists, for creating the contemporary 'celibriculture' that has seemingly tainted the entire journalistic profession. There were promises of new standards and criteria, with questions of whether or not the paparazzi should even be considered journalists at all, and vows to disown them entirely. But in reality the paparazzi are mostly photojournalists covering what the market wants, photographing celebrities just as they might other newsworthy subjects; if the journalistic climate is to change, it will have to be reformed from within. Just three weeks after Diana was buried, the sordid sex trial of the US television sportscaster Marv Albert began, and its lurid details instantly became front page news in the USA. It remains to be seen what, if anything, will change in the future.

Books

Top 10 Best-Selling Hardback Fiction Titles of the Year in the UK

1997

Rank	Title	Author and publisher
1	Jingo	Terry Pratchett (Gollancz)
2	The God of Small Things	Arundhati Roy (Flamingo)
3	10-lb Penalty	Dick Francis (Michael Joseph)
4	Unnatural Exposure	Patricia D Cornwell (Little, Brown)
5	Remote Control	Andy McNab (Bantam Press)
6	Birds of Prey	Wilbur Smith (Macmillan)
7	The Partner	John Grisham (Century)
8	A Certain Justice	P D James (Faber)
9	Road Rage	Ruth Rendell (Hutchinson)
10	Excalibur	Bernard Cornwell (Michael Joseph)

Source: Bookwatch

Top 10 Best-Selling Paperback Fiction Titles of the Year in the UK

1997

Rank	Title	Author and publisher
1	Bridget Jones's Diary	Helen Fielding (Picador)
2	Evening Class	Maeve Binchy (Orion)
3	High Fidelity	Nick Hornby (Indigo)
4	The Runaway Jury	John Grisham (Arrow)
5	The Upstart	Catherine Cookson (Corgi)
6	Captain Corelli's Mandolin	Louis de Bernières (Minerva)
7	Appassionata	Jilly Cooper (Corgi)
8	The Woman Who Walked Into Doors	Roddy Doyle (Minerva)
9	Cause of Death	Patricia D Cornwell (Warner)
10	Hogfather	Terry Pratchett (Corgi)

Source: Bookwatch

Top 10 Best-Selling Paperback Reference and General Non-Fiction Titles of the Year in the UK

1997

Rank	Title	Author and publisher
1	Delia's Red Nose Collection	Delia Smith (New Crane Publishing)
2	The Highway Code	TSO
3	Notes from a Small Island	Bill Bryson (Black Swan)
4	The Little Book of Calm	Paul Wilson (Penguin)
5	Angela's Ashes	Frank McCourt (Flamingo)
6	Men Are from Mars, Women Are from Venus	John Gray (Thorsons)
7	Fever Pitch	Nick Hornby (Indigo)
8	Official Theory Test: Cars and Motorcycles (2nd Edition)	Driving Standards Agency (TSO)
9	The Nation's Favourite Poems	edited by Griff Rhys Jones (BBC Books)
10	The Art Book	Phaidon

Source: Bookwatch

Top 10 Best-Selling Hardback Reference and General Non-Fiction Titles of the Year in the UK

1997

Rank	Title	Author and publisher
1	Full Circle	Michael Palin (BBC)
2	Diana: Her True Story in Her Own Words	Andrew Morton (O'Mara)
3	A Walk in the Woods	Bill Bryson (Doubleday)
4	My Autobiography	'Dickie' Bird (Hodder)
5	The Guinness Book of Records 1998	Guinness
6	Longitude	Dava Sobel (Fourth Estate)
7	Diana, Princess of Wales: A Tribute	Tim Graham (Weidenfeld)
8	My Autobiography	Kevin Keegan (Little, Brown)
9	Moab is My Washpot	Stephen Fry (Hutchinson)
10	Two Fat Ladies Ride Again	Jennifer Paterson and Clarissa Dickson-Wright (Ebury)

Source: Bookwatch

Top 10 Best-Selling Children's Hardbacks of the Year in the UK

1997

Rank	Title	Author and publisher
1	The Beano Book 1998	D C Thomson
2	The Teletubbies Play Hide and Seek	BBC
3	Totally 100% Unofficial Special Spice Girls	Granddreams
4	The Dandy Book 1998	D C Thomson
5	Guess How Much I Love You?	Sam McBratney and Anita Jeram (Walker)
6	Diana, Princess of Wales	Audrey Daly (Ladybird)
7	Goosebumps Wailing Special	R L Stine (Scholastic)
8	Letterland ABC	Richard Carlisle and Lyn Wendon (HarperCollins)
9	Boyzone: Living the Dream	Eddie Rowley (Ebury)
10	The Roald Dahl Treasury	Roald Dahl (Cape)

Source: Bookwatch

The World's Top 10 Producers of Books

(Figures include school textbooks, children's books, and government publications.)

1995

Rank	Country	Number of titles
1	UK	101,764
2	China	100,951[1]
3	Germany	74,174
4	USA	62,039[2][3]
5	Spain	48,467
6	Korea, South	35,864
7	France	34,766
8	Italy	34,470
9	Netherlands	34,067
10	Russia	33,623

[1] Number refers to books published in 1994.
[2] This figure does not include US government publications and university theses.
[3] This figure does not include school textbooks.

Source: Used with permission from © UNESCO 1997

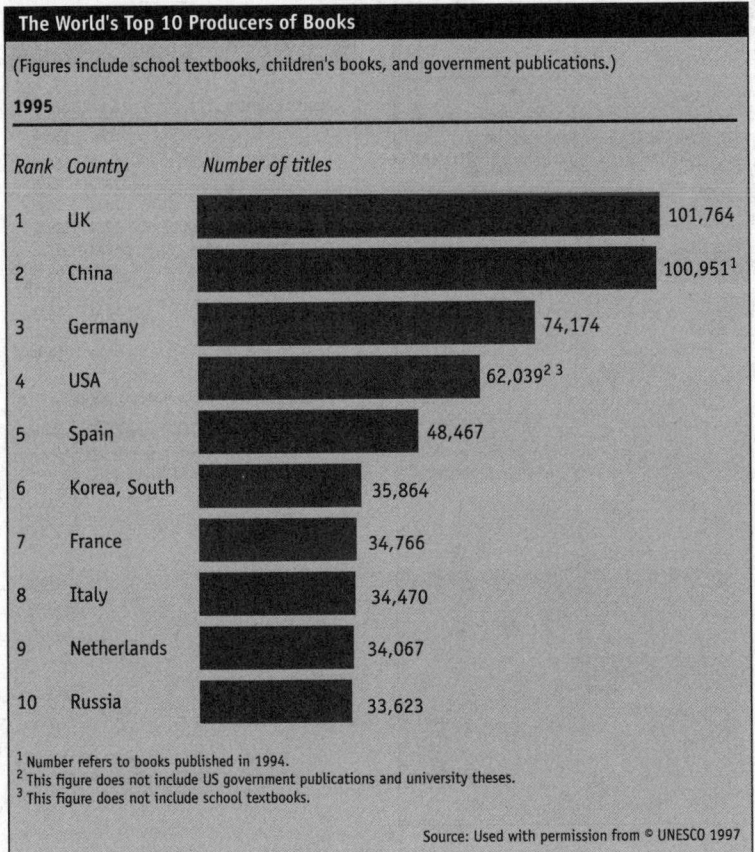

Some of the World's Most Translated Authors

(— = not applicable.)

Name	Dates
Various (The Bible)	—
Vladimir Ilyich Lenin	1870–1924
Agatha Christie	1890–1976
Jules Verne	1828–1905
William Shakespeare	1564–1616
Enid Blyton	1897–1968
Leo Nikolaievich Tolstoy	1828–1910
Charles Perrault	1628–1703
Georges Simenon	1903–1989
Karl Marx	1818–1883
Fyodor Mikhailovich Dostoievsky	1821–1881
Barbara Cartland	1901–
Hans Christian Andersen	1805–1875
Jacob and Wilhelm Grimm	1785–1863 and 1786–1859
Konstantin Ustinovich Chernenko	1911–1985
Issac Asimov	1920–1992
Friedrich Engels	1820–1895
Jack London (John Griffith Chaney)	1876–1916
Arthur Conan Doyle	1859–1930
Mark Twain (Samuel Langhorne Clemens)	1835–1910
Charles Dickens	1812–1870
Robert Louis Stevenson	1850–1894
Walt Disney Productions (collective)	—
Graham Greene	1904–1991
Pope John Paul II (Karol Wojtyła)	1920–

© Danish Tourist Board

Hans Christian Andersen

Some of the World's Most Reprinted Books

(All figures are approximate. – = not applicable)

Title	Author	Number of copies
The Bible	Various translations	over 6,000,000,000
Little Red Book	Mao Zedong (Mao Tse Tung) (1893–1976)	over 800,000,000
Eclectic Readers (The McGuffey Readers)	William Holmes McGuffey (1800–1873)	up to 122,000,000
A Grammatical Institute of the English Language (Webster's Spelling Book, or American Spelling Book)	Noah Webster (1758–1843)	100,000,000
The Guinness Book of Records	–	79,000,000[1]
A Message to Garcia	Elbert Hubbard (1856–1915)	up to 50,000,000
The World Almanac	–	over 40,000,000[1]
The Common Sense Book of Baby and Child Care	Benjamin Spock (1903–1998)	over 39,200,000
The Valley of the Dolls	Jacqueline Susann (c. 1926–1974)	30,000,000
In His Steps: What Would Jesus Do?	Charles Monroe Sheldon (1857–1946)	28,500,000

[1] Figures represent aggregate sales of annual publication.

The World's Top 10 Producers of Children's Books

1995

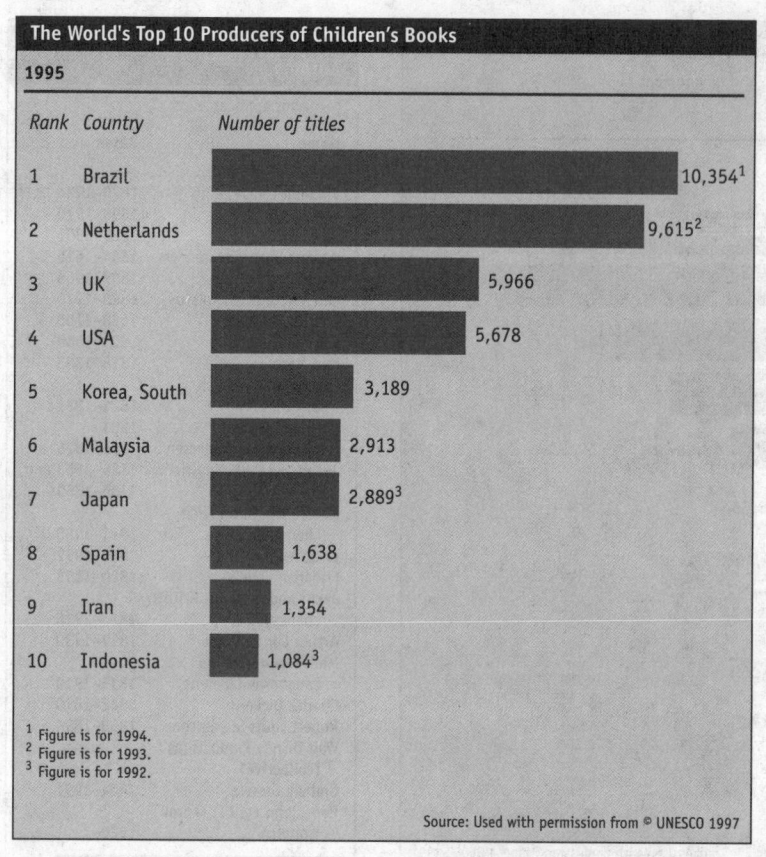

Rank	Country	Number of titles	
1	Brazil		10,354[1]
2	Netherlands		9,615[2]
3	UK		5,966
4	USA		5,678
5	Korea, South		3,189
6	Malaysia		2,913
7	Japan		2,889[3]
8	Spain		1,638
9	Iran		1,354
10	Indonesia		1,084[3]

[1] Figure is for 1994.
[2] Figure is for 1993.
[3] Figure is for 1992.

Source: Used with permission from © UNESCO 1997

Top 10 UK Export Markets for Books by Value

Rank	Country	£ millions[1]	
		1994	**1996**
1	USA	153.8	184.6
2	Germany	79.9	82.6
3	Australia	74.0	78.0
4	Ireland, Republic of	57.7	65.8
5	Netherlands	48.8	65.2
6	France	47.5	63.9
7	Spain	45.6	48.1
8	Japan	44.6	44.2
9	South Africa	35.8	41.7
10	Italy	33.6	39.9

[1] Figures are based on Customs and Excise data.

Source: The British Council/DTI

Top 10 Best-Selling Children's Paperbacks of the Year in the UK

1997

Rank	Title	Author and publisher	Rank	Title	Author and publisher
1	Teletubbies: The Flying Toast	BBC	6	Matilda	Roald Dahl (Puffin)
2	Teletubbies: Laa Laa's Ball	BBC	7	Goosebumps Flashing Special	R L Stine (Scholastic)
3	Teletubbies: The Magic Flag	BBC	8	Junk	Melvyn Burgess (Puffin)
4	Teletubbies: Tinky Winky's Bag	BBC	9	Northern Lights	Philip Pullman (Scholastic)
5	Goosebumps: The Headless Ghost	R L Stine (Scholastic)	10	Goosebumps: Say Cheese and Die Again	R L Stine (Scholastic)

Source: Bookwatch

Top 10 Highest Prices Paid for Books and Manuscripts Sold at Auction

Rank	Work	Place and date of sale	Price ($)
1	The Codex Hammer	Christie's, New York, 11 November 1994	30,800,000
2	The Gospels of Henry the Lion (c. 1173–75)	Sotheby's, London, 6 December 1983	10,841,000
3	Chaucer's Canterbury Tales (printed by William Caxton c. 1476)	Christie's, London, 8 July 1998	6,890,000
4	The Gutenberg Bible (1455)	Christie's, New York, 22 October 1987	5,390,000
5	The Northumberland Bestiary (c. 1250–60)	Sotheby's, London, 29 November 1990	5,049,000
6	Autographed manuscript of nine symphonies by Mozart (c. 1773–74)	Sotheby's, London, 22 May 1987	3,854,000
7	John James Audubon's The Birds of America (1827–38)	Sotheby's, New York, 6 June 1989	3,600,000
8	The Bible in Hebrew	Sotheby's, London, 5 December 1989	2,932,000
9	The Moneypenny Breviary, illuminated manuscript (c. 1490–95)	Sotheby's, London, 19 June 1989	2,639,000
10	The Hours and Psalter of Elizabeth de Bohun (c. 1340–45)	Sotheby's, London, 21 June 1988	2,530,000

Source: Art Sales Index

Libraries

Top 10 Most Borrowed Fiction Titles of the Year in the UK

July 1996–June 1997

Rank	Title	Author	Publisher and year of publication
1	*A Ruthless Need*	Catherine Cookson	Bantam Press, 1995
2	*Justice is a Woman*	Catherine Cookson	Bantam Press, 1994
3	*The Year of the Virgins*	Catherine Cookson	Bantam Press, 1993
4	*The Obsession*	Catherine Cookson	Bantam Press, 1995
5	*The Upstart*	Catherine Cookson	Bantam Press, 1996
6	*The Tinker's Girl*	Catherine Cookson	Bantam Press, 1994
7	*The Rag Nymph*	Catherine Cookson	Bantam Press, 1991
8	*The House of Women*	Catherine Cookson	Bantam Press, 1992
9	*Come to Grief*	Dick Francis	Michael Joseph, 1995
10	*The Golden Straw*	Catherine Cookson	Bantam Press, 1993

Source: Registrar of Public Lending Right

Top 20 Most Borrowed Authors in the UK

July 1996–June 1997

Rank	Author	Rank	Author
1	Catherine Cookson	11	Wilbur Smith
2	Danielle Steele	12	Dean R Koontz
3	Dick Francis	13	Barbara Taylor Bradford
4	Ruth Rendell	14	Bernard Cornwell
5	Agatha Christie	15	Rosamunde Pilcher
6	Jack Higgins	16	Elizabeth Ferrars
7	Josephine Cox	17	Stephen King
8	Terry Pratchett	18	Ed McBain
9	Ellis Peters	19	Emma Blair
10	Virginia Andrews	20	Maeve Binchy

Source: Registrar of Public Lending Right

Top 10 Most Borrowed Non-Fiction Titles in the UK

July 1996–June 1997

Rank	Title	Author	Publisher and year of publication
1	*Immediate Action*	Andy McNab	Bantam, 1995
2	*Delia Smith's Winter Collection*	Delia Smith (photographs Flo Bayley)	BBC Books, 1995
3	*Wild Swans: Three Daughters of China*	Jung Chang	HarperCollins, 1991
4	*Eyewitness Guide: Ancient Rome*	Simon James	Dorling Kindersley, 1990
5	*Delia Smith's Summer Collection*	Delia Smith (photographs Peter Knab)	BBC Books, 1993
6	*A Brief History of Time*	Stephen Hawking	Bantam, 1988
7	*The Complete Theory Test for Cars and Motorcycles*	Driving Standards Agency	HMSO, 1996
8	*The Children's Step-by-Step Cook Book*	Angela Wilkes	Dorling Kindersley, 1994
9	*Driving Manual*	Driving Standards Agency	HMSO, 1992
10	*Bravo Two Zero*	Andy McNab	Bantam, 1993

Source: Registrar of Public Lending Right

Top 20 Most Borrowed Classic Authors in the UK

July 1996–June 1997

Rank	Author	Rank	Author
1	Beatrix Potter	11	Rudyard Kipling
2	Daphne Du Maurier	12	George Orwell
3	Jane Austen	13	D H Lawrence
4	A A Milne	14	Arthur Conan Doyle
5	William Shakespeare	15	George Eliot
6	Thomas Hardy	16	Louisa M Alcott
7	Charles Dickens	17	Charlotte Brontê
8	J R R Tolkien	18	John Buchan
9	Anthony Trollope	19	Virginia Woolf
10	E M Forster	20	W Somerset Maugham

Source: Registrar of Public Lending Right

Top 20 Most Borrowed Children's Authors in the UK

July 1996–June 1997

Rank	Author	Rank	Author
1	R L Stine	11	Martin Waddell
2	Janet and Allan Ahlberg	12	Kate William
3	Roald Dahl	13	Mick Inkpen
4	Ann M Martin	14	Tony Bradman
5	Enid Blyton	15	Jamie Suzanne
6	Dick King-Smith	16	Nick Butterworth
7	Goscinny	17	Colin and Jacqui Hawkins
8	Eric Hill	18	Rev W Awdry
9	John Cunliffe	19	David McKee
10	Shirley Hughes	20	Jill Murphy

Source: Registrar of Public Lending Right

Top 10 Most Borrowed Children's Fiction Titles of the Year in the UK

July 1996–June 1997

Rank	Title	Author/illustrator	Publisher and year of publication
1	*A Quiet Night In*	Jill Murphy	Walker, 1993
2	*Spot Makes a Cake*	Eric Hill	Warne, 1994
3	*Matilda*	Roald Dahl/Quentin Blake	Cape, 1988
4	*Esio Trot*	Roald Dahl/Quentin Blake	Cape, 1980
5	*The Twits*	Roald Dahl/Quentin Blake	Cape, 1980
6	*Scarecrow Walks at Midnight*	R L Stine	Scholastic, 1995
7	*Five Minutes' Peace*	Jill Murphy	Walker, 1986
8	*Where's Wally: in Hollywood*	Martin Handford	Walker, 1993
9	*Return of the Mummy*	R L Stine	Scholastic, 1995
10	*Matilda*	Roald Dahl/Quentin Blake	Puffin, 1989

Source: Registrar of Public Lending Right

Library Loans by Category in the UK

(In percentages.)

Category	1988–89	1995–96	1996–97
Adult Fiction			
General fiction	17.8	21.2	21.0
Historical	3.5	3.4	3.1
Mystery and detection	12.8	13.2	12.8
Horror	0.7	0.5	0.5
Science fiction	0.8	0.9	0.1
War	1.8	1.2	1.2
Humour	0.7	0.2	0.3
Light romance	14.1	11.1	10.4
Westerns	1.2	0.7	0.7
Short stories	0.5	0.2	0.3
Total	53.9	52.6	50.4
Adult Non-Fiction			
Science and technology	1.3	0.1	1.1
History	3.5	2.7	2.7
Travel and foreign countries	2.9	2.5	2.6
Social sciences	2.5	2.2	2.2
Religion	0.9	0.8	0.8
Nature and country life	1.5	1.1	1.1
Domestic and leisure	4.7	4.1	4.2
Health	1.7	1.8	1.9
Arts	1.2	0.9	1.0
Biography	2.6	2.6	2.6
Humour	0.7	0.2	0.2
Literature	0.9	0.8	0.9
Total	24.4	19.8	21.3
Adult total	78.3	72.4	71.7
Children's fiction	17.5	23.0	22.3
Children's non-fiction	4.2	4.6	6.0
Children's total	21.7	27.6	28.3
TOTAL	100.0	100.0	100.0

Major World Libraries

Library	Date founded
Alexandrian Library, Alexandria, Egypt	c. 300 BC
Vatican Library, Rome, Italy	4th century
Bibliothèque nationale, Paris, France (Bibliothèque du Roi until 1795)	15th century
Bodleian Library, Oxford, England	1602[1]
British Library, London, England	1759
Library of Congress, Washington, DC, USA	1800
The New York Public Library, New York City, USA	1895

[1] Duke Humphrey's Room housed a book collection on the site from 1450.

Films and Videos

50 Notable Films of the Year in the UK (1997)

The 1997 date is for UK release; year of release in country of origin can be significantly different.

L'Appartment/The Apartment (France/Spain/Italy) *Director:* Gilles Mimouni; *Actors:* Vincent Cassel, Romane Bohringer, Monica Bellucci, Jean-Philippe Ecoffey

Austin Powers: International Man of Mystery (USA) *Director:* Jay Roach; *Actors:* Mike Myers, Elizabeth Hurley, Michael York, Mimi Rogers

Big Night (USA) *Director:* Stanley Tucci and Campbell Scott; *Actors:* Stanley Tucci, Tony Shalhoub, Minnie Driver, Isabella Rossellini, Ian Holm

Le bonheur est dans le pré/Happiness is in the Field (France) *Director:* Etienne Chatiliez; *Actors:* Michel Serrault, Eddy Mitchell, Carmen Maura

Bound (USA) *Director:* Andy and Larry Wachowski; *Actors:* Jennifer Tilly, Gina Gershon, Joe Pantoliano

Career Girls (UK) *Director:* Mike Leigh; *Actors:* Katrin Cartlidge, Lynda Steadman, Mark Benton

Carla's Song (UK/Germany/Spain) *Director:* Ken Loach; *Actors:* Robert Carlyle, Oyanka Cabezas, Scott Glenn

Chasing Amy (USA) *Director:* Kevin Smith; *Actors:* Ben Affleck, Joey Lauren Adams, Jason Lee, Dwight Ewell

Le Cinquième Elément/The Fifth Element (France) *Director:* Luc Besson; *Actors:* Bruce Willis, Gary Oldman, Ian Holm, Milla Jovovich

Cop Land (USA) *Director:* James Mangold; *Actors:* Sylvester Stallone, Harvey Keitel, Ray Liotta, Robert De Niro, Annabella Sciorra

Crash (Canada) *Director:* David Cronenberg; *Actors:* James Spader, Holly Hunter, Deborah Kara Unger, Rosanna Arquette

The Crucible (USA) *Director:* Nicholas Hytner; *Actors:* Daniel Day-Lewis, Winona Ryder, Paul Scofield, Joan Allen

Donnie Brasco (USA) *Director:* Mike Newell; *Actors:* Johnny Depp, Al Pacino, Michael Madsen, Bruno Kirby

The English Patient (USA) *Director:* Anthony Minghella; *Actors:* Ralph Fiennes, Juliette Binoche, Willem Dafoe, Kristin Scott Thomas

Everyone Says I Love You (USA) *Director:* Woody Allen; *Actors:* Alan Alda, Woody Allen, Drew Barrymore, Goldie Hawn

Evita (USA) *Director:* Alan Parker; *Actors:* Madonna, Antonio Banderas, Jonathan Pryce

Face/Off (USA) *Director:* John Woo; *Actors:* John Travolta, Nicolas Cage, Joan Allen, Alessandro Nivola, Gina Gershon

Fengyue/Temptress Moon (Hong Kong/China) *Director:* Chen Kaige; *Actors:* Leslie Cheung, Gong Li, Kevin Lin

Flirting with Disaster (USA) *Director:* David O Russell; *Actors:* Ben Stiller, Patricia Arquette, Téa Leoni

The Full Monty (USA/UK) *Director:* Peter Cattaneo; *Actors:* Robert Carlyle, Tom Wilkinson, Mark Addy, Leslie Sharp, Steve Huison, Paul Barber, Emily Woof

Grosse Point Blank (USA) *Director:* George Armitage; *Actors:* John Cusack, Minnie Driver, Dan Aykroyd, Joan Cusack, Alan Arkin

Hamlet (UK) *Director:* Kenneth Branagh; *Actors:* Kenneth Branagh, Kate Winslet, Robin Williams, Julie Christie

Un héro très discret/A Self-Made Hero (France). *Director:* Jacques Audiard; *Actors:* Mathieu Kassovitz, Anouk Grinberg, Sandrine Kiberlain

Irma Vep (France) *Director:* Olivier Assayas; *Actors:* Maggie Cheung, Jean-Pierre Léaud, Nathalie Richard

Jerry Maguire (USA) *Director:* Cameron Crowe; *Actors:* Tom Cruise, Cuba Gooding Jr, Renee Zellweger, Kelly Preston

Kansas City (USA/France) *Director:* Robert Altman; *Actors:* Jennifer Jason Leigh, Miranda Richardson, Harry Belafonte

Kolya (Czech Republic/UK/France) *Director:* Jan Svěrák; *Actors:* Zdeněk Svěrák, Andrej Chalimon, Libuše Safránkova

L.A. Confidential (USA) *Director:* Curtis Lee Hanson; *Actors:* Russell Crowe, Guy Pearce, Kevin Spacey, James Cromwell, Kim Basinger

A Life Less Ordinary (UK) *Director:* Danny Boyle; *Actors:* Ewan McGregor, Cameron Diaz, Holly Hunter, Delroy Lindo, Ian Holm, Dan Hedaya

Looking for Richard (USA) *Director:* Al Pacino; *Actors:* Al Pacino, Harris Yulin, Kevin Spacey

Lost Highway (USA) *Director:* David Lynch; *Actors:* Bill Pullman, Patricia Arquette, Balthazar Getty, Robert Blake

Ma vie en rose/My Life in Pink (France/Belgium/UK/Switzerland) *Director:* Alain Berliner; *Actors:* Michèle Laroque, Jean-Philippe Ecoffey, Hélène Vincent, Georges du Fresne

Men in Black (USA) *Director:* Barry Sonnenfeld; *Actors:* Tommy Lee Jones, Will Smith, Linda Fiorentino

Top 20 Films at the UK Box Office

This ranking only includes films released in the UK in 1997.

1997

Rank	Title	Country	Distributor	Box office (£)
1	The Full Monty	UK/USA	Fox	51,866,206
2	Men in Black	USA	Columbia Tristar	35,820,921
3	The Lost World: Jurassic Park	USA	UIP	25,799,961
4	Tomorrow Never Dies	UK/USA	UIP	19,768,150
5	Bean	UK	Polygram	17,902,161
6	Star Wars (Reissue 1997)	USA	Fox	16,343,172
7	Batman & Robin	USA	Warner	14,676,429
8	Ransom	USA	Buena Vista	12,859,705
9	The English Patient	USA	Buena Vista	12,729,802
10	Liar Liar	USA	UIP	11,785,973
11	Space Jam	USA	Warner	11,648,511
12	Hercules	USA	Buena Vista	11,413,518
13	SpiceWorld: The Movie	UK	Polygram	11,270,905
14	Sleepers	USA	Polygram	10,148,370
15	Jerry Maguire	USA	Columbia Tristar	9,429,212
16	My Best Friend's Wedding	USA	Columbia Tristar	8,764,980
17	Scream	USA	Buena Vista	8,276,247
18	The Borrowers	UK/USA	Polygram	7,765,945
19	Romeo + Juliet	USA	Fox	7,438,055
20	Alien Resurrection	USA	Fox	7,349,146

Source: BFI/EDI

Mrs Brown (UK/USA/Ireland) *Director:* John Madden; *Actors:* Judi Dench, Billy Connolly, Antony Sher, Geoffrey Palmer

Nil by Mouth (UK/USA) *Director:* Gary Oldman; *Actors:* Raymond Winstone, Kathy Burke, Charlie Creed-Miles

One Night Stand (USA) *Director:* Mike Figgis; *Actors:* Wesley Snipes, Nastassja Kinski, Kyle MacLachlan, Ming-na Wen

The Portrait of a Lady (UK/USA) *Director:* Jane Campion; *Actors:* Nicole Kidman, John Malkovich, Barbara Hershey, Mary Louise Parker

Ransom (USA) *Director:* Ron Howard; *Actors:* Mel Gibson, Rene Russo, Garry Sinise, Delroy Lindo

She's the One (USA) *Director:* Edward Burns; *Actors:* Jennifer Aniston, Maxine Bahns, Edward Burns, Cameron Diaz, John Mahoney

Shine (Australia/UK) *Director:* Scott Hicks; *Actors:* Geoffrey Rush, Noah Taylor, Armin Mueller-Stahl, Lynn Redgrave

Sleepers (USA) *Director:* Barry Levinson; *Actors:* Jason Patric, Brad Pitt, Kevin Bacon, Robert De Niro, Dustin Hoffman

SubUrbia (USA) *Director:* Richard Linklater; *Actors:* Jayce Bartok, Amie Carey, Nicky Katt, Ajay Naidu, Parker Posey

The Sweet Hereafter (Canada) *Director:* Atom Egoyan; *Actors:* Ian Holm, Maury Chaykin, Gabrielle Rose, Peter Donaldson, Bruce Greenwood

Ridicule (France) *Director:* Patrice Leconte; *Actors:* Fanny Ardant, Charles Berling, Bernard Girandeau

Tierra (Spain) *Director:* Julio Medem; *Actors:* Carmelo Gómez, Emma Suárez, Karra Elejalde

Twin Town (UK) *Director:* Kevin Allen; *Actors:* Llyr Evans, Rhys Ifans, Dorien Thomas, Dougray Scott

L'uomo delle stelle/The Starmaker (Italy) *Director:* Giuseppe Tornatore; *Actors:* Sergio Castellitto, Tiziana Lodato, Lopoldo Trieste

Welcome to the Dollhouse (USA) *Director:* Todd Solondz; *Actors:* Bill Buell, Heather Matarazzo, Victoria Davis

William Shakespeare's Romeo + Juliet (USA) *Director:* Baz Luhrmann; *Actors:* Leonardo DiCaprio, Claire Danes, John Leguizamo, Harold Perrineau

When We Were Kings (USA) *Director:* Leon Gast; *Actors:* Muhammad Ali, George Foreman, Don King

Top 10 Retail Videos in the UK

1997

Rank	Title	Distributor
1	*Independence Day*	FoxVideo
2	*Star Wars – Trilogy*	FoxVideo
3	*101 Dalmatians*	Walt Disney
4	*The Hunchback of Notre Dame*	Walt Disney
5	*Spice – The Official Video – Volume 1*	Virgin
6	*Matilda*	Columbia Tristar
7	*Oliver and Company*	Walt Disney
8	*Teletubbies – Here Come the Teletubbies*	BBC
9	*Teletubbies – Dance with the Teletubbies*	BBC
10	*Space Jam*	Warner Home Video

Source: Chart Information Network

Top 10 Video Rentals in the UK

1997

Rank	Title	Distributor
1	*The Rock*	Hollywood
2	*Ransom*	Touchstone
3	*Independence Day*	Fox Pathé
4	*Twister*	CIC
5	*Mission Impossible*	CIC
6	*The Nutty Professor*	CIC
7	*Jerry Maguire*	Columbia Tristar
8	*Eraser*	Warner
9	*Phenomenon*	Touchstone
10	*Sleepers*	PolyGram Video

Source: MRIB

Attendances at Cultural Events in the UK

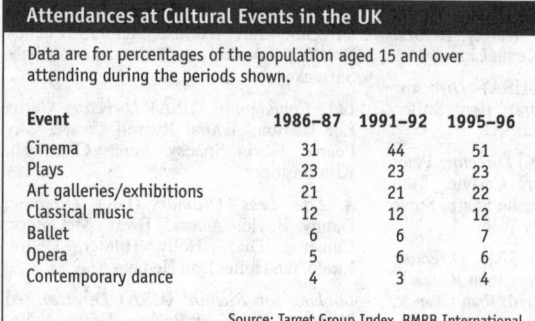

Data are for percentages of the population aged 15 and over attending during the periods shown.

Event	1986–87	1991–92	1995–96
Cinema	31	44	51
Plays	23	23	23
Art galleries/exhibitions	21	21	22
Classical music	12	12	12
Ballet	6	6	7
Opera	5	6	6
Contemporary dance	4	3	4

Source: Target Group Index, BMRB International

Trends in Cinema-Going in the UK

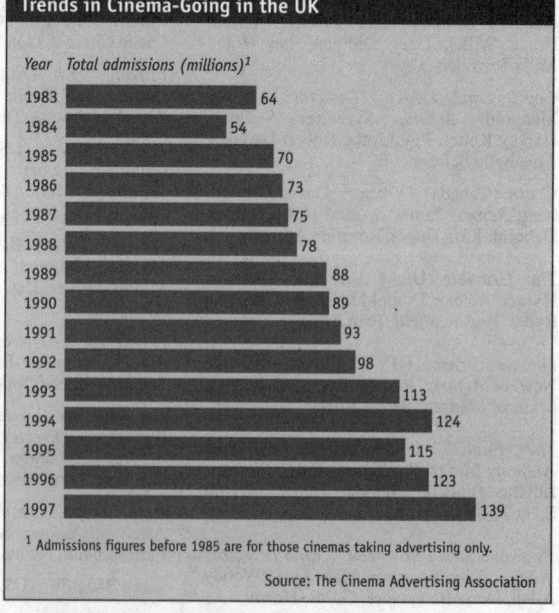

Year	Total admissions (millions)[1]
1983	64
1984	54
1985	70
1986	73
1987	75
1988	78
1989	88
1990	89
1991	93
1992	98
1993	113
1994	124
1995	115
1996	123
1997	139

[1] Admissions figures before 1985 are for those cinemas taking advertising only.

Source: The Cinema Advertising Association

HAS HOLLYWOOD LOST THE PLOT WITH *TITANIC*?

BY RICHARD MARTIN

James Cameron's film *Titanic* made waves for any number of reasons. It became both a commercial success and a media event, raising questions about the role being played by the Hollywood film industry today and about film's status both as commerce and art. Indeed, among the more serious charges levelled against the film – and mainstream cinema in general – is that the Hollywood blockbuster, although undoubtedly a source of entertainment, both diminishes film's value as art and, in its efforts to conform to what independent film guru John Pierson has termed 'the lowest common denominator mentality,' succeeds in doing little more than infantilizing its audience.

Mainstream Cinema

Mainstream American cinema of the 1980s and 1990s, as served up by such filmmakers as Steven Spielberg (*ET: The Extra-Terrestrial*, *Jurassic Park*), John McTiernan (*Die Hard*, *Last Action Hero*), Robert Zemeckis (*Who Framed Roger Rabbit?*, *Forrest Gump*), Paul Verhoeven (*Total Recall*, *Starship Troopers*), and James Cameron (*Terminator* and *Terminator 2*, *True Lies*), among many others, has been generically formulaic, ideologically conservative fare characterized by cartoonlike universes in which everything is black and white, governed by clear moral boundaries that separate good from evil. Valuing the image above all else, these filmmakers frequently produce beautifully photographed, visually stylish films, in which character and plot become secondary to visual pyrotechnics and exorbitant special effects.

Of course, mainstream American cinema's tendency towards the epic in length, spectacle, and budget dates back to such silent pioneers as D W Griffith, Cecil B De Mille, and Eric von Stroheim, with films like *The Birth of a Nation*, *The Ten Commandments*, and *Greed*; the very filmmakers and works that paradoxically helped establish the cinema as an art form, albeit one that depended heavily on those most 'unartistic' of bedfellows, the worlds of commerce and science.

Cinema's conversion to sound in the late 1920s ushered in the 'golden era' of Hollywood studio filmmaking. Technical developments made it possible to add dialogue and background sound to the previously silent images projected on to the silver screen. The involvement of the Wall Street banks made the wholesale conversion to this new form of filmmaking a financial viability. Finally, the well-oiled studio system of film production operated by major studios such as MGM and Warner Bros put the whole process into effect. As cars were manufactured in the conveyor-belt system in the Ford factories, films were assembled by being passed through the capable hands of clearly departmentalized contract personnel (script development, direction, musical soundtrack, editing); shaped by following established generic formulae (western, musical, horror film, screwball comedy); and marketed according to the star status of the actors who featured in it.

Blockbusters

One blockbuster like *Titanic*, both in its production costs and its box office returns, was *Gone with the Wind*. Surprisingly, for such an archetypal Hollywood A feature, the film also signalled the development of a new type of American film production policy that would have an enduring legacy in film history. Although released and partly financed by MGM, the film was in fact produced by Selznick International, an independent production company which had close ties with the major studio.

As the number of independent production companies increased throughout the 1940s, the majors (and the banks that financed them) began to assume the roles of financiers, farming out packages and facilities to the independents, gaining an increased level of input at all levels of supposedly 'independent' production, and gradually enforcing their own conservative filmmaking policies in this briefly vibrant sector. For all that, the mid-1940s were one of the most exciting and innovative periods in American film history, paralleled only by the emergence of the 'Movie Brats' in the film industry in the early 1970s, and the revitalization of the independent filmmaking sector in the 1990s.

The more memorable films of the forties, led by Orson Welles' landmark film *Citizen Kane*, which would exercise an enormous influence on many B- and A-feature filmmakers (most notably on those working in the *film noir* genre), were characterized by their expression of a personal artistic vision, their stylistic experimentation (including the fusion of different genres), and their almost self-conscious difference in comparison with the mainstream films of the Depression years.

The post-war years, however, saw a reversion to more traditional Hollywood values and styles. It also saw the industry as a whole competing with the latest form of popular entertainment – television – and seeking to maintain its appeal for a mobile middle class. The advent of television as a major force in American popular culture saw the film industry renew its commitment to grandiosity. This would involve the enlargement of the cinematic image itself, the introduction of advanced sound systems, and a brief experimentation with 3D. It would also see the 1950s and early 1960s dominated by the production of lavish, visual spectacles such as *The Robe*, *The Searchers*, *South Pacific*, and *El Cid*, which were filmed in widescreen and colour, contrasting sharply with the small black-and-white image served up by television.

In a series of takeovers and mergers during the 1960s lay the foundations for a huge cross-media culture industry. The immediate effect, as the old movie moguls of the past, many of whom had founded major studios such as Columbia and Warner Bros, were now replaced by out-and-out moneymen, was that the film industry was dominated by the 'blockbuster mentality'. Studios began to throw millions of dollars into the production of a single film, in the expectation that they would reap huge financial returns; successful films were then imitated for years to come, prompting a practice that continues today with countless remakes and sequels. The policy had near catastrophic consequences for some in the 1960s. Twentieth Century Fox, for example, enjoyed a huge commercial success with *The Sound of Music*, which prompted a cycle of epic musical productions, including *Dr Doolittle* and *Star!*, all of which flopped at the box office.

Movie Brats

If it had not been for the commercial success of low-budget, non-mainstream productions like *Butch Cassidy and the Sundance*

(continued)

Kid and *M*A*S*H*, Fox would probably have gone bankrupt. In fact, such films signalled a reaction against the inherent conservatism of Hollywood cinema, consolidated and enhanced as it had been by the corporatism that had now gripped the industry. They also marked the emergence of the first generation of television-educated Movie Brats, a 'new wave' of cine-literate American filmmakers who were entering the film industry direct from film school or from an apprenticeship in television production. The brief period in the late 1960s and early 1970s, in which filmmakers such as Francis Ford Coppola, Brian DePalma, George Lucas, Martin Scorsese, and Steven Spielberg first made their name, commodifying European new wave film techniques for American consumption, borrowing as much from European cinema and the B film as from their mainstream Hollywood heritage, ushered in the second period of innovation and experimentation in American filmmaking.

As in the forties, however, the 'innovators' largely had to co-exist with their mainstream counterparts. Indeed, the blockbuster mentality still prevailed in some quarters, and a cycle of megabudget disaster films populated by stellar casts, including *The Towering Inferno*, *The Poseidon Adventure*, and *Airport* – they were a significant feature of the 1970s.

The late 1970s would also witness a fascinating division between the Movie Brats, which would have consequences that still largely affect the film industry today. Simplistically put, in the latter half of the 1970s the Spielberg–Lucas faction embraced the 'blockbuster mentality', serving up huge critical and box office successes with *Jaws* and *Star Wars*, films which would spawn a whole series of imitators similarly drawn to a visual, formulaic style of cinema that catered explicitly for the mass consumption market. On the other hand, many of the independent filmmakers who would rise to prominence in the 1980s and 1990s, such as

Scorsese, John Sayles, and Alan Rudolph, were drawn to a less formulaic, art-house style of cinema. In the work of such filmmakers there was a greater level of stylistic experimentation, where character, plot, and dialogue were frequently valued above the image, and the narrative worlds depicted were far more complex than the cartoon-like universes of the mainstream films.

The Future for Independent Cinema

The co-existence of these two forms of American cinema has seen the film industry successfully catering for a wide variety of niche markets. Furthermore, in recent years the mainstream has relied heavily on the independent sector to supply original material that it can then imitate (as in the way that Hollywood executives strove to emulate the success of films such as *Pulp Fiction*). The worry is that if it is eventually left with no competitors, then the mainstream will churn out a series of *Titanics* which will sink the industry itself.

The production of blockbuster films fosters a whole array of spin-off products (soundtrack CDs, T-shirts, posters, books, computer games, toys, even television animation spin-offs) and promotional events (often in conjunction with fast food chains such as McDonald's and Burger King). In the particular case of *Titanic*, there has even been an auction of props used in the film at prices that far exceed the going rate for the originals on which they were modelled. But if cinema really does fall in thrall to grandiosity and franchising to the exclusion of all else, then the independent/art-house sector, and very possibly the industry as a whole, will suffer the consequences. A cinema of superficiality and special effects may well survive, but cinema as an art form will sink without a trace. For every *Titanic*, there has to be a *She's Gotta Have It*, *Blood Simple*, *sex, lies and videotape*, *Reservoir Dogs*, or *Clerks* to maintain cinema as art. Such films inject new life and ideas into a medium that has the potential to be forever evolving.

Television and Radio

Top 30 Programmes on Terrestrial Television in the UK

(Data exclude programmes shorter than 15 minutes, and multiple occurrences.)

1997

Rank	Programme	Channel	Transmission date	Number of viewers
1	Funeral of Diana, Princess of Wales	BBC1	6 September	19,294,000
2	Heartbeat	ITV	16 November	18,354,000
3	Touch of Frost	ITV	16 February	18,224,000
4	EastEnders	BBC1	2 January	18,055,000
5	Coronation Street	ITV	17 November	18,032,000
6	Casualty	BBC1	22 February	16,421,000
7	Men Behaving Badly	BBC1	25 December	16,342,000
8	One Foot in the Xmas Grave	BBC1	25 December	15,756,000
9	Before They Were Famous	BBC1	31 March	15,345,000
10	It'll be Alright on the Night 8	ITV	4 January	14,888,000
11	Procession to Westminster Abbey	BBC1	6 September	14,781,000
12	Emmerdale	ITV	20 February	14,234,000
13	The Bill	ITV	17 January	14,153,000
14	London's Burning	ITV	2 February	14,101,000
15	Police, Camera, Action	ITV	7 January	13,663,000
16	National Lottery Live	BBC1	15 March	13,607,000
17	Midsomer Murders	ITV	23 March	13,633,000
18	Ballykissangel	BBC1	5 January	13,470,000
19	Ronnie Barker: A Life in Comedy	BBC1	1 January	13,219,000
20	Peak Practice	ITV	18 February	13,114,000
21	National TV Awards	ITV	8 October	12,960,000
22	It'll be Alright on the Night 5	ITV	2 February	12,665,000
23	Where the Heart is	ITV	20 April	12,646,000
24	Jane Eyre	ITV	9 March	12,522,000
25	Vicar of Dibley	BBC1	26 December	12,453,000
26	The Driving School	BBC1	15 July	12,448,000
27	Birds of a Feather, Christmas special	BBC1	27 December	12,356,000
28	This is Your Life	BBC1	3 February	12,341,000
29	Mrs Doubtfire	BBC1	30 December	12,337,000
30	The Wingless Bird	ITV	29 April	12,330,000

Source: Taylor Nelson AGB/BARB

Top 30 Drama Programmes Shown on Terrestrial Television in the UK

Ratings are for the highest rated episode of each drama during 1997. The data exclude multiple occurrences.

1997

Rank	Programme	Channel	Transmission date	Number of viewers	Rank	Programme	Channel	Transmission date	Number of viewers
1	Heartbeat	ITV	16 November	18,354,000	16	The Student Prince	BBC1	29 November	12,258,000
2	Touch of Frost	ITV	16 February	18,224,000	17	Emmerdale Special	ITV	1 April	12,073,000
3	EastEnders	BBC1	2 January	18,055,000	18	Inspector Morse	ITV	19 November	12,060,000
4	Coronation Street	ITV	17 November	18,032,000	19	Midsommer Murders	ITV	14 December	12,028,000
5	Casualty	BBC1	22 February	16,421,000	20	Reckless	ITV	13 March	11,947,000
6	Emmerdale	ITV	20 February	14,234,000	21	The Vanishing Man	ITV	2 April	11,927,000
7	The Bill	ITV	17 January	14,153,000	22	Taggart	ITV	16 January	11,803,000
8	London's Burning	ITV	2 February	14,101,000	23	McCallum	ITV	17 February	11,717,000
9	Midsomer Murders	ITV	23 March	13,533,000	24	Kavanagh QC	ITV	14 April	11,501,000
10	Ballykissangel	BBC1	5 January	13,470,000	25	Crime Traveller	BBC1	1 March	11,456,000
11	Peak Practice	ITV	18 February	13,114,000	26	The Knock	ITV	27 April	11,366,000
12	Where the Heart Is	ITV	20 April	12,646,000	27	Wycliffe	ITV	29 June	11,278,000
13	Jane Eyre	ITV	9 March	12,522,000	28	Gold	ITV	27 October	11,252,000
14	Touching Evil	ITV	29 April	12,330,000	29	Poirot	ITV	16 March	11,178,000
15	The Wingless Bird	ITV	26 January	12,324,000	30	The Grand	ITV	4 April	11,058,000

Source: TARIS Ratings Analyser

Top 30 Light Entertainment Programmes on Terrestrial Television in the UK

1997

Rank	Programme	Channel	Transmission date	Number of viewers	Rank	Programme	Channel	Transmission date	Number of viewers
1	Men Behaving Badly	BBC1	25 December	16,342,000	15	Audience with Elton John	ITV	27 September	11,783,000
2	One Foot in the Xmas Grave	BBC1	25 December	15,766,000	16	Blind Date	ITV	11 January	11,727,000
3	Before They Were Famous	BBC1	31 March	15,345,000	17	It'll Be Alright on the Night 7	ITV	1 March	11,379,000
4	It'll Be Alright on the Night 8	ITV	4 January	14,888,000	18	Alright/Cock-up Trip	ITV	21 September	11,334,000
5	National Lottery Live	BBC1	15 March	13,607,000	19	You've Been Framed	ITV	9 November	11,315,000
6	National TV Awards	ITV	8 October	12,960,000	20	Auntie's New Bloomers	BBC1	29 December	11,302,000
7	It'll Be Alright on the Night 5	ITV	2 February	12,665,000	21	Wheel of Fortune	ITV	3 January	11,276,000
8	Vicar of Dibley	BBC1	26 December	12,453,000	22	Only Fools and Horses	BBC1	12 June	11,180,000
9	Birds of a Feather, Christmas special	BBC1	27 December	12,356,000	23	Audience with the Spice Girls	ITV	29 November	11,074,000
10	This is Your Life	BBC1	3 February	12,341,000	24	Royal Variety Performance	ITV	6 December	10,909,000
11	They Think It's All Over	BBC1	25 December	12,309,000	25	Another Freddie Starr	ITV	11 October	10,726,000
12	Big Birthday Party	BBC1	22 November	12,029,000	26	Auntie's Natural Bloomers	BBC1	14 July	10,694,000
13	Dennis Norden's 2nd Laughter File	ITV	4 October	11,886,000	27	Strike It Rich	ITV	2 January	10,671,000
14	It'll Be Alright on the Night 10	ITV	15 November	11,810,000	28	Stars in Your Eyes	ITV	7 June	10,609,000
					29	Comic Relief	BBC1	14 March	10,582,000
					30	Audience with Bruce Forsyth	ITV	1 February	10,579,000

Source: TARIS Ratings Analyser

Top 30 Films Shown on Terrestrial Television in the UK

1997

Rank	Programme	Channel	Transmission date	Number of viewers	Rank	Programme	Channel	Transmission date	Number of viewers
1	Mrs Doubtfire	BBC1	30 December	12,337,000	16	Clear and Present Danger	BBC1	23 December	8,668,000
2	Hocus Pocus	ITV	29 October	10,357,000	17	Hostile Waters	BBC1	26 July	8,665,000
3	The Bodyguard	ITV	24 February	10,323,000	18	The Chase	BBC1	22 November	8,439,000
4	Airport	BBC1	24 July	10,184,000	19	Another Stakeout	ITV	15 February	8,364,000
5	Sister Act 2	ITV	30 March	10,132,000	20	Lethal Weapon	ITV	16 December	8,323,000
6	True Lies	BBC1	26 December	10,071,000	21	Home Alone 2	ITV	25 December	8,245,000
7	In the Line of Fire	ITV	12 November	9,730,000	22	Under Siege	BBC1	24 January	8,240,000
8	Made in America	BBC1	9 March	9,710,000	23	Ghost	BBC1	9 May	8,239,000
9	Addams Family Values	BBC1	26 April	9,671,000	24	City Heat	ITV	2 January	8,204,000
10	Father of the Bride	ITV	3 September	9,579,000	25	My Girl	ITV	28 March	8,199,000
11	Pelican Brief	ITV	26 March	9,560,000	26	Bitter Vengeance	BBC1	1 November	8,192,000
12	Tightrope	ITV	9 January	9,459,000	27	Unforgiven	ITV	17 December	8,171,000
13	Die Hard	ITV	1 January	9,207,000	28	Don't Talk to Strangers	BBC1	13 December	8,147,000
14	Beethoven's Second	BBC1	26 December	9,139,000	29	Cracker – The Movie	ITV	15 March	8,062,000
15	Pretty Woman	ITV	22 December	8,799,000	30	Naked Gun 33 $\frac{1}{3}$	BBC1	24 December	8,047,000

Source: TARIS Ratings Analyser

Top 30 Sports Programmes on Terrestrial Television by Rating in the UK

(Figures exclude multiple occurrences.)

1997

Rank	Programme	Channel	Transmission date	Number of viewers	Rank	Programme	Channel	Transmission date	Number of viewers
1	Grand National	BBC1	7 April	12,017,000	17	FA Cup Round 6	BBC1	9 March	6,662,000
2	FA Cup Final (Chelsea – Middlesborough)	BBC1	17 May	11,100,000	18	Rugby Highlights	BBC1	18 January	6,616,000
3	Champions League Live	ITV	5 March	11,069,000	19	Final Score	BBC1	11 January	6,596,000
4	FA Cup Final-Post Match	BBC1	17 May	10,572,000	20	Wimbledon (Henman – Krajicek)	BBC2	1 July	6,595,000
5	The European Match	ITV	19 March	10,323,000	21	Rugby Union	BBC1	1 February	6,341,000
6	Road to Wembley	BBC1	5 January	10,219,000	22	Boat Race	BBC1	29 March	6,186,000
7	Match of the Day	BBC1	26 January	9,986,000	23	Argentine Grand Prix	ITV	13 April	6,055,000
8	Sportsnight	BBC1	18 March	9,084,000	24	World Athletics Championships	BBC1	3 August	5,923,000
9	Sportsnight Special	BBC1	4 March	8,964,000	25	Canadian Grand Prix	ITV	15 June	5,920,000
10	Grandstand	BBC1	7 April	8,493,000	26	Wimbledon (Henman – Stich)	BBC1	3 July	5,835,000
11	Sports Review of the Year	BBC1	14 December	8,232,000	27	Tennis	BBC2	28 June	5,715,000
12	Match of the Day Live	BBC1	4 November	8,028,000	28	Spanish Grand Prix	ITV	26 October	5,679,000
13	The Match Live	ITV	26 February	7,841,000	29	Snooker	BBC2	5 May	5,647,000
14	International Football	ITV	11 October	7,069,000	30	FA Cup Draw Live	ITV	7 December	5,611,000
15	Brazilian Grand Prix	ITV	30 March	6,836,000					
16	Champions League Final	ITV	28 May	6,812,000					

Source: Taylor Nelson AGB/BARB

Average Daily Television Usage per Household in the UK

(– = not applicable. In hours.)

Year	Total[1]	ITV	BBC1	BBC2	Channel 4	Year	Total[1]	ITV	BBC1	BBC2	Channel 4
1969	4.5	2.4	2.1	–	–	1990	5.1	2.3	1.9	0.5	0.5
1972	4.8	2.7	1.9	0.3	–	1993	5.8	2.3	1.9	0.6	0.7
1976	5.1	2.7	2.1	0.4	–	1994	5.8	2.3	1.9	0.7	0.7
1980	5.1	2.5	2.0	0.6	–	1995	5.9	2.2	1.9	0.7	0.7
1982	4.9	2.4	1.9	0.6	–	1996	5.8	2.0	1.9	0.7	0.7
1986	5.3	2.4	1.9	0.6	0.5						

[1] Totals may not add due to rounding and the small percentage of other (non-terrestrial) viewing.

Source: Taylor Nelson AGB/BARB

Average Daily Hours of Viewing by Age and Social Grade in the UK

(In hours.)

Category	1994	1997
All individuals	3.6	3.53
Socio-economic group		
ABC1	3.2	3.07
C2	3.7	3.57
DE	4.2	4.16
Age		
4–9	2.6	2.47
10–15	2.7	2.51
16–24	2.8	2.54
25–34	3.5	3.33
35–44	3.4	3.33
45–54	3.6	3.63
≥55	4.8	4.74

Source: TARIS Ratings Analyser

Proportion of Factual Programmes in Peak-Time Television in the UK

(Figures are percentages.)

Channel	1995–96	1996–97
BBC1	49	46
BBC2	51	51
ITV	28	29
Channel 4	52	49

Source: *BBC Annual Report 1997*

Household Penetration of TV Sets and VCRs in the UK

(– = not applicable.)

Year	All households	TV households	TV households %	Receiving colour %	2+ TV sets %	VCR %	Teletext %
1970	18,364,000	16,895,000	92	2	3	–	–
1980	20,322,000	19,916,000	98	71	19	–	–
1990	22,122,000	21,458,000	97	93	46	61	33
1995	23,902,000	23,212,000	97	98	55	76	57
1997	24,340,000	23,627,000	97	99	59	81	66

Source: Taylor Nelson AGB/BARB

BBC Licence Fee Budget Breakdown

The BBC licence fee income was £1,820 million in 1995–96 and £1,915 million in 1996–97.

Area	1995–96 (£ millions)	1996–97 (£ millions)		Non-Broadcast		
Television				Licence fee collection	95.0	96.9
BBC1	648.4	652.5		Restructuring costs	35.2	81.7
BBC2	327.5	346.8		Corporate Centre[1]	53.5	55.6
Regional	154.4	161.1		Resources, transmission, and services net		
Television total	1,130.3	1,160.4		surplus	–1.3	–15.3
				Other[2]	62.8	86.9
Radio						
Radio 1	37.3	37.7		*Non-Broadcast total*	245.2	305.8
Radio 2	39.0	42.0				
Radio 3	56.6	58.8		*TOTAL*	1,756.5	1,854.7
Radio 4	79.7	79.2		Gross operating		
Radio 5 Live	45.8	46.3		expenditure	1,813.1	1,910.4
Regional	46.6	48.9		Less funded from		
Local	76.0	75.6		external income	–56.6	–55.7
Radio total	381.0	388.5		*TOTAL*	1,756.5	1,854.7

[1] Includes Corporate Finance, Personnel, Policy and Planning, Corporate Affairs, Legal Adviser, Research and Development, and expenditure which cannot be meaningfully charged against other areas.
[2] Includes corporate provisions and accounting adjustments.

Source: *BBC Annual Report 1997*

Television Companies in the UK

Anglia Television Ltd Anglia House, Norwich, NR1 3JG; phone: (01603) 615151; fax: (01603) 763 1032; www.angliatv.co.uk

BBC Network Television Television Centre, Wood Lane, London W12 7RJ; phone: (0181) 743 8000; fax: (0181) 749 7520; www.bbc.co.uk

BBC Worldwide Television Woodlands, 80 Wood Lane, London W12 0TT; phone: (0181) 576 2992; fax: (0181) 576 3040; www.bbc.co.uk

Border Television The Television Centre, Carlisle CA1 3NT; phone: (01228) 525101; fax: (01228) 541384

Carlton Broadcasting 101 St Martin's Lane, London, WC2N 4AZ; phone: (0171) 240 4000; fax: (0171) 240 4171; www.carltontv.co.uk

Central Television Central House, Broad Street, Birmingham B1 2JP; phone: (0121) 643 9898; fax (press office): (0121) 634 4606; www.centraltv.co.uk

Channel 4 124 Horseferry Road, London SW1P 2TX; phone: (0171) 396 4444; fax (press office): (0171) 306 8353; www.channel4.com

Channel 5 Broadcasting 22 Long Acre, London WC2E 9LY; phone: (0171) 497 5225; fax: (0171) 497 5620; www.channel5.co.uk

Channel Television Television Centre, St Helier, Jersey, Channel Islands JE2 3ZD; phone: (01534) 816816; fax: (01534) 816817; www.channeltv.co.tv

GMTV London Television Centre, Upper Ground, London SE1 9TT; phone: (0171) 827 7000; fax (press office): (0171) 827 7069

Grampian Television Queen's Cross, Aberdeen AB15 4XJ; phone: (01224) 846846; fax: (01224) 846800; www.grampiantv.co.uk

Granada Television The Television Centre, Quay Street, Manchester M60 9EA; phone: (0161) 832 7211; fax: (0161) 827 2029; www.granadatv.co.uk

HTV Group The Television Centre, Culverhouse Cross, Cardiff CF5 6XJ; phone: (01222) 590590; fax: (01222) 597183; www.htv.co.uk

London Weekend Television (LWT) The London Television Centre, Upper Ground, London SE1 9LT; phone: (0171) 620 1620; fax: (0171) 261 1290; www.lwt.co.uk

Meridian Broadcasting Television Centre, Northam, Southampton SO14 0PZ; phone: (01703) 222555; fax: (01703) 335050; www.meridiantv.co.uk

Scottish Television Cowcaddens, Glasgow G2 3PR; phone: (0141) 300 3000; fax: (0141) 300 3030; www.stv.co.uk

Tyne Tees Television The Television Centre, City Road, Newcastle upon Tyne NE1 2AL; phone: (0191) 261 0181; fax: (0191) 269 2302; www.tynetees.tv.co.uk

Ulster Television (UTV) Havelock House, Ormeau Road, Belfast BT17 1EB; phone: (01232) 328122; fax: (01232) 246695; www.utvlive.com

Westcountry Television Western Wood Way, Plymouth PL7 5BG; phone: (01752) 333333; fax: (01752) 333444; www.westcountry.co.uk

Yorkshire Television The Television Centre, Leeds LS3 1JS; phone: (0113) 243 8283; fax: (0113) 244 5107; www.york-shiretv.co.uk

Satellite and Cable Television Companies in the UK

Bloomberg International TV Citygate House, 39-45 Finsbury Square, London EC2A 1PQ; phone: 0171 330 7500; fax: 0171 392 6000; www.bloomberg.com\uk

Bravo, The Discovery Channel, Trouble, UK Gold, UK Living 160 Great Portland Street, London W1N 5TB; phone: 0171 299 5000; fax: 0171 299 6000; www.flextech.co.uk

Carlton Select, Carlton Food Network 45 Fouberts Street, London W1V 2DN; phone: 0171 432 9000; fax: 0171 432 3151

Cartoon Network 18 Soho Square, London W1V 5FD; phone: 0171 478 1000; fax: 0171 478 1010; www.cartoon.network.co.uk

CNN International CNN House, 19-22 Rathbone Place, London W1P 1DF; phone: 0171 637 6800; fax: 0171 637 6868; www.cnn.com

Disney Channel UK Beaumont House, Kensington Village, Avonmore Road, London W14 8TS; phone: 0181 222 1300; fax: 0181 222 1144; www.disneychannel.co.uk

Eurosport UK 55 Drury Lane, London WC2B 5SQ; phone: 0171 468 7777; fax: 0171 468 0023

Good Life, Granada Plus Granada Sky Broadcasting, Franciscan Court, 16 Hatfields, London SE1 8DJ; phone: 0171 578 4040; fax: 0171 578 4176

L!ve TV 24th Floor, One Canada Square, London E14 5DJ; phone: 0171 293 3900; fax: 0171 293 2151; www.l!vetv.co.uk

MTV Europe Hawley Crescent, London NW1 8TT; phone: 0171 284 7777; fax: 0171 284 7788; www.mtv.com

News 24 Stage 5, Television Centre, Shephard's Bush, London W12 7RJ; phone: 0181 743 8000; fax: 0181 225 8080

Nickleodeon 15-18 Rathbone Place, London W1P 1DF; phone: 0171 462 1000; fax: 1071 462 1030; www.nickleodeon @cix.compulink.co.uk

The Sci-Fi Channel 77 Charlotte Street, London W1P 2DD; phone: 0171 805 6100; fax: 0171 805 6150; www.scifi.com

Sky (including the Movie Channel, Sky 1, Sky Movies 1, Sky Movies Gold, Sky Sports (1, 2 and 3), Sky News, National Geographic Channel) 6 Centaurs Business Park, Grant Way, Isleworth TW7 5QD; phone: 0171 705 3000; fax: 0171 705 3030; www.sky.co.uk

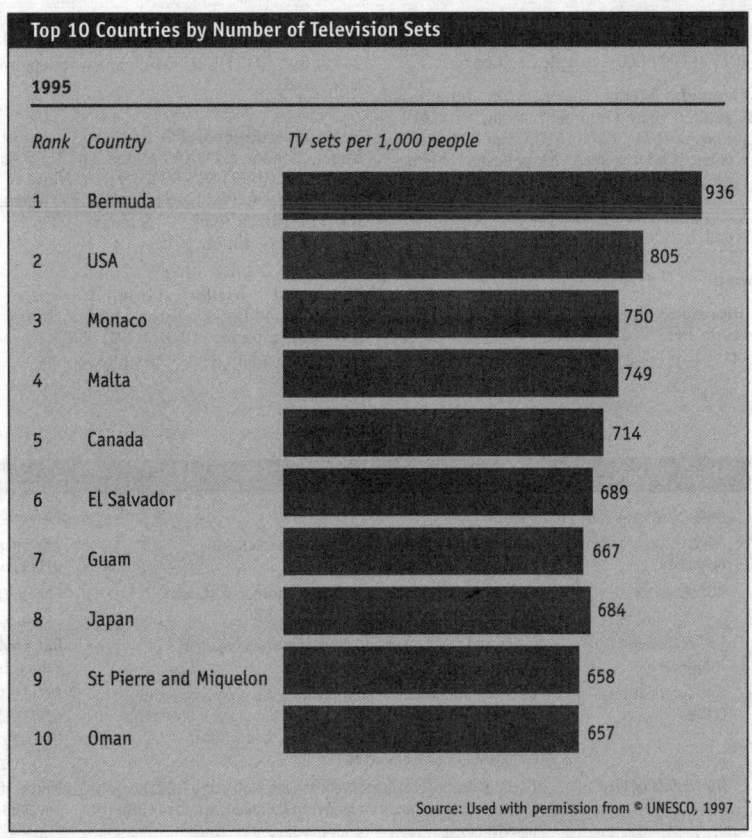

Top 10 Countries by Number of Television Sets

1995

Rank	Country	TV sets per 1,000 people
1	Bermuda	936
2	USA	805
3	Monaco	750
4	Malta	749
5	Canada	714
6	El Salvador	689
7	Guam	667
8	Japan	684
9	St Pierre and Miquelon	658
10	Oman	657

Source: Used with permission from © UNESCO, 1997

National Radio Stations in the UK

BBC Network Radio Broadcasting House, Portland Place, London W1A 1AA; phone (publicity office): (0171) 765 2265; **Radio 1** phone (publicity office): (0171) 765 4575; **Radio 2** phone (publicity office): (0171) 765 4330; **Radio 3** phone (publicity office): (0171) 765 2722; **Radio 4** phone (publicity office): (0171) 765 5337; **Radio 5 Live** phone (publicity office): (0171) 765 4095; **Classic FM** Academic House, 24–28 Oval Road, London NW1 7DQ; phone: (0171) 284 3000; fax: (0171) 713 2630; **Talk Radio** PO Box 1089, London W1A 1PP; phone: (0171) 636 1089; fax: (0171) 636 1053; **Virgin Radio** 1 Golden Square, London W1R 4DJ; phone: (0171) 434 1215; fax: (0171) 434 1197; www.virginradio.co.uk

Main Media Groups in the UK

BBC Corporate HQ Broadcasting House, London W1A 1AA; phone: (0171) 580 4468; fax: (0171) 637 1630; www.bbc.co.uk

Capital Radio 30 Leicester Square, London WC2H 7LA; phone: (0171) 766 6000; fax: (0171) 766 6100; www.capitalradio.co.uk

Carlton Communications 15 St George Street, London W1R OLU; phone: (0171) 663 6363; fax: (0171) 663 6300; www.carltonplc.co.uk

Associated Press/Daily Mail 2 Derry Street, London W8 5TT; phone: (0171) 938 6000; fax: (0171) 938 4626; www.dailymail.co.uk

Flextech 160 Great Portland Street, London W1N 3HA; phone: (0171) 299 5000; fax: (0171) 299 6000; www.flextech.co.uk

Granada Media The London Television Centre, Upper Ground, London SE1 9LT; phone: (0171) 620 1620; The Television Centre, Quay Street, Manchester; phone: (0161) 832 7211

Guardian Media Group 119 Farringdon Road, London EC1R 3ER; phone: (0171) 278 2332; fax: (0171) 837 2114; www.guardian.co.uk

Johnstone Press 53 Manor Place, Edinburgh EH3 7EG; phone: (0131) 225 3361; fax: (0131) 225 4580; www.johnstone.co.uk

Mirror Group 1 Canada Square, Canary Wharf, London E14 5AP; phone: (0171) 239 2435; fax: (0171) 293 3405; www.independent.co.uk

News International PO Box 495, Virginia Street, London E1 9XY; phone: (0171) 782 6000; fax: (0171) 895 9020; Sun & News of the World: www.lineone.net; The Times: www.the_times.co.uk; Sunday Times: www.sunday_times.co.uk

Newsquest Media Group Newspaper House, 33–44 London Road, Morden, Surrey SM4 5BR; phone: (0181) 640 8989; fax: (0181) 646 6306; www.newsquest .co.uk

Pearson 3 Burlington Gardens, London W1X 1LE; phone: (0171) 411 2000; fax: (0171) 411 2390; www.pearson.com

Telegraph 1 Canada Square, Canary Wharf, London E14 5DT; phone: (0171) 538 5000; fax: (0171) 538 6242; www.telegraph.co.uk

Trinity Holdings 6 Heritage Court, Chester CH1 1RD; phone: (01244) 687000; fax: (01255) 687100

United News and Media 48 Leicester Square, London WC2H 7LY; phone: (0171) 579 4400; fax: (0171) 925 0665; www.unm.com

Media Watchdogs in the UK

Agency/programme	Details	Address
Advertising Standards Authority	deals with complaints about advertisements in newspapers and magazines	2 Torrington Place, London WC1E 7HW; phone: (0171) 580 5555
BBC *Biteback*	a monthly TV programme (Sunday afternoons) takes comments to be broadcast about the BBC	phone: (0181) 741 3715
BBC Engineering Information	for TV and radio reception advice; leave a daytime phone number	BBC Engineering, Villiers House, The Broadway, Ealing, London W5 2PA; phone: 0345 010313 (local rate)
BBC Information Offices	general information: if possible give the programme title, transmission date, and time; a daily summary of comments is seen by senior programme-makers, and written comments will be answered	*TV:* phone: (0181) 743 8000, (answerphone 62959/62848); *Radio:* phone: (0171) 580 4468; Minicom: (0181) 576 8988
BBC *Points of View*	TV programme (broadcast Wednesdays 8.30 p.m., BBC1) takes complaints and comments to be broadcast about BBC television	Points of View, BBCTV, London W12 7RJ; e-mail: pov@bbc.co.uk
BBC Programme Complaints Unit	deals with complaints of specific and serious injustice or inaccuracy, or a serious breach of accepted standards in a BBC broadcast	Fraser Steel, Head of the BBC Programme Complaints Unit, BBC Broadcasting House, London W1A 1AA
BBC Viewer and Listener Correspondence	deals with all BBC output, and all written comments receive a reply	Viewer and Listener Correspondence, BBC, Villiers House, The Broadway, Ealing, London W5 2PA
Broadcasting Standards Commission	for complaints about violence, sexual conduct, decency, and taste in TV and radio programmes and advertisements	7 The Sanctuary, London SW1P 3JS; phone: (0171) 233 0544; fax: (0171) 233 0397
Channel 4 *Right to Reply*	takes complaints and suggestions about television programmes for discussion at 6.30 p.m. on Saturdays	Right to Reply, 124 Horseferry Road, London SW1P 2TX; phone: (0171) 306 8582; fax: (0171) 306 8373; e-mail: righttoreply@channel4.co.uk
Independent Television Commission	deals with complaints about ITV, Channel 4, cable, and satellite	33 Foley Street, London W1P 7LB; phone: (0171) 255 3000
Press Complaints Commission	deals with complaints about newspaper and magazine editorials	1 Salisbury Square, London EC4Y 8AE; phone: (0171) 353 1248
Press Radio Authority	deals with programmes and advertising on independent (non-BBC) radio	Holbrook House, 14 Great Queen Street, London WC2B 5DG; phone: (0171) 430 2724

Advertising

Top 20 Advertisers by Spend Across All Media in the UK

Figures include press, television, radio, cinema, and outdoor. Outdoor excludes tobacco advertising and 'moving transport advertising'.

1997

Rank	Company	Amount (£ millions)
1	British Telecom	159.308
2	Procter and Gamble	117.814
3	Dixon's	107.689
4	Ford	81.602
5	Vauxhall	74.846
6	Kellogg	71.314
7	Procter and Gamble Health and Beauty	69.765
8	Renault UK	58.780

Vic Reeves, Bob Mortimer, and 'Nicole' in the 1998 Renault advertising campaign

© Richard Watt

Rank	Company	Amount
9	Mars	55.922
10	Unilever Elida Faberge	55.755
11	Unilever Lever Brothers	54.230
12	Rover	52.495
13	Nissan GB	46.333
14	Peugeot Talbot	44.407
15	Volkswagen UK	42.470
16	Boots	41.417
17	McDonald's	41.266
18	Golden	41.189
19	Mattel UK	40.627
20	Coca Cola GB and Ireland	38.683

Source: AC Nielsen MEAL, 1998

Top 20 Brands by Advertising Spend Across All Media in the UK

Figures include press, television, radio, cinema, and outdoor. Outdoor excludes tobacco advertising and 'moving transport advertising'. Figures show spend in £ millions.

1997

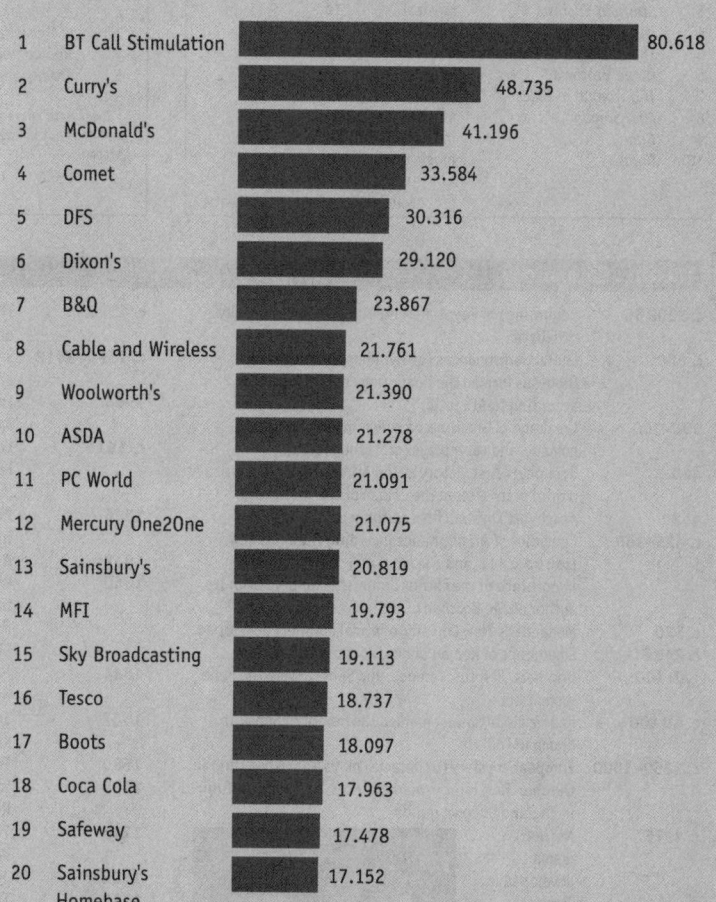

1	BT Call Stimulation	80.618
2	Curry's	48.735
3	McDonald's	41.196
4	Comet	33.584
5	DFS	30.316
6	Dixon's	29.120
7	B&Q	23.867
8	Cable and Wireless	21.761
9	Woolworth's	21.390
10	ASDA	21.278
11	PC World	21.091
12	Mercury One2One	21.075
13	Sainsbury's	20.819
14	MFI	19.793
15	Sky Broadcasting	19.113
16	Tesco	18.737
17	Boots	18.097
18	Coca Cola	17.963
19	Safeway	17.478
20	Sainsbury's Homebase	17.152

Source: AC Nielsen MEAL, 1998

Top 10 Advertising Agencies in the UK

1996

Rank	Agency	HQ	Billings (£ millions)[1]	Rank	Agency	HQ	Billings (£ millions)[1]
1	J Walter Thompson Company	London	370.0	6	Ogilvy & Mather	London	255.3
2	Saatchi & Saatchi Advertising	London	325.0	7	Resource Advertising	Poole, Dorset	250.0
3	Abbott Mead Vickers BBDO	London	283.0	8	Bartle Bogle Hegarty	London	244.0
4	Grey Advertising	London	277.0	9	Bates Dorland	London	235.0
5	Lowe Howard-Spink	London	267.0	10	Leo Burnett Company	London	225.0

[1] Billings are as declared by the agency to *Advertisers Annual*.

Source: *Advertisers Annual*

Theatre

Top 10 Longest-Running West End Theatre Productions

(As at February 1998.)

Rank	Production	Category	Years	Months
1	*The Mousetrap*	whodunnit	45	3
2	*Cats*	musical	16	9
3	*Starlight Express*	musical	13	11
4	*Les Misérables*	musical	12	4
5	*The Phantom of the Opera*	musical	11	4
6	*Blood Brothers*	musical	9	6
7	*The Woman in Black*	thriller	9	0
8	*Miss Saigon*	musical	8	5
9	*Buddy*	musical	8	4
10	*Grease*	musical	4	6

Source: Society of London Theatre

Top 5 Shakespeare Plays by Tickets Sold

April 1996–March 1997

Rank	Production	Tickets sold[1]
1	*Macbeth*	166,232
2	*As You Like It*	154,651
3	*A Midsummer Night's Dream*	96,906
4	*Romeo and Juliet*	74,276
5	*Troilus and Cressida*	35,470

[1] These data cover all theatre activity within the subsidized sector in England and does not include the rest of the UK, the West End, or the commercial sector.

Source: Arts Council of England

Theatre: Chronology

c. 3200 BC — Beginnings of Egyptian religious drama, essentially ritualistic.

c. 600 — Choral performances (dithyrambs) in honour of Dionysus formed the beginnings of Greek tragedy, according to Aristotle.

500–300 — Great age of Greek drama which included tragedy, comedy, and satyr plays (grotesque farce).

468 — Sophocles' first victory at the Athens festival. His use of a third actor altered the course of the tragic form.

458 — Aeschylus' *Oresteia* first performed.

c. 425–388 — Comedies of Aristophanes including *The Birds* 414, *Lysistrata* 411, and *The Frogs* 405. In tragedy the importance of the chorus diminished under Euripides, author of *The Bacchae* c. 405.

c. 320 — Menander's 'New Comedy' of social manners developed.

c. 240 BC–AD 100 — Emergence of Roman drama, adapted from Greek originals. Plautus, Terence, and Seneca were the main dramatists.

c. AD 400 — Kālidāsa's *Sakuntalā* marked the height of Sanskrit drama in India.

c. 1250–1500 — European mystery (or miracle) plays flourished, first in the churches, later in marketplaces, and were performed in England by town guilds.

c. 1375 — Nō (Noh) drama developed in Japan.

c. 1495 — *Everyman*, the best known of all the morality plays, was first performed.

Nō theatre

Japanese National Tourist Organization

1525–1750 — Italian commedia dell'arte troupes performed popular, improvised comedies; they were to have a large influence on Molière and on English harlequinade and pantomime.

c. 1540 — Nicholas Udall wrote *Ralph Roister Doister*, the first English comedy.

c. 1576 — The first English playhouse, The Theatre, was built by James Burbage in London.

c. 1587 — Christopher Marlowe's play *Tamburlaine the Great* marked the beginning of the great age of Elizabethan and Jacobean drama in England.

c. 1588 — Thomas Kyd's play *The Spanish Tragedy* was the first of the 'revenge' tragedies.

c. 1590–1612 — Shakespeare's greatest plays, including *Hamlet* and *King Lear*, were written.

1604 — Inigo Jones designed *The Masque of Blackness* for James I, written by Ben Jonson.

c. 1614 — Lope de Vega's *Fuenteovejuna* marked the Spanish renaissance in drama. Other writers included Calderón de la Barca.

1636 — Pierre Corneille's *Le Cid* established classical tragedy in France.

1642 — An act of Parliament closed all English theatres.

1660 — With the restoration of Charles II to the English throne, dramatic performances recommenced. The first professional actress appeared as Desdemona in Shakespeare's *Othello*.

1664 — Molière's *Tartuffe* was banned for five years by religious factions.

1667 — Jean Racine's first success, *Andromaque*, was staged.

1680 — The Comédie Française was formed by Louis XIV.

1700 — William Congreve, the greatest exponent of Restoration comedy, wrote *The Way of the World*.

1716 — The first known American theatre was built in Williamsburg, Virginia.

1728 — John Gay's *The Beggar's Opera* was first performed.

1737 — The Stage Licensing Act in England required all plays to be approved by the Lord Chamberlain before performance.

1747 — The actor David Garrick became manager of the Drury Lane Theatre, London.

1773 — In England, Oliver Goldsmith's *She Stoops to Conquer* and Richard Sheridan's *The Rivals* 1775 established the 'comedy of manners'. Goethe's *Götz von Berlichingen* was the first *Sturm und Drang* play (literally, storm and stress).

1781 — Friedrich Schiller's *Die Räuber/The Robbers*.

1784 — Beaumarchais' *Le Mariage de Figaro/The Marriage of Figaro* (written 1778) was first performed.

1830 — Victor Hugo's *Hernani* caused riots in Paris. His work marked the beginning of a new Romantic drama, changing the course of French theatre.

1878 — Henry Irving became actor-manager of the Lyceum with Ellen Terry as leading lady.

Theatre: Chronology (continued)

1879	Henrik Ibsen's *A Doll's House,* an early example of realism in European theatre.
1888	August Strindberg wrote *Miss Julie.*
1893	George Bernard Shaw wrote *Mrs Warren's Profession* (banned until 1902 because it deals with prostitution). Shaw's works brought the new realistic drama to Britain and introduced social and political issues as subjects for the theatre.
1895	Oscar Wilde's comedy *The Importance of Being Earnest.*
1896	The first performance of Anton Chekhov's *The Seagull* failed. Alfred Jarry's *Ubu Roi,* a forerunner of Surrealism, produced in Paris.
1904	Chekhov's *The Cherry Orchard.* The Academy of Dramatic Art (Royal Academy of Dramatic Art 1920) was founded in London to train young actors. The Abbey Theatre, Dublin, opened by W B Yeats and Lady Gregory, marked the beginning of an Irish dramatic revival.
1919	The Theater Guild was founded in the USA to perform less commercial new plays.
1920	*Beyond the Horizon,* Eugene O'Neill's first play, marked the beginning of serious theatre in the USA.
1921	Luigi Pirandello's *Six Characters in Search of an Author* introduced themes of the individual and exploration of reality and appearance.
1927	*Show Boat,* composed by Jerome Kern with libretto by Oscar Hammerstein II, laid the foundations of the US musical.
1928	Bertolt Brecht's *Die Dreigroschenoper/The Threepenny Opera* with score by Kurt Weill; other political satires by Karel Čapek and Elmer Rice. In the USA musical comedies by Cole Porter, Irving Berlin, and George Gershwin were popular.
1930s	US social-protest plays of Clifford Odets, Lillian Hellman, Thornton Wilder, and William Saroyan.
1935	T S Eliot's *Murder in the Cathedral.*
1935–39	WPA Federal Theater Project in the USA.
1938	Publication of Antonin Artaud's *Theatre and Its Double.*
1943	The first of the Rodgers and Hammerstein musicals, *Oklahoma!,* opened.
1944	Jean-Paul Sartre's *Huis Clos/In Camera;* Jean Anouilh's *Antigone.*
post-1945	Resurgence of German-language theatre, including Wolfgang Borchert, Max Frisch, Friedrich Dürrenmatt, and Peter Weiss.
1947	Tennessee Williams' *A Streetcar Named Desire.* First Edinburgh Festival, Scotland, with fringe theatre events.
1949	Bertolt Brecht and Helene Weigel founded the Berliner Ensemble in East Germany.
1953	Arthur Miller's *The Crucible* opened in the USA; *En attendant Godot/Waiting for Godot* by Samuel Beckett exemplified the Theatre of the Absurd.
1956	The English Stage Company was formed at the Royal Court Theatre to provide a platform for new dramatists. John Osborne's *Look Back in Anger* was included in its first season.
1957	Leonard Bernstein's *West Side Story* opened in New York.
1960	Harold Pinter's *The Caretaker* was produced in London.
1960s	Off-off-Broadway theatre, a more daring and experimental type of drama, began to develop in New York. Fringe theatre developed in Britain.
1961	The Royal Shakespeare Company was formed in the UK under the directorship of Peter Hall.
1963–64	The UK National Theatre Company was formed at the Old Vic under the directorship of Laurence Olivier.
1964	Théâtre du Soleil, directed by Ariane Mnouchkine, founded in Paris.
1967	Athol Fugard founded the Serpent Players as an integrated company in Port Elizabeth, South Africa; success in the USA of *Hair,* the first of the 'rock' musicals; Tom Stoppard's *Rosencrantz and Guildenstern are Dead* was produced in London.
1968	Abolition of pre-censorship theatre in the UK.
1970	Peter Brook founded his international company, the International Centre for Theatre Research, in Paris; first festival of Chicano theatre in the USA.
1970s	Women's theatre movement developed in the USA and Europe.
1972	Sam Shepherd's *The Tooth of Crime* performed in London.
1974	Athol Fugard's *Statements After an Arrest under the Immorality Act* performed in London.
1975	*A Chorus Line,* to become the longest-running musical, opened in New York; Tadeusz Kantor's *Dead Class* produced in Poland.
1980	Howard Brenton's *The Romans in Britain* led in the UK to a private prosecution of the director for obscenity; David Edgar's *The Life and Times of Nicholas Nickleby* performed in London.
1985	Peter Brook's first production of *The Mahabharata* produced at the Avignon Festival.
1987	The Japanese Ninagawa Company performed Shakespeare's *Macbeth* in London.
1989	Discovery of the remains of the 16th-century Rose and Globe theatres, London.
1990	The Royal Shakespeare Company suspended its work at the Barbican Centre, London, for six months, pleading lack of funds.
1992	Ariane Mnouchkine's production of *Les Atrides* performed in Paris and the UK; Robert Wilson's production of *Alice* performed in Germany.
1993	Construction of the new Globe Theatre, a replica of the Elizabethan Globe Playhouse, began in London, approximately 183 m/600 ft from the site of the original Globe.
1994	The Abbey Theatre in Dublin produced Frank McGuinness's *Observe the Sons of Ulster Marching Towards the Somme* as a gesture of peace and reconciliation following the declaration of the Northern Ireland ceasefire.
1995	The National Lottery in the UK began to distribute millions of pounds to the theatre. However, most was allocated to the large prestigious concerns, and many small and medium-scale touring companies were left disappointed.
1996	Trevor Nunn was appointed director of the Royal National Theatre in London. The Prologue Season at the new Globe Theatre in London opened with *The Two Gentlemen of Verona.*
1998	London theatre played host to many Hollywood stars, including Liam Neeson, Kevin Spacey, and Juliet Binoche.

Top 10 Most Performed Playwrights

April 1996–March 1997

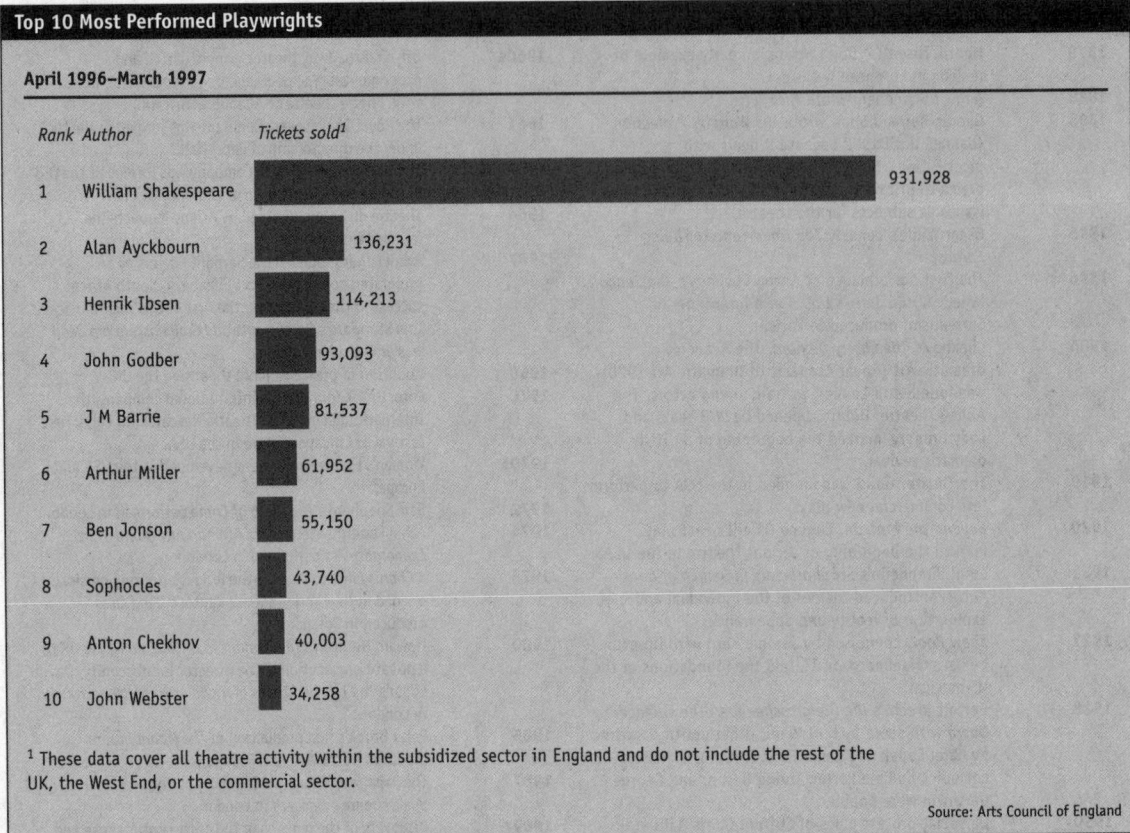

Rank	Author	Tickets sold[1]
1	William Shakespeare	931,928
2	Alan Ayckbourn	136,231
3	Henrik Ibsen	114,213
4	John Godber	93,093
5	J M Barrie	81,537
6	Arthur Miller	61,952
7	Ben Jonson	55,150
8	Sophocles	43,740
9	Anton Chekhov	40,003
10	John Webster	34,258

[1] These data cover all theatre activity within the subsidized sector in England and do not include the rest of the UK, the West End, or the commercial sector.

Source: Arts Council of England

Shakespeare's Plays

Title	First performed/written (approximate)	Title	First performed/written (approximate)
Early Plays		**The 'Great' or 'Middle' Comedies**	
Henry VI Part I	1589–92	A Midsummer Night's Dream	1594–95
Henry VI Part II	1590–91	The Merchant of Venice	1596–98
Henry VI Part III	1590–92	Much Ado About Nothing	1598
The Comedy of Errors	1591–93	As You Like It	1599–1600
The Taming of the Shrew	1593–94	The Merry Wives of Windsor	1597
Titus Andronicus	1593–94	Twelfth Night	1600–02
The Two Gentlemen of Verona	1590–95		
Love's Labour's Lost	1593–95	**The Great Tragedies**	
Romeo and Juliet	1594–95	Hamlet	1601–02
		Othello	1604
Histories		King Lear	1605–06
Richard III	1592–93	Macbeth	1606
Richard II	1595–97	Timon of Athens	1607–08
King John	1595–97		
Henry IV Part I	1596–97	**The 'Dark' Comedies**	
Henry IV Part II	1596–97	Troilus and Cressida	1601–02
Henry V	1599	All's Well That Ends Well	1602–03
		Measure for Measure	1604
Roman Plays			
Julius Caesar	1599	**Late Plays**	
Antony and Cleopatra	1606–07	Pericles	1606–08
Coriolanus	1608	Cymbeline	1609–10
		The Winter's Tale	1611
		The Tempest	1611
		Henry VIII	1613

Theatres and Theatre-Going in the UK

Item	1991	1992	1993	1994	1995	1996
Number of performances	28,870	29,832	27,053	26,123	23,931	22,628
Number of tickets sold	12,152,791	12,119,531	11,342,495	11,285,791	9,499,491	8,769,493
Seats offered for sale	20,885,597	21,202,862	18,934,387	19,309,381	16,818,785	15,594,179
% of tickets sold	58.2	57.2	59.9	58.4	56.5	56.2
Value of tickets sold (£)	101,755,958	110,643,218	113,940	120,968,507	104,576,349	94,456,887
Value of tickets offered for sale (£)	179,334,654	201,915,987	199,250,618	212,511,859	191,328,404	179,662,566
% of cash value achieved	56.7	54.8	57.2	56.9	54.7	52.6
Average number of seats sold per performance	421	406	419	432	397	388
Average number of seats offered per performance	723	711	700	739	703	689
Total income retained after deduction of VAT (£)	88,483,442	94,164,441	96,970,504	102,951,921	89,001,148	80,388,840
VAT to government on tickets alone (£)	13,272,516	16,478,777	16,969,838	18,016,586	15,575,201	14,068,047

Source: Theatrical Managers Association

Major Film Stars Who Have Recently Appeared on the UK Stage

Name	Play	Theatre	Date
Juliette Binoche	Naked	Almeida, London	winter 1998
Julie Christie	Suzanna Andler	Chichester	summer 1997
Ralph Fiennes	Ivanov	Almeida, London	spring 1997
Isabelle Huppert	Mary Stuart	Lyttleton, London	spring 1996
Ben Kingsley	Waiting for Godot	Old Vic, London	autumn 1997
Jessica Lange	A Streetcar Named Desire	Haymarket, London	spring 1997
Liam Neeson	The Judas Kiss	Playhouse, London	spring 1998
Kevin Spacey	The Iceman Cometh	Almeida, London	spring 1998
Kathleen Turner	Tallulah, Our Betters	Chichester	summer 1997
Gene Wilder	Laughter on the 23rd Floor	Queen's, London	winter 1996

Andrew Lloyd Webber Productions Showing around the World

(As at March 1998.)

Show	Country/region	City
Aspects of Love	Hungary[1]	Budapest
	Germany[1]	Dresden
	Finland[1]	Seinajoen Kaupunginteatteri
Cats	UK	London
	USA	New York (NY)
	USA	National tour
	Germany	Hamburg
	Hungary[1]	Budapest
Jesus Christ Superstar	UK	London
	Czech Republic	Prague
Joseph and the Amazing Technicolour Dreamcoat	Canada	National tour
	Hungary[1]	Budapest
	Slovak Republic[1]	Bratislava
	Germany	Essen
	USA[1]	Carousel National Tour
	Southeast Asia	Tour
Starlight Express	UK	London
	Germany	Bochum
	Mexico[1]	Mexico City
Sunset Boulevard	Germany	Frankfurt
The Phantom of the Opera	UK	London
	USA	New York (NY)
		San Francisco (CA)
	Japan	Nagoya
	Canada	Toronto
	Germany	Hamburg
	Australia	Melbourne

[1] Non-replica shows.

Source: Really Useful Group

Some Important Regional Theatres in the UK

Birmingham Repertory Theatre Centenary Square, Broad Street, Birmingham B1 2EP; phone: (0121) 236 6771; artistic director: Bill Alexander

Theatre Royal King Street, Bristol BS1 4ED; phone: (0117) 949 3993; artistic director: Andy Hay

Royal Lyceum Theatre Grindlay Street, Edinburgh EH3 9AX; phone: (0131) 229 7404; artistic director: Kenny Ireland

Citizen's Theatre Gorbals, Glasgow G5 9DS; phone: (0141) 429 5561; artistic director: Giles Havergal

West Yorkshire Playhouse Playhouse Square, Quarry Hill, Leeds LS2 7UP; phone: (0113) 244 2141; artistic director: Jude Kelly

Haymarket Theatre Belgrave Gate, Leicester LE1 3YQ; phone: (0116) 253 0021; artistic director: Paul Kerryson

Royal Exchange Theatre Upper Campfield Market, Liverpool Road, Manchester M2 5HD; phone: (0161) 833 9333; artistic directors: Braham Murray, Greg Hersov

Nottingham Playhouse Wellington Circus, Nottingham NG1 5AF; phone: (0115) 947 4361; artistic director: Martin Duncan

Theatre Royal Royal Parade, Plymouth, Devon PL1 2TR; phone: (01752) 668282

Stephen Joseph Theatre Westborough, Scarborough YO11 1JW; phone: (01723) 370540; artistic director: Alan Ayckbourn

Music

Top 40 Singles of the Year in the UK

1997

Rank	Title	Artist (label)
1	'Something About the Way/ Candle in the Wind, 1997'	Elton John (Rocket)
2	'Barbie Girl'	Aqua (Universal)
3	'I'll Be Missing You'	Puff Daddy & Faith Evans (Puff Daddy)
4	'Perfect Day'	Various artists (Chrysalis)
5	'Teletubbies Say Eh-Oh!'	Teletubbies (BBC Worldwide Music)
6	'Men in Black'	Will Smith (Columbia)
7	'Don't Speak'	No Doubt (Interscope)
8	'Torn'	Natalie Imbruglia (RCA)
9	'Tubthumping'	Chumbawamba (EMI)
10	'Spice Up Your Life'	Spice Girls (Virgin)
11	'Mmm Bop'	Hanson (Mercury)
12	'D'You Know What I Mean?'	Oasis (Creation)
13	'Never Ever'	All Saints (London)
14	'I Believe I Can Fly'	R Kelly (Jive)
15	'Mama/Who Do You Think You Are'	Spice Girls (Virgin)
16	'I Wanna be the Only One'	Eternal featuring Bebe Winans (EMI)
17	'Freed from Desire'	Gala (Big Life)
18	'Where Do You Go'	No Mercy (Arista)
19	'Sunchyme'	Dario G (Eternal)
20	'Free'	Ultra Nate (AM:PM)
21	'Encore une fois'	Sash! (Multiply)
22	'Too Much'	Spice Girls (Virgin)
23	'Time to Say Goodbye (Con te partiro)'	Sarah Brightman/Andrea Bocelli (Coalition)
24	'Bellissima'	DJ Quicksilver (Positiva)
25	'As Long as You Love Me'	Backstreet Boys (Jive)
26	'Baby Can I Hold You/ Shooting Star'	Boyzone (Polydor)
27	'Ecuador'	Sash! featuring Rodriguez (Multiply)
28	'Wind Beneath My Wings'	Steven Houghton (RCA)
29	'Don't Let Go (Love)'	En Vogue (East West)
30	'Stay'	Sash! featuring La Trec (Multiply)
31	'Lovefool'	Cardigans (Stockholm)
32	'The Drugs Don't Work'	Verve (Hut)
33	'Tell Him'	Barbra Streisand and Celine Dion (Epic)
34	'Together Again'	Janet Jackson (Virgin)
35	'2 Become 1'	Spice Girls (Virgin)
36	'You Might Need Somebody'	Shola Ama (WEA)
37	'You're Not Alone'	Olive (RCA)
38	'Everybody (Backstreet's Back)'	Backstreet Boys (Jive)
39	'Angels'	Robbie Williams (Chrysalis)
40	'C U When U Get There'	Coolio Feat 40 Thevz (Tommy Boy)

Source: Chart Information Network

Top 40 Albums of the Year in the UK

1997

Rank	Title	Artist (label)
1	Be Here Now	Oasis (Creation)
2	Urban Hymns	Verve (Hut)
3	Spice	Spice Girls (Virgin)
4	White on Blonde	Texas (Mercury)
5	Spiceworld	Spice Girls (Virgin)
6	The Fat of the Land	Prodigy (XL Recordings)
7	Let's Talk About Love	Celine Dion (Epic)
8	OK Computer	Radiohead (Parlophone)
9	Greatest Hits	Eternal (EMI)
10	The Best Of	Wham (Epic)
11	Ocean Drive	Lighthouse Family (Wild Card)
12	Backstreet's Back	Backstreet Boys (Jive)
13	Older	George Michael (Virgin)
14	Postcards from Heaven	Lighthouse Family (Wild Card)
15	Sheryl Crow	Sheryl Crow (A&M)
16	Travelling Without Moving	Jamiroquai (Sony S2)
17	Fresco	M People (M People)
18	Lennon Legend – The Very Best Of	John Lennon (Parlophone)
19	Paint the Sky with Stars – The Best Of	Enya (WEA)
20	All Saints	All Saints (London)
21	Blue Is the Colour	Beautiful South (Go! Discs)
22	Like You Do...Best Of	Lightning Seeds (Epic)
23	Evita	Original cast recording (Warner Bros)
24	Everything Must Go	Manic Street Preachers (Epic)
25	Pop	U2 (Island)
26	Tragic Kingdom	No Doubt (Interscope)
27	Falling into You	Celine Dion (Epic)
28	Secrets	Toni Braxton (Laface)
29	Blur	Blur (Food)
30	Their Greatest Hits	Hot Chocolate (EMI)
31	Marchin' Already	Ocean Colour Scene (MCA)
32	Do It Yourself	Seahorses (Geffen)
33	Stoosh	Skunk Anansie (One Little Indian)
34	Always on My Mind – Ultimate Love Songs	Elvis Presley (RCA)
35	(What's the Story) Morning Glory?	Oasis (Creation)
36	Glow	Reef (Sony S2)
37	The Big Picture	Elton John (Rocket)
38	Tellin' Stories	Charlatans (Beggars Banquet)
39	K	Kula Shaker (Columbia)
40	It's My Life – The Album	Sash! (Multiply)

Source: Chart Information Network

Top 40 Classical Albums of the Year in the UK

1997

Rank	Title	Artist (label)
1	*Most Relaxing Classical Album...Ever!*	Various Artists (Virgin/EMI)
2	*Diana, Princess of Wales 1961–1997*	Various Artists (BBC Worldwide Music)
3	*Adiemus II – Cantata Mundi*	Adiemus (Venture)
4	*A Soprano Inspired*	Lesley Garrett (Conifer Classics)
5	*Songs of Sanctuary*	Adiemus (Venture)
6	*Shine (soundtrack)*	David Hirschfelder (Philips)
7	*Best Opera Album in the World...Ever!*	Various Artists (Virgin)
8	*Salva Nos*	Mediaeval Baebes (Venture)
9	*Agnus Dei*	Choir of New College, Oxford/Edward Higginbottom (Erato)
10	*100 Popular Classics*	Various Artists (Castle Communication)
11	*Braveheart (soundtrack)*	London Symphony Orchestra/Horner (Decca)
12	*The Greatest Classical Movie Album*	Various Artists (Telstar)
13	*The Ultimate Collection*	Luciano Pavarotti (Decca)
14	*The English Patient (soundtrack)*	(Fantasy)
15	*Best Classical Album in the World...Ever!*	Various Artists (Virgin/EMI)
16	*Dies Irae – Essential Choral Collection*	Various Artists (Deutsche Grammophon)
17	*Paul McCartney's Standing Stone*	London Symphony Orchestra/Foster (EMI Classics)
18	*Tavener – Innocence*	Soloists/Westminster Abbey Choir/Neary (Sony Classical)
19	*The Soprano's Greatist Hits*	Lesley Garrett (Silva Classics)
20	*The Piano (soundtrack)*	Michael Nyman (Venture)
21	*Classic Hits*	Various Artists (Erato)
22	*The Voice of the Century*	Maria Callas (EMI)
23	*Brassed Off (soundtrack)*	Grimethorpe Colliery Band (RCA Victor)
24	*Silence*	Various Artists (Sony TV)
25	*Gregorian Moods*	Monks and Choirboys of Downside Abbey (Virgin/EMI)
26	*The Classical Album 1*	Vanessa-Mae (EMI Classics)
27	*The No 1 Classical Album*	Various Artists (Decca/DG/Philips/PTV)
28	*Elgar – Violin Concerto*	Nigel Kennedy/City of Birmingham Symphony Orchestra/Simon Rattle (EMI Classics)
29	*The Voice*	Luciano Pavarotti (Hallmark)
30	*Wings of a Dove*	Anthony Way (Decca)
31	*Rachmaninov – Piano Concerto 3*	David Helfgott (Red Seal)
32	*The Entertainer – The Very Best of Scott Joplin*	(Nonesuch)
33	*Stars Wars – A New Hope (soundtrack)*	London Symphony Orchestra/John Williams (RCA Victor)
34	*The Greatest Opera Show on Earth*	Various Artists (Decca)
35	*Vivaldi – Four Seasons*	Nigel Kennedy (EMI Classics)
36	*Prokofiev – Peter and the Wolf*	Dame Edna Everage/Mel So/Lanchbery (Naxos)
37	*Something Wonderful*	Bryn Terfel (Deutsche Grammophon)
38	*Ultimate Carol Collection*	Anthony Way/King's College Choir, Cambridge (Decca)
39	*A Lasting Inspiration*	Jacqueline du Pre (EMI Classics)
40	*Blow the Wind Southerly – The Art of Kathleen Ferrier*	(Decca)

Luciano Pavarotti

© Polygram

Source: Chart Information Network

Top Grossing North American Concerts of the Year

1997

Rank	Artist	Venue	Location	Total number of performances	Total gross ($ millions)
1	The Rolling Stones	Oakland Stadium	Oakland (CA)	4	10.86
2	'3 Tenors' (Carreras, Domingo, Pavarotti)	Toronto Skydome	Toronto (ONT)	1	8.16
3	The Rolling Stones	Giants Stadium	East Rutherford (NJ)	2	6.82
4	Luis Miguel	Auditorio Nacional	Mexico City	17	6.77
5	U2	Giants Stadium	East Rutherford (NJ)	3	6.50
6	The Rolling Stones	Soldier Field Stadium	Chicago (IL)	2	6.26
7	U2	Soldier Field Stadium	Chicago (IL)	3	5.96
8	The Rolling Stones	Dodger Stadium	Los Angeles (CA)	2	5.34
9	The Rolling Stones	Foxboro Stadium	Foxboro (MA)	2	4.84
10	U2	Foxboro Stadium	Foxboro (MA)	2	4.79

Source: Pollstar

Top Grossing North American Concert Tours of the Year

1997

Rank	Artist	Number of cities	Number of shows	Total gross ($ millions)
1	The Rolling Stones	26	33	89.3
2	U2	37	46	79.9
3	Fleetwood Mac	40	44	36.3
4	Metallica	65	77	34.1
5	Brooks and Dunn/Reba McEntire	66	69	33.0
6	Garth Brooks	28	110	26.9
7	Tina Turner	56	70	24.8
8	The Artist (formerly known as Prince)	71	73	24.6
9	Jimmy Buffett	31	44	24.4
10	Aerosmith	60	63	22.3

Source: Pollstar

Selected Symphony and Chamber Orchestras in the UK

Orchestra	Director
The Academy of Ancient Music	Christopher Hogwood
Academy of London	Richard Stamp
Academy of St Martin in the Fields	Neville Marriner
Academy of the London Mozarteum	Robert Hamwee
Ambache Chamber Orchestra	Diana Ambache
BBC Concert Orchestra	Barry Wordsworth
BBC National Orchestra of Wales	Mark Wigglesworth
BBC Philharmonic	Yan Pascal Tortelier
BBC Scottish Symphony Orchestra	Osmo Vänskä
BBC Symphony Orchestra	Andrew Davis
Bournemouth Sinfonietta	Alexander Polianichko
Bournemouth Symphony Orchestra	Yakov Kreizberg
The Brandenburg Consort	Roy Goodman
The Brandenburg Orchestra	Robert Porter
The Britten Sinfonia	Nicholas Cleobury
CBSO (City of Birmingham Symphony Orchestra)	Simon Rattle

Simon Rattle

© EMI

Orchestra	Director
Charivari Agréable Simfonie	Kah-Ming Ng
City of London Sinfonia	Richard Hickox
City of Oxford Orchestra	Marios Papadopoulos
Corydon Orchestra	Matthew Best
East of England Orchestra	Nicholas Kok
English Baroque Orchestra	Leon Lovett
English Camerata	Elizabeth Altman
English Classical Players	Jonathan Brett
English National Opera Orchestra	Paul Daniel
English Northern Philharmonia	Richard Mantle
English Sinfonia	Bramwell Tovey
English String Orchestra	William Boughton

Orchestra	Director
English Symphony Orchestra	William Boughton
European Women's Orchestra	Odaline de la Martinez
Fiori Musicali	Penelope Rapson
Gabrieli Consort and Players	Paul McCreesh
Glyndebourne Touring Opera Orchestra	Ivor Bolton
Guildford Philharmonic Orchestra	En Shao
The Hallé Orchestra	Kent Nagano
The Hanover Band	Caroline Brown
The King's Consort	Robert King
London Chamber Orchestra	Christopher Warren-Green
London Handel Orchestra	Denys Darlow
London Jupiter Orchestra	Gregory Rose
London Mozart Players	Matthias Bamert
London Philharmonic Orchestra	Bernard Haitink
London Pro Arte Orchestra	Murray Stewart
London Sinfonietta	Markus Stenz
London Symphony Orchestra	Colin Davis
Manchester Camerata	Sachio Fujioka
Mozart Orchestra	Gordon Heard
New London Orchestra	Ronald Corp
New Queen's Hall Orchestra	John Boyden
Northern Sinfonia	Jean-Bernard Pommier
Orchestra da Camera	Kenneth Page
Orchestra of St John's Smith Square	John Lubbock
Orchestra of the Age of Enlightenment	Marshall Marcus
Orchestre Révolutionnaire et Romantique	John Eliot Gardiner
Oxford Orchestra da Camera	Patricia Bavaud
Philharmonia Orchestra	Christoph von Dohnányi
Philomusica of London	David Littaur
The Royal Liverpool Philharmonic Orchestra	Petr Altrichter
Royal Opera House Orchestra	Bernard Haitink
Royal Philharmonic Concert Orchestra	Thomas Siracusa
Royal Scottish National Orchestra	Alexander Lazarev
The Scottish Chamber Orchestra	Joseph Swensen
Sinfonia 21	Dennis Stevenson
Taverner Players	Andrew Parrott
Ulster Orchestra	Michael Henson
Welsh Chamber Orchestra	Anthony Hose
Welsh National Opera Orchestra	Carlo Rizzi
Welsh Philharmonic Orchestra	G J Harries

Classical Music Festivals in the UK

Festival	Box office phone number	Date
England		
Aldeburgh Festival of Music and the Arts	(01728) 453543	June
Arundel Festival	(01903) 883690	August–September
Bath International Music Festival	(01225) 463362	May
Buxton Festival	(01298) 72190	July
Cheltenham International Festival of Music	(01242) 227979	July
Dartington International Summer School	(01803) 865988	July–August
Garsington Opera	(01865) 361636	June–July
Glyndebourne Festival Opera	(01273) 813813	May–August
Harrogate International Festival	(01423) 565757	July–August
Henley Festival of Music and the Arts	(01491) 411353	July
Leicester International Music Festival	(0116) 247 3043	June
London BBC Henry Wood Promenade Concerts	(0171) 589 8212	July–September
London Greenwich and Docklands International Festival	(0181) 305 1818	July[1]
London Festival of Chamber Music	(0171) 435 6232	September–October
London Handel Festival	(0181) 563 0618	March–May
London St Ceciliatide International Festival of Music	(01327) 361380	November
Malvern Elgar Festival	(01684) 892277	May–June
Manchester Hallé Proms Festival	(0161) 907 9000	June–July
Manchester RNCM Manchester International Cello Festival	(0161) 273 4504	April–May (biennially)
Norfolk and Norwich Festival	(01603) 764764	October
Oxford Festival of Contemporary Music	(01865) 261384	March–April, October–November
Salisbury Festival	(01722) 320333	May–June
Stratford upon Avon The English Music Festival	(01789) 261577	October
Three Choirs Festival[2]	(01452) 529819	August
Warwick and Leamington Festival	(01926) 496277	July
York Early Music Festival	(01904) 584123	July
Scotland		
Ayton Summer Music at Ayton Castle	(0141) 339 2708	July
Edinburgh International Festival	(0131) 473 2000	August–September
Glasgow International Early Music Festival	(0141) 333 1178	August (biennially)
Highland Festival	(01463) 719000	May–June
Orkney Islands St Magnus Festival	(01856) 872669	June
Scottish Proms	(0141) 226 3868	May–June
Wales		
Aberystwyth Musicfest	(01970) 622882	July
Beaumaris Festival	(01248) 440541	May–June
Cardiff Summer Festival	(01222) 873913	July–August
Carmarthen Festival/Gwyl Caerfyrddin	(01267) 290343	June–July
Llangollen International Musical Eisteddfod	(01978) 861501	July
Presteigne Festival of Music and the Arts	(01544) 267800	August
St David's Cathedral Festival	(01437) 720271	May
Swansea Festival	(01792) 475715	October
Wrexham Arts Festival	(01978) 292015	N/A
Northern Ireland		
Belfast Festival of Early Music	(01232) 335205	October (biennially)
Belfast Sonorities	(01232) 335105	May
Belfast Festival at Queen's	(01232) 665577	November
Castleward Opera Festival	(01232) 661090	June
Derry Two Cathedrals Festival	(01504) 262412	October
Portstewart Flowerfield Arts Festival	(01265) 833959	October[1]

[1] This date is provisional.
[2] Worcester 1999, Hereford 2000.

Selected Symphony Orchestras in Europe

Country	Orchestra	Director
Austria	Mozarteum Orchester	Hubert Soudant
	Wiener Philharmoniker	Clemens Hellsberg
	Wiener Symphoniker	Rainer Bischof
Belgium	Orchestre National de Belgique	Alain Pierlot
Bulgaria	Bulgarian National Radio Symphony Orchestra	Milen Natchev
Croatia	Dubrovnik Symphony Orchestra	Pero Glavinic
Czech Republic	Czech Philharmonic Orchestra	Ing Jiri Kovár
	Czech Symphony Orchestra	Jiri Kauders
Denmark	Danish National Radio Symphony Orchestra	Per Erik Veng
	Royal Danish Orchestra	Elaine Padmore
Estonia	Estonian National Symphony Orchestra	Neeme Kuningas
Finland	Finnish Radio Symphony Orchestra	Jukka-Pekka Saraste
France	Orchestre National de France	Charles Dutoit
	Orchestre Philharmonique de Radio-France	Marek Janowski
Germany	Bayerische Staatsorchester	Zubin Mehta
	Leipziger Gewandhausorchester	Kurt Masur
	Radio-Sinfonie-Orchester Frankfurt	Dmitrij Kitajenko
Hungary	Hungarian National Philharmonic Orchestra	Gilbert Varga
Ireland, Republic of	National Symphony Orchestra of Ireland	Kasper de Roo
	RTE Concert Orchestra	Proinnsias O Duinn
Italy	Orchestra dell'Arena	Paula Bonnetti
	Toscanini Symphony Orchestra	Antonello Zangrandi
	Orchestra Sinfonica di Roma della Radiotelevisione Italiana	Michelangelo Zurletti
	Orchestra Sinfonica Nazionale della RAI	Sergio Sablich
Latvia	Latvian National Symphony Orchestra	Terje Mikkelsen
Lithuania	Lithuanian National Symphony Orchestra	Juozas Domarkas
	Lithuanian State Symphony Orchestra	Gintaras Rinkevicius
Luxembourg	Orchestre Philharmonique du Luxembourg	Jacques Mauroy
Moldova	National Orchestra for Radio and Television	Gheorghe Ion Mustea
Monaco	Orchestre Philharmonique de Monte-Carlo	James DePreist
Netherlands	Netherlands Philharmonic Orchestra	Jan Willem Loot
	Netherlands Radio Philharmonic	Edo de Waart
	Royal Concertgebouw Orchestra	Riccardo Chailly
Norway	Oslo Philharmonic Orchestra	Trond Okkelmo
Poland	Polish Radio National Symphony Orchestra	Antoni Wit
	Warsaw Philharmonic	Kazimierz Kord
Portugal	Gulbenkian Orchestra	Muhai Tang
	Lisbon Metropolitan Orchestra	Miguel Graça Moura
Russia	Bolshoi Symphony Orchestra	Aleksandr Lazarev
	Russian National Symphony Orchestra	Mikhail Pletnev
	Russian State Philharmonic Orchestra	Valery Poliansky
Slovak Republic	Slovak Radio Symphonic Orchestra	R Stankovsky
Slovenia	Slovenian Philharmonic	Boris Sinigoj
Spain	Bilbao Symphony Orchestra	Theo Alcántara
	National Orchestra and Chorus of Spain	Tomás Marco
	Orquesta Sinfónica de Barcelona i Nacional de Catalunya	Lawrence Foster
Sweden	Royal Stockholm Philharmonic Orchestra	Gennady Rozhdestvensky
	Swedish Radio Symphony Orchestra	Esa-Pekka Salonen
Switzerland	Berner Symphonie-Orchester	Dmitrij Kitajenko
	Orchestre de la Suisse Romande	Armin Jordan
	Tonhalle-Orchester Zürich	David Zinman
Ukraine	National Symphony Orchestra of Ukraine	Theodore Kuchar
	Ukrainian TV and Radio Symphony Orchestra	V Ph Syrenko

Some Major Opera Companies in the UK

Company	Director	Company	Director
British Youth Opera	Timothy Dean	New Sussex Opera	David Angus
Central Festival Opera Ltd	Tom Hawkes	Northern Opera Ltd	Richard Bloodworth
City of Birmingham Touring Opera	Graham Vick	Opera Box Ltd	Fraser Goulding
Dorset Opera	Patrick Shelley	Opera da Camera	Derek Barnes
English Festival Opera	Simon Gray	Opera Europa	John Gibbons
English National Opera	Dennis Marks	Opera Factory	David Freeman
English Touring Opera	Andrew Greenwood	Opera North	Richard Mantle
European Chamber Opera	Stefan Paul Sanchez	Opera Northern Ireland	Stephen Barlow
First Act Opera International	Elaine Holden	Opera Restor'd	Peter Holman
Garsington Opera Ltd	Leonard Ingrams	Pimlico Opera	Wasfi Kani
Glyndebourne Festival Opera	Andrew Davis	Pocket Opera	Michael Armitage
Glyndebourne Touring Opera	Louis Langrée	Royal Opera	Bernard Haitink
London Chamber Opera	David Wordsworth	Scottish Early Music Consort	Warwick Edwards
London Community Opera	Peter Bridges	Scottish Opera	Richard Armstrong
Midsummer Opera	David Roblou	South Yorkshire Opera Ltd	Nita White
Millenium Opera	James Kelleher	Surrey Opera	Jonathan Butcher
Music Theatre London	Tony Britten	Travelling Opera	Peter Knapp
Music Theatre Wales	Michael Rafferty	Welsh National Opera	Carlo Rizzi
National Youth Music Theatre	Jeremy James Taylor		
New Chamber Opera	Gary Cooper		

Bernard Haitink

© EMI

Some Major World Opera Companies

(N/A = not available.)

Country	Company	Director	Country	Company	Director
Argentina	Teatro Colon	Kive Staiff	Ireland, Republic of	Opera Ireland	Fergus Shiel
Australia	Opera Australia	Moffatt Oxenbould	Italy	L'Arena di Verona	Mauro Trombetta
	The State Opera of South Australia	Bill Gillespie		Teatro Alla Scala	Riccardo Muti
	West Australian Opera	Richard Mills		Teatro di San Carlo	Filippo Zigante
Austria	Salzburger Landestheater	Lutz Hochstraate		Teatro La Fenice	Francesco Siciliani
	Wiener Staatsoper	Ioan Holender	Japan	Opera Theatre/Konnyakuza	Hikaru Hayashi
	Wiener Volksoper	Ioan Holender	Monaco	L'Opéra de Monte-Carlo	John Mordler
Bulgaria	Opera National de Sofia	Rouslan Raichev	Netherlands	De Nederlandse Opera	Pierre Audi
Canada	Calgary Opera	David Speers		International Opera Centrum Nederland	Hans Nieuwenhuis
	Edmonton Opera	Irving Guttman	New Zealand	Auckland Opera Company	Stephen Morrison
	L'Opéra de Montréal	Bernard Uzan		Wellington City Opera	Patricia Hurley
	Opéra de Québec	Bernard Labadie	Norway	Den Norske Opera	Bernt E Bauge
	Opera Ontario	Daniel Lipton	Poland	National Theatre/Teatr Narodowy	Grzegorz Nowak
	Vancouver Opera	David Agler		Warsaw Chamber Opera	Stefan Sutowski
China	Central Opera Theatre	Wang Shi-guang	Russia	Bolshoi Theatre of Opera and Ballet	N/A
Czech Republic	The National Theatre Opera/ Národní Divadlo	Josef Prudek		Mariisky Theatre	Valery Gergyev
Denmark	The Royal Danish Opera	Elaine Padmore	Slovak Republic	Slovak National Theatre	Ondrej Lenárd
Finland	Finnish National Opera	Okko Kamu	South Africa	Opera of the Cape Performing Arts	Angelo Gobbato
France	L'Opéra Comique	Pierre Medecin	Sweden	Royal Swedish Opera	Walton Grönroos
	Opéra National de Paris-Bastille	Pierre Bergé		Swedish Folkopera	Claes Fellbom
Germany	Bayerische Staatsoper	Zubin Mehta	Switzerland	Grand Théâtre de Genève	Renée Auphan
	Deutsche Oper Berlin	Christian Tuielemann		Opernhaus Zürich	Franz Welser-Möst
	Komische Oper	Yakov Kreizberg	USA	Baltimore Opera Company	William Yannuzzi
	Staatsoper Unter den Linden	Daniel Barenboim		Cleveland Opera	David Bamberger
Hungary	The Hungarian State Opera	Géza Oberfrank		The Metropolitan Opera	James Levine

Major Operas and their First Performances

Date	Opera	Composer	Librettist	Location[1]
1607	Orfeo	Monteverdi	Striggio	Mantua, Italy
1642	The Coronation of Poppea	Monteverdi	Busenello	Venice, Italy
1689	Dido and Aeneas	Purcell	Tate	London, UK
1724	Julius Caesar in Egypt	Handel	Haym	London, UK
1762	Orpheus and Eurydice	Gluck	Calzabigi	Vienna, Austria
1786	The Marriage of Figaro	Mozart	Da Ponte	Vienna, Austrua
1787	Don Giovanni	Mozart	Da Ponte	Prague, Czech Republic
1790	Così fan tutte	Mozart	Da Ponte	Vienna, Austria
1791	The Magic Flute	Mozart	Schikaneder	Vienna, Austria
1805	Fidelio	Beethoven	Sonnleithner	Vienna, Austria
1816	The Barber of Seville	Rossini	Sterbini	Rome, Italy
1821	Der Freischütz	Weber	Kind	Berlin, Germany
1831	Norma	Bellini	Romani	Milan, Italy
1835	Lucia di Lammermoor	Donizetti	Cammarano	Naples, Italy
1836	Les Huguenots	Meyerbeer	Scribe	Paris, France
1842	Ruslan and Lyudmila	Glinka	Shirkov/Bakhturin	St Petersburg, Russia
1850	Lohengrin	Wagner	Wagner	Weimar, Germany
1851	Rigoletto	Verdi	Piave	Venice, Italy
1853	Il Trovatore	Verdi	Cammarano	Rome, Italy
	La Traviata	Verdi	Piave	Venice, Italy
1859	Faust	Gounod	Barbier/Carré	Paris, France
1865	Tristan und Isolde	Wagner	Wagner	Munich, Germany
1866	The Bartered Bride	Smetana	Sabina	Prague, Czech Republic
1868	Die Meistersinger von Nürnberg	Wagner	Wagner	Munich, Germany
1871	Aida	Verdi	Ghislanzoni	Cairo, Egypt
1874	Boris Godunov	Mussorgsky	Mussorgsky	St Petersburg, Russia
	Die Fledermaus	Johann Strauss II	Haffner/Genée	Vienna, Austria
1875	Carmen	Bizet	Meilhac/Halévy	Paris, France
1876	The Ring of the Nibelung	Wagner	Wagner	Bayreuth, Germany
1879	Eugene Onegin	Tchaikovsky	Tchaikovsky/Shilovsky	Moscow, Russia
1881	The Tales of Hoffman	Offenbach	Barbier	Paris, France
1882	Parsifal	Wagner	Wagner	Bayreuth, Germany
1885	The Mikado	Sullivan	Gilbert	London, UK
1887	Otello	Verdi	Boito	Milan, Italy
1890	Cavalleria Rusticana	Mascagni	Menasci/Targioni-Tozzetti	Rome, Italy
	Prince Igor	Borodin	Borodin	St Petersburg, Russia
1892	I Pagliacci	Leoncavallo	Leoncavallo	Milan, Italy
	Werther	Massenet	Blau/Milliet/Hartman	Vienna, Austria
1896	La Bohème	Puccini	Giacosa/Illica	Turin, Italy
1900	Tosca	Puccini	Giacosa/Illica	Rome, Italy
1902	Pelléas et Mélisande	Debussy	Maeterlinck	Paris, France
1904	Jenufa	Janáček	Janáček	Brno, Czech Republic
	Madame Butterfly	Puccini	Giacosa/Illica	Milan, Italy
1905	Salome	Richard Strauss	Wilde/Lachmann	Dresden, Germany
1909	The Golden Cockerel	Rimsky-Korsakov	Bel'sky	Moscow, Russia
1911	Der Rosenkavalier	Richard Strauss	Hofmannsthal	Dresden, Germany
1918	Duke Bluebeard's Castle	Bartók	Balázs	Budapest, Hungary
1925	Wozzeck	Berg	Berg	Berlin, Germany
1935	Porgy and Bess	Gershwin	Ira Gershwin/Heyward	Boston, USA
1937	Lulu	Berg	Berg	Zürich, Switzerland
1945	Peter Grimes	Britten	Slater	London, UK
1946	War and Peace	Prokofiev	Prokofiev/Mendelson	St Petersburg, Russia
1951	The Rake's Progress	Stravinsky	Auden/Kallman	Venice, Italy
1978	Paradise Lost	Penderecki	Fry	Chicago, USA
1984	Akhnaten	Glass	Glass	Stuttgart, Germany
1986	The Mask of Orpheus	Birtwistle	Zinovieff	London, UK
1989	New Year	Tippett	Tippett	Houston, USA
1992	Dienstag aus LICHT	Stockhausen	Stockhausen	Lisbon, Portugal

[1] Present-day city and country names are given.

Some Musical Expressions

Expression	Meaning	Expression	Meaning
accelerando	gradually faster	*mezzo*	quite
adagio, adagietto	easy-going	*misterioso*	mysteriously
alla breve	four beat as two to the bar	*molto*	much, very
allargando	spreading out in tempo	*pesante*	weightily
allegro, allegretto	with lightness of action	*pianissimo*	very soft
andante, andantino	with movement	*piano*	soft
cantabile	singing	*poco, pochissimo*	a little, very little
con brio	with spirit	*portamento*	lifting (note to note)
con fuoco	with fire	*presto, prestissimo*	at speed, at high speed
crescendo	gradually louder	*ritardando*	gradually coming to a stop
da capo	from the top (beginning)	*ritenuto*	pulling back
diminuendo	gradually softer	*rubato*	borrowed (time)
divisi a 2, 3, etc.	divided in 2, 3, etc. parts	*segue*	follow on
dolce, dolcissimo	soft and sweetly	*sempre*	always
espressivo	with expression	*sforzato, sforzando*	with a forced tone
forte	loud	*smorzando*	smothering, stifling the tone
fortissimo	very loud	*sotto voce*	in an undertone
giocoso	with fun	*spiccato*	bounced (of the bow off the string)
grave	with gravity	*staccato, staccatissimo*	short, very short
largo, larghetto	expansively	*subito*	sudden, suddenly
legato	smoothly	*tenuto*	holding back
lento	slowly	*tranquillo*	calmly
loco	in (its usual) place	*vivo, vivace*	with life
lungo, lunga	long		

Top 5 Most Popular Operas Performed in the UK

April 1996–March 1997

Rank	Opera	Tickets sold
1	*La Bohème*	105,436
2	*La Traviata*	92,608
3	*The Marriage of Figaro*	72,294
4	*Rigoletto*	61,287
5	*Madame Butterfly*	46,987

Source: Arts Councils of England, Scotland, Wales, and Northern Ireland

Dance

Top 10 Most Popular Ballet Productions in the UK

April 1996–March 1997

Rank	Repertoire	Company	Tickets sold
1	*Nutcracker*	English National Ballet	80,430
2	*Nutcracker*	Kirov Ballet	47,690
3	*Alice in Wonderland*	English National Ballet	41,100
4	*Sleeping Beauty*	Birmingham Royal Ballet	39,217
5	*Dracula*	Northern Ballet Theatre	36,651
6	*Coppelia*	English National Ballet	35,579
7	*Nutcracker*	Birmingham Royal Ballet	32,869
8	*A Christmas Carol*	Northern Ballet Theatre	32,723
9	*Swan Lake*	Birmingham Royal Ballet	27,657
10	*Sleeping Beauty*	Royal Ballet	21,255

Source: Arts Councils of England, Scotland, Wales, and Northern Ireland

Top 5 Ballets by Repertoire in the UK

April 1996–March 1997

Rank	Repertoire	Tickets sold[1]
1	*Nutcracker*	172,966
2	*Swan Lake*	80,279
3	*Sleeping Beauty*	60,472
4	*Cinderella*	40,838
5	*Romeo and Juliet*	35,963

[1] This figure is a combined total from performances throughout the year by different ballet companies.

Source: Arts Councils of England, Scotland, Wales, and Northern Ireland

Top 5 Dance Companies by Budget in the UK

1 **Birmingham Royal Ballet** Birmingham Hippodrome, Thorp Street, Birmingham B5 4AU; phone: (0121) 622 2555; artistic director: David Bintley
2 **English National Ballet** Markova House, 39 Jay Mews, London SW7 2ES; phone: (0171) 581 1245; artistic director: Derek Deane
3 **Northern Ballet Theatre** West Park Centre, Spen Lane, Leeds LS16

5BE; phone: (0113) 274 5355; artistic director: Christopher Gable
4 **The Royal Ballet** Royal Opera House, Covent Garden, London WC2E 9DD; phone: (0171) 240 1200; artistic director: Anthony Dowell
5 **The Scottish Ballet** 261 West Princes Street, Glasgow G4 9EE; phone: (0141) 331 2931; acting artistic director: Ken Burke

Source: Arts Councils of England, Scotland, Wales, and Northern Ireland

Ballets and their First Performances

Date	Ballet	Composer	Choreographer	Location[1]
1670	Le Bourgeois Gentilhomme	Lully	Beauchamp	Chambord, France
1735	Les Indes galantes	Rameau	Blondy	Paris, France
1761	Don Juan	Gluck	Angiolini	Vienna, Austria
1778	Les Petits Riens	Mozart	Noverre	Paris, France
1801	The Creatures of Prometheus	Beethoven	Viganò	Vienna, Austria
1828	La Fille mal gardée	Hérold	Aumer	Paris, France
1832	La Sylphide	Schneitzhoeffer	F Taglioni	Paris, France
1841	Giselle	Coralli	Perrot	Paris, France
1842	Napoli	Gade/Helsted/Lumbye/Paulli	Bournonville	Copenhagen, Denmark
1844	La Esmeralda	Pugni	Perrot	London, UK
1869	Don Quixote	Minkus	M Petipa	Moscow, Russia
1870	Coppélia	Delibes	Saint-Léon	Paris, France
1877	La Bayadère	Minkus	M Petipa	St Petersburg, Russia
	Swan Lake	Tchaikovsky	Reisinger	Moscow, Russia
1890	The Sleeping Beauty	Tchaikovsky	M Petipa	St Petersburg, Russia
1892	Nutcracker	Tchaikovsky	M Petipa/Ivanov	St Petersburg, Russia
1898	Raymonda	Glazunov	M Petipa	St Petersburg, Russia
1905	The Dying Swan	Saint-Saëns	Fokine	St Petersburg, Russia
1909	Les Sylphides/Chopiniana	Chopin	Fokine	St Petersburg, Russia
1910	The Firebird	Stravinsky	Fokine	Paris, France
1911	Petrushka	Stravinsky	Fokine	Paris, France
	Le Spectre de la rose	Weber	Fokine	Monte Carlo
1912	L'Après-midi d'un faune	Debussy	Nijinsky	Paris, France
1913	Le Sacre du printemps/The Rite of Spring	Stravinsky	Nijinsky	Paris, France
1917	Parade	Satie	Massine	Paris, France
1919	The Three-Cornered Hat	Falla	Massine	London, UK
1923	Les Noces	Stravinsky	Nijinska	Paris, France
1924	Les Biches	Poulenc	Nijinska	Monte Carlo
1927	The Red Poppy	Glière	Lashchilin/Tikhomirov	Moscow, Russia
1928	Apollo	Stravinsky	Balanchine	Paris, France
1929	The Prodigal Son	Prokofiev	Balanchine	Paris, France
	La Valse	Ravel	Nijinska	Monte Carlo
1931	Façade	Walton	Ashton	London, UK
1937	Checkmate	Bliss	de Valois	Paris, France
	Les Patineurs	Meyerbeer/Lambert	Ashton	London, UK
	Romeo and Juliet	Prokofiev	Psota	Brno, Czech Republic
1938	Billy the Kid	Copland	Loring	Chicago, USA
1942	The Miraculous Mandarin	Bartók	Milloss	Milan, Italy
	Rodeo	Copland	deMille	New York, USA
1944	Fancy Free	Bernstein	Robbins	New York, USA
1949	Carmen	Bizet	Petit	London, UK
1951	Pineapple Poll	Sullivan/Mackerras	Cranko	London, UK
1956	Spartacus	Khachaturian	Jacobson	St Petersburg, Russia
1957	Agon	Stravinsky	Balanchine	New York, USA
1962	Pierrot lunaire	Schoenberg	Tetley	New York, USA
1964	The Dream	Mendelssohn/Lanchbery	Ashton	London, UK
1965	The Song of the Earth	Mahler	MacMillan	Stuttgart, Germany
1966	Romeo and Juliet	Prokofiev	MacMillan	London, UK
1968	Enigma Variations	Elgar	Ashton	London, UK
1969	The Taming of the Shrew	Scarlatti/Stolze	Cranko	Stuttgart, Germany
1972	Duo Concertante	Stravinsky	Balanchine	New York, USA
1974	Elite Syncopations	Joplin and others	MacMillan	London, UK
1976	A Month in the Country	Chopin/Lanchbery	Ashton	London, UK
1978	Mayerling	Liszt/Lanchbery	MacMillan	London, UK
	Symphony of Psalms	Stravinsky	Kylian	Scheveningen, Netherlands
1980	Gloria	Poulenc	MacMillan	London, UK
	Rhapsody	Rachmaninov	Ashton	London, UK
1982	The Golden Age	Shostakovich	Grigorovich	Moscow, Russia
1984	Different Drummer	Webern/Schoenberg	MacMillan	London, UK
1986	The Snow Queen	Tovey/Mussorgsky	Bintley	Birmingham, UK
1988	L'allegro, il penseroso ed il moderato	Handel	Morris	Brussels, Belgium
1989	The Prince of the Pagodas	Britten	MacMillan	London, UK
1991	Winter Dreams	Tchaikovsky	MacMillan	London, UK
1992	Making of Maps	Hatzis/Ramamani/MacDonald	Jeyasingh	London, UK
	The Judas Tree	Elias	MacMillan	London, UK
1993	Body as Site	Fisher Turner/Cusack	Butcher	Glasgow, UK
	Delicious Arbour	Purcell (incidental music to Abdelazar)	Alston	Nottingham, UK
1994	Fearful Symmetries	Adams	Page	London, UK
	Metacholica	Madden	Anderson	London, UK
1995	Enter Achilles	DV8 Physical Theatre	Newson	Newcastle, UK
	Firstext	Bach	Forsythe	London, UK
1996	Swan Lake	Stravinsky	Bourne	London, UK
	Affections	Handel/Barry	Davies	London, UK
1997	Decoy Landscapes	Cowton	Maliphant	London, UK

[1] Present-day city and country names are given.

Art and Architecture

Top 10 Highest Prices Paid for Paintings Sold at Auction

Rank	Work	Artist	Place and date of sale	Price ($)
1	*Portrait of Dr Gachet*	Vincent van Gogh	Christie's, New York, 15 May 1990	75,000,000
2	*Au Moulin de la Galette*	Pierre-Auguste Renoir	Sotheby's, New York, 17 May 1990	71,000,000
3	*Les Noces de Pierette*	Pablo Picasso	Binoche et Godeau, Paris, 30 November 1989	51,671,920
4	*Irises*	Vincent van Gogh	Sotheby's, New York, 11 November 1987	49,000,000
5	*Le Rêve*	Pablo Picasso	Christie's, New York, 10 November 1997	44,000,000
6	*Self Portrait: Yo Picasso*	Pablo Picasso	Sotheby's, New York, 9 May 1989	43,500,000
7	*Au Lapin Agile*	Pablo Picasso	Sotheby's, New York, 15 November 1989	37,000,000
8	*Sunflowers*	Vincent van Gogh	Christie's, London, 30 March 1987	36,225,000
9	*Acrobate et Jeune Arlequin*	Pablo Picasso	Christie's, London, 28 November 1988	35,000,000
10	*Portrait of Duke Cosimo I de' Medici*	Jacopo Carucci (also known as Pontormo)	Christie's, New York, 31 May 1989	32,000,000[1]

[1] This is the record price for an Old Master.

Source: Art Sales Index

Top 5 Highest Prices Paid for Paintings at Auction by Living Artists

Rank	Work	Artist	Place and date of sale	Price ($)
1	*False Start*	Jasper Johns	Sotheby's, New York, 10 November 1988	15,500,000
2	*Two Flags*	Jasper Johns	Sotheby's, New York, 8 November 1989	11,000,000
3	*Corpse and Mirror*	Jasper Johns	Christie's, New York, 10 November 1997	7,600,000
4	*White Numbers*	Jasper Johns	Christie's, New York, 10 November 1997	7,200,000
5	*Rebus*	Robert Rauschenberg	Sotheby's, New York, 30 April 1991	6,600,000

Source: Art Sales Index

Top 10 Single-Owner Art Sales

(As of February 1998.)

Rank	Collection	Place and date of sale	Price (£)
1	the collection of Victor and Sally Ganz	Christie's, New York, 10 November 1997	111,022,783
2	John T Dorrance's collection of oil paintings and watercolours	Sotheby's, New York, 18 October 1989	70,624,937
3	paintings and watercolours from Madame Bourdon's collection	Christie's, London, 27 November 1989	70,063,000
4	the collection of John and Frances L Loeb	Christie's, New York, 12 May 1997	51,714,727
5	the collection of Lydia Winston Malbin	Sotheby's, New York, 16 May 1990	39,684,024
6	Jaime Ortiz-Patino's collection of Impressionist paintings	Sotheby's, New York, 9 May 1989	37,834,358
7	Paul Mellon's Impressionist and modern collection	Christie's, New York, 14 November 1989	30,116,131
8	Impressionist and modern art, including paintings from the estate of Joseph H Hazen	Sotheby's, New York, 8 November 1995	30,000,001
9	German and Austrian art '97, including the Ravenborg Collection	Christie's, London, 9 October 1997	28,252,800
10	Old Master paintings, including the Henle Collection	Sotheby's, London, 3 December 1997	27,987,200

Source: Art Sales Index

Painting: Chronology of Western Painting

27000–13000 BC	Cave art in southwest Europe expressed the concerns of hunters.
3000–100	Egyptian wall paintings combined front, three-quarter and side views of the human body in a flat 'diagrammatic' style.
2000–1450	The Minoan civilization, based at Knossos in Crete, evolved bright wall paintings.
1000–400	Greek painting by the finest artists survived mainly as vase decorations.
AD 79	Volcanic ash from Vesuvius preserved fine examples of Roman domestic painting and mosaics.
230–450	Early Christian murals painted in catacombs and as mosaics in churches.
330–1453	Byzantine art expressed Orthodox Christian values in formalized mosaics and painted icons.
680–800	Celtic Christian art illuminated religious texts such as the *Lindisfarne Gospel* and the *Book of Kells*.
1290–1337	Italian painting emerged from the Byzantine style with the new depth and realism of Giotto, the first great painter of the Italian Renaissance period.
1315–1425	Italian Gothic and then International Gothic evolved an elegant and decorative style.
1420–1492	Fra Angelico, Piero della Francesca and Botticelli brought a new freshness of vision to Italian painting.
1425–50	A new and vivid realism, owing much to the established use of high quality oil paints, appears in the early Renaissance painters of the North such as Jan van Eyck.
c.1428	Masaccio incorporated Brunelleschi's laws of perspective in his grand and austere *Holy Trinity*, creating an illusion of depth never seen before in painting.
1470–1569	The Northern Renaissance produced a series of disparate geniuses, including Dürer, Bosch, and Brueghel, who expressed the religious anxieties of the age.
1472–1519	Leonardo da Vinci brought a new sense of mystery and psychological depth to painting.
1500–1564	Michelangelo rediscovered classical grandeur and harnessed it to Christian subjects as in the Sistine Chapel frescoes.
1504–1520	Raphael's short career expressed the Florentine Renaissance ideals with an unsurpassed harmony.
1506–1594	The Venetian Renaissance is manifested in the warm sensuality of Titian, Giorgione, Tintoretto, and Veronese.
1520–1600	Mannerists, such as Romano, Pontormo and Parmigianino, applied the discoveries of the High Renaissance in more stylized forms.
1525–1792	The tradition of portrait painting in Britain began with Holbein and continued to Reynolds and Gainsborough.
1560–1609	Caravaggio, a master of dramatic light and shade, led the way towards the Baroque style.
1570–1682	The great age of Spanish painting lasted from the tortured religious idealism of El Greco through to Velázquez.
1577–1640	Rubens was the supreme master of the Baroque grand style.
1620–1670	Dutch genre painting produced masters of portraiture, interiors, landscapes and still life.
1624–82	Poussin and Claude established the idealized classical landscape painting.
1626–1669	Rembrandt brought an unparalled psychological and emotional depth to biblical scenes and portraits.
1706–1806	The elegance of French rococo is captured by Watteau, Boucher and Fragonard.
1780–1851	The Romantic spirit was expressed in the vision of

Michelangelo's The Holy Family
© Italian State Tourist Office

Goya's Carnival Scene (the Burial of the Sardine)
© Spanish Tourist Office

	painters such as Goya, Turner, Constable and Delacroix.
1780–1867	Ingres and David sustained the classicism of the French revolutionary and post-revolutionary periods.
1840–1877	Courbet developed a radical realism in his work.
1863	Eschewing half-tones and contemporary pictorial conventions, Manet heralded a new era in art.
1870–1890	Symbolists and Pre-Raphaelites portrayed visionary ideas through the use of symbols and rich colours.
1874	Monet, Renoir and Degas exhibited at the first Impressionist exhibiton with paintings composed of broken surfaces of light.
1883–1891	Seurat carried the discoveries of the Impressionists further with his pointillist techniques of dots of colour.
1883–1903	Gauguin's spiritual and sensual odyssey to Tahiti looked forward to expressionism and fauvism.
1885–90	Van Gogh's personal vision invested ordinary scenes with unparalleled emotion and spirituality through broad strokes of bright colour.
1886–1906	Cézanne created a new kind of painting with solid forms built with a mosaic of brush strokes. His concentration on geometric forms inspired the Cubist movement.
1892–1926	Munch, and later the Expressionists, used colour and form to express their inner emotions.
1905	Matisse and the Fauves showed compositions where form was defined by subjective choice of colour.
1907	*Les Demoiselles d'Avignon* by Picasso heralded the Cubist movement by rejecting conventional naturalistic representation from only one viewpoint and conventional ideas of beauty.
1910–1914	Kandinsky developed a purely abstract art.
1913	The Armory Show in New York is often regarded as the beginning of public interest in progressive art in the USA.
1913–1944	A geometrical abstract art was developed by Malevitch, Tatlin, Rodchenko and Mondrian.
From 1914	Duchamp and the Dadaists brought an anarchist element to painting that questioned traditional notions of art.
1914–1940	Klee's figurative painting was built out of abstract patterns.
From 1924	Surrealist painters, notably Dali, Magritte and Miro, reached for unconscious sources of inspiration.
1940s	Abstract Expressionism, developed in New York by Jackson Pollock and Arshile Gorky, added the element of uninhibited expression to pure abstraction.
From World War II	Painting became increasingly pluralistic, with a broad range of styles flourishing, including abstract and figurative.
Late 1940s–1950s	European post-war anxiety finds expression in the *art brut* of Jean Dubuffet (France), and the Expressionism of the COBRA group, including Karel Appel (Holland).
Late 1950s–1960s	Pop Art returned to representation, drawing on popular images and commercial techniques. Artists included Richard Hamilton (UK), David Hockney (UK), Jasper Johns (USA), and Andy Warhol (USA).
From late 1950s	The broadly based 'London School' continue the British figurative tradition: Francis Bacon, Frank Auerbach, and Lucien Freud.
From 1960s	In the USA, super-Realist artists (Malcolm Morley and Richard Estes) strive for a photographic realism. Op art extends the range of abstraction, with Bridget Riley (UK) a leading figure.
Mid-1970s–1980s	In the USA, graffiti, seen as an urban folk art, exploited by artists such as Keith Haring and Jean-Michel Basquiat.
Late 1970s–1980s	Neo-Expressionism flourished in Germany (Anselm Keifer and Georg Baselitz), Italy (Francesco Clemente and Enzo Cucchi), and the USA (Julian Schnabel).
1980s–1990s	A multiplicity of styles with no dominant tendency. The self-conscious use of style and images from a broad range of sources – from pop culture to old masters – is common.
1997	The controversial and provocative *Sensation* exhibition was held at the Royal Acadamy, London. It included works such as Damien Hirst's 'pickled animal' sculptures, and a portrait of child murderer Myra Hindley

Top 10 Highest Prices Paid for Sculptures Sold at Auction

Rank	Work	Artist	Place and date of sale	Price ($)
1	*Petite Danseuse de Quatorze Ans*	Edgar Degas	Sotheby's, New York, 12 November 1996	10,800,000
2	*The Dancing Faun*	Adriaen de Vries	Sotheby's, London, 7 December 1989	9,796,000
3	*Petite Danseuse de Quatorze Ans* (resold later, see above)	Edgar Degas	Christie's, New York, 14 November 1988	9,250,000
4	*Petite Danseuse de Quatorze Ans* (resold later, see above)	Edgar Degas	Sotheby's, New York, 10 May 1988	9,200,000
5	*La Negresse Blonde*	Constantin Brancusi	Sotheby's, New York, 16 May 1990	8,000,000
6	*La Muse Endormie III*	Constantin Brancusi	Christie's, New York, 14 November 1989	7,500,000
7	*Mlle Pogany II*	Constantin Brancusi	Christie's, New York, 14 May 1997	6,400,000
8	*L'Homme Qui Marche I*	Alberto Giacometti	Christie's, London, 28 November 1988	6,358,000
9	*La Muse Endormie II*	Constantin Brancusi	Christie's, New York, 11 November 1997	6,000,000
10	*Grande Femme Debout I*	Alberto Giacometti	Christie's, New York, 14 November 1989	4,500,000

Source: Art Sales Index

Top 10 Exhibitions at the British Museum, London, by Total Attendance

Figures are for temporary exhibitions as at March 1998.

Rank	Name	Date	Total attendance number
1	Treasures of Tutankhamun	1972	1,694,117
2	Turner Watercolours	1975–76	585,046
3	The Vikings	1980	465,000
4	Thracian Treasures from Bulgaria	1976	424,465
5	From Manet to Toulouse-Lautrec: French Lithographs 1860–1900	1978	355,354
6	The Ancient Olympic Games	1980–81	334,354
7	Treasures for the Nation – Conserving our Heritage	1988–89	297,837
8	Excavating in Egypt: The Egypt Exploration Fund 1882–1992	1982–83	285,736
9	Heraldry: British Heraldry from its Origins to 1800	1978	262,183
10	Drawings by Michelangelo	1975	250,000

Source: The British Museum

Is Modern Art 'a Load of Rubbish'?

BY IAN CHILVERS

Art rarely makes front page headlines. When it does, it is usually for one of two reasons: either because a work has been sold for a gigantic sum, or because a work or exhibition has caused shock or outrage. There is a long tradition of artistic rebels or outsiders whose work has baffled or offended their contemporaries, but it was not until the early 19th century that it became commonplace for artists to believe it was part of their role deliberately to flout conventions.

The notion of artistic rebellion gathered strength during the 19th century, notably with the Impressionists, whose work seemed crude and garish to many contemporaries. However, although the Impressionists challenged many traditional ideas, they did not question the fundamental assumption that painting and sculpture were concerned with depicting the real world in a recognizable way. It was not until the years between the turn of the century and the outbreak of World War I in 1914 that this assumption was completely overthrown. This was a period of unprecedented artistic experimentation, when Cubism, Expressionism, Fauvism, and abstract art were all developed. Although it is hard to give a precise definition of 'modern art', it is reasonable to place its birth in this period.

Dada and Duchamp

The early 20th-century developments were followed during World War I by a movement that was even more radical, for it questioned the very nature and validity of art. This was Dada, in which artists went to extremes of provocative behaviour to express their disillusionment with the values of the society that had created the war. It was an enormously influential movement, for it subsequently became virtually obligatory for leaders of avant-garde art to debunk traditional cultural values.

The most influential of the Dadaists was Marcel Duchamp, whose works included 'ready-mades', in which he selected a mass-produced object (the first was a bicycle wheel) and displayed it with no – or very slight – alteration, as a work of art. Duchamp's ideas lie at the root of Conceptual art, which became a major force in the art world in the 1960s. The essential notion behind this kind of art is that the ideas in the artist's mind are more important than any physical expression they are given. This is a notion that many find hard to accept, for the visual arts have traditionally involved skilful craftsmanship as well as original ideas; the UK painter Keith Vaughan wrote in 1972 that the term Conceptual art 'is a contradiction in itself, art being the realization of concepts, not just having them'.

Damien Hirst

© Richard Watt

'It's Art Because I Say So'

By the time that Conceptual art came on the scene, modern art had already gone through a bewildering variety of movements and 'isms', and subsequently the range of what has been described as art has expanded even further. For example, in 1976 the US artist Mary Kelly had an exhibition at London's Institute of Contemporary Arts at which she displayed imprints of soiled nappies as part of an ongoing work aimed at exploring the relationship between mother and child. She said 'I am trying to show the reciprocity of the process of socialization in the first few years of life', and declared that the exhibits 'are art because I say so'. Not surprisingly, she attracted a good deal of criticism. A report in *The Daily Telegraph* of 15 November was fairly representative in quoting a visitor at the exhibition saying 'I think it's a load of rubbish. Taxpayers should not be asked to subsidize this sort of rubbish.'

It is easy to cite other works or activities that seem pointless or offensive to the man or woman in the street, but which are hailed by many critics as important and original statements. For example, the American Jeff Koons, perhaps the most controversial artist of the 1980s, made his name with deliberately banal works, such as vacuum cleaners exhibited in plastic display cases. A large exhibition of such provocative art was held at the Royal Academy, London, in 1997. Entitled *Sensation*, it featured – among much else – 'pickled animal' sculptures by Damien Hirst, who is the most talked-about UK artist of his generation, and a giant portrait (by Marcus Harvey) of the 1960s child murderer Myra Hindley, which was defaced by protestors. All the works in the exhibition came from the collection of the wealthy businessman Charles Saatchi, the UK's leading buyer of contemporary art. One of the artists represented in the exhibition, Chris Ofili, was quoted at the time as saying that 'a lot of young artists . . . just want to get the attention of this buyer overnight and make a bit of money', adding that some of those with pieces already in his collection can produce 'half-hearted' work knowing he will take it off their hands. Ofili himself specializes in pictures incorporating pieces of elephant dung.

A Confidence Trick?

Some people have argued that many modern artists (and their supporters) are charlatans and confidence tricksters, fooling gullible people who are so afraid of being labelled philistines

(Continued)

or reactionaries that they refuse to believe what common sense tells them. There is probably a good deal of cynicism in certain parts of the art world (just as there is in most spheres where large sums of money are involved), and it is obvious that outrageous flamboyance in an artist is likely to gain much more attention than dedicated craftsmanship. However, there seems no reason to doubt the sincerity of many avant-garde artists (some of whom shun rather than court publicity), so if there is deception taking place it is self-deception as much as anything.

Some contemporary artists whose work is dismissed as rubbish like to claim a kinship with great figures from the past, believing that their work – like that of the Impressionists – will be vindicated when the public's taste catches up with it. Taste undoubtedly does change, and it is true that some artists who are now considered geniuses were once once derided. And artists who were once mocked become cultural icons. The US artist Jackson Pollock – the leading exponent of 'action' painting – was facetiously labelled 'Jack the Dripper' in his lifetime, but he is now widely regarded as one of the outstanding artists of the century. However, it is a myth that most great artists have been misunderstood in their own time.

It is only in the 20th century that 'advanced' art has diverged so sharply from what the majority of the public likes or understands.

The Test of Time

In the 20th century, the art world has seen so many movements and trends that to some observers it seems more and more like the fashion world. Certainly the sheer amount of art being produced today is enormous. This in itself makes it overwhelmingly likely that a great deal of contemporary art will prove to be ephemeral, for talent is a rare commodity and genius even rarer. The paintings and sculptures that we see in the great galleries of the world or reproduced in art books usually represent the cream of the past, which is why they have been preserved and studied. The average products of any age fall far short of these masterpieces, so we tend to be much less aware of them. Thus it is easy to have a rosy image of the art of the past. Today's masterpieces, if they exist, may take time to emerge from the flood of mediocrity.

Top 10 Exhibitions at the National Gallery of Art, Washington, DC, by Total Attendance

In 1963, when Leonardo da Vinci's *Mona Lisa* was shown for 27 days, the average daily attendance was 19,205. However, the short duration of the showing means that the total attendance number is not large enough to be included here.

Rank	Name	Date	Total attendance number	Average daily attendance
1	Rodin Rediscovered	1981–82	1,053,223	3,431
2	Treasure Houses of Britain	1985–86	990,474	6,190
3	Treasures of Tutankhamun	1976–77	835,924	7,145
4	Archaeological Finds of the People's Republic of China	1974–75	684,238	6,455
5	Ansel Adams: Classic Images	1985–86	651,652	5,871
6	The Splendor of Dresden	1978	620,089	6,459
7	The Art of Paul Gauguin	1988	596,058	6,479
8	Circa 1492: Art in the Age of Exploration	1991–92	568,192	6,244
9	Andrew Wyeth: The Helga Pictures	1987	558,433	4,397
10	Post-Impressionism: Cross-Currents in European & American Painting	1980	557,533	5,575

Source: National Gallery of Art, Washington DC

Fine Art Museums and Galleries in the UK

Abbot Hall Art Gallery Abbot Hall, Kendal, Cumbria LA9 5AL; phone: (01539) 722464. Collection of both national and local importance from 18th to mid-20th century. Includes work by Romney, Turner, Ruskin, and Kurt Schwitters.

Ashmolean Museum of Art & Archaeology Beaumont Street, Oxford OX1 2PH; phone: (01865) 278000. World class collection of Old Master drawings and paintings, including Raphael, Michelangelo, and Ucello.

Astley Cheetham Art Gallery Trinity Street, Stalybridge SK15 2BN; phone:

(0161) 338 2708. Italian Old Masters, British art of the 19th and 20th centuries, including Gertler, Burne-Jones, and Duncan Grant.

Atkinson Art Gallery Lord Street, Southport PR8 1DH; phone: (01704) 533133 x 2110. British art of the 17th to 20th centuries, including work by Cotman, Lely, Ford Madox Brown, and Sickert.

Bankfield Museum Akroyd Park, Boothtown Road, Halifax HX3 6HG; phone: (01422) 354823. Old Master drawings and British works from the 19th and 20th centuries, including Rowlandson, Ruskin, Sickert, and Matthew Smith.

Barber Institute of Fine Arts The University of Birmingham, Birmingham B15 2TS; phone: (0121) 414 7333. West European painting, 13th to early-20th

century; Old Master drawings and small sculpture, Roman Imperial and Byzantine coins.

Ben Uri Art Society and Gallery 4th Floor, 21 Dean Street, London W1V 6NE; phone: (0171) 482 1234. Features the work of Jewish artists, including Bomberg, Gertler, Epstein, Kitaj, Kossoff, and Auerbach.

Berwick-upon-Tweed Museum & Art Gallery Berwick Barracks, Ravensdowne, Berwick-upon-Tweed TD15 1DQ; phone: (01289) 330044. Includes 18th-century portraits and 19th-century paintings, including Gericault, Degas, and Boudin.

Birmingham Museum & Art Gallery Chamberlain Square, Birmingham B3 3DH; phone: (0121) 303 2834. Major collections of fine and decorative arts, including Old

Masters and an outstanding collection of Pre-Raphaelite paintings.

Blackburn Museum & Art Gallery Museum Street, Blackburn BB1 7AJ; phone: (01254) 667130. 19th-century British paintings, including Turner, Girtin, Cox, and Lord Leighton; also featured is a large collection of Japanese prints and illuminated manuscripts.

Bolton Museum & Art Gallery Le Mans Crescent, Bolton BL1 1SE; phone: (01204) 522311 x 2191. Italian baroque paintings and a representative British collection, including Turner, the Bloomsbury group, and bronze busts by Epstein.

Bowes Museum Barnard Castle, Co Durham DL12 8NP; phone: (01833) 690606. Extensive collections of European and British fine and decorative arts, 15th to 19th centuries. Includes paintings by El Greco, Goya, Tiepolo, Boucher, Courbet, and Canaletto.

Brighton Museum & Art Gallery Church Street, Brighton BN1 1EE; phone: (01273) 290900. European and British paintings from the 16th century to the present day; artists represented include Phillippe de Champaigne, Jan Lievens, Lawrence, and Alma-Tadema.

Burrell Collection 2060 Pollokshaws Road, Glasgow G43 1AT; phone: (0141) 649 7151. Outstanding collection of European and Middle and Far Eastern fine and decorative art.

Bury Art Gallery & Museum Moss Street, Bury, Lancs. BL9 0DR; phone: (0161) 253 5878. Thomas Wrigley collection of Victorian oil and watercolour paintings, including works by Turner, Constable, and Landseer; there is also work by contemporary artists.

Cartright Hall Lister Park., Bradford BD9 4NS; phone: (01274) 493313. 19th- and 20th-century British art, including local-born David Hockney; also shows other European works.

Castle Museum Norwich, Norfolk NR1 4JU; phone: (01603) 223624. Fine collection of paintings from the Norwich school, including Crome and Cotman.

Castle Museum & Art Gallery Castle Road, Nottingham NG1 6EL; phone: (0115) 915 3700. Paintings from the European Renaissance and Dutch 17th century plus British art from the 18th to 20th centuries.

Cecil Higgins Art Gallery & Museum Castle Close, Castle Lane, Bedford MK40 3RP; phone: (01234) 211222. One of Britain's best collections of watercolours, including works by Cozens, Cotman, Dadd, Turner, and Stanley Spencer.

Cheltenham Art Gallery & Museum Clarence Street, Cheltenham GL50 3JT; phone: (01242) 237431. 17th-century Dutch and Flemish paintings, 19th-century Dutch and Belgian paintings, and local topographical collection.

Christ Church Picture Gallery Christ Church, Oxford OX1 1DP; phone: (01865) 276172. Important Italian 14th- to 18th-century collection of Old Master paintings and drawings, including works by Michelangelo, Leonardo, Tintoretto and Carracci, Raphael, Rubens, and Durer.

City Art Gallery Civic Centre, Southampton SO14 7LP; phone: (01703) 832277. Old Masters, French Impressionists, British 19th- and 20th-century works, including work by Anthony Gormley and Richard Long.

City Museum & Art Gallery Queen's Road, Bristol BS8 1RL; phone: (0117) 922 3571. Fine European and British paintings from the 15th to 20th centuries, including Bristol artists.

City of Salford Art Gallery Peel Park, The Crescent, Salford M5 4WU; phone: (0161) 736 2649. Predominately the work of L S Lowry, plus other 19th- and 20th-century paintera, including Watts, Maclise, and Ivon Hitchens.

Cooper Gallery Church Street, Barnsley S70 2AH; phone: (01226) 242905. Dutch works of the 17th century; French and Italian painters of the 18th and 19th centuries; also British art of the 18th century.

Courtauld Institute Galleries Somerset House, Strand, London WC2R 0RN; phone: (0171) 873 2526. Northern European paintings, drawings, and prints from the 14th to the 20th centuries; includes important collection of Old Masters and French Impressionist paintings.

Derby Museum & Art Gallery The Strand, Derby DE1 1BS; phone: (01332) 716659. Paintings and drawing by Joseph Wright of Derby, plus other British artists.

Dulwich Picture Gallery College Road, London SE21 7AD; phone: (0181) 693 5254. Old Master collection housed in a gallery designed for it by Sir John Soane.

Falmouth Art Gallery Municipal Buildings, The Moor, Falmouth, Cornwall TR11 2RT; phone: (01326) 313863. Victorian paintings and prints together with maritime paintings and prints.

Ferens Art Gallery Queen Victoria Square, Hull HU1 3RA; phone: (01482) 613902. Old Masters, principally Dutch, and other European painters; British art from the 16th century to the present day, including sculpture, marine paintings, and local views.

Fitzwilliam Museum Trumpington Street, Cambridge CB2 1RB; phone: (01223) 332900. Outstanding collections of fine and decorative arts, including European paintings from the Middle Ages to the 20th century; collection also includes French Impressionists and Post-Impressionists.

Gainsborough's House 46 Gainsborough Street, Sudbury, Suffolk CO10 6EU; phone: (01787) 372958. Devoted to the work of Gainsborough, who was born in the house,

and the work of his contemporaries and followers.

Gallery of Modern Art Queen Street, Glasgow G1 3AZ; phone: (0141) 229 1996. Predominately the work of living artists, mostly post-war; includes painting, sculpture, craft, and interactive computer art.

Graves Art Gallery Surrey Street, Sheffield S1 1XZ; phone: (0114) 273 5158. British and European art of the 16th to 20th centuries.

Guildhall Art Gallery The Corporation of London, Guildhall, London EC2P 2EJ; phone: (0171) 606 3030. Pre-Raphaelite and 19th-century genre painting and landscape; paintings of London interest from the 17th century to present day.

Harris Museum & Art Gallery Market Square, Preston, Lancs PRI 2PP; phone: (01772) 258248. 19th- and 20th-century British paintings by Samuel Palmer, Holman Hunt, Landseer, Sickert, and Stanley Spencer.

Hatton Gallery Department of Fine Art, The University, Newcastle upon Tyne NE1 7RU; phone: (0191) 222 6057. Old Master paintings, 19th- and 20th- century drawings and prints; includes work by Kurt Schwitters and a good collection of African sculpture.

Herbert Art Gallery & Museum Jordan Well, Coventry CV1 5QP; phone: (01203) 832381. British watercolours and 20th-century art, including Graham Sutherland's studies for Coventry Cathedral.

Huddersfield Art Gallery Princess Alexandra Walk, Huddersfield HD1 2SU; phone: (01484) 221964. British works of art from the 18th century onwards; 20th-century artists include Sickert, Bacon, Auerbach. Blackadder, and the Camden Town Group.

Hunterian Art Gallery 82 Hillhead Street, Glasgow G12 8QQ; phone: (0141) 330 5431. Work by Whistler, C R Mackintosh; European prints from the 15th to 20th centuries; European and Scottish painting from the 16th to the 20th centuries.

Iveagh Bequest Kenwood, Hampstead Lane, London NW3 7JR; phone: (0181) 348 1286. Major collection of paintings by Rembrandt, Vermeer, Gainsborough, Reynolds, and others, housed in one of Robert Adam's finest villas.

Kettle's Yard Castle Street, Cambridge CB3 0AQ; phone: (01223) 352124. Personal collection housed in the home of the collector, Jim Ede. Includes work by Brancusi, Gaudier-Brzeska, Christopher Wood, and Alfred Wallis.

Lady Lever Art Gallery Port Sunlight Village, Wirral L62 5EQ; phone: (0151) 478 4136. Outstanding collection of Victorian painting and decorative arts.

Laing Art Gallery Higham Place, Newcastle upon Tyne NE1 8AG; phone: (0191) 232 7734. Very good collection of 18th- and 19th-century British paintings, sculpture, prints, and drawings, and also decorative arts; special reference to arts and crafts from the northeast of England.

Leamington Spa Art Gallery Avenue Road, Leamington Spa, Warks CV31 3PP; phone: (01926) 426559. British art from the 19th century onwards, including paintings by Terry Frost, Patrick Caulfield, and L S Lowry.

Leeds City Art Gallery The Headrow, Leeds LS1 3AA; phone: (0113) 247 8248. Victorian paintings, early English watercolours, and one of the finest collections of 20th-century British paintings and sculpture outside London.

Leicester Museum and Art Gallery New Walk, Leicester LE1 7EA; phone: (0116) 255 4100. Old Master paintings, European and modern British art, and a fine collection of German Impressionist and Expressionist art.

Manchester City Art Galleries Mosley Street, Manchester M23JL; phone: (0161) 236 5244. Outstanding collection of Old Masters, British and Continental paintings, and sculpture, including Gainsborough, Stubbs, Turner, and the Pre-Raphaelites.

Mead Gallery Warwick Arts Centre, Coventry CV4 7AL; phone: (01203) 522589. Post-war British and US art.

Mercer Art Gallery Crown Place, Harrogate HG1 2RX; phone: (01423) 503340. British art of the 19th and 20th centuries. Works range from Turner, Frith, and Burne-Jones to Andy Goldsworthy and David Mach.

Middlesborough Art Gallery 320 Linthorpe Road, Middlesborough TS1 4AW; phone: (01642) 247445. Collection of major established artists of the 20th century; work includes a collection of work by leading women artists.

National Gallery Trafalgar Square, London WC2N 5DN; phone: (0171) 839 3321. Internationally important collection of Western European painting from the 13th to the early 20th centuries.

National Gallery of Scotland The Mound, Edinburgh EH2 2EL; phone: (0131) 556 8921. Outstanding collection of paintings, drawings, and prints by the greatest artists from the Renaissance to Post-Impressionism.

National Museum & Gallery, Cardiff Cathays Park, Cardiff CF1 3NP; phone: (01222) 397951. Multidisciplinary collection of fine art, including major Impressionist works.

National Portrait Gallery St Martin's Place, London, WC2H 0HE; phone: (0171) 306 0055. Portraits of British men and women; the most comprehensive collection of its kind in the world.

Pallant House 9 North Pallant, Chichester, West Sussex PO19 1TJ; phone: (01243) 774557. Mainly 20th-century British art, including work by Graham Sutherland, John Piper, Ceri Richards, and Chagall.

Pier Arts Centre 28–30 Victoria Street, Stromness, Orkney KW16 3AA; phone: (01856) 850209. Major collection of 20th-century paintings, including work by Ben Nicolson, Peter Lanyon, and Barbara Hepworth.

Plymouth City Museum & Art Gallery Drake Circus, Plymouth PL4 8AJ; phone: (01752) 304774. Old Master and British drawings, including local-born Joshua Reynolds and portraits of his family.

Preston Hall Museum Yarm Road, Stockton-on-Tees TS18 3RH; phone: (01642) 781184. European paintings and 19th-century British watercolours, including work by Turner.

Queen's Gallery Buckingham Palace, London SW1A 1AA; phone: (0171) 799 2331. Annual exhibitions based on various aspects of the Royal Collection.

Rochdale Art Gallery Esplanade Arts & Heritage Centre, Esplanade, Rochdale OL16 IAQ; phone: (01706) 342154. British art of the 18th to 20th centuries, and 17th-century European portraits.

Royal Albert Memorial Museum Queen Street, Exeter EX4 3RX; phone: (01392) 265858. Mainly 18th- to 20th-century British paintings, which include works by Hayman, Richard Wilson, and Devon artists, such as Joshua Reynolds and Thomas Hudson; also includes work by the Camden Town School.

Royal Cornwall Museum 25 River Street, Truro, Cornwall TR1 2SJ; phone: (01872) 272205. Old Master drawings, including work by Rembrandt, Rubens, van Dyck, Constable, Cranach, and Gericault; also paintings from the Newlyn School.

Royal Museum & Art Gallery 18 High Street, Canterbury, Kent CT1 2RA; phone: (01227) 452747. Major Old Master drawings and other works by Gainsborough, Laura Knight, and Piper.

Russell-Cotes Art Gallery & Museum East Cliff, Bournemouth, Dorset BH1 3AA; phone: (01202) 451800. Victorian and Edwardian fine and decorative arts in a major arts building; also contemporary sculpture and crafts.

Saatchi Gallery 98a Boundary Road, London NW8 0RH; phone: (0171) 624 8299. International and European contemporary art.

Sainsbury Centre for the Visual Arts University of East Anglia, Norwich, Norfolk NR4 7TJ; phone: (01603) 592467. Modern and Western art, African, Oceanic, and indigenous American art and antiquities; includes important holdings of Giacometti, Bacon, and Moore.

Scottish National Gallery of Modern Art Belford Road, Edinburgh EH4 3DR; phone: (0131) 556 8921. Work of established masters of the 20th century and the leading figures of the contemporary international scene.

Scottish National Portrait Gallery 1 Queen Street, Edinburgh EH2 1JD; phone: (0131) 556 8921. Portraits of people who have played an important part in Scottish history, from the 16th century to the present, recorded by the most famous artists of the day.

Shipley Art Gallery Prince Consort Road, Gateshead, Tyne & Wear NE8 4JB; phone: (0191) 477 1495. 17th-century Dutch and Flemish paintings; work by Tintoretto, Ricci, and Schauffelein, as well as British artists.

Smith Art Gallery Halifax Road, Brighouse, West Yorkshire HD6 2AF; phone: (01484) 719222. Victorian paintings by Atkinson, Grimshaw, Thomas Faed, Lord Leighton, and Frith.

Stanley Spencer Gallery King's Hall, High Street, Cookham, Berks SL6 9SJ; phone: (01628) 520890. Gallery devoted to the work of Stanley Spencer, who lived in Cookham.

Sunderland Museum & Art Gallery Borough Road, Sunderland SR1 IPP; phone: (0191) 565 0723. Strong collection of 19th- and 20th-century British artists, including work by Rossetti, Clarkson Stanfield, Burra, and Lowry.

Swindon Museum & Art Gallery Bath Road, Swindon SN1 4BA; phone: (01793) 466556. Modern British art, including work by Gillian Ayres, John Bellany, John Hoyland, and Graham Sutherland.

Tate Gallery Albert Dock, Liverpool L3 4BB; phone: (0151) 709 3223. Changing displays from the national collection of modern art alongside major loan exhibitions.

Tate Gallery Millbank, London SW1P 4RG; phone: (0171) 887 8000. Houses the national collections of British art and international 20th-century art.

Tate Gallery St Ives Porthmeor Beach, St Ives, Cornwall TR26 ITG; phone: (01736) 796226. Changing displays of 20th-century art in the Cornish context, focusing on the modern tradition with which St Ives is associated.

Torre Abbey Historic House & Gallery The King's Drive, Torquay TQ2 5JX; phone: (01803) 293593. Works by Holman Hunt and Burne-Jones, and sculpture by Frederick Thrupp.

Towneley Hall Art Gallery & Museum Burnley BB11 3RQ; phone: (01282) 424213. Former home of the famous 18th-century art collector Charles Towneley. 18th- and 19th-century British paintings and watercolours, including Zoffany and Alma-Tadema.

Towner Art Gallery & Museum Manor Gardens, High Street, Old Town, Eastbourne, East Sussex BN22 8BB; phone: (01323) 417961. Mainly 19th- and 20th-century British art, including Eric Ravilious and Christopher Wood.

Tullie House Museum & Art Gallery Castle Street, Carlisle, Cumbria CA3 8TP; phone: (01228) 534781. Displays include the Pre-Raphaelites and other 19th- and 20th-century artists.

University Art Collection The Middleton Hall, Hull HU6 TRX; phone: (01482) 465035. Specializes in art produced in Britain in 1890–1940; collection includes Gaudier-Brzeska, Augustus John, Stanley Spencer, and Henry Moore.

Victoria Art Gallery Bridge Street, Bath, Avon BA2 4AT; phone: (01225) 477772. European Old Masters, British paintings, watercolours, and drawings from the 18th–20th centuries; noted for topographical views.

Wakefield Art Gallery Wentworth Terrace, Wakefield WF1 3QW; phone: (01924) 305796. Mostly 20th-century British painting and sculpture, including works by Henry Moore, Barbara Hepworth, Caro, Epstein, and Hockney.

Walker Art Gallery William Brown Street, Liverpool L3 8EL; phone: (0151) 478 4199. Wide variety of art from the Renaissance to the present day; includes European masterpieces, such as work by Poussin, as well as an expansive British art collection.

Wallace Collection Hertford House, Manchester Square, London W1M 6BN; phone: (0171) 935 0687. Outstanding collection of French, Spanish, Italian, Dutch, and British paintings, and other works of art bequeathed to the nation by Lady Wallace in 1897.

Walsall Museum & Art Gallery Litchfield, Walsall WS1 1TR; phone: (01922) 653116. Important collection of art, including bronzes by Epstein, Impressionist paintings by Monet, and other works by van Gogh, Picasso, Freud, and Matthew Smith.

Warrington Museum & Art Gallery Bold Street, Warrington, Cheshire WA1 1JG; phone: (01925) 442392. Large collection of well-known local artists, plus Victorian art and 19th-century watercolours.

Williamson Art Gallery & Museum Slatey Road, Birkenhead L43 4UE; phone: (0151) 652 4177. British landscape paintings and watercolours, including works by Stanley Spencer.

Whitworth Art Gallery University of Manchester, Oxford Road, Manchester M15 6ER; phone: (0161) 275 7450. Internationally famous collection of British drawings and watercolours, contemporary painting, and sculpture.

Wolverhampton Art Gallery Litchfield Street, Wolverhampton, WV1 1DU; phone:

(01902) 552055. Wide-ranging collection with a strong 20th-century collection of British and US art.

Worthing Museum & Art Gallery Chapel Road, Worthing, West Sussex BN11 IHP; phone: (01903) 239999 x 2528. 19th- and 20th-century British paintings, including Holman Hunt, Sickert, Pissaro, and Hitchens.

York City Art Gallery Exhibition Square, York Y01 7EW; phone: (01904) 551861. Collection includes paintings by Parmigianino, Lely, Reynolds, and Gwen John.

Notable Buildings of the Post-War Era

(All dates given are dates of completion.)

Eames House, Pacific Palisades, Los Angeles, California, USA (Charles and Ray Eames, 1949)
Partially engaged to its hillside site and personalized by its owner-builders, this house provided a model to a generation of young architects, showing that modernism could be humanized and still adhere to a strict set of principles. Modernism, or the Modern Movement, was a conscious attempt to break with the artistic traditions of the 19th century. It was based on a concern with form and the expression of technique, as opposed to content and narrative; functionalism ousted decorativeness as a central objective.

Lever House, New York City, New York, USA (Skidmore, Owings, and Merrill, 1952)
The building commercialized the language of the Modern Movement; the design provided the model for buildings throughout the world.

Church of Nôtre-Dame-du-Haut, Ronchamp, Vosges, France (Le Corbusier, 1955)
This building was revolutionary for its expressive use of massive concrete walls and a concrete shell roof; for the first time, concrete was used in a sculptural way to create a fluid structure. It was a departure from Le Corbusier's rectilinear work, which had been seen as archetypal of the Modern Movement.

Seagram Building, New York City, New York, USA (Ludwig Mies van der Rohe and Philip Johnson, 1958)
This building provided a compelling image for the skyscraper in the urban context that conformed to the new post-war corporate image of sleekness, sophistication, cool elegance, and control.

Guggenheim Museum, New York City, New York, USA (Frank Lloyd Wright, 1959)
This was the most important building of Wright's last period, a low-rise circular tower in the high-rise cityscape of New York. The round, spiralling ramp took the visitor and the works of modern art to the full height of the building and provided a revolutionary circulation model for museums.

Richards Medical Research Building, University of Pennsylvania, Philadelphia, Pennsylvania, USA (Louis Kahn, 1960)
Stretched the modernist invocation against historicism by evoking vernacular images of an Italian hill town that inspired the architect, whilst also accentuating the function of the various elements of the building in a meaningful way. Historicism is the copying of styles from the past. It implies a detailed imitation, rather than the ironic reference that is common in Post-Modernism (see **House, Chestnut Hill**).

TWA Terminal, John F Kennedy International Airport, New York City, New York, USA (Eero Saarinen, 1962)
Served as a model of originality and elegance in concrete construction, showing the fluid possibilities of concrete, in this instance used as a metaphor for flight.

Faculty of Engineering, Leicester University, Leicester, UK (James Stirling and James Gowan, 1963)
Refined the language of Modernism and reinvigorated the Modernist style.

House, Chestnut Hill, Philadelphia, USA (Robert Venturi and John Rausch, 1964)
Changed perceptions about the principle of form following function, as advocated by modernists. The exterior symbolically expressed a domestic image that was detached from interior use; it is considered to be the first Post-Modern building. Post-Modernism rejects the preoccupation of Modernism with purity of form and techniques. Post-Modernists use an amalgam of style elements from the past, such as Classical and Baroque, and apply them to spare modern forms, often with ironic effect.

Modena Cemetery, Modena, Italy (Aldo Rossi, 1971)
A major nationalistic statement using the arcade typology and blending of rationalism (an architecture derived from logic rather than empiricism) with metaphorical symbols.

Willis Faber and Dumas Office Building, Ipswich, Suffolk, UK (Norman Foster and Associates, 1975)
A sensitive application of the high-tech approach to an urban environment. Its hung glass façade provided two faces: a slick black covering that reflects its surroundings by day and a transparent skin that seems to disappear when lit from inside by night.

Pompidou Centre, Paris, France (Richard Rogers and Renzo Piano, 1977)
With its external escalators snaking up the walls, it brought high-tech architecture at mega-scale into the city. It became a symbol of the museum as a cultural centre and the power of a modern building in regenerating an urban centre.

Abteiburg Museum, Mönchen-Gladbach, Germany (Hans Hollein, 1982)
This building helped to define the role of the museum, with its sculptural interior and innovative circulation pattern.

AT&T Building, New York City, New York, USA (Philip Johnson and John Burgee, 1982)
The first Post-Modern building that became memorable to the public. The use of a broken pediment defining the building's roof profile provoked controversy about the use and interpretation of traditional and modern forms.

National Commercial Bank Headquarters, Jeddah, Sa.udi Arabia (Skidmore, Owings, and Merrill, 1982)
Two enormous rectangular openings in the plain, monumental exterior walls and a triangular plan gave this skyscraper a dramatic appearance unlike any other high-rise building to date. The building was innovative in its control of glare and air circulation. Removing the elevator and stairs from their usual positions in the middle of the building to the outside walls, the architect created atrium-like courtyards.

Haj Terminal, Jeddah, Saudi Arabia (Skidmore, Owings, and Merrill, 1982)
High-technology materials were used – teflon-impregnated fibreglass fabric – to create an elegant tent structure that ameliorated harsh climatic conditions and was an appropriate cultural expression using traditional forms. The research on new materials for tent structures formed the basis for works by architects throughout the world.

Public Service Building, Portland, Oregon, USA (Michael Graves, 1983)
This building galvanized opinions among architects about Post-Modernism; until the design of this building, Post-Modernism had been considered an exercise in the avant-garde rather than a mainstream movement in architecture.

Staatsgalerie, Stuttgart, Germany (James Stirling and Michael Wilford, 1984)
A skilful application of Post-Modern aesthetics to the urban context. Reformed the museum for the 1980s and 1990s by making it a popular playground with plazas and galleries.

Hong Kong and Shanghai Bank, Hong Kong, Special Administrative Region of China (Norman Foster, 1986)
Redefined the skyscraper by using an innovative suspension structure (inspired by the Golden Gate Bridge in San Francisco, USA), allowing for a soaring atrium space inside.

Petronas Towers, Kuala Lumpur, Malaysia (Cesar Pelli, 1996 (main structure))
The tallest building in the world, it expands skyscraper design to the category of megastructure.

Bilbao Guggenheim Museum, Bilbao, Spain (Frank Gehry, 1997)
A colossal, shimmering edifice located on a waterfront site, this building was seen as

Hong Kong and Shanghai Bank

inspirational by many critics. Outside, the building's curving forms, together resembling a boat, are coated with titanium panels. Inside, the fluid spaces include an atrium of glass and flowing white plaster walls. The fluidity of the design and interior spaces might not have been attempted without the latest computer-aided technology; specifically, a program used by a French aeronautical company in designing jet aircraft.

Web Sites

BalletWeb

URL: 'http://www.novia.net/~jlw/index.html'

Site devoted to classical ballet, with commentary on dance issues, photo-essays, and the Electronic Ballerina – a computer animation illustrating ballet steps.

Baroque Music

URL: 'http://www.geocities.com/Paris/Rue/1663/music.html'

Description of Baroque music. The Web site consists of descriptions of the important composers of the period, including Handel, Bach, and Vivaldi. A links section which draws together the scattered sites dealing with this subject.

Blues Access Online

URL: 'http://www.he.net/~blues/'

Online version of *Blues Access* magazine, with sample features, festival listings, and lists of other blues-related sites.

Bolshoi in History

URL: 'http://www.bolshoi-theatre.com/tbtih.html'

History of the Bolshoi Theatre from its inception in 1776 through many trials and tribulations until the present day..

Brass Bands – The Official Brass Band Site

URL: 'http://www.smsltd.demon.co.uk/'>

Information for the British brass band movement. There are details of a brass band mailing list and brass band RealAudio concerts. There are samples from all the best known pieces in the brass band repertoire and latest news of bands.

Carry Online

URL: 'http://www.carryonline.com/'

Tribute to the Carry On films and their cast.

Celebration of Women's Writers

URL: 'http://www.cs.cmu.edu/People/mmbt/women/writers.html'

Extensive site, still under development and dedicated to all aspects of women's contribution to literature. There is extensively linked biographical information, as well as access to essays about, and text by, the various authors.

Centennial Salute to Cinema

URL: 'http://photo2.si.edu/cinema/cinema.html'

Presentations of the first magic lantern broadsides, the first frame by frame movement experiments, and early motion picture advertisements.

Children's Literature Web Guide

URL: 'http://www.ucalgary.ca/~dkbrown/index.html'

Information about recommended titles, reviews of children's books, lists of book awards and best-sellers, as well as a host of links on where to find children's literature online.

Classics for Young People

URL: 'http://www.acs.ucalgary.ca/~dkbrown/storclas.html'

Some of the most popular and increasingly difficult to find classic stories for children and young adults.

Complete Works of Shakespeare

URL: 'http://the-tech.mit.edu/Shakespeare/works.html'

Complete works of William Shakespeare. Text searching is available across all poems and plays, and plays are also accessible by act and scene. This site also contains an index of other Shakespeare sites on the Web.

Cyfarwydd – Storyteller

URL: 'http://snowcrash.cymru.net/~nwi/cfarwydd.htm'

Collection of tales retold from *The Mabinogion* and from Welsh folklore, including 'the changeling of Llanfabon' and 'Pryderi son of Pwyll'.

Early Music by Women Composers

URL: `http://150.252.8.92/www/iawm/pages/`

Presentation of medieval, Renaissance, and baroque women composers. It includes a chronology, a CD discography, MIDI soundfiles, reference sources, and illustrations by early women artists.

English Literature Main Page

URL: `http://humanitas.ucsb.edu/shuttle/english.html`

Base site if you are searching for works of literature written in English. It begins with resources on Anglo-Saxon literature. The site also includes resources on related fields such as cultural studies and creative writing.

Folk Music Home Page

URL: `http://www.jg.org/folk/`

This site primarily provides an organized set of pointers to other pages but also includes some original material.

GramoFile Home Page

URL: `http://www.gramofile.co.uk`

Over 20,000 reviews of classical music releases are available at this site.

Greek Tragedies

URL: `http://www.classics.cam.ac.uk/Faculty/tragedy.html`

A complete listing (and links to) the 33 extant works of Aeschylus, Euripides, and Sophocles, with an introduction to the social and historical context in which tragedy was born, the structured form of Greek tragedy, the symbolic and physical spaces in which they were enacted, and the language employed.

Gregorian Chants

URL: `http://www.music.princeton.edu:80/chant_html/`>

Dedicated to early Christian music.

International Lyrics Server

URL: `http://www.lyrics.ch`

Non-profit database with flexible searching facilities, located in Switzerland and providing the lyrics, artists, and albums of 59,000 songs across an extended range of music genres. Additions and requests are welcome.

Internet Beatles Album

URL: `http://www.primenet.com/~dhaber/bmain.html`

Extensive collection of Beatles information, photos, and sound clips. Biographical sections are provided on the four members and on Stu Sutcliffe, Brian Epstein, George Martin, and Pete Best.

Inventing Entertainment: The Early Motion Pictures of the Edison Company

URL: `http://lcweb2.loc.gov/ammem/edhtml/edhome.html`

Part of the American Memory presentation of the US Library of Congress, this collection was designed in celebration of US inventor Thomas Edison's 150th birthday. It includes eight motion pictures produced by the Edison Manufacturing Company, including *The Great Train Robbery*.

Jazz Central Station

URL: `http://jazzcentralstation.com/jcs/station/`

Jazz site in the style of a train journey. 'Trains' depart regularly for jazz festivals all over the globe.

Motown

URL: `http://www.motown.com/motown/`

Introduction to Motown. Each month three artists are featured – click link for access. The site also includes a history of Motown's first 25 years and a link to trivia questions.

Movieweb

URL: `http://movieweb.com/movie/movie.html`

US-based site dedicated to (mainly current) films. Links to all the major studios on the Web, plus previews and trailers of upcoming films.

OperaGlass Database

URL: `http://rick.stanford.edu/opera/main.html`

Reference material on opera, including individual operas, composers, performance histories, synopses, and librettists.

Punk Page

URL: `http://www.webtrax.com/punk/`

Access to punk music lyrics, pictures, sounds, magazines, and record labels, as well as hyperlinks to other relevant sites.

Reggae Update

URL: `http://www.earthchannel.com/reggaesupersite/`

The latest news from the reggae scene is presented, together with biographies of Bob Marley, Peter Tosh, and other Wailers.

RootsWorld

URL: `http://www.rootsworld.com/rw/`

Online magazine of world music, roots, and folk, with a wealth of feature articles, reviews, and sound samples.

Roughstock's History of Country Music

URL: `http://www.roughstock.com/history/`

This site features some of the most influential artists and songs of country music from the 1930s through to the present day, with photos, sound, and video.

Royal Academy of Dramatic Art

URL: `http://rada.drama.ac.uk/`

Includes details of the various courses offered by RADA.

Royal Court Theatre

URL: `http://www.royal-court.org.uk/`>

Information on the work of the theatre noted for showcasing new productions and innovation in the British theatre.

Royal Opera House

URL: `http://195.26.96.12/house/welcome.html`

In addition to providing practical information on current performances and bookings, the site has a history of the Royal Opera. An education section has a host of practical activities designed to interest young people in opera and ballet.

Royal Shakespeare Company

URL: `http://www.stratford.co.uk/rsc/`>

Site of the British theatre company. In addition to full details of the RSC's current repertoire in London and Stratford, there is access to sources of information about William Shakespeare.

Sci-Fi Channel: the Dominion

URL: `http://www.scifi.com/`

The site offers an abundance of graphics, video and audio-clips available for downloading, and a link to *Science-Fiction Weekly,* featuring reviews, soundbites, and videoclips from classic scientific fiction titles, cinema productions, and TV releases.

Theatre Arts Library

URL: `http://www.perspicacity.com/elactheatre/index.html`

Plays, papers, historical documents, and other theatre links useful for the study of all aspects of the theatre.

UK Theatre Web

URL: `http://www.uktw.co.uk/`

Includes information on current amateur theatre, dance, opera, and gossip, as well as a fully searchable database on what's on in theatres across the UK.

Welsh Literature: Introduction

URL: `http://www.britannia.com/wales/lit/intro.html`

Introduction to the antiquity and continuity of the literature of Wales. The site provides numerous links to essays on chronologically arranged topics from the heroic poetry of the 6th century AD to 20th-century writing.

LANGUAGE AND LANGUAGES

Languages of the World

Language

Linguists estimate that there are about 6,000 distinct languages in the world. The number is uncertain because: (1) it is not always easy to establish whether a speech form is a distinct language or a dialect of another language; (2) some parts of the world remain incompletely explored (such as New Guinea); and (3) the rate of language death is often unknown (for example, in Amazonia, where many undescribed Native American languages have died out). It is also difficult to estimate the precise number of speakers of many languages, especially where communities mix elements from several languages elsewhere used separately (as in parts of India).

One of the world's richest language banks is Papua New Guinea. In 1995 it was estimated that there were more than 100 languages in Papua New Guinea threatened with extinction. This trend is linked largely to the destruction of natural habitat by foreign commercial exploitation. In the Americas, 100 languages, each of which has fewer than 300 speakers, are all close to extinction. North America, which once had several hundreds of languages, had only about 100 languages left in 1995.

Languages Spoken or Understood by More Than Ten Million People: Introduction

Source: *The Linguasphere Register of the World's Languages and Linguistic Communities* (Linguasphere Press, Hebron, Wales, 1998)

The table overleaf is based on provisional estimates established in the course of preparation of the *Linguasphere Register of the World's Languages and Linguistic Communities*. As world populations rise, more lan-

guages reach and pass the total of ten million speakers each year. Estimates often depend on national census figures of varying reliability, which may or may not include sub-totals by language. Figures for past censuses or estimates have been increased to allow for growth of population to 1998.

Totals include an allowance, where appropriate, for estimated totals of competent second-language speakers and listeners. Totals of first-language speakers would often have given a false picture of linguistic reality, for example, 6 million for Swahili (as opposed to 55 million including second-language speakers) or a maximum 500 million for English (as opposed to 1,200 million).

Pairs of very closely related languages are treated together for the purpose of assessing realistic totals, for example, Hindi/Urdu, Malay/Indonesian, Croatian/Serbian, and Czech/Slovak. This is not to imply that they are the 'same' languages but that they are sufficiently close to form an extended speech-community in each case. For the same reason, the figure for Turkish includes also the Azeri and Turkmen languages, for Persian also the Tajik language. In Africa, the collective name Manding covers the continuum of Mandinka/Malinka/Maninka, Bambara, and Jula, whereas Berber covers a chain of fragmented languages extending from Morocco to Tunisia, including Kabyle and Riff. A case could be made also for treating Swedish, Norwegian, and Danish together, providing a combined total of 19 million, but Swedish has been included on its own in the following list (with an increase from 8 to 12 million) to allow for the many speakers of Danish and Norwegian who are also competent speakers or listeners of Swedish.

Frequent competence in speaking and/or understanding a language closely related to a speaker's first language has been allowed for also in other estimates, for example, in Spanish among speakers of Portuguese, in Russian among speakers of Ukrainian and Belorussian, in Polish among speakers of Czech and

Slovak, and in Hindi/Urdu (where competence in listening and understanding is more widespread than that in speaking, due in part to the great popularity of Hindi-speaking films in Southern Asia). In some cases, there is a continuum between two or more very closely related languages, for example, Hindi/Urdu, or Malay/Indonesian, such cases being treated as a single language in the following estimates.

In other cases, it has been necessary to establish separate figures for adjacent languages which share a common name without being readily interintelligible, as in the case of the Min languages in China, the Luba languages in Zaire or the Quechua/Quichua languages in South America (not represented in this ten million plus list).

'Language writers or readers' must not be confused with 'language speakers or listeners', not only because of varying literacy rates, but also because of the differential distribution of certain writing systems. Croatian and Serbian (formerly under the composite name of Serbo-Croat) are still to be treated together as spoken languages but are written in different alphabets (Roman and Cyrillic). In Asia, Hindi and Urdu overlap as spoken languages but are written in different scripts (Devanagari and Perso-Arabic), whereas the major Chinese languages (not readily interintelligible when spoken) are the 'same' language in writing, through the use of identical 'meaning-based' characters.

Speakers of individual Chinese languages are estimated separately, those who are bilingual in the official national language (Putong-hua or Mandarin) and in one other Chinese language being therefore counted twice. The related but distinct languages known collectively as 'Chinese' include: Putong-hua (literally 'commonly understood language', Wu, Yue (Cantonese), Hakka, Zhuang, Xiang, Gan, Min-nang ('South Min'), Min-pei ('North Min'), North Coastal Min, and Ping (Gui).

Languages Spoken or Understood by More Than Ten Million People

Language	Speakers in millions	Where spoken
English	1,200	UK, USA, Canada, Ireland, Australia, New Zealand, South Africa, Gibraltar, Hong Kong, India, Bahamas, Grenada, Jamaica, Barbados, Grenada, Trinidad and Tobago, Belize, St Lucia, Suriname, Guyana, Malta, St Kitts and Nevis, St Vincent, Virgin Islands, Dominica, Fiji, Guam, Kiribati, Federated States of Micronesia, Nauru, Papua New Guinea, Philippines, Solomon Islands, Tuvalu, Vanuatu, Western Samoa, Botswana, Cameroon, Gambia, Ghana, Kenya, Lesotho, Liberia, Malawi, Mauritius, Namibia, Nigeria, Seychelles, Sierra Leone, Swaziland, Tanzania, Tonga, Uganda, Zambia, Zimbabwe
Mandarin (Chinese)	1,000	China, Taiwan, Thailand, Malaysia, Hong Kong, Singapore, Vietnam
Hindu/Urdu	550	India, Fiji, Pakistan
Spanish	450	Spain, Mexico, Venezuela, Colombia, Ecuador, Peru, Bolivia, Chile, Argentina, Paraguay, Uruguay, Panama, Costa Rica, Nicaragua, Honduras, El Salvador, Guatemala, Cuba, Dominican Republic, Puerto Rico, Canary Islands, Morocco, Equatorial Guinea, USA
Russian	320	Russia, Ukraine, Kazakhstan, Belarus, Azerbaijan, Georgia, Turkmenistan, Armenia, USA, Uzbekistan, Latvia, Kyrgystan, Moldova, Estonia, Tajikistan, Lithuania, Canada
Arabic	250	Saudi Arabia, Yemen, United Arab Emirates, Oman, Kuwait, Bahrain, Qatar, Iraq, Syria, Jordan, Lebanon, Djibouti, Egypt, Somalia, Sudan, Libya, Tunisia, Mauritania, Algeria, Morocco, Comoros, Israel
Bengali	200	Bangladesh, India
Portuguese	180	Portugal, Brazil, Angola, Cape Verde, Guinea-Bissau, Macau, Mozambique, São Tomé and Príncipe
Malay/Indonesian	160	Indonesia, Malaysia, Singapore, Brunei
Japanese	130	Japan, USA, Brazil
German	120	Germany, Austria, Switzerland, France, Italy, Belgium, Luxembourg, Liechtenstein, USA, Canada, Namibia, Kazakhstan, Romania, Russia, Brazil, Argentina
French	90	France, Canada, Belgium, Switzerland, French Guiana, Luxembourg, Haiti, St Pierre and Miquelon, Guadeloupe, Martinique, French Polynesia, Réunion, New Caledonia, Tahiti, Morocco, Tunisia, Algeria, Lebanon, Syria, Laos, Cambodia, Vietnam, and former French and Belgian colonies in Africa (Benin, Burkina Faso, Côte d'Ivoire, Burundi, Cameroon, Central African Republic, Chad, Comoros, Republic of the Congo, Djibouti, Gabon, Guinea, Madagascar, Mali, Mauritiana, Niger, Rwanda, Senegal, Seychelles, Togo, Democratic Republic of Congo)
Panjabi	85	Pakistan, India
Wu (Chinese)	85	China
Javanese	80	Indonesia
Korean	75	North Korea, South Korea, China, Japan, USA
Italian	70	Italy, Switzerland, USA, Canada, Argentina, Brazil, San Marino
Marathi	70	India
Yue (Chinese)	70	China
Telugu	69	India
Tamil	66	India, Sri Lanka, Malaysia, Singapore, Fiji, Mauritius, Trinidad and Tobago
Vietnamese	65	Vietnam
Bihari/Bhojpuri	60	India, Nepal, Mauritius
Turkish (includes Azeri and Turkmen)	60	Turkey, Bulgaria, Greece, Cyprus, Turkmenistan, Kazakhstan, Uzbekistan, Iran, Azerbaijan
Min-nan (Chinese)	55	China, Taiwan, Malaysia, Singapore
Swahili	55	Tanzania, Kenya, Uganda, Rwanda, Burundi, Democratic Republic of Congo
Ukrainian	50	Ukraine, Canada, USA
Xiang (Chinese)	48	China
Polish	47	Poland, USA, Lithuania, Ukraine, Canada, Brazil
Gujarati	45	India
Hausa	42	Nigeria, Niger
Kannada	42	India
Persian (includes Tajik)	40	Iran, Tajikistan, Afghanistan
Thai	40	Thailand
Malayalam	39	India
Hakka (Chinese)	35	China
Burmese	33	Myanmar
Oriya	32	India
Sundanese	30	Indonesia
Tagalog	30	Philippines
Romanian	27	Romania, Moldova
Yoruba	26	Nigeria, Benin
Amharic	25	Ethiopia
Pashto	25	Afghanistan, Pakistan
Dutch/Flemish	23	Netherlands, Belgium, Suriname, Netherlands Antilles
Assamese	22	India, Bhutan, Bangladesh
Lao/Isan	21	Thailand, Laos
Igbo	19	Nigeria
Serbian/Croatian	19	Serbia, Croatia, Bosnia-Herzegovina
Sindhi	18	Pakistan, India
Uzbek	18	Uzbekistan, Tajikistan, Afghanistan, Kyrgyzstan, Kazakhstan
Cebuano	17	Philippines

Languages Spoken or Understood by More Than Ten Million People *(continued)*

Language	Number in millions	Where spoken
Nepali	17	Nepal, Sikkim, India, Bhutan
Czech/Slovak	16	Czech Republic, Slovak Republic
Fula	16	Nigeria, Guinea, Guinea-Bissau, Senegal, Gambia, Mauritania, Mali, Burkina Faso, Niger, Cameroon
Hungarian	15	Hungary, Romania, Slovak Republic
Kurdish	15	Turkey, Iraq, Iran, Syria
Zhuang/Bouyei	15	China
Lingala	14	Republic of the Congo, Democratic Republic of Congo
Oromo	14	Ethiopia, Kenya
Rwanda/Rundi	14	Rwanda, Burundi, Democratic Republic of Congo, Tanzania
Sinhalese	14	Sri Lanka
Madura	13	Indonesia
Malagasy	13	Madagascar
Manding (includes Mandinka, Bambara, and Jula)	13	Gambia, Guinea-Bissau, Guinea, Mali, Côte d'Ivoire, Senegal, Burkina Faso, Sierra Leone, Liberia
Greek	12	Greece, Cyprus
Min-pei (Chinese)	12	China
Swedish	12	Sweden, Denmark, Norway
Catalan	11	Spain, France, Andorra
Zulu/Swazi/Ndebele	11	Zimbabwe, South Africa

Source: *The Linguasphere Register of the World's Languages and Linguistic Communities* (Linguasphere Press, Hebron, Wales, 1998)

Indo-European Languages: Common Roots

Similarities between six words in Indo-European languages contrasted with their differences to other language groups, for six sample words.

Indo-European languages

English	month	mother	new	night	nose	three
English	month	mother	new	night	nose	three
Welsh	mis	mam	newydd	nos	trwyn	tri
Gaelic	mí	máthair	nua	oíche	srón	trí
French	mois	mère	nouveau	nuit	nez	trois
Spanish	mes	madre	nuevo	noche	nariz	tres
Portuguese	mês	mãe	novo	noite	nariz	três
Italian	mese	madre	nuovo	notte	naso	tre
Latin	mensis	mater	novus	nox	nasus	tres
German	Monat	Mutter	neu	Nacht	Nase	drei
Dutch	maand	moeder	nieuw	nacht	neus	drie
Icelandic	mánudur	módir	nýr	nótt	nef	brír
Swedish	månad	moder	ny	natt	näsa	tre
Polish	miesiąc	matka	nowy	noc	nos	trzy
Czech	měśc	matka	nový	noc	nos	tři
Romanian	lună	mamă	nou	noapte	nas	trei
Albanian	muaj	nênê	iri	natê	hundê	tre,tri
Greek	men	meter	neos	nux	rhïs	treis
Russian	mesyats	mat	novy	noch	nos	tri
Lithuanian	menuo	motina	naujas	naktis	nosis	trys
Armenian	amis	mayr	nor	kisher	kit	yerek
Persian	mãh	mãdar	nau	shab	bini	se
Sanskrit	mãs	matar	nava	nakt	nãs	trayas

Non-Indo-European languages

Basque	hilabethe	ama	berri	gai	sãdãr	hirur
Basque	hilabethe	ama	berri	gai	sãdãr	hirur
Finnish	kuukausi	äiti	uusi	yö	nenä	kolme
Hungarian	hónap	anya	új	éjszaka	orr	három
Turkish	ay	anne	yeni	gece	burun	úç

Dictionaries: Chronology

10th century	Byzantine *Lexicon* of Suidas (first A–Z).	1730	Nathan Bailey published his *Dictionarium Britannicum*.
1225	John Garland used the term dictionarius.		
1530	The first English–English dictionary appeared (appendix to William Temple's *Pentateuch*).	1755	Samuel Johnson's dictionary of standard English, *A Dictionary of the English Language*, appeared.
1538	Thomas Elyot's *Shorte Dictionarie for Yonge Begynners* (English–Latin) was published.	1773	William Kenrick published the first dictionary to indicate pronunciations.
16th century	The first vernacular–vernacular dictionaries were prepared by William Salesbury, Welsh–English 1547, and Giovanni Florio, Italian–English 1599.	1828	Noah Webster published *An American Dictionary of the English Language*.
		1852	Peter Mark *Roget's Thesaurus of English Words* was published.
1604	Robert Cawdrey's *Table Alphabeticall of hard usuall English wordes* aimed at converting Latin to Latinate English.	1884–1928	The *Oxford English Dictionary* was compiled.
		1992	The *Oxford English Dictionary* was published on CD-ROM.

Usage

Selected Eponyms

atlas a book of maps; named after the Titan Atlas, who was depicted holding up the universe on the frontispiece of early books of maps, notably by the Flemish geographer Mercator in the 16th century

beef stroganoff beef cooked with onions and a sauce of sour cream, mushrooms, and spices; named after the Russian diplomat Count Paul Stroganoff (1772–1817)

biro a trademark for a type of ball-point pen; named after Lazlo Biró (1900–1985), the Hungarian inventor who devised it

bowdlerize to expurgate a book or piece of writing; named after Thomas Bowdler (1754–1825), who produced an expurgated edition of Shakespeare in 1818

boycott to cut off social or commercial dealings with a person or country; named after Captain C C Boycott (1832–97), an Irish land agent who suffered this treatment because of the high rents he charged

cardigan a knitted jacket fastened with buttons at the front; named after the 7th Earl of Cardigan (1797–1868), who led the Charge of the Light Brigade at the Battle of Balaclava

chauvinism an excessive or intolerant patriotism; named after Nicolas Chauvin, a French soldier who showed unthinking loyalty to Napoleon Bonaparte and was ridiculed in a number of contemporary plays

derrick a crane or hoisting apparatus with a long horizontal arm; also a framework built over an oil well; named after a 17th-century hangman named Derrick who is said to have executed over 3,000 people; his name was originally applied to the gallows, and then to the crane because it resembled the gallows

diesel a type of internal-combustion engine; after Rudolf Diesel (1858–1913), the German engineer who invented it

Ferris wheel a fairground amusement consisting of a large power-driven upright wheel with passenger cars hung on its outer edge; after George Washington Gale Ferris (1859–1896), the American civil engineer who invented it

fuchsia an ornamental shrub with drooping flowers; named after the German botanist Leonhard Fuchs (1501–1566)

gargantuan huge, enormous; after Gargantua, a giant in Rabelais's comic book of the same name (1534)

gerrymander to rig political boundaries in one's own favour; named after Elbridge Gerry (1744–1814), who as governor of Massachusetts produced a political map on which the shape of one district resembled that of a salamander, the name of which was then merged with his name

guillotine a machine for executing criminals by beheading; also a device for cutting paper, and a parliamentary procedure for limiting discussion of a bill; named after Joseph Ignace Guillotin (1738–1814), who proposed use of the executing machine to avoid excessive pain to victims

jackanapes a pretentious upstart who apes his superiors; from the nickname Jack Napes given to William de la Pole, Duke of Suffolk (1396–1450), when he was arrested and beheaded for treason against Henry VI of England; his emblem, a clog and chain, was associated with training apes for entertainment

leotard a one-piece, close-fitting garment worn by dancers and gymnasts; named after the French trapeze artist Jules Léotard (1830–1870), who devised it

machiavellian politically cunning and immoral; named after the Italian statesman and writer Nicolò Machiavelli (1469–1527), whose treatise on government, **Il Principe/ The Prince**, advocated ruthless principles of rule

Mach number the ratio of the speed of a body to the speed of sound in air; named after the German scientist Ernst Mach (1838–1916), who investigated supersonic speed and the shock waves it produces, and from whose investigations the Mach measurement was developed

mesmerize to entrance or fascinate; named after the Austrian physician and hypnotist Friedrich Anton Mesmer (1734–1815), who claimed to exert 'animal magnetism' over his patients

pasteurize to sterilize milk or other substances by a process of heating followed by rapid cooling; named after the French chemist Louis Pasteur (1822–1895), who developed the process in the 1850s

platonic denoting spiritual as distinct from sexual love; named after the Greek philosopher Plato (427–347 BC), who described this form of love with particular reference to his teacher Socrates

Queensberry rules a code of rules followed in modern boxing; named after the eighth Marquis of Queensberry (1844–1900), who greatly reduced the brutality of the sport by means of rules introduced in 1869

quixotic romantically chivalrous; named after Don Quixote, hero of the romantic story by the Spanish writer Miguel de Cervantes (1547–1616)

raglan an overcoat cut with the arms continuing up to the neck without shoulder seams; named after Lord Raglan (1788–1855), who wore a coat designed in this way so as to disguise his loss of an arm from a battle wound

sandwich a snack consisting of two pieces of bread with a filling between; named after the 4th Earl of Sandwich (1718–92), who is said to have ordered this kind of food for eating at the gaming table

Selected Eponyms (*continued*)

silhouette a representation of a figure in outline; named after the French politician and writer Etienne de Silhouette (1709–1767), who was noted for his meanness and gave his name first to things made cheaply and then to this particular form of economy

teddy bear a toy bear; named after Teddy, the nickname of US President Theodore Roosevelt

(1858–1919), who was a well-known hunter of bears and was shown sparing the life of a bear cub in a cartoon of 1906

titanic great, colossal; named after the Titans, an early pre-Olympian family of gods in Greek mythology

volt a unit of electrical force; named after Count Alessandro Volta (1745–1827), an

Italian physicist who invented the first electric battery that had a continuous current

zinnia an annual plant with elaborate and strongly coloured flowers; named after the German botanist Johann Gottfried Zinn (1727–1759)

Some New Words in English

alcopop any of various alcoholic drinks that are flavoured and marketed like soft drinks

bad hair day a day that starts badly for someone, when they feel depressed at the prospect of the day ahead, think their hair is in a mess, can't find the right clothes, and so on

breakbeat a short snatch of a rhythm on drums or other instruments, played repeatedly as a tape loop to create a special rhythm

Britpop popular music that emphasizes melody and draws on the pop music of the 1960s

browser also referred to as a **Web Browser,** an application that enables users to access information on the Internet in the form of pages combining text, graphics, and, increasingly, interactive contents

business park an area on the outskirts of a town or city that is designed for business premises and light industry

challenged used with a preceding word to form a supposedly politically correct (PC) alternative to a term that is regarded as offensive or discriminatory, such as **intellectually challenged** for 'backward' and **vertically challenged** for 'short'; frequently used in a jokey way

channel surfing browsing through the various channels of a television network or cable television to find what one wants; an extension of the idea of 'surfing the Net (or Internet)'

distance learning a system of educational courses taught by means of correspondence, television broadcasts, electronic communication, and so on, for people who are unable to attend a university or college regularly

downsize to reduce the size and scale of a business operation, usually by making redundancies

emoticon a sequence of ordinary keyboard symbols used in e-mail to form an icon representing anger, pleasure, shock, or other basic emotions of the sender; for example, the sequence of colon, hyphen, and closing parenthesis resembles a smiling face (called a **smiley**) when turned on its side

fast track a quick way to get something done, to make progress, or to succeed in life

feel-good factor a feeling of optimism and prosperity in people's financial and material circumstances

flame to send aggressive or abusive e-mail messages; the practice is called **flaming** and the message is sometimes referred to as **flame mail;** it is possibly a revival (conscious or otherwise) of an older use of **flame** meaning 'intense emotion' and (as a verb) 'to excite emotion', 'to become violently angry'

gangsta a style of rap or beat music with strong rhythms and aggressive lyrics; it is a fanciful variation of the word **gangster,** because of its violent associations

glass ceiling the limit that a person, especially a woman or a member of an ethnic minority, can reach in their career; it is so called because what is on the other side can be seen but can't be reached

hypermedia a combination of **multimedia** and **hypertext;** information presented in a format designed for viewing on the computer screen and which may combine text, graphics, sound, and video, where the components of the presentation may be integrated by means of links or **hyperlinks** to allow the reader to navigate between them; the presentation media include CD-ROM and Internet (HTML) pages

infobahn another name for the information superhighway, and including telecommunications, the Internet, the World Wide Web, and associated resources; it is a fanciful variation of the German **Autobahn** (motorway), extended by the use of the prefix **info-** which is also found in **infomania** (a craving for electronic information), **infomercial** (an information film used for commercial purposes), and other words

microfibre a closely woven synthetic fibre used in telecommunications

must-have something that a fashionable person has to have, such as a fashion accessory or the latest advance in computer technology

nanny state the government regarded as having an excessive or intrusive influence on people's lives

newsgroup a forum for discussion and exchange of information by users of the Internet, especially **Usenet** which comprises thousands of newsgroups dealing with a wide range of topics

one-stop involving only one call or point of reference, especially of a shop or store providing everything that customers are likely to need

on-line shopping a shopping service using a telecommunication or computer link to enable customers to order goods from their homes

outsource to subcontract work to another company or to buy in components from another supplier

peace dividend the financial benefit resulting from a reduction in military expenditure during a time of international peace

power dressing dressing in a way that helps to reinforce a person's business position and authority

road rage uncontrolled rage among road-users, usually leading to physical violence and in some cases severe injury or even death; the concept is being extended to other areas of human activity, such as **trolley rage** (in supermarkets) and **golf rage**

safe haven a demilitarized area in a war zone that is set aside by international agreement for refugees, especially ethnic minorities and other oppressed people, often maintained by the UN or some other neutral organization

smart card a plastic card like a credit card but with information stored in an intergrated circuit instead of in a strip, used in electronic and telecommunications applications

smart drug a drug that is supposed to improve a person's mental powers and enhance perception of their surroundings

soundbite a short extract from a speech or interview, chosen for its effectiveness in making a point and often disregarding the context in which it was originally made

spam to send an unsolicited e-mail message to hundreds or thousands of recipients, usually for commercial reasons, although sometimes for purely mischievous reasons

spin doctor a senior marketing or public-relations official who seeks to project a particular image for a party or politician

swipe card a plastic card such as a charge card or credit card with information stored in a magnetic strip on the back, which can be read when it is passed or 'swiped' through an electronic reading device

(continued)

Some New Words in English (continued)

tabloid television television broadcasting that consists mainly of short popular programmes and sensational news stories in the manner of tabloid newspapers; a **tabloid** was originally a tradename for a type of medicine tablet, then came to mean a small-format highly illustrated newspaper, and is now working its way into the information superhighway

-tastic a combining form made from the ending of **fantastic** and used to build other words meaning 'something fantastic', usually in the domain of youth culture in words such as **poptastic** and **rocktastic**

techno a style of dance music in which the rhythm is enhanced by electronic means, producing a loud hectic effect

video wall a series of VDT (visual display terminal) screens arranged geometrically to cover a large surface, showing the same picture in each or making a large composite picture for use in exhibitions and presentations

virtual used to denote a transaction or activity done as a simulation of an ordinary-life activity within the context of electronic networks such as the Internet, for example **virtual payment;** it is an extension of the use in **virtual reality,** which denotes the electronic simulation of a person's (real or imagined) immediate environment

voice mail a system for handling and storing verbal messages transmitted over a conventional telephone line, and for providing information and access to the caller

-zine a combining form denoting a magazine or newspaper devoted to a particular readership or age group, for example a **popzine** or **teenzine;** it is developed from the original use in **fanzine,** and **zine** is also occasionally used by itself to mean any kind of special-interest magazine

Some Commonly Misspelled Words

accommodation	conscientious	exercise	install	omit	separate
achieve	controversial	exhilarate	instalment	oneself	sergeant
acquittal	definitely	extravagant	jewellery	parallel	siege
address	dependant (noun)	February	league	paraphernalia	sieve
aggressive	dependent	foreign	liaise	permissible	sincerely
amount	(adjective)	friend	library	personnel	soldier
anemone	describe	fulfil	liquefy	Pharaoh	solemn
appearance	desiccate	gauge	literature	poisonous	supersede
asphalt	desperate	gazetteer	longitude	possess	targeted
attach	detach	government	manoeuvre	potatoes	terrestrial
banister	diarrhoea	grammar	Mediterranean	practice (noun)	tomatoes
beautiful	diphtheria	guarantee	millennium	practise (verb)	tranquillity
beginning	disappear	guard	millionaire	precede	traveller
bicycle	disappoint	handkerchief	mischievous	prejudice	unnecessary
biscuit	dissect	harass	mortgage	privilege	until
budgeted	dissipated	height	necessary	profession	unusual
business	ecstasy	hygiene	neither	pronunciation	unwieldy
cemetery	eighth	hypocrisy	niece	publicly	vetoed
cigarette	embarrass	idiosyncrasy	noticeable	questionnaire	vicious
collapsible	exaggerate	immediately	nuisance	receive	videoed
committee	excellent	independent (noun	occasion	repellent	Wednesday
competition	excitement	and adjective)	occurrence	seize	yield

Some Commonly Confused Words

accept to take, acknowledge (*We accept credit cards.*)

except to exclude, excluding (*Open daily except Sundays.*)

adjacent next to, lying near, though not necessarily in contact (*The school was adjacent to the church.*)

adjoining next to and in contact with another (*The offices are to the left, with a snack bar adjoining.*)

admission the right to enter a place (*Admission to the exhibition is by invitation only.*)

admittance the act of entering a place (*No admittance except on business.*)

adverse hostile, harmful (*The medicine has no adverse effects.*)

averse opposed, disinclined (*Are you averse to the idea?*)

affect to produce a change or alteration (*Smoking can affect your health.*)

effect to bring about, accomplish (*The treatment effected an immediate improvement in the patient's health.*)

affection fondness for a person or thing (*I remember our times together with great affection.*)

affectation pretentious or unnatural behaviour (*Try to avoid affectation when speaking in public.*)

allusion indirect reference (*The poem is full of allusions to nature.*)

delusion mistaken belief (*He had the delusion of being watched.*)

illusion false perception (*Magic is a mixture of illusion and belief.*)

alternate to take turns; happening in turns (*The two television channels agreed to alternate coverage of the matches; each would show a game on alternate days.*)

alternative choice between possibilities (*There are several alternatives: we could walk, we could go by bus, or we could take a taxi.*)

Some Commonly Confused Words (*continued*)

ambiguous obscure (*The message was perfectly clear and not in the least ambiguous.*)

ambivalent having an uncertain attitude or feeling (*Young people have an ambivalent attitude to religion.*)

amend to alter something (*The referee amended the rules to make it easier for new players.*)

emend alter a text to improve it (*The editor has emended the last five lines, which were corrupt.*)

amuse to cause to smile or laugh (*The clowns amused the audience.*)

bemuse bewilder (*The children were bemused by the strange surroundings.*)

appraise to evaluate or assess (*They appraised the proposed budget.*)

apprise to inform (*We will be apprised of the committee's decision.*)

ascent rise, climb (*The ascent of the hill proved too exhausting for some of the walkers.*)

assent agree (*The director assented to the new proposal.*)

assume to take for granted without proof (*The teacher assumed she could read.*)

presume to suppose (*When he did not return from the war, he was presumed dead.*)

assure to state positively, guarantee (*She assured him the tickets were ready.*)

ensure to make something certain (*The builder ensured the walls were safe.*)

insure to cover by insurance (*Are your belongings insured?*)

aural of hearing (*The doctor arranged an aural examination for the patient.*)

oral spoken; concerning the mouth (*Many of the stories were passed down by oral tradition, rather than in writing.*)

averse see **adverse**

avoid to take action not to encounter someone or experience something (*Have you been avoiding me? I try to avoid the centre of town on Saturdays.*)

evade to escape an obligation or difficulty by cunning (*The Chancellor managed to evade all questions about the recent rise in interest rates.*)

baleful gloomy or menacing (*He gave a baleful glance in my direction.*)

baneful harmful or lethal (*The new tenants exercised a baneful influence on the community. We were warned of the baneful effects of too much alcohol.*)

bemuse see **amuse**

biannual happening twice a year (*We make biannual visits to the in-laws: once at Christmas and again in the summer.*)

biennial happening every two years (*The school was due for its biennial inspection that year.*)

breach a break or violation (*The action amounted to a serious breach of contract.*)

breech the lower or back part of something, especially a gun (*They loaded new shells into the breech.*)

cannon a large gun (*The enemy was bombarded by cannons from the castle walls.*)

canon a rule; a priest living under church rule (*Canon law has detailed rules on marriage. He has just been appointed canon.*); also musical piece

censor to ban or suppress (*The authorities censored part of the play because of its bad language.*)

censure to criticize, find fault with (*The tennis player was censured for his unsporting behaviour on court.*)

childish silly or immature, as a child can be (*It was childish of him to stomp out of the room like that.*)

childlike innocent or endearing like a child (*She has many delightful, childlike qualities.*)

classic first or finest of its kind; regarded as standard (*This book is the classic authority on bee-keeping.*)

classical traditional; having links with the culture of Greece and Rome (*The statue had a classical simplicity and beauty.*)

complement to suit, complete (*That shirt complements your suit nicely.*)

compliment to praise (*She complimented the child on his good manners.*)

confidant person to whom secrets are told (*The teacher became the confidant of many of the pupils.*)

confident bold, trusting (*After a while the pupils became more confident in their approach to exams.*)

continual happening constantly or repeatedly (*The families suffered continual attacks from vandals.*)

continuous going on without interruption (*The job was finished after three weeks' continuous work.*)

co-respondent person cited in divorce proceedings (*He was embarrassed to find himself named as co-respondent.*)

correspondent regular writer of letters (*My pen friend and I have been correspondents since we were teenagers.*)

council body of people who meet for discussion or consultation (*The council meets once a month.*)

counsel advice, guidance; the person who provides it, especially a barrister (*He listened to counsel's advice, then acted upon it.*)

credible believable (*The actor gave a credible portrayal of Iago.*)

creditable bringing honour (*The gymnast gave a highly creditable performance.*)

currant a dried fruit (*She added currants to the cake mix.*)

current present, of the moment (*The current crisis is more serious than the last one.*); also movement of electrically charged particles (**electric current**)

definite exact, clear, certain (*There was a definite chill in the air.*)

definitive decisive, authoritative (*This is the definitive version of the story.*)

delusion see **allusion**

depraved morally bad or corrupt (*He was utterly depraved, and had a bad influence on many of his colleagues.*)

deprived lacking life's necessities (*He suffered a deprived childhood.*)

deprecate to express disapproval of (*She deprecated smoking and drinking.*)

depreciate to lose or lower value (*The value of the property depreciated over the years.*)

diagnosis identification of a condition or problem (*My diagnosis of the poor sales is that people are ignoring our advertisements.*)

prognosis forecast (*The economic prognosis this month is more favourable.*)

discreet modest or cautious (*We must be discreet about this in case he suspects something.*)

discrete distinct, separate (*The work can be divided into several discrete tasks.*)

disinterested not involved, impartial (*A disinterested observer of the scene would have wondered what all the fuss was about.*)

uninterested not interested, indifferent (*The artist was uninterested in the public reaction to his work.*)

doubtful causing doubt (*It is doubtful whether we will arrive on time.*)

dubious having doubts (*She feels very dubious about the whole idea.*)

effect see **affect**

elicit to draw or bring out (*To elicit the information, she asked the troubled teenager subtle questions.*)

illicit unlawful (*The crew were involved in the illicit import of alcohol.*)

(*continued*)

Some Commonly Confused Words (continued)

emend see **amend**

eminent famous, distinguished (The actor had an eminent career.)

imminent impending, about to happen (A storm was imminent.)

ensure see **assure**

except see **accept**

explicit clearly and directly stated (The instructions were explicit but the driver still lost his way.)

implicit suggested, implied (The implicit message in the politician's speech made voters feel uncomfortable.)

extant still existing (The historic documents were extant in the library.)

extent range, scope (The full extent of the damage caused by the fire had not been fully estimated.)

evade see **avoid**

flaunt to parade ostentatiously (He loved flaunting his knowledge on the subject.)

flout to openly disobey (The school's lack of discipline meant that many pupils flouted the rules.)

flounder to struggle, stumble (My next question made him flounder.)

founder to collapse, sink (The project foundered when we no longer had the funds to support it.)

forbear to refrain or abstain from (It was hard to forbear from mentioning his bad behaviour.)

forebear ancestor (He was a carpenter as his forebears had been.)

forego to go before, precede (Choose an item from the foregoing list. It was a foregone conclusion.)

forgo to do without (Lack of money meant that he had to forgo many luxuries.)

fortunate lucky, having good fortune (It was fortunate that the weather stayed fine.)

fortuitous happening by chance (It was fortuitous that everyone arrived together.)

founder see **flounder**

hereditary handed down by inheritance (She suffers from a hereditary blood condition.)

heredity genetic transmission of traits from one generation to another (Heredity is an important factor in determining character.)

historic memorable, momentous (The two heads of state signed a historic agreement.)

historical concerning history; based on historical events (King Arthur is generally believed to be a historical figure, though some regard him as legendary.)

illicit see **elicit**

illusion see **allusion**

imminent see **eminent**

implicit see **explicit**

imply to mean, suggest without direct statement (He didn't actually say I took the money, but he implied it.)

infer to deduce (I think we can infer from his repeated absences that he is not really interested in the subject.)

inapt not fitting or suitable (They gave her the inapt name of Patience.)

inept not skilful, awkward (They were extremely inept at finding names for their children.)

inequity unfairness, injustice (Some members grumbled about the inequity of the voting system.)

iniquity wickedness, immorality (The nightclub was said to be a den of iniquity, with alcohol and drugs freely available.)

ingenious clever or well thought out (Sally had an ingenious method of keeping the bread fresh.)

ingenuous honest and open (He was ingenuous enough to admit that he'd been wrong.)

insidious gradually and stealthily harmful or destructive (Cancer is often an insidious disease.)

invidious liable to cause resentment (Teachers are often faced with invidious duties.)

insure see **assure**

inter to bury a dead person (The body will be interred after a short service.)

intern to imprison someone for political reasons (Suspected terrorists were interned for several months.)

militate to adversely influence (The bad weather militated against the planned outing.)

mitigate to moderate, make less severe (The offence was mitigated by the fact that the offender had not seen the warning notice.)

moral concerned with behaviour (Who is responsible for the morals of society?)

morale confidence (Morale was high as the team carried off the trophy.)

mythical imaginary, belonging to myth (Unicorns are mythical creatures.)

mythological relating to the study of myths (He compares the mythological content of the world's main religions.)

oral see **aural**

ordinance law, guideline (The people were afraid of the king's harsh ordinances.)

ordnance weapons, military supplies (The Board of Ordnance considered purchasing a new type of gun.)

persecute to cause to suffer (The Christians were persecuted by the Romans.)

prosecute to bring to trial (The criminal was prosecuted for the offence.)

precede to go before in place or time (The talk was preceded by drinks in the foyer.)

proceed to go forward, continue (The government intends to proceed with its proposal for a referendum.)

prescribe order the use of (The doctor prescribed a course of antibiotics.)

proscribe ban, prohibit, outlaw (In earlier times adultery was proscribed by law.)

presume see **assume**

prevaricate to avoid saying what should be said (The doctor prevaricated, not wanting to tell the patient the truth.)

procrastinate to put off doing something (We cannot procrastinate any longer; we must get on with it.)

principal chief, most important (My principal objection is the cost.)

principle belief or rule (It would be against my principles to do such a thing.)

proceed see **precede**

procrastinate see **prevaricate**

prognosis see **diagnosis**

proscribe see **prescribe**

prosecute see **persecute**

sociable friendly, companionable (She was a sociable old lady, and liked a good chat.)

social relating to society (I'm not doing this out of a sense of social duty.)

stalactite tapering formation of calcite hanging down in limestone caves

stalagmite tapering formation of calcite pointing up in limestone caves

stationary not moving (The train was stationary in the station.)

stationery paper goods (There was plenty of paper in the office stationery store.)

tortuous full of twists and turns (We climbed the tortuous path up the hill.)

torturous causing torture (Families of the trapped men waited in torturous silence for news.)

Some Commonly Confused Words (*continued*)

unexceptionable that cannot be faulted (*Their views on race relations seem unexceptionable.*)

unexceptional ordinary, not exceptional (*The house was small and unexceptional.*)

uninterested see **disinterested**

unwanted not wanted (*What do you do with your unwanted presents?*)

unwonted not usual (*That was an unwonted liberty on your part.*)

urban relating to towns or town life (*I prefer to live in an urban environment.*)

urbane having a refined or cultivated manner; suave (*My uncle is urbane and witty, and likes fine wines.*)

venal corrupt; mercenary (*The candidate committed the venal offence of bribing colleagues to vote for him.*)

venial pardonable (*Some dogs are punished for relatively venial offences.*)

waive to give up or disclaim (*The prisoner waived his right to appeal against the sentence.*)

wave to move a hand in greeting or as a signal; to move back and forth (*The flag waved in the breeze.*)

Some Foreign Words and Phrases Used in English

agent provocateur (French 'instigating agent') person employed during political or social conflicts, someone who in the guise of a supporter, infiltrates a political or social movement in order to provoke action that will damage that movement

ahimsa (Sanskrit 'non-injury') the Hindu, Buddhist, and Jain doctrine of harming no living being; non-violence

aide-de-camp (French 'camp assistant') (ADC) officer who acts as private secretary to a general, commander-in-chief, or air marshal, and would normally accompany them on any duty

aide-mémoire (French 'memory aid') outline of a discussion or agreement; something that serves as an aid to memory

apartheid (Afrikaans 'separateness') in South Africa, the former government system of economic, political, and legal discrimination and rigorous separation between people of European descent and others; often applied to similar systems elsewhere

apropos (French 'to the purpose') relevant to; with respect to; by the way

arête (French 'fishbone') sharp mountain ridge between two gorges

au pair (French 'at par, even') a usually young person serving as a domestic, caregiver, or companion in return for room and board

avant-garde (French 'vanguard') in the arts, those artists or works that are in the forefront of new developments in their media

ayatollah (Persian, from āya Arabic 'miracle' + Allah) the title for a Shiite religious leader

bar mitzvah (Hebrew 'man of duty') the ceremony in a synagogue for a Jewish boy who has reached 13, the age of religious responsibility; the boy himself at the time of the ceremony

belles-lettres (French 'fine letters') literature that is appreciated more for its aesthetic qualities than for its content

bête noire (French 'black beast') something particularly disliked

bhangra (Punjabi) a style of music that combines traditional Punjabi music with rock music

billabong (Aboriginal *billa bong* 'dead river') a dry streambed filled in the rainy season; a branch of a river that comes to a dead end; a stagnant pond

billet-doux (French 'sweet note') a love letter

biltong (Afrikaans 'buttock-tongue') strips of lean meat dried in the sun

blitzkrieg (German 'lightning war') swift military campaign combining air and land forces

bloc (French 'block') united group, generally used to describe politically allied people, parties, or countries, as in the former 'Soviet bloc'

bola or **bolas** (Spanish 'ball') device consisting of two or more heavy balls fastened to the ends of a long rope, used to entrap cattle and other animals by hurling it at their legs and entangling them

bon mot (French 'good word') witty remark

bonsai (Japanese 'bowl cultivation') art of producing miniature trees in small pots by selective pruning

bon voyage (French 'good journey') an expression meaning 'have a good journey'

bourgeois (French 'townsman') a member of the middle class, implying that a person is unimaginative, conservative, and materialistic

bric-a-brac (French) odds and ends, usually old, ornamental, and less valuable than antiques, and often having sentimental value

cachet (French, from Old French *cacher*, to press) a quality or mark of distinction or authenticity

caftan or **kaftan** (Russian from Turkish) a garment consisting of a long tunic with or without a belt and long sleeves. Worn mainly in eastern Mediterranean countries

canaille (French, from Italian *canaglia*, 'pack of dogs') the mob, rabble

carte blanche (French 'blank paper') no instructions, complete freedom to do as one wishes

ceilidh (Irish Gaelic 'companion') an informal social gathering, with conversation, music, dancing and story-telling

c'est la vie (French) that's life

chacun à son goût (French) each to their own taste

chakra (Sanskrit 'wheel') in yoga, one of the centres of spiritual or physical power in the human body

chef d'oeuvre (French 'leading work') a masterpiece, particularly in literature or art

chinook (Native American) warm, dry wind of the eastern slopes of the Rocky Mountains

comme il faut (French 'as it should be') socially correct and acceptable

conquistador (Spanish 'conqueror') any of the early Spanish explorers and adventurers in the Americas, such as Hernán Cortés (Mexico) and Francisco Pizarro (Peru)

coup d'état (French 'stroke of state') or **coup** forcible takeover of the government of a country, generally carried out by violent or illegal means

crème de la crème (French 'the cream of the cream') the elite, the very best

cri de coeur (French 'cry from the heart') a fervent outcry

cul-de-sac (French 'bottom of the bag') street closed off at one end; an inescapable situation

cwm (Welsh 'valley') a valley or deep rounded hollow on the side of a hill

déjà vu (French 'already seen') the feeling that something encountered for the first time has in fact been experienced before

denouement (French *dénouer* 'to untie') the unravelling of the plot of a work of fiction; the result of a complicated sequence of events

(continued)

Some Foreign Words and Phrases Used in English (*continued*)

de rigueur (French 'of strictness') demanded by current rules of etiquette or fashion

détente (French 'a loosening') reduction of political tension and the easing of strained relations between nations

de trop (French 'too much') not needed; superfluous

diaspora (Greek 'dispersal') the scattering of the Jews after being exiled to Babylonia; the breaking up of a homogeneous group of people

doppelgänger (German 'double-goer') apparition of a living person; a person's double

double entendre (French 'double meaning') an ambiguous word or phrase often with sexual reference

ecru (French 'raw, unbleached') a neutral pale brown colour, as of an unbleached fabric

effendi (Turkish 'master') a title of respect originally applied to learned people and government officials in Turkey; now refers to a respected or educated man in eastern Mediterranean countries

eisteddfod (Welsh 'session') a festival of poetry, singing, and music; a congress of Welsh bards and minstrels

embarras de richesses (French 'embarrassment of riches') more than one needs or can use

éminence grise (French 'gray eminence') a power behind a throne: that is, a manipulator of power without immediate responsibility

enchanté (French 'enchanted') delighted, charmed

encore (French 'again') in music, an unprogrammed extra item, usually short and well known, played at the end of a concert at the request of an enthusiastic audience

enfant terrible (French 'terrible child') person whose rash and unconventional behaviour shocks and embarrasses others

en masse (French 'in a mass') as a group, in a body, all together

en passant (French 'in passing') incidentally

en route (French) on the way

ersatz (German 'substitute') artificial; generally inferior imitation or substitute

fait accompli (French 'accomplished fact') something that has been done and cannot be undone

fatwa (Arabic) a formal ruling given by an Islamic religious authority

faux pas (French 'false step') a social blunder

felucca (Italian from Arabic *fuluk*, pl. of *fulk*, 'ship') type of sailing vessel used in the Mediterranean or on the Nile

femme fatale (French 'fatal woman') a seductive woman who brings about the ruin of her lovers

finale (Italian 'final') the conclusion of an opera or instrumental composition; the close or end of something

fin de siècle (French 'end of century') referring to the end of the 19th century, especially its art and literature

force majeure (French 'superior force') circumstances beyond one's control; irresistible or overwhelming force

futon (Japanese) a mattress, usually made of cotton, used on the floor or on a frame and designed to be folded when not in use

gaucho (American Spanish) cowboy of the pampas of South America

geisha (Japanese *gei* 'art' and *sha* 'person') a Japanese woman skilled in the arts of entertaining men with music, dance, and conversation

glasnost (Russian 'publicity') in the former Soviet Union, the policy of introducing greater freedom of expression and information and opening up relations with Western countries

goy (Hebrew 'nation') a colloquial Yiddish name for a non-Jew, usually used disparagingly. The plural is **goyim**

gravure (French *graver* 'to engrave') photogravure; engraving; engraved item

gulag (Russian) the system of prisons and forced-labour camps used to silence dissidents and opponents of the Soviet regime

hafiz (Arabic 'to guard') Muslim who knows the Koran by heart; a title of respect for such a person

hara-kiri (Japanese 'belly-cut') ceremonial suicide by disembowelling, formerly practised by samurai faced with disgrace; also known as **seppuku**

hosanna (Hebrew 'save us, we pray') shout of praise to God; originally an appeal to God for deliverance

intelligentsia (Russian, from Latin *intelligentia*, 'intelligence') the top echelon of intellectuals in a society

je ne sais quoi (French 'I don't know what') a certain indescribable quality

jihad or **jehad** (Arabic) holy war; crusade

joie de vivre (French 'joy of living') the joy of being alive

kabuki (Japanese *kabu* 'music and dancing' plus *ki* 'style') popular Japanese theatrical form, with music and dancing performed in a stylized manner

kamikaze (Japanese 'divine wind') from a mythical wind that destroyed a fleet of invading Mongols; Japanese airmen who made suicidal crashes onto enemy targets during World War II; now used to imply recklessness

karaoke (Japanese 'empty orchestra') a form of entertainment in which people sing well-known songs to an accompaniment of pre-recorded music

karma (Sanskrit 'action') in Hinduism and Buddhism, the total of a person's actions in one incarnation, which determines their fate in the next; fate, destiny

khaki (Urdu 'dust-coloured') a dull yellow-brown colour; cloth of this colour used for military uniforms

kibbutz (Hebrew 'gathering') an Israeli collective farming community. The plural is **kibbutzim**

kimono (Japanese *ki* 'wearing' and *mono* 'thing') a long sashed Japanese robe with loose sleeves; a similar garment worn in the West

kohl (Arabic) powdered antimony sulphide, used in Asia and the Middle East to darken the area around the eyes

kosher (Hebrew 'proper') used to describe food that is prepared in accordance with Jewish law; slang for legitimate, authentic

kvetch (Yiddish 'squeeze') to complain, gripe; a complainer

laager (Afrikaans 'camp') an encampment defended by a circle of wagons

laissez faire (French 'let do') theory that the state should not intervene in economic affairs beyond the minimum necessary for the government to operate

lèse-majesté (French from Latin 'injured majesty') treason; offence against the sovereign

lingua franca (Italian 'Frankish tongue') any language that is used as a means of communication by groups who speak different languages; for example, English is a lingua franca used by Japanese doing business in Finland

litotes (Greek) rhetorical understatement, in particular, affirming something by denying its opposite, as in 'It was no small matter'

macramé (Turkish, from Arabic *miqramah*, 'striped cloth') (the art of making) knotted and woven cord used as patterned ornaments

maharaja or **maharajah** (Hindi, from Sanskrit 'great king') the title of certain Indian princes who rank above rajas

mah-jong (Chinese) popular Chinese game, played with tiles marked in suits

major-domo (Spanish *mayordomo*, from Medieval Latin *majordomus*, 'head of the house') chief steward, head servant

malapropos (French *mal à propos*, 'ill(-suited) to the purpose') inappropriate(ly); out of place

Some Foreign Words and Phrases Used in English (*continued*)

mañana (Spanish) morning; tomorrow; an unspecified time in the future

mantra (Sanskrit 'sacred utterance') in Hinduism, a sacred formula, such as from the Vedas, used as a prayer or incantation; a sacred word or syllable used for meditation

mestizo (Spanish, from Latin *mixticius*, 'mixed') person of mixed blood, especially of mixed Native American and European ancestry

meze (Turkish) an hors d'oeuvre, served especially with an aperitif

mikado (Japanese 'exalted gate') formerly the title of the emperor of Japan

mise en scène (French 'stage setting') in cinema, the composition and content of the frame in terms of background scenery, actors, costumes, props, camera movement, and lighting

mot juste (French) the right word, just the word to suit the occasion

narghile or **nargileh** (Persian 'coconut') an oriental pipe in which the smoke bubbles through scented water before being inhaled through a tube

necropolis (Greek *nekropolis*, from *nekros* 'dead body' and *polis* 'city') cemetery; burial ground

née (French 'born') followed by a surname, indicating the name of a woman before marriage

nirvana (Sanskrit 'blowing out') the extinction of individual existence with its desires and passions, a religious goal in Hinduism and Buddhism; place or state of bliss

noblesse oblige (French 'nobility obliges') notion that the aristocracy ought to behave honourably

nom de plume (French 'pen name') a writer's pseudonym

nouveau riche (French, literally 'new rich') person who recently became wealthy

oeuvre (French 'work') work of art or literary work; collected works of a person

origami (Japanese *ori* 'to fold' and *kami* 'paper') the art of folding paper into decorative shapes

outré (French *outrer* 'to go beyond') extreme, beyond the bounds of acceptability

padre (Italian 'father') a priest

parvenu (French 'arrived') a social upstart

passé (French) out of date

pastiche (French, from Italian *pasticcio*) a work of art that mixes styles, motifs, and materials, often in imitation of the work of other artists

perestroika (Russian 'restructuring') in the former Soviet Union, the wide-ranging restructuring and reforming of the economic and political system initiated from 1985 by Mikhail Gorbachev

piazza (Italian, from Latin *platea*, 'broad street') square or open area, especially in an Italian town; marketplace

pièce de résistance (French 'piece with staying power') the most outstanding item in a collection; the main dish of a meal

pied-à-terre (French 'foot on the ground') a convenient second home, usually small and in a town or city

pique (French *piquer* 'to prick') a feeling of irritation or resentment; to arouse by challenge or provocation

piqué (French *piquer* 'to prick, quilt') stitched; embossed or nubby fabric, usually cotton

plus ça change, plus c'est la même chose (French) the more things change, the more they stay the same

poste restante (French 'waiting mail') a postal system whereby mail is sent to a post office and kept there until collected by the person to whom it is addressed

poteen (Irish Gaelic 'little pot') an Irish alcoholic spirit, illegally brewed, usually from potatoes

prêt-à-porter (French 'ready to wear') ready-to-wear clothing

raison d'être (French) reason for existence

raj (Hindi from Sanskrit *rājan* 'king') government or rule. The raj refers to British dominance in the Indian subcontinent before 1947

Realpolitik (German) practical politics

recherché (French 'sought after') rare, hard to find; often used to mean highly refined, exotic, or pretentious

roman à clef (French, literally 'novel with a key') a novel in which a real story is told using fictitious names

samovar (Russian 'self-boiling') metal urn with a tap spout, traditionally heated by charcoal, used for making tea

samurai (Japanese) in the 11th–19th centuries in Japan, a warrior retainer of a prince or nobleman; a member of the military caste

sang-froid (French 'cold blood') coolness, composure

sari or **saree** (Hindi) a long strip of cloth worn generally as a garment by Indian women

savoir-faire (French 'know how to do') knowing what to do, how to behave

schlemiel (Yiddish) a fool; unlucky person

serape or **sarape** (Mexican Spanish *sarape*) a heavy blanket worn as a shawl or wrap

sierra (Spanish 'saw') mountain range with a jagged outline

siesta (Spanish) an afternoon nap; rest

sjambok (Afrikaans) a heavy strip made of rhinoceros or hippopotamus hide, used in South Africa for driving cattle or administering punishment

slalom (Norwegian 'sloping track') a downhill ski race on a zigzag course between upright poles

sobriquet or **soubriquet** (French) nickname

sortie (French, from *sortir*, 'to go out') quick attack; a military mission or flight

sushi (Japanese) a Japanese dish of shaped balls of cold rice with slices of raw fish

swami (Hindi, from Sanskrit 'lord') a Hindu mystic or religious teacher; used especially as a title

Swaraj (Sanskrit 'self-rule') in British India, self-government or independence

swastika (Sanskrit 'mark of well-being') an equal-armed cross with right-angled ends, a symbol of good fortune; adopted as an Aryan symbol by the German Nazi Party in 1935

Taoiseach (Irish Gaelic 'chieftan') the title of the prime minister of the Republic of Ireland

tepee, teepee, or **tipi** (Sioux *thípi*, 'dwelling') a conically shaped dwelling, constructed from poles covered with bark or skins, once used by certain Native American peoples

tête-à-tête (French 'head-to-head') private conversation between two people

tour de force (French 'feat of strength') a remarkable accomplishment

trek (Afrikaans 'march' from Middle Dutch *trecken* 'to pull') (one stage of) a long journey across country, originally by ox wagon; to make such a journey

tsunami (Japanese *tsu* 'harbor' and *nami* 'wave') a large wave produced by an earthquake or volcanic eruption on the ocean floor

vamoose (Spanish *vamos*, 'let's go') to depart or leave quickly

veld or **veldt** (Afrikaans 'field') unenclosed country or open grassland, especially of southern Africa

vérité (French 'truth'), as in *cinéma vérité*, used to describe a realistic or documentary style

virtuoso (Italian 'skilled') in music, a performer of unusual interpretive and technical skill; a person skilled in a particular endeavour, especially in the arts or sciences

vis-à-vis (French 'face-to-face') with regard to; as compared with

voilà (French 'see there') used to express satisfaction with something or to call attention to something

Weltanschauung (German 'world-view') a philosophy of life

yarmulke (Yiddish, from Polish and Ukranian *yarmulka*) a skullcap worn by Jewish men, especially at worship or prayer

yeti (Tibetan) the abominable snowman

yoga (Hindi, from Sanskrit 'yoke, union') a Hindi system of philosophy using physical and mental exercises to attain control, well-being, and spiritual insight

Zeitgeist (German 'time spirit') spirit of the age

A Selection of Latin Phrases

ab ovo from the beginning

ad astra per aspera to the stars through difficulties

addendum something to be added, usually in writing, which qualifies a foregoing thesis or statement

ad infinitum to infinity, endlessly

ad nauseam to the point of disgust

animus will or intention

carpe diem 'seize the day'; live for the present

casus belli justification for war, grounds for a dispute

caveat emptor 'let the buyer beware'; dictum that professes the buyer is responsible for checking that the goods or services they purchase are satisfactory

cave canem beware of the dog

cogito, ergo sum 'I think, therefore I am'; quotation from French philosopher René Descartes

cognomen surname or family name; nickname

compos mentis of sound mind

corrigendum something to be corrected

curriculum vitae (CV) 'the course of life'; account of a person's education and previous employment, attached to a job application

de facto in fact

de gustibus non est disputandum there is no accounting for taste

de jure according to law; legally

deus ex machina 'a god from the machinery'; far-fetched or unlikely event that resolves an intractable difficulty

dramatis personae the characters in a play

emeritus someone who has retired from an official position but retains their title on an honorary basis, for example, a professor emeritus

ergo therefore; hence

erratum an error

et alia or **et al.** and other things

ex cathedra 'from the throne'; term describing a statement by the pope, taken to be indisputably true, and which must be accepted by Catholics

ex libris 'from among the books of'; used on bookplates to identify the owner

factotum 'do everything'; someone employed to do all types of work

fiat 'let it be done'; authoritative decree or order, especially one given by a person or group holding absolute power

in loco parentis 'in place of a parent'; in a parental capacity

ipse dixit '(he) himself said (it)'; the master has spoken

in situ in place, on the spot, without moving from position

inter alia among other things

in vino veritas in wine (there is) the truth

ipso facto by that very fact

literati educated or cultured people; literary persons

magnum opus a great work of art or literature

mea culpa 'my fault'; an admission of guilt

modus operandi a method of operating

modus vivendi 'way of living'; a compromise between opposing points of view

mores the customs and manners of a society

mutatis mutandis with changes being made; with alterations to fit a new set of circumstances

ne plus ultra no further; the furthest point possible; limit

nil desperandum never despair

nolo contendere plea of no defense; no contest; equivalent to plea of guilty

non sequitur 'it does not follow'; statement that has little or no relevance to the one that preceded it

obiter dictum incidental remark; remark made by a judge on a matter not within his or her jurisdiction

passim 'in many places'; indicates that a reference occurs repeatedly throughout the work

per se in itself

postmortem 'after death'; autopsy

post scriptum (PS) something written below the signature on a letter

prima facie at first sight

pro rata in proportion

pro tem(pore) for the time being

quantum 'as much, how much'; an indivisible physical quantity

quidnunc 'what now?'; gossip; busybody

quid pro quo 'something for something'; an exchange of one thing in return for another

quod erat demonstrandum (QED) 'which was to be proved'; added at the end of a geometry proof

quo vadis? where are you going?

q.v. abbreviation for *quod vide* ('which see'), indicating a cross-reference

sic 'thus', 'so'; sometimes found in brackets within a printed quotation to show that the original has been quoted accurately even though it contains an apparent error

sine die 'without a day being appointed'; indefinitely

sine qua non 'without which not'; absolutely essential

status quo 'the state in which'; the current situation, without change

sub judice 'under a judge'; of judicial proceedings, not yet decided by a court of law or judge: as long as a matter is sub judice all discussion is prohibited elsewhere

tabula rasa 'scraped tablet' (from the Romans' use of wax-covered tablets which could be written on with a pointed stick and cleared by smoothing over the surface); a mind without any preconceived ideas

tempus fugit time flies

terra firma dry land; solid ground

vade mecum 'go with me'; a useful handbook carried about for reference

versus (abbreviation v. or vs.) against

vice versa the other way around

viva voce 'with living voice'; by word of mouth; an oral examination

BRITISH AND AMERICAN ENGLISH

BY R E ALLEN

The great playwright, George Bernard Shaw, once supposedly said that Britain and the USA are 'two countries divided by a common language'. But as is the case when any cultures meet, borrowed words can enrich a language, help identify new activities and experiences, and introduce colourful and entertaining metaphors and phrases.

Vocabulary

Some names for things are totally different, such as *lift–elevator, pavement–sidewalk, caravan–trailer, queue–line, chemist's–drugstore, windscreen–windshield;* others are simply different ways of saying things, such as *planning permission–building permit;* others have minor variations, such as *driving licence–driver's license, maths–math;* and others again exist in addition to words that are shared, such as American *fall* and British–American *autumn,* American *faucet* and British–American *tap,* and American *outlet,* British *power point,* and shared *socket.*

Some words have a different meaning that can be confusing, such as *mean* ('stingy' in Britain, 'nasty' in the USA) and *purse* (a container for coins in Britain, a handbag/pocketbook in the United States). In Britain *pants* are *underpants,* in the USA they are *trousers.*

British English would surely be the poorer without *baby sitter, commuter, gimmick, punchline, snoop, teenager,* and without colourful expressions such as *face the music, be out on a limb, pull the wool over someone's eyes,* and *take a back seat.* Other American terms include *reliable* and *grapevine,* and verbs such as *to advocate, to park,* and *to interview.*

New words are assimilated because they serve a purpose, and without them something could not be said so effectively or interestingly. There are various reasons for this process. One is the political importance of the USA in the world, allowing it to export its culture and language as Britain did in the past. In this way American English finds its way into World English as well as British English. American films and television are seen all over the world, and American food is eaten just as widely, especially by the young. So *burgers, chewing gum,* and *pastrami,* are now familiar to most World English speakers, as are *game shows* and *motels.*

The most famous American term is *OK,* which is found not only in British English but in all varieties of English and as a loanword in many other languages. Some words are easily recognized as American: *bimbo, cop-out,* and *guy,* for example. The word *scam,* meaning a swindle, was thought to be sufficiently foreign to need quotation marks round it when it was used in an article in *The Times* in 1994. Since then it has become rapidly assimilated.

The influence is less strong in the other direction, although British terms that have crossed the Atlantic include *miniskirt, gay* (homosexual) and *gamesmanship.* Some words went to the USA years ago and were then forgotten in Britain, only to reappear as American terms. Examples include *teen, mugging,* and *moonshine* (illicit whiskey). American English has borrowed widely from the languages of its original inhabitants and its immigrants, notably *cookie* (which comes from Dutch), *patio* (Mexican Spanish), and many food terms including *bologna* (sausage, Italian) and *chowder* (from the French, *chaudière).*

It is not surprising to find many computer terms used on both sides of the Atlantic. *GIGO,* an acronym that stands for 'garbage in, garbage out', sums up a basic principle of computer use. With the arrival of the Internet, a universal terminology is developing, and all English-speaking Internet users know about *browsing, cyberspace, downloading, flaming, spamming,* and *surfing.*

Major political events in the USA are news in most countries. From *Watergate,* which was brought to everyone's attention by the events of 1972, came a new combining form *-gate,* which can be added to any name that emerges at the centre of a political scandal, such as *Irangate.* For a brief period British newspapers were full of *Dianagate* (and even *Squidgygate)* when an alleged tape recording of a private conversation of Princess Diana hit the newspaper headlines.

Some words are familiar on one side of the Atlantic but totally unknown on the other. In Britain, only someone who knows the USA well will have heard of the *boondocks* (rural area or wilderness), *duplex* (a two-family dwelling or an apartment on two floors), or *revenue sharing,* and the reverse is true of British terms such as *VAT* (value added tax). In 1993 the popular American film *Groundhog Day* made a hitherto unknown word and idea widely familiar throughout Britain.

Grammar

Grammatical differences between British and American English tend to be fairly minor, and sometimes reflect older structures that have disappeared in British usage. Many of the differences are rapidly disappearing as a result of increased communication between the two cultures. *Shall* and *should* are less commonly used for *will* and *would* in the USA, and *Did you collect your ticket yet?* is still more usual than British *Have you collected your ticket yet?* The American *Do you have...?* is more common than British *Have you got...?* But even these differences are less clearcut than they used to be.

A few verbs are different: British English has *sneaked* and *dived;* American English has *snuck* and *dove.* Most people are aware of *gotten,* which is used in American English as an alternative for *got,* although its use is criticized by some Americans.

Idiom

There are various differences of construction and idiom. American English frequently uses *different than,* which is sometimes used in British English but often deplored. Some Americans would say that JFK Airport in New York is *named for* John F Kennedy, but a British speaker would say it is *named after* him. British speakers have a *home from home* and *sweep things under the carpet* while Americans have a *home away from home* and *sweep things under the rug.* Americans live *on* a street and not *in* it, and *cater to* people instead of *catering for* them. There are several differences in expressing time: *Monday to Friday* is British, *Monday through Friday* American; *a week on Sunday* and *Sunday week* are British; *a quarter of nine* and *ten after six* denote times to Americans only.

Spelling

Differences of spelling persist, and are the most noticeable characteristics that distinguish a piece of writing as American or British. Some differences relate to particular words, for example British *gaol* vs. American *jail* (although *jail* is now common in Britain too), and British *cheque* vs. American *check.* Others are systematic, and apply to whole classes of words. The principal systematic differences are:

American English prefers to keep a single final *-l* where British English doubles it in verb inflection *rivaled/rivalled, traveling/travelling, traveler/traveller.*

However, the following words are preferred with a double *-ll* in American English but retain a single *-l* in British English: *enroll/enrol, enrollment/enrolment, fulfill/fulfil, fulfillment/fulfilment, installment/instalment.* British English is inconsistent, preferring *install* for example to *instal.*

British English uses *-our* where American English uses *-or* as follows: *colour/color, harbour/harbor, humour/humor, parlour/parlor, tumour/tumor.*

Words that end in *-er* in American English often end in *-re* in British English as follows: *center/centre, theater/theatre*. However, *-re* is used in both American English and British English in *acre, lucre,* and *ogre*.

American English tends to simplify the digraphs *ae* and *oe* to *e*: *archeology/archaeology, hemoglobin/haemoglobin, fetus/foetus* (although *fetus* is standard in British English too in medical usage).

British English prefers *-ise* to *-ize* (and their derivatives) as a verbal ending when there is a choice: *civilisation/civilization, organise/organize, privatise/privatize,* except that several influential publishing houses have *-ize* as their house style.

British English prefers *analyse* and *cosy;* American English prefers *analyze* (but *analysis*) and *cozy.*

American English uses *-ense* for British *-ence* as follows: *defense, license* (noun and verb), *offense, pretense;* British English *defence, licence,* (used as nouns) *offence, pretence.*

American English simplifies the ending *-ogue* to *-og,* and simplifies other endings: *catalog/catalogue, epilog/epilogue, program/programme.* In computing, however, the American English spelling *program* is used also in British English, as are other variants such as *disk* for *disc.*

Web Sites

Acronyms and Abbreviations

URL: "http://www.ucc.ie/acronyms/"

Immense, searchable database of abbreviations, acronyms, and their expanded forms. There are currently about 15,500, searchable by abbreviation or key word. It is also possible to submit new additions.

Arabic

URL: "http://philae.sas.upenn.edu/Arabic/arabic.html"

Twelve dialogue lessons from which to learn Arabic. If your computer doesn't support the audio capability, this site is still worth a visit for the library of Arabic images.

Braille and Moon

URL: "http://www.rnib.org.uk/braille/welc.htm"

Information about Braille and Moon from Britain's Royal National Institute for the Blind. You can see how Braille works by typing text and seeing it translated. There are downloadable Braille and Moon truetype fonts.

Brief History of the English Language

URL: "http://www.m-w.com/about/look.htm"

A brief history of the English language, showing its evolution through the three periods of Old, Middle, and Modern English.

Chinese Characters

URL: "http://zhongwen.com/"

Extensive Web site covering Chinese character genealogy. This Web-based etymological dictionary for learning Chinese characters covers over 4,000 characters, including several types of pronunciation for each and a 'family tree' diagram to demonstrate the character's genealogy. The site also includes a rough Chinese-English dictionary containing many thousands of entries.

Elements of Style

URL: "http://www.columbia.edu/acis/bartleby/strunk/"

William Strunk's guide provides a succinct and effective insight into the elementary rules and principles of English grammar.

Esperanto – The International Language

URL: "http://esperanto.org/angle/"

Official source of information (in many languages) on the international language spoken by two million people.

Etymological Dictionary of the Gaelic Language

URL: "http://www.smo.uhi.ac.uk/gaidhlig/faclair/macbain/"

Text of an etymology of Gaelic compiled by Alexander MacBain and published by Gairm Publications, Glasgow.

Foreign Languages for Travellers

URL: "http://www.travlang.com/languages/"

Extensive site to help you out if you are travelling abroad.

Foundation for Endangered Languages

URL: "http://www.bris.ac.uk/Depts/Philosophy/CTLL/FEL/"

Bristol University site bringing together latest information and research on the world's endangered languages.

Hindi Language and Literature

URL: "http://www.cs.colostate.edu/~malaiya/hindiint.html"

Exploration of Hindi language and culture providing links to information about Hindi-speaking regions, dialects, traditional songs, authors, and poets.

Little Venture's Latin Pages

URL: "http://www.compassnet.com/mrex/index.html"

Online aid to learning or brushing up Latin. Operated by an experienced teacher of the language, this non-commercial site answers e-mailed grammar and vocabulary inquiries.

Modern English to Old English Vocabulary

URL: "http://www.mun.ca/Ansaxdat/vocab/wordlist.html"

Comprehensive online dictionary of modern English words paired with their Old English counterparts.

Online English Grammar

URL: "http://www.edunet.com/english/grammar/index.html"

Course on English grammar, with a section dedicated to the use of verbs.

Punctuation

URL: "http://sti.larc.nasa.gov/html/Chapt3/Chapt3-TOC.html"

Handbook aimed at technical writers and editors, but which could help anyone to punctuate correctly.

Roget's Thesaurus

URL: "http://humanities.uchicago.edu/forms_unrest/ROGET.html"

Online version of Roget's Thesaurus (last updated in 1991).

Sign Writing Site

URL: "http://www.signwriting.org/"

Information about sign language with lessons, dictionaries, stories, and computer programs in sign language.

Welsh Course

URL: "http://www.cs.brown.edu/fun/welsh/home.html"

Course on the Welsh language that contains a lexicon and glossary as well as a set of graded lessons.

Wordbot

URL: "http://www.cs.washington.edu/homes/kgolden/wordbot.html"

Linguistic site offering filters which can not only translate foreign language pages into your own language, but also link words to dictionary definitions, or look up synonyms and antonyms.

World Wide Words

URL: "http://www.quinion.demon.co.uk/words/index.htm"

Site listing neologisms in the English language. Topical words, turns of phrase, and weird words too new to be found in dictionaries are listed and defined.

LAW ENFORCEMENT AND CRIME

The Year in Review

15 July 1997–23 July 1997 One of the largest manhunts in US history takes place for the serial killer Andrew Cunanan, wanted for murdering fashion designer Gianni Versace in Florida. The search ends when his body is found in a Miami Beach apartment after an apparent suicide.

25 July 1997 Brendan Smyth, a Roman Catholic priest in Ireland, is sentenced to 12 years in prison for sexually abusing children 74 times over a 36-year period. He recently completed a four-year prison sentence in Northern Ireland for similar crimes.

8 October 1997 The European Commission rejects US proposals for global rules permitting law enforcement officials to unscramble coded messages transmitted over telephone lines and computer networks.

12 October 1997 Ramzi Ahmed Yousef and Eyad Ismoil are convicted in the USA of the 1993 World Trade Center bombing in New York.

14 October 1997 Keith Hellawell, chief constable of West Yorkshire Police, is made 'drugs tsar' (head of the British government's new antidrugs task force).

30 October 1997 The British nanny Louise Woodward is found guilty of the murder of baby Matthew Eappen by a court in Cambridge, Massachusetts; the following day she is sentenced to life imprisonment.

10 November 1997 US Judge Hiller Zobel reduces the second degree murder charge against the British nanny Louise Woodward to involuntary manslaughter and frees her, deeming the 279 days she has spent in jail awaiting trial sufficient punishment; Woodward must remain in the USA pending an appeal by the prosecution. Zobel also publishes his ruling on the Internet – he is the first judge to do so.

20 November 1997 British Home Secretary Jack Straw announces plans to increase the electronic tagging of convicts to help reduce the prison population. The plan would enable criminals serving short sentences to be released up to two months ahead of schedule, fitted with electronic bracelets to record their movements.

23 December 1997 Venezuelan Ilich Ramírez Sánchez, known as Carlos the Jackal, is sentenced to life imprisonment in Paris for the murder in 1975 of two French secret service agents and a Lebanese informer.

27 December 1997 Billy Wright, presumed leader of the Loyalist Volunteer Force, a militant Protestant group in Northern Ireland, is shot and killed by Roman Catholic inmates at the Maze prison near Lisburn, Northern Ireland. The killers are members of the Irish National Liberation Army (INLA), a guerilla group that had broken off from the Irish Republican Army (IRA).

29 December 1997 The number of recorded murders for the year (1997) in New York is the lowest since 1967. The total is 756; in 1992 it was 2262.

7 January 1998 Terry Nichols, who was convicted in December 1997 of conspiracy and involuntary manslaughter in the 1995 bombing of the Alfred P Murrah federal building in Oklahoma City, escapes the death penalty after the jury sentencing him could not reach a consensus.

21 January 1998 John Gotti, Jr, son of Mafia crime boss John J Gotti, is arrested in New York, on charges of extortion, fraud, money laundering, and racketeering. The arrest follows a five-year federal investigation.

26 January 1998 A law banning the possession of all handguns goes into effect in Britain.

28 January 1998 A court in Poonamallee, Tamil Nadu, India, condemns 26 people to death by hanging for their roles in the assassination of former Prime Minister Rajiv Gandhi in 1991. The sentencing ends India's longest-ever assassination trial.

29 January 1998 A bomb explodes outside an abortion clinic in Birmingham, Alabama, killing one person and seriously injuring another. This is the first time that a bombing of a clinic causes a death. A religious anti-abortion group called the Army of God takes responsibility.

2 February 1998 Guy Snowdon, head of lottery firm Gtech Holdings Corp, is found guilty by a jury in London, of libeling British entrepreneur Richard Branson. Snowdon is fined £100,000 and ordered to pay Branson's legal fees, estimated at more than £1,000,000.

12 February 1998 The Cuban government announces that it will free more than 200 prisoners, including some political prisoners, on 'humanitarian grounds'. The release was sparked by Pope John Paul II's plea during his visit to the island.

9 March 1998 British Home Secretary Jack Straw announces that Britain will not extradite Roisin McAliskey, a suspect in an IRA bombing at a British base in Osnabruck, Germany, in June 1996. McAliskey was suffering from health problems, including serious postnatal depression.

9 March 1998 US prosecutors and defence attorneys appeal against the 1997 manslaughter conviction of British nanny Louise Woodward, who was initially sentenced to murder after eight-month-old Matthew Eappen died in her care.

24 March 1998 Mitchell Johnson, 13, and Andrew Golden, 11, pupils at Westside Middle Schhol in Jonesboro, Arkansas, open fire on the school playground from nearby woods, killing four students and one teacher and injuring ten others.

4 May 1998 US Dictrict Judge Garland Burrell Jr sentences Theodore Kaczynski, the 'Unabomber', to four life sentences plus 30 years for four bombings that killed three people and wounded 11 others. Authorities suspected that Kaczynski was responsible for 16 bombings over 17 years.

21 May 1998 A 15-year-old student opens fire with a semiautomatic rifle in the cafeteria of his secondary school in Springfield, Oregon, killing two students and injuring 22 others.

7 June 1998 Three white men, two with white-supremacist tattoos, are arrested in Texas, accused of murdering a black man, James Byrd Jr, by dragging him behind their truck for two miles.

10 June 1998 In part of Scotland Yard's biggest anti-corruption campaign in the UK for 25 years, detectives raid the homes of suspected officers.

16 June 1998 The Supreme Court of Massachusetts votes 4–3 to uphold the trial judge's decision to reduce the sentence of British nanny Louise Woodward, who was accused of murdering Matthew Eappen, an 18-month-old baby in her care, from second-degree murder to manslaughter.

17 June 1998 Ian Johnston, the assistant commissioner of the Metropolitan Police publicly apologizes to the parents of Stephen Lawrence, a black teenager who died in a racist attack in 1993, for failing to bring his killers to justice.

World Law and Crime

Number of Recorded Crimes by Selected Countries

(N/A = not available.)

Offence	1994
Austria	
Murder	198
Sex offence	3,961
Serious assault	203
Robbery and violent theft	4,615
Drug offence	11,963
Belgium	
Murder	315
Sex offence	2,218
Serious assault	33,329
Robbery and violent theft	5,659
Drug offence	14,959
Chile	
Murder	1,545
Sex offence	3,458
Serious assault	13,471
Robbery and violent theft	4,915
Drug offence	3,737
China	
Murder	2,553
Sex offence	N/A
Serious assault	67,864
Robbery and violent theft	N/A
Drug offence	38,033
France	
Murder	2,696
Sex offence	29,279

Offence	1994
Serious assault	63,435
Robbery and violent theft	73,310
Drug offence	70,735
Germany	
Murder	3,751
Sex offence	45,339
Serious assault	88,037
Robbery and violent theft	57,752
Drug offence	132,389
Ireland, Republic of	
Murder	25
Sex offence	645
Serious assault	433
Robbery and violent theft	2,307
Drug offence	95
Japan	
Murder	1,279
Sex offence	5,196
Serious assault	18,097
Robbery and violent theft	2,684
Drug offence	23,059
Russia	
Murder	32,288
Sex offence	17,919
Serious assault	67,706
Robbery and violent theft	186,450
Drug offence	74,798

Offence	1994
Sweden	
Murder	837
Sex offence	7,679
Serious assault	4,290
Robbery and violent theft	5,331
Drug offence	31,601
Turkey	
Murder	1,794
Sex offence	2,843
Serious assault	N/A
Robbery and violent theft	N/A
Drug offence	N/A
USA	
Murder	23,310
Sex offence	N/A
Serious assault	1,119,950
Robbery and violent theft	618,820
Drug offence	N/A
Zimbabwe	
Murder	549
Sex offence	123
Serious assault	21,294
Robbery and violent theft	10,382
Drug offence	9,109

Source: International Crime Statistics (Interpol)

Average Sentences Handed Down for Assault by Selected Countries

Figures have been rounded up or down to the nearest month. (In months. N/A = not available.)

Country/territory	1986	1988	1990
Australia	5	4	6
Croatia	8	6	8
England and Wales	8	9	10
Hong Kong	11	14	9
Israel	N/A	9	12
Jordan	18	18	18
Latvia	60	55	80
Rwanda	36	36	36
Swaziland	6	8	10
Switzerland	9	9	11
Syria	12	12	12
Turkey	24	24	20
Vanuatu	9	2	18

Source: United Nations Survey of Crime Trends and Operations of Criminal Justice Systems

Average Sentences Handed Down for Drugs Crimes by Selected Countries

Figures have been rounded up or down to the nearest month. (In months. N/A = not available.)

Country/territory	1986	1988	1990
Australia	7	5	8
Croatia	9	8	12
England and Wales	10	12	13
Hong Kong	19	20	29
Israel	N/A	15	17
Latvia	72	72	82
Swaziland	16	20	24
Switzerland	9	9	9
Syria	120	120	120
Turkey	72	72	60

Source: United Nations Survey of Crime Trends and Operations of Criminal Justice Systems

Average Sentences Handed Down to Convicted Murderers by Selected Countries

Figures have been rounded up or down to the nearest month. (In months. N/A = not available.)

Country/territory	1986	1988	1990
Australia	55	38	39
Bulgaria	1,897	1,554	1,445
Croatia	38	49	37
Hong Kong	55	49	61
Israel	N/A	26	33
Latvia	204	204	260
Rwanda	122	122	122
Switzerland	33	33	42
Turkey	115	115	96
Vanuatu	78	144	84

Source: United Nations Survey of Crime Trends and Operations of Criminal Justice Systems

Countries that Have Abolished the Death Penalty for All Crimes

(N/A = not applicable)

Country	Date of abolition	Date of last execution	Country	Date of abolition	Date of last execution	Country	Date of abolition	Date of last execution
Andorra	1990	1943	Hungary	1990	1988	Panama	N/A	1903 [3]
Angola	1992	N/A	Iceland	1928	1830	Portugal	1976	1849 [3]
Australia	1985	1967	Ireland, Republic of	1990	1954	Romania	1989	1989
Austria	1968	1950	Italy	1994	1947	San Marino	1865	1468 [3]
Belgium	1996	1950	Kiribati	N/A [4]		São Tomé and		
Cambodia	1989	N/A	Liechtenstein	1987	1785	Príncipe	1990 [4]	
Cape Verde	1981	1835	Luxembourg	1979	1949	Slovak Republic	1990 [1]	N/A
Colombia	1910	1909	Macedonia, Former			Slovenia	1989	N/A
Costa Rica	1877	N/A	Yugoslav Republic of	N/A	N/A	Solomon Islands	N/A [4]	
Croatia	1990	N/A	Marshall Islands	N/A [4]		Spain	1995	1975
Czech Republic	1990 [1]	N/A	Mauritius	1995	1987	Sweden	1972	1910
Denmark	1978	1950	Micronesia	N/A [4]		Switzerland	1992	1944
Dominican Republic	1966	N/A	Moldova	1995	N/A	Tuvalu	N/A [4]	
Ecuador	1906	N/A	Monaco	1962	1847	UK	1965 [5]	1964
Finland	1972	1944	Mozambique	1990	1986	Uruguay	1907	N/A
France	1981	1977	Namibia	1990	1988[3]	Vanuatu	N/A [4]	
Germany	1949/1987 [2]	1949 [2]	Netherlands, the	1982	1952	Vatican City State	1969	N/A
Greece	1993	1972	New Zealand	1989	1957	Venezuela	1863	N/A
Guinea-Bissau	1993	1986 [3]	Nicaragua	1979	1930			
Haiti	1987	1972 [3]	Norway	1979	1948			
Honduras	1956	1940	Palau	N/A	N/A			

[1] The death penalty was abolished in the Czech and Slovak Federal Republic in 1990. On 1 January 1993 the Czech and Slovak Federal Republic divided into two states, the Czech Republic and the Slovak Republic. The last execution in the Czech and Slovak Federal Republic was in 1988.

[2] The death penalty was abolished in the Federal Republic of Germany (FRG) in 1949 and in the German Democratic Republic (GDR) in 1987. The last execution in the FRG was in 1949; the date of the last execution in the GDR is not known. The FRG and the GDR were unified in October 1990.

[3] Date of last known execution.

[4] No executions since independence.

[5] The death penalty was abolished for all crimes except treason.

Source: Amnesty International

Average Sentences Handed Down to Convicted Rapists by Selected Countries

Figures have been rounded up or down to the nearest month. (In months. N/A = not available.)

Country/territory	1986	1988	1990
Australia	22	22	20
Bulgaria	1,225	1,179	959
Croatia	12	27	23
England and Wales	26	30	30
Ghana	37	N/A	N/A
Hong Kong	129	74	72
Israel	N/A	24	23
Jordan	60	60	60
Latvia	90	90	100
Panama	30	33	35
Rwanda	63	63	63
Swaziland	60	72	72
Switzerland	16	29	30
Syria	60	60	60
Turkey	24	24	20
Vanuatu	72	120	84

Source: United Nations Survey of Crime Trends and Operations of Criminal Justice Systems

Average Sentences Handed Down for Robbery by Selected Countries

Figures have been rounded up or down to the nearest month. (In months. N/A = not available.)

Country/territory	1986	1988	1990
Australia	24	24	24
Bulgaria	828	724	676
Croatia	41	24	20
England and Wales	19	22	23
Ghana	90	N/A	N/A
Hong Kong	58	53	49
Jordan	108	108	108
Latvia	72	64	80
Panama	40	41	43
Rwanda	150	150	150
Swaziland	48	60	72
Switzerland	22	21	24
Syria	84	84	84
Turkey	48	48	40

Source: United Nations Survey of Crime Trends and Operations of Criminal Justice Systems

Some Infamous Crimes and Criminals of the 20th Century

Berkowitz, David murderer of six people who claimed he had been instructed to commit the murders by the spirit of his neighbour's dog. He began his criminal career as an arsonist, and was also believed to be a Satanist. He was nicknamed the 'Son of Sam' by the police and the media. He was arrested on 10 August 1977 and currently resides in prison in the USA.

Bonnie and Clyde Clyde Barrow and Bonnie Parker, a notorious couple who committed many robberies in the USA in the early 1930s. They and their gang are also believed to have committed numerous murders. Soon after they had met, Bonnie helped Clyde escape from prison, but within a month Bonnie found herself in jail for a failed robbery. Bonnie was released by a grand jury, and the couple spent the rest of their lives living in stolen cars, carrying out robberies for pocket money. In October 1932 they killed a man for $28 and a few vegetables. The couple was finally caught and shot to death in an ambush by officers on 23 May 1934 in Louisiana.

Brink's security firm robbery a seven-man team, including Adolph 'Jazz' Maffey, Henry J Baker, 'Specs' O'Keefe, and Anthony 'Fats' Pino, who robbed the Brink's security firm in Boston, USA, in 1950. On 17 January 1950 the team stole $2,775,395, nearly half of it in cash. It took the team just 17 minutes to carry out the robbery, and the police had no leads as to who had committed the crime. 'Specs' O'Keefe threatened to inform the police when another gang member refused to return $90,000 he had been given for safe-keeping. A contract was put out on his life, but it failed and O'Keefe did go to the police in January 1956. All members of the gang were sent to prison.

Bundy, Ted serial killer convicted of 30 homicides, but who claimed to have murdered over 100 people. Having been imprisoned in Colorado, USA, he escaped on 30 December 1977. On 15 January 1978 he killed two girls and wounded two others. Two weeks later he murdered Kimberley Leach. He was finally caught and having unsuccessfully defended himself, was sentenced to death by electrocution.

Capone, Al builder of an organized crime empire who was known worldwide for his racketeering during the prohibition period in Chicago. Born in New York City, Al Capone made Chicago the bootleg capital of the USA. He was brutal and merciless in extinguishing all competition. Responsible for the deaths of friends, enemies, and employees alike, Capone was unstoppable in his pursuit of dominance. He was finally imprisoned for ten years in 1931 for tax evasion, the only charge that could be sustained against him. Released in 1939 on health grounds, Capone retired to his estate in Florida.

Chikatilo, Andrei Romanovich Ukrainian who confessed to killing 53 adults and children over a 12-year period. Sentenced to death in 1992, he appeared at his trial in a metal cage.

Dahmer, Jeffrey cannibalistic murderer who killed gay black men in the USA before abusing them sexually or eating their corpses. He was captured and imprisoned in 1991, and was attacked and killed by fellow inmate Christopher Scarver on 28 November 1994. Contrary to his mother's wish that his brain be preserved in formaldehyde, he was cremated.

DeSalvo, Albert Henry the Boston Strangler who terrorized the city of Boston during the mid-1960s. He posed as a workman and then raped and strangled his victims. Also accredited with the assault and rape crimes of 'The Measuring Man' and 'The Green Man', De Salvo was judged insane after confessing to the murders and could not be tried for them. Instead, he stood trial as 'The Green Man' in 1966. He was sentenced to life imprisonment and was stabbed to death by a fellow inmate in November 1973.

Dillinger, John Herbert one of the USA's most notorious gangsters who specialized in armed bank robbery. Dillinger led his gang on a series of bank raids throughout the Midwest during the 1930s. He and his gang were caught and imprisoned in January 1934, but Dillinger escaped and formed a new gang. More bank robberies took place until June 1934, and in July he was ambushed by FBI agents and reportedly shot dead. There were discrepan-

cies between the dead man and what was known about Dillinger: the dead man had brown eyes, Dillinger's were blue; the dead man wore prescription glasses and Dillinger had never worn glasses; the dead man's face was not scarred, Dillinger's was. Many people believe that Dillinger escaped and spent the rest of his life in Los Angeles, but the truth will probably never be known.

Ferguson, Arthur Scottish conman who, over a six-week period in 1925, sold Buckingham Palace, London, for £2,000, Big Ben for £1,000, and Nelson's Column for £6,000 to US tourists. Arthur Ferguson himself emigrated to the USA in late 1925, and proceeded to attempt to rent out the White House to a Texas cattleman for $100,000 a year. He was finally arrested during negotiations for the sale of the Statue of Liberty to an Australian tourist. Jailed for five years, Ferguson died a wealthy man in 1938.

Gacy, John Wayne child murderer who, by dressing up as a clown, was able to trick children into putting on handcuffs, after which he would rape and murder them. He was arrested in Chicago, USA, in 1978 and spent much of his remaining life in prison as a painter. He was executed by lethal injection in 1994.

Ganev, Galtscho Bulgarian who held the coffin of Charlie Chaplin to ransom. Charlie Chaplin was buried in a small cemetery overlooking Lake Geneva in Switzerland in 1977. In March 1978, his coffin disappeared. Galtscho Ganev claimed responsibility, demanding a ransom of £330,000 from the Chaplin family. Ganev and his accomplice were caught and the ransom was never paid, but they could not remember where they had hidden the coffin. Police finally found it using mine detectors. Chaplin's coffin is now protected by a concrete lining.

Gein, Ed psychopathic murderer and grave digger, who was the inspiration for the films *Psycho* and *The Texas Chainsaw Massacre*. He was declared criminally insane in December 1957 and was committed to a mental hospital in the USA.

Gray, Barry Edward English conman who bought a pair of shoes from a junk shop in the USA for $3.50 and proceeded to sell them to the *New York Times* for $50,000, convincing the newspaper that the shoes belonged to the US Teamster boss James R Hoffa, who had been kidnapped in 1975.

Great Train Robbery, the robbery of the London–Glasgow mail train. On 8 August 1963 the train was stopped and robbed of more than £2,500,000 in used banknotes. Most of the gang were caught and imprisoned for long terms. Sentenced to 30 years, the most famous member of the gang, Ronald Biggs, escaped from Wandsworth prison in July 1965 and fled, first to Australia and later to Rio de Janeiro in Brazil. Never recaptured, owing to Brazilian extradition laws being in his favour, he still resides there today.

Green River Killer, the serial killer who murdered 48 women from 1982 to 1984. Their corpses were found along the banks of the

Green River near Seattle, USA. Many of the women were prostitutes, but others were runaways and hitchhikers. No one has ever been convicted for these murders.

Hamilton, Thomas murderer who entered the gym of a primary school in Dunblane, Scotland, on 13 March 1996 and shot dead 16 children and a teacher. Many other children were injured in the attack. The killings were thought to be Hamilton's reaction to being fired from his position of Boy Scout Master. Hamilton shot and killed himself after the attack. Directly as a result of this crime, the British Government banned the ownership of handguns in the UK in 1997.

Hauptmann, Bruno Richard kidnapper who abducted and held to ransom the son of aviation hero Charles A Lindbergh. On 1 March 1932 Charles A Lindbergh Jr, the 19 month-old baby, was abducted from his home in Hopewell, USA. The Lindberghs received and paid ransom demands, but on 12 May the baby's body was found in woods just miles from the Lindbergh's home. He had been killed within hours of his abduction. It was two years before the ransom money was traced to Bruno Richard Hauptmann, a German carpenter. Hauptmann was tried and convicted in 1935, and was executed in the electric chair in April 1936.

Hearst, Patty the 19 year-old daughter of the multi-millionaire newspaper magnate Randolf Hearst who was kidnapped from her home by the Symbionese Liberation Army in February 1974. The SLA demanded a ransom of $3,250,00 to fund food programmes for the poor. Two months later her family were informed of Patty's release but she stunned them by announcing that she was joining her captors. She was converted to violent revolution, taking part in a bank robbery and she publicly rejected her family. In a violent battle at the SLA hideout in May 1974, the police and FBI found Patty Hearst unharmed. At her trial she convinced the jury that she had been forced to join the SLA and admitted taking part in the bank raid. In the light of her traumatic kidnap, she received only a light prison sentence.

Hickman, William Edward US kidnapper and murderer who returned two year-old Marion Parker in December 1927 after her father agreed to a $1,500 ransom. At the handover, the father paid the ransom before realizing that the child had been killed and her body dismembered. Hickman was executed in February 1928.

Hindley, Myra and Brady, Ian British couple who were found guilty of the murder of two children and a 17 year-old youth between 1963 and 1965. They were known as 'The Moors Murderers' because they buried most of their victims on Saddleworth Moor in the Pennines. They abducted and sexually abused the children before killing them. In a case that horrified the British public, Brady and Hindley documented their activities, to the extent of taking photographs and recording the torment of their victims. They were arrested after Hindley's brother-in-law witnessed a murder and went to the police. During the mid-1980s, Brady and Hindley separately confessed to the murder of two other children.

Kemper, Ed serial killer, cannibal, and necrophiliac. As a young teenager, Kemper was sent to a hospital for the criminally insane for the murder of his grandparents. Released in the early 1970s, he went on to murder numerous others, mostly students from his mother's college. On Easter Sunday 1973 he decapitated his mother before confessing to his crimes. He currently resides in Vacaville Prison, USA.

Kray, Ronald and Reginald British twins who controlled the East End of London with a Mafia-style operation during the 1960s. Their gang ran drinking clubs and protection rackets, and organized illegal gambling operations. Ronnie Kray shot dead a rival gang member and Reggie stabbed another to death for threatening his brother. They were convicted of murder in 1969, and sentenced to life imprisonment with the recommendation that they serve not less than 30 years.

Kujau, Conrad German forger of the Hitler diaries during the late 1970s and early 1980s. Kujau persuaded the German *Stern* magazine to pay 2 million marks for 27 diaries that in reality Hitler never wrote; he then copied sections from Hitler's *Speeches and Proclamations*, sprinkled the pages with tea to make them look old, and produced the diaries. Kujau kept up this work until he had produced 58 'diaries'. *Stern* magazine eventually paid a total of 9.3 million marks for their 'scoop'. Fooling revered historians and investigative journalists alike, the diaries were serialized for publication in the *Sunday Times* in the UK. The fraud was not established until after serialization had begun. Kujau received a four-year jail sentence in 1985.

Lopez, Pedro Alonso serial killer nicknamed 'The Monster of the Andes' who carried out hundreds of killings in Peru, Colombia, and Ecuador. It is believed that his actions were largely a result of childhood trauma, connected with his being frequently sexually abused. A flash flood in 1980 began to uncover his buried victims which in turn led to his arrest. It is estimated that he killed over 300 people, mostly young girls.

Lucas, Henry Lee and Toole, Ottis a sadist and incestuous necrophiliac and a cannibal who were believed to have killed around 200 people between them, many of them hitchhikers. They parted as a result of Lucas's relationship with Toole's niece, who was later found dismembered. Lucas is awaiting a death sentence, while Toole died of liver failure in a US prison hospital on 15 September 1996.

Luciano, Charles 'Lucky' the head of an organized crime empire in New York City. Born Salvatore Lucania in 1897 in Sicily, Italy, Luciano moved with his family to New York City in 1906. Soon becoming involved in crime, he went on to become the head of organized crime in New York City. Luciano's empire included drug smuggling, extortion, and prostitution. Famed for restructuring the Mafia and laying the foundations for modern organized crime, Luciano was finally tried and convicted of extortion and running prostitution in 1936. Sentenced to 30–50 years in the notorious Sing Sing prison in New York, Luciano set up and ran the Crime Syndicate of Mafia families from his cell. He was released from prison in 1942 for helping the US naval authorities by arranging for partisan cover for the Allied landings on Sicily. Although he was released from prison, he was also deported to Italy.

Lustig, 'Count' Victor Czechoslovakian-born conman who sold the Eiffel Tower in Paris, not once, but twice. Conning a scrap merchant into believing he could buy the rights for the Tower's demolition and its haul of 7,000 tons of metal, Lustig's ruse went unreported, and he did it again a year later. Years later, he also rashly duped Al Capone out of $50,000, but had second thoughts and went back to Capone with the money and an apology. Capone gave him $5,000 for being so honest. Lustig received his final conviction in 1945 for distributing $134 million in forged bank notes.

Manson, Charles convicted of murder after his arrest in 1969, along with eight members of his cult, 'The Family'. Manson was born in Kentucky, USA, the unwanted child of a prostitute. He spent much of his youth in jail. When released in 1967, Manson moved to San Francisco where he led a cult of 20, consisting mainly of women. The cult took hallucinogenic drugs and prepared themselves for 'Helter Skelter', the nuclear and race war that Manson predicted. As the cult grew in size, Manson began to exercise revenge against those he felt had hindered his earlier musical career. In July 1969 a record producer was killed and his car stolen. In an attempt to set off 'Helter Skelter', Manson sent several cultists to the house of film director Roman Polanski. Actress Sharon Tate, the wife of Polanski, and four others were murdered. Manson recently came up for parole, but said he was not ready to be released as he was too busy working on his Internet web site.

Maxwell, Robert Czechoslovakian-born British media tycoon who was involved in a number of fraudulent practices. He was found dead at sea in November 1991, having last been seen on his yacht off the Canary Islands. After his death, startling revelations of his fraudulent business practices began to come to light. Most serious was the loss of hundreds of millions of pounds in Maxwell company pension funds. It transpired that Maxwell himself had siphoned money from the pension funds to preserve his financial empire.

Nilsen, Dennis British serial killer who was convicted for murdering between 12 and 16 people between 1978 and 1983. A lonely homosexual, Nilsen murdered his victims so that they would 'stay with him', and kept the bodies under floorboards in his home. He was sentenced to life imprisonment, with a recommendation that he serve a minimum of 25 years.

Paulin, Thierry and Mathurin, Jean-Thierry French serial killers known as the 'Old Ladies Killer' and the 'Monster of Montmartre'. Paulin and his boyfriend, Mathurin, murdered over 20 elderly women in Montmartre in the years 1984–87. All their victims were women between the ages of 60 and 95. While Paulin escaped a mass round-up by the Parisian police, he was eventually caught after a description of him was given by a victim he had left for dead. Thierry was later named and caught. Paulin died of AIDS in 16 April 1989 before his trial had been concluded.

Perruggia, Vincenzo house-painter who stole the *Mona Lisa* from the Louvre in Paris in August 1911. Working alone in the gallery where the painting hung, he simply removed it from the wall, and left the building with the canvas hidden under his smock. Perruggia kept the painting under his bed for two years, before trying to sell it for a reported $95,000 to an Italian art dealer. The art dealer recognized the *Mona Lisa* and went to the police. Perruggia received only a light prison sentence for his crime.

Sams, Michael kidnapper and murderer who abducted Stephanie Slater, a young estate agent from Birmingham, England. She was abducted in January 1992 after meeting Michael Sams who was pretending to be a prospective house-buyer. She was kept for eight days in a coffin, itself contained in a large bin. She was gagged, handcuffed, and blindfolded. Sams made a ransom demand of £175,000. Slater was released, and Sams was later convicted of her kidnap and the murder of Julie Dart, a prostitute from Leeds.

Société Générale robbery French bank robbed in 1976 in a bank raid masterminded by Albert Spaggiari. He worked with a gang from Marseilles, and together they spent nearly two months tunnelling and drilling beneath the bank in Nice before they found themselves in the bank's strongroom. Over a weekend, they removed a haul worth up to $US 75 million in money, jewels, gold, and securities. The police investigating the theft were so impressed with the tunnelling that at first they suspected miners to be responsible. Spaggiari was only caught after police traced Dom Miguel cigar butts, littered in the strongroom, to him. While in court in 1977, Spaggiari broke free and escaped, never to be recaptured. Like Ronald Biggs of the Great Train Robbery in England, Spaggiari fled to Rio de Janeiro, Brazil. He died, on the run, from natural causes.

Sutcliffe, Peter murderer of at least 13 women in northern England between 1975 and 1984 who was known as 'The Yorkshire Ripper'. He was finally caught sitting in a car with a prostitute. While in custody he confessed. He is suspected of having killed and maimed several other women in France and Sweden during his travels in Europe. He is currently in prison, where he has been attacked by fellow prisoners on a number of occasions.

Twin Cities Killer one or possibly two serial killers who murdered in Minneapolis and St Paul between 1986 and 1994. Around 34 corpses were discovered during this period in the Twin Cities, many of the victims being prostitutes. Several corpses were mutilated, dismembered, and occasionally decapitated. The identity of the murderer or murderers remains unknown.

West, Fred and Rosemary English couple accused of murdering 12 women and girls over a 16-year period. They were arrested in 1994, and their home was excavated to reveal many bodies, including that of Fred West's 16 year-

old daughter. Other excavations revealed the bodies of West's first wife and child, plus other bodies. West hung himself in prison on New Year's Day in 1995. Rosemary West was convicted of the murders, and is now in prison.

Zodiac Killer serial killer active in the USA, so named because of the zodiac signs left with victims. The number of victims is

unknown, but is believed to be around 50 according to some estimates. The killer was active in the San Francisco area between 1966 and the mid-1970s, but his or her identity is unknown, and no suspect has ever been convicted.

Terrorist Attacks

Some Major Recent Terrorist Attacks in the UK

1994–97

Date	Details	Injuries/fatalities
4 January 1994	The Ulster Volunteer Force (UVF) sent two letter bombs to Sinn Féin office in Dublin	none
9–13 March 1994	The Irish Republican Army (IRA) launched three separate mortar attacks on Heathrow airport in a five-day period	none
27 July 1994	Car bomb detonated outside a London office building housing the headquarters of several Jewish organizations in the UK	5 injured
6 December 1994	Two letter bombs exploded at branches of Barclays Bank at Hampstead High Street and Ladbroke Grove, London; four other bombs at Hammersmith, Kensington High Street, Gloucester Road, and Edgware Road, London, were defused. The bombs were hidden in video cassette boxes in Christmas wrapping bearing a label reading 'Welcome to the Mardi Gra Experience'; this was the first attack of the so-called Mardi Gra bomber who has since targeted Barclays Bank and the supermarket giant Sainsbury	1 injured
24 January 1995	A Sikh newspaper editor killed by an unknown assailant	1 killed
9 February 1996	IRA bomb attack on the South Quay Plaza office buildings in the Docklands area, London	2 killed; 29 injured
15 February 1996	Police defused a small IRA bomb left in a telephone box in the heart of London's theatreland in the West End; a telephone warning had been given	none
18 February 1996	An IRA terrorist, Edward O'Brien, blew himself up and injured nine people when the bomb he was carrying in a briefcase detonated prematurely; the bomb exploded as the bus he was travelling on was passing through the Aldwych area of London's West End	1 killed, 9 injured
17 April 1996	An IRA bomb exploded outside a house in a fashionable street in West London known as 'The Boltons'; this happened shortly after a coded warning had been received by the Associated Press News Agency	none
24 April 1996	Two IRA bombs planted under Hammersmith Bridge, London, failed to go off (detonators had exploded but failed to ignite the bombs); police officials stated that the bombs had been designed to kill and to cause serious structural damage	none
15 June 1996	A massive IRA bomb weighing in excess of 1 ton planted in a Ford lorry exploded causing extensive damage to the Arndale Centre in Manchester; the cost of damage exceeded £100 million	none
14 July 1996	An IRA bomb exploded outside the Killykelrin Hotel in Enniskillen; the bomb was made of 1,250 lb of explosive and had been parked in a 4-wheel-drive vehicle; the hotel had been hosting a wedding reception when the bomb exploded at midnight	17 injured
29 September 1996	A 250 lb car bomb was defused in Belfast; a group known as the Continuity Council of the IRA was associated with planting the device	none
7 October 1996	A car bomb exploded in a car park within army headquarters in Northern Ireland at Lisburn; a second car bomb exploded 5–10 minutes later outside the barracks' medical centre; Warrant Officer James Bradwell died of wounds on 11 October 1996. The IRA claimed responsibility	1 killed, 30 injured
31 December 1996	A massive bomb was planted at Belfast Castle by the IRA; a wedding reception had been taking place inside the castle; security forces defused the bomb	none
13 January 1997	Two security guards were injured when a letter bomb exploded at the offices of the *Al Hayat* newspaper in Hammersmith, West London. No group claimed responsibility	2 injured
9 March 1997	A small IRA bomb left in rubbish bins in west London exploded; the blast shattered nearby windows but no serious injuries followed	none
26 March 1997	Two IRA bombs exploded at Wilmslow railway station in Cheshire in the early morning; police believe that the second bomb was timed to go off to cause loss of life to security forces who were cordoning off the area following the first blast some 35 minutes earlier	none
26 March 1997	A false alarm at Doncaster railway station; this was coordinated to cause havoc by being timed to coincide with the bomb attack at Wilmslow; a coded warning from the IRA had been received by the police	none
3 April 1997	Two terrorist bombs planted by the IRA beneath junctions of the M6, together with a hoax warning of a bomb beside the M1, created chaos on the motorway network; the two bombs were found at junctions 8 and 9 of the M6; some 250,000 vehicles were trapped in the ensuing traffic jams	none
5 April 1997	The Grand National horse race was postponed following two coded bomb warnings believed to be from the IRA	none

England and Wales: Law and Crime

Strength of the Police Service in England and Wales

Office	1991	1992	1993	1994	1995	1996	1997
Constables	95,609	95,662	96,591	97,010	97,107	97,651	98,132
Civilians	49,621	50,766	53,187	53,703	54,709	52,933	53,011
Specials	15,881	18,073	19,243	20,573	20,026	19,736	19,252

Source: The Home Office

Number of Recorded Crimes in England and Wales

Offence	1992	1993	1994	1995	1996
Violent Crime					
Violence against the person	201,777	205,102	218,354	212,588	239,109
Sexual offences	29,528	31,284	31,971	30,274	31,247
Robbery	52,894	57,845	60,007	68,074	73,957
Violent crime total	284,199	294,231	310,332	310,936	344,313
Burglary					
Burglary in a dwelling	708,231	727,276	678,882	643,645	601,992
Burglary other than in a dwelling	647,043	642,308	577,800	595,839	562,372
Burglary total	1,355,274	1,369,584	1,256,682	1,239,484	1,164,364
Theft and Handling Stolen Goods					
Theft from the person	39,111	47,743	51,119	59,692	59,302
Theft of bicycle	222,242	190,685	176,825	169,476	148,799
Theft from shops	288,672	275,607	269,017	275,802	281,982
Theft from vehicle	961,340	925,819	842,680	813,094	799,445
Theft of motor vehicle	587,856	597,519	541,749	508,450	493,302
Other	752,417	714,528	683,218	625,595	600,126
Theft total	2,851,638	2,751,901	2,564,608	2,452,109	2,382,956
Fraud and forgery	168,600	162,836	145,289	133,016	135,902
Criminal damage	892,623	906,746	928,329	913,991	950,698
Other notifiable offences	39,383	40,957	47,740	50,705	55,595
TOTAL	5,591,717	5,526,255	5,252,980	5,100,241	5,033,828

Source: The Home Office

Number of Crimes Cleared Up in England and Wales

Category	1986	1988	1990	1992	1993	1994	1995	1996
Method of Clear-Up								
Charge/summons	592,000	637,000	687,000	644,000	604,000	604,000	558,000	576,000
Caution	118,000	136,000	151,000	197,000	197,000	187,000	181,000	166,000
Taken into consideration	182,000	212,000	209,000	209,000	183,000	153,000	127,000	132,000
No Further Action								
Interview of convicted prisoner	175,000	188,000	221,000	230,000	221,000	236,000	235,000	211,000
Other	89,000	76,000	111,000	110,000	124,000	151,000	176,000	203,000
Total[1]	1,156,000	1,249,000	1,379,000	1,390,000	1,329,000	1,331,000	1,277,000	1,288,000

[1] Excluding criminal damage of value £20 and under.

Source: The Home Office

Notifiable Offences Recorded by the Police by Police Force Area in England and Wales

(N = nil or negligible.)

Police force area	1995	1996	Change Number	%
England				
Avon and Bath	152,886	156,557	3,671	2.4
Bedfordshire	51,104	52,005	901	1.8
Cambridgeshire	67,652	69,532	1,880	2.8
Cheshire	73,202	66,214	−6,988	−9.5
Cleveland	79,719	78,608	−1,111	−1.4
Cumbria	41,230	39,739	−1,491	−3.6
Derbyshire	82,380	78,896	−3,484	−4.2
Devon and Cornwall	102,193	103,121	928	0.9
Dorset	54,582	49,731	−4,851	−8.9
Durham	57,817	51,849	−5,968	−10.3
Essex	98,097	100,758	2,661	2.7
Gloucestershire	55,448	53,675	−1,773	−3.2
Greater Manchester	327,994	327,976	−18	N
Hampshire	134,319	135,915	1,596	1.2
Hertfordshire	55,891	54,441	−1,450	−2.6
Humberside	128,393	126,932	−1,461	−1.1
Kent	155,251	147,980	−7,271	−4.7
Lancashire	124,921	122,487	−2,434	−1.9
Leicestershire	93,607	94,125	518	0.6
Lincolnshire	48,015	47,077	−938	−2.0
London, City of	5,727	4,831	−896	−15.6
Merseyside	153,385	145,956	−7,429	−4.8
Metropolitan Police	817,082	841,784	24,702	3.0
Norfolk	51,716	55,314	3,598	7.0
Northamptonshire	56,524	57,378	854	1.5
Northumbria	194,141	169,656	−24,485	−12.6
England				
North Yorkshire	63,539	56,919	−6,620	−10.4
Nottinghamshire	151,371	141,307	−10,064	−6.6
South Yorkshire	154,293	151,577	−2,716	−1.8
Staffordshire	91,495	92,155	660	0.7
Suffolk	38,233	37,094	−1,139	−3.0
Surrey	44,313	42,014	−2,299	−5.2
Sussex	110,300	118,086	7,786	7.1
Thames Valley	178,702	172,194	−6,508	−3.6
Warwickshire	38,906	38,926	20	0.1
West Mercia	80,013	82,254	2,241	2.8
West Midlands	318,087	317,892	−195	−0.1
West Yorkshire	283,938	268,716	−15,222	−5.4
Wiltshire	36,428	35,911	−517	−1.4
Wales				
Dyfed-Powys	19,419	19,072	−347	−1.8
Gwent	33,034	44,572	11,538	34.9
North Wales	41,645	41,024	−621	−1.5
South Wales	153,249	141,578	−11,671	−7.6
Total metropolitan forces	2,254,647	2,228,388	−26,259	−1.2
Total non-metropolitan forces	2,845,594	2,805,440	−40,154	−1.4
TOTAL	5,100,241	5,033,828	−66,413	−1.3

Source: The Home Office

Percentage of Crimes Cleared Up by Police Force Area in England and Wales

Data are in percentages and exclude offences of 'other criminal damage' of value £20 and under.

Police force area	1992	1993	1994	1995	1996
Avon and Somerset	17	17	21	23	24
Bedfordshire	20	21	22	22	33
Cambridgeshire	27	25	25	19	24
Cheshire	29	26	30	31	34
Cleveland	32	27	19	25	24
Cumbria	37	38	37	40	36
Derbyshire	22	21	21	20	21
Devon and Cornwall	18	25	27	27	30
Dorset	32	33	30	28	27
Durham	30	30	32	30	30
Essex	29	32	36	33	29
Gloucestershire	24	20	24	27	23
Greater Manchester	35	34	34	24	17
Hampshire	26	26	27	28	28
Hertfordshire	26	21	24	28	30
Humberside	23	16	17	19	20
Kent	27	25	29	26	32
Lancashire	37	35	33	34	33
Leicestershire	30	28	30	29	31
Lincolnshire	39	37	32	39	42
London, City of	20	22	27	23	27
Merseyside	42	39	33	27	29
Metropolitan Police	16	17	23	25	24
Norfolk	34	28	34	31	32
Northamptonshire	30	27	31	28	34
Northumbria	17	20	22	23	24
North Yorkshire	33	30	25	23	25
Nottinghamshire	26	29	28	23	28
South Yorkshire	26	20	24	24	23
Staffordshire	30	29	31	32	34
Suffolk	39	37	35	34	33
Surrey	22	20	30	31	29
Sussex	23	24	24	28	29
Thames Valley	19	21	22	23	25
Warwickshire	23	21	24	25	24
West Mercia	34	29	29	28	26
West Midlands	27	27	25	24	23
West Yorkshire	25	28	20	21	24
Wiltshire	37	35	36	32	29
England average	25	25	26	26	26
Dyfed-Powys	53	50	53	57	58
Gwent	44	45	47	50	50
North Wales	33	36	39	32	33
South Wales	30	28	24	29	32
Wales average	35	34	34	32	37

Source: The Home Office

Metropolitan Police have a lower than average crime clean-up rate

Photo Disc Ltd.

Murder and Manslaughter Recorded by the Police by Offence in England and Wales

(– = not applicable. Percentages in brackets are based on totals of less than 100.)

Offence	Offences recorded							Offences cleared up 1996[1]	
	1990	1991	1992	1993	1994	1995	1996	Number	%
Homicide (murder, manslaughter, infanticide)	669	725	687	670	726	745	681	635	93
Attempted murder	476	555	568	661	651	634	674	598	89
Threat or conspiracy to murder	4,162	4,712	5,487	5,638	6,844	7,044	8,533	7,112	83
Child destruction	0	2	0	3	7	8	2	2	(100)
Causing death by dangerous driving or by careless driving when under the influence of drink and drugs	419	416	277	292	278	242	320	309	97
Causing death by aggravated vehicle taking[2]	–	–	19	17	14	21	34	28	(82)

[1] Offences cleared up in current year may have been initially recorded in an earlier year.
[2] Offence introduced on 1 April 1992.

Source: The Home Office

Selected Sex Offences Recorded by the Police in England and Wales

(– = not applicable.)

Offence		Offences recorded (found guilty or cautioned in brackets)							Offences cleared up 1996	
		1990	1991	1992	1993	1994	1995	1996	Number	%
Buggery		1,120 (336)	1,127 (302)	1,255 (277)	1,279 (245)	1,258 (245)	818 (191)	728 (132)	648	89
Indecent assault	on a male	3,043 (831)	3,070 (710)	3,119 (720)	3,340 (667)	3,205 (635)	3,150 (668)	3,130 (631)	2,715	87
	on a female	15,783 (3,990)	15,792 (3,791)	16,235 (3,695)	17,350 (3,471)	17,579 (3,390)	16,876 (3,321)	17,643 (3,344)	12,558	71
Rape	of a male[1]	–	–	–	–	–	150 (9)	231 (24)	164	71
	of a female	3,391 (561)	4,045 (559)	4,142 (529)	4,589 (482)	5,032 (460)	4,986 (578)	5,759 (573)	4,418	77
Unlawful sexual intercourse with a girl under 16		2,140 (1,288)	1,949 (1,073)	1,563 (924)	1,443 (723)	1,446 (705)	1,260 (603)	1,261 (576)	1,135	90

[1] The Criminal Justice and Public Order Act 1994 introduced a specific offence of rape of a male. Following this change in legislation, male victims of forced buggery are now classified as male rape.

Source: The Home Office

Victims of Violence by Gender in England and Wales

Because of differing proportions of men and women in the sample to the population, the numbers of incidents against men and women do not add up to percentage totals. Survey rates are grossed up to population estimates: i.e. by 19,968,400 for men, and by 21,198,800 for women.

1995–96

Type of violence	Number of incidents			Type of violence as a proportion of all types of violence for men/women		Type of violence as a proportion of all types of violence		
	Men	Women	All	Men (%)	Women (%)	Men (%)	Women (%)	All (%)
Domestic	290,000	680,000	990,000	12	43	7	17	24
Mugging	230,000	160,000	390,000	9	10	6	4	10
Stranger	750,000	220,000	950,000	30	14	18	5	23
Acquaintance	1,240,000	510,000	1,730,000	50	32	31	13	43
Total contact crime	2,510,000	1,580,000	4,050,000	100	100	62	39	100

Source: 1996 British Crime Survey: England and Wales

Police Assaulted in the Line of Duty in England and Wales

Degree of injury	1989	1990	1991	1992	1993	1994/95	1995/96
Fatal	2	1	5	0	2	1	1
Serious	1,062	1,572	1,275	963	886	652	654
Other	16,963	16,705	17,870	17,145	17,062	14,904	14,411
Total	18,027	18,278	19,150	18,108	17,950	15,587	15,066

Source: The Home Office

Reasons Given by Victims for Not Reporting Offences in England and Wales

(In percentages.)

1996

Reason	Vandalism	Burglary	Vehicle thefts[1]	Bike theft	Assault	Robbery	Theft from person	Other thefts[2]	All offences
Too trivial/no loss	45	45	45	30	22	28	50	46	40
Police could do nothing	35	32	41	38	16	30	33	24	29
Police would not be interested	22	21	26	24	12	23	15	21	20
Dealt with matter ourselves	11	16	9	12	47	21	12	11	19
Reported to other authorities	2	3	1	1	8	6	5	9	5
Inconvenient to report	3	2	6	6	2	2	6	4	4
Fear reprisals	2	2	<1	0	11	11	<1	4	4
Fear/dislike police	<1	1	<1	0	1	0	1	<1	<1
Other	4	7	3	6	9	11	4	6	5

[1] Thefts from vehicles and attempted thefts of and from them.
[2] Other household thefts and thefts of personal property.

Source: The Home Office

Population in Prison Under Sentence by Sex and Offence Group in England and Wales

Offence group	1991	1992	1993	1994	1995	1996
Men						
Offences with immediate custodial sentence						
Violence against the person	6,945	6,893	7,273	7,715	8,491	9,230
Rape	1,508	1,582	1,593	1,638	1,781	1,926
Other sexual offences	1,585	1,564	1,572	1,629	1,875	2,013
Burglary	5,082	5,349	4,690	5,096	5,896	6,342
Robbery	3,990	4,174	4,856	5,090	5,264	5,591
Theft and handling	2,910	2,910	2,578	3,030	3,450	3,591
Fraud and forgery	791	800	826	879	1,071	1,099
Drugs offences	2,584	2,899	2,900	3,186	3,858	5,269
Motoring offences	861	967	1,045	1,527	1,660	1,720
Other offences	2,311	2,490	2,448	2,301	2,514	2,952
Offence not recorded	5,002	4,402	1,794	1,869	1,547	1,454
All offences	33,569	34,030	31,375	33,960	37,407	41,187
In default of a fine	397	359	522	514	490	136
Total	33,966	34,389	31,897	34,474	37,897	41,323
Women						
Offences with immediate custodial sentence						
Violence against the person	189	184	216	277	290	355
Sexual offences	16	10	15	12	12	12
Burglary	39	51	39	39	57	80
Robbery	46	56	77	95	108	124
Theft and handling	175	190	207	227	279	314
Fraud and forgery	42	53	64	65	96	119
Drugs offences	272	259	308	326	398	486
Motoring offences	2	3	7	20	18	14
Other offences	174	155	118	112	114	150
Offence not recorded	181	191	74	93	84	73
All offences	1,136	1,152	1,125	1,266	1,482	1,727
In default of payment of a fine	12	23	24	23	26	5
Total	1,148	1,175	1,149	1,289	1,482	1,732
TOTAL	35,114	35,564	33,046	35,763	39,379	43,055

Source: The Home Office

Complaints against the Police in England and Wales

(– = not applicable.)

Complaints	1993			1994			1995/96			1996/97		
	Number	% of all complaints	% of investigated complaints	Number	% of all complaints	% of investigated complaints	Number	% of all complaints	% of investigated complaints	Number	% of all complaints	% of investigated complaints
Total complaints												
All complaints	34,894	–	–	36,521	–	–	35,840	–	–	36,731	–	–
Investigated	10,484	–	–	9,590	–	–	8,653	–	–	10,820	–	–
Substantiated	750	2	7.2	793	2	8.3	749	2	8.7	834	2	7.7
Unsubstantiated	9,734	28	92.8	8,797	24	91.7	7,904	23	91.3	9,986	27	92.3
Withdrawn	14,284	41	–	14,658	40	–	15,535	43	–	14,286	39	–
Informally resolved	10,126	29	–	12,273	34	–	11,652	33	–	11,625	32	–

Substantiated Complaints by Reason for Complaint

Oppressive behaviour												
Assault	94					82			71			94
Oppressive conduct/harassment	41					40			43			46
Unlawful/unnecessary arrest/detention	72					61			52			67
Oppressive behaviour total	207					183			166			207
Racially discriminatory behaviour	5					4			2			6
Malpractice												
Perjury/irregularity in evidence	24					22			29			21
Corrupt practice	7					2			5			2
Mishandling of property	34					39			29			36
Malpractice total	65					63			63			59
Failures in duty												
Neglect of duty	208					237			206			254
Impropriety in connection with search of premises	27					29			30			23
Irregularity in procedure	130					147			153			178
Failures in duty total	365					413			389			455
Incivility	62					84			93			78
Traffic irregularity	8					11			8			7
Other	38					35			28			22
TOTAL	750					793			749			834

Source: The Home Office

Young Offenders under an Immediate Custodial Sentence by Age, Sex, and Offence Group in England and Wales

Age and offence group		1990	1991	1992	1993	1994	1995	1996
Men								
Aged under 18	violence against the person	350	309	385	425	424	546	665
	sexual offences	52	44	35	47	33	46	62
	burglary	1,203	1,112	1,056	1,070	1,211	1,258	1,284
	robbery	314	276	293	330	378	521	704
	theft and handling	761	874	726	1,004	1,192	1,268	1,219
	fraud and forgery	7	2	4	4	10	8	14
	drugs offences	22	19	36	32	26	43	63
	other offences	507	545	543	555	625	721	789
	offence not recorded	493	440	266	97	72	94	271
	Total	3,709	3,621	3,344	3,564	3,971	4,505	5,071
Aged 18–20	violence against the person	1,384	1,261	1,208	1,221	1,378	1,434	1,623
	sexual offences	133	130	102	108	81	119	90
	burglary	2,686	2,730	2,552	2,335	2,535	2,665	2,468
	robbery	743	665	731	709	669	726	977
	theft and handling	1,980	2,253	1,737	2,083	2,586	2,737	2,693
	fraud and forgery	69	78	45	66	79	72	123
	drugs offences	193	214	299	287	296	391	518
	other offences	1,820	2,052	1,901	2,098	2,516	2,812	2,833
	offence not recorded	1,282	1,615	911	315	336	219	485
	Total	10,290	10,998	9,486	9,222	10,476	11,175	11,810
Total men		13,999	14,619	12,830	12,786	14,447	15,680	16,881

(continued)

Young Offenders under an Immediate Custodial Sentence by Age, Sex, and Offence Group in England and Wales (*continued*)

Age and offence group		1990	1991	1992	1993	1994	1995	1996
Women								
Aged under 18	violence against the person	20	13	18	34	54	48	68
	sexual offences	0	1	0	0	0	3	0
	burglary	7	14	8	4	15	21	15
	robbery	14	18	15	22	28	28	40
	theft and handling	23	20	15	20	31	39	43
	fraud and forgery	0	0	2	3	0	0	2
	drugs offences	0	3	4	2	3	4	4
	other offences	13	8	6	15	13	20	31
	offence not recorded	18	20	11	2	5	3	11
	Total	95	97	79	102	149	166	214
Aged 18–20	violence against the person	38	42	41	59	74	67	81
	sexual offences	4	2	2	0	0	1	0
	burglary	19	24	18	35	30	30	34
	robbery	24	23	17	24	30	32	46
	theft and handling	77	76	72	86	113	129	179
	fraud and forgery	11	11	10	13	9	23	23
	drugs offences	26	23	23	24	31	43	58
	other offences	52	43	45	53	56	56	61
	offence not recorded	35	68	37	23	17	17	16
	Total	286	312	265	317	360	398	498
Total women		381	409	344	419	509	564	712

Source: The Home Office

Fear of Crime: by Type of Crime and Ethnic Group in England and Wales

This table reports the percentage of people aged 16 and over in each ethnic group who were 'very worried' about each type of crime.

1996

Type of crime	White	Black	Indian	Pakistani/Bangladeshi
Rape[1]	31	43	51	49
Theft from car[2]	24	42	40	40
Burglary	21	40	47	44
Theft of car[2]	20	35	35	33
Mugging	18	32	40	38
Racially motivated attacks	7	27	35	38

[1] Figures refer to females only.
[2] Figures show the percentage of car owners who reported a fear of car crime.

Source: The Home Office

Police Complaints Authority

In the UK, an independent group of a dozen people set up under the Police and Criminal Evidence Act 1984 to supervise the investigation of complaints against the police by members of the public.

When the investigation of a complaint is completed the authority must make a public declaration of its decision. It can order disciplinary action to be taken against police officers. The total number of complaints in 1989 was 11,155, of which 1.7% resulted in disciplinary charges. Alternatively, a complainant may take a case to court. The number of successful civil actions against the police rises every year. In England and Wales in 1992 there were 35,000 recorded complaints against the police, but not all of these were forwarded to the authority.

© Richard Watt

Police at Stonehenge, *during summer solstice celebrations there*

Offences against Prison Discipline and Punishment Given in England and Wales

1996

Offence[1][2]	All offences[5]	Type of punishment[3]							
		Average number of punishments per offence	Cellular confinement	Forfeiture of privileges	Stoppage or reduction of earnings	Caution	Other[4]	Additional days	All punishments[5]
Violence	3,104	8,203	5,067	422	1,009	10,159	27,894	12,853	2.2
Escape/abscond	99	298	154	1	119	1,170	1,841	1,150	1.6
Disobedience/disrespect	7,819	21,578	19,917	2,916	2,668	25,771	80,669	45,832	1.8
Wilful damage	931	2,965	4,009	210	375	2,777	11,267	5,804	1.9
Unauthorized transactions	2,150	11,009	12,003	1,362	960	31,072	58,556	38,265	1.5
Other offences	876	3,726	5,429	934	741	6,372	18,078	11,568	1.6
TOTAL	14,889	47,779	46,599	5,845	5,872	77,321	198,305	115,472	1.4

[1] Includes offences committed at one establishment and punished at another.
[2] Includes attempting, inciting and assisting under Rule 47(22), except for attempted escapes, which are shown separately.
[3] Including suspended and prospective punishments.
[4] Includes exclusion from associated work (prisons and remand centres only), and removal from activities, removal from wing or living area, and extra work or fatigues (all young offender institutions only).
[5] The number of offences punished and punishments given are not equal because in many cases two or more punishments are given for a single offence.

Source: The Home Office

Employment in the Criminal Justice System in England and Wales

(N/A = not available.)

Service[1]		1988/89	1990/91	1992/93	1993/94	1995/96	1996/97[2]
Police	officers	125,631	127,495	128,290	127,897	126,878	N/A
	civilians[3]	42,767	46,361	49,518	50,299	52,933	N/A
Magistrates' courts		9,882	10,182	10,112	10,086	10,727	N/A
Probation[4]	officers	6,787	7,188	7,832	8,070	7,813	7,500
	support staff[5]	8,952	9,774	10,526	10,526	10,679	10,209
Prisons[6]	31,180	35,040	39,193	38,903	40,360	38,310	
Lord Chancellor's Department[7]		1,866	1,958	2,086	2,074	2,041	N/A
Crown Prosecution Service		4,676	5,316	6,307	6,675	6,577	6,175

[1] Average strength.
[2] Estimated.
[3] Excluding traffic wardens and cadets.
[4] At 31 December, full- and part-time staff.
[5] Excludes hostel staff.
[6] Prison officers, other industrial and non-industrial staff.
[7] Criminal work only.

Source: The Home Office

Expenditure on the Criminal Justice System in England and Wales

(In millions of current pounds. N/A = not available.)

Service	1990/91	1992/93	1993/94	1995/96	1996/97[1]
Police	3,806	5,860	6,181	6,749	7,060
Magistrates' courts	300	356	410	416	321
Probation	329	424	480	491	N/A
Prisons	1,453	1,610	1,507	1,667	1,522
Lord Chancellor's Department[2]	528	707	716	744	1,003
Crown Prosecution Service	211	276	283	296	288
Total[3]	6,627	9,233	9,577	10,363	N/A

[1] Estimated.
[2] Criminal work only.
[3] Total expenditure by central and local government only, capital and current.

Source: The Home Office

Scotland: Law and Crime

Actual Strength of the Police Service in Scotland

Figures exclude domestic staff and cadets and include clerical and technical staff in Scottish Criminal Record Office and Scottish Crime Squad. Part-time police support staff are included as 0.5 unit.
(As of 31 March 1996.)

Year	Regular police officers (including additional)			Support staff (whole-time equivalent)	
	Total	Men	Women	Traffic wardens	Clerical and technical
1993	12,581	1,558	544.5	3,301.0	17,984.5
1994	12,631	1,680	535.5	3,490.5	18,337.0
1995–96	12,634	1,883	494.5	3,686.0	18,697.5

Source: The Scottish Office Home Department

Crimes and Offences Recorded by the Police in Scotland

Category		1992	1993	1994	1995	1996	% change 1995–1996
Crimes							
Non-sexual crimes of violence	serious assault	7,709	6,527	6,705	6,920	6,988	1
	handling offensive weapons	6,536	5,152	5,282	6,465	6,822	6
	robbery	6,807	5,582	5,297	5,330	5,254	–1
	other	2,248	2,143	2,490	2,404	2,473	3
	Total	23,300	19,404	19,774	21,119	21,537	2
Crimes of indecency	sexual assault	1,604	1,626	1,603	1,638	1,729	6
	lewd and libidinous practices	2,596	2,721	2,655	2,381	2,465	4
	other	1,950	1,700	1,740	1,528	1,482	–3
	Total	6,150	6,047	5,998	5,547	5,676	2
Crimes of dishonesty	housebreaking	113,160	97,829	88,394	74,235	64,470	–13
	theft by opening lockfast places	92,226	84,795	74,862	66,539	60,472	–9
	theft of a motor vehicle	47,433	42,816	41,962	37,514	34,161	–9
	shoplifting	29,736	26,746	26,573	27,952	26,927	–4
	other theft	98,794	93,327	88,900	87,716	82,576	–6
	fraud	22,564	19,125	17,670	17,093	16,081	–6
	other	11,079	10,299	11,985	10,152	10,754	6
	Total	414,992	374,937	350,346	321,201	295,441	–8
Fire-raising, vandalism	fire-raising	4,666	4,118	3,589	3,299	3,306	>1
	vandalism, etc	87,571	80,076	84,954	83,247	85,719	3
	Total	92,237	84,194	88,543	86,546	89,025	3
Other	crimes against public justice	14,411	14,515	16,004	16,359	16,148	–1
	drugs	13,568	17,986	19,281	24,773	23,992	–3
	other	232	164	164	152	137	–10
	Total	28,211	32,665	35,449	41,284	40,277	–2
	Total crimes	564,890	517,247	500,110	475,697	451,956	–5
Offences							
Motor vehicle offences	dangerous and careless driving	22,461	19,951	21,088	18,729	17,347	–7
	drunk driving	11,260	10,905	10,835	10,719	11,796	10
	speeding	93,574	85,398	85,799	85,141	82,355	–3
	unlawful use of vehicle	79,863	85,826	88,652	83,416	79,123	–5
	vehicle defect offences	47,775	51,387	56,943	56,321	53,451	–5
	other	51,508	61,652	67,407	63,175	61,830	–2
	Total	306,441	315,119	330,724	317,501	305,902	–4
Other	petty assault	42,469	41,339	45,083	46,604	47,605	2
	breach of the peace	60,003	61,370	65,514	66,088	70,830	7
	drunkenness	10,393	10,144	10,289	9,737	9,608	–1
	other	14,590	13,740	12,307	11,939	18,043	51
	Total	127,455	126,593	133,193	134,368	146,086	9
	Total offences	433,896	441,712	463,917	451,869	451,988	>1
TOTAL		998,786	958,959	964,027	927,566	903,944	–3

Source: The Scottish Office Home Department

Crimes and Offences Recorded by Police Force Area per 10,000 Population in Scotland

1996

Category		Central	Dumfries and Galloway	Fife	Grampian	Lothian and Borders	Northern	Strathclyde	Tayside	Scotland average
Crimes										
Non-sexual crimes of violence	serious assault	12	9	3	7	12	3	20	9	14
	handling offensive weapons	11	13	10	6	8	7	18	18	13
	robbery	3	3	3	4	10	1	16	6	10
	other	3	3	3	3	6	3	5	7	5
	Total[1]	30	28	20	20	36	13	59	40	42
Crimes of indecency	sexual assault	2	2	2	4	5	2	3	4	3
	lewd and libidinous practices	3	1	5	4	6	3	5	6	5
	other	1	1	1	4	1	1	4	1	3
	Total[1]	7	4	8	12	12	6	12	12	11
Crimes of dishonesty	housebreaking	88	80	112	129	106	39	148	153	126
	theft by opening lockfast places	56	29	103	116	116	33	140	143	118
	theft of a motor vehicle	36	17	38	31	60	17	95	65	67
	shoplifting	42	41	37	55	59	33	53	68	52
	other theft	109	116	129	192	178	110	160	200	161
	fraud	21	27	19	47	27	30	34	23	31
	other	18	29	7	15	42	15	14	35	21
	Total[1]	370	339	444	584	588	275	646	688	575
Fire-raising, vandalism	fire-raising	4	2	4	4	7	3	8	8	6
	vandalism, etc	123	112	167	173	159	101	176	222	167
	Total[1]	127	114	172	177	166	103	184	230	173
Other	crimes against public justice	34	31	20	24	21	31	38	36	31
	drugs	37	44	48	43	36	44	54	41	47
	other	0	1	0	0	0	0	0	0	0
	Total[1]	71	76	68	67	57	75	92	77	78
	Total crimes	604	561	712	859	860	473	993	1,047	880
Offences										
Motor vehicle offences	dangerous and careless driving	19	39	60	59	14	49	29	46	34
	drunk driving	22	21	18	22	23	32	23	24	23
	speeding	201	618	271	222	143	135	110	125	160
	unlawful use of vehicle	160	173	146	122	141	148	166	153	154
	vehicle defect offences	199	86	181	72	110	114	96	48	104
	other	67	191	126	143	141	76	119	89	120
	Total[1]	669	1,128	802	642	573	553	543	484	596
Other	petty assault	92	81	93	96	92	80	97	78	93
	breach of the peace	151	110	111	149	76	151	165	118	138
	drunkenness	15	14	11	6	3	39	28	12	19
	other	20	25	16	27	9	64	51	25	35
	Total[1]	278	230	232	278	180	333	341	233	284
TOTAL[1]		1,551	1,919	1,745	1,779	1,612	1,360	1,877	1,764	1,760

[1] Due to rounding, figures may not add up to the totals.

Source: The Scottish Office Home Department

Number of Crimes Recorded by the Police by Council and Clear-Up Rates in Scotland

1996

Council	Non-sexual crimes of violence	Crimes of indecency	Crimes of dishonesty	Fire-raising and vandalism	Other crimes	Total crimes	% of crimes cleared up
Aberdeen City	619	373	21,369	3,797	1,984	28,142	32
Aberdeenshire	296	175	6,766	3,736	1,177	12,150	34
Angus[1]	308	135	4,060	2,154	833	7,490	42
Argyll and Bute	274	68	3,032	1,106	578	5,058	45
Clackmannanshire	134	34	1,280	613	344	2,405	65
Dumfries and Galloway	418	59	5,008	1,687	1,119	8,291	62
Dundee City[1]	847	252	16,332	4,676	1,395	23,502	31
East Ayrshire	469	79	6,414	1,948	751	9,661	33
East Dunbartonshire	300	51	4,727	1,390	333	6,801	27
East Lothian	149	80	2,535	1,227	287	4,278	35
East Renfrewshire	258	30	4,934	1,314	283	6,819	21
Edinburgh, City of	2,128	700	36,615	8,353	2,941	50,737	33
Falkirk	410	75	5,627	2,066	1,005	9,183	58
Fife	697	275	15,607	6,037	2,404	25,020	46
Glasgow City	6,164	1,653	60,132	15,131	10,421	93,501	35
Highland	307	136	6,697	2,260	1,794	11,194	62
Inverclyde	507	102	5,272	1,300	913	8,094	36
Midlothian	223	69	2,442	1,215	456	4,405	42
Moray	147	86	2,986	1,887	388	5,494	38
North Ayrshire	623	118	6,810	2,500	1,022	11,073	35
North Lanarkshire	1,373	222	15,472	4,967	2,060	24,094	32
Orkney Islands	18	12	154	104	85	373	76
Perth and Kinross[1]	424	69	6,823	2,287	829	10,432	36
Renfrewshire	1,118	132	12,607	3,879	1,216	18,952	26
Scottish Borders	207	89	2,765	1,155	467	4,683	47
Shetland Islands	14	8	347	235	112	716	75
South Ayrshire	388	79	6,432	1,625	736	9,260	42
South Lanarkshire	1,368	214	13,986	4,698	1,801	22,067	32
Stirling	278	75	3,219	792	600	4,964	60
West Dunbartonshire	631	72	7,597	2,085	980	11,365	33
Western Isles	34	7	518	292	124	975	64
West Lothian	406	147	6,876	2,509	839	10,777	33
Total[1]	21,537	5,676	295,441	89,025	40,277	451,956	37

[1] Figures for the period prior to local government reorganization (Quarter 1, 1996) for the councils in Tayside were estimated from the information submitted for old districts.

Source: The Scottish Office Home Department

Outcome of Recorded Crime by Main Penalty in Scotland

Penalty	1990	1991	1992	1993	1994	1995
Absolute discharge	709	698	775	773	601	682
Admonition or caution	16,593	17,195	17,431	16,982	16,231	15,854
Probation	4,182	4,916	5,326	5,674	6,091	6,071
Permit to children's hearing	52	82	72	83	124	172
Community service order	4,811	5,306	5,576	5,185	5,456	5,506
Fine	135,302	135,185	131,872	116,928	112,763	110,346
Compensation order	1,749	1,663	1,672	1,695	1,672	1,671
Insanity, hospital, guardianship order	152	153	133	138	133	136
Prison	8,810	9,235	10,103	10,843	11,592	11,571
Young offender's institution	4,175	4,371	4,501	4,475	4,479	4,650
Detention of child	23	32	22	30	36	48
Total persons with charge proved	176,558	178,836	177,483	162,806	159,178	156,707

Source: The Scottish Office Home Department

Crimes and Offences Cleared Up by the Police as a Percentage of Those Recorded in Scotland

(In percentages.)

Crime/offence category		1992	1993	1994	1995	1996
Total crimes		29	31	34	35	37
Non-sexual crimes of violence	serious assault, etc	57	57	57	54	57
	handling offensive weapons	100	99	99	99	99
	robbery	24	27	29	29	29
	other	84	83	83	82	84
Crimes of indecency	sexual assault	63	63	68	66	69
	lewd and libidinous practices	56	62	65	67	68
	other	98	97	97	96	98
Crimes of dishonesty	housebreaking	14	16	17	17	18
	theft by opening lockfast places	12	12	15	13	15
	theft of a motor vehicle	19	21	24	24	25
	shoplifting	78	77	80	79	78
	other theft	16	17	18	18	19
	fraud	73	75	82	81	79
	other	85	86	84	87	82
Fire-raising, vandalism, etc	fire-raising	17	19	19	19	20
	vandalism, etc	19	19	20	21	21
Other crimes	crimes against public justice	100	100	100	100	100
	drugs	99	100	100	100	99
	other	83	79	84	80	82
Miscellaneous offences	petty assault	71	73	73	74	75
	breach of the peace	92	90	92	93	94
	drunkenness	100	100	100	100	100
	other	88	89	92	95	97

Source: The Scottish Office Home Department

Cases of Homicide Recorded by Crime and Status in Scotland

Crime/status		1990	1992	1993	1994	1995[1]
All homicide cases		80	131	115	108	135
Solved cases	murder	33	65	73	62	83
	culpable homicide	45	65	41	42	51
	Total	78	130	114	104	134
Unsolved cases		2	1	1	4	1

[1] The classification as murder or culpable homicide reflects the position as at 31 July 1996 but may change where cases have not been finally disposed of.

Source: The Scottish Office Home Department

Young Offenders: Average Daily Sentenced Prison Population in Scotland

Sentence	1990	1992	1993	1994	1995
Less than 18 months	438	492	473	387	427
18 months to less than 4 years	169	170	211	205	164
4 years and over (excluding life)	77	85	105	103	98
Life	7	12	17	15	14

Source: The Scottish Office Home Department

Complaints Cases and Allegations against the Police in Scotland

		1995–96
Number of complaint cases	outstanding at beginning of year	545
	received during the year	1,444
	disposed of during the year	1,403
	standing over at end of year	586
Number of allegations	withdrawn by complainer	93
	abandoned due to non-cooperation of complainer	29
	found to be unsubstantiated	580
	resolved by conciliation or explanation to complainer	124
	leading to police officers being charged with criminal offences	11
	leading to criminal proceedings	29
	leading to 'No Proceedings' decision by Procurator Fiscal	1,406
	leading to criminal convictions	5
	resulting in disciplinary hearings	9
	resulting in formal warnings in terms of disciplinary regulations	22
	resulting in corrective advice to officers	138
	Total allegations disposed of during year	2,361

Average Daily Prison Population and Receptions in Scotland

Category	1990	1991	1992	1993	1994	1995
Average Daily Population						
Men	4,587	4,696	5,099	5,466	5,408	5,451
Women	137	143	158	171	177	175
Total	4,724	4,839	5,257	5,637	5,585	5,626
Analysis by Type of Custody						
Remand	751	770	876	948	1,015	998
Persons under sentence adult prisoners	3,202	3,322	3,552	3,795	3,785	3,823
young offenders	707	684	769	819	720	719
persons recalled from supervision/licence	40	39	32	40	37	44
others	13	12	21	32	28	38
Total	3,962	4,057	4,374	4,686	4,570	4,624
Persons sentenced by court martial	11	12	6	2	1	3
Civil prisoners	1	1	1	1	1	0
Receptions[1] to Penal Establishments						
Men	14,323	12,360	12,722	12,478	13,985	13,377
Women	845	769	824	934	937	876
Persons under sentence men	16,235	17,033	18,856	20,741	19,697	17,737
women	899	1,193	1,110	1,416	1,414	1,293
imprisoned directly	7,551	7,951	8,543	9,444	9,349	8,730
imprisoned in default of fine	5,182	6,336	6,603	7,956	7,377	6,299
imprisoned in default of compensation order	23	6	40	41	26	13
Total	17,134	18,226	19,966	22,157	21,111	19,030
Persons sentenced to young offenders' institution						
directly	2,719	2,356	3,041	3,052	2,855	2,772
in default of fine	1,653	1,573	1,736	1,660	1,498	1,210
in default of compensation order	3	2	2	4	6	4
Recalled to young offenders' institutions/ from Borstal supervision	1	1	1	0	0	0
Other sentences	2	1	0	0	0	0
Persons sentenced by court martial	10	1	2	7	5	4
Civil prisoners[2]	21	25	34	37	27	25
Total remand	15,168	13,129	13,546	13,412	14,922	14,253

[1] Total receptions cannot be calculated by adding together receptions in each category because there is double counting. This arises because a person received on remand and then under sentence in relation to the same set of charges, is counted in both categories.
[2] For 1995, data are estimated.

Source: The Scottish Office Home Department

Breaches of Prison Discipline in Scotland

1996–97

Population	Prisons		Young offenders' institutions		All establishments[1]	
	Men	Women	Men	Women	Men	Women
Average daily number of prisoners and young offenders	5,026	158	776	32	5,802	189
Breaches of discipline	19,264	578	9,571	195	28,835	773
Breaches of discipline committed per head of average population	2.9	3.9	6.1	6.0	3.3	4.3

[1] Components do not add to total due to rounding.

Source: The Scottish Office Home Department

Expenditure on Penal Establishments in Scotland

Figures are for 31 March in year shown and are in pounds.

Expenditure	1990/91	1991/92	1992/93	1993/94	1994/95	1995/96	1996/97
Manpower and associated services	110,454	124,898	129,597	135,301	140,009	135,941	143,107
Prisoner and associated costs	8,446	8,504	10,274	10,795	11,679	12,373	13,377
Capital expenditure	12,866	13,032	13,681	11,845	15,636	15,377	22,577
Total gross expenditure	131,766	146,434	153,552	157,941	167,324	163,691	179,061

Source: The Scottish Office Home Department

Northern Ireland: Law and Crime

Notifiable Offences Recorded by the Police in Northern Ireland

Crime category		1990	1991	1992	1993	1994	1995	1996
Violence against the person	murder	71	114	108	101	82	22	35
	manslaughter and infanticide	11	7	3	5	4	2	4
	attempted murder	225	360	311	416	255	35	71
	other	3,067	3,474	3,680	4,075	4,452	5,091	5,530
	Total	3,374	3,955	4,102	4,597	4,793	5,150	5,640
Sexual offences	rape	94	117	116	151	168	229	264
	attempted rape	31	38	38	42	40	30	28
	incest	38	25	35	20	24	13	15
	indecent assault	401	413	493	597	698	932	991
	other	226	284	291	377	403	475	447
	Total	790	877	973	1187	1333	1679	1745
Burglary	in a dwelling	6,505	7,206	7,461	8,005	9,454	9,774	8,530
	in a building other than a dwelling	7,311	8,281	8,677	6,675	6,480	6,499	7,426
	other[1]	1,001	1,076	979	1,055	968	184	158
	Total	14,817	16,563	17,117	15,735	16,902	16,457	16,114
Robbery	armed robbery	579	686	866	751	657	620	655
	hijacking	425	519	339	365	194	331	439
	other	626	643	646	607	716	588	631
	Total	1,630	1,848	1,851	1,723	1,567	1,539	1,725
Theft	from the person	219	304	242	217	257	330	235
	in a dwelling	428	304	356	436	427	618	628
	from a motor vehicle	6,443	7,227	7,117	6,729	6,555	6,715	6,554
	shoplifting	3,984	3,737	4,549	4,625	4,510	5,410	5,291
	of, or unauthorized taking of, motor vehicles	7,042	8,455	9,376	9,011	8,974	7,794	8,404
	other	11,151	12,006	12,616	12,143	12,510	12,605	11,660
	Total	29,267	32,033	34,256	33,161	33,233	33,472	32,772
Fraud and forgery	frauds	3,895	4,533	4,991	4,922	4,127	4,204	3,707
	forgery	282	278	495	631	973	680	374
	Total	4,177	4,811	5,486	5,553	5,100	4,884	4,081
Criminal damage	arson	691	805	860	901	940	1,132	1,490
	explosives offences	90	112	117	88	65	13	7
	other[2]	1,410	1,477	1,525	1,867	2,072	2,627	3,350
	Total	2,191	2,394	2,502	2,856	3,077	3,772	4,847
Offences against the state	offences under the NI Emergency Provisions Act	133	151	103	87	106	18	61
	firearms offences	119	114	73	76	98	42	47
	other	333	327	302	273	236	279	292
	Total	585	592	478	436	440	339	400
Other	drug	216	287	619	811	1,286	1,426	1,093
	other	151	132	148	169	155	90	132
	Total	367	419	767	980	1,441	1,516	1,225
	TOTAL	57,198	63,492	67,532	66,228	67,886	68,808	68,549

[1] From 1995 'other' excludes attempted burglary, which is included in 'burglary in a dwelling' or 'burglary in a building other than a dwelling'.
[2] 'Other criminal damage' excludes offences where damage was under £200.

Source: Northern Ireland Office

Crimes Recorded and Crimes Cleared Up by the Police in Northern Ireland

(N/A= not available.)

Crime category	1990	1991	1992	1993	1994	1995	1996
Notifiable crimes recorded	57,198	63,492	67,532	66,228	67,886	68,808	68,549
Number of crimes cleared	21,475	22,675	23,253	24,088	24,342	24,838	23,103
Clear-up rate (%)	38	36	34	36	36	36	34

% of Crimes Recorded that Were Cleared Up[1]

	1990	1991	1992	1993	1994	1995	1996
Violence against the person							
Murder	28	60	51	52	58	64	63
Manslaughter and infanticide	109	43	200	160	75	100	125
Attempted murder	28	27	34	35	31	74	49
Other violence against the person	65	66	67	65	69	67	63
Sexual offences							
Rape	88	80	80	76	69	83	81
Attempted rape	77	97	71	81	73	70	79
Incest	89	84	106	80	71	115	87
Indecent assault	89	83	73	80	82	81	80
Other sexual offence	100	94	90	63	112	82	98
Burglary							
Burglary in a dwelling	20	18	16	15	16	18	17
Burglary in a building other than a dwelling	22	21	19	22	22	19	17
Other burglary[2]	44	54	46	43	43	98	99
Robbery							
Armed robbery	20	18	17	14	18	17	19
Hijacking	13	9	24	13	22	10	5
Other robbery	19	21	19	18	21	27	21
Theft							
Theft from the person	23	24	17	19	16	15	23
Theft from dwelling	65	54	57	66	63	57	54
Theft from motor vehicles	14	12	9	10	8	10	8
Shoplifting	89	92	85	83	86	83	80
Theft or unauthorized taking of motor vehicles	31	29	27	30	19	18	15
Other thefts	31	31	29	31	30	28	26
Fraud and forgery							
Frauds	74	68	43	64	71	66	66
Forgery	77	52	63	45	38	39	46
Criminal damage							
Arson	22	20	22	19	20	18	12
Explosive offences	37	33	12	31	26	62	29
Other criminal damage[3]	43	38	41	43	43	39	34
Offences against the state							
Offences under the NI Emergency Provisions Act	97	101	97	95	90	167	84
Firearms offences	84	73	79	66	59	52	66
Other offences against the state	78	67	75	74	86	91	82
Other notifiable offences							
Drug offences[4]	N/A	99	92	91	93	94	97
Other notifiable offences	72	47	58	57	70	74	54

[1] From 1995 excludes 'Attempted burglary' which is included in 'Burglary in a dwelling' or 'Burglary in a building other than a dwelling'.
[2] Other criminal damage excludes offences where damage was under £200.
[3] Drug offences not available separately prior to 1991 – included in 'Other notifiable offences'.
[4] Offences cleared up in the current year may have been initially recorded in an earlier year.

Source: Northern Ireland Office

Royal Ulster Constabulary Staffing Levels

Figures for 31 December for each year.

Year	Regular RUC	Full-time reserve	Part-time reserve	Civilian support
1990	8,233	2,990	1,555	2,623
1991	8,217	3,042	1,518	2,363
1992	8,478	3,160	1,433	2,361
1993	8,464	3,184	1,389	2,421
1994	8,493	3,199	1,491	2,466

Source: Royal Ulster Constabulary, Chief Constable's Reports

Outcome of Recorded Crime – Disposal Given to Those Convicted by Court in Northern Ireland

(– = not applicable.)

Outcome	1990	1991	1992	1993	1994	1995	1996
Magistrates Court – All Offences							
Prison	1,009	960	830	1,027	945	1,046	1,003
Young offenders' centre (YOC)	370	502	588	575	499	483	443
Training school	153	177	120	125	193	169	147
Total immediate custody	1,532	1,639	1,538	1,727	1,637	1,698	1,593
Prison suspended	1,513	1,379	1,420	1,529	1,558	1,674	1,722
YOC suspended	310	432	507	447	447	385	444
Attendance centre	118	90	66	94	89	101	91
Probation/supervision	854	742	849	881	1,017	1,137	1,134
Community supervision order	575	547	464	536	551	547	591
Fine	26,644	19,569	23,418	25,166	24,390	22,726	20,612
Recognizance	399	514	713	858	961	1,001	1,203
Conditional discharge	1,982	2,102	1,965	2,021	1,830	1,928	1,679
Absolute discharge	1,274	845	732	690	661	608	509
Disqualification	4,335	4,211	640	6	6	2	5
Other	28	24	12	7	11	8	10
Crown Court – All Offences							
Prison	493	493	447	555	471	533	469
Young offenders' centre (YOC)	106	125	119	130	87	76	106
Training school	4	13	5	2	5	6	–
Total immediate custody	603	631	571	687	563	615	575
Prison suspended	295	238	249	211	277	265	253
YOC suspended	78	46	63	37	43	63	71
Attendance centre	–	–	–	–	1	–	–
Probation/supervision	85	103	95	73	58	60	49
Community Supervision order	105	89	79	48	59	60	54
Fine	33	23	17	33	23	27	39
Recognizance	8	7	9	5	16	–	7
Conditional discharge	37	53	36	19	15	64	30
Absolute discharge	2	5	8	3	2	1	–
Disqualification	10	6	2	–	–	–	–
Other	–	8	6	6	1	2	3

Source: Northern Ireland Office

Complaints Against the Police in Northern Ireland

1996

Offence alleged	Substantiated	Not substantiated	Informally resolved	Withdrawn	Incapable of investigation	Total
Assault	17	832	107	802	313	2,071
Incivility	13	336	348	99	80	876
Oppressive conduct/harassment	6	154	150	54	86	450
Irregularity in procedure	17	161	101	54	33	366
Neglect of duty	22	109	149	40	19	339
Unlawful arrest/detention	3	141	13	38	148	343
Irregularity in connection with search of premises	3	23	22	12	13	73
Mishandling of property	1	16	5	11	7	40
Irregularity in relation to evidence/perjury	0	18	4	8	13	43
Traffic irregularity	0	16	20	2	5	43
Corrupt practice	0	7	0	2	4	13
Discriminatory behaviour	0	1	5	0	1	7
Other	5	110	6	27	23	171
Total	87	1,924	930	1,149	745	4,835

Source: Northern Ireland Office

Average Population in Prison Establishments by Type of Prisoner in Northern Ireland

Type of prisoner			1990	1991	1992	1993	1994	1995	1996
Men	remand	aged under 21	87	79	93	96	106	72	69
		aged 21 or over	259	254	307	322	321	240	249
		Total	346	333	400	418	427	312	318
	fine defaulter	aged under 21	6	8	6	7	4	5	5
		aged 21 or over	23	23	27	23	23	23	19
		Total	29	31	33	30	27	28	24
	immediate custody	young offenders' centre	134	141	145	153	133	118	115
		young prisoners	140	116	102	100	91	87	66
		adult prisoners	1,105	1,136	1,088	1,192	1,179	1,177	1,076
		Total	1,379	1,393	1,335	1,445	1,403	1,382	1,257
	non-criminal		1	1	1	1	1	5	11
	Total		1,755	1,758	1,769	1,894	1,858	1,727	1,610
Women	remand	aged under 21	6	6	6	2	5	2	2
		aged 21 or over	8	10	7	6	7	3	6
		Total	14	16	13	8	12	5	8
	fine defaulter	aged under 21	0	0	0	1	1	0	0
		aged 21 or over	1	1	1	1	2	1	0
		Total	1	1	1	2	3	1	0
	immediate custody	young offenders' centre	2	2	4	3	4	6	4
		young prisoners	1	1	2	3	3	2	1
		adult prisoners	12	18	21	24	19	21	16
		Total	15	21	27	30	26	29	21
	non-criminal		0	0	0	0	0	0	0
	Total		30	38	41	40	41	35	29
Both sexes	remand		360	349	413	426	439	317	326
	fine defaulter		30	32	34	32	30	29	24
	immediate custody		1,394	1,414	1,362	1,475	1,429	1,411	1,278
	non-criminal		1	1	1	1	1	5	11
	TOTAL		1,785	1,796	1,810	1,934	1,899	1,762	1,639

Source: Northern Ireland Office

Juveniles Found Guilty at All Courts by Offence Group in Northern Ireland

Offence	1990	1991	1992	1993	1994	1995	1996
Violence against the person	44	38	46	43	49	51	75
Sexual offences	17	8	11	7	8	7	4
Burglary	232	194	165	155	180	170	137
Robbery	10	7	8	4	9	22	13
Theft	329	328	247	280	283	345	338
Fraud and forgery	10	10	16	14	14	21	14
Criminal damage	90	92	82	94	117	116	121
Offences against the state	6	5	6	1	8	9	6
Other indictable	10	11	8	2	6	14	24
Total indictable[1]	748	693	589	600	674	755	732
Summary	138	111	113	125	131	180	182
Motoring[2]	92	71	40	44	74	74	58
TOTAL[3]	978	875	742	769	879	1,009	972

[1] Excludes indictable motoring offences.
[2] Includes indictable motoring offences.
[3] Juveniles are aged 10–16 years inclusive.

Source: Northern Ireland Office

Expenditure on the Criminal Justice System in Northern Ireland

(In millions of pounds.)

Item	Expenditure
Law, Order, Protective, and Miscellaneous Services (LOPMS)	929.0[1]
Courts of Criminal Jurisdiction	17.6[2]
Criminal Legal Aid	7.0[3]
Total	953.6

[1] The 1993–94 LOPMS budget excludes Ministry of Defence funding for the army, courts, and legal aid expenditure which are funded by the Northern Ireland Court Service.
[2] Estimated Northern Ireland Court Service expenditure on criminal business from an overall total of £30.4 million.
[3] Consists of fees and administrative costs.

Source: Northern Ireland Office

Number of Deaths Due to the Security Situation in Northern Ireland

Year	Royal Ulster Constabulary	Royal Ulster Constabulary Reserves	Army	Ulster Defence Regiment/ Royal Irish Regiment[1]	Civilian	Total
1969	1	0	0	0	13	14
1970	2	0	0	0	23	25
1971	11	0	43	5	115	174
1972	14	3	105	26	322	470
1973	10	3	58	8	173	252
1974	12	3	30	7	168	220
1975	7	4	14	6	216	247
1976	13	10	14	15	245	297
1977	8	6	15	14	69	112
1978	4	6	14	7	50	81
1979	9	5	38	10	51	113
1980	3	6	8	9	50	76
1981	13	8	10	13	57	101
1982	8	4	21	7	57	97
1983	9	9	5	10	44	77
1984	7	2	9	10	36	64
1985	14	9	2	4	26	55
1986	10	2	4	8	37	61
1987	9	7	3	8	68	95
1988	4	2	21	12	55	94
1989	7	2	12	2	39	62
1990	7	5	7	8	49	76
1991	5	1	5	8	75	94
1992	2	1	4	2	76	85
1993	3	3	6	2	70	84
1994	3	0	1	2	56	62
1995	1	0	0	0	8	9
1996	0	0	1	0	14	15
Total	196	101	450	203	2,262	3,212

[1] Figures include Royal Irish Regiment (Home Service Battalions).

Source: Northern Ireland Office

Terrorism: Security Situation Incidents in Northern Ireland

Year	Shootings	Bombings (explosions/defusings)	Incendiaries (ignitions/defusings)	Year	Shootings	Bombings (explosions/defusings)	Incendiaries (ignitions/defusings)
1969	73	10	0	1984	334	248	10
1970	213	170	0	1985	238	215	36
1971	1,756	1,515	0	1986	392	254	21
1972	10,631	1,853	0	1987	674	384	9
1973	5,019	1,520	0	1988	538	458	8
1974	3,208	1,113	270	1989	566	420	7
1975	1,803	635	56	1990	557	286	33
1976	1,908	1,192	236	1991	499	368	237
1977	1,081	535	608	1992	506	371	126
1978	755	633	115	1993	476	289	61
1979	728	564	60	1994	348	222	115
1980	642	400	2	1995	50	2	10
1981	1,142	529	49	1996	125	25	4
1982	547	332	36	Total	35,233	14,910	2,152
1983	424	367	43				

Source: Northern Ireland Office

SCIENCE AND TECHNOLOGY

The Year in Review

4 July 1997 The US spacecraft *Mars Pathfinder* lands on Mars. Two days later the probe's rover *Sojourner*, a six-wheeled vehicle that is controlled by an Earth-based operator, begins to explore the area around the spacecraft.

10 July 1997 Japanese astronomer Makoto Hattori and colleagues report the discovery of a knot of mass, which they call a 'dark cluster'. It has the chemical and gravitational properties of a cluster of galaxies, but is optically invisible. A new type of cosmic entity, it helps explain how light from a particular quasar has been distorted and challenges the theories of galaxy formation.

11 July 1997 Teams of researchers from Germany and the USA use mitochondrial DNA (deoxyribonucleic acid) extracted from the original fossils of Neanderthal Man, discovered in the Neander Valley near Düsseldorf, Germany, in 1856, to confirm that Neanderthal Man and modern humans diverged evolutionarily about 600,000 years ago. It supports the theory that modern humans arose recently in Africa as a distinct species and replaced Neanderthals with little or no interbreeding, the Neanderthals becoming extinct without evolving into modern humans.

18 July 1997 Japanese scientist Yoshinori Kuwabara announces that his team has successfully grown goat embryos in an acrylic tank. The embryos, removed from their mother at 17 weeks into pregnancy, are placed in the tank filled with liquid which simulates amniotic fluid. The placenta is replaced by a machine to pump oxygen and nutrients into the embryo's blood. At 20 weeks' gestation the goat is 'born'. At present the procedure can only be done late in development.

24 July 1997 Canadian researcher Richard Bottomley and colleagues date the 100-km/62-mi-wide Popigai impact crater in Siberia, thought to be the fifth largest impact crater on Earth, to 35.7 million years old. They suggest that the meteorite that created it may be responsible for the mass extinction that occurred at the end of the Eocene and the start of the Oligocene geological periods, which is dated to about the same time.

25 July 1997 US researcher Joseph L Kirschvink and colleagues, by examining the record of remnant magnetism in very ancient rocks, discover that the outer layers of the Earth shifted by 90 degrees relative to the core between about 535 and 520 million years ago. It is suggested that this major reorganization of the continents may have led to the Cambrian Explosion – the rapid appearance of abundant fossils in the geological record in the Cambrian Period, which began 540 million years ago.

31 July 1997 Japanese researcher Akira Fujishima and colleagues describe a self-cleaning and antifogging coating for glass and other hard surfaces. The coating, a thin layer of titanium dioxide, causes water, in the presence of ultraviolet light, to form a film instead of a droplet on the surface and allows the water to wash away oil and dirt.

4 August 1997 Using computer models, British meteorologist Alan O'Neill demonstrates a connection between the collapse of anchovy fishing in Peru, drought in Australia, the late arrival of India's monsoons, and El Niño, the warm water current off South America's west coast.

7 August 1997 The US *Mars Global Surveyor* spacecraft reports the discovery of bacteria on Mars.

11 September 1997 Israeli physicist Rafi de-Picciotto demonstrates the formation, within semiconductor materials, of 'quasiparticles', which have a charge one-third that of an electron. Quasiparticles are not true particles in the sense that an electron, or proton, is but a stable association between particles that behaves as if it were a separate entity. They challenge the idea that charge always comes in discrete units based on the charge of a single electron.

12 September 1997 The US spacecraft *Mars Global Surveyor* goes into orbit around Mars to conduct a detailed photographic survey of the planet, commencing in March 1998. The spacecraft uses a previously untried technique called 'aerobraking' to turn its initially highly elongated orbit into a 400-km/249-mi circular orbit by dipping into the outer atmosphere of the planet.

9 October 1997 US scientist Richard Superfine and colleagues, using atomic force microscopy, demonstrate that carbon nanotubes, sheets of carbon atoms rolled into concentric tubes a few millionths of a millimetre in diameter, are the stiffest and strongest materials known. The nanotubes which are bent almost double without breaking, return to their original shapes when the bending force is removed.

13 November 1997 Chinese palaeontologists Zhexi Luo and Chuankui Li describe the fossil skeleton of *Zhangheotherium*, a 145-million-year-old rat-sized creature discovered in northern China. Belonging to an extinct group of mammals called the symmetrodonts which lived in the shadow of the dinosaurs, it possesses both monotreme and mammalian features and represents one of the first steps towards modern mammals.

22 November 1997 Australian scientists demonstrate a 5-mm/0.2-in-long car – the world's smallest – by making it circle some Australian 10-cent coins. The car drives itself and travels at 0.36 kph/0.22 mph.

25 November 1997 US astronaut Winston Scott and Japanese astronaut Takao Doi, on board the US space shuttle *Columbia*, succeed in retrieving the *Spartan* satellite which had gone out of control the previous week when it was hit by *Columbia*'s robotic arm as it was being released into space. They retrieve it by hand.

1997 'Sakurai's object', a new star named after the amateur Japanese astronomer who discovered it in 1996 in the constellation of Sagittarius, has expanded since its discovery from an Earth-sized hot dwarf, with a surface temperature of 50,000°C/90,032°F, to a bright yellow supergiant about 80 times wider than the Sun and no hotter than 6,000°C/10,832°F. 'Sakurai's object' may be a red giant star that had previously shrunk, the contraction of its core triggering nuclear reactions and subsequent reinflation.

1997 A credit card-sized version of the plastic battery is introduced by its US inventors in Baltimore, Maryland. It produces 2.5 volts of electricity.

1997 A study presented at the Division of Planetary Sciences of the American Astronomical Society says that the Moon was created by debris thrown off from Earth after a collision with a planet three times as large as Mars.

1997 Most cameramakers release quality digital cameras that shoot pixels instead of film, making them a low-cost alternative to 35 mm cameras. Sales nearly double from the previous year.

1997 The Solar Heliospheric Observatory (SOHO) reveals that Venus's ion-packed tail is 45 million km/27,963,000 mi in length. Discovered in the late 1970s, it stretches away from the Sun and is caused by the bombardment of the ions in Venus's upper atmosphere by the solar wind.

1997 The US company Dragon Systems releases 'Naturally Speaking', the world's first voice recognition software program that recognizes and creates text from normal continuous speech. Spoken words are transcribed immediately onto the computer screen at up to 160 words per minute or higher with over 95% accuracy.

1997 US microbiologists bring to life a previously unknown *Staphylococcus* bacterium species from spores preserved in amber.

1997 US physicists display the first atomic laser. It emits atoms that act like light-waves.

6 January 1998 The US spacecraft *Lunar Prospector* is launched to gather information on the Moon's resources, structure, and origin.

8 January 1998 US astronomers present evidence that the universe will never stop expanding and that it is about 15 billion years old, much older than previous estimates.

16 January 1998 The National Aeronautics and Space Administration (NASA) announces that John Glenn, a Democratic senator from Ohio who became the first American in orbit in 1962, will be part of the space shuttle *Discovery* team on a 10-day mission to study life sciences. Glenn, who will be 77, will become the oldest space traveller.

20 January 1998 Veterinaries in Dubai, United Arab Emirates, announce the birth of Rama the 'cama', the first cross between a camel and a llama. It has the long fleece of llama but the strength of a camel; it has no hump.

24 January 1998 The US space shuttle *Endeavour* successfully docks with the Russian space station *Mir*. US astronaut S W Thomas replaces US astronaut David Wolf on the space station.

26 January 1998 Analysis of high resolution images from the *Galileo* spacecraft suggests that the icy crust of Europa, Jupiter's fourth largest moon, may hide a vast ocean that might be warm enough to support life.

27 January 1998 Al Schultz of the Space Science Institute in Baltimore, using the Hubble Space Telescope, announces the discovery of a giant planet, larger than the Sun, orbiting Proxima Centauri, the closest star to Earth. It is the first planet outside the Solar System to be directly observed.

30 January 1998 After five years of DNA testing the Russian government affirms that the human remains excavated at Yekaterinburg, Russia, in 1991 are those of Tsar Nicholas.

30 January 1998 US scientist Angela Christiano of Columbia University, New York, New York, publishes a study that identifies a 'hairless' gene that causes severe hair loss.

5 February 1998 Paleontologists led by Shuhai Xiao of Harvard University, Cambridge, Massachusetts, and Li Chia-wei of Tsing Hua University, Taiwan, discover animal and plant fossils that could be up to 580 million years old, in Guizhou province, China.

7 February 1998 Swiss balloonist Bertrand Piccard, in the balloon *Breitling Orbiter*, sets a record for the longest non-stop, nonrefuelled flight by an aircraft: 9 days, 17 hours and 55 minutes.

10 February 1998 The US food company Frito-Lay begins selling fat-free crisps made with olestra, a synthetic fat substitute produced by US company Proctor and Gamble.

12 February 1998 British archaeologist Elizabeth Moore announces that radar surveys of Angkor, Cambodia, reveal remains of temples from 8th–13th centuries AD, much older than other ruins previously found on the site. The radar pictures also show ancient canals, dikes, and reservoirs.

20 February 1998 Researchers at the University of Texas in conjunction with the British company SmithKline Beecham publish a study in which they identify a hormone that triggers hunger in humans. Scientists hope the discovery will lead to potential treatments of appetite disorders.

2 March 1998 US scientist Dennis McFadden and his team of researchers from the University of Texas in Austin report a physiological difference between lesbians and heterosexual women that could influence sexual orientation. Echoes produced in the ears of lesbians in response to clicking sounds were weaker than those of their heterosexual counterparts.

5 March 1998 US scientists announce that the *Lunar Prospector* satellite has detected 11 million tonnes of water on the Moon. It is in the form of ice.

11 March 1998 Australian palaeontologists announce the discovery of 800,000–900,000 year-old stone tools made by *Homo erectus* on the Indonesian island of Flores. They suggest that *H. erectus* were seafarers and had the language abilities and social structure to organize the movements of large groups to colonize new islands.

11 March 1998 US astronomer Brian Marsden predicts that an asteroid will pass within 48,000 km/30,000 mi of the earth in the year 2028, raising the possibility that it could hit the earth. The following day, however, scientists from the US National Aeronautics and Space Administration (NASA) refute his theory, saying that the asteroid is not likely to come closer than 960,000 km/600,000 mi to the earth.

12 March 1998 Astronomers in Mauna Kea, Hawaii, announce the sighting of a new galaxy, named 0140+326RD1, which is around 90 million light years farther away than the previously known furthest galaxy from Earth.

15 March 1998 *Psychology Today* magazine reports that 5 million Americans are addicted to the Internet.

26 March 1998 Italian scientists Cristiano del Sasso and Marco Signore report their research on a 113 million-year-old baby dinosaur fossil of an unknown species, complete with several organs including the intestines, liver, and windpipe. The fossil was found in the Matese mountains, north of Naples, Italy.

2 April 1998 US software company Knowledge Adventure introduce a product called 'JumpStart Baby' which is designed for nine-month-old babies to play on their parents' laps. 'Lapware' is the fastest-growing sector in the software market.

6 April 1998 The US National Aeronautics and Space Administration (NASA) releases a new picture of a rock formation on Mars. A previous picture made the formation look like a face, fuelling the theory that the formation was constructed by a Martian civilization. The new picture, which does not look like a face, refutes this theory.

13 April 1998 Dolly, the sheep who was cloned in 1996, gives birth to a female lamb at the Roslin Institute in Edinburgh, Scotland.

16 April 1998 US scientists at the National Renewable Energy Laboratory develop a solar cell that can split water into hydrogen and oxygen. It is seen as a breakthrough in the generation of alternative fuels.

23 April 1998 The first cash machines to use 'iris recognition technology' to identify the user and dispense money, enter service in Swindon, England.

April 1998 A US study of six major search engines for finding information on the Internet concludes that the best (HotBot) only accesses 34% of relevant pages, whilst the worst (Lycos) finds only 3%.

16 June 1998 Some 10,000 people log on to watch the first birth recorded live on the Internet. The baby, Sean, is born in Arnold Palmer Hospital, Orlando, Florida.

June 1998 Scientists report the discovery at least 300 species of insects and spiders never before documented in the rainforest in British Columbia, Canada. The results of the report will influence policy on the preservation of the area, which is being considered for logging.

The Elements

| 1 Hydrogen **H** 1.00794 | — atomic number — name — symbol — relative atomic mass |

element

| 1 Hydrogen **H** 1.00794 |

Period	I	II								
1	1 Hydrogen **H** 1.00794									
2	3 Lithium **Li** 6.941	4 Beryllium **Be**								
3	11 Sodium **Na** 22.98977	12 Magnesium **Mg** 24.305								
4	19 Potassium **K** 30.098	20 Calcium **Ca** 40.06	21 Scandium **Sc** 44.9559	22 Titanium **Ti** 47.90	23 Vanadium **V** 50.9414	24 Chromium **Cr** 51.996	25 Manganese **Mn** 54.9380	26 Iron **Fe** 55.847	27 Cobalt **Co** 58.9332
5	37 Rubidium **Rb** 85.4678	38 Strontium **Sr** 87.62	39 Yttrium **Y** 88.9059	40 Zirconium **Zr** 91.22	41 Niobium **Nb** 92.9064	42 Molybdenum **Mo** 95.94	43 Technetium **Tc** 97.9072	44 Ruthenium **Ru** 101.07	45 Rhodium **Rh** 102.9055
6	55 Caesium **Cs** 132.9054	56 Barium **Ba** 137.34	**La**	72 Hafnium **Hf** 178.49	73 Tantalum **Ta** 180.9479	74 Tungsten **W** 183.85	75 Rhenium **Re** 186.207	76 Osmium **Os** 190.2	77 Iridium **Ir** 192.22
7	87 Francium **Fr** 223.0197	88 Radium **Ra** 226.0254	**Ac**	104 Rutherfordium **Rf** 261.109	105 Dubnium **Db** 262.114	106 Seaborgium **Sg** 263.120	107 Bohrium **Bh** 262	108 Hassium **Hs** 265	109 Meitnerium **Mt** 266

Lanthanide series

| 57 Lanthanum **La** 138.9055 | 58 Cerium **Ce** 140.12 | 59 Praeseodymium **Pr** 140.9077 | 60 Neodymium **Nd** 144.24 | 61 Promethium **Pm** 144.9128 | 62 Samarium **Sm** 150.36 |

Actinide series

| 89 Actinium **Ac** 227.0278 | 90 Thorium **Th** 232.0381 | 91 Protactinium **Pa** 231.0359 | 92 Uranium **U** 238.029 | 93 Neptunium **Np** 237.0482 | 94 Plutonium **Pu** 244.0642 |

Periodic table of the elements *The periodic table of the elements arranges the elements into horizontal rows (called periods) and vertical columns (called groups) according to their atomic numbers. The elements in a group or column all have similar properties – for example, all the elements in the far right-hand column are inert gases. Nonmetals are shown in dark grey, metals in mid-grey and the metalloid (metal-like) elements in pale grey. The elements in white are called transition elements.*

U

III	IV	V	VI	VII	2 Helium **He** 4002.60
5 Boron **B** 10.81	6 Carbon **C** 12.011	7 Nitrogen **N** 14.0067	8 Oxygen **O** 15.9994	9 Fluorine **F** 18.99840	10 Neon **Ne** 20.179
13 Aluminium **Al** 26.98154	14 Silicon **Si** 28.066	15 Phosphorus **P** 30.9738	16 Sulphur **S** 32.06	17 Chlorine **Cl** 35.453	18 Argon **Ar** 39.948

28 Nickel **Ni** 58.70	29 Copper **Cu** 63.546	30 Zinc **Zn** 65.38	31 Gallium **Ga** 69.72	32 Germanium **Ge** 72.59	33 Arsenic **As** 74.9216	34 Selenium **Se** 78.96	35 Bromine **Br** 79.904	36 Krypton **Kr** 83.80
46 Palladium **Pd** 106.4	47 Silver **Ag** 107.868	48 Cadmium **Cd** 112.40	49 Indium **In** 114.82	50 Tin **Sn** 118.69	51 Antimony **Sb** 121.75	52 Tellurium **Te** 127.75	53 Iodine **I** 126.9045	54 Xenon **Xe** 131.30
78 Platinum **Pt** 195.09	79 Gold **Au** 196.9665	80 Mercury **Hg** 200.59	81 Thallium **Tl** 204.37	82 Lead **Pb** 207.37	83 Bismuth **Bi** 207.2	84 Polonium **Po** 210	85 Astatine **At** 211	86 Radon **Rn** 222.0176
110 Ununnilium **Uun** 269	111 Unununium **Uuu** 272							

63 Europium **Eu** 151.96	64 Gadolinium **Gd** 157.25	65 Terbium **Tb** 158.9254	66 Dysprosium **Dy** 162.50	67 Holmium **Ho** 164.9304	68 Erbium **Er** 167.26	69 Thulium **Tm** 168.9342	70 Ytterbium **Yb** 173.04	71 Lutetium **Lu** 174.97

95 Americium **Am** 243.0614	96 Curium **Cm** 247.0703	97 Berkelium **Bk** 247	98 Californium **Cf** 251.0786	99 Einsteinium **Es** 252.0828	100 Fermium **Fm** 257.0951	101 Mendelevium **Md** 258.0986	102 Nobelium **No** 259.1009	103 Lawrencium **Lr** 260.1054

The Chemical Elements

An element is a substance that cannot be split chemically into simpler substances. The atoms of a particular element all have the same number of protons in their nuclei (their atomic number).
(– = not applicable.)

Name	Symbol	Atomic number	Atomic mass (amu)[1]	Relative density[2]	Melting or fusing point (°C)
Actinium	Ac	89	227[3]	–	–
Aluminium	Al	13	26.9815	2.58	658
Americium	Am	95	243[3]	–	–
Antimony	Sb	51	121.75	6.62	629
Argon	Ar	18	39.948	gas	–188
Arsenic	As	33	74.9216	5.73	volatile, 450
Astatine	At	85	210[3]	–	–
Barium	Ba	56	137.34	3.75	850
Berkelium	Bk	97	249[3]	–	–
Beryllium	Be	4	9.0122	1.93	1,281
Bismuth	Bi	83	208.9806	9.80	268
Bohrium	Bh	107	262[3]	–	–
Boron	B	5	10.81	2.5	2,300
Bromine	Br	35	79.904	3.19	–7.3
Cadmium	Cd	48	112.40	8.64	320
Caesium	Cs	55	132.9055	1.88	26
Calcium	Ca	20	40.08	1.58	851
Californium	Cf	98	251[3]	–	–
Carbon	C	6	12.011	3.52	infusible
Cerium	Ce	58	140.12	6.68	623
Chlorine	Cl	17	35.453	gas	–102
Chromium	Cr	24	51.996	6.5	1,510
Cobalt	Co	27	58.9332	8.6	1,490
Copper	Cu	29	63.546	8.9	1,083
Curium	Cm	96	247[3]	–	–
Dubnium	Db	105	262[3]	–	–
Dysprosium	Dy	66	162.50	–	–
Einsteinium	Es	99	254[3]	–	–
Erbium	Er	68	167.26	4.8	–
Europium	Eu	63	151.96	–	–
Fermium	Fm	100	253[3]	–	–
Fluorine	F	9	18.9984	gas	–223
Francium	Fr	87	223[3]	–	–
Gadolinium	Gd	64	157.25	–	–
Gallium	Ga	31	69.72	5.95	30
Germanium	Ge	32	72.59	5.47	958
Gold	Au	79	196.9665	19.3	1,062
Hafnium	Hf	72	178.49	12.1	2,500
Hassium	Hs	108	265[3]	–	–
Helium	He	2	4.0026	gas	–272
Holmium	Ho	67	164.9303	–	–
Hydrogen	H	1	1.0080	gas	–258
Indium	In	49	114.82	7.4	155
Iodine	I	53	126.9045	4.95	114
Iridium	Ir	77	192.22	22.4	2,375
Iron	Fe	26	55.847	7.86	1,525
Krypton	Kr	36	83.80	gas	–169
Lanthanum	La	57	138.9055	6.1	810
Lawrencium	Lr	103	260[3]	–	–
Lead	Pb	82	207.2	11.37	327
Lithium	Li	3	6.941	0.585	186
Lutetium	Lu	71	174.97	–	–
Magnesium	Mg	12	24.305	1.74	651
Manganese	Mn	25	54.9380	7.39	1,220
Meitnerium	Mt	109	266[3]	–	–
Mendelevium	Md	101	256[3]	–	–
Mercury	Hg	80	200.59	13.596	–38.9
Molybdenum	Mo	42	95.94	10.2	2,500
Neodymium	Nd	60	144.24	6.96	840
Neon	Ne	10	20.179	gas	–248.6
Neptunium	Np	93	237[3]	–	–
Nickel	Ni	28	58.71	8.9	1,452
Niobium	Nb	41	92.9064	8.4	1,950
Nitrogen	N	7	14.0067	gas	–211
Nobelium	No	102	254[3]	–	–
Osmium	Os	76	190.2	22.48	2,700
Oxygen	O	8	15.9994	gas	–227
Palladium	Pd	46	106.4	11.4	1,549
Phosphorus	P	15	30.9738	1.8–2.3	44
Platinum	Pt	78	195.09	21.5	1,755
Plutonium	Pu	94	242[3]	–	–
Polonium	Po	84	210[3]	–	–
Potassium	K	19	39.102	0.87	63
Praseodymium	Pr	59	140.9077	6.48	940
Promethium	Pm	61	145[3]	–	–
Protactinium	Pa	91	231.0359	–	–
Radium	Ra	88	226.0254	6.0	700
Radon	Rn	86	222[3]	gas	–150
Rhenium	Re	75	186.2	21	3,000
Rhodium	Rh	45	102.9055	12.1	1,950
Rubidium	Rb	37	85.4678	1.52	39
Ruthenium	Ru	44	101.07	12.26	2,400
Rutherfordium	Rf	104	262[3]	–	–
Samarium	Sm	62	150.4	7.7	1,350
Scandium	Sc	21	44.9559	–	–
Seaborgium	Sg	106	263[3]	–	–
Selenium	Se	34	78.96	4.5	170–220
Silicon	Si	14	28.086	2.0–2.4	1,370
Silver	Ag	47	107.868	10.5	960
Sodium	Na	11	22.9898	0.978	97
Strontium	Sr	38	87.62	2.54	800
Sulphur	S	16	32.06	2.07	115–119
Tantalum	Ta	73	180.9479	16.6	2,900
Technetium	Tc	43	99[3]	–	–
Tellurium	Te	52	127.60	6.0	446
Terbium	Tb	65	158.9254	–	–
Thallium	Tl	81	204.37	11.85	302
Thorium	Th	90	232.0381	11.00	1,750
Thulium	Tm	69	168.9342	–	–
Tin	Sn	50	118.69	7.3	232
Titanium	Ti	22	47.90	4.54	1,850
Tungsten	W	74	183.85	19.1	2,900–3,000
Ununnilium	Uun[4]	110	269[3]	–	–
Unununium	Uuu[4]	111	272[3]	–	–
Uranium	U	92	238.029	18.7	–
Vanadium	V	23	50.9414	5.5	1,710
Xenon	Xe	54	131.30	gas	–140
Ytterbium	Yb	70	173.04	–	–
Yttrium	Y	39	88.9059	3.8	–
Zinc	Zn	30	65.37	7.12	418
Zirconium	Zr	40	91.22	4.15	2,130

[1] Atomic mass units.
[2] Also known as specific gravity.
[3] The number given is that for the most stable isotope of the element.
[4] Elements as yet unnamed; temporary identification assigned until a name is approved by the International Union for Pure and Applied Chemistry.

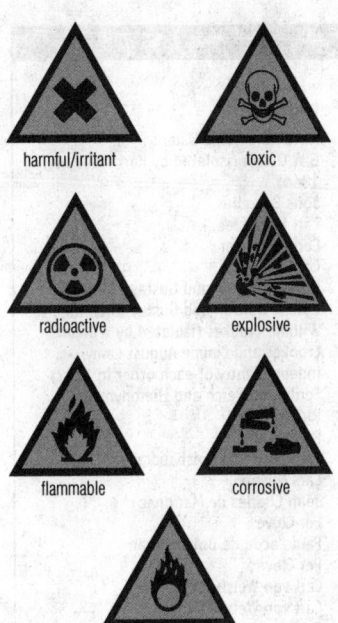

harmful/irritant   toxic

radioactive   explosive

flammable   corrosive

oxidizing/supports fire

Hazard labels

Common Alloys

Name	Approximate composition	Uses
brass	35–10% zinc, 65–90% copper	decorative metalwork, plumbing fittings, industrial tubing
bronze – common	2% zinc, 6% tin, 92% copper	machinery, decorative work
bronze – aluminium	10% aluminium, 90% copper	machinery castings
bronze – coinage	1% zinc, 4% tin, 95% copper	coins
cast iron	2–4% carbon, 96–98% iron	decorative metalwork, engine blocks, industrial machinery
dentist's amalgam	30% copper, 70% mercury	dental fillings
duralumin	0.5 % magnesium, 0.5% manganese, 5% copper, 95% aluminium	framework of aircraft
gold – coinage	10% copper, 90% gold	coins
gold – dental	14–28% silver, 14–28% copper, 58% gold	dental fillings
lead battery plate	6% antimony, 94% lead	car batteries
manganin	1.5% nickel, 16% manganese, 82.5% copper	resistance wire
nichrome	20% chromium, 80% nickel	heating elements
pewter	20% lead, 80% tin	utensils
silver – coinage	10% copper, 90% silver	coins
solder	50% tin, 50% lead	joining iron surfaces
steel – stainless	8–20% nickel, 10–20% chromium, 60–80% iron	kitchen utensils
steel – armour	1–4% nickel, 0.5–2% chromium, 95–98% iron	armour plating
steel – tool	2–4% chromium, 6–7% molybdenum, 90–95% iron	tools

The Transuranic Elements

A transuranic element is a chemical element with an atomic number of 93 or more – that is, with a greater number of protons in the nucleus than uranium. All transuranic elements are radioactive.
(– = not applicable.)

Atomic number	Name	Symbol	Year discovered	Source of first preparation identified	Isotope	Half-life of first isotope identified
Actinide series						
93	neptunium	Np	1940	irradiation of uranium-238 with neutrons	Np-239	2.35 days
94	plutonium	Pu	1941	bombardment of uranium-238 with deuterons	Pu-238	86.4 years
95	americium	Am	1944	irradiation of plutonium-239 with neutrons	Am-241	458 years
96	curium	Cm	1944	bombardment of plutonium-239 with helium nuclei	Cm-242	162.5 days
97	berkelium	Bk	1949	bombardment of americium-241 with helium nuclei	Bk-243	4.5 h
98	californium	Cf	1950	bombardment of curium-242 with helium nuclei	Cf-245	44 min
99	einsteinium	Es	1952	irradiation of uranium-238 with neutrons in first thermonuclear explosion	Es-253	20 days
100	fermium	Fm	1953	irradiation of uranium-238 with neutrons in first thermonuclear explosion	Fm-235	20 h
101	mendelevium	Md	1955	bombardment of einsteinium-253 with helium nuclei	Md-256	76 min
102	nobelium	No	1958	bombardment of curium-246 with carbon nuclei	No-255	2.3 sec
103	lawrencium	Lr	1961	bombardment of californium-252 with boron nuclei	Lr-257	4.3 sec
Transactinide elements						
104	rutherfordium	Rf	1969	bombardment of californium-249 with carbon-12 nuclei	Db-257	3.4 sec
105	dubnium	Db	1970	bombardment of californium-249 with nitrogen-15 nuclei	Unp-260	1.6 sec
106	seaborgium	Sg	1974	bombardment of californium-249 with oxygen-18 nuclei	Rf-263	0.9 sec
107	bohrium	Bh	1977	bombardment of bismuth-209 with nuclei of chromium-54	Uns	102 millisec
108	hassium	Hs	1984	bombardment of lead-208 with nuclei of iron-58	Uno-265	1.8 millisec
109	meitnerium	Mt	1982	bombardment of bismuth-209 with nuclei of iron-58	Une	3.4 millisec
110	unununilium[1]	Uun	1994	bombardment of lead nuclei with nickel nuclei	–	–
111	unununium[1]	Uuu	1994	bombardment of bismuth-209 with nickel nuclei	–	–

[1] Temporary names as proposed by the International Union for Pure and Applied Chemistry.

Discovery of the Elements

(– = not applicable.)

Date	Element (symbol)	Discoverer
Prehistoric knowledge	antimony (Sb)	–
	arsenic (As)	
	bismuth (Bi)	
	carbon (C)	
	copper (Cu)	
	gold (Au)	
	iron (Fe)	
	lead (Pb)	
	mercury (Hg)	
	silver (Ag)	
	sulphur (S)	
	tin (Sn)	
	zinc (Zn)	
1557	platinum (Pt)	Julius Scaliger
1674	phosphorus (P)	Hennig Brand
1730	cobalt (Co)	Georg Brandt
1751	nickel (Ni)	Axel Cronstedt
1755	magnesium (Mg)	Joseph Black (oxide isolated by Humphry Davy in 1808; pure form isolated by Antoine-Alexandre-Brutus Bussy in 1828)
1766	hydrogen (H)	Henry Cavendish
1771	fluorine (F)	Karl Scheele (isolated by Henri Moissan in 1886)
1772	nitrogen (N)	Daniel Rutherford
1774	chlorine (Cl)	Karl Scheele
	manganese (Mn)	Johann Gottlieb Gahn
	oxygen (O)	Joseph Priestley and Karl Scheele, independently of each other
1781	molybdenum (Mo)	named by Karl Scheele (isolated by Peter Jacob Hjelm in 1782)
1782	tellurium (Te)	Franz Müller
1783	tungsten (W)	isolated by Juan José Elhuyar and Fausto Elhuyar
1789	uranium (U)	Martin Klaproth (isolated by Eugène Péligot in 1841)
	zirconium (Zr)	Martin Klaproth
1790	titanium (Ti)	William Gregor
1794	yttrium (Y)	Johan Gadolin
1797	chromium (Cr)	Louis-Nicolas Vauquelin
1798	beryllium (Be)	Louis-Nicolas Vauquelin (isolated by Friedrich Wöhler and Antoine-Alexandre-Brutus Bussy in 1828)
1801	vanadium (V)	Andrés del Rio (disputed), or Nils Sefström in 1830
	niobium (Nb)	Charles Hatchett
1802	tantalum (Ta)	Anders Ekeberg
1804	cerium (Ce)	Jöns Berzelius and Wilhelm Hisinger, and independently by Martin Klaproth
	iridium (Ir)	Smithson Tennant
	osmium (Os)	Smithson Tennant
	palladium (Pd)	William Wollaston
	rhodium (Rh)	William Wollaston
1807	potassium (K)	Humphry Davy
	sodium (Na)	Humphry Davy
1808	barium (Ba)	Humphry Davy
	boron (B)	Humphry Davy, and independently by Joseph Gay-Lussac and Louis-Jacques Thénard
	calcium (Ca)	Humphry Davy
	strontium (Sr)	Humphry Davy
1811	iodine (I)	Bernard Courtois
1817	cadmium (Cd)	Friedrich Strohmeyer
	lithium (Li)	Johan Arfwedson
	selenium (Se)	Jöns Berzelius
1823	silicon (Si)	Jöns Berzelius
1824	aluminium (Al)	Hans Oersted (also attributed to Friedrich Wöhler in 1827)
1826	bromine (Br)	Antoine-Jérôme Balard
1827	ruthenium (Ru)	G W Osann (isolated by Karl Klaus in 1844)
1828	thorium (Th)	Jöns Berzelius
1839	lanthanum (La)	Carl Mosander
1843	erbium (Er)	Carl Mosander
	terbium (Tb)	Carl Mosander
1860	caesium (Cs)	Robert Bunsen and Gustav Kirchhoff
1861	rubidium (Rb)	Robert Bunsen and Gustav Kirchhoff
	thallium (Tl)	William Crookes (isolated by William Crookes and Claude August Lamy, independently of each other in 1862)
1863	indium (In)	Ferdinand Reich and Hieronymus Richter
1868	helium (He)	Pierre Janssen
1875	gallium (Ga)	Paul Lecoq de Boisbaudran
1876	scandium (Sc)	Lars Nilson
1878	ytterbium (Yb)	Jean Charles de Marignac
1879	holmium (Ho)	Per Cleve
	samarium (Sm)	Paul Lecoq de Boisbaudran
	thulium (Tm)	Per Cleve
1885	neodymium (Nd)	Carl von Welsbach
	praseodymium (Pr)	Carl von Welsbach
1886	dysprosium (Dy)	Paul Lecoq de Boisbaudran
	gadolinium (Gd)	Paul Lecoq de Boisbaudran
	germanium (Ge)	Clemens Winkler
1894	argon (Ar)	John Rayleigh and William Ramsay
1898	krypton (Kr)	William Ramsay and Morris Travers
	neon (Ne)	William Ramsay and Morris Travers
	polonium (Po)	Marie and Pierre Curie
	radium (Ra)	Marie Curie
	xenon (Xe)	William Ramsay and Morris Travers
1899	actinium (Ac)	André Debierne
1900	radon (Rn)	Friedrich Dorn
1901	europium (Eu)	Eugène Demarçay
1907	lutetium (Lu)	Georges Urbain and Carl von Welsbach, independently of each other
1913	protactinium (Pa)	Kasimir Fajans and O Göhring
	hafnium (Hf)	Dirk Coster and Georg von Hevesy
1925	rhenium (Re)	Walter Noddack, Ida Tacke, and Otto Berg
1937	technetium (Tc)	Carlo Perrier and Emilio Segrè
1939	francium (Fr)	Marguérite Perey
1940	astatine (At)	Dale R Corson, K R MacKenzie, and Emilio Segrè
	neptunium (Np)	Edwin McMillan and Philip Abelson
	plutonium (Pu)	Glenn Seaborg, Edwin McMillan, Joseph Kennedy, and Arthur Wahl
1944	americium (Am)	Glenn Seaborg, Ralph James, Leon Morgan, and Albert Ghiorso
	curium (Cm)	Glenn Seaborg, Ralph James, and Albert Ghiorso
1945	promethium (Pm)	J A Marinsky, Lawrence Glendenin, and Charles Coryell
1949	berkelium (Bk)	Glenn Seaborg, Stanley Thompson, and Albert Ghiorso
1950	californium (Cf)	Glenn Seaborg, Stanley Thompson, Kenneth Street Jr, and Albert Ghiorso
1952	einsteinium (Es)	Albert Ghiorso and co-workers
1955	fermium (Fm)	Albert Ghiorso and co-workers
	mendelevium (Md)	Albert Ghiorso, Bernard G Harvey, Gregory Choppin, Stanley Thompson, and Glenn Seaborg
1958	nobelium (No)	Albert Ghiorso, Torbjørn Sikkeland, J R Walton, and Glenn Seaborg
1961	lawrencium (Lr)	Albert Ghiorso, Torbjørn Sikkeland, Almon Larsh, and Robert Latimer
1964	dubnium (Db)	claimed by Soviet scientist Georgii Flerov and co-workers (disputed by US workers)

Discovery of the Elements (*continued*)

Date	Element (symbol)	Discoverer	Date	Element (symbol)	Discoverer
1967	unnilpentium (Unp)	claimed by Georgii Flerov and co-workers (disputed by US workers)	1976	bohrium (Bh)	Georgii Flerov and Yuri Oganessian (confirmed by German scientist Peter Armbruster and co-workers)
1969	rutherfordium (Rf)	claimed by US scientist Albert Ghiorso and co-workers (disputed by Soviet workers)	1982	meitnerium (Mt)	Peter Armbruster and co-workers
			1984	hassium (Hs)	Peter Armbruster and co-workers
1970	dubnium (Db)	claimed by Albert Ghiorso and co-workers (disputed by Soviet workers)	1994	ununnilium (Uun)	team at GSI heavy-ion cyclotron, Darmstadt, Germany
1974	seaborgium (Sg)	claimed by Georgii Flerov and co-workers, and independently by Albert Ghiorso and co-workers		unununium (Uuu)	team at GSI heavy-ion cyclotron, Darmstadt, Germany

Inventions and Discoveries

Scientific Discoveries

Discovery	Date	Discoverer	Nationality
Absolute zero, concept	1851	William Thomson, 1st Baron Kelvin	Irish
Adrenalin, isolation	1901	Jokichi Takamine	Japanese
Alizarin, synthesized	1869	William Perkin	English
Allotropy (in carbon)	1841	Jöns Jakob Berzelius	Swedish
Alpha rays	1899	Ernest Rutherford	New Zealand-born British
Alternation of generations (ferns and mosses)	1851	Wilhelm Hofmeister	German
Aluminium, extraction by electrolysis of aluminium oxide	1886	Charles Hall, Paul Héroult	US, French
Aluminium, improved isolation	1827	Friedrich Wöhler	German
Anaesthetic, first use (ether)	1842	Crawford Long	US
Anthrax vaccine	1881	Louis Pasteur	French
Antibacterial agent, first specific (Salvarsan for treatment of syphilis)	1910	Paul Ehrlich	German
Antiseptic surgery (using phenol)	1865	Joseph Lister	English
Argon	1892	William Ramsay	Scottish
Asteroid, first (Ceres)	1801	Giuseppe Piazzi	Italian
Atomic theory	1803	John Dalton	English
Australopithecus	1925	Raymond Dart	Australian-born South African
Avogadro's hypothesis	1811	Amedeo Avogadro	Italian
Bacteria, first observation	1683	Anton van Leeuwenhoek	Dutch
Bacteriophages	1916	Felix D'Herelle	Canadian
Bee dance	1919	Karl von Frisch	Austrian
Benzene, isolation	1825	Michael Faraday	English
Benzene, ring structure	1865	Friedrich Kekulé	German
Beta rays	1899	Ernest Rutherford	New Zealand-born British
Big-Bang theory	1948	Ralph Alpher, George Gamow	US
Binary arithmetic	1679	Gottfried Leibniz	German
Binary stars	1802	William Herschel	German-born English
Binomial theorem	1665	Isaac Newton	English
Blood, circulation	1619	William Harvey	English
Blood groups, ABO system	1900	Karl Landsteiner	Austrian-born US
Bode's law	1772	Johann Bode, Johann Titius	German
Bohr atomic model	1913	Niels Bohr	Danish
Boolean algebra	1854	George Boole	English
Boyle's law	1662	Robert Boyle	Irish
Brewster's law	1812	David Brewster	Scottish
Brownian motion	1827	Robert Brown	Scottish
Cadmium	1817	Friedrich Strohmeyer	German
Caesium	1861	Robert Bunsen	German
Carbon dioxide	1755	Joseph Black	Scottish
Charles' law	1787	Jacques Charles	French
Chlorine	1774	Karl Scheele	Swedish
Complex numbers, theory	1746	Jean d'Alembert	French
Conditioning	1902	Ivan Pavlov	Russian
Continental drift	1912	Alfred Wegener	German

(continued)

Scientific Discoveries (*continued*)

Discovery	Date	Discoverer	Nationality
Coriolis effect	1834	Gustave-Gaspard Coriolis	French
Cosmic radiation	1911	Victor Hess	Austrian
Decimal fractions	1576	François Viète	French
Dinosaur fossil, first recognized	1822	Mary Ann Mantell	English
Diphtheria bacillus, isolation	1883	Edwin Krebs	US
DNA	1869	Johann Frederick Miescher	Swiss
DNA and RNA	1909	Phoebus Levene	Russian-born US
DNA, double-helix structure	1953	Francis Crick, James Watson	English, US
Doppler effect	1842	Christian Doppler	Austrian
Earth's magnetic pole	1546	Gerardus Mercator	Flemish
Earth's molten core	1916	Albert Michelson	German-born US
Earth's molten core, proof	1906	Richard Oldham	Welsh
Earth's rotation, demonstration	1851	Léon Foucault	French
Eclipse, prediction	585 BC	Thales of Miletus	Greek
Electrolysis, laws	1833	Michael Faraday	English
Electromagnetic induction	1831	Michael Faraday	English
Electromagnetism	1819	Hans Christian Oersted	Danish
Electron	1897	J J Thomson	English
Electroweak unification theory	1967	Sheldon Lee Glashow, Abdus Salam, Steven Weinberg	US, Pakistani, US
Endorphins	1975	John Hughes	US
Enzyme, first animal (pepsin)	1836	Theodor Schwann	German
Enzyme, first (diastase from barley)	1833	Anselme Payen	French
Enzymes, 'lock and key' hypothesis	1899	Emil Fischer	German
Ether, first anaesthetic use	1842	Crawford Long	US
Eustachian tube	1552	Bartolomeo Eustachio	Italian
Evolution by natural selection	1858	Charles Darwin	English
Exclusion principle	1925	Wolfgang Pauli	Austrian-born Swiss
Fallopian tubes	1561	Gabriello Fallopius	Italian
Fluorine, preparation	1886	Henri Moissan	French
Fullerines	1985	Harold Kroto, David Walton	English
Gay-Lussac's law	1808	Joseph-Louis Gay-Lussac	French
Geometry, Euclidean	300 BC	Euclid	Greek
Germanium	1886	Clemens Winkler	German
Germ theory	1861	Louis Pasteur	French
Global temperature and link with atmospheric carbon dioxide	1896	Svante Arrhenius	Swedish
Gravity, laws	1687	Isaac Newton	English
Groups, theory	1829	Evariste Galois	French
Gutenberg discontinuity	1914	Beno Gutenberg	German-born US
Helium, production	1896	William Ramsay	Scottish
Homo erectus	1894	Marie Dubois	Dutch
Homo habilis	1961	Louis Leakey, Mary Leakey	Kenyan, English
Hormones	1902	William Bayliss, Ernest Starling	English
Hubble's law	1929	Edwin Hubble	US
Hydraulics, principles	1642	Blaise Pascal	French
Hydrogen	1766	Henry Cavendish	English
Iapetus	1671	Giovanni Cassini	Italian-born French
Infrared solar rays	1801	William Herschel	German-born English
Insulin, isolation	1921	Frederick Banting, Charles Best	Canadian
Insulin, structure	1969	Dorothy Hodgkin	English
Interference of light	1801	Thomas Young	English
Irrational numbers	450 BC	Hipparcos	Greek
Jupiter's satellites	1610	Galileo	Italian
Kinetic theory of gases	1850	Rudolf Clausius	German
Krypton	1898	William Ramsay, Morris Travers	Scottish, English
Lanthanum	1839	Carl Mosander	Swedish
Lenses, how they work	1039	Ibn al-Haytham Alhazen	Arabic
Light, finite velocity	1675	Ole Römer	Danish
Light, polarization	1678	Christiaan Huygens	Dutch
Linnaean classification system	1735	Linnaeus	Swedish
'Lucy', hominid	1974	Donald Johanson	US
Magnetic dip	1576	Robert Norman	English
Malarial parasite in *Anopheles* mosquito	1897	Ronald Ross	British
Malarial parasite observed	1880	Alphonse Laveran	French
Mars, moons	1877	Asaph Hall	US
Mendelian laws of inheritance	1866	Gregor Mendel	Austrian
Messenger RNA	1960	Sydney Brenner, François Jacob	South African, French
Microorganisms as cause of fermentation	1856	Louis Pasteur	French

Scientific Discoveries (*continued*)

Discovery	Date	Discoverer	Nationality
Monoclonal antibodies	1975	César Milstein, George Köhler	Argentinean-born British, German
Motion, laws	1687	Isaac Newton	English
Natural selection	1859	Charles Darwin	English
Neon	1898	William Ramsay, Morris Travers	Scottish, English
Neptune	1846	Johann Galle	German
Neptunium	1940	Edwin McMillan, Philip Abelson	US
Nerve impulses, electric nature	1771	Luigi Galvani	Italian
Neutron	1932	James Chadwick	English
Nitrogen	1772	Daniel Rutherford	Scottish
Normal distribution curve	1733	Abraham De Moivre	French
Nuclear atom, concept	1911	Ernest Rutherford	New Zealand-born British
Nuclear fission	1938	Otto Hahn, Fritz Strassman	German
Nucleus, plant cell	1831	Robert Brown	Scottish
Ohm's law	1827	Georg Ohm	German
Organic substance, first synthesis (urea)	1828	Friedrich Wöhler	German
Oxygen	1774	Joseph Priestley	English
Oxygen, liquefaction	1894	James Dewar	Scottish
Ozone layer	1913	Charles Fabry	French
Palladium	1803	William Hyde Wollaston	English
Pallas (asteroid)	1802	Heinrich Olbers	German
Pendulum, principle	1581	Galileo	Italian
Penicillin	1928	Alexander Fleming	Scottish
Penicillin, widespread preparation	1940	Ernst Chain, Howard Florey	German, Australian
Pepsin	1836	Theodor Schwann	German
Periodic law for elements	1869	Dmitri Mendeleyev	Russian
Period–luminosity law	1912	Henrietta Swan	US
Phosphorus	1669	Hennig Brand	German
Piezoelectric effect	1880	Pierre Curie	French
Pi meson (particle)	1947	Cecil Powell, Giuseppe Occhialini	English, Italian
Pistils, function	1676	Nehemiah Grew	English
Planetary nebulae	1790	William Herschel	German-born English
Planets, orbiting Sun	1543	Copernicus	Polish
Pluto	1930	Clyde Tombaugh	US
Polarization of light by reflection	1808	Etienne Malus	French
Polio vaccine	1952	Jonas Salk	US
Polonium	1898	Marie and Pierre Curie	French
Positron	1932	Carl Anderson	US
Potassium	1806	Humphry Davy	English
Probability theory	1654	Blaise Pascal, Pierre de Fermat	French
Probability theory, expansion	1812	Pierre Laplace	French
Proton	1914	Ernest Rutherford	New Zealand-born British
Protoplasm	1846	Hugo von Mohl	German
Pulsar	1967	Jocelyn Bell Burnell	English
Pythagoras' theorem	550 BC	Pythagoras	Greek
Quantum chromodynamics	1972	Murray Gell-Mann	US
Quantum electrodynamics	1948	Richard Feynman, Seymour Schwinger, Shin'chiro Tomonaga	US, US, Japanese
Quark, first suggested existence	1963	Murray Gell-mann, George Zweig	US
Quasar	1963	Maarten Schmidt	Dutch-born US
Rabies vaccine	1885	Louis Pasteur	French
Radioactivity	1896	Henri Becquerel	French
Radio emissions, from Milky Way	1931	Karl Jansky	US
Radio waves, production	1887	Heinrich Hertz	German
Radium	1898	Marie and Pierre Curie	French
Radon	1900	Friedrich Dorn	German
Refraction, laws	1621	Willibrord Snell	Dutch
Relativity, general theory	1915	Albert Einstein	German-born US
Relativity, special theory	1905	Albert Einstein	German-born US
Rhesus factor	1940	Karl Landsteiner, Alexander Wiener	Austrian, US
Rubidium	1861	Robert Bunsen	German
Sap circulation	1846	Giovanni Battista	Italian
Sap flow in plants	1733	Stephen Hales	English
Saturn, 18th moon	1990	Mark Showalter	US
Saturn's satellites	1656	Christiaan Huygens	Dutch
Smallpox inoculation	1796	Edward Jenner	English
Sodium	1806	Humphry Davy	English
Stamens, function	1676	Nehemiah Grew	English

(*continued*)

Scientific Discoveries (*continued*)

Discovery	Date	Discoverer	Nationality
Stars, luminosity sequence	1905	Ejnar Hertzsprung	Danish
Stereochemistry, foundation	1848	Louis Pasteur	French
Stratosphere	1902	Léon Teisserenc	French
Sunspots	1611	Galileo, Christoph Scheiner	Italian, German
Superconductivity	1911	Heike Kamerlingh-Onnes	Dutch
Superconductivity, theory	1957	John Bardeen, Leon Cooper, John Schrieffer	US
Thermodynamics, second law	1834	Benoit-Pierre Clapeyron	French
Thermodynamics, third law	1906	Hermann Nernst	German
Thermoelectricity	1821	Thomas Seebeck	German
Thorium-X	1902	Ernest Rutherford, Frederick Soddy	New Zealand-born British, English
Titius–Bode law	1772	Johan Bode, Johann Titius	German
Tranquilliser, first (reserpine)	1956	Robert Woodward	US
Transformer	1831	Michael Faraday	English
Troposphere	1902	Léon Teisserenc	French
Tuberculosis bacillus, isolation	1883	Robert Koch	German
Tuberculosis vaccine	1923	Albert Calmette, Camille Guérin	French
Uranus	1781	William Herschel	German-born English
Urea cycle	1932	Hans Krebs	German
Urease, isolation	1926	James Sumner	US
Urea, synthesis	1828	Friedrich Wöhler	German
Valves, in veins	1603	Geronimo Fabricius	Italian
Van Allen radiation belts	1958	James Van Allen	US
Virus, first identified (tobacco mosaic disease, in tobacco plants)	1898	Martinus Beijerinck	Dutch
Vitamin A, isolation	1913	Elmer McCollum	US
Vitamin A, structure	1931	Paul Karrer	Russian-born Swiss
Vitamin B, composition	1955	Dorothy Hodgkin	English
Vitamin B, isolation	1925	Joseph Goldberger	Austrian-born US
Vitamin C	1928	Charles Glen King, Albert Szent-Györgi	US, Hungarian-born US
Vitamin C, isolation	1932	Charles Glen King	US
Vitamin C, synthesis	1933	Tadeus Reichstein	Polish-born Swiss
Wave mechanics	1926	Erwin Schrödinger	Austrian
Xenon	1898	William Ramsay, Morris Travers	Scottish, English
X-ray crystallography	1912	Max von Laue	German

Inventions

Invention	Date	Inventor	Nationality
Achromatic lens	1733	Chester Moor Hall	English
Adding machine	1642	Blaise Pascal	French
Aeroplane, powered	1903	Orville and Wilbur Wright	US
Air conditioning	1902	Willis Carrier	US
Air pump	1654	Otto Guericke	German
Airship, first successful	1852	Henri Giffard	French
Airship, rigid	1900	Ferdinand von Zeppelin	German
Amniocentesis test	1952	Douglas Bevis	English
Aqualung	1943	Jacques Cousteau	French
Arc welder	1919	Elihu Thomson	US
Armillary ring	125	Zhang Heng	Chinese
Aspirin	1899	Felix Hoffman	German
Assembly line	1908	Henry Ford	US
Autogiro	1923	Juan de la Cierva	Spanish
Automatic pilot	1912	Elmer Sperry	US
Babbitt metal	1839	Isaac Babbitt	US
Bakelite, first synthetic plastic	1909	Leo Baekeland	US
Ballpoint pen	1938	Lazlo Biró	Hungarian
Barbed wire	1874	Joseph Glidden	US
Bar code system	1970	Monarch Marking, Plessey Telecommunications	US, English
Barometer	1642	Evangelista Torricelli	Italian
Bathysphere	1934	Charles Beebe	US
Bessemer process	1856	Henry Bessemer	British
Bicycle	1839	Kirkpatrick Macmillan	Scottish
Bifocal spectacles	1784	Benjamin Franklin	US
Binary calculator	1938	Konrad Zuse	German
Bottling machine	1895	Michael Owens	US
Braille	1837	Louis Braille	French
Bunsen burner	1850	Robert Bunsen	German
Calculator, pocket	1971	Texas Instruments	US
Camera film (roll)	1888	George Eastman	US
Camera obscura	1560	Battista Porta	Italian
Carbon fibre	1963	Leslie Phillips	English
Carbon-zinc battery	1841	Robert Bunsen	German
Carburettor	1893	Wilhelm Maybach	German
Car, four-wheeled	1887	Gottlieb Daimler	German
Car, petrol-driven	1885	Karl Benz	German
Carpet sweeper	1876	Melville Bissell	US
Cash register	1879	James Ritty	US
Cassette tape	1963	Philips	Dutch
Catapult	c. 400 BC	Dionysius of Syracuse	Greek
Cathode ray oscilloscope	1897	Karl Braun	German
CD-ROM	1984	Sony, Fujitsu, Philips	Japanese, Japanese, Dutch
Cellophane	1908	Jacques Brandenberger	Swiss
Celluloid	1869	John Wesley Hyatt	US
Cement, Portland	1824	Joseph Aspidin	English
Centigrade scale	1742	Anders Celsius	Swedish
Chemical symbols	1811	Jöns Jakob Berzelius	Swedish
Chronometer, accurate	1762	John Harrison	English
Cinematograph	1895	Auguste and Louis Lumière	French
Clock, pendulum	1656	Christiaan Huygens	Dutch
Colt revolver	1835	Samuel Colt	US
Compact disc	1972	RCA	US
Compact disc player	1984	Sony, Philips	Japanese, Dutch
Compass, simple	1088	Shen Kua	Chinese
Computer, bubble memory	1967	A H Bobeck and Bell Telephone Laboratories team	US
Computer, first commercially available (UNIVAC 1)	1951	John Mauchly, John Eckert	US

Invention	Date	Inventor	Nationality
Computerized axial tomography (CAT) scanning	1972	Godfrey Hounsfield	English
Contraceptive pill	1954	Gregory Pincus	US
Cotton gin	1793	Eli Whitney	US
Cream separator	1878	Carl de Laval	Swedish
Crookes tube	1878	William Crookes	English
Cyclotron	1931	Ernest O Lawrence	US
DDT	1940	Paul Müller	Swiss
Diesel engine	1892	Rudolf Diesel	German
Difference engine (early computer)	1822	Charles Babbage	English
Diode valve	1904	Ambrose Fleming	English
Dynamite	1866	Alfred Nobel	Swedish
Dynamo	1831	Michael Faraday	English
Electric cell	1800	Alessandro Volta	Italian
Electric fan	1882	Schuyler Wheeler	US
Electric generator, first commercial	1867	Zénobe Théophile Gramme	French
Electric light bulb	1879	Thomas Edison	US
Electric motor	1821	Michael Faraday	English
Electric motor, alternating current	1888	Nikola Tesla	Croatian-born US
Electrocardiography	1903	Willem Einthoven	Dutch
Electroencephalography	1929	Hans Berger	German
Electromagnet	1824	William Sturgeon	English
Electron microscope	1933	Ernst Ruska	German
Electrophoresis	1930	Arne Tiselius	Swedish
Fahrenheit scale	1714	Gabriel Fahrenheit	Polish-born Dutch
Felt-tip pen	1955	Esterbrook	English
Floppy disc	1970	IBM	US
Flying shuttle	1733	John Kay	English
FORTRAN	1956	John Backus, IBM	US
Fractal images	1962	Benoit Mandelbrot	Polish-born French
Frozen food	1929	Clarence Birdseye	US
Fuel cell	1839	William Grove	Welsh
Galvanometer	1820	Johann Schwiegger	German
Gas mantle	1885	Carl Welsbach	Austrian
Geiger counter	1908	Hans Geiger, Ernest Rutherford	German, New Zealand-born British
Genetic fingerprinting	1985	Alec Jeffreys	British
Glider	1877	Otto Lilienthal	German
Gramophone	1877	Thomas Edison	US
Gramophone (flat discs)	1887	Emile Berliner	German
Gyrocompass	1911	Elmer Sperry	US
Gyroscope	1852	Jean Foucault	French
Heart, artificial	1982	Robert Jarvik	US
Heart-lung machine	1953	John Gibbon	US
Helicopter	1939	Igor Sikorsky	US
Holography	1947	Dennis Gabor	Hungarian-born British
Hovercraft	1955	Christopher Cockerell	English
Hydrogen bomb	1952	US government scientists	US
Hydrometer	1675	Robert Boyle	Irish
Iconoscope	1923	Vladimir Zworykin	Russian-born US
Integrated circuit	1958	Jack Kilby, Texas Instruments	US
Internal-combustion engine, four-stroke	1877	Nikolaus Otto	German
Internal-combustion engine, gas-fuelled	1860	Etienne Lenoir	Belgian
In vitro fertilization	1969	Robert Edwards	Welsh
Jet engine	1930	Frank Whittle	English

(continued)

Inventions (*continued*)

Invention	Date	Inventor	Nationality
Jumbo jet	1969	Joe Sutherland and Boeing team	US
Laser, prototype	1960	Theodore Maiman	US
Lightning rod	1752	Benjamin Franklin	US
Linoleum	1860	Frederick Walton	English
Liquid crystal display (LCD)	1971	Hoffmann-LaRoche Laboratories	Swiss
Lock (canal)	980	Ciao Wei-yo	Chinese
Lock, Yale	1851	Linus Yale	US
Logarithms	1614	John Napier	Scottish
Loom, power	1785	Edmund Cartwright	English
Machine gun	1862	Richard Gatling	US
Magnifying glass	1250	Roger Bacon	English
Map	c. 510 BC	Hecataeus	Greek
Map, star	c. 350 BC	Eudoxus	Greek
Maser	1953	Charles Townes and Arthur Schawlow	US
Mass-spectrograph	1918	Francis Aston	English
Microscope	1590	Zacharias Janssen	Dutch
Miners' safety lamp	1813	Humphry Davy	English
Mohs' scale for mineral hardness	1822	Frederick Mohs	German
Morse code	1838	Samuel Morse	US
Motorcycle	1885	Gottlieb Daimler	German
Neutron bomb	1977	US military	US
Nylon	1934	Wallace Carothers	US
Paper chromatography	1944	Archer Martin, Richard Synge	English
Paper, first	105	Ts'ai Lun	Chinese
Particle accelerator	1932	John Cockcroft, Ernest Walton	English, Irish
Pasteurization (wine)	1864	Louis Pasteur	French
Pen, fountain	1884	Lewis Waterman	US
Photoelectric cell	1904	Johann Elster	German
Photograph, first colour	1881	Frederic Ives	US
Photograph, first (on a metal plate)	1827	Joseph Niepce	French
Piano	1704	Bartelommeo Cristofori	Italian
Planar transistor	1959	Robert Noyce	US
Plastic, first (Parkesine)	1862	Alexander Parkes	English
Plough, cast iron	1785	Robert Ransome	English
Punched-card system for carpet-making loom	1805	Joseph-Marie Jacquard	French
Radar, first practical equipment	1935	Robert Watson-Watt	Scottish
Radio	1901	Guglielmo Marconi	Italian
Radio interferometer	1955	Martin Ryle	English
Radio, transistor	1952	Sony	Japanese
Razor, disposable safety	1895	King Gillette	US
Recombinant DNA, technique	1973	Stanley Cohen, Herbert Boyer	US
Refrigerator, domestic	1918	Nathaniel Wales, E J Copeland	US
Richter scale	1935	Charles Richter	US
Road locomotive, steam	1801	Richard Trevithick	English
Road vehicle, first self-propelled (steam)	1769	Nicolas-Joseph Cugnot	French
Rocket, powered by petrol and liquid oxygen	1926	Robert Goddard	US
Rubber, synthetic	1909	Karl Hoffman	German
Scanning tunnelling microscope	1980	Heinrich Rohrer, Gerd Binning	Swiss, German
Seed drill	1701	Jethro Tull	English
Seismograph	1880	John Milne	English
Shrapnel shell	1784	Henry Shrapnel	English
Silicon transistor	1954	Gordon Teal	US
Silk, method of producing artificial	1887	Hilaire, Comte de Chardonnet	French
Spinning frame	1769	Richard Arkwright	English
Spinning jenny	1764	James Hargreaves	English
Spinning mule	1779	Samuel Crompton	English
Stainless steel	1913	Harry Brearley	English
Steam engine	50 BC	Heron of Alexandria	Greek
Steam engine, first successful	1712	Thomas Newcomen	English
Steam engine, improved	1765	James Watt	Scottish
Steam locomotive, first effective	1814	George Stephenson	English
Steam turbine, first practical	1884	Charles Parsons	English
Steel, open-hearth production	1864	William Siemens, Pierre Emile Martin	German, French
Submarine	1620	Cornelius Drebbel	Dutch
Superheterodyne radio receiver	1918	Edwin Armstrong	US
Tank	1914	Ernest Swinton	English
Telephone	1876	Alexander Graham Bell	Scottish-born US
Telescope, binocular	1608	Johann Lippershey	Dutch
Telescope, reflecting	1668	Isaac Newton	English
Television	1926	John Logie Baird	Scottish
Terylene (synthetic fibre)	1941	John Whinfield, J T Dickson	English
Thermometer	1607	Galileo	Italian
Thermometer, alcohol	1730	Réné Antoine Ferchault de Réaumur	French
Thermometer, mercury	1714	Gabriel Fahrenheit	Polish-born Dutch
TNT	1863	J Willbrand	German
Toaster, pop-up	1926	Charles Strite	US
Toilet, flushing	1778	Joseph Bramah	English
Transistor	1948	John Bardeen, Walter Brattain, William Shockley	US
Triode valve	1906	Lee De Forest	US
Tunnel diode	1957	Leo Esaki, Sony	Japanese
Tupperware	1944	Earl Tupper	US
Type, movable earthenware	1045	Pi Shêng	Chinese
Type, movable metal	1440	Johannes Gutenberg	German
Ultrasound, first use in obstetrics	1958	Ian Donald	Scottish
Velcro	1948	Georges de Mestral	Swiss
Video, home	1975	Matsushita, JVC, Sony	Japanese
Viscose	1892	Charles Cross	English
Vulcanization of rubber	1839	Charles Goodyear	US
Wind tunnel	1932	Ford Motor Company	US
Wireless telegraphy	1895	Guglielmo Marconi	Italian
Word processor	1965	IBM	US
Zinc-carbon battery	1868	George Leclanché	French
Zip	1891	Whitcombe Judson	US

Gene Technology

DOLLY: THE CLONING DEBATE

BY STEPHEN WEBSTER

Dolly, the most famous sheep in the world, has been the subject of debate ever since her existence was announced in February 1997. For Dolly is a clone, produced without sex from a single cell scraped from the udder of an adult sheep. The experiments that produced Dolly were done at the Roslin Institute, a research establishment just outside Edinburgh, but there has been interest in cloning animals for several decades. The intense publicity that surrounded Dolly arose because, as a mammal, she is closely related to humans. And if genetically identical individuals, or clones, can be produced from adult sheep cells, then it seems likely that the same process could be applied to humans. Very soon after Dolly met the world's photographers, a House of Commons committee summoned Ian Wilmut, the team leader of Roslin's Dolly project, to explain the meaning of his work. Wilmut confirmed that his technology could be applied to humans, and given the resources, might lead to cloned humans 'within a couple of years'. He said, however, that such a use of the technique would be 'pointless'; and Wilmut declared himself glad that there were laws in the UK banning the cloning of humans.

Advantages of Cloning

It is important, therefore, in assessing the significance of Dolly, to understand the background to cloning, and to appreciate why Wilmut's small agricultural research institute persisted for so long in its attempts to clone an adult mammal. The motive is simple, and relates to the commercial breeding of animals. If a farmer has a successful animal, for example a cow that produces a great quantity of excellent milk, similar cows would also be welcome. Normally, breeders obtain the animals they want by mating one favoured individual with another. Yet sexual reproduction produces variation among animals, so the offspring are always a little different from the parents. If it were possible to reproduce an animal without using sex, then the offspring would be identical to its single parent: a clone. Any useful characteristics in the parent would then be found in its genetically identical offspring.

With plants the application was obvious: tomatoes, strawberries, and carrots can all be cloned from individuals judged successful by farmer and consumer – and have been. It is harder to clone animals, yet soon another scientific development made cloning even more attractive: genetic engineering. Much time and money has been invested in making transgenic animals: creatures that contain one or more genes from another species, particularly humans. The Roslin Institute, with its commercial links to the pharmaceutical company PPL Therapeutics, was interested in making sheep with genes that altered the composition of the milk, so that it contained valuable medicines. Clones of such sheep would be guaranteed to have the same ability, and the investment would be secure.

The basis of cloning is that all the cells of an organism, with the exception of the sex cells, contain a full set of genes. A liver cell, for example, contains all the genes for making a brain, the skin, the skeleton, and indeed every other part of the body, yet when a liver cell reproduces it only ever makes other liver cells. It is as if all the other genes it contains were permanently switched off. Therefore, in order to grow an animal from a single cell, a way had to be found to switch back on every gene.

Early Cloning Experiments

Embryo cells differ from adult cells in that their genes have not yet been switched off. This is why cloning experiments have tended to use cells taken from an embryo. The method always followed is this: take the nucleus (where the genes are found) out of a cell and then inject it into a fertilized egg – one that has been prepared by having its own nucleus removed. Success came in 1952 in Philadelphia, Pennsylvania, when Robert Briggs and Tom King took a frog embryo, separated out all the cells, and inserted each nucleus into a prepared egg. Twenty-seven tadpoles developed, each genetically identical. It was a world first: an animal had been experimentally cloned.

Frogs are not economically important; mammals are. If a sheep or cow could be cloned after its excellence had been established, in other words when it was fully developed, the technique would be highly lucrative. However, efforts to clone mammals were at first unsuccessful. Then, in the mid-1980s scientists at the University of Wisconsin, funded by the US beef giant W R Grace and Company, made a breakthrough – they managed to clone cow embryo cells, with the cloned embryos growing into adults. The same procedure was followed: take the nucleus from an embryo cell, inject it into a prepared egg, and look for signs of development. If all went well the growing egg, now itself an embryo, would be implanted into a surrogate mother and after the normal gestation period the cow would be born. Venture capitalists saw an opportunity here, related to the beef industry's requirements for productive, disease-resistant cows. Yet while the technique worked, the cloned cows were expensive. The quality of American beef was good enough using ordinary breeding techniques. Cloning cattle was an expensive luxury and within just a few years, research money for cloning was once more in short supply. Furthermore, it was considered most unlikely that any mammal could ever be cloned from an adult cell, however much money was available.

Triumph at Roslin

Researchers at the Roslin Institute had meanwhile been developing their interest in transgenic sheep. Sheep embryos

(continued)

were being injected with human genes, and some of these genes were finding their way into the sheep genetic apparatus. One such gene caused the sheep to produce in their milk the drug alpha-1 antitrypsin, used in treating some lung diseases. However, the technique is hit-and-miss: the sheep embryos only incorporate the human genes occasionally. Yet if it were possible to clone transgenic sheep, especially from those individuals with a proven drug-producing history, then the offspring would be guaranteed to contain the gene, and there would be no need for those gene injections with their low success rates. Ian Wilmut had already had success with cloning from embryonic cells, but believed that it should be possible to use adult cells instead. He argued that all the genes contained within an adult nucleus could be reactivated; it was just a matter of finding the right method. Oddly enough, a period of starvation was found to produce the desired effect. Cells taken from a sheep's udder were starved for a short period and this produced in the nucleus a change: the genes became active again. Egg cells were prepared by having their own nuclei removed and replaced by the udder nuclei. Out of 277 eggs that received the nuclei, just 29 developed into embryos, all of which were implanted in surrogate mothers. Fourteen pregnancies began, but most miscarried; only one pregnancy went through to term – this was Dolly.

Ethical Issues

It is no exaggeration to say that the scientific world was astonished by the achievement. Scientists' widespread feeling had been that cloning from adult mammals was impossible; indeed, throughout the long-running but sporadic debate about the ethics of cloning, running since the 1970s, scientific commentators tended to downplay the possibility of cloning from adults. In any event, with the attention of the media focused on the concept of human cloning, scientists have had little opportunity to explain that Dolly is not simply an example of scientists in white coats 'playing God' but might constitute instead a serious medical advance.

Ever since the birth of Dolly, the public debate has been dominated by this question: will humans be cloned? The prospect of dictators cloning themselves and of women giving birth to their father were all discussed as serious possibilities. One reader, writing to the *The Times*, suggested that if his son, who had died in a car accident, were cloned 'he would be able to resume his relationship with my wife and myself and our younger son in a meaningful way and our family would be complete again'. Yet a clone of a person would have their own personality, wrought by the environment. They would have their own identity. In reality no-one could clone themselves and predict the outcome, any more than one can predict the future. Yet there are more straightforward uses for human cloning. One such application might be in the cloning of tissues, not individuals. Cloned bone marrow, genetically identical to the patient in need, would save lives. More lives would be saved if whole organs could be grown, genetically matched to someone with heart or kidney disease. For the moment, because of the wider ethical issues, research in such areas is banned in the UK.

Recent Developments

Dolly returned to the headlines in April 1998 when she gave birth to a lamb, Bonnie, conceived in the normal way. This was good news for the Roslin scientists because it showed that a cloned sheep can be fully healthy and able to pass on her genetic characteristics in the simplest and easiest way – by sexual reproduction. However, there was less welcome publicity too. The simple fact is that, Dolly remains unique. Neither Roslin nor any other laboratory has managed to repeat the original feat of cloning a mammal from an adult cell. In science repeatability is an important part of the process by which a scientific result becomes not a fluke but a useful advance. Dolly was the single success from 277 attempts and this has raised the question that perhaps the original udder cell was unusual in some respect. Among the possibilities are that the cell was undifferentiated or, if the original sheep was pregnant, fetal in origin. The research carries on therefore, and several laboratories, both in Europe and the USA, are striving to produce adult clones of sheep and cows. Given the doubts about Dolly, and the strength of the debate over cloning, it is certain that the next cloned adult animal will generate another rash of headlines.

Genetics: Chronology

1856	Austrian monk and botanist Gregor Mendel begins experiments breeding peas that will lead him to the laws of heredity.
1865	Gregor Mendel publishes a paper in the *Proceedings* of the Natural Science Society of Brünn that outlines the fundamental laws of heredity.
1869	Swiss biochemist Johann Miescher discovers a nitrogen and phosphorous material in cell nuclei that he calls nuclein but which is now known as the genetic material DNA.
1888	Dutch geneticist Hugo Marie de Vries uses the term 'mutation' to describe varieties that arise spontaneously in cultivated primroses.
1902	US geneticist Walter Sutton and German zoologist Theodor Boveri found the chromosomal theory of inheritance when they show that cell division is connected with heredity.

1906	English biologist William Bateson introduces the term 'genetics'.
1910	US geneticist Thomas Hunt Morgan discovers that certain inherited characteristics of the fruit fly *Drosophila melanogaster* are sex linked. He later argues that because all sex-related characteristics are inherited together they are linearly arranged on the X-chromosome.
1934	Norwegian biochemist Asbjrn Fölling discovers the genetic metabolic defect phenylketonuria, which can cause retardation; his discovery stimulates research in biochemical genetics and the development of screening tests for carriers of deleterious genes.
1944	The role of deoxyribonucleic acid (DNA) in genetic inheritance is first demonstrated by US bacteriologist Oswald Avery, US biologist Colin MacLeod, and US biologist Maclyn McCarthy; it opens the door to the elucidation of the genetic code.

Genetics: Chronology (*continued*)

1945 Working in Japan, US geneticist Samuel G Salmon discovers Norin 10, a semidwarf wheat variety which grows quickly, responds well to fertilizer, does not fall over from the weight of the grains, and when crossed with disease-resistant strains in the USA results in a wheat strain that increases wheat harvests by more than 60% in India and Pakistan.

25 April 1953 English molecular biologist Francis Crick and US biologist James Watson announce the discovery of the double helix structure of DNA, the basic material of heredity. They also theorize that if the strands are separated then each can form the template for the synthesis of an identical DNA molecule. It is perhaps the most important discovery in biology.

1954 Russian-born US cosmologist George Gamow suggests that the genetic code consists of the order of nucleotide triplets in the DNA molecule.

1958 US geneticists George Beadle, Edward Tatum, and Joshua Lederberg share the Nobel Prize for Physiology or Medicine: Beadle and Tatum for their discovery that genes act by regulating definite chemical events; and Lederberg for his discoveries concerning genetic recombination.

1961 French biochemists François Jacob and Jacques Monod discover messenger ribonucleic acid (mRNA), which transfers genetic information to the ribosomes, where proteins are synthesized.

1967 US scientist Charles Caskey and associates demonstrate that identical forms of messenger RNA produce the same amino acids in a variety of living beings, showing that the genetic code is common to all life forms.

1967 US biochemist Marshall Nirenberg establishes that mammals, amphibians, and bacteria all share a common genetic code.

October 1968 US geneticists Mark Ptashne and Walter Gilbert separately identify the first repressor genes.

1969 US geneticist Jonathan Beckwith and associates at Harvard Medical School isolate a single gene for the first time.

1969 The Nobel Prize for Physiology or Medicine is awarded jointly to US physiologists Max Delbrück, Alfred Hershey, and Salvador Luria for their discoveries concerning the replication mechanism and genetic structure of viruses.

1970 US geneticist Hamilton Smith discovers type II restriction enzyme that breaks the DNA strand at predictable places, making it an invaluable tool in recombinant DNA technology.

1970 US biochemists Howard Temin and David Baltimore separately discover the enzyme reverse transcriptase, which allows some cancer viruses to transfer their RNA to the DNA of their hosts turning them cancerous – a reversal of the common pattern in which genetic information always passes from DNA to RNA.

1972 US microbiologist Daniel Nathans uses a restriction enzyme that splits DNA (deoxyribonucleic acid) molecules to produce a genetic map of the monkey virus (SV40), the simplest virus known to produce cancer; it is the first application of these enzymes to an understanding of the molecular basis of cancer.

1972 Venezuelan-born US immunologist Baruj Benacerraf and Hugh O'Neill McDevitt show immune response to be genetically determined.

1973 US biochemists Stanley Cohen and Herbert Boyer develop the technique of recombinant DNA (deoxyribonucleic acid). Strands of DNA are cut by restriction enzymes from one species and then inserted into the DNA of another; this marks the beginning of genetic engineering.

1975 The gel-transfer hybridization technique for the detection of specific DNA (deoxyribonucleic acid) sequences is developed; it is a key development in genetic engineering.

1976 US biochemist Herbert Boyer and venture capitalist Robert Swanson found Genentech in San Francisco, California, the world's first genetic engineering company.

28 August 1976 Indian-born US biochemist Har Gobind Khorana and his colleagues announce the construction of the first artificial gene to function naturally when inserted into a bacterial cell. This is a major breakthrough in genetic engineering.

1977 US scientist Herbert Boyer, of the firm Genentech, fuses a segment of human DNA (deoxyribonucleic acid) into the bacterium *Escherichia coli* which begins to produce the human protein somatostatin; this is the first commercially produced genetically engineered product.

1980 A new vaccine for the prevention of hepatitis B is tested in the USA. It is the first genetically engineered vaccine and has a success rate of 92%. It wins Federal Drug Administration approval in 1986.

16 June 1980 The US Supreme Court rules that a microbe created by genetic engineering can be patented.

1981 The US Food and Drug Administration grants permission to Eli Lilley and Co to market insulin produced by bacteria, the first genetically engineered product to go on sale.

1981 The genetic code for the hepatitis B surface antigen is discovered, creating the possibility of a bioengineered vaccine.

1981 US geneticists Robert Weinberg, Geoffrey Cooper, and Michael Wigler discover that oncogenes (genes that cause cancer) are integrated into the genome of normal cells.

1982 Using genetically engineered bacteria, the Swedish firm Kabivitrum manufactures human growth hormone.

1983 Geneticist James Gusella identifies the gene for Huntington's disease.

1984 British geneticist Alec Jeffreys discovers that a core sequence of DNA (deoxyribonucleic acid) is almost unique to each person; this examination of DNA, known as 'genetic fingerprinting', can be used in criminal investigations and to establish family relationships.

1986 The US Department of Agriculture permits the Biological Corporation of Omaha to market a virus produced by genetic engineering; it is the first living genetically altered organism to be sold. The virus is used against a form of swine herpes.

1986 The US Department of Agriculture permits the first outdoor test of genetically altered high-yield plants (tobacco plants).

1987 German-born British geneticist Walter Bodmer and associates announce the discovery of a marker for a gene that causes cancer of the colon.

1987 The first genetically altered bacteria are released into the environment in the USA; they protect crops against frost.

1987 Foxes in Belgium are immunized against rabies by using bait containing a genetically engineered vaccine, dropped from helicopters. The success of the experiment leads to a large-scale vaccination programme.

April 1987 The US Patent and Trademark Office announces its intention to allow the patenting of animals produced by genetic engineering.

10 October 1987 The *New York Times* announces Dr Helen Donis-Keller's mapping of all 23 pairs of human chromosomes, allowing the location of specific genes for the prevention and treatment of genetic disorders.

April 1988 The US Patent and Trademark Office grants Harvard University a patent for a mouse developed by genetic engineering.

1989 Scientists in Britain introduce genetically engineered white blood cells into cancer patients, to attack tumours.

1991 British geneticists Peter Goodfellow and Robin Lovell-Badge discover the gene on the Y chromosome that determines sex.

1992 The US biotechnology company Agracetus patents transgenic cotton, which has had a foreign gene added to it by genetic engineering.

(continued)

Genetics: Chronology (continued)

1992	US biologist Philip Leder receives a patent for the first genetically engineered animal, the oncomouse, which is sensitive to carcinogens.
1993	US geneticist Dean Hammer and colleagues at the US National Cancer Institute publish the approximate location of a gene that could predispose human males to homosexuality.
1994	Trials using transfusions of artificial blood begin in the USA. The blood contains genetically engineered haemoglobin.
February 1994	The US Food and Drug Administration approves the use of genetically engineered bovine somatotropin (BST), which increases a cow's milk yield by 10–40%. It is banned in Europe.
May 1994	The first genetically engineered food goes on sale in California and Chicago, Illinois. The 'Flavr Savr' tomato is produced by the US biotechnology company Calgene.
1995	A genetically engineered potato is developed that contains the gene for Bt toxin, a natural pesticide produced by a soil bacterium. The potato plant produces Bt within its leaves.
1995	US embryologists Edward Lewis and Eric Wieschaus and German embryologist Christiane Nüsslein-Volhard are jointly awarded the Nobel Prize for Physiology or Medicine for their discoveries concerning the genetic control of early embryonic development.
1995	Australian geneticists produce a genetically engineered variety of cotton that contains a gene from a soil bacteria that kills the cotton bollworm and native budworm.
1995	Trials begin in the USA to treat breast cancer by gene therapy. The women are injected with a virus genetically engineered to destroy their tumours.
April 1995	US surgeons report the successful transplant of genetically altered hearts of pigs into baboons, a notable advance in trans-species operations.
July 1995	The US government approves experimentation of genetically altered animal organs in humans.
August 1995	The US Environmental Protection Agency approves the sale of genetically modified maize, which contains a gene from a soil bacterium that produces a toxin fatal to the European corn borer, a pest that causes approximately $1 billion damages annually.
January 1996	The first genetically engineered salmon are hatched, at Loch Fyne in Scotland. The salmon contain genes from the ocean pout as well as a salmon growth hormone gene that causes them to grow five times as fast as other salmon.
9 May 1996	Scientists at the National Institute of Allergy and Infectious Disease discover a protein, 'fusin', which allows the HIV virus to fuse with a human immune system cell's outer membrane and inject genetic material. Its presence is necessary for the AIDS virus to enter the cell.
August 1996	US geneticists clone two rhesus monkeys from embryo cells.
27 February 1997	Scottish researcher Ian Wilmut of the Roslin Institute in Edinburgh, Scotland, announces that British geneticists have cloned an adult sheep. A cell was taken from the udder of the mother sheep and its DNA (deoxyribonucleic acid) combined with an unfertilized egg that had had its DNA removed. The fused cells were grown in the laboratory and then implanted into the uterus of a surrogate mother sheep. The resulting lamb, Dolly, came from an animal that was six years old. This is the first time cloning has been achieved using cells other than reproductive cells. The news is met with international calls to prevent the cloning of humans.
February 1997	US genetic scientist Don Wolf announces the production of monkeys cloned from embryos. It is a step closer to cloning humans and raises acute philosophical issues.
16 May 1997	US geneticists identify a gene *clock* in chromosome 5 in mice that regulates the circadian rhythm.
3 June 1997	US geneticist Huntington F Wilard constructs the first artificial human chromosome. He inserts telomeres (which consist of DNA (deoxyribonucleic acid) and protein on the tips of chromosomes) and centromeres (specialized regions of DNA within a chromosome) removed from white blood cells into human cancer cells which are then assembled into chromosomes which are about one-tenth the size of normal chromosomes. The artificial chromosome is successfully passed on to all daughter cells.
11 June 1997	English behavioural scientist David Skuse claims that boys and girls differ genetically in the way they acquire social skills. Girls acquire social skills intuitively and are 'pre-programmed', while boys have to be taught. This has important implications for education.
August 1997	US geneticist Craig Venter and colleagues publish the genome of the bacterium *Helicobacter pylori*, a bacterium that infects half the world's population and which is the leading cause of stomach ulcers. It is the sixth bacterium to have its genome published, but is the most clinically important. It has 1,603 putative genes, encoded in a single circular chromosome that is 1,667,867 nucleotide base-pairs of DNA long. Complete genomes are increasingly being published as gene-sequencing techniques improve.
18 September 1997	US geneticist Bert Vogelstein and colleagues demonstrate that the p53 gene, which is activated by the presence of carcinogens, induces cells to commit suicide by stimulating them to produce large quantities of poisonous chemicals, called 'reactive oxygen species' (ROS). The cells literally poison themselves. It is perhaps the human body's most effective way of combating cancer. Many cancers consist of cells with a malfunctioning p53 gene.
November 1997	The US Food and Drug Administration (FDA) approves Rituxan, the first anticancer monoclonal antibody made from genetically engineered mouse antibodies. The antibody binds itself to non-Hodgkin's lymphoma (a cancer of the lymph system) cancer cells and triggers the immune system to kill the cells.

Astronomy

The Planets

(– = not applicable.)

Planet	Main constituents	Atmosphere	Average distance from the Sun		Orbital period (Earth yrs)	Diameter		Average density (water = 1 unit)
			km (millions)	mi (millions)		km (thousands)	mi (thousands)	
Mercury	rock, ferrous	–	58	36	0.241	4.88	3.03	5.4
Venus	rock, ferrous	carbon dioxide	108	67	0.615	12.10	7.51	5.2
Earth	rock, ferrous	nitrogen, oxygen	150	93	1.00	12.76	7.92	5.5
Mars	rock	carbon dioxide	228	141	1.88	6.78	4.21	3.9
Jupiter	liquid hydrogen, helium	–	778	483	11.86	142.80	88.73	1.3
Saturn	hydrogen, helium	–	1,427	886	29.46	120.00	74.56	0.7
Uranus	ice, hydrogen, helium	hydrogen, helium	2,870	1,783	84.00	50.80	31.56	1.3
Neptune	ice, hydrogen, helium	hydrogen, helium	4,497	2,794	164.80	48.60	30.20	1.8
Pluto	ice, rock	methane	5,900	3,666	248.50	2.25	1.39	~2

Photo Disc Ltd.

Saturn is encircled by bright and easily visible equatorial rings

Largest Natural Planetary Satellites

Satellite	Planet	Diameter		Mean distance from centre of primary planet		Orbital period (Earth days)	Reciprocal mass (planet = 1)
		km	mi	km	mi		
Ganymede	Jupiter	5,262	3,300	1,070,000	664,898	7.16	12,800
Titan	Saturn	5,150	3,200	1,221,800	759,226	15.95	4,200
Callisto	Jupiter	4,800	3,000	1,883,000	1,170,096	16.69	17,700
Io	Jupiter	3,630	2,240	421,600	261,982	1.77	21,400
Moon	Earth	3,476	2,160	384,400	238,866	27.32	81.3
Europa	Jupiter	3,138	1,900	670,900	416,897	3.55	39,700

The Largest Asteroids

An asteroid is a small body, composed of rock and iron, that orbits the Sun. Most lie in a belt between the orbits of Mars and Jupiter, and are thought to be fragments left over from the formation of the Solar System.

Name	Diameter km	mi	Average distance from Sun (Earth = 1)	Orbital period (years)
Ceres	940	584	2.77	4.6
Pallas	588	365	2.77	4.6
Vesta	576	358	2.36	3.6
Hygeia	430	267	3.13	5.5
Interamnia	338	210	3.06	5.4
Davida	324	201	3.18	5.7

The 20 Brightest Stars

A star's brightness is referred to as its 'magnitude'. 'Apparent magnitude' is brightness as seen from Earth. 'Absolute magnitude' is measured at a standard distance of 32.6 light-years or 10 parsecs from the star.
In October 1997 astronomers at the University of California identified the biggest and brightest star in the universe so far and named it the Pistol Star. The star was detected using NASA's Hubble Space Telescope. Its distance from the Earth is yet to be determined, although its diameter is estimated as 4 light-years.

Scientific name	Common name	Distance (light years)
Alpha Canis Majoris	Sirius	9
Alpha Carinae	Canopus	1,170
Alpha Centauri	Rigil Kent	4
Alpha Boötis	Arcturus	36
Alpha Lyrae	Vega	26
Alpha Aurigae	Capella	42
Beta Orionis	Rigel	910
Alpha Canis Minoris	Procyon	11
Alpha Eridani	Achernar	85
Alpha Orionis	Betelgeuse	310
Beta Centauri	Hadar	460
Alpha Aquilae	Altair	17
Alpha Tauri	Aldebaran	25
Alpha Crucis	Acrux	360
Alpha Scorpii	Antares	330
Alpha Virginis	Spica	260
Beta Geminorum	Pollux	36
Alpha Piscis Austrini	Fomalhaut	22
Alpha Cygni	Deneb	1,830
Beta Crucis	Mimosa	420
Alpha Leonis	Regulus	85

Constellations

A constellation is one of the 88 areas into which the sky is divided for the purposes of identifying and naming celestial objects. The first constellations were simple, arbitrary patterns of stars in which early civilizations visualized gods, sacred beasts, and mythical heroes. (– = not applicable.)

Constellation	Abbreviation	Popular name	Constellation	Abbreviation	Popular name	Constellation	Abbreviation	Popular name	Constellation	Abbreviation	Popular name
Andromeda	And	–	Cygnus	Cyn	Swan	Pavo	Pav	Peacock
Antlia	Ant	Airpump	Delphinus	Del	Dolphin	Pegasus	Peg	Flying Horse
Apus	Aps	Bird of Paradise	Dorado	Dor	Goldfish	Perseus	Per	–
Aquarius	Aqr	Water-bearer	Draco	Dra	Dragon	Phoenix	Phe	Phoenix
Aquila	Aqi	Eagle	Equuleus	Equ	Foal	Pictor	Pic	Painter
Ara	Ara	Altar	Eridanus	Eri	River	Pisces	Psc	Fishes
Aries	Ari	Ram	Fornax	For	Furnace	Piscis Austrinus	PsA	Southern Fish
Auriga	Aur	Charioteer	Gemini	Gem	Twins	Puppis	Pup	Poop
Boötes	Boo	Herdsman	Grus	Gru	Crane	Pyxis	Pyx	Compass
Caelum	Cae	Chisel	Hercules	Her	–	Reticulum	Ret	Net
Camelopardalis	Cam	Giraffe	Horologium	Hor	Clock	Sagitta	Sge	Arrow
Cancer	Cnc	Crab	Hydra	Hya	Watersnake	Sagittarius	Sgr	Archer
Canes Venatici	CVn	Hunting Dogs	Hydrus	Hyi	Little Snake	Scorpius	Sco	Scorpion
Canis Major	CMa	Great Dog	Indus	Ind	Indian	Sculptor	Scl	–
Canis Minor	CMi	Little Dog	Lacerta	Lac	Lizard	Scutum	Sct	Shield
Capricornus	Cap	Sea-goat	Leo	Leo	Lion	Serpens	Ser	Serpent
Carina	Car	Keel	Leo Minor	LMi	Little Lion	Sextans	Sex	Sextant
Cassiopeia	Cas	–	Lepus	Lep	Hare	Taurus	Tau	Bull
Centaurus	Cen	Centaur	Libra	Lib	Balance	Telescopium	Tel	Telescope
Cepheus	Cep	–	Lupus	Lup	Wolf	Triangulum	Tri	Triangle
Cetus	Cet	Whale	Lynx	Lyn	–	Triangulum Australe	TrA	Southern Triangle
Chamaeleon	Cha	Chameleon	Lyra	Lyr	Lyre	Tucana	Tuc	Toucan
Circinus	Cir	Compasses	Mensa	Men	Table	Ursa Major	UMa	Great Bear
Columba	Col	Dove	Microscopium	Mic	Microscope	Ursa Minor	UMi	Little Bear
Coma Berenices	Com	Berenice's Hair	Monoceros	Mon	Unicorn	Vela	Vel	Sails
Corona Australis	CrA	Southern Crown	Musca	Mus	Southern Fly	Virgo	Vir	Virgin
Corona Borealis	CrB	Northern Crown	Norma	Nor	Rule	Volans	Vol	Flying Fish
Corvus	Crv	Crow	Octans	Oct	Octant	Vulpecula	Vul	Fox
Crater	Crt	Cup	Ophiuchus	Oph	Serpent-bearer			
Crux	Cru	Southern Cross	Orion	Ori	–			

Some Major Comets

A comet is a small, icy body orbiting the Sun, usually on a highly elliptical path. Comets consist of a central nucleus a few kilometres across, and are often likened to dirty snowballs because they consist mostly of ice mixed with dust.
(– = not applicable.)

Name	First recorded sighting	Orbital period (yrs)	Interesting facts
Halley's comet	240 BC	76	parent of Eta Aquarid and Orionid meteor showers
Comet Tempel-Tuttle	AD 1366	33	parent of Leonid meteors
Biela's comet	1772	6.6	broke in half in 1846; not seen since 1852
Encke's comet	1786	3.3	parent of Taurid meteors
Comet Swift-Tuttle	1862	130	parent of Perseid meteors; reappeared 1992
Comet Ikeya-Seki	1965	880	so-called 'Sun-grazing' comet, passed 500,000 km/300,000 mi above surface of the Sun on 21 October 1965
Comet Kohoutek	1973	–	observed from space by *Skylab* astronauts
Comet West	1975	500,000	nucleus broke into four parts
Comet Bowell	1980	–	ejected from Solar System after close encounter with Jupiter
Comet IRAS-Araki-Alcock	1983	–	passed only 4.5 million km/2.8 million mi from the Earth on 11 May 1983
Comet Austin	1989	–	passed 32 million km/20 million mi from the Earth in 1990
Comet Shoemaker-Levy 9	1993	–	made up of 21 fragments; crashed into Jupiter in July 1994
Comet Hale-Bopp	1995	1,000	spitting out of gas and debris produced a coma, a surrounding hazy cloud of gas and dust, of greater volume than the Sun; the bright coma is due to an outgassing of carbon monoxide; clearly visible with the naked eye in March 1997
Comet Hyakutake	1996	–	passed 15 million km/9,300,000 mi from the Earth

Phases of the Moon 1999

Phases of the Moon shown to the nearest hour with timings given in Greenwich Mean Time (GMT).

New moon			First quarter			Full moon			Last quarter		
Month	Day	Time	Month	Day	Time	Month	Day	Time	Month	Day	Time
January	17	16:00	January	24	19:00	January	2	03:00	January	9	15:00
February	16	07:00	February	23	03:00	January	31	16:00	February	8	12:00
March	17	19:00	March	24	10:00	March	2	07:00	March	10	09:00
April	16	05:00	April	22	19:00	March	31	23:00	April	9	03:00
May	15	12:00	May	22	06:00	April	30	15:00	May	8	18:00
June	13	19:00	June	20	18:00	May	30	07:00	June	7	04:00
July	13	03:00	July	20	09:00	June	28	22:00	July	6	12:00
August	11	11:00	August	19	02:00	July	28	12:00	August	4	18:00
September	9	22:00	September	17	20:00	August	26	24:00	September	2	22:00
October	9	12:00	October	17	15:00	September	25	11:00	October	2	04:00
November	8	04:00	November	16	09:00	October	24	21:00	October	31	12:00
December	7	23:00	December	16	01:00	November	23	07:00	November	29	23:00
						December	22	18:00	December	29	14:00

Astronomical Constants

Constant	Value	Constant	Value
Astronomical unit (au)	149,597,870 km	Light year (ly)	9.4605×10^{12} km (or 0.30660 pc)
Speed of light in a vacuum (*c*)	299,792.458 km/sec	Parsec (pc)	30.857×10^{12} km (or 3.26161 ly)
Solar parallax	8.794148 arc seconds	Obliquity of the elliptic (2000)	23° 26' 21.448"
Mass of the Sun	1.9891×10^{30} kg	General precession (2000)	50.290966 arc seconds/year
Mass of the Earth	5.9742×10^{24} kg	Constant of nutation (2000)	9.2025 arc seconds
Mass of the Moon	7.3483×10^{22} kg	Constant of aberration (2000)	20.49552 arc seconds

Solar and Lunar Eclipses

This table does not include partial eclipses of the Moon.

Month	Day	Type of eclipse	Duration of maximum eclipse	Region for observation
1999				
February	16	Sun annular	6 hr 35 min	southern Indian Ocean, Antarctica, Australia
August	11	Sun total	11 hr 4 min	Europe, North Africa, Arabia, western Asia
2000				
January	21	Moon total	4 hr 44 min	the Americas, Europe, Africa, western Asia
February	5	Sun partial	12 hr 50 min	Antarctica
July	1	Sun partial	19 hr 34 min	southeastern Pacific Ocean
July	16	Moon total	13 hr 56 min	southeastern Asia, Australasia
July	31	Sun partial	2 hr 14 min	Arctic regions
December	25	Sun partial	17 hr 36 min	USA, eastern Canada, Central America, Caribbean
2001				
January	9	Moon total	20 hr 21 min	Africa, Europe, Asia
June	21	Sun total	12 hr 4 min	central and southern Africa
December	14	Sun annular	20 hr 52 min	Pacific Ocean

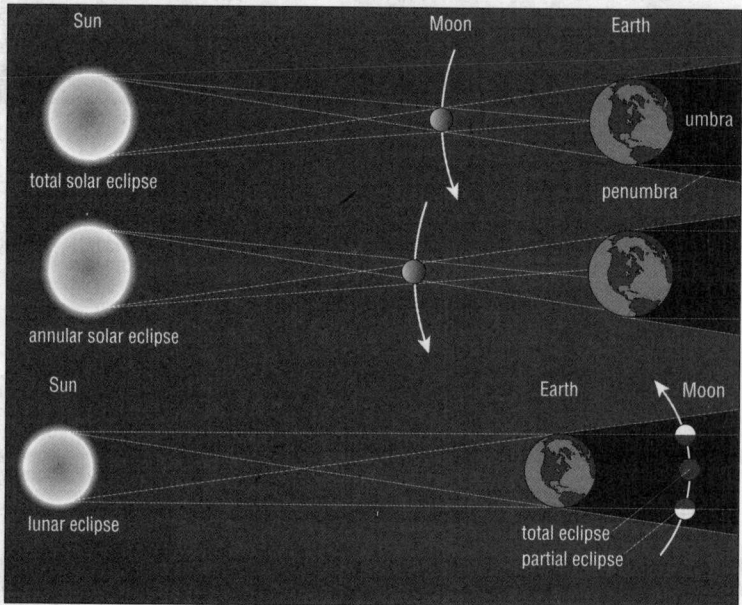

Eclipse *A diagram to show the passage of the Moon between the Earth and Sun in a solar eclipse, and passage of the Earth between the Moon and Sun in a lunar eclipse.*

Seasons 1999

Times are in GMT, to the nearest hour.

Vernal (Spring) equinox			Summer solstice			Autumnal equinox			Winter solstice		
Month	Day	Time	Month	Day	Time	Month	Day	Time	Month	Day	Time
1999											
March	21	02:00	June	21	20:00	September	23	12:00	December	22	08:00

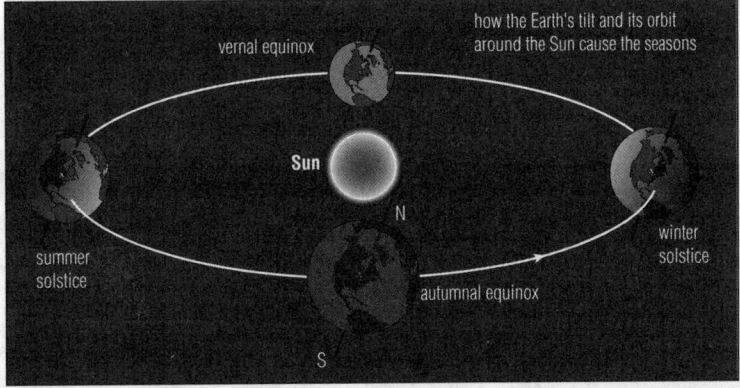

Seasons *As the Earth orbits the Sun, its axis of rotation always points in the same direction. This means that during the northern hemisphere summer solstice (21 June), the Sun is overhead in the northern hemisphere. At the northern hemisphere winter solstice (22 December), the Sun is overhead in the southern hemisphere.*

Space Flight

Notable Uncrewed Space Flights

Date	Remarks
Interplanetary missions	
September 1959	first craft to reach the Moon, by USSR's *Luna 2*
October 1959	first pictures of lunar far side from *Luna 3*
December 1962	first fly-by of Venus by US *Mariner 2*
July 1964	first close-up images of the Moon from *Ranger 7*
July 1965	first successful fly-by of Mars with first images of the planet from *Mariner 4*
January 1966	first 'soft' lunar landing and surface images from *Luna 9*
April 1966	first lunar orbiter, *Luna 10*
October 1967	first successful exploration of Venus's atmosphere by *Venera 4*
September 1968	first spacecraft to fly round the Moon and return to Earth, *Zond 5*
September 1970	first return of sample from Moon by unmanned craft, *Luna 16*
November 1970	first lunar rover, *Lunakhod 1*
December 1970	first successful Venus landing by *Venera 7*
November 1971	first Mars orbiter, *Mariner 9*
December 1973	first craft to explore Jupiter, *Pioneer 10*
March 1974	first fly-by of Mercury by *Mariner 10*
October 1975	first craft to orbit Venus and return surface pictures, *Venera 9*
July 1976	first soft landing on Mars by *Viking 1*
September 1979	first exploration of Saturn by *Pioneer 11*
October 1983	first mapping of Venus by radar, *Venera 15*
January 1986	first exploration of Uranus, *Voyager 2*
March 1986	first encounter with coma of comet (Halley) by *Giotto*
August 1989	first exploration of Neptune by *Voyager 2*

Date	Remarks
October 1991	first fly-by of a comet, Gaspra, by *Galileo*
February 1992	*Ulysses* flies past Jupiter
July 1992	*Giotto* flies to within 200 km/124 mi of comet Grigg-Skellerup
December 1995	first craft to enter Jupiter's atmosphere, *Galileo* probe
	first Jupiter orbiter, *Galileo*
November 1997	launch of the US $3.4 billion Cassini probe to orbit Saturn
Satellites	
October 1957	first artificial Earth satellite, Soviet Union's Sputnik 1
November 1957	first living being (dog, Laika) in orbit aboard Sputnik 2
January 1958	first US satellite, first science satellite, *Explorer 1*
December 1958	first experimental communications satellite, *Score 1*
April 1959	first military spy satellite, *Discoverer 2*
April 1960	first weather satellite, *Tiros 1*
	first navigation satellite, *Transit 1B*
August 1960	first recovery of craft from orbit, *Discoverer 13*
	first recovery of living creatures (two dogs) from orbit, *Sputnik 5*
July 1962	first commercial communications satellite, *Telstar 1*
July 1963	first geostationary orbiting communications satellite, *Syncom 2*
April 1966	first astronomical satellite, *OAO 1*
December 1966	first French satellite launch, *A1*
October 1967	first automatic, unmanned docking in orbit, *Cosmos 186* and *188*

(continued)

Notable Uncrewed Space Flights (*continued*)

Date	Remarks	Date	Remarks
February 1970	first Japanese satellite launch, *Ohsumi*	May 1984	first fully commercial satellite launch by Arianespace, *Spacenet1*
April 1970	first Chinese satellite launch, *Tungfanghung*	November 1985	first satellite capture and return to Earth, *Palapa* and *Westar*
October 1971	first British satellite launch, *Prospero*		
July 1972	first Earth resources remote sensing satellite, *Landsat 1*	February 1986	first privately operated, commercial, remote-sensing craft, *Spot 1*
February 1976	first maritime mobile communications satellite, *Marisat 1*	September 1988	first Israeli satellite launch, *Ofeq 1*
July 1980	first Indian satellite launch, *Rohini*	December 1988	first privately operated, commercial TV satellite, *Astra 1A*
June 1981	first European operational satellite launch by *Ariane, Meteosat 2*	April 1990	first optical telescope in orbit, Hubble Space Telescope
April 1984	first satellite to be captured, repaired, and redeployed, *SMM 1*		

Space Probes: Recent Chronology

8 February 1992	*Ulysses* flew past Jupiter at a distance of 380,000 km/ 236,000 mi from the surface, just inside the orbit of Io and closer than 11 of Jupiter's 16 moons.	1997	The US space probe *Galileo* began orbiting Jupiter's moons. It took photographs of Europa for a potential future landing site, and detected molecules containing carbon and nitrogen on Callisto, suggesting that life once existed there.
10 July 1992	*Giotto* (USA) flew at a speed of 14 kms/8.5 mps to within 200 km/124 mi of comet Grigg-Skellerup, 12 light years (240 million km/150 mi) away from Earth.	1997	The US Near Earth Asteroid Rendezvous (NEAR) spacecraft flew within 1,200 km/746 mi of the asteroid Mathilde, taking high-resolution photographs and revealing a 25-km /15.5-mi crater covering the 53-km/33-mi asteroid.
25 September 1992	*Mars Observer* (USA) launched from Cape Canaveral, the first US mission to Mars for 17 years.		
10 October 1992	*Pioneer-Venus 1* burned up in the atmosphere of Venus.	1997	The US spacecraft *Mars Global Surveyor* went into orbit around Mars to conduct a detailed photographic survey of the planet, commencing in March 1998, and reported the discovery of bacteria there.
21 August 1993	*Mars Observer* disappeared three days before it was due to drop into orbit around Mars.		
28 August 1993	*Galileo* flew past the asteroid Ida.	1998	The US probe *Lunar Prospector* was launched to go into low orbits around the Moon and transmit data on the composition of its crust, record gamma rays, and map its magnetic field. The satellite detected 11 million tonnes of water on the Moon in the form of ice.
December 1995	*Galileo's* probe entered the atmosphere of Jupiter. It radioed information back to the orbiter for 57 minutes before it was destroyed by atmospheric pressure.		
1996	NASA's Near Earth Asteroid Rendezvous (NEAR) was launched to study Eros.	1998	Analysis of high resolution images from the *Galileo* spacecraft suggested that the icy crust of *Europa*, Jupiter's fourth largest moon, may hide a vast ocean warm enough to support life.
4 July 1997	The US spacecraft *Mars Pathfinder* landed on Mars. Two days later the probe's rover *Sojourner*, a six-wheeled vehicle controlled by an Earth-based operator, began to explore the area around the spacecraft.		

Successful Satellite Launches

(Data as of January 1998.)

Country	Launch site	First success date	Number of successes 1957–97
Russia/CIS	Tyuratam (Baikonur), Kazakhstan	4 October 1957	1,012
	Kapustin Yar, Russia	16 March 1962	83
	Plesetsk, Russia	17 March 1966	1,445
	Svobodny, Russia	8 March 1997	2
USA	Cape Canaveral (Eastern Test Range) and Kennedy Space Center	1 February 1958	569
	Vandenberg AFB (Western Test Range)	28 February 1959	522
	Wallops Island	16 February 1961	19
	US operated air-launch	5 April 1990	21
France	Hammaguir	26 November 1965 (closed since April 1967)	4
USA/Italy	Indian Ocean Platform (San Marco)	26 April 1967	9
Australia/UK	Woomera	29 November 1967 (closed since 1976)	2
Japan	Uchinoura (Kagoshima)	11 February 1970	23
	Tanegashima (Osaki)	9 September 1975	30
France/Europe	Kourou	10 March 1970	104
China	Jiuquan	24 April 1970	23
	Xichang	29 January 1984	23
	Taiyuan	6 September 1988	4
India	Sriharikota	18 July 1980	8
Israel	Palmachim	19 September 1988	3

Space: News Review

BY TIM FURNISS

Space in the past year has been dominated by three events: the landing on the planet Mars of the NASA *Mars Pathfinder* and its tiny rover, the *Sojourner,* on 4 July 1997; the hyped-up, infamous incidents on the Russian *Mir* space station; and the successful test flight of Europe's *Ariane 5* rocket.

Mars Pathfinder Lands

The landing of the low-cost *Mars Pathfinder* and the images it returned – 21 years after the last touchdowns on the Red Planet by the *Vikings 1* and *2* – was made all the more spectacular by the access to its pictures by users of the Internet. The Web revolution even resulted in home-based addicts getting daily weather reports from Mars. The *Sojourner,* about the size of a microwave oven and the precursor of slightly larger and more sophisticated rovers on future missions in the *Mars Surveyor* programme, caught the imagination of the public with its explorations and analysis of rocks with such names as Yogi and Barnacle Bill.

Both craft continued to operate well beyond their design lives and provided more evidence that water once flowed across the now barren, ruddy coloured, rocky surface. The mission formally ended in November after four months.

Mir Space Station

Closer to home, the remarkable Russian *Mir 1* space station continued manned operations – also beyond its design life – providing a wealth of data and experience about operating larger space stations. The Russians' invaluable expertise in this area of space utilization was sadly underplayed by the extraordinary media reaction to certain incidents on the station, which were highlighted because US astronauts were on board at the time.

A fire that broke out in February was not the first to occur on the station, but the collision of the *Progress* tanker craft with the *Spektr* module in June could have been a disaster. The collision was more of a glancing blow, but the *Spektr* module lost the use of a solar panel and was depressurized as a result. The incident was a reminder that space travel is dangerous, and risks have to be accepted. Most of the media attention was given to the age of the Mir station, and the fact that it was apparently a 'wreck'. In fact, while the core module of *Mir* was launched in 1986, the final module of the space complex was launched in 1996! Running a space station for that long is bound to involve things breaking down, but part of the Russian way of working is to treat these events as operational, not emergency, situations, which is a different culture altogether from NASA Space Shuttle missions. Regular spacewalks and maintenance on the Mir station will contribute towards keeping the *Mir* in working order and ready to house many more crews until it is retired, perhaps in 1999.

During spacewalks in 1997 and early 1998, the veteran Russian cosmonaut Anatoli Solovyov became the first to make 14 spacewalks, all outside the *Mir* station on various missions. He has accumulated 63 hours of spacewalk time, compared with the individual US record of 29 hours. Another *Mir* spacewalk marked the first by a Russian and US astronaut together, an occasion later repeated aboard the Space Shuttle. Once the International Space Station is operational, NASA and the other partners will owe a debt to the operational space-station experience database provided by Russia.

Ariane 5 Launched

The successful flight of the *Ariane 5* from Kourou on 31 October was a great relief to the European space industry. The first *Ariane 5* failed dramatically in an explosion in June 1996, and another problem could have been a disaster. It is now hoped that Ariane 5 can go on to forge a successful commercial career, allowing the old workhorse, the *Ariane* 4, to retire in about 2003. Eleven *Ariane 4*s made successful commercial flights in 1997.

Notable Satellite Launches

Brazil, making its first attempt to join the 'space league' of nations that have launched national satellites on indigenously-developed boosters, failed when its VLS booster had to be destroyed after an engine fault. A spectacular failure of a US Delta rocket, which had people running for cover at Cape Canaveral in January, illustrated that losses can be experienced by veteran space nations as well. Another Delta featured in the successful launch of the first in a series of satellites, opening a new era in communications. Sixty-six iridium satellites will eventually enable users of mobile telephones to make calls from anywhere in the world to anywhere in the world. By the end of the year, 41 iridiums had been launched, and the network should have been completed in mid-1998.

Successes and Some Failures

A new era in planetary exploration began in 1997, too, with the launch in October of the first spacecraft – the *Cassini/ Huygens* – to orbit the planet Saturn in 2004 after its long route around the solar system. The *Huygens* lander is to touch down on the surface of the Saturnian moon, Titan. Another planetary spacecraft, the *Mars Global Surveyor,* reached Mars orbit in September, but its manoeuvring to operational mapping orbit was interrupted by some malfunctions and, as a result, its mission may be limited.

The launch of a new crew to operate a shift aboard the *Mir* space station in July marked the 200th manned spaceflight launch in history since April 1961 (not including the failed *Challenger* Shuttle mission in 1986). The USA also launched eight Space Shuttle missions in 1997, three of them to dock with the Mir space station to deliver a new astronaut and return

(continued)

one home. As the year closed, the US resident *Mir* astronaut was David Wolf, who clambered aboard the *Mir* in October and was replaced by another astronaut early in 1998.

The year also marked a Shuttle record. One mission, STS 83, had to be aborted after three days due to a fuel cell failure but was reflown in July with the entire crew returning to space in a record 84 days. The Russian *Proton* launcher completed its second commercial launch in May 1997, carrying a Telstar satellite into orbit for the joint US/Russian International Launch Services (ILS). The company's link-up with the USA has transformed the commercial career of the *Proton*, which is now fully booked until 2001 for commercial launches. But the *Proton* blotted the copy book by failing on 25 December 1997. Overall, in 1997, there were 86 satellite launches, 38 by the USA, 28 by Russia, 12 by Europe, 6 by China, 2 by Japan and 1 by India, involving almost 140 satellites.

Not all the satellites performed well, however. A Japanese earth-observation satellite suffered a solar panel malfunction and was lost, two US Earth-observation satellites were also lost, and a communications satellite was stranded in the wrong orbit.

One of the 28 Russian satellite launches inaugurated a new launch site at Svobodny in far-eastern Russia. The former top-secret military base and missile launch complex has been converted into a launch base for small satellites into low Earth orbit, using converted military missiles. In the business world, the proposed merger of the UK/French Matra Marconi Space company and Germany's Diamler-Benz Aerospace space division, announced in 1997, will result in the formation of a large pan-European company to compete on equal terms with the giant US satellite manufacturers, Hughes, Lockheed Martin, and Space Systems Loral. 1998 promises to be a very significant year in the history of space exploration – the start of the assembly of the first International Space Station.

Notable Crewed Space Flights

Launch date	Spacecraft	Crew	Duration	Remarks
12 April 1961	*Vostok* 1	Yuri Gagarin	1 hr 58 min	first man in space; Gagarin landed separately from the spacecraft after ejecting at 1 hr 48 min, in a procedure followed by all *Vostok* pilots
5 May 1961	*Freedom* 7	Alan Shepard	15 min 28 sec	first American in space; suborbital flight ended in planned splashdown
6 August 1961	*Vostok* 2	Gherman Titov	1 day 1 hr 18 min	at 25, Titov was the youngest person in space; he was spacesick and the first to sleep in space
20 February 1962	*Friendship* 7	John Glenn	4 hr 55 min	first American to orbit the Earth
11 August 1962	*Vostok* 3	Andrian Nikolyev	3 days 22 hr 25 min	long duration flight
12 August 1962	*Vostok* 4	Pavel Popovich	2 days 22 hr 59 min	flew to within 6.4 km/4 mi of *Vostok* 3
15 May 1963	*Faith* 7	Gordon Cooper	1 day 10 hr 19 min	final US one-man flight
14 June 1963	*Vostok* 5	Valeri Bykovsky	4 days 23 hr 7 min	solo flight record-holder
16 June 1963	*Vostok* 6	Valentina Tereshkova	2 days 22 hr 50 min	first woman in space, flew close to *Vostok* 5
12 October 1964	*Voskhod* 1	Vladimir Komarov, Konstantin Feoktistov, Boris Yegerov	1 day 17 min	first multi-crewed spaceflight without spacesuits or ejection seats, flying in stripped down one-man *Vostok*
18 March 1965	*Voskhod* 2	Pavel Belyayev, Alexei Leonov	1 day 2 hr 2 min	Leonov made first walk in space
25 March 1965	*Gemini* 3	Gus Grissom, John Young	4 hr 52 min	first US two-man flight; Grissom first man to return to space
3 June 1965	*Gemini* 4	James McDivitt, Edward White	4 days 1 hr 56 min	White makes first American spacewalk
4 December 1965	*Gemini* 7	Frank Borman, James Lovell	13 days 18 hr 35 min	acted as rendezvous target for *Gemini* 6; broke endurance record
15 December 1965	*Gemini* 6	Wally Schirra, Tom Stafford	1 day 1 hr 51 min	first rendezvous in space
16 March 1966	*Gemini* 8	Neil Armstrong, David Scott	10 hr 41 min	emergency landing after first space docking
12 September 1966	*Gemini* 11	Charles Conrad, Richard Gordon	2 days 23 hr 17 min	docking on first orbit; spacewalk; re-boost to altitude of 1368 km/850 mi; automatic landing
11 November 1966	*Gemini* 12	James Lovell, Edwin Aldrin	3 days 22 hr 34 min	record spacewalk of over 2 hr by Aldrin
23 April 1967	*Soyuz* 1	Vladimir Komarov	1 day 2 hr 47 min	Komarov killed when parachute failed after emergency landing; intended to dock with *Soyuz 2*
11 October 1968	*Apollo* 7	Wally Schirra, Donn Eisele, Walt Cunningham	10 days 20 hr 9 min	Earth orbit maiden flight of Apollo Command/service modules
21 December 1968	*Apollo* 8	Frank Borman, James Lovell, William Anders	6 days 3 hr	first crewed craft to orbit the Moon
14 January 1969	*Soyuz* 4	Vladimir Shatalov	2 days 23 hr 20 min	launched with one man, returned with three
15 January 1969	*Soyuz* 5	Boris Volynov, Alexei Yeleseyev, Yevgeny Khrunov	3 days 54 min	Yeleseyev and Khrunov spacewalk to *Soyuz* 4 after docking with it
18 May 1969	*Apollo* 10	Tom Stafford, John Young, Eugene Cernan	8 days 3 min	lunar module tested in lunar orbit and flew to 14.5 km/9 mi from the Moon
16 July 1969	*Apollo* 11	Neil Armstrong, Michael Collins, Edwin Aldrin	8 days 3 hr 18 min	first crewed lunar landing; Armstrong and Aldrin walked on the Moon for over 2 hr
14 November 1969	*Apollo* 12	Charles Conrad, Richard Gordon, Alan Bean	10 days 4 hr 36 min 25 sec	pinpoint landing near uncrewed *Surveyor* craft on the Moon; two moonwalks

Notable Crewed Space Flights (*continued*)

Launch date	Spacecraft	Crew	Duration	Remarks
11 April 1970	Apollo 13	James Lovell, Jack Swigert, Fred Haise	5 days 22 hr 54 min	service module exploded 55 hr into mission; crew limped home using lunar module as lifeboat
31 January 1971	Apollo 14	Alan Shepard, Stuart Roosa, Edgar Mitchell	9 days 1 min	third Moon landing; samples collected
6 June 1971	Soyuz 11	Georgi Dobrovolsky, Vladislav Volkov, Viktor Patsayev	23 days 18 hr 21 min	crew died as craft depressurized before re-entry; they were not wearing spacesuits
26 July 1971	Apollo 15	David Scott, Alfred Worden, James Irwin	12 days 7 hr 11 min	use of first lunar rover
16 April 1972	Apollo 16	John Young, Ken Mattingly, Charles Duke	11 days 1 hr 51 min	Mattingly in lunar orbit makes longest solo US flight; three moonwalks were taken
7 December 1972	Apollo 17	Eugene Cernan, Ron Evans, Jack Schmitt	12 days 13 hr 51 min	last crewed expedition to the Moon this century
25 May 1973	Skylab 2	Charles Conrad, Joe Kerwin, Paul Weitz	28 days 49 min	spacewalk to repair severely disabled Skylab 1 space station
16 November 1973	Skylab 4	Gerry Carr, Edward Gibson, Bill Pogue	84 days 1 hr 15 min	longest US crewed spaceflight until 1996
24 May 1975	Soyuz 18	Pyotr Klimuk, Vitali Sevastyanov	62 days 23 hr 20 min	record stay on Salyut 4
15 July 1975	Soyuz 19	Alexei Leonov, Valeri Kubasov	5 days 22 hr 30 min	docked with Apollo 18 in joint Apollo-Saturn Test Project (ASTP) mission
5 July 1975	Apollo 18	Tom Stafford, Vance Brand, Donald 'Deke' Slayton	9 days 1 hr 28	docked with Soyuz 19; first US-Soviet space link-up
10 December 1977	Soyuz 26	Yuri Romanenko, Georgi Grechko	96 days 10 hr	aboard Salyut 6; broke endurance record
2 March 1978	Soyuz 28	Alexei Gubarev, Vladimir Remek	7 days 22 hr 16 min	Remek was from Czechoslovakia, the first non-American, non-Soviet in space; visit to Salyut 6
15 June 1979	Soyuz 29	Vladimir Kovalyonok, Alexander Ivanchenkov	139 days 14 hr 47 min	record duration on Salyut 6
15 November 1979	Soyuz 32	Vladimir Lyakhov, Valeri Ryumin	175 days 0 hr 35 min	record duration on Salyut 6 broken
9 April 1980	Soyuz 35	Leonid Popov, Valeri Ryumin	184 days 20 hr 11 min	another record Salyut 6 mission, with Ryumin achieving 361 days' space experience
12 April 1981	Columbia STS 1	John Young, Bob Crippen	2 days 6 hr 20 min	maiden flight of Space Shuttle
13 May 1982	Soyuz T5	Anatoli Berezevoi, Valentin Lebedev	211 days 9 hr 4 min	first record-breaking visit to Salyut 7
27 June 1982	Columbia STS 4	Ken Mattingly, Hank Hartsfield	7 days 1 hr 9 min	military flight; final Shuttle test flight
19 August 1982	Soyuz T7	Leonid Popov, Alexander Serebrov, Svetlana Savitskaya	7 days 21 hr 52 min	Savitskaya becomes second woman in space
11 November 1982	Columbia STS 5	Vance Brand, Robert Overmyer, Joe Allen, William Lenoir	5 days 2 hr 14 min	first commercial mission of Shuttle; deployed two communications satellites; first four-person flight
18 June 1983	Challenger STS 7	Bob Crippen, Rick Hauck, John Fabian, Sally Ride, Norman Thagard	6 days 2 hr 24 min	satellite deployment mission; first with five-person crew and first US woman in space
28 November 1983	Columbia STS 9	John Young, Brewster Shaw, Owen Garriott, Robert Parker, Byron Lichtenberg, Ulf Merbold	10 days 7 hr 47 min	flight of European Spacelab 1; Merbold from West Germany; first six-person flight
3 February 1984	Challenger STS 41B	Vance Brand, Robert Gibson, Bruce McCandless, Robert Stewart, Ronald McNair	7 days 23 hr 15 min	first independent spacewalk using Manned mission Manoeuvring Unit (MMU) by McCandless; first space mission to end at launch site (Kennedy/Canaveral);
8 February 1984	Soyuz T10	Leonid Kizim, Vladimir Solovyov, Oleg Atkov	236 days 22 hr 9 min	longest crewed space mission to date; Kizim and Solovyov made record six spacewalks
6 April 1984	Challenger STS 41C	Bob Crippen, Dick Scobee, George Nelson, Terry Hart, James van Hoften	6 days 23 hr 40 min	repaired Solar Max; with Soyuz T10 and T11 crews in space; 11 people in space at once
17 July 1984	Soyuz T12	Vladimir Dhzanibekov, Svetlana Savitskaya, Oleg Volk	11 days 19 hr 14 min	Savitskaya became first woman space-walker, outside Salyut 7
30 August 1984	Discovery STS 41	Hank Hartsfield, Michael Coats, Judy Resnik, Steven Hawley, Michael Mullane, Charlie Walker	6 days 56 min	100th crewed spaceflight
5 October 1984	Challenger STS 41G	Bob Crippen, Jon McBride, Sally Ride, Kathy Sullivan, David Leestman, Marc Garneau, Paul Scully Power	8 days 5 hr 23 min	first seven-person flight; first carrying two women; Sally Ride first woman in space twice; Sullivan first US woman to spacewalk; Garneau from Canada
8 November 1984	Discovery STS 51A	Rick Hauck, Dave Walker, Joe Allen, Dale Gardner, Anna Fisher	7 days 23 hr 45 min	two spacewalks to retrieve lost communications satellites and return them to Earth
6 June 1985	Soyuz T13	Vladimir Dzhanibekov, Viktor Savinykh	112 days 3 hr 12 min	complete overhaul of Salyut 7 after systems failures
17 September 1985	Soyuz T14	Vladimir Vasyutin, Georgi Grechko, Alexander Volkov	64 days 21 hr 52 min	mission cut short after Vasyutin suffered depression and anxiety

(continued)

Notable Crewed Space Flights (*continued*)

Launch date	Spacecraft	Crew	Duration	Remarks
28 January 1986	*Challenger* STS 51	Dick Scobee, Mike Smith, Judith Resnik, Ronald McNair, Ellison Onizuka, Christa McAuliffe, Gregory Jarvis	73 sec	broke apart at 14,325 m/47,000 ft; crew killed; first flight to take off but not to reach space; first American in-flight fatalities
13 March 1986	*Soyuz* T15	Leonid Kizim, Vladimir Solovyov	125 days 1 min	first mission to new space station *Mir 1*; also docked with *Salyut* 7; Kizim achieved over a year in space experience
5 February 1987	*Soyuz* TM2	Yuri Romanenko, Alexander Laveikin	326 days 11 hr 37 min	record duration mission by Romanenko aboard *Mir 1*; Laveikin, 200th person in space, returned after 174 days
21 December 1987	*Soyuz* TM4	Vladimir Titov, Musa Manarov, Anatoli Levchenko	365 days 22 hr 39 min	longest duration mission by Titov and Manarov
29 September 1988	*Discovery* STS 26	Rick Hauck, Dick Covey, Mike Lounge, David Hilmers, George Nelson	4 days 1 hr	USA's return to space 32 months after *Challenger* disaster
26 November 1988	*Soyuz* TM7	Alexander Volkov, Sergei Krikalev, Jean-Loup Chretien	151 days 11 hr 10 min	visit to *Mir*; Frenchman Chretien is first non-US, non-USSR astronaut to make two space flights, to make spacewalk, and the oldest spacewalker at 50; Chretien returned in TM6 after 25 days
4 May 1989	*Atlantis* STS 30	David Walker, Ron Grabe, Norman Thagard, Mary Cleave, Mark Lee	4 days 57 min	deployed *Magellan* for its journey to orbit the planet Venus; first deployment of a planetary spacecraft from a crewed spacecraft
18 October 1989	*Atlantis* STS 34	Donald Williams, Michael McCulley, Shannon Lucid, Franklin Chang-Diaz, Ellen Baker	4 days 23 hr 39 min	deployed Jupiter orbiter *Galileo*
24 April 1990	*Discovery* STS 31	Loren Shriver, Charles Bolden, Steven Hawley, Bruce McCandless, Kathryn Sullivan	5 days 1 hr 16 min	deployed Hubble Space Telescope; reached record 532 km/319 mi Shuttle altitude
18 May 1991	*Soyuz* TM12	Anatoli Artsebarski, Sergei Krikalev, Helen Sharman	144 days 15 hr 22 min	Sharman first non-Soviet, non-US woman and first Briton in space, returned in TM11 after seven days; Krikalev stayed aboard *Mir* and returned after 311 days; Artsebarski and Krikalev made a record six spacewalks in 33 days
22 January 1992	*Discovery* STS 42	Ronald Grabe, Stephen Oswald, Norman Thagard, David Hilmers, William Readdy, Roberta Bondar, Ulf Merbold	8 days 1 hr 14 min	International Microgravity Laboratory mission; Bondar from Canada and Merbold from Germany; Thagard achieves record 25-day Shuttle flight time on fourth mission
7 May 1992	*Endeavour* STS 49	Dan Brandenstein, Kevin Chilton, Rick Heib, Bruce Melnick, Pierre Thuot, Kathryn Thornton, Tom Akers	8 days 21 hr 17 min	retrieved *Intelsat* 6 and reboosted it into geostationary orbit; record breaking 8 hr 29 min extra-vehicular activity (EVA) by Thuot, Hieb, and Akers
31 July 1992	*Atlantis* STS 46	Loren Shriver, Andrew Allen, Claude Nicollier, Marsha Ivins, Jeff Hoffman, Franklin Chang-Diaz, Franco Malerba	7 days 23 hr 15 min	deployed *Eureca* and tethered satellites; Nicollier first Swiss astronaut and first non-US NASA mission specialist; Malerba first Italian in space; 12 people in space at once, with record five space nations being represented, with *Mir* mission
2 December 1992	*Discovery* STS 53	David Walker, Robert Cabana, Guion Bluford, James Voss, Michael Clifford	7 days 7 hr 19 min	final US Department of Defence Shuttle mission
2 December 1993	*Endeavour* STS 61	Richard Covey, Ken Bowersox, Claude Nicollier, Story Musgrave, Jeff Hoffman, Tom Akers, Kathryn Thornton	10 days 19 hr 58 min	Hubble Space Telescope servicing and repair mission; Musgrave, first to fly five Shuttle missions, achieves record 35 days' flight time
8 January 1994	*Soyuz* TM18	Viktor Afanasyev, Yuri Usachev, Valeri Poliakov	182 days 27 min	new residency aboard *Mir 1* space station; Poliakov remained on *Mir* and landed on 22 March 1995 with a flight time of 437 days
3 February 1994	*Discovery* STS 60	Charles Bolden, Kenneth Reightler, Franklin Chang-Diaz, Jan Davis, Ron Sega, Sergei Krikalev	8 days 7 hr 9 min	Krikalev first Russian to fly on US rocket
3 October 1994	*Soyuz* TM20	Alexander Viktorenko, Yelena Kondakova, Ulf Merbold	169 days 5 hr 21 min	new crew to *Mir*, including Kondakova, the first woman to make a long duration flight, and German European Space Agency (ESA) visitor Merbold, the first non-US, non-Soviet spaceperson to make three flights and first Western European to fly both US and Russian rockets; with Shuttle in space, 12 people in orbit at once; Merbold landed in TM19 after 31 days

Notable Crewed Space Flights (*continued*)

Launch date	Spacecraft	Crew	Duration	Remarks
3 February 1995	*Discovery* STS 63	James Wetherbee, Eileen Collins, Michael Foale, Bernard Harris, Janice Ford, Vladimir Titov	8 days 6 hr 28 min	*Spacelab* science rendezvous mission with *Mir* space station and spacewalk – first by British-born astronaut, Foale; Collins first female Shuttle pilot; Titov from Russia
14 March 1995	*Soyuz* TM21	Vladimir Dezhurov, Gennady Strekalov, Norman Thagard	115 days 8 hr 44 min	mission to *Mir 1* with first US astronaut to ride a Russian rocket; record 13 people in space at same time on 14–18 March; crew landed in STS 71
27 June 1995	*Atlantis* STS 71	Robert Gibson, Charles Precourt, Ellen Baker, Bonnie Dundar, Gregory Harbaugh, Anatoli Solovyov, Nikolai Budarin	9 days 19 hr 23 min	100th US crewed flight including Thagard's *Soyuz* to TM21 launch; Shuttle/*Mir 1* mission 1; 5 days joined *Mir*; delivered Solovyov and Budarin and returned with the TM21 crew; first time ten people on board one spacecraft (223 tonnes) in orbit
12 November 1995	*Atlantis* STS 74	Ken Cameron, James Halsall, Jerry Ross, Bill McArthur, Chris Hadfield	8 days 4 hr 30 min	Shuttle/*Mir* mission 2; carried docking module to be left at Mir; Hadfield NASA mission specialist from Canada
22 February 1996	*Columbia* STS 75	Andrew Allen, Scott Horowitz, Maurizio Cheli, Claude Nicollier, Jeff Hoffman, Franklin Chang-Diaz, Umberto Guidoni	15 days 17 hr 40 min	tethered satellite system reflight, satellite lost when tether broke; 12 people, five nations (two from Italy) in space with TM22 and TM23 crews also orbiting
22 March 1996	*Atlantis* STS 76	Kevin Chilton, Richard Searfoss, Ronald Sega, Ric hr Clifford, Linda Godwin, Shannon Lucid	9 days 5 hr 15 min	Shuttle/*Mir* mission 3, delivered Shannon Lucid for extended stay on *Mir*; returned 26 September aboard STS 79; after stay of 188 days, a record for a woman; spacewalk
20 June 1996	*Columbia* STS 78	Tom Henricks, Kevin Kregal, Susan Helms, Charles Brady, Richard Linnehan, Jean-Jaques Favier, Robert Thirsk	16 days 21 hr 47 min	*Spacelab* Life and Microgravity science mission; Favier from France, Thirsk from Canada
17 August 1996	*Soyuz* TM24	Valeri Korzun, Alexander Kaleri, Claudie Andre-Deshays	196 days 16 hr 26 min	new crew for *Mir 1* with Deshays, the first French woman in space, as commercial crew-person on 15-day flight, landing in TM23; Korzun and Kaleri first back-up crew to fly since *Soyuz 11* in 1971 after prime commander Gennady Manakov hospitalized (if one crew member unable to fly, back-up crew takes over) with heart attack
17 September 1996	*Atlantis* STS 79	William Readdy, Terence Wilcutt, Tom Akers, Jerome Apt, Carl Waltz, John Blaha	10 days 13 hr 18 min	Shuttle/*Mir* mission 4, delivered John Blaha and returned Shannon Lucid from *Mir*
19 November 1996	*Columbia* STS 80	Ken Cockrell, Kent Rominger, Tamara Jernigan, Thomas Jones, Story Musgrave	17 days 15 hr 53 min	Musgrave oldest person in space at 61, flying longest Shuttle mission
12 January 1997	*Atlantis* STS 81	Mike Baker, Brent Jett, John Grunsfield, Jeff Wisoff, Marsha Ivins, Jerry Linenger	10 days 4 hr 55 min	Shuttle/*Mir* mission 5, delivered Jerry Linenger and returned John Blaha from *Mir* after 128 days; Lineger made first US-Russian spacewalk with Tsiblyev, wearing Russian spacesuit
10 February 1997	*Soyuz* TM25	Vasili Tsiblyev, Alexander Lazutkin, Reinhold Ewald	184 days 22 hr 7 min	new crew for *Mir* with German Ewald flying shorter commercial mission; this crew experienced a fire on the space station and a collision with the *Progress* M34 supply ship
11 February 1997	*Discovery* STS 82	Ken Bowersox, Scott Horowitz, Steven Hawley, Mark Lee, Joe Tanner, Greg Harbaugh, Steve Smith	9 days 23 hr 37 min	second mission to service the Hubble Space Telescope; featured five spacewalks

Photo Disc Ltd.

Space Shuttle launch

(continued)

Notable Crewed Space Flights (continued)

Launch date	Spacecraft	Crew	Duration	Remarks
15 May 1997	Atlantis STS 84	Charles Precourt, Eileen Collins, Carlos Noregia, Jean Francois Clervoy, Ed Lu, Michael Foale, Yelena Kondakova	9 days 5 hr 19 min	Shuttle/Mir mission 6, delivered Michael Foale and returned Jerry Linenger after 132 days; crew the most cosmopolitan in history: Precourt and Collins from USA, Noregia born in Chile, Clervoy from France, Lu born of Chinese parents, Foale British-born, Kondakova from Russia
5 August 1997	Soyuz TM26	Anatoli Solovyov, Pavel Vinogradev	in flight	200th launched crewed spaceflight in history; new crew to Mir to carry out major repair work to the damaged space station
26 September 1997	Atlantis STS 86	James Wetherbee, Mike Bloomfield, Scott Parazinsky, Titov, Jean-Loup Chretien, Wendy Lawrence, David Wolf	10 days 19 hr 20 min	Shuttle/Mir mission 7, delivered David Wolf and returned Michael Foale after 144 days; featured spacewalk by Parazinsky and Titov – the first Russian to wear US EVA suit
23 January 1998	Endeavour STS 89	Terence Willcutt, Joe Frank Edwards, Bonnie Dunbar, Michael Anderson, James Reilly, Andrew Thomas	8 days, 19 hr 46 min	Shuttle/Mir mission 8, returned David Wolf (with flight time of 127 days) and delivered Andrew Thomas

Crewed Spacecraft Accidents

16 March 1966 *Gemini 8* Command pilot Neil Armstrong and pilot Dave Scott had just completed the first space docking with an Agena target rocket when the combination went into a spin. One of the spacecraft's thrusters was firing continuously due to a short circuit. Armstrong undocked from the Agena and the spinning got worse. An emergency set of thrusters on *Gemini 8* was fired to bring the capsule under control and an immediate return to Earth was ordered.

27 January 1967 *Apollo 1* A fire in the spacecraft, during pre-launch testing in preparation for an Earth orbital test flight on 21 February, killed three astronauts at Cape Canaveral's Pad 34. The Apollo programme was delayed by 21 months. The astronauts killed were Gus Grissom, one of the *Mercury 7* crew, who made America's second crewed spaceflight in 1961; Edward White, America's first spacewalker from *Gemini 4* in June 1965; and newcomer Roger Chaffee.

24 April 1967 *Soyuz 1* The maiden crewed flight of this new Soviet spaceship, piloted by lone cosmonaut Vladimir Komarov, hit serious technical problems soon after reaching orbit on 23 April. The launch of *Soyuz 2* to dock with *Soyuz 1* was cancelled and attempts to return Komarov to Earth were made. With the spacecraft tumbling in orbit, Komarov re-entered the Earth's atmosphere on the 18th orbit. The craft's main parachute failed to deploy properly and *Soyuz 1* plummeted to Earth, catching fire on impact. Komarov was killed instantly. The accident delayed crewed *Soyuz* flights for 17 months.

13 April 1970 *Apollo 13* A routine flight to the Moon to complete the third crewed land-ing was dramatically interrupted by an explosion in a fuel cell oxygen tank in the service module. With power dwindling from the command module, the crew – Jim Lovell, Jack Swigert, and Fred Haise – were extremely fortunate that they were still attached to the lunar module which provided power and propulsion to allow the spacecraft to limp back home during a dramatic few days watched by an anxious world. The astronauts just made it with their lives and had to endure a very uncomfortable mission.

30 June 1971 *Soyuz 11* Having completed a record-breaking 23 days in space, most of it aboard the USSR's first space station, *Salyut 1*, Georgi Dobrovolsky, Vladimir Volkov, and Viktor Patsayev were killed in space just before re-entry when the cabin of *Soyuz 11* sprang a leak (causing depressurization and loss of oxygen). The cosmonauts were not equipped with spacesuits, which could have saved them. The craft made an automatic re-entry and landing and the crew was found dead inside.

5 April 1975 *Soyuz 18-1* A long-duration visit to the *Salyut 4* space station was on the schedule for cosmonauts Vasili Lazarev and Oleg Makarov as they lifted off aboard their *Soyuz* spacecraft atop a booster of the same name. The second stage failed to separate properly from the first stage booster section and the vehicle went off course. A computer-controlled emergency landing was made close to the border with China after a flight lasting 21 minutes 27 seconds. It could have been worse; a parachute line that snarled on a branch of a tree saved the capsule from plunging over a ravine.

27 September 1983 *Soyuz T10-1* Cosmonauts Vladimir Titov and Gennady Strekalov were on board their spacecraft awaiting launch to *Salyut 7*, for a long duration shift aboard the *Salyut* space station, when the *Soyuz* launcher caught fire before ignition of the rocket engines. Moments before the rocket exploded, the *Soyuz* craft's emergency escape rockets fired, hauling the spacecraft away towards a safe landing far from the blazing launch pad. During the five-minute abort flight, Titov and Strekalov endured a record 20g-plus acceleration force.

28 January 1986 *Challenger STS-51L* The 25th space shuttle mission was launched from Pad 39B at the Kennedy Space Center, carrying six astronauts, Dick Scobee, Mike Smith, Judith Resnick, Ellison Onizuka, Ron McNair, and Gregory Jarvis, plus a teacher, Christa McAuliffe, who was to become the first US 'citizen' in space. The right hand solid rocket booster suffered a severe mechanical fault at lift off and 73 seconds later the shuttle broke apart and all the crew were killed instantly. The accident caused a major redesign to the solid rocket boosters and other shuttle systems and delayed the programme until September 1988.

25 June 1997 *Mir* The Russian space station *Mir* was hit by the unmanned *Progress M34* supply ship when it went out of control during a docking practice manually-controlled by cosmonauts inside the space station. The *Progress* broke one of the solar panels on the *Spektr* module of the space station and its impact depressurized the *Spektr* module. The hatch of the *Spektr* module was open and had it not been closed rapidly, the whole space station could have lost pressure and air, killing the three-person crew – Russians Vasili Tsiblyev and Alexander Lazutkin, with visiting US astronaut Michael Foale – or at least resulted in an emergency evacuation to the *Soyuz* ferry vehicle for return to Earth.

The Longest Spacewalks

(As of March 1998.)

Duration	Name(s)	Country	Mission	Spacecraft
Men				
8 hr 29 min	Pierre Thuot, Rick Hieb, Tom Akers	USA	Earth orbit	STS 49
7 hr 37 min	Eugene Cernan, Jack Schmitt	USA	Moon	Apollo 17
7 hr 16 min	Anatoli Solovyov, Alexander Balandin	Russia	Earth orbit	Soyuz TM9
5 hr 57 min	Jean-Loup Chretien	France	Earth orbit	Soyuz TM7
1 hr 24 min	Ken Mattingly	USA	Transfer orbit around Earth	Apollo 16
1 hr 22 min	Bruce McCandless	USA	Earth orbit (independent spacewalk using untethered Manned Manoeuvring Unit, MMU)	STS 41B
Women				
7 hr 49 min	Kathryn Thornton	USA	Earth orbit	STS 49
3 hr 55 min	Svetlana Savitskaya	Russia	Earth orbit	Soyuz T12

The Most Experienced Space Travellers

(As of March 1998.)

Duration (days in space)	Name	Country	Number of flights
Men			
678	Valeri Poliakov	USSR/Russia/CIS	2
179	Thomas Reiter	Germany	1
170	Michael Foale	USA (born in the UK)	4
Women			
223	Shannon Lucid	USA	5
169	Yelena Kondakova	USSR/Russia/CIS	1
15	Claudie Andre-Deshays	France	1

The Most Spaceflights

(As of March 1998.)

Number of flights	Name	Country
Men		
6	John Young, Story Musgrave	USA
5	Vladimir Dzhanibekov	USSR/Russia/CIS
	Anatoli Solovyov	USSR/Russia/CIS
	Gennady Strekalov	USSR/Russia/CIS
3	Ulf Merbold	Germany
	Claude Nicollier	Switzerland
	Jean-Loup Chretien	France
Women		
5	Shannon Lucid	USA
	Bonnie Dunbar	USA
2	Svetlana Savitskaya	USSR/Russia/CIS
	Yelena Kondakova	USSR/Russia/CIS

The Longest Spaceflights

(As of March 1998.)

Duration (days)	Name	Country	Spacecraft
Men			
437	Valeri Poliakov	USSR/Russia/CIS	Soyuz TM18/Mir 1/TM20
179	Thomas Reiter	Germany	Soyuz TM22/Mir 1
144	Michael Foale	USA (born in UK)	STS 84/Mir 1/STS 86
Women			
188	Shannon Lucid	USA	STS 76/Mir 1/STS 79
169	Yelena Kondakova	USSR/Russia/CIS	Soyuz TM20
15	Claudie Andre-Deshays	France	Soyuz TM24/23

Selected Forthcoming Missions of the European Space Agency

Proposed date	Mission	Remarks
December 1999	XMM	X-ray multi-mirror mission, an ESA satellite for observations at X-ray wavelengths
April 2001	Integral	international gamma-ray laboratory, an ESA satellite for observations at gamma-ray wavelengths
2002	Columbus	pressurized laboratory 6.7 m/22 ft long and 4.5 m/15 ft in diameter, to be launched by the Space Shuttle
January 2003	*Rosetta*	ESA space probe to rendezvous with comet Wirtanen in 2011; *Rosetta* will release two landers which will sample the comet's nucleus
2003	Mars Express	Mars orbiter that will land craft to analyse the surface
end 2005	First/Planck	far infrared and submillimetric space telescope and cosmic ray observatory combined into one mission

Highlights of Proposed US Space Missions

Date	Spacecraft	Remarks
1998		
September	STS 88	first US assembly flight for the International Space Station to join equipment to a Russian module scheduled to be launched in August
December	STS 93	Shuttle will deploy NASA's next great space observatory, after the Hubble Space Telescope, called the X-Ray Astrophysics Facility
December	*Mars Surveyor Lander*	next series of NASA's assault on the planet Mars will be a new lander to touch down near one of the poles of Mars and will sample and make simple analysis of the soil; it will be launched on a Delta
1999		
January	*Mars Surveyor Orbiter*	another Delta launch; this soft-lander will touch down near one of the poles of Mars and will sample and make a simple analysis of the soil
February	*Stardust*	first attempt to fly a mission to return to Earth with samples of interplanetary dust and material from a comet; it will be launched on a Delta
May	STS 98	fifth Shuttle mission to assemble the International Space Station; carries the US laboratory module
August	STS 100	100th Shuttle flight since April 1981 will be the ninth mission to assemble the International Space Station, construction of which will be completed in 2002
December	STS 103	third mission to service and add new instruments to the Hubble Space Telescope

Space Agencies

Commonwealth of Independent States Some of the countries of the former USSR, particularly Russia, continue to have very active space programmes. Besides Russia, Kazakhstan and the Ukraine are the countries with the most active involvement in space activities. The Russian Space Agency (RKA) was established in 1992. (**Russian Space Agency,** Shchepkin Street 42, 129857 Moscow; phone: +7 095 971 9176; fax: +7 095 975 6936)

Europe Space research and technology in Europe are organized by the European Space Agency (ESA), whose participant countries are Austria, Belgium, Denmark, France, Germany, Ireland, Italy, the Netherlands, Norway, Spain, Sweden, Switzerland, and the UK. It was founded in 1975, with headquarters in Paris. (**European Space Agency,** 8-10 rue Mario-Nikis, 75015 Paris; phone: +33 1 42 73 76 54; fax: +33 1 42 73 75 60)

France France established the French space agency Centre National d'Etudes Spatiales (CNES) in 1961. CNES is responsible for preparing and proposing the long-term objectives of French space activity and for managing the space programmes (both national and international). The government commissioner for CNES is appointed by the Ministry for Research and Space, the authority to which

CNES reports. Military programmes are coordinated by the Délégation Générale à l'Armament (DGA) and, more particularly, by the Direction des Missiles et de l'Espace (DME). (**Centre National d'Etudes Spatiales,** 2 place Maurice Quentin, 75039 Paris; phone: +33 1 45 08 75 00; fax: +33 1 45 08 76 76)

Germany Since 1989 German space activities have been coordinated by the Federal Cabinet Committee on Space, chaired by the chancellor. The German space agency, Deutsche Argentur für Raumfahrtangelegenheiten (DARA), was also created in 1989 and concentrates on management tasks related to space technological research and represents Germany on an international level. DARA has represented Germany at ESA since 1989. (**Deutsche Argentur für Raumfahrtangelegenheiten,** Königswinterer Strasse 522-524, 5300 Bonn 3; phone: +49 228 447 0; fax: +49 228 447 700)

Ireland, Republic of Ireland's space activities are coordinated by the Department of Industry and Energy (Direction for Scientific and Technological Affairs). Since 1993 the Forbairt Science and Technology Directorate has been responsible for the formulation of Ireland's space activities, which are focused on the participation in the European Space Agency. (**Forbairt Science and Technology Directorate,** Glasnevin, Dublin 9; phone: +353 1 808 2000; fax: +353 1 808 2587)

Italy The Italian space agency, Agenzia Spaziale Italiana (ASI) was created in 1988. Italian space activities are approved by the International Committee for Economic Planning (CIPE) and coordinated by the Ministry for Scientific and Technological Research (MRST). (**Agenzia Spaziale Italiana,** Via di Villa Patrizi 13, 00161 Rome; phone: +39 6 85 679; fax: +39 6 44 04 212)

UK Funding and implementation of space programmes are ensured by several ministries and institutions, including the Department of Trade and Industry (DTI) and the Ministry of Defence (MOD), and coordinated by the British National Space Centre (BNSC) created in 1985. (**British National Space Centre,** Dean Bradley House, 52 Horseferry Road, London SW1P 2AG; phone: 0171 276 2688; fax: 0171 276 2377)

USA The National Aeronautics and Space Administration (NASA) was established in 1958. It is constitutionally responsible for civil and peaceful activities alone, all military space programmes coming under the aegis of the Department of Defense (DOD). NASA Headquarters exercises management over the Space Flight Centers, Research Centers and other installations that constitute NASA. (**National Aeronautics and Space Administration,** Headquarters, Washington, DC 20546; phone: +1 202 358-0000; fax: +1 202 358-0037)

Computing and Telecommunications

Some Internet Terms

acceptable use set of rules enforced by a service provider or backbone network restricting the use to which their facilities may be put

access provider another term for Internet Service Provider

ack radio-derived term for 'acknowledge', used on the Internet as a brief way of indicating agreement with or receipt of a message or instruction

alt hierarchy 'alternative' set of newsgroups on USENET, set up so that anyone can start a newsgroup on any topic

anonymous remailer service that allows Internet users to post to USENET and send e-mail without revealing their true identity or e-mail address

Archie software tool for locating information on the Internet

bang path list of routing that appears in the header of a message sent across the Internet, showing how it travelled from the sender to its destination

Big Seven hierarchies original seven hierarchies of newsgroups on USENET. They are: **comp.** – computing; **misc.** – miscellaneous; **news.** – newsgroups; **rec.** – recreation; **sci.** – science; **soc.** – social issues; and **talk.** – debate

blocking software any of various software programs that work on the World Wide Web to block access to categories of information considered offensive or dangerous

blue-ribbon campaign campaign for free speech launched to protest against moves towards censorship on the Internet

'bot (short for robot) automated piece of software that performs specific tasks on the Internet. 'Bots are commonly found on multi-user dungeons (MUDs) and other multi-user role-playing game sites, where they maintain a constant level of activity even when few human users are logged on

bozo filter facility to eliminate messages from irritating users

browser any program that allows the user to search for and view data; Web browsers allow access to the World Wide Web

bulletin board centre for the electronic storage of messages; bulletin board systems are usually dedicated to specific interest groups, and may carry public and private messages, notices, and programs

cancelbot automated software program that cancels messages on USENET; Cancelbot is activated by the CancelMoose, an anonymous individual who monitors newsgroups for complaints about spamming

crawler automated indexing software that scours the Web for new or updated sites

crossposting practice of sending a message to more than one newsgroup on USENET

cybersex online sexual fantasy spun by two or more participants via live, online chat

cyberspace the imaginary, interactive 'worlds' created by networked computers; often used interchangeably with 'virtual world'

Telecommunications: Chronology

1794	Claude Chappe in France built a long-distance signalling system using semaphore.
1839	Charles Wheatstone and William Cooke devised an electric telegraph in England.
1843	Samuel Morse transmitted the first message along a telegraph line in the USA, using his Morse code of signals – short (dots) and long (dashes).
1858	The first transatlantic telegraph cable was laid.
1876	Alexander Graham Bell invented the telephone.
1877	Thomas Edison invented the carbon transmitter for the telephone.
1878	The first telephone exchange was opened at New Haven, Connecticut.
1884	The first long-distance telephone line was installed, between Boston and New York.
1891	A telephone cable was laid between England and France.
1892	The first automatic telephone exchange was opened, at La Porte, Indiana.
1894	Guglielmo Marconi pioneered wireless telegraphy in Italy, later moving to England.
1900	Reginald Fessenden in the USA first broadcast voice by radio.
1901	Marconi transmitted the first radio signals across the Atlantic.
1904	John Ambrose Fleming invented the thermionic valve.
1907	Charles Krumm introduced the forerunner of the teleprinter.
1920	Stations in Detroit and Pittsburgh began regular radio broadcasts.
1922	The BBC began its first radio transmissions, for the London station 2LO.
1932	The Telex was introduced in the UK.
1956	The first transatlantic telephone cable was laid.
1962	Telstar pioneered transatlantic satellite communications, transmitting live TV pictures.
1966	Charles Kao in England advanced the idea of using optical fibres for telecommunications transmissions.
1969	Live TV pictures were sent from astronauts on the Moon back to Earth.
1975	Prestel, the world's first viewdata system, using the telephone lines to link a computer data bank with the TV screen, was introduced in the UK.
1977	The first optical fibre cable was installed in California.
1984	First commercial cellphone service started in Chicago, USA.
1988	International Services Digital Network (ISDN), an international system for sending signals in digital format along optical fibres and coaxial cable, was launched in Japan.
1989	The first transoceanic optical fibre cable, capable of carrying 40,000 simultaneous telephone conversations, was laid between Europe and the USA.
1991	ISDN was introduced in the UK.
1992	Videophones, made possible by advances in image compression and the development of ISDN, introduced in the UK.
1993	Electronic version of the *Guardian* newspaper, for those with impaired vision, launched in the UK. The newspaper is transmitted to the user's home and printed out in braille or spoken by a speech synthesizer.
1995	The USA's main carrier of long-distance telecommunications, AT&T, processed 160 million calls daily, an increase of 50% since 1990.
1996	Researchers in Tokyo and California used lasers to communicate with an orbiting satellite, the first time lasers had been used to provide two-way communications with space.
1996	Work began on laying the world's longest fibreoptic cable, which will follow a 17,000-mi/27,300-km route around the globe from Europe, through the Suez Canal, across the Indian Ocean, and around the Pacific.
1996	Computer scientists in Japan and the USA transmitted information along optical fibre at a rate of one trillion bits. At this rate, 300 years' worth of a daily newspaper could be transmitted in one second.
1997	There were 300 active artificial satellites in orbit around Earth, the majority of which were used for communications purposes.

cypherpunk passionate believer in the importance of free access to strong encryption on the Internet, in the interests of guarding privacy and free speech

digital city area in cyberspace, either text-based or graphical, that uses the model of a city to make it easy for visitors and residents to find specific types of information

e-zine (contraction of **electronic magazine**) periodical sent by e-mail. E-zines can be produced very cheaply as there are no production costs for design and layout, and minimal costs for distribution

FAQ (abbreviation for **frequently asked questions**) file of answers to commonly asked questions on any topic

firewall security system built to block access to a particular computer or network while still allowing some types of data to flow in and out on to the Internet

flame angry public or private electronic mail message used to express disapproval of breaches of netiquette or the voicing of an unpopular opinion

follow-up post publicly posted reply to a USENET message; unlike a personal e-mail reply, follow-up post can be read by anyone

FurryMUCK popular MUD site where the players take on the imaginary shapes and characters of furry, anthropomorphic animals

Gopher menu-based server on the Internet that indexes resources and retrieves them according to user choice via any one of several built-in methods such as FTP or Telnet. Gopher servers can also be accessed via the World Wide Web and searched via special servers called Veronicas

Gopherspace name for the knowledge base composed of all the documents indexed on all the Gophers in the world

hit request sent to a file server. Sites on the World Wide Web often measure their popularity in numbers of hits

home page opening page on a particular site on the World Wide Web

hop intermediate stage of the journey taken by a message travelling from one site to another on the Internet

HTTP (abbreviation for **Hypertext Transfer Protocol**) protocol used for communications between client (the Web browser) and server on the World Wide Web

hypermedia system that uses links to lead users to related graphics, audio, animation, or video files in the same way that hypertext systems link related pieces of text

in-line graphics images included in Web pages that are displayed automatically by Web browsers without any action required by the user

Internet Relay Chat (IRC) service that allows users connected to the Internet to chat with each other over many channels

Internet Service Provider (ISP) any company that sells dial-up access to the Internet

Jughead (acronym for **Jonzy's Universal Gopher Hierarchy Excavation and Display**) search engine enabling users of the Internet server Gopher to find keywords in Gopherspace directories

killfile file specifying material that you do not wish to see when accessing a newsgroup. By entering names, subjects or phrases into a killfile, users can filter out tedious threads, offensive subject headings, spamming, or contributions from other subscribers

link image or item of text in a World Wide Web document that acts as a route to another Web page or file on the Internet

lurk read a USENET newsgroup without making a contribution

MBONE (contraction of **multicast backbone**) layer of the Internet designed to deliver packets of multimedia data, enabling video and audio communication

MIME (acronym for **Multipurpose Internet Mail Extensions**) standard for transferring multimedia e-mail messages and World Wide Web hypertext documents over the Internet

moderator person or group of people that screens submissions to certain newsgroups and mailing lists before passing them on for wider circulation

MUD (acronym for **multi-user dungeon**) interactive multi-player game, played via the Internet or modem connection to one of the participating computers. MUD players typically have to solve puzzles, avoid traps, fight other participants, and carry out various tasks to achieve their goals

Number of Hosts on the Internet

Year	Number of hosts
1981	213
1985	1,961
1990	313,000
1991	535,000
1992	992,000
1993	1,776,000
1994	3,212,000
1995	6,642,000
1996	12,881,000

Source: Key Note

Categories of Hosts on the Internet

1996

Category	Hosts
Commercial	3,323,647
Educational	2,114,851
Networks	1,232,902
Government	361,065
Organizations	327,148
International organizations	1,930
Other	5,519,156
Total	**12,880,699**
% of which UK	4.5

Source: Key Note

Acronyms and Abbreviations in Common Use Online

Abbreviation	Meaning	Abbreviation	Meaning
AFAICR	As Far As I Can Recall	OIC	Oh I See
AFAICT	As Far As I Can Tell	OLR	Off Line Reader
AIUI	As I Understand It	OTOH	On The Other Hand
ATM	At The Moment	OTT	Over The Top
BTDT	Been There Done That	OTTH	On The Third Hand
BTW	By The Way	OVSN	Out Very Soon Now
DQM	Don't Quote Me	PIM	Personal Information Manager
DWIM	Do What I Mean	PMFJI	Pardon Me For Jumping In
FAQ	Frequently Asked Question	PMJI	Pardon Me Jumping In
FOAF	Friend Of A Friend	POV	Point Of View
FOC	Free Of Charge	ROTFL	Rolling On The Floor Laughing
FOCL	Falls Off Chair Laughing	RSN	Real Soon Now
FUD	Fear, Uncertainty, and Doubt	SO	Significant Other
FWIW	For What It's Worth	SOTA	State Of The Art
FYI	For Your Information	TIA	Thanks In Anticipation
IIRC	If I Recall/Remember Correctly	TIC	Tongue In Cheek
IKWYM	I Know What You Mean	TLA	Three Letter Abbreviation/Acronym
IMO	In My Opinion		
IOW	In Other Words	TPTB	The Powers That Be
ISTM	It Seems To Me	TTBOMK	To The Best of My Knowledge
ISTR	I Seem To Recall/Remember	TTFN	Ta Ta For Now
IYKWIM	If You Know What I Mean	TTYL	Talk To You Later
IYSWIM	If You See What I Mean	TYVM	Thank You Very Much
LCW	Loud, Confident, and Wrong	UKP	United Kingdom Pounds (sterling)
LOL	Lots Of Luck/Laughing Out Loud	WRT	With Respect To
NAFAIK	Not As Far As I Know	WYSIWYG	What You See Is What You Get
NALOPKT	Not A Lot Of People Know That	YHM	You Have Mail
NIMBY	Not In My Back Yard	YKWIM	You Know What I Mean

MUSE (abbreviation for **multi-user shared environment**) type of MUD

MUSH (acronym for **multi-user shared hallucination**) a MUD (multi-user dungeon) that can be altered by the players

netiquette behaviour guidelines evolved by users of the Internet including: no messages typed in upper case (considered to be the equivalent of shouting); new users, or new members of a newsgroup, should read the frequently asked questions (FAQ) file before asking a question; and no advertising via USENET newsgroups

net police USENET readers who monitor and 'punish' postings which they find offensive or believe to be in breach of netiquette. Many newsgroups are policed by these self-appointed guardians

newbie insulting term for a new user of a USENET newsgroup

newsgroup discussion group on the Internet's USENET. Newsgroups are organized in seven broad categories: **comp.** – computers and programming; **news.** – newsgroups themselves; **rec.** – sports and hobbies; **sci.** – scientific research and ideas; **talk.** – discussion groups; **soc.** – social issues and **misc.** – everything else. In addition, there are alternative hierarchies such as the wide-ranging and anarchic **alt.** (alternative). Within these categories there is a hierarchy of subdivisions

newsreader program that gives access to USENET newsgroups, interpreting the standard commands understood by news servers in a simple, user-friendly interface

news server computer that stores USENET messages for access by users. Most Internet Service Providers (ISPs) offer a news server as part of the service

off-line browser program that downloads and copies Web pages onto a computer so that they can be viewed without being connected to the Internet

off-line reader program that downloads information from newsgroups, FTP servers, or other Internet resources, storing it locally on a hard disc so that it can be read without running up a large phone bill

Pretty Good Privacy (PGP) strong encryption program that runs on personal computers and is distributed on the Internet free of charge

proxy server server on the World Wide Web that 'stands in' for another server, storing and forwarding files on behalf of a computer which might be slower or too busy to deal with the request itself

pseudonym name adopted by someone on the Internet, especially to participate in USENET or discussions using IRC (Internet Relay Chat)

signature (or **.sig**) personal information appended to a message by the sender of an e-mail message or USENET posting in order to add a human touch

spamming advertising on the Internet by broadcasting to many or all newsgroups regardless of relevance

spider program that combs the Internet for new documents such as Web pages and FTP files. Spiders start their work by retrieving a document such as a Web page and then following all the links and references contained in it

surfing exploring the Internet. The term is rather misleading: the glitches, delays, and complexities of the system mean the experience is more like wading through mud

sysop (contraction of **system operator**) the operator of a bulletin board system (BBS)

trolling mischievously posting a deliberately erroneous or obtuse message to a newsgroup in order to tempt others to reply – usually in a way that makes them appear gullible, intemperate, or foolish

URL (abbreviation for **Uniform Resource Locator**) series of letters and/or numbers specifying the location of a document on the World Wide Web. Every URL consists of a domain name, a description of the document's location within the host computer, and the name of the document itself, separated by full stops and backslashes

USENET (acronym for **users' network**) the world's largest bulletin board system, which brings together people with common interests to exchange views and information. It consists of e-mail messages and articles organized into newsgroups

vertical spam on USENET, spam which consists of many, often repetitive, messages per day posted to the same newsgroup or small set of newsgroups. The effect is to drown out other, more useful, conversation in the newsgroup

wAreZ slang for pirated games or other applications that can be downloaded using FTP

Web authoring tool software for creating Web pages. The basic Web authoring tool is HTML, the source code that determines how a Web page is constructed and how it looks

Web browser client software that allows you to access the World Wide Web

Webmaster system administrator for a server on the World Wide Web

Web page hypertext document on the World Wide Web

webzine magazine published on the World Wide Web, instead of on paper

World Wide Web (WWW) hypertext system for publishing information on the Internet. World Wide Web documents ('Web pages') are text files coded using HTML to include text and graphics, stored on a special computer (a Web server) connected to the Internet. Web pages may also contain Java applets for enhanced animation, video, sound, and interactivity

COMPUTER INDUSTRY STANDARDS

BY JACK SCHOFIELD

Why Standards are Needed

In computing, standards are vital in two areas: compatibility and interoperability. Compatibility affects both hardware and software, but if two machines are 'software compatible' then they will run the same programs. Interoperability refers to the ability of two computers to work together, usually by exchanging data. For example, two incompatible computers can interoperate if they both support the same networking protocol, such as the Internet's TCP/IP. Compatibility is the basis of the computer industry, while interoperability is the basis of the World Wide Web.

The computer industry recognizes two sorts of standard, known as de jure and de facto standards. The *de jure standards* have been discussed and ratified by recognized standards bodies such as America's IEEE (Institution of Electrical and Electronics Engineers) and the ISO (International Standards Organization). The *de facto standards* are the ones that have been accepted by a compelling proportion of the marketplace. Personal computers based on Intel processors running Microsoft's MS-DOS and Windows operating systems are a de facto standard, even though the elements that make up a PC are proprietary (owned by their manufacturers) and not 'open' or based on agreed standards.

Standards are an important way of avoiding 'lock in'. A proprietary product that cannot be obtained from alternative sources 'locks' users to a particular supplier. Also, the availability of written standards means that products can be designed and tested to see whether they meet a known specification, and given a certificate or brand label if they do. Such products should then be compatible or able to interoperate with each other, though this is not always the case. (Products designed to the same specifica-tion sometimes fail to interoperate because the specification has been written too loosely, or because vendors have interpreted it differently.)

With de facto standards there are rarely any 'test suites' to ensure compatibility, and buyers have to rely on manufacturers' claims, press reports, and their own experience. An early 'test' for IBM PC-compatibility, for example, was the ability to run a game, Microsoft's *Flight Simulator*.

Drawbacks

The drawback with standards is that the computer industry develops very rapidly while standards bodies are notoriously slow-moving. Also, standards bodies often include too many options and compromises to satisfy the competing manufacturers represented on their various committees. The resulting standard may be too late, too unwieldy, or too expensive to achieve success in the marketplace, as happened with the ISO's highly-touted OSI (Open Systems Interconnection) standards for networking. Real customers will often buy a cheaper, faster, proprietary solution if it is readily available and meets their needs.

However, because manufacturers of key products can demand large sums for proprietary systems (thanks to 'lock in'), and because they sometimes go bust, the industry recognizes the value of standards. These provide a choice of products and this tends to drive down prices, which everyone likes. Also, developing an industry standard product can still be extremely profitable, and suppliers sometimes put their proprietary designs under a standards umbrella to encourage their adoption – as Microsoft has done with its object-oriented software architecture, ActiveX.

Computers Per-Household in Selected Countries

(N/A = not available.)

1995

Country	PC penetration (%)	Modem penetration (%)	
		of all households	of PC households
USA	37	20	54
Australia	32	6	18
Singapore	32	4	13
Germany	29	4	14
Sweden	27	5	17
UK	25	2	8
Canada	23	N/A	N/A
France	15	2	9
Japan	7	1	20

Source: Department of Trade and Industry

Trends in Computer Sales in the UK

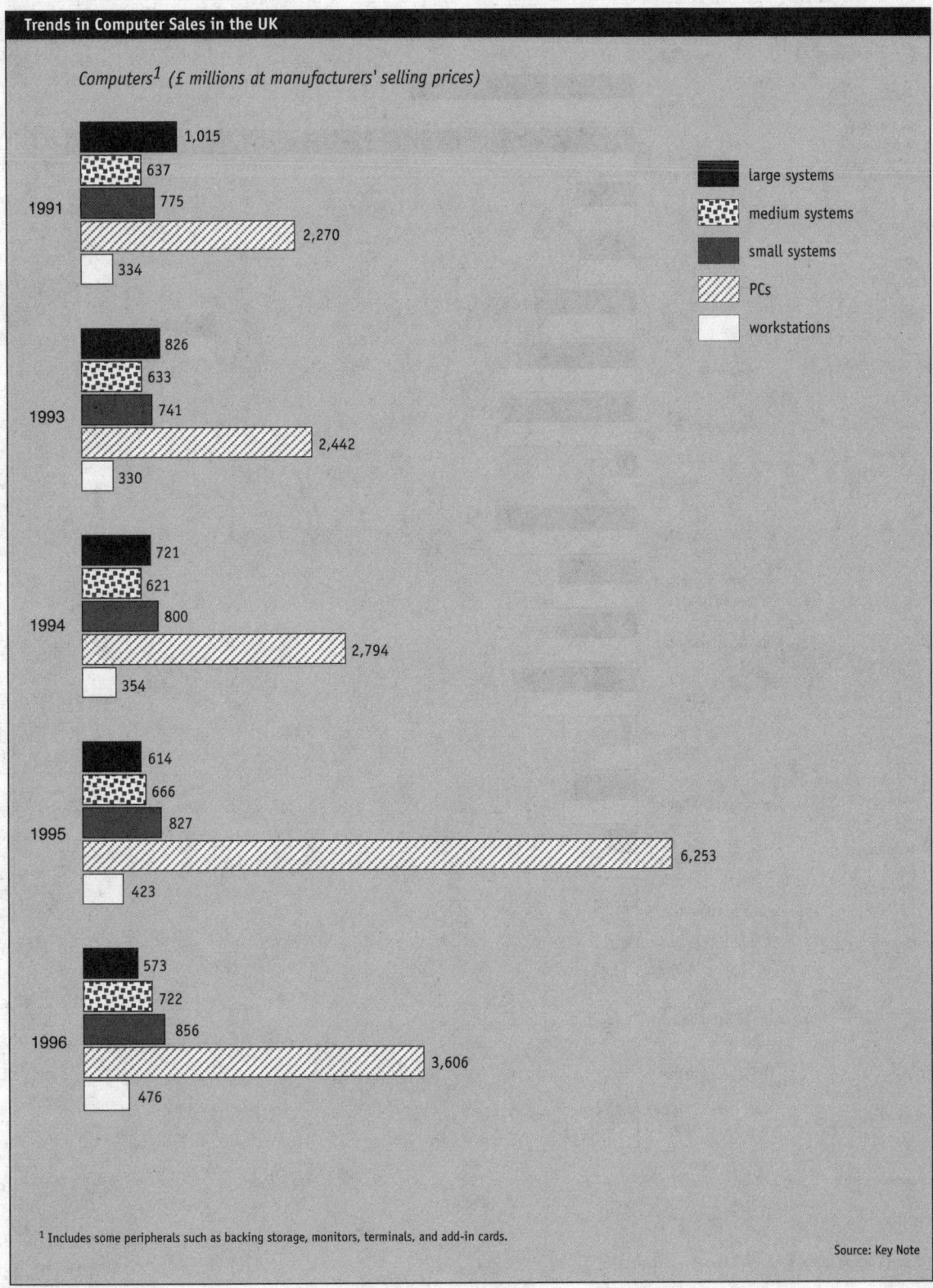

Computers[1] (£ millions at manufacturers' selling prices)

1991
- large systems: 1,015
- medium systems: 637
- small systems: 775
- PCs: 2,270
- workstations: 334

1993
- large systems: 826
- medium systems: 633
- small systems: 741
- PCs: 2,442
- workstations: 330

1994
- large systems: 721
- medium systems: 621
- small systems: 800
- PCs: 2,794
- workstations: 354

1995
- large systems: 614
- medium systems: 666
- small systems: 827
- PCs: 6,253
- workstations: 423

1996
- large systems: 573
- medium systems: 722
- small systems: 856
- PCs: 3,606
- workstations: 476

Legend:
- large systems
- medium systems
- small systems
- PCs
- workstations

[1] Includes some peripherals such as backing storage, monitors, terminals, and add-in cards.

Source: Key Note

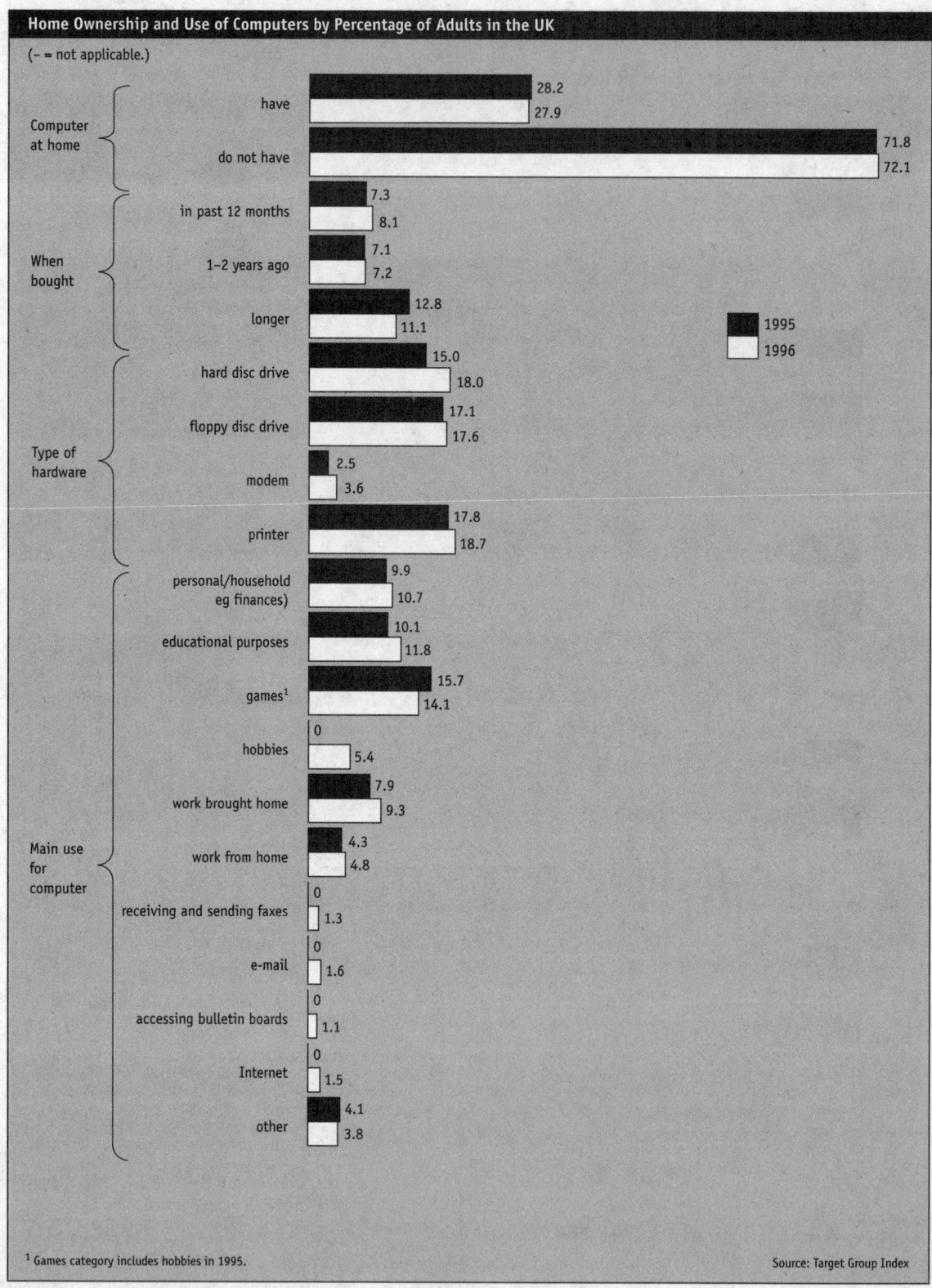

Home Ownership and Use of Computers by Percentage of Adults in the UK

(– = not applicable.)

Computer at home
- have: 28.2 (1995), 27.9 (1996)
- do not have: 71.8 (1995), 72.1 (1996)

When bought
- in past 12 months: 7.3 (1995), 8.1 (1996)
- 1–2 years ago: 7.1 (1995), 7.2 (1996)
- longer: 12.8 (1995), 11.1 (1996)

Type of hardware
- hard disc drive: 15.0 (1995), 18.0 (1996)
- floppy disc drive: 17.1 (1995), 17.6 (1996)
- modem: 2.5 (1995), 3.6 (1996)
- printer: 17.8 (1995), 18.7 (1996)

Main use for computer
- personal/household eg finances): 9.9 (1995), 10.7 (1996)
- educational purposes: 10.1 (1995), 11.8 (1996)
- games[1]: 15.7 (1995), 14.1 (1996)
- hobbies: 0 (1995), 5.4 (1996)
- work brought home: 7.9 (1995), 9.3 (1996)
- work from home: 4.3 (1995), 4.8 (1996)
- receiving and sending faxes: 0 (1995), 1.3 (1996)
- e-mail: 0 (1995), 1.6 (1996)
- accessing bulletin boards: 0 (1995), 1.1 (1996)
- Internet: 0 (1995), 1.5 (1996)
- other: 4.1 (1995), 3.8 (1996)

■ 1995
□ 1996

[1] Games category includes hobbies in 1995.

Source: Target Group Index

Top Suppliers of Desktop Computers in the UK

Desktop computers include PCs and workstations.

1995

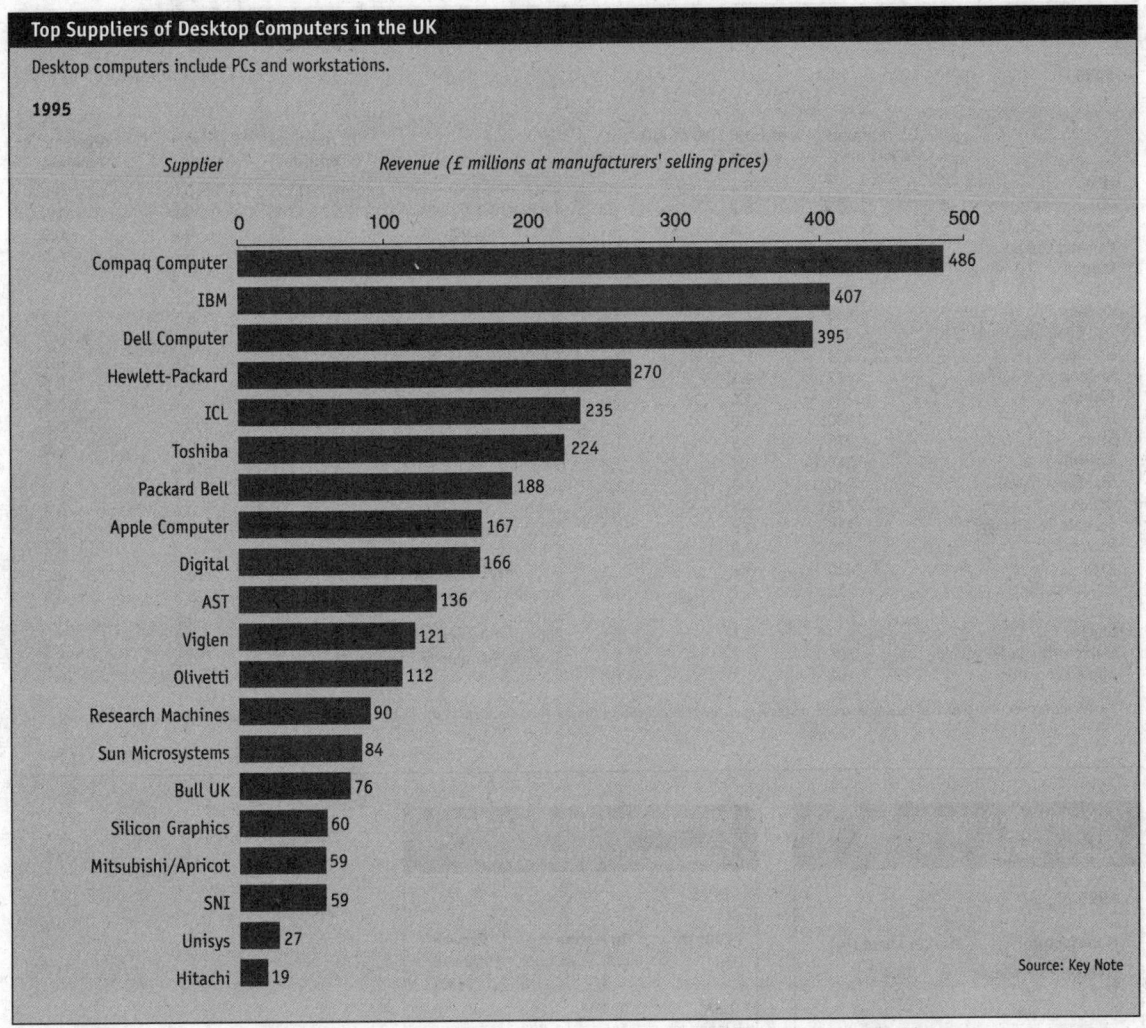

Supplier   *Revenue (£ millions at manufacturers' selling prices)*

Supplier	Revenue
Compaq Computer	486
IBM	407
Dell Computer	395
Hewlett-Packard	270
ICL	235
Toshiba	224
Packard Bell	188
Apple Computer	167
Digital	166
AST	136
Viglen	121
Olivetti	112
Research Machines	90
Sun Microsystems	84
Bull UK	76
Silicon Graphics	60
Mitsubishi/Apricot	59
SNI	59
Unisys	27
Hitachi	19

Source: Key Note

CD-ROM and Multimedia CD Publishers by Major Countries of Origin

(– = not applicable. Percentages may not add to 100 due to rounding.)

Country/ territory	1994		1995		1996	
	Number of publishers	%	Number of publishers	%	Number of publishers	%
USA	554	45	863	46	1,326	49
UK	206	17	321	17	465	17
Germany	102	8	173	9	201	7
France	80	7	96	5	175	7
Japan	55	4	84	5	124	5
Benelux	80	7	89	5	107	4
Canada	44	4	74	4	95	4
Italy	44	4	53	3	62	2
Australia	29	2	42	2	58	2
Switzerland	16	1	36	2	39	1
Spain	19	2	25	1	38	1
Total	1,229	–	1,856	–	2,690	–

Source: TFPL Multimedia

Top Computer Companies by UK Market Share

1995

	UK revenues (£ millions)	% of total market	% of relevant[1] market		UK revenues (£ millions)	% of total market	% of relevant[1] market
IBM	1,869	6.4	9.6	Cisco	193	0.6	0.9
ICL	1,520	5.2	7.8	Packard Bell	188	0.6	1.0
Hewlett-Packard	1,000	3.4	5.1	British Telecom	180	0.6	0.9
Compaq Computer	728	2.5	3.7	Canon	170	0.6	0.9
Digital	616	2.1	3.2	Logica	163	0.6	0.8
EDS	525	1.8	2.7	Misys PLC	159	0.5	0.8
Reuters	435	1.5	2.2	AST	136	0.5	0.7
Dell Computer	395	1.4	2.0	Delphi	127	0.4	0.7
Bull UK	373	1.3	1.9	Bay Networks	127	0.4	0.7
Andersen Consulting	322	1.1	1.6	Quantum	125	0.4	0.6
Toshiba	296	1.0	1.5	Viglen	121	0.4	0.6
Olivetti	280	1.0	1.4	Hitachi	121	0.4	0.6
Sema	275	0.9	1.4	Sun Microsystems	120	0.4	0.6
Hoskyns	246	0.8	1.3	Sequent	115	0.4	0.6
GEC-Marconi S31	240	0.8	1.2	Amdahl	115	0.4	0.6
Unisys	239	0.8	1.2	Parity	112	0.4	0.6
Seagate Technology	235	0.8	1.2	Silicon Graphics/Cray Research	111	0.4	0.6
Microsoft	230	0.8	1.2	Tandem	110	0.4	0.6
AT&T	210	0.7	1.1	McDonnal Information Systems	105	0.4	0.5
CSC Consulting	210	0.7	1.1	Mitsubishi/Apricot	100	0.3	0.5
3Com	209	0.7	1.0	Intel	95	0.3	0.5
Oracle	208	0.7	1.1	Computer Associates	92	0.3	0.5
Siemens-Nixdorf/Pyramid	204	0.7	1.0	Storage Technology	90	0.3	0.5
Apple Computer	198	0.7	1.0				

[1] Relevant market = total market less expenditure on personnel and telecommunications charges (ie share of the market in which the above companies operate effectively).

Source: Key Note

Top Computer Companies by PC Sales in the UK

1995

Manufacturer	Market share (%)
Compaq Computer	14.4
IBM	10.4
Dell Computer	7.4
Apple Computer	5.8
Packard Bell/Zenith	5.1
Toshiba	4.8
AST	3.7
Digital	2.8
ICL	2.7
Other	42.9
Total	**100.0**

Source: *Computer Weekly*

Estimated Investment in IT Per Employee in Selected Countries

1996

Country	Investment $	Investment £	Growth 1992–96 (%)
USA	2,021	1,296	8
Japan	1,565	1,003	4
Sweden	1,521	975	7
France	1,243	797	3
UK	1,075	689	6
Germany	1,056	677	4

Source: Department of Trade and Industry

Computing: Chronology

1614	John Napier invented logarithms.
1615	William Oughtred invented the slide rule.
1623	Wilhelm Schickard (1592–1635) invented the mechanical calculating machine.
1645	Blaise Pascal produced a calculator.
1672–74	Gottfried Leibniz built his first calculator, the Stepped Reckoner.
1801	Joseph-Marie Jacquard developed an automatic loom controlled by punch cards.
1820	The first mass-produced calculator, the Arithometer, was developed by Charles Thomas de Colmar (1785–1870).
1822	Charles Babbage completed his first model for the difference engine.
1830s	Babbage created the first design for the analytical engine.
1890	Herman Hollerith developed the punched-card ruler for the US census.
1936	Alan Turing published the mathematical theory of computing.
1938	Konrad Zuse constructed the first binary calculator, using Boolean algebra.
1939	US mathematician and physicist J V Atanasoff (1903–1995) became the first to use electronic means for mechanizing arithmetical operations.
1943	The Colossus electronic code-breaker was developed at Bletchley Park, England. The Harvard University Mark I or Automatic Sequence Controlled Calculator (partly financed by IBM) became the first program-controlled calculator.
1946	ENIAC (acronym for electronic numerator, integrator, analyser, and computer), the first general purpose, fully electronic digital computer, was completed at the University of Pennsylvania, USA.
1948	Manchester University (England) Mark I, the first stored-program computer, was completed. William Shockley of Bell Laboratories invented the transistor.
1951	Launch of Ferranti Mark I, the first commercially produced computer. Whirlwind, the first real-time computer, was built for the US air-defence system. Grace Murray Hopper of Remington Rand invented the compiler computer program.
1952	EDVAC (acronym for electronic discrete variable computer) was completed at the Institute for Advanced Study, Princeton, USA (by John Von Neumann and others).
1953	Magnetic core memory was developed.
1958	The first integrated circuit was constructed.
1963	The first minicomputer was built by Digital Equipment (DEC). The first electronic calculator was built by Bell Punch Company.
1964	Launch of IBM System/360, the first compatible family of computers. John Kemeny and Thomas Kurtz of Dartmouth College invented BASIC (Beginner's All-purpose Symbolic Instruction Code), a computer language similar to FORTRAN.
1965	The first supercomputer, the Control Data CD6600, was developed.
1971	The first microprocessor, the Intel 4004, was announced.
1974	CLIP–4, the first computer with a parallel architecture, was developed by John Backus at IBM.
1975	Altair 8800, the first personal computer (PC), or microcomputer, was launched.
1981	The Xerox Star system, the first WIMP system (acronym for windows, icons, menus, and pointing devices), was developed. IBM launched the IBM PC.
1984	Apple launched the Macintosh computer.
1985	The Inmos T414 transputer, the first 'off-the-shelf' microprocessor for building parallel computers, was announced.
1988	The first optical microprocessor, which uses light instead of electricity, was developed.
1989	Wafer-scale silicon memory chips, able to store 200 million characters, were launched.
1990	Microsoft released Windows 3, a popular windowing environment for PCs.
1992	Philips launched the CD-I (Compact-Disc Interactive) player, based on CD audio technology, to provide interactive multimedia programs for the home user.
1993	Intel launched the Pentium chip containing 3.1 million transistors and capable of 100 MIPs (millions of instructions per second). The Personal Digital Assistant (PDA), which recognizes users' handwriting, went on sale.
November 1995	Intel launched the Pentium Pro microprocessor (formerly codenamed P6).
1996	IBM's computer Deep Blue beat grand master Gary Kasparov at chess, the first time a computer has beaten a human grand master.
1997	In the USA, an attempt to bring legislation to control the Internet, intended to prevent access to sexual material, is rejected as unconstitutional.
1997	The US Justice Department ruled that Microsoft's bundling of its web browser with its operating system was unfair trading and an attempt to dominate the market. Microsoft was ordered to sell the browser separately to prevent it from building a monopoly.
1997	A computer employee in Virginia ignored malfunction warnings and caused seven of the world's nine root servers to corrupt all of the data sent to them, causing the Internet to break down. Millions of e-mail messages were returned all over the world, prompting speculation about the dangers of the over-centralization of information.
1998	Plans were announced in the USA for Internet2, a high-speed data communications backbone, that will run on a second network called Abilene. Serving the main US research universities, it will enable them to bypass congestion on the Internet and should be operational by 1999.
23 June 1998	The US Court of Appeals lifted the injunction against Microsoft, allowing it to tie its internet browser to its Windows 95 operating system.

ASCII Codes

Character	Binary code	Character	Binary code	Character	Binary code	Character	Binary code
A	1000001	H	1001000	O	1001111	V	1010110
B	1000010	I	1001001	P	1010000	W	1010111
C	1000011	J	1001010	Q	1010001	X	1011000
D	1000100	K	1001011	R	1010010	Y	1011001
E	1000101	L	1001100	S	10100111	Z	1011010
F	1000110	M	1001101	T	1010100		
G	1000111	N	1001110	U	1010101		

Structures

Remarkable Structures

Temple of Ammon (Karnak, Egypt; built c. 1524–1212 BC)

The largest religious building ever constructed, built in granite, sandstone, and limestone. The Temple's Great Court measures 8,918 sq m/10,668 sq yds.

Pyramid of Cholula (Puebla, Mexico; built 2nd–8th centuries)

Legendary Mexican tomb and the world's largest pyramid. Built of adobe (sundried brick), it is 60 m/195 ft in height and 130 sq m/1,400 sq ft at the base.

Krak des Chevaliers (Western Syria; built 11th–13th centuries; successively strengthened)

Principal stronghold of the Crusaders which never fell to force of arms. Concentric in plan, it has two circles of walls with a series of towers. Its design epitomized the concept of defence in depth. Its maximum wall thickness is 24 m/80 ft.

Forbidden City (Beijing, China; built 1406–20; mostly rebuilt)

The Chinese Imperial Palace; a huge complex of buildings. No ordinary citizen was allowed to step within its walls. Built in wood and tiles, it has 9,000 rooms.

Vatican Palace (Vatican City, Italy; built 1507–1612)

Home to the greatest concentration of Renaissance art in the world. Includes the Vatican Museum and St Peter's Basilica, the world's second largest church, designed by Bramante and Michelangelo. It covers an area of 5,054 sq m/54,402 sq ft.

Taj Mahal (Agra, India; built c. 1632–49)

Erected by Shah Jahan in memory of his favourite wife, Mahal, it is a celebrated example of Indo-Islamic architecture. Over 20,000 workers were employed to build the mausoleum. The entire complex took 22 years to complete and measures 580m by 305 m/1,902ft by 1,002 ft.

Crystal Palace (London, UK; built 1850–51)

Designed by Joseph Paxton, it was the world's first exhibition building constructed of glass and iron, covering 76,879 sq m/19 acres of Hyde Park. Its design was revolutionary, paving the way for modern steel-framed buildings.

La Sagrada Familia (Barcelona, Spain; built 1882–)

The world's most unorthodox cathedral. Designed by Antonio Gaudí, the unfinished cathedral is unlike any other building in style or concept. Gaudí planned for it to have a dozen tower-like spires (eight of which are complete) and a giant central dome. The cathedral is 170 m/557 ft in height and seats over 13,000 people.

Eiffel Tower (Paris, France; built 1887–89)

This distinctive tower was built to commemorate the centenary of the French Revolution. Its height of 320 m/1,050 ft made it the world's tallest building at the time. A structure of wrought-iron ribs, it weighed 9,700,229 kg/9,547 tons and was built of 18,000 components, held together with 2.5 million rivets.

Chrysler Building (New York, New York, USA; built 1926–30)

An Art Deco skyscraper and one of the most striking features of the Manhattan skyline. At 319.4 m/1,048 ft in height, it was briefly the world's tallest building, until the construction of the Empire State Building in 1931. Its sleek design is typical of the modernism of the 1920s.

Sydney Opera House (Sydney, Australia; built 1959–73)

One of the world's most distinctive buildings. It was built in pre-stressed concrete and glass; the open ends of the shells from which the roof is constructed are filled with 6,224 sq m/67,000 sq ft of specially made glass. The roof, covered with 1 million ceramic tiles, weighs 27,230,140 kg/26,800 tons.

Epcot Center (Orlando, Florida, USA; built 1966–82)

Built by Walt Disney World, it is the largest privately-financed construction project ever undertaken. The theme park covers 1,052,184 sq m/260 acres and cost $1 billion to construct.

Louisiana Superdome (New Orleans, Louisiana, USA; built 1971–75)

The world's largest indoor stadium, covered by the world's biggest dome. Built in steel and concrete, the multi-purpose building can accommodate up to 75,000 people. Its dome is 207 m/680 ft across and 83 m/273 ft high in the centre. Optimum seating arrangements for the football and baseball fields were determined by computer analysis of 200 schemes.

CN Tower (Toronto, Ontario, Canada; built 1973–76)

The world's tallest unsupported structure. A product of the television age, the tower rises 555 m/1,822 ft from its base to the tip of its lightening rod, and weighs 132,086,500 kg/130,000 tons. It was built by Canadian National Railways at a cost of $57 million.

Sultan of Brunei's Palace (26 km/16 mi southwest of Bandar, Seri Begawan, Brunei; built 1982–86)

Istana Nurul Iman, the palace of Sultan Hassanal Bolkiah, is the world's largest occupied palace. Its floor area covers 202,343 sq m/50 acres and contains 1,778 rooms. There are four thrones (an extra two to accommodate visiting royal couples) behind which is a 18 m/60 ft Islamic arch covered in 20-carat gold tiles. The banqueting hall can seat 4,000 people and is by far the largest in the world. The palace was designed by Filipino architect Leandro V Locsin.

Basilica of Our Lady of Peace (Yamoussoukro, Ivory Coast; built 1987–89)

It is the largest church in the world and was modelled on St Peter's in Rome. The basilica is 158 m/520 ft in height, 193 m/632 ft in length, and seats 7,000 people. It was built in just under three years. The church was created by President Houphouêt-Boigny as a declaration of faith. Only about 15 percent of the Ivory Coast's population is Roman Catholic.

Biosphere II (64 km/40 miles north of Tucson, Arizona, USA; built 1987–90)

The first large-scale attempt to replicate the Earth's environment and behaviour. Constructed of glass and steel, the 12,545.3 sq m/3.1 acre sealed structure contained simulations of a number of different habitats (tropical rain forest, salt marsh, desert, etc.) and representatives of nearly 4,000 species, including eight humans.

Gigaworld (Kuala Lumpur, Malaysia; approval granted September 1996)

To be built near the world's tallest office blocks, Petronas Towers, it will be the world's longest building. A 1.8 km/1.1 mi cylindrical structure, it will be built on stilts above the river Klang in Kuala Lumpur.

The Tallest Buildings in the World

(N/A = not available.)

Building/structure	City	Height m	Height ft
Inhabited Buildings			
Miglin-Beitler Tower[1]	Chicago (IL), USA	609	1,999
Chongqing Tower	Chongqing, China	460[2]	1,509[2]
Petronas Tower II[3]	Kuala Lumpur, Malaysia	452[2]	1,483[2]
Sears Tower	Chicago (IL), USA	442[2]	1,450[2]
Jin Mao Building	Shanghai, China	421	1,380
Two World Trade Centre	New York (NY), USA	415	1,362[2]
Empire State Building	New York (NY), USA	381[2]	1,250[2]
Bank of China	Hong Kong, China	368	1,209
Amoco Building	Chicago (IL), USA	346	1,136
John Hancock Centre	Chicago (IL), USA	344	1,127
Chrysler Building	New York (NY), USA	319	1,046
Nations Bank Tower	Atlanta (GA), USA	312	1,023
First Interstate World Center	Los Angeles (CA), USA	310	1,017
Stratosphere Tower	Las Vegas (NV), USA	308	1,012
Texas Commerce Tower	Houston (TX), USA	305	1,002
Allied Bank Plaza	Houston (TX), USA	302	992
Two Prudential Plaza	Chicago (IL), USA	298	978
311 South Waker Drive	Chicago (IL), USA	295	969
First Canadian Place	Toronto, Ontario, Canada	290	952
American International	New York (NY), USA	290	952
Bay/Adelaide Centre	Toronto, Ontario, Canada	288	945
One Liberty Place	Philadelphia (PA), USA	288	945
Columbia Seafirst Center	Seattle (WA), USA	287	943
40 Wall Tower	New York (NY), USA	283	927
Nations Bank Plaza	Dallas (TX), USA	281	921
Citicorp Center	New York (NY), USA	279	915
Scotia Plaza	Toronto, Ontario, Canada	275	902
One Peach Tree Center	Atlanta (GA), USA	275	902
Transco Tower	Houston (TX), USA	274	901
Society Center	Cleveland (OH), USA	271	888
Two Union Square	Seattle (WA), USA	270	886
AT&T Corporate Center	Chicago (IL), USA	270	885
Mellon Bank Center	Philadelphia (PA), USA	268	880
Nations Bank Corporate Center	Charlotte (NC), USA	267	875
900 North Michigan	Chicago (IL), USA	265	871
Canada Trust Tower	Toronto, Ontario, Canada	263	863
Water Tower Place	Chicago (IL), USA	262	859

Building/structure	City	Height m	Height ft
First Interstate Bank	Los Angeles (CA), USA	261	858
Transamerica Pyramid	San Francisco (CA), USA	260	853
G E Building, Rockefeller Center	New York (NY), USA	259	850
One First National Plaza	Chicago (IL), USA	259	851
Two Liberty Place	Philadelphia (PA), USA	258	845
USX Towers	Pittsburgh (PA), USA	256	841
One Atlantic Center	Atlanta (GA), USA	251	825
Cityspire	New York (NY), USA	248	814
One Chase Manhattan	New York (NY), USA	248	813
Metlife Building	New York (NY), USA	246	808
John Hancock Tower	Boston (MA), USA	244	800
Tallest Structures			
Warszawa Radio Maszt[4]	Konstantynów, Poland	646	2,120
KTHI-TV Mast	Fargo (ND), USA	629	2,063
CN Tower	Toronto, Ontario, Canada	555	1,822

[1] Planned; this will become the tallest inhabited building when completed.
[2] Excluding TV antennas.
[3] Tallest tower in building listed.
[4] Collapsed during renovation, August 1991.

Photo Disc Ltd.

The World Trade Center, New York

The Longest Bridges by Span in the World

Bridge	Location	Date built/opened	Length m	ft
Suspension Spans				
Akashi–Kaikyo	Honshu–Awaji Islands, Japan	1998	1,990	6,529
Store Baelt	Zealand–Funen, Denmark	1998	1,624	5,328
Humber Bridge	Kingston-upon-Hull, UK	1973–81	1,410	4,626
Verrazono Narrows	Brooklyn–Staten Island, New York Harbor (NY), USA	1959–64	1,298	4,260
Golden Gate	San Francisco (CA), USA	1937	1,280	4,200
Mackinac Straits	Michigan (MI), USA	1957	1,158	3,800
Bosporus	Golden Horn, Istanbul, Turkey	1973	1,074	3,524
George Washington	Hudson River, New York (NY), USA	1927–31	1,067	3,500
Ponte 25 Abril (Salazar)	Tagus River, Lisbon, Portugal	1966	1,013	3,323
Firth of Forth (road)	South Queensferry, UK	1958–64	1,006	3,300
Severn Bridge	Beachley, UK	1961–66	988	3,240
Cable-Stayed Spans				
Pont de Normandie	Seine Estuary, France	1995	2,200	7,216
Skarnsundet	near Trondheim, Norway	1991	530	1,740
Cantilever Spans				
Howrah (railroad)	Hooghly River, Calcutta, India	1936–43	988	3,240
Pont de Quebec (railroad)	St Lawrence, Canada	1918	549	1,800
Ravenswood	Ravenswood (WV) USA	1981	525	1,723
Firth of Forth (rail)	South Queensferry, UK	1882–90	521	1,710
Commodore Barry	Chester (PA), USA	1974	494	1,622
Greater New Orleans	Mississippi River (LA), USA	1958	480	1,575
Steel Arch Spans				
New River Gorge	Fayetteville (WV), USA	1977	518	1,700
Bayonne (Killvan Kull)	New Jersey–Staten Island (NY), USA	1932	504	1,652
Sydney Harbour	Sydney, Australia	1923–32	503	1,500

Photo Disc Ltd.

The Golden Gate Bridge, San Francisco

Notable Railway Bridges in the World

The world's highest railway bridge (above ground) spans the Mala Rijeka Gorge near Kolasin in Yugoslavia. It consists of five steel spans on concrete piers and took 25 years to build. The table consists of other bridges that are over 100 m/328 ft above ground level. (N/A = not available.)

Bridge	Railway	Location	Date opened	Height m	ft
Mala Rijeka Viaduct	Yugoslav Railways	Kolasin on Belgrade–Bar line	1976	198	650
Vresk	Iranian State	220 km/137 mi from Bandar Shah on Caspian Sea Trans Iranian line	1938	152	500
Fades Viaduct	French National	Clermont-Ferrand–Montluçon line	1909	133	435
Khotur	Iranian State	Khotur River near Khoi	1973	131	430
Victoria Falls	Rhodesia Railways	Livingstone	1904	128	420
Pfaffenberg–Zwenberg	Austrian Federal	Mallnitz–Spittal	1971	120	394
Viaur	French National	Tanus, Rodez–Albi	1902	116	381
Garabit Viaduct	French National	Neussargues–Mallnitz	1884	112	367
Müngstner	German Federal	Mügsten, over River Wupper	1897	107	350
Rio Grande	Costa Rica	near San José	N/A	105	346
Vance Creek	Simpson Timber Co	Shelton, west of Tacoma (WA), USA	1928	105	346
Tramo Sobre	Former Buenos Aires Great Southern, Argentina	Rio Negro	N/A	104	344
Viaduct No 2	Turkish State	between Konakler and Günaykoy on Izmir–Afyonkarahisar line, 199.3 km/123.8 mi from Izmir	1900	103	338
Faux-Mau-Ti	China	Yunnan section	1910	102	335
Rio Chinipas	Chihuahua–Pacific Mexico	on Ojinago–Topolobampo line	N/A	101	330
Corte	Corsica	Corte	1894	100	328
Lindischgraben	Austrian Federal	Tauern Railway Obervellach–Penk	1977	100	328
Ten Tze	China	Yunnan section	1910	approx. 100	approx. 328

The Longest Vehicular Tunnels in the World

Tunnel	Location	Year opened	Length km	Length mi
Saint Gotthard	Switzerland	1980	16.3	10.1
Arlberg	Austria	1978	14.0	8.7
Fréjus	France–Italy	1980	12.9	8.0
Mont Blanc	France–Italy	1965	11.7	7.3
Gran Sasso	Italy	1976	10.0	6.2
Seelisberg	Switzerland	1979	9.3	5.8
Mount Ena	Japan	1976	8.5	5.3
Rokko 11	Japan	1974	6.9	4.3
San Bernardino	Switzerland	1967	6.6	4.1
Tauren	Austria	1974	6.4	4.0

The Longest Railway Tunnels in the World

Tunnel	Location	Year opened	Length km	Length mi
Seikan	Japan	1985	54	34
Channel Tunnel	UK–France	1994	50	31
Dai-Shimizu	Japan	1979	23	14
Simplon Nos 1 and 2	Switzerland–Italy	1906, 1922	19	12
Kanmon	Japan	1975	19	12
Apennine	Italy	1934	18	11
Rokko	Japan	1972	16	10
Mt MacDonald	Canada	1989	15	9
Gotthard	Switzerland	1882	14	9
Lotschberg	Switzerland	1913	14	9
Hokuriku	Japan	1962	14	9
Mont Canis (Frejus)	France–Italy	1871	13	8
Shin-Shimizu	Japan	1961	13	8
Aki	Japan	1975	13	8
Cascade	USA	1929	13	8
Flathead	USA	1970	13	8
Keijo	Japan	1970	11	7
Lierasen	Norway	1973	11	7
Santa Lucia	Italy	1977	10	6
Arlberg	Austria	1884	10	6
Moffat	USA	1928	10	6
Shimizu	Japan	1931	10	6

The Highest Dams in the World

Dam	Location	Height above lowest formation m	Height above lowest formation ft	Dam	Location	Height above lowest formation m	Height above lowest formation ft
Rogun[1]	Tajikistan	335	1,099	Ertan[1]	China	240	787
Nurek	Tajikistan	300	984	Mauvoisin	Switzerland	237	778
Grand Dixence	Switzerland	285	935	Chivor	Colombia	237	778
Inguri	Georgia	272	892	El Cajon	Honduras	234	768
Boruca[1]	Costa Rica	267	875	Chirkey	Russia	233	765
Chicoasen	Mexico	261	856	Oroville	USA	230	754
Tehri[1]	India	261	856	Bekhme[1]	Iraq	230	754
Kambaratinsk[1]	Kyrgyzstan	255	836	Bhakra	India	226	741
Kishau[1]	India	253	830	Hoover	USA	221	726
Sayano-Shushensk[1]	Russia	245	804	Contra	Switzerland	220	722
Guavio	Colombia	243	797	Mratinje	Yugoslavia	224	722
Mica	Canada	242	794				

[1] Under construction.

Source: Institute of Civil Engineers, London

The Largest Embankment Dams by Volume in the World

Dam	Location	Year completed	Volume cubic m	Volume cubic yd
Tarbela	Pakistan	1976	148,500,000	194,223,000
Fort Peck	USA	1937	96,050,000	125,624,000
Tucurui	Brazil	1984	85,200,000	111,433,000
Atatürk	Turkey	1992	85,000,000	111,172,000
Yacireta[1]	Argentina		81,000,000	105,939,000
Rogun[1]	Tajikistan		75,500,000	98,746,000
Oahe	USA	1958	70,339,000	91,996,000
Guri	Venezuela	1986	70,000,000	91,553,000
Parambikulam	India	1967	69,165,000	90,461,000
High Island West	Hong Kong	1978	67,000,000	87,629,000
Gardiner	Canada	1968	65,000,000	85,014,000
Afsluitdijk	Netherlands	1932	63,400,000	82,921,000
Mangla	Pakistan	1967	63,379,000	82,893,000
Oroville	USA	1968	59,635,000	77,997,000
San Luis	USA	1967	59,559,000	77,897,000
Nurek	Tajikistan	1980	58,000,000	75,858,000
Tanda	Pakistan	1967	57,250,000	74,877,000
Garrison	USA	1953	50,843,000	66,498,000
Cochiti	USA	1975	50,228,000	65,693,000
Ôosterschelde	Netherlands	1986	50,000,000	65,395,000

[1] Under construction.

The Largest Reservoirs by Volume in the World

Reservoir	Location	Year completed	Volume cubic m (millions)	Volume cubic yd (millions)
Owen Falls[1]	Uganda	1954	204,800	266,240
Bratsk	Russia	1964	169,000	219,700
High Aswan	Egypt	1970	162,000	210,600
Kariba	Zimbabwe/Zambia	1959	160,368	208,478
Akosombo	Ghana	1965	147,960	192,348
Daniel Johnson	Canada	1968	141,851	184,406
Guri	Venezuela	1986	135,000	175,500
Krasnoyarsk	Russia	1967	73,300	95,290
W A C Bennett	Canada	1967	70,309	91,402
Zeya	Russia	1978	68,400	88,920
Cabora Bassa	Mozambique	1974	63,000	81,900
La Grande 2 Barrage	Canada	1978	61,715	80,230
La Grande 3 Barrage	Canada	1981	60,020	78,026
Ust-Ilim	Russia	1977	59,300	77,090
Boguchany[2]	Russia		58,200	75,660
Kuibyshev	Russia	1955	58,000	75,400
Serra de Mesa[2]	Brazil		54,400	70,720
Caniapiscau Barrage K A 3	Canada	1980	53,790	69,927
Bukhtarma	Kazakhstan	1960	49,800	64,740
Atatürk	Turkey	1992	48,700	63,310

[1] This volume is not fully obtainable by the dam: the major part of it is the natural capacity of the lake. Owen Falls is not the largest man-made lake.
[2] Under construction.

Source: Institute of Civil Engineers, London

Web Sites

Allstar Network – Principles of Flight

URL: 'http://www.allstar.fiu.edu/aero/princl.htm'

Three-level guide to flight and aviation, involving images, explanations, and experiments to demonstrate the physics behind flight.

Cameras: The Technology of Photographic Imaging

URL: 'http://www.mhs.ox.ac.uk/cameras/index.htm'

The camera collection at the Museum of the History of Science, Oxford, including some very early photographs, the photographic works of Sarah A Acland, and the cameras of T E Lawrence.

Chemistry Of Carbon

URL: 'http://cwis.nyu.edu/pages/math-mol/modules/carbon/carbon1.html'

Introduction to carbon, the element at the heart of life.

Computer Museum

URL: 'http://www.net.org/'

Examines the history, development, and future of computer technology.

Constellations and Their Stars

URL: 'http://www.vol.it/mirror/constellations/'

Notes on the constellations (listed alphabetically, by month, and by popularity), plus lists of the 25 brightest starts and the 32 nearest stars, and photographs of the Milky Way.

Dictionary of Cell Biology

URL: 'http://www.mblab.gla.ac.uk/~julian/Dict.html'

Searchable database of more than 5,000 terms frequently encountered in reading modern biology literature.

E-mail: An Introduction

URL: 'http://www.webfoot.com/advice/email.top.html'

Explains e-mail to the uninitiated. The site includes information on layout, expressing gestures and intonations, and an appendix of e-mail jargon.

Evolution: Theory and History

URL: 'http://www.ucmp.berkeley.edu/history/evolution.html'

Dedicated to the study of the history and theories associated with evolution, this site explores topics on classification, taxonomy, and dinosaur discoveries.

Franklin Institute Science Museum

URL: 'http://sln.fi.edu/'

Virtual museum of science with exhibits especially designed for online presentation.

Hello Dolly

URL: 'http://whyfiles.news.wisc.edu/034clone/'

Imaginative look at the issue of cloning, presented by the *Why Files*, an online magazine on the science behind the news.

History of Space Exploration

URL: 'http://www.hawastsoc.org/solar/eng/history.htm'

Contains information on the history of rocketry, and chronologies of exploration by the USA, Russia, Japan, and Europe.

Human Genome Project Information

URL: 'http://www.ornl.gov/TechResources/Human_Genome/home.html'

US-based site devoted to this mammoth project – with news, progress reports, and a molecular genetics primer.

Internet Starter Kit

URL: 'http://206.246.131.227/resources/geninternet/iskm/iskw2/index.html'

The full text of a recent book that covers advice on getting connected and recommendations about the best shareware. It also includes some information on how to start creating Web pages yourself.

Learning Centre for Young Astronomers

URL: 'http://heasarc.gsfc.nasa.gov/docs/StarChild/StarChild.html'

Introduction to the universe for young astronomers. The presentation covers a wide range of issues with discussions of quasars, comets, meteoroids, the Milky Way, black holes, the Hubble space telescope, space wardrobes, and space probes.

Microbe Zoo

URL: 'http://commtechlab.msu.edu/sites/dlc-me/zoo/'

Colourful and interactive zoo of some of the microbes that surround us.

Mineral Gallery

URL: 'http://mineral.galleries.com/'

Collection of descriptions and images of minerals, organized by mineral name, class (sulphides, oxides, carbonates, etc.), and grouping (such as gemstones, birth stones, and fluorescent minerals).

Molecule of the Month

URL: 'http://www.bris.ac.uk/Depts/Chemistry/MOTM/motm.htm'

Pages on interesting – and sometimes hypothetical – molecules, contributed by university chemistry departments throughout the world.

Museum of Palaeontology

URL: 'http://www.ucmp.berkeley.edu/exhibit/exhibits.html'

Explore palaeontology through phylogeny, geology, and evolution.

NASA Shuttle Web

URL: 'http://shuttle.nasa.gov/reference/'

Official NASA site for all shuttle missions. There is extensive technical and non-technical information, both textual and graphic. Questions can be sent to shuttle crew members during missions.

Natural History of Genetics

URL: 'http://raven.umnh.utah.edu/'

An accessible and well designed introduction to genetics. It includes several guided projects with experiments and explanations.

Neuroscience for Kids

URL: 'http://weber.u.washington.edu/~chudler/neurok.html'

Explore the nervous system – your brain, spinal cord, nerve cells, and senses – by means of this site, designed for primary and secondary school pupils and teachers.

Nuclear Energy: Frequently Asked Questions

URL: 'http://www-formal.stanford.edu/jmc/progress/nuclear-faq.html'

Answers to the most commonly asked questions about nuclear energy. It contains many links to related pages and is a personal opinion that openly asks for comment from visitors.

Particle Adventure

URL: 'http://pdg.lbl.gov/cpep/adventure.html'

Introduction to the theory of fundamental particles and forces, called the Standard Model. It explores the experimental evidence and the reasons physicists want to go beyond this theory. In addition, it provides information on particle decay and a brief history section.

Practical Guide to Astronomy

URL: "http://www.aardvark.on.ca/space/"

Guide to astronomy, containing explanations of many aspects of the subject, including the 'Big Bang' theories of Stephen Hawking, a list of early astronomers and their key discoveries, and an in-depth look at all the main elements of our solar system.

Radioactivity in Nature

URL: "http://www.sph.umich.edu/group/
eih/UMSCHPS/natural.htm"

Detailed explanation of the different types of radiation found naturally on Earth and in its atmosphere, as well as those produced by humans.

Robotic Telescope

URL: "http://www.telescope.org:80/rti/"

Web site based around a robot-controlled telescope high on the Yorkshire Moors, from which you can request a picture of anything in the northern sky. This site contains a library of images to download and details of current academic research (and an opportunity to get involved).

Royal Greenwich Observatory

URL: "http://www.ast.cam.ac.uk/RGO/"

In addition to a history and guide for visitors to the observatory's museum, there are comprehensive details of current RGO research (no longer carried out in Greenwich).

Science Web Goes to the Movies

URL: "http://scienceweb.dao.nrc.ca/
movies/movies.html"

Explains the real-life science behind the often dubious science depicted in films and suggests experiments to try at home.

Solar System

URL: "http://www.hawastsoc.org/
solar/eng/"

Educational tour of the Solar System. It contains information and statistics about the Sun, Earth, planets, moons, asteroids, comets, and meteorites found within the Solar System.

Technology of Compact Discs

URL: "http://www.ee.washington.edu/
class/ConsElec/cd.html"

Introduction to the technology behind the compact-disc player, including music and its relation to frequency, and an explanation of the differences between analogue and digital signals.

Virtual Chemistry Lab

URL: "http://www.burningpress.org/
bphome.html"

Series of interactive chemistry experiments for A-level and university-level students hosted by this site from Oxford University.

Web Elements

URL: "http://www.shef.ac.uk/~chem/
web-elements/web-elements-home.html"

Periodic table on the Web, with 12 different categories of information available for each element – from its physical and chemical characteristics to its electronic configuration.

Welcome to the Mars Missions, Year 2000 and Beyond!

URL: "http://marsweb.jpl.nasa.gov/"

Well presented NASA site with comprehensive information on current and future missions to Mars. There are accounts of Pathfinder and Global Surveyor, and large numbers of images of the red planet.

What Is Virtual Reality?

URL: "http://www.cms.dmu.ac.uk/
~cph/VR/whatisvr.html"

Text-based introduction to VR and an information resource list.

MEDICINE AND HEALTH

The Year in Review

4 August 1997 US researchers Sidney Altman, Cecilia Guerreir-Takada, and Reza Salavati discover a gene-transfer method of disabling the genes in disease organisms which allow them to neutralize common antibiotics. This makes the bacteria vulnerable, once again, to treatment with antibiotics and combats the growing problem of bacterial drug-resistance. The biomedical company Innovir Laboratories works on developing the process to combat viruses such as those responsible for hepatitis B and C.

12 August 1997 Nebraska's Hudson Meats Ltd recalls 25 million pounds of ground beef, the biggest such recall in history, after the meat is found to be contaminated with *E. coli* bacteria.

28 August 1997 Researchers at the University of Utah report the development of a nontoxic, temperature-sensitive hydrogel (a drug-delivering sac) which can be injected into the body to deliver the required dose of a medicine at an appointed time, for a specified duration, and which is biodegradable. It will revolutionize the administration of complicated drugs such as insulin.

August 1997 US geneticist Craig Venter and colleagues publish the genome of the bacterium *Helicobacter pylori*, a bacterium that infects half the world's population and which is the leading cause of stomach ulcers. It is the sixth bacterium to have its genome published, but is clinically the most important. It has 1,603 putative genes, encoded in a single circular chromosome that is 1,667,867 nucleotide base-pairs of DNA long. Complete genomes are increasingly being published as gene-sequencing techniques improve.

18 September 1997 US geneticist Bert Vogelstein and colleagues demonstrate that the p53 gene, which is activated by the presence of carcinogens, induces cells to commit suicide by stimulating them to produce large quantities of poisonous chemicals, called 'reactive oxygen species' (ROS). The cells literally poison themselves. It is perhaps the human body's most effective way of combating cancer. Many cancers consist of cells with a malfunctioning p53 gene.

September 1997 The fen/phen fad diet ends when doctors discover that taking a mixture of the appetite suppressants fenfluramine and phentermine can cause permanent heart damage.

2 October 1997 UK scientists Moira Bruce and, independently, John Collinge and their colleagues show that the new variant form of the human brain-wasting Creutzfeldt-Jakob disease (CJD) is the same disease as bovine spongiform encephalopathy (BSE or 'mad cow disease') in cows.

November 1997 The National Health Service (NHS) Confederation in the UK reports a growing increase in the number of treatments involving physical manipulation, especially aromatherapy (massage with essential oils), and reflexology (massage of hands and feet). Physiotherapy treatments on the NHS have increased by 26% since 1995.

November 1997 The US Food and Drug Administration (FDA) approves Rituxan, the first anti-cancer monoclonal antibody made from genetically engineered mouse antibodies. The antibody binds itself to non-Hodgkin's lymphoma (a cancer of the lymph system) cancer cells and triggers the immune system to kill the cells. It has few side effects.

2 December 1997 The US Food and Drug Administration (FDA) approves the irradiation of pork, beef, and lamb following cases of contaminated hamburger meat from Nebraska.

29 December 1997 Hong Kong begins killing 1.25 million chickens – the entire population – for fear of a pandemic of 'bird flu'. To date 12 people have contracted the disease and four have died.

1997 The British Medical Association updates the Hippocratic Oath. Changes concern issues of modern medical ethics, such as abortion and treating the terminally ill.

1997 US scientists at the National Human Genome Research Institute announce the discovery of a gene that causes Parkinson's disease. The gene produces a protein called alpha synuclein. When the instructions of the gene go wrong, the protein's structure is affected and this causes the build-up of deposits on brain cells that is usually seen in Parkinson's sufferers.

7 January 1998 Doctors meeting at the World Medical Association's conference in Hamburg, Germany, call for a worldwide ban on human cloning. US President Clinton calls for legislation banning cloning the following day.

16 January 1998 The World Health Organization announces an outbreak of Rift Valley fever in northeast Kenya. Thousands are affected and more than 300 die. The outbreak is triggered by flooding and a subsequent explosion in the mosquito population.

9 February 1998 US scientist David Ho reports the discovery of the AIDS virus in a 1959 blood sample and suggests that the transfer from ape to human occurred in the late 1940s or early 1950s.

16 February 1998 'Billy', weighing 4 kg/8.8 lb, is born in Tarzana, California, 7.5 years after being conceived. It is the longest time a human embryo has been frozen and later implanted in a woman's uterus.

17 February 1998 US manufacturer Dow Corning Corp agrees to pay a total of $3 billion in compensation to around 177,000 women who claimed that their silicone breast implants, made by the company, had caused them some injury.

26 February 1998 British Health Secretary Frank Dobson announces a ban on the use of British plasma in blood products for medical procedures because of the threat of Creutzfeldt-Jakob disease, the human disease linked to the bovine 'mad cow' disease.

13 March 1998 Mary Morgan, the wife of child care expert and author of *Baby and Child Care* Benjamin Spock, makes a public plea for funds to help pay for her 94-year-old husband's health care costs, which include 24-hour nursing, special food, yoga, massage, and other therapies.

27 March 1998 The US manufacturing company Pfizer gets approval from the US Food and Drug Administration (FDA) for its pill Viagra, which can cure male impotence. It becomes the fastest-selling prescription drug in US history.

6 April 1998 A report from the US National Cancer Institute reveals that a study has shown that tamoxifen, a synthetic hormone, could prevent breast cancer, but might have serious side effects, including uterine cancer and blood clots, in women over 50.

10 April 1998 The US National Cancer Institute issues a report that claims that cigar smoking, which is on the increase, could be as harmful as cigarette smoking, increasing the risks of mouth, throat, and lung cancer.

20 April 1998 The American Society of Clinical Oncology reports that two studies show that Raloxifene, a drug used to prevent osteoporosis, might prevent breast cancer, without the risks associated with tamoxifen, another drug recently discovered to prevent the disease.

22 April 1998 Scientists at the Public Health Laboratory Service in London, report the discovery of a bacterium *Pseudonas aeruginosa* that is resistant to all known antibiotics. It causes a wide range of infections in people with impaired immune systems.

28 April 1998 UK researchers at Guy's Hospital in London, announce the development of a vaccine against *Streptococcus mutans* the bacterium that causes tooth decay. They hope it will be incorporated into toothpaste to eradicate decay.

April 1998 US doctor Judah Folkman of Children's Hospital in Boston, Massachusetts, discovers that a combination of two drugs, angiostatin and endostatin, completely eliminates cancerous tumours in mice. The National Cancer Institute plans to begin trials on humans by the end of the year.

June 1998 The European Commission recommends that the two-year-old export ban on British beef, costing Britain some £1.5 billion, be lifted. The ban was put in place after the discovery of 'mad cow' disease in British herds.

General Medical Information

First Aid

Emergency		Treatment
Allergic reactions		call an ambulance; make the casualty comfortable and carefully monitor[1]; check for a warning bracelet, syringe of adrenaline, or other medication (see also anaphylactic shock, below)
Amputation		control any blood loss by applying direct pressure and elevating the injured part (do not use a tourniquet); apply a sterile dressing; treat the casualty for shock; call an ambulance, stating that amputation is involved; if the amputated part has been recovered, wrap the severed part in kitchen foil, cling film, or a plastic bag (do not wash); once the severed part is wrapped, re-wrap this in a container filled with crushed ice (the ice must not make direct contact with the severed part); mark the package with the time of the injury, the name of the casualty, and the severed part
Anaphylactic shock		call an ambulance; check for a syringe of adrenaline or other medication; if the casualty is conscious, help him/her sit up to relieve breathing difficulties; if unconscious, open the airway, check breathing and pulse, place in the recovery position[2], be prepared to resuscitate
Angina pectoris		help the casualty sit down; reassure him/her; if the casualty has tablets for angina or a puffer aerosol, let him/her administer it, be prepared to help if necessary; if the pain persists or returns, suspect a heart attack and treat accordingly
Animal bites	superficial bites	wash the wound thoroughly with soap and warm water; pat the wound dry with gauze and cover with an adhesive dressing or a small sterile dressing; advise casualty to see a doctor in case inoculation is needed
	serious wounds	control bleeding by applying pressure and elevating the injured part; cover the wound with a sterile dressing or a clean pad bandaged in place; take or send the casualty to hospital
Asthma attack		make the casualty comfortable; let him/her use an inhaler; encourage casualty to breathe slowly; if the inhaler has no effect after 5–10 minutes, call an ambulance
Back injury		steady and support the casualty's head and neck; call an ambulance; do not move the casualty unless he/she is in danger or becomes unconscious, if the casualty is unconscious, place in the recovery position for back injury[3] or recovery position for a child[2]
Bacterial meningitis		early recognition is crucial; symptoms include: fever, vomiting or loss of appetite, headache (in babies, the sign is slight tenseness of the soft parts of the skull, or *fontanelles*), sensitivity to light, stiffness in the neck, convulsions, a change for the worse in a child who has recently had an infection, and a rash of purple blood spots ('purpuric rash'; press the side of a glass lightly against the rash: if the rash does not disappear under pressure, it is a purpuric rash; contact the doctor immediately; casualty must be taken into hospital as quickly as possible)
Bleeding		apply pressure to the wound; raise and support the injured part; dress and bandage the wound; call an ambulance if bleeding persists; treat for shock and monitor the casualty
Broken bones		steady and support the injured part; protect the injury with padding; take or send casualty to hospital; do not give anything to eat or drink
Burns	general action	cool the burn by pouring cold liquid on injury for at least ten minutes; remove any constrictions (clothing, jewellery, watches); cover burn; take or send casualty to hospital
	fires	call an ambulance; remove the casualty from danger if it is safe to do so; if clothing is on fire, 'stop, drop, wrap, and roll' casualty on the ground or lay the casualty down and douse with water
	electrical injuries	make sure that contact with the electrical source is broken; do not go within 18 m/20 yards of live high-voltage electrical sources; proceed carefully as in general action
	chemical spills	protect yourself from corrosive chemicals; do not delay starting treatment by searching for an antidote; never attempt to neutralize acid or alkali burns; try to identify the substance spilled; proceed carefully as in general action
Choking	adult	give up to five back slaps; hold the casualty from behind; give up to five abdominal thrusts; repeat sequence until obstruction clears
	child	give up to five back slaps; give up to five chest thrusts; repeat the back slaps; give up to five abdominal thrusts; call an ambulance if necessary; repeat the sequence
	baby	give up to five back slaps; check baby's mouth; give up to five chest thrusts; call an ambulance if necessary; repeat the sequence
	yourself	locate a firm, rigid, non-moveable object; rest your abdomen across it; quickly and forcefully press your weight downwards so that the object works to thrust upwards into your abdomen; repeat until the obstacle is dislodged
Convulsions	adult	support the casualty; protect the casualty; loosen his/her clothing; place casualty into the recovery position[2]; never use force to restrain the casualty; if he/she is unconscious for more than ten minutes, is having repeated fits, or it is his/her first fit, call an ambulance
	child	cool the child; protect the child from injury; sponge with tepid water; put the child into the recovery position[2]; call an ambulance

First Aid (*continued*)

Emergency		Treatment
Cramp	in the foot	help the casualty to stand with his/her weight on the front of the foot; when the first spasm has passed, massage the foot
	in the calf	straighten the casualty's knee, and draw the foot firmly and steadily upwards towards the shin; massage the muscles
	in the thigh	straighten the casualty's knee by raising the leg; bend the knee for cramp in front of the thigh; in all cases, massage the affected muscle firmly until the pain eases
Crush injuries	for a casualty crushed for less than ten minutes	attempt to release the casualty as quickly as possible; control any external bleeding, and cover any wounds; secure and support any suspected fractures; monitor for signs of shock (see section below); call an ambulance
	for a casualty crushed for more than ten minutes	do not attempt to release the casualty; call an ambulance and give clear details of the incident; comfort and reassure the casualty until help arrives; treat for shock if necessary
Drowning		get the casualty onto dry land, with minimum danger to yourself; open the airway; check breathing and pulse, and be prepared to resuscitate; treat the casualty for hypothermia; call an ambulance
Eye injury		support casualty's head; give eye dressing to casualty; take or send casualty to hospital; never touch the eye or any contact lens;; never allow the casualty to rub the eye
Fainting		lay the casualty down; raise and support the legs; ensure the casualty has plenty of fresh air; reassure him/her upon recovery; help the casualty sit up gradually; look for and treat any injury that might have been sustained through falling
Fever		make the casualty comfortable, preferably in bed with a light cover; encourage him/her to rest, give plenty of cool, bland drinks; an adult may take his/her usual medicine (do not exceed the stated dose); give a child the recommended dose of paracetamol syrup (not aspirin); call a doctor if in doubt about the casualty's condition
Foreign bodies in the skin	splinters	gently clean the area with soap and warm water; sterilize a pair of tweezers by passing them through a flame; draw out the splinter at the angle it went in; squeeze the wound to encourage a little bleeding, clean the area, and apply an adhesive dressing; if in any doubt as to whether the casualty's tetanus immunization is up to date, advise him/her to see a doctor immediately; if the splinter does not come out easily, treat as embedded foreign body, and seek medical advice
	fish hooks	when medical aid is expected, cut the fishing line as close as possible to the hook, and gently cover the area with gauze and bandage, taking care not to push the hook any further; when medical aid is not readily available, cut the barb away and carefully withdraw the hook by its eye, clean the wound, pad around it with gauze and bandage it; ensure the tetanus immunity is up to date; do not pull out a hook unless the barb is cut off (if the barb is not visible, push the hook forwards through the wound until the barb emerges from the skin, then cut the barb and proceed as above)
Frostbite		very gently remove gloves, rings, boots, or any other constrictions; warm the affected part with your hands, in your lap, or in the casualty's armpit (avoid rubbing); move, or carry, the casualty into warmth; place the affected part in warm (not hot) water; do not put affected part by direct heat, or thaw where there is a danger of refreezing; dry carefully, apply a light dressing; raise and support the limb to reduce swelling; take or send the casualty to hospital if necessary
Hanging, strangling, and throttling		quickly remove any constriction from around the casualty's neck, supporting the body if it is still hanging; lay the casualty on the floor; open the airway; check breathing and pulse; if the casualty is not breathing, be prepared to resuscitate; if he/she is breathing, place him/her in the recovery position[2]; call an ambulance in all cases
Head injury		control any bleeding; replace any displaced skin flaps if needed; secure dressing with bandage; lay casualty down; take or send casualty to hospital; if the casualty becomes unconscious, place him/her in the recovery position[2] and be ready to resuscitate if necessary; if the casualty is unconscious for more than three minutes, call an ambulance; if the bleeding does not stop, re-apply pressure on the wound and add another padded bandage on top of the first
Heart attack		make casualty comfortable, preferably in a half-sitting position; if the casualty has tablets or a puffer aerosol for angina let him/her administer it to him- or herself (assist if necessary); call an ambulance and say that you suspect a heart attack; encourage the casualty to rest; monitor and record the casualty's breathing and pulse; give casualty aspirin to be chewed slowly; do not give any fluids; if the casualty becomes unconscious, be prepared to resuscitate
Heat exhaustion		help the casualty to a cool place, lay him/her down and raise the legs; give plenty of water and follow with weak salt solution, if available (one teaspoon of salt per litre of water); if condition deteriorates, put casualty in the recovery position[2], be prepared to resuscitate and call an ambulance; ensure the casualty sees a doctor in all cases
Heatstroke		quickly remove the casualty to a cool place; remove his/her outer clothing; call an ambulance; wrap the casualty in a cold, wet sheet and keep it wet until the temperature falls to 38°C/100.4°F under the tongue or 37.5°C/99.5°F under the armpit (if no sheet is available, constantly fan the casualty or sponge with cold water); when the safe temperature has been reached, replace the wet sheet with a dry one; monitor the casualty until help arrives; if condition deteriorates, open the casualty's airway, check breathing and pulse, be prepared to resuscitate if necessary
Hyperventilation		may accompany hysteria or a panic attack; reassure the casualty; lead him/her into a quiet place; let him/her re-breathe own expired air from a paper bag; encourage the casualty to see a doctor

First Aid (*continued*)

Emergency		Treatment
Hypothermia	casualty indoors	replace any wet clothing if brought from outside; if not elderly, bathe in warm water (40°C/104°F); put the casualty in bed and cover well; give warm drinks, soup, and high-energy foods such as chocolate; do not give any alcohol; do not place direct heat sources close to the casualty; call a doctor if the casualty is elderly, or an infant, or if you have any doubts about his/her condition
	casualty outdoors	insulate the casualty with extra clothing or blankets and cover the head; take to a sheltered place; protect the casualty from the ground and the elements: put him/her in a dry sleeping bag, wrap in blankets, or survival bag, or papers; send for help but do not leave the casualty alone; give casualty warm drinks and high-energy foods; if casualty is unconscious, open the airway, check breathing, and resuscitate if necessary
Impalement		never attempt to lift the casualty off; call an ambulance, explaining the incident clearly to alert the emergency services, giving full details, so that the necessary cutting equipment can be brought to the scene; support the casualty's weight; do not give the casualty anything by mouth; constantly reassure him/her
Insect bites		if the casualty shows signs of anaphylactic shock, call an ambulance; if the sting is in the skin, pluck it out with tweezers, apply a cold compress, and advise the casualty to see a doctor if pain and swelling persists; if the sting is in the mouth, give the casualty cold water to sip or an ice cube to suck to minimize swelling, call an ambulance, and reassure the casualty
Internal bleeding		help the casualty to lie down; raise and support the legs; loosen any tight clothing; keep the casualty warm; call an ambulance; monitor and record breathing, pulse, and level of response; note the type, amount, and source of any blood loss from body orifices (if possible, keep a sample)
Marine stings		if the casualty shows signs of anaphylactic shock, call an ambulance immediately; reassure the casualty, sit him/her down, and pour a copious amount of vinegar or sea water over the injury to incapacitate stinging cells that have not yet released venom; dust a dry powder (talcum powder, meat tenderizer used in barbecue cooking) over the area, and gently brush it off; if the injuries are severe, call an ambulance
Meningitis		(see bacterial meningitis)
Nosebleeds		sit the casualty down, with the head held well forward (do not tip the head back); ask the casualty to breathe through the mouth, and to pinch the nose just below the bridge; tell the casualty not to blow the nose, sniff, cough, spit, swallow, or speak; after ten minutes, tell the casualty to release the pressure; if the bleeding has not stopped, repeat the cycle; if the nosebleed persists for more than 30 minutes, send or take the casualty to hospital
Poisoning		check airway and breathing; place casualty in the recovery position[2]; call an ambulance giving as much information as possible about the swallowed poison so that an antidote can be sought; monitor and record breathing, pulse, and level of response; never attempt to induce vomiting; if the casualty stops breathing, be prepared to resuscitate (using a face shield to protect yourself)
Resuscitation	assessing the casualty	check response; if there is no response, open airway; check breathing: if breathing is present, place the casualty in the recovery position[2]; if breathing is absent, breathe for the casualty
	the recovery position[2]	open airway and straighten limbs; bring the furthest arm from you across the casualty's chest; place his/her hand, palm outwards, against his/her cheek; using your other hand, pull up the casualty's far leg just above the knee; roll the casualty towards you until he/she is lying on his/her side; steady the casualty's body by bending the upper leg at the knee so that it is at a right angle to the body; make any adjustments necessary to ensure that the airway is open by tilting the head back[2][3]
	breathing for the casualty	remove any obvious obstruction; open airway; pinch casualty's nose; give mouth-to-mouth ventilation; if breathing returns, place the casualty in the recovery position[2]; if the pulse is present, continue with mouth-to-mouth ventilation, checking the pulse every ten breaths; if the pulse is absent, commence cardio-pulmonary resuscitation (CPR)
	cardio-pulmonary resuscitation (CPR)	if you cannot find the pulse, or there are no other signs of recovery (such as return of skin colour or any movement), begin CPR immediately; place the middle finger of your lower hand (your hand furthest from the patient's head) over the point where the lowermost ribs meet the breastbone; place your index finger above it on the breastbone; place the heel of your other hand on the breastbone, slide it down to meet your index finger; place the heel of your first hand on top of the other hand, and interlock your fingers; lean well over the casualty with your arms straight; press down vertically on the breastbone and depress it by approximately 4–5 cm/1.5–2 in; complete 15 chest compressions, aiming for about 100 per minute; give two breaths of mouth-to-mouth ventilation; continue alternating 15 chest compressions with two breaths of mouth-to-mouth ventilation[4]
Shock		lay casualty down; loosen tight clothing; prop up legs as high as possible; keep the casualty warm; call an ambulance; monitor breathing, pulse, and level of response every ten minutes; be prepared to resuscitate if necessary; do not leave the casualty alone, except to call an ambulance; do not let the casualty eat, move, smoke, or drink
Snake bites		lay the casualty down, tell him/her to remain calm and still; wash the wound and pat dry with clean swabs; call an ambulance; lightly compress the limb above the wound with a rolled-up bandage and immobilize the injury; if casualty stops breathing, be prepared to resuscitate; do not apply a tourniquet, or slash the wound with a blade, or suck out the venom

First Aid (*continued*)

Emergency		Treatment
Stroke	for an unconscious casualty	open the airway; check breathing and pulse; be prepared to resuscitate if necessary; place in the recovery position[2]; monitor and record breathing, pulse, and level of response every ten minutes; loosen any tight clothing; call an ambulance
	for a conscious casualty	lay the casualty down, with the head and shoulders slightly raised and supported; loosen any tight clothing; incline the head to one side; do not give anything by mouth; call an ambulance
Unconsciousness		assess the casualty's response; open airway, and check breathing and pulse; examine and, if necessary and possible, treat the casualty for any injury sustained; place the casualty in the recovery position[2]; call an ambulance if the casualty does not regain full consciousness within three minutes; do not leave the casualty alone, except to call an ambulance; do not give the casualty anything by mouth
Vomiting and diarrhoea		reassure the casualty while he/she is being sick; give the casualty a warm damp cloth to wash himself/herself; give the casualty plenty of bland fluids to sip slowly and often (water, still 'isotonic' drinks, or a solution of 1 teaspoonful salt and 4–5 teaspoonfuls sugar per litre of water or diluted orange juice); when appetite returns, give the casualty only bland, starchy, or sugary food for the first 24 hours; if in doubt, or if the condition persists, call a doctor

[1] Monitoring the casualty involves checking his/her breathing, pulse, and levels of response (speech, movement, and visual response).
[2] The recovery position for a baby (under one year old): cradle the baby in your arms with the head tilted downwards to prevent him/her from choking on the tongue or inhaling vomit; for child (aged 1–7): the procedure is the same as for an adult (see table).
[3] Precaution: if back or neck injury is suspected, modify the recovery position – ensure that the head and neck are supported at all times, and place the arm furthest from you over the casualty's chest, not under his/her cheek.
[4] CPR for baby (under one year old): place the tips of two fingers one finger's breadth below the nipple line of the baby; press down sharply at this point to a third of the depth of the chest; do this five times at a rate of about 100 compressions per minute; give one breath of mouth-to-mouth ventilation. Alternate five chest compressions with one ventilation for one minute before calling an ambulance, and while waiting for help. To give CPR to a child (aged 1–7), position your hands as you would for an adult but use the heel of one hand only; press down sharply to a third of the depth of the chest; do this five times at a rate of about 100 per minute; give one breath of mouth-to-mouth ventilation; alternate five chest compressions with one ventilation for one minute before calling an ambulance, and while waiting for help.

Medicine, Western: Chronology

c. 400 BC	Hippocrates recognized that disease had natural causes.
c. AD 200	Galen consolidated the work of the Alexandrian doctors.
1543	Andreas Vesalius gave the first accurate account of the human body.
1628	William Harvey discovered the circulation of the blood.
1768	John Hunter began the foundation of experimental and surgical pathology.
1785	Digitalis was used to treat heart disease; the active ingredient was isolated in 1904.
1798	Edward Jenner published his work on vaccination.
1877	Patrick Manson studied animal carriers of infectious diseases.
1882	Robert Koch isolated the bacillus responsible for tuberculosis.
1884	Edwin Klebs isolated the diphtheria bacillus.
1885	Louis Pasteur produced a vaccine against rabies.
1890	Joseph Lister demonstrated antiseptic surgery.
1895	Wilhelm Röntgen discovered X-rays.
1897	Martinus Beijerinck discovered viruses.
1899	Felix Hoffman developed aspirin; Sigmund Freud founded psychiatry.
1900	Karl Landsteiner identified the first three blood groups, later designated A, B, and O.
1910	Paul Ehrlich developed the first specific antibacterial agent, Salvarsan, a cure for syphilis.
1922	Insulin was first used to treat diabetes.
1928	Alexander Fleming discovered penicillin.
1932	Gerhard Domagk discovered the first antibacterial sulphonamide drug, Prontosil.
1937	Electro-convulsive therapy (ECT) was developed.
1940s	Lithium treatment for manic-depressive illness was developed.
1950s	Antidepressant drugs and beta-blockers for heart disease were developed. Manipulation of the molecules of synthetic chemicals became the main source of new drugs. Peter Medawar studied the body's tolerance of transplanted organs and skin grafts.
1950	Proof of a link between cigarette smoking and lung cancer was established.
1953	Francis Crick and James Watson announced the structure of DNA. Jonas Salk developed a vaccine against polio.
1958	Ian Donald pioneered diagnostic ultrasound.
1960s	A new generation of minor tranquillizers called benzodiazepines was developed.
1967	Christiaan Barnard performed the first human heart-transplant operation.
1971	Viroids, disease-causing organisms even smaller than viruses, were isolated outside the living body.
1972	The CAT scan, pioneered by Godfrey Hounsfield, was first used to image the human brain.
1975	César Milstein developed monoclonal antibodies.
1978	World's first 'test-tube baby' was born in the UK.
1980s	AIDS (acquired immunodeficiency syndrome) was first recognized in the USA. Barbara McClintock's discovery of the transposable gene was recognized.
1980	The World Health Organization reported the eradication of smallpox.
1983	The virus responsible for AIDS, now known as human immunodeficiency virus (HIV), was identified by Luc Montagnier at the Institut Pasteur, Paris; Robert Gallo at the National Cancer Institute, Maryland, USA discovered the virus independently in 1984.
1984	The first vaccine against leprosy was developed.
1987	The world's longest-surviving heart-transplant patient died in France, 18 years after his operation.
1989	Grafts of fetal brain tissue were first used to treat Parkinson's disease.
1990	Gene for maleness discovered by UK researchers.
1991	First successful use of gene therapy (to treat severe combined immune deficiency) was reported in the USA.
1993	First trials of gene therapy against cystic fibrosis took place in the USA.
1996	An Australian man, Ben Dent, was the first person to end his life by legally sanctioned euthanasia.

Transplant: Chronology

1771 Scottish surgeon John Hunter describes his experiments in the transplantation of tissues, including a human tooth into a cock's comb in *Treatise on the Natural History of Human Teeth*

1905 Corneal grafting, which may restore sight to a diseased or damaged eye, was pioneered.

1950s The kidneys were first transplanted successfully; kidney transplants were pioneered by British surgeon Roy Calne. Peter Medawar conducted vital research into the body's tolerance of transplanted organs and skin grafts.

1964 Chimpanzee kidneys were transplanted into humans in the USA, but with little success; in the UK a pig's heart valve was transplanted successfully and the operation became routine.

1967 South African surgeon Christiaan Barnard performed the first human heart transplant. The 54-year-old patient lived for 18 days.

1969 The world's first heart and lung transplant is performed at the Stanford Medical Center, California, USA.

1970 The first successful nerve transplant is achieved in West Germany.

1978 Cyclosporin, an immunosuppressive drug derived from a fungus revolutionized transplant surgery by reducing the incidence and severity of rejection of donor organs.

1982 Jarvik 7, an artificial heart made of plastic and aluminium was transplanted; the recipient lived another 112 days.

1986 British surgeons John Wallwork and Roy Calne perform the first triple transplant – heart, lung, and liver – at Papworth Hospital, Cambridge, England.

1987 The world's longest-surviving heart-transplant patient died in France, 18 years after his operation. A three-year-old girl in the USA receives a new liver, pancreas, small intestine, and parts of the stomach and colon; the first successful five-organ transplant.

1989 Grafts of fetal brain tissue were first used to treat Parkinson's disease.

1990 Nobel Prize for Medicine or Physiology was awarded to two US surgeons, Donnall Thomas and Joseph Murray, for their pioneering work on organ and tissue transplantation.

1995 The first experiments to use genetically altered animal organs in humans were given US government approval July – genetically altered pig livers were attached to the circulatory systems of patients whose livers had failed. An AIDS patient received a bone marrow transplant from a baboon but the graft failed to take.

COMPLEMENTARY THERAPY

BY PAMELA MORLEY

The term 'complementary therapy' is used to encompass any practice or system of beliefs about treatment that is not included in what is generally understood as Western scientific medicine. Science and much of Western medical practice is incompatible with many of the practices of complementary therapy, as such practices do not have a scientific basis, though this should not be seen as an obstacle to its understanding and acceptance. Practitioners of complementary therapy are seeing their role increasingly as offering something that Western scientific medicine does not, and something that adds to it without denying that scientific medicine has an essential role.

Medical intervention is restricted to qualified medical practitioners in many Western countries and a significant proportion of them use complementary therapy. Not all complementary practitioners are regulated and this has caused concern as complementary therapy grows in popularity. However, organizations concerned with the training and registration of complementary practitioners have developed at a rapid rate recently to meet the growing demands of the public for a pluralist, holistic, effective, and safe approach to health care.

Homeopathy

The roots of homeopathy lie in the work of Samuel Hahnemann, an 18th-century German physician. The brutalities of medical practice, which included purging, bleeding, and the use of poisons, were instrumental in his decision to explore other avenues in which he could use his skills. He was prompted to investigate the use of cinchona bark in the treatment of fever while he was working on a *Materia Medica*. Cinchona bark produced many of the symptoms associated with fever without inducing pyrexia. This led him to speculate that a substance that was effective against a disease would produce symptoms resembling those of that disease if it was given to a healthy person.

Homeopathy recognizes a need for balance and harmony. Disturbances in the harmony of the body due to illness can precede the appearance of symptoms as the body reacts to the illness. Symptoms of the same illness differ between individuals, and the establishment of a detailed profile of the patient and a complete symptom picture are an essential part of the diagnosis. Homeopathic remedies are intended to stimulate the resources of the body to restore its natural harmony, following Hahnemann's principle that the appropriate treatment is one that produces the same symptoms in a healthy person. Many of these principles pose a problem to the scientist, but the greatest obstacle to scientific acceptance is the observation that homeopathic remedies become more potent when subject to serial dilution and mechanical shock in the process known as 'succussion'. Theories have been developed in an attempt to explain why more dilute preparations are more powerful, but none of these have yet been proven.

Herbal Medicine

A wide range of medical practices that use unrefined and refined plant materials for treatment is encompassed by the term 'herbal medicine'. They do not necessarily have a common belief system and they range from traditional herbal medicine to many ethnic medical systems, such as Chinese and Ayurvedic medicine.

Plants were used medicinally in China, Egypt, Greece, Rome, and other ancient civilizations up to 5,000 years ago. The central position of herbalism in health care was challenged by changes in medical thinking in Renaissance Europe, and by the consequent emphasis on the management of symptoms with specific remedies by the emerging medical establishment.

Samuel Thomson, an American physician, documented much of this early herbalist knowledge in the early 19th century, and he is now credited as the founder of Western herbal medicine. He developed a theory resembling that of the four humours, in which life and health were represented by heat; illness and death by cold; motion by air; and energy or life force by fire. He believed that the fever associated with infection was a healthy sign and, unlike his contemporaries, he wanted to facilitate it rather than to suppress it. He considered that coughing, vomiting, and diarrhoea were healthy signs of the body removing toxins.

The underlying belief in herbalism is that health depends on maintaining the natural state of the body. The natural state of the body, or 'vital pulse', is represented by the rhythmic variation in tissue and cell activity, which protects, regulates, and renews the body. A herbal remedy is a preparation of the entire plant rather than an active ingredient extracted from it. The constituent components may have many different activities that restore the balance of the body, which is lost with the onset of illness. They are not specific for a particular symptom and they are thought to act by stimulating the natural defences of the body and enhancing the elimination of toxins. Attention to diet is often used as an adjunct to treatment by herbalists.

Aromatherapy

The therapeutic use of volatile oils can be traced back to the ancient civilizations of India, China, Egypt, Babylon, and Greece, and their use in medicine survived until challenged by the advent of scientific chemistry in the 17th century.

Aromatherapists believe that health depends on a balance of mental, emotional, and physical processes which is disturbed in illness. A holistic approach is taken to diagnosis and treatment. The volatile oils used in aromatherapy are complex mixtures of chemicals that occur naturally in plants. Specific disorders are treated with particular oils. They are believed to be absorbed through the skin or by inhalation before exerting their subtle effects on physical symptoms and emotional well being. The pleasant smell and application of the oils by massage can enhance the beneficial effects of aromatherapy through reduction of tension and pain, increased relaxation, and improved circulation. Aromatherapy is widely used as an adjunct to conventional care in patients who are terminally ill.

Acupuncture

Traditional Chinese medicine is based on the fundamental principle that a life force known as *qi* flows around the body in 12 channels known as meridians. The flow of *qi* is important for good health. The balance between *yin* and *yang*, qualities possessed by all things including the internal functions and processes of the body and the meridians, is also vital to health. *Yin* is cold, dark, passive, and negative; *yin* organs include the heart, spleen, kidney, and liver. *Yang* is warm, light, active, and positive; *yang* organs include the small intestine, stomach, bladder, and gall bladder. Illness occurs when either *yin* or *yang* is dominant, and treatment helps to restore their balance.

Acupuncture is one form of treatment used in traditional Chinese medicine. It involves the insertion of fine needles into the skin at particular points on the body to correct the imbalances between *yin* and *yang*. There are about 2,000 acupoints that lie on the meridians through which *qi* flows. The imbalance between *yin* and *yang* may be associated with many factors, such as stress, emotion, diet, or injury, and these are considered in conjunction with the medical history of the patient, and examination of the 12 pulses and the condition of the tongue before a diagnosis is made. The acupoints to be stimulated are then selected and needles are inserted to a depth of about 6 mm/$\frac{1}{4}$ of an inch and rotated. The direction of insertion and rotation of the needles regulates the flow of *qi* and the collection or dispersion of energy.

Acupuncture can be used to treat a wide range of acute and chronic illnesses, such as pain, anxiety, asthma, migraine, menstrual disorders, and gastrointestinal complaints. It can also be used as an aid to dieting and giving up smoking.

Osteopathy

Osteopaths perceive the function of muscles and the skeletal system to be central to a range of health problems. Osteopathy was conceived as a system of diagnosis and treatment by Andrew Taylor Still in the USA in the 19th century. He believed that a lack of balance in the mechanical functioning of the body, such as muscle groups being too tense or joints moving incorrectly, may cause illness. He developed a range of manipulative techniques to correct the imbalances and claimed therapeutic success. These include massage, passive movement, and stretching of the limbs. Despite opposition from the medical profession, osteopathy has slowly achieved success because it can produce a dramatic improvement in disorders that are difficult to treat by conventional medicine, such as chronic back pain and sciatica.

Bones of the Human Body

Bone	Number
Cranium (Skull)	
Occipital	1
Parietal: 1 pair	2
Sphenoid	1
Ethmoid	1
Inferior nasal conchae	2
Frontal: 1 pair, fused	1
Nasal: 1 pair	2
Lacrimal: 1 pair	2
Temporal: 1 pair	2
Maxilla: 1 pair, fused	1
Zygomatic: 1 pair	2
Vomer	1
Palatine: 1 pair	2
Mandible (jawbone): 1 pair, fused	1
Total	21
Ears	
Malleus (hammer)	2
Incus (anvil)	2
Stapes (stirrups)	2
Total	6
Vertebral Column (Spine)	
Cervical vertebrae	7
Thoracic vertebrae	12
Lumbar vertebrae	5
Sacral vertebrae: 5, fused to form the sacrum	1
Coccygeal vertebrae: between 3 and 5, fused to form the coccyx	1
Total	26
Ribs	
Ribs, 'true': 7 pairs	14
Ribs, 'false': 5 pairs, of which 2 pairs are floating	10
Total	24
Sternum (Breastbone)	
Manubrium	1
Sternebrae	1
Xiphisternum	1
Total	3
Throat	
Hyoid	1
Total	1
Pectoral Girdle	
Clavicle: 1 pair (collar-bone)	2
Scapula (including coracoid): 1 pair (shoulder blade)	2
Total	4

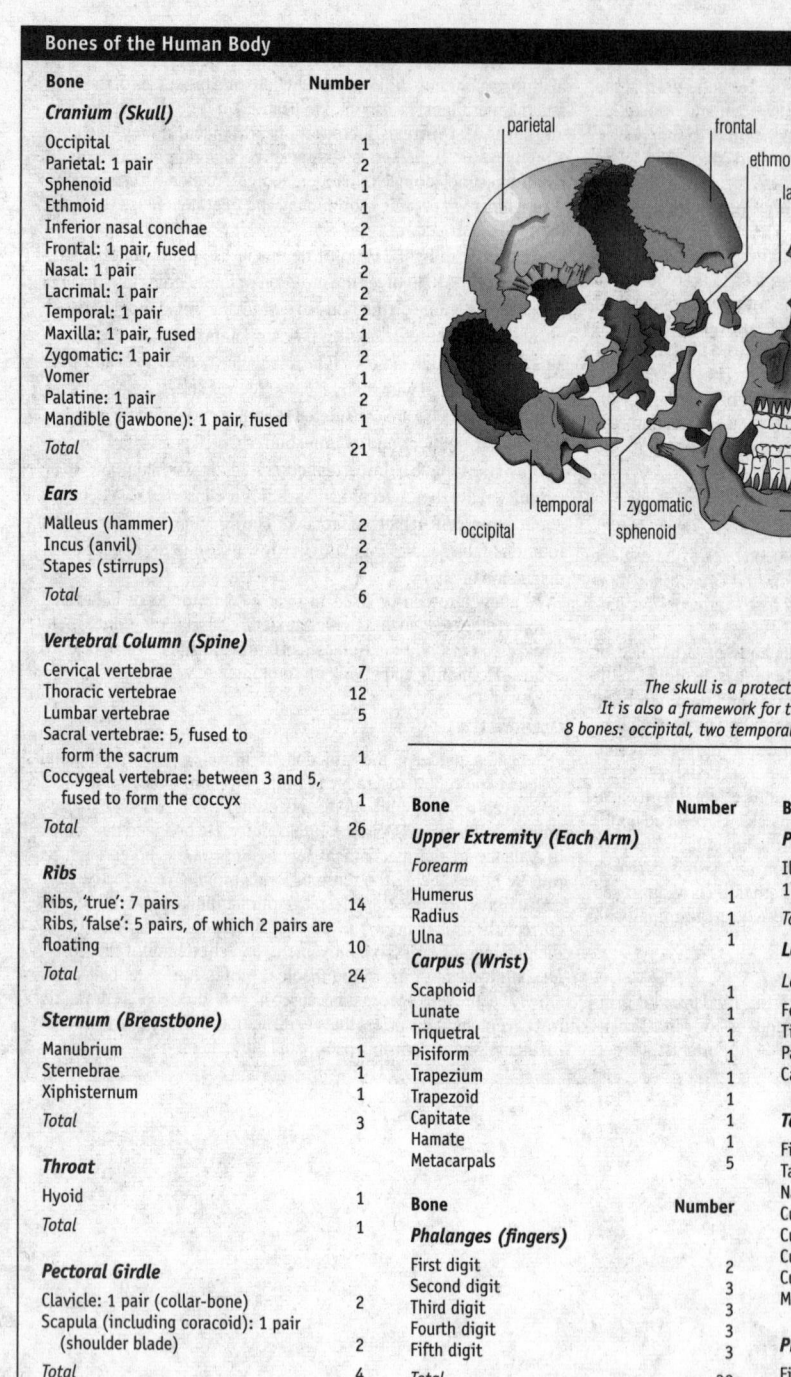

Skull

The skull is a protective box for the brain, eyes, and hearing organs. It is also a framework for the teeth and flesh of the face. The cranium has 8 bones: occipital, two temporal, two parietal, frontal, sphenoid, and ethmoid.

Bone	Number
Upper Extremity (Each Arm)	
Forearm	
Humerus	1
Radius	1
Ulna	1
Carpus (Wrist)	
Scaphoid	1
Lunate	1
Triquetral	1
Pisiform	1
Trapezium	1
Trapezoid	1
Capitate	1
Hamate	1
Metacarpals	5

Bone	Number
Phalanges (fingers)	
First digit	2
Second digit	3
Third digit	3
Fourth digit	3
Fifth digit	3
Total	30

Bone	Number
Pelvic Girdle	
Ilium, ischium, and pubis (combined): 1 pair of hip bones, innominate	2
Total	2
Lower Extremity (Each Leg)	
Leg	
Femur (thighbone)	1
Tibia (shinbone)	1
Patella (kneecap)	1
Calcaneus	1
Tarsus (Ankle)	
Fibula	1
Talus	1
Navicular	1
Cuneiform, medial	1
Cuneiform, intermediate	1
Cuneiform, lateral	1
Cuboid	1
Metatarsals (foot bones)	5
Phalanges (Toes)	
First digit	2
Second digit	3
Third digit	3
Fourth digit	3
Fifth digit	3
Total	30
TOTAL	207

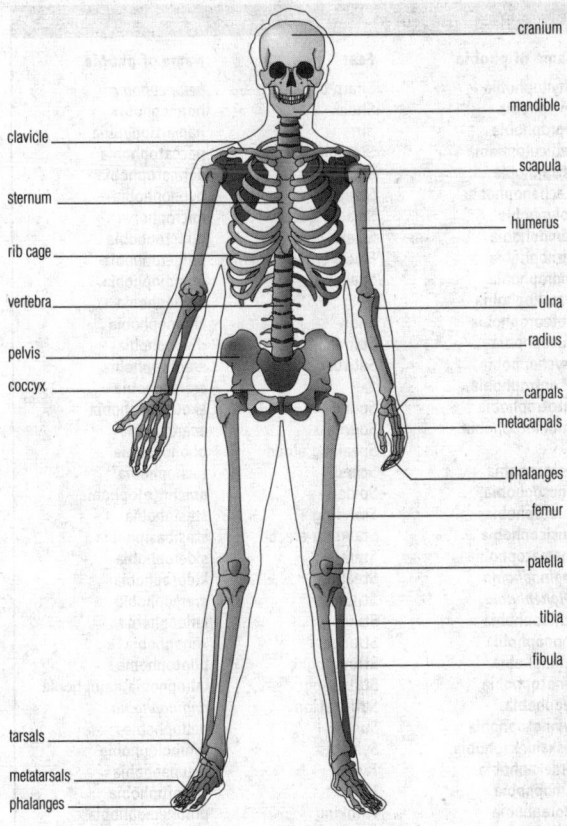

cranium
mandible
scapula
humerus
ulna
radius
carpals
metacarpals
phalanges
femur
patella
tibia
fibula

clavicle
sternum
rib cage
vertebra
pelvis
coccyx

tarsals
metatarsals
phalanges

Skeleton
*The human skeleton is made up of 207 bones and provides
a strong but flexible supportive framework for the body.*

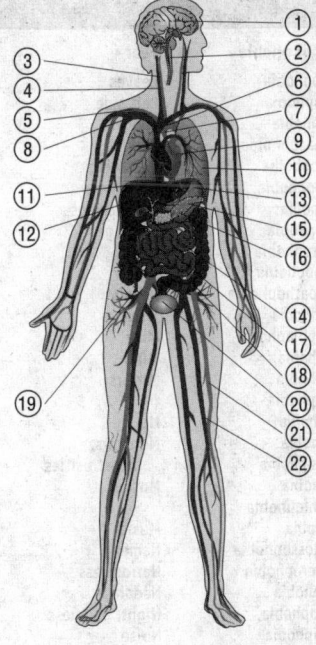

Key
1. brain
2. spinal cord
3. carotid artery
4. jugular vein
5. subclavian artery
6. superior vena cava
7. aorta
8. subclavian vein
9. heart
10. lungs
11. diaphragm
12. liver
13. stomach
14. gall bladder
15. kidney
16. pancreas
17. small intestine or ileum
18. large intestine or colon
19. appendix
20. bladder
21. popliteal artery
22. popliteal vein

Organs
*The adult human body has approximately 650 muscles,
100,000 km/60,000 mi of blood vessels and 13,000 nerve cells.*

Phobias

Fear	Name of phobia	Fear	Name of phobia	Fear	Name of phobia
Animals	zoophobia	Cancer	cancerophobia, carcinophobia	Crossing bridges	gephyrophobia
Bacteria	bacteriophobia, bacillophobia	Cats	ailurophobia, gatophobia	Crossing streets	dromophobia
Beards	pogonophobia			Crowds	demophobia, ochlophobia
Bees	apiphobia, melissophobia	Chickens	alektorophobia	Darkness	achulophobia, nyctophobia, scotophobia
Being alone	monophobia, autophobia, eremophobia	Childbirth	tocophobia, parturiphobia		
		Children	paediphobia	Dawn	eosophobia
Being buried alive	taphophobia	Cold	cheimatophobia, frigophobia	Daylight	phengophobia
Being seen by others	scopophobia			Death, corpses	necrophobia, thanatophobia
Being touched	haphephobia, aphephobia	Colour	chromatophobia, chromophobia, psychrophobia	Defecation	rhypophobia
				Deformity	dysmorphophobia
Birds	ornithophobia	Comets	cometophobia	Demons	demonophobia
Blood	h(a)ematophobia, hemophobia	Computers	computerphobia, cyberphobia	Dirt	mysophobia
				Disease	nosophobia, pathophobia
Blushing	ereuthrophobia, erythrophobia	Contamination	misophobia, coprophobia	Disorder	ataxiophobia
Books	bibliophobia	Criticism	enissophobia	Dogs	cynophobia

(continued)

Phobias (*continued*)

Fear	Name of phobia	Fear	Name of phobia	Fear	Name of phobia
Draughts	anemophobia	Leaves	phyllophobia	Sharp objects	*belonephobia*
Dreams	oneirophobia	Left side	levophobia	Shock	hormephobia
Drinking	dipsophobia	Leprosy	leprophobia	Sin	hamartiophobia
Drugs	pharmacophobia	Lice	pediculophobia	Sinning	peccatophobia
Duration	chronophobia	Lightning	astraphobia	Skin	dermatophobia
Dust	amathophobia,	Machinery	mechanophobia	Sleep	hypnophobia
	koniphobia	Many things	polyphobia	Small objects	microphobia
Eating	phagophobia	Marriage	gamophobia	Smell	olfactophobia
Enclosed spaces	claustrophobia	Meat	carnophobia	Smothering, choking	pnigerophobia
Everything	pan(t)ophobia	Men	androphobia	Snakes	ophidiophobia,
Facial hair	trichopathophobia	Metals	metallophobia		ophiophobia
Faeces	coprophobia	Meteors	meteorophobia	Snow	chionophobia
Failure	kakorrphiaphobia	Mice	musophobia	Soiling	rhypophobia
Fatigue	kopophobia,	Mind	psychophobia	Solitude	eremitophobia,
	ponophobia	Mirrors	eisoptrophobia,		eremophobia
Fears	phobophobia		catotrophobia	Sound	akousticophobia
Fever	febriphobia	Money	chrometophobia	Sourness	acerophobia
Fire	pyrophobia	Monsters,		Speaking aloud	phonophobia
Fish	ichthyophobia	monstrosities	teratophobia	Speed	tachophobia
Flying, the air	aerophobia	Motion	kinesophobia,	Spiders	arachn(e)ophobia
Fog	homichlophobia		kinetophobia	Standing	stasiphobia
Food	sitophobia	Music	musicophobia	Standing erect	stasibasiphobia
Foreign languages	xenoglossophobia	Names	onomatophobia	Stars	siderophobia
Freedom	eleutherophobia	Narrowness	*anginaphobia*	Stealing	kleptophobia
Fun	cherophobia	Needles	*belonephobia*	Stillness	eremophobia
Germs	spermophobia,	Night, darkness	achluophobia	Stings	cnidophobia
	bacillophobia	Noise	phonophobia	Strangers	xenophobia
Ghosts	phasmophobia	Novelty	cainophobia,	Strong light	photophobia
Glass	hyalophobia		cenotophobia,	Stuttering	laliophobia, lalophobia
God	theophobia		neophobia	Suffocation	*anginophobia*
Going to bed	clinophobia	Nudity	gymnotophobia	Sun	heliophobia
Graves	taphophobia	Number 13	triskaidekaphobia,	Symbols	symbolophobia
Hair	chaetophobia,		terdekaphobia	Taste	geumaphobia
	trichophobia,	Odours	osmophobia	Teeth	odontophobia
	hypertrichophobia	Open spaces	agoraphobia	Thinking	phronemophobia
Heart conditions	cardiophobia	Pain	algophobia,	Thrown objects	ballistophobia
Heat	thermophobia		odynophobia	Thunder	astraphobia,
Heaven	ouranophobia	Parasites	parasitophobia		brontophobia,
Heights	acrophobia, altophobia	Physical love	erotophobia		keraunophobia
Hell	hadephobia,	Pins	enetophobia	Touch	aphephobia,
	stygiophobia	Places	topophobia		haptophobia,
Home	domatophobia,	Pleasure	hedonophobia		haphephobia
	oikophobia	Pointed instruments	aichmophobia	Travel	hodophobia
Horses	hippophobia	Poison	toxiphobia,	Travelling by train	siderodromophobia
Human beings	anthrophobia		toxophobia, iophobia	Trees	dendrophobia
Ice, frost	cryophobia	Poverty	peniaphobia	Trembling	tremophobia
Ideas	ideophobia	Precipices	cremnophobia	Vehicles	amaxophobia,
Illness	nosemaphobia,	Pregnancy	maieusiophobia		ochophobia
	nosophobia	Punishment	poinephobia	Venereal disease	cypridophobia
Imperfection	atelophobia	Rain	ombrophobia	Void	kenophobia
Infection	mysophobia	Reptiles	batrachophobia	Vomiting	emetophobia
Infinity	apeirophobia	Responsibility	hypegiaphobia	Walking	basiphobia
Injustice	dikephobia	Ridicule	katagalophobia	Wasps	spheksophobia
Inoculations,		Rivers	potamophobia	Water	hydrophobia,
injections	trypanophobia	Robbery	harpaxophobia		aquaphobia
Insanity	lyssophobia,	Ruin	atephobia	Weakness	asthenophobia
	maniaphobia	Rust	iophobia	Wind	ancraophobia
Insects	entomophobia	Sacred things	hierophobia	Women	gynophobia
Itching	acarophobia,	Satan	satanophobia	Words	logophobia
	scabiophobia	School	scholionophobia	Work	ergophobia,
Jealousy	zelophobia	Sea	thalassophobia		ergasiophobia
Knowledge	epistemophobia	Semen	spermatophobia	Worms	helminthophobia
Lakes	limnophobia	Sex	genophobia	Wounds, injury	traumatophobia
Large objects	macrophobia	Sexual intercourse	coitophobia	Writing	graphophobia
		Shadows	sciophobia		

Common Drugs Derived from Plants

These plants are poisonous and if swallowed can cause serious illness or unconsciousness. They should only be used if administered by a medically trained professional.

Plant	Drug	Use	Plant	Drug	Use
Amazonian liana	curare	muscle relaxant	Indian snakeroot	reserpine	antihypertensive
Annual mugwort	artemisinin	antimalarial	Meadowsweet	salicylate	analgesic
Autumn crocus	colchicine	antitumour agent	Mexican yam	diosgenin	birth control pill
Coca	cocaine	local anaesthetic	Opium poppy	codeine, morphine	analgesic (and antitussive)
Common thyme	thymol	antifungal			
Deadly nightshade (belladonna)	atropine	anticholinergic	Pacific yew	taxol	antitumour agent
			Recured thornapple	scopolamine	sedative
Dog button (nux-vomica)	strychnine	central nervous system stimulant	Rosy periwinkle	vincristine, vinblastine	antileukaemia
			Velvet bean	L-dopa	antiparkinsonian
Ergot fungus	ergotamine	analgesic	White willow	salicylic acid	topical analgesic
Foxglove	digitoxin, digitalis	cardiotonic	Yellow cinchona	quinine	antimalarial, antipyretic

Medical Prefixes

a(n)- lacking
ab- away from
abdomin(o)- abdominal
ad- towards, near
andr(o)- male
angi(o)- blood or lymph vessel
ant(i)- against, counteracting
ante- before
arthr(o)- joint
aut(o)- self
bi- twice, two
brachi(o)- arm
brachy- shortness
brady- slowness
bronch(o)- bronchial tube
carcin(o)- cancer
cardi(o)- heart
cerebr(o)- brain
cholecyst- gall bladder
circum- surrounding
colp(o)- vagina
contra- against
crani(o)- skull
cry(o)- cold
crypt- hidden, concealed
cyst(o)- bladder
cyt(o)- cell
dent- tooth
derm- skin
di- double
dys- difficult, painful, abnormal
end(o)- within, inner
enter(o)- intestine
epi- above, upon
ex(o)- outside, outer

extra- outside, beyond
gastr(o)- stomach
gyn- female
haem- blood
hepat(o)- liver
hist(o)- tissue
hyper- above
hypno- sleep
hypo- below
hyster(o)- uterus
immuno- immunity
infra- below
intra- within
laryng(o)- larynx
mal- abnormal, diseased
mast- breast
muco- mucus
my(o)- muscle
necro- death
neo- new
nephr(o)- kidney
neur(o)- nerve
noct- night
oculo- eye
olig(o)- deficiency, few
ophthalm(o)- eye
oro- mouth
ortho- straight, normal
osteo- bone
ot(o)- ear
paed- children
path(o)- disease
peri- around, enclosing
pharmac(o)- drugs
phleb(o)- vein
phot(o)- light
pneumon- lung

poly- many, excessive
post- after
pre-(pro-) before
ren- kidney
retro- behind
rhin- nose
sclero- thickening
ser(o)- serum
spondyl- vertebra, spine
supra- above
syn- together, union
tachy- fast
tetra- four
therm(o)- heat, temperature
trache(o)- trachea
uni- one
urin- urine, urinary system
utero- uterus
vaso- vessel
vesico- bladder

Medical Suffixes

-aemia condition of blood
-algia pain
-ase enzyme
-blast formative cell
-cele tumour, swelling
-centesis puncture
-cide destructive, killing
-coccus spherical bacterium
-cyte cell
-derm skin
-dynia pain
-ectasis dilation, extension
-ectomy surgical removal of
-facient making, causing

-fuge expelling
-genesis origin, development
-genic causing, produced by
-gram tracing, record
-iasis diseased condition
-iatric practice of healing
-itis inflammation of
-kinesis movement
-lith calculus, stone
-lysis breaking down, dissolution
-malacia softening
-megaly enlargement
-oid likeness, resemblance
-oma tumour
-opia eye defect
-osis disease, condition
-ostomy surgical opening or outlet
-otomy surgical incision into an organ or part
-pathy disease
-penia lack of, deficiency
-pexy surgical fixation
-phage ingesting
-philia affinity for, morbid attraction
-phobia fear
-plasty reconstructive surgery
-plegia paralysis
-pnoea condition of breathing
-poiesis formation
-ptosis prolapse
-scopy visual examination
-stasis stagnation, stoppage of flow
-tome cutting instrument
-uria condition of urine

Medical Abbreviations and Acronyms

A & E accident and emergency department

ABP arterial blood pressure

ADLs activities of daily living

adm. admission

aet. aetiology

AI artificial insemination

AIDS acquired immune deficiency syndrome

ALG antilymphocyte globulin

ALS antilymphocyte serum

ARM artificial rupture of membranes (for delivery)

BCG bacille Calmette-Guérin (TB vaccine)

BMI body mass index

BMR basal metabolic rate

BP blood pressure

BPD bronchopulmonary dysplasia

CA cancer

CABG coronary artery bypass graft

CAPD continuous ambulatory peritoneal dialysis

CAT computerized axial tomography

CCU coronary care unit

CJD Creutzfeldt-Jakob disease

CMV cytomegalovirus

CNS central nervous system

COAD chronic obstructive airways disease

CPAP continuous positive airways pressure

CPR cardiopulmonary resuscitation

CSF cerebrospinal fluid

CT computerized tomography

CV cardiovascular

CVA cardiovascular accident

CVP central venous pressure

CVS chorionic villus sampling

CXR chest X-ray

D & C dilation and curettage

DHA district health authority

DI donor insemination

DIC disseminated intravascular coagulation

disch. discharge

DL danger list

DMD Duchenne's muscular dystrophy

DNA deoxyribonucleic acid

DOA dead on arrival

DPT combined vaccine against diphtheria, pertussis (whooping cough), and tetanus

Dr doctor

DRG diagnostic related group

DTs delirium tremens

DVT deep vein thrombosis

ECG electrocardiogram

ECT electroconvulsive therapy

EEG electroencephalograph

EMG electromyograph

ENT ear, nose, and throat

EPO erythropoietin

ET endotracheal tube (used for patient on ventilator)

GH growth hormone

GIFT gamete intrafallopian transfer

GP general practitioner

GVHD graft-versus-host disease

HBIG hepatitis B immunoglobulin

HCG human chorionic gonadotrophin

HIV human immunodeficiency virus

HLA human leucocyte antigen system

HMO health maintenance organization

HRT hormone replacement therapy

IBS irritable bowel syndrome

ICD international classification of diseases

ICP intracranial pressure

ICU intensive care unit

IHD ischaemic heart disease

IMR infant mortality rate

IMV intermittent mandatory ventilation

IOP intraocular pressure

IPPV intermittent positive pressure ventilation

IQ intelligence quotient

IUD intrauterine device

IV intravenous

IVP intravenous pyelogram

IZS insulin zinc suspension

K & M kaolin and morphine

LBW low birth weight

LP lumbar puncture

LSD lysergic acid diethylamide

MAB monoclonal antibody

MAOI monoamine oxidase inhibitor

MAP mean arterial pressure

MBD minimal brain dysfunction

MD doctor of medicine

ME myalgic encephalomyelitis

MHC major histocompatibility complex

MI myocardial infarction

MLD minimum lethal dose

MMR combined vaccine against measles, mumps, and rubella (German measles)

MND motor neurone disease

MO medical officer

MRI magnetic resonance imaging

MRS magnetic resonance spectroscopy

MRSA methicillin-resistant *Staphylococcus aureus*

MS multiple sclerosis

MSU mid-stream urine specimen

NHS National Health Service (in the UK)

NPO nil per orem (nothing by mouth)

NTD neural tube defect

O & G obstetrics and gynaecology

OA osteoarthritis

OD overdose

OP outpatient

ORT oral rehydration therapy

OT occupational therapy

PA physician's assistant

paed. paediatrics

path. pathology

PCOD polycystic ovary disease

PE pleural effusion

PET positron-emission tomography

PICU paediatric intensive care unit

PID pelvic inflammatory disease

PIH pregnancy-induced hypertension

PKU phenylketonuria

PM postmortem

PMS premenstrual stress disorder

PO per orem (by mouth)

PoP plaster of Paris

pre-op pre-operative

PTA post-traumatic amnesia

RA rheumatoid arthritis

RDS respiratory distress syndrome

REM sleep rapid eye movement sleep

RES reticuloendothelial system

RN registered nurse

RNA ribonucleic acid

RQ respiratory quotient

RSI repetitive strain injury

RSV respiratory syncytial virus

Rx treatment/prescription

SAD seasonal affective disorder

SAH subarachnoid haemorrhage

SIDS sudden infant death syndrome

SLE systemic lupus erythematous

STD sexually transmitted disease

TAB combined vaccine against typhoid, paratyphoid A, and paratyphoid B

TAT thematic apperception test

TATT tired all the time

TB tuberculosis

TENS transcutaneous electrical nerve stimulation

TIA transient ischaemic attack

tPA tissue plasminogen activator (heart drug)

TPR temperature, pulse, and respiration

TS Tourette's syndrome

TSH thyroid-stimulating hormone

Tx transfusion, transplant

URTI upper respiratory tract infection

UTI urinary tract infection

VA visual acuity

VD venereal disease

VF ventricular fibrillation

WHO World Health Organization

World Health

The Leading Causes of Mortality in the World

1993

Rank	Cause	Deaths (thousands)	% of overall deaths
1	Infectious and parasitic diseases	16,445	32
2	Diseases of the circulatory system	9,676	19
3	Unknown causes	8,124	16
4	Malignant tumours (neoplasms)	6,013	12
5	External causes	3,996	8
6	Perinatal and neonatal causes	3,180	6
7	Chronic lower respiratory diseases	2,888	6
8	Maternal causes	508	1
9	Other causes	170	0.3

Source: World Resources Institute

Newly Recognized Infectious Diseases

Year of recognition	Agent	Type	Disease/comments
1973	Rotavirus	virus	major cause of infantile diarrhoea worldwide
1975	Parvovirus B19	virus	aplastic crisis in chronic haemolytic anaemia
1976	*Cryptosporidium parvum*	parasite	acute and chronic diarrhoea
1977	Ebola virus	virus	Ebola haemorrhagic fever
1977	*Legionella pneumophila*	bacterium	legionnaires' disease
1977	Hantaan virus	virus	haemorrhagic fever with renal syndrome (HRFS)
1977	*Campylobacter jejuni*	bacterium	enteric pathogen distributed globally
1980	human T-lymphotropic virus 1 (HTLV-1)	virus	T-cell lymphoma-leukaemia
1981	toxin-producing strains of *Staphylococcus aureus*	bacterium	toxic shock syndrome
1982	*Escherichia coli* O157:H7	bacterium	haemorrhagic colitis; haemolytic uraemic syndrome
1982	HTLV-2	virus	hairy cell leukaemia
1982	*Borrelia burgdorferi*	bacterium	Lyme disease
1983	human immunodeficiency virus (HIV)	virus	acquired immunodeficiency syndrome (AIDS)
1983	*Helicobacter pylori*	bacterium	peptic ulcer disease
1985	*Enterocytozoon bieneusi*	parasite	persistent diarrhoea
1986	*Cyclospora cayetanensis*	parasite	persistent diarrhoea
1986	BSE agent (uncertain)	non-conventional agent	bovine spongiform encephalopathy in cattle and possibly variant Creutzfeldt-Jakob disease (vCJD) in humans
1988	human herpes virus 6 (HHV-6)	virus	exanthem subitum
1988	hepatitis E virus	virus	enterically transmitted non-A, non-B hepatitis
1989	*Ehrlichia chaffeensis*	bacterium	human ehrlichiosis
1989	hepatitis C virus	virus	parenterally transmitted non-A, non-B liver hepatitis
1991	Guanarito virus	virus	Venezuelan haemorrhagic fever
1991	*Encephalitozoon hellem*	parasite	conjunctivitis, disseminated disease
1991	new species of *Babesia*	parasite	atypical babesiosis
1992	*Vibrio cholerae* O139	bacterium	new strain associated with epidemic cholera
1992	*Bartonella henselae*	bacterium	cat-scratch disease causing flu-like fever; bacillary angiomatosis
1993	Sin Nombre virus	virus	Hantavirus pulmonary syndrome
1993	*Encephalitozoon cuniculi*	parasite	disseminated disease
1994	Sabia virus	virus	Brazilian haemorrhagic fever
1995	human herpes virus 8	virus	associated with Kaposi's sarcoma in AIDS patients

Source: World Health Organization

World Mortality from Chronic Diseases, and Preventive Measures

1993

Disease	Deaths	Dietary and lifestyle preventive measures
Heart disease	5,400,000[1]	avoid obesity; exercise regularly; reduce fat intake, especially intake of saturated and animal fat; reduce animal protein; maintain low cholesterol level; increase fruit and vegetable consumption; moderate alcohol intake; eliminate smoking; treat hypertension and diabetes
Stroke	3,900,000	reduce salt intake; reduce body weight; eliminate smoking; treat hypertension and diabetes
Diabetes mellitus	170,000	reduce body weight; improve nutrition
Cancers		
Lung	1,040,000	eliminate smoking
Stomach	734,000	increase fruit and vegetable consumption; reduce salt intake
Colon and rectum	468,000	reduce fat and protein consumption; increase vegetable consumption
Larynx, lip, and mouth	458,000	eliminate smoking; reduce alcohol consumption
Liver	367,000	reduce alcohol consumption; vaccinate against hepatitis B
Breast	358,000	reduce fat and animal protein consumption; avoid obesity
Oesophagus	328,000	eliminate smoking; reduce alcohol consumption
Pancreas	214,000	eliminate smoking; reduce alcohol consumption
Bladder	135,000	eliminate smoking; reduce alcohol consumption

[1] Includes all forms of heart disease.

Source: Worldwatch Institute

Mortality Distribution by Age in the World

Figures are rounded down.

1990–95

Major area or region	Deaths (in thousands)	0–4	5–14	15–64	>64
Africa					
Eastern Africa	16,740	45	13	29	13
Middle Africa	5,789	44	13	28	15
Northern Africa	6,517	32	8	30	29
Southern Africa	1,996	30	5	35	30
Western Africa	15,647	46	14	28	13
Total	46,691	43	12	29	16
Asia					
Eastern Asia	49,922	12	2	31	55
Southcentral Asia	65,150	36	7	29	28
Southeast Asia	18,725	24	6	37	33
Western Asia	5,790	30	5	30	34
Total	139,588	25	5	31	39
Europe					
Eastern Europe	18,931	2	1	35	62
Northern Europe	5,253	1	0	19	80
Southern Europe	6,837	2	0	21	77
Western Europe	9,463	1	0	20	78
Total	40,484	2	1	27	71
Latin America and Caribbean					
Caribbean	1,312	17	3	31	49
Central America	3,383	26	5	34	35
South America	10,862	21	4	34	41
Total	15,556	22	4	34	40
North America					
Total	12,425	2	1	24	73
Oceania					
Australia and New Zealand	789	2	1	21	76
Melanesia	253	26	6	45	23
Micronesia	13	29	6	34	30
Polynesia	16	28	4	32	35
Total	1,071	8	2	27	63
World					
More developed regions	58,398	2	1	26	72
Less developed regions	197,432	30	7	31	33
Least developed regions	40,002	45	12	28	15
Total	255,830	23	5	30	42

Mortality, Morbidity, and Disability for Selected Infectious Diseases in the World

In thousands. (N/A = not available.)

1995

Disease by main mode of transmission	Deaths	New cases (incidence)	All cases (prevalence)	Permanent and long-term affected cases
Person to Person				
Acute lower respiratory infection (ALR)[1]	4,416	394,750[2]	N/A	N/A
Tuberculosis	3,072	8,888	22,000	N/A
Hepatitis B, viral	1,156	4,149	350,000[3]	N/A
Measles	1,066	N/A	42,000	5,590
AIDS	1,063	1,125	1,538	N/A
Whooping cough (pertussis)	355	N/A	40,000	N/A
Meningococcal meningitis	35	350	N/A	45
Poliomyelitis, acute	9	N/A	82	85
Leprosy	2	561	1,833	3,000
Gonorrhoea	N/A	62,000	N/A	N/A
Syphilis, venereal	N/A	12,000	N/A	N/A
Chancroid	N/A	7,000	N/A	N/A
Trachoma	N/A	20,540	153,832	5,583
Diphtheria[4]	N/A	N/A	35	N/A
Food-, Water-, and Soil-borne				
Diarrhoea[5]	3,115	4,002,000[2]	N/A	N/A
Neonatal tetanus	459	N/A	N/A	N/A
Hookworm diseases	65	N/A	151,000	N/A
Ascariasis	60	N/A	250,000	N/A
Schistosomiasis	20	N/A	200,000	N/A
Cholera[4]	11	384	N/A	N/A
Trichuriasis	10	N/A	45,530	N/A
Trematode infections (foodborne only)	10	N/A	40,000	N/A
Dracunculiasis (guinea-worm infection)	N/A	122	122	N/A
Insect-borne				
Malaria	2,100	approx. 400,000	N/A	N/A
Leishmaniasis	80	1,750	12,000	N/A
Onchocerciasis (river blindness)	47	N/A	18,000	360
Chagas' disease (American trypanosomiasis)	45	800	18,000	N/A
Dengue/dengue haemorrhagic fever	24	592	N/A	N/A
Sleeping sickness (African trypanosomiasis)	20	N/A	300	N/A
Japanese encephalitis	11	43	N/A	9
Plague[4]	0.2	2	N/A	N/A
Yellow fever[4]	0.2	0.5	N/A	N/A
Filariasis (lymphatic)	N/A	N/A	120,000	43,000
Animal-borne				
Rabies (dog-mediated)	60	N/A	N/A	N/A
Total	17,312	N/A	N/A	N/A

[1] Figures do not include lower respiratory infections related to measles, pertussis, and HIV infections.
[2] Incidence figure refers to episodes.
[3] Figure refers to chronic hepititas B virus carriers.
[4] Officially reported figures only.
[5] Figures relate to acute watery diarrhoea, persistent diarrhoea, and dysentery, but do not include measles- and HIV-related diarrhoea.

Source: World Health Organization

Reported Cases for Infectious Diseases by Country in the World

Estimates are obtained or derived from relevant WHO programmes or from responsible international agencies for the areas of their concern. (N/A = not available.)

Country/territory	AIDS[1]	Tuberculosis[2]	Malaria[3]	Polio[1,4]	Measles[2]	Neonatal tetanus[2]
Afghanistan	N/A	N/A	N/A	N/A	N/A	N/A
Albania	2	707	N/A	0	3	N/A
Algeria	N/A	13,725	85	4	5,913	21
Angola	35	7,157	N/A	4	5,480	814
Antigua and Barbuda	1	N/A	N/A	0	0	0
Argentina	686	13,683	758	0	86	9
Armenia	N/A	753	N/A	3	149	0
Australia	110	1,020	N/A	0	N/A	0
Austria	113	1,264	N/A	0	N/A	N/A
Azerbaijan	1	2,839	N/A	5	6,138	N/A
Bahamas	165	N/A	N/A	0	0	0
Bahrain	8	N/A	258	0	0	0
Bangladesh	6	48,724	125,402	207	9,343	469
Barbados	49	N/A	N/A	0	0	0
Belarus	2	4,348	N/A	0	685	N/A
Belgium	73	1,521	320	0	N/A	N/A
Belize	N/A	59	8,586	0	0	N/A
Benin	N/A	2,119	N/A	7	5,963	76
Bhutan	0	1,159	28,116	0	680	1
Bolivia	4	9,431	27,475	0	719	21
Bosnia-Herzegovina	N/A	1,595	N/A	0	N/A	N/A
Botswana	194	4,756	14,778	0	2,004	1
Brazil	2,698	87,280	466,190	0	35	151
Brunei	N/A	N/A	21	0	N/A	N/A
Bulgaria	1	5,296	N/A	0	73	N/A
Burkina Faso	N/A	N/A	N/A	12	2,824	19
Burundi	N/A	3,840	N/A	0	7,192	26
Cambodia	76	15,172	99,189	98	946	147
Cameroon	N/A	7,312	N/A	2	1,548	69
Canada	489	N/A	394	0	503	N/A
Cape Verde	N/A	N/A	N/A	0	30	2
Central African Republic	173	N/A	N/A	4	N/A	8
Chad	592	N/A	N/A	192	9,373	614
Chile	114	N/A	2	0	0	1
China	12	363,804	68,594	91	76,204	N/A
Colombia	181	8,901	129,377	0	525	61
Comoros	N/A	494	N/A	0	2	9
Congo, Democratic Republic of	N/A	N/A	N/A	475	12,573	306
Congo, Republic of the	N/A	3,080	N/A	0	226	8
Cook Islands	N/A	4	N/A	0	0	0
Costa Rica	112	325	5,033	0	7	0
Côte d'Ivoire	N/A	N/A	N/A	87	N/A	N/A
Croatia	12	2,217	N/A	0	138	1
Cuba	31	1,681	10	0	0	0
Cyprus	N/A	37	2	1	0	0
Czech Republic	10	1,960	N/A	0	9	0
Denmark	151	494	N/A	0	18	N/A
Djibouti	119	3,311	1,007	0	N/A	N/A
Dominica	N/A	12	N/A	0	0	N/A
Dominican Republic	207	3,783	967	0	3	5
Ecuador	24	9,685	46,859	0	3,668	57
Egypt	7	3,911	17	47	1,444	993
El Salvador	256	3,901	3,887	0	0	8
Equatorial Guinea	98	356	N/A	0	270	5
Eritrea	370	N/A	N/A	10	541	N/A
Estonia	2	645	N/A	0	230	0
Ethiopia	3,867	99,329	N/A	199	1,133	N/A
Fiji	N/A	280	N/A	0	N/A	N/A
Finland	25	539	N/A	0	N/A	N/A
France	2,453	9,093	N/A	0	N/A	N/A
Gabon	265	1,034	N/A	N/A	N/A	N/A
Gambia	42	N/A	N/A	0	N/A	N/A
Georgia	N/A	N/A	N/A	0	136	N/A
Germany	637	12,982	N/A	0	N/A	0
Ghana	904	8,894	N/A	28	34,821	128
Greece	115	N/A	N/A	0	87	N/A
Grenada	N/A	3	N/A	0	0	N/A
Guatemala	N/A	2,976	41,868	0	204	17
Guinea	133	3,241	N/A	26	437	16
Guinea-Bissau	N/A	1,647	158,748	0	378	18
Guyana	96	266	33,172	0	0	N/A
Haiti	N/A	N/A	853	0	N/A	N/A
Honduras	219	4,291	44,513	0	1	9
Hungary	24	4,163	N/A	0	11	0
Iceland	2	18	N/A	0	N/A	N/A
India	1,210	1,114,374	2,207,431	2,993	48,607	2,285
Indonesia	22	49,647	140,559	21	6,798	45
Iran	7	N/A	64,581	90	506	21
Iraq	6	N/A	49,823	34	10,657	89
Ireland, Republic of	14	N/A	N/A	0	775	N/A
Israel	23	395	58	0	1,574	N/A
Italy	3,231	5,816	N/A	0	5,082	0
Jamaica	286	109	N/A	6	0	0
Japan	173	44,590	N/A	0	N/A	N/A
Jordan	1	443	266	0	516	5
Kazakhstan	N/A	10,519	N/A	1	1,787	N/A
Kenya	637	22,930	N/A	12	4,180	50
Kiribati	0	253	N/A	0	299	0
Korea, North	N/A	N/A	N/A	7	0	N/A
Korea, South	5	38,155	N/A	0	7,883	N/A
Kuwait	3	237	1,379	0	432	0
Kyrgyzstan	N/A	2,726	N/A	0	186	0
Laos	3	1,135	41,787	11	1,385	10
Latvia	N/A	1,470	N/A	0	10	0
Lebanon	8	940	4	1	51	3
Lesotho	N/A	4,334	N/A	0	573	0
Liberia	N/A	1,764	N/A	0	571	59
Libya	N/A	N/A	136	0	N/A	N/A
Lithuania	1	2,135	N/A	0	286	0
Luxembourg	10	33	N/A	0	0	0
Macedonia, Former Yugoslav Republic of	N/A	728	N/A	0	229	0
Madagascar	4	10,671	N/A	5	14,164	6
Malawi	3,386	N/A	N/A	0	2,164	14
Malaysia	70	11,708	39,890	0	346	9
Maldives	1	249	29	0	2	0
Mali	N/A	3,076	295,737	26	2,183	18
Malta	1	N/A	N/A	0	5	N/A
Marshall Islands	N/A	N/A	N/A	0	0	0
Mauritania	16	N/A	N/A	1	2,668	4
Mauritius	N/A	149	N/A	0	10	0
Mexico	3,406	16,353	15,793	0	108	81
Micronesia	N/A	173	N/A	0	905	0
Moldova	2	2,626	N/A	0	3,951	0
Monaco	3	1	N/A	N/A	N/A	N/A
Mongolia	0	1,730	N/A	0	177	4
Morocco	31	30,316	198	0	3,512	9
Mozambique	455	27,885	N/A	0	9,618	56
Myanmar	185	15,583	113,000	18	1,855	48
Namibia	N/A	N/A	N/A	28	133	9
Nauru	0	4	N/A	0	N/A	N/A
Nepal	16	15,572	16,380	2	775	4
Netherlands	241	1,811	223	0	302	0
New Zealand	28	352	N/A	0	33	0
Nicaragua	9	2,750	44,037	0	3	4
Niger	N/A	3,784	N/A	40	48,685	28
Nigeria	N/A	8,449	N/A	92	95,915	419
Norway	37	242	N/A	0	4	N/A
Oman	7	304	16,873	0	163	0
Pakistan	6	N/A	92,634	460	1,421	1,842
Palau	N/A	N/A	N/A	0	0	0

Reported Cases for Infectious Diseases by Country in the World (continued)

Country/ territory	AIDS[1]	Tuber- culosis[2]	Malaria[3]	Polio[1 4]	Measles[2]	Neonatal tetanus[2]	Country/ territory	AIDS[1]	Tuber- culosis[2]	Malaria[3]	Polio[1 4]	Measles[2]	Neonatal tetanus[2]
Panama	105	827	481	0	3	2	Sweden	116	537	N/A	0	0	N/A
Papua New							Switzerland	188	924	N/A	0	77	0
Guinea	32	5,335	66,797	0	6,821	159	Syria	N/A	5,127	961	0	1,334	74
Paraguay	9	1,850	436	0	122	18	Tajikistan	0	892	N/A	0	429	N/A
Peru	189	48,601	95,222	0	665	129	Tanzania	N/A	34,799	1,243,217	17	3,558	25
Philippines	37	180,044	64,974	4	3,006	336	Thailand	3,379	47,767	115,220	1	38,336	62
Poland	53	16,653	N/A	0	864	N/A	Togo	853	1,137	N/A	5	4,721	16
Portugal	249	5,619	N/A	0	3,038	N/A	Tonga	N/A	23	N/A	0	N/A	0
Qatar	5	N/A	370	0	12	0	Trinidad and						
Romania	393	21,422	N/A	0	6,228	N/A	Tobago	149	129	8	0	0	0
Russia	21	70,822	N/A	152	68,672	0	Turkey	8	N/A	47,156	28	21,995	N/A
Rwanda	N/A	N/A	N/A	1	5,999	0	Turkmenistan	N/A	N/A	N/A	8	2,552	N/A
St Kitts and							Tunisia	46	2,376	45	0	597	7
Nevis	2	2	N/A	0	0	N/A	Tuvalu	N/A	19	N/A	0	0	0
St Lucia	7	24	N/A	0	0	N/A	Uganda	N/A	26,994	N/A	85	46,192	494
St Vincent and							UK	718	6,196	1,922	0	23,525	N/A
the Grenadines	5	0	N/A	0	0	N/A	Ukraine	16	20,622	N/A	1	N/A	N/A
Samoa	1	45	N/A	0	0	0	United Arab						
San Marino	N/A	2	N/A	0	N/A	N/A	Emirates	N/A	426	3,735	0	518	0
São Tomé							Uruguay	101	666	N/A	0	N/A	0
and Príncipe	4	N/A	N/A	0	319	3	USA	37,509	24,361	1,074	0	958	0
Saudi Arabia	37	2,518	18,380	3	1,283	33	Uzbekistan	N/A	14,890	N/A	1	N/A	N/A
Senegal	128	6,913	N/A	0	5,944	24	Vanuatu	0	152	10,377	0	0	0
Seychelles	N/A	N/A	N/A	0	0	0	Venezuela	453	4,877	12,539	0	15,364	14
Sierra Leone	29	2,564	N/A	0	114	53	Vietnam	79	51,763	156,069	104	11,853	422
Singapore	22	1,677	354	0	159	0	Yemen	9	11,464	39,396	46	35	3
Slovak Republic	2	1,760	N/A	0	29	0	Yugoslavia	N/A	N/A	N/A	N/A	N/A	N/A
Slovenia	10	526	N/A	0	60	N/A	Zambia	N/A	N/A	N/A	6	13,352	4
Solomon Islands	0	332	126,123	0	406	0	Zimbabwe	2,746	N/A	877,734	0	N/A	N/A
Somalia	N/A	2,023	3,049	N/A	N/A	N/A							
South Africa	1,120	90,292	N/A	0	3,390	19							
Spain	2,901	N/A	N/A	0	3,300	N/A							
Sri Lanka	11	6,372	363,200	0	200	5							
Sudan	174	N/A	N/A	22	963	70							
Suriname	20	53	N/A	0	N/A	N/A							
Swaziland	58	N/A	N/A	0	610	0							

[1] Data as of 1995.
[2] Data as of 1994.
[3] Data as of 1993.
[4] Totals exclude vaccine-associated and imported cases.

Source: World Health Organization

Creutzfeldt–Jakob disease (CJD)

Creutzfeldt-Jakob disease (CJD) is a rare brain disease that causes progressive physical and mental deterioration, leading to death usually within a year of onset. It claims one person in every million and is universally fatal. It has been linked with bovine spongiform encephalopathy (BSE), and there have also been occurrences in people treated with pituitary hormones derived from cows for growth or fertility problems.

CJD is one of a group of human and animal diseases known as the transmissible spongiform encephalopathies since they are characterized by the appearance of spongy changes in brain tissue. Some scientists believe that all these conditions, including BSE in cattle and scrapie in sheep, are in effect the same disease. In 1993 CJD was linked to a genetic trait predisposing individuals to the disease; about 10–15% of cases are inherited. Like BSE, CJD is caused by the presence of an altered form of the brain protein PrP, that plays a role in sleep rhythms and in maintaining the brain cells called Purkinje cells. Once a small amount of the abnormal protein is present it begins to convert all the normal PrP. In 1996 the discovery of similarities in the PrP of humans and bovines that are not found in other mammals heightened concern over transmission of BSE to humans.

Bovine Spongiform Encephalopathy: Chronology

1970s	Feeds containing animal products, including sheep remains, were developed.
1985	The first cases of bovine spongiform encephalopathy (BSE) were recorded by vets. UK government epidemiologists announced that the source was probably scrapie in sheep.
July1988	The practice of feeding cattle on the brains of other cattle and sheep was abandoned.
1989	Diseased cattle brains and spinal cords continued to be used in human food products until November.
1990	The Creutzfeldt-Jakob disease (CJD) Surveillance Unit was set up in Edinburgh to monitor any changes in CJD occurrence that may be linked to BSE.
1992	There is a peak in the number of cases of BSE in cattle, with 700 cases per week.
1995	Around 147,000 cases of BSE had been recorded in UK cows – 18,000 of these had been born since the feed ban – with about 220 new cases per week.
1996	The government announced in March that 10 young people had died from a variant of CJD probably caused by eating infected meat. A worldwide ban on UK beef products was put in place by the European Union. Government scientists admitted that cows can pass BSE to their calves.
1997	Research published by British pathologists proved that the new variant of CJD (vCJD), is caused by the same agent that causes BSE, indicating that the disease has jumped species, from cattle to humans.

BSE: THE DEBATE GOES ON

BY SUE DUDLEY AND NIGEL STOLTON

BSE (bovine spongiform encephalopathy) is the cattle version of a group of diseases known as TSEs (transmissible spongiform encephalopathies), which degenerate the nerve cells in mammals. The human version is known as Creutzfeldt-Jakob Disease or CJD, and causes brain degeneration and death.

BSE was first identified in 1985. In 1988, UK government epidemiologists announced that the source was probably scrapie, the form of TSE in sheep. They linked the emergence of the cattle disease to changes in industrial plants where protein was recovered from animal carcasses to produce cattle feed. Feeds containing animal products were developed in the 1970s, when scientists found that they could bypass the rumination process in cows and get protein – from fishmeal or animal remains – into the animals' first 'true' stomach, which had the result that production was increased. As the price of soya and fishmeal rose, feed-makers turned to sheep remains.

Government action to deal with the initial crisis involved a ban on animal remains (except fishmeal) being included in sheep and cattle feed, the slaughter of animals suspected of having the disease, and the removal from the human food chain of types of offal believed to carry the disease such as the spinal cord and brain. However, beef itself is not the only product affected. Food which contains beef, beef bone stock, mechanically recovered meat, suet, gelatine, or animal fats includes such products as chicken gravy granules, Christmas pudding, frankfurters, baby food, cakes, and jellies.

The government was initially confident that these steps would contain the problem. By April 1995, however, there had been approximately 147,000 cases of BSE recorded in UK cows – 18,000 of which had been born since the feed ban – with about 220 new cases being reported each week. It was obvious that things were not as simple as had been hoped. One problem was the UK government's failure to carry out research to assess the scrapie/BSE link. The government's reported view was that a single, highly resilient strain of scrapie must have escaped inactivation in the rendering plants, and was thus passed onto cattle. However, a variety of other hypotheses are now emerging. Robert Rohwer, who studies spongiform encephalopathies in the US, suggests that BSE is a new disease that first arose in a few British cows and then built over several years as the carcasses were repeatedly recycled in animal feed. Another theory is that the routine use of organophosphate insecticides to eradicate warble fly has affected the nervous system of treated cattle and made them more susceptible to disease.

The Human Link

A new crisis was triggered by the government announcement in March 1996 that 10 young people had died from a variant of CJD probably caused by eating infected meat. Stephen Dorrell, the Health Secretary, stated that although there was no actual 'scientific proof' that BSE can be transmitted to humans, the scientists concluded that 'the most likely explanation' for the 10 cases was exposure to BSE before the offal ban in 1989. Although the government tried to persuade processors, retailers, and consumers that eating beef had become progressively safer since the controls introduced in 1989, the statements that the risk from eating beef was only 'extremely small' did little to reduce people's fears. Nor did it ally fears in the European Union, which imposed a bitterly contested ban on beef from the UK.

By November 1997 a further 12 cases of new variant CJD had come to light and the Spongiform Encephalopathy Advisory Committee in the UK recommended that white blood cells be removed from donor blood, by a process known as leucodepletion. This advice follows research published by Professor Adriano Aguzzi of Zurich University, Switzerland – who had been working on the problem of how the disease could transmit itself from the gut to the brain – which suggests that white blood cells, lymphocytes, could play an important role in transmitting the infection.

Other scientists, notably Dr Bruno Oesch of the company Prionics in Zurich, Switzerland, have been busy developing tests that could screen for the disease agent – abnormal prion proteins – in milk and blood, but a lot of work still needs to be done.

The situation remains unclear. There have been over 400 times as many reported cases of BSE in the UK compared to the rest of the world put together, but there is no evidence that CJD-related deaths are more prevalent in the UK. This, however, could be because of the long lead time for development of CJD. Researchers are still not precisely sure how BSE developed in the British cattle herd. The number of cases are rising elsewhere and some observers believe that countries have been underreporting the level of incidence to prevent a public panic.

Undoubtedly, earlier British complacency about the risks to humans in government assurances that the situation was under control, in conjunction with poor implementation of controls, has not helped further our knowledge of the disease. The Spongiform Encephalopathy Research Campaign has argued that by the year 2000 the British could have eaten as many as 1.8 million infected beasts. The disease has already cost the government an estimated £3,300 million.

The Reaction

Fears over safety of beef has brought the £500 million per annum UK beef industry to its knees, and had repercussions throughout the world. Schools have taken beef off dinner menus and burger chains are sourcing beef products from outside the UK. A ban on UK beef products was put in place by the European Union. Much discussion has also ensued about wide-scale slaughter policies and who will provide the farmers with financial compensation. Perhaps more importantly, in the long term, the issue has focused attention on the the safety aspects of modern, intensive agricultural practice.

UK Health Care

National Health Service Hospital Waiting Lists

Comprises NHS patients on waiting lists but excludes private patients. Figures exclude patients undergoing a series of repeat admissions and those who are temporarily suspended from the waiting list for medical or social reasons.
(N/A = not available.)

Patients' region of residence[1]	Ordinary admissions					Day case admissions				
	Total waiting	Months waited (%)			Patients admitted from the waiting list per month[3]	Total waiting	Months waited (%)			Patients admitted from the waiting list per month[3]
		Less than 6	6 but less than 12	12 or over			Less than 6	6 but less than 12	12 or over	
Northern and Yorkshire	65,500	70.7	26.6	2.7	17,600	69,300	79.4	19.5	1.1	22,400
North West	78,600	71.3	27.8	0.9	17,000	91,100	80.2	19.6	0.2	27,300
Trent	56,400	72.4	23.8	3.8	9,200	50,100	78.2	19.4	2.4	11,600
West Midlands	38,000	86.8	13.0	0.2	10,300	46,100	90.0	9.9	0.1	14,600
Anglia and Oxford	58,300	73.0	25.6	1.4	12,500	50,400	80.6	18.7	0.7	15,200
North Thames	77,600	70.8	26.8	2.4	15,900	74,600	80.7	18.2	1.1	25,800
South Thames	73,600	71.3	27.0	1.7	16,300	77,800	80.0	19.4	0.6	22,800
South and West	68,700	77.6	20.5	1.9	15,300	61,900	84.6	14.8	0.6	19,900
England	516,900	73.4	24.6	1.9	114,100	521,200	81.4	17.8	0.8	159,600
Wales[2]	41,100	N/A	N/A	11.6	11,900	26,100	N/A	N/A	5.8	16,800
Scotland	46,100	81.9	16.7	1.4	21,500	33,7900	89.4	9.9	0.7	20,600
Northern Ireland	22,900	61.5	25.9	12.6	5,900	18,400	71.2	20.2	8.6	7,200

[1] Region of treatment for Wales, Scotland, and Northern Ireland.
[2] Figures for Wales relate to 31 March 1997.
[3] Average for the 3 months ending 30 September 1996 for England, for the 12 months ending 30 September 1996 for Scotland and Northern Ireland, and for the 6 months ending 31 March 1997 for Wales. The figures relate to admissions from waiting lists plus booked admissions.

Source: Department of Health. © Crown copyright 1997

Treatment for Patients Purchased by Health Authorities and GP Fundholders in the UK

Figures are on a 'purchaser basis' and relate to activity purchased, using NHS funds, by health authorities and GP fundholders for their patients. Figures include activity purchased from private hospitals and NHS hospitals but exclude private patients.
(N/A = not available.)

1995–96

Region of purchaser	Finished consultant episodes	Accident and emergency attendances	Out-patient first attendances	Community and paramedical contacts	Ambulance journeys (emergency and urgent)	Learning disabilities		Mental illness	
						Hospital bed days	Community bed days[1]	Hospital bed days	Community bed days[1]
Northern and Yorkshire	1,552,000	2,014,000	1,408,000	16,761,000	586,000	630,000	691,000	1,798,000	339,000
North West	1,648,000	2,220,000	1,391,000	20,337,000	655,000	128,000	959,000	1,638,000	566,000
Trent	1,052,000	1,267,000	1,039,000	12,766,000	393,000	281,000	552,000	1,159,000	349,000
West Midlands	1,078,000	1,679,000	1,045,000	11,936,000	441,000	354,000	463,000	989,000	207,000
Anglia and Oxford	976,000	1,079,000	1,058,000	12,456,000	298,000	444,000	331,000	1,156,000	281,000
North Thames	1,332,000	2,000,000	1,459,000	14,636,000	550,000	593,000	675,000	2,243,000	624,000
South Thames	1,313,000	2,092,000	1,498,000	16,275,000	515,000	727,000	1,291,000	1,630,000	761,000
South and West	1,403,000	1,770,000	1,332,000	16,487,000	403,000	430,000	858,000	1,440,000	266,000
England	10,354,000	14,121,000	10,229,000	121,655,000	3,842,000	3,588,000	5,820,000	12,054,000	3,392,000
Scotland	976,000	1,546,000	1,327,000	N/A	435,000	1,105,000	N/A	3,325,000	N/A

[1] In nursing homes, residential care homes and group homes.

Source: Department of Health. © Crown copyright 1997

Private Medical Insurance by Age in Great Britain

(Figures are given in percentages.)

1995–96

Region	0–15	16–44	45–64	65 or over	All ages	Region	0–15	16–44	45–64	65 or over	All ages
North East	6	7	9	2	7	South East (GOR)	17	18	22	11	18
North West (GOR) and Merseyside	5	8	11	3	7	South West	6	9	10	5	8
Yorkshire and the Humber	5	7	12	3	7	England	8	11	13	6	10
East Midlands	9	10	10	7	9	Wales	2	2	8	1	4
West Midlands	6	8	11	8	8	Scotland	4	5	6	2	5
Eastern	8	10	12	6	10	Great Britain	8	10	12	5	9
London	10	13	11	6	11						

Source: Office for National Statistics. © Crown copyright 1997

Deaths Analysed by Cause in the UK

The figures relate to the number of deaths registered during each calendar year. However, from 1993 onwards, the figures for England and Wales represent occurrences. This change has little effect on annual totals. Changes in coding practices for England and Wales, particularly coding of underlying cause of death, from January 1993 have led to some differences in the pattern of cause of death as compared with previous years. (N/A = not available.)

Cause	1990[1]	1991[1]	1992[1]	1993[1]	1994	1995	1996
England and Wales							
Deaths from natural causes[2]							
infectious and parasitic diseases[3]	2,446	2,406	2,633	3,257	3,318	3,590	3,662
intestinal infectious diseases	187	169	240	194	222	276	338
neoplasms	144,577	145,355	145,963	142,535	141,747	140,791	140,120
endocrine, nutritional, and metabolic diseases and immunity disorders	10,249	10,538	10,605	7,924	7,430	7,839	7,551
other metabolic and immunity disorders[3]	1,512	1,664	1,747	1,119	1,052	1,130	1,060
diseases of the blood and blood-forming organs	2,427	2,446	2,417	1,974	1,898	1,922	1,992
mental disorders	13,395	13,500	12,950	7,780	8,042	9,030	9,354
diseases of the nervous system and sense organs	11,644	11,889	11,577	9,143	9,010	9,646	9,809
meningitis	203	233	208	218	170	207	247
diseases of the circulatory system	259,247	261,834	254,683	257,989	242,213	241,871	238,855
diseases of the respiratory system	61,018	63,273	60,388	90,981	81,485	90,094	89,216
diseases of the digestive system	18,429	18,508	18,742	18,399	18,635	19,390	19,958
diseases of the genito-urinary system	3,919	3,234	2,072	3,401	3,246	3,272	6,788
complications of pregnancy, childbirth, etc	57	45	45	36	50	46	47
diseases of the skin and subcutaneous tissue	823	930	907	1,019	1,107	1,081	1,089
diseases of the musculo-skeletal system	5,286	5,417	5,376	3,559	3,406	3,599	3,540
congenital anomalies	1,621	1,643	1,565	1,338	1,301	1,288	1,238
certain conditions originating in the perinatal period	249	250	242	259	147	151	151
signs, symptoms, and ill-defined conditions	4,897	5,208	5,278	6,729	7,754	9,672	10,842
sudden infant death syndrome	1,079	912	456	391	371	322	337
Total	543,682	594,706	535,722	561,725	537,103	549,773	546,887
Deaths from injury and poisoning[2]							
all accidents	11,721	11,049	12,729	10,396	10,219	10,202	10,438
motor vehicle accidents	4,968	4,470	4,114	3,437	3,279	3,203	3,217
suicide and self-inflicted injury	3,950	3,893	3,952	3,719	3,619	3,547	3,455
all other external causes	2,272	2,344	2,294	2,959	2,253	2,380	2,227
Total	17,943	17,286	16,681	17,074	16,091	16,129	16,120
TOTAL	564,846	570,044	555,358	578,799	553,194	565,902	563,007
Scotland							
Deaths from natural causes[2]							
infectious and parasitic diseases[3]	258	310	270	340	306	326	493
intestinal infectious diseases	13	14	18	19	19	17	22
neoplasms	15,137	15,031	15,312	15,619	15,394	15,462	15,419
endocrine, nutritional, and metabolic diseases and immunity disorders	733	776	742	775	768	738	722
other metabolic and immunity disorders[3]	156	197	193	215	217	235	140

Deaths Analysed by Cause in the UK (*continued*)

Cause	1990[1]	1991[1]	1992[1]	1993[1]	1994	1995	1996
diseases of the blood and blood-forming organs	169	170	183	173	121	129	180
mental disorders	986	1,110	1,133	1,322	1,306	1,583	1,595
diseases of the nervous system and sense organs	890	947	877	879	853	832	852
meningitis	26	26	27	17	24	18	14
diseases of the circulatory system	29,437	29,166	28,776	29,909	27,138	27,079	26,728
diseases of the respiratory system	7,231	7,068	6,999	8,409	6,981	7,668	7,863
diseases of the digestive system	2,035	2,059	2,122	2,162	2,192	2,252	2,440
diseases of the genito-urinary system	817	805	888	857	816	928	839
complications of pregnancy, childbirth, etc	4	9	7	7	9	6	6
diseases of the skin and subcutaneous tissue	79	82	82	100	101	80	75
diseases of the musculo-skeletal system	301	270	306	269	279	303	252
congenital anomalies	206	193	209	216	170	176	192
certain conditions originating in the perinatal period	206	213	216	174	191	178	181
signs, symptoms, and ill-defined conditions	371	300	280	344	311	365	337
sudden infant death syndrome	132	90	64	58	48	48	43
Total	58,887	58,509	58,402	61,560	56,956	58,105	58,174
Deaths from injury and poisoning[2]							
all accidents	1,784	1,734	1,580	1,469	1,413	1,439	1,497
motor vehicle accidents	547	513	468	402	354	422	363
suicide and self-inflicted injury	535	525	569	615	624	623	596
all other external causes	321	273	386	405	335	333	404
Total	2,640	2,532	2,535	2,489	2,372	2,395	2,497
TOTAL	61,527	61,041	60,937	64,049	59,328	60,500	60,671

Northern Ireland

	1990[1]	1991[1]	1992[1]	1993[1]	1994	1995	1996
Deaths from natural causes[2]							
infectious and parasitic diseases[3]	46	44	41	55	39	44	14,620
intestinal infectious diseases	3	1	N/A	N/A	2	1	1
neoplasms	3,525	3,552	3,621	3,705	3,665	3,585	3,715
endocrine, nutritional, and metabolic diseases and immunity disorders	51	38	38	55	47	51	81
other metabolic and immunity disorders[3]	27	23	26	25	20	38	28
diseases of the blood and blood-forming organs	35	31	18	29	29	29	22
mental disorders	58	68	52	56	91	78	100
diseases of the nervous system and sense organs	177	168	181	189	187	224	236
meningitis	15	10	7	15	4	1	7
diseases of the circulatory system	7,110	6,986	7,112	7,137	7,011	6,929	6,633
diseases of the respiratory system	2,781	2,493	2,423	2,756	2,398	2,656	2,749
diseases of the digestive system	392	395	405	445	424	449	483
diseases of the genito-urinary system	251	272	238	261	250	251	254
complications of pregnancy, childbirth, etc	N/A	1	N/A	N/A	N/A	N/A	1
diseases of the skin and subcutaneous tissue	21	36	27	33	27	37	29
diseases of the musculo-skeletal system	59	54	43	35	31	40	35
congenital anomalies	85	90	77	116	87	91	72
certain conditions originating in the perinatal period	68	82	63	62	69	93	68
signs, symptoms, and ill-defined conditions	41	40	46	40	44	55	88
sudden infant death syndrome	14	15	11	6	7	9	15
Total	14,727	14,377	14,407	14,994	14,426	14,647	14,620
Deaths from injury and poisoning[2]							
all accidents	456	492	376	391	430	391	402
motor vehicle accidents	186	195	165	152	172	140	121
suicide and self-inflicted injury	158	129	107	129	138	122	124
all other external causes	85	98	98	119	120	150	72
Total	699	719	581	639	688	663	598
TOTAL	15,426	15,096	14,988	15,633	15,114	15,310	15,218

[1] On 1 January 1986, a new certificate for deaths within the first 28 days of life was introduced. It is not possible to assign one underlying cause of death from this certificate. The 'cause' figures in this table exclude all deaths at ages under 28 days.
[2] Within certain main categories only selected causes of death are shown
[3] Deaths assigned to AIDS and AIDS-related diseases are included in immunity disorders for England and Wales up to 1992 and Scotland up to 1995. Northern Ireland has always assigned such deaths to Infectious Diseases. England and Wales adopted this practice from 1993 onwards.

Immunization

ANTIBIOTIC RESISTANCE: A RISING TOLL

BY PAULETTE PRATT

When, in 1969, the US Surgeon-General announced that we could soon 'close the book' on infectious diseases, he was speaking prematurely. For already, two years earlier, first reports had surfaced of penicillin resistance developing in *Pneumococcus*, a bacterium which causes a number of potentially fatal diseases, including pneumonia and meningitis. Within little more than a decade, epidemics of pneumococcal disease were breaking out in many countries.

In 1995, when workers from the Centers for Disease Control in Atlanta looked at samples taken from patients with severe pneumonia, they found that a quarter had been hit by pneumococcal (*Staphylococcus pneumoniae*) strains resistant to penicillin; some 15% were also resistant to erythromycin. Today, growing resistance of this and other organisms to antibiotics is a global public health problem.

Rise of the Superbugs

Bacteria vary greatly in their sensitivity to antibiotics, and there is no such thing as a 'magic bullet' with blanket activity against all pathogens. The trouble is that, after more than half a century of antibiotic use, bacteria are mutating faster than new drugs can be found. The growth of super-resistance is being hastened by the indiscriminate use of antibiotics, including overprescribing.

In the developed world, the danger is greatest in hospitals, where people are already very sick. Currently some 14,000 Americans are dying each year from hospital-acquired infections caused by resistant bacteria. Most at risk are people whose immune systems are in some way impaired, including the very young or the frail elderly, AIDS patients, organ transplant recipients, and patients receiving chemotherapy for cancer.

Most notorious of the so-called 'superbugs' stalking hospital floors is methicillin-resistant *Staphylococcus aureus* (MRSA), a pathogen with an awesome talent for acquiring resistance traits from its microscopic neighbours. So far outbreaks of MRSA, which can cause temporary closure of operating rooms and intensive care units, have been met with vancomycin, a 'last resort' antibiotic normally reserved for life-threatening infections. But in spring of 1997, the Japanese reported the most convincing evidence yet of the appearance of vancomycin-resistant strains.

The Japanese report brings one step closer the spectre of the unstoppable 'superbug' overrunning hospitals. In fact, microbiologists have been predicting just this scenario, not least because strains of the intestinal bacterium *Enterococcus* have for some time been defying all existing antibiotics, including vancomycin and the closely related teicoplanin. In the laboratory, it has been shown that genes for resistance can pass from *Enterococcus* to the more deadly *S. aureus* by plasmid transfer.

It was fear of an epidemic of untreatable infections that prompted the recent European ban on avoparcin, a drug administered to farm animals to promote growth. The rationale for antibiotic use in this context is that it improves feeding efficiency. However, avoparcin is close in chemical structure to vancomycin, and many scientists argue that its use as a growth promoter in livestock creates a potential reservoir of vancomycin-resistant bacteria that would be transmissible to human beings.

Return of Old-Time Diseases

The phenomenon of super-resistance means also that many one-time killer diseases, including tuberculosis (TB), typhoid, cholera, and diphtheria, are returning in force. TB, always a major problem in the Third World, is the biggest threat, since now it is making a comeback in countries where previously it had been brought under control. Moreover, some strains of the bacterium have become resistant. Parts of the US worst affected are deprived inner-city areas such as Newark, New Jersey, and Brooklyn, the Bronx, and Harlem in New York, where resistance is widespread.

A big factor in the spread of multi-drug-resistant tuberculosis (MDRTB) has been the failure of control programs in the industrialized countries, including the US. This has meant that many patients starting out on medication lapse before the six-month course is completed. If a patient carrying a resistant strain takes only one drug instead of the prescribed combination, or fails to complete the course, the effect is to promote resistant strains.

Bacteria developing the ability to foil an antibiotic can become permanently resistant, according to researchers at Emory University in Atlanta. They demonstrated this in another rising superbug, *Escherichia coli*, which causes gastrointestinal infections. This finding implies that, contrary to what many doctors previously believed, reducing antibiotic use will not eliminate resistant strains.

While the quest for new drugs to fight infection is now paramount, many researchers are developing fresh strategies. These include: tinkering with the structure of antibiotics to add in helper molecules; seeking to disable genes for resistance; and developing laser-activated chemical compounds to blitz the superbugs. Some teams, too, are reviving the old idea of turning bacteriophages (bacteria-eating viruses) loose on resistant bacteria.

All these strategies and more may be needed to overcome the rising toll exacted by antibiotic resistance. Certainly, with infectious diseases claiming more than 17 million lives a year worldwide, we are still no nearer to 'closing the book'.

Mechanisms of Resistance

Bacteria may be naturally resistant to some antibiotics, or resistance may be acquired, mostly by the phenomenon of plasmid transfer. A plasmid is a free-floating fragment of DNA adrift in the cell cytoplasm. It carries some genetic material, including data governing the cell's resistance to antibiotics. Plasmids can be transmitted from one bacterium to another.

Occasionally resistance may be due to spontaneous mutation, which is the result of an error in replication of the cell's nuclear material during reproduction. Further reproduction causes the development of a resistant strain.

Bacteria demonstrate resistance in two ways. One way is by producing enzymes that disable drugs. A drug-defying enzyme is not always expressed by the organism targeted by therapy. The normally innocuous *Staphylococcus epidermidis* produces an enzyme that disables penicillin before it can act against harmful staphylococcal species; or some bacteria can contrive metabolic changes that foil the action of drugs. Sulphonamides – antibacterials introduced before the discovery of antibiotics – are often defeated by these metabolic readjustments on the part of bacteria.

Immunization: Chronology

AD 23–79	Pliny the Elder suggested using liver from mad dogs as protection against rabies.
1500s	Asian physicians immunized against smallpox using the crusts from pustules. This was only partially successful.
1720s	Lady Mary Wortley Montagu introduced smallpox immunization into Europe from Turkey.
1796	British physician Edward Jenner developed a safe smallpox vaccine using the cowpox virus.
1853	Vaccination against smallpox was made compulsory in Britain.
1885	French microbiologist Louis Pasteur developed a vaccine for rabies.
1894–1904	German immunologist Emil von Behring and Japanese bacteriologist Kitasato Shibasaburo successfully tested vaccines for diphtheria and tetanus.
1896	A E Wright developed typhoid vaccine.
1914	Tetanus vaccine became available on a large scale.
1920s	Tuberculosis vaccine produced.
1937	South African-born US microbiologist Max Theiler developed vaccine 17-D, still the main form of protection against yellow fever.
1949	Whooping cough vaccine licensed.
1952	US microbiologist Jonas Salk developed the first successful vaccine for poliomyelitis.
1960s	Measles and rubella vaccines produced.
1961	The oral vaccine for poliomyelitis, developed by Russian-born virologist Albert Sabin, became widely available.
1967	The World Health Organization (WHO) began its global campaign against smallpox.
1970s	Vaccines produced for meningococcal diseases and chickenpox. The WHO began constructing its 'cold chain' to ensure adequate transport and refrigeration for vaccines, which can take up to two years to reach their target in a developing country.
1974	WHO launched the Expanded Programme on Immunization, as fewer than 5% of children in developing countries were currently immunized.
1978	Pulmonary disease vaccine was developed.
1980s	Vaccine for hepatitis B, and a combination vaccine for measles, mumps, and rubella (MMR) became available.
1980	Smallpox virtually eradicated.
1984	Leprosy vaccine developed.
1989–1990	More than 100 children died when a measles epidemic swept through several large cities in the USA, highlighting the failure of the immunization programme. Three-quarters of the 45,000 children affected had not been vaccinated.
1990	Vaccine introduced for *Hemophilus influenzae*, a cause of meningitis.
1991	WHO estimated 80% of the world's children were immunized against diphtheria, whooping cough, tetanus, measles, polio, and tuberculosis. A US survey of nine major cities found that less than half of school-age children had been fully vaccinated against infectious diseases by their second birthday.
1994	Fear of a measles epidemic in the UK led to a vaccination programme for all children aged 5–16.
1995	First human trials of a vaccine administered by eating genetically-engineered potatoes.
1996	Heat-sensitive chemical monitors used on polio vaccine containers from January. If the monitor changes colour health workers will know that high temperatures have destroyed the vaccine. A vaccine for salmonella for use in poultry was approved in Australia.

Immunization for Travellers

(– = not applicable.)

Disease	Immunization	Timing	Reaction	Protection	Duration of protection	Other precautions	Notes
Cholera	2 injections not less than 1 week apart	at least 2 weeks before travel	soreness where injected, fever, headache	50–60%	6 months	avoid food or water that may be dirty	low risk in reasonable tourist accommodation; not recommended for children under 1 year
Hepatitis A	injection of immunoglobulin	just before travel	14 days	prevents illness	3 months	see typhoid	vaccine is not recommended for children under 10 years
	vaccine consisting of 2 doses 1 before travel, then a 2nd dose 6–12 months later	before travel		lessens its severity	10 years		
Hepatitis B	2 injections of vaccine 1 month apart, then booster 4 months later	last injection 1 month before travel	soreness where injected	very variable	about 5 years	–	usually only given to those at high risk, such as health workers
Malaria	none; take preventative tablets from 1 week before travel to 4 weeks after leaving malaria area	order tablets 2 weeks before travel	–	90%	only while tablets are taken	use anti-mosquito sprays, mosquito nets; keep arms and legs covered after sunset	some anti-malarial drugs are not recommended for pregnant mothers or children under 1 year
Polio	unimmunized adults: 3 doses each 1 month apart	4 months before travel	fever, flu-like symptoms	>95%	10 years	–	not usually given in first months of pregnancy

(continued)

Immunization for Travellers (*continued*)

Disease	Immunization	Timing	Reaction	Protection	Duration of protection	Other precautions	Notes
	immunized adults: 1 booster dose	just before travel					
Rabies	2 injections 1 month apart, booster 12 months later and as needed from then on	5 weeks before travel	soreness where injected, headache, muscle pains, vomiting possible within 48 hours	opinion is divided as to whether vaccine prevents rabies or promotes a faster response to treatment	3 months	avoid bites, scratches, or licks from any animal; wash any bite or scratch with antiseptic or soap as quickly as possible and get immediate medical treatment	–
Tetanus	normally given in childhood with booster every 10 years unimmunized adults: 2 injections 1 month apart then 3rd injection 6 months later	not critical	headache, lethargy in rare cases	>95%	about 10 years	wash any wounds with antiseptic	–
Typhoid	1–2 injections 4–6 weeks apart single injection 3 daily oral doses	5–7 weeks before departure	soreness where injected, nausea, headache (worst in those over 35 and on repeat immunizations) may last 36 hours	70–90%	1–3 years 3 years 1 year	avoid food or milk that may be contaminated by sewage or by flies	–
Yellow fever	1 injection	at least 10 days before departure	possible slight headache and low fever 5–10 days later	almost 100%	10 years	as malaria	may only be available from special centres

Immunization for Infants and Children in the UK

(Table indicates ages at which children should be immunized.)

Disease[1]	Immunization	Timing								Notes
		2 months	4 months	6 months	12–15 months	12–18 months	4–6 years	11–12 years	14–16 years	
Chicken pox	varicella zoster virus vaccine (VZV) in 1 dose					yes		yes		children who have not been vaccinated as infants should be vaccinated at 11–12 years; children of 13 years and older should receive 2 doses of the vaccine 4–8 weeks apart
Diphtheria, Tetanus (lockjaw), Pertussis (whooping cough)	DTP vaccine in 5 doses	yes	yes	yes		yes	yes			children who have not been vaccinated before 15 months may be given DTP vaccine
Diphtheria, Tetanus (lockjaw)	Td vaccine in 2 doses							yes	yes	must be 5 years from last booster of DTP and repeated every 10 years throughout life
Measles, Mumps, Rubella (German measles)	MMR vaccine in 2 doses				yes		yes			2nd dose can be given at 4–6 years or 11–12 years

Immunization for Infants and Children in the UK (*continued*)

Disease[1]	Immunization	Timing								Notes
		2 months	4 months	6 months	12–15 months	12–18 months	4–6 years	11–12 years	14–16 years	
Meningitis, Pneumonia	HbOC or PRP-T vaccine against *Haemophilus influenzae* type b virus in 3 doses	yes	yes	yes						
	PRP-OMP vaccine against *Haemophilus influenzae* type b virus in 2 doses	yes	yes							
Polio	IPV (inactivated polio virus) in 3 doses	yes	yes			yes				recommended for children with congenital or acquired immune deficiency disease; the 2nd dose must be 4 weeks after the 1st and the 3rd dose must be 6 months after the 2nd
	or OPV (oral polio virus) in 4 doses	yes	yes	yes			yes			

[1] Hepatitis B not included on chart. The vaccine dose is based on the Hepatitis B status of the mother.

Source: British Medical Association

Immunization Programme Recommended for Cats in the UK

(As of October 1997.)

Disease	Age at first vaccination (weeks)	Age at second vaccination (weeks)	Revaccination intervals (months)
Panleukopenia	8–10	12–16	12
Viral rhinotracheitis	8–10	12–16	12
Caliciviral disease	8–10	12–16	12
Pneumonitis (chlamydiosis)	8–10	12–16	12
Rabies	12	64	12 or 36[1]
Feline leukaemia	10	12–24[1]	13–14[1]

[1] Check with your veterinarian as to type of vaccine.

Source: American Veterinary Medicine Association

Immunization Programme Recommended for Dogs in the UK

(– = not applicable. As of October 1997.)

Disease	Age at first vaccination (weeks)	Age at second vaccination (weeks)	Age at third vaccination (weeks)	Revaccination intervals (months)
Distemper	6–10	10–12	14–16	12
Infectious canine hepatitis (CAV-1 or CAV-2)	6–8	10–12	14–16	12
Parvovirus infection	6–8	10–12	14–16	12
Bordetellosis	6–8	10–12	14–16	12
Parainfluenza	6–8	10–12	14–16	12
Leptospirosis	10–12	14–16	–	12
Rabies	12	64	–	12 or 36[1]
Coronavirus	6–8	10–12	12–14	12

[1] Check with your veterinarian as to type of vaccine.

Source: American Veterinary Medicine Association

HIV/AIDS

Estimated Number of Deaths from HIV/AIDS in the World

AIDS deaths in 1997 totalled 2.3 million, of which 1.8 million were among adults aged 15 and above. Since the beginning of the epidemic there have been an estimated 11.7 million deaths from AIDS. The total number of AIDS orphans is near 8 million.

1996

Region	Estimated deaths	Region	Estimated deaths
East Asia and Pacific	1,200	North America	61,300
Central and eastern Europe and central Asia	1,000	Latin America	70,900
Australia and New Zealand	1,000	Caribbean	14,500
North Africa and Middle East	10,800	Sub-Saharan Africa	783,700
Western Europe	21,000		
South and Southeast Asia	143,700		

Source: World Health Organization

History of Reported AIDS Cases by Continent

(As of December 1995.)

Continent	1979	1980	1981	1982	1983	1984	1985	1986	1987
Africa	0	0	0	2	19	206	727	6,165	23,019
America	2	187	509	1,665	5,017	11,697	24,379	45,701	80,263
Asia	0	1	2	3	11	19	46	132	282
Europe	0	17	37	117	412	982	2,457	4,852	14,492
Oceania	0	0	0	91	97	173	315	567	891
Total	2	205	548	1,878	5,556	13,077	27,924	57,417	118,947

Continent	1988	1989	1990	1991	1992	1993	1994	1995
Africa	51,231	92,526	147,054	219,810	293,441	360,565	426,249	442,735
America	127,960	184,162	249,203	327,782	427,663	528,394	611,869	659,662
Asia	458	746	1,224	2,062	4,101	11,469	23,176	28,630
Europe	25,303	39,658	56,969	75,906	96,603	118,656	142,197	154,103
Oceania	1,489	2,188	2,958	3,855	4,721	5,600	6,506	6,680
Total	206,441	319,280	457,408	629,415	826,529	1,024,684	1,209,997	1,291,810

Source: World Health Organization

AIDS Cases in the UK by Region and Year of Report

Country and region of report	1985 or earlier	1986	1987	1988	1989	1990	1991	1992	1993	1994	1995	1996	1997	Total
England														
Northern and Yorkshire	7	17	21	41	34	64	36	43	65	48	40	72	52	540
Trent	2	7	10	21	14	24	25	43	30	72	42	55	54	399
Anglia and Oxford	4	7	42	45	46	53	89	91	115	104	88	65	35	784
North Thames	183	187	388	379	461	703	715	829	812	925	791	868	401	7,642
South Thames	24	38	86	111	124	192	215	218	278	282	256	325	253	2,402
South and West	18	4	23	36	30	49	64	73	70	83	91	88	45	674
West Midlands	4	7	9	15	22	32	33	27	38	38	48	35	33	341
North West	9	19	24	51	35	64	73	48	53	71	59	230	79	815
Total	251	286	603	699	766	1,181	1,250	1,372	1,461	1,623	1,415	1,738	952	13,597
Wales	5	4	9	16	14	13	12	17	20	21	18	12	17	178
Northern Ireland	1	1	2	5	5	8	4	7	9	7	13	11	0	73
Scotland	7	8	24	34	57	62	85	77	111	120	132	95	59	871
TOTAL UK	264	299	638	754	842	1,264	1,351	1,473	1,601	1,771	1,578	1,856	1,028	14,719
Channel Isles/Isle of Man	0	0	0	2	1	2	0	0	1	0	0	0	1	7

Source: Communicable Disease Surveillance Centre

Current Total of Reported AIDS Cases in the World

There are currently an estimated 30.6 million people living with HIV/AIDS and 5.8 million new infections occurred in 1997. If current global trends continue, it is estimated that more than 40 million people will be living with HIV/AIDS in the year 2000.

1996

Category	Group		Number (millions)	Category	Group		Number (millions)
New HIV infections	adults		2.70	Cumulative HIV infections	adults	male	15.50
	children		0.40			female	11.30
	TOTAL		3.10		*Total*		26.80
					children		2.60
People living with HIV/AIDS	adults	male	12.60		*TOTAL*		29.40
		female	9.20				
	Total		21.80	Cumulative AIDS cases	adults	male	3.90
	children		0.83			female	2.80
	TOTAL		22.60		*Total*		6.70
					children		1.70
HIV/AIDS associated deaths	adults	male	0.65		*TOTAL*		8.40
		female	0.47				
	Total		1.10	Cumulative HIV/AIDS deaths	adults	male	2.90
	children		0.35			female	2.10
	TOTAL		1.50		*Total*		5.00
					children		1.40
					TOTAL		6.40

Source: World Health Organization

AIDS: RECENT DEVELOPMENTS

BY PAUL MOSS

The global count of people infected with the human immunodeficiency virus (HIV) continues to increase at an alarming rate. Despite some notable successes with health education campaigns, millions are infected, with the worst infection rates being in the developing world. Nevertheless, there are signs that the enormous scientific effort that has been mobilized against the disease is now paying dividends. Current drug regimes are able to prolong life and are even allowing scientists to debate the prospect of cure.

When HIV enters the body, the main cell type infected is the CD4+ T lymphocyte, a circulating white cell that plays an important role in controlling immune responses. In addition, the virus can enter a variety of other cell types that have the CD4 molecule on their surface. The net result of infection is a relentless fall in the number of CD4+ T cells and a gradual dismantling of the immune system's ability to fight off infectious agents such as bacteria, fungi, and other viruses. This process leaves patients very susceptible to a wide variety of infections, many of which are virtually never seen in people with a normally functioning immune system. One important advance in the last few years has been the use of molecular assays to measure the amount of virus in the blood of infected patients. This procedure is valuable in predicting how rapidly they are likely to progress to an advanced state of the disease.

Early Treatment

The initial successes in the drug treatment of HIV infection were with agents that could treat or prevent the infectious complications of the disease. These drugs remain very valuable but do not have any activity against HIV itself. The first drug with proven activity against HIV was zidovudine (AZT). Zidovudine resembles one of the building blocks of DNA, and when HIV undergoes replication, zidovudine can bind to an essential HIV enzyme and prevent the virus from completing its life cycle. Zidovudine can improve the symptoms of HIV infection, is valuable in asymptomatic patients with low CD4+ T lymphocyte counts, and is effective at reducing the rate of transmission of HIV from pregnant women to their babies. However, when zidovudine is used alone, the virus is usually able to escape from the effects of zidovudine by mutating its DNA sequence. There is now an increasing appreciation of the need to use zidovudine in combination with some of the new antiviral drugs.

New Developments

At the moment, probably the most exciting class of drugs that inhibit HIV replication is the protease inhibitors. When HIV replicates inside a cell it has to make a copy of its DNA, and then this genetic message is decoded into a protein. Some HIV proteins need to be broken down into smaller pieces in order to function, and this is done by a protease molecule. Normal function of the HIV protease appears to be vital for efficient replication of the virus, and over the last few years researchers have spent a great deal of effort in developing drugs that can block its function.

At least four protease inhibitors have been tried in clinical practice: saquinavir, ritonavir, nelfinavir, and indinavir. All have slightly different properties and different side effects. In clinical trials, these drugs have demonstrated a spectacular ability to reduce the amount of virus in the body. Sensitive molecular assays such as the polymerase chain reaction (PCR) have shown that the amount of HIV in blood can be reduced by over a thousandfold and sometimes may reach undetectable levels. Although effective on their own, most of the current drive in HIV therapeutics is to use these agents in combination with other anti-HIV agents. Typically this would include zidovudine, a protease inhibitor, and another agent such as didanosine. In a recent trial this combination led to the virus being undetectable in 60 % of patients after 24 weeks of treatment. A very encouraging observation with protease inhibitors is that they can be used at a very advanced state of the disease. It seems that the drugs should be used at quite large doses, to avoid the development of a resistant virus, and unfortunately they do have several side effects. Although most of these effects are not serious, many patients are unable to tolerate a particular drug combination; in these cases a change to another combination is indicated.

The Role of Combination Therapy

The exact role of combination therapy in the overall management of HIV infection is a subject of considerable debate at present. In an attempt to achieve consensus, a panel of the International AIDS Society-USA met in 1996. After results from many clinical trials, the group suggested that combination therapy was now the treatment of choice. It remains unclear, however, whether or not protease inhibitors should be used with all patients or just those at particular risk of rapid progression to full-blown AIDS based on measurement of the amount of HIV in their blood. Patients with symptoms should be offered treatment, but for those who are asymptomatic the situation is less clear and the decision will be based on the CD4+ count and the viral load in the blood. There are relatively little data to recommend how to treat patients who have been infected in the last month or two and are suffering from the typical symptoms of acute infection: fever, swollen lymph nodes, and headaches. As this is a time of intense viral replication, there is a theoretical advantage in using the strongest available treatment to limit the initial multiplication of the virus. This may also reduce the chance of the virus making mutations that would allow it to resist drug treatment.

The last few years have seen valuable advances in the treatment of HIV infection. Several powerful drugs are now available and are being tested in trials around the world. The human immunodeficiency virus has an astounding ability to mutate itself in order to evade drugs, and there are likely to be setbacks ahead. It is too soon to say whether or not some patients may be offered the prospect of complete cure. Nevertheless, many AIDS researchers are hoping that they can now maintain the upper hand in the battle against this formidable virus.

AIDS: Chronology

1977	Two homosexual men in New York, are diagnosed as having the rare cancer Kaposi's sarcoma. They are thought to be the first victims of AIDS.
1979	The Center for Disease Control in Atlanta, Georgia, reports the first cases of the disease later known as AIDS.
1981	The US Center for Disease Control in Atlanta, Georgia, first conclusively identifies AIDS; doctors realize that they have previously seen similar cases among drug users and homosexuals.
1983	US medical researcher Robert Gallo at the US National Cancer Institute, Maryland, and French medical researcher Luc Montagnier at the Pasteur Institute in Paris, isolate the virus thought to cause AIDS; it becomes known as the HIV virus (human immunodeficiency virus).
1984	Bath houses are closed in San Francisco, California, to slow the spread of the AIDS virus.
1985	Screening blood donations for the AIDS virus begins in Britain.
2 October 1985	Rock Hudson, US film actor, the first celebrity to have announced publicly that he had AIDS, dies in Beverly Hills, California, aged 59.
11 November 1985	*An Early Frost*, the first television drama about AIDS, is shown on US television, starring Aidan Quinn, Gena Rowlands, and Ben Gazzara.
1986	There are 25,000 diagnosed cases of AIDS in the USA.
1986	The US writer Larry Kramer completes *The Normal Heart*, a play dealing with the issue of AIDS.
1986	In the USA, gay activist Cleve Jones conceives the idea of a huge patchwork quilt to commemorate the victims of AIDS.
22 October 1986	The US surgeon general urges education, abstinence, and greater use of condoms in the fight against AIDS.
4 February 1987	US entertainer Liberace dies of AIDS in Palm Springs, California, aged 67.
20 March 1987	The AIDS treatment drug AZT is given approval by the US Food and Drug Administration. Treatment costs $10,000 per year per patient. The treatment does not cure the disease but it does relieve some symptoms and extend victims' lives.
31 December 1989	Since 1981, 10,611 women in the USA have reported having AIDS. Between 1984 and 1988, the proportion of US AIDS sufferers who are women has increased from 6.4% to 10.4%
1991	The red ribbon signifying AIDS awareness is designed for the Tony Awards in New York.
25 January 1991	US federal health officials announce that 100,777 people have died from AIDS since the discovery of the disease in 1981.
9 October 1991	The US Food and Drug Administration approves DDI, a drug to combat AIDS that is much cheaper than AZT, and which can be taken by those who cannot tolerate AZT.
7 November 1991	Basketball star Earvin 'Magic' Johnson retires on discovering that he is infected with the HIV virus that causes AIDS.
24 November 1991	Freddie Mercury, lead singer and songwriter of the British rock group Queen, dies of AIDS in London aged 45.
1993	The film *Philadelphia*, directed by Jonathan Demme, is released in the USA. The first mainstream Hollywood film to deal with the subject of AIDS, it stars Tom Hanks.
1993	AIDS becomes the leading cause of death among men aged between 25 and 44 in the USA.
31 December 1994	The number of AIDS cases worldwide exceeds 1 million for the first time, when the World Health Organization reports that there are 1,025,073 officially reported AIDS cases.
1995	US researchers estimate that HIV reproduces at a rate of a billion viruses a day, even in otherwise healthy individuals, but is held at bay by the immune system producing enough white blood cells to destroy them. Gradually, the virus mutates so much that the immune system is overwhelmed and the victim develops AIDS.
1996	The death rate from AIDS in the USA falls from 15.6 per 100,000 people to 11.6, a 26% decline. It is the first decline in the 15 years since the pandemic began.
1996	*This Wild Darkness*, US writer Harold Brodkey's journal about his experience of AIDS, is published posthumously.
9 May 1996	Scientists discover a protein, 'fusin', which allows the HIV virus to fuse with a human immune system cell's outer membrane and inject genetic material. Its presence is necessary for the AIDS virus to enter the cell.
January 1997	The World Health Organization (WHO) estimates that 22.6 million men, women, and children have to date been infected by HIV, the virus responsible for causing AIDS. Approximately 42% of adult sufferers are female, with the proportion of women infected steadily increasing.
February 1997	The Centers for Disease Control and Prevention in Atlanta, Georgia, report that deaths among people with AIDS declined 13% during the first six months of 1996 over the same period the year before.
8 May 1997	US AIDS researcher David Ho and colleagues show how aggressive treatment of HIV-1 infection with a cocktail of three antiviral drugs can drive the virus to below the limits of conventional clinical detection within eight weeks.
9 February 1998	US scientist David Ho reports the discovery of the AIDS virus in a 1959 blood sample and suggests that a transfer of the virus from ape to human occurred in the late 1940s or early 1950s.

Cancer and Heart Disease

Factors that Contribute to an Individual's Risk of Developing Cancer

Source: American Cancer Society

Current research shows that attention to diet and stopping smoking reduce an individual's risk of developing cancer.

Smoking
Cigarette smoking is responsible for 90 per-cent of lung cancers among men and 79 per-cent among women – about 87 percent overall. Smoking accounts for about 30 per-cent of all cancer deaths. Those who smoke two or more packs of cigarettes a day have lung cancer mortality rates 12 to 25 times greater than that of nonsmokers.

Nutrition and Diet
Nutrition plays an import-ant role in prevent-ing cancer. Research indicates that people may reduce their cancer risk by observing these nutrition guidelines:

Maintain a desirable weight. For people who are obese, weight reduction is a good way to lower cancer risk. Weight mainten-ance can be accomplished by reducing intake of calories and by maintaining a physically active lifestyle.

Eat a varied diet. A varied diet eaten in moderation offers the best hope for lowering the risk of cancer.

Include a variety of vegetables and fruits in the daily diet. Studies have shown that daily consumption of vegetables and fresh fruits is associated with a decreased risk of lung, prostate, bladder, oesophagus, colorectal, and stomach cancers.

Eat more high-fibre foods, such as whole grain cereals, breads, pasta, vegetables, and fruits. High-fibre diets are a healthy substi-

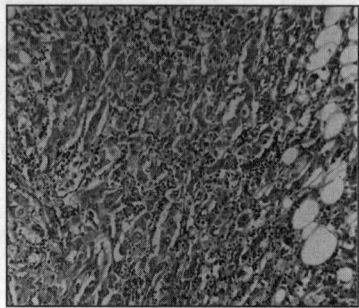

Breast cancer cell: *A diet full of fatty foods may contribute to the development of certain cancers, including breast cancer*
Photo Disc Ltd.

tute for fatty foods and may reduce the risk of colon cancer.

Cut down on total fat intake. A diet high in fat may be a factor in the development of cer-tain cancers, particularly breast, colon, and prostate cancers.

Limit consumption of alcohol, if you drink at all. Heavy drinking, especially when accompanied by cigarette smoking or smoke-less tobacco use, increases risk of cancers of the mouth, larynx, throat, oesophagus, and liver. Limit consumption of salt-cured, smoked, and nitrite-cured foods. In areas of the world where salt-cured and smoked foods are eaten frequently, there is higher incidence of cancer of the oesophagus and stomach. Modern methods of food processing and pre-serving appear to avoid the cancer-causing by-products associated with older methods of food treatment.

Sunlight
Epidemiological evidence shows that sun exposure is a major factor in the development of melanoma and that incidence increases for those living near the equator.

Alcohol
Oral cancer and cancers of the larynx, throat, oesophagus, and liver occur more frequently among heavy drinkers of alcohol especially when accompanied by smoking cigarettes or chewing tobacco.

Smokeless Tobacco
Use of chewing tobacco or snuff increases the risk of cancer of the mouth, larynx, throat, and oesophagus, and is a highly addictive habit.

Oestrogen
Oestrogen treatment to control menopausal symptoms can increase risk of endometrial cancer. However, using progesterone with the oestrogen helps to minimize this risk. Consultation with a physician will help each woman to assess personal risks and benefits. Continued research is needed in the area of oestrogen use and breast cancer.

Occupational Hazards
Exposure to several different industrial agents, such as nickel, chromate, asbestos, vinyl chloride, increases risk of various can-cers. Risk of lung cancer from asbestos is greatly increased when combined with ciga-rette smoking.

Ionizing Radiation
Excessive exposure to ionizing radiation can increase cancer risk. Most medical and dental x-rays are adjusted to deliver the lowest dose possible without sacrificing image quality. Excessive radon exposure (emitted by rocks in the Earth's crust) in homes may increase risk of lung cancer, especially in cigarette smokers. If levels are found to be too high, remedial actions should be taken.

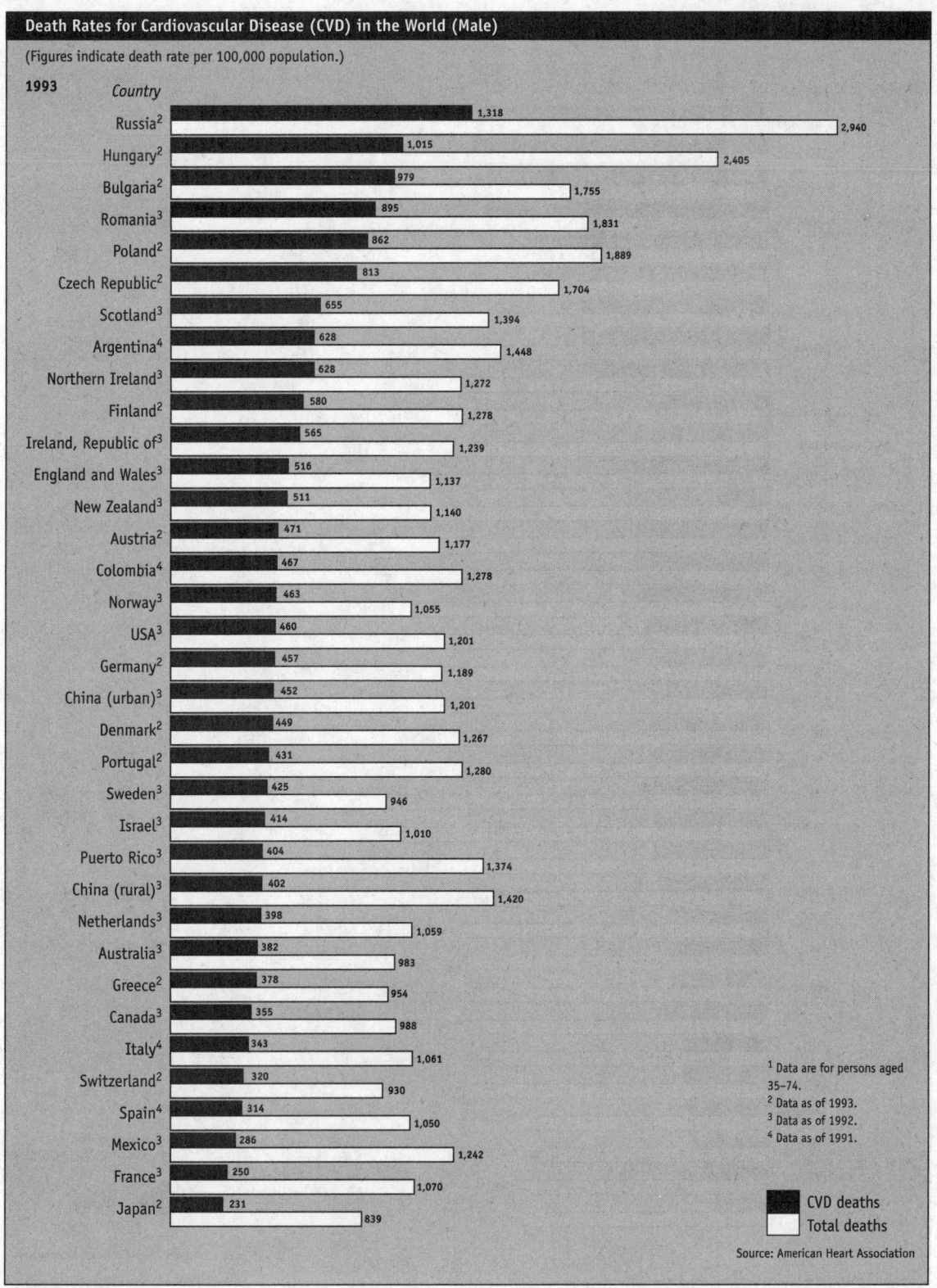

Death Rates for Cardiovascular Disease (CVD) in the World (Male)

(Figures indicate death rate per 100,000 population.)

1993

Country	CVD deaths	Total deaths
Russia[2]	1,318	2,940
Hungary[2]	1,015	2,405
Bulgaria[2]	979	1,755
Romania[3]	895	1,831
Poland[2]	862	1,889
Czech Republic[2]	813	1,704
Scotland[3]	655	1,394
Argentina[4]	628	1,448
Northern Ireland[3]	628	1,272
Finland[2]	580	1,278
Ireland, Republic of[3]	565	1,239
England and Wales[3]	516	1,137
New Zealand[3]	511	1,140
Austria[2]	471	1,177
Colombia[4]	467	1,278
Norway[3]	463	1,055
USA[3]	460	1,201
Germany[2]	457	1,189
China (urban)[3]	452	1,201
Denmark[2]	449	1,267
Portugal[2]	431	1,280
Sweden[3]	425	946
Israel[3]	414	1,010
Puerto Rico[3]	404	1,374
China (rural)[3]	402	1,420
Netherlands[3]	398	1,059
Australia[3]	382	983
Greece[2]	378	954
Canada[3]	355	988
Italy[4]	343	1,061
Switzerland[2]	320	930
Spain[4]	314	1,050
Mexico[3]	286	1,242
France[3]	250	1,070
Japan[2]	231	839

[1] Data are for persons aged 35–74.
[2] Data as of 1993.
[3] Data as of 1992.
[4] Data as of 1991.

■ CVD deaths
□ Total deaths

Source: American Heart Association

Death Rates for Cardiovascular Disease (CVD) in the World (Female)

(Figures indicate death rate per 100,000 population.)

1993

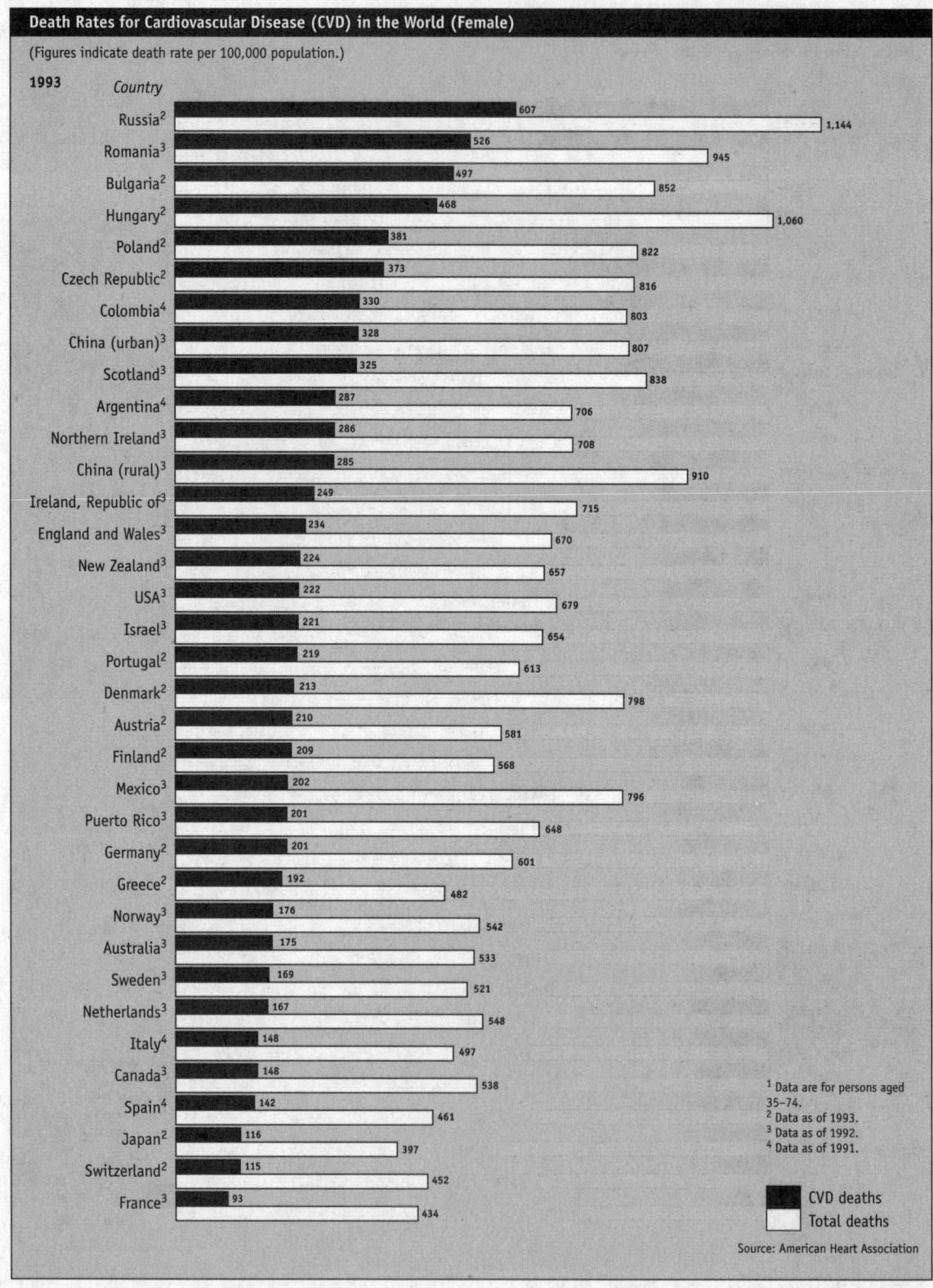

Country	CVD deaths	Total deaths
Russia[2]	607	1,144
Romania[3]	526	945
Bulgaria[2]	497	852
Hungary[2]	468	1,060
Poland[2]	381	822
Czech Republic[2]	373	816
Colombia[4]	330	803
China (urban)[3]	328	807
Scotland[3]	325	838
Argentina[4]	287	706
Northern Ireland[3]	286	708
China (rural)[3]	285	910
Ireland, Republic of[3]	249	715
England and Wales[3]	234	670
New Zealand[3]	224	657
USA[3]	222	679
Israel[3]	221	654
Portugal[2]	219	613
Denmark[2]	213	798
Austria[2]	210	581
Finland[2]	209	568
Mexico[3]	202	796
Puerto Rico[3]	201	648
Germany[2]	201	601
Greece[2]	192	482
Norway[3]	176	542
Australia[3]	175	533
Sweden[3]	169	521
Netherlands[3]	167	548
Italy[4]	148	497
Canada[3]	148	538
Spain[4]	142	461
Japan[2]	116	397
Switzerland[2]	115	452
France[3]	93	434

[1] Data are for persons aged 35–74.
[2] Data as of 1993.
[3] Data as of 1992.
[4] Data as of 1991.

■ CVD deaths
□ Total deaths

Source: American Heart Association

Incidence of Lung Cancer in the UK (Male)

Figures relate to malignant neoplasms of the trachea, bronchus, and lung registered by 31 December 1995 for England, Wales, and Northern Ireland and registered by 12 September 1996 for Scotland. Cancer registration rates are standardized to the European Standard Population for the purpose of comparison with other European countries.

Registrations of lung cancer (rates per 100,000 population) (N/A = not available.)

Area	1981	1991
Northern	132.0	114.0
North Western	127.2	102.8
Yorkshire	109.8	94.9
Mersey	125.2	113.2
Trent	108.6	84.5
West Midlands	113.5	94.8
East Anglian	93.0	69.1
Oxford	102.3	84.4
North East Thames	112.4	92.9
North West Thames	97.8	81.8
South West Thames	109.5	78.3
South East Thames	111.3	86.5
Wessex	101.6	77.6
South Western	93.4	72.5
England	110.5	89.4
Wales[1]	104.0	N/A
Scotland	135.8	118.4
Northern Ireland[2]	87.2	88.5

Year: 1981, 1991

[1] The Welsh Cancer and Intelligence Surveillance Unit is in the process of validating these data, which may be subject to amendment in the future.
[2] All rates for Northern Ireland are likely to be underestimates due to incompleteness of the registry.

Source: Office for National Statistics; General Register Office for Scotland; Northern Ireland Statistics and Research Agency. © Crown copyright 1997

Incidence of Lung Cancer in the UK (Female)

Figures relate to malignant neoplasms of the trachea, bronchus, and lung registered by 31 December 1995 for England, Wales, and Northern Ireland and registered by 12 September 1996 for Scotland. Cancer registration rates are standardized to the European Standard Population for the purpose of comparison with other European countries.

Registrations of lung cancer (rates per 100,000 population) (N/A = not available.)

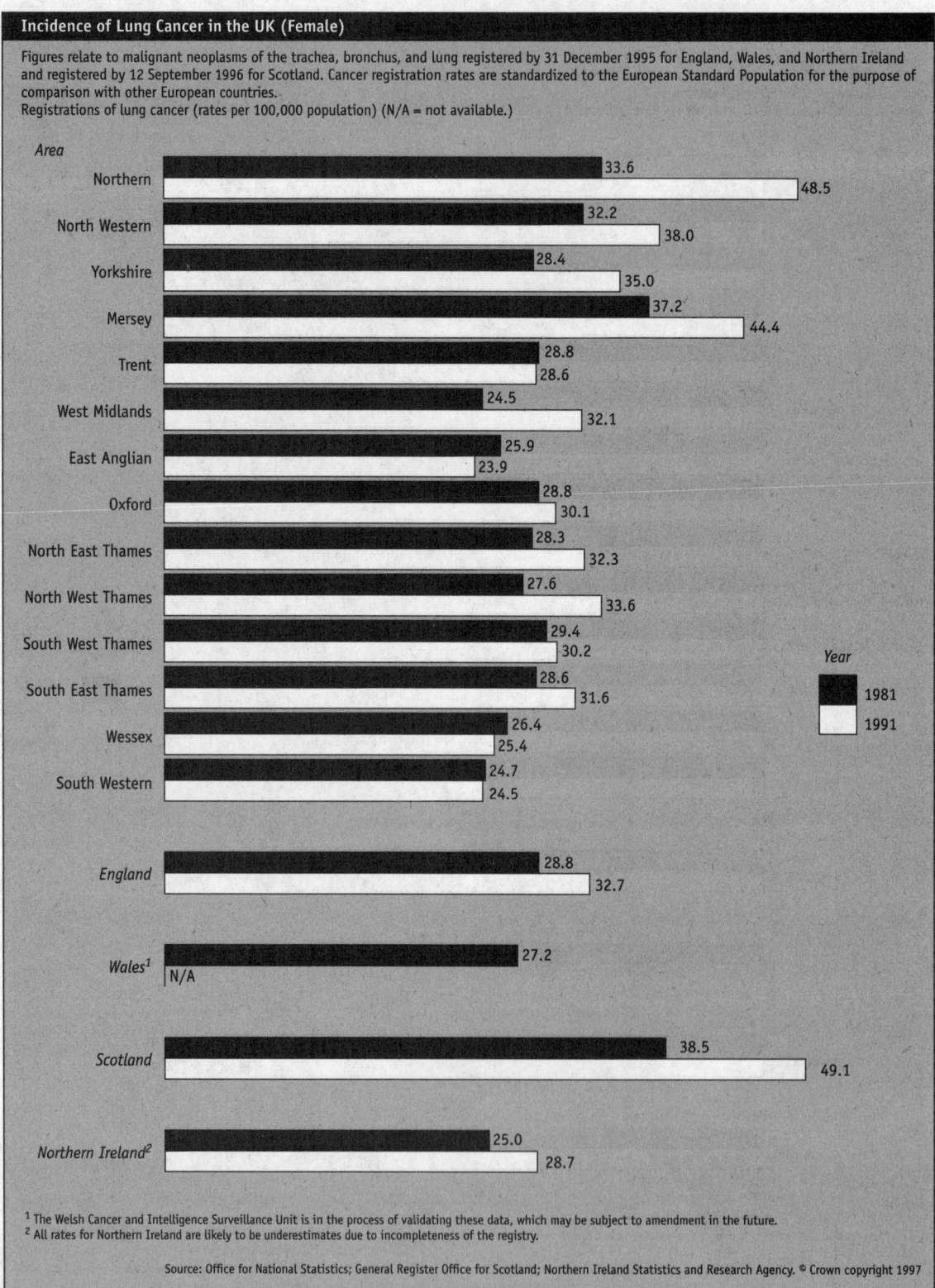

Area	1981	1991
Northern	33.6	48.5
North Western	32.2	38.0
Yorkshire	28.4	35.0
Mersey	37.2	44.4
Trent	28.8	28.6
West Midlands	24.5	32.1
East Anglian	25.9	23.9
Oxford	28.8	30.1
North East Thames	28.3	32.3
North West Thames	27.6	33.6
South West Thames	29.4	30.2
South East Thames	28.6	31.6
Wessex	26.4	25.4
South Western	24.7	24.5
England	28.8	32.7
Wales[1]	27.2	N/A
Scotland	38.5	49.1
Northern Ireland[2]	25.0	28.7

[1] The Welsh Cancer and Intelligence Surveillance Unit is in the process of validating these data, which may be subject to amendment in the future.
[2] All rates for Northern Ireland are likely to be underestimates due to incompleteness of the registry.

Source: Office for National Statistics; General Register Office for Scotland; Northern Ireland Statistics and Research Agency. © Crown copyright 1997

Prevalence of Smoking in some Countries of the World

Data are for men and women 15 years or older and are given in order of male smoking prevalence. (N/A = not available.)

Country/ territory	Year of survey	Men (% of population)	Women (% of population)	Country/ territory	Year of survey	Men (% of population)	Women (% of population)
South Korea	1989	68.2	6.7	India	1980s	40.0	3.0
Latvia	1993	67.0	12.0	Iraq	1990	40.0	5.0
Russia	1993	67.0	30.0	Malta	1992	40.0	18.0
Dominican Republic	1990	66.3	13.6	Mongolia	1990	40.0	7.0
Tonga	1991	65.0	14.0	Uzbekistan	1989	40.0	1.0
Turkey	1988	63.0	24.0	Brazil	1989	39.9	25.4
China	1984[1]	61.0	7.0	Egypt	1986	39.8	1.0
Bangladesh	1990	60.0	15.0	Morocco	1990	39.6	9.1
Fiji	1988	59.3	30.6	Lesotho	1989	38.3	1.0
Japan	1994	59.0	14.8	Mexico	1990	38.3	14.4
Sri Lanka	1988	54.8	0.8	El Salvador	1988	38.0	12.0
Algeria	1980	53.0	10.0	Italy	1994	38.0	26.0
Indonesia	1986	53.0	4.0	Portugal	1994	38.0	15.0
Samoa	1994	53.0	18.6	Chile	1990	37.9	25.1
Saudi Arabia	1990	52.7	N/A	Guatemala	1989	37.8	17.7
Estonia	1994	52.0	24.0	Denmark	1993	37.0	37.0
Kuwait	1991	52.0	12.0	Germany	1992	36.8	21.5
Lithuania	1992	52.0	10.0	Norway	1994	36.4	35.5
South Africa	1995	52.0	17.0	Honduras	1988	36.0	11.0
Poland	1993	51.0	29.0	Netherlands	1994	36.0	29.0
Seychelles	1989	50.9	10.3	Switzerland	1992	36.0	26.0
Bolivia	1992	50.0	21.4	Colombia	1992	35.1	19.1
Albania	1990	49.8	7.9	Costa Rica	1988	35.0	20.0
Cuba	1990	49.3	24.5	Slovenia	1994	35.0	23.0
Bulgaria	1989	49.0	17.0	Swaziland	1989	33.0	8.0
Thailand	1995	49.0	4.0	Luxembourg	1993	32.0	26.0
Spain	1993	48.0	25.0	Singapore	1995	31.9	2.7
Mauritius	1992	47.2	3.7	Belgium	1993	31.0	19.0
Greece	1994	46.0	28.0	Canada	1991	31.0	29.0
Papua New Guinea	1990	46.0	28.0	Iceland	1994	31.0	28.0
Israel	1989	45.0	30.0	Australia	1993	29.0	21.0
Cook Islands	1988	44.0	26.0	Ireland	1993	29.0	28.0
Czech Republic	1994	43.0	31.0	USA	1991	28.1	23.5
Jamaica	1990	43.0	13.0	UK	1994	28.0	26.0
Philippines	1987	43.0	8.0	Pakistan	1980	27.4	4.4
Slovak Republic	1992	43.0	26.0	Finland	1994	27.0	19.0
Cyprus	1990	42.5	7.2	Turkmenistan	1992	26.6	0.5
Austria	1992	42.0	27.0	Nigeria	1990	24.4	6.7
Malaysia	1986	41.0	4.0	Paraguay	1990	24.1	5.5
Peru	1989	41.0	13.0	Bahrain	1991	24.0	6.0
Uruguay	1990	40.9	26.6	New Zealand	1992	24.0	22.0
Argentina	1992	40.0	23.0	Sweden	1994	22.0	24.0
France	1993	40.0	27.0	Bahamas	1989	19.3	3.8
Hungary	1989	40.0	27.0				

[1] More recent data collected in 1991 on the smoking habits of men and women for a study of the health effects of smoking in China suggest that there has been little change in smoking prevalence since 1984.

Source: World Health Organization

Cigarette Smoking Status of Adults in England

(Figures are in percentages and are from weighted data where a sample of the population has been used to represent the full population.)

1996

Age

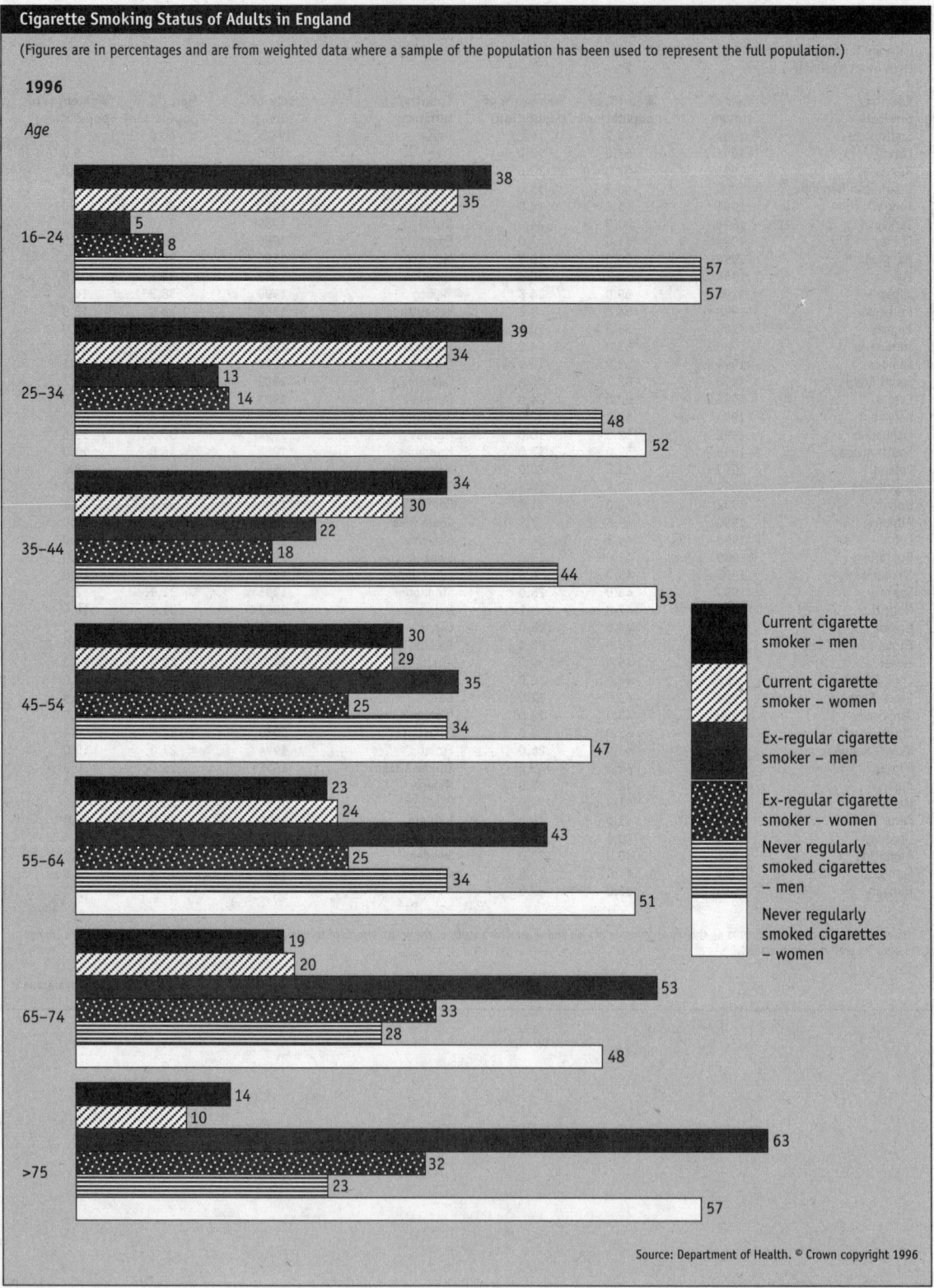

Current cigarette smoker – men

Current cigarette smoker – women

Ex-regular cigarette smoker – men

Ex-regular cigarette smoker – women

Never regularly smoked cigarettes – men

Never regularly smoked cigarettes – women

16–24
- 38
- 35
- 5
- 8
- 57
- 57

25–34
- 39
- 34
- 13
- 14
- 48
- 52

35–44
- 34
- 30
- 22
- 18
- 44
- 53

45–54
- 30
- 29
- 35
- 25
- 34
- 47

55–64
- 23
- 24
- 43
- 25
- 34
- 51

65–74
- 19
- 20
- 53
- 33
- 28
- 48

>75
- 14
- 10
- 63
- 32
- 23
- 57

Source: Department of Health. © Crown copyright 1996

Cigarette Smoking Status of Children in England

(Totals may not add to 100 percent due to rounding. Figures are in percentages and are from weighted data where a sample of the population has been used to represent the full population.)

1996

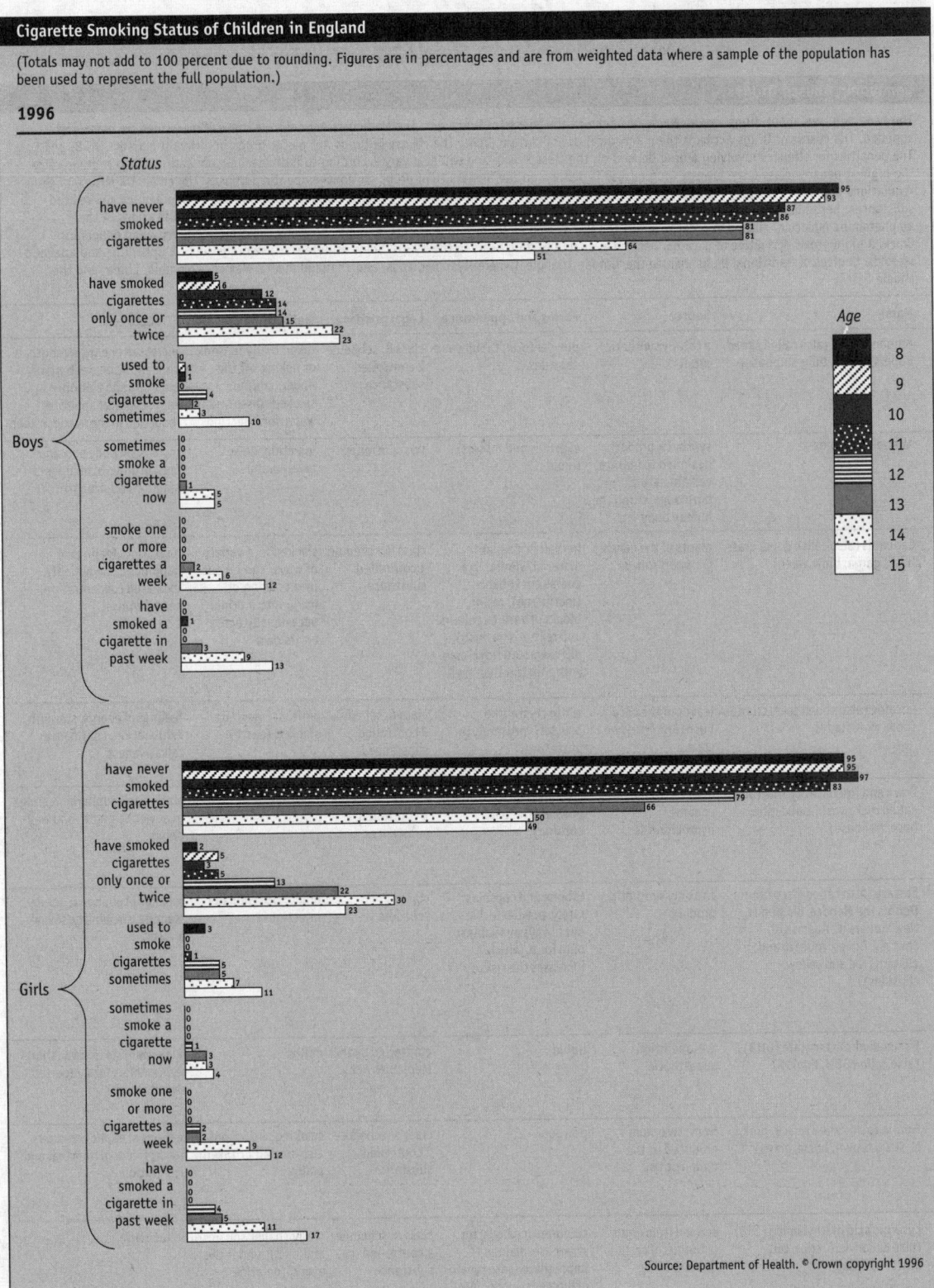

Source: Department of Health. © Crown copyright 1996

Drug Use/Misuse

Commonly Abused Drugs

The two main laws about drugs are the Medicines Act and the Misuse of Drugs Act. The Medicines Act controls the way medicines are made and supplied. The Misuse of Drugs Act bans the nonmedical use of certain drugs. The Misuse of Drugs Act places drugs in different classes – A, B, and C. The penalties for offences involving a drug depend on the class it is in and will also vary according to individual circumstances. Class A drugs carry the highest penalty, class C the lowest. Drug misuse is defined on the illegal use of drugs for nontherapeutic purposes. Under the UK Misuse of Drugs regulations drugs used illegally include: narcotics, such as heroin, morphine, and the synthetic opioids; barbiturates; amphetamines and related substances; benzodiazepine tranquillizers; cocaine, LSD, and cannabis. *Designer drugs,* for example ecstasy, are usually modifications of the amphetamine molecule, altered in order to evade the law as well as for different effects, and may be many times more powerful and dangerous. Crack, a highly toxic derivative of cocaine, became available to drug users in the 1980s. Some athletes misuse drugs such as ephedrine and anabolic steroids. Sources of traditional drugs include the 'Golden Triangle' (where Myanmar, Laos, and Thailand meet), Mexico, Colombia, China, and the Middle East.

Name	Source	Forms and appearance	Legal position	Methods of use	Effects of use
Amphetamine (also called speed, uppers, whizz, billy, sulphate)	a totally synthetic product	powder form; tablets and capsules	class B, schedule 2 controlled substance	taken orally in drink or licking off the finger; sniffed; smoked; dissolved in water for injecting	increased energy, strength, concentration, feelings of euphoria and elation; suppression of appetite; reduction in the need for sleep
Anabolic steroids	synthetic products designed to imitate certain natural hormones within the human body	capsules and tablets; liquid	not controlled	injections; also taken orally	increase in body bulk and muscle growth; feelings of stamina and strength
Cannabis (also called dope, grass, hash, ganja, blow, weed)	plants of the genus *Cannabis saliva*	herbal: dried plant material, similar to a coarse cut tobacco (marijuana); resin: blocks of various colours and texture (hashish); oil: extracted from resin, with a distinctive smell	class B, schedule 1 controlled substance	smoked in a variety of ways; can be put into cooking or made into a drink; occasionally eaten on its own	relaxation, feelings of happiness, congeniality, increased concentration, sexual arousal
Cocaine (also called coke, charlie, snow, white lady)	leaves of the coca bush, *Erythroxylum coca*	white crystalline powder; very rarely in paste form	class A, schedule 2 controlled substance	sniffed; injected; smoked (paste)	feelings of energy, strength, exhilaration, confidence; talkativeness
Crack and freebase cocaine (also called rock, wash, cloud nine; base, freebase)	derived from cocaine hydrochloride	crystals (crack cocaine); powder (freebase cocaine)	class A, schedule 2 controlled substances	smoking	elation and euphoria, feelings of power, strength, and well-being
Ecstasy (also called disco burgers, Dennis the Menace, diamonds, New Yorkers, E, Adam, XTC, Fantasy, Doves, rhubarb and custard (red and yellow capsules))	a totally synthetic product	tablets and capsules; rarely, powder; ecstasy is not always available in pure form, which increases the risks	class A, schedule 1	orally; occasionally injections	feelings of euphoria, energy, stamina, sociability, sexual arousal
Gammahydroxybutyrate (GHB) (also called GBH, liquid X)	pre-operation anaesthetic	liquid	controlled by the Medicines Act	orally	relaxation, sleepiness, short-term memory loss; reported sexual arousal
Heroin (also called smack, junk, H, skag, brown, horse, gravy)	from raw opium produced by the opium poppy	powder	class A, schedule 2 controlled substance	smoking; injections; also sniffed or taken orally	feelings of euphoria, inner peace, freedom from fear and deprivation
Lysergic acid diethylamide (LSD) (also called acid, trips, tab, blotters, dots)	derived from ergot (a fungus of certain cereal grains)	colourless crystals; for street use, mainly impregnated into squares of blotted paper or into squares of clear gelatine; or into tiny pills	class A, schedule 1 controlled substance	orally (paper squares and pills); under the eyelid (gelatine squares)	hallucinations

Commonly Abused Drugs

Name	Adverse effects	Tolerance potential	Habituation potential	Withdrawal effects	Overdose potential
Amphetamine (also called speed, uppers, whizz, billy, sulphate)	increased blood pressure with risk of stroke; diarrhoea or increased urination; disturbance of sleep patterns; weight loss; depression; paranoia; psychosis	tolerance develops rapidly	physical dependence: rare; psychological dependence: common	mental agitation, depression, panic; no physical symptoms	fatal overdose possible, even at low doses
Anabolic steroids	bone growth abnormalities; hypertension and heart disease; liver and kidney malfunction; hepatitis; sexual abnormalities and impotence; damage to foetal development	tolerance may develop	no physical dependence; profound psychological dependence	sudden collapse of muscle strength and stamina; irritability, violent mood swings	overdose can lead to collapse, convulsions, coma, and death
Cannabis (also called dope, grass, hash, ganja, blow, weed)	impaired judgement; loss of short-term memory; dizziness; confusion; anxiety; paranoia; potential for cancer and breathing disorders	tolerance develops rapidly	true physical dependence: rare; psychological dependence: common	disturbed sleep patterns; anxiety, panic	it is not thought possible to overdose fatally
Cocaine (also called coke, charlie, snow, white lady)	agitation, panic, feelings of being threatened; damage to nasal passages, exhaustion,, weight loss; collapsed veins, ulceration; delusions, violence	tolerance develops rapidly	strong physical and psychological dependence	severe cravings; feelings of anxiety and panic; depression	it is possible to overdose fatally
Crack and freebase cocaine (also called rock, wash, cloud nine; base, freebase)	depression, feelings of being threatened; paranoia, psychosis; violence	some tolerance develops	strong physical and psychological dependence; babies born to pregnant users may also be dependent	severe depression; aggression, panic; risk of suicide	overdose can lead to coma and death
Ecstasy (also called disco burgers, Dennis the Menace, diamonds, New Yorkers, E, Adam, XTC, Fantasy, Doves, rhubarb and custard (red and yellow capsules))	mood swings, nausea and vomiting, overheating, dehydration, convulsions, sudden death	tolerance develops	physical dependence: none; psychologist dependence: low	no physical symptoms; irritability, depression	overdose can lead to coma and death
Gammahydroxybutyrate (GHB) (also called GBH, liquid X)	nausea and vomiting; muscle stiffness; disorientation; collapse; risks from mixing with alcohol and unknown concentration of the drug	little tolerance develops	little dependence	few withdrawal symptoms	overdose can lead to convulsions and collapse, and, rarely, death
Heroin (also called smack, junk, H, skag, brown, horse, gravy)	depressed breathing, severe constipation, nausea, and vomiting; effect on general state of health, lower immunity; vein collapse and ulceration; risk of infection from needles	tolerance develops rapidly	profound physical and psychological dependence	sweating, flu-like symptoms 'going cold turkey'; severe cravings; professional assistance necessary	overdose can lead to coma and death
Lysergic acid diethylamide (LSD) (also called acid, trips, tab, blotters, dots)	risk of accident while hallucinating; flashbacks; risk of developing a latent psychiatric disorder	tolerance develops and disappears rapidly	no physical dependence; some psychological dependence	no physical effect; few psychological effects	it is not thought possible to overdose

Commonly Abused Drugs					
Name	**Source**	**Forms and appearance**	**Legal position**	**Methods of use**	**Effects of use**
Magic (hallucinogenic) mushrooms (also called shrooms, mushies)	natural mushrooms (mainly fly agaric and liberty cap)	several varieties; identification is difficult	possession and eating of fresh mushrooms is not an offence; preparation is[1]	eaten; infused to make a drink	hallucinations; feelings of euphoria, well-being, gaiety
Methadone (also called doll, dolly, red rock, tootsie roll; phy-amps, phy (ampoules))	a totally synthetic product	powder; tablets, ampoules, linctus, mixture	class A, schedule 2 controlled substance	orally; injections	feelings of relaxation, bodily warmth, freedom from pain and worry
Methylamphetamine (also called ice, meth, crystal, glass, ice-cream (crystal form); meth, Methedrine (powder or tablets))	a totally synthetic drug, closely related to amphetamine sulphate	crystals or, less commonly, tablets or powder	class B, schedule 2 controlled substance	burning crystals and inhaling the fumes; drinking, sniffing, licking off the finger (powder and tablets)	feelings of euphoria, great strength and energy, sustained for long periods without rest or food
Nitrites (poppers) (also called nitro, nitrite)	various synthetic volatile chemicals	in small glass bottles under trade names of Liquid Gold, Hi-Tech, Rave, Locker Room, Ram, Rush, etc	controlled by the Medicines Act	inhalation	feelings of excitement and exhilaration; sexual arousal and increased sensitivity of sexual organs
Over-the-counter medicines	range of proprietary medicines	mostly tablets	some are controlled	taken orally; injected	vary
Solvents (also called glue, gas, can, cog (depending on substance and container))	domestic and commercial products	liquid petroleum gases (LPGs): aerosols, camping gas cylinders, lighter gas refills; liquid solvents: fire extinguisher fluid, corrective fluids, certain paints and removers, nail polish and remover, anti-freeze, petrol; solvent-based glues: impact adhesives used for wood, plastic, laminate surfaces, vinyl floor tiles	not controlled	sprayed into the mouth and inhaled (LPGs); sniffing	deep intoxication, hallucinations, excitability
Tranquillizers (also called tranx, barbs, barbies, blockers, tueys, traffic lights, golf balls (tranquillizers); jellies, jelly beans, M&Ms, rugby balls (temazepam in jelly capsules))	pharmaceutical drugs aimed at treating patients with problems of anxiety, insomnia, and depression; based on benzodiazepine or barbiturate	tablets or capsules	benzodiazepine based: class C controlled substances; barbiturate based: class B controlled substances	taken orally or injected	in higher doses: feelings of euphoria, elimination of fear and feeling of deprivation

[1] Preparation (such as crushing, slicing, drying, etc) is punishable as an offence relating to psilocin and psilocybin – the active ingredients of most hallucinogenic mushrooms, both class A, schedule 1 controlled substances.

Commonly Abused Drugs

Name	Adverse effects	Tolerance potential	Habituation potential	Withdrawal effects	Overdose potential
Magic (hallucinogenic) mushrooms (also called shrooms, mushies)	long-term mental problems; risk of poisoning	tolerance develops rapidly	no dependence	few withdrawal effects	little overdose potential
Methadone (also called doll, dolly, red rock, tootsie roll; phy-amps, phy (ampoules))	sweating, nausea, itching, tiredness; disruption of menstrual cycle in women	tolerance develops slowly	strong physical and psychological dependence	fever, flu-like symptoms; diarrhoea; aggression	overdose can lead to respiratory depression, collapse, coma, and death
Methylamphetamine (also called ice, meth, crystal, glass, ice-cream (crystal form); meth, Methedrine (powder or tablets))	increased blood pressure with risk of stroke and heart failure, diarrhoea or increased urination, severe disturbance of sleep patterns, hallucinations, aggression, psychosis, delusions, paranoia	tolerance develops rapidly	physical dependence: not uncommon; psychological dependence: profound	severe cravings; depression; fear; panic and mental agitation	serious risk of fatal overdose, even at very low levels
Nitrites (poppers) (also called nitro, nitrite)	nausea and vomiting; headaches and dizziness; skin problems; damage to vision if touches the eyes; poisonous if swallowed	tolerance develops rapidly	no significant physical or psychological dependence	no significant effects	little risk of overdose
Over-the-counter medicines	vary	tolerance develops quickly	physical and psychological dependence may develop	possible effects	overdose can lead to health disturbances and death
Solvents (also called glue, gas, can, cog (depending on substance and container))	over-stimulation of the heart, and death; asphyxiation from swelling of throat tissues or inhalation of vomit; danger of accidents whilst hallucinating; problems with speech, balance, short-term memory, cognitive skills; possible personality changes	tolerance may develop	no physical dependence; strong psychological dependence	no physical symptoms; anxiety and mood swings	overdose can lead to collapse, coma, and death
Tranquillizers (also called tranx, barbs, barbies, blockers, tueys, traffic lights, golf balls (tranquillizers); jellies, jelly beans, M&Ms, rugby balls (temazepam in jelly capsules))	violent mood swings, bizarre sexual behaviour, deep depression, disorientation, lethargy	tolerance develops rapidly	profound physical and psychological tolerance	confusion, violent headaches, deep depression; sudden withdrawal may lead to convulsions and death	overdose can lead to convulsions, depression of breathing, collapse, coma, and death (more common for barbiturate-based products; generally increased if combined with alcohol)

[1] Preparation (such as crushing, slicing, drying, etc) is punishable as an offence relating to psilocin and psilocybin – the active ingredients of most hallucinogenic mushrooms, both class A, schedule 1 controlled substances.

Numbers of New Drug Addicts in the UK

Figures give the number of new addicts as a percentage of all addicts notified throughout the year. Under the Misuse of Drugs (Notification of and Supply to addicts) Regulations 1973, doctors were required to notify the Chief Medical Officer at the Home Office with particulars of persons whom they considered, or suspected, to be addicted to any of the 14 controlled drugs.

Country/region	1991	1992	1993	1994	1995	Country/region	1991	1992	1993	1994	1995
England						South East (GOR)	39	40	43	42	39
North East	50	52	53	49	56	South West	42	44	49	47	43
North West (GOR)	44	44	42	39	37	*Total*	38	38	41	38	39
Merseyside	30	27	28	23	22						
Yorkshire and the Humber	49	59	55	52	52	*Wales*	42	41	47	39	41
East Midlands	37	34	40	43	43	*Scotland*	48	47	47	49	41
West Midlands	37	37	49	43	49	*Northern Ireland*	28	54	52	62	56
Eastern	30	34	32	33	40						
London	37	35	37	34	35	*AVERAGE UK*	38	39	41	40	40

Source: The Home Office. © Crown copyright 1996

Numbers of Notified Drug Addicts in the UK

Figures give the number of addicts notified throughout the year. Under the Misuse of Drugs (Notification of and Supply to addicts) Regulations 1973, doctors were required to notify the Chief Medical Officer at the Home Office with particulars of persons whom they considered, or suspected, to be addicted to any of the 14 controlled drugs.

Country/Region	All addicts notified[1]				
	1991	1992	1993	1994	1995
England					
North East	125	168	418	399	621
North West (GOR)	3,106	3,713	4,608	5,636	6,463
Merseyside	2,979	3,124	2,853	2,957	2,367
Yorkshire and the Humber	953	1,557	2,205	3,228	4,245
East Midlands	404	663	699	781	971
West Midlands	966	1,160	1,218	1,511	1,812
Eastern	1,159	1,324	1,416	1,656	1,944
London	6,423	7,011	7,682	8,321	8,307
South East (GOR)	1,499	1,953	2,044	2,476	2,814
South West	1,147	1,567	1,904	2,524	3,153
Total	18,761	22,240	25,047	29,489	32,697
Wales	528	579	659	735	886
Scotland	1,499	1,849	2,220	3,691	3,542
Northern Ireland	32	35	50	37	39
TOTAL UK	20,820	24,703	27,976	33,952	37,164

[1] Figures are in the cumulative register.

Source: The Home Office. © Crown copyright 1996

Alcohol Consumption Levels for Adults in England

(Figures show estimated usual weekly levels. Totals may not add to 100 percent due to rounding. Results are in percentages and come from weighted data where a sample of the population has been used to represent the full population.)

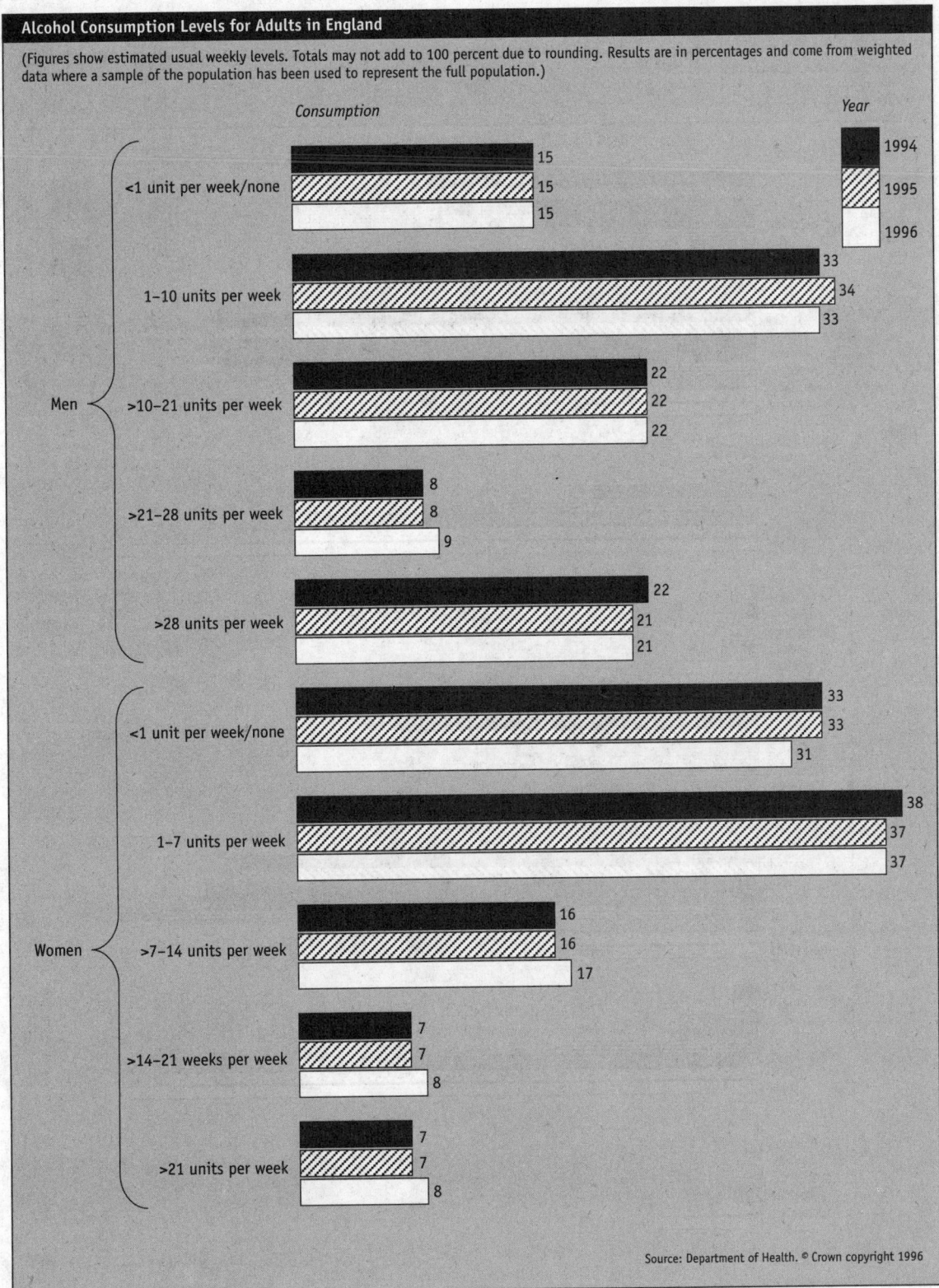

Consumption

Year

1994
1995
1996

Men

<1 unit per week/none
15
15
15

1–10 units per week
33
34
33

>10–21 units per week
22
22
22

>21–28 units per week
8
8
9

>28 units per week
22
21
21

Women

<1 unit per week/none
33
33
31

1–7 units per week
38
37
37

>7–14 units per week
16
16
17

>14–21 weeks per week
7
7
8

>21 units per week
7
7
8

Source: Department of Health. © Crown copyright 1996

Experience of Alcohol in Children in England

(Totals may not add to 100 percent due to rounding. Results are given in percentages and come from weighted data where a sample of the population has been used to represent the full population.)

1996

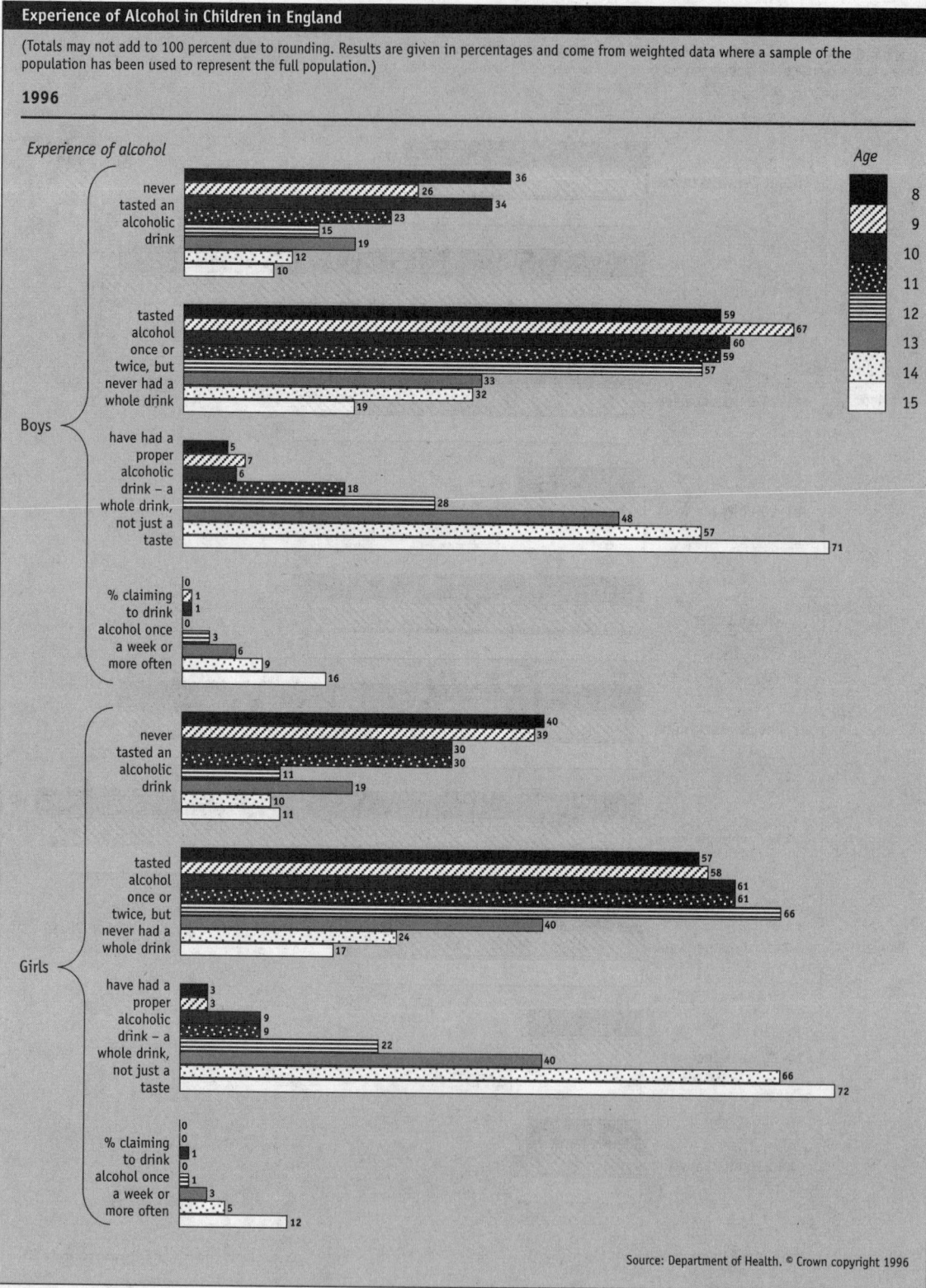

Source: Department of Health. © Crown copyright 1996

Food and Nutrition

Human Body: Composition

Chemical element or substance	Body weight (%)	Chemical element or substance	Body weight (%)
Pure elements		**Water and solid matter**	
oxygen	65	water	60–80
carbon	18	total solid material	20–40
hydrogen	10		
nitrogen	3	**Organic molecules**	
calcium	2		
phosphorus	1.1	protein	15–20
potassium	0.35	lipid	3–20
sulphur	0.25	carbohydrate	1–15
sodium	0.15	other	0–1
chlorine	0.15		
magnesium, iron, manganese, copper, iodine, cobalt, zinc	traces		

Recommended Daily Intake of Nutrients

(– = not applicable.)

Sex and Age		Energy		Protein (g)	Calcium (mg)	Iron (mg)	Vitamin A (µg)	Thiamine (retinol equivalent) (mg)	Riboflavin (mg)	Niacin (mg)	Vitamin C (mg)	Vitamin D[1] (µg)
		MJ	kcal									
Boys												
<1		3.25	780	19	600	6	450	0.3	0.4	5	20	7.5
1		5.00	1,200	30	600	7	300	0.5	0.6	7	20	10
2		5.75	1,400	35	600	7	300	0.6	0.7	8	20	10
3–4		6.50	1,560	39	600	8	300	0.6	0.8	9	20	10
5–6		7.25	1,740	43	600	10	300	0.7	0.9	10	20	–
7–8		8.25	1,980	49	600	10	400	0.8	1.0	11	20	–
9–11		9.50	2,280	56	700	12	575	0.9	1.2	14	25	–
12–14		11.00	2,640	66	700	12	725	1.1	1.4	16	25	–
15–17		12.00	2,880	72	600	12	750	1.2	1.7	19	30	–
Girls												
<1		3.00	720	18	600	6	450	0.3	0.4	5	20	7.5
1		4.50	1,100	27	600	7	300	0.4	0.6	7	20	10
2		5.50	1,300	32	600	7	300	0.5	0.7	8	20	10
3–4		6.25	1,500	37	600	8	300	0.6	0.8	9	20	10
5–6		7.00	1,680	42	600	10	300	0.7	0.9	10	20	–
7–8		8.00	1,900	48	600	10	400	0.8	1.0	11	20	–
9–11		8.50	2,050	51	700	12[2]	575	0.8	1.2	14	25	–
12–14		9.00	2,150	53	700	12[2]	725	0.9	1.4	16	25	–
15–17		9.00	2,150	53	600	12[2]	750	0.9	1.7	19	30	–
Men												
18–34	sedentary	10.50	2,510	62	500	10	750	1.0	1.6	18	30	–
	moderately active	12.00	2,900	72	500	10	750	1.2	1.6	18	30	–
	very active	14.00	3,350	84	500	10	750	1.3	1.6	18	30	–
35–64	sedentary	10.00	2,400	60	500	10	750	1.0	1.6	18	30	–
	moderately active	11.50	2,750	69	500	10	750	1.1	1.6	18	30	–
	very active	14.00	3,350	84	500	10	750	1.3	1.6	18	30	–
65–74		10.00	2,400	60	500	10	750	1.0	1.6	18	30	–
>74		9.00	2,150	54	500	10	750	0.9	1.6	18	30	–
Women												
18–54	most occupations	9.00	2,150	54	500	12[2]	750	0.9	1.3	15	30	–
	very active	10.50	2,500	62	500	12[2]	750	1.0	1.3	15	30	–
Pregnant		10.00	2,400	60	1,200	13	750	1.0	1.6	18	60	10
Lactating		11.50	2,750	69	1,200	15	1,200	1.1	1.8	21	60	10
55–74		8.00	1,900	47	500	10	750	0.8	1.3	15	30	–
>74		7.00	1,680	42	500	10	750	0.7	1.3	15	30	–

[1] Most people who go out in the sun need no dietary source of vitamin D, but children and adolescents in winter, and housebound adults, are recommended to take 10 µg vitamin D daily.

[2] These iron recommendations may not cover heavy menstrual losses.

Main Dietary Minerals

Mineral	Main dietary sources	Major functions in the body	Deficiency symptoms
Calcium	milk, cheese, green vegetables, dried legumes	constituent of bones and teeth; essential for nerve transmission, muscle contraction, and blood clotting	tetany
Chromium	vegetable oils, meat	involved in energy metabolism	impaired glucose metabolism
Copper	drinking water, meat	associated with iron metabolism	anaemia
Fluoride	drinking water, tea, seafoods	helps to keep bones and teeth healthy	increased rate of tooth decay
Iodine	seafoods, dairy products, many vegetables, iodized table salt	essential for healthy growth and development	goitre
Iron	meat (especially liver), legumes, green vegetables, whole grains, eggs	constituent of haemoglobin; involved in energy metabolism	anaemia
Magnesium	whole grains, green vegetables	involved in protein synthesis	growth failure, weakness, behavioural disturbances
Manganese	widely distributed in foods	involved in fat synthesis	not known in humans
Molybdenum	legumes, cereals, offal	constituent of some enzymes	not known in humans
Phosphorus	milk, cheese, meat, legumes, cereals	formation of bones and teeth, maintenance of acid–base balance	weakness, demineralization of bone
Potassium	milk, meat, fruits	maintenance of acid–base balance, fluid balance, nerve transmission	muscular weakness, paralysis
Selenium	seafoods, meat, cereals, egg yolk	role associated with that of vitamin E	not known in humans
Sodium	widely distributed in foods	as for potassium	cramp, loss of appetite, apathy
Zinc	widely distributed in foods	involved in digestion	growth failure, underdevelopment of reproductive organs

fruit market
Fresh fruit and vegetables contain many of the dietary minerals and vitamins that we require to stay healthy. Corel

Recommended Weight Tables

Height		Small frame weight		Medium frame weight		Large frame weight	
m	ft/in	kg	lbs	kg	lbs	kg	lbs
Men Aged 25 and Over							
1.55	5'1'	48–51	105–13	50–55	111–22	54–61	119–34
1.57	5'2'	49–53	108–16	52–57	114–26	55–62	122–37
1.60	5'3'	50–54	111–19	53–59	117–29	57–64	125–41
1.63	5'4'	52–55	114–22	54–60	120–32	58–66	128–45
1.65	5'5'	53–57	117–26	56–62	123–36	59–68	131–49
1.68	5'6'	55–59	121–30	58–64	127–40	61–70	135–54
1.70	5'7'	57–61	125–34	59–66	131–45	64–72	140–59
1.73	5'8'	59–68	129–49	61–68	135–49	65–74	144–63
1.75	5'9'	60–65	133–43	63–69	139–53	67–76	148–67
1.78	5'10'	62–67	137–47	65–72	143–58	69–78	152–72
1.80	5'11'	64–69	141–51	67–74	147–63	71–80	157–77
1.83	6'0'	66–70	145–55	69–76	151–68	73–83	161–82
1.85	6'1'	68–73	149–60	70–79	155–73	76–85	168–87
1.88	6'2'	69–74	153–64	73–81	160–78	78–87	171–92
1.91	6'3'	71–76	157–68	75–83	165–83	79–89	175–97
Women Aged 25 and Over							
1.45	4'9'	41–44	90–97	43–48	94–106	46–54	102–18
1.47	4'10'	42–45	92–100	44–49	97–109	48–55	106–21
1.50	4'11'	43–47	95–103	45–51	100–12	49–56	108–24
1.52	5'0'	45–48	98–106	47–53	103–16	50–58	111–27
1.55	5'1'	46–49	101–09	48–54	106–18	52–59	114–30
1.57	5'2'	47–51	104–12	49–51	109–12	53–61	117–34
1.60	5'3'	49–52	107–15	51–57	112–26	55–63	121–38
1.63	5'4'	50–54	110–19	53–59	116–31	57–64	125–42
1.65	5'5'	52–56	114–23	54–62	120–36	59–66	129–46
1.68	5'6'	54–58	118–27	56–63	124–39	60–68	133–50
1.70	5'7'	55–59	122–31	58–65	128–43	62–70	137–54
1.73	5'8'	57–62	126–36	60–67	132–47	64–72	141–59
1.75	5'9'	59–64	130–40	62–69	136–51	66–74	145–64
1.78	5'10'	61–65	134–44	64–70	140–55	68–77	149–69

Source: Metropolitan Life Insurance Company

Rules for Safe Food Production

Source: World Health Organization

The World Health Organization (WHO) regards illness due to contaminated food as one of the most widespread health problems in the contemporary world. For infants, immunocompromised people, pregnant women, and the elderly, the consequences of such an illness can be fatal. WHO data indicate that a small number of factors related to food handling are responsible for a large proportion of food-borne disease episodes everywhere. Common errors include: preparation of food several hours prior to consumption, combined with storage of that food at temperatures that favour growth of bacteria and/or formation of toxins; insufficient cooking or reheating of food and so failing to reduce or eliminate pathogens; cross contamination; handling of the food by people with poor personal hygiene. The WHO has devised Ten Golden Rules in response to these errors, offering advice that can reduce the risk of food-borne pathogens being able to contaminate, survive, or multiply. By following these basic rules, the risk of food-borne disease will be significantly reduced.

1. Choose foods processed for safety

While many foods, such as fruits and vegetables, are best in their natural state, others simply are not safe unless they have been processed. For example, always buy pasteurized as opposed to unpasteurized milk, and if you have the choice, select fresh or frozen poultry treated with ionizing radiation. When shopping, keep in mind that food processing was invented to improve safety as well as to prolong shelf-life. Certain foods eaten raw, such as lettuce, need thorough washing.

2. Cook food thoroughly

Many raw foods, most notably poultry, meats, eggs, and unpasteurized milk, may be contaminated with disease-causing organisms. Thorough cooking will kill the bacteria, but remember that the temperature of all parts of the food must reach at least 70°C/158°F. If cooked chicken is still raw, put it back in the oven until it is done – all the way through. Frozen meat, fish, and poultry must be thoroughly thawed before cooking.

3. Eat cooked foods immediately

When cooked foods cool to room temperature, microbes begin to proliferate. The longer the wait, the greater the risk. To be on the safe side, eat cooked foods just as soon as they come off the heat.

4. Store cooked foods carefully

If you must prepare foods in advance or want to keep leftovers, be sure to store them under either hot (near or above 60°C/140°F) or cool (near or below 10°C/50°F) conditions. This rule is of vital importance if you plan to store foods for more than four or five hours. Foods for infants should preferably not be stored at all. A common error, responsible for countless cases of food-borne disease, is putting too large a quantity of warm food in the refrigerator. In an overburdened refrigerator, cooked foods cannot cool to the core as quickly as they must. When the centre of food remains warm (above 10°C/50°F) for too long, microbes thrive, quickly proliferating to disease-causing levels.

5. Reheat cooked foods thoroughly

This is your best protection against microbes that may have developed during storage (proper storage slows down microbial growth but does not kill the organisms). Once again, thorough reheating means that all parts of the food must reach at least 70°C/158°F.

6. Avoid contact between raw foods and cooked foods

Safely cooked food can become contaminated through even the slightest contact with raw food. This cross-contamination can be direct, as when raw poultry meat comes into contact with cooked foods. It can also be more subtle. For example, do not prepare a raw chicken and then use the same unwashed cutting board and knife to carve the cooked bird. Doing so can reintroduce the disease-causing organisms.

7. Wash hands repeatedly

Wash hands thoroughly before you start preparing food and after every interruption – especially if you have to change a baby or have been to the toilet. After preparing raw foods such as fish, meat, or poultry, wash again before you start handling other foods. And if you have an infection on your hand, be sure to bandage or cover it before preparing food. Remember too that household pets – dogs, cats, birds, and especially turtles – often harbour dangerous pathogens that can pass from your hands into food.

8. Keep all kitchen surfaces meticulously clean

Since foods are so easily contaminated, any surface used for food preparation must be kept absolutely clean. Think of every food scrap, crumb, or spot as a potential reservoir of germs. Cloths that come into contact with dishes and utensils should be changed frequently and boiled before re-use. Separate cloths for cleaning the floors also require frequent washing.

9. Protect foods from insects, rodents, and other animals

Animals frequently carry pathogenic micro-organisms that cause food-borne disease. Storing foods in closed containers is your best protection against contamination against animals.

10. Use safe water

Safe water is just as important for food preparation as for drinking. If you have any doubts about the water supply, boil water before adding it to food or making ice for drinks. Be especially careful with any water used to prepare an infant's meal.

Nutritive Value of Foods

The energy value of each food is given in kilojoules (kJ) and kilocalories (kcal), and both have been calculated from the protein, fat, and carbohydrate content per 100 g of edible portion.

Food	Energy kJ	Energy kcal	Protein (g)	Fat (g)	Saturated fat (g)	Carbohydrate (g)
Cereal and Cereal Products						
Bread, brown	927	218	8.5	2.0	0.4	44.3
Bread, white	1,002	235	8.4	1.9	0.4	49.3
Flour, plain, white	1,450	341	9.4	1.3	0.2	77.7
Flour, wholemeal	1,318	310	12.7	2.2	0.3	63.9
Oats, porridge, raw	1,587	375	11.2	9.2	1.6	66.0
Rice, brown, boiled	597	141	2.6	1.1	0.3	32.1
Rice, white, boiled	587	138	2.6	1.3	0.3	30.9
Spaghetti, white, boiled	442	104	3.6	0.7	0.1	22.2
Dairy Products						
Butter	3,031	737	0.5	81.7	54.0	0.0
Cheddar cheese	1,708	412	25.5	34.4	21.7	0.1
Cottage cheese	413	98	13.8	3.9	2.4	2.1
Cream, fresh, heavy	1,849	449	1.7	48.0	30.0	2.7
Cream, fresh	817	198	2.6	19.1	11.9	4.1
Eggs, boiled	612	147	12.5	10.8	3.1	0.0
Low-fat spread	1,605	390	5.8	40.5	11.2	0.5
Margarine, polyunsaturated	3,039	739	0.2	81.6	16.2	1.0
Milk, semi-skimmed	195	46	3.3	1.6	1.0	5.0
Milk, skimmed	140	33	3.3	0.1	0.1	5.0
Milk, whole	275	66	3.2	3.9	2.4	4.8
Yoghurt, whole milk, plain	333	79	5.7	3.0	1.7	7.8
Fish						
White fish, steamed, flesh only	417	98	22.8	0.8	0.2	0.0
Shrimps, boiled	451	107	22.6	1.8	0.4	0.0
Fruit						
Apples	199	47	0.4	0.1	0.0	11.8
Apricots	674	158	4.0	0.6	0.0	36.5
Avocados	784	190	1.9	19.5	4.1	1.9
Bananas	403	95	1.2	0.3	0.1	23.2
Cherries	203	48	0.9	0.1	0.0	11.5
Grapefruit	126	30	0.8	0.1	0.0	6.8
Grapes	257	60	0.4	0.1	0.0	15.4
Mangoes	245	57	0.7	0.2	0.1	14.1
Melon	119	28	0.6	0.1	0.0	6.6
Oranges	158	37	1.1	0.1	0.0	8.5
Pears	169	40	0.3	0.1	0.0	10.0
Plums	155	36	0.6	0.1	0.0	8.8
Raspberries	109	25	1.4	0.3	0.1	4.6
Strawberries	113	27	0.8	0.1	0.0	6.0
Meat						
Beef, lean only, raw	517	123	20.3	4.6	1.9	0.0
Chicken, meat and skin, raw	954	230	17.6	17.7	5.9	0.0
Lamb, lean only, raw	679	162	20.8	8.8	4.2	0.0
Pork, lean only, raw	615	147	20.7	7.1	2.5	0.0
Vegetables						
Aubergine	64	15	0.9	0.4	0.1	2.2
Beetroot	195	46	2.3	0.0	0.0	9.5
Cabbage	109	26	1.7	0.4	0.1	4.1
Celery	32	7	0.5	0.2	0.0	0.9
Courgettes	74	18	1.8	0.4	0.1	1.8
Cucumber	40	10	0.7	0.1	0.0	1.5
Lettuce	59	14	0.8	0.5	0.1	1.7
Mushrooms	55	13	1.8	0.5	0.1	0.4
Onions	150	36	1.2	0.2	0.0	7.9
Parsnips	278	66	1.6	1.2	0.2	12.9
Peas	291	69	6.0	0.9	0.2	9.7
Peppers	65	15	0.8	0.3	0.1	2.6
Potatoes, new, flesh only	298	70	1.7	0.3	0.1	16.1
Potatoes, old, flesh only	318	75	2.1	0.2	0.0	17.2
Spinach	90	21	301	0.8	0.1	0.5
Sweetcorn kernels	519	122	2.9	1.2	0.2	26.6
Sweet potatoes	358	84	1.1	0.3	0.1	20.5
Tofu, soya bean, steamed	304	73	8.1	4.2	0.5	0.7
Watercress	94	22	3.0	1.0	0.3	0.4

Source: UK Ministry of Agriculture, Fisheries and Food

Vitamins

Vitamin	Name	Main dietary sources	Established benefit	Deficiency symptoms
A	retinol	dairy products, egg yolk, liver; also formed in body from ß-carotene, a pigment present in some leafy vegetables	aids growth; prevents night blindness and xerophthalmia (a common cause of blindness among children in developing countries); helps keep the skin and mucous membranes resistant to infection	night blindness; rough skin; impaired bone growth
B_1	thiamin	germ and bran of seeds and grains, yeast	essential for carbohydrate metabolism and health of nervous system	beriberi; Korsakov's syndrome
B_2	riboflavin	eggs, liver, milk, poultry, broccoli, mushrooms	involved in energy metabolism; protects skin, mouth, eyes, eyelids, mucous membranes	inflammation of tongue and lips; sores in corners of the mouth
B_6	pyridoxine/ pantothenic acid/biotin	meat, poultry, fish, fruits, nuts, whole grains, leafy vegetables, yeast extract	important in the regulation of the central nervous system and in protein metabolism; helps prevent anaemia, skin lesions, nerve damage	dermatitis; neurological problems; kidney stones
B_{12}	cyanocobalamin	liver, meat, fish, eggs, dairy products, soybeans	involved in synthesis of nucleic acids, maintenance of myelin sheath around nerve fibres; efficient use of folic acid	anaemia; neurological disturbance
	folic acid	green leafy vegetables, liver, peanuts; cooking and processing can cause serious losses in food	involved in synthesis of nucleic acids; helps protect against cervical dysplasia (precancerous changes in the cells of the uterine cervix)	megaloblastic anaemia
	nicotinic acid (or niacin)	meat, yeast extract, some cereals; also formed in the body from the amino acid tryptophan	maintains the health of the skin, tongue, and digestive system	pellagra
C	ascorbic acid	citrus fruits, green vegetables, tomatoes, potatoes; losses occur during storage and cooking	prevents scurvy, loss of teeth; fights haemorrhage; important in synthesis of collagen (constituent of connective tissue); aids in resistance to some types of virus and bacterial infections	scurvy
D	calciferol, cholecalciferol	liver, fish oil, dairy products, eggs; also produced when skin is exposed to sunlight	promotes growth and mineralization of bone	rickets in children; osteomalacia in adults
E	tocopherol	vegetable oils, eggs, butter, some cereals, nuts	prevents damage to cell membranes	anaemia
K	phytomenadione, menaquinone	green vegetables, cereals, fruits, meat, dairy products	essential for blood clotting	haemorrhagic problems

Useful Addresses

Societies and Institutions for Health and Related Issues

Action for Blind People 14–16 Verney Road, London SE16 3DZ; phone: (0171) 732 8771

Action Research Vincent House, Horsham, West Sussex RH12 2DP; phone: (01403) 210406

Age Concern England: Astral House, 1268 London Road, London SW16 4ER; phone: (0181) 679 8000; Northern Ireland: 3 Lower Crescent, Belfast BT7 1NR; phone: (01232) 245729; Scotland: 113 Rose Street, Edinburgh EH2 3DT; phone: (0131) 220 3345; Wales: 1 Cathedral Road, Cardiff CF1 9SD; phone: (01222) 371566

Alcoholics Anonymous PO Box 1, Stonebow House, Stonebow, York YO1 2NJ; phone: (01904) 644026

Alzheimer's Disease Society Gordon House, 10 Greencoat Place, London SW1P 1PH; phone: (0171) 306 0606

Association for Spina Bifida and Hydrocephalus (ASBAH) 42 Park Road, Peterborough PE1 2UQ; phone: (01733) 555988

Association of Anaesthetists of Great Britain and Ireland 9 Bedford Square, London WC1B 3RA; phone: (0171) 631 1650

Association of British Dispensing Opticians 6 Hurlingham Business Park, Sulivan Road, London SW6 3DU; phone: (0171) 736 0088

Association of Dental Hospitals of the United Kingdom Birmingham Dental Hospital, St Chad's Queensway, Birmingham B4 6NN; phone: (0121) 236 8611 ext 5732

Arthritis and Rheumatism Council for Research Copeman House, St Mary's Court, St Mary's Gate, Chesterfield, Derbyshire S41 7TD; phone: (01246) 558033

Arthritis Care 18 Stephenson Way, London NW1 2HD; phone: (0171) 916 1500

Biochemical Society 59 Portland Place, London W1N 3AJ; phone: (0171) 580 5530

British Association of Cancer United Patients (BACUP) 3 Bath Place, Rivington Street, London EC2A 3JR; phone: (0171) 696 9003; Cancer Information Service: (0800) 181199 or (0171) 613 2121

British Association of the Hard of Hearing *see* **Hearing Concern**

British Chiropractic Association 29 Whitley Street, Reading, Berkshire RG2 0EG; phone: (01734) 757557

British Deaf Association 1 Worship Street, London EC2A 2AB; phone: (0171) 588 3520

British Dental Association 64 Wimpole Street, London W1M 8DQ; phone: (0171) 935 0875

British Diabetic Association 10 Queen Anne Street, London W1M 0BX; phone: (0171) 323 1531

British Epilepsy Association Anstey House, Hanover Square, Leeds LS3 1BE; phone: (0113) 243 9393/(0800) 309030

British Health Care Association 24a Main Street, Garforth, Leeds LS25 1AA; phone: (0113) 232 0903

British Heart Foundation 14 Fitzhardinge Street, London W1H 4DH; phone: (0171) 935 0185

British Homeopathic Association 27a Devonshire Street, London S1N 1RJ; phone: (0171) 935 2163

British Institute of Radiology 36 Portland Place, London W1N 4AT; phone: (0171) 580 4317

British Lung Foundation 78 Hatton Garden, London EC1N 8JR; phone: (0171) 387 2353

British Migraine Association 178a High Road, Byfleet, West Byfleet, Surrey KT14 7ED; phone: (01932) 352468

British Nutrition Foundation High Holborn House, 52–54 High Holborn, London WC1V 6RQ; phone: (0171) 404 6504

British Orthopaedic Association c/o The Royal College of Surgeons, 35–43 Lincoln's Inn Fields, London WC2A 3PN; phone: (0171) 405 6507

British Polio Fellowship Ground Floor, Unit A, Eagle Office Centre, The Runway, South Ruislip, Middlesex HA4 6SE; phone: (0181) 842 1898

British Red Cross 9 Grosvenor Crescent, London SW1X 7EJ; phone: (0171) 235 5454

Cancer Research Campaign 10 Cambridge Terrace, London NW1 4JI; phone: (0171) 224 1333

Chartered Society of Physiotherapy 14 Bedford Row, London WC1R 4ED; phone: (0171) 306 6666

Chest, Heart and Stroke Association *see* **Stroke Association**

Children's Society Edward Rudolf House, Margery Street, London WC1X 0JL; phone: (0171) 837 4299

Christian Aid PO Box 100, London SE1 7RT; phone: (0171) 620 4444

College of Optometrists 10 Knaresborough Place, London SW5 0TG; phone: (0171) 373 7765

Commonwealth Society for the Deaf (Sound Seekers) 134 Buckingham Palace Road, London SW1W 9SA; phone: (0171) 259 0200

Council for Complementary and Alternative Medicine 179 Gloucester Place, London NW1 6DX; phone: (0171) 724 9103

Cystic Fibrosis Trust Alexandra House, 5 Blyth Road, Bromley, Kent BR1 3RS; phone: (0181) 464 7211

Downs Syndrome Association 155 Mitcham Road, London SW17 9PG; phone: (0181) 682 4001

Dyslexia Institute 133 Gresham Road, Staines, Middlesex TW18 2AJ; phone: (01784) 463851

Eating Disorders Association Sackville Place, 44 Magdalen Street, Norwich NR3 1JE; phone: (01603) 619090; helpline: (01603) 621414

ENABLE (Scottish Society for the Mentally Handicapped) 7 Buchanan Street, Glasgow G1 3HL; phone: (0141) 226 4541

Family Planning Association 2–12 Pentonville Road, London N1 9FP; phone: (0171) 837 5432

Foley House Residential Home for Deaf People Foley House, 115 High Garrett, Braintree, Essex CM7 5NU; phone: (01376) 326652

Foundation for the Study of Infant Deaths 14 Halkin Street, London SW1X 7DB; phone: (0171) 235 0965

Friends of the Elderly 42 Ebury Street, London SW1W 0LZ; phone: (0171) 730 8263

General Council and Register of Osteopaths 56 London Street, Reading, Berkshire RG1 4SQ; phone: (01734) 576585

General Dental Council 37 Wimpole Street, London W1M 8DQ; phone: (0171) 486 2171

General Medical Council 178 Great Portland Street, London W1N 6JE; phone: (0171) 580 7642

General Optical Council 41 Harley Street, London W1N 2DJ; phone: (0171) 580 3898

Guide Dogs for the Blind Hillfields, Burghfield Common, Reading, Berks RG7 3YG; phone: (0118) 983 5555

Guild of Health Edward Wilson House, 26 Queen Anne Street, London W1M 9LB; phone: (0171) 580 2492

Haemophilia Society Chesterfield House, 385 Euston Road, London NW1 3AU; phone: (0171) 380 0600

Hearing Concern (British Association for the Hard of Hearing) 7–11 Armstrong Road, London W3 7JL; phone: (0181) 743 1110

Help the Aged St James's Walk, Clerkenwell Green, London EC1R 0BE; phone: (0171) 253 0253

Imperial Cancer Research Fund PO Box 123, Lincoln's Inn Fields, London WC2A 3PX; phone: (0171) 242 0200

Institute for Complementary Medicine PO Box 194, London SE16 1QZ; phone: (0171) 237 5165

Institute for the Study of Drug Dependence (ISDD) 32 Loman Street, London SE1 0EE; phone: (0171) 928 1211

Institute of Biology 20–22 Queensbury Place, London SW7 2DZ; phone: (0171) 581 8333

Institute of Food Science and Technology 5 Cambridge Court, 210 Shepherd's Bush Road, London W67 NJ; phone: (0171) 603 6316

Institute of Health Education Department of Oral Health and Development, University Dental Hospital, Higher Cambridge Street, Manchester M15 6FH; phone: (0161) 275 6610

Institute of Health Services Management 39 Chalton Street, London NW1 1JD; phone: (0171) 388 2626

International Hospital Federation 4 Abbot's Place, London NW6 4NP; phone: (0171) 372 7181

Leprosy Mission (England and Wales) Goldhay Way, Orton Goldhay, Peterborough PE2 5GL; phone: (01733) 370505

Leukaemia Research Fund 43 Great Ormond Street, London WC1N 3JJ; phone: (0171) 405 0101

London College of Osteopathic Medicine 8–10 Boston Place, London NW1 6QH; phone: (0171) 262 5250

Macmillan Cancer Relief Anchor House, 15–19 Brittan Street, London SW3 3TZ; phone: (0171) 351 7811

Marie Curie Cancer Care 28 Belgrave Square, London SW1X 8QG; phone: (0171) 235 3325

Maternity Alliance 45 Beech Street, London EC2P 2LX; phone: (0171) 588 8583

ME Association 4 Corringham Road, Stanford-le-Hope, Essex SS17 1EF; phone: (01375) 642466

Medical Society for the Study of Venereal Diseases The Royal Society of Medicine, 1 Wimpole Street, London W1M 8AE; phone: (0171) 290 3904

Medical Society of London Lettsom House, 11 Chandos Street, London W1M 0EB; phone: (0171) 580 1043

MENCAP (The Royal Society for Mentally Handicapped Children and Adults) 123 Golden Lane, London EC1Y 0RT; phone: (0171) 454 0454

Mental After Care Association 25 Bedford Square, London WC1B 3HW; phone: (0171) 580 0145

Mental Health Foundation 37 Mortimer Street, London W1N 8JU; phone: (0171) 580 0145

Migraine Trust 45 Great Ormond Street, London WC1N 3HZ; phone: (0171) 278 2676

MIND (The National Association for Mental Health) Granta House, 15–19 Broadway, London E15 4BQ; phone: (0181) 519 2122

Multiple Sclerosis Society 25 Effie Road, London SW6 1EE; phone: (0171) 610 7171

National Association of Carers Ruth Pitter House, 20–25 Glasshouse Yard, London EC1A 4JS; phone: (0171) 490 8818

National Association of Citizen's Advice Bureaux Myddelton House, 115–123 Pentonville Road, London N1 9LZ; phone: (0171) 833 2181

National Association for Colitis and Crohn's Disease PO Box 205, St Albans, Hertfordshire AL1 1AB; phone: (01727) 844296

National Association of Health Authorities and Trusts Birmingham Research Park, Vincent Drive, Birmingham B15 2SQ; phone: (0121) 471 4444

National Association for Maternal and Child Welfare Ltd 1st Floor, 40–42 Osnaburgh Street, London NW4 3ND; phone: (0171) 383 4117

National Association for Mental Health *see* **MIND**

National Asthma Campaign Providence House, Providence Place, London N1 0NT; phone: (0171) 226 2260

National Blood Service Oak House, Reeds Crescent, Watford, Hertfordshire WD1 1QH; phone: (01923) 486800

National Childbirth Trust Alexandra House, Oldham Terrace, London W3 6NH; phone: (0181) 992 8637

National Library for the Blind Far Cromwell Road, Bredbury, Stockport, Cheshire SK6 2SG; phone: (0161) 494 0217

National Osteoporosis Society PO Box 10, Radstock, Bath, BA3 3YB; phone: (01761) 471771

National Schizophrenia Fellowship (NSF) 28 Castle Street, Kingston upon Thames, Surrey, KT1 1SS; phone: (0181) 547 3937

Nutrition Society 10 Cambridge Court, 210 Shepherds Bush Road, London W6 7NJ; phone: (0171) 602 0228

OPSIS (National Association for the Education, Training and Support of Blind and Partially Sighted People) Gretton House, 43 Hatton Garden, London EC1N 8EE; phone: (0171) 405 6697

Patients Association 8 Guilford Street, London WC1N 1DT; phone: (0171) 242 3460

Princess Royal Trust for Carers 16 Byward Street, London EC3R 5BA; phone: (0171) 480 7788

Psoriasis Association 7 Milton Street, Northampton NN2 7JG; phone: (0171) 235 2351

QUIT (National Society of Non-Smokers) Victory House, 170 Tottenham Court Road, London W1P 0HA; phone: (0171) 388 5775

RADAR (Royal Association for Disability and Rehabilitation) 12 City Forum, 250 City Road, London EC1V 8AF; phone: (0171) 250 3222

Red Cross Society *see* **British Red Cross**

Royal Association in Aid of Deaf People 27 Old Oak Road, London W3 7HN; phone: (0181) 743 6187

Royal Cancer Hospital, Institute of Cancer Research 17a Onslow Gardens, London SW7 3AL; phone: (0171) 352 8133

Royal College of General Practitioners 14 Princes Gate, London SW7 1PU; phone: (0171) 581 3232

Royal College of Midwives 15 Mansfield Street, London W1M 0BE; phone: (0171) 872 5100

Royal College of Nursing 20 Cavendish Square, London W1M 0AB; phone: (0171) 409 3333

Royal College of Obstetricians and Gynaecologists 27 Sussex Place, London NW1 4RG; phone: (0171) 262 5425

Royal College of Paediatrics and Child Health 5 St Andrews Place, Regents Park, London NW1 4 LB; phone: (0171) 486 6151

Royal College of Pathologists 2 Carlton House Terrace, London SW1Y 5AF; phone: (0171) 930 5863

Royal College of Physicians 11 St Andrews Place, London NW1 4LE; phone: (0171) 935 1174

Royal College of Physicians and Surgeons of Glasgow 232–242 St Vincent Street, Glasgow G2 5RJ; phone: (0141) 221 6072

Royal College of Physicians of Edinburgh 9 Queen Street, Edinburgh EH2 1JQ; phone: (0131) 225 7324

Royal College of Psychiatrists 17 Belgrave Square, London SW1X 8PG; phone: (0171) 235 2351

Royal College of Radiologists 38 Portland Place, London W1N 4JQ; phone: (0171) 636 4432

Royal College of Surgeons of Edinburgh Nicolson Street, Edinburgh EH8 9DW; phone: (0131) 527 1600

Royal College of Surgeons of England 35–43 Lincoln's Inn Fields, London WC2A 3PN; phone: (0171) 405 3474

Royal Commonwealth Society for the Blind *see* **Sight Savers International**

Royal Institute of Public Health and Hygiene 28 Portland Place, London W1N 4DE; phone: (0171) 580 2731

Royal London Society for the Blind Dorton House, Seal, Sevenoaks, Kent TN15 0ED; phone: (01732) 761477

Royal National College for the Blind College Road, Hereford, HR1 1EB; phone: (01432) 265725

Royal National Institute for Deaf People 19–23 Featherstone Street, London EC1Y 8SL; phone: (0171) 296 8000

Royal National Institute for the Blind 224 Great Portland Street, London W1N 6AA; phone: (0171) 388 1266

Royal School for Deaf Children Victoria Road, Margate, Kent CT9 1NB; phone: (01843) 227561

Royal Society for the Prevention of Accidents Edgbaston Park, 353 Bristol Road, Birmingham B5 7ST; phone: (0121) 248 2000

Royal Society of Health 38 St George's Drive, London SW1V 4BH; phone: (0171) 630 0121

Royal Society of Medicine 1 Wimpole Street, London W1M 8AE; phone: (0171) 290 2901

Royal Society of Tropical Medicine and Hygiene Manson House, 26 Portland Place, London W1N 4EY; phone: (0171) 580 2127

St John Ambulance 1 Grosvenor Crescent, London SW1X 7EF; phone: (0171) 235 5231

SANE – The Mental Health Charity 199–205 Old Marleybone Road, London NW1 5QP; phone: (0171) 724 6520; helpline: (0345) 678000

Save the Children Fund 17 Grove Lane, London SE5 8RD; phone: (0171) 703 5400

Sargent Cancer Care for Children 14 Abingdon Road, London W8 6AF; phone: (0171) 565 5100

Scottish Association for Mental Health Cumbrae House, 15 Carlton Court, Glasgow G5 9JP; phone: (0141) 429 4800

Scottish National Blood Transfusion Association c/o Scottish National Blood Transfusion Service, Ellen's Glen Road, Edinburgh EH17 7QT; phone: (0131) 2317

Scottish Society for the Mentally Handicapped *see* **ENABLE**

SENSE (The National Deafblind and Rubella Association) 11–13 Clifton Terrace, London N4 3SR; phone: (0171) 272 7774

Sight Savers International (Royal Commonwealth Society for the Blind) Grosvenor Hall, Bolnore Road, Haywards Heath, West Sussex RH16 4BX; phone: (01444) 412424

Society of Apothecaries of London 14 Black Friars Lane, London EC4V 6EJ; phone: (0171) 236 1189

Society of Chiropodists and Podiatrists 53 Welbeck Street, London W1M 7HE; phone: (0171) 486 3381

Stroke Association Stroke House, Whitecross Street, London EC1V 8JJ; phone: (0171) 490 7999

Terrence Higgins Trust 52–54 Grays Inn Road, London WC1X 8JU; phone: (0171) 831 0330; helpline: (0171) 242 1010

Web Sites

Acupuncture.com

URL: `"http://www.acupuncture.com/"`

Introduction to acupuncture with descriptions of the main notions and powers of herbology, yoga, Qi Gong, and Chinese nutrition.

AIDS and HIV Information

URL: `"http://www.thebody.com/"`

AIDS/HIV site offering safe sex and AIDS prevention advice, information about treatments and testing, and health/nutritional guidance for those who have contracted the disease.

Allergy Facts

URL: `"http://www.sig.net/~allergy/facts.html"`

Extended fact sheet about allergies. It provides basic information about the causes, symptoms, and treatment of allergy attacks, and helps clarify typical misunderstandings about allergy sufferers.

Alzheimer's Disease Web Page

URL: `"http://med-www.bu.edu/Alzheimer/home.html"`

Information for families, caregivers, and investigators.

Ancient Medicine/Medicina Antiqua

URL: `"http://web1.ea.pvt.k12.pa.us/medant/"`

Ancient Greek and Roman medicine. Containing hypertext editions of Greco-Roman medical texts.

Antibiotics: How Do Antibiotics Work

URL: `"http://ericir.syr.edu/Projects/Newton/12/Lessons/antibiot.html"`

Introduction to the use and importance of antibiotics in easy to understand language.

Asthma Tutorial for Children and Parents

URL: `"http://sln.fi.edu/inquirer/warming.html"`

Online tutorial for parents and children on asthma. It provides an explanation of what happens during an asthma attack, a description of the symptoms normally registered during an attack, and a discussion of the available medications. Video and audio clips of asthmatic breathing are also included.

Basic Principles of Chinese Medicine

URL: `"http://www.healthy.net/library/books/modacu/mod1.htm"`

Comprehensive guide to Chinese medicine. The conceptual basis of Chinese medicine is fully explained, together with a description of how particular organs fit within the overall system.

Cancer: The Facts

URL: `"http://www.icnet.uk/research/factsheet/index.html"`

Information on cancer from the Imperial Cancer Research Fund. There is a simple explanation of what cancer is, followed by links to different types of cancer – bowel, leukaemia, lung, pancreatic, skin, and multiple myeloma cancers, as well as cancers specific to either men or women, or prevalent within families.

Dentistry Now

URL: `"http://www.DentistryNow.com/Mainpage.htm#Main Part"`

Canadian-based site that includes an index of dentists worldwide. There is also an index of university courses where dentistry can be studied. In addition, there is a section on common dental problems and a site for children called 'tooth fairy' to introduce them to the importance of cleaning their teeth.

Ear Anatomy

URL: `"http://weber.u.washington.edu/~otoweb/ear_anatomy.html"`

Concise medical information on the anatomy and function of the ear. It includes separate sections on perforated eardrums and their treatment, ear tubes and their use, tinnitus, and a series of different hearing tests.

Experimental Psychology Lab

URL: "http://www.uni-tuebingen.de/uni/sii/Ulf/Lab/WebExpPsyLab.html"

Take part in online psychology experiments carried out by the University of Tübingen's Psychology Institute.

Grey Wings Herbal

URL: "http://www.geocities.com/Athens/4177/herbal.htm"

Information about herbal medicine. Instructions are provided on preparing a range of herbal medicines and using herbs in food.

Heart: An Online Exploration

URL: "http://sln.fi.edu/biosci/heart.html"

Explore the heart: discover its complexities, development, and structure; follow the blood on its journey through the blood vessels; learn how to maintain a healthy heart; and look at the history of cardiology.

HEBSWeb

URL: "http://www.hebs.scot.nhs.uk/"

Information service run by the Health Education Board of Scotland. The site is devoted to the promotion of public health issues and includes factcards, posters, booklets, and statistics on smoking, mental and sexual health, dietary issues, accidents, and alcohol and drug misuse.

Home, Bacteria-Ridden Home

URL: "http://www.sciam.com/explorations/072197bacteria/mirsky.html"

Part of a larger site maintained by *Scientific American*, this page examines the increasing threat of bacteria that have become resistant to antibiotics.

Homeopathy Home Page

URL: "http://www.homeopathyhome.com/"

Information on the homeopathic treatment of a variety of ailments and results of research into its efficacy. The online edition (and back issues) of *Homeopathy Online* have articles on the application of homeopathy.

Human Anatomy Online

URL: "http://www.innerbody.com/indexbody.html"

Interactive and educational site on the human body.

Human Genetic Disease: A Layman's Approach

URL: "http://mcrcr2.med.nyu.edu/murphp01/lysosome/hgd.htm"

Comprehensive manual of cell biology for the family. It includes discussions about cell structure, DNA, chromosomes, and the detection of genetic defects. It also outlines the main goals of genetic research.

International Travel and Health

URL: "http://jupiter.who.ch/yellow/welcome.htm"

World Health Organization database of vaccination requirements for every country in the world. The site contains a mass of practical advice for international travellers. Information is regularly updated.

Internet Drug Index

URL: "http://www.rxlist.com/"

Online list of prescription and non-prescription drugs, with a search engine to help find specific types of products and access to information about indications and side effects too.

It's All in the Brain

URL: "http://www.hhmi.org/senses/a/a110.htm"

As part of a much larger site called 'Seeing, Hearing, and Smelling the World', this is a set of pages introducing the way in which we perceive the world through our senses.

Lifeblood

URL: "http://sln2.fi.edu/biosci/blood/blood.html"

Introduction to blood, with links to other pages where you will find out everything you have ever thought to ask about blood.

Marijuana as a Medicine

URL: "http://www.calyx.com/~olsen/MEDICAL/"

Campaigning site arguing for the legalization of cannabis for medical purposes. A wide range of research evidence is produced to show cannabis is effective in the treatment of everything from glaucoma to menstrual cramps. There is information about ongoing legal controversies around the issue, and links to a large number of similar sites.

MedicineNet

URL: "http://www.medicinenet.com/"

Immense US-based site dealing with all current aspects of medicine in plain language. There is a dictionary of diseases, cures, and medical terms. The site also includes an 'ask the experts' section, lots of current medical news, and some important first aid advice.

Multimedia Medical Reference Library

URL: "http://www.med-library.com/medlibrary/"

Huge medical reference work on the Web, with detailed text, diagrams, and explanations of a great range of ailments and other medical matters. A full search engine is available to help you locate your section of interest quickly.

Odyssey of Life

URL: "http://www.pbs.org/wgbh/nova/odyssey/"

Companion to the US Public Broadcasting Service (PBS) television programme *Nova*, this page examines the formation of embryos. It includes time-lapse video sequences of growing embryos.

Oriental Therapies

URL: "http://acupuncture.com/"

Different levels of information on alternative Oriental therapies – for the patient, the student, and the practitioner.

Royal National Institute for the Blind United Kingdom

URL: "http://www.rnib.org.uk/"

Site of Britain's leading organization for the visually impaired. RNIB's work is clearly explained. Advice and general information on loss of eyesight is provided.

Shiatsu – Japanese Massage

URL: "http://www1.tip.nl/~t283083/e_index.htm"

Introduction to the theory and practice of shiatsu. The origins of this ancient Japanese pressure technique are explained with reference to the theory of yin and yang.

Tobacco Alert

URL: "http://www.who.ch/programmes/psa/toh/Alert/apr96/index.html"

Special 1996 No Smoking Day edition of the World Health Organization's tobacco report. It is unabashedly dedicated to remedying a global health problem which accounts for 6 percent of all fatalities worldwide.

United Nations International Drug Control Programme

URL: "http://www.undcp.org/undcp.html"

Informative source of information on the work of the UN agency charged with coordinating international efforts to control the narcotics trade. There are details of international treaties and projects to discourage the use, manufacture, and distribution of drugs.

Virtual Hospital

URL: "http://indy.radiology.uiowa.edu/
        VirtualHospital.html"

Virtual Hospital with multimedia instructional tools, contents of a wide series of medical publications, simulations of patients, patient textbooks, peer-reviewed Web resources on common medical problems, and an online continuing education service for health care providers and patients.

Visible Embryo

URL: "http://visembryo.ucsf.edu/"

Learn about the first four weeks of human development.

Visible Human Project

URL: "http://www.nlm.nih.gov/research/
        visible/visible_gallery.html"

Sample images from a long-term US project to collect a complete set of anatomically detailed, three-dimensional representations of the human body.

THE MILITARY AND DEFENCE

The Year in Review

8 July 1997 At a summit meeting in Madrid, Spain, leaders of the North Atlantic Treaty Organization (NATO) formally invite the Czech Republic, Hungary, and Poland to join their military alliance in 1999.

10 July 1997 During a raid in Prijedor, Bosnia-Herzegovina, British troops in the command of NATO kill a Bosnian-Serb, Simo Drljaca, who was accused of committing war crimes. Drljaca is shot after resisting arrest and firing at and wounding a British soldier.

14 August 1997 The US Congress general accounting office announces that the B-2 Stealth bomber's special coating of radar-absorbent paint deteriorates when the plane is left out in the rain or exposed to heat or humidity, making the plane no longer invisible to radar.

August 1997 The largest sex scandal in US Army history is uncovered at Aberdeen Proving Ground in Maryland, involving sexual assault and abuse. It prompts an investigation at army installations worldwide. The ensuing report discovers that sexual harassment and discrimination are pervasive in the army.

24 September 1997 The military wing of the main Islamic opposition group in Algeria instructs its members to lay down their arms for the first time in six years of civil war.

2 October 1997 NATO officials report that the Muslim-led Bosnian government is secretly rearming and training its military to attack the Bosnian Serbs.

29 October 1997 Iraq threatens to end cooperation with the United Nations Special Commission (UNSCOM), responsible for ensuring Iraq's nuclear, chemical, and biological disarmament, unless UNSCOM's US personnel are withdrawn. UNSCOM suspends operations in Iraq.

4 December 1997 More than 125 countries sign an international treaty in Ottawa, Canada, banning land mines.

22 December 1997 After three years of delays, the defense ministers of the UK, Germany, Italy, and Spain sign an agreement to begin producing a new military aeroplane, the 'Eurofighter'.

26 January 1998 US federal judge Stanley Sporkin rules that the US Navy is forbidden to discharge senior chief petty officer Timothy McVeigh (not related to the man who was convicted of the 1995 bombing of a federal building in Oklahoma) because he is homosexual. Although McVeigh did not reveal his sexual orientation to the Navy, officers discovered his homosexuality through a listing on the Internet service America Online.

3 February 1998 A US military aircraft flying low severs a ski-lift cable at a ski resort in Italy's Dolomite mountains, killing 20 people in a cable car that falls 90m/300 ft to the ground.

10 February 1998 For the first time in nearly 30 years, Australia commits armed ground forces to a foreign military endeavour. Prime Minister John Howard pledges military support to the USA if it attacks Iraq for hindering US-led United Nations arms inspections.

27 February 1998 US Vice President Al Gore announces that the USA is ending its 35-year ban on the sale of weapons to South Africa. The ban started as a sanction against the white minority government during apartheid.

13 March 1998 A military jury at Fort Belvoir, Virginia, acquits army Sergeant Major Gene McKinney of all charges of sexual misconduct brought by six female colleagues, but is demoted for obstructing justice by trying to tell one of the accusers what to say to investigators.

March 1998 The US armed forces begin trials to replace metal dog tags with smartcards. The plastic cards have computer chips embedded in them which contain information on the enlisted person's blood group, allergies, and so on, which medical personnel can read with a hand-held computer.

6 April 1998 At a United Nations ceremony, the UK and France ratify the Comprehensive Test Ban Treaty (CTBT), which prohibits all testing of nuclear weapons; they are the first countries with nuclear capabilities to ratify the ban.

22 April 1998 The UK army introduces 'gender-free' physical recruitment tests to give women a better chance of entering the armed forces.

30 April 1998 The United States Senate votes to admit the Czech Republic, Hungary, and Poland into NATO. The last country previously admitted was Spain in 1982.

3 May 1998 Allegations surface that British government officials from the Foreign Office gave secret permission to the British weapons company Sandline International to supply arms to rebels in Sierra Leone, in direct violation of a United Nations resolution.

13 May 1998 The government of India detonates five nuclear weapons in the Thar Desert, Rajasthan. The international community condemns the action, fearing a south Asian arms race.

28 May 1998 Pakistan conducts five underground nuclear tests, escalating the nuclear arms race in South Asia.

30 May 1998 Pakistan detonates another underground nuclear device, despite appeals for restraint from the international community.

World Military and Defence

Conventional Armed Forces in Europe (CFE)

Data show manpower and Treaty-limited equipment (TLE) current holdings and CFE limits on the forces of the treaty members. Current holdings are derived from data declared as at 1 January 1997.

Country	Manpower		Tanks[1]		Armoured combat vehicles		Artillery		Attack helicopters		Combat aircraft[2]	
	Holding	Limit	Holding	Limit	Holding	Limit	Holding	Limit	Holding	Limit	Holding	Limit
Budapest/Tashkent Group												
Armenia	54,658	60,000	102	220	218	220	225	285	7	50	6	100
Azerbaijan	69,254	70,000	270	220	557	220	301	285	15	50	48	100
Belarus	83,817	100,000	1,778	1,800	2,518	2,600	1,533	1,615	71	80	286	294
Bulgaria	93,731	104,000	1,475	1,475	1,985	2,000	1,750	1,750	43	67	235	235
Czech Republic	61,647	93,333	952	957	1,367	1,367	767	767	36	50	144	230
Georgia	30,000	40,000	79	220	102	220	92	285	3	50	6	100
Hungary	49,958	100,000	797	835	1,300	1,700	840	840	59	108	142	180
Moldova	11,075	20,000	0	210	209	210	155	250	0	50	27	50
Poland	227,860	234,000	1,729	1,730	1,442	2,150	1,581	1,610	94	130	384	460
Romania	228,195	230,000	1,375	1,375	2,091	2,100	1,466	1,475	16	120	372	430
Russia[3]	817,139	1,450,000	5,541	6,400	10,198	11,480	6,011	6,415	812	890	2,891	3,416
Slovakia	45,483	46,667	478	478	683	683	383	383	19	25	113	115
Ukraine	370,847	450,000	4,063	4,080	4,847	5,050	3,764	4,040	294	330	940	1,090
North Atlantic Treaty Group												
Belgium	44,057	70,000	334	334	678	1,099	312	320	46	46	166	232
Canada[4]	0	10,660	0	77	0	277	0	38	0	0	0	90
Denmark	29,629	39,000	343	353	286	316	503	553	12	12	74	106
France	281,647	325,000	1,156	1,306	3,574	3,820	1,192	1,292	326	396	650	800
Germany	285,326	345,000	3,248	4,166	2,537	3,446	2,058	2,705	205	306	560	900
Greece	158,621	158,621	1,735	1,735	2,325	2,534	1,878	1,878	20	30	486	650
Italy	245,575	315,000	1,283	1,348	3,031	3,339	1,932	1,955	132	139	516	650
Netherlands	43,856	80,000	722	743	610	1,080	448	607	12	50	181	230
Norway	24,421	32,000	170	170	199	225	246	527	0	0	74	100
Portugal	45,731	75,000	186	300	346	430	320	450	0	26	105	160
Spain	180,063	300,000	725	794	1,194	1,588	1,230	1,310	28	90	200	310
Turkey[3]	527,670	530,000	2,563	2,795	2,424	3,120	2,843	3,523	25	103	362	750
UK	224,351	260,000	521	1,015	2,411	3,176	436	636	289	371	624	900
USA	107,481	250,000	1,115	4,006	1,849	5,372	612	2,492	126	431	220	784

[1] Includes TLE with land-based maritime forces (Marines, Naval Infantry, etc).
[2] Does not include land-based maritime aircraft, for which a separate limit has been set.
[3] Manpower and TLE are for the Atlantic to the Urals (ATTU) zone only.
[4] Canada has now withdrawn all its TLE from the ATTU.

Source: *The Military Balance 1997/98*, International Institute for Strategic Studies (by permission of Oxford University Press)

Arms Control Agreements

Treaty	Dates	Parties	Details
Agreements (Nuclear)			
Antarctic Treaty	signed 1 December 1959; entered into force 23 June 1961	37 nations	prohibited any use of Antarctica for military purposes; specifically prohibited nuclear testing and nuclear waste
Partial Test Ban Treaty	signed 5 August 1963; entered into force 10 October 1963	124 nations; an additional 11 nations have signed the treaty, but have not ratified it	prohibited nuclear weapon tests in outer space, in the atmosphere, and underwater
Outer Space Treaty	signed 27 January 1967; entered into force 10 October 1967	98 nations; an additional 28 nations have signed the treaty, but have not ratified it	prohibited nuclear weapons in Earth orbit and outer space
Treaty of Tlatelolco	signed 14 February 1967; entered into force 22 April 1968	31 nations; the USA, the UK, France, Russia, China, and the Netherlands have signed the relevant protocols to the treaty	prohibited nuclear weapons in Latin America and required safeguards on facilities

Arms Control Agreements (*continued*)

Treaty	Dates	Parties	Details
Non-proliferation Treaty	signed 1 July 1968; entered into force 5 March 1970; renewed indefinitely in 1995	187 nations; all nations that have signed have also formally adopted the treaty; the principal non-signatories are Israel, India, and Pakistan	divided the world into nuclear and non-nuclear weapon states based on status in 1968; obliged non-nuclear states to refrain from acquiring nuclear weapons and to accept International Atomic Energy Agency (IAEA) safeguards on their nuclear energy facilities; obliged nuclear states to refrain from providing nuclear weapons to non-nuclear states, to assist in the development of nuclear energy in non-nuclear states, and to work toward global nuclear disarmament
Seabed Arms Control Treaty	signed 11 February 1971; entered into force 18 May 1972	93 nations; an additional 20 nations have signed the treaty, but have not ratified it	prohibited placement of nuclear weapons on the seabed and ocean floor beyond a 19 km/12 mi coastal limit
Accident Measures Agreement	signed and entered into force 30 September 1971	USA and USSR (Russia)	measures to prevent accidental nuclear war, including agreement to notify each other of planned missile launches and the detection of unidentified objects
SALT I – Interim Agreement	signed 26 May 1972; entered into force 3 October 1972	USA and USSR (Russia); USA dropped commitment to agreement in 1986	froze at existing levels the number of strategic ballistic missile launchers on each side; permitted an increase in submarine-launched ballistic missiles (SLBMs) up to an agreed level only with the dismantling or destruction of a corresponding number of older intercontinental ballistic missile (ICBM) or SLBM launchers
ABM Treaty	signed 26 May 1972; entered into force 3 October 1972	USA and USSR (Russia)	prohibited nationwide anti-ballistic missile (ABM) defences, limiting each side to 2 deployment areas (1 to defend the national capital and 1 to defend an ICBM field) of no more than 100 ABM launchers and interceptor missiles each
Prevention of Nuclear War Agreement	signed and entered into force 22 June 1973	USA and USSR (Russia)	agreed to make the removal of the danger of nuclear weapons and their use an 'objective of their policies'; committed to consult with each other in case of danger of nuclear confrontation between them or other countries
ABM Protocol	signed 3 July 1974; entered into force 24 May 1976	USA and USSR (Russia)	limited each side to a single ABM deployment area
Threshold Test Ban Treaty	signed 3 July 1974; entered into force 11 December 1990	USA and USSR (Russia)	limited nuclear tests on each side to a 150 kiloton threshold
US–International Atomic Energy Agency Safeguards Agreement	signed 18 November 1977; entered into force 9 December 1980	USA and the IAEA	agreed to apply IAEA safeguards in designated facilities in the USA
SALT II Treaty	signed 18 June 1979	USA and USSR (Russia); USA dropped commitment to the agreement in 1986	never ratified, but both nations pledged to comply with the treaty's provisions; provided for broad limits on strategic offensive nuclear weapons systems, including equal numbers of strategic nuclear delivery vehicles, and restraints on qualitative developments that could threaten future stability; superceded by START in 1991
Convention on the Physical Protection of Nuclear Material	signed 3 March 1980; entered into force 8 February 1987	28 nations; an additional 23 nations have signed the treaty, but have not ratified it	provided for certain levels of physical protection during international transport of nuclear materials
Treaty of Rarotonga	signed 6 April 1985; entered into force 11 December 1986	11 nations are party to the treaty; all 5 declared nuclear weapons states have signed the relevant protocols to the treaty; the USA signed the protocols on 25 March 1996, but has yet to ratify the treaty	established a nuclear-weapons-free zone in the South Pacific
Missile Technology Control Regime	informal association formed in April 1987	28 nations	established export control guidelines and annexed listing nuclear-capable ballistic missile equipment and technologies that would require export licenses

(continued)

Arms Control Agreements (*continued*)

Treaty	Dates	Parties	Details
Nuclear Risk Reduction Centres	signed and entered into force 15 September 1987	USA and USSR (Russia)	established centres designed to reduce the risk of nuclear war
Intermediate-Range Nuclear Forces Treaty	signed 8 December 1987; entered into force 1 June 1988	USA and USSR (Russia)	eliminated all US and Soviet ground-launched ballistic and cruise missiles with ranges of 500–5,500 km/310–3,418 mi, their launchers, associated support structures, and support equipment
Ballistic Missile Launch Notification Agreement	signed and entered into force 31 May 1988	USA and USSR (Russia)	agreement to notify each other, through nuclear risk reduction centres, no less than 24 hours in advance, of the planned date, launch area, and area of impact for any launch of an ICBM or SLBM
START I Treaty	signed 31 July 1991; entered into force 5 December 1994	USA and USSR (Russia)	Russia formally accepted all of the USSR's arms control treaty obligations after the dissolution of the USSR. Because strategic nuclear weapons affected by the START I Treaty remained on the soil of Ukraine, Kazakhstan, and Belarus after the USSR's demise, an additional agreement was necessary to guarantee their removal; this was assured under the Lisbon protocol of May 1992. START established limits on deployed strategic nuclear weapons, and required the USA and Russia to make phased reductions in their offensive strategic nuclear forces over a 7 year period
START II Treaty	signed 3 January 1993; ratified by USA 26 January 1996	USA and Russia; still awaiting ratification by Russia	limited each side to 3,000–3,500 deployed strategic nuclear weapons each by the year 2003; banned multiple-warhead land-based missiles
Treaty of Bangkok	signed 15 December 1995	10 nations; none of the acknowledged nuclear powers have signed the relevant protocols	established a nuclear-weapons-free zone in Southeast Asia
Treaty of Pelindaba	signed 11 April 1996; the USA signed on 11 May 1996	53 signatories; the 5 acknowledged nuclear weapons states have signed the relevant protocols to the treaty	established a nuclear-weapons-free zone in Africa
Comprehensive Test Ban Treaty	signed 24 September 1996	as of late April 1997, 144 nations had signed the treaty, but only 2 nations (Qatar and Fiji) had formally ratified it – to enter into force, the 44 nations that have nuclear electrical-generating and research reactors are required to sign and ratify the treaty; included in the 44 are India, Pakistan, and North Korea, none of which have signed the treaty	banned all explosive nuclear tests

Agreements (Non-Nuclear)

Treaty	Dates	Parties	Details
Geneva Protocol	signed 17 June 1925; entered into force 8 February 1928; ratified by USA 22 January 1975	135 nations	prohibited in war the use of asphyxiating or poisonous gas and liquids and all bacteriological (biological) methods of warfare; essentially a 'no first use' agreement, because many signatories ratified it with the reservation that it would cease to be binding if an enemy failed to observe the prohibitions
Biological Weapons Convention	signed 10 April 1972; entered into force 26 March 1975	157 nations	prohibited development, production, stockpiling, acquisition, or retention of biological agents not associated with peaceful uses, biological or toxin weapons, and their delivery systems; required destruction or diversion of all prohibited agents to peaceful purposes within 9 months after entry into force; prohibited transfer of, or assistance to manufacture, prohibited agents
Incidents at Sea Agreement	signed and entered into force 25 May 1972	USA and USSR (Russia)	agreement on the prevention of incidents on and over the high seas, including steps to avoid collision and the avoidance of manoeuvres in areas of heavy sea traffic

Arms Control Agreements (*continued*)

Treaty	Dates	Parties	Details
Environmental Modification Prevention	signed 18 May 1977; entered into force 5 October 1978	67 nations; an additional 17 nations have signed the treaty, but have not ratified it	prohibited deliberate manipulation of natural processes for hostile or other military purposes
Convention on Certain Conventional Weapons (The Inhumane Weapons Convention)	opened for signature 10 April 1981; entered into force 2 December 1983; signed by the USA 2 April 1982 and ratified 24 March 1995	63 nations	banned the use of non-metallic fragmentation weapons and blinding lasers, and imposed restrictions on the use of land mines and incendiary weapons
Australia Group	informal association formed in 1984 in response to chemical weapons use in the Iran–Iraq War	30 nations	established voluntary export controls on certain chemicals
Stockholm Conference	signed and entered into force 19 September 1986	54 nations	established security and confidence-building measures designed to increase openness and predictability with regard to military activities in Europe
US–Soviet Bilateral Memorandum of Understanding	signed and entered into force September 1989	USA and USSR (Russia)	agreement to exchange data on size, composition, and location of chemical weapon stockpiles and storage, production, and destruction facilities, and to conduct reciprocal visits and both routine and challenge inspections
US–Soviet Bilateral Destruction Agreement	signed June 1990; has not yet entered into force	USA and USSR (Russia); currently abandoned by Russia	agreement to stop producing chemical weapons and to reduce their stockpiles to no more than 5,000 agent tons, with destruction to begin by 31 December 1992 and to be completed by 31 December 2002
Conventional Forces in Europe (CFE) Treaty	signed 19 November 1990; entered into force 9 November 1992	30 nations	established limits on the numbers of tanks, armoured combat vehicles, artillery combat aircraft, and helicopters in Europe
Open Skies Treaty	signed 24 March 1992	27 nations; the USA and 23 other nations have ratified the treaty; ratifications by Russia, Belarus, and Ukraine are still required for entry into force	permitted unarmed reconnaissance flights designed to promote military transparency and confidence among former NATO and Warsaw Pact adversaries
CFE 1A Treaty	signed 10 July 1992; entered into force 9 November 1992	30 nations	established limits on the number of troops in Europe
Chemical Weapons Convention	opened for signature 12 January 1993; entered into force 29 April 1997	165 nations; at the time of entry into force, 87 of the signatories had ratified the treaty	prohibited the development, production, acquisition, stockpiling, retention, transfer, and use of chemical weapons – required declaration of chemical weapons or chemical weapon capabilities, including those primarily associated with commercial use; required destruction of declared chemical weapons and associated production facilities; provided for routine inspections of relevant facilities and challenge inspections upon request
Ottawa Treaty	signed 3–4 December 1997	122 countries	banned the production, use, and export of anti-personnel mines; also committed signatories to the destruction of stockpiles of mines within 4 years, and to clear existing minefields as well as relieving the suffering of the victims of land mines

Source: US Center for Defense Information

LAND MINES: DEFUSING A GLOBAL TIME BOMB

BY DAVID SHUKMAN

Almost every 20 minutes, somewhere in the world, a land mine blows up. A farmer working her fields or a schoolboy heading home or a toddler playing will step onto a particular patch of ground, unwittingly trigger the pressure sensor of a bomb hidden underneath, and set off an explosion that causes severe injury. Often the blast is fatal. Every year, in the aftermath of conflicts in Asia, Africa, and Europe, an average of 15,000 people are killed or wounded by land mines. They have been described as 'nuclear weapons in slow motion'.

Types of Land Mine

Land mines come in hundreds of different designs. Some, meant to destroy heavy armoured vehicles, can be as large as a cooking pot. Iraq's President Saddam Hussein ordered the laying of thousands of big anti-tank mines along the border between Saudi Arabia and Kuwait in preparation for the 1991 Gulf War. Fortunately, US and other allied forces had little trouble locating the weapons. They also had the equipment and know-how to destroy or defuse them. Military personnel are trained to expect the enemy to lay land mines. Civilians are not so well prepared.

By far the largest category of land mines is so-called anti-personnel weapons. Of course, they cannot distinguish between a passing soldier and a civilian. These weapons can be similar in size and shape to either a pancake or a grapefruit, with over 350 different models in production over the past 25 years. The devices are planted in the ground with the purpose of disrupting the progress of the opposing side's foot soldiers. In Afghanistan in the 1980s, the Soviet army laid anti-personnel mines along tracks and pathways to try to kill or injure Mujaheddin rebels. One type of Soviet land mine, known as the 'butterfly', was specifically designed to cause wounds rather than death because, if one fighter lost a foot or leg in the blast, two of his colleagues would then be obliged to carry him – that meant three soldiers temporarily out of action.

The Campaign to Ban Land Mines

For years after the conflict is over, civilians in Afghanistan and other war zones – including Angola, Cambodia, Ethiopia, Mozambique, Somalia, and Bosnia – continue to suffer casualties. A stretch of territory that formed a front line during a war may, in peacetime, be a family's only plot of cultivable land. A track once used by rebel forces may be a village's only route to a supply of clean water. Alongside, the land mines remain poised to explode. The statistics speak for themselves: whereas in the USA, only one person in every 22,000 has lost a limb through an accident, in Angola, there is one amputee for every 334 members of the population. Artificial feet, legs, and arms are all too common a sight in many countries of the developing world. Experts estimate that land mines have been planted in a total of over 70 different nations and, despite several initiatives to clear them, as many as 100 million remain in the ground.

A campaign to outlaw land mines has been running for years but until recently its success had been limited. Although an international convention was drawn up in 1980 to control the trade in and use of land mines, it had little or no effect. Only in the last few years have signficant steps been taken. In 1992, the USA declared a self-imposed ban on exports of US-made anti-personnel mines. In 1993, the United Nations General Assembly called for a worldwide ban on exports of the weapons. At the same time, Belgium, France, the Netherlands, and South Africa announced they would all stop trading in land mines. Yet all this fell short of an outright global prohibition.

It took the intervention of the late Diana, Princess of Wales, to highlight the problem and galvanize public opinion. Television pictures and press photographs of Diana, dressed in body armour and posing near a minefield in Angola in 1997, were broadcast and published around the world. The fight against land mines gained popular support in many countries. A huge boost was given to a coordinating organization, the US-based International Campaign to Ban Land Mines, when it was awarded the 1997 Nobel Peace Prize jointly with its American organizer Jody Williams.

Reaching a Treaty

Crucially, negotiations towards a worldwide ban on land mines gathered momentum. Originally supported by around fifty countries, work on a new treaty suddenly attracted the interest of twice that number. In December 1997, four months after the death of the princess, 125 countries met in Ottawa, Canada, where they signed an agreement prohibiting the production, export, and use of anti-personnel land mines. Many observers praised the contribution of Diana. Canada's foreign minister, Lloyd Axworthy, declared: 'People power has moved to the international stage and we should all be thankful for it.'

Yet several key countries, including the USA, would not sign the accord. Many Middle Eastern countries have entirely refused to take part. US officials insist on the right to deploy land mines along the front line between North and South Korea, citing that region's sensitivity and the need to prevent a sudden attack by North Korean forces. Russia claims that the cost of implementing the treaty is too high: stocks of land mines must be destroyed within four years and mines already laid must be cleared within ten years. Finland, with its long border with Russia, has said that it needs more time to destroy existing stocks of mines.

The treaty itself faces formidable challenges. The cost of clearing up existing minefields has been estimated at about $500 million. Weapons which cost between $3 and $30 each to deploy can cost at least $1,000 to remove, in a slow and dangerous operation requiring highly trained personnel. A special fund has been established to help the poorest countries meet the costs of land-mine clearance, but contributions are slow to materialize. One British government study concludes that unless the current rate of work is accelerated, it will take 1,000 years to free the world of mines.

The Leading Suppliers of Major Conventional Weapons

Countries are ranked according to 1992–96 aggregate exports. Figures are trend-indicator values expressed in millions of constant 1990 dollars.

Rank 1992–96	Rank 1991–95	Supplier	1992	1993	1994	1995	1996	1992–96
1	1	USA	14,187	14,270	12,029	10,972	10,228	61,686
2	2	Russia	2,918	3,773	763	3,505	4,512	15,471
3	3	Germany	1,527	1,727	2,448	1,549	1,464	8,715
4	4	UK	1,315	1,300	1,346	1,568	1,773	7,302
5	5	France	1,302	1,308	971	785	2,101	6,467
6	6	China	883	1,234	718	949	573	4,357
7	7	Netherlands	333	395	581	430	450	2,189
8	8	Italy	434	447	330	377	158	1,746
9	9	Czech Republic[1]	214	267	371	195	152	1,199
10	10	Israel	192	271	207	352	168	1,190
11	11	Canada	131	146	330	387	157	1,151
12	14	Ukraine	256	119	178	193	185	931
13	13	Uzbekistan	0	0	406	464	0	870
14	12	Switzerland	363	75	37	95	105	675
15	17	Sweden	123	45	54	174	274	670
16	15	Korea, North	86	423	48	48	21	626
17	21	Belgium	0	0	55	310	110	475
18	19	Spain	64	53	138	78	57	390
19	20	Poland	0	1	117	178	60	356
20	18	Norway	0	93	186	52	0	331

[1] For 1992, the data refer to the former Czechoslovakia.

Source: Ian Anthony, Pieter Wezeman, Siemon Wezeman, in *SIPRI Yearbook 1997*, Stockholm International Peace Research Institute (Oxford University Press)

The Leading Recipients of Major Conventional Weapons

Countries are ranked according to 1992–96 aggregate imports. Figures are trend-indicator values expressed in millions of constant 1990 dollars.

Rank 1992–96	Rank 1991–95	Recipient	1992	1993	1994	1995	1996	1992–96
1	1	Saudi Arabia	1,105	2,889	1,577	1,401	1,611	8,583
2	4	Turkey	1,590	2,171	1,591	1,015	1,066	7,433
3	3	Egypt	1,255	1,339	1,773	2,150	803	7,320
4	11	Taiwan	211	1,058	835	1,305	3,234	6,643
5	2	Japan	2,016	1,992	621	925	679	6,233
6	9	China	1,172	1,277	529	935	1,957	5,870
7	6	Greece	2,467	893	1,055	737	274	5,426
8	10	Korea, South	387	483	611	1,909	1,727	5,117
9	7	India	1,417	604	429	1,092	1,317	4,859
10	5	Germany	1,677	1,636	797	178	96	4,384
11	12	Kuwait	998	657	44	1,048	1,363	4,110
12	8	Israel	1,343	613	905	246	48	3,155
13	14	Thailand	866	152	807	785	355	2,965
14	15	USA	489	626	689	552	130	2,846
15	18	Spain	190	602	768	465	458	2,483
16	16	Iran	239	1,151	327	235	437	2,389
17	22	Indonesia	69	367	792	483	537	2,248
18	19	Finland	698	785	385	155	192	2,215
19	13	Canada	876	350	673	155	137	2,191
20	20	United Arab Emirates	163	618	591	368	271	2,011

Source: Ian Anthony, Pieter Wezeman, Siemon Wezeman, in *SIPRI Yearbook 1997*, Stockholm International Peace Research Institute (Oxford University Press)

Largest Arms-Producing Companies

1995

Company/country	Arms sales ($ millions)
Lockheed Martin/USA	13,800
McDonnell Douglas/USA	9,620
British Aerospace/UK	6,720
Loral/USA	6,500
General Motors (GM)/USA	6,250
Hughes Electronics (GM)[1]/USA	5,950
Northrop Grumman/USA	5,700
Thomson/France	4,630
Thomson-CSF (Thomson)[2]/France	4,620
Boeing/USA	4,200
GEC/UK	4,100
Raytheon/USA	3,960
United Technologies (UTC)/USA	3,650
Daimler Benz (DB)/Germany	3,350
DCN International/France	3,280
Daimler-Benz Aerospace[3]/Germany	3,250
Litton/USA	3,030
General Dynamics/USA	2,930
TRW/USA	2,800
IRI/Italy	2,620
Westinghouse Electric/USA	2,600
Aerospatiale Groupe/France	2,550
Mitsubishi Heavy Industries/Japan	2,430
Rockwell International/USA	2,430
Finmeccanica (IRI)[4]/Italy	2,380
Rolls Royce/UK	2,050
Alcatel Alsthom/France	2,000
Pratt & Whitney (UTC)[5]/USA	1,840
CEA/France	1,740
Texas Instruments/USA	1,740

[1] Subsidiary of General Motors.
[2] Subsidiary of Thomson.
[3] Subsidiary of Daimler Benz.
[4] Subsidiary of IRI.
[5] Subsidiary of United Technologies.

Source: Elisabeth Sköns, Renaud Bellais, and the SIPRI Arms Industry Network, in
SIPRI Yearbook 1997, Stockholm International Peace Research Institute (Oxford University Press)

Biological Weapons: The Germ Genie

By David Shukman

The joint American–British military strike force marshalled in the Gulf in early 1998 was one of the most powerful the region had ever seen. The latest-technology cruise missiles were ready for launch beside dozens of fighter-bombers equipped with precision-guided munitions. And the cause of this vast deployment? Some of the tiniest weapons ever invented: the biological (or germ) weapons secretly produced in Iraq under the regime of Saddam Hussein.

Invisible weapons

According to General Colin Powell, America's military chief during the 1991 Gulf War, biological weaponry is 'the one that scares me the most, even more than tactical nuclear weapons'. The Cold War threat of atomic annihilation may have receded but a new nightmare of massacre by bioweapons has taken its place. Official calculations of the effect of an attack on a typical city make chilling reading: a nuclear bomb weighing 181 kg/400lbs could kill up to 40,000 people, but a device containing just 32 kg/70lbs of deadly anthrax could kill twice that number.

Biological armaments are essentially 'disease-bombs'. They come in many different forms, the simplest being 'spores', microscopic life forms which induce fatal illnesses. Some, such as anthrax, occur naturally. Initial contact with the airborne anthrax spores causes a grotesque inflammation of the skin; the spores quickly lodge in the lungs and multiply rapidly, producing toxins that spread throughout the body; choking and fever lead to death within a few days. The lethal dose is just one billionth of a gram. Little wonder that when Western intelligence established that Iraq had stockpiles of anthrax, the Pentagon ordered all its personnel to be inoculated against the threat, as did Britain for its forces serving in the Gulf.

Early use of germ weapons

The first large-scale use of germ weapons came in China in World War II, when Japan's invasion force released cholera and plague to devastating effect. At the same time, Japanese scientists carried out gruesome germ warfare experiments on Allied prisoners at the notorious Camp 731 in Manchuria. Britain came close to dropping anthrax on Germany in an attempt to infect dairy cattle but the plan was scrapped.

But such was the revulsion felt by the public and by many in the military that the USA and Britain voluntarily gave up their own biological weapons during the 1950s. Years later, in 1972, the international community agreed to a general prohibition under the Biological Weapons Convention. Yet this agreement lacked any means of checking to prevent cheating and it has done little to halt a biological arms race. By its own admission, the USSR continued a clandestine programme of research and development, and, even after the collapse of communism, defectors warned that Russia maintained a secret germ warfare operation known as Biopreparat, with a huge budget and over 30,000 staff.

Cheap to produce, easy to hide

US officials believe that about a dozen countries are investing in biological weapons, including (besides Iraq) China, Iran, Israel, North Korea, and Syria. Potentially more worrying, according to US congressional researchers, is that well over 100 countries have the industrial expertise to pursue the option of biological weaponry. The fact is, unlike with nuclear weapons, the production of biological weapons is simple and cheap; it is also easy to hide. At the most basic level, all that is required is the same know-how and equipment for brewing beer or manufacturing antibiotics.

It is no surprise that a dictator such as Saddam Hussein should find these weapons appealing. The United Nations inspections of Iraq after the Gulf War uncovered an extensive network of germ warfare research and production. The Iraqis obscured much of this effort, disguising it as work for civilian purposes. The plant at Al-Hakem near Baghdad was one of several officially declared to be producing animal vaccines. Yet because of the unusually large quantities of biological supplies found at the site, and with the Iraqis unwilling to be more open, the UN inspectors concluded that the facility was also being used to make weapons and eventually ordered its demolition.

But the fear is that almost any laboratory – in a university, factory, or even hospital – could be turned to military use. Iraq's so-called 'presidential sites', which Saddam tried to keep off-limits to the UN, are certainly large enough to house the necessary equipment for germ warfare production. As one British inspector commented: 'They could brew this stuff up almost anywhere and we'd never know.'

This search becomes all the more pressing given the sheer difficulty of defending against a germ weapon attack. Inoculations can be effective – but only against one particular type of weapon. For some biological agents, a preventative injection can be extremely debilitating and, as seen with the so-called Gulf War Syndrome, a mixture of inoculations can itself cause sickness. And despite the huge levels of military spending during the Cold War, the military lack any system for warning of a biological attack. The US Army has special 'sniffer' vehicles that can detect the presence of germ agents – but only once they have been released. A long-range detector system, carried by helicopter, is being tested but it can only spot that a cloud of spores or bacteria is approaching; it cannot distinguish one type of threat from another, let alone destroy the microscopic weapons before they arrive.

An ever-increasing menace

The future holds even greater threats. In the same year that the Biological Weapons Convention was signed, scientists carried out the first successful experiments in genetic engineering – rearranging the genetic codes of DNA to change an organism's characteristics. For the most part, this development has been heralded as beneficial, with huge strides made against previously incurable diseases. Yet the same science has a darker side too. Russian researchers apparently managed to 'splice together' the genes of the disease smallpox with those of the killer virus Ebola to produce a terrifyingly new biological weapon. American analysts warn that the technique could also combine snake venom with a highly infectious virus such as influenza. Or the microscopic 'appearance' of a biological weapon such as anthrax could be disguised to look like that of a harmless organism to evade detection. Worse still, weapons could even be developed to target particular ethnic groups – in effect, ethnic cleansing by test-tube.

The biological menace is now high on the international agenda. Western governments realize that in the hands of a dictator or a terrorist group biological weapons could cause incalculable harm. The micro-organisms used in an attack would be deadly but hard to identify. Existing defence systems offer little protection to the military and none to civilians. And the diseases themselves may have no known cure. Over the years, many have cursed the release of the genie of atomic warfare; far more may come to curse that of germ warfare instead.

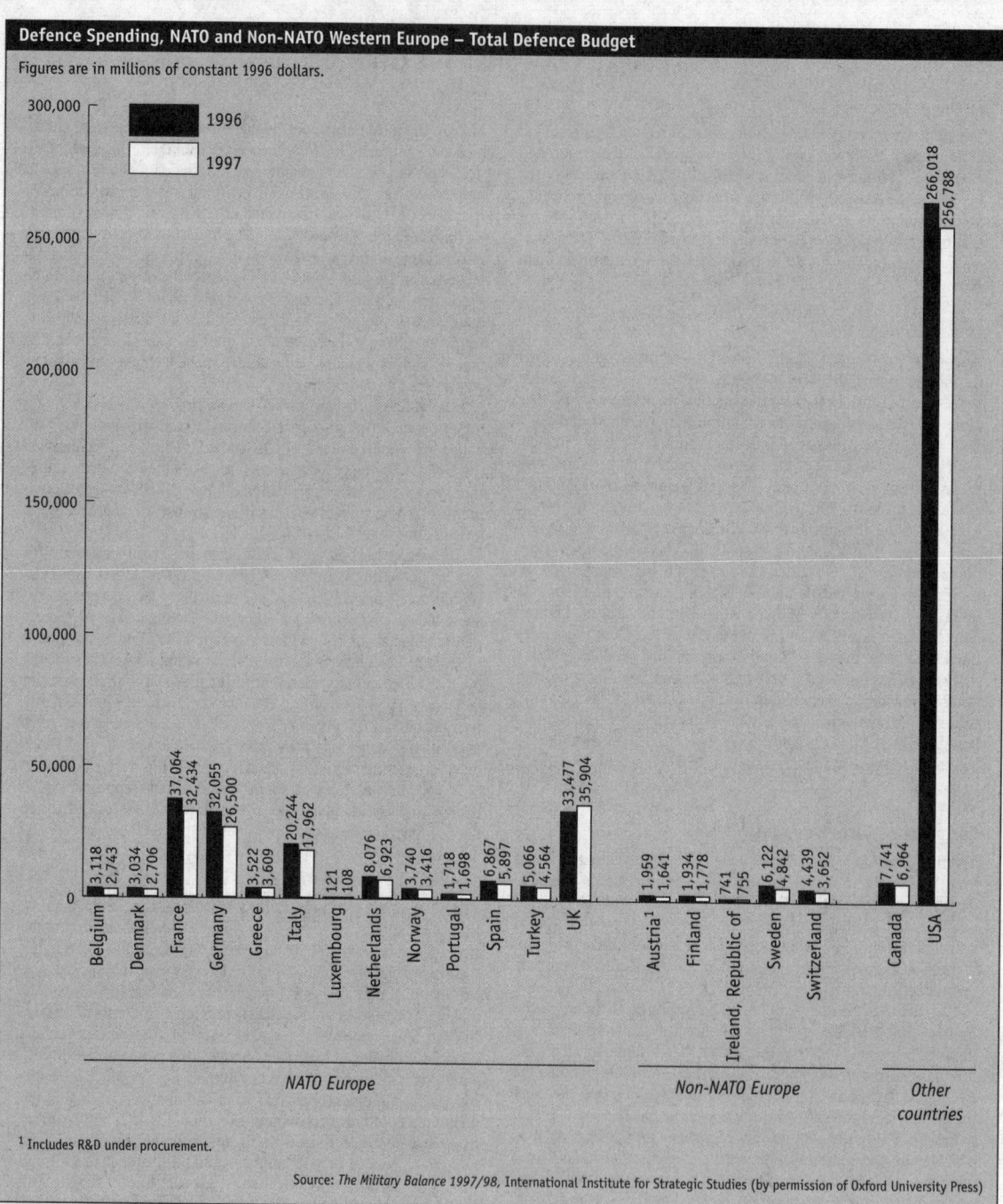

Defence Spending, NATO and Non-NATO Western Europe – Total Defence Budget

Figures are in millions of constant 1996 dollars.

- ■ 1996
- □ 1997

Country	1996	1997
Belgium	3,118	2,743
Denmark	3,034	2,706
France	37,064	32,434
Germany	32,055	26,500
Greece	3,522	3,609
Italy	20,244	17,962
Luxembourg	121	108
Netherlands	8,076	6,923
Norway	3,740	3,416
Portugal	1,718	1,698
Spain	6,867	5,897
Turkey	5,066	4,564
UK	33,477	35,904
Austria[1]	1,959	1,641
Finland	1,934	1,778
Ireland, Republic of	741	755
Sweden	6,122	4,842
Switzerland	4,439	3,652
Canada	7,741	6,964
USA	266,018	256,788

NATO Europe   *Non-NATO Europe*   *Other countries*

[1] Includes R&D under procurement.

Source: *The Military Balance 1997/98*, International Institute for Strategic Studies (by permission of Oxford University Press)

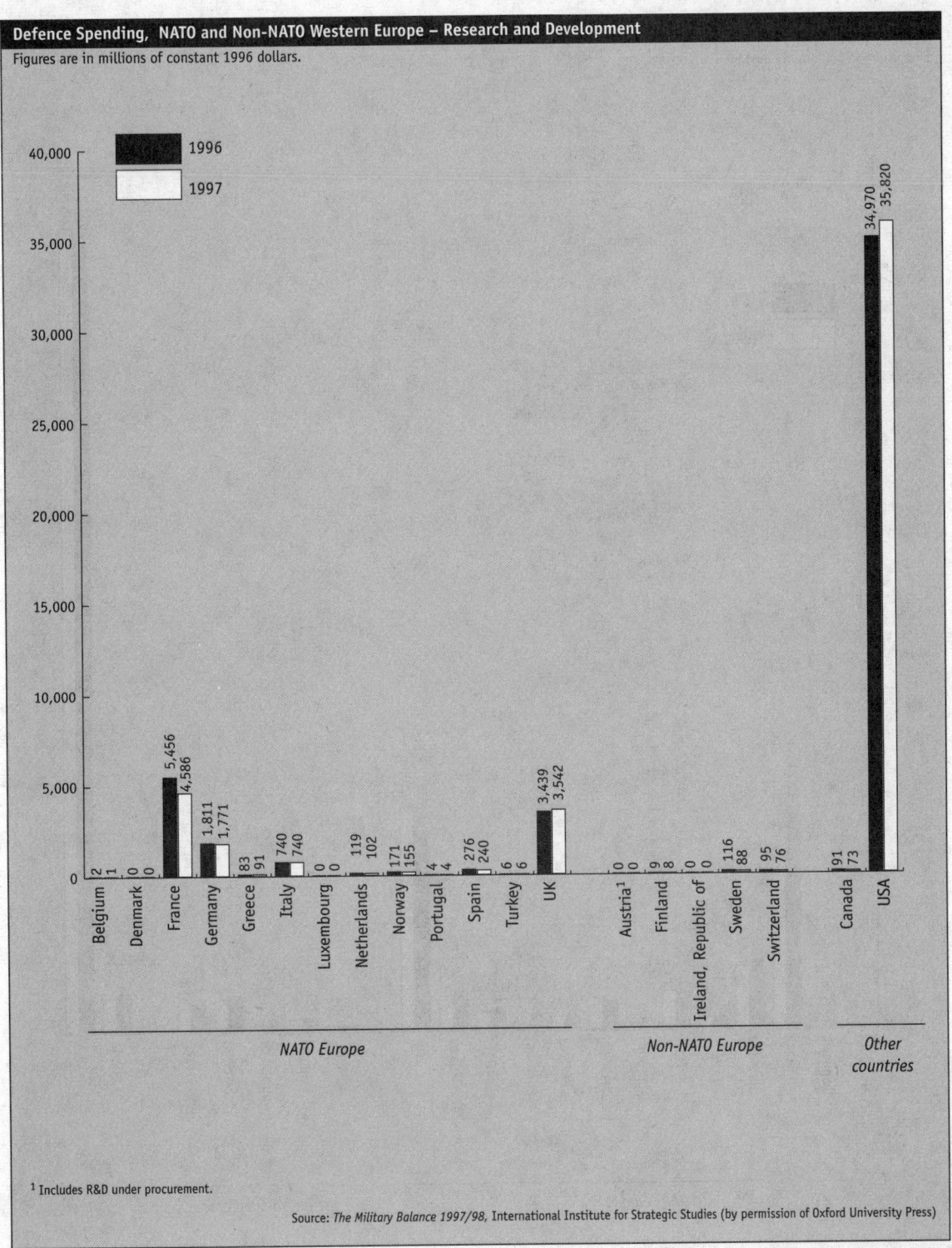

Defence Spending, NATO and Non-NATO Western Europe – Research and Development

Figures are in millions of constant 1996 dollars.

■ 1996
□ 1997

Belgium 2 / 1
Denmark 0 / 0
France 5,456 / 4,586
Germany 1,811 / 1,771
Greece 83 / 91
Italy 740 / 740
Luxembourg 0 / 0
Netherlands 119 / 102
Norway 171 / 155
Portugal 4 / 4
Spain 276 / 240
Turkey 6 / 6
UK 3,439 / 3,542

NATO Europe

Austria¹ 0 / 0
Finland 9 / 8
Ireland, Republic of 0 / 0
Sweden 116 / 88
Switzerland 95 / 76

Non-NATO Europe

Canada 91 / 73
USA 34,970 / 35,820

Other countries

¹ Includes R&D under procurement.

Source: *The Military Balance 1997/98,* International Institute for Strategic Studies (by permission of Oxford University Press)

Defence Spending, NATO and Non-NATO Western Europe – Procurement

Figures are in millions of constant 1996 dollars.

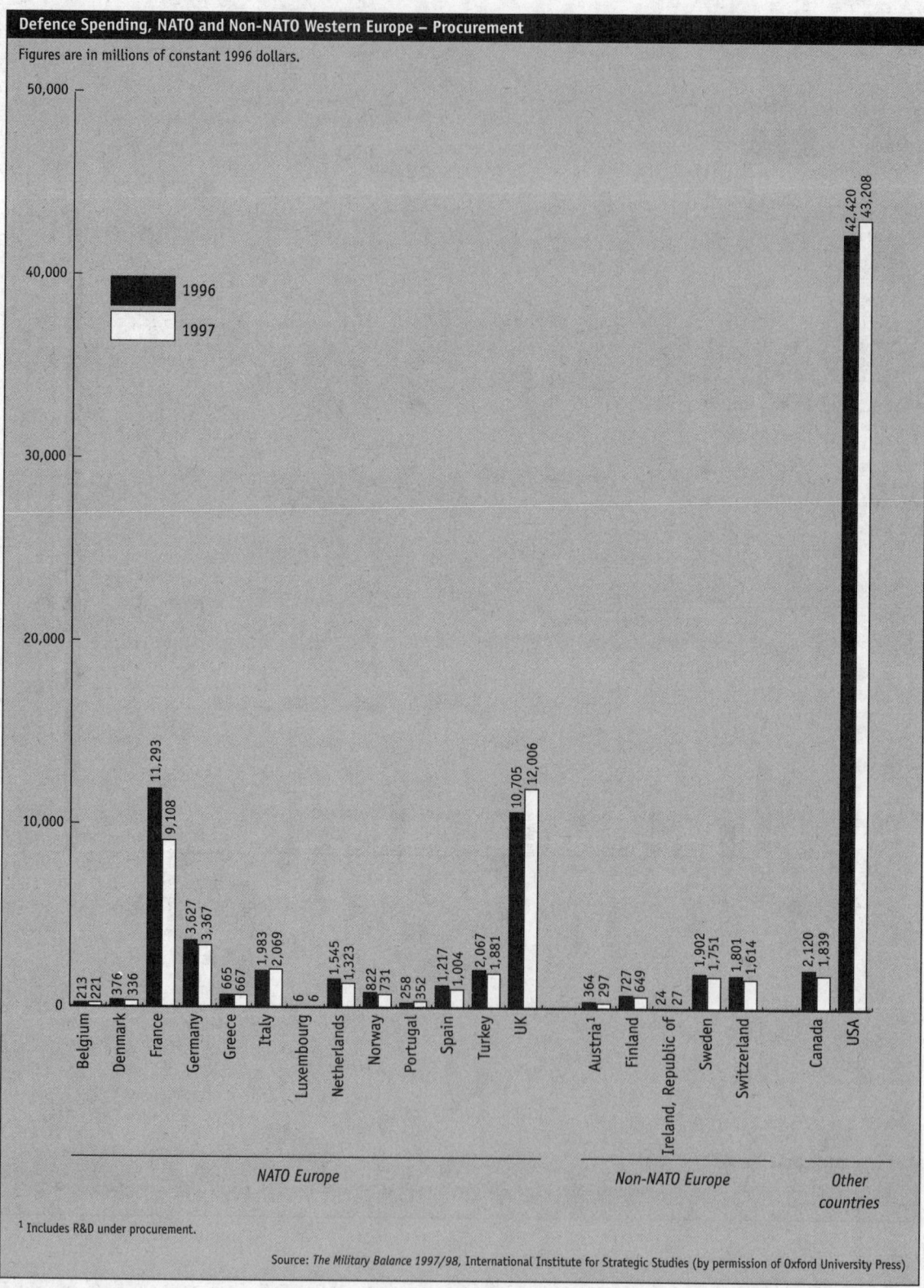

[1] Includes R&D under procurement.

Source: *The Military Balance 1997/98*, International Institute for Strategic Studies (by permission of Oxford University Press)

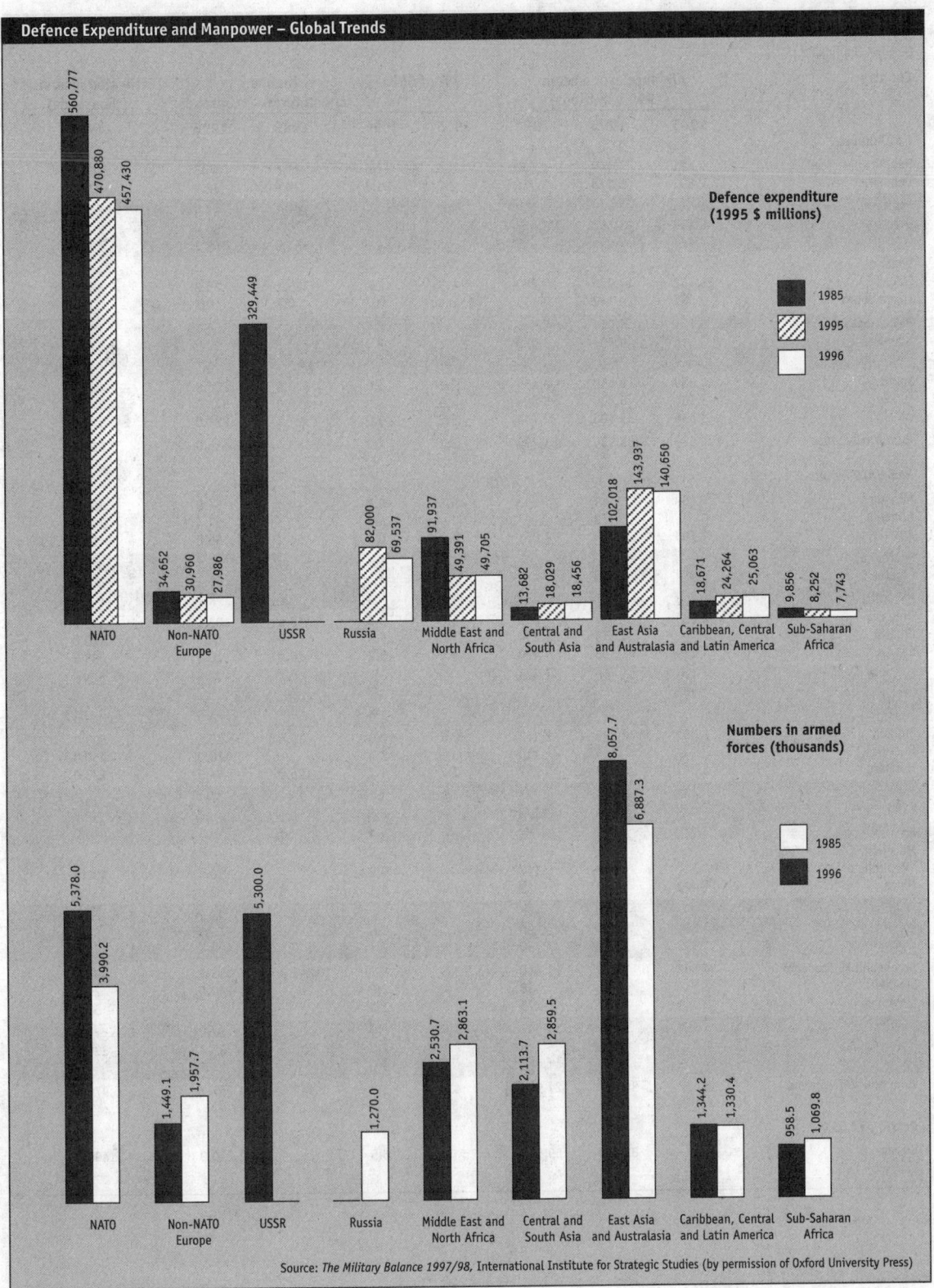

Defence Expenditure and Manpower – Global Trends

Defence expenditure
(1995 $ millions)

1985
1995
1996

Numbers in armed
forces (thousands)

1985
1996

Source: *The Military Balance 1997/98*, International Institute for Strategic Studies (by permission of Oxford University Press)

European Defence: Expenditure and Manpower

(– = not applicable.)

Country	Defence expenditure (1995 $ millions)			% of GDP		Numbers in armed forces (thousands)		Estimated reservists (thousands)
	1985	1995	1996	1985	1996	1985	1996	1996
NATO Europe								
Belgium	5,621	4,449	4,190	3.0	1.6	91.6	46.3	60.0
Denmark	2,855	3,118	2,978	2.2	1.7	29.6	32.9	70.4
France	44,604	47,746	46,217	4.0	3.1	464.3	398.9	337.0
Germany	48,149	41,157	38,432	3.2	1.7	478.0	358.4	304.9
Greece	3,180	5,056	5,465	7.0	4.8	201.5	168.3	291.0
Iceland[1]	–	–	–	–	–	–	–	–
Italy	23,462	19,376	23,289	2.3	2.2	385.1	325.2	584.0
Luxembourg	87	142	133	0.9	0.7	0.7	0.8	–
Netherlands	8,121	8,011	7,915	3.1	2.1	105.5	63.1	81.0
Norway	2,826	3,508	3,689	3.1	2.4	37.0	30.0	255.0
Portugal	1,674	2,670	2,853	3.1	2.8	73.0	54.2	210.0
Spain	10,289	8,652	8,439	2.4	1.5	320.0	206.8	420.0
Turkey	3,134	6,606	6,856	4.5	3.9	630.0	525.0	378.7
UK	43,536	33,406	32,764	5.2	3.0	327.1	226.0	327.4
Total NATO Europe	197,539	183,920	183,219	3.1	2.2	3,143.4	2,435.9	3,319.4
Non-NATO Europe								
Albania	258	89	98	5.3	6.7	40.4	54.0	155.0
Armenia	–	79	87	–	6.2	–	57.4	300.0
Austria	1,763	2,129	2,011	1.2	0.9	54.7	55.8	91.8
Azerbaijan	–	107	131	–	5.8	–	70.7	560.0
Belarus	–	496	480	–	4.2	–	85.5	289.5
Bosnia-Herzegovina	–	600	245	–	6.3	–	92.0	100.0
Bulgaria	2,235	417	335	6.6	3.3	148.5	103.5	303.0
Croatia	–	1,773	1,254	–	6.8	–	64.7	220.0
Cyprus	119	368	420	3.6	5.2	10.0	10.0	88.0
Czech Republic	–	1,120	988	–	2.4	–	70.0	240.0
Czechoslovakia	3,200	–	–	8.2	–	203.3	–	–
Estonia	–	101	106	–	2.4	–	3.5	6.0
Finland	2,051	2,385	2,162	2.8	2.0	36.5	32.5	500.0
Georgia	–	106	110	–	3.4	–	10.0	250.0
Hungary	3,241	613	757	7.2	1.7	106.0	64.3	173.0
Ireland, Republic of	437	688	725	1.8	1.1	13.7	12.7	15.6
Latvia	–	121	130	–	3.5	–	8.0	16.5
Lithuania	–	115	122	–	4.3	–	5.1	11.0
Macedonia, Former Yugoslav Republic of	–	116	117	–	9.2	–	10.4	100.0
Malta	22	32	32	1.4	1.1	0.8	2.0	–
Moldova	–	43	46	–	4.2	–	11.9	66.0
Poland	7,864	2,753	3,020	8.1	2.8	319.0	248.5	466.0
Romania	1,905	872	730	4.5	2.3	189.5	228.4	427.0
Serbia and Montenegro	4,562	3,111	1,440	3.8	8.7	241.0	113.9	400.0
Slovakia	–	455	438	–	2.6	–	42.6	20.0
Slovenia	–	277	275	–	1.8	–	9.6	53.0
Sweden	4,359	6,035	5,941	3.3	2.9	65.7	62.6	729.0
Switzerland	2,636	4,952	4,479	2.1	1.6	20.0	27.3	396.0
Ukraine	–	1,005	11,306	–	3.0	–	400.8	1,000.0
Total non-NATO Europe	34,652	30,960	27,986	4.8	3.8	1,449.1	1,957.7	6,976.4
Russia and USSR								
Russia	–	82,000	69,537	–	6.5	–	1,270.0	2,400.0

NATO Common-Funded Budgets

There has been zero real growth for the past four years in NATO's common-funded budgets. The Security Investment Programme almost halved from over $1.3 billion in 1989 to $787 million in 1996. Figures are in millions of dollars, except percentages.
(− = not applicable.)

1996

Country	Civil budget	Military budget	Security and investment	NATO AEW&C[1]	Total	% common funding	Total defence spending	% defence spending on NATO common-funded budgets
Belgium	5.0	19.5	35.8	7.7	68.0	3.8	4,278	0.01
Canada	10.2	38.3	34.5	21.3	104.3	5.9	8,564	0.02
Denmark	2.9	11.5	28.7	4.5	47.6	2.7	3,041	0.01
France	30.1	29.3	37.1	−	96.5	5.4	47,190	0.02
Germany	28.4	106.4	198.6	63.5	396.9	22.3	39,240	0.08
Greece	0.7	2.6	7.2	1.4	11.9	0.7	5,580	0.00
Iceland	0.1	0.3	0.0	−	0.4	0.0	0.0	0.00
Italy	10.5	40.5	65.2	16.4	132.6	7.4	23,779	0.03
Luxembourg	0.2	0.6	1.7	0.2	2.7	0.2	135	0.00
Netherlands	5.0	19.5	39.8	8.5	72.8	4.1	8,082	0.02
Norway	2.0	7.9	24.4	3.3	37.6	2.1	3,766	0.01
Portugal	1.2	4.3	2.4	1.6	9.5	0.5	2,913	0.00
Spain	6.4	7.2	7.2	−	20.8	1.2	8,617	0.00
Turkey	2.9	10.9	7.7	3.7	25.2	1.4	7,000	0.01
UK	34.3	120.4	90.4	0.2	245.3	13.8	33,453	0.05
USA	42.6	165.2	206.8	93.7	508.3	28.5	271,417	0.11
Total	182.5	584.4	787.5	226.0	1,780.4	100.0	467,056	0.38

[1] Airborne early warning and control.

NATO International Commands

(As of January 1998.)

Command	Commander/branch of service
Supreme Allied Commander, Europe (SACEUR)	General Wesley K Clark (US Army) (concurrently Commander in Chief, US European Command)
Deputy Supreme Allied Commander, Europe (DSACEUR)	General Sir Jeremy MacKenzie (UK Army)
Supreme Allied Commander, Atlantic (SACLANT)	Admiral Harold W Gehman, Jr (US Navy)
Commander-in-Chief, Allied Forces, Southern Europe (AFSOUTH)	Admiral Thomas J Lopez (US Navy)
Commander-in-Chief, Allied Forces, Central Europe (AFCENT)	General Dieter Stockmann (German Army)
Commander-in-Chief, Allied Forces, Northwestern Europe (AFNORTHWEST)	Air Chief Marshal Sir John Cheshire (UK Royal Air Force)
Chairman, Military Committee (MC)	General Klaus Naumann (German Army)

Source: US Department of Defense

Estimated Number of World Nuclear Explosions

(− = not applicable. As of January 1997.)

Explosion	USA	USSR/ Russia	UK	France	China	India	Total
Year of first explosion	1945	1949	1952	1960	1964	1974	−
Atmospheric explosions	217[1]	219[2]	21[3]	50	23	0	530
Underground explosions	815	496	24[3]	160	22	1	1,518
Total	1,032	715	45	210	45	1	2,048

[1] Four were underwater explosions.
[2] Three were underwater explosions.
[3] All UK tests since 1962 have been conducted jointly with the USA. Thus, the US tests are higher than the US figures given above.

Source: Ragnhild Ferm, in *SIPRI Yearbook 1997*, Stockholm International Peace Research Institute (Oxford University Press)

Major Armed Conflicts Worldwide

Data show regional distribution of locations with at least one major armed conflict, for the period 1989–96.

Region	1989	1990	1991	1992	1993	1994	1995	1996
Africa	9	10	10	7	7	6	6	5
Asia	11	10	8	11	9	9	9	10
Central and South America	5	5	4	3	3	3	3	3
Europe	2	1	2	4	5	4	3	2
Middle East	5	5	5	4	4	5	4	4
Total	32	31	29	29	28	27	25	24

Source: Margareta Sollenberg and Peter Wallensteen, Uppsala Conflict Data Project (Uppsala University), in *SIPRI Yearbook 1997*, Stockholm International Peace Research Institute (Oxford University Press)

MILITARY CONFLICTS: REVIEW

BY IAN DERBYSHIRE

There were no significant inter-state wars during 1997–98, although there were border skirmishes between Armenia and Azerbaijan and between India and Pakistan in disputed Kashmir. Continuing recent trends, conflicts were chiefly confined within states, involving sometimes long-running, insurrections by ethnic, religious, and political groups. These occurred in around 40 states. The bloodiest conflicts were in Africa, notably in Algeria, the Democratic Republic of Congo, Rwanda, and Sudan.

Europe

In Western Europe, violence was limited to sporadic kidnappings and bombings by regionally-based terrorist organizations: the National Liberation Front of Corsica in France; the Basque separatist group Euskadi to Askatasuna (ETA) in Spain; and the nationalist Irish Republican Army (IRA) in Northern Ireland, in the UK. By 1998, there were hopeful signs of a waning of the threat posed by these groups. In Spain, following the wave of public outrage over ETA's assassination in July 1997 of a popular young local councillor, the government moved decisively, imprisoning the entire leadership of ETA's political wing. In the UK, a second IRA cease-fire was announced in July 1997 and, after months of all party talks, in which Sinn Féin, the IRA's political wing, participated, an agreement was reached on Northern Ireland's future in April 1998 and was to be voted on in a May 1998 referendum.

In eastern Europe, peace continued in Bosnia-Herzegovina, where a 35,000-strong NATO-led Stabilization Force was deployed. However, in Albania, an armed rebellion in the south, triggered by the collapse of pyramid investment schemes, overthrew the northern-based president, Sali Berisha, in July 1997. In the neighbouring Albanian-peopled Yugoslav province of Kosovo, the separatist activities of the Kosovo Liberation Army resulted in a brutal crackdown by the Serb army in March 1998, claiming over 80 lives. Meanwhile, in the Caucasus region, there was heavy border fighting between Armenia and Azerbaijan in April–May 1997, on the third anniversary of a cease-fire.

The Middle East

In Algeria, the uprising against President Liamine Zeroual by Muslim guerrillas, based in areas south and west of Algiers, continued into 1998; by February, according to Western sources, massacres of civilians had taken around 65,000 lives since 1992. In Egypt, the Gema's Islamiyah (Islamic Group) was responsible for the slaughter, in November 1997, of 58 foreign tourists in Luxor.

In northern Iraq, conflict erupted in November 1997 between the principal Kurdish factions – the Patriotic Union of Kurdistan (PUK) and the Kurdistan Democratic Party (KDP) – after a year's truce. Earlier, in May and September–November 1997, 50,000 Turkish troops had entered northern Iraq in pursuit of the radical Kurdistan Workers Party (PKK). A potentially more serious international conflict was averted in February 1998, following Iraqi President Saddam Hussein's refusal to cooperate with UN weapons inspectors, and the subsequent build-up of US military strength in the Gulf. As tensions escalated, Kofi Annan, the UN secretary-general, secured an agreement from Hussein to allow the inspectors unconditional access to any site suspected of containing materials for producing chemical, biological, or nuclear weapons. By April 1998, however, the inspection team reported little progress in achieving verification that such facilities had been closed down.

Israeli-Palestinian peace talks, under US auspices, resumed in November 1997, after a seven-month break. This was despite a series of suicide bombings in Jerusalem by Hamas Islamic activists and clashes, in June 1997, between Israeli forces and Hezbollah guerrillas in Israel's self-declared 'security zone' in southern Lebanon. The new talks soon stalled, as the Palestinians demanded that Israel stop building settlements on occupied land.

The Americas

Conflicts in Latin America were restricted to those between chiefly left-wing guerrillas and repressive governments abetted by right-wing militias. In Colombia, atrocities attributed to the left-wing National Liberation Army (ELN) and Revolutionary Armed Forces of Colombia (FARC) claimed hundreds of lives. The government countered with aerial bombardment campaigns, but in March 1998 more than 80 government troops were killed by the FARC in the southern province of Caqueta. However, the ELN agreed to preliminary peace talks.

In Mexico, in the southern state of Chiapas, the centre of a 1994 Zapatist rebellion by local Indians, armed groups, allegedly linked to the ruling Institutional Revolutionary Party (PRI), massacred 45 villagers, mostly women and children, in December 1997.

In Peru, the left-wing Tupac Amaru guerrillas held the world's attention during a 126-day siege of the Japanese embassy in Lima, which was ended in April 1997 by a lightning raid by government commandos, freeing 72 hostages. The Sendero Luminoso (Shining Path) radical guerrillas, believed to have been crushed by the authorities in 1992, resurfaced with terrorist attacks in July and October 1997.

Asia

Two major long-running civil wars in Asia, in Afghanistan and Sri Lanka, continued during 1997. A third, in Tajikistan, ended, while a fourth, in Cambodia, re-started. In Afghanistan, the extremist Talibaan Islamic militia, in control of Kabul and the south, suffered reverses in 1997 against the Tajikistan-backed 'northern alliance' of Ahmed Shah Masoud and the Uzbek militia of General Abdul Rashid Dostam, and in April 1998 agreed to a US-brokered truce.

In Sri Lanka, the government, whilst seeking a political settlement, launched Operation Jaya Sikuru (Sure Victory) in May 1997, a military offensive against the northern-based separatist Tamil Tigers (LTTE). This claimed the lives of over 400 rebels during its first month, and provoked LTTE retaliatory bombings in Kandy and the capital, Colombo. In January 1998 the government formally outlawed the LTTE and the following month more than 300 rebels were killed in renewed fighting in the north.

In Tajikistan, the Russian-backed President Rakhmonov signed a peace accord in June 1997 with the United Tajik Opposition (UTO) Muslim rebels to end the five-year civil war.

In Cambodia, a July 1997 coup by the communists against their royalist coalition partners claimed over 40 lives. The royalists and the much depleted Khmer Rouge resumed the guerrilla war, ending four years of peace; but in March 1998 the ousted Prince Norodom Ranariddh returned to contest elections, set for July 1998.

In the disputed region of Kashmir, over 50 people were killed in September cross-border shelling in September 1997.

Africa

The overthrow in Zaire (now the Democratic Republic of Congo) of President Mobutu in May 1997 by Laurent Kabila had far-reaching repercussions on the power balances within neighbouring states. The idiosyncratic Mobutu had, for example, supported the UNITA rebel movement in Angola, providing it with bases, and had also backed Hutu militia in Rwanda and the Lord's Resistance Army rebels in northern Uganda. In contrast, Kabila, a pragmatic ex-Marxist, was a close ally of the Uganda- and Tutsi-dominated Rwanda and Burundi governments. He came to power in May 1997, following a seven-month armed rebellion against Mobutu, during which, it was alleged, his Tutsi-led forces massacred up to 200,000 Hutu refugees. Immediately, the Angolan government moved against UNITA guerrillas based in the diamond fields of northeast Angola. By January 1998, UNITA's position was so weakened that its leader, Jonas Savimbi, agreed finally to implement the 1994 Lusaka agreement, which provided for demobilization of the rebel army, based in central Angola. UNITA did not, however, keep to the agreed March 1998 deadline.

In both Burundi and Rwanda there were bloody ethnic clashes, in which thousands died, involving Hutu extremists and counter-reprisals by the Tutsi-led armies; by January 1998 the weekly death toll exceeded 100. In the eastern Democratic Republic of Congo, the Mai Mai, a local ethnic movement, fanned fresh unrest.

Elsewhere in Africa, in Liberia the formerly warring factions were disarmed by international peacekeepers, and the July 1997 presidential election was won decisively by Charles Taylor, the warlord who had launched and dominated Liberia's seven-year civil war. In Sierra Leone, the elected government was overthrown in May 1997 in a coup by junior-ranking army officers. This prompted the Nigerian army, with UN blessing, to intervene and in March 1998 the military junta was expelled, enabling the ousted President Ahmad Tejan Kabbah to return from exile. In the Republic of the Congo, President Pascal Lissouba was overthrown in October 1997, after a four-month military struggle with militia loyal to his predecessor General Denis Sassou-Nguesso.

Meanwhile, the 14- and 6-year-old civil wars in Sudan and Somalia continued. In Sudan, the southern-based rebel Sudan People's Liberation Army (SPLA) – which receives backing from Ethiopia, Eritrea, Uganda, the Democratic Republic of Congo, and, allegedly, the USA – continued to grow in strength and formed an alliance with the Sudan Alliance Forces, based in the northeast. During 1997 the SPLA seized control of garrison towns in the African animist and Christian south, where more than one million have been killed during the war against Khartoum's Islamist regime.

However, in December 1997 an agreement was signed in Cairo by Somalia's contending political-military groups – the National Salvation Council, led by Ali Mahdi, and the Somali National Alliance, led by Hussein Aideed – which covered arrangements for choosing a transitional government.

Wars and Casualties

Military Casualties in World War I

World War I casualty statistics vary greatly from source to source. Official records are often lacking and based on differing criteria and these figures remain open to interpretation and debate. Figures are for 1914–18 and are rounded to the nearest 250.
(N/A = not available.)

Country	Mobilized	Deaths (all causes)	Wounded	Total casualties	Prisoners/missing
Allied Powers					
Belgium	207,000	13,750	44,000	57,750	67,750
British Empire[1]					
UK	5,397,000	702,500	1,662,750	2,365,250	170,500
Australia	330,000	59,250	152,250	211,500	4,000
Canada	552,000	56,750	149,750	206,500	3,750
India[2]	1,216,000	64,500	69,250	133,750	11,250
Newfoundland	N/A	1,250	2,250	3,500	250
New Zealand	N/A	16,750	41,250	58,000	500
South Africa	N/A	7,000	12,000	19,000	1,500
Other colonies	N/A	500	750	1,250	N/A
Total British Empire	>7,495,000	908,500	2,090,250	2,998,750	191,750
France (including colonial territories)	7,500,000	1,385,250	2,675,000–4,266,000[3]	4,060,250–5,651,250	446,250
Greece	230,000	5,000	21,000	26,000	1,000
Italy	5,500,000	460,000	947,000	1,407,000	530,000
Japan	800,000	250	1,000	1,250	0
Montenegro	50,000	3,000	10,000	13,000	7,000
Portugal	100,000	7,250	15,000	22,250	12,250
Romania	750,000	200,000	120,000	320,000	80,000
Russia	12,000,000	1,700,000	4,950,000	6,650,000	2,500,000
Serbia	707,250	127,500	133,250	260,750	153,000
USA	4,272,500	116,750	204,000	320,750	4,500
Central Powers					
Austria-Hungary	6,500,000	1,200,000	3,620,000	4,820,000	2,200,000
Bulgaria	400,000	101,250	152,500	253,750	11,000
Germany	11,000,000	1,718,250	4,234,000	5,952,250	1,073,500
Turkey[4]	1,600,000	>335,750	>400,000	>735,750	>200,000

[1] Figures for the British Empire and constituent countries are for 1914–20.
[2] Includes 4,912 British casualties: British drafts and units serving with the Indian Army.
[3] Official records for the number of French wounded are not available.
[4] There are no official records available for Turkish casualties.

World War I: Chronology

1914

June — Assassination of Archduke Franz Ferdinand of Austria, 28 June.

July — German government issued 'blank cheque' to Austria, offering support in war against Serbia. Austrian ultimatum to Serbia. Serbs accepted all but two points. Austria refused to accept compromise and declared war. Russia began mobilization to defend Serbian ally. Germany demanded Russian demobilization.

Aug — Germany declared war on Russia. France mobilized to assist Russian ally. Germans occupied Luxembourg and demanded access to Belgian territory, which was refused. Germany declared war on France and invaded Belgium. Britain declared war on Germany, then on Austria. Dominions within the British Empire, including Australia, automatically involved. Battle of Tannenburg between Central Powers and Russians. Russian army encircled.

Sept — British and French troops halted German advance just short of Paris, and drove them back. First Battle of the Marne, and of the Aisne. Beginning of trench warfare.

Oct–Nov — First Battle of Ypres. Britain declared war on Turkey.

1915

April–May — Gallipoli offensive launched by British and dominion troops against Turkish forces. Second Battle of Ypres. First use of poison gas by Germans. Italy joined war against Austria. German submarine sank ocean liner *Lusitania* on 7 May, later helping to bring USA into the war.

Aug–Sept — Warsaw evacuated by the Russians. Battle of Tarnopol. Vilna taken by the Germans. Tsar Nicholas II took supreme control of Russian forces.

1916

Jan — Final evacuation of British and dominion troops from Gallipoli.

Feb — German offensive against Verdun began, with huge losses for little territorial gain.

May — Naval battle of Jutland between British and German imperial fleets ended inconclusively, but put a stop to further German naval participation in the war.

June — Russian (Brusilov) offensive against the Ukraine began.

July–Nov — First Battle of the Somme, a sustained Anglo-French offensive which won little territory and lost a huge number of lives.

Aug — Hindenburg and Ludendorff took command of the German armed forces. Romania entered the war against Austria but was rapidly overrun.

Sept — Early tanks used by British on Western Front.

Nov — Nivelle replaced Joffre as commander of French forces. Battle of the Ancre on the Western Front.

Dec — French completed recapture of Verdun fortifications. Austrians occupied Bucharest.

1917

Feb — Germany declared unrestricted submarine warfare. Russian Revolution began and tsarist rule overthrown.

March — British seizure of Baghdad and occupation of Persia.

March–April — Germans retreated to Siegfried Line (Arras-Soissons) on Western Front.

April–May — USA entered the war against Germany. Unsuccessful British and French offensives. Mutinies among French troops. Nivelle replaced by Pétain.

July–Nov — Third Ypres offensive including Battle of Passchendaele.

Sept — Germans occupied Riga.

Oct–Nov — Battle of Caporetto saw Italian troops defeated by Austrians.

Dec — Jerusalem taken by British forces under Allenby.

1918

Jan — US President Woodrow Wilson proclaimed 'Fourteen Points' as a basis for peace settlement.

March — Treaty of Brest-Litovsk with Central Powers ended Russian participation in the war, with substantial concessions of territory and reparations. Second Battle of the Somme began with German spring offensive.

July–Aug — Allied counter-offensive, including tank attack at Amiens, drove Germans back to the Siegfried Line.

Sept — Hindenburg and Ludendorff called for an armistice.

Oct — Armistice offered on the basis of the 'Fourteen Points'. German naval and military mutinies at Kiel and Wilhelmshaven.

Nov — Austria-Hungary signed armistice with Allies. Kaiser Wilhelm II of Germany went into exile. Provisional government under social democrat Friedrich Ebert formed. Germany agreed armistice. Fighting on Western Front stopped.

1919

Jan — Peace conference opened at Versailles.

May — Demands presented to Germany.

June — Germany signed peace treaty at Versailles, followed by other Central Powers: Austria (Treaty of St Germain-en-Laye, Sept), Bulgaria (Neuilly, Nov), Hungary (Trianon, June 1920), and Turkey (Sèvres, Aug 1920).

World War II Casualties

Figures are for 1939–45 and are rounded to the nearest 250.
(– = not applicable. N/A = not available.)

Country	Personnel[1]	Military killed	Military wounded	Prisoners of war	Civilian dead
Allied Powers					
Australia	680,000	23,250	39,750	26,250	–
Belgium	800,000	7,750	14,500	N/A	75,000 [2]
Brazil	200,000	1,000	4,250	–	–
Canada	780,000	37,500	53,250	9,750	–
China	5,000,000	1,324,500[3]	1,762,000	N/A	N/A [4]
Czechoslovakia	180,000	6,750	8,000	–	310,000 [5]
Denmark	15,000	4,250	N/A	–	–
Estonia	–	–	–	–	140,000
France	5,000,000	205,750	390,000	765,000	300,000
Greece	150,000	16,250	50,000	N/A	337,000 [6]
India	2,394,000	24,250	64,250	79,500	–
Latvia	–	–	–	–	120,000
Lithuania	–	–	–	–	170,000
Netherlands	500,000	13,750	2,750	N/A	236,250 [7]
New Zealand	157,000	12,250	19,250	8,500	–
Norway	25,000	4,750	N/A	N/A	5,500 [8]
Poland	1,000,000	320,000	530,000	–	6,028,000 [10]
South Africa	140,000	8,750	14,250	14,500	–
UK	4,683,000	264,500	277,000	172,500[9]	60,500
USA	16,353,750	405,500	671,750	105,000	–
USSR	20,000,000	13,600,000	5,000,000	N/A	7,720,000
Yugoslavia	3,741,000	305,000	425,000	–	1,355,000 [11]
Axis Powers					
Austria	800,000	380,000	N/A	N/A	145,000 [12]
Finland	250,000	79,000	N/A	–	–
Germany	10,000,000	3,300,000	N/A	630,000[13]	3,063,000 [14]
Hungary	350,000	147,500	N/A	–	280,000 [15]
Italy	4,500,000	262,500	N/A	1,478,000	93,000 [16]
Japan	N/A	1,140,500	N/A	11,600[17]	953,000 [18]
Romania	600,000	300,000	N/A	N/A	145,000 [19]

[1] Peak strength of armed forces during World War II.
[2] Includes approximately 25,000 Jews.
[3] Estimates vary for Chinese military killed.
[4] Estimates for Chinese civilian dead vary very widely, from 700,000 to 10,000,000.
[5] Includes approximately 250,000 Jews.
[6] Includes approximately 260,000 deaths due to starvation.
[7] Includes approximately 104,000 Jews, 25,000 civilian underground workers, and 15,000 deaths due to starvation.
[8] Includes approximately 2,000 resistance fighters and 750 Norwegians serving in the German army.
[9] 7,250 British prisoners of war died while in German captivity; 12,500 died while in Japanese captivity.
[10] Includes approximately 3,200,000 Jews.
[11] Includes approximately 55,000 Jews.
[12] Includes approximately 60,000 Jews.
[13] Excludes those in the USSR.
[14] Includes approximately 170,000 Jews.
[15] Includes approximately 200,000 Jews.
[16] Includes approximately 8,000 Jews.
[17] Excludes those in the USSR.
[18] Includes approximately 668,000 killed in air raids on home islands.
[19] Includes approximately 60,000 Jews.

Costs to Individual Nations Directly Related to World War II

Country	Cost ($ millions)	Country	Cost ($ millions)	Country	Cost ($ millions)
USA	288,000	Italy	21,072	Sweden	2,344
Germany	212,336	Canada	20,104	South Africa	2,152
France	111,272	Australia	10,036	Turkey	1,924
USSR	93,012	Netherlands	9,624	Switzerland	1,752
UK	57,254	Belgium	6,324	Norway	992
China	49,072	India	4,804	Portugal	320
Japan	41,272	New Zealand	2,560		

Source: US Department of Defense

World War II: Chronology

1939

Sept	German invasion of Poland; Britain and France declared war on Germany; the USSR invaded Poland; fall of Warsaw (Poland divided between Germany and USSR).
Nov	The USSR invaded Finland.

1940

March	Soviet peace treaty with Finland.
April	Germany occupied Denmark, Norway, the Netherlands, Belgium, and Luxembourg. In Britain, a coalition government was formed under Churchill.
May	Germany outflanked the defensive French Maginot Line.
May–June	Evacuation of 337,131 Allied troops from Dunkirk, France, across the Channel to England.
June	Italy declared war on Britain and France; the Germans entered Paris; the French Prime Minister Pétain signed an armistice with Germany and moved the seat of government to Vichy.
July–Oct	Battle of Britain between British and German air forces.
Sept	Japanese invasion of French Indochina.
Oct	Abortive Italian invasion of Greece.

1941

April	Germany occupied Greece and Yugoslavia.
June	Germany invaded the USSR; Finland declared war on the USSR.
July	The Germans entered Smolensk, USSR.
Dec	The Germans came within 40 km/25 mi of Moscow, with Leningrad (now St Petersburg) under siege. First Soviet counteroffensive. Japan bombed Pearl Harbor, Hawaii, and declared war on the USA and Britain. Germany and Italy declared war on the USA.

1942

Jan	Japanese conquest of the Philippines.
June	Naval battle of Midway, the turning point of the Pacific War.
Aug	German attack on Stalingrad (now Volgograd), USSR.
Oct–Nov	Battle of El Alamein in North Africa, turn of the tide for the Western Allies.
Nov	Soviet counteroffensive on Stalingrad.

1943

Jan	The Casablanca Conference issued the Allied demand of unconditional surrender; the Germans retreated from Stalingrad.
March	The USSR drove the Germans back to the river Donetz.
May	End of Axis resistance in North Africa.
July	A coup by King Victor Emmanuel and Marshal Badoglio forced Mussolini to resign.
Aug	Beginning of the campaign against the Japanese in Burma (now Myanmar); US Marines landed on Guadalcanal, Solomon Islands.
Sept	Italy surrendered to the Allies; Mussolini was rescued by the Germans who set up a Republican Fascist government in northern Italy; Allied landings at Salerno; the USSR retook Smolensk.
Oct	Italy declared war on Germany.
Nov	The US Navy defeated the Japanese in the Battle of Guadalcanal.
Nov–Dec	The Allied leaders met at the Tehran Conference.

1944

Jan	Allied landing in Nazi-occupied Italy: Battle of Anzio.
March	End of the German U-boat campaign in the Atlantic.
May	Fall of Monte Cassino, southern Italy.
6 June	D-day: Allied landings in Nazi-occupied and heavily defended Normandy.
July	The bomb plot by German generals against Hitler failed.
Aug	Romania joined the Allies.
Sept	Battle of Arnhem on the Rhine; Soviet armistice with Finland.
Oct	The Yugoslav guerrilla leader Tito and Soviets entered Belgrade.
Dec	German counteroffensive, Battle of the Bulge.

1945

Feb	The Soviets reached the German border; Yalta conference; Allied bombing campaign over Germany (Dresden destroyed); the US reconquest of the Philippines was completed; the Americans landed on Iwo Jima, south of Japan.
April	Hitler committed suicide; Mussolini was captured by Italian partisans and shot.
May	German surrender to the Allies.
June	US troops completed the conquest of Okinawa (one of the Japanese Ryukyu Islands).
July	The Potsdam Conference issued an Allied ultimatum to Japan.
Aug	Atom bombs were dropped by the USA on Hiroshima and Nagasaki; Japan surrendered.

Tank Production During World War II

Country	Number of tanks
USA	60,973
USSR	54,500
UK	23,202
Germany	19,926
Italy	4,600
Japan	2,464

Source: US Department of Defense

Merchant Shipping Losses During World War II

(Ships over 200 tons.)

Country	Number of ships
UK	3,194
Japan	2,346
USA	866
Neutral	902
Other Allied	1,467

Source: US Department of Defense

Aircraft Production During World War II

Figures indicate number of aircraft produced.

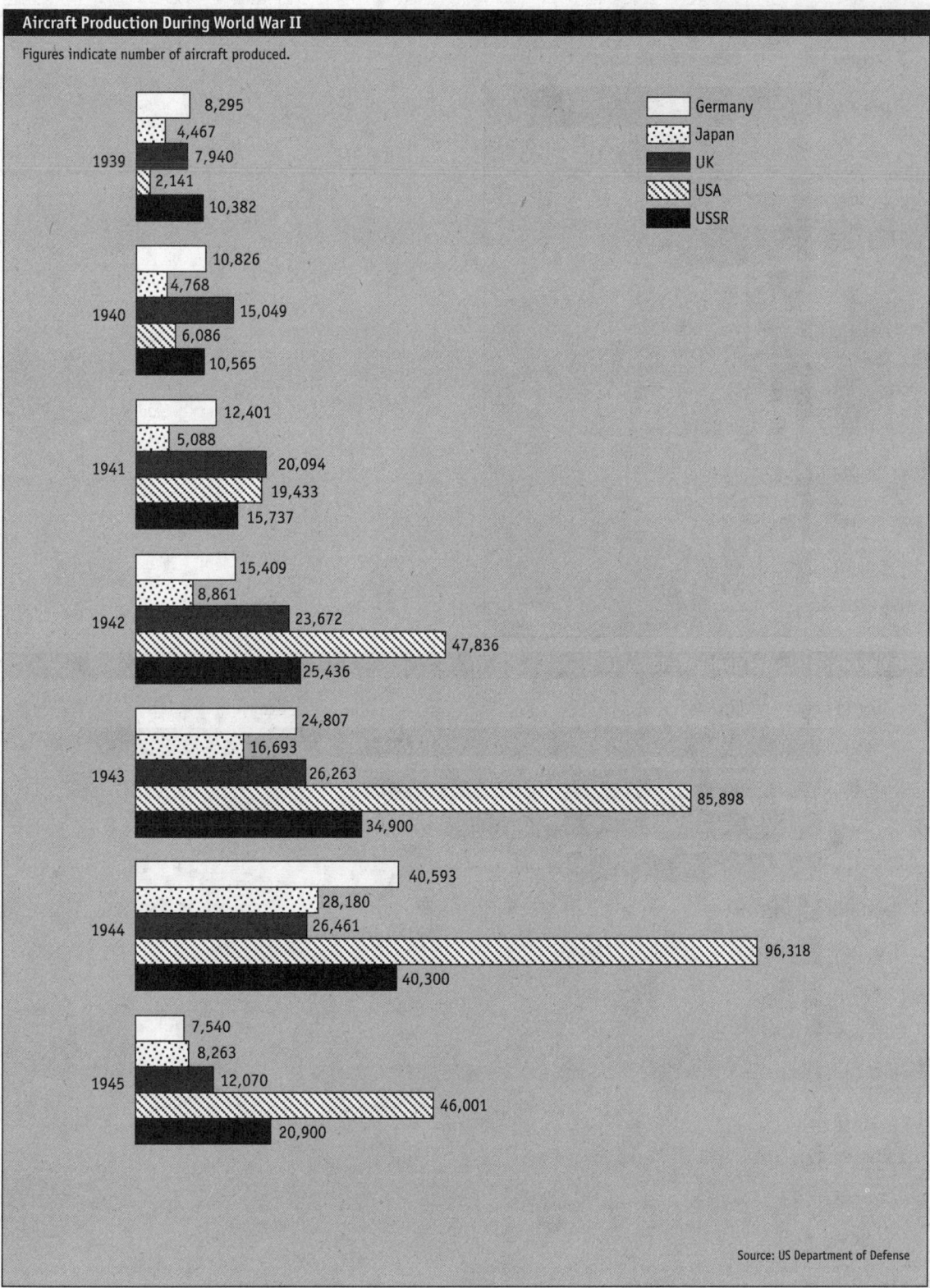

Legend:
- Germany
- Japan
- UK
- USA
- USSR

1939
- Germany: 8,295
- Japan: 4,467
- UK: 7,940
- USA: 2,141
- USSR: 10,382

1940
- Germany: 10,826
- Japan: 4,768
- UK: 15,049
- USA: 6,086
- USSR: 10,565

1941
- Germany: 12,401
- Japan: 5,088
- UK: 20,094
- USA: 19,433
- USSR: 15,737

1942
- Germany: 15,409
- Japan: 8,861
- UK: 23,672
- USA: 47,836
- USSR: 25,436

1943
- Germany: 24,807
- Japan: 16,693
- UK: 26,263
- USA: 85,898
- USSR: 34,900

1944
- Germany: 40,593
- Japan: 28,180
- UK: 26,461
- USA: 96,318
- USSR: 40,300

1945
- Germany: 7,540
- Japan: 8,263
- UK: 12,070
- USA: 46,001
- USSR: 20,900

Source: US Department of Defense

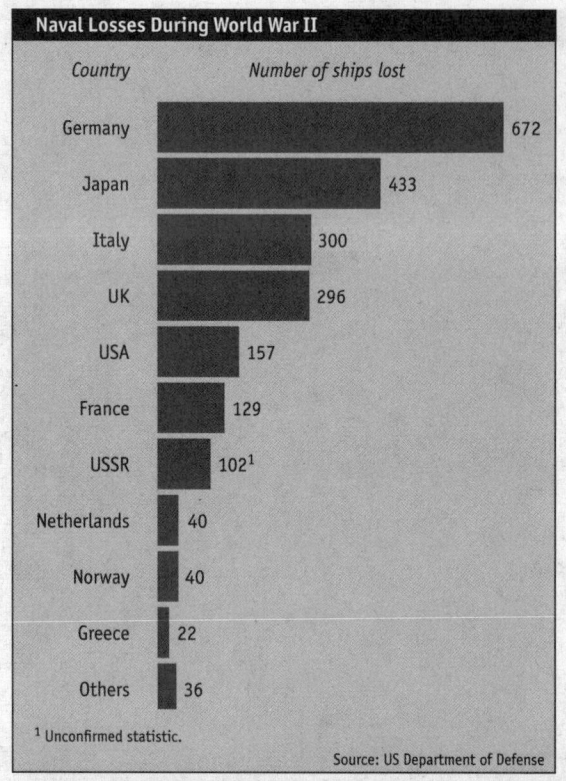

Naval Losses During World War II

Country	Number of ships lost
Germany	672
Japan	433
Italy	300
UK	296
USA	157
France	129
USSR	102[1]
Netherlands	40
Norway	40
Greece	22
Others	36

[1] Unconfirmed statistic.

Source: US Department of Defense

Military Aircraft Losses During World War II

Country	Number of aircraft lost
Germany	95,000
USA	59,296
Japan	49,485
UK	33,090
Australia	7,160
Italy	4,000
Canada	2,389
France	2,100
New Zealand	684
India	527
Sweden	272
Denmark	154
USSR	N/A[1]

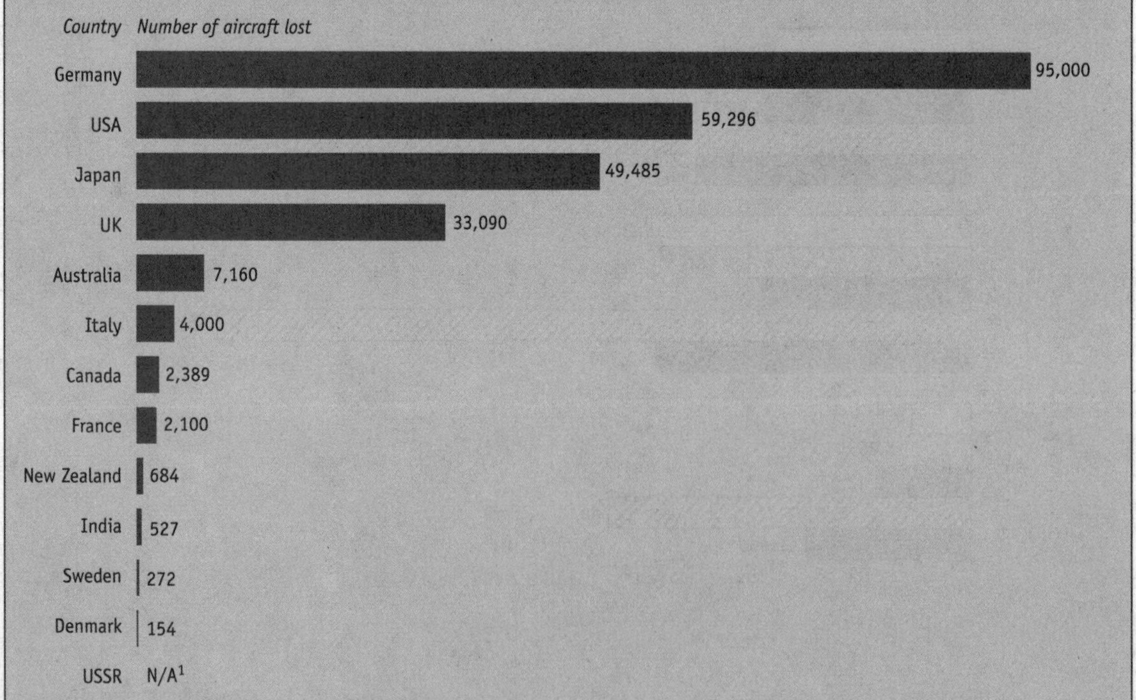

[1] USSR losses were extremely high, but they were undisclosed by the Soviet government

Source: US Department of Defense

World War II: Declarations of War

Declared by	Against	Date	Declared by	Against	Date
Germany	Poland	none; invaded 1 September 1939	USA	Germany, Italy	11 December 1941
UK, France, Australia, New Zealand	Germany	3 September 1939	Germany, Italy	USA	11 December 1941
			Hungary	USA	11 December 1941
			Brazil	Germany, Italy	22 August 1942
Canada	Germany	10 September 1939	Bolivia	Germany, Italy, Japan	7 April 1943
USSR	Poland	none; invaded 17 September 1939	Iran	Germany	9 September 1943
			Italy	Germany	13 October 1943
USSR	Finland	13 November 1939	Liberia	Germany, Japan	26 January 1944
Germany	Denmark, Norway	none; invaded 9 April 1940	Romania	Germany	25 August 1944
			Bulgaria	Germany	7 September 1944
Germany	Holland, Belgium	none; invaded 10 May 1940	Ecuador	Germany, Japan	2 February 1945
			Peru	Germany, Japan	11 February 1945
Italy	UK, France	10 June 1940	Chile	Japan	14 February 1945
Italy	Greece	none; invaded 28 October 1940	Venezuela	Germany, Japan	16 February 1945
			Uruguay	Germany, Japan	22 February 1945
Bulgaria	Allies	6 April 1941	Turkey	Germany, Japan	23 February 1945
Germany	Greece, Yugoslavia	none; invaded 6 April 1941	Egypt	Germany, Japan	24 February 1945
			Syria	Germany, Japan	26 February 1945
Italy	Yugoslavia	none; invaded 6 April 1941	Lebanon	Germany, Japan	27 February 1945
			Saudi Arabia	Germany, Japan	1 March 1945
Germany	USSR	none; invaded 22 June 1941	Iran	Japan	1 March 1945
			Finland	Germany	4 March 1945, but a state of war was held to have existed from 15 September 1944
USSR	Germany	22 June 1941			
Italy, Romania	USSR	22 June 1941			
Finland	USSR	26 June 1941			
Hungary, Slovakia	USSR	27 June 1941	Argentina	Germany, Japan	27 March 1945
UK	Finland, Hungary, Romania	5 December 1941	Brazil	Japan	6 June 1945
			USSR	Japan	8 August 1945
Japan	UK, USA	7 December 1941			
USA	Japan	8 December 1941			

Source: US Department of Defense

UK Casualties in Post-1945 Conflicts

The number of wounded refers to those detained in hospital, and may represent a lower figure than that reported operationally; the number of wounded and killed refers to officers and soldiers in all services. (N/A = not available.)

Conflict/campaign	Number killed	Number wounded	Total
Indonesia (1945–46)	50	N/A	N/A
Palestine (1945–48)	223	478	701
Malaya (1948–61)	509	921	1,430
British units	340	613	953
Brigade of Gurkhas	169	308	477
Korea (1950–53)	865	2,589	3,454
Egypt (1951–54)	53	N/A	N/A
Kenya (1952)	12	69	81
Cyprus (1955–58)	79	414	493
Egypt (1956)	12	63	75
Borneo and Malaya (1962–66)	59	123	182
British units	16	36	52
Brigade of Gurkhas	43	87	130
Radfan (1964–67)	24	188	212
Aden (1964–67)	68	322	390
Falklands (1982)	255[1]	777	1,032
Gulf (1991)	42[2]	43	85

[1] Includes five civilians.
[2] Includes nine killed accidentally by US 'friendly fire'.

UK Armed Forces and Defence Expenditure

Armed Forces in the UK

General Information

The armed forces of the UK are made up of the Army, the Royal Navy, and the Royal Air Force. The Queen is the commander-in-chief for all branches of the armed forces. The Ministry of Defence (MoD) is concerned with the control, administration, equipment, and support of the armed forces of the Crown. The research, development, production, and purchase of weapons is the concern of the Procurement Executive of the MoD.

The Chief of Staff of the Defence Staff is the professional head of the armed forces and under him each Service's Chief of Staff is responsible for the fighting effectiveness,

Formation of the UK Armed Forces: Front Line and Support Units

The number of personnel and the amount of equipment in each vessel, regiment, battalion, or squadron vary according to the roles currently assigned. (N/A = not available. As of 1 April 1997.)

Front Line Units

Royal Navy

Trident/Polaris submarines	vessels	3
Fleet submarines	vessels	12
Carriers	vessels	3
Assault ships	vessels	3
Destroyers	vessels	12
Frigates	vessels	23
Mine counter measure	vessels	19
Patrol ships and craft	vessels	34
Fixed wing aircraft	squadrons	3
Helicopters	squadrons	15

Royal Marines

Commandos		3

Army

Combat arms	armour	regiments	11
	infantry	battalions	40
	special forces	regiments	1
	aviation	regiments	5
Combat support	artillery	regiments	16
	engineers	regiments	10
	signals	regiments	11

Home Service Forces[1]

Combat arms	infantry	battalions	7

Territorial Army

Combat arms	armour	regiments	6
	infantry	battalions	33
	special forces	regiments	2
	aviation	regiment	1
Combat support	artillery[2]	regiments	6
	engineers	regiments	9
	signals	regiments	11

Royal Air Force

Strike/attack	squadrons	6
Offensive support	squadrons	5
Reconnaissance	squadrons	5

Royal Air Force (continued)

Maritime patrol		squadrons	3
Air defence		squadrons	6
Airborne Early Warning		squadrons	2
Air transport, tankers, and helicopters[3]		squadrons	13
Search and Rescue		squadrons	2
RAF regiments	surface to air missiles	squadrons	6
	ground defence	squadrons	5
Royal Auxiliary Air Force	ground defence	squadrons	5

Support Units

Royal Navy and Royal Fleet Auxiliary Service

Support ships[4]	vessels	1
Survey ships	vessels	6
Ice patrol ships	vessels	1
Tankers[5]	vessels	9
Fleet replenishment ships[5]	vessels	5
Aviation training ship[5]	vessels	1
Landing ships[5]	vessels	5
Forward repair ships[6]	vessels	1

Royal Marines

Logistic Unit	regiments	1

Army

Combat service support	equipment support[6]	battalions	5
	logistics	regiments	24
	field ambulances/ field hospitals	number	12

Territorial Army

Combat service support	equipment support[6]	battalions	5
	logistics	regiments	N/A
	field ambulances/ field hospitals	number	18

[1] Includes Royal Irish Regiment (Home Service) battalions (formed under the Ulster Defence Regiment in 1992) and home defence units raised in the Dependent Territories. Excludes the Home Service Force which was not organized into battalion-size units.
[2] Includes Operational Conversion Units.
[3] Includes UK and Germany-based squadrons.
[4] The one support ship since 1 April 1994 is HMY Britannia.
[5] Ships of the Royal Fleet Auxiliary Service.
[6] The REME Order of Battle did not include regiment or battalion equivalents until 1993.

Source: *UK Defence Statistics 1997*, Ministry of Defence (HMSO)

A British Aerospace Tornado F2 swing-wing (variable-geometry) fighter-bomber.

© British Aerospace

efficiency, and morale of his Service. They and other senior officers and officials at the head of the department's main functions form the MoD's corporate board, chaired by the Permanent Under-Secretary. The Secretary of State chairs the Defence Council (established 1964) and is responsible to Parliament for the formulation and conduct of defence policy, and the provision of the means to implement it.

The defence and security of the UK are pursued through membership of the European Union (EU), the Western European Union (WEU), the Organization for Security and Cooperation in Europe (OSCE), and the United Nations (UN). The majority of the armed forces are committed to NATO. The UK contributes significantly to the peacekeeping work of the UN both financially and in terms of the deployment of personnel.

All three armed services are professionals, with no conscript element.

Royal Navy

Control of the Royal Navy is vested in the Defence Council and is exercised through the Admiralty Board, chaired by the Secretary of State for Defence. Naval members of the Defence Council are the Chief of Naval Staff (First Sea Lord), responsible for management, planning, fighting efficiency, and operational advice; the combined Second Sea Lord and Commander-in-Chief Naval Home Command, responsible for procurement of ships, their weapons, and equipment; the Chief of Fleet Support, responsible for logistic support, fuels and transport, naval dockyards, and auxiliary services; the Commander-in-Chief Fleet and the Assistant Chief of Staff, responsible for coordinating advice on certain policy and operational matters.

The principal roles of the Royal Navy are to deploy the national strategic nuclear deterrent, to provide maritime defence of the UK and its dependent territories, to contribute to the maritime elements of NATO forces, and to meet national maritime objectives outside the NATO area. The Commander-in-Chief Fleet, with headquarters at Northwood, is responsible for the command of the fleet, while command of naval establishments in the UK is exercised by the Commander-in-Chief Home Command from Portsmouth.

Royal Marines

The British Corps of Royal Marines was founded in 1664. It is primarily a military force also trained for fighting at sea, and providing commando units, landing craft, crews, and frogmen. The Royal Marines corps provides a commando brigade comprising three commando groups. Each commando group is approximately 1,000 strong, with artillery, engineering and logistic support, air defence, and three helicopter squadrons. The Royal Marine corps' strength is completed by the Special Boat Squadron and specialist defence units.

Royal Naval Reserve and Royal Marines Reserve

The Royal Naval Reserve (RNR) and the Royal Marines Reserve (RMR) are volunteer forces that provide trained personnel in war to supplement regular forces. The RMR principally provides reinforcement and other specialist tasks with the UK-Netherlands Amphibious Force.

Personnel who have completed service in the Royal Navy and the Royal Marines have a commitment to serve in the Royal Fleet Reserve.

Queen Alexandra's Royal Naval Nursing Service

Nursing sisters were first appointed to naval hospitals in 1884. The Queen Alexandra's Royal Nursing Service (QARNNS) gained its title in 1902. Men were integrated into the Service in 1982; female medical assistants were introduced in 1987. QARNNS ratings, both male and female, enlist on the 'Open Engagement' to complete 22 years of active service with the option to leave at 18 months notice at the completion of a minimum of $2\frac{1}{2}$ years productive service.

Army

Control of the British Army is vested in the Defence Council and is exercised through the Army Board. The Secretary of State is Chairman of the Army Board. The military members of the Army Board are the Chief of the General Staff, the Adjutant General, the Quartermaster General, the Master General of the Ordnance, the Commander-in-Chief Land Command, and the Assistant Chief of the General Staff.

Women serve throughout the Army in the same regiments and corps as men. There are only a few roles in which they are not employed, such as the Infantry and Royal Armoured Corps.

Territorial Army

The Territorial Army (TA) is a force of volunteer soldiers, created from volunteer regiments (incorporated in 1872) as the Territorial Force in 1908. It was raised and administered by county associations, and intended primarily for home defence. It was renamed Territorial Army in 1922. Merged with the Regular Army in World War II, it was revived in 1947, and replaced by a smaller, more highly trained Territorial and Army Volunteer Reserve, again renamed Territorial Army in 1979. The Army Chief of the General Staff is responsible for the TA.

The role of the TA is to act as a general reserve for the Army, reinforcing it, as required, with individuals, sub-units, and other units, both overseas and in the UK. It also provides the framework and basis for regeneration and reconstruction in the event of unforeseen needs in times of national emergency.

Queen Alexandra's Royal Army Nursing Corps

Founded in 1902 as Queen Alexandra's Imperial Military Nursing Service, the Queen Alexandra's Royal Army Nursing Corps (QARANC) gained its current title in 1949. The Corps has trained nurses and trains and employs health care assistants. Members of the QARANC serve in Ministry of Defence hospital units in the UK and in military hospitals both in the UK and abroad. Service in the Corps was opened to men in 1992.

Royal Air Force

The Royal Air Force (RAF) was formed in 1918 by the merger of the Royal Naval Air Service and the Royal Flying Corps. The RAF is administered by the Air Force Board, which is chaired by the Secretary of State for Defence. Other members of the Board include the Chief of the Air Staff, Air Member for Personnel, Air Member for Logistics, and Air Officer Commanding-in-Chief Strike Command. The RAF is organized into three commands: Strike Command, Personnel and Training Command, and Logistics Command.

Royal Auxiliary Air Force

The Royal Auxiliary Air Force (RAUXAF) was formed in 1924, and merged with the Royal Air Force Volunteer Reserve in 1997. It supports the RAF in air and ground defence of airfields, air movements, maritime air operations, and medical evacuations by air.

Princess Mary's Royal Air Force Nursing Service

The Princess Mary's Royal Air Force Nursing Service (PMRAFNS) offers commissions to Registered General Nurses.

Relative Ranks in the UK Armed Forces		
Royal Navy	**Army**	**Royal Air Force**
Admiral of the Fleet	Field Marshal	Marshal of the RAF
Admiral	General	Air Chief Marshal
Vice Admiral	Lieutenant General	Air Marshal
Rear Admiral	Major General	Air Vice Marshal
Commodore	Brigadier	Air Commodore
Captain	Colonel	Group Captain
Commander	Lieutenant Colonel	Wing Commander
Lieutenant Commander	Major	Squadron Leader
Lieutenant	Captain	Flight Lieutenant
Sub Lieutenant	Lieutenant	Flying Officer
Acting Sub Lieutenant	Second Lieutenant	Pilot Officer

Source: Ministry of Defence

UK Defence Expenditure

Figures are VAT-inclusive at current prices and are in million of pounds, except for percentages.
(– = not applicable.)

Type of Expenditure		1975/76	1985/86	1990/91	1993/94	1995/96	1996/97[1]	1997/98[1]
Expenditure on personnel	of the armed forces	1,305	3,510	4,811	6,907	6,150	6,191	5,993
	of the retired armed forces	255	899	1,406	–	–	–	–
	of civilian staff	970	1,970	2,594	2,928	2,374	2,325	2,286
	Total	2,530	6,379	8,811	9,835	8,524	8,516	8,279
Expenditure on equipment	sea	440	2,499	2,955	2,589	2,110	1,999	2,016
	land	413	1,887	1,927	1,806	1,576	1,594	1,525
	air	752	3,296	3,197	3,245	3,356	3,444	4,079
	other	187	511	759	1,559	1,495	1,423	1,361
	Total	1,792	8,193	8,838	9,200	8,537	8,460	8,981
Other expenditure	works, buildings, and land	394	1,413	2,067	2,073	2,065	1,858	1,212
	miscellaneous stores and services	630	1,958	2,582	2,316	2,391	2,591	2,650
	Total	1,024	3,371	4,649	4,389	4,456	4,449	3,862
	Total expenditure/budget	5,346	17,943	22,298	23,424	21,517	21,425	21,122
	Total expenditure at 1995/96 prices	26,053	29,917	27,946	25,049	21,517	20,666	19,974
Percentage of Total Expenditure/Budget								
Expenditure on personnel	of the armed forces	24.4	19.6	21.6	29.5	28.6	28.9	28.4
	of the retired armed forces	4.8	5.0	6.3	–	–	–	–
	of civilian staff	18.1	11.0	11.6	12.5	11.0	10.9	10.8
	Total	47.3	35.6	39.5	42.0	39.6	39.8	39.2
Expenditure on equipment	sea	8.2	13.9	13.3	11.0	9.8	9.3	9.5
	land	7.7	10.5	8.6	7.7	7.3	7.4	7.2
	air	14.1	18.4	14.3	13.9	15.6	16.1	19.3
	other	3.5	2.8	3.4	6.7	7.0	6.6	6.5
	Total	33.5	45.6	39.6	39.3	39.7	39.4	42.5
Other expenditure	works, buildings, and land	7.4	7.9	9.3	8.9	9.6	8.7	5.7
	miscellaneous stores and services	11.8	10.9	11.6	9.8	11.1	12.1	12.6
	Total	19.2	18.8	20.9	18.7	20.7	20.8	18.3

[1] Estimate.

Source: Defence Analytical Services Agency

UK Ministry of Defence Contracts over £100 Million

(Data for 1996–97. Includes suppliers of food, fuels, and services.)

Over £250 million

British Aerospace plc
Building and Property Defence Ltd
DERA
General Electric Co plc
GKN plc
Hunting plc
Lockheed Martin Corp
Rolls Royce plc
VSEL plc
Vickers plc

£100–250 million

Babcock International Group plc
British Telecommunications plc
Devonport Management Ltd
ICL plc
John Mowlem and Co plc
Other UK government departments
Racal Electronics Ltd
Sema Group plc
Serco Group plc
Siemens plc
Valuation Office Agency
WS Atkins Ltd

Source: Defence Analytical Services Agency

Highest Ranking UK Officers

UK Chiefs of Staff

Source: Ministry of Defence, © Crown copyright 1998
(Date of appointment given in parentheses.)

Chief of the General Staff
Chief of the General Staff General Sir Roger Wheeler, GCB, CBE (Gen) (1995); **Assistant Chief of the General Staff** Major General M A Willcocks, CB (1992); **Director-General Development and Doctrine** Major General A D Pigott, CBE (1992)

Chief of the Naval Staff
Chief of the Naval Staff and First Sea Lord Admiral Sir Jock Slater, GCB, LVO, ADC (1991); **Assistant Chief of the Naval Staff** Rear Admiral J Band (1997)

Chief of the Air Staff
Chief of the Air Staff Air Chief Marshal Sir Richard Johns, GCB, CBE, LVO, ADC (1994); **Assistant Chief of the Air Staff** Air Vice-Marshal T I Jenner, CB (1994)

Defence Council

Source: Ministry of Defence, © Crown copyright 1998
(As of end of 1997.)

Secretary of State for Defence (Chairman of the Defence Council) The Right Honourable George Robertson MP; **Minister of State for the Armed Forces** Dr John Reid MP; **Minister of State for Defence Procurement** The Right Honourable Dr The Lord Gilbert; **Parliamentary Undersecretary of State for Defence** Mr John Spellar MP; **Chief of the Defence Staff** General Sir Charles Guthrie, GCB, LVO, OBE, ADC (Gen); **Permanent Undersecretary of State** R C Mottram; **Chief of the Naval Staff and First Sea Lord** Admiral Sir Jock Slater, GCB, LVO, ADC; **Chief of the General Staff** General Sir Roger Wheeler, GCB, CBE, ADC (Gen); **Chief of the Air Staff** Air Chief Marshal Sir Richard Johns, GCB, CBE, LVO, ADC; **Vice Chief of the Defence Staff** Air Chief Marshal Sir John Willis, KCB, CBE; **Chief of Defence Procurement** Vice Admiral Sir Robert Walmsley, KCB; **Chief Scientific Advisor** Professor Sir David Davies, CBE; **Second Permanent Undersecretary of State** Mr Roger Jackling, CB, CBE

The UK Royal Navy: Highest-Ranking Officers

Source: Ministry of Defence, © Crown copyright 1998

Lord High Admiral of the United Kingdom: HM The Queen

Admirals of the Fleet (Year Appointed)
HRH The Prince Philip, Duke of Edinburgh, KG, KT, OM, GBE, AC, QSO (1953); The Lord Hill-Norton, GCB (1971); Sir Michael Pollock, GCB, LVO, DSC (1974); Sir Edward Ashmore, GCB, DSC (1977); The Lord Lewin, KG, GCB, LVO, DSC (1979); Sir Henry Leach, GCB (1982); Sir William Staveley, GCB (1989); Sir Julian Oswald, GCB (1992); Sir Benjamin Bathurst, GCB (1995)

Admirals (Year of Rank)
Sir Jock Slater, GCB, LVO, ADC (Chief of Naval Staff and First Sea Lord) (1991); Sir Michael Boyce, KCB, OBE, ADC (Second Sea Lord and Commander-in-Chief Naval Home Command) (1995); Sir Peter Abbott, KCB (Commander-in-Chief Fleet, Commander-in-Chief Eastern Atlantic Area) (1995)

Vice Admirals (Year of Rank)
Sir Michael Moore, KBE, LVO (Chief of Staff to Commander, Allied Naval Forces Southern Europe) (1994); Michael Peter Gretton (SACLANT Representative Europe) (1994); John Hugh Dunt (Chief of Fleet Support) (1995); John Richard Brigstocke, KCB (Flag Officer Surface Flotilla) (1995); Ian D G Garnett (Deputy SACLANT) (1995); Jeremy J Blackham (Deputy Commander Fleet) (1997)

The UK Royal Air Force: Highest-Ranking Officers

Source: Ministry of Defence, © Crown copyright 1998

Air Commodore-in-Chief HM The Queen
Marshals of the Royal Air Force (Year Appointed)
HRH The Prince Philip, Duke of Edinburgh, KG, KT, OM, GBE, AC, QSO (1953); Sir John Grandy, GCB, GCVO, KBE, DSO (1971); Sir Denis Spotswood, GCB, CBE, DSO, DFC (1974); Sir Michael Beetham, GCB, CBE, DFC, AFC (1982); Sir Keith Williamson, GCB, AFC (1985); The Lord Craig of Radley, GCB, OBE (1988)

Air Chief Marshals (Year of Rank)
HRH Princess Alice, Duchess of Gloucester, GCB, CI, GCVO, GBE (1990); Sir Michael Graydon, GCB, CBE (1991); Sir Richard Johns, KCB, CBE, LVO (Chief of the Air Staff) (1994); Sir William Wratten, KBE, CB, AFC (Air Officer Commanding-in-Chief Strike Command) (1994); Sir John Willis, KCB, CBE (Vice Chief of the Defence Staff) (1995); Sir John Allison, KCB, CBE (Air Officer Commanding-in-Chief Strike Command) (1996); Sir John Cheshire, KBE, CB (Commander-in-Chief Allied Forces Northwestern Europe) (1997)

Air Marshals (Year of Rank)
Ian D Macfadyen, CB, OBE (Director-General Saudi Armed Forces Projects) (1994); Sir David Cousins, KCB, AFC (Air Officer Commanding-in-Chief Personnel and Training Command) (1995); Sir Peter Squire, KCB, DFC, AFC (Deputy Chief of the Defence Staff (Programmes and Personnel)) (1996); Graeme A Robertson, CBE (Chief of Staff and Deputy Commander-in-Chief Strike Command) (1996); Anthony J C Bagnall, CB, OBE (Deputy Commander-in-Chief Allied Forces Central Europe 1996); John R Day, OBE (Deputy Chief of the Defence Staff (Commitments)) (1997); Colin G Terry, CB, OBE (Air Officer Commanding-in-Chief Logistics Command and Chief Engineer (RAF)) (1997)

The UK Army: Highest-Ranking Officers

Source: Ministry of Defence, © Crown copyright 1998

HM The Queen
Field Marshals (Year Appointed)
HRH The Prince Philip, Duke of Edinburgh, KG, KT, OM, GBE, AC, QSO (1953); The Lord Carver, GCB, CBE, DSO, MC (1973); Sir Roland Gibbs, GCB, CBE, DSO, MC (1979); The Lord Bramall, KG, GCB, OBE, MC (1982); Sir John Stanier, GCB, MBE (1985); Sir Nigel Bagnall, GCB, CVO, MC (1988); Sir Richard Vincent, GBE, KCB, CBE (1991); Sir John Chapple, GCB, CBE (1992); HRH The Duke of Kent, KG, GCMG, GCVO (1993); Sir Peter Inge, GCB (Col Green Howards) (1994)

Generals (Year of Rank)
Sir Charles Guthrie, GCB, LVO, OBE, ADC (Gen) (Chief of the Defence Staff); (1992); Sir Jeremy MacKenzie, KCB, OBE, ADC (Gen) (Deputy Supreme Allied Commander

Europe/Colonel Commandant Adjutant General's Corps) (1994); Sir Roger Wheeler, GCB, CBE, ADC (Gen) (Chief of the General Staff) (1995); Sir Michael Rose (Hon Colonel Officers Training Corps, Oxford) (1995); Sir Michael Walker (Colonel Commandant AAC/Commander-in-Chief, Land) (1997)

UK Central Staffs and Commands

Source: Ministry of Defence, © Crown copyright 1998
(As of end of 1997.)

Armed Forces

Defence Policy Staff

Deputy Undersecretary of State (Policy) Richard Hatfield; **Assistant Chief of Defence Staff (Policy)** Air Vice Marshal J C French, CBE; **Director Defence Policy** John Day; **Director Force Development** Commodore S E Saunders (RN); **Director Nuclear Policy** Commodore J M Parkinson; **Assistant Undersecretary of State (Policy)** G W Hopkinson; **Director International Organization** Brigadier A A Milton, OBE; **Director for Central and Eastern Europe** Paul Ryan; **Director Proliferation and Arms Control Secretary** P W D Hatt; **Head Protocol** Captain M Bickley (RN) (retired)

Defence Programmes and Personnel Staff

Deputy Chief of Defence Staff (Programmes and Personnel) Air Marshal P T Squire, KCB, DFC, AFC; **Assistant Chief of Defence Staff (Programmes)** Rear Admiral N R Essenhigh; **Director Programmes** Brigadier F R Dannatt, OBE, MC; **Director Navy Plans** Commodore R A I McClean, OBE; **Director Army Plans** Brigadier A M D Palmer, CBE; **Director Air Plans** Air Commodore S M Nicholl, CBE, AFC, BA (RAF); **Assistant Chief of Defence Staff (Logistics)** Major General G A Ewer, CBE; **Director Defence Logistics (Programmes)** Colonel C A Hewitt, MBE, CGIA; **Director Defence Logistics (Operations/Policy)** Group Captain D M Wesley, OBE; **Director Defence Logistics (Movements)** Colonel R I Harrison, OBE; **Defence Services Secretary** Air Vice Marshal P J Harding, CB, CBE, APC; **Assistant Undersecretary of State (State Personnel Policy)** Miss A D Walker; **Director Service Personnel Policy 1** Commodore D R S Lewis, CBE; **Director Service Personnel Policy 2** Dr N F Price; **Director Service Personnel Policy (Projects)** Brigadier R C Walker, CBE; **Director Service Personnel Policy (Pensions)** J C Robb; **Director Resettlement** Air Commodore N I Hamilton; **Director Reserve Forces and Cadets** Brigadier D A K Biggart, OBE

Defence Commitments Staff

Deputy Chief of the Defence Staff (Commitments) Air Marshal J R Day, OBE, BSC,
FRAeS (RAF); **Assistant Chief of Defence Staff (Operations)** Air Vice Marshal A J Harrison CBE (RAF); **Director Overseas Military Assistance** Commodore J de Halpert (RN); **Director Defence Material Policy** Air Commodore C F Cooper (RAF); **Director Naval Operations** Commodore M D Macpherson, OBE (RN); **Director Military Operations** Brigadier J G Reith, CBE; **Director Air Operations** Air Commodore K D Filbey, CBE (RAF); **Director Joint Warfare** Commodore R P Stevens (RN); **Assistant Undersecretary of State, Home and Overseas** Dr E V Buckley

Defence Systems Staff

Deputy Chief of the Defence Staff (Systems) Lieutenant General E Burton, OBE; **Director Defence Systems** Air Commodore T W Rimmer, OBE; **Assistant Chief of Defence Staff Operational Requirements (Sea)** Rear Admiral R T R Phillips; **Director Operational Requirements (Sea)** Commodore R G J Ward (RN); **Assistant Chief of Defence Staff Operational Requirements (Land)** Major General P J Russell-Jones, OBE; **Director Operational Requirements (Land)** Brigadier D M O'Callaghan; **Assistant Chief of Defence Staff Operational Requirements (Air)** Air Vice-Marshal C C C Coville, CB (RAF); **Director Operational Requirements (Air)** Air Commodore A A Nicholson, LVO (RAF)

Information and Communication

Director-General Information and Communications Major General W J P Robins, OBE; **Director Policy (ICS)** Air Commodore R J Holt (RAF); **Director Operational Requirements (ICS)** Commodore S J B Newsom (RN); **Director (DFTS)** Air Commodore A M Ferguson

Defence Medical Services Directorate

Surgeon General Surgeon Vice Admiral A L Revell, QHS; **Director Medical Policy** Air Commodore C Sharples, QHP (RAF)

Defence Information Division

Press Secretary and Chief of Information Ms G Samuel

Defence Scientific Staff

Chief Scientific Adviser Professor Sir David Davis, CBE; **Chief Scientist** Mr P Ewins; **Assistant Chief Scientific Adviser (Nuclear)** R W Roper; **Deputy Chief Scientist (Systems and Technology)** A F Everett; **Deputy Chief Scientist (Scrutiny and Analysis)** M Earweather; **Director Science (Ballistic Missile Defence)** Dr M Rance

Procurement Executive

Chief of Defence Procurement Vice Admiral Sir Robert Walmsley, KCB; **Deputy Chief of Defence Procurement (Operations)/Master General of the Ordnance** Lieutenant General Sir Robert Hayman-Joyce, KCB, CBE; **Director-**
General Land Systems Major General D J M Jenkins, CBE; **Director-General Communications and Information Systems** J D Maines; **Director-General Weapons and Electronic Systems** Mr G N Beaven

Royal Navy

Sea Lord/Commander-in-Chief Naval Home Command

Second Sea Lord and Commander-in-Chief Naval Home Command Admiral Sir Michael Boyce, KCB, OBE; **Chief of Staff to Second Sea Lord and Commander-in-Chief Naval Home Command** Rear Admiral R B Lees; **Flag Officer Training and Recruiting** Rear Admiral J H S McAnally, LVO; **Naval Secretary/Director-General Naval Manning** Rear Admiral F M Malbon ; **Director-General Naval Medical Services** Surgeon Rear Admiral M P W H Paine; **Director-General Naval Chaplaincy Service** Reverend Dr C E Stewart

Naval Support Command

Chief of Fleet Support Vice Admiral J H Dunt; **Director-General Fleet Support (Operations and Plans)** Rear Admiral B B Perowne, OBE; **Director-General Ships** R V Babington; **Director-General Naval Bases and Supply/Chief Executive Naval Bases and Supply Agency** Rear Admiral J A Trewby; **Director-General Aircraft (Navy)** Rear Admiral D J Wood; **Flag Officer Scotland, Northern England and Northern Ireland** Rear Admiral J G Tolhurst, CB

Commander-in-Chief Fleet

Commander-in-Chief Fleet, Eastern Atlantic Area and Commander Naval Forces North Western Europe Admiral Sir Peter Abbott, KCB; **Deputy Commander Fleet/Chief of Staff** Vice Admiral J J Blackham; **Flag Officer Submarines/Chief of Staff (Operations)** Rear Admiral J F Perowne, OBE; **Flag Officer Surface Flotilla** Vice Admiral J R Brigstocke, KCB, OBE; **Flag Officer Sea Training** Rear Admiral P M Franklyn, MVO; **Commander UK Task Group and Commander Anti-Submarine Warfare Striking Force** Rear Admiral A W J West, DSE; **Flag Officer Naval Aviation** Rear Admiral T W Loughran, CB; **Commandant General, Royal Marines** Major General D A S Pennefather, CB, OBE

Army

Quartermaster-General's Department

Quartermaster-General Lieutenant General Sir Sam Cowan, CBE; **Chief of Staff Headquarters Quartermaster-General** Major General K O'Donoghue, CBE; **Chief**

Executive of Logistic Information Systems Agency Brigadier A W Pollard; **Director-General Logistic Support (Army)** Major General M S White, CBE; **Director-General Equipment Support (Army)** Major General P V R Besgrove, CBE

Adjutant General's Department

Adjutant General General Sir Alex Harley, KCB, CB; **Chief of Staff** Major General R A Oliver, OBE; **Command Secretary** W A Perry; **Chaplain-General (Army)** The Reverend D V Dobbin, MBE; **Director-General**

Army Medical Services Major General W R Short; **Director Army Legal Services** Major General A P V Rogers; **Director-General Army Personnel Centre** Major General D L Burden; **Military Secretary** Major General M I E Scott; **Director-General Individual Training and Chief Executive, Army Individual Training Organization** Major General C L Elliott; **Commandant, Royal Military Academy, Sandhurst** Major General J F Deverell, OBE; **Commandant, Royal Military College of Science** Major General D J M Jenkins, CBE

Commander-in-Chief Land Command

Commander-in-Chief General Sir Michael Walker, KCB, GCB, CBE; **Deputy Commander-in-Chief/Inspector General Territorial Army** Lieutenant General H W R Pike, DSO, MBE; **Chief of Staff Headquarters** Major General C G C Vyvyan, CBE; **Deputy Chief of Staff Headquarters (Land)** Major General R A Gordy-Simpson, CB, OBE; **Brigadier General Staff Headquarters (Land)** Brigadier A E G Truluck

Strength of UK Regular Forces by Gender and Rank

The ranks shown are in army terms. Prior to 1990 the figures relate to 1 January; from 1990 they relate to 1 April.

Rank	1975	1985	1990	1992	1994	1996	1997
Total female officers[1]	2,079	2,157	2,537	2,864	2,738	2,478	2,380
Major General and above	0	0	0	0	0	0	0
Brigadier	6	6	7	4	5	2	2
Colonel	28	23	24	25	21	19	16
Lieutenant Colonel	62	47	60	81	88	95	80
Major	336	292	309	394	399	411	424
Captain	864	936	1,172	1,429	1,402	1,265	1,181
Lieutenant and below	783	853	965	931	823	686	677
Total female other ranks	12,496	14,244	14,672	16,784	15,024	13,204	12,451
Warrant Officer	127	117	144	157	171	161	174
Staff Sergeant	189	262	361	409	369	363	372
Sergeant	682	963	1,386	1,426	1,396	1,274	1,169
Corporal	1,481	2,903	2,979	3,187	3,161	2,718	2,357
Lance Corporal	860	1,156	1,288	1,445	1,282	1,095	1,076
Private (including juniors)	9,157	8,843	8,514	10,150	8,645	7,593	7,303
Total male officers[1]	44,900	39,986	40,332	39,531	34,749	31,628	30,295
Major General and above	254	212	203	195	180	160	149
Brigadier	414	381	381	385	339	355	347
Colonel	1,587	1,421	1,459	1,432	1,272	1,124	1,066
Lieutenant Colonel	4,841	4,378	4,556	4,589	4,109	3,928	3,785
Major	12,457	11,660	11,491	11,452	10,311	9,833	9,522
Captain	17,336	13,987	13,891	13,773	12,992	12,008	11,305
Lieutenant and below	8,011	7,947	8,351	7,705	5,546	4,220	4,121
Total male other ranks	283,046	270,462	248,170	234,265	201,977	174,506	165,697
Warrant Officer	11,777	11,416	11,407	11,280	9,801	8,729	8,614
Staff Sergeant	27,102	23,241	22,352	21,778	19,317	17,618	16,638
Sergeant	37,794	35,042	34,045	32,829	28,451	25,563	24,129
Corporal	48,645	52,764	52,587	50,356	45,152	38,206	34,660
Lance Corporal	22,100	22,973	22,553	20,982	18,091	15,682	15,292
Private (including juniors)	135,628	125,026	105,226	97,040	81,165	68,762	66,364

[1] Prior to 1987, professionally qualified female officers serving in the medical, dental, veterinary, and legal specializations are included with the male officer numbers.

Source: Defence Analytical Services Agency

© Richard Watt

Soldiers of the Royal Logistics Corps *While the number of men in the British armed forces has fallen dramatically since the 1970s, the number of women in the forces has remained stable.*

Royal Air Force

Strike Command – Command Headquarters

Air Officer Commanding-in-Chief Air Chief Marshal Sir John Allison, KCB, CBE; **Chief of Staff and Deputy Commander-in-Chief** Air Marshal G A Robertson, CBE; **Senior Air Staff Officer and Air Officer Commanding No. 38 Group** Air Vice-Marshal D A Hurrell, AFC; **Air Officer Engineering and Supply** Air Vice-Marshal D J Saunders, CBE; **Air Officer Administration and Air Officer Commanding Directly Administered Units** Air Vice-Marshal I M Stewart, AFC; **Air Officer Commanding No. 1 Group** Air Vice-Marshal G E Stirrup, AFC; **Air Officer Commanding No. 11/18 Group** Air Vice-Marshal C R Spink, CBE; **Command Secretary** J P Thatcher

Headquarters Logistics Command

Air Officer Commanding-in-Chief, Air Member for Logistics and Chief Engineer (RAF) Air Marshal C G Terry, CB, OBE; **Chief of Staff, Deputy Commander-in-Chief and Air Officer Commanding Directly Administered Units** Air Vice-Marshal M D Pledger, OBE, AFC; **Air Commodore Plans** Air Commodore A J Pye; **Air Commodore Logistics Policy** Air Commodore R Brumpton; **Command Secretary** Mr H Griffiths; **Acting Chief Executive RAF Maintenance Group Defence Agency** Air Commodore K J M Procter; **Director-General Support Management (RAF)** Air Vice-Marshal M van der Veen

RAF Personnel and Training Command

Air Member for Personnel and Air Officer Commanding-in-Chief Air Marshal Sir David Cousins, KCB, AFC; **Chief of Staff/Air Member for Personnel** Air Vice-Marshal M D Smart; **Air Officer Administration and Air Officer Commanding Directly Administered Units** Air Commodore O D L Delany, OBE; **Chief Executive Training Group Defence Agency and Air Officer Commanding Training Group** Air Vice-Marshal A J Stables, CBE; **Air Secretary/Chief Executive Personnel Management Agency** Air Vice-Marshal R P O'Brien, CB, OBE; **Director-General Medical Services (RAF)** Air Vice-Marshal C J Sharples, QHP; **Director Legal Services (RAF)** Air Vice-Marshal G W Carleton, CB; **Chaplain-in-Chief** The Venerable (Air Vice-Marshal) P R Turner; **Command Secretary** Mrs L D Kyle

Ethnic Composition of UK Regular Forces by Rank

For 'All Services' the ranks are shown in army terms. Figures are as of 1 April 1997.
(– = not applicable.)

Rank	Total	White		Ethnic minorities		Unknown	
		Number	%	Number	%	Number	%
All services	210,823	206,279	97.84	2,184	1.04	2,360	1.12
Officers							
Total	32,675	31,843	97.45	317	0.97	515	1.58
Lieutenant Colonel and above	5,200	5,137	98.79	49	0.94	14	0.27
Major and below	27,475	26,706	97.20	268	0.98	501	1.82
Other ranks							
Total	178,148	174,436	97.92	1,867	1.05	1,845	1.04
Sergeant and above	48,979	48,269	98.55	648	1.32	62	0.13
Corporal and below	129,169	126,167	97.68	1,219	0.94	1,783	1.38
Naval services	45,146	44,797	99.23	349	0.77	–	–
Officers							
Total	7,914	7,840	99.06	74	0.94	–	–
Commander and above	1,467	1,460	99.52	7	0.48	–	–
Lieutenant Commander and below	6,447	6,380	98.96	67	1.04	–	–
Other ranks							
Total	37,232	36,957	99.26	275	0.74	–	–
Petty Officer and above	14,082	13,975	99.24	107	0.76	–	–
Leading rate and below	23,150	22,982	99.27	168	0.73	–	–
Army	108,810	105,969	97.39	1,064	0.98	1,777	1.63
Officers							
Total	13,720	13,297	96.92	112	0.82	311	2.27
Lieutenant Colonel and above	2,207	2,182	98.87	24	1.09	1	0.05
Major and below	11,513	11,115	96.54	88	0.76	310	2.69
Other ranks							
Total	95,090	92,672	97.46	952	1.00	1,466	1.54
Sergeant and above	22,145	21,793	98.41	332	1.50	20	0.09
Corporal and below	72,945	70,879	97.17	620	0.85	1,446	1.98
Royal Air Force	56,867	55,513	97.62	771	1.36	583	1.03
Officers							
Total	11,041	10,706	96.97	131	1.19	204	1.85
Wing Commander and above	1,526	1,495	97.97	18	1.18	13	0.85
Squadron Leader and below	9,515	9,211	96.81	113	1.19	191	2.01
Other ranks							
Total	45,826	44,807	97.78	640	1.40	379	0.83
Sergeant and above	12,752	12,501	98.03	209	1.64	42	0.33
Corporal and below	33,074	32,306	97.68	431	1.30	337	1.02

Source: Defence Analytical Services Agency

UK Service Personnel

Deployment of UK Military Personnel in the UK

Figures show deployment of UK regular forces and Ministry of Defence civilians, including Royal Navy and Royal Marines personnel on board ships in home waters. Figures are as of 1 July for the year shown.

Personnel	1980	1985	1990	1992	1993	1994	1995	1996
UK[1]								
Total	496,300	397,200	351,100	342,500	326,300	313,500	290,200	280,000
Service	238,100	229,600	215,900	210,700	204,300	199,500	182,200	177,400
Civilian	231,200	167,700	135,200	131,800	122,000	114,000	108,000	102,600
England								
Total	396,700	333,700	294,200	286,000	269,500	257,000	239,000	232,000
Service	200,000	193,300	179,600	174,200	167,100	162,100	149,400	146,600
Civilian	196,600	140,400	114,600	111,800	102,400	95,000	89,600	85,400
Wales								
Total	16,400	12,800	10,800	10,700	10,100	10,400	10,000	9,100
Service	6,900	6,300	5,300	5,200	5,100	5,500	5,200	4,300
Civilian	9,500	6,500	5,500	5,500	5,000	4,900	4,800	4,700
Scotland								
Total	40,000	38,200	31,600	30,600	31,200	29,300	27,500	25,000
Service	18,100	20,100	19,300	18,800	19,400	18,000	16,900	15,500
Civilian	21,900	18,100	12,300	11,800	11,800	11,200	10,600	9,500
Northern Ireland[2]								
Total	15,100	12,400	14,200	15,200	15,400	14,600	12,900	13,500
Service	11,900	9,700	11,500	12,600	12,500	11,600	9,900	10,500
Civilian	3,200	2,700	2,700	2,600	2,900	2,900	3,000	3,000

[1] The figures for service personnel in England, Scotland, and Wales are obtained from a different source from that used to obtain the UK total; consequently, the sum of the national figures may differ from the UK total.
[2] Includes all personnel serving on emergency tours of duty, but excludes the former Ulster Defence Regiment, now the Home Service element of the Royal Irish Regiment.

Source: Defence Analytical Services Agency

Strengths of UK Regular Forces

(Figures include trainees.)

Year[1]		Officers			Other ranks		
	Total	Total	Males	Females	Total	Males	Females
All services							
1993	274,849	40,403	37,599	2,804	234,446	218,333	16,113
1994	254,488	37,487	34,749	2,738	217,001	201,977	15,024
1995	233,340	35,545	32,956	2,589	197,795	183,776	14,019
1996	221,870	34,106	31,628	2,478	187,764	174,560	13,204
1997	211,047	32,791	30,284	2,507	178,256	165,270	12,986
Naval services[1]							
1993	59,357	9,802	9,307	495	49,555	45,564	3,991
1994	55,779	9,182	8,688	494	46,597	42,841	3,756
1995	50,893	8,760	8,287	473	42,133	38,696	3,437
1996	48,307	8,370	7,913	457	39,937	36,763	3,174
1997	44,651	7,810	7,357	453	36,841	34,041	2,800
Army							
1993	134,583	16,129	14,959	1,170	118,454	112,030	6,424
1994	123,028	14,840	13,669	1,171	108,188	102,307	5,881
1995	111,693	13,956	12,851	1,105	97,737	92,265	5,472
1996	108,840	13,757	12,677	1,080	95,083	89,709	5,374
1997	110,140	13,971	12,831	1,140	96,169	90,074	6,095

(continued)

Strengths of UK Regular Forces (*continued*)

(Figures include trainees.)

Year[1]	Total	Officers			Other ranks		
		Total	Males	Females	Total	Males	Females
Royal Air Force							
1993	80,909	14,472	13,333	1,139	66,437	60,739	5,698
1994	75,681	13,465	12,392	1,073	62,216	56,829	5,387
1995	70,754	12,829	11,818	1,011	57,925	52,815	5,110
1996	64,723	11,979	11,038	941	52,744	48,088	4,656
1997	56,256	11,010	10,096	914	45,246	41,155	4,091

[1] Figures are as of 1 April, except for 1997 figures, which are as of 1 December and are provisional.

Source: Defence Analytical Services Agency

Deployment of UK Military Personnel Overseas

Figures are as of 1 April for the year shown.

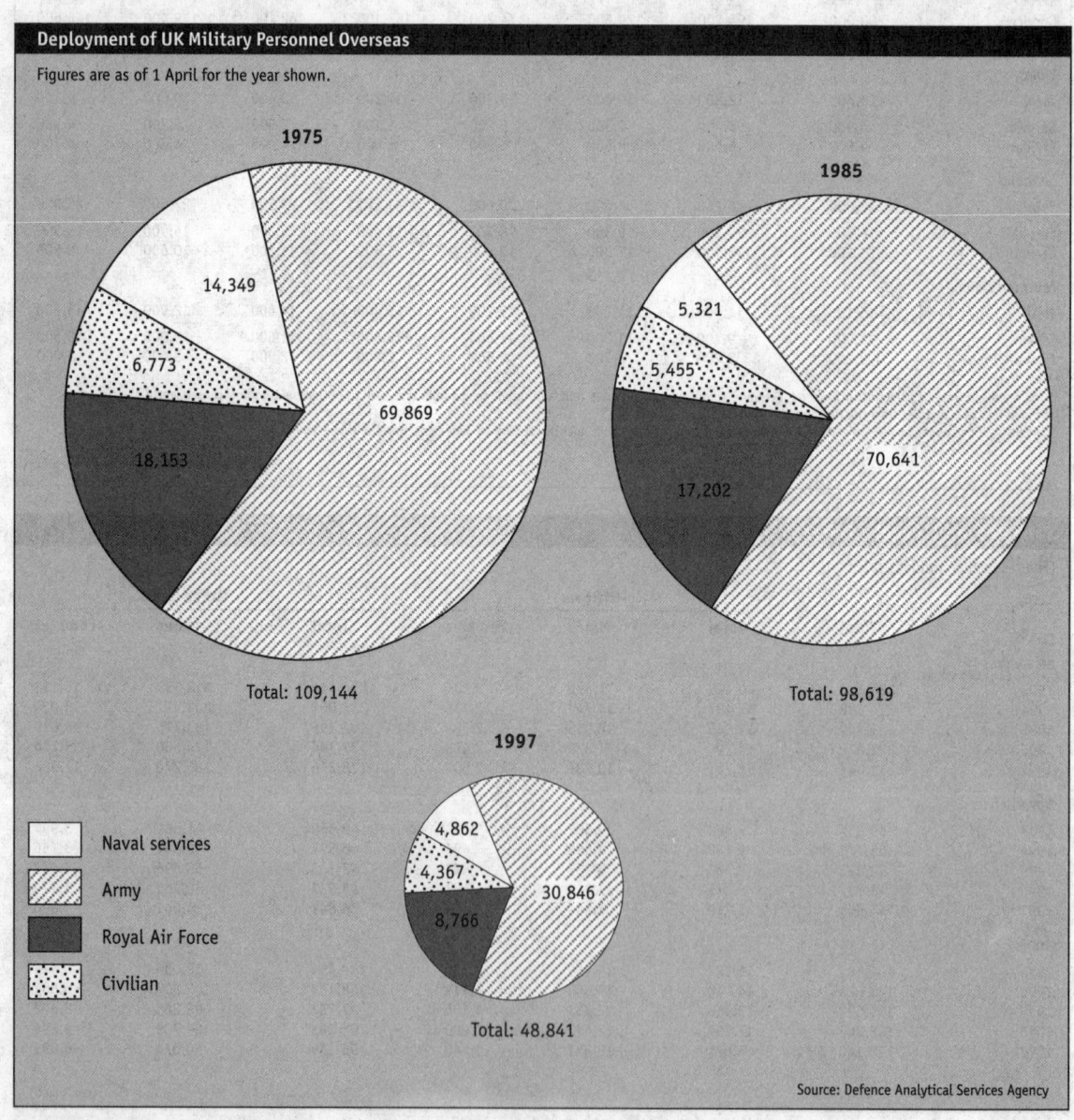

1975

14,349
6,773
18,153
69,869

Total: 109,144

1985

5,321
5,455
17,202
70,641

Total: 98,619

1997

4,862
4,367
8,766
30,846

Total: 48,841

Naval services
Army
Royal Air Force
Civilian

Source: Defence Analytical Services Agency

Strengths of UK Reserves and Auxiliary Forces

Volunteer reserves and auxiliary forces comprise personnel in civilian occupations who undertake to give a certain amount of their time to train in support of the regular forces.
(– = not applicable.)

Service/force	1985	1990	1993	1995	1996	1997
Total regular reserves	205,600	252,000	259,600	262,900	263,500	258,400
Total volunteer reserves and auxiliary forces	88,600	90,600	76,100	64,700	62,200	63,300
Naval services	31,900	35,400	31,100	25,800	26,200	26,600
Regular reserves	25,600	28,400	25,500	22,100	22,700	23,100
Volunteer reserves and auxiliary forces	6,300	7,000	5,600	3,700	3,500	3,500
Army	231,200	265,400	258,800	255,000	254,700	247,700
Regular reserves	150,200	183,500	190,100	195,300	196,000	190,100
Territorial Army	73,700	72,500	68,500	59,700	57,300	57,600
Ulster Defence Regiment[1]	6,400	6,200	–	–	–	–
Home Service Force[2]	900	3,200	200	–	–	–
Royal Air Force	31,200	42,000	47,800	46,800	46,400	46,600
Regular reserves	29,900	40,200	46,100	45,500	45,200	45,300
Volunteer reserves and auxiliary forces	1,300	1,800	1,700	1,300	1,200	1,400

[1] On 1 July 1992, the UDR merged with the Royal Irish Rangers to form the Royal Irish Regiment, members of which are no longer counted as reserves.
[2] By 1 April 1994, the Home Service Force had been disbanded.

Source: Defence Analytical Services Agency

Salaries in the UK Armed Forces

Figures are for Army ranks, starting salaries, and for lowest class and band within rank.
(For equivalent ranks in Royal Navy, Royal Marines, and Royal Air Force see Ranks of the Armed Forces.)

1997–98

Army rank	Salary (£)
Field marshal	128,911
General	103,510
Lieutenant general	77,493
Major general	67,627
Brigadier	62,353
Colonel	50,837
Lieutenant colonel	43,738
Major	31,062
Captain	24,488
Lieutenant	20,222
Second lieutenant	13,802
Officer designate	10,198
Warrant officer class 1	23,809
Warrant officer class 2	20,666
Staff sergeant	19,345
Sergeant	18,308
Corporal	15,257
Lance corporal	13,260
Private (classes 1–3)	10,285
Private (class 4)/Junior	9,110

Source: Defence Analytical Services Agency, Ministry of Defence

Military Colleges in the UK

Source: Ministry of Defence

Royal College of Defence Studies
Commandant: Lieutenant General S C Grant, CB
Seaford House, 37 Belgrave Square, London SW1X 8NS; (0171) 915 4800

Joint Services Command and Staff Training College
Commandant: Major General T J Granville-Chapman, CBE
Bracknell, Berkshire RG12 9DD; (01344) 454593

Joint Service Defence College Greenwich
Commandant: Rear Admiral N J Wilkinson, CB
Greenwich, London SE10 9NN; (0181) 858 2154

Royal Naval Military Colleges
Britannia Royal Naval College
Commandant: Commodore R A G Clare
Dartmouth, Devon TQ6 0HJ; (01803) 832141

Military Colleges (Army)
Staff College
Commandant: Major General A D Piggott, CBE
Camberley, Surrey GU15 4NP; (01276) 63344

Royal Military College of Science Shrivenham
Commandant: Major General A S H Irwin, CBE
Swindon, Wiltshire SN6 8LA; (01793) 784455

Royal Military Academy Sandhurst
Commandant: Major General J F Deverell, OBE
Camberley, Surrey GU15 4PQ; (01276) 63344

Royal Air Force Colleges
Royal Air Force Staff College, Bracknell
Commandant: Air Vice-Marshal M Van der Veen
Bracknell, Berkshire RG12 3DD; (01344) 454593

Royal Air Force Staff College, Cranwell
Commandant: Air Commodore A J Stables
Cranwell, Sleaford, Lincolnshire NG34 8GZ; (01400) 261201

Web Sites

Atlantic Charter

URL: "http://www.yale.edu/lawweb/
avalon/wwii/atlantic.htm"

Part of the Avalon Project at the Yale Law School, this page provides the text of the agreement made between Prime Minister Churchill and President Roosevelt on 14 August 1941, in which they assert to 'common principles in the national policies of their respective countries'.

Atomic Bomb: Decision

URL: "http://www.peak.org/~danneng/
decision/decision.html"

Documentation regarding the US government's decision to drop atomic bombs on Japan in August 1945.

Atomic Bombings of Hiroshima and Nagasaki

URL: "http://www.yale.edu/lawweb/
avalon/abomb/mpmenu.htm"

United States Army describing the effects of the atomic bombs dropped on Hiroshima and Nagasaki during August 1945.

Battle of Britain

URL: "http://www.geocities.com/
Pentagon/4143/"

A history of the battle is included, with detailed notes on the pilots, the aircraft, and the aircraft losses.

Battle of the Skagerrak

URL: "http://www.wtj.com/arcdocs/
scheer10.htm"

Full account of the World War I naval battle. Written by the German commander, Reinhard Scheer, it is part of the online version of the translation of his history of Germany's High Sea Fleet.

Battles of World War II – An Overview

URL: "http://www.cyberplus.ca/
~chrism/battles.htm"

Accounts of the major battles of World War II. The descriptions are divided into three sections – land, sea, and air.

British Army

URL: "http://www.army.mod.uk/"

Home page of the British Army. There is extensive information on the structure of the army, weapons systems, current deployments, and career opportunities.

Campaign Against Arms Trade

URL: "http://www.gn.apc.org/caat/"

Work of the British organization campaigning to end the international arms trade and Britain's role in it.

Chemical and Biological Warfare Chronicle

URL: "http://www.stimson.org/
cwc/chron.htm"

Features on biological- and chemical-warfare issues, where policy, technology, and politics intersect. It includes information on current treaties as well as maps of biological and chemical weapon sites.

D-Day

URL: "http://www.pbs.org/wgbh/
pages/amex/dday/index.html"

Companion to the US Public Broadcasting Service (PBS) television programme *The American Experience*, this page tells the story of the allied invasion of Normandy during World War II.

Desert-Storm.Com

URL: "http://www.desert-storm.com/
index.html"

Archive Web site 'created by a student to honour those who participated in Operation Desert-Storm'. The Web site features hoards of information, media clips, articles and other related details of the war.

Franklin D Roosevelt: Pearl Harbor Speech

URL: "http://odur.let.rug.nl/~usa/P/
fr32/speeches/ph.htm"

Part of a larger site on historical documents, this page is the text of the speech US President Franklin D Roosevelt delivered to US Congress on 8 December 1941, following the Japanese attack on the US naval base at Pearl Harbor, Hawaii.

Gallipoli 1915

URL: "http://www.focusmm.com.au/
~focus/anzac_01.htm"

Illustrated historical account of the 1915 events at Gallipoli during World War I.

German Surrender Documents – WWII

URL: "http://www.msstate.edu/Archives/
History/USA/WWII/german-surrender"

Full and complete English transcript of the German surrender documents from World War II.

Great War and the Shaping of the 20th Century

URL: "http://www.pbs.org/greatwar/"

A comprehensive multimedia exploration of the history and effects of World War I.

Great War Statistics

URL: "http://www.d-n-a.net/users/
dnetDkjs/figures.htm"

Part of a larger site about World War I, this site includes numerous tables and statistics relating to soldiers, casualties, ammunitions and materials, and financial costs of the war.

Gulf War Frontline

URL: "http://www2.pbs.org/wgbh/pages/
frontline/gulf/index.html"

Includes transcripts of interviews with key figures – decision-makers, commanders, and analysts – maps, and a chronology.

Imperial War Museum

URL: "http://www.iwm.org.uk/"

Guide to the Imperial War Museum, the Cabinet War Rooms, and the historic ship *HMS Belfast*.

International Committee of the Red Cross

URL: "http://www.icrc.org/unicc/
icrcnews.nsf/DocIndex/home_eng?
OpenDocument"

Introduction to the Red Cross Movement. There are frequently updated reports on ICRC operations in more than 50 states. The coverage of issues surrounding international humanitarian law and campaigning issues of current concern to the Red Cross is extensive.

Japanese Surrender Documents

URL: "http://www.yale.edu/lawweb/
avalon/wwii/jmenu.htm"

Part of the Avalon Project at the Yale Law School, this page contains seven documents regarding the surrender of Japanese forces during World War II. It includes several instruments of surrender and a translation of Emperor Hirohito's receipt of the surrender documents.

Maps and Pictures of the Western Front

URL: "http://www.d-n-a.net/users/dnet-
Dkjs/maps_pix.htm"

Part of a larger site about World War I, this site includes several maps and photographs relating to the war on the Western Front.

Medical Front, World War I

URL: "http://raven.cc.ukans.edu/~kan-
site/ww_one/medical/medtitle.htm"

Part of a larger site concerning World War I
documents, this page features all manner of
medical-related documents from the Great
War, including articles on military surgery
and on the treatment of influenza and trench
fever.

NATO

URL: "http://www.nato.int/"

NATO site with thousands of pages of information on NATO's structure, history, and
current role. Frequently updated press
releases set out NATO policy on issues of
current concern.

Nazi Occupation of Poland

URL: "http://www.ibiscom.com/
poland.htm"

Information on the German invasion of
Poland in 1939 featuring excerpts from the
journal of Dr Zygmunt Klukowski, chief
physician of a small hospital in the village
of Szczebrzeszyn, in which he describes the
brutality of Nazi occupation.

News About Chemical and
Biological Agents and Threats

URL: "http://www.outbreak.org/cgi-
unreg/dynaserve.exe/cb/bionews.html"

US-based page on news on chemical and
biological weapons.

Nuclear Test Ban Treaty

URL: "http://www.ctbt.rnd.doe.gov/
ctbt/index.html"

US Department of Energy site with sections
on monitoring methods, including hydroa-
coustic, seismic, radio nuclides, and infra-
sound, as well as onsite inspections.

Out There News Explores the
Middle East Conflict

URL: "http://www.megastories.com/
mideast/index.htm"

Site describing the wars of the Arab–Israeli
conflict.

Pearl Harbor

URL: "http://www.execpc.com/~dschaaf/
mainmenu.html"

Short account of the attack on Pearl Harbor,
plus maps, a timeline of events, a list of
casualties, and a survivor's story.

Potsdam Conference

URL: "http://www.yale.edu/lawweb/
avalon/decade/decade17.htm"

Part of the Avalon Project at the Yale Law
School, this page features the text of conclusions arrived at by Truman, Churchill, and
Stalin during the Berlin Conference, held
from 17 July to 2 August 1945.

Radio Broadcast of the D-Day
Landing at Normandy

URL: "http://www.otr.com/hicks.html"

Part of a larger site paying homage to the glory
days of radio, this site features audio of
George Hicks's on-the-scene news report of
the D-day invasion of Normandy, including
the account of a German air attack on the *USS
Ancon* during which the furious sounds of war
nearly drown out the sound of Hicks' report.

Report on the Marne

URL: "http://www.lib.byu.edu/~rdh/wwi/
1914/joffre.html"

Part of a larger site concerning World War I
documents, this page features the text of the
official French report of Marshal Joseph
Joffre regarding events of August and September 1914 at the Marne. Marshal Joffre's
report analyzes the successes and failures of
the French armies engaged in the first battle
of the Marne.

Royal Air Force

URL: "http://www.raf.mod.uk/"

Site of Britain's air force. In addition to information for would-be recruits, there is extensive information on the role of the RAF and
profiles of all RAF aircraft, weapons systems, and bases.

Royal British Legion

URL: "http://www.britishlegion.org.uk/"

There is comprehensive information about
the history of the British Legion, its current
activities and its annual Poppy Appeal. A
'lost trails' section helps reunite ex-servicemen.

Royal Navy

URL: "http://www.royal-navy.mod.uk/"

Official guide to the Royal Navy that
includes information about the latest training, deployments worldwide, and career
opportunities, as well as a 'future' section for
each of the four arms of the service and history
of the navy from its humble beginnings.

START II Treaty Fact Sheet

URL: "http://www.state.gov/www/regions/
nis/russia_start2_treaty.html"

Site published by the US Bureau of Public
Affairs explaining the START II treaty of
1993 which was designed to further reduce
and limit strategic offensive weapons.

Versailles Treaty Contents

URL: "http://ac.acusd..edu/History/text/
versaillestreaty/vercontents.html"

Full text, maps, cartoons, photos, and suggested reading on the Treaty of Versailles.

War Crimes Agreement and Interna-
tional Military Tribunal Charter

URL: "http://www.trincoll.edu/
pols312/LA.HTML"

Reproduction of the 1945 War Crimes Agreement and the Charter of the International Military Tribunal.

World War I Document Archive

URL: "http://www.lib.byu.edu/~rdh/wwi/"

Archive of primary documents from the Great
War, including conventions, treaties, and official papers.

World War II – Day by Day

URL: "http://www.cyberplus.ca/
~chrism/chrono.htm"

Large and detailed chronology of World War
II. It has been divided by year and places an
emphasis on the navy although all major
events have been included.

World War II Images

URL: "http://earthstation1.simplenet.
com/wwiipics/wwiipics.html"

Images of the World War II. Over a hundred
pictures are shown here as thumbnails, clicking on one will load the full size image.

World War II Warship Images

URL: "http://earthstation1.simplenet.
com/warships/wwii/wwiiship.html"

Image only site with images of World War II
warships. The images are composed mainly of
US navy vessels, but several of the more
important ships from other navies are also featured.

World War I: The War at Sea

URL: "http://www.ukans.edu/~kansite/
ww_one/naval/n0000000.htm"

Part of a larger site concerning World War I
documents, this page provides a comprehensive look at the role of the navy in the this war.

TRANSPORT AND TRAVEL

9 July 1997–12 July 1997 British Airways flight attendants go on strike in protest at planned changes to the company's work policy. The disruption leads to widespread delays and cancellations of flights.

31 July 1997 The US government lifts a 10-year-old ban on travel by US tourists to Lebanon. The ban was initiated in 1987 during the hostage crisis.

6 August 1997 A Korean Airlines Boeing 747 crashes on the island of Guam, killing more than 225 people.

19 August 1997 After a week of ethnic violence in Mombasa, Kenya, the country suffers a decline in tourism, its most profitable industry.

28 August 1997 The United Nations Security Council passes a resolution that imposes air and travel sanctions against the National Union for Total Liberation of Angola (UNITA), an armed rebel group that controls some parts of Angola.

8 September 1997 Around 600 people are killed when the ferry *Fierte Gonaivience* capsizes off Port-au-Prince, Haiti.

14 September 1997 A train derails on a bridge in Madyah Pradesh, India, killing more than 80 people and injuring hundreds more.

26 September 1997 An A300 B-4 Airbus crashes at Medan in southern Sumatra, killing 234 people; smog from forest fires is blamed as the probable cause.

30 September 1997 A Federal Bureau of Investigation/Central Intelligence Agency (FBI/CIA) investigation into the explosion aboard TWA Flight 800 in July 1996 concludes it was caused by a build-up of pressure in a fuel tank.

10 October 1997 A DC-9 airliner from Argentina crashes in Uruguay, killing all of the 75 people on board.

26 October 1997 Italy joins the Schengen group, a zone with open borders in the European Union with seven other member countries.

6 December 1997 A Russian Antonov 124 military transport ploughs into a residential area in Irkutsk, Russia, shortly after takeoff, killing 70 people.

10 December 1997 The Chinese government announces that Australia is an 'approved destination' for Chinese tourists; Australia is the first non-Asian country to achieve the status.

15 December 1997 A Tajik charter airliner crashes in the United Arab Emirates, killing 85 passengers.

4 January 1998–6 January 1998 US car manufacturers exhibit several new cars, with advanced fuel-efficient technology that would reduce polluting emissions, at the North American International Auto Show in Detroit, Michigan.

5 January 1998 The German car manufacturer Volkswagen introduces its New Beetle, an up-to-date version of its original Beetle, the most popular car in history.

2 February 1998 A Cebu Pacific DC-9 crashes in the southern Philippines, killing all 104 people aboard.

4 February 1998 The Federal Aviation Administration (FAA) admits that it is behind in its effort to sort out computer glitches before 2000. If computers are not repaired before the Millennium, air-traffic control systems could be inoperable, threatening airline safety.

16 February 1998 A China Airways jet crashes near Taipei, Taiwan, killing all 196 people on board as well as 7 people on the ground. One of the victims was the head of Taiwan's central bank, Sheu Yuan-dong, who was returning from an economic conference in Bali.

20 March 1998 British Deputy Prime Minister John Prescott announces that the government seeks £7 billion in private funding to renovate the London Underground.

8 June 1998 British Deputy Prime Minister John Prescott announces plans for the privatization of Britain's air-traffic control.

15 June 1998 London Underground workers begin a 48-hour walkout over job security. The strike causes several tube stations in London, to close and around 40% of morning rush hour trains to be cancelled.

23 June 1998 British Prime Minister Tony Blair opens a £450 million high-speed train service to Heathrow airport. A single ticket costs £10 and it takes 15 minutes to travel the 17 miles from London Paddington station to the airport.

World Aviation

Aircraft Operating Statistics

The figures are averages for the most commonly used models.

1995

Aircraft	Number of seats	Average cargo payload (tons)	Speed (airborne)		Flight length		Fuel (US gallons per hour)	Aircraft operating cost per hour ($)
			kpm	mph	km	mi		
B747-400	396	8.69	866	538	7,916	4,919	3,420	6,686
B747-100	395	7.98	838	521	5,233	3,252	3,626	6,235
B747-200/300	342	9.12[1]	861	535	6,674	4,147	3,752	7,435
B747F	0	30.05	822	511	3,674	2,283	3,669	6,981
B777	291	7.79	824	512	4,067	2,527	1,995	3,923
DC10 40	288	6.04	814	506	3,185	1,979	2,644	4,056
L-1011-100/200	285	2.96	789	490	2,119	1,317	2,356	3,861
DC10 10	283	8.15	805	500	2,472	1,536	2,225	4,866
DC10 30	277	6.93[1]	834	518	4,596	2,856	2,625	5,530
A300-600	267	9.11	758	471	1,859	1,155	1,691	4,277
MD-11	261	9.96[1]	842	523	6,135	3,812	2,344	5,528
L-1011-500	222	3.81	843	524	5,270	3,275	2,504	4,028
B767-300ER	219	6.73	798	496	3,763	2,338	1,572	3,191
B757-200	186	2.34	748	465	1,862	1,157	1,036	2,465
B767-200ER	180	4.27	784	487	3,437	2,136	1,425	2,845
A310-300	172	2.55	801	498	3,843	2,388	1,506	3,479
MD-90	150	0.42	715	444	1,281	796	800	1,887
B727-200	149	0.67	706	439	1,178	732	1,285	2,266
B727-200F	0	15.57	718	446	925	575	1,346	5,213
A320-100/200	147	0.85	731	454	1,674	1,040	802	1,967
B737-400	146	0.47	666	414	1,073	667	754	2,044
MD-80	139	0.48	694	431	1,241	771	906	1,843
B737-300	131	0.39	661	411	927	576	763	1,834
DC9 50	121	0.46	602	374	546	339	894	1,838
B737-100/200	112	0.37	628	390	684	425	799	1,629
B737-500	111	0.34	669	416	916	569	738	1,609
DC9 40	109	0.43	624	388	769	478	825	1,883
DC9 30	100	0.43	626	389	727	452	811	1,419
F-100	97	0.22	621	386	800	497	755	1,698
DC9 10	71	0.44	613	381	668	415	736	1,414

[1] Cargo carriers have been excluded.

Air Distances Between Major World Cities

(In miles.)

City	Bangkok	Beijing	Berlin	Cairo	Cape Town	Caracas	Chicago	Hong Kong	London	Los Angeles	Madrid	Melbourne	Mexico City	Montreal	Moscow	New York	Paris	Rio de Janeiro	Rome	San Francisco	Singapore	Stockholm	Tokyo	Washington, DC
Bangkok		2,046	5,352	4,523	6,300	10,555	8,570	1,077	5,944	7,637	6,337	4,568	9,793	8,338	4,389	8,669	5,877	9,994	5,494	7,931	883	5,089	2,865	8,807
Beijing	2,046		4,584	4,698	8,044	8,950	6,604	1,217	5,074	6,250	5,745	5,643	7,753	6,519	3,607	6,844	5,120	10,768	5,063	5,918	2,771	4,133	1,307	6,942
Berlin	5,352	4,584		1,797	5,961	5,238	4,414	5,443	583	5,782	1,165	9,918	6,056	3,740	1,006	3,979	548	6,209	737	5,672	6,164	528	5,557	4,181
Cairo	4,523	4,698	1,797		4,480	6,342	6,141	5,066	2,185	7,520	2,087	8,675	7,700	5,427	1,803	5,619	1,998	6,143	1,326	7,466	5,137	2,096	5,958	5,822
Cape Town	6,300	8,044	5,961	4,480		6,366	8,491	7,376	5,989	9,969	5,308	6,425	8,519	7,922	6,279	7,803	5,786	3,781	5,231	10,248	6,008	6,423	9,154	7,895
Caracas	10,555	8,950	5,238	6,342	6,366		2,495	10,165	4,655	3,632	4,346	9,717	2,234	2,438	6,177	2,120	4,732	2,804	5,195	3,902	11,402	5,471	8,808	2,047
Chicago	8,570	6,604	4,414	6,141	8,491	2,495		7,797	3,958	1,745	4,189	9,673	1,690	745	4,987	714	4,143	5,282	4,824	1,859	9,372	4,331	6,314	596
Hong Kong	1,077	1,217	5,443	5,066	7,376	10,165	7,797		5,990	7,240	6,558	4,595	8,788	7,736	4,437	8,060	5,990	11,009	5,774	6,905	1,605	5,063	1,791	8,155
London	5,944	5,074	583	2,185	5,989	4,655	3,958	5,990		5,439	785	10,500	5,558	3,254	1,564	3,469	214	5,750	895	5,367	6,747	942	5,959	3,674
Los Angeles	7,637	6,250	5,782	7,520	9,969	3,632	1,745	7,240	5,439		5,848	7,931	1,542	2,427	6,068	2,451	5,601	6,330	6,326	347	8,767	5,454	5,470	2,300
Madrid	6,337	5,745	1,165	2,087	5,308	4,346	4,189	6,558	785	5,848		10,758	5,643	3,448	2,147	3,593	655	5,045	851	5,803	7,080	1,653	6,706	3,792
Melbourne	4,568	5,643	9,918	8,675	6,425	9,717	9,673	4,595	10,500	7,931	10,758		8,426	10,395	8,950	10,359	10,430	8,226	9,929	7,856	3,759	9,630	5,062	10,180
Mexico City	9,793	7,753	6,056	7,700	8,519	2,234	1,690	8,788	5,558	1,542	5,643	8,426		2,317	6,676	2,090	5,725	4,764	6,377	1,887	10,327	6,012	7,035	1,885
Montreal	8,338	6,519	3,740	5,427	7,922	2,438	745	7,736	3,254	2,427	3,448	10,395	2,317		4,401	331	3,432	5,078	4,104	2,543	9,203	3,714	6,471	489
Moscow	4,389	3,607	1,006	1,803	6,279	6,177	4,987	4,437	1,564	6,068	2,147	8,950	6,676	4,401		4,683	1,554	7,170	1,483	5,885	5,228	716	4,660	4,876
New York	8,669	6,844	3,979	5,619	7,803	2,120	714	8,060	3,469	2,451	3,593	10,359	2,090	331	4,683		3,636	4,801	4,293	2,572	9,534	3,986	6,757	205
Paris	5,877	5,120	548	1,998	5,786	4,732	4,143	5,990	214	5,601	655	10,430	5,725	3,432	1,554	3,636		5,684	690	5,577	6,673	1,003	6,053	3,840
Rio de Janeiro	9,994	10,768	6,209	6,143	3,781	2,804	5,282	11,009	5,750	6,330	5,045	8,226	4,764	5,078	7,170	4,801	5,684		5,707	6,613	9,785	6,683	11,532	4,779
Rome	5,494	5,063	737	1,326	5,231	5,195	4,824	5,774	895	6,326	851	9,929	6,377	4,104	1,483	4,293	690	5,707		6,259	6,229	1,245	6,142	4,497
San Francisco	7,931	5,918	5,672	7,466	10,248	3,902	1,859	6,905	5,367	347	5,803	7,856	1,887	2,543	5,885	2,572	5,577	6,613	6,259		8,448	5,399	5,150	2,441
Singapore	883	2,771	6,164	5,137	6,008	11,402	9,372	1,605	6,747	8,767	7,080	3,759	10,327	9,203	5,228	9,534	6,673	9,785	6,229	8,448		5,936	3,300	9,662
Stockholm	5,089	4,133	528	2,096	6,423	5,471	4,331	5,063	942	5,454	1,653	9,630	6,012	3,714	716	3,986	1,003	6,683	1,245	5,399	5,936		5,053	4,183
Tokyo	2,865	1,307	5,557	5,958	9,154	8,808	6,314	1,791	5,959	5,470	6,706	5,062	7,035	6,471	4,660	6,757	6,053	11,532	6,142	5,150	3,300	5,053		6,791
Washington, DC	8,807	6,942	4,181	5,822	7,895	2,047	596	8,155	3,674	2,300	3,792	10,180	1,885	489	4,876	205	3,840	4,779	4,497	2,441	9,662	4,183	6,791	

International Aircraft Registration Prefixes

Most civil aircraft carry one or two letters or a number and a letter to identify their nationality. This nationality mark is painted on both sides of the fuselage or tail. It is also displayed on the underside of the wing. Numbers or letters following the nationality mark on a plane are the registration mark issued to that particular plane in its own country. Each country that belongs to the International Civil Aviation Organization (ICAO) reports its nationality mark to the organization.
(As of January 1998.)

Country	ICAO mark	Country	ICAO mark	Country	ICAO mark
Afghanistan	YA	Greece	SX	Oman	A40
Albania	ZA	Grenada	J3	Pakistan	AP
Algeria	7T	Guatemala	TG	Panama	HP
Andorra	C3	Guinea	3X	Papua New Guinea	P2
Angola	D2	Guinea-Bissau	J5	Paraguay	ZP
Antigua and Barbuda	V2	Guyana	8R	Peru	OB
Argentina	LQ, LV	Haiti	HH	Philippines	RP
Armenia	EK	Honduras	HR	Poland	SP
Australia	VH	Hungary	HA	Portugal	CS
Austria	OE	Iceland	TF	Qatar	A7
Azerbaijan	4K	India	VT	Romania	YR
Bahamas	C6	Indonesia	PK	Russia	RA
Bahrain	A9C	Iran	EP	Rwanda	9XR
Bangladesh	S2, S3	Iraq	YI	St Kitts and Nevis	V4
Barbados	8P	Ireland, Republic of	EI	St Lucia	J6
Belarus	EW	Israel	4X	St Vincent and the Grenadines	J8
Belgium	OO	Italy	I	Samoa	5W
Belize	V3	Jamaica	6Y	San Marino	T7
Benin	TY	Japan	JA	São Tomé and Príncipe	S9
Bhutan	A5	Jordan	JY	Saudi Arabia	HZ
Bolivia	CP	Kazakhstan	UN	Senegal	6W
Bosnia-Herzegovina	T9	Kenya	5Y	Seychelles	S7
Botswana	A2	Kiribati	T3	Sierra Leone	9L
Brazil	PP, PT	Korea, North	P	Singapore	9V
Brunei	V8	Korea, South	HL	Slovak Republic	OM
Bulgaria	LZ	Kuwait	9K	Slovenia	S5
Burkina Faso	XT	Kyrgyzstan	EX	Solomon Islands	H4
Burundi	9U	Laos	RDPL	Somalia	60
Cambodia	XU	Latvia	YL	South Africa	ZS, ZT, ZU
Cameroon	TJ	Lebanon	OD	Spain	EC
Canada	C, CF	Lesotho	7P	Sri Lanka	4R
Cape Verde	D4	Liberia	EL	Sudan	ST
Central African Republic	TL	Libya	5A	Suriname	PZ
Chad	TT	Liechtenstein	HB	Swaziland	3D
Chile	CC	Lithuania	LY	Sweden	SE
China	B	Luxembourg	LX	Switzerland	HB
Colombia	HK	Macedonia, Former		Syria	YK
Comoros	D6	Yugoslav Republic of	Z3	Taiwan	B
Congo, Democratic Republic of	9Q, 9T	Madagascar	5R	Tajikistan	EY
Congo, Republic of the	TN	Malawi	7Q	Tanzania	5H
Costa Rica	TI	Malaysia	9M	Thailand	HS
Côte d'Ivoire	TU	Maldives	8Q	Togo	5V
Croatia	9A	Mali	TZ	Tonga	A3
Cuba	CU	Malta	9H	Tunisia	TS
Cyprus	5B	Marshall Islands	V7	Turkey	TC
Czech Republic	OK	Mauritania	5T	Turkmenistan	EZ
Denmark	OY	Mauritius	3B	Tuvalu	T2
Djibouti	J2	Mexico	XA, XB, XC	Uganda	5X
Dominica	J7	Micronesia	V6	UK	G
Dominican Republic	HI	Moldova	ER	Ukraine	UR
Ecuador	HC	Monaco	3A	United Arab Emirates	A6
Egypt	SU	Mongolia	BNMAU, MONGOL, MT	United Nations	4N
El Salvador	YS	Morocco	CN	Uruguay	CX
Equatorial Guinea	3C	Mozambique	C9	USA	N
Eritrea	E3	Myanmar	XY, XZ	Uzbekistan	UK
Estonia	ES	Namibia	V5	Vanuatu	YJ
Ethiopia	ET	Nauru	C2	Vatican City State	HV
Fiji	DQ	Nepal	9N	Venezuela	YV
Finland	OH	Netherlands	PH	Vietnam	VN
France	F	New Zealand	ZK, ZL, ZM	Yemen	70
Gabon	TR	Nicaragua	YN	Yugoslavia	YU
Gambia	C5	Niger	5U	Zambia	9J
Georgia	4L	Nigeria	5N	Zimbabwe	Z
Germany	D	Norway	LN		
Ghana	9G				

Source: International Civil Aviation Organization

The World's Busiest Airports by Passenger Traffic

The figures are for airports participating in the Airports Council International (ACI) Monthly Airport Traffic Statistics Collection. Data are for the period January–September 1997.

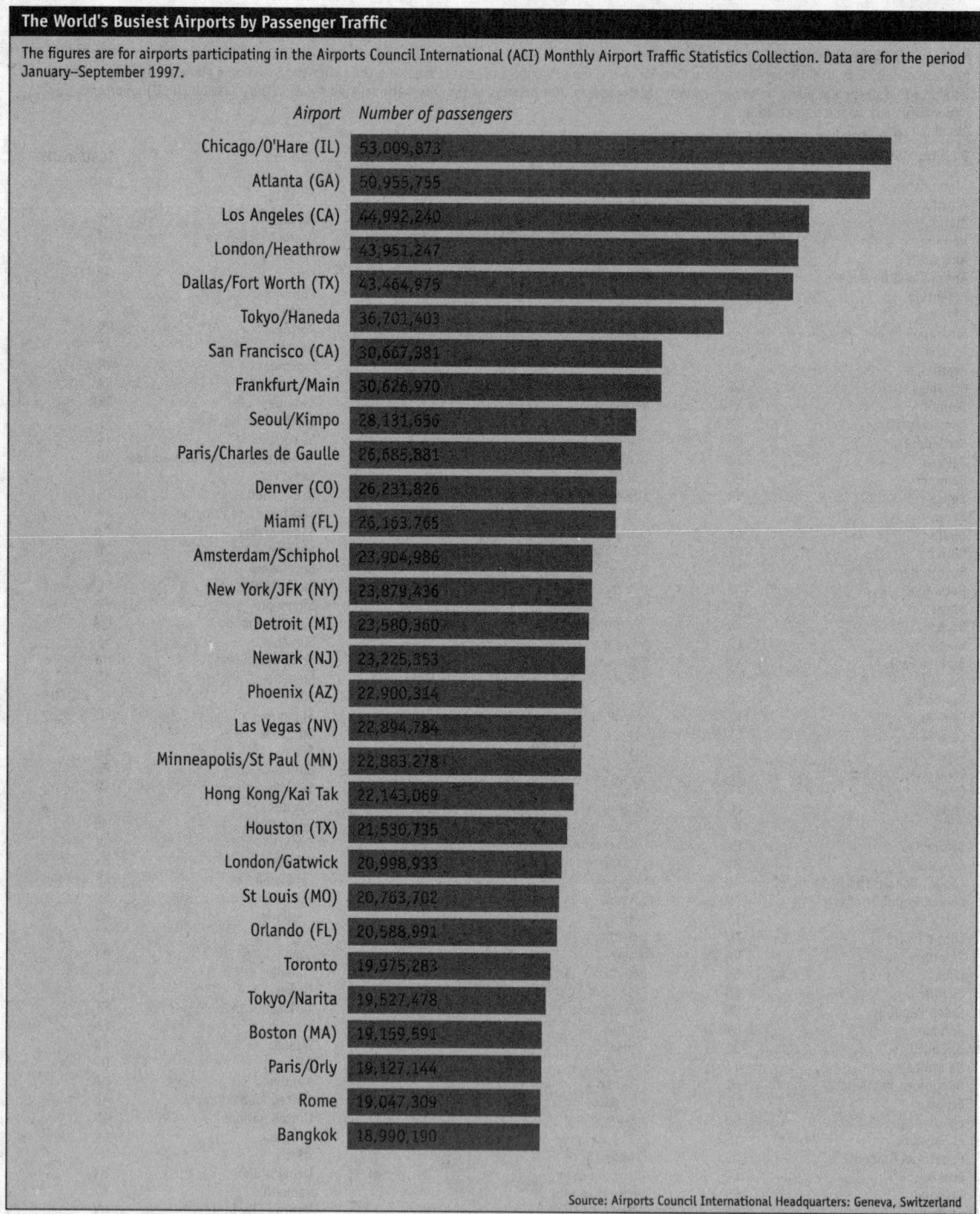

Airport	Number of passengers
Chicago/O'Hare (IL)	53,009,873
Atlanta (GA)	50,955,755
Los Angeles (CA)	44,992,240
London/Heathrow	43,951,247
Dallas/Fort Worth (TX)	43,464,975
Tokyo/Haneda	36,701,403
San Francisco (CA)	30,667,381
Frankfurt/Main	30,626,970
Seoul/Kimpo	28,131,650
Paris/Charles de Gaulle	26,685,881
Denver (CO)	26,231,826
Miami (FL)	26,163,765
Amsterdam/Schiphol	23,904,986
New York/JFK (NY)	23,879,436
Detroit (MI)	23,580,360
Newark (NJ)	23,225,353
Phoenix (AZ)	22,900,314
Las Vegas (NV)	22,894,784
Minneapolis/St Paul (MN)	22,883,278
Hong Kong/Kai Tak	22,143,069
Houston (TX)	21,530,735
London/Gatwick	20,998,933
St Louis (MO)	20,763,702
Orlando (FL)	20,588,991
Toronto	19,975,283
Tokyo/Narita	19,527,478
Boston (MA)	19,159,591
Paris/Orly	19,127,144
Rome	19,047,309
Bangkok	18,990,190

Source: Airports Council International Headquarters: Geneva, Switzerland

The World's Busiest Airports by Cargo Volume

The figures are for airports participating in the Airports Council International (ACI) Monthly Airport Traffic Statistics Collection. Data are for the period January–September 1997.

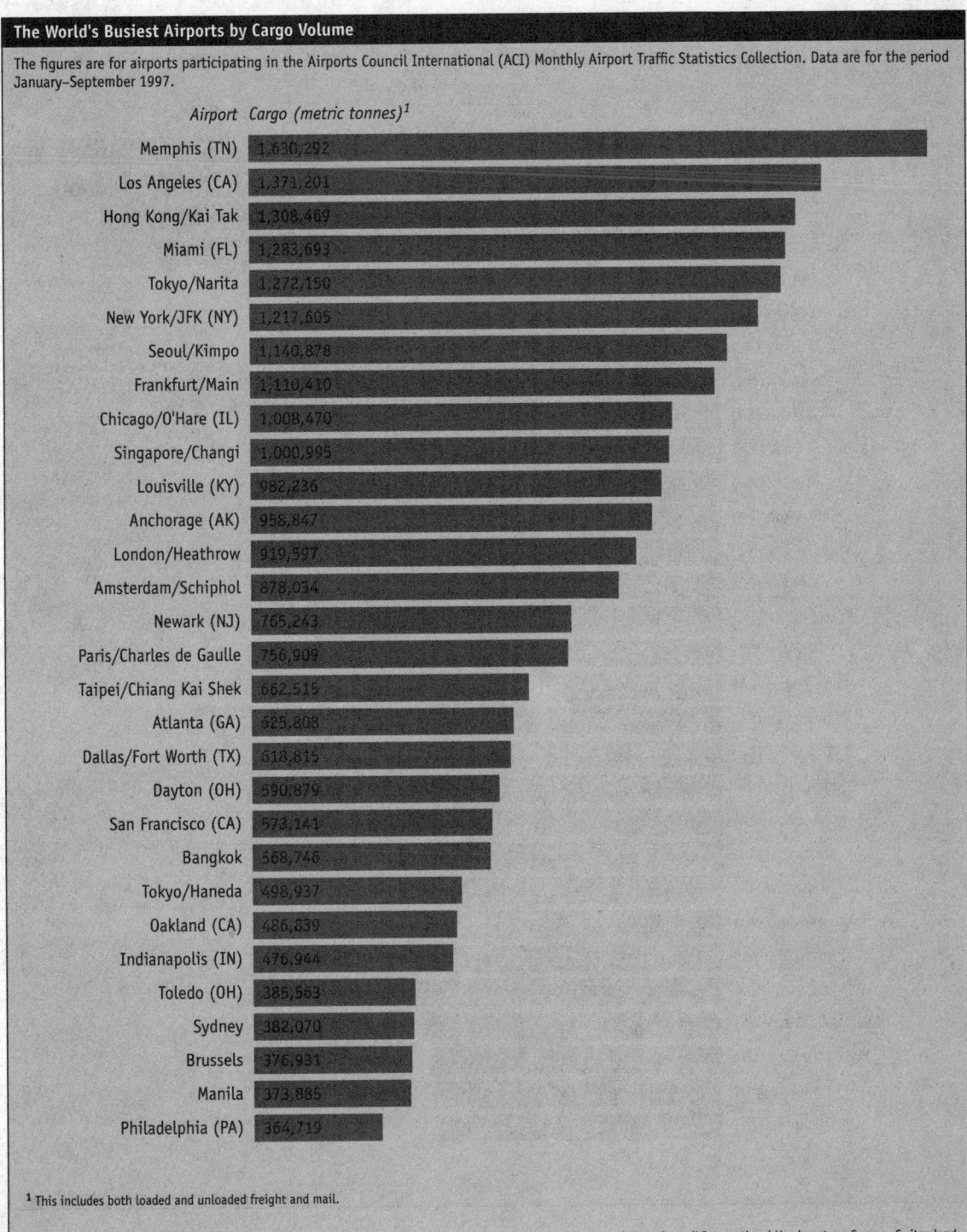

Airport	Cargo (metric tonnes)[1]
Memphis (TN)	1,630,292
Los Angeles (CA)	1,371,201
Hong Kong/Kai Tak	1,308,469
Miami (FL)	1,283,693
Tokyo/Narita	1,272,150
New York/JFK (NY)	1,217,605
Seoul/Kimpo	1,140,878
Frankfurt/Main	1,110,410
Chicago/O'Hare (IL)	1,008,470
Singapore/Changi	1,000,995
Louisville (KY)	982,236
Anchorage (AK)	958,847
London/Heathrow	919,597
Amsterdam/Schiphol	878,034
Newark (NJ)	765,243
Paris/Charles de Gaulle	756,909
Taipei/Chiang Kai Shek	662,515
Atlanta (GA)	625,808
Dallas/Fort Worth (TX)	618,815
Dayton (OH)	590,879
San Francisco (CA)	573,141
Bangkok	588,746
Tokyo/Haneda	498,937
Oakland (CA)	486,839
Indianapolis (IN)	476,944
Toledo (OH)	386,563
Sydney	382,070
Brussels	376,931
Manila	373,885
Philadelphia (PA)	364,719

[1] This includes both loaded and unloaded freight and mail.

Source: Airports Council International Headquarters: Geneva, Switzerland

The World's Busiest Airports by Take-Offs and Landings

The figures are for airports participating in the Airports Council International (ACI) Monthly Airport Traffic Statistics Collection. Data are for the period January–September 1997.

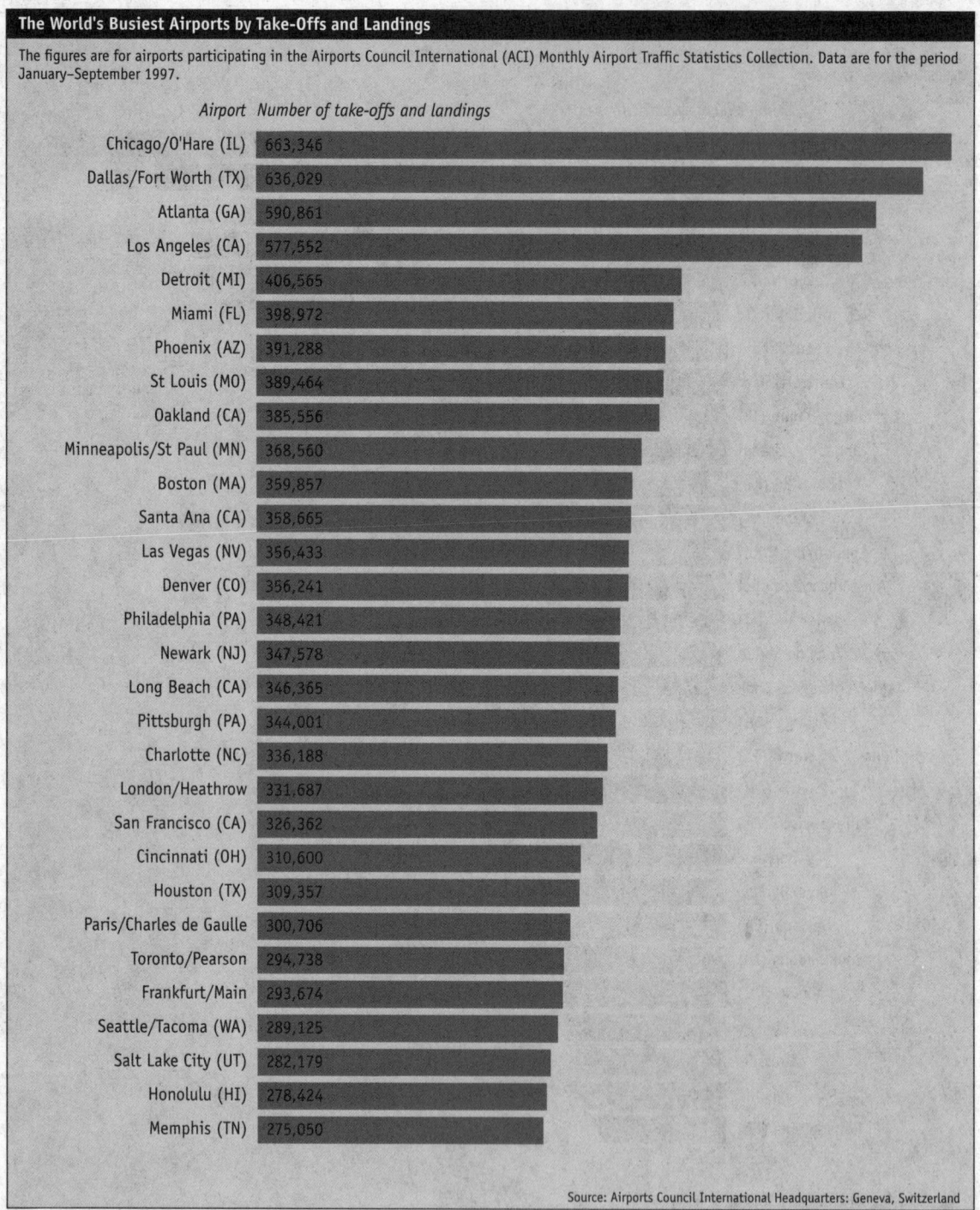

Airport	Number of take-offs and landings
Chicago/O'Hare (IL)	663,346
Dallas/Fort Worth (TX)	636,029
Atlanta (GA)	590,861
Los Angeles (CA)	577,552
Detroit (MI)	406,565
Miami (FL)	398,972
Phoenix (AZ)	391,288
St Louis (MO)	389,464
Oakland (CA)	385,556
Minneapolis/St Paul (MN)	368,560
Boston (MA)	359,857
Santa Ana (CA)	358,665
Las Vegas (NV)	356,433
Denver (CO)	356,241
Philadelphia (PA)	348,421
Newark (NJ)	347,578
Long Beach (CA)	346,365
Pittsburgh (PA)	344,001
Charlotte (NC)	336,188
London/Heathrow	331,687
San Francisco (CA)	326,362
Cincinnati (OH)	310,600
Houston (TX)	309,357
Paris/Charles de Gaulle	300,706
Toronto/Pearson	294,738
Frankfurt/Main	293,674
Seattle/Tacoma (WA)	289,125
Salt Lake City (UT)	282,179
Honolulu (HI)	278,424
Memphis (TN)	275,050

Source: Airports Council International Headquarters: Geneva, Switzerland

Aviation Firsts

(– = not applicable.)

Date	Name	Achievement
1804	George Cayley (UK)	first modern-configuration airplane prototype in history ('Cayley's glider')
1891	Otto Lilienthal (Germany)	first successful crewed glider flight
1896	Samuel Pierpont Langley (USA)	first steam-driven pilotless airplane (12,082 m/24,000 ft over the Potomac River)
1903	Orville and Wilbur Wright (USA)	first successful flight of a powered aircraft, Kitty Hawk (NC) (59 seconds; 259 m/850 ft)
1906	Alberto Santos-Dumos (Brazil)	first successful European flight (Bagatelle Field, Paris, France)
1908	Frank P Lahm (USA)	first airplane passenger (with Wilbur Smith piloting)
	Samuel Franklin Cody (UK)	first powered flight in the UK
1909	Louis Blériot (France)	first successful flight across the English Channel
1910	Raymonde de la Roche (France)	first licensed female pilot
	Henri Faber (France)	first take-off from water
1911	Harriet Quimby (USA)	first US female pilot
1912	Harriet Quimby (USA)	first crossing of the English Channel by female pilot
	–	first automatic pilot in service
1913	Ivan Sikorsky (Russia)	first multi-engined aircraft
1914		first scheduled passenger airline service (St Petersburg–Tampa, Florida)
1914–18	–	first military use of aircraft; developments in speed and power of aircrafts triggered by World War I
1918	–	first airmail service established in the USA (Washington–New York City)
1919	Walter Hinton (USA)	first transatlantic flight (Trepassy Bay, Newfoundland–Lisbon, Portugal via Horta, Azores, and Ponta Delgada)
	John W Alcock, Arthur Whitten Brown (UK)	first nonstop transatlantic flight (St John's, Newfoundland–Clifden, Ireland; 3,058 km/1,900 mi; 16 hr 12 min)
	Ross Smith, Keith Smith (Australia)	first flight from the UK to Australia
	–	first scheduled London, UK–Paris, France passenger service
	–	first airline food served
1923	John A Macready, Oakley Kelly (USA)	first nonstop transcontinental flight (New York–San Diego, USA; 4,023 km/2,500 mi; 26 hr 50 min)
1924	Lowell Smith, Erik Nelson (USA)	first round-the-world flight
1926	Richard E Byrd, Floyd Bennett (USA)	first flight over the North Pole
1927	Charles Augustus Lindbergh (USA)	first solo nonstop transatlantic flight
1928	Charles K Smith, C T P Ulm	first transpacific flight (San Francisco, USA–Brisbane, Australia)
1929	James H Doolittle (USA)	first take-off and landing relying solely on instruments ('blind')
	Richard E Byrd, Nernt Balchen, Harold I June, A C McKinley (USA)	first flight over the South Pole
1930	Frank Whittle (UK)	jet engine patented
	Amy Johnson (UK)	first female pilot to fly from the UK to Australia
	Ellen Church (USA)	first flight attendant
1931	Hugh Herndon, Clyde Pangborn (USA)	first nonstop transpacific flight (Sabishiro Beach, Japan–near Wenatchee (WA), USA; 41 hr 13 min)
1932	Amelia Earhart (USA)	first transatlantic solo flight by a female pilot (Harbor Grace, Newfoundland–Ireland; around 15 hr)
1933	Wiley Post (USA)	first round-the-world solo flight
1937	Amelia Earhart (USA)	first attempt at a round-the-world flight by a female pilot (Earhart disappeared in the Pacific, between New Guinea and Howland Island)
	–	first fully pressurized aircraft (*Lockheed XC-35*)
1939	Erich Warsitz (Germany)	first turbojet flight, Germany (*Heinkel He 178*)
1939–45	–	developments related to World War II (*Hawker Hurricane* and *Supermarine Spitfire* fighters; *Avro Lancaster* and *Boeing Flying Fortress* bombers)
1941	–	first UK jet aircraft (*Gloster e.28/39*)
1942	Robert Stanley (USA)	first US jet plane flight
1944		first rocket-engine fighter plane operational, Germany (Messerschmitt Me 163B *Komet*)
1947	Charles E ('Chuck') Yeager (USA)	first piloted supersonic flight (*Bell X-1* rocket-powered aircraft)
1949	James Gallagher (USA)	first round-the-world nonstop flight
	–	first jet airliner in service (de Havilland *Comet*)
1950	David C Schilling (USA)	first nonstop transatlantic jet flight (UK to Limestone, Maine)
1952	–	first jetliner service (London, UK–Johannesburg, South Africa)
1953	–	first vertical take-off aircraft tested (Rolls-Royce *Flying Bedstead*)
	Jacqueline Cochran (USA)	first female pilot to break the sound barrier
1957	Archie J Old Jr (USA)	first nonstop round-the-world jet plane flight (45 hr 19 min)
1958	–	first domestic jet passenger service (New York–Miami, USA); first transatlantic jet passenger service (New York, USA–London, UK, and Paris, France)
1960	–	first supersonic bomber (*Convair B-58*)
1968	–	first supersonic plane (*Tupolev Tu-144*; supersonic speed achieved: Mach 2, c. 1,924 kph/1,200 mph)
1970	–	Mach 2 exceeded (*Tupolev Tu-144*; 2,140 kph/1,335 mph)
	–	*Boeing 747* jumbo jet in service
1976	–	first commercial supersonic flights (*Concorde*)
1977	Paul MacCready (USA)	first succcessful human-powered aircraft (*Gossamer Condor*)
1979	Bryan Allen (USA)	first crossing of the English Channel by a human-powered aircraft (*Gossamer Albatross*)
1980	Janice Brown (USA)	first successful long-distance solar-powered flight (*Solar Challenger*; 10 km/6 mi in 22 min)
1986	Dick Rutan, Jeana Yeager (USA)	first nonstop around-the-world flight without refuelling (*Voyager*; 216 hr 3 min 44 sec)
1988	Kaneilos Kanellopoulos (Greece)	first flight of a human-powered aircraft across the Aegean Sea
1992	–	first radio-controlled ornithopter (aircraft propelled and manoeuvred by flapping wings; model demonstrated in the USA)
1993	Barbara Harmer (UK)	first female co-pilot of a commercial supersonic plane
	–	automatic on-board collision avoidance system (TCAS-2) mandatory in US airspace

Recent Aircraft Disasters Throughout the World

Date	Aircraft	Location	Details	Fatalities
3 July 1988	Iranian A300 Airbus	Persian Gulf	shot down by US Navy warship *Vincennes*	290
21 December 1988	US Boeing 747	Lockerbie, Scotland	exploded and crashed	270[1]
8 February 1989	Boeing 707	Azores Islands, Portugal	crashed into mountain	144
7 June 1989	Suriname DC8	Paramaribo Airport, Suriname	crashed	168
19 July 1989	US DC10	Sioux City (IA) USA	crashed while landing with a faulty hydraulic system	111
19 September 1989	French DC10	Tenere desert, Niger	exploded in air	171
1 February 1991	US Boeing 737-300 and Metro SA-227-AC	Los Angeles (CA) USA	collision	34
26 May 1991	Austrian Boeing 767-329ER	Phu Khao Chan, Thailand	crashed in jungle	223
11 July 1991	Nigerian DC8	Jiddah, Saudi Arabia	crashed while landing	261
31 July 1992	Airbus A310-304, Thai Airways Int	Kathmandu, Nepal	crashed on descent	113
31 July 1992	Yakovlev 42D, China General Aviation Corporation	near Nanjing, China	crashed during initial climb	106
28 September 1992	Airbus A300B4-203	Kathmandu, Nepal	crashed on descent	167
24 November 1992	Boeing 737-3Y0, China Southern Airlines	Guilin, China	crashed into mountain on descent	141
22 December 1992	Boeing 727-2L5, Libyan Arab Airlines	Souk al-Sabt, Libya	collided with a MIG-23UB at 1,067 m/ 3,500 ft and crashed	157
26 April 1994	Chinese A300-600R Airbus	Nagoya, Japan	crashed while landing	264
18 December 1995	Lockheed L-188C Electra, Trans Service Airlift	Kahengula, Angola	crashed after take-off (aircraft over-loaded)	141
20 December 1995	Boeing 757-223, American Airlines	Buga, Colombia	crashed on approach	160
17 July 1996	US Boeing 747	Long Island (NY) USA	crashed after take-off	230
12 November 1996	Saudi Arabian Boeing 747-100 and Kazakh Ilyushin 76TD	Charki Dadri, India	mid-air collision	349
6 August 1997	Korean Boeing 747-300	Guam, Mariana Islands	crashed into mountain	227
26 September 1997	Indonesian Airbus A300B	near Medan, Indonesia	crashed and burst into flames; visibility was reduced due to smog from forest fires	234
10 October 1997	Argentinian DC9	near Nuevo Berlin, Uruguay	crashed in swamp land on the banks of the Uruguay River	74
15 December 1997	Tajikistani Tupolev 154B	near Sharjah, United Arab Emirates	crashed and burst into flames while approaching Sharjah	85
17 December 1997	Ukrainian Yakovlev 42	Thessaloniki, Greece	crashed while holding at 10,067 m/35,000 ft near Thessaloniki due to heavy traffic in the area	70
19 December 1997	Indonesian 737	near Palembang, Indonesia	crashed nose-down into the river bed of the River Musi; one of the wings broke off during the plunge	104
13 January 1998	Antonov 24/26, Ariana Afghan Airlines	Khojak Pass area, Pakistan	crashed after fuel exhaustion	51
2 February 1998	DC-9-32 RP-1507, Cebu Pacific Air	near Cagayan de Oro, Philippines	crashed into a volcano (Mt Balatucan)	104
16 February 1998	Airbus A300-600R, China Airlines	Tapei International Airport	crashed in thick fog during a second attempt to land and burst into flames	205[2]

[1] Figure includes 11 on the ground.
[2] Figure includes 9 on the ground.

The 10 Worst Aircraft Disasters in Aviation History

Fatalities	Date	Airline	Aircraft	Location
582	27 March 1977	Pan American and KLM (Royal Dutch Airlines)	Two Boeing 747s	Tenerife, Canary Islands
520	12 August 1985	Japan Airlines	Boeing 747	Mount Ogura, Japan
349	12 November 1996	Saudi Arabian Air and Kazak Airlines	Boeing 747 and Ilyushin 76TD	Charki Dadri, India
346	3 March 1974	Turkish Air	DC10	northeast of Paris
329	23 June 1985	Air India	Boeing 747	Republic of Ireland coast, Atlantic Ocean
301	19 August 1980	Saudi Arabian Air	Lockheed L-1011	Riyadh, Saudi Arabia
290	3 July 1988	Iran Air	A300 Airbus	Persian Gulf
275	25 May 1979	American Airlines	DC10	Chicago (IL) USA
270	21 December 1988	Pan American	Boeing 747	Lockerbie, Scotland
269	1 September 1983	Korean Airlines	Boeing 747	near Sakhalin Island, Okhokst Sea

Source: National Transportation Safety Board, US Department of Transportation

World Airliner Accident Statistics

All civil aircraft capable of carrying 19 or more passengers are included (freighter aircraft are also included if the original passenger version is capable of carrying 19 or more passengers). Accidents with aircraft owned and operated by Air Forces, etc, are not included. Accidents with aircraft owned by Air Forces, etc, but operating on a passenger flight are included.

Year	Fatalities	Third-party fatalities[1]	Total	Occupants[2]	Fatality rate	Fatal accidents per type of aircraft			
						jet	prop	piston	Total
1970	1,583	13	1,596	2,138	0.74	16	34	19	69
1971	1,453	1	1,454	1,763	0.82	12	23	15	50
1972	2,556	16	2,572	2,877	0.89	23	25	25	73
1973	2,135	38	2,173	2,627	0.81	31	21	16	68
1974	2,082	7	2,089	2,355	0.88	18	19	20	57
1975	1,174	12	1,186	1,427	0.82	12	18	19	49
1976	1,807	110	1,917	2,058	0.88	22	24	11	57
1977	1,736	14	1,750	2,138	0.81	20	21	14	55
1978	1,288	24	1,312	2,430	0.53	17	23	21	61
1979	1,855	38	1,893	2,051	0.92	22	34	13	69
1980	1,358	0	1,358	1,912	0.71	17	11	15	43
1981	920	2	922	1,130	0.81	9	19	12	40
1982	1,164	35	1,199	2,280	0.52	14	18	3	35
1983	1,355	22	1,377	1,763	0.78	21	11	3	35
1984	624	55	679	742	0.91	5	22	7	34
1985	2,367	1	2,368	2,481	0.95	14	20	6	40
1986	926	23	949	1,429	0.66	14	17	10	41
1987	1,351	52	1,403	1,510	0.93	14	25	3	42
1988	1,734	12	1,746	2,490	0.70	24	29	10	63
1989	1,855	74	1,929	2,659	0.72	21	33	7	61
1990	781	22	803	1,432	0.55	16	18	5	39
1991	1,161	5	1,166	1,597	0.73	14	30	10	54
1992	1,552	60	1,612	2,076	0.75	17	33	7	57
1993	1,275	6	1,281	1,839	0.69	18	29	6	53
1994	1,493	5	1,498	1,867	0.80	21	28	5	54
1995	1,167	6	1,173	1,624	0.72	11	32	8	51
1996	1,945	349	2,234	2,428	0.80	23	23	6	52
1997	1,226	3	1,229	1,551	0.79	12	23	2	37

[1] These include fatalities on the ground as well as fatalities aboard light aircraft, after colliding with an airliner.

[2] This refers to number of people involved in fatal airliner accidents.

Source: Aviation Safety Web Pages (web.inter.nl.net/users/H.Ranter)

Notable Military Aircraft Disasters throughout the World

Date	Aircraft	Location	Details	Fatalities
23 August 1944	US Air Force B-24	Freckleton, England	crashed into school	76[1]
28 July 1945	US Army B-25	New York (NY) USA	crashed into Empire State Building	141
20 December 1952	US Air Force C-124	Moses Lake, Washington, DC, USA	crashed and burned	87
18 June 1953	US Air Force C-124	Tokyo, Japan	crashed and burned	129
24 December 1966	US military-chartered CL-44	South Vietnam	crashed into village	129[1]
30 July 1971	Japanese Boeing and Japanese Air Force F-86	Morioka, Japan	airliner-fighter collision; pilot of fighter parachuted to safety	162
4 April 1975	Air Force Galaxy C-5B	Saigon, South Vietnam	crashed after take-off	172
15 May 1982	Sea King MK4 helicopter	South Atlantic	crashed into sea whilst transferring SAS troops back to HMS Hermes following Pebble Island raid during Falkland Islands war	18
11 September 1982	US Army CH-47 Chinook helicopter	Mannheim, West Germany	crashed during air show	46
June 1994	Chinook helicopter	Mull of Kintyre, Scotland	helicopter carrying military and police personnel crashed en route to an anti-terrorism conference	29
3 February 1998	American EA-6B Prowler	Cavalese, Italian Dolomites	cut through wires of a mountain cable car killing those inside	20

[1] Figures includes fatalities on the ground and in buildings.

Recent International Airline Terrorism

Not every hijacking or bombing can be categorized as a terrorist act. This table excludes hijackings and bombings carried out for ransom or other personal motives rather than for political reasons.

Date	Terrorist act	Airline	Flight	Description
2 April 1986	bombing	TransWorld Airlines	Rome, Italy–Athens, Greece–Cairo, Egypt	landed safely; 4 killed, 9 injured; explosive left by a woman carrying a Lebanese passport, acting on behalf of a Palestinian terrorist
3 May 1986	bombing	Air Lanka	Colombo, Sri Lanka	explosion on the ground; 16 killed, 41 injured
26 October 1986	bombing	Thai Airways	Bangkok, Thailand–Manila, Philippines–Osaka, Japan	aircraft landed in Osaka; 62 injured
29 November 1987	bombing	Korean Air, flight 858	Abu Dhabi, UAE–Bangkok, Thailand	aircraft destroyed in flight; 115 killed; North Korean agent planted the bomb to discourage people from attending the 1988 Seoul Olympics
1 March 1988	bombing	BOP Air	Phadabawa–Johannesburg, South Africa	aircraft destroyed in flight; 17 killed
21 December 1988	bombing	Pan American, flight 103	London, UK–New York, USA	aircraft destroyed in flight over Lockerbie, UK; 270 killed
19 September 1989	bombing	Union des Transport	Brazzaville, Congo–N'Djamena, Chad–Paris, France	aircraft destroyed in flight; 171 killed
27 November 1989	bombing	Avianca	Bogota–Cali, Colombia	aircraft destroyed in flight; 107 killed
18 March 1991	bombing	Aeroflot	Moscow, Novokuznetsk, Russia	incendiary device; aircraft landed safely
19 July 1994	bombing	Alas Airline	Colon City–Panama City, Panama	explosion in flight; aircraft crashed over the Santa Rita mountains; 21 killed
3 November 1994	hijacking	Scandinavian Airlines	Bardfoss–Oslo, Norway	80 passengers held hostage; hijacker demanded peace corridor in Bosnia and later surrendered
11 December 1994	bombing	Philippines Airlines 747	Manila, Philippines–Tokyo, Japan	explosion in flight; 1 killed, 10 injured; aircraft landed safely; Abu Sayyaf Group (ASG) responsible
24 December 1994	hijacking; bombing	Air France Airbus 400	Algiers, Algeria–Marseilles, France	Algerian hijackers demanded that 2 leaders of Islamic Salvation Front be released; in Marseilles police stormed the aircraft and killed all terrorists; dynamite discovered in cabin; 3 hostages had been killed by the terrorists
23 November 1996	hijacking	Ethiopian Airlines	Ethiopia–Kenya	aircraft ran out of fuel on redirected route and crashed near a beach on the Comoros Islands; 125 killed, including the hijackers

Source: Federal Aviation Administration

UK Aviation

Total Fleet for UK Airlines

This table shows the number of aircraft in service at the end of each year.
(– = not applicable. N/A = not available.)

Fleet	1986	1987	1988	1989	1990	1991	1992	1993	1994	1995	1996
British Airways[1]	189	192	200	215	233	233	225	225	227	212	212
British Airways (Euro Ops)[2]	51	40	45	50	40	39	12	15	16	26	28
British International Helicopters[3]	29	29	31	26	27	27	24	25	28	25	21
Air Europe	4	9	14	21	–	–	–	–	–	–	–
Air UK	19	22	21	25	25	29	28	34	36	37	41
Bond Helicopters	30	33	36	35	45	50	45	43	N/A	N/A	N/A
Bristow Helicopters	65	62	62	57	65	63	59	56	N/A	N/A	N/A
Britannia Airways	29	31	33	40	32	39	33	28	29	29	28
British World Airline[4]	19	16	11	16	17	17	19	20	21	18	17
British Midland Airways	16	17	19	21	29	30	31	34	34	34	34
Loganair	15	16	18	18	17	22	22	24	14	14	13
Monarch	5	8	12	9	17	18	21	16	18	22	24
Virgin Atlantic	2	2	2	4	6	8	8	9	13	12	15

[1] Prior to 1988 the data include British Caledonian Airways as well as British Airways and British Airtours.
[2] This was formerly Dan Air Services until taken over by British Airways in November 1992.
[3] This was formerly British Airways Helicopters until 12 October 1986.
[4] This was formerly British Air Ferries until 1993.

Source: Department of the Environment, Transport and the Regions, Transport Statistics Great Britain, © Crown copyright

Total Cargo Tonnage Handled at UK Airports

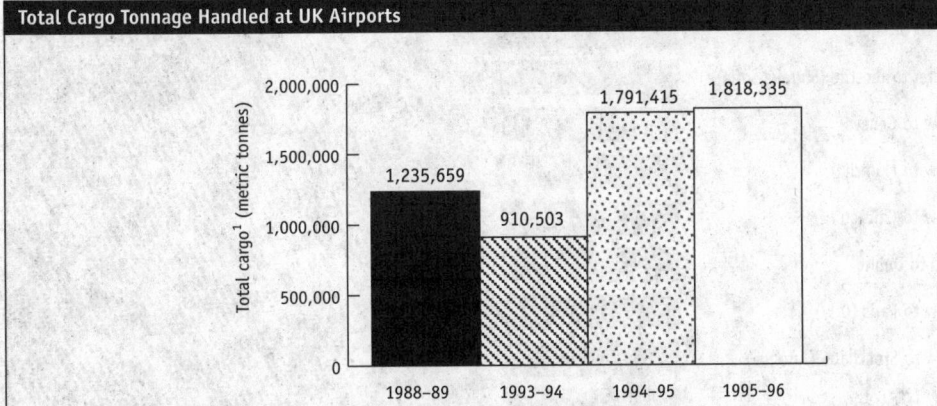

[1] Cargo consists of air cargo plus mail.

Source: From the UK Airports Industry-Airport Statistics, 1995–6 published by CRI (The Centre for the Study of Regulated Industries) a research centre of CIPFA (The Chartered Institute of Public Finance and Accountancy)

Top 30 UK Airline Routes

Rank	Route	Passengers carried (1995)
1	Heathrow to New York (JFK)	2,305,349
2	Heathrow to Paris (Charles de Gaulle)	1,972,251
3	Heathrow to Amsterdam	1,832,418
4	Heathrow to Dublin	1,704,582
5	Heathrow to Frankfurt am Main	1,308,781
6	Heathrow to Los Angeles International	1,085,258
7	Heathrow to Tokyo (Norita)	987,349
8	Heathrow to Rome (Fiumicino)	986,426
9	Heathrow to Brussels	964,310
10	Heathrow to Zurich	892,887
11	Gatwick to Malaga	855,307
12	Heathrow to Milan (Linate)	852,129
13	Heathrow to San Francisco	837,237
14	Heathrow to Hong Kong	826,483
15	Heathrow to Toronto	776,638
16	Gatwick to Orlando	758,866
17	Manchester to Tenerife (Surreira Sofia)	742,207
18	Heathrow to Geneva	741,684
19	Heathrow to Munich	723,896
20	Heathrow to Chicago	711,914
21	Stansted to Dublin	711,230
22	Heathrow to Paris (Orly)	697,919
23	Heathrow to Stockholm (Arlonda)	696,463
24	Heathrow to Copenhagen	693,617
25	Heathrow to Washington	688,691
26	Heathrow to Düsseldorf	669,708
27	Gatwick to Tenerife (Surreira Sofia)	631,582
28	Gatwick to Faro	628,018
29	Heathrow to Madrid	615,345
30	Gatwick to Mallorca	583,054

UK Airports Ranked by Passenger Traffic

(N = Negligible)

Rank for 1997	Airport	1996		1997	
		Terminal[1] passengers (thousands)	% of passengers at UK airports	Terminal[1] passengers (thousands)	% of passengers at UK airports
1	Heathrow	55,047	41.4	56,928	40.1
2	Gatwick	23,216	17.5	25,628	18.0
3	Manchester	14,405	10.8	15,183	10.7
4	Glasgow	5,474	4.1	5,733	4.0
5	Birmingham	5,323	4.0	5,613	4.0
6	Stansted	4,476	3.4	5,115	3.6
7	Edinburgh	3,563	2.7	3,993	2.8
8	Luton	2,026	1.5	2,933	2.1
9	Newcastle	2,453	1.8	2,501	1.8
10	Aberdeen	2,307	1.7	2,493	1.8
11	Belfast International	2,369	1.8	2,383	1.7
12	East Midlands	1,862	1.4	1,819	1.3
13	Bristol	1,407	1.1	1,492	1.1
14	Belfast City	1,361	1.0	1,301	0.9
15	Leeds/Bradford	981	0.7	1,173	0.8
16	Cardiff Wales	1,017	0.8	1,078	0.8
17	London City	598	0.4	996	0.7
18	Liverpool	575	0.4	655	0.5
19	Isle of Man	569	0.4	652	0.5
20	Southampton	531	0.4	591	0.4
21	Prestwick	465	0.3	543	0.4
22	Teesside	433	0.3	497	0.4
23	Sumburgh	433	0.3	368	0.3
24	Inverness	274	0.2	340	0.2
25	Humberside	279	0.2	310	0.2
26	Norwich	268	0.2	260	0.2
27	Bournemouth	116	0.1	225	0.1
28	Exeter	195	0.1	212	0.1
29	Isles of Scilly (St Mary's)	121	0.1	130	0.1
30	Penzance Heliport	97	0.1	110	0.1
31	Scatsta	41	0.0	102	0.1
32	Plymouth	91	0.1	101	0.1
33	Stornoway	96	0.1	95	0.1
34	Kirkwall	95	0.1	88	0.1
35	Blackpool	81	0.1	83	0.1
36	Londonderrry	70	0.1	59	N
37	Benbecula	39	N	37	N
38	Isles of Scilly (Tresco)	24	N	27	N
39	Wick	30	N	25	N
40	Cambridge	32	N	22	N
41	Islay	19	N	19	N
42	Dundee	14	N	14	N
43	Campbeltown	3	N	9	N
44=	Barra	8	N	8	N
44=	Southend	4	N	8	N
46=	Biggin Hill	6	N	6	N
46=	Battersea Heliport	4	N	6	N
48	Tiree	5	N	5	N
49	Lerwick (Tingwall)	4	N	4	N
50=	Kent International	2	N	3	N
50=	Shoreham	3	N	3	N
52=	Coventry	3	N	2	N
52=	Gloucestershire	2	N	2	N
52=	Unst	50	N	2	N
55	Hawarden	N	N	1	N
56=	Lydd	N	N	N	N
56=	Carlisle	1	N	N	N
56=	Barrow-in-Furness	N	N	N	N
56=	Sheffield City	N	N	N	N
Total UK airports		132,969		141,989	

[1] Terminal refers to both embarking and disembarking passengers.

Domestic Passenger Traffic at UK Airports

This table provides statistics on domestic terminal (both embarking and disembarking) passenger traffic at UK airports as of August 1997. Domestic traffic is counted at both the airport of arrival and the airport of departure. The total of domestic traffic is, therefore, only a measure of airport activity. (– = not applicable.)

Airport		1996 Total	1997 Scheduled	1997 Charter	1997 Total	% change
London area airports	Gatwick	209,103	240,606	798	241,404	15
	Heathrow	669,138	660,428	1,046	661,474	-1
	London City	2,660	8,289	64	8,353	214
	Luton	46,105	68,788	638	69,426	51
	Southend	820	0	1,157	1,157	41
	Stansted	105,489	116,834	631	117,465	11
Total		1,033,315	1,094,945	4,334	1,099,279	6
Battersea Heliport		393	0	318	318	-19
Other UK airports	Aberdeen	144,596	133,683	17,414	151,097	4
	Barra	886	962	12	974	10
	Barrow-in-Furness	0	0	1	1	–
	Belfast City	133,999	128,514	709	129,223	-4
	Belfast International	167,628	185,177	30	185,207	10
	Benbecula	3,199	2,990	133	3,123	-2
	Biggin Hill	27	0	180	180	567
	Birmingham	90,458	98,425	1,608	100,033	11
	Blackpool	9,961	8,928	56	8,984	-10
	Bournemouth	1,903	103	2,362	2,465	30
	Bristol	25,240	31,887	410	32,297	28
	Cambridge	980	0	450	450	-54
	Campbeltown	903	775	69	844	-7
	Cardiff Wales	10,963	11,127	322	11,449	4
	Carlisle	8	0	38	38	375
	Coventry	66	0	47	47	-29
	Dundee	943	694	404	1,098	16
	East Midlands	42,443	36,236	1,023	37,259	-12
	Edinburgh	286,704	305,466	1,162	306,628	7
	Exeter	10,059	10,632	411	11,043	10
	Glasgow	271,069	288,841	1,321	290,162	7
	Gloucestershire	380	0	399	399	5
	Hawarden	0	0	0	0	–
	Humberside	3,420	2,078	1,392	3,470	1
	Inverness	27,960	38,235	690	38,925	39
	Islay	2,284	2,047	125	2,172	-5
	Isle of Man	62,752	66,946	165	67,111	7
	Isles of Scilly (St Mary's)	22,344	20,829	0	20,829	-7
	Isles of Scilly (Tresco)	0	4,097	0	4,097	–
	Kent International	345	0	317	317	-8
	Kirkwall	8,928	8,264	363	8,627	-3
	Leeds/Bradford	38,761	44,212	869	45,081	16
	Lerwick (Tingwall)	480	214	279	493	3
	Liverpool	32,686	32,590	947	33,537	3
	Londonderry	7,913	5,963	341	6,304	-20
	Lydd	16	0	12	12	-25
	Manchester	215,210	201,878	6,452	208,330	-3
	Newcastle	73,521	69,904	2,463	72,367	-2
	Norwich	7,184	6,594	34	6,628	-8
	Penzance Heliport	17,664	16,033	0	16,033	-9
	Plymouth	8,090	6,405	109	6,514	-19
	Prestwick	25,957	30,071	502	30,573	18
	Scatsta	4,486	0	4,247	4,247	-5
	Sheffield City	0	0	26	26	–
	Shoreham	242	0	136	136	-44
	Southampton	49,387	49,963	3,369	53,332	8
	Stornoway	8,036	8,195	35	8,230	2
	Sumburgh	24,033	10,699	9,457	20,156	-16
	Teesside	20,861	18,779	1,222	20,001	-4
	Tiree	568	515	3	518	-9
	Unst	104	146	0	146	40
	Wick	2,213	2,053	8	2061	-7
Total		1,867,860	1,891,150	62,124	1,953,274	5
Total reported UK airports	2,901,568	2,986,095	66,776	3,052,871	5	
Channel Islands airports	Alderney	13,747	11,797	34	11,831	-14
	Guernsey	88,908	94,790	1,838	96,628	9
	Jersey	199,266	184,831	26,677	211,508	6
Total		301,921	291,418	28,549	319,967	6

Source: Civil Aviation Authority, UK Airports: Monthly Statements of Movements, Passenger and Cargo, July 1997

Air Traffic between the UK and Abroad

This table shows the combined total of passenger arrivals and departures by country of embarkation or landing.

Country/Region	1986	1991	1996	Country/Region	1986	1991	1996
EC[1]				**Rest of world**			
Austria	381,000	845,000	1,161,000	USSR[3]	168,000	276,000	399,000
Belgium	986,000	1,352,000	1,925,000	Rest of Eastern Europe	375,000	805,000	1,565,000
Denmark	622,000	910,000	1,598,000	North Africa	734,000	604,000	1,148,000
France	3,667,000	5,915,000	6,399,000	South Africa[5]	395,000	614,000	1,043,000
Finland	206,000	343,000	618,000	Rest of Africa	859,000	927,000	969,000
Germany	3,820,000	5,112,000	6,939,000	Israel	445,000	416,000	885,000
Greece	3,349,000	3,459,000	3,589,000	Persian Gulf States	314,000	304,000	363,000
Ireland, Republic of	2,107,000	3,947,000	6,938,000	Saudi Arabia	296,000	255,000	357,000
Italy	2,714,000	3,076,000	4,941,000	United Arab Emirates	190,000	334,000	698,000
Luxembourg	106,000	141,000	161,000	Rest of Near and Middle East	364,000	314,000	605,000
Netherlands	2,312,000	3,159,000	4,941,000	USA	6,335,000	9,699,000	14,402,000
Portugal and Madeira[2]	2,044,000	2,418,000	2,674,000	Canada	1,501,000	1,846,000	2,543,000
Spain and Canary Islands	12,678,000	11,653,000	17,789,000	South America	106,000	286,000	466,000
Sweden	566,000	833,000	1,306,000	Central America	–	48,000	471,000
Total	35,558,000	43,163,000	60,979,000	Carribean	419,000	678,000	1,116,000
Other Western Europe				Australia	409,000	605,000	714,000
Norway	706,000	767,000	1,283,000	New Zealand	85,000	147,000	158,000
Switzerland	2,112,000	2,536,000	2,870,000	India	312,000	472,000	970,000
Yugoslavia[3]	899,000	258,000	173,000	Pakistan	211,000	237,000	340,000
Gibraltar	174,000	218,000	158,000	Rest of Indian sub-continent[6]	196,000	304,000	449,000
Cyprus	617,000	1,319,000	1,521,000	Japan	357,000	821,000	1,348,000
Turkey	257,000	525,000	2,368,000	Hong Kong	516,000	700,000	1,023,000
Malta	746,000	1,012,000	948,000	Singapore	429,000	503,000	765,000
Other[4]	72,000	99,000	161,000	Thailand	144,000	259,000	441,000
				Rest of Asia	252,000	526,000	1,162,000
Total	5,583,000	6,735,000	9,481,000				
Total Western Europe	41,142,000	49,899,000	70,460,000	*Total rest of world*	15,411,000	21,981,000	34,400,000
				All air passenger movements	56,554,000	71,879,000	104,861,000

[1] Austria, Finland, and Sweden joined the EC in 1995, but are included in the EC total for all years to show the time series on a consistent basis.
[2] This includes the Azores and Cape Verde Islands.
[3] Former constituent states.
[4] This includes Iceland and the Faroe Islands.
[5] This includes Botswana, Zimbabwe, and the Republic of South Africa.
[6] This includes the Indian Ocean Islands.

Source: Department of the Environment, Transport and the Regions, © Crown copyright

Aircraft Near-Miss Incidents in UK Airspace

Aircraft type	Risk level	1985	1986	1987	1988	1989	1990	1991	1992	1993	1994	1995
Civil and military aircraft	risk of collision	14	21	20	33	30	25	22	25	15	16	17
	safety not assured	52	50	58	59	55	67	70	51	79	62	57
	Total dangerous incidents	66	71	78	92	85	92	92	76	94	78	74
	no risk of collision	77	104	113	120	118	152	119	141	123	137	134
	TOTAL	143	175	191	212	203	244	211	217	217	215	208
Commercial air transport aircraft	risk of collision	1	4	2	4	2	6	1	5	3	5	3
	safety not assured	11	8	9	11	9	18	19	11	17	20	21
	Total dangerous incidents	12	12	11	15	11	24	20	16	20	25	24
	no risk of collision	37	49	44	58	51	78	67	77	56	57	71
	TOTAL	49	61	55	73	62	102	87	93	76	82	95

Source: Department of the Environment, Transport and the Regions; Transport Statistics Great Britain, © Crown copyright

Casualties Caused by Aviation Accidents in UK Airspace

Aircraft and casualty categories				1986	1987	1988	1989	1990	1991	1992	1993	1994	1995	1996
Casualties caused by accidents involving UK registered aircraft in UK airspace	Airline (includes air taxis)	Fixed-wing – crew	Fatal	1	2	1	0	0	0	0	2	1	3	1
			Total	2	7	1	8	2	2	1	5	2	3	3
		Fixed-wing – passengers	Fatal	0	0	0	47	0	0	0	0	0	9	0
			Total	14	0	0	118	1	0	1	0	2	14	2
		Total fixed-wing[1]		16	7	2	126	4	2	4	6	4	18	7
		Rotary-wing – crew	Fatal	2	0	0	1	2	0	2	0	0	0	0
			Total	3	0	0	1	2	1	3	1	0	0	1
		Rotary-wing – passengers	Fatal	43	0	0	4	4	0	11	0	0	0	0
			Total	45	1	1	5	11	4	19	0	0	0	2
		Total rotary-wing[1]		48	1	1	6	13	5	24	1	1	0	3
	Other (general aviation)	Crew	Fatal	13	21	11	14	18	16	15	13	18	10	25
			Total	38	42	53	51	63	59	49	51	38	32	49
		Passengers	Fatal	9	19	4	4	13	5	8	9	9	7	10
			Total	19	20	21	20	39	29	37	33	25	12	29
		Total		57	67	79	72	103	88	86	91	63	45	80
		TOTAL[1]	Fatal	68	42	16	71	39	21	38	25	28	29	37
			Total	121	75	82	204	120	95	114	98	68	63	90
Casualties caused by accidents involving aircraft registered overseas in UK airspace	Airline	Fixed-wing – crew	Fatal	0	0	16	0	0	0	0	0	5	0	0
			Total	0	0	16	0	1	0	1	0	5	0	0
		Fixed-wing – passengers	Fatal	0	0	243	0	0	0	0	0	0	0	0
			Total	13	0	243	1	29	0	0	0	0	0	0
		Total fixed-wing[1]		13	0	275	2	33	0	1	0	6	2	0
	Other (general aviation)	Crew	Fatal	1	4	0	1	3	1	1	0	2	0	2
			Total	1	4	0	2	4	1	3	0	5	0	4
		Passengers	Fatal	0	5	0	0	0	0	2	0	2	0	0
			Total	2	5	0	2	0	0	4	0	3	0	4
		Total[1]		3	11	0	4	4	1	7	0	8	0	9
		TOTAL[1]	Fatal	1	11	270	1	3	1	3	0	9	0	2
			Total	16	11	275	6	37	1	8	0	14	2	9

[1] These totals include 'third-party' casualties on the ground, not shown separately.

Source: Department of the Environment, Transport, and the Regions, Transport Statistics Great Britain, © Crown copyright

Air Distances between UK Cities

(– = not applicable.)

City	Aberdeen		Belfast		Birmingham		Bristol		Cambridge		Cardiff		Carlisle		Edinburgh		Glasgow		Liverpool	
	km	mi	km	mi	km	mi	km	mi	km	mi	km	mi	km	mi	km	mi	km	mi	km	mi
Aberdeen	–	–	372	231	520	323	633	393	567	352	631	392	256	159	151	94	196	122	418	260
Belfast	372	231	–	–	356	221	415	258	482	300	389	242	196	122	229	142	176	109	232	144
Birmingham	520	323	356	221	–	–	122	76	142	88	139	86	277	172	393	244	405	252	128	80
Bristol	633	393	415	258	122	76	–	–	204	127	43	27	383	238	499	310	500	311	221	137
Cambridge	567	352	482	300	142	88	204	127	–	–	241	150	361	224	467	290	495	308	250	155
Cardiff	631	392	389	242	139	86	43	27	241	150	–	–	377	234	492	306	487	303	214	133
Carlisle	256	159	196	122	277	172	383	238	361	224	377	234	–	–	166	103	135	84	163	101
Edinburgh	151	94	229	142	393	244	499	310	467	290	492	306	166	103	–	–	66	41	279	173
Glasgow	196	122	176	109	405	252	500	311	495	308	487	303	135	84	66	41	–	–	281	175
Liverpool	418	260	232	144	128	80	221	137	250	155	214	133	163	101	279	173	281	175	–	–
London	640	398	519	322	164	102	171	106	80	50	214	133	421	262	532	331	554	344	290	180
Londonderry	403	250	101	63	455	283	506	314	583	362	477	296	282	175	281	175	216	134	333	207
Newcastle	240	149	283	176	283	176	401	249	332	206	404	251	86	53	144	89	192	119	199	124
Norwich	546	339	525	326	219	136	297	185	94	58	333	207	375	233	468	291	508	316	301	187
Nottingham	468	291	362	225	75	47	195	121	122	76	214	133	243	151	354	220	377	234	132	82
Oxford	602	374	444	276	92	57	98	61	106	66	138	86	366	227	481	299	496	308	220	137
Plymouth	761	473	482	300	276	172	159	99	357	222	138	86	505	314	617	383	605	376	344	214
Portsmouth	712	442	536	333	198	123	130	81	180	112	169	105	475	295	590	367	602	374	323	201
Sheffield	421	262	321	199	104	65	226	140	170	106	238	148	193	120	304	189	327	203	100	62
York	372	231	322	200	160	99	282	175	201	125	294	183	164	102	266	165	298	185	130	81

City	London		Londonderry		Newcastle		Norwich		Nottingham		Oxford		Plymouth		Portsmouth		Sheffield		York	
	km	mi	km	mi	km	mi	km	mi	km	mi	km	mi	km	mi	km	mi	km	mi	km	mi
Aberdeen	640	398	403	250	240	149	546	339	468	291	602	374	761	473	712	442	421	262	372	231
Belfast	519	322	101	63	283	176	525	326	362	225	444	276	482	300	536	333	321	199	322	200
Birmingham	164	102	455	283	283	176	219	136	75	47	92	57	276	172	198	123	104	65	160	99
Bristol	171	106	506	314	401	249	297	185	195	121	98	61	159	99	130	81	226	140	282	175
Cambridge	80	50	583	362	332	206	94	58	122	76	106	66	357	222	180	112	170	106	201	125
Cardiff	214	133	477	296	404	251	333	207	214	133	138	86	138	86	169	105	238	148	294	183
Carlisle	421	262	282	175	86	53	375	233	243	151	366	227	505	314	475	295	193	120	164	102
Edinburgh	532	331	281	175	144	89	468	291	354	220	481	299	617	383	590	367	304	189	266	165
Glasgow	554	344	216	134	192	119	508	316	377	234	496	308	605	376	602	374	327	203	298	185
Liverpool	290	180	333	207	199	124	301	187	132	82	220	137	344	214	323	201	100	62	130	81
London	–	–	619	385	402	250	159	99	178	111	83	52	307	191	106	66	228	142	269	167
Londonderry	619	385	–	–	367	228	626	389	463	288	543	337	556	345	631	392	422	262	421	262
Newcastle	402	250	367	228	–	–	325	202	228	142	362	225	539	335	472	293	182	113	133	83
Norwich	159	99	626	389	325	202	–	–	170	106	200	124	451	280	265	165	205	127	212	132
Nottingham	178	111	463	288	228	142	170	106	–	–	136	85	351	218	245	152	50	31	96	60
Oxford	83	52	543	337	362	225	200	124	136	85	–	–	251	156	110	68	181	112	232	144
Plymouth	307	191	556	345	539	335	451	280	351	218	251	156	–	–	219	136	376	234	432	268
Portsmouth	106	66	631	392	472	293	265	165	245	152	110	68	219	136	–	–	291	181	341	212
Sheffield	228	142	422	262	182	113	205	127	50	31	181	112	376	234	291	181	–	–	56	35
York	269	167	421	262	133	83	212	132	96	60	232	144	432	268	341	212	56	35	–	–

World Shipping

Merchant Fleets of the World

1997

Country of registry	Total number of ships	Number of combination passenger and cargo ships	Number of general cargo ships	Number of bulk carriers	Number of tankers
Antigua and Barbuda	378	0	264	9	11
Bahamas	954	47	443	142	241
Brazil	188	1	31	53	83
Bulgaria	105	1	44	34	14
China: mainland	1,513	33	791	354	233
Cyprus	1,476	18	610	555	165
Denmark	315	0	163	11	71
Egypt	110	1	69	18	14
Germany	404	11	172	1	31
Greece	874	19	132	406	286
Honduras	256	3	208	10	28
Hong Kong	223	0	45	124	15
India	305	2	64	140	83
Indonesia	446	9	287	18	118
Iran	123	0	45	47	28
Italy	352	17	503	36	194
Japan	744	15	148	162	299
Korea, South	449	0	151	124	105
Liberia	1,587	38	269	461	642
Malaysia	303	0	121	50	96
Malta	1,113	9	441	337	265
Netherlands	4,454	9	302	8	71
Norway (NIS)	626	14	177	102	285
Panama	3,988	54	1,528	1,086	893
Philippines	534	6	199	232	65
Poland	125	1	47	69	4
Romania	223	0	161	39	12
Russia	1,655	10	1,203	129	271
St Vincent and the Grenadines	683	1	420	121	99
Singapore	753	1	166	126	331
Spain	81	0	29	1	16
Sweden	198	4	88	10	88
Taiwan	202	0	40	55	19
Thailand	288	1	160	35	82
Turkey	516	7	238	177	74
UK	140	20	27	6	60
Ukraine	415	8	326	21	29
USA	495	15	147	15	173
Vanuatu	98	0	48	32	12
World total [1]	26,858	427	11,471	5,694	6,384

[1] This total includes other ships and is not simply a total of all ships accounted for in this table.

Source: Marine Administration, US Department of Transportation

Merchant ship in port: The total number of merchant ships

The Shortest Navigable Distances between Selected World Ports

From	To	Distance		From	To	Distance	
		Nautical mi	Statute mi			Nautical mi	Statute mi
Cape Town, South Africa	Jakarta, Indonesia	6,067	5,276	New York (NY), USA	Barcelona, Spain	4,271	3,714
					Cape Town, South Africa	7,804	6,786
	Melbourne, Australia	7,590	6,600		Cherbourg, France	3,604	3,134
	Singapore	6,456	5,614		Copenhagen, Denmark	4,278	3,720
Colón, Panama	Buenos Aires, Argentina	6,193	5,385		Galveston (TX) USA	2,225	1,935
	Galveston (TX), USA	1,734	1,508		Glasgow, UK	3,692	3,210
	Gibraltar	4,982	4,332		Hamburg, Germany	4,202	3,654
	Hamburg, Germany	5,820	5,061		Havana, Cuba	1,364	1,186
	Helsinki, Finland	6,866	5,970		Helsinki, Finland	4,896	4,257
	Lagos, Nigeria	5,808	5,050		Oslo, Norway	4,191	3,644
	Lisbon, Portugal	4,775	4,152		Piraeus, Greece	5,391	4,688
	Oslo, Norway	5,811	5,053		Southampton, UK	3,644	3,169
	Piraeus, Greece	6,623	5,759	Panama, Panama	Jakarta, Indonesia	12,193	10,603
	Port Said, Egypt	7,189	6,251	Port Said, Egypt	Ho Chi Minh City, Vietnam	6,537	5,684
	St John's, Newfoundland	3,099	2,695		Hong Kong	7,462	6,489
	Southampton, UK	5,262	4,576		Manila, Philippines	7,320	6,365
Montreal, Canada	Algiers, Algeria	4,418	3,842		Melbourne, Australia	9,069	7,886
	Barcelona, Spain	4,530	3,939		Singapore	5,790	5,035
	Cape Town, South Africa	8,186	7,118		Yokohama, Japan	9,113	7,924
	Gibraltar	3,943	3,429	San Francisco (CA), USA	Bombay, India	11,263	9,794
	Halifax, Nova Scotia	1,029	895				
	Havana, Cuba	3,825	3,326		Calcutta, India	10,792	9,384
	Istanbul, Turkey	6,010	5,226		Colón, Panama	3,778	3,285
	Kingston, Jamaica	3,759	3,269	Vancouver, Canada	Calcutta, India	10,036	8,727
	Lagos, Nigeria	7,481	6,505		Melbourne, Australia	8,470	7,365
	Marseilles, France	4,733	4,116				
	Naples, Italy	5,067	4,406				
	Oslo, Norway	4,551	3,957				
	Piraeus, Greece	5,584	4,856				
	Port Said, Egypt	6,150	5,348				
	Southampton, UK	3,907	3,397				

Source: Defense Mapping Agency, US

Notable Shipwrecks and Disappearances at Sea

Date	Vessel	Location	Fatalities
Atlantic Ocean and surrounding seas			
6 or 7 September 1622	at least 12 ships of the Tierra Firme Armada and the New Spain Fleet	wrecked by hurricane in the Florida Keys	thousands
22 August 1711	eight English transports	wrecked in storm at Egg Island, Labrador	around 2,000
1740	*Invencible*, galleon	struck by lightning in Havana harbour and exploded	unknown
6 September 1776	100 merchant vessels	wrecked by hurricane at Point Bay, Martinique	around 6,000
9 October 1780	seven Dutch ships	wrecked by hurricane at St Eustatius, Lesser Antilles	around 5,000
September 1788	at least 50 French vessels	wrecked by hurricane at Martinique, Lesser Antilles	unknown
22 December 1810	*Minotaur*, British frigate	lost off a reef off the coast of the Netherlands	570
26 February 1852	*Birkenhead*, British frigate	struck a rock and sank off Cape Town, South Africa	455
29 September 1853	*Annie Jane*, immigrant ship	lost off the Hebrides, UK	348
27 September 1854	*Arctic*, liner, and *Vesta*, French steamer	collided off Cape Race, Newfoundland	322
12 September 1857	*Central America*, American mail steamship	sank off Florida coast	427
25 March 1865	*General Lyon*, steamship	caught fire off Cape Hatteras, North Carolina	400
5 November 1872	*Marie Celeste*, US half-brig	abandoned in the Atlantic Ocean	unknown
22 January 1873	*Northfleet*, British steamer	foundered off Dungeness, UK	300
1 April 1873	*Atlantic*, British steamer	wrecked off Nova Scotia, Canada	585
23 November 1873	*Ville du Havre*, French steamer, and *Loch Earn*, British sailing ship	collided off south coast, UK	226
7 May 1875	*Schiller*, German steamer	wrecked off the Scilly Isles	312
24 March 1878	*Eurydice*, British frigate	sank off the Isle of Wight	398
19 January 1883	*Cimbria*, German steamer and *Sultan*, British steamer	collided in the North Sea	389
17 March 1891	*Utopia*, liner, and a battleship	collided in the Bay of Gilbraltar	576
30 January 1895	*Elbe*, German steamer and *Craithie*, British steamer	collided in the North Sea	332
15 February 1898	*Maine*, US battleship	blown up in Havana Harbour	260
4 July 1898	*La Bourgogne*, French steamer, and *Cromartyshire*, British sailing ship	collided off Nova Scotia, Canada	549
26 November 1898	*Portland*, US steamer	wrecked off Cape Cod, USA	157

Notable Shipwrecks and Disappearances at Sea (continued)

Date	Vessel	Location	Fatalities
28 June 1904	Norge, Danish steamer	wrecked on Rockall Island, Scotland	651
4 August 1906	Sirio, Italian steamer	wrecked off Cape Palos, Spain	350
14–15 April 1912	Titanic, British steamer	sank after hitting iceberg in the North Atlantic	1,517
7 May 1915	Lusitania, British (Cunard Line) steamer	torpedoed and sunk by German submarine off Ireland	1,198
9 July 1917	Vanguard, British battleship	Scapa Flow, Scotland	804
6 December 1917	Mont Blanc, French ammunition ship, and Imo, Belgian steamer	collided in Halifax Harbor, Canada	1,600
9 September 1919	Valbanera, Spanish steamer	lost off Florida coast	500
26 August 1922	Niitaka, Japanese cruiser	sank in storm off Kamchatka, former USSR	300
25 October 1927	Principessa Mafalda, Italian steamer	blew up, sank off Porto Seguro, Brazil	314
12 November 1928	Vestris, British steamer	sank in gale off Virginia	113
8 September 1934	Morro Castle, US steamer	burned off Asbury Park (NJ), USA	134
23 May 1939	Squalus, US submarine	sank off Portsmouth (NH), USA	26
1 June 1939	Thetis, British submarine	sank in Liverpool Bay, England	99
18 February 1942	Truxtun, US destroyer, and Pollux, cargo ship	ran aground and sank off Newfoundland, Canada	204
2 October 1942	Curaçao, British cruiser	sank after collision with liner Queen Mary, Atlantic Ocean	338
16 April 1947	Grandcamp, French freighter	exploded in Texas City (TX), USA	510
17 September 1949	Noronic, Canadian Great Lakes Cruiser	burned at Toronto dock, Canada	130
26 April 1952	Hobson, US destroyer, and Wasp, aircraft carrier	collided in the Atlantic Ocean	176
31 January 1953	Princess Victoria, British ferry	sank off northern Irish coast	133
25 July 1956	Andrea Doria, Italian liner, and Stockholm, Swedish liner	collided off Nantucket (MA), USA	52
10 April 1963	Thresher, US Navy atomic submarine	sank in the North Atlantic	129
13 November 1965	Yarmouth Castle, Panamanian registered cruise ship	burned and sank off Nassau, Bahamas	90
late May, 1968	Scorpion, US nuclear submarine	sank in the Atlantic Ocean near the Azores	99
11 January 1977	Grand Zenith, Panamanian-registered tanker	sank off Cape Cod (MA), USA	38
6 March 1987	Herald of Free Enterprise, British ferry	capsized off Zeebrugge, Belgium	188
17 February 1993	Neptune, ferry	capsized off Port-au-Prince, Haiti	>500
28 September 1994	Estonia, ferry	sank in the Baltic Sea when water entered bow door	1,049

Pacific Ocean and surrounding seas

Date	Vessel	Location	Fatalities
4 August 1846	Cataraqui, immigrant ship	ran aground in a storm in the Bass Strait between Australia and Tasmania	414
4 November 1875	Pacific, US steamer	sank after collision off Cape Flattery (WA), USA	236
19 September 1890	Ertogrul, Turkish frigate	foundered off Japan	587
23 March 1908	Matsu Maru, Japanese steamer	sank after collision near Hakodate, Japan	300
28 September 1912	Kichemaru, Japanese steamer	sank off Japanese coast	1,000
29 August 1916	Hsin Yu, Chinese steamer	sank off Chinese coast	1,000
25 April 1918	Kiang-Kwan, Chinese steamer	sank after collision off Hankow, China	500
12 July 1918	Kawachi, Japanese battleship	blew up in Tokayama Bay, Japan	500
25 October 1918	Princess Sophia, Canadian steamer	sank off Alaskan coast	398
18 March 1921	Hong Koh, steamer	sank near Swatow	1,000
3 December 1948	Kiangya, Chinese refugee ship	wrecked in explosion south of Shanghai, China	>1,100
November 1949	Chinese army evacuation ship	exploded and sank off South Manchuria	6,000
26 September 1954	Toyo Maru, Japanese ferry	sank in Tsugaru Strait, Japan	2,750
10 February 1964	Voyager, Australian destroyer, and Melbourne, Australian aircraft carrier	collided off New South Wales, Australia	82
15 December 1970	Namyong-Ho, South Korean ferry	sank in the Korea Strait	308
27 January 1981	Tamponas II, Indonesian passenger ship	caught fire and sank in the Java Sea	580
20 December 1987	Dona Paz, Philippine ferry, and Victor, oil tanker	collided in the Tablas Strait, Philippines	3,000
10 October 1993	West Sea Ferry, ferry	capsized during storm in the Yellow Sea near South Korea	285

Indian Ocean and surrounding seas

Date	Vessel	Location	Fatalities
1 February 1807	Blenheim, 74-gun war ship	wrecked by hurricane near the island of Rodriguez	≈600
1 February 1807	Java	wrecked by hurricane near the island of Rodriguez	280
15 November 1887	Wah Yeung, British steamer	burned at sea, Indian Ocean	400
17 February 1890	Duburg, British steamer	wrecked in China Sea	400
28 July 1909	Waratah, British steamer	vanished in Indian Ocean	300
December 1944	3 US Third Fleet destroyers	sank during typhoon in the Philippine Sea	790
8 July 1961	Save, Portuguese ship	ran aground off Mozambique	259
8 April 1962	Dara, British liner	sank when time-bomb exploded, Persian Gulf	236
2 June 1969	Evans, US destroyer	cut in half by Australian carrier Melbourne, in the South China Sea	74
25 December 1976	Patria, Egyptian liner	caught fire and sank in the Red Sea	≈100
14 December 1991	Salem Express, ferry	rammed coral reef off Egyptian coast	462

Notable Shipwrecks and Disappearances at Sea (*continued*)

Date	Vessel	Location	Fatalities
Mediterranean sea			
17 March 1800	*Queen Charlotte,* British frigate	burned off Livorno, Italy	700
23 October 1850	*Neiri-Shevket,* Turkish warship	exploded at Constantinople	>500
18 December 1878	*Byzantin,* French steamer	sank after collision, Dardanelles, Turkey	210
17 March 1891	*Utopia,* British steamer, and *Anson,* British ironclad	collided off Gibraltar coast	562
11 March 1895	*Reina Regenta,* Spanish cruiser	foundered off Gibraltar	400
9 February 1910	*General Chanzy,* French steamer	wrecked off Minorca, Spain	93
25 September 1911	*Liberté,* French battleship	exploded at Toulon, France	285
26 February 1916	*Provence,* French cruiser	sank in the Mediterranean sea	3,100
17 January 1919	*Chaonia,* French steamer	lost in the Straits of Messina, Italy	460
19 January 1947	*Himera,* Greek steamer	sank after hitting a mine off Athens	392
25 January 1968	*Dakar,* Israeli submarine	vanished in the Mediterranean Sea	69
27 January 1968	*Minerve,* French submarine	vanished in the Mediterranean Sea	52
4 March 1970	*Eurydice,* French submarine	sank near Toulon, France	57
10 April 1991	auto ferry and oil tanker	collided outside Livorno harbour, Italy	140
26–27 April 1865	*Sultana,* US side-wheeled steamer	exploded and burned near Memphis, Tennessee	>1,500
World waterways and rivers			
3 September 1878	*Princess Alice,* British steamer	sank after collision in the River Thames, UK	645
24 May 1881	*Victoria,* Canadian steamer	capsized in Thames River, Canada	200
15 June 1904	*General Slocum,* excursion steamer	burned in Hudson River, New York (NY), USA	1,030
29 May 1914	*Empress of Ireland,* British steamer, and Norwegian collier	collided in St Lawrence River, Canada	1,014
24 July 1915	*Eastland,* excursion steamer	capsized in Chicago River	852
14 July 1957	*Eshghabad,* Soviet ship	ran aground in Caspian Sea	270
29 July 1967	*Forrestal,* US aircraft carrier	caught fire off North Vietnam	134
26 September 1974	Soviet destroyer	burned and sank in the Black Sea	>200
20 October 1976	*George Prince,* ferryboat and *Frosta,* Norwegian tanker	collided on the Mississippi River at Luling (LA), USA	77
25 May 1983	*10th of Ramadan,* Nile steamer	caught fire and sank in Lake Nasser, Egypt	357
31 August 1986	*Admiral Nakhimov,* Soviet passenger ship, and *Pyotr Vasev,* Soviet freighter	collided in the Black Sea	398
6 August 1988	Indian ferry	capsized on the Ganges River, India	>400
20 August 1989	*Bowbelle,* British barge, and *Marchioness,* British pleasure cruiser	collided on the River Thames, UK	56
10 September 1989	Romanian pleasure boat and barge	collided on the Danube River, Austria, Hungary, Romania, and Serbia	161
21 May 1996	*Bukoba,* ferry	sank in Lake Victoria, Uganda, Kenya, and Tanzania	500

Major Navigation Canals and Waterways of the World

Canal	Route	Year opened	Length	
			km	mi
Karakum Canal, Turkmenistan	Caspian Sea inland	1954–81	1,100	683
Volga-Baltic, Russia	River Volga to Baltic Sea	1964	850	528
New York State Barge Canal (Erie Canal), USA	Lake Erie to Hudson River	1918	873	520
Rajasthan Canal, India	River Indus (Punjab) to Myajlan	1955	649	403
St Lawrence Seaway, Canada–USA[1]	Montreal to Lake Ontario	1959	304	189
Main-Danube Canal, Germany	Main River (Bamberg) to Danube River	1992	171	106
Suez Canal, Egypt	Mediterranean Sea to Red Sea	1869	162	101
Albert Canal, Belgium	River Meuse (Maes) to River Scheld	1939	129	80
Volga-Don, Russia	River Volga to Black Sea	1952	101	63
Kiel Canal, Germany	North Sea to Baltic Sea	1895	99	62
Alfonso XIII Canal, Spain	Seville to Gulf of Cadiz	1926	85	53
Panama Canal, Panama	Pacific Ocean to Caribbean Sea	1914	81	50
Sabine-Neches Waterway, USA[2]	Beaumont to Gulf of Mexico	1916	72	45
Houston Ship Canal, USA	Houston to Gulf of Mexico	1914	69	43
Manchester Ship Canal, UK	Manchester to Mersey estuary	1894	58	36
Welland Canal, Canada	Lake Ontario to Lake Erie	1933	44	28
North Sea Canal (Noordzeekanaal), Netherlands	Amsterdam to Ijmuiden on the North Sea	1876	27	17
Chesapeake and Delaware Canal, USA	Chesapeake Bay to Delaware River	1829	22	14

[1] The canalized section of the St Lawrence Seaway enables shipping to sail 3,769 km/2,342 mi from the North Atlantic up the St Lawrence estuary and through the Great Lakes to Duluth (MN).

[2] This is part of a series of artificial and natural channels, collectively called the Gulf Intercoastal Waterway with a total length of 1,770 km/1,100 mi, providing a discontinuous navigation, linking the Texan Gulf coast ports with the Mississippi Delta and Florida.

UK Shipping

The UK Fleet's Proportion of World Tonnage

Data are given as percentages of the world total, which includes the US reserve fleet, estimated at 2.1 million gt (2.87 million dwt), and US Great Lakes ships, amounting to 0.9 million gt (1.7 million dwt), respectively, all as of 1 January 1997. Dates are mid-year values except for 1997 which is as of 1 January.

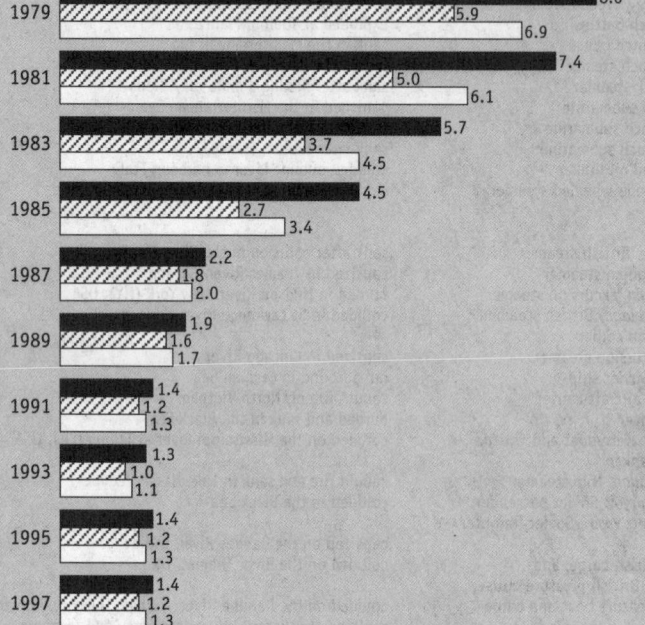

Source: Department of the Environment, Transport and the Regions, Transport Statistics Report: Merchant Fleet Statistics 1996 © Crown copyright

Ports Ranked by Cargo Tonnage in the UK

This table represents all foreign and domestic traffic in 1996.

Rank	Port	Traffic (tonnes)	(%)
1	London	52,869,000	9.6
2	Grimsby and Immingham	46,813,000	8.5
3	Forth	45,583,000	8.3
4	Tees and Hartlepool	44,639,000	8.1
5	Sullom Voe	38,162,000	6.9
6	Milford Haven	36,587,000	6.6
7	Southampton	34,193,000	6.2
8	Liverpool	30,874,000	5.6
9	Felixstowe	25,778,000	4.7
10	Medway	14,111,000	2.6
11	Dover	13,224,000	2.4
12	Belfast	12,480,000	2.3
13	Port Talbot	12,208,000	2.2
14	Orkneys	11,448,000	2.1
15	Hull	9,721,000	1.8
16	Manchester	8,529,000	1.5
17	Clyde	7,201,000	1.3
18	Rivers Hull and Humber	6,464,000	1.2
19	Bristol	5,907,000	1.1
20	Glensanda	4,486,000	0.8
	All above ports	461,277,000	83.8
	Other major UK ports	51,556,000	9.4
	Other UK ports	38,410,000	7.0
	All UK ports	551,243,000	

Source: Department of the Environment, Transport and the Regions, Port Statistics 1996, © Crown copyright

Accompanied Passenger Vehicles on Ships in UK Ports

(N/A = not available. In thousands.)

Vehicle	Route		1988	1989	1990	1991	1992	1993	1994	1995[1]	1996
Cars	overseas route by ship	France	2,020	2,642	2,900	3,329	3,594	4,058	4,575	4,233	4,147
		Belgium	440	492	482	514	463	413	404	400	279
		Netherlands	335	346	356	399	413	410	328	331	353
		Germany	26	26	29	34	35	44	48	46	46
		Ireland, Republic of	413	507	551	611	577	621	634	667	710
		Denmark	48	52	64	44	39	32	39	34	27
		Scandinavia and Baltic	67	44	32	56	52	53	42	49	53
		Spain and Portugal	28	38	45	47	40	70	79	79	83
		Total	3,378	4,148	4,460	5,034	5,213	5,701	6,148	5,838	5,700
	hovercraft services	France	262	245	230	189	109	158	181	169	233
		All overseas routes	3,640	4,393	4,690	5,223	5,322	5,859	6,330	6,008	5,933
	coastwise route by ship[2]	Northern Ireland	612	707	734	760	870	977	1060	1178	1101
		Isle of Man	58	69	72	75	71	70	125	70	76
		Orkneys and Shetlands	80	97	102	100	106	99	103	107	119
		Channel Islands	74	95	100	96	86	98	81	85	122
		other	107	119	124	126	124	121	122	126	137
		Total	932	1,088	1,131	1,159	1,256	1,365	1,490	1,566	1,555
		Total cars	4,572	5,481	5,821	6,382	6,578	7,223	7,820	7,574	7,488
Coaches	overseas route by ship	France	119	136	142	142	168	167	184	182	175
		Belgium	20	18	19	17	15	13	13	13	11
		Netherlands	11	11	12	13	14	13	11	9	9
		Germany	N/A	N/A	N/A	N/A	N/A	N/A	N/A	N/A	N/A
		Ireland, Republic of	9	9	10	10	11	12	14	15	17
		Denmark	1	1	1	N/A	N/A	N/A	N/A	N/A	N/A
		Scandinavia and Baltic	1	1	N/A	1	1	1	1	N/A	N/A
		Spain and Portugal	N/A	N/A	N/A	N/A	N/A	N/A	1	1	1
		Total	160	177	185	182	208	207	223	221	214
	hovercraft services	France	1	1	N/A	N/A	N/A	N/A	N/A	N/A	N/A
		All overseas routes	161	177	185	182	208	207	223	221	214
	coastwise route by ship[2]	Northern Ireland	23	30	33	20	12	19	19	12	13
		Isle of Man	N/A	N/A	N/A	N/A	N/A	N/A	N/A	1	N/A
		Orkneys and Shetlands	N/A	N/A	N/A	N/A	N/A	N/A	N/A	N/A	N/A
		Channel Islands	N/A	N/A	N/A	N/A	N/A	N/A	N/A	N/A	N/A
		other	N/A	N/A	N/A	1	1	1	1	1	1
		Total	23	31	33	22	13	21	22	14	16
		Total coaches	185	208	218	204	222	228	245	235	229

[1] From 1995, estimates for vehicles at smaller ports are included.
[2] Traffic to the Isle of Wight is not included.

Source: Department of the Environment, Transport and the Regions, Transport Statistics Report © Crown copyright

International Sea Passenger Movements to and from the UK

(N/A = not available. In thousands.)

Country/region	1988	1989	1990	1991	1992	1993	1994	1995	1996
Republic of Ireland, European continent, and Mediterranean sea area									
Belgium	3,232	3,444	3,588	3,510	3,239	2,958	2,878	2,480	2,053
France	15,975	19,246	20,104	21,248	22,874	24,643	27,224	25,164	25,470
Ireland, Republic of	2,434	2,737	2,773	3,037	3,123	3,407	3,478	3,632	3,887
Netherlands	2,218	2,365	2,524	2,610	2,693	2,550	1,987	1,837	1,956
other EC[1]	815	855	922	886	838	1,010	1,052	1,056	1,014
other countries	159	161	177	130	146	145	148	188	191
Total	24,833	28,807	30,088	31,419	32,912	34,713	36,767	34,355	34,571
Rest of world									
USA	30.7	29.3	18.0	29.6	22.5	33.7	31.1	29.9	20.4
Canada	N/A	N/A	N/A	N/A	0.5	0.1	N/A	N/A	N/A
Australia	1.1	0.4	1.6	1.7	1.6	1.0	1.0	1.2	1.0
New Zealand	0.3	0.2	0.3	0.4	0.1	0.2	0.3	0.2	0.4
South Africa	0.6	0.1	0.8	0.8	0.8	0.7	0.6	0.6	0.4
West Africa	0.3	0.2	0.3	0.5	0.1	0.2	0.2	0.1	0.1
British West Indies and Bermuda	N/A	N/A	N/A	0.1	N/A	N/A	N/A	N/A	0.3
other countries	0.6	1.0	0.5	0.9	0.7	1.1	1.1	0.6	1.3
Total	33.6	31.2	21.6	33.9	26.5	37.0	34.2	32.6	23.9
Pleasure cruises beginning and/or ending at UK seaports[2]	127	129	153	172	138	193	236	207	233
Total sea passenger movements	24,994	28,968	30,263	31,625	33,076	34,943	37,038	34,595	34,828

[1] Finland and Sweden have been included in this grouping throughout even though they did not join the EC until 1995.

[2] Cruise passengers, like other passengers, are counted at both departure and arrival if their journeys begin and end at a UK seaport.

Source: Department of the Environment, Transport and the Regions, Transport Statistics Report: Port Statistics 1996 © Crown copyright

Number of UK-Owned Ships

This chart shows the total number of UK-owned ships of 100 gt and over at 31 December 1996.

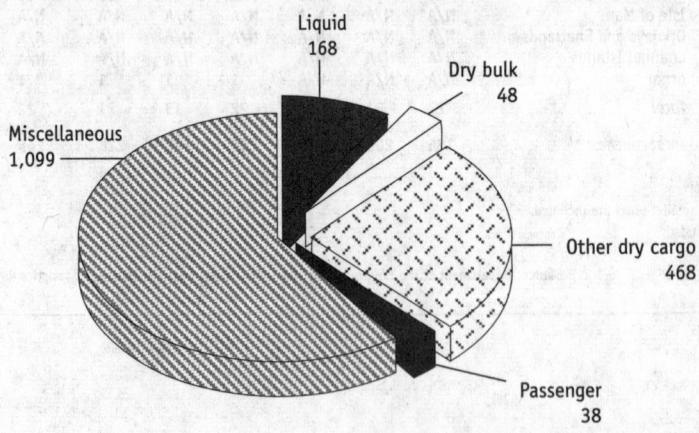

Liquid
168

Dry bulk
48

Miscellaneous
1,099

Other dry cargo
468

Passenger
38

Source: Department of the Environment, Transport and the Regions, Transport Statistics Report: Merchant Fleet Statistics 1996 © Crown copyright

Traffic on Major Rivers and Inland Waterways in the UK

(N = nil or negligible. In billions of tonne-kilometres.)

River/waterway	Internal traffic						Seagoing traffic					
	1991	1992	1993	1994	1995	1996[1]	1991	1992	1993	1994	1995	1996[1]
Goods Moved												
River Thames	0.07	0.08	0.08	0.10	0.09	0.07	0.85	0.82	0.79	0.83	0.70	0.57
River Medway	N	N	N	N	N	N	0.08	0.05	0.05	0.06	0.06	0.04
River Severn (including Gloucester and Sharpness canal)	N	N	N	N	N	N	0.01	N	0.01	0.01	0.01	0.01
River Mersey	N	0.01	0.02	0.01	0.02	0.02	0.11	0.10	0.09	0.09	0.10	0.10
Manchester Ship Canal	0.01	0.01	0.02	0.01	0.02	0.01	0.10	0.11	0.10	0.10	0.10	0.10
River Clyde	N	N	N	N	N	N	0.10	0.08	0.08	0.09	0.10	0.10
River Forth	N	N	N	N	N	N	0.19	0.18	0.20	0.19	0.19	0.18
River Humber	0.02	0.02	0.02	0.02	0.01	0.01	0.28	0.27	0.27	0.29	0.31	0.30
River Ouse	0.01	N	N	N	N	N	0.03	0.03	0.03	0.04	0.04	0.04
Aire and Calder Navigation	0.03	0.03	0.03	0.02	0.03	0.02	N	N	N	N	N	N
River Trent	0.02	0.02	0.02	0.02	0.02	0.02	0.03	0.03	0.03	0.04	0.04	0.03
River Orwell	N	N	N	N	N	N	0.08	0.08	0.07	0.08	0.06	0.04
Total	0.16	0.17	0.18	0.20	0.18	0.15	1.86	1.76	1.73	1.81	1.70	1.52
Goods Lifted												
River Thames	1.83	1.84	1.87	2.83	2.24	1.75	21.83	20.89	20.39	21.30	21.94	18.12
River Medway	0.11	0.01	0.06	0.19	0.23	0.20	4.02	2.60	2.52	2.84	2.68	2.12
River Severn (including Gloucester and Sharpness canal)	N	N	0.02	N	N	N	0.33	0.34	0.39	0.31	0.30	0.30
River Mersey	0.22	1.01	1.20	1.09	1.03	1.00	6.31	6.11	5.22	5.52	5.95	6.10
Manchester Ship Canal	0.33	1.12	1.32	1.09	1.41	1.06	6.31	6.11	5.22	5.52	5.95	6.10
River Clyde	N	N	N	N	N	N	2.55	2.06	2.10	2.44	2.51	2.45
River Forth	N	N	N	N	N	N	8.46	8.28	8.94	8.41	8.40	8.32
River Humber	0.70	0.47	0.60	0.59	0.48	0.46	6.41	6.16	6.29	6.24	6.82	6.55
River Ouse	0.33	0.23	0.23	0.25	0.26	0.27	2.19	2.17	2.24	2.56	2.82	2.95
Aire and Calder Navigation	2.54	2.33	2.41	2.32	2.11	2.02	N	N	N	N	N	N
River Trent	0.30	0.25	0.25	0.26	0.2	0.23	2.82	2.67	2.69	3.01	3.10	2.69
River Orwell	N	N	N	N	N	N	4.61	4.53	4.13	4.59	3.49	2.07
Total[2]	5.41	5.91	6.36	7.05	6.59	5.45	57.68	53.98	53.18	54.81	54.13	48.09

[1] The data are preliminary.

[2] This total includes other waterways. However, it may be less than the sum of the waterways because goods lifted on more than one waterway are counted only once in the overall total.

Source: Department of the Environment, Transport and the Regions, Transport Statistics Great Britain, 1997 © Crown copyright

World Road Transport

Road Network Measures for Selected Countries

1995

Country	Major roads			Secondary roads			All roads		
	total km	km per 1,000 persons	km per sq km	total km	Km per 1,000 persons	km per sq km	total km	km per 1,000 persons	km per sq km
Canada	268,000	9.30	0.03	753,000	26.13	0.08	1,021,000	35.43	0.10
France	37,700	0.65	0.07	775,000	13.29	1.42	817,700	14.02	1.49
Germany	52,900	0.63	0.15	597,800	7.16	1.67	650,700	7.79	1.82
Japan	63,360	0.51	0.19	1,081,000	8.62	3.20	1,144,360	9.12	3.39
Mexico	51,520	0.54	0.03	198,000	2.07	0.10	247,410	2.58	0.13
Sweden	15,676	1.76	0.03	121,588	13.66	0.27	136,233	15.31	0.30
UK	18,600	0.32	0.08	404,916	6.92	1.65	367,000	6.27	1.50
USA	693,829	2.64	0.08	5,602,278	21.29	0.61	6,296,107	23.92	0.69

Source: Office of Highway Information Management

Road Vehicle Use for Selected Countries

1995

Country	Total vehicle km of travel				Average vehicle km of travel			
	cars (millions)	motorcycles (millions)	buses (millions)	trucks (millions)	per automobile	per motorcycle	per bus	per truck
Canada[1]	168,000	N/A	N/A	80,000	11,765	N/A	N/A	11,034
France[2]	351,000	6,000	2,500	102,000	13,984	2,007	31,646	19,937
Germany[3]	507,000	11,500	3,600	58,400	12,519	4,991	42,138	14,062
Japan	417,000	N/A	6,870	263,000	9,267	N/A	28,041	11,895
Mexico[4]	38,000	1,074	537	16,000	4,562	4,007	4,099	4,570
Sweden	56,762	612	2,034	5,241	15,634	5,214	139,535	17,032
UK	353,200	4,110	4,700	68,900	16,997	6,821	43,925	26,258
USA	2,480,736	15,767	10,272	1,392,303	18,232	4,186	14,985	21,493

[1] The data in this column are for 1993.
[2] The data in this column for motorcycles are for 1993.
[3] The data in this column on trucks include truck-tractors only.
[4] The data in this column for automobiles and trucks are for 1993 and for motorcycles and buses are for 1991.

Source: Office of Highway Information Management

Transportation Indicators for Selected Countries

1995

Country	Total number				Number per 1,000 persons			
	cars	motorcycles and mopeds	buses	trucks	Cars	Motorcycles and mopeds	Buses	Trucks[2]
Canada	14,280,000	30,600	65,600	7,250,000	495.5	1.1	2.3	251.6
France	25,100,000	2,990,000[3]	79,000	5,116,000	430.4	51.3	1.4	87.7
Germany	40,499,442	2,304,253	85,434	4,153,086	484.8	27.6	1.0	49.7
Japan	45,000,000	15,340,000	245,000	22,111,000	358.7	122.3	2.0	176.3
Mexico	8,330,000	268,000	131,000	3,501,043[1]	87.0	2.8	1.4	36.6
Sweden	3,630,760	117,387	14,577	307,709[1]	407.9	13.2	1.6	34.6
UK	20,780,000	601,000	107,000	2,624,000	355.3	10.3	1.8	44.9
USA	136,066,045	3,767,029	685,504	64,778,472	517.0	14.3	2.6	246.1

[1] This figure excludes tractor trailers.
[2] This figure is for 1993.

Source: Office of Highway Information Management

Motor Vehicle Nationality Abbreviations

Many road vehicles display one or more letters to identify their nationality. These letters are in accordance with the 1968 (United Nations) UN Convention on Road Traffic and the 1949 UN Convention on Road Traffic.

Country	Abbreviation	Country	Abbreviation	Country	Abbreviation
Aden	ADN	Grenada	WG	Pakistan	PAK
Albania	AL	Guatemala	GCA	Papua New Guinea	PNG
Alderney	GBA	Guernsey	GBG	Paraguay	PY
Algeria	DZ	Guyana	GUY	Peru	PE
Andorra	AND	Haiti	RH	Philippines	RP
Argentina	RA	Hong Kong	HK	Poland	PL
Australia	AUS	Hungary	H	Portugal	P
Austria	A	Iceland	IS	Romania	RO
Bahamas	BS	India	IND	Russia	RUS
Bahrain	BRN	Indonesia	RI	Rwanda	RWA
Bangladesh	BD	Iran	IR	St Lucia	WL
Barbados	BDS	Ireland, Republic of	IRL	St Vincent	WV
Belarus	SU[1]	Isle of Man	GBM	Samoa	WS
Belgium	B	Israel	IL	San Marino	RSM
Belize	BH	Italy	I	Senegal	SN
Benin	DY	Jamaica	JA	Seychelles	SY
Bosnia-Herzegovina	BIH	Japan	J	Sierra Leone	WAL
Botswana	RB	Jersey	GBJ	Singapore	SGP
Brazil	BR	Jordan	HKJ	Slovak Republic	SK
Brunei	BRU	Kazakhstan	KZ	Slovenia	SLO
Bulgaria	BG	Kenya	EAK	South Africa	ZA
Cambodia	K	Korea, South	ROK	Spain (including African	
Canada	CDN	Kuwait	KWT	localities and provinces)	E
Central African Republic	RCA	Kyrgyzstan	KS	Sri Lanka	CL
Chile	RCH	Laos	LAO	Suriname	SME
China	RC	Latvia	LV	Swaziland	SD
Congo, Democratic Republic of	ZRE	Lebanon	RL	Sweden	S
Congo, Republic of the	RCB	Lesotho	LS	Switzerland	CH
Costa Rica	CR	Lithuania	LT	Syria	SYR
Côte d'Ivoire	CI	Luxembourg	L	Tajikistan	TJ
Croatia	HR	Macedonia, Former Yugoslav		Tanzania	EAT
Cyprus	CY	Republic of	MK	Thailand	T
Czech Republic	CZ	Malawi	MW	Togo	TG
Denmark	DK	Malaysia	MAL	Trinidad and Tobago	TT
Dominican Republic	DOM	Mali	RMM	Tunisia	TN
Ecuador	EC	Malta	M	Turkey	TR
Egypt	ET	Mauritius	MS	Turkmenistan	TM
Estonia	EST	Mexico	MEX	Uganda	EAU
Faroe Islands	FO	Monaco	MC	Ukraine	UA
Fiji	FJI	Morocco	MA	Uruguay	ROU
Finland	FIN	Myanmar	BUR	USA	USA
France	F	Namibia	NAM	Uzbekistan	UZ
Gambia	WAG	Netherlands	NL	Vatican City State	V
Georgia	GE	Netherlands Antilles	NA	Venezuela	YV
Germany	D	New Zealand	NZ	Yugoslavia	YU
Ghana	GH	Nicaragua	NIC	Zambia	RNR
Gibraltar	GBZ	Niger	RN	Zanzibar	EAZ
Great Britain	GB	Nigeria	WAN	Zimbabwe	ZW
Greece	GR	Norway	N		

[1] Belarus has not yet announced its new distinguishing sign. Therefore the sign 'SU' still appears on this list.

Source: United Nations

Countries that Drive on the Left

Anguilla	Grenada	Montserrat	South Africa
Antigua	Guyana	Mozambique	Sri Lanka
Australia	Hong Kong	Namibia	Suriname
Bahamas	India	Nepal	Swaziland
Bangladesh	Indonesia	New Zealand	Tanzania
Barbados	Ireland, Republic of	Norfolk Island	Thailand
Bermuda	Jamaica	Pakistan	Tonga
Bhutan	Japan	Papua New Guinea	Trinidad and Tobago
Botswana	Kenya	St Kitts and Nevis	Tuvalu
Brunei	Kiribati	St Lucia	Uganda
Cook Islands	Lesotho	St Vincent and the Grenadines	UK (including Guernsey, Jersey,
Cyprus	Malawi	Seychelles	and the Isle of Man)
Dominica	Malaysia	Singapore	Virgin Islands (British)
Falkland Islands	Malta	Solomon Islands	Zambia
Fiji	Mauritius	Somalia	Zimbabwe

Road Accident Fatalities and Fatality Rates for OECD Countries

(N/A = not available.)

Country	1985	1986	1987	1988	1989	1990	1991	1992	1993	1994	1995	Rate of road deaths per 100,000 population[1]	Rate of car user deaths per billion car km
Great Britain	5,165	5,382	5,125	5,052	5,373	5,217	4,568	4,229	3,814	3,650	3,621	6	5
Northern Ireland	177	236	214	178	181	185	185	150	143	157	144	9	8[3]
UK	5,342	5,618	5,339	5,230	5,554	5,402	4,753	4,379	3,957	3,807	3,765	6	5[3]
Austria	1,524	1,495	1,469	1,620	1,570	1,558	1,551	1,403	1,283	1,338	1,210	15	15
Belgium	1,801	1,951	1,922	1,967	1,993	1,976	1,873	1,672	1,660	1,692	1,449	14	N/A
Denmark	772	723	698	713	670	634	606	577	559	546	582	11	8[3]
Finland	541	612	581	653	734	649	632	601	484	480	441	9	6
France	11,387	11,947	10,742	11,497	11,476	11,215	10,483	9,900	9,568	9,019	8,891	15	N/A
Germany	10,070	10,620	9,498	9,862	9,779	11,046	11,300	10,631	9,949	9,814	9,454	12	12
Greece	1,960	1,669	1,727	1,738	1,954	1,998	2,058	2,103	2,104	2,195	N/A	21[2]	N/A
Ireland, Republic of	410	387	462	463	460	478	445	415	431	404	437	12	8
Italy	7,700	7,642	7,327	7,494	6,923	7,151	8,098	8,029	7,177	7,104	7,033	12	N/A
Luxembourg	79	79	68	84	67	70	80	73	76	74	68	19[2]	N/A
Netherlands	1,438	1,527	1,485	1,366	1,456	1,376	1,281	1,285	1,252	1,298	1,334	9	6[3]
Portugal	2,437	2,577	2,985	3,294	3,087	3,017	3,217	3,084	2,700	2,504	2,710	29	N/A
Spain	6,374	7,045	7,615	8,252	9,344	9,032	8,836	7,818	6,378	5,615	5,751	15	N/A
Sweden	808	844	787	813	904	772	745	759	632	589	572	6	7
Czech Republic	1,008	915	924	982	1,084	1,307	1,355	1,545	1,524	1,637	1,588	15	36[3]
Hungary	1,756	1,632	1,571	1,706	2,164	2,532	2,120	2,101	1,678	1,562	1,589	16	N/A
Iceland	24	24	24	29	28	24	27	21	17	N/A	N/A	N/A	N/A
Norway	402	452	398	378	381	332	323	325	281	283	305	7	9
Switzerland	881	1,003	923	917	897	925	834	834	723	679	692	10	N/A
Turkey	7,229	9,509	9,789	8,902	8,258	8,212	8,105	8,078	8,394	N/A	N/A	N/A	N/A
Australia	2,941	2,888	2,772	2,887	2,801	2,331	2,113	1,981	1,953	1,937	N/A	11[2]	N/A
Canada	4,364	4,068	4,286	4,154	4,246	3,960	3,691	3,501	3,615	3,260	N/A	11[2]	N/A
Japan	12,039	12,112	12,151	13,447	14,412	14,595	14,436	14,886	13,269	12,768	12,670	10	8[3]
New Zealand	746	766	799	728	762	729	650	646	600	580	581	16	N/A
USA	43,825	46,056	46,390	47,087	45,582	44,529	41,462	39,235	40,150	40,716	41,798	16	10[3]

[1] Population and car kilometres taken from the OECD's (Organization of Economic Cooperation and Development) international Road and Traffic Accidents Database.

[2] 1994 deaths and population.

[3] 1994 deaths and car kilometres.

Source: Department of the Environment, Transport and the Regions, Transport Statistics Great Britain, 1997, © Crown copyright

UK Road Transport

Top 20 UK New Car Registrations by Model Range

1997

Rank	Model range	Registrations	Market share (%)
1	Ford Fiesta	119,471	5.50
2	Ford Escort	113,522	5.23
3	Ford Mondeo	107,239	4.94
4	Vauxhall Vectra	93,778	4.32
5	Vauxhall Astra	89,537	4.12
6	Vauxhall Corsa	79,898	3.68
7	Peugeot 306	66,888	3.08
8	Rover 200 Series	62,365	2.87
9	Rover 400 Series	61,913	2.85
10	Renault Clio	58,033	2.67
11	Renault Megane	57,654	2.66
12	Volkswagen Polo	56,235	2.59
13	Peugeot 106	50,069	2.31
14	Peugeot 406	47,395	2.18
15	Fiat Punto	45,551	2.10
16	Nissan Micra	42,858	1.97
17	Renault Laguna	40,324	1.86
18	BMW 3 Series	40,312	1.86
19	Volkswagen Golf	39,986	1.84
20	Citroën Saxo	36,855	1.70
	Total top 20	1,309,883	60.34
	Total market	2,170,725	100.00

Source: Society of Motor Manufacturers and Traders Ltd

Top 10 Automatic Cars in the UK by Model Range

1997

Rank	Model range	Sales	Market share (%)
1	Mercedes C Class	14,639	4.93
2	Mercedes E Class	14,143	4.76
3	Vauxhall Vectra	9,626	3.24
4	BMW 5 Series	8,920	3.00
5	Ford Mondeo	8,666	2.92
6	BMW 3 Series	8,001	2.69
7	Vauxhall Astra	7,579	2.55
8	Honda Civic	7,312	2.55
9	Vauxhall Omega	7,156	2.41
10	Nissan Micra	6,809	2.29
	Total top 10	92,860	31.25
	Total automatics	297,190	13.69
	Total car market	2,170,725	100.00

Source: Society of Motor Manufacturers and Traders Ltd

Top 10 Diesel Cars in the UK by Model Range

1997

Rank	Model range	Sales	Market share (%)
1	Peugeot 306	36,427	10.38
2	Ford Mondeo	24,831	7.08
3	Peugeot 406	23,903	6.81
4	Vauxhall Astra	19,386	5.52
5	Vauxhall Vectra	16,780	4.78
6	Ford Escort	14,536	4.14
7	Land Rover Discovery	14,079	4.01
8	Citroën Xantia	12,309	3.51
9	Rover 400 Series	12,237	3.49
10	Peugeot 106	12,069	3.44
	Total top 10	186,557	53.16
	Total diesels	350,913	16.17
	Total market	2,170,725	100.00

Source: Society of Motor Manufacturers and Traders Ltd

Seat Belt Laws in the UK

This table shows what is required by UK seat belt laws as of February 1998.
(– = not applicable.)

Vehicle occupants	Front seat	Rear seat	Who is responsible
Driver	seat belt must be worn if available	–	driver
Children aged under 3 years	appropriate child restraint[1] must be used	appropriate child restraint[1] must be used if available	driver
Children aged 3–11 years, and under 1.5 m (approximately 5ft) in height	appropriate child restraint[1] must be worn if available; if not, adult seat belt must be used	appropriate child restraint[1] must be worn if available; if not, adult seat belt must be worn if available	driver
Children aged 12 or 13 or younger children 1.5 m (approximately 5 ft) or more in height	adult seat belt must be worn if available	adult seat belt must be worn if available	driver
Adult passengers	seat belt must be worn if available	seat belt must be worn if available	passenger

[1] An appropriate child restraint is a baby carrier, child seat harness, or booster seat suitable for the weight of the child using it.

Distance Travelled per Person per Year by Mode of Transport in Great Britain

These data relate to the region of the traveller's residence and therefore some journeys may have been undertaken outside this region. The journeys included were within Great Britain only. (In miles.)

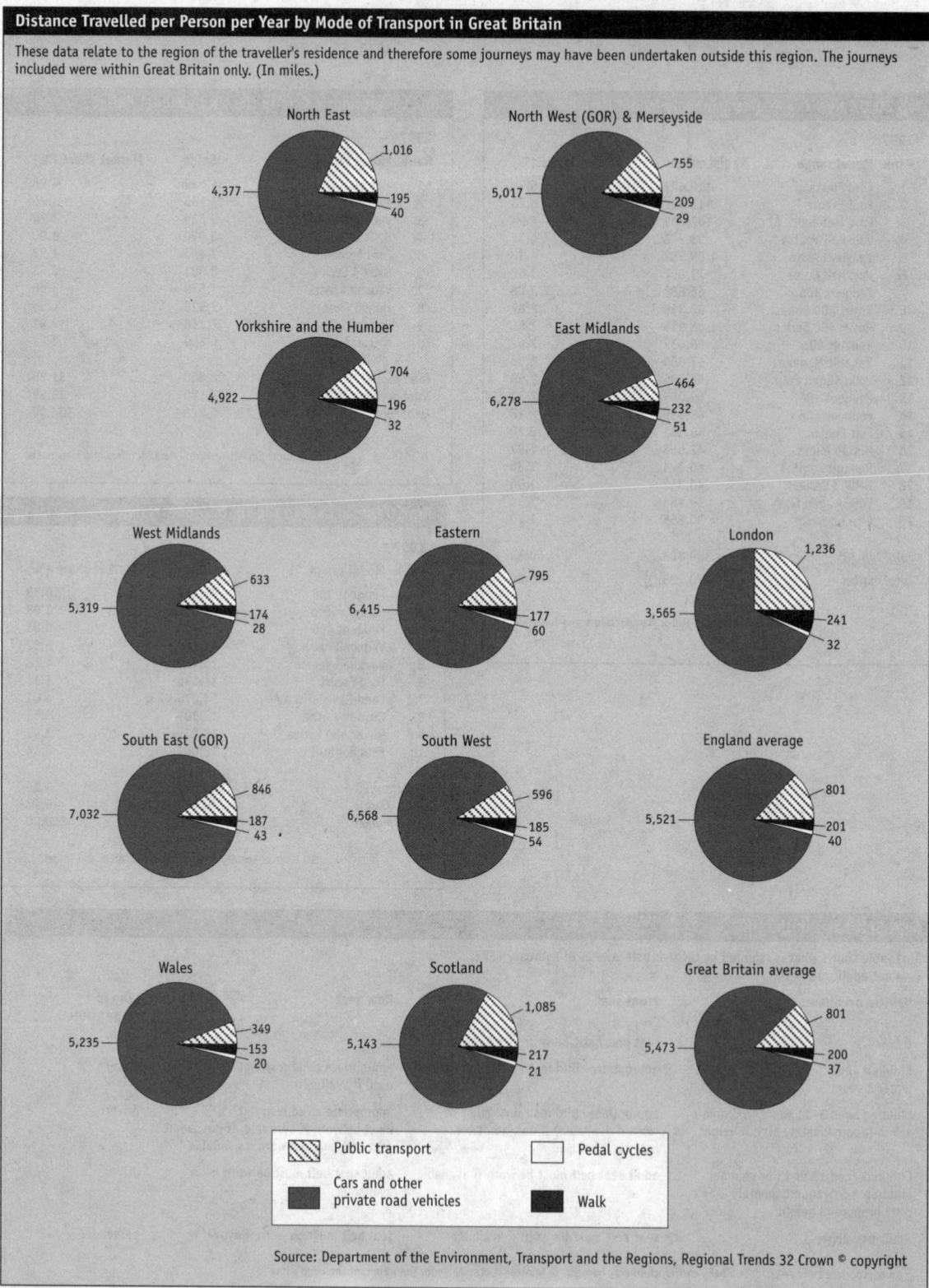

North East
1,016
4,377
195
40

North West (GOR) & Merseyside
755
5,017
209
29

Yorkshire and the Humber
704
4,922
196
32

East Midlands
464
6,278
232
51

West Midlands
633
5,319
174
28

Eastern
795
6,415
177
60

London
1,236
3,565
241
32

South East (GOR)
846
7,032
187
43

South West
596
6,568
185
54

England average
801
5,521
201
40

Wales
349
5,235
153
20

Scotland
1,085
5,143
217
21

Great Britain average
801
5,473
200
37

Legend:
- Public transport
- Cars and other private road vehicles
- Pedal cycles
- Walk

Source: Department of the Environment, Transport and the Regions, Regional Trends 32 Crown © copyright

Road Traffic Forecasts by Vehicle Type for Great Britain

Traffic in Great Britain is forecast to grow to levels shown by the index numbers in the table below, where 1996 = 100. The figure given for each year represents the central forecast; this estimate is considered to be the most likely outcome.

Traffic Forecast/% growth	Year/range	Cars	Light goods vehicles	Rigid heavy goods vehicles[1]	Articulated heavy goods vehicles[2]	Passenger service vehicles	Average
Traffic Index	2001	109	115	104	114	103	109
	2006	118	129	108	129	107	119
	2011	127	144	112	146	111	128
	2016	136	161	117	165	115	138
	2021	143	179	123	186	120	146
	2026	148	198	129	208	126	153
	2031	153	218	136	231	133	160
Annual % growth rates	1996–2001	1.65	2.87	0.72	2.63	0.68	1.74
	2001–06	1.65	2.27	0.77	2.55	0.68	1.69
	2006–11	1.46	2.17	0.80	2.44	0.69	1.53
	2011–16	1.37	2.29	0.91	2.52	0.77	1.48
	2016–21	1.01	2.21	0.94	2.39	0.87	1.19
	2021–26	0.69	2.06	0.99	2.27	0.97	0.91
	2026–31	0.67	1.89	1.00	2.13	1.06	0.89

[1] Rigid HGV = Other Goods Vehicle, Category 1 (large rigid vehicles, except for axles).
[2] Artic HGV = Other Goods Vehicle, Category 2 (all articulated vehicles and 4 axle rigid vehicles).

Source: Department of the Environment, Transport and the Regions, National Road Traffic Forecasts (Great Britain) © Crown copyright

London bus: Passenger service vehicle traffic is set to increase over the coming decades, but at a slower rate than for other types of vehicle

Principal Motorways in the UK

For roads consisting of motorway and other types of road, the length is given for the motorway part only.

Motorway	Destinations	Length	Motorway	Destinations	Length
M1	London–Leeds	189 mi/304 km	M56	Manchester–Chester	24 mi/39 km
M11	London–Cambridge	61 mi/98 km	M6	Rugby–Killington	162 mi/261 km
M18	Rotherham–Goole	35 mi/56 km	M6, A74(M)	Killington–Glasgow	156 mi/251 km
M180	Doncaster–Grimsby	51 mi/82 km	M61	Manchester–Preston	31 mi/50 km
M2	Gravesend–Faversham	33 mi/53 km	M62	Liverpool–Kingston Upon Hull	128 mi/206 km
M20	London–Folkestone	73 mi/117 km	M63	Salford–Stockport	20 mi/32 km
M23	London–Crawley	28 mi/45 km	M65	Bamber Bridge–Colne	28 mi/45 km
M25	London Orbital	117 mi/188 km	M66	Ramsbottom–Stockport	22 mi/35 km
M27	Lyndhurst–Portsmouth	34 mi/55 km	M8	Edinburgh–Greenock	68 mi/109 km
M3	London–Southampton	80 mi/129 km	M9	Edinburgh–Dunblane	40 mi/64 km
M4	London–Llanelli	202 mi/325 km	M90	Rosyth–Perth	30 mi/48 km
M40	London–Birmingham	120 mi/193 km	A1(M)	London–Newcastle	143 mi/230 km
M42	Bromsgrove–Ashby-de-la-Zouch	49 mi/79 km			
M5	Birmingham–Exeter	165 mi/266 km	*Ireland*		
M53	Wallasey–Chester	24 mi/39 km	M1	Belfast–Dungannon	41 mi/66 km
M54	Wolverhampton–Telford	23 mi/37 km	M2	Belfast–Ballymena	26 mi/42 km
M55	Preston–Blackpool	18 mi/29 km			

New Car Registrations in the UK by Manufacturer

This chart does not include export vehicles, vehicles supplied under the Home Delivery Scheme for ultimate export within a period of 12 months, or used vehicles (those imported into the UK after use abroad). 'Country of origin' indicates the place of final assembly. Percentages in brackets indicate total registration.
(– = not applicable.)

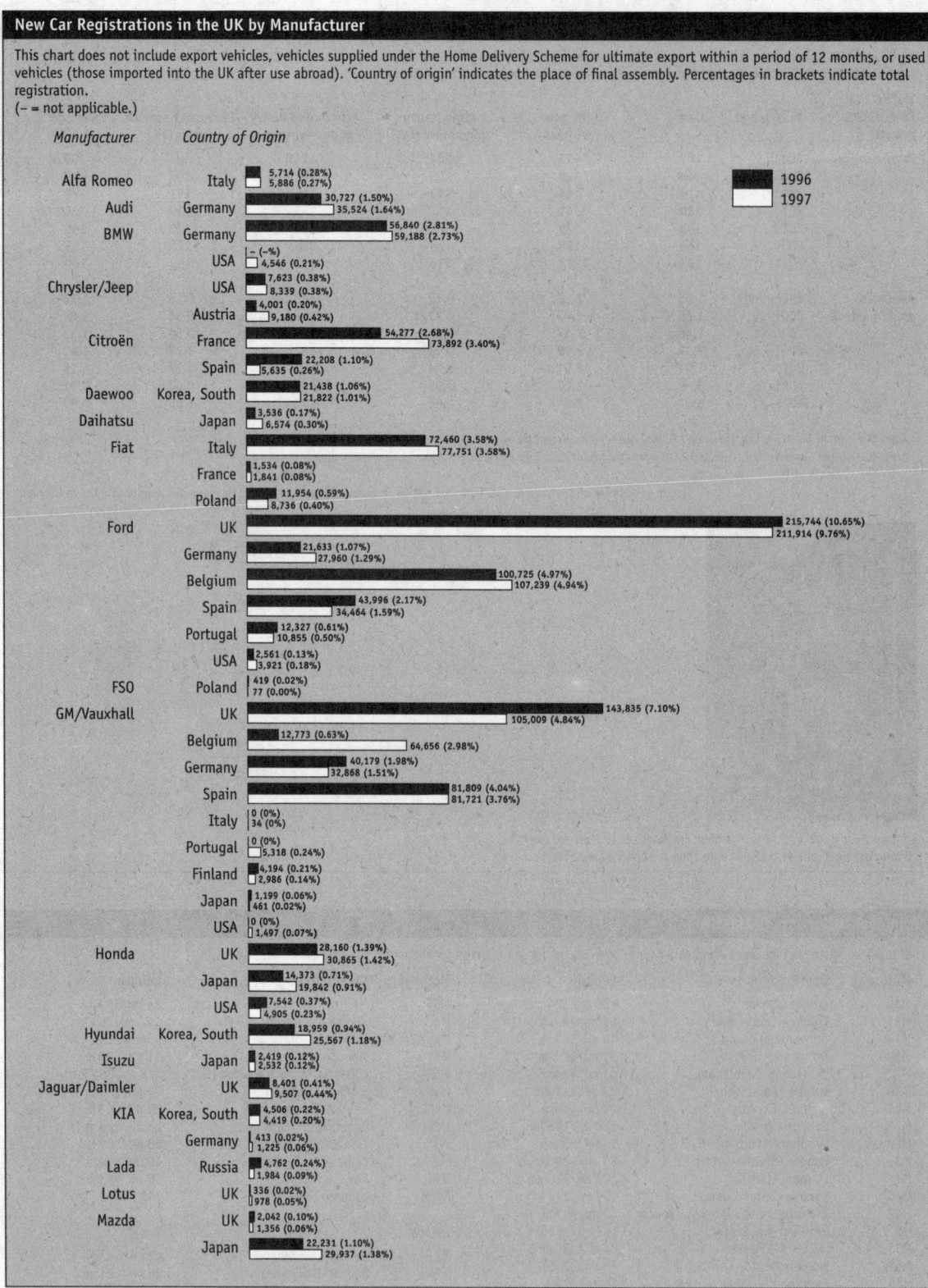

Manufacturer	Country of Origin	1996	1997
Alfa Romeo	Italy	5,714 (0.28%)	5,886 (0.27%)
Audi	Germany	30,727 (1.50%)	35,524 (1.64%)
BMW	Germany	56,840 (2.81%)	59,188 (2.73%)
	USA	– (–%)	4,546 (0.21%)
Chrysler/Jeep	USA	7,623 (0.38%)	8,339 (0.38%)
	Austria	4,001 (0.20%)	9,180 (0.42%)
Citroën	France	54,277 (2.68%)	73,892 (3.40%)
	Spain	22,208 (1.10%)	5,635 (0.26%)
Daewoo	Korea, South	21,438 (1.06%)	21,822 (1.01%)
Daihatsu	Japan	3,536 (0.17%)	6,574 (0.30%)
Fiat	Italy	72,460 (3.58%)	77,751 (3.58%)
	France	1,534 (0.08%)	1,841 (0.08%)
	Poland	11,954 (0.59%)	8,736 (0.40%)
Ford	UK	215,744 (10.65%)	211,914 (9.76%)
	Germany	21,633 (1.07%)	27,960 (1.29%)
	Belgium	100,725 (4.97%)	107,239 (4.94%)
	Spain	43,996 (2.17%)	34,464 (1.59%)
	Portugal	12,327 (0.61%)	10,855 (0.50%)
	USA	2,561 (0.13%)	3,921 (0.18%)
FSO	Poland	419 (0.02%)	77 (0.00%)
GM/Vauxhall	UK	143,835 (7.10%)	105,009 (4.84%)
	Belgium	12,773 (0.63%)	64,656 (2.98%)
	Germany	40,179 (1.98%)	32,868 (1.51%)
	Spain	81,809 (4.04%)	81,721 (3.76%)
	Italy	0 (0%)	34 (0%)
	Portugal	0 (0%)	5,318 (0.24%)
	Finland	4,194 (0.21%)	2,986 (0.14%)
	Japan	1,199 (0.06%)	461 (0.02%)
	USA	0 (0%)	1,497 (0.07%)
Honda	UK	28,160 (1.39%)	30,865 (1.42%)
	Japan	14,373 (0.71%)	19,842 (0.91%)
	USA	7,542 (0.37%)	4,905 (0.23%)
Hyundai	Korea, South	18,959 (0.94%)	25,567 (1.18%)
Isuzu	Japan	2,419 (0.12%)	2,532 (0.12%)
Jaguar/Daimler	UK	8,401 (0.41%)	9,507 (0.44%)
KIA	Korea, South	4,506 (0.22%)	4,419 (0.20%)
	Germany	413 (0.02%)	1,225 (0.06%)
Lada	Russia	4,762 (0.24%)	1,984 (0.09%)
Lotus	UK	336 (0.02%)	978 (0.05%)
Mazda	UK	2,042 (0.10%)	1,356 (0.06%)
	Japan	22,231 (1.10%)	29,937 (1.38%)

New Car Registrations in the UK by Manufacturer (*continued*)

Manufacturer   Country of Origin

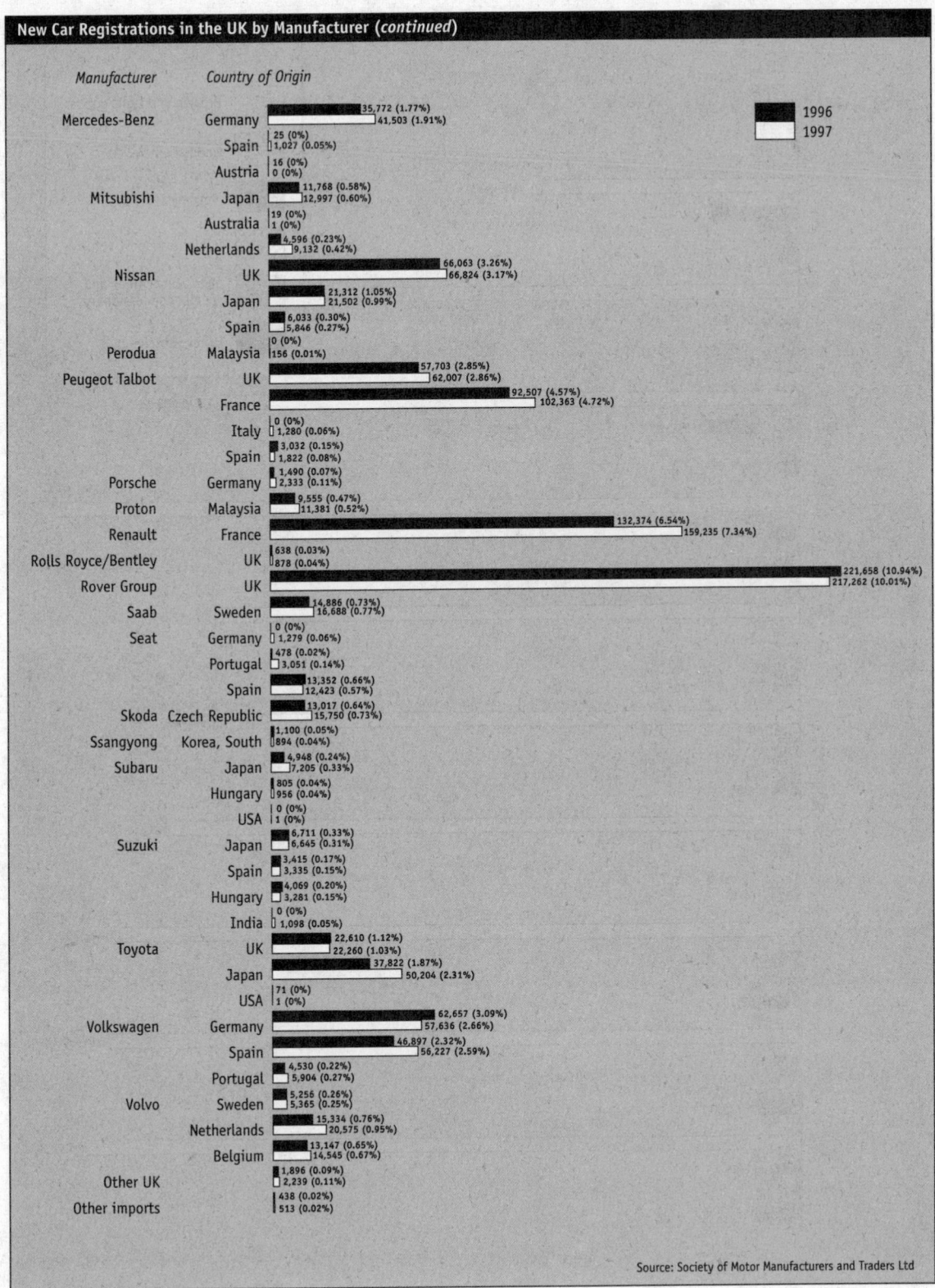

■ 1996
□ 1997

Manufacturer	Country of Origin	1996	1997
Mercedes-Benz	Germany	35,772 (1.77%)	41,503 (1.91%)
	Spain	25 (0%)	1,027 (0.05%)
	Austria	16 (0%)	0 (0%)
Mitsubishi	Japan	11,768 (0.58%)	12,997 (0.60%)
	Australia	19 (0%)	1 (0%)
	Netherlands	4,596 (0.23%)	9,132 (0.42%)
Nissan	UK	66,063 (3.26%)	66,824 (3.17%)
	Japan	21,312 (1.05%)	21,502 (0.99%)
	Spain	6,033 (0.30%)	5,846 (0.27%)
Perodua	Malaysia	0 (0%)	156 (0.01%)
Peugeot Talbot	UK	57,703 (2.85%)	62,007 (2.86%)
	France	92,507 (4.57%)	102,363 (4.72%)
	Italy	0 (0%)	1,280 (0.06%)
	Spain	3,032 (0.15%)	1,822 (0.08%)
Porsche	Germany	1,490 (0.07%)	2,333 (0.11%)
Proton	Malaysia	9,555 (0.47%)	11,381 (0.52%)
Renault	France	132,374 (6.54%)	159,235 (7.34%)
Rolls Royce/Bentley	UK	638 (0.03%)	878 (0.04%)
Rover Group	UK	221,658 (10.94%)	217,262 (10.01%)
Saab	Sweden	14,886 (0.73%)	16,688 (0.77%)
Seat	Germany	0 (0%)	1,279 (0.06%)
	Portugal	478 (0.02%)	3,051 (0.14%)
	Spain	13,352 (0.66%)	12,423 (0.57%)
Skoda	Czech Republic	13,017 (0.64%)	15,750 (0.73%)
Ssangyong	Korea, South	1,100 (0.05%)	894 (0.04%)
Subaru	Japan	4,948 (0.24%)	7,205 (0.33%)
	Hungary	805 (0.04%)	956 (0.04%)
	USA	0 (0%)	1 (0%)
Suzuki	Japan	6,711 (0.33%)	6,645 (0.31%)
	Spain	3,415 (0.17%)	3,335 (0.15%)
	Hungary	4,069 (0.20%)	3,281 (0.15%)
	India	0 (0%)	1,098 (0.05%)
Toyota	UK	22,610 (1.12%)	22,260 (1.03%)
	Japan	37,822 (1.87%)	50,204 (2.31%)
	USA	71 (0%)	1 (0%)
Volkswagen	Germany	62,657 (3.09%)	57,636 (2.66%)
	Spain	46,897 (2.32%)	56,227 (2.59%)
	Portugal	4,530 (0.22%)	5,904 (0.27%)
Volvo	Sweden	5,256 (0.26%)	5,365 (0.25%)
	Netherlands	15,334 (0.76%)	20,575 (0.95%)
	Belgium	13,147 (0.65%)	14,545 (0.67%)
Other UK		1,896 (0.09%)	2,239 (0.11%)
Other imports		438 (0.02%)	513 (0.02%)

Source: Society of Motor Manufacturers and Traders Ltd

Number of Motor Vehicles Registered in the UK for the First Time

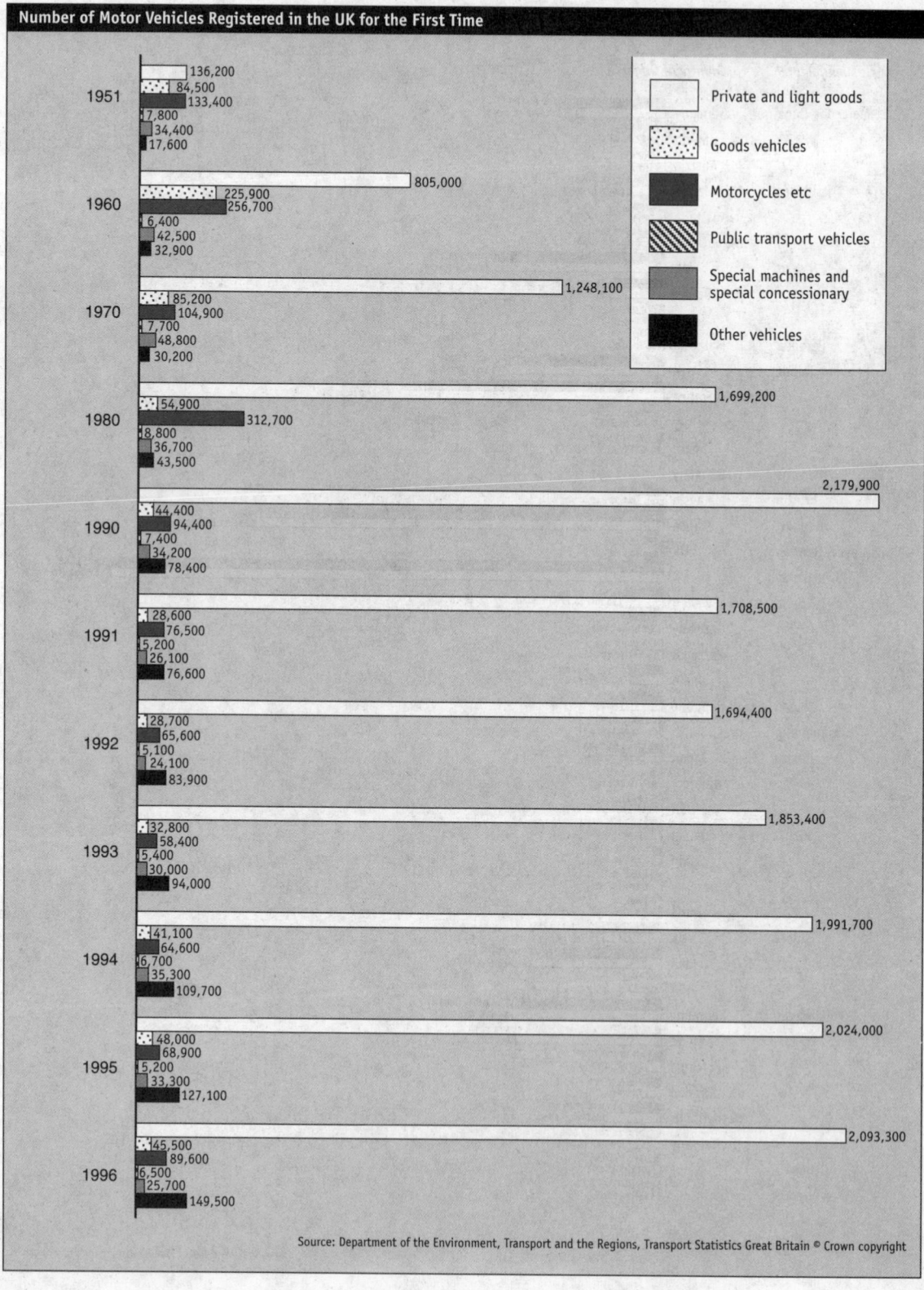

Legend:
- Private and light goods
- Goods vehicles
- Motorcycles etc
- Public transport vehicles
- Special machines and special concessionary
- Other vehicles

1951
- 136,200
- 84,500
- 133,400
- 7,800
- 34,400
- 17,600

1960
- 805,000
- 225,900
- 256,700
- 6,400
- 42,500
- 32,900

1970
- 1,248,100
- 85,200
- 104,900
- 7,700
- 48,800
- 30,200

1980
- 1,699,200
- 54,900
- 312,700
- 8,800
- 36,700
- 43,500

1990
- 2,179,900
- 144,400
- 94,400
- 7,400
- 34,200
- 78,400

1991
- 1,708,500
- 28,600
- 76,500
- 5,200
- 26,100
- 76,600

1992
- 1,694,400
- 28,700
- 65,600
- 5,100
- 24,100
- 83,900

1993
- 1,853,400
- 32,800
- 58,400
- 5,400
- 30,000
- 94,000

1994
- 1,991,700
- 41,100
- 64,600
- 6,700
- 35,300
- 109,700

1995
- 2,024,000
- 48,000
- 68,900
- 5,200
- 33,300
- 127,100

1996
- 2,093,300
- 45,500
- 89,600
- 6,500
- 25,700
- 149,500

Source: Department of the Environment, Transport and the Regions, Transport Statistics Great Britain © Crown copyright

Public Road Measures in the UK

Road type		Length (km)										
		1986	**1987**	**1988**	**1989**	**1990**	**1991**	**1992**	**1993**	**1994**	**1995**	**1996**
Trunk motorway		2,820	2,874	2,891	2,903	2,993	3,033	3,063	3,061	3,092	3,118	3,181
Principal motorway		101	101	102	92	77	68	71	78	76	72	45
Built-up major roads	trunk	1,744	1,631	1,631	1,628	1,532	1,455	1,431	1,400	1,344	1,297	1,313
	principal	12,460	12,442	12,447	12,452	12,457	12,575	12,627	12,681	12,737	12,750	12,961
	Total	14,204	14,073	14,078	14,080	13,989	14,030	14,058	14,081	14,081	14,047	14,274
Non built-up major roads	trunk	10,796	10,889	10,950	11,087	11,142	10,867	10,865	10,803	10,767	10,811	11,046
	principal	22,408	22,546	22,492	22,587	22,692	23,005	23,014	23,034	23,054	23,207	22,896
	Total	33,204	33,435	33,442	33,674	33,834	33,872	33,879	33,837	33,821	34,018	33,941
Minor roads	B roads	29,121	29,766	29,666	29,706	29,838	30,106	30,227	30,308	30,347	30,286	30,196
	C roads	80,360	80,004	80,264	80,542	80,716	81,073	81,334	81,824	82,105	82,540	82,528
	unclassified	191,267	192,442	193,872	195,606	196,588	197,783	199,679	201,024	201,445	202,918	204,656
	Total roads	351,076	352,695	354,315	356,602	358,034	359,966	362,310	364,212	364,966	366,999	368,821

Source: Department of the Environment, Transport and the Regions, Transport Statistics Great Britain © Crown copyright

Road Haulage Traffic in the UK

Loading Region	Road haulage traffic[1] (million tonnes)					
	1991	**1992**	**1993**	**1994**	**1995**	**1996**
England	1,265	1,221	1,278	1,347	1,352	1,369
Wales	92	87	89	96	100	98
Scotland	148	157	158	155	157	162
Northern Ireland	41	41	50	43	49	54
Total UK	1,547	1,505	1,575	1,641	1,658	1,685

[1] This refers to traffic carried by UK registered vehicles only. International road haulage is considered to be loaded at the port of entry. Includes weight of containers.

Source: Department of the Environment, Transport and the Regions, Regional Trends 32 © Crown copyright

Road Distances in Great Britain

(In miles.)

Destination	London	Aberdeen	Aberystwyth	Ayr	Barnstaple	Berwick	Birmingham	Blackpool	Bournemouth	Brighton	Bristol	Cambridge	Cardiff	Carlisle	Dover	Edinburgh	Exeter	Fishguard	Fort William	Glasgow	Gloucester	Harwich	Holyhead	Inverness	Kendal	Kingston Upon Hull
Aberdeen	548	–	470	190	606	187	433	336	578	608	516	464	536	234	589	125	589	526	157	148	481	548	462	106	281	360
Aberystwyth	238	470	–	341	222	323	123	167	213	290	132	215	118	236	325	335	206	56	446	334	110	309	105	496	190	228
Ayr	419	190	341	–	477	130	304	307	449	479	387	364	407	105	506	82	460	397	136	35	352	448	333	216	152	276
Barnstaple	216	606	222	477	–	435	178	303	121	202	100	267	137	372	272	471	55	243	582	469	126	312	341	632	326	322
Berwick	351	187	323	130	435	–	273	189	417	415	364	296	384	87	420	57	448	379	192	105	330	380	315	219	134	187
Birmingham	120	433	123	304	178	273	–	130	161	170	88	98	108	199	208	298	161	177	409	296	53	192	168	459	153	141
Blackpool	245	336	167	307	303	189	130	–	274	304	212	229	232	102	332	201	286	223	312	199	178	316	159	362	56	142
Bournemouth	108	578	213	449	121	417	161	274	–	95	82	205	128	344	179	443	84	233	554	441	101	206	313	604	298	258
Brighton	59	608	290	479	202	415	170	304	95	–	169	120	205	374	81	474	172	310	585	472	155	132	344	634	328	282
Bristol	120	516	132	387	100	364	88	212	82	169	–	124	48	206	200	373	84	112	379	356	35	251	251	542	236	232
Cambridge	61	464	215	364	267	296	98	229	205	120	124	–	205	259	124	336	250	292	469	399	150	69	260	519	253	140
Cardiff	155	536	118	407	137	384	108	232	128	205	48	205	–	302	241	401	121	112	512	346	44	251	206	561	256	252
Carlisle	314	234	236	105	372	87	199	102	344	374	206	259	302	–	401	99	355	347	210	150	247	343	228	259	47	171
Dover	78	589	325	506	272	420	208	332	179	81	200	124	241	401	–	461	244	391	611	454	251	136	370	661	355	264
Edinburgh	413	125	335	82	471	57	298	201	443	474	373	336	401	99	461	–	454	454	133	46	346	420	327	157	146	232
Exeter	200	589	206	460	55	448	161	286	84	172	84	250	121	355	244	454	–	227	566	454	110	297	325	616	310	306
Fishguard	261	526	56	397	243	379	177	223	233	310	112	292	112	347	391	454	227	–	502	390	171	357	161	552	246	285
Fort William	524	157	446	136	582	192	409	312	554	585	379	469	512	210	611	133	566	502	–	102	458	553	439	65	258	382
Glasgow	412	148	334	35	469	105	296	199	441	472	356	399	346	150	454	46	454	390	102	–	344	440	325	174	144	268
Gloucester	103	481	110	352	126	330	53	178	101	155	35	150	44	247	251	346	110	171	458	344	–	136	216	507	201	197
Harwich	82	548	309	448	312	380	192	316	206	132	251	69	251	343	136	420	297	357	553	440	136	–	355	603	340	224
Holyhead	283	462	105	333	341	315	168	159	313	344	251	260	206	228	370	327	325	161	439	325	216	355	–	487	181	220
Inverness	574	106	496	216	632	219	459	362	604	634	542	519	561	259	661	157	616	552	65	174	507	603	487	–	307	431
Kendal	268	281	190	152	326	134	153	56	298	328	236	253	256	47	355	146	310	246	258	144	201	340	181	307	–	165
Kingston Upon Hull	188	360	228	276	322	187	141	142	258	282	232	140	252	171	264	232	306	285	382	268	197	224	220	431	165	–

Road Distances in Great Britain (continued)

(In miles.)

Destination	Kingston Hull	Kendal	Inverness	Holyhead	Harwich	Gloucester	Glasgow	Fort William	Fishguard	Exeter	Edinburgh	Dover	Carlisle	Cardiff	Cambridge	Bristol	Brighton	Bournemouth	Blackpool	Birmingham	Berwick	Barnstaple	Ayr	Aberystwyth	Aberdeen
Leeds	60	72	383	165	232	177	220	333	230	286	200	272	123	231	148	212	262	264	87	121	160	302	228	174	328
Lincoln	48	177	443	205	179	150	280	394	254	259	261	219	183	204	94	185	215	240	154	88	221	274	288	199	389
Liverpool	129	79	386	102	288	149	223	336	167	258	225	303	126	204	193	184	277	246	56	101	213	274	231	111	360
Manchester	99	74	380	122	245	137	218	331	187	246	220	291	121	191	161	172	264	234	51	89	211	261	226	131	355
Middlesbrough	89	83	307	235	284	235	191	280	300	344	147	325	94	289	200	269	320	321	133	178	102	359	199	244	275
Newcastle	145	92	267	268	317	267	153	240	333	376	108	357	59	322	233	302	352	354	152	211	63	392	161	277	236
Norwich	151	277	543	305	74	212	380	493	372	313	360	173	283	266	63	233	169	220	253	159	320	329	388	277	488
Nottingham	93	149	449	174	171	110	286	399	215	219	266	218	189	165	87	145	195	197	126	54	226	235	294	160	394
Oban	371	246	115	427	542	447	92	50	492	556	123	601	199	501	458	481	574	543	301	398	181	571	126	436	182
Oxford	190	225	532	239	145	48	368	482	215	154	370	146	271	109	100	74	109	93	201	68	323	170	376	159	505
Penzance	415	419	725	433	406	219	562	676	337	109	564	356	465	231	361	194	283	196	396	271	548	109	570	316	699
Perth	277	195	114	375	465	395	62	103	440	504	42	549	147	459	381	430	522	492	250	347	104	520	104	384	86
Peterborough	111	224	490	225	122	140	327	440	300	248	307	162	230	194	38	158	158	184	200	87	267	264	335	205	435
Plymouth	346	351	657	365	338	151	494	607	268	45	496	287	397	162	292	125	215	127	327	203	479	61	502	247	631
Portsmouth	284	310	616	324	168	119	453	567	266	133	456	141	356	160	135	97	49	53	101	153	418	161	461	245	591
Sheffield	66	125	431	158	207	148	268	381	223	257	236	256	171	202	123	183	233	235	111	91	196	272	276	167	364
Shrewsbury	163	134	441	104	235	97	278	391	128	205	280	251	181	110	140	131	224	193	268	48	268	221	286	74	415
Southampton	257	291	597	305	179	100	434	548	247	112	437	152	337	141	131	76	63	32	279	134	390	140	442	226	572
Southend	211	302	608	316	63	154	445	559	320	229	408	94	348	214	71	179	90	163	86	155	368	275	453	272	536
Stoke	130	109	415	123	235	97	252	366	171	206	254	251	155	151	140	131	224	193	210	48	242	221	260	115	389
Stranraer	279	154	266	335	451	355	85	186	400	464	132	509	107	409	367	390	482	452	268	307	171	479	52	344	240
Swansea	287	291	597	182	287	100	434	548	72	157	436	277	337	42	240	83	240	163	417	143	420	173	442	78	571
Ullapool	486	362	57	542	658	562	229	112	607	671	212	716	314	616	574	597	689	659	465	514	274	687	271	551	161
Wick	535	410	105	590	706	611	277	168	655	719	261	765	363	665	622	645	738	707	514	562	322	735	319	599	210
York	38	91	376	191	241	191	213	326	256	300	193	281	116	245	157	226	276	278	114	134	153	315	221	200	321

Road Distances in Great Britain (*continued*)

(In miles.)

Destination	York	Wick	Ullapool	Swansea	Stranraer	Stoke	Southend	Southampton	Shrewsbury	Sheffield	Portsmouth	Plymouth	Peterborough	Perth	Penzance	Oxford	Oban	Nottingham	Norwich	Newcastle	Middlesbrough	Manchester	Liverpool	Lincoln	Leeds
London	212	677	629	191	422	163	44	80	163	169	75	241	86	462	309	56	514	131	115	288	256	204	216	142	199
Aberdeen	321	210	161	571	240	389	536	572	415	364	591	631	435	86	699	505	182	394	488	236	275	355	360	389	328
Aberystwyth	200	599	551	78	344	115	272	226	74	167	245	247	205	384	316	159	436	160	277	277	244	131	111	199	174
Ayr	221	319	271	442	52	260	453	442	286	276	461	502	335	104	570	376	126	294	388	161	199	226	231	288	228
Barnstaple	315	735	687	173	479	221	275	140	221	272	161	61	264	520	109	170	571	235	329	392	359	261	274	274	302
Berwick	153	322	274	420	171	242	368	390	268	196	418	479	267	104	548	323	181	226	320	63	102	211	213	221	160
Birmingham	134	562	514	143	307	48	155	134	48	91	153	203	87	347	271	68	398	54	159	211	178	89	101	88	121
Blackpool	114	465	417	268	210	86	279	268	111	101	287	327	200	250	396	201	301	126	253	152	133	51	56	154	87
Bournemouth	278	707	659	163	452	193	163	32	193	235	53	127	184	492	196	93	543	197	220	354	321	234	246	240	264
Brighton	276	738	689	240	482	224	90	63	224	233	49	215	158	522	283	109	574	195	169	352	320	264	277	215	262
Bristol	226	645	597	83	390	131	179	76	131	183	97	125	158	430	194	74	481	145	233	302	269	172	184	185	212
Cambridge	157	622	574	240	367	140	71	131	140	123	135	292	38	381	361	100	458	87	63	233	200	161	193	94	148
Cardiff	245	665	616	42	409	151	214	141	110	202	160	162	194	459	231	109	501	165	266	322	289	191	204	204	231
Carlisle	116	363	314	337	107	155	348	337	181	171	356	397	230	147	465	271	199	189	283	59	94	121	126	183	123
Dover	281	765	716	277	509	251	94	152	251	256	141	287	162	549	356	146	601	218	173	357	325	291	303	219	272
Edinburgh	193	261	212	436	132	254	408	437	280	236	456	496	307	42	564	370	123	266	360	108	147	220	225	261	200
Exeter	300	719	671	157	464	206	229	112	205	257	133	45	248	504	109	154	556	219	313	376	344	246	258	259	286
Fishguard	256	655	607	72	400	171	320	247	128	223	266	268	300	440	337	215	492	215	372	333	300	187	167	254	230
Fort William	326	168	112	548	186	366	559	548	391	381	567	607	440	103	676	482	50	399	493	240	280	331	336	394	333
Glasgow	213	277	229	434	85	252	445	434	278	268	453	494	327	62	562	368	92	286	380	153	191	218	223	280	220
Gloucester	191	611	562	100	355	97	154	100	97	148	119	151	140	395	219	48	447	110	212	267	235	137	149	150	177
Harwich	241	706	658	287	451	235	63	179	235	207	168	338	122	465	406	145	542	171	74	317	284	245	288	179	232
Holyhead	191	590	542	182	335	123	316	305	104	158	324	365	225	375	433	239	427	174	305	268	235	122	102	205	165
Inverness	376	105	57	597	266	415	608	597	441	431	616	657	490	114	725	532	115	449	543	267	307	380	386	443	383
Kendal	91	410	362	291	154	109	302	291	134	125	310	351	224	195	419	225	246	149	277	92	83	74	79	177	72
Kingston Upon Hull	38	535	486	287	279	130	211	257	163	66	284	346	111	277	415	190	371	93	151	145	89	99	129	48	60

Road Distances in Great Britain (*continued*)

(In miles.)

Destination	Leeds	Lincoln	Liverpool	Manchester	Middlesbrough	Newcastle	Norwich	Nottingham	Oban	Oxford	Penzance	Perth	Peterborough	Plymouth	Portsmouth	Sheffield	Shrewsbury	Southampton	Southend	Stoke	Stranraer	Swansea	Ullapool	Wick	York
Leeds	–	73	74	44	64	97	173	74	322	171	395	245	120	327	265	36	118	237	220	93	230	277	438	486	24
Lincoln	73	–	141	85	125	157	103	36	383	128	368	306	50	299	217	47	125	213	166	92	291	240	498	546	81
Liverpool	74	141	–	35	145	177	241	108	325	173	367	273	188	299	258	80	66	239	250	57	233	176	440	489	101
Manchester	44	85	35	–	115	147	185	71	320	160	355	268	132	286	246	38	70	227	238	45	228	227	435	484	71
Middlesbrough	64	125	145	115	–	39	224	130	269	228	452	191	171	384	322	100	189	294	272	163	202	324	361	410	50
Newcastle	97	157	177	147	39	–	257	163	230	260	484	153	204	416	354	132	221	327	304	196	164	356	322	371	90
Norwich	173	103	241	185	224	257	–	119	482	143	422	405	77	354	206	147	202	193	100	174	391	302	598	648	181
Nottingham	74	36	108	71	130	163	119	–	388	103	328	311	58	259	197	44	86	170	165	52	297	200	504	552	87
Oban	322	383	325	320	269	230	482	388	–	471	665	94	430	597	556	371	381	537	548	355	176	537	161	217	316
Oxford	171	128	173	160	228	260	143	103	471	–	264	420	86	195	85	141	121	66	108	121	380	140	587	635	184
Penzance	395	368	367	355	452	484	422	328	665	264	–	613	358	77	244	366	315	223	340	315	573	266	780	828	409
Perth	245	306	273	268	191	153	405	311	96	420	613	–	352	545	504	281	329	485	496	303	154	485	169	217	238
Peterborough	120	50	188	132	171	204	77	58	430	86	358	352	–	289	160	94	130	157	109	102	337	230	545	593	127
Plymouth	327	299	299	286	384	416	354	259	597	195	77	545	289	–	176	298	246	155	272	246	505	198	712	760	341
Portsmouth	265	217	258	246	322	354	205	197	556	85	244	504	160	176	–	235	207	21	126	207	465	196	672	721	278
Sheffield	36	47	80	38	100	132	147	44	371	141	366	281	94	298	235	–	114	207	203	53	278	237	485	534	56
Shrewsbury	118	125	66	70	189	221	202	86	381	121	315	329	130	246	207	114	–	187	198	38	288	118	495	544	145
Southampton	237	213	239	227	294	327	193	170	537	66	223	485	157	155	21	207	187	–	136	188	446	177	653	702	250
Southend	220	166	250	238	272	304	100	165	548	108	340	496	109	272	126	203	198	136	–	198	456	250	663	712	228
Stoke	93	92	57	45	163	196	174	52	355	121	315	303	102	246	207	53	38	188	198	–	263	187	470	518	119
Stranraer	230	291	233	228	202	164	391	297	176	380	573	154	337	505	465	278	288	446	456	263	–	445	321	369	224
Swansea	277	240	176	227	324	356	302	200	537	140	266	485	230	198	196	237	118	177	250	187	445	–	652	701	281
Ullapool	438	498	440	435	361	322	598	504	161	587	780	169	545	712	672	485	495	653	663	470	321	652	–	115	431
Wick	486	546	489	484	410	371	648	552	217	635	828	217	593	760	721	534	544	702	712	518	369	701	115	–	479
York	24	81	101	71	50	90	181	97	316	184	409	238	127	341	278	56	145	250	228	119	224	281	431	479	–

Number of Road Accident Casualties in the UK

Road user type	Severity	1986	1987	1988	1989	1990	1991	1992	1993	1994	1995	1996
Child pedestrians	killed	279	264	282	254	242	225	180	165	160	132	131
	killed or severely injured	6,459	5,887	5,897	5,836	5,914	5,096	4,901	4,231	4,610	4,400	4,132
	all severities	23,396	21,507	21,839	22,154	22,860	20,707	20,123	18,249	19,263	18,590	18,509
Adult pedestrians	killed	1,561	1,435	1,454	1,439	1,434	1,263	1,163	1,072	953	897	858
	killed or severely injured	12,414	11,563	11,781	11,460	11,228	9,726	9,119	8,256	8,108	7,712	7,297
	all severities	36,367	35,014	36,008	36,820	36,318	32,204	30,333	28,727	28,091	27,128	26,775
Child pedal cyclists	killed	58	79	62	73	59	50	48	37	42	48	54
	killed or severely injured	1,643	1,757	1,576	1,623	1,490	1,345	1,195	1,146	1,234	1,249	1,231
	all severities	8,629	9,010	8,616	9,327	8,720	8,182	7,725	7,386	8,075	8,133	8,216
Adult pedal cyclists	killed	212	201	165	220	197	192	156	148	129	164	148
	killed or severely injured	3,568	3,339	3,272	3,477	3,075	2,800	2,751	2,597	2,709	2,672	2,514
	all severities	17,148	16,863	16,922	18,749	17,311	16,190	16,477	16,097	16,074	16,109	15,737
Motorcyclists[1] and passengers	killed	762	723	670	683	659	548	469	427	444	445	440
	killed or severely injured	16,466	13,896	12,654	12,488	11,121	8,501	7,335	6,879	6,665	6,613	6,193
	all severities	52,280	45,801	42,836	42,630	39,048	30,736	26,873	25,066	24,309	23,480	23,044
Car drivers and passengers	killed	2,231	2,206	2,142	2,426	2,371	2,053	1,978	1,760	1,764	1,749	1,806
	killed or severely injured	29,686	29,086	29,346	29,684	29,120	25,393	25,124	22,831	23,891	23,459	24,045
	all severities	159,178	159,468	170,705	184,688	190,558	179,357	185,645	187,457	195,109	193,992	205,277
Bus/coach drivers and passengers	killed	24	15	17	20	19	25	19	35	21	35	11
	killed or severely injured	859	826	892	835	807	725	655	725	815	835	695
	all severities	9,518	9,088	9,501	10,200	9,954	8,870	9,099	9,294	10,082	9,269	9,338
LGV drivers and passengers	killed	156	111	146	144	129	119	117	91	64	69	61
	killed or severely injured	1,782	1,810	1,845	1,827	1,627	1,427	1,308	1,082	1,101	1,106	989
	all severities	8,990	8,842	9,669	10,101	9,728	8,673	8,127	7,417	7,554	7,196	7,213
HGV drivers and passengers	killed	83	75	73	82	67	75	70	59	41	57	63
	killed or severely injured	770	780	792	846	772	695	659	635	571	635	555
	all severities	3,319	3,487	3,670	4,063	3,844	3,603	3,326	3,333	3,370	3,330	3,245
All road users[2]	killed	5,382	5,125	5,052	5,373	5,217	4,568	4,229	3,814	3,650	3,621	3,598
	killed or severely injured	74,134	69,418	68,543	68,531	65,658	56,173	53,474	48,823	50,181	49,144	48,071
	all severities	321,451	311,473	322,305	341,592	341,141	311,269	310,673	306,020	315,189	310,506	320,302

[1] These figures include mopeds and scooters.
[2] These figures include other motor or non-motor road users, and unknown vehicle type and casualty age.

Source: Department of the Environment, Transport and the Regions, Transport Statistics Great Britain © Crown copyright

Drink Driving Legislation and Statistics in the UK

The legal alcohol limits in the UK are as follows: 35 microgrammes of alcohol in 100 millilitres of breath, 80 milligrammes of alcohol in 100 millilitres of blood, and 107 milligrammes of alcohol in 100 millilitres of urine. Within the EC, about half the member states have an 80 milligramme limit. France, the Netherlands, Belgium, Greece, and Finland have 50; Portugal has 40; Sweden has 20. (N/A = not available.)

Measures	1989	1990	1991	1992	1993	1994	1995	1996
Fatal casualties in accidents where one driver or passenger was over the legal limit	810	760	660	600	540	540	540	540[1]
% of drivers and riders killed in Great Britain whose blood alcohol level was known, who were over the legal limit	19	18	19	20	19	21	19	N/A
Breath tests administered in England and Wales								
number of tests	541,000	597,000	562,000	531,000	600,000	678,500	702,700	781,000
proportion positive/refused (%)	20	17	16	16	15	14	13	13
Breath tests administered in injury accidents in Great Britain								
number of tests	102,000	113,000	110,000	109,000	106,000	110,000	119,000	159,000
proportion positive (%)	10	9	8	7	7	7	6	5
Convictions for alcohol-related driving offences	114,000	113,000	104,000	95,000	91,000	90,000	93,000	N/A

[1] This figure is preliminary.

Source: Drink Driving Campaign, Department of the Environment, Transport and the Regions © Crown copyright

Rail Transport

International Comparisons of Rail Infrastructures

(N/A = not available.)

Country	Rail network[1] in operation (km thousands)		Of which electrified (km thousands)		Rail network per 1,000 sq km	
	1984	*1994*	*1984*	*1994*	*1984*	*1994*
UK	17.20	16.90	3.80	5.10	70	69
Belgium	3.70	3.40	1.90	2.40	123	111
Denmark	2.50	2.30	0.10	0.40	57	55
France	34.70	32.30	11.40	13.70	63	59
Germany	45.40	41.40	13.90	17.70	127	116
Greece	2.50	2.50	N/A	N/A	19	19
Ireland, Republic of	1.90	1.90	N/A	N/A	28	28
Italy	16.10	16.10	10.30	10.10	53	53
Luxembourg	0.30	0.30	0.20	N/A	104	106
Netherlands	2.90	2.80	1.80	2.00	70	68
Portugal	3.60	3.10	0.50	0.50	39	33
Spain	15.10	12.61	6.40	7.01	30	25
Austria	5.70	5.60	3.10	3.30	68	67
Croatia	2.40	2.70	0.80	0.80	43	48
Czech Republic	13.10	9.40	3.30	2.60	166	119
Finland	6.00	5.90	1.40	2.00	18	17
Hungary	7.80	7.80	1.90	2.30	84	84
Norway	4.20	4.00	2.40	2.40	13	12
Slovak Republic	N/A	3.70	N/A	1.50	0	75
Sweden	12.10	10.30	7.60	7.20	27	23
Switzerland	5.10	5.10	5.10	5.12	123	124
Australia	N/A	36.20	N/A	3.60	N/A	5
Japan	21.10	20.30	11.20	11.90	56	54
USA	244.60	176.00	1.70	1.70	26	19

[1] This refers to national railways only.

Source: Department of the Environment, Transport and the Regions, Transport Statistics Great Britain, 1997 © Crown copyright

National Rail Length and London Underground Statistics in the UK

(N/A = not available.)

Year	Length of National Rail[1] route			Passengers on National Rail[2]		London Underground	
	total route (km)	electrified route (km)	open to passenger traffic (km)	passenger journeys (millions)	passenger kilometres (billions)	passenger journeys (millions)	passenger kilometres (billions)
1900	29,783	N/A	N/A	N/A	N/A	N/A	N/A
1923	32,462	1,122	N/A	1,772	N/A	N/A	N/A
1946	31,963	N/A	N/A	1,266	47.0	569	N/A
1955	30,676	1,577	23,820	994	32.7	676	5.6
1965	24,011	2,886	17,516	865	30.1	657	4.7
1975	18,118	3,655	14,431	730	30.9	601	4.8
1984/85	16,816	3,798	14,304	701	29.5	672	5.4
1989/90	16,587	4,546	14,318	758	33.3	765	6.0
1990/91	16,584	4,912	14,317	762	33.2	775	6.2
1991/92	16,558	4,886	14,291	741	32.5	751	5.9
1992/93	16,528	4,910	14,317	745	31.7	728	5.8
1993/94	16,536	4,968	14,357	713	30.4	735	5.8
1994/95	16,542	4,970	14,359	702	28.7	764	6.1
1995/96	16,666	5,163	15,002	788	30.0	784	6.3
1996/97	16,666	5,176	15,034	N/A	32.2	772	6.2

[1] From 1994/95 route length is for Railtrack.
[2] From 1995/96 passenger traffic is for National Rail and former British Rail Train Operating Companies.

Source: Department of the Environment, Transport and the Regions, Transport Statistics Great Britain, 1997 © Crown copyright

Channel Tunnel Traffic to and from Europe

Tunnel traffic	1994	1995	1996
Passenger vehicles on shuttles[1]	82,000	1,246,000	2,135,000
Freight vehicles on shuttles[1]	65,000	391,000	519,000
All vehicles on shuttles[1]	147,000	1,637,000	2,654,000
Number of passengers on shuttles and through trains[2]	315,000	7,081,000	12,799,000
Through-train freight (tonnes)	452,000	1,692,000[3]	2,334,000

[1] The figures include non-commercial vehicles.
[2] The figures exclude non-commercial vehicles.
[3] The figure has been revised downward.

Source: Department of the Environment, Transport and the Regions, Transport Statistics Great Britain, 1997 © Crown copyright

Channel Tunnel Express A 7,600 hp/5.6 MW locomotive heads a Eurotunnel shuttle. Each shuttle is made up of 24 specially designed wagons, and carries an estimated 800 passengers in a load of 120 cars and 12 coaches.

© Channel Tunnel Group Ltd.

Channel Tunnel: Chronology

1751   French farmer Nicolas Desmaret suggested a fixed link across the English Channel.

1802   French mining engineer Albert Mathieu-Favier proposed to Napoleon I a Channel tunnel through which horse-drawn carriages might travel. Discussions with British politicians ceased in 1803 when war broke out between the two countries.

1834   Aim de Gamond of France suggested the construction of a submerged tube across the Channel.

1842   De la Haye of Liverpool designed an underwater tube, the sections of which would be bolted together underwater by workers without diving apparatus.

1851   Hector Horeau proposed a tunnel that would slope down towards the middle of the Channel and up thereafter, so that the carriages would be propelled downhill by their own weight and for a short distance uphill, after which compressed air would take over as the motive power.

1876   An Anglo-French protocol was signed laying down the basis of a treaty governing construction of a tunnel.

1878   Borings began from the French and British sides of the Channel.

1882   British government forced abandonment of the project after public opinion, fearing invasion by the French, turned against the tunnel.

1904   Signing of the Entente Cordiale between France and the UK enabled plans to be reconsidered. Albert Sartiaux and Francis Fox proposed a twin-tunnel scheme.

1930   A Channel-tunnel bill narrowly failed in British parliament.

1930–40   British Prime Minister Winston Churchill and the French government supported the digging of a tunnel.

1955   Defence objections to a tunnel were lifted in the UK by Prime Minister Harold Macmillan.

1957   Channel Tunnel Study Group established.

1961   Study Group plans for a double-bore tunnel presented to British government.

1964   Ernest Marples, minister of transport, and his French counterpart gave go-ahead for construction.

1967   British government invited tunnel-building proposals from private interests.

1973   Anglo-French treaty on trial borings signed.

1974   New tunnel bill introduced in British Parliament but was not passed before election called by Harold Wilson.

1975   British government cancelled project because of escalating costs.

1981   Anglo-French summit agreed to investigation of possible tunnel.

1982   Intergovernmental study group on tunnel established.

1984   Construction of tunnel agreed in principle at Anglo-French summit.

1986   Anglo-French treaty signed; design submitted by a consortium called the Channel Tunnel Group accepted.

1987   Legislation completed, Anglo-French treaty ratified; construction started in November.

1990   First breakthrough of service tunnel took place in December.

1991   Breakthrough of first rail tunnel in May; the second rail tunnel was completed in June.

1994   6 May: The Queen and President Mitterrand officially inaugurated the Channel Tunnel. November: Limited commercial Eurostar services (for foot passengers) commenced. December: Limited commercial shuttle services (for cars) commenced.

1995   April: Eurotunnel chairman Alistair Morton warned of the risk of financial collapse. Cost of project reported at £8 billion. Complete service for cars started. September: Eurotunnel suspended interest payments on its £8 billion debt. November: The millionth car was carried through the tunnel.

1996   London and Continental Railways (LCR) awarded the agreement to build the 68-mile Channel Tunnel rail link. 18 November: A fire broke out in a freight train injuring 34 people, and resulting in the tunnel being closed for repair.

1998   January: Labour government turned down an appeal by LCR for £1.2 billion of state aid to help complete the rail link. April 1998: LCR was given a deadline of mid-May to tell the government how it intended to raise £5 billion needed to complete the link.

Rail Freight by Commodity in the UK

(N/A = not available.)

Commodity	1986/87	1987/88	1988/89	1989/90	1990/91	1991/92	1992/93	1993/94	1994/95	1995/96	1996/97
Freight moved (billion tonne-kilometres)											
Coal	5.0	4.6	4.8	4.6	5.0	5.0	5.4	3.9	3.3	2.9	N/A
Metals	2.5	2.7	2.8	2.5	2.3	2.4	2.3	2.1	1.7	2.1	N/A
Construction	2.9	2.9	3.3	3.2	2.7	2.5	2.5	2.3	2.5	2.1	N/A
Oil and petroleum	2.1	2.0	2.2	2.1	2.0	2.0	2.0	1.9	1.8	1.7	N/A
Other commodities	4.0	5.2	4.9	4.2	3.8	3.4	3.3	3.5	3.8	4.3	N/A
Total	16.6	17.5	18.1	16.7	16.0	15.3	15.5	13.8	13.0	13.0	N/A
Freight lifted (million tonnes)											
Coal	77.2	78.8	79.2	75.8	74.7	75.1	67.9	49.0	42.5	46.1	51.0
Metals	17.3	19.6	20.6	18.9	18.0	17.8	15.9	15.8	16.9	17.8	N/A
Construction	18.1	19.5	22.9	23.5	20.2	17.7	15.8	16.1	16.8	13.4	N/A
Oil and petroleum	9.8	10.1	10.8	10.2	10.0	10.0	9.5	9.0	8.1	7.6	N/A
Other traffic	16.0	16.3	16.1	14.7	15.1	15.3	13.2	13.4	13.0	16.4	50.0
Total	138.4	144.4	149.5	143.1	138.2	135.8	122.4	103.3	97.3	101.3	101.0

Source: Department of the Environment, Transport and the Regions, Transport Statistics Great Britain, 1997 © Crown copyright

Railway Disasters throughout the World

The worst train disaster ever is considered to be that in Bihar, India, when a train plunged off a bridge over the Bagmati River. The official death toll was given as 268 but as the train was very overcrowded the number of deaths was probably in excess of 800.

Date	Location	Fatalities	Date	Location	Fatalities
8 September 1900	Bolivar (TX)	85	14 November 1960	Pardubice, Czech Republic	110
1 March 1910	Wellington (WA)	96	8 January 1962	Woerden, Netherlands	91
22 May 1915	near Gretna, Scotland	227	3 May 1962	Tokyo, Japan	163
12 December 1917	Modane, France	>540	26 July 1964	Oporto, Portugal	94
9 July 1918	Nashville (TN)	101	4 February 1970	Buenos Aires, Argentina	236
2 November 1918	Brooklyn (NY)	92	16 June 1972	Vierzy, France	107
23 December 1933	Lagny-Polponne, France	230	21 July 1972	Seville, Spain	76
16 July 1937	near Patna, India	107	6 October 1972	Saltillo, Mexico	208
22 December 1939	near Magdeburg, Germany	132	30 August 1974	Zagreb, Yugoslavia	153
	near Friedrichshafen, Germany	99	18 January 1977	Granville, Australia	82
16 January 1944	Leon Province, Spain	>500	6 June 1981	Bihar, India	>800
2 March 1944	near Salerno, Italy	521	27 January 1982	El Asnam, Algeria	130
20 March 1946	Aracaju, Mexico	185	11 July 1982	Tepic, Mexico	120
22 October 1949	near Dwor, Poland	>200	19 February 1983	Empalme, Mexico	100
6 February 1951	Woodbridge (NJ)	84	12 December 1988	London, UK	115
4 March 1952	near Rio de Janeiro, Brazil	119	15 January 1989	Maizdi Khan, Bangladesh	>110
9 July 1952	Rzepin, Poland	160	4 June 1989	Chelyabinsk, former USSR	>600
8 October 1952	Harrow, UK	112	4 January 1990	Sindh Province, Pakistan	>210
3 April 1955	Guadalajara, Mexico	300	14 May 1991	Shigaraki, Japan	42
1 September 1957	Kendal, Jamaica	178	8 March 1994	Durban, South Africa	63
29 September 1957	Montgomery, Pakistan	>250	22 September 1994	Tolunda, Angola	>300
4 December 1957	London, UK	90	20 August 1995	Firozabad, India	>300
8 May 1958	Rio de Janeiro, Brazil	128	3 June 1998	Eschede, Germany	98

Train Casualties by Type of Accident in the UK

Type of accident		1987[1]	1988	1989	1990	1991[2]	1991/92	1992/93	1993/94	1994/95	1995/96	1996/97[3]
Train accidents (collisions, derailments)												
Killed	Passengers	3	34	6	0	2	2	0	0	3	1	1
	Railway staff	1	2	6	1	0	2	1	0	5	1	0
	Others	6	4	6	3	1	7	4	6	4	5	0
	Total	10	40	18	4	3	11	5	6	12	7	1
Major injuries	Passengers	13	75	39	13	34	18	3	5	11	1	0
	Railway staff	5	6	18	6	4	6	5	4	8	15	9
	Others	7	3	1	3	0	6	5	2	5	7	0
	Total	25	84	58	22	38	30	13	11	24	23	9
Minor injuries	Passengers	297	540	272	144	515	289	63	129	179	61	182
	Railway staff	60	62	53	67	14	59	69	91	75	60	52
	Others	14	19	21	10	2	13	8	15	18	22	14
	Total	371	621	346	221	531	361	140	235	272	143	248
Accidents through movement of railway vehicles (entering or alighting from trains, opening or closing carriage doors)												
Killed	Passengers	36	34	25	35	6	28	16	14	12	7	11
	Railway staff	11	11	8	19	5	9	5	3	3	2	2
	Others	10	8	8	15	2	12	6	9	12	8	7
	Total	57	53	41	69	13	49	27	26	27	17	20
Major injuries	Passengers	80	102	97	107	19	73	79	41	58	52	0
	Railway staff	34	36	28	48	8	39	34	23	14	18	31
	Others	1	1	6	2	1	1	3	2	1	5	0
	Total	115	139	131	157	28	113	116	66	73	75	31
Minor injuries	Passengers	2,609	2,619	2,601	2,551	375	2,181	2,335	2,168	2,157	2,808	559
	Railway staff	50	49	35	68	9	65	106	134	187	188	222
	Others	2	3	2	1	0	1	1	5	0	7	16
	Total	2,661	2,671	2,638	2,620	384	2,247	2,442	2,307	2,344	3,003	797
Accidents on railway premises (ascending or descending steps at stations, falling over packages on platforms)												
Killed	Passengers	29	1	2	2	0	1	2	2	2	2	3
	Railway staff	4	3	4	2	0	6	5	5	1	2	0
	Others	1	0	4	1	0	1	0	1	0	0	1
	Total	34	4	10	5	0	8	7	8	3	4	4
Major injuries	Passengers	84	132	132	104	39	101	156	159	135	161	0
	Railway staff	199	231	231	252	64	233	245	235	230	192	270
	Others	11	10	17	15	3	18	6	13	23	20	0
	Total	294	373	380	371	106	352	407	407	388	373	270
Minor injuries	Passengers	3,566	3,903	4,297	3,543	587	3,318	3,727	4,309	4,250	4,601	1,710
	Railway staff	2,562	2,911	2,770	2,916	775	3,102	3,173	3,365	3,149	3,896	1,568
	Others	192	164	181	198	21	128	217	163	146	176	121
	Total	6,320	6,978	7,248	6,657	1,383	6,548	7,117	7,837	7,545	8,673	3,399
Overall Totals												
Killed	Passengers	68	69	33	37	8	31	18	16	17	10	15
	Railway staff	16	16	18	22	5	17	11	8	9	5	2
	Others	17	12	18	19	3	20	10	16	16	12	8
	Total	101	97	69	78	16	68	39	40	42	27	25
Major injuries	Passengers	177	309	268	224	92	192	238	205	204	214	0
	Railway staff	238	273	277	306	76	278	284	262	252	225	310
	Others	19	14	24	20	4	25	14	17	29	32	0
	Total	434	596	569	550	172	495	536	484	485	471	310
Minor injuries	Passengers	6,472	7,062	7,170	6,238	1,477	5,788	6,125	6,606	6,586	7,470	2,451
	Railway staff	2,672	3,022	2,858	3,051	798	3,226	3,348	3,590	3,411	4,144	1,842
	Others	208	186	204	209	23	142	226	183	164	205	151
	Total	9,352	10,270	10,232	9,498	2,298	9,156	9,699	10,379	10,161	11,819	4,444

Train Casualties by Type of Accident in the UK (*continued*)

Type of accident	1987[1]	1988	1989	1990	1991[2]	1991/92	1992/93	1993/94	1994/95	1995/96	1996/97[3]
Trespassers and suicides											
Deaths	317	334	298	311	63	300	264	262	254	246	251
Injured	101	129	92	123	23	119	89	97	85	82	106

[1] Figures include casualties arising from the King's Cross underground fire.
[2] Figures are for the period January to March 1991.
[3] Under the new accident reporting regulations (RIDDOR 95) brought into force on 1 April 1996, there is no longer a distinction between major and minor injury to members of the public. All injuries to members of the public are now shown as either minor or killed. The reporting trigger for minor injuries is that the person is taken to hospital for treatment.

Source: Department of the Environment, Transport and the Regions, Transport Statistics Great Britain, 1997 © Crown copyright

Train Accidents in the UK

(N/A = not available)

Type of accident	1986	1987	1988	1989	1990	1991/92	1992/93	1993/94	1994/95	1995/96	1996/97[1]
Collisions	266	290	296	329	290	187	154	135	125	123	120
Derailments	192	193	231	192	183	144	205	113	149	104	118
Running into level crossing gates and other obstructions	451	391	486	510	473	340	532	445	397	488	749
Fires	174	191	229	283	257	225	202	247	217	256	323
Missiles through cab windscreens[2]	N/A	N/A	N/A	N/A	N/A	N/A	N/A	N/A	N/A	N/A	468
Miscellaneous	88	101	88	120	80	64	59	37	19	18	3
Total	1,171	1,166	1,330	1,434	1,283	960	1,152	977	907	989	1,781

[1] New accident reporting regulations (RIDDOR 95) came into force on 1 April 1996.
[2] Category now reportable under RIDDOR 95.

Source: Department of the Environment, Transport and the Regions, Transport Statistics Great Britain, 1997 © Crown copyright

Tourism

UK Travellers' Favourite Destinations

Country	Numbers of travellers					% change 1992–96
	1992	1993	1994	1995	1996[1]	
France	7,887,000	8,485,000	9,009,000	9,710,000	9,910,000	25.6
Spain	5,675,000	6,491,000	7,705,000	8,302,000	7,548,000	33.0
USA	2,450,000	2,661,000	2,509,000	2,739,000	3,250,000	32.7
Ireland, Republic of	2,134,000	2,225,000	2,491,000	2,809,000	2,846,000	33.4
Germany	1,777,000	1,883,000	1,898,000	1,922,000	1,932,000	8.7
Netherlands	1,364,000	1,354,000	1,414,000	1,393,000	1,600,000	17.3
Italy	1,223,000	1,241,000	1,540,000	1,625,000	1,588,000	29.8
Belgium	928,000	1,057,000	964,000	1,085,000	1,472,000	58.6
Portugal	1,232,000	1,096,000	1,188,000	1,231,000	1,262,000	2.4
Turkey	329,000	660,000	721,000	865,000	1,030,000	213.1
Cyprus	934,000	789,000	977,000	679,000	727,000	−22.2
Switzerland	629,000	571,000	575,000	526,000	525,000	−16.5
Austria	638,000	690,000	590,000	604,000	450,000	−29.5
Subtotal	27,200,000	29,203,000	31,581,000	33,490,000	34,140,000	25.5
Other countries	6,636,000	7,517,000	8,316,000	8,383,000	9,392,000	41.5
World Total	33,836,000	36,720,000	39,897,000	41,873,000	43,532,000	28.7

[1] 1996 figures are estimates.

Source: Information Research Network

Numbers of International Visitors to the UK by Country of Origin

Country	Number of visitors					% change 1992–96
	1992	1993	1994	1995	1996[1]	
France	2,483,000	2,605,000	2,779,000	3,217,000	4,027,000	62.2
USA	2,748,000	2,849,000	2,979,000	3,258,000	3,207,000	16.7
Germany	2,268,000	2,457,000	2,517,000	2,682,000	3,004,000	32.5
Ireland, Republic of	1,416,000	1,464,000	1,677,000	1,988,000	2,131,000	50.5
Netherlands	996,000	1,268,000	1,204,000	1,441,000	1,694,000	70.1
Belgium	771,000	935,000	979,000	1,302,000	1,636,000	112.2
Italy	784,000	810,000	826,000	941,000	962,000	22.7
Spain	684,000	720,000	681,000	786,000	906,000	32.5
Australia	507,000	507,000	562,000	628,000	688,000	35.7
Canada	629,000	594,000	571,000	626,000	651,000	3.5
Japan	554,000	492,000	588,000	640,000	643,000	16.1
Sweden	507,000	503,000	517,000	560,000	620,000	22.3
Switzerland	433,000	503,000	474,000	549,000	618,000	42.7
Norway	297,000	312,000	336,000	433,000	445,000	49.8
Subtotal	15,077,000	16,019,000	16,690,000	19,051,000	21,232,000	40.8
Other countries	3,458,000	3,844,000	4,344,000	4,957,000	4,793,000	38.6
World total	18,535,000	19,863,000	21,034,000	24,008,000	26,025,000	40.4

[1] 1996 figures are estimates.

Source: Information Research Network

Visits to and Expenditure in the UK by Overseas Residents

(– = not applicable.)

Measure	1992	1993	1994	1995	1996[1]	% change 1992–96
Numbers of visits	18,535,000	19,863,000	21,034,000	24,008,000	26,025,000	40.4
% change year-on-year	–	7.2	5.9	14.1	8.4	
Expenditure in UK (£ million)	7,891	9,487	9,919	12,092	12,672	60.6
% change year-on-year	–	20.2	4.6	21.9	4.8	
Real expenditure at 1992 prices (£ million)	7,891	9,337	9,525	11,218	11,515	45.9

[1] 1996 figures are estimates.

Source: Information Research Network

Countries whose Inhabitants Spend the Most on Tourism

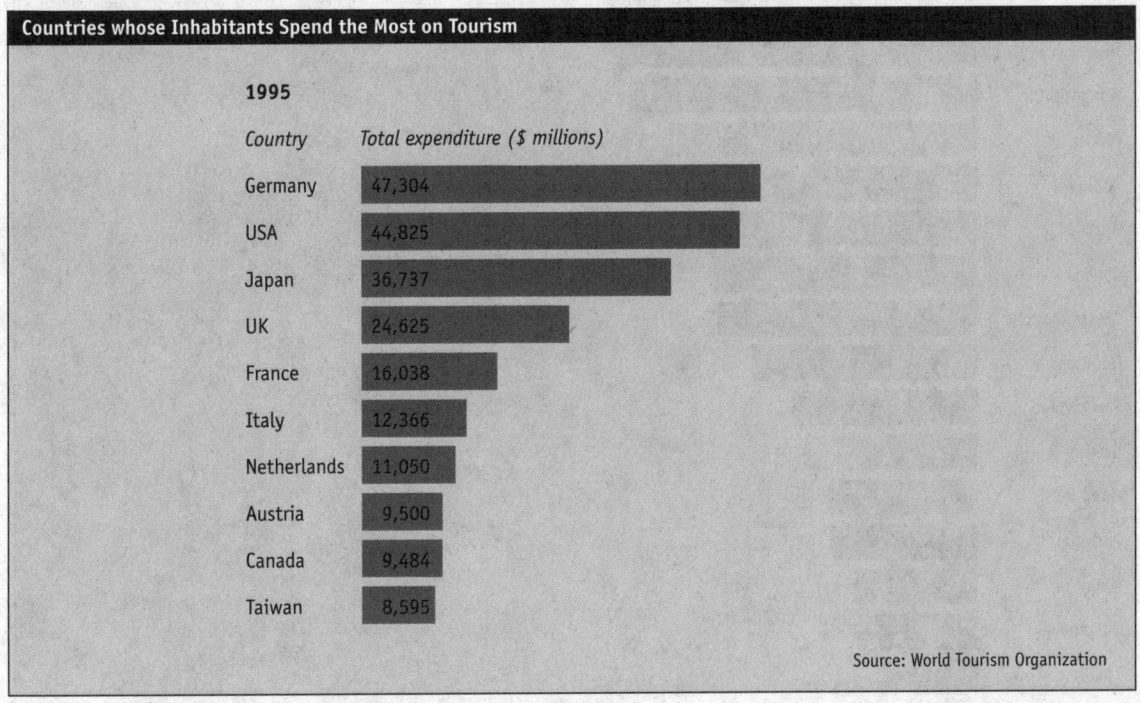

1995

Country	Total expenditure ($ millions)
Germany	47,304
USA	44,825
Japan	36,737
UK	24,625
France	16,038
Italy	12,366
Netherlands	11,050
Austria	9,500
Canada	9,484
Taiwan	8,595

Source: World Tourism Organization

The World's Top 20 Tourism Destinations

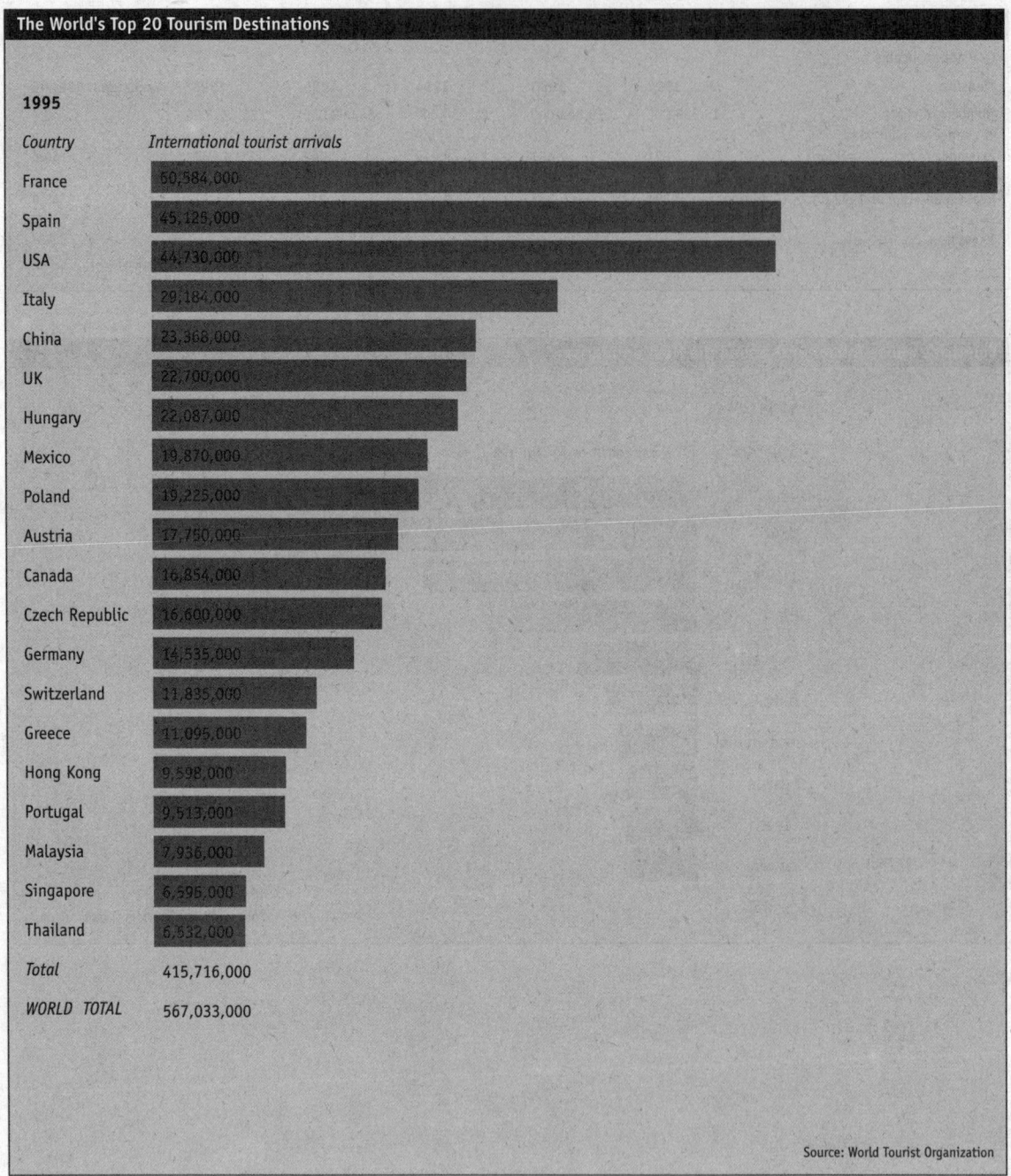

1995

Country	International tourist arrivals
France	60,584,000
Spain	45,125,000
USA	44,730,000
Italy	29,184,000
China	23,368,000
UK	22,700,000
Hungary	22,087,000
Mexico	19,870,000
Poland	19,225,000
Austria	17,750,000
Canada	16,854,000
Czech Republic	16,600,000
Germany	14,535,000
Switzerland	11,835,000
Greece	11,095,000
Hong Kong	9,598,000
Portugal	9,513,000
Malaysia	7,936,000
Singapore	6,596,000
Thailand	6,532,000
Total	415,716,000
WORLD TOTAL	567,033,000

Source: World Tourist Organization

Web Sites

Automotive Learning Online

URL: "http://www.innerbody.com/
innerauto/Default.htm"

Interactive and educational site on the car. It is a good training resource for engineering minds but also suited to all those who would simply like to know how their car works.

Aviation Enthusiasts' Corner

URL: "http://www.brooklyn.cuny.edu/
rec/air/air.html"

Forum dedicated to furthering interest in aviation-related hobbies. It includes links to museums and displays, features on key events in aviation history, and indexes of aircraft by type and manufacturer.

Cyberider Cycling Web Site

URL: "http://blueridge.databolts.
ibm.com/bikes/"

More than 50 megabytes of searchable information on equipment, advice, places, events, news, and archives, with hyperlinks to over 600 other cycling sites.

European Railway Server

URL: "http://mercurio.iet.unipi.it/
home.html"

Complete source of information on the railways of Europe. The needs of travellers, railway enthusiasts, and students of public transport are provided for. There are links to all Europe's railway operators.

Helicopter Aviation Home Page

URL: "http://www.copters.com/"

Contents include a history of the helicopter, technical aerodynamic details of what keeps them in the air, profile of mechanical components, advice to novice helicopter pilots, and manuals of various kinds of helicopters.

Home Page for Lighter-Than-Air Craft

URL: "http://spot.colorado.edu/
~dziadeck/airship.html"

Comprehensive site devoted to airships and all lighter-than-air craft, including of course the Zeppelin.

International Civil Aviation Organization

URL: "http://www.icao.int"

Site of the specialized UN agency regulating civil aviation. The role and history of the ICAO are well presented. There is information on rules of the air, international conventions, and standardization of safety standards. There are also links to all the online airlines, airports, and pilot training centres in the world.

National Railway Museum York

URL: "http://www.nmsi.ac.uk/nrm/
page2.html"

Excellent source of information for railway enthusiasts. In addition to information about the National Railway Museum and its exhibitions, there is news of railway matters from around the world. There is a listing of other sites for train buffs.

Radio Broadcast of the Hindenburg Disaster

URL: "http://www.otr.com/
hindenburg.html"

Part of a larger site paying homage to the glory days of radio, this site features audio of the chilling, live news coverage of the Hindenburg disaster as the giant airship exploded into flames at Lakehurst, New Jersey, on 6 May 1937.

Railtrack – The Heart of the Railway

URL: "http://www.railtrack.co.uk/
home.html"

User-friendly Railtrack site. Input your planned destination and time of departure and a schedule rapidly appears. The site also includes corporate information. There are plans to include frequent updates of operational difficulties and advice to travellers.

Rec.Motorcycles.Reviews Archives

URL: "http://rmr.cecm.sfu.ca/RMR/"

Plethora of motorbike (and accessories) reviews, written by motorcyclists and based on their own experiences.

Transportation: Panoramic Photographs, 1851–1991

URL: "http://lcweb2.loc.gov/cgi-
bin/query/r?ammem/pan:(@field
(SUBJ+@band(Airplanes+Biplanes+
Seaplanes+Airships+Railroad+Railro
ads+Automobiles+Motorcycles.+)))"

Part of the Panoramic Photo Collection of the US Library of Congress, this page features more than 200 panoramic photographs of various modes of transportation, including aeroplanes, biplanes, seaplanes, airships, trains, automobiles, motorcycles, mostly taken at the turn of the 20th century.

THE ENVIRONMENT

The Year in Review

7 July 1997 The Chilean government grants permission to US businessman and conservationist, Douglas Tompkins, to create a national park on a 677,000 acre/274,000 ha area of land he owns in southern Chile.

25 July 1997 The US Senate votes unanimously to pass a resolution that urges President Clinton not to agree to an international treaty that limits emissions of greenhouse gases by industrialized countries, warning that such a pact could pose a threat to the US economy.

July 1997 Flooding in central Europe causes more than 100 deaths in Poland and the Czech Republic and forces hundreds of thousands of people to evacuate their homes. The flood, caused by the overflow of the Oder River, is the worst to hit the area in 200 years.

7 August 1997 Canadian researcher Suzanne W Simard and colleagues announce the discovery that trees use the thread-like growths of fungi called mycorrhizae which infest their roots and connect the trees together underground to exchange food resources. It suggests that forest trees succeed as co-operative communities rather than competing individuals.

7 August 1997 The space shuttle *Discovery* blasts off from Cape Canaveral, Florida, on a 12-day ozone research mission to gather environmental data and test new equipment to be used on a future international space station.

22 August 1997 Scientists from the World Wide Fund for Nature (WWF) announce the discovery of a new species of muntjac deer in Vietnam. A dwarf species weighing only about 16 kg/35 lb, it has antlers the length of a thumbnail and lives at altitudes of 457–914 m/1,500–3,000 ft.

26 August 1997 At the World Climate Research Program meeting in Geneva, Switzerland, weather experts predict that El Niño could cause extreme weather conditions during the first six months of 1998 in Asia, Africa, and the USA.

7 September 1997 Australian researcher William de la Mare, using old whaling records which record data on every whale caught since the 1930s, including the ship's latitude, announces the discovery that Antarctic sea-ice could have decreased by up to a quarter between the mid-1950s and the 1970s. The finding has major implications, both for global climate conditions as well as for whaling.

26 September 1997 Two earthquakes strike central Italy, killing at least 11 people and injuring more than 120. The worst in Italy since 1980, the earthquakes also damaged important frescoes at the Basilica of St Francis in Assisi.

September 1997 Forest fires in Indonesia cause dense smog throughout the region; a state of emergency is declared in eastern Malaysia on 19 September.

8 October 1997–9 October 1997 Hurricane Pauline hits Mexico's southern coast, killing at least 230 people and leaving around 20,000 homeless. The strength of the storm, which causes extensive damage to the tourist resort of Acapulco, is blamed on El Niño.

22 October 1997 US President Bill Clinton announces a proposal to fight global warming by introducing $5 billion in tax breaks to companies who agree to reduce their greenhouse emissions.

3 November 1997 Typhoon Linda hits the southern coast of Vietnam, killing more than 100 people and destroying around 13,000 homes in Ca Mau and the neighbouring province of Ben Tre.

November 1997 Three weeks of rain causes severe flooding in Somalia, killing over 2,000 people and leaving 250,000 people homeless. A cholera outbreak follows the floods.

3 January 1998–4 January 1998 Violent storms sweep through Britain and Ireland, bringing winds up to 160 kph/100 mph and claiming two lives. Damage from this and other recent storms is estimated at £500 million.

10 January 1998 An earthquake measuring 6.2 on the Richter scale erupts in Hebei, a northeastern province of China, killing 50 people and injuring more than 11,000. It shakes some buildings in the capital, Beijing, which is 225 km/140 mi away, and cracks the Great Wall.

22 January 1998 The Australian government bans Japanese fishing boats from its waters after Japan refuses to limit its fishing of bluefin tuna, a probable endangered species.

4 February 1998 An earthquake measuring 6.1 on the Richter scale kills some 4,500 people in northeastern Afghanistan.

24 March 1998 A tornado carrying winds of 185 kph/115 mph strikes the eastern states of Orissa and West Bengal in India, killing at least 105 people and injuring some 1,100.

March 1998–April 1998 A series of tornadoes hits the southeastern USA, killing more than 60 people, spurred by the warmed ocean currents of El Niño.

8 April 1998 The International Union for the Conservation of Nature (IUCN), based in Switzerland, publishes a survey which reports that one in every eight known plant species in the world is in danger of becoming extinct.

10 April 1998–11 April 1998 The eastern and central regions of England experience the worst flooding in 50 years, resulting in five deaths and estimated damage of up to £500 million.

14 April 1998 Toxic algae in the waters off Hong Kong kill fish and result in beaches being closed. Environmentalists claim this 'red tide' is at least partly caused by pollution from southern China, but the Hong Kong government claims it developed naturally.

5 June 1998 British Deputy Prime Minister John Prescott announces proposals to protect Britain's national parks following concern about traffic congestion, pollution, and soil erosion. Traffic free-zones, bicycle lanes, and cheap bus fares are being considered for the park areas.

June 1998 The British government announces that it is considering a proposal to tax households according to how much rubbish they produce. The move would be designed to encourage recycling.

Animals and Plants

Classification of Living Things

Classification is the grouping of organisms based on similar traits and evolutionary histories. Taxonomy and systematics are the two sciences that attempt to classify living things. In taxonomy, organisms are generally assigned to groups based on their characteristics. In modern systematics, the placement of organisms into groups is based on evolutionary relationships among organisms. Thus, the groupings are based on evolutionary relatedness or family histories called phylogenies.

The groups into which organisms are classified are called taxa (singular, taxon). The taxon that includes the fewest members is the species, which identifies a single type of organism. Closely related species are placed into a genus (plural, genera). Related genera are placed into families, families into orders, orders into classes, classes into phyla (singular, phylum) or – in the case of plants and fungi – into divisions, and phyla into divisions or kingdoms. The kingdom level, of which five are generally recognized, is the broadest taxonomic group and includes the greatest number of species. The table below provides an example of the classification of an organism representative of the animal kingdom and the plant kingdom.

Taxonomic Groups[1]

Common name	Kingdom	Phylum/division[2]	Class	Order	Family	Genus[3]	Species[3]
human	Animalia	Chordata	Mammalia	Primates	Hominoidea	Homo	sapiens
Douglas fir	Plantae	Tracheophyta	Gymnospermae	Coniferales	Pinaceae	Pseudotsuga	douglasii

[1] Intermediate taxonomic levels can be created by adding the prefixes 'super-' or 'sub-' to the name of any taxonomic level.
[2] The term division is generally used in place of phylum/phyla for the classification of plants and fungi.
[3] An individual organism is given a two-part name made up of its genus and species names. For example, Douglas fir is correctly known as *Pseudotsuga douglasii*.

Major Invertebrate and Vertebrate Groups

Invertebrates

Taxon[1]	Name	Examples
P	Porifera	all sponges
P	Cnidaria	corals, sea anemones, *Hydra*, jellyfishes
P	Ctenophora	sea gooseberries, comb jellies
P	Platyhelminthes	flatworms, flukes, tapeworms
P	Nemertina	nemertine worms, ribbon worms
P	Nematoda	roundworms
P	Mollusca	clams, oysters, snails, slugs, octopuses, squids, cuttlefish
P	Annelida	ringed worms, including lugworms, earthworms, and leeches
P	Arthropoda	(subdivided into classes below)
C	Arachnida	spiders, ticks, scorpions, mites
C	Branchiopoda	water fleas
C	Cirripedia	barnacles
C	Malacostraca	crabs, lobsters, shrimp, woodlice
C	Diplopoda	millipedes
C	Chilopoda	centipedes
C	Insecta	silverfish, dragonflies, mayflies, stoneflies, cockroaches, earwigs, web spinners, termites, booklice, lice, grasshoppers, thrips, lace-wings, scorpion flies, caddis-flies, moths, butterflies, beetles, house flies, fleas, stylopids, ants, bees
P	Echinodermata	sea stars, brittle stars, sea urchins, sand dollars, sea cucumbers
P	Hemichordata	acorn worms, pterobranchs, graptolites

Vertebrates

Taxon[1]	Name	Examples
C	Agnatha	(jawless fishes) lampreys
C	Chondrichthyes	(cartilaginous fishes) dogfish, sharks, rays, skates
C	Osteichthyes	(bony fishes) salmon, catfishes, perches, flatfishes including flounder and halibut
C	Amphibia	frogs, toads, newts, salamanders, caecilians
C	Reptilia	tuatara, tortoises, turtles, lizards, snakes
C	Aves	rheas, ostriches, moa, penguins, ducks, pheasants, gulls, swifts, kingfishers, sparrows, woodpeckers, pelicans, flamingoes, herons, falcons, cranes, divers, pigeons, parrots, cuckoos, owls
C	Mammalia	duck-billed platypuses, echidnas, kangaroos, opossums, shrews, bats, dogs, seals, whales, dolphins, rats, rabbits, pigs, camels, deer, horses, tapirs, elephants, hyraxes, anteaters, manatees, pangolins, lemurs, monkeys, humans

West Indian (Florida) manatee

Corel

[1] P represents phylum; C represents class.

The Five Kingdoms of Living Things

Kingdom	Main features of organisms	Number of species
Monera[1]	all are bacteria; single-celled; prokaryotic (lack a membrane-bound nucleus); autotrophic (photosynthesis and chemosynthesis) and heterotrophic; all reproduce asexually, some also reproduce sexually	>10,000
Protista	single-celled or multicelled; eukaryotic (have a membrane-bound nucleus and membrane-bound organelles); autotrophic (photosynthesis in algae and Euglenoids) and heterotrophic; may reproduce asexually or sexually	>65,000
Fungi	single-celled and multicellular; eukaryotic; heterotrophic; form spores at all stages of their life cycle; usually reproduce asexually, many reproduce sexually by conjugation	about 100,000
Plantae	all are multicellular; eukaryotic; most are autotrophic (via photosynthesis); reproduce sexually; in some life cycle includes an alternation of generations (a haploid gametophyte stage and a diploid sporophyte stage)	about 500,000
Animalia	all are multicellular; eukaryotic; all are heterotrophic; reproduce sexually; develop from a blastula; most have tissues organized into organs	>795,000

[1] The Kingdom Monera is sometimes called the Kingdom Prokaryotae.

Animal Kingdom

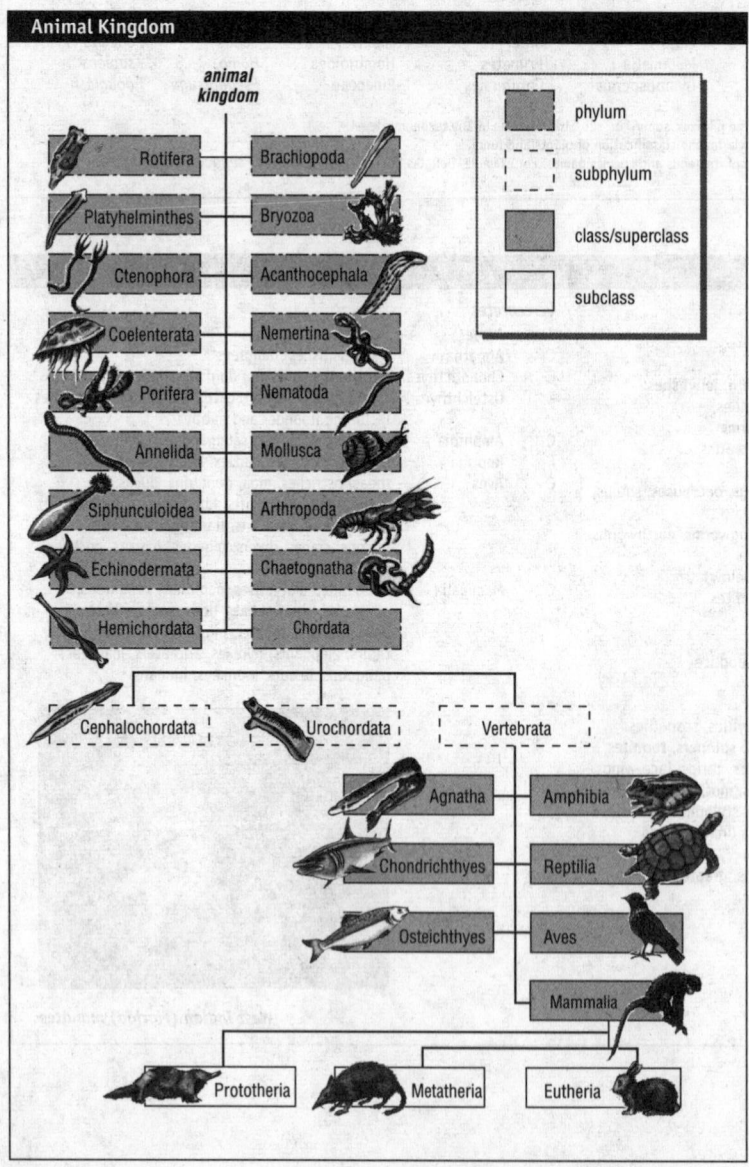

Classification of Mammals

Order	Number of species	Examples
Class: Mammalia		
Subclass: Prototheria (egg-laying mammals)		
Monotremata	3	echidna, platypus
Subclass: Theria		
Infraclass: Metatheria (pouched mammals)		
Marsupiala	266	kangaroo, koala, opossum
Infraclass: Eutheria (placental mammals)		
Rodentia	1,700	rat, mouse, squirrel, porcupine
Chiroptera	970	all bats
Insectivora	378	shrew, hedgehog, mole
Carnivora	230	cat, dog, weasel, bear
Primates	180	lemur, monkey, ape, human
Artiodactyla	145	pig, deer, cattle, camel, giraffe
Cetacea	79	whale, dolphin
Lagomorpha	58	rabbit, hare, pika
Pinnipedia	33	seal, walrus
Edentata	29	anteater, armadillo, sloth
Perissodactyla	16	horse, rhinoceros, tapir
Hyracoidea	11	hyrax
Pholidota	7	pangolin
Sirenia	4	dugong, manatee
Dermoptera	2	flying lemur
Proboscidea	2	elephant
Tubulidentata	1	aardvark

Classification of Major Bird Groups

Order	Examples
Tinamiformes	tinamous
Rheiformes	rhea
Struthioniformes	ostrich,
Casuariiformes	cassowary, emu
Apterygiformes	kiwi
Podicipediformes	grebe
Procellariiformes	albatross, petrel, shearwater, storm petrel
Sphenisciformes	penguin
Pelecaniformes	pelican, booby, gannet, frigate bird
Anseriformes	duck, goose, swan
Phoenicopteri-formes	flamingo
Ciconiiformes	heron, ibis, stork, spoonbill
Falconiformes	falcon, hawk, eagle, buzzard, vulture
Galliformes	grouse, partridge, pheasant, turkey
Gruiformes	crane, rail, bustard, coot
Charadriiformes	wader, gull, auk, oyster-catcher, plover, puffin, tern
Gaviiformes	diver
Columbiformes	dove, pigeon, sandgrouse
Psittaciformes	parrot, macaw, parakeet
Cuculiformes	cuckoo, roadrunner
Strigiformes	owl
Caprimulgiformes	nightjar, oilbird
Apodiformes	swift, hummingbird
Coliiformes	mousebird
Trogoniformes	trogon
Coraciiformes	kingfisher, hoopoe
Piciformes	woodpecker, toucan, puffbird
Passeriformes	finch, crow, warbler, sparrow, weaver, jay, lark, blackbird, swallow, mockingbird, wren, thrush

Corel

Bald eagle

Classification of Fish

Order	Number of species	Examples
Class Agnatha (jawless fishes)		
Sublass Cyclostomota (scaleless fish with round mouths)		
Petromyzoniformes	30	lamprey
Myxiniformes	15	hagfish
Superclass Pisces (jawed fishes)		
Class Chondrichthyes (cartilaginous fishes)		
Subclass Elasmobranchii (sharks and rays)		
Hexanchiformes	6	frilled shark, comb-toothed shark
Heterodontiformes	10	Port Jackson shark
Lamniformes	200	'typical' shark
Rajiformes	300	skate, ray
Subclass Holocephali (rabbitfishes)		
Chimaeriformes	20	chimaera, rabbitfish
Class Osteichthyes (bony fishes)		
Subclass Sarcopterygii (lobe-finned fishes)		
Coelacanthiformes	1	coelacanth
Ceratodiformes	1	Australian lungfish
Lepidosireniformes	4	South American and African lungfish
Subclass Actinopterygii (ray-finned fishes)		
Polypteriformes	11	bichir, reedfish
Acipensiformes	25	paddlefish, sturgeon
Amiiformes	8	bowfin, garpike
Superorder Teleostei		
Elopiformes	12	tarpon, tenpounder
Anguilliformes	300	eel
Notacanthiformes	20	spiny eel
Clupeiformes	350	herring, anchovy
Osteoglossiformes	16	arapaima, African butterfly fish
Mormyriformes	150	elephant-trunk fish, featherback
Salmoniformes	500	salmon, trout, smelt, pike
Gonorhynchiformes	15	milkfish
Cypriniformes	350	carp, barb, characin, loache
Siluriformes	200	catfish
Myctophiformes	300	deep-sea lantern fish, Bombay duck
Percopsiformes	10	pirate perch, cave-dwelling amblyopsid
Batrachoidiformes	10	toadfish

(continued)

Classification of Fish (*continued*)

Order	Number of species	Examples	Order	Number of species	Examples
Gobiesociformes	100	clingfish, dragonets	Channiformes	5	snakeshead
Lophiiformes	150	anglerfish	Synbranchiformes	7	cuchia
Gadiformes	450	cod, pollack, pearlfish, eelpout	Scorpaeniformes	700	gurnard, miller's thumb, stonefish
Atheriniformes	600	flying fish, toothcarp, halfbeak	Dactylopteriformes	6	flying gurnard
			Pegasiformes	4	sea-moth
Lampridiformes	50	opah, ribbonfish	Pleuronectiformes	500	flatfish
Beryciformes	150	squirrelfish	Tetraodontiformes	250	puffer fish, triggerfish, sunfish
Zeiformes	60	John Dory, boarfish			
Gasterosteiformes	150	stickleback, pipefish, seahorse	Perciformes	6,500	perch, cichlid, damsel fish,

Classification of Insects

(N/A = not available.)

Order	Number of species	Examples	Order	Number of species	Examples
Class insecta					
Subclass Apterygota (wingless insects)			*Exopterygota (young resemble adults but have externally-developing wings)*		
Thysanura	350	three-pronged bristletails, silverfish	Psocoptera	1,600	booklice, barklice, psocids
Diplura	400	two-pronged bristletails, campodeids, japygids	Mallophaga	2,500	biting lice, mainly parasitic on birds
Protura	50	minute insects living in soil	Anoplura	250	sucking lice, mainly parasitic on mammals
Collembola[1]	1,500	springtails	Hemiptera	55,000	true bugs, including shield- and bedbugs, froghoppers, pond skaters, water boatmen
Subclass Pterygota (winged insects or forms secondary wingless)			Homoptera	N/A	aphids, cicadas
			Thysanoptera	5,000	thrips
Superorder Exopterygota (young resemble adults but have externally-developing wings)			*Superorder Endopterygota (young, unlike adults, undergo sudden metamorphosis)*		
Ephemeroptera	1,000	mayflies			
Odonata	5,000	dragonflies, damselflies	Neuroptera	4,500	lacewings, alder flies, snake flies, ant lions
Plecoptera	3,000	stoneflies			
Grylloblattodea	12	wingless soil-living insects of North America	Mecoptera	300	scorpion flies
Orthoptera	20,000	crickets, grasshoppers, locusts, mantids, roaches	Lepidoptera	165,000	butterflies, moths
			Trichoptera	3,000	caddis flies
Phasmida	2,000	stick insects, leaf insects	Diptera	80,000	true flies, including bluebottles, mosquitoes, leatherjackets, midges
Dermaptera	1,000	earwigs			
Embioptera	150	web-spinners			
Dictyoptera	5,000	cockroaches, praying mantises	Siphonaptera	1,400	fleas
			Hymenoptera	100,000	bees, wasps, ants, sawflies, chalcids
Isoptera	2,000	termites			
Zoraptera	16	tiny insects living in decaying plants	Coleoptera	350,000	beetles, including weevils,

[1] Some zoologists recognize the Collembola taxon as a class rather than an order.

EXTINCTION: A RACE AGAINST TIME

BY COLIN TUDGE

About a million different living species have been identified so far. Recent studies in tropical forests – where biodiversity is greatest – suggest the total number of species in the world is nearer 30 million. Most are animals, and most of those are insects. Because the tropical forests are threatened, at least half the animal species could become extinct within the next century.

There is conflict within the conservation movement over what is to be done about this. Some believe that *habitats* (the places where animals and plants live) should be conserved; others prefer to concentrate upon individual *species*. Both approaches have strengths and weaknesses, and they must operate in harmony.

Habitat Protection

Habitat protection has obvious advantages. Many species benefit if land is preserved. Animals need somewhere to live; unless the habitat is preserved it may not be worth saving the individual animal. Habitat protection *seems* cheap; for example, tropical forest can often be purchased for only a few dollars per hectare. Only by habitat protection can we save more than a handful of the world's animals.

But there are difficulties. Even when a protected area is designated a 'national park', its animals may not be safe. All five remaining species of rhinoceros are heavily protected in the wild, but are threatened by poaching. Early in 1991 Zimbabwe had 1,500 black rhinos – the world's largest population. Patrols of game wardens shoot poachers on sight. Yet by late 1992, 1,000 of the 1,500 had been poached. In many national parks worldwide, the habitat is threatened by the local farmers' need to graze their cattle.

Computer models and field studies show that wild populations need several hundred individuals to be viable. Smaller populations will eventually go extinct in the wild, because of accidents to key breeding individuals, or epidemics. The big predators need vast areas. One tiger may command hundreds of square kilometres; a viable population of tigers needs an area as big as Wales or Holland.

Only one of the world's five remaining subspecies of tiger – a population of Bengals in India – occupies an area large enough to be viable. All the rest (Indo-Chinese, Sumatran, Chinese, and Siberian) seem bound to die out. Three other subspecies have gone extinct in the past 100 years – the latest, the Javan, in the 1970s.

Mosaic

Ecologists now emphasize the concept of *mosaic*. All animals need different things from their habitat, and a failure of supply

Greater panda *Reserves in which rare animals live must contain all the elements an animal needs to survive*

Corel

of any one is disastrous. For example giant pandas feed mainly on bamboo, but give birth in old hollow trees – of which there is a shortage.

Nature reserves must either contain all essentials for an animal's life, or else allow access to such areas elsewhere. For many animals in a reserve, these conditions are not fulfilled. Interest is increasing in *captive breeding*, carried out mainly by the world's 800 zoos. Their task is formidable; each captive species should include several hundred individuals. Zoos maintain such numbers through *cooperative breeding*, organized regionally and coordinated by the Captive Breeding Specialist Group or the World Conservation Union, based in Minneapolis, Minnesota. Each programme is underpinned by a studbook, showing which individuals are related to which.

Breeding for conservation is different from breeding for livestock improvement. Livestock breeders breed *uniform* creatures by selecting animals conforming to some prescribed ideal. Conservation breeders maintain *maximum genetic diversity:* by encouraging every individual to breed, including those reluctant to breed in captivity; by equalizing family size, so one generation's genes are all represented in the next; and by swapping individuals between zoos to prevent inbreeding.

Cooperative Breeding

Cooperative breeding programmes are rapidly diversifying; by the year 2000 there should be several hundred. They can only make a small impression on the 15 million endangered species, but they can contribute greatly to particular groups of animals, especially the land vertebrates – mammals, birds, reptiles, and amphibians. Land vertebrates include most of the world's largest animals, animals which have greatest impact on their habitats. There are 24,000 species of land vertebrate, of which 2,000 probably require captive breeding to survive.

Captive breeding is not intended to establish 'museum' populations, but to provide a temporary 'lifeboat'. Things are hard for wild animals, but over the next few decades, despite the growing human population, it should be possible to establish more and safer national parks. The Arabian oryx, California condor, black-footed ferret, red wolf, and Mauritius kestrel are among the creatures so far saved from extinction by captive breeding and returned to the wild. In the future, we can expect to see many more.

Major Divisions in the Plant Kingdom

Phylum	Examples
Bryophyta	mosses, liverworts, hornworts
Psilophyta	whisk ferns
Sphenophyta	horsetails
Filicinophyta	ferns
Cycadophyta	cycads
Gingkophyta	*Gingko*
Coniferophyta	cedar, cypress, juniper, pine, redwood
Anthophyta	flowering plants

Classes of flowering plants

Dicotyledons	magnolia, laurel, water lily, buttercup, poppy, pitcher plant, nettle, walnut, cacti, peonies, violet, begonia, willow, primrose, rose, maple, holly, grape, honeysuckle, African violet, daisy
Monocotyledons	flowering rush, eel grass, lily, iris, banana, orchid, sedge, pineapple, grasses, palms, cat tail

Classification of Carnivorous Plants

Plants that obtain at least some of their nutrition by capturing and digesting prey are called carnivorous plants. Such plants have adaptations that allow them to attract, catch, and break down or digest prey once it is caught. Estimates of the number of species of carnivorous plants number from 450 to more than 600. Generally, these plants are classified into genera based upon the mechanism they have for trapping and capturing their prey. The major genera of these plants are listed in the table.

Common name	Genus	Scientific name	Trapping mechanism
bladderwort	*Utricularia*	*Utricularia vulgaris*	active trap; shows rapid motion during capture
butterwort	*Pinguicula*	*Pinguicula vulgaris*	semi-active trap; two-stage trap in which prey is initially caught in sticky fluid
calf's head pitcher plant	*Darlingtonia*	*Darlingtonia californica*	passive trap; attracts prey with nectar and then drowns prey in fluid contained within plant
flypaper plant	*Byblis*	*Byblis liniflora*	passive trap; attracts prey with nectar and then drowns prey in fluid contained within plant
sundew	*Drosera*	*Drosera linearis*	semi-active trap; two-stage trap in which prey is initially caught in sticky fluid
Venus flytrap	*Dionaea*	*Dionaea muscipula*	active trap; shows rapid motion during capture

Venus flytrap

Selected Animals on the Endangered and Threatened Species List for the World

(Data as of April 1997.)

Common name	Scientific name	Range	When listed
Mammals			
armadillo, giant	*Priodontes maximus (= giganteus)*	South America	24 June 1976
bear, brown	*Ursus arctos arctos*	Europe	24 June 1976
bear, brown	*Ursus arctos pruinosus*	Asia	24 June 1976
bear, Mexican grizzly	*Ursus arctos (= U. a. nelsoni)*	North America	2 June 1970
bison, wood	*Bison bison athabascae*	North America	2 June 1970
bobcat	*Felis rufus escuinapae*	North America	24 June 1976
camel, Bactrian	*Camelus bactrianus (=ferus)*	Asia	24 June 1976
cat, leopard	*Felis bengalensis bengalensis*	Asia	24 June 1976
deer, pampas	*Ozotoceros bezoarticus*	South America	24 June 1976
dugong	*Dugong dugon*	Africa	2 December 1970
duiker, Jentink's	*Cephalophus jentinki*	Africa	25 June 1979
eland, western giant	*Taurotragus derbianus derbianus*	Africa	25 June 1979
elephant, African	*Loxodonta africana*	Africa	12 May 1978
elephant, Asian	*Elephas maximus*	Asia	24 June 1974
gazelle, Clark's (Dibatag)	*Ammodorcas clarkei*	Africa	2 June 1970
gorilla	*Gorilla gorilla*	Africa	2 June 1970
kangaroo, Tasmanian forester	*Macropus giganteus tasmaniensis*	Australia	4 June 1973
lemurs	*Lemuridae*	Africa	2 June 1970, 14 June 1976, 24 June 1976
leopard	*Panthera pardus*	Africa, Asia	2 June 1970, 30 March 1972, 28 January 1982

Selected Animals on the Endangered and Threatened Species List for the World (*continued*)

Common name	Scientific name	Range	When listed
leopard, snow	*Panthera uncia*	Asia	30 March 1972
manatee, Amazonian	*Trichechus inunguis*	South America	2 June 1970
manatee, West African	*Trichechus senegalensis*	Africa	20 July 1979
monkey, black howler	*Alouatta pigra*	North America	19 October 1976
monkey, red-backed squirrel	*Saimiri oerstedii*	South America	2 June 1970
monkey, spider	*Ateles geoffroyi frontatus*	South America	2 June 1970
mouse, Shark Bay	*Pseudomys praeconis*	Australia	2 December 1970
orangutan	*Pongo pygmaeus*	Asia	2 June 1970
panda, giant	*Ailuropoda melanoleuca*	Asia	23 January 1984
rat-kangaroo, Queensland	*Bettongia tropica*	Australia	2 December 1970
rhinoceros, black	*Diceros bicornis*	Africa	14 July 1980
rhinoceros, great Indian	*Rhinoceros unicornis*	Asia	2 December 1970
seal, Saimaa	*Phoca hispida saimensis*	Europe	28 July 1993
sloth, Brazilian three-toed	*Bradypus torquatus*	South America	2 June 1970
tapir, Asian	*Tapirus indicus*	Asia	24 June 1974
tapir, mountain	*Tapirus pinchaque*	South America	2 June 1970
tiger	*Panthera tigris*	Asia	2 June 1970, 30 March 1972
tiger, Tasmanian (thylacine)	*Thylacinus cynocephalus*	Australia	2 June 1970
wallaby, banded hare	*Lagostrophus fasciatus*	Australia	2 December 1970
whale, blue	*Balaenoptera musculus*	Oceanic	2 June 1970
whale, bowhead	*Balaena mysticetus*	Oceanic	2 June 1970
whale, finback	*Balaenoptera physalus*	Oceanic	2 June 1970
whale, humpback	*Megaptera novaeangliae*	Oceanic	2 June 1970
whale, right	*Balaena glacialis* (incl. *australis*)	Oceanic	2 June 1970
whale, sperm	*Physeter macrocephalus* (=*catodon*)	Oceanic	2 June 1970
wombat, hairy-nosed (Barnard's and Queensland hairy-nosed)	*Lasiorhinus krefftii* (formerly *L. Barnardi* and *L. gillespiei*)	Australia	2 December 1970, 4 June 1973
zebra, Grevy's	*Equus grevyi*	Africa	21 August 1979
zebra, mountain	*Equus zebra zebra*	Africa	24 June 1976, 10 February 1981

Birds

Common name	Scientific name	Range	When listed
booby, Abbott's	*Sula abbotti*	Asia	24 June 1976
condor, Andean	*Vultur gryphus*	South America	2 December 1970
crane, hooded	*Grus monacha*	Asia	2 December 1970
crane, Japanese	*Grus japonenis*	Asia	2 June 1970
crane, whooping	*Grus americana*	North America	11 March 1967, and other dates
eagle, harpy	*Harpia harpyja*	South America	24 June 1976
egret, Chinese	*Egretta eulophotes*	Asia	2 June 1970
falcon, American peregrine	*Falco peregrinus anatum*	North America	13 October 1970
hawk, Galapagos	*Buteo galapagoensis*	South America	2 June 1970
ibis, Japanese crested	*Nipponia nippon*	Asia	2 June 1970
ibis, northern bald	*Geronticus eremita*	Africa, Asia, Europe	28 September 1990
macaw, glaucous	*Anodorhynchus glaucus*	South America	24 June 1976
macaw, indigo	*Anodorhynchus leari*	South America	24 June 1976
ostrich, Arabian	*Struthio camelus syriacus*	Asia	2 June 1970
ostrich, West African	*Struthio camelus spatzi*	Africa	2 June 1970
parakeet, gold-shouldered (hooded)	*Psephotus chrysopterygius*	Australia	2 June 1970
parakeet, Norfolk Island	*Cyanoramphus novaezelandiae cookii*	Australia	28 September 1990
parrot, ground	*Pezoporus wallicus*	Australia	4 June 1973
parrot, red-capped	*Pionopsitta pileata*	South America	24 June 1976
stork, oriental white	*Ciconia ciconia boyciana*	Asia	2 June 1970
woodpecker, imperial	*Campephilus imperialis*	North America	2 June 1970
woodpecker, Tristam's	*Drycopus javensis richardsi*	Asia	2 June 1970

Reptiles

Common name	Scientific name	Range	When listed
alligator, Chinese	*Alligator sinensis*	Asia	24 June 1976
caiman, Apaporis River	*Caiman crocodilus apaporiensis*	South America	24 June 1976
crocodile, African dwarf	*Osteolaemus tetraspis tetraspis*	Africa	24 June 1976
crocodile, African slender-snouted	*Crocodylus cataphractus*	Africa	30 March 1972
crocodile, Morelet's	*Crocodylus moreletii*	South America	2 June 1970
iguana, Barrington land	*Conolophus pallidus*	South America	2 June 1970
lizard, Hierro giant	*Gallotia simonyi simonyi*	Europe	29 February 1984
lizard, Ibiza wall	*Podarcis pityusensis*	Europe	29 February 1984

(continued)

Selected Animals on the Endangered and Threatened Species List for the World (*continued*)

Common name	Scientific name	Range	When listed
monitor, Bengal	*Varanus bengalensis*	Asia	24 June 1976
monitor, desert	*Varanus griseus*	Africa	24 June 1976
monitor, yellow	*Varanus flavescens*	Asia	24 June 1976
python, Indian	*Python molurus molurus*	Asia	24 June 1976
tartaruga	*Podocnemis expansa*	South America	2 June 1970
tortoise, Bolson	*Gopherus flavomarginatus*	North America	17 April 1979
tortoise, Galapagos	*Geochelone elephantopus*	South America	2 June 1970
tuatara	*Sphenodon punctatus*	Australia	2 June 1970
turtle, aquatic box	*Terrapene coahuila*	North America	4 June 1973
turtle, green sea	*Chelonia mydas* (incl. *agassizi*)	North America (circumglobal)	28 July 1978
viper, Lar Valley	*Vipera latiffi*	Asia	22 June 1983
Amphibians			
frog, Goliath	*Conraua goliath*	Africa	8 December 1994
frog, Israel painted	*Discoglossus nigriventer*	Europe	2 June 1970
frog, Panamanian golden	*Atelopus varius zeteki*	South America	24 June 1976
frog, Stephen Island	*Leiopelma hamiltoni*	Australia	2 June 1970
salamander, Chinese giant	*Andrias davidianus davidianus*	western China	24 June 1976
salamander, Japanese giant	*Andrias davidianus japonicus*	Japan	24 June 1976
toad, African viviparous	*Nectophrynoides* spp.	Africa	24 June 1976
toad, Cameroon	*Bufo superciliaris*	Africa	24 June 1976
toad, Monte Verde	*Bufo periglenes*	South America	24 June 1976

Source: US Fish and Wildlife Service and World Conservation Monitoring Centre

Threatened Animals of the World: Numbers of Species

The table consists of the number of threatened species for each taxonomic class listed.

1996

Class	Extinct species	Species extinct in the wild	Sub-total	Critically endangered species	Endangered species	Vulnerable species[1]	Sub-total	Conserv-ation dependent	Near threatened	Data-deficient[2]
Mammalia (mammals)	86	3	89	169	315	612	1,096	75	598	209
Aves (birds)	104	4	108	168	235	704	1,107	11	875	66
Reptilia (reptiles)	20	1	21	41	59	153	253	1	79	74
Amphibia (amphibians)	5	0	5	18	31	75	124	2	25	42
Cephalaspidomorphi (lampreys)	1	0	1	0	1	2	3	0	5	3
Elasmobranchii (sharks)	0	0	0	1	7	7	15	0	0	2
Actinopterygii (ray-finned fish)	80	11	91	156	125	434	715	12	96	250
Sarcopterygii (lobe-finned fish)	0	0	0	0	1	0	1	0	0	0
Echinoidea (sea urchins)	0	0	0	0	0	0	0	0	1	0
Arachnida (arthropods)	0	0	0	0	1	9	10	0	1	7
Chilopoda (centipedes)	0	0	0	0	0	1	1	0	0	0
Crustacea (crustaceans)	9	1	10	54	73	280	407	9	1	31
Insecta (insects)	72	1	73	44	116	377	537	3	77	40
Merostomata (class of aquatic arthropods)	0	0	0	0	0	0	0	0	1	3
Onychophora (phylum of terrestrial arthropods)	3	0	3	1	3	2	6	0	1	1
Hirudinea (leeches)	0	0	0	0	0	0	0	0	1	0
Oligochaeta (earthworms)	0	0	0	1	0	4	5	0	1	0
Polychaeta (bristleworms)	0	0	0	1	0	0	1	0	0	1
Bivalvia (bivalves)	12	0	12	81	22	11	114	5	62	5
Gastropoda (snails)	216	9	225	176	190	440	806	16	172	541
Enopla (nematodes)	0	0	0	0	0	2	2	0	1	3
Turbellaria (flatworms)	1	0	1	0	0	0	0	0	0	0
Anthozoa (cnidaria)	0	0	0	0	0	2	2	0	0	1

[1] Facing a high risk of extinction in the medium-term future.
[2] Information is inadequate to make a direct or indirect assessment of risk.

Source: World Conservation Monitoring Centre

Endangered Species

Species	Observation	Species	Observation
plants	a quarter of the world's plants are threatened with extinction by the year 2010	invertebrates	about 100 species are lost each day due to deforestation; half the freshwater snails in the southeastern USA are now extinct or threatened; a quarter of German invertebrates are threatened
amphibians	worldwide decline in numbers; half of New Zealand's frog species are now extinct; 25% of species threatened with extinction 1996	mammals	half of Australia's mammals are threatened; 40% of mammals in France, the Netherlands, Germany, and Portugal are threatened; 25% of species are threatened with extinction 1996
birds	three-quarters of all bird species are declining; 11% are threatened with extinction 1996	primates	two-thirds of primate species are threatened
carnivores	almost all species of cats and bears are declining in numbers	reptiles	over 40% of reptile species are threatened; 20% with extinction 1996
fish	one-third of North American freshwater fish are rare or endangered; half the fish species in Lake Victoria, Africa's largest lake, are close to extinction due to predation by the introduced Nile perch; 33% of species are threatened with extinction 1996		

Some Threatened Plants and Animals Used in the World Wildlife Trade

International trade in live plants and animals, and in wildlife products such as skins, horns, shells, and feathers has made some species virtually extinct, and whole ecosystems (for example, coral reefs) are threatened. Wildlife trade is to some extent regulated by CITES (Convention on International Trade in Endangered Species). Species almost eradicated by trade in their products include many of the largest whales, crocodiles, marine turtles, and some wild cats. Until recently, some two million snake skins were exported from India every year. Populations of black rhino and African elephant have collapsed because of hunting for their horns and tusks (ivory), and poaching remains a problem in cases where trade is prohibited.

Common name	Scientific name	Range	Reason threatened
alligator snapping turtle	*Macroclemys temminckii*	North America	used in canned turtle soup, a delicacy in some countries; also sold as pets
beluga sturgeon	*Huso huso*	Caspian Sea	caviar is a delicacy in many countries; the long life cycle of the fish makes the population more vulnerable
big leaf mahogany	*Swietenia macrophylla king*	Central and South America	mahogany wood is used for furniture in many countries
black rhino	*Diceros bicornis*	Africa	hunted for their horns, which are used in powdered form in oriental medicine
giant panda	*Ailuropoda melanaleca*	China	destruction of the bamboo forests, the natural habitat for pandas, makes the population more vulnerable; as does poaching and demand as zoo animals
goldenseal	*Hydrastis canadensis*	North America	used in herbal medicine as a 'natural antibiotic'; demand has increased as herbal medicine becomes more widespread
green-cheeked parrot	*Amazona viridiginohs*	Mexico	hunted and captured for pet trade; many birds die in transit
hawksbill turtle	*Eretmochelys imbricata*	tropical seas	the shell is used as tortoiseshell, although under an official ban in most places; the slow reproductive cycle of the turtle makes the population more vulnerable
mako shark	*Isurus oxyrinchus*	Atlantic, Pacific, and Indian oceans	shark meat is a delicacy in some countries; the slow reproductive cycle makes the population more vulnerable
tiger	*Panthera tigis*	Asia	destruction of jungle; hunted for bones and other parts for use in oriental medicine

Source: Convention on International Trade in Endangered Species, World Wide Fund for Nature

Some Plants and Animals Removed from the World Endangered and Threatened Species List

Common name	Scientific name	Range	Reason removed from list
dove, Palau	*Gallicolumba canifrons*	West Pacific–Palau Islands	recovered
falcon, Arctic peregrine	*Falco peregrinus tundris*	nests from northern Alaska to Greenland; winters to Central and South America	recovered
fantail, Palau (Old World flycatcher)	*Rhipidura lepida*	West Pacific–Palau Islands	recovered
kangaroo, eastern gray	*Macropus giganteus* (all subspecies except *tasmaniensis*)	Australia	recovered
kangaroo, red	*Macropus rufus*	Australia	recovered
kangaroo, western gray	*Macropus fuliginosus*	Australia	recovered
owl, Palau	*Pyrroglaux podargina*	West Pacific–Palau Islands	recovered
turtle, Indian flap-shelled	*Lissemys punctata punctata*	India, Pakistan, Bangladesh	better data
whale, gray (eastern North Pacific population)	*Eschrichtius robustus*	North Pacific Ocean–coastal and Bering Sea, formerly North Atlantic Ocean	recovered

Source: US Fish and Wildlife Service and World Conservation Monitoring Centre

Whaling: Chronology

11th/12th century	Basque villagers began hunting right whales in the Bay of Biscay, severely depleting local stocks by the 13th century.	**1960–61**	All-time peak in whaling; 64,000 cetaceans caught worldwide.
1610	Greenland bowhead whale fishery began. Stocks were reduced to the brink of extinction by the 19th century.	**1962**	Whaling reduced the humpback whale population to an estimated 1,000.
1789	The first commercial whalers entered the Pacific.	**1967**	IWC prohibited the hunting of blue, right, grey, and humpback whales.
1848	Arctic bowhead whales discovered and quickly exploited; stocks were almost totally depleted by 1914.	**1979**	IWC banned the hunting of sperm whales.
		1985	IWC officially banned all commercial whaling; however, whaling continued under the guise of 'scientific' expeditions.
1864	Norwegian engineer Sven Foyn invents the gun-launched harpoon with an explosive head. It permits hunting the faster and more plentiful fin, sei, and blue whales and ushers in the era of modern whaling.	**1988–89**	Boycott of Icelandic fishing products, in protest against the country's continuation of commercial whaling, cost the Icelandic fishing industry $30 million.
1890	Californian grey whale believed to be extinct after 40 years of hunting; however, some individuals survived and are now protected.	**1993**	Greenpeace conducted a boycott campaign against Norwegian products to discourage Norway's continued whaling.
1904	Whaling operations began in the Southern Ocean.	**1994**	Russia revealed that the former Soviet Union fleet had secretly continued large-scale commercial whaling for 40 years, without declaring catch numbers to IWC. The IWC established a whale sanctuary in Antarctica.
1925	First factory ships used by whalers, doing away with the need to return to shore-based stations and so increasing catches.		
1946	International Whaling Commission (IWC) established.	**1995**	Japan and Norway continued their commercial whaling, despite an international moratorium. Norway was openly whaling commercially; Japan claimed it was doing so for scientific research.
1950s	First commercial whale-watching tours began, observing migrating grey whales off southern California.		

Average Animal Gestation Periods and Incubation Times

Animal	Gestation[1]/ incubation[2] (days)	Animal	Gestation[1]/ incubation[2] (days)	Animal	Gestation[1]/ incubation[2] (days)
Mammals					
Ass	365	Deer (white-tailed)	201	Lion	108
Baboon	187	Dog (domestic)	58–70	Llama	330
Bear (black)	210	Elephant (Asian)	645	Mink	40–75
Bear (grizzly)	225	Elk (Wapiti)	240–250	Monkey (rhesus)	164
Bear (polar)	60	Fox (red)	52	Moose	240–250
Beaver	122	Giraffe	420–450	Mouse (domestic white)	19
Buffalo (American)	270	Goat (domestic)	145–155	Mouse (meadow)	21
Camel (Bactrian)	410	Gorilla	257	Muskrat	28–30
Cat (domestic)	58–65	Guinea pig	68	Opossum (American)	12–13
Chimpanzee	23	Hippopotamus	225–250	Otter	270–300
Chinchilla	110–120	Horse	330–342	Pig (domestic)	112–115
Chipmunk	31	Kangaroo	42	Porcupine	112
Cow	279–292	Leopard	92–95	Puma	90

Average Animal Gestation Periods and Incubation Times (*continued*)

Animal *Mammals*	Gestation[1]/ incubation[2] (days)	Animal	Gestation[1]/ incubation[2] (days)	Animal	Gestation[1]/ incubation[2] (days)
Rabbit (domestic)	30–35	Whale (sperm)	480–500	*Birds*	
Raccoon	63	Wolf	60–68		
Rhinoceros (black)	450	Zebra (Grant's)	365	Chicken	20–22
Seal	330			Duck	26–28
Sea lion (California)	350			Finch	11–14
Sheep (domestic)	144–151			Goose	25–28
Squirrel (grey)	30–40			Parrot	17–31
Tiger	105–113			Pheasant	24
				Pigeon	10–18
				Quail	21–23
				Swan	33–36
				Turkey	28

[1] Mammals.
[2] Birds.

Animal Lifespans

(N/A = not available.)

Animal	Average longevity (years)	Maximum longevity (years)[1]	Animal	Average longevity (years)	Maximum longevity (years)[1]
Ass	12	35.8	Guinea pig	4	7.5
Baboon	20	35.5	Hippopotamus	45	49
Bear (black)	18	36.8	Horse	20	46
Bear (grizzly)	25	47	Kangaroo	12	28
Bear (polar)	20	34.7	Leopard	12	19.3
Beaver	10	20.5	Lion	15	25
Buffalo (American)	15	N/A	Monkey (rhesus)	15	N/A
Camel (Bactrian)	12	N/A	Moose	12	N/A
Cat (domestic)	12	28	Mouse (domestic white)	1	3.5
Chimpanzee	40	44.5	Mouse (meadow)	3	N/A
Chipmunk	6	8	Opossum (American)	2	8
Cow	15	30	Pig (domestic)	10	27
Deer (white-tailed)	8	N/A	Puma	12	19
Dog (domestic)	12	20	Rabbit (domestic)	5	13
Elephant (African)	60	80	Rhinoceros (black)	15	N/A
Elephant (Asian)	60	80	Rhinoceros (white)	20	N/A
Elk	15	26.5	Sea lion (California)	12	28
Fox (red)	7	14	Sheep (domestic)	12	20
Giraffe	25	33.5	Squirrel (grey)	10	N/A
Goat (domestic)	8	8	Tiger	16	26.3
Gorilla	35	50	Wolf (grey)	12	20
			Zebra (Grant's)	15	35

[1] Maximum longevity figures refer to animals in captivity; an animal's potential life span is rarely attained in nature.

Names for Animal Young

Animal	Name for young	Animal	Name for young	Animal	Name for young
Bear	cub	Duck	duckling	Rabbit	bunny, kitten
Beaver	pup, kit, kitten	Elephant	calf	Rhinoceros	calf
Bird	nestling	Fish	fry	Seal	pup, whelp, cub
Bobcat	kitten, cub	Frog	polliwog, tadpole	Sea lion	pup
Buffalo	calf, yearling, spike-bull	Giraffe	calf	Sheep	lamb, lambkin
Camel	calf, colt	Goat	kid	Squirrel	pup
Canary	chick	Goose	gosling	Swan	cygnet
Cat	kitten	Horse	foal, yearling, colt (male), filly (female)	Tiger	cub, whelp
Cattle	calf			Turkey	chick
Chicken	chick	Kangaroo	joey	Turtle	chicken
Chimpanzee	infant	Lion	cub	Walrus	calf
Cod	coling, scrod	Louse	nit	Whale	calf
Condor	chick	Owl	owlet	Wolf	cub, pup
Deer	fawn	Partridge	cheeper, chick	Zebra	colt, foal
Dog	pup, puppy, whelp	Penguin	fledgling, chick		

Speeds of Animals

Animal	Speed		Animal	Speed		Animal	Speed	
	kph	mph		kph	mph		kph	mph
Cheetah	103	64	Greyhound	63	39	Human	45	28
Wildebeest	98	61	Whippet	57	35.5	Elephant	40	25
Lion	81	50	Rabbit (domestic)	56	35	Black mamba snake	32	20
Horse	76	47.5	Jackal	56	35	Squirrel	19	12
Elk	72	45	Reindeer	51	32	Pig (domestic)	18	11
Cape hunting dog	72	45	Giraffe	51	32	Chicken	14	9
Coyote	69	43	White-tailed deer	48	30	Giant tortoise	0.27	0.17
Grey fox	68	42	Wart hog	48	30	Three-toed sloth	0.24	0.15
Hyena	64	40	Grizzly bear	48	30	Garden snail	0.05	0.03
Zebra	64	40	Cat (domestic)	48	30			

Biology: Chronology

c. 500 BC	First studies of the structure and behaviour of animals, by the Greek Alcmaeon of Croton.
c. 450	Hippocrates of Kos undertook the first detailed studies of human anatomy.
c. 350	Aristotle laid down the basic philosophy of the biological sciences and outlined a theory of evolution.
c. 300	Theophrastus carried out the first detailed studies of plants.
c. AD 175	Galen established the basic principles of anatomy and physiology.
c. 1500	Leonardo da Vinci studied human anatomy to improve his drawing ability and produced detailed anatomical drawings.
1628	William Harvey described the circulation of the blood and the function of the heart as a pump.
1665	Robert Hooke used a microscope to describe the cellular structure of plants.
1672	Marcelle Malphigi undertook the first studies in embryology by describing the development of a chicken egg.
1677	Anton van Leeuwenhoek greatly improved the microscope and used it to describe spermatozoa as well as many microorganisms.
1736	Carolus (Carl) Linnaeus published his systematic classification of plants, so establishing taxonomy.
1768–79	James Cook's voyages of discovery in the Pacific revealed an undreamed-of diversity of living species, prompting the development of theories to explain their origin.
1796	Edward Jenner established the practice of vaccination against smallpox, laying the foundations for theories of antibodies and immune reactions.
1809	Jean-Baptiste Lamarck advocated a theory of evolution through inheritance of acquired characteristics.
1839	Theodor Schwann proposed that all living matter is made up of cells.
1857	Louis Pasteur established that microorganisms are responsible for fermentation, creating the discipline of microbiology.
1859	Charles Darwin published 'On the Origin of Species', expounding his theory of the evolution of species by natural selection.
1865	Gregor Mendel pioneered the study of inheritance with his experiments on peas, but achieved little recognition.
1883	August Weismann proposed his theory of the continuity of the germ plasm.
1900	Mendel's work was rediscovered and the science of genetics founded.
1935	Konrad Lorenz published the first of many major studies of animal behaviour, which founded the discipline of ethology.
1953	James Watson and Francis Crick described the molecular structure of the genetic material, DNA.
1964	William Hamilton recognized the importance of inclusive fitness, so paving the way for the development of sociobiology.
1975	Discovery of endogenous opiates (the brain's own painkillers) opened up a new phase in the study of brain chemistry.
1976	Har Gobind Khorana and his colleagues constructed the first artificial gene to function naturally when inserted into a bacterial cell, a major step in genetic engineering.
1982	Gene databases were established at Heidelberg, Germany, for the European Molecular Biology Laboratory, and at Los Alamos, USA, for the US National Laboratories.
1985	The first human cancer gene, retinoblastoma, was isolated by researchers at the Massachusetts Eye and Ear Infirmary and the Whitehead Institute, Massachusetts.
1988	The Human Genome Organization (HUGO) was established in Washington DC with the aim of mapping the complete sequence of DNA.
1991	Biosphere 2, an experiment that attempts to reproduce the world's biosphere in miniature within a sealed glass dome, was launched in Arizona, USA.
1992	Researchers at the University of California, USA, stimulated the multiplication of isolated brain cells of mice, overturning the axiom that mammalian brains cannot produce replacement cells once birth has taken place. The world's largest organism, a honey fungus with underground hyphae (filaments) spreading across 600 hectares/1,480 acres, was discovered in Washington State, USA.
1994	Scientists from Pakistan and the USA unearthed a 50-million-year-old fossil whale with hind legs that would have enabled it to walk on land.
1995	New phylum identified and named Cycliophora. It contains a single known species, *Symbion pandora*, a parasite of the lobster.
1996	The sequencing of the genome of brewer's yeast *Saccharomyces cerevisiae* is completed, the first time this has been achieved for an organism more complex than a bacterium. The 12 million base pairs took 300 scientists six years to map. A new muscle was discovered by two US dentists. It is 3 cm/1 in long, and runs from the jaw to behind the eye socket.
1997	The first mammal to be cloned from a non-reproductive cell was born. The lamb (named Dolly) had been cloned from an udder cell from a six-year-old ewe.

Collective Names for Animals

Animal	Collective name	Animal	Collective name	Animal	Collective name
Ants	colony, swarm, nest	Gnats	cloud, horde	Oysters	bed
Bears	sleuth, sloth	Goats	tribe, trip, herd	Partridge	covey
Bees	grist, swarm, hive, nest, colony	Goldfinches	charm	Peacocks	muster, ostentation
Birds	flight, volery, flock	Gorillas	band	Pheasants	nest, nide
Cats	clowder, clutter, litter	Greyhounds	leash	Pigs	litter
Cattle	drove, herd	Hares	down, husk	Quails	bevy, covey
Chicks	brood, clutch	Hawks	cast	Rhinoceroses	crash
Clams	bed	Horses	pair, team, herd, stable	Seals	pod, herd, rookery
Crows	murder	Hounds	pack, cry, mute	Sheep	drove, flock
Deer	herd	Kangaroos	mob, troop, herd	Swans	bevy, wedge
Dogs	litter, kennel, pack (wild)	Larks	exaltation	Termites	colony, nest, swarm
Ducks	brace, team, flock	Leopards	leap	Toads	knot
Elephants	herd	Lions	pride	Turtles	bale, dole, rafter
Elks	gang	Monkeys	troop	Vipers	nest
Fishes	school, shoal, draught	Nightingales	watch	Whales	gam, pod, herd
Foxes	leash, skulk	Oxen	yoke, drove, herd	Wolves	pack
Geese	flock, gaggle, skein				

Dogs Registered with the Kennel Club

Year	Sporting	Non-sporting	Total	Year	Sporting	Non-sporting	Total
1980	90,075	111,545	201,620	1989	135,016	148,899	283,915
1981	75,398	96,960	172,358	1990	131,811	138,958	270,769
1982	75,110	97,410	172,520	1991	126,997	125,527	252,524
1983	78,663	106,236	184,899	1992	121,709	118,448	240,157
1984	77,784	106,259	184,043	1993	119,689	116,204	235,893
1985	84,608	113,682	198,290	1994	125,328	121,379	246,707
1986	83,101	106,315	189,416	1995	136,679	127,412	264,091
1987	79,674	101,762	181,436	1996	144,124	129,217	273,341
1988	75,562	90,988	166,550				

Source: The Kennel Club

Crufts Supreme Champions

(Ch = Champion. Sh Ch = Show Champion. D = dog. B = bitch. N = neutered.)

Year	Dog's name	Breed	Sex	Owner	Breeder
1980	Ch Shargleam Blackcap	Flat coated retriever	D	Miss P Chapman	owner
1981	Ch Astley's Portia of Rua	Irish setter	B	Mrs and Miss Tuite	Mrs M Korbel
1982	Ch Grayco Hazelnut	Toy poodle	B	Mrs L A Howard	owner
1983	Ch Montravia-Kaskarak Hitari	Afghan hound	D	Mrs P Gibbs	Mrs L Race
1984	Ch Saxonsprings Hackensack	Llaso Apso	D	Mrs J Blyth	owner
1985	Ch Montravia Tommy-Gun	Standard poodle	D	Miss M Gibbs	Mrs C Coxall
1986	Ch Ginger Xmas Carol	Airedale terrier	B	Mrs A Livraghi	owner
1987	Ch Viscount Grant	Afghan hound	D	Mr C Amoo	owner
1988	Ch Starlight Express of Valsett	English setter	B	Mr and Mrs J W Watkin	Mrs A R Wick
1989	Ch Potterdale Classic of Moonhill	Bearded collie	B	Mrs B R White	Mr and Mrs M Lewis
1990	Ch Olac Moon Pilot	West Highland white terrier	D	Mr D Tattersall	owner
1991	Sh Ch Raycroft Socialite	Clumber spaniel	D	Mr R Dunne	Mrs R Furness
1992	Ch Penglow Dutch Gold	Whippet	N	Miss Bolton	owner
1993	Sh Ch Dunnaway Debonair	Irish setter	N	Mrs Carrimer	owner
1994	Ch Perston Hit and Miss from Brocalita	Welsh terrier	N	Mrs B Halliwell	owner
1995	Sh Ch Starshell Chicago Bear	Irish setter	N	Miss Rachael Shaw	owner
1996	Sh Ch Canigou Cambrai	Cocker spaniel	N	Ms Tricia Bentley	owner
1997	Ch Ozmilion Mystification	Yorkshire terrier	D	Mr Osman Adam Sameja	owner
1998	Ch Saredon Forever Young	Welsh Terrier	D	Mr D Scawthorn and Mrs J Averis	owner

Source: The Kennel Club

Climate and Weather

EL NIÑO: THE CHRISTMAS CHILD

BY NIGEL DUDLEY

In 1997, more tropical forest burned than at any other time in recorded history. Vast fires in Indonesia and the Amazon appeared on television screens all over the world, but fires also blazed throughout Africa, Papua New Guinea, and Australia. Unlike some temperate and boreal forests, most tropical moist forests do not readily burn under natural conditions. Reasons for the increase are complex, and include changes to the forest through over-logging and uncontrolled use of fire as a land management tool. However, the 1997 fires were given a fresh impetus by a catastrophic drought that affected vast areas of Africa, Asia, and South America. This drought was, in turn, associated with a hitherto fairly obscure climatic event – known as El Niño (literally 'The Child') – that principally affects large parts of the Pacific coast of South America.

Theory

El Niño is a current of warm water in the southeastern Pacific, which usually reaches the Pacific coast of South America around Christmas. Although normally benign, it can periodically become extremely damaging when it is associated with another climatic phenomenon known as the Southern Oscillation, a complex series of events including changes in wind temperature, ocean currents, and sea levels. The combination, often known as an El Niño/Southern Oscillation or ENSO event, produces an invasion of warm water into usually cool areas, causing wet and stormy weather in the west Pacific and sometimes as far as North America, and drought conditions in Africa, Brazil, Australia, and parts of Asia and the Pacific.

Immediate Impact

The immediate impact on the Latin American coastline can be catastrophic. Warmer water kills plankton, squid, and smaller fish such as anchovy and sardine. Lack of food in turn kills larger fish such as herring and hake. This sometimes causes extreme short-term declines in the seabird colonies found along the coast and on offshore islands. Seabirds may also have their nests inundated by rising waters and coral reefs sometimes suffer bleaching – perhaps as a result of warmer water. In human terms, fisheries face extreme hardship and agricultural crops are likely to fail. Along the coasts of Chile and off the southern USA, sardine populations can virtually disappear for a period. Particularly spectacular ENSO events occurred in 1940–41, 1957–58, and 1982–83. Loss of sardines caused a collapse in the industry in California during the 1940s, as recorded in John Steinbeck's *Cannery Row*.

Wider Implications

The wider climatic conditions have other impacts. The greater number of forest fires has been mentioned above, but it is only in recent years that their full significance has been recognized. For example, over several months in the summer of 1997, and continuing into 1998, an area of Southeast Asia from the Philippines to Australia was enveloped in smog caused by forest fires in the Indonesian islands of Java, Borneo, Sulawesi, Irian Jaya, and Sumatra. Over two million hectares of forests and other land were destroyed. More than 40,000 Indonesians became ill as a result and over a million suffered eye infections. Primary forest and at least 19 protected areas were damaged in Indonesia. Rains after the fire caused soil erosion and consequent damage to offshore fisheries as coral was smothered with debris. Business, including tourism, suffered badly and initial estimates put costs at a massive US$20 billion. Although most fires were started deliberately – often illegally – by commercial interests such as plantation owners, impacts were exacerbated by the El Niño climatic effect. ENSO events are also associated started particularly bad burning seasons in Australia and the Amazon.

Drought also causes direct human hardship as a result of crop failures. At the end of 1997, hundreds of thousands of people in the Indonesian-controlled area of Irian Jaya and in neighbouring Papua New Guinea were facing starvation after the worst drought for 50 years. Associated fires in Papua New Guinea created such a dense pall of smoke that pilots bringing in emergency food supplies were sometimes unable to land.

The Future

Currently, El Niño and the associated ENSO events appear to be growing both more frequent and more severe. An increasing number of scientists are linking this change to changes caused by pollution-related climatic change, although others think that it may be largely the result of natural fluctuations. Whatever the cause, the impacts are becoming more intense, and off the coast of western South America and the southern USA marine life seems to be undergoing longer-term changes. Since the 1950s, there has been an 80 percent decline in zooplankton along California's coast between San Diego and San Francisco, accompanied by a 1.2–1.6°C temperature rise. This decline in plankton is also having an effect on seabird populations, particularly the sooty shearwater. The population of this bird has declined by 90 percent.

Timing of ENSO events is also becoming more erratic. In the past, severe El Niño events tended to last around 18 months, and would be separated by long breaks so that marine and bird life could become re-established. However, the current ENSO event began in 1990 and appears to be continuing, with a series of unpredictable peaks and troughs. It apparently reached maturity in early 1992 and started to decline in the expected manner, but by the following November it had increased in strength again. It continued through 1994 and it appears as if the 1997 events may be simply another continuation..

Climate change specialists are also interested in El Niño because the main oceanic effects – a rise in sea level, higher water temperatures, and reduced offshore flow – are those most often associated with predictions relating to climate change. Scientists and fisheries experts have studied El Niño to find out what might happen elsewhere on the globe under conditions of global warming. Scientists are currently using the occurrence of a temperature-sensitive algae, *Emiliana huxleyi*, in layers of sediment to create an accurate profile of changing sea temperatures in the eastern Pacific between 1915 and 1988.

A Summary of World Weather Records

(Data as of April 1997. N/A = not applicable.)

Record	Location	Details
Highest amount of rainfall in 24 hours (not induced by the presence of mountains)	Dharampuri, India	99 cm/39 in
Highest amount of rainfall in 24 hours	Cilaos, La Reunion Island	188 cm/74 in
Highest amount of rainfall over 5 days	Cilaos, La Reunion Island	386 cm/152 in
Highest amount of rainfall in 12 hours	Belouve, La Reunion Island	135 cm/53 in
Highest amount of rainfall in 20 minutes	Curtea-de-Arge, Romania	21 cm/8.1 in
Highest yearly number of days of rainfall	Bahia Felix, Chile	325 days
Longest period without rainfall	Arica, Chile	14 years
Highest yearly average period of thunderstorms	Kampala, Uganda	242 days per year
Highest sustained yearly average period of thunderstorms	Bogor, Indonesia	322 days per year from 1916 to 1919
Highest yearly average rainfall in Africa	Debundscha, Cameroon	1,029 cm/405 in (with an average variability of 191 cm/75 in)
Lowest yearly average rainfall in Africa	Wadt Halfa, Sudan	3 mm/0.1 in
Lowest yearly average rainfall in Asia	Aden, South Yemen	5 cm/1.8 in
Highest yearly average rainfall in Europe	Crkvice, Yugoslavia	465 cm/183 in
Lowest yearly average rainfall in Europe	Astrakhan, Russia	16 cm/6.4 in
Highest amount of rainfall in Australia in 24 hours	Crohamhurst, Queensland	91 cm/36 in
Highest yearly average rainfall in Australia	Tully, Queensland	455 cm/179 in
Lowest yearly average rainfall in Australia	Mulka, South Australia	10 cm/4.1 in
Highest yearly average rainfall in South America	Quibdo, Colombia	899 cm/354 in
Lowest yearly average rainfall in South America	Arica, Chile	0.7 mm/0.03 in
Highest yearly average rainfall in North America	Henderson Lake, British Columbia, Canada	665 cm/262 in
Lowest yearly average rainfall in North America	Bataques, Mexico	3 cm/1.2 in
Highest temperature ever recorded in the world	El Aisisa, Libya	58°C/136°F
Lowest temperature ever recorded in the world	Vostok, Antarctica	−88°C/−127°F
Highest yearly average temperature in world	Dallol, Ethiopia	34°C/94°F
Highest yearly average temperature range	Eastern Sayan Region, Russia	through 63°C/146°F
Highest average temperature sustained over a long period	Marble Head, Australia	38°C/100°F for 162 consecutive days
Highest temperature in Antarctica	N/A	near 16°C/60°F
Lowest temperature in Africa	Ifrane, Morocco	−24°C/−11°F
Highest temperature in Asia	Tirat Tsvi, Israel	54°C/129°F
Highest temperature in Australia	Cloncurry, Queensland	53°C/128°F
Lowest temperature in Australia	Charlotte Press	−22°C/−8°F
Highest temperature in Europe	Seville, Spain	50°C/122°F
Lowest temperature in Europe	Ust 'Shchugor, USSR	−55°C/−67°F
Lowest temperature in Greenland	Northice	−66°C/−87°F
Lowest temperature in North America (excluding Greenland)	Snag, Yukon Territory, Canada	−63°C/−81°F
Lowest temperature in northern hemisphere	Verkhoyansk, Oimekon, USSR	−68°C/−90°F
Highest temperature in South America	Rivadavia, Argentina	49°C/120°F
Lowest temperature in South America	Sarmiento, Argentina	−33°C/−27°F
Highest temperature in western hemisphere	Death Valley (CA)	57°C/134°F
Highest peak wind	Thule Air Base, Greenland	333 kph/207 mph
Highest average wind speed in 24 h	Port Martin, Antarctica	173 kph/108 mph
Highest peak wind gust	Mt Washington (NH)	372 kph/231 mph
Highest monthly average wind speed	Port Martin, Antarctica	104 kph/65 mph

Source: National Weather Service; National Oceanic and Atmospheric Administration

Retired Hurricane and Tropical Storm Names

The names used for tropical storms and hurricanes are reused on a four- or six-year cycle, depending upon the part of the world in which the storm strikes. However, the names of tropical storms and hurricanes that cause severe damage or result in great loss of life are retired and not used again. Storm names that have been retired appear in the table with the year of their retirement.

Name	Year	Name	Year	Name	Year
Agnes	1972	Celia	1970	Frederic	1979
Alicia	1983	Cleo	1964	Gilbert	1988
Allen	1980	Connie	1955	Gloria	1985
Andrew	1992	David	1979	Gracie	1959
Anita	1977	Diana	1990	Hattie	1961
Audrey	1957	Diane	1955	Hazel	1954
Betsy	1965	Dona	1960	Hilda	1964
Beulah	1967	Dora	1964	Hugo	1989
Bob	1991	Edna	1954	Inez	1966
Camille	1969	Elena	1985	Ione	1955
Carla	1961	Eloise	1975	Janet	1955
Carmen	1974	Fifi	1974	Joan	1988
Caro	1954	Flora	1963	Klaus	1990

Photo Disc Ltd.

Aeriel view of a collapsed thunderstorm

Source: National Weather Service, NOAA (National Oceanic and Atmospheric Administration), US Department of Commerce

The Worst Storms, Floods, and Hurricanes in the UK

Date	Location	Details
26–27 November 1703	southwest England	one of the worst storms in British history (called The Great Storm); it occurred before records were kept, but sources show that 125 people were killed on land and 8,000 at sea
16 January 1841	River Till	following heavy snow in the first week of 1841, the temperature rose to 5°C/41°F and meltwater burst the banks of the River Till
29 December 1897	Tay Bridge	part of the bridge collapsed during gale force winds, causing a train to plunge into the water below, drowning 75 people
26 August 1912	Norwich	torrential rain amounting to the equivalent of 3 months' rainfall in a single day caused severe flooding, damaging or destroying about 3,650 buildings
29 May 1920	Louth	thunderstorms, where 115 mm/4.5 in of rain fell in 2.5 hours, caused severe flooding and devastated the town
28 January 1927	Glasgow	gale force winds caused extensive damage and 11 people were killed and over 100 injured
6 January 1928	London	torrential rain and meltwater from snow caused widespread flooding of the Thames and its tributaries; 14 people were drowned in the basements of their houses
21 May 1950	Berkshire	tornado with a wind speed of up to 370 kph/230 mph blazed a trail of destruction for nearly 161 km/100 mi in approximately 4 hours
15 August 1952	Lynmouth	torrential rainfall measuring 386 mm/15.2 in in 12 hours on Exmoor caused flood water to flow down the river Lyn and devastate Lynmouth; 34 people were killed
1–7 December 1952	London	anticyclone prevented the passage of clean air clearing fog over London; it is believed that up to 4,000 deaths in 1952 were a direct result of the black smoke from chimneys, or 'smog', which had settled in the air
4 November 1957	Hatfield	gale force winds caused damage to 26 houses
16 February 1962	Sheffield	severe gale with gusts of up to 154 kph/96 mph caused extensive damage to buildings; a crane was uprooted and crashed onto the new technical college and 100,000 homes were damaged, including 100 beyond repair
21 July 1965	Wisley	tornado lasting about 10 minutes caused destruction 10–30 m/32–98 ft-wide for a distance of 3 km/2 mi
1 November 1965	Ferrybridge	gusting winds caused 3 cooling towers to collapse
27 December 1965	Sea Gem Oil Rig	high winds created waves 6 m/20 ft high, and caused oil rig to collapse; 9 people died
24 June 1967	Mossdale	heavy rains filled the caves drowning 6 people inside
15 January 1968	Glasgow	gale force winds gusting up to 161 km/100 mph caused extensive damage; over 100,000 homes were damaged
16 September 1968	River Mole	150–200 mm/5.9–7.9 in of rainfall over 3 days caused the River Mole to burst its banks
21 November 1971	Cairngorms	snow blizzard caused deaths of 6 members of a school party on a climbing expedition
16 October 1987	south England	the worst storm since 1703, causing extensive damage to tree areas and a total of 17 deaths
10 April 1998	Eastern and central England	the worst flooding in 50 years, resulting in 5 deaths and estimated damage of up to £500 million

© Richard Watt

Flooding *At Easter 1998 huge amounts of rainfall in a very short period of time led to severe floods in England*

Average Monthly High and Low Temperatures for UK Cities and Weather Stations

1961–90

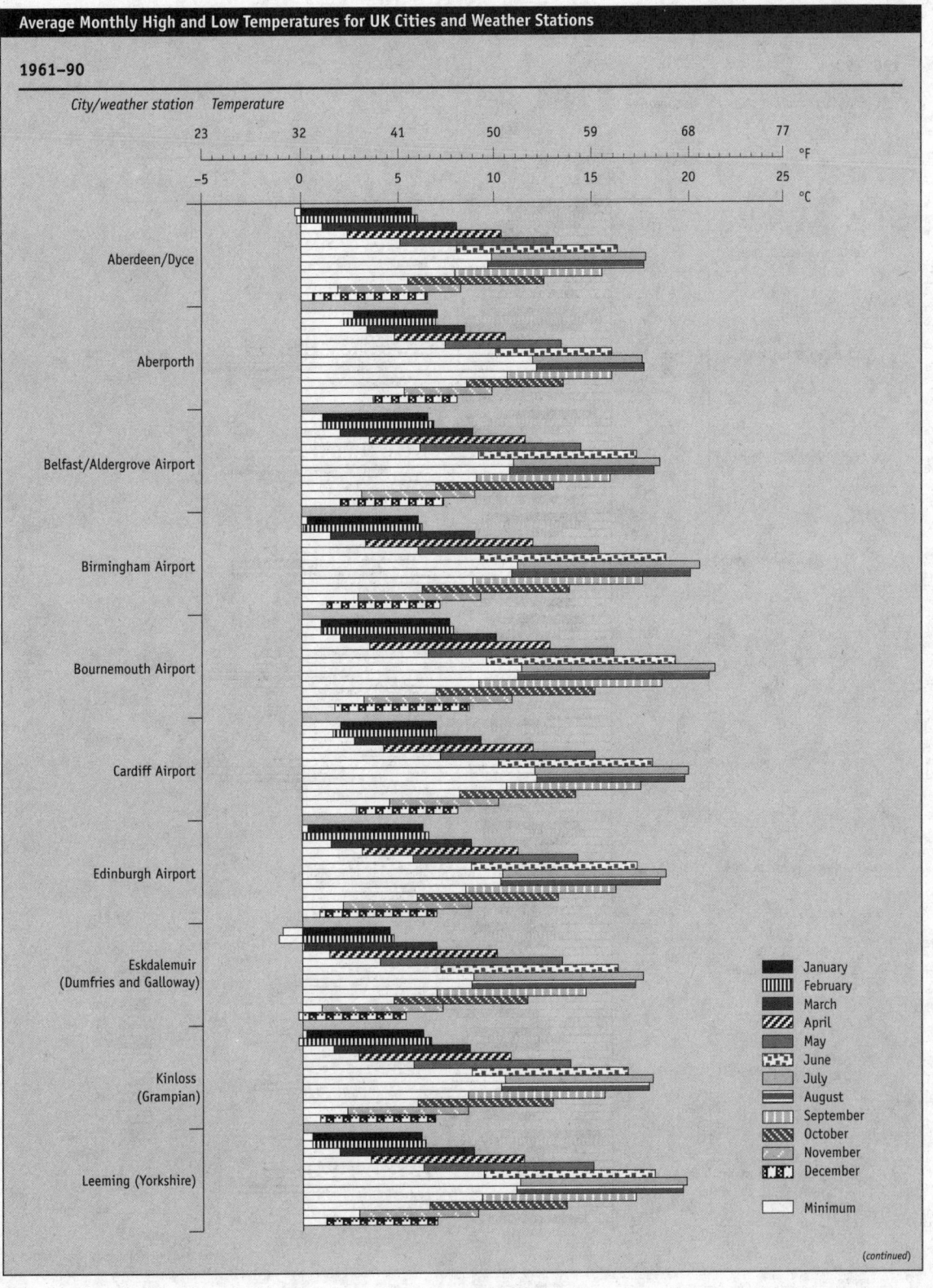

City/weather station   Temperature

Aberdeen/Dyce

Aberporth

Belfast/Aldergrove Airport

Birmingham Airport

Bournemouth Airport

Cardiff Airport

Edinburgh Airport

Eskdalemuir
(Dumfries and Galloway)

Kinloss
(Grampian)

Leeming (Yorkshire)

January
February
March
April
May
June
July
August
September
October
November
December

Minimum

(continued)

Average Monthly High and Low Temperatures for UK Cities and Weather Stations (*continued*)

1961–90

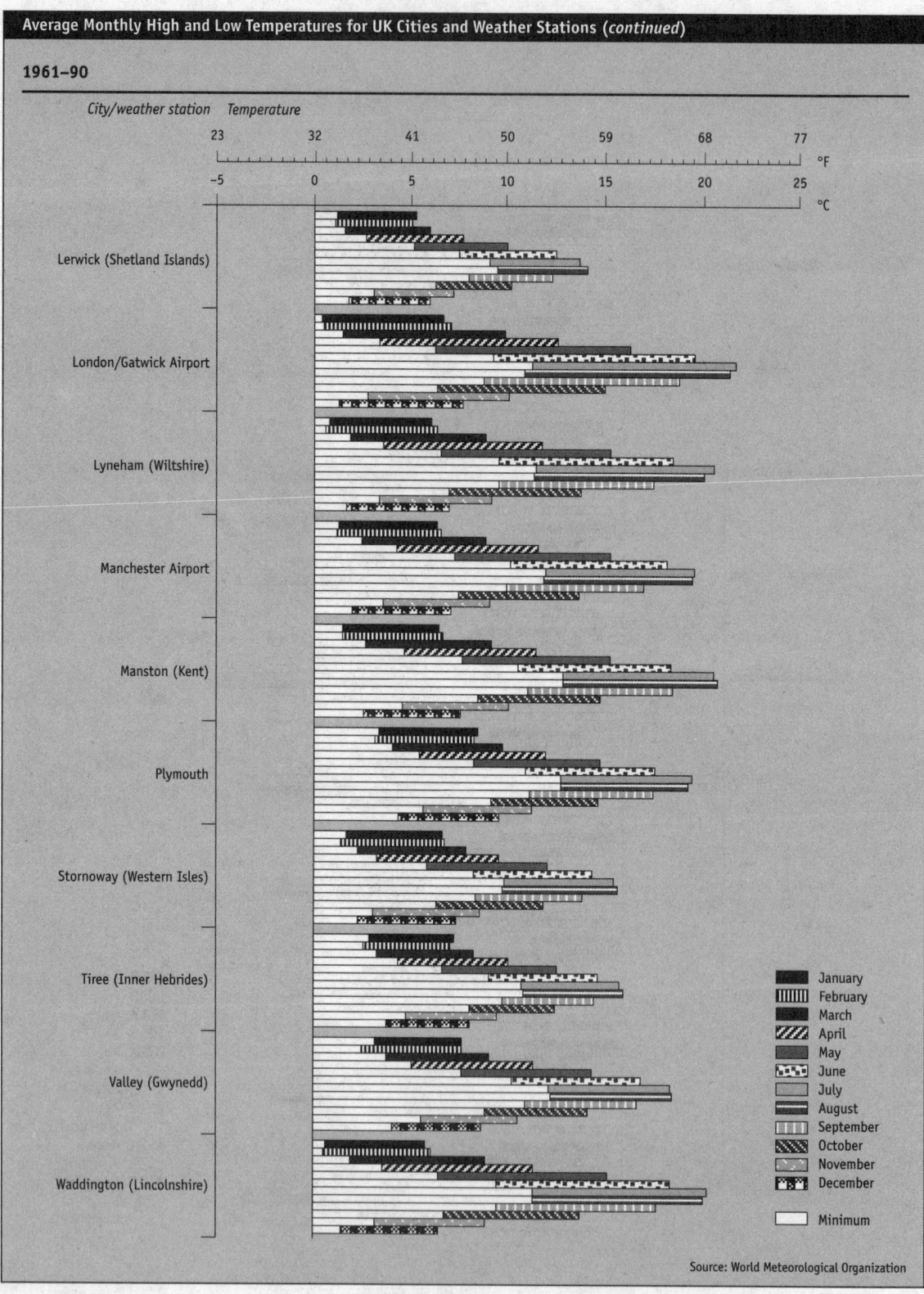

City/weather station   Temperature

Lerwick (Shetland Islands)
London/Gatwick Airport
Lyneham (Wiltshire)
Manchester Airport
Manston (Kent)
Plymouth
Stornoway (Western Isles)
Tiree (Inner Hebrides)
Valley (Gwynedd)
Waddington (Lincolnshire)

January
February
March
April
May
June
July
August
September
October
November
December

Minimum

Source: World Meteorological Organization

Average Monthly Duration of Sunshine for UK Cities and Weather Stations

1961–90

City/weather station   Duration of sunshine (hours)

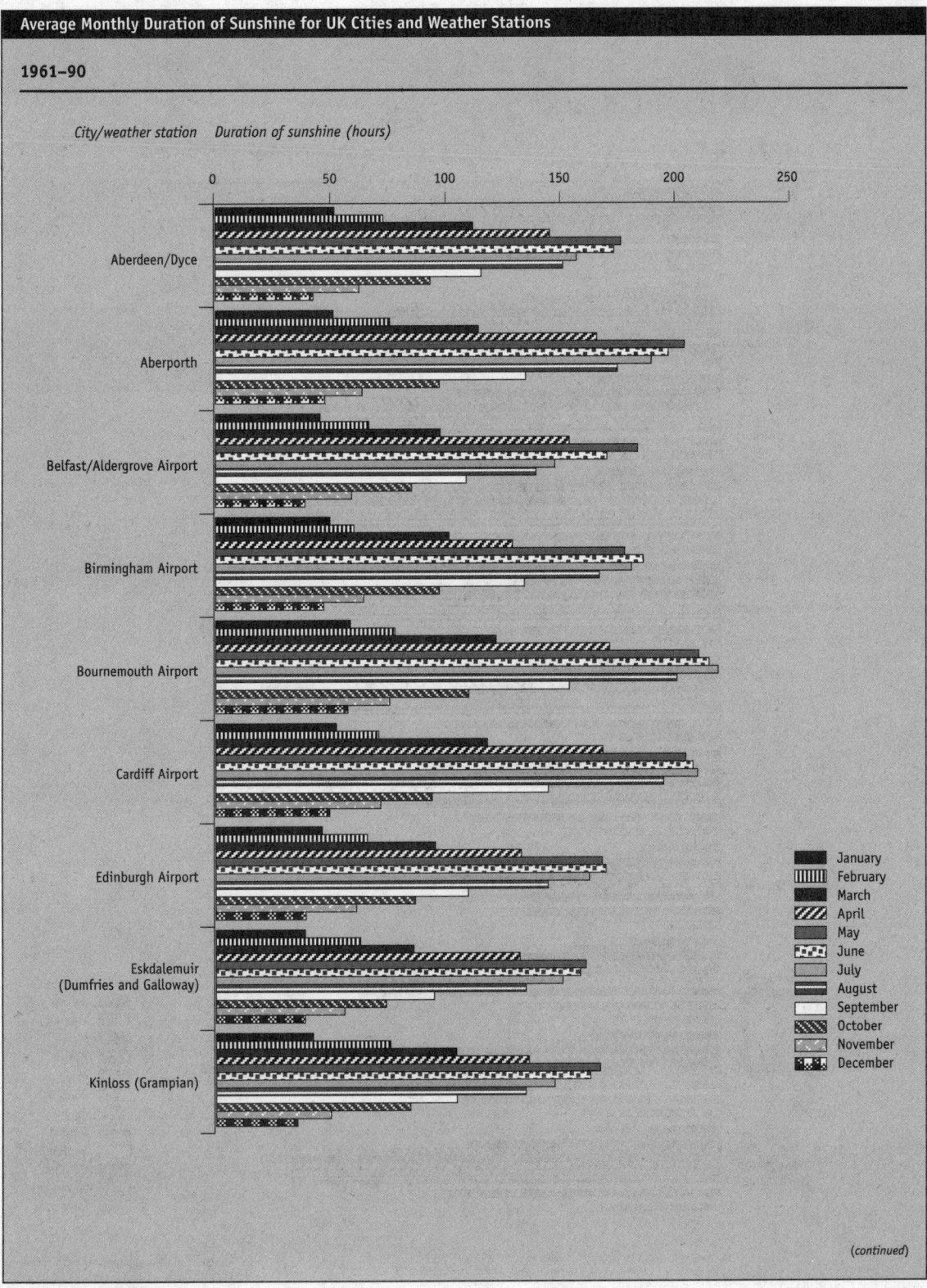

Legend:
- January
- February
- March
- April
- May
- June
- July
- August
- September
- October
- November
- December

City/weather stations:
- Aberdeen/Dyce
- Aberporth
- Belfast/Aldergrove Airport
- Birmingham Airport
- Bournemouth Airport
- Cardiff Airport
- Edinburgh Airport
- Eskdalemuir (Dumfries and Galloway)
- Kinloss (Grampian)

(continued)

Average Monthly Duration of Sunshine for UK Cities and Weather Stations (*continued*)

1961–90

City/weather station   Duration of sunshine (hours)

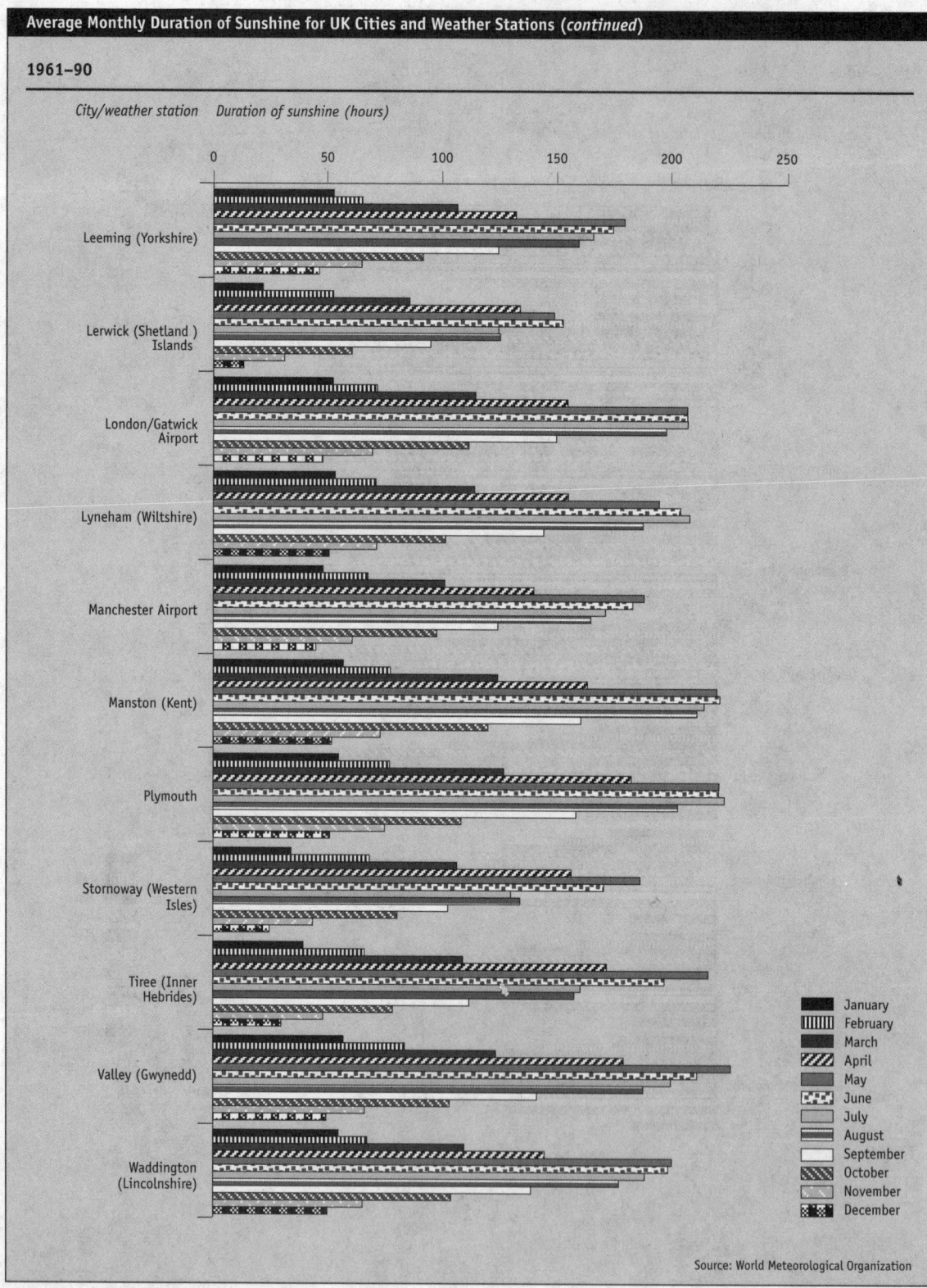

Source: World Meteorological Organization

Average Monthly Rainfall for UK Cities and Weather Stations

1961–90

City/weather station   Average monthly rainfall

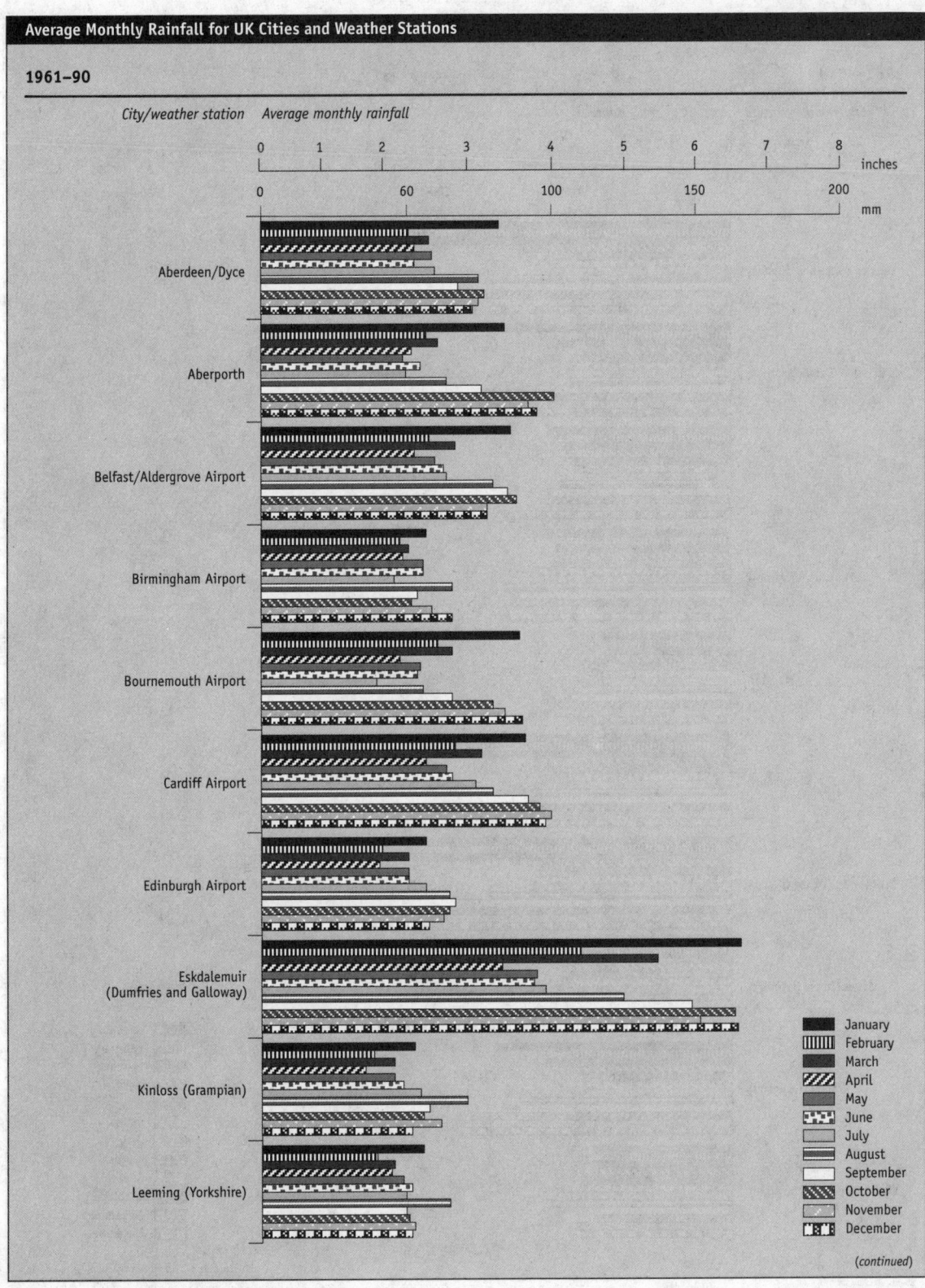

(continued)

Average Monthly Rainfall for UK Cities and Weather Stations (*continued*)

1961–90

City/weather station   *Average monthly rainfall*

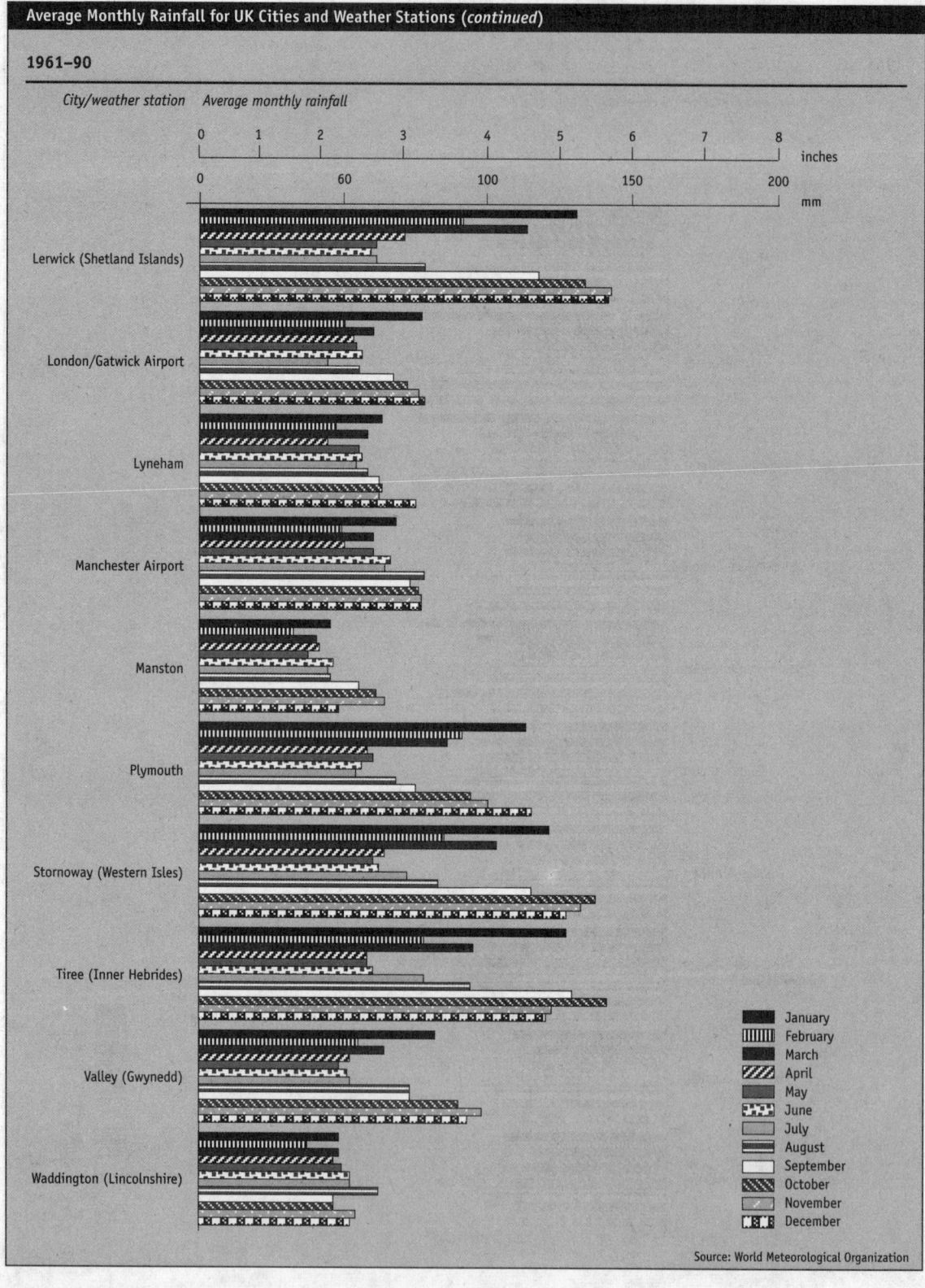

Source: World Meteorological Organization

Average Monthly Rainfall for Major Cities of the World (Adelaide – Belfast)

As of January 1997.

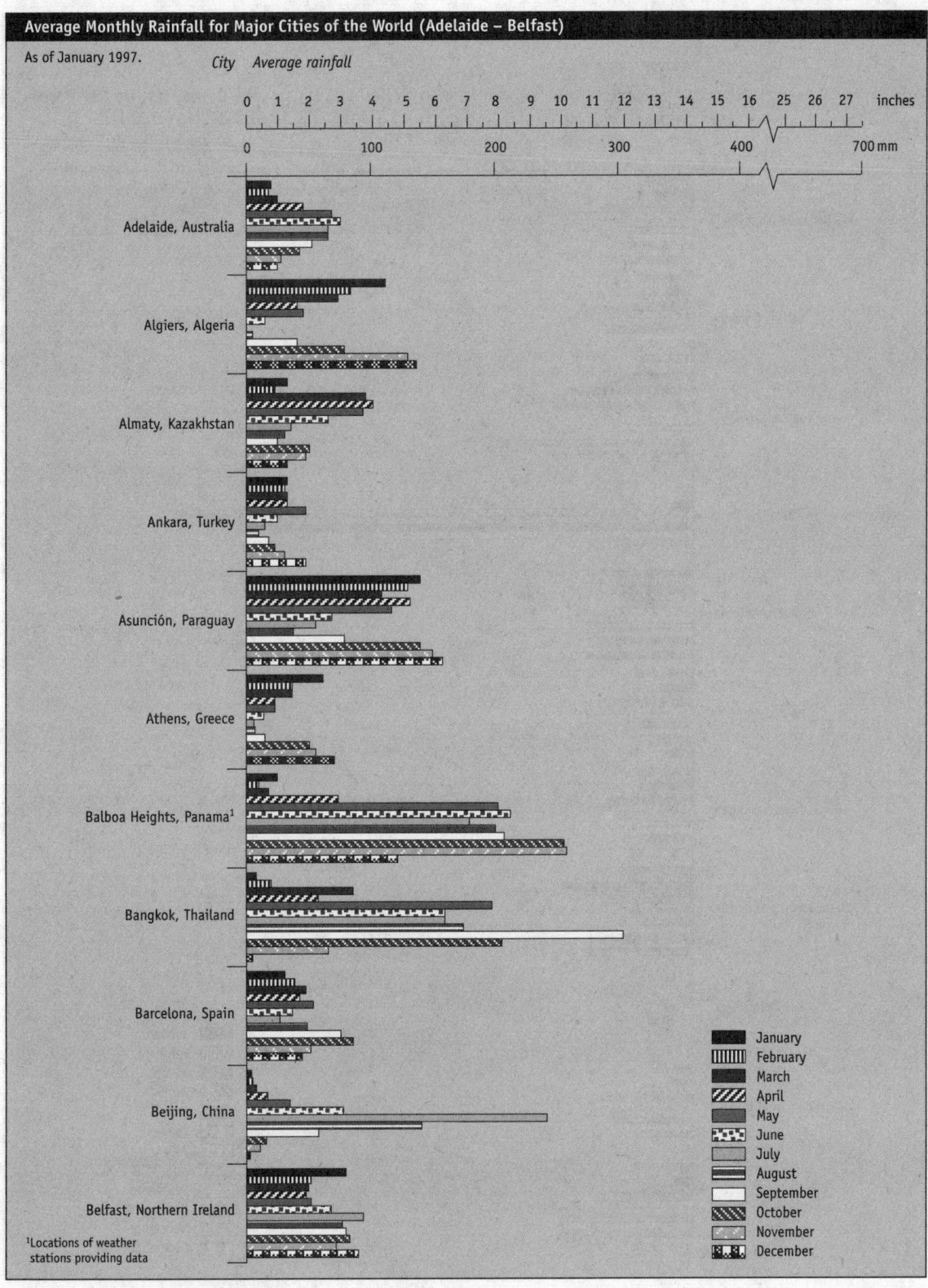

¹Locations of weather
 stations providing data

Average Monthly Rainfall for Major Cities of the World (Belgrade – Caracas)

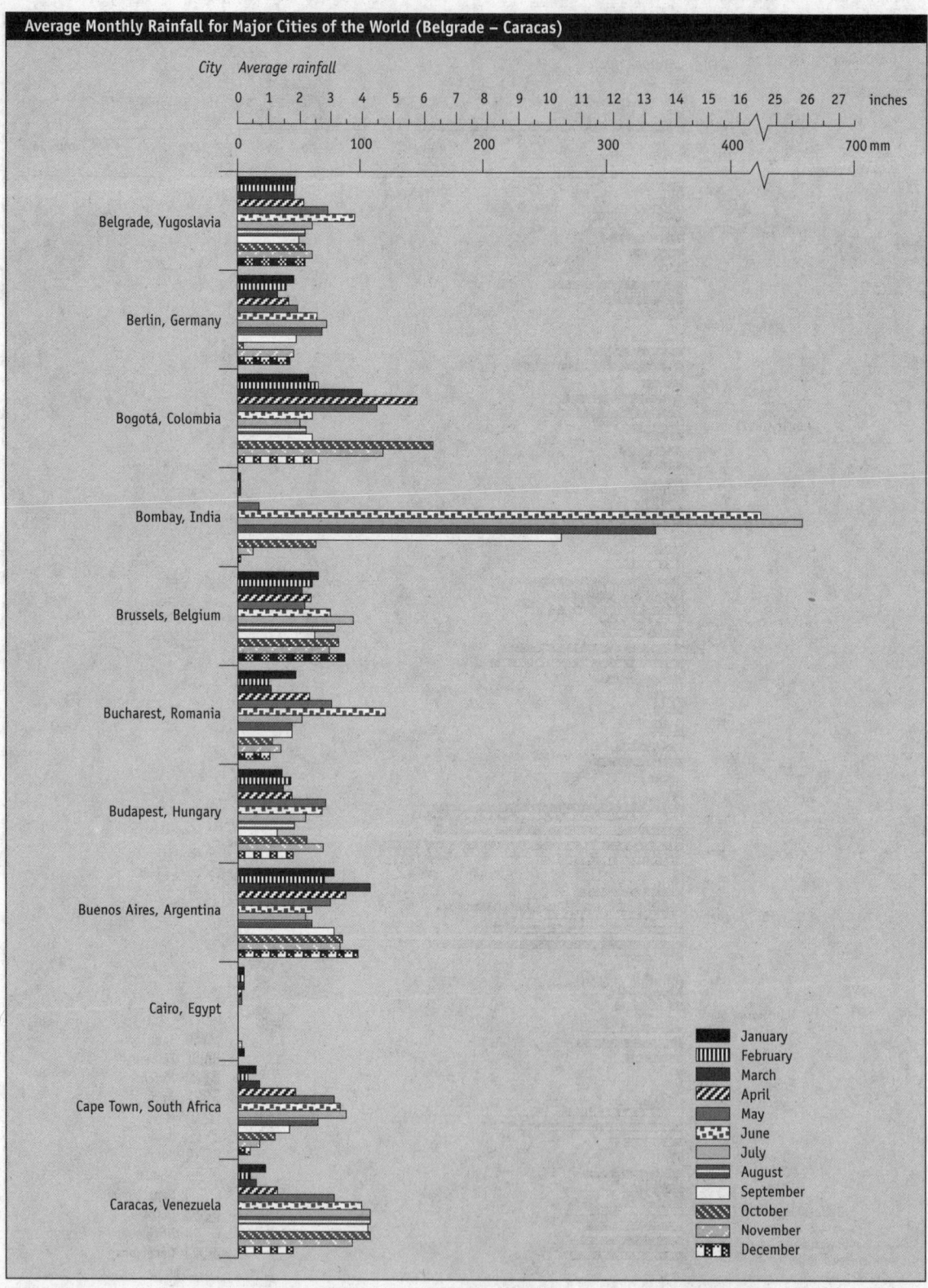

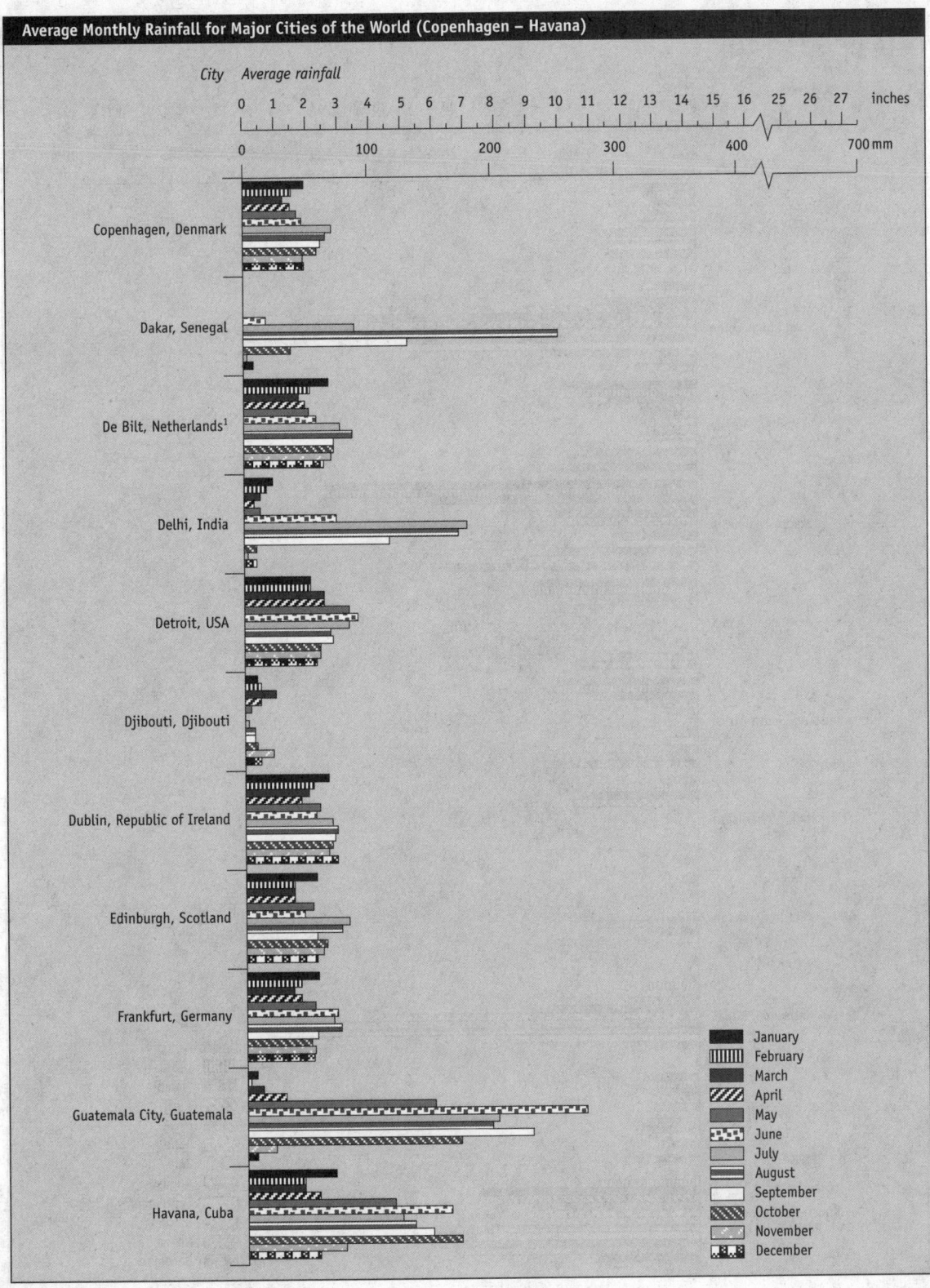

Average Monthly Rainfall for Major Cities of the World (Copenhagen – Havana)

City   Average rainfall

Copenhagen, Denmark

Dakar, Senegal

De Bilt, Netherlands[1]

Delhi, India

Detroit, USA

Djibouti, Djibouti

Dublin, Republic of Ireland

Edinburgh, Scotland

Frankfurt, Germany

Guatemala City, Guatemala

Havana, Cuba

January
February
March
April
May
June
July
August
September
October
November
December

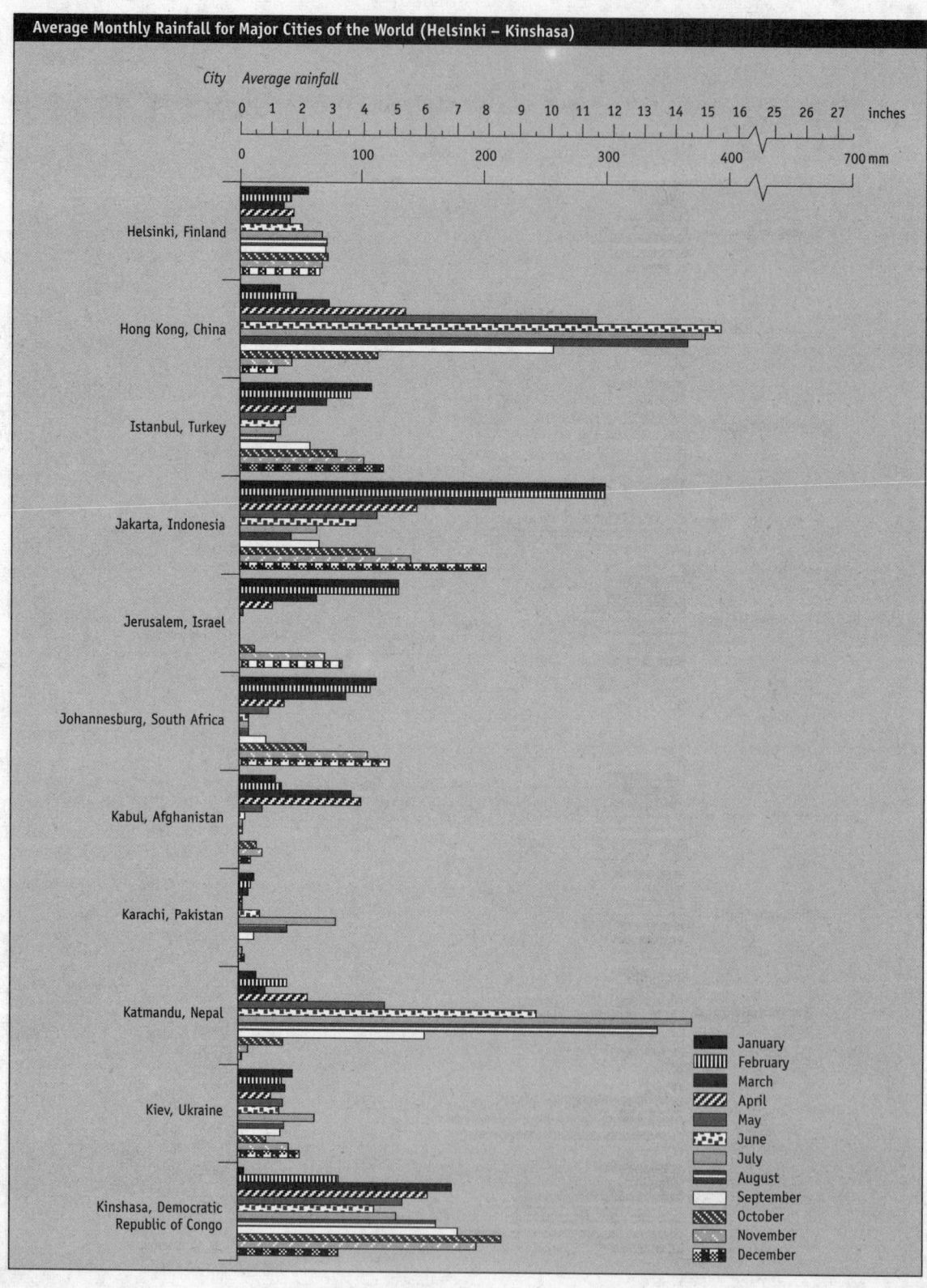

Average Monthly Rainfall for Major Cities of the World (Helsinki – Kinshasa)

Average Monthly Rainfall for Major Cities of the World (Lagos – Mexico City)

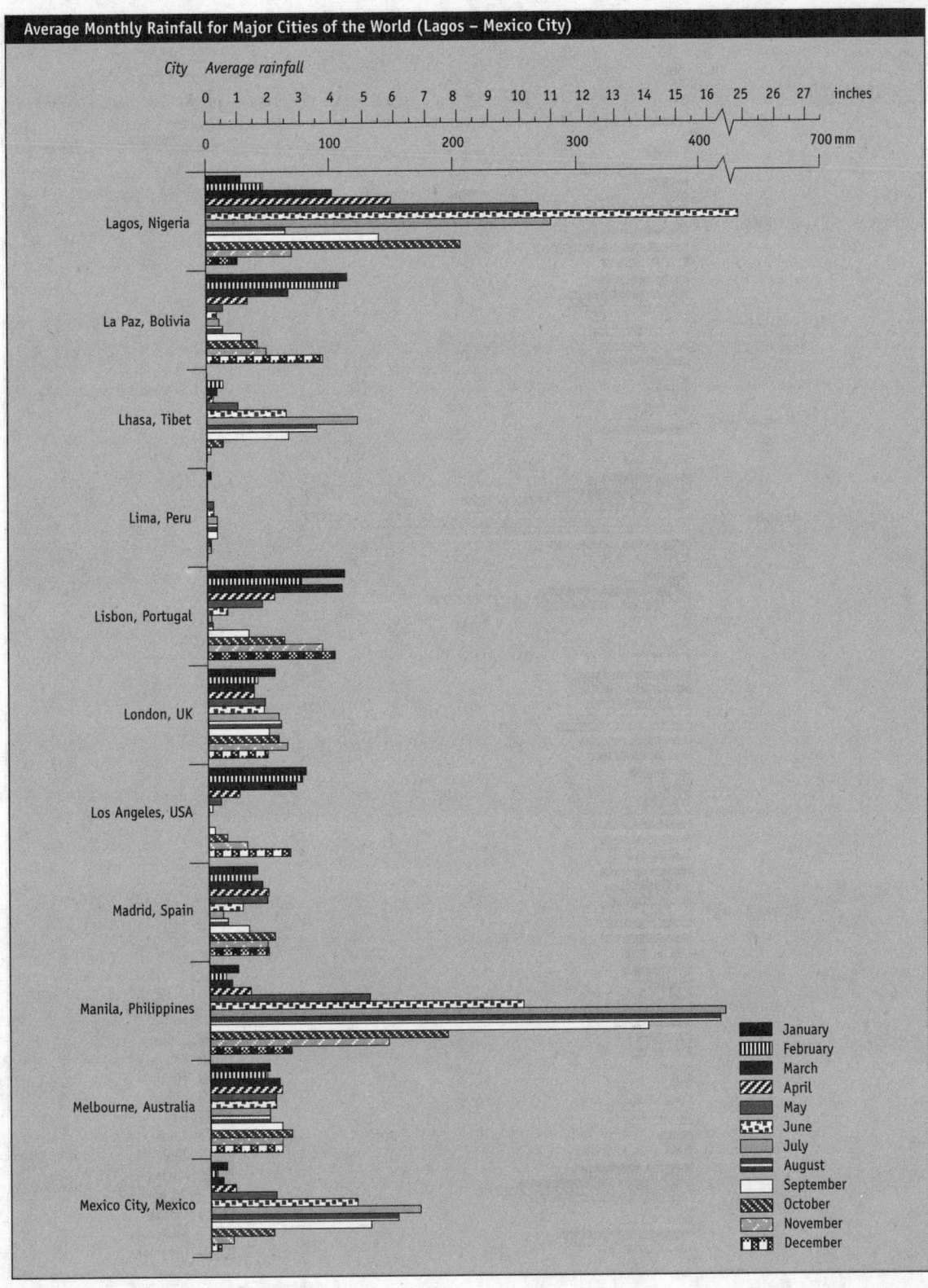

City   Average rainfall

0 1 2 3 4 5 6 7 8 9 10 11 12 13 14 15 16 25 26 27   inches

0   100   200   300   400   700 mm

Lagos, Nigeria

La Paz, Bolivia

Lhasa, Tibet

Lima, Peru

Lisbon, Portugal

London, UK

Los Angeles, USA

Madrid, Spain

Manila, Philippines

Melbourne, Australia

Mexico City, Mexico

January
February
March
April
May
June
July
August
September
October
November
December

Average Monthly Rainfall for Major Cities of the World (Milan – Quito)

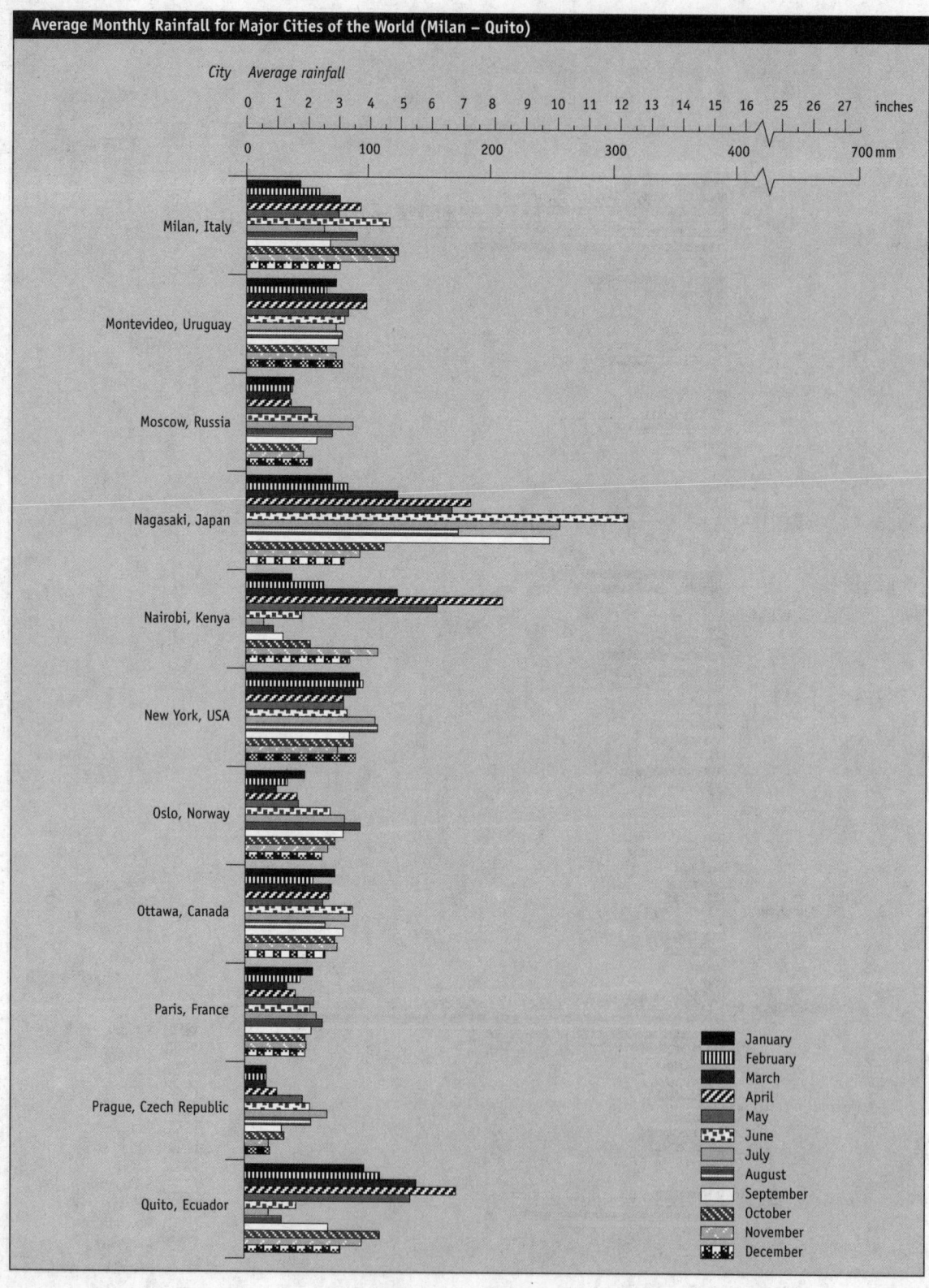

Average Monthly Rainfall for Major Cities of the World (Reykjavik – Stockholm)

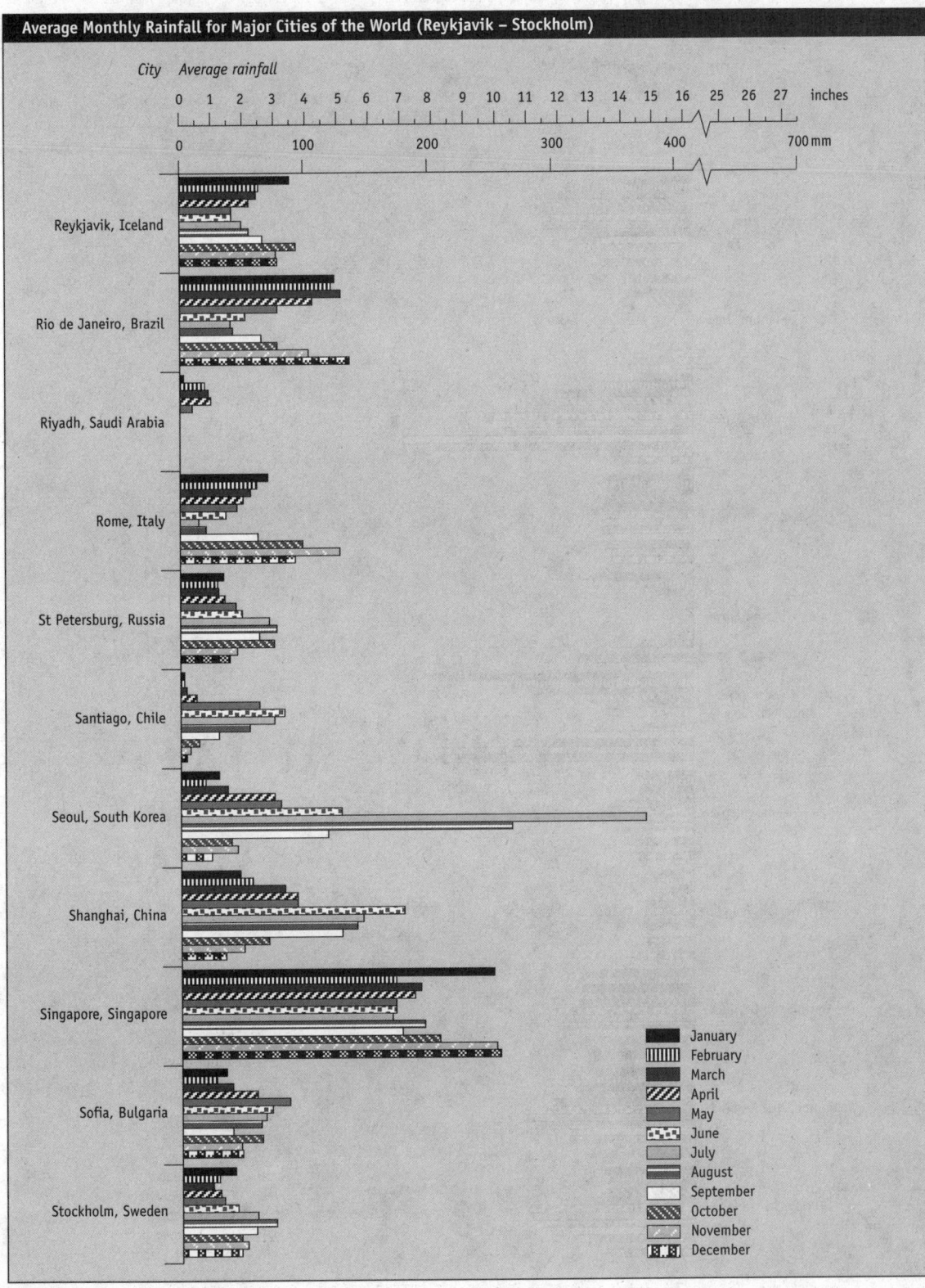

Average Monthly Rainfall for Major Cities of the World (Sydney – Zürich)

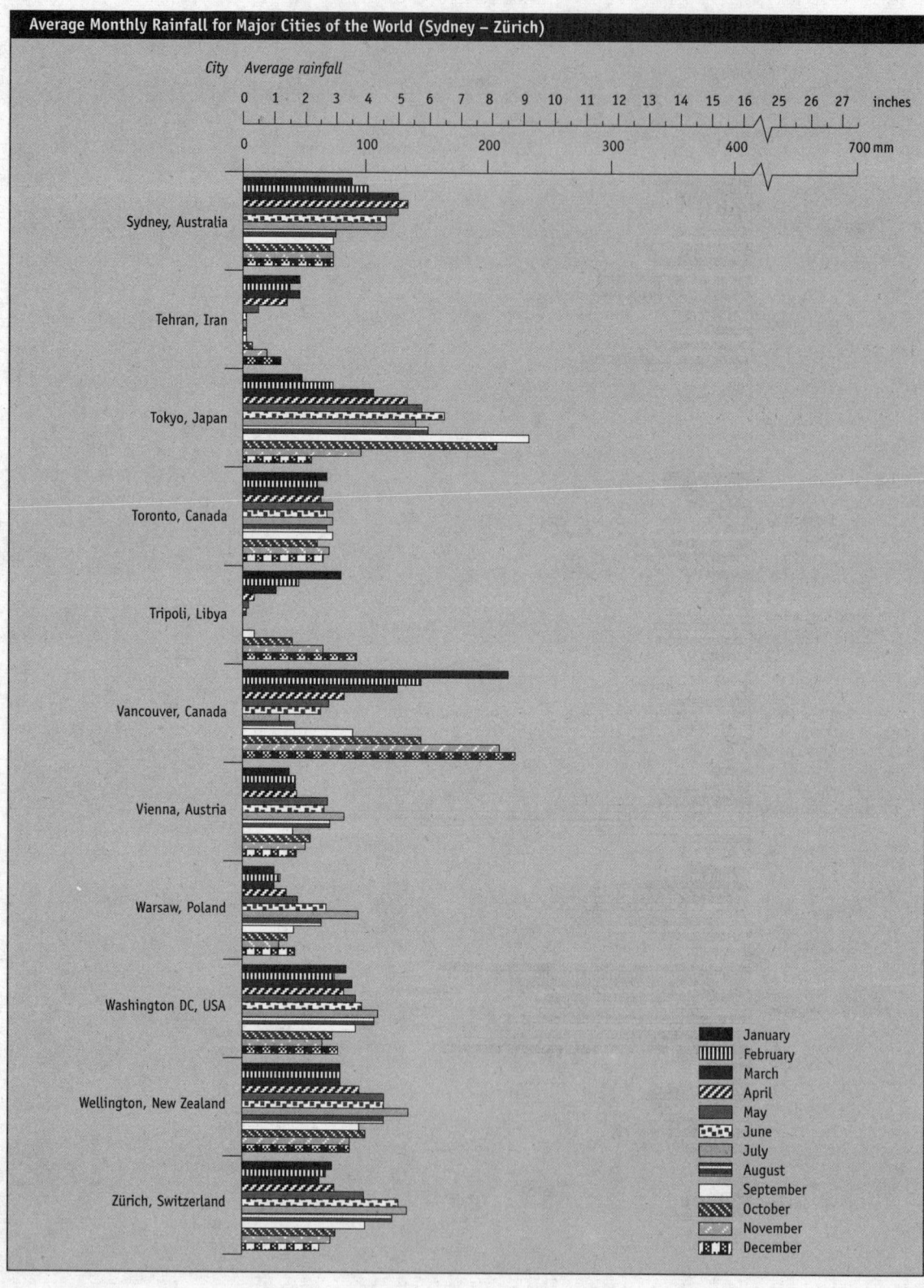

City   Average rainfall

Sydney, Australia

Tehran, Iran

Tokyo, Japan

Toronto, Canada

Tripoli, Libya

Vancouver, Canada

Vienna, Austria

Warsaw, Poland

Washington DC, USA

Wellington, New Zealand

Zürich, Switzerland

January
February
March
April
May
June
July
August
September
October
November
December

Average Monthly High and Low Temperatures for Major Cities of the World (Adelaide – Kinshasa)

Data is given in °C. To convert from °C to °F, use the equation F = (C × 180/100) + 32. (Data as of January 1997.)

City	January		February		March		April		May		June	
	°C max	°C min	°C max	°C min	°C max	°C min	°C max	°C min	°C max	°C min	°C max	°C min
Adelaide, Australia	30	16	30	17	27	15	23	13	19	10	16	8
Algiers, Algeria	15	9	16	9	17	11	20	13	23	15	26	18
Almaty, Kazakhstan	−5	−14	−3	−13	4	−6	13	3	20	10	24	14
Ankara, Turkey	4	−4	6	−3	11	−1	17	4	23	9	26	12
Asunción, Paraguay	35	22	34	22	33	21	29	18	25	14	22	12
Athens, Greece	13	6	14	7	16	8	20	11	25	16	30	20
Balboa Heights, Panama[1]	31	22	32	22	32	22	31	23	30	23	31	23
Bangkok, Thailand	32	20	33	22	34	24	35	25	34	26	33	24
Barcelona, Spain	13	6	14	7	16	9	18	11	21	14	25	18
Beijing, China	1	−10	4	−8	11	−1	21	7	27	13	31	18
Belfast, Northern Ireland	6	2	7	2	9	3	12	4	15	6	18	9
Belgrade, Yugoslavia	3	−3	5	−2	11	2	18	7	23	12	26	15
Berlin, Germany	2	−3	3	−3	8	0	13	4	19	8	22	12
Bogotá, Colombia	19	9	20	9	19	10	19	11	19	11	18	11
Bombay, India	28	19	28	19	30	22	32	24	33	27	32	26
Brussels, Belgium	4	−1	7	0	10	2	14	5	18	8	22	11
Bucharest, Romania	1	−7	4	−5	10	−1	18	5	23	10	27	14
Budapest, Hungary	1	−4	4	−2	10	2	17	7	22	11	26	15
Buenos Aires, Argentina	29	17	28	17	26	16	22	12	18	8	14	5
Cairo, Egypt	18	8	21	9	24	11	28	14	33	17	35	20
Cape Town, South Africa	26	16	26	16	25	14	22	12	19	9	18	8
Caracas, Venezuela	24	13	25	13	26	14	27	16	27	17	26	17
Copenhagen, Denmark	2	−2	2	−3	5	−1	10	3	16	8	19	11
Dakar, Senegal	26	18	27	17	27	18	27	18	29	20	31	23
De Bilt, Netherlands[1]	4	−1	5	−1	10	1	13	4	18	8	21	11
Delhi, India	21	7	24	9	31	14	36	20	41	26	39	28
Detroit, USA	−1	−7	0	−8	6	−3	13	3	19	9	25	14
Djibouti, Djibouti	29	23	29	24	31	25	32	26	34	28	37	30
Dublin, Republic of Ireland	8	1	8	2	10	3	13	4	15	6	18	9
Edinburgh, Scotland	6	1	6	1	8	2	11	4	14	6	17	9
Frankfurt, Germany	3	−2	5	−1	11	2	16	6	20	9	23	13
Guatemala City, Guatemala	23	12	25	12	27	14	28	14	29	16	27	16
Havana, Cuba	26	18	26	18	27	19	29	21	30	22	31	23
Helsinki, Finland	−3	−9	−4	−10	0	−7	6	−1	14	4	19	9
Hong Kong, China	18	13	17	13	19	16	24	19	28	23	29	26
Istanbul, Turkey	8	3	9	2	11	3	16	7	21	12	25	16
Jakarta, Indonesia	29	23	29	23	30	23	31	24	31	24	31	23
Jerusalem, Israel	13	5	13	6	18	8	23	10	27	14	29	16
Johannesburg, South Africa	26	14	25	14	24	13	22	10	19	6	17	4
Kabul, Afghanistan	2	−8	4	−6	12	1	19	6	26	11	31	13
Karachi, Pakistan	25	13	26	14	29	19	32	23	34	26	34	28
Katmandu, Nepal	18	2	19	4	25	7	28	12	30	16	29	19
Kiev, Ukraine	−4	−10	−2	−8	3	−4	14	5	21	11	24	14
Kinshasa, Democratic Republic of Congo	31	21	31	22	32	22	32	22	31	22	29	19

(continued)

Average Monthly High and Low Temperatures for Major Cities of the World (Adelaide – Kinshasa) (continued)

(Data as of January 1997.)

City	July °C max	July °C min	August °C max	August °C min	September °C max	September °C min	October °C max	October °C min	November °C max	November °C min	December °C max	December °C min
Adelaide, Australia	15	7	17	8	19	9	23	11	26	13	28	15
Algiers, Algeria	28	21	29	22	27	21	23	17	19	13	16	11
Almaty, Kazakhstan	27	16	27	14	22	8	13	2	4	−5	−2	−9
Ankara, Turkey	30	15	31	15	26	11	21	7	14	3	6	−2
Asunción, Paraguay	23	12	26	14	28	14	30	17	32	18	34	21
Athens, Greece	33	23	33	23	29	19	24	15	19	12	15	8
Balboa Heights, Panama[1]	31	23	30	23	29	23	29	23	29	23	31	23
Bangkok, Thailand	32	24	32	24	32	24	31	24	34	22	31	20
Barcelona, Spain	28	21	28	21	25	19	21	15	16	11	13	8
Beijing, China	31	21	30	20	26	14	20	6	9	−2	3	−8
Belfast, Northern Ireland	18	11	18	11	16	9	13	7	9	4	7	3
Belgrade, Yugoslavia	28	17	28	17	24	13	18	8	11	4	5	0
Berlin, Germany	24	14	23	13	20	10	13	6	7	2	3	−1
Bogotá, Colombia	18	10	18	10	19	9	19	10	19	10	19	9
Bombay, India	29	25	29	25	29	24	32	24	32	23	31	21
Brussels, Belgium	23	12	22	12	21	11	15	7	9	3	6	0
Bucharest, Romania	30	16	30	15	25	11	18	6	10	2	4	−3
Budapest, Hungary	28	16	27	16	23	12	16	7	8	3	4	−1
Buenos Aires, Argentina	14	6	16	6	18	8	21	10	24	13	28	16
Cairo, Egypt	36	21	35	22	32	20	30	18	26	14	20	10
Cape Town, South Africa	17	7	18	8	18	9	21	11	23	13	24	14
Caracas, Venezuela	26	16	26	16	27	16	26	16	25	16	26	14
Copenhagen, Denmark	22	14	21	14	18	11	12	7	7	3	4	1
Dakar, Senegal	31	24	31	24	32	24	32	24	30	23	27	19
De Bilt, Netherlands[1]	22	13	22	13	19	10	14	7	9	3	5	1
Delhi, India	36	27	34	26	34	24	34	18	29	11	23	8
Detroit, USA	28	17	27	17	23	13	16	7	8	1	2	−4
Djibouti, Djibouti	41	31	39	29	36	29	33	27	31	25	29	23
Dublin, Republic of Ireland	20	11	19	11	17	9	14	6	10	4	8	3
Edinburgh, Scotland	18	11	18	11	16	9	12	7	9	4	7	2
Frankfurt, Germany	25	15	24	14	21	11	14	7	8	3	4	0
Guatemala City, Guatemala	26	16	26	16	26	16	24	16	23	14	22	13
Havana, Cuba	32	24	32	24	31	24	29	23	27	21	26	19
Helsinki, Finland	22	13	20	12	15	8	8	3	3	−1	−1	−5
Hong Kong, China	31	26	31	26	29	25	27	23	23	18	20	15
Istanbul, Turkey	28	18	28	19	24	16	20	13	15	9	11	5
Jakarta, Indonesia	31	23	31	23	31	23	31	23	30	23	29	23
Jerusalem, Israel	31	17	31	18	29	17	27	15	21	12	15	7
Johannesburg, South Africa	17	4	20	6	23	9	25	12	25	13	26	14
Kabul, Afghanistan	33	16	33	15	29	11	23	6	17	1	8	−3
Karachi, Pakistan	33	27	31	26	31	25	33	22	31	18	27	14
Katmandu, Nepal	29	20	28	20	28	19	27	13	23	7	19	3
Kiev, Ukraine	25	15	24	14	20	10	13	6	6	0	−1	−6
Kinshasa, Democratic Republic of Congo	27	18	29	18	31	20	31	21	31	22	30	21

Average Monthly High and Low Temperatures for Major Cities of the World (Lagos – Zürich)

City	January °C max	January °C min	February °C max	February °C min	March °C max	March °C min	April °C max	April °C min	May °C max	May °C min	June °C max	June °C min
Lagos, Nigeria	31	23	32	25	32	26	32	25	31	24	29	23
La Paz, Bolivia	17	6	17	6	18	6	18	4	18	3	17	1
Lhasa, Tibet	7	−10	9	−7	12	−2	16	1	19	5	24	9
Lima, Peru	28	19	28	19	28	19	27	17	23	16	20	14
Lisbon, Portugal	14	8	15	8	17	10	20	12	21	13	25	15
London, UK	6	2	7	2	10	3	13	6	17	8	20	12
Los Angeles, USA	18	8	19	8	19	9	21	10	22	12	24	13
Madrid, Spain	9	2	11	2	15	5	18	7	21	10	27	15
Manila, Philippines	30	21	31	21	33	22	34	23	34	24	33	24
Melbourne, Australia	26	14	26	14	24	13	20	11	17	8	14	7
Mexico City, Mexico	19	6	21	6	24	8	25	11	26	12	24	13
Milan, Italy	5	0	8	2	13	6	18	10	23	14	27	17
Montevideo, Uruguay	28	17	28	16	26	15	22	12	18	9	15	6
Moscow, Russia	−9	−16	−6	−14	0	−8	10	1	19	8	21	11
Nagasaki, Japan	9	2	10	2	14	5	19	10	23	14	26	18
Nairobi, Kenya	25	12	26	13	25	14	22	13	21	12	21	11
New York City, USA	3	−4	3	−4	7	−1	14	6	20	12	25	16
Oslo, Norway	−2	−7	−1	−7	4	−4	10	1	16	6	20	10
Ottawa, Canada	−6	−16	−6	−16	1	−9	11	−1	19	7	24	12
Paris, France	6	1	7	1	12	4	16	6	20	10	23	13
Prague, Czech Republic	0	−5	1	−4	7	−1	12	3	18	8	21	11
Quito, Ecuador	22	8	22	8	722	8	21	8	21	8	22	7
Reykjavik, Iceland	2	−2	3	−2	4	−1	6	1	10	4	12	7
Rio de Janeiro, Brazil	29	23	29	23	28	22	27	21	25	19	24	18
Riyadh, Saudi Arabia	21	8	23	9	28	13	32	18	38	22	42	25
Rome, Italy	11	5	13	5	15	7	19	10	23	13	28	17
St Petersburg, Russia	−7	−13	−5	−12	0	−8	8	0	15	6	20	11
Santiago, Chile	29	12	29	11	27	9	23	7	18	5	14	3
Seoul, South Korea	0	−9	3	−7	8	−2	17	5	22	11	27	16
Shanghai, China	8	1	8	1	13	4	19	10	25	15	28	19
Singapore, Singapore	30	23	31	23	31	24	31	24	32	24	31	24
Sofia, Bulgaria	2	−4	4	−3	10	1	16	5	21	10	24	14
Stockholm, Sweden	−1	−5	−1	−5	3	−4	8	1	14	6	19	11
Sydney, Australia	26	18	26	18	24	17	22	14	19	11	16	9
Tehran, Iran	7	−3	10	0	15	4	22	9	28	14	34	19
Tokyo, Japan	8	−2	9	−1	12	2	17	8	22	12	24	17
Toronto, Canada	−1	−9	−1	−9	3	−5	10	1	17	7	23	12
Tripoli, Libya	16	8	17	9	19	11	22	14	24	16	27	19
Vancouver, Canada	5	0	7	1	10	3	14	4	18	8	21	11
Vienna, Austria	1	−4	3	−3	8	−1	15	6	19	10	23	14
Warsaw, Poland	0	−6	0	−6	6	−2	12	3	20	9	23	12
Washington DC, USA	6	−3	7	−2	12	2	18	7	24	12	28	17
Wellington, New Zealand	21	13	21	13	19	12	17	11	14	8	13	7
Zürich, Switzerland	2	−3	5	−2	10	1	15	4	19	8	23	12

[1] Locations of weather stations providing data.

(continued)

Average Monthly High and Low Temperatures for Major Cities of the World (Lagos – Zürich) (*continued*)

City	July		August		September		October		November		December	
	°C max	°C min	°C max	°C min	°C max	°C min	°C max	°C min	°C max	°C min	°C max	°C min
Lagos, Nigeria	28	23	28	23	28	23	29	23	31	24	31	24
La Paz, Bolivia	17	1	17	2	18	3	19	4	19	6	18	6
Lhasa, Tibet	23	9	22	9	21	7	17	1	13	−5	9	−9
Lima, Peru	19	14	19	13	20	14	22	14	23	16	26	16
Lisbon, Portugal	27	17	28	17	26	17	22	14	17	11	15	9
London, UK	22	14	21	13	19	11	14	8	10	5	7	4
Los Angeles, USA	27	16	28	16	27	14	24	12	23	10	19	8
Madrid, Spain	31	17	30	17	25	14	19	10	13	5	9	2
Manila, Philippines	31	24	31	24	31	24	31	23	31	22	30	21
Melbourne, Australia	13	6	15	6	17	8	19	9	20	11	24	12
Mexico City, Mexico	23	12	23	12	23	12	21	10	20	8	19	6
Milan, Italy	29	20	28	19	24	16	17	11	10	6	6	2
Montevideo, Uruguay	14	6	15	6	17	8	20	9	23	12	26	15
Moscow, Russia	23	13	22	12	16	7	9	3	2	−3	−5	−10
Nagasaki, Japan	29	23	31	23	27	20	22	14	17	1	12	4
Nairobi, Kenya	21	11	24	11	24	13	23	13	23	13	23	13
New York City, USA	28	19	27	19	26	16	21	9	11	3	5	−2
Oslo, Norway	22	13	21	12	16	8	9	3	3	−1	0	−4
Ottawa, Canada	27	14	25	13	20	9	12	3	4	−3	−4	−13
Paris, France	25	15	24	14	21	12	16	8	10	5	7	2
Prague, Czech Republic	23	13	22	13	18	9	12	5	5	1	1	−3
Quito, Ecuador	22	7	23	7	23	7	22	8	22	7	22	8
Reykjavik, Iceland	14	9	14	8	11	6	7	3	4	0	2	−2
Rio de Janeiro, Brazil	24	17	24	18	24	18	25	19	26	20	28	22
Riyadh, Saudi Arabia	42	26	42	24	39	22	34	16	29	13	21	9
Rome, Italy	30	20	30	20	26	17	22	13	16	9	13	6
St Petersburg, Russia	21	13	20	13	15	9	9	4	2	−2	−3	−8
Santiago, Chile	15	3	17	4	19	6	22	7	26	9	28	11
Seoul, South Korea	29	31	31	22	26	15	19	7	11	0	3	−7
Shanghai, China	32	23	32	23	28	19	23	14	17	7	12	2
Singapore, Singapore	31	24	31	24	31	24	31	23	31	23	31	23
Sofia, Bulgaria	27	16	26	15	22	11	17	8	9	3	4	−2
Stockholm, Sweden	22	14	20	13	15	9	9	5	5	1	2	−2
Sydney, Australia	16	8	17	9	19	11	22	13	23	16	25	17
Tehran, Iran	37	22	36	22	32	18	24	12	17	6	11	1
Tokyo, Japan	28	21	30	22	26	19	21	13	16	6	11	1
Toronto, Canada	26	15	25	14	21	11	13	4	6	−1	1	−6
Tripoli, Libya	29	22	30	22	29	22	27	18	23	14	18	9
Vancouver, Canada	23	12	23	12	18	9	14	7	9	4	6	2
Vienna, Austria	25	15	24	15	20	11	14	7	7	3	3	−1
Warsaw, Poland	24	15	23	14	19	10	13	5	6	1	2	−3
Washington DC, USA	31	20	29	19	26	15	19	9	13	3	7	−2
Wellington, New Zealand	12	6	12	6	14	8	16	9	17	10	19	112
Zürich, Switzerland	25	14	24	13	20	11	14	6	7	2	3	−2

[1] Locations of weather stations providing data.

The Greenhouse Effect

The greenhouse effect is a phenomenon of the Earth's atmosphere by which solar radiation, trapped by the Earth and re-emitted from the surface as infrared radiation, is prevented from escaping by various gases in the air. Greenhouse gases trap heat because they readily absorb infrared radiation. The result is a rise in the Earth's temperature (global warming). The main greenhouse gases are carbon dioxide, methane, and chlorofluorocarbons (CFCs) as well as water vapour. Fossil-fuel consumption and forest fires are the principal causes of carbon dioxide build-up; methane is a byproduct of agriculture (rice, cattle, sheep).

The United Nations Environment Pro-gramme estimates that, by 2025, average world temperatures will have risen by 1.5°C/2.7°F with a consequent rise in the sea level of 20 cm/7.9. Low-lying areas and entire countries would be threatened by flooding and crops would be affected by the change in climate. However, predictions about global warming and its possible climatic effects are tentative and often conflict with each other.

At the 1992 Earth Summit it was agreed that by 2000 countries would stabilize carbon dioxide emissions at 1990 levels. However, to halt the acceleration of global warming, emissions would probably need to be cut by 60%. Any increases in carbon dioxide emissions are expected to come from transport. The Berlin Mandate, agreed unanimously at the climate conference in Berlin in 1995, committed industrial nations to the continuing reduction of greenhouse gas emissions after 2000, when the existing pact to stabilize emissions runs out. The stabilization of carbon dioxide emissions at 1990 levels by 2000 will not be achieved by a number of developed countries, including Spain, Australia, and the USA, according to 1997 estimates. Australia is in favour of different targets for different nations, and refused to sign a communiqué at the South Pacific Forum meeting in the Cook Islands in 1997 which insisted on legally binding reductions in greenhouse gas emissions.

Dubbed the 'greenhouse effect' by Swedish scientist Svante Arrhenius, it was first predicted in 1827 by French mathematician Joseph Fourier.

Global Warming: Chronology

1967	US scientists Syukuvo Manabe and R T Wetherald warned that the increase in carbon dioxide in the atmosphere, produced by human activities, was causing a 'greenhouse effect', which would raise atmospheric temperatures and cause a rise in sea levels.
1980	A ten-year World Climate Research Programme was launched to study and predict climate changes and human influence on climate change.
1989	1989 was the warmest year on record worldwide; environmentalists suggested this was due to the 'greenhouse effect'.
3 June 1992	The United Nations Conference on Environment and Development was held in Rio de Janeiro, Brazil, attended by delegates from 178 countries, most of whom signed binding conventions to combat global warming.
1993	An ice core drilled in Greenland, providing evidence of climate change over 250,000 years, suggested that sudden fluctuations have been common and that the recent stable climate is unusual.
1995	The Prince Gustav Ice Shelf and the northern Larsen Ice Shelf in Antarctica began to disintegrate as a result of global warming.
11 December 1997	Delegates at the Kyoto, Japan, conference on global warming agreed to cut emissions of greenhouse gases by 5.2% from 1990 levels during the years 2008 and 2012.
17 April 1998	An iceberg 40 km/25 mi long and 4.8 km/3 mi wide broke off from the Larson B Ice Shelf in Antarctica.

Ultraviolet Index

The Ultraviolet Index (UVI) is a measurement used to forecast the potential strength of the sun's rays during specific periods. There are four types of UV radiation (see below), each having different wavelengths. Specifically, the UVI measures UV-B radiation, the most dangerous and damaging type of UV radiation because it is not blocked by the earth's ozone layer. Using UVI measurements, a forecast can be made indicating the potential danger resulting from exposure to UV radiation for peak hours of sunlight.

Wavelengths of UV Radiation by Type

UV category	Wavelengths (nm)
UV-A	320–400
UV-B	280–320
UV-C	200–280
UV-D	<200

The UVI uses a scale of 0–10+ to indicate the potential danger of the sun's rays on a given day. The index is issued on a daily basis. From the index, an estimate can be made of how long (in minutes) an individual can be exposed to the sun's rays before damage to exposed skin may result. These values are presented in the following table.

Ultraviolet Index and Skin Damage Estimates

UVI	Exposure level	Minutes before skin damage
0–2	minimal	>60
3–4	low	45
5–6	moderate	30
7–9	high	15
>10	very high	<10

Source: National Weather Service; National Oceanic and Atmospheric Administration; US Environmental Protection Agency

CLIMATE CHANGE

BY NIGEL DUDLEY

Every year it seems as if a new climatic record is made – the warmest annual temperature on record, the wettest October since records began, the driest summer, the highest winds...

Worldwide temperatures in 1997 climbed to their highest average levels since record-keeping began in 1880. This wasn't a one-off freak occurrence; the decade previously saw 9 of the 11 hottest years in the century. The world is half a degree warmer than it was in the 1860s and average temperatures will soon be the highest for 10,000 years. Yet there are also a growing number of extreme weather events including storms and hurricanes. The timing and frequency of monsoons is changing. The world's climate seems to be entering an unprecedented period of extremes, and a growing number of scientists put these extremes down to changes we have brought about ourselves, by releasing air pollutants known as 'greenhouse gases' leading to an overall global warming.

The Greenhouse Effect

The theory is simple. Much of the solar energy reaching the Earth should be reflected straight back to space again. However, some of the gases found in the atmosphere – such as carbon dioxide – can 're-reflect' some of this energy back to Earth again, acting like the glass in a greenhouse. The higher the concentration of these gases, the more solar energy is trapped in the atmosphere and the higher becomes the average temperature. During the industrial age, our own actions have created a dramatic increase in the amount of some greenhouse gases. In particular, by burning fossil fuels such as coal and gas and by deliberately burning forests, humans have doubled the amount of carbon dioxide in the atmosphere. Currently, the rich countries of the world release around 5 billion tonnes of carbon dioxide every year. Many of the things we take for granted – car and air travel, disposable plastic goods, and even electricity – contribute to the problem. Other important greenhouse gases include chlorofluorocarbons, (CFCs) which have been used in refrigerators and pressurized spray cans; nitrous oxides from artificial fertilizers and industrial emissions; and methane from rubbish and as a by-product of cattle rearing.

The Consequences

The results, according to scientists who have studied the phenomenon, are likely to be extremely serious. Higher average temperatures could lead to a melting of some of the polar ice caps, raising average sea levels and flooding low-lying land. For example, several Pacific Island nations could disappear altogether, and cities such as Sydney, Bangkok, Venice, and Shanghai could all be at risk. The changing climate will alter and damage ecosystems as conditions are likely to change more quickly than species are able to adapt, risking large-scale extinctions. Some habitats – including northern boreal forests, mangroves, and wetlands – will be particularly threatened, and rising sea temperatures are being linked to die-back of coral in places.

There will be direct impacts on people as well. Areas suitable for large-scale agriculture – such as grain production – could shift dramatically, with implications for food security and national economies. Warmer conditions could also result in the spread of infectious diseases; for example, malaria mosquitoes could spread back into Europe and North America and outbreaks of dengue fever have already occurred in northern Australia.

Perhaps even more importantly, the consequences are unpredictable. Visions of previously cold areas basking in warm sunshine are unlikely to materialize. Climate change will result in the climate becoming both more variable and more extreme – storms, heat-waves, cold spells, rainstorms, and droughts are all likely to increase – as is the severity of the occasional weather event known as El Niño, which is responsible for many of the world's worst droughts. Perhaps 'global change' or 'climate change' are better terms than simply global warming.

Predictions for Climate Change

Modelling the world's climate is notoriously difficult – as anyone who has tried to plan their lives around weather forecasts will know! Predictions of climate change were initially met with widespread scepticism, and there are still scientists who think that the problems have been greatly exaggerated. In fact, it will be impossible to be absolutely certain about the overall trends one way or another for many decades in the future. Yet as studies continue, the weight of opinion is increasingly supporting the climate change theory – even in institutions that have previously been cautious. For example, in January 1998, Elbert Friday, assistant administrator of the US National Oceanic and Atmospheric Administration, said: 'For the first time, I feel confident in saying there's a human component (in climate change)'.

Tackling Climate Change

Tackling climate change poses enormous problems for industrial society with its heavy reliance on oil, coal, and the other fossil fuels, which are the main sources of greenhouse gases. It is the rich countries that are responsible for the lion's share of the problem. Perhaps there is nowhere where this is more true than in the USA, which is currently responsible for almost a quarter of all greenhouse gas emissions. Steps towards reducing pollution include energy conservation, replacing fossil fuels with renewable solar sources of energy, reversing deforestation, changing farming practices, finding substitutes for processes that are likely to increase global warming, and – most difficult of all – perhaps also changes to lifestyles. None of these steps is easy. Nor are they likely to be popular: attempts to address the problem of global warming have been met with massive resistance from industry and some governments.

Some steps have been made. In 1992, the Earth Summit in Rio de Janeiro agreed a Climate Change Convention, in which countries pledged to gradually reduce their greenhouse gas emissions. Unfortunately, since then many countries have ignored or fallen short of their targets. Even worse, at a major conference in Kyoto, Japan, in December 1997, some of the largest polluters refused to honour original agreements and said that it was impossible to reduce emissions at the rate previously decided.

It appears as if the world is still in denial about the seriousness of climate change. Yet taking concrete steps now could avoid panic measures in the future. The problem will certainly not be going away. As we enter a new century, the climatic implications of our actions will take on an ever greater significance.

Pollution

Waste Generated in OECD Countries

(Data as of January 1997. N = nil or negligible. N/A = not available.)

Country	Industrial waste per unit of GDP[1] (tonnes per $ millions)	Municipal waste (kg per capita)	Nuclear waste per unit of energy[2] (tonnes per Mtoe[3])	Country	Industrial waste per unit of GDP[1] (tonnes per $ millions)	Municipal waste (kg per capita)	Nuclear waste per unit of energy[2] (tonnes per Mtoe[3])
Australia	125	N/A	N	Japan	61	410	1.9
Austria	53	430	N	South Korea	67	390	1.8
Belgium	76	470	2.0	Luxembourg	164	530	N
Canada	N/A	630	7.4	Mexico	70	320	0.1
Czech Republic	232	230	1.1	Netherlands	30	540	0.2
Denmark	24	520	N	New Zealand	N/A	N/A	N
Finland	201	410	2.2	Norway	39	620	N
France	100	560	5.1	Poland	117	290	N/A
Germany	60	360	1.4	Portugal	N/A	350	N
Greece	44	310	N	Spain	28	370	1.6
Hungary	104	420	N/A	Sweden	95	440	4.8
Iceland	2	660	N	Switzerland	5	380	3.0
Ireland, Republic of	N/A	N/A	N	Turkey	86	390	N
Italy	22	470	N	UK	59	350	5.2
				USA	142	730	1.2

[1] GDP = gross domestic product.
[2] Wastes from spent fuel in nuclear power plants, in tonnes of heavy metal per million tonnes of oil equivalent (primary energy supply).
[3] Mtoe = million tonnes.

Source: Organization for Economic Corporation and Development

Air Pollution: Major Pollutants

Air pollution is contamination of the atmosphere caused by the discharge, accidental or deliberate, of a wide range of toxic airborne substances. Often the amount of the released substance is relatively high in a certain locality, so the harmful effects become more noticeable. The cost of preventing any discharge of pollutants into the air is prohibitive, so attempts are more usually made to reduce the amount of discharge gradually and to disperse it as quickly as possible by using a very tall chimney, or by intermittent release.

Possibly the world's worst ever human-made air pollution disaster occurred in Indonesia in September 1997. It was caused by forest clearance fires. Smoke pollution in the city of Palangkaraya reached 7.5 mg per cu m (nearly 3 mg more than in the London smog of 1952). The pollutants spread to Malaysia and other countries of the region.

The 1997 Kyoto protocol commits the industrialized nations of the world to cutting their levels of harmful gas emissions to 5.2% by 2012. Europe is expected to take the biggest cut of 8%, the USA 7%, and Japan 6%. The agreement covers Russia and eastern Europe as well.

Corel

Air and water pollution Pollutants pour from a pulp mill in Tacoma, Washington, USA.

Pollutant	Sources	Effects
sulphur dioxide SO_2	oil, coal combustion in power stations	acid rain formed, which damages plants, trees, buildings, and lakes
oxides of nitrogen NO, NO_2	high-temperature combustion in cars, and to some extent power stations	acid rain formed
lead compounds	from leaded petrol used by cars	nerve poison
carbon dioxide CO_2	oil, coal, petrol, diesel combustion	greenhouse effect
carbon monoxide CO	limited combustion of oil, coal, petrol, diesel fuels	poisonous, leads to photochemical smog in some areas
nuclear waste	nuclear power plants, nuclear weapon testing, war	radioactivity, contamination of locality, cancers, mutations, death

Ozone Destroyers

A Class I substance is any chemical with an ozone-depleting potential (ODP) of 0.2 or greater. Class II substances include all of the hydrochlorofluorocarbons (HCFCs).
(– = not applicable.)

Substance	Chemical name	ODP[1]	GWP[2]
Class I Ozone-Depleting Substances			
Group I			
CFC-11	trichlorofluoromethane	1.0	4,000
CFC-12	dichlorodifluoromethane	1.0	8,500
CFC-113	1,1,1-trichlorotrifluoroethane	0.8	5,000
	1,1,2-trichlorotrifluoroethane	0.8	–
CFC-114	dichlorotetrafluoroethane	1.0	9,300
CFC-115	monochloropentafluoroethane	0.6	9,300
Group II			
Halon 1211	bromochlorodifluoromethane	3.0	–
Halon 1301	bromotrifluoromethane	10.0	5,600
Halon 2402	dibromotetrafluoroethane	6.0	–
Group III			
CFC-13	chlorotrifluoromethane	1.0	11,700
CFC-111	pentachlorofluoroethane	1.0	–
CFC-112	tetrachlorodifluoroethane	1.0	–
CFC-211	heptachlorofluoropropane	1.0	–
CFC-212	hexachlorodifluoropropane	1.0	–
CFC-213	pentachlorotrifluoropropane	1.0	–
CFC-214	tetrachlorotetrafluoropropane	1.0	–
CFC-215	trichloropentafluoropropane	1.0	–
CFC-216	dichlorohexafluoropropane	1.0	–
CFC-217	chloroheptafluoropropane	1.0	–
Group IV			
CC14	carbon tetrachloride	1.1	1,400
Group V			
Methyl chloroform	1,1,1-trichloroethane	0.1	110
Group VI			
CH_3Br	methyl bromide	0.7	–
Group VII			
$CHFBr_2$		1.0	–
$CHF_2Br(HBFC-22B1)$		0.74	–
CH_2FBr		0.73	–

Substance	Chemical name	ODP[1]	GWP[2]
Group VII (continued)			
C_2HFBr_4		0.3–0.8	–
$C_2HF_2Br_3$		0.5–1.8	–
$C_2HF_3Br_2$		0.4–1.6	–
C_2HF_4Br		0.7–1.2	–
$C_2H_2FBr_3$		0.1–1.1	–
$C_2H_2F_2Br_2$		0.2–1.5	–
$C_2H_2F_3Br$		0.7–1.6	–
$C_2H_3FBr_2$		0.1–1.7	–
$C_2H_3F_2Br$		0.2–1.1	–
C_2H_4Br		0.07–0.1	–
C_3HFBr_6		0.3–1.5	–
$C_3HF_2Br_5$		0.2–1.9	–
$C_3HF_3Br_4$		0.3–1.8	–
$C_3HF_4Br_3$		0.5–2.2	–
$C_3HF_5Br_2$		0.9–2.0	–
C_3HF_6Br		0.7–3.3	–
$C_3H_2FBr_5$		0.1–1.9	–
$C_3H_2F_3Br$		30.2–5.6	–
$C_3H_2F_4Br_2$		0.3–7.5	–
$C_3H_2F_5Br$		0.9–1.4	–
$C_3H_3FBr_4$		0.08–1.9	–
$C_3H_3F_2Br_3$		0.1–3.1	–
$C_3H_3F_3Br_2$		0.1–2.5	–
$C_3H_3F_4Br$		0.3–4.4	–
$C_3H_4FBr_3$		0.03–0.3	–
$C_3H_4F_2Br_2$		0.1–1.0	–
$C_3H_4F_3Br$		0.07–0.8	–
$C_3H_5FBr_2$		0.04–0.4	–
$C_3H_5F_2Br$		0.07–0.8	–
C_3H_6FB		0.02–0.7	–
Selected Class II[3] Ozone-depleting Substances			
HCFC-22	chlorodifluoromethane	0.05	1,700
HCFC-123	2,2-dichloro-1,1,1-trifluoroethane	0.02	93
HCFC-124	2-chloro-1,1,1,2-tetrafluoroethane	0.02	480
HCFC-141b	1,1-dichloro-1-fluoroethane	0.1	630
HCFC-142b	1-chloro-1,1-difluoroethane	0.06	2,000

[1] ODP (ozone depletion potential) is a ratio of a chemical's impact on ozone compared with the impact of a similar mass of CFC-11.
[2] GWP (global warming potential) represents a ratio of the warming caused by a substance to the warming caused by the same mass of carbon dioxide (CO_2).
[3] Although all HCFCs are included in Class II, only commonly used HCFCs are listed.

Source: Stratospheric Protection Division of the US Environmental Protection Agency

Major Oilspills Throughout the World

(Data as of January 1997.)

Date	Location	Description	Amount tonnes	millions of gallons
March 1967	off Cornwall, England	grounding of *Torrey Canyon*	118,000	35.4
June 1968	off South Africa	Hull failure of *World Glory*	37,000	11.0
December 1972	Gulf of Oman	collision of *Sea Star* with another ship	103,500	31.0
May 1976	La Caruña, Spain	grounding of the *Urquioia*	60–70,000	18.0–21.0
December 1976	Nantucket (MA), USA	grounding of *Argo Merchant*	25,000	7.5
February 1977	mid-Pacific	*Haiwaiian Patriot* develops leak and catches fire	100,000	30.0
April 1977	North Sea	blow-out of well in *Ekofisk* oil field	270,000	81.0
March 1978	Portsall, Brittany, France	grounding of the *Amoco Cadiz*	226,000	68.0
June 1979	Gulf of Mexico	blow-out of well in *Ixtoc 1* oil field	600,000	180.0
July 1979	off Tobago, Caribbean	collision of the *Atlantic Empress* and *Aegean Captain*	370,000	111.0
February 1983	Persian Gulf	blow-out of well in *Nowruz* oil field	600,000	180.0
August 1983	off Cape Town, South Africa	fire on board the *Castillo de Beliver*	250,000	75.0
September 1985	Delaware River (DE), USA	grounding of *Grand Eagle*	1,500	0.5
January 1988	Floreffe (PA), USA	collapsing of *Ashland* oil storage tank	2,400–2,500	0.7–0.8
March 1989	Prince William Sound, off Alaskan Coast	grounding of *Exxon Valdez*	37,000	11.0
June 1989	Canary Islands	fire on board the *Kharg 5*	65,000	19.5
January 1991	Sea Island Terminal of Persian Gulf	deliberate release of oil by Iraqi troops at end of Persian Gulf War	799,120	240.0
January 1993	Shetland Islands, Scotland	grounding of *Braer*	130,000	39.0
August 1993	Tampa Bay (FL), USA	collision of two barges and a Philippine freighter	984	0.3
January 1996	Pembrokeshire coastline of Wales, British Isles	grounding of *Sea Empress*	>100,000	19.0
January 1996	south shore of Rhode Island (RI), USA	grounding of the tugboat *Scandia* and *North Cape* tanker it was towing	1,000	0.3

© British Petroleum

Oil spill containment *Oil spills became a major environmental problem in the 1960s and 1970s as a result of oil exploration along the continental shelf*

Sulphur Oxide and Nitrogen Oxide Emissions for OECD Countries

N/A = Not Available

1990

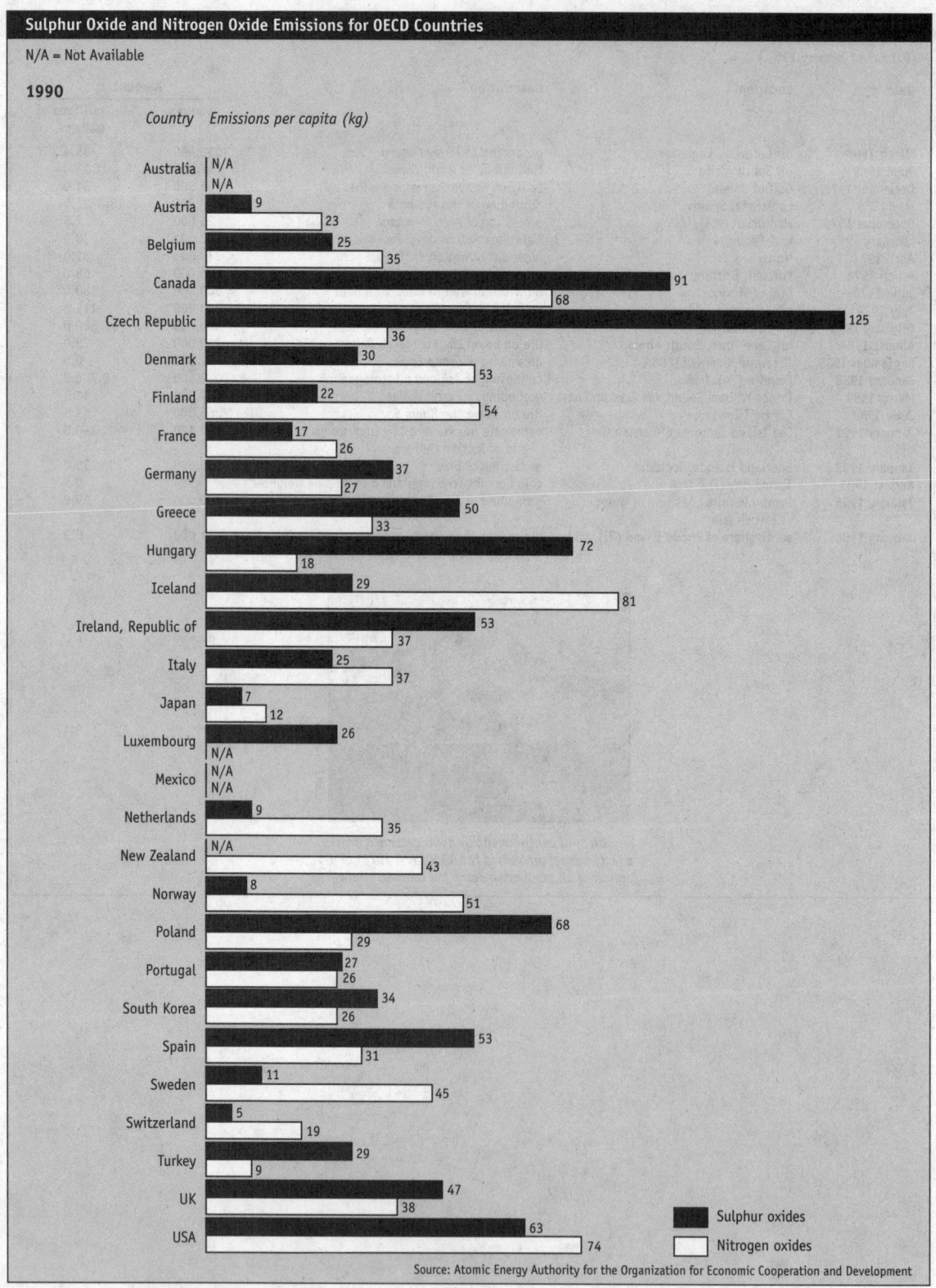

Country	Emissions per capita (kg)	Sulphur oxides	Nitrogen oxides
Australia		N/A	N/A
Austria		9	23
Belgium		25	35
Canada		91	68
Czech Republic		125	36
Denmark		30	53
Finland		22	54
France		17	26
Germany		37	27
Greece		50	33
Hungary		72	18
Iceland		29	81
Ireland, Republic of		53	37
Italy		25	37
Japan		7	12
Luxembourg		26	N/A
Mexico		N/A	N/A
Netherlands		9	35
New Zealand		N/A	43
Norway		8	51
Poland		68	29
Portugal		27	26
South Korea		34	26
Spain		53	31
Sweden		11	45
Switzerland		5	19
Turkey		29	9
UK		47	38
USA		63	74

Source: Atomic Energy Authority for the Organization for Economic Cooperation and Development

Carbon Dioxide Emissions for OECD Countries

As of January 1997.

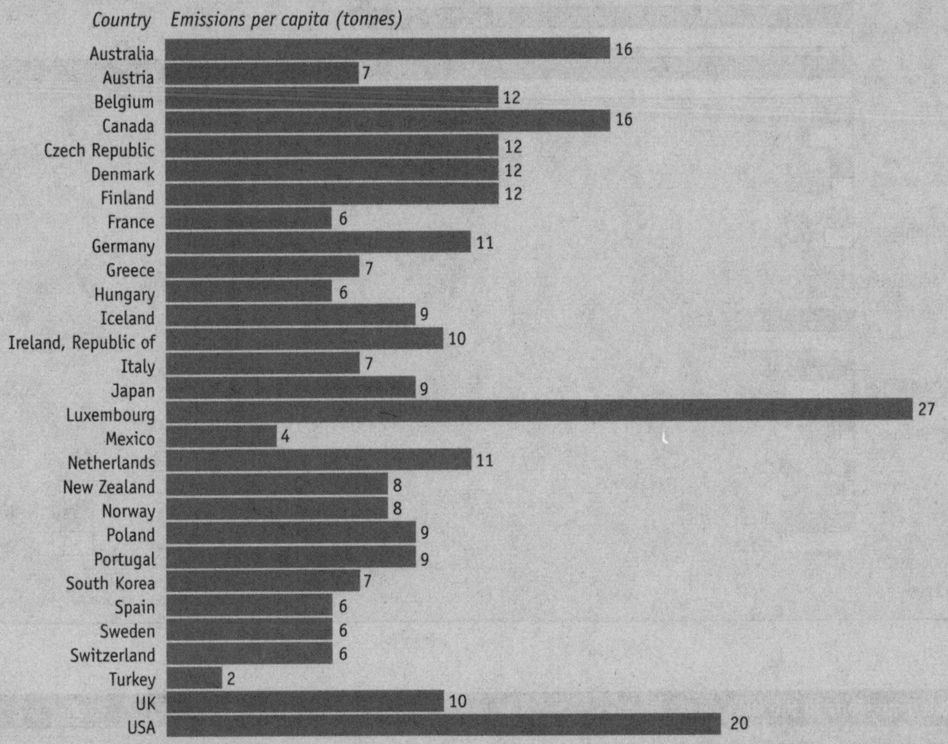

Country	Emissions per capita (tonnes)
Australia	16
Austria	7
Belgium	12
Canada	16
Czech Republic	12
Denmark	12
Finland	12
France	6
Germany	11
Greece	7
Hungary	6
Iceland	9
Ireland, Republic of	10
Italy	7
Japan	9
Luxembourg	27
Mexico	4
Netherlands	11
New Zealand	8
Norway	8
Poland	9
Portugal	9
South Korea	7
Spain	6
Sweden	6
Switzerland	6
Turkey	2
UK	10
USA	20

Source: Atomic Energy Authority for the Organization for Economic Cooperation and Development

Methane Emissions in the UK

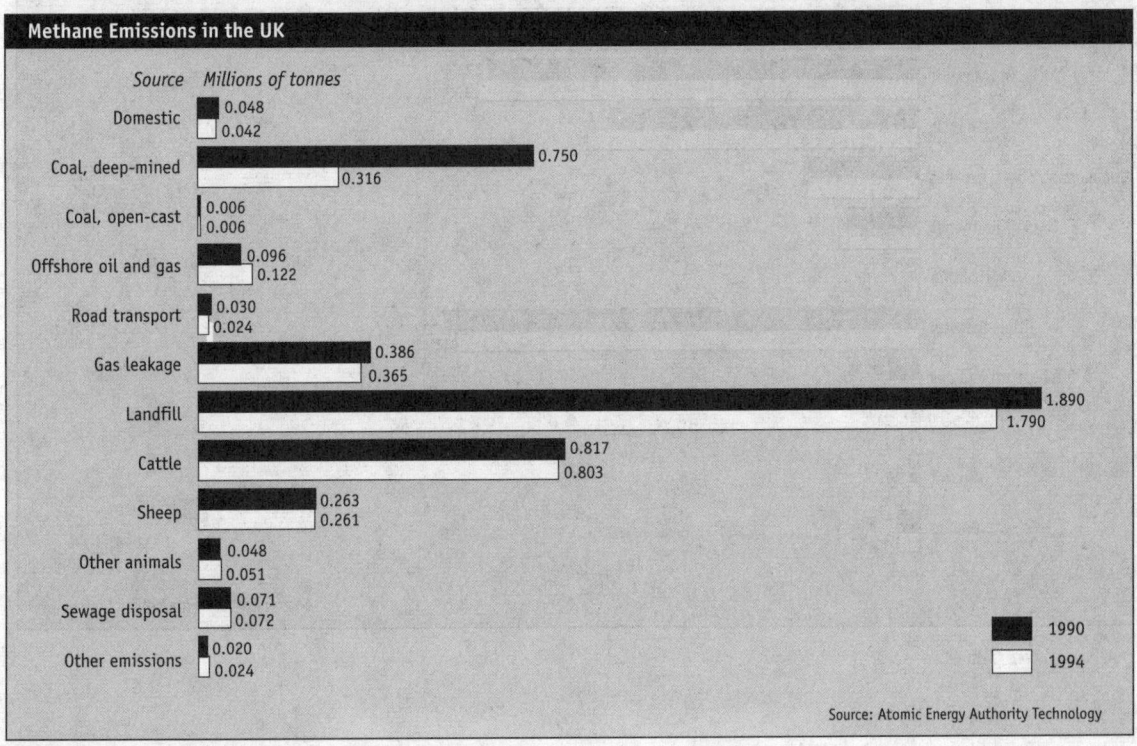

Source	Millions of tonnes	
	1990	1994
Domestic	0.048	0.042
Coal, deep-mined	0.750	0.316
Coal, open-cast	0.006	0.006
Offshore oil and gas	0.096	0.122
Road transport	0.030	0.024
Gas leakage	0.386	0.365
Landfill	1.890	1.790
Cattle	0.817	0.803
Sheep	0.263	0.261
Other animals	0.048	0.051
Sewage disposal	0.071	0.072
Other emissions	0.020	0.024

Source: Atomic Energy Authority Technology

Nitrogen Oxide Emissions in the UK

Source   *Millions of tonnes*

Source	1990	1994
Power stations	0.781	0.526
Road transport	1.339	1.095
Domestic	0.064	0.069
Commercial/public services	0.035	0.034
Refineries	0.040	0.045
Agriculture	0.003	0.003
Other industry	0.205	0.185
Offshore oil and gas	0.082	0.109
Railways	0.021	0.021
Aircraft	0.014	0.015
Shipping	0.117	0.115

1990
1994

Source: Atomic Energy Authority Technology

Carbon Dioxide Emissions in the UK

(Carbon dioxide (CO_2) given as carbon (C) in millions of tonnes.)

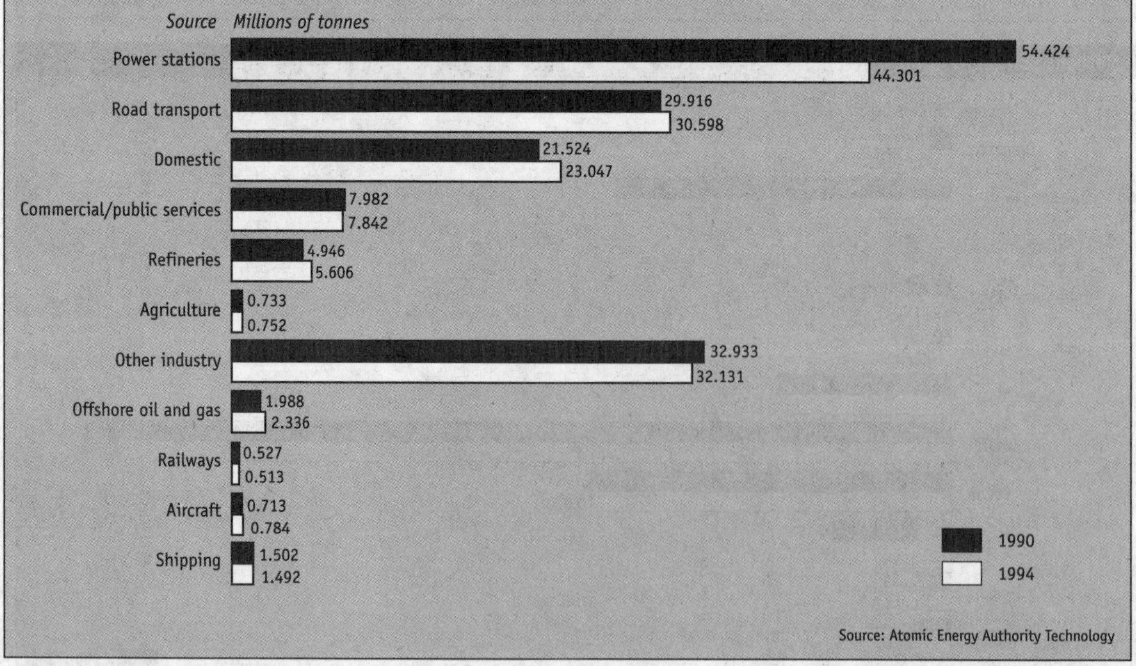

Source   *Millions of tonnes*

Source	1990	1994
Power stations	54.424	44.301
Road transport	29.916	30.598
Domestic	21.524	23.047
Commercial/public services	7.982	7.842
Refineries	4.946	5.606
Agriculture	0.733	0.752
Other industry	32.933	32.131
Offshore oil and gas	1.988	2.336
Railways	0.527	0.513
Aircraft	0.713	0.784
Shipping	1.502	1.492

1990
1994

Source: Atomic Energy Authority Technology

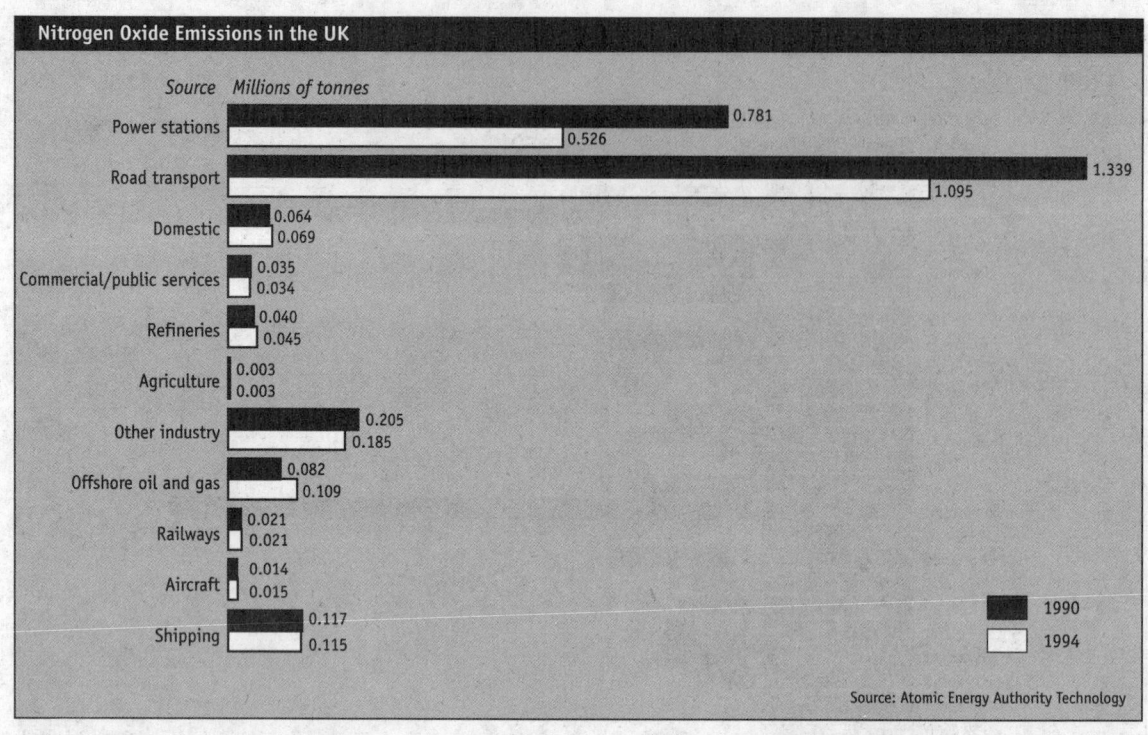

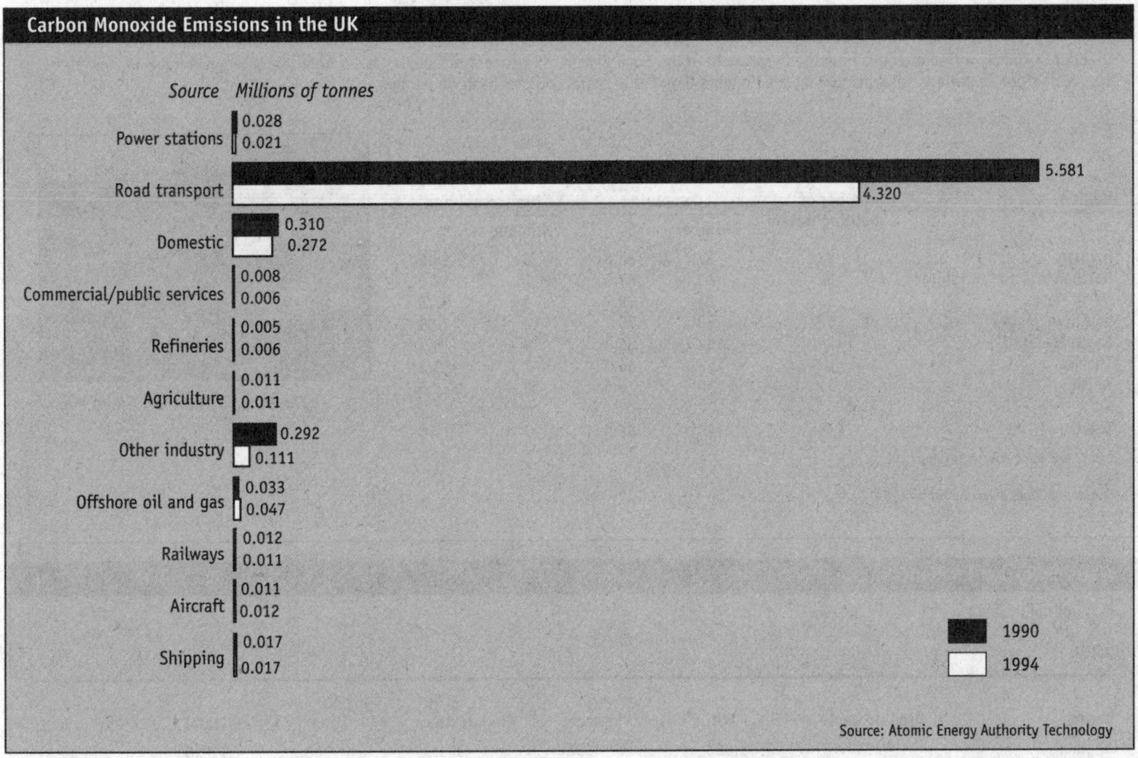

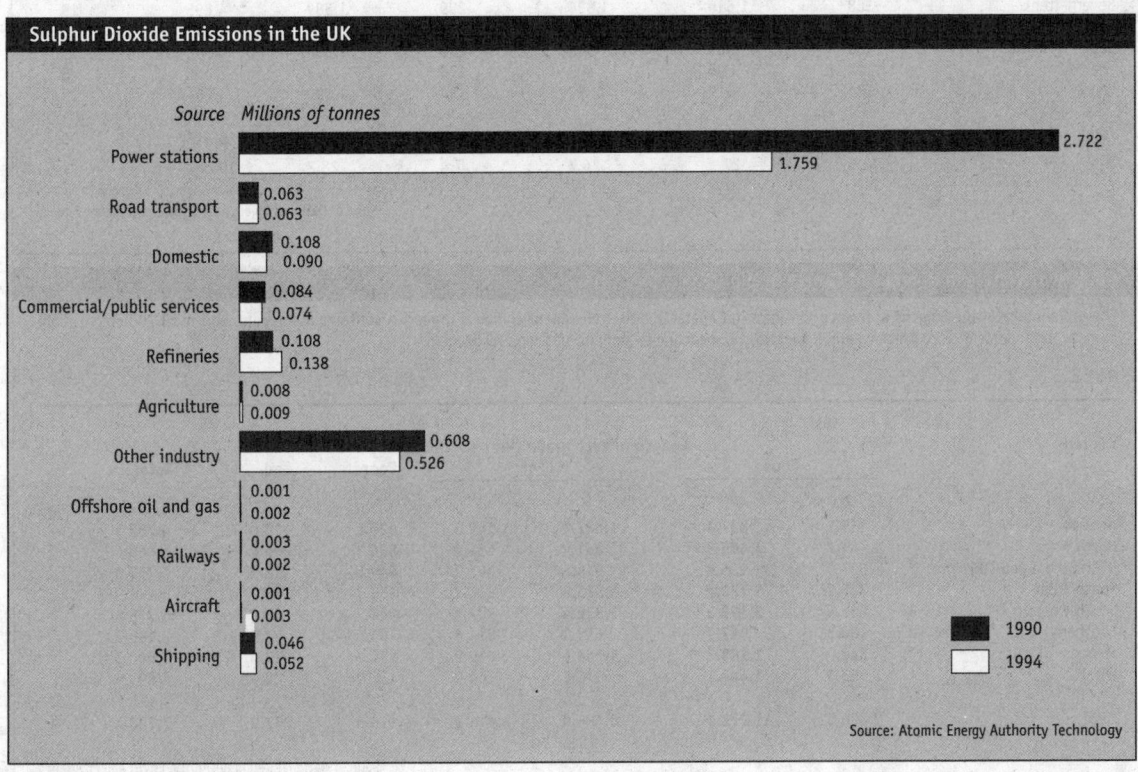

Carbon Monoxide Emissions in the UK

Source	Millions of tonnes
Power stations	0.028 / 0.021
Road transport	5.581 / 4.320
Domestic	0.310 / 0.272
Commercial/public services	0.008 / 0.006
Refineries	0.005 / 0.006
Agriculture	0.011 / 0.011
Other industry	0.292 / 0.111
Offshore oil and gas	0.033 / 0.047
Railways	0.012 / 0.011
Aircraft	0.011 / 0.012
Shipping	0.017 / 0.017

1990
1994

Source: Atomic Energy Authority Technology

Sulphur Dioxide Emissions in the UK

Source	Millions of tonnes
Power stations	2.722 / 1.759
Road transport	0.063 / 0.063
Domestic	0.108 / 0.090
Commercial/public services	0.084 / 0.074
Refineries	0.108 / 0.138
Agriculture	0.008 / 0.009
Other industry	0.608 / 0.526
Offshore oil and gas	0.001 / 0.002
Railways	0.003 / 0.002
Aircraft	0.001 / 0.003
Shipping	0.046 / 0.052

1990
1994

Source: Atomic Energy Authority Technology

Quality of Seaside Bathing Waters in the UK

In order to comply with a directive from the Department of the Environment, 95 per cent of samples taken from sea water must have no more than 10,000 coliform bacteria in total per 100 ml and no more than 2,000 faecal coliform bacteria per ml.

1994

The beach at Ventnor, Isle of Wight

Region	Number of bathing waters	Complying		Non-complying	
		Number	%	Number	%
Anglian	33	27	81.8	6	18.2
Northumbria and Yorkshire	56	49	87.5	7	12.5
North West	33	24	72.7	9	27.3
Southern	67	53	79.1	14	20.9
South Western[1]	175	151	86.3	24	13.7
Thames	3	2	66.7	1	33.3
Welsh	51	39	76.5	12	23.5
Total[1]	418	345	82.5	73	17.5

[1] Data exclude Lyme Regis (Church) Beach.

Source: National Rivers Authority (NRA)

Water Pollution Incidents in the UK

(– = not applicable.)

1994

Region	Organic waste	Oil	Sewage	Chemicals	Other	Total	%
Anglian	311	1,023	596	301	588	2,819	11
Northumbria and Yorkshire	291	705	992	251	1,004	3,243	13
North West	479	895	894	383	881	3,532	14
Severn-Trent	368	1,519	1,320	299	1,389	4,895	19
Southern	102	488	322	129	275	1,316	5
South Western	938	865	930	209	1,398	4,340	17
Thames	92	896	403	178	437	2,006	8
Welsh	584	517	830	134	1,199	3,264	13
Total	3,165	6,908	6,287	1,884	7,171	25,415	100
%	12.5	27.2	24.7	7.4	28.2	100.00	–

Source: National Rivers Authority, Environment Agency

Quality of Waters in Rivers and Canals in the UK

The table indicates the lengths of rivers and canals in General Quality Assessment chemical grades. A contains 80 percent oxygen, B 70 percent, C 60 percent, D 50 percent, E 20 percent, and F contains no measurable amount of dissolved oxygen.

1992

Region	Length in each grade (km)						
	Good		Fair		Poor	Bad	Total
	A	B	C	D	E	F	
Anglian	139.7	897.4	1,527.1	1,149.5	920.6	118.0	4,752.3
North West	1,481.2	1,405.9	861.9	654.9	836.1	206.6	5,446.6
Nottingham and Yorkshire	627.9	1,925.8	916.8	397.2	749.6	138.0	4,755.3
South Trent	365.7	1,721.4	1,523.2	917.2	733.3	173.7	5,434.5
South Western	2,025.6	2,399.5	1,359.4	307.1	241.7	42.6	6,375.9
Southern	180.3	937.7	658.8	214.6	165.9	22.9	2,180.2
Thames	246.8	1,188.3	1,264.4	619.9	335.5	27.4	3,682.3
Welsh	2,753.3	1,447.1	376.4	154.9	135.9	28.0	4,895.6
Total	7,820.5	11,923.1	8,488.0	4,415.3	4,118.6	757.2	37,522.7

Source: National Rivers Authority, Environment Agency

Background Radiation

Some radiation is always present in the environment. By far the greater proportion (87%) of it is emitted from natural sources. Alpha and beta particles, and gamma radiation are radiated by the traces of radioactive minerals that occur naturally in the environment and even in the human body, and by radioactive gases such as radon and thoron, which are found in soil and may seep upwards into buildings. Radiation from space (cosmic radiation) also contributes to the background level.

Average Radiation Exposure of the UK Population

The table covers the exposure of the entire population from all sources of ionizing radiation, natural and artificial. The annual collective dose (ie the dose for the whole population) is 150,000 man sieverts (mSv) and the average dose (for each individual) about 2.6 µSv. Radon is the dominant average source of human exposure in the home and at work. Exposure of patients to X-rays is next in magnitude, while exposure from nuclear discharges is negligible. Totals are rounded.

Source	Annual collective dose (man Sv)	Average annual dose (µSv)	Source	Annual collective dose (man Sv)	Average annual dose (µSv)
Natural			*Artificial*		
Cosmic	15,000	260	Medical	21,000	370
Gamma	20,000	350	Occupational[1]	430	7
Internal	17,000	300	Fallout	290	5
Radon	75,000	1,300	Discharges[2]	20	0.4
			Products	20	0.4
			Total	150,000	2,600

[1] Some 80 percent from natural sources.
[2] Some 20 percent from natural activity.

Source: National Radiological Protection Board

Radon-Affected Areas in England

Radon is a colourless, odourless, gaseous, radioactive, nonmetallic element, symbol Rn, atomic number 86, relative atomic mass 222. It is grouped with the inert gases and was formerly considered nonreactive, but is now known to form some compounds with fluorine. Of the 20 known isotopes, only three occur in nature; the longest half-life of radon is 3.82 days (Rn-222). Radon is the densest gas known and occurs in small amounts in spring water, streams, and the air, being formed from the natural radioactive decay of radium. Ernest Rutherford discovered the isotope Rn-220 in 1899, and Friedrich Dorn did so in 1900. After several other chemists discovered additional isotopes, William Ramsay and R W Whytlaw-Gray isolated the element, which they named niton in 1908. The name radon was adopted in the 1920s.

This table shows the results of a number of surveys of radon levels in English homes; data are for 1996. (AM = arithmetic mean; GM = geometric mean; AL = action level (taken as 200 Becquerels per cubic metre).)

Local authority code[1]	County or metropolitan area	Dwellings Total	Dwellings Number of results	Results (Becquerels per cubic metre) AM	Results (Becquerels per cubic metre) GM	Number of dwellings at or above AL
1	Inner London	1,146,500	113	12	<10	0
2	Outer London	1,791,000	316	23	16	0
3	Greater Manchester	1,105,400	676	24	16	6
4	Merseyside	595,400	149	14	11	0
5	South Yorkshire	558,000	1,255	38	26	25
6	Tyne and Wear	494,800	136	19	13	0
7	West Midlands	1,089,400	265	24	17	2
8	West Yorkshire	889,100	534	45	27	17
9	Avon	406,700	1,344	67	43	74
10	Bedfordshire	226,800	384	31	25	0
11	Berkshire	313,100	287	31	23	2
12	Buckinghamshire	275,500	647	39	30	9
13	Cambridgeshire	290,200	997	34	26	6
14	Cheshire	413,900	706	23	18	1
15	Cleveland	233,800	140	33	19	4
16	Cornwall	219,400	61,079	168	101	15,237
17	Cumbria	219,000	2,247	67	40	136
18	Derbyshire	412,100	34,337	82	40	3,111
19	Devon	463,700	71,426	81	48	5,674
20	Dorset	308,600	738	38	26	10
21	Durham	261,200	394	30	20	4
22	East Sussex	324,900	502	30	21	5
23	Essex	678,700	638	23	19	0
24	Gloucestershire	239,900	1,667	86	55	122

(continued)

Radon-Affected Areas in England (*continued*)

Local authority code[1]	County or metropolitan area	Dwellings		Results (Becquerels per cubic metre)		Number of dwellings at or above AL
		Total	Number of results	AM	GM	
25	Hampshire	671,300	817	34	24	10
26	Hereford and Worcester	293,400	936	45	33	20
27	Hertfordshire	423,600	341	33	25	0
28	Humberside	377,100	688	31	23	5
29	Isle of Wight	60,800	107	28	21	0
30	Kent	656,500	689	33	24	3
31	Lancashire	607,700	569	31	20	5
32	Leicestershire	376,000	2,469	86	50	230
33	Lincolnshire	271,500	6,645	77	48	517
34	Norfolk	353,200	974	31	24	4
35	Northamptonshire	256,900	66,203	65	37	4,171
36	Northumberland	136,600	890	41	27	20
37	North Yorkshire	314,000	1,711	49	30	67
38	Nottinghamshire	440,100	1,510	49	31	50
39	Oxfordshire	238,600	3,068	105	63	393
40	Shropshire	178,100	1,104	55	36	44
41	Somerset	208,900	30,778	59	40	1,169
42	Staffordshire	436,300	1,020	50	30	42
43	Suffolk	288,300	710	31	24	3
44	Surrey	434,500	310	27	20	1
45	Warwickshire	212,700	667	43	31	9
46	West Sussex	325,700	468	34	25	4
47	Wiltshire	251,400	837	44	28	26

[1] Local authority codes as used by the Office of Population Censuses & Surveys in the 1991 census.

Source: National Radiological Protection Board

Conservation

Conservation: Chronology

1627 Last surviving aurochs, long-horned wild cattle that previously roamed Europe, southwest Asia, and North Africa, became extinct in Poland.

1664 A Dutch mandate drawn up to protect forest in Cape Colony, South Africa.

1681 The last dodo, a long-standing symbol of the need for species conservation, died on the island of Mauritius.

1764 The British established forest reserves on Tobago, after deforestation in Barbados and Jamaica resulted in widespread soil erosion.

1769 The French passed conservation laws in Mauritius.

1868 First laws passed in the UK to protect birds.

1948 The International Union for Conservation of Nature and Natural Resources (IUCN) was founded, with its sister organization, the World Wildlife Fund (WWF).

1970 The Man and the Biosphere Programme was initiated by UNESCO, providing for an international network of biosphere reserves.

1971 The Convention on Wetlands of International Importance (especially concerned with wildfowl habitat) signed in Ramsar, Iran and started a List of Wetlands of International Importance.

1972 The Convention Concerning the Protection of the World Cultural and Natural Heritage adopted in Paris, France, providing for the designation of World Heritage Sites.

1972 The UN Conference on the Human Environment held in Stockholm, Sweden, lead to the creation of the UN Environment Programme (UNEP).

1973 The Convention on International Trade in Endangered Species of Wild Fauna and Flora (CITES) signed in Washington DC.

1974 The world's largest protected area, the Greenland National Park covering 97 million hectares, created.

1980 The World Conservation Strategy launched by the IUCN, with the WWF and UNEP, showed how conservation contributes to development.

1982 The first herd of 10 Arabian oryx bred from a 'captive breeding' programme released into the wild in Oman. The last wild oryx had been killed 1972.

1986 The first 'Red List' of endangered animal species compiled by IUCN.

1989 International trade in ivory banned under CITES legislation in an effort to protect the African elephant from poachers.

1992 The UN convened the 'Earth Summit' in Rio de Janeiro, Brazil, to discuss global planning for a sustainable future. The Convention on Biological Diversity and the Convention on Climate Change were opened for signing.

1993 The Convention on Biological Diversity came into force.

1995 The Arabian oryx conservation programme (began 1962), the most successful attempt at reintroducing zoo-bred animals to the wild, came to an end as the last seven animals were flown from the USA to join the 228-strong herd in Oman.

1996 The World Wide Fund for Nature had 5 million members in 28 countries.

1997 The world ban on the ivory trade was lifted in June 1997 at the tenth CITES convention. Trade is scheduled to resume in 1999 with Zimbabwe, Botswana, and Namibia the only countries allowed to export.

Earth Summit (*official name* United Nations Conference on Environment and Development)

The first Earth Summit took place in Rio de Janeiro, Brazil, in June 1992. Treaties were made to combat global warming and protect wildlife ('biodiversity') (the latter was not signed by the USA). The second Earth Summit was held in New York in June 1997 to review progress on the environment. The meeting agreed to work towards a global forest convention in 2000 with the aim of halting the destruction of tropical and old-growth forests.

The Rio summit, which cost $23 million to stage (of which 60% was spent on security), was attended by 10,000 official delegates, 12,000 representatives of nongovernmental organizations, and 7,000 journalists.

In 1993, the Clinton administration overturned certain decisions made by George Bush at the Earth Summit. The USA, which had failed to ratify the Convention of Biological Diversity pact along with other nations, came under renewed pressure to endorse it in April 1995 after India threatened to prevent US pharmaceutical and cosmetic companies from gaining access to its natural resources.

By 1996 most wealthy nations estimated that they would exceed their emissions targets, including Spain by 24%, Australia by 25%, and the USA by 3%. Britain and Germany were expected to meet their targets.

The second summit (1997) failed to agree a new deal to address the world's escalating environmental crisis. Dramatic falls in aid to the so-called Third World countries, which the 1992 Earth Summit promised to increase, were at the heart of the breakdown. British prime minister Tony Blair condemned the USA, Japan, Canada and Australia for failing to deliver on commitments to stabilize rising emissions of climate-changing greenhouse gases. The European Community as a whole was on target to meet its stabilization commitment because of cuts in emissions in Germany and the UK.

Deforestation was the main problem tackled at the second summit. The World Bank and the World Wide Fund for Nature signed an agreement aimed at protecting 250 million hectares/617 million acres of forest (10% of the world's forests). The importance of the issue was highlighted by the fact that deforestation increased rapidly in developing countries since the first summit, with 15,000 sq km/9,300 sq mi a year lost in the Amazon region.

Montréal Protocol

This international agreement was signed in 1987 to stop the production of ozone-depleting chemicals by the year 2000.

Originally the agreement was to reduce the production of ozone depleters by 35% by 1999. The green movement criticized the agreement as inadequate, arguing that an 85% reduction in ozone depleters would be necessary just to stabilize the ozone layer at 1987 levels. The protocol (under the Vienna Convention for the Protection of the Ozone Layer) was reviewed 1992. Amendments added another 11 chemicals to the original list of eight chemicals suspected of harming the ozone layer. A controversial amendment concerns a fund established to pay for the transfer of ozone-safe technology to poor countries.

Deforestation of Tropical and Temperate Forests Worldwide

(In hectares.)

Region	Forest area		Total change 1990–95	Annual change	Annual change (%)
	1990	1995			
Africa	538,978,000	520,237,000	–18,741,000	–3,748,000	–0.7
Asia	490,812,000	474,172,000	–16,640,000	–3,328,000	–0.7
Europe[1]	144,044,000	145,988,000	1,944,000	389,000	0.3
Former USSR[1]	813,381,000	816,167,000	2,786,000	557,000	0.1
North and Central America	537,898,000	536,529,000	–1,369,000	–274,000	–0.1
Oceania	91,149,000	90,695,000	–454,000	–91,000	–0.1
South America	894,466,000	870,594,000	–23,872,000	–4,774,000	–0.5

[1] No tropical forests exist in these regions, thus totals represent only temperate forests.

Source: Food and Agriculture Organization of the United Nations

Deforestation of Tropical Forests Worldwide

(In hectares.)

Region	Forest area		Total change 1990–95	Annual change	Annual change (%)
	1990	1995			
Africa	523,376,000	504,901,000	–18,475,000	–3,695,000	–0.7
Asia	295,041,000	279,766,000	–15,275,000	–3,055,000	–1.1
North and Central America	84,628,000	79,443,000	–5,185,000	–1,037,000	–1.3
Oceania	48,490,000	48,792,000	302,000	60,000	0.1
South America	851,223,000	827,946,000	–23,277,000	–4,655,000	–0.6

Source: Food and Agriculture Organization of the United Nations

Countries Losing Greatest Areas of Forest

1990–95

Rank	Country	Area of lost forest (hectares)	Rank	Country	Area of lost forest (hectares)
1	Brazil	2,554,000	21	Laos	148,000
2	Indonesia	1,084,000	22	Vietnam	135,000
3	Congo, Democratic Republic of	740,000	23	Papua New Guinea	133,000
4	Bolivia	581,000	24	Madagascar	130,000
5	Mexico	508,000	25	Cameroon	129,000
6	Venezuela	503,000	26	Central African Republic	128,000
7	Malaysia	400,000	27	Nigeria	121,000
8	Myanmar	387,000	28	Afghanistan	118,000
9	Sudan	353,000	29	Ghana	117,000
10	Thailand	329,000	30	Mozambique	116,000
11	Paraguay	327,000	31	Guinea-Bissau	114,000
12	Tanzania	323,000	32	Honduras	102,000
13	Zambia	264,000	33	Chad	94,000
14=	Colombia	262,000	34	Gabon	91,000
	Philippines	262,000	35	Argentina	89,000
16	Angola	237,000	36	Hong Kong, China	87,000
17	Peru	217,000	37	Guatemala	82,000
18	Ecuador	189,000	38	Guinea	75,000
19	Cambodia	164,000	39	Botswana	71,000
20	Nicaragua	151,000	40	Panama	64,000

Source: Food and Agriculture Organization of the United Nations

Afforestation

Planting of trees in areas that have not previously held forests. (*Reafforestation* is the planting of trees in deforested areas.) Trees may be planted (1) to provide timber and wood pulp; (2) to provide firewood in countries where this is an energy source; (3) to bind soil together and prevent soil erosion; and (4) to act as windbreaks.

Afforestation is a controversial issue because while many ancient woodlands of mixed trees are being lost, the new plantations consist almost exclusively of conifers. It is claimed that such plantations acidify the soil and conflict with the interests of biodiversity (they replace more ancient and ecologically valuable species and do not sustain wildlife).

Top 10 Countries with the Fastest Forest Depletion Rates

1990–95

Rank	Country	Average (annual loss) (%)
1	Lebanon	7.8
2	Jamaica	7.2
3	Afghanistan	6.8
4	Comoros	5.6
5	Virgin Islands (British)	4.4
6	St Lucia	3.6
7	Philippines	3.5
8	Haiti	3.4
9	El Salvador	3.3
10=	Costa Rica	3.0
	Sierra Leone	3.0

Source: Food and Agriculture Organization of the United Nations

Freshwater Resources and Withdrawals

Country by continent	Annual internal renewable water resources[1]			Annual withdrawals		
	Total (cubic km)	1995 per capita (cubic metres)	Year of data	Total (cubic km)	% of water resources[1][2]	Per capita (cubic metres)
World[3]	41,022.0	7,176	1987	3,240.00	8	645
Africa[3]	3,996.0	5,488	1995	145.14	4	199
Asia[3]	13,206.7	3,189	1987	1,633.85	12	542
Europe[3]	6,234.6	8,576	1995	455.29	7	626
North and Central America[3]	6,443.7	15,369	1995	608.44	9	1,451
Oceania[3]	1,614.3	56,543	1995	16.73	1	586
South America[3]	9,526.0	29,788	1995	106.21	1	332

[1] Annual internal renewable water resources usually include river flows from other countries.
[2] Total withdrawals may exceed 100% due to groundwater drawdowns or river inflows.
[3] Regional and world totals may include countries not listed.

Source: World Resources Institute

DID WE SAVE THE WORLD AT RIO DE JANEIRO?

BY NIGEL DUDLEY

The Earth Summit

The United Nations Conference on Environment and Development – usually called UNCED or the Earth Summit – took place in Rio de Janeiro, Brazil, in June 1992. It was the largest gathering of heads of state in history and almost certainly also the largest assembly of professional environmentalists and non-governmental organizations. In a historic meeting, the world's leaders agreed two important conventions to combat environmental destruction – on climate change and biodiversity – along with a comprehensive environmental strategy called 'Agenda 21' and a carefully-worded set of 'Forest Principles'. The meeting raised high expectations. It was hailed as a new start for the environment – indeed as a step towards a safer, more equitable world. Yet did anything really change? Five years on, in June 1997, a follow-up meeting took place in New York. Some of the results make depressing reading.

The Climate Change Convention has made extremely slow progress. After agreeing targets for reducing greenhouse gases that many experts believed were too low, several of the richer countries have failed to meet even these aims, and, instead, pollution continues to increase. The Convention on Biological Diversity has, in turn, become mired in infighting about rights to genetic material and has suffered from chronic underfunding: if anything, threats of widespread extinctions are greater now than they were in 1992. Debates about the need for a global forest convention – rejected at the time of the Earth Summit – are still going on today, against a background of continuing deforestation and forest degradation. Worse still, there has been a well-orchestrated backlash against the environment, promoted by some business interests intent on preventing their short-term profits being affected by long-term environmental planning.

Decisions into Practice

Yet the bad news has to be balanced by some good. While global negotiations have sometimes seemed like little more than an excuse for a handful of people to fly around the world for talking sessions, changes at the national, regional, and grassroots levels have been more encouraging. A 'Local Agenda 21' initiative has challenged community groups, non-governmental organizations, individuals, and local authorities to put the principles of the Earth Summit into practice. Literally thousands of projects have sprung up around the world, ranging from neighbourhood energy conservation schemes to community forest management and introduction of new techniques to enable resources to be used sustainably. These are important not only because of their practical impact, but because they have enabled the environmental message to be carried into thousands of schools and colleges, women's groups, religious organizations, trade unions, and so on.

Indeed, if there is one fundamental change that can be identified since the Rio meeting, it is that social issues have become much more fundamentally related to environmental concerns. Whereas early environmental projects sometimes virtually ignored people – leading, for example, to local people being expelled from their traditional areas to establish nature reserves – today there is increasing effort to integrate human and environmental needs, leading to stronger and more durable solutions. Rather than impose solutions from above, experience has also shown that results are likely to be far better if local people are involved in both the planning and the management of conservation projects, instead of being left to gaze at them from the outside. Such changes make the conservationist's role more complicated, and involve some inevitable give and take, but ultimately result in ways of reducing our impact on the environment that invite general support rather than opposition.

Things are working better at a regional level as well. Although we have no global forest convention, there have been several regional initiatives to define and implement 'sustainable forest management', where timber needs are balanced with other requirements, such as biodiversity conservation, environmental services such as control of soil erosion, production of food, medicinal herbs, and a range of non-timber forest products, recreational uses of forests, and even the spiritual and religious importance of particular forests.

Global Partnerships

In the absence of global leadership, local and national partnerships have been developing to fill the vacuum. Some of them are unexpected. For example, sections of the timber trade have been working with non-governmental organizations in several countries to develop 'certification of good forest management'; a forest gains a certificate if it is judged to be well-managed by an independent inspector against an agreed set of standards. Consumers have the chance to buy timber that they know has been produced without damaging the environment or local human communities. Efforts are being co-ordinated by the Forest Stewardship Council, an international organization based in Mexico which had not even been thought of at Rio, and already over 5 million hectares of forest have been certified around the world.

Conditions Are Still Getting Worse

These and other similar developments are certainly signs of hope. But down at the sharp end of environmental problems, it is hard to avoid the conclusion that, for many countries, conditions are still getting worse. Almost every developing country is still losing its forests. Desertification – the creation of new deserts as a result of overgrazing, poor irrigation schemes, climate change, and forest loss – is occurring in over a hundred countries. Forest fires are increasing in intensity, particularly in the tropical moist forests that should almost never burn under natural conditions. Commercially important fish species have, in many cases, been over-caught to the extent that stocks have collapsed, and the loss of mangroves in coastal regions has resulted in a similar rapid decline in the coastal species that rely on them to provide cover for breeding. The ozone hole continues to grow, and the evidence for climate change is increasing: extreme weather events appear to be growing in strength and frequency. At the moment we stand at a crossroads. Awareness of the importance of environmental issues has never been stronger. Governments and local communities are becoming increasingly willing to take action. But at the same time, ground continues to be lost – literally – and efforts at conservation and restoration will, in the future, be played out against a backdrop of a planet that will probably be far poorer in species and habitats than it was when the 20th century began.

Projected Water Stress Index

The water stress index was established by Population Action International to provide a rough guide to future water scarcity. Renewable freshwater resources of 1,000 cubic metres per capita per year are considered the benchmark below which most countries are likely to experience chronic water scarcity on a scale sufficient in certain circumstances to impede development and cause harm to human health. The projected future water stress index figures for the countries listed below have been calculated using United Nations population projections and relevant renewable water resources (assuming the latter remain constant).
(Data as of 1995.)

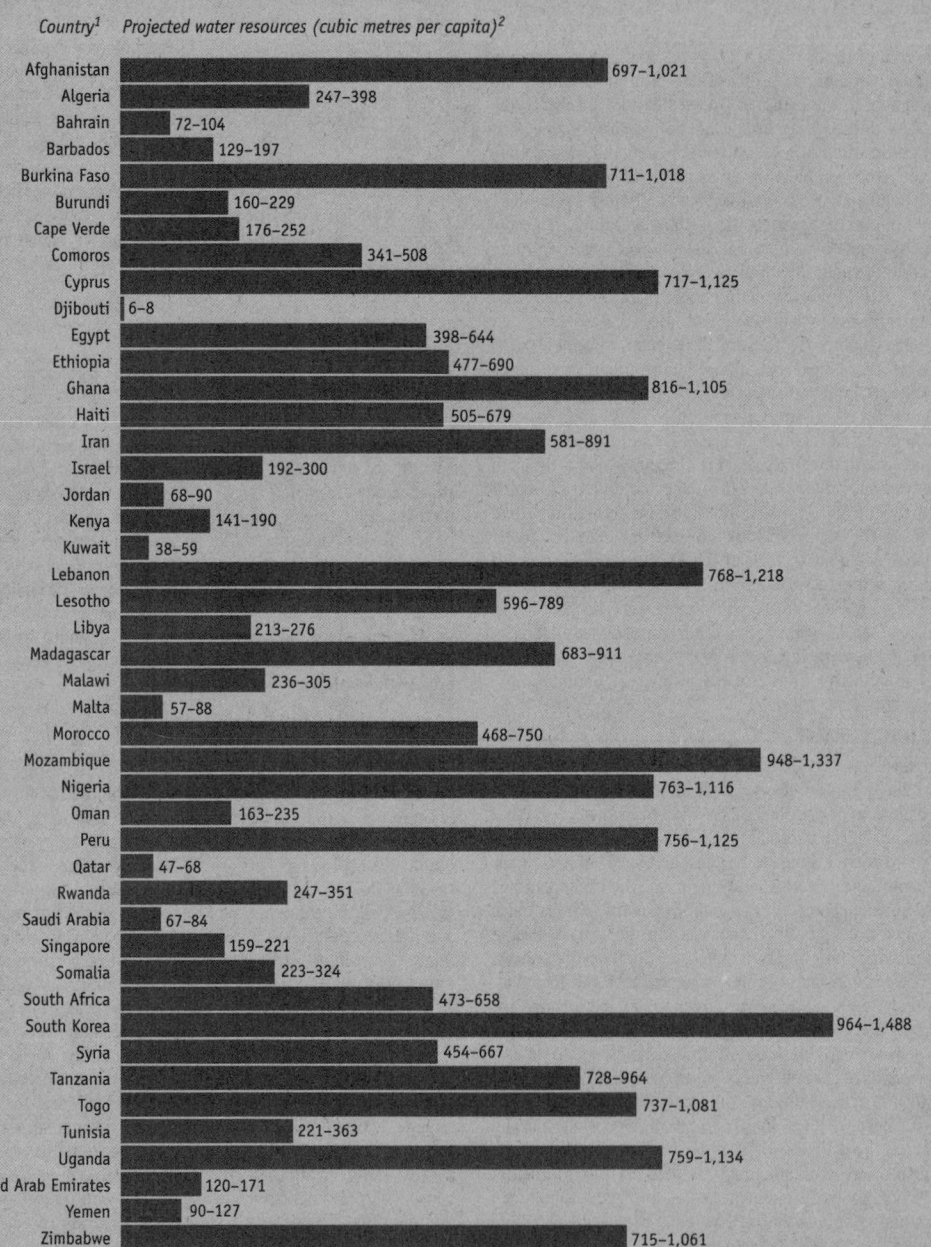

Country[1]   *Projected water resources (cubic metres per capita)*[2]

Country	Projected water resources (cubic metres per capita)
Afghanistan	697–1,021
Algeria	247–398
Bahrain	72–104
Barbados	129–197
Burkina Faso	711–1,018
Burundi	160–229
Cape Verde	176–252
Comoros	341–508
Cyprus	717–1,125
Djibouti	6–8
Egypt	398–644
Ethiopia	477–690
Ghana	816–1,105
Haiti	505–679
Iran	581–891
Israel	192–300
Jordan	68–90
Kenya	141–190
Kuwait	38–59
Lebanon	768–1,218
Lesotho	596–789
Libya	213–276
Madagascar	683–911
Malawi	236–305
Malta	57–88
Morocco	468–750
Mozambique	948–1,337
Nigeria	763–1,116
Oman	163–235
Peru	756–1,125
Qatar	47–68
Rwanda	247–351
Saudi Arabia	67–84
Singapore	159–221
Somalia	223–324
South Africa	473–658
South Korea	964–1,488
Syria	454–667
Tanzania	728–964
Togo	737–1,081
Tunisia	221–363
Uganda	759–1,134
United Arab Emirates	120–171
Yemen	90–127
Zimbabwe	715–1,061

[1] Includes countries with projected annual renewable resources of less than 1,000 cubic metres per capita per year.
[2] Figures are given for both the low and the high United Nations population growth projections.

Source: Population Action International

Land and Protected Areas

Ecology: Chronology

c. 325 BC	Greek scholar Theophrastus wrote about the relationship between organisms, and between organisms and their environment – the first ecological study.
1735	Swedish naturalist Carl Linnaeus developed his system for classifying and naming plants and animals.
1798	English cleric Thomas Malthus produced the earliest theoretical study of population dynamics.
1859	English naturalist Charles Darwin published his 'On the Origin of Species'.
1869	German zoologist Ernst Haeckel first defined the term 'ecology'.
1899	US botanist Henry Cowles published his classic paper on succession in sand dunes on Lake Michigan, USA.
1913	British Ecological Society founded.
1915	Ecological Society of America founded.
1916	US ecologist Frederic Clements coined the phrase 'climax communities' for large areas of rather uniform vegetation which he attributed to climactic factors.
1926	Russian botanist N I Vavilov published *Centres of Origin of Cultivated Plants*, concluding that there are relatively few such centres, many of which are located in mountainous areas.
1934	Russian ecologist G F Gause first stated the principles of competitive exclusion, related to a species' niche.
1935	British ecologist Arthur Tansley first coined the term 'ecosystem'.
1938	The coelacanth, a marine fish believed to have become extinct 65 million years ago, was 'rediscovered' in the Indian Ocean.
1940	Population biologist Charles Elton developed the idea of trophic levels in a community of organisms.
1950	The theory that natural selection may favour either individuals with high reproductive rates and rapid development (*r*-selection) or individuals with low reproductive rates and better competitive ability (*k*-selection) was first discussed.
1967	US biologists MacArthur and Wilson proposed their 'Theory of Island Biogeography' which related population and community size to island size. The theory is still widely used in the design of nature reserves today.
1979	English naturalist James Lovelock proposed his Gaia hypothesis, viewing the planet as a single organism.
1993	UN Convention on Biological Diversity came into force.

Top 10 Countries in the World with the Greatest Land Area Protected

The International Union for the Conservation of Nature and Natural Resources (IUCN) identifies a protected area as an area of land and/or sea dedicated to the protection and maintenance of biological diversity and natural and associated cultural resources that are managed through legal or other effective means. The main purposes of management of a region or area as a protected area are: for scientific research; wilderness protection; preservation of species and genetic diversity; maintenance of environmental services; protection of specific natural and cultural features; tourism and recreation; education; sustainable use of resources from natural ecosystems; and maintenance of cultural and traditional attributes. The number of protected areas in the UK is 191 and the area protected is 51,280 sq km (19,799 sq mi). This represents 20.94% of the land area.

1996

Country	Area		Number of protected areas	Area protected		Land area protected (%)[1]
	sq km	sq mi		sq km	sq mi	
USA	9,368,900	3,618,770	1,494	1,042,380	402,463	11.12
Greenland	2,186,000	844,014	2	982,500	379,344	44.95
Australia	7,682,300	2,966,136	892	935,455	361,180	12.18
Canada	9,970,610	3,849,674	640	825,455	318,708	8.32
Russia	17,075,500	6,591,100	199	655,368	253,038	3.84
China	9,596,960	3,599,975	463	580,666	224,195	6.05
Brazil	8,511,965	3,285,618	273	321,898	124,285	3.78
Venezuela	912,100	352,162	100	263,223	101,631	28.86
Indonesia	1,191,443	740,905	175	185,653	71,680	9.67
India	3,166,829	1,222,396	374	143,507	55,408	4.53

[1] The figures in the percentage of land area protected column may be inflated due to the inclusion of protected marine areas in the calculation.

Source: US Fish and Wildlife Service

Top 10 Countries in the World with the Greatest Percentage of Land Area Protected

Only includes those areas greater than 10 sq km/4 sq mi in extent, or completely protected islands of more than 1 sq km/0.4 sq mi, classified in any of the IUCN management categories.

1996

Country	Area		Number of protected areas	Area protected		Land area protected (%)[1]
	sq km	sq mi		sq km	sq mi	
Seychelles	453	175	3	379	146	93.79
Slovak Republic	49,035	18,940	40	10,155	3,921	72.36
Greenland	2,186,000	844,014	2	982,500	379,344	44.95
Kiribati	717	277	3	266	103	38.93
Liechtenstein	160	62	1	60	23	37.50
Denmark	43,075	16,627	113	13,888	5,362	32.24
Venezuela	912,100	352,162	100	263,223	101,631	28.86
Germany	357,041	137,853	504	91,957	35,505	25.77
Ecuador	461,475	178,176	15	111,139	42,910	24.08
Austria	83,500	32,374	170	20,058	7,744	23.92

[1] The figures in the percentage of land area protected column may be inflated due to the inclusion of protected marine areas in the calculation.

Source: US Fish and Wildlife Service

Areas of Outstanding Natural Beauty and National Scenic Areas in the UK

The Countryside Commission designates Areas of Outstanding Natural Beauty in England. In Wales, similar areas are the responsibility of the Countryside Council for Wales. No Areas of Outstanding Natural Beauty are designated in Scotland; the Scottish Natural Heritage recognizes equivalent sites called National Scenic Areas.
(N/A = not available.)

Name	Region	Established (year)	Area	
			sq km	sq mi
England				
Arnside and Silverdale	Cumbria, Lancashire	1972	75	29
Blackdown Hills	Devon, Somerset	1991	370	143
Cannock Castle	Staffordshire	1958	68	26
Chichester Harbour	Hampshire, west Sussex	1964	74	29
Chilterns	Bedfordshire, Buckinghamshire, Hertfordshire, Oxfordshire	1965; extended 1990	833	322
Cornwall	Cornwall	1959; Camel estuary 1983	958	370
Cotswolds	south Gloucestershire, Bath and northeast Somerset, Gloucestershire, Hereford and Worcester, Oxfordshire, Wiltshire, Warwickshire	1966	2,038	787
Cranborne Chase and West Wiltshire Downs	Dorset, Hampshire, Somerset, Wiltshire	1983	983	379
Dedham Vale	Essex, Suffolk	1970; extended 1978, 1991	90	35
Dorset	Dorset, Somerset	1959	1,129	436
East Devon	Devon	1963	268	103
East Hampshire	Hampshire	1962	383	148
Forest of Bowland	Lancashire, north Yorkshire	1964	802	310
High Weald	Sussex, Kent, Surrey	1983	1,460	564
Howardian Hills	north Yorkshire	1987	204	79
Isle of Wight	Isle of Wight	1963	189	73
Isles of Scilly	Isles of Scilly	1976	16	6
Kent Downs	Bromley, Kent	1968	878	339
Lincolnshire Wolds	northeast Lincolnshire	1973	558	215
Malvern Hills	Gloucestershire, Hereford and Worcester	1959	105	40
Mendip Hills	northwest Somerset, Bath and northeast Somerset	1972	198	76
Nidderdale	north Yorkshire	1994	603	233
Norfolk Coast	Norfolk	1968	451	174
North Devon	Devon	1960	171	66
North Pennines	Cumbria, Durham, Northumberland	1988	1,983	766
Northumberland Coast	Northumberland	1958	135	52
North Wessex Downs	Berkshire, Hampshire, Oxfordshire, Wiltshire	1972	1,730	668
Quantock Hills	Somerset	1957	99	38
Shropshire Hills	Shropshire	1959	804	310
Solway Coast	Cumbria	1964	115	44

Areas of Outstanding Natural Beauty and National Scenic Areas in the UK (*continued*)

Name	Region	Established (year)	Area sq km	Area sq mi
South Devon	Devon	1960	337	130
South Hampshire Coast	Hampshire	1967	77	30
Suffolk Coast and Heaths	Suffolk	1970	403	156
Surrey Hills	Surrey	1958	419	162
Sussex Downs	Sussex	1966	983	379
Tamar Valley	Devon, Cornwall	1995	195	115
Wye Valley (England)	Gloucestershire, Hereford and Worcester	1971	209	126
Northern Ireland				
Antrim Coast and Glens	Co. Antrim	1988	706	273
Causeway Coast	Co. Antrim	1989	42	16
Lagan Valley	Co. Down	1965	21	8
Lecale Coast	Co. Down	1967	31	12
Mourne	Co. Down	1986	570	220
North Derry	Co. Londonderry	1966	130	50
Ring of Gullion	Co. Armagh	1991	154	59
Sperrin	Co. Tyrone, Co. Londonderry	1968	1,010	390
Strangford Lough	Co. Down	1972	186	72
Wales				
Anglesey	Anglesey	1967	221	85
Clwydian Range	Denbighshire, Flintshire	1985	157	60
Gower	Swansea	1956	189	73
Llyn	Gwynedd	1957	161	62
Scotland				
Assynt-Coigach	Highland	N/A	902	348
Ben Nevis and Glen Coe	Highland, Argyll and Bute, Perthshire and Kinross	N/A	1,016	392
Cairngorm Mountains	Highland, Aberdeenshire, Moray	N/A	672	259
Cuillin Hills	Highland	N/A	219	85
Deeside and Lochnagar	Aberdeenshire, Angus	N/A	400	154
Dornoch Firth	Highland	N/A	75	29
East Stewartry Coast	Dumfries and Galloway	N/A	45	17
Eildon and Leaderfoot	Borders	N/A	36	14
Fleet Valley	Dumfries and Galloway	N/A	53	20
Glen Affric	Highland	N/A	193	75
Glen Strathfarrar	Highland	N/A	38	15
Hoy and West Mainland	Orkney Islands	N/A	148	57
Jura	Argyll and Bute	N/A	218	84
Kintail	Highland	N/A	155	60
Knapdale	Argyll and Bute	N/A	198	76
Knoydart	Highland	N/A	395	153
Kyle of Tongue	Highland	N/A	185	71
Kyles of Bute	Argyll and Bute	N/A	44	17
Lochna Keal, Mull	Argyll and Bute	N/A	127	49
Loch Lomond	Argyll and Bute, Stirling, West Dumbartonshire	N/A	274	106
Loch Rannoch and Glen Lyon	Perthshire and Kinross, Stirling	N/A	484	187
Loch Shiel	Highland	N/A	134	52
Loch Tummel	Perthshire and Kinross	N/A	92	36
Lynn of Lorn	Argyll and Bute	N/A	48	19
Morar, Moidart, and Ardnamurchan	Highland	N/A	135	52
Ninth estuary	Dumfries and Galloway	N/A	93	36
North Arran	North Ayrshire	N/A	238	92
North-West Sutherland	Highland	N/A	205	79
River Earn	Perthshire and Kinross	N/A	30	12
River Tay	Perthshire and Kinross	N/A	56	22
St Kilda	Western Isles	N/A	9	3
Scarra, Lunga, and the Garvellachs	Argyll and Bute	N/A	19	7
Shetland	Shetland Islands	N/A	116	45
Small Isles	Highland	N/A	155	60
South Lewis, Harris, and North Uist	Western Isles	N/A	1,096	423
South Uist Machair	Western Isles	N/A	61	24
The Trossachs	Stirling	N/A	46	18
Trotternish	Highland	N/A	50	19
Upper Tweeddale	Borders	N/A	105	41
Wester Ross	Highland	N/A	1,453	561

National Parks in England and Wales

The Countryside Commission is responsible for designating areas in England and Wales as National Parks, and advises Government on policy towards them. There are seven National Parks which, together with The Broads, are managed by a special Authority and cover 7.6 percent (9,934 sq km/3,836 mi) of England.

Name	Region	Established (year)	Area sq km	Area sq mi	Natural features	Activities
England						
The Broads[1]	between Norwich and Great Yarmouth, Norfolk	1989	303	117	fens, waterways, marshes, woodlands	walking, sailing, fishing, birdwatching
Dartmoor	Devon	1951	954	368	boggy plateaux, rocky land, river valleys; prehistoric remains	walking, fishing, riding
Exmoor	Somerset and Devon	1954	693	268	moorlands, cliffs; prehistoric remains	walking, riding, cycling, fishing
Lake District	Cumbria	1951	2,292	885	lakes, mountains, moorlands, fells	walking, climbing, sailing
The New Forest[2]	Hampshire	1990	376	117	forest, woodlands, heathlands	walking, riding, cycling
Northumberland	Northumberland	1956	1,049	405	grass moorlands, deep burn valleys, hills, mountains; Roman antiquities	walking, rock-climbing, canoeing, riding
North York Moors	north Yorkshire, Redcar, Cleveland	1952	1,436	554	open heather moorlands; unique wildlife	walking, riding
Peak District	Derbyshire, Staffordshire, south Yorkshire, Cheshire, west Yorkshire, Greater Manchester	1951	1,438	555	dales, hills, peat moorlands	walking, rock-climbing
Yorkshire Dales	north Yorkshire, Cumbria	1954	1,769	683	limestone cliffs, gorges, and pavements; valleys, waterfalls, caves	walking, caving
Wales						
Breacon Beacons	Powys, Carmarthenshire, Rhondda, Cynon, Taff, Merthyr Tydfil, Blaneau, Gwent, Monmouthshire	1957	1,351	522	mountains, valleys	walking, riding
Pembrokeshire Coast	Pembrokeshire	1952 and 1995	584	225	cliffs, moorlands; includes Skomer Islands	walking, birdwatching, marine life watching
Snowdonia	Gwynedd, Conwy	1951	2,142	827	deep valleys, rugged mountains	hill walking, rock-climbing, riding

[1] The Broads are considered to have equivalent status to National Parks due to Statutory designation.
[2] The New Forest does not enjoy Statutory designation, despite planning protection that recognizes its high landscape qualities. Therefore the area does not have equivalent administration or funding to a National Park. 1990 is the date of the establishment of the New Forest Committee.

Heritage Coasts in England

England has many popular coastal resorts but 32 percent (1,027 km/638 mi) of scenic English coastline is conserved as Heritage Coasts. These special coastlines are managed so that their natural beauty is conserved and, where appropriate, the accessibility for visitors is improved. The first Heritage Coast to be defined was the famous white chalk cliffs of Beachy Head in Sussex.
(– = not applicable.)

Coast	Defined[1] (year)	Length km	mi	Location	Coast	Defined[1] (year)	Length km	mi	Location
Dover-Folkestone[2]	1975	7	4	Kent	South Devon	1986	75	47	Devon
East Devon	1984	27	17	Devon	South Foreland[2]	1975	7	4	Kent
Exmoor	1991	45	28	Devon/Somerset	Spurn	1988	18	11	East Riding of Yorkshire
Flamborough Headland	1989	19	12	East Riding of Yorkshire/north Yorkshire	Suffolk	1979	57	35	Suffolk
					Sussex	1973	13	8	Sussex
Godrevy-Portreath	1986	9	6	Cornwall	Tennyson	1988	34	21	Isle of Wight
Gribbin Head-Polperro	1986	24	15	Cornwall	The Lizard	1986	27	17	Cornwall
Hamstead	1988	11	7	Isle of Wight	The Roseland	1986	53	33	Cornwall
Hartland (Cornwall only)	1986	11	7	Cornwall	Trevose Head	1986	4	2	Cornwall
Hartland (Devon)	1990	37	23	Devon	West Dorset	1984	41	25	Dorset
Isles of Scilly	1974	64	40	Isles of Scilly	**Total**	–	**1,041**	**647**	–
Lundy	1990	14	9	Devon					
North Devon	1992	32	20	Devon					
North Norfolk	1975	64	40	Norfolk					
North Northumberland	1992	110	68	Northumberland					
North Yorkshire and Cleveland	1981	57	35	North Yorkshire/Redcar and Cleveland					
Pentire Point-Widemouth	1986	52	32	Cornwall					
Penwith	1986	54	34	Cornwall					
Purbeck	1981	50	31	Dorset					
Rame Head	1986	8	5	Cornwall					
St Agnes	1986	11	7	Cornwall					
St Bees Head	1992	6	4	Cumbria					

[1] Date of completion definition.
[2] Coastal frontage only defined

Chalk cliffs, Sussex

National Trails in England

The first National Trail was the 412 km/256 mi Pennine Way opened in 1965. The longest is the 962 km/598 mi South West Coast Path which meanders through Somerset, Devon, Cornwall, and Dorset. The latest is Thames Path (344 km/214 mi) which was opened in July 1997. It is unique in that it follows the course of a river – the Thames – from its source in Gloucestershire to its end at the Thames Barrier in London.
(– = not applicable.)

National Trail	Opened (year)	Length km	mi	Location
Cleveland Way	1969	176	109	north Yorkshire/Redcar and Cleveland; 44 km/27 mi of the trail is open to both horse riders and cyclists, while 3.4 km/2.1 mi is open to motorized vehicles
North Downs Way	1978	246	153	Surrey/Kent; 122 km/76 mi of the trail is open to both horse riders and cyclists, while 74 km/46 mi is open to motorized vehicles
Offa's Dyke Path	1971	285	177	Gloucestershire/Hereford and Worcester/Shropshire (includes 198 km/123 mi in Wales); 22 km/14 mi of the trail is open to horse riders, 49 km/30 mi to cyclists, and 57 km/35 mi to motorized vehicles
Peddars Way/Norfolk Coast Path	1986	150	93	Norfolk/Suffolk; 70 km/43 mi of the trail is open to horse riders, cyclists, and motorized vehicles
Pennine Way	1965	412	256	Derby/north Yorkshire/Kirklees/Calderdale/Bradford/Rochdale/Oldham/Durham/Cumbria/Northumberland (includes 16 km/10 mi in Scotland); 83 km/52 mi of the trail is open to both horse riders and cyclists, while 38 km/24 mi is open to motorized vehicles
Ridgeway	1973	137	85	Wiltshire/Oxfordshire/Berkshire/Buckinghamshire/Hertfordshire; 101 km/63 mi of the trail is open to both horse riders and cyclists, while 83 km/52 mi is open to motorized vehicles
South Downs Way	1972	171	106	Hampshire/west and east Sussex; 171 km/106 mi of the trail is open to both horse riders and cyclists, while 25 km/16 mi is open to motorized vehicles
South West Coast Path	1973–78	962	598	Somerset/Devon/Cornwall/Dorset; 35 km/22 mi of the trail is open to cyclists, while 45 km/28 mi is open to motorized vehicles
Thames Path	1997	344	214	Gloucestershire/Wiltshire/Oxfordshire/ Berkshire/Buckinghamshire/Surrey/Greater London; 14 km/9 mi of the trail is open to horse riders, 16 km/10 mi to cyclists, and 0.6 km/0.4 mi to motorized vehicles
Wolds Way	1982	130	81	East Riding of Yorkshire/North Yorkshire; 44 km/27 mi of the trail is open to both horse riders and cyclists, while 20 km/12 mi is open to motorized vehicles

International Environmental Groups and Initiatives

Atmospheric Research and Information Centre

Organization that aims to research into urban air quality and to increase awareness of acid rain and the greenhouse effect through education and public information.

Date established 1984
Address c/o Manchester Metropolitan University, Department of Environmental and Geographical Sciences, Chester Street, Manchester M1 5GD; phone: (0161) 247 1590/1/2/3; fax: (0161) 247 6332; e-mail: aric@mmu.ac.uk
Web site www.doc.mmu.ac.uk/aric/arichome.html

British Hydropower Association

Association that aims to protect and promote the use of water to generate energy. It is believed that it is in the nation's and the world's interest to extend the use of water power and to save fossil fuels. The association is affiliated with the European Small Hydro-Power Association and the Association of Independent Electricity Producers.

Date established 1996
Address 52 Bramhall Lane South, Bramhall, Stockport, Cheshire SK7 1AH; phone: (0161) 440 9196; fax: (0161) 440 9273; e-mail: brithydro@aol.com

British Trust for Conservation Volunteers

Major practical conservation organization and the largest in the UK. It has numerous affiliations including BCTV Enterprises, the National Trust, Green Alliance, Groundwork, Wildlife Link, and the Environmental Council.

Date established 1959
Membership 8,728
Address 36 St Mary's Street, Wallingford, Oxfordshire OX10 0EU; phone: (01491) 839766; fax: (01491) 839646; e-mail: information@btcv.org.uk
Web site www.btcv.org.uk

British Wind Energy Association

Organization that aims to promote excellence in wind energy research, development, and deployment. It is affiliated with the European Wind Energy Association, Eurosolar, AEP, and the Irish Wind Energy Association.
Date established 1977
Membership c. 900
Address 26 Spring Street, London W2 1JA, UK; phone: (0171) 402 7107; fax: (0171) 402 7102; e-mail: bwea@gn.apc.org
Web site www.bwea.com

Butterfly Conservation

Organization formed for the purpose of the conservation of butterflies and their habitats by owning, managing, and advising on habitat management and reserves. It is affiliated with English Nature, JCCBI, and Wildlife Link.

Date established 1968
Membership 10,000
Address PO Box 222, Dedham, Colchester, Essex CO7 6EY; phone: (01206) 322342; fax: (01206) 322739; e-mail: butterfly@cix.compulink.co.uk

Centre for Alternative Technology

Organization set up to invesigate, use, demonstrate, and promote environmentally and socially appropriate technologies for energy generation and conservation, food production, and building design.

Date established 1974
Membership 3,500
Address Machynlleth, Powys SY20 9AZ; phone: (01654) 702400; fax: (01654) 702782; e-mail: cat@gn.apc.org
Web site www.foe.co.uk/cat

Conservation International

Organization established in order to conserve the Earth's living natural heritage and global biodiversity, and to demonstrate, through science, economics, policy, and community involvement, that human societies can live in harmony with nature. The organization has members in 22 countries.

Date established 1987
Membership 40,000
Address 2501 M Street NW, Suite 200, Washington, DC 20037; phone: (202) 429 5660; fax: (202) 887-0192
Web site www.conservation.org/

Countryside Commission

Organization working to conserve the natural beauty of the English countryside. An advisory and promotional body, rather than an executive one, the Commission owns no land and manages no facilities but achieves its objectives through collaboration with other organizations. It has seven regional offices.

Date established 1968
Address John Dower House, Crescent Place, Cheltenham, Gloucestershire GL50 3RA; phone: (01242) 521381; fax: (01242) 584270
Web site www.countryside.gov.uk

The Earth Council

Organization that aims to support and empower people in building a more secure, equitable, and sustainable future, to promote awareness and support, encourage public participation, and build bridges of understanding between citizens and government. Funding comes through the Earth Council Foundation's sponsoring institutions, foundations, corporations, and individuals.

Date established 1992
Membership covers 22 countries
Address Deputy Executive Director, Apartado 2323-1002, San José, Costa Rica; phone: (506) 256 1611; fax: (506) 255 2197; e-mail: eci@terra.ecouncil.ac.cr
Web site www.terra.ecouncil.ac.cr/

Earthwatch

Charity organization that aims to build a sustainable world through active partnership between scientists and citizens, by gathering data and communicating information to empower people and governments to act wisely as global citizens. It is funded through membership dues and donor organizations and individuals. The organization has members in over 118 countries.

Date established 1971
Membership 70,000
Address Earthwatch Europe, 57 Woodstock Road, Oxford, OX2 6HJ, UK; phone: (44 1865) 311600; fax: (44 1865) 311383; e-mail: info@uk.earthwatch.org
Web site www.gaia.earthwatch.org

Energy and Environmental Programme

Part of the Royal Institute of International Affairs (RIIA), the Programme researches and publishes reports on strategic and economic planning.

Date established 1985
Membership 5,000 (RIIA)
Address Chatham House, 10 St James's Square, London SW1Y 4LE; phone: (0171) 957 5711; fax: (0171) 957 5710; e-mail: eepriia@gn.apc.org
Web site www.riia.org

Friends of the Earth

Charity organization that aims to protect the planet from environmental degradation, to preserve biological, cultural, and ethnic diversity, and to empower citizens to have an influential voice in decisions affecting the quality of their environment and their lives. It is funded through membership dues, donations, and subsidies.

Date established 1969
Membership 35,000
Address: Headquarters Friends of the Earth International, PO Box 19199, NL-1000 GD, Amsterdam; phone: (31 20) 622-1369; fax: (31 20) 639-2181; e-mail: foeint@ antenna.nl
Address in UK Friends of the Earth, 56–58 Alma Street, Luton, Bedfordshire, LU1 2YZ; e-mail: info- request@foe.co.uk
Web site www.foe.org; www.xs4all.nl/~-foeint/

Green Alliance

Organization that works on environmental policy and politics. Its main activities fall into three areas; greening government, greening business and finance, and greening science. It is affiliated with the European Environment Bureau, Wildlife Link, and the National Council for Voluntary Organizations.

Date established 1978
Membership 380
Address 49 Wellington Street, London WC71 7BN; phone: (0171) 836 0341; fax: (0171) 240 9205; e-mail: gralliance@ gn.apc.org

Greenpeace International

Independent organization that aims to protect biodiversity in all its forms, to prevent pollution and abuse of the Earth's ocean, land, air, and fresh water, to end all nuclear threats, and to promote peace, global disarmament, and non-violence. It is funded through donations, voluntary contributions from the public, and sales of merchandise. Greenpeace does not accept funds from business interests or governments. The organization has offices in 30 countries.

Date established 1971
Membership 4,500,000
Address: Headquarters Keizersgracht 176, NL-1016 DW, Amsterdam, The Netherlands; phone: (31 20) 523 6222; fax: (31 20) 523 6200; e-mail: greenpeace.international-@greenz.dat.de
Web site www.greenpeace.org

Institute of Terrestrial Ecology

Organization that undertakes specialist ecological research in all aspects of the terrestrial environment and seeks to understand the ecology of species and of human-made communities. The Institute is part of the National Environment Research Council and has six research stations based in the UK.

Date established 1973
Address Monk's Wood, Abbots Ripton, Huntingdon, Cambridgeshire PE17 2LS; phone: (01487) 773381; fax: (01487) 773467; e-mail: eic@itc.ac.uk
Web site www.nmw.ac.uk/ite

Institute of Wastes Management

Organization that aims to advance the scientific, technical, and professional aspects of waste management for the safeguarding of the environment.

Date established 1898
Address 9 Saxon Court, St Peter's Gardens, Northampton, Northamptonshire NN1 1SX; phone: (01604) 20426; fax: (01604) 21339; e-mail: iwm.technical@dial.pipex.com

International Energy Agency (IEA)

Autonomous agency linked with the OECD that aims to foster cooperation among participating countries to increase energy security through diversification of energy supply, more efficient and cleaner use of energy, energy conservation, and the development of alternative energy sources. The governments of the 23 OECD member states form the membership of the International Energy Agency.

Date established 1974
Membership governments of 23 OECD countries
Address: Headquarters 9 rue de la Fédération, 75739 Paris Cedex 15, France; phone: (33 1) 4057 6554; fax: (33 1) 4057 6559
Web site www.iea.org/

International Wildlife Coalition (home of Whale Adoption Project)

Organization that aims to preserve wildlife all over the world.

Date established 1983
Membership c.150,000 individual members in five countries
Address PO Box 73, Hartfield, East Sussex, TN7 4EY; phone: (44 1342) 825482; fax: (44 1342) 824716
Web site www.webcom.com/iwcwww/

Marine Conservation Society

Organization that aims to protect the marine environment for both wildlife and future generations by promoting its sustainable and environmentally sensitive management.

Date established 1983
Address 9 Gloucester Road, Ross on Wye, Hereford HR9 5BU; phone: (01989) 566017; fax: (01989) 567815

National Association for Environmental Education

Association set up to promote and encourage environmental education through all levels of the education system.

Date established 1960
Address Wolverhampton University, Walsall Campus, Gorway, West Midlands WS1 3BD; phone: (01922) 31200; fax: (01922) 31200

New Economics Foundation

Organization that aims to build a just and sustainable economy, with ideas and action that put people and the environment first. The Foundation has close links with Friends of the Earth, GreenNet, and the Centre for Employment Initiatives.

Date established 1986
Membership 2,000
Address 1st Floor, Vine Court, 112–116 Whitechapel Road, London E1 1JE; phone: (0171) 377 5696; fax: (0171) 377 5720; e-mail: neweconomics@gn.apc.org
Web site soslq.ac.uk/New Economic-s/newe-con.html

Population Action International

Organization that aims to advance policies and programs that slow the world's population growth in order that the quality of life for all people can be enhanced.

Date established 1965
Address 1120 19th Street NW, Suite 550, Washington, DC 20036; phone: (202) 659 1833; fax: (202) 293 1795; e-mail: pai@ popact.org
Web site www.populationaction.org/

Rainforest Action Network (RAN)

Non-profit volunteer and member-based organization that aims to protect tropical rainforests and support the rights of indigenous peoples. It is financed by membership dues, foundation grants and donations, and special events.

Date established 1985
Membership 30,000 individual and 150 organizations and groups, covering 74 countries and territories
Address 221 Pine Street, Suite 500, San Francisco, CA 94104; phone: (415) 398 4404; fax: (415) 398 2732; e-mail: rainforest@ran.org
Web site www.ran.org/ran/

Royal Society for the Protection of Birds

Organization acting for the protection of wild birds and their habitats. This includes the buying of land to create new nature reserves and protecting existing bird sites from any type of environmental encroachment.

Date established 1889
Address The Lodge, Sandy, Bedfordshire SG19 2DL; phone: (01767) 680551; fax: (01767) 692365

Trees for Life

Charity organization that aims to help people in Third World countries become self-sufficient by providing funding, planning, management, materials, and information on the planting, cultivation, and harvest of food-bearing trees. It is funded by membership dues and donations.

Date established 1984
Membership 5,000
Address 1103 Jefferson, Wichita, KS 67203; phone: (316) 263-7294; fax: (316) 263-5293; e-mail: info@treesforlife.org
Web site www.treesforlife.org

Waste Management Information Bureau

The UK's national referral centre for advice and information on waste management.

Date established 1973
Address National Environmental Technology Centre, AEA Technology plc, F6 Culham, Abingdon, Oxfordshire OX14 3DB; phone: (01235) 463162; fax: (01235) 463004; e-mail: wmib@aeat.co.uk

Waste Watch

Organization that aims to promote recycling and waste reduction, with particular reference to the interests of the voluntary sector.

Date established 1987
Address Gresham House, 24 Holborn Viaduct, London EC1A 2BN; phone: (0171) 248 1816; fax: (0171) 248 1404

The Wildfowl and Wetlands Trust

Organization that aims to promote the conservation of wildfowl and their wetland habitats through research, conservation, and education programmes. The Trust's Mission Statement is to save wetlands for wildlife and people.

Membership 75,000
Date established 1946
Address Slimbridge, Gloucestershire GL2 7BT; phone: (01453) 890333 ext 279; fax: (01453) 890627

World Conservation Union

Organization that aims to influence, encourage, and assist societies throughout the world to conserve the integrity and diversity of nature, and to ensure that any use of natural resources is equitable and ecologically sustainable.

Date established 1948
Membership 74 governments and more than 700 NGOs

 Green Movement: Chronology

1798   Thomas Malthus's *Essay on the Principle of Population* published, setting out the idea that humans are also bound by ecological constraints.

1824   Society for the Prevention of Cruelty to Animals founded.

1835–39 Droughts and famine in India resulted in the first connections being made between environmental damage (deforestation) and climate change.

1864   George Marsh's 'Man and Nature' was the first comprehensive study of humans' impact on the environment.

1865   Commons Preservation Society founded, raising the issue of public access to the countryside, taken further by the mass trespasses of the 1930s.

1872   Yellowstone National Park created in the USA; a full system of national parks was established 40 years later.

1893   National Trust founded in the UK to buy land in order to preserve places of natural beauty and cultural landmarks.

1930   Chlorofluorocarbons (CFCs) invented; they were hailed as a boon for humanity as they were not only cheap and nonflammable but were also thought not to be harmful to the environment.

1934   Drought exacerbated soil erosion, causing the 'Dust Bowl Storm' in USA, during which some 350 million tons of topsoil were blown away.

1948   United Nations created special environmental agency, the International Union for the Conservation of Nature (IUCN).

1952   Air pollution caused massive smog in London, killing some 4,000 people and leading to clean-air legislation.

1968   Garret Hardin's essay 'The Tragedy of the Commons' challenged individuals to recognize their personal reponsibility for environmental degradation as a result of lifestyle choices.

1969   Friends of the Earth launched in USA as a breakaway group from increasingly conservative Sierra Club; there was an upsurge of more radical active groups within the environmental movement over the following years.

1972   *Blueprint for Survival,* a detailed analysis of the human race's ecological predicament and proposed solutions, published in UK by Teddy Goldsmith and others from the *Ecologist* magazine.

1974   First scientific warning of serious depletion of protective ozone layer in upper atmosphere by CFCs.

1980   US president Jimmy Carter commissioned *Global 2000* report, reflecting entry of environmental concerns into mainstream of political issues.

1983   German Greens (Die Grünen) won 5% of vote, giving them 27 seats in the Bundestag.

1985   Greenpeace boat *Rainbow Warrior* sunk by French intelligence agents in a New Zealand harbour during a protest against French nuclear testing in the South Pacific. One crew member was killed.

1988   NASA scientist James Hansen warned US Congress of serious danger of global warming: 'The greenhouse effect is here'.

1989   European elections put green issues firmly on political agenda as Green parties across Europe attracted unprecedented support; especially in the UK, where the Greens received some 15% of votes cast (though not of seats).

1989   *The Green Consumer Guide* published in the UK, one of many such books worldwide advocating 'green consumerism'.

1991   The Gulf War had massive environmental consequences, primarily as a result of the huge quantity of oil discharged into the Persian Gulf from Kuwait's oilfields. Many felt this was just the start of a grim future of wars over ever decreasing resources.

1992   United Nations Earth Summit in Rio de Janeiro aroused great media interest but achieved little progress in tackling difficult global environmental issues because many nations feared possible effects on trade.

1994   Protests against roadbuilding in many parts of the UK; for example, in 'Battle of Wanstonia', green activists occupied buildings and trees in East London in attempt to halt construction of M11 motorway.

1995   Animal-rights activists campaigned against the export of live animals; activist Jill Phipps was killed 1 Feb during a protest at Coventry airport. In May Greenpeace's London headquarters were raided by the Ministry of Defence and files and computer discs were confiscated.

1996   A new political force, Real World, was formed from a coalition of 32 campaigning charities and pressure groups.

1997   The second Earth Summit took place in New York. Delegates reported on progress since the 1992 Rio Summit, but failed to agree on a deal to address the world's escalating environmental crisis. Delegates at the Kyoto, Japan, conference on global warming agreed to cut emission of greenhouse gases by 5.2% from 1990 levels during the years 2008 and 2012.

Address Rue Mauverney 28, CH-1196 Gland, Switzerland; phone: (41) 22 999 00 01; fax: (41) 22 999 00 02; e-mail: mail@hq.iucn.org
Web site w3.iprolink.ch/iucnlib/

World Society for the Protection of Animals (WSPA)

Organization that aims to end the exploitation of animals through practical projects, educational campaigns, and representations at government level. WSPA policy states that it aims to 'encourage respect for animals, and responsible stewardship and laws and enforcement structures to provide legal protection for animals'. It is a charity that relies on member societies, individual membership dues, donations, and bequests. It accepts no financial aid from governments. It has a network of 350 member societies in more than 70 countries.

Date established 1981 (previously active in another name for over 40 years)
Address: Eastern Hemisphere Headquarters 2 Langley Lane, London, SW8 1TJ, UK; phone: (44 171) 793 0540; fax: (44 171) 793 0208; e-mail: wspa@wspa.org.uk
Address: Western Hemisphere Headquarters PO Box 190, 29 Perkins Street, Boston, MA 02130; phone: (617) 522-7000; fax: (617) 522-7077; e-mail: wspa@world. std.com
Web site www.way.net/wspa/

World Wide Fund for Nature (WWF)

International organization that aims to protect the biological resources upon which human well-being depends and to preserve endangered and threatened species of wildlife and plants as well as habitats and natural areas of the world. It is funded through membership dues, legacies, bequests, corporate subscriptions, governments and aid agencies, foundation grants, and other earned income.

Date established 1961
Membership 1.2 million
Address WWF International (World Wide Fund for Nature), Avenue du Mont-Blanc, CH-1196 Gland; phone: (41 22) 364 9111; fax: (41 22) 364 5358
Web site www.panda.org

Web Sites

Air Pollution – Committee on the Medical Aspects of Air Pollutants

URL: 'http://www.open.gov.uk/doh/hef/airpol/airpolh.htm'

Comprehensive report on the state of Britain's air from the Ministry of Health. There is a large amount of textual and statistical information on all aspects of air pollution, description of improved warning and detection measures, and details of how the general public may access advice and information.

Bioenergy Information Network

URL: 'http://www.esd.ornl.gov/bfdp/'

US government site about the possibilities and research into producing energy from rapidly replaced trees and grasses.

Biomass

URL: 'http://www.nrel.gov/research/industrial_tech/biomass.html'

Information on biomass from the US Department of Energy. There is a clear explanation of the chemical composition of biomass and development of technologies to transform it into usable fuel sources.

Centre for Alternative Technology

URL: 'http://www.cat.org.uk/'

Dedicated to the Centre For Alternative Technology in Wales and includes a virtual tour of the site, pictures, and maps.

Chemistry of the Ozone Layer

URL: 'http://pooh.chem.wm.edu/chemWWW/courses/chem105/projects/group2/page1.html'

Step-by-step introduction to the ozone layer for those wishing to understand the chemistry of ozone depletion, the role of chlorofluorocarbons, the consequences of increased radiation for life on earth.

Countryside Commission

URL: 'http://www.countryside.gov.uk/'

Information on all of Britain's national parks and officially-designated areas of outstanding beauty.

English Heritage

URL: 'http://www.english-heritage.org.uk/dminterface/dmindex.asp'

Site of the public body charged with protecting England's historic environment. A clickable map accesses information on historic properties.

English Nature – Facts and Figures

URL: 'http://www.english-nature.org.uk/facts.htm'

Outline of the role of the government agency charged with conserving wildlife and natural features in England. There is information about Sites of Special Scientific Interest (SSSIs), national and marine nature reserves, and protection of wetlands.

Environmental Education Network

URL: 'http://envirolink.org/enviroed/'

Collaborative effort to place environmental information on the Internet. It is divided into sections for teachers and students. These are further subdivided into sections such as geology, archaeology, and exploration/travel.

Fish – Endangered Species

URL: 'http://www.nmfs.gov/tmcintyr/fish/anadromo.html'

Endangered or threatened species of fish in the US. There are also hypertext, links to page descriptions of the biology, distribution, and threat to each of the twelve species listed.

Friends of the Earth Home Page

URL: 'http://www.foe.co.uk/'

The site hosts lengthy accounts of several campaigns undertaken by FoE on climate, industry, transport, and sustainable development. It also maintains an archive of press releases from FoE on some of the most controversial environmental problems encountered in the course of last year around the world.

Geothermal Technologies

URL: 'http://www.eren.doe.gov/geothermal/'

Home page of the US Department of Energy. There is a description of various geothermal energy sources and technologies being developed to exploit them. There is information about a number of energy authorities across the world tapping geothermal energy.

Global Warming

URL: 'http://pooh.chem.wm.edu/chemWWW/courses/chem105/projects/group1/page1.html'

Step-by-step explanation of the chemistry behind global warming. There is information on the causes of global warming, the environmental effects, and the social and economic consequences.

International Global Atmospheric Chemistry

URL: 'http://web.mit.edu/afs/athena.mit.edu/org/i/igac/www/intro.html'

Examination of the complex chemistry of the atmosphere and how it is being affected by human development.

Intermediate Technology Development Group

URL: 'http://www.oneworld.org/itdg/'

Account of the work of the British aid organization working with rural poor to develop relevant and sustainable technologies.

National Wind Technology Centre

URL: "http://www.nrel.gov/wind/"

Source of information on the importance of wind power. This US Department of Energy site has reports on the latest research.

Ocean Planet

URL: "http://seawifs.gsfc.nasa.gov/ocean_planet.html"

Oceans and the environmental issues affecting their health, based on the Smithsonian Institute's travelling exhibition of the same name. Use the exhibition floor plan to navigate your way around the different 'rooms' – with themes ranging from Ocean Science and Immersion to Heroes and Sea People.

People for the Ethical Treatment of Animals – PETA Online

URL: "http://www.envirolink.org/arrs/peta/frontpage.html"

PETA's mission, history, and role are described together with reports of campaigns, a comprehensive listing of resources, and a children's section.

Problem of ChloroFluoroCarbons

URL: "http://pooh.chem.wm.edu/chemWWW/courses/chem105/projects/group2/page5.html"

Graphical presentation of the effect of CFCs on the ozone layer. The information can be readily understood by a general reader wishing to learn more about the chemistry of ozone depletion and why more ultraviolet radiation is reaching the surface of the earth.

Recycle City

URL: "http://www.epa.gov/recyclecity/"

Child-friendly site of the US Environmental Protection Agency designed to help people to live more ecologically. The site includes a host of fun games.

State of the Environment

URL: "http://www.environment-agency.gov.uk/gui/new_index.html"

Britain's Environment Agency's page on the environment with access to data collected and studied by the Agency on the topics of 'bathing water quality', 'river habitats', and 'river gauging stations'.

Sustainable Architecture: Eco Design and Landscaping

URL: "http://www.aloha.net/~laumana/"

This site is an archive of information about sustainable architecture, which includes ecological planning, design, integrated architecture, and landscaping for tropical, sub-tropical or temperate climates.

Sustainable Development

URL: "http://iisd1.iisd.ca/"

This site reports on global initiatives to encourage sustainability, in a way that is easy to understand.

Technology Summary

URL: "http://www.yahoo.com/headlines/compute/"

Daily online magazine specializing in features associated with technology.

Welcome to Four Seasons!

URL: "http://www.4seasons.org.uk/"

Several environment-related Web projects, written by and for teachers. According the site: 'by using data collected nationally and linking it with locally collected data, using simple equipment, pupils can participate in national projects, while immediately seeing the relevance to their own immediate environment'.

What Hath Man Wrought

URL: "http://sln.fi.edu/inquirer/warming.html"

Extensive account of the state of global warming. The site has also incorporated links to a series of space institutes, climate centres, and environmental agencies which conduct related research.

Woods Hole Oceanographic Institution Home Page

URL: "http://www.whoi.edu/index.html"

Site run by a Massachusetts-based oceanographic institute. As well as containing details of their research programmes and an overview of the organization, there is a gallery of marine pictures and videos, and contacts for their education programmes.

World Heritage List

URL: "http://www.unesco.org/whc/heritage.htm"

United Nations list of 506 sites all across the world that are considered to be an essential part of the 'world's cultural and natural heritage'.

Worldwide Fund for Nature

URL: "http://www.panda.org/"

Online base of the international wildlife charity.

ECONOMY AND BUSINESS

The Year in Review

2 July 1997 Chancellor of the Exchequer Gordon Brown presents the first budget plan of the new Labour Party government. The plan features a reduction in taxes on business profits and an increase in social spending, as well as a plan for an overhaul of the benefits system.

2 July 1997 The Bank of Thailand abandons its attempt to support the baht, which loses 17% of its value, beginning a Southeast Asian economic crisis.

9 July 1997 The chief executive of US computer company Apple Computer Inc, Gilbert Amelio, resigns as sales hit a downturn. He was only in the job for 18 months. The resignation signals the ongoing financial difficulties of the company.

23 July 1997 The European Commission accepts the $14 billion merger of the US aerospace companies Boeing Co and McDonnell Douglas Corp. The merger, which would result in annual revenues of $40 billion, is the largest ever in aerospace history.

28 July 1997 The White House and the US Congress agree on a final version of a plan to balance the budget by 2002. The plan comprises a balanced budget bill and a tax cuts bill.

3 August 1997 Union workers for United Parcel Service (UPS) go on a 16-day strike over the issue of part-time work, paralysing the world's largest parcel delivery company, creating havoc for those who rely on the service, and causing ripple effects throughout the business community. Nearly 185,000 members of the Teamster's Union go on strike – the biggest strike in more than a decade.

6 August 1997 US computer company Apple Computer Inc announce that their rival Microsoft Corp would invest $150 million in Apple and pay the company $100 million for cross-licensing.

11 August 1997 For the first time, US President Bill Clinton uses the line-item veto (a power granted by Congress to the president in April 1996) to deal with taxation and expenditure bills.

19 August 1997 The Teamsters Union reaches a five-year contract agreement with the delivery company United Parcel Service (UPS) in the USA, ending a 15-day strike by 185,000 workers. The contract includes wage increases and the creation of more full-time work.

8 September 1997 The online company Compuserve, 80% of which is owned by H & R Block, announces that it will be sold to America Online (AOL) and WorldCom Inc.

11 September 1997 The result of a Scottish referendum is that the new Scottish parliament will have some control over local interest rates; they will have the power to raise or lower tax rates by up to three percentage points.

18 September 1997 'Big Six' accounting firms Coopers & Lybrand and Price Waterhouse announce a merger which would make them the world's largest accounting and consulting firm, with 8,600 partners and around $12 billion in annual revenues.

23–25 September 1997 The World Bank and the International Monetary Fund (IMF) hold their annual plenary session of their boards of governors in Hong Kong. They address such issues as corruption and liberalization of global markets.

29 September 1997 Chancellor of the Exchequer Gordon Brown, in a speech at the Labour Party conference 29 September–3 October, announces that the public-sector salary freeze initiated by the previous Tory government would extend for another two years.

1 October 1997 US telecommunications firm WorldCom Inc makes an unsolicited $30 billion offer for MCI Communications Corp, which outbids a previous offer by British Telecom by $11 billion. If successful, it would be the largest takeover in history.

10 October 1997 Four major US tobacco companies, Brown & Williamson, Lorillard, Philip Morris, and R J Reynolds, announce a $349 million settlement with flight attendants who claimed health problems resulting from secondhand smoke in the workplace. This is the first class-action suit involving liability for secondhand smoke.

14 October 1997 Vietnam devalues its currency, the dong, in response to the Southeast Asian economic crisis.

15 October 1997 The US Telecommunications company GTE joins the bidding for the takeover of MCI Communications Corp with a cash offer of $28 billion. If successful, it would be the largest cash takeover in history.

20 October 1997 'Big Six' accounting firms KPMG Peat Marwick and Ernst & Young announce a merger to create the world's largest consulting and accounting firm, one month after the merger of Coopers & Lybrand and Price Waterhouse.

22 October 1997 The South Korean government announces that it will take over Kia Motors Corp, which declared bankruptcy earlier in the year. Kia is South Korea's third-largest car manufacturer.

27 October 1997 In a speech before parliament, Chancellor of the Exchequer Gordon Brown says that the government does not plan to join the European Union's economic and monetary union (EMU) until at least 2002. The EMU plans to launch the new European currency, the euro, in 1999.

27 October 1997 The Dow Jones index makes its biggest drop in history – 554 points – triggering the first ever automatic trading cut-off.

31 October 1997 After Indonesian President Suharto agreed to major economic reforms and anti-corruption measures in the banking industry, including the closure of 16 banks, the International Monetary Fund (IMF) announces a $33 billion loan package to stabilize Indonesia's economy.

October 1997 The Hang Seng, Hong Kong's share index, falls 20% because of currency speculation against the Hong Kong dollar. On 24 October it recovers to rise 7%.

October 1997 US unemployment reaches a record low of 4.7%.

1 November 1997 Tory Shadow Agriculture Minister David Curry resigns in protest at party leader William Hague's firm opposition to Britain joining the European monetary union. The move marks a growing dispute within the Conservative party between those who are for and against joining the union.

4–7 November 1997 French lorry drivers blockade roads and ports until a negotiated settlement ends their dispute over pay and conditions.

5 November 1997 The UK government confirms that it is exempting Formula One motor racing from a ban on tobacco advertising in sports events. A scandal erupts after links are revealed between the government and high level Formula One officials.

10 November 1997 US telecommunications giant MCI agrees to accept a $37 billion takeover bid from WorldCom Inc. WorldCom increased its offer from October by $7 billion, outbidding British Telecom and GTE. The merger will be the largest in US history to date.

17 November 1997 Hokkaido Takushoku, Japan's tenth largest commercial bank, ceases operations; on 24 November, Yamaichi Securities, the fourth largest securities house, becomes Japan's biggest ever corporate failure.

17 November 1997 Richard Hu, Finance Minister of Singapore, announces measures to liberalize the financial sector in anticipation of the deregulation of the country's economy in 1998.

18 November 1997 Chief Operating Officer David Hoare replaces Ann Iverson as chief executive of UK textiles and clothing company Laura Ashley Holdings PLC.

21 November 1997 South Korea, the world's tenth largest economy, seeks International Monetary Fund (IMF) assistance in response to financial crisis and a fall in value of its currency, the won.

24 November 1997 The Japanese Yamaichi Securities Co announces that it will cease business after a serious liquidity crisis. The failure of the 100-year-old company causes concern about the health of Japanese business.

25 November 1997 Chancellor of the Exchequer Gordon Brown announces plans to reduce Britain's corporate tax rate from 31% to 30%, to take effect in April 1999, which would result in a £2 billion tax cut for business over the next few years.

25 November 1997 Leaders of the Asia-Pacific Economic Cooperation (APEC) issue a bulletin at the close of their annual trade meeting in Vancouver, Canada, in which they they outline plans for reducing tariffs and liberalizing trade restrictions in an effort to stabilize the floundering Southeast Asian economies. They also agreed that the International Monetary Fund (IMF) would be in charge of the bailout.

November 1997 The US Justice Department sees Microsoft's integration its Web browser, Internet Explorer, with its operating system, Windows 95, as unfair trading and an attempt to dominate the market, and orders the company to pay $1 million a day. The fine is waived in December.

3 December 1997 The International Monetary Fund (IMF) and the South Korean government formally agree to terms of a $57 billion bailout to help recover the country's failing economy.

7 December 1997 The Histadrut labour union in Israel agrees to terms with the Treasury to end a four-day nationwide strike that involved around 700,000 workers, mostly civil servants. The strike, mainly over pensions and privatization issues, was one of the largest and longest in Israel's history and shut down many public services.

8 December 1997 Swiss Bank Corp and Union Bank of Switzerland confirm plans of a merger, which will make them the largest bank in Switzerland and the second-largest financial institution in the world, after the Bank of Tokyo-Mitsubishi in Japan.

12 December 1997 The US Justice Department orders Microsoft to sell its Internet browser separately from its Windows operating system to prevent it from building a monopoly of Web access programs.

15 December 1997 The US Federal Trade Commission (FTC) approves the £23.8 billion merger of Guinness and Grand Met. This enables the new company, Diageo, to be traded on the London Stock Exchange.

16 December 1997 The Japanese government announces measures to prevent further financial crises and to stimulate the economy. The measures include issuing government bonds worth 10 trillion yen and tax cuts of 850 billion yen.

29 December 1997 Intel Corp's chairman and chief executive officer Andrew Grove is named *Time* magazine's 1997 'Man of the Year' for his contribution in developing microchips.

1997 Apple computer sales fall to about 3% of the market; down from 20% ten years earlier.

1997 The US software company Microsoft's stock more than doubles during the year as the company becomes the major player on the Internet.

1 January 1998 The Russian government revalues the ruble, making it 1,000 times its previous value.

5 January 1998 The British venture-capital company Cinven and other investors announce that they will buy the IPC consumer magazine group, Britain's largest, from British publisher Reed Elsevier.

5 January 1998 US President Bill Clinton announces that he will propose a balanced budget for 1999, three years earlier than planned.

6 January 1998 The credit card company Visa International reports that personal bankruptcy in the USA rose by 19.5% in 1997.

8 January 1998 At a meeting in New York, a group of 16 banks from around the world agree to extend South Korea's debt repayment deadline until 31 March.

9 January 1998 French premier Lionel Jospin announces plans for an emergency one billion franc fund for poor people, prompted by weeks of demonstrations by unemployed workers.

12 January 1998 The largest investment bank in Hong Kong, Peregrin Investments Holdings Ltd, collapses following an unsuccessful sale of shares to Zurich Group of Switzerland and formally files for liquidation the following day.

14 January 1998 The European Commission recommends relaxing the ban on beef exports from the UK by allowing exports from Northern Ireland. The ban was instituted in March 1996 after reports of a high incidence of 'mad cow' disease in British herds.

15 January 1998 Indonesian President Suharto signs a pact with the International Monetary Fund (IMF) promising major economic reforms and anti-corruption measures to help save his country's floundering economy.

16 January 1998 In the largest tobacco industry legal payout to date, eight tobacco companies and three trade groups agree to a $15.3 billion settlement in a suit brought by the state of Texas which sought compensation for money spent on treating smoking-related illnesses. The companies are required to pay the settlement to the state over the next 25 years.

22 January 1998 The US computer company Microsoft makes an initial out-of-court settlement with the US government, who sued the company to prevent it from attaining a monopoly on Internet browser software. Microsoft agrees to make the companion browser to its Windows 95 system more difficult to install.

23 January 1998 The Royal Bank of Canada, Canada's largest bank, and the Bank of Montreal, the country's third-largest bank, announce plans for a merger, which will create the second largest bank in North America.

26 January 1998 US company Compaq Computer Corporation announces that it will take over its rival, Digital Equipment Corporation, for $9.6 billion, which will make it the world's second-largest computer company after IBM.

2 February 1998 US President Bill Clinton presents the 1999 $1.73 trillion budget, balanced for the first time since 1969, to Congress.

3 February 1998 The British government announces that it is changing its method of recording unemployment figures to be in line with international labour-monitoring groups. The current method only categorizes people receiving benefit as unemployed.

5 February 1998 The German government announces that the unemployment rate has risen to 12.6%, with the highest number of people unemployed in more than 50 years, which prompts unemployed workers to demonstrate.

18 February 1998 The first budget of Hong Kong since its return to Chinese sovereignty includes tax cuts of HK$100 billion, the largest in Hong Kong's history.

19 February 1998 British supermarket chains Somerfield's and Kwik-Save announce plans to merge, which would make them Britain's sixth largest super-

market company with £6 billion in annual sales.

20 February 1998 In a trade deal with the USA, the government of Taiwan agrees to reduce import taxes on a range of US goods and services.

20 February 1998 Indonesian President Suharto abandons plans to link his country's currency to the US dollar. The plans were opposed by the International Monetary Fund (IMF), who promised a loan package to help stabilize the country's economy.

24 February 1998 Canadian Finance Minister Paul Martin presents the country's first balanced budget since 1969.

25 February 1998 British insurance companies Commercial Union and General Accident announce plans to merge.

5 March 1998 The German medical supplier Fresenius Medical Care announces that it will withdraw from a deal to provide dialysis equipment to a military hospital in Guangzhou, China, because of evidence that the hospital was selling kidneys removed from executed prisoners.

9 March 1998 Publishers Reed Elsevier and Wolters Kluwer abandon plans to merge after US and European regulators imply that they would require the companies to sell off many of their assets.

10 March 1998 US President Bill Clinton lifts a trade restriction, the Jackson-Vanik Amendment, that prohibits US companies doing business in Vietnam in order to get US Export-Import Bank financing.

12 March 1998 Amidst mounting corruption scandals in Japanese financial institutions, the central bank of Japan is raided and the head of its capital markets division, Yasuyuki Yoshizawa, is arrested for accepting bribes, prompting Yasuo Matsushita, the bank's governor, to resign.

15 March 1998 Australian Prime Minister John Howard announces plans to sell the government's majority shares in Telstra Corp, the country's largest telecommunications company, if his Liberal-National coalition government is reelected. Proceeds would go to repay around 40% of Australia's national debt.

16 March 1998 European Union agriculture ministers approve plans to export beef from Northern Ireland. This will be the first export of beef from the UK since the ban imposed in March 1996 because of the threat of 'mad cow' disease.

17 March 1998 Chancellor Gordon Brown presents the Labour government's

1998–99 budget to Parliament, which includes changes in the tax and benefit systems. Under the new budget, businesses will benefit from tax relief on profits, but taxes on petrol, alcohol, and cigarettes will increase. Changes to the benefit system are designed to encourage employment. Brown also announces that the budget is likely to be balanced by 2000.

23 March 1998 The German media company Bertelsmann AG announces that it will buy Random House Inc from the US publisher Advance Publications for $1.5 billion. Bertelsmann is already the world's third largest media company, behind Walt Disney and Time Warner.

25 March 1998 The European Commission officially recommends 11 European Union countries – Austria, Belgium, Finland, France, Germany, Ireland, Italy, Luxembourg, the Netherlands, Portugal, and Spain – to join the European economic and monetary union (EMU), for the launch of the European currency, the euro, in 1999. Of the other four European Union countries, Greece would not meet the economic criteria, and Britain, Denmark, and Sweden had already chosen not to participate in the euro launch.

30 March 1998 British spirits company Bacardi Ltd, based in Bermuda, agrees to buy the Bombay gin and Dewar's whiskey brands from British liquor company Diageo plc, the company that was created in 1997 from the merger between Guiness and Grand Metropolitan.

31 March 1998 The Organization of Petroleum Exporting Countries (OPEC) agrees to reduce its oil production by 1,250,000 barrels a day to help stop plunging oil prices.

3 April 1998 During a summit in Brussels, Belgium, European Union government ministers settle a long-standing dispute that threatened to delay the launch of the new European currency, the euro, over who will head of the new European Central Bank. The job goes to Wim Duisenberg, former president of the Dutch central bank.

6 April 1998 US consumer bank Citicorp and US investment bank and insurance firm Travelers Group announce plans to merge. The deal is estimated at $83 billion, which is the world's largest merger deal to date.

8 April 1998 The Indonesian government announces that it has reached a new financial agreement with the International Monetary Fund (IMF), the third such agreement in six months. The

IMF had postponed any payment of loans after Indonesian president Suharto failed to stick to terms mapped out in previous agreements.

8 April 1998 The South Korean government sells $4 billion worth of government bonds to international investors. Analysts view the high demand for the bonds as increased confidence in the South Korean economy after the country's financial crisis in 1997.

10 April 1998 The central bank of Japan announces that it disciplined 98 bank employees for accepting gifts from commercial banks. The move was part of an internal corruption investigation, started in April when a senior bank official was arrested for accepting bribes.

13 April 1998 US bank BankAmerica announces plans to take over NationsBank in a deal valued at $60 billion, the second largest proposed deal to date after the merger plans announced in April between US banks Citicorp and Travelers Group.

15 April 1998 On the opening day of their annual meeting in Washington DC, finance officials from the Group of Seven (G-7) industrialized nations – comprising Canada, Germany, France, Italy, Japan, the UK, and the USA – call on Japan to take strong financial measures and make structural reforms to boost its floundering economy.

15 April 1998 The South Korean car manufacturer Kia Motors Corp is put in court receivership, where it is protected from creditors until it develops a plan for financial recovery. Workers strike from 16 to 20 April in protest at the court-appointed administrator of the plan, Yoo Chong Yul, whom they fear will sell the company.

17 April 1998 British cable television company Telewest Communications announces that it will take over its rival General Cable for £635 million.

17–19 April 1998 Thousands of workers demonstrating in Seoul, South Korea, clash with riot police. The workers are protesting against massive job cuts since the country's economic crisis began in 1997.

24 April 1998 British mail-order company Great Universal Stores clinches a deal to buy its rival Argos for £1.6 billion, to form one of Britain's largest retail companies.

7 May 1998 British company Vickers announces that it will sell its luxury car manufacturer, Rolls-Royce Motor Cars, to German car manufacturer Volkswagen AG for £430 million. Vickers agreed to sell Rolls-Royce to Bayerische Motoren Werke (BMW) in April, but Volkswagen outbid BMW by £90 million.

7 May 1998 German manufacturer Daimler-Benz, makers of Mercedes-Benz cars, announces plans to merge with US car manufacturer Chrysler Corp to form a new company, Daimler-Chrysler. The deal is valued at $38.3 billion.

7 May 1998 The US Senate votes unanimously to pass a reform bill for the Internal Revenue Service (IRS), after hearings that cited corruption, abuse of power, and poor customer service.

8 May 1998 Tobacco companies agree to pay the state of Minnesota and Blue Cross and Blue Shield of Minnesota $6.6 billion to settle a law suit filed to compensate for the cost of treating smoking-related illnesses.

11 May 1998 US telephone service provider SBC Communications Inc announces plans to take over another telecommunications firm, Ameritech Corp, in a deal worth $56.18 billion. The merger would be the largest-ever in the telecommunications industry.

18 May 1998 French businessman and art collector Francois Pinault announces that he will buy British auction house Christie's.

18 May 1998 The US federal government and 20 states file lawsuits in Washington, DC, against US computer software company Microsoft for allegedly violating anti-trust laws by using its Windows operating system to try to monopolize sales of other kinds of software.

9 June 1998 Air France pilots, rail workers, and police strike on the opening day of the World Cup football tournament in Paris. They resume work the following day.

17 June 1998 The New York based investment bank Goldman Sachs announces plans to float on the stock market, which will award the executive committee the biggest bonus in Wall Street history. The six committee members are likely to own shares worth some $4 billion in total.

18 June 1998 The British government announces that the new UK minimum wage will be set at £3.60 per hour, to go into effect in April 1999.

22 June 1998 The Hong Kong government announces an emergency £2.5 billion rescue package in an effort to prevent the country's failing economy from affecting the rest of the world.

25 June 1998 The US software company Microsoft releases its operating system Windows '98.

June 1998 Unemployment in the UK increases for the first time in two years.

General Information

The Top 50 Banking Companies in the World

Data are based on total at year-end 1996, or latest fiscal year-end, for bank holding companies and commercial and savings banks.

Rank	Company	Total assets ($ millions)	Rank	Company	Total assets ($ millions)
1	Bank of Tokyo-Mitsubishi Ltd, Japan	648,161	26	Tokai Bank Ltd, Nagoya, Japan	273,430
2	Deutsche Bank AG, Frankfurt, Germany	575,072	27	Swiss Bank Corp, Basel, Switzerland	268,519
3	Credit Agricole Mutuel, Paris, France	479,963	28	Bayerische Vereinsbank, Munich, Germany	260,848
4	Dai-Ichi Kangyo Bank Ltd, Tokyo, Japan	434,115	29	Mitsui Trust & Banking Co Ltd, Tokyo, Japan	254,189
5	Fuji Bank Ltd, Tokyo, Japan	432,992	30	Lloyds TSB Group Inc, London, UK	252,292
6	Sanwa Bank Ltd, Osaka, Japan	427,689	31	Sumitomo Trust & Banking Co Ltd, Osaka, Japan	248,418
7	Sumitomo Bank Ltd, Osaka, Japan	426,103	32	BankAmerica Corp, San Francisco, USA	247,892
8	Sakura Bank Ltd, Tokyo, Japan	423,017	33	Long-Term Credit Bank of Japan Ltd, Tokyo, Japan	231,761
9	HSBC Holdings Plc, London, UK	404,979	34	Asahi Bank Ltd, Tokyo, Japan	230,080
10	Norinchukin Bank, Tokyo, Japan	375,210	35	Bayerische Landesbank Girozentrale, Munich, Germany	223,496
11	Dresdner Bank, Frankfurt, Germany	358,829	36	JP Morgan & Co Inc, New York, USA	221,814
12	Banque Nationale de Paris, France	357,322	37	Bayerische Hypotheken-und Wechsel Bank, Munich, Germany	220,100
13	Industrial Bank of Japan Ltd, Tokyo, Japan	350,468	38	Credit Suisse First Boston, Zürich, Switzerland	218,870
14	ABN-AMRO Bank NV, Amsterdam, Netherlands	341,916	39	Bankgesellschaft Berlin AG, Berlin, Germany	218,226
15	Société Générale, Paris, France	341,867	40	Daiwa Bank Ltd, Osaka, Japan	212,967
16	Chase Manhattan Corp,.New York, USA	333,777	41	Abbey National Plc, London, UK	212,307
17	Union Bank of Switzerland, Zürich, Switzerland	326,190	42	Deutsche Genossenschaftsbank, Frankfurt, Germany	212,061
18	NatWest Group, London, UK	317,295	43	Yasuda Trust & Banking Co Ltd, Tokyo, Japan	196,520
19	Crédit Lyonnais, Paris, France	311,747	44	Toyo Trust & Banking Co Ltd, Tokyo, Japan	192,802
20	Barclays Plc, London, UK	308,710	45	NationsBank Corp, Charlotte, North Carolina, USA	184,886
21	Westdeutsche Landesbank Girozentrale, Düsseldorf, Germany	298,455	46	Rabobank Nederland, Utrecht, Netherlands	180,960
22	Compagnie Financière de Paribas, Paris, France	292,320	47	ING Bank, Amsterdam, Netherlands	178,886
23	Commerzbank, Frankfurt, Germany	290,300	48	Halifax Building Society, Halifax, UK	175,111
24	Mitsubishi Trust & Banking Corp, Tokyo, Japan	284,528	49	Generale Bank, Brussels, Belgium	174,639
25	Citicorp, New York, USA	278,941	50	Istituto Bancario San Paolo di Torino, Italy	172,540

Source: *American Banker* magazine, 29 July 1997

Annual Percentage Change in Consumer Prices by Country

(N/A = not available. Figures are percentage change from previous year.)

Country	1992	1993	1994	1995	1996	Country	1992	1993	1994	1995	1996
Argentina	24.9	10.6	4.2	3.4	0.2	Malaysia	4.8	3.5	3.7	5.3	3.5
Australia	1.0	1.8	1.9	4.6	2.6	Mexico	15.5	9.8	7.0	35.0	34.4
Belgium	2.4	2.8	2.4	1.5	2.1	Netherlands	1.4	2.1	1.8	2.8	4.0
Brazil	1,009.0	2,148.0	2,669.0	84.0	18.0	Nigeria	44.6	57.2	57.0	72.8	29.3
Canada	1.5	1.8	0.2	2.2	1.6	Norway	2.3	2.3	1.4	2.5	1.3
Chile	15.4	12.7	11.4	8.2	7.4	Pakistan	9.5	10.0	12.4	12.3	10.4
Colombia	27.0	22.6	23.8	21.0	20.2	Philippines	8.9	7.6	9.1	8.1	8.4
France	2.4	2.1	1.7	1.8	2.0	Romania	211.0	255.0	137.0	32.0	N/A
Germany	4.0	5.0	3.0	1.8	1.5	South Africa	13.9	9.7	9.0	8.7	7.4
India	11.8	6.4	10.2	10.2	9.0	Spain	5.9	4.6	4.7	4.7	3.6
Indonesia	7.5	9.7	8.5	9.4	7.9	Sweden	2.3	4.6	2.2	2.5	0.5
Iran	25.6	21.2	31.5	49.6	28.9	Switzerland	4.1	3.3	0.8	1.8	0.8
Israel	11.9	10.9	12.3	10.0	11.3	Turkey	70.1	66.1	106.3	88.1	80.3
Italy	5.1	4.5	4.0	5.2	4.0	UK	3.7	1.6	2.5	3.4	2.4
Japan	1.7	1.3	0.7	-0.1	0.1	USA	3.0	3.0	2.6	2.8	2.9
Korea, South	6.2	4.8	6.3	4.5	5.0	Venezuela	31.4	38.1	60.8	59.9	99.9

Source: International Monetary Fund

ECONOMIC CRISIS IN ASIA

BY RICHARD THOMSON

When financial crisis suddenly struck the 'tiger' economies of Southeast Asia in the late summer of 1997, it came as a surprise to most Western investors. For most of the decade the region had produced staggering rates of growth of 6–8% and was regarded as the most dynamic part of the world economy. Japanese, European, and American banks, in particular, vied to get a slice of the new markets, pouring in money in the form of direct loans and bond issues. Few lending institutions seriously questioned the received wisdom about the region's fundamental economic strength. They failed to notice that they were helping to fuel a vast speculative boom.

The first sign of trouble was a sharp fall in Thailand's currency, the baht. This was soon followed by similar currency weakness in Malaysia and Indonesia. South Korea also began to crack and by the autumn the currencies of Indonesia, Malaysia, South Korea, and Thailand were in free fall. Most fell between 40% and 60%, but severe problems in Indonesia caused its currency to plunge by 80% by March 1998.

Speculation against the currencies of these countries was one of the immediate causes of the crisis. But although Western speculators were involved, the largest players were local businesses desperate to sell local currency and buy dollars to enable them to pay off substantial dollar loans. The more currency they sold, the further it fell.

The currency crisis, however, was the result of serious fundamental economic problems in Southeast Asia which had been building up for years. Each country had somewhat different problems. In South Korea, for example, there was a closed economic system that kept out many foreign goods and services. Within this system, banks often formed a part of industrial conglomerates, called *chaebols*, and often lent to other companies in their group at uneconomic rates for uneconomic projects. Strong government control of the economy also meant that many loans were invested in uneconomic projects.

Indonesia, however, suffered from massive corruption and cronyism led by President Suharto and his family, who controlled a substantial portion of the country's entire economy. Suharto is also believed to have plundered at least $30 billion from the country, which he deposited in banks abroad. As in Korea, much of the apparent economic growth was an illusion. Massive borrowing from overseas flooded the country with cash but it was not being invested in businesses that could repay the loans. Instead, it went into inflating asset values, such as property prices, which spiralled out of control.

A problem common to most Southeast Asian countries was that to avoid high local interest rates, businesses borrowed in dollars, for which interest rates were lower. But this left them with a massive foreign exchange exposure which went heavily against them when their currencies collapsed.

A further problem in the region was the poor quality of financial information. In many cases, information officially put out by governments themselves was simply wrong. South Korea was forced to admit that until the crisis hit, it had been putting out figures for its foreign debt that were far too low. The disinformation was one reason why Western creditors failed to see that a crisis was brewing.

Once the crisis had begun, the West was stunned when South Korea announced, towards the end of 1997, that it could not meet all of its external debt repayments. South Korea had until then been regarded as the region's strongest economy. By the end of 1997, 70,000 Korean businesses had gone bankrupt while unemployment soared from 2.5% to 8.5%. Growth fell from 5.5% in 1997 to an expected 0.2% the following year. Economic decline was as bad or worse in other Asian economies.

The West quickly stepped in with offers to help, motivated partly by political reasons (the USA was worried about South Korea's relationship with North Korea), but there were real fears that the crisis would spread to other markets and ultimately to Western economies. At first several countries, including South Korea, rejected outside interference, but eventually they recognized the need for help. The International Monetary Fund arranged an $8 billion bailout for South Korea and $45 billion for Indonesia. Regional currencies were stabilized and the crisis halted. But in return for its help, the West insisted on policy changes in the region, more open economies, and better information on business.

There are few hopes of a rapid rebound from economic disaster in Southeast Asia, however, because Japan, Asia's largest economy, is unable to provide the necessary engine for recovery. After the 'bubble' economy of the 1980s burst in the early 1990s, Japan has been in the most prolonged slump since World War II.

Japan's Economy

Despite its huge industrial success, Japan had a relatively closed economy, with strong government intervention which enabled the government to stoke up a speculative economic environment. During the 1980s the Ministry of Finance had encouraged share prices, and other asset values, to rise far beyond realistic levels. Bank lending mushroomed, overheating the economy. Much of the boom of the 1980s was an illusion fed by excessive borrowing – and it could not last.

When the boom ended, the stock market fell by more than 50%. Exports were not enough to sustain growth as domestic demand collapsed. The banking sector was in left in a state of crisis, with too little capital and massive bad loans. The Japanese economic miracle ended in a morass of serious structural problems which needed to be urgently addressed.

Yet it was almost as if the country could not face up to what had happened to it. The government refused, or was unable, to take effective action to turn the economy around. One 'stimulus' package after another failed because it was too little or the wrong policy. Instead of cutting taxes, deregulating large parts of the economy, and encouraging growth, the government futilely poured public money into propping up insolvent banks and cut back spending to reduce its massive deficit. Not even its support of the banks could prevent some spectacular collapses such as that of Yamaichi, Japan's oldest investment bank, which further damaged confidence in the financial sector.

Meanwhile, Japanese economic growth sank to below 2% a

(continued)

(continued)

year and any recovery is clearly going to take years. The West has come to see Japan as part of the Asian problem rather than the solution.

The once roaring Asian tigers, therefore, look likely to remain subdued for the foreseeable future. Even Hong Kong, Taiwan, and Singapore, which did not suffer a serious crisis, will be slowed down by the wider problems in the Pacific region. When the problem countries do revive, they are likely to be different and more efficient than before, thanks to the changes forced on them by the West.

In the meantime, there is deep uncertainty in the West as to how badly affected it will be by the 'Asian flu'. Now that the crisis has been contained, the fear that it could spread has subsided. But many Western industries had come to rely increasingly on the Asian markets for their growth in the early 1990s. Inevitably, some sectors such as the US computer industry suffered quickly from the loss of business in Asia. But in general, the Asian crisis had little immediate impact for Britain, America, and most other Western economies. To the surprise of many economists, economic growth in those countries was barely affected in the first half of 1998.

The most visible effect is on the banking sector. Japanese banks had the biggest exposure in Southeast Asia. The losses they have made there have weakened them further. The next largest lenders were European banks. Britain, for example, was Indonesia's largest creditor. Deutsche Bank, Commerzbank, Crédit Lyonnais, and many other European lenders began to write off large amounts against bad loans in Asia as early as the beginning of 1998. The USA had the smallest exposure, since many US banks had begun scaling back their lending in the region two years before the crisis.

But even if the effect of 'Asian flu' on the West is not immediately dramatic, over the long term it is likely to be a dampening influence. Asian customers can no longer afford to buy as much as before from the West. Big losses may also force Western banks to raise their lending rates to their customers at home. The only ones to gain from one of the worst financial panics in recent years were a few lucky speculators and Western businesses who rushed in to buy stricken Asian companies on the cheap.

International Consumer Price Comparisons by Cities of the World

(Zürich = 100.)

1994

City	Prices including rent	City	Prices including rent	City	Prices including rent
Tokyo, Japan	142.7	Vienna, Austria	77.0	Rio de Janeiro, Brazil	60.6
Zürich, Switzerland	100.0	Los Angeles (CA), USA	75.4	Toronto, Canada	60.3
Hong Kong	97.5	Luxembourg, Luxembourg	75.2	Kuala Lumpur, Malaysia	59.9
Oslo, Norway	95.8	Taipei, Taiwan	74.6	Cairo, Egypt	59.5
Geneva, Switzerland	94.9	London, UK	74.1	Montréal, Canada	59.2
Singapore, Singapore	94.8	Brussels, Belgium	72.0	Athens, Greece	56.7
New York (NY), USA	93.8	Jakarta, Indonesia	70.6	Lisbon, Spain	55.9
Copenhagen, Denmark	92.0	Milan, Italy	70.4	Mexico City, Mexico	54.6
Lagos, Nigeria	91.8	Amsterdam, the Netherlands	70.3	Bogotá, Colombia	54.4
Seoul, South Korea	87.3	Bangkok, Thailand	70.1	Manila, Philippines	51.0
Paris, France	87.0	Houston (TX), USA	65.8	Nicosia, Cyprus	48.5
Stockholm, Sweden	85.2	Tel Aviv, Israel	65.8	Johannesburg, South Africa	46.1
Chicago (IL), USA	81.2	Madrid, Spain	63.5	Budapest, Hungary	43.4
Frankfurt, Germany	79.8	Manama, Bahrain	63.4	Caracas, Venezuela	39.9
Düsseldorf, Germany	79.4	Sydney, Australia	63.0	Bombay, India	38.8
Helsinki, Finland	79.3	Dublin, Republic of Ireland	62.6	Prague, Czech Republic	34.8
Abu Dhabi, United Arab Emirates	78.1	São Paulo, Brazil	61.1	Nairobi, Kenya	30.2
Buenos Aires, Argentina	77.0	Panama, Panama	60.8		

Source: Prices and Earnings Around the Globe 94

Countries with the Fastest Economic Growth

(Percentage of average real growth of GDP.)

1990–95

Rank	Country	Average	Rank	Country	Average	Rank	Country	Average	Rank	Country	Average
1	Lebanon	12.4	10=	Syria	7.4	21=	Oman	5.8	31=	Bahrain	5.0
2	China	12.0	12	Guyana	7.3	21=	Lesotho	5.8	31=	Mauritius	5.0
3	Malaysia	8.7	13	Indonesia	7.1	23=	Hong Kong	5.5	33=	Argentina	4.9
4	Thailand	8.6	14	Maldives	6.8	23=	Peru	5.5	33=	Ghana	4.9
5	Singapore	8.5	15	Uganda	6.7	25=	Sri Lanka	5.4	35=	Namibia	4.8
6	Vietnam	8.2	16=	Taiwan	6.6	25=	Nepal	5.4	35=	Pakistan	4.8
7	Kuwait	7.7	16=	Israel	6.6	27=	Malawi	5.3	37=	Iran	4.7
8=	Jordan	7.5	18=	El Salvador	6.2	27=	Ireland, Republic of	5.3	37=	Costa Rica	4.7
8=	Korea, South	7.5	18=	Belize	6.2	29	Panama	5.2	39=	India	4.6
10=	Chile	7.4	20	Myanmar	5.9	30	Malta	5.1	39=	Cyprus	4.6

Source: UN Statistics Division

Countries with the Slowest Economic Growth

(Percentage of average real growth of GDP.)

1990–95

Rank	Country	Average	Rank	Country	Average	Rank	Country	Average	Rank	Country	Average
1	Iraq	-28.2	12	Kyrgyzstan	-12.2	20	Estonia	-7.7	31	Afghanistan	-2.6
2	Georgia	-27.0	13	Yugoslavia (Serbia		21	Somalia	-7.2	32	Albania	-2.5
3	Moldova	-17.7		and Montenegro)	-11.2	22	Cuba	-7.1	33=	Slovak Republic	-2.3
4	Armenia	-17.2	14	Turkmenistan	-10.3	23	Croatia	-6.3	33=	Hungary	-2.3
5	Azerbaijan	-17.0	15	Belarus	-9.2	24	Uzbekistan	-4.8	35	Cameroon	-1.7
6	Tajikistan	-16.6	16=	Congo, Democratic		25=	Romania	-3.4	36=	Finland	-0.7
7	Rwanda	-15.1		Republic of	-9.1	25=	Bulgaria	-3.4	36=	Zambia	-0.7
8	Kazakhstan	-13.9	16=	Macedonia, Former		27	Haiti	-3.2	38	Slovenia	-0.6
9	Bosnia-Herzegovina	-13.7		Yugoslav Republic of	-9.1	28	Czech Republic	-3.1	39=	Barbados	-0.5
10	Ukraine	-13.5	16=	Russia	-9.1	29	Korea, North	-3.0	39=	Sierra Leone	-0.5
11	Latvia	-13.2	19	Lithuania	-7.9	30	Mongolia	-2.8			

Source: UN Statistics Division

Exchange Rates of the British Pound Against the US Dollar and Deutsche Mark

(Figures show averages for the month.)

Month	1988	1989	1990	1991	1992	1993	1994	1995	1996	1997	1998
Sterling/US Dollar											
January	1.7981	1.7748	1.6523	1.9348	1.8127	1.5325	1.4940	1.5747	1.5306	1.6587	1.6353
February	1.7578	1.7541	1.6962	1.9655	1.7781	1.4386	1.4799	1.5720	1.5364	1.6246	1.6407
March	1.8324	1.7146	1.6246	1.8265	1.7328	1.4625	1.4917	1.6005	1.5271	1.6063	1.6620
April	1.8765	1.7022	1.6374	1.7502	1.7576	1.5472	1.4837	1.6074	1.5145	1.6295	1.6733
May	1.8694	1.6295	1.6778	1.7252	1.8109	1.5481	1.5029	1.5868	1.5152	1.6334	
June	1.7790	1.5532	1.7094	1.6499	1.8556	1.5099	1.5252	1.5949	1.5418	1.6446	
July	1.7042	1.6244	1.8081	1.6503	1.9186	1.4963	1.5463	1.5953	1.5539	1.6702	
August	1.6983	1.5955	1.8998	1.6841	1.9412	1.4911	1.5427	1.5681	1.5502	1.6034	
September	1.6833	1.5715	1.8786	1.7249	1.8559	1.5261	1.5651	1.5584	1.5597	1.6015	
October	1.7382	1.5882	1.9454	1.7226	1.6577	1.5037	1.6057	1.5779	1.5862	1.6329	
November	1.8090	1.5724	1.9647	1.7787	1.5275	1.4806	1.5886	1.5623	1.6626	1.6890	
December	1.8282	1.5957	1.9257	1.8258	1.5536	1.4904	1.5595	1.5398	1.6647	1.6597	
Sterling/Deutsche Mark											
January	2.977	3.256	2.793	2.920	2.856	2.475	2.604	2.409	2.236	2.660	2.971
February	2.983	3.245	2.843	2.908	2.877	2.362	2.567	2.360	2.252	2.722	2.974
March	3.072	3.199	2.769	2.931	2.865	2.407	2.523	2.249	2.256	2.726	3.036
April	3.138	3.181	2.761	2.979	2.895	2.468	2.520	2.218	2.282	2.788	3.032
May	3.166	3.172	2.790	2.963	2.936	2.488	2.491	2.239	2.323	2.782	
June	3.124	3.072	2.879	2.940	2.917	2.496	2.484	2.232	2.356	2.840	
July	3.144	3.074	2.962	2.947	2.860	2.566	2.426	2.214	2.336	2.992	
August	3.207	3.074	2.983	2.936	2.816	2.529	2.413	2.264	2.298	2.950	
September	3.142	3.065	2.950	2.925	2.683	2.472	2.424	2.276	2.349	2.863	
October	3.160	2.963	2.965	2.911	2.455	2.463	2.441	2.232	2.424	2.868	
November	3.162	2.877	2.917	2.884	2.424	2.517	2.446	2.215	2.513	2.926	
December	3.207	2.776	2.879	2.856	2.455	2.549	2.451	2.218	2.583	2.952	

Source: Bank of England. © Crown copyright 1998

Countries with the Highest Per Capita GDP

Data are for most recent figures available for all countries shown. There are different systems for calculating GDP per capita. The rates in this and the following table are based on official exchange rates for the year shown, and not on the purchasing power parity (PPP) system. (The latter system converts the GDP per capita of a country into US dollars on the basis of the purchasing power parity of the country's currency; this system allows for more accurate international comparisons of GDP and its components, and is the one used in the articles for individual countries in this book.)

1995

Rank	Country/Region	Per capita GDP ($)	Rank	Country/Region	Per capita GDP ($)	Rank	Country/Region	Per capita GDP ($)	Rank	Country/Region	Per capita GDP ($)
1	Switzerland	42,416	14	Netherlands	25,635	26	Brunei	16,683	39	Netherlands Antilles	9,039
2	Japan	41,718	15	Singapore	25,581	27	Kuwait	15,757	40	Malta	8,793
3	Luxembourg	35,109	16	Finland	24,453	28	Spain	14,111	41	Greece	8,684
4	Norway	33,734	17	Hong Kong	22,898	29	Qatar	14,013	42	Argentina	8,055
5	Denmark	33,191	18	Australia	20,046	30	Bahamas	12,545	43	Seychelles	7,272
6	Bermuda	32,495	19	Italy	19,121	31	Taiwan	12,359	44	Barbados	7,173
7	Germany	29,632	20	Canada	18,943	32	Puerto Rico	12,213	45	Antigua and Barbuda	6,966
8	Austria	29,006	21	UK	18,913	33	Cyprus	11,459	46	Saudi Arabia	6,583
9	Belgium	26,582	22	United Arab Emirates	17,690	34	Iraq	11,308	47	Oman	6,232
10	France	26,444	23	Ireland, Republic of	17,419	35	Portugal	10,428	48	Uruguay	5,602
11	Sweden	26,253	24	New Zealand	16,866	36	Korea, South	9,736	49	Libya	5,498
12	Iceland	26,217	25	Israel	16,738	37	Slovenia	9,652	50	Cook Islands	5,432
13	USA	26,037				38	Bahrain	9,073			

Source: UN Statistics Division

Countries with the Lowest Per Capita GDP

1995

Rank	Country	Per capita GDP ($)	Rank	Country	Per capita GDP ($)	Rank	Country	Per capita GDP ($)
1	Sudan	36	8	Tajikistan	122	15	Chad	187
2	São Tomé and Príncipe	49	9	Cambodia	130	16	Nepal	203
3	Mozambique	77	10	Guinea-Bissau	131	17	Burundi	205
4=	Ethiopia	96	11	Tanzania	139	18	Niger	207
4=	Eritrea	96	12	Malawi	142	19	Madagascar	215
6	Congo, Democratic Republic of	117	13	Burkina Faso	165	20	Mali	223
7	Somalia	119	14	Bhutan	166			

Source: UN Statistics Division

The Largest Economies of the World

1995

Rank	Country	GDP ($ billions)	Rank	Country	GDP ($ billions)	Rank	Country	GDP ($ billions)	Rank	Country	GDP ($ billions)
1	USA	6,955	14	Australia	358	27	Thailand	169	40	Singapore	85
2	Japan	5,218	15	India	339	28	Norway	146	41	Columbia	79
3	Germany	2,418	16	Switzerland	304	29	Hong Kong	140	42	Venezuela	76
4	France	1,536	17	Argentina	280	30	South Africa	134	43	Philippines	74
5	UK	1,103	18	Belgium	269	31	Finland	125	44	Pakistan	69
6	Italy	1,094	19	Taiwan	263	32	Saudi Arabia	120	45	Chile	67
7	Brazil	717	20	Mexico	246	33	Poland	118	46	Nigeria	66
8	China	698	21	Austria	233	34	Myanmar	108	47	Ireland, Republic of	62
9	Canada	561	22	Sweden	231	35	Iran	106	48=	Egypt	60
10	Spain	559	23	Iraq	227	36	Portugal	102	48=	New Zealand	60
11	Korea, South	437	24	Indonesia	201	37	Israel	92	50	Peru	59
12	Netherlands	397	25	Denmark	173	38	Greece	91			
13	Russia	364	26	Turkey	171	39	Malaysia	87			

Source: UN Statistics Division

Gold Reserves: Industrial Countries

(– = not applicable. In million fine troy ounces.)

Country	1990	1992	1994	1996[1]	1997[2]	Country	1990	1992	1994	1996[1]	1997[2]
Europe						Spain	15.61	15.62	15.62	15.63	15.63
Austria	20.39	19.93	18.34	10.75	10.10	Sweden	6.07	6.07	6.07	4.70	4.70
Belgium	30.23	25.04	25.04	15.32	15.32	Switzerland	83.28	83.28	83.28	83.28	83.28
Denmark	1.65	1.66	1.63	1.66	1.66	UK	18.94	18.61	18.44	18.43	18.43
Finland	2.00	2.00	2.00	1.60	1.60						
France	81.85	81.85	81.85	81.85	81.85	**North America**					
Germany	95.18	95.18	95.18	95.18	95.18	USA	261.91	261.84	261.73	261.66	261.72
Greece	3.40	3.43	3.45	3.47	3.47	Canada	14.76	9.94	3.89	3.09	3.09
Iceland	0.05	0.05	0.05	0.05	0.05						
Ireland, Republic of	0.36	0.36	0.36	0.36	0.36	**Pacific**					
Italy	66.67	66.67	66.67	66.67	66.67	Australia	7.93	7.93	7.90	7.90	7.90
Luxembourg	0.34	0.34	0.31	0.31	0.31	Japan	24.23	24.23	24.23	24.23	24.23
Netherlands	43.94	43.94	34.77	34.77	25.14	New Zealand	–	–	–	–	–
Norway	1.18	1.18	1.18	1.18	1.18						
Portugal	15.83	16.06	16.07	16.07	16.07	*Total*	795.81	785.24	768.05	748.16	737.94

[1] Fourth quarter.
[2] First quarter.

Source: International Monetary Fund

The Dow Jones World Index by Country and Industry

Indexes based on 30 June 1982 = 100 for USA; 31 December, 1991 = 100 for world. Based on share prices denominated in US dollars. Stocks in countries that impose significant restrictions on foreign ownership are included in the world index in the same proportion that shares are available to foreign investors. (As of 31 December.)

	Country	1995	1996		Country	1995	1996
By country					Ireland, Republic of	152.83	196.04
					Italy	103.51	113.62
Americas	USA	581.43	700.56		Netherlands	167.30	207.58
	Canada	108.25	135.41		Norway	129.21	159.87
	Mexico	77.96	94.31		Spain	114.31	149.44
	Total	143.61	173.40		Sweden	163.14	213.88
					Switzerland	232.62	236.03
Asia/Pacific	Australia	127.90	148.78		UK	124.49	152.02
	Hong Kong	223.67	299.50		*Total*	136.54	162.41
	Indonesia	172.48	187.42				
	Japan	114.08	95.63		*TOTAL*	133.46	147.57
	Malaysia	223.08	265.49				
	New Zealand	176.17	203.35	**By industry**			
	Singapore	195.91	199.84		Basic materials	130.91	136.62
	Thailand	196.76	126.66		Conglomerate	146.57	171.32
	Total	119.80	108.93		Consumer, cyclical	135.13	148.64
					Consumer, noncyclical	130.19	152.04
Europe	Austria	101.29	110.00		Energy	132.32	163.27
	Belgium	142.56	158.64		Financial services	134.62	142.64
	Denmark	112.42	137.26		Industrial	118.38	122.31
	Finland	202.88	280.72		Technology	168.07	197.94
	France	120.03	142.38		Utilities	118.44	123.90
	Germany	138.24	161.41				

Source: Dow Jones & Company, Inc, New York; *Wall Street Journal,* selected issues

Stock Markets: Market Capitalization and Value of Shares Traded by Country

Market capitalization is defined as the total amount of the various securities (bonds, debentures, and stock) issued by corporations. (N/A = not available. In millions of dollars.)

Country	Market capitalization[1]			Value of shares traded[2]		
	1990	1995	1996	1990	1995	1996
Argentina	3,268	37,783	44,679	852	4,594	4,382
Australia	107,611	245,218	311,988	39,333	97,884	145,482
Austria	11,476	32,513	33,953	18,609	25,759	20,528
Belgium	65,449	104,960	119,831	6,425	15,249	26,120
Brazil	16,354	147,636	216,990	5,598	79,186	112,108
Canada	241,920	366,344	486,268	71,278	183,686	265,360
Chile	13,645	73,860	65,940	783	11,072	8,460
China	N/A	42,055	113,755	N/A	49,774	256,008
Colombia	1,416	17,893	17,137	71	1,254	1,360
Czech Republic	N/A	15,664	18,077	N/A	3,630	8,431
Denmark	39,063	56,223	71,688	11,105	25,942	34,667
Finland	22,721	44,138	63,078	3,933	19,006	22,422
France	314,384	522,053	591,123	116,893	364,550	277,100
Germany	355,073	577,365	670,997	501,805	573,549	768,745
Greece	15,228	17,060	24,178	3,924	6,091	8,283
Hong Kong	83,397	303,705	449,381	34,633	106,888	166,419
India	38,567	127,199	122,605	21,918	13,738	109,448
Indonesia	8,081	66,585	91,016	3,992	14,403	32,142
Italy	148,766	209,522	258,160	42,566	86,904	102,351
Japan	2,917,679	3,667,292	3,088,850	1,602,388	1,231,552	1,251,998
Korea, South	110,594	181,955	138,817	75,949	185,197	177,266
Luxembourg	10,456	30,443	32,692	87	205	534
Malaysia	48,611	222,729	307,179	10,871	76,822	173,568
Mexico	32,725	90,694	106,540	12,212	34,377	43,040
Netherlands	119,825	356,481	378,721	40,199	248,606	339,500
New Zealand	8,835	31,950	38,288	1,933	8,407	9,871
Norway	26,130	44,587	57,423	13,996	24,420	35,882
Pakistan	2,850	9,286	10,639	231	3,210	6,054
Peru	812	11,795	12,291	99	3,935	3,805
Philippines	5,927	58,859	80,649	1,216	14,727	25,519
Portugal	9,201	18,362	24,660	1,687	4,233	7,147
South Africa	137,540	280,526	241,571	8,158	17,048	27,202
Spain	111,404	197,788	242,779	40,967	59,791	249,128
Sweden	92,102	178,049	247,217	15,718	93,197	136,898
Switzerland	160,044	433,621	402,104	N/A	310,928	392,783
Taiwan	100,710	187,206	273,608	715,005	383,099	470,193
Thailand	23,896	141,507	99,828	22,894	57,000	44,365
Turkey	19,065	20,772	30,020	5,841	51,392	36,831
UK	848,866	1,407,737	1,740,246	278,740	510,131	578,471
USA	3,059,434	6,857,622	8,484,433	1,815,476	5,108,591	7,121,487
Venezuela	8,361	3,655	10,055	2,232	510	1,275

[1] Year-end total market values of listed domestic companies.
[2] Annual turnover of listed company shares.

Source: International Finance Corporation

Merchandise Trade Balance by Country

(N/A = not available. In millions of dollars.)

Country	1995
Algeria	N/A
Argentina	2,237
Australia	−4,166
Austria	−5,103
Bangladesh	−2,324
Belgium	10,206
Brazil	−3,157
Burma	N/A
Cameroon	N/A
Canada	22,341
Chile	1,383
China	18,050
Colombia	−2,548
Congo, Democratic Republic of	N/A
Côte d'Ivoire	1,345
Denmark	6,820
Ecuador	354
Egypt	−7,597
Finland	12,346
France	11,175
Germany	66
Ghana	N/A
Greece	−14,425
Hungary	−2,433
India	N/A
Indonesia	5,710
Ireland, Republic of	13,125
Israel	−7,694
Italy	44,082
Japan	131,790
Kenya	−738
Korea, South	−4,746
Kuwait	5,478
Libya	N/A
Malaysia	−100
Mexico	7,089
Morocco	−2,397
Nepal	−961
Netherlands	20,979
Nigeria	N/A
Norway	N/A
Pakistan	N/A
Peru	−2,111
Philippines	−8,944
Poland	−3,224
Portugal	−8,484
Romania	−1,231
Saudi Arabia	24,390
Singapore	1,625
South Africa	1,610
Spain	−17,661
Sri Lanka	−880
Sudan	−510
Sweden	15,973
Switzerland	3,237
Syria	−143
Thailand	−7,968
Trinidad and Tobago	588
Turkey	−13,212
UK	−18,390
USA	−171,990
Venezuela	7,290

Source: International Monetary Fund

World Trade and Aid

Net Flow of Financial Resources to Developing Countries of the World

Net flow covers loans, grants, and grant-like flows minus amortization on loans. Military flows are excluded. Developing countries cover countries designated by the Development Assistance Committee (DAC) as developing. Official development assistance covers all flows to developing countries and multilateral institutions provided by official agencies, including state and local governments, or by their executive agencies, which are administered with the promotion of economic development and welfare of developing countries as their main objective and whose financial terms are intended to be concessional in character with a grant element of at least 25 percent. Other official flows cover export credits and portfolio investment from the official sector. (N/A = not available. In billions of dollars.)

Origin and type of resource	1980	1990	1995
DAC Countries[1]			
Official development assistance	27.3	53.0	58.9
Other official flows	5.3	8.6	9.8
Private flows at market terms	40.4	9.8	92.0
Private voluntary agencies	2.4	5.1	6.0
Total	75.4	76.4	166.7
Total Net Flow to Developing Countries, by DAC Country[1]			
Australia	0.9	1.5	2.5
Austria	0.3	0.6	0.9
Belgium	2.9	0.1	-0.2
Canada	3.2	3.5	4.7
Denmark	0.8	1.1	1.8
Finland	0.2	1.0	0.6
France	11.6	5.7	12.8
Germany[2]	10.6	13.6	21.2

Origin and type of resource	1980	1990	1995
Total Net Flow to Developing Countries, by DAC Country[1] (continued)			
Ireland, Republic of	[3]	0.2	0.2
Italy	4.0	3.2	2.8
Japan	6.8	17.2	42.3
Luxembourg	N/A	N/A	0.1
Netherlands	2.4	4.0	6.8
New Zealand	0.1	0.1	0.2
Norway	0.9	1.2	1.5
Portugal	N/A	0.3	0.3
Spain	N/A	1.0	1.6
Sweden	1.9	2.8	2.2
Switzerland	2.7	3.4	0.9
UK	12.2	6.5	15.5
USA	13.9	11.1	47.8
Total	75.4	76.4	166.7

[1] Includes flows to OPEC countries: Algeria, Ecuador, Gabon, Iran, Iraq, Kuwait, Libya, Nigeria, Qatar, Saudi Arabia, United Arab Emirates, and Venezuela. Country totals may not add to DAC total because debt forgiveness of non-official development assistance claims is not included in DAC totals.
[2] Former West Germany.
[3] Less than $50 million.

Source: Organization for Economic Cooperation and Development

Merchandise Trade of the European Union, the USA, and Japan with the Least Developed Countries of the World

Type of trade	Value ($ millions)					Share (%)	
	1990	1993	1994	1995	1996	1990	1996
Imports							
European Union							
Agricultural products	2,486	1,824	2,421	3,201	2,896	25.7	31.1
Mining products	4,378	1,563	1,527	1,480	1,626	45.3	17.5
Manufactures	2,664	3,166	3,574	4,592	4,697	27.6	50.4
European total	9,660	6,654	7,593	9,397	9,311	100.0	100.0
USA							
Agricultural products	363	305	400	343	409	7.9	7.2
Mining products	3,033	2,782	2,752	2,843	3,356	65.9	59.0
Manufactures	1,127	1,310	1,454	1,765	1,892	24.5	33.3
US total	4,603	4,417	4,631	4,981	5,685	100.0	100.0
Japan							
Agricultural products	541	614	724	825	810	43.3	48.1
Mining products	645	551	435	658	722	51.6	42.9
Manufactures	55	51	66	80	149	4.4	8.9
Japanese total	1,250	1,301	1,259	1,579	1,683	100.0	100.0

Type of trade	Value ($ millions)					Share (%)	
	1990	1993	1994	1995	1996	1990	1996
Exports							
European Union							
Agricultural products	2,024	1,788	1,814	2,162	2,276	20.1	24.1
Mining products	286	255	281	270	272	2.8	2.9
Manufactures	7,623	5,774	5,338	6,499	6,770	75.6	71.6
European total	10,077	7,907	7,532	9,109	9,460	100.0	100.0
USA							
Agricultural products	631	687	859	1,059	808	34.3	36.6
Mining products	19	11	10	34	38	1.0	1.7
Manufactures	1,067	965	728	1,074	1,231	58.1	55.8
US total	1,837	1,744	1,686	2,291	2,205	100.0	100.0
Japan							
Agricultural products	30	27	28	39	34	1.8	2.1
Mining products	5	6	5	4	5	0.3	0.3
Manufactures	1,666	1,564	1,440	1,637	1,607	97.5	97.2
Japanese total	1,708	1,602	1,484	1,689	1,654	100.0	100.0

Source: World Trade Organization

Leading Exporters and Importers of Commercial Services in the World

(N/A = not available. In billions of dollars, except percentages.)

1996

Exporters

Rank	Country	Value ($)	Share (%)	Annual change (%)
1	USA	202.0	16.2	7
2	France	87.2	7.0	-4
3	Germany	82.8	6.4	3
4	UK	74.9	6.0	6
5	Italy	69.1	5.6	6
6	Japan	66.4	5.3	4
7	Netherlands	48.1	3.9	2
8	Spain	44.0	3.5	11
9	Hong Kong	38.9	3.1	9
10	Austria	35.1	2.9	6
11	Belgium-Luxembourg	34.6	2.8	2
12	Singapore[1]	29.4	2.4	0
13	Switzerland[1]	27.1	2.1	N/A
14	Korea, South[1]	25.3	2.0	1
15	Canada	23.1	1.9	9
16	China[1]	20.5	1.7	11
17	Australia	18.1	1.5	17
18	Thailand[1]	17.3	1.4	18
19	Sweden	17.0	1.4	12
20	Taipei, Chinese	16.5	1.3	7
21	Denmark	15.5	1.3	6
22	Norway[1]	15.2	1.2	N/A
23	Turkey[1]	15.0	1.2	N/A
24	Malaysia[1]	14.1	1.1	27
25	Russia	10.6	0.9	6
	Total	1,047.8	83.2	N/A
	World total	1,260.0	100.0	5

Importers

Rank	Country	Value ($)	Share (%)	Annual change (%)
1	USA	135.3	10.8	5
2	Germany	132.3	10.5	0
3	Japan	128.7	10.2	6
4	France	70.4	5.6	-2
5	Italy	66.9	5.3	3
6	UK	61.9	5.0	7
7	Netherlands	44.6	3.5	-2
8	Belgium-Luxembourg	33.2	2.6	1
9	Korea, South[1]	31.7	2.5	15
10	Canada	31.5	2.5	7
11	Austria	30.5	2.4	7
12	China[1]	26.3	2.1	7
13	Taipei, Chinese	24.5	1.9	3
14	Spain	23.9	1.9	11
15	Hong Kong	22.3	1.8	4
16	Thailand[1]	20.9	1.7	12
17	Sweden	18.8	1.5	10
18	Singapore[1]	18.6	1.5	13
19	Australia	18.1	1.4	10
20	Russia	17.2	1.4	-9
21	Malaysia[1]	16.9	1.3	18
22	Norway[1]	16.5	1.3	N/A
23	Switzerland[1]	15.8	1.3	N/A
24	Brazil[1]	15.2	1.2	15
25	Denmark	14.7	1.2	5
	Total	1,036.7	81.8	N/A
	World total	1,265.0	100.0	5

[1] Estimates.

Source: World Trade Organization

Tourism Receipts: Leading Countries of the World

Country	Total receipts ($ millions)			% change (1995–96)	% of world total	
	1990	1995	1996		1990	1996
USA	43,007	61,137	64,373	5.29	16.16	15.22
Spain	18,593	25,343	28,428	12.17	6.98	6.72
France	20,185	27,527	28,241	2.59	7.58	6.68
Italy	20,016	27,451	27,349	-0.37	7.52	6.47
UK	14,940	19,133	20,415	6.70	5.61	4.83
Austria	13,410	14,618	15,095	3.26	5.04	3.57
Germany	11,471	12,810	13,168	2.79	4.31	3.11
Hong Kong	5,032	9,604	11,200	16.62	1.89	2.65
China	2,218	8,733	10,500	20.23	0.83	2.48
Switzerland	7,411	9,459	9,892	4.58	2.78	2.34
Singapore	4,596	8,212	9,410	14.59	1.73	2.22

Country	Total receipts ($ millions)			% change (1995–96)	% of world total	
	1990	1995	1996		1990	1996
Canada	6,339	8,012	8,727	8.92	2.38	2.06
Thailand	4,326	7,664	8,600	12.21	1.63	2.03
Australia	4,088	7,100	8,264	16.39	1.54	1.95
Poland	358	6,400	7,000	9.38	0.13	1.65
Mexico	5,467	6,164	6,898	11.91	2.05	1.63
Turkey	3,225	4,957	6,536	31.85	1.21	1.55
Korea, South	3,559	5,579	6,315	13.19	1.34	1.49
Belgium	3,721	5,719	5,893	3.04	1.40	1.39
Netherlands	3,636	5,762	5,877	2.00	1.37	1.39
Total	266,207	393,278	423,022	7.56	100.00	100.00

Source: World Tourism Organization

See Also   Tourism (Transport and Travel)

Leading Exporters and Importers of Merchandise in the World

1996

Exporters					*Importers*				
Rank	Country	Value ($)	Share (%)	Annual change (%)	Rank	Country	Value ($)	Share (%)	Annual change (%)
1	USA	624.5	11.8	7	1	USA	817.8	15.1	6
2	Germany	521.2	9.9	0	2	Germany	456.3	8.4	−2
3	Japan	410.9	7.8	−7	3	Japan	349.2	6.4	4
4	France	290.5	5.5	1	4	UK	278.5	5.3	8
5	UK	262.0	5.0	8	5	France	275.6	5.1	0
6	Italy	250.8	4.8	7	6	Italy	207.0	3.8	0
7	Canada	201.6	3.8	5	7	Hong Kong			
8	Netherlands	197.5	3.7	0		retained imports[5]	47.8	0.9	−8
9	Hong Kong					*Total*	201.3	3.7	3
	domestic exports	27.4	0.5	−8	8	Netherlands	180.7	3.3	2
	re-exports	153.5	2.9	7	9	Canada	175.2	3.2	4
	Total	180.9	3.4	4	10	Belgium-Luxembourg	157.5	2.9	1
10	Belgium-Luxembourg	169.4	3.2	0	11	Korea, South	150.2	2.8	11
11	China	151.1	2.9	2	12	China	138.8	2.6	5
12	Korea, South	129.8	2.5	4	13	Singapore			
13	Singapore					retained imports[5]	79.8	1.5	5
	domestic exports	73.5	1.4	6		*Total*	131.3	2.4	5
	re-exports	51.5	1.0	6	14	Spain	121.9	2.2	6
	Total	125.0	2.4	6	15	Taipei, Chinese	101.4	1.9	−2
14	Taipei, Chinese	115.9	2.2	4	16	Mexico[1]	90.2	1.7	24
15	Spain	102.1	1.9	11	17	Switzerland	79.3	1.5	−1
16	Mexico[1]	96.0	1.8	21	18	Malaysia	78.6	1.4	1
17	Sweden	84.5	1.6	6	19	Thailand	73.5	1.4	4
18	Switzerland	80.8	1.5	−1	20	Austria	66.7	1.2	1
19	Malaysia	78.4	1.5	6	21	Sweden	66.6	1.2	3
20	Russia[2]	68.7	1.3	8	22	Australia	65.4	1.2	7
21	Australia	60.5	1.1	15	23	Brazil	56.9	1.1	6
22	Saudi Arabia[3]	59.0	1.1	18	24	Denmark	45.2	0.8	−1
23	Austria	57.1	1.1	−1	25	Indonesia	42.9	0.8	6
24	Thailand	55.7	1.1	−1		*Total[4]*	4,417.1	81.5	4
25	Denmark	50.7	1.0	0					
	Total[4]	4,424.6	83.9	3		*World total[4]*	5,420.0	100.0	5
	World total[4]	5,270.0	100.0	4					

[1] Includes shipments through processing zones.
[2] Excludes trade with the Baltic States and the CIS. Including trade with these states would lift Russian exports and imports to $88 billion and $61 billion respectively.
[3] Estimates.
[4] Includes significant re-exports or imports for re-export.
[5] Retained imports are defined as imports less re-exports.

Source: World Trade Organization

Corel

The UK is the world's fifth-largest exporter and fourth-largest importer

World Energy and Minerals

Coal Production by Major Producing Country

(– = not applicable. In millions of short tons.)

Country	1986	1987	1988	1989	1990	1991	1992	1993	1994	1995
China	985.5	1,022.9	1,080.1	1,161.9	1,190.4	1,198.7	1,230.6	1,330.5	1,410.4	1,478.1
USA	890.3	918.8	950.3	980.7	1,029.1	996.0	997.5	945.4	1,033.5	1,033.0
India	207.4	208.6	214.5	221.4	233.4	252.7	262.6	290.1	295.6	311.1
Russia	–	–	–	–	–	–	405.9	364.0	320.3	310.0
Germany	–	–	–	–	–	388.4	346.1	315.2	291.8	274.2
Australia	186.8	208.9	196.4	216.1	225.8	235.9	249.0	247.6	249.2	268.0
South Africa	194.8	194.6	199.9	194.5	193.2	196.4	191.9	203.0	215.8	227.3
Poland	285.9	293.4	293.8	275.0	237.3	231.2	218.8	218.9	220.9	217.7
Kazakhstan	–	–	–	–	–	–	139.4	123.5	115.1	91.7
Ukraine	–	–	–	–	–	–	147.3	127.6	104.2	91.4
Canada	63.7	67.5	77.9	77.7	75.4	78.4	72.3	76.1	80.3	82.6
Czech Republic	–	–	–	–	–	–	–	77.2	82.1	78.6
Korea, North	60.6	62.3	66.1	69.1	71.3	72.8	73.9	77.7	77.7	78.1
Greece	42.0	49.2	53.3	57.2	57.2	58.1	60.7	60.4	62.5	64.1
Turkey	51.0	51.6	43.2	57.6	52.3	50.8	56.7	53.5	59.9	59.7
UK	119.2	115.1	114.8	111.4	106.0	106.6	94.9	76.3	54.0	52.4
Serbia and Montenegro	–	–	–	–	–	–	46.9	40.9	40.6	44.4
Romania	52.4	56.8	64.8	68.5	42.1	35.7	42.2	42.8	45.3	43.9
Indonesia	3.1	3.6	4.6	9.2	11.9	15.1	23.3	30.4	32.5	41.5
Spain	52.4	47.3	45.1	48.4	39.6	37.0	36.9	34.8	32.7	31.5
World total[1]	5,022.3	5,131.3	5,235.4	5,324.2	5,356.3	5,033.3	5,030.4	4,958.2	5,040.5	5,090.9

[1] Includes countries not shown separately.

Source: US Energy Information Administration

Crude Oil Imports and Exports by Area of the World

(– = not applicable.)

1991

Exporting area	Total[1]	Importing area							
		North America		Central and South America	Western Europe	Eastern Europe	Middle East and Africa	Japan	Other Far East and Oceania
		USA	Canada						
Middle East	12,947	1,770	89	682	3,567	246	731	3,034	2,828
Africa	4,969	1,160	59	147	3,101	95	323	11	73
Western Europe	2,939	183	348	11	2,374	0	23	0	0
Far East and Oceania	2,267	239	0	12	12	0	18	967	1,019
North America except USA	2,121	1,502	15	58	346	0	32	157	11
Central and South America	1,842	927	35	615	208	0	0	9	48
Eastern Europe and USSR	1,205	1	0	5	637	493	16	2	51
USA	116	–	5	111[2]	0	0	0	0	0
World total	28,406	5,782	551	1,641	10,245	834	1,143	4,180	4,030

[1] Includes stocks at sea, exchanges, transshipments, and other statistical discrepancies not shown separately.
[2] Includes shipments to Puerto Rico and Virgin Islands.

Source: US Energy Information Administration

Crude Oil Production by Major Producing Country

Figures indicate number of barrels produced per day. (– = not applicable. N/A = not available.)

Country	1980	1985	1989	1990	1991	1992	1993	1994	1995
Saudi Arabia	9,900,000	3,388,000	5,064,000	6,410,000	8,115,000	8,332,000	8,198,000	8,120,000	8,231,000
USA	8,597,000	8,971,000	7,613,000	7,355,000	7,417,000	7,171,000	6,847,000	6,662,000	6,560,000
Russia	–	–	–	–	–	7,632,000	6,730,000	6,135,000	5,995,000
Iran	1,662,000	2,250,000	2,810,000	3,088,000	3,312,000	3,429,000	3,540,000	3,618,000	3,643,000
China	2,114,000	2,505,000	2,757,000	2,774,000	2,835,000	2,845,000	2,890,000	2,939,000	2,990,000
Norway	N/A	N/A	1,554,000	1,704,000	1,890,000	2,230,000	2,350,000	2,521,000	2,768,000
Venezuela	2,168,000	1,677,000	1,907,000	2,137,000	2,375,000	2,371,000	2,450,000	2,588,000	2,750,000
Mexico	1,936,000	2,745,000	2,520,000	2,553,000	2,680,000	2,669,000	2,673,000	2,685,000	2,618,000
UK	1,622,000	2,530,000	1,802,000	1,820,000	1,797,000	1,825,000	1,915,000	2,375,000	2,489,000
United Arab Emirates	1,709,000	1,193,000	1,860,000	2,117,000	2,386,000	2,266,000	2,159,000	2,193,000	2,279,000
Kuwait	1,656,000	1,023,000	1,783,000	1,175,000	190,000	1,058,000	1,852,000	2,025,000	2,057,000
Nigeria	2,055,000	1,495,000	1,716,000	1,810,000	1,892,000	1,943,000	1,960,000	1,931,000	1,993,000
Canada	1,435,000	1,471,000	1,560,000	1,553,000	1,548,000	1,605,000	1,679,000	1,746,000	1,805,000
Indonesia	1,577,000	1,325,000	1,409,000	1,462,000	1,592,000	1,504,000	1,511,000	1,510,000	1,503,000
Libya	1,787,000	1,059,000	1,150,000	1,375,000	1,483,000	1,433,000	1,361,000	1,378,000	1,390,000
Algeria	1,106,000	1,037,000	1,095,000	1,175,000	1,230,000	1,214,000	1,162,000	1,180,000	1,202,000
World total[1]	59,599,000	53,981,000	59,863,000	60,566,000	60,207,000	60,216,000	60,647,000	61,003,000	62,446,000

[1] Includes countries not shown separately.

Source: US Energy Information Administration

Electricity Production by Country, Region, and Fuel (OECD)

Data include production from pumped storage. (– = not applicable. In percentages except as indicated.)

1994[1]

Country/Region	Nuclear	Hydro	Geothermal	Solar/Wind[2]	Combustible fuels[3]	Total terawatt hours[4]
Australia	–	10.06	–	–	89.94	167.1
Austria	–	69.21	–	–	30.79	53.3
Belgium	56.24	1.64	–	0.01	42.11	72.2
Canada	19.60	59.89	–	0.02	20.49	550.2
Denmark	–	0.07	–	2.85	97.08	38.0
Finland	29.38	18.14	–	0.01	52.47	65.1
France	75.53	16.91	–	0.12	7.45	475.8
Germany	28.64	4.30	–	0.04	67.03	528.0
Greece	–	6.99	–	0.06	92.94	40.6
Iceland	–	94.51	5.41	–	0.08	4.8
Ireland, Republic of	–	7.00	–	0.11	92.89	17.1
Italy	–	20.55	1.46	0.13	77.85	232.1
Japan	27.45	7.57	0.19	0.00	64.78	968.1
Luxembourg	–	59.27	–	–	40.73	1.1
Mexico	3.08	14.59	4.07	0.00	78.25	137.4
Netherlands	4.99	0.13	–	0.30	94.58	79.5
New Zealand	–	76.93	5.98	–	17.10	34.3
Norway	–	99.32	–	0.01	0.67	113.6
Portugal	–	34.32	0.11	0.04	65.54	31.2
Spain	34.91	17.89	–	–	47.21	158.5
Sweden	51.59	41.43	–	0.05	6.92	142.6
Switzerland	37.19	60.98	–	0.00	1.83	65.5
Turkey	–	39.07	0.10	–	60.83	78.3
UK	26.65	1.89	–	0.06	71.40	331.3
USA	19.61	7.47	0.52	0.12	72.28	3,455.9
Europe	32.26	19.69	0.15	0.11	47.79	2,528.8
Pacific	22.73	9.96	0.34	0.00	66.98	1,169.6
North America	19.06	14.67	0.57	0.10	65.60	4,143.4
Total OECD	23.87	15.58	0.40	0.09	60.06	7,841.8

[1] Preliminary.
[2] Includes tide, wave, ocean, and other (fuel cells).
[3] Total production from electricity and CHP plants using coal and coal products, oil and oil products, gas and combustible renewables, and waste. The term combustible fuels refers to fuels that are capable of igniting or burning, i.e. reacting with oxygen to produce a significant rise in temperature.
[4] A terrawatt hour = one trillion watt hours.

Source: International Energy Agency and Organization for Economic Cooperation and Development (OECD), OECD/IEA 1994

Energy Consumption by Country

(− = not applicable. In British thermal units (Btu).)

Country	Primary energy consumed				Country	Primary energy consumed			
	Total (quadrillion Btu)		Per capita (million Btu)			Total (quadrillion Btu)		Per capita (million Btu)	
	1990	1995	1990	1995		1990	1995	1990	1995
Algeria	1.1	1.3	45	44	Kuwait	0.5	0.6	208	323
Argentina	1.8	2.5	56	71	Libya	0.5	0.5	123	103
Australia	4.0	4.4	233	245	Malaysia	1.0	1.6	55	77
Austria	1.2	1.3	150	147	Mexico	4.9	5.6	57	59
Bahrain	0.3	0.3	532	536	Morocco	0.3	0.4	13	15
Bangladesh	0.3	0.4	2	3	Netherlands	3.4	3.8	228	244
Belarus	−	1.0	−	98	New Zealand	0.7	0.9	218	240
Belgium	2.2	2.4	216	233	Nigeria	0.7	0.8	6	6
Brazil	5.7	6.8	39	43	Norway	1.8	1.7	373	390
Bulgaria	1.3	1.0	141	118	Pakistan	1.2	1.5	11	12
Canada	11.0	11.7	413	396	Philippines	0.7	1.0	12	13
Chile	0.6	0.7	43	51	Poland	3.9	3.8	103	97
China	27.0	35.7	24	29	Portugal	0.8	0.9	77	79
Colombia	1.0	1.2	30	35	Romania	2.9	2.0	124	87
Cuba	0.5	0.4	46	37	Russia	−	26.8	−	181
Czech Republic	−	2.2	−	210	Saudi Arabia	3.2	3.7	212	208
Denmark	0.8	0.9	159	179	South Africa	4.3	5.5	116	134
Egypt	1.4	1.6	27	26	Spain	3.9	4.5	100	114
Finland	1.2	1.1	233	219	Sweden	2.2	2.2	251	244
France	8.9	9.4	157	162	Switzerland	1.2	1.2	174	165
Germany	−	13.7	−	168	Syria	0.6	0.7	50	52
Greece	1.0	1.2	103	111	Taiwan	2.0	2.7	100	126
Hong Kong	0.5	0.6	85	96	Thailand	1.3	2.0	22	33
Hungary	1.3	1.1	120	107	Turkey	1.9	2.5	34	41
India	7.7	10.5	9	11	UK	9.4	9.9	163	169
Indonesia	2.2	3.1	12	16	Ukraine	−	6.3	−	122
Iran	3.1	3.9	57	64	United Arab Emirates	1.2	1.6	735	817
Iraq	0.9	1.3	51	61	USA	82.0	88.3	328	335
Ireland, Republic of	0.4	0.5	104	134	Venezuela	2.1	2.5	108	117
Israel	0.5	0.7	96	118	Vietnam	0.3	0.5	4	7
Italy	7.0	7.4	121	127					
Japan	18.0	21.4	146	171	World total [1]	343.0	362.2	65	63
Korea, North	2.1	2.1	96	87					
Korea, South	3.7	6.3	87	140					

[1] Includes countries not shown separately.

Source: US Energy Information Administration

World Primary Energy Production by Region

(N/A = not available. In quadrillion British thermal units.)

Region	1980	1985	1987	1988	1989	1990	1991	1992	1993	1994
Africa	18.05	19.29	19.45	20.57	21.41	22.42	23.41	23.50	23.46	24.05
America, Central and South	12.11	13.59	14.44	15.29	15.86	16.81	17.64	17.73	18.32	N/A
America, North	80.85	84.55	84.73	86.83	86.85	88.80	89.31	89.12	88.52	N/A
Europe, Eastern, and former USSR	66.72	74.96	79.67	82.02	80.83	78.93	72.53	68.25	64.15	59.67
Europe, Western	30.66	37.30	38.54	38.75	38.40	38.14	38.54	38.80	39.42	40.27
Far East and Oceania	35.82	48.69	52.62	54.37	57.17	59.45	61.11	62.39	66.19	68.98
Middle East	42.17	25.77	32.21	36.12	39.72	41.04	40.33	43.59	45.80	47.39

Source: US Energy Information Administration

Commercial Nuclear Power Generation by Country

Generation is for calender years; other data are as of December. (N/A = not available. N = nil or negligible.)

Country	Reactors				Gross electricity generated (billion kilowatt hours)				Gross capacity (million kilowatts)			
	1980	1990	1994	1995	1980	1990	1994	1995	1980	1990	1994	1995
Argentina	1	2	2	2	2.3	7.0	8.2	7.0	357	1,005	1,005	1,005
Belgium	3	7	7	7	12.5	42.7	40.6	41.3	1,744	5,740	5,824	5,911
Brazil	N	1	1	1	N	2.0	0.1	2.5	N	657	657	657
Bulgaria	N/A	N/A	6	6	N/A	N/A	14.9	17.1	N/A	N/A	3,760	3,760
Canada	9	19	22	22	40.4	74.0	110.6	100.2	5,588	13,855	16,699	16,699
Czech Republic	N/A	N/A	N/A	N/A	N/A	N/A	N/A	N/A	N/A	N/A	N/A	N/A
Finland	4	4	4	4	7.0	18.9	19.1	18.9	2,296	2,400	2,400	2,400
France	22	58	57	56	61.2	314.1	359.0	377.2	15,412	58,862	61,234	60,674
Germany	11	22	21	21	43.7	147.2	151.1	154.1	8,996	23,973	23,934	24,035
Hungary	N	4	4	4	N	13.6	14.0	14.0	N	1,760	1,840	1,840
India	4	6	9	10	2.9	6.0	4.9	7.6	860	1,330	2,035	2,270
Italy	4	2	N/A	N/A	2.2	N	N/A	N/A	1,490	1,132	N/A	N/A
Japan	22	40	49	50	81.0	191.9	253.7	286.0	15,117	31,645	40,531	41,356
Korea, South	1	9	9	10	3.5	52.8	58.3	63.9	587	7,616	7,616	8,615
Mexico	N	1	1	2	N	2.1	4.2	7.9	N	675	675	1,350
Netherlands	2	2	2	2	4.2	3.4	3.9	4.0	529	540	540	540
Pakistan	1	1	1	1	0.1	0.4	0.5	0.5	137	137	137	137
Russia	N/A	N/A	29	29	N/A	N/A	97.6	98.7	N/A	N/A	21,316	21,266
Slovenia[1]	N	1	1	1	N	4.6	4.6	4.7	N	664	664	664
South Africa	N	2	2	2	N	8.9	10.2	11.9	N	1,930	1,930	1,930
Spain	3	10	9	9	5.2	54.3	55.2	55.4	1,117	7,984	7,400	7,400
Sweden	8	12	12	12	26.7	68.2	72.7	69.9	5,770	10,344	10,434	10,442
Switzerland	4	5	5	5	14.3	23.6	24.2	24.8	2,034	3,079	3,135	3,200
Taiwan	2	6	6	6	8.2	32.9	34.8	35.3	1,272	5,146	5,144	5,144
UK	33	42	35	34	37.2	68.8	89.4	84.7	9,012	15,274	14,252	14,022
Ukraine	N/A	N/A	14	15	N/A	N/A	68.3	70.5	N/A	N/A	12,880	13,880
USA	74	112	110	109	265.2	606.4	672.4	705.7	56,529	105,998	105,548	105,810
Total	208	368	418	423	617.8	1,743.9	2,173.6	2,274.7	128,847	301,745	351,588	358,414

[1] Formerly Yugoslavia.

Natural Gas Production by Major Producing Country

(– = not applicable. In quadrillion British thermal units.)

Country	1980	1985	1989	1990	1991	1992	1993	1994	1995
USA	19.91	16.98	17.85	18.36	18.23	18.38	18.58	19.27	19.33
Russia	–	–	–	–	–	20.60	19.87	19.41	19.01
Canada	2.80	3.08	3.85	3.90	4.12	4.60	4.99	5.45	5.80
UK	1.37	1.57	1.64	1.92	2.01	2.01	2.40	2.57	2.77
Netherlands	3.04	2.69	2.39	2.41	2.72	2.73	2.78	2.63	2.66
Indonesia	0.66	1.29	1.57	1.53	1.72	1.79	1.97	2.21	2.23
Algeria	0.44	1.44	1.81	1.90	2.05	2.09	2.02	1.92	2.18
Saudi Arabia	0.39	0.75	1.10	1.13	1.18	1.26	1.33	1.39	1.49
Iran	0.26	0.63	0.83	0.88	0.97	0.93	1.01	1.19	1.31
Norway	0.99	1.02	1.18	1.06	1.05	1.14	1.06	1.16	1.20
Mexico	0.97	0.92	0.94	0.96	1.14	1.13	1.10	1.11	1.15
Australia	0.34	0.49	0.59	0.76	0.79	0.87	0.92	0.98	1.13
Venezuela	0.56	0.70	0.88	0.91	0.95	0.91	0.97	1.04	1.11
United Arab Emirates	0.21	0.51	0.85	0.82	0.96	1.07	0.98	0.95	1.11
Malaysia	0.04	0.45	0.63	0.68	0.78	0.83	0.92	0.96	1.10
World total[1]		52.58	61.42	71.49	72.53	73.29	73.70	75.17	75.81	77.42

[1] Includes other countries not shown separately.

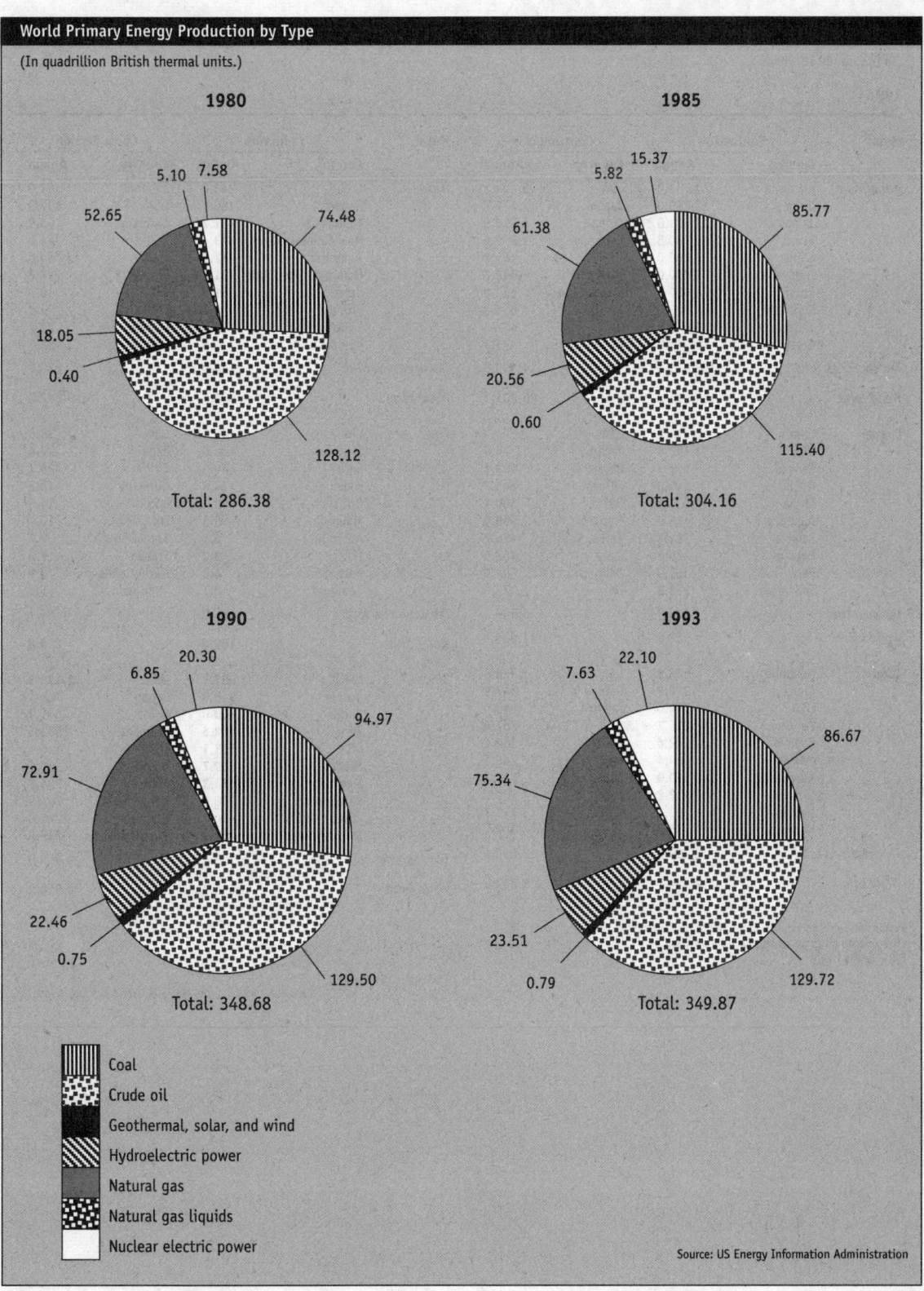

World Primary Energy Production by Type

(In quadrillion British thermal units.)

1980

5.10   7.58
52.65
74.48
18.05
0.40
128.12

Total: 286.38

1985

15.37
5.82
85.77
61.38
20.56
0.60
115.40

Total: 304.16

1990

20.30
6.85
94.97
72.91
22.46
0.75
129.50

Total: 348.68

1993

22.10
7.63
86.67
75.34
23.51
0.79
129.72

Total: 349.87

Coal
Crude oil
Geothermal, solar, and wind
Hydroelectric power
Natural gas
Natural gas liquids
Nuclear electric power

Source: US Energy Information Administration

Production and Consumption of Selected Metals: Top Ten Countries

(In thousands of tonnes.)

1994

Metal	Production		Consumption		Metal	Production		Consumption	
	Country	Annual	Country	Annual		Country	Annual	Country	Annual
Aluminium[1]	Australia	41,733.0	USA	5,407.1	Nickel	USSR[2]	243.0	Japan	164.9
	Guinea	17,040.0	Japan	2,174.8		Canada	150.1	USA	137.3
	Jamaica	11,571.0	China	1,318.0		Indonesia	81.2	Germany	93.9
	Brazil	8,280.8	Germany	1,300.0		New Caledonia	73.6	USSR[2]	64.0
	China	7,260.0	USSR[2]	1,185.0		Australia	71.9	Italy	44.6
	India	5,280.0	France	665.0		Dominican Republic	31.6	France	42.2
	Russia	4,000.0	Korea, South	557.0		Cuba	31.0	UK	38.0
	Suriname	3,200.5	Italy	554.0		China	30.7	China	26.8
	Venezuela	2,540.0	UK	477.3		South Africa	30.1	Finland	23.4
	Greece	2,168.0	India	475.3		Colombia	20.8	Sweden	23.0
Ten countries total		103,073.6		14,113.5	Ten countries total		764.0		829.9
World total		111,024.2		20,201.1	World total		802.5		882.0
Copper	Chile	2,219.9	USA	2,674.3	Tin	China	46.0[3]	USA	33.5
	USA	1,795.4	Japan	1,374.9		Indonesia	30.6	Japan	29.4
	Canada	617.3	Germany	983.1		Peru	20.0	China	26.1
	USSR[2]	540.0[3]	China	745.7[3]		Brazil	17.0	Germany	18.2
	China	432.1	USSR[2]	560.0[3]		Bolivia	16.1	USSR[2]	14.5[3]
	Australia	415.6	France	495.0		Malaysia	6.5	UK	10.4
	Zambia	384.4	Korea, South	476.2		Australia	6.4	Korea, South	9.8
	Poland	376.8	Italy	467.9		USSR[2]	5.0[3]	France	9.2
	Peru	359.9	Belgium	404.9		Portugal	4.3	Netherlands	7.9
	Indonesia	333.8	UK	377.3		Thailand	3.1	Thailand	5.1
Ten countries total		7,475.2		8,559.3	Ten countries total		155.0		164.1
World total		9,522.6		11,084.2	World total		169.4		216.8
Lead	Australia	523.8	USA	1,374.8	Zinc[3]	Canada	1,007.3	USA	1,118.3
	China	376.2	Germany	347.9		Australia	945.0	Japan	723.1
	USA	374.0	Japan	345.0		China	900.0	China	611.9
	Peru	216.7	UK	267.6		Peru	602.6	Germany	531.6
	Canada	172.6	Italy	262.2		USA	513.1	Italy	336.1
	Mexico	164.4	France	246.7		Mexico	369.7	USSR[2]	330.0
	Kazakhstan	160.0	China	214.1		Sweden	173.3	France	296.7
	Sweden	112.8	USSR[2]	200.0		Kazakhstan	250.0	Korea, South	264.9
	Namibia	93.1	Korea, South	175.1		Korea, North	210.0	Belgium	225.0
	Morocco	75.7	Mexico	162.0		Ireland, Republic of	210.0	Australia	215.4
Ten countries total		2,269.3		3,595.4	Ten countries total		5,181.0		4,653.0
World total		2,764.7		5,342.2	World total		6,895.1		6,950.3

[1] Production refers to bauxite, consumption to aluminium.
[2] Data refer to all components of the former USSR.
[3] Data are for 1993.

Source: *World Resources 1997–97*, World Resources Institute

World Production of Major Mineral Commodities

(N/A = not available.)

Country	Units	1990	1993	1994	1995	Leading producers, 1994
Mineral Fuels[1]						
Coal	million short tons	5,356	4,958	5,041	5,091	China, USA, Russia
Dry natural gas	trillion cubic feet	73.6	76.3	76.7	78.3	Russia, USA, Canada
Natural gas plant liquids[2]	million barrels[3]	1,691	1,887	1,928	1,998	USA, Saudi Arabia, Canada
Petroleum, crude	million barrels[3]	22,107	21,990	22,266	22,793	Saudi Arabia, USA, Russia
Petroleum, refined	million barrels[3]	23,791	N/A	24,512	N/A	USA, Japan, Russia
Nonmetallic Minerals						
Cement, hydraulic	million tonnes	1,148	1,300	1,370	1,390	China, Japan, USA
Diamond, gem and industrial	thousand carats	110,919	105,000	111,000	N/A	Australia, Russia, Democratic Republic of Congo
Nitrogen in ammonia	million tonnes	97.1	92.0	92.0	96.0	China, USA, India
Phosphate rock	million tonnes	162	120	128	137	USA, China, Morocco
Potash, marketable	million tonnes	27.8	21.0	22.5	26.2	Canada, Germany, Belarus
Salt	million tonnes	184	190	180	185	USA, China, Germany
Sulphur, elemental basis	million metric tons	58.1	52.0	51.0	52.0	USA, Canada, China
Metals						
Aluminium[4]	million tonnes	19.3	20.0	19.1	19.3	USA, Russia, Canada
Bauxite, gross weight	million tonnes	108.6	110.0	107.0	109.0	Australia, Guinea, Jamaica
Chromite, gross weight[2]	thousand metric tons	12,968	10,001	9,570	10,600	South Africa, Kazakhstan, India
Copper, metal content[5]	thousand metric tons	9,017	9,400	9,430	9,800	Chile, USA, Canada
Gold, metal content	tonnes	2,133	2,300	2,300	2,200	South Africa, USA, Australia
Iron ore, gross weight[6]	million metric tons	982	1,000	1,000	1,000	China, Brazil, Russia
Lead, metal content[5]	thousand metric tons	3,353	2,900	2,800	2,800	Australia, USA, China
Manganese ore, gross weight	million metric tons	25.3	21.8	21.2	21.0	China, Ukraine, South Africa
Nickel, metal content[5]	thousand metric tons	965	900	906	920	Russia, Canada, New Caledonia
Steel, crude	million tonnes	771	730	726	760	European Union, Japan, China
Tin, metal content[5]	thousand metric tons	222	180	184	180	China, Indonesia, Brazil
Zinc, metal content[5]	thousand metric tons	7,184	6,900	6,810	7,070	Australia, Canada, China

[1] 1995 data are preliminary.
[2] Excludes China.
[3] Barrels hold 42 gallons.
[4] Unalloyed ingot metal.
[5] Mine output.
[6] Includes iron ore concentrates and iron ore agglomerates.

Source: Energy Information Administration; nonmetallic minerals and metals through 1994, US Bureau of Mines, thereafter, US Geological Survey

Oil and Gas Reserves of the World

1994

Oil

Region	Thousand million tonnes	Thousand million barrels	Share of total (%)	Reserves/ production ratio[1]
Middle East	89.4	660.3	65.4	93.4
North America	12.0	88.3	8.7	18.9
South and Central America	11.2	78.3	7.8	41.4
Africa	8.3	62.2	6.2	25.2
Eastern Europe	8.1	59.2	5.9	21.6
Asia and Australia	6.1	44.5	4.4	17.6
Western Europe	2.2	16.5	1.6	7.6
World total	137.3	1,009.3	100.0	43.0

Gas

Region	Trillion cubic feet	Trillion cubic metres	Share of total (%)	Reserves/ production ratio[1]
Eastern Europe	2,001.9	56.7	40.2	76.9
Middle East	1,594.3	45.2	32.0	[2]
Asia and Australia	350.7	9.9	7.1	49.7
Africa	341.6	9.6	6.8	[2]
North America	311.3	8.8	6.3	12.7
Western Europe	191.4	5.4	3.8	24.7
South and Central America	189.1	5.4	3.8	76.1
World total	4,980.3	141.0	100.0	66.4

[1] If the reserves remaining at the end of any year are divided by the production in that year, the result is the length of time that those remaining reserves would last if production were to continue at the current level.
[2] More than 100 years.

Source: *Oil and Gas Journal*, 26 December 1994

World Industry

Growth of Industrial Output by Country

1990–95

High growth		Low growth	
Country	**Average annual % growth**	**Country**	**Average annual % growth**
China	18.1	Georgia	−34.1
Papua New Guinea	17.8	Armenia	−28.7
Panama	14.9	Latvia	−25.1
Lesotho	12.3	Ukraine	−21.6
Cambodia	11.3	Kazakhstan	−19.2
Malaysia/Uganda	11.0	Rwanda	−17.0
Thailand	10.8	Albania	−15.6
Indonesia	10.1	Estonia	−14.9
Myanmar	9.4	Belarus	−10.9
Nepal	9.3	Slovak Republic	−10.4

Source: *World Development Indicators*, 1997, The World Bank

Corel

Industrial output
The countries of the former USSR are among those at the bottom of the league of annual growth

Index of Industrial Production by Country

Industrial production index measures output in the manufacturing, mining, and electric and gas utilities industries. (N = nil or negligible. N/A = not available.)

Country	Index (1990 = 100)								Annual % change				
	1980	1985	1991	1992	1993	1994	1995	1996	1991–92	1992–93	1993–94	1994–95	1995–96
OECD total	78.9	86.3	99.6	99.4	98.8	102.9	106.1	108.1	−0.2	−0.6	4.1	3.1	1.9
Australia	N/A	N/A	N/A	97.8	100.4	105.8	105.5	108.8	N/A	2.7	5.4	−0.3	3.1
Austria	76.1	82.5	101.9	100.5	99.0	102.4	107.9	N/A	−1.4	−1.5	3.4	5.4	N/A
Belgium	82.1	85.5	98.0	98.0	92.9	94.6	98.6	99.1	N	−5.2	1.8	4.2	0.5
Canada[1]	81.5	94.5	95.8	96.9	101.2	108.3	112.0	113.9	1.1	4.4	7.0	3.4	1.7
Finland	75.3	87.8	90.3	92.4	97.2	108.3	116.4	120.7	2.3	5.2	11.4	7.5	3.7
France	89.2	89.3	98.9	98.9	93.9	97.4	99.4	100.0	N	−5.1	3.7	2.1	0.6
Germany[2]	83.0	85.6	103.6	101.0	93.6	96.9	98.9	99.0	−2.5	−7.3	3.5	2.1	0.1
Greece	90.8	98.2	98.6	97.4	95.4	96.3	98.5	98.6	−1.2	−2.1	0.9	2.3	0.1
Ireland, Republic of	54.2	69.5	103.3	112.7	119.0	133.2	158.3	170.9	9.1	5.6	11.9	18.8	8.0
Italy	87.5	84.8	99.1	97.8	95.7	101.7	107.9	104.8	−1.3	−2.1	6.3	6.1	−2.9
Japan	67.3	79.8	101.9	96.0	92.0	93.1	96.2	98.8	−5.8	−4.2	1.2	3.3	2.7
Luxembourg	69.7	84.7	100.1	99.3	95.2	100.9	102.3	100.6	−0.8	−4.1	6.0	1.4	−1.7
Mexico[3]	N/A	N/A	N/A	106.5	108.2	113.4	104.6	115.5	N/A	1.6	4.8	−7.8	10.4
Netherlands	86.8	91.7	101.7	101.6	100.3	104.6	106.7	110.2	−0.1	−1.3	4.3	2.0	3.3
Norway	58.3	79.0	102.1	108.6	112.1	120.0	127.2	134.1	6.4	3.2	7.0	6.0	5.4
Portugal	62.8	73.9	100.0	97.7	95.2	95.0	99.4	100.8	−2.3	−2.6	−0.2	4.6	1.4
Spain	83.3	86.1	99.3	96.5	92.0	98.7	103.3	102.6	−2.8	−4.7	7.3	4.7	−0.7
Sweden[4]	82.5	91.5	94.9	93.5	94.3	105.5	115.1	117.5	−1.5	0.9	11.9	9.1	2.1
Switzerland[5]	82.0	84.8	100.8	99.0	97.0	102.0	104.0	103.0	−1.8	−2.0	5.2	2.0	−1.0
UK	81.6	88.2	96.4	96.3	98.4	103.4	105.9	107.3	−0.1	2.2	5.1	2.4	1.3
USA	79.3	89.0	98.0	101.1	104.6	109.8	113.4	116.5	3.2	3.4	5.0	3.3	2.7

[1] Gross domestic product in industry at factor cost and 1986 prices.
[2] 1980–90 former West Germany; later data use 1990 annual average data for West Germany as base year.
[3] Includes construction.
[4] Mining and manufacturing.
[5] Excludes mining and quarrying.

Source: Organization for Economic Cooperation and Development (OECD)

Leading Producers of Selected Commodities: World and Developing World

(– = not applicable.)

1994

World leading countries		Leading developing countries		World leading countries		Leading developing countries		World leading countries		Leading developing countries	
Country or area	Share (%)[1]	Country or area	Share (%)[2]	Country or area	Share (%)[1]	Country or area	Share (%)[2]	Country or area	Share (%)[1]	Country or area	Share (%)[2]
Food Products				**Non-Electrical Machinery**				**Other Chemicals**			
USA	24.5	Brazil	12.6	USA	32.0	Brazil	22.2	USA	27.3	Korea, South	14.4
Japan	15.0	Argentina	11.2	Japan	19.3	Korea, South	16.5	Japan	17.7	Brazil	14.0
France	6.5	Korea, South	6.6	Germany, western	12.2	India	10.2	Germany, western	10.1	Mexico	11.4
Germany, western	6.2	Mexico	6.3	Italy	6.2	Singapore	8.3	France	5.8	Argentina	9.7
UK	4.8	India	5.6	UK	5.2	Taiwan	7.9	UK	5.2	India	7.9
Italy	4.1	Indonesia	5.0	France	4.3	Argentina	7.1	Switzerland	3.2	Taiwan	4.3
Spain	3.4	Philippines	4.2	Brazil	2.0	Mexico	4.8	Spain	2.9	Turkey	4.1
Canada	2.6	Taiwan	4.1	Canada	1.8	Turkey	4.4	Italy	2.8	Philippines	3.9
Brazil	2.5	Turkey	4.0	Korea, South	1.5	Iran	3.2	Korea, South	2.3	Thailand	2.6
Argentina	2.2	Thailand	3.1	Spain	1.4	Hong Kong	2.2	Brazil	2.2	Indonesia	2.5
Netherlands	1.8	Chile	2.9	Sweden	1.1	Malaysia	2.1	Canada	1.9	Pakistan	2.3
Australia	1.8	Peru	2.0	India	0.9	Chile	0.9	Mexico	1.8	Chile	2.2
Belgium	1.5	Egypt	1.7	Netherlands	0.9	Venezuela	0.6	Argentina	1.6	Venezuela	2.1
Korea, South	1.3	Colombia	1.7	Austria	0.8	Algeria	0.5	India	1.3	Singapore	1.8
Mexico	1.3	Pakistan	1.6	Mexico	0.7	Colombia	0.4	Sweden	1.2	Peru	1.8
Total	79.5	Total	72.6	Total	90.3	Total	91.3	Total	87.2	Total	85.0
Textiles				**Electrical Machinery**				**Iron and Steel**			
USA	19.8	India	15.9	Japan	25.7	Korea, South	23.1	Japan	23.0	Korea, South	15.5
Japan	12.9	Brazil	9.8	USA	24.0	Taiwan	20.9	USA	15.3	India	14.8
Italy	10.4	Taiwan	9.5	Germany, western	12.5	Brazil	13.6	Germany, western	8.7	Brazil	14.0
India	5.2	Korea, South	8.3	Italy	4.8	Mexico	6.4	Italy	7.5	Taiwan	11.7
Germany, western	4.9	Turkey	7.0	France	4.7	Malaysia	5.9	France	4.5	Mexico	10.9
France	4.3	Argentina	4.8	UK	3.4	India	5.7	Korea, South	3.7	Indonesia	6.5
Brazil	3.2	Pakistan	4.3	Korea, South	3.0	Singapore	5.1	India	3.5	Turkey	4.5
Taiwan	3.1	Iran	3.5	Taiwan	2.7	Turkey	2.7	Brazil	3.3	Argentina	3.2
UK	3.0	Hong Kong	3.4	Brazil	1.8	Argentina	2.1	UK	3.3	Venezuela	1.8
Korea, South	2.7	Indonesia	3.3	Spain	1.6	Hong Kong	1.9	Spain	2.8	Malaysia	1.2
Spain	2.4	Mexico	3.0	Netherlands	1.3	Philippines	1.9	Taiwan	2.8	Philippines	1.2
Turkey	2.3	Egypt	1.7	Canada	1.3	Iran	1.1	Mexico	2.6	Peru	1.0
Canada	1.6	Colombia	1.7	Austria	1.1	Indonesia	0.5	Canada	1.7	Chile	0.9
Argentina	1.6	Peru	1.7	Sweden	1.1	Algeria	0.5	Indonesia	1.5	Colombia	0.9
Pakistan	1.4	Malaysia	1.1	Mexico	0.8	Colombia	0.5	Austria	1.5	Egypt	0.8
Total	78.7	Total	79.1	Total	89.8	Total	92.0	Total	85.7	Total	88.8
Wearing Apparel				**Industrial Chemicals**							
USA	26.0	Brazil	14.5	USA	25.0	Taiwan	14.3				
Japan	11.3	Hong Kong	11.2	Japan	15.6	Mexico	13.1				
Italy	8.7	Korea, South	8.8	Germany, western	13.1	Brazil	12.9				
France	5.7	Argentina	6.0	UK	5.1	India	12.0				
UK	4.2	Turkey	3.4	France	4.9	Korea, South	11.4				
Germany, western	3.9	Taiwan	2.9	Italy	3.8	Saudi Arabia	6.6				
Brazil	3.8	Philippines	2.7	Netherlands	2.9	Turkey	3.6				
Hong Kong	2.9	India	2.2	Taiwan	2.7	Argentina	3.3				
Spain	2.8	Sri Lanka	2.1	Mexico	2.4	Malaysia	2.3				
Canada	2.4	Mexico	2.0	Brazil	2.4	Indonesia	1.8				
Korea, South	2.3	Tunisia	1.7	India	2.2	Pakistan	1.7				
Argentina	1.6	Iraq	1.6	Korea, South	2.1	Venezuela	1.6				
Portugal	1.5	Malaysia	1.3	Belgium	2.0	Singapore	1.6				
Belgium	1.3	Morocco	1.3	Spain	1.9	Colombia	1.2				
Australia	1.2	Algeria	1.2	Canada	1.6	Philippines	1.0				
Total	79.6	Total	62.9	Total	87.9	Total	88.3				

[1] In world total value added (excluding eastern Europe and the former USSR) at constant 1990 prices.
[2] In total value added of developing countries at constant 1990 prices.

Source: UNIDO, *United Nations International Yearbook of Industrial Statistics*, 1997

Motor Vehicle Production of the World

As far as possibly can be determined, production in this table refers to vehicles locally manufactured.

1995

Country	Passenger cars	Commercial vehicles	Total	Country	Passenger cars	Commercial vehicles	Total
Argentina	226,658	58,779	285,435	Malaysia	195,000	0	195,000
Australia	314,142	29,709	343,851	Mexico	699,312	235,705	935,017
Austria	43,466	3,217	46,683	Netherlands	100,434	32,036	132,470
Belgium	385,894	81,555	467,449	Poland	380,000	27,000	407,000
Brazil	1,296,586	327,555	1,624,141	Russia	831,500	165,500	997,000
Canada	1,339,490	1,080,644	2,420,134	Spain	2,130,540	203,247	2,333,787
China	325,461	1,127,236	1,452,697	Sweden	387,659	102,483	490,142
Czech Republic	208,490	7,909	216,399	Taiwan	282,006	124,474	406,480
France	3,050,929	423,776	3,474,705	Turkey	233,412	49,028	282,440
Germany	4,360,235	307,129	4,667,364	UK	1,532,084	233,001	1,765,085
Hungary	42,000	2,058	44,058	USA	6,351,255	5,634,724	11,985,979
India	329,879	306,382	636,261	Yugoslavia	7,502	1,809	9,311
Italy	1,422,359	244,911	1,667,270				
Japan	7,610,533	2,585,003	10,195,536	*Total*	36,089,970	13,918,124	50,008,094
Korea, South	2,003,146	523,254	2,526,400				

Source: *World Motor Vehicle Data*

See Also **World Road Transport (Transport and Travel)**

World Agriculture

Countries Most and Least Economically Dependent on Agriculture

1996

Most Dependent				Least dependent				
Country	**% of GDP**	**Country**	**% of GDP**	**Country**	**% of GDP**	**Country**	**% of GDP**	
Georgia	86.81	Côte d'Ivoire	30.56	Singapore	0.17	Mauritius	9.39	
Tanzania	68.30	India	29.48	Kuwait	0.43	Lesotho	10.09	
Albania	65.82	Kenya	29.08	Bahrain	0.94	Congo, Republic of the	10.32	
Burundi	65.71	Nigeria	28.16	Djibouti	3.43	Panama	10.87	
Cambodia	51.27	Vietnam	27.55	Trinidad and Tobago	3.49	Thailand	10.95	
Uganda	49.73	Papua New Guinea	26.40	South Africa	4.68	Lithuania	10.98	
Moldova	49.55	Pakistan	26.02	Slovenia	4.76	Grenada	10.99	
Ghana	46.27	Iran	25.19	Botswana	5.09	Eritrea	11.08	
Mali	46.09	Guinea	24.14	Venezuela	5.33	St Vincent and the Grenadines	11.21	
Guinea-Bissau	45.94	Sri Lanka	23.01	Slovak Republic	6.64	Tunisia	11.85	
Armenia	44.28	Zambia	22.34	Argentina	5.99	Ecuador	11.92	
Kyrgyzstan	43.68	Philippines	21.66	Poland	6.49	Croatia	12.38	
Sierra Leone	42.00	Honduras	21.00	Peru	7.50	Angola	12.44	
Malawi	41.81	Romania	20.91	Hungary	7.52	Kazakhstan	12.49	
Nepal	41.77	China	20.59	Mexico	7.73	Algeria	12.84	
Cameroon	39.15	Senegal	19.93	Estonia	8.06	Bulgaria	12.87	
Comoros	38.74	Egypt	19.87	Jamaica	8.73	Malaysia	13.02	
Rwanda	37.22	Ukraine	17.53	Uruguay	8.87	Belarus	13.35	
Madagascar	33.82	Costa Rica	17.38	Swaziland	9.03	El Salvador	13.65	
Bangladesh	30.88	Indonesia	17.19	Latvia	9.26	Morocco	14.34	

Source: *World Economic Indicators*, 1997, The World Bank

Commercial Catch of Fish, Crustaceans, and Molluscs by Major Fishing Areas of the World

The data indicate live-weight and do not include marine mammals or aquatic plants. (In tonnes.)

Area	1991	1992	1993	1994	1995
Marine Areas					
Atlantic Ocean	23,792,000	24,372,000	23,748,000	23,720,000	24,690,000
Indian Ocean	6,879,000	7,356,000	7,857,000	7,818,000	8,031,000
Pacific Ocean	52,358,000	52,844,000	54,334,000	59,975,000	59,185,000
Total	83,029,000	84,572,000	85,939,000	91,513,000	91,906,000
Inland Waters					
Africa	1,808,000	1,832,000	1,855,000	1,849,000	1,908,000
America, North	551,000	583,000	578,000	573,000	549,000
America, South	331,000	352,000	376,000	391,000	415,000
Asia	10,798,000	11,627,000	13,336,000	15,188,000	17,091,000
Europe	493,000	504,000	497,000	510,000	528,000
Oceania	23,000	25,000	23,000	24,000	24,000
Former USSR	764,000	682,000	568,000	490,000	489,000
Total	14,768,000	15,605,000	17,233,000	19,025,000	21,004,000
TOTAL	97,797,000	100,177,000	103,172,000	110,538,000	112,910,000

Source: US Department of Commerce

Global Food Production

(In millions of tonnes.)

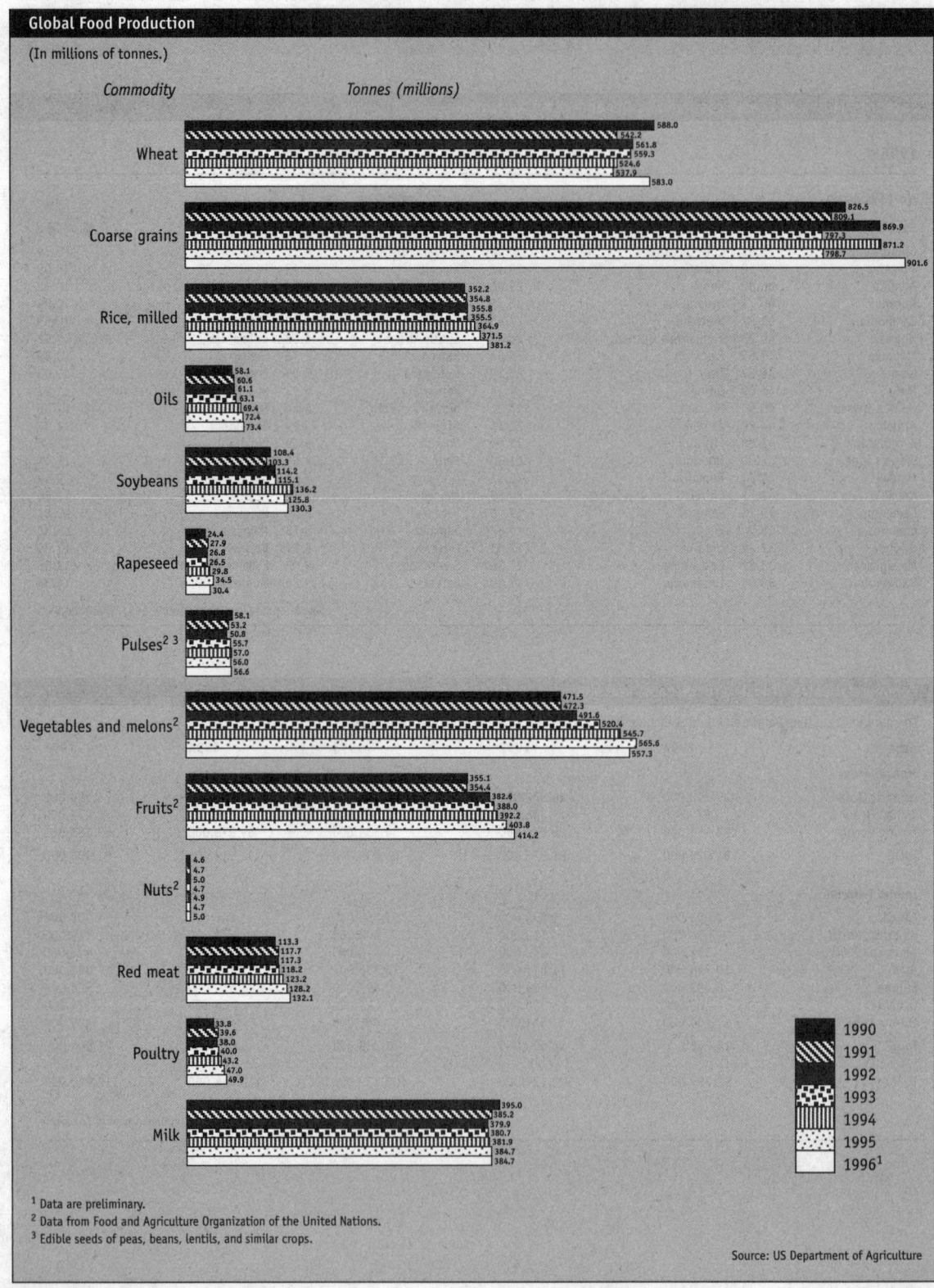

Commodity   Tonnes (millions)

Wheat
- 588.0
- 542.2
- 561.8
- 559.3
- 524.6
- 537.9
- 583.0

Coarse grains
- 826.5
- 809.1
- 869.9
- 797.3
- 871.2
- 798.7
- 901.6

Rice, milled
- 352.2
- 354.8
- 355.8
- 355.5
- 364.9
- 371.5
- 381.2

Oils
- 58.1
- 60.6
- 61.1
- 63.1
- 69.4
- 72.4
- 73.4

Soybeans
- 108.4
- 103.3
- 114.2
- 115.1
- 136.2
- 125.8
- 130.3

Rapeseed
- 24.4
- 27.9
- 26.8
- 26.5
- 29.8
- 34.5
- 30.4

Pulses[2][3]
- 58.1
- 53.2
- 50.8
- 55.7
- 57.0
- 56.0
- 56.6

Vegetables and melons[2]
- 471.5
- 472.3
- 491.6
- 520.4
- 545.7
- 565.6
- 557.3

Fruits[2]
- 355.1
- 354.4
- 382.6
- 388.0
- 392.2
- 403.8
- 414.2

Nuts[2]
- 4.6
- 4.7
- 5.0
- 4.7
- 4.9
- 4.7
- 5.0

Red meat
- 113.3
- 117.7
- 117.3
- 118.2
- 123.2
- 128.2
- 132.1

Poultry
- 33.8
- 39.6
- 38.0
- 40.0
- 43.2
- 47.0
- 49.9

Milk
- 395.0
- 385.2
- 379.9
- 380.7
- 381.9
- 384.7
- 384.7

Legend:
- 1990
- 1991
- 1992
- 1993
- 1994
- 1995
- 1996[1]

[1] Data are preliminary.
[2] Data from Food and Agriculture Organization of the United Nations.
[3] Edible seeds of peas, beans, lentils, and similar crops.

Source: US Department of Agriculture

Imports and Exports of Fishery Commodity Groups By Leading Countries

Data on imports and exports cover the international trade of 176 countries or areas. The total value of exports is consistently less than the total value of imports, probably because charges for insurance, freight, and similar expenses were included in the import value but not in the export value. The seven fishery commodity groups covered by this table are: fish, fresh, chilled, or frozen; fish, dried, salted, or smoked; crustaceans and molluscs, fresh, dried, salted, etc; fish products and preparations, whether or not in airtight containers; crustacean and mollusc products and preparations, whether or not in airtight containers; oils and fats, crude or refined, of aquatic animal origin; and meals, solubles, and similar animal foodstuffs of aquatic animal origin. (– = not applicable. Value in thousands of dollars.)

Imports

Country	1991	1992	1993	1994	1995
Japan	12,085,125	12,831,760	14,187,149	16,140,465	17,853,481
USA	5,999,580	6,024,064	6,290,233	7,043,431	7,141,428
France	2,925,994	2,934,588	2,556,151	2,796,719	3,221,298
Spain	2,748,304	2,898,232	2,629,799	2,638,737	3,105,684
Germany	2,114,720	2,190,892	1,884,301	2,316,449	2,478,817
Italy	2,689,639	2,643,440	2,131,181	2,257,462	2,281,316
UK	1,911,905	1,906,861	1,628,852	1,880,350	1,910,091
Hong Kong	1,232,076	1,398,181	1,376,856	1,642,105	1,827,691
Denmark	1,148,255	1,197,370	1,094,253	1,415,239	1,573,732
Netherlands	867,511	888,606	791,608	1,017,635	1,191,857
Belgium	775,966	828,086	730,459	920,918	1,035,818
Canada	675,242	686,876	821,404	913,404	1,034,070
China	438,090	680,844	575,929	855,706	941,293
Thailand	1,052,918	942,090	830,480	815,616	825,606
Korea, South	568,229	498,036	537,346	718,451	824,817
Portugal	757,843	734,928	627,713	669,888	763,245
Singapore	460,545	543,769	566,502	619,595	659,681
Taiwan	458,830	491,029	544,243	560,799	589,723
Sweden	441,490	467,773	371,756	448,661	546,076
Other	4,137,182	4,467,246	4,394,097	5,391,889	6,034,407
Total	43,489,444	45,254,671	44,570,312	51,063,519	55,840,131

Exports

Country	1991	1992	1993	1994	1995
Thailand	2,901,360	3,071,780	3,404,268	4,190,036	4,449,457
USA	3,281,746	3,582,545	3,179,474	3,229,585	3,383,589
Norway	2,282,247	2,436,832	2,302,346	2,718,132	3,122,662
China	1,181,989	1,559,977	1,542,429	2,320,125	2,854,373
Denmark	2,302,299	2,319,917	2,150,665	2,359,034	2,459,629
Taiwan	1,524,735	1,802,097	2,369,422	2,213,259	2,328,105
Canada	2,168,122	2,085,495	2,055,438	2,182,078	2,314,413
Chile	1,066,781	1,252,364	1,124,679	1,303,974	1,704,260
Indonesia	1,186,062	1,178,552	1,419,492	1,583,416	1,666,752
Russia	–	826,299	1,471,446	1,720,459	1,628,204
Korea, South	1,490,659	1,359,050	1,335,238	1,411,052	1,564,878
Netherlands	1,356,885	1,405,567	1,296,340	1,435,824	1,447,239
Iceland	1,280,006	1,252,713	1,137,638	1,264,615	1,342,552
India	647,652	673,369	835,980	1,125,440	1,240,603
UK	1,121,885	1,146,138	1,036,674	1,180,158	1,195,477
Spain	772,651	712,729	813,750	1,021,015	1,190,676
France	925,560	955,379	857,752	909,734	993,364
Argentina	448,012	559,029	709,292	728,091	917,580
Germany	715,975	692,954	652,956	790,357	899,248
Other	12,262,841	11,341,410	11,712,740	13,576,105	15,041,899
Total	38,917,467	40,214,196	41,408,019	47,262,489	51,744,960

Source: US Department of Commerce

Leading Producers and Consumers of Fruit in the World

(N/A = not available. In tonnes. Including melon and watermelon.)

Country	1991	1992	1993	1994	1995	1996
Production						
China	35,805,950	42,127,420	51,478,260	55,843,280	62,557,730	65,703,530
India	33,145,050	34,993,360	37,220,860	39,977,070	40,196,070	40,197,070
Brazil	32,660,940	34,170,340	34,148,670	33,336,970	35,197,770	37,436,400
USA	28,860,030	31,633,070	33,928,440	34,046,880	34,764,380	34,311,270
Italy	20,582,360	24,074,460	22,339,430	21,433,340	19,550,340	20,262,230
Turkey	15,745,360	15,339,340	15,156,940	15,811,000	15,825,200	15,572,190
Spain	15,762,890	18,197,250	15,798,560	14,535,220	13,375,200	15,145,560
Iran	9,950,748	11,479,000	11,888,720	13,541,050	13,513,870	13,743,830
Mexico	10,674,180	11,070,720	11,774,660	12,425,380	13,100,200	13,692,800
France	9,788,916	14,647,370	12,097,850	12,982,150	13,116,340	13,063,500
Consumption						
China	31,360,530	36,937,690	45,240,340	49,036,360	55,156,250	N/A
USA	30,882,990	32,783,720	35,480,780	35,244,480	35,186,520	N/A
India	28,230,660	29,825,750	31,698,510	34,502,350	35,128,970	N/A
Brazil	15,981,580	16,355,690	13,592,500	13,217,590	17,953,250	N/A
Nigeria	15,219,250	15,393,080	15,815,040	16,022,980	16,235,930	N/A
France	10,311,660	11,589,730	11,126,010	11,551,990	11,833,770	N/A
Germany	12,160,940	14,846,570	12,473,640	12,762,760	11,451,220	N/A
Iran	8,175,335	9,620,131	9,872,316	11,023,460	11,199,020	N/A
Italy	12,490,180	12,958,890	12,958,890	12,457,560	11,096,080	N/A
Mexico	8,209,982	8,960,619	8,960,619	10,079,980	10,234,500	N/A

Source: Food and Agriculture Organization of the United Nations

Leading Producers and Consumers of Meat in the World

(– = not applicable. N/A = not available. In tonnes.)

Country	1991	1992	1993	1994	1995	1996
Production						
China	31,443,350	34,307,390	38,406,370	44,991,660	52,299,800	58,168,800
USA	29,553,660	30,859,070	31,174,480	32,846,500	33,902,000	34,563,510
Brazil	8,460,203	8,712,318	9,183,951	9,419,637	10,086,890	10,964,890
France	5,995,692	6,019,128	6,025,135	6,110,871	6,312,493	6,325,500
Germany	6,609,283	6,101,572	5,922,789	5,757,194	5,742,749	5,840,349
Russia	–	8,265,400	7,518,000	6,814,900	5,748,200	5,272,000
India	3,945,217	3,974,462	4,080,232	4,183,529	4,272,429	4,294,579
Italy	3,962,465	4,029,396	4,029,426	3,994,813	3,982,803	4,071,782
Spain	3,603,188	3,651,233	3,764,753	3,823,709	3,991,801	3,800,313
Mexico	3,040,828	3,148,089	3,300,125	3,543,209	3,799,026	3,682,136
Consumption						
China	30,839,660	34,013,400	37,963,120	44,497,290	52,041,370	N/A
USA	29,401,960	30,519,770	30,580,460	31,511,010	31,669,330	N/A
Brazil	7,911,928	7,929,163	8,170,616	8,576,899	9,435,759	N/A
Russia	–	8,956,583	8,677,279	8,261,716	7,867,060	N/A
Germany	7,099,309	7,113,228	6,916,651	6,930,990	6,710,716	N/A
France	5,855,648	5,611,446	5,408,744	5,487,398	5,676,443	N/A
Japan	4,751,990	4,925,710	4,975,670	5,054,288	5,480,386	N/A
Italy	4,905,931	4,915,620	4,997,810	4,698,406	4,838,392	N/A
UK	4,187,850	4,359,211	4,176,159	4,271,336	4,277,479	N/A
Mexico	3,391,146	3,578,748	3,763,796	4,112,159	4,129,188	N/A

Source: Food and Agriculture Organization of the United Nations

Leading Producers and Consumers of Rice in the World

(N/A = not available. In tonnes.)

Country	1991	1992	1993	1994	1995	1996
Production						
China	183,381,000	186,222,000	177,514,000	175,933,000	185,226,000	188,000,000
India	112,042,000	109,001,200	120,600,000	121,559,200	119,442,000	120,012,000
Indonesia	44,688,240	48,240,010	48,181,090	46,641,500	49,744,140	51,165,000
Bangladesh	27,377,460	27,510,420	27,048,000	25,311,800	26,398,500	28,008,000
Vietnam	19,621,900	21,590,300	22,836,600	23,528,300	24,963,700	26,300,000
Thailand	20,400,000	19,917,000	18,447,000	21,111,000	21,130,000	21,800,000
Myanmar	13,201,400	14,837,400	16,759,650	18,195,030	19,568,450	20,865,000
Japan	12,005,000	13,216,000	9,793,000	14,976,000	13,435,000	13,000,000
Philippines	9,673,262	9,513,000	9,434,208	10,538,050	10,540,650	11,283,570
Brazil	9,495,938	9,961,899	10,142,930	10,499,460	11,225,990	10,035,400
Consumption						
China	164,113,300	167,707,000	165,817,000	162,347,800	161,812,700	N/A
India	106,046,300	105,512,600	107,047,500	107,781,200	108,499,600	N/A
Indonesia	40,657,770	41,153,670	42,218,050	42,702,300	43,186,750	N/A
Bangladesh	26,361,190	26,310,450	26,082,090	27,123,880	25,940,300	N/A
Vietnam	15,718,560	16,476,310	17,011,250	17,359,920	18,073,190	N/A
Myanmar	13,040,910	13,456,060	13,751,510	14,053,030	14,393,950	N/A
Japan	12,787,120	12,777,970	12,746,830	12,227,060	12,751,120	N/A
Thailand	9,985,858	10,752,370	10,926,320	10,817,250	9,615,474	N/A
Brazil	9,005,368	9,087,296	10,066,320	9,574,531	9,329,073	N/A
Philippines	8,454,783	8,922,573	8,585,584	8,735,625	9,195,880	N/A

Source: Food and Agriculture Organization of the United Nations

Leading Producers and Consumers of Vegetables in the World

(– = not applicable. N/A = not available. In tonnes.)

Country	1991	1992	1993	1994	1995	1996
Production						
China	115,758,200	127,768,200	150,970,300	168,148,000	179,439,100	180,069,100
India	60,469,810	64,363,790	63,385,500	64,769,640	64,828,540	64,828,540
USA	30,199,570	30,198,610	29,661,070	33,854,260	32,579,600	32,801,490
Turkey	13,750,310	14,299,070	14,009,160	14,687,310	16,817,110	15,871,830
Italy	14,503,250	14,400,420	14,090,390	13,941,350	13,634,410	13,634,410
Japan	13,098,600	13,321,770	12,769,230	12,478,540	12,676,320	12,676,320
Russia	–	10,018,000	9,827,000	9,621,000	11,151,000	10,716,000
Korea, South	8,916,135	9,096,055	10,235,680	9,079,910	9,661,394	9,489,394
Spain	9,118,807	9,117,218	8,872,489	9,277,154	8,916,372	9,033,772
Egypt	7,488,350	8,257,396	8,395,387	8,309,462	8,465,231	8,216,546
Consumption						
China	102,423,400	113,083,900	133,718,000	149,084,800	158,993,500	N/A
India	54,339,640	58,068,020	57,622,170	58,904,640	60,536,270	N/A
USA	27,199,650	26,704,600	26,589,310	30,356,170	29,492,240	N/A
Japan	13,170,740	13,455,120	13,166,400	13,268,760	13,650,860	N/A
Russia	–	11,216,880	11,109,860	10,289,490	12,134,760	N/A
Turkey	9,206,318	9,769,251	9,640,027	9,963,400	11,692,750	N/A
Italy	9,779,665	10,151,190	8,599,472	9,296,768	8,551,862	N/A
Korea, South	7,703,212	7,876,244	8,847,310	7,992,936	8,423,441	N/A
Egypt	6,629,544	7,230,130	7,383,972	7,209,162	7,382,572	N/A
France	7,068,513	6,610,338	6,839,176	6,995,448	7,269,806	N/A

Source: Food and Agriculture Organization of the United Nations

Leading Producers and Consumers of Wheat in the World

(– = not applicable. N/A = not available. In tonnes.)

Country	1991	1992	1993	1994	1995	1996
Production						
China	95,950,000	101,587,000	106,390,000	99,297,000	102,207,000	109,000,000
India	55,134,500	55,689,500	57,210,100	59,840,000	65,767,000	62,620,000
USA	53,890,000	67,136,000	65,222,000	63,168,000	59,400,000	62,099,000
France	34,344,610	32,545,880	29,252,200	30,549,000	30,879,000	35,946,000
Russia	–	46,166,700	43,546,550	32,128,600	30,117,600	34,900,000
Canada	31,945,600	29,879,000	27,231,500	22,933,000	25,017,000	30,495,000
Australia	10,557,400	14,738,680	16,543,800	9,035,530	17,262,700	23,497,000
Germany	16,611,970	15,541,660	15,766,500	16,538,600	17,816,000	18,921,700
Turkey	20,418,500	19,318,000	21,016,000	17,514,000	18,015,000	18,515,000
Pakistan	14,565,000	15,684,200	16,156,500	15,213,000	17,002,400	16,907,400
Consumption						
China	94,728,140	95,884,190	98,270,980	97,240,620	95,080,400	N/A
India	49,534,120	48,262,900	49,244,760	51,212,180	53,661,270	N/A
USA	20,954,780	21,671,690	22,636,700	23,144,920	22,766,860	N/A
Russia	–	20,216,410	19,702,590	20,051,450	20,678,010	N/A
Pakistan	15,254,310	16,985,780	16,694,570	17,694,350	17,371,740	N/A
Turkey	11,549,070	11,795,630	12,136,970	12,757,840	12,370,330	N/A
Iran	10,422,870	10,669,690	11,177,890	12,009,970	11,813,460	N/A
Egypt	8,495,301	8,626,253	8,636,915	8,843,073	9,032,486	N/A
Italy	8,628,568	8,351,280	8,149,972	8,023,140	8,454,597	N/A
Ukraine	N/A	7,763,080	7,633,286	7,892,074	7,269,342	N/A

Grain production

Source: Food and Agriculture Organization of the United Nations

World Employment

Agricultural and Non-Agricultural Employment by Country

Data based on US labour force definitions except that the minimum age for population base varies as follows: USA, France, Sweden, and UK, 16 years; Australia, Canada, Germany, Italy (1995), and Japan, 15 years; and Italy (1990), 14 years. For the USA and Italy the data are not comparable between 1990 and 1995. (N/A = not available.)

Industry			Australia	Canada	France	Germany	Italy	Japan	Sweden	UK	USA
Total Employment (thousands)											
1990	Agriculture, forestry, fishing		440	551	1,248	965	1,879	4,270	178	567	3,394
	Industry[1]	manufacturing	1,170	2,105	4,708	8,839	4,755	15,010	943	5,358	21,346
		Total	1,865	3,117	6,425	10,875	6,842[2]	20,890	1,268	7,470	29,834
	Services		5,554	9,497	14,425	16,112	12,355	36,550	3,056	18,603	85,565
	Total		7,859	13,165	22,098	27,952	21,080	61,710	4,501	26,639	118,793
1995	Agriculture, forestry, fishing		412	555	1,015	786[3]	1,482	3,510	143	565[3]	3,592
	Industry[1]	manufacturing	1,117	2,061	N/A	N/A	N/A	14,520	770	N/A	20,493
		Total	1,805	2,957	5,564	9,719[3]	6,488[2]	21,160	1,011	6,391[3]	28,788
	Services		6,018	9,994	15,419	17,399[3]	12,003	39,230	2,891	18,206[3]	92,520
	Total		8,235	13,506	21,998	27,905[3]	19,974	63,900	4,044	25,163[3]	124,900
Percentage Distribution											
1990	Agriculture, forestry, fishing		6	4	6	3	9	7	4	2	3
	Industry[1]	manufacturing	15	16	21	32	23	24	21	20	18
		Total	24	24	29	39	32[2]	34	28	28	25
	Services		71	72	65	58	59	59	68	70	72
	Total		100	100	100	100	100	100	100	100	100
1995	Agriculture, forestry, fishing		5	4	5	3[3]	7	6	3	2[3]	3
	Industry[1]	manufacturing	14	15	N/A	N/A	N/A	23	19	N/A	16
		Total	22	22	25	35[3]	33[2]	33	25	25[3]	23
	Services		73	74	70	62[3]	60	61	72	72[3]	74
	Total		100	100	100	100[3]	100	100	100	100[3]	100

[1] Includes mining and construction.
[2] Public utilities included in industry.
[3] 1994 data.

Source: US Bureau of Labor Statistics

Civilian Employment by Sex in Selected Countries

Country	Civilian employment–population ratio[1]							
	Women				Men			
	1980	1985	1990	1995	1980	1985	1990	1995
Australia	41.9	42.9	49.3	50.3	75.1	70.4	71.2	68.1
Canada	46.7	49.2	54.0	52.1	73.1	69.0	70.1	65.5
France	40.3	40.5	41.6	40.6[2]	68.9	62.4	61.3	58.0[2]
Germany[3]	38.9	37.6[4]	40.9	41.2[2 5]	69.9	65.8[4]	65.6	60.0[2 5]
Italy	27.9	27.8	29.2	28.4[2 4]	66.0	62.5	60.0	56.5[2 4]
Japan	45.7	46.3	48.0	47.7	77.9	75.9	75.4	75.0
Sweden	58.0	59.7	61.8[4]	54.9	73.6	70.5	70.6[4]	62.2
UK	44.8	44.3	49.6	49.0[2 5]	72.8	67.0	69.7	64.7[2 5]
USA	47.7	50.4	54.3[4]	55.6[4]	72.0	70.9	72.0[4]	70.8[2]

[1] Civilian employment as a percentage of the civilian working-age population.
[2] Preliminary.
[3] Former West Germany.
[4] Break in series. Data not comparable with prior years.
[5] 1994 data.

Source: US Bureau of Labor Statistics

Average Remuneration of Chief Executive Officers by Country

(In estimated dollars per annum.)

1997

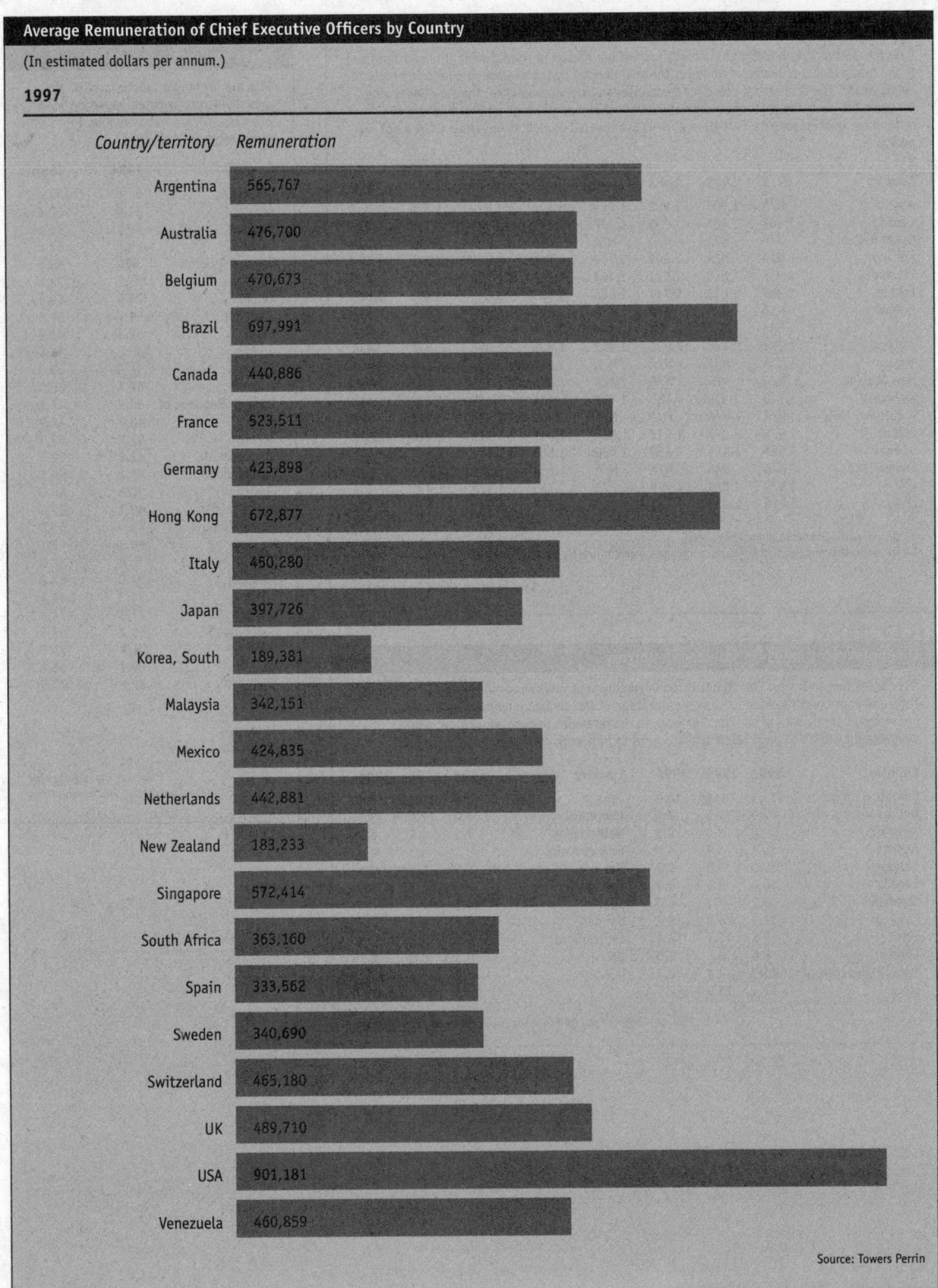

Country/territory	Remuneration
Argentina	565,767
Australia	476,700
Belgium	470,673
Brazil	697,991
Canada	440,886
France	523,511
Germany	423,898
Hong Kong	672,877
Italy	450,280
Japan	397,726
Korea, South	189,381
Malaysia	342,151
Mexico	424,835
Netherlands	442,881
New Zealand	183,233
Singapore	572,414
South Africa	363,160
Spain	333,562
Sweden	340,690
Switzerland	465,180
UK	489,710
USA	901,181
Venezuela	460,859

Source: Towers Perrin

Number of Hours Worked in Selected Countries

Data for are average annual hours actually worked per person in employment. The concept used is the total number of hours worked over the year divided by the average numbers of people in employment. The data are intended for comparisons of trends over time; they are unsuitable for comparisons of the level of average annual hours of work for a given year because of differences in their sources. Part-time workers are covered as well as full-time. (N/A = not available.)

Country	1973	1979	1983	1990	1993	1994	1995	1996
Australia	N/A	1,904	1,852	1,869	1,874	1,879	1,876	1,867
Canada	1,867	1,802	1,731	1,738	1,718	1,735	1,737	1,732
Czech Republic	N/A	N/A	N/A	N/A	N/A	N/A	2,065	2,072
Finland[1]	N/A	N/A	1,809	1,764	1,744	1,780	1,775	1,790
Finland[2]	1,915	1,868	1,821	1,764	1,754	1,768	1,773	N/A
France	1,904	1,813	1,711	1,668	1,639	1,635	1,638	1,645
Germany	N/A	N/A	N/A	N/A	1,607	1,602	1,583	1,578
Italy	1,885	1,788	1,764	N/A	N/A	N/A	N/A	N/A
Japan	2,201	2,126	2,095	2,031	1,905	1,898	N/A	N/A
Mexico	N/A	N/A	N/A	N/A	1,804	N/A	1,834	1,955
New Zealand	N/A	N/A	N/A	1,820	1,844	1,851	1,843	1,838
Norway	1,712	1,516	1,485	1,432	1,434	1,430	1,417	1,410
Portugal	N/A	N/A	N/A	N/A	2,000	2,009	N/A	N/A
Spain	N/A	2,022	1,912	1,824	1,815	1,815	1,814	1,810
Sweden	1,557	1,451	1,453	1,480	1,501	1,532	1,544	1,554
Switzerland	N/A	N/A	N/A	N/A	1,633	1,639	1,643	N/A
UK	1,929	1,821	1,719	1,773	1,715	1,728	1,735	1,732
USA	1,924	1,905	1,882	1,943	1,946	1,945	1,952	1,951

[1] Data estimated from the Labour Force Survey.
[2] Data estimated from National Accounts; total employment figure for 1994 is preliminary.

Source: International Energy Agency

Unemployment Rates by Selected Countries

Data are annual averages. The standardized unemployment rates shown here are calculated as the number of unemployed persons as a percentage of the civilian labour force. The unemployed are persons of working age who, in the reference period, are without work, available for work, and have taken specific steps to find work. (N/A = not available.)

Country	1994	1995	1996	Country	1994	1995	1996
European Union	11.1	10.8	10.9	Japan	2.9	3.1	3.4
OECD	7.9	7.5	7.6	Luxembourg	3.2	2.9	3.1
Australia	9.8	8.6	8.6	Netherlands	7.1	6.9	6.3
Austria	N/A	3.9	4.4	New Zealand	8.1	6.3	6.1
Belgium	10.0	9.9	9.8	Norway	5.5	5.0	4.9
Canada	10.4	9.5	9.7	Portugal	7.0	7.3	7.3
Denmark	8.2	7.1	6.0	Spain	24.1	22.9	22.2
Finland	17.9	16.6	15.7	Sweden	9.8	9.2	10.0
France	12.3	11.7	12.4	Switzerland	3.6	3.3	3.3
Germany	8.4	8.2	9.0	UK	9.6	8.8	8.2
Ireland, Republic of	14.3	12.4	12.3	USA	6.1	5.6	5.4
Italy	11.4	11.9	12.0				

Source: Organization for Economic Cooperation and Development

Female Labour Force Participation Rates by Country

Data are for female labour force of all ages divided by female population 15–64 years old. (N/A = not available. In percentages.)

Country	1984	1994
Australia	52.8	63.4
Austria	51.5	62.1
Belgium	48.7[1]	55.1[2]
Canada	63.5	67.8
Czech Republic	N/A	65.6
Denmark	73.8	73.8
Finland	72.9	69.9
France	54.7	59.6
Germany	52.3[3]	61.8
Greece	40.9	44.6
Hungary	N/A	53.0
Iceland	62.7	80.0
Ireland, Republic of	36.9	47.2
Italy	40.7	42.9
Japan	57.2	62.1
Korea, South	43.8	52.7
Luxembourg	42.2	56.5
Mexico	N/A	40.0
Netherlands	40.7	57.4
New Zealand	46.0	65.0
Norway	66.3	71.1
Poland	N/A	62.0
Portugal	56.0	62.2
Spain	33.2	44.1
Sweden	77.3	74.4
Switzerland	55.7	67.5
Turkey	N/A	33.7
UK	59.1	66.2
USA	62.8	70.5

[1] 1983 data.
[2] 1993 data.
[3] Former West Germany.

Source: Organization for Economic Cooperation and Development

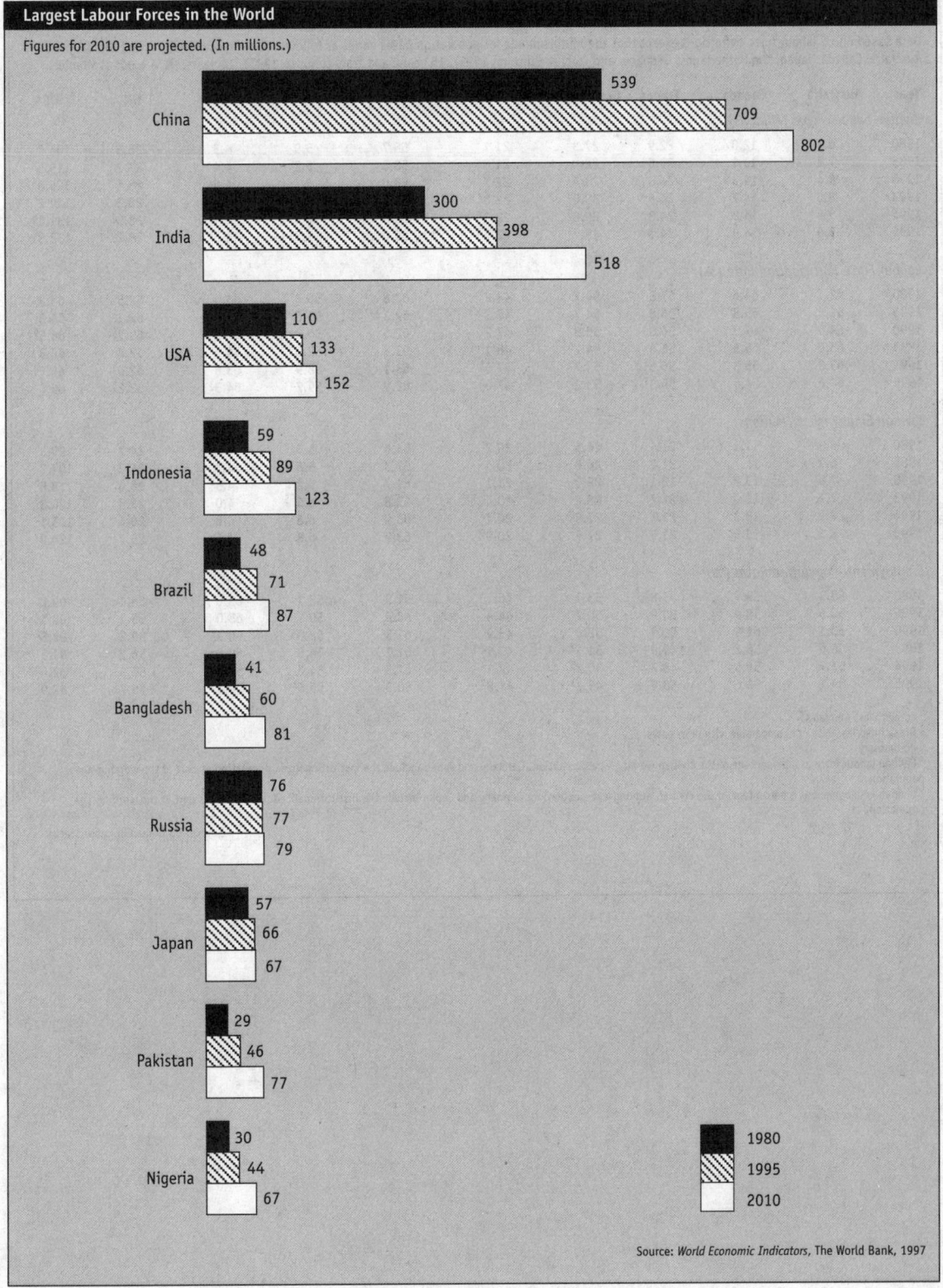

Largest Labour Forces in the World

Figures for 2010 are projected. (In millions.)

China — 539, 709, 802
India — 300, 398, 518
USA — 110, 133, 152
Indonesia — 59, 89, 123
Brazil — 48, 71, 87
Bangladesh — 41, 60, 81
Russia — 76, 77, 79
Japan — 57, 66, 67
Pakistan — 29, 46, 77
Nigeria — 30, 44, 67

■ 1980
▨ 1995
□ 2010

Source: *World Economic Indicators*, The World Bank, 1997

Civilian Labour Force and Employment by Country

Data based on US labour force definitions except that the minimum age for population bases varies as follows: USA, France, Sweden, and UK, 16 years; Australia, Canada, Japan, the Netherlands, Germany, and Italy (beginning 1993), 15 years; and Italy (prior to 1993), 14 years. (N/A = not available.)

Year	Australia	Canada	France	Germany[1]	Italy	Japan	Netherlands	Sweden	UK	USA
Civilian Labour Force (Millions)										
1980	6.7	12.0	22.9	27.3	21.1	55.7	5.9	4.3	26.5	106.9
1985	7.3	13.1	23.6	28.0	21.8	58.8	6.2	4.4	27.2	115.5
1990	8.4	14.3	24.3	29.4	22.7	63.0	6.7	4.6[2]	28.5	125.8[2]
1993	8.6	14.7	24.6	30.0[3]	22.8[2][3]	65.5	7.1	4.4	28.3	129.2
1994	8.8	14.8	24.8	29.8[3]	22.6[3]	65.8	7.2	4.4	28.3	131.1[2]
1995	9.0	14.9	24.8	29.7[3]	22.7[3]	66.0	7.3	4.5	28.2	132.3
Labour Force Participation Rate (%)[4]										
1980	62.1	64.6	57.5	54.7	48.2	62.6	55.4	66.9	62.5	63.8
1985	61.6	65.8	56.8	54.7	47.2	62.3	55.5	66.9	62.1	64.8
1990	64.6	67.3	56.0	55.3	47.2	62.6	56.3	67.4[3]	63.7	66.5[2]
1993	63.6	65.5	55.6	54.2[3]	48.1[2][3]	63.3	58.6	64.5	62.8	66.3
1994	63.9	65.3	55.5[3]	53.7[3]	47.5[3]	63.1	58.9	63.8	62.6[3]	66.6[2]
1995	64.6	64.8	55.3[3]	53.1[3]	47.6[3]	62.9	59.7[3]	64.3[3]	62.2[3]	66.6
Civilian Employment (Millions)										
1980	6.3	11.1	21.4	26.5	20.2	54.6	5.5	4.2	24.7	99.3
1985	6.7	11.7	21.2	26.0	20.5	57.3	5.6	4.3	24.2	107.2
1990	7.9	13.2	22.1	28.0	21.1	61.7	6.2	4.5[2]	26.6	118.8[2]
1993	7.7	13.0	21.7	28.2[3]	20.4[2][3]	63.8	6.6	4.0	25.3	120.3
1994	7.9	13.3	21.7	27.9[3]	20.1[3]	63.9	6.6	4.0	25.6[3]	123.1[2]
1995	8.2	13.5	21.9	27.7[3]	20.0[3]	63.9	6.8	4.1	25.7[3]	124.9
Employment–Population Ratio (%)[5]										
1980	58.3	59.7	53.8	53.1	46.1	61.3	52.1	65.6	58.1	59.2
1985	56.5	58.9	50.9	50.7	44.4	60.6	50.1	65.0	55.1	60.1
1990	60.1	61.9	50.9	52.6	43.9	61.3	52.8	66.1[2]	59.2	62.8[2]
1993	56.6	58.2	49.0	51.1[3]	43.1[2][3]	61.7	54.8	58.5	56.2	61.7
1994	57.7	58.5	48.7	50.2[3]	42.1[3]	61.3	54.6	57.6	56.5[3]	62.5[2]
1995	59.1	58.6	48.8[3]	49.7[3]	41.8[3]	60.9	55.4[3]	58.4[3]	56.7[3]	62.9

[1] Former West Germany.
[2] Break in series. Data not comparable with prior years.
[3] Preliminary.
[4] Civilian labour force as a percentage of the civilian working-age population. Germany and Japan include the institutionalized population as part of the working-age population.
[5] Civilian employment as a percentage of the civilian working-age population. Germany and Japan include the institutionalized population as part of the working-age population.

Source: US Bureau of Labor Statistics

International Economic Organizations

African Development Bank (ADB) Bank founded in 1963 by the Organization of African Unity to promote and finance economic development across the African continent. Its members include 52 African and 25 non-African countries. Its headquarters are in Abidja'n, Côte d'Ivoire.

Arab Monetary Fund (AMF) Money reserve established in 1976 by 20 Arab states plus the Palestine Liberation Organization to provide a mechanism for promoting greater stability in exchange rates and to coordinate Arab economic and monetary policies. It operates mainly by regulating petrodollars within the Arab community to make member countries less dependent on the West for the handling of their surplus money. The Fund's headquarters are in Abu Dhabi in the United Arab Emirates.

Asian Development Bank (ADB) Bank founded in 1966 to stimulate growth in Asia and the Far East by administering direct loans and technical assistance. Members include 40 countries within the region and 16 countries of western Europe and North America. The Bank's headquarters are in Manila, the Philippines.

Asia-Pacific Economic Cooperation (APEC) Trade group comprising 18 Pacific Asian countries, formed in November 1989 to promote multilateral trade and economic cooperation between member states. Its members are the USA, Canada, Japan, Australia, New Zealand, South Korea, Brunei, Indonesia, Malaysia, the Philippines, Singapore, Thailand, China, Hong Kong, Taiwan, Papua New Guinea, Chile, and Mexico. In 1995 APEC members accounted for more than 50 percent of the world's economic production and 41 percent of its overall trade value. The group's headquarters are in Singapore, Singapore.

Bank for International Settlements (BIS) Organization established in 1930 whose function is to promote cooperation between central banks and to facilitate international financial settlements; it is also a centre for economic and monetary research. Central banks of the main trading states are members, each providing a director to the board, which meets at least ten times a year. The Bank was largely superseded by the International Monetary Fund. Its liaising role among central banks is its primary function today. The BIS is based in Basel, Switzerland.

Central American Common Market (CACM)/Mercado Común Centro-americana (MCCA) Economic alliance established in 1960 by El Salvador, Guatemala, Honduras, and Nicaragua (seceded 1970); Costa Rica joined in 1962. Formed to encourage economic development and cooperation between the smaller Central American nations and to attract industrial capital, CACM failed to live up to early expectations: nationalist interests remained strong and by

the mid-1980s political instability in the region and border conflicts between members were hindering its activities. Its offices are in Guatemala City, Guatemala.

Colombo Plan Plan for cooperative economic and social development in Asia and the Pacific, established in 1950. The 26 member countries are Afghanistan, Australia, Bangladesh, Bhutan, Cambodia, Canada, Fiji, India, Indonesia, Iran, Japan, South Korea, Laos, Malaysia, Maldives, Myanmar, Nepal, New Zealand, Pakistan, Papua New Guinea, the Philippines, Singapore, Sri Lanka, Thailand, the UK, and the USA. They meet annually to discuss economic and development plans such as irrigation, hydroelectric schemes, and technical training.

Comecon Acronym for Council for Mutual Economic Assistance (CMEA). Economic organization in operation 1949–91 which linked the Union of Soviet Socialist Republics (USSR) with Bulgaria, Czechoslovakia, Hungary, Poland, Romania, East Germany (1950–90), Mongolia (from 1962), Cuba (from 1972), and Vietnam (from 1978), with Yugoslavia as an associated member. Albania also belonged 1949–61. Its establishment was prompted by the Marshall Plan. Comecon was formally disbanded in June 1991.

Commonwealth of Independent States (CIS) Successor body to the Union of Soviet Socialist Republics (USSR), initially formed as a new commonwealth of Slav republics on 8 December 1991, by the presidents of the Russian Federation, Belarus, and Ukraine. On 21 December, eight of the nine remaining non-Slav republics – Moldova, Tajikistan, Armenia, Azerbaijan, Turkmenistan, Kazakhstan, Kyrgyzstan, and Uzbekistan – joined the CIS at a meeting held in Kazakhstan's capital, Alma-Ata (now Almaty). The CIS formally came into existence in January 1992 when President Gorbachev resigned and the Soviet government voted itself out of existence. Georgia joined in 1994. Its headquarters are in Minsk (Mensk), Belarus.

The CIS has no real, formal political institutions and its role is uncertain. The main objectives in founding the Commonwealth were to ensure that some measure of cooperation continued in economic, financial, and monetary matters in order to avert a collapse in inter-republican trade and to coordinate price liberalization and market reform; to maintain some degree of coordination in foreign (and especially military) policy, and in such areas as transport and communications; and to ensure recognition of borders and thus prevent inter-republican conflicts. CIS decisions are arrived at through the holding of regular summits of heads of state and through the formation of ministerial committees, with, in theory, all CIS members being equals; however, some members have complained of its domination by Russia.

Communauté Économique des États de l'Afrique Centrale (CEEAC)/Economic Community of Central African States Organization formed in 1983 to foster economic cooperation between member states, which include Burundi, Cameroon, the Central African Republic, Chad, the Republic of the Congo, Equatorial Guinea, Gabon, Rwanda, São Tomé and Principe, and the Democratic Republic of Congo (formerly Zaire). Angola has observer status. The Community's headquarters are in Libreville, Gabon.

Communauté Économique des États de l'Afrique de l'Ouest/Economic Community of West African States (ECOWAS) Organization promoting economic cooperation and development, established in 1975 by the Treaty of Lagos. Its members include Benin, Burkina Faso, Cape Verde, the Gambia, Ghana, Guinea, Guinea-Bissau, Côte d'Ivoire, Liberia, Mali, Mauritania, Niger, Nigeria, Senegal, Sierra Leone, and Togo. Its headquarters are in Lagos, Nigeria.

Economic Cooperation Organization (ECO) Islamic regional grouping formed in 1985 by Iran, Pakistan, and Turkey to reduce customs tariffs and promote commerce, with the aim of eventual customs union. In 1992 the newly independent republics of Azerbaijan, Kyrgyzstan, Tajikistan, Turkmenistan, and Uzbekistan were admitted into the ECO. The headquarters are in Tehran, Iran.

European Bank for Reconstruction and Development (EBRD) International bank established in 1991, with an initial capital of 10 billion European Currency Units (ECUs), to assist the economic reconstruction of central and eastern Europe. The Bank aims to help central and eastern European countries to implement structural and sectoral economic reform, including demonopolization, decentralization, and privatization. The EBRD has 60 members: 58 countries, including 26 countries in central and eastern Europe and the Commonwealth of Independent States, the European Union and the European Investment Bank. Each member appoints a Governor and an Alternate. The Board of Governors delegates power to a Board of Directors, responsible for the direction of the general operations of the Bank. The President is elected by the Board of Governors. The Bank's headquarters are in London, UK.

European Economic Area Agreement 1991 between the European Community and the European Free Trade Association (EFTA) to create a zone of economic cooperation, allowing their 380 million citizens to transfer money, shares, and bonds across national borders and to live, study, or work in one another's countries. The pact, which took effect Jan 1994, was seen as a temporary arrangement since most EFTA members hoped, eventually, to join the EU.

European Free Trade Association (EFTA)
Organization established in 1960 consisting of Iceland, Norway, Switzerland, and Liechtenstein (from 1991), previously a nonvoting associate member. There are no import duties between members. Of the original EFTA members, the UK and Denmark left in 1972 to join the European Community (EC), as did Portugal in 1985; Austria, Finland, and Sweden joined the EC's successor, the European Union, in 1995. In 1973 the EC signed agreements with EFTA members, setting up a free-trade area of over 300 million consumers. Trade between the two groups amounted to over half of total EFTA trade. A further pact signed in October 1991 between the EC and EFTA provided for a European Economic Area (EEA), allowing EFTA greater access to the EC market by ending many restrictions. The EEA came into effect in January 1994.

European Monetary System (EMS)
Attempt by the European Union (formerly the European Community) to bring financial cooperation and monetary stability to Europe. It was established in 1979 in the wake of the 1974 oil crisis, which brought growing economic disruption to European economies because of floating exchange rates. Central to the EMS is the Exchange Rate Mechanism (ERM), a voluntary system of semi-fixed exchange rates based on the European Currency Unit (ECU).

European Monetary Union (EMU) The proposed European Union policy for a single currency and common economic policies. The proposal was announced by what was then a European Community (EC) committee headed by EC Commission president Jacques Delors in April 1989. Three stages are envisaged for EMU. In the first stage, all controls on individual nations' capital flow would be ended, and the European System of Central Banks (ESCB) created. In stage two, the ESCB would begin to regulate money supply. Finally, exchange rates between member states would be fixed; a single European currency would be created; and the ESCB would take over the function of the member nations' central banks.

European Union (EU) Formerly (to 1993) the European Community (EC). Political and economic alliance consisting of the European Coal and Steel Community (1952), the European Economic Community (EEC, popularly called the Common Market, 1957), and the European Atomic Energy Community (Euratom, 1957). The original six members – Belgium, France, West Germany, Italy, Luxembourg, and the Netherlands – were joined by the UK, Denmark, and the Republic of Ireland in 1973, Greece in 1981, and Spain and Portugal in 1986. East Germany was incorporated on German reunification in 1990. Membership terms were agreed in March 1994 for Norway, but membership was rejected by referendum in November 1994. Austria, Finland, and Sweden joined in 1995. Association agreements, providing for free trade within ten years and the possibility of full membership, were signed with Czechoslovakia, Hungary, and Poland in 1991, Romania in 1992, and later with Bulgaria and Slovakia. Estonia and Latvia applied for full membership in 1995. A customs pact with Turkey, which was approved in December 1995, was seen as the first step towards Turkey's full membership; however, the move has been criticized by human-rights activists. In July 1997 the European Commission agreed that Estonia, Poland, the Czech Republic, Hungary, Slovenia, and Cyprus, should commence entry talks for the EU's expansion into central and eastern Europe. There are more than 360 million people in the EU countries.

A European Charter of Social Rights was approved at the Maastricht summit in December 1991 by all members except the UK. The same meeting secured agreement on a treaty framework for European union, including political and monetary union, and for a new system of police and military cooperation. After initial rejection by Denmark in a national referendum in June 1992, the Maastricht Treaty on European union came into effect on 1 November 1993, and the new designation European Union was adopted, embracing not only the various bodies of its predecessor, the EC, but also two intergovernmental 'pillars', covering common foreign and security policy and cooperation on justice and home affairs. In September 1995 the EU's member nations stated their commitment to the attainment of monetary union by 1999, and in December of the same year they agreed to call the new currency the 'euro'.

The aims of the EU include the expansion of trade, reduction of competition, the abolition of restrictive trading practices, the encouragement of free movement of capital and labour within the alliance, and the establishment of a closer union among European people. A single market with free movement of goods and capital was established in January 1993. The EU reached agreement on closer economic and political cooperation with 12 Middle Eastern and North African countries in the Barcelona Declaration in November 1995, and an agreement between the USA and the EU to move towards closer economic and political cooperation was signed in December 1995.

The EU has the following institutions: the European Commission of 20 members (two members each from France, Germany, Italy, Spain, and the UK; and one each from Austria, Belgium, Denmark, Finland, Greece, the Republic of Ireland, Luxembourg, the Netherlands, Portugal, and Sweden) pledged to independence of national interests, who initiate Union action; the Council of Ministers of the European Union, which makes decisions on the Commission's proposals; the European Parliament, directly elected from 1979; the Economic and Social Committee, a consultative body; the Committee of Permanent Representatives consisting of civil servants temporarily seconded by member states to work for the Commission; and the European Court of Justice, to safeguard interpretation of the Rome Treaties (1957) that established the original alliance. The European Commission is based in Brussels, Belgium.

General Agreement on Tariffs and Trade (GATT) Organization within the United Nations founded in 1948 with the aim of encouraging free trade between nations by reducing tariffs, subsidies, quotas, and regulations that discriminate against imported products. GATT was effectively replaced by the World Trade Organization in January 1995. During the last round of talks, begun in 1986 in Uruguay, the USA opposed European Community (EC) restrictions on agricultural imports, but argued to maintain restrictions on textile imports to the USA. Talks repeatedly stalled over a plan to reduce farm subsidies, but the round eventually ended in 1993 when negotiators from the European Union (formerly, to 1993, the EC) and USA reached agreement, and the resulting Final Act was signed on 15 April 1994, in Marrakesh, Morocco.

Group of Seven (G7) Group made up of the seven leading industrial nations of the world: the USA, Japan, Germany, France, the UK, Italy, and Canada, which together account for more than three-fifths of global GDP. Since 1975 their heads of government have met once a year to discuss economic and, increasingly, political matters. The Group formed with the aim of coordinating international management of exchange rates following the collapse of the Bretton Woods system of fixed rates. However, its intervention in the mid-1980s was later blamed for the 1987 stock-market crash. The annual summits are also attended by the president of the European Commission and, from 1991, Russia. Russia has been an equal partner in political consultations since 1994.

Inter-American Development Bank (IADB) Bank founded in 1959, at the instigation of the Organization of American States, to finance economic and social development, particularly in the less wealthy regions of the Americas. Its 46 members include the states of Central and Southern America, the Caribbean, and the USA, as well as Austria, Belgium, Canada, Denmark, Finland, France, Germany, Israel, Italy, Japan, the Netherlands, Norway, Portugal, Spain, Sweden, Switzerland, and the UK. The Bank's headquarters are in Washington, DC.

International Monetary Fund (IMF) Specialized agency of the United Nations with its headquarters in Washington, DC, established under the 1944 Bretton Woods agreement and operational since 1947. It seeks to promote international monetary cooperation and the growth of world trade, and to smooth multilateral payment arrangements among member states. IMF standby loans are available to members in balance-of-payments difficulties (the amount being governed by the member's quota), usually on the basis that the country must agree to take certain corrective measures. The IMF also operates other drawing facilities, including several designed to provide preferential credit to developing countries with liquidity problems. Having previously operated in US dollars linked to gold, since 1972 the IMF has used the special drawing right (SDR) as its standard unit of account, valued in terms of a weighted 'basket' of currencies. Since 1971, IMF rules have been progressively adapted to floating exchange rates.

Asociación Latino-Americana de Integración (ALADI)/Latin American Integration Association (LAIA) Organization established to create a common market in Latin America. To promote trade, it applies tariff reductions preferentially on the basis of the different stages of economic development that individual member countries have reached. Formed in 1980 to replace the Latin American Free Trade Association, it has 11 members: Argentina, Bolivia, Brazil, Chile, Colombia, Ecuador, Mexico, Paraguay, Peru, Uruguay, and Venezuela. Its headquarters are in Montevideo, Uruguay.

Lomé Convention Convention in 1975 that established economic cooperation between the European Community (now the European Union) and African, Caribbean, and Pacific countries. It was renewed in 1979 and 1985.

Mercado Comun del Cono Sur (Mercosur)/Southern Cone Common Market Free-trade organization, founded in 1991 on the signing of the Asunción Treaty by Argentina, Brazil, Paraguay, and Uruguay, and formally inaugurated on 1 January 1995. With a GNP of $800,000 million and a population of more than 190 million, Mercosur constitutes the world's fourth-largest free-trade bloc after the European Economic Area, the North American Free Trade Area, and the Asia-Pacific Economic Cooperation. Mercosur's headquarters are in Buenos Aires, Argentina.

North American Free Trade Agreement (NAFTA) Trade agreement between the USA, Canada, and Mexico, agreed in August 1992 and effective from January 1994. The first trade pact of its kind to link two highly-industrialized countries to a developing one, it created a free market of 360 million people, with a total GDP of $6.45 trillion. Tariffs were to be progressively eliminated over a 10–15 year period and investment into low-wage Mexico by Canada and the USA progressively increased. Chile was invited to join in December 1994.

Organisation Commune Africaine et Mauricienne (OCAM)/Joint African and Mauritian Organization Organization founded in 1965 to strengthen the solidarity and close ties between member states, raise living standards, and coordinate economic policies. OCAM works closely with the Organization of African Unity. The membership includes Benin, Burkina Faso, the Central African Republic, Côte d'Ivoire, Niger, Rwanda, Senegal, and Togo. Through the organization, members share an airline, a

merchant fleet, and a common postal and communications system. The headquarters of OCAM are in Bangui in the Central African Republic.

Organization for Economic Cooperation and Development (OECD) International organization of 30 industrialized countries that provides a forum for discussion and coordination of member states' economic and social policies. Founded in 1961, the OECD superseded the Organization for European Economic Cooperation, which had been established in 1948 to implement the Marshall Plan. The Commission of the European Union also participates in the OECD's work. The OECD's subsidiary bodies include the International Energy Agency which was set up in 1974 in the face of a world oil crisis. The scope of the OECD also includes development aid. Members are: Australia, Austria, Belgium, Canada, the Czech Republic, Denmark, Finland, France, Germany, Greece, Iceland, the Republic of Ireland, Italy, Japan, Luxembourg, Mexico, the Netherlands, New Zealand, Norway, Portugal, Spain, Sweden, Switzerland, Turkey, the UK, and the USA; Hungary, Poland, and Slovakia joined in 1996, and South Korea in 1997. The headquarters are in Paris, France.

Organization of African Unity (OAU) Association established in 1963 to eradicate colonialism and improve economic, cultural, and political cooperation in Africa. There are now 53 members representing virtually the whole of central, southern, and northern Africa. The French-speaking Organisation Commune Africaine et Mauricienne/Joint African and Mauritian Organization works within the framework of the OAU for African solidarity. The OAU's headquarters are in Addis Ababa, Ethiopia.

Organization of Arab Petroleum Exporting Countries (OAPEC) Body established in 1968 to safeguard the interests of its members and encourage economic cooperation within the petroleum industry. Its members are Algeria, Bahrain, Egypt, Iraq, Kuwait, Libya, Qatar, Saudi Arabia, Syria, and the United Arab Emirates. OAPEC's headquarters are in Safat, Kuwait.

Organization of Petroleum Exporting Countries (OPEC) Body established in 1960 to coordinate price and supply policies of oil-producing states. Its concerted action in raising prices in the 1970s triggered worldwide recession but also lessened demand so that its influence was reduced by the mid-1980s. OPEC members in 1996 were: Algeria, Gabon, Indonesia, Iran, Iraq, Kuwait, Libya, Nigeria, Qatar, Saudi Arabia, the United Arab Emirates, and Venezuela. Its headquarters are in Vienna, Austria.

Common Market for Eastern and Southern African Countries (COMESA) Organization established in 1981 as the Preferential Trade Area of Eastern and Southern African States (PTA) with the object of increasing economic and commercial cooperation between member states, har-

monizing tariffs, and reducing trade barriers. The PTA developed into a common market in 1993. The countries signing the treaty were: Eritrea, Ethiopia, Kenya, Lesotho, Madagascar, Malawi, Mauritius, Mozambique, Namibia, Rwanda, Sudan, Swaziland, Tanzania, Uganda, Zambia, and Zimbabwe.

Southern African Development Community (SADC) Formerly (to 1992) Southern African Development Coordination Conference (SADCC). Established in April 1980, SADCC's original aim was to promote regional independence from the economic dominance of the Republic of South Africa. With the adoption of the new name, the organization recast its objective as increased regional coordination and cooperation for mutual benefit. The community comprises 12 member states. The Republic of South Africa joined in 1994. Its headquarters are in Gaborone, Botswana.

South Asian Association for Regional Cooperation   (SAARC) Organization established in 1985 by India, Pakistan, Bangladesh, Nepal, Sri Lanka, Bhutan, and the Maldives to cover agriculture, telecommunications, health, population, sports, art, and culture. In 1993 a preferential trade agreement was adopted to reduce tariffs on intra-regional trade. SAARC's headquarters are in Kathmandu, Nepal.

World Bank Popular name for the International Bank for Reconstruction and Development, a specialized agency of the United Nations that borrows in the commercial market and lends on commercial terms. It was established in 1945 under the 1944 Bretton Woods agreement, which also created the International Monetary Fund. The International Development Association is an arm of the World Bank. Control of the bank is vested in a board of executives representing national governments, whose votes are apportioned according to the amount they have funded the bank. Thus, the USA has nearly 20 percent of the vote and always appoints the board's president. In 1992 the World Bank made a net transfer of $49.7 million to developing countries. The World Bank is based in Washington, DC.

World Trade Organization (WTrO) World trade monitoring body established in January 1995, on approval of the Final Act of the Uruguay round of the General Agreement on Tariffs and Trade (GATT). Under the Final Act, the WTrO, a permanent trading body with a status commensurate with that of the International Monetary Fund or the World Bank, effectively replaced GATT. The WTrO monitors agreements to reduce barriers to trade, such as tariffs, subsidies, quotas, and regulations which discriminate against imported products. All members of GATT were automatically to become members of the WTrO on their parliaments' ratification of the Uruguay round; new members, without exception, would have to meet the criteria established by the Uruguay round. WTrO headquarters are in Geneva, Switzerland.

See Also   International Political Organizations (The World)

UK Economy

Balance of Payments of the UK

(In millions of pounds.)

Category		1986	1988	1990	1992	1994	1996
Current Account							
Trade in goods	exports[1]	72,627	80,346	101,718	107,343	134,664	166,340
	imports[1]	82,186	101,826	120,527	120,447	145,793	178,938
	Balance	−9,559	−21,480	−18,809	−13,104	−11,129	−12,598
Services balance		6,223	3,957	3,689	4,950	4,776	7,142
Investment income		4,629	4,566	1,269	3,124	9,667	9,652
Transfers balance		−2,157	−3,518	−4,896	−5,102	−4,969	−4,631
Current balance		−864	−16,475	−18,746	−10,133	−1,655	−435
Transactions in External Assets and Liabilities[2]							
Investment overseas by UK residents	direct	−11,649	−20,863	−10,490	−10,850	−21,982	−28,560
	portfolio	−22,288	−11,209	−17,206	−27,346	−18,448	−60,691
	Total	−33,937	−32,072	−27,696	−38,196	−3,534	−89,251
Investment in the UK by overseas residents	direct	5,837	12,006	18,514	9,184	6,087	20,758
	portfolio	11,982	20,603	11,763	24,616	32,928	27,701
	Total	17,819	32,609	30,277	33,800	39,015	48,459
Foreign currency lending abroad by UK banks		−47,288	−14,176	−35,980	−16,066	−48,487	−55,589
Foreign currency borrowing abroad by UK banks		59,811	19,570	34,318	18,598	41,255	78,136
Net foreign currency transactions of UK banks		12,523	5,394	−1,662	2,532	−7,232	22,547
Sterling lending abroad by UK banks		−5,822	−4,609	−3,805	−10,767	308	−7,737
Sterling borrowing and deposit liabilities abroad by UK banks		5,317	13,724	12,658	2,610	6,128	3,411
Net sterling transactions of UK banks		−505	9,115	8,853	−8,157	6,436	−11,148
Deposits with and lending to banks abroad by the UK non-bank private sector		−3,094	−4,026	−8,491	−6,151	−7,904	−10,821
Borrowing from banks abroad by	UK non-bank private sector	3,816	3,977	10,388	9,998	−1,381	33,629
	public corporations	−31	−253	−124	−440	−118	−14
	general government	100	−10	−496	1,221	−133	−79
Official reserves (− = additions to; + = drawings on)		−2,891	−2,761	−76	1,407	−1,045	1,966
Other external assets of	UK non-bank private sector and public corporations	1,848	1,036	−3,342	−11,145	26,416	−55,751
	general government	−509	−887	−1,025	−682	−619	−653
Other external liabilities of	UK non-bank private sector and public corporations	871	1,823	8,757	23,393	−53,908	61,088
	general government	171	974	1,180	−2,596	633	−713
Net transactions in assets and liabilities		−3,820	14,917	16,543	4,986	−3,374	−2,198
Balancing item		4,684	1,558	2,203	5,147	5,029	2,633

[1] On free on board (f.o.b.) basis.
[2] Assets: − = increase; + = decrease. Liabilities: + = increase; − = decrease.

Source: Office for National Statistics. © Crown copyright 1998

See Also   **UK Population and Demography (The United Kingdom)**

UK Economy: Review

Hannah Beecham

One Year – Two Governments

Five months into 1997 the UK Labour Party won the general election and took over from 18 years of Conservative government. At that time, economic recovery had been sustained for five years. Consumer spending was up, house prices recovering, unemployment falling, and Britain's economy was seen to outpace those of other major European countries. Despite such optimism, Labour won voters' hearts on the promise of no more 'stop-go, boom-bust' economic rides. Halfway through the year, the new chancellor, Gordon Brown, delivered his first budget announcing government spending and borrowing plans which fell well within the budget-deficit and government debt criteria for European single currency membership (although there is little intention to join up for another five years). The economy gathered momentum and ended the year in robust form.

The Golden Twins of Fiscal Policy

Chancellor Gordon Brown's July budget promised two fiscal-policy 'golden rules': first, that the government would only borrow to invest and, second, the ratio of government debt to GDP would be 'stable and prudent'. By the year end, public finances seemed to be in good shape and set to improve further, thanks to tight control of government spending and a buoyant economy.

In 1997, public spending accounted for 41 percent of GDP (a tightening of 2.5 percent). Although the public sector borrowing requirement (PSBR) was forecast by the previous government for 1997–98 to be £19 billion, the 'New Labour' government's projected plan for public spending and revenues anticipates the deficit to fall over the next five years. Proving that such an ambition might be possible, the budget deficit was reduced from £22.7 billion (April 1997) to £5 billion (April 1998). Such success was won through the economy pushing up tax revenues, an increase in the oil surplus, and a tighter control on public spending which included a squeeze on social security spending.

The Bank's in Charge

The new government, cautious about sterling's strength and GDP growth of 3.7 percent by year end, spent the year seeking methods to ease inflationary pressures. In a surprise move, the Chancellor handed over to the Bank of England's Monetary Policy Committee operational independence in setting interest rates with an overall goal to keep inflation (excluding mortgage interest payments) to 2.5 percent. Between May and November there were five quarter-point increases in interest rates leading up to 7.25 percent and by the year end inflation was 2.8 percent.

Unemployment's Record Plummet

By the end of 1997, Britain's unemployment rate had taken its 21st consecutive fall to a 17-year low of 5.1 percent – the lowest figure since 1980. The July budget introduced a welfare-to-work programme financed to the tune of £3.5 billion by a windfall tax on excess profits of the privatized utilities (bringing in a total of £5.2 billion). Inducements for companies to hire unemployed young people came in the form of subsidies and additional funding for training. Average wages throughout 1997 continued to grow by about 4.2 percent year-on-year, but the rate of increase was expected to slow by 1998.

Taking Stock of Sales

Despite sales rising by 4.8 percent over the course of 1997, it was a bumpy ride for retailers. Buoyed by the promise of a summer surge in spending, as consumers clutched around £25 million in cash windfalls from the conversion of mutual societies into limited companies, this fillip to consumer spending was short-lived. Autumn's sales figures were completely distorted following the death of the Princess of Wales, as shoppers stayed away to mourn. This, coined the Diana effect, meant retailers had to hold out for a busy Christmas season, but the mild weather discounted much interest in winter clothing, and hopes were not realized until the new year's January sales.

A Bull Run ... For Some

Investors were bullish about the UK equity markets throughout 1997 and were rewarded by seeing the stock market reach an all-time high, pushing through the 5,000 barrier and finishing the year end up 29.2 percent.

Corporate-earnings growth for the year wasput between 8.5 and 9 percent, but the fall-out from the economic crisis in Asia took its toll on some sectors. Still, the UK fared better than some exporting competitors since, during the first quarter of 1997, all of Asia (excluding Japan) only accounted for 9 percent of Britain's exports. However, worries persisted for those companies with huge investments in Asia: in the latter half of 1997 Britain's exports to Thailand were down 22 percent on the previous year, and sales to South Korea decreased by 5 percent. Those sectors with more than 20 percent of their total sales in the Asia/Pacific region are extractive industries, chemicals, and retail banks.

Across the general industrials group, only one sector, buildings and construction, saw earnings upgraded over the year. This sector, dominated by the domestic economy, found relief in the residential housing market, where the outlook remained positive.

The FTSE 100 stocks led the pack, thanks to a strong performance amongst financials, oils, and pharmaceuticals, while mid-cap stocks remained broadly unchanged over the year. UK smaller companies picked up, but only just, as the FTSE Smaller Companies Index rose by 2.6 percent. Much of the improvement on a generally flat year occurred in October, when their larger counterparts were hurt by the Asian crisis. This disparity in performance reflected concerns that sterling's strength would be worse for smaller and mid-cap stocks given their export bias, coupled with investor preference to support the relative earnings security of the larger companies.

What Next?

The government forecast a growth in the economy through 1998 of 2–2.5 percent and by 1.75–2.25 percent in 1999. Underlying inflation is forecast at 2.75 percent over 1998, falling to the 1999 target of 2.5 percent. Extra spending will test budgeting skills as 1998 will see £500 million more spent on health and an extra £250 million on education. Over the next three years, the 'green budget' has allotted an extra £500 million for public transport. Clouds that could blot the government's vista include a further strengthening of sterling – a very real concern given that it has appreciated by about 25 percent in real terms in the past two years – and a runaway economy before measures encouraging private sector saving take hold.

Consumer Expenditure by Commodity in the UK

(In millions of pounds at 1990 prices.)

Commodity	1986	1987	1988	1989	1990	1991	1992	1993	1994	1995	1996
Durable Goods											
Cars, motorcycles, and other vehicles	15,552	16,525	19,410	21,031	19,034	15,782	14,767	16,140	17,259	17,582	18,666
Furniture and floor coverings	5,573	6,043	6,858	6,748	6,422	6,070	6,137	6,680	7,186	6,912	7,168
Other durable goods	6,802	7,829	8,785	9,090	9,220	9,355	9,906	10,635	11,711	13,170	14,580
Other Goods											
Food (household expenditure)	39,610	40,621	41,542	42,247	41,817	41,869	42,384	42,801	43,458	43,581	44,862
Beer	11,595	11,822	11,960	11,956	11,904	11,438	10,724	10,375	10,675	10,429	10,601
Other alcoholic drink	9,293	9,443	9,700	9,550	9,455	9,129	8,983	9,269	9,589	9,396	9,964
Tobacco	8,771	8,706	8,729	8,730	8,649	8,437	7,969	7,562	7,431	7,219	6,994
Clothing other than footwear	15,618	16,582	17,234	17,096	17,245	17,387	17,906	18,936	19,835	20,833	22,378
Footwear	3,551	3,622	3,546	3,566	3,631	3,430	3,549	3,729	4,019	4,019	4,138
Energy products	21,420	21,871	22,482	22,335	22,422	23,151	22,889	23,021	22,720	22,198	23,122
Other goods	31,035	33,490	36,308	38,486	39,566	38,550	38,739	40,225	41,349	41,705	42,784
Services											
Rents, rates, and water charges	36,896	37,407	37,959	38,428	38,916	39,325	39,648	40,219	40,803	41,403	41,868
Other services	89,906	97,273	110,078	116,143	119,246	116,114	116,051	118,572	121,810	125,599	129,523
Total	295,622	311,234	334,591	345,406	347,527	340,037	339,652	348,164	357,845	364,046	376,648

Source: *United Kingdom National Accounts*, 1997. © Crown copyright 1998

General Government: Current Income and Expenditure in the UK

(– = not applicable. In millions of pounds.)

Item	1986	1987	1988	1989	1990	1991	1992	1993	1994	1995	1996
Receipts											
Taxes on income	51,973	55,658	61,723	70,000	76,875	75,178	73,716	73,248	80,675	90,694	94,685
Taxes on expenditure	62,872	68,971	76,039	79,980	78,298	85,416	87,521	90,336	96,418	103,697	108,484
Social security contributions	26,165	27,663	30,682	33,333	34,457	36,216	36,975	39,267	42,086	44,371	46,270
Community charge/council tax	–	–	–	586	8,629	8,128	7,907	8,038	8,450	9,151	9,906
Gross trading surplus	155	–75	–32	199	12	–36	206	193	495	623	681
Rent, dividends, and interest, etc	9,839	10,149	10,188	10,892	10,652	10,228	9,983	10,205	10,612	10,894	11,096
Miscellaneous current transfers	266	363	394	431	504	545	419	617	704	713	632
Imputed charge for consumption of non-trading capital	2,583	2,804	3,110	3,448	3,806	3,763	3,603	3,354	3,287	3,455	3,653
Total	153,853	165,533	182,104	198,869	213,233	219,438	220,330	225,258	242,727	263,598	275,407
Expenditure											
Final consumption	80,911	87,045	93,641	101,796	112,934	124,105	131,875	137,756	144,068	149,208	155,732
Subsidies	6,301	6,265	6,037	5,782	6,066	5,995	6,737	7,203	7,484	7,631	9,100
Social security benefits	40,860	41,961	43,056	44,965	48,898	57,381	65,902	71,784	74,356	77,132	80,021
Other current grants to personal sector	8,594	8,837	9,119	9,068	10,041	11,906	14,150	16,753	18,274	19,036	18,590
Current grants paid abroad (net)	2,233	3,277	3,248	4,278	4,596	1,083	4,834	4,908	5,077	7,089	4,933
Debt interest	17,243	18,026	18,279	19,010	18,786	17,022	17,120	18,515	22,250	25,917	27,159
Total	156,142	165,411	173,380	184,899	201,321	217,492	240,618	256,919	271,509	286,013	295,535
Balance: current surplus	–2,289	122	8,724	13,970	11,912	1,946	–20,288	–31,661	–28,782	–22,415	–20,128

Source: *United Kingdom National Accounts*, 1997. © Crown copyright 1998

Gross National Product by Category in the UK

(In millions of pounds at 1990 prices. – = not applicable.)

Category	1975	1980	1985	1990	1992	1994	1995	1996
At 1990 Market Prices								
Consumers' expenditure	224,580	247,185	276,742	347,527	339,652	357,845	364,046	376,648
General government final consumption								
central government	59,156	63,207	66,241	70,108	72,039	75,506	76,114	78,752
local authorities	36,552	37,791	38,856	42,826	43,693	42,574	43,464	43,666
Total	95,748	101,005	105,097	112,934	115,732	118,080	119,578	122,418
Gross domestic fixed capital formation	71,720	71,764	81,575	107,577	95,973	100,778	102,249	104,090
Value of physical increase in stocks and work progress	–4,103	–4,064	990	–1,800	–1,699	2,890	4,119	2,635
Total domestic expenditure	386,710	414,792	464,316	566,238	549,658	579,593	589,992	605,791
Exports of goods and services								
goods	52,293	67,475	80,250	101,718	105,457	120,481	129,942	138,681
services	25,891	27,917	28,883	31,447	32,588	35,608	38,260	41,124
Total	77,179	94,918	109,163	133,165	138,045	156,089	168,202	179,805
Total final expenditure	461,473	509,274	573,567	699,403	687,703	735,682	758,194	785,596
Expenditure 'less' imports of goods and services[1]								
goods	–56,643	–66,827	–84,825	–120,527	–121,629	–131,841	–137,792	–149,550
services	–17,420	–20,055	–21,189	–27,758	–28,626	–31,540	–32,490	–35,121
Total	–73,752	–86,469	–105,957	–148,285	–150,255	–163,381	–170,282	–184,671
Statistical discrepancy (expenditure adjustment)[2]	–4,001	–1,420	–	–	–	–	–	795
Gross domestic product[3]	386,867	423,490	468,071	551,118	537,448	572,301	587,912	601,720
Net property income from abroad	2,281	–273	2,458	1,269	3,116	8,633	6,599	8,007
Gross national product[3]	388,949	422,188	469,976	552,387	540,564	580,934	594,511	609,728
At 1990 Factor Cost								
Gross domestic product at market prices[3]	386,867	423,490	468,071	551,118	537,448	572,301	587,912	601,720
'Less' factor-cost adjustment[4]	–48,158	–55,347	–60,310	–72,232	–70,992	–74,070	–75,977	–77,172
Gross domestic product at factor cost	338,138	368,216	407,844	478,886	466,456	498,231	511,935	524,548
Net property income from abroad	2,281	–273	2,458	1,269	3,116	8,633	6,599	8,007
Gross national product at factor cost	340,152	366,889	409,714	480,155	469,572	506,864	518,534	532,556
'Less' capital consumption	–40,752	–48,878	–56,214	–61,261	–62,970	–65,676	–66,536	–68,224
Net national product at factor cost ('national income')	301,074	319,554	353,208	418,894	406,602	441,188	451,998	464,332

[1] Excluding taxes on expenditure levied on imports.
[2] The difference between gross domestic product and the total of its expenditure components at 1990 prices.
[3] Including taxes on expenditure levied on imports.
[4] This adjustment represents taxes on expenditure, less subsidies valued at constant rates.

Source: *United Kingdom National Accounts*, 1997. © Crown copyright 1998

National and Domestic Product of the UK

(In millions of pounds at current prices, except as indicated.)

The main aggregates (1990 = 100)

	1975	1980	1985	1990	1992	1994	1995	1996
GDP at current market prices ('money GDP')[1]	19.2	42.1	64.8	100.0	108.7	121.4	127.8	134.7
GDP at current factor cost	20.0	42.0	64.3	100.0	108.2	121.1	127.0	134.3
GDP at 1990 market prices	70.2	76.8	84.9	100.0	97.5	103.8	106.7	109.2
GDP at 1990 factor cost	70.6	76.9	85.2	100.0	97.4	104.0	106.9	109.5
GNDI at 1990 market prices[2]	68.9	76.4	85.4	100.0	98.5	105.6	107.2	110.7
Index of total home costs[3]	28.3	54.6	75.5	100.0	111.1	116.4	118.8	122.6

At Current Prices

		1975	1980	1985	1990	1992	1994	1995	1996
At market prices	gross domestic product at market prices ('money GDP')[1]	105,852	231,772	357,344	551,118	598,916	669,069	704,156	742,300
	net property income from abroad	891	–182	2,296	1,269	3,124	9,667	7,920	9,652
	gross national product at market prices[1]	106,743	231,590	359,640	552,387	602,040	678,736	712,076	751,952
	net transfer income from abroad	–475	–1,984	–3,111	–4,896	–5,102	–4,969	–6,887	–4,631
	gross national disposable income[1]	106,268	229,606	356,529	547,491	596,938	673,767	705,189	747,321
At factor cost	gross domestic product at market prices	105,852	231,772	357,344	551,118	598,916	669,069	704,156	742,300
	adjustment to factor cost	–10,265	–30,755	–49,442	–72,232	–80,784	–88,934	–96,066	–99,384
	gross domestic product at factor cost	95,587	201,017	307,902	478,886	518,132	580,135	608,090	642,916
	net property income from abroad	891	–182	2,296	1,269	3,124	9,667	7,920	9,652
	gross national product at factor cost	96,478	200,835	310,198	480,155	521,256	589,802	616,010	652,568
	'less' capital consumption	–11,621	–27,952	–41,883	–61,261	–62,485	–68,298	–73,014	–77,372
	net national product at factor cost ('national income')	84,857	172,883	268,315	418,894	458,771	521,504	542,996	575,196

[1] This series is affected by the abolition of domestic rates and the introduction of the community charge.
[2] GNDI = gross national disposable GNDI = real national income.
[3] Expenditure-based deflator at factor cost.

Source: *United Kingdom National Accounts*, 1997. © Crown copyright 1998

National Product by Category of Expenditure in the UK

(N/A = not available. In millions of pounds at current prices.)

Category		1975	1980	1985	1990	1992	1995	1996
At Current Market Prices								
Consumer's expenditure[1]		65,590	138,564	217,485	347,527	383,490	446,169	473,509
General government final consumption	central government	14,055	31,033	47,341	70,108	82,259	96,027	101,140
	local authorities	9,597	18,951	27,926	42,826	49,616	53,181	54,592
	Total	23,652	49,984	75,267	112,934	131,875	149,208	155,732
Gross domestic fixed capital formation		21,035	41,561	60,718	107,577	93,642	108,736	114,623
Value of physical increase in stocks and work in progress		–1,354	–2,572	821	–1,800	–1,937	4,748	2,917
Total domestic expenditure[1]		108,923	227,537	354,291	566,238	607,070	708,861	746,781
Exports of goods and services	goods	19,185	47,149	77,991	101,718	107,343	153,077	166,340
	services	7,678	15,467	24,050	31,447	35,154	46,598	50,807
	Total	26,863	62,616	102,041	133,165	142,497	199,675	217,147
Total final expenditure[1]		135,786	290,153	456,332	699,403	749,567	908,536	963,928
'Less' imports of goods and services[2]	goods	–22,440	–45,792	–81,336	–120,527	–120,447	–164,659	–178,938
	services	–6,363	–11,814	–17,652	–27,758	–30,204	–39,721	–43,665
	Total	–28,803	–57,606	–98,988	–148,285	–150,651	–204,380	–222,603
Statistical discrepancy (expenditure adjustment)[3]		–1,131	–775	N/A	N/A	N/A	N/A	975
Gross domestic product[1][4]		105,852	231,772	357,344	551,118	598,916	704,156	742,300
Net property income from abroad		891	–182	2,296	1,269	3,124	7,920	9,652
Gross national product[1][4]		106,743	231,590	359,640	552,387	602,040	712,076	751,952
Factor Cost Adjustment								
Taxes on expenditure		14,036	36,474	56,667	78,298	87,521	103,697	108,484
Subsidies		3,771	5,719	7,225	6,066	6,737	7,631	9,100
Factor cost adjustment (taxes less subsidies)		10,265	30,755	49,442	72,232	80,874	96,066	99,384

National Product by Category of Expenditure in the UK (*continued*)

Category	1975	1980	1985	1990	1992	1995	1996
At Current Factor Cost							
Consumer's expenditure	57,871	116,962	180,811	295,939	325,088	376,874	401,987
General government final consumption	22,686	46,392	70,851	106,130	123,214	138,576	144,652
Gross domestic capital formation	18,871	36,334	57,011	98,252	84,655	105,368	109,164
Total domestic expenditure	99,428	199,688	308,673	500,321	532,957	620,818	655,803
Exports of goods and services	26,093	59,710	98,217	126,850	135,826	191,652	208,741
Total final expenditure	125,521	259,398	406,890	627,171	668,783	812,470	864,544
'Less' imports of goods and services	−28,803	−57,606	−98,988	−148,285	−150,651	−204,380	−222,603
Statistical discrepancy (expenditure adjustment)[3]	−1,131	−775	N/A	N/A	N/A	N/A	975
Gross domestic product	95,587	201,017	307,902	478,886	518,132	608,090	642,916
Net property income from abroad	891	−182	2,296	1,269	3,124	7,920	9,652
Gross national product	96,478	200,835	310,198	480,155	521,256	616,010	652,568
'Less' capital consumption	−11,621	−27,952	−41,883	−61,261	−62,485	−73,014	−77,372
Net national product at factor cost ('national income')	84,857	172,883	268,315	418,894	458,771	542,996	575,196

[1] This series is affected by the abolition of domestic rates and the introduction of the community charge.
[2] Excluding taxes on expenditure levied on imports.
[3] The statistical discrepancy (expenditure adjustment) is part of the residual error.
[4] Including taxes on expenditure levied on imports.

Source: *United Kingdom National Accounts,* 1997. © Crown copyright 1998

General Government Expenditure by Function, as a Percentage of GDP in the UK

Spending includes contributions to the European Union and activities required for the general maintenance of government, such as tax collection and the registration of population. (– = not applicable.)

Function	1978–79 outturn	1983–84 outturn	1985–86 outturn	1987–88 outturn	1989–90 outturn	1991–92 outturn	1992–93 outturn	1993–94 outturn	1994–95 outturn	1995–96 outturn	1996–97 estimated outturn
Defence	4.5	5.2	5.1	4.4	4.0	3.9	3.8	3.6	3.3	3.0	2.8
Overseas services, including overseas aid	0.6	0.6	0.5	0.5	0.5	0.5	0.6	0.5	0.5	0.5	0.5
Agriculture, fisheries, food, and forestry	0.6	0.8	0.8	0.6	0.4	0.5	0.5	0.6	0.5	0.6	0.8
Trade, industry, energy, and employment	2.4	2.4	2.3	1.6	1.6	1.7	1.7	1.7	1.5	1.4	1.3
Transport	1.8	1.8	1.6	1.3	1.3	1.6	1.8	1.6	1.5	1.3	1.2
Housing	2.6	1.4	1.1	1.0	1.0	1.0	1.0	0.8	0.8	0.7	0.5
Other environmental services	1.6	1.5	1.3	1.3	1.3	1.4	1.5	1.3	1.4	1.4	1.3
Law, order, and protective services	1.5	1.9	1.8	1.9	2.0	2.2	2.3	2.3	2.3	2.2	2.2
Education	5.4	5.2	4.7	4.8	4.8	5.0	5.2	5.2	5.2	5.1	4.9
National heritage	0.4	0.4	0.4	0.4	0.4	0.5	0.4	0.4	0.4	0.4	0.4
Health and personal social services											
health	4.6	5.1	4.9	4.9	4.8	5.4	5.7	5.6	5.6	5.6	5.5
Total	5.4	6.0	5.8	5.7	5.7	6.5	6.8	6.7	6.8	6.9	6.9
Social security	9.9	12.0	12.1	11.4	10.2	12.1	13.1	13.6	13.2	13.1	13.1
Miscellaneous expenditure	1.6	1.1	1.1	1.3	1.3	1.0	1.3	1.3	1.1	1.4	1.0
Total expenditure on services	38.3	40.4	38.7	36.1	34.5	37.8	39.8	39.5	38.3	37.8	36.8
General government net debt interest	2.6	3.1	3.2	2.8	2.3	1.9	2.1	2.3	2.6	2.8	3.0
Other accounting adjustments	1.3	1.4	1.4	1.5	1.5	1.3	1.5	1.5	1.7	1.8	1.8
Allowance for shortfall	–	–	–	–	–	–	–	–	–	−0.1	−0.2
General government expenditure	42.2	44.8	43.2	40.5	38.3	41.0	43.4	43.3	42.6	42.3	41.3

Source: *Public Expenditure: Statistical Analyses,* 1997–98. © Crown copyright 1998

THE EURO: BRITAIN STAYS OUT

BY DAVID SHUKMAN

Britain, Euro So Alone

On New Year's Day in 1999 a new type of money will be born in Europe. For the first time in history, nearly a dozen countries are clubbing together to create a shared currency. It has been given an inelegant name, the 'euro'. This new currency – the product of the European Union's latest development, Economic and Monetary Union (EMU) – will replace currencies as wide-ranging as the French franc, the German mark, and the Spanish peseta. From Ireland in the far west of Europe to Austria in the east, and from Finland in the north to Portugal in the south, the euro is set to become the common currency. Of the major economies in Europe, only Britain is staying on the sidelines.

For so many countries to choose to bind themselves together so closely is unprecedented. Europeans have only previously witnessed a single currency when it was forced on them: under the Roman Empire and Hitler's Third Reich. This time, the 11 governments committing themselves to this momentous step all believe the benefits are self-evident. The immediate cancellation of the costs of currency exchange between euro-members will allow businesses to make huge savings. Gone too will be the uncertainties of shifting exchange rates, with companies no longer seeing their projected profits falling victim to volatile currency markets.

Union Member in Name Only?

Yet the greatest benefit claimed for the euro is its political impact in Europe and beyond. After a three-year transition period in which banks, companies, and governments will use the euro electronically, the first euro notes and coins will appear on the streets on 1 January 2002. From that date, the different members of the European Union will suddenly share one of the most tangible features of life – money. Each country will still have a 'national' symbol on its own version of the euro notes and coins. But every time EU citizens open their purses and wallets, they will be reminded that they are part of the same Union. Advocates of the single currency point out that British people, despite being fully paid-up citizens of the EU, will not of course experience the same sentiment.

Outside Europe too the euro will make its mark. Until now, the most important global currencies have been the American dollar and the Japanese yen, each backed by a formidably large economy. The advent of the European single currency will add another player to this international scene. By putting the weight of most of Europe's richest economies into one basket, the euro is set to acquire the status of a so-called 'reserve' currency, a safe bet for the world's top financial institutions. For that reason, influential voices in the European Commission claim that Europe's representatives (currently France, Germany, Italy, and the UK) at the annual G7 meetings of the world's seven richest nations could soon be replaced by a single figure, speaking on behalf of euro countries. The UK, which is likely to be left out of such a scheme, objects.

Blair's Double Dilemma

The British government faces a very awkward dilemma. Tony Blair wants Britain to reclaim 'a leading role in Europe' after the open hostility felt by the Conservatives. Yet the single biggest project currently underway in the EU is one about which Mr Blair and his ministers share uncertainties, even doubts. John Major's policy of 'wait and see' has been turned into the more positive one of 'prepare and decide'. But the effect is the same: Britain will not take part for the lifetime of this Parliament – which means not until 2002 or 2003 at the very earliest.

One worry for Britain is whether the new currency will actually work. The test for membership was set in the Maastricht Treaty of 1991 with five criteria for sound economic management, including the size of each participant's deficit and debt, and its rates of inflation and interest. In a last-minute scramble to qualify, governments have resorted to desperate measures, including selling off gold reserves, using 'creative accountancy' to maximize privatization proceeds, even – in the case of Italy – raising a one-off 'euro-tax'. Not surprisingly, many observers have cried foul, claiming the figures have been fudged and that the euro will not be as soundly based as its founders intended.

Beyond that lies British unease about harnessing a huge variety of different economies. While the participating countries will share a common currency, they will also share a common interest rate. And critics wonder whether that will be manageable. For example, if the British economy were to need a reduction in the interest rate at a particular time – perhaps to stave off the threat of recession – there could well be a clash with other countries demanding a higher rate to prevent their economies from overheating. The question asked by many is whether the UK, with an economic cycle slightly ahead of the continent's, can afford to lock itself permanently into a Europe-wide interest rate.

Preserving the Pound ... But at What Price?

Ultimately, the choice for Britain represents a balance between maintaining sovereignty and exerting influence. By staying out, Britain will retain sovereign control of its own economic affairs. But it will also lose the chance of a say in decisions concerning the management of the new currency – even though those decisions will affect the British economy anyway. In practical terms, Britain will be denied a place on the key decision-making bodies. The governor of the Bank of England will not have a seat on the governing council of the new and all-powerful European Central Bank, while the Chancellor of the Exchequer will not be allowed to attend every meeting of the so-called 'euro-x' group of participating countries.

This dilemma will become more acute if British businesses and the City of London, shut out of the euro-zone, start to lose trade to continental rivals. Critics of the single currency say the threat to British jobs and earnings is being exaggerated, and that Britain anyway looks more to business opportunities in America and Asia than in Europe. Yet major foreign investors (such as Japanese car and electronics manufacturers) clearly regard euro membership as a factor in their future investment decisions. If the euro is a success, there will certainly be a risk that Britain will lose out. The question is whether that is a price worth paying for preserving the pound.

Many commentators regard the euro as the most important issue facing the UK since World War II. Assuming the Labour Party wins the next general election, perhaps in 2001 or 2002, the Cabinet will be under pressure to make a quick decision on membership and then put its view to the public in a referendum. By then, the single currency will be up and running. Businesses operating outside the euro-zone may be feeling the competitive edge of those inside it; and the British government may find itself excluded from some of the EU's most significant decisions. Against that, ministers will have to decide whether they want to be remembered as the men and women who ended one thousand years of British history by consigning sterling to oblivion.

SEX SCANDAL PUTS PRESSURE ON PRESIDENT
Monica Lewinsky – leaves the office of her lawyer Jacob Stein after it was announced in July 1998 that she had agreed to give evidence against the US President Bill Clinton in exchange for immunity from prosecution.
In August 1998 Clinton admitted having 'a relationship' with Lewinsky 'that was not appropriate'.
Rex Features Ltd. (© Robert Trippett / SIPA Press)

ARMS INSPECTION CRISES

Right In February 1998, the Iraqi Deputy Prime Minister Tariq Aziz (*left*) and the United Nations Secretary-General Kofi Annan (*right*) agreed terms by which United Nations inspectors would be allowed access to Iraqi weapons sites. This agreement lifted the immediate threat of air strikes by the USA and Britain against Iraq. However, in early August 1998, President Saddam Hussein (*pictured below on his 61st birthday*) broke off co-operation with the inspectors in protest at the UN's failure to lift the sanctions imposed following the invasion of Kuwait by Iraq in 1990.
Aziz, Annan: Frank Spooner Pictures (© William Stevens / Gamma); Hussein: Rex Features Ltd. (© SIPA Press)

NETANYAHU VISITS AUSCHWITZ

Benjamin Netanyahu and Jerzy Buzek, prime ministers of Israel and Poland respectively, lead a 'March of the Living', organized to commemorate the victims of Auschwitz. Some 7,000 Jews came to the march from all over the world.

Frank Spooner Pictures (© Laski Diffusion / Gamma)

VIOLENCE IN ALGERIA

The civil war which has been raging in Algeria since the government cancelled a general election in 1992 – because of fears of victory by Islamic parties – continued with massacres at the end of 1997 and into 1998. In one attack, 31 people were killed in the village of Larbaa (*above*), southeast of Algiers.

Frank Spooner Pictures (© Menouar / Gamma)

KOSOVO FUNERAL

Mourners gather at the funeral of Qerim Muriqi, an Albanian killed during a demonstration in Kosovo, southern Serbia. Tens of thousands of ethnic Albanians fled fighting in Kosovo in 1998 between Serb forces and the Kosovo Liberation Army who want Kosovo to secede from Serbia. In Kosovo there are some 1.8 million Albanians and 210,000 Serbs.

Frank Spooner (© Art Zamur)

ITALIAN MUDSLIDE

More than 100 people died when a mudslide hit the Italian village of Sarno near Naples in May 1998. Following a period of heavy rain, mud had cascaded down from Mount Sarno into nearby villages. Within days, the mud had solidified. Environmentalists blamed the disaster on erosion of the mountain due to poor forestry practices.
Frank Spooner Pictures (© Livio Anticoli)

SUFFERING THE EFFECTS OF EL NIÑO

Hurricane devastation in Florida. In February 1998, at least 38 people were killed when winds of over 320 kph / 200 mph hit the Orlando area. The hurricane was blamed on El Niño, the movement of warm water towards the west coast of South America.
Rex Features Ltd. (© Tony Ranze)

MICROSOFT LEGAL BATTLE

In early 1998, Bill Gates, chief executive of Microsoft, argued for Microsoft's right to bundle its Web browser with its operating system, Windows 98. An injunction against Microsoft in 1997 had ruled that it was unfair for the company to tie the two products together. However in June 1998 the injunction was lifted.

Frank Spooner Pictures (© Gamma Liaison)

CLINTON AND MANDELA VISIT ROBBEN ISLAND PRISON
In March 1998, President Clinton and first lady Hillary Clinton – with President Nelson Mandela and Graca Machel, now Mandela's wife – visited the cell on Robben Island in which Mandela was imprisoned during the years of apartheid.
Rex Features Ltd. (© Julian Kuus / SIPA Press)

DEATH OF SINATRA
The coffin of Frank Sinatra, who died in May 1998, is carried from the church in Beverly Hills where his funeral took place. Among the invited mourners were Jack Nicholson, Jack Lemmon, Gregory Peck, Liza Minnelli, Anthony Quinn, Sophia Loren, and Mia Farrow.
Frank Spooner Pictures (© Eric Rohmer / Gamma Liaison)

Index of Gross Domestic Product by Industry in the UK

(1990 = 100.)

Industry		1986	1989	1992	1995	1996
Agriculture, hunting, forestry, and fishing		95.5	96.7	107.7	97.1	95.4
Production	*Mining and Quarrying*					
	mining of coal and nuclear fuel	122.9	109.9	91.4	50.4	49.5
	extraction of mineral oil and natural gas	136.0	102.4	114.3	170.0	178.3
	other mining and quarrying	95.5	110.3	92.1	89.7	79.9
	Total mining and quarrying	129.2	104.6	107.6	138.7	143.3
	Manufacturing					
	food and beverages	93.9	98.5	101.1	106.2	107.3
	tobacco products	87.4	96.2	107.3	102.8	106.9
	textiles and leather products	101.1	101.4	90.2	90.1	89.2
	wood and wood products	83.3	103.2	88.0	91.2	89.4
	pulp, paper products, printing, and publishing	78.1	97.7	96.5	102.5	101.1
	solid and nuclear fuels, oil refining	114.2	104.8	114.3	131.2	117.0
	chemicals and man-made fibres	84.0	100.2	106.0	116.9	119.3
	rubber and plastic products	75.5	97.3	96.5	114.5	113.3
	other non-metallic mineral products	91.0	106.6	86.5	92.3	88.7
	basic metals and metal products	84.1	100.8	86.3	89.0	88.9
	machinery and equipment	88.4	99.6	85.7	90.9	89.4
	electrical and optical equipment	78.6	99.1	97.6	121.6	124.8
	transport equipment	79.6	102.2	91.7	92.0	95.5
	other manufacturing	85.0	98.7	87.1	89.6	91.1
	Total manufacturing (revised definition)	85.7	100.1	94.9	102.5	102.8
	Electricity, Gas, and Water Supply	95.1	97.4	107.4	116.3	123.6
	Total production	90.1	100.3	97.0	106.7	107.9
Construction		76.0	97.6	87.9	90.0	91.1
Service industries	wholesale and retail trade; repairs	85.3	101.7	96.5	108.5	111.9
	hotels and restaurants	85.9	99.1	89.3	93.9	97.5
	transport and storage	85.6	100.8	99.1	115.6	115.9
	post and telecommunication	81.1	96.3	98.9	122.9	135.9
	financial intermediation	75.9	95.6	94.9	104.0	109.7
	real estate, renting, and business activities	84.3	97.9	95.1	116.0	125.4
	ownership of dwellings	98.1	98.7	102.1	106.1	107.2
	public administration, national defence, social security	100.2	98.5	100.4	94.5	92.5
	education	96.0	101.3	100.3	101.8	102.9
	health and social work	90.6	98.7	103.6	110.8	113.1
	other services	85.3	99.6	100.8	125.0	131.9
	adjustment for financial services	78.1	96.9	94.3	108.2	116.3
	Total services	88.6	99.2	98.4	108.9	112.6
Gross Domestic Product		88.6	99.4	97.4	106.9	109.5

Source: *United Kingdom National Accounts*, 1997. © Crown copyright 1998

General Government: Total Expenditure on Goods and Services in the UK

(In millions of pounds at 1990 prices.)

Item				1994	1995	1996
Central government	final consumption	military defence	pay	7,567	7,021	7,657
			procurement	11,825	11,053	11,040
			capital consumption	68	68	71
			Total	19,460	18,142	18,768
		National Health Service	pay	3,188	2,026	1,809
			procurement	26,320	28,773	30,152
			capital consumption	109	117	96
			Total	29,617	30,916	32,057
		other	pay[1]	9,867	9,911	9,987
			procurement[1]	9,438	9,428	9,656
			capital consumption[1]	1,097	1,100	1,103
			education grants	6,027	6,617	7,181
			Total	26,429	27,056	27,927
		Total	pay	20,622	18,958	19,453
			procurement	47,583	49,254	50,848
			capital consumption	1,274	1,285	1,270
			education grants	6,027	6,617	7,181
			Total	75,506	76,114	78,752
	capital expenditure	gross domestic fixed capital formation		6,912	5,966	4,144
		value of physical increase in stocks		−256	−150	120
		Total		6,656	5,816	4,264
	Total expenditure			82,162	81,930	83,016
Local authorities	final consumption	education[2]		17,351	17,278	17,245
		other		25,223	26,186	26,421
		Total		42,574	43,464	43,666
	capital expenditure	gross domestic fixed capital formation	expenditure on fixed assets	10,350	9,795	8,446
			less sales of council housing	−1,167	−1,067	−940
			less other sales	−1,661	−1,320	−1,240
			Total capital expenditure	7,522	7,408	6,266
	Total expenditure			50,096	50,872	49,932
General government	final consumption			118,080	119,578	122,418
		gross domestic fixed capital formation		14,434	13,374	10,410
		value of physical increase in stocks		−256	−150	120
	Total expenditure			132,258	132,802	132,948

[1] Including education elements.
[2] Including school meals and milk.

Source: *United Kingdom National Accounts,* 1997. © Crown copyright 1998

Average House Prices at Mortgage Completion in the UK

(− = not applicable. N/A = not available. In pounds.)

1996

Region	First-time buyers	Other	All buyers	% of dwellings in council tax bands A–C	Region	First-time buyers	Other	All buyers	% of dwellings in council tax bands A–C
North East	36,100	68,200	51,000	88	South East	58,400	108,600	87,600	51
North West	41,500	77,000	57,400	80	South West	49,400	82,600	68,000	66
Merseyside	41,800	76,700	58,400	86	*England*	50,100	93,000	72,200	68
Yorkshire and the Humber	39,930	74,300	55,900	83					
East Midlands	40,900	76,700	58,900	81	*Wales*	42,000	69,600	54,900	−
West Midlands	44,800	83,200	64,300	78					
Eastern	50,900	92,500	73,400	64	*Scotland*	37,700	76,100	56,700	−
London	67,200	123,000	94,100	44	*Northern Ireland*	34,900	63,000	47,700	N/A
					Total UK	48,700	91,200	70,600	N/A

Source: Department of the Environment, Transport, and the Regions. © Crown copyright 1998

County Court Actions for Mortgage Possessions in the UK

Data are for local authority and private actions. The figures do not indicate the number of houses repossessed through the courts; not all warrants will have resulted in the issue and execution of warrants of possession. The regional breakdown relates to the location of the court rather than the address of the property. Data exclude Scotland. (N/A = not available.)

Region	1991			1994			1995			1996		
	Actions entered	Suspended orders	Orders made	Actions entered	Suspended orders	Orders made	Actions entered	Suspended orders	Orders made	Actions entered	Suspended orders	Orders made
North East	6,000	2,900	1,900	3,200	2,400	1,200	3,300	2,100	1,000	3,500	2,000	1,100
North West	17,900	6,900	6,100	9,700	5,400	3,100	10,200	5,500	3,400	9,900	6,300	3,500
Merseyside	4,400	1,700	1,400	2,500	800	600	2,600	1,200	600	2,800	1,400	500
Yorkshire and the Humber	14,100	5,100	5,700	7,600	3,200	2,300	7,400	3,600	2,200	7,600	3,900	2,600
East Midlands	13,500	4,500	5,200	6,000	3,200	2,400	6,500	3,300	2,100	5,900	3,000	2,000
West Midlands	17,700	6,500	6,900	8,600	4,400	2,600	8,200	4,200	2,400	7,600	3,900	2,100
Eastern	18,600	6,000	8,400	9,300	4,200	3,600	8,500	4,300	3,400	8,300	4,000	3,400
London	35,300	13,100	14,400	15,500	8,400	6,800	12,100	6,700	6,000	11,400	6,400	4,800
South East	32,200	13,200	13,200	13,600	7,900	5,600	13,000	7,600	5,300	11,600	6,600	4,000
South West	16,700	5,800	6,500	7,400	3,500	2,500	7,100	3,400	2,400	6,300	3,300	2,400
England	176,400	65,600	69,900	83,500	43,300	30,700	78,900	41,900	28,800	74,900	40,700	26,400
Wales	10,200	3,500	4,000	4,400	2,300	1,500	5,300	2,700	1,600	4,900	2,700	1,400
Northern Ireland[1]	3,100	N/A	N/A	1,400	N/A	N/A	1,200	N/A	N/A	1,200	N/A	N/A

[1] Mortgage possession actions are heard in the Chancery Division of the Northern Ireland High Court.

Source: The Court Service; Northern Ireland Court Service. © Crown copyright 1998

Housing Expenditure by Tenure Group and Region in the UK

Average weekly household expenditure in pounds. Expenditure includes such items as rent, water, and council tax; repairs, maintenance and decorations; and dwelling insurance and mortgage repayments in the case of owner-occupied housing. Data are given after the deduction of housing benefit, rebates, and any other financial reductions. (N/A = not available.)

1996–97

Type of tenure	UK	North East	North West and Merseyside	Yorkshire and the Humber	East Midlands	West Midlands	Eastern	London	South East	South West	England	Wales	Scotland	Northern Ireland
Rented unfurnished														
local authority housing	24.71	21.48	22.46	26.07	26.58	23.23	33.90	27.82	32.01	23.64	26.10	20.76	21.45	12.70
association	28.52	22.27	24.10	27.73	24.04	29.23	24.06	34.08	25.55	43.88	28.72	25.77	27.72	N/A
other rented unfurnished	55.87	−44.31	52.22	45.14	37.40	45.02	75.18	65.98	69.77	64.90	57.77	−47.70	41.40	N/A
Total	29.34	22.96	27.63	27.86	27.97	27.14	38.83	32.59	37.76	39.57	31.17	23.69	23.12	13.38
Rented furnished	60.05	30.70	44.48	56.71	53.98	52.39	−56.85	73.22	82.46	50.25	60.93	60.80	55.52	N/A
Rent free	10.56	N/A	−9.17	N/A	11.41	−13.35	−13.53	−6.46	6.63	−16.22	10.21	N/A	−17.14	N/A
Owner occupied														
in process of purchase	74.18	67.52	68.46	61.20	67.47	65.50	80.84	96.19	90.24	68.35	75.71	77.74	60.37	51.02
owned outright	27.06	34.21	25.87	25.24	20.51	27.39	25.83	28.87	33.00	26.72	27.53	23.56	29.17	11.09
Total	57.68	56.73	53.97	48.72	49.40	50.14	62.65	77.11	70.39	52.63	58.85	54.91	51.10	36.83

Source: *Family Spending*, 1996–97. © Crown copyright 1998

Individual Insolvencies in the UK

(N/A = not available.)

Type of insolvency	1986	1987	1988	1989	1990	1991	1992	1993	1994	1995	1996
England and Wales											
Bankruptcies[1][2]	7,093	6,994	7,717	8,138	12,058	22,632	32,106	31,016	25,634	21,933	21,803
Individual voluntary arrangements[3]	N/A	404	779	1,224	1,927	3,002	4,686	5,679	5,103	4,384	4,466
Deeds of arrangement	62	29	11	3	2	6	2	8	2	2	2
Total	7,155	7,427	8,507	9,365	13,987	25,640	36,794	36,703	30,739	26,319	26,271
Scotland											
Sequestrations[4]	437	808	1,401	2,301	4,350	7,665	10,845	6,828	2,182	2,188	2,503
Northern Ireland											
Bankruptcies[5][6]	193	134	164	238	286	367	406	474	438	399	415
Individual voluntary arrangements[7]	N/A	N/A	N/A	N/A	N/A	2	42	67	84	64	101
Total	193	134	164	238	286	369	448	541	522	463	516

[1] Comprise receiving and administration orders under the Bankruptcy Act, 1914, and bankruptcy orders under the Insolvency Act, 1986.
[2] Orders later consolidated or rescinded are included in these figures.
[3] Introduced under the Insolvency Act, 1986.
[4] Sequestrations awarded but not brought into operation are included in these figures.
[5] Comprise bankruptcy adjudication orders, arrangement protection orders, and orders for the administration of estates of deceased insolvents.
[6] Orders later set aside or dismissed are included in these figures.
[7] Introduced under the insolvency Northern Ireland order, 1989.

Source: Department of Trade and Industry. © Crown copyright 1998

Public Expenditure on Overseas Aid in the UK

(In millions of pounds.)

Expenditure	1989	1990	1991	1992	1993	1994	1995	1996
Bilateral								
Project aid								
Department for International Development, excluding ATP	178.0	225.6	146.6	129.4	95.0	114.8	107.7	106.9
Aid and Trade Provision (ATP)	51.7	74.3	113.0	77.2	68.9	82.9	49.0	60.4
Commonwealth Development Corporation	150.7	136.8	159.7	168.4	217.8	227.8	273.9	225.4
Total	380.5	436.8	419.3	375.0	381.7	425.4	430.6	392.7
Non-project aid	275.9	151.3	256.2	309.5	210.2	370.9	257.1	256.8
Technical cooperation	407.2	425.6	528.9	528.5	530.1	544.1	618.9	665.5
Administrative costs	65.7	56.1	57.0	61.7	66.6	71.3	74.1	90.4
Bilateral total	1,129.2	1,069.8	1,261.5	1,274.6	1,188.6	1,411.8	1,380.7	1,405.5
Multilateral								
European Community	305.3	312.7	437.7	482.9	584.9	593.5	542.8	598.9
World Bank Group	208.2	185.2	224.5	236.2	279.8	278.1	257.7	264.6
UN agencies	89.5	86.0	116.2	125.0	107.6	103.2	121.6	134.2
Other multilateral	75.3	74.6	63.5	105.4	113.0	104.4	25.7	56.5
Multilateral total	678.3	658.5	842.0	949.5	1,085.3	1,079.3	947.8	1,054.3
Total	1,807.5	1,728.3	2,103.4	2,224.1	2,274.0	2,491.1	2,328.5	2,459.7

Source: Department for International Development. © Crown copyright 1998

Official Reserves of the UK

(N/A = not available.)

| Year | UK (£ millions) | | | | | | | | US ($ millions) | | | | |
| | Drawings on (+) or additions to (−) official reserves | Reevaluations and other changes | Changes in levels (incr −) | End of period[1] | | | | | End of period[2] | | | | |
				Total	Gold	IMF special drawing rights	Reserve position in the IMF	Convertible currencies	Total	Gold	IMF special drawing rights	Reserve position in the IMF	Convertible currencies
1991	−2,680	−1,010	−3,690	23,625	2,698	660	928	19,339	44,126	5,039	1,232	1,733	36,122
1992	1,404	−5,273	−3,869	27,494	3,149	356	1,325	22,664	41,654	4,770	539	2,007	34,338
1993	−700	−849	−1,549	29,043	3,084	195	1,265	24,499	42,926	4,558	289	1,869	36,210
1994	−1,043	2,027	984	28,059	3,397	297	1,212	23,153	43,898	5,314	465	1,896	36,223
1995	198	−3,900	−3,702	31,761	4,610	267	1,615	25,269	46,986	5,242	417	2,518	38,809
1996	509	3,923	4,432	27,329	4,006	209	1,430	21,684	46,300	5,477	361	2,468	37,994
1997	N/A	N/A	N/A	22,849	N/A	N/A	N/A	N/A	38,418	N/A	N/A	N/A	N/A

[1] Pre-December 1995: translated from official dollar valuations using end-period $/£ market rate. Post December 1995: translated from original currencies using end-period market rates.
[2] Amounts outstanding are revalued at end of March each year.

Personal Income by Region of England

(N/A = not available. In pounds. As of April 1996.)

Region	Average gross weekly full-time earnings			Region	Average gross weekly full-time earnings		
	Men	Women	Average		Men	Women	Average
North East	347.7	252.4	314.1	Former county of Humberside[1]			
North West	369.0	262.4	330.5	East Riding of Yorkshire UA	354.0	244.8	319.7
Merseyside	361.7	271.3	325.4	Kingston upon Hull UA	343.4	257.8	314.1
Yorkshire and the Humber	350.7	252.5	316.4	North East Lincolnshire UA	367.7	N/A	327.0
East Midlands	352.9	248.7	317.9	North Lincolnshire UA	388.5	220.0	336.9
West Midlands	360.1	256.9	324.3	Former county of North Yorkshire[1]			
Eastern	382.3	279.9	345.7	York UA	362.9	240.6	317.7
London	514.3	364.9	454.3	North Yorkshire	333.3	240.0	302.3
South East	412.7	292.7	367.4	Former county of Avon[1]			
South West	364.8	261.1	326.5	Bath and North East Somerset UA	373.5	N/A	334.7
Former county of Cleveland[1]				Bristol UA	377.9	274.0	339.1
Hartlepool UA	N/A	N/A	N/A	North Somerset UA	362.9	249.8	321.0
Middlesbrough UA	360.4	N/A	327.5	South Gloucestershire UA	395.2	262.5	358.6
Redcar and Cleveland UA	401.4	N/A	370.0	Total England	396.2	286.6	356.0
Stockton-on-Tees UA	367.6	209.2	329.8	Total UK	389.9	282.3	350.3

[1] A new local government structure was created with effect from 1 April 1996. UA = Unitary Authority.

Source: Office for National Statistics. © Crown copyright 1998

Producer Price Index Numbers of Materials and Fuels Purchased in the UK

Data are annual averages and give the index of prices paid by manufacturers to buy in items such as materials and fuel. (1990 = 100. n.e.c. = not elsewhere classified.)

	1994	1995	1996
All Manufacturing			
Materials and fuel purchased by manufacturing industry	104.4	114.4	113.1
Materials purchased by manufacturing industry	104.0	116.0	115.5
Fuel purchased by manufacturing industry	107.3	102.8	96.3
Materials and fuel purchased by manufacturing industry, seasonally adjusted	104.4	114.4	113.1
Materials and fuel purchased by manufacturing industry other than the food, beverages, petroleum, and tobacco manufacturing industries, unadjusted	102.6	113.6	109.1
Materials and fuel purchased by manufacturing industry other than the food, beverages, petroleum, and tobacco manufacturing industries, seasonally adjusted	102.6	113.6	109.1
Materials purchased by manufacturing industry other than the food, beverages, petroleum, and tobacco manufacturing industries	100.5	114.7	109.7
Fuel purchased by manufacturing industry other than the food, beverages, petroleum, and tobacco manufacturing industries	107.1	105.4	102.5
Materials and fuel purchased by the food, beverages, petroleum, and tobacco manufacturing industries	111.7	121.0	121.2
Materials purchased by the food, beverages, petroleum, and tobacco manufacturing industries	111.8	121.6	122.1
Fuel purchased by the food, beverages, petroleum, and tobacco manufacturing industries	109.4	109.0	106.2
Output of Selected Sub-Sectors of Industry			
Other mining and quarrying products	119.4	125.2	126.9
Food products and beverages	113.5	123.2	123.2
Food manufacturing	111.2	120.4	120.8
Tobacco products	107.1	114.1	114.5
Textiles and textile products	103.0	115.9	114.9
Textiles	99.1	113.7	112.3
Wearing apparel: dressing and dyeing of fur	105.4	114.3	115.3
Leather and leather products	90.4	91.4	91.5
Wood and wood products	114.8	119.3	116.0
Pulp, paper, and paper products; publishing, printing	94.4	111.0	107.6
Pulp, paper, and paper products	94.8	113.4	103.7
Publishing, printing, and reproduction of recorded media	95.0	113.2	115.5
Coke, refined petroleum products, and nuclear fuel	88.8	91.9	108.1
Chemicals, chemical products, and man-made fibres	107.2	116.9	115.6
Rubber and plastic products	103.3	122.9	116.7
Other non-metallic mineral products	107.8	113.1	114.2
Basic metals and fabricated metal products	102.0	113.0	107.2
Basic metals	100.3	110.0	103.4
Fabricated metal products, except machinery and equipment	108.2	118.4	114.7
Metal goods, engineering, and vehicles	108.9	118.2	115.8
Machinery and equipment n.e.c	112.8	119.9	119.6
Electrical and optical equipment	109.7	118.9	118.1
Office machinery and computers	103.0	106.5	108.2
Electrical machinery and apparatus n.e.c	105.3	114.6	113.0
Radio, television, and communications equipment and apparatus	108.8	113.4	114.2
Medical, precision and optical instruments, watches, and clocks	105.1	110.3	111.3
Transport equipment	112.1	118.6	119.2
Vehicles, trailers, and semi-trailers	111.5	118.3	118.8
Other transport equipment	109.8	115.2	115.9
Manufacturing n.e.c.	107.2	115.2	113.4

Source: Office for National Statistics. © Crown copyright 1998

Personal Income, Expenditure, and Saving in the UK

(Q =yearly quarter. In millions of pounds, unless otherwise indicated.)

Year	Personal income before tax					Deductions from personal income				Total personal disposable income	Consumers' expenditure		Balance: personal saving	Saving ratio
	Wages, salaries, and forces' pay	Employers' contributions	Current grants from general government	Other personal income	Total	UK taxes on income (payments)	Social security contributions	Community charge/council tax	Miscellaneous current deductions		Total	Durable goods		
Not Seasonally Adjusted														
1992	301,449	41,159	80,052	125,553	548,213	65,178	36,975	7,907	2,607	435,546	383,490	33,068	52,056	12.0
1993	307,975	43,586	88,537	132,875	572,973	63,636	39,267	8,038	2,807	459,225	406,569	36,007	52,656	11.5
1994	318,709	46,326	92,630	141,248	598,913	68,274	42,086	8,450	2,872	477,231	427,394	38,963	49,837	10.4
1995	333,558	47,650	96,168	158,721	636,097	74,265	44,371	9,151	2,909	505,401	446,169	41,106	59,232	11.7
1996	349,742	51,078	98,212	170,076	669,108	75,386	46,589	9,906	2,868	534,361	473,845	45,212	60,516	11.3
1997 1st quarter	92,100	13,251	25,086	39,824	170,261	21,790	12,046	2,525	731	133,169	118,206	11,814	14,963	11.2
2nd quarter	92,150	12,824	25,704	49,236	179,914	17,955	12,260	2,704	693	146,302	122,566	11,279	23,736	16.2
3rd quarter	93,486	13,052	25,586	44,939	177,063	19,554	12,439	2,704	709	141,657	130,779	15,132	10,878	7.7
Seasonally Adjusted														
1995 1st quarter	82,122	11,752	24,004	38,479	156,357	17,905	10,962	2,158	724	124,608	109,902	10,122	14,706	11.8
2nd quarter	82,785	12,026	23,827	38,460	157,098	18,534	11,028	2,331	730	124,475	110,924	10,060	13,551	10.9
3rd quarter	83,487	12,051	23,950	39,758	159,246	18,445	11,122	2,331	737	126,611	112,036	10,482	14,575	11.5
4th quarter	85,164	11,821	24,387	42,024	163,396	19,381	11,259	2,331	718	129,707	113,307	10,442	16,400	12.6
1996 1st quarter	85,862	12,603	23,957	43,109	165,531	19,227	11,537	2,331	729	131,707	116,166	10,815	15,541	11.8
2nd quarter	86,676	12,727	24,616	41,277	165,296	19,663	11,440	2,525	684	131,984	117,270	11,194	14,714	11.1
3rd quarter	87,933	12,838	24,666	42,544	167,981	18,366	11,673	2,525	691	134,726	119,087	11,398	15,639	11.6
4th quarter	89,271	12,910	24,973	43,146	170,300	19,130	11,939	2,525	762	135,944	121,322	11,805	14,622	10.8
1997 1st quarter	91,242	12,961	25,361	43,046	172,610	20,127	12,103	2,525	705	137,150	122,938	11,945	14,212	10.4
2nd quarter	92,576	12,913	25,554	47,717	178,760	19,606	12,247	2,704	706	143,497	125,404	12,741	18,092	12.6
3rd quarter	93,942	13,013	25,394	46,035	178,384	19,907	12,379	2,704	713	142,681	127,257	12,823	15,424	10.8

Source: Office for National Statistics. © Crown copyright 1998

Producer Price Index Numbers of Output in the UK

Data are annual averages and give the index of 'factory-gate' prices charged to customers such as wholesalers. (1990 = 100. n.e.c. = not elsewhere classified.)

All Manufacturing

	1994	1995	1996
Output of manufactured products	115.8	120.6	123.8
All manufacturing excluding duty	113.8	118.9	121.7
All manufacturing excluding duty, seasonally adjusted	113.8	118.9	121.7
Products of manufacturing industry other than the food, beverages, petroleum, and tobacco manufacturing industries	112.5	117.5	119.8
Products of manufacturing industry other than the food, beverages, petroleum, and tobacco manufacturing industries, seasonally adjusted	112.5	117.5	119.8
Products of the food, beverages, petroleum, and tobacco manufacturing industries	121.8	126.1	130.7

Output of Selected Sub-Sectors of Industry

	1994	1995	1996
Other mining and quarrying products	113.9	120.0	125.9
Food products and beverages	119.3	122.3	125.8
Food manufacturing	117.5	120.1	123.3
Tobacco products	144.2	155.9	166.4
Textiles and textile products	112.6	116.7	119.4
Textiles	110.7	114.9	117.5
Wearing apparel: dressing and dyeing of fur	115.4	118.5	121.4
Leather and leather products	114.5	118.3	121.5
Wood and wood products	114.9	119.8	118.7
Pulp, paper, and paper products; publishing, printing	111.1	119.8	122.4
Pulp, paper, and paper products	107.6	126.3	127.6
Publishing and paper	109.7	115.3	118.6
Chemicals, chemical products, and man-made fibres	113.2	120.0	121.2
Rubber and plastic products	111.9	120.9	122.5
Other non-metallic mineral products	109.7	114.6	116.2
Basic metals and fabricated metal products	112.7	121.4	122.9
Base metals	110.6	122.2	121.3
Fabricated metal products, except machinery and equipment	111.1	115.9	119.0
Machinery and equipment n.e.c	114.3	118.0	121.6
Electrical and optical equipment	106.3	108.3	110.3
Office machinery and computers	88.5	86.0	82.5
Electrical machinery and apparatus n.e.c	117.3	124.6	128.7
Radio, television, and communications equipment and apparatus	99.3	100.9	102.3
Medical, precision and optical instruments, watches, and clocks	119.3	120.0	123.1
Transport equipment	116.9	121.3	124.5
Motor vehicles, trailers, and semi-trailers	117.5	122.5	126.2
Other transport equipment	118.4	124.0	126.3
Manufacturing n.e.c.	121.3	125.9	128.7

Source: Office for National Statistics. © Crown copyright 1998

Retail Prices Index Summary in the UK

(− = not applicable.)

Period	Annual average	Jan	June	Dec	Period	Annual average	Jan	June	Dec	Period	Annual average	Jan	June	Dec
January 1962=100					**January 1974=100**					**January 1987=100**				
1962	101.6	100.0	102.9	102.3	1974	108.5	100.0	108.7	116.9	1987	101.9	100.0	101.9	103.3
1963	103.6	102.7	103.9	104.2	1975	134.8	119.9	137.1	146.0	1988	106.9	103.3	106.6	110.3
1964	107.0	104.7	107.4	109.2	1976	157.1	147.9	156.0	168.0	1989	115.2	111.0	115.4	118.8
1965	112.1	109.5	112.7	114.1	1977	182.0	172.4	183.6	188.4	1990	126.1	119.5	126.7	129.9
1966	116.5	114.3	117.1	118.3	1978	197.1	189.5	197.2	204.2	1991	133.5	130.2	134.1	135.7
1967	119.4	118.5	119.9	121.2	1979	223.5	207.2	219.6	239.4	1992	138.5	135.6	139.3	139.2
1968	125.0	121.6	125.4	128.4	1980	263.7	245.3	265.7	275.6	1993	140.7	137.9	141.0	141.9
1969	131.8	129.1	132.1	134.4	1981	295.0	277.3	295.8	308.8	1994	144.1	141.3	144.7	146.0
1970	140.2	135.5	139.9	145.0	1982	320.4	310.6	322.9	325.5	1995	149.1	146.0	149.8	150.7
1971	153.4	147.0	154.3	158.1	1983	335.1	325.9	334.7	342.8	1996	152.7	150.2	153.0	154.4
1972	164.3	159.0	163.7	170.2	1984	351.8	342.6	351.9	358.5	1997	−	154.4	157.5	160.0
1973	179.4	171.3	178.9	188.2	1985	373.2	359.8	376.4	378.9	1998	−	159.5	−	−
1974	−	191.8	−	−	1986	385.9	379.7	385.8	393.0					
					1987	−	394.5	−	−					

Source: Office for National Statistics. © Crown copyright 1998

Purchasing Power of the Pound within the UK

To find the purchasing power of the pound in 1993, given that it was 100 pence in 1980, select the column headed 1980 and look at the 1993 row. The result is 48 pence. These figures are calculated by taking the inverse ratio of the respective annual averages of the Retail Prices Index. (Based on the Retail Price Index. In pence.)

Year	1980	1981	1982	1983	1984	1985	1986	1987	1988	1989	1990	1991	1992	1993	1994	1995	1996
1980	100	112	122	127	133	142	146	152	160	172	189	200	207	210	216	223	228
1981	89	100	109	114	119	127	131	136	143	154	169	179	185	188	193	199	204
1982	82	92	100	105	110	116	120	125	132	142	155	164	171	173	177	184	188
1983	79	88	96	100	105	111	115	120	126	136	148	157	163	166	170	176	180
1984	75	84	91	95	100	106	110	114	120	129	141	150	155	158	162	167	171
1985	71	79	86	90	94	100	103	108	113	122	133	141	146	149	152	158	161
1986	68	76	83	87	91	97	100	104	109	118	129	136	142	144	147	152	156
1987	66	73	80	83	88	93	96	100	105	113	124	131	136	138	141	146	150
1988	63	70	76	79	83	88	92	95	100	108	118	125	130	132	135	139	143
1989	58	65	71	74	77	82	85	88	93	100	109	116	120	122	125	129	133
1990	53	59	64	67	71	75	78	81	85	91	100	106	110	112	114	118	121
1991	50	56	61	64	67	71	73	76	80	86	94	100	104	105	108	112	114
1992	48	54	59	61	64	68	71	74	77	83	91	96	100	102	104	108	110
1993	48	53	58	60	63	67	70	72	76	82	90	95	98	100	102	106	109
1994	46	52	56	59	62	66	68	71	74	80	88	93	96	98	100	103	106
1995	45	50	54	57	60	63	66	68	72	77	85	90	93	94	97	100	102
1996	44	49	53	56	58	62	64	67	70	75	83	87	91	92	94	98	100

Source: Office for National Statistics. © Crown copyright 1998

Retail Prices Index Rate of Change in the UK

Item	% change on the previous year					
	1991	1992	1993	1994	1995	1996
Housing	−1.8	−0.7	−5.4	3.3	6.7	1.3
Food	5.2	2.1	1.8	1.0	3.9	3.2
Motoring expenditure	7.4	6.8	4.3	3.5	1.8	3.0
Alcohol	12.4	6.4	4.5	2.5	3.8	2.9
Household goods	6.2	3.3	1.2	0.3	3.7	3.3
Leisure services	11.5	8.1	4.5	3.7	3.2	3.6
Clothing and footwear	3.0	0.3	0.8	0.5	0.2	−0.7
Household services	8.3	5.8	3.6	0.1	−0.3	0.1
Catering	10.0	6.3	5.2	4.2	4.3	4.0
Leisure goods	4.7	2.6	1.4	−0.6	−0.1	1.6

Item	% change on the previous year					
	1991	1992	1993	1994	1995	1996
Fuel and light	7.9	2.2	−1.3	4.4	2.1	0.2
Personal goods and services	8.7	6.6	4.0	3.7	3.2	3.7
Tobacco	14.3	11.0	8.5	7.5	6.7	6.7
Fares and other travel	9.8	6.2	5.2	2.6	2.5	3.0
Total	5.9	3.7	1.6	2.4	3.5	2.4
All items except housing	7.6	4.7	3.1	2.3	2.7	2.7
All items except mortgage interest payments	6.7	4.7	3.0	2.3	2.9	3.0

Source: Office for National Statistics. © Crown copyright 1998

Household Participation in the National Lottery by Social Class in the UK

In the two-week diary-keeping period following interview between January and March each year for Saturday draw, and between February and March for Wednesday draw. (In percentages.)

Social group	Saturday draw			Wednesday draw
	1995	1996	1997	1997
Professional	63	55	54	21
Managerial and technical	70	70	62	33
Skilled non-manual	82	83	67	31
Skilled manual	89	80	80	47
Partly skilled	75	80	69	40
Unskilled	79	79	68	29
Economically inactive	62	62	52	29
Average	72	69	62	33

Source: Office for National Statistics. © Crown copyright 1998

Length of Time Necessary to Work to Pay for Selected Commodities and Services in the UK

Figure indicate length of time necessary for a person on average hourly adult earnings for all industries and services to work so that his/her net income pays for various goods. The earnings figures are based on full-time employees on adult rates whose pay was not affected for the survey period by absence. Net income also includes child benefit payments. (In hours and minutes.)

Commodity	Married couple with husband only working[1]		Working single mother with child		Commodity	Married couple with husband only working[1]		Working single mother with child	
	1971	1997	1971	1997		1971	1997	1971	1997
800 g white sliced wrapped bread	9 min	4 min	14 min	5 min	1 kg rump steak	1 hr 54 min	1 hr 8 min	2 hr 49 min	1 hr 22 min
1 pint milk	5 min	3 min	8 min	3 min	1 pint of beer (bitter)	14 min	13 min	20 min	15 min
Dozen eggs, first quality, size 2	21 min	12 min	32 min	14 min	20 cigarettes (king size filter)	22 min	22 min	33 min	27 min
1 kg potatoes	4 min	5 min	6 min	6 min	Road fund tax	40 hr	18 hr	59 hr	22 hr
1 kg cod fillets	1 hr 1 min	43 min	1 hr 30 min	53 min		20 min	26 min	54 min	26 min
					First class stamp	3 min	2 min	4 min	2 min

[1] Married man with non-earning wife and two children under 11.

Source: Office for National Statistics; DVLA; Postal Museum. © Crown copyright 1998

UK Taxation

Average Council Tax by Region of England and Wales (including Council Tax Bands for Scotland)

Council Tax assessment is performed in the following way: having taken into account its budgeted expenditure and precepts levelled by County Councils, the billing authority (that is, the District Council) then deducts whatever income it derives from the Business Rate, Rate Support Grant, and any other items of income; the amount then remaining is that raised by the Council Tax. This is divided among the number of houses in the District. The amount actually payable per house is adjusted by the proportions listed in the Bands A–H. Amounts shown below for Council Tax are headline Council Tax for the area of each billing authority for Band D, 2 adults, before transitional relief and benefit. The ratios of other bands are: A 6/9, B 7/9, C 8/9, E 11/9, F 13/9, G 15/9, and H 18/9. The revenue raised in these proportions has to equal the total sum required to meet that needed from the Council Tax. Averages are calculated by dividing the sum of the tax requirement for each area by the tax base for the area. The tax base is calculated by weighting each dwelling on the valuation list to take account of exemptions, discounts, and disabled relief, and the valuation bands it falls into. It therefore represents the number of Band D equivalent (fully chargeable) dwellings. (UA = Unitary Authority.)

	England	Wales	Scotland		England	Wales	Scotland
Band A	up to £40,000	up to £30,000	up to £27,000	Band E	£88,001–£120,000	£66,001–£90,000	£58,001–£80,000
Band B	£40,001–£52,000	£30,001–£39,000	£27,001–£35,000	Band F	£120,001–£160,000	£90,001–£120,000	£80,001–£106,000
Band C	£52,001–£68,000	£39,001–£51,000	£35,001–£45,000	Band G	£160,001–£20,000	£120,001–£240,000	£106,001–£212,000
Band D	£68,001–£88,000	£51,001–£66,000	£45,001–£58,000	Band H	£320,001 or over	£240,001 or over	£212,001 or over

England

Region	Council tax (£) April 1996
North East	
Cleveland[1]	763
Durham	689
Northumberland	679
Tyne and Wear	737
Average	724
North West and Merseyside	
North West	
Cheshire	676
Cumbria	711
Greater Manchester	746
Lancashire	716
Average	721
Merseyside	847
Average	745
Yorkshire and the Humber	
Humberside[1]	744
North Yorkshire[1]	587
South Yorkshire	674
West Yorkshire	665
Average	667
East Midlands	
Derbyshire	681
Leicestershire	635
Lincolnshire	622
Northamptonshire	628
Nottinghamshire	728
Average	665
West Midlands	
Hereford and Worcester	584
Shropshire	636
Staffordshire	599
Warwickshire	673
West Midlands (Met County)	704
Average	656

Region	Council tax (£) April 1996
Eastern	
Bedfordshire	643
Cambridgeshire	554
Essex	609
Hertfordshire	595
Norfolk	591
Suffolk	610
Average	600
London	616
South East	
Berkshire	606
Buckinghamshire	612
East Sussex	622
Hampshire	593
Isle of Wight UA[2]	640
Kent	598
Oxfordshire	604
Surrey	590
West Sussex	615
Average	603
South West	
Avon[1]	730
Cornwall and the Isles of Scilly	614
Devon	591
Dorset	585
Gloucestershire	597
Somerset	629
Wiltshire	604
Average	625

New Local Government Structure with Effect from 1 April 1996

Region	Council tax (£) April 1996
Former County of Cleveland	
Hartlepool UA	837
Middlesbrough UA	854
Redcar and Cleveland UA	640
Stockton-on-Tees UA	749

Region	Council tax (£) April 1996
Former County of Humberside	
East Riding of Yorkshire UA	742
Kingston upon Hull UA	655
North East Lincolnshire UA	735
North Lincolnshire UA	887
Former County of North Yorkshire	
York UA	581
North Yorkshire	589
Former County of Avon	
Bath and North East Somerset UA	673
Bristol UA	871
North Somerset UA	616
South Gloucestershire UA	653
Average England	646

Wales[3]

	Council tax (£) April 1996
Blaenau Gwent	428
Bridgend	500
Caerphilly	467
Cardiff	425
Carmarthenshire	553
Ceredigion	510
Conwy	401
Denbighshire	459
Flintshire	500
Gwynedd	481
Isle of Anglesey	417
Merthyr Tydfil	495
Monmouthshire	409
Neath Port Talbot	543
Newport	391
Pembrokeshire	436
Powys	434
Rhondda, Cynon, Taff	495
Swansea	455
Torfaen	438
The Vale of Glamorgan	435
Wrexham	489
Average Wales	462

[1] New local government structure came into effect on 1 April 1996.
[2] The Isle of Wight became a Unitary Authority on 1 April 1995.
[3] 1 April to December 1996 only.

Source: Department of the Environment, Transport, and the Regions; Welsh Office. © Crown copyright 1997

Estimated Average Incomes of Households Before and After Tax in the UK

Original income is the total income in cash and kind of the household before the deduction of taxes or the addition of state benefits. The addition of cash benefits (retirement pensions, child benefit, etc) and the deduction of income tax, council tax, water charges, domestic rates, and employees' National Insurance contributions give disposable income. By further allowing for taxes paid on goods and services purchased, such as value added tax (VAT), an estimate of 'post-tax' income is derived.

1995–96

Households	Retired households		Non-retired households[1]								All house-holds
	One adult	Two or more adults	One adult	Two adults	Three or more adults	One adult with children[2]	Two adults with one child[2]	Two adults with two children[2]	Two adults with three or more children[2]	Three or more adults with children[2]	
Number of households in sample	955	827	870	1,383	471	434	568	727	334	228	6,797
Average per household (£ per year)											
Original income	3,103	7,711	11,969	24,500	30,818	4,786	24,154	25,463	22,443	30,574	17,203
Disposable income	6,554	11,969	10,615	20,278	26,531	9,212	20,206	21,209	20,788	26,802	16,166
Post-tax income	5,931	9,236	8,404	16,181	20,705	7,202	16,078	16,985	16,536	20,936	12,819

[1] A retired household is defined as one where the combined income of retired members amounts to at least half the total gross income of the household, where a retired person is defined as anyone who describes themselves as 'retired' or anyone over the minimum National Insurance pension age describing themselves as 'unoccupied' or 'sick or injured but not intending to seek work'.
[2] Children are defined as persons aged under 16 or aged between 16 and 18, unmarried and receiving non-advanced further education.

Source: Office for National Statistics. © Crown copyright 1998

Income Tax in the UK

Source: Office for National Statistics. © Crown copyright 1998

Taxes on individual incomes are generally progressive in that larger incomes are subject to a greater amount of tax. Income tax is imposed for the year of assessment beginning on 6 April. According to the government's announcement, the basic and upper rates of income tax – 23 and 40 percent respectively – will not be raised in the current Parliament. The government has also announced its long-term objective of introducing a lower starting rate of tax of 10 percent. Of nearly 26 million income taxpayers, around 7.2 million are expected to pay only lower rate tax in 1997–98, about 16.2 million will be basic rate taxpayers, and 2.2 million will be in the higher rate tax band.

Allowances and reliefs reduce an individual's income tax liability. All taxpayers are entitled to a personal allowance against income from all sources. In addition, there is a married couple's allowance, which may be allocated to either partner, or they may receive half each. Tax relief for some allowances, including the married couple's allowance, is restricted to 15 percent.

Among the most important reliefs is that for mortgage interest payments on borrowing for house purchase up to a limit of £30,000. Relief, which is now (from April 1998) 10 percent, is usually given 'at source', that is, repayments that the borrower makes to the lender are reduced to take account of tax relief and the tax refund is passed directly by the tax authorities to the lender rather than to the individual borrower. Employees' contributions to their pension schemes also qualify for tax relief.

In general, income tax is charged on all income that originates in the UK – although some forms of income are exempt, such as child benefit – and on all income arising abroad of people resident in the UK. The UK has entered into agreements with many countries to provide relief from double taxation; where such agreements are not in force, unilateral relief is often allowed. British residents working abroad for the whole year may benefit from 100 percent tax relief. The 1998 budget included a measure whereby the 'foreign earnings deduction' would be eliminated for all but seafarers with effect from 6 April 1998.

Most wage and salary earners pay their income tax under the Pay-As-You-Earn (PAYE) system whereby tax is deducted and accounted for to the Inland Revenue by the employer, in a way that enables most employees to pay the correct amount of tax during the year.

A new self-assessment system for collecting personal taxation has been introduced. The first 'new style' tax returns were sent out in April 1997 to around 8 million people who regularly complete a tax return – primarily higher-rate taxpayers, the self-employed, and those receiving investment income (particularly where this is paid without tax being deducted). Taxpayers are now able to calculate their own tax liability, although they can choose to have the calculations done by the Inland Revenue. There is a new legal requirement to keep records of income and capital gains from all sources.

National Insurance Contributions in the UK

Source: Office for National Statistics. © Crown copyright 1998

Entitlement to National Insurance benefits such as Retirement Pension, Incapacity Benefit, contributory Jobseeker's Allowance, Maternity Allowance, and Widow's Benefit, is dependent upon the payment of contributions. There are five classes of National Insurance contributions. The rates given below are effective from April 1997 to April 1998.

Class 1

Class 1 contributions are paid by employees and their employers. Employees with earnings below £64 a week do not pay Class 1 contributions. Contributions on earnings of £64 a week and over are at the rate of 2 percent of the first £64 of total earnings and 10 percent of the balance, up to the upper earnings limit of £485 a week. Employers' contributions are subject to the same threshold. On earnings above the threshold, contributions rise in stages from 3 percent of total earnings up to a maximum of 10 percent when earnings are £210 or more a week; there is no upper earnings limit. The contribution is lower if the employer operates a 'contracted-out' occupational pension scheme.

Class 1A

Class 1A contributions are paid by employers who provide their employees with fuel and/or a car for private use. A Class 1A contribution is payable on the cash equivalent of the benefit provided.

Rates of Income Tax in the UK

(– = not applicable.)

Tax year	Taxable income	Lower rate	Basic rate	Higher rate	Additional rate applicable to trusts[2]	Rate applicable to trusts[2]
1991–92	bands of taxable income[1] (£)	–	1–23,700	over 23,700		
	rate of tax (%)		25	40	10	
1992–93	bands of taxable income[1] (£)	1–2,000	2,001–23,700	over 23,700	–	–
	rate of tax (%)	20	25	40	10	–
1993–94	bands of taxable income[1] (£)	1–2,500	2,501–23,700	over 23,700	–	–
	rate of tax (%)	20	25[3]	40	–	35
1994–95	bands of taxable income[1] (£)	1–3,000	3,001–23,700	over 23,700	–	–
	rate of tax (%)	20	25[3]	40	–	35
1995–96	bands of taxable income[1] (£)	1–3,200	3,201–24,300	over 24,300	–	–
	rate of tax (%)	20	25[3]	40	–	35
1996–97	bands of taxable income[1] (£)	1–3,900	3,901–25,500	over 25,500	–	–
	rate of tax (%)	20	24[4]	40	–	34
1997–98	bands of taxable income[1] (£)	1–4,100	4,101–26,100	over 26,100	–	–
	rate of tax (%)	20	23[4]	40	–	34
1998–99	bands of taxable income[1] (£)	1–4,300	4,301–27,100	over 27,100	–	–
	rate of tax (%)	20	23[4]	40	–	33

[1] Taxable income is defined as gross income for income tax purposes less any allowances and reliefs available at the taxpayer's marginal rate.
[2] Applies to the income of discretionary and accumulation trusts. Prior to 1993–94 trusts paid tax at the basic rate, with an additional rate of 10 percent.
[3] The basic rate of tax on dividend income is 20 percent.
[4] The basic rate of tax on dividends and saving income is 20 percent.

Source: Inland Revenue, 1998. © Crown copyright 1998

Income Tax Personal Allowances and Reliefs in the UK

(In pounds, unless otherwise indicated.)

Allowances and reliefs	1992–93	1993–94	1994–95	1995–96	1996–97	1997–98	1998–99
Personal allowance[1]	3,445	3,445	3,445	3,525	3,765	4,045	4,195
Married couple's allowance[2]	1,720	1,720	1,720	1,720	1,790	1,830	1,900
Age allowance[3]							
personal (aged 65–74)	4,200	4,200	4,200	4,630	4,910	5,220	5,410
personal (aged 75 or over)	4,370	4,370	4,370	4,800	5,090	5,400	5,600
married couple's (either partner between 65–74 but neither partner 75 or over)	2,465	2,465	2,665	2,995	3,115	3,185	3,305
married couple's (either partner 75 or over)	2,505	2,505	2,705	3,035	3,155	3,225	3,345
income limit	14,200	14,200	14,200	14,600	15,200	15,600	16,200
marginal fraction	$\frac{1}{2}$	$\frac{1}{2}$	$\frac{1}{2}$	$\frac{1}{2}$	$\frac{1}{2}$	$\frac{1}{2}$	$\frac{1}{2}$
Additional personal allowance[4]	1,720	1,720	1,720	1,720	1,790	1,830	1,900
Widow's bereavement allowance[5]	1,720	1,720	1,720	1,720	1,790	1,830	1,900
Blind person's allowance[6]							
single, or married (one spouse blind)	1,080	1,080	1,200	1,200	1,250	1,280	1,330
married (both spouses blind)	2,160	2,160	2,400	2,400	2,500	2,560	2,660
Life assurance relief (% of gross premium)[7]	12.5% or 0	12.5% or 0	12.5% or 0	12.5% or 0	12.5% or 0	12.5% or 0	12.5% or 0

[1] Every individual taxpayer is entitled to a personal allowance. The personal allowance is an amount you can receive without having to pay any tax, and can be set against any type of income. Where an individual's total income is less than the allowance, their tax liability is reduced to nil. However, any unused part of the personal allowance cannot be transferred to any other person.
[2] In the year of marriage the allowance is reduced by one twelfth for each complete month (beginning on the sixth day of each calendar month) prior to the date of marriage. The married couple's allowance, and allowances linked to it, that is, the additional personal allowance and the widow's bereavement allowance, are restricted to 20 percent in 1994–95 and 15 percent from 1995–96. In 1998–99 the maximum value of the allowance is £1,900 x 15% = £285.
[3] The amount of the personal allowance depends on the age of the individual taxpayer. The amount of the married couple's allowance depends on the age of the elder of the husband or wife. The maximum value of these age-related allowances will be given provided the individual taxpayer's total income is below the income limit shown. For incomes in excess of the limit, the allowance is reduced by £1 for each additional £2 of income until the basic levels of the personal and married couple's allowances are reached.
[4] The additional personal allowance may be claimed by a single person who has a child resident with him or her during the year (or by a married man with children if his wife is totally incapacitated).
[5] Widow's bereavement allowance is due to a widow in the year of her husband's death and in the following year provided the widow has not remarried before the beginning of that year.
[6] You can claim the blind person's allowance if you are registered as blind with a local authority in England or Wales, or live in Scotland or Northern Ireland, and are unable to perform any work in which eyesight is essential. Surplus blind person's allowance may be transferred to a husband or wife.
[7] From 1984–85 life assurance premium relief is confined to policies made before 14 March 1984.

Source: Inland Revenue, 1998. © Crown copyright 1998

Class 2

Class 2 contributions are paid by the self-employed. These contributions are at a flat rate of £6.35 a week. The self-employed may claim exemption from Class 2 contributions if their profits are expected to be below £3,590 for the 1998–99 tax year. Self-employed people are not eligible for unemployment and industrial injuries benefits.

Class 3

Class 3 contributions are paid voluntarily to safeguard rights to some benefits and for pension purposes. Contributions are at a flat rate of £6.25 a week.

Class 4

Class 4 contributions are paid by self-employed people on their taxable profits between £7,310 and £25,220 a year (in addition to their Class 2 contribution). Class 4 contributions are payable at the rate of 6 percent.

Employees who work after pensionable age (60 for women and 65 for men) do not pay contributions but the employer continues to be liable. Self-employed people over pensionable age do not pay contributions.

Capital Gains Tax in the UK

Source: Inland Revenue, 1998; Office for National Statistics. © Crown copyright 1998

Capital gains tax (CGT) is payable by individuals and trusts on gains realized from the disposal of assets. It is payable on the amount by which total chargeable gains for a year exceed the exempt amount (£6,800 for individuals and £3,400 for trusts in 1998–99). For individuals, CGT is calculated at income tax rates, as if the amount were additional taxable income, while there are special rates for trusts. Only gains arising since 1982 are subject to tax. Indexation relief is given to take account of the effects of inflation. Gains on some types of asset are exempt from CGT. These include the

Rates of Capital Gains Tax in the UK

Tax Year	Annual exempt amount (£)	
	Individuals	Trusts
1980–81 and 1981–82	3,000	1,500
1982–83	5,000	2,500
1983–84	5,300	2,650
1984–85	5,600	2,800
1985–86	5,900	2,950
1986–87	6,300	3,150
1987–88	6,600	3,300
1988–89 to 1990–91	5,000	2,500
1991–92	5,500	2,750
1992–93 to 1994–95	5,800	2,900
1995–96	6,000	3,000
1996–97	6,300	3,150
1997–98	6,500	3,250
1998–99	6,800	3,400

Source: Inland Revenue, 1998. © Crown copyright 1998

Rates of Corporation Tax in the UK

(– = not applicable)

Financial year commencing 1 April	Full rate (%)	Advance rate on distributions	Capital gains relief (general[1])	Small companies Rate (%)	Range of profit for marginal relief Lower limit (£)	Range of profit for marginal relief Upper limit (£)	Marginal relief fraction	Cooperative and building societies rate (%[2])
1980	52	$\frac{3}{7}$	$\frac{11}{26}$	40	80,000	200,000	$\frac{2}{25}$	40
1981	52	$\frac{3}{7}$	$\frac{11}{26}$	40	90,000	225,000	$\frac{2}{25}$	40
1982	52	$\frac{3}{7}$	$\frac{11}{26}$	38	100,000	500,000	$\frac{7}{200}$	40
1983	50	$\frac{3}{7}$	$\frac{2}{5}$	30	100,000	500,000	$\frac{1}{20}$	40
1984	45	$\frac{3}{7}$	$\frac{1}{3}$	30	100,000	500,000	$\frac{3}{80}$	40
1985	40	$\frac{3}{7}$	$\frac{1}{4}$	30	100,000	500,000	$\frac{1}{40}$	–
1986	35	$\frac{29}{71}$	$\frac{1}{7}$	29	100,000	500,000	$\frac{3}{200}$	–
1987	35	$\frac{29}{73}$	–	27	100,000	500,000	$\frac{1}{50}$	–
1988	35	$\frac{25}{75}$	–	25	100,000	500,000	$\frac{1}{40}$	–
1989	35	$\frac{25}{75}$	–	25	150,000	750,000	$\frac{1}{40}$	–
1990	34	$\frac{25}{75}$	–	25	200,000	1,000,000	$\frac{9}{400}$	–
1991	33	$\frac{25}{75}$	–	25	250,000	1,250,000	$\frac{1}{50}$	–
1992	33	$\frac{25}{75}$	–	25	250,000	1,250,000	$\frac{1}{50}$	–
1993	33	$\frac{9}{31}$	–	25	250,000	1,250,000	$\frac{1}{50}$	–
1994	33	$\frac{20}{80}$	–	25	300,000	1,500,000	$\frac{1}{50}$	–
1995	33	$\frac{20}{80}$	–	25	300,000	1,500,000	$\frac{1}{50}$	–
1996	33	$\frac{20}{80}$	–	24	300,000	1,500,000	$\frac{9}{400}$	–
1997	31	$\frac{20}{80}$	–	21	300,000	1,500,000	$\frac{1}{40}$	–
1998	31	$\frac{20}{80}$	–	21	300,000	1,500,000	$\frac{1}{40}$	–

[1] Chargeable gains realized after 16 March 1987 are taxed at the same rate as income.
[2] Normal corporation tax rates apply from 1985 after abolition of the special rate.

Source: Inland Revenue 1998; Office for National Statistics. © Crown copyright 1998

principal private residence, government securities, certain corporate bonds, and gains on shares and corporate bonds owned under Personal Equity Plans (PEPs). For companies, capital gains are charged to corporation tax, although there is no annual exempt amount. The table gives the annual amount exempt from tax. The rate of tax chargeable on the excess of gains over the annual exempt amount was 30 percent from 1980–81 to 1987–88. Thereafter the rate has been the same as income tax.

Rates of Corporation Tax in the UK

Source: Inland Revenue, 1998; Office for National Statistics. © Crown copyright 1998

The rates of company tax in the UK are lower than in most other industrialized countries. Companies pay corporation tax on their income and capital gains after deduction of certain allowances and reliefs. A company that distributes profits to its shareholders is required to pay advance corporation tax (ACT) on these distributions to the Inland Revenue. ACT is set against the company's liability to corporation tax, subject to a limit. In the budget of March 1998 the government announced the abolition of advance corporation tax from April 1998, and its intention to introduce a new instalment system for the payment of large companies' corporation tax. Shareholders (except pension schemes and companies) resident in the UK receiving distributions from UK-resident companies are treated as having some or all their liability to income tax satisfied for such income. The main rate of corporation tax is 31 percent (reducing to 30 percent from April 1999), with a reduced rate of 21 percent (reducing to 20 percent from April 1999) for small companies (those with profits below £300,000 a year). Relief is allowed for companies with profits between £300,000 and £1.5 million, so that the company's overall rate is between the main rate and the small companies' rate. Some capital expenditure may qualify for relief in the form of capital allowances. Examples include expenditure on machinery and plant, industrial buildings, agricultural buildings, and scientific research. Expenditure on machinery or plant by small or medium-sized businesses qualifies for a first-year allowance, normally of 50 percent if expenditure is incurred in the year to July 1998.

Rates of Inheritance Tax/Capital Transfer Tax in the UK

Source: Inland Revenue, 1998; Office for National Statistics. © Crown copyright 1998

Rates of Stamp Duty in the UK

(– = not applicable)

Commencing date	Threshold and rates of stamp duty				
	Nil rate	0.5%	1%	1.5%	2%
	Considerations up to £	Considerations exceeding £	£	£	£
6 April 1980	20,000	20,000	25,000	30,000	35,000
22 March 1982	25,000	25,000	30,000	35,000	40,000
13 March 1984	30,000	–	30,000	–	–
20 December 1991	250,000	–	250,000	–	–
20 August 1992	30,000	–	30,000	–	–
16 March 1993	60,000	–	60,000	–	–
8 July 1997	60,000	–	60,000	250,000	500,000
24 March 1998	60,000	–	60,000	250,000	500,000

Inheritance tax is essentially charged on estates at the time of death and on gifts made within seven years of death; most other lifetime transfers are not taxed. There are several important exemptions. Generally, transfers between spouses are exempt, and gifts and bequests to British charities, major political parties, and heritage bodies are also normally exempt. In general, business assets and farmland are exempt from inheritance tax, so that most family businesses can be passed on without a tax charge. Tax is charged at a single rate of 40 percent above a threshold, currently £223,000. Only about 2 percent of estates a year become liable for an inheritance tax bill. The table gives the lower limit of the slice of chargeable capital/transfer.

Rates of Stamp Duty in the UK

Source: Inland Revenue, 1998; Office for National Statistics. © Crown copyright 1998

Certain kinds of transfer are subject to stamp duty. Transfers of shares attract duty at 0.5 percent of the cost, while certain instruments, such as declarations of trust, have small fixed duties of 50p or £1. Transfers by gift and transfers to charities are exempt. The March 1998 Budget raised the rate of stamp duty on the transfers of property (except shares) over £250,000, in order to encourage stability in the housing market. Duty is now payable at 1 percent of the total price above £60,000, 2 percent for property above £250,000, and 3 percent for property where the price exceeds £500,000. The table shows conveyances and transfers of land, buildings, and property other than stocks and shares.

Value Added Tax in the UK

Source: Office for National Statistics. © Crown copyright 1998

Value Added Tax (VAT) is a broadly based expenditure tax, with a standard rate of 17.5 percent and a reduced rate of 5 percent on domestic fuel and power. It is collected at each stage in the production and distribution of goods and services by taxable persons. The final tax is payable by the consumer. The annual level of turnover above which traders must register for VAT is £50,000. Certain goods and services are relieved from VAT, either by being charged at a zero rate or by being exempt.

Zero Rating

Under zero rating, a taxable person does not charge tax to a customer but reclaims any input tax paid to suppliers. Among the main categories where zero-rating applies are: goods exported to other countries; most food; water and sewerage for non-business use; domestic and international passenger transport; books, newspapers, and periodicals; construction of new residential buildings; young children's clothing and footwear; drugs and medicines supplied on prescription; specified aids for handicapped people; and certain supplies by or to charities.

Exemptions

For exempt goods or services, a taxable person does not charge any output tax but is not entitled to reclaim the input tax. The main categories where exemption applies are: many supplies of land and buildings; insurance and other financial services; postal services; betting; gaming (with certain important exceptions); lotteries; much education and training; and health and welfare.

Rates of Inheritance Tax/Capital Transfer Tax in the UK

(– = not applicable. In pounds unless otherwise indicated.)

Rates of tax (%)	15.3.83–12.3.84	13.3.84–5.4.85	6.4.85–17.4.86	18.3.86–16.3.87	17.3.87–14.3.88	15.3.88–5.4.89	6.4.89–5.4.90	6.4.90–5.4.91	6.4.91–9.3.92	10.3.92–5.4.95	6.4.95–6.4.96	6.4.96–5.4.97	6.4.97–5.4.98	From 6.4.98
						Threshold above which tax is charged								
On Transfers on Death														
30	60,000	64,000	67,000	71,000	90,000	–	–	–	–	–	–	–	–	–
35	80,000	85,000	89,000	95,000	–	–	–	–	–	–	–	–	–	–
40	110,000	116,000	122,000	129,000	140,000	110,000	118,000	128,000	140,000	150,000	154,000	200,000	215,000	223,000
45	140,000	148,000	155,000	164,000	–	–	–	–	–	–	–	–	–	–
50	175,000	185,000	194,000	206,000	220,000	–	–	–	–	–	–	–	–	–
55	220,000	232,000	243,000	257,000	–	–	–	–	–	–	–	–	–	–
60	270,000	285,000	299,000	317,000	330,000	–	–	–	–	–	–	–	–	–
65	700,000	–	–	–	–	–	–	–	–	–	–	–	–	–
70	1,325,000	–	–	–	–	–	–	–	–	–	–	–	–	–
75	2,650,000	–	–	–	–	–	–	–	–	–	–	–	–	–
Lifetime Transfers														
15.0	60,000	64,000	67,000	71,000	90,000	–	–	–	–	–	–	–	–	–
17.5	80,000	85,000	89,000	95,000	–	–	–	–	–	–	–	–	–	–
20.0	110,000	116,000	122,000	129,000	140,000	110,000	118,000	128,000	140,000	150,000	154,000	200,000	215,000	223,000
22.5	140,000	148,000	155,000	164,000	–	–	–	–	–	–	–	–	–	–
25.0	175,000	185,000	194,000	206,000	220,000	–	–	–	–	–	–	–	–	–
27.5	220,000	232,000	243,000	257,000	–	–	–	–	–	–	–	–	–	–
30.0	270,000	285,000	299,000	317,000	330,000	–	–	–	–	–	–	–	–	–
35.0	700,000	–	–	–	–	–	–	–	–	–	–	–	–	–
40.0	1,325,000	–	–	–	–	–	–	–	–	–	–	–	–	–
42.5	2,650,000	–	–	–	–	–	–	–	–	–	–	–	–	–
45.0	–	–	–	–	–	–	–	–	–	–	–	–	–	–
50.0	–	–	–	–	–	–	–	–	–	–	–	–	–	–

Source: Inland Revenue, 1998; Office for National Statistics. © Crown copyright 1998

UK Investment and Banking

Assets and Liabilities of the Bank of England

(In millions of pounds.)

Year	Issue Department				Banking Department							
	Liabilities		Assets		Liabilities				Assets			
	Notes in circulation	Notes in Banking Department	Government securities	Other securities	Total	Public deposits	Bankers deposits	Reserves and other accounts	Government securities	Advances and other accounts	Premises equipment and other securities	Notes and coin
1989	16,849	11	13,946	2,914	5,398	69	1,750	3,565	1,354	726	3,307	11
1990	17,283	7	14,672	2,618	8,613	44	1,842	6,713	1,432	2,146	5,030	7
1991	17,466	4	11,791	5,679	5,825	104	1,813	3,894	1,346	2,443	2,031	5
1992	17,542	8	7,808	9,742	5,623	97	1,553	3,959	1,237	3,935	443	8
1993	18,218	12	6,816	11,414	11,095	6,205	1,700	3,175	1,174	9,411	498	12
1994	20,055	5	11,468	8,592	6,192	938	1,855	3,385	1,050	4,696	441	5
1995	21,262	7	14,552	6,717	7,114	1,159	2,001	3,941	1,090	5,499	518	7
1996	22,407	12	16,524	5,896	6,229	1,001	2,021	3,193	1,232	2,339	2,646	12

Source: Bank of England. © Crown copyright 1998

Assets and Liabilities of Banks in the UK

UK banks comprise offices in Great Britain and Northern Ireland of authorized institutions under the Banking Act 1987, together with certain institutions in the Channel Islands and Isle of Man, the Banking Department of the Bank of England, and, from 1993, in accordance with the Second Banking Co-Ordination Directive, UK branches of 'European Authorized Institutions' entitled to accept deposits in the UK and covered by the UK's Deposits Protection Scheme. Inter-bank items are netted with the resulting differences allocated to appropriate sectors, and adjustments (to deposits and loans) are made to allow for transit items. Figures for other currencies are affected by changes in exchange rates. Figures given are for the end of the year. (In millions of pounds.)

Assets and liabilities		1991	1992	1993	1994	1995	1996
Assets							
Lending to public sector	sterling	14,276	14,358	17,708	25,887	34,791	29,941
	other currencies	443	5,438	5,903	1,732	1,595	2,614
Lending to private sector	sterling[1]	411,633	415,805	426,836	438,096	493,367	547,734
	other currencies	62,268	69,481	76,949	83,432	110,002	134,330
Lending to overseas sector	sterling	42,700	52,294	62,760	62,690	66,424	77,076
	other currencies	479,760	596,308	620,690	674,564	774,480	754,729
Total		1,011,080	1,153,685	1,210,846	1,286,401	1,480,658	1,546,424
Liabilities							
Public sector deposits	sterling	11,615	14,996	18,563	13,005	17,104	17,660
	other currencies	238	391	344	340	585	628
Private sector deposits	sterling[1]	324,776	329,451	346,044	356,489	412,539	468,037
	other currencies	38,216	53,253	58,517	70,241	94,304	112,850
Overseas sector deposits	sterling	74,940	76,470	77,992	84,022	92,086	90,193
	other currencies	491,442	601,738	624,564	668,458	760,900	741,391
Non-deposit liabilities (net)		69,853	77,385	84,823	93,796	103,141	115,664
Total		1,011,080	1,153,685	1,210,846	1,286,401	1,480,658	1,546,424

[1] Revised rules on netting of customers' credit balances against their borrowing increased the UK private sector's outstanding balances of deposits and borrowing by £2.5 billion at end-December 1993. Re-netting during 1994 amounted to £1.7 billion.

Source: Bank of England. © Crown copyright 1998

Selected Banks' Base Rate in the UK

Percentage rates operative between the dates shown. The base rate is the rate of interest which forms the basis for the charges for bank loans and overdrafts, or deposit rates.

Date of change	New rate	1986 confirmed Date of change	New rate	1988 confirmed Date of change	New rate	1992 confirmed Date of change	New rate
1984		8 April	11.00–11.50	28 June	9.00–9.50	19 October	8.00
7 March	8.75–9.00	9 April	11.00	29 June	9.50	13 November	7.00
15 March	8.50–8.75	21 April	10.50	4 July	9.50–10.00		
10 May	9.00–9.25	23 May	10.00–10.50	5 July	10.00	**1993**	
27 June	9.25	27 May	10.00	18 July	10.00–10.50	26 January	6.00
6 July	9.25–10.00	14 October	10.00–11.00	19 July	10.50	23 November	5.50
9 July	10.00	15 October	11.00	8 August	10.50–11.00		
11 July	10.00–12.00			9 August	11.00	**1994**	
12 July	12.00	**1987**		25 August	11.00–12.00	8 February	5.25
9 August	11.50	10 March	10.50	26 August	12.00	12 September	5.75
10 August	11.00	18 March	10.00–10.50	25 November	13.00	7 December	6.25
17 August	10.50–11.00	19 March	10.00				
20 August	10.50	28 April	9.50–10.00	**1989**		**1995**	
7 November	10.00	29 April	9.50	24 May	14.00	2 February	6.25–6.75
20 November	9.75–10.00	11 May	9.00	5 October	15.00	3 February	6.75
23 November	9.50–9.75	6 August	9.00–10.00			13 December	6.50
		7 August	10.00	**1990**			
1985		23 October	9.50–10.00	8 October	14.00	**1996**	
11 January	10.50	29 October	9.50			18 January	6.25
14 January	12.00	4 November	9.00–9.50			8 March	6.00
28 January	14.00	5 November	9.00	**1991**		6 June	5.75
20 March	13.50–14.00	4 December	8.50	13 February	13.50	30 October	5.75–6.00
21 March	13.50			27 February	13.00	31 October	6.00
29 March	13.00–13.50	**1988**		22 March	12.50		
3 April	13.00–13.25	2 February	9.00	12 April	12.00	**1997**	
12 April	12.75–13.00	17 March	8.50–9.00	24 May	11.50	6 May	6.25
19 April	12.50–12.75	18 March	8.50	12 July	11.00	6 June	6.25–6.50
12 June	12.50	11 April	8.00	4 September	10.50	9 June	6.50
15 July	12.00–12.50	17 May	7.50–8.00			10 July	6.75
16 July	12.00	18 May	7.50	**1992**		7 August	7.00
29 July	11.50–12.00	2 June	7.50–8.00	5 May	10.00	6 November	7.25
30 July	11.50	3 June	8.00	16 September	12.00		
		6 June	8.00–8.50	17 September	10.00–12.00		
1986		7 June	8.50	18 September	10.00		
9 January	12.50	22 June	8.50–9.00	22 September	9.00		
19 March	11.50	23 June	9.00	16 October	8.00–9.00		

Source: Bank of England. © Crown copyright 1998

Corel

The Lloyd's Building in the City of London, designed by Richard Rogers

Top 10 Largest Banks in the UK

This table is ranked by market capitalization. Market capitalization is the market value of a company's issued share capital, that is the quoted price of its shares multiplied by the number of shares issued. (As of 22 January 1998.)

1997

Rank	Bank	Market capitalization (£ million)
1	HSBC Holdings	56,986.0
2	Lloyds TSB Group	44,980.0
3	Barclays	25,352.8
4	Halifax	18,323.0
5	National Westminster Bank	16,044.6
6	Abbey National	13,475.8
7	Standard Chartered	8,400.6
8	Bank of Scotland	6,147.1
9	Royal Bank of Scotland Group	5,972.8
10	Woolwich	4,976.0

Source: FT500, FT Surveys, Financial Times

Top 20 Largest Banks in Europe

This table is ranked by market capitalization. Market capitalization is the market value of a company's issued share capital, that is the quoted price of its shares multiplied by the number of shares issued. (As of 22 January 1998.)

1997

Rank	Bank	Country	Market capitalization ($ million)
1	HSBC Holdings	UK	91,339.4
2	Lloyds TSB Group	UK	72,094.9
3	Barclays	UK	40,636.1
4	Deutsche Bank	Germany	36,991.1
5	Union Bank of Switzerland	Switzerland	29,632.6
6	Halifax	UK	29,368.5
7	ABN Amro Holding	Netherlands	27,863.9
8	CS Holding	Switzerland	26,062.5
9	National Westminster Bank	UK	25,716.7
10	Dresdner Bank	Germany	24,825.4
11	Abbey National	UK	21,599.3
12	Swiss Bank Corporation	Switzerland	20,911.0
13	Banco Bilbao Vizcaya	Spain	20,616.9
14	Commerzbank	Germany	15,991.9
15	Banco de Santander	Spain	15,543.5
16	Société Générale	France	13,663.1
17	Bayerische Vereinsbank	Germany	13,577.9
18	Standard Chartered	UK	13,464.7
19	Bayerische Hypo & Wechsel Bank	Germany	10,861.8
20	Banque Nationale de Paris	France	10,613.0

Source: FT500, FT Surveys, Financial Times

Capital Issues and Redemptions of Borrowers in the UK

The table gives data on the value of securities issued to raise cash for companies. Redemptions cover 'partial redemptions' on instruments (where a bond, for example, pays out before reaching maturity) and payments on maturity. (N/A = not available. N = nil or negligible. LSE = London Stock Exchange. USM = Unlisted Securities Market. In millions of pounds.)

Year	Net issues of share and loan capital								Ordinary shares				
	Of which[1]			Comprising			Gross issues		Redemptions	Net issues			
	Total	Listed on LSE	Listed on USM	Local authorities and public corporations	Industrial and commercial companies	Financial institutions	Total	Of which: rights issues		Total	Listed on LSE	Listed on USM
1992	14,088	2,535	149	1	8,453	5,634	6,253	3,200	29	6,224	5,951	138
1993	29,933	9,723	248	-1	16,680	13,254	16,672	10,918	N	16,672	16,321	234
1994	26,199	8,246	507	N	13,496	12,703	14,994	4,958	2	14,992	13,751	505
1995	17,077	14,151	247	N	16,069	1,008	9,821	4,597	36	9,785	5,687	250
1996	25,916	N/A	N/A	N	13,659	12,257	10,810	3,884	400	10,410	N/A	N/A

[1] Ceased to be compiled as from February 1996.

Source: Bank of England. © Crown copyright 1998

Building Societies in the UK

The figures for each year relate to accounting years ending on dates between 1 February of that year and 31 January of the following year. (N/A = not available.)

Building societies	1988[1]	1990	1992	1994	1996[2]
Societies on register (number)	130	117	105	96	88
Share investors (£)	43,816,000	36,948,000	37,533,000	38,150,000	37,768,000
Depositors (£)	4,306,000	4,299,000	3,879,000	5,369,000	6,718,000
Borrowers (£)	7,369,000	6,724,000	7,005,000	7,222,000	6,586,000
Liabilities (£ millions)					
shares	149,791.1	160,538.2	187,108.4	201,812.2	196,546.4
deposits and loans	26,528.5	40,695.5	57,067.5	69,925.2	73,919.1
taxation and other	2,953.4	3,768.8	2,559.5	2,939.2	3,727.4
general reserves	8,466.0	10,206.1	12,634.4	16,312.3	17,940.3
other capital	1,105.1	1,639.7	3,144.7	4,125.7	4,762.3
Assets (£ millions)					
mortgages	153,015.4	175,745.4	210,994.5	240,297.2	241,472.9
investments	20,964.9 ⎫	35,050.9	42,909.1	50,786.7	51,016.7
cash	11,748.1 ⎭				
other	3,115.7	6,052.0	8,610.1	4,030.7	4,405.9
Total	188,844.2	216,848.3	262,514.5	295,114.6	296,895.5

Transactions	1988[1]	1990[3]	1992	1994	1996[2]
Shares (£ millions)					
received	111,716.9	N/A	N/A	N/A	N/A
interest thereon	9,852.6	N/A	N/A	N/A	N/A
withdrawn (including interest)	100,991.8	N/A	N/A	N/A	N/A
Deposits (£ millions)					
received	58,637.2	N/A	N/A	N/A	N/A
interest thereon	2,170.0	N/A	N/A	N/A	N/A
withdrawn (including interest)	54,924.7	N/A	N/A	N/A	N/A
Mortgages (£ millions)					
advances	47,374.9	43,081.0	34,989.0	34,829.0	38,488.0
repayments of principal	25,002.8	N/A	N/A	N/A	N/A
interest[4]	15,965.1	N/A	N/A	N/A	N/A
Management expenses (£ millions)	2,074.7	2,363.0	2,723.7	3,136.7	3,555.3
Rate of interest (%)[5]					
paid on shares	7.04	N/A	N/A	N/A	N/A
paid on deposits	9.21	N/A	N/A	N/A	N/A
received on mortgage advances	11.25	N/A	N/A	N/A	N/A

[1] 1988 and subsequent years include Northern Ireland societies, responsibility for which was acquired under the Building Societies Act 1986.
[2] The conversions to the banking sector of Cheltenham and Gloucester in August 1995 and National and Provincial in August 1996 have resulted in the following statistical treatment being adopted. The societies have been included in the flow figures (using flows up to date of conversion) but have been omitted from end year balances.
[3] Apart from mortgage advances and management expenses no new data are available for 1990 onwards. This is due to procedural changes.
[4] Includes amounts recoverable from HM Government under Option Mortgage Scheme and Mortgage Interest Relief at Source (MIRAS).
[5] Based on the mean of the amounts outstanding at the end of previous and the current year.

Source: Building Societies Commission. © Crown copyright 1998

Share Ownership in the UK

(For the end of the given year. In billions of pounds.)

Share ownership	1989	1990	1991	1992	1993	1994
Pension funds	154.8	140.4	165.7	199.5	251.5	211.8
Insurance companies	93.9	91.0	110.2	119.8	159.8	167.2
Unit trusts	29.7	27.3	30.4	38.0	52.7	51.8
Banks	3.3	3.2	1.1	3.0	4.7	3.0
Investments trusts	7.9	6.9	7.8	12.8	19.8	15.0
Other financial institutions	5.8	3.0	4.4	2.7	4.5	9.8
Individuals	104.3	90.5	105.3	125.4	141.1	154.6
Other personal sector	11.7	8.2	12.8	11.2	12.5	9.9
Public sector	10.2	9.0	6.8	11.3	10.2	5.8
Industrial and commercial companies	19.3	12.7	17.6	11.3	11.7	8.7
Overseas	64.5	52.7	68.1	80.7	130.2	124.3
Total	505.5	445.0	530.2	615.5	798.8	761.9

Source: Office for National Statistics. © Crown copyright 1998

Investment of Overseas Companies in the UK

Data show net investment analysed by area and main country; includes unremitted profits. Unremitted profits are profits that are not repatriated for the UK home company. (N = nil or negligible. - = net disinvestment overseas, i.e. a decrease in the amount due to the investor's home country. In millions of pounds.)

Country		1992	1993	1994	1995	1996
Western Europe						
EU[1]	Belgium and Luxembourg	65	-427	357	520	-73
	Denmark	91	97	76	58	67
	Germany	1,261	656	71	2,090	74
	France	802	-37	310	1004	356
	Greece	N	N	N	N	N
	Ireland, Republic of	N	N	224	-35	185
	Italy	-37	80	177	328	-171
	Netherlands	1,135	1,244	1,915	-633	2,677
	Portugal	N	N	N	N	N
	Spain	3	14	21	17	66
	Austria	-45	13	60	21	20
	Finland	54	-42	32	-36	2
	Sweden	129	-56	119	1,874	-374
	Total	3,433	1,590	3,367	3,555	3,891
EFTA[2]	Norway	-34	49	-131	124	1,060
	Switzerland	710	501	-44	912	1,817
	Total	674	548	-176	1,036	2,877
Other Western Europe		17	15	18	1	7
Total		4,124	2,154	3,208	4,592	6,775

Country	1992	1993	1994	1995	1996
North America					
Canada	-45	33	-246	-438	487
USA	3,748	5,142	2,138	9,293	6,994
Total	3,703	5,175	1,891	8,853	7,481
Other Developed Countries					
Australia	340	995	260	-708	1,037
Japan	-21	277	4	-39	390
New Zealand	-17	0	127	60	-104
South Africa	85	58	50	125	109
Total	385	1,330	441	-902	1,430
Rest of the World					
Africa	N	N	13	-8	9
Asia	651	293	183	190	319
Caribbean, Central and South America	17	818	453	-102	30
Other countries[3]	-76	N	-142	34	41
World total	8,816	9,871	6,046	12,654	16,084

[1] Figures include data for Austria, Finland, and Sweden.
[2] Figures exclude data for Austria, Finland, and Sweden.
[3] Includes the countries of the former USSR, the Baltic states, Albania, other Eastern European countries, and returns received with no country breakdown.

Source: Office for National Statistics. © Crown copyright 1998

Investment Overseas by Companies of the UK (by Country)

Data show net investment analysed by area and main country; includes unremitted profits. Unremitted profits are profits that are not repatriated for the UK home company. A minus sign indicates a net disinvestment overseas, i.e. a decrease in the amount due to the UK. (N = nil or negligible. In millions of pounds.)

Country		1992	1993	1994	1995	1996
Western Europe						
EU[1]	Belgium and Luxembourg	−191	160	132	438	953
	Denmark	47	273	64	416	−175
	Germany	536	1,333	1,261	1,478	1,277
	France	628	471	423	1,515	2,235
	Greece	167	44	84	163	680
	Ireland, Republic of	895	1,082	100	776	680
	Italy	222	282	298	406	343
	Netherlands	1,585	2,436	4,615	2,953	6,423
	Portugal	237	25	169	159	59
	Spain	217	−31	460	431	745
	Austria	16	13	102	90	86
	Finland	7	10	26	112	29
	Sweden	249	84	546	522	280
	Total	4,613	6,146	8,278	9,457	13,046
EFTA[2]	Norway	156	92	662	−255	92
	Switzerland	−1	−177	−16	−338	−139
	Total	163	−84	645	−594	−46
Other Western Europe	Cyprus	0	92	662	−255	92
	Gibraltar	46	−31	−6	−10	−17
	Malta	11	16	1	0	12
	Turkey	17	30	21	68	42
	Total	106	55	34	89	127
Total		4,882	6,116	8,985	8,950	13,126

North America

Country	1992	1993	1994	1995	1996
Canada	−106	5	−4	244	−169
USA	1,321	7,975	6,549	11,840	2,044
Total	1,214	7,980	6,544	12,084	1,874

Other Developed Countries

Country	1992	1993	1994	1995	1996
Australia	989	655	625	2,258	1,550
Japan	13	−49	245	169	324
New Zealand	110	71	264	67	249
South Africa	72	314	170	466	−28
Total	1,184	991	1,304	2,960	2,094

Rest of the World

		1992	1993	1994	1995	1996
Africa	Cameroon	−9	2	7	6	12
	Egypt	−48	19	10	10	28
	Ghana	28	36	23	83	42
	Kenya	23	33	9	67	24
	Malawi	3	5	6	14	18
	Mauritius	−7	0	0	38	108
	Nigeria	138	347	−197	−271	−94
	Sierra Leone	N	N	0	8	12
	Swaziland	N	2	8	20	17
	Tanzania	1	2	2	10	15
	Zambia	14	0	0	26	19
	Zimbabwe	59	36	28	16	25
	Total	228	−50	157	243	586

Country		1992	1993	1994	1995	1996
Asia						
Middle East	Jordan	N	0	0	1	1
	Saudi Arabia	4	−17	5	−4	13
	other Gulf states[3]	61	−228	232	−9	18
	Total	44	−236	253	154	27
other	Bangladesh	3	7	3	24	27
	Hong Kong	−18	456	128	734	590
	India	−27	139	87	61	107
	Indonesia	−59	69	92	−28	155
	Malaysia	272	363	286	28	181
	Pakistan	8	27	34	46	43
	Philippines	N	74	85	38	57
	Singapore	569	528	590	−48	537
	South Korea	37	44	27	47	33
	Sri Lanka	12	9	10	11	27
	Taiwan	−48	−5	68	69	38
	Thailand	51	103	177	245	194
	Total	902	1,885	1,551	1,334	2,286

Caribbean, Central and South America

Country	1992	1993	1994	1995	1996
Argentina	55	104	65	29	87
Bahamas	45	38	−9	11	13
Barbados	−15	11	9	10	11
Bermuda	506	586	349	291	153
Brazil	121	38	291	473	689
Cayman Islands	−36	−13	15	16	6
Chile	−22	101	76	220	89
Colombia	N	−245	204	123	100
Dominica	−22	24	15	3	6
Jamaica	13	34	145	52	38
Mexico	114	44	42	79	116
Netherlands Antilles	90	−5	329	−161	−14
Panama	211	−100	94	75	103
Trinidad and Tobago	6	4	27	4	5
Venezuela	24	34	145	52	38
Total	1,443	694	1,920	1,376	1,614

Other Countries[4]

Country	1992	1993	1994	1995	1996
Oceania	N	43	52	79	68
Total	209	−19	353	502	408

	1992	1993	1994	1995	1996
World total	10,107	17,358	21,040	27,604	22,014
Commonwealth total	2,840	3,381	2,740	3,896	3,734
Developing countries total[5]	2,799	2,224	3,952	3,387	4,633
Oil-exporting countries total[6]	203	231	192	−38	341

[1] Figures include data for Austria, Finland, and Sweden.
[2] Figures exclude data for Austria, Finland, and Sweden.
[3] Figures prior to 1995 include returns for Abu Dhabi, Bahrain, Dubai, and Oman; from 1995 returns for these countries are held separately.
[4] Includes the countries of the former USSR, the Baltic states, Albania, and other Eastern European Countries, and returns received with no country breakdown.
[5] Rest of the world, excluding the countries of the former USSR, the Baltic states, Albania, and other Eastern European countries.
[6] Abu Dhabi, Algeria, Dubai, Gabon, Indonesia, Iran, Iraq, Kuwait, Libya, Nigeria, Qatar, Bahrain, Saudi Arabia, and Venezuela.

Investment Overseas by Companies of the UK (by Category)

Assets are shown as positive; liabilities as negative. Investments are at market value. (N = nil or negligible. In millions of pounds.)

Item	1992	1993	1994	1995	1996
Investment Trust Companies					
Short-term assets and liabilities					
cash and UK bank deposits	820	992	1,006	1,660	1,424
other short-term assets	460	887	555	518	799
short-term liabilities	–706	–825	–1,301	–1,450	–848
Total (net)	574	1,054	260	728	1,375
Medium and long-term liabilities and capital					
issued share and loan capital	–4,827	–8,286	–10,978	–13,250	–8,330
foreign currency borrowing	–500	–595	–482	–703	–637
other borrowing	–919	–843	–752	–604	–135
reserves and provisions, etc	–22,859	–26,532	–27,494	–28,949	–41,120
Total	–29,105	–36,256	–39,706	–43,506	–51,222
Investments					
British government securities	996	1,013	2,490	1,194	1,422
UK company securities: loan capital and preference shares	814	854	1,000	846	832
UK company securities: ordinary and deferred shares	12,825	14,892	15,926	19,384	25,046
overseas company securities: loan capital and preference shares	514	533	896	740	279
overseas company securities: ordinary and deferred shares	11,943	16,886	17,873	19,485	21,047
other investments	1,494	1,122	1,401	1,761	1,408
Total	28,586	35,300	39,586	43,410	50,034
Unit Trusts					
Short-term assets and liabilities					
cash and UK bank deposits	2,506	3,141	3,791	3,556	4,113
other short-term assets	920	1,013	1,364	986	1,201
short-term liabilities	–890	–1,331	–1,381	–1,506	–1,370
Total	2,536	2,823	3,774	3,036	3,944
Foreign currency borrowing	–8	–39	–21	–1	N
Investments					
British government securities	664	959	1,414	1,774	2,716
UK company securities: loan capital and preference shares	1,664	2,906	2,970	3,298	5,029
UK company securities: ordinary and deferred shares	33,356	49,657	43,335	59,122	67,509
overseas company securities: loan capital and preference shares	570	864	1,001	2,145	1,288
overseas company securities: ordinary and deferred shares	21,862	32,904	33,473	36,062	47,346
other assets	669	1,189	1,302	1,668	1,953
Total	58,785	88,479	83,495	104,069	125,841
Property Unit Trusts					
Short-term assets and liabilities	103	237	119	280	255
Property	1,373	1,492	2,197	1,807	2,582
Other assets	34	60	11	11	11
Long-term borrowing	–42	–42	N	–131	–45

Source: Office for National Statistics. © Crown copyright 1998

Currency in the UK

The monetary unit in use in the UK is the **pound sterling** (£). The unit is divided into 100 **pence** (p).

Notes

UK notes are issued by the Bank of England in the following denominations: £5, £10, £20, and £50. Series D £10 note was withdrawn on 20 May 1994. Series E £50 note came into circulation on 20 April 1994.

Coins

Coins in general circulation are: nickel-brass £1, cupro-nickel 5p, 10p, 20p and 50p, and bronze 1p and 2p. 1p and 2p coins (from September 1992) are issued in copper-plated steel. Another legal tender is the nickel-brass £2 coin. It was, however, issued as a commemorative coin and as such is not intended for general circulation.

Coins that remain a legal tender and can sometimes be found in circulation are silver or cupro-nickel crowns dating from 1816 onwards. These had been equivalent to 25p; in 1990 the face value of the crown changed from 25p to £5.

Gold coins dating from 1838 onwards in denominations of 10 shillings (=50p), £1, £2, and £5 are legal tender but only at face value. Gold coins introduced in October 1987 as Britannia Gold Bullion Coins, in denominations of £10, £20, £50, and £100 are not found in general circulation.

Average *Financial Times*/Stock Exchange (FTSE) Actuaries Share Indices

FTSE Actuaries share indices	1992	1993	1994	1995	1996
FTSE 100[1]					
January	2,520.19	2,790.29	3,431.29	3,028.27	3,715.78
February	2,543.31	2,840.17	3,396.40	3,051.68	3,738.08
March	2,495.24	2,897.07	3,206.10	3,078.24	3,697.50
April	2,549.44	2,837.45	3,130.94	3,198.38	3,792.32
May	2,702.34	2,830.13	3,089.23	3,288.31	3,758.41
June	2,604.44	2,874.70	2,980.32	3,351.55	3,734.02
July	2,443.25	2,850.73	3,036.57	3,426.50	3,707.21
August	2,344.11	3,019.28	3,178.50	3,486.95	3,841.75
September	2,452.41	3,028.12	3,098.35	3,534.27	3,927.10
October	2,587.09	3,125.15	3,046.77	3,531.80	4,020.99
November	2,712.92	3,111.59	3,086.85	3,580.31	3,969.54
December	2,777.08	3,313.68	3,026.62	3,650.05	4,038.89
FT Non-Financials[1]					
January	1,353.77	1,496.94	1,818.98	1,631.29	1,919.36
February	1,374.45	1,522.74	1,818.96	1,631.03	1,941.86
March	1,354.06	1,552.97	1,745.46	1,631.47	1,953.49
April	1,387.84	1,522.32	1,708.89	1,690.67	2,021.61
May	1,476.08	1,522.69	1,690.44	1,738.74	2,013.00
June	1,419.66	1,539.22	1,618.42	1,767.52	1,999.60
July	1,319.06	1,521.63	1,642.28	1,806.86	1,958.89
August	1,258.02	1,614.52	1,726.77	1,846.24	2,002.27
September	1,301.02	1,623.43	1,680.38	1,868.17	2,043.06
October	1,364.42	1,653.67	1,639.72	1,851.30	2,069.12
November	1,425.57	1,643.34	1,654.73	1,854.75	2,040.44
December	1,473.45	1,733.10	1,622.39	1,879.54	2,056.24
Financials[1]					
January	1,385.89	1,718.78	2,619.71	2,084.15	2,916.24
February	1,384.60	1,822.76	2,607.79	2,125.71	2,942.72
March	1,346.68	1,888.45	2,324.02	2,170.51	2,837.38
April	1,353.29	1,901.37	2,240.03	2,264.66	2,866.93
May	1,505.57	1,926.91	2,164.18	2,350.00	2,898.78
June	1,452.21	2,011.94	2,111.15	2,411.52	2,867.16

FTSE Actuaries share indices	1992	1993	1994	1995	1996
Financials[1]					
July	1,352.32	2,065.80	2,129.92	2,466.78	2,886.69
August	1,267.47	2,175.74	2,197.58	2,526.20	3,078.43
September	1,348.16	2,174.42	2,181.71	2,599.72	3,149.04
October	1,483.95	2,310.58	2,137.44	2,691.46	3,292.82
November	1,622.84	2,289.99	2,188.27	2,805.33	3,300.68
December	1,645.58	2,502.99	2,134.40	2,879.80	3,418.82
Investment Trusts[1]					
January	1,822.17	2,064.63	3,058.15	2,609.12	3,079.31
February	1,825.74	2,217.35	3,056.69	2,604.17	3,142.90
March	1,808.41	2,244.24	2,901.35	2,583.43	3,106.91
April	1,826.01	2,225.74	2,844.45	2,648.57	3,216.41
May	1,945.40	2,256.79	2,812.57	2,762.00	3,237.58
June	1,837.53	2,330.08	2,709.20	2,791.09	3,170.26
July	1,726.09	2,372.09	2,725.64	2,874.20	3,075.76
August	1,626.22	2,563.16	2,882.04	2,938.91	3,147.91
September	1,688.05	2,549.64	2,831.12	2,969.59	3,182.58
October	1,801.19	2,663.51	2,732.79	2,924.52	3,204.46
November	1,933.38	2,669.09	2,732.46	2,932.60	3,137.47
December	2,000.31	2,880.07	2,686.29	2,998.07	3,129.25
FTSE All Share[1]					
January	1,203.08	1,351.60	1,710.35	1,501.87	1,818.72
February	1,218.70	1,384.99	1,709.09	1,506.17	1,839.78
March	1,199.04	1,415.40	1,619.80	1,511.04	1,836.04
April	1,225.16	1,393.70	1,582.06	1,566.98	1,892.47
May	1,310.73	1,397.10	1,559.27	1,614.69	1,889.96
June	1,260.28	1,419.94	1,497.44	1,643.59	1,875.05
July	1,171.62	1,413.38	1,517.70	1,680.80	1,844.67
August	1,114.82	1,498.55	1,591.47	1,718.13	1,899.46
September	1,156.91	1,505.06	1,554.01	1,743.26	1,938.37
October	1,221.44	1,544.80	1,516.65	1,739.84	1,973.94
November	1,284.96	1,535.11	1,533.46	1,755.17	1,951.91
December	1,324.08	1,628.88	1,502.42	1,783.30	1,976.41

[1] Working day average.

Source: Bank of England. © Crown copyright 1998

Glossary of Stock Market Terms

Source: The Stock Exchange

After hours dealing dealing done after the mandatory quote period which is treated as dealing done on the following business day

AGM Annual General Meeting of shareholders which a company must call every year

AIM Alternative Investment Market – the Exchange's new market which began trading in June 1995 for smaller and growing companies

Allotment letter see *renounceable documents*

APCIMS Association of Private Client Investment Managers and Stockbrokers

Arbitrage buying securities in one country, currency, or market, and selling in another to take advantage of price differences

Bear an investor who has sold a security in the hope of buying it back at a lower price as he thinks the market will go down

Bear market a falling market in which bears would prosper

Bed and breakfast deal selling shares one day and buying them back the next for tax purposes at the end of the financial year

Best execution brokers are advised to take reasonable care to find out the price which is the best available for their customers

Bid (1) the price at which the market maker will buy shares; (2) an approach made by one company wishing to buy the majority of another company's shares

Big Bang 27 October 1986, when the Exchange's new regulations took effect and the new automated price quotation system was introduced

Blue chip term for the most highly regarded shares; originally an American term, from the highest value poker chip

Bonus issue see Capitalization issue

Broker/dealer a London Stock Exchange member firm which provides advice and dealing services to the public and which can deal on its own account

Bull an investor who has bought a security in the hope of selling it at a higher price as he thinks the market will go up

Bull market a rising market in which bulls would prosper

Call the amount due to be paid to a company by the buyer of new or partly-paid shares

Call option the right (but not the obligation) to buy stock or shares at an agreed price up to a date in the future

Capital adequacy requirement for firms conducting investment business to have sufficient funds

Capitalization issue money from a company's reserves is converted into issued capital, which is then distributed to shareholders in place of a cash dividend; also known as a bonus or scrip issue

Commission the fee that a broker may charge clients for dealing on their behalf

Commodity any item that can be bought and sold; taken to refer to Exchange-traded items, including sugar, wheat, coffee, tin, etc

Consideration the money value of a transaction (number of shares multiplied by the price) before adding or deducting commission, stamp duty, etc

Contract note on the same day as a transaction takes place a member firm sends to the client a contract note detailing the transaction, including full title of the stock, price, stamp duty (if applicable), consideration, commission, time of deal, etc

Coupon (1) on bearer stocks, the detachable part of the certificate exchangeable for dividends; (2) denotes the rate of interest on a fixed interest security – a 10 percent coupon pays interest of 10 percent on the face value of the stock

Covered warrants covered warrants allow the buyer the right – but not the obligation – to buy or sell an asset at a specified price on, or before, a specified date

CREST the new paperless share settlement system, introduced by CRESTCo in 1996

Cum Latin for 'with', used in the abbreviations cum cap, cum div, cum rights, etc to indicate that the buyer of a security is entitled to participate in the forthcoming capitalization issue, dividend, or rights issue

Daily Official List the Daily Official List is the register of listed securities and gives the prices at which all stocks were traded on the previous day; it is produced by Extel

Debenture a loan raised by a company, paying a fixed rate of interest and secured on the assets of the company

Depositary receipts marketed internationally to sophisticated investors, these are negotiable certificates that give evidence of ownership of a company's shares. They are a good medium for international investors because they may be more liquid and more easily traded than the shares they represent

Discount when the market price of a newly issued security is lower than the issue price

Dividend that part of a company's profits after tax distributed to shareholders, usually expressed in pence per share; see *final dividend* and *interim dividend*

EDS Electronic Data Services – an historical turnover information service representing trading on the London Stock Exchange

EGM Extraordinary General Meeting – any meeting of a company's shareholders other than its AGM

Equity the risk sharing part of a company's capital, usually referred to as ordinary shares

Eurobond a long-term loan issued in a currency other than that of the country or market in which it is issued; interest is paid without the deduction of tax

Ex the opposite of *cum*, and used to indicate that the buyer is not entitled to participate in whatever forthcoming event is specified. Ex cap, ex dividend, ex rights, etc

FESE Federation of European Stock Exchanges

FIBV Fédération Internationale des Bourses de Valeurs (World Federation of Stock Exchanges)

Final dividend the dividend paid by a company at the end of the financial year

Fixed interest loans issued by a company, the government (gilts or gilt-edged), or a local authority, where the amount of interest to be paid each year is set on issue; usually the date of repayment is included in the title

Flotation the occasion on which a company's shares are offered on the market for the first time

FTSE indices figures that show the performance of the UK and the European markets over a period of time, the FTSE indices are run by FTSE International Ltd; they are:

    FTSE 100
    FTSE 250
    FTSE Small Cap
    FTSE 350 Yield
    FTSE All-Share
    FTSE Fledgling
    FTSE Eurotrack 100
    FTSE Eurotrack 200

Futures securities or goods bought or sold at a fixed price for future delivery; there may be no intention to take them up but to rely upon price changes in order to sell at a profit before delivery

Gearing a company's debts expressed as a percentage of its equity capital. High gearing means debts are high in relation to equity capital

GDRs Global Depositary Receipts are negotiable certificates that give evidence of ownership of a company's shares; they are marketed internationally, mainly to financial institutions

GEMMS Gilt-Edged Market Makers

Gilts or gilt-edged securities loans issued on behalf of the government to fund its spending; they fall into the following categories:
    'longs': those with a redemption date greater than 15 years
    'mediums': those with a redemption date between 5 and 15 years
    'shorts': those with a redemption date within five years

Gross before deduction of tax

Index linked gilt a gilt whose interest and capital change in line with the retail price index

Insider dealing the purchase or sale of shares by someone who possesses 'inside' information about the company. This is the information on the company's performance and prospects which has not yet been made available to the market as a whole, and which, if available, might affect the share price. In the UK such deals are a criminal offence

Interim dividend a dividend declared part-way through a company's financial year, authorized solely by the directors

Investment trust company whose sole business consists of buying, selling, and holding shares

IOSCO International Organization of Securities Commissions

Issuing house an organization, usually a merchant bank, that arranges the details of an issue of stocks or shares; it will also make sure the listing of that issue complies with Exchange regulations

LCAC Listed Companies Advisory Committee

Letter of renunciation this applies to a rights issue and is the form attached to an allotment letter which is completed should the original holder wish to pass entitlement to someone else, or to renounce rights absolutely

LIFFE London International Financial Futures and Options Exchange

Liquidity ease with which an item can be traded on the market

Listed company a company whose shares have been admitted to the Daily Official List; it has had to comply with the Exchange's listing regulations

Listing particulars the details a company must publish about itself and any securities it issues before these can be listed in the Daily Official List; often called a prospectus

Loan stock stock bearing a fixed rate of interest; unlike a debenture, loan stocks may be unsecured

London Market Information Link the Exchange's new main source of UK financial data for market professionals and information vendors; it is part of the Exchange's Sequence programme

Mandatory quote period the period of time from Monday to Friday when all registered market makers in a security must display their prices; for SEAQ the period is from 8.30 a.m.–4.30 p.m., and for SEAQ International, 9.30 a.m.–4.00 p.m.

Market maker an Exchange member firm which is obliged to offer to buy and sell securities in which it is registered throughout the mandatory quote period

Member firm a trading firm of the London Stock Exchange which may deal in shares on behalf of its clients or on behalf of the firm itself

Mid-price the price half-way between the two prices shown in the Daily Official list under 'Quotation', or the average of both buying and selling prices offered by the market makers; the prices found in newspapers are normally the mid-prices

Minimum quote size (MQS) the minimum number of shares in which market makers are obliged to display prices on SEAQ for securities in which they are registered

Net asset value the value of a company after all debts have been paid, expressed in pence per share

New issue a company coming to the market for the first time or issuing extra shares

Nil paid a new issue of shares, usually as the result of a rights issue, on which no payment has yet been made

Nil value shares shares newly issued by a company; these shares can usually be transferred on renounceable documents

Nominated adviser a London Stock Exchange approved adviser for AIM companies

Nominee name name in which a security is registered and held in trust on behalf of the rightful owner

Normal market size (NMS) the SEAQ classification system that replaced the old alpha, beta, gamma system; NMS is a value expressed as a number of shares used to calculate the minimum quote size for each security

Offer the price at which the market maker will sell shares to investors

Offer for sale a method of bringing a company to the market. The public can apply for shares directly at a fixed price; a prospectus containing details of the sale must be printed in a national newspaper

Option the right (but not the obligation) to buy or sell securities at a fixed price within a specified period

Ordinary shares the most common form of share; holders receive dividends which vary in amount in line with the profitability of the company and recommendation of directors; the holders are the owners of the company

Par the nominal value of a security

PEP a Personal Equity Plan, allowing investment in a number of shares. It carries various tax benefits including receiving dividends without paying income tax on the income, and sales free from capital gains tax on the profit

PIA Personal Investment Authority – the self-regulating organization responsible for personal pensions and unit trusts

Portfolio a collection of securities owned by an investor

POTAM the Panel on Take-Overs and Mergers regulates conduct of take-overs and is non-statutory

Preference shares these are normally fixed-income shares whose holders have the right to receive dividends before ordinary shareholders but after debenture and loan stock holders have received their interest

Preferential form the London Stock Exchange allows companies offering shares to the public to set aside up to 10 percent of the issue for application from employees and, where a parent company is floating off a subsidiary, from shareholders of the parent company; separate application forms, usually pink (hence the nickname pink forms), are used for this

Premium (1) if the market price of a new security is higher than the usual price, the difference is the premium; if it is lower, the difference is called the discount; (2) the cost of purchasing a trading option

Price/Earnings ratio (P/E ratio) a measure of the level of confidence investors have in a company (rightly or wrongly); generally, the higher the figure, the higher the confidence. It is worked out by dividing the current share price by the last published earnings per share which is net profit divided by the number of ordinary shares

Price sensitive information information that has to be reported to the Exchange's Regulatory News Service, that may have an effect on a company's share price

Primary market the function of a stock exchange in bringing securities to the market for the first time; money is being raised either for the founders of the company or to fund future growth

Private company a company that is not a public company and which is not allowed to offer its shares to the general public

Privatization conversion of a state run company to a public limited company status often accompanied by a sale of its shares to the public

ProShare an independent organization that promotes share ownership among individual investors, including employees

Prospectus document giving the details that a company is required to make public to support a new issue of shares; see *listing particulars*

Proxy a person empowered by a shareholder to vote on his behalf at company meetings

Public limited company (plc) A company whose shares may be purchased by the public and traded freely on the open market and whose share capital is not less than a statutory minimum

Put option the right (but not the obligation) to sell at an agreed price at or within a stated future time

Quote vendors screen-based computer system providing instant information on prices of shares, foreign exchanges, and commodities

Redemption date the date on which a security (usually a fixed interest stock) is due to be repaid by the issuer at its full face value; the year is included in the title of the security; the actual redemption date is that on which the last interest is due to be paid

Registrar an organization that takes responsibility for maintaining a company's share register

Regulatory News Service (RNS) a service operated by the Exchange, in its role as competent authority for listing, which ensures that price-sensitive information from listed companies is collected and then disseminated to all RNS subscribers at the same time

Renounceable documents temporary evidence of ownership, of which there are three main types: when a company offers shares to the public, it sends an allotment letter to the successful applicants; if it makes a rights issue, it sends a provisional allotment letter to its shareholders; in the case of a capitalization issue, it sends a renounceable certificate.

All of these are in effect bearer securities, and are valuable. Each includes full instructions on what should happen if the holder wishes to have the newly issued shares registered in their own name, or if they wish to renounce them in favour of somebody else

RIE Recognized Investment Exchange – an investment exchange that meets the Securities Investment Board's requirements for recognition

Rights issue an invitation to existing shareholders to purchase additional shares in the company

SAEF SEAQ Automated Execution Facility – this enables small trades in UK shares to be carried out automatically at a computer terminal instead of over the telephone

Scrip issue see *capitalization issue*

SEAQ The Stock Exchange Automated Quotations system for UK securities; this is a continuously updated computer database containing price quotations and trade reports in UK securities. SEAQ carries the market makers' bids and offers for the UK securities and is part of the Exchange's Sequence programme

SEAQ International the Exchange's electronic price quotation system for non-UK equities; similar to SEAQ, it is part of the Exchange's Sequence programme

SEATS PLUS a service which supports the trading of listed UK equities in which turnover is insufficient for the market making system. It is distributed via a number of screen-based information

10 Most Active Stocks in the UK

1997

Rank	Company	Turnover value (£ millions)	Shares traded (millions)
1	HSBC Holdings	48,267.4	2,888.1
2	British Telecommunications	39,977.4	9,228.9
3	Shell Transport and Trading	25,879.0	4,242.8
4	British Petroleum Company	25,247.0	3,033.2
5	Glaxo Wellcome	24,313.1	1,961.6
6	Lloyds TSB Group	20,788.2	3,344.6
9	SmithKline Beecham	19,761.5	2,269.5
8	Barclays plc	19,462.1	1,555.8
9	National Westminster Bank	15,448.4	1,881.2
10	BAT Industries	14,764.4	2,700.2

Source: London Stock Exchange Fact File (1998), London Stock Exchange Ltd. Reproduced with permission.

services; it shows current orders, company information, historical trading activity for each stock and the sole market maker, where only one is registered; it is part of the Exchange's Sequence programme

Secondary market marketplace for trading in securities that are not new issues

Securities general name for stocks and shares of all types; in common usage, stocks are fixed interest securities and shares are the rest

Securities and Futures Authority (SFA) the self-regulating organization (previously known as the Securities Association)

responsible for regulating the conduct of brokers and dealers in securities, options, and futures, including most member firms of the Exchange

Securities and Investments Board (SIB) agency appointed by the government under the Financial Services Act to oversee the regulation of the investment industry, including the SROs, RIEs, and clearing houses

Self-regulating Organization (SRO) an organization recognized by the SIB and responsible for monitoring the conduct of business by, and capital adequacy of, investment firms

SEPON the Stock Exchange Pool Nominee – an account into which stock is registered during the course of settlement

Sequence an integrated, reliable computer system developed by the Exchange to deliver a wider range of better quality trading and information services to market participants; the SEAQ, SEATS PLUS, and SEAQ international trading services operate on the new system

Average Zero Coupon Yields in the UK

Zero coupon yields	1992	1993	1994	1995	1996	Zero coupon yields	1992	1993	1994	1995	1996
Nominal 5 Year Yield[1]						*Nominal 20 Year Yield*[1] (continued)					
January	9.37	7.14	5.84	8.68	6.85	July	8.80	8.31	8.25	8.38	8.41
February	9.14	6.78	6.19	8.57	7.13	August	8.95	7.70	8.37	8.30	8.34
March	9.56	6.66	6.93	8.49	7.47	September	9.12	7.49	8.51	8.21	8.34
April	9.32	6.97	7.58	8.30	7.53	October	9.91	7.36	8.43	8.45	8.06
May	8.91	7.23	8.00	7.98	7.54	November	9.49	7.30	8.37	8.14	7.92
June	8.91	7.15	8.47	7.81	7.48	December	9.36	6.77	8.27	7.95	7.78
July	8.92	6.83	8.31	7.92	7.31						
August	9.31	6.44	8.52	7.73	7.21	*Real 10 Year Yield*[1]					
September	9.00	6.43	8.75	7.50	7.19	January	4.21	3.62	2.76	3.90	3.49
October	7.71	6.30	8.69	7.58	6.98	February	4.15	3.34	2.89	3.87	3.62
November	7.08	6.28	8.53	7.23	7.19	March	4.24	3.17	3.13	3.87	3.75
December	7.35	5.86	8.54	6.90	7.21	April	4.40	3.28	3.34	3.78	3.69
						May	4.31	3.37	3.59	3.60	3.77
Nominal 10 Year Yield[1]						June	4.25	3.34	3.82	3.61	3.82
January	9.23	8.37	6.35	8.60	7.48	July	4.34	3.26	3.87	3.65	3.76
February	9.13	8.11	6.79	8.52	7.82	August	4.53	3.21	3.80	3.51	3.65
March	9.46	7.80	7.48	8.47	8.10	September	4.52	3.12	3.84	3.48	3.45
April	9.21	7.93	7.88	8.33	8.08	October	3.79	3.05	3.84	3.68	3.29
May	8.84	8.21	8.33	8.08	8.12	November	3.47	2.98	3.84	3.57	3.33
June	8.86	7.99	8.73	8.05	8.11	December	3.72	2.81	3.86	3.49	3.35
July	8.79	7.62	8.53	8.23	7.98						
August	9.02	7.12	8.59	8.10	7.87	*Real 20 Year Yield*[1]					
September	8.96	7.01	8.79	7.95	7.87	January	4.30	3.85	3.01	3.85	3.58
October	8.68	6.92	8.68	8.12	7.58	February	4.29	3.65	3.16	3.87	3.69
November	8.24	6.94	8.53	7.80	7.59	March	4.48	3.51	3.37	3.87	3.79
December	8.31	6.43	8.46	7.53	7.55	April	4.55	3.50	3.44	3.80	3.74
						May	4.39	3.60	3.62	3.62	3.83
Nominal 20 Year Yield[1]						June	4.30	3.57	3.84	3.63	3.87
January	9.30	9.46	6.76	8.41	7.99	July	4.37	3.50	3.87	3.66	3.81
February	9.18	9.18	7.11	8.35	8.30	August	4.57	3.35	3.79	3.57	3.74
March	9.47	8.83	7.70	8.33	8.50	September	4.47	3.25	3.81	3.57	3.73
April	9.31	8.78	7.92	8.25	8.41	October	3.93	3.19	3.80	3.71	3.59
May	9.00	8.92	8.25	8.08	8.47	November	3.78	3.20	3.79	3.61	3.60
June	9.10	8.75	8.40	8.15	8.49	December	3.96	3.06	3.81	3.55	3.59

[1] Working day average.

Source: Bank of England. © Crown copyright 1998

SETS Stock Exchange Electronic Trading Service

Settlement once a deal has been made, the settlement process transfers stock from seller to buyer and arranges the corresponding movement of money between buyer and seller (see *Talisman*)

Settlement day day on which bought stock is due for delivery to the buyer and the appropriate payment to the seller

Shares see *Securities*

Shorts See *Gilts*

Stag one who applies for a new issue in the hope of being able to sell the shares allotted to him/her at a profit as soon as dealing starts

Stamp duty a UK tax currently levied on the purchase of shares

Stocks see *Securities*

Talisman the computerized settlement system used by the Exchange until April 1997, which acted as a central clearing house for transactions in equities (see *CREST*)

Tender offer in an offer by tender, buyers of shares specify the price at which they are willing to buy

Touch the best buying and selling prices available from a market maker on SEAQ and SEAQ International in a given security at any one time

Traded Options transferable options with the right to buy and sell a standardized amount of a security at a fixed price within a specified period

Transaction a deal made on the Exchange or subject to the rules of the Exchange

Transfer the form signed by the seller of a security authorizing the company to remove

his/her name from the register, and substitute that of the buyer

Underwriting an arrangement by which a company is guaranteed that an issue of shares will raise a given amount of cash; the underwriters undertake to subscribe for any of the issue not taken up by the public; they charge commission for this service

Unit trust a portfolio of holdings in various companies, divided into units and managed by professionals

White knight a company that rescues another company which is in financial difficulty, especially one which saves a company from an unwelcome take-over bid

Yield the return earned on an investment taking into account the annual income and its present capital value; there are a number of different types of yield, and in some cases different methods of calculating each type

Average Rates on Representative British Government Stocks

Rate	1992	1993	1994	1995	1996	Rate	1992	1993	1994	1995	1996
5 Year Conventional Rate[1]						**20 Year Conventional Rate[1] (continued)**					
January	9.57	6.88	5.76	8.61	6.78	July	8.85	7.98	8.35	8.30	8.21
February	9.34	6.72	6.05	8.52	7.02	August	9.06	7.46	8.46	8.19	8.12
March	9.75	6.62	6.72	8.44	7.56	September	9.08	7.31	8.65	8.06	8.11
April	9.54	6.91	7.33	8.26	7.43	October	9.15	7.18	8.56	8.26	7.84
May	9.09	7.10	7.74	7.96	7.61	November	8.78	7.12	8.46	7.93	7.77
June	9.12	7.01	8.22	7.79	7.52	December	8.78	6.57	8.39	7.70	7.67
July	9.13	6.70	8.06	7.90	7.35						
August	9.50	6.35	8.31	7.69	7.21	**10 Year Index-Linked Rate[1]**					
September	9.13	6.34	8.61	7.45	7.20	January	4.29	3.60	2.70	3.89	3.42
October	7.80	6.17	8.57	7.54	7.01	February	4.18	3.23	2.81	3.87	3.57
November	7.15	6.09	8.44	7.16	7.22	March	4.29	3.07	3.07	3.86	3.70
December	7.38	5.66	8.49	6.83	7.26	April	4.47	3.11	3.25	3.79	3.66
						May	4.41	3.30	3.51	3.58	3.74
10 Year Conventional Rate[1]						June	4.40	3.31	3.78	3.58	3.80
January	9.47	8.22	6.23	8.66	7.42	July	4.51	3.22	3.85	3.61	3.82
February	9.32	7.91	6.61	8.59	7.75	August	4.76	3.16	3.82	3.52	3.59
March	9.67	7.66	7.29	8.53	8.05	September	4.68	3.09	3.85	3.46	3.57
April	9.43	7.82	7.68	8.39	8.05	October	3.82	3.03	3.84	3.65	3.41
May	9.06	8.06	8.13	8.12	8.08	November	3.40	2.96	3.84	3.54	3.42
June	9.14	7.87	8.54	8.08	8.04	December	3.61	2.75	3.85	3.45	3.41
July	9.08	7.49	8.37	8.23	7.91						
August	9.35	6.98	8.52	8.10	7.81	**20 Year Index-Linked Rate[1]**					
September	9.17	6.90	8.80	7.92	7.80	January	4.34	3.84	2.96	3.91	3.58
October	8.68	6.81	8.70	8.08	7.51	February	4.32	3.64	3.11	3.89	3.70
November	8.26	6.77	8.57	7.75	7.56	March	4.49	3.50	3.35	3.89	3.82
December	8.38	6.29	8.53	7.45	7.54	April	4.59	3.51	3.45	3.81	3.77
						May	4.42	3.62	3.64	3.64	3.84
20 Year Conventional Rate[1]						June	4.35	3.57	3.88	3.67	3.88
January	9.23	8.74	6.53	8.45	7.73	July	4.42	3.48	3.90	3.71	3.72
February	9.12	8.44	6.88	8.43	8.04	August	4.61	3.32	3.83	3.62	3.75
March	9.44	8.19	7.49	8.40	8.28	September	4.55	3.22	3.87	3.60	3.74
April	9.25	8.42	7.81	8.30	8.26	October	4.00	3.15	3.86	3.74	3.60
May	8.93	8.58	8.18	8.09	8.31	November	3.77	3.14	3.85	3.62	3.59
June	8.99	8.36	8.48	8.08	8.31	December	3.94	2.98	3.86	3.55	3.58

[1] Working day average.

Source: Bank of England. © Crown copyright 1998

Futures Market: Contract Records in the UK

The data give the record number of contracts exchanged for products on the London International Financial Futures and Options Exchange (LIFFE). (As of June 1998. N/A = not available.)

Exchange	Daily volume		Monthly volume		Daily open interest	
	Amount	Date	Amount	Date	Amount	Date
Total	1,986,892	9 October 1997	25,719,682	October 1997	8,800,419	18 February 1998
Short-Term Interest Rate Products						
Futures						
Three month Sterling	552,954	17 June 1998	2,746,650	January 1998	832,635	27 February 1998
Three month Euromark	582,185	9 October 1997	6,614,051	October 1997	2,229,691	27 February 1998
One month Euromark	14,665	15 January 1997	43,547	January 1997	36,168	17 February 1997
Three month Eurolira	214,517	3 March 1998	2,102,969	October 1997	874,410	27 February 1998
Three month Euroswiss	83,390	8 June 1998	573,261	October 1997	191,381	7 November 1997
Three month ECU	8,927	21 October 1993	107,091	March 1995	41,147	5 September 1997
Three month Euroyen	24,150	26 September 1997	49,715	March 1997	N/A	N/A
Options						
Three month Sterling	117,876	17 June 1998	537,360	September 1994	696,690	21 September 1994
Three month Euromark	98,818	9 October 1997	679,924	October 1997	905,479	9 December 1996
Three month Euroswiss	10,300	27 March 1998	9,841	February 1998	19,844	17 June 1996
Three month Eurolira	64,819	14 October 1997	508,811	February 1998	611,804	27 February 1998
Medium- and Long-Term Bond Products						
Futures						
Long Gilt	236,433	6 May 1997	2,733,630	February 1994	271,926	28 February 1997
German Government Bond (Bund)	419,700	4 March 1998	5,066,606	February 1996	340,585	28 February 1997
German Government Bond (Bobl)	32,460	3 October 1997	333,343	October 1997	37,714	12 January 1998
Italian Government Bond (BTP)	185,241	3 March 1998	1,675,263	February 1997	155,437	18 February 1998
Japanese Government Bond (JGB)	12,082	21 May 1997	124,033	May 1997	N/A	N/A
Options						
Long Gilt	52,882	13 April 1992	415,060	N/A	177,002	N/A
German Government Bond (Bund)	125,820	22 October 1997	1,468,684	N/A	643,490	N/A
German Government Bond (Bobl)	13,338	30 October 1997	96,442	October 1997	58,828	7 November 1997
Italian Government Bond (BTP)	54,852	3 October 1996	382,047	October 1996	411,885	21 November 1996
Equity Products	184,960	9 May 1997	1,599,999	June 1997	N/A	N/A
Futures						
FTSE 100 Index Future	55,158	18 June 1997	525,470	N/A	92,471	N/A
FTSE 250 Index Future	5,162	24 May 1995	14,030	December 1997	10,099	16 December 1997
Options						
FTSE 100 Index Options	116,890	5 November 1996	804,705	October 1996	N/A	N/A
FTSE 100 Index Options (SEI)	94,946	5 November 1996	429,818	November 1996	398,687	15 November 1996
FTSE 100 Index Options (ESX)	58,621	13 June 1997	470,141	July 1997	656,251	20 June 1997
FTSE 100 Index FLEX Options	6,650	27 July 1995	20,589	July 1995	65,167	20 December 1996
Equity Options	114,400	21 October 1987	1,229,271	June 1987	1,243,765	19 October 1987
Commodity Products						
Futures						
No 7 cocoa	49,662	22 June 1993	253,224	September 1993	203,302	17 November 1997
Robusta coffee	21,759	27 June 1994	186,720	January 1997	54,988	29 May 1997
No 5 white sugar	8,696	25 September 1997	98,180	September 1997	45,086	21 January 1998
Wheat	1,759	18 April 1996	16,606	April 1997	11,104	29 August 1997
Barley	869	24 November 1997	3,904	October 1992	3,056	23 October 1992
BIFFEX	1,758	19 May 1988	15,947	May 1988	5,360	19 March 1996
Potato	1,020	9 March 1994	6,713	March 1994	3,259	2 March 1994
Options						
No 7 cocoa	5,470	27 June 1995	21,936	May 1990	43,673	18 November 1993
Robusta coffee	6,010	21 January 1993	33,880	March 1994	61,025	14 June 1994
No 5 white sugar	2,200	26 February 1997	8,999	February 1998	10,111	28 January 1998
Wheat	515	29 March 1995	2,560	November 1995	7,637	7 December 1995
Barley	100	18 September 1992	400	October 1992	400	9 October 1992
BIFFEX	120	25 July 1995	300	February 1998	331	15 July 1996
Potato	20	2 December 1996	20	December 1996	40	19 February 1997

Source: London International Financial Futures and Options Exchange (LIFFE)

Futures Market: Total Contracts Exchanged in the UK

The table gives the total number of contracts exchanged on the London International Financial Futures and Options Exchange (LIFFE). (– = not applicable. Annual total volume as of February 1998.)

Exchange	1996	1997
Total	167,940,452	209,427,578
Short-Term Interest Rate Products		
Futures		
Three month Sterling	15,793,775	20,370,846
Three month Euromark	36,231,178	43,326,030
One month Euromark	48,644	113,408
Three month Eurolira	6,936,873	14,894,163
Three month Euroswiss	3,299,058	4,746,234
Three month ECU	602,518	534,457
Three month Euroyen	242,413	162,686
Options		
Three month Sterling	2,213,494	2,662,716
Three month Euromark	4,888,942	4,225,874
Three month Euroswiss	45,568	31,390
Three month Eurolira	953,558	2,402,371
Total	71,256,021	93,470,175
Long-Term Bond Products		
Futures		
Long Gilt	15,408,010	19,653,565
German Government Bond (Bund)	39,801,928	44,984,029
German Government Bond (Bobl)	–	731,865
Italian Government Bond (BTP)	12,603,754	15,260,072
Japanese Government Bond (JGB)	816,059	813,241
US T-Bond	–	58,180
Options		
Long Gilt	1,361,344	1,799,660
German Government Bond (Bund)	8,462,806	10,082,217
German Government Bond (Bobl)	–	196,128
Italian Government Bond (BTP)	2,456,177	2,544,870
US T-Bond	–	6,868
Total	80,910,078	96,130,695

Exchange	1996	1997
Equity Products		
Futures		
FTSE 100 Index Future	3,627,044	3,698,368
FTSE 250 Index Future	34,068	68,280
Options		
FTSE 100 Index Options (SEI)	3,764,079	2,988,158
FTSE 100 Index Options (ESX)	2,974,876	4,200,191
FTSE 100 Index FLEX Options	65,701	32,985
Equity Options (individual)	4,298,010	4,295,877
Total	14,763,778	15,283,859
Commodity Products		
Futures		
No 7 cocoa	403,715	1,857,065
Robusta coffee	332,770	1,544,193
No 5 white sugar	150,713	686,302
Wheat	35,104	128,411
Barley	5,112	15,325
BIFFEX	21,778	45,059
Potato	4,020	22,933
Options		
No 7 cocoa	12,088	27,838
Robusta coffee	37,575	184,975
No 5 white sugar	4,653	21,062
Wheat	2,891	9,326
Barley	0	206
BIFFEX	131	149
Potato	25	5
Total	1,010,575	4,542,849

Source: London International Financial Futures and Options Exchange (LIFFE)

Securities Quoted on the Stock Exchange of the UK

The stock exchanges of the UK and the Republic of Ireland form one exchange (The Stock Exchange). (At last working day of March. In millions of pounds.)

Item	1986	1987	1988	1989	1990	1991	1992	1993	1994	1995	1996
British government and government guaranteed stocks											
nominal values	128,850	138,777	142,857	133,780	117,857	118,702	130,143	150,803	200,282	217,283	262,246
market values	138,417	147,550	151,207	137,195	109,431	121,183	132,806	172,114	221,960	228,242	292,057
Other securities at market values											
Irish government stocks	8,398	9,727	11,026	10,730	11,834	11,878	13,359	14,003	15,366	14,445	17,320
corporation stocks, public boards, etc	1,149	912	644	763	309	276	246	213	423	434	671
dominion and foreign government and corporation stocks	83,656	104,460	102,703	142,501	123,575	138,957	138,977	205,555	282,018	335,613	355,169
Company securities											
loan capital	9,004	12,013	11,820	13,621	16,788	14,129	15,164	16,407	22,216	21,758	24,872
preference and preferred capital	8,259	22,438	26,887	35,459	39,859	32,918	26,822	15,226	13,124	11,390	14,673
ordinary and deferred capital[2]	998,697	1,250,745	1,123,110	1,520,822	1,804,351	1,875,872	1,727,553	2,181,575	2,670,814	2,730,499	3,389,664
Total	1,015,960	1,285,196	1,161,817	1,569,902	1,860,998	1,922,919	1,769,539	2,213,208	2,706,154	2,763,647	3,429,210
Total of all securities at market values	1,247,580	1,547,845	1,427,397	1,861,091	2,106,147	2,195,213	2,054,927	2,605,093	3,225,921	3,342,381	4,077,109

1 Excluding marketable unlisted securities; including all outstanding amounts of 4% Victory Bonds and 4% Funding Loan, 1960–90 (that is, amounts for death duties and held by the National Debt Commissioners are included).
2 From 1978 shares of no par value are no longer distinguished separately.

Source: Council of the Stock Exchange. © Crown copyright 1998

UK Energy and Minerals

Coal Supply and Demand in the UK

(N = nil or negligible. In millions of tonnes.)

Supply/demand	1986	1988	1990	1992	1993	1994	1995	1996
Supply								
Production of deep-mined coal	90.4	83.8	72.9	65.8	50.5	31.9	35.2	32.2
Production of opencast coal	14.3	17.9	18.1	18.2	17.0	16.8	16.4	16.3
Total	104.6	101.7	91.0	84.0	67.5	48.7	51.5	48.5
Recovered slurry, fines, etc	3.5	2.4	1.7	0.5	0.7	0.3	1.5	1.7
Imports	10.6	11.7	14.8	20.3	18.4	15.1	15.9	17.8
Total	118.7	115.8	107.5	104.8	86.6	64.0	68.9	68.0
Change in colliery stocks	0.3	0.7	-0.9	2.2	1.8	-4.2 }	-4.2	-3.0
Change in stocks at opencast sites	-0.8	0.5	-0.1	0.6	0.5	-0.5		
Total supply	119.2	114.6	108.5	102.0	84.5	68.7	73.1	71.0
Home Consumption								
Electricity supply industry[1]	82.7	84.3	84.0	78.5	66.2	62.4	59.6	54.9
Coke ovens	11.1	10.9	10.9	9.0	8.5	8.6	8.7	8.6
Low temperature carbonization plants	1.0	0.8	0.8	0.6	0.5	0.5	0.4 }	0.9
Manufactured fuel plants	1.0	1.2	0.8	0.7	0.8	0.7	0.6	
Collieries	0.3	0.2	0.1	0.1	N	N	N	N
Industry[2][3]	8.2	7.2	6.3	6.6	5.3	4.9	4.5	3.6
Domestic								
house coal[3][4]	5.7	3.7	2.5	2.9	2.7	1.9	1.2	1.3
anthracite and dry steam coal[4][5][6]	1.5	1.3	1.2	1.3	1.9	2.0	1.5	1.4
miners' coal	1.3	0.8	0.6	0.4	N	N	N	N
Public services	1.3	0.9	0.9	0.7	0.6	0.5	0.3	0.4
Miscellaneous	0.2	0.2	0.3	0.2	0.2	0.2	0.2	0.2
Total home consumption	114.2	111.5	108.3	100.6	86.7	81.8	76.9	71.4
Overseas shipments and bunkers	2.7	1.8	2.5	1.0	1.1	1.2	0.9	1.0
Total consumption and shipments	116.9	113.3	110.8	101.6	87.9	82.9	77.8	72.4
Change in distributed stocks[7]	4.0	1.7	-0.4	1.2	-3.6	-14.6	-4.6	-1.1
Balance[8]	-1.7	-0.4	1.9	-0.8	0.2	0.4	-0.1	-0.3
Stocks at End of Year								
Distributed[7]	29.8	28.8	28.7	33.5	29.9	15.3	10.7	9.6
At collieries	6.0	5.6	6.0	10.9	12.7	8.5 }	7.1	4.2
At opencast sites	2.7	1.7	3.0	2.8	3.3	2.8		
Total stocks	38.5	36.2	37.8	47.2	45.9	26.6	17.8	13.8

[1] Includes quantities used in the production of steam for sale.
[2] Includes colliery and opencast disposals to industry.
[3] Includes estimated proportions of steam coal imports.
[4] Includes colliery and opencast disposals to merchants.
[5] Includes cncludes disposals of imported anthracite.
[6] Anthracite is also consumed under other categories, including miners' coal and manufactured fuel plants.
[7] Data are for Great Britain. Stock change excludes industrial and domestic stocks.
[8] This is the balance between supply and consumption, shipments, and changes in known distributed stocks.

Source: Department of Trade and Industry. © Crown copyright 1998

Electricity Distributed by Regional Company in the UK

The figures for the area and number of customers are taken from the Office of Electricity Regulation's (OFFER) *Report on Distribution and Transmission Performance 1994/95*. The figures for electricity distributed were taken from the Regional Electricity Companies' (REC) 1994–95 accounts. The two Scottish companies and Northern Ireland Electricity have separately given their permission for this information to be published. Northern Ireland data relate to the calendar year 1995.

1994–95

Region	Area (sq km)	Number of customers	Customer density (number per sq km)	Electricity distributed (gigawatt hours)
Eastern	20,300	3,156,000	156	29,898
East Midlands	16,000	2,200,000	138	24,156
London	665	1,933,000	2,907	19,666
MANWEB	12.200	1,346,000	110	18,485
Midlands	13,300	2,220,000	165	24,079
Northern	14,400	1,418,000	99	14,950
Northern Ireland	13,506	645,000	44	6,624
NORWEB	12,500	2,160,000	173	22,076
Scottish Hydro-Electric	54,390	640,000	12	7,700
Scottish Power	22,950	1,770,000	77	20,822
SEEBOARD	8,200	1,977,000	241	17,655
Southern	16,900	2,573,000	152	26,808
SWALEC	11,800	960,000	81	11,164
South Western	14,400	1,289,000	90	12,979
Yorkshire	10,700	2,026,000	189	22,631
Total	242,211	26,293,000	109	279,693

Source: Department of Trade and Industry. © Crown copyright 1998

Electricity Generation, Supply, and Consumption in the UK

(N/A = not available. N = nil or negligible. In gigawatt hours.)

Category	1986	1988	1990	1992	1994	1996
Electricity Generated						
Major power producers[1]						
conventional steam stations	221,426	222,887	230,376	217,228	175,362	160,565
combined cycle gas turbine stations	N/A	N/A	N/A	2,991	36,971	65,880
nuclear stations	54,005	58,867	61,306	73,269	83,944	91,040
gas turbines and oil engines	508	464	432	358	244	266
hydro-electric stations						
natural flow	4,098	4,171	4,393	4,591	4,317	2,801
pumped storage	2,221	2,121	1,982	1,697	1,463	1,556
renewables other than hydro[2]	1	1	4	45	506	1,087
Total	282,258	288,511	298,495	300,177	302,807	323,155
Other generators[3]						
conventional steam stations[4]	13,057	14,294	15,014	15,049	14,866	17,200
combined cycle gas turbine stations	N/A	N/A	292	409	902	1,232
nuclear stations	5,074	4,589	4,441	3,538	4,338	3,631
hydro-electric stations (natural flow)	682	762	814	840	777	560
renewables other than hydro[2]	N	659	683	1,028	1,707	1,591
Total	18,813	20,314	21,244	20,864	22,590	24,214
All generating companies						
conventional steam stations	234,483	237,181	245,390	232,277	190,228	177,765
combined cycle gas turbine stations	N/A	N/A	292	3,400	37,873	67,112
nuclear stations	59,079	63,456	65,749	76,807	88,282	94,671
gas turbines and oil engines	508	464	432	358	244	226
hydro-electric stations						
natural flow	4,780	4,933	5,207	5,431	5,094	3,361
pumped storage	2,221	2,121	1,982	1,697	1,463	1,556
renewables other than hydro[2]	1	670	687	1,073	2,213	2,678
Total	301,071	308,825	319,739	321,043	325,397	347,369

(continued)

Electricity Generation, Supply, and Consumption in the UK (*continued*)

Category	1986	1988	1990	1992	1994	1996
Electricity used on works						
major generating companies[1]	18,105	18,694	17,891	18,485	15,921	16,064
other generators[3]	1,497	1,532	1,720	1,752	1,583	1,664
Total	19,602	20,226	19,611	20,237	17,504	17,728
Electricity Supplied (Gross)						
Major power producers[1]						
conventional steam stations	209,977	211,502	218,957	205,897	167,289	N/A
combined cycle gas turbine stations	N/A	N/A	N/A	2,964	36,815	65,604
nuclear stations	47,484	51,699	54,964	66,269	76,412	82,871
gas turbines and oil engines	475	430	403	311	233	216
hydro-electric stations						
natural flow	4,087	4,160	4,384	4,579	4,265	2,763
pumped storage	2,129	2,025	1,892	1,635	1,417	1,507
renewables other than hydro	1	1	3	37	455	960
Total	264,154	269,817	280,604	281,692	286,886	307,091
Other generators[3]						
conventional steam stations[4]	12,278	13,442	14,082	14,033	14,183	16,340
combined cycle gas turbine stations	N/A	N/A	280	394	866	1,180
nuclear stations	4,359	3,942	3,700	2,866	3,550	2,949
hydro-electric stations (natural flow)	679	669	806	832	769	554
renewables other than hydro[2]	N	643	656	987	1,639	1,527
Total	17,316	18,782	19,524	19,112	21,007	22,550
All generating companies						
conventional steam stations[4]	222,255	224,944	233,039	219,930	181,472	169,510
combined cycle gas turbine stations	N/A	N/A	280	3,358	37,681	66,784
nuclear stations	51,843	55,642	58,664	69,135	79,962	85,820
gas turbines and oil engines	475	430	403	311	233	216
hydro-electric stations						
natural flow	4,766	4,914	5,190	5,411	5,034	3,317
pumped storage	2,129	2,025	1,892	1,635	1,417	1,507
renewables other than hydro[2]	1	644	659	1,024	2,094	2,487
Total	281,469	288,599	300,128	300,804	307,893	329,641
Electricity Used in Pumping						
major power producers[1]	2,993	2,888	2,626	2,257	2,051	2,430
Electricity Supplied (Net)						
major power producers[1]	261,160	266,929	277,978	279,435	284,835	304,659
other generators[3]	17,316	18,782	19,524	19,112	21,007	22,550
Total	278,476	265,711	297,502	298,547	305,842	327,209
Net imports	4,256	12,830	11,990	16,694	16,887	16,677
Electricity available	282,732	298,540	309,408	315,241	322,729	343,866
Losses in transmission, etc	22,914	24,036	24,988	23,788	30,947	29,601
Electricity consumption						
fuel industries	9,505	9,163	9,986	9,984	7,518	8,629
final users						
industrial sector	88,800	97,143	100,643	95,277	95,067	103,129
domestic sector	91,826	92,362	93,793	99,482	101,407	107,513
other sectors	69,687	75,837	79,997	86,711	87,790	95,014
Total	250,313	265,342	274,434	281,468	284,264	305,656
Total	259,818	274,505	284,420	291,453	291,782	314,285

[1] Represents generating companies corresponding to the old public sector supply system, i.e. National Power, PowerGen, Nuclear Electric, First Hydro Ltd, Scottish Power, Scottish Hydro-Electric, Scottish Nuclear, Premier Power Ltd, Coolkeeragh Power Ltd, Midland Power (UK) Ltd, South Western Electricity, NIGEN, and new independent generators, i.e. Teeside Power Ltd, Lakeland Power Ltd, Corby Power Ltd, Peterborough Power Ltd, Regional Power Ltd, Fibropower Ltd, Fibrogen Ltd, Fellside Heat and Power Ltd, Kead by Generation Ltd, Barking Power Ltd, Elm Energy and Recycling (UK) Ltd, South East London Combined Heat and Power Ltd, Derwent Cogeneration Ltd, Medway Power Ltd.
[2] Includes wind and biofuels.
[3] Represents larger establishments in the industrial and transport sectors generating one gigawatt-hour or more a year. Reactors operated by the United Kingdom Atomic Energy Authority and by British Nuclear Fuels plc are included.
[4] For other generators, conventional steam stations cover all types of station not separately listed.

Source: Department of Trade and Industry. © Crown copyright 1998

Energy Production and Consumption in the European Union

(N = nil or negligible. In millions of tonnes of oil equivalent unless otherwise indicated.)

1995

Country	Production	Imports	Exports	Gross inland consumption	Final consumption	Import dependency[1] (%)	Energy ratio[2] (tonnes of oil equivalent per $1,000 GDP)
Austria	9.1	19.4	2.0[3]	26.7[3]	21.6[3]	65.1[3]	0.16
Belgium	10.8	62.9	19.4	50.0	34.2	80.6	0.24
Denmark	15.5	19.0	11.1	20.6	15.0	35.7	0.14
Finland	13.2	19.6	4.1	29.0	22.2	52.9	0.22
France	121.2	138.4	22.4	234.8	141.6	48.9	0.14
Germany	142.6	217.3	22.2	338.6	219.6[3]	57.3	0.19
Greece	10.2	22.4	4.2	24.7	16.3	64.6	0.27
Ireland, Republic of	4.2[3]	8.4[3]	1.0[3]	10.9[3]	7.6[3]	67.1[3]	0.18
Italy	30.7	152.0	17.3	162.7	116.6	81.6	0.14
Luxembourg	N	3.3	0.1	3.3	3.2	97.7	0.27
Netherlands	66.0	105.9	89.6	73.4	48.7	19.3	0.23
Portugal	3.2	21.8	4.0	20.1	13.5	86.6	0.27
Spain	31.4	83.9	8.4	102.3	64.0	71.5	0.19
Sweden	31.0	29.7	10.6	49.8	33.5	37.6	0.21
UK	250.9	73.2	109.3	220.0	141.2	−16.2	0.21

[1] (Imports − exports) divided by gross inland consumption and bunkers.
[2] Gross inland consumption divided by GDP where GDP is expressed in billions of US dollars at 1990 prices.
[3] Data are provisional.

Source: *The Energy Report.* © Crown copyright 1998

Nuclear Power Plants in the UK

(Magnox – named after the magnesium oxide casing surrounding the uranium fuel rod. PWR – pressure water reactor. AGR – advanced gas reactor.)

Station name	Company	Fuel	Installed capacity (megawatts)	Year of commission
Hinkley Point B	Nuclear Electric	AGR	1,270	1978
Torness	Scottish Nuclear	AGR	1,265	1988
Heysham 2	Nuclear Electric	AGR	1,250	1988
Sizewell B	Nuclear Electric	PWR	1,188	1995
Hunterston B	Scottish Nuclear	AGR	1,170	1976
Heysham 1	Nuclear Electric	AGR	1,150	1984
Hartlepool	Nuclear Electric	AGR	1,150	1984
Dungeness B	Nuclear Electric	AGR	1,170	1985
Wylfa	Magnox Electric	Magnox	950	1971
Hinkley Point A	Magnox Electric	Magnox	470	1965
Dungeness A	Magnox Electric	Magnox	440	1965
Oldbury	Magnox Electric	Magnox	424	1967
Sizewell A	Magnox Electric	Magnox	420	1966
Brodwell	Magnox Electric	Magnox	245	1962
Calder Hall	British Nuclear Fuels	Magnox	198	1956
Chapelcross	British Nuclear Fuels	Magnox	188	1959

Source: Department of Trade and Industry. © Crown copyright 1998

Renewable Energy Utilization in the UK

(Includes some waste of fossil fuel origin. In tonnes of oil equivalent.)

Used to Generate Electricity[1]

Source	1991	1993	1995
Onshore wind	900,000	18,800,000	30,200,000
Hydro			
small scale	12,200,000	13,700,000	18,200,000
large scale[2]	385,400,000	356,200,000	436,100,000
Biofuels			
landfill gas	68,200,000	146,600,000	185,500,000
sewage sludge			
digestion[3]	107,600,000	123,800,000	120,200,000
municipal solid waste			
combustion[4]	111,900,000	186,800,000	298,800,000
other[5]	600,000	64,600,000	140,000,000
Total	686,800,000	910,500,000	1,229,000,000

Used to Generate Heat

Source	1991	1993	1995
Active solar heating[6]	8,000,000	8,800,000	9,500,000
Biofuels			
landfill gas	36,300,000	15,000,000	20,300,000
sewage sludge			
digestion[3]	43,500,000	34,000,000	53,300,000
wood combustion[7]	174,100,000	174,100,000	174,100,000
straw combustion[8]	71,700,000	71,700,000	71,700,000
municipal solid waste			
combustion[4]	53,200,000	44,800,000	51,400,000
other[9]	80,100,000	93,800,000	102,500,000
Geothermal aquifiers	800,000	800,000	800,000
Total	467,700,000	443,000,000	483,600,000

Total Use of Renewable Sources

Source	1991	1993	1995
Active solar heating[6]	8,000,000	8,800,000	9,500,000
Onshore wind	900,000	18,800,000	30,200,000
Hydro			
small scale	12,200,000	13,700,000	18,200,000
large scale[2]	385,400,000	356,200,000	436,100,000
Biofuels			
landfill gas	104,500,000	161,600,000	205,800,000
sewage sludge			
digestion[3]	151,100,000	157,800,000	173,500,000
wood combustion[7]	174,100,000	174,100,000	174,100,000
straw combustion[8]	71,700,000	71,700,000	71,700,000
municipal solid waste			
combustion[4]	165,100,000	231,600,000	350,200,000
other[5][9]	80,700,000	158,400,000	242,500,000
Geothermal aquifiers	800,000	800,000	800,000
Total	1,154,400,000	1,353,500,000	1,712,600,000

[1] For wind and hydro, the figures represent the energy content of the electricity supplied, but for biofuels the figures represent the energy content of the fuel used.
[2] Excluding pumped storage stations.
[3] No estimate is made for digestors where gas is used to heat the sludge.
[4] Includes combustion of refuse-derived fuel pellets.
[5] Includes electricity from farm waste digestion, poultry litter combustion, and waste tyre combustion.
[6] Figures are based on a survey carried out in 1994.
[7] Figures are an approximate estimate of domestic combustion based on a survey carried out in 1989; a moisture content of five percent is assumed. Industrial wood combustion is included under 'other'.
[8] An approximate estimate based on a limited survey carried out in 1994 and on information collected in 1990.
[9] Includes heat from industrial wood waste combustion, waste tyre combustion, hospital waste combustion, general industrial waste combustion, and farm waste digestion.

Source: Department of Trade and Industry. © Crown copyright 1998

Total Inland Energy Consumption in the UK

(In millions of tonnes of oil equivalent.)

Category	1986	1988	1990	1992	1994	1996
Inland Energy Consumption of Primary Fuels and Equivalents[1]						
Coal[2]	70.0	70.1	67.4	63.6	52.2	46.7
Petroleum[3]	72.3	74.7	78.3	78.3	78.0	78.6
Primary electricity[4]	16.2	18.1	17.7	20.4	23.1	23.8
Natural gas[5]	52.7	51.5	50.6	54.5	64.8	82.4
Less energy used by fuel producers and losses in conversion and distribution	−65.5	−65.8	−67.6	−66.8	−66.2	−70.8
Total consumption by final users[1]	145.7	148.6	146.4	150.0	151.9	160.8
Total internal energy consumption[1]	211.2	214.4	214.1	216.8	218.1	231.6
Final Energy Consumption by Type of Fuel						
Coal (direct use)	12.3	9.7	8.1	8.1	6.9	5.0
Coke and breeze	4.9	5.6	4.3	3.9	3.9	4.3
Other solid fuel[6]	1.1	1.3	1.2	1.1	1.0	1.0

Category	1986	1988	1990	1992	1994	1996
Final Energy Consumption by Type of Fuel (continued)						
Coke oven gas	0.8	0.8	0.6	0.5	0.6	0.6
Natural gas (direct use)[5]	46.7	46.4	45.3	47.5	48.7	56.2
Electricity	20.8	22.8	23.6	24.2	24.4	26.3
Petroleum (direct use)[6]	59.2	62.0	63.3	64.6	66.2	67.3
Final Energy Consumption by Class of Consumer						
Agriculture	1.4	1.4	1.3	1.4	1.4	1.4
Iron and steel industry	7.0	8.2	6.9	6.5	7.7	8.1
Other industries	33.9	32.7	30.9	29.1	29.0	29.5
Railways[7]	1.1	1.0	1.0	1.0	1.0	1.0
Road transport	32.6	36.2	38.8	39.4	40.0	41.0
Water transport	1.2	1.2	1.4	1.4	1.3	1.3
Air transport	6.1	6.9	7.3	7.4	8.1	9.0
Domestic	43.7	42.3	40.8	44.0	44.0	48.1
Public administration	8.9	8.3	7.7	9.1	8.3	9.0
Commercial and other services[8]	9.8	10.3	10.3	10.5	11.0	12.1

[1] Includes, from 1988, small amounts of primary heat sources (solar, geothermal, etc). Up to 1988 includes natural gas used for non-energy purposes (e.g. petrochemicals).
[2] Includes net trade and stock change in other solid fuels. Includes, from 1988, solid renewable sources (wood, waste, etc).
[3] Figures give refinery throughput of crude oil, plus net foreign trade and stock change in petroleum products. Petroleum products not used as fuels (chemical feedstock, industrial and white spirits, lubricants, bitumen, and wax) are excluded.
[4] Primary electricity comprises nuclear, natural flow hydro, net imports of electricity, and, from 1988, generation of wind stations.
[5] Natural gas includes colliery methane, non-energy use of natural gas up to 1988, and, from 1988, landfill gas and sewage gas.
[6] Includes products such as briquettes, ovoids, Phurnacite, and Coalite, and, from 1988, wood, waste, and other materials used for heat generation.
[7] Figures include fuel used at transport premises from 1990.
[8] Figures include fuel used at transport premises prior to 1990.

Source: Department of Trade and Industry. © Crown copyright 1998

Minerals Production in the UK

(N/A = not available. N = nil or negligible. In tonnes.)

Mineral	1990	1992	1994	1996
Great Britain				
Limestone	9,775,000	86,000,000	102,844,000	82,442,000
Sandstone	14,952,000	11,586,000	13,494,000	12,581,000
Igneous rock	49,542,000	48,630,000	50,014,000	43,731,000
Clay/shale	15,864,000	12,155,000	12,464,000	11,804,000
Industrial sand	4,132,000	3,615,000	4,038,000	4,861,000
Chalk	13,129,000	9,171,000	10,236,000	9,239,000
Fireclay	892,000	572,000	679,000	536,000
Barium sulphate	67,600	76,700	34,000	93,000
Calcium fluoride	118,500	76,100	49,900	N/A
Copper	1,000	N	N	N
Lead	1,400	N/A	1,800	N/A
Tin	3,400	2,000	1,900	2,100
Zinc	6,700	N/A	N/A	N/A
Iron ore, crude	4,000	4,000	2,000	1,000
Iron ore, iron content	2,000	2,000	1,000	1,000
Calcspar	34,000	4,000	3,000	N/A
China clay	4,042,000	2,732	2,977,000	2,654,000
Ball clay		N/A	913,000	N/A
Chert and flint	14,000	N/A	N/A	N/A
Fuller's earth	228,000	203,000	193,000	183,000
Lignite	5,000	3,000	2,000	N
Rock salt	815,000	N/A	N/A	N/A

Mineral	1990	1992	1994	1996
Salt in brine	N/A	3,401,000	4,009,000	3,512,000
Anhydrite	N/A	N/A	N/A	N
Dolomite	20,674,000	18,539,000	17,616,000	16,555,000
Gypsum	N/A	N/A	N/A	N
Slate[1]	359,000	326,000	402,000	408,000
Soapstone and talc	15,000	5,000	5,000	5,000
Sand and gravel, land-won	98,993,000	78,341,000	86,341,000	70,489,000
Sand and gravel, marine dredged	17,179,000	10,557,000	11,331,000	11,508,000
Northern Ireland				
Clay and shale	N/A	N/A	N/A	N
Sand and gravel	4,030,000	3,697,000	5,109,000	7,684,000
Basalt and igneous rock, other than granite	7,691,000	9,024,000	6,480,000	6,974,000
Limestone	2,866,000	3,398,000	N/A	4,122,000
Sandstone[2]	3,090,000	3,304,000	5,480,000	4,941,000
Granite	N/A	N/A	N/A	N
Others[3]	N/A	N/A	896,000	1,392,000

[1] 'Slate' includes waste used for constructional fill, and powder and granules used in manufacturing.
[2] Prior to 1993 the 'Sandstone' heading was called 'Grit and conglomerate'. The new heading is all-encompassing.
[3] Includes rock salt, chalk, diatomite, and fireclay.

Indigenous Production, Refinery Receipts, Imports, and Exports of Oil in the UK

The term 'indigenous' is used for convenience to include oil from the UK continental shelf as well as the small amounts produced on the mainland. (In tonnes.)

Category		1986	1988	1990	1992	1993	1994	1995	1996
Petroleum Production[1]									
Crude petroleum[2]									
net foreign arrivals		39,880,000	42,613,000	51,065,000	56,485,000	59,868,000	51,170,000	47,590,000	48,275,000
refinery receipts	indigenous[3]	38,780,000	40,582,000	37,754,000	35,472,000	36,680,000	42,174,000	44,872,000	47,029,000
	other[4]	1,006,000	730,000	916,000	832,000	852,000	427,000	1,110,000	997,000
	Total	79,666,000	83,925,000	89,735,000	92,789,000	97,400,000	93,771,000	93,572,000	96,301,000
Foreign trade									
imports		41,209,000	44,272,000	52,710,000	57,683,000	61,701,000	53,096,000	48,749,000	50,099,000
exports	indigenous	83,341,000	69,965,000	54,022,000	54,441,000	60,165,000	77,466,000	77,930,000	76,030,000
	other[5]	1,635,000	1,967,000	1,878,000	1,536,000	2,225,000	2,359,000	1,757,000	2,200,000
Total indigenous production		127,053,000	114,459,000	91,604,000	94,251,000	100,188,000	126,938,000	130,324,000	129,838,000
Petroleum Products									
Foreign trade									
imports		11,767,000	9,219,000	11,005,000	10,567,000	10,064,000	10,441,000	9,878,000	9,230,000
exports		17,726,000	17,176,000	18,002,000	21,899,000	24,890,000	24,644,000	24,418,000	26,018,000
net imports		−5,959,000	−7,957,000	−6,997,000	−11,332,000	−14,826,000	−14,203,000	−14,540,000	−16,788,000
bunkers[6]		2,091,000	1,831,000	2,538,000	2,546,000	2,478,000	2,313,000	2,465,000	2,665,000

[1] Data include crude oil plus condensates and petroleum gases derived at onshore treatment plants.
[2] Includes process (partly refined) oils.
[3] Includes condensates for distillation.
[4] Includes mainly recycled products.
[5] Represents re-exports of imported crude, which may include some indigenous oil in blend.
[6] International marine bunkers.

Source: Department of Trade and Industry. © Crown copyright 1998

UK Industry and Business

Construction: Value of New Orders Obtained by Contractors in Great Britain

(In millions of pounds.)

Item	1988	1990	1992	1994	1996
New housing					
public housing	882	683	1,246	1,386	1,073
private housing[1]	7,893	4,855	4,016	5,721	5,416
Total	8,775	5,538	5,263	7,106	6,487
Infrastructure					
water	157	321	669	412	640
sewerage	332	491	469	389	481
electricity	154	187	281	170	294
roads	1,101	1,425	1,322	1,356	1,710
gas, communications, air	230	391	554	494	745
railways	128	160	200	412	524
harbours	206	216	252	218	270
Total public	1,908	2,029	1,690	2,211	1,671
private	399	1,161	2,056	1,240	2,993
Total	2,307	3,190	3,746	3,451	4,664
Other public non-housing					
factories	237	149	128	111	91
warehouses	21	14	54	38	14
oil, steel, coal	180	81	47	12	4
schools and colleges	435	527	584	658	708
universities	66	146	203	376	355
health	711	663	644	752	674
offices	414	570	499	469	381
entertainment	341	283	189	308	253

Item	1988	1990	1992	1994	1996
Other public non-housing					
garages	88	56	28	49	28
shops	38	24	23	14	11
agriculture	18	5	14	22	8
other	659	601	351	844	419
Total	3,209	3,117	2,763	3,654	2,945
Private industrial[1]					
factories	2,099	2,094	1,006	1,451	1,603
warehouses	786	648	426	498	663
oil, steel, coal	56	108	72	51	71
Total	2,941	2,850	1,503	1,999	2,337
Private commercial[1]					
schools, universities	191	169	121	115	156
health	191	271	193	255	277
offices	4,585	4,215	1,691	1,777	2,169
entertainment	1,356	1,195	747	928	1,407
garages	375	364	234	300	265
shops	2,048	1,345	1,034	1,453	1,795
agriculture	157	127	94	120	123
other	163	109	103	127	198
Total	9,066	7,796	4,218	5,075	6,390
Total	26,298	22,491	17,493	21,285	22,834

[1] Figures for private sector include work to be carried out by contractors on their own initiative for sale.

Source: Department of the Environment, Transport, and the Regions. © Crown copyright 1998

Construction: Value of Output in Great Britain

Data comprise output by contractors, including unrecorded estimates by small firms and self-employed workers, and output by public sector direct labour departments. (In millions of pounds.)

Item				1988	1990	1992	1994	1996
New Work	new housing	for public sector		880	934	1,243	1,671	1,421
		for private sector		7,775	5,746	4,841	5,746	5,592
		Total		8,655	6,680	6,084	7,417	7,013
	infrastructure			3,367	4,965	5,716	5,149	6,338
	other new work	for public sector		3,075	4,414	4,181	4,384	4,441
	(excluding infrastructure)	for private sector	private industrial	2,763	3,394	2,234	2,489	3,119
			private commercial	6,903	11,310	6,600	5,648	7,015
		Total		12,741	19,118	13,015	12,521	14,575
	Total			24,763	30,762	24,814	25,086	27,926
Repair and Maintenance	housing	for public sector		4,485	5,384	4,991	5,963	6,637
		for private sector		7,045	8,455	7,595	7,804	8,398
		Total		11,530	13,839	12,586	13,767	15,035
	public other work			4,488	5,488	5,087	5,211	5,252
	private other work			4,073	5,218	4,985	5,375	7,030
	Total			20,090	24,544	22,658	24,353	27,317
Total (all work)				44,853	55,307	47,472	49,439	55,243

Source: Department of the Environment, Transport, and the Regions. © Crown copyright 1998

Growth Rate of Manufacturing Sales in the UK

'Intermediate' and 'major' refer to size of companies' turnover.

Manufacturing	Growth rate (%)			Compound growth (%)
	1991/92–1992/93	1992/93–1993/94	1993/94–1995/96	1991–95
Electronic component manufacturers	11.1	19.5	27.6	19.2
Computer equipment manufacturers	21.0	21.0	14.2	18.7
Printed circuit manufacturers	6.2	18.2	22.6	15.4
Pharmaceutical manufacturers and developers	16.0	16.3	10.0	14.1
Leather manufacturers and processors	−1.4	18.9	19.6	11.9
Toy industry	7.7	15.9	9.9	11.1
Motor component and accessory manufacturers	5.3	12.2	14.6	10.6
Spring manufacturers	2.9	2.3	26.2	9.9
Computer software houses	13.8	13.8	2.1	9.8
Record industry	7.3	8.5	13.2	9.7
Food processors (intermediate)	10.4	11.0	7.6	9.7
Soap and detergent industry	15.2	7.5	6.1	9.6
Medical equipment industry	13.1	10.0	5.7	9.6
Timber trade	0.6	12.5	15.9	9.5
Toiletries and cosmetics	9.5	10.5	7.8	9.2
Steel processors	−6.3	17.8	18.0	9.2
Agricultural equipment	−1.2	17.8	10.0	8.6
Consumer electronics	1.2	11.5	12.4	8.2
Compound animal feedstuffs	7.6	10.0	6.9	8.2
Dairy industry	13.7	3.9	6.1	7.8
Industrial chemical manufacturers (intermediate)	3.4	6.2	13.9	7.7
Wire and wire products	3.0	5.7	14.7	7.7
Plastics processors	0.5	8.0	15.0	7.7
Meat processors	9.7	5.7	7.4	7.6
Poultry processors	6.1	12.7	3.9	7.5
Domestic furniture manufacturers	5.0	8.0	9.0	7.3
Frozen food producers	5.7	8.3	7.6	7.2
Joinery manufacturers	−0.2	9.0	13.2	7.2
Carpet industry	2.3	10.2	8.4	6.9
Scientific and electrical installations manufacturers	2.6	7.5	10.8	6.9
Office equipment industry	3.9	6.5	10.4	6.9
Plastics packaging manufacturers	6.0	3.0	11.8	6.8
Architectural ironmongers	8.6	7.1	4.7	6.8
Confectionery manufacturers	4.5	9.2	6.1	6.6
Switchgear, motors, and control systems	4.0	6.8	8.6	6.4
Dyers and finishers	9.9	2.7	6.7	6.4
Sports equipment industry	0.6	8.0	10.0	6.1
Lighting equipment	3.3	7.0	8.1	6.1
Machine tool manufacturers	−1.9	−0.6	22.1	6.0
Rubber and tyre industry	4.6	6.7	6.2	5.8
Electrical installation equipment manufacturers	4.5	−0.8	13.8	5.7
Iron founders	−1.7	−2.2	22.7	5.6
Soft drinks manufacturers	5.6	2.4	9.0	5.6
Hydraulic and pneumatic equipment	−3.5	5.2	16.0	5.6
Glass industry	0.2	13.1	3.7	5.5
Industrial fastener manufacturers	0.2	3.1	13.6	5.5
Window and door manufacturers	0.1	9.7	6.8	5.5
Jewellery trade	−5.5	13.9	8.9	5.4
Photographic industry	2.4	6.6	7.2	5.4
Kitchen and bathroom furniture	3.8	2.5	9.6	5.2
Mechanical power transmissions manufacturers	1.5	3.7	10.6	5.2
Sign and street furniture manufacturers	2.2	3.5	9.8	5.1
Footwear industry	0.0	7.0	8.5	5.1
Wool industry	1.0	3.6	10.9	5.1
Contract and office furniture	0.0	0.4	15.5	5.0
Caravan industry	3.0	2.7	9.6	5.0
Ceramics manufacturers	1.2	5.5	8.5	5.0
Cotton and man-made fibre	3.2	4.2	7.5	5.0
Stationery manufacturers	1.7	4.0	9.2	4.9
Food processors (major)	1.1	8.3	4.9	4.7
Hosiery and knitwear	5.6	5.3	2.3	4.4
Paper and board manufacturers	−0.4	3.6	9.9	4.3
Refrigeration equipment	6.3	3.3	3.2	4.3
Mining and quarrying	−4.4	8.1	9.5	4.2
Valve manufacturers	2.2	1.5	8.6	4.1

Growth Rate of Manufacturing Sales in the UK (*continued*)

Manufacturing	Growth rate (%)			Compound growth (%)
	1991/92–1992/93	1992/93–1993/94	1993/94–1995/96	1991–95
Distillers	4.4	2.1	5.7	4.0
Brewers	4.0	4.2	3.5	3.9
Domestic electrical appliances	−0.3	6.3	5.7	3.9
Industrial chemical manufacturers (major)	2.4	4.4	4.8	3.9
Constructional steelwork manufacturers	2.4	1.2	7.9	3.8
Bakeries	0.4	−2.2	13.5	3.7
Paper and board packaging manufacturers	3.3	4.1	3.1	3.5
Paint and printing ink manufacturers	−5.2	7.5	8.5	3.4
Ready mixed concrete	−7.4	3.4	15.4	3.4
Oil and gas industry	1.0	11.0	−3.5	2.7
Pumps industry	−3.1	2.3	9.1	2.7
Heating and ventilating equipment	−1.5	7.2	2.3	2.6
Mining equipment manufacturers	5.1	−0.8	3.0	2.4
Forging industry	−10.5	9.1	9.8	2.4
Heating and ventilating contractors	−1.2	−1.7	8.0	1.6
Agrochemical and fertilizer industry	−0.3	1.0	4.1	1.6
Precast concrete manufacturers	−14.8	6.9	15.1	1.6
Greeting card industry	7.6	5.9	−10.0	0.9
Aerospace industry	−3.5	−1.8	8.1	0.8
Non-ferrous founders	−9.4	0.7	9.6	0.0
Defence industry	−2.7	3.2	−1.0	−0.2
Fire protection equipment	7.4	−1.7	−7.8	−0.9

Source: ICC Business Publications, Suppliers of Company Financial Information. Tel: (0181) 481 8720

Growth Rate of Services Sales in the UK

'Intermediate' and 'major' refer to size of companies' turnover.

Services and distributors	Growth rate (%)			Compound growth (%)
	1991/92–1992/93	1992/93–1993/94	1993/94–1995/96	1991–95
Services				
Employment agencies	7.2	18.7	31.4	18.7
Unit trust managers	−8.5	175.2	−34.7	18.0
Travel agents and tour operators	19.6	14.8	13.7	16.0
Waste and scrap merchants	14.9	13.8	19.1	15.9
Telecommunications	5.4	16.6	23.7	15.0
Security industry	11.7	11.1	18.6	13.7
Market research	9.9	14.4	12.0	12.1
Computer services	6.1	17.7	12.8	12.1
Car dealers	3.6	15.9	15.0	11.3
Book publishers	10.1	13.4	9.3	10.9
Water companies	14.2	10.4	6.3	10.3
Contract cleaners	10.3	9.2	11.0	10.2
Housebuilders (major)	2.2	12.0	16.4	10.0
Private healthcare	12.3	12.5	5.5	10.0
Insurance brokers	9.9	14.4	5.3	9.8
Airlines and airports	8.2	11.4	8.7	9.4
Direct marketing	3.3	9.0	16.0	9.3
Optical industry	9.8	6.7	11.3	9.3
Management consultants	6.7	11.6	6.0	8.1
Printers (intermediate)	3.3	10.5	9.5	7.7
Freight forwarders	5.3	6.8	10.7	7.6
Plant hire	−1.5	10.5	14.0	7.5
Vehicle rental and leasing	5.6	9.8	6.5	7.3
Periodical publishers	−1.1	14.3	8.6	7.1
Film and television	−3.5	9.9	15.6	7.0
Road hauliers	4.7	8.1	8.2	7.0
Steel stockholders	−3.2	8.2	16.4	6.8
New car industry	1.9	15.1	2.5	6.3
Design consultancies	3.9	1.5	13.9	6.3
Passenger shipping	6.5	9.0	3.3	6.2

(*continued*)

Growth Rate of Services Sales in the UK (*continued*)

Services and distributors	Growth rate (%)			Compound growth (%)
	1991/92–1992/93	1992/93–1993/94	1993/94–1995/96	1991–95
Services (continued)				
Shopfitters	−6.9	6.0	20.1	5.8
Couriers and despatch services	−6.8	11.2	13.2	5.5
Advertising agencies	1.6	8.2	6.6	5.4
Printers (major)	1.8	7.0	4.8	4.5
Newspaper publishers	2.2	5.3	6.1	4.5
Antiques and fine art	−7.9	15.6	4.2	3.5
Bus and coach operators	4.5	1.9	4.2	3.5
Housebuilders (intermediate)	−11.9	10.1	14.1	3.4
Automatic vending industry	5.1	4.0	0.3	3.1
Launderers and dry cleaners	0.8	0.4	8.2	3.1
Pollution control	7.8	4.0	−2.9	2.9
Betting and gaming	0.2	6.3	2.0	2.8
Electrical contractors	−3.6	4.3	7.3	2.6
Building and civil engineering (intermediate)	−5.8	2.8	9.7	2.0
Roofing contractors	−11.8	7.7	10.2	1.5
Hotel industry	5.2	4.7	−6.2	1.1
Air conditioning industry	−6.2	1.4	8.3	1.0
Public relations consultants	−12.9	9.1	7.5	0.7
Non-ferrous metal stockholders	−8.2	−17.2	26.7	−1.3
Building and civil engineering (major)	−6.9	−3.6	3.3	−2.5
Finance houses	−11.0	−6.7	−2.5	−6.8
Distributors				
Computer equipment distributors	11.4	17.2	22.9	17.1
Industrial fastener distributors	10.3	11.7	18.7	13.5
Stationery distributors	4.5	15.7	17.2	12.4
Booksellers	9.9	10.4	13.0	11.1
Catering industry	11.7	6.0	13.2	10.3
Retail and wholesale chemists	9.7	6.8	12.1	9.5
Chemical distributors	5.0	10.3	13.1	9.4
Mail order and catalogue houses	11.7	7.0	9.0	9.2
Supermarkets	6.0	9.5	11.8	9.1
Giftware industry	8.5	8.7	9.6	9.0
Engineering distributors	3.9	10.4	11.8	8.6
Home furnishing retailers	4.2	9.0	11.6	8.2
Clothing retailers	6.4	10.2	6.6	7.7
Paper merchants	2.3	2.0	18.9	7.5
Horticulture and garden centres	8.7	6.6	6.0	7.1
Department stores	1.6	9.7	9.9	7.0
DIY industry	2.5	8.8	9.4	6.9
Retail industry	7.7	6.9	5.8	6.8
Meat wholesalers	9.2	9.2	0.7	6.3
Electrical wholesalers	2.8	5.7	10.5	6.3
Frozen food distributors	3.9	6.6	8.2	6.2
Wine and spirit merchants	8.5	3.7	4.8	5.6
Fruit, flower, and vegetable merchants	1.0	2.1	13.6	5.4
Builders merchants	−4.2	5.4	15.0	5.1
Grocery wholesalers	3.7	4.0	4.1	3.9
Cash and carry	3.7	2.3	5.0	3.7
Food ingredients industry	2.5	3.7	3.1	3.1
Motor goods distributors	−9.8	−5.1	14.6	−0.7

Source: ICC Business Publications, Suppliers of Company Financial Information. Tel: (0181) 481 8720

Number of Furnaces and Production of Steel in the UK

(N = nil or negligible.)

Item		1989	1991	1993	1995	1996
Steel furnaces (in existence at end of period)[1]						
	open hearth	N	N	N	N	N
	oxygen converters	14	14	11	11	11
	electric	215	195	191	181	181
	stock and tropenas	N	N	N	N	N
	Total	229	209	202	192	192
Production of crude steel (thousand tonnes)						
by process	open hearth	N	N	N	N	N
	oxygen converters	13,627	12,540	12,330	13,082	13,758
	electric	5,113	3,934	4,295	4,522	4,234
	stock and tropenas	N	N	N	N	N
by cast method	cast to ingot	3,469	2,201	2,140	2,174	1,892
	continuously cast	15,031	14,085	14,319	15,250	15,912
	steel for castings	240	189	166	180	188
by quality	non-alloy steel	17,371	15,496	15,558	16,243	16,708
	stainless and other alloy steel	1,369	978	1,067	1,361	1,284
	Total	18,740	16,474	16,625	17,604	17,992
Production of finished steel products (thousand tonnes)						
	rods and bars for reinforcement (in coil and lengths)	1,219	1,151	1,229	1,154	1,246
	wire rods and other rods and bars in coil	1,417	1,272	1,427	1,642	1,536
	hot rolled bars in lengths	1,243	1,192	1,140	1,311	1,499
	bright steel bars[2]	340	257	295	424	357
	light sections other than rails	326	324	294	286	298
	heavy and light rails and accessories and other heavy sections	2,540	2,297	2,408	2,549	2,557
	hot rolled plates, sheets, and strip in coil and lengths	8,076	7,270	7,230	8,077	8,512
	cold rolled plates and sheet in coil and lengths	3,976	3,592	3,635	4,100	4,221
	cold rolled strip[2]	388	286	229	267	246
	tinplate	960	742	829	791	739
	other coated sheet	1,568	1,647	1,865	2,306	2,366
	tubes and pipes[2]	1,519	1,260	1,155	1,183	1,317
	forged bars[2]	16	7	2	3	3

[1] Includes steel furnaces at steel foundries.
[2] Figures are based on producers' deliveries.

Source: Iron and Steel Statistics Bureau. © Crown copyright 1998

Production and Consumption of Non-Ferrous Metals in the UK

(N/A = not available. N = nil or negligible. In thousands of tonnes.)

Item			1989	1991	1993	1995
Copper	production of refined copper	primary	48.6	16.6	10.6	12.0
		secondary	70.4	53.5	35.9	43.0
	home consumption	refined	324.7	269.4	325.0	397.9
		scrap (metal content)	129.7	118.5	77.9	81.0
		stocks (end of period)[1][2]	14.5	9.3	9.3	7.5
	analysis of home consumption (refined and scrap)	wire[3]	221.7	191.9	253.9	306.8
		rods, bars, and sections	55.5	52.7	53.2	59.0
		sheet, strip, and plate	59.2	37.1	30.7	37.1
		tubes	77.7	65.5	65.2	75.7
		castings and miscellaneous	40.4	40.7	N/A	N/A
		Total[4]	454.4	387.9	403.0	478.6
Zinc	slab zinc	production	79.8	100.7	102.4	106.0
		home consumption	194.5	183.7	195.9	198.4
		stocks (end of period)	13.9	11.2	11.4	9.8
	other zinc (metal content)	consumption	49.6	49.5	45.4	46.8
	analysis of home consumption (slab and scrap)	brass	51.1	47.2	41.6	45.2
		galvanized products	104.3	96.6	105.1	110.7
		zinc sheet and strip	4.0	3.6	4.0	3.0
		zinc alloy die castings	43.1	45.4	46.5	46.5
		zinc oxide	21.7	20.3	20.7	21.6
		other products	19.8	20.2	23.4	18.2
		Total	244.1	233.2	241.3	245.2
Lead, refined	production[5][6]		350.0	311.0	363.8	320.7
	home consumption[6][7]	refined lead	301.3	263.8	263.6	285.4
		scrap and remelted lead[6]	35.0	33.6	35.2	41.6
	stocks (end of period)[8]	lead bullion	17.0	22.8	20.7	9.5
		refined soft lead at consumers' premises	25.7	21.8	25.0	24.9
		in London Metals Exchange warehouses	11.0	8.0	9.5	0.4
	analysis of home consumption (refined and scrap)	cables	12.6	8.6	8.9	9.8
		batteries (excluding oxides)	50.5	51.9	48.7	52.7
	oxides and compounds	batteries	51.7	54.2	53.9	56.2
		other uses	72.6	55.0	56.3	53.8
		sheets and pipes	98.1	79.8	82.7	101.2
		solder	9.1	7.7	7.4	7.4
		alloys	13.4	12.2	14.1	15.9
		other uses	28.4	28.0	26.8	30.0
		Total	336.4	297.4	298.8	327.0
Tin	tin ore (metal content)	production	4.0	2.3	2.2	2.1
	tin metal[10]	production[9]	10.8	5.2	N	N
		home consumption[10]	10.2	10.3	10.4	10.5
		exports and re-exports[11]	5.4	2.9	0.3	2.7
		stocks (end of period) consumers	1.0	1.0	1.0	1.0
		merchants and others	N/A	N/A	N/A	N/A
	analysis of home consumption (excluding scrap)	tinplate	3.6	3.6	3.6	3.6
		alloys	3.4	3.3	3.4	3.4
		solder	1.0	1.1	1.1	1.1
		other uses	2.2	2.3	2.3	2.4
		Total	10.2	10.3	10.4	10.5
Aluminium	primary aluminium[12]	production	297.3	293.5[11]	239.1	237.9
		despatches to customers	494.2	485.4	815.3	459.4
	secondary aluminium	production	220.0	195.1	236.2	229.7
		exports	61.2	64.8	98.3	145.8
	fabricated aluminium	rolled products[13]	236.2	269.4	309.3	359.2
		extrusions and tubes[14]	163.1	129.1	136.2	142.1
		wire products	24.5	22.2	13.5	N/A
		castings	121.0	97.3	133.0	147.0
		Total despatches[15]	544.8	518.0	592.0	648.3
Nickel, refined	production (including ferro-nickel)		26.1	28.6	28.0	35.1

[1] Unwrought copper (electrolytic, fire refined, and blister).
[2] Reported stocks of refined copper held by consumers, and those held in London Metal Exchange warehouses in the UK.
[3] Consumption of high-conductivity copper and cadmium copper wire represented by consumption of wire rods; production of wire rods for export is also included.
[4] Copper content.
[5] Includes lead reclaimed from secondary and scrap material and lead refined from bullion and domestic ores.
[6] Figures for production and consumption of refined lead include antimonial lead, and for scrap and remelted lead, exclude secondary antimonial lead.
[7] Includes toll transactions involving fabrication.
[8] Excludes government stocks.
[9] Includes production from imported scrap and residues refined on toll.
[10] Includes primary and secondary metal.
[11] Includes re-exports on toll transactions.
[12] Includes primary alloys. Despatches to consumers are calculated as the despatches by UK industry plus imports, minus exports; deliveries to London Metals Exchange warehouses are not included.
[13] Includes foil stock and excludes foil products.
[14] Excluding forging bars, wirebars, and almost two-thirds of despatches of hot rolled rod.
[15] Includes wrought and cast products, and excludes foil products.

Source: World Bureau of Metal Statistics; Aluminium Federation. © Crown copyright 1998

Summary of Industrial Production in the UK

(N = nil or negligible. N/A = not available.)

Category	Year	Estimates for All Firms							
		(£ millions)							
		Gross output (production)[1]	Gross value added	Stocks and work in progress		Capital expenditure less disposals	Wages and salaries	Average number of persons employed[2]	Gross value added per person employed (£)
				At end of year	Change of value during year				
Main Production and Construction	1993	465,085.9	146,293.5	N/A	N/A	19,464.9	79,026.9	5,399,300	27,751
	1994	497,553.9	160,070.3	N/A	N/A	20,491.6	81,794.8	5,368,900	29,813
	1995	N/A	168,453.9	75,052.0	N/A	22,875.2	83,374.7	5,383,700	31,289
Production Industries (Revised Definitions)	1993	388,023.5	127,135.6	N/A	N/A	18,371.4	66,973.2	4,487,000	29,124
	1994	428,751.8	140,720.7	N/A	2,865.6	19,284.2	69,354.1	4,495,500	31,301
	1995	452,615.7	145,505.1	57,314.2	4,680.8	21,593.2	68,704.6	4,416,000	32,950
Mining and Quarrying of energy producing materials	1993	2,205.5	751.3	N/A	N/A	134.8	792.7	29,400	25,555
	1994	1,992.5	747.2	N/A	−78.3	72.4	335.0	13,900	53,664
	1995	2,357.7	856.4	352.1	−96.1	89.7	386.1	16,400	52,319
except energy producing materials	1993	2,954.5	1,077.1	184.9	0.4	125.5	477.0	30,500	35,320
	1994	3,081.1	1,043.6	187.2	−5.9	193.0	493.7	30,400	34,277
	1995	2,940.0	1,240.6	187.8	15.5	188.6	451.2	28,100	44,190
Total	1993	5,160.0	1,828.3	N/A	N/A	260.3	1,269.7	59,900	30,522
	1994	5,073.6	1,790.8	N/A	−266.1	265.4	828.7	44,300	40,361
	1995	5,297.8	2,102.8	539.9	−80.6	278.3	841.6	44,800	46,961
Manufacturing of food, beverages, and tobacco	1993	65,323.6	16,472.6	6,174.0	−39.0	2,285.2	7,134.1	560,800	29,373
	1994	67,221.4	17,280.0	6,181.5	266.3	2,220.2	7,388.3	551,500	30,617
	1995	70,482.4	17,138.5	6,543.1	367.0	2,371.5	7,172.8	520,500	32,927
of textiles and textile products	1993	14,528.8	5,706.5	2,265.1	117.1	390.7	3,515.6	384,500	14,841
	1994	15,541.1	6,034.6	2,861.8	419.7	461.8	3,555.8	361,400	16,698
	1995	16,635.6	6,238.4	2,812.4	184.8	457.1	3,663.1	374,100	16,677
of leather and leather products	1993	2,503.1	950.2	376.7	18.4	51.8	608.3	57,100	16,640
	1994	2,683.2	953.6	464.7	50.7	63.9	579.5	57,700	16,527
	1995	2,173.8	745.1	336.0	23.3	57.4	539.5	52,200	14,460
of wood and wood products	1993	4,423.3	1,379.6	553.3	35.4	127.8	853.5	74,900	18,420
	1994	5,292.5	1,528.0	654.1	78.3	125.4	991.8	79,200	19,293
	1995	5,018.4	1,561.6	625.0	11.9	140.7	932.2	74,500	20,955
of pulp, paper, and paper products; publishing and printing	1993	31,444.6	13,255.7	2,285.5	65.1	1,606.4	7,029.6	443,200	29,909
	1994	34,742.0	14,445.5	2,678.6	325.1	1,718.4	7,796.7	456,700	31,630
	1995	36,048.1	14,892.5	2,903.4	404.3	1,935.4	7,350.4	438,100	33,997
of coke, refined petroleum products, and nuclear fuel	1993	22,093.0	2,342.6	1,375.2	−96.3	720.7	668.9	29,600	79,141
	1994	21,832.1	2,264.9	1,089.4	25.5	579.6	672.4	27,700	81,764
	1995	21,547.0	2,845.5	1,177.9	220.2	739.1	657.7	26,700	106,466
of chemicals, chemical products, and man-made fibres	1993	37,437.1	12,443.4	4,849.6	140.0	1,859.7	5,179.4	270,400	46,018
	1994	39,865.0	13,307.0	5,010.7	236.7	1,870.3	5,239.4	265,000	50,215
	1995	43,690.6	15,121.3	5,691.3	438.9	2,274.5	5,624.9	276,500	54,679
of rubber and plastic products	1993	14,667.9	5,710.4	1,493.9	51.3	752.8	3,196.0	232,000	24,614
	1994	16,302.3	6,244.7	1,637.5	162.8	750.6	3,365.7	233,200	26,778
	1995	17,244.9	6,244.5	1,736.7	163.2	906.0	3,443.1	235,700	26,488
of other non-metalic mineral products	1993	8,949.6	3,611.6	1,185.1	−80.2	406.7	2,084.3	148,500	24,321
	1994	10,501.9	4,458.1	1,321.1	91.3	416.7	2,238.9	156,400	28,504
	1995	11,427.7	4,759.7	1,389.6	117.1	577.6	2,318.9	159,000	29,931
of basic iron and non-ferro alloys	1993	33,122.7	11,883.1	3,877.4	59.6	935.6	7,588.2	513,800	23,128
	1994	37,162.2	13,190.7	4,110.6	243.9	1,093.2	7,853.8	521,600	25,289
	1995	40,057.0	14,507.0	5,678.2	473.8	1,263.8	7,854.9	526,700	27,540
of machinery and equipment not elsewhere specified	1993	25,762.6	9,408.3	4,620.8	−67.6	702.2	6,071.5	386,600	24,336
	1994	28,232.0	10,334.1	4,866.3	155.4	856.3	6,415.2	393,100	26,289
	1995	32,134.5	11,392.5	5,380.5	350.1	1,026.0	6,628.6	400,800	28,421
of electrical and optical equipment	1993	40,292.8	13,275.7	6,583.2	313.5	1,440.7	8,069.7	514,700	25,793
	1994	44,846.9	15,482.1	6,871.4	557.7	1,767.6	8,465.4	533,000	29,035
	1995	48,883.4	16,239.1	7,123.2	697.3	2,338.4	8,196.5	518,600	31,314
of transport equipment	1993	40,253.0	12,929.2	10,776.0	94.2	1,294.6	7,180.7	417,100	30,998
	1994	45,245.9	13,549.0	10,707.6	1,081.4	1,503.1	7,187.6	404,300	33,512
	1995	46,820.5	13,355.0	12,253.8	1,289.4	2,301.6	7,372.8	406,200	32,881
not elsewhere classified	1993	N/A	N/A	1,203.9	72.6	235.9	2,203.7	185,100	N/A
	1994	12,026.1	4,213.0	1,488.4	122.4	318.2	2,672.5	213,600	19,724
	1995	12,035.8	4,135.9	1,515.7	117.8	378.8	2,417.6	195,700	21,139
Total	1993	340,832.1	109,368.7	47,619.6	684.1	12,810.8	61,383.5	4,218,300	26,767
	1994	381,494.9	123,285.4	49,943.7	3,817.2	13,743.5	64,423.0	4,254,400	28,977
	1995	404,199.8	129,185.7	55,167.2	4,859.0	16,768.1	64,173.0	4,205,200	30,719

(continued)

Summary of Industrial Production in the UK (*continued*)

Category	Year	Estimates for All Firms							
		(£ millions)							
		Gross output (production)[1]	Gross value added	Stocks and work in progress		Capital expenditure less disposals	Wages and salaries	Average number of persons employed[2]	Gross value added per person employed (£)
				At end of year	Change of value during year				
Electricity, Gas, and Water Supply	1993	42,031.4	15,938.6	2,403.6	−262.6	5,300.3	4,319.8	208,800	76,334
	1994	42,183.3	15,644.5	1,737.1	−661.2	5,275.3	4,102.2	196,800	79,494
	1995	43,118.3	14,216.7	1,607.1	−97.6	4,546.7	3,690.0	165,800	85,728
Construction	1993	77,062.4	19,157.8	N	N	1,093.5	12,053.7	912,300	17,843
	1994	68,802.1	19,349.6	N	N	1,207.4	12,440.7	873,400	22,154
	1995	79,186.7	22,948.8	14,737.8	N/A	1,281.9	14,670.0	967,600	23,714

[1] Figures for gross output include a substantial amount of duplication represented by the total value of partly manufactured goods sold by one industrial establishment to another. The extent of duplication varies from one census industry to another.
[2] The figures include working proprietors but exclude outworkers.

Source: Office for National Statistics. © Crown copyright 1998

Motor Vehicle Production in the UK

	1986	1987	1988	1989	1990	1991	1992	1993	1994	1995	1996
Passenger cars											
< 1,001 cc	162,090	153,214	129,446	133,135	93,039	26,621	22,037	98,034	98,178	95,198	108,645
1,001 cc–1,600 cc	665,093	718,046	764,289	716,784	809,219	830,530	793,307	709,615	729,397	814,873	845,084
1,601 cc–2,800 cc	134,802	205,067	260,231	375,309	325,116	338,530	437,951	515,487	573,357	528,444	635,861
> 2,800 cc	56,977	66,356	72,869	73,854	68,236	40,872	38,585	52,388	65,891	93,569	96,544
Total	1,018,962	1,142,683	1,226,835	1,299,082	1,295,610	1,236,900	1,291,880	1,375,524	1,466,823	1,532,084	1,686,134
Commercial vehicles											
light commercial vehicles	175,825	188,858	250,053	267,135	230,510	184,005	216,477	171,141	197,285	199,346	205,372
trucks											
< 7.5 tonnes	12,451	15,697	19,732	17,687	10,515	8,833	9,558	4,755	8,154	9,523	8,913
> 7.5 tonnes	22,718	22,834	24,887	21,083	13,674	11,766	11,113	8,269	10,016	11,717	10,128
motive units for articulated vehicles	5,351	5,343	6,171	5,827	3,327	2,700	2,788	2,283	2,794	3,476	2,631
buses, coaches, and minibuses	12,340	13,996	16,500	14,858	12,320	9,837	8,517	7,019	9,566	8,939	11,270
Total	228,685	246,728	317,343	326,590	270,346	217,141	248,453	193,467	227,815	233,001	238,314

Source: Office for National Statistics. © Crown copyright 1998

Retail Businesses in the UK

The figures in this table include retail outlets and retail turnover of sales by mail-order, party-plan, automatic vending machines, market stalls, roadside pitches, and door-to-door. (N = nil or negligible.)

1994

		Number of businesses	Number of outlets	Number of persons engaged	Total turnover [2] (£ millions)[1]	VAT in total turnover (£ millions)
Non-specialized stores						
retail sales	mainly food, drinks, or tobacco	20,604	32,786	750,000	57,803	3,830
	other	542	4,123	168,000	11,210	1,339
	Total	21,146	36,910	917,000	69,014	5,169
Specialized stores						
retail sales of food,	fruit and vegetables	6,280	7,357	35,000	1,064	12
drinks, or tobacco	meat and meat products	10,566	12,634	54,000	2,447	10
	fish	848	928	3,000	120	N
	bread, cakes, flour, and sugar confectionery	3,794	6,915	45,000	1,046	37
	alcoholic and other drinks	9,835	14,377	56,000	4,032	544
	tobacco products	13,605	16,358	71,000	4,073	426
	other	1,044	1,244	7,000	322	17
	Total	45,971	59,814	270,000	13,103	1,047
retail sales of	dispensing chemists	6,300	10,404	68,000	4,762	225
pharmarceutical and	medical and orthopaedic goods	976	510	1,000	59	6
medical goods, cosmetics,	cosmetics and toilet articles	1,616	19,000	1,039	144	
and toilet articles	*Total*	7,275	12,529	88,000	5,860	375
other sales of new goods	textiles	3,336	5,261	22,000	734	103
	clothing	12,256	30,107	294,000	19,124	2,289
	footwear and leather goods	2,936	9,665	66,000	2,629	324
	furniture, lighting, and household articles	8,879	13,368	76,000	5,535	811
	electrical household appliances, radio and television goods	5,192	9,793	65,000	6,536	929
	hardware, paints, and glass	4,577	6,117	68,000	5,101	755
	books, newspapers, and stationery	13,940	17,822	135,000	6,005	403
	floor coverings	3,423	4,363	22,000	1,480	211
	photographic, optical, and precision equipment, office supplies and equipment (including computers, etc)	1,162	2,116	12,000	766	108
	other	56,801	75,646	412,000	20,980	2,859
	Total	81,809	133,195	949,000	57,278	7,203
retail sales of second-hand goods		5,870	6,460	15,000	1,258	64
retail sales not in stores	mail order houses	3,068	3,542	46,000	6,199	792
	stalls and markets	12,442	18,676	44,000	1,702	82
	other	17,659	17,546	44,000	2,081	105
	Total	33,169	39,764	133,000	9,981	979
repair of personal and household goods		1,322	1,324	6,000	156	16
Retail hire		638	3,676	28,000	1,426	272
Total businesses selling food, drinks, or tobacco		66,575	92,600	1,020,000	70,906	4,876
Total retail businesses (excluding retail hire businesses)		196,563	289,996	2,379,000	156,649	14,852

[1] Includes retail hire from non-hire retail businesses.
[2] Inclusive of VAT.

Source: Office for National Statistics. © Crown copyright 1998

Sales by Selected Manufacturing Industy in the UK

(N/A = not available. In millions of pounds.)

Industry	1994	1996
Chemicals and Chemical Products		
Dyes and pigments	1,316	1,250
Explosives	122	121
Fertilizers and nitrogen compounds	776	933
Industrial gases	445	475
Man-made fibres	738	805
Paints, varnishes, and similar coatings; printing ink and mastic	2,412	2,771
Perfumes and toilet preparations	2,536	2,836
Pesticides and other agro-chemical products	1,459	1,646
Pharmaceutical preparations	5,529	5,987
Plastics in primary forms	3,701	4,166
Soaps and detergents, cleaning and polishing preparations	2,297	2,318
Synthetic rubber in primary forms	361	N/A
Electrical Machinery and Apparatus Not Elsewhere Classified		
Electric motors, generators, and transformers	2,041	2,337
Electricity: distribution and control apparatus	2,237	2,387
Lighting equipment and electric lamps	989	1,186
Food Products, Beverages, and Tobacco		
Bacon and ham production	1,218	1,513
Bread, fresh pastry goods, and cakes	3,741	3,567
Cocoa, chocolate, and sugar confectionery	2,903	3,195
Dairies, operation of	6,191	6,082
Fish and fish products, processing and preserving of	1,251	1,486
Fruit and vegetable juice	506	528
Grain mill products	2,727	2,911
Ice cream	448	536
Margarine and similar edible fats	496	492
Meat, production and preserving of	3,616	3,811
Oils and fats, refined	378	350
Potatoes, processing and preserving of	1,058	1,376
Poultry meat, production and preserving of	1,603	1,834
Prepared feeds for farm animals	2,328	2,636
Prepared pet foods	1,143	1,259
Sugar	1,325	1,413
Beer	3,190	2,976
Mineral waters and soft drinks	2,101	N/A
Tea and coffee, processing of	1,568	1,496
Tobacco products	2,711	2,588
Furniture and Manufacturing Not Elsewhere Classified		
Chairs and seats	1,767	2,046
Coins and metals, striking of	114	112
Games and toys	610	628
Jewellery and related articles not elsewhere classified	468	781
Jewellery, imitation	43	46
Mattresses	340	391
Musical instruments	47	55
Sports goods	231	258
Luggage, Handbags, Saddlery, Harnesswear, and Footwear		
Footwear	1,149	1,251
Luggage, handbags, and other bags, saddlery, harnesswear	231	257
Machinery and Equipment Not Elsewhere Classified		
Agricultural tractors	878	1,124
Compressors	770	1093
Earth-moving equipment	703	897
Electric domestic appliances	1,712	1,984

Industry	1994	1996
Machinery and Equipment Not Elsewhere Classified (continued)		
Engines and turbines, except aircraft, vehicles, and cycle engines	1,301	1,081
Furnaces and furnace burners	322	315
Lifting and handling equipment	2,109	2,531
Machine tools	1,493	1,823
Machinery for food, beverage, and tobacco processing	612	801
Machinery for mining	358	407
Machinery for paper and paperboard production	266	385
Machinery for textile, apparel, and leather production	436	375
Pumps	784	996
Weapons and ammunition	1,020	2,364
Medical, Precision, and Optical Instruments; Watches and Clocks		
Medical and surgical equipment and orthopaedic appliances	1,113	1,608
Optical instruments and photographic equipment	760	880
Watches and clocks	77	84
Metals, Basic		
Aluminium production	2,153	2,394
Casting of iron	723	866
Casting of light metals	146	222
Casting of steel	165	257
Cast-iron tubes	152	106
Copper production	1,041	1,138
Lead, zinc, and tin production	398	465
Other non-ferrous metal production	410	597
Precious metals production	376	315
Steel tubes	1,095	1,397
Wire drawing	386	365
Metal Products, Fabricated, Except Machinery and Equipment		
Builders' carpentry and joinery of metal	607	1,012
Central heating radiators and boilers	443	544
Cutlery	164	186
Locks and hinges	608	693
Tools	935	1,129
Mineral Products, Non-metallic		
Bricks, tiles, and construction products in baked clay	621	548
Ceramic household and ornamental items	659	728
Ceramic sanitary fixtures	192	205
Ceramic insulators and insulating fittings	47	35
Cement	642	704
Concrete products for construction purposes	1,395	1,456
Cutting, shaping, and finishing of stone	135	209
Flat glass	110	259
Ready mixed concrete	939	922
Mining and Quarrying		
Mining of chemical and fertilizer minerals	125	46
Operation of gravel and sand pits	1,841	1,296
Quarrying of stone for construction	11	23
Office Machinery and Computers		
Computers and other information processing equipment	7,255	9,460
Office machinery	1,117	1,113
Publishing, Printing, and Reproduction of Recorded Media		
Publishing of books	2,871	3,250
Publishing of journals and periodicals	4,728	5,575
Publishing of newspapers	3,284	3,180
Publishing of sound recordings	88	143

Sales by Selected Manufacturing Industy in the UK (continued)

Industry	1994	1996
Publishing, Printing, and Reproduction of Recorded Media (continued)		
Printing of newspapers	232	233
Reproduction of computer media	54	99
Reproduction of sound recording	278	352
Reproduction of video recording	114	156
Pulp, Paper, and Paper Products		
Paper and paperboard	3,269	4,112
Paper stationery	849	1,022
Household and sanitary goods, toilet requisites	1,542	1,725
Radio, Television, and Communication Equipment and Apparatus		
Electronic valves and tubes, and other electronic components	3,144	3,949
Telegraph and telephone apparatus and equipment	1,987	2,854
Television and radio receivers, sound or video recording equipment	3,093	3,502
Rubber and Plastic Products		
Rubber tyres and tubes	1,214	1,197
Retreading and rebuilding of rubber tyres	169	201
Builders' ware of plastic	1,957	3,090
Plastic packing goods	2,213	2,747
Textiles		
Carpets and rugs	1,013	1,183
Household textiles	700	1,016
Knitted and crocheted pullovers, cardigans, and other garments	924	917
Preparation and spinning of textile fibres	1,445	1,596
Soft furnishings	394	398
Textile weaving	1,681	1,323

Industry	1994	1996
Transport: Motor Vehicles, Trailers, and Semi-Trailers		
Bodies (coachwork) for motor vehicles (excluding caravans)	567	669
Caravans	367	379
Motor vehicles	16,344	20,760
Parts and accessories for motor vehicles and their engines	6,594	8,185
Trailers and semi-trailers	617	875
Transport: Other Equipment		
Aircraft and spacecraft	8,615	9,755
Bicycles	135	148
Invalid carriages	70	93
Motorcycles	59	95
Railway and tramway locomotives and rolling stock	1,184	1,001
Wearing Apparel		
Hats	88	94
Leather clothes	24	N/A
Men's outerwear	937	1,033
Men's underwear	481	537
Workwear	275	256
Women's outerwear	1,334	1,702
Women's underwear	978	1,009
Wood and Products of Wood, Except Furniture		
Builders' carpentry and joinery	1,298	1,813
Sawmilling and planing of wood, impregnation of wood	884	840

Source: Office for National Statistics. © Crown copyright 1998

Summary of the UK Service Sector

(N/A = not available. Net capital expenditure and turnover in millions of pounds.)

Category	Net capital expenditure 1990	Net capital expenditure 1994	Turnover 1990	Turnover 1994	Number of businesses 1990	Number of businesses 1994
Retail businesses[1]						
food retailers	2,634	N/A	48,171	N/A	65,169	N/A
drink, confectionery, and tobacco retailers	189	N/A	12,834	N/A	48,376	N/A
clothing, footwear, and leather goods retailers	209	N/A	12,716	N/A	30,688	N/A
household goods retailers	556	N/A	20,619	N/A	51,379	N/A
other non-food retailers	291	N/A	12,749	N/A	41,707	N/A
mixed retail businesses	521	N/A	24,286	N/A	2,877	N/A
hire and repair businesses	156	N/A	1,330	N/A	1,508	N/A
Total	4,555	N/A	132,704	N/A	241,704	N/A
Wholesaling and dealing						
wholesaling of food[2] and drink	602	521	47,286	52,539	16,435	15,754
wholesaling of petroleum products	533	467	21,660	37,871	969	938
wholesaling of clothing, furs, textiles, and footwear	102	92	9,587	11,142	10,217	9,813
wholesaling of other goods	1,081	1,061	79,495	117,520	60,685	62,271
coal and oil merchants	17	22	2,340	2,948	3,210	2,681
builders' merchants	113	139	8,540	9,415	4,381	3,989
corn, seed, and agricultural merchants; dealers in livestock	48	51	8,351	8,183	3,083	2,812
dealing in industrial materials	167	150	26,967	26,827	6,016	5,527
dealing in scrap and other waste materials	74	60	2,922	2,062	3,946	3,084
dealing in industrial and agricultural machinery	300	272	15,218	25,806	8,778	8,663
operational leasing	275	457	3,095	2,582	2,860	2,239
Total	3,313	3,291	225,461	296,896	120,580	117,771

(continued)

Summary of the UK Service Sector (*continued*)

Category	Net capital expenditure		Turnover		Number of businesses	
	1990	1994	1990	1994	1990	1994
Catering and allied trades						
hotels and other residential establishments	1,231	418	6,370	6,997	14,444	12,002
holiday camps, camping, and holiday caravan sites	125	94	939	1,188	2,027	2,038
restaurants, cafes, and snack bars selling food for consumption on the premises only	289	203	3,906	4,920	17,842	16,160
fish and chip shops, sandwich and snack bars, and other establishments selling food partly or wholly for consumption off the premises	198	120	4,162	4,449	30,921	26,340
public houses[3]	588	665	10,154	13,364	40,155	36,591
clubs (excluding sports clubs and gaming clubs)	118	172	2,587	3,002	16,806	14,740
catering contractors	43	41	2,059	2,451	2,704	2,324
Total	2,593	1,713	30,178	36,371	124,900	110,195
Motor trades						
retail distributors	502	341	42,869	47,295	28,060	22,160
wholesale distributors	98	100	16,709	24,650	3,687	5,450
repair and servicing	124	132	4,758	5,705	36,468	32,062
petrol filling stations	170	140	9,663	11,508	8,518	7,591
Total	894	713	73,999	89,157	76,733	67,262
Road transport and ancillary transport services; postal and telecommunications						
omnibus and tramway services	137	277	1,909	3,320	3,612	3,776
taxis and private hire cars	568	1,172	2,462	3,195	5,691	4,495
road haulage contracting for general hire or reward, other road haulage	734	1,257	11,082	14,579	44,871	38,354
postal and telecommunications	3,066	3,413	14,579	19,201	1,397	1,973
shipping agents and forwarding agents, travel agents, driving instruction, operation of car parks, toll roads and toll bridges, other miscellaneous transport services and storage	496	740	13,811	21,073	16,521	16,651
Total	5,001	6,856	43,843	61,368	72,092	65,249
Business services						
advertising and market research	155	170	N/A	11,096	10,304	10,282
industrial and commercial valuers, auctioneers and transfer agents	43	23	706	569	3,232	2,694
chartered or company secretaries (firms acting as)	1	1	20	23	173	170
computer services	534	634	9,085	14,458	37,740	44,957
contract cleaning	48	45	1,254	1,828	5,935	5,162
management consultants	102	118	2,042	398	16,469	20,454
staff bureaux and employment agencies	52	76	3,991	6,015	6,569	5,779
duplicating, calculating, and typewriting agencies	11	5	158	114	1,070	715
other business services	649	565	11,001	15,953	36,240	40,889
Total	1,595	1,637	N/A	53,554	117,732	131,102
Professional and scientific services						
opticians	36	59	732	1,122	2,511	2,619
accountancy	244	159	5,155	6,290	17,031	17,503
miscellaneous private educational services	98	192	1,473	5,115	3,034	3,694
legal services	265	209	6,573	8,355	17,460	19,721
private hospitals	74	87	750	1,152	119	81
private nursing homes	170	234	1,460	2,769	3,498	4,404
research and development services	295	437	2,393	3,537	1,785	1,707
surveying (various kinds)	130	73	2,737	2,512	10,386	9,661
architects (private practice)	82	45	1,939	1,302	8,099	6,878
draughtsmen	13	17	360	240	6,415	3,924
consultant engineers	174	110	4,123	5,007	19,945	16,894
research chemists, analytical chemists, assayers, non-medical bacteriologists, metallurgists, and geologists (private practices)	16	24	235	323	800	823
artists, sculptors, designers, authors, journalists (freelance), and composers	133	83	2,885	2,339	20,702	18,719
other professional and scientific services	174	168	3,324	4,185	22,570	22,162

Summary of the UK Service Sector (*continued*)

Category	Net capital expenditure		Turnover		Number of businesses	
Personal and miscellaneous services						
cinemas, theatres, music halls, radio and television services, film recording studios, performers and performing groups, drama, music, variety	812	759	8,906	11,702	18,622	19,083
dance halls and dancing schools, sport, other recreations, betting, gaming	667	807	8,247	11,242	16,173	18,100
launderettes, laundries, hire of towels, linen, and industrial clothing, dry cleaning, job dyeing and carpet beating, and photography	119	155	2,235	1,719	11,115	9,473
hairdressing and manicure, repair of boots and shoes, funeral direction, cemeteries and crematoria	61	35	985	1,106	12,197	7,466
other personal and miscellaneous services[4]	631	1,623	9,353	11,699	51,940	61,562
Total	2,290	3,379	29,726	37,468	110,046	115,684
Property						
land or estate company	4,040	894	N/A	N/A	14,527	25,091
property developer	2,388	−212	N/A	N/A	5,186	4,086
property dealer	−2	244	N/A	N/A	1,547	2,308
property nominee company	1,109	382	N/A	N/A	4,460	7,683
property and estate management	1,011	1,582	N/A	N/A	10,355	15,808
Total	8,546	2,890	N/A	N/A	36,075	54,976

[1] Improvements to employment data have led to increased coverage of non-retail businesses in the 1990 inquiry. This coverage has resulted in a discontinuity in the series of sales by non-retail businesses.
[2] 'Wholesaling of food' excludes slaughterhouses.
[3] These figures include managed public houses owned by breweries.
[4] The 1994 figures for personal and miscellaneous services include data relating to 'sewage disposal' provided by the privatized water companies for the first time.

Source: *Business Monitor*, 1996. © Crown copyright 1997

UK Employment

Average Weekly Earnings by Region and Gender in England

Data are gross earnings of full-time employees; as of April 1996 (See following page for UK data). Data relate to full-time employees on adult rates whose pay for the survey pay-period was not affected by absence. (In pounds.)

Region	Manual male employees	Non-manual male employees	All full-time male employees	Manual female employees	Non-manual female employees	All full-time female employees
England						
North East	298.4	406.0	347.7	184.8	270.2	252.4
North West and Merseyside						
North West	300.2	433.6	369.0	191.7	279.7	262.4
Merseyside	308.3	409.6	361.7	184.4	284.0	271.3
Yorkshire and the Humber	292.8	410.0	350.7	182.6	270.4	252.5
East Midlands	294.1	413.1	352.9	181.8	271.1	248.7
West Midlands	297.1	425.0	360.1	191.5	276.4	256.9
Eastern	308.7	442.6	382.3	197.0	296.7	279.9
London	336.8	585.7	514.3	239.5	379.5	364.9
South East	307.7	477.9	412.7	204.0	309.5	292.7
South West	282.7	431.4	364.8	185.5	277.0	261.1
Average	302.8	468.9	369.2	196.5	305.6	286.6

Source: © Crown copyright 1997

Average Weekly Earnings by Region and Gender in the UK

Data are gross earnings of full-time employees; as of April 1996. Data relate to full-time employees on adult rates whose pay for the survey pay-period was not affected by absence. (In pounds.)

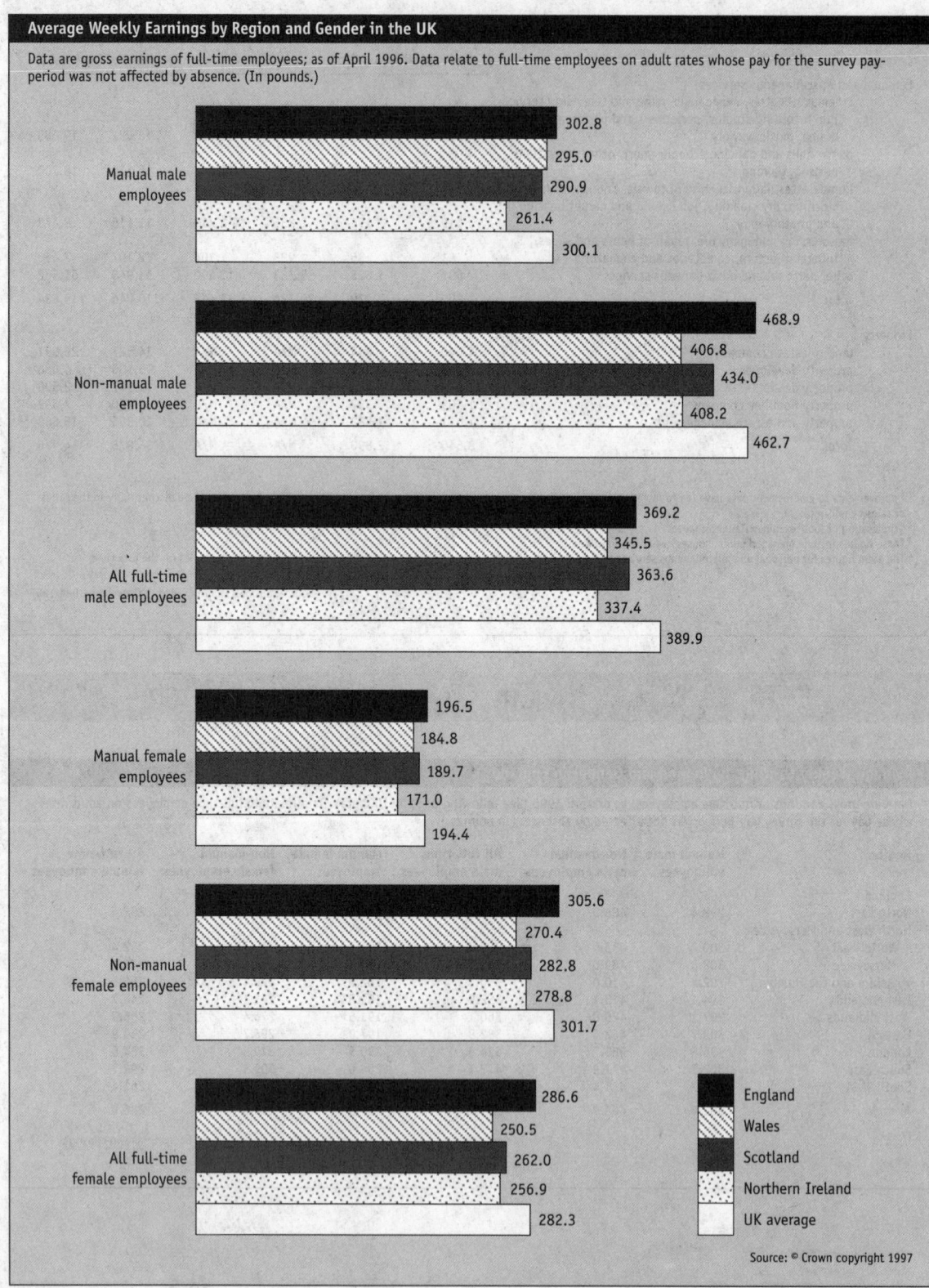

Manual male employees
- 302.8
- 295.0
- 290.9
- 261.4
- 300.1

Non-manual male employees
- 468.9
- 406.8
- 434.0
- 408.2
- 462.7

All full-time male employees
- 369.2
- 345.5
- 363.6
- 337.4
- 389.9

Manual female employees
- 196.5
- 184.8
- 189.7
- 171.0
- 194.4

Non-manual female employees
- 305.6
- 270.4
- 282.8
- 278.8
- 301.7

All full-time female employees
- 286.6
- 250.5
- 262.0
- 256.9
- 282.3

Legend:
- England
- Wales
- Scotland
- Northern Ireland
- UK average

Source: © Crown copyright 1997

Average Weekly Earnings and Hours of Full-Time Employees on Adult Rates in the UK

| Year | Manufacturing industries | | | | | All industries and services | | | | |
| | Weekly earnings (£) | | | Hourly earnings (£)[1] | | Weekly earnings (£) | | | Hourly earnings (£)[1] | |
	Including those whose pay was affected by absence	Excluding those whose pay was affected by absence	Hours[1]	Including overtime pay and overtime hours	Excluding overtime pay and overtime hours	Including those whose pay was affected by absence	Excluding those whose pay was affected by absence	Hours[1]	Including overtime pay and overtime hours	Excluding overtime pay and overtime hours
Men										
1987	217.0	222.3	43.0	5.11	5.07	219.4	224.0	41.9	5.27	5.26
1988	236.3	242.3	43.3	5.50	5.44	240.6	245.8	42.1	5.74	5.73
1989	257.3	264.6	43.6	5.98	5.94	263.5	269.5	42.3	6.28	6.29
1990	282.2	289.2	43.4	6.55	6.50	290.2	295.6	42.2	6.88	6.89
1991	299.5	308.1	42.1	7.20	7.15	312.9	318.9	41.5	7.55	7.57
1992	319.8	328.3	42.3	7.62	7.58	333.6	340.1	41.4	8.07	8.10
1993	334.8	342.7	42.1	7.99	7.95	347.3	353.5	41.3	8.44	8.47
1994	343.0	350.9	42.5	8.16	8.12	355.6	362.1	41.6	8.61	8.65
1995	358.0	364.0	43.0	8.44	8.41	369.0	374.6	41.9	8.91	8.97
1996	373.5	380.0	42.7	8.86	8.81	385.9	391.3	41.7	9.33	9.38
1997	386.7	392.7	42.8	9.17	9.12	403.2	408.7	41.8	9.76	9.82
Women										
1987	128.2	133.4	39.0	3.39	3.36	144.9	148.1	37.5	3.88	3.86
1988	138.4	144.3	39.2	3.66	3.62	160.1	164.2	37.6	4.31	4.29
1989	152.7	159.1	39.1	4.04	4.00	178.1	182.3	37.6	4.80	4.78
1990	170.3	177.1	39.1	4.48	4.44	197.0	201.5	37.5	5.30	5.28
1991	184.2	192.9	38.8	4.94	4.91	217.2	222.4	37.4	5.91	5.89
1992	199.3	207.1	38.9	5.28	5.24	235.8	241.1	37.3	6.40	6.38
1993	211.0	220.0	38.9	5.61	5.57	246.9	252.6	37.4	6.70	6.68
1994	218.3	226.8	39.1	5.76	5.72	255.8	261.5	37.6	6.89	6.88
1995	229.2	236.7	39.4	6.01	5.96	264.2	269.8	37.6	7.15	7.14
1996	239.2	246.7	39.3	6.27	6.23	277.9	283.0	37.6	7.51	7.49
1997	251.5	258.8	39.2	6.60	6.56	291.7	297.2	37.6	7.90	7.88
Average										
1987	196.0	202.0	42.0	4.74	4.68	194.9	198.9	40.4	4.85	4.81
1988	212.7	219.4	42.3	5.09	5.02	213.6	218.4	40.6	5.29	5.26
1989	231.7	239.5	42.5	5.55	5.48	234.3	239.7	40.7	5.81	5.79
1990	255.1	262.8	42.4	6.09	6.01	258.0	263.1	40.5	6.37	6.34
1991	271.3	280.7	41.3	6.69	6.62	278.9	284.7	40.0	7.00	6.98
1992	290.7	299.7	41.5	7.09	7.02	298.5	304.6	39.9	7.50	7.49
1993	304.8	313.7	41.3	7.45	7.39	310.9	316.9	39.8	7.84	7.83
1994	312.7	321.6	41.7	7.62	7.55	319.3	325.7	40.1	8.03	8.03
1995	327.1	334.3	42.2	7.92	7.85	330.4	336.3	40.3	8.31	8.32
1996	341.9	349.3	41.9	8.29	8.22	346.0	351.5	40.2	8.70	8.71
1997	354.8	361.7	42.0	8.61	8.53	361.8	367.6	40.3	9.12	9.13

[1] Excluding those whose pay was affected by absence.

Source: Office for National Statistics

Average Earnings Index in the UK

(1990 = 100. n.e.c = not elsewhere classified.)

Industry	1995	1996	Industry	1995	1996
Agriculture and forestry	126.4	133.7	Electrical and optical equipment	132.9	140.2
Mining and quarrying	139.0	142.2	Transport equipment	133.2	140.4
Food products, beverages, and tobacco	136.2	140.9	Electricity, gas, and water supply	133.6	138.7
Textiles	132.6	138.8	Construction	123.5	127.8
Clothing, leather, and footwear	129.3	134.1	Wholesale trade	124.4	130.2
Wood, wood products, and other manufacturing n.e.c	123.9	131.2	Retail trade and repairs	118.3	123.2
Pulp, paper products, printing, and publishing	128.5	133.9	Hotels and restaurants	122.3	125.3
Chemicals and chemical products	131.7	137.1	Transport, storage, and communication	128.2	132.5
Rubber and plastic products	133.7	137.7	Financial intermediation	133.4	140.5
Other non-metallic mineral products	124.8	128.7	Real estate renting and business activities	119.3	124.3
Basic metals	131.8	137.8	Public administration	126.0	128.7
Fabricated metal products (excluding machinery)	133.4	139.0	Education, health, and social work	124.6	128.5
Machinery and equipment n.e.c	134.3	139.8	Other services	129.5	136.1

Source: Office for National Statistics © Crown copyright 1998

Highest Qualification Levels Attained by Sex and Socioeconomic Group in Great Britain

Data are for economically active persons aged 25–69 not in full-time education. (Data are for 1994 and 1995 combined. In percentages.)

Highest qualification level attained[1]		Socioeconomic group[2]							
		Professional	Employers and managers	Intermediate non-manual	Junior non-manual	Skilled manual and own account non-professional	Semi-skilled manual and personal service	Unskilled manual	Total
Degree or equivalent	men	61	23	30	9	2	1	1	15
	women	67	21	21	4	3	1	0	10
	Total	62	23	24	5	2	1	1	13
Higher education below degree level	men	17	18	20	12	10	6	4	13
	women	9	18	28	4	5	4	1	11
	Total	15	18	25	6	9	5	2	12
GCE A-level or equivalent[3]	men	9	17	17	23	13	10	2	14
	women	9	13	10	11	9	6	2	9
	Total	9	16	12	14	13	8	2	12
GCSE grades A–C or equivalent[3]	men	7	21	20	29	25	20	18	21
	women	7	25	23	39	28	23	15	28
	Total	7	22	22	37	25	22	16	24
GCSE grades D–G or equivalent/commercial qualifications/apprenticeship	men	2	5	3	7	13	14	11	9
	women	3	8	7	18	12	13	11	12
	Total	2	6	6	16	13	14	11	10
Foreign or other qualifications	men	3	3	4	3	2	2	3	3
	women	6	2	3	2	2	3	2	2
	Total	3	3	3	2	2	3	2	3
No qualifications	men	2	12	6	16	35	47	60	25
	women	0	14	9	22	40	49	68	27
	Total	2	13	8	21	36	48	66	26
Bases = 100%	men	779	2,189	1,005	595	3,148	1,090	295	9,101
	women	206	1,113	1,719	2,520	661	1,479	565	8,263
	Total	985	3,302	2,724	3,115	3,809	2,569	860	17,364

[1] Those who never went to school are excluded.
[2] Excludes members of the armed forces, full-time students, and those who had never worked.
[3] Including further-education qualifications.

Source: Living in Britain 1996. © Crown copyright 1996

Average Hours Worked per Week by Gender in the European Union

1996

Country	Men			Women		
	Full-time	Part-time	All	Full-time	Part-time	All
Austria	40.2	22.3	39.6	39.8	22.0	34.7
Belgium	38.8	21.5	38.3	37.1	21.5	31.7
Denmark	39.4	13.5	36.5	37.6	21.2	31.9
Finland	39.4	19.0	38.2	38.0	21.3	35.7
France	40.5	22.5	39.6	38.8	22.7	34.0
Germany	40.4	16.5	39.6	39.3	19.1	32.5
Greece	41.4	28.6	41.0	38.9	22.5	37.9
Ireland, Republic of	42.0	20.4	40.9	38.0	18.5	33.8
Italy	39.8	29.8	39.5	36.4	22.6	34.7
Luxembourg	40.4	30.8	40.3	37.7	19.6	34.5
Netherlands	39.5	19.3	36.3	39.0	18.5	25.0
Portugal	42.7	32.3	42.6	39.3	20.9	37.8
Spain	41.0	19.4	40.5	39.6	17.6	36.0
Sweden	40.1	18.7	38.1	39.9	24.9	33.1
UK	45.8	16.2	43.5	40.6	18.0	30.6
EU average	41.3	19.3	40.1	39.0	19.8	32.8

Source: Labour Force Surveys, Eurostat © Crown copyright 1998

Homeworkers by Gender and Occupation in the UK

Data show percentages of those in employment in each occupation who were homeworkers excluding those on government training and employment schemes. Homeworkers covers those who work mainly in their own home but excludes those who work in the same grounds or buildings as their home, those who work in different places using their home as a base, and those who sometimes do work at home. (N/A = not available. As of spring 1997.)

Occupation	Men	Women	All employees
Professional	2.8	2.4	2.7
Managers and administrators	1.9	5.8	3.2
Associate professional and technical	4.6	4.8	4.7
Clerical and secretarial	1.3	4.8	3.9
Personal and protective services	N/A	5.2	3.7
Sales	1.3	0.8	1.0
Craft and related	0.5	10.5	1.3
Plant and machine operatives	N/A	3.0	0.7
Average[1]	1.4	4.0	2.6

[1] Includes those with other occupations and those who did not state their occupation.

Source: Labour Force Survey, Office for National Statistics. © Crown copyright 1998

Economic Activity of Women with Children in the UK

(In percentages unless otherwise indicated.) As of spring 1997.

Status	Age of youngest dependent child			No dependent children[1]	All women[2]
	0–4	5–10	11–15		
Working full-time	18.0	23.0	34.0	48.0	38.0
Working part-time	33.0	43.0	40.0	24.0	29.0
Unemployed[3]	4.0	5.0	4.0	4.0	4.0
Economically inactive	45.0	29.0	22.0	25.0	29.0
All women[2] (millions)	3.0	2.2	1.5	10.3	17.0

[1] Aged under 16.
[2] Aged 16 to 59.
[3] Based on the International Labour Organization definition.

Source: Labour Force Survey, Office for National Statistics. © Crown copyright 1998

Part-Time Employees by Region and Gender in the UK

Data are based on employees' own definition of part-time and show part-time employees as a percentage of all employees. (As of spring 1996.)

Region	Men			Women		
	Manual	Non-manual	Average	Manual	Non-manual	Average
England						
North East	7.1	7.2	7.2	61.6	38.5	46.2
North West	8.0	6.5	7.2	58.4	38.9	45.0
Merseyside	7.7	8.4	8.0	61.7	39.7	46.8
Yorkshire and the Humber	7.3	8.1	7.7	62.1	41.2	48.6
East Midlands	6.6	7.7	7.1	54.9	41.2	46.1
West Midlands	6.2	5.8	6.1	58.2	39.7	46.1
Eastern	9.3	6.4	7.6	61.0	40.2	46.2
London	11.6	7.9	9.2	52.7	28.0	33.0
South East	10.0	7.0	8.1	61.8	38.9	45.2
South West	11.7	7.8	9.3	61.8	45.5	50.2
Average	8.6	7.2	7.8	59.3	38.4	44.7
Northern Ireland	6.5	4.1	5.3	52.7	36.0	40.5
Scotland	7.2	7.0	7.1	54.2	36.9	42.2
Wales	7.9	7.2	7.7	59.9	42.2	48.7
UK average	8.4	7.1	7.7	58.7	38.4	44.5

Source: Office for National Statistics; Department of Economic Development, Northern Ireland. © Crown copyright 1997

Employees by Region, Industry, and Gender in the UK

(N = nil or negligible. As of September 1995. In percentages unless otherwise indicated.)

Region	Agriculture, hunting, forestry, and fishing	Mining and quarrying (including oil and gas extraction)	Manufacturing	Electricity, gas, and water	Construction	Distribution, hotels and catering, repairs	Transport, storage, and communication	Financial and business services	Public administration and defence	Education, social work, and health services	Other	Whole economy = 100 %
Men												
England												
North East	1.1	0.7	30.8	1.4	9.3	16.1	7.7	10.5	7.6	10.7	4.1	432,000
North West and Merseyside												
North West	1.5	0.2	31.4	1.2	6.7	19.5	8.6	13.5	5.6	8.2	3.5	1,049,000
Merseyside	0.4	0.1	25.5	0.7	6.4	18.6	9.9	13.5	7.1	12.7	5.1	206,000
Yorkshire and the Humber	1.8	0.6	30.6	1.1	7.1	20.5	8.4	12.1	5.7	8.6	3.5	958,000
East Midlands	2.5	0.7	35.1	1.3	5.5	20.0	7.5	11.0	4.9	8.5	3.1	785,000
West Midlands	1.1	0.3	38.1	1.1	5.7	18.9	7.0	11.9	5.2	7.6	3.1	1,059,000
Eastern	3.8	0.4	25.7	1.2	5.6	21.0	9.6	16.1	5.2	8.1	3.3	972,000
London	0.1	0.3	10.7	0.5	4.4	21.1	11.8	29.8	7.6	7.7	6.0	1,646,000
South East	2.5	0.2	20.9	1.2	4.8	22.5	9.4	19.3	6.3	9.5	3.4	1,437,000
South West	3.3	0.6	25.3	1.6	5.6	21.6	7.3	14.6	7.5	9.1	3.4	865,000
Total	1.8	0.4	25.8	1.1	5.7	20.5	9.0	16.9	6.2	8.6	3.9	9,407,000
Wales	3.0	0.9	31.6	1.6	6.6	17.5	7.1	9.2	8.3	10.2	4.0	476,000
Scotland	3.2	1.7	22.3	1.6	10.9	17.4	8.4	12.4	7.0	10.5	4.6	987,000
Northern Ireland	6.0	0.6	24.2	1.5	7.4	17.9	5.9	7.0	12.7	12.0	4.8	288,000
UK total	2.1	0.5	25.7	1.2	6.3	20.0	8.7	15.9	6.6	8.9	4.0	11,158,000
Women												
England												
North East	0.3	N	12.8	0.4	1.4	23.1	2.3	12.1	8.4	33.8	5.5	439,000
North West and Merseyside												
North West	0.5	N	13.1	0.4	1.1	25.7	2.9	15.8	6.3	29.9	4.3	1,009,000
Merseyside	0.1	N	8.9	0.1	0.8	23.3	2.2	15.2	7.2	36.0	6.2	233,000
Yorkshire and the Humber	0.4	0.1	12.1	0.3	1.4	26.2	2.7	15.0	6.2	31.1	4.3	917,000
East Midlands	0.7	0.1	17.2	0.4	1.5	24.0	2.5	12.6	5.4	31.8	4.0	762,000
West Midlands	0.3	N	14.7	0.5	1.3	25.0	2.5	15.7	5.5	30.1	4.3	949,000
Eastern	1.0	0.1	10.9	0.3	1.2	26.1	3.2	17.6	5.4	29.9	4.4	927,000
London	0.1	0.1	6.1	0.2	1.1	22.7	4.7	29.3	6.6	22.8	6.4	1,546,000
South East	0.7	N	8.4	0.4	1.1	25.1	3.5	19.6	5.2	31.6	4.4	1,426,000
South West	1.0	0.1	9.3	0.5	1.2	27.0	2.4	16.5	5.9	31.8	4.3	877,000
Total	0.5	0.1	10.9	0.4	1.2	24.9	3.1	18.4	6.0	29.8	4.7	9,086,000
Wales	1.0	0.1	12.4	0.4	1.1	24.1	1.8	11.9	7.5	34.9	4.9	470,000
Scotland	0.8	0.2	9.7	0.4	1.4	26.6	2.6	16.9	6.6	30.2	4.6	1,012,000
Northern Ireland	0.8	0.1	11.9	0.2	0.9	21.8	1.8	8.9	8.2	41.2	4.4	288,000
UK total	0.6	0.1	10.9	0.4	1.2	25.0	3.0	17.7	6.2	30.3	4.7	10,856,000

Source: Office for National Statistics; Department of Economic Development, Northern Ireland. © Crown copyright 1997

Temporary Employees by Region, Type of Work, and Gender in the UK

(N/A = not available. As of spring 1996. In percentages unless otherwise indicated.)

Region	Seasonal work, agency temping, and other casual and temporary work		Contract for fixed period/fixed task		All temporary employees[1]	All temporary employees as a percentage of all employees
	Men	Women	Men	Women		
England						
North East	17.4	21.6	40.6	20.4	80,000	8.4
North West and Merseyside						
North West	16.2	27.2	26.3	30.3	130,000	6.3
Merseyside	N/A	N/A	N/A	N/A	26,000	5.6
Yorkshire and the Humber	19.4	25.2	26.4	29.1	130,000	6.8
East Midlands	22.2	28.3	19.7	29.8	102,000	6.1
West Midlands	21.4	24.1	25.9	28.6	126,000	6.2
Eastern	24.0	27.1	20.7	28.1	144,000	6.8
London	21.0	30.3	20.9	27.8	228,000	8.8
South East	21.0	30.3	23.0	25.6	217,000	6.9
South West	23.4	32.3	17.1	27.2	133,000	7.4
Average	20.7	28.1	23.5	27.7	1,317,000	7.0
Wales	17.1	34.6	24.9	23.4	84,000	8.4
Scotland	18.9	25.3	31.3	24.5	156,000	7.9
Northern Ireland	N/A	N/A	N/A	N/A	29,000	5.7
UK average	20.3	28.2	24.3	27.1	1,586,000	7.1

[1] Includes those who did not state type of temporary work but percentages are based on totals excluding them.

Source: Office for National Statistics; Department of Economic Development, Northern Ireland. © Crown copyright 1997

Labour Force by Gender and Age in the UK

The former civilian labour force definition has been used to produce estimates for 1971 and 1981; in later years the International Labour Organization definition has been used and members of the armed forces excluded. (In millions.)

Year	16–24	25–44	45–54	55–59	60–64	65 and over	All aged 16 and over
Men							
1971	3.0	6.5	3.2	1.5	1.3	0.6	16.0
1981	3.2	7.1	3.0	1.4	1.0	0.3	16.0
1991	3.1	8.1	3.0	1.1	0.8	0.3	16.4
1997	2.4	8.1	3.4	1.1	0.7	0.3	16.0
2001[1]	2.4	8.2	3.4	1.3	0.7	0.3	16.3
2006[1]	2.6	7.8	3.5	1.4	0.8	0.3	16.4
Women							
1971	2.3	3.5	2.1	0.9	0.5	0.3	10.0
1981	2.7	4.6	2.1	0.9	0.4	0.2	10.9
1991	2.6	6.1	2.4	0.8	0.3	0.2	12.4
1997	2.0	6.4	2.9	0.8	0.4	0.2	12.7
2001[1]	2.1	6.4	3.0	0.9	0.4	0.2	13.1
2006[1]	2.2	6.4	3.2	1.1	0.5	0.2	13.6

[1] Data for 2001 and 2006 are based on the spring 1996 Labour Force Survey and mid-1994 based population projections.

Source: Census and Labour Force Survey, Office of National Statistics; Department of Economic Development, Northern Ireland. © Crown copyright 1998

Unemployment Rates by Gender and Age in the UK

At spring each year. Unemployment is based on the International Labour Organization definition as a percentage of all economically active. (N/A = not available. In percentages.)

Age	1991	1992	1993	1994	1995	1996	1997	Age	1991	1992	1993	1994	1995	1996	1997
Males								*Females*							
16–19	16.4	18.6	22.0	20.9	19.6	20.6	18.2	16–19	12.7	13.6	15.9	16.0	14.8	14.6	14.0
20–24	15.2	18.9	20.3	18.3	17.0	16.2	14.0	20–24	10.1	10.2	11.8	10.7	10.6	8.9	8.9
25–44	8.0	10.5	10.9	10.2	9.0	8.7	7.0	25–44	7.1	7.3	7.3	7.0	6.7	6.3	5.4
45–54	6.3	8.4	9.4	8.6	7.4	6.4	6.1	45–54	4.6	5.0	5.0	5.0	4.5	4.1	3.8
55–59	8.4	11.2	12.3	11.6	10.2	9.9	8.0	55–59	5.5	4.5	6.0	6.5	4.7	4.2	4.8
60–64	9.9	10.2	14.2	11.6	9.9	8.9	7.6	60 and over	4.4	3.1	3.9	2.9	N/A	N/A	2.0
65 and over	5.9	4.9	4.6	3.7	N/A	4.1	4.0								
Average	9.2	11.5	12.4	11.4	10.1	9.7	8.1	*Average*	7.2	7.3	7.6	7.3	6.8	6.3	5.8

Source: Labour Force Survey, Office for National Statistics. © Crown copyright 1998

Unemployment by Region of the UK

Data are the number of unemployment-related benefit claimants as a percentage of the estimated total workforce (the sum of claimants, employees in employment, self-employed, participants on work related government training programmes, and HM Forces) at mid-year. Data are seasonally adjusted and exclude claimants under 18. (N/A = not available. Annual averages. In percentages.)

Region		1986	1987	1988	1989	1990	1991	1992	1993	1994	1995	1996
Great Britain												
England	North East	N/A	15.3	13.0	10.9	9.6	11.2	12.1	12.9	12.4	11.6	10.6
	North West	N/A	10.6	8.6	6.9	6.2	7.9	9.4	9.5	8.7	7.6	6.9
	Merseyside	N/A	18.3	16.0	13.7	12.7	14.2	15.0	15.1	14.9	13.7	13.1
	Yorkshire and the Humber	12.4	11.3	9.3	7.3	6.6	8.7	9.9	10.2	9.6	8.7	8.0
	East Midlands	9.9	8.9	7.1	5.4	5.1	7.2	9.0	9.5	8.7	7.6	6.8
	West Midlands	12.8	11.3	8.8	6.5	5.7	8.4	10.3	10.8	9.9	8.3	7.4
	Eastern	N/A	7.1	4.9	3.4	3.6	6.4	8.7	9.4	8.1	6.9	6.1
	London	9.1	8.2	6.6	5.1	5.0	8.0	10.5	11.6	10.7	9.7	8.9
	South East	N/A	6.0	4.1	2.8	3.0	5.8	8.0	8.6	7.3	6.2	5.4
	South West	9.2	8.0	6.0	4.3	4.2	6.9	9.2	9.5	8.1	7.0	6.2
Scotland		13.5	13.1	11.2	9.4	8.2	8.8	9.4	9.7	9.3	8.1	7.9
Wales		13.7	12.1	9.9	7.3	6.7	9.0	10.0	10.3	9.3	8.7	8.2
Average Great Britain		10.9	9.8	7.8	6.0	5.6	7.9	9.6	10.2	9.2	8.1	7.4
Northern Ireland		16.8	16.4	15.0	14.0	12.8	12.9	13.8	13.7	12.6	11.4	10.9
Average UK		11.1	9.9	8.0	6.2	5.8	8.0	9.7	10.3	9.3	8.2	7.5

Source: Office for National Statistics; Labour Market Statistics. © Crown copyright 1998

Major Job Eliminations in the UK

Major announcements from the beginning of 1995.

Company	Number of jobs to be shed	Date	Company	Number of jobs to be shed	Date
Royal Sun Alliance	4,000	August 1996	Carlsberg	1,500	September 1997
Northern Foods	3,450	June 1995	British Energy	1,460	October 1997
Safeway	3,000	May 1995	Tarmac	1,400	September 1996
Commercial Union/General Accident	3,000	February 1998	Ford	1,300	February 1997
Transco	2,500	September 1997	Electrolux	1,300	October 1997
Refuge Assurance/United Friendly	2,200	April 1997	Kingfisher	1,200	January 1997
BNFL/Magnox Electric	2,000	December 1997	Scottish Power	1,100	December 1996
Kwik Save	1,900	November 1996	Barclays	1,000	March 1996
Midland	1,745	March 1995	House of Fraser	1,000	January 1997
Unigate	1,500	June 1995			

Duration of Unemployment by Gender and Age in the UK

Data exclude those who did not state their duration of unemployment. Unemployment is based on the International Labour Organization definition. (N/A = not available. In percentages.)

1997

Age	Less than three months	More than three months but less than six months	More than six months but less than one year	More than one year but less than two years	More than two years but less than three years	Three years or more
Men						
16–19	40	23	21	13	N/A	N/A
20–29	26	16	16	17	9	15
30–39	22	11	13	16	9	28
40–49	22	15	14	15	7	27
50–64	18	12	14	11	8	37
Total[1]	25	15	15	15	8	22
Women						
16–19	45	21	20	11	N/A	N/A
20–29	42	16	19	11	6	6
30–39	33	17	17	15	7	11
40–49	38	15	16	13	N/A	10
50–59	27	16	14	15	N/A	19
Total[2]	38	17	17	13	6	9

[1] Includes males aged 65 and over who were unemployed.
[2] Includes females aged 60 and over who were unemployed.

Source: Labour Force Survey, Office for National Statistics. © Crown copyright 1998

Standardized Unemployment Rates in Western Europe

Adjusted for comparability between countries except Austria, Cyprus, Denmark, Greece, Iceland, Luxembourg, Malta, Switzerland, and Turkey. (Percentage of labour force.)

Country	1992	1993	1994	1995	Country	1992	1993	1994	1995
Austria	3.6	4.2	3.7	3.6	Malta	4.0	4.5	4.1	3.4
Belgium	7.7	8.6	9.7	9.9	Netherlands	5.6	6.2	6.8	6.5
Cyprus	1.8	2.6	2.7	2.6	Norway	5.9	6.0	5.4	4.9
Denmark	11.2	12.3	12.1	10.0	Portugal	4.1	5.5	6.8	7.1
Finland	13.0	17.7	18.2	17.0	Spain	18.1	22.4	23.8	22.6
France	10.4	11.6	12.3	11.6	Sweden	5.8	9.5	9.8	9.2
Germany	6.6	7.9	8.4	8.2	Switzerland	2.5	4.5	4.7	4.2
Greece	8.7	9.7	9.6	9.8	Turkey	7.9	8.7	10.9	10.2
Iceland	3.1	4.4	4.8	5.2	UK	10.1	10.4	9.5	8.7
Ireland, Republic of	15.5	15.6	14.3	12.9					
Italy	10.5	10.3	11.4	11.8	Total	9.2	10.3	10.9	10.5
Luxembourg	2.1	2.7	3.5	3.9					

Source: OECD, Eurostat, UN/ECE secretariat estimates

Youth Unemployment Rates in the European Union

Data show unemployment of 15 to 24 year olds (except for the UK where figures are for 16 to 24 year olds) as a percentage of the economically active population. (– = not applicable.)

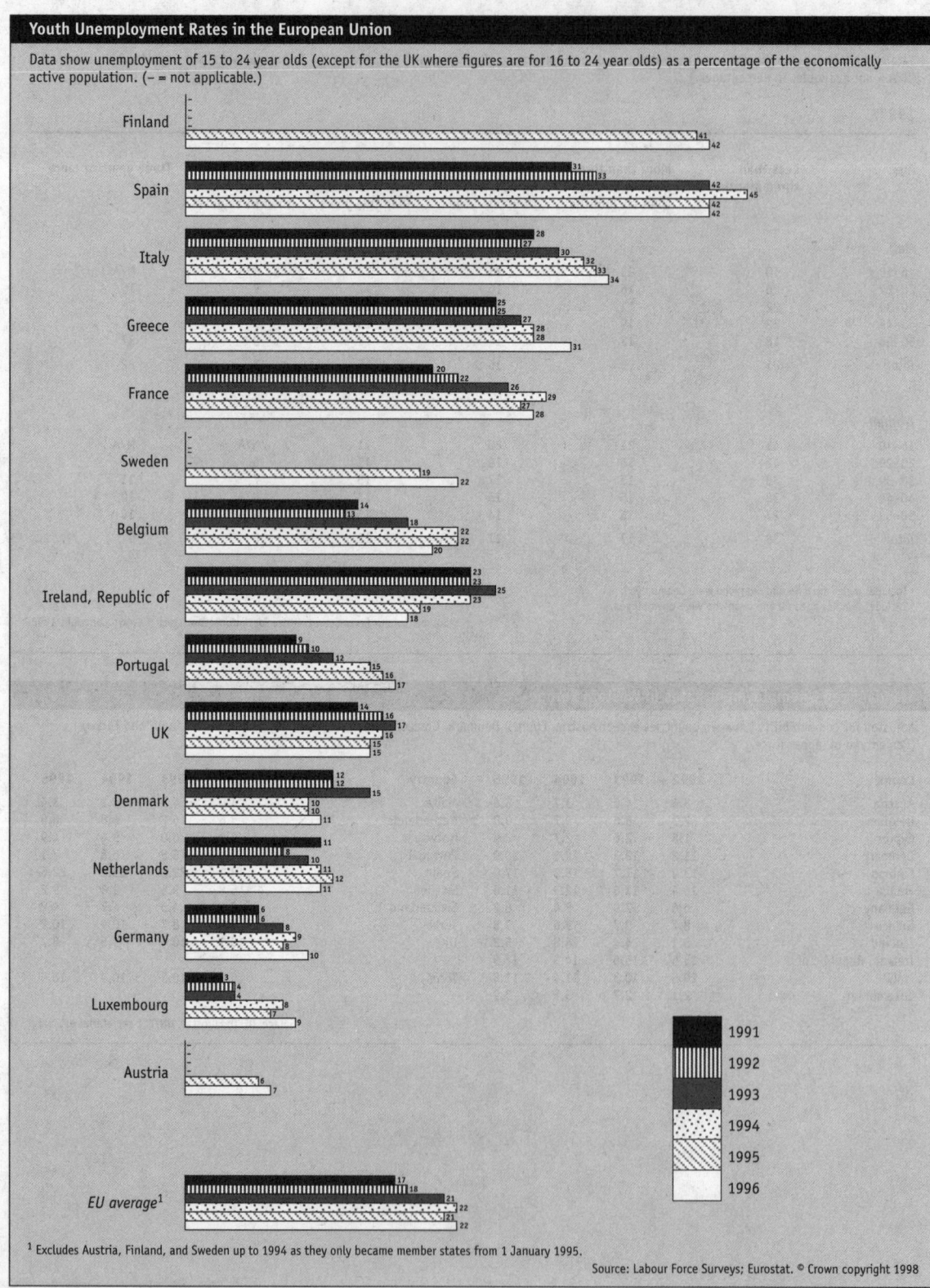

Finland — 41 — 42

Spain — 31 — 33 — 42 — 45 — 42 — 42

Italy — 28 — 27 — 30 — 32 — 33 — 34

Greece — 25 — 25 — 27 — 28 — 28 — 31

France — 20 — 22 — 26 — 29 — 27 — 28

Sweden — 19 — 22

Belgium — 14 — 13 — 18 — 22 — 22 — 20

Ireland, Republic of — 23 — 23 — 25 — 23 — 19 — 18

Portugal — 9 — 10 — 12 — 15 — 16 — 17

UK — 14 — 16 — 17 — 16 — 15 — 15

Denmark — 12 — 12 — 15 — 10 — 10 — 11

Netherlands — 11 — 8 — 10 — 11 — 12 — 11

Germany — 6 — 6 — 8 — 9 — 8 — 10

Luxembourg — 3 — 4 — 4 — 8 — 7 — 9

Austria — 6 — 7

Legend:
- 1991
- 1992
- 1993
- 1994
- 1995
- 1996

EU average[1] — 17 — 18 — 21 — 22 — 21 — 22

[1] Excludes Austria, Finland, and Sweden up to 1994 as they only became member states from 1 January 1995.

Source: Labour Force Surveys; Eurostat. © Crown copyright 1998

Redundancies by Occupation in the UK

It is assumed that people do not change occupation when starting employment after having been made redundant. (N = less than 10,000; estimate not shown.)

Date	Managers and administrators	Professional	Associate professional and technical	Clerical and secretarial	Craft and related	Personal and protective services	Sales	Plant and machine operatives	Other
Redundancies									
Summer 1996	33,000	11,000	12,000	28,000	37,000	17,000	23,000	30,000	16,000
Autumn 1996	26,000	11,000	11,000	28,000	30,000	15,000	19,000	22,000	20,000
Winter 1996	22,000	N	11,000	30,000	31,000	16,000	17,000	32,000	19,000
Spring 1997	26,000	N	12,000	32,000	43,000	14,000	15,000	36,000	19,000
Summer 1997	20,000	N	13,000	38,000	33,000	12,000	15,000	32,000	16,000
Redundancy Rates (Redundancies per 1,000 Employees)									
Summer 1996	10	5	6	8	17	7	12	14	9
Autumn 1996	8	5	6	8	14	6	10	10	11
Winter 1996	7	N	5	8	14	6	9	15	10
Spring 1997	8	N	6	9	19	5	7	17	10
Summer 1997	6	N	6	10	15	5	8	15	9

Source: *Labour Market Trends.* © Crown copyright

Redundancies by Region in the UK

(N = less than 10,000; estimate not shown.)

Date	Great Britain	Northern	Yorkshire and Humberside	East Midlands	East Anglia	South East excluding Greater London	South East	Greater London	South West	West Midlands	North West	Wales	Scotland
Redundancies													
Summer 1996	208,000	12,000	22,000	N	19,000	17,000	19,000	21,000	16,000	27,000	16,000	13,000	23,000
Autumn 1996	185,000	N	16,000	N	20,000	15,000	15,000	13,000	21,000	30,000	15,000	N	22,000
Winter 1996	186,000	N	23,000	N	13,000	18,000	19,000	21,000	15,000	27,000	12,000	N	23,000
Spring 1997	206,000	13,000	23,000	N	20,000	18,000	18,000	18,000	21,000	28,000	13,000	11,000	18,000
Summer 1997	187,000	N	21,000	N	16,000	15,000	22,000	20,000	20,000	23,000	13,000	N	19,000
Redundancy Rates (Redundancies per 1,000 Employees)													
Summer 1996	9	12	10	N	10	10	9	10	6	8	9	13	11
Autumn 1996	8	N	8	N	11	9	7	6	8	9	8	N	11
Winter 1996	8	N	11	N	7	10	9	10	6	8	6	N	11
Spring 1997	9	13	11	N	11	10	9	8	8	9	7	11	9
Summer 1997	8	N	10	N	8	9	10	9	7	7	7	N	9

Source: *Labour Market Trends.* © Crown copyright

Labour Disputes in the UK

These figures exclude details of stoppages involving fewer than ten workers or lasting less than one day except any in which the aggregate number of working days lost exceeded 100. There may be some under-recording of small or short stoppages. Some stoppages that affected more than one industry group have been counted under each of the industries but only once in the totals. The figures have been rounded and consequently the sum of the constituent items may not agree with the totals. Classifications by size are based on the full duration of stoppages where these continue into the following year. Working days lost per 1,000 employees are based on the latest available mid-year (June) estimates of employees in employment. (N = nil or negligible.)

Item	1986	1987	1988	1989	1990	1991	1992	1993	1994
Working Days Lost Through All Stoppages in Progress									
analysis by industry									
coal extraction	143,000	217,000	222,000	50,000	59,000	29,000	8,000	27,000	N
other energy and water	6,000	9,000	16,000	20,000	39,000	4,000	26,000	N	N
metals, minerals, and chemicals	192,000	60,000	70,000	42,000	42,000	27,000	14,000	6,000	8,000
engineering and vehicles	744,000	422,000	1,409,000	617,000	922,000	160,000	63,000	91,000	36,000
other manufacturing industries	135,000	115,000	151,000	91,000	106,000	35,000	16,000	13,000	15,000
construction	33,000	22,000	17,000	128,000	14,000	14,000	10,000	1,000	5,000
transport and communication	190,000	1,705,000	1,491,000	624,000	177,000	60,000	13,000	160,000	87,000
public administration, sanitary services, and education	449,000	939,000	254,000	2,237,000	175,000	362,000	328,000	339,000	92,000
medical and health services	11,000	6,000	36,000	151,000	345,000	1,000	1,000	2,000	1,000
all other industries and services	20,000	53,000	30,000	167,000	20,000	69,000	50,000	9,000	35,000
analysis by number of working days lost in each stoppage									
under 250 days	48,000	48,000	33,000	30,000	28,000	15,000	7,000	10,000	11,000
250–499 days	50,000	54,000	34,000	28,000	24,000	16,000	15,000	9,000	6,000
500–999 days	89,000	88,000	78,000	51,000	45,000	34,000	22,000	15,000	24,000
1,000–4,999 days	369,000	360,000	310,000	221,000	216,000	123,000	114,000	74,000	53,000
5,000–24,999 days	381,000	388,000	325,000	365,000	286,000	205,000	156,000	78,000	68,000
25,000–49,999 days	258,000	118,000	127,000	234,000	216,000	190,000	115,000	149,000	N
50,000 days and over	726,000	2,490,000	2,795,000	3,198,000	1,087,000	178,000	98,000	314,000	117,000
Total	1,920,000	3,546,000	3,702,000	4,128,000	1,903,000	761,000	528,000	649,000	278,000
Working days lost per 1,000 employees, all industries and services	90,000	164,000	166,000	182,000	83,000	34,000	24,000	30,000	13,000
Workers Directly and Indirectly Involved									
analysis by industry									
coal extraction	87,000	98,000	92,000	25,000	15,000	6,000	3,000	14,000	N
other energy and water	2,000	2,000	2,000	10,000	18,000	2,000	6,000	N	N
metals, minerals, and chemicals	17,000	9,000	10,000	7,000	5,000	2,000	2,000	2,000	2,000
engineering and vehicles	147,000	174,000	137,000	99,000	92,000	34,000	21,000	25,000	17,000
other manufacturing industries	30,000	19,000	29,000	12,000	11,000	15,000	3,000	3,000	4,000
construction	8,000	4,000	4,000	20,000	5,000	6,000	4,000	1,000	1,000
transport and communication	72,000	207,000	321,000	112,000	68,000	12,000	7,000	71,000	25,000
public administration, sanitary services, and education	348,000	361,000	161,000	414,000	70,000	87,000	92,000	261,000	39,000
medical and health services	4,000	4,000	31,000	9,000	10,000	N	2,000	N	1,000
all other industries and services	6,000	10,000	4,000	19,000	3,000	11,000	9,000	7,000	18,000
analysis by duration of stoppage									
not more than 5 days	369,000	308,000	381,000	194,000	185,000	133,000	111,000	364,000	75,000
6–10 days	47,000	66,000	280,000	97,000	24,000	2,000	8,000	5,000	5,000
11–20 days	24,000	153,000	19,000	388,000	27,000	11,000	4,000	13,000	1,000
21–30 days	58,000	25,000	22,000	8,000	21,000	3,000	1,000	N	6,000
31–50 days	17,000	23,000	57,000	12,000	22,000	1,000	12,000	N	N
51 days and over	206,000	313,000	32,000	29,000	19,000	26,000	11,000	3,000	20,000
Total	720,000	887,000	790,000	727,000	298,000	176,000	148,000	385,000	107,000

Source: Office for National Statistics; Labour Market Statistics. © Crown copyright 1998

The Largest Labour Unions in the UK

Rank	1990 Union	Membership	1995 Union	Membership	Male (%)	Female (%)
1	Transport and General Workers Union	1,224,000	UNISON – The Public Service Union	1,355,000	28	72
2	GMB	865,000	Transport and General Workers Union	897,000	81	19
3	National and Local Government Officers Association	744,000	GMB	740,000	64	36
4	Amalgamated Engineering Union	702,000	Amalgamated Engineering and Electrical Union	726,000	94	6
5	Manufacturing Science and Finance Union	653,000	Manufacturing Science and Finance Union	446,000	69	31
6	National Union of Public Employees	579,000	Royal College of Nursing of the UK	300,000	8	92
7	Electrical Electronic Telecommunication and Plumbing Union	367,000	Union of Shop Distributive and Allied Workers	283,000	42	58
8	Union of Shop Distributive and Allied Workers	362,000	Communication Workers Union	275,000	81	19
9	Royal College of Nursing of the UK	289,000	National Union of Teachers	248,000	25	75
10	National Union of Teachers	218,000	National Association of School Masters and Union of Women Teachers	234,000	47	53

Source: Labour Force Survey

Labour Union Membership in the UK by Job-Related Characteristic

(N = base too low to provide a reliable estimate. In percentages.)

1996

Characteristic	All (%)	Full time (%)	Part time (%)	Characteristic	All (%)	Full time (%)	Part time (%)
All employees[1]	31	35	20				
				Managerial Status			
Length of Service				Manager	27	27	25
Less than 1 year	12	14	8	Foreman or supervisor	40	41	35
1 to 2 years	17	20	11	No managerial duties	31	37	19
2 to 5 years	23	25	17				
5 to 10 years	37	38	30	**Employment Status**			
10 to 20 years	48	50	40	Permanent	33	36	21
20 years or more	58	61	40	Temporary	20	22	16
Occupational Group				**Special Working Arrangements**			
Managers and administrators	20	20	14	Flexitime	45	49	29
Professional	52	53	45	Job sharing	34	N	34
Associate professional/technical	47	45	53	Term-time working	46	76	24
Clerical and secretarial	27	30	19	Annualized hours contract	51	56	34
Craft and related	36	37	16	9-day fortnight/4.5-day week	49	49	N
Personal and protective	28	38	17	Work mainly in own home	4	10	2
Sales	11	13	10				
Plant and machine operatives	41	43	19				
Other occupations	26	38	16				

[1] Includes all employees, except for those in the armed forces.

Source: Labour Force Survey

Labour Union Membership in the UK by Type of Employee

(In percentages.)

1996

Employees	All	Male	Female	Employees	All	Male	Female
All employees[1]	31	33	29	**Highest Qualification**			
				Degree or equivalent	38	33	46
Age Group				Other higher education	47	36	57
Under 20 years	6	6	6	A-level or equivalent	32	36	24
20 to 29 years	23	23	24	GCSE or equivalent	24	27	22
30 to 39 years	34	35	33	Other	29	34	24
40 to 49 years	39	44	35	No qualifications	26	31	22
50 years and over	35	38	32				
				Marital Status			
Ethnic Origin				Single, never married	22	22	23
White		31	33	29	Married or cohabiting	34	37	32
Non-white	Black	36	33	39	Divorced or separated	32	35	30
	Indian	29	30	28	Widowed	29	34	27
	Pakistani/Bangladeshi	17	15	21				
	Other	26	27	25				
	Total	29	28	31				

[1] Includes all employees, except for those in the armed forces.

Source: Labour Force Survey

See Also | **UK Population and Demography (The United Kingdom)**

Trade Unions Directory of the UK

Source: Trades Unions Congress

The following member organizations are listed alphabetically by full union title. Unions' details are based on information given to the TUC (Trade Unions Congress) in late autumn 1997. Membership figures are those filed with the TUC for 1 January 1997. The TUC membership now stands at 74 unions, representing nearly 6.8 million people. (GS = General Secretary; m = male; f = female.)

Abbey National Staff Association (ANSA) ANSA House, 15b Mile End Road, Colchester, Essex CO4 5BT; phone: (01206) 577545; fax: (01206) 540085

Amalgamated Engineering and Electrical Union (AEEU) Hayes Court, West Common Road, Bromley, Kent BR2 7AU; phone: (0181) 462 7755; fax: (0181) 315 8234. Membership: m 678,139; f 46,958; total 725,097. GS: Ken Jackson

Associated Metalworkers Union (AMU) 92 Worsley Road North, Worsley, Manchester M28; phone: (01204) 793245; fax: (01204) 793245. Membership: total 805. GS: R Marron

Associated Society of Locomotive Engineers and Firemen (ASLEF) 9 Arkwright Road, London NW3 6AB; phone (0171) 317 8600; fax: (0171) 794 6406. Membership: m 15,100; f 300; total 15,400. GS: Lew Adams (from January 1999, Dave Rix)

Association of First Division Civil Servants (FDA) 2 Caxton Street, London SW1H 0QH; phone: (0171) 343 1111; fax: (0171) 343 1105. Membership: total 10,137. GS: Jonathan Baume

Association of Flight Attendants (AFA) AFA Council 07, United Airlines Cargo Centre, Shoreham Road East, Heathrow Airport, Hounslow, Middx TW6 3RD; phone: (0181) 750 9723; fax: (0181) 750 9706. Membership: total 776. LEC president: Kevin P Creighan

Association of Magisterial Officers (AMO) 231 Vauxhall Bridge Road, London SW1V 1EG; phone: (0171) 630 5455; fax: (0171) 630 1989. Membership: m 1,458; f 3,822; total 5,280. GS: Rosie Eagleson

Association of University Teachers (AUT) United House, 9 Pembridge Road, London W11 3JY; phone: (0171) 221 4370; fax: (0171) 727 6547. Membership: m 31,496; f 5,558; total 37,054. GS: David Triesman

Bakers, Food, and Allied Workers Union (BFAWU) Stanborough House, Great North Road, Stanborough, Welwyn Garden City, Herts AL8 7TA; phone: (01707) 260150; fax: (01707) 261570. Membership: m 12,560; f 15,564; total 28,124. GS: Joe Marino

Banking, Insurance, and Finance Union (BIFU) Sheffield House, 1b Amity Grove, London SW20 0LG; phone: (0181) 946 9151; fax: (0181) 879 7916. Membership: m 47,649; f 68,516; total 116,165. GS: Ed Sweeney

Barclays Bank Union for Financial Staff (UniFI) Oathall House, Oathall Road, Haywards Heath, West Sussex RH16 3DG; phone: (01444) 458811; fax: (01444) 416248. Membership: m 18,338; f 27,459; total 45,797. GS: Paul Snowball

British Actors Equity Association (EQUITY) Guild House, Upper St Martin's Lane, London WC2H 9EG; phone: (0171) 379 6000; fax: (0171) 379 7001. Membership: m 17,354; f 17,377; total 34,731. GS: Ian McGarry

British Air Line Pilots Association (BALPA) 81 New Road, Harlington, Hayes, Middlesex UB3 5BG; phone: (0181) 476 4000; fax: (0181) 476 4077. Membership: m 5,546; f 117; total 5,723. GS: Chris Darke

British Association of Colliery Management (BACM) 17 South Parade, Doncaster DN1 2DR; phone: (01302) 815551; fax: (01302) 815552. Membership: m 4,394; f 216; total 4,610. GS: Patrick Carragher

British Dietetic Association (BDA) 7th floor, Elizabeth House, 22 Suffolk Street Queensway, Birmingham B1 1LS; phone: (0121) 643 1431; fax: (0121) 633 4399. Membership: m 64; f 3,149; total 3,213. Industrial relations officer: David Wood

British Orthoptic Society (BOS) Tavistock House North, Tavistock Square, London WC1H 9HX; phone: (0171) 387 7992; fax: (0171) 383 2584. Membership: m 22; f 951; total 973. Executive secretary: Joanna Brown

Annual Days Off Work Due to Work-Related Illnesses in the UK

Data provide median projections for the whole population based on sample groups. (N/A = not available; sample group did not provide sufficient information.)

1995

Illness	Days lost	Average days lost per case	Illness	Days lost	Average days lost per case
Stress, depression, or anxiety	5,032,000	21.21	Pneumoconiosis	N/A	N/A
Stress-ascribed heart disease, hypertension, or stroke	875,000	16.63	Skin disease	661,000	13.71
			Back	3,745,000	10.34
Stress-ascribed diseases of the digestive system	354,000	7.84	Upper limbs, or neck (ULN)	3,756,000	14.56
Stress-ascribed other conditions	905,000	10.91	Lower limbs (LL)	896,000	14.31
Headache or eyestrain	69,000	1.61	Back and ULN	252,000	7.14
Deafness, tinnitus, or other ear conditions	6,000	0.12	Back and LL	657,000	33.22
Vibration white finger	111,000	5.46	ULN and LL	740,000	47.88
Asthma symptoms	265,000	9.81	Back and ULN and LL or whole body	682,000	78.24
Asthma and chronic bronchitis symptoms	55,000	2.84	Internal	352,000	12.47
Other lower respiratory disease or unspecified	143,000	4.34	Trauma	978,000	34.09
			Other illnesses	211,000	4.63
			Total	19,515,000	14.96

Source: Health and Safety Executive. © Crown copyright 1995

Broadcasting, Entertainment, Cinematograph, and Theatre Union (BECTU) 111 Wardour Street, London W1V 4AY; phone: (0171) 437 8506; fax: (0171) 437 8268. Membership: m 19,310; f 10,525; total 29,835. GS: Roger Bolton

Card Setting Machine Tenters Society (CSMT) 48 Scar End Lane, Staincliffe, Dewsbury, West Yorkshire WF12 4NY; phone: (01924) 400206; fax: (01924) 400206. Membership: m 88; f 0; total 88. GS: Anthony John Moorhouse

Ceramic and Allied Trades Union (CATU) Hillcrest House, Garth Street, Hanley, Stoke-on-Trent ST1 2AB; phone: (01782) 272755; fax: (01782) 284902. Membership: m 12,524; f 9,299; total 21,823. GS: Geoff Bagnall

Chartered Society of Physiotherapy (CSP) 14 Bedford Row, London WC1R 4ED; phone: (0171) 306 6666; fax: (0171) 306 6611. Membership: m 2,176; f 26,849; total 29,025. Joint directors of industrial relations: Jocelyn Prudence and Richard Griffin

Communication Managers Association (CMA) CMA House, Ruscombe Business Park, Twyford, Reading, Berks RG10 9JD; phone: (0118) 934 2300; fax: (0118) 934 2087. Membership: m 11,743; f 2,254; total 13,997. GS: Terry Deegan

Communication Workers Union (CWU) 150 The Broadway, Wimbledon, London SW19 1RX; phone: (0181) 971 7200; fax: (0181) 971 7300. Membership: m 220,043; f 54,777; total 274,820. Joint GSs: Derek Hodgson and Tony Young

Community and District Nursing Association (CDNA) Thames Valley University, 8 University House, Ealing Green, London W5 5ED; phone: (0181) 231 2776; fax: (0181) 231 2782. Membership: m 71; f 3,982; total 4,053. GS: Ann Keen

The Community and Youth Workers' Union (CYWU) Unit 302, The Argent Centre, 60 Frederick Street, Birmingham B1 3HS; phone: (0121) 244 3344; fax: (0121) 244 3345. Membership: m 1,190; f 1,340; total 2,530. GS: Doug Nicholls

Educational Institute of Scotland (EIS) 46 Moray Place, Edinburgh EH3 6BH; phone: (0131) 225 6244; fax: (0131) 220 3151. Membership: m 14,575; f 35,610; total 50,185. GS: Ronald A Smith

Engineering and Fastener Trade Union (EFTU) 42 Galton Road, Warley, West Midlands B67 5JU; phone: (0121) 429 2594. Membership: m 188; f 52; total 240. GS: James Burdis

Engineers and Managers Association (EMA) Flaxman House, Gogmore Lane, Chertsey, Surrey KT16 9JS; phone: (01932) 577007; fax: (01932) 567707. Membership: m 29,309; f 748; total 30,057. GS: Tony Cooper

Fire Brigades Union (FBU) Bradley House, 68 Coombe Road, Kingston-upon-Thames, Surrey KT2 7AE; phone: (0181) 541 1765; fax: (0181) 546 5187. Membership: m 53,732; f 1,609; total 55,341. GS: Ken Cameron

General Union of Loom Overlookers (GULO) 9 Wellington Street, St John's, Blackburn BB1 8AF; phone: (01254) 51760; fax: (01254) 51760. Membership: total 352. GS: Don Rishton

GMB 22/24 Worple Road, London SW19 4DD; phone: (0181) 947 3131; fax: (0181) 944 6552. Membership: m 459,227; f 258,912; total 718,139. GS: and Treasurer John Edmonds

Graphical, Paper, and Media Union (GPMU) Keys House, 63/67 Bromham Road, Bedford MK40 2AG; phone: (01234) 351521; fax: (01234) 270580. Membership: m 174,583; f 35,317; total 209,900. GS: Tony Dubbins

Guinness Brewing Staff Association (GBSA) Sun Works Cottage, Park Royal Brewery, London NW10 7RR; phone: (0181) 965 7700; fax: (0181) 963 5184. GS: Jim Collins

Hospital Consultants and Specialists Association (HCSA) 1 Kingsclere Road, Overton, Basingstoke, Hampshire RG25 3JA; phone: (01256) 771777; fax: (01256) 770999. Membership: m 2,023; f 253; total 2,276. GS: Stephen Charkham

Independent Union of Halifax Staff (IUHS) Simmons House, 46 Old Bath Road, Charvil, Reading, Berks RG10 9QR; phone: (0118) 934 1808; fax: (0118) 932 0208. Membership: m 6,489; f 18,635; total 25,124. GS: Ged Nichols

Institution of Professionals, Managers, and Specialists (IPMS) 75–79 York Road, London SE1 7AQ; phone: (0171) 902 6600; fax: (0171) 902 6667. Membership: m 64,454; f 13,364; total 77,818. GS: Bill Brett

Iron and Steel Trades Confederation (ISTC) Swinton House, 324 Gray's Inn Road, London WC1X 8DD; phone: (0171) 837 6691/2/3; fax: (0171) 278 8378. Membership: m 47,383; f 2,618; total 50,001. GS: Keith Brookman

Managerial and Professional Officers (MPO) Terminus House, The High, Harlow, Essex CM20 1TZ; phone: (01279) 434444; fax: (01279) 451176. Membership: m 9,064; f 1,833; total 10,897. GS: Graham Corless

Manufacturing, Science, and Finance (MSF) MSF Centre, 33–37 Moreland Street, London EC1V 8BB; phone: (0171) 505 3000; fax: (0171) 505 3030. Membership: m 291,876; f 133,227; total 425,103. GS: Roger Lyons

Occupational Injuries to Workers in the UK by Industry and Severity of Injury

(n.e.c. = not elsewhere reported.)

Industry	Fatal			Major[1]			Over three days[2]		
	1993/94	1994/95	1995/96	1993/94	1994/95	1995/96	1993/94	1994/95	1995/96
Agriculture, hunting, forestry, and fishing[3]	38	46	40	579	514	476	1,403	1,401	1,373
Energy and water supply industries[4]	17	5	18	671	492	525	4,954	3,951	3,187
Mining and quarrying[4]	16	4	16	435	299	341	1,968	1,453	1,404
of energy-producing materials	10	3	10	322	204	226	1,295	704	779
except energy-producing materials	6	1	6	113	95	115	673	749	625
Electricity, gas, and water supply	1	1	2	236	193	184	2,986	2,498	1,783
Manufacturing									
of food products, beverages, and tobacco	5	7	4	1,070	1,012	983	11,245	11,320	10,051
of textile and textile products	2	3	1	283	241	236	2,021	2,074	1,942
of leather and leather products	1	1	0	22	18	16	276	270	198
of wood and wood products	6	4	3	281	286	231	1,302	1,440	1,235
of pulp, paper and paper products; publishing and printing	6	3	5	370	352	348	3,081	3,112	2,829
of coke, refined petroleum products, and nuclear fuel	0	1	0	32	26	33	302	240	182
of chemicals, chemical products, and man-made fibres	6	1	3	366	338	386	2,707	2,682	2,309
of rubber and plastic products	4	2	1	304	338	386	2,909	3,253	3,140
of other non-metallic mineral products	6	5	5	312	309	268	2,492	2,727	2,470
of basic metals and fabricated metal products	11	12	10	898	1,001	963	6,302	6,432	6,268
of machinery and equipment n.e.c.	6	8	2	502	514	499	3,578	3,820	3,581
of electrical and optical equipment	5	2	3	263	286	244	2,361	2,360	2,174
of transport equipment	3	2	6	458	452	440	4,649	4,634	4,382
Manufacturing n.e.c.	1	3	0	209	268	248	1,102	1,448	1,540
Construction	91	83	79	2,574	2,627	2,477	11,073	11,174	9,695
Wholesale and retail trade, and repairs	21	20	23	1,765	2,008	1,918	13,995	15,054	15,554
Hotels and restaurants	1	2	1	489	533	490	2,628	2,709	2,482
Transport, storage, and communication[5]	29	27	22	1,389	1,428	1,295	16,856	17,723	16,525
Financial intermediation	0	0	0	103	94	81	608	672	591
Real estate, renting, and business activities	13	11	11	426	417	375	1,905	2,006	1,994
Public administration and defence	7	9	10	1,332	1,314	1,298	15,695	16,299	14,495
Education	5	1	2	1,241	1,210	1,089	5,066	5,156	4,702
Health and social work	4	1	0	1,047	1,191	1,130	12,774	13,753	12,996
Other community, social, and personal services activities	8	13	9	546	585	599	3,964	4,125	3,624
Unclassified	0	0	0	447	500	700	2,211	2,353	3,457
Total	296	272	258	17,979	18,354	17,734	137,449	142,218	132,976

[1] Major injuries include fractures to the skull, spine, or pelvis; loss of sight; amputation; injuries requiring immediate medical attention.
[2] Injuries causing incapacity for normal work for more than three days.
[3] Excludes sea fishing.
[4] Includes the number of injuries in the oil and gas industry collected under offshore installations safety legislation.
[5] Injuries arising from shore-based services only. Excludes incidents reported under merchant shipping legislation.

Source: Health and Safety Executive. © Crown copyright 1998

Musicians Union (MU) 60/62 Clapham Road, London SW9 0JJ; (0171) 582 5566; fax: (0171) 582 9805. Membership: m 23,266; f 6,697; total 29,963. GS: Dennis Scard

National Association of Colliery Overmen, Deputies, and Shotfirers (NACODS) Simpson House, 48 Nether Hall Road, Doncaster, South Yorkshire DN1 2PZ; phone: (01302) 368015; fax: (01302) 341945. Membership: m 783; f 0; total 783. GS: Peter McNestry

National Association of Cooperative Officials (NACO) Coronation House, Arndale Centre, Manchester M4 2HW; phone: (0161) 834 6029; fax: (0161) 832 0671. Membership: m 2,618; f 614; total 3,232. GS: Lindsay Ewing

National Association of Probation Officers (NAPO) 4 Chivalry Road, London SW11 1HT; phone: (0171) 223 4887; fax: (0171) 223 3503. Membership: m 2,861; f 3,918; total 6,779. GS: Judy McKnight

National Association of Schoolmasters, Union of Women Teachers (NASUWT) 5 King Street, London WC2E 8HN; phone: (0171) 379 9499; fax: (0171) 497 8262. Membership: m 66,889; f 98,612; total 165,501. GS: Nigel de Gruchy

National League of the Blind and Disabled (NLBD) 2 Tenterden Road, London N17 8BE; phone: (0181) 808 6030; fax: (0181) 885 3235. Membership: m 1,563; f 512; total 2,075. GS: Joe Mann

National Union of Domestic Appliances and General Operatives (NUDAGO) 7–8 Imperial Buildings (first floor), Corporation Street, Rotherham, South Yorkshire S60 1PB; phone: (01709) 382820; fax: (01709) 362826. Membership: m 1,609; f 641; total 2,250. GS: Tony McCarthy

National Union of Insurance Workers (NUIW) 27 Old Gloucester Street, London WC1N 3AF; phone: (0171) 405 6798; fax: (0171) 404 8150. Membership: m 8,363; f 2,019; total 10,382. GS: Ken Perry

National Union of Journalists (NUJ) Acorn House, 314–320 Gray's Inn Road, London WC1X 8DP; phone: (0171) 278 7916; fax: (0171) 837 8143. Membership: m 12,326; f 7,058; total 19,384. GS: John Foster

National Union of Knitwear, Footwear, and Apparel Trades (KFAT) 55 New Walk, Leicester LE1 7EB; phone: (0116) 255 6703; fax: (0116) 254 4406. Membership: m 16,953; f 23,577; total 40,530. GS: Paul Gates

National Union of Lock and Metal Workers (NULMW) Bellamy House, Wilkes Street, Willenhall, West Midlands WV13 2BS; phone: (01902) 366651; fax: (01902) 368035. Membership: m 2,337; f 2,310; total 4,647. GS: Ray Ward

National Union of Marine, Aviation, and Shipping Transport Officers (NUMAST) Oceanair House, 750/760 High Road, London E11 3BB; phone: (0181) 989 6677; fax: (0181) 530 1015. Membership: m 18,190; f 185; total 18,375. GS: Brian Orrell

National Union of Mineworkers (NUM) Miners' Offices, 2 Huddersfield Road, Barnsley, South Yorkshire S70 2LS; (01226) 215555; fax: (01226) 215561. Membership: m 9,565; f 0; total 9,565. President Arthur Scargill

National Union of Rail, Maritime, and Transport Workers (RMT) Unity House, 205 Euston Road, London NW1 2BL; phone: (0171) 387 4771; fax: (0171) 387 4123. Membership: m 55,801; f 4,341; total 60,142. GS: Jimmy Knapp

National Union of Teachers (NUT) Hamilton House, Mabledon Place, London WC1H 9BD; phone: (0171) 388 6191; fax: (0171) 387 8458. Membership: m 47,336 f 140,877; total 188,213. GS: Doug McAvoy

Northern Carpet Trades Union (NCTU) 22 Clare Road, Halifax HX1 2HX; phone: (01422) 360492; fax: (01422) 321146. Membership: m 518; f 110; total 628. GS: Keith Edmondson

Power Loom Carpet Weavers and Textile Workers Union (PLCWTWU) 148 Hurcott Road, Kidderminster, Worcestershire DY10 2RL; phone: (01562) 823192; fax: (01562) 861469. Membership: total 1,439. GS: Gordon Rudd

Prison Officers Association (POA) Cronin House, 245 Church Street, London N9 9HW; phone: (0181) 803 0255; fax: (0181) 803 1761. Membership: m 23,798; f 3,524; total 27,322. GS: David Evans

Professional Footballers Association (PFA) 2 Oxford Court, Bishopsgate, Manchester M2 3WQ; phone: (0161) 236 0575; fax: (0161) 228 7229. Membership: total 1,473 Chief executive: Gordon Taylor

Public and Commercial Services Union (PCS) 160 Falcon Road, London SW11 2LN; phone: (0171) 924 2727; fax: (0171) 924 1847. Membership: m 108,707; f 157,236; total 265,943. Joint GSs: Barry Reamsbottom and John Sheldon

Scottish Prison Officers' Association (SPOA) 21 Calder Road, Edinburgh EH11 3PF; phone: (0131) 443 8105; fax: (0131) 444 0657. Membership: m 2,866; f 352; total 3,218. GS: Derek Turner

Scottish Union of Power-Loom Overlookers (SUPLO) 3 Napier Terrace, Dundee, Tayside DD2 2SL; phone: (01382) 612196. Membership: m 42; f 0; total 42. GS: Jim Reilly

Sheffield Wool Shear Workers Union (SWSWU) 5 Collin Avenue, Sheffield S6 4ES. Membership: m 9; f 2; total 11. GS: B Bell

Society of Chiropodists and Podiatrists (SCP) 53 Welbeck Street, London W1M 7HE; phone: (0171) 486 3381; fax: (0171) 935 6359. Membership: m 1,814; f 4,343; total 6,157. GS: M Paulson

Society of Radiographers (SoR) 2 Carriage Row, 183 Eversholt Street, London NW1 1BU; phone: (0171) 391 4500; fax: (0171) 391 4533/4504. Membership: total 13,620. GS and Chief Executive: Stephen Evans

Society of Telecom Executives (STE) Arthur Willitt House, 1 Park Road, Teddington, Middlesex TW11 0AR; phone: (0181) 943 5181; fax: (0181) 943 2532. Membership: m 15,289; f 2,141; total 17,430. GS: Simon Petch

Transport and General Workers Union (TGWU) Transport House, Palace Street, Victoria, London SW1E 5JD; phone: (0171) 828 7788; fax (0171) 630 5861. Membership: m 717,369; f 173,550; total 890,919. GS: Bill Morris

Transport Salaried Staffs Association (TSSA) Walkden House, 10 Melton Street, London NW1 2EJ; phone: (0171) 387 2101; fax: (0171) 383 0656. Membership: m 23,042; f 8,574; total 31,616. GS: Richard Rosser

Undeb Cenedlaethol Athrawon Cymru (UCAC) Pen Roc, Rhodfa'r Mor, Aberystwyth SY23 2AZ; phone: (01970) 615577; fax: (01970) 626765. Membership: m 876; f 2,737; total 3,613. GS: G Wyn James

Union of Construction, Allied Trades, and Technicians (UCATT) UCATT House, 177 Abbeville Road, London SW4 9RL; phone: (0171) 622 2442; fax: (0171) 720 4081. Membership: m 110,895; f 1,006; total 111,901. GS: George Brumwell

Union of Shop, Distributive, and Allied Workers (USDAW) Oakley, 188 Wilmslow Road, Fallowfield, Manchester M14 6LJ; phone: (0161) 224 2804; fax: (0161) 257 2566. Membership: m 119,554; f 170,616; total 290,170. GS: Bill Connor

Union of Textile Workers (UTW) Foxlowe, Market Place, Leek, Staffordshire ST13 6AD; phone: (01538) 382068; fax: (01538) 382068. Membership: m 820; f 781; total 1,601. GS: Alf Hitchmough

UNISON 1 Mabledon Place, London WC1H 9AJ; phone: (0171) 388 2366; fax: (0171) 387 6692. Membership: m 384,883; f 989,700; total 1,374,583. GS: Rodney Bickerstaffe

The University and College Lecturers' Union (NATFHE) 27 Britannia Street, London WC1X 9JP; phone: (0171) 837 3636; fax: (0171) 837 4403. Membership: m 39,575; f 30,352; total 69,927. GS: Paul Mackney

The Writers' Guild of Great Britain (WGGB) (incorporating the Theatre Writers' Union) 430 Edgware Road, London W2 1EH; phone: (0171) 723 8074; fax: (0171) 706 2413. Membership: m 1,133; f 528; total 1,661. GS: Alison Gray

Political Funds of Trade Unions in the UK

1995

Trade union	Number of members contributing to the political fund[1]	Number of members exempt from contributing to the political fund[1]	Income	Expenditure	Fund at beginning of year	Fund at end of year
				Political fund (£)		
Amalgamated Engineering and Electrical Union	480,637	58,729	1,551,000	1,321,000	829,000	1,059,000
Associated Society of Locomotive Engineers and Firemen	15,265	476	58,376	64,587	82,067	75,856
Association of Her Majesty's Inspectors of Taxes	2,262	106	7,050	0	37,757	44,807
Association of University Teachers	28,918	413	24,695	12,013	44,789	57,471
Bakers, Food, and Allied Workers Union	27,390	7	56,643	53,589	−4,223	−1,169
Broadcasting, Entertainment, Cinematograph, and Theatre Union	27,657	99	49,686	71,064	49,534	28,156
Ceramic and Allied Trades Union	22,016	190	90,920	71,114	160,636	180,442
Civil and Public Services Association	0	0	0	0	−4,368	−4,368
Communication Managers Association	12,620	883	15,588	21,814	25,604	19,378
Communication Workers Union	221,550	31,954	933,698	1,058,076	521,740	457,362
Educational Institute of Scotland	46,407	2,086	75,027	6,018	327,718	396,727
Fire Brigades Union	40,434	13,973	140,560	138,730	220,194	222,024
General Union of Associations of Loom Overlookers	267	183	1,108	247	267	1,128
GMB	683,032	57,287	2,649,000	2,561,000	385,000	473,000
Graphical, Paper, and Media Union	86,044	130,947	312,080	295,863	635,382	651,599
Inland Revenue Staff Federation	46,560	2,061	115,889	280,011	164,122	0
Institution of Professionals, Managers, and Specialists	67,742	1,699	40,645	19,214	60,506	81,937
Iron and Steel Trades Confederation	27,203	6,352	142,109	130,301	66,612	78,420
Manufacturing, Science, and Finance Union	177,674	268,326	567,000	445,000	93,000	215,000
Musicians Union	30,051	981	30,525	29,003	3,427	4,949
National Association of Colliery Overmen, Deputies, and Shotfirers	745	2	4,874	7,166	43,430	41,138
National Association of Schoolmasters and Union of Women Teachers	132,503	101,343	65,815	53,474	111,500	123,841
National Association of Teachers in Further and Higher Education	59,908	2,700	79,294	192,583	194,681	81,392
National League of the Blind and Disabled	908	1,096	2,666	3,063	8,905	8,508
National Union of Civil and Public Servants	101,704	1,117	172,169	187,930	648,765	633,004
National Union of Domestic Appliances and General Operatives	590	8	1,224	1,168	1,299	1,355
National Union of Insurance Workers	8,260	2,207	13,267	7,529	78,497	84,235
National Union of Knitwear, Footwear, and Apparel Trades	43,067	736	114,074	128,656	75,625	61,043
National Union of Lock and Metal Workers	0	0	32	13,571	13,539	0
National Union of Mineworkers	6,955	598	80,955	95,489	224,973	210,439
National Union of Rail, Maritime, and Transport Workers	58,380	870	222,000	203,000	74,000	93,000
Power Loom Carpet Weavers and Textile Workers Union	1,703	2	1,788	1,049	7,053	7,792
Retained Firefighters Union	0	0	0	0	5	5
Rossendale Union of Boot, Shoe, and Slipper Operatives	0	15	10	63	1,390	1,337
Scottish Carpet Workers Union	732	0	608	208	2,515	2,915
Society of Telecom Executives	10,376	8,175	43,227	11,765	143,043	174,505
Transport and General Workers Union	842,366	10,754	2,537,000	2,194,000	3,578,000	3,921,000
Transport Salaried Staffs Association	31,622	3,792	95,385	81,292	92,354	106,447
Union of Construction, Allied Trades, and Technicians	80,577	27,295	209,000	207,000	6,000	8,000
Union of Democratic Mineworkers	3,054	0	2,088	1,412	8,986	9,662
Union of Shop Distributive and Allied Workers	260,159	23,096	874,229	710,463	838,450	1,002,216
Union of Textile Workers	1,503	26	2,913	4,375	1,811	349
Unison – The Public Service Union	1,248,786	106,527	4,298,000	5,558,000	5,383,000	4,123,000
Total for the 43 unions with political funds for 1995	4,937,627	867,111	15,742,217	16,241,900	15,236,585	14,736,902
Total for the 47 unions with political funds for 1994[2]	5,079,654	983,715	18,121,218	18,401,195	15,486,916	15,206,939

[1] These columns do not necessarily add up to a union's total membership. This is because, in the case of some trade unions, total membership includes various classes of special category members (for example, honorary, retired, unemployed) who are members under the union's rules but who are neither required to pay the political levy nor to seek formal exemption.

[2] The figures for 1994 are distorted due to the inclusion of figures for UNISON covering an 18 month period.

Source: Certification Officer for Trade Unions and Employers' Association, © Crown copyright

UK Public Spending

Benefit Expenditure by Recipient Group in the UK

(In millions of pounds.)

Group	1982–83	1987–88	1992–93	1993–94	1994–95	1995–96	1996–97
Total benefit expenditure	31,628	46,697	75,337	82,421	84,854	88,666	92,846
Contributory	18,210	25,311	37,320	39,539	39,825	40,702	42,337
Non-contributory	13,418	21,386	38,016	42,882	45,029	47,964	50,509
Total benefit paid to:							
Elderly	16,105	22,873	34,154	36,568	37,365	38,751	40,799
Sick and disabled							
short-term sick	615	1,171	1,323	1,295	714	954	1,108
long-term sick and disabled	3,527	6,642	14,802	17,809	19,662	21,074	22,392
Total	4,142	7,813	16,125	19,104	20,375	22,028	23,500
Family lone parents	1,394	2,972	7,112	8,127	8,886	9,609	10,029
Total	5,598	8,108	13,893	15,149	16,089	17,198	18,051
Unemployed	4,767	6,594	9,357	9,768	9,153	8,643	8,271
Widows and others	1,016	1,313	1,808	1,832	1,872	2,046	2,225

Source: *Social Security Statistics,* 1997. © Crown copyright 1997

Child Benefit in the UK

Data are for 31 December of each year.)

Type of family	1982	1987	1992	1993	1994	1995	1996
Families with							
1 child	2,912,000	2,870,000	2,906,000	2,920,000	2,941,000	2,970,000	2,983,000
2 children	2,942,000	2,744,000	2,752,000	2,772,000	2,781,000	2,783,000	2,794,000
3 children	907,000	832,000	894,000	908,000	920,000	928,000	929,000
4 children	216,000	200,000	226,000	231,000	228,000	231,000	236,000
5 children	49,000	46,000	55,000	57,000	60,000	60,000	59,000
6 or more children	19,000	21,000	24,000	24,000	24,000	24,000	23,000
Total	7,045,000	6,712,000	6,857,000	6,913,000	6,955,000	6,996,000	7,024,000
Total children attracting benefit	12,750,000	12,015,000	12,425,000	12,555,000	12,632,000	12,698,000	12,745,000

Source: *Social Security Statistics,* 1997. © Crown copyright 1997

Family Credit in the UK

Average amount of payments on awards at 30 November of each year. (In pounds per week.)

Year	All families	Couples			Lone parent		
		Main earner is		All couples	Main earner is		All lone parents
		Male	Female		Male	Female	
1991	34.89	34.09	36.01	34.41	36.18	35.59	35.61
1992	42.10	38.15	45.35	40.35	39.44	44.72	44.53
1993	46.03	41.97	49.02	44.15	41.37	48.70	48.45
1994	49.73	45.58	54.37	47.95	44.21	52.34	52.04
1995	54.80	52.79	58.07	54.17	51.08	55.76	55.58
1996	56.92	54.94	59.90	56.15	53.76	58.02	57.85

Source: *Social Security Statistics,* 1997. © Crown copyright 1997

Government Expenditure on Social Security Benefits in the UK

(– = not applicable. Years ending 31 March. In millions of pounds.)

Government current expenditure	1986–87	1987–88	1988–89	1989–90	1990–91	1991–92	1992–93	1993–94	1994–95	1995–96	1996–97
National insurance fund											
retirement pensions	18,006	18,884	18,679	20,757	22,725	25,691	27,076	28,481	28,925	37,769	39,990
lump sums to pensioners	107	107	109	112	114	114	115	122	123	124	119
widows' and guardians' allowances	827	840	881	896	893	884	1,014	1,041	1,034	1,018	1,070
unemployment benefit	1,734	1,468	1,318	752	892	1,627	1,761	1,623	1,277	1,099	590
jobseeker's allowance[1]	–	–	–	–	–	–	–	–	–	–	314
sickness benefit	179	193	217	209	222	278	365	294	426	12	–
invalidity benefit	2,673	2,968	3,820	3,935	4,544	5,461	6,198	7,146	8,042	271	–
incapacity benefit[2]	–	–	–	–	–	–	–	–	–	7,615	7,605
maternity benefit	168	51	45	32	35	40	42	32	17	28	31
death grant	18	3	–	–	–	–	–	–	–	–	–
disablement benefit	440	453	504	475	526	–	–	–	–	–	–
industrial death benefit	61	56	70	61	62	–	–	–	–	–	–
statutory sick pay	779	852	892	996	966	725	688	688	24	24	28
statutory maternity pay	–	199	263	292	344	396	416	440	498	480	492
payments in lieu of benefits foregone	–	2	–	–	–	–	–	–	–	–	–
Total	24,992	26,076	26,798	28,474	31,323	35,216	37,675	39,867	40,366	40,825	42,320
Maternity fund	71	31	–	–	–	–	–	–	–	–	–
Redundancy fund	256	92	80	71	130	276	321	110	208	128	156
Social fund	–	33	76	101	123	130	175	189	183	216	204
Non-contributory benefits											
war pensions	562	562	572	641	688	844	976	913	1,083	1,247	1,343
family benefits											
child benefit	4,696	4,796	4,720	4,751	4,840	5,433	5,950	6,347	6,294	6,332	6,603
one parent benefit	148	163	180	200	227	249	275	282	289	310	348
family credit	–	–	397	424	466	626	929	1,208	1,441	1,739	2,047
family income supplement	175	180	–	–	–	–	–	–	–	–	–
maternity grants	14	–	–	–	–	–	–	–	–	–	–
income support/supplementary benefits											
supplementary pensions	1,178	1,321	–	–	–	–	–	–	–	–	–
supplementary allowances	7,151	6,983	–	–	–	–	–	–	–	–	–
income support	–	–	7,810	8,257	9,106	12,325	15,578	16,997	16,387	16,650	14,584
other											
old persons' pensions	37	37	37	35	38	36	36	36	35	36	36
lump sums to pensioners	8	9	7	9	8	11	13	14	13	15	17
attendance allowance	812	911	1,315	1,262	1,698	1,706	1553	1795	1963	2194	2421
invalid care allowance	104	184	152	184	229	285	345	442	526	617	768
mobility allowance	514	596	675	770	895	1,063	68	–	–	–	–
disability living allowance	–	–	–	–	–	–	1973	2772	3125	3802	4361
disability working allowance	–	–	–	–	–	–	3	7	11	19	25
severe disablement allowance	285	295	320	347	407	596	640	703	776	820	893
industrial injury benefits	–	–	–	–	142	655	668	687	706	731	716
retail price index adjustment	–	94	–	–	–	–	–	–	–	–	–
housing benefit	3,398	3,511	3,711	4,095	4,735	6,053	7,670	9,163	10,345	10,868	10,764
Administration	1,860	2,117	2,527	2,813	3,206	3,617	3,998	4,273	4,190	4,076	3,998
Total government expenditure	46,261	47,991	49,377	52,434	58,261	69,121	78,846	85,805	87,941	90,625	91,604
Total government expenditure as % of GDP[3]	11.99	11.24	10.39	10.14	10.47	11.89	12.99	13.40	12.96	12.70	12.18

[1] Jobseeker's allowance was introduced in October 1996 to replace unemployment benefit and income support for the unemployed.
[2] Sickness benefit and invalidity benefit were replaced by a single incapacity benefit in 1995.
[3] GDP is adjusted to take account of change from rates to community charge.

Source: Office for National Statistics. © Crown copyright 1998

Number of Recipients of Social Security Benefits in the UK

Number of recipients relates to number of awards in the year. (– = not applicable. N = nil or negligible.)

Benefit	1982	1987	1992	1993	1994	1995	1996
Income-Related Benefits							
Family Credit[1][2]	–	–	356,000	485,000	536,000	602,000	676,000
Income Support[3]	–	–	5,088,000	5,643,000	5,675,000	5,670,000	5,549,000
Rent Rebate (local authority tenants)	3,580,000[4]	3,665,000[4]	3,032,000	3,035,000	3,009,000	2,922,000	2,849,000
Rent Allowance (private tenants)	851,000[4]	1,195,000[4]	1,358,000	1,496,000	1,702,000	1,838,000	1,860,000
Rate Rebate	6,950,000[4]	6,875,000[4]					
Community Charge Benefit	–	–	6,723,000	6,872,000[5]	–	–	–
Council Tax Benefit	–	–	–	5,406,000	5,641,000	5,696,000	5,587,000
Retirement Pension	9,234,000	9,772,000	10,125,000	10,131,000	10,167,000	10,289,000	10,451,000
Unemployment Benefit[6]	975,000	675,000	654,000	584,000	458,000	387,000	397,000
Sickness and Invalidity Benefits							
Sickness Benefit	393,000	110,000	138,000	147,000	127,000	127,000	–
Invalidity Benefit	683,000	968,000	1,439,000	1,580,000	1,681,000	1,767,000	–
Incapacity Benefit	–	–	–	–	–	–	1,813,000
Severe Disablement Allowance[7]	143,000	260,000	302,000	316,000	329,000	348,000	344,000
Disability Benefits							
Attendance Allowance	364,000	641,000	1,059,000	890,000	962,000	1,046,000	1,108,000
Mobility Allowance	253,000	512,000	699,000	–	–	–	–
Disability Living Allowance	–	–	–	1,145,000	1,038,000	1,491,000	1,688,000
Disability Working Allowance[2]	–	–	–	2,000	4,000	6,000	9,000
Invalid Care Allowance	8,000	91,000	189,000	230,000	274,000	316,000	357,000
War Pensions	327,000	266,000	260,000	293,000	309,000	315,000	327,000
Industrial Injuries Disablement Benefit	189,000	186,000	204,000	212,000	226,000	235,000	245,000[8]
Reduced Earnings Allowance	144,000	147,000	160,000	156,000	154,000	152,000	151,000[8]
Industrial Death Benefit	30,000	30,000	24,000	22,000	21,000	21,000	19,000
Workmen's Compensation	4,000	2,000	1,000	1,000	1,000	1,000	1,000
Pneumoconiosis, byssinosis, and miscellaneous diseases	1,000	1,000	1,000	N	N	N	N
Family Benefits							
Child Benefit	7,014,000	6,762,000	6,857,000	6,913,000	6,995,000	6,996,000	7,024,000
One Parent Benefit	513,000	681,000	855,000	898,000	941,000	994,000	1,027,000
Widow's Benefit	412,000	367,000	340,000	334,000	324,000	314,000	301,000
Child's Special Allowance	900	600	100	100	100	100	N
Guardian's Allowance	3,000	2,000	2,000	2,000	2,000	2,000	2,000
Maternity Allowance	115,000	109,000	11,000	11,000	11,000	12,000	13,000

[1] Family Income Supplement before April 1998.
[2] Family Credit and Disability Working Allowance figures are for March of each year.
[3] Supplementary Benefit before April 1998. Figures for Income Support are for May of each year.
[4] Figures apply to the financial years 1982–83 and 1987–88 and include Supplementary Benefit recipients receiving housing assistance. Figures are estimated.
[5] Community Charge and Community Charge Benefit ran until 31 March 1993. The recipients figure here is as at 26 February 1993.
[6] Source: Quarterly analysis of registered Unemployed Claimants as at November. (Figures for 1994 and before are based on a 100 percent count, figures for 1995 and 1996 are based on a 5 percent sample.)
[7] Non-Contributory Invalidity Pension and Housewives Non-Contributory Invalidity Pension before 29 November 1984.
[8] Includes an allowance for late returns.

Source: *Social Security Statistics*, 1997. © Crown copyright 1997

Income Support: Average Weekly Amounts of Benefit in the UK

(As of May 1997. Pounds per week.)

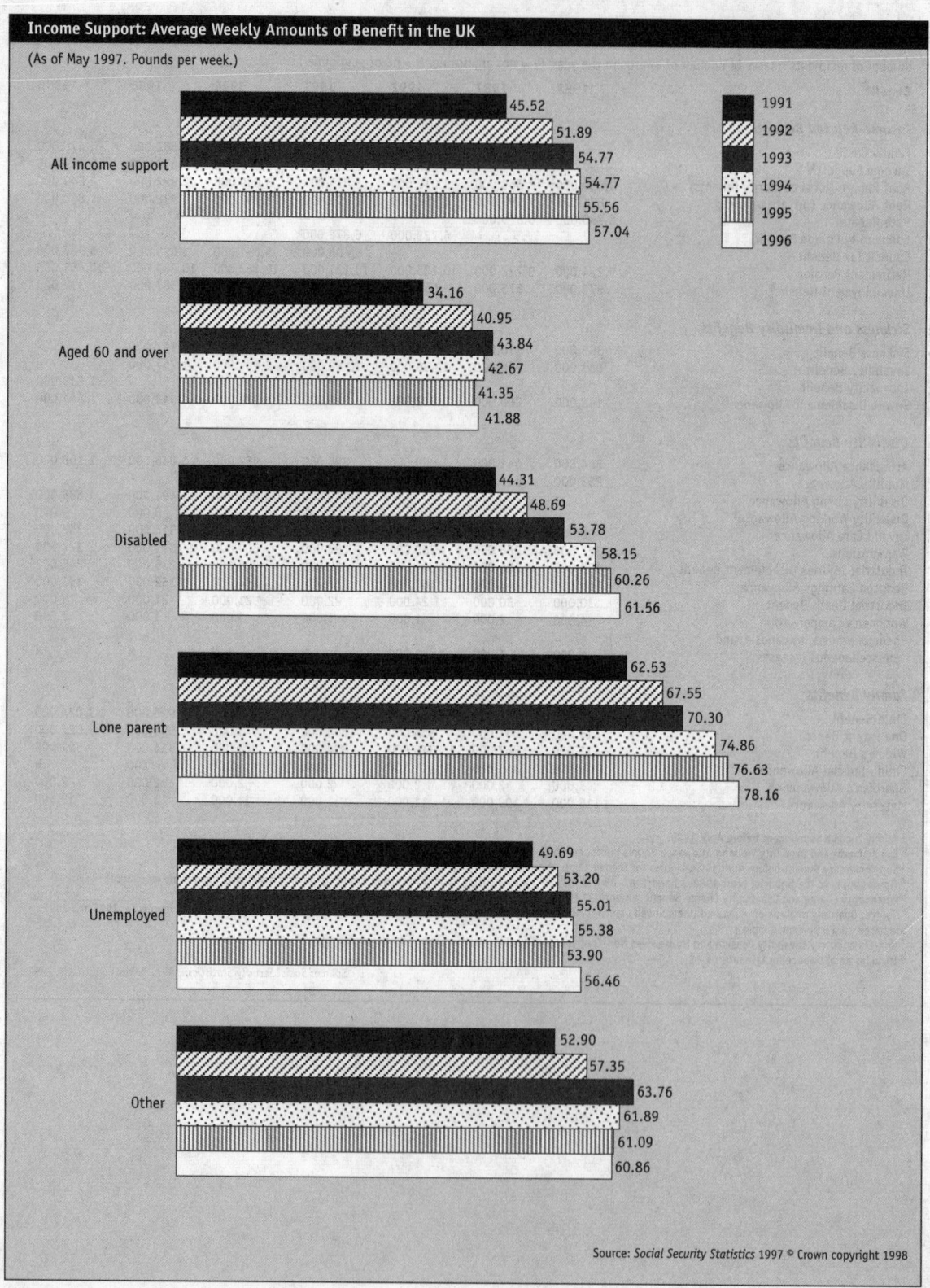

All income support
- 45.52 (1991)
- 51.89 (1992)
- 54.77 (1993)
- 54.77 (1994)
- 55.56 (1995)
- 57.04 (1996)

Aged 60 and over
- 34.16
- 40.95
- 43.84
- 42.67
- 41.35
- 41.88

Disabled
- 44.31
- 48.69
- 53.78
- 58.15
- 60.26
- 61.56

Lone parent
- 62.53
- 67.55
- 70.30
- 74.86
- 76.63
- 78.16

Unemployed
- 49.69
- 53.20
- 55.01
- 55.38
- 53.90
- 56.46

Other
- 52.90
- 57.35
- 63.76
- 61.89
- 61.09
- 60.86

Legend:
- 1991
- 1992
- 1993
- 1994
- 1995
- 1996

Source: *Social Security Statistics* 1997 © Crown copyright 1998

Government Spending on Education in the UK

(N/A = not available. Years ending 31 March. In millions of pounds. Due to rounding constituent figures may not sum to totals.)

Expenditure	1984–85	1985–86	1986–87	1987–88	1988–89	1989–90	1990–91	1991–92	1992–93[1]	1993–94[2]	1994–95[2][3]
Current Expenditure											
Nursery schools	70	74	81	4,743	5,259	5,889	6,458	7,247	8,262	8,712	9,094
Primary schools	3,483	3,702	4,157								
Secondary schools	4,850	5,061	5,583	5,991	6,437	6,832	7,147	7787	8,347	8,615	8,875
Special schools	620	667	727	812	888	1,008	1,121	1,245	1,354	1,420	1,451
Universities[4]	1,562	1,605	1,654	1,824	1,958	2,104	2,265	2,437	3,361	N/A	N/A
Other higher, further, and adult education[5]	2,348	2,475	2,716	2,971	3,277	3,729	4,128	4,454	4,136	N/A	N/A
Higher Education Funding Council[5][6]	N/A	N/A	N/A	N/A	N/A	N/A	N/A	N/A	N/A	4,908	5,192
Further Education Funding Council[7]	N/A	N/A	N/A	N/A	N/A	N/A	N/A	N/A	N/A	3,072	3,200
Continuing education	N/A	N/A	N/A	N/A	N/A	N/A	N/A	N/A	N/A	380	294
Other education expenditure	697	736	871	900	1,009	1,191	1,325	1,361	1,009	905	963
Related Current Expenditure											
Training of teachers: residence[8]	18	19	19	N/A	N/A	N/A	N/A	N/A	N/A	N/A	N/A
School welfare[9]	33	37	40	57	70	91	155	214	270	346	359
Meals and milk	527	532	559	547	469	485	506	556	161	149	147
Youth service and physical training	227	239	211	246	277	328	348	360	393	392	401
Maintenance grants and allowances to pupils and students[10][11]	850	838	806	843	900	934	1,028	1,379	1,705	1,972	2,204
Transport of pupils	268	279	290	302	311	335	393	442	417	444	486
Miscellaneous expenditure	5	5	5	6	10	17	2	3	8	10	31
Total current expenditure[12]	15,558	16,267	17,719	19,240	20,865	22,943	24,876	27,485	29,424	31,325	32,697
Capital Expenditure											
Nursery schools	7	8	7	192	246	314	353	376	384	414	517
Primary schools	154	164	180								
Secondary schools	217	233	187	213	195	397	465	493	518	485	565
Special schools	12	17	23	11	33	38	36	35	32	31	37
Universities[4]	121	140	156	158	172	196	211	231	236	N/A	N/A
Other higher, further, and adult education[5]	147	151	152	177	180	248	230	293	285	N/A	N/A
Higher Education Funding Council[5][6]	N/A	N/A	N/A	N/A	N/A	N/A	N/A	N/A	N/A	406	412
Further Education Funding Council[7]	N/A	N/A	N/A	N/A	N/A	N/A	N/A	N/A	N/A	194	201
Continuing education	N/A	N/A	N/A	N/A	N/A	N/A	N/A	N/A	N/A	6	8
Other education expenditure	12	11	10	32	22	41	39	33	25	12	45
Related capital expenditure	23	23	24	21	25	32	26	20	17	23	25
Total capital expenditure	693	737	739	804	873	1,266	1,359	1,481	1,496	1,571	1,810
VAT refunds to local authorities	266	284	345	357	399	455	493	584	656	579	639

(continued)

Government Spending on Education in the UK (*continued*)

Expenditure	1984–85	1985–86	1986–87	1987–88	1988–89	1989–90	1990–91	1991–92	1992–93[1]	1993–94[2]	1994–95[2][3]
Total Expenditure											
Central government	2,283	2,378	2,567	2,746	3,025	4,337	4,582	4,288	4,722	8,186	9,490
Local authorities	14,233	14,911	16,235	17,655	19,112	20,325	22,146	25,261	26,853	25,285	25,653
Total government expenditures[12]	16,517	17,288	18,803	20,401	22,137	24,664	26,728	29,550	31,576	33,475	35,146
Total government expenditures as % of GDP[13]	5.06	4.82	4.87	4.78	4.66	4.77	4.80	5.08	5.20	5.23	5.18

[1] Includes 1991–92 data for Wales.
[2] Data are provisional.
[3] Includes 1993–94 data for Wales.
[4] Includes expenditure on University Departments of Education for England and Wales.
[5] Including tuition fees.
[6] Includes expenditure on higher education institutions in Northern Ireland.
[7] Includes expenditure on further education institutions in Northern Ireland.
[8] With effect from 1987–88 included with maintenance grants and allowances.
[9] Expenditure on the school health service is included in the National Health Service.
[10] From 1992–93 expenditures on meals and milk have been recharged across other expenditure settings.
[11] From 1990–91, includes student loans expenditure.
[12] Excludes additional adjustment to allow for capital consumption made for National Accounts purposes amounting to £928 million in 1994–95.
[13] GDP includes adjustments to remove the distortion caused by the abolition of domestic rates which have led to revisions to the historical series.

Source: Department for Education and Employment; Office for National Statistics. © Crown copyright 1998

See Also | **UK Schools and Teachers (Education)**

Expenditure on Prisons in Great Britain

(N/A = not available. In pounds.)

Operating cost and total capital employed		1993–94[1]	1994–95	1995–96	1996–97
England and Wales					
Expenditure	staff costs	833,900,000	866,600,000	895,700,000	948,700,000
	accommodation costs	163,800,000	127,100,000	122,400,000	113,900,000
	other operating costs	295,500,000	323,400,000	369,000,000	373,900,000
	depreciation	4,100,000	90,300,000	159,300,000	123,600,000
	cost of capital	N/A	201,800,000	211,500,000	225,500,000
	Total expenditure	1,297,300,000	1,609,200,000	1,757,900,000	1,785,600,000
Income	contributions from industries	–4,700,000	–4,600,000	–6,400,000	–6,600,000
	other operating income	–4,300,000	–3,300,000	–4,900,000	–5,300,000
	Total income	–9,000,000	–7,900,000	–11,300,000	–11,900,000
Net operating costs		1,288,300,000	1,601,300,000	1,746,600,000	1,773,700,000
Total capital employed		N/A	3,452,000,000	3,580,700,000	3,920,900,000
Scotland					
Expenditure	manpower and associated services	135,301,000	140,009,000	135,941,000	143,107,000
	prisoner and associated costs	10,795,000	11,679,000	12,373,000	13,377,000
	capital expenditure	11,845,000	15,636,000	15,377,000	22,577,000
	Total gross expenditure	157,941,000	167,324,000	163,691,000	179,061,000
Less receipts		–3,598,000	–3,042,000	–2,800,000	–2,600,000
Net operating costs		154,343,000	164,282,000	160,891,000	176,461,000

[1] 1993–94 figures are not directly comparable with subsequent years. No figure is available for cost of capital or capital employed, as no balance sheet was produced.

Source: Home Office; The Scottish Office Home Department. © Crown copyright 1998

See Also | **England and Wales, Scotland (Law Enforcement and Crime)**

Government Spending on the National Health Service in the UK

(– = not applicable. Years ending 31 March. In millions of pounds.)

Expenditure	1986–87	1987–88	1988–89	1989–90	1990–91	1991–92	1992–93	1993–94	1994–95	1995–96	1996–97
Current Expenditure											
Central government hospitals, Community Health Services[1], and Family Health Services[2]	17,086	18,870	21,110	22,197	25,276	29,061	32,195	35,567	37,698	38,514	39,425
administration[3]	553	627	682	855	979	1,119	1,258	–	–	–	–
less payments by patients											
hospital services	–99	–106	–347	–407	–510	–540	–505	–368	–111	–42	–42
pharmaceutical services	–204	–256	–202	–242	–247	–270	–297	–324	–342	–383	–376
dental services	–261	–290	–282	–340	–441	–477	–470	–440	–464	–494	–447
ophthalmic services	–1	–1	–	–	–	–	–	–	–	–	–
Total	–565	–653	–831	–989	–1,198	–1,287	–1,272	–1,132	–917	–919	–865
Departmental administration	171	193	206	202	268	293	319	270	256	242	265
Other central services	577	632	604	693	738	865	1,301	1,651	2,304	2,538	3,124
Total current expenditure	17,822	19,669	21,771	22,958	26,063	30,051	33,801	36,356	39,341	40,375	41,949
Capital Expenditure											
Central government	1,160	1,212	1,309	2,071	1,848	1,791	1,612	903	538	316	434
Total Expenditure											
Central government	18,982	20,881	23,080	25,029	27,911	31,842	35,413	37,259	39,879	40,691	42,383
Total government expenditure as % of GDP[4]	4.92	4.89	4.85	4.84	5.01	5.48	5.84	5.82	5.88	5.70	5.63

[1] Includes the school health service.
[2] General medical services have been included in the expenditure of the Health Authorities. Therefore, hospitals and Community Health Services and Family Practitioner Services (now Family Health Services) are not identifiable separately.
[3] Administration costs are not separately identifiable from 1993–94.
[4] GDP is adjusted to take account of change from rates to community charge.

Source: Office for National Statistics. © Crown copyright 1998

Government Expenditure on Welfare Services in the UK

(N = nil or negligible. Years ending 31 March. Does not include school meals and milk. In millions of pounds.)

Item	1986–87	1987–88	1988–89	1989–90	1990–91	1991–92	1992–93	1993–94	1994–95	1995–96	1996–97
Personal social services											
central government current expenditure	124	126	127	143	163	190	202	216	197	140	101
local authorities current expenditure: running expenses	3,271	3,650	4,056	4,521	5,236	5,852	6,363	7,113	8,400	9,531	9,996
capital expenditure	137	133	163	213	227	200	189	190	235	229	221
Total	3,532	3,909	4,346	4,877	5,626	6,242	6,754	7,519	8,832	9,900	10,318
Welfare foods service											
central government current expenditure on welfare foods (including administration)	120	124	105	108	120	142	171	182	185	228	264
less receipts from the public	N	N	N	N	–1	–1	–1	–1	–1	–1	–1
Total	120	124	105	108	119	141	170	181	184	227	263
Total government expenditure	3,652	4,033	4,451	4,985	5,745	6,383	6,924	7,700	9,016	10,127	10,581
Total government expenditure as % of GDP[1]	0.95	0.94	0.94	0.96	1.03	1.10	1.14	1.20	1.33	1.42	1.41

[1] GDP is adjusted to take account of change from rates of community charge.

Source: Office for National Statistics. © Crown copyright 1998

Government and Other Public Sector Expenditure on Housing in the UK

(N = nil or negligible. Years ending 31 March. In millions of pounds.)

Type of expenditure	1986–87	1987–88	1988–89	1989–90	1990–91	1991–92	1992–93	1993–94	1994–95	1995–96	1996–97
Government Expenditure											
Current expenditure											
central government											
housing subsidies											
to local authorities	513	496	603	714	1,273	1,144	992	874	814	752	655
to public corporations	298	306	304	285	284	260	208	214	228	216	221
to housing associations	29	41	43	53	67	40	135	180	207	212	228
grants to housing associations	8	7	8	7	85	117	59	13	3	1	1
local authorities housing											
subsidies	538	492	554	487	3	N	1	N	N	N	3
administration	211	251	250	249	320	373	394	364	405	402	425
Total	1,597	1,593	1,763	1,794	2,032	1,934	1,789	1,645	1,657	1,584	1,533
Capital expenditure											
investment in housing by											
local authorities	948	1,031	79	1,387	1,322	822	913	780	842	1,009	710
capital grants to housing											
associations	804	931	956	552	1,495	2,045	2,583	2,136	1,774	1,329	1,407
improvement grants	614	757	809	886	862	1,150	1,240	1,287	1,105	842	845
net lending for house purchase	–448	–283	–148	–259	–596	–782	–211	–402	–141	–136	–719
capital grants to public											
corporations	20	38	65	241	774	482	631	439	387	771	321
net lending to public											
corporations	599	1,018	855	672	176	–104	39	34	10	7	–1
Total	2,537	3,492	2,616	3,479	4,033	3,613	5,195	4,274	3,977	3,822	2,563
Total expenditure											
central government	2,325	2,923	3,023	2,547	3,835	3,697	4,595	3,839	3,409	3,277	2,247
local authorities	1,809	2,162	1,356	2,726	2,230	1,850	2,389	2,080	2,225	2,129	1,849
Total government expenditure	4,134	5,085	4,379	5,273	6,065	5,547	6,984	5,919	5,634	5,406	4,096
Public Corporations' Capital Expenditure											
Investment in housing	293	305	285	451	519	673	549	568	560	559	557
Net lending to private sector	–16	–10	–8	–2	–3	–4	3	1	–1	–5	–5
Total	277	295	277	449	516	669	552	569	559	554	552
Total public sector expenditure[1]	3,792	4,324	3,736	4,809	5,631	5,838	6,866	6,015	5,796	5,182	4,328
Total public sector expenditure as % of GDP[2]	0.98	1.01	0.79	0.93	1.01	1.00	1.13	0.94	0.85	0.73	0.58

[1] Figures show total government expenditure less grants and loans to public corporations, plus public corporations' capital expenditure.
[2] GDP is adjusted to take account of change from rates to community charge.

Source: Office for National Statistics, © Crown copyright 1998

Financing Requirements of Nationalized Industries in the UK

'Financing requirements' excludes central government grants and subsidies that are generally available to the private sector; these grants and subsidies are treated as contributing to internal resources and are included in central government's own expenditure. (– = not applicable. In millions of pounds.)

Industry	1991–92 outturn	1992–93 outturn	1993–94 outturn	1994–95 outturn	1995–96 outturn	1996–97 estimated outturn	1997–98 plans	1998–99 plans	1999–2000 plans
Department of Trade and Industry									
British Coal[1]	605	791	1,400	742	48	104	71	1	1
British Nuclear Fuels	–	–392	–653	–422	–13	–29	–67	–44	–83
British Shipbuilders	–9	–10	–9	10	–1	–1	–1	–21	–1
Nuclear Electric/Magnox Electric[2]	1,180	991	726	483	235	–176	307	222	192
Post Office	–74	–80	–186	–235	–245	–268	–330	–335	–345
Total	1,702	1,300	1,278	577	25	–370	–19	–176	–235
Department of Transport									
National Railways	1,135	1,673	1,033	–657	–1,663	–1,056	70	97	107
Union Railways	21	26	36	46	30	19	–	–	–
European Passenger Services	308	365	392	178	288	15	–	–	–
Civil Aviation Authority	33	51	91	46	34	–13	–34	–39	–23
London Transport	554	883	693	783	903	973	701	350	161
Total	2,051	2,998	2,244	396	–408	–64	736	409	244
Department of the Environment									
British Waterways Board	50	48	49	48	50	50	51	51	51
Scotland									
Highlands and Islands Airports	4	5	6	8	11	9	7	6	5
Scottish Hydro-Electric	–23	–	–	–	–	–	–	–	–
Scottish Power	–48	–	–	–	–	–	–	–	–
Scottish Nuclear	25	14	–28	–46	–43	–	–	–	–
Caledonian MacBrayne	9	13	12	11	11	11	15	10	10
Scottish Transport Group	–2	–	44	–	–	–	–	–	–
Total	–34	32	34	–27	–22	20	22	17	16
Total external finance	3,768	4,378	3,605	995	–335	–364	789	300	75

[1] Figures for 1995–96 onwards largely reflect departmental costs of meeting coal related liabilities.
[2] Figures up to 1996–97 include Nuclear Electric, which was privatized in July 1996.

Source: Her Majesty's Treasury. © Crown copyright 1998

Debt of the Public Sector in the UK

(N = nil or negligible. N/A = not available. Nominal amount outstanding as of 31 March in each year. In millions of pounds.)

Item	1986	1987	1988	1989	1990	1991	1992	1993	1994	1995	1996
Central Government											
Sterling national debt											
sterling debt[1]	167,730	179,909	192,716	192,051	185,870	190,474	205,360	228,949	289,000	331,045	372,857
less official holdings[2][3]	13,159	16,483	19,364	30,146	32,293	34,646	33,645	22,039	31,207	42,041	45,704
Foreign currency national debt											
foreign currency debt	3,861	5,915	4,724	5,272	6,675	8,268	9,399	20,178	18,308	18,488	18,329
less official holdings[2]	N	N	N	N	221	383	751	1,285	1,448	1,575	1,540
Total market holdings of national debt[4]	158,432	169,341	178,076	167,177	160,031	163,713	180,363	225,803	274,653	305,917	343,942
Other liabilities											
net indebtedness to Banking Department	N	319	583	969	1,451	1,223	1,258	437	729	869	N
deposits with National Savings Bank ordinary account	1,686	1,668	1,657	1,632	1,555	1,474	1,435	1,438	1,444	1,446	1,432
liability to trustee savings banks	105	N	N	N	N	N	N	N	N	N	N
accrued interest on national savings	5,229	5,754	6,109	5,440	4,645	3,897	3,525	3,478	3,103	3,316	3,517
notes and coin in circulation	14,539	14,232	16,105	16,907	17,678	18,670	17,582	18,520	21,447	21,771	23,427
Northern Ireland government debt	255	231	168	165	172	155	150	154	128	128	119
public corporations' balances with the Pay Master General	72	53	79	77	44	41	25	52	124	224	190
borrowing from UK banks	N	N	N	N	N	N	N	12	N	6	N/A
Other sectors											
local authorities	96	98	120	147	181	150	94	81	124	149	155
public corporations	1,740	1,181	1,669	2,088	1,883	2,218	1,508	2,454	3,043	4,446	6,602
domestic private sector[4]	159,871	168,311	176,824	162,618	156,444	158,270	168,058	199,606	240,253	272,896	307,703
overseas	18,611	22,008	24,164	27,514	27,068	28,535	34,678	47,785	58,236	56,219	58,207
Total held by other sectors[4]	180,318	191,598	202,777	192,367	185,576	189,173	204,338	249,894	301,628	333,677	N/A
Local Authorities											
Sterling debt	42,041	44,287	46,989	50,101	50,986	53,076	53,707	48,301	48,728	48,785	49,208
Foreign currency debt	614	719	768	742	733	642	599	621	536	470	384
Other sectors											
central government	29,660	35,560	39,677	44,404	47,124	48,814	49,173	41,527	40,977	40,707	41,266
public corporations	1,004	876	965	960	821	838	808	910	945	911	215
domestic private sector[4]	11,120	7,767	6,264	4,692	3,081	3,399	3,638	5,783	6,501	6,779	7,224
overseas	871	803	851	787	693	667	687	702	841	858	887
Total held by other sectors[4]	42,655	45,006	47,757	50,843	51,719	53,730	54,306	48,922	49,264	49,255	N/A
Public Corporations											
Sterling debt	25,574	23,180	23,397	19,580	13,340	9,279	10,719	15,618	23,354	26,542	26,350
Foreign currency debt	5,149	4,548	3,001	2,276	1,421	1,160	790	576	513	373	245
Other sectors											
central government	23,838	22,069	22,182	18,598	12,787	8,842	10,312	15,227	22,951	26,278	25,980
public corporations	804	454	291	247	36	26	29	11	69	3	N
domestic private sector[4]	2,218	1,713	1,026	769	566	460	414	396	340	276	383
overseas	3,863	3,492	2,899	2,242	1,372	1,111	754	560	507	358	232
Total held by other sectors[4]	30,723	27,728	26,398	21,856	14,761	10,439	11,509	16,194	23,867	26,915	26,595
Public Sector Debt Held Outside the Public Sector											
Sterling debt held by											
domestic private sector	170,492	173,663	181,271	167,229	158,895	160,735	170,913	201,397	243,841	277,361	312,941
overseas	16,438	19,249	22,264	23,103	21,721	22,020	27,279	33,345	44,927	42,269	44,277
Foreign currency debt held by											
domestic private sector	2,217	4,128	2,843	850	1,196	1,394	1,197	4,388	3,253	2,590	2,369
overseas	6,907	7,054	5,650	7,440	7,412	8,293	8,840	15,702	14,657	15,166	15,049
Total	196,554	204,094	212,028	198,622	189,224	192,442	208,229	254,832	306,678	337,386	374,636

Debt of the Public Sector in the UK (*continued*)

Item	1986	1987	1988	1989	1990	1991	1992	1993	1994	1995	1996
Debt Excluded from Public Sector Borrowing Requirement Financing [5]											
Central government[6]	497	537	636	764	843	877	1,006	1,263	1,608	1,834	1,803
Contingent Liabilities of Central Government											
Export credit guarantees	38,389	37,213	36,128	36,552	40,106	41,818	38,291	29,350	32,964	34,081	35,943
Assistance to industry, guaranteed loans	2,053	1,801	1,788	1,947	2,490	2,420	1,978	1,668	1,442	1,427	1,241
Overseas development, guaranteed loans	40	32	5	5	4	5	4	4	4	4	3
National heritage acts, guaranteed loans	209	301	881	1,172	1,629	2,043	2,696	2,030	2,733	3,059	2,198
Other identified	63	64	65	23	19	21	16	16	20	18	17
Total	40,754	39,411	38,867	39,699	44,248	46,307	42,985	33,068	37,163	38,589	39,402
% of total debt held outside the public sector	77.5	77.2	76.6	74.9	75.1	76.0	77.1	80.9	81.8	82.3	83.5
Debt held outside the public sector as a % of GDP[7]	52.0	49.5	46.3	39.2	34.7	34.6	35.8	42.0	47.9	49.8	52.9
Debt held overseas as a % of debt held outside the public sector	11.9	12.9	13.2	15.4	15.4	15.8	17.3	19.2	19.4	17.0	15.8
Debt held overseas as a % of GDP[7]	6.2	6.4	6.1	6.0	5.3	5.4	6.2	8.1	9.3	8.5	8.4
Foreign currency debt as a % of debt held outside the public sector	4.9	5.5	4.0	4.2	4.5	5.0	4.8	7.9	5.8	5.3	4.6

[1] Includes British government guaranteed stocks of nationalized industries.
[2] At 31 March 1994 official holdings comprised: (in millions of pounds) British Government Stocks 12,408; National Investment and Loans Office Stocks 1,275; Sterling Treasury Bills 1,181; Ways and Means advances 18,739; Debt to Bank of England Issue Department 11; Temporary Deposit 31; ECU Treasury Bills 205; ECU Ten-Year Bond 178; ECU Treasury Notes 356.
[3] Excludes gilts held temporarily by the Issue Department under purchase and resale agreements with the monetary sector.
[4] Includes gilts held temporarily by the Issue Department under purchase and resale agreements with the monetary sector.
[5] Not included in the main body of the table, which is confined to liabilities that finance the public sector borrowing requirement.
[6] Comprises liability to Post Office Superannuation Fund and court funds.
[7] GDP (average measure) at current market prices for the 12 months centred on 31 March.

Source: Office for National Statistics. © Crown copyright 1998

Public Sector Financial Account of the UK

(N = nil or negligible. N/A = not available. In millions of pounds.)

Financial account	1986–87	1987–88	1988–89	1989–90	1990–91	1991–92	1992–93	1993–94	1994–95	1995–96	1996–97
Financial Surplus or Deficit											
Public sector total	−8,150	−3,247	6,986	2,458	−3,616	−18,863	−46,106	−49,990	−42,676	−34,783	−28,659
Transactions in Financial Liabilities											
Public sector borrowing requirement total	3,567	−3,504	−14,652	−7,958	−599	13,760	36,285	45,421	35,903	31,709	22,518
Contributions											
central government	10,452	839	−7,142	−5,628	−2,459	12,924	36,316	48,949	38,346	35,529	25,051
local authorities	−5,609	−2,875	−4,601	−930	1,860	951	1,532	−2,126	−570	−1,614	−2,353
public corporations	−1,276	−1,468	−2,909	−1,400	N	−115	−1,563	−1,402	−1,873	−2,220	−106
Other financial liabilities	1,349	1,428	2,187	2,991	1,918	329	1,177	480	893	−55	−1,930
Total	4,934	−2,088	−12,467	−5,040	1,312	14,086	37,449	45,901	36,802	31,363	20,738

(continued)

Public Sector Financial Account of the UK (*continued*)

Financial account	1986–87	1987–88	1988–89	1989–90	1990–91	1991–92	1992–93	1993–94	1994–95	1995–96	1996–97
Transactions in Financial Assets											
Net lending to private sector and overseas											
central government	−3,599	−5,109	−6,136	−3,602	−5,435	−8,125	−7,784	−5,016	−5,772	−1,542	−3,751
public corporations	88	−182	−98	108	−170	2	N	55	−56	−1,328	−1,403
Other financial assets	−132	228	−1,250	2,739	2,720	3,252	856	1,375	987	1,092	−2,305
Total	−4,028	−5,195	−7,610	−811	−3,165	−5,308	−7,071	−3,904	−4,927	−1,854	−7,497
Total financial transactions	−8,962	−3,107	4,857	4,229	−4,477	−19,394	−44,520	−49,805	−41,729	−33,490	−28,235
Balancing item	812	−140	2,129	−1,771	861	531	−1,586	−185	−947	−1,293	−424

Source: Office for National Statistics. © Crown copyright 1998

Expenditure on Social Protection in the European Union

(N/A = not available; – = not applicable. Austria, Finland, and Sweden joined the EU in 1995.)

Country	1990	1991	1992	1993	1994	1995
Index of Total Expenditure on Social Protection per Person; ECU at 1990 Prices. 1990 = 100						
Austria	100	111	114	118	123	124
Belgium	100	103	106	107	105	113
Denmark	100	–	–	–	123	123
Finland	100	109	116	118	120	121
France	100	103	106	110	111	113
Germany	100	96	104	106	107	112
Greece	100	97	95	98	101	–
Ireland, Republic of	100	106	112	118	123	–
Italy	100	104	109	109	109	108
Luxembourg	100	108	112	121	126	–
Netherlands	100	101	103	103	101	99
Portugal	100	113	130	143	152	154
Spain	100	109	116	122	119	–
Sweden	–	–	–	–	2	–
UK	100	109	118	127	129	130
Total Expenditure on Social Protection at Current Prices as a % of GDP						
Austria	–	–	–	–	30.2	N/A
Belgium	26.9	27.4	27.0	27.0	27.1	N/A
Denmark	29.8	30.9	32.2	33.3	33.7	N/A
Finland	25.4	30.1	34.2	35.2	34.8	N/A
France	27.7	28.4	29.2	30.9	30.5	N/A
Germany	26.9	28.8	30.1	31.0	30.8	N/A
Greece	16.1	15.3	14.9	15.8	16.0	N/A
Ireland, Republic of	19.4	20.5	21.3	21.5	21.1	N/A
Italy	23.6	24.1	25.5	25.7	25.3	N/A
Luxembourg	22.5	23.6	24.0	24.6	24.9	N/A
Netherlands	32.2	32.3	32.9	33.4	32.3	N/A
Portugal	15.0	17.3	18.1	18.5	19.5	N/A
Spain	20.7	21.8	23.0	24.5	23.6	N/A
Sweden	–	–	–	–	–	N/A
UK	22.7	25.3	27.0	27.8	28.1	N/A

Source: Eurostat 1997

UK Companies and Corporations

Business Registrations and Deregistrations in the UK

Figures show enterprises registered for VAT. An enterprise is defined as a legal unit, person, or group of people producing goods or services under their own control and with their own legal identity. A branch or office of a larger organization is not in itself an enterprise. There may be one or more VAT units within an enterprise.

Region	1994						1995					
	Registrations	Deregistrations	Net change	Registration rates (%)[1]	Deregistration rates (%)[1]	End-year stock	Registrations	Deregistrations	Net change	Registration rates (%)[1]	Deregistration rates (%)[1]	End-year stock
England												
North East	4,500	4,800	−300	10.4	11.1	43,400	4,100	5,100	−1,000	9.5	11.7	42,400
North West	14,400	15,500	−1,200	10.3	11.2	137,600	13,600	15,400	−1,700	9.9	11.2	135,800
Merseyside	2,600	2,700	−100	11.4	11.8	22,400	2,500	2,900	−400	11.0	12.8	22,000
Yorkshire and the Humber	11,900	12,700	−800	9.8	10.5	120,600	11,300	13,500	−2,200	9.3	11.2	118,300
East Midlands	11,200	11,200	0	10.1	10.1	110,400	10,800	11,700	−900	9.8	10.6	109,600
West Midlands	14,100	14,300	−200	10.3	10.5	136,700	13,600	14,800	−1,300	9.9	10.8	135,400
Eastern	16,400	17,000	−600	10.4	10.8	156,900	16,100	16,800	−700	10.2	10.7	156,200
London	34,000	30,300	3,700	14.1	12.5	245,200	33,500	29,400	4,100	13.7	12.0	249,200
South East	28,000	28,100	100	11.7	11.7	239,800	26,500	27,600	−1,100	11.0	11.5	238,600
South West	14,500	15,800	1,300	9.6	10.5	149,500	13,000	15,800	−2,800	8.7	10.6	146,700
Total	151,500	152,400	−900	11.1	11.2	1,362,300	144,900	152,900	−8,100	10.6	11.2	1,354,300
Wales	6,400	7,700	−1,300	8.2	9.8	77,300	6,000	7,200	−1,200	7.8	9.3	76,100
Scotland	11,600	11,500	100	9.8	9.7	118,900	11,200	12,000	−700	9.4	10.1	118,100
Northern Ireland	3,500	2,800	700	6.7	5.3	52,900	3,700	3,000	700	6.9	5.6	53,600
Total UK	173,100	174,400	−1,300	10.7	10.8	1,611,400	165,800	175,100	−9,300	10.3	10.9	1,602,100

[1] Registrations and deregistrations during the year as a percentage of the stock figure at the end of the previous year.

Source: Department of Trade and Industry. © Crown copyright 1997

Companies Spending the Most on Research and Development in the UK

Total expenditure on scientific research and development in 1995 was £14,300 million – 2.05% of GDP (compared to 2.11% in 1994). Expenditure on civil research and development was £12,200 million in 1995, the rest going to defence projects.

1995

Rank	Company	Annual investment (£ millions)	As % of sales	Rank	Company	Annual investment (£ millions)	As % of sales
1	Glaxo Wellcome	1,161	13.9	7	Ford Motors	320	4.5
2	SmithKline Beecham	764	9.6	8	British Telecommunications	282	2.0
3	Zeneca	602	11.2	9	Reuters	202	6.9
4	Unilever	600	1.8	10	Rolls-Royce	199	4.6
5	Shell Transport and Trading	449	0.5	11	Imperial Chemicals Industries	191	1.8
6	General Electric	432	6.9	12	British Aerospace	156	2.4

Source: Office for National Statistics. © Crown copyright 1998

Top 25 Companies in Europe

This table is ranked by market capitalization. Market capitalization is the market value of a company's issued share capital, that is the quoted price of its shares multiplied by the number of shares issued. (As of 22 January 1998.)

1997

Rank	Company	Country	Market capitalization ($ millions)	Rank	Company	Country	Market capitalization ($ millions)
1	Royal Dutch/Shell	Netherlands/UK	191,002.3	14	Ericsson (Telefonaktiebolaget LM)	Sweden	46,174.0
2	Novartis	Switzerland	104,467.4				
3	HSBC Holdings	UK	91,339.4	15	Daimler-Benz	Germany	42,709.9
4	British Petroleum	UK	85,905.0	16	British Telecommunications	UK	42,017.5
5	Roche Holding	Switzerland	85,852.8	17	Barclays	UK	40,636.1
6	Glaxo Wellcome	UK	79,715.9	18	Siemens AG	Germany	37,357.7
7	Lloyds TSB Group	UK	72,094.9	19	ING Groep	Netherlands	37,345.8
8	Unilever	Netherlands/UK	57,484.2	20	Deutsche Bank	Germany	36,991.1
9	Allianz Holding	Germany	56,013.3	21	Elf Aquitaine	France	35,997.4
10	Nestlé	Switzerland	54,315.6	22	Telecom Italia	Italy	34,666.1
11	SmithKline Beecham	UK	53,304.1	23	Gazprom	Russia	31,947.1
12	Deutsche Telecom	Germany	52,515.4	24	Zeneca	UK	30,753.3
13	Ente Nazionale Idrocarburi (ENI)	Italy	49,876.9	25	Astra	Sweden	29,673.2

Source: *FT500, FT Surveys, Financial Times*

Top 25 Companies in the UK

This table is ranked by market capitalization. Market capitalization is the market value of a company's issued share capital, that is the quoted price of its shares multiplied by the number of shares issued. (As of 22 January 1998.)

1997

Rank	Company	Market capitalization ($ millions)	Rank	Company	Market capitalization ($ millions)
1	HSBC Holdings	56,986.6	14	Unilever	14,782.8
2	British Petroleum	53,596.1	15	Abbey National	13,475.8
3	Glaxo Wellcome	49,734.7	16	Prudential Corporation	13,362.6
4	Shell Transport and Trading	45,093.8	17	Grand Metropolitan	12,489.5
5	Lloyds TSB Group	44,980.0	18	Reuters Holdings	12,439.6
6	SmithKline Beecham	33,256.4	19	Cable & Wireless	11,981.2
7	British Telecommunications	26,214.7	20	BG	11,960.0
8	Barclays	25,352.8	21	Guinness	11,075.4
9	Zeneca	19,175.7	22	General Electric Company	10,900.8
10	Halifax	18,323.0	23	Rio Tinto	10,617.0
11	Marks and Spencer	18,064.5	24	Tesco	10,282.0
12	BAT Industries	16,868.5	25	Vodaphone Group	10,214.7
13	National Westminster Bank	16,044.6			

Source: *FT500, FT Surveys, Financial Times*

Company Bankruptcies by Industry in England and Wales

Industry		1992	1993	1994	1995	1996
Self-Employed						
Agriculture and horticulture		313	277	231	218	168
Manufacturing	food, drink, and tobacco	56	34	33	30	31
	chemicals	9	7	23	8	5
	metals and engineering	634	612	523	396	411
	textiles and clothing	174	160	95	114	91
	timber and furniture	317	207	176	158	118
	paper, printing, and publishing	205	161	142	142	117
	other	125	169	133	146	117
	Total	1,520	1,350	1,125	994	890
Construction and transport	construction	4,692	4,361	3,362	2,783	2,713
	transport and communication	2,038	1,754	1,402	1,138	1,227
Wholesaling	food, drink, and tobacco	114	114	94	103	77
	motor vehicles	48	21	28	33	36
	other	220	191	160	122	101
	Total	382	326	282	258	214
Retailing	food, drink, and tobacco	1,001	1,107	981	782	662
	motor vehicles and filling stations	399	412	343	316	327
	other	2,159	2,087	1,615	1,566	1,268
	Total	3,559	3,606	2,939	2,664	2,257
Services	financial institutions	266	292	241	185	125
	business services	1,859	1,843	1,537	1,354	1,176
	hotels and catering	2,366	2,437	2,102	1,956	1,736
	Total	4,491	4,572	3,880	3,495	3,037
Other		2,530	2,315	1,893	1,732	2,161
Total self-employed		19,525	18,561	15,114	13,282	12,667
Other Individuals						
Employees		2,588	2,507	2,279	1,981	2,471
No occupation and unemployed		4,325	4,816	3,696	2,859	3,294
Directors and promoters of companies		965	862	628	484	368
Occupation unknown		4,703	4,270	3,917	3,327	3,003
Total other individuals		12,581	12,455	10,520	8,651	9,136
Total bankruptcies and deeds of arrangement		32,106	31,016	25,634	21,933	21,803

Source: Department of Trade and Industry. © Crown copyright 1998

Major Foreign Acquisitions of UK Companies

1995–97

Acquirer	Target	Value (£)	Date
Merrill Lynch, USA	Mercury Asset Management	3.1 billion	November 1997
Lafarge, France	Redland	1.8 billion	November 1997
Central and South West, USA	Seeboard	1.6 billion	November 1995
American Electric Power, USA	Yorkshire Electricity	1.5 billion	February 1997
Dominion Resources, USA	East Midlands Electricity	1.3 billion	November 1996
Entergy, USA	London Electricity	1.27 billion	December 1996
Southern Electric International, USA	South Western Electricity	1.1 billion	July 1995
Lyonnaise des Eaux, France	Northumbrian Water	823 million	November 1995
CalEnergy Electric, USA	Northern Electric	782 million	December 1996
Clear Channel, USA	More Group	446 million	March 1998

Fastest-Growing Companies in Great Britain

(Ranked by growth of turnover.)

1997

Rank	Company	Business activity	Turnover (£ millions)	Profit (£ millions)	Profit (%)	Profit growth (%)	Turnover growth (%)
1	Hanover International plc	hoteliers	8,865,000	857,000	9.67	517	707
2	Queensborough Holdings plc	holding company	30,328,000	3,586,000	11.82	460	595
3	P G A European Tour Courses plc	leisure industry	4,884,000	2,769,000	56.70	479	518
4	American Port Services plc	port operators	28,118,000	7,182,000	25.54	387	509
5	Time Out Group Ltd	'what's on' magazine	17,347,526	−115,427	−0.67	103	481
6	Bulkbag LTD	flexible bulk plastic container manufacturers	4,201,508	386,315	9.19	438	452
7	M A T Davies Holdings Ltd	holding company	29,895,241	1,999,278	6.69	381	376
8	The Television Corporation plc	film producers	25,098,000	3,069,000	12.23	213	359
9	Eidos plc	computer video editing equipment manufacturers	3,706,000	−1,949,000	−52.59	711	358
10	Expamet International plc	holding company	115,664,000	16,079,000	13.90	313	357
11	Ravenhead Ltd	glass tableware manufacturers	9,619,000	0	0.00	0.00	344
12	Lay & Wheeler Ltd	wine traders	10,200,745	151,451	1.48	332	333
13	W R M Group Ltd	holding company	38,626,000	−1,410,000	−3.65	697	328
14	R G B Holdings Ltd	holding company	4,853,025	1,350,875	27.84	347	322
15	Fortune Oil plc	holding company	391,853,000	3,480,000	0.89	60	321
16	Cantab Pharmaceuticals plc	research	3,115,000	−4,493,000	0.00	27	313
17	The Equine & Livestock Insurance Co Ltd	insurance company	4,484,000	419,000	9.34	230	312
18	Tillbrook Poland Ltd	holding company	10,619,480	189,266	1.78	254	302
19	Lambert Smith Hampton plc	property consultancy	32,987,000	1,610,000	4.88	227	299
20	Green Pharmacies Ltd	chemists and perfumery retailers	3,584,737	−96,399	−2.69	30	289
21	Gardner Avon Ltd	diesel engine manufacturers	21,976,000	2,528,000	11.50	816	279
22	John Dickie Group Ltd	general building contractors	27,460,000	825,000	3.00	143	274
23	Bisichi Mining plc	investment company	3,341,000	161,000	4.82	41	272
24	Regal Hotel Group plc	holding company	66,332,000	10,429,000	15.72	259	266
25	Menzies Hotels plc	hotel proprietors	3,485,006	455,469	13.07	219	266

Reproduced from *National Star Performers 1997/98* with permission of the publisher, Commerce Directories Ltd. Tel: (01908) 614 477.

Company Insolvencies by Industry in England and Wales

Industry	1992	1993	1994	1995	1996
Agriculture and horticulture	191	157	166	99	89
Manufacturing					
food, drink, and tobacco	215	213	142	130	163
chemicals	141	91	108	69	65
metals and engineering	1,621	1,381	932	681	658
textiles and clothing	1,120	917	736	567	568
timber and furniture	508	333	252	267	249
paper, printing, and publishing	830	777	579	452	438
other	1,014	878	859	681	599
Total	5,449	4,590	3,608	2,847	2,740
Construction and transport					
construction	3,830	3,189	2,401	1,844	1,610
transport and communication	1,261	1,082	774	706	682
Total	5,091	4,271	3,175	2,550	2,292

Industry	1992	1993	1994	1995	1996
Wholesaling					
food, drink, and tobacco	388	231	244	205	183
motor vehicles	186	142	112	83	95
other	672	639	638	678	429
Total	1,246	1,012	994	966	707
Retailing					
food, drink, and tobacco	406	388	299	246	236
motor vehicles and filling stations	339	229	226	195	227
other	1,732	1,388	1,186	1,127	956
Total	2,477	2,055	1,711	1,568	1,419
Services					
financial institutions	563	421	259	198	222
business services	2,788	2,415	1,807	1,525	1,500
hotels and catering	1,010	912	777	692	708
Total	4,361	3,748	2,843	2,415	2,430
Other	5,610	4,925	4,231	4,091	3,784
Total	24,425	20,708	16,728	14,536	13,461

Source: Department of Trade and Industry. © Crown copyright 1998

Top 25 Unlisted Companies in the UK

Unlisted or 'unquoted' companies are those not on the 'official list' of the London Stock Exchange, which comprises the main market of the Exchange. The companies below may be public companies, but their shares will not be traded on the unlisted securities markets. They are not listed at Companies House as official subsidiaries of companies on the official list. Companies are ranked according to sales.

1997

Company	Sales (£)	Profit (£)	Company	Sales (£)	Profit (£)
Cantor Fitzgerald Gilts	77,096,893,000	−287,000	Mitsui & Co (UK) Plc	3,699,259,000	7,473,000
Shell International Petroleum Co Ltd	22,219,600,000	338,200,000	Texaco North Sea UK Co Ltd	3,659,941,000	59,033,000
Ford Motor Co Ltd	7,111,000,000	−389,000,000	Rank Xerox Ltd	3,617,000,000	526,000,000
Shell UK Ltd	6,053,000,000	405,000,000	Esso Exploration & Production (UK) Ltd	2,982,300,000	524,200,000
Wittington Investments Ltd	5,740,000,000	444,000,000	ICI Plc	2,916,900,000	−2,500,000
Rover Group Ltd	5,535,500,000	40,100,000	Itochu Europe Plc	2,899,457,000	−7,612,000
IBM (UK) Holdings Ltd	5,118,500,000	272,000,000	John Lewis Partnership Plc	2,849,700,000	135,400,000
Tomen (UK) Plc	5,075,755,000	460,000	Morgan Grenfell Unit Trust Managers Ltd	2,844,200,000	−35,446,000
Texaco Ltd	4,725,309,000	−41,837,000	Conoco (UK) Ltd	2,823,500,000	394,600,000
Gallaher Ltd	4,478,300,000	296,200,000	Motorola Ltd	2,797,562,000	−46,124,000
IBM (UK) Ltd	4,315,600,000	203,400,000	Sumitomo Corp (UK) Plc	2,596,177,000	510,000
Vauxhall Motors Ltd	4,115,900,000	10,100,000	Compaq Computer Group Ltd	2,519,266,000	126,080,000
General Motors Holdings (UK)	3,966,400,000	22,800,000			

Source: ICC Business Publications, Suppliers of
Company Financial Infomation. Tel: (0181) 481 8720

Major Mergers and Major Bids in the UK

1995–98

Companies	Value ($ billions)	Year	Companies	Value ($ billions)	Year
Glaxo Wellcome/SmithKline Beecham[1]	100	1998	Hambros/Guinness Mahon	9	1997
Commercial Union/General Accident	14.2	1998	Coopers & Lybrand/Price Waterhouse[2]	8	1997
Guinness/Grand Metropolitan	24	1997	British Telecommunications/Cable & Wireless[1]	34	1996
Reed Elsevier/Wolters Kluwer[1]	17.5	1997	British Telecommunications/MCI	13	1996
Ernst and Young/KPMG	11.5	1997	Lloyds/TSB	15	1995
Asda/Safeway[1]	9	1997			

[1] Called off.
[2] Currently under investigation (as of 1 May 1998).

Gross Profits and Other Trading Income by Industry in the UK

(Data include rent. In millions of pounds.)

Industry	1990	1991	1992	1993	1994
Agriculture, hunting, forestry, and fishing	6,127	5,858	6,259	6,976	8,251
Mining and quarrying, including oil and gas extraction	8,151	7,361	7,460	8,703	9,516
Manufacturing	33,242	26,502	28,646	32,465	38,628
Electricity, gas, and water supply	5,822	7,323	7,629	9,179	10,433
Construction	19,179	14,818	14,677	14,440	16,043
Wholesale and retail trade, repairs, and hotels and restaurants	27,881	30,005	26,935	29,825	32,821
Transport, storage, and communication	12,740	13,514	14,750	15,871	18,681
Financial intermediation, real estate, renting, and business activities	67,617	67,077	76,892	83,917	94,851
Education, health, and social work	5,318	5,768	7,343	8,351	9,541
Other services, including sewage and refuse disposal	6,564	6,091	6,744	7,551	7,715
All industries	192,640	184,318	197,335	217,278	246,480

Source: © Crown copyright 1996

Privatization Proceeds in the UK

(– = not applicable. In millions of pounds.)

Company	1979–80 to 1982–83	1983–84	1984–85	1985–86	1986–87	1987–88	1988–89	1989–90	1990–91	1991–92	1992–93	1993–94	1994–95	1995–96	1996–97[1]
Amersham International	64	–	–	–	–	–	–	–	–	–	–	–	–	–	–
Associated British Ports Holdings Plc	46	–	51	–	–	–	–	–	–	–	–	–	–	–	–
Atomic Energy Authority Technology	–	–	–	–	–	–	–	–	–	–	–	–	–	–2	215
BAA Plc	–	–	–	–	–	534	689	–	–	–	–	–	–	–	–
Belfast International Airport	–	–	–	–	–	–	–	–	–	–	–	–	47	–	–
British Aerospace Plc	43	–	–	347	–	–	–	–	–	–	–	–	–	–	–
British Airways Plc	–	–	–	–	435	419	–	–	–	–	–	–	–	–	–
British Coal	–	–	–	–	–	–	–	–	–	–	–	–	811	3	111
British Gas Plc															
sale of shares	–	–	–	1,820	1,758	1,555	4	150	4	–	–	–	–	–	–
redemption of debt	–	–	–	–	750	–	250	800	350	–	350	–	–	–	–
British Petroleum Plc	284	543	–	–	–	863	3,000	1,363	–	–	–	–	–	–	–
British Steel Plc	–	–	–	–	–	–	1,138	1,287	–	–	–	–	–	–	–
British Sugar Corporation	44	–	–	–	–	–	–	–	–	–	–	–	–	–	–
British Telecommunications Plc															
sale of shares	–	–	1,358	1,246	1,081	–	–	–	–	1,666	3,544	3,773	1,519	–	–
loan stock	–	–	44	61	53	23	85	92	100	106	113	124	130	130	140
redemption of preference shares	–	–	–	–	250	250	250	–	–	–	–	–	–	–	–
Britoil Plc	334	293	–	426	–	–	–	–	–	–	–	–	–	–	–
BTG	–	–	–	–	–	–	–	–	25	–	–	–	–	–	–
Cable and Wireless Plc	181	–	–	–	–	–	–	–	–	–	–	–	–	–	–
Chessington Computer Centre	–	263	–	577	–	–	–	–	–	–	–	–	–	–	–
DTELs	–	–	–	–	–	–	–	–	–	–	–	5	–	–	–
DVOIT	–	–	–	–	–	–	–	–	–	–	–	12	–	–	–
Electricity industries															
sale of shares (England and Wales)	–	–	–	–	–	–	–	–	3,134	2,329	1,465	13	1,724	1,029	796
sale of shares (Scotland)	–	–	–	–	–	–	–	–	–	1,112	907	703	–	–	–
redemption of debt	–	–	–	–	–	–	–	–	–	1,106	110	654	390	–	–
Enterprise Oil Plc	–	–	384	–	–	–	–	–	–	–	–	–	–	–	–
Forestry Commission	14	21	28	15	16	13	12	15	11	16	10	17	11	–	–
Forward	–	–	–	–	–	–	–	–	–	–	–	4	–	–	–
General Practice Finance Corporation	–	–	–	–	–	–	67	–	–	–	–	–	–	–	–
Harland and Wolff	–	–	–	–	–	–	–	8	–	–	–	–	–	–	–
HMSO	–	–	–	–	–	–	–	–	–	–	–	–	–	–	2
Insurance Services Group	–	–	–	–	–	–	–	–	–	12	–	–	–	–	5
Land Settlement	–	2	12	5	2	–	–	–	1	–	–	–	–	–	–
Motorway Service Area leases	4	1	–	–	2	1	–	2	5	5	4	–	–	–	–
National Enterprise Board Holdings	122	–	168	30	34	–	–	–	–	–	–	–	–	–	–
National Freight Consortium	5	–	–	–	–	–	–	–	–	–	–	–	–	–	–
National Ireland Electricity															
sale of shares	–	–	–	–	–	–	–	–	–	–	350	148	187	2	8
redemption of debt	–	–	–	–	–	–	–	–	–	–	–	–	70	–	–
National Seed Development Organization	–	–	–	–	–	65	–	–	–	–	–	–	–	–	–
National Transcommunications Ltd	–	–	–	–	–	–	–	–	–	70	–	–	–	–	–
Nuclear Power Industry															
sale of shares	–	–	–	–	–	–	–	–	–	–	–	–	–	–8	525
redemption of debt	–	–	–	–	–	–	–	–	–	–	–	–	–	–	160
Privatized companies' debt	–	–	–	–	–	–	–	–	–	–	1,337	–	1,617	517	663
PSA (building management)	–	–	–	–	–	–	–	–	–	–	–	–	–	15	6
Professional and Executive Recruitment	–	–	–	–	–	–	5	–	–	–	–	–	–	–	–
Railtrack															
sale of shares	–	–	–	–	–	–	–	–	–	–	–	–	–	–10	910
redemption of debt	–	–	–	–	–	–	–	–	–	–	–	–	–	–	282

Privatization Proceeds in the UK (*continued*)

Company	1979–80 to 1982–83	1983–84	1984–85	1985–86	1986–87	1987–88	1988–89	1989–90	1990–91	1991–92	1992–93	1993–94	1994–95	1995–96	1996–97[1]
Recruitment and Assessment Services	–	–	–	–	–	–	–	–	–	–	–	–	–	–	7
Residual Share Sales	–	–	–	–	–	–	–	–	–	–	–	–	–	750	560
Rolls-Royce Plc	–	–	–	–	–	–	1,029	3	–	–	–	–	–	–	–
Rover Group Plc	–	–	–	–	–	–	–	150	–	–	–	–	–	–	–
Royal Ordnance	–	–	–	–	–	186	–	–	–	–	–	–	–	–	–
Short Brothers	–	–	–	–	–	–	–	30	–	–	–	–	–	–	–
Transport Research Laboratories	–	–	–	–	–	–	–	–	–	–	–	–	–	–1	4
Water companies															
sale of shares	–	–	–	–	–	–	–	423	1,487	1,485	–	–	–	–	–
redemption of debt	–	–	–	–	–	–	–	73	–	–	–	–	–	–	–
Wytch Farm	–	–	–	–	18	–	–	–	130	–	–	–	–	–	–
Miscellaneous	394	16	5	–1	–3	–1	15	–22	–21	–12	–1	–70	–9	14	95
Total	1,535	1,139	2,050	2,706	4,458	5,140	7,069	4,225	5,347	7,924	8,189	5,453	6,429	2,439	4,500

[1] Figures are estimates.

Source: Her Majesty's Treasury. © Crown copyright 1997

Wealthiest Executives in the UK

(N/A = not available.)

Director	Company	Financial year ending	Pay (£)	% change
Top 10 Pay Increases for Directors of Publicly Quoted Companies				
Harvey Lipsith	Allders	September 1996	736,000	+222.8
Antony Collyer	Allders	September 1996	552,000	+203.2
Roger Head	Vickers	December 1996	659,944	+121.7
Jean Pierre-Garnier	SmithKline Beecham	December 1996	1,965,000	+107.5
Mike Smith	Ladbroke	December 1996	800,000	+98.5
Carol Galley	Mercury Asset Management	March 1997	2,211,000	+97.9
Jonathan Leslie	RTZ	December 1996	632,000	+90.9
Robert Adams	RTZ	December 1996	701,000	+80.2
James Walsh	Laura Ashley	January 1997	648,000	+80.0
Stanley Fink	ED & F Man	March 1997	969,000	+78.4
Directors of Publicly Quoted Companies (£1 Million or More a Year)				
Jim Fifield	EMI	March 1997	5,768,200	−11.4
Sam Chisholm	British Sky Broadcasting	June 1996	3,823,037	−18.9
Bill Harrison	Barclays	December 1996	3,032,000	N/A
David Chance	British Sky Broadcasting	June 1996	2,629,832	N/A
Lawrence Fish	Royal Bank of Scotland	September 1996	2,487,000	+68.7
Stephen Zimmerman	Mercury Asset Management	March 1997	2,236,000	+67.4
Carol Galley	Mercury Asset Management	March 1997	2,211,000	+97.9
Jan Leschley	SmithKline Beecham	December 1996	2,096,000	+16.2
Jean Pierre-Garnier	SmithKline Beecham	December 1996	1,965,000	+107.5
Charles Brady	Amvesco	December 1996	1,954,000	+35.7
Top Paid Private Company Directors (£2 Million or More a Year)				
Highest paid	Deutsche Morgan Grenfell	December 1996	7,141,684	N/A
Bernie Ecclestone	International Sportsworld/ Formula One Promotions	December and March 1995	6,569,221	−77.7
Sir Cameron Mackintosh	Cameron Mackintosh & Co	March 1996	5,614,667	−1.1
John Madejski	Hurst Publishing	March 1996	4,380,606	−20.3
Ashley Levett	Winchester Commodities	April 1996	4,316,667	N/A
Highest paid	NTL Group	December 1995	4,004,117	N/A
Highest paid	Princes	December 1995	3,787,378	N/A
Paul Raymond	Paul Raymond Organization	December 1995	3,784,493	+392.5
Director	Deutsche Morgan Grenfell	December 1996	3,665,000	N/A
Highest paid	Morgan Stanley Group (Europe)	November 1996	3,416,127	N/A
The Celebrity Top 10				
Elton John	Happenstance/J Bondi	July 1996	35,491,366	+240.7
John Reid	John Reid Enterprises	March 1996	10,629,123	+151.5
Sting	Steerpike/Overseas	July 1995	10,229,390	+659.1
Eric Clapton	Marshbrook	September 1995	9,322,500	+58.5
Phil Collins	Philip Collins	December 1995	8,780,160	+48.4
George Harrison	Apple	January 1996	3,980,000	+51.4
Yoko Ono	Apple	January 1996	3,980,000	+51.4
Paul McCartney	MPL/Apple	December 1995/January 1996	3,567,903	+134.7
David Gilmour	David Gilmour Music/Overseas	June 1996	2,994,904	+4.9
Mark Knopfler	Chariscourt	March 1996	1,690,076	−38.7

Source: Reproduced from *Labour Research* magazine

UK Agriculture

Agricultural Land Use in the UK

The data in this table cover all holdings (including minor holdings) in England, Wales, and Northern Ireland but exclude minor holdings in Scotland. (Area given is that at the annual June agricultural census. In hectares. N/A = not available.)

Land use	1986	1987	1988	1989	1990	1991	1992	1993	1994	1995	1996
Agricultural area											
crops	5,240,000	5,272,000	5,255,000	5,138,000	5,013,000	4,956,000	4,981,000	4,519,000	4,469,000	4,544,000	4,721,000
bare fallow	48,000	42,000	58,000	65,000	64,000	64,000	53,000	47,000	44,000	40,000	35,000
Total	18,670,000	18,672,000	18,634,000	18,580,000	18,563,000	18,498,000	18,511,000	18,530,000	18,503,000	18,406,000	18,401,000
Tillage											
all grass under 5 years old	1,721,000	1,690,000	1,613,000	1,538,000	1,582,000	1,586,000	1,562,000	1,561,000	1,436,000	1,387,000	1,376,000
Total	5,288,000	5,314,000	5,313,000	5,203,000	5,077,000	5,020,000	5,033,000	4,566,000	4,513,000	4,584,000	4,756,000
Arable land											
all grass 5 years old and over	5,075,000	5,107,000	5,159,000	5,239,000	5,272,000	5,261,000	5,213,000	5,209,000	5,322,000	5,309,000	5,289,000
Total	7,008,000	7,003,000	6,926,000	6,741,000	6,659,000	6,605,000	6,595,000	6,127,000	5,949,000	5,971,000	6,133,000
Tillage and grass											
sole right rough grazing	4,826,000	4,790,000	4,763,000	4,739,000	4,715,000	4,685,000	4,680,000	4,611,000	4,551,000	4,516,000	4,489,000
set aside[1]	N/A	N/A	N/A	N/A	72,000	97,000	160,000	677,000	728,000	633,000	509,000
all other land on agricultural holdings, including woodland	544,000	555,000	571,000	624,000	609,000	616,000	632,000	678,000	708,000	729,000	745,000
Total	12,083,000	12,110,000	12,085,000	11,980,000	11,931,000	11,866,000	11,808,000	11,335,000	11,271,000	11,280,000	11,241,000
Land on agricultural holdings											
common rough grazing	1,216,000	1,216,000	1,216,000	1,236,000	1,236,000	1,233,000	1,230,000	1,229,000	1,246,000	1,248,000	1,237,000
Total	17,454,000	17,456,000	17,419,000	17,344,000	17,327,000	17,264,000	17,281,000	17,301,000	17,258,000	17,158,000	17,164,000
Crops											
Cereals											
wheat	1,997,000	1,994,000	1,886,000	2,083,000	2,013,000	1,980,000	2,067,000	1,759,000	1,811,000	1,859,000	1,976,000
barley	1,917,000	1,831,000	1,879,000	1,652,000	1,516,000	1,393,000	1,297,000	1,164,000	1,106,000	1,192,000	1,267,000
oats	97,000	99,000	120,000	118,000	106,000	103,000	100,000	92,000	109,000	112,000	96,000
mixed corn	7,000	6,000	5,000	5,000	4,000	4,000	4,000	3,000	3,000	3,000	3,000
rye[2]	7,000	7,000	7,000	7,000	8,000	9,000	8,000	6,000	7,000	8,000	8,000
triticale[3]	N/A	N/A	N/A	8,000	9,000	11,000	11,000	7,000	6,000	7,000	7,000
Total	4,025,000	3,936,000	3,898,000	3,874,000	3,657,000	3,500,000	3,487,000	3,031,000	3,042,000	3,180,000	3,357,000
Other arable crops (excluding potatoes)											
oilseed rape	299,000	388,000	347,000	321,000	390,000	440,000	421,000	377,000	404,000	354,000	356,000
sugar beet not for stock feeding[2]	205,000	203,000	201,000	197,000	194,000	196,000	197,000	197,000	195,000	196,000	199,000
hops[4]	4,000	4,000	4,000	4,000	4,000	4,000	4,000	3,000	3,000	3,000	3,000
peas for harvesting dry and field beans	150,000	208,000	260,000	215,000	216,000	203,000	208,000	244,000	228,000	195,000	178,000

(continued)

Agricultural Land Use in the UK (*continued*)

Land use	1986	1987	1988	1989	1990	1991	1992	1993	1994	1995	1996
Other arable crops (excluding potatoes) (*continued*)											
linseed[5]	N/A	N/A	N/A	17,000	34,000	92,000	144,000	150,000	58,000	54,000	49,000
others	165,000	156,000	156,000	128,000	133,000	142,000	143,000	159,000	187,000	204,000	217,000
Total	824,000	958,000	968,000	882,000	971,000	1,076,000	1,117,000	1,130,000	1,076,000	1,005,000	1,003,000
Potatoes	177,000	178,000	180,000	174,000	177,000	176,000	180,000	170,000	164,000	171,000	177,000
Horticultural	214,000	200,000	209,000	208,000	208,000	204,000	197,000	187,000	189,000	187,000	189,000
Vegetables grown in the open	146,000	132,000	141,000	141,000	142,000	139,000	135,000	126,000	127,000	130,000	132,000
Orchard fruit	38,000	38,000	37,000	36,000	34,000	34,000	33,000	32,000	32,000	28,000	28,000
Soft fruit	15,000	15,000	15,000	15,000	15,000	15,000	14,000	13,000	13,000	12,000	12,000
Ornamentals[6]	12,000	12,000	13,000	14,000	14,000	14,000	14,000	14,000	14,000	15,000	14,000
Glasshouse crops	2,000	2,000	2,000	2,000	2,000	2,000	2,000	2,000	2,000	2,000	2,000

[1] Figures are for England only in 1990 and 1991, and Great Britain only in 1992.
[2] Figures are for England and Wales only.
[3] Figures are for Great Britain only.
[4] Figures are for England and Wales only for 1989 and England only from 1990.
[5] Figures are for England and Wales only from 1989 to 1991, and for Great Britain only in 1992.
[6] Includes non-commercial orchards.

Source: Agricultural Departments. © Crown copyright 1998

Agricultural Employment in the UK

The data in this table exclude school children, farmers, partners and directors, their spouses, and most trainees. The figures include estimates for minor holdings in England, Wales, and Northern Ireland. Data are for June of each year.

Year	Regular workers					Seasonal or casual workers			All workers			Salaried managers[1]
	Full time		Part time									
	Male	Female	Male	Female	Total	Male	Female	Total	Male	Female	Total	
1986	134,100	14,800	32,200	29,100	210,300	57,200	38,100	95,300	223,500	82,100	305,500	8,300
1987	127,400	14,500	31,400	28,800	202,100	55,900	37,700	93,500	214,700	81,000	295,700	7,900
1988	120,700	14,500	31,800	29,200	196,100	56,400	36,700	93,100	208,900	80,400	289,300	7,900
1989	114,600	15,100	31,100	27,900	188,700	54,200	34,300	88,600	199,900	77,300	277,200	7,800
1990	109,700	15,500	31,900	28,300	185,400	55,800	35,000	90,800	197,400	78,800	276,200	8,100
1991	104,600	14,900	31,600	27,700	178,900	54,000	32,800	86,900	190,300	75,500	265,800	7,800
1992	99,800	14,700	31,000	26,400	171,900	54,600	31,900	86,500	185,300	73,000	258,400	7,800
1993	96,400	13,600	31,800	25,500	167,300	55,300	30,400	85,700	183,500	69,600	253,000	7,600
1994	93,500	13,100	31,900	24,400	162,900	54,200	28,400	82,500	179,500	65,900	245,400	7,600
1995	90,300	12,900	31,900	24,300	159,400	56,700	27,200	84,000	178,900	64,400	243,400	7,600
1996	89,000	12,600	33,000	23,600	158,200	55,800	25,900	81,700	177,900	62,000	239,900	7,900

[1] These figures are for Great Britain only.

Source: Agricultural Departments. © Crown copyright 1998

Index of Producer Prices of Agricultural Products in the UK

(Annual averages. 1990 = 100.)

Product				Index weights	1986	1988	1992	1994	1996
Crop products	cereals	wheat for	breadmaking	3.9	108.1	102.8	116.6	102.3	108.6
			other milling	0.5	102.3	98.1	110.6	96.4	103.6
			feeding	6.6	99.8	95.2	105.7	93.5	102.5
		barley for	feeding	2.9	101.6	95.0	105.4	98.1	101.3
			malting	1.7	97.7	99.2	102.1	97.9	110.8
		oats for	milling	0.2	91.4	102.6	108.2	100.6	100.3
			feeding	0.1	93.9	100.5	109.6	101.0	100.6
		Total		15.9	101.8	97.7	108.1	97.2	104.7
	root crops	potatoes	early	0.3	140.7	127.7	100.7	257.7	139.1
			main crop	3.3	79.8	73.6	72.4	119.2	94.4
		sugar beet		2.1	96.2	91.5	105.5	107.6	123.1
		Total		5.6	88.8	82.9	86.0	121.7	107.2
	fresh vegetables	cauliflowers		0.5	78.2	84.8	95.7	106.6	107.7
		lettuce		1.0	90.9	93.3	121.2	124.3	106.1
		tomatoes		0.7	91.7	102.4	80.4	84.8	98.5
		carrots		0.8	67.0	84.4	67.1	100.1	121.0
		cabbage		0.7	72.9	85.3	85.6	94.5	112.1
		beans		0.2	59.1	68.1	57.2	93.1	87.6
		onions		0.5	71.9	71.8	78.2	108.6	75.5
		mushrooms		1.6	98.7	101.1	96.4	104.3	111.6
		Total		7.8	85.5	91.0	90.5	101.9	108.4
	fresh fruit	dessert apples		0.7	91.8	93.2	124.7	74.8	112.6
		dessert pears		0.1	69.5	60.8	90.3	78.9	82.9
		cooking apples		0.3	79.9	89.3	78.0	86.9	105.6
		strawberries		0.5	111.7	107.0	105.3	103.0	94.1
		raspberries		0.2	114.5	88.8	69.0	93.1	156.8
		Total		2.1	92.4	90.7	100.5	87.0	107.5
	seeds			1.1	91.8	93.8	101.1	107.3	122.7
	flowers and plants			3.8	96.2	101.1	99.3	104.4	114.6
	other			4.1	96.6	82.8	73.7	62.6	66.8
	Total			40.4	95.0	92.7	96.7	98.4	103.5
Animals and animal products	animals for slaughter	calves		0.3	84.0	135.0	114.8	145.4	93.6
		clean cattle		11.7	88.9	101.9	102.7	114.6	98.2
		cows and bulls		2.1	90.5	110.5	131.8	118.1	106.6
		clean pigs		7.7	87.6	80.8	102.3	88.6	121.9
		sows and boars		0.3	95.7	81.6	121.4	95.4	131.0
		sheep		4.3	109.6	101.5	105.1	135.4	163.2
		ewes and rams		0.3	125.2	136.3	109.9	125.9	172.0
		Total		33.8	92.5	94.9	102.1	109.1	115.5
	poultry	chickens		5.0	94.5	89.3	94.0	99.3	104.8
		turkeys		1.6	87.4	76.6	95.9	107.2	117.4
		Total		7.0	92.6	86.5	95.0	101.5	108.4
	cow's milk			21.7	83.9	93.4	109.6	117.7	134.3
	eggs			3.6	76.7	72.9	86.2	99.4	107.6
	wool (clip)			0.6	107.2	105.5	86.4	92.1	114.5
	Total			59.6	88.6	93.1	103.8	111.5	121.9
Total				100.0	91.2	92.9	100.9	106.2	114.4

Source: Ministry of Agriculture, Fisheries, and Food. © Crown copyright 1998

Agricultural Outputs, Inputs, Net Products, and Incomes in the UK

(N = nil or negligible. Figures are given in calendar years. 1996 figures are provisional. In millions of pounds.)

1995–96

Category		England		Wales		Scotland		Northern Ireland	
		1995	**1996**	**1995**	**1996**	**1995**	**1996**	**1995**	**1996**
Outputs[1]									
1	Total cereals	2,530	2,628	18	24	353	369	21	22
2	Total other crops	908	1,005	4	6	52	54	3	2
3	Total potatoes	745	434	22	11	181	103	34	15
4	Total horticulture	1,923	1,929	18	18	83	88	52	55
5	Total livestock[2][3]	4,244	4,152	715	649	1,028	981	690	656
6	Total livestock products	2,874	2,927	382	376	339	347	385	393
7	Own account capital formation: livestock	−80	−52	−21	1	−7	4	11	6
8	Total output (1+2+3+4+5+6+7)	13,144	13,024	1,138	1,086	2,029	1,946	1,196	1,150
9	Other direct receipts[3][4]	264	577	13	78	40	98	5	93
10	Total receipts (8+9)	13,408	13,601	1,151	1,164	2,069	2,044	1,201	1,242
11	Total value of physical increase in output stocks	−5	137	−25	6	43	−5	−6	−12
12	Gross output (10+11)	13,403	13,738	1,126	1,169	2,112	2,039	1,195	1,230
Inputs									
13	Total expenditure[2]	6,188	6,582	637	682	946	977	641	679
14	Value of physical increase in input stock[5]	29	−10	1	1	−12	N	1	N
15	Gross input (13–14)	6,159	6,592	636	681	959	977	640	679
16	Gross product (12–15)	7,244	7,146	490	488	1,154	1,062	555	551
17	Total depreciation	1,309	1,391	145	155	228	231	161	172
18	Net product (16–17)	5,936	5,755	345	334	926	831	394	379
19	Interest[6]	416	386	48	45	89	82	34	36
20	Net rent	122	125	10	11	15	15	N	N
21	Income from agriculture of total labour (18–19–20)	5,397	5,244	287	278	822	734	360	343
22	Labour: hired[7][8]	1,403	1,405	56	57	204	214	32	34
23	Total income from farming (21–22)	3,994	3,839	231	221	617	519	328	309
24	Labour: family, partners, and directors[9][10]	761	776	116	111	73	76	63	72
25	Farming income[10] (23–24)	3,233	3,063	115	110	545	443	265	237

[1] Output is net of VAT collected on the sale of non-edible products. Figures for total output include subsidies but not 'other direct receipts'.

[2] In this table, total livestock includes sale of stock between England, Wales, and Scotland. Similarly, total expenditure includes the purchases of such stock. The sum of the four countries will therefore not match the UK total for some items.

[3] Compensation payments to farmers paid for the Over Thirty Months Scheme and the Calf Processing Aid Scheme are included in 'other direct receipts'.

[4] These receipts include compensation for set-aside land and milk quota cuts.

[5] Input stocks comprise fertilisers and purchased feed.

[6] Figures include interest charges on loans for current farming purposes and buildings and works, less interest on money held on short term deposit.

[7] Includes employers' national insurance contributions, perks, and other payments (including the payment by farmers of rates on farm cottages occupied by farm workers and of their council tax).

[8] Excludes the value of work done by farm labour on own account capital formation in buildings and works.

[9] The estimate in respect of family workers, non-principal partners, and directors (and their spouses) is calculated on the basis of the earnings of hired labour.

[10] Income is calculated as the return to farmers (and their spouses) for their labour, management skills, and own capital invested after providing for depreciation.

Source: *Farm Incomes in the United Kingdom, 1995/6.* © Crown copyright 1996

Farm Assets and Liabilities in the UK

(Averages per farm in pounds at opening (March) and closing (February) of the farm year.)

1995–96

Category			England Opening	England Closing	Wales Opening	Wales Closing	Scotland Opening	Scotland Closing	Northern Ireland Opening	Northern Ireland Closing
Number of farms in sample			2,088	2,088	484	484	443	443	355	355
Assets										
	fixed assets	land and buildings	360,000	390,600	276,600	281,200	171,100	196,700	190,400	197,400
		breeding livestock	33,300	32,900	42,100	42,300	33,800	34,500	22,500	23,700
		machinery and equipment	53,500	58,100	33,600	36,400	39,800	42,500	17,600	18,900
	Total		455,200	490,100	368,400	376,000	244,700	273,700	230,400	239,900
	current assets	crops and livestock	38,400	39,600	23,700	24,700	51,800	51,800	30,000	30,600
		liquid assets	27,900	32,900	9,400	10,900	61,400	64,400	2,300	2,800
	Total		76,000	83,600	34,100	36,600	113,200	116,200	32,200	33,400
Total assets			531,200	573,700	402,400	412,600	358,000	389,900	262,700	273,300
External liabilities										
	bank term loans		11,700	12,000	9,700	9,900	4,700	5,900	4,800	5,800
	other long and medium term loans		20,200	20,400	7,800	7,300	9,600	8,700	200	100
	bank overdraft		20,100	19,100	14,600	15,200	29,900	28,200	6,600	6,800
	other short term loans		18,800	19,300	3,000	3,400	13,300	15,300	1,700	2,300
	Total		70,800	70,800	35,100	35,700	57,600	58,000	13,200	15,000
Net worth			460,300	502,900	367,300	376,900	300,400	331,800	249,500	258,400

Source: *Farm Incomes in the United Kingdom, 1995/6.* © Crown copyright 1996

Cattle, Sheep, Pigs, and Poultry on Agricultural Holdings in the UK

The data in this table cover all holdings (including minor holdings) in England, Wales, and Northern Ireland but exclude minor holdings in Scotland. Data are for June of each year. (N/A = not available.)

Type of livestock	1986	1987	1988	1989	1990	1991	1992	1993	1994	1995	1996
Cattle and Calves											
Dairy cows	3,138,000	3,042,000	2,912,000	2,865,000	2,847,000	2,770,000	2,682,000	2,667,000	2,175,000	2,602,000	2,587,000
Beef cows	1,312,000	1,348,000	1,379,000	1,499,000	1,603,000	1,669,000	1,699,000	1,751,000	1,775,000	1,805,000	1,829,000
Heifers in calf	880,000	775,000	835,000	794,000	757,000	733,000	762,000	797,000	771,000	771,000	813,000
Total	12,554,000	12,189,000	11,902,000	11,993,000	12,079,000	11,885,000	11,804,000	11,729,000	11,834,000	11,733,000	11,913,000
Sheep and Lambs											
Ewes and shearlings	17,405,000	18,132,000	19,086,000	20,050,000	20,424,000	20,334,000	20,385,000	20,563,000	20,544,000	20,507,000	20,277,000
Lambs under 1 year old	18,387,000	19,386,000	20,600,000	21,576,000	22,036,000	21,950,000	22,341,000	22,132,000	21,510,000	21,093,000	20,168,000
Total	37,031,000	38,776,000	41,028,000	43,012,000	43,828,000	43,639,000	43,998,000	43,901,000	43,295,000	42,771,000	41,530,000
Pigs											
Sows in pig and other sows for breeding	716,000	714,000	704,000	661,000	660,000	678,000	672,000	687,000	680,000	644,000	639,000
Gilts in pig	109,000	107,000	101,000	97,000	109,000	107,000	108,000	115,000	104,000	100,000	105,000
Total	7,939,000	7,945,000	7,983,000	7,510,000	7,450,000	7,597,000	7,609,000	7,754,000	7,797,000	7,534,000	7,496,000
Fowls											
Table fowls including broilers	63,807,000	70,869,000	75,437,000	70,176,000	73,588,000	75,701,000	73,298,000	79,451,000	75,205,000	76,621,000	N/A
Laying fowls[1]	38,116,000	38,553,000	37,439,000	33,971,000	33,489,000	33,286,000	33,206,000	32,824,000	32,543,000	31,692,000	N/A
Growing pullets	12,502,000	12,238,000	11,243,000	9,414,000	10,452,000	11,016,000	10,764,000	10,653,000	10,293,000	10,098,000	N/A
Total	120,760,000	128,825,000	131,018,000	120,366,000	124,636,000	127,241,000	124,013,000	130,175,000	125,718,000	125,981,000	N/A

[1] Excludes fowl laying eggs for hatching.

Source: Office for National Statistics. © Crown copyright 1998

Estimated Quantity of Crops and Grass Harvested in the UK

For vegetables, figures give the output marketed for the calendar year; for horticultural crops, figures give the output marketed for the crop year. Except for sugar beet and hops, the production area for England and Wales is the area returned at the June census together with estimates for very small holdings (known as minor holdings). In Scotland and Northern Ireland the area returned in June is also the production area, except that estimates for minor holdings are included in Scotland for potatoes, and in Northern Ireland for barley, oats, and potatoes. (N/A = not available. In tonnes.)

Crop		1992	1993	1994	1995	1996
Cereals	wheat	14,095,000	12,890,000	13,314,000	14,310,000	16,102,000
	barley	7,365,000	6,038,000	5,945,000	6,834,000	7,784,000
	oats	502,000	479,000	597,000	617,000	589,000
	mixed corn for threshing	16,000	13,000	13,000	16,000	12,000
	rye for threshing	37,000	30,000	43,000	43,000	51,000
	maize for threshing	1,975,000	2,730,000	N/A	N/A	N/A
Potatoes	early crop	411,000	426,000	337,000	372,000	324,000
	main crop	7,391,000	6,639,000	6,194,000	6,026,000	6,896,000
Fodder crops	beans for stockfeeding	445,000	612,000	454,000	319,000	318,000
	turnips and swedes	760,000	620,000	N/A	N/A	N/A
	fodder beet and mangolds	710,000	655,000	N/A	N/A	N/A
	kale, cabbage, savoys, and kohl rabi	515,000	485,000	N/A	N/A	N/A
	peas harvested dry for stockfeeding	209,000	266,000	249,000	229,000	240,000
Other crops	sugar beet	10,148,000	9,666,000	8,720,000	8,431,000	9,555,000
	rape grown for oil seed	1,166,000	1,100,000	1,253,000	1,235,000	1,410,000
	hops	5,000	6,000	5,000	4,000	6,000

Horticultural Crops

		1992	1993	1994	1995	1996
Vegetables grown in the open	Brussels sprouts	115,000	98,000	105,000	79,000	81,000
	cabbage (including savoys and spring greens)	402,000	381,000	403,000	340,000	353,000
	cauliflowers	341,000	309,000	289,000	244,000	239,000
	carrots	608,000	592,000	633,000	517,000	617,000
	parsnips	60,000	64,000	70,000	63,000	75,000
	turnips and swedes	158,000	141,000	137,000	148,000	150,000
	beetroot	74,000	93,000	87,000	72,000	72,000
	onions, dry bulb	235,000	274,000	274,000	255,000	260,000
	onions, salad	28,000	24,000	25,000	24,000	28,000
	leeks	72,000	60,000	61,000	57,000	52,000
	broad beans	17,000	11,000	12,000	11,000	9,000
	runner beans (including French)	39,000	46,000	36,000	30,000	35,000
	peas, green for market	6,000	6,000	6,000	8,000	9,000
	peas, green for processing	211,000	209,000	181,000	191,000	210,000
	celery	44,000	41,000	43,000	39,000	38,000
	lettuce	206,000	145,000	178,000	214,000	190,000
	rhubarb	20,000	20,000	21,000	20,000	20,000
Protected crops	tomatoes	122,000	110,000	108,000	113,000	116,000
	cucumbers	90,000	104,000	83,000	88,000	86,000
	lettuce	44,000	37,000	33,000	30,000	28,000
Fruit crops	dessert apples	178,100	180,200	167,700	118,500	116,600
	culinary apples	178,900	114,900	142,600	127,200	106,900
	pears	23,400	38,700	25,600	35,300	40,100
	plums	21,300	11,900	11,100	14,500	19,700
	cherries	3,800	2,400	1,300	3,500	3,600
	soft fruit	94,100	93,500	77,200	74,400	80,600

Number and Size of Farms in the UK

(As of June 1996.)

Number and area of holdings

		< 2	2–5	5–10	10–20	20–30	30–40	40–50	Hectares 50–100	100–200	200–300	300–500	500–700	700 and over	Total[1]
England	number of holdings	9,935	12,068	18,749	21,353	13,509	10,425	8,685	24,956	16,436	4,838	3,108	861	714	145,637
	%	6.8	8.3	12.9	14.7	9.3	7.2	6.0	17.1	11.3	3.3	2.1	0.6	0.5	100.0
	area of holdings (ha)	10,023	40,777	139,089	308,109	333,558	362,367	387,557	1,783,398	2,282,062	1,166,552	1,174,096	501,397	761,471	9,250,456
	%	0.1	0.4	1.5	3.3	3.6	3.9	4.2	19.3	24.7	12.6	12.7	5.4	8.2	100.0
Scotland	number of holdings	1,930	3,509	2,942	3,443	2,382	1,825	1,708	5,952	4,888	1,642	1,127	468	1,177	32,993
	%	5.8	10.6	8.9	10.4	7.2	5.5	5.2	18.0	14.8	5.0	3.4	1.4	3.6	100.0
	area of holdings (ha)	2,296	11,465	21,211	49,558	58,760	63,546	76,255	430,115	678,758	395,263	428,773	273,921	2,775,951	5,265,872
	%	0.0	0.2	0.4	0.9	1.1	1.2	1.4	8.2	12.9	7.5	8.1	5.2	52.7	100.0
Wales	number of holdings	658	1,639	3,796	4,796	3,191	2,514	2,147	5,625	2,761	533	298	68	64	28,090
	%	2.3	5.8	13.5	17.1	11.4	8.9	7.6	20.0	9.8	1.9	1.1	0.2	0.2	100.0
	area of holdings (ha)	714	5,630	28,379	69,155	78,683	87,401	96,034	397,013	372,748	129,147	112,725	39,177	69,842	1,486,648
	%	0.0	0.4	1.9	4.7	5.3	5.9	6.5	26.7	25.1	8.7	7.6	2.6	4.7	100.0
Northern Ireland	number of holdings	500	864	3,570	6,591	4,668	3,194	2,184	4,466	1,253	166	69	12	10	27,547
	%	1.8	3.1	13.0	23.9	16.9	11.6	7.9	16.2	4.5	0.6	0.3	0.0	0.0	100.0
	area of holdings (ha)	342	3,033	27,350	96,488	114,835	110,394	97,292	303,335	164,587	39,142	25,053	7,202	11202	1,000,256
	%	0.0	0.3	2.7	9.6	11.5	11.0	9.7	30.3	16.5	3.9	2.5	0.7	1.1	100.0
Total UK	number of holdings	13,023	18,080	29,057	36,183	23,750	17,958	14,724	40,999	25,338	7,179	4,602	1,409	1,965	234,267
	%	5.6	7.7	12.4	15.4	10.1	7.7	6.3	17.5	10.8	3.1	2.0	0.6	0.8	100.0
	area of holdings (ha)	13,374	60,905	216,030	523,310	585,836	623,709	657,138	2,913,861	3,498,155	1,730,104	1,740,648	821,696	3,618,466	17,003,232
	%	0.1	0.4	1.3	3.1	3.4	3.7	3.9	17.1	20.6	10.2	10.2	4.8	21.3	100.0

[1] Totals may not necessarily agree with the sum of their components, due to rounding.

Source: *Digest of Agricultural Statistics*. © Crown copyright 1997

Fishing Fleet of the UK

Prior to 1990 the figures refer to vessels that were active; after 1990 the figures refer to vessels in the registered fleet for which the data are currently under review. (– = not applicable. N/A = not available. Figures are for 31 December each year.)

Fleet by size and segment	1991	1992	1993	1994	1995	1996
By size (metres)						
10 and under	N/A	7,376	7,666	7,194	6,319	5,606
10.00–12.19	N/A	1,450	1,361	1,167	1,016	800
12.20–17.00	N/A	787	751	680	622	540
17.01–18.29	N/A	232	220	193	187	164
18.30–24.38	N/A	697	657	610	574	509
24.39–30.48	N/A	200	210	211	212	223
30.49–36.58	N/A	120	124	126	127	114
> 36.58	N/A	117	119	116	117	117
Total >10 m	N/A	3,603	3,442	3,103	2,855	2,467
Total UK fleet (excluding Islands)	10,862	10,979	11,108	10,297	9,174	8,073

Fleet by size and segment	1991	1992	1993	1994	1995	1996
By segment						
pelagic gears	88	76	69	68	67	58
beam trawls	200	227	240	212	220	215
demersal trawls	1,105	1,039	988	854	856	N/A
nephrop trawls	648	566	560	593	528	411
seines	274	255	203	197	165	N/A
demersal trawls and seines	N/A	N/A	N/A	N/A	N/A	1,040
lines and nets	343	339	329	300	267	224
shellfish: mobile	169	214	181	206	194	265
shellfish: fixed	137	306	312	305	283	339
distant water	17	16	14	13	12	15
under 10 metres	7,538	7,831	8,128	7,607	6,757	6,091
non-active/ non-TAC[1]	892	692	668	472	371	–
Total UK fleet[2]	11,411	11,561	11,692	10,827	9,720	8,658

[1] TAC = Total Allowable Catch; this is for fish species for which there are quotas.
[2] The UK figures here include Channel Islands and Isle of Man.

Source: Ministry of Agriculture, Fisheries, and Food. © Crown copyright 1998

Landings of Fish by UK Vessels in the UK

(– = not applicable. N/A = not available.)

Species of fish	Quantity (tonnes)						Value (£ millions)					
	1991	1992	1993	1994	1995	1996	1991	1992	1993	1994	1995	1996
Demersal (Living Near the Sea Bottom)												
brill	400	500	400	500	500	500	1.4	1.6	1.5	1.9	2.2	2.6
catfish	2,000	1,900	1,700	1,400	1,000	1,100	1.9	1.9	1.9	1.7	1.5	1.4
cod	65,700	62,200	64,800	65,700	74,400	75,700	76.4	71.6	64.9	65.1	65.8	69.8
dogfish	12,400	14,100	10,400	8,200	10,900	9,700	8.6	10.0	7.3	6.3	7.7	7.0
haddock	53,300	53,900	87,100	92,900	85,300	89,100	53.3	40.1	54.7	61.0	54.7	54.3
hake	5,700	46,000	4,300	3,200	3,100	2,800	13.4	10.8	11.5	8.4	7.4	7.3
lemon soles	6,100	5,600	5,000	4,800	4,600	5,100	11.3	11.2	11.1	11.9	10.1	11.9
ling	5,400	6,100	7,700	8,100	9,800	9,200	4.1	4.9	5.2	5.8	7.5	6.9
megrims	4,000	4,100	4,300	4,700	5,100	6,000	6.8	8.3	8.5	9.2	9.2	10.4
monks or anglers	14,100	15,000	16,700	17,700	22,200	29,700	27.6	30.9	32.3	34.3	39.5	51.5
plaice	25,400	24,100	19,400	17,500	15,500	12,500	28.6	24.3	21.5	19.9	17.6	16.0
pollack (lythe)	2,600	3,100	3,400	2,900	3,300	2,900	2.5	3.0	3.1	2.6	2.9	2.6
saithe	15,900	13,000	12,200	12,500	12,800	13,300	7.9	5.7	4.7	4.9	5.6	5.7
sand eels	8,300	4,200	2,900	8,700	7,300	9,300	0.4	0.2	0.1	0.4	0.4	1.0
skates and rays	7,800	7,900	7,300	7,300	7,600	8,300	5.2	5.9	5.9	6.3	6.5	7.5
soles	3,400	2,900	2,600	2,800	2,800	2,500	13.8	13.2	12.8	13.5	14.2	14.1
turbot	600	800	900	1,000	800	800	2.2	3.9	4.5	5.2	4.7	5.0
whiting	46,400	44,200	45,600	41,800	39,800	37,300	22.9	21.7	20.7	20.1	18.9	19.0
whiting, blue	3,900	6,500	2,300	1,900	3,400	3,500	0.2	0.3	0.1	0.1	0.2	0.2
whitches	2,400	2,100	2,000	2,100	2,300	2,300	2.8	2.5	2.3	2.9	2.9	3.1
other	8,100	8,600	8,900	8,900	12,900	13,300	7.3	7.0	8.7	10.7	17.0	16.6
Total[1]	293,900	285,200	310,100	314,700	325,400	334,800	299.8	278.9	283.9	292.3	296.5	313.4
Pelagic (Living in the Upper Layers of the Open Sea)												
herring[2]	94,000	88,800	87,200	86,100	95,900	72,300	10.1	9.3	9.7	9.8	11.1	8.7
horse mackerel	4,500	1,700	3,900	9,500	26,200	22,000	0.4	0.4	0.4	0.8	2.6	3.0
mackerel[2]	125,400	150,700	161,800	155,900	140,400	60,800	16.3	19.4	22.1	21.2	20.9	15.6
pilchards	3,000	4,200	4,800	2,100	6,800	6,800	0.3	0.5	0.6	0.3	0.7	1.0
sprats	6,000	10,000	7,000	7,600	5,900	7,200	0.9	1.0	1.0	1.5	1.1	1.2
tuna	100	100	300	400	100	N/A	0.2	0.1	0.7	0.7	0.2	0.1
other	100	200	500	100	200	300	–	0.0	0.2	0.1	0.1	0.1
Total	233,100	255,800	265,600	261,700	275,600	169,500	28.3	30.7	34.6	34.4	36.7	29.7
Shellfish												
cockles	46,600	32,100	21,400	22,300	25,400	24,200	4.0	3.3	3.4	3.1	3.5	3.3
crabs	17,700	17,200	15,200	19,200	21,700	20,300	18.0	17.0	15.8	20.4	21.3	22.2
lobsters	1,200	1,100	1,000	1,100	1,300	1,300	9.6	9.2	9.4	10.7	11.9	11.9
mussels	9,400	7,000	7,800	10,300	9,500	12,300	1.7	1.5	1.4	2.0	3.0	4.6
nephrops	26,800	24,800	28,400	29,800	31,100	29,000	47.7	40.0	48.9	56.4	60.7	57.2
periwinkles	2,300	2,000	1,900	2,300	2,400	2,400	1.2	1.2	1.2	1.6	2.0	2.0
queens	7,700	8,600	7,500	3,000	2,900	2,300	2.8	3.2	2.9	1.8	1.9	1.2
scallops	7,400	7,900	9,300	14,000	15,700	17,100	12.1	12.4	13.8	21.2	24.3	27.0
shrimps/prawns	800	700	1,500	1,400	2,700	2,700	1.2	1.0	1.9	2.0	3.5	3.3
squid	1,400	2,100	1,700	1,300	1,600	1,400	2.3	3.4	2.5	2.8	3.8	3.0
other	3,300	4,500	6,800	6,200	10,400	18,700	3.4	3.6	6.5	5.9	9.1	12.3
Total	124,500	108,000	102,500	111,100	124,600	131,600	104.2	95.7	107.6	127.7	145.0	148.0
Total	651,500	649,000	678,200	687,600	725,600	635,900	432.3	405.3	425.6	454.5	478.2	491.0

[1] Includes fish roes.
[2] Includes transshipments, that is those caught by UK boats but not actually landing at UK ports. These quantities are transshipped to foreign vessels in coastal waters and are later recorded as exports.

Source: Agricultural Departments. © Crown copyright 1998

Forestry in the UK

(Years ending 31 March. Area: thousands of hectares; volume: millions of cubic metres.)

Item	1986–87	1987–88	1988–89	1989–90	1990–91	1991–92	1992–93	1993–94	1994–95	1995–96	1996–97
Forest Area[1]											
Great Britain	2,265	2,285	2,307	2,326	2,336	2,350	2,361	2,377	2,390	2,405	2,423
Northern Ireland	72	72	73	74	75	77	77	78	79	80	81
Total UK	2,337	2,357	2,380	2,400	2,411	2,427	2,438	2,455	2,469	2,485	2,504
Forestry Commission (Great Britain)											
Productive woodland	889	888	888	864[5]	859	855	845	827	815	804	795
Net disposals of forestry land[2]	3.7	4.7	2.5	4.5	0.8	4.2	6.5	14.1	9.6	8.2	9.6
New planting[3]	5.3	5.0	4.1	4.1	3.5	3.0	2.4	1.4	0.9	0.4	0.5
Restocking[3]	8.0	8.1	8.5	7.9	7.6	8.3	8.5	7.9	7.9	7.5	7.7
Volume of timber removed[4]	3.3	3.4	3.6	3.5	3.4	3.9	4.1	4.3	4.3	4.2	4.7
Total estates	1,157	1,148	1,143	1,140	1,133	1,128	1,115	1,100	1,089	1,080	1,073
Private Forestry (Great Britain)											
Productive woodland	1,195	1,227	1,231	1,266	1,281	1,298	1,317	1,344	1,367	1,392	1,417
New planting[3]	19.4	24.0	25.4	15.6	15.5	14.3	15.5	16.1	18.5	15.3	16.4
Restocking[3]	4.6	5.0	4.9	6.3	7.2	7.9	8.1	8.5	6.2	5.8	6.6
Volume of timber removed[4]	2.7	2.8	3.2	3.6	3.3	3.1	2.9	3.0	3.8	4.2	4.0
State Afforestation in Northern Ireland											
Land under plantation	57.9	58.4	58.3	58.5	58.8	60.6	60.8	60.8	61.0	61.0	60.9
Plantable land acquired during year	0.5	0.4	0.4	0.6	0.4	0.3	0.4	0.4	0.1	0.1	0.1
Total area planted during year	1.0	1.0	1.0	1.0	1.0	0.9	0.9	0.8	0.8	0.8	0.6
Total estates	73.9	74.1	74.3	74.6	74.8	75.1	75.2	75.5	75.5	75.3	75.5

[1] Includes unproductive woodland.
[2] Data represent disposals less acquisitions, for plantations and plantable land.
[3] New planting is planting on ground not previously carrying forest; restocking is replacing trees after felling.
[4] Figures represent standing volume overbark; private forestry figures are for calendar years ending the previous December.
[5] The apparent decrease in 1989–90 is mainly the result of the reclassification of certain woodland types within the Forestry Commission.

Source: Department of Agriculture (Northern Ireland); Forestry Commission. © Crown copyright 1998

UK Trade and Transportation

Agricultural Imports and Exports of the UK

(N = nil or negligible. n.e.c. = not elsewhere classified. In millions of pounds.)

Industry			Imports[1]		Exports[2]	
			1995	1996	1995	1996
Agriculture, hunting, and related services	crops, market gardening, and horticulture	cereals and other crops n.e.c	1,438	1,578	780	849
		vegetables, horticultural, and nursery products	1,300	1,332	77	82
		fruit, nuts, beverage, and spice crops	2,001	2,160	112	108
		Total	4,739	5,069	969	1,039
	farming of animals	cattle and dairy farming	39	28	91	17
		sheep, goats, horses, asses, mules, and hinnies	288	315	258	260
		swine	11	24	35	31
		poultry	19	23	62	62
		other animals	49	61	22	23
		Total	406	451	467	393
	growing of crops combined with farming of animals (mixed farming)		N	N	N	N
	agricultural and animal husbandry services, except veterinary	agricultural service activities	N	N	N	N
		animal husbandry services, except veterinary	N	N	N	N
	hunting and game rearing, including related services		N	N	N	N
	Total		5,146	5,521	1,436	1,432
Forestry, logging, and related services	forestry and logging		121	118	31	28
	forestry and logging related services		N	N	N	N
	Total		121	118	31	28
Fishing	fishing, fish hatcheries, and services	fishing	125	154	288	286
		operation of fish hatcheries and farms	4	5	5	5
		Total	129	159	293	291

[1] Calculated on a cost, insurance, and freight basis.
[2] Calculated on a free on board basis.

Source: *Business Monitor MQ10.* © Crown copyright 1997

Goods Transport in Great Britain

(N/A = not available.)

Item		1986	1987	1988	1989	1990	1991	1992	1993	1994	1995	1996
In tonne km (billions)												
Road[1]		105.4	113.3	130.2	137.8	136.3	130.0	126.5	134.5	143.7	149.6	153.9
Rail		16.6	17.5	18.1	16.7	16.0	15.3	15.5	13.8	13.0	13.1	N/A
Water	coastwise oil[2]	33.9	31.4	34.2	34.1	32.1	31.2	29.4	28.9	28.9	31.4	37.7[3]
	other	20.9	22.7	25.1	23.8	23.6	26.5	25.5	22.3	23.3	21.2	17.4[3]
Pipelines[4]		10.4	10.5	11.1	9.8	11.0[5]	11.1	11.0	11.6	12.0	12.2	13.3
Total		187.2	195.2	218.8	222.8	218.8	214.1	208.3	210.9	220.8	N/A	N/A
In million tonnes												
Road[1]		1,473	1,542	1,758	1,812	1,749	1,600	1,555	1,615	1,689	1,701	N/A
Rail		138	144	150	143	138	136	122	103	97	101[5]	101
Water	coastwise oil[2]	46	43	47	46	44	44	43	42	43	47	54[3]
	other	98	99	109	109	108	100	97	92	97	98	85[3]
Pipelines[4]		79	83	99	93	121[6]	105	106	125	125	181	N/A
Total		1,836	1,909	2,163	2,206	2,163	1,984	1,923	1,984	2,051	N/A	N/A

[1] Includes all road freight by goods vehicles (over 3.5 tonnes gross vehicle weight) and small commercial vehicles.
[2] Oil comprises crude oil and all petroleum products. 'Coastwise' includes all sea traffic within the UK, Isle of Man, and Channel Islands. 'Other' means coastwise plus inland waterway traffic and one-port traffic (one-port traffic is largely crude oil direct from rigs).
[3] Water figures are provisional for 1996.
[4] These data exclude movements of gases by pipelines.
[5] This figure is provisional.
[6] The increase, as compared with the corresponding figure for 1989, is believed to be largely due to changes in coverage.

Source: Department of the Environment, Transport, and the Regions. © Crown copyright 1998

Exports of the European Union

Percentage of total exports.

Country/region	Belgium/Luxembourg		Denmark		Germany[1]		Greece		Spain		France	
	1958	1994	1958	1994	1958	1994	1958	1994	1958	1994	1958	1994
Export to												
Belgium/Luxembourg	–	–	1.2	1.9	6.6	6.7	1.0	1.6	2.1	2.8	6.3	8.5
Denmark	1.6	0.9	–	–	3.0	1.8	0.2	0.8	1.7	0.6	0.7	0.9
Germany	11.6	20.8	20.0	23.0	–	–	20.5	21.1	10.2	13.4	10.4	17.7
Greece	0.8	0.6	0.3	0.7	1.3	0.8	–	–	0.1	0.9	0.6	0.7
Spain	0.7	2.9	0.8	1.8	1.2	3.2	0.2	2.2	–	–	1.6	6.9
France	10.6	19.3	3.0	5.6	7.6	12.0	12.8	5.4	10.1	19.0	–	–
Ireland, Republic of	0.3	0.4	0.3	0.5	0.3	0.5	0.4	0.3	0.3	0.4	0.2	0.6
Italy	2.3	5.2	5.3	4.0	5.0	7.6	6.0	13.9	2.7	8.7	3.4	9.8
Netherlands	20.7	13.0	2.2	4.3	8.1	7.5	2.0	2.5	3.2	3.6	2.0	4.5
Portugal	1.1	0.8	0.3	0.5	0.9	0.9	0.3	0.4	0.4	7.4	0.8	1.4
UK	5.7	8.3	25.9	8.8	3.9	8.0	7.6	5.9	15.9	7.6	4.9	9.8
Total intra-EC trade	55.4	72.1	59.3	52.3	37.9	48.9	50.9	54.2	46.8	64.5	30.9	60.7
Other European OECD countries	8.7	5.8	16.6	22.2	22.7	16.9	10.3	8.1	12.4	5.8	9.0	7.8
USA	9.4	4.9	9.3	5.5	7.3	7.9	13.6	4.8	10.1	4.6	5.9	7.0
Canada	1.1	0.4	0.7	0.5	1.2	0.6	0.3	0.5	1.3	0.5	0.8	0.7
Japan	0.6	1.3	0.2	4.0	0.9	2.6	1.4	1.0	1.7	1.1	0.3	1.9
Australia	0.5	0.3	0.3	0.6	1.0	0.7	0.1	0.4	0.3	0.4	0.5	0.4
Developing countries												
OPEC	3.3	1.7	2.3	1.8	4.8	2.6	0.9	4.0	2.6	3.0	21.3	3.7
other developing countries	14.7	9.6	7.0	9.1	16.1	10.1	6.3	13.2	15.8	17.7	25.6	14.3
Total	18.0	11.3	9.3	10.9	20.9	12.7	7.2	17.2	18.4	20.7	46.9	18.0
Rest of the world and unspecified	6.3	3.9	4.3	5.1	8.1	9.7	16.2	13.8	9.0	2.4	5.7	3.5
World (excluding EC)	44.6	27.9	40.7	48.8	62.1	51.1	49.1	45.8	53.2	35.5	69.1	39.3
World (including EC)	100	100	100	100	100	100	100	100	100	100	100	100

[1] 1958: West Germany; 1994: unified Germany.

Imports and Exports of Manufactured Goods of the UK

(In millions of pounds. n.e.c. = not elsewhere classified.)

Item	Imports[1]		Exports[2]	
	1995	1996	1995	1996
Food products and beverages	12,631	12,981	9,106	8,722
Tobacco products	222	241	1,127	1,201
Textiles	5,286	5,525	3,448	3,497
Wearing apparel; dressing and dyeing of fur	4,386	5,073	2,534	2,616
Tanning and dressing of leather; luggage, handbags, saddlery, harness, and footwear	2,184	2,471	953	1,053
Wood and products of wood and cork, except furniture; articles of straw and plaiting materials	2,211	2,212	242	273
Pulp and paper products	6,281	5,462	2,430	2,360
Publishing, printing, and reproduction of recorded media	1,453	1,575	2,436	2,445
Coke, petroleum products, and nuclear fuel	1,753	2,091	2,974	3,535
Chemicals and chemical products	18,374	18,525	21,925	22,903
Rubber and plastic products	4,545	4,551	3,889	4,040
Other non-mineral products	1,779	1,804	1,986	2,098
Basic metals	8,485	8,280	8,091	7,536
Fabricated metal products, except machinery	3,414	3,524	3,206	3,410
Machinery and equipment n.e.c.	14,212	14,420	16,250	17,418
Office machinery and computers	12,401	12,627	11,799	12,007
Electrical machinery and apparatus n.e.c.	6,497	6,744	5,657	6,276
Radio and television equipment	12,000	14,886	12,228	12,963
Medical and precision instruments	5,175	5,779	5,470	5,974
Motor vehicles, trailers, and similar vehicles	19,167	22,918	13,380	15,990
Other transport equipment	5,041	6,054	6,946	8,243
Furniture; manufacturing n.e.c.	4,753	5,275	3,427	3,632

[1] Calculated on a cost, insurance, and freight basis.
[2] Calculated on a free on board basis.

Source: *Business Monitor MQ10*. © Crown copyright 1997.

Exports of the European Union (*continued*)

Percentage of total exports.

Country/region	Ireland, Republic of		Italy		Netherlands		Portugal		UK		EUR12	
	1958	1994	1958	1994	1958	1994	1958	1994	1958	1994	1958	1994
Export to												
Belgium/Luxembourg	0.8	3.9	2.2	3.0	15.0	13.9	3.7	3.7	1.9	5.5	4.8	6.0
Denmark	0.1	1.1	0.8	0.8	2.6	1.6	1.2	2.3	2.4	1.4	2.0	1.3
Germany	2.2	14.1	14.1	19.0	19.0	28.6	7.7	18.7	4.2	12.9	7.6	13.6
Greece	0.1	0.5	1.9	1.8	0.6	1.0	0.6	0.5	0.7	0.7	0.8	0.9
Spain	0.8	2.3	0.7	4.6	0.8	2.5	0.7	14.3	0.8	3.8	1.0	3.8
France	0.8	9.2	5.3	13.1	4.9	10.6	6.6	14.7	2.4	10.2	4.7	10.6
Ireland, Republic of	–	–	0.1	0.3	0.4	0.6	0.3	0.5	3.5	5.4	1.1	1.1
Italy	0.4	3.9	–	–	2.7	5.5	4.3	3.3	2.1	5.1	3.1	6.1
Netherlands	0.5	5.5	2.0	2.9	–	–	2.5	5.2	3.2	7.1	5.3	5.7
Portugal	0.1	0.4	0.7	1.3	0.4	0.8	–	–	0.4	1.0	0.8	1.3
UK	76.8	27.5	6.8	6.5	11.9	9.6	11.3	11.7	–	–	5.9	7.7
Total intra-EC trade	82.4	70.0	34.5	53.4	58.3	74.7	38.9	75.1	21.7	54.1	37.2	58.4
Other European OECD countries	0.9	6.9	18.9	11.3	11.9	6.7	5.1	8.1	9.1	8.2	13.7	10.7
USA	5.7	8.1	9.9	7.8	5.6	4.0	8.3	5.3	8.8	12.0	7.9	7.3
Canada	0.7	0.9	1.2	0.9	0.8	0.4	1.1	0.8	5.8	1.4	2.3	0.7
Japan	0.0	3.1	0.3	2.1	0.4	1.0	0.5	0.8	0.6	2.3	0.6	2.1
Australia	0.1	0.6	0.8	0.7	0.7	0.4	0.6	0.3	7.2	1.4	2.4	0.7
Developing countries												
OPEC	0.2	1.4	7.5	3.8	4.5	1.8	2.0	0.8	7.0	3.6	7.6	2.9
other developing countries	1.4	5.3	18.7	13.3	13.1	6.5	40.3	7.1	26.6	12.8	19.8	11.3
Total	1.6	6.7	26.2	17.1	17.6	8.3	42.3	7.9	33.6	16.4	27.4	14.2
Rest of the world and unspecified	8.6	3.7	8.2	6.7	4.7	4.5	3.2	1.8	13.2	4.2	8.5	5.9
World (excluding EC)	417.6	30.0	65.5	46.6	41.7	25.3	61.1	24.9	78.3	45.9	62.8	41.6
World (including EC)	1100	100	100	100	100	100	100	100	100	100	100	100

Export from

[1] 1958: West Germany; 1994: unified Germany.

Source: European Commission

International Seaborne Trade of the UK

Exports plus imports by sea		Total seaborne trade[1]							Percentage of total trade carried by UK vessels		
		1990	1991	1992	1993	1994	1995	1996	1990	1991	1992
Weight (million tonnes)	dry bulk cargo	77.7	79.7	82.2	78.5	84.7	87.7	89.8	22	21	21
	other dry cargo	86.3	86.8	91.9	101.2	110.0	112.2	113.5	24	23	24
	tanker cargo	136.5	134.8	137.2	146.5	156.7	154.2	151.0	14	12	14
Total		300.5	301.4	311.3	326.2	351.5	354.1	354.3	19	18	19
Value (£ billions)	dry bulk cargo	7.7	6.9	6.9	7.2	7.4	8.5	8.5	16	16	16
	other dry cargo	151.7	149.9	160.3	176.7	195.7	223.4	236.2	37	37	38
	tanker cargo	13.8	12.4	11.8	13.3	13.3	13.9	16.2	15	14	15
Total		173.2	169.2	179.0	197.2	216.4	245.7	260.9	34	35	36

[1] Comprises exports (including re-exports) plus imports.

Source: Department of the Environment, Transport, and the Regions. © Crown copyright 1998

See Also   UK Shipping (Transport and Travel)

Imports of the European Union

Percentage of total imports.

Country/region	Import from											
	Belgium/ Luxembourg		Denmark		Germany[1]		Greece		Spain		France	
Import to	1958	1994	1958	1994	1958	1994	1958	1994	1958	1994	1958	1994
Belgium/Luxembourg	–	–	3.8	3.7	4.5	7.1	3.3	3.8	1.8	3.9	5.4	10.3
Denmark	0.5	0.6	–	–	3.4	1.9	0.7	1.5	1.3	0.8	0.6	1.0
Germany[1]	17.2	18.9	19.9	21.8	–	–	20.3	16.4	8.7	15.3	11.6	20.4
Greece	0.1	0.1	0.0	0.2	0.7	0.5	–	–	0.2	0.3	0.6	0.2
Spain	0.5	1.6	0.7	1.2	1.6	2.8	0.1	3.1	–	–	1.2	6.0
France	11.6	15.2	3.4	5.4	7.6	11.3	5.4	8.1	6.8	18.0	–	–
Ireland, Republic of	0.1	1.0	0.0	0.8	0.1	1.1	0.0	0.9	0.6	0.9	0.0	1.3
Italy	2.1	4.1	1.7	4.2	5.5	8.4	8.8	16.7	1.8	8.9	2.4	9.9
Netherlands	15.7	17.0	7.3	6.9	8.1	10.5	4.8	7.5	2.6	4.5	2.5	6.5
Portugal	0.4	0.5	0.3	1.3	0.4	0.9	0.3	0.4	0.3	2.8	0.4	1.1
UK	7.4	9.1	22.8	6.7	4.3	6.3	9.9	6.2	7.8	8.0	3.5	8.2
Total intra-EC trade	55.5	68.1	60.0	52.1	36.3	50.7	53.7	64.4	31.8	63.5	28.3	65.0
Other European OECD countries	7.7	6.8	18.6	25.5	15.2	16.5	11.5	6.6	8.4	5.5	6.7	7.6
USA	9.9	5.9	9.1	4.3	13.6	5.9	13.7	3.2	21.6	6.2	10.0	7.3
Canada	1.4	0.7	0.2	0.4	3.1	0.6	0.8	0.3	0.5	0.4	1.0	0.6
Japan	0.6	2.7	1.5	3.1	0.6	4.8	2.0	3.8	0.7	2.8	0.2	2.5
Australia	1.7	0.3	0.0	0.2	1.2	0.2	0.3	0.0	0.8	0.3	2.4	0.3
Developing countries												
OPEC	5.7	1.4	0.3	0.7	6.7	2.1	1.7	5.3	17.7	6.1	19.7	3.8
other developing countries	13.5	8.6	5.6	7.6	17.2	8.9	7.9	8.3	14.3	10.9	25.9	8.8
Total	19.2	10.0	5.9	8.3	23.9	11.0	9.6	13.6	32.0	17.0	45.6	12.6
Rest of the world and unspecified	4.0	5.5	4.7	6.1	6.1	10.3	8.4	8.1	4.2	4.3	5.8	4.1
World (excluding EC)	44.5	31.9	40.0	47.9	63.7	49.3	46.3	35.6	68.2	36.5	71.7	35.0
World (including EC)	100	100	100	100	100	100	100	100	100	100	100	100

[1] 1958: West Germany; 1994: unified Germany.

(continued)

Visible Trade of the UK

Category	1986	1988	1990	1992	1994	1996
Value (£ millions)						
Exports of goods	72,627	80,346	101,718	107,343	134,664	166,340
Imports of goods	82,186	101,826	120,527	120,447	145,793	178,938
Balance on trade in goods	–9,559	–21,480	–18,809	–13,104	–11,129	–12,598
Price Index Numbers (1990 = 100)						
Exports of goods	88.3	92.4	100.0	103.5	118.6	128.4
Imports of goods	91.9	93.7	100.0	102.1	116.1	128.3
Terms of trade[1]	96.1	98.6	100.0	101.4	102.2	100.1
Volume Index Number (1990 = 100)						
Exports of goods	82.2	89.0	100.0	103.7	118.5	136.3
Imports of goods	75.5	92.4	100.0	100.9	109.4	124.1

[1] Terms of trade are the export price index as a percentage of the import price index.

Source: Office for National Statistics. © Crown copyright 1998

Imports of the European Union

Percentage of total imports.

Country/region	Import from											
	Ireland, Republic of		Italy		Netherlands		Portugal		UK		EUR12	
	1958	1994	1958	1994	1958	1994	1958	1994	1958	1994	1958	1994
Import to												
Belgium/Luxembourg	1.8	1.6	2.0	4.7	17.8	10.7	7.3	3.5	1.6	4.6	4.4	6.2
Denmark	0.7	0.7	2.2	1.0	0.7	1.1	0.8	0.8	3.1	1.4	2.0	1.2
Germany	4.0	7.0	12.0	19.2	19.5	20.9	17.6	14.0	3.6	14.2	8.7	13.4
Greece	0.2	0.1	0.4	0.8	0.2	0.1	0.1	0.1	0.2	0.2	0.4	0.3
Spain	0.4	0.9	0.4	3.8	0.4	1.6	0.4	19.8	1.0	2.4	0.9	3.2
France	1.6	3.4	4.8	13.6	2.8	6.9	7.7	12.7	2.7	9.8	4.4	9.5
Ireland, Republic of	–	–	0.0	0.9	0.0	1.1	0.1	0.7	2.9	4.7	0.9	1.5
Italy	0.8	2.0	–	–	1.8	3.4	3.7	8.5	2.1	4.9	2.7	6.2
Netherlands	2.9	3.3	2.6	5.7	–	–	2.9	4.4	4.2	6.5	5.2	7.5
Portugal	0.2	0.3	0.4	0.8	0.2	0.5	–	–	0.4	0.8	0.3	0.9
UK	56.3	41.2	5.5	6.1	7.4	8.5	12.9	6.7	–	–	5.4	6.8
Total intra-EC trade	68.9	63.3	30.2	56.2	50.7	54.8	53.4	71.4	21.8	49.9	35.2	57.0
Other European OECD countries	3.4	4.8	13.1	11.6	7.2	9.0	8.6	6.0	8.7	10.8	10.1	11.1
USA	7.0	16.9	16.4	4.6	11.3	8.7	7.0	3.6	9.4	12.8	11.4	7.4
Canada	3.0	0.6	1.5	0.9	1.4	0.7	0.5	0.3	8.2	1.2	3.6	0.7
Japan	1.1	4.3	0.4	2.4	0.8	4.4	0.0	2.8	0.9	5.9	0.7	3.9
Australia	1.2	0.1	3.0	0.5	0.2	0.4	0.9	0.1	5.4	0.7	2.6	0.4
Developing countries												
OPEC	0.7	0.3	13.9	5.3	11.5	5.3	6.3	5.8	11.3	2.4	10.8	3.2
other developing countries	8.6	7.0	15.5	8.9	12.9	12.0	21.3	7.5	23.4	10.8	18.7	9.6
Total	9.3	7.3	29.4	14.2	24.4	17.3	27.6	13.3	34.7	13.2	29.5	12.8
Rest of the world and unspecified	6.1	2.7	6.0	9.6	4.0	4.7	2.0	2.5	10.9	5.5	6.9	6.7
World (excluding EC)	31.1	36.7	69.8	43.8	49.3	45.2	46.6	28.6	78.2	50.1	64.8	43.0
World (including EC)	100	100	100	100	100	100	100	100	100	100	100	100

[1] 1958: West Germany; 1994: unified Germany.

Source: European Commission

Imports and Exports by Selected Country and the UK

(N/A = not available. In millions of pounds. Seasonally adjusted.)

Country/region	Imports to the UK				Exports from the UK			
	1990	1992	1994	1996	1990	1992	1994	1996
European Union	72,895	72,022	83,627	99,988	59,937	65,610	77,309	95,915
Germany	20,151	19,153	22,192	27,202	13,272	15,337	17,447	20,752
France	11,851	12,305	15,228	17,719	10,988	11,608	13,734	17,119
Italy	6,783	6,808	7,607	8,783	5,637	6,196	6,869	8,048
Netherlands	10,559	9,969	10,215	12,418	7,548	8,573	9,654	13,481
Belgium and Luxembourg	5,773	5,771	7,187	8,625	5,673	5,761	7,400	8,548
Denmark	2,294	2,397	2,206	2,352	1,419	1,573	1,830	2,217
Republic of Ireland	4,531	5,095	5,987	7,222	5,332	5,788	7,202	8,669
Greece	403	372	357	394	684	777	939	1,150
Portugal	1,184	1,177	1,303	1,658	1,038	1,176	1,265	1,680
Spain	2,992	3,039	3,734	5,043	3,860	4,552	5,165	6,737
Sweden	3,620	3,300	4,262	4,770	2,724	2,459	3,424	4,432
Finland	1,788	1,687	2,306	2,650	1,054	1,007	1,324	1,817
Austria	966	949	1,043	1,152	708	803	1,056	1,265
Other Western Europe	9,388	8,602	9,656	11,838	4,580	4,318	5,729	7,383
Norway	4,235	3885	3,823	4,982	1,291	1,421	2,034	2,066
Switzerland	4,254	3,919	4,816	5,411	2,359	1,845	2,461	3,205
Turkey	551	456	629	933	609	691	815	1,566
Iceland	258	241	240	268	89	93	109	155
North America	16,924	15,872	19,940	25,747	15,235	14,262	19,523	22,435
USA	14,357	13,715	17,729	22,812	12,999	12,231	16,908	19,831
Canada	2,258	1,898	1,883	2,484	1,902	1,584	1,917	1,975
Mexico	173	154	241	334	262	292	390	319
Other OECD countries	9,871	10,441	12,594	14,357	5,816	5,494	7,662	10,923
Japan	6,760	7,443	8,898	8,994	2,632	2,233	2,990	4,265
Australia	1,036	1,014	1,064	1,296	1,646	1,377	1,920	2,467
South Korea	963	932	1,096	2,039	621	660	972	1,303
Poland	357	356	545	601	221	606	704	1,352
New Zealand	485	429	538	633	440	263	411	473
Czech Republic	N/A	N/A	278	375	N/A	N/A	375	716
Oil exporting countries	2,974	3,078	3,267	3,750	5,572	6,014	5,738	8,095
Saudi Arabia	795	964	812	753	2,013	1,966	1,519	2,484
Kuwait	108	128	238	181	181	263	314	580
Iran	279	163	134	119	385	583	290	398
Nigeria	298	166	124	296	501	622	458	433
Rest of the world	13,996	15,549	20,384	28,213	12,515	12,533	18,702	22,662
Eastern Europe	1,219	1,022	1,766	2,535	1,017	747	1,484	2,274
South America	1,583	2,226	2,472	3,167	1,000	1,467	2,377	2,678
China	585	953	1,643	2,203	471	428	845	739
Hong Kong	1,970	2,398	3,082	4,074	1,237	1,612	2,299	2,925
India	800	864	1,289	1,610	1,264	946	1,313	1,706
Israel	506	486	572	832	568	587	1,034	1,267
Malaysia	776	1,104	1,204	2,381	602	636	1,310	1,160
Pakistan	237	273	360	391	253	312	354	344
Singapore	1,024	1,193	1,896	2,574	1,041	1,147	1,769	2,144
South Africa	1,079	866	971	1,222	1,112	1,079	1,416	1,880
Taiwan	1,210	1,395	1,584	2,088	431	559	736	941
Thailand	484	643	914	1,189	417	475	749	974

Source: Office for National Statistics. © Crown copyright 1998

Web Sites

Bank for International Settlements

URL: "http://www.bis.org/"

Full source of official information on the BIS and its role to promote cooperation among central banks. The history and structure of BIS is well explained. BIS reviews, press releases, and publications may be accessed. There is a listing of all the world's central banks which have Web sites.

Bank of England – Banknote Printing

URL: "http://www.bankofengland.co.uk/print.htm#top"

History of legal tender and the stages the Bank of England goes through to produce new notes. This easily-navigable site is well linked and contains details of the origins of money and the complex printing process involved in the manufacture of new notes.

Budget

URL: "http://www.hm-treasury.gov.uk/pub/html/budget.html"

Frequently updated information on Britain's Budget from the Treasury. There is an index of official press releases relating to the budget. Accompanying documents provide a picture of the state of Britain's public finances.

Business Ethics Magazine Online

URL: "http://condor.depaul.edu/ethics/bizethics.html"

Online version of a print magazine which combines two aspects sometimes thought to sit uncomfortably together: business and ethics.

CA Net

URL: "http://www.dss.gov.uk/ca/index.htm"

Guide to Britain's national insurance system provided by the Contributions Agency of the Department of Social Security.

European Bank for Reconstruction and Development

URL: "http://www.ebrd.com/"

Explanation of the role and structure of the London-based group that finances 'the economic transition in central and eastern Europe and the CIS'. The text is principally of interest for economists interested in developments in central Europe and the former Soviet Union or countries wishing to find about the mechanisms of obtaining EBRD support.

European Free Trade Association

URL: "http://www.imf.org/external/np/sec/decdo/efta.htm"

Introduction to the work of EFTA. There is a history, an explanation of its structures, contact addresses, and a description of its relationship with the European Union.

European Monetary Union – The Legal Framework

URL: "http://www.cliffordchance.com/library/publications/emu_legal/section1.html"

Analysis of the background to the introduction of a single European currency. The history of the European Monetary System is examined, along with progress on implementation of the Maastricht Treaty. There is also a timetable of the stages towards full monetary union.

Grameen Bank

URL: "http://www.citechco.net/grameen/bank/"

Information about the pioneering work of the Grameen Bank, which extends credit without collateral to the poor of Bangladesh.

International Fund for Agricultural Development

URL: "http://www.unicc.org/ifad/home.html"

Site of the UN agency charged with tackling rural poverty and hunger. Its work and structures are explained, there are details of international conferences, and an overview of the agency's first twenty years.

International Monetary Fund

URL: "http://www.imf.org/external/index.htm"

The IMF explains its role promoting international monetary cooperation and assisting states with balance of payments difficulties.

London Stock Exchange

URL: "http://www.londonstockex.co.uk/"

London Stock Exchange Web site that tells you how the exchange and its markets work and how to get in touch. The site includes details on what the LSE does, how the exchange is organized, a brief history, and planned future developments. The site also holds information on how the stock market is regulated.

OECD – Organization for Economic Cooperation and Development

URL: "http://www.oecd.org"

Regularly updated site with information on the role, structure, and history of OECD.

Office of Fair Trading

URL: "http://www.oft.gov.uk/"

Site of the agency charged with protecting consumers and enforcing UK competition policy. Its mandate, structure, and history are set out, together with advice to consumers, information on publications, and a large number of news items dealing with current investigations and matters of concern.

164 Currency Converter

URL: "http://www.oanda.com/cgi-bin/ncc"

Simple to use and effective site allowing you to do automatic conversions to and from a wide range of currencies, from the Afghanistan Afghani to the Zimbabwe dollar.

Stockmarket – the UK's Personal Finance Web Site

URL: "http://www.moneyworld.co.uk/stocks/index.html"

Constantly updated financial information from the leading stock exchanges. You can follow the fortunes of the FTSE and the Dow and the latest currency fluctuations.

World Bank Home Page

URL: "http://www.worldbank.org/"

Includes sections on current events, press releases and bank news, country information, publications, and research studies.

World Trade Organization

URL: "http://www.wto.org/wto/index.htm"

Extensive information on the functions of the UN agency charged with administering international trade agreements.

WTO and GATT

URL: "http://www.wto.org/wto/about/facts6.htm"

Account of the evolution of the General Agreement on Tariffs and Trade into the specialized UN agency, the World Trade Organization. The information is provided by the WTO and chronicles the increasing determination of the international community to regularize global trade.

CONSUMER AND CITIZENSHIP INFORMATION

General Information

Forms of Address in the UK

Two dashes indicate first name and surname; one dash indicates surname or place; C – indicates first name only. Honourable is abbreviated to Hon. Formal ceremonial styles for closing letters are provided where appropriate. Spoken address is provided where a special style is followed, and only in selected instances. For the royal family, it is more normal practice to address letters to the private secretary, lady-in-waiting, or equerry of the relevant member of the family. Both formal and social forms of address are given for the peerage, where usage differs in some cases. In general, the social form is now generally preferred to the formal. For formal forms of address used for official documents and on very formal occasions, as well as for more detailed information on forms of address, see Debrett's *Correct Form* and Black's *Titles and Forms of Address*.

Addressee	Address	Salutation
Government Officers		
Cabinet minister	The Right Hon – –	Dear Minister
Member of Parliament	– –, Esq, adding MP after title or name and honours	Dear Minister
Minister of the Crown	if a Privy Counsellor, see relevant section below; otherwise, Member of Parliament or grade of peerage below	Dear Secretary of State, or Dear Minister if the matters concerns the department
Prime Minister	The Right Hon – –	Dear (Mr) Prime Minister
Privy Counsellor	The Right Hon – –, if not a peer; The Right Hon, the Earl of –, PC (PC after all orders and decorations)	according to rank
Secretary of State	The Right Hon – –, MP, Secretary of State for –, or The Secretary of State for –; otherwise according to rank	Dear Secretary of State
Diplomatic Officials		
Ambassador	His/Her Excellency the Ambassador of –, or HM Ambassador to –	Your Excellency; close letter: I have the honour to be, Sir/Madam (or according to rank), Your Excellency's obedient servant; spoken address: Your Excellency at least once, and then Sir or Madam by name
Consul	– –, Esq, HM Consul-General (Consul, or Vice-Consul, as the case may be)	Sir
Governor of a country	His Excellency (preceding all ranks and titles); if knighted: His Excellency Mr – –	according to rank; close letter: have the honour to be, Sir (or My Lord, if a peer), Your Excellency's obedient servant; spoken address: Your Excellency
Governor-General	His Excellency (preceding all ranks and titles) followed by ordinary designation, Governor-General of –. (The Governor-General of Canada has the rank of Right Hon, which he retains for life)	as for Governor
Governor-General's wife	the style Her Excellency is confined to wives of Governor-Generals of Commonwealth countries within the country administered by her husband	

(continued)

Forms of Address in the UK (*continued*)

Addressee	Address	Salutation
High Commissioner	His Excellency (preceding all ranks and titles) the High Commissioner of –	as for Ambassador
Lieutenant-Governor	Isle of Man, Jersey, and Guernsey	as for Governor
Civic Titles		
Lady Mayoress	as for Lord Mayor's wife	
Lord Mayor	the Lord Mayors of London, York, Belfast, Cardiff, Dublin, and also Sydney, Melbourne, Adelaide, Brisbane, and Hobart are styled: The Right Hon the Lord Mayor of –. Other Lord Mayors are styled: The Right Worshipful the Lord Mayor of –	My Lord Mayor, or Dear Lord Mayor
Lord Mayor's wife	The Lady Mayoress of –	My Lady Mayoress
Mayor	The Right Worshipful the Mayor of – (if mayor of a city); The Worshipful the Mayor of – (if mayor of a borough or town mayor)	Dear Mr Mayor (may be used for a man or woman); Mr Mayor, or Sir/Madam
Lord Provost	the Lord Provosts of Edinburgh and Glasgow are styled: The Right Hon the Lord Provost; the Lord Provosts of Perth, Aberdeen, and Dundee are styled: The Lord Provost of –	My Lord Provost
Provost	The Provost of –	Dear Lord Provost
Aldermen	Mr/Miss/Mrs Alderman –	Dear Sir; Dear Alderman; Dear Alderman –
Councillor	Councillor –; Miss/Mrs Councillor –	Dear Councillor; Dear Councillor –; Dear Miss/Mrs Councillor –; never Mr Councillor
The Bench		
Judge of City of London Court	as for Circuit Judge	
Judge, Circuit	His or Her Honour Judge –; if a Knight, His Honour Judge Sir – –	Dear Sir or Madam; spoken address: when on the bench, Your Honour; otherwise Sir
Judge of High Court (men)	The Hon Mr Justice –	Dear Sir; spoken address: when on the bench, My Lord or Your Lordship; otherwise Sir
Judge of High Court (women)	The Hon Mrs (or Miss) Justice –	Dear Madam; spoken address: when on the bench, My Lady or Your Ladyship; otherwise Madam
Justice of the Peace	as for Esquire (see peerage)	spoken address: when on the bench, Your Worship; otherwise as for Esquire
Lord Advocate	The Right Hon the Lord Advocate, or The Right Hon – –	as for Esquire (see peerage)
Lord Chancellor	The Right Hon the Lord High Chancellor	as for peer, according to rank (see peerage)
Lord Chief Justice	The Lord Chief Justice of England or The Right Hon Lord –, Lord Chief Justice of England	Dear Lord Chief Justice
Lord Justice Clerk and Lord Justice General	The Right Hon the Justice Clerk, and The Right Hon the Lord Justice General	My Lord, Dear Lord Justice General/Clerk, or Dear Lord –
Lord Justice of Appeal	The Right Hon Lord Justice –, or The Right Hon Sir – –	as for Judge of High Court
Lord of Appeal-in-Ordinary	as for Baron (see peerage)	
Lord of Session, Scottish	The Hon Lord/Lady –	My Lord/Lady/Madam, or Dear Lord/Lady/Madam –
Lord of Session's wife or widow	Lady –	as for a Baron's wife
Master of the Rolls	The Right Hon the Master of the Rolls, or The Right Hon –, according to rank	Dear Sir; spoken address: when on the bench, My Lord or Your Lordship; otherwise Sir
Queen's Counsel	– – Esq, QC	as for Esquire (see Peerage and Other Titles)
Sheriff	Sheriff Principal –	Dear Sheriff

Forms of Address in the UK (*continued*)

Addressee	Address	Salutation
Peerage and Other Titles		
Baron	The Right Hon Lord – (formal), The Lord – (social)	The Lord – (formal), Dear Lord – (social); spoken address: Lord –
Baroness in her own right	The Right Hon the Baroness – (formal), The Baroness – (social)	My Lady (formal), Dear Lady – (social); spoken address: Lady –
Baron's wife	The Right Hon Lady – (formal), The Lady – (social)	as for Baroness in her own right
Baron's children	The Hon – –	Dear Mr/Miss/Madam –
Baronet	Sir – –, Bt	Dear Sir (formal), Dear Sir C– (social); spoken address: Sir C–
Baronet's wife	Lady –	Dear Madam (formal), Dear Lady – (social); spoken address: Lady –
Countess	The Right Hon the Countess of –	as for Baroness in her own right
Courtesy titles	while his father is alive, the heir apparent to a Duke, Earl, or Marquess takes the highest of his father's other titles as a courtesy title; these courtesy titles are not preceded by The Most Hon or The Right Hon; in correspondence the title is not preceded by The	
Dames of Orders of Chivalry	Dame – –, followed by appropriate post-nominal letters	Dear Madam (formal), Dear Dame C– (social); spoken address: Dame C–
Duchess	Her Grace the Duchess of – (formal), The Duchess of – (social)	Dear Madam (formal), Dear Duchess (social); spoken address: Duchess
Duke	His Grace the Duke of – (formal), The Duke of – (social)	My Lord Duke (formal), Dear Duke (social); spoken address: Your Grace (formal), Duke (social)
Duke's daughter	Lady – – (formal), Dear Madam (social)	Dear Lady C–; spoken address: Lady C–
Duke's eldest son	see Courtesy titles	
Duke's younger son	Lord – –	My Lord (formal); Dear Lord C– (social); spoken address: My Lord (formal), Lord C– (social)
Earl	The Right Hon the Earl of – (formal), The Earl of – (social)	My Lord (formal), Dear Lord – (social); spoken address: My Lord (formal), Lord – (social)
Earl's daughter	as for Duke's daughter	
Earl's eldest son	see Courtesy titles	
Earl's wife	The Right Hon the Countess of – (formal), The Countess of – (social)	Madam (formal), Lady – (social); spoken address: Madam (formal), Lady – (social)
Earl's younger son	The Hon – –	as for Baron's children
Esquire	– – Esq	Sir; spoken address: Sir
Knight Bachelor	Sir – –	Dear Sir (formal), Dear Sir C– (social); spoken address: Sir C–
Knight's wife	as for a Baronet's wife	as for Knight Bachelor
Knight of an Order of Chivalry	Sir – –, followed by appropriate post-nominal letters	
Life Peer	as for Baron	
Life Peeress	as for Baroness in her own right	
Life Peer's children	as for Baron's children	
Life Peer's wife	as for Baron's wife	
Marchioness	The Most Hon the Marchioness of – (formal), The Marchioness of – (social)	as for Baroness
Marquess	The Most Hon the Marquess of – (formal), The Marquess of – (social)	My Lord (formal), Dear Lord – (social); spoken address: My Lord (formal), Lord – (social)
Marquess's daughter	Lady – –	as for Duke's daughter

(*continued*)

Forms of Address in the UK (*continued*)

Addressee	Address	Salutation
Marquess's eldest son	see Courtesy titles	
Marquess's younger son	Lord – –	as for Duke's younger son
Master	The Master of –; the title is used in Scottish peerage by the heir apparent or presumptive of a peer; heirs apparent of the senior grades of the peerage usually use a courtesy title	Dear Sir (formal), Dear Master of – (social); spoken address: Master, or Sir (formal), Master, or Mr – (social)
Master's wife	according to her husband's rank	
Prince	His Royal Highness the Duke of –, if a duke; His Royal Highness the Prince C–, if the son of a sovereign; otherwise His Royal Highness Prince C–	Sir; close letter: I have the honour to be, Your Royal Highness's most humble and obedient servant; spoken address: Your Royal Highness
Princess	Her Royal Highness the Duchess of –, if the wife of a Royal duke; Her Royal Highness The Princess C–; otherwise Her Royal Highness the Princess C–	Madam; close letter: I have the honour to be, Madam, Your Royal Highness's most humble and obedient servant; spoken address: Your Royal Highness
Queen Mother	Her Gracious Majesty Queen Elizabeth The Queen Mother, for state and formal documents; otherwise Her Majesty Queen – The Queen Mother	as for Queen Regent
Queen Regent	The Queen's Most Excellent Majesty, for state and formal documents; otherwise Her Majesty The Queen	Madam, May it please your Majesty; close letter: I have the honour to remain Madam, or, Majesty's most humble and obedient servant; spoken address: Your Majesty
Viscount	The Right Hon the Viscount – (formal), The Viscount – (social)	My Lord (formal), Dear Lord – (social); spoken address: Lord –
Viscount's wife	The Right Hon the Viscountess – (formal), The Viscountess – (social)	Madam (formal), Dear Lady – (social); spoken address: Lady –
Viscount's children	as for Baron's children	
Widow and Divorcee	widows and divorcees keep their husbands' titles until remarriage; the wife of the holder of a peerage becomes a dowager on the death of her husband or on the marriage of the new peer if unmarried at the time of succession; she is addressed as The Dowager Lady; the same title can be held by more than one person, hence the term is used less frequently today, and an alternative form, eg, The Right Hon C–, Countess of – is used, distinction being made by the use of the first name; the ex-wives of Marquesses and below are not styled The Most Hon or The Right Hon	

Clerical Titles

Addressee	Address	Salutation
Archbishop (Anglican)	Most Reverend the Lord Archbishop of –; (the Archbishops of Canterbury and York are Privy Counsellors, and should be addressed as The Most Reverend and Right Hon the Lord Archbishop of –)	Your Grace (more formal), Dear Archbishop, or My Lord Archbishop; spoken address: Your Grace
Archbishop (Roman Catholic)	His Grace the Archbishop of –	My Lord Archbishop; spoken address: Your Grace
Archdeacon	The Venerable the Archdeacon of –	Dear Archdeacon, Dear Mr Archdeacon, or Venerable Sir; spoken address: Archdeacon
Bishop (Anglican)	The Right Reverend the Lord Bishop of –; (the Bishop of London is a Privy Counsellor and should be addressed as The Right Reverend and Right Hon the Lord Bishop of London; the Bishop of Meath is styled The Most Reverend)	Dear Bishop or My Lord; spoken address: Bishop
Bishop (Episcopal Church in Scotland)	The Right Reverend – –, Bishop of –	as for Anglican bishop
Bishop (Roman Catholic)	His Lordship the Bishop of –, or The Right Reverend – –, Bishop of –; in Ireland, The Most Reverend is used instead of The Right Reverend	My Lord, or My Lord Bishop; spoken address: My Lord, or My Lord Bishop
Canon (Anglican)	The Reverend Canon – –	Dear Canon, or Dear Canon –; spoken address: Canon, or Canon –
Canon (Roman Catholic)	The Very Reverend Canon – –	Very Reverend Sir; spoken address: Canon –
Cardinal	His Eminence Cardinal –; if an archbishop, His Eminence the Cardinal Archbishop of –	Your Eminence, My Lord Cardinal, or Dear Cardinal –; spoken address: Your Eminence
Dean and priest	The Reverend – –	Dear Mr/Mrs/Miss/Ms – (or Father – if a male priest prefers, or if Roman Catholic)
Monsignor	The Very Reverend Monsignor – –	Reverend Sir or Dear Monsignor; spoken address: Monsignor –
Pope	His Holiness the Pope	Your Holiness or Most Holy Father; close letter: if Roman Catholic: I have the honour to be Your Holiness's most devoted and obedient child (or, most humble child); if not Roman Catholic: I have the honour to be (or remain) Your Holiness's obedient servant; spoken address: Your Holiness

Forms of Address in the UK (*continued*)

Addressee	Address	Salutation
Prebendary (Anglican)	The Very Reverend Prebendary – –	Dear Prebendary, or Dear Prebendary –; spoken address: Prebendary, or Prebendary –
Prebendary (Roman Catholic)	The Very Reverend Prebendary – –	Very Reverend Sir; spoken address: Prebendary –
Rabbi	Rabbi – –; with a doctorate, Rabbi Doctor – –	Dear Sir, Dear Rabbi, or Dear Doctor; spoken address: Rabbi –, or Doctor –
Armed Forces	professional rank always precedes any other rank or title, for example, Admiral the Right Hon the Earl of, Air Marshal Sir –; officers below the rank of Rear-Admiral and Marshall of the Royal Air Force are entitled to RN and RAF respectively after their name; officers in the women's services add WRNS, WRAF, or WRAC	
Academic		
Chancellor of University	The Chancellor of the University of –	Dear Sir/Madam, My Lord (if a peer), or Dear Chancellor
Dean, Director, Master, Mistress, President, Principal, Provost, Rector, and Warden of university college	The Dean/Director, etc, of – College, University of –, or title/status – – (position) of – College, University of –	as for Chancellor, substituting relevant position
High Steward	The High Steward of the University of –	Dear High Steward
Professor	Professor – –; if in holy orders, The Reverend Professor	Dear Sir/Madam, or Dear Professor; spoken address: according to rank
Vice-Chancellor	The Vice-Chancellor of the University of –; The Reverend the Vice-Chancellor of Oxford, and The Right Worshipful the Vice-Chancellor of the University of Cambridge	Dear Vice-Chancellor

See Also **The Peerage (The United Kingdom)**

Associations and Societies in the UK

(ind = individuals; f = firms; org = organizations; soc = societies; where not specified, figures refer to numbers of individual members; data given is year organization was founded.)

Arts, Culture, and Media

Actors' Equity Association, British (EQUITY) (45,000), Guild House, Upper St Martins Lane, London WC2M 9EG; 1930

Arts Ltd, National Campaign for the (900 ind; 100 f; 550 org), Francis House, Francis Street, London SW1P 1DE

Arts, Royal Academy of (RA) (85 ind; 71,000 friends of the RA), Burlington House, Piccadilly, London W1V 0DS; 1768

Authors' Licensing & Collecting Society (10,000), 74 New Oxford Street, London WC1A 1EF; 1977

Authors, Society of (5,500), 84 Drayton Gardens, London SW10 9SB; 1884

Broadcasting Entertainment, Cinematograph, & Theatre Union (29,300), 111 Wardour Street, London W1V 4AY; 1991

Contemporary Arts, Institute of (ICA) (7,000), Nash House, The Mall, London SW1Y 5AH; 1947

Dancing, Royal Academy of (RAD) (20,000), 36 Battersea Square, London SW11 3RA; 1920

Decorative and Fine Arts Societies, National Association of (73,000), NADFAS House, 8 Guildford Street, London WC1N 1DT; 1968

Dickens Fellowship (5,500 ind; 5 affiliated societies), 48 Doughty Street, London WC1N 2LF; 1902

Entertainment Unions, Federation of (140,000 ind; 6 org), 1 Highfield, Twyford, Winchester, Hants SO21 1QR; 1990

Film and Television Arts, British Academy of (BAFTA) (3,300), 195 Piccadilly, London W1V 0LN; 1963

Film Institute, British (BFI) (41,500 ind; 356 f; 255 film soc), 21 Stephen Street, London W1P 2LN; 1933

Fine Arts, Royal Glasgow Institute of the (1,500), 5 Oswald Street, Glasgow G1 4QR; 1861

Flute Society, British (2,000), Flat B, 336 Alexandra Park Road, London N22 4BD; 1982

Folk Dance and Song Society, English (5,800 ind; 135 clubs; 450 org), Cecil Sharpe House, 2 Regent's Park Road, London NW1 7AY; 1932

Humanist Association, British (3,050 ind; 30 org), 47 Theobalds Road, London WC1X 8SP; 1963

Jane Austen Society (2,100 ind; 45 libraries), Carlton House, Redwood Lane, Medstead, Alton, Hants GU34 5PE; 1940

Journalists, Chartered Institute of (2,000), 2 Dock Offices, Surrey Quays, Lower Road, London SE16 2XU; 1884

Musicians, Incorporated Society of (4,550 ind; 150 f), 10 Stratford Place, London W1N 9AE; 1882

Newspaper Editors, Guild of British (450), 74–77 Great Russell Street, London WC1B 3DA; 1946

Operatic & Dramatic Association, National (NODA) (4,500), 1 Crestfield Street, London WC1H 8AU; 1899

Organists, Incorporated Association of (6,000), 11 Stonehill Drive, Bromyard HR7 4XB; 1927

Poetry Society (2,700), 22 Betterton Street, London WC2H 9BU; 1909

Publishers' Association (180 f), 19 Bedford Square, London WC1B 3HJ; 1896

Publishers' Association, Scottish (68 f), Scottish Book Centre, 137 Dundee Street, Edinburgh EH11 1BG; 1974

Recorded Music Societies, Federation of (10,000 ind; 252 f), 29 Brockenhurst Close, Gillingham ME8 0HG; 1936

Songwriters, Composers, and Authors, British Academy of (4,000), Hanway Street, London W1P 9DE; 1947

Talking Newspaper Association of the United Kingdom (150,000), National Recording Centre, 10 Browning Road, Heathfield, East Sussex TN21 8DB; 1974

Television Society, Royal (3,500 ind; 103 f), Holborn Hall, 100 Gray's Inn Road, London WC1X 8AL; 1927

Voice of the Listener and Viewer (VLV) (2,530 ind; 40 colleges and university departments; 24 soc), 101 King's Drive, Gravesend, Kent DA12 5BQ; 1983

Women Writers & Journalists, Society of (500), 110 Whitehall Road, Chingford, London E4 6DW; 1894

Writers' Guild of Great Britain (2,000), 430 Edgware Road, London W2 1EH; 1959

Business, Professional, and Labour

Accountants, Association of International (8,000), South Bank Building, Kingsway, Gateshead, Newcastle upon Tyne NE1 0JS; 1928

Accountants, Chartered Association of Certified (153,000), 29 Lincoln's Inn Fields, London WC2A 3EE; 1900

Accountants, Institute of Financial (8,000), Burford House, 44 London Road, Sevenoaks TN13 1AS; 1916

Accounting Technicians, Association of Authorised (21,000 ind; 68,000 f), 154 Clerkenwell Road, London EC1R 5AD; 1981

Actuaries, Institute of (8,506), Staple Inn Hall, High Holborn, London WC1V 7QJ; 1848

Administrative Management, Institute of (10,000), 40 Chatsworth Parade, Petts Wood, Orpington BR5 1RW; 1915

Advertising, Institute of Practitioners in (IPA) (1,168 ind; 230 f), 44 Belgrave Square, London SW1X 8QS; 1917

Aeronautical Society, Royal (18,000), 4 Hamilton Place, London W1V 0BQ; 1866

Agricultural Botany, National Institute of (3,500 ind; 500 f), Huntingdon Road, Cambridge CB3 0LE; 1919

Agricultural Society of England, Royal (17,227), National Agricultural Centre, Stoneleigh Park CV8 2LZ; 1838

Aircraft Engineers, Association of Licensed (1,400), The Old Court House, London Road, Ascot SL5 7EN; 1970

Aircraft Owners' and Pilots' Association of the United Kingdom (4,500 ind; 146 f), 50a Cambridge Street, London SW1V 4QQ; 1966

Air Line Pilots' Association, British (BALPA) (8,000), 81 New Road, Harlington, Hayes UB3 5BG; 1937

Arboricultural Association (2,300 ind; 300 f), Ampfield House, Ampfield, Romsey SO51 9PA; 1964

Architects, Royal Institute of British (RIBA) (28,000), 66 Portland Place, London W1N 4AD; 1834

Architects in Scotland, Royal Incorporation of (3,800), 15 Rutland Square, Edinburgh EH1 2BE; 1916

Architects' & Surveyors' Institute (ASI) (6,500), St Mary House, 15 St Mary Street, Chippenham, Wilts SN15 3WD; 1989

Astrological Association of Great Britain (1,500), 396 Caledonian Road, London N1 1DN; 1958

Astronomical Society, Royal (3,000), Burlington House, Piccadilly, London W1V 0NL; 1820

Bakers, Food, and Allied Workers' Union (BFAWU) (32,000), Stanborough House, Great North Road, Stanborough, Welwyn Garden City Al8 7TA; 1849

Bank Customers, National Association of (4,000 ind; 12,000 f; 25 org), Llantony Secunda Manor, Church Road, Caldicot, Gwent NP6 4HT; 1992

Bankers, Chartered Institute of (85,000), 10 Lombard Street, London EC3V 9AS; 1879

Biochemical Society (9,000), 59 Portland Place, London W1N 3AJ; 1911

Biologists, Association of Applied (1,190), c/o Horticulture Research International, Wellesbourne, Stratford-upon-Avon CV35 9EF; 1904

Booksellers' Association of Great Britain & Ireland (3,500 f), Minster House, 272–274 Vauxhall Bridge Road, London SW1V 1BA; 1895

Building Employers' Confederation (4,000), 82 New Cavendish Street, London W1M 8AD; 1878

Building Services Engineers, Chartered Institution of (15,500), 222 Balham High Road, London, SW12 9BS; 1897

Business Executives, Association of (2,000 ind; 18,000 org), William House, 14 Worple Road, London SW19 4DD; 1973

Business & Professional Women, International Federation of (60,000), 16 Cloisters House, 8 Battersea Park Road, London SW8 4BG; 1930

Business & Professional Women UK (5,000), 23 Ansdell Street, London W8 5BN; 1938

Chemical Engineers, Institution of (21,000), Davis Building, 165–189 Railway Terrace, Rugby CV21 3HQ; 1922

Chemistry, Royal Society of (45,000), Burlington House, Piccadilly, London W1V 0BN; 1841

Civil Engineers, Institution of (79,756), 1–7 Great George Street, London SW1P 3AA; 1818

Computer Professionals, Association of (4,000), 204 Barnett Wood Lane, Ashtead KT21 2DB; 1994

Computer Society, British (33,000), 1 Sanford Street, Swindon SN1 1HJ; 1957

Computer Users' Forum (4,700 ind; 4,300 f), 1 Stuart Road, Thornton Heath CR7 8RA; 1984

Concrete Society (7,000 f), 112 Windsor Road, Slough SL1 2AY; 1966

Economic Society, Royal (3,000), Department of Economics, London Business School, Sussex Place, Regent's Park, London NW1 4SA; 1890

Electrical Engineers, Institution of (130,000), Savoy Place, London WC2R 0BL; 1871

Electronics & Electrical Incorporated Engineers, Institution of (27,000), Savoy Hill House, Savoy Hill, London WC2R 0BS; 1990

Encouragement of the Arts, Manu-factures, and Commerce, Royal Society for the (RSA) (19,000), 8 John Adam Street, London WC2N 6EZ; 1754

Engineers, Association of Municipal (11,500), c/o The Institution of Civil Engineers, 1 Great George Street, London SW1P 3AA; 1984

Engineers, Institution of Gas (5,800 ind; 3,588 f), 21 Portland Place, London W1N 3AF; 1863

Engineers, Institution of Mechanical (77,000), 1 Birdcage Walk, London SW1H 9JJ; 1847

Engineers, Institution of Structural (23,000), 11 Upper Belgrave Street, London SW1X 8BH; 1908

Engineers' & Managers' Association (32,000), Flaxman House, Gogmore Lane, Chertsy KT16 9JS; 1913

Engineers & Technicians, Institute of (5,500), 100 Grove Vale, London SE22 8DR; 1948

Entomological Society, Royal (2,000), 41 Queen's Gate, London SW7 5HR; 1833

Estate Agents, National Association of (10,000), Arbon House, 21 Jury Street, Warwick CV34 4EH; 1962

Farmers' Union, National (100,000), 22 Long Acre, London WC2E 9LY; 1908

Fire Brigades' Union (FBU) (50,000), 68 Coombe Road, Kingston–upon-Thames KT2 7AE; 1918

Fire Engineers, Institution of (10,500), 148 New Walk, Leicester LE1 7QB; 1918

Forensic Science Society (2,000 ind; 75 f), Clarke House, 18a Mount Parade, Harrogate HG1 1BX; 1959

Foresters, Institute of Chartered (1,434 ind; 836 f), 7A St Colme Street, Edinburgh EH3 6AA; 1925

Forestry Society, Royal Scottish (1,400), 62 Queen Street, Edinburgh EH2 4NA; 1854

Freight Transport Association (12,000), Hermes House, St John's Road, Tunbridge Wells TN4 9UZ; 1890

Frozen Food Corp, British (350 f), 2nd Floor, Barclays Bank Chambers, 55 High Street, Grantham NG31 6NE; 1948

Geographers, Institute of British (2,000), 1 Kensington Gore, London SW7 2AR; 1933

Geographical Association (5,176 ind; 5,723 f), 343 Fulwood Road, Sheffield S10 3BP; 1893

Geological Society (7,874 ind; 1,532 f), Burlington House, Piccadilly, London W1V 0JU; 1807

Geologists' Association (2,200 ind; 300 f), Burlington House, Piccadilly, London W1V 9AG; 1858

GMB (formerly General, Municipal, Boilermakers' and Allied Trades' Union) (800,000), 22–24 Worple Street, London SW19 4DD; 1889

Hairdressers' Federation, National (7,000), 11 Goldington Road, Bedford, Beds MK40 3JY; 1942

Hairdressing Council (18,000), 12 David House, 45 High Street, London SE25 6HJ; 1964

Highland & Agricultural Society of Scotland, Royal (14,500), Royal Highland Centre, Ingliston, Edinburgh EH28 8NF; 1784

Highways & Transportation, Institution of (10,500), 3 Lygon Place. London SW1W 0JS; 1930

Hospitality Association, British (23,000 f), Queens House, 55–56 Lincoln's Inn Fields, London WC24 3BH; 1910

Hotel and Catering International Management Association (23,000), 191 Trinity Road, London SW17 7HN; 1971

House Builders' Federation (3,000), 82 New Cavendish Street, London W1M 8AD; 1947

Industrial Retailers & Businesses, Alliance of (20,000), Alliance House, 14 Pierpont Street, Worcester WR1 1TA; 1983

Industrial Society (12,000 f), Peter Runge House, 3 Carlton House Terrace, London SW1Y 5DG; 1918

Industry, Confederation of British (CBI) (240,000 f), Centre Point, 103 New Oxford Street, London WC1A 1DU; 1965

Insurance Institute, Chartered (70,000), 20 Aldermanbury, London EC2V 7HY; 1912

Iron and Steel Trades' Confederation (32,000), Swinton House, 324 Gray's Inn Road, London WC1X 8DD; 1917

Librarians, Association of Assistant (8,787), c/o Library Association, 7 Ridmount Street, London WC1E 7AE; 1895

Life Insurance Association (14,000), Citadel House, Chorleywood, Rickmans-worth WD3 5PF; 1972

Locomotive Engineers & Firemen, Associated Society of (18,612), 9 Arkwright Road, Hampstead, London NW3 6AB; 1880

Management Accountants, Chartered Institute of (40,000), 63 Portland Place, London W1N 4AB; 1919

Managerial and Professional Officers, Federated Union of (14,000), Terminus House, The High, Harlow CM20 1TZ; 1986

Marketing, Chartered Institute of (26,000), Moor Hall, Cookham, Maidenhead SL6 9QH; 1911

Market Traders' Federation, National (38,650), Hampton House, Hanshaw Lane, Hoyland, Barnsley S74 0HA; 1899

Master Builders, Federation of (17,500), Gordon Fisher House, 14–15 Great James Street, London WC1N 3DP; 1941

Mathematical Association (6,000 ind; 2,000 schools), 259 London Road, Leicester LE2 3BE; 1872

Medical Secretaries, Practice Administrators, & Receptionists, Association of (2,400), Tavistock House North, Tavistock Square, London WC1H 9LN; 1964

Meteorological Society, Royal (3,000), 104 Oxford Road, Reading RG1 7LJ; 1850

Microbiology, Society for General (5,200), Marlborough House, Basingstoke Road, Spencers Wood, Reading RG1 1AE; 1945

Mining & Metallurgy, Institution of (4,800), 44 Portland Place, London W1N 4BR; 1892

Motor Industry, Institute of the (29,500), Fanshaws, Brickendon, Hertford SG13 8PQ; 1920

Motor Vehicle Retail & Repair Industry, National Joint Council for (200,000), 201 Great Portland Street, London W1N 6AB; 1945

Museums' Association (3,000 ind; 900 museums), 42 Clerkenwell Close, London EC1R 0PA; 1889

Naval Architects, Royal Institution of (5,600), 10 Upper Belgrave Street, London SW1X 8BQ; 1860

Occupational Safety & Health, Institution of (14,300), The Grange, Highfield Drive, Wigston, Leicester LE18 1NN; 1945

Performing Rights Society (24,000 ind; 2,344 f), 29–33 Berners Street, London W1P 4AA; 1914

Petroleum, Institute of (7,800 ind; 380 f), 61 New Cavendish Street, London W1M 8AR; 1913

Photographic Society, Royal (10,000), The Octagon, Milsom Street, Bath BA1 1DN; 1853

Photography, British Institute of Professional (4,200), 2 Amwell End, Ware SG12 9HN; 1901

Physics, Institute of (21,000), 76 Portland Place, London W1N 4AA; 1970

Plant Engineers, Institution of (6,000), 77 Great Peter Street, London SW1P 2EZ; 1946

Police Federation of England & Wales (125,000), 15–17 Langley Road, Surbiton KT6 6LP; 1919

Poultry Meat Federation, British (95 percent of UK poultry meat producers; 7 trade associations), High Holborn House, 52–52 High Holborn, London WC1V 6SX; 1991

Professionals, Managers & Specialists, Institution of (90,434), 75–79 York Road, London SE1 7AQ; 1919

Public Finance & Accountancy, Chartered Institute of (12,000), 3 Robert Street, London WC2N 6BH; 1885

Purchasing & Supply, Chartered Institute of (20,550), Easton House, Easton-on-the-Hill, Stamford PE9 3NZ; 1932

Qualified Private Secretaries, Institute of (3,000), 68 Longmoor Road, Long Eaton, Nottingham NG10 4FP; 1957

Retail Motor Industry Federation (12,000), 201 Great Portland Street, London W1N 6AB; 1913

Retail Newsagents, National Federation of (28,500), Yeoman House, Sekforde Street, London EC1R 0HD; 1919

Soil Association (5,000), Organic Food & Farming Centre, 86–88 Colston Street, Bristol BS1 5BB; 1946

Statistical Society, Royal (6,000), 12 Errol Street, London EC1Y 8LX; 1834

Surveyors, Royal Institution of Chartered (90,000; 70,000 f), 12 Great George Street, London SW1P 3AD; 1868

Taxation, Chartered Institute of (9,500), 12 Upper Belgrave Street, London SW1X 8BB; 1930

Textile Institute (8,900 ind; 350 f), International Headquarters, 10 Blackfriars Street, Manchester M3 5DR; 1910

Timber Growers' Association (1,796 ind; 69 f), 5 Dublin Street, Lane South, Edinburgh EH1 3PX; 1984

Town Planning Institute, Royal (17,000), 26 Portland Place, London W1N 4BE; 1914

Trades Union Congress (TUC) (7,200,000; 69 trade unions), Congress House, 23–28 Great Russell Street, London WC13 3LS; 1868

Transport, Chartered Institute of (21,000), 80 Portland Place, London W1N 4DP; 1919

Travel Agents, Association of British (3,500 f), 55–57 Newman Street, London W1P 4AH; 1950

Travel & Tourism, Institute of (3,000 ind; 125 f), 113 Victoria Street, St Albans AL1 3TJ; 1956

Veterinary Association, British (8,850), 7 Mansfield Street, London W1M 0AT; 1882

Veterinary Surgeons, Royal College of (16,800), Belgravia House, 62–64 Horseferry Road, London SW1P 2AG; 1844

Water & Environmental Management, Chartered Institution of (12,000), 15 John Street, London WC1N 2EB; 1895

Welding Institute (5,000 ind; 2,600 f), Abington Hall, Abington, Cambridge CB1 6AL; 1946

Legal

Bar Association, International (17,000), 2 Harewood Place, Hanover Square, London W1R 9HB; 1947

Bar, General Council of the (over 9,000), 3 Bedford Row, London WC1R 4DB; 1894

Criminal Bar Association of England & Wales (2,000), Rooms 15–18 (ground floor), Chancery House, London WC2A 1QX; 1969

Environmental Law Association, UK (1,056 ind; 119 f), Honeycroft House, Pangbourne Road, Upper Basildon RG8 8LP; 1987

JUSTICE (1,500), 59 Carter Lane, London EC4V 5AQ; 1957

Law Agents' Society, Scottish (2,000), Ground Floor, 79 West Regent Street, Glasgow G2 2AW; 1884

Law Society (58,431), 113 Chancery Lane, London W2A 1PL; 1831

Law Society of Northern Ireland (1,450 ind; 550 f), 98 Victoria Street, Belfast BT1 3JZ; 1922

Law Society of Scotland (8,000), 26 Drumsheugh Gardens, Edinburgh EH3 7YR; 1949

Legal Action Group (1,200), 242–244 Pentonville Road, London N1 9UN; 1971

Legal Association, British (1,700), 2 Princess Way, Swansea SA1 3LW; 1964

Legal Executives, Institute of (22,000), Kempston Manor, Kempston, Bedford MK42 7AB; 1963

Magistrates' Association (28,500), 28 Fitzroy Square, London W1P 6DD; 1920

Penal Reform, Howard League for (3,000), 708 Holloway Road, London N19 3NL; 1866

Public Teachers of Law, Society of (2,200), All Souls College, Oxford OX1 4AL; 1908

Solicitors' Family Law Association (4,000), PO Box 302, Orpington, Kent BR6 8QX; 1912

Women Barristers, Association of (500), PO Box 11750, London WC2A 3RX; 1991

Women Solicitors, Association of (over 5,500), The Law Society, 50 Chancery Lane, London WC2A 1SX; 1919

Special Interest and Social

Abortion Campaign, National (3,500 ind; 250 org and unions), The Print House, 18 Ashwin Street, London E8 3DL; 1975

Adoption and Fostering, British Agencies for (1,644 ind; 168 agencies; 52 associations), Skyline House, 200 Union Street, London SE1 0LY; 1980

Age Discrimination in Employment, Campaign Against (6,000), 395 Barlow Road, Altrincham, Cheshire WA14 5HW; 1989

Amnesty International Ltd (1,000,000), 1 Easton Street, London WC1X 8DJ; 1961

Amnesty International – UK Section (120,000), 99–119 Roseberry Avenue, London EC1R 4RE; 1961

Arms Trade, Campaign Against (3,500 ind; 300 org), 11 Goodwin Street, London N4 3HQ; 1974

CAMRA (Campaign for Real Ale Ltd) (44,000), 230 Hatfield Road, St Albans AL1 4LW; 1971

Carers' National Association (11,000), 20–25 Glasshouse Yard, London EC1A 4JS; 1988

Children's Bureau, National (1,000 ind; 500 f), 8 Wakley Street, London EC1V 7QE; 1963

Civic Trust Societies, National Council of (240,000), c/o Carlton House Terrace, London SW1Y 5AW; 1919

Civil Service Retirement Fellowship (120,000), 1b Deal's Gateway, Blackheath Road, London SE10 8BW; 1968

CLEANAIR – Campaign for a Smoke-free Environment (1,500), 20 Church Path, Emsworth, Hants PO16 7DP; 1982

Community Workers, Association of (300 ind; 100 f), Stephenson Building, Elswick Road, Newcastle upon Tyne NE4 6SQ; 1968

Counselling, British Association for (11,750 ind; 690 f), 1 Regent Place, Rugby CV21 2PJ; 1977

Cruelty to Children, National Society for the Prevention of (NSPCC) (50,000 voluntary workers), NSPCC National Centre, 42 Curtain Road, London EC2A 3NH; 1884 **NSPCC Child Protection Helpline:** (0800 800500)

Divorced and Separated, National Council for the (10,000), 8 South Knighton Road, Leicester LE2 3LN; 1974

Family Therapy, Association for (1,404), 18 Winnipeg Drive, Lakeside, Cardiff CF2 6ET; 1979

Foster Care Association, National (10,000 ind; 180 f), Leonard House, 5–7 Marshalsea Road, London SE1 1EP; 1974

Homosexual Equality, Campaign for (5,000), PO Box 342, London WC1X 0DU; 1970

Immigrants, Joint Council for the Welfare of (300 ind; 450 corporate), 115 Old Street, London EC1V 9JR; 1967

Lesbian & Gay Employment Rights (LAGER) (6,500), Unit 1G, Leroy House, 436 Essex Road, London N1 3QP; 1984

Liberty (National Council for Civil Liberties) (7,000 ind; 700 org), 21 Tabard Street, London SE1 4LA; 1934

LIFE (30,500), LIFE House, Newbold Terrace, Leamington Spa, Warwicks CV32 4EA; 1970

Mothers' Union (500,000), 24 Tufton Street, London SW1P 3RB; 1876

Nonsmokers' Rights, Association for, Melgund Centre, Melgund Terrace, Edinburgh EH7 4BU; 1981

Nuclear Disarmament, Campaign for (CND) (45,000 ind; 627 org), 162 Holloway Road, London N7 8DQ; 1958

Peace Pledge Union (1,185 ind; 1,162 org), 41B Brecknock Road, London N7 0BT; 1934

Press & Broadcasting Freedom, Campaign for (1,550 ind; 50 org), 8 Cynthia Street, London N1 9JF; 1979

Protection of Unborn Children, Society for the, (50,000), 5–6 Matthew Street, London SW1P 2JT; 1967

Right to Enjoy Smoking Tobacco, Freedom Organisation for the (FOREST) (5,000), 2 Grosvenor Gardens, London SW1W 0DH; 1979

Rotary International in Great Britain & Ireland (65,000), Kinwarton Road, Alcester, Warwicks; 1914

Royal Society, The (1,170), 6 Carlton House Terrace, London SW1Y 5AG; 1660

Sailors' Society, British & International (50,000 ind; 30,000 f), Orchard Place, Southampton SO14 3AT; 1818

Service to the Elderly, British Association for (700 ind; 150 f), 119 Hassell Street, Newcastle under Lyme ST5 1AX; 1982

Social Care Association (4,000 ind; 100 f), 23a Victoria Road, Surbiton KT6 4JZ; 1949

Social Workers, British Association of (10,000), 16 Kent Street, Birmingham B5 6RD; 1970

Sociological Association, British (2,300 ind; 2 f), Unit 3G, Mountjoy Research Centre, Stockton Road, Durham DH1 3UR; 1950

Spiritualist Association of Great Britain (3,000), 33 Belgrave Square, London SW1X 8QB; 1872

Stonewall (15,000), 16 Clerkenwell Close, London EC1R 0AA; 1989

Taxpayers' Association, British (2,500 ind; 500 f), Harcourt House, 19 Cavendish Square, London W1M 9AB; 1919

Third World First (5,500), 232 Cowley Road, Oxford OX4 1VH; 1969

United Grand Lodge of England (about 343,000), Freemason's Hall, Great Queen Street, London WC2B 5AZ; 1813

Victims' Support National Office (432 f), National Office, Cranmer House, 39 Brixton Road, London SW9 6DZ; 1979

Welfare Officers, Institute of (2,000), 254 Hanging Ditch, Corn Exchange, Manchester M4 3BQ; 1945

Women of Great Britain, National Council of (52 branches; about 90 affiliates), 36 Danbury Street, Islington, London N1 8JU; 1895

Women's Institutes National Federation of (NFWI) (296,000), 104 New Kings Road, London SW9 4LY; 1915

Educational

Adult Continuing Education, National Institute of (269 ind; 204 f), 21 De Montfort Street, Leicester LE1 7GE; 1983

Commonwealth Universities, Association of (448 universities and f), John Foster House, 36 Gordon Square, London WC1H 0PF; 1913

Early Childhood Education, British Association for (5,000), 111 City View House, 463 Bethnal Green Road, London E2 9QY; 1923

Educational Inspectors, Advisers, & Consultants, National Association of (2,500), 1 Heath Square, Boltro Road, Haywards Heath RH16 1BL; 1918

Educational Institute of Scotland (EIS) (49,371), 46 Moray Place, Edinburgh EH3 6BH; 1847

Environmental Education, National Association for (2,000), c/o Wolverhampton University, Walsall Campus, Gorway, Walsall WS1 3BD; 1960

Geographical Society, Royal (12,357), 1 Kensington Gore, London SW7 2AR; 1830

Geographical Society, Royal Scottish (2,000), Graham Hills Building, University of Strathclyde, Glasgow G1 1QE; 1884

Gifted Children, National Association for (2,000 ind; 80 f), c/o Park Campus, Boughton Green Road, Northampton NN2 7AL; 1966

Head Teachers & Deputies, National Association of (38,500) 1 Heath Square, Boltro Road, Haywards Heath RH16 1BL; 1897

Independent Schools Careers Organisation (80,000 ind; 381 f), 12A–18A Princess Way, Camberley GU15 3SP; 1942

International Schools, European Council of (563 ind; 807 f), 21 Lavant Street, Petersfield GU32 3EL; 1965

Local Education Authorities, Council of (115 LEAs), 66a Eaton Square, London SW1W 9BH; 1974

MBAs, Association of (8,000 ind; 448 f), 15 Duncan Terrace, London N1 8BZ; 1967

Music Education, International Society for (1,600 ind; 50 f), International Centre for Research in Music Education, University of Reading, Bulmershe Court, Reading RG6 1HY; 1953

Preceptors, College of (3,500), Coppice Row, Theydon Bois, Epping CM16 7DN; 1846

Primary Education, National Association for (1,000 ind; 150 f), Queens Building, Leicester University, Barrack Road, Northampton NN2 6AF; 1980

Science Education, Association for (22,000 ind; 52 f), College Lane, Hatfield AL10 9AA; 1902

Special Educational Needs, National Association for (9,000), York House, Exhall Grange, Wheelwright Lane, Coventry CV7 9HP; 1992

Teaching of the Social Sciences, Association for the (700 ind; 400 f), PO Box 461, Sheffield S2 2RH; 1965

Teachers & Lecturers, Association of (ATL) (165,000), 7 Northumberland Street, London WC2N 5DA; 1979

Teachers of Mathematics, Association of (2,400 ind; 1,540 f), 7 Shaftesbury Street, Derby DE23 8YB; 1955

Townswomen's Guilds (90,000) Chamber of Commerce House, 75 Harborne Road, Birmingham B15 3DA; 1928

United Kingdom Reading Association (1,200), c/o Warrington Road County Primary School, Naylor Road, Widnes WA80BP; 1963

University Administrators, Association of (3,200), University of Manchester, Oxford Road, Manchester M13 9PL; 1993

University Teachers, Association of (31,000), 9 Pembridge Road, London W11 3JY; 1919

University Teachers (Scotland), Association of (4,800), 6 Castle Street, Edinburgh EH2 3AT; 1919

Women Graduates, British Federation of (2,250), 4 Maudeville Courtyard, 142 Battersea Park Road, London SW11 4NB; 1907

Workers' Education Association (150,000), 17 Victoria Square, London E2 9PB; 1903

Environmental Preservation and Animals

Abolition of Vivisection, British Union for the (8,200), 16a Crane Grove, London N7 8LB; 1898

Advocates for Animals (over 3,000), 10 Queensferry Street, Edinburgh EH2 4PG; 1912

Anglers' Conservation Association (14,500 ind; 234 f; 764 org), 23 Castlegate, Grantham, Lincs NG31 6SW; 1948

Animal Aunts (6,500), 45 Fairview Road, Headley Down, Hants GU35 8HQ; 1987

Animal Behaviour, Association for the Study of (1,350), School of Biology, University of St Andrews, Fife KY6 9TS; 1936

Animal Welfare, University Federation for (1,690 ind; 50 f), 8 Hamilton Close, Potters Bar, Herts EN6 3QD; 1926

Aviculture, National Council for/ National Bird Theft Register (7,500), 4 Haven Crescent, Werrington, Stoke-on-Trent, Staffs ST9 0EY; 1935

Bat Conservation Trust (2,000), London Ecology Centre, 45 Shelton Street, London WC2H 9HJ; 1990

Born Free Foundation (10,000), Coldharbour, Dorking, Surrey RH5 6HA; 1991

Butterfly Conservation (10,000), Box 222 Dedham, Colchester CO7 6EY; 1968

Canine Defence League, National (30,250 ind; 826 f; 125,624 supporters), 17 Wakley Street, London EC1V 7LT; 1891

Care for the Wild (60,000), 1 Ashfolds, Horsham Road, Rusper, W Sussex RH12 4QX; 1984

Cats' Protection League (46,000), 17 Kings Road, Horsham RH13 5PN; 1927

Clean Air and Environmental Protection, National Society for (395 ind; 111 f; 284 local authorities), 136 North Street, Brighton BN1 1RG; 1899

Compassion in World Farming (12,000), 5a Charles Street, Petersfield, Hants GU32 3EH; 1967

Conservation of Artistic and Historic Works, United Kingdom Institute for (1,500 ind; 530 f), 6 Whitehorse Mews, Westminster Bridge Road, London SE1 7QD; 1979

Conservation of Plants & Gardens, National Council for the (over 7,000 ind; 50 org), The Pines, Wisley Garden, Woking, Surrey GU23 6QP; 1978

Conservation Volunteers, British Trust for (12,000), 36 St Mary's Street, Wallingford OX10 0EU; 1959

Cruel Sports, League Against (35,000), Sparling House, 83–87 Union Street, London SE1 1SG; 1924

EarthKind (3,500), Humane Education Centre, Bounds Green Road, London N22 4EU; 1955

Ecological Society, British (4,800), 26 Blades Court, Deodar Road, Putney, London SW15 2NU; 1913

Endangered Species, People's Trust for (about 50,000 supporters),15 Cloisters Business Centre, 8 Battersea Park Road, London SW8 4BG; 1997

Environmental Transport Association (10,000 ind; 110 f), The Old Post House, Heath Road, Weybridge KT13 8RS; 1990

Environment and Nature Conservation, Young People's Trust for the (250,000), 8 Leapale Road, Guildford, Surrey GU1 4JX; 1981

Environment Network, Women's (3,550 ind; 35 f; 10 org), 3D Aberdeen Studios, 22 Highbury Grove, London N5 2EA; 1988

Fauna and Flora Preservation Society (5,000), 1 Kensington Gore, London SW7 2AR; 1903

Friends of the Earth (200,000), 26–28 Underwood Street, London N1 7JQ; 1971

Friends of the Earth, Scotland (4,000) Bonnington Mill, 72 Newhaven Road, Edinburgh EH 5QE

Goat Society, British (3,200), 34–36 Fore Street, Bovey Tracey, Newton Abbot, Devon TQ13 9AD; 1879

Greenpeace (UK: 200,000; World: 2,000,000), Canonbury Villas, London N1 2PN; UK: 1979; World: 1971

Hedgehog Preservation Society, British (10,300), Knowbury House, Ludlow SY8 3LQ; 1982

Horse Society, British (63,500 ind; 138 f; 43,000 riding clubs affiliated), British Equestrian Centre, Stoneleigh Park, Kenilworth, Warks CV8 2LR; 1947

Humane Research, Dr Hadwen Trust for (9,000), 22 Bancroft, Hitchin, Herts SG5 1JW; 1970

Inland Waterways Association (20,000 ind; 100 f; 200 org), 114 Regent's Park Road, London NW1 8UQ; 1946

Marine Conservation Society (5,700), 9 Gloucester Road, Ross-on-Wye, Herefordshire HR9 5BU; 1983

National Trust for Places of Historic Interest or Natural Beauty (2,555,000), 36 Queen Anne's Gate, London SW1H 9AS; 1895

National Trust for Scotland (237,880 ind; 781 f & org), 5 Charlotte Square, Edinburgh EH2 4DV; 1931

Naturalists' Association, British (8,300), 48 Russell Way, Higham Ferrers, Wellingborough NN9 8EJ; 1905

Nature Conservation, Royal Society for (260,000), The Green, Witham Park, Waterside South, Lincoln LN5 7JR; 1912

Noise Abatement Society (4,000 ind; 250 f; 1,000 org), PO Box 518, Eynsford, Dartford, Kent DA4 0LL; 1959

Open Spaces Society – Commons, Open Spaces, and Footpaths Preservation Society (2,500 ind; 1,101 f), 25a Bell Street, Henley-on-Thames RG9 2BA; 1865

Ornithology, British Trust for (9,500 ind; 320 org), The National Centre for Ornithology, The Nunnery, Thetford, Norfolk IP24 2PU; 1933

Pet Trade & Industry Association (1,400 f), Bedford Business Centre, 17 Mile Road, Bedford MK42 9TW; 1963

Pony Club (126,000), British Equestrian Centre, Stoneleigh Park, Kenilworth, Warks CV8 2LR; 1929

Prevention of Cruelty to Animals, Royal Society for the (RSPCA) (20,000), Causeway, Horsham, W Sussex RH12 1HG; 1824

Prevention of Cruelty to Animals, Scottish Society for the (SSPCA) (8,400), Braehead Mains, 603 Queensferry Road, Edinburgh EH6 5EQ; 1839

Protection of Animals, World Society for the (100,000), 2 Langley Lane, London SW8 1TJ; 1981

Protection of Birds, Royal Society for the (850,000), The Lodge, Sandy, Beds SG19 2DL; 1889

Protection of Horses, International League for the (85,000), Anne Colvin House, Shetterton, Norwich NR16 2LR; 1927

Pure Water Association, National, 17 Sycamore Lane, West Bretton, Wakesfield WF4 4JR; 1960

Rabbit Council, British (5,042), Purefoy House, 7 Kirk Gate, Newark NG24 1AD; 1934

Rare Breeds Survival Trust (10,500 ind; 114 org), National Agricultural Centre, Kenilworth, Warks CV35 0EY; 1973

Replacement of Animals in Medical Experiments, Fund for the (FRAME) (1,600 ind; 170 f; 120 org), Russell & Burch House, 96–98 North Sherwood Street, Nottingham NG1 4EE; 1969

Rural England, Council for the Protection of (45,000), 25 Buckingham Palace Road, London SW1W 0PP; 1926

Rural Scotland, Association for the Protection of (980 ind; 3 f), Gladstone's Land, 3rd floor, Lawnmarket, Edinburgh EH1 2NT; 1926

Tanker Owners' Pollution Federation, International (3,800 f), Staple Hall, Stonehouse Court, 87–90 Houndsditch, London EC3A 7AX; 1968

Vegan Society (4,000), Donald Watson House, 7 Battle Road, St Leonards-on-Sea, E Sussex TN37 7AA; 1944

Water Quality, International Association on (4,950 ind; 530 f), 1 Queen Anne's Gate, London SW1H 9BT; 1965

World Wildlife Fund (WWF) (185,000), Panda House, Weyside Park, Godalming, Surrey GU7 1XR; 1961

Zoological Society of London (40,000), Regent's Park, London NW1 4RY; 1826

See Also	**International Environmental Groups and Initiatives (The Environment)**

Ethnic and National

African Society, Royal (756 ind; 25 f), SOAS/University of London, Thornhaugh Street, Russell Square, London WC1H 0XG; 1901

ARHAG H A Ltd (1,500; to promote the welfare of African refugees), 2nd Floor, St Margaret's, 25 Leighton Road, London NW5 2QD; 1979

Black European Community Development Federation (2,500), Unit 2, 150 Townmead Road, London SW6 2RA; 1975

Caribbean Community Centre (3,000), 416 Seven Sisters Road, Manor House, London N4 2LX; 1971

Ghana Welfare Association (2,000), Greater London House, 547–551 High Road, London E11 4PB; 1983

Greek Cypriot Brotherhood (1,045), Shropshire House, 5th Floor, 179 Tottenham Court Road, London W1P 9LF; 1934

Gypsy Council, National (Romani Kris) (50,000), Greenacres Caravan Park, Hapsford, Helsby, Warrington WA6 0JS; 1966

Honourable Society of Cymmrodorion (900 ind; about 180 org), 30 Eastcastle Street, London W1N 7PD; 1751

Indian Organizations, Confederation of (125 org), 5 Westminster Bridge Road, London SE1 7XW; 1975

Indian Workers' Association (7,000), 112a The Green, Southall, Middx UB2 4BQ; 1956

Muslim Council of Britain (over 250 Muslim org), PO Box 168, Bradford, BD7 3YS; 1997

Pakistan Welfare Association (4,000), 10a Stoke Newington High Street, London N16 7PL; 1967

Race Relations, Institute of (400 ind; 90 f), 2–6 Leeke Street, London WC1X 9HS; 1958

Sikh Cultural Society of Great Britain (1,000), 88 Mollison Way, Edgware, Middx HA8 5QW; 1960

Southern Africa, Action for (7,000), 28 Penton Street, London N1 9SA; 1994

Spanish Organisations, Federation of (15,000), Office 3, Canalside House, 383 Ladbroke Road, London W10 5AA; 1975

Synagogues, Federation of (9,000), 65 Watford Way, London NW4 3AQ; 1887

Zionist Federation of Great Britain & Ireland (45,000), 741 High Road, London N12 0BQ; 1899

Historical and Archaeological

Anthropological Institute of Great Britain & Ireland, Royal (2,100), 50 Fitzroy Street, London W1P 5HS; 1843

Antiquaries of London, Society of (1,700 ind; 300 org), Burlington House, Piccadilly, London W1V 0HS; 1717

Antiquaries of Scotland, Society of (234,500 ind; 400 org), National Museums, York Buildings, Queen Street, Edinburgh EH2 1JD; 1780

Archaeological Institute, Royal (about 1,700 ind; 384 libraries and institutions), c/o Society of Antiquaries, Burlington House, Piccadilly, London W1V 0HS; 1844

Archaeology, Council of British (3,000 ind; 410 org), 11 Walmgate, York YO1 2UA; 1944

Art Historians, Association of (1,500 ind; 1,250 institutions), Dog & Partridge House, Byley, Cheshire CW10 9NJ; 1974

Field Archaeologists, Institute of (IFA) (1,330), University of Manchester, Oxford Road, Manchester M13 9PL; 1982

Historical Society, Royal (2,200 ind; 700 f), c/o University College London, Gower Street, London WC1E 6BT; 1868

Local History, British Association for (2,500), 24 Lower Street, Harnham, Salisbury, Wilts SP2 8EY; 1982

Prehistoric Society (2,000 ind; 400 org), c/o University College London, Institute of Archaeology, 31–34 Gordon Square, London WC1H 0PY; 1935

Recreational and Hobbies

Allotment and Leisure Gardeners, National Association of (104,000), O'Dell House, Hunters Road, Corby, Northants NN17 5JE; 1930

Alpine Club (1,150), 55–56 Charlotte Road, London EC2A 3QT; 1857

Antique Collectors' Club (10,000), 5 Church Street, Woodbridge IP12 1DS; 1966

Army Cadet Force Association (40,000), E Block, Duke of York's Headquarters, London SW3 4RR; 1930

Automobile Association (over 9,200,000), Norfolk House, Priestly Road, Basingstoke, Hants RG24 9NY; 1905

Boat Owners, National Association of (1,500), 111 Maas Road, Northfield, Birmingham B31 2PP; 1992

Boys' and Girls' Club of Northern Ireland (135 clubs), 2nd Floor, 38 Dublin Road, Belfast BT2 7HN; 1940

Boys' and Girls' Club of Scotland (11,000 ind; 5 federations), 88 Giles Street, Edinburgh EH6 6BZ; 1928

Camping & Caravanning Club Ltd (about 250,000), Greenfields House, Westwood Way, Coventry CV4 8JH; 1901

Chess Federation, British (1,200), 9a Grand Parade, St Leonard's on Sea, E Sussex TN39 4DY; 1904

Cyclists' Touring Club (40,000 ind; 200 f), Cotterall House, 69 Meadrow, Godalming GU7 3HS; 1878

Guide Association (750,000), 17–19 Buckingham Palace Road, London SW1W 0PT; 1910

Health and Beauty, Women's League of (22,000), 52 London Street, Chertsey, Surrey KT16 8AJ; 1930

Horticultural Society, Royal (190,000), 80 Vincent Square, London SW1P 2PE; 1804

Keep Fit Association (20,000), Francis House, Francis Street, London SW1P 1DE; 1956

Kids' Clubs Network (about 800 clubs), Bellerive House, 3 Muirfield Crescent, London E14 9SZ; 1981

Long Distance Walkers Association (6,500), 21 Upcroft, Windsor, Berks SL4 3NH; 1971

Magic Circle (1,350), Victory Services Club, 63–79 Seymour Street, London W2 2HF; 1905

Motorcycle Action Group (20,300 ind; 325 clubs), PO Box 750, Kings Norton, Birmingham B30 3BA; 1973

Naturism, Central Council for British (20,000), 30–32 Wycliffe Road, Northampton NN1 5JF; 1964

Numismatic Societies, British Association of (about 2,000), c/o Bush Boake Allen Ltd, Blackhorse Lane, London E17 5QP; 1953

Numismatic Society, Royal (1,100), c/o Dept of Coins and Medals, British Museum, Great Russell Street, London WC1B 3DG; 1836

Philatelic Society, Royal (1,600), 41 Devonshire Place, London W1N 1PE; 1869

Rose Society, Royal National (20,000 ind; 50 f), Chiswell Green Lane, St Albans AL2 3NR; 1876

Sail Training Association (2,000), 2a The Hard, Portsmouth PO1 3PT; 1956

Scout Association (657,073), Baden-Powell House, Queen's Gate, London SW7 5JS; 1908

Scrabble Clubs (UK) (5,000), Richard House, Enstone Road, Enfield, Middx EN3 7TB; 1993

Sea Anglers, National Federation of (35,000), 51A Queen Street, Newton Abbot, Devon TQ12 2QJ; 1904

Sea Cadets Corps (21,000), 202 Lambeth Road, London SE1 7JF; 1895

Sports Association for the Disabled, British (50,000), The Mary Glen Haig Suite, Solecast House, 13–27 Brunswick Place, London N1 6DX; 1961

Sub-Aqua Club, British (50,000), Telford's Quay, Ellesmere Port L65 4FY; 1953

Tenpin Bowling Association, British (30,000), 114 Balfour Road, Ilford IG1 4JD; 1962

Veteran Car Club of Great Britain (1,550 ind; 10 f; 25 org), Jessamine House, High Street, Ashwell, Herts SG7 5NL; 1930

Vintage Motor Cycle Club Ltd (12,650 ind; over 50,000 affiliated clubs), Allen House, Westmore Road, Burton-upon-Trent, Staffs DE14 1TR; 1946

Vintage Sports Car Club Ltd (about 6,000), 121 Russell Road, Newbury, Berks RG14 5JX; 1934

Wine and Food Society, International (9,000), 9 Fitzmaurice Place, London W1X 6JD; 1933

Youth Clubs Scotland (75,000 ind; 12 regional arms), 19 Bonnington Grove, Edinburgh EH6 4BL; 1911

Youth Clubs UK (650,000 young people; 44,000 adult volunteers; 41 local associations), 11 St Bride Street, London EC4A 4AS; 1911

Youth Hostels' Association (England & Wales) (265,000), Trevelyan House, 8 St Stephen's Hill, St Albans, Herts AL1 2DY; 1930

See Also **Sports Organizations (Sport)**

Medical and Health

Alcoholics Anonymous (AA) (40–45,000), PO Box 1, Stonebow House, Stonebow, York YO1 2NJ; 1947

Allergy, Action Against, 24–26 High Street, Hampton Hill, Middx TW12 1PD; 1978

Alzheimer's Disease Society (18,000), 10 Greencoat Place, London SW1P 1PH; 1979

Anaesthetists of Great Britain and Ireland, Association of (5,720), 9 Bedford Square, London WC1B 3RA; 1932

Arthritis Care (70,000), 18 Stephenson Way, London NW1 2HD; 1947

Asthma Campaign, National (20,000), Unit 1304, The Custard Factory, Gibb Street, Birmingham B9 4AA; 1982

Autistic Society, National (4,960 ind; 45 f), 276 Willesden Lane, London NW2 5RB; 1962

Back Pain Association, National (4,750 ind; 50 org), 16 Elmtree Road, Teddington, Middx TW11 8ST; 1968

Bone Marrow Trust, Anthony Nolan (250,000), The Royal Free Hospital, London NW3 2QG; 1974

Blind, National Federation of the (1,400 ind; 400 associates), Unity House, Smyth Street, Westgate, Wakefield WF1 1ER; 1947

Blind, Royal National Institute for the (RNIB) (subscribers), 224 Great Portland Street, London W1N 6AA; 1868

Cancer Relief Macmillan Fund (7,500), Anchor House, 15–19 Britten Street, London SW3 3TZ; 1911

Childbirth Trust, National (55,000), Alexandra House, Oldham Terrace, Acton, London W3 6NH; 1956

Child Psychology and Psychiatry, Association for (2,400), 70 Borough High Street, London SE1 1XF; 1956

Chiropody & Podiatry Association (11,000), 149 Bath Road, Maidenhead, Berks SL6 4LA; 1959

Complementary & Alternative Medicine, Council for (2,000), 179 Gloucester Place, London NW1 6DX; 1984

Cystic Fibrosis Research Trust (16,000), 5 Blyth Road, Bromley BR1 3RS; 1964

Deaf Association, British (4,000), 38 Victoria Place, Carlisle CA1 1HU; 1890

Dental Association, British (16,100), 64 Wimpole Street, London W1M 8AL; 1880

Diabetic Association, British (about 150,000), 10 Queen Anne's Street, London W1M 0BD; 1934

Disability Alliance (250 f), Universal House, 88–94 Wentworth Street, London E1 7SA; 1974

Down's Syndrome Association (5,150), 153–155 Mitchan Road, London SW17 9PG; 1970

Dyslexia Association, British (14,000), 98 London Road, Reading RG1 5AU; 1972

Eating Disorders Association (750), Sackville Place, 44 Magdalen Street, Norwich NR3 1JU; 1989

Epilepsy Association, British (16,000), Anstey House, 40 Hanover Square, Leeds LS3 1BE; 1950

General Practitioners, Royal College of (17,575), 48–49 Russell Square, London WC1B 4JY; 1952

Geriatrics Society, British (1,700), 1 Saint Andrew's Place, Regent's Park, London NW1 4LB; 1947

Guide Dogs for the Blind Association (2,500), Hillfields, Burghfield, Reading RG7 3YG; 1931

Health, Royal Society of (10,000), RSH House, 38a St George's Drive, London SW1V 4BH; 1876

Health Visitors' Association (17,000), 50 Southwark Street, London SE1 1UN; 1896

Hearing Concern (5,000), 7–11 Armstrong Road, London W3 7JL; **Helpline:** 0800 626216; 1947

Homoeopathic Association, British (5,000), 27a Devonshire Street, London W1N 1RG; 1902

Leukaemia Care Society (6,500), 14 Kingfisher Court, Venny Bridge, Pinhoe, Exeter EX4 8JN; 1967

Marie Curie Cancer Care (6,600), 28 Belgrave Square, London SW1X 8QG; 1948

Medical Society, Royal (2,500), Student Centre, 5/5 Bristo Square, Edinburgh EH8 9AL; 1737

Medicine, Royal Society of (18,000), 1 Wimpole Street, London W1M 8AE; 1805

Mencap (Royal Society for Mentally Handicapped Children and Adults) (55,000), 123 Golden Lane, London EC1Y 0RT; 1946

Midwives, Royal College of (36,000), 15 Mansfield Street, London W1M 0BE; 1881

MIND – National Association for Mental Health (2,000), Granta House, 15–19 Broadway, London E15 4BQ; 1946

Motor Neurone Disease Association (6,200), PO Box 246, Northampton NN1 2PR; 1979

Multiple Sclerosis Society of Great Britain & Northern Ireland (60,000), 25 Effie Road, London SW6 1EE; 1953

Muscular Dystrophy Group of Great Britain (2,000), 7–11 Prescott Place, London SW4 6BS; 1959

Myalgic Encephalomyelitis Association (9,000), Stanhope House, High Street, Stanford-le-Hope, Essex SS17 0HA; 1976

Narcotics Anonymous (NA), UK Service Office, PO Box 1980, London N19 3LS; 1980

Nursing of the UK, Royal College of (300,000), 20 Cavendish Square, London W1M 0AB; 1916

Obstetricians & Gynaecologists, Royal College of (8,938), 27 Sussex Place, London NW1 4RG; 1929

Ophthalmologists, Royal College of (2,824), 17 Cornwall Terrace, London NW1 4QW; 1988

Osteoporosis Society, National (17,000), PO Box 10 Radstock, Bath BA3 3YB; 1986

Paediatric Association, British (3,000), 5 St Andrew's Place, Regent's Park, London NW1 4LB; 1928

Parkinson's Disease Society of the UK (40,000), 22 Upper Woburn Place, London WC1H 0RA; 1969

Pathologists, Royal College of (6,634), 2 Carlton House Terrace, London SW1Y 5AF; 1962

Pharmaceutical Society of Great Britain, Royal (38,000), 1 Lambeth High Street, London SE1 7JN; 1841

Physicians, Royal College of (12,000), 11 St Andrew's Place, London NW1 4LE; 1518

Psychological Society, British (22,442), St Andrews House, 48 Princess Road East, Leicester LE1 7DR; 1901

Radiologists, Royal College of (4,300), 38 Portland Place, London W1N 4JQ; 1975

Red Cross Society, British (100,000), 9 Grosvenor Crescent, London SW1X 7EJ; 1870

Retinitis Pigmentosa Society, British (3,000), PO Box 350, Buckingham MK18 5EL; 1976

Schizophrenia Fellowship, National (7,500), 28 Castle Street, Kingston upon Thames, Surrey KT1 1SS; 1972

SCOPE (formerly The Spastics Society) (208 groups), 12 Park Crescent, London W1N 4EQ; 1952

Spina Bifida & Hydrocephalus, Association for (15,000), 42 Park Road, Peterborough PE1 2UQ; 1966

Stammering Association, British (1,350), 15 Old Ford Road, London E2 9PJ; 1978

Surgeons of England, Royal College of (8,560), 35–43 Lincoln's Inn Fields, London WC2A 3PN; 1800

Tinnitus Association, British (5,000 ind; 4,000 f), Room 6, 14–18 West Bar Green, Sheffield S1 2DA; 1979

Tropical Medicine & Hygiene, Royal Society of (3,000), 26 Portland Street, London W1N 4EY; 1907

See Also Useful Addresses (Medicine and Health)

Military

1940 Dunkirk Veterans Association (6,000), White Wickets, Parkgate Road, Neston, South Wirral L64 6QQ; 1953

Air Training Corps (46,000), Headquarters Air Cadets, RAF Cranwell, Sleaford, Lincs NG34 8HB; 1941

Army Cadet Force Association (40,000), E Block, Duke of York's Headquarters, London SW3 4RR; 1930

Frontiersmen of the Commonwealth, Legion of – UK Command (6,000), 4 Edwards Road, Belvedere, Kent DA1 5AL; 1904

Jewish ex-Servicemen & Women, Association of (5,000), Ajax House, East Bank, London N16 5RT; 1930

'Not Forgotten' Association (2,500), 158 Buckingham Place Road, London SW1W 9TR; 1920

Royal Air Forces Association (102,000), 43 Grove Park Road, London W4 3RX; 1943

Royal British Legion (760,000), 48 Pall Mall, London SW1Y 5JY; 1921

Royal British Legion Women's Section (103,000), 48 Pall Mall, London SW1Y 5JY; 1921

Royal Naval Benevolent Society (1,400), 1 Fleet Street, London EC4Y 1BD; 1739

Soldiers, Sailors, Airmen, & Families Association – Forces Help (5,000), SSAFA Central Office, 19 Queen Elizabeth Street, London SE1 2LP; 1885

Political and Governmental

300 Group (over 1,400; campaign to bring more women into Parliament), PO Box 353, Uxbridge, Middx UB10 0UN; 1980

Charter 88 (over 60,000), Exmouth House, 3–11 Pine Street, London EC1R 05H; 1988

Conservative Party (about 500,000), 32 Smith Square, Westminster, London SW1P 3HH; 1870 as Conservative Central Office

Co-operative Party (about 10,000 ind; 50 soc with about 7.75 million affiliated members), Victory House, 10–15 Leicester Square, London WC2H 7QH; 1917

Green Party (about 4,020), 1a Waterloo Road, London Sw1P 3HH; 1973 as the Ecology Party

Independent Britain, Campaign for an (2,500), 81 Ashmole Street, London SW8 1NF; 1989

Labour Party (365,000 ind; total ind and affiliated membership 3,965,00 in 1995), 150 Walworth Road, London SE17 1JT; 1900

Liberal Democrats (about 100,500), 4 Cowley Street, London SW1P 3NB; 1988

Plaid Cymru (Welsh National Party) (10,000), 18 Park Grove, Cardiff CF1 3BN; 1925

Politics Association (1,200), Studio 16, 1 Innex Business Park, Hamilton Road, Manchester M13 0PD; 1969

Socialist Workers' Party (SWP) (about 9,000), PO Pox 82, London E3 3LH; 1950

United Kingdom Independence Party (16,000), 80 Regent Street, London W1R 5PE; 1993

United Nations Association (6,000), 3 Whitehall Court, London SW1A 2EL; 1945

Religious and Charitable

ACTIONAID (about 108,00 sponsors; over 200,000 supporters), Hamlyn House, MacDonald Road, London N19 5PG; 1972

Bible Lands Society (68,000), PO Box 50, High Wycombe, Bucks HP15 7QU; 1854

Bible Reading Fellowship (100,000), Peters Way, Sandy Lane West, Oxford OX4 5HG; 1922

Bible Society, British & Foreign (sometimes known as the Bible Society) (157,000), Stonehill Green, Westlea, Swindon SN5 7DG; 1804

Bible Society of Scotland, National (20,000), 7 Hampton Terrace, Edinburgh EH12 5XV; 1861

Boys' Brigade (153,000), Felden Lodge, Felden Lane, Hemel Hempstead, Herts HP3 0BL; 1883

CARE (Cooperative for American Relief to Everywhere, Inc) (aid programmes in 61 developing countries), 36–38 Southampton Street, London WC2E 7AF; 1945

Catholic Mothers, Union of (9,500), 1 Petersfinger Cottages, Clarendon Park, Salisbury SP5 3DA; 1913

Catholic Women's League (9,000), 164 Stockwell Road, London SW9 9TQ; 1906

Child Poverty Action Group (6,000), 4th Floor, 1–5 Bath Street, London EC1V 9PY; 1965

Christian Children's Fund of Great Britain (17,000), 4 Bath Place, Rivington Street, London EC2A 3DR; 1983

Christians and Jews, Council of (4,900), Drayton House, 30 Gordon Street, London WC1H 0AN; 1942

Church's Ministry Among the Jewish People (6,000), 30c Clarence Road, St Albans, Herts AL1 4JJ; 1809

Girls' Brigade (38,500), Girls' Brigade House, Foxhall Road, Didcot, Oxon OX11 7BQ; 1893

Help the Aged (1,200), St James's Walk, London EC1R 0BE; 1961

Hunger Project (418,405), 11 Carteret Street, London SW1H 9DL; 1980

Jewish Care (12,000), Stuart Young House, 221 Golders Green Road, London NW11 9DQ; 1990

Jewish Refugees in Great Britain & AJR Charitable Trust, Association of (4,000), 1 Hampstead Gate, 1a Frognal, London NW3 6AL; 1941

Jewish Women, League of (4,900), 24–32 Stephenson Way, London NW1 2JW; 1943

Jewish Youth, Association for (30,000), AJY House, 128 East Lane, Wembley, Middx HA0 3NL; 1899

Latin Mass Society (for the Preservation of the Tridentine Mass) (4,500), 11–13 Macklin Street, London WC2B 5NH; 1965

Maccabi Associations in Great Britain & Northern Ireland, Union of (10,000), Gildesgame House, 73a Compayne Gardens, London NW6 3RS; 1935

Methodist Local Preachers' Mutual Aid Association (13,500), Chorleywood Close, Rickmansworth, Herts WD3 4EG; 1849

Oxfam (emergency programmes in some 70 developing countries), 274 Banbury Road, Oxford OX2 7DZ; 1942

Pagan Federation (2,500), BM 7097, London WC1N 3XX; 1971

Prison Fellowship England & Wales (4,145), PO Box 945, Chelmsford CM2 7RD; 1980

Samaritans (23,500), 10 The Grove, Slough SL1 1QP; 1953

Seekers Trust (4,300), The Close, Addington, West Malling, Kent ME19 5BL; 1925

Shelter (The National Campaign for Homeless People) (about 150,000 supporters), 88 Old Street, London EC1V 9HU; 1966

Survival International (15,000), 11–15 Emerald Street, London WC1N 3QL; 1969

Terrence Higgins Trust (1,400), 52–54 Gray's Inn Road, London WC1X 8JU; 1983

Voluntary Service, Women's Royal (about 140,000) 234–244 Stockwell Road, London SW9 9SP; 1938

Young Men's Christian Associations, National Council of (YMCA) (80,000), 640 Forest Road, London E17 3DZ; 1844

Young Women's Christian Association of Great Britain (about 20,000), 52 Cornmarket Street, Oxford OX1 3EJ; 1855

See Also	Religions in the UK (Religion and Belief)

Consumer Complaints in the UK

Source: Office of Fair Trading © Crown copyright 1997

When you complain, get your facts right and always keep calm. You are probably more likely to get matters resolved if you do not lose your temper.

Goods
Return to the shop as soon as possible with your receipt or proof of purchase (bank or credit card statement showing the amount paid through your account); explain the problem and what you expect to be done, setting a deadline; if the outcome is not satisfactory, put your complaint in writing; address your letter to the customer services manager, chairman or, where the shop is part of a chain, the head office; if the problem is still not resolved, get further advice and/or consider going to court.

Services
Complain verbally to the supplier and provide an opportunity for the supplier to resolve the problem; complain in writing if the matter is not resolved and provide a deadline for it to be corrected; consider withholding payment until the problem is resolved, but beware: check the small print of any contract you have signed and obtain further advice before refusing to pay, especially if you have a credit agreement. Note: if you continue to pay for a service you are not happy with under a credit agreement, you still have legal redress against the lender for providing an unsatisfactory service; keep a diary of events, notes of telephone calls, and copies of any relevant documentation, such as letters. Also take photographs where necessary, these records will all help in case you have to bring legal action to resolve the matter; consider obtaining an expert opinion to support your complaint.

Complaints over the Phone
Make a note beforehand of what you want to say; have receipts and any other documents handy; note the name of the person you speak to; write down the date and time of the call and what was said; follow up your call with a letter, particularly if the complaint is a serious one.

Complaints in Writing
Type your letter if possible, if your letter is handwritten, make sure it is clear and legible; include your name, address, and home and work telephone numbers; keep your letter brief, polite, and to the point, avoid repetition and personal remarks; describe the item or service; say where and when you bought the item, or when the service was done, and how much it cost; explain what is wrong, any action you have already taken, to whom you spoke, and what happened; say what you want done to remedy the situation – for example, a refund or repair, or the job done again without charge; set a deadline by which you want a response from the other party; use special delivery so you can check that your letter has been delivered; keep copies of any letters you send; do not send original documents, such as receipts and guarantees – send copies instead; be persistent: if you fail to get what you want at your first attempt, write another letter of complaint setting out your dissatisfaction.

Model Complaint Letter
[Your name and address]
[Date] [Name of person, if known, or 'Customer Services Manager' or 'Chairman'] [The person's title, if name is known] [Company name] [Full address, including postal code] Dear [Person's surname, if known, or 'Dear Sir or Madam'] Re: [Order, account, or reference number] On [full date], I [ordered, bought, rented, leased, had repaired, sought a service] [a name of the product with its serial and/or model number or service performed] at/from [company, location, catalogue, and other important details relevant to the transaction] price [£...]. Unfortunately, your product [does not correspond with its description, was damaged in transit, showed serious defects, etc.] [or the service was inadequate]. I am disappointed because [describe why the product or service was faulty or inadequate, misrepresented, and so on, or why you believe the billing was incorrect]. To resolve this problem, I would appreciate your [state the specific action you want: reimbursement, charge-card credit, replacement, repair, exchange, the service done or improved, etc.] within [... days]. Enclosed are copies of my records (include copies, not originals, of any relevant documents). I look forward to [your reply, your cheque for £..., receiving a replacement, etc.]. I will wait until [date] before seeking help from [my local trading standards or consumer protection department]. Please contact me at the above address or by telephone at [give home and work numbers with their area codes]. Yours sincerely/faithfully [Your name] Enclosure(s) cc: [Name(s) of any person(s) to whom you are sending a copy of this letter]

Taking Further Action
If you are struggling to get a complaint addressed satisfactorily, you can take further action. Just telling a trader who is being unhelpful or obstructive that you will go to court could be enough to get your complaint resolved. If you do have to take legal action, it can be much easier than it sounds and could well be worth the effort. Before going to arbitration or to court, you may wish to seek an impartial opinion on the merits of your case. This opinion is best obtained from a solicitor. Some solicitors work in law centres or advice agencies that offer free advice. Many solicitors in private practice offer a low-cost initial interview. Your local Citizens' Advice Bureau can help you find such a solicitor.

Conciliation and Arbitration
If the trader is a member of a trade association, there may be a conciliation or arbitration scheme you can use. Some associations have both. Such schemes are informal and generally inexpensive. However, arbitration may not necessarily be cheaper than going to court under the small claims procedure. Check what fees you will be expected to pay if you lose the case. You have to choose between court and arbitration – you cannot do both. If you do not like an arbitrator's decision, you cannot then go to court (except in special circumstances). Under the Consumer Arbitration Agreements Act 1988, a clause in a contract which says that you have to go to arbitration cannot bind you as long as the value of your dispute is not greater than the small claims limit.

Going to Court
If, after trying to resolve your complaint by telephone and in writing, you remain unsatisfied, you can take further action by going to court. If the threat of court action is not sufficient to make a trader/service provider address your problem seriously, you can proceed with legal action and go to

court to sue for the return of your money or for compensation. In the UK, outside Scotland, a claim of £3,000 or less can be dealt with as a 'small claim'; in Scotland, small claims of up to £750 can be taken to the Sheriff Court. You do not require the services of a solicitor to pursue a small claim, and even if your opponent employs the services of one, you are not liable for their legal costs if you lose the case (unless you are found to have made an unreasonable claim, caused unnecessary expense costs, or do not attend a hearing). The necessary forms for filing a small claim are available from County Court offices (Sheriff Court in Scotland). The court will then serve the summons and advise you on what to do next. There are court fees which are payable by your opponent if you win your case. Outside Scotland, the fees are 10 pence for every £1 claimed, with a minimum fee of £10 and a maximum of £65 for claims of £1,000–3,000. In Scotland the fees are £6 for claims up to £50 and £32 for claims of £50–750.

Major Consumer Organizations

Citizens' Advice Bureaux (CAB) CABs provide a wide range of advice and can help resolve many consumer problems, including complaints about goods and services. Details on contacting your nearest branch can be found in the telephone book under Citizens' Advice Bureaux.

Trading Standards departments Trading Standards departments have the powers to investigate complaints about goods and services and can advise on everyday consumer issues. Details on contacting your local Trading Standards department can be found in the telephone book under Trading Standards Service.

Office of Fair Trading The Office of Fair Trading is a non-ministerial government department responsible for a wide range of issues of fair trading in the UK. It has powers to protect consumers in the following ways: identifying and correcting trading practices which are against the consumer's interests; regulating the provision of consumer credit; investigating and acting to prevent anti-competitive practices; encouraging competitive behaviour.

Utilities regulators If you have a complaint about utilities services, that is gas, electricity, water, or telephones, you can take the matter to the relevant regulatory body if your problem is not resolved by the company. Each of the four utilities has a regulator that can help solve consumer problems: OFFER, Office of Electricity Regulation; OFWAT, Office of Water Services; OFTEL, Office of Telecommunications; Gas Consumers' Council. Contact information for these bodies can be found in the telephone book.

The Ombudsmen Ombudsmen exist to deal with complaints from citizens about certain public bodies or private sector services. There are 23 recognized Ombudsman schemes, most of which are established by statute. The schemes vary in the procedures they use and the powers that they have. Using the services of an Obmudsman is a last resort. The party against which a complaint is being made must first be given reasonable time to resolve the complaint; indeed, many organizations have their own complaints procedures, which normally resolve problems satisfactorily. It is only if and when a complaint has not been resolved by going through the normal channels that an Obudsman will consider it. Ombudsmen schemes include: The Health Service Ombudsman; Police Complaints Authority; The Legal Services Ombudsman; Broadcasting Standards Commission; The Independent Housing Ombudsman; The Parliamentary Ombudsman. There are also Ombudsmen schemes for banking, pensions, and investments.

Other organizations Other organizations from which help and advice can be obtained include environmental health departments (for advice on health matters) law centres, and trade associations. Contact information for many consumer organizations can be found here, or consult your telephone book.

Guide for Consumers in the UK

Source: Office of Fair Trading. © Crown copyright 1997

In General
Before you buy, ask yourself:
- Is it what I am looking for?
- Can I afford it?
- Is this the best place to buy it?
- Can I take it back if I do not like it?
- How will I pay for it?
- Have I seen what other shops have to offer?
- Does the trader have a good reputation for treating customers fairly?

Statutory Rights
As a customer purchasing goods, you have certain statutory rights, whether what you are buying is new or second-hand. Under the Sale and Supply of Goods Act 1994, goods must fit any description given, whether on a label, packaging, in an advertisement, or anywhere else; be in good condition, free from any minor or major faults, and capable of doing the job expected of them for a reasonable length of time; be fit for the purpose for which they are intended: if you have told a retailer that you need the goods for a specific purpose, they must be fit for that purpose as well as for general use; correspond with any samples you have been shown.

If goods fail to meet the above criteria, you are legally entitled to reject them and to receive your money back, in cash. It is illegal for a retailer or supplier to insist on providing a credit note or a replacement instead of a cash repayment, unless you agree to accept it. You have a 'reasonable' time in which to reject goods that fail to meet with the above requirements, if you do not reject goods in such time you may only be able to insist on to have an item repaired at no cost. Current legislation does not specify the length of 'reasonable' time, but it can be as little as a few days.

Under hire purchase or conditional sale agreement terms, you have the same basic rights as if you had paid cash, but your contract is with the finance company, not the retailer. If, however, the goods are faulty, your rights last for the length of time of the hire purchase agreement, not just for a 'reasonable' length of time.

Guarantees and Warranties
Guarantees provide you with additional rights over and above your statutory rights. A guarantee does not take away or replace your statutory rights. Guarantees are required by law to state that your 'statutory rights are not affected'. Traditional guarantees – those provided by manufacturers with their new products – are often subject to conditions of use. They promise to repair any faults that occur due to defects from the manufacture of an item, during a specified period. These guarantees are dependent on the proper use, servicing, maintenance, and so on, of a product. It is not a legal requirement for manufacturers to provide a guarantee with their products.

Guarantees are also sometimes given with second-hand goods, but may only be a verbal statement by the seller, or be written on the receipt. If something goes wrong with a second-hand product, there is no legal way to enforce a verbal or even a written guarantee, but you could sue for breach of contract under civil law. It is not a criminal offence to renege on a verbal agreement.

When you purchase goods from a retailer, you may be offered an extended warranty. Warranties usually have to be purchased from a specialist insurance or warranty company; they are sold to you in addition to the goods you purchase and, as with guarantees, have terms and conditions with which you must comply in order to obtain any benefit from them. They tend to cover problems with goods, such as the failure of components within the period of the warranty, and do not cover failures due to general wear and tear. Insurance-backed warranties can mean that you have to pay the trader to carry out repairs and then claim the cost back from the insurers.

Guarantees usually last for one year, during which time the manufacturer of a product is legally obliged to repair any faults that are due to manufacturing or material defects. If faults occur very soon after purchasing an item, you can claim your money back, under your statutory rights, without having to have the item repaired under guarantee. Make sure, where there is a registration card for return to the manufacturer, that the seller has filled in details of the purchase; the registration may not be valid without this having been done. For the guarantee to be effective you may need to ensure that you return the registration card to a stated address. Make sure you retain the documentation that is supplied with the goods and tells you how to make a claim under your guarantee. It is important to note that a guarantee or warranty is only as good as the company that issues it; if the company stops trading, the guarantee or warranty is worthless.

Trade Associations

Trade associations and professional bodies can develop and enforce their own codes of conduct, or practice guidelines, for their members. If a trader, for example a builder, carries out unsatisfactory work, he or she can be reported to the trade association of which he or she is a member. If traders are found to be in breach of their trade association's code of conduct, they can be excluded from the association. However, membership of a trade association is not always a guarantee of quality; not all trade associations regulate their members. It is always advisable to check the membership status of a trader and to find out any benefits there may be in choosing a supplier belonging to a particular trade association or professional body.

Buying on Credit

Most people at some time will enter an agreement to purchase goods or services on credit. Before entering a credit agreement you should take the following actions:

Work out what the total cost of the loan will be.

Shop around for credit: how much will a loan cost to repay each month and for how long? Check also the annual percentage rate of charge (normally referred to as APR). Generally speaking, the lower the APR the better the deal. Some traders offer interest-free credit (0% APR) but you will need to take care that you are not paying higher amounts in other ways; for example, it may be a higher cash price than you would pay for the same goods elsewhere.

Make absolutely sure you have read and understood all credit agreements before signing them. If there is anything you do not understand, ask.

Make sure you can afford to pay back the loan and the interest – and still have enough to cover all your other commitments. Check whether the loan has a variable rate of interest. If it has, your repayments can go up as well as down.

Make sure you can really afford the purchase. If you are refused credit you have certain rights. You have the right to know the name and address of the credit reference agency that the lender contacted for details about you; the right to see any information held about you by that agency; and the right to correct any inaccurate information. Some loans are only given if they are secured on your home. These loans are not available if you rent. A secured loan gives security to the lender, not to you. If you cannot keep up with the repayments, the lender can sell your home to cover any loss. You might get a lower rate of interest with a secured loan, but you could have a lot at stake.

Right to Cancel a Credit Deal

If you change your mind and want to cancel a credit deal, you should be able to do so if: the deal was made within the last few days; you talked to the lender or supplier in person (not on the telephone); when you signed the credit agreement you were not on the lender's or supplier's business premises, including an exhibition stand (agreements signed in shops, etc are not normally cancellable, but agreements signed at home usually are).

When you sign, you should always be given a copy of the credit agreement, which sets out your cancellation rights. You should also receive, by post, a second copy or a notice of your cancellation rights. If you change your mind, and the lender has not yet signed the agreement, you have the right to withdraw from a credit deal.

Credit Brokers' Fees

If you use a credit broker to get a loan, including a mortgage or a loan secured on your home, you will probably be charged a fee for the service. Make sure you know what this fee will be before you commit yourself. If, however, you do not enter into an agreement within six months of being introduced to a possible lender, the broker can only charge a fee or commission of £3, and if you have already paid more you can recover the excess. Similarly, other fees, such as a survey fee, or insurance premium paid to a credit broker in connection with a loan that you do not eventually take up, are also refundable to you for credit agreements up to £15,000.

Shopping by Mail, Telephone, and Television

Before you send any money, take note of these points:

If ordering by mail, check that the newspaper, magazine, or catalogue is up-to-date.

If you buy through a newspaper, magazine, or television advertisement, check whether you are covered by a protection scheme. If you are not, and you pay in advance, you could lose your money if the trader goes out of business.

Try to avoid sending cash by post. Use credit cards, cheques, or postal orders, and make sure you retain cheque stubs or counterfoils as a record of payment. If you have to send cash, use registered post.

Be careful when giving out your credit card details. Make sure that you know who the trader is, and that you have a business address of the trader before giving the information.

Keep a copy or record of your order and note the date it was sent or placed.

Keep a copy of the advertisement. If this isn't possible, keep a note of the advertiser's name and address, where and when the advertisement appeared and any other details. Make sure there is a full postal address given for the trader – be wary of dealing with any company which only has a post office box number.

If you intend to purchase a product based on a telephone call from a company, make sure you have asked for the company's name, address, and telephone number, as well as the name of the sales representative who contacted you, before you consider the offer and decide whether to call and place your order.

If you are joining a book or record club, make sure you know what commitment you are making and the cancellation terms. Find out exactly what you have to buy and over how long a period in order to qualify for any introductory offer.

Before buying a product from a television shopping programme, check the cost of the same item sold by shops and mail order catalogues.

Paying by Credit

You have some extra protection if you buy the goods with a credit card. This protection applies to goods costing £100 or more for one item, even if you only pay a deposit. If you have a claim against the seller because, for example, the goods are not what you asked for or are faulty, you may also have a claim against the credit card company. This claim could be useful if the seller were to go out of business.

Untrue Claims

It is a criminal offence for a trader to say or write something untrue about what is being offered for sale. If, when you have bought the goods, you feel that you have been seriously misled, tell your local Trading Standards or Consumer Protection Department, which may decide to prosecute the trader. If the trader is convicted, a claim for compensation may be considered in court, except in Northern Ireland, where you would have to sue separately.

Delivery

If you insist on, or are given, a delivery date when you send for the goods, and this date is not met, you can cancel your order and ask for your money back. Even if no definite date is given, goods should be delivered within a reasonable time, usually 28 days, or as specified in the advertisement or by the telephone sales representative. If they are not delivered within such a time, contact the seller to say that if the goods have not arrived by a certain date (for example, within two weeks) you will not accept them and will ask for your money back. But if you agree to give the seller extra time (for example, another month), you cannot change your mind and try to cancel your order before that extra time is up.

Unsolicited Goods

If you receive goods you have not ordered, you do not have to accept them. If you do nothing and do not hear any more from the trader for six months, the goods will become yours. Or you can write to the trader saying that the goods were 'unsolicited' (unasked for). If the trader does not then collect them within 30 days, the goods are yours. You must, of course, allow unsolicited goods to be collected, provided that the trader comes to collect them at a reasonable time after prior notice. You must also take care of the goods until they are collected.

Price

Make sure you know all the conditions regarding price. You may have agreed to pay any increase which takes place between ordering and delivery, or perhaps you will have agreed a fixed price. Be sure you know whether there are extra charges for postage and packing, and if so, what they are.

Unfair Contract Terms

If you have entered into a contract on the trader's standard terms of business, the law says that certain types of terms which act against the consumer's interest may be unfair and unenforceable. If you think a term is unfair, you may wish to seek advice from your local Trading Standards service or Citizens' Advice Bureau. You can also write to the Director General of Fair Trading. He can take court action to stop the use of an unfair term in future contracts. He cannot, however, get involved with individual cases.

Counterfeit Products

An increasing range of products are being copied and sold, including video and audio tapes, 'designer' clothes, perfume, cosmetics, toys, computer software, etc. The practice of counterfeiting is illegal and it infringes on the intellectual property rights of those who own the copyright, designs, patents, and trade marks of these products. The production, distribution, and sale of fake goods purporting to be original is viewed very seriously by Trading Standards Departments; counterfeit goods can be seized and those responsible prosecuted, resulting in large fines and prison sentences. To control counterfeiting, UK trade marks, copyright, and trade descriptions legislation is provided for under the Trades Descriptions Act of 1968 and specifies the following: a trade mark can be a name, logo, word, or signature that connects a person/company to a product; therefore, they have the right to use the mark; copyright provides rights to the creator of literary, dramatic, musical, or artistic work; a trade description can be applied to anything that a person is likely to think applies to the goods and which conduces to a belief in the authenticity of a product's origin or the quality of an item.

Under UK trade descriptions legislation it is therefore illegal to: apply a registered trade mark to goods or packaging without the consent or licence of the trade mark owner; infringe copyright by copying work without the authorization or licence of the copyright owner; apply any kind of identity to products or packaging which is likely to mislead a consumer as to the origin of manufacture or the identity of the producer.

Directory of Consumer Bodies in the UK

Arbitration

Chartered Institute of Arbitrators 24 Angel Gate, City Road, London EC1V 2RS; phone: (0171) 837 4483

Scottish Council for Arbitration 27 Melville Street, Edinburgh EH3 7JF; phone: (0131) 220 4776

Ombudsmen

Banking Ombudsman 70 Grays Inn Road, London WC1X 8NB; phone: (0171) 404 9944

Building Societies Ombudsman Millbank Tower, Millbank, London SW1P 4XJ; phone: (0171) 931 9944

Corporate Estate Agents Ombudsman Beckett House, 4 Bridge Street, Salisbury, Wiltshire SP1 2LX; phone: (01722) 333306

Funeral Ombudsman 31 Southampton Row, London WC1B 5HJ; phone: (0171) 430 1112

Insurance Ombudsman City Gate One, 135 Park Street, London SE1 9EA; phone: (0171) 928 7600

Legal Services Ombudsman 22 Oxford Court, Oxford Street, Manchester M2 3WQ; phone: (0161) 236 9532

Pensions Ombudsman 11 Belgrave Road, London SW1V 1RB; phone: (0171) 834 9144

Personal Investment Authority Ombudsman 3rd Floor, Centre Point, 103 New Oxford Street, London WC1 1QH; phone: (0171) 240 3838

Doorstep and Party Plan Selling

Direct Selling Association Ltd 29 Floral Street, London WC2E 9DP; phone: (0171) 497 1234

Electrical Goods

The Association of Manufacturers of Domestic Electrical Appliances Rapier House, 40–46 Lambs Conduit Street, London WC1N 3NW; phone: (0171) 405 0666

The Radio, Electrical, and Television Retailers' Association Ltd RETRA House, St John's Terrace, 1 Ampthill Street, Bedford MK42 9EY; phone: (01234) 269110

Furniture

Qualitas National Conciliation Service Chief Conciliation Officer, Maxwell Street, Stevenage, Herts SG1 2EW; phone: (01438) 316100

Holidays

Air Travel Organizer's Licence (ATOL) Civil Aviation Authority, 45–59 Kingsway, London WC2B 1RG; phone: (0171) 832 5620/6600

Association of British Travel Agents (ABTA) 55–57 Newman Street, London W1P 4AH; phone: (0171) 637 2444

Association of Independent Tour Operators (AITO) 133a St Margarets Road, Twickenham, Middlesex TW1 1RG; phone: (0181) 744 9280

The Timeshare Council 23 Buckingham Gate, London SW1E 6LB; phone: (0171) 821 8845

Home Maintenance and Improvements

Glass and Glazing Federation 44–48 Borough High Street, London SE1 1XB; phone: (0171) 403 7177

Mail Order

British Telecom phone: (0800) 398893

Direct Marketing Association 1 Oxendon Street, London SW1Y 4EE; phone: (0171) 321 2525

Mailing/Telephone Preference Service FREEPOST 22, London W1E 7EZ; phone: (0171) 738 1625

Mail Order Protection Scheme 16 Tooks Court, London EC4A 1LB; phone: (0171) 405 6806

Mail Order Traders' Association 100 Old Hall Street, Liverpool L3 9TD; phone: (0151) 227 4181

Mercury phone: (0500) 398893. Customers of other companies should call the customer services number on their bill.

Motor Trade

Complaints About Used Cars, Repairs, and Servicing in England, Wales, and Northern Ireland
The National Conciliation Service, Retail Motor Industry Federation 9 North Street, Rugby CV21 2AB; phone: (01788) 576465

Complaints About Cars Still Under a Manufacturer's Warranty
The Customer's Relation Adviser, Society of Motor Manufacturers and Traders Forbes House, Halkin Street, London SW1X 7DS; phone: (0171) 235 7000

Complaints About Car Body Repair
The Conciliation Service, The Vehicle Builders' and Repairers' Association Belmont House, 102 Finkle Lane, Gildersome, Leeds LS27 7TW; phone: (0113) 253 8333

Complaints About Used Cars, Repairs and Servicing in Scotland
Customer Complaints Service, Scottish Motor Trade 3 Palmerston Place, Edinburgh EH12 5AF; phone: (0131) 225 3643

Vehicle Checks
HPI Autodata PO Box 61, Dolphin House, New Street, Salisbury, Wiltshire SP1 2TB; phone: (01722) 422422

Small Claims Procedure
Lord Chancellor's Department, Civil Operations Southside, 105 Victoria Street, London SW1E 6QT; phone: (0171) 210 1689

Scottish Courts Service Hayweight House, 23 Lauriston House, Edinburgh EH3 9DQ; phone: (0131) 229 9200

General Consumer and Advisory Bodies
Advice Services Alliance (ASA) Universal House, 2nd Floor, 88–94 Wentworth Street, London E1 7SA; phone: (0171) 247 2441

Citizens' Advice Scotland (CAS) 26 George Square, Edinburgh EH8 9LD; phone: (0131) 667 0156

Consumers' Association (CA) 2 Marylebone Road, London NW1 4DF; phone: (0171) 830 6000

Department of Trade and Industry (DTI) Consumer Affairs Enquiry Unit DTI, 1 Victoria Street, London SW1H 0ET; phone (0171) 215 5000

Federation of Independent Advice Centres (FIAC) 13 Stockwell Road, London SW9 9AU; phone: (0171) 274 1839

General Consumer Council for Northern Ireland (GCCNI) Elizabeth House, 116 Holywood Road, Belfast BT4 1NY; phone: (01232) 672488

Institute of Consumer Affairs (ICA) 21 Wood Street, Woburn Sands, Milton Keynes, Bucks MK17 8PH; phone: (01908) 585618

Law Centres Federation Duchess House, 28–29 Warren Street, London W1P 5DB; phone: (0171) 387 8570

National Association of Citizens' Advice Bureaux (NACAB) Myddleton House, 115–123 Pentonville Road, London N1 9LZ; phone: (0171) 833 2181

National Consumer Council (NCC) 20 Grosvenor Gardens, London SW1W 0DH; phone: (0171) 730 3469

National Federation of Consumer Groups 527 Leeds Road, Scholes, Leeds LS15 4RD; phone: (0113) 283 2600

Office of Fair Trading (OFT) Field House, 15–25 Breams Buildings, London EC4A 1PR; phone: (0171) 242 2858

OFT Consumer Information Line (0345) 224499 (local call rates apply on BT lines within the UK)

Scottish Consumer Council (SCC) Royal Exchange House, 100 Queen Street, Glasgow G1 3DN; phone: (0141) 226 5261

Welsh Consumer Council (WCC)/ Cyngor Defnyddwyr Cymru (CDC) Castle Buildings, Womanby Street, Cardiff CF1 2BN; phone: (01222) 396056

Postal Information

Summary of First and Second Class Mail in the UK

As of April 1998.

First Class costs 26p up to 60 g, and 39p up to 100 g. Rates continue to increase according to weight up to 1 kg, which costs £2.75; each extra 250 g above 1 kg costs 70p.

Second Class costs 20p up to 60 g, and 31p up to 100 g. Rates continue to increase according to weight up to 750 g, which costs £1.55 and is the maximum weight that can be sent by Second Class.

Summary of International Delivery Times from the UK

As of April 1998.

Surface mail delivery times noted by Royal Mail are 2 weeks within Western Europe (all European countries not part of the former USSR or Eastern Europe); 8 weeks to other parts of Europe; and up to 12 weeks for places outside Europe.

Airmail delivery times are 3 days within Western Europe; 4–6 days to Canada and the USA; 5 days to Hong Kong; 5–7 days to a range of countries including former USSR countries, Eastern Europe, Bangladesh, Japan, New Zealand, Singapore, South Africa, and Zimbabwe; and 6–8 days to a range of countries including Ghana, Argentina, India, and Venezuela.

Airmail distinctions outside Europe are categorized as either Zone 1 or Zone 2. The Post Office supplies full lists of the zones into which individual countries fall.

Summary of International Letter Rates from the UK

As of April 1998.

Surface mail and postcards outside Europe only items up to 20 g cost 31p, up to 60 g cost 52p; and up to 100 g cost 75p. Rates increase with each extra 50 g up to 500 g, which costs £3.18; thereafter rates increase with each extra 500 g up to a maximum of 2 kg, which costs £12.21.

Airmail Europe items up to 20 g cost 26p if sent within the European Union, and 31p within the rest of Europe. Items over 20 g are charged at the same rate for both areas, and rates increase with each extra 20 g up to 500 g, which costs £3.33; thereafter rates increase with each extra 500 g up to a maximum of 2 kg, which costs £13.08.

Airmail zone 1 items up to 10 g cost 43p, and 63p up to 20 g. Rates increase with each extra 20 g up to 500 g, which costs £8.66; thereafter rates increase with each extra 500 g up to a maximum of 2 kg, which costs £33.41.

Airmail zone 2 items up to 10 g cost 43p, and 63p up to 20 g. Rates increase with each extra 20 g up to 500 g, which costs £11.17; thereafter rates increase with each extra 500 g up to a maximum of 2 kg, which costs £44.17.

Summary of International Printed Papers Service from the UK

As of April 1998.
The International Printed Papers service is for sending printed material (such as books, newspapers, pamphlets) other than personalised material (such as personal correspondence). Items intended for this service should be marked 'Printed Papers', and those sent by Airmail should be marked 'Par Avion – By Airmail'. Delivery times are normally the same as for letters.

Customs labels are not usually obligatory. For items just containing books, a Customs declaration is required for the following countries: Algeria; Dominican Republic. For all Printed Papers items a Customs declaration is required for the following countries: Bangladesh; Djibouti; India; Japan; Zimbabwe. For Venezuela, please consult a Post Office. Customs labels are available from a Post Office.

Rates

Surface mail costs 50p up to 20 g. Rates increase by 16–17p per extra 50 g up to 500 g, which costs £1.84, and thereafter by 17p per extra 20 g up to a maximum of 2 kg for printed material other than books and pamphlets, which costs £6.91; and a maximum of 5 kg for books and pamphlets (2 kg for books and pamphlets sent to Canada).

Airmail Europe costs 61p up to 100 g. Rates increase by 6–7p per extra 20 g up to 500 g, which costs £1.86, and thereafter by 7p per extra 20 g up to a maximum of 2 kg for printed material other than books and pamphlets, which costs £7.11; and a maximum of 5 kg for books and pamphlets.

Airmail zone 1 costs £1.06 up to 100 g. Rates increase by 15–16p per extra 20 g up to 500 g, which costs £4.19, and thereafter by 16p per extra 20 g up to a maximum of 2 kg for printed material other than books and pamphlets, which costs £16.19; and a maximum of 5 kg for books and pamphlets (2 kg for books and pamphlets sent to Canada or Cambodia).

Airmail zone 2 costs £1.18 up to 100 g. Rates increase by 18–19p per extra 20 g up to 500 g, which costs £4.95, and thereafter by 19p per extra 20 g up to a maximum of 2 kg for printed material other than books and pamphlets, which costs £19.20; and a maximum of 5 kg for books and pamphlets.

Add-On Services

International Recorded costs £2.50 plus the normal postage rate. Advice of delivery is available for an extra 40p, and compensation for a lost item is up to £28.

Swiftair costs £2.70 plus the airmail postage rate, and is for express delivery of items.

Summary of International Small Packets Service from the UK

As of April 1998.

The International Small Packets service is for sending gifts or goods worldwide. Items intended for this service should be marked 'Small Packet', and those sent by Airmail should be marked 'Par Avion – By Airmail'. It is permissible to include a letter in the Small Packet if it relates to the contents. Delivery times are normally the same as for letters. Small Packets sent to countries in the Commonwealth of Independent States must be unsealed and the contents must not include any correspondence or be worth over £19.

Customs declarations are obligatory for all Small Packets unless they are sent within the European Union. The required declaration varies according to the value of the Packet's contents; information is available from a Post Office.

Rates

Surface mail costs 50p up to 100 g. Rates increase by 16–17p per extra 50 g up to 500 g, which costs £1.84, and thereafter by 17p per extra 20 g up to a maximum of 2 kg, which costs £6.91.

Airmail Europe costs 75p up to 100 g. Rates increase by 7–8p per extra 20 g up to 500 g, which costs £2.22, and thereafter by 8p per extra 20 g up to a maximum of 2 kg, which costs £8.22.

Airmail zone 1 costs £1.06 up to 100 g. Rates increase by 15–16p per extra 20 g up to 500 g, which costs £4.19, and thereafter by 16p per extra 20 g up to a maximum of 2 kg, which costs £16.19.

Airmail zone 2 costs £1.18 up to 100 g. Rates increase by 18–19p per extra 20 g up to 500 g, which costs £4.95, and thereafter by 19p per extra 20 g up to a maximum of 2 kg, which costs £19.20; for Papua New Guinea the maximum is 500 g.

Add-On Services

International Recorded costs £2.50 plus the normal postage rate. Advice of delivery is available for an extra 40p, and compensation for a lost item is up to £28.

International Registered is available in two price brackets: £3.00 plus the normal postage rate, with advice of delivery available for an extra 40p, and compensation for a lost item up to £500; and £4.00 plus the normal postage rate, with advice of delivery available for an extra 40p, and compensation for a lost item up to £1,000.

Swiftair costs £2.70 plus the airmail postage rate, and ensures that items arrive at least one day in advance of normal Airmail.

Summary of Royal Mail Special International Services from the UK

As of April 1998.

International Recorded costs £2.50 plus Airmail postage. Advice of delivery (a copy of the signature taken on delivery) is available for an extra 40p, and compensation for a lost item is up to £28. Items must have an International Recorded label, available from a Post Office.

International Registered is for items of monetary value, and costs £3.00 plus Airmail postage for compensation cover up to £500, and £4.00 plus Airmail postage for compensation cover up to £2,200. Advice of delivery (a copy of the signature taken on delivery) is available for an extra 40p. Items must have an International Registered label attached, with 'Insured for xxx pounds' written in ink above the address. Secure sealing is advisable, and for some countries a signed customs declaration is required. The maximum weight is 2 kg.

Swiftair is for packages that require priority handling, so that they are sent on the first available flight to their destination countries. It is not a guaranteed courier service. It costs £2.70 per item plus Airmail postage. Items must have a Swiftair label attached, available from a Post Office. The maximum weight for letters and Small Packages is 2 kg, and for books and pamphlets 5 kg. Swiftair is available from the UK to most destinations worldwide.

Swiftair Plus Recorded combines Swiftair with International Recorded, and costs £3.30 plus Airmail postage. Advice of delivery is available for an extra 40p. The maximum weight is 2 kg for letters and Small Packets, and 5 kg for books and pamphlets.

Swiftair Plus Registered combines Swiftair with International Registered, and costs £3.80 for compensation cover up to £500 and £4.50 for compensation cover up to £2,200. Advice of delivery is available for an extra 40p. The maximum weight is 2 kg.

Summary of Royal Mail Domestic Services in the UK

As of April 1998.

Sending Mail

First Class costs from 26p, and is usually delivered the next working day after posting. A certificate of posting is available free on request, and compensation for a lost item is either the market value of the item or up to £26, whichever is lower.

Second Class costs from 20p, and is usually delivered within 3 working days after posting. A certificate of posting is available free on request, and compensation for a lost item is either the market value of the item or up to £26, whichever is lower.

Recorded costs 60p plus the first or second class postage, and is delivered within the usual first or second class period. A certificate of posting is available free on request, and compensation for a lost item is either the market value of the item or up to £26, whichever is lower.

Special Delivery costs from £3.20, and delivery to 99 percent of UK addresses is guaranteed by 12.30 p.m. on the next working day. Proof of posting and delivery is provided, and compensation for a lost item is either the market value of the item or up to £50, whichever is lower; a Consequential Loss service is available at extra cost.

Registered costs from £3.50, and delivery to 99 percent of UK addresses is guaranteed by 12.30 p.m. on the next working day. Proof of posting and delivery is provided, and compensation for a lost item is either the market value of the item or up to £500, whichever is lower; a Consequential Loss service is available at extra cost. A Registered Plus service is also available at greater cost and provides a greater level of compensation.

Receiving Mail

Caller Service allows you to collect items from your local delivery office before the delivery round begins.

Keepsafe Royal Mail stores your mail while you are away and delivers it on your return.

Poste Restante allows you to select a Post Office from which to collect your mail while travelling in the UK. There is a maximum duration of 3 months in any town, and there is no charge.

Private Box (PO Box) provides you with an alternative address and holds your mail for collection from your local delivery office.

There is no maximum duration, and the cost is £42 for 6 months and £52 for 1 year.

Redirection (personal mail) Royal Mail forwards your personal mail to a new permanent or temporary address, either in the UK or abroad. There is a maximum duration of 2 years, and the cost (per surname) ranges from £6 for 1 month to £60 for 1 year.

Redirection (business mail) Royal Mail forwards your business mail to a new permanent or temporary address, either in the UK or abroad. There is a maximum duration of 2 years, and the cost (per business name) ranges from £12 for 1 month to £60 for 1 year.

Telephone Information

Public Telecommunications Operators in the UK

Source: Oftel

The UK was one of the first countries in the world to break up telecommunications and postal services within its state-owned monopoly and allow competition by issuing licences to new Public Telecommunications Operators (PTOs) of fixed networks and mobile networks.

Two events in 1981 heralded the beginning of deregulation and increased competition in the UK telecommunications industry: the government sold shares in Cable; and postal and telecommunications services, which had both been run by the Post Office, were

separated and British Telecommunications plc (BT) was formed.

Privatization of BT took place in stages, beginning in 1984 when the Government sold 51 percent of its shares in BT to the public. In the same year, BT lost its monopoly on telecommunications provision and services in the UK when Mercury Communications was granted an operator's licence. The introduction of Vodafone and Cellnet cellular radio networks in 1985 provided the BT and Mercury duopoly with some competition, encouraging the development of new markets. Cable television operators were also granted licences to provide telecommunications services, but only as agents for BT and Mercury.

The BT/Mercury duopoly on fixed services continued until 1991 when the Government decided to accept applications for licences

from new operators. Vodafone and Cellnet were issued with licences to provide fixed services, and cable television networks were allowed to offer services in their own right.

Restrictions on the use of leased lines for the provision of international services were lifted in 1991. Further competition was encouraged with the creation of International Simple Resale (ISR). This system allows operators of international leased lines to interconnect with public networks between designated countries and re-sell their services to both residential and business customers.

In 1996 the Department of Trade and Industry removed the BT/Mercury duopoly on the provision of international telecommunications services and opened the telecommunications industry to full competition.

BT General Services in the UK

Service		Details	Contact (service is free unless stated otherwise)
Customer services	residential customers	to enquire about any BT service or product, to change your phone book entry, or to make a complaint; 8 a.m. to 6 p.m., Monday to Saturday	from a BT line: 150; from a mobile phone or non-BT line: 0800 800150
	business customers	Sales Office: to make an enquiry about a BT product or service; Service Centre: to make an after-sales enquiry, to change your phone book entry or to make a complaint; 8 a.m. to 6 p.m., Monday to Saturday	from a BT line: 152; from a mobile phone or non-BT line: 0800 800152
	general enquiries	to enquire about BT media relations, schools liaison, building services, land planning, wayleaves (concerning access to properties for building work, etc), or personnel; 8 a.m. to 6 p.m., Monday to Friday	from any line: 0800 309409; from a mobile phone or non-BT line: 0800 309409
Fault reporting	residential customers	24 hours a day, 7 days a week	from a BT line: 151; from a mobile phone or non-BT line: 0800 800151
	business customers	24 hours a day, 7 days a week	from any line: 0800 800154; from a mobile phone: 0800 800154
Bill enquiries	residential customers	8 a.m. to 6 p.m., Monday to Saturday	from a BT line: 150; from a mobile phone or non-BT line: 0800 800150
	business customers	8 a.m. to 6 p.m., Monday to Saturday	from any line: 0800 800156; from a mobile phone: 0800 800156
Making a complaint		contact customer services (see above) for complaints about any BT services	contact customer services (see above)
Operator services		for help making a call, 24 hours a day, 7 days a week	local and national calls, and calls to the Republic of Ireland: 100; international calls: 155
Directory enquiries		for help finding a number or code, 24 hours a day, 7 days a week	local and national numbers and numbers for the Republic of Ireland: 192[1]; international numbers: 153[1]; for those who cannot hold, handle, or read *The Phone Book*, contact 195 for free directory enquiry service

BT General Services in the UK (*continued*)

Service	Details	Contact (service is free unless stated otherwise)
Customers with special needs	details of BT services for customers with special needs, including people with impaired hearing, speech difficulties, restricted vision, and limited mobility, can be found in *The Phone Book*	
Malicious calls	customer services will provide simple advice on the most suitable action to take	150
	adviceline: BT provides information on how to deal with unwanted phone calls and what BT can offer to help tackle the problem, 24 hours a day, 7 days a week	0800 666700
	specialist bureau: specially trained investigators will help tackle the problem. In extreme cases, they can work with the police to trace calls	0800 661441

[1] Unless calls are made from a public payphone, users are charged 21p (excluding VAT) per use for directory enquiries services for both residential and business lines.

Source: British Telecommunications plc

BT Select Services in the UK

Service	Details
Call Minder	network-based call answering service; answers up to two calls simultaneously; answers calls if you are already using the phone or modem; messages can be up to 5 minutes long; maximum 30 messages or 15 minutes; retrieve messages free from your home phone; store and replay messages; requires connection to a BT digital exchange; to use Call Minder from your own phone, dial 1571 and follow the voice prompts; to use Call Minder from another phone, dial your own number and when Call Minder answers dial ** followed by your PIN; will not work with Call Diversion or Call Barring; to rent, Call Minder costs £5.00 per quarter
Caller Display	see the number of the person calling before you pick up the phone; use with any caller-display equipment, for example, Caller Display 50 or Relate 1000 telephones; requires connection to a BT digital exchange; users should note that numbers from some payphones, chargecards, switchboards, and non-BT networks may not be displayed; dial 141 before your call if you want to withhold your number; to rent, Caller Display costs £4.00 per quarter
Call Barring	prevents access to certain types of number, for example international, premium-rate, or mobile-phone numbers; requires the use of a PIN; to activate, dial *34, you will then be given an option-list of 7 types of number; select the type of number you wish to bar access to, then dial to set the command; to reactivate access dial 34, select the type of number, dial *, enter your PIN, dial; Call Barring can also be used for incoming calls; the basic rental for Call Barring is £7.00 per quarter.
Call Waiting	important calls get through when your phone is engaged; bleep indicates when a call is coming in; facility for switching between calls; requires connection to a BT digital exchange; to switch on Call Waiting, dial *43; to put your current call on hold and take the other one, press 'Recall' and then 2 when you hear the dial tone; to finish the call you are on and talk to the other caller, hang up; your phone will ring you back; to switch off Call Waiting, dial 43 (do this before using a fax or modem to avoid data interruptions); to check whether Call Waiting is active, dial *43; to rent, Call Waiting costs £4.00 per quarter
Call Diversion	calls follow you to another location; divert calls to anywhere in the UK; can divert to mobile phones or pager bureaux; requires connection to a BT digital exchange; to rent, Call Diversion costs £7.00 per quarter
Three-Way Calling	talk to two other people at once; one number can be international; requires connection to a BT digital exchange; to set up a three-way call, make your first call and once connected, explain what you are doing; press 'Recall' and then dial the second person; when they answer, press 'Recall' followed by 3 to start an open three-way call, 2 to switch between private calls, 5 to end the first call, or 7 to end the second call; to end an open three-way call, hang up; all parties will be disconnected; to end a private call, hang up, your phone will ring and you will be returned to the other caller; Three-Way Calling costs 50p per use, or to rent, £4.00 per quarter, plus the normal cost of the calls
Ring Back	your phone lets you know when a previously-engaged number is free; to use, dial 5 when you hear an engaged tone; wait for a confirmation message and then hang up; when your phone rings, pick it up and wait for the other person to answer; can stack up to 5 ring backs; dial 37 to cancel all Ring Back requests; dial 37* 'telephone number' to cancel individual Ring Back requests; Ring Back is automatically cancelled if not connected within 45 minutes; requires connection to a BT digital exchange; will not work with calls to some multi-line switchboards; Ring Back costs 10p per use, plus the normal cost of the calls
Call Return	dial 1471 to hear the number of the last person to call you, whether answered or not; also includes time and date of call; press 3 to dial the stored number straight away; works with pulse or tone-dialled phones; requires connection to a BT digital exchange; Call Return is a free service – there are no set-up or rental charges
Charge Advice	exchange rings you back with your last call's approximate cost and duration; before you make a call, dial *40* followed by the phone number and ; on some exchanges you may have to dial *40 followed by the phone number instead, without the final ; to book charge advice during a call, press 'Recall' and then dial *40 when you hear the dial tone; to book Charge Advice for all calls, dial *411; to cancel Charge Advice for all calls, dial 411; requires connection to a BT digital exchange; Charge Advice is a free service – there are no set-up or rental charges
Reminder Calls	use the phone as an alarm clock; for single Reminder Calls, dial *55*, then time in 24-hour format; to cancel a Reminder Call, dial 55; to check a Reminder Call, dial *55; Reminder Calls cost 20p per use and there are no set-up or rental charges

Source: British Telecommunications plc

Operator-Connected Calls in the UK

Help Making Calls
The Operator can provide help in making calls, 24 hours a day, 7 days a week. For help making local and national calls and calls to the Republic of Ireland, call free on 100. For help with international calls, call free on 155. The operator can help with the following services: calls to someone else in the UK; calls to someone abroad; calls from abroad; calls to or from a ship.

Alarm Calls
The Operator can arrange for you to be called at a set time. Users of this service will be charged £2.70.

Telemessages
The Operator can arrange for a message given over the phone to be delivered by post the next day. Telemessages within the UK cost £8.99 for 50 words. For special occasions, such as weddings or birthdays, a telemessage card with up to 50 words can be sent for £9.99. For more information, contact Freefone: 0800 190190.

Emergency Telephone Numbers in the UK

For emergency services in the UK
Fire, Police, Ambulance, Coastguard (sea and cliff rescue), Mountain Rescue, and Cave Rescue, dial: 999. 112 can also be dialled as an alternative.

The operator asks callers which emergency service they require and then connects the caller to the service. Callers should tell the emergency service: where the trouble is; what the trouble is; where the caller is, and the number of the telephone they are using.

Textphone users should contact Typetalk's emergency relay service on: 0800 112999 text.

It is against the law to make false calls to the emergency services. Callers making false calls can be traced immediately to the telephone that they are calling from.

International Direct Dialling Codes from the UK

When dialling overseas from the UK, prefix the country codes below with the international network access code: 00; then dial the area code, followed by the number that you wish to call.

Country/territory	Code	Country/territory	Code	Country/territory	Code	Country/territory	Code
Afghanistan	93	China	86	Guinea	224	Marshall Islands	692
Albania	355	Colombia	57	Guinea-Bissau	245	Martinique	596
Algeria	213	Comoros	269	Guyana	592	Mauritania	222
American Samoa	684	Congo, Democratic		Haiti	509	Mauritius	230
Andorra	376	Republic of	243	Honduras	504	Mexico	52
Angola	244	Congo, Republic of the	242	Hong Kong	852	Micronesia	691
Anguilla	809	Costa Rica	506	Hungary	36	Moldova	373
Antarctica (Scott Base)	672	Côte d'Ivoire	225	Iceland	354	Monaco	377
Antigua and Barbuda	1 268	Croatia	385	India	91	Mongolia	976
Argentina	54	Cuba	53	Indonesia	62	Montserrat	1 664
Armenia	374	Cyprus	357	Iran	98	Morocco	212
Aruba	297	Czech Republic	42	Iraq	964	Mozambique	258
Ascension Island	247	Denmark	45	Ireland, Republic of	353	Myanmar	95
Australia	61	Djibouti	253	Israel	972	Namibia	264
Austria	43	Dominica	1 809	Italy	39	Nauru	674
Azerbaijan	994	Dominican Republic	1 809	Jamaica	1 876	Nepal	977
Bahamas	1 242	Ecuador	593	Japan	81	Netherlands	31
Bahrain	973	Egypt	20	Jordan	962	New Caledonia	687
Bangladesh	880	El Salvador	503	Kazakhstan	7	New Zealand	64
Barbados	1 246	Equatorial Guinea	240	Kenya	254	Nicaragua	505
Belarus	375	Eritrea	291	Kiribati	686	Niger	227
Belgium	32	Estonia	372	Korea, North	850	Nigeria	234
Belize	501	Ethiopia	251	Korea, South	82	Northern Mariana	
Benin	229	Falkland Islands	500	Kuwait	965	Islands	670
Bermuda	1 441	Fiji	679	Kyrgyzstan	7	Norway	47
Bhutan	975	Finland	358	Laos	856	Oman	968
Bolivia	591	France	33	Latvia	371	Pakistan	92
Bosnia-Herzegovina	387	French Antilles	596	Lebanon	961	Palau	680
Botswana	267	French Guiana	594	Lesotho	266	Panama	507
Brazil	55	French Polynesia	689	Liberia	231	Papua New Guinea	675
Brunei	673	Gabon	241	Libya	218	Paraguay	595
Bulgaria	359	Gambia	220	Liechtenstein	4175	Peru	51
Burkina Faso	226	Georgia	995	Lithuania	370	Philippines	63
Burundi	257	Germany	49	Luxembourg	352	Poland	48
Cambodia	855	Ghana	233	Macau	853	Portugal	351
Cameroon	237	Gibraltar	350	Macedonia, Former		Puerto Rico	1 787
Canada	1	Greece	30	Yugoslav Republic of	389	Qatar	974
Cape Verde	238	Greenland	299	Madagascar	261	Romania	40
Cayman Islands	1 345	Grenada	1 809	Malawi	265	Russia	7
Central African		Guadeloupe	590	Malaysia	60	Rwanda	250
Republic	236	Guam	671	Maldives	960	St Kitts and Nevis	1 869
Chad	235	Guantanamo Bay	5399	Mali	223	St Lucia	1 758
Chile	56	Guatemala	502	Malta	356	St Vincent and	
						the Grenadines	1 809

International Direct Dialling Codes from the UK (*continued*)

Country/territory	Code	Country/territory	Code	Country/territory	Code	Country/territory	Code
Samoa	685	Spain	34	Tonga	676	USA	1
San Marino	378	Sri Lanka	94	Trinidad and Tobago	1 868	Uzbekistan	7
São Tomé and Principe	239	Sudan	249	Tunisia	216	Vanuatu	678
Saudi Arabia	966	Suriname	597	Turkey	90	Vatican City	39
Senegal	221	Swaziland	268	Turkmenistan	7	Venezuela	58
Seychelles	248	Sweden	46	Turks and Caicos		Vietnam	84
Sierra Leone	232	Switzerland	41	Islands	1 649	Virgin Islands, British	1 809 49
Singapore	65	Syria	963	Tuvalu	688	Virgin Islands, US	1 340
Slovakia	42	Taiwan	886	Uganda	256	Yemen	967
Slovenia	386	Tajikistan	7	UK	44	Yugoslavia	381
Solomon Islands	677	Tanzania	255	Ukraine	380	Zambia	260
Somalia	252	Thailand	66	United Arab Emirates	971	Zimbabwe	263
South Africa	27	Togo	228	Uruguay	598		

US State Dialling Codes

For states with more than one area code, callers should consult International Directory Enquiries (call 153).

State	Area code	State	Area code	State	Area code
Alabama	205 or 334	Kansas	316 or 913	Ohio	216, 330, 419, 513, 614, or 937
Alaska	907	Kentucky	502 or 606		
Arizona	520 or 602	Louisiana	318 or 504	Oklahoma	405 or 918
Arkansas	501	Maine	207	Oregon	503 or 541
California	209, 213, 230, 310, 408, 415, 510, 562, 619, 707, 714, 760, 805, 818, 907, 909, or 916	Maryland	301 or 410	Pennsylvania	215, 412, 610, 717, 724, or 814
		Massachusetts	413, 508, or 617		
		Michigan	313, 517, 616, 810, or 906	Rhode Island	401
				South Carolina	803 or 864
Colorado	303, 719, or 970	Minnesota	218, 320, 507, or 612	South Dakota	605
Connecticut	203 or 860	Mississippi	601	Tennessee	423, 615, or 901
Delaware	302	Missouri	314, 417, 573, or 816	Texas	210, 214, 281, 409, 512, 713, 806, 817, 903, 915, or 972
District of Columbia	202	Montana	406		
Florida	305, 352, 407, 561, 813, 904, 941, or 954	Nebraska	308 or 402		
		Nevada	702	Utah	801
Georgia	404, 706, 770, or 912	New Hampshire	603	Vermont	802
Hawaii	808	New Jersey	201, 609, or 908	Virginia	540, 703, 757, or 804
Idaho	208	New Mexico	505	Washington	206, 360, or 509
Illinois	217, 309, 618, 630, 639, 708, 815, or 847	New York	212, 315, 516, 518, 607, 716, 718, or 914	West Virginia	304
				Wisconsin	414, 608, or 715
Indiana	219, 317, or 812	North Carolina	704, 910, or 919	Wyoming	307
Iowa	319, 515, or 712	North Dakota	701		

Source: US Department of Commerce

Citizenship and Immigration Information

Customs Allowances of the UK

Source: HM Customs and Excise. © Crown copyright 1997

If travellers are entering the UK from another European Union (EU) country, they no longer need to go through the red ('something to declare') or green ('nothing to declare') channels at Customs. EU travellers usually go through a separate exit, sometimes called the blue channel, and do not have to pass through Customs at all.

While travellers may not see any Customs officers on arrival in the UK, it is important to remember that Customs do carry out selective checks to look for prohibited and restricted goods.

The EU countries are: Austria, Belgium, Denmark, Finland, France, Germany, Greece, the Republic of Ireland, Italy, Luxembourg, the Netherlands, Portugal, Spain (but not the Canary Islands), Sweden, and the UK (but not the Channel Islands).

Prohibited and Restricted Goods

Certain goods are restricted or banned completely from being brought into the UK from any country. Restricted goods are those which cannot be imported into the

UK without an appropriate authority, such as a licence. Within the EU, these restrictions may vary slightly. Travellers are advised to contact the Customs departments of the countries they are leaving to enquire whether particular goods are banned or restricted in the UK. The table below provides examples of banned and restricted goods from outside the EU, together with contact details for enquiries.

Goods Bought in the EU – Duty-Free and Tax-Free Goods

Travellers to EU countries can purchase goods in the quantities shown below from duty-free and tax-free shops. Under EU law, it is illegal for these shops to sell you more, in total, than these quantities. However, these quantities can be purchased on each journey to an EU country and brought back into the UK as long as they are for personal use.

The duty-free and tax-free goods are: 200 cigarettes or 100 cigarillos or 50 cigars or 250 gms of tobacco; 2 litres of still table wine; 1 litre of spirits or strong liqueurs over 22 percent volume or 2 litres of fortified wine, sparkling wine, or other liqueurs; 60 cc/ml of perfume; 250 cc/ml of

toilet water; £75 worth of all other goods including souvenirs and gifts.

Note: people aged under 17 do not have a tobacco or alcohol allowance, they are not allowed to bring tobacco or alcohol into the country.

Duty-Paid and Tax-Paid Goods

If goods are bought within the EU and have had the duty or tax paid on them, the allowances are different. The law states that these allowances are a guide; it is permitted to bring more than the below allowances into the country, but if more than the following levels are brought into the UK, Customs officers must completely satisfied that the goods are for personal use and not for resale: 800 cigarettes; 400 cigarillos; 200 cigars; 1 kg of smoking tobacco; 10 litres of spirits; 20 litres of fortified wine (such as port or sherry); 90 litres of wine (of which not more than 60 litres can be sparkling wine); 110 litres of beer.

Note: these quantities include anything bought duty- or tax-free. Personal use includes gifts (i.e. goods bought for others are included in your personal allowance). The selling on of duty-free or duty-paid goods can be a criminal offence. Anyone caught committing such an offence can face the seizure of their goods and up to seven years in prison. If

Prohibited and Restricted Goods

(– = not applicable.)

Type of goods	Details	Contact for further information
Prohibited (Banned) Goods		–
Unlicensed drugs	such as heroin, morphine, cocaine, cannabis, amphetamines, barbiturates, and LSD	–
Offensive weapons	such as flick knives, swordsticks, knuckledusters, and some martial arts equipment	–
Obscene material	such as pornographic material in the form of books, magazines, films, video tapes, laser discs, and computer software, and indecent or obscene material featuring children	
Counterfeit and copied goods	such as watches, clothes, and CDs. Also any fake goods with false marks of their origin, e.g. fake designer labels on clothes	–
Restricted Goods		
Firearms, explosives, and ammunition	including electric shock devices (such as stunguns) and gas canisters	Excise and Inland Customs Advice Centre (see below)
Dogs, cats, and other animals	including rabbits, gerbils, rats, and mice; a British import (rabies) licence is vital	Ministry of Agriculture, Fisheries and Food: (0181) 330 4411
Live birds	including family pets, unless they are covered by a British health import licence	Ministry of Agriculture, Fisheries and Food: (0181) 330 4411
Endangered species	including birds and plants, whether alive or dead. Also goods, such as fur, ivory, or leather, that have been taken from endangered species	Department of the Environment: (0117) 987 8202
Meat and poultry	including most products made from them, such as bacon, ham, sausages, paté, eggs, milk, and cream; 1 kg of meat per person is allowed as long as it is fully cooled and in airtight containers	Ministry of Agriculture, Fisheries and Food: (0181) 330 4411
Certain plants and their produce	including trees, shrubs, potatoes, certain fruit, bulbs, and seeds	Ministry of Agriculture, Fisheries and Food: (01904) 455195
Radio transmitters	such as CB radios that are not approved for use in the UK	Radio Communications Agency: (0171) 215 2297

an individual is being paid for buying alcohol or tobacco for somebody else (including receiving only travel expenses), Customs must be contacted and arrangements made to pay any duty and tax owed.

Goods Bought Outside the EU

Travellers arriving in the UK from a country that is not part of the EU must go through customs; through the red channel if they have something to declare; through the green channel if they are confident that they have no more than the Customs allowances and are not carrying any prohibited, restricted, or commercial goods.

For travellers arriving from outside the EU, the following allowances apply: 200 cigarettes or 100 cigarillos or 50 cigars or 250 gms of tobacco; 2 litres of still table wine; 1 litre of spirits or strong liqueurs over 22 percent volume or 2 litres of fortified wine, sparkling wine, or other liqueurs; 60 cc/ml of perfume; 250 cc/ml of toilet water; £145 worth of all other goods including souvenirs and gifts.

Note: people aged under 17 do not have a tobacco or alcohol allowance, they are not allowed to bring tobacco or alcohol into the country.

Money

There are no legal limits to the amount of money that travellers can bring into the UK from either within or outside the EU. However, if a traveller is found be in possession of more than £10,000 sterling in cash or items transferable to cash, such as traveller's cheques or share certificates, they will be challenged to explain why and to provide proof of their explanation.

Further Information

For further information about UK Customs rules and allowances, contact one of the Excise and Inland Customs Advice Centres below:

Belfast Custom House, Queens Square, Belfast BT1 3ET; phone: (01232) 562600; fax: (01232) 562971; open: 9.00 a.m.–5.00 p.m.

Birmingham Two Broadway, Broad Street, Five Ways, Birmingham B15 1BG; phone: (0121) 697 4000; fax: (0121) 697 4002; open: 9.00 a.m.–4.00 p.m.

Bristol Froomsgate House, Rupert Street, Bristol BS1 2QP; phone: (0117) 900 2000; fax: (0117) 900 2006; open 9.00 a.m.–4.30 p.m.

Cardiff Portcullis House, 21 Cowbridge Road East, Cardiff CF1 9SS; phone: (01222) 386200; fax: (01222) 386222; open: 9.00 a.m.–4.30 p.m.

Cheadle Boundary House, Cheadle Point, Cheadle, Cheshire SK8 2JZ; phone: (0161) 912 7300; fax: (0161) 912 7399; open: 9.00 a.m.–4.30 p.m.

Chester Eden House, Lakeside, Chester Business Park, Wrexham Road, Chester CH4 9QY; phone: (01244) 684200; fax: (01244) 684299; open: 9.00 a.m.–4.30 p.m.

Dundee Caledonian House, Greenmarket, Dundee DD1 1HD; phone: (0345) 442266; fax: (01382) 313247; open: 9.00 a.m.–4.00 p.m.

Glasgow Portcullis House, 21 India Street, Glasgow G2 4PZ; phone: (0345) 442266; fax: (0141) 308 3416; open: 9.00 a.m.–4.30 p.m.

Gloucester Elmbridge Court, Cheltenham Road, Gloucester GL3 1JX; phone: (01452) 306522; fax: (01452) 302258; open: 9.00 a.m.–4.30 p.m.

Ipswich Haven House, 17 Lower Brook Street, Ipswich, Suffolk IP4 1DN; phone: (01473) 235951; fax: (01473) 235921; open: 9.00 a.m.–4.30 p.m.

London Central Berkeley House, 304 Regents Park Road, Finchley, London N3 2JY; phone: (0171) 865 4400; fax: (0181) 346 9154; open: 9.00 a.m.–4.30 p.m.

London South Dorset House, Stamford Street, London SE1 9PY; phone: (0171) 202 4227; fax: (0171) 202 4216; open: 9.00 a.m.–5.00 p.m; non-UK phone: (44) 171 202 4227; non-UK fax: (44) 171 202 4216

Newcastle-upon-Tyne Custom House, 39 Quayside, Newcastle-upon-Tyne NE1 3ES; phone: (0191) 261 0981; fax: (0191) 223 1425; open: 9.00 a.m.– 4.00 p.m.

Nottingham Bowman House, 100–102 Talbot Street, Nottingham NG1 5NG; phone: (0115) 971 2100; fax: (0115) 948 3487; open: 9.00 a.m.–4.00 p.m.

Plymouth Crownhill Court, Tailyour Road, Crownhill, Plymouth PL6 5BZ; phone: (01752) 777123; fax: (01752) 765807; open: 10.00 a.m.–4.00 p.m.

Reading Eldon Court, 75 London Road, Reading RG1 5BS; phone: (0118) 964 4200; fax: (0118) 964 4208; open: 9.00 a.m.–5.00 p.m.

Redhill Warwick House, 67 Station Road, Redhill, Surrey RH1 1QU; phone: (08450) 199199; fax: (01737) 734600; open: 9.00 a.m.–5.00 p.m.

Southampton Custom House, Orchard Place, Southampton SO14 3NS; phone: (01703) 827068; fax: (01703) 827048; open: 9.00 a.m.–5.00 p.m. Contact details can also be found in the phone book under Customs and Excise. For advice on Air Passenger Duty, please contact the Excise and Inland Customs Advice Centre office: 1 Park Road, Uxbridge, Middx UB8 1PW; phone: (0189) 584 2226; fax: (0189) 581 4305 (not open to the public)

Web site: www.open.gov.uk/customs

Passport Regulations and Requirements of the UK

Source: The UK Passport Agency. © Crown copyright 1997

Eligibility for a UK Passport

As of 1 January 1983, under the British Nationality Act 1981, UK passports are issued to British citizens; British subjects; British Dependent Territories citizens; British Overseas citizens; British Protected Persons; British Nationals (Overseas). British Nationals (Overseas) passports can be acquired only by people with a connection to Hong Kong.

The most usual ways to qualify as one of the above (excluding British Nationals (Overseas)), are by birth in the UK or a British Colony; by naturalization in the UK or a British Colony; by registration as a citizen of the UK and Colonies; by legitimate descent from a father to whom one of the above applies.

Women who marry UK citizens do not automatically acquire British nationality by marriage (see 'Immigration Rules of the UK').

Anyone who is unsure about their eligibility to hold a UK passport should contact a Passport Office for advice (see below).

While the holder of a UK passport can generally travel anywhere in the world, travellers are not exempt from immigration rules in other countries. Nor are they exempt from obtaining any necessary visas.

Passport Applications

UK passports are issued in the UK by the six Regional Passport Offices of the United Kingdom Passport Agency, an Executive Agency of the Home Office. Passport application forms can be obtained from the Regional Passport Offices (see over page), main Post Offices, Lloyds Bank, and ARTAC WorldChoice Travel Agents. Until recently, three types of passport were available in the UK: the standard ten-year passport, the British Visitor's Passport, valid for travel to EU countries for one year, and the Collective Passport, valid for a single journey for sponsored parties of young people under the age of 18. The British Visitor's Passport has been abolished, and the standard ten-year passport is now required to travel abroad. The Collective Passport is still available. The following table gives details of the current types of passports available, together with information on validity, postal application fees, and the forms required to make applications. (Fees are current as of 28 March 1998.)

Notes

Family passports have now been discontinued, but existing ones may still be used until they expire. Applications that are made in person to Passport Offices will incur a handling charge of £10 per application in addition to the fees listed above. Personal applications do not guarantee a priority service.

Women who are getting married and want to change their names on their passports in time for their honeymoon can do so by requesting special forms PD1 and PD2. Applications must not be made more than three months before the wedding. For further information, contact a Passport Office (see table). It should be noted that some countries will not grant visas on these passports.

UK Passports

Type of passport	Validity/details	Application fee (£)	Application form required
New Passports			
Standard passport (30 pages)	normally valid for ten years	21	Form A
Large standard passport (48 pages)	for persons who travel widely, valid for 10 years	31	Form A
Standard passport for minors under 16	valid initially for 5 years	11	Form B
Collective passports	valid on a single journey for organized trips for school children or young people under the age of 18	40	contact Passport Office for application form
Additions/Amendments to Existing Passports			
Standard passport	if replacing and surrendering a ten-year passport	11	Form R
Standard passport	to make changes or add children to a UK passport	11	Form C
Standard passport for minors under 16	to extend a passport (total possible life is ten years)	no fee[1]/11[2]	Form D

[1] For passports issued before 28 March 1998.
[2] For passports issued after 28 March 1998.

Travellers are advised to contact the Embassy or High Commission of the country concerned for further information. Married women can also amend their passport details after their marriage to show their new name, if applicable, using Form C.

If a passport is lost or stolen, an application for a replacement can be made using Forms A or B. Details of the lost passport will need to be given and photographs, relevant documents, and the usual fee will have to be submitted. Initially, a replacement passport, valid for one year, might be issued, to enable enquiries about the lost passport to be made.

Completing Passport Applications

Instructions for completing applications are provided on the forms. Original documents proving status and eligibility for a UK passport must be sent with an application; copies are not acceptable. The type of documents required with an application are detailed on application forms and vary according to the type of application. Documents to be produced may include any of the following: birth certificate; marriage certificate; proof of a name change; adoption certificate; divorce decree; old passport; registration document; naturalization document.

Where photographic evidence of identity is required with a passport application, two identical copies of a recent photograph should be included. These should be unmounted, printed on normal thin photographic paper, and should measure 45 mm x 35 mm/1.77 in x 1.38 in. The photograph should show the full face, without a hat, and should be taken against a light background. One copy of the photograph must be signed by someone else to confirm the identity of the applicant. This person must be one of the following Member of Parliament; Justice of the Peace; Minister of Religion; professionally qualified person (for example, doctor, lawyer, teacher, etc); Local Councillor;

Bank Officer; Civil Servant; Police Officer; or someone of similar standing who has known you for at least two years, and who is either a British citizen, British Dependent Territories citizen, British National (Overseas), British Overseas citizen, British Subject, or a citizen of a Commonwealth country. A relative cannot countersign a passport application.

Passport applications should be made at least one month before the passport is needed. The time of year that an application is made can affect the speed with which it is processed. The UK Passport Agency explains in its leaflet *Answers to Questions People Ask Us* (included with all passport application forms) that passports can be issued within two weeks between the months of September and December. Between January and August, applications can take up to four weeks to be processed. If a passport is needed more quickly than in two to four weeks, it is possible to process properly completed applications if they are submitted together with a photocopy of proof of travel, for example, a flight ticket. It is not normally possible to obtain a passport on the day of application. However, in cases of emergency, travellers are advised to contact a Passport Office for advice (see below).

Regional Passport Offices and Areas Covered

(Minicom numbers are for the deaf and hard of hearing.)

Liverpool Passport Office, 5th Floor, India Buildings, Water Street, Liverpool L2 0QZ; phone: (0151) 237 3010; minicom: (0151) 236 6292

Areas covered by the Liverpool Passport Office:

Cheshire; Cleveland; Clwyd; Cumbria; Derbyshire; Durham; Greater Manchester; Humberside; Lancashire; Merseyside; Northumberland; North Yorkshire; South Yorkshire; Staffordshire; Tyne and Wear; West Yorkshire

London Passport Office, 70 Petty France, London SW1H 9HD; phone: (0171) 799 2290; minicom: (0171) 271 8808

The London Office only deals with personal callers. Postal applications from residents of Greater London should be sent to the Glasgow Passport Office.

Newport Passport Office, Olympia House, Upper Dock Street, Newport, Gwent NP9 1XA; phone: (01633) 244500; minicom: (01633) 473701

Areas covered by the Newport Passport Office:

Avon; Berkshire; Cornwall; Devon; Dorset; Dyfed; East Sussex; Gloucestershire; Gwent; Hampshire; Hereford; Isle of Wight; Mid Glamorgan; Oxfordshire; Powys; Shropshire; Somerset; South Glamorgan; Surrey (less London Boroughs); West Glamorgan; West Sussex; Wiltshire; Worcestershire

Peterborough Passport Office, Aragon Court, Northminster Road, Peterborough PE1 1QG; phone: (01733) 895555; minicom: (01733) 555688

Areas covered by the Peterborough Passport Office:

Bedfordshire; Buckinghamshire; Cambridgeshire; Essex (less London Boroughs); Hertfordshire (less London Boroughs); Kent (less London Boroughs); Leicestershire; Lincolnshire; Norfolk; Northamptonshire; Nottinghamshire; Suffolk; Warwickshire; West Midlands

Belfast Passport Office, Hampton House, 47–53 High Street, Belfast BT1 2QS; phone: (01232) 232371; minicom: (01232) 330214

The Belfast Passport Office deals with all applications in Northern Ireland.

Glasgow Passport Office, 3 Northgate, 96 Milton Street, Cowcaddens, Glasgow G4 0BT; phone: (0141) 332 0271; minicom: (0141) 332 4621

The Glasgow Passport Office deals with all applications in Scotland and those from Greater London.

Visa Requirements for Travel to and from the UK

Source: Foreign and Commonwealth Office; Home Office Immigration and Nationality Directorate. © Crown copyright 1997

(See also 'Visiting and Immigration to the UK'.)

Foreign Visitors Travelling to the UK

All overseas nationals wishing to enter the UK must satisfy immigration officers on arrival in this country that they meet the requirements of UK immigration law. Where necessary, people must have a valid entry clearance (visa or entry certificate) before arriving in the UK. Nationals of the countries or territories listed below must have a valid UK visa each time they enter the country:

Afghanistan; Albania; Algeria; Angola; Armenia; Azerbaijan; Bahrain; Bangladesh; Belarus; Benin; Bhutan; Bosnia-Herzegovina; Bulgaria; Burkina Faso; Burundi; Cambodia; Cameroon; Cape Verde; Central African Republic; Chad; China; Colombia; Comoros; Congo, Democratic Republic of; Congo, Republic of the; Côte d'Ivoire; Cuba; Cyprus, Turkish Republic of Northern; Djibouti; Dominican Republic; Ecuador; Egypt; Equatorial Guinea; Eritrea; Ethiopia; Fiji; Former Yugoslav Republic of Macedonia; Gabon; Gambia; Georgia; Ghana; Guinea; Guinea-Bissau; Guyana; Haiti; India; Indonesia; Iran; Iraq; Jordan; Kazakhstan; Kenya; Kyrgyzstan; Korea, North; Kuwait; Laos; Lebanon; Liberia; Libya; Madagascar; Maldives; Mali; Mauritania; Mauritius; Moldova; Mongolia; Morocco; Mozambique; Myanmar; Nepal; Niger; Nigeria; Oman; Pakistan; Papua New Guinea; Peru; Philippines; Qatar; Romania; Russia; Rwanda; São Tomé and Príncipe; Saudi Arabia; Senegal; Sierra Leone; Somalia; Sri Lanka; Sudan; Suriname; Syria; Taiwan; Tajikistan; Tanzania; Thailand; Togo; Tunisia; Turkey; Turkmenistan; Uganda; Ukraine; United Arab Emirates; Uzbekistan; Vietnam; Yemen; Yugoslavia (documents issued by former SFR of Yugoslavia or by present Yugoslav authorities); Zambia

Nationals of any country not listed above do not need a UK visa for a visit or to study in the UK. However, an entry clearance must be obtained if they wish to do one of the following: settle in the UK; work in the UK (unless a work permit is held); set up business in the UK; live in the UK as a person of independent means; accompany or join someone going to the UK for any of the above purposes.

Applicants for entry clearance to the UK must fill in all necessary official forms. These forms are available from British Missions in foreign countries offering entry clearance services. Applicants should check with their nearest British Mission for information and advice.

For more information about British immigration and visa requirements, see the Internet Service of the Foreign and Commonwealth Office: www.fco.gov.uk/visa/ or contact the Immigration and Nationalisation Directorate (IND) at:

Lunar House, 40 Wellesley Road, Croydon, Surrey CR9 2BY; phone: (0181) 686 0688 (general enquiries)

Alternatively, contact the Immigration Advisory Service (IAS). The IAS is an independent charity that gives free and confidential advice, assistance and representation to anyone applying for an entry clearance to the UK. Their address is:

County House, 190 Great Dover Street, London SE1 4YB; phone: (0171) 357 6917; duty office 24 hrs: (0181) 814 1559; fax: (0171) 378 0665

British Nationals Travelling Overseas

British nationals wishing to travel abroad should enquire about any visa requirements at the Embassy, High Commission, or consulate of the country they plan to visit. Tourists can check with their travel agents. Business and tourist visa requirements in foreign countries change constantly, sometimes at short notice. They also vary according to the length of stay and purpose of the visit.

There are some countries to which UK nationals are advised against travelling.

The Travel Advice Unit of the Foreign and Commonwealth Office advises against all travel to the following destinations (as of February 1998): Afghanistan, Algeria, Burundi, Chechen Republic (Russian Federation), Iraq, Jammu and Kashmir (India), North West Cameroon, Papua New Guinea, Republic of the Congo, Sierra Leone, Somalia, Tajikistan, Western Sahara.

Unless on essential business, the Travel Advice Unit advises against travel to the following destinations (as of February 1998): Albania, Angola, Central African Republic, Liberia, Montserrat, Rwanda, South Eastern Turkey, South Sudan.

Travellers wanting up-to-date information or advice from the Foreign and Commonwealth Office about travelling abroad can use the Internet Service of the Foreign and Commonwealth Office – www.fco.gov.uk/visa/ – or contact the British Embassy of the country to which they wish to travel.

Visiting and Immigration to the UK

Source: Home Office Immigration and Nationality Directorate. © Crown copyright 1997

(See also 'Visa Requirements for Travel to and from the UK'.)

General Information

People wishing to visit the UK must be able to prove that they wish to visit the country for no more than six months, that they plan to leave the UK at the end of their visit, and that they have enough funds to finance their visit

without applying for social security benefits. Multiple-entry visas (valid for two years) can be applied for by frequent business visitors. People wishing to visit the UK on business can do so if they satisfy the criteria above, with an additional proviso that they live and work abroad and do not intend to move their business base to this country, or plan to take employment, produce goods, or provide services in the UK. There is no strict limit to the number of visits to the UK. However, a visitor is not normally expected to spend more than six months out of any twelve month period in the country.

Students

People who wish to come to the UK to study must show that they have been accepted for a course of study at a publicly funded institution of further or higher education, a bona fide private education institution, or an independent fee-paying school. They must also show that they will be undertaking an appropriate educational course, such as a recognised full-time degree course, a weekday course with a minimum of 15 hours' organised daytime study per week, or a full-time course of study at an independent fee-paying school. Students must be able to meet the costs of their course and maintain and accommodate themselves (and any dependants) without working or applying for benefits. Students must be intending to leave the UK on completion of their studies.

Au Pairs

An au pair placement is an arrangement whereby a single person aged between 17 and 27 comes to the UK to study English and live as a member of an English-speaking family. The au pair helps in the home for a maximum of five hours a day with a minimum of two full days off each week. In return, the au pair receives a reasonable allowance and the use of his or her own room. An au pair placement is for a maximum of two years. The following countries are included in the au pair scheme:

Andorra; Bosnia-Herzegovina; Croatia; Cyprus; Czech Republic; Faroe Islands; Former Yugoslav Republic of Macedonia; Greenland; Hungary; Malta; Monaco; San Marino; Slovak Republic; Slovenia; Switzerland; Turkey

Nationals of the European Economic Area (EEA) can enter the UK to work or study without any formalities (see details on the European Economic Area below). Visas have to be obtained by nationals of the following countries applying to work in the UK as an au pair:

Bosnia-Herzegovina; Former Yugoslav Republic of Macedonia; Turkey

Anyone who wishes to come to the UK as an au pair must show that they want to enter the country having arranged an au pair placement and that they are not married; they have no dependants; they do not intend to stay in the UK for more than two years as an au pair; they are able to maintain and accommodate themselves without applying for benefits; they intend to leave the country on completion of their stay as an au pair.

Permission to extend a stay in the UK for more than the normal two-year period will only be granted to someone who entered the UK as an au pair; permission will not be granted to anyone who did not enter the UK as an au pair.

Working Holidaymakers

In the UK, there is a working holidaymaker scheme. This is an arrangement whereby a single person aged between 17 and 27 comes to the UK for an extended holiday (maximum two years) before settling down in their own country. Part-time or casual employment is allowed as part of the conditions of being in the UK as a working holidaymaker. Working holidaymakers must show that they: are a Commonwealth citizen, British Dependent Territories citizen, or British Overseas citizen; are seeking entry for an extended holiday; are unmarried or married to a person who at the same time qualifies for entry as a working holidaymaker, and that they intend to take a holiday together; do not have any dependent children who are five years of age or over, or who will reach five years of age before they complete their holiday; only intend to take employment that will be incidental (casual or part-time) to their holiday; are able to support and accommodate themselves without applying for benefits; have the means to pay for their onward journey; intend to leave the UK on completion of their holiday.

Spouses and Fiancé(e)s

A person's spouse or fiancé(e) can apply to join or accompany the person in the UK so long as the person is lawfully living in the UK themselves. Alternatively, they must be returning to settle in the UK on the same occasion as their spouse or fiancé(e). Spouses must show that they: are lawfully married; intend to live together permanently; have met each other; can support themselves and any dependants without applying for benefits; have adequate accommodation where they and their dependants can live without applying for benefits; are not under the age of 16.

On arrival in the UK, a spouse will be given permission to stay and work for 12 months. Near the end of the 12 months, if the couple are still married and intend to live together, the spouse may apply to remain here permanently. Fiancé(e)s must show that they: plan to marry within a reasonable time (usually six months); both plan to live together permanently after they are married; have met each other; have somewhere to live until they are married, without needing to apply for benefits; are able to support themselves and any dependants without applying for benefits.

A fiancé(e) will be given permission to stay in the UK for six months without permission to work. Once married, the fiancée can apply to stay. If granted, permission will be given to stay and work for 12 months after

which time an application to stay in the UK permanently can be made.

Children

To qualify to bring children to the UK, the parents must show that they: are present and settled in the UK, meaning that they live here lawfully, with no time limit on their stay; have adequate accommodation in which the family can all live without applying for benefits; are the child's parent (this includes the stepfather/mother of a child whose father/mother is dead, both the father and mother of an illegitimate child, and an adoptive parent in certain defined circumstances).

For children to qualify to join their parents in the UK, children must show that they: are not leading a life independent of their parents, are not married, or have not formed an independent family unit; are less than 18 years old.

Children cannot normally come to live in the UK if one parent lives abroad, unless the parent here has had sole responsibility for the child's upbringing, or there are serious and compelling reasons which make it undesirable not to allow the child to come here. Provided that the parents of children are settled in the UK, or that the person applying for children to be allowed into the country has sole responsibility for the children, children will normally be allowed to remain permanently in the UK from the date of their arrival. If children are accompanying a spouse into the country, they will normally be given permission to remain in the country for one year, the same period as the spouse. If the spouse is given permission to remain in the country permanently, the children will normally also be allowed to remain permanently in the country.

Adopted Children

Different rules apply to the admission of adopted children into the UK. For information, contact the Immigration and Nationality Directorate of the Home Office: (0181) 686 0688

Right of Abode in the UK (British Citizenship)

The right of abode means that a person is entirely free from UK immigration control; they do not need to obtain the permission of an immigration officer to enter the UK; and they may live and work without restriction. To apply for or to obtain further information about British citizenship contact: Nationality Directorate, 3rd Floor, India Buildings, Water Street, Liverpool L2 0QN; phone: (0151) 237 5200

Relatives

Immigration rules in the UK allow for the admission of widowed mothers and fathers aged 65 or over and the parents or grandparents travelling together, of whom at least one is aged 65 or over. In certain circumstances sons, daughters, sisters, brothers, uncles, and aunts over the age of 18, and also parents and grandparents under 65 may be granted entrance to the UK. People who would like relatives to join them in the UK must be law-

fully living in the country with no time limit on their stay. They must be able to show that they have sufficient funds to support and accommodate their relatives without applying for benefits, and that their relatives are: wholly or mainly financially dependent on them; without other close relatives to turn to for financial support.

Children over 18, sisters, brothers, aunts, uncles, and other parents and grandparents may come if they meet the requirements set out above, and if they can show that they live alone in 'exceptional circumstances'.

Nationals of the European Economic Area (EEA)

If you are a national of one of the following countries, you are a national of the EEA;

Austria; Belgium; Denmark; Finland; France; Germany; Greece; Iceland; Ireland, Republic of; Italy; Liechtenstein; Luxembourg; Netherlands; Norway; Portugal; Spain; Sweden

Note: Iceland, Liechtenstein, and Norway are not members of the European Union (EU). However, under the European Economic Area Agreement, nationals of these countries have the same rights as EU citizens. European Community law grants EEA nationals a right to live and work in the UK. This right is called a right of residence. EEA nationals have a right of residence in the UK if they are working in the UK, or if they are not working in the UK, but have enough funds to support themselves throughout their stay in the country without needing assistance through applying for benefits. Family members of EEA nationals in the UK have the same rights to live and work here. Further information about rights of residence of EEA nationals and their family members can be obtained by writing to: EC Group, European Directorate, Immigration and Nationality Directorate, Room 1204, Apollo House, 36 Wellesley Road, Croydon CR9 3RR.

Further Information

For further information about immigration rules on the above and other categories of immigrants to the UK, contact the Immigration and Nationality Directorate (IND) at: Immigration and Nationality Directorate, Lunar House, 40 Wellesley Road, Croydon, Surrey CR9 2BY. The IND's Telephone Enquiry Bureau (TEB) deals with general enquiries: (0181) 686 0688. The TEB is open from 9 a.m. to 4.45 p.m., Monday to Wednesday, 10 a.m. to 4.45 p.m. Thursday, and from 9 a.m. to 4.30 p.m. on Fridays. In addition, there are a number of public recorded-information lines: overseas visitors call: (0181) 760 1600; overseas students call: (0181) 760 1622; work-permit holders call: (0181) 760 1644; au pairs call: (0181) 760 1666. There are also regional offices which deal with personal enquiries only:

Belfast Belfast Immigration Office, Olive Tree House, Fountain Street, Belfast BT1 5EA; phone: (01232) 322547; open: Tuesday to Thursday 2.00 p.m.–4.00 p.m.

Birmingham Birmingham Public Enquiry Office, Dominion Court, 41 Station Road, Solihull B91 3RT; phone: (0121) 606 7345; open: Monday to Friday 9.00 a.m.–3.00 p.m.

Glasgow Glasgow Immigration Office, Dumbarton Court Argyll Avenue, Glasgow Airport, Paisley PA3 2TD; phone: (0141) 887 2255; open: Monday to Friday 9.30 a.m.–12.30 p.m. and 2.00 p.m–4.00 p.m.

Liverpool Liverpool Immigration Office, Graeme House, Derby Square, Liverpool L2 7SF; phone: (0151) 236 4909; open: Tuesday to Friday 2.00 p.m.–4.00 p.m.

Birth, Marriage, and Death

Birth, Marriage, and Death Registration and Records in the UK

Source: Office of National Statistics. © Crown copyright 1998

Births
In England, Wales, and Northern Ireland, a child's birth must be registered within six weeks of the event. In Scotland, a birth must be registered within three weeks. If the parents are married, either parent should go to their district Registrar of Births, Deaths, and Marriages and provide details of the child and of both parents. It is not a requirement to provide proof of the birth. If the parents are not married, both parents must visit the Registrar if they wish both their details to appear on the birth certificate. Otherwise, only the mother's details will be entered on the certificate. Alternatively, the father can send a sworn testimonial stating that he is the father of the child.

Marriages
Marriages are registered at the time of the event, and a certificate is given to the couple getting married.

Deaths
A death must be registered with the local Registrar of Births, Marriages, and Deaths within five days of the event. When registering a death, the registrar will require the following information about the deceased: full name (including maiden name if applicable) and home address; full

Births in the UK

(N/A = not available. Annual averages or calendar years. Figures have been rounded.)

Year(s)	Live births			Sex ratio[1]	Rates		Total period fertility rate[4]	Stillbirths[5]	Stillbirth rate[5]
	Male	Female	Total		Crude birth rate[2]	General fertility rate[3]			
1900–02	558,000	537,000	1,095,000	1,037	28.6	115.1	N/A	N/A	N/A
1910–12	528,000	508,000	1,037,000	1,039	24.6	99.4	N/A	N/A	N/A
1920–22	522,000	496,000	1,018,000	1,052	23.1	93.0	N/A	N/A	N/A
1930–32	383,000	367,000	750,000	1,046	16.3	66.5	N/A	N/A	N/A
1940–42	372,000	351,000	723,000	1,062	15.0	N/A	1.89	26,000	N/A
1950–52	413,000	390,000	803,000	1,061	16.0	73.7	2.21	18,000	N/A
1960–62	487,000	459,000	946,000	1,063	17.9	90.3	2.80	18,000	N/A
1970–72	453,000	427,000	880,000	1,064	15.8	82.5	2.36	12,000	13
1980–82	377,000	358,000	735,000	1,053	13.0	62.5	1.83	5,000	7
1981	375,000	356,000	731,000	1,053	13.0	62.1	1.81	5,000	7
1982	369,000	350,000	719,000	1,054	12.8	60.6	1.78	5,000	6
1983	371,000	351,000	721,000	1,058	12.8	60.2	1.77	4,000	6
1984	373,000	356,000	730,000	1,049	12.9	60.3	1.77	4,000	6
1985	385,000	366,000	751,000	1,053	13.3	61.4	1.80	4,000	6
1986	387,000	368,000	755,000	1,053	13.3	61.1	1.78	4,000	5
1987	398,000	378,000	776,000	1,053	13.6	62.3	1.82	4,000	5
1988	403,000	384,000	788,000	1,049	13.8	63.2	1.84	4,000	5
1989	398,000	379,000	777,000	1,051	13.6	62.4	1.81	4,000	5
1990	409,000	390,000	799,000	1,049	13.9	64.2	1.84	4,000	5
1991	406,000	386,000	793,000	1,052	13.7	63.6	1.82	4,000	5
1992	400,000	380,000	781,000	1,052	13.5	63.4	1.80	3,000	4
1993	391,000	371,000	762,000	1,054	13.1	62.4	1.76	4,000	6
1994	385,000	365,000	751,000	1,054	12.9	61.6	1.74	4,000	6
1995	375,000	357,000	732,000	1,052	12.5	60.1	1.71	4,000	6
1996	376,000	357,000	733,000	1,055	12.5	60.1	1.72	4,000	6

[1] Sex ratio is the number of male births per 1,000 female births.
[2] Rate per 1,000 population (male and female).
[3] Rate per 1,000 women aged 15–44.
[4] Total period fertility rate is the average number of children which would be born per woman if women experienced the age-specific fertility rates of the period in question throughout their child-bearing life span. Figures for the years 1970–72 and earlier are estimates.
[5] Figures given are based on stillbirths of 28 or more completed weeks of gestation. On 1 October 1992, the legal definition of a stillbirth was altered to include babies born dead between 24 and 27 completed weeks' gestation. Between 1 October and 31 December 1992 in the UK, there were 258 babies born dead between 24 and 27 completed weeks' gestation (216 in England and Wales, 35 in Scotland, and 7 in Northern Ireland). If these babies were included in the stillbirth figures given, the UK stillbirth rates would be 5. Stillbirth rate = number of still births ÷ by total births (stillbirths + total live births) × 1,000.

Source: Office for National Statistics. © Crown copyright 1998

details of date and place of birth, and sex; date of birth of surviving husband or wife, if applicable; occupation of the deceased; date and place of death.

The registrar will also need the following documents: a doctor's certificate of cause of death; the deceased's NHS card; details of any state benefits the deceased was receiving; war pension order book, if applicable.

Whoever goes to register a death with the registrar must also supply their own details. Certificates registering the death and allowing a burial are then issued.

How to Obtain a Copy of a Birth, Death, or Marriage Certificate

Copies of birth, marriage, and death certificates can be obtained from the Register Office in the area where the event took place. This can be done by post or in person. If you don't know where the event occurred, you can obtain copies of certificates by searching the indexes to records held at the Family Records Centre. All the indexes to births, deaths, and marriages from 1837 in England and Wales

are held at the Centre and are available for public searches. The address of the Family Records Centre is: 1 Myddleton Place, London EC1R 1UW. Obtaining a copy of a certificate from the Family Records Centre can be done in one of four ways:

In person

The Family Records Centre is open Monday–Friday, between 8.30 a.m. and 4.30 p.m. (except for public holidays), and you can search the indexes of records held there. If you make your application in person, there are two services available: a 24-hour priority service allows you to collect a certificate one clear working day after the day of application; alternatively, you can collect the certificate on the fourth working day. Otherwise, it will be posted to you within four working days.

By post

You can make an order for certificates by post. Again, there are two services available: a priority service, through which your order will be posted to you within two working days, and a standard service,

through which the order will be posted within 22 working days. If you can provide the volume reference number for the certificate from the General Register Office index, your order will be posted to you within ten working days.

By telephone

Certificates can be ordered by telephone at the following number: (0151) 471 4800. Telephone orders must be paid for by credit or debit card when the order is placed. Again, there are priority and standard services, and dispatch times are the same as orders by post.

By fax

Orders can also be made by fax on (01704) 550013. You must quote your credit or debit card details. For an application form and a list of fees, contact: General Register Office, PO Box 2, Merseyside PR8 2JD; phone: (0151) 471 4800. Many public libraries and local public record offices keep microfilm copies of the indexes that are available for public use.

Marriages in the UK

Category	1985	1986	1987	1988	1989	1990	1991	1992	1993	1994	1995
Marriages											
Men											
under 21	30,243	25,828	24,269	20,608	19,070	15,930	13,271	11,031	8,767	7,091	6,302
21–24	123,242	119,464	118,355	109,482	102,977	92,270	79,877	74,458	65,129	56,877	48,432
25–29	109,896	114,007	119,808	120,939	123,491	122,800	115,637	118,255	114,101	111,108	105,218
30–34	47,594	49,287	51,389	53,865	56,442	56,966	56,970	62,470	63,848	65,490	68,245
35–44	46,265	48,583	48,598	51,329	51,411	49,984	48,147	51,125	50,553	51,310	53,350
45–54	19,652	20,376	19,788	21,544	22,329	21,996	20,915	23,290	23,841	24,136	24,786
55 and over	16,225	16,394	15,730	16,282	16,322	15,464	14,922	15,384	15,369	15,220	14,918
Women											
under 21	82,209	72,466	68,629	59,284	54,256	45,626	38,305	32,618	26,839	22,903	20,643
21–24	137,437	138,219	140,509	134,122	128,411	119,037	105,505	102,494	93,125	84,171	75,071
25–29	80,105	85,316	90,911	95,338	100,531	103,209	99,851	105,223	104,517	102,803	100,644
30–34	33,424	35,237	36,643	39,680	41,989	42,794	43,617	48,514	49,546	52,359	54,819
35–44	35,380	37,515	36,978	39,534	40,290	38,983	37,582	40,075	40,090	41,213	43,115
45–54	14,892	15,414	15,001	16,570	17,172	16,825	16,473	18,504	18,800	19,280	19,720
55 and over	9,670	9,772	9,260	9,521	9,393	8,936	8,406	8,585	8,691	8,503	8,239
Total	393,117	393,939	397,937	394,049	392,042	375,410	349,739	356,013	341,608	331,232	322,251
Persons marrying per 1,000 resident population	13.9	13.9	14.0	13.8	13.7	13.1	12.1	12.3	11.7	11.3	11.0
Previous Marital Status											
Bachelors	291,171	290,144	296,290	289,493	288,478	276,512	256,538	258,567	245,996	236,619	227,717
Divorced men	88,981	91,006	89,814	92,755	92,033	88,199	83,069	87,419	85,824	85,261	85,743
Widowers	12,965	12,789	11,833	11,801	11,531	10,699	10,132	10,027	9,788	9,352	8,791
Spinsters	296,797	294,564	301,073	293,551	291,516	279,442	259,084	260,252	248,063	237,241	228,462
Divorced women	83,921	87,080	85,238	89,066	89,234	85,608	81,224	86,361	84,268	85,220	85,396
Widows	12,399	12,295	11,626	11,612	11,294	10,360	9,431	9,400	9,277	8,771	8,393
First marriage for both partners	256,594	254,237	260,459	253,150	251,572	240,729	222,369	222,142	210,567	200,910	192,078
First marriage for one partner only	74,780	76,254	76,445	76,744	76,850	74,496	70,884	74,535	72,925	72,040	72,023
Remarriage for both partners	61,743	63,458	61,033	64,155	63,620	60,185	56,486	59,336	58,116	58,282	58,150

Source: Office for National Statistics. © Crown copyright 1998

Deaths by Age and Sex in the UK

(Annual averages or calendar years.)

Year(s)	All ages[1]	Under 1 year old	1–4 year old	5–9 year old	10–14 year old	15–19 year old	20–24 year old	25–34 year old	35–44 year old	45–54 year old	55–64 year old	65–74 year old	75–84 year old	85 and over
Men														
1900–02	340,664	87,242	37,834	8,429	4,696	7,047	8,766	19,154	24,739	30,488	37,610	39,765	28,320	6,563
1910–12	303,703	63,885	29,452	7,091	4,095	5,873	6,817	16,141	21,813	28,981	37,721	45,140	29,397	7,283
1920–22	284,876	48,044	19,008	6,052	3,953	5,906	6,572	13,663	19,702	29,256	40,583	49,398	34,937	7,801
1930–32	284,249	28,840	11,276	4,580	2,890	5,076	6,495	12,327	16,326	29,376	47,989	63,804	45,247	10,022
1940–42	314,643	24,624	6,949	3,400	2,474	4,653	4,246	11,506	17,296	30,082	57,076	79,652	59,733	12,900
1950–52	307,312	14,105	2,585	1,317	919	1,498	2,289	5,862	11,074	27,637	53,691	86,435	79,768	20,131
1960–62	318,850	12,234	1,733	971	871	1,718	1,857	3,842	8,753	26,422	63,009	87,542	83,291	26,605
1970–72	335,166	9,158	1,485	1,019	802	1,778	2,104	3,590	7,733	24,608	64,898	105,058	82,905	30,027
1980–82	330,495	4,829	774	527	652	1,999	1,943	3,736	6,568	19,728	54,159	105,155	98,488	31,936
1990–92	312,521	3,315	623	372	396	1,349	2,059	4,334	6,979	15,412	40,424	87,849	106,376	43,032
1981	329,145	4,759	771	517	666	2,008	1,919	3,761	6,544	19,740	53,770	104,950	97,881	31,859
1982	329,971	4,555	760	456	632	1,966	1,971	3,661	6,462	18,867	53,531	103,426	101,281	32,403
1983	328,824	4,230	695	469	609	1,834	1,899	3,601	6,537	18,238	54,493	100,469	103,038	32,712
1984	321,095	3,995	725	423	580	1,708	1,999	3,595	6,425	17,647	53,715	95,420	102,513	32,350
1985	331,562	4,003	728	393	583	1,612	2,031	3,452	6,728	17,316	52,502	97,458	109,241	35,515
1986	327,160	4,219	653	384	444	1,676	2,067	3,668	6,712	16,814	50,352	95,987	108,123	36,061
1987	318,282	4,105	657	377	470	1,612	2,125	3,776	6,793	15,950	47,675	93,348	105,773	35,621
1988	319,119	4,110	680	433	460	1,525	2,160	3,983	6,860	16,016	46,001	91,893	107,082	37,916
1989	320,193	3,799	699	414	398	1,537	2,118	3,968	6,832	15,560	43,693	90,304	109,450	41,421
1990	314,601	3,614	674	376	406	1,487	2,197	4,354	6,991	15,507	41,983	88,458	107,451	41,103
1991	314,427	3,377	636	395	404	1,417	2,049	4,270	7,102	15,493	40,256	88,014	107,416	43,598
1992	308,535	2,954	559	346	377	1,144	1,932	4,379	6,845	15,236	39,033	87,075	104,261	44,394
1993	317,796	2,746	582	325	401	1,072	1,907	4,442	6,672	15,631	38,734	90,160	105,693	49,431
1994	303,333	2,660	497	319	400	1,041	1,829	4,741	6,661	14,983	36,469	86,896	98,982	47,855
1995	310,722	2,595	447	314	388	1,115	1,810	4,748	6,754	15,644	36,068	85,459	103,324	52,056
1996	305,323	2,562	489	267	352	1,104	1,693	4,746	6,789	15,796	35,033	81,333	102,092	53,069
Women														
1900–02	322,058	68,770	36,164	8,757	5,034	6,818	8,264	18,702	21,887	25,679	34,521	42,456	34,907	10,099
1910–12	289,608	49,865	27,817	7,113	4,355	5,683	6,531	15,676	19,647	24,481	32,813	46,453	37,353	11,828
1920–22	274,772	35,356	17,323	5,808	4,133	5,729	6,753	14,878	18,121	24,347	34,026	48,573	45,521	14,203
1930–32	275,336	21,072	9,995	3,990	2,734	4,721	5,931	12,699	15,373	24,695	39,471	59,520	56,250	18,886
1940–42	296,646	17,936	5,952	2,743	2,068	4,180	5,028	11,261	14,255	23,629	42,651	70,907	71,377	24,658
1950–52	291,597	10,293	2,098	880	625	1,115	1,717	5,018	8,989	18,875	37,075	75,220	92,848	36,844
1960–62	304,871	8,887	1,334	627	522	684	811	2,504	6,513	16,720	36,078	73,118	105,956	51,117
1970–72	322,968	6,666	1,183	654	459	718	900	2,110	5,345	15,594	36,177	75,599	109,539	68,024
1980–82	330,269	3,561	585	355	425	733	772	2,099	4,360	12,206	32,052	72,618	117,760	82,743
1990–92	328,218	2,431	485	259	255	520	714	1,989	4,340	9,707	25,105	61,951	115,467	104,994
1981	328,829	3,402	599	352	424	738	737	2,083	4,309	12,275	31,625	72,476	117,458	82,351
1982	332,830	3,342	561	304	410	689	767	2,057	4,312	11,759	32,183	71,705	119,362	85,379
1983	330,277	3,126	568	318	374	719	698	1,914	4,318	11,384	32,197	69,266	118,940	86,455
1984	323,823	3,005	537	304	344	665	722	1,932	4,269	10,947	32,262	66,432	116,649	85,756
1985	339,094	3,027	574	314	355	626	729	1,852	4,397	10,581	32,010	68,505	122,445	93,679
1986	333,575	2,961	561	275	307	635	769	1,882	4,387	10,211	29,954	67,313	120,663	93,657
1987	326,060	2,972	550	265	288	614	733	1,974	4,454	10,177	29,037	65,570	117,266	92,160
1988	330,059	2,951	552	264	251	612	745	1,915	4,615	9,887	28,154	65,020	117,731	97,362
1989	337,540	2,743	551	271	268	598	773	1,955	4,506	9,834	27,324	64,575	120,975	103,167
1990	327,198	2,658	489	249	273	534	700	1,967	4,463	9,718	26,350	62,019	116,357	101,421
1991	331,754	2,448	512	280	264	538	738	2,005	4,295	9,699	24,952	62,200	116,924	106,899
1992	325,703	2,187	455	249	228	489	704	1,994	4,262	9,705	24,013	61,635	113,119	106,663
1993	340,685	2,084	436	239	283	465	659	2,121	4,204	9,973	23,900	63,767	114,905	117,649
1994	324,303	1,989	410	205	232	406	626	2,053	4,285	10,081	22,401	62,069	106,816	112,730
1995	334,771	1,931	370	224	250	449	592	2,140	4,203	10,389	22,093	60,988	110,247	120,895
1996	330,701	1,904	355	214	224	493	589	2,140	4,215	10,301	21,406	57,889	109,578	121,393

[1] In some years, the totals include a small number of persons whose age was not stated.

Source: Office for National Statistics. © Crown copyright 1998

See Also   UK Health Care (Medicine and Health)

Divorces in England and Wales, and Scotland

(N/A = not available.)

Item	1985	1986	1987	1988	1989	1990	1991	1992	1993	1994	1995	1996
England and Wales												
Decrees absolute, granted[1] (rate per 1,000 married couples[1])	13.4	12.9	12.7	12.8	12.7	13.0	13.5	13.7	13.9	13.4	13.1	N/A
Total[1]	160,300	153,903	151,007	152,633	150,872	153,386	158,745	160,385	165,018	158,175	155,499	N/A
Duration of marriage (years)												
0–4	45,776	38,637	35,423	35,582	35,719	36,299	37,779	36,898	37,252	35,695	34,507	N/A
5–9	41,537	42,187	43,150	42,617	42,108	42,061	42,735	43,745	46,536	44,769	44,304	N/A
10–14	27,087	26,718	26,194	26,545	26,281	27,310	28,791	29,285	30,156	28,073	27,365	N/A
15–19	18,460	19,547	19,576	20,132	19,418	19,819	20,127	20,160	20,233	19,200	18,943	N/A
20 and over	26,427	26,805	26,664	27,747	27,327	27,881	29,294	30,290	30,836	30,431	30,370	N/A
not stated	13	9	N/A	10	19	16	19	7	5	N/A	N/A	N/A
Age of wife at marriage (years)												
16–19	52,858	48,621	46,097	44,693	42,612	41,116	40,594	39,731	38,810	34,068	31,319	N/A
20–24	69,663	68,387	68,345	69,489	69,424	71,489	74,050	74,698	76,580	73,287	71,355	N/A
25–29	18,689	18,990	19,049	20,267	20,369	21,701	24,025	25,172	27,177	28,358	29,439	N/A
30–34	8,544	8,189	7,983	8,441	8,590	8,909	9,608	9,939	10,593	11,007	11,585	N/A
35–39	4,612	4,497	4,403	4,501	4,643	4,880	5,024	5,200	5,673	5,615	5,800	N/A
40–44	2,609	2,378	2,416	2,530	2,541	2,598	2,727	2,872	3,091	3,064	3,121	N/A
45 and over	3,325	2,841	2,714	2,712	2,693	2,693	2,717	2,766	2,819	2,769	2,870	N/A
Age of wife at divorce (years)												
16–24	26,170	21,713	19,066	17,693	16,628	15,454	14,960	13,482	12,924	10,956	9,783	N/A
25–29	35,680	34,478	34,209	34,504	34,483	35,121	35,582	34,853	35,362	32,608	30,563	N/A
30–34	28,668	28,452	28,995	29,406	29,757	31,295	33,195	34,901	36,300	35,848	35,538	N/A
35–39	26,554	25,956	24,934	24,685	24,170	24,421	25,661	26,577	28,162	27,195	27,550	N/A
40–44	17,767	18,519	19,403	20,873	20,647	21,263	21,979	21,783	21,891	20,765	20,739	N/A
45 and over	25,448	24,776	24,400	25,462	25,168	25,816	27,349	28,782	30,374	30,796	31,316	N/A
not stated	13	9	N/A	10	19	16	19	7	5	7	10	N/A
Divorces involving no children[2]	51,912	47,330	46,770	47,049	46,910	47,119	48,115	46,979	47,652	48,286	48,560	N/A
Divorces involving 1 or more children[2]	108,388	106,573	104,237	105,584	103,962	106,267	110,630	113,406	117,366	109,889	106,939	N/A
Scotland												
Decrees absolute, granted[3][4] (rate per 1,000 married couples[5])	11.1	10.7	10.2	9.8	10.0	10.5	10.6	10.8	11.1	11.5	10.8	9.9
Total[1]	13,371	12,800	12,133	11,472	11,659	12,272	12,399	12,479	12,787	13,133	12,249	11,123
Duration of marriage (years)												
0–4	2,364	2,233	2,173	1,986	2,013	2,208	2,142	2,085	2,092	2,095	1,908	1,731
5–9	3,882	3,735	3,544	3,353	3,420	3,546	3,508	3,610	3,722	3,790	3,399	3,112
10–14	2,684	2,536	2,351	2,227	2,245	2,361	2,484	2,454	2,539	2,592	2,407	2,087
15–19	1,868	1,804	1,670	1,592	1,633	1,617	1,718	1,675	1,745	1,786	1,698	1,547
20 and over	2,573	2,492	2,395	2,314	2,348	2,540	2,547	2,655	2,689	2,870	2,837	2,637
Age of wife at marriage (years)												
16–20	7,143	6,767	6,134	5,660	5,565	5,600	5,592	5,378	5,406	5,306	4,600	3,987
21–24	3,914	3,768	3,778	3,577	3,708	4,185	4,147	4,198	4,252	4,532	4,336	3,920
25–29	1,246	1,257	1,274	1,236	1,363	1,377	1,545	1,685	1,812	1,926	1,887	1,755
30–34	461	458	423	466	479	497	514	575	612	628	654	631
35–39	247	250	224	219	235	275	249	301	312	329	338	362
40–44	143	120	142	124	131	139	148	138	152	163	196	205
45 and over	170	174	158	153	143	159	142	153	164	166	166	180
not stated	49	6	N/A	37	35	40	62	51	77	83	72	78

Divorces in England and Wales, and Scotland (*continued*)

Item	1985	1986	1987	1988	1989	1990	1991	1992	1993	1994	1995	1996
Age of wife at divorce (years)												
16–24	1,881	1,674	1,504	1,285	1,139	1,199	1,038	963	844	767	622	524
25–29	3,152	3,001	2,920	2,676	2,818	2,938	2,932	2,807	2,775	2,750	2,353	2,052
30–34	2,628	2,597	2,443	2,378	2,442	2,611	2,741	2,785	3,037	3,045	2,747	2,446
35–39	2,183	2,136	1,942	1,917	1,927	1,891	2,037	2,092	2,212	2,390	2,290	2,074
40–44	1,440	1,370	1,482	1,381	1,436	1,614	1,665	1,685	1,771	1,788	1,734	1,565
45 and over	2,040	2,016	1,842	1,798	1,862	1,979	1,924	2,096	2,071	2,310	2,431	2,344
age not stated	49	6	N/A	37	35	40	62	51	77	83	72	118
Actions involving no children[6]	6,040	6,046	5,989	5,887	6,091	6,555	6,521	6,927	6,951	7,390	7,515	7,334
Actions involving 1 or more children[6]	7,331	6,754	6,144	5,585	5,568	5,717	5,878	5,552	5,836	5,743	4,734	3,789

[1] Data include decrees of divorce and of nullity.
[2] Children of the family as defined by the Matrimonial Causes Act, 1973.
[3] For divorces under pre-1976 legislation, these figures relate only to persons who were married in Scotland, and obtained their decree of divorce from the Court of Session. Also with effect from 1 May 1984, the jurisdiction of the Sheriff Courts was extended to include divorce.
[4] With effect from 1984, these statistics have been collected on the basis of divorces granted only, and any difference in the number of divorces brought and granted relates to nullity of marriages.
[5] Rates are calculated using the average of the estimated married male and female populations.
[6] These actions relate to all persons divorced or separated in Scotland, irrespective of the country of marriage.

Source: Office for National Statistics; General Register Office (Scotland); Scottish Courts Administration. © Crown copyright 1998

Marriage Laws and Procedure in the UK

Source: The Wedding Guide UK

(This articles includes some information on Guernsey, Jersey and the Isle of Man. Please note that these territories are not part of the UK, but are British Crown Dependencies.)

Minimum Age and Parental Consent

The minimum legal age for getting married throughout the UK is 16. In England, Wales, Northern Ireland, Guernsey, and the Isle of Man, the written consent of parents or legal guardians is required if you are under 18 years of age. In Jersey, parental consent is required if you under 20 years of age. In Scotland, no parental consent is required.

Marriage in England and Wales

As long as the legal requirements are met, anyone from anywhere in the world can get married in England or Wales, either by civil or religious ceremony. Marriages in England and Wales must take place between 8 a.m. and 6 p.m. Most ceremonies, civil or religious, are governed by the opening times of register offices and the times of church services.

Civil marriage Marriage at a register office or other licensed venue (see below) can take place anywhere in England or Wales and does not have to be the place of residence of one or both of the people wishing to marry. If you wish to marry by civil ceremony you should contact the Superintendent Registrar of the district in which you wish to get married to discuss any arrangements that must be made.

Details of your nearest register office can be found in your local telephone directory under 'Registration of Births, Deaths, and Marriages'.

To start civil marriage proceedings, you must 'give notice'. This can be done in one of three ways:

Marriage by Certificate without Licence. This is the most common form of notice. After 21 days, you will be issued with a certificate of marriage to enable you to get married. You must get married within three months of the date of entry in the notice book.

Marriage by Certificate and Licence. This allows couples to marry more quickly, but it is more expensive. One whole day after giving notice, the Superintendent Registrar will issue a certificate of marriage. Your marriage must then take place within three months of the date of entry in the notice book.

Marriage by Registrar General's Licence. This licence is available for couples where one partner cannot attend a place where marriages can be legally solemnized. This situation would apply to those who are seriously ill at home or in hospital, or those who are in prison. The marriage can take place at any time and at any place, as long as it is within three months of the date of entry in the notice book.

Civil marriage: at a licensed venue Since April 1995, it has been possible to arrange for a civil marriage ceremony to take place at a specially licensed venue. Buildings such as hotels, stately homes, and castles can now be licensed to allow civil ceremonies to take place on their premises. No religious content is allowed at all, but in addition to the statutory declaratory and contracting words that you are required to say in a civil ceremony, it is also possible to

make your own choice of vows and promises. The legal requirements for getting married at such a venue are the same as those for getting married by civil ceremony at a register office, but with the additional requirement of arranging for the attendance of a Registrar at the venue. You do not have to give formal notice of your marriage to the Superintendent Registrar of the registration district in which the venue is situated. However, once you have chosen your venue, you should contact the local Superintendent Registrar as his or her attendance is required to solemnize the marriage. You can obtain a full list of the addresses and telephone numbers of approved premises by sending a cheque or postal order for £5.00, made payable to 'Office for National Statistics', to: Local Services Office for National Statistics, Smedley Hydro, Trafalgar Road, Southport PR8 2HH; phone: (0151) 471 4458 (telephone orders are not acceptable)

Civil marriage: further information For more information on legal civil marriage issues in England and Wales, you can contact the Marriages Section of the Registrar General for England and Wales by telephoning: (01704) 569824. Alternatively you can write to the Marriages Section at the same address as the Office for National Statistics (above).

Religious marriage You don't have to be regular churchgoer to be married in the Church of England or the Church in Wales. If you wish to be married in either Church, you should visit the minister of the church in which you want to get married to discuss your plans. There are four ways of getting married in accordance with the procedures of the Church of England:

Publication of banns. This simply means

announcing aloud your intention to marry. It is the traditional and most popular method, used by most couples, and is equivalent to the civil method of getting married by certificate. Church congregations are invited to register objections, if they have any. Couples are usually required to be in attendance on at least one of the three occasions when banns are read. If couples live in different parishes, the banns are read in both parishes.

Marriage by common licence. This is equivalent in timing to the civil method of getting married by certificate and licence. Banns are not required to be published. The bishop of the diocese in which you wish to marry approves the application to marry, and one whole day's notice is required before the ceremony can take place. To be married by common licence, one of the couple must have lived in the parish during the fifteen days before the application for the licence. One of the couple must also have been baptized. A common licence lasts for three months from the date of issue.

Marriage by special licence. This is very unusual and must be approved by the Archbishop of Canterbury. If granted, a special licence allows couples to marry at any time within three months and in any place without any residence requirement. For more information on getting married by special licence, you should contact the Registrar of Court Faculties: The Sanctuary, London SW1P 3JT; phone: (0171) 222 5381

Marriage by Superintendent Registrar's Certificate without Licence. This is a rarely used method of getting married in church, as ministers will prefer you to marry by either publication of banns or by common licence.

Religious marriage: further information If you would like more information about getting married in a church of the Church of England or Church in Wales, you should either see your minister, or you can contact the Enquiry Centre of the General Synod of the Church of England. The address is: Church House, Great Smith Street, London SW1P 3NZ; phone: (0171) 222 9011

Religious marriage: Roman Catholic marriages The legal requirements that have to be fulfilled for a Roman Catholic wedding are the same that apply to civil marriages. However, if the church is in a different registration district and you cannot prove the church is your normal place of worship, you will be required to give notice in the registration district in which the church is situated. For more information, you should talk to your priest or contact either of following organizations: Marriage Care, 1 Blythe Mews, Blythe Road, London W14 0NW; phone: (0171) 371 1341; The Catholic Enquiry Office, The Chase Centre, 114 West Heath Road, London NW3 7TX; phone: (0181) 455 9871 fax: (0181) 905 5780

Cost of marriage By civil ceremony: as of 1st April 1998, to be married by certificate without licence, the cost of giving notice is £21. If you both live in different districts, you will both have to pay £21. The fee for the Superintendent Registrar to solemnize your marriage at a register office is £36. To be married by certificate and licence, the fee is an additional £46.50. Your marriage certificate will cost £3.50 (£6.50 if purchased at a later date).

For a marriage at a specially licensed venue, the Registrar is paid an additional fee for attending and solemnizing your marriage. Local authorities set these fees, and you should expect to pay between £100–£150, plus the hire fee for the marriage room at the venue. You do not have to pay the Superintendent Registrar's register office attendance fee of £36.

By religious ceremony: Fees payable for religious marriages are not fixed and are decided by the religious celebrant solemnizing your marriage. You should discuss fees with the minister, priest, or celebrant of the church in which you intend to marry.

Marriage in Scotland

Civil marriage A civil marriage can only be solemnized in a register office by a Registrar or an Assistant Registrar who has been authorized by the Registrar General. In Scotland, there are no time-of-day restrictions for marriage ceremonies, although ceremonies are restricted to the opening times of register offices. Some remote Scottish communities have their own Parlour Registrars, who are authorized to perform civil marriages in their home. These marriages can take place at any time, at the discretion of the Parlour Registrar.

Religious marriage Religious ceremonies can take place at any time and in any place in Scotland, as long as an authorized celebrant can attend and officiate, and there are two witnesses present. Scottish churches make no provision for marriage by the publication of banns.

Residency requirements Scotland is the only country in the UK where there is no residency requirement to be fulfilled. Instead, at least one of the couple must visit the Registrar from the district in which the marriage is to take place during the seven days before the date of the wedding. In the case of civil marriages, this is to make arrangements with the Registrar; in the case of religious marriages, it is to collect the marriage schedule.

Giving notice Couples must both submit a marriage notice to the Registrar for the district in which they intend to marry during the three months before the wedding date, and not later than 15 days before the date.

The marriage schedule No marriage can take place in Scotland without a marriage schedule (the licence to marry), which must

be presented to the person performing the ceremony before it commences.

Marriage at Gretna Green Possibly the world's most famous wedding venue, Gretna Green is a small town in Dumfriesshire. In 1996, it was host to more than 4,000 weddings, about 13 percent of all weddings held in Scotland. The minimum age for getting married in Scotland has been 16, without parental consent, since the eighteenth century. Once the first stage-coach stop over the English/Scottish border, Gretna Green became the place for young English couples wishing to elope and marry without their parents' consent.

Cost of marriage From April 1997, the cost of giving notice to get married by either civil or religious ceremony is £12. For the solemnization of a civil marriage, the fee is £40. For Saturday afternoon ceremonies, there is sometimes a surcharge which can be in the region of £50. The marriage certificate will cost £8. The cost of marriage by religious ceremony is not fixed and is decided by the religious celebrant solemnizing the marriage. Couples should speak to the minister in charge of their chosen venue to discuss fees.

Further information For further information and advice about getting married in Scotland and to obtain a list of all register offices in Scotland, contact the General Register Office: Marriages Section, New Register House, Edinburgh EH1 3YT; phone: (0131) 334 0380; e-mail: gros@gtnet.gov.uk (Mark e-mail correspondence 'For Marriages Section'.)

Marriage in Northern Ireland

Civil marriage Civil marriages can take place in Northern Ireland by either a registrar's certificate or by a registrar's licence. The marriage of house-bound or detained persons can only take place on the authority of a licence issued by the Registrar General.

Civil marriage: by certificate A registrar's certificate authorizes you to marry in a register office, church, or other registered building, providing at least one of you resides in the district in which you wish to marry. A certificate allowing the marriage to take place is issued 21 days after notice of intent to marry is given.

Civil marriage: by licence A registrar's licence allows you to get married a little quicker: seven days after giving notice.

Civil marriage: by Registrar General's licence This licence allows you to marry if one of you is either house-bound or detained as a prisoner. A Registrar General's licence cannot be issued for a marriage between two people of the Roman Catholic, Jewish, or Quaker religions.

Religious marriage Church of Ireland: marriage according to the rites and ceremonies of the Church of Ireland can take place by the publications of banns, licence, special licence, or a registrar's certificate. Provided that one or both people are members of the Church of Ireland, or other Protestant Episcopal Church, a licence is available from a Church of Ireland licensing minister. Names and addresses of licensing ministers can be obtained from any member of the Church of Ireland clergy.

Special licences may be granted by a bishop of the Church of Ireland, provided that one or both of you are members of that Church or other Protestant Episcopal Church. The marriage may then take place at any time and in any place within the diocese of the bishop granting the licence. To obtain a registrar's certificate to authorize your marriage, one or both of you must belong to the Church of Ireland. Marriage by any of these means can be advised on by your minister.

Presbyterian Church Marriages: the governing bodies of the Presbyterian Church in Northern Ireland are the General Assembly of the Presbyterian Church in Ireland, the Remonstrant Synod of Ulster (non-subscribing), the Presbytery of Antrim, and the Reformed Presbyterian Synod of Ireland. Marriages according to the disciplines of these bodies can take place by licence, special licence, or publication of banns. You should discuss with your Presbyterian minister which method would be most suitable, according to your circumstances.

Roman Catholic Church: where both of you are Roman Catholics, the marriage procedure is governed by the laws of the Roman Catholic Church. Information and guidance on your marriage should be obtained from a member of the Roman Catholic clergy. According to the Irish Marriage Acts, marriage in a Roman Catholic church can also take place by licence or registrar's certificate. These methods apply where one of you is not a Roman Catholic.

Religious marriage: other Church marriages Marriages according to the customs of other religious bodies can take place in Northern Ireland by registrar's licence (except for Jews and Quakers), by registrar's certificate, or by special licence. Information about these marriages can be obtained from the registrar in the district in which you wish to marry.

Cost of marriage If your marriage is on the authority of a licence issued by a licensing minister of the Church of Ireland or Presbyterian Church, giving notice of your marriage will cost £4.50. The licence will cost £10.50. To give notice to marry by licence or certificate issued by a Registrar of Marriages costs £4.50. A registrar's certificate costs £3; a registrar's licence costs £10.50. The solemnization of your marriage in the presence of a registrar will cost £11. For ceremonies taking place in a church, the celebrant will charge a fee for the church service. These fees are set by the relevant church authorities. Couples should consult their church minister for information.

Further information For information about getting married in Northern Ireland, contact the registrar of marriages in the registration district in which you wish to get married. Alternatively, contact the General Register Office: Oxford House, 49–55 Chichester Road, Belfast BT1 4HL; phone: (01232) 252000

Other Religions and Interfaith Marriages

For information and advice about Jewish weddings, contact the Jewish Marriage Council: 23 Ravenhurst Avenue, London NW4 4EE; phone: (0171) 203 6311

For information about Quaker marriages, contact the Religious Society of Friends: 173–177 Euston Road, London NW1 2BJ; phone: (0171) 387 3601

For advice when partners are practising members of different Churches, contact: Association of Interchurch Families, 35–41 Lower Marsh, London SE1 7RL; phone: (0171) 620 4444; fax: (0171) 928 0010

Documents Required for Marriage

To be married in the UK you must produce your birth certificate. If you have been married before, you must produce your decree absolute of divorce (dissolution or annulment papers in Northern Ireland) or, if you are widowed, the death certificate of your former spouse. For marriages in Scotland and Northern Ireland you must obtain from your own marriage authority a certificate stating that there is no impediment to marry, i.e. that you are both free to marry. If you do not live in the UK, you will have to produce your passport. Travel documents may also be required to prove you have met the necessary residency requirements. For further information, contact the registrar of the registration district in which you wish to get married.

Same-Sex Marriages in the UK

It is not possible for gay and lesbian couples to have a legally solemnized marriage. UK marriage laws prohibit people of the same sex from marrying. However, the marriage laws refer to sex at birth. It is therefore possible for transsexuals legally to marry someone who was of the same sex as them at birth.

Marriage Prohibitions

A man cannot marry his: mother, including adoptive mother or former adoptive mother; daughter, including adoptive daughter or former adoptive daughter; father's mother (grandmother); mother's mother (grandmother); son's daughter (granddaughter); daughter's daughter (granddaughter); sister; father's daughter (step-sister); mother's daughter (step-sister); former wife's daughter (former step-daughter); father's wife (step-mother); son's wife (daughter-in-law); father's father's mother (great grandmother); mother's father's wife (step-grandmother); former wife's father's mother (former grandmother-in-law); former wife's mother's mother (former grandmother-in-law); former wife's son's daughter (former step-granddaughter); former wife's daughter's daughter (former step-granddaughter); son's son's wife (grandson's wife); daughter's son's wife (grandson's wife); father's sister (aunt); mother's sister (aunt); brother's daughter (niece); sister's daughter (niece).

A woman cannot marry her: father, including adoptive father or former adoptive father; son, including adoptive son or former adoptive son; father's father (grandfather); mother's father (grandfather); son's son (grandson); daughter's son (grandson); brother's father's son (step-brother); mother's son (step-brother); former husband's son (former step-son); mother's husband (step-father); former husband's father (former father-in-law); daughter's husband (son-in-law); mother's mother's husband (step-grandfather); father's mother's husband (step-grandfather); former husband's father's father (former grandfather-in-law); former husband's mother's father (former grandfather-in-law); former husband's son's son (former step-grandson); former husband's daughter's son (former step-grandson); daughter's daughter's husband (granddaughter's husband); son's daughter's husband (granddaughter's husband); father's brother (uncle); mother's brother (uncle); brother's son (nephew); sister's son (nephew).

Exceptions for step-relatives and relatives-in-law: In England, Scotland, and Wales (not Northern Ireland, Isle of Man, Guernsey, or Jersey), the Marriage Act of 1986 allows for the following relatives to marry:

Step-relatives can marry provided they are at least 21 years of age. The younger of the couple must not ever have lived in the same house as the older of the couple before the age of 18, nor must they ever have been treated as the child of the older person's family.

Relatives-in-law can marry provided they are at least 21 years of age, and that the family members involved in creating the in-law relationship are both dead. For example, if a man wishes to marry his daughter-in-law, both his son and his son's mother must be dead. In England and Wales, marriages under this Act are not permitted with the calling of banns but can take place in a church on the authority of a licence issued by a superintendent registrar.

Marriage of cousins: It is not illegal to marry a cousin. However, cousins who wish to marry should visit their GP to ensure that there are no factors in their family health records that might make a decision to have children inadvisable on medical grounds.

Divorce Laws and Procedure in the UK

Source: Gordon Bancks & Co, Solicitors, Worcester; Terry Co, Solicitors, London

According to UK divorce law, there is essentially one basis for divorce: that a marriage has 'irretrievably broken down'. To satisfy a court that a marriage has reached this condition, one or more of the following five grounds must be proved:

A spouse has committed adultery. It is no longer necessary to name a third party in this case. If no third party is named, a defendant can admit to adultery on a form called an 'Acknowledgement of Service'. If a defendant will not admit to adultery, other forms of proof may be necessary to satisfy a court that adultery has been committed.

The couple have been living apart for two years or more, and both agree to a divorce.

The couple have lived apart for five years, and one partner wants a divorce.

One partner deserted the marriage more than two years before. (Note: desertion is not the same as agreed separation.)

One partner has behaved in such a way that the other partner can no longer be expected to tolerate living with them. 'Unreasonable behaviour' covers a very broad range of acts: physical and/or verbal abuse, drunkenness, public humiliation, mental cruelty, financial irresponsibility, excessive jealousy; even excessive DIY, and failure to help with household work.

It is not possible to get divorced unless you have been married for at least one year.

The legal procedure for obtaining a divorce in England begins with issuing a divorce petition to any divorce county court, or, in London, the Principle Registry. In Scotland, divorces are generally conducted in the Sheriff Court. Less commonly, they can also be issued in the Court of Session in Edinburgh, Scotland's supreme court. In Northern Ireland, the majority of divorces are issued in the High Court, although it is possible to seek divorce through the county courts. After a divorce petition is successful, a Decree Nisi is granted, and a further six or more weeks after this, a Decree Absolute, which finalizes the dissolution of the marriage.

It is not a legal requirement to employ the services of a solicitor when you wish to get divorced. A free booklet on obtaining an undefended divorce, 'DIY Divorce', can be obtained from any county court.

Professional advice is recommended, however. The advice of a professional can help determine whether there are grounds for a divorce. Legal advice can also be essential in guiding couples through the legal processes involved in divorce, as well as settling matters such as financial support for children. It is not recommended that you pursue a divorce without professional advice if children are involved, and/or extra financial settlement is being sought.

Common-Law Marriage

Contrary to popular and widespread belief, there is no such thing as common-law marriage. It is often believed that if man and a woman live together, after a certain length of time they acquire similar rights to an actual wife or husband. Where cohabiting couples (both heterosexual or same-sex partnerships) end their relationship, the law in the UK is not the same as for married couples. Property rights are unaffected between unmarried couples, i.e. the distinction between 'his', 'hers', and 'theirs' remains the same as beforehand when a relationship breaks down; each is entitled to keep their own property. The position for married couples is that the courts can divide all property whichever way they think best, regardless of who actually owns it.

If a couple live together, and they have children, the situation can become more complex if the relationship fails. An unmarried mother has legal responsibility for her children; an unmarried father has to ask the courts to give him joint responsibility. However, whether the father has joint responsibility or not, he is still responsible for maintaining his children, and this responsibility can be enforced.

Arrangements for Children

The Children Act resulted in a change in the arrangements for children of divorced parents. Parents are now encouraged to agree access and living arrangements without the need for the courts to step in. If this attempt fails, the courts will intervene to make a decision on behalf of the children; the Children Act requires that courts put the good of the children first. Children now have the right to have their wishes heard when decisions are made about them.

In 1993 a system for child maintenance was introduced in England, Wales, Scotland, and Northern Ireland. A government agency called the Child Support Agency (CSA) operates the scheme. Under the Child Support Act, 1991, child support maintenance is an amount of money that absent parents pay regularly as a contribution to the financial support of their children. Absent parents must now, by law, support their children, whether the couple are married, divorced, separated, formerly lived together, or had a child during a very brief relationship. The courts no longer decide on the financial contributions that absent parents must make towards their children; the CSA has been given these decision-making powers. The amount that absent parents pay is calculated by the CSA; the agency also assesses and reviews the amounts of child support maintenance needed. The CSA is empowered to collect money from an absent parent and pass it on to the guardian parent. The Child Support Agency can be contacted at the following address: PO Box 55, Brierley Hill, West Midlands DY5 1YL; National Enquiry Line: (0345) 133133

Counselling

The National Marriage Guidance Council (Relate), Herbert Gray College, Little Church Street, Rugby, Warwickshire CV21 3AP; phone: (01788) 573241 fax: (01788) 535007. Relate provides help with marital and relationship problems. There are over 130 branches nationwide. For your nearest branch, look in your local telephone directory.

Marriage Care, Clitherow House, 1 Blythe Mews, Blythe Road, London W14 0NW; phone: (0171) 371 1341; fax: (0171) 371 4921; e-mail: knight@enterprise.net Web site: www.fertilizeuk.org Marriage Care is a relationship counselling service largely serving the Roman Catholic community. The organization also runs marriage preparation courses and provides fertility and family planning advice.

Mortgage and Financial Information

Types of Mortgages in the UK

Source: Council of Mortgage Lenders; Office of Fair Trading

Outlined below are the most popular types of mortgage taken out by borrowers in the UK. However, other types of mortgage can sometimes be made available to borrowers, and anyone needing more information on finding a mortgage to suit their financial circumstances should visit a mortgage lender for advice.

Repayment Mortgage

The repayment mortgage provides for regular monthly repayments of the amount borrowed, over the whole term of the mortgage (usually 25 years). Monthly repayments are made up of interest on the loan and repayments on the capital amount. During the first few years, most of each monthly repayment goes towards paying the interest on the loan. As the mortgage term reduces, the capital payments increase, and the interest payments reduce. At the time of writing it is possible to claim tax relief on the interest payments of the first £30,000 of a loan; the relief rate is currently 15%. As the amount of interest paid through monthly repayments decreases, so does the amount of tax relief. Monthly repayments are calculated taking into account the tax relief entitlement; this is known as MIRAS (Mortgage Interest Relief at Source).

Most repayment mortgages are taken out on a variable rate of interest. That is, monthly payments vary according to changes in general interest rates. Some lenders, however, adjust mortgage repayments on an annual basis, taking into account the previous year's interest rates. Borrowers on a variable rate mortgage do have options for altering their repayments in some cases. For example, if interest rates increase, borrowers may be given an option not to increase their payments. This depends on the length of the term and the amount outstanding. Failure to increase repayments in line with current interest rates can result in not paying enough to meet interest charges on the loan. Conversely, when interest rates decease, borrowers can opt not to reduce their monthly payments and thereby reduce the term of their mortgage.

Endowment Mortgage

An endowment policy is one of a variety of investment-linked mortgages available to home buyers. Investment-linked mortgages allow for interest payments on a loan to be paid and leave the capital sum borrowed unpaid. The borrower makes an investment over the term of the loan which, when matured, is used to repay the capital at the end of the term. With an endowment policy, borrowers pay a monthly premium into an endowment insurance policy, commonly a with-profits or unit-linked policy. On a with-profits policy, profit bonuses are normally added each year. These bonuses cannot be removed or reduced. Over the term of the policy it may be possible to increase the amount insured so that when the time comes to pay off the capital on the loan, there may be more money in the policy than required. With a unit-linked policy, the premiums are paid into investments such as stocks and shares. The potential benefits of investing premiums into these investments are clear, but it is important to remember that investing in this way can be risky. Most insurers conduct regular reviews of the performance of unit trusts in order to monitor whether the projected maturity will be sufficient to cover the loan.

Another form of endowment policy, known as a unitized policy, is a combination of the with-profits and the unit-linked policies. Part of the premium is invested in a with-profits endowment and the rest is invested in stocks and shares.

Endowment-linked mortgages may have an additional benefit of providing for a loan to be paid off in full in the event of the death of the borrower. Some policies may, however, require additional life cover.

Unlike the repayment mortgage, endowment mortgages do not usually offer a facility to extend the term of a mortgage if interest rates increase; higher payments need to be met in full. It is also important to note that endowment policies have a low surrender value in the early years of a policy. However, most mortgages do not run to their full term, ie they are paid off when home owners sell and move home. In such cases, an existing endowment policy can usually be used to secure a new mortgage.

Personal Equity Plan (PEP)

PEPs can also be linked to mortgage loans and have the advantage that they may bring high returns for relatively small contributions. However, investing in a PEP can be a high-risk option as it does not guarantee a minimum level of return. Separate life cover in addition to a PEP will be required by a lender. As of early 1998, PEP-linked mortgages are still an option, but the current government is proposing to end the PEP as a form of investment. Alternative investments will become available and borrowers are advised to contact their mortgage lender for information on linking these to mortgage loans.

Pension-Linked Mortgage

For the self-employed or holders of personal pensions, a loan can be linked to a pension plan. The borrower pays interest on the loan to the lender and pays contributions to their pension fund. At the end of the term of the loan, part of the proceeds of the pension fund are used to pay off the mortgage. For those eligible for tax relief on pension contributions and interest payments, this can be an attractive option. However, it is important to remember that this sort of mortgage will reduce the amount of pension available to the borrower when they retire.

Fixed Rate Mortgage

Many lenders offer mortgages with fixed interest rates over a period of years, generally between one and five years. After the term of the fixed rate, the interest reverts to current rates, or a new fixed rate term can be taken out on the loan. The advantage of fixed interest payments is that monthly mortgage repayments are guaranteed and borrowers can budget for their mortgage payments for a definite period. On the other hand, while fixed interest rates will protect the borrower from increases in general interest rates, borrowers may also find themselves paying more if rates decrease. There can also be high financial penalties for redeeming a fixed interest rate mortgage early.

Discount Rate Mortgage

A popular option for first time buyers, the discount rate mortgage offers a loan with interest at a discounted rate, generally for the first year or two of the loan. The rate is discounted by 1 percent or more and can make a big difference to mortgage payments. Borrowers should remember, though, that once the term of the discounted rate is over, the mortgage payments will revert to the current interest rate; the difference between repayments on a discounted rate mortgage and current rates over two years can be quite considerable. As with the fixed rate mortgage, borrowers can be subject to financial penalties if they redeem a discount rate mortgage early.

Capped Rate Mortgage

Capped interest on a mortgage means that, for a certain period, borrowers can arrange for maximum and minimum interest rates to be charged on a loan. Capped rate mortgages benefit borrowers when interest rates are high, because interest payments on their loan will not exceed the capped rate. However, if interest rates decrease, the minimum rate of interest set on the loan may be higher than the general rate of interest.

Monthly Repayments on a £30,000 Mortgage at Various Rates

Calculations for a repayment, assuming no change in the applicable percentage rate of 15 percent (the Mortgage Interest Relief at Source (MIRAS) rate). Mortgage rate figures in parentheses are net values, that is the figure after MIRAS has been deducted.

Mortgage rate (%)	20 year term (£)	25 year term (£)	30 year term (£)
5.00 (4.25)	188.05	164.29	149.00
5.50 (4.67)	195.12	171.65	156.65
6.00 (5.10)	202.31	179.16	164.49
6.50 (5.52)	209.63	186.83	172.49
7.00 (5.95)	217.08	194.64	180.65
7.50 (6.37)	224.64	202.59	188.97
8.00 (6.80)	232.33	210.68	197.43
8.50 (7.22)	240.12	218.89	206.04
9.00 (7.65)	248.03	227.24	214.78
9.50 (8.07)	256.05	235.70	223.64
10.00 (8.50)	264.18	244.28	232.63
10.50 (8.92)	272.40	252.97	241.72
11.00 (9.35)	280.73	261.77	250.93
11.50 (9.77)	289.15	270.67	260.23
12.00 (10.20)	297.67	279.67	269.63
12.50 (10.62)	306.27	288.76	279.12
13.00 (11.05)	314.97	297.93	288.69
13.50 (11.47)	323.74	307.20	298.34
14.00 (11.90)	332.60	316.54	308.06

Source: Council of Mortgage Lenders

Annual Repayments on a £30,000 Mortgage over 25 Years

Calculations for a repayment mortgage, assuming no change in the interest rate payable or in the applicable MIRAS percentage rate of 15 percent. Based on a mortgage at 7 percent (5.95 percent after MIRAS has been deducted).

Year	Constant net annual repayment (£)	Principal (£)	Interest (£)	Balance at end of year (£)
1	2,335.66	550.66	1,785.00	29,449.34
2	2,335.66	583.43	1,752.23	28,865.91
3	2,335.66	618.14	1,717.52	28,247.77
4	2,335.66	654.92	1,680.74	27,592.85
5	2,335.66	693.89	1,641.78	26,898.96
6	2,335.66	735.18	1,600.49	26,163.78
7	2,335.66	778.92	1,556.74	25,384.86
8	2,335.66	825.26	1,510.40	24,559.60
9	2,335.66	874.37	1,461.29	23,685.23
10	2,335.66	926.39	1,409.28	22,758.84
11	2,335.66	981.51	1,354.15	21,777.33
12	2,335.66	1,039.91	1,295.75	20,737.41
13	2,335.66	1,101.79	1,233.88	19,635.63
14	2,335.66	1,167.34	1,168.32	18,468.28
15	2,335.66	1,236.80	1,098.86	17,231.48
16	2,335.66	1,310.39	1,025.27	15,921.09
17	2,335.66	1,388.36	947.31	14,532.73
18	2,335.66	1,470.97	864.70	13,061.77
19	2,335.66	1,558.49	777.17	11,503.28
20	2,335.66	1,651.22	684.45	9,852.06
21	2,335.66	1,749.47	586.19	8,102.60
22	2,335.66	1,853.56	482.10	6,249.04
23	2,335.66	1,963.85	371.82	4,285.19
24	2,335.66	2,080.69	254.97	2,204.50
25	2,335.73	2,204.50	131.16	0
Total	58,391.57	30,000.00	28,391.57	0

Source: Council of Mortgage Lenders

Sources of Finance for Small Business in the UK

Source: © 1997 Project North East

Introduction

There are three sources of funds for any business: equity, loans, and retained earnings. Most businesses rely largely on loan finance, obtaining loans and overdrafts from the major banks. As commercial lenders, the banks are concerned with getting a good return on their investments and do not want to lose their investors' money on businesses that go bankrupt. Banks are increasingly responsive to the needs of small businesses, but there are many occasions where the risk of lending is considered too high. This is usually because the business is being started by someone with little previous business experience and not much of their own capital to invest, and there is insufficient security.

Small businesses often need other sources of financial help if they are to grow and develop. Financial assistance and advice to small businesses is available all over the country, especially in areas of high unemployment and economic deprivation. Funds may come from the government (at European Union, national, and local level) and from a number of organizations such as Local Enterprise Agencies. Many major private companies collaborate with such organisations to provide finance in the form of grants and loans. Banks are more likely to help small businesses who are receiving support and advice from these agencies.

Small Business Support Networks

The networks of organizations that make financial support and advice available to small firms is constantly changing. Identifying the right package of support can be complicated. Several regional networks – Business Links (England), Business Shops (Scotland), Business Connects (Wales), and the Local Enterprise Development Unit (LEDU) Regional Offices in Northern Ireland – have recently been established to clarify matters. All of these networks provide 'one stop shops', bringing together information on all the most important local and national business support services for small and medium-sized businesses.

Every area now has a local Business Link (or equivalent) office. The main services provided by these networks are business information, Personal Business Advisers (PBAs), and a range of more specialized consultancy services. Anyone starting a business or needing further assistance should first contact their local Business Link (or equivalent), which should signpost them to relevant local and national sources of advice and financial assistance. Business Link (or equivalent) services are mostly free or subsidized.

Financial assistance is often provided for specific purposes, for example marketing or rent relief; specific types of business, for example manufacturing, technology; for particular types of people, for example unemployed or young people; or for specific areas, for example rural areas or areas of industrial decline. Anyone starting or developing a business and looking for financial assistance must produce a comprehensive business plan clearly setting out the financial case. PBAs can assist with this and can also refer clients to other agencies for more in-depth advice and training. An experienced PBA will know how best to put together a package of support to suit the needs of small businesses and will guide clients through the application process. So many different types of finance and assistance are available that it is worth looking for relevant programmes which may be relatively under-subscribed.

Types of Financial Support

Loan funds Terms and conditions for loans funds are often 'soft' – less stringent than for commercial loans. Interest is often fixed for the period of the loan or charged below bank rates. Less security than a bank would seek is usually required. The repayment period can be flexible, with repayment 'holidays' usually available. Soft loan funds are often 'revolving' – repayments go back into the main fund. Loans are often only available to businesses that are viable, but cannot raise all the finance required from banks. Most funds require borrowers to be monitored for the period of the loan and some integrate loan finance with advisory schemes. PBA's are usually familiar with application procedures and should advise clients on the most suitable loan funds to apply for.

Grants and awards Grants and awards do not need to be repaid. Grants are usually 'one-off' payments providing a percentage of the costs towards specific purposes, for example marketing, refurbishing premises, capital equipment. They are rarely available to retail businesses. Many local authorities provide grants to encourage small firms. Awards usually recognize achievement and can be either local or national. Awards bring publicity and prizes in cash or in kind. LiveWIRE runs an annual competition for young entrepreneurs and the Department of Trade and Industry runs SMART – the Small Firms Merit Award for Science and Technology for UK firms with less than 50 employees.

Venture capital Venture capital is a means of financing a growing business where a portion of the share capital or equity is sold in return for a major investment in the business. Whilst some measure of personal control over the business is lost to the new shareholder, the amount of finance gained can be very large indeed. Some schemes combine loan and equity finance. The British Venture Capital Association publishes a list of Venture Capital Funds.

The Enterprise Investment Scheme allows businesses to raise up to £1 million per tax year. Individuals are encouraged to invest up to £100,000 per tax year in a company by receiving tax relief on that sum. Investors previously unconnected to the company can become paid directors. The aim is to encourage 'business angels' – wealthy people with extensive business experience – to provide finance and expertise. Most regions of the UK now have 'business angel' matching services, which encourage local investment and mentoring on a smaller scale. The Local Investment Networking Company (LINC) works across the country matching investors with small business requiring £10,000 to £250,000, and is sponsored by several banks.

Sources of Financial Support

This section is a starting point to sources of business finance and is in no way exhaustive. Business Links, etc., should have details on what is available locally.

Business start-up The Training and Enterprise Councils (TECs) in England and Wales, Local Enterprise Companies (LECs) in Scotland, and the LEDU in Northern Ireland administer a variety of schemes to help support new businesses. Each TEC and LEC uses its own discretion in the way that the scheme is run and conditions vary from place to place. Most schemes include business planning, training, and some form of financial support.

Department of Trade and Industry (DTI) The DTI runs a variety of schemes offering financial help to businesses in areas such as technology, research and development, and export.

The Small Firms Loan Guarantee Scheme (SFLGS) Bank loans usually require some security, which not all small businesses can provide. Through the SFLGS, the government acts as a guarantor to a certain percentage of loans made by banks or other financial institutions to small businesses. The SFLGS is not available if a conventional loan can be obtained. Available only to established businesses that have traded for over two years, the maximum loan which can be covered is £250,000. There are restrictions on the types of companies eligible for SFLGS. Details are available from most banks.

Young people The Prince's Youth Business Trust (PYBT), or PSYBT in Scotland, assists unemployed young people aged 18–29 to start up in business. PYBT is aimed at disadvantaged young people, who often find it difficult to obtain finance from conventional sources. It operates from regional offices, arranging advice and training as well as grants and loans. Grants are also available for pre-start market testing.

LiveWIRE, sponsored by Shell UK Ltd, aims to assist young people who are interested in starting their own business. The LiveWIRE Business Start Up awards provide over £200,000 of cash and in-kind support to owner managers aged 16–25 in their first year of trading. Entrants must provide a comprehensive business plan to their local co-ordinator.

Former industrial areas British Steel (Industry) Ltd provides assistance in areas affected by the decline in the steel industry. It helps business to start up, expand, or relocate to the designated areas. Finance can take the form of loans or shared capital.

Rural areas The Rural Development Commission provides grants towards the redevelopment of redundant rural buildings for commercial purposes. Advice and training for craft businesses is also available.

Local sources of funding Most areas have funds available for local businesses, often provided through Local Authorities, Local Enterprise Agencies, TECs, LECs, etc. There may also be less well publicized independent funds and trusts.

European funding Various European funding schemes are available to businesses, mainly supporting research and development.

Useful Tips

Funding for small businesses is frequently raised most effectively as a package of support from several sources. Backing from one source can inspire the confidence of another. The best way to assemble a suitable package of support is through an experienced PBA's acting as an intermediary. A comprehensive business plan is essential before seeking any financial help. The business plan should contain financial forecasts detailing exactly how much money is required and what it will be used for. Business Advisers and bank managers can advise on business plan preparation. Financial assistance, especially for business start-ups, is often associated with business skills courses. Undertaking business training not only improves personal skills, but will increase the confidence of potential investors in the business.

Useful Contacts

Business Link Hotline; phone: (0345) 567765

Business Connect Wales; phone: (0345) 969798

Scottish Business Shops; phone: (0800) 787878

LEDU (Northern Ireland); phone: (01232) 491031

TEC Information Line; phone: (0114) 259 4776

The above numbers should give you local contact details.

Local Investment Networking Company (LINC) 4 Snow Hill, London EC1A 2BS; phone: (0171) 236 3000

British Venture Capital Association (BVCA) Essex House, 12–13 Essex Street, London WC2R 3AA; phone: (0171) 240 3846

DTI Loan Guarantee Section Level 2, St Mary's House, c/o Moorfoot, Sheffield S1 4PQ; phone: (0114) 259 7308

Prince's Youth Business Trust 18 Park Square East, London NW1 4LH; phone: (0800) 842842

Prince's Scottish Youth Business Trust Mercantile Chambers, 6th Floor, 53 Bothwell Street, Glasgow G2 6TS; phone: (0141) 248 4999

LiveWIRE Freepost NT805, Newcastle upon Tyne NE1 1BR; phone: (0345) 573252 (lo-call hotline)

British Steel (Industry) Ltd Bridge House, Bridge Street, Sheffield S3 8NS; phone: (0114) 273 1612

Rural Development Commission 141 Castle Street, Salisbury SP1 3TP; phone: (01722) 336255

There are government offices throughout the UK, under DTI in the phone book. For Enterprise Agencies, TECs, and LECs, look under Business Enterprise Agencies in Yellow Pages.

Compound Interest

This table assumes that interest is calculated annually and takes no account of taxation.

Interest rate	Value of £100 after:											
	4%	5%	6%	7%	8%	9%	10%	11%	12%	13%	14%	15%
3 months	101.0	101.3	101.5	101.8	102.0	102.3	102.5	102.8	103.0	103.3	103.5	103.8
6 months	102.0	102.5	103.0	103.5	104.0	104.5	105.0	105.5	106.0	106.5	107.0	107.5
1 year	104.0	105.0	106.0	107.0	108.0	109.0	110.0	111.0	112.0	113.0	114.0	115.0
2 years	108.2	110.3	112.4	114.5	116.6	118.8	121.0	123.2	125.4	127.7	130.0	132.3
3 years	112.5	115.8	119.1	122.5	126.0	129.5	133.1	136.8	140.5	144.3	148.2	152.1
4 years	117.0	121.6	126.2	131.1	136.0	141.2	146.4	151.8	157.4	163.0	168.9	174.9
5 years	121.7	127.6	133.8	140.3	146.9	153.9	161.1	168.5	176.2	184.2	192.5	201.1
6 years	126.5	134.0	141.9	150.1	158.7	167.7	177.2	187.0	197.4	208.2	219.5	231.3
7 years	131.6	140.7	150.4	160.6	171.4	182.8	194.9	207.6	221.1	235.3	250.2	266.0
8 years	136.9	147.7	159.4	171.8	185.1	199.3	214.4	230.5	247.6	265.8	285.3	305.9
9 years	142.3	155.1	168.9	183.8	199.9	217.2	235.8	255.8	277.3	300.4	325.2	351.8
10 years	148.0	162.9	179.1	196.7	215.9	236.7	259.4	283.9	310.6	339.5	370.7	404.6
15 years	180.1	207.9	239.7	275.9	317.2	364.2	417.7	478.5	547.4	625.4	713.8	813.7
20 years	219.1	265.3	320.7	387.0	466.1	560.4	672.7	806.2	964.6	1,152.3	1,374.3	1,636.7
25 years	266.6	338.6	429.2	542.7	684.8	862.3	1,083.5	1,358.5	1,700.0	2,123.1	2,646.2	3,291.9

See Also UK Taxation (Economy and Business)

Copyright, Patents, Trade Marks, and Designs

Copyright: National Law and International Protection in the UK

Source: The British Council Copyright Office; The UK Copyright Directorate; The UK Copyright Licensing Agency; The UK Patent Office. © Crown copyright 1997

What is Copyright?

Copyright is a form of protection that gives rights to creators of certain kinds of material. These rights control the unauthorized use or exploitation of the literary or artistic work. Material protected by copyright includes original literary, dramatic, musical, and artistic works, sound recordings, films, and video, broadcasts including cable and satellite, computer software, and databases. Anyone who creates a literary, dramatic, musical, or artistic work in the UK is automatically the copyright owner and holds the rights to his or her work. Broadly, an author holds rights to cover copying, adapting, lending, or renting copies, performing in public, and broadcasting. The copyright owner has exclusive rights to do a number of things with his or her work, known as 'restrictive acts'. These include copying the work; issuing copies to the public; presenting the work to the public, in any form; adapting the work.

How Long Does Copyright Last?

UK copyright lasts until 70 years after the death of the author for a literary, dramatic, musical, or artistic work. Some works are subject to more limited terms of copyright, for example, films. Copyright in a film lasts until 70 years after the death of the last surviving person out of the following: principal director, screenplay and dialogue author, and composer of the film's music score. For computer-generated works, sound recordings, broadcasts, and cable programmes, copyright lasts for 50 years. Rights for performing artists last for 50 years; these rights cover the broadcasting and recording of live performances, the renting and lending of recordings of their performances, and the broadcasting and performing of sound recordings.

Exceptions to Copyright

In some circumstances, copyright material can be used without permission. Some acts, which are within the scope of the 'restricted acts', can be carried out without infringing copyright. The Copyright, Designs and Patents Act of 1988 provides for Fair Dealing and Library Privilege in the following ways:

Fair Dealing

Use or copying of literary, dramatic, musical, or artistic works is permitted for the purposes of research or private study without infringing upon the rights of the copyright holder.

The 1988 Act does not state explicitly what fair dealing is, but it would be reasonable to assume that if the amount of copying done does not threaten the economic inter-ests of the copyright holder (as, for example, making a complete copy of a work and not purchasing it would) then it can be considered fair. Although there is no legislation that stipulates the amount of material that can be copied from a work, the British Copyright Council has published a set of guidelines for use when photocopying from books: the copyright holder would consider it fair dealing if, for the purposes of research or private study, a single photocopy of up to one chapter from a book is photocopied. If several extracts are copied, not more than five percent of the whole book would be acceptable. It is never fair dealing to make multiple copies of the same material.

The above guidelines do not cover journal articles. Increasingly, individual-article supply services are making journal articles available to anyone who wishes to purchase a copy. A copyright fee is paid to the holder by the supplier and therefore even a single photocopy of a journal article is not considered fair dealing because it damages the economic interests of the copyright holder.

With the rapid advance of electronic publishing, there is currently no official consensus as to what constitutes fair dealing regarding this manner of dissemination. UK copyright laws apply to information sent over the Internet, stored on web servers, or recorded on CD-ROM. It is therefore advisable to ask the copyright holder directly for permission to use or distribute works electronically.

Library Privilege

The Copyright, Designs and Patents Act of 1998 provides certain privileges to libraries. The librarian of a prescribed library has the right to provide a service to readers, for the purposes of research or private study, whereby they can be supplied with either one copy of one article from a journal publication or one copy of a reasonable proportion of a book. A 'reasonable proportion' of a book is considered by the British Copyright Council to be one chapter or 10 percent of its contents.

Note: According to the British Copyright Council's guidelines, ten percent is reasonable under library privilege, 5 percent is reasonable under fair dealing.

How to Register UK Copyright

There is no legal requirement in the UK to register copyright; copyright protection is automatic and there is no system for registration, nor are there any fees to pay. In case of proceedings against infringement of copyright, which will require the copyright owner to proof ownership, it is advisable to protect an original literary, dramatic, musical, or artistic work in the following way:

Mark up a copy of the original work with: year of publication (copyright subsists in work, whether published or unpublished; in the case of unpublished work, mark a copy with the date of completion); name of the author/owner; the international copyright symbol © (it is not essential in the UK to mark up original work with the international copyright symbol, although it is advisable in the case of infringement proceedings).

Deposit the copy with a bank or solicitor, or send a copy of the work to yourself, by registered post and keep the envelope sealed. This will prove that the work existed at the time it was deposited.

European Copyright Protection

The provisions of the Copyright, Designs and Patents Act of 1988 form the main legislation on copyright in the UK. Information technology developments in recent years have led the European Community to adopt Directives in response to the need to adapt existing copyright and intellectual property rights legislation to technological advances. These Directives have resulted in the following additions to UK copyright legislation:

Directive 91/250/EEC on the legal protection of computer programs, implemented by the Copyright (Computer Programs) Regulations 1992 [Statutory Instrument (SI) 1992 No. 3233], which came into force on 1 January 1993; Directive 92/100/EEC on rental, lending, and other rights in the copyright field, and Directive 93/83/EEC on copyright and related rights in relation to cable and satellite broadcasting, both implemented by the Copyright and Related Rights Regulations 1996 (SI 1996 No. 2967), which came into force on 1 December 1996; Directive 93/98/EEC on the duration of copyright and related rights, implemented (with the exception of Article 4) by the Duration of Copyright and Rights in Performances Regulations 1995 (SI 1995 No. 3297), which came into force on 1 January 1996. Article 4 of this Directive is implemented by SI 1996 No. 2967. There is also an adopted EC Directive (96/9/EC) on the legal protection of databases, but this has not yet been implemented in the UK.

Currently, a proposal for an EC Directive on artists' resale right or *droit de suite* is also under discussion, but it is not as yet clear if or when this will be adopted. The European Commission has also recently published a Communication (COM (95) 282) setting out its plans for legislative proposals as regards copyright and related rights in the information society.

International Copyright Protection

Although 'international copyright' does not exist in itself, there are global and multilateral copyright treaties which protect the rights of authors against unauthorized use in foreign countries. The Berne Convention for the Protection of Literary Artistic Works and the Universal Copyright Convention (UCC) are two international conventions that protect the rights of authors. Copyright material created by UK authors is protected by the national copyright law of each member country. The UK is a party to both of these conventions and to the UCC, which is administered by the United Nations Educational, Scientific, and Cultural Organization (UNESCO). The UK is also a member of the World Trade Organization (WTO) and, therefore, adheres to the agreement on Trade-Related Aspects of Intellectual Property Rights (TRIPS), which lays down minimum standards of protection in all areas of intellectual property, including copyright and related rights.

Berne Convention The International Convention for the Protection of Literary and Artistic Works was established in Berne, Switzerland, in 1886; it is known as the

---

Parties to the Berne Convention for the Protection of Literary and Artistic Works

As of 24 September 1997.

Albania	Costa Rica	Haiti	Mali	St Vincent and the
Argentina	Côte d'Ivoire	Honduras	Malta	Grenadines
Australia	Croatia	Hungary	Mauritania	Senegal
Austria	Cuba	Iceland	Mauritius	Slovak Republic
Bahamas	Cyprus	India	Mexico	Slovenia
Bahrain	Czech Republic	Indonesia	Moldova	South Africa
Barbados	Denmark	Ireland, Republic of	Monaco	Spain
Belarus	Dominican Republic	Israel	Morocco	Sri Lanka
Belgium	Ecuador	Italy	Namibia	Suriname
Benin	Egypt	Jamaica	Netherlands	Sweden
Bolivia	El Salvador	Japan	New Zealand	Switzerland
Bosnia-Herzegovina	Equatorial Guinea	Kenya	Niger	Tanzania
Brazil	Estonia	Korea, South	Nigeria	Thailand
Bulgaria	Fiji	Latvia	Norway	Togo
Burkina Faso	Finland	Lebanon	Pakistan	Trinidad and Tobago
Cameroon	France	Lesotho	Panama	Tunisia
Canada	Gabon	Liberia	Paraguay	Turkey
Cape Verde	Gambia	Libya	Peru	UK
Central African Republic	Georgia	Liechtenstein	Philippines	Ukraine
Chad	Germany	Lithuania	Poland	Uruguay
Chile	Ghana	Luxembourg	Portugal	USA
China	Greece	Macedonia, Former	Romania	Vatican City State
Colombia	Guatemala	Yugoslav Republic of	Russia	Venezuela
Congo, Democratic	Guinea	Madagascar	Rwanda	Yugoslavia
Republic of	Guinea-Bissau	Malawi	St Kitts and Nevis	Zambia
Congo, Republic of the	Guyana	Malaysia	St Lucia	Zimbabwe

Parties to the Universal Copyright Convention

As of 17 March 1997.

Algeria	China	Haiti	Mexico	Saudi Arabia
Andorra	Colombia	Hungary	Monaco	Senegal
Argentina	Costa Rica	Iceland	Morocco	Slovak Republic
Australia	Croatia	India	Netherlands	Slovenia
Austria	Cuba	Ireland, Republic of	New Zealand	Spain
Bahamas	Cyprus	Israel	Niger	Sri Lanka
Bangladesh	Czech Republic	Italy	Nigeria	Sweden
Barbados	Denmark	Japan	Norway	Switzerland
Belarus	Dominican Republic	Kazakhstan	Pakistan	Tajikistan
Belgium	Ecuador	Kenya	Panama	Trinidad and Tobago
Belize	El Salvador	Korea, South	Paraguay	Tunisia
Bolivia	Fiji	Laos	Peru	UK
Bosnia-Herzegovina	Finland	Lebanon	Philippines	Ukraine
Brazil	France	Liberia	Poland	Uruguay
Bulgaria	Germany	Liechtenstein	Portugal	USA
Cambodia	Ghana	Luxembourg	Russia	Vatican City State
Cameroon	Greece	Malawi	Rwanda	Venezuela
Canada	Guatemala	Malta	St Vincent and the	Yugoslavia
Chile	Guinea	Mauritius	Grenadines	Zambia

Berne Convention. Member countries of the Berne Convention provide each others' authors with copyright protection as if they were nationals of their own country. Copyright does not depend on formalities such as the registration of a work. However, in cases of infringement, a member country can take into account any registration procedures an author may have carried out to protect his or her work. The minimum term for copyright protection under the Berne Convention is the duration of the life of the author plus a further 50 years after their death. Member countries of the Convention can provide for longer terms, according to their national copyright laws. Each member country must provide minimum exclusive rights for the protection of an author's rights in translation, reproduction, public performance, adaptation, paternity, and integrity.

Universal Copyright Convention (UCC)
The UCC came into effect in 1955. The most recent revision of the Convention was in Paris in 1971; hence, it is often referred to as the Paris Convention.

The UCC's objective is to protect the rights of authors; it also operates on the principle of national copyright law. The UCC differs slightly from the Berne Convention. It allows for national signatories to require copyright notice and registration under their national law. Copyright duration must be for at least 25 years after either the author's death or first publication, depending on member countries' individual laws. The UCC's provisions for minimum rights for authors are for reproduction, adaptation, or public performance or broadcasting of works; considerably less demanding than the provisions of the Berne Convention. The UCC recognizes the Berne Convention and where countries are signatories of both conventions, the Berne Convention controls apply.

Other international copyright and related rights treaties include the Rome Convention

(the International Convention for the Protection of Performers, Producers of Phonograms, and Broadcasting Organizations), administered by the World Intellectual Property Organization (WIPO); the WIPO Copyright Treaty and the WIPO Performances and Phonograms Treaty.

If an author wishes to protect his or her work in a specific country it is advisable that they find out the extent to which foreign works are protected in that particular country. If a country is not a signatory to any international treaty, its own copyright laws may provide protection for a foreign author.

Patents: National Law and International Protection in the UK

Source: The UK Patent Office. © Crown copyright 1997

What is a Patent?
A patent is a form of protection granting its holder the exclusive right to an invention, preventing others from making, using, or selling the invention without the permission of the inventor. The inventor has this right for a limited period (20 years), during which time he or she is protected from competition and can control the exploitation of his or her invention.

Patents are territorial rights, i.e. a UK patent will only give the holder rights within the UK. Concerned mainly with how things work, what they do, and how they are made, patents are generally applied to new functional or technical aspects of products or processes. To be eligible for a UK patent, an invention must not have been made public in the UK in any way before a patent application is filed.

All patents are published. Patent documents cover almost every area of technology and provide a comprehensive source of technical information in the world. The patent system plays a major part in the transfer of

technology, which acts as a stimulus to technical innovation. Patents indicate the level of innovative activity in a particular market. They generate new investment and are a motivating force behind technical progress.

An invention is patentable if it is new; it involves an innovation; it can be applied to some form of industry (i.e. anything that is not simply an intellectual or aesthetic activity. This does not necessarily mean that it must involve the use of machinery or the manufacture of goods).

An invention is not patentable if it is a discovery; it is a scientific theory or mathematical model; it is a literary, dramatic, or artistic work (these are covered by copyright); it is a plan or a method for performing a mental act, playing a game, or doing business; it is the presentation of information, or a computer program; it is a new animal or plant species; it is a method of surgical or therapeutic treatment of the human body, or animals; it is a method of diagnosis.

Patent Rights
A patent gives an inventor the right to prevent anyone from using his or her invention, unless he or she chooses to let others use it under agreed terms. In cases of infringement, the possession of a patent provides the right to take legal action. A patent provides negative rights, i.e. it protects against anyone else making, using, or selling an invention.

It is not a legal requirement for an inventor to obtain a patent in order to put his or her invention into practice. However, once an invention is made public, there will be no protection against others using it. Obtaining a patent will provide the inventor with time to develop his or her invention, perhaps by establishing a business. Alternatively, the patent holder can allow someone else to exploit the invention and receive royalties under a licensing agreement.

Filing for a UK Patent
To file an application for a patent, a patent

Member States of the Patent Copyright Treaty

As of 26 February 1997.

Albania	Congo, Republic of the	Italy	Mauritania	Spain
Armenia	Côte d'Ivoire	Japan	Mexico	Sri Lanka
Australia	Cuba	Kazakhstan	Moldova	Sudan
Austria	Czech Republic	Kenya	Monaco	Swaziland
Azerbaijan	Denmark	Korea, North	Mongolia	Sweden
Barbados	Estonia	Korea, South	Netherlands	Switzerland
Belarus	Finland	Kyrgyzstan	New Zealand	Tajikistan
Belgium	France	Latvia	Niger	Togo
Benin	Gabon	Lesotho	Norway	Trinidad and Tobago
Bosnia-Herzegovina	Georgia	Liberia	Poland	Turkey
Brazil	Germany	Liechtenstein	Portugal	Turkmenistan
Bulgaria	Ghana	Lithuania	Romania	Uganda
Burkina Faso	Greece	Luxembourg	Russia	UK
Cameroon	Guinea	Macedonia, Former	St Lucia	Ukraine
Canada	Hungary	Yugoslav Republic of	Senegal	USA
Central African Republic	Iceland	Madagascar	Singapore	Uzbekistan
Chad	Ireland, Republic of	Malawi	Slovak Republic	Vietnam
China	Israel	Mali	Slovenia	Yugoslavia

specification must be prepared to describe the invention. A UK patent application is a legal document called a Specification. Its contents determine whether a patent can be granted. The Specification must include all the necessary information about the invention, including drawings if appropriate.

Completing a Specification requires technical and legal skills and it is advisable to employ the services of a registered patent agent (or chartered patent agent). It is vital that all the necessary information about an invention is included in the description; changes cannot be made once an application has been filed. It is also essential that copies of all application documents are kept by the inventor.

A 'Request for Grant of a Patent', Patents Form 1/77 must be completed to file an application. Application documents should then be taken or sent to the Patent Office. At the same time, the relevant application fees must be paid. The fee for filing Patents Form 1/77 is £25.00. A detailed list of fees relating to UK patents is available from the UK Patent Office. If you use a patent agent in preparing and applying for a patent, there will be additional professional fees to pay.

International Patent Protection

An inventor may want to consider filing for protection of an invention abroad if he or she wants to plan for expansion into foreign markets or if there are possibilities for licensing rights abroad.

The first thing to do when seeking international patent protection is to file a UK patent application. The inventor then has 12 months in which to file any foreign, European, or world patent application. It is not a legal requirement to file a patent application in the UK first, but there are advantages: an early and inexpensive search report from the UK Patent Office can be obtained; an inventor can use a national application made under the

Patents Act 1977 as a basis for claiming priority for an application filed in most other countries; security clearance from the UK Patent Office has to be obtained before an application for a patent abroad can be made; the UK search report can be used to make a first assessment of an invention before starting the costly process of obtaining protection abroad.

The UK and most other Western European countries are parties to the European Patent Convention (EPC), administered by the European Patent Office (EPO). A patent application granted under the EPC will be effective in each country listed on the application. A fee is payable for each country on the application. This method of obtaining a European patent may be cheaper than applying separately to each country in which protection is desired.

When granted, the European patent provides protection in the same way as a number of separate national patents, and is subject to the national law of each country. You can therefore obtain a patent valid in the UK by filing a European application and making the UK a designated country. You can file a European patent application at the UK Patent Office, or at the EPO.

Another international patent treaty is the Patent Cooperation Treaty (PCT) of 1970. Signatory countries of the Universal Copyright Convention can become members of the PCT. Under the PCT it is possible to file for patent protection for an invention in a large number of countries simultaneously. This is an 'international' patent application and it can be filed by anyone who is a national or resident of a member country. As with a European patent application, an inventor can indicate which countries he or she wishes his or her international application to have effect ('designated States').

Residents of the UK must obtain permission from the UK Patent Office before applying for any international patent, unless they have already applied

for a patent for the same invention in the UK. The Patent Office can prohibit or restrict the publication or communication of a patent application if it is considered that the application contains information that might be prejudicial to the defence of the realm or the safety of the public. If a UK application has been made, you must not make an application abroad until at least six weeks after the UK filing date.

Trade Marks: National Law and International Protection in the UK

Source: The UK Patent Office. © Crown copyright 1997

What is a Trade Mark?

Trade marks are used as marketing tools to make the product of a particular trader recognizable to the public. A trade mark is any sign that can distinguish between the goods and services of one trader from those of another, and that can be represented graphically. The sign of a trade mark can include words, three-dimensional shapes, or even sounds and smells. The essential criterion for a trade mark is that is must be distinctive.

A trade mark must not be descriptive of the goods or services to which it applies; a word that other traders might legitimately want to use for their own products; indicative of the kind, quality, quantity, purpose, or value of a product; a geographic name or common surname.

A trade mark cannot be registered if it is a sign that consists exclusively of a shape that results from the nature of a product; serves a utilitarian purpose; adds value to the product because of its visual appeal.

A trade mark also cannot be registered if it is of such a nature as to deceive the public, e.g. if the mark suggests a certain quality of product or service which does not exist; if it is the same as or similar to an earlier mark, whether registered or applied for, for the

Members of the Madrid System of Trade Mark Registration

As of September 1997. (A) = party to the Madrid Agreement, (P) = party to the Madrid Protocol, and (AP) = party to both the Agreement and the Protocol.

Albania (A)	Cuba (AP)	Korea, North (AP)	Mongolia (A)	Slovenia (A)
Algeria (A)	Czech Republic (AP)	Kyrgyzstan (A)	Morocco (A)	Spain (AP)
Armenia (A)	Denmark (P)	Latvia (A)	Netherlands (A)	Sudan (A)
Austria (A)	Egypt (A)	Liberia (A)	Norway (P)	Sweden (P)
Azerbaijan (A)	Finland (P)	Liechtenstein (A)	Poland (AP)	Switzerland (AP)
Belarus (A)	France (AP)	Lithuania (P)	Portugal (AP)	Tajikistan (A)
Belgium (A)	Germany (AP)	Luxembourg (A)	Romania (A)	UK (P)
Bosnia Herzegovina (A)	Hungary (AP)	Macedonia, Former	Russia (A)	Ukraine (A)
Bulgaria (A)	Iceland (P)	Yugoslav Republic of (A)	San Marino (A)	Uzbekistan (A)
China (AP)	Italy (A)	Moldova (AP)	Sierra Leone (A)	Vietnam (A)
Croatia (A)	Kazakhstan (A)	Monaco (AP)	Slovak Republic (AP)	Yugoslavia (A)

same or a similar product; priority will always be given to an earlier mark.

The above criteria prevent the trade mark system from providing an indefinite extension of the rights conferred by a patent, a registered design, or copyright. A trade mark can last indefinitely; normal procedure is to register a trade mark initially for ten years. It can be renewed every ten years by paying a renewal fee. Details of renewal fees can be obtained from the UK Patent Office.

Trade Mark Rights
Registration of a trade mark allows the holder to use that mark on the goods or services for which it is registered. Under trade mark law, it also provides the right to take legal action in cases of infringement.

Trade Mark Registration
Trade mark registration is not compulsory in the UK; however, if a trade mark is not registered, it is not possible to bring any legal action against infringement to protect the mark.

Any trade mark owner can apply for registration of a trade mark and you do not have to be British subject to do so. You do, however, have to be using, or intending to use, the mark in the UK. To apply for registration of a trade mark you must file Form TM3 and pay the appropriate fee, details of which can be obtained from the UK Patent Office. You have two months in which to pay the fee from the filing date. You can send the application by post or deliver it by hand to the Trade Marks Registry at the Patent Office (Newport) or the Patent Office (London).

Registering trade marks is a specialized area of work and you may find it helpful to employ the services of a trade mark agent. Some patent agents also specialize in trade mark law. If you use a professional agent in preparing and applying for a trade mark, there will be additional professional fees to pay. To obtain information about professional agents who can help with the legal and technical aspects of applying for a trade mark, contact the Chartered Institute of Patent Agents.

If an application to register a trade mark is approved, it will be published in the next available edition of the *Trade Mark Journal*. If there is no third party opposition to it during a period of three months, the trade mark will then be entered onto the Register. UK trade marks do not offer protection abroad. However, you can use a UK application or registration as the basis for an application overseas, covering any or all of the countries party to the Madrid Protocol (see below).

International Trade Mark Registration
If you want to use your trade mark in countries other than the UK, you can acquire protection for your trade mark in more than one country using a single application. This can be done in one of three ways: by applying direct to the trade mark office in each country; by applying for a European Community trade mark with the Office for Harmonization in the Internal Market (Trade Marks and Designs). The Community trade mark gives protection in all EU countries.

Community trade marks can also be applied for through the UK Patent Office. Based in Alicante, Spain, the Office for Harmonization in the Internal Market (OHIM) is the Community body responsible for administering the Community trade marks Regulations. It provides the legal basis of a trade mark registration that has rights across the entire Community.

Procedures of OHIM differ from the procedures of the UK Patent Office, but there is close similarity in the legal basis: both the UK trade marks legislation (Trade Marks Act 1994) and the Council Regulation (EC No. 40/94) are based on Council Directive 89/104 to harmonize the trade mark laws of Community member states; by applying to register your trade mark in countries party to the Madrid system of trade mark registration. This system is governed by two treaties; the Madrid Agreement Concerning the International Registration of Marks, dating from 1891, and the Protocol Relating to the Madrid Agreement which came into effect on 1 April 1996. They are administered by the International Bureau of the World Intellectual Property Organization (WIPO), based in Geneva, Switzerland. Some of the countries party to the Madrid system are also members of the EU.

To register a trade mark under the Madrid system, all applications which use a UK application or registration as basis must be filed through the UK Patent Office. Each designated country on the application examines the application against its own criteria for registration. Each has up to 18 months to notify WIPO of any objections.

Designs: National Law and International Protection in the UK

Source: The UK Patent Office. © Crown copyright 1997

There are two kinds of design protection in the UK; registered designs and the new design right. Design right is automatic in its protection and, as such, has many similarities to copyright. The Copyright Directorate in the UK is responsible for policy on design right. The UK Patent Office's Design Registry administers and grants applications for registered designs.

Design Right
Design right in the UK gives automatic protection for designs, without the need for registration. It is a new intellectual property right provided for in the Copyright, Designs and Patents Act 1988, which applies to original and non-commonplace designs of the shape or configuration of articles. Design right is not a monopoly right, rather a right to prevent copying of a design. As with any other business commodity, a design right can be bought, sold, or licensed to others. It is effective for 10 years after first marketing or making articles to the design, subject to an overall limit of 15 years from the creation of the design. The protection provided is weaker than that attending registration.

Although there is no requirement to register for design right, it is advisable to keep records of when the design was first created and when the design was first used to make an article for sale or hire. This information can help in cases of infringement. Not all designs qualify for design right. Two-dimensional designs such as wall paper and greeting card designs do not qualify for design right. Design right applies only to three-dimensional articles.

Design Right Protection

Design right is an 'exclusive right' for five years after first marketing. It then becomes subject to licences of right for the remaining five years of its term. The design right owner has the right to take legal action in cases of infringement during the first five years. During the final five years, anyone is entitled to a licence to make and sell articles copying the design. However, the rights owner is not obliged to make design drawings or know-how available to the copier. Normally the party wishing to obtain a licence will seek to come to an agreement with the owner, but if negotiations break down the Patent Office has the power to intervene and to fix terms on the basis of arguments put forward by the parties.

A new European Community Directive protects designs of semiconductor chips. Exclusive rights to these designs last for the full ten year term and cannot be licensed during the last five years.

Under the terms of the Copyright, Designs and Patents Act 1988, nationals, residents, or companies of the European Community, New Zealand, and UK colonies are protected by design right.

Design Right Exceptions

If a design feature enables an article to be functionally fitted or aesthetically matched to another article, it has no protection. These are known as the 'must-fit' and 'must-match' exceptions and they mean that competitors cannot be prevented from copying any features of a protected design that enable their own design to be connected to or matched with existing equipment designed by someone else. However, design right can still be infringed upon if features of a protected design are copied where there is no need to do so.

International Design Right Protection

Unlike copyright, design right is only effective in the countries where design right applies. It may be possible to obtain protection in other countries under petty patent or registered design systems, but it is not usually automatic and must be applied for.

Registered Designs

A registered design provides a monopoly right to its holder for the outward appearance of an item or items of manufacture. This right can last for a maximum of 25 years and can be bought, sold, hired, or licensed. A registered design is separate and additional to any copyright protection that may exist automatically in the creation of the design.

To be registrable, a design must be truly aesthetic and stand-alone so that competitors will not have to copy the design in order to compete; materially different from any other published design for the same or any other type of item.

A design must not be purely functional; determined by the shape of the whole article. For example, a design for a car panel cannot be registered because its shape and configuration is determined by the overall design of the car; a work of sculpture; a wall plaque, medal, or medallion; printed matter, primarily of a literary or artistic nature, for example greeting cards, leaflets, brochures, book jackets, etc. (copyright is the intellectual property right for items such as these).

Registering a Design

Before filing an application to register a design it is vital that the design has not been disclosed to the public in any way; if it has, a registered design may later be invalid.

To apply to register a design you must provide clear representations of the design, these must include a series of drawings and views of the design, together with a statement of novelty. A completed application form DF2A (available from the Design Registry at the UK Patent Office) must be submitted together with the appropriate filing fee. It may be advisable to use the services of a professional design registration agent, to receive advice on the legal and technical aspects of presenting a design registration application. If you do so, professional fees will of course have to paid as well as filing fees.

Once a design has been registered, the registration can be kept in force for up to 25 years by paying a renewal fee every five years.

Rights of a Registered Design Holder

A registered design in the UK provides exclusive rights to the holder to make, import, sell, or hire any article to which the design has been applied. The rights holder also has the right to licence the use of the design by others, subject to agreed terms, within the UK and the Isle of Man. Registering a design also provides the right to take legal action in cases of infringement of the design.

International Registered Design Protection

There is no such thing as international registration for designs. In general, separate applications must be made in each country where protection is sought. It is possible however, to extend UK protection for registered designs to some countries, mainly members of the Commonwealth. In these countries a UK-registered design is accepted as being equivalent to an independent registration in the country concerned.

If an application is made abroad, it must comply with the requirements of the country concerned. Further information concerning overseas regulations should be sought either from professional agents or from Embassies or Trade Missions of the countries concerned. Alternatively, contact the UK Patent Office. The following countries/territories extend protection to UK-registered designs without the need for local registration:

Anguilla; Antigua; Belize; Bermuda; Botswana; British Indian Ocean Territory;

Countries Deemed to be Convention Countries for the Purposes of Design Registration

Algeria	Chile	Ghana	Korea, North	New Zealand	Sudan
Argentina	China	Greece	Korea, South	Niger	Suriname
Australia	Congo, Democratic	Guinea	Lebanon	Nigeria	Swaziland
Austria	Republic of	Guinea-Bissau	Lesotho	Norway	Sweden
Bahamas	Congo, Republic of	Haiti	Libya	Pakistan	Switzerland
Bangladesh	the	Hong Kong	Liechtenstein	Philippines	Syria
Barbados	Côte d'Ivoire	Hungary	Luxembourg	Poland	Tanzania
Belarus	Croatia	Iceland	Madagascar	Portugal	Togo
Belgium	Cuba	India	Malawi	Romania	Trinidad and Tobago
Benin	Cyprus	Indonesia	Malaysia	Russia	Tunisia
Brazil	Czech Republic	Iran	Mali	Rwanda	Turkey
Bulgaria	Denmark	Iraq	Malta	San Marino	Uganda
Burkina Faso	Dominican Republic	Ireland, Republic of	Mauritania	Senegal	Ukraine
Burundi	Egypt	Israel	Mauritius	Singapore	USA
Cameroon	Finland	Italy	Mexico	Slovak Republic	Uruguay
Canada	France	Japan	Monaco	Slovenia	Vatican City State
Central African	Gabon	Jordan	Mongolia	South Africa	Vietnam
Republic	Gambia	Kazakhstan	Morocco	Spain	Zambia
Chad	Germany	Kenya	Netherlands	Sri Lanka	Zimbabwe

British Virgin Islands; Brunei (awaiting confirmation); Cyprus; Dominica; Falkland Islands; Fiji; Gambia; Ghana; Gibraltar; Grenada; Guyana; Hong Kong; Kenya; Kiribati; Malaysia (including Sabah and Sarawak); St Kitts and Nevis; St Helena; St Lucia; St Vincent; Sierra Leone; Singapore; Solomon Islands; Swaziland; Tuvalu; Uganda; Vanuatu; Yemen.

The following countries extend protection by local re-registration of a UK design within 4 months of filing the UK application: Malta within 3 years of UK registration: Jersey; Tanzania; Trinidad and Tobago at any time during the life of the UK design: Guernsey; Montserrat.

It is important to note that countries may terminate or change the extension of protection of UK designs at any time. There are some countries in which UK protection cannot be extended, or there is no provision in local law for protection of designs by local registration. These include the Cayman Islands, the Seychelles, and Mauritius.

International Convention

A number of countries have signed an International Convention whereby designs can be protected in each other's countries. This Convention is not administered by any one particular organization. If an application to register a design is made in a country that has signed the Convention, priority can be claimed to protect the same design in another Convention country from the earliest application made. There is a time limit of six months from the earliest Convention country filing date for claiming priority.

If priority is claimed, an application has to be supported with appropriate Convention documents. These documents certify details of the earlier application and must include a copy of original representations made to the Design Registry at the UK Patent Office. Alternatively, a request can be made to the Design Registry to make photocopies of the documents. The necessary Convention documents can be obtained by filing form DF23 with the UK Patent Office.

Intellectual Property: Directory of Organizations

British Copyright Council (for publications relating to copyright issues) Copyright House, 29–33 Berners St, London W1P 4AA, UK; phone: (0171) 405 9450

Chartered Institute of Patent Agents (for information about professional agents who can help with the legal and technical aspects of a trade mark) Staple Inn Buildings, High Holborn, London WC1V 7PZ, UK; phone: (0171) 405 9450; fax: (0171) 430 0471; e-mail: mailcipa.org.uk/; Web site: www.cipa.org.uk/

Copyright Directorate (for queries on copyright issues) The Patent Office, Room 150, 25 Southampton Buildings, London WC2A 1AY, UK; phone: (0171) 438 4777; fax: (0171) 438 4780; e-mail: copyrightpatent.gov.uk/

Copyright Licensing Agency (reproduction rights organization, representing copyright owners' rights, and licensing major users of copyright material) 90 Tottenham Court Road, London W1P 0LP, UK; phone: (0171) 436 5931; fax: (0171) 436 3986; Web site: www.cla.co.uk/

Copywatch hotline (for reporting infringements of copyright) phone: (0171) 436 4242

EUROPA (for details of copyright Directives, their measures and objectives) European Union's Web site: www.europa.eu.int/

European Patent Office (for further information about European patents) Erhardtstrasse 27, D-80331 Munich, Germany; phone: 0049 89 23 990; fax: 0049 89 23 99 44 65; Web site: www.european-patent-office.org/; relevant publications: *How to Get a European Patent*

UK Patent Office (for information about patents, the International Convention for designs and design registrations in general, and registering trade marks, both in the UK and internationally)

Patent Office (London) 25 Southampton Buildings, Chancery Lane, London WC2 1AY, UK

Patent Office (Newport) Concept House, Cardiff Road, Newport, South Wales NP9 1RH, UK

UK Patent Offices Central Enquiry Unit phone: (0645) 500505 (charged at local rates); fax: (01633) 813611; e-mail: enquiriespatent.gov.uk/; if you have hearing difficulties, you can contact the Central Enquiry Unit by text telephone on (0645) 222250; relevant publications: *Application for a Community Trade Mark, The Madrid Protocol – Applying for an International Trade Mark, International Trade Mark Registration*

World Intellectual Property Organization (for more information about international patents) PO Box 18, CH-1211, Geneva 20, Switzerland; phone: 0041 22 33 89 111; fax: 0041 22 73 35 428; Web site: www.wipo.int/; relevant publications: *Basic Facts about the PCT, PCT Applicant's Guide.*

Web Sites

Alt.Culture: an A–Z of the 90s

URL: 'http://cgi.pathfinder.com/ @@BE@ANAUA29KAOo6s/cgi-bin/altculture/home.cgi'

'Lively encyclopaedia of 1990s youth culture that spans grunge and gangsta, indie rock and indie film, cyberpunk and street fashion, extreme sports and political correctness, infomercials and zines'.

British Immigration and Visa Requirements

URL: 'http://www.fco.gov.uk/visa/'

Explanation of UK entry requirements provided by the Foreign and Commonwealth Office. Addresses of all British consular offices are provided and it is possible to download application forms and a variety of explanatory leaflets.

Charity Commission for England and Wales

URL: 'http://www.charity-commission.gov.uk/'

Functions of the body charged with supervising the 160,000 registered charities in England and Wales are fully explained.

Citizen's Charter Unit

URL: 'http://www.open.gov.uk/ charter/ccuhome.htm'

Provides discussion documents, explains how to complain about government services, and invites public feedback.

Cultural Exchange

URL: 'http://www.oceanintl.org/ newsletter.htm'

Bimonthly magazine produced by a non-profit-making US organization dedicated to promoting cultural exchange between students of different countries.

54 Ways to Help The Homeless

URL: 'http://earthsystems.org/ways/'

Begins by debunking many myths about who the homeless actually are, before moving on to a series of wide-ranging pragmatic approaches to this problem.

Gay and Lesbian Pride Trust

URL: 'http://www.pride.org.uk/'

Home page of the UK-based gay rights group. The site has extensive details of the annual gay pride parade in London.

Human Rights Caravan

URL: "http://rights.amnesty.org/"

Comprehensive review by Amnesty International of the effect of the Universal Declaration of Human Rights fifty years after its inception.

NHS Story

URL: "http://www.nhs50.nhs.uk/
nhsstory-index.htm"

History of Britain's National Health Service. Written as part of the NHS's 50th birthday celebration, this account conveys the excitement generated in 1948 by the first ever provision of a free comprehensive health service.

Rural Development Commission's World Wide Web Pages

URL: "http://www.argonet.co.uk/rdc/"

Description of the role of the agency charged with the wellbeing of those who live and work in the English countryside.

Welcome to the Rotary International Web Site

URL: "http://www.rotary.org./"

Central source of information on the worldwide Rotary movement.

Welcome to the Samaritans Online

URL: "http://www.samaritans.org.uk/"

Site of the UK voluntary organization providing support to the suicidal and despairing. There are statistics on suicide in the UK and an analysis of trends.

Women's Web

URL: "http://www.womweb.com/"

Site dedicated to women in business, and women's issues generally.

PEOPLE

Architects, Artists, Photographers, and Fashion Designers

Noteworthy Architects

Aalto (Hugo) Alvar Henrik (1898–1976) Finnish architect and designer who pioneered the Modern Movement in Finland

Adam William (1689–1748) and son Robert (1728–1792) family of Scottish architects and designers

Alberti Leon Battista (1404–1472) Italian Renaissance architect and theorist who set the principles of Classical style

Asam Cosmas Damian (1686–1739) and his brother Egid Quirin (1692–1750) German architects famous for their churches in flamboyant Late Baroque style

Barragán Luis (1902–1988) Mexican architect who combined Modernism with vernacular South American styles

Barry Charles (1795–1860) English architect whose work includes the Neo-Gothic Houses of Parliament in London, UK

Behrens Peter (1868–1940) German architect who adapted architecture to industry

Belluschi Pietro (1899–1994) Italian-born modernist architect who designed the Juilliard School of Music in New York, New York, and St Mary's Cathedral in San Francisco, California

Bernini Gianlorenzo (Giovanni Lorenzo) (1598–1680) Italian sculptor, architect, and painter who developed the Baroque style and designed the Roman papal monuments

Borromini Francesco (Castelli) (1599–1667) Swiss-born Italian Baroque architect in the Classical style whose work includes the churches of San Carlo alle Quatro Fontane and Sant'Ivo della Sapienza

Boullée Étienne Louis (1728–1799) French architect who drew on Neo-Classicism, his best-known project (unrealized) being a vast monument to Sir Isaac Newton

Bramante Donato (1444–1514) Italian Renaissance artist and architect who designed the circular Tempietto of San Pietro and rebuilt part of the Vatican, both in Rome, Italy

Breuer Marcel Lajos (1902–1981) Hungarian-born architect and designer with an affinity for natural materials who designed the Bijenkorf in Rotterdam, Netherlands

Brunelleschi Filippo (1377–1446) Italian Renaissance architect who pioneered the scientific use of perspective and designed the Florence Cathedral dome, Italy

Bulfinch Charles (1763–1844) American architect who designed the State House in Boston, Massachusetts, and part of the Capitol in Washington, DC

Bunshaft Gordon (1909–1990) US architect who applied the International Style to US glass skyscrapers

Burges William (1827–1881) English Gothic Revival architect and designer, known for sumptuous interiors, who designed Cork Cathedral, Ireland

Burlington Richard Boyle, Earl of Burlington (1695–1753) Anglo-Irish architectural patron and architect in the Palladian style who strictly adhered to Classical rules

Butterfield William (1814–1900) English architect who was a leading figure in the Gothic Revival

Callicrates (5th century BC) Athenian architect who designed, with Ictinus, the Parthenon, Greece

Campbell Colen (1676–1729) Scottish architect, principal figure of British Palladian architecture and author of *Vitruvius Britannicus*

Chambers William (1723–1796) Swedish-born English architect who designed the Chinese-style pagoda in Kew Gardens, London, UK, and the Neo-Palladian Somerset House, also in London

Coates Nigel (1949–) English architect who spurred regeneration of London's derelict areas

Duiker Johannes (1890–1935) Dutch architect whose work demonstrates structural vigour, and who designed the Zonnestraal Sanatorium in Hilversum and the Open Air School in Amsterdam, both in the Netherlands

Eiffel (Alexandre) Gustave (1832–1923) French engineer who constructed the Eiffel Tower in Paris

Engel (Johann) Carl Ludwig (1778–1840) German architect of the Neo-Classical Senate Square in Helsinki, Finland

Esquivel Adolfo (1932–) Argentinian sculptor and architect who won the 1980 Nobel Peace Prize

Farrell Terry (1938–) English architect in the Post-Modern style

Fathy Hassan (1900–1989) Egyptian architect who used indigenous building technology and natural materials to solve contemporary housing problems

Fontana Domenico (1543–1607) Italian architect who designed the Lateran Palace and the Vatican Library in Rome, Italy

Foster Norman (Robert) (1935–) English architect of the High Tech school

Fuller (Richard) Buckminster (1895–1983) US architect, engineer, and social philosopher who invented the geodesic dome

Gaudí Antonio (1852–1926) Spanish architect with a flamboyant Art Nouveau style, noted for his unusual materials and technical innovation

Geddes Patrick (1854–1932) Scottish town planner who established the importance of surveys and research work

Gehry Frank Owen (1929–) US architect whose use of collage and montage techniques approaches abstract art

Gibbs James (1682–1754) Scottish Neo-Classical architect who designed the Radcliffe Camera in Oxford, England

Gilbert Cass (1859–1934) US architect who designed the Woolworth Building, New York, New York

Graves Michael (1934–) US architect who blends Classical and Modern styles; his works include a commission to design the addition to the Whitney Museum of American Art in Manhattan, New York, New York

Grimshaw Nicholas (Thomas) (1939–) English architect of a distinctly industrial, High Tech style

Gropius Walter Adolf (1883–1969) German-born US architect who was an early exponent of the International style

Hardouin-Mansart Jules (1646–1708) French architect who designed lavish extensions to the Palace of Versailles and the Grand Trianon, both in France

(continued)

Noteworthy Architects (*continued*)

Haussmann Georges Eugène (1809–1891) French administrator who replanned Paris with long wide boulevards and parks

Hawksmoor Nicholas (1661–1736) English architect who developed a distinctive style incorporating elements from both Gothic and Classical sources

Hoban James C (1762–1831) Irish-born US architect who designed the White House in Washington, DC, and other public buildings

Hoffmann Josef (1870–1956) Austrian architect, influenced by Art Nouveau, who designed the Purkersdorf Sanatorium, Austria

Hood Raymond (Mathewson) (1881–1934) US architect who co-designed the Rockefeller Center, New York, New York

Howard Ebenezer (1850–1928) English town planner who pioneered the garden city ideal

Isozaki Arata (1931–) Japanese architect who blends Western Post-Modernism with elements of traditional Japanese architecture; his designs include the Museum of Contemporary Art, Los Angeles, California

Johnson Philip Cortelyou (1906–) US architect, who coined the term International style and designed the AT&T building in New York, New York

Jones Inigo (1573–1652) English Classical architect who introduced the Palladian style to England, and whose work includes the Banqueting House in Whitehall, London, UK

Juvarra Filippo (1678–1736) Italian architect and designer of the Late Baroque best known for his churches and his innovations in stage design

Kahn Louis Isadore (1901–1974) US architect with a classically Romantic style and imaginative use of concrete and brick, whose work includes the Yale Art Gallery, Connecticut

Kent William (1684–1748) English architect, landscape gardener, and interior designer whose work excelled in richly carved interiors and furnishings, as in Holkham Hall in Norfolk, England; he was also a pioneer in Romantic landscape gardening

Lasdun Denys Louis (1914–) English Modernist architect whose work includes the University of East Anglia, Norwich, England, and London's National Theatre, UK

Latrobe Benjamin Henry (1764–1820) English-born US architect whose works include the Bank of Pennsylvania, Philadelphia, Pennsylvania, and the Roman Catholic cathedral in Baltimore, Maryland

Le Corbusier (Charles-Edouard Jeanneret) (1887–1965) Swiss-born French architect who was influential in the Modern movement and advocated 'vertical garden cities' as a solution to urban chaos

L'Enfant Pierre Charles (1754–1825) French-born US architect who is principally remembered for his plan for Washington, DC

Le Vau Louis (1612–1670) French architect of Vaux-le-Vicomte château outside Paris, France, whose work also includes the inspired remodelling of Versailles

Loos Adolf (1870–1933) Austrian architect who designed private houses on Lake Geneva, Switzerland, and the Steiner House in Vienna, Austria

Lorimer Robert Stodart (1864–1929) Scottish architect in Scotland's Arts and Crafts movement whose work includes Ardkinglas House, Argyll, Scotland, and Rowallan House, Ayrshire, Scotland

Lutyens Edwin Landseer (1869–1944) English architect best known for his country houses in the Arts and Crafts style, and for his work planning New Delhi in India

McKim Charles Follen (1847–1909) US architect who designed Boston Public Library, Massachusetts, and co-founded the firm that became McKim, Mead, and White

Mackintosh Charles Rennie (1868–1928) Scottish architect, designer, and painter, and one of the leading figures in Art Nouveau

Mendelsohn Erich (1887–1953) German Expressionist architect who designed the Einstein Tower in Potsdam, Germany, and the Schocken Stores in Stuttgart, Germany

Meier Richard Alan (1934–) US architect whose abstract style is exemplified in the Museum für Kunsthandwerk in Frankfurt, Germany

Michelozzo di Bartolommeo (1396–1472) Italian architect and sculptor of the Early Renaissance

Mies van der Rohe Ludwig (1886–1969) German-born US architect and leading exponent of the International style whose work includes the Seagram building in New York, New York, and the National Gallery in Berlin, Germany

Mills Robert (1781–1855) US architect who designed the Washington Monument, Washington, DC, and other classically inspired works

Nash John (1752–1835) English architect who designed Regent's Park in London, UK, with its grandiose scheme of terraces, crescents, and palatial-style houses; other work includes Trafalgar Square and St James's Park, also in London

Nervi Pier Luigi (1891–1979) Italian engineer who used steel mesh within concrete to create flowing form; his work includes the cathedral at New Norcia, near Perth, Australia, and the Turin Exhibition Hall, Italy

Neutra Richard Joseph (1892–1970) Austrian-born US architect who was a leading exponent of the International style

Niemeyer (Soares Filho) Oscar (1907–) Brazilian architect and joint designer of the United Nations headquarters in New York, New York, whose work includes the Catholic cathedral in Brasília, Brazil

Nouvel Jean (1945–) French architect in the High Tech style who adapted traditional Islamic motifs to technological ends in the Institut du Monde Arabe in Paris, France

Oud J(acobus) J(ohannes) P(ieter) (1890–1963) Dutch architect and designer, and one of the leading figures of the De Stijl movement

Palladio Andrea (1508–1580) Italian Renaissance architect who used Roman Classical forms, symmetry, and proportion

Paxton Joseph (1801–1865) English architect who designed the Great Exhibition building in London, UK, revolutionary in its structural use of glass and iron

Pei Ieoh Ming (1917–) Chinese-born US Modernist architect known for innovative High Tech structures and glass walls, whose work includes the Bank of China, Hong Kong, and the Pyramid in The Louvre, Paris, France

Piranesi Giambattista (Giovanni Battista) (1720–1778) Italian architect and graphic artist who was an influential theorist of architecture, imaginatively using Roman models

Pugin Augustus Welby Northmore (1812–1852) English architect whose work instigated the Gothic Revival in England; he collaborated on the design of the Houses of Parliament in London, UK

Rastrelli Bartolomeo Francesco (1700–1771) Italian architect who became a major figure in the creation of St Petersburg in Russia

Richardson Henry Hobson (1838–1886) US architect who revived the Romanesque style; his works include Trinity Church in Boston, Massachusetts

Rietvelt Gerrit Thomas (1888–1964) Dutch architect associated with the De Stijl group, whose work includes the Schroeder House in Utrecht, Netherlands

della Robbia Italian family of sculptors in Florence during the 15th century: Luca della Robbia (1400–1482) created the marble *cantoria* (singing gallery) in Florence Cathedral, Italy

Rogers Richard George (1933–) English High Tech architect whose work includes the Pompidou Centre, Paris, France, the Lloyd's of London building, and the Reuters building at Blackwell Yard, London, UK (RIBA award)

Rossi Aldo (1931–1997) Italian architect and theorist, leader of Neo-Rationalism, whose design theories offer an alternative to Modernism

Saarinen Eero (1910–1961) Finnish-born US architect renowned for innovative Modernist designs, whose work includes the US Embassy in London, UK, the TWA Kennedy terminal in New York, New York, and Dulles Airport in Washington, DC

Saarinen (Gottlieb) Eliel (1873–1950) Finnish-born US architect and town planner, and founder of the Finnish Romantic school, whose work includes Helsinki railway station, Finland, the Cranbrook

Noteworthy Architects (continued)

Academy of Art in Bloomfield Hills, Michigan, and Christ Church in Minneapolis, Minnesota

Sansovino (Jacopo d'Antonio Tatti) (1486–1570) Italian architect who introduced the High Renaissance style to Venice, Italy

Schinkel Karl Friedrich (1781–1841) German architect and designer noted for his grandiose public buildings in the Neo-Classical style

Scott Gilbert (1880–1960) English architect who designed Liverpool Anglican cathedral, Cambridge University Library, and Waterloo Bridge, London, all in England; he also supervised the rebuilding of the House of Commons, London, after World War II

Sinan (1489–1588) Ottoman architect who designed hundreds of buildings including the Suleimaniye Mosque complex in Istanbul and Selimiye Mosque in Adrianople, both in Turkey

Smythson Robert (c. 1535–1614) English architect and builder of Elizabethan country houses

Soane John (1753–1837) English architect whose Neo-Classical designs anticipated contemporary taste, and whose work includes the Soane Museum, London, UK

Speer Albert (1905–1981) German architect and Nazi minister during World War II who worked as Hitler's architect, and whose overblown Classicism glorified the state

Spence Basil Urwin (1907–1976) Scottish architect whose work includes Coventry Cathedral, England and the British Embassy in Rome

Stern Robert (1939–   ) US architect who is a leading exponent of Post-Modernism

Stirling James Frazer (1926–1992) Scottish architect whose masterpiece the Staatsgalerie in Stuttgart, Germany, blends Constructivism, Modernism, and strands of Classicism

Stone Edward Durell (1902–1978) US architect who designed the US Embassy, Delhi, India

Sullivan Louis Henry (1856–1924) US architect who was a leader of the Chicago School and an early developer of the skyscraper, including the Wainwright Building, St Louis, Missouri

Tange Kenzo (1913–   ) Japanese architect who helped to introduce Modernism to Japan

Vanbrugh John (1664–1726) English Baroque architect and dramatist who designed Blenheim Palace, Oxfordshire, and Castle Howard, Yorkshire, both in England

Vasari Giorgio (1511–1574) Italian architect and painter who designed the Uffizi Palace, Florence, Italy

Venturi Robert Charles (1925–   ) US architect who pioneered Post-Modernism and whose work includes the Sainsbury Wing extension to the National Gallery in London, UK

Vignola (Jacopo Barozzi) (1507–1573) Italian architect whose late works (in particular the church of Il Gesù in Rome, Italy) anticipate the Baroque style

Vitruvius (Marcus Vitruvius Pollio) (1st century AD) Roman architect whose book *De Architectural/On Architecture* had a profound effect on Renaissance and Neo-Classical architecture

Voysey Charles Francis Annesley (1857–1941) English architect and designer of asymmetrical country houses with massive buttresses, long sloping roofs, and roughcast walls

Wagner Otto (1841–1918) Viennese architect who rejected ornament for Rationalism, and whose work includes the Post Office Savings Bank in Vienna, Austria

Waterhouse Alfred (1830–1905) English architect and leading exponent of the Victorian Neo-Gothic style, whose work includes the National History Museum in London, UK

Webb Philip Speakman (1831–1915) English architect involved in the revival of 19th-century English domestic architecture

White Stanford (1853–1906) US architect who co-founded the firm of McKim, Mead, and White; his designs include the original Madison Square Garden and the Washington Square Arch, both in New York, New York

Wilkins William (1778–1839) English architect who pioneered the Greek Revival in England with his design for Downing College, Cambridge, UK; other work includes the National Gallery, London, UK

Wren Christopher (1632–1723) English architect with a refined and sober Baroque style, whose work includes St Paul's Cathedral, London, UK

Wright Frank Lloyd (1869–1959) US architect known for 'organic architecture', in which buildings reflect their natural surroundings, as in his prairie-house style; he designed the Museum of Modern Art in New York, New York

Yamasaki Minoru (1912–1986) US architect who designed the World Trade Center, New York, New York

Noteworthy Artists

Alma-Tadema Lawrence (1836–1912) Dutch-born English painter of Romantic, idealized scenes of ancient Greek, Roman, and Egyptian life

Altdorfer Albrecht (c. 1480–1538) German painter, noted in particular for his dramatic, panoramic battle scenes

Andrea del Sarto (originally Andrea d'Agnolo di Francesco) (1486–1530) Italian Renaissance portraitist and religious painter

Angelico Fra (originally Guido di Pietro) (c. 1400–1455) Italian monk and painter of religious scenes who created the frescoes at the monastery of San Marco, Florence, Italy

Antonello da Messina (c. 1430–1479) Italian painter of portraits and religious themes who helped to introduce the use of oil paints to Italian Renaissance art

Apelles (4th century BC) Greek painter known for his startling realism

Arcimboldo Giuseppe (c. 1530–1593) Italian painter and designer known for fantastical, symbolic portraits

Audubon John James (1785–1851) US painter and naturalist famous for his series *Birds of America*

Bacon Francis (1909–1992) Irish-born painter of distorted, blurred figures in loosely defined space, including *Study after Velázquez's Portrait of Pope Innocent X*

Balthus (adopted name of Balthazar Klossowski de Rola) (1908–   ) Polish-born French painter of self-absorbed figures, frequently languid, pubescent girls, clothed or nude, such as *Le nu avec un chat/Nude with Cat*

Bartolommeo Fra (originally Baccio della Porta) (c. 1472–1517) Italian religious painter of classic simplicity and order, as in *The Mystical Marriage of St Catherine*

Beardsley Aubrey Vincent (1872–1898) English illustrator of meticulous, often erotic, black-and-white drawings

Beckmann Max (1884–1950) German Expressionist painter and graphic artist whose themes focused on human cruelty, as in *Night*

Bellini Jacopo (c. 1400–1470/71) and his sons, Gentile (c. 1429–1507) and Giovanni (c. 1430–1516) Venetian family of artists, and founders of the Venetian school

Bellows George Wesley (1882–1925) US painter noted for his scenes of everyday life and his boxing scenes, such as *Stag at Sharkey's*

Beuys Joseph (1921–1986) German sculptor and performance artist who created/performed *How to Explain Pictures to a Dead Hare*

Bewick Thomas (1753–1828) English illustrator who made many small, expressive engravings of birds and animals

(continued)

Noteworthy Artists (continued)

Bierstadt Albert (1830–1902) German-born US painter of spectacular panoramas of the American wilderness, such as *Thunderstorm in the Rocky Mountains*

Blake Peter (1932–) English painter who designed the Beatles' album cover *Sergeant Pepper's Lonely Hearts Club Band*

Blake William (1757–1827) English poet, artist, engraver, and visionary, and one of the most important figures of English Romanticism

Bomberg David (Garshen) (1890–1957) English painter who moved from semi-abstraction to more representational work, such as *The Mud Bath*

Bonnard Pierre (1867–1947) French painter, designer, and graphic artist, known for his series of nudes, including *Le nu à la baignoire/Nude in the Bath*

Bosch Hieronymus (Jerome) (c. 1460–1516) Netherlandish painter of bizarre, cruel images of a sinful, tormented world, such as the triptych *The Garden of Earthly Delights*

Botticelli Sandro Filipepi (adopted name of Alessandro di Mariano Filipepi) (1445–1510) Florentine painter of religious and mythological subjects, such as *The Birth of Venus*

Boucher François (1703–1770) French Rococo painter who was popular for light-hearted, playfully erotic scenes, such as *Diana Bathing*

Boudin Louis Eugène (1824–1898) French artist known for luminous seaside scenes, such as *Harbour of Trouville*

Bouts Dirk (Dierick) (c. 1420–1475) Netherlandish painter of portraits and religious scenes, such as *The Last Supper*

Braque Georges (1882–1963) French painter decisive in developing Cubism

Bronzino Agnolo (1503–1572) Italian Mannerist painter known for elegant portraits and the allegory *Venus, Cupid, Folly, and Time*

Brown Ford Madox (1821–1893) English painter who used elaborate symbolism and realistic detail, as in *Work*

Brueghel or **Bruegel** Pieter (c. 1525–1569) one of a family of Flemish painters who captured peasant life, as in *Hunters in the Snow*

Burne-Jones Edward Coley (1833–1898) English painter associated with the Pre-Raphaelite movement and symbolism

Caillebotte Gustave (1848–1894) French painter and supporter of the Impressionists; he painted *Rainy Day*

Callot Jacques (c. 1592–1635) prolific French engraver and painter whose *Great Miseries of War* is full of horrific detail

Campin Robert (Master of Flémalle) (c. 1378–1444) early Netherlandish painter, one of the founders of the Netherlandish school

Canaletto Antonio (Giovanni Antonio Canal) (1697–1768) Italian painter of highly detailed views of Venice, London, and the river Thames, such as *Venice: Regatta on the Grand Canal*

Caravaggio Michelangelo Merisi da (1573–1610) Italian early Baroque painter known for dramatic contrasts of light and shade

Carpaccio Vittore (c. 1450–c. 1525) Italian painter famous for scenes of Venice whose works include *The Legend of St Ursula*

Carracci Lodovico (1555–1619) and his two cousins, Agostino (1557–1602) and Annibale (1560–1609) three Italian painters who were leaders in developing early Baroque

Cassatt Mary (1845–1926) US Impressionist painter and printmaker of colourful images of mothers and children, such as *The Bath*

Castagno Andrea del (Andrea di Bartolo de Bargilla) (c. 1421–1475) Italian Renaissance painter whose images are almost sculptural in effect, as in *David*

Cézanne Paul (1839–1906) French Post-Impressionist painter whose paintings include *Cardplayers*

Chagall Marc (1887–1985) Belarusian-born French painter and designer inspired by village life and Jewish and Russian folk traditions, as in *I and the Village*

Champaigne Philippe de (1602–1674) French painter of elegant and restrained portraits, such as *Ex Voto*

Chardin Jean-Baptiste-Siméon (1699–1779) French painter of naturalistic still lifes and quiet domestic scenes

Chirico Giorgio de (1888–1978) Greek-born Italian painter, founder of the school of Metaphysical Painting whose paintings include *Nostalgia of the Infinite*

Cimabue Giovanni (Cenni di Peppi) (c. 1240–1302) Italian painter often considered the 'father of Italian painting' whose works include *Crucifix*

Claude Lorrain (Claude Gelée) (1600–1682) French Classical painter of luminous landscapes, such as *The Enchanted Castle*

Clouet François (c. 1515–1572) French artist who was court painter under four French kings

Colville Alex (1920–) Canadian painter of smooth, broad-bodied nudes, working men, and animals, as in *Hound in Field*

Constable John (1776–1837) English landscape artist whose paintings include *The Haywain*

Copley John Singleton (1738–1815) US artist who painted *Brook Watson and the Shark*

Corot Jean-Baptiste Camille (1796–1875) French painter of soft, low-key landscapes and romanticized paintings of women

Correggio (Antonio Allegri) (c. 1494–1534) Italian painter of the High Renaissance who placed emphasis on movement, soft forms, and contrasts of light and shade

Cotman John Sell (1782–1842) English landscape painter whose paintings (mostly watercolours) include *Greta Bridge*

Courbet Gustave (1819–1877) French realist artist who depicted ordinary life with unflattering frankness, as in *Burial at Ornans*

Cranach the Elder Lucas (Lucas Müller) (1472–1553) German painter, etcher, and woodcut artist of religious scenes, allegories, and precise portraits, such as *Martin Luther*

Crome John (1768–1821) English landscape painter whose works include *The Poringland Oak*

Cuyp Aelbert (1620–1691) Netherlandish painter of serene landscapes, seascapes, and portraits, such as *A Herdsman with Cows by a River*

Dadd Richard (1817–1887) English painter of minutely detailed fantasies and fairy tales, such as *The Fairy Feller's Master-Stroke*

Dalí Salvador (Felippe Jacinto) (1904–1989) Spanish Surrealist painter and designer known for hallucinatory images and distorted figures, such as *The Persistence of Memory*

Daumier Honoré (1808–1879) French painter and caricaturist noted as a political satirist and a leading Realist

David Gerard (c. 1450–c. 1523) Netherlandish painter with a taste for Italianate ornament, as in *The Marriage at Cana*

David Jacques-Louis (1748–1825) French Neo-Classical painter of politically significant works, such as *Death of Marat*

Davis Stuart (1894–1964) US abstract painter who foreshadowed Pop art

Degas (Hilaire Germain) Edgar (1834–1917) French Impressionist painter, and sculptor, who specialized in informal studies of ballet, horse racing, and young women working

De Kooning Willem (1904–1997) Dutch-born US Abstract Expressionist painter whose paintings include *Women*

Delacroix (Ferdinand Victor) Eugène (1798–1863) French Romantic painter of historical and literary subjects, such as *The Death of Sardanapalus*

Delaunay Robert (1885–1941) French pioneer of abstract painting who developed Orphism

Delaunay-Terk Sonia (1885–1979) French pioneer of abstract painting and textile designer

Derain André (1880–1954) French Fauvist painter whose strong colours can be seen in *Pool of London*

Dine Jim (James) (1935–) US Pop artist and pioneer of 'happenings' and environment art

Dix Otto (1891–1969) German Realist painter who depicted the hell of trench warfare, as in *Flanders: After Henri Barbusse 'Le Feu'*

Domenichino (Domenico Zampieri) (1581–1641) Italian Baroque painter and architect who was a pioneer of landscape painting

Doré Gustave (1832–1883) French artist who illustrated editions of *Don Quixote* and Dante's *Inferno*

Drysdale (George) Russell (1912–1981) Australian artist who recorded the bleakness of life in the Australian outback, as in *The Gatekeeper's Wife*

Dubuffet Jean (Philippe Arthur) (1901–1985) French artist and originator of Art Brut, 'raw' or 'brutal' art

Duccio di Buoninsegna (*c.* 1255–*c.* 1311) influential Italian painter whose paintings include the altarpiece *Maestà*

Duchamp Marcel (1887–1968) French-born US artist and exponent of Dada whose paintings include *Nude Descending a Staircase No. 2*

Dufy Raoul (1877–1953) French painter and designer of bright scenes of gaiety and leisure

Dürer Albrecht (1471–1528) German graphic artist and painter who perfected a technique of woodcut and engraving; his works include *Apocalypse*

Dyck Anthony van (1599–1641) Flemish painter of religious works and portraits, such as *Charles I on Horseback*

Eakins Thomas (1844–1916) US Realist painter of medical and sporting scenes, such as *The Gross Clinic*

Ensor James (Sidney, Baron Ensor) (1860–1949) Belgian painter and printmaker who created a surreal, macabre world in vivid colours, as in *Entry of Christ into Brussels*

Ernst Max (1891–1976) German artist and major figure in Dada and Surrealism; his paintings include *The Elephant Celebes*

Escher M(aurits) C(ornelis) (1898–1972) Dutch graphic artist who created prints containing paradoxes and illusions, such as *Ascending and Descending*

Eyck Jan van (*c.* 1390–1441) Netherlandish painter of meticulous religious scenes and portraits, such as *The Arnolfini Wedding*

Fantin-Latour (Ignace) Henri Jean Théodore (1836–1904) French painter of delicate still lifes, flowers, and portraits, such as *Homage à Delacroix*

Feininger Lyonel (Charles Adrian) (1871–1956) US abstract artist and early Cubist

Fischl Eric (1948–) US Realist painter of frequently disturbing scenes of suburban Americans at play, as in *Bad Boy*

Fragonard Jean-Honoré (1732–1806) French Rococo painter of light-hearted, often erotic works, such as *The Swing*

Frankenthaler Helen (1928–) US Abstract Expressionist painter who invented the colour-staining technique

Freud Lucian (1922–) German-born British figurative artist who combined meticulous accuracy with disquieting intensity, as in *Portrait of Francis Bacon*

Friedrich Caspar David (1774–1840) German Romantic landscape painter whose paintings include *The Cross in the Mountains*

Fuseli (John) Henry (originally Johann Heinrich Füssli) (1741–1825) Swiss-born British Romantic painter of macabre and dream-like images, such as *The Nightmare*

Gaddi Italian family of artists: Gaddo (*c.* 1260–1332) painter and mosaic worker, and his sons Taddeo (*c.* 1300–1366) painter of frescoes, and Agnola (active 1369–1396) painter of frescoes

Gainsborough Thomas (1727–1788) English landscape and society portrait painter whose paintings include *The Blue Boy*

Gauguin (Eugène Henri) Paul (1848–1903) French Post-Impressionist painter of sensuously coloured, heavily symbolic, and decorative style, such as *The Yellow Christ*

Gentile da Fabriano (Niccolo di Giovanni di Massio) (*c.* 1370–*c.* 1427) Italian painter of frescoes and altarpieces in the International Gothic style, such as *Adoration of the Magi*

Gentileschi Artemisia (*c.* 1593–*c.*1652) Italian Baroque artist who painted *Judith Decapitating Holofernes*

Géricault (Jean Louis André) Théodore (1791–1824) French Romantic painter and graphic artist of energy and emotional intensity, as seen in *The Raft of the Medusa*

Ghirlandaio Domenico (Domenico di Tommaso Bigordi) (*c.* 1449–1494) Italian fresco painter whose painting was characterized by contemporary domestic detail

Giorgione da Castelfranco (Giorgio Barbarelli) (*c.* 1475–1510) Italian Renaissance painter who created the Renaissance poetic landscape

Giotta di Bondone (*c.* 1267–1337) Italian painter and architect who broke from the Byzantine style and introduced a new naturalism, painting saints as real people

Goes Hugo van der (*c.* 1440–1482) early Flemish painter, with a style rich in symbolism and naturalistic detail, as in his *Portinari Altarpiece*

Gogh Vincent Willem van (1853–1890) Dutch Post-Impressionist painter who used intense colour and expressive brushwork, as in his *Sunflowers* series

Goncharova Natalia (1881–1962) Russian painter and designer who created designs for Diaghilev's ballets

Gorky Arshile (Vosdanig Manoüg Adoian) (1904–1948) Armenian-born US painter who combined organic shapes and vigorous brushwork with a sense of fantasy, as in *The Liver Is the Cock's Comb*

Goya Francisco José de Goya y Lucientes (1746–1828) Spanish painter and engraver who depicted Spanish life with often strange, nightmarish works, such as the *Caprichos*

Gozzoli Benozzo (*c.* 1421–1497) Florentine painter in International Gothic style, known for his fresco *The Procession of the Magi*

Grant Duncan (James Corrowr) (1885–1978) Scottish painter and designer of great fluency and subtle use of colour, as seen in *Snow Scene*

Greco, El (originally Doménikos Theotokopoulos) (1541–1614) Greek-born Spanish painter of elegant portraits and intensely emotional religious scenes with distorted figures and unearthly light, such as *The Burial of Count Orgaz*

Gris Juan (José Vittoriano Gonzalez) (1887–1927) Spanish Cubist painter with distinctive geometrical style

Grosz George (1893–1959) German-born US Expressionist painter, graphic artist, and founder of Berlin Dada

Grünewald Matthias (Mathis Gothardt-Neihardt) (*c.* 1475–1528) German painter, architect, and engineer whose paintings expressed intensity of feeling, as in the Isenheim altarpiece

Guardi Francesco (1712–1793) Italian painter who produced atmospheric views of his native Venice

Guston Philip (1913–1980) US painter who moved from abstraction to cartoon-like figurative works

Hals Frans (*c.* 1581–1666) Flemish-born painter of vibrant portraits, such as *Laughing Cavalier*

Hamilton Richard (1922–) English pioneer of typically humorous and satirical Pop art, such as *Just What Is It That Makes Today's Homes So Different, So Appealing?*

Henri Robert (1865–1929) US painter who, as a leading figure in the Ashcan school, painted scenes from everyday city life

Hirst Damien (1965–) English artist who was awarded the Turner Prize in 1995 for *Mother and Child Divided*, a bisected cow and calf presented in a glass case

Hilliard Nicholas (*c.* 1547–1619) English miniaturist who painted leading figures of Tudor and Stuart society

Hobbema Meindert (1638–1709) Netherlandish landscape artist who painted *The Avenue at Middelharnis*

Hockney David (1937–) English Pop and graphic artist whose paintings include *Mr and Mrs Clark and Percy*

Hogarth William (1697–1764) English engraver and painter of portraits and moralizing genre scenes, such as *A Rake's Progress*

Hokusai Katsushika (1760–1849) Japanese artist and exponent of ukiyo-e (colour prints depicting scenes from everyday life), such as *36 Views of Mount Fuji*

Holbein the Elder Hans (*c.* 1464–1524) German painter of mainly religious works, such as the altarpiece *St Sebastian*

Holbein the Younger Hans (1497–1543) German Renaissance portrait painter who depicted the court of Henry VIII

Homer Winslow (1836–1910) US Realist painter of vivid seascapes and lithographer, whose paintings include *The Gulf Stream*

Honthorst Gerrit van (1590–1656) Netherlandish painter of biblical, mythological, and genre pictures who brought Italian influences into Netherlandish art

Hooch Pieter de (1629–1684) Netherlandish painter of harmonious domestic interiors and courtyards, such as *The Courtyard of a House in Delft*

(continued)

Noteworthy Artists (*continued*)

Hopper Edward (1882–1967) US Realist painter and etcher whose paintings are characterized by a brooding sense of emptiness and solitude, as in *Nighthawks*

Hunt William Holman (1827–1910) English painter who created works characterized by a meticulous attention to detail and a clear moral and religious symbolism, such as *The Awakening Conscience*

Ingres Jean-Auguste-Dominique (1780–1867) French Neo-Classical painter of meticulously detailed portraits and sensuous female nudes

Israëls Jozef (1824–1911) Netherlandish leader of the Hague school of landscape painters

Jawlensky Alexei von (1864–1941) Russian Expressionist painter

John Gwen(dolen) (Mary) (1876–1939) Welsh painter who depicted young women, nuns, and calm, muted interiors

John Augustus (Edwin) (1878–1961) Welsh painter of vivacious portraits, such as *The Smiling Woman*

Johns Jasper (1930–   ) US Pop artist and printmaker who painted the series *Flags* and *Targets*

Jones Allen (1937–   ) English Pop artist, painter, sculptor, and printmaker whose works include *Perfect Match*

Jordaens Jacob (1593–1678) Flemish painter of exuberant and large scale scenes of peasant life, mythological scenes, altarpieces, and portraits

Kahlo Frida (1907–1954) Mexican surrealist painter who painted a series of frank and disturbing self-portraits

Kandinsky Wasily (1866–1944) Russian-born painter who was a pioneer of abstract art and originator of the Expressionist Blaue Reiter movement

Kauffmann (Maria Anna Catherina) Angelica (1741–1807) Swiss Neo-Classical painter of portraits and mythological scenes

Kiefer Anselm (1945–   ) German Neo-Expressionist painter of landscapes that relate to recent German history

Kirchner Ernst Ludwig (1880–1938) German Expressionist painter of city scenes and portraits

Kitaj R(onald) B(rooks) (1932–   ) US painter and graphic artist who uses allusions to art, history, and literature, as in *The Autumn of Central Paris (After Walter Benjamin)*

Klee Paul (1879–1940) inventive and playful Swiss painter and graphic artist whose paintings suggest child-like innocence, as in *Twittering Machine*

Klimt Gustav (1862–1918) Austrian painter who created often sensual and erotic works, such as *The Kiss*

Kneller Godfrey (Gottfried Kniller) (1646–1723) German-born portrait painter working in England during the late 17th and early 18th centuries

Kokoschka Oskar (1886–1980) Austrian Expressionist painter of vivid landscapes and highly charged allegories and portraits, such as *The Bride of the Wind (The Tempest)*

Kollwitz Käthe (born Schmidt) (1867–1945) German Expressionist graphic artist and sculptor who was concerned with social injustice and human suffering, as in *Never Again War!*

Landseer Edwin Henry (1802–1873) English painter, sculptor, and engraver of animal studies whose works are often sentimental and moralistic, such as *Dignity and Impudence*

La Tour Georges de (1593–1652) French painter who used deep contrasts of light and shade, as in *Joseph the Carpenter*

Lawrence Thomas (1769–1830) English painter of portraits, such as *Queen Charlotte*

Léger Fernand (1881–1955) French painter and designer associated with Cubism

Leighton Frederic (1830–1896) English painter who became famous for his lavish depictions of life in ancient Greece and Rome, such as *Garden of the Hesperides*

Leonardo da Vinci (1452–1519) Italian painter, sculptor, architect, engineer, and scientist, perhaps the greatest figure of the Italian Renaissance, whose paintings include *The Last Supper* and *Mona Lisa*

Lewis (Percy) Wyndham (1882–1957) English writer and artist who pioneered Vorticism and sought to reflect the age of industry

Lichtenstein Roy (1923–1997) US Pop artist who uses comic-strip techniques and popular ideals of romance and heroism, as in *Whaam!*

Lippi Filippino (c. 1457–1504) Italian painter of religious scenes

Lippi Fra Filippo (c. 1406–1469) Italian painter of frescoes depicting religious scenes

Lochner Stephan (c. 1400–1451) German painter and master of the International Gothic style, as seen in *The Adoration of the Magi*

Long Richard (1945–   ) English conceptual artist who works in the natural landscape, for example creating large patterns with stones

Lotto Lorenzo (c. 1480–1556) Italian High Renaissance painter of religious works and portraits

Lowry L(aurence) S(tephen) (1887–1976) English painter who depicted life in the industrial towns of northern England, as in *The Pond*

Lucas van Leyden (1494–1533) Dutch painter and engraver; he was a pioneer of genre scenes and his paintings include *The Chess Players*

Mabuse Jan (adopted name of Jan Gossaert) (c. 1478–c. 1533) Flemish painter who started a vogue for Classical detail, as in *Neptune and Amphitrite*

Macke August (1887–1914) German Expressionist painter of simple, brightly coloured paintings of park and street scenes

Magritte René François Ghislain (1898–1967) Belgian Surrealist painter who focused on visual paradoxes and everyday objects taken out of context, as in *Golconda*

Malevich Kasimir Severinovich (1878–1935) Russian abstract painter who launched Suprematism, and whose paintings include *White on White*

Manet Édouard (1832–1883) French painter who developed a clear and unaffected Realist style close to that of the Impressionists, as in *A Bar at the Folies-Bergère*

Mantegna Andrea (c. 1431–1506) Italian early Renaissance painter and engraver of religious and mythological subjects, such as *The Agony in the Garden*

Marc Franz (1880–1916) German Expressionist painter of bold semi-abstracts of red and blue animals

Martin John (1789–1854) English Romantic painter whose paintings are characterized by an apocalyptic, nightmarish style and massive perspectives, as in *The Great Day of His Wrath*

Masaccio (adopted name of Tommasco di Giovanni di Simone Guidi) (1401–c. 1428) Florentine early Italian Renaissance painter of frescoes who pioneered the use of perspective

Matisse Henri (1869–1954) French painter, sculptor, and illustrator, and a leading figure in Fauvism; his paintings include *Dance*

Memling or **Memlinc** Hans (c. 1430–1494) Flemish painter of religious subjects and portraits, such as *Tommaso Portinari and His Wife*

Millais John Everett (1829–1896) English painter and founding member of the Pre-Raphaelite Brotherhood; his paintings include *Ophelia*

Millet Jean François (1814–1875) French painter of peasant life and landscapes, such as *The Angelus*

Miró Joan (1893–1983) Spanish Surrealist painter and sculptor who developed a witty abstract style, as in *Birth of the World*

Modersohm-Becker Paula (1876–1907) German painter of self-portraits, children, and women, whose works anticipate Expressionism

Modigliani Amedeo (1884–1920) Italian painter and sculptor of graceful, sensual nudes and portraits

Noteworthy Artists (*continued*)

Mondrian Piet (originally Pieter Cornelis Mondriaan) (1872–1944) Dutch abstract painter and exponent of Neo-Plasticism, based on simple geometric forms and pure colours, as seen in *Composition in Red, Yellow, and Blue*

Monet Claude (1840–1926) French painter and pioneer of Impressionism whose paintings include *Impression, Sunrise*, and *Water Lilies*

Morisot Berthe (Marie Pauline) (1841–1895) French Impressionist painter of sensitive pictures of women and children, such as *The Cradle*

Moses Grandma (adopted name of Anna Mary Robertson) (1860–1961) US primitive painter of colourful scenes depicting rural American life, such as *What a Farmwife Painted*

Motherwell Robert (1915–1991) US Action painter and Abstract Expressionist whose paintings include *Elegies to the Spanish Republic*

Mucha Alphonse Maria (1860–1939) Czech Art Nouveau painter and designer who created theatre posters, such as *Gismonda*

Munch Edvard (1863–1944) Norwegian painter and graphic artist who focused on intense emotional states, as in *The Scream*

Murillo Bartolomé Esteban (c. 1618–1682) Spanish painter of self-portraits, sentimental pictures depicting the Immaculate Conception, and street urchins

Nash Paul (1889–1946) English painter who promoted the Avant-Garde style, as in *Dead Sea*

Newman Barnett (1905–1970) US painter who was one of the founders of Abstract Expressionism

Nicholson Ben (1894–1982) English abstract artist who developed a style of geometric reliefs

Nolan Sidney (Robert) (1917–1992) Australian painter of the outback and Australian history

Noland Kenneth (Clifton) (1927–   ) US painter concerned with geometry, colour, and symmetry

O'Keeffe Georgia (1887–1986) US painter of semi-abstract studies of flowers and bones, such as *Black Iris*

Oldenburg Claes (Thure) (1929–   ) Swedish-born US Pop artist who creates gigantic replicas of everyday objects and foods, such as *Lipstick*

Orozco José Clemente (1883–1949) Mexican muralist who painted social and political works in public buildings in the USA and Mexico

Palmer Samuel (1805–1881) English landscape painter and etcher of small pastoral scenes

Parmigianino (Girolamo Francesco Mazzola) (1503–1540) Italian Mannerist artist who painted *Portrait in a Convex Mirror*

Perugino Pietro (adopted name of Pietro di Cristoforo Vannucci) (c. 1446–1523) Italian painter with a graceful figure style, as seen in the altarpiece *Virgin and Child with St Michael and St Raphael*

Picasso Pablo (Ruiz y) (1881–1973) Spanish artist of inventive and prolific talents whose Blue Period and Rose Period preceded Cubism; his paintings include *Les Demoiselles d'Avignon* and *Guernica*

Piero della Francesca (c. 1420–1492) Italian painter of solemn stillness and solid figures in luminous colour, as in *The Flagellation of Christ*

Piero di Cosimo (c. 1462–c. 1521) Italian painter of inventive pictures of mythological and religious subjects, such as *Mythological Scene*

Pietro da Cortona (originally Pietro Berrettini) (1596–1669) Italian painter and architect whose paintings include *Allegory of Divine Providence*, which gives a convincing illusion of reality

Pinturicchio or **Pintoricchio** (adopted name of Bernardino di Betto) (c. 1454–1513) Italian painter of frescoes in the Borgia Apartments in the Vatican

Piranesi Giambattista (Giovanni Battista) (1720–1778) Italian engraver and architect who made powerful etchings of Roman antiquities

Pisanello (adopted name of Antonio Pisano) (c. 1395–c. 1455) Italian painter and medallist in the International Gothic style whose paintings include *Madonna and Child with St George and St Anthony Abbot*

Pisarro Camille (1830–1903) French Impressionist painter of the French countryside, peasant life, and street scenes, as in *Boulevard Montmartre*

Pollaiuolo Antonio del (c. 1432–1498) and Piero (c. 1441–1496) Italian brothers, painters, sculptors, goldsmiths, engravers, and designers; the painting *The Martyrdom of St Sebastian* is considered a joint project

Pollock (Paul) Jackson (1912–1956) US painter who was a pioneer of Abstract Expressionism

Poussin Nicolas (1594–1665) French painter known for mythological and literary scenes done in austere Classical style, such as *Et in Arcadia Ego*

Raeburn Henry (1756–1823) Scottish artist noted for his sensitive portraits

Raphael Sanzio (Raffaello Sanzio) (1483–1520) great Italian High Renaissance painter of portraits and mythological and religious works, such as *The School of Athens*

Rauschenberg Robert (adopted name of Milton Rauschenberg) (1925–   ) US Pop artist who created 'happenings' and multimedia works called 'combined painting', such as *Monogram*

Redon Odilon (1840–1916) French painter and graphic artist known for fantastic and dream-like images

Rembrandt (Harmensz) van Rijn (1606–1669) Netherlandish painter and etcher of penetrating self-portraits and religious subjects, whose works include *The Night Watch*

Reni Guido (1575–1642) Italian painter prominent in the development of the Baroque style whose paintings include *Aurora*

Renoir Pierre-Auguste (1841–1919) French Impressionist painter who created a 'rainbow' style, using lively, colourful, and feathery brushwork to depict scenes of everyday life, such as *The Luncheon of the Boating Party*

Reynolds Joshua (1723–1792) English portrait painter in the 'Grand Manner' style, as seen in *Mrs Siddons as the Tragic Muse*

Ribera José (Jusepe) de (1591–1652) Spanish painter of full-length versions of saints, mythological figures, and genre scenes

Ricci Sebastiano (1659–1734) Venetian decorative painter whose paintings include *Resurrection*

Riley Bridget Louise (1931–   ) English painter and pioneer of Op art, as seen in *Fission*

Rivera Diego (1886–1957) Mexican painter of murals and exponent of Social Realism who was influenced by Mexican folk art

Rossetti Dante Gabriel (1828–1882) English painter of romantic mediaeval scenes and idealized portraits of women, such as *Beata Beatrix*; he was a founding member of the Pre-Raphaelite Brotherhood

Rothko Mark (adopted name of Marcus Rothkovich) (1903–1970) Russian-born US Abstract Expressionist painter and pioneer of Colour Field painting, as in *Light Red over Black*

Rouault Georges Henri (1871–1958) French religious painter, etcher, illustrator, and designer who used rich, dark colours, heavy outlines, and subjects including clowns and prostitutes, as in *Christ Mocked*

Rousseau Henri (Julien Félix) (known as Le Douanier) (1844–1910) French Naive painter of Parisian suburbs, portraits, and exotic scenes, as in *Tropical Storm with a Tiger*

Rubens Peter Paul (1577–1640) Flemish painter of the Baroque who created religious and allegorical paintings that revealed a mastery of drama and movement, as in *The Rape of the Daughters of Leucippus*

Rublev or **Rublyov** Andrei (c. 1360–c. 1430) Russian icon painter whose finest surviving work is *Old Testament Trinity*

Ruisdael Jacob Isaakszoon van (c. 1628–1682) Netherlandish landscape painter of atmospheric style who concentrated on dramatic aspects of nature, as in *The Jewish Cemetery*

(*continued*)

Noteworthy Artists (*continued*)

Ryder Albert Pinkham (1847–1917) US painter of romantic, dream-like landscapes, moonlit seascapes, and scenes from Shakespeare and Wagner, such as *Death on a Pale Horse*

Sargent John Singer (1856–1925) US portrait painter who depicted affluent late Victorian and Edwardian society in Britain and the USA, as in *Madame X*

Schiele Egon (1890–1918) Austrian painter of portraits and openly erotic nudes in an angular, contorted style using garish colours; he was a pioneer of Expressionism

Schwitters Kurt (1887–1948) German artist, poet, and leading member of the Dada movement who created increasingly elaborate collages

Sebastiano del Piombo (originally Sebastiano Luciani) (*c.* 1485–1547) Italian High Renaissance painter whose paintings include *The Resurrection of Lazarus*

Seurat Georges (Pierre) (1859–1891) French Post-Impressionist artist who painted with small dabs rather than long brushstrokes, as in *A Sunday Afternoon on the Island of La Grande Jatte*

Shahn Ben(jamin) (1898–1969) Lithuanian-born US Social Realist painter and graphic artist, concerned with social and political issues, who painted a series on the Sacco-Vanzetti case

Sickert Walter (Richard) (1860–1942) English artist who worked in a broadly Impressionist style, depicting shabby music halls, streets, and interiors, as in *Ennui*

Signac Paul (1863–1935) French artist known for landscapes and seascapes painted in mosaic-like blocks of pure colour

Simone Martini (*c.* 1284–1344) Italian painter and master of the Sienese school whose paintings included *The Annunciation*

Sisley Alfred (1839–1899) French Impressionist painter of lyrical, harmonious landscapes, such as *The Canal*

Soutine Chaïm (1893–1943) Lithuanian-born French Expressionist painter who created intense, emotionally charged landscapes and portraits, such as *Page Boy*

Spencer Stanley (1891–1959) English painter of meticulously detailed, often humorous depictions of everyday life with elaborate religious symbolism, such as *The Resurrection, Cookham*

Steen Jan (Havickszoon) (*c.* 1626–1679) Netherlandish painter of humorous genre scenes, portraits, and landscapes, such as *The Prince's Birthday*

Steer Philip Wilson (1860–1942) Leader of the English Impressionist painters, noted for his landscapes, such as *The Beach at Walberswick*

Stella Frank (Philip) (1936–   ) US painter who was a pioneer of a severe, geometric style

Stubbs George (1724–1806) English artist renowned for paintings of horses, such as *Lion Attacking a Horse*

Sutherland Graham (Vivian) (1903–1980) English painter of portraits, landscapes, and religious subjects, often in a semi-abstract style

Taeuber-Arp Sophie (1889–1943) Swiss artist, sculptor, and designer active in the Dada movement and abstraction groups

Tamayo Rufino (1899–1991) Mexican painter and printmaker, known for vibrant colours and cryptic, semi-abstract figures, such as *Women Reaching for the Moon*

Tanguy Yves (1900–1955) French Surrealist painter of dream-like desert landscapes

Tàpies Antoni (1923–   ) Spanish artist who creates abstract, wall-like canvases using earth, plaster, and discarded materials

Teniers the Younger David (1610–1690) Flemish painter who depicted peasant life

Tiepolo Giovanni Battista (Giambattista) (1696–1770) Italian Rococo painter of warmly coloured, monumental decorative schemes

Tintoretto (adopted name of Jacopo Robusti) (1518–1594) Italian Mannerist painter of portraits and religious works of great intensity and unearthly light, such as *St George and the Dragon*

Tissot James (Joseph Jacques) (1836–1902) French painter known for detailed depictions of Victorian high society, such as *Ball on Shipboard*

Titian (adopted name of Tiziano Vecellio) (*c.* 1487–1576) Italian High Renaissance painter of portraits and religious and mythological scenes, such as *Venus and Adonis*

Toulouse-Lautrec Henri Marie Raymond de (1864–1901) French artist of brilliant technical skill whose work was vital to the development of poster art

Turner (Joseph Mallord) William (1775–1851) English landscape painter whose paintings anticipated Impressionism; they include *Rain, Steam and Speed*

Uccello Paolo (Paolo di Dono) (1397–1475) Italian painter who experimented with perspective, as in *St George and the Dragon*

Utamaro Kitagawa (1753–1806) Japanese artist who created colour prints of women engaged in everyday activities

Utrillo Maurice (1883–1955) French painter of views of Montmartre who developed a style of pale tones and muted colours

Vasarély Victor (1908–   ) Hungarian-born French artist and exponent of Op art

Velázquez Diego Rodríguez de Silva y (1599–1660) Spanish painter of portraits, and religious and genre scenes, such as *The Maids of Honour*

van de Velde Essaias (*c.* 1591–1630), his brother, Willem the Elder (*c.* 1610–1693), and Willem's sons, Willem the Younger (1633–1707) and Adriaen (1636–1672) family of Netherlandish landscape painters

Vermeer Jan (1632–1675) Netherlandish painter of quiet, everyday scenes characterized by his remarkable ability to capture light on objects, as in *Maidservant Pouring Milk*

Veronese Paolo (*c.* 1528–1588) Italian painter of grand decorative themes celebrating the power and splendour of Venice

Vlaminck Maurice de (1876–1958) French artist who was a leading figure in Fauvism

Vuillard (Jean) Édouard (1868–1940) French printmaker and decorative painter of intimate domestic interiors with figures

Warhol Andy (adopted name of Andrew Warhola) (1928–1987) US Pop artist and film-maker known for painting Campbell's soup cans, Coca-Cola bottles, and film stars

Watteau (Jean-)Antoine (1684–1721) French Rococo painter of fanciful outdoor scenes with elegant young people, such as *The Embarkation for Cythera*

Watts George Frederick (1817–1904) English painter of biblical and Classical subjects and moralizing allegories, such as *Hope*

Wearing Gillian (1963–   ) English video artist who was awarded the Turner Prize in 1997; her work inludes *60 Minutes Silence*, an hour-long video of police officers posing for a group photograph

West Benjamin (1738–1820) US Neo-Classical painter of historical themes whose paintings include *The Death of General Wolfe*

Weyden Rogier van der (*c.* 1399–1464) Netherlandish painter of portraits and religious subjects in an elegant Realist style, such as *The Last Judgement*

Whistler James (Abbott) McNeill (1834–1903) US painter, etcher, and leading figure in the Aesthetic movement whose paintings include *Arrangement in Grey and Black: Portrait of the Painter's Mother*

Wilson Richard (1714–1782) Welsh painter of landscapes infused with Italianate atmosphere and painted in a Classical manner

Wood Grant (1892–1942) US artist who painted *American Gothic*

Wright Joseph (Wright of Derby) (1734–1797) English painter of dramatically lit portraits, landscapes, and groups performing scientific experiments

Wyeth Andrew Newell (1917–   ) US painter of naturalistic and minutely detailed portraits and landscapes, such as *Christina's World*

Yeats Jack Butler (1871–1957) Irish painter of spirited portrayals of Irish life and landscapes, such as *Back from the Races*

Zeuxis (5th century BC) Greek painter who was regarded as the greatest artist of ancient Greece

Noteworthy Sculptors

Andre Carl (1935–) US Minimalist sculptor who created the controversial *Equivalent VIII* (a collection of bricks)

Archipenko Alexander (1887–1964) Ukrainian-born US sculptor noted for Cubist sculptures, including *Woman Combing Her Hair*

Arp Hans, or Jean (1887–1966) French abstract painter, poet, and sculptor who was a founder of the Dada movement

Barlach Ernst (1870–1938) German Expressionist sculptor who drew inspiration from Russian peasant art

Bartholdi Frédéric Auguste (1834–1904) French sculptor who designed the Statue of Liberty

Bernini Gianlorenzo (Giovanni Lorenzo) (1598–1680) Italian sculptor, architect, and painter who was a leading figure in developing the Baroque style

Boccioni Umberto (1882–1916) Italian Futurist artist who sculpted *Unique Forms of Continuity in Space*

Borglum (John) Gutzon (de la Mothe) (1867–1941) US sculptor who created the group of giant heads of four US presidents carved into the mountainside at Mount Rushmore

Brancusi Constantin (1876–1957) Romanian pioneer of abstract sculpture who reduced forms to their most essential, simplified nature, as in *Bird in Space*

Calder Alexander (Stirling) (1898–1976) US abstract sculptor who is most famous for his mobiles

Canova Antonio (Marquese d'Ischia) (1757–1822) Italian Neo-Classical sculptor of highly-finished marble busts and groups of figures

Caro Anthony (Alfred) (1924–) English abstract sculptor who often uses prefabricated metal parts painted with bright colours, as in *Early One Morning*

Cellini Benvenuto (1500–1571) Italian Mannerist sculptor and goldsmith who created the graceful bronze *Perseus*

César (full name César Baldaccini) (1921–) French sculptor of imaginary insects and animals from iron, scrap metal, and crushed car bodies

Christo (full name Christo Javacheff) (1935–) Bulgarian-born US sculptor known for wrapping buildings and other large structures in fabric tied down with rope

Donatello (Donato di Niccolo) (c. 1386–1466) Italian early Renaissance sculptor who revived the Classical style, as in the bronze *David* and the equestrian statue *Gattamelata*

Epstein Jacob (1880–1959) US-born British sculptor who created monumental figures, including *St Michael and the Devil*, and muscular nudes, such as *Genesis*

Flaxman John (1755–1826) English sculptor of monumental public works who created monuments to the English Admiral Nelson and Scottish poet Robert Burns

Frink Elisabeth (1930–1993) English sculptor of rugged naturalistic bronzes of human and animal forms, such as *Running Man*

Gabo Naum (adopted name of Naum Neemia Pevsner) (1890–1977) Russian-born US abstract sculptor and exponent of Constructivism and kinetic sculpture, such as *Linear Construction*

Gaudier-Brzeska Henri (adopted name of Henri Gaudier) (1891–1915) French sculptor of angular, semi-abstract style, as in *Birds Erect*

Ghiberti Lorenzo (1378–1455) Italian sculptor and goldsmith who created a pair of gilded doors for Florence Cathedral

Giacometti Alberto (1901–1966) Swiss sculptor of thin, rough-textured, single bronze figures, such as *Man Pointing*

Giambologna (Giovanni da Bologna or Jean de Boulogne) (1529–1608) Flemish-born Mannerist sculptor whose works contain muscular, contorted figures, as in *The Rape of the Sabine Women*

Gill (Arthur) Eric (Rowton) (1882–1940) English graphic designer, engraver, writer, and sculptor of monumental stone works, including *Prospero and Ariel*

González Julio (1876–1942) Spanish sculptor and painter who used wrought and welded iron, as in *Woman with a Mirror*

Gormley Anthony (1950–) English sculptor best known for his *Angel of the North* and *Derry Sculpture*

Greenough Horatio (1805–1852) US sculptor who was one of the first US Neo-Classicists, and whose work includes a colossal statue of George Washington for the Rotunda of the US Capitol

Hepworth (Jocelyn) Barbara (1903–1975) English abstract sculptor of wood or stone whose works feature slender, upright, or round hollowed forms, such as *Pelagos*

Lipchitz Jacques (1891–1973) Lithuanian-born early Cubist sculptor whose works include *Man with Guitar*

Lysippus or **Lysippos** (4th century BC) Greek sculptor of *Apoxyomenos* and the colossal *Hercules* (lost)

Michelangelo (Michelangelo di Lodovico Buonarroti) (1475–1564) dominant Italian High Renaissance sculptor, painter, architect, and poet; his marble *David* set a new standard in nude sculpture

Moore Henry (Spencer) (1898–1986) English sculptor of reclining nudes, mother-and-child groups, warriors, and interlocking abstract forms, such as *Reclining Figure*

Myron (c. 500–c. 440 BC) Greek sculptor who excelled at representing movement, as in *Discobolus/Discus-Thrower*

Nevelson Louise (1899–1988) Russian-born US artist who created sculptures using discarded wooden objects, mostly bits from furniture

Noguchi Isamu (1904–1988) US sculptor and designer whose work includes *Khmer*

Paolozzi Eduardo (Luigi) (1924–) Scottish sculptor of sinister, robot-like figures from bronze casts of machinery, such as *Cyclops*

Phidias or **Pheidias** (mid-5th century BC) Greek sculptor of the colossal *Zeus* at Olympia

Praxiteles (mid-4th century BC) Greek sculptor of life-size, free-standing female nudes, such as *Aphrodite of Cnidus*

Ray Man (adopted name of Emmanuel Rabinovich Rudnitsky) (1890–1976) US photographer, painter, and sculptor of *The Gift*; he was associated with the Dadaists and Surrealism

Robbia Luca della (c 1400–1482) Italian sculptor best known for his glazed terracotta sculptures

Rodin (René François) Auguste (1840–1917) French sculptor who is considered the greatest of his time; his work includes *The Thinker*

Roubiliac or **Roubillac** Louis François (c. 1705–1762) French sculptor of a statue of German composer George Handel

Rysbrack Jan Michiel (1694–1770) Netherlandish-born English monumental sculptor of a restrained Baroque style who created a monument to scientist Isaac Newton

Saint-Gaudens Augustus (1848–1907) Irish-born US sculptor who was one of the leading Neo-Classical sculptors, and whose work includes *Admiral Farragut*

Segal George (1924–) US sculptor who creates sculptures using plaster casts of people, as in *The Restaurant Window*

Serra Richard (1939–) US Minimalist sculptor of metal whose works include *Tilted Arc*

Sluter Claus (c. 1350–1406) northern European sculptor whose realism marked a break from the International Gothic style, as in *Well of Moses*

Smith David (Roland) (1906–1965) US sculptor of large, openwork, metal abstracts, such as *Cubi XXVII*

Tatlin Vladimir Yevgrapovich (1885–1953) Russian highly abstract sculptor and co-founder of Constructivism

Turnbull William (1922–) Scottish painter and sculptor of totem-like figures and austere, vertical structures grouped in mathematical repetition, such as *5 × 1*

Verrocchio Andrea del (Andrea di Cione) (c. 1435–1488) Italian sculptor, painter, and goldsmith who created the vigorous equestrian statue of *Bartolomeo Colleoni* and the painting *The Baptism of Christ*

Westmacott Richard (1775–1856) English Neo-Classical sculptor of monuments to politicians and heroes of the Napoleonic Wars

Noteworthy Photographers

Abbott Berenice (1898–1991) US photographer and exponent of realism best known for her portrait studies of artists in the 1920s and for her comprehensive documentation of New York City in the 1930s

Adams Ansel Easton (1902–1984) US photographer whose images of dramatic landscapes and organic forms of the American West have made him a legend in the field of photography

Adamson Robert (1821–1848) Scottish photographer who collaborated with David Octavius Hill

Arbus Diane (1923–1971) US fashion photographer who is best known for her later work which examined the fringes of US society: the misfits, the eccentrics, and the bizarre

Arnold Eve (c. 1925–) US photographer resident in the UK, member of the Magnum Agency and best known for her sensitive photojournalism

Atget Eugène (1857–1927) French photographer discovered by Berenice Abbott, who documented urban Paris in some 10,000 images

Avedon Richard (1923–) leading US photographer whose animated portraits are shot in a studio against a white background

Bailey David (1938–) English fashion photographer whose gritty black-and-white portraits of fashionable celebrities did much to define the image of 'swinging London' in the 1960s

Beaton Cecil Walter Hardy (1904–1980) English fashion and society photographer whose elaborate portraits, having the quality of *tableaux vivants*, set the style for *Vogue* up to the 1950s

Beaufoy Merlin Henry (1803–1873) Australian documentary photographer who recorded everyday life in small pioneer settlements in Australia

Bourke-White Margaret (1906–1971) US photographer who was an important innovator of the photo essay and the first woman photographer attached to US armed forces in World War II

Brady Matthew B (c. 1823–1896) US photographer whose portraiture and military photography recorded the American Civil War

Brandt Bill (Hermann Wilhelm) (1904–1983) German-born British photographer famous for highly contrasted, atmospheric pictures such as the landscape *Top Withens*

Brassäi (adopted name of Gyula Halasz) (1899–1984) Hungarian-born French photographer who recorded the nightlife of Paris: the prostitutes, street cleaners, and criminals

Bravo Manuel Alvarez (1902–) Mexican photographer who conveys an essentially tragic vision of his native land

Cameron Julia Margaret (born Pattle) (1815–1879) British photographer who made lively and dramatic portraits of the Victorian intelligentsia, often posed as historical or literary figures

Capa Robert (adopted name of André Friedmann) (1913–1954) Hungarian-born US photographer who specialized in war photography, covering the Spanish Civil War and World War II

Cartier-Bresson Henri (1908–) French photograher who is considered one of the greatest photographic artists, shooting documentary work in black and white, master of the 'captured moment' and founder of the Magnum Agency

Cazneaux Harold (1878–1953) Australian photographer known for his portraits and landscapes

Claudet Antoine François Jean (1797–1867) French-born pioneer of photography whose experiments led to greatly reduced exposure time, the earliest light meter, and the introduction of painted backgrounds into studio portraits

Cunningham Imogen (1883–1976) US photographer who, with Ansel Adams and Edward Weston, was a founder member of the 'f/64' group which advocated precise definition

Curtis Edward Sheriff (1868–1952) US photographer who recorded the disappearing life of the American Indians

Daguerre Louis Jacques Mandé (1787–1851) French pioneer of photography who, with Joseph Niépce, is credited with the invention of photography

Dalton Stephen (Neal) (1937–) English nature photographer whose innovative techniques in high speed photography have produced definitive pictures of birds and animals caught in motion

Demachy Robert (1859–1936) French photographer who, by differing printing techniques, produced hazy and impressionistic images, largely of young women in landscape or 'backstage' settings

Doisneau Robert (1912–1994) French photographer who is known for his sensitive and often witty depictions of ordinary people and everyday situations within the environs of Paris

Dupain Max (1911–) leading Australian photographer famous for industrial landscapes

Eastman George (1854–1932) US entrepreneur and inventor who founded the Eastman Kodak photographic company in 1892; he patented flexible film, invented the Kodak box camera, and introduced daylight-loading film

Eggleston William (1937–) US photographer whose colour photographs of commonplace scenes in the deep south are transformed by his use of the dye transfer technique

Eickemeyer Rudolph Jr (1862–1932) US photographer who became the leader in the pictorial movement of the late 19th century and received more than 100 awards and medals

Eisenstaedt Alfred (1898–1995) US photographer who is especially recognized for his photographs of celebrities, such as Winston Churchill, Charlie Chaplin, Marilyn Monroe, and John F Kennedy

Emerson Peter Henry (1856–1936) English landscape photographer whose aim was to produce uncontrived naturalistic images of the countryside

Erwitt Elliot (1928–) US photographer born in Paris whose candid shots, often featuring dogs, are stamped with humour

Evans Walker (1903–1975) one of the USA's finest documentary photographers, famous for his portraits of people in the rural American South during the Great Depression

Fenton Roger (1819–1869) English photographer who is best known for his comprehensive documentation of the Crimean War, and who was a founder member of the Photographic Society (later the Royal Photographic Society) in London

Frank Robert (1924–) Swiss-born US photographer famous for his informal and unromanticized pictures of street life in America and Europe

Freund Gisèle (1912–) German-born French portrait photographer of literary subjects and the first woman to be a member of the Magnum Agency

Gerster Georg (Anton) (1928–) Swiss photographer, master of aerial photography that shows the beauty integral to objects which is not always obvious from the ground; author of *Grand Design: the Earth from Above*

Godwin Fay (1931–) English photographer whose powerful landscapes have illustrated books such as *Remains of Elmet* (with Ted Hughes)

Halsman Phillippe (1906–1979) US photographer born in Latvia, master of the psychological portrait

Hardy Bert (1913–) English photojournalist who captured British life for *Picture Post* during World War II and in the 1950s

Herschel John Frederick William (1792–1871) English scientist, astronomer, and photographer who coined the terms 'photography', 'negative', and 'positive'

Hill David Octavius (1802–1870) Scottish photographer who worked with Robert Adamson photographing leading members of the Free Church of Scotland, Edinburgh, and the Scottish fishing village of Newhaven

Hine Lewis Wickes (1874–1940) US sociologist and photographer whose dramatic photographs of child labour conditions in US factories at the beginning of the 20th century led to changes in state and local labour laws

Noteworthy Photographers (*continued*)

Hosking Eric John (1909–1991) English wildlife photographer who is known for his documentation of British birds

Hurley James Francis (1885–1962) Australian photographer and film-maker best known for Antarctic work done on expeditions with Douglas Mawson and Ernest Shackleton and for documentaries made in Papua New Guinea

Jackson William Henry (1843–1942) US photographer of the American West

Karsh Yousuf (1908–) Armenian-born Canadian portrait photographer who is known for his formal and dramatically lit studies of the famous in which he attempts to capture their 'inward power'

Kertész André (1894–1986) Hungarian-born US photographer whose spontaneity and pioneering use of the hand-held camera had a great impact on photojournalism

Koudelka Josef (1938–) Czech photographer who has recorded the vanishing way of life of East European gypsies

Land Edwin Herbert (1909–1991) US inventor of the Polaroid Land camera in 1947, which developed the film in one minute inside the camera and produced an 'instant' photograph

Lange Dorothea (born Nutzhorn) (1895–1965) US photographer who documented the westward migration of farm families from the Dust Bowl of southern central USA

Lartigue Jacques-Henri (Charles Auguste) (1894–1986) French photographer who took over 40,000 photographs documenting people and everyday situations, often catching his subjects off-guard

Le Gray Gustave (1820–1882) French photographer who invented the waxed paper negative, a more efficient version of the calotype, and experimented with printing images using more than one negative, notably in his detailed seascapes

Leibovitz Annie (1950–) US photographer whose elaborately staged portraits of US celebrities appeared first in *Rolling Stone* magazine and later in *Vanity Fair*

Lewinsky Jorge (Jerzy) (1921–) Polish-born British photographer, known for his literary landscapes and portraits of artists

Lichfield Patrick Anson (1939–) English photographer who is best known for his travel and publicity shots as well as his royal portraits

McBean Angus (1904–1990) Leading British theatre photographer of his day

McCullin Don(ald) (1935–) English war photographer whose coverage of hostilities in the Congo, Vietnam, Biafra, and Cambodia are notable for their pessimistic vision

Man Felix H (1893–1985) German-born British photojournalist famous for the candid shot

Mapplethorpe Robert (1946–1989) US art photographer who was known for his use of racial and homo-erotic imagery, chiefly in fine platinum prints

Marey Etienne-Jules (1830–1904) French photographer who devised a photographic gun for taking serial pictures and also invented the 'chronophotograph' from which modern cinematography was developed

Meiselas Susan (1948–) US freelance war photographer who has covered conflicts in Nicaragua and El Salvador, and whose uncompromising realism makes powerful viewing

Modotti Tina (1896–1942) Italian photographer who made sensitive studies of Mexican women, Mexican muralists, and near-abstract prints of stairs and flowers

Morimoto Hiromitsu (1942–) Japanese-born US photographer and teacher who uses silver liquid emulsion on rag paper in the production of his photographs

Morse Samuel Finley Breese (1791–1872) US inventor and a noted photographer whose 1840 picture of his class reunion was said to be the first group portrait made

Mortensen William (1897–1965) US photographer who perfected the Metalchrome process and pigment painting and was the first to shoot movie stills with a small-format camera

Munkácsi Martin (1896–1963) Hungarian-born US photographer who worked as a fashion photographer pioneering a more lively and natural style of photograph for such magazines as *Harper's Bazaar* and *Ladies' Home Journal*

Muybridge Eadweard (adopted name of Edward James Muggeridge) (1830–1904) English-born US photographer who made a series of animal locomotion photographs in the 1870s and proved that when a horse trots there are times when all its feet are off the ground

Nadar (adopted name of Gaspard-Félix Tournachon) (1820–1910) French portrait photographer and caricaturist who took the first aerial photographs (from a balloon) and was the first to take flash photographs (using magnesium bulbs)

Namuth Hans (1915–1990) German-born US photographer who specialized in portraits and documentary work including documentation of artists at work

Nègre Charles (1820–1880) French photographer who began by producing everyday street scenes as studies for his paintings but soon embarked on a series of documentary projects such as Chartres Cathedral in France

Newton Helmut (1920–) German-born Australian photographer of fashion in a decadent style which exploits sexuality

Parer Damien (1912–1944) Australian photographer noted particularly for his World War II work photographing troops in action in Tobruk, Syria, and Greece

Parkinson Norman (adopted name of Ronald William Smith) (1913–1990) highly influential English fashion and portrait photographer, best known for his colour work and his official portraits of the royal family

Parks Gordon Alexander Buchanan (1912–) self-taught African-American photographer who worked for the Office of War Information in 1944 and was with *Life* magazine (1948–72)

Penn Irving (1917–) leading US fashion and fine art photographer who works in black and white and with the platinum process; he was associated for many years with *Vogue* magazine

Plage (Götz) Dieter (1936–1993) German wildlife photographer known especially for his films for the English television company Anglia's *Survival* series

Ray Man (Emmanuel Rudnitky) (1890–1976) US experimental photographer and leading exponent of Dadaism who 'discovered' Rayographs and Solarizations

Renger-Patzsch Albert (1897–1966) German photographer who was a leading figure of the New Photography movement which emphasized objectivity of vision

Riboud Marc (1923–) French photographer with great talent in composition and design, best known for his photographs taken in China

Robinson Henry Peach (1830–1901) English photographer who, by careful composition and the combination of several negatives in one print, produced images that closely imitated the effects and subject matter of Victorian painting

Rodchenko Aleksander Mikhailovich (1891–1956) Russian avant-garde painter, designer, and photographer whose photographs of everyday objects were presented in close-up from strange angles or from high viewpoints and document the early years of the Soviet era

St Joseph (John) Kenneth (Sinclair) (1912–1994) British pioneer of aerial photography in archaeology who was responsible for the discovery of thousands of previously unknown archaeological sites

Salgado Sabastio Ribeiro (1944–) Brazilian photographer, resident in Paris, whose monotone pictures of workers in Brazil and India are among the masterworks of 20th century photography

(*continued*)

Noteworthy Photographers (*continued*)

Sander August (1876–1964) German portrait photographer who concentrated on German society in a way that combined the individual with the archetypal

Sherman Cindy (1954–) leading experimental US art photographer who has specialized in taking pictures of herself in various roles suggested by cinema and advertising

Siskind Aaron (1903–1991) US art photographer who began as a documentary photographer and in 1940 made a radical change towards a poetic exploration of forms and planes, often working on Martha's Vineyard off the Massachusetts coast

Snowdon Anthony (Charles Robert) Armstrong-Jones, 1st Earl of Snowdon (1930–) English photographer once known for his fashion photography and portraits of celebrities, now working on social issues

Smith W(illiam) Eugene (1918–1978) US photojournalist and war correspondent who is remembered for numerous *Life* photo essays

Stackpole Peter (1913–1997) US photojournalist who invented and built underwater equipment for still and movie photography, a variation of which remains standard in film-making

Steichen Edward Jean (1879–1973) Luxembourg-born US photographer who, with Alfred Stieglitz, helped to establish photography as an art form

Steinert Otto (1915–1978) German photographer teacher and physician who was a master of photographic technique in all its forms and a leader in the field of art photography

Stieglitz Alfred (1864–1946) Hugely influential US photographer who formed the Photo Secession group in 1903 and started up the magazine *Camera Work*

Strand Paul (1890–1976) US photographer and film-maker who concentrated on predominantly rural subjects that celebrate human dignity in a clear and straightforward manner

Sutcliffe Frank Meadow (1853–1941) English photographer who photographed the inhabitants and environs of Whitby, England, in a consistently naturalistic style

Talbot William Henry Fox (1800–1877) English pioneer of photography who invented the paper-based calotype process and the first negative/positive method

Turbeville Deborah (1937–) US Post-Modernist photographer of fashion for magazines such as *Vogue* and *Marie Claire* using theatrical backgrounds and grainy, scratched surfaces

Uelsmann Jerry N(orman) (1934–) US photographer in the Symbolist school whose dream-like images are created by combining or layering many elements into one with great technical skill

Weegee (born Arthur Fellig) (1899–1968) US photographer born in Austro-Hungary who became the archetypal press photographer of the seamy side of life in 1940s New York; author of *Naked City*

Weston Brett (Theodore) (1911–1993) US photographer working in black and white; master of abstract expressionism while using nature as his subject

Weston Edward (1886–1958) US photographer who is noted for the technical mastery, composition, and clarity in his California landscapes, clouds, gourds, cacti, and nude studies

White Minor (Martin) (1908–1976) US photographer who was known for his sharply focused black-and-white prints of metaphysical significance; editor of *Aperture*

Woolcott Marion Post (1910–1990) US documentary photographer who is best known for her work for the Farm Security Administration showing the conditions of poor farmers in the late 1930s in Kentucky and the deep South

Noteworthy Cartoonists

Addams Charles Samuel (1912–1988) US cartoonist who created a ghoulish family featured in the *New Yorker*

Bairnsfather (Charles) Bruce (1888–1959) British cartoonist who created the famous World War II character Old Bill

Bancks James Charles (1889–1952) Australian cartoonist who created the comic strip *Ginger Meggs*

Bateman H(enry) M(ayo) (1887–1970) Australian cartoonist who depicted scenes of social embarrassment and confusion in *The Man Who* series

Crumb Robert (1943–) US underground cartoonist

Day Clarence Shepard Jr (1874–1935) US cartoonist and author

Disney Walt(er Elias) (1901–1966) US cartoonist and film producer who created Mickey Mouse and full-length animations such as *Snow White and the Seven Dwarfs*

Fleischer Max (1889–1972) Austrian-born US cartoonist, creator of Betty Boop and Popeye, and producer of films such as *Talkartoons*

Giles (Carl Ronald) (1916–1995) British cartoonist who for *Express* Newspapers developed the dysfunctional Giles Family headed by Grandma

Goldberg Rube (Reuben Lucius) (1883–1970) US Pulitzer prizewinning cartoonist whose cartoons featured ridiculously complicated inventions

Gould H(enry) M(ayo) (1900–1985) US cartoonist who created detective Dick Tracy

Herblock Chester (1900–) US Pulitzer prizewinning cartoonist

Hopkins Livingston (1846–1927) Australian cartoonist, watercolorist, and etcher

Keene Charles Samuel (1823–1891) English book illustrator and cartoonist contributing to *Punch* magazine

Lancaster Osbert (1908–1986) English writer and creator of the 'pocket cartoons' published in the *Daily Express*, satirizing current social mores

Larson Gary (1950–) US cartoonist and creator of *The Far Side*

Leech John (1817–1864) English caricaturist and illustrator who recorded Victorian political and social life

Lindsay Norman Alfred William (1879–1969) Australian artist and writer, known for political cartoons and erotic illustrations

Low David (Alexander Cecil) (1891–1963) New Zealand-born British political cartoonist on the staff of London's *Evening Standard* who created Colonel Blimp

May Phil(ip) William (1864–1903) English artist and cartoonist, contributor to *Punch* and creator of cockney characters

Nast Thomas (1840–1902) German-born US illustrator and cartoonist for *Harper's Weekly* who established the donkey and elephant as symbols of the Democrats and Republicans

Petty Bruce Leslie (1929–) Australian cartoonist, caricaturist, and film director

Raven-Hill Leonard (1867–1942) English painter and illustrator known for his *Punch* drawings

Ripley Robert LeRoy (1893–1949) US cartoonist and creator of the syndicated column *Believe It or Not!*

Robinson W(illiam) Heath (1872–1944) English cartoonist and illustrator famous for drawings of bizarre machinery performing simple tasks

Sagendorf Forrest (Bud) (1915–1994) US cartoonist and creator of Popeye with Elsie Segar

Scarfe Gerald (1936–) English cartoonist and animator whose savage cartoons of the uglier side of life found a home in the satirical magazine *Private Eye*

Noteworthy Cartoonists (*continued*)

Schulz Charles M(onroe) (1922–) US cartoonist who created the *Peanuts* strip featuring Snoopy, Linus, and Charlie Brown

Searle Ronald (William Fordham) (1920–) English cartoonist, illustrator, and creator of the horrible girls of St Trinians

Segar Elsie Crisler (1894–1938) US cartoonist and creator of Popeye with Forrest Sagendorf

Shepard E(rnest) H(oward) (1879–1976) English illustrator and cartoonist who illustrated children's classics, including *Winnie the Pooh* and *The Wind in the Willows*

Shuster Joe (Joseph) (1914–1992) Canadian-born US cartoonist who collaborated on the first comic-strip superhero, Superman

Spiegelman Art (1948–) US cartoonist who won a Pulitzer Prize for the *Maus* novels

Steinberg Saul Jacobson (1914–) Romanian-born US artist of cartoons with allusions to the irrational and absurd

Sullivan Pat(rick) (1887–1933) Australian-born US animator and cartoonist who created the first cartoon film hero, Felix the Cat

Tenniel John (1820–1914) English illustrator and cartoonist who illustrated Lewis Carroll's *Alice's Adventures in Wonderland*

Trudeau Garry (1948–) American cartoonist and creator of the Doonesbury comic strip known for scathing social and political commentary

Vicky (pen name of Victor Weisz) (1913–1966) Hungarian cartoonist resident in Britain whose cartoons attacking power and privilege appeared in papers such as the *Daily Mirror* and *Evening Standard*

Noteworthy Fashion Designers

Amies Hardy (1909–) British couturier to the Queen, holder of a royal warrant, known for the simple elegance of his designs

Anthony John (1938–) US fashion designer noted for cardigans, trousers, and evening dresses in satin and sheer wool

Armani Giorgio (1935–) Italian fashion designer known for understated styles and fine fabrics

Ashley Laura (born Mountney) (1925–1985) Welsh designer of neo-Victorian country style

Balenciaga Cristóbal (1895–1972) innovative Spanish couturier of women's clothing

Banks Jeff (1943–) popular Welsh-born designer, founder of Warehouse, also known for presenting TV fashion shows

Blahnik Manolo (1943–) of mixed Czech-Spanish origin, Blahnik is famous for his inventive, exotic shoe designs

Cardin Pierre (1922–) French pioneering fashion designer who launched menswear and designed ready-to-wear collections

Chanel Coco (Gabrielle) (1883–1971) French fashion designer and trendsetter who created the 'little black dress'

Claiborne Liz (1929–) US designer of clothing for professional women

Comme des Garçons (trade name of Rei Kawakubo) (1942–) unconventional Japanese fashion designer who combines Eastern and Western ideas of clothing

Conran Jasper (1960–) British designer of linear and sophisticated clothing

Courrèges André (1923–) French fashion designer who is credited with inventing the miniskirt, and is famous for his futuristic, 'space age' style

de la Renta Oscar (1932–) US fashion designer who is noted for the use of opulent fabrics in evening clothes

Dior Christian (1905–1957) French couturier whose 'New Look' had impact following World War II austerity

Emanuel David (1952–) and Elizabeth (1953–) British fashion designers of opulent evening wear and gowns for English royalty

Farhi Nicole (1946–) French-born designer of clean-cut, modern clothing for French Connection

Fassett Kaffe (1937–) US knitwear and textile designer

Ferré Gianfranco (1944–) Italian designer who translates his knowledge of architecture to fashion

Galliano John (1960–) visionary British designer working in Paris, currently (since 1996) for the house of Dior, inspired by

mythology and historical costume

Gaultier Jean-Paul (1952–) French fashion designer who is influential in the ready-to-wear market and has designed costumes for American entertainers

Givenchy Hubert James Marcel Taffin de (1927–) French fashion designer, creator of the 'Bettina blouse', and known for simple, reasonably priced mix-and-match wear

Halston (trade name of Roy Halston Frowick) (1932–1990) US fashion designer and the first American to break into international haute couture

Hamnett Katharine (1948–) English fashion designer of inexpensive unisex designs and oversized T-shirts

Herrera Carolina (1939–) Venezuelan-born designer of sophisticated, elegant fashions

Hulanicki Barbara (1936–) Polish-born, English-educated designer, she established the Biba boutique in the 1960s

Jackson Betty (1949–) British designer of functional womenswear

Karan Donna (1948–) US designer of women's business clothing, casuals, and sportswear, owner of the DKNY emporium

Kenzo (trade name of Kenzo Takada) (1940–) Japanese fashion designer known for unconventional designs based on traditional Japanese clothing

Klein Calvin (Richard) (1942–) US fashion designer who made designer jeans a status symbol

Lacroix Christian (1951–) French couturier famous for his frivolous style and sumptuous designs

Lagerfeld Karl (1938–) cosmopolitan, German-born designer known as much for personal eccentricity as for his luxurious, spectacular collections

Lanvin Jeanne (1867–1946) French fashion designer known for mother-and-daughter ensembles, fine craft, and embroidery

Laroche Guy (1923–1989) French designer of women's clothing and menswear known for their flawless cut

Lauren Ralph (adopted name of Ralph Lipschitz) (1939–) US fashion designer of the Polo label of menswear

Lisi Ben de (1955–) US-born designer working currently in the UK, specializing in separates and evening clothes

McQueen Alexander (1969–) British designer, who since 1996 has worked for Givenchy where he replaced John Galliano

Miyake Issey (1938–) Japanese fashion designer whose 'anti-fashion', theatrical looks combine Eastern and Western influences

(*continued*)

Noteworthy Fashion Designers (*continued*)

© Gemma Levine

Jean Muir

Montana Claude (1949–) French fashion designer who promoted the broad-shouldered look

Muir Jean Elizabeth (1928–1995) English designer of impeccably cut, flowing evening gowns and sophisticated dresses

Oldfield Bruce (1950–) English fashion designer famous for his evening wear

Ozbek Rifat (1953–) Turkish-born British designer famous for ornate, colourful creations

Patou Jean (1880–1936) French clothes designer who greatly influenced the couture and ready-to-wear sectors of the fashion world

Quant Mary (1934–) English fashion designer who popularized the miniskirt in the UK

Rhodes Zandra (1940–) English fashion designer known for her extravagant dress creations

Ricci Nina (1883–1970) prominent Italian designer famous for her impeccable taste and elegance

Rocha John (1953–) Hong-Kong born Irish designer of Chinese-Portuguese parentage, who produces softly tailored, attractively textured clothing for men and women

Rykiel Sonia (1930–) French designer of women's ready-to-wear fashion who pioneered the inside-out look

Saint-Laurent Yves (Henri Donat Mathieu) (1936–) French fashion designer who creates a 'power-dressing' look of classic, stylish city clothes for men and women

Schiaparelli Elsa (*c.* 1890–1973) Italian couturier and knitwear designer famous for padded shoulders, 'shocking pink', and pioneering use of synthetic fabrics

Smith Paul (1946–) English designer of stylistically simple and practical clothes, commercially successful abroad (particularly in Japan)

Ungaro Emanuel Maffeolti (1933–) French designer who uses specially produced fabrics; he moved from a preference for stark silhouettes to promoting softer, more fluid lines

Valentino (trade name of Valentino Garavani) (1933–) Italian fashion designer of elegantly tailored suits and coats

Versace Gianni (1946–1997) Italian designer of provocative clothing using unusual fabric combinations, strong colours, and simple shapes

Westwood Vivienne (1941–) bold and visionary English designer, creator of punk style, known for her eclectic and iconoclastic taste

Worth Charles Frederick (1825–1895) English tailor established in Paris, who was one of the first couturiers to sell his designs to manufacturers for mass production

Classical Music

Noteworthy Composers of Classical Music

Albeniz Isaac (1860–1909) Spanish composer and pianist whose numerous works include zarzuelas, operas, orchestral suites, and 250 piano works

Albinoni Tommaso (1671–1751) Italian composer whose numerous operas and sonatas helped establish the Baroque style

Arnold Malcolm Henry (1921–) English composer of orchestral, chamber, ballet, and vocal music, as well as numerous film scores

Auric Georges (1899–1983) French composer whose works include a comic opera, several ballets, and incidental music for films

Babbitt Milton (1916–) US composer and theorist who pioneered the application of information theory to music

Bach Carl Philip Emmanuel (1714–1788) German composer who introduced a new 'homophonic' style that influenced Mozart, Haydn, and Beethoven

Bach Johann Christian (1735–1782) German musician who became celebrated in Italy as a composer of operas

Bach Johann Sebastian (1685–1750) German musician and one of the world's great composers whose music epitomizes the Baroque polyphonic style

Bach Wilhelm Friedemann (1710–1784) German composer, organist, and improviser who was a master of counterpoint

Balakirev Mily Alexeyevich (1837–1910) Russian composer of orchestral works, piano music, songs, and a symphonic poem *Tamara*

Barber Samuel (1910–1981) US Neo-Classical composer whose compositions include *Adagio for Strings* and the opera *Vanessa*

Bartók Béla (1881–1945) Hungarian composer whose works combine folk elements with mathematical concepts of tonal and rhythmic proportion

Bax Arnold Edward Trevor (1883–1953) English composer whose works, often based on Celtic legends, include seven symphonies and two tone poems

Beethoven Ludwig van (1770–1827) German composer and pianist who was the dominant influence on 19th-century music, and whose *Ode to Joy* from the 9th Symphony is the anthem of the European Union

Bellini Vincenzo (1801–1835) Italian composer of operas who helped develop a new simplicity of melodic expression for classic themes

Bennett Richard Rodney (1936–) English composer of jazz, film music, symphonies, and operas

Berg Alban (1885–1935) Austrian composer who developed a personal 12-tone idiom of great emotional and stylistic versatility and wrote the operas *Wozzeck* and *Lulu*

Berio Luciano (1925–) Italian composer whose work combines serial techniques with commedia dell'arte and antiphonal practices

Berkeley Lennox Randal Francis (1903–1989) English composer whose works include verses from Spenser's *The Faerie Queene* set for an eight-part unaccompanied chorus

Berlioz (Louis) Hector (1803–1869) French Romantic composer known as the founder of modern orchestration

Bernstein Leonard (1918–1990) US composer, conductor, and pianist whose works include symphonies, ballets, and scores for musicals, such as *West Side Story*

Noteworthy Composers of Classical Music (*continued*)

Birtwistle Harrison (1934–) English avant-garde composer who specializes in chamber music, and whose chamber operas include *Punch and Judy*

Bizet Georges (Alexandre César Léopold) (1838–1875) French composer of operas whose operatic masterpiece is *Carmen*

Borodin Alexander Porfir'yevich (1833–1887) Russian composer of symphonies, songs, and chamber music whose principal work is the opera *Prince Igor*

Boulez Pierre (1925–) French composer who is the founder and director of IRCAM, a music research studio in Paris

© Polygram

Pierre Boulez

Brahms Johannes (1833–1897) German composer who is considered one of the greatest composers of symphonic music and songs

Britten (Edward) Benjamin (1913–1976) English composer whose works include *Young Person's Guide to the Orchestra* and the oratorio *War Requiem*

Brown Earle (1926–) US composer who pioneered graph notation and mobile form

Bruckner (Josef) Anton (1824–1896) Austrian Romantic composer whose works include numerous choral pieces and 11 symphonies

Bull John (c. 1562–1628) English composer and organist whose works include *God Save the King*

Busoni Ferruccio Dante Benvenuto (1866–1924) Italian composer and pianist who wrote for the piano and composed several operas, including *Doktor Faust*

Buxtehude Diderik (1637–1707) Danish composer of organ works, cantatas, and trio sonatas for two violins, viola da gamba, and harpsichord

Byrd William (1543–1623) English composer whose sacred and secular choral music exemplifies the English polyphonic style

Cage John (1912–1992) US composer who experimented with randomness and inexactitude to produce ultra-modern sounds

Carter Elliott Cook (1908–) US composer who created structured works in Schoenbergian serial idiom incorporating 'metrical modulation'

Cavalli (Pietro) Francesco (1602–1676) Italian composer, pupil of Monteverdi, and the first to make opera a popular entertainment

Chopin Frédéric François (1810–1849) Polish composer and pianist who revolutionized the technique of pianoforte playing

Copland Aaron (1900–1990) US composer whose works include the ballets *Billy the Kid* and *Appalachian Spring*

Corelli Arcangelo (1653–1713) Italian composer and one of the first virtuoso exponents of the Baroque violin, whose works include a set of *concerto grossi*

Couperin François le Grand (1668–1733) French composer of numerous chamber concertos and harpsichord suites

Davies Peter Maxwell (1934–) English composer and conductor whose music combines mediaeval and serial codes of practice with a heightened Expressionism

Debussy (Achille-)Claude (1862–1918) French composer, traditionally regarded as one of the musical Impressionists, who introduced qualities of melody and harmony based on the whole-tone scale

Delibes (Clement Philibert) Leo (1836–1891) French composer whose works include the ballet *Coppélia* and the opera *Lakmé*

Delius Frederick Theodore Albert (1862–1934) English composer of operas, choral pieces, chamber music, orchestral works, and pastoral songs

Dessau Paul (1894–1979) German composer whose works include incidental music to Bertolt Brecht's theatre pieces

Dohnányi Ernst (Ernö) von (1877–1960) Hungarian pianist, conductor, and composer whose works include *Variations on a Nursery Song*

Donizetti (Domenico) Gaetano (Maria) (1797–1848) Italian composer who created more than 60 operas, including *Lucrezia Borgia*

Dowland John (c. 1563–c. 1626) English composer of lute songs who introduced refinements of harmony and ornamentation to English Renaissance style

Dufay Guillaume (c. 1400–1474) Flemish composer whose masses and motets were very influential in the Renaissance

Dukas Paul Abraham (1865–1935) French composer whose works include the animated orchestral scherzo *L'Apprenti sorcier/The Sorcerer's Apprentice*

Dunstable John (c. 1385–1453) English composer who was an early exponent of counterpoint

Dvořák Antonin Leopold (1841–1904) Czech composer whose works include the *New World Symphony*

Elgar Edward (William) (1857–1934) English composer who wrote *The Dream of Gerontius* and *Pomp and Circumstance* marches

Falla Manuel de (full name Manuel Maria de Falla y Matheu) (1876–1946) Spanish composer whose works include *Noches en los jardines de España/Nights in the Gardens of Spain* and *El sombrero de tres picos/The Three-Cornered Hat*

Fauré Gabriel (Urbain) (1845–1924) French composer who wrote songs, chamber music, and a choral *Requiem*

Gershwin George (born Jacob) (1898–1937) US composer whose works include *Rhapsody in Blue* and the opera *Porgy and Bess*

Glass Philip (1937–) US composer whose work is characterized by repeated figures that are continually expanded and modified

Gluck Christoph Willibald von (1714–1787) German composer who revolutionized opera by giving free scope to dramatic effect, most notably in *Orfeo*

Gounod Charles François (1818–1893) French composer and organist whose operas and songs combine graceful melody and elegant harmonization

Grieg Edvard (Hagerup) (1843–1907) Norwegian national composer whose works include *Piano Concerto in A Minor* and *Peer Gynt*

Handel Georg Friedrich (originally Händel) (1685–1759) German-born British composer whose prolific operas and oratorios include the *Messiah*

Haydn (Franz) Joseph (1732–1809) Austrian composer who was a major exponent of the classical symphony, and who influenced Mozart and Beethoven

Henze Hans Werner (1926–) German composer whose works include an opera *Elegy for Young Lovers*

Hindemith Paul (1895–1963) German composer of the operas *Cardillac* and *Mathis der Maler/Mathis the Painter*

Hoffman Amadeus (Ernst Theodor Wilhelm) (1776–1822) German composer of the opera *Undine* and author of advanced musical criticism, novels, and stories

Holst Gustav(us) Theodore von (1874–1934) English composer of operas, ballets, choral works, orchestral suites, and songs; his work includes *The Planets*

Honegger Arthur (1892–1955) Swiss composer who was one of the group of composers known as 'Les Six'

Ives Charles Edward (1874–1954) US composer who experimented with atonality, quarter tones, clashing time signatures, and quotations from popular music

(*continued*)

Noteworthy Composers of Classical Music (*continued*)

Janáček Leoš (1854–1928) Czech composer whose work was influenced by Moravian folk music

Janequin Clément (*c.* 1472–*c.* 1560) French composer of chansons and psalms

Josquin Desprez (or des Prés) (1440–1521) Franco-Flemish composer whose polyphonic masses and motets mark a peak in Renaissance vocal music

Khachaturian Aram Ilich (1903–1978) Armenian composer who used folk themes in works such as *Sabre Dance*

Kodály Zoltán (1882–1967) Hungarian composer whose works include the cantata *Psalmus Hungaricus* and a comic opera *Háry János*

Lehár Franz (1870–1948) Hungarian composer whose many operettas include *Die Lustige Witwe/The Merry Widow* and *Das Land des Lächelns/The Land of Smiles*

Leoncavallo Ruggiero (1858–1919) Italian operatic composer whose works include *I Pagliacci/The Strolling Players* and *Zaza*

Ligeti György Sándor (1923–   ) Hungarian-born Austrian composer who has developed a highly chromatic polyphonic style in his works

Liszt Franz (1811–1886) Hungarian keyboard virtuoso and composer who developed the symphonic poem

Luening Otto (1900–1996) US composer who pioneered compositions for instruments and synthesizer

Lully Jean-Baptiste (adopted name of Giovanni Battista Lulli) (1632–1687) Italian-born French composer who established French opera with such works as *Alceste*

Lutosławski Witold (1913–1994) Polish composer whose works are technically refined, yet remain expressive and lyrical

Mahler Gustav (1860–1911) Czechoslovakian-born Austrian composer and conductor whose melancholic style reaches full expression in the *5th Symphony*

Martinu Bohuslav Jan (1890–1959) Czech composer whose works include *Julietta* and *The Greek Passion*

Massenet Jules Emile Frédéric (1842–1912) French composer of operas, oratorios, and orchestral suites

Mendelssohn(-Bartholdy) (Jakob Ludwig) Felix (1809–1847) German composer whose works include the *Fingals Höhle/Fingal's Cave* overture and *A Midsummer Night's Dream*, from which comes the famous *Wedding March*

Messiaen Olivier Eugène Prosper Charles (1908–1992) French composer whose works include *Quatuor pour la fin du temps/Quartet for the End of Time*

Meyerbeer Giacomo (adopted name of Jakob Liebmann Meyer Beer) (1791–1864) German composer whose operas include *Robert le Diable/Robert the Devil* and *Les Huguenots/The Huguenots*

Morley Thomas (*c.* 1557–1602) English composer who wrote consort music, madrigals, and airs

Mozart (Johann Chrysostom) Wolfgang Amadeus (1756–1791) Austrian composer, child prodigy, and musical genius, whose vast output included over 40 symphonies and operas, including *The Magic Flute*

Mussorgsky Modest Petrovich (1839–1881) Russian nationalist composer whose operatic masterpiece is *Boris Godunov*

Nancarrow Conlon (1912–   ) US composer whose compositions experiment with mathematically derived combinations of rhythm and tempo

Nielsen Carl August (1865–1931) Danish composer whose works include the opera *Maskarade/Masquerade* and six programmatic symphonies

Nono Luigi (1924–1990) Italian composer whose works include *Suspended Song* and *Intolerance*

Nyman Michael (1944–   ) English composer whose music is characterized by the repetition of complex musical formulae

Offenbach Jacques (1819–1880) French composer who wrote light operas, such as *Orfée aux enfers/Orpheus in the Underworld*

Orff Carl (1895–1982) German composer whose music is characterized by sharp dissonances and percussion

Palestrina Giovanni Pierluigi da (*c.* 1525–1594) Italian composer and papal choirmaster whose many liturgical choral works had a great influence on later composers

Pärt Arvo (1935–   ) Estonian composer resident in Germany whose music fuses traditional and modern styles to express contemporary spirituality

Penderecki Krzysztof (1933–   ) Polish composer whose works include *Magnificat* and *Die schwarze Maske/The Black Mask*

Peri Jacopo (1561–1633) Italian composer whose opera *Euridice* established the operatic form

Poulenc Francis Jean Marcel (1899–1963) French composer and pianist whose works include the ballet *The Little Darlings*

Prokofiev Sergei Sergeievich (1891–1953) Soviet composer whose works include *Romeo and Juliet* and *Peter and the Wolf*

Puccini Giacomo (Antonio Domenico Michele Secondo Maria) (1858–1924) Italian composer whose popular operas include *La Bohème*, *Tosca*, and *Madam Butterfly*

Purcell Henry (*c.* 1659–1695) English court musician and organist at the Chapel Royal, London, whose works include the opera *Dido and Aeneas* and *The Fairy Queen*

Rachmaninov Sergei Vasilevich (1873–1943) Russian Romantic composer, conductor, and pianist whose works include three symphonies and four piano concertos

Rameau Jean-Philippe (1683–1764) French organist and composer whose *Traité de l'harmonie/Treatise on Harmony* established academic rules for harmonic progression

Ravel (Joseph) Maurice (1875–1937) French composer and pianist whose work is characterized by sensuousness, exotic harmonics, and dazzling orchestral effects, as in *Boléro*

Reich Steve (1936–   ) US composer whose Minimalist music employs simple patterns, as in *Music for Percussion and Keyboards*

Rimsky-Korsakov Nikolai Andreievich (1844–1908) Russian nationalist composer whose operas include *Pskovitianka/The Maid of Pskov* and *Snegurochka/The Snow Maiden*

Rossini Gioacchino Antonio (1792–1868) Italian composer and 19th century master of the comic opera, particularly noted for long and exciting overtures

Rubbra Edmund (1901–1986) English composer whose work includes 11 symphonies, chamber music, and songs

Saint-Saëns (Charles) Camille (1835–1921) French composer, pianist, and organist whose works include the orchestral *Le carnaval des animaux/Carnival of the Animals*

Satie Erik (Alfred Leslie) (1866–1925) French composer whose piano works include *Gymnopedies* and *Messe des pauvres/Poor People's Mass*

Scarlatti (Giuseppe) Domenico (1685–1757) Italian composer who wrote over 500 sonatas for the harpsichord

Scarlatti (Pietro) Alessandro (Gaspare) (1660–1725) Italian Baroque composer who wrote more than 100 operas that contributed to the development of the operatic genre, as well as hundreds of liturgical choral works

Schoenberg Arnold Franz Walter (1874–1951) Austro-Hungarian-born US composer who developed the 12-tone system of musical composition

Schubert Franz Peter (1797–1828) Austrian composer who combined Romantic expression of emotion with pure melody and is best known for his Lieder

Schumann Robert Alexander (1810–1856) German composer whose works include four symphonies, a violin concerto, and a piano concerto

Noteworthy Composers of Classical Music (*continued*)

Shostakovich Dmitri Dmitrievich (1906–1975) Soviet composer whose work includes 15 symphonies

Sibelius Jean Julius Christian (1865–1957) Finnish composer whose works include *En saga* and *Finlandia*

Skriabin or **Scriabin** Aleksander Nikolaievich (1872–1915) Russian composer and pianist whose works include *Prometheus* and *Bozhestvennaya poema/Divine Poem*

Stockhausen Karlheinz (1928–) German composer of avant-garde music whose major works include *Gesang de Jünglinge* and *Sirius*

Strauss Johann (Baptist) (1825–1899) Austrian conductor and composer of operettas and waltzes, including *An der schönen blauen Donau/The Blue Danube*

Strauss Richard (1864–1949) German Neo-Romantic composer best known for his symphonic poems, such as *Also sprach Zarathustra/Thus Spake Zarathustra*, and his opera *Der Rosenkavalier/The Knight of the Rose*

Stravinsky Igor (1882–1971) Russian-born French and US composer whose works include *The Firebird* and *The Rite of Spring*

Sullivan Arthur Seymour (1842–1900) English composer whose operettas with William Gilbert include *HMS Pinafore* and *The Mikado*

Tallis Thomas (*c.* 1505–1585) English composer whose works include *Tallis's Canon* and the 40-part motet *Spem in alium*

Tartini Giuseppe (1692–1770) Italian composer and violinist who composed numerous sonatas and concertos for strings

Tavener John Kenneth (1944–) English composer whose works, such as *Hymn to Athene*, show the influence of the Eastern Orthodox Church

Taverner John (*c.* 1490–1545) English organist and composer who wrote masses and motets in polyphonic style

Tchaikovsky Piotr Ilich (1840–1893) Russian composer whose works include *The Nutcracker* and *Romeo and Juliet*

Telemann Georg Philipp (1681–1767) German Baroque composer whose prolific output includes both instrumental and vocal music

Tippett Michael Kemp (1905–1998) English composer whose works include three operas, four symphonies, and compositions of choral music

Vaughan Williams Ralph (1872–1958) English composer and first nationalist composer since the 16th century, whose work includes nine symphonies and *Fantasia on a Theme of Tallis*

Verdi Giuseppe Fortunino Francesco (1813–1901) master of Italian opera whose works include *Otello* and *Falstaff*

Vivaldi Antonio Lucio (1678–1741) Italian Baroque composer whose prolific number of symphonies, sonatas, concertos, operas, and sacred music includes *The Four Seasons*

Wagner (Wilhelm) Richard (1813–1883) German composer of *The Ring Cycle* opera and founder of the Bayreuth Theatre

Walton William Turner (1902–1983) English composer whose works include *Façade* and *Belshazzar's Feast*

Weber Carl Maria Friedrich Ernst von (1786–1826) German composer who established the Romantic school of opera with *Der Freischütz/The Marksman* and other works

Webern Anton (Friedrich Wilhelm von) (1883–1945) Austrian composer whose constructivist aesthetic influenced the post-war generation of advanced composers

Weill Kurt Julian (1900–1950) German-born US composer who tried to evolve a new form of music theatre

Wolf Hugo (Filipp Jakob) (1860–1903) Austrian composer of late-Romantic Lieder whose works include *Mörike-Lieder/Mörike Songs* and *Italienisches Liederbuch/Italian Songbook*

Noteworthy Classical Musicians

Anda Géza (1921–1976) Hungarian-born Swiss pianist who excelled in sensitive performances, especially of Mozart, Brahms, and Bartók

Argerich Martha (1941–) Argentinian pianist who is admired in the Romantic repertory and in partnership with violinist Gidon Kremer

Arrau Claudio (1903–1991) Chilean pianist who was particularly respected as an individualistic interpreter of Beethoven and Romantic works

Ashkenazy Vladimir (1937–) Russian-born pianist and conductor who has excelled as a performer of Romantic Russian works

Badura-Skoda Paul (1927–) Austrian pianist and musicologist who has concentrated on the music of 18th-century Vienna

Bartók Béla (1881–1945) Hungarian pianist and leading composer of the 20th century, whose recordings still survive

© Polygram

Vladimir Ashkenazy

Bell Joshua (1967–) US violinist who made his debut in 1982; he has played both the standard repertory and modern works

Berman Lazar (1930–) Russian pianist who is known for his powerful interpretations of the Russian Romantic repertory

Biggs E(dward George) Power (1906–1977) English-born US organist who was the most influential performer of his generation

Bolet Jorge (1914–1990) Cuban-born US pianist who was particularly admired as an interpreter of Liszt

Brain Dennis (1921–1957) English horn player for whom several composers, including Britten and Hindemith, wrote concertos

Bream Julian (1933–) English guitarist and lutenist who studied with Segovia; he plays much modern music

Brendel Alfred (1931–) Austrian pianist who is highly respected, especially for his interpretations of the Classical-period repertory

Busch Adolf (1891–1952) German violinist and composer who founded the Marlboro School of Music in Vermont, USA, in 1950

Casals Pablo (1876–1973) Catalan cellist who was one of the great artists of this century; he was particularly famous for his interpretations of Bach

Chang Sarah (1980–) US violinist who made her debut at the age of eight with the New York Philharmonic Orchestra

Cortot Alfred (1877–1962) French pianist and conductor who was also influential as a teacher in Paris

Curzon Clifford (1907–1982) English pianist who received the greatest acclaim for his sensitive interpretations of Mozart, Schubert, and Brahms

Douglas Barry (1960–) British pianist who, since winning the 1986 Tchaikovsky Competition, has excelled in the standard repertory

Du Pré Jacqueline (1945–1987) English cellist admired especially for her interpretation of the Elgar concerto

Entremont Philippe (1934–) French pianist and conductor who has been noted for his beautifully shaped phrasing

Fischer Annie (1914–1995) Hungarian pianist whose career was built upon performances of Mozart, Beethoven, Schubert, and Brahms

(continued)

Noteworthy Classical Musicians (*continued*)

Fleischer Leon (1928–) US pianist whose career was devastated by an injury to his right hand; he made a return after 1981

Fodor Eugene (1950–) US violinist who came to fame in 1972 after winning the Paganini Competition

Fournier Pierre (1906–1986) French cellist who was renowned for his chamber-music playing; he also premiered several concertos

Galway James (1939–) Irish flautist who has played to popular acclaim on his 18-carat gold instrument

Gilels Emil (1916–1985) Russian pianist who is remembered for his convincing performances of Russian and Classical-period music

Goldberg Szymon (1909–1993) Polish-born US violinist and conductor who was noted especially for his performances of Mozart

Goodman Benny (1909–1986) US clarinettist, composer, and band leader who excelled both in jazz and classical music

Gould Glenn (1932–1982) Canadian pianist who specialized in the interpretation of Bach; he was also renowned for his eccentric personality

Greenhouse Bernhard (1916–) US cellist who is best known as a member of the Beaux Arts Trio

Grumiaux Arthur (1921–1986) Belgian violinist who was admired for his performances in Classical-period and modern music

Haimovitz Matt (1970–) Israeli cellist who has gained a name for his recordings of the Lalo, Haydn, and Saint-Saëns concertos

Harrell Lynn (1944–) US cellist who, after beginning his career as an orchestral player, turned soloist in 1971

Heifetz Jascha (1901–1987) Russian-born US violinist, a child prodigy, who became one of the great virtuosos of this century

Hess Myra (1890–1965) English pianist who was famous especially for her wartime concerts at the National Gallery

Hindemith Paul (1895–1963) German composer and violist who, as a performing musician, premiered the Walton Viola Concerto in London

Horowitz Vladimir (1904–1989) Russian, later US, pianist, who was one of the great virtuosos of the 20th century

Hurford Peter (1930–) English organist who has done much to promote the organ as a concert instrument; he is also an influential editor

Isserlis Steven (1958–) English cellist who is well respected for his interpretations of 20th-century music and the standard repertory

Kaplan Mark (1953–) US violinist who is known equally as a chamber music player and a soloist

Kempff Wilhelm (1895–1991) German pianist who was a thoughtful interpreter, particularly of Classical-period repertory

Kennedy Nigel (1956–) English violinist who is perhaps better known for his unconventionality than his characterful playing

King Thea (1925–) English clarinettist who has supported much 20th-century British music

Kipnis Igor (1930–) US harpsichordist who has had a wide and varied career; he is an expert in Baroque performance practice

Kissin Evgeny (1971–) Russian pianist who is probably the most promising virtuoso of his generation; he excels especially in Chopin

Kocsis Zoltán (1952–) Hungarian pianist who is a sensitive and powerful interpreter, particularly of Bach, Schubert, and Bartók

Kolisch Rudolph (1896–1978) Austrian violinist who knew Schoenberg, Berg, and Bartók; he gave first performances of their works

Kreisler Fritz (1875–1962) Austrian-born US violinist and one of the great artists of his era

Kremer Gidon (1947–) Russian violinist who is one of most respected players of our time in both the standard and modern repertory

Landowska Wanda (1877–1959) Polish harpsichordist who revived the popularity of the instrument in the modern age

Laredo Jaime (1941–) Bolivian-born US violinist who is best known as a chamber music player

Little Tasmin (1965–) English violinist active as both a soloist and chamber musician; she is best known for her interpretations of Beethoven

Lupu Radu (1945–) Romanian pianist who has concentrated on the 18th- and 19th-century repertory

Ma Yo Yo (1955–) US cellist whose rich, singing tone is unequalled among his contemporaries

Maisky Mischa (1948–) Latvian cellist who is noted for his intense, romantic playing

Marsalis Wynton (1961–) US trumpeter whose formidable technique has been noted in both classical music and jazz

Menuhin Yehudi (1916–) US-born British violinist, conductor, and teacher whose distinguished career has lasted over 70 years

Messiaen Olivier (1908–1992) French organist and leading avant-garde composer of the 20th century who was organist at La Trinité, Paris

Mutter Anne-Sophie (1963–) German violinist, one of the outstanding virtuosos of her generation in both standard and modern repertory

Ogdon John (1937–1989) English pianist who enjoyed both the standard and modern repertory; he was also active as a composer

Oistrakh David (1908–1974) Russian violinist who gave many first performances of concertos by Russian composers

Oistrakh Igor (1931–) Russian violinist, son of David Oistrakh, whose interpretations of the standard repertory are well respected

Paderewski Ignacy Jan (1860–1941) Polish pianist and statesman whose performances were renowned for their gripping emotion, if not for their technique

Perahia Murray (1947–) US pianist who has built his reputation upon well-crafted interpretations of Mozart and Beethoven

Perlman Itzhak (1945–) Israeli violinist who is one of the foremost virtuosos of our time

Piatigorsky Gregor (1903–1976) Russian-born US cellist who was most renowned for forming chamber music ensembles with great violinists and pianists

Pinnock Trevor (1946–) English harpsichordist and conductor who has been an exponent of 'authentic' performances of early music

Pleeth William (1916–) English cellist who is best known as a chamber musician and teacher

Pogoreli Ivo (1958–) Serbian pianist who possesses a formidable technique and control; he excels in the 19th-century repertory

Pollini Maurizio (1942–) Italian pianist who won the 1960 Chopin Competition and has since shown additional interest in modern music

Preston Simon (1938–) English organist who is famous as a virtuoso of the instrument

Rachmaninov Sergei Vasilevich (1873–1943) Russian pianist and late-Romantic composer whose awe-inspiring performances were captured on early recordings

Rampal John-Pierre (1922–) French flautist who has specialized in 18th-century music; he has also published a book on the subject

Richter Sviatoslav (1914–1997) Russian pianist whose magnificent technique and fine musicianship place him at the forefront of 20th-century artists

Rogé Pascal (1951–) French pianist who has been noted as a discerning interpreter of French composers

Rose Leonard (1918–1984) US cellist who was distinguished as a soloist, teacher, and orchestral musician

Rostal Max (1905–1991) Austrian-born British violinist who was one of the leading players of his day; he was also famous as a teacher

Noteworthy Classical Musicians (*continued*)

Rostropovich Mstislav (1927–) Russian cellist and conductor who is one of the greatest artists of this century

Rubinstein Arthur (1887–1982) Polish-born US pianist who undoubtedly ranks among the great figures of this century; he was particularly famous for his interpretations of Chopin

Schiff Heinrich (1951–) Austrian cellist and conductor who has engaged in a wide range of musical activities

Schnabel Artur (1882–1951) Austrian pianist whose thoughtful (if sometimes technically inaccurate) interpretations inspired a century's pianists

Segovia Andrés (1893–1987) Spanish guitarist, undoubtedly the greatest of this century, who made the guitar an accepted concert instrument

Serkin Rudolf (1903–1991) US pianist who was renowned for his intellectually rigorous interpretations

Shaham Gil (1971–) US violinist whose talents are best revealed in the Romantic repertory

Shankar Ravi (1920–) Indian sitar player who successfully brought the music of his native country to the West

Starker János (1924–) Hungarian-born US cellist who gained experience as an orchestral player before becoming a soloist

Stern Isaac (1920–) US violinist of Russian origin; he is one of the most musical and human of modern virtuosos

Stoltzman Richard (1942–) US clarinettist who has a wide repertory both as a soloist and ensemble player

Suk Joseph (1929–) Czech violinist, grandson of the composer Josef Suk and great-grandson of Dvořák

Szeryng Henryk (1918–1988) Polish-born Mexican violinist who was renowned for his interpretations of Bach and Beethoven

Szigeti Joseph (1892–1973) Hungarian-born US violinist who supported the cause of modern music, giving many important premieres

Tan Melvyn (1956–) Malaysian-born British keyboard player who has done much to bring the fortepiano to a wider audience

Tortelier Paul (1914–1990) French cellist who was noted for his individualistic temperament; he was also famous for his masterclasses

Tuckwell Barry (1931–) Australian-born British horn player who has inspired several contemporary composers to write for the instrument

Uchida Mitsuko (1948–) Japanese pianist who has specialized in Mozart; he has played and directed all of Mozart's concertos

Vanessa-Mae (stage name of Vanessa-Mae Vanakorn Nicholson) (1978–) Singaporean-born British violinist known for both her classical and pop performances

Watts André (1946–) US pianist who is best known as a performer of big Romantic works

Williams John (Christopher) (1942–) Australian guitarist and a sensitive performer

Zimerman Krystian (1956–) Polish pianist whose profound interpretations are put to best effect in the Romantic repertory

Zukerman Pinchas (1948–) Israeli violinist and violist who is well respected in the standard repertory, especially for his interpretation of Elgar's Violin Concerto

Noteworthy Opera Singers

Adam Theo (1926–) German bass-baritone and producer who is best known for interpretations of Wagner and 20th-century composers

Allen Thomas (1944–) English baritone who has been based at Covent Garden, London, since 1971; he is also active as a concert artist

Ameling Elly (1934–) Dutch soprano who is best known for her work in Lieder and oratorio, especially in Bach's cantatas

Anderson Marian (c. 1897–1993) US contralto who was the first black singer at the New York Metropolitan Opera

Baker Janet (1933–) English mezzo-soprano, one of the greatest of her generation, who concentrated on the Baroque opera and concert repertory

Bartoli Cecilia (1966–) Italian mezzo-soprano known mainly for her interpretation of Mozart's and Rossini's operas

Battle Kathleen (1948–) US soprano whose agile voice is especially well-suited to Baroque and Classical-period music

Björling Jussi (Johan Jonaton) (1911–1960) Swedish tenor whose repertoire was mainly Italian

Borg Kim (1919–) Finnish bass who, over his long career, has boasted a wide-ranging concert and operatic repertory

Brilioth Helge (1931–) Swedish tenor, formerly baritone, whose career has centred on Wagner's characters: Siegmund, Siegfried, Tristan, and Parsifal

Caballé Montserrat (1933–) Spanish soprano whose fine technique has been applied in a wide range of operatic roles

Callas Maria (adopted name of Maria Anna Sofia Cecilia Kalogeropoulos) (1923–1977) US soprano of Greek descent who is best remembered for her versatile and emotionally-charged operatic interpretations

Carreras José (1946–) Spanish tenor who was one of the most popular lyric tenors of his generation

Caruso Enrico (1873–1921) Italian tenor, the greatest of the early 20th century, whose voice has survived on early recordings

Curtin Phyllis (1921–) US soprano who, since retiring in 1984, has also become well respected as a teacher

Deller Alfred (1912–1979) English counter-tenor who, entirely self-trained, revived counter-tenor singing in the modern age

Dernesch Helga (1939–) Austrian soprano, later mezzo, who has excelled in Wagner's operas; her roles have included Brünnhilde and Isolde

Domingo Placido (1941–) Spanish tenor who is arguably the best lyric-dramatic tenor of our day; he boasts a formidable repertory

Evans Anne (1941–) English soprano whose beautiful, rich voice has been best applied to big Romantic roles, especially in the works of Wagner

Ferrier Kathleen (1912–1953) English contralto whose voice is still heard on many old recordings

Fischer-Dieskau Dietrich (1925–) German baritone, the outstanding Lieder singer of his generation, who was equally successful in opera

Garrett Lesley (1955–) English soprano whose versatile voice has been most effective in lighter operatic roles, including the works of Mozart and Handel

Gedda Nicolai (1925–) Swedish tenor of Russian descent whose operatic career has included an eclectic range of roles

Gorchakova Galina (1962–) Russian soprano whose career has been built on dramatic performances of 19th- and 20th-century opera

Hampson Thomas (1955–) US baritone with a wide operatic and concert repertory; he has a particular interest in Mahler

Hvorostovsky Dmitri (1962–) Russian baritone, active both as a recitalist and an opera singer, who made his debut in 1982

Jones Gwyneth (1936–) Welsh soprano who has excelled in the heavy Romantic roles of 19th-century opera

Kirkby Emma (1949–) English soprano who has applied her light, vibrato-free voice to early music, both in opera and recital

Langridge Philip (1939–) English tenor whose operatic interests extend from Monteverdi and Rameau to Schoenberg and Birtwistle

(continued)

Noteworthy Opera Singers (*continued*)

Lind Jenny (Johanna Maria) (1820–1887) Swedish soprano with a remarkable range, who was known as the 'Swedish nightingale'

Los Angeles Victoria de (1923–) Spanish soprano whose versatile operatic career has lasted half a century

Lott Felicity (1947–) English soprano who is best known for her operatic interpretations of Mozart and Richard Strauss

Ludwig Christa (1924–) German mezzo-soprano with a truly great voice who is perhaps best loved for her Richard Strauss and Mahler

McNair Sylvia (1956–) US soprano who has been successful in Classical-period opera and 'authentic' productions of Baroque works

Murray Ann (1949–) Irish mezzo-soprano who is highly regarded as a concert singer; her opera interests include Mozart

Nilsson Birgit (1918–) Swedish soprano, the greatest Wagnerian soprano of the century, known particularly for her Isolde and Brünnhilde

Norman Jessye (1945–) US soprano with a beautifully rich and flexible voice who has excelled in both opera and Lieder

Otter Anne Sofie von (1955–) Swedish mezzo-soprano who is highly regarded in Mozart's and Haydn's operas, as well as in concert repertory

Pavarotti Luciano (1935–) Italian tenor, arguably the greatest lyric tenor of our time; he has also helped bring opera to a wider audience

Pears Peter (1910–1986) English tenor who was the life companion and inspiration of the composer Benjamin Britten

Price Leontyne (1927–) US soprano, retired in 1985, who enjoyed singing in a variety of styles from Verdi to 20th-century music

Ramey Samuel (1942–) US bass-baritone whose operatic career has included a range of roles from Mozart and other composers

Rolfe Johnson Anthony (1940–) English tenor who has been closely associated with the English National Opera and Covent Garden, London

Schreier Peter (1935–) German tenor and conductor whose sensitive interpretations are well suited to Lieder and sacred works

Schwarzkopf Elisabeth (1915–) German soprano who is best loved for her operatic interpretations of Mozart and Richard Strauss

Shirley-Quirk John (1931–) English bass-baritone who is best known for creating several roles in the operas of Benjamin Britten

Sills Beverly (1929–) US soprano who first performed on radio at the age of three; she was director of the New York City Opera (1979–89)

Stade Frederica von (1945–) US mezzo-soprano whose operatic interests extend from Monteverdi to Richard Strauss and the 20th century

Sutherland Joan (1926–) Australian soprano, retired 1990, whose light coloratura voice was best loved in 18th- and 19th-century Italian opera

Tear Robert (1939–) Welsh tenor who created several roles in Britten's operas; he has also concentrated on other modern works

Te Kanawa Kiri (1944–) New Zealand-born British soprano who has been admired for the lyric beauty of her voice

Vickers Jon (1926–) Canadian tenor who was noted for his dramatic performances of Wagner and Verdi

Watts Helen (1927–) Welsh contralto who was best known as a singer of Lieder and oratorios, especially in the works of Mahler and Elgar

Noteworthy Classical Music Conductors

Abbado Claudio (1933–) Italian conductor who became music director of the Berlin Philharmonic in 1989, following Karajan's death

Ansermet Ernest (1883–1969) Swiss conductor and theoretician of music, originally a mathematician, who was particularly well-known for his interpretations of Stravinsky

Barbirolli John (1899–1970) English conductor who was an exponent of late Romantic music, especially the works of Elgar

Barenboim Daniel (1942–) Argentinian-born Israeli conductor and pianist with many interests ranging from opera to chamber music

Beecham Thomas (1879–1961) the first English conductor to gain international repute; he founded the Royal Philharmonic Orchestra in 1947

Bernstein Leonard (1918–1990) US conductor, composer, pianist, and teacher who endowed his performances with vigour and passion

Böhm Karl (1894–1981) Austrian conductor whose weighty interpretations were best suited to the works of Richard Strauss, Wagner, and Beethoven

Boulez Pierre (1925–) French conductor who, until the 1960s, was more famous as a leading composer of the avant garde

Leonard Bernstein

Boult Adrian (1889–1983) English conductor best known for his interpretation of late Romantic and modern music, especially Vaughan Williams

Davis Colin (1927–) English conductor, the first Briton to conduct at Bayreuth, who has also excelled in the modern repertory

Dohnányi Christoph von (1929–) German-born conductor who has specialized in modern music; he is the grandson of Hungarian composer Ernö Dohnányi

Dutoit Charles (1936–) Swiss conductor who is best known for building up the Montreal Symphony into a world-class orchestra

Fiedler Arthur (1894–1979) US conductor who founded the Boston Pops Orchestra in 1930

Fischer Ivan (1951–) Hungarian conductor who has excelled in both symphonic and operatic media; he is noted for his energy and precision

Fricsay Ferenc (1914–1963) Hungarian conductor who spent much of his life in the USA; he made a large number of recordings

Furtwängler Wilhelm (1886–1954) German conductor who was the greatest interpreter of Romantic composers, particularly Wagner, of his generation

Gardiner John Eliot (1943–) English conductor who has stressed the use of original instruments; he is noted for his vibrant and 'authentic' interpretations

Giulini Carlo Maria (1914–) Italian conductor who, in a limited repertory, has divided his time between opera and symphonic repertory

Haitink Bernhard (1929–) Dutch conductor best known for his long and close relationship with Amsterdam's Concertgebouw Orchestra

Noteworthy Classical Music Conductors (*continued*)

Hickox Richard (1948–) English conductor with a wide range of interests, particularly Baroque and operatic works

Hogwood Christopher (1941–) English conductor and harpsichordist who, since the late 1960s, has led the 'authentic' performance movement

Järvi Neeme (1937–) Estonian conductor who is best recognized for his performances of modern Russian works

Jochum Eugen (1902–1987) German conductor who is known for his many recordings of the 1960s and 1970s

Karajan Herbert von (1908–1989) Austrian conductor who excelled in Romantic interpretations; in recordings he is the leading conductor of his generation

Klemperer Otto (1885–1973) German conductor whose particularly broad, expansive interpretations were best suited to Romantic music

Koussevitzky Sergey (1874–1951) Russian-born US conductor who, as director of the Boston Symphony, commissioned many works from contemporary composers

Leinsdorf Erich (1912–1993) Austrian-born US conductor who was famous for his recordings of the 1960s and 1970s

Levine James (1943–) US conductor who has concentrated on operatic works and Mahler's symphonies

Maazel Lorin (1930–) French-born US conductor who first led the New York Philharmonic at the age of nine

Marriner Neville (1924–) English conductor who has concentrated on Baroque music, founding the Academy of St Martin-in-the-Fields

Masur Kurt (1927–) Silesian-born German conductor who has been admired for his interpretations of Beethoven and Bruckner

Mehta Zubin (1936–) Indian conductor best known for his work with the New York Philharmonic

Munch Charles (1891–1968) French conductor, also active in the USA, who helped found the Orchestre de Paris in 1967

Muti Riccardo (1941–) Italian conductor who has been successful in both operatic and orchestral music

Nagano Kent (1951–) US conductor who has excelled in his performances of opera

Norrington Roger (1934–) English conductor who has been an exponent of 'authentic' performance, especially in vocal music

Ormandy Eugene (originally Jenö Ormandy Blau) (1899–1985) Hungarian-born US conductor who was associated with the Philadelphia Symphony Orchestra for half a century

Ozawa Seiji (1935–) Japanese conductor who has spent most of his life in the USA, particularly with the Boston Symphony

Previn André (adopted name of Andreas Priwin) (1929–) German-born US conductor and pianist who has travelled widely and made many recordings

Rattle Simon (1955–) leading English conductor of his generation who has excelled in late 19th- and 20th-century works

Reiner Fritz (1888–1963) Hungarian-born US conductor who led many of the world's greatest ensembles in operatic and orchestral works

Shaw Robert (1916–) US conductor who has concentrated on non-operatic vocal music, especially music by Bach and Handel

Shostakovich Maksim (1938–) Russian conductor, the son of composer Dmitri Shostakovich, who has gained a name especially in opera

Slatkin Leonard (1944–) US conductor who has often been noted for his performances of modern music

Solti Georg (1912–1997) Hungarian-born British conductor and pianist who has excelled in every genre, including opera, symphony, and chamber music

Stokowski Leopold (1882–1977) US conductor who was extremely influential in the early years of the recording industry

Szell Georg (1897–1970) Hungarian-born US conductor who became the long-standing leader of the Cleveland Orchestra

Thomas Michael Tilson (1944–) US conductor and pianist who has supported modern music, in addition to the standard repertory

Toscanini Arturo (1867–1957) Italian conductor, one of the great figures of his era, who emigrated to the USA in order to escape the Nazis

Walter Bruno (1876–1962) German conductor, noted for his richly textured performances, who escaped to the USA in 1939

Wood Henry (Joseph) (1869–1944) English conductor and founder of the Promenade Concerts with Robert Newman

Popular Music

Noteworthy Rock and Pop Music Artists

Abba (1973–*c.* 1980) Swedish pop group

Allman Brothers Band (1968–) US southern-rock band led by brothers Duane and Gregg Allman

All Saints (1994–) English pop group whose songs include 'Under the Bridge' and 'Never Ever'

Ama Shola (1979–) English soul singer whose songs include 'You Might Need Somebody'

Amos Tori (1964–) US pop singer, songwriter, and pianist

Anderson Ian (1947–) Scottish lead singer, guitarist, and flautist for the bluesy, folk-rock band Jethro Tull, whose songs include 'Living in the Past'

Animals, the (1960–66; reformed in 1976 and 1983) English rock and rhythm-and-blues group whose songs include 'House of the Rising Sun'

Anka Paul (1941–) Canadian teen idol, pop singer, and songwriter whose songs include 'My Way'

Armatrading Joan (1950–) West Indies-born folk singer and songwriter

B-52s (1976–) US new-wave group

Bacharach Burt (1928–) US pop songwriter, composer, and arranger

Baez Joan (1941–) US folk singer and activist

Band, the (*c.* 1965–) Canadian-US rock band who also backed Bob Dylan

Bassey Shirley (1937–) Welsh cabaret singer

Beach Boys, the (1961–) US harmonizing surf-rock and pop band led by Brian Wilson whose songs include 'Good Vibrations'

Beatles, the (1960–70) the dominant English pop band of the 1960s whose popularity continues today

Beck Jeff (1944–) English rock guitarist; member of the Yardbirds

Bee Gees, the (1967–) British-Australian pop and disco vocal group whose songs include 'Massachusetts'

Belafonte Harry (1927–) US calypso singer and actor

Bennett Richard Rodney (1936–) English composer of jazz, film music, symphonies, and operas

Bennett Tony (1925–) enduring US pop singer and entertainer

(*continued*)

Noteworthy Rock and Pop Music Artists (continued)

Berry Chuck (1926–) US guitarist, singer, and songwriter who was the founder of rock music, and whose songs include 'Roll Over, Beethoven'

Blondie (1975–82) US new-wave band fronted by singer and songwriter Deborah Harry whose songs include 'Heart of Glass'

Blur (1989–) English band whose songs include *Song 2*

Bolton Michael (1953–) soul-inspired US pop singer

Bowie David (adopted name of David Robert Jones) (1947–) versatile English pop singer, songwriter, and actor whose songs include 'Space Oddity'

Boyzone (1993–) Irish pop group whose songs include 'Words'

Bread (1969–) US soft-rock band

Brel Jacques (1929–1978) Belgian balladeer and songwriter

Brown James (1933–) US rhythm-and-blues, soul, and funk singer, known as the 'Godfather of Soul', whose songs include 'Sex Machine'

Browne Jackson (1948–) US rock singer and songwriter whose songs include 'The Pretender'

Buffet Jimmy (1946–) US singer and songwriter of 'beach bum' music

Bush Kate (1958–) English pop singer, songwriter, and pianist whose songs include 'Wuthering Heights'

Byrds, the (1964–73) US influential folk- and country-rock band of the 1960s whose songs include 'Mr Tambourine Man'

Byrne David (1952–) Scottish-born singer, songwriter, composer, and film director who was lead singer for the US avant-garde group the Talking Heads, and whose songs include 'Psycho Killer'

Carey Mariah (1970–) US pop singer

Carpenters, the Richard (1946–) and Karen (1950–83) US pop duo whose songs include 'Close to You'

Chapin Harry (1942–1981) US folk singer and songwriter whose songs include 'Cat's in the Cradle'

Charles Ray (1930–) US pianist, singer, and songwriter of blues, soul, gospel, rock, and rhythm-and-blues

Chicago (1967–) US jazz-rock group whose songs include 'If You Leave Me Now'

Chumbawamba (1982–) English anarchic pop group who gained fame with the song 'Tubthumping'

Clapton Eric (1945–) English rock and blues guitarist, singer, and songwriter whose songs include 'Layla'

Clark (Harold) Gene (1941–91) US rock and folk singer, songwriter, and guitarist who was a founding member of the Byrds (1964–66)

Clash, the (1976–85) British new wave band influenced by punk, reggae, and rockabilly whose songs include 'Should I Stay or Should I Go?'

Cobain Kurt (1967–1994) US singer, songwriter, and guitarist for the grunge-rock band Nirvana whose songs include 'Smells Like Teen Spirit'

Cochran Eddie (1938–1960) US rock singer, songwriter, and guitarist whose songs include 'C'mon Everybody'

Cohen Leonard (1934–) Canadian poet, novelist, singer, and songwriter whose songs include 'Suzanne'

Cole Nat King (1919–1965) US pianist and balladeer whose songs include 'Unforgettable'

Collins Phil(lip) David Charles (1951–) English pop drummer, singer, songwriter, actor, and a member of Genesis whose solo songs include 'One More Night'

Como Perry (1912–) US pop singer and entertainer whose hits include 'Some Enchanted Evening'

Cooder Ry(land Peter) (1947–) US guitarist, singer, composer, and session musician

Cooke Sam (1935–1964) US soul and pop singer whose songs include 'You Send Me'

Cooper Alice (1948–) eccentric US rock singer and songwriter

Costello Elvis (stage name of Declan Patrick McManus) (1954–) English rock singer, songwriter, and guitarist whose songs include 'Oliver's Army'

Creedence Clearwater Revival (1967–72) US rock and rockabilly group led by Fogerty brothers Tom and John, whose songs include 'Bad Moon Rising'

Croce Jim (1943–1973) US folk-pop singer, songwriter, and guitarist

Crosby Bing (Harry Lillis) (1904–77) US crooner and actor

Crosby, Stills & Nash (1968–71) David Crosby, Stephen Stills, Graham Nash, US soft-rock group whose songs include 'Suite: Judy Blue Eyes'

Crow Sheryl (1962–) US Grammy-winning pop singer

Cure, the (1976–) English rock band fronted by Robert Smith whose songs include 'Friday I'm in Love '

Darin Bobby (stage name of Walden Robert Cassotto) (1936–1973) US rock idol, singer, songwriter, and actor

Dave Clark Five, the (1963–71) English pop group whose songs include 'Bits and Pieces'

Denver John (stage name of John Henry Deutschendorf) (1943–1997) US folk-pop singer, songwriter, and guitarist whose songs include 'Take Me Home, Country Roads'

Depeche Mode (1980–) English synth-rock group

Diamond Neil (stage name of Noah Kaminsky) (1941–) US pop singer and songwriter whose songs include 'I Should Have Known Better'

Diddley Bo (stage name of Ellas Bates McDaniel) (1928–) US blues-rock guitarist, singer, and songwriter whose songs include 'Who Do You Love'

Dion Celine (1968–) Canadian singer whose songs include 'Tell Him', a duet with Barbra Streisand

Dion & the Belmonts (1958–) US vocal group whose songs include 'The Wanderer'

Dire Straits (1977–) English rock band fronted by guitarist and lead singer Mark Knopfler whose songs include 'Brothers in Arms'

Domino Fats (Antoine) (1929–) influential US rock-and-roll pianist and singer whose songs include 'Blueberry Hill'

Donovan (1946–) Scottish pop singer and songwriter whose songs include 'Mellow Yellow'

Doobie Brothers, the (1970–) US rock and rhythm-and-blues group whose songs include 'Long Train Running'

Doors, the (1965–73) psychedelic US rock band fronted by Jim Morrison whose songs include 'Light My Fire'

Dr Dre (stage name of Andre Young) (1996–) influential US gangsta rapper and founder member of NWA (Niggers With Attitude)

Duran Duran (1978–) English synth-pop band, led by singer Simon Le Bon, whose songs include 'Rio'

Dylan Bob (adopted name of Robert Allen Zimmerman) (1941–) US folk-rock singer, songwriter, and guitarist whose songs include 'Like a Rolling Stone'

Eagles, the (1971–81) US country-rock band led by Don Henley and Glen Frey whose songs include 'Hotel California'

Earth, Wind & Fire (1969–) US rhythm-and-blues and funk vocal group whose songs include 'Shining Star'

Estefan Gloria (1957–) Cuban-born Latin-American pop singer and songwriter

Eurythmics, the (1980–) English synth-pop duo of Annie Lennox and Dave Stewart whose songs include 'Here Comes the Rain Again'

Eternal (1992–) English soul group whose songs include 'I Wanna Be the Only One'

Everly Brothers, the Don (1937–) and Phil (1939–) US singers, songwriters, and guitarists whose songs include 'Bye Bye Love'

Fabian (adopted name of Fabiano Forte) (1943–) US teen idol and singer

Fagen Donald (1948–) US rock singer, songwriter, and musician who was a member of Steely Dan

Faithfull Marianne (1946–) English pop singer and teen star

Noteworthy Rock and Pop Music Artists (*continued*)

Ferry Bryan (1945–) English pop singer; lead singer of Roxy Music whose songs include 'Virginia Plain'

Fleetwood Mac (1967–) English blues-influenced rock group; members included Peter Green, Stevie Nicks, and Lindsey Buckingham

Fogelberg Dan (1951–) US pop singer and songwriter

Frampton Peter (1950–) English rock singer, songwriter, and guitarist who was a member of Humble Pie

Franklin Aretha (1942–) US soul singer who is known as the 'Queen of Soul', and whose songs include 'I Say a Little Prayer'

Gabriel Peter (1950–) English rock and pop singer and songwriter who was a member of Genesis (1966–75), and whose songs include 'Biko'

Gaye Marvin (1939–1984) US soul and pop singer and songwriter whose songs include 'Heard it Through the Grapevine'

Geldof Bob (1954–) Irish rock singer and leader of the Boomtown Rats (1975–86) whose songs include 'I Don't Like Mondays'

Gladys Knight & the Pips (1952–) US vocal group whose songs include 'Midnight Train to Georgia'

Glitter Gary (stage name of Paul Gadd) (1944–) English rock singer and songwriter, known as the 'King of Glam Rock', whose songs include 'I'm the Leader of the Gang (I Am)'

Go-Gos, the (1978–84) US all-female rock group fronted by Belinda Carlisle

Grateful Dead, the (1967–) US acid- and country-rock band known for live performances, led by Jerry Garcia (1942–1995)

Greco Juliette (1927–) French avant-garde singer of post-World War II Paris

Green Al (1946–) US soul and gospel singer and songwriter whose songs include 'Tired of Being Alone'

Guthrie Woody (Woodrow Wilson) (1912–1967) US folk and protest singer and songwriter whose songs include 'This Train is Bound for Glory'

Haley Bill (1925–1981) US singer, songwriter, and pioneer of rock music whose songs include 'Rock Around the Clock'

Hall & Oates Daryl Hall (Hohl) (1948–) and John Oates (1949–) US pop singers and songwriters

Hamlisch Marvin (1944–) US pianist, composer, arranger, and conductor

Hammer (Stanley Kirk Burrell) (1963–) US pop-rap vocalist, songwriter, and dancer whose songs include 'You Can't Touch This'

Hendrix Jimi (James Marshall) (1942–1970) US virtuoso rock guitarist, singer, and songwriter whose songs include 'Voodoo Chile'

Herman's Hermits (1963–) English pop group led by Peter 'Herman' Noone whose songs include 'Mrs Brown, You've Got a Lovely Daughter'

Hollies, the (1962–) English pop and rock group whose songs include 'He Ain't Heavy, He's My Brother'

Holly Buddy (stage name of Charles Hardin Holley) (1936–1959) influential US rock-and-roll singer and songwriter whose songs include 'Peggy Sue'

Houston Whitney (1963–) US soul and pop singer whose songs include 'I Wanna Dance with Somebody (Who Loves Me)'

Humperdinck Engelbert (1936–) English pop singer and entertainer whose songs include 'Release Me'

Hunter Ian (1946–) English rock singer and songwriter who was a member of Mott the Hoople

Ice Cube (stage name of O'Shea Jackson) (1969–) US rapper and member of NWA (Niggers With Attitude)

Idol Billy (stage name of William Broad) (1955–) English punk and rock singer; lead singer of Generation X, whose songs include 'Hot in the City'

Iglesias Julio (1943–) Spanish pop singer

Isley Brothers, the O'Kelly (1937–1986), Rudolph (1939–), and Ronald (1941–) US soul-rock singers

Jackson Joe (1954–) versatile English pianist of rock, new-wave, pop, reggae, and jazz styles whose songs include 'Steppin' Out'

Jackson Michael (1958–) US pop singer and performer whose songs include 'Thriller'

Jagger Mick (Michael Philip) (1943–) English singer and songwriter who is lead singer of the Rolling Stones

Jamiroquai (1992–) English jazz, funk, and pop group whose work includes 'Cosmic Girl'

Jefferson Airplane (later **Jefferson Starship**) (1965–) US psychedelic rock band associated with the counterculture movement of the 1960s; their songs include 'White Rabbit'

Joel Billy (1949–) US pop pianist, singer, and songwriter whose songs include 'Uptown Girl'

Johansen David (1950–) US singer and songwriter who created the Buster Poindexter persona and was lead singer of the New York Dolls

John Elton (stage name of Reginald Kenneth Dwight) (1947–) English pop singer, pianist, and songwriter whose songs include 'Rocket Man'

Elton John

Jones Rickie Lee (1954–) jazz-influenced US pop-rock singer and songwriter whose songs include 'Chuck E's in Love'

Jones Tom (stage name of Thomas Jones Woodward) (1940–) Welsh pop singer whose songs include 'Delilah'

Joplin Janis (1943–1970) US blues-rock singer whose songs include 'Piece of My Heart'

Journey (1973–) US rock group led by singer Steve Perry and guitarist Neal Schon

KC & The Sunshine Band (1973–) US disco band

King Carole (stage name of Carol Klein) (1942–) US composer, pop singer, and pianist whose songs include 'It's Too Late'

Kinks, the British pop-rock group led by the Davies brothers Ray (1944–) and David (1947–), whose songs include 'Waterloo Sunset'

Kiss (1972–) US glam-rock band whose songs include 'Crazy Nights'

Kristofferson Kris (1936–) US singer, songwriter, and actor whose songs include 'Help Me Make it Through the Night'

Kula Shaker (1995–) English rock group whose songs include 'Sound of Drums'

Kuti Fela Anikulapo (1938–1997) Nigerian singer, songwriter, and musician of big-band African funk whose songs include 'Mr Who Are You'

Led Zeppelin (1968–80) groundbreaking English rock band led by singer Robert Plant (1947–) and guitarist Jimmy Page (1945–), whose songs include 'Whole Lotta Love'

Lennon John Winston Ono (1940–1980) English rock singer, songwriter, and a member of the Beatles, who formed one of the most successful songwriting partnerships ever with Paul McCartney; his solo songs include 'Imagine'

Lewis Jerry Lee (1935–) US rock-and-roll pianist and singer whose songs include 'Great Balls of Fire'

Liberace (stage name of Wladziu Valentino) (1919–1987) flamboyant US pianist whose work includes *Rhapsody by Candlelight*

Lightfoot Gordon (1938–) Canadian folk-pop singer and songwriter whose songs include 'The Wreck of the Edmund Fitzgerald'

Little Richard (stage name of Richard Wayne Penniman) (1932–) US rock-and-roll singer and pianist whose songs include 'Tutti Frutti'

LL Cool J (James 'Ladies Love Cool James' Smith) (1969–) US rapper

Lowe Nick (1949–) English pop singer and songwriter whose songs include 'I Love the Sound of Breaking Glass'

(*continued*)

Noteworthy Rock and Pop Music Artists (*continued*)

Lynn Vera Margaret Lewis (1917–) English singer famous for World War II songs, including 'We'll Meet Again'

Lynyrd Skynyrd (1966–) US southern-rock band fronted by Ronnie Van Zant whose songs include 'Sweet Home Alabama'

McCartney (James) Paul (1942–) English rock singer, composer, and a member of the Beatles, who formed one of the most successful songwriting partnerships ever with John Lennon; he also founded Wings, and his songs include 'Yesterday'

Madonna (stage name of Madonna Louise Veronica Ciccone) (1958–) US pop singer, songwriter, and actress whose songs include 'Like a Virgin'

Makeba Miriam Zenzile (1932–) South African singer known as the 'Empress of African Song'

Mamas and the Papas, the (1965–) US folk-pop vocal group whose songs include 'California Dreamin''

Mangione Chuck (1940–) US jazz and pop flugelhorn-player and composer

Manic Street Preachers (1988–) Welsh multi-award-winning rock band whose work includes 'Everything Must Go' and 'Kevin Carter'

Manilow Barry (stage name of Barry Alan Pinkus) (1946–) sentimental US pop pianist, singer, and songwriter whose songs include 'Mandy'

Marley Bob (Robert) Nesta (1945–1981) Jamaican singer and songwriter who popularized reggae internationally, and whose songs include 'No Woman, No Cry'

Marriot Steve (1947–) English pop singer, guitarist, and lead singer of the Small Faces, whose songs include 'All or Nothing'

Mason Dave (1945–) English rock singer, songwriter, and member of Traffic

Mathis Johnny (1935–) US pop singer of romantic ballads

Mayall John (1943–) English blues and rhythm-and-blues performer who fronted John Mayall and the Blues Breakers

Michael George (1963–) (stage name of Georgios Kyriacos Panayiotou) English pop singer and songwriter who was a member of Wham!, and whose songs include 'Careless Whisper'

Miller Steve (1943–) US rock singer and songwriter whose songs include 'The Joker'

Mills Brothers Herbert (1912–), Harry (1913–1982), John (1889–1935), and Donald (1915–) US close-harmony vocal group whose songs include 'Lazy River'

Mitchell Joni (stage name of Roberta Joan Anderson) (1943–) Canadian confessional pop/folk singer, songwriter, and guitarist whose songs include 'Big Yellow Taxi'

Monkees, the (1966–) US pop group whose songs include 'Daydream Believer'

Moody Blues, the (1964–) innovative English rock band whose songs include 'Blue Guitar'

Morrison Van (George Ivan) (1945–) Northern Irish jazz- and soul-influenced rock singer and songwriter whose songs include 'Moondance'

M People (1991–) English dance group whose songs include 'Open Your Heart'

N'Dour Youssou (1959–) Senegalese singer, songwriter, and musician who combines African and electronic instruments, and whose songs include 'Xalis Money'

Nelson Rick(y) (1940–1985) US teen idol, pop singer, and actor whose songs include 'Hello Mary Lou'

Neville Brothers, the (1954–) US New Orleans-style rhythm-and-blues group whose songs include 'Bony Maronie'

Newman Randy Gary (1944–) US pop singer, satirical songwriter, and pianist whose songs include 'Gone Dead Train'

Newton-John Olivia (1948–) English-born Australian pop singer and actress whose songs include 'Heart Attack'

Nilsson Harry (stage name of Harry Edward Nelson III) (1941–1994) US singer and songwriter who wrote the soundtrack to *Midnight Cowboy*

Nirvana (1987–94) US rock band who popularized 'grunge' but were disbanded after the singer Kurt Cobain's death in 1994; their songs include 'Smells Like Teen Spirit'

Oasis (1994–) English pop group, featuring brothers Liam and Noel Gallagher, whose songs include 'Supersonic'

Ocean Colour Scene (1990–) English pop and rock band whose songs include 'The Riverboat Song'

O'Connor Sinead (1967–) Irish pop singer whose hits include the cover of the Prince song, 'Nothing Compares 2 U'

Orbison Roy (1936–1988) US pop balladeer and songwriter whose songs include 'Oh, Pretty Woman'

Paul Les (1915–) US guitarist and inventor of the solid-body electric guitar whose songs include 'Vaya con Dios'

Perkins Carl (1932–1998) US rockabilly guitarist, singer, and songwriter whose songs include 'Blue Suede Shoes'

Peter, Paul & Mary (1961–) Peter Yarrow, Paul Stookey, and Mary Travers, US folk-rock vocal group whose hits include the children's song 'Puff The Magic Dragon'

Piaf Edith (stage name of Edith Giovanna Gassion) (1915–1963) French cabaret singer and songwriter whose songs include 'La Vie en Rose'

Pickett Wilson (1941–) US soul, pop, and rhythm-and-blues singer whose songs include 'In the Midnight Hour'

Pink Floyd (1965–) British psychedelic rock group whose songs include 'Shine on You Crazy Diamond'

Platters, the (1954–67) US pop vocal group whose songs include 'Twilight Time'

Pop Iggy (stage name of James Newell Osterberg) (1947–) US rock singer and songwriter, whose songs include 'The Passenger', and lead singer of proto-punk band the Stooges (1967–74)

Presley Elvis Aron (1935–1977) influential US rock singer who is known as 'The King of Rock 'n' Roll'

Pretenders, the (1978–) English rock group fronted by American lead singer Chrissie Hynde, whose songs include '2,000 Miles'

Prince (Prince Rogers Nelson) (1958–) US pop musician, singer, composer, and producer whose songs include '1999'

Prodigy (1990–) English dance group whose songs include 'Firestarter' and 'Breathe'

Public Enemy influential US rap group lead by Chuck D (Carlton Ridenhauer)

Puff Daddy US rap artist whose songs include 'No Way Out'

Queen (1971–91) theatrical English rock group known for layered vocals, who were fronted by Freddie Mercury, and whose songs include 'Bohemian Rhapsody'

Radiohead (1987–) English band whose songs include 'Creep' and 'Paranoid Android'

Raitt Bonnie (1949–) US blues-rock singer and guitarist

Ramones, the (1974–96) influential US punk group whose songs include 'Do You Remember Rock 'n' Roll Radio?'

Rawls Lou (1935–) jazz-influenced US soul singer whose songs include 'You'll Never Find Another Love Like Mine'

Redding Otis (1941–1967) US soul singer and songwriter whose songs include 'Sittin' on the Dock of the Bay'

Reddy Helen (1941–) Australian-born pop singer whose songs include 'I am Woman'

Reed Lou (1944–) US rock singer, songwriter, and guitarist who was a member of avant-garde group the Velvet Underground, and whose solo songs include 'Walk on the Wild Side'

REM (1980–) US rock band fronted by lead singer Michael Stipe, whose songs include 'Nightswimming'

Richard Cliff (stage name of Harry Roger Webb) (1940–) English pop singer and star of musical films, whose songs include 'Livin' Doll'

Noteworthy Rock and Pop Music Artists (*continued*)

Richie Lionel (1949–) US soul-pop saxophonist, pianist, singer, songwriter, and a member of the Commodores, whose solo songs include 'Hello'

Righteous Brothers, the (1962–) Bill Medley and Bobby Hatfield, US soul duo whose songs include 'You've Lost that Lovin' Feelin''

Robinson Smokey (William) (1940–) US soul and pop singer and songwriter, lead singer of the Miracles, whose songs include 'The Tears of a Clown'

Rolling Stones, the (1962–) English rock-and-roll institution led by singer Mick Jagger (1943–) and Keith Richards (1943–), whose songs include 'Satisfaction'

Ronstadt Linda (Maria) (1946–) versatile US country-rock singer whose songs include 'You're No Good'

Ross Diana (stage name of Diane Earle) (1944–) silk-voiced US pop singer who was a member of the Supremes, and whose solo songs include 'Upside Down'

Ruffin David (1941–1991) US pop singer and lead baritone for the Temptations, whose songs include 'What Becomes of the Brokenhearted'

Run-DMC (1983–) US rap pioneers

Rush (1969–) Canadian rock band led by Geddy Lee

Santana Carlos (1947–) Mexican-born US Latin-rock and jazz-fusion guitarist and singer whose songs include 'Soul Sacrifice'

Sedaka Neil (1939–) US pop singer, songwriter, and pianist whose songs include 'Calendar Girl'

Seeger Pete(r) (1919–) US folk singer and protest songwriter whose songs include 'The Lion Sleeps Tonight'

Sex Pistols, the (1975–78, 1996–) English punk group led by sneering singer Johnny Rotten (John Lydon) whose songs include 'Anarchy in the UK'

Shore Dinah (Frances Rose) (1917–1994) US pop singer, actress, and television talk-show hostess

Simon Carly (1945–) US pop singer and songwriter whose songs include 'You're So Vain'

Simon Paul (1942–) US pop singer and songwriter who was a member of folk-rock duo Simon and Garfunkel, and whose solo songs include 'You Can Call Me Al'

Simple Minds (1977–) Scottish rock band fronted by Jim Kerr, whose songs include 'Don't You (Forget about Me)'

Sinatra Frank (Francis) Albert (1915–1998) US pop singer, entertainer, and film actor

Smith Patti (1946–) US poet, influential new-wave rock singer, and songwriter whose songs include 'Because the Night'

Smiths, the (1982–87) UK quartet fronted by Morrissey (stage name of Steven Patrick Morrisset) (1959–) and guitarist Johnny Marr (1959–), whose songs include 'What Difference Does it Make?'

Spice Girls (1996–) British vocal pop quintet whose debut single 'Wannabe' was a simultaneous number one hit in the US and UK charts

Springsteen Bruce (1949–) US rock singer, songwriter, and guitarist known as 'The Boss', whose songs include 'Born in the USA'

Stevens Cat (born Steven Georgiou, now Yusef Islam) (1947–) English singer and songwriter whose songs include 'Peace Train'

Stewart Rod (David) (1945–) English rock singer and songwriter who was lead singer of the Faces, and whose solo songs include 'Maggie May'

Sting (stage name of Gordon Sumner) (1951–) English pop singer, songwriter, bass player, and actor who was a member of the Police (1977–83), and whose solo songs include 'An Englishman in New York'

Streisand Barbra (1942–) US pop singer and actress

Summer Donna (stage name of Adrian Donna Gaines) (1948–) US disco and pop singer known as the 'Queen of Disco' whose songs include 'Last Dance'

Supremes, the (1959–76) Florence Ballard, Diana Ross, and Mary Wilson, US rhythm-and-blues and pop vocal group whose songs include 'Stop! In the Name of Love'

Taylor James (1948–) US soft-rock singer, songwriter, and musician whose songs include 'Fire and Rain'

Temptations, the (1960–) premiere US pop and soul vocal group whose songs include 'I Can't Get Next to You'

Texas (1989–) Scottish pop group whose songs include 'Black Eyed Boy' and 'Say What You Want'

Thompson Richard (1949–) English virtuoso guitarist, songwriter, and singer who was a member of folk-rock group Fairport Convention (1966–71), and whose songs include 'Valerie'

Thunders Johnny (stage name of John Anthony Genzale) (1952–1991) US rock guitarist, singer, and songwriter who was lead guitarist for glam-garage band the New York Dolls (1971–75)

Tone Loc (Anthony 'Antonio Loco' Smith) gravel-voiced US rapper

T Rex (1968–77) influential English glam rock band fronted by lead singer and songwriter Marc Bolan, whose songs include 'Ride a White Swan'

Turner Tina (stage name of Annie Mae Bullock) (1940–) US pop and rhythm-and-blues singer whose songs include 'River Deep, Mountain High'

Turtles, the (1965–70) US pop-rock group whose songs include 'It Ain't Me Babe'

UB40 (1978–) English reggae group whose hits include the cover of Neil Diamond's 'Red Red Wine'

U2 (1977–) Irish rock group fronted by Bono (Paul Hewson) and guitarist The Edge (Dave Evans), whose songs include 'With or Without You'

Vallee Rudy (Hubert Prior) (1901–1986) US crooner, actor, and leader of the Connecticut Yankees

Vandross Luther (1951–) US soul singer, songwriter, and producer

Van Halen (1974–) US rock band fronted by singer David Lee Roth (Sammy Hagar after 1985) and guitarist Eddie Van Halen, whose songs include 'Jump'

Velvet Underground, the (1965–75) influential US avant-garde rock band fronted by Lou Reed, whose songs include 'Venus in Furs'

Verve, the (1990–95; reformed 1997–) English pop group whose songs include 'Bitter Sweet Symphony' and 'The Drugs Don't Work'

Waits Tom (1949–) gravel-voiced, jazz-inspired US singer, songwriter, musician, and actor

Warwick Dionne (Marie) (1940–) US soul and pop singer

Wells Mary Esther (1943–1992) US pop and rhythm-and-blues singer whose hits include the Smokey Robinson song 'My Guy'

Westerberg Paul (1960–) US lead singer, songwriter, and guitarist for raucous, anti-establishment rock band the Replacements (1980–92)

White Barry (1944–) US soul singer, songwriter, pianist, and producer whose songs include 'Can't Get Enough of Your Love, Babe'

Who, the English rock group fronted by singer Roger Daltrey (1944–) and guitarist and songwriter Pete Townshend (1945–), whose songs include 'My Generation'

Williams Robbie (1974–) English pop singer and ex-member of pop group Take That; his songs as a solo singer include 'Old Before I Die'

Wonder Stevie (stage name of Steveland Judkins Morris) (1950–) US pop singer, songwriter, and versatile musician whose songs include 'Superstition'

Yes (1968–*c.* 1987) English progressive rock band fronted by Jon Anderson

Young Neil (1945–) Canadian-born rock and country-rock singer, songwriter, and guitarist whose songs include 'Like a Hurricane'

Young Paul (1956–) soul-inspired English rock singer whose songs include 'Love of the Common People'

Zappa Frank (1940–1993) US experimental rock musician, singer, and composer who founded the avant-garde group The Mothers of Invention, and whose biggest hit was 'Valley Girl'

Noteworthy Blues and Jazz Artists

Adderley Cannonball (Julian Edwin) (1928–1975) US jazz alto saxophonist

Armstrong Louis ('Satchmo') (1901–1971) US jazz trumpet and cornet player and scat singer

Bailey Mildred (1907–1951) US blues singer

Baker Chet (Chesney) (1929–1988) US jazz trumpet player

Baker Joséphine (1906–1975) US-born French blues singer and dancer

Baker LaVern (1928–1997) US jazz, blues, and pop singer

Barber Chris (1930–) English trombonist and pioneer of 'trad' jazz who formed the Chris Barber Blues and Jazz Band in the 1960s

Basie Count (William) (1904–1984) US jazz pianist and big-band leader

Bechet Sidney (1897–1959) US jazz soprano saxophonist and clarinetist

Beiderbecke Bix (stage name of Leon Bismarck) (1903–1931) US jazz cornetist, pianist, and composer

Benford Tommy (1906–1994) US jazz drummer

Berigan Bunny (Roland Bernard) (1909–1942) US jazz trumpet player and singer

Bigard Barney (1906–1980) US jazz clarinetist

Bilk Acker (stage name of Bernard Stanley Bilk) (1929–) English jazz clarinetist, popular during the 1960s for such hits as 'Stranger on the Shore'

Blackwell Ed (1929–1992) US jazz drummer

Blakey Art (Abdullah ibn Buhaina) (1919–1990) US jazz drummer and bandleader; leader of the Jazz Messengers

Blanton Jimmy (1921–1942) US jazz bassist

Bolden Buddy (Charles) (1868–1931) US jazz cornetist

Broonzy Big Bill (William Lee Conley) (1893–1958) US blues guitarist and singer

Brubeck Dave (David Warren) (1920–) US jazz pianist and composer, leader of the Dave Brubeck Quartet

Byas Don (Carlos Wesley) (1912–1972) US jazz tenor saxophonist

Calloway Cab(ell) (1907–1994) US jazz singer and bandleader at the Cotton Club

Carmichael Hoagy (Hoagland) Howard (1899–1981) US jazz pianist, singer, and composer

Carney Harry (1910–1974) US jazz baritone saxophonist

Carter Benny (Bennett Lester Carter) (1907–) US alto-saxophonist and trumpeter who also composed for Benny Goodman

Catlett Big Sid (Sidney) (1910–1951) US jazz drummer

Charles Ray (adopted name of Ray Charles Robinson) (1930–) US singer, songwriter, and pianist who has recorded blues, jazz, and a variety of other styles

Cherry Don (1936–1995) US jazz trumpet player

Christian Charlie (1919–1942) US jazz guitarist

Clarke Kenny 'Klook' (1914–1985) US jazz drummer

Clayton Buck (Wilbur) (1911–1991) US jazz trumpet player

Cohn Al(vin) Gilbert (1925–1988) US jazz tenor saxophonist and composer

Cole Cozy (William) (1909–1981) US jazz drummer

Coleman Ornette (1930–) US avant-garde alto saxophonist and jazz composer

Collins Albert (1932–1993) US blues guitarist, singer, and songwriter

Coltrane John William (1926–1967) innovative US jazz tenor saxophonist

Condon Eddie (1905–1973) US Dixieland jazz guitarist and bandleader

Corea Chick (Armando Anthony) (1941–) US jazz keyboard player

Dameron Tadd (Tadley) (1917–1965) US jazz pianist and composer

Dankworth John Philip William (1927–) English jazz musician, composer, and bandleader

Davis Lockjaw (Eddie) (1922–1986) US jazz tenor saxophonist

Davis Miles (1926–1991) US jazz trumpet player and a pioneer of bebop, cool, and jazz fusion styles

Davison Wild Bill (1906–1989) US Chicago-style jazz cornetist

Desmond Paul (1924–1977) US jazz alto saxophonist

Dickenson Vic (1906–1984) US jazz trombone player and composer

Dixon Willie (1915–1992) US blues bassist, songwriter, and pioneer of Chicago blues

Dodds Baby (William) (1898–1959) US Dixieland jazz drummer

Dodds Johnny (1892–1940) US jazz clarinetist

Domino Fats (stage name of Antoine Domino) (1928–) US rhythm and blues pianist and singer famous for 'Ain't That a Shame' and 'Blueberry Hill'

Dorsey Jimmy (1904–1957) US jazz clarinetist, alto saxophonist, and bandleader

Dorsey Tommy (1905–1956) US jazz trombone player and bandleader

Eckstine Billy (stage name of William Clarence Eckstein) (1914–1993) US jazz singer, bandleader, and trumpet player

Eldridge (David) Roy (1911–1989) US jazz trumpet player, drummer, and singer

Ellington Duke (Edward Kennedy) (1899–1974) US jazz pianist, bandleader, and composer

Evans Bill (1929–1980) US jazz pianist

Evans Gil (1912–1988) US jazz pianist, composer, and arranger

Fitzgerald Ella (1917–1996) lyrical US jazz vocalist, renowned for her scat singing

Freeman Bud (Lawrence) (1906–1991) US Chicago-style jazz saxophonist

Gaillard Slim (Bulee) (1916–1991) US jazz singer, songwriter, actor, and musician

Garbarek Jan (1947–) Norwegian avant-garde tenor saxophonist, renowned for fusing jazz with classical, folk, and ethnic elements

Garland Red (William M) (1923–1984) US jazz pianist

Garner Erroll (1921–1977) US jazz pianist and composer

Getz Stan (stage name of Stanley Gayetzby) (1927–1991) US tenor saxophonist, exponent of cool, bossa nova, and jazz fusion styles

Gillespie Dizzy (stage name of John Birks) (1917–1993) US bebop jazz trumpet player and composer

Goodman Benny (1909–1986) US jazz clarinetist and bandleader known as the 'King of Swing'

Gordon Dexter (1923–1990) US jazz tenor saxophonist

Grappelli Stéphane (1908–1997) French jazz violinist known for romantic improvization

Hackett Bobby (1915–1976) US jazz trumpet and cornet player

Hampton Lionel (1909–) US jazz bandleader and vibraphone, drums, and piano player

Hancock Herbie (1940–) US jazz pianist, composer, and arranger

Handy William Christopher (1873–1958) US blues composer known as the 'Father of the Blues'

Hawkins Coleman (c. 1901–1969) influential US jazz tenor saxophonist

Henderson Fletcher James (1897–1952) US jazz orchestra leader and arranger

Herman Woody (Woodrow Charles) (1913–1987) US jazz clarinetist, alto saxophonist, and bandleader

Higginbotham Jay C (Jack) (1906–1973) US jazz trombone player

Hines Earl Kenneth (Fatha) (1903–1983) US jazz pianist and songwriter

Hodges Johnny (1905–1983) US jazz pianist and songwriter

Holiday Billie (stage name of Eleanora Fagan) (1915–1959) US jazz singer

Noteworthy Blues and Jazz Artists (*continued*)

Hooker John Lee (1917–) US blues guitarist and singer

Hopkins Lightnin' (Sam) (1912–1982) US blues guitarist and singer

Howlin' Wolf (stage name of Chester Arthur Burnett) (1910–1976) US blues singer, songwriter, harmonica player, and guitarist

Humes Helen (1913–1981) US blues singer

Hunter Alberta (1895–1984) US blues singer, songwriter, and actress

Ibrahim Abdullah (originally known as Dollar Brand) (1934–) South African pianist and composer who fuses African rhythms and jazz

Jackson Mahalia (1911–1972) US gospel singer

James Elmore (1918–1963) US electric-slide blues guitarist, singer, and songwriter

Jarrett Keith (1945–) innovative US jazz pianist and composer

Jefferson Blind Lemon (1897–1929) US blues guitarist and singer

John Little Willie (William Edgar) (1937–1968) US blues singer and songwriter

Johnson Bunk (William Geary) (1879–1949) US jazz cornet and trumpet player

Johnson James P (1891–1955) US jazz pianist and composer

Johnson Robert (1912–1938) US blues guitarist, singer, and songwriter

Jones Jo (1911–1985) US jazz drummer

Jones Philly Joe (Joseph Rudolph) (1923–1985) US jazz drummer

Jones Thad (1923–1986) US jazz trumpet and cornet player

Joplin Scott (1868–1917) US ragtime jazz pianist and composer

Jordan Louis (1908–1975) US jazz singer and alto saxophonist

Kenton Stan (Stanley Newcomb) (1912–1979) progressive US jazz orchestra leader, pianist, and composer

King Albert (stage name of Albert Nelson) (1923–1992) US blues guitarist and singer

King B B (Riley B) (1925–) US blues guitarist and singer who has influenced rock music

Krupa Gene (1909–1973) US jazz drummer and band leader

LaFaro Scott (1936–1961) US jazz bass player

Laine Cleo (stage name of Clementina Dinah Campbell) (1927–) English jazz and scat singer who rose to fame singing with her husband Johnny Dankworth's jazz band

Lead Belly (stage name of Hudson (Huddie) William Ledbetter) (1889–1949) US blues guitarist and singer

Lee Peggy (stage name of Norma Deloris Egstrom) (1920–) US jazz singer famous for her smokey-voiced renditions of songs like 'Fever' and 'He's a Tramp'

Lewis John (1920–) US jazz musician and founder, in 1951, of the Modern Jazz Quartet whose distinctive style was characterized by Lewis on vibraphone

Lewis Mel (stage name of Melvin Sokoloff) (1929–1990) US jazz drummer and orchestra leader

Lunceford Jimmie (1902–1947) US jazz saxophonist and bandleader

Lyttelton Humphrey (1921–) English jazz trumpet player and bandleader

McLaughlin John (1942–) English jazz guitarist

McPartland Jimmy (James Duigald) (1907–1991) US jazz trumpet player

McRae Carmen (1920–1994) US jazz singer

Marsalis Branford (1960–) US jazz saxophonist

Marsalis Wynton (1961–) US jazz and classical trumpet player, bandleader, and composer

Metheny Pat (1954–) US jazz-rock guitarist

Miller (Alton) Glenn (1904–1944) US swing jazz trombone player and big-band leader

Mingus Charles (1922–1979) US jazz composer, pianist, bass player, and bandleader

Monk Thelonius (1917–1982) US bebop jazz pianist, composer, and bandleader

Montgomery Wes (John Leslie) (1923–1968) US jazz guitarist

Morton Jelly Roll (stage name of Ferdinand Joseph La Menthe) (1890–1941) US New Orleans-style jazz pianist, singer, and composer

Moten Bennie (1894–1935) US jazz pianist

Mulligan Gerry (Gerald) (1927–1996) US jazz baritone saxophonist and songwriter

Murphy Turk (Melvin) (1915–1987) US jazz trombone player and bandleader

Navarro Fats (Theodore) (1923–1950) US jazz trumpet player

Nichols Red (Ernest Loring) (1905–1965) US jazz cornetist and combo leader

Oliver Joe (Joseph) 'King' (1885–1938) US jazz cornet player and bandleader

Oliver Sy (Melvin James) (1910–1988) US swing jazz arranger, composer, and conductor

Ory Kid (Edward) (1886–1973) US jazz trombone player

Parker Charlie 'Bird' (also 'Yardbird') (1920–1955) US bebop jazz alto saxophonist, composer, and renowned improviser

Pass Joe (1929–1994) US jazz guitarist

Pepper Art (Edward) (1925–1982) US jazz alto saxophonist

Peterson Oscar (1925–) Canadian jazz pianist

Pettiford Oscar (1922–1960) US bebop jazz bassist

Powell Bud (Earl) (1924–1966) US modern jazz pianist

Puente Tito (Ernest Anthony) Jr (1923–) US Latin-jazz percussionist and bandleader

Pullen Don (1944–1995) US jazz pianist

Ra Sun (stage name of Herman P Blount) (1915–1993) US experimental jazz pianist, composer, and bandleader

Rainey Ma (stage name of Gertrude Melissa Nix Pridgett) (1886–1939) US blues singer

Redman Don (1900–1964) US jazz composer and arranger

Reed Jimmy (1925–1976) US Chicago blues guitarist and singer

Reinhardt Django (Jean Baptiste) (1910–1953) Belgian jazz guitarist and composer

Rich Buddy (Bernard) (1917–1987) US jazz drummer and bandleader

Rodney Red (stage name of Robert Roland Chudnick) (1928–1994) US jazz trumpet player

Rollins Sonny (Theodore Walter) (1929–) US 'hard bop' tenor saxophonist and jazz composer

Rosollino Frank (1926–1978) US jazz trombone player

Ross Annie (stage name of Annabelle Short Lynch) (1930–) English jazz singer who opened a jazz club, Annie's Room, in London in the 1960s

Rowles Jimmy (Charles) (1918–1996) US jazz composer and accompanist

Rushing Jimmy (James) (1902–1972) US blues singer

Russell Pee Wee (Charles) (1906–1969) US jazz clarinet player

Shaw Artie (stage name of Arthur Arshawsky) (1910–) US swing jazz clarinetist, bandleader, and composer

Silver Horace (1928–) US jazz pianist and tenor saxophonist who formed the Jazz Messengers with Art Blakey in 1953

Simone Nina (Eunice Waymon) (1933–) US jazz and blues singer

Sims Zoot (John Haley) (1925–1985) US jazz alto and tenor saxophonist and clarinetist

Singleton Zutty (Arthur James) (1898–1975) US Dixieland jazz drummer

Smith Bessie (1894–1937) US singer, the 'Empress of the Blues'

(continued)

Noteworthy Blues and Jazz Artists (*continued*)

Smith Pinetop (Clarence) (1904–1929) US 'boogie woogie' pianist and singer

Smith Willie 'The Lion' (1897–1973) US jazz pianist

Spanier Muggsy (Francis) (1906–1967) US jazz cornetist and bandleader

Strayhorn Billy (1915–1967) US jazz composer and pianist

Stitt Sonny (1924–1982) US jazz alto and tenor saxophonist

Tatum Art(hur) (1910–1956) technically brilliant US jazz pianist

Taylor Art (1929–1995) US jazz drummer and bandleader

Teagarden Jack (Weldon John) (1905–1964) US jazz trombone player and singer

Tormé Mel (1925–) US singer and song writer who worked with some of the great 1950s jazz bands, notable for his smooth style

Tough Dave (adopted name of David Jarvis) (1908–1948) US jazz drummer

Tristano Lennie (Leonard) Joseph (1919–1978) US jazz pianist and composer

Turner Big Joe (Joseph Vernon) (1911–1985) US blues singer who influenced early rock-and-roll

Vaughan Sarah Lois (1929–1990) US jazz singer of broad range

Vaughan Stevie Ray (1954–1990) US blues guitarist and singer

Venuti Joe (Giuseppe) (1903–1978) US jazz violinist

Walker T-Bone (Aaron Thibeaux) (1910–1975) US pioneer of the electric blues guitar

Waller Fats (Thomas Wright) (1904–1943) US jazz pianist, singer, and composer

Washington Dinah (stage name of Ruth Lee Jones) (1924–1963) US blues singer

Waters Ethel (1896–1977) US jazz and blues singer and actress

Waters Muddy (stage name of McKinley Morganfield) (1915–1983) US blues guitarist, singer, and songwriter

Watson Johnny 'Guitar' (1935–1996) US rhythm and blues guitarist

Webb Chick (William) (1902–1939) US jazz drummer and band leader

Webster Ben (1909–1973) US jazz tenor saxophonist

Whiteman Paul (1890–1967) US jazz orchestra leader

Williams Cootie (Charles Melvin) (c. 1908–1985) US jazz trumpet player and bandleader

Williams Mary Lou (1914–1981) US jazz pianist and composer

Wilson Nancy (1937–) US jazz singer who began her career singing with Cannonball Adderly and George Shearing and later fused her jazz style with popular music

Wilson Teddy (1912–1986) US jazz pianist and composer

Winding Kai (1922–1983) Danish-born US trombone player and composer

Witherspoon Jimmy (1923–97) US blues singer who made the transition to jazz in the 1950s and later became an inspiration to many younger musicians

Yancey Jimmy (1894–1951) US jazz pianist

Young Lester Willis 'the Pres' (1909–1959) US jazz tenor saxophonist and composer

Noteworthy Country Music Artists

Acuff Roy (Claxton) (1903–1992) US country music guitarist singer and songwriter

Arnold Eddy (1918–) US country music singer known as the 'Tennessee Ploughboy'

Atkins Chet (1924–) US country music performer and pioneer of the 'Nashville Sound'

Autry (Orvon) Gene (1907–) US country and western singer who popularized 'singing cowboy' films

Black Clint (1962–) US country music singer and songwriter

Brooks Garth (1962–) US country music and pop singer and songwriter

Bryant (Diadorius) Boudleaux (1920–1987) US country music singer and songwriter

Campbell Glen (1938–) US country music and pop singer and guitarist

Carson 'Fiddlin' John (1868–1949) US fiddle player and singer who popularized country music on the radio in the 1920s

Carter 'Mother' Maybelle (1909–1978), A P (1891–1960), and Sara (1898–1979) family of US country music singers

Cash Johnny (1932–) US country music singer, songwriter, and guitarist

Cline Patsy (adopted name of Virginia Patterson Hensley) (1932–1963) US country music singer

Dalhart Vernon (1883–1948) US country music singer

Flatt Lester (1914–1979) US country music singer and guitarist; member of the Foggy Mountain Boys

Foley Red (1910–1968) US country music singer

Ford Tennessee Ernie (Ernest Jennings) (1919–1991) US country music singer

Frizzell Lefty (William Orville) (1928–1975) US country music guitarist and singer

Gill Vince (1957–) US country music singer and guitarist; member of the Pure Prairie League

Haggard Merle (1937–) US country music singer and songwriter

Harris Emmylou (1947–) US country music singer

Hayes Kendall L (1936–1995) US country music songwriter

John Olivia Newton (1948–) English-born Australian singer who fused country and popular music

Jones George (1931–) US country music singer and songwriter

lang k(athryn) d(awn) (1962–) Canadian country music and pop singer

Lovett Lyle (1957–) US country music singer, songwriter, and musician

Lynn Loretta (stage name of Loretta Webb) (1935–) US country music singer

McEntire Reba (Nell) (1955–) US country music singer

Macon Uncle Dave (1870–1952) US country music banjo player and singer

Miller Jay D (1923–1996) US country music and cajun singer, songwriter, and producer

Miller Roger (1936–1992) US country music singer and songwriter

Nelson Willie (Hugh) (1933–) US 'outlaw' country music singer and songwriter

Parton Dolly (1946–) US country music singer and songwriter

Pierce Webb (1926–1991) US honky-tonk country singer and songwriter

Pride Charley (1938–) US country music singer

Reeves Jim (James Travis) (1923–1964) US country music singer

Rich Charlie 'Silver Fox' (1932–1995) US country music singer and songwriter

Ritter Tex (Woodward Maurice) (1907–1974) US country music singer and actor

Noteworthy Country Music Artists (*continued*)

Robbins Marty (stage name of Martin David Robinson) (1925–1982) US country music singer and songwriter

Rodgers Jimmie (James) Charles 'The Singing Brakeman' (1897–1933) US country music singer, songwriter, and guitarist who popularized yodelling

Rogers Kenny (Kenneth Donald) (1937–) US country singer and songwriter

Rose Fred (1898–1954) US country music singer, songwriter, and musician whose songs include 'Blues Eyes Cryin' in the Rain'

Sons of the Pioneers Len Slyle (1912–); Bob Nolan (1908–1980); Tim Spencer (1905–1974); Hugh Farr (1903–1980); Karl Farr (1909–1961); Lloyd Perryman (1917–1977) US country music singers and songwriters

Strait George (1952–) US country music singer and songwriter

Travis Merle (Robert) (1917–1983) US country music guitarist, singer, and songwriter

Travis Randy (stage name of Randy Bruce Traywick) (1959–) US country music singer and songwriter

Tubb Ernest (1914–1984) US country music singer

Tucker Tanya (1958–) US country and country-rock singer

Twitty Conway (stage name of Harold Lloyd Jenkins) (1933–1993) US country music singer and songwriter

West Dottie (adopted name of Dorothy Marie Marsh) (1932–1991) US country music singer and songwriter

Whitman Slim (Otis Dewey Whitman Jr) (1924–) yodelling US country music singer

Williams Hank Sr (1923–1953) US country music singer and songwriter whose songs include 'Your Cheatin' Heart'

Wills Bob (James Robert) (1905–1975) US country music fiddle player and composer who was a pioneer of 'Western Swing'

Wynette Tammy (stage name of Virginia Wynette Pugh) (1942–1998) US country music singer

Noteworthy Composers of Operettas, Musicals, and Popular Music

Adamson Harold (1906–) US composer who wrote Broadway revues, and whose songs include 'An Affair to Remember'

Arlen Harold (adopted name of Hyman Arluck) (1905–1986) US composer who, with various collaborators, wrote songs including 'Stormy Weather'; his Broadway shows include *St Louis Woman*

Bacharach Burt (1928–) US composer, pianist, conductor, and arranger who, with lyricist Hal David, wrote many songs, including 'I'll Never Fall in Love Again' and 'Raindrops Keep Fallin' on My Head' (1969 Oscar)

Barry John (adopted name of John Barry Prendergast) (1933–) English composer of film scores including those for *Out of Africa* and *Dances With Wolves*; he also composed the original James Bond theme

Berlin Irving (adopted name of Israel Baline) (1888–1989) Russian-born US songwriter whose works include the song 'White Christmas' and the musicals *Top Hat* and *Annie Get Your Gun*

Bernstein Elmer (1922–) US film composer and conductor who has written many film and TV scores, including those for *The Man with the Golden Arm*, Cecil B De Mille's *Ten Commandments*, and *Thoroughly Modern Millie*, for which he won an Oscar

Bernstein Leonard (1918–1990) US composer, conductor, arranger, and educator whose musicals include *On the Town* and *West Side Story*; he also wrote ballets and symphonies

Bock Jerry (1928–) US composer who collaborated with US lyricist Sheldon Harnick (1924–) on musicals such as *Fiddler on the Roof*

Boubil and Schönberg Alain Boubil (1941–) and Claude-Michel Schönberg (1944–) French musicians and composers whose works include *Les Misérables*, *Miss Saigon*, and *Martin Guerre*

Bricusse Leslie (1931–) English composer and lyricist who wrote songs, stage shows such as *Stop the World – I Want to Get Off*, and scores for films, including *Doctor Dolittle* and *Scrooge*

Carmichael Hoagy (Hoagland) Howard (1899–1981) US composer, pianist, singer, and actor whose songs include 'Stardust' and 'Georgia on My Mind'

Cohan George M(ichael) (1878–1942) US composer of the Broadway hit musical *Little Johnny Jones*; he was associated with popular patriotism through songs like 'You're a Grand Old Flag'

Coleman Cy (born Seymour Kaufman) (1929–) US composer and jazz pianist whose songs include 'Witchcraft' and 'If They Could See Me Now'

Coward Noël Peirce (1899–1973) English dramatist, actor, director, and composer whose musical works include the operetta *Bitter Sweet*

and songs such as 'Mad Dogs and Englishmen' and 'I'll See You Again'

Ellington Duke (Edward Kennedy) (1899–1974) US pianist who composed numerous pieces including 'Mood Indigo' and 'Solitude'

Fain Sammy (1902–1989) US composer, pianist, and singer whose songs include 'I'll Be Seeing You' and 'Love is a Many-Splendoured Thing'

Forrest Chet (George) (1915–) US composer and lyricist who collaborated with Robert Wright on Broadway scores

Friml Rudolf (1879–1972) Czech-born US composer and pianist whose operettas include *Rose Marie* and *The Three Musketeers*

Gershwin George (1898–1937) US composer whose collaborations with his brother Ira include 'I Got Rhythm' and 'They Can't Take That Away From Me'; he also wrote the opera *Porgy and Bess* and the orchestral work *Rhapsody in Blue*

Gilbert and Sullivan W(illiam) S(chwenk) Gilbert (1836–1911) and Arthur Seymour Sullivan (1842–1900) English composers who wrote operettas such as *The Pirates of Penzance* and *The Mikado*

Goffin and King Gerry Goffin (1939–) and Carole King (1942–) US song composers who had a string of successful hits in the 1960s, such as 'Will You Still Love Me Tomorrow?' and 'Take Good Care of My Baby'

Goldsmith Jerry (1929–) US film and TV composer and conductor whose film scores include *Stagecoach*, *Alien*, and *Basic Instinct*

Hamlisch Marvin (1944–) US composer and conductor who wrote scores to Broadway shows including *A Chorus Line* and films such as *The Sting*

Herbert Victor (1859–1924) Dublin-born US operetta composer whose Broadway scores include *Babes in Toyland*

Herman Jerry (1933–) US composer and lyricist who scored, among others, *Hello Dolly!* and *La Cage aux Folles*

Herrmann Bernard (1911–1975) US symphonic and film composer and conductor who composed several ballets, operas, and cantatas, but is most famous for his motion picture scores, ranging from *Citizen Kane* in 1941 to *Taxi Driver* in 1975

Jarre Jean-Michel (1948–) (son of Maurice Jarre) French composer of electronic music, notably his 'concept' album *Oxygene*

Jarre Maurice (1924–) French-born US film composer who wrote film scores for both French and English-language films, including *Lawrence of Arabia*, *Doctor Zhivago*, and *A Passage to India* – for all of which he won Oscars

Joplin Scott (1868–1917) US ragtime pianist and composer whose 'Maple Leaf Rag' was the first instrumental sheet music to sell a million copies; his music was successfully revived with the 1973 film *The Sting*

(*continued*)

Noteworthy Composers of Operettas, Musicals, and Popular Music (*continued*)

Kern Jerome (1885–1945) US composer whose scores include *Show Boat* and *Very Warm for May*; he also wrote various songs with different collaborators, including 'Ol' Man River'

Korngold Erich Wolfgang (1897–1957) Czech-born US film composer who wrote operas, violin and piano concertos, and sonatas, but is most famous for his work on the scores of Warner Bros films

Larsen Jonathan (1961–1996) US composer and lyricist whose only work, *Rent*, a contemporary rock opera derived from *La Bohème*, became a cultural phenomenon in the late 1990s

Legrand Michel Jean (1932–) French-born US composer, pianist, and arranger whose film scores include *The Thomas Crown Affair*, *The Go-Between*, and *Summer of '42*

Lehár Franz (1870–1948) Hungarian composer of operettas, such as *The Merry Widow*

Livingston Jay (Harold) (1915–) US composer who, with longtime collaborator US lyricist Ray Evans (1915–), wrote songs such as 'Qué Sera Sera' and the theme to TV's *Bonanza*

Lloyd Webber Andrew (1948–) English composer who wrote (with Tim Rice) lavish musicals such as *Evita*, *Cats*, and *Phantom of the Opera*

Loesser Frank (1910–1969) US composer and lyricist whose Broadway shows include *Guys and Dolls*

Loewe Frederick (1901–1988) German-born US composer who is best remembered for his collaborations with lyricist Alan Jay Lerner on shows such as *My Fair Lady* and *Gigi*

McHugh Jimmy (1894–1969) US composer, pianist, and publisher whose songs with various collaborators include 'On the Sunny Side of the Street' and 'I Can't Give You Anything But Love, Baby'

Mancini Henry (Enrico) (1924–1994) US composer whose works include *Breakfast at Tiffany's* and the theme to *The Pink Panther* films

Menken Alan (1950–) US composer who has written scores and songs for Disney, including *Beauty and the Beast*, *Aladdin*, and *The Hunchback of Notre Dame*

Morricone Ennio (1928–) Italian film composer whose prolific output includes *A Fistful of Dollars*, *The Mission*, and *Cinema Paradiso*

Newman Alfred (1901–1970) US composer, conductor, and pianist who has scored over 200 films including *All About Eve* and *Love Is a Many-Splendoured Thing*

Newman Randy (1943–) US songwriter whose works include 'I Think It's Gonna Rain Today' and 'Mamma Told Me Not to Come'

Novello Ivor (stage name of David Ivor Davies) (1893–1951) Welsh actor and composer of popular World War I songs and musical plays, such as *The Dancing Years*

Offenbach Jacques (Jakob Eberst) (1819–1880) German composer of light operetta, notably *La Belle Hélène* and *Tales of Hoffman*

Pomus and Shuman Doc (Jerome Solon Felder) Pomus (1925–1991) and Mort Shuman (1936–) US pop songwriting partners whose songs include 'Save the Last Dance for Me'

Porter Cole (1891–1964) US composer and lyricist who wrote sophisticated songs, primarily for the stage and films, including 'I've Got You Under My Skin' and 'Night and Day'

Rainger Ralph (1901–1942) US composer, pianist, and arranger who worked with various collaborators for Paramount in the 1930s, and whose songs include 'Thanks for the Memory'

Rodgers Richard Charles (1902–1979) US composer who collaborated with Lorenz Hart on musicals such as *Pal Joey*, and after Hart's death with Oscar Hammerstein II on many more musicals, including *Oklahoma!*, *South Pacific*, and *The Sound of Music*

Romberg Sigmund (1887–1951) Hungarian-born US composer and conductor who wrote chiefly operettas, such as *The Student Prince* and *Rosalie*

Rome Harold (1908–1993) US composer, lyricist, pianist, and artist whose Broadway scores include *Call Me Mister* and *Destry Rides Again*

Rozsa Miklos (1907–1995) Hungarian-born US composer, violinist, and conductor who was a child prodigy, and who later scored Hollywood films, including *Ben-Hur*

Schmidt Harvey (1929–) US composer who, with US lyricist Tom Jones, created the longest running stage musical in American theatre history, *The Fantasticks*

Schwartz Arthur (1900–1984) US composer, producer, and lawyer who wrote for film and TV, as well as Broadway shows, such as *The Band Wagon*

Simon Carly (1945–) US singer, author, and composer who wrote songs, such as 'You're So Vain', 'That's the Way I've Always Heard It Should Be', and 'The Right Thing to Do'; her film scores include *Heartburn*, *Working Girl*, and *This Is My Life*

Sondheim Stephen Joshua (1930–) US composer and lyricist who wrote the lyrics of Leonard Bernstein's *West Side Story*; his own musicals include *A Little Night Music*, *Sweeney Todd*, and *Sunday in the Park with George*

Steiner Max (Maximilian) Raoul (1888–1971) Austrian-born US film composer and conductor who scored more than 200 films, including *Gone With the Wind* and *Since You Went Away*

Stock, Aitken, and Waterman Mike Stock (1951–), Matt Aitken (1956–), and Pete Waterman (1947–) British songwriters and composers who produced a string of hits during the 1980s

Stoller Mike (1933–) US composer and record producer who collaborated with Jerry Leiber on many early classics, including 'Jailhouse Rock'

Strouse Charles (1928–) US composer whose main collaborator was US lyricist Lee Adams; their Broadway shows include *Shoestring*, *Bye Bye Birdie*, and *Golden Boy*

Strauss Johann the Younger (1825–) Austrian composer of waltzes, songs, and operettas, such as *Die Fledermaus*

Styne Jule (Julius) Kerwin (1905–1994) English-born US composer of songs, mainly for musicals and films, whose work includes the musicals *Gentlemen Prefer Blondes* and *Funny Girl*

Tiomkin Dimitri (1894–1979) Russian-born US film composer and music director who scored numerous films, including *High Noon* and *The Old Man and the Sea*

Vangelis (adopted name of Evangalos Odyssy Papathanassiou) (1943–) Greek composer of electronic-based music who rose to fame with the success of his scores for the films *Chariots of Fire* and *Bladerunner*

Van Heusen James (adopted name of Edward Chester Babcock) (1913–1990) US composer, publisher, and pianist whose songs include 'Swinging on a Star' and 'High Hopes'

Warren Harry (adopted name of Salvatore Guaragna) (1883–1981) US composer of stage and film songs and scores, including *42nd Street*, *Footlight Parade*, the *Gold Diggers* films, and 20th Century Fox's Betty Grable films

Waxman Franz (adopted name of Franz Wachsmann) (1906–1967) German-born US film composer who scored a number of films, including *Sunset Boulevard* and *Rear Window*

Weill Kurt (1900–1950) US classically-trained composer who collaborated with Bertolt Brecht on the modern operas *Little Mahagonny* and *The Threepenny Opera*

Williams John Towner (1932–) US composer and conductor who, after an early career as a jazz pianist and film and TV composer, became famous as a composer of symphonic film scores, including *Jaws*, the *Star Wars* trilogy, *E.T.*, and *Schindler's List*

Willson Meredith (adopted name of Robert Meredith Reiniger) (1902–1984) US composer, lyricist, conductor, and author who scored Chaplin's *The Great Dictator* and the Bette Davis film *The Little Foxes*

Noteworthy Composers of Operettas, Musicals, and Popular Music (*continued*)

Wright Robert Craig (1914–) US composer and lyricist who collaborated with George Forrest on Broadway scores, mainly based on classical works, such as *Song of Norway* (Grieg), *Magdalena* (Villa Lobos), and *Anya* (Rachmaninoff)

Wrubel Allie (1905–1973), US composer whose songs include 'As You Desire Me', 'Music, Maestro, Please', and 'Zip-a-Dee-Doo-Dah'

Yeston Maury (1945–) US composer, lyricist, and author who was associate professor in music at Yale; his Broadway musicals include *Nine*, *Phantom*, and *Titanic*

Youmans Vincent (1898–1946) US composer and producer who wrote shows such as *No! No! Nanette*, and whose songs include 'Tea for Two' and 'More Than You Know'

Young Victor (1900–1956) US composer, conductor, arranger, and violinist who wrote film scores, such as *For Whom the Bell Tolls* and *Around the World in 80 Days*

Noteworthy Lyricists

Adams Lee (Richard) (1924–) US lyricist whose main collaborator was US composer Charles Strouse; their Broadway shows include *Shoestring* and *Golden Boy*, and their songs together include 'Put on a Happy Face'

Bergman Marilyn Keith (1929–) and Alan (1925–) US lyricists who have written songs for revues, nightclubs, and films, including scores to Streisand's *A Star is Born* and *Yentyl*

Burke Johnny (1908–1964) US staff composer at Paramount in the 1930s and 1940s whose songs include 'Pennies From Heaven' and 'Swinging on a Star', and who collaborated with Jimmy Van Heusen on many songs for Bing Crosby

Caesar Irving (1895–1996) US lyricist who collaborated with George Gershwin and many others on 'Swanee' and 'Tea for Two'

Cahn Sammy (1913–1993) US lyricist whose career is noted for his long association with Frank Sinatra, including 'Come Fly With Me' and 'My Kind of Town'

Comden Betty (1919–) US lyricist who collaborated with Adolph Green on the films *Singin' in the Rain* and *Auntie Mame*; her songs include 'New York, New York' (with Leonard Bernstein)

David Hal (1921–) US songwriter who collaborated on some of the notable pop songs of the 1960s and 1970s, including 'I'll Never Fall in Love Again' and 'Raindrops Keep Fallin' on My Head' (1969 Oscar)

Dietz Howard (1896–1983) US songwriter who, primarily with composer Arthur Schwartz, wrote the Broadway shows *The Gay Life* and *Jennie* and songs including 'Alone Together' and 'That's Entertainment'

Ebb Fred (1936–) US lyricist who worked with US composer John Kander on shows such as *Cabaret* and *Chicago*; their most famous movie score was for *New York, New York*

Evans Ray(mond) B (1915–) US lyricist who, with longtime collaborator Jay (Harold) Livingston wrote songs, such as 'Buttons and Bows' and 'Qué Sera Sera', and the theme to TV's *Bonanza*

Fields Dorothy (1904–1974) US lyricist whose songs include 'On the Sunny Side of the Street' and 'The Way You Look Tonight' (1936 Oscar with Jerome Kern), and who also wrote Broadway musicals such as *Sweet Charity*

Gershwin Ira (1896–1983) US lyricist who chiefly collaborated with his brother George; the songs he wrote with other collaborators are 'My Ship' and 'The Man that Got Away'

Green Adolph (1915–) US lyricist who collaborated with Betty Comden

Hammerstein Oscar II (1895–1960) US lyricist who collaborated with Jerome Kern (*Show Boat*) and later with Richard Rodgers on seminal Broadway shows, such as *Oklahoma!* and *The Sound of Music*

Harburg E Y 'Yip' (Edgar) (1896–1981) US songwriter whose songs include 'Over the Rainbow' (1939 Oscar with Harold Arlen) and several Broadway musicals, such as *Ziegfeld Follies of 1934*

Harnick Sheldon (1924–) US lyricist who collaborated with US composer Jerry Bock on such Broadway musical scores as *Fiorello!* and *Fiddler on the Roof*

Hart Lorenz (Milton) (1895–1943) US librettist, closely associated with Richard Rodgers, whose shows include *A Connecticut Yankee* and *Pal Joey*, and whose songs include 'Blue Moon', 'The Lady is a Tramp', and 'My Funny Valentine'

Jones Tom (1928–) US lyricist who, with US composer Harvey Schmidt, created the longest-running stage musical in US theatre history, *The Fantasticks*; the team's other musicals include *I Do! I Do!*

Lane Burton (1912–) US lyricist who wrote songs for *Finian's Rainbow* and collaborated with Harold Arlen, Alan Jay Lerner, Richard Rodgers, Ira Gershwin, Frank Loesser, and Al Dubin

Leiber Jerry (1933–) US lyricist and record producer who collaborated with Mike Stoller on many early classics for Elvis Presley, including 'Jailhouse Rock' and 'Hound Dog'

Leigh Carolyn (1926–) US lyricist who wrote TV specials, such as *Heidi*, and Broadway scores, such as *Peter Pan*; her songs include 'Young at Heart'

Lerner Alan Jay (1918–1986) US lyricist who collaborated with Frederick Loewe on musicals such as *Paint Your Wagon* and *My Fair Lady*

Mercer Johnny (John H Emdon) (1909–1976) prodigious lyricist who won Oscars for 'Moon River' and 'Days of Wine and Roses' (both with Henry Mancini)

Rice Tim (Timothy Miles Bindon) (1944–) English lyricist who collaborated with Andrew Lloyd-Webber on *Joseph and the Amazing Technicolour Dreamcoat*, *Jesus Christ Superstar*, and *Evita*, and has more recently written for Disney films, Abba, and Cliff Richard

Robin Leo (1900–1984) US lyricist on stage, screen, and TV whose stage scores include *Gentlemen Prefer Blondes*, and whose songs include 'Thanks for the Memory' (1938 Oscar with Ralph Rainger)

Sager Carol Bayer (1946–) US lyricist and singer who wrote a number of the signature songs of the 1970s and 1980s, including 'Nobody Does It Better' and 'Arthur's Theme (Best That You Can Do)' (1982 Oscar with husband Burt Bacharach, Peter Allen, and Christopher Cross)

Washington Ned (1901–1976) US lyricist who wrote the film score to Disney's *Pinocchio* with Leigh Harline and the title song to the TV western series *Rawhide*

Webster Paul Francis (1907–1984) US lyricist who began in films in 1935 writing for Shirley Temple and later wrote scores for other films, including Doris Day's *Calamity Jane* (with Ray Heindorf)

Dance

Noteworthy Ballet Choreographers and Dancers

Alonso Alicia (born Alicia Ernestina de la Caridad dei Cobre Martínez Hoyo) (1921–) Cuban ballerina and director who became prima ballerina and director of the National Ballet of Cuba

Amboise Jacques d' (1934–) US dancer who created roles in many of George Balanchine's greatest works as a principal dancer with New York City Ballet

Angiolini Gasparo (pseudonym of Angelo Gasparini) (1731–1803) Italian choreographer who was one of the first to create dramatic ballets integrating music, dance, and story

Ashton Frederick William Mallandaine (1904–1988) English choreographer and dancer who was director of the Royal Ballet, London, (1963–70) and contributed to the worldwide reputation of British ballet

Balanchine George (born Georgi Melitonovich Balanchivadze) (1904–1983) Russian-born US choreographer who was the most influential 20th-century choreographer of ballet in the USA

Baryshnikov Mikhail Nikolayevich (1948–) Latvian-born dancer now based in the USA who joined the American Ballet Theater (ABT) as principal dancer partnering Gelsey Kirkland

Béjart Maurice (adopted name of Maurice Jean Berger) (1927–) French choreographer and ballet director who has staged huge spectacular productions, such as *Romeo and Juliet*

Beriosova Svetlana (1932–) Latvian-born British ballerina who danced with the Royal Ballet from 1952, excelling in *Ondine* and *Giselle*

Bessmertnova Natalya (1941–) Russian ballerina renowned for her interpretation of all the great classical roles who has appeared in ballets choreographed by her husband Yuri Grigorovich

Blasis Carlo (1795–1878) Italian ballet teacher whose celebrated treatise on the art of dancing forms the basis of classical dance training

Bournonville August (1805–1879) Danish dancer and choreographer who was director of the Royal Danish Ballet, for which he both danced and created ballets

Bujones Fernando (1955–) US ballet dancer who has danced leading roles in both the major classics and contemporary ballets, including *Swan Lake* and *Fancy Free*

Bussell Darcey Andrea (1969–) English ballerina who joined the Royal Ballet in 1988 and is particularly noted for her roles in George Balanchine's ballets

Camargo Marie-Anne de Cupis de (1710–1770) French ballerina who was the first ballerina to attain the 'batterie' (movements involving beating the legs together), previously danced only by men

Cecchetti Enrico (1850–1928) Italian ballet master who evolved a system of teaching that greatly improved the technical standards of the dance and is still widely used

Collier Lesley Faye (1947–) English ballerina who became a principal dancer of the Royal Ballet in 1972

Coralli Jean (originally Jean Coralli Peracini) (1779–1854) French dancer and choreographer who made his debut as a dancer in 1802

Cranko John Cyril (1927–1973) South African-born British choreographer who was a pivotal figure in the ballet boom of the 1960s, turning the Stuttgart Ballet into a world-class company

de Valois Ninette (adopted name of Edris Stannus) (1898–) Irish choreographer, dancer, and teacher, and one of the architects of British ballet, who set up the Vic-Wells Ballet in 1931 (later the Royal Ballet and Royal Ballet School) with choreographer Frederick Ashton

Diaghilev Sergei Pavlovich (1872–1929) Russian ballet impresario who founded the Ballets Russes/Russian Ballet, which he directed for 20 years, introducing and encouraging an array of dancers, such as Anna Pavlova and Vatslav Nijinsky

Didelot Charles-Louis (1767–1837) Swedish-born French choreographer, teacher, and dancer who taught in both London and St Petersburg, and devised over 50 ballets, notably *Zephyr Flora*, in which he pioneered the use of wires to lift dancers and create the illusion of flying

Dolin Anton (stage name of Patrick Healey-Kay) (1904–1983) English dancer and choreographer who was the first British male dancer to win an international reputation as a leading member of Diaghilev's company (1924–29) and guest soloist with the American Ballet Theater (1940–46)

Dowell Anthony James (1943–) English classical ballet dancer who was principal dancer with the Royal Ballet (1966–86) and its director from 1986

Eagling Wayne John (1950–) Canadian dancer who joined the Royal Ballet in London, becoming a soloist and a principal dancer before becoming artistic director of the Dutch National Ballet in 1991

Elssler Fanny (1810–1884) Austrian ballerina and choreographer noted for introducing elements of folk dance to the ballet; she was one of the first European ballerinas to tour the USA (in the 1840s)

Feld Eliot (1942–) US dancer, choreographer, and artistic director who formed the Eliot Feld Ballet in 1974 (now Ballet Tech) and started the New Ballet School for inner-city youngsters

Feuillet Raoul-Auger (c. 1675–1710) French dancer and teacher who devised a dance notation system *Choréographie ou l'art de décrire la danse/Choreography or the Art of Describing the Dance*, which was published in 1700

Fokine Michel (originally Mikhail Mikhailovich Fokin) (1880–1942) Russian-born US choreographer and dancer who was chief choreographer to the Ballets Russes (1909–14) and, with Diaghilev, revitalized and reformed the art of ballet

Fonteyn Margot (stage name of Margaret Hookham) (1919–1991) English ballet dancer who created many roles in Frederick Ashton's ballets and formed a legendary partnership with Rudolf Nureyev

Genée Adeline (stage name of Anina Margarete Kristina Petra Jensen) (1878–1970) Danish-born British dancer who was president of the Royal Academy of Dancing (1920–54)

Grey Beryl (1927–) English dancer who was prima ballerina with the Sadler's Wells Company (1942–57) and then artistic director of the London Festival Ballet (1968–79)

Guillem Sylvie (1965–) French ballerina, originally with the Paris Opera, and since 1989 principal guest artist of the Royal Ballet, who is noted for her extremely sinuous style of dance, which she has put to good effect in both classical ballets, such as *Manon* and *Romeo and Juliet*, as well as more innovative ballets, such as *In the middle somewhat elevated*

Helpmann Robert Murray (1909–1986) Australian dancer, choreographer, and actor who was the leading male dancer with the Sadler's Wells Ballet London (1933–50) and partner of Margot Fonteyn in the 1940s

Jeanmaire Renée ('Zizi') (1924–) French ballerina who performed with Petit's Les Ballets de Paris from the late 1940s and has also made several Hollywood films, including *Hans Christian Andersen*, with its ballet of 'The Little Mermaid'

Karsavina Tamara Platonova (1885–1978) Russian ballerina and leading light of Diaghilev's Ballets Russes (1909–22), who most famously partnered Nijinsky in ballets choreographed by Fokine, such as *Le Spectre de la rose*, *Petrushka*, and *Firebird*

Noteworthy Ballet Choreographers and Dancers (*continued*)

Kirkland Gelsey (1953–) US ballerina who joined the New York City Ballet and then the American Ballet Theater with Mikhail Baryshnikov

Kschessinska Mathilde (Mathilde-Maria Feliksovna Kshesinskaya) (1872–1971) Russian *prima ballerina assoluta* of the St Petersburg Imperial Ballet who was the first Russian ballerina to achieve 32 *fouettés* (a quick whipping movement of the raised leg)

Lifar Serge (1905–1986) Ukrainian dancer and choreographer who was artistic director and principal dancer of the Paris Opéra, completely revitalizing the company and reversing the diminished fortunes of French ballet

MacMillan Kenneth (1929–1992) Scottish choreographer who was director and then principal choreographer of the Royal Ballet, and whose works include *Romeo and Juliet* for Margot Fonteyn and Rudolf Nureyev

Makarova Natalia Romanovna (1940–) Russian ballerina who became one of the greatest international dancers of the ballet boom of the 1960s and 1970s

Markova Alicia (adopted name of Lilian Alicia Marks) (1910–) English ballet dancer who was the first resident ballerina of the Vic-Wells Ballet; a dancer of delicacy and lightness, she is associated with the great classical ballets, such as *Giselle*

Martins Peter (1946–) Danish-born US dancer, choreographer, and ballet director who was principal dancer with the New York City Ballet from 1969 and its director from 1990

Massine Léonide (adopted name of Leonid Fiodorovich Miassin) (1895–1979) Russian choreographer and dancer with the Ballets Russes who was a creator of comedy in ballet and also of symphonic ballet, using concert music

Mitchell Arthur (1934–1990) US dancer who was a principal dancer with the New York City Ballet, creating many roles in Balanchine's ballets, such as *Agon*

Mukhamedov Irek (1960–) Russian-born dancer who trained at the Bolshoi and then joined the Royal Ballet as a principal in 1990; he has demonstrated his power and athleticism in roles such as *Spartacus, Don Quixote*, and *Apollo*

Nijinska Bronislava (1891–1972) Russian choreographer and dancer who was the first major female choreographer to work in classical ballet, creating several dances for Diaghilev's Ballets Russes

Nijinsky Vatslav Fomich (1890–1950) Russian dancer and choreographer who was a legendary member of Diaghilev's Ballets Russes in ballets such as *L'Après-midi d'un faun* and *Le Spectre de la rose*

Noverre Jean-Georges (1727–1810) French choreographer, writer, and ballet reformer who is often considered the creator of modern classical ballet

Nureyev Rudolf Hametovich (1938–1993) Russian dancer and choreographer who is mainly associated with the Royal Ballet, London; as Margot Fonteyn's principal partner, he was one of the most brilliant dancers of the 1960s and 1970s

Park Merle Florence (1937–) Rhodesian-born English ballerina who joined the Sadler's Wells Ballet in 1954 and by 1959 was a principal soloist with the Royal Ballet

Pavlova Anna (1881–1931) Russian dancer who was one of the world's most celebrated exponents of classical ballet, influencing dancers worldwide with roles such as Michel Fokine's *The Dying Swan* solo

Perrot Jules Joseph (1810–1894) French ballet master and choreographer, one of the first great choreographers of the Romantic school, who devised Giselle's dances for the 1841 ballet; of his many ballets, he is best known for *Pas de quatre*

Petipa Marius (1822–1910) French choreographer who created some of the most important ballets in the classical repertory, such as *The Sleeping Beauty* and *Swan Lake*

Petit Roland (1924–) French choreographer and artistic director, generally considered the foremost figure in French ballet, who became an international star with his choreographic version of *Carmen*

Plisetskaia Maia Mikhailovna (1925–) Soviet ballerina and actress who became prima ballerina of the Bolshoi Ballet in 1945 and is noted for her fast spins, scissor-like jumps, and head-to-heel backward kicks

Rambert Marie (adopted name of Cyvia Myriam Rambam) (1888–1982) Polish-born British ballet dancer and teacher who was one of the major innovative and influential figures in modern ballet, founding and directing the Ballet Rambert

Robbins Jerome (1918–) US dancer and choreographer who was co-director of the New York City Ballet (1969–83) with George Balanchine and is considered the greatest US-born ballet choreographer

Saddler Donald Edward (1920–) US choreographer and dancer who, with Ballet Company NYC, danced *Swan Lake*; he was later artistic director of Harkness Ballet (1964–70)

Seymour Lynn (born Lynn Springbett) (1939–) Canadian ballerina who was made principal dancer of the Royal Ballet in 1959 and artistic director of the Munich State Opera Ballet (1978–80)

Shearer Moira (1926–) Scottish ballerina of great poise and beauty whose career in dance was brief, but who was immortalized in the great Powell and Pressburger ballet film *The Red Shoes* in 1948

Sibley Antoinette (1939–) English dancer whose roles include Odette/Odile in *Swan Lake*, and who formed an ideal partnership with Anthony Dowell

Somes Michael George (1917–1994) British ballet dancer, teacher, and *répétiteur* who was guardian of the Royal Ballet's Frederick Ashton repertoire and also an important long-time partner of Margot Fonteyn

Taglioni Marie (1804–1884) Italian dancer who was the first to use pointe work (dancing on the toes) as an expressive part of ballet rather than as sheer technique

Ulanova Galina Sergeyevna (1910–1998) Soviet dancer and prima ballerina of the Bolshoi Ballet (1944–62) who created the role of Katerina in Prokofiev's *The Stone Flower*

Vigano Salvatore (1878–1949) Italian choreographer and dancer whose dramatic ballets, dubbed 'coreodramma', were a synthesis of pantomime and dance

Noteworthy Modern Dance Choreographers and Dancers

Ailey Alvin (1931–1989) US dancer, choreographer, and director who formed the first truly multiracial modern dance company in 1958, and whose works include *Blues Suite*

Alston Richard (John William) (1948–) English Modernist choreographer whose pieces include *Bell High* and *Midsummer*

Amaya Carmen (1913–1963) Spanish Romany dancer who performed in public from the age of seven; her inspired, fiery, and passionate style made her a popular performer, especially in Argentina

Antonio (stage name of Antonio Ruiz Soler) (1921–1996) Spanish dancer, choreographer, and director who established a National Ballet Company in 1953 and is remembered primarily for his pure Spanish dance technique

Argentina La (stage name of Antonia Merce) (1890–1936) Argentine Spanish dancer, choreographer, and director who became one of the most famous exponents of Spanish dance and was also known for her castanet playing

Astaire Fred (adopted name of Frederick Austerlitz) (1899–1987) US dancer, actor, singer, and choreographer who starred in numerous films, including *Top Hat* and *Funny Face*

Bausch Pina (1940–) German avant-garde dance choreographer and director of the Wuppertal Tanztheater (dance theatre) from 1974 whose works include *Le Sacre du printemps/The Rite of Spring* by Igor Stravinsky

Bennett Michael (adopted name of Michael Bennet Difiglia) (1943–1987) seminal US Broadway choreographer of the 1970s and 1980s who won Tony Awards for *A Chorus Line*

Berkeley Busby (stage name of William Berkeley Enos) (1895–1976) US choreographer and film director famed for creating song and dance sequences that formed large-scale kaleidoscopic patterns when filmed from above, as in the *Gold Diggers* series

Bojangles (Luther Robinson) (1878–1949) US dancer and vaudeville star who developed the art of the soft-shoe shuffle, and whose tap dancing routines, in particular his famous *stair dance*, were the inspiration for many later dancers

Bolger Ray (1904–1987) US dancer who appeared as a specialty dancer in several films before attaining his signature screen role as the rubber-legged scarecrow in *The Wizard of Oz*

Brown Trisha (1936–) US dancer and choreographer who is one of the leading Post-Modernist choreographers, and who founded the improvisational Grand Union (1970–76). Her works include *Roof Piece*, *Accumulation*, and *Glacial Decoy*

Bruce Christopher (1945–) English choreographer and dancer who became artistic director of the Rambert Dance Company in 1992, and whose work includes *Ghost Dances*

Butcher Rosemary (1947–) English choreographer and dancer who is a leading exponent of the avant-garde; often performed in unorthodox settings, her pieces include *Flying Lines*

Champion Gower (1921–1980) US choreographer who won seven Tony Awards and later choreographed and directed *Hello Dolly!*

Clark Michael (1962–) Scottish avant-garde dancer who formed his own company in the mid-1980s and in 1991 played Caliban in Peter Greenaway's film *Prospero's Books* and premiered his *Mmm ... Modern Masterpiece*

Cohan Robert Paul (1925–) US choreographer who was the founding artistic director of the London Contemporary Dance Theatre (1969–89); his works include *Video-Life*

Cunningham Merce (1919–) US choreographer and dancer who is recognized as the father of Post-Modernist, or experimental, dance, liberating dance from its relationship with music; he formed his own avant-garde dance company and school in New York in 1953, and his works include *The Seasons*

Davies Siobhan Susan (1950–) English choreographer and dancer who was a founding member of the London Contemporary Dance Theatre; her Siobhan Davies Company was premiered during the 10th Dance Umbrella festival, and her other works include *Bridge the Distance*

Davis Sammy, Jr (1925–1990) US entertainer and dancer who starred in the Broadway show *Mr Wonderful*

Delsarte (François) Alexandre Nicolas Chéri (1811–1871) French music teacher and theoretician; at the Paris Conservatoire he devised a system of body movements designed to develop coordination, grace, and expressiveness; these movements greatly inspired modern dance

DeMille Agnes George (1909–1993) US dancer and choreographer who choreographed *Oklahoma!* and *Carousel*

Donen Stanley (1924–) US director who directed and choreographed musicals, such as *On the Town* (with Gene Kelly), *Seven Brides for Seven Brothers*, and *Singin' in the Rain*

Duncan Isadora (originally Angela) (1877–1927) US dancer who was a pioneer of modern dance and adopted an emotionally expressive free form, dancing to classic composers

Dunham Katherine (1910–) US dancer and choreographer who was noted for employing her extensive knowledge of anthropology as a basis for dance techniques and choreography

Fosse Bob (Robert) Louis (1927–1987) US dancer, choreographer, and director of such works as *Sweet Charity*, *Cabaret*, and *All that Jazz*

Gennaro Peter (1924–) US master of modern jazz movement in dance who choreographed *West Side Story* with Jerome Robbins

Glover Savion (1973–) leading African-American US dancer who appeared in *Tap* and won a Tony Award for choreographing *Bring in da Noise! Bring in da Funk!*, in which he starred

Graham Martha (1894–1991) US dancer, choreographer, teacher, and director who was regarded as the greatest exponent of modern dance in the USA, and who developed a distinctive vocabulary of movement designed to express inner emotion and intention

Hines Gregory (1946–) US dancer who won a Tony for *Jelly's Last Jam* and danced and starred with Baryshnikov in *White Nights* and with Sammy Davis Jr in *Tap*

Humphrey Doris (1895–1958) US choreographer, dancer, teacher, and one of the pioneers of modern dance; her movement technique was based on the shifting imbalance of weight; her work includes *The Shakers*

Jooss Kurt (1901–1979) German choreographer and teacher who attempted to synthesize ballet with modern dance in works such as *The Green Table*

Keeler Ruby (1909–1993) US singer and tap dancer famous for her dancing-singing routines in the classic backstage film *42nd Street* and other musicals of the 1930s, such as *Gold Diggers*, *Dames*, and *Go to Your Dance*

Kelly Gene (1912–1996) US actor, choreographer, dancer, and director who was a major star of a series of MGM musicals, including *On the Town*, *An American in Paris*, and *Singin' in the Rain*

Kidd Michael (1919–) US dancer, choreographer, director, and actor whose works include *Guys and Dolls*

Laban Rudolf von (1879–1958) Hungarian dance theoretician who is known as the leader of modern dance theory; he invented Labanotation – an accurate and detailed system of recording steps and movements – and also tried to order the principles of human motion into specific systems

Lee Gypsy Rose (Rose Louise Hovick) (1914–1970) US burlesque singer and dancer who perfected the art of striptease dance between the wars

Lubovitch Lar (1943–) US modern dance choreographer who founded the Lar Lubovitch Dance Company and was the first to use Minimalist music in works like *Marimba*

Lynne Gillian (her d.o.b. is a closely guarded secret, c. 1937–) UK choreographer of some of the most popular international stage musicals, including *Cats*, *Phantom of the Opera*, and *Aspects of Love*

Noteworthy Modern Dance Choreographers and Dancers (*continued*)

Mattox Matt (1921–) US jazz dancer and teacher who pioneered jazz dance in the USA and has appeared in many films, including *Seven Brides for Seven Brothers*

Morris Mark (1956–) US choreographer and dancer whose ballets merge various styles; he was artistic director of the Théâtre de la Monnaie in Brussels (1988–91) and is now the director of his own company in New York

Newson Lloyd (1954–) Australian avant-garde choreographer and dancer who is the co-founder and director of the DV8 Physical Theatre; his ballets are frequently provocative, such as *My Body Your Body*

Nicholas Fayard (Antonio) (1914–) and his brother Harold (1921–) African-American dance team who made over 30 films, notably *Pie Pie Blackbird*

Primus Pearl (1919–1994) US dancer, choreographer, and teacher who pioneered an awareness and understanding of the African-American tradition in dance and was awarded the National Medal of the Arts in 1991

Rand Sally Helen Gould Beck (1904–1979) US exotic dancer who worked in Chicago during the 1930s and developed her trademark nude-dance-with-ostrich-feathers routine

Rivera Chita (1933–) US dancer, actress, and singer who was nominated for six Tonys, the first for her role in *West Side Story*

Rogers Ginger (1911–1995) legendary US Hollywood musical star and dance partner of Fred Astaire in a series of classic 1930s musicals, including *The Gay Divorcee*, *Top Hat*, and *Shall We Dance?*

Ross Herbert (1927–) US choreographer who choreographed such Broadway musicals as *I Can Get It for You Wholesale* and such films as *Funny Girl*

Schlemmer Oskar (1888–1943) German choreographer, sculptor, painter, teacher, and designer who, during the 1920s, was a member of the Bauhaus school of artists, which influenced his choreography; his dances include *Triadic Ballet*

Sleep Wayne (1948–) English dancer who was a principal dancer with the Royal Ballet (1973–83); he then formed his own company, Dash, and in 1983 adapted his TV *Hot Shoe Show* for the stage; he also appeared in the musical *Cats*

Taylor Paul Belville (1930–) US choreographer and dancer whose works include *Aureole*, and who founded his own modern dance company in 1954

Tetley Glen (1926–) US choreographer and dancer who was the first to attempt the blending of ballet with modern dance idioms and whose works include *Pierrot lunaire* by Arnold Schoenberg

Tharp Twyla (1942–) US modern dance choreographer and dancer who fused many dance styles; her works, frequently set to popular music, include *Eight Jelly Rolls*

Tudor Antony (stage name of William Cook) (1908–1987) English choreographer, dancer, and teacher who was one of the founding choreographers for the American Ballet Theater in 1940, and whose works include *Romeo and Juliet*

Tune Tommy (Thomas) James (1939–) US Broadway choreographer, dancer, and director who danced in the film *Hello Dolly!* before choreographing and directing stage musicals, such as *The Club*

Wigman Mary (adopted name of Marie Wiegmann) (1886–1973) German dancer and choreographer who was noted for her solos exploring the darker melancholic sides of human nature

Stage, TV, and Film

Noteworthy Actors

Adjani Isabel (1955–) enigmatic French film actress who has been one of the leading performers in European cinema since the 1970s

Allen Woody (adopted name of Allen Stewart Konigsberg) (1935–) US film actor, writer, and director known for his comically neurotic screen persona

Arbuckle Fatty (adopted name of Roscoe Conkling Arbuckle) (1887–1933) US silent-film comedian, screenwriter, and director whose career was ruined by a sex scandal

Astaire Fred (adopted name of Frederick Austerlitz) (1899–1987) US actor, singer, and dancer who enjoyed a successful Hollywood career, frequently in partnership with Ginger Rogers

Auteuil Daniel (1950–) Algerian-born French film actor who first won international recognition for his performance in *Jean de Florette*

Bacall Lauren (adopted name of Betty Joan Perske) (1924–) US film and stage actress who rose to fame opposite her future husband Humphrey Bogart in *To Have and Have Not*

Bardot Brigitte (adopted name of Camille Javal) (1934–) French film actress who was a celebrated sex symbol of the 1950s and 1960s

Bassett Angela (1958–) US stage and screen actress who has established herself as one of the leading female performers of her generation, lending her characters a sense of moral strength and indomitability

Bates Alan (1934–) English actor who is a prolific and versatile performer on both the stage and screen

Béart Emmanuelle (1965–) French actress who was one of the leading French screen actresses of the 1980s and 1990s

Beatty Warren (stage name of Warren Beaty) (1937–) US film actor and director who established himself as a leading Hollywood player in such 1960s films as *Bonnie and Clyde*

Belmondo Jean-Paul (1933–) French actor who, with his performance in *A bout de souffle/Breathless*, established himself as an icon of post-war cinema

Bergman Ingrid (1915–1982) multiple Academy award-winning Swedish stage and screen actress who starred in several 1940s Hollywood classics, including *Casablanca* and *Gaslight*

Bernhardt Sarah (1844–1923) French actress celebrated for her performances at the Comédie Française in Paris

Binoche Juliet (1964–) French actress who has appeared in Krzysztof Kieslowski's *Three Colours* trilogy of films, as well as *The English Patient*

Bogarde Dirk (stage name of Derek Niven van den Bogaerde) (1921–) English actor and writer who gained international recognition for accomplished screen performances in the 1960s and 1970s in such films as *The Servant*

Bogart Humphrey DeForest (1899–1957) US film actor whose tough screen persona in such films as *Casablanca* and *The Big Sleep* established him as a cult figure of US cinema

(continued)

Noteworthy Actors (*continued*)

Branagh Kenneth Charles (1960–) Northern Irish actor, director, and writer who has won acclaim for his performances in a series of Shakespearean adaptations

Brando Marlon (1924–) Academy award-winning US stage and film actor who was an early exponent of the Method style of acting, winning acclaim for his performances in such films as *On the Waterfront* and *The Godfather*

Bronson Charles (adopted name of Charles Buchinsky) (1922–) US film actor known for his 'hard-boiled' screen persona

Brooks Louise (1906–1985) US film actress who remains an enduring icon of silent cinema

Brynner Yul (adopted name of Taidje Khan) (1915–1985) US theatre and film actor best known for his role in the stage and screen productions of *The King and I*

Burton Richard (stage name of Richard Walter Jenkins Jr) (1925–1984) Welsh stage and screen actor celebrated for his rich voice and imposing dramatic presence

Cagney James Francis Jr (1899–1986) US film actor who rose to fame in the 1930s with a series of comic, musical, and gangster roles

Caine Michael (stage name of Maurice Joseph Micklewhite) (1933–) prolific English film actor whose performance in *Alfie* established his reputation

Carlyle Robert (1961–) Scottish actor who gained prominence as a result of his roles in *Trainspotting* and *The Full Monty*

Chaplin Charlie (Charles) Spencer (1889–1977) English film actor and director who was one of the leading figures in US silent cinema

Christie Julie Frances (1940–) Indian-born English stage and screen actress who rose to prominence in the 1960s, winning an Academy Award for *Darling*

Cleese John Harwood (1939–) English comic actor who rose to fame as a member of the Monty Python team

Clift (Edward) Montgomery (1920–1966) US film and theatre actor who won international acclaim for a series of accomplished film performances in the 1940s and 1950s

Close Glenn (1947–) one of the leading US stage and screen actresses of the 1980s and 1990s

Colbert Claudette (stage name of Lily Claudette Chauchoin) (1903–1996) French-born US film actress who starred in a series of romantic comedies, including *It Happened One Night*

Connery Sean Thomas (1930–) Scottish film actor who gained fame as the first James Bond, and has gone on to enjoy a successful Hollywood career

Cooper Gary (Frank James) (1901–1961) US film actor who won Academy Awards for his performances in *Sergeant York* and *High Noon*

Costner Kevin (1955–) US film actor and director who won acclaim for his film *Dances with Wolves*

Coward Noël Peirce (1899–1973) English dramatist and actor known for his dry wit and sophistication

Crawford Joan (stage name of Lucille Fay Le Sueur) (1908–1977) US film actress who won an Academy Award for her eponymous role in *Mildred Pierce*

Crawford Michael (1942–) English actor and singer who has enjoyed a successful career on stage and in TV

Crosby Bing (Harry Lillis) (1904–1977) US actor and singer who enjoyed a popular screen partnership with comedian Bob Hope in the 'Road to' movies

Cruise Tom (adopted name of Thomas Cruise Mapother IV) (1962–) US film actor who established himself as one of the major box office attractions of the 1980s and 1990s

Cusack Cyril James (1910–1993) Irish actor who won international acclaim for his stage performances, notably in Beckett's *Krapp's Last Tape*

Davis Bette (Ruth Elizabeth) (1908–1989) US film actress best known for her dramatic roles in such films as *Jezebel* and *All About Eve*

Day Doris (stage name of Doris von Kappelhoff) (1924–) US film actress best known for her musical and comedy work in the 1950s and 1960s

Day-Lewis Daniel (1958–) English stage and screen actor who, since winning an Academy Award for *My Left Foot*, has enjoyed a successful career in Hollywood

Dean James (adopted name of James Byron) (1931–1955) US stage and film actor whose handful of film roles established him as an icon of teenage rebellion

de Filippo Eduardo (1900–1984) Italian actor and dramatist responsible for a series of celebrated comedies

De Havilland Olivia Mary (1916–) US film actress who specialized in dramatic roles in such films as *Gone With the Wind*

Delon Alain (1935–) French film actor who gained international recognition for his accomplished performances in European cinema of the 1960s

Dench Judi (Judith) Olivia (1934–) English actress of the stage and screen who has established herself as a leading Shakespearean performer and was awarded a 1998 BAFTA award for *Mrs Brown*

Deneuve Catherine (adopted name of Catherine Dorléac) (1943–) French film actress known for her elegant and graceful screen presence in films such as *Belle de Jour* and *Indochine*

De Niro Robert (1943–) US film actor who won two Academy Awards for *The Godfather Part II* and *Raging Bull*, establishing himself as one of the leading screen actors of his generation

Depardieu Gérard (1948–) French film actor who won international acclaim for his performances in such films as *Jean de Florette* and *Cyrano de Bergerac*

Depp Johnny (1964–) US film actor who has proved to be one of the most exciting talents to emerge in the cinema of the 1990s

DiCaprio Leonardo (Wilhelm) (1974–) US actor who rose to stardom through the films *Titanic* and *William Shakespeare's Romeo + Juliet*

Dietrich Marlene (stage name of Maria Magdalene Dietrich von Losch) (1901–1992) German-born US film actress who gained fame starring in a series of films directed by Josef von Sternberg

Douglas Kirk (stage name of Issur Danielovitch, later Isidore Demsky) (1916–) US film actor known for his dynamic, edgy performances in films such as *Lust for Life* and *Spartacus*

Du Maurier Gerald Hubert Edward (1873–1934) English stage actor who was the original Captain Hook in the first production of *Peter Pan* in 1904

Dunaway (Dorothy) Faye (1941–) US film actress who rose to prominence with accomplished performances in *Bonnie and Clyde*, *Chinatown*, and *Network*

Dunne Irene (1904–1990) US film actress who featured in a range of musicals, romantic comedies, and melodramas

Eastwood Clint(on) (1930–) US screen actor who rose to fame as the 'Man with No Name' in Sergio Leone's 1960s spaghetti Western trilogy

Elliott Denholm Mitchell (1922–1992) English stage and screen actor who specialized in playing eccentric, upper-class characters

Fairbanks Douglas Sr (stage name of Douglas Elton Ulman) (1883–1939) US film actor remembered for his acrobatic performances in the silent cinema of the 1920s

Fields W C (stage name of William Claude Dukenfield) (1880–1946) comic US actor who was one of the first stars of sound cinema in the 1930s

Fiennes Ralph (Nathaniel) (1962–) English actor who has appeared in *Schindler's List*, *Quiz Show*, and *The English Patient*

Noteworthy Actors (*continued*)

Finch Peter (William Mitchell) (1916–1977) Australian-raised English actor who won an Academy Award for his performance in *Network*

Finney Albert (1936–) English actor who rose to prominence in the 1960s, winning acclaim for his work both on the stage and in film

Flynn Errol (Leslie Thomson) (1909–1959) Australian-born US film actor who created an enduring swashbuckling screen persona in such films as *Robin Hood*

Fonda Henry (1905–1982) US film actor whose screen persona was founded on pioneering American ideals and moral rectitude, as in *Young Mr Lincoln* and *The Grapes of Wrath*

Fonda Jane (Seymour) (1937–) versatile US film actress who won Academy Awards for *Klute* and *Coming Home*

Fontaine Joan (stage name of Joan De Beauvoir De Havilland) (1917–) US film actress who won an Academy Award for her performance in *Suspicion*

Fontanne Lynn (1887–1983) US actress who, in partnership with her husband Alfred Lunt, won acclaim for her sophisticated comedy performances

Ford Glenn (stage name of Gwyllym Samuel Newton) (1916–) Canadian-born US film actor who starred in such Hollywood productions as *Gilda* and *The Big Heat*

Ford Harrison (1942–) US film actor who rose to international prominence as Han Solo in *Star Wars*, going on to feature in a series of Hollywood blockbusters

Formby George (1904–1961) English stage and screen actor who built his reputation as a ukelele-playing comedian

Foster Jodie (stage name of Alicia Christian Foster) (1962–) US film actress and director who established herself as one of the leading performers of her generation, winning two Academy Awards

Freeman Morgan (1937–) US film, stage, and TV actor who won acclaim for his performances in such films as *Driving Miss Daisy* and *Unforgiven*

Gabin Jean (stage name of Jean-Alexis Moncorgé) (1904–1976) leading French film actor celebrated for his accomplished performances in such films as *Pépé le Moko*

Gable (William) Clark (1901–1960) popular US film actor who remained a star for over 30 years, featuring in films as diverse as *It Happened One Night*, *Gone With the Wind*, and *The Misfits*

Garbo Greta (stage name of Greta Lovisa Gustafsson) (1905–1990) enigmatic Swedish-born US film actress whose career spanned both the silent and early sound eras

Gardner Ava (stage name of Lucy Johnson) (1922–1990) US film actress who rose to fame in such films as *The Killers* and *Mogambo*

Garland Judy (stage name of Frances Gumm) (1922–1969) US film actress and singer best remembered for her performance in *The Wizard of Oz*

Gassman Vittorio (1922–) Swiss-born Italian actor, and founder of the Italian Popular Theatre

Gibson Mel (1956–) US-born Australian film actor and director who became an international star after *Mad Max*

Gielgud John (1904–) English actor who has been a stalwart of both the stage and screen since the 1920s, earning a reputation as one of the great Shakespearean actors of the 20th century

Gish Lillian (stage name of Lillian Diana de Guiche) (1899–1993) US film and stage actress who featured in such landmark films as *The Birth of a Nation*

Sir John Gielgud

© Richard Watt

Grant Cary (stage name of Archibald Alexander Leach) (1904–1986) English-born US film actor remembered for his witty, debonair characters in such films as *The Awful Truth* and *North by Northwest*

Grimaldi Joseph (1779–1837) English actor and clown who lent his name, 'Joey', to subsequent generations of clowns

Guinness Alec (1914–) English actor who was one of the most versatile performers of his generation, enjoying a prolific career both on stage and in film

Guitry Sacha (1885–1957) French dramatist, actor, and film director known for his witty comedies

Hackman Gene (Eugene) (1931–) US film actor who won Academy Awards for his roles in *The French Connection* and *Unforgiven*

Hanks Tom (1956–) US film actor who won two Academy awards in the 1990s for his roles in *Philadelphia* and *Forrest Gump*

Harlow Jean (stage name of Harlean Carpenter) (1911–1937) US film actress remembered as a wisecracking sex symbol of the 1930s

Hardwicke Cedric Webster (1893–1964) English character actor who enjoyed a prolific career in both the UK and the USA

Harris Richard St Johns (1933–) Irish stage and screen actor who rose to fame in the 1960s in such films as *This Sporting Life*

Harrison Rex (Reginald Carey) (1908–1990) English theatre and film actor who made a career out of playing eccentric sophisticates

Hayworth Rita (stage name of Margarita Carmen Cansino) (1918–1987) US dancer and film actress remembered for her vivacious and erotic screen roles, as in *Gilda*

Hepburn Audrey (stage name of Edda van Heemstra Hepburn-Ruston) (1929–1993) Belgian-born British actress who rose to stardom with an Academy award-winning performance in *Roman Holiday*

Hepburn Katharine (1907–) leading US stage and screen actress who won 4 Academy Awards and was nominated on 12 separate occasions

Heston Charlton (stage name of Charles Carter) (1924–) US film actor who made his name starring in a series of biblical and historical epics

Hoffman Dustin (1937–) Academy award-winning US film actor who rose to fame with *The Graduate* and *Midnight Cowboy*, establishing himself as one of the most accomplished and versatile performers of his generation

Hope Bob (stage name of Leslie Townes Hope) (1903–) British-born US comedian and film actor who starred in the 'Road to' series of films with Dorothy Lamour and Bing Crosby

Hopkins Anthony Philip (1937–) Welsh stage and screen actor whose Academy award-winning performance in *The Silence of the Lambs* brought him to the attention of an international audience

Hopper Dennis (1936–) cult US film actor and director who won acclaim with *Easy Rider*

Hordern Michael Murray (1911–1995) English character actor who enjoyed a lengthy and well-respected stage and film career

Hoskins Bob (Robert) William (1942–) English stage and film actor who won international recognition in the 1980s with such films as *Mona Lisa*

Howard Leslie (stage name of Leslie Howard Stainer) (1893–1943) English actor acclaimed for his performances in *The Scarlet Pimpernel* and *Gone With the Wind*

Howerd Frankie (stage name of Francis Alex Howard) (1922–1992) English comic actor remembered for his rambling, suggestive monologues and his role in the TV series *Up Pompeii*

Hudson Rock (stage name of Roy Harold Scherer Jr) (1925–1985) US film star of the 1950s and 1960s who enjoyed success in a range of romantic comedies and melodramas

(continued)

Noteworthy Actors (*continued*)

Humphries (John) Barry (1934–) Australian actor and author best known for his comic role as Dame Edna Everage

Hunter Holly (1958–) versatile US film actress who won an Academy Award for her mute performance in *The Piano*

Irons Jeremy (1948–) English film actor who won international recognition in the 1980s and 1990s with films such as *Reversal of Fortune*

Jackson Glenda (1936–) English actress and politician who first won fame for her Shakespearean roles on stage and a series of film appearances in the 1960s and 1970s

Jacobi Derek George (1938–) English stage, film, and TV actor, best known for his Shakespearean performances and his eponymous role in *I, Claudius*

Jannings Emil (stage name of Theodor Friedrich Emil Janenz) (1884–1950) Swiss-born Austrian actor celebrated for his accomplished performances in films such as *Der letzte Mann/The Last Laugh*

Jolson Al (stage name of Asa Yoelson) (1886–1950) Russian-born US singer and actor who starred in Hollywood's first sound feature, *The Jazz Singer*

Keaton Buster (Joseph Francis) (1895–1966) US silent-film comedian and actor who was one of the great pioneers of early cinema

Keitel Harvey (1939–) prolific US film actor celebrated for his intense performances in *Mean Streets* and *Reservoir Dogs*

Kelly Emmett (1898–1979) US clown and circus performer best known for his 'Weary Willie' clown act

Kelly Gene (Eugene) Curran (1912–1996) US film actor, director, and dancer who is remembered for a series of colourful musicals, including *Singin' in the Rain*

Kelly Grace Patricia (1929–1982) US film actress who, before marrying Prince Rainier III of Monaco, was one of the leading Hollywood stars of the 1950s, featuring in such films as *High Noon* and *Rear Window*

Kerr Deborah Jane (1921–) Scottish film actress who rose to stardom in the British cinema before featuring in such Hollywood films as *From Here to Eternity*

Kingsley Ben (stage name of Krishna Banji) (1943–) British film actor who won an Academy Award for his eponymous role in *Gandhi*

Lancaster Burt (Burton) Stephen (1913–1994) athletic US film actor who won acclaim with his first screen role in *The Killers*

Laughton Charles (1899–1962) English film and theatre actor who had an imposing presence on both stage and screen

Lawrence Gertrude Alexandra Dagma (1898–1952) English actress who specialized in musical comedies

Lee Bruce (stage name of Lee Yuen Kam) (1941–1973) US 'Chinese Western' film actor who popularized oriental martial arts in the West with pictures such as *Enter the Dragon*

Leigh Vivien (1913–1967) English actress who won Academy Awards for her performances in *Gone with the Wind* and *A Streetcar Named Desire*

Lemmon Jack (stage name of John Uhler III) (1925–) award-winning US film actor who has proved an enduring favourite of US cinema, adept at both drama and comedy

Lewis Jerry (stage name of Joseph Levitch) (1926–) comic US film actor and director who enjoyed a lengthy screen partnership with Dean Martin

Lombard Carole (stage name of Jane Alice Peters) (1908–1942) US film actress who rose to stardom in such comedies as *Twentieth Century* and *My Man Godfrey*

Loren Sophia (stage name of Sofia Scicolone) (1934–) glamorous Italian film actress who won an Academy Award for *La Ciociara/Two Women*

Loy Myrna (stage name of Myrna Williams) (1905–1993) accomplished US film actress who enjoyed success in partnership with William Powell in a range of MGM comedies

Lunt Alfred (1893–1977) US actor who gained fame appearing on stage with his wife Lynn Fontanne in a series of sophisticated comedies

McGregor Ewan (Gordon) (1971–) Scottish actor who rose to fame in *Trainspotting*, and has also starred in *A Life Less Ordinary* and *Brassed Off*

McKellen Ian Murray (1939–) English actor who, as one of the leading Shakespearean players of his generation, won acclaim for his stage and film portrayals of Richard III in the 1990s

MacLaine Shirley (stage name of Shirley MacLean Beaty) (1934–) versatile US film actress who has featured in a range of comic, dramatic, and musical roles since the 1950s

McQueen Steve (Terrence Steven) (1930–1980) US film actor noted both for his strong, taciturn screen persona and for performing his own stunts

Marceau Marcel (1923–) French mime artist and creator of the clown-harlequin Bip

Marvin Lee (1924–1987) accomplished US film actor who created a tough, violent screen persona in such films as *Point Blank*

Marx Brothers Chico (Leonard) (1891–1961), Harpo (Arthur) (1893–1964), Groucho (Julius) (1895–1977), and Zeppo (Herbert) (1901–1979) US comedians who starred in zany comic films such as *Animal Crackers* and *Duck Soup*

Mason James Neville (1909–1984) English film actor who enjoyed a successful career in both the British cinema and Hollywood, frequently playing intelligent, romantically troubled characters

Mastroianni Marcello (1923–1996) popular Italian film actor who first won international acclaim in Federico Fellini's *La dolce vita/The Sweet Life*

Meyerhold Vsevolod Yemilevich (1874–1940) Russian actor and director who developed the system of actor training known as 'biomechanics'

Mifune Toshiro (1920–) Chinese-born Japanese film actor who rose to international prominence as the star of several films directed by Akira Kurosawa

Mills John (Lewis Ernest Watts) (1908–) versatile English actor who won an Academy Award for his performance in *Ryan's Daughter*

Mirren Helen (1945–) English stage, film, and TV actress who, in the 1990s, has won international recognition for her performances in the TV crime drama series *Prime Suspect*

Mitchum Robert (Charles Duran) (1917–1997) US film actor who achieved stardom in the late 1940s, and whose career spanned more than 50 years

Monroe Marilyn (stage name of Norma Jean Mortenson) (1926–1962) US film actress who was a celebrated sex symbol of the 1950s and early 1960s, starring in films such as *Some Like It Hot* and *Gentlemen Prefer Blondes*

Moore Demi (born Demi Guynes) (1962–) US film actress who, with *Ghost*, established herself as one of the leading box-office attractions of the 1990s

Moreau Jeanne (1928–) French film actress who first achieved international stardom in such films as *Les Amants/The Lovers* and *Jules et Jim*, becoming an icon of 'new wave' cinema

Murphy Eddie (Edward) Regan (1951–) comic US film actor who enjoyed a succession of box-office successes during the 1980s

Neeson Liam (1952–) Irish film and stage actor who played Oskar Schindler in *Schindler's List*

Newman Paul (1925–) US film actor who, with a string of acclaimed performances, including *The Hustler* and *Hud*, rose to stardom in the 1960s

Nicholson Jack (1937–) US film actor and director who won Academy Awards for *One Flew Over the Cuckoo's Nest* and *Terms of Endearment*

Niven (James) David Graham (1909–1983) Scottish-born US film actor who established himself as a suave and sophisticated leading man

Noteworthy Actors (*continued*)

Novak Kim (Marilyn Pauline) (1933–) US film actress who rose to stardom in the 1950s, winning acclaim for her performance in *Vertigo*

O'Toole Peter Seamus (1932–) Irish-born film actor who won international recognition for his title role in *Lawrence of Arabia*

Olivier Laurence Kerr (1907–1989) English actor who was one of the leading stage performers of his generation, and who is particularly remembered for his Shakespearean roles both on stage and on screen

Pacino Al(fredo) James (1940–) award-winning US stage and screen actor who rose to stardom in the 1970s in *The Godfather* films

Peck (Eldred) Gregory (1916–) US film actor who won an Academy Award for his performance in *To Kill a Mocking Bird*

Pfeiffer Michelle (1959–) versatile US film actress who has become one of the leading stars of the 1990s

Phoenix River (1970–1993) US film actor who gave a series of intense portrayals of disaffected youth prior to his untimely death

Pickford Mary (stage name of Gladys Mary Smith) (1893–1979) Canadian-born US film actress who was one of the major stars of the silent screen

Pitt (William) Brad(ley) (1964–) US film actor who has reached an international audience through such films as *Thelma and Louise*

Pleasance Donald (1919–1995) English character actor who specialized in playing sinister villains

Poitier Sidney (1924–) elegant US film actor and director who won an Academy Award for his performance in *Lilies of the Field*

Powell William (1892–1984) US film actor who played suave leading roles in films such as *Life with Father*

Quayle (John) Anthony (1913–1989) English actor and director who enjoyed a prolific career on stage and in film

Rains Claude (1889–1967) British-born US film actor best known for his performance as an endearingly corrupt police chief in *Casablanca*

Redford (Charles) Robert (1937–) US film actor and director who rose to international stardom in the 1970s in such films as *Butch Cassidy and the Sundance Kid*

Redgrave Michael Scudamore (1908–1985) English stage and screen actor who featured in such films as *The Lady Vanishes* and *Goodbye, Mr Chips*

Redgrave Vanessa (1937–) English theatre and film actress who won an Academy Award for her performance in *Julia*

Richardson Miranda (1958–) English actress who has proved herself an accomplished and versatile performer in a variety of theatrical, film, and TV productions

Richardson Ralph David (1902–1983) English actor who was one of the leading stage performers of his generation and gained a reputation for his deadpan humour

Rigg Diana (1938–) English stage and TV actress who starred in the cult TV programme *The Avengers*

Robson Flora McKenzie (1902–1984) English stage and screen actress who starred as Queen Elizabeth I in the film *Fire Over England*

Rogers Ginger (stage name of Virginia Katherine McMath) (1911–1995) US film actress, dancer, and singer who co-starred with Fred Astaire in a number of Hollywood musicals

Ryder Winona (stage name of Winona Laura Horowitz) (1971–) leading US film actress who rose to stardom as the heroine of *Heathers*

Rylance Mark (1960–) English actor and director who appeared in several Royal Shakespeare Company productions before being named the first artistic director of the restored Globe Theatre in 1995

Sarandon Susan (stage name of Susan Abigail Tomalin) (1946–) versatile US film actress who won an Academy Award for her performance in *Dead Man Walking*

Schwarzenegger Arnold (1947–) Austrian-born US film actor who, in a series of violent action movie roles, has become one of Hollywood's biggest box-office attractions

Scofield (David) Paul (1922–) English stage and film actor much lauded for his performances in both the stage and film productions of Robert Bolt's *A Man for All Seasons*

Sellers Peter (adopted name of Richard Henry Sellers) (1925–1980) English comedian and film actor who made his name on the radio programme *The Goon Show*

Shearer (Edith) Norma (1900–1983) Canadian-born US actress who was a leading film star of the 1930s

Sher Anthony (1949–) South-African born British actor who has established himself as one of the leading British stage actors of the 1980s and 1990s

Sinatra Frank (Francis) Albert (1915–) US singer and film actor who won an Academy Award for his performance in *From Here to Eternity*

Sinden Donald Alfred (1923–) versatile English stage and TV actor

Smith Maggie (Margaret Natalie) (1934–) English theatre, film, and TV actress who won an Academy Award for her performance in *The Prime of Miss Jean Brodie*

Stallone (Michael) Sylvester (1946–) US film actor, writer, and director who rose to international stardom with *Rocky*

Stanislavsky Konstantin Sergeyevich Alekseyev (1863–1938) Russian actor and director who developed a style of acting based on the psychological development of character

Stanwyck Barbara (stage name of Ruby Stevens) (1907–1990) commanding US film actress who was one of the leading female stars of the classical Hollywood era

Steiger Rod(ney) Steven (1925–) US Method actor who won an Academy Award for his performance in *In the Heat of the Night*

Stevenson Juliet Anne Virginia (1956–) English stage and film actress best known for her acclaimed performance in the film *Truly, Madly, Deeply*

Stewart James Maitland (1908–1997) award-winning US film actor who was one of Hollywood's most enduring stars, skilled at both drama and comedy

Strasberg Lee (stage name of Israel Strassberg) (1901–1982) US actor and artistic director of the Actors' Studio, where he developed the theory and practice of Method acting

Streep Meryl Mary Louise (1949–) US film actress, recognized as one of the leading actors of her generation, who won Academy Awards for her performances in *Kramer vs Kramer* and *Sophie's Choice*

Swanson Gloria (adopted name of Gloria Josephine Mae Swenson) (1897–1983) US film actress renowned for her glamour; her films include *Male and Female* and *Sunset Boulevard*

Sydow Max Carl Adolf von (1929–) Swedish film actor who won international acclaim featuring in a series of films directed by Ingmar Bergman

Tandy Jessica (1909–1994) English theatre and film actress who began her career as a leading Shakespearean actor

Tati Jacques (stage name of Jacques Tatischeff) (1908–1982) comic French film actor and director best remembered for his portrayal of the bumbling character Monsieur Hulot

Taylor Elizabeth Rosemond (1932–) English-born US film actress who was one of Hollywood's most glamorous stars of the 1950s and 1960s

Temple Shirley (1928–) US film actress who was perhaps the most celebrated child actress in film history

Terry (Alice) Ellen (1847–1928) English actress who was one of the leading stage performers of her day

Thompson Emma (1959–) English stage and screen actress who has won Academy Awards for both her acting and her screenwriting

(continued)

Noteworthy Actors (*continued*)

Thorndike (Agnes) Sybil (1882–1976) English actress for whom George Bernard Shaw wrote the play *St Joan*

Tracy Spencer (1900–1967) award-winning US film actor who appeared in nine films with off-screen partner Katharine Hepburn

Travolta John (1954–) US film actor who began his career as a teen idol, going on to win critical acclaim in the 1990s for his role in *Pulp Fiction*

Turner Lana (Julia Jean Mildred Frances) (1920–1995) US film actress who starred in such melodramas as *Imitation of Life*

Ustinov Peter (1921–) English actor, writer, and director who has enjoyed success on both the stage and screen, winning two Academy Awards in the 1960s

Valentino Rudolph (adopted name of Rodolfo Alfonso Raffaele Pierre Philibert Guglielmi) (1895–1926) Italian-born US film actor and dancer who established himself as the archetypal romantic lover of the silent screen

Veidt Conrad (1893–1943) German film actor who appeared in *Casablanca*

Voight Jon (1938–) US film actor who won an Academy Award for his portrayal of a Vietnam veteran in *Coming Home*

Wayne John (stage name of Marion Michael Morrison) (1907–1979) US film actor whose name became synonymous with the Western film genre

Weigel Helene (1900–1971) Austrian stage actress who, with her husband Bertolt Brecht, co-founded the Berliner Ensemble

Welles (George) Orson (1915–1985) US film and theatre actor, writer, and director who, with *Citizen Kane*, announced himself as one of the greats of world cinema

West Mae (1892–1980) US stage and screen actress best remembered for her employment of verbal innuendo and her status as a provocative sex symbol

Williams Robin (1952–) comic US TV and film actor who has created a hyperactive screen persona whose rapid dialogue often verges on the surreal

Willis Bruce (1955–) US TV and film actor who has cultivated a tough, wisecracking image in such films as *Die Hard*

Winslett Kate (1975–) English actress who starred in *Titanic* alongside Leonardo DiCaprio, and has also appeared in *Jude* and *Sense and Sensibility*

UK Television Personalities

Abbott Russ (stage name of Russ Roberts) (1948–) English comedian and comic actor who emerged in the 1980s as one of Britain's most popular TV entertainers

Alexander Jean (1926–) English actress who played Hilda Ogden in the ITV soap opera *Coronation Street* (1964–87)

Allen Dave (1936–) (stage name of David Tynan O'Mahony) Irish comedian whose sharply observed humour has been popular on British TV since the late 1960s

Anderson Clive (1953–) English chat show host and presenter who has chaired the Channel 4 improvisation game show *Whose Line is it Anyway?* since 1988

Andrews Eamonn (1922–1987) Irish presenter, chat show host, and sports commentator who rose to prominence in British TV in the 1950s as the host of panel game *What's My Line?*

Aspel Michael (stage name of Michael Terence) (1933–) laidback English presenter and chat show host who has presented *This Is Your Life* since its revival in 1994

Atkinson Rowan (1955–) English comedian and comic actor who starred in the hit TV comedies *Blackadder* and *Mr Bean*

Attenborough David Frederick (1926–) English TV naturalist who has made an unrivalled contribution to the BBC's natural history coverage; the brother of the film actor and director Richard Attenborough

Baker Richard Douglas James (1925–) English newsreader and classical music presenter who, in 1954, became one of BBC TV's first 'in-vision' newsreaders, a position he held until 1982

Bakewell Joan (born Joan Dawson) (1933–) distinguished English broadcaster who presents the BBC moral issue series *Heart of the Matter*

Barker Ronnie (1929–) English comedian, comic actor, and writer who co-starred with Ronnie Corbett in the long-running BBC series *The Two Ronnies* and also starred in the BBC sitcoms *Porridge* and *Open All Hours*

Barrymore Michael (1952–) energetic English comedian and entertainer who hosts the ITV game show *Strike It Lucky*

Baxter Stanley (1926–) inventive Scottish TV comedian renowned for his elaborate parodies of the film world

Beadle Jeremy (1948–) English TV entertainer who presents humorous excerpts from viewers' home videos on ITV's peak-time show *You've Been Framed*

Bellamy David James (1933–) popular English TV naturalist and environmental campaigner

Berry Nick (1963–) English actor who starred as PC Nick Rowan in the popular ITV drama series *Heartbeat*

Bewes Rodney (1938–) English actor who co-starred with James Bolam in the BBC sitcom *The Likely Lads*

Black Cilla (stage name of Priscilla White) (1943–) English presenter, entertainer, and former pop star who hosts two of ITV's most popular programmes, *Blind Date* and *Surprise, Surprise*

Braden Bernard (1916–1993) Canadian actor and presenter who pioneered consumer programming on British television in the late 1960s with his show *Braden's Week*

Bragg Melvin (1939–) English presenter, TV executive, and author who presents and edits the long-running ITV arts documentary series *The South Bank Show*

Brambell Wilfrid (1912–1985) Irish-born actor who is famous for his role as the coarse, manipulative father Albert Steptoe in the BBC sitcom *Steptoe and Son*

Bremner Rory (1961–) inventive Scottish-born TV impressionist who specializes in topical and political satire

Briers Richard (1934–) English actor who is best known as the co-star with Felicity Kendal in the BBC sitcom *The Good Life*

Burnet Alastair (adopted name of James William Alexander) (1928–) distinguished Scottish current affairs presenter and journalist who anchored ITN's *News at Ten* for many years

Carpenter Harry (1925–) esteemed English sports commentator who commentated on boxing and other sports on BBC TV for over 40 years

Carrott Jasper (stage name of Robert Davies) (1945–) English comedian who has been popular on British TV since the 1970s

Carson Violet (1898–1983) English actress who played the formidable Ena Sharples for over 20 years in the ITV soap opera *Coronation Street*

Castle Roy (1933–1994) English entertainer, musician, and actor who presented the BBC children's programme *Record Breakers* for 22 years

UK Television Personalities (*continued*)

Chalmers Judith (1935–) English presenter who hosted the ITV holiday programme *Wish You Were Here* for over 20 years

Clarkson Jeremy (1960–) English motoring journalist, star presenter of BBC's car programme *Top Gear*

Cleese John (1939–) English comic actor who rose to fame on TV and film as a member of *Monty Python's Flying Circus*

Cole George (1925–) English actor best known for his portrayal of the spiv entrepreneur Arthur Daley in the ITV comedy drama *Minder*

Coleman David (1926–) veteran English sports presenter and commentator who also hosted the popular BBC quiz show *A Question of Sport* for over 20 years

Collins Joan (1936–) English film and TV actress who is best known for her role as Alexis Carrington/Colby in the US soap opera *Dynasty*

Coltrane Robbie (stage name of Anthony McMillan) (1950–) Scottish comedian and actor who won a BAFTA Best Actor award for his starring role in the ITV thriller *Cracker*

Connolly Billy (1942–) Scottish comedian and actor who, after successfully translating his uproarious stage act to TV in the 1970s, has diversified into comic and straight acting roles on TV and film

Coogan Steve (1958–) English comic actor and writer whose 1997 BBC comedy *It's Alan Partridge* has confirmed his reputation as one of British TV's brightest new talents

Cook Peter (1937–1995) English comedian and writer with a genius for improvisation whose 1960s BBC show *Not Only…But Also*, co-starring Dudley Moore, is regarded as a masterpiece of British TV comedy

Cook Roger (1943–) New Zealand-born investigative reporter famous for his face-to-face confrontations with fraudsters and other criminals on his long-running ITV series *The Cook Report*

Cooper Tommy (1922–1984) Welsh comedian whose deliberately bad jokes and hilariously unsuccessful magic tricks performed in his trademark fez made him one of British TV's most adored personalities

Corbett Ronnie (1930–) diminutive Scottish comedian who co-starred with Ronnie Barker in the long-running BBC series *The Two Ronnies*

Cotton Billy (1899–1969) English bandleader and entertainer who was a permanent fixture of BBC TV's variety revues in the 1950s and 1960s

Cradock Fanny (Phyllis) (1909–1994) pioneering English TV cook who is less remembered for her recipes than for her comically strident manner and brusque on-screen treatment of her embattled husband Johnny

Crawford Michael (stage name of Michael Dumble-Smith) (1942–) English actor and musical star who played the part of the accident-prone simpleton Frank Spencer in the BBC sitcom *Some Mothers Do 'Ave 'Em*

Daniels Paul (1938–) English magician and entertainer who won the Golden Rose of Montreaux award in 1985 for *The Paul Daniels Magic Show*

Davidson Jim (1953–) English comedian and entertainer who hosts the BBC game shows *Big Break* and *Jim Davidson's Generation Game*

Dawson Les (1934–1993) English comedian whose brand of dry, deadpan wit brought him high ratings on British TV in the 1980s

Day Robin (1923–) eminent English broadcast journalist who pioneered the probing political interview on British TV in the 1950s

Deayton Angus (1956–) English actor, writer, and presenter who has hosted the humorous topical quiz show *Have I Got News For You* on BBC TV since 1990

Dennis Les (1954–) English comedian and impressionist who has hosted the ITV game show *Family Fortunes* since 1987

Dimbleby David (1938–) English BBC current affairs broadcaster and newspaper proprietor, the son of Richard Dimbleby and brother of Jonathan Dimbleby

Dimbleby Jonathan (1944–) English current affairs broadcaster and writer, the son of Richard Dimbleby and brother of David Dimbleby

Dimbleby Richard Frederick (1913–1965) eminent BBC radio and TV current affairs broadcaster and presenter, the father of David and Jonathan Dimbleby

Doonican Val (1929–) wholesome Irish singer and entertainer who enjoyed peak-time success on British TV in the 1960s and early 1970s

Edmonds Noel (1948–) English entertainer and former radio disc jockey who hosts the highly popular BBC TV show *Noel's House Party*

Elton Ben(jamin) Charles (1959–) English stand-up comedian who is also one of British TV's leading comedy writers, with the award-winning *Blackadder* among his credits

Emery Dick (1917–1983) English comic actor whose *Dick Emery Show* was a mainstay of BBC TV's comedy output in the 1960s and 1970s

Enfield Harry (1961–) English comedian and writer who displays his talent for comic characterization on his BBC TV show *Harry Enfield and Chums*

Evans Chris (1966–) English radio disc jockey and TV entertainer who made his reputation on TV as a presenter of Channel 4's *The Big Breakfast* (1992–94)

Ford Anna (1943–) English broadcaster who has been one of British TV's leading newsreaders since the late 1970s

Forsyth Bruce (Bruce Forsyth Johnson) (1928–) English comedian and entertainer who hosted *The Generation Game* (1971–77) and *Bruce Forsyth's Generation Game* (1992–94)

French Dawn (1957–) English comedienne and comic actress who emerged in the 1980s in partnership with Jennifer Saunders as one of British TV's most inventive comic talents

Frost David Paradine (1939–) English broadcaster and producer who has enjoyed a long and varied career on both British and US TV as a political interviewer, chat show host, and presenter

Fry Stephen (1957–) English actor, comedian, and writer who came to the fore in the 1980s on British TV alongside comedy partner Hugh Laurie

Gascoigne Bamber (1935–) author and broadcaster who chaired the student quiz show *University Challenge* (1962–87)

Gordon Noele (1923–1985) English actress who starred as motel proprietress Meg Richardson in the ITV soap opera *Crossroads* (1964–81)

Grayson Larry (1923–1995) camp English comedian and entertainer who enjoyed peak time success as a host of BBC's *Generation Game* (1978–82)

Greene Hughie (1920–1997) Canadian-born presenter and quiz show host who compered the ITV talent show *Opportunity Knocks* for 21 years from 1956

Hancock Tony (1924–1968) brilliant English comedian and comic actor whose *Hancock's Half Hour* (later *Hancock*) pioneered situation comedy on British TV in the 1950s

Harding Gilbert (1907–1990) English broadcaster who, as an outspoken panellist on the TV quiz *What's My Line?*, became perhaps the leading personality on British TV in the 1950s

Harris Rolf (1930–) Australian entertainer and presenter who has enjoyed a long and successful career on British TV

Harty Russell (1934–1988) English presenter who was one of Britain's leading chat show hosts in the 1980s

Henry Lenny (Lenworth) (1958–) English comedian and comic actor who emerged in the 1980s as one of British TV's finest talents

Hill Benny (stage name of Alfred Hawthorne Hill) (1925–1992) English comedian and comic actor whose blend of sauce and slapstick humour on the long-running *Benny Hill Show* won him international success

Howerd Frankie (stage name of Francis Howard) (1917–1992) acclaimed English comedian and comic actor, perhaps best remembered for his starring role as the slave Lurcio in the sitcom *Up Pompeii!*

Humphries Barry (1934–) Australian comedian who has enjoyed great success on stage and TV in the guise of Australian 'housewife megastar' Dame Edna Everage

(*continued*)

UK Television Personalities (continued)

Inman John (1935–) English comic actor who is best known for his portrayal of the camp menswear assistant Mr Humphries in the BBC sitcom *Are You Being Served?*

James Clive Vivian Leopold (1939–) Australian presenter, chat show host, and author whose British TV programmes (taking a humorous look at TV around the world) have been much imitated

Jason David (stage name of David White) (1949–) award-winning English actor who is best known as the cockney wideboy Del Boy Trotter in the BBC sitcom *Only Fools And Horses*

Kennedy Ludovic (1919–) British current affairs journalist, presenter, and author whose distinguished career on British TV began in the 1950s

Lawley Sue (Susan) (1946–) English current affairs presenter and host of the BBC radio series *Desert Island Discs*

Lowe Arthur (1915–1982) English actor best known for his portrayal of the bumptious Captain Mainwaring in the BBC sitcom *Dad's Army*

Lumley Joanna (1946–) English actress who came to the fore in the 1970s TV action drama *The New Avengers*, but who has achieved cult status in the 1990s for her role in the BBC comedy *Absolutely Fabulous*

Lynham Des (Desmond) Michael (1942–) suave, Irish-born BBC sports presenter

Lyndhurst Nicholas (1961–) English comic actor, a star of the BBC sitcoms *Only Fools and Horses* and *Goodnight Sweetheart*

MacDonald Trevor (1939–) Trinidadian-born newsreader who is the main presenter of ITV's *News at Ten*

McGoohan Patrick (1928–) US-born British actor who created and starred in the cult British TV drama *The Prisoner*

McNee Patrick (1922–) English actor who starred as the suave gentleman agent in the ITV action drama *The Avengers* (1961–69) and in *The New Avengers* (1976–77)

Magnussen Magnus (1929–) Icelandic broadcaster who chaired the BBC quiz show *Mastermind* (1972–97)

Mayall Rik (1958–) English comic actor who rose to prominence in the 1980s alongside regular comedy partner Adrian Edmondson in the BBC sitcom *The Young Ones*

Michelmore Cliff (Clifford) Arthur (1919–) English current affairs journalist, presenter, and producer who enjoyed a long and distinguished career on BBC TV

Miller Jonathan (1934–) multi-talented English director, writer, broadcaster, and doctor who has made a significant contribution to British TV in the arts and other fields

Milligan Spike (stage name of Terence Milligan) (1918–) Indian-born British comedian and writer who rose to fame on the 1950s radio programme *The Goon Show* before successfully translating his absurd, inventive humour to TV

Mitchell Warren (1926–) English actor whose bigoted cockney Alf Garnett in the long running sitcom *Till Death Us Do Part* became a national institution

Monkhouse Bob (1928–) English comedian, actor, writer, and entertainer whose long and varied career on British TV began in 1954

Moore Patrick (originally Patrick Caldwell-Moore) (1923–) English presenter of the BBC astronomy programme *The Sky at Night* since 1957

Morecambe Eric Bartholomew (1926–1984) acclaimed English comedian who, in partnership with Ernie Wise, achieved a degree of popularity in the 1960s and 1970s perhaps unrivalled on British TV

Morris Johnny (1916–) Welsh-born broadcaster who made the animals talk on the long-running BBC children's programme *Animal Magic*

Muggeridge Malcolm (1903–1990) English journalist and broadcaster who, despite an avowed aversion to TV, made a significant contribution to the medium as a presenter and interviewer

Muir Frank (1920–1998) English broadcaster and leading comedy writer on radio and TV who is best remembered on TV as a panellist on the BBC quiz show *Call My Bluff*

Norden Denis (1922–) English broadcaster and leading comedy writer best known on TV for his humorous compilations of TV out-takes on ITV's *It'll Be Alright on the Night*

Norman Barry Leslie (1933–) English broadcaster, writer, and journalist who has presented BBC TV's *Film* movie review series since the early 1970s

O'Connor Des (1932–) English singer and entertainer who has established himself as a leading celebrity chat show host with his series *Des O'Connor Tonight*, which began in the 1980s on BBC and later transferred to ITV in the 1990s

Owen Bill (stage name of William John Owen Rowbotham) (1914–) veteran English actor who plays the part of the jovial scruff Compo in the whimsical BBC sitcom *Last of the Summer Wine*

Palin Michael (1943–) English comic actor and presenter who rose to prominence in TV and film as a member of *Monty Python's Flying Circus*, and who in recent years has enjoyed high ratings for his globe-trotting TV travelogues

Parkinson Michael (1935–) English journalist and chat show host whose long-running BBC chat show *Parkinson* was revived in 1998 after a gap of 15 years

Paxman Jeremy (1950–) English current affairs presenter and writer who presents BBC's *Newsnight* and chairs the quiz show *University Challenge*

Phoenix Pat (stage name of Patricia Pilkington) (1923–1986) Irish-born English actress who played the part of Elsie Tanner in the ITV soap opera *Coronation Street* (1960–84)

Rantzen Esther Louise (1940–) English broadcaster who presented and edited the long-running BBC consumer programme *That's Life* (1973–84)

Reeves Vic (stage name of Jim Moir) (1959–) English comedian who hosts the award-winning alternative celebrity quiz show *Shooting Stars* with regular comedy partner Bob Mortimer

Rhys Jones Griff (1953–) Welsh-born comedian and comic actor who has enjoyed a long and successful TV comedy partnership with Mel Smith

Rippon Angela (1944–) English broadcaster who in the 1970s became BBC TV's first female newsreader

Roache William (1932–) English actor who, in the role of Ken Barlow, is the only surviving original cast member of the ITV soap opera *Coronation Street*

Ross Jonathan (1960–) English broadcaster and producer who rose to prominence in the late 1980s as the host of the Channel 4 chat show *The Last Resort*

Rossiter Leonard (1926–1984) English actor who enjoyed great success in the 1970s in the title role of the BBC comedy *The Fall and Rise of Reginald Perrin*, and as the seedy landlord Rigsby in the ITV sitcom *Rising Damp*

Savile Jimmy (1926–) radio disc jockey and TV presenter who is best known on TV for his BBC series *Jim'll Fix It*

Saunders Jennifer (1958–) English comedienne and comic actress who, as well as enjoying a highly successful comedy partnership with Dawn French, stars in the award-winning BBC sitcom *Absolutely Fabulous*

Secombe Harry Donald (1921–) Welsh-born singer, entertainer, presenter, and comedian who rose to fame in the 1950s radio show *The Goon Show*

Singleton Valerie (1937–) English presenter who came to the fore in the 1960s as a presenter of the BBC children's programme *Blue Peter*

Sykes Eric (1923–) English comedian, comic actor, and writer whose BBC sitcom *Sykes*, co-starring Hattie Jacques, ran for 16 years between 1961 and 1979

Thaw John (1942–) English actor who is best known for his police detective roles in the ITV dramas *The Sweeney* and *Inspector Morse*

Turner Anthea (1960–) English TV presenter who was the first presenter of the *National Lottery Live*, and has also appeared on *Blue Peter* and *GMTV*

Walden Brian (Alistair Brian) (1932–) English current affairs broadcaster and former Labour MP who became one of British TV's toughest political interviewers

UK Television Personalities (*continued*)

Warner Jack (stage name of Horace John Waters) (1895–1981) English actor who played the part of the reliable neighbourhood bobby George Dixon in the BBC drama *Dixon of Dock Green* for 21 years from 1955

Wax Ruby (1953–   ) sassy US comedian, TV editor, and presenter who specializes in 'at home' TV interviews of celebrities

Whelden Huw (1916–1986) eminent Welsh broadcaster who made a long and lasting contribution to the BBC as a presenter, editor, producer, and senior executive

Whicker Alan Donald (1925–   ) globe-trotting English broadcaster who, in 1993, became the first person to be named in the Royal Television Society's Hall of Fame for making an outstanding creative contribution to British TV

Whitehouse Paul (1958–   ) English comedian and writer who stars in the cult BBC TV comedy sketch show *The Fast Show*

Wilson Richard (1936–   ) Scottish actor who has become famous in the 1990s for his portrayal of the grumpy pensioner Victor Meldrew in the BBC sitcom *One Foot in the Grave*

Wogan Terry (Michael Terence) (1938–   ) Irish presenter and radio disc jockey who was British TV's leading chat show host in the 1980s

Worth Harry (stage name of Harry Illingsworth) (1920–1989) English comedian and comic actor who was a mainstay of British TV in the 1960s and 1970s

Wood Victoria (1953–   ) English comedienne and singer who rose to prominence in the 1980s in partnership with Julie Walters as one of British TV's leading comics

Yarwood Mike (1941–   ) English impressionist who enjoyed high ratings on British TV in the 1970s

Noteworthy Film Directors

Aldrich Robert (1918–1983) US director and producer whose films include *Kiss Me Deadly* and *Whatever Happened to Baby Jane?*

Allen Woody (adopted name of Allen Stewart Konigsberg) (1935–   ) US director, actor, and writer whose films include *Annie Hall*, *Manhattan*, and *Hannah and Her Sisters*

Almodóvar Pedro (1951–   ) Spanish director and screenwriter whose films include *Qué he hecho yo para merecer esto?/What Have I Done to Deserve This?* and *Mujeres al borde de un ataque de nervios/Women on the Verge of a Nervous Breakdown*

Altman Robert (1925–   ) US director and producer whose lengthy oeuvre, including *M*A*S*H*, *Nashville*, and *The Player*, serves up an irreverent critique of US society

Anderson Lindsay (1932–1994) British director whose films include *This Sporting Life* and *If...*

Ang Lee (1954–   ) Taiwanese director, screenwriter, and producer whose films include *The Wedding Banquet* and *Eat Drink Man Woman*

Antonioni Michelangelo (1912–   ) Italian director whose art-house films include *L'Avventura* and *Blow-Up*

Armstrong Gillian May (1950–   ) Australian writer and film and documentary director whose films include *My Brilliant Career* and *Little Women*

Attenborough Richard (1923–   ) English director, actor, and producer who appeared in such films as *Brighton Rock* and who directed *Gandhi* and *Cry Freedom*

Avery Tex (Frederick Bean) (1907–1980) US animator and director whose works are characterized by comic, frequently surreal, scenes of violence; at Warner Bros he helped develop Bugs Bunny and Daffy Duck

Beatty Warren (stage name of Warren Beaty) (1937–   ) US actor, director, and producer who won an Academy Award for his direction of *Reds*, in which he also starred

Beresford Bruce (1940–   ) Australian screenwriter and director whose films include *Breaker Morant* and *Driving Miss Daisy*

Bergman (Ernst) Ingmar (1918–   ) Swedish stage and film director whose films include *Det sjunde inseglet/The Seventh Seal* and *Fanny och Alexander/Fanny and Alexander*

Berkeley Busby (stage name of William Berkeley Enos) (1895–1976) US choreographer and director famed for choreographing large-scale dance numbers in such films as *42nd Street*

Bertolucci Bernardo (1940–   ) Italian director whose works include *Strategia del ragno/The Spider's Stratagem* and *Il conformista/The Conformist*

Bogdanovich Peter (1939–   ) US director, screenwriter, and producer who won critical acclaim for his *The Last Picture Show*

Bondarchuk Sergei Feodorovich (1920–1994) Soviet actor and director who, in 1967, directed an eight-hour version of Leo Tolstoy's novel *War and Peace*

Boorman John (1933–   ) English director, screenwriter, and producer whose films include *Point Blank* and *Deliverance*

Branagh Kenneth Charles (1960–   ) Northern Irish stage and film actor, director, and producer whose films include *Henry V* and *Hamlet*

Bresson Robert (1907–   ) French director whose works include *Pickpocket* and *Le Procès de Jeanne d'Arc/The Trial of Joan of Arc*

Brest Martin (1951–   ) US filmmaker whose works include *Beverly Hills Cop* and *Scent of a Woman*

Brooks Mel (stage name of Melvin Kaminsky) (1926–   ) US director and comedian, whose films include *The Producers* and *Blazing Saddles*

Buñuel Luis (1900–1983) Spanish-born director, famed for such films as *Los Olvidados/The Young and the Damned*, *Viridiana*, and *Belle de Jour*

Burton Tim (1960–   ) US director and producer whose works include *Edward Scissorhands* and *Ed Wood*

Cameron James (1954–   ) Canadian-born US filmmaker whose stylish and special-effects-based films include *The Terminator* and *Titanic*

Campion Jane (1954–   ) New Zealand director and screenwriter whose work includes *An Angel at My Table* and *The Piano*

Capra Frank (1897–1991) Italian-born US director whose credits include *It Happened One Night* and *It's a Wonderful Life*

Carné Marcel (1909–   ) French director of such films as *Le Jour se lève/Daybreak* and *Les Enfants du paradis/The Children of Paradise*

Carpenter John Howard (1948–   ) US director whose works include *Assault on Precinct 13* and *Halloween*

Cassavetes John (1929–1989) US director and actor who made such experimental, low-budget films as *Shadows* and *A Woman Under The Influence*

Chabrol Claude (1930–   ) French New Wave director responsible for *Les Bonnes Femmes* and *Le Boucher/The Butcher*

Chaplin Charlie (Charles) Spencer (1889–1977) English actor and director who was one of the pioneers of silent cinema and whose films include *The Gold Rush* and *Modern Times*

Chen Kaige (1952–   ) Chinese director whose films include *Huang Tudi/Yellow Earth* and *Bawang Bie Ji/Farewell My Concubine*

Cimino Michael (1943–   ) US director and screenwriter whose films include *The Deer Hunter* and the financially disastrous *Heaven's Gate*

Clayton Jack (1921–1995) English filmmaker whose films include *Room at the Top* and *The Lonely Passion of Judith Hearne*

Cocteau Jean (1889–1963) French poet, dramatist, and director who was a leading figure in European Modernism; his films include *Orphée/Orpheus*

(*continued*)

Noteworthy Film Directors (*continued*)

Coen Joel (1954–) US director who, with his brother Ethan (1957–), has been responsible for *Blood Simple*, *Miller's Crossing*, and *Fargo*

Coppola Francis Ford (1939–) US filmmaker who directed *The Godfather* trilogy, *The Conversation*, and *Apocalypse Now*

Corman Roger (William) (1926–) US filmmaker with over 200 films to his credit, including *The Little Shop of Horrors* and *The Raven*

Cukor George (1899–1983) US director whose films include *The Philadelphia Story*, *Gaslight*, and *Born Yesterday*

Curtiz Michael (adopted name of Mihaly Kertész) (1888–1962) Hungarian-born US director whose films include *The Adventures of Robin Hood* and *Casablanca*

Dassin Jules (1911–) US filmmaker who directed *Naked City*, *Du Rififi chez les hommes/Rififi Among Men*, and *Topkapi*

Davies Terence (1945–) British film director whose works include *Distant Voices, Still Lives*, and *The Long Day Closes*

De Mille Cecil B(lount) (1881–1959) US director and producer whose films include *The Cheat*, *The Ten Commandments*, and *The Greatest Show on Earth*

Demme Jonathan (1944–) US director, screenwriter, and producer whose films include *Something Wild* and *The Silence of the Lambs*

De Palma Brian Russell (1940–) US film director whose works include *Carrie*, *Dressed to Kill*, and *Mission: Impossible*

De Sica Vittorio (1901–1974) Italian director and actor who was a pioneer of neorealism; his films include *Ladri di biciclette/Bicycle Thieves* and *Umberto D*

Disney Walt(er) Elias (1901–1966) US filmmaker and animator, who established his own studio in Hollywood, and whose celebrated work includes the Mickey Mouse cartoons

Dmytryk Edward (1908–) Canadian-born US film director whose work includes *Murder, My Sweet*, *Crossfire*, and *The Caine Mutiny*

Donen Stanley (1924–) US director and a former dancer who directed a number of musicals and comedies, including *Singin' in the Rain* (with Gene Kelly), *Funny Face*, and *Charade*

Dreyer Carl Theodor (1889–1968) Danish director whose films include *La Passion de Jeanne d'Arc/The Passion of Joan of Arc* and *Vredens Dag/Day of Wrath*

Duvivier Julien Henri Nicolas (1896–1967) French film director whose work includes two classics of French 'poetic realism', *Pépé le Moko* and *Un Carnet de bal*

Eastwood Clint(on) Jr (1930–) US film actor and director whose films include *Play Misty for Me* and *Unforgiven*

Edwards Blake (adopted name of William Blake McEdwards) (1922–) US director and writer whose films include *The Pink Panther* and *Breakfast at Tiffany's*

Egoyan Atom (1960–) Egyptian-born Canadian director and screenwriter whose films include *Family Viewing* and *Exotica*

Eisenstein Sergei Mikhailovich (1898–1948) Latvian-born Soviet filmmaker and theoretician whose *Battleship Potemkin* remains a landmark achievement in film history

Erice Victor (full name Victor Erice Aras) (1940–) Spanish director and screenwriter whose films include *El espíritu de la colmena/The Spirit of the Beehive* and *El sol del membrillo/The Quince Tree Sun*

Eyre Richard (Charles Hastings) (1943–) English stage and film director whose films include *The Ploughman's Lunch*

Fassbinder Rainer Werner (1946–1982) West German director who made more than 40 films, including *Die bitteren Tränen der Petra von Kant/The Bitter Tears of Petra von Kant* and *Angst essen Seele auf/Fear Eats the Soul*

Fellini Federico (1920–1993) Italian director and screenwriter whose films include *La strada/The Street*, *La dolce vita/The Sweet Life*, and *Otto e Mezzo/8½*

Flaherty Robert Joseph (1884–1951) US director who was one of the pioneers of documentary filmmaking, particularly in his notable film of Inuit life, *Nanook of the North*

Forbes Bryan John Clarke (1926–) English producer, director, and screenwriter who directed *Whistle Down the Wind* and *The Stepford Wives*

Ford John (adopted name of Sean Aloysius O'Feeney) (1895–1973) influential US director whose films include *Stagecoach*, *The Searchers*, and *The Grapes of Wrath*

Forman Milos (1932–) Czech-born film director whose work includes *Hori, Ma Panenko/The Firemen's Ball* and *One Flew Over the Cuckoo's Nest*

Forsyth Bill (1947–) Scottish director and screenwriter whose films include *Gregory's Girl* and *Local Hero*

Fosse Bob (Robert) Louis (1927–1987) US director who began his career as a dancer and choreographer and then directed such films as *Cabaret* and *All That Jazz*

Frankenheimer John Michael (1930–) US director whose films include *The Manchurian Candidate* and *Seven Days in May*

Frears Stephen Arthur (1931–) English director whose films include *My Beautiful Laundrette* and *The Grifters*

Friedkin William (1939–) US director whose films include *The French Connection* and *The Exorcist*

Fuller Sam(uel) Michael (1911–1997) US director, screenwriter, producer, and novelist whose films include *Park Row*, *Pickup on South Street*, and *The Naked Kiss*

Gance Abel (1889–1981) French director whose *Napoléon* was one of the most innovative and ambitious films of the silent era

Gibson Mel (1956–) US-born Australian film actor and director who directed and starred in *Man Without a Face* and *Braveheart*

Gilliam Terry Vance (1940–) US-born director, actor, writer, and animator whose films include *Brazil* and *Twelve Monkeys*

Godard Jean-Luc (1930–) French New Wave film director responsible for *A bout de souffle/Breathless* and *Le Mépris/Contempt*

Greenaway Peter (1942–) Welsh director whose highly visual, cerebral films include *The Draughtsman's Contract* and *Prospero's Books*

Griffith D(avid) (Lewelyn) W(ark) (1875–1948) US director and pioneer of silent film whose work includes *The Birth of a Nation* and *Intolerance*

Guitry Sacha (1885–1957) French dramatist, actor, and director whose films include *Les Perles de la couronne/The Pearls of the Crown*

Hall Ken (1901–1994) Australian film and TV director and producer who was a pioneer of feature film production in Australia, with 19 credits to his name between 1932 and 1946

Hartley Hal (1960–) US director, screenwriter, editor, and producer whose films include *The Unbelievable Truth* and *Amateur*

Hawks Howard Winchester (1896–1977) influential US filmmaker whose works include *Scarface*, *Bringing Up Baby*, *The Big Sleep*, and *Rio Bravo*

Herzog Werner (adopted name of Werner Stipetic) (1942–) German director whose films include *Aguirre der Zorn Gottes/Aguirre Wrath of God* and *Fitzcarraldo*

Hitchcock Alfred Joseph (1899–1980) English-born director whose films include *The Thirty-Nine Steps*, *Notorious*, *Vertigo*, and *Psycho*

Hopper Dennis (1936–) US actor and director who caused a sensation with the anti-establishment *Easy Rider*

Howard Ron (1954–) US director whose films include *Splash* and *Apollo 13*

Hughes John (1950–) US filmmaker responsible for such youth-oriented films as *Weird Science* and *Ferris Bueller's Day Off*

Huston John Marcellus (1906–1987) US director, screenwriter, and actor whose works include *The Maltese Falcon*, *The Asphalt Jungle*, and *The Dead*

Ichikawa Kon (1915–) Japanese director and screenwriter whose films include *Biruma no tategoto/The Burmese Harp* and *Nobi/Fires on the Plain*

Noteworthy Film Directors (*continued*)

Ince Thomas Harper (1882–1924) US director and producer who brought realism into the silent Western genre, notably in a series of films featuring William S Hart

Ivens Joris (adopted name of Georg Henri Anton) (1898–1989) Dutch filmmaker whose documentary works include *Nieuve Gronden/New Earth*

Ivory James (1928–) US director whose long-term collaboration with producer Ismail Merchant has produced such films as *Shakespeare Wallah* and *Howard's End*

Jancsó Miklós (1921–) Hungarian director and screenwriter whose films include *Szegénylegények/The Round-up* and *Még kér a nép/Red Psalm*

Jarman Derek (1942–1994) English avant-garde director whose work includes including *Sebastiane, Caravaggio*, and *Wittgenstein*

Jarmusch Jim (1953–) US independent director and screenwriter whose films include *Stranger Than Paradise* and *Dead Man*

Jewison Norman (1926–) Canadian-born US filmmaker responsible for *In the Heat of the Night* and *Moonstruck*

Jones Chuck (Charles) Martin (1912–) US animator and cartoon director who was responsible for a wide range of Warner Bros and MGM animated shorts

Jordan Neil (1950–) Irish director, screenwriter, and novelist whose films include *Mona Lisa* and *Michael Collins*

Kasdan Lawrence (1949–) US producer, writer, and director whose films include *Body Heat* and *The Big Chill*

Kazan Elia (born Kazanjoglou) (1909–) Turkish-born US stage and film director whose films include *A Streetcar Named Desire* and *On the Waterfront*

Kelly Gene (Eugene Curran) (1912–1996) US filmmaker and major Hollywood star whose directorial credits include *On the Town* and *Singin' in the Rain*

Kieślowski Krzysztof (1941–1996) Polish director and screenwriter whose work includes the ten-part *Dekalog/Decalogue* and the *Trzy kolory/Three Colours* trilogy

Korda Alexander Laszlo (1893–1956) Hungarian-born British producer and director whose films as director include *Marius* and *The Private Life of Henry VIII*

Kramer Stanley (1913–) US director and producer whose works include *The Defiant Ones* and *Inherit the Wind*

Kubrick Stanley (1928–) US director, producer, and screenwriter whose films include *The Killing, Lolita*, and *2001: A Space Odyssey*

Kurosawa Akira (1910–) Japanese director whose films include *Rashōmon* and *Shichinin no samurai/Seven Samurai*

Landis John (1950–) US director responsible for *The Blues Brothers* and *Trading Places*

Lang Fritz (Friedrich) Christian Anton (1890–1976) Austrian-born director whose films include *Metropolis, M, Fury*, and *The Big Heat*

Lean David (1908–1991) English director whose films include *Brief Encounter, Great Expectations*, and *Lawrence of Arabia*

Lee Spike (stage name of Shelton Jackson) (1957–) US director, actor, and writer whose films include *Do The Right Thing* and *Clockers*

Leigh Mike (1943–) English director and writer whose work includes *Secrets & Lies* and *Life Is Sweet*

Leone Sergio (1929–1989) Italian director and screenwriter responsible for *The Good, the Bad, and the Ugly* and *Once Upon a Time in the West*

Lester Richard (1942–) US director who filmed *A Hard Day's Night* and *The Three Musketeers*

Levinson Barry (1932–) US director and screenwriter whose films include *Diner* and *Sleepers*

Lewis Jerry (stage name of Joseph Levitch) (1926–) US comic actor and director whose directorial credits include *The Nutty Professor*

Loach Ken(neth) (1936–) British film and TV director who is known for his realistic treatment of social issues in such films as *Kes* and *Riff Raff*

Longford Raymond John Walter Hollis (1878–1959) Australian actor, director, and producer whose directorial work includes *Ginger Mick* and *The Man They Could Not Hang*

Losey Joseph Walton III (1909–1984) US director who was blacklisted in the USA for political reasons and settled in the UK, where he made such films as *The Servant* and *The Go-Between*

Lubitsch Ernst (1892–1947) German director who worked in the USA from 1921, directing such films as *Ninotchka* and *Heaven Can Wait*

Lucas George (1944–) US director and producer responsible for *American Graffiti* and the *Star Wars* franchise

Lumet Sidney (1924–) US director whose films on social issues include *12 Angry Men, Network*, and *Q & A*

Lupino Ida (1918–) English-born US actress and director whose low-budget films include *The Bigamist* and *The Hitch-Hiker*

Lynch David (1946–) US director whose surreal works include *Eraserhead, Blue Velvet*, and the cult television series *Twin Peaks*

Mackendrick Alexander (1912–1993) US-born Scottish director and teacher whose films include *Whisky Galore!, The Ladykillers*, and *Sweet Smell of Success*

Malle Louis (1932–1995) French director whose films include *Les Amants/The Lovers, Atlantic City*, and *Au revoir, les enfants/Goodbye, Children*

Mamet David Alan (1947–) US dramatist, screenwriter, and director whose films include *House of Games* and *Homicide*

Mamoulian Rouben (1897–1987) Armenian-born US stage and film director whose films include *Dr Jekyll and Mr Hyde* and *The Mark of Zorro*

Mann Anthony (pseudonym of Emil Anton Bundmann) (1906–1967) US director whose films include *T-Men, Raw Deal*, and *The Naked Spur*

Marshall Garry (originally Marscharelli) (1934–) US producer, director, and writer who filmed *Pretty Woman* and *Frankie & Johnny*

Marshall Penny (originally Marscharelli) (1943–) US director whose films include *Big* and *The Preacher's Wife*

Menzies William Cameron (1896–1957) US production designer, director, and producer whose credits include the futuristic *Things to Come*

Milius John Frederick (1944–) US director and screenwriter whose films include *The Wind and the Lion* and *Conan the Barbarian*

Miller George (1945–) Australian director responsible for the *Mad Max* trilogy, *The Witches of Eastwick*, and *Lorenzo's Oil*

Miller George Turnbull (1945–) Scottish-born US film and TV director whose credits include *The Man From Snowy River*

Minnelli Vincente (1903–1986) US director whose films include *Meet Me in St Louis, An American in Paris*, and *The Bad and the Beautiful*

Mizoguchi Kenji (1898–1956) Japanese director whose works include *Naniwa Ereji/Osaka Elegy* and *Ugetsu monogatari*

Murnau F W (adopted name of Friedrich Wilhelm Plumpe) (1889–1931) German director of silent films whose work includes *Der letzte Mann/The Last Laugh* and *Sunrise*

Nichols Mike (adopted name of Michael Igor Peschkowsky) (1931–) German-born US film and stage director whose films include *Who's Afraid of Virginia Woolf?* and *The Graduate*

Olivier Laurence Kerr (1907–1989) English actor and director whose films include *Henry V* and *Hamlet*

Ophüls Max (adopted name of Max Oppenheimer) (1902–1957) German director who worked in Europe and the USA on such films as *Letter from an Unknown Woman* and *Lola Montès*

Oshima Nagisa (1932–) Japanese director whose violent and sexually explicit *Ai no corrida/In the Realm of the Senses* caused controversy when first released

Ozu Yasujirō (1903–1963) Japanese director who was one of the masters of world cinema; his works include *Tōkyō monogatari/Tokyo Story* and *Samma No Aji/An Autumn Afternoon*

(*continued*)

Noteworthy Film Directors (*continued*)

Pabst G(eorg) W(ilhelm) (1885–1967) German director whose films include *Die Büchse der Pandora/Pandora's Box* and *Die Dreigroschenoper/The Threepenny Opera*

Pakula Alan J(ay) (1928–) US director whose films include *Klute*, *The Parallax View*, and *All the President's Men*

Parker Alan William (1944–) British director whose work includes *Midnight Express*, *Angel Heart*, and *Evita*

Pasolini Pier Paolo (1922–1975) Italian Marxist director, poet, and novelist whose films include *Accatone!* and *Il vangelo secondo Mateo/The Gospel According to St Matthew*

Peckinpah (David) Sam(uel) (1926–1984) US director whose violent, controversial films include *The Wild Bunch* and *Straw Dogs*

Penn Arthur (1922–) US director whose films include *Bonnie and Clyde*, *Little Big Man*, and *Night Moves*

Polanski Roman (1933–) Polish-born French director whose films include *Repulsion*, *Rosemary's Baby*, and *Chinatown*

Porter Edwin S(tratton) (1869–1941) US silent-film pioneer whose 1903 film *The Great Train Robbery* was one of the first Westerns and offered a significant advancement in film technique

Powell Michael Latham (1905–1990) English director and producer whose films include *A Matter of Life and Death*, *The Red Shoes*, and *Peeping Tom*

Preminger Otto Ludwig (1906–1986) Austrian-born US producer, director, and actor whose films include *Laura* and *The Man with the Golden Arm*

Pudovkin Vsevolod Illarionovich (1893–1953) Russian director and theoretician whose films include *Mat'/Mother*

Rafelson Bob (Robert) (1933–) US director whose films include *Five Easy Pieces* and *The Postman Always Rings Twice*

Ray Nicholas (adopted name of Raymond Nicholas Kienzle) (1911–1979) US director who made such films as *They Live by Night*, *In a Lonely Place*, and *Rebel Without a Cause*

Ray Satyajit (1921–1992) Indian director and screenwriter who gained international recognition for his Apu trilogy: *Pather Panchali*, *Aparajito*, and *The World of Apu*

Redford (Charles) Robert (1937–) US actor and director whose films include *Ordinary People* and *Quiz Show*

Reed Carol (1906–1976) English producer and director whose films include *Odd Man Out*, *The Fallen Idol*, and *The Third Man*

Reiner Carl (1922–) US director of such film comedies as *The Jerk* and *Dead Men Don't Wear Plaid*

Reiner Rob (1945–) US comedy actor who successfully turned to directing with *This Is Spinal Tap* and *When Harry Met Sally*

Reisz Karel (1926–) Czech-born British director whose films include *Saturday Night and Sunday Morning* and *The French Lieutenant's Woman*

Renoir Jean (1894–1979) French film director, a master of the medium, whose works include *La Grande Illusion/Grand Illusion* and *La Règle du jeu/Rules of the Game*

Resnais Alain (1922–) French director whose films include *Hiroshima, mon Amour/Hiroshima, My Love* and *L'Année dernière à Marienbad/Last Year at Marienbad*

Richardson Tony (Cecil Antonio) (1928–1991) English director and producer whose films include *Look Back in Anger* and *Tom Jones*

Roeg Nicolas Jack (1928–) English director and writer who was initially a cinematographer; his films include *Performance* and *Don't Look Now*

Rohmer Eric (adopted name of Jean-Marie Maurice Scherer) (1920–) French filmmaker and critic whose films include *Ma nuit chez Maud/My Night at Maud's* and *Le Genou de Claire/Claire's Knee*

Rossellini Roberto (1906–1977) Italian director and a pioneer of Italian Neorealism whose films include *Roma città aperta/Rome, Open City* and *Paisà/Paisan*

Rudolph Alan (1943–) US director, screenwriter, and producer whose directing credits include *The Moderns* and *Mrs Parker and the Vicious Circle*

Russell (Henry) Ken(neth) Alfred (1927–) English director whose work, typified by stylistic extravagance, includes *Women in Love* and *Tommy*

Saura Carlos (1932–) Spanish director and screenwriter whose films include *Los golfos/The Hooligans* and *Carmen*

Sayles John Thomas (1950–) US director, screenwriter, actor, producer, and novelist whose films include *The Return of the Secaucus Seven* and *Lone Star*

Schepisi Frederic Alan (1939–) Australian director whose films include *The Chant of Jimmy Blacksmith* and *Roxanne*

Schlesinger John Richard (1926–) English film and TV director whose films include *Billy Liar*, *Darling*, and *Midnight Cowboy*

Schumacher Joel (1939–) US director whose films include *Falling Down* and *Batman and Robin*

Scorsese Martin (1942–) US director, screenwriter, and producer, an influential figure whose films include *Mean Streets*, *Raging Bull*, and *The Age of Innocence*

Scott Ridley (1939–) English director and producer who directed *Alien*, *Blade Runner*, and *Thelma and Louise*

Scott Tony (1944–) English director whose films include *Top Gun* and *True Romance*

Sembene Ousmane (1923–) Senegalese director, producer, and writer whose films include *Xala* and *Ceddo/The People*

Sennett Mack (adopted name of Mikall Sinnott) (1880–1960) Canadian-born US director who, in 1912, founded his own film production company, the Keystone Company, which specialized in short slapstick comedies

Siegel Don(ald) (1912–1991) US director whose films include *Invasion of the Body Snatchers* and *Dirty Harry*

Singleton John (1968–) US writer-director who won international acclaim with his debut film *Boyz N the Hood*

Siodmak Robert (1900–1973) German-raised US director whose films include *The Spiral Staircase* and *The Killers*

Sirk Douglas (adopted name of Claus Detlef Sierck) (1900–1987) German-born stage and film director who made such Hollywood melodramas as *All that Heaven Allows* and *Written on the Wind*

Skolimowski Jerzy (1938–) Polish director and screenwriter whose films include *The Shout* and *Moonlighting*

Spheeris Penelope (1945–) US director whose films include the documentary *The Decline of Western Civilization* and *Wayne's World*

Spielberg Steven (1947–) US film director, writer, and producer whose many commercial successes include *Jaws*, *Jurassic Park*, and *Schindler's List*

Sternberg Josef von (1894–1969) Austrian director whose films include *Der blaue Engel/The Blue Angel* and *Blonde Venus*

Stevens George (1904–1975) US director who began as a director of photography and went on to make such films as *Swing Time*, *Shane*, and *Giant*

Stone Oliver (1946–) US director, screenwriter, and producer whose films include *Platoon* and *JFK*

Stroheim Erich von (assumed name of Erich Oswald Stroheim) (1885–1957) Austrian-born US actor and director whose films include *Greed* and *The Wedding March*

Sturges Preston (adopted name of Edmund Preston Biden) (1898–1959) US director and writer whose films include *Sullivan's Travels* and *The Lady Eve*

Tarantino Quentin (1963–) US director and screenwriter whose films include *Reservoir Dogs* and *Pulp Fiction*

Tarkovsky Andrei Arsenevich (1932–1986) Soviet director whose films include *Solaris* and *Offret/The Sacrifice*

Noteworthy Film Directors (*continued*)

Tati Jacques (stage name of Jacques Tatischeff) (1908–1982) French comic actor, director, and writer whose films include *Les Vacances de M Hulot/Monsieur Hulot's Holiday* and *Mon Oncle/My Uncle*

Truffaut François (1932–1984) French New Wave director and actor whose films include *Les Quatre cents coups/The 400 Blows*, *Jules et Jim/Jules and Jim*, and *La Nuit américaine/Day for Night*

Ustinov Peter Alexander (1921–) English stage and film actor, writer, and director who wrote, produced, directed, and acted in several films, including *Romanoff and Juliet* and *Billy Budd*

Varda Agnès (1928–) French director whose films include *Cléo de Cinq à Sept/Cleo from Five to Seven* and *Jacquot de Nantes*

Verhoven Paul (1938–) Dutch-born filmmaker whose films include *RoboCop* and *Basic Instinct*

Vertov Dziga (adopted name of Denis Arkadevich Kaufman) (1896–1954) Polish-born Soviet director, editor, and theoretician whose films include *Kino-Glaz/Cinema-Eye* and *Chelovek s Kinoapparatom/The Man with a Movie Camera*

Vidor King Wallis (1894–1982) US film director who made such epics as *The Big Parade* and *Duel in the Sun*

Vigo Jean (adopted name of Jean Almereyda) (1905–1934) French director who made only two feature films, *Zéro de conduite/Zero for Conduct* and *L'Atalante*

Visconti Luchino (1906–1976) Italian film, opera, and theatre director whose films include *Ossessione/Obsession* and *Il Gattopardo/The Leopard*

Wajda Andrzej (1926–) Polish film and theatre director whose films include *Popiół i Diament/Ashes and Diamonds* and *Danton*

Walsh Raoul (1887–1980) US film director and actor whose lengthy career spanned both the silent and the sound eras, and whose films include *The Thief of Bagdad*, *High Sierra*, and *White Heat*

Weir Peter Lindsay (1944–) Australian director whose films include *Picnic at Hanging Rock*, *Dead Poets' Society*, and *Fearless*

Welles (George) Orson (1915–1985) US actor, screenwriter, and film and theatre director; a hugely influential filmmaker, his works include *Citizen Kane*, *The Magnificent Ambersons*, and *Touch of Evil*

Wellman William A(ugustus) (1896–1975) US director whose films include *Wings*, *The Public Enemy*, and *The Ox-Bow Incident*

Wenders Wim (Wilhelm) (1945–) German director, screenwriter, and producer who has worked in both Germany and the USA, and whose films include *Paris, Texas* and *Der Himmel über Berlin/Wings of Desire*

Wertmuller Lina (adopted name of Arcangela Felice Assunta Wertmuller von Elgg) (1928–) Italian director whose films include *Mimi Metallurgio Ferito nell'Onore/The Seduction of Mimi* and *Pasqualino Settebellezze/Seven Beauties*

Whale James (1886–1957) English director whose films include *Frankenstein* and *Show Boat*

Wiene Robert (1881–1938) German director whose reputation rests solely on a single film, the exceptional psychological horror film *Das Kabinett des Dr Caligari/The Cabinet of Dr Caligari*

Wilder Billy Samuel (1906–) Austrian-born US director and screenwriter whose films include the pioneering film noir *Double Indemnity*, *Some Like It Hot*, and *The Apartment*

Wise Robert Earl (1914–) US director and editor whose films include *The Day the Earth Stood Still* and *West Side Story*

Wyler William (1902–1981) German-born US director whose films include *Roman Holiday* and *Ben Hur*

Young Terence (1915–1994) British director responsible for three of the early James Bond action films, including *Dr No*

Zeffirelli Franco Corsi (1923–) Italian theatre, opera, and film director and stage designer whose films include *Romeo and Juliet* and *Hamlet*

Zemeckis Robert (1952–) US director and screenwriter whose films include *Back to the Future* and *Forrest Gump*

Zetterling Mai Elisabeth (1925–1994) Swedish actress and director whose credits include *Alksande Par/Loving Couples*

Zhang Yimou (1950–) Chinese director whose films include *Hong Gaoliang/Red Sorghum* and *Houzhe/To Live*

Zinnemann Fred(erick) (1907–1997) Austrian-born US director whose films include *High Noon*, *From Here to Eternity*, and *A Man For All Seasons*

Writers

Noteworthy Fiction Writers

Achebe Chinua (Albert Chinualumogo) (1930–) Nigerian novelist whose novels explore the impact of European colonialism on Africans, such as in *Things Fall Apart*

Adams Richard (George) (1920–) English novelist whose books, often about animals, contain a social message, such as *Watership Down*

Aesop (7th or 6th century BC) Greek storyteller, of whom little is known, and whose existence is not even certain, although the moral anecdotes, or *Fables*, with animal protagonists which are attributed to him are known worldwide

Alain-Fournier (pen name of Henri-Alban Fournier) (1886–1914) French novelist and author of the novel *Le Grand Meaulnes/The Lost Domain*

Alcott Louisa May (1832–1888) US author of the novel *Little Women*

Amis Kingsley (William) (1922–1995) English novelist and poet whose novels include *Lucky Jim* and *The Old Devils*

Amis Martin (Louis) (1949–) English novelist whose novels include *Time's Arrow* and *The Information*

Andersen Hans Christian (1805–1875) Danish writer of fairy tales including 'The Snow Queen' and 'The Tinder Box'

Angelou Maya (adopted name of Marguerite Annie Johnson) (1928–) US writer and poet who writes about her struggles as a black woman, such as in *I Know Why the Caged Bird Sings*

Asimov Isaac (1920–1992) Russian-born US author and editor of science fiction and nonfiction; his fiction includes *I, Robot* and *The Foundation Trilogy*

Asturias Miguel Ángel (1899–1974) Guatemalan author, diplomat, and Nobel prizewinner who attacked Latin-American dictatorships and 'Yankee Imperialism' in novels such as *El señor presidente/The President*

Atwood Margaret (Eleanor) (1939–) Canadian novelist, short story writer, and poet who treats feminist themes with wit and irony, as in *Cat's Eye*

Austen Jane (1775–1817) English novelist whose ironic and shrewd observations of manners and society can be seen in her novels, including *Sense and Sensibility* and *Pride and Prejudice*

(*continued*)

Noteworthy Fiction Writers (*continued*)

Baldwin James (Arthur) (1924–1987) US writer whose works portray the suffering of blacks in US society, as in *Go Tell it on the Mountain*

Ballard J(ames) G(raham) (1930–) English novelist whose works include *Crash* and *Empire of the Sun*

Balzac Honoré de (1799–1850) French novelist whose novel series *La Comédie humaine/The Human Comedy* was planned to depict every aspect of 19th-century French society

Barnes Julian (Patrick) (1946–) English novelist whose reputation was made by the novel *Flaubert's Parrot*

Bates H(erbert) E(rnest) (1905–1974) English writer of compassionate characterization, as in *The Jacaranda Tree*

Beckett Samuel (Barclay) (1906–1989) Irish dramatist and novelist whose novels include *Mallone* and *The Unnamable*

Behn Aphra (1640–1689) English dramatist and novelist, and the first Englishwoman to earn her living by writing, whose novels included *Oroonoko*

Bellow Saul (1915–) Canadian-born US Nobel prizewinning novelist, author of *Herzog* and *Humboldt's Gift*

Bennett (Enoch) Arnold (1867–1941) English writer of novels set in industrial towns, such as *Anna of the Five Towns*

Bernières Louis de (1954–) English author whose work includes the award-winning *Captain Corelli's Mandolin*

Bierce Ambrose (Gwinett) (1842–*c.* 1914) US author and master of the short story, whose collection *Tales of Soldiers and Civilians* explores war and the supernatural

Binchy Maeve (1940–) Irish novelist whose work includes *Evening Class*

Blackmore R(ichard) D(oddridge) (1825–1900) English author of the classic romance novel *Lorna Doone*

Boccaccio Giovanni (1313–1375) Italian writer and poet who raised the status of vernacular literature largely through his collection of tales entitled *Decameron*

Böll Heinrich (Theodor) (1917–1985) German Nobel prizewinning novelist whose novels, such as *Group Portrait with Lady*, were critical of German society

Borges Jorge (Luis) (1899–1986) Argentine short story writer and poet, and an exponent of magic realism, as in *Ficciones/Fictions*

Bowles Paul (Frederick) (1910–) US writer and composer who wrote the novel *The Sheltering Sky*

Boyd William (1952–) Ghanaian-born English novelist and short-story writer whose work includes *The Blue Afternoon*

Bradbury Ray (Douglas) (1920–) US science-fiction writer whose novels include *Fahrenheit 451*

Braine John (Gerard) (1922–1986) English novelist who created northern working-class antiheroes in the novel *Room at the Top*

Brontê three English novelists: Charlotte (1816–1855) author of *Jane Eyre*; Emily (1818–1848) author of *Wuthering Heights*; and Anne (1820–1849) author of *The Tenant of Wildfell Hall*

Brookner Anita (1928–) English novelist who won the Booker Prize for *Hotel du Lac*

Buck Pearl S(ydenstricker) (1892–1973) US Nobel prizewinning novelist who wrote about life in China and won a Pulitzer prize for *The Good Earth*

Bunyan John (1628–1688) English writer of the allegorical story *The Pilgrim's Progress*

Burgess Anthony (pen name of John Anthony Burgess Wilson) (1917–1993) versatile English novelist and composer who wrote *A Clockwork Orange*

Burney Fanny (Frances) (1752–1840) English novelist and letter writer whose novels include *Evelina*

Burroughs Edgar Rice (1875–1950) US novelist who wrote *Tarzan of the Apes*

Burroughs William S(eward) (1914–1997) US experimental writer and author of the anti-novel *Naked Lunch*

Butler Samuel (1835–1902) English writer who attacked Victorian hypocrisy in *The Way of all Flesh*

Byatt A(ntonia) S(usan) (1936–) English novelist and critic who wrote the Booker prizewinning *Possession*

Camus Albert (1913–1960) Algerian-born French Nobel prizewinning, existential writer and author of *L'Etranger/The Outsider*

Capote Truman (pen name of Truman Streckfus Persons) (1924–1984) US novelist, journalist, playwright, and author of the 'nonfiction novel' *In Cold Blood*

Carroll Lewis (pen name of Charles Lutwidge Dodgson) (1832–1898) English author of children's classics, such as *Alice in Wonderland*

Carter Angela (1940–1992) English writer of the magic realist school whose novels include *The Magic Toyshop*

Cather Willa (Sibert) (1873–1947) US novelist and short story writer whose novels include *My Ántonia* and the Pulitzer prizewinning *One of Ours*

Cervantes Saavedra, Miguel de (1547–1616) Spanish novelist, dramatist, poet, and author of *Don Quixote de la Mancha* (in full, *El ingenioso hidalgo Don Quixote de la Mancha*)

Chandler Raymond (Thornton) (1888–1959) US detective novelist who created the quintessential private eye, Philip Marlowe, a character who featured in novels such as *The Big Sleep*

Cheever John (1912–1982) US Pulitzer prizewinning writer whose novels, such as *The Wapshot Chronicle*, focus on suburban America

Chesterton G(ilbert) K(eith) (1874–1936) English novelist and essayist, who was the creator of the detective Father Brown, and whose other works include *The Man Who Was Thursday*

Christie Agatha (Mary Clarissa) (born Miller) (1890–1976) English detective novelist who created the characters Hercule Poirot and Miss Marple; her many books include *The Body in the Library*

Clarke Arthur C(harles) (1917–) English science-fiction and nonfiction writer, author of the short story 'The Sentinel', which was made into the film *2001: A Space Odyssey*

Coetzee J(ohn) M(ichael) (1940–) South African author who wrote the Booker prizewinning novel *The Life and Times of Michael K*

Colette (Sidonie-Gabrielle) (1873–1954) French writer of sensitive novels about love, such as *Gigi*

Collins (William) Wilkie (1824–1889) English author of mystery and suspense novels, such as *The Woman in White*

Compton-Burnett Ivy (1884–1969) English novelist who depicted the tyranny of family relationships, as in *Pastors and Masters*

Conrad Joseph (adopted name of Józef Teodor Konrad Nałecz Korzeniowski) (1857–1924) Polish-born English novelist, known for evocative landscapes and the scrutiny of moral dilemmas, as in *Lord Jim* and *Heart of Darkness*

Cookson Catherine (1906–1998) English novelist whose work includes *The Dwelling Place* and *Kate Hannigan*

Cooper James Fenimore (1789–1851) US writer and author of *The Last of the Mohicans*

Crane Stephen (1871–1900) US writer who introduced grim realism into American fiction, as in *The Red Badge of Courage*

Dahl Roald (1916–1990) British writer, celebrated for children's books and the collection of short stories with a twist, *Tales of the Unexpected*

Defoe Daniel (1660–1731) English writer and author of *Robinson Crusoe* and *Moll Flanders*

Deighton Len (Leonard Cyril) (1929–) English author of spy fiction whose books include *The Ipcress File*

Dickens Charles John Huffam (1812–1870) English novelist who portrayed social evils in Victorian England, as in *David Copperfield* and *Oliver Twist*

Noteworthy Fiction Writers (*continued*)

Dinesen Isak (pen name of Karen Christence Blixen-Finecke) (1885–1962) Danish writer known for short stories, such as *Seven Gothic Tales*, and for her autobiography *Out of Africa*

Döblin Alfred (1878–1957) German novelist who wrote a panoramic depiction of Weimar Germany in *Berlin-Alexanderplatz*

Dos Passos John (Roderigo) (1896–1970) US author whose major work is the innovative trilogy *U.S.A.*

Dostoevsky Fyodor Mikhailovich (1821–1881) Russian psychological novelist whose novels include *Crime and Punishment* and *The Idiot*

Doyle Arthur Conan (1859–1930) Scottish writer who created the detective Sherlock Holmes, a character who featured in many short stories and the novel *The Hound of the Baskervilles*

Doyle Roddy (1958–) Irish novelist and dramatist who won the Booker Prize in 1993 for *Paddy Clarke Ha Ha Ha;* his other works include the novel *The Commitments*

Drabble Margaret (1939–) English writer whose books portray intelligent modern women, as in *The Millstone*

Dumas Alexandre (1802–1870) French writer who collaborated on historical romances, and whose books include *Le Comte de Monte Cristo/The Count of Monte Cristo*

Du Maurier Daphne (1907–1989) English writer whose romantic fiction includes *Rebecca*

Duras Marguerite (assumed name of Marguerite Donnadieu) (1914–1996) French writer, dramatist, and filmmaker who wrote the novels *Le Vice-Consul/The Vice-Consul* and *L'Amant/The Lover*

Eco Umberto (1932–) Italian writer, semiologist, and literary critic who wrote the 'philosophical thriller' *The Name of the Rose*

Eliot George (pen name of Mary Ann Evans) (1819–1880) English novelist whose books include *Silas Marner* and *Middlemarch*

Ellison Ralph (Waldo) (1914–1994) US novelist who wrote the book *Invisible Man* about race relations in postwar America

Faulkner William (Cuthbert) (1897–1962) US Nobel prizewinning novelist whose books, such as *The Sound and the Fury*, are concerned with the American South

Fielding Henry (1707–1754) English novelist whose picaresque novels include *The History of Tom Jones, a Foundling*

Fitzgerald F(rancis) Scott (Key) (1896–1940) US novelist and short story writer who captured the jazz age in *The Great Gatsby*

Flaubert Gustave (1821–1880) French realist writer whose novels include *Madame Bovary*

Fleming Ian (Lancaster) (1908–1964) English author of suspense novels and the creator of the spy James Bond, who features in such books as *Goldfinger*

Forster E(dward) M(organ) (1879–1970) English novelist, short story writer, and critic whose novels include *A Room with a View* and *A Passage to India*

France Anatole (pen name of Jacques Anatole François Thibault) (1844–1924) French Nobel prizewinning writer of wit, urbanity, and style, as in *Le Crime de Sylvestre Bonnard/The Crime of Sylvestre Bonnard*

Fuentes Carlos (1928–) Mexican novelist, lawyer, and diplomat whose novels include *The Death of Artemio Cruz*

Galsworthy John (1867–1933) English novelist and dramatist whose novels, such as *The Forsyte Saga*, examine the social issues of the Victorian and Edwardian eras

García Márquez Gabriel (Gabo) (1928–) Colombian magic-realist novelist whose books include *Cien Años de Soledad/One Hundred Years of Solitude*

Gaskell Elizabeth (Cleghorn) (born Stevenson) (1810–1865) English novelist whose books are concerned with social issues and include *Cranford*

Gide André (Paul Guillaume)(1869–1951) French Nobel prizewinning novelist whose novels, such as *L'Immoraliste/The Immoralist*, are concerned with the conflict between desire and morality

Gogol Nikolay Vasilevich (1809–1852) Russian writer who wrote the comic novel *Dead Souls*

Goethe Johann Wolfgang von (1749–1832) German Romantic poet, dramatist, and novelist whose novels include *The Sorrows of Young Werther*

Golding William (Gerald) (1911–1993) English novelist whose works are chiefly concerned with corruption and evil in human nature, as in the allegorical *Lord of the Flies*

Goldsmith Oliver (1728–1774) Irish writer and author of the novel *The Vicar of Wakefield*

Goncharov Ivan Aleksandrovich (1812–1891) Russian novelist and author of the satirical masterpiece *Oblomov*

Gordimer Nadine (1923–) South African Nobel prizewinning novelist and opponent of apartheid and censorship, whose work includes *The Conservationist*

Grahame Kenneth (1859–1932) Scottish writer who wrote the children's classic *The Wind in the Willows*

Grass Günter (Wilhelm) (1927–) German writer of grotesque humour and socialist feeling, as typified by *Die Blechtrommel/The Tin Drum*

Greene (Henry) Graham (1904–1991) English writer whose books, such as *Brighton Rock*, deal with the religious themes of guilt, despair, and penitence

Grey (Pearl) Zane (1872–1939) US author with a prolific output who principally created the Western as a literary genre with books such as *Riders of the Purple Sage*

Grisham John (1955–) US writer whose work includes *The Firm*, *The Pelican Brief*, and *The Rainmaker*, all of which have also been made into films

Haggard H(enry) Rider (1856–1925) English romantic adventure novelist whose books include *King Solomon's Mines*

Hall Radclyffe (Marguerite Radclyffe-Hall) (1880–1943) English novelist whose book *The Well of Loneliness* deals with lesbianism

Hammett (Samuel) Dashiell (1894–1961) US crime novelist who introduced the tough detective character to fiction, as in *The Maltese Falcon*

Hamsun Knut (pseudonym of Knut Pedersen) (1859–1952) Norwegian Nobel prizewinning novelist who tried to capture 'the unconscious life of the soul', as in *Hunger* and *Growth of the Soil*

Hardy Thomas (1840–1928) English novelist and poet who portrayed intense human relationships, as in *Far From the Madding Crowd* and *Jude the Obscure*

Harris Joel Chandler (1848–1908) US writer who created the folk character Uncle Remus

Hartley L(eslie) P(oles) (1895–1972) English novelist who wrote *The Go-Between*

Hawthorne Nathaniel (1804–1864) US writer who wrote a classic allegorical novel *The Scarlet Letter*

Heinlein Robert A(nson) (1907–) US science-fiction writer and author of the utopian cult novel *Stranger in a Strange Land*

Heller Joseph (1923–) US novelist who satirized war in his novel *Catch-22*

Hemingway Ernest (Miller) (1899–1961) US Pulitzer prizewinning writer, author of *A Farewell to Arms* and *The Old Man and the Sea*

Henry O (pen name of William Sydney Porter) (1862–1910) US short story writer, skilled at surprise endings, as in *Cabbages and Kings*

Hesse Hermann (1877–1962) German-born Swiss Nobel prizewinning short story writer, poet, and novelist whose books include *Siddhartha* and *Steppenwolf*

(*continued*)

Noteworthy Fiction Writers (*continued*)

Hornby Nick (1957–) English novelist who grew to fame with *High Fidelity*

Hugo Victor (Marie) (1802–1885) French novelist, poet, and dramatist, leader of French Romanticism, whose novels include *Les Misérables*

Huxley Aldous (Leonard) (1894–1963) English writer of novels, essays, and verse who wrote the science-fiction novel *Brave New World*

Ibáñez Vicente Blasco (1867–1928) Spanish novelist and politician whose books include *Los cuatro jinetes del Apocalipsis/The Four Horsemen of the Apocalypse*

Irving Washington (1783–1859) US author who wrote the story 'Rip Van Winkle'

Isherwood Christopher (Christopher William Bradshaw-Isherwood) (1904–1986) English-born US novelist who wrote *Goodbye to Berlin*

Ishiguro Kazuo (1954–) Japanese-born British novelist who won the Booker Prize for *The Remains of the Day*

James Henry (1843–1916) US novelist and master of psychological realism, as in *The Portrait of a Lady* and *The Turn of the Screw*

James P(hyllis) D(orothy) (1920–) English detective novelist whose books include *Death of an Expert Witness*

Jerome Jerome K(lapka) (1859–1927) English journalist and writer who wrote the humorous novel *Three Men in a Boat*

Jhabvala Ruth Prawer (1927–) British novelist, born in Germany of Polish parents, who lived in India 1951–75, and whose works explore the blend of East and West in the Indian middle class; she won the Booker Prize for *Heat and Dust*

Joyce James (Augustine Aloysius) (1882–1941) Irish writer who pioneered innovative literary technique in such novels as *A Portrait of the Artist as a Young Man* and *Ulysses*

Kafka Franz (1883–1924) Czech-born Austrian allegorical novelist and author of *Der Prozess/The Trial* and the short story 'Die Verwandlung/The Metamorphosis'

Kawabata Yasunari (1899–1972) Japanese novelist and Nobel prizewinner whose books include *A Thousand Cranes*

Kazantzakis Nikos (1885–1957) Greek author and poet whose novels include *Zorba the Greek* and the controversial *The Last Temptation of Christ*

Kelman James (1946–) Scottish novelist and short story writer of angry, compassionate, and ironic works, such as the Booker prizewinning *How Late It Was, How Late*

Keneally Thomas (Michael) (1935–) Australian novelist who won the Booker Prize with *Schindler's Ark*

Kerouac Jack Jean-Louis (1922–1969) US novelist who named and epitomized the Beat Generation and whose books include *On the Road*

King Stephen (Edwin) (1947–) US writer of best-selling horror novels, such as *Carrie* and *The Shining*

Kingsley Charles (1819–1875) English author who wrote historical novels, including *Westward Ho!*, social novels, and children's books

Kipling (Joseph) Rudyard (1865–1936) English writer and Nobel prizewinner who depicted Anglo-Indian society in poems, short stories, and children's books, including *The Jungle Book* and *Kim*

Koestler Arthur (1905–1983) Hungarian-born British writer whose *Darkness at Noon* is a fictional account of Stalinist purges

Koontz Dean (Ray) (1945–) US writer whose work includes *Intensity* and *Watchers*

Kundera Milan (1929–) Czech writer whose novels include *Zert/The Joke* and *Nesnesitelná lehkost bytí/The Unbearable Lightness of Being*

Laclos Pierre (-Ambroise-François) Choderlos de (1741–1803) French author of *Les Liaisons Dangereuses/Dangerous Liaisons*, an analysis of moral corruption

La Fayette (Marie-Madeleine, comtesse) Madame de (1634–1693) French writer who published the novel *La Princesse de Clèves*

Lagerlöf Selma (Ottiliana Lovisa) (1858–1940) Swedish novelist and Nobel prizewinner whose books include *Gösta Berling's saga/The Story of Gösta Berling*

Lawrence D(avid) H(erbert) (1885–1930) English writer who believed that the passionate life was threatened by the modern world; his novels include *Sons and Lovers* and *Lady Chatterley's Lover*

Le Carré John (pen name of David John Moore Cornwell) (1931–) English writer of complex espionage novels, including *The Spy Who Came in From the Cold* and *Tinker, Tailor, Soldier, Spy*

Lee (Nelle) Harper (1926–) US author who wrote the novel *To Kill a Mockingbird*

Le Guin Ursula K(roeber) (1929–) US writer of science fiction and fantasy whose books include *The Dispossessed*

Leonard Elmore (John Jr) (1925–) US author of Westerns and thrillers, including *La Brava* and *Get Shorty*

Lessing Doris (May) (born Tayler) (1919–) English novelist whose works, such as *Children of Violence*, have social and political themes

Levi Primo (1919–1987) Italian novelist who wrote of his experiences during World War II, as in *If This Is a Man*

Lewis (Harry) Sinclair (1885–1951) US Nobel prizewinning author of social documentary novels, such as *Main Street* and *Babbitt*

London Jack (John Griffith Chaney) (1876–1916) US author of naturalistic novels, adventure stories, and socialist reportage whose books include *The Call of the Wild*

Luo Guan Zhong or **Luo Kuan-chung** (lived 14th century) Chinese novelist who reworked popular tales, as in *The Romance of the Three Kingdoms*

McCullers (Lula) Carson (born Smith) (1917–1967) US 'Southern Gothic' novelist whose books include *The Heart is a Lonely Hunter*

McEwan Ian (Russell) (1948–) English author of sinister and macabre novels and short stories, such as *The Comfort of Strangers*

Machado de Assis Joaquim Maria (1839–1908) Brazilian writer and poet, sceptical and ironic, whose works include *Mémorias pósthumos de Bras Cubas/Epitaph for a Small Winner*

Maclean Alistair (1922–1987) Scottish adventure novelist whose books include *The Guns of Navarone*

Mahfouz Naguib (1911–) Egyptian Nobel prizewinning novelist and playwright whose novels, such as *The Cairo Trilogy*, are concerned with the urban working class

Mailer Norman (Kingsley) (1923–) US writer and journalist whose novels include *The Naked and the Dead*

Malamud Bernard (1914–1986) US novelist and short story writer, concerned with moral redemption, as in *The Natural* and *God's Grace*

Malory Thomas (c. 1410–1471) English author of the prose romance *Le Morte D'Arthur*

Malraux André (Georges) (1901–1976) French writer, art critic, and politician whose novels include *La Condition Humaine/Man's Estate*

Mann Heinrich (1871–1950) German novelist whose books include *Professor Unrat/The Blue Angel*

Mann Thomas (1875–1955) German Nobel prizewinning novelist and critic whose novels are preoccupied with the artist's relation to society, such as *Der Zauberberg/The Magic Mountain* and *Der Tod in Venedig/Death in Venice*

Mansfield Katherine (pen name of Kathleen Beauchamp) (1888–1923) New Zealand short story writer whose collections include *The Garden Party*

Marsh (Edith) Ngaio (1899–1982) New Zealand detective fiction writer whose books include *A Man Lay Dead*

Maugham (William) Somerset (1874–1965) English anti-romantic writer whose novels include *Of Human Bondage*; he also wrote many short stories

Maupassant (Henry René Albert) Guy de (1850–1893) French author of short stories and novels including the story 'Boule de Suif/Ball of Fat'

Noteworthy Fiction Writers (continued)

Mauriac François (1885–1970) French novelist whose books are concerned with the psychological and moral problems of Catholics, as in *Le Baiser au Lépreux/A Kiss for the Leper*

Melville Herman (1819–1891) US writer whose novels are drawn from his experiences as a sailor and include *Moby Dick*

Miller Henry (Valentine) (1891–1980) US writer of controversial, sexually explicit novels, such as *Tropic of Cancer*

Mishima Yukio (pen name of Kimitake Hiraoka) (1925–1970) Japanese novelist whose works, such as *Confessions of a Mask*, deal with sexual desire

Mitchell Margaret (1900–1949) US Pulitzer prizewinning author of *Gone With the Wind*

Moorcock Michael (John) (1939–) English science-fiction writer whose books include *The Cornelius Chronicles*

Moravia Alberto (pen name of Alberto Pincherle) (1907–1991) Italian writer whose short stories and novels give a frank account of Italian life, as in the novel *La ciociara/Two Women*

Morrison Toni (Chloe Anthony) (born Wofford) (1931–) US Pulitzer and Nobel prizewinning novelist whose novels, such as *Beloved*, record black life in the South

Murakami Haruki (1949–) Japanese surrealist novelist and translator whose novels include *Norwegian Wood*

Murasaki Shikibu (c. 978–c. 1015) Japanese writer of what is possibly the world's first novel, *The Tale of Genji*

Murdoch (Jean) Iris (1919–) English novelist whose books combine philosophical speculation with tangled relationships and include *The Sea, The Sea*

Nabokov Vladimir (Vladimirovich) (1899–1977) Russian-born US writer best known for his novel *Lolita*, the story of a middle-aged man's infatuation with a 12-year-old girl

Naipaul V(idiadhar) S(urajprasad) (1932–) Trinidadian novelist whose novels include *A Bend in the River*

Narayan R(asipuram) K(rishnaswami) (1906–) Indian novelist and short story writer whose novels include *A Tiger for Malgudi*

Nerval Gérard de (pen name of Gérard Labrunie) (1808–1855) French writer and poet who was a precursor of French Symbolism and Surrealism; his short stories include the collection *Les Filles du feu/The Daughters of Fire*

Ngugi wa Thiong'o (born James Ngugi) (1938–) Kenyan writer of essays, plays, short stories, and novels, including *The River Between* and dealing with the effects of colonialism

Norris Frank (Benjamin Franklin) (1870–1902) US naturalist novelist whose novels include *The Octopus*

O'Connor (Mary) Flannery (1925–1964) US novelist and short story writer whose books explore evil, sin, and the religious sensibility of the Deep South, such as *The Violent Bear It Away*

Okri Ben (1959–) Nigerian novelist, broadcaster, and journalist who wrote the Booker prizewinning *The Famished Road*

Orwell George (pen name of Eric Arthur Blair) (1903–1950) British writer with a deep social conscience and antipathy for dictatorships who is known for his political satires, such as *1984*, and the allegorical *Animal Farm*

Pasternak Boris (Leonidovich) (1890–1960) Russian poet and Nobel prizewinning author of the novel *Dr Zhivago*

Paton Alan (Stewart) (1903–1988) South African author who wrote the novel *Cry, The Beloved Country*

Pilcher Rosamunde (1924–) English-born Scottish novelist whose work includes *The Shell Seekers*

Poe Edgar Allan (1809–1849) US writer and poet who created horrific atmospheres, as in the short story 'The Fall of the House of Usher'

Powell Anthony (Dymoke) (1905) English novelist who wrote the 12-volume novel sequence *A Dance to the Music of Time*

Powys John Cowper (1872–1963) English writer of historic, mystic, and erotic books, such as *Wolf Solent*

Pratchett Terry (1948–) English author of fantasy novels who became well-known for his *Discworld* novels

Priestley J(ohn) B(oynton) (1894–1984) English dramatist and novelist, author of the novel *The Good Companions*

Proust Marcel (1871–1922) French novelist and critic who is best known for his series of novels *A la Recherche du temps perdu/Remembrance of Things Past*

Pynchon Thomas (1937–) US novelist who uses fantastic imagery in his novels such as *Gravity's Rainbow*

Rabelais François (c. 1495–1553) bawdy French satirist, monk, and physician, author of satirical allegories, including *La vie inestimable de Gargantua/The Inestimable Life of Gargantua*

Remarque Erich Maria (1898–1970) German author who wrote the war novel *All Quiet on the Western Front*

Rendell Ruth (Barbara) (1930–) English novelist and short-story writer whose work includes *Lake of Darkness*; she also writes under the pseudonym Barbara Vine

Richardson Dorothy M(iller) (1873–1957) English novelist who wrote the multi-volume, stream-of-consciousness novel *Pilgrimage*

Richardson Henry Handel (Ethel Florence Lindesay Robertson) (1870–1946) Australian writer who wrote the novel *The Getting of Wisdom*

Richardson Samuel (1689–1761) English novelist who is considered a founder of the modern novel because of his epistolary work *Pamela*

Robbe-Grillet Alain (1922–) French writer and theorist of the 'new novel' who wrote *La Jalousie/Jealousy*

Roth Philip (Milton) (1933–) US novelist whose books depict moral and sexual anxieties, as in *Portnoy's Complaint*

Roy Arundhati (1961–) Indian author who won the Booker Prize in 1997 for *The God of Small Things*, her debut novel

Runyon (Alfred) Damon (1880–1946) US journalist who wrote short stories dealing with the seamier side of New York City, such as 'Guys and Dolls'

Rushdie (Ahmed) Salman (1947–) Indian-born British writer who wrote the controversial *The Satanic Verses*

Sade (Donatien Alphonse François, Comte de) Marquis de Sade (1740–1814) French writer whose work, which includes *Juliette*, deals explicitly with sexual subject matter

Saint-Exupéry Antoine (Marie Roger de) (1900–1944) French author and pilot who wrote the allegorical children's book *Le Petit Prince/The Little Prince* and the novel *Terre des hommes/Wind, Sand, and Stars*

Saki (Hector Hugh Munro) (1870–1916) Scottish writer best known for wittily cruel short stories, as in the collection *Beasts and Super-Beasts*

Salinger J(erome) D(avid) (1919–) reclusive US writer of the classic adolescent novel *The Catcher in the Rye*

Sand George (pen name of Amandine Aurore Lucie Dupin) (1804–1876) French author whose *Indiana* was a plea for women's independence

Sartre Jean-Paul (1905–1980) French existentialist author and philosopher whose novels include the trilogy *Les Chemins de la Liberté/Roads to Freedom*

Sayers Dorothy L(eigh) (1893–1957) English crime novelist whose books include *Strong Poison*

Scott Walter (1771–1832) Scottish historical novelist and poet whose novels include *Ivanhoe*

Sewell Anna (1820–1878) English writer and author of the children's classic *Black Beauty*

Shelley Mary Wollstonecraft (born Godwin) (1797–1851) English writer and author of the Gothic horror *Frankenstein*

Sillitoe Alan (1928) English novelist and short story writer whose novels include *Saturday Night and Monday Morning*

(continued)

Noteworthy Fiction Writers (*continued*)

Simenon Georges (Joseph Christian) (1903–1989) Belgian crime writer and creator of the Inspector Maigret series of popular detective novels

Singer Isaac Bashevis (1904–1991) Polish-born US Nobel prizewinning novelist and short story writer whose novels include *The Family Moskat*

Smith Wilbur (1933–) African-born author whose novels include *The Seventh Scroll*

Solzhenitsyn Aleksander (Isayevich) (1918–) Soviet novelist whose work, such as *One Day in the Life of Ivan Denisovich*, is highly critical of the communist system

Sōseki Natsume (pen name of Natsume Kinnosuke) (1867–1916) Japanese novelist of deep psychological studies of urban intellectual lives, such as *Light and Darkness*

Spark Muriel (Sarah) (born Camberg) (1918–) Scottish-born satirical novelist whose books include *The Prime of Miss Jean Brodie*

Staêl (Anne Louise Germaine Necker), Madame de (1766–1817) French critic and writer whose novels include *Delphine*

Stein Gertrude (1874–1946) US writer who evolved a 'continuous present' style, as in *The Autobiography of Alice B Toklas*

Steinbeck John (Ernst) (1902–1968) US realist novelist and Pulitzer prizewinner whose novels include *Of Mice and Men* and *The Grapes of Wrath*

Stendhal (pen name of Marie-Henri Beyle) (1783–1842) French novelist who wrote the masterpiece of psychological analysis *Le Rouge et le Noir/The Red and the Black*

Sterne Laurence (1713–1768) Irish writer who created a bawdy, comic anti-hero in *The Life and Opinions of Tristram Shandy*

Stevenson Robert Louis (Balfour) (1850–1894) Scottish novelist and poet whose adventure novels include *Treasure Island*

Stoker Bram (Abraham) (1847–1912) Irish novelist, actor, theatre manager, and author who crystallized the traditional vampire legend with the novel *Dracula*

Stowe Harriet (Elizabeth) Beecher (1811–1896) US suffragist, abolitionist, and author of the antislavery novel *Uncle Tom's Cabin*

Swift Jonathan (1667–1745) Irish satirist and Anglican cleric who wrote *Gulliver's Travels*

Tanizaki Jun-ichirō (1886–1965) Japanese novelist whose books include *The Key*

Tarkington (Newton) Booth (1869–1946) US novelist who wrote classic, young-adult novels, such as *Penrod*

Thackeray William Makepeace (1811–1863) English essayist and sentimental novelist whose first novel was *Vanity Fair*

Thurber James (Grover) (1894–1961) US humorist and writer whose short stories include 'The Secret Life of Walter Mitty'

Tolkien J(ohn) R(onald) R(euel) (1892–1973) English writer of fantasy novels such as the trilogy *The Lord of the Rings*

Tolstoy Leo (Nikolaievich) (1828–1910) Russian novelist whose works include *War and Peace* and *Anna Karenina*

Trollope Anthony (1815–1882) English novelist who portrayed provincial middle-class society in novels such as *Barchester Towers*

Turgenev Ivan (Sergeievich) (1818–1883) Russian writer whose novels include *Fathers and Sons*

Twain Mark (pen name of Samuel Langhorne Clemens) (1835–1910) US writer who wrote the classic novels *The Adventures of Tom Sawyer* and *The Adventures of Huckleberry Finn* in American dialect

Updike John (Hoyer) (1932–) US writer known for polished prose, poetry, and criticism who wrote *Couples* and *The Witches of Eastwick*

Vargas Llosa (Jorge) Mario Pedro (1936–) Peruvian novelist and politician whose novels include *La ciudad y los perros/The Time of the Hero*

Verne Jules (1828–1905) French author of adventure tales that anticipated future scientific developments, such as *Voyage au centre de la terre/Journey to the Centre of the Earth*

Vidal Gore (pen name of Eugene Luther Vidal) (1925–) US writer, critic, and author of satiric histories and political novels, such as *Myra Breckinridge* and *Empire*

Vonnegut Kurt Jr (1922–) US writer of science fiction, fantasy, and absurdist anarchy, such as *Slaughterhouse-Five* and *Galapagos*

Walker Alice (Malsenior) (1944–) US novelist, poet, critic, and essay writer who wrote the Pulitzer prizewinning novel *The Color Purple*

Waugh Evelyn (Arthur St John) (1903–1966) English writer of socially satirical novels such as *Vile Bodies* and *Brideshead Revisited*

Weldon Fay (1931–) English feminist novelist and dramatist whose works are often comic or ironic, including the novels *The Fat Woman's Joke* and *The Life and Loves of a She-Devil*

Wells H(erbert) G(eorge) (1866–1946) English pioneer of science fiction whose books include *The Time Machine* and *War of the Worlds*

Welty Eudora (1909–) US novelist and short story writer whose work, such as *The Optimist's Daughter*, reflects life in the American South

West Nathanael (pen name of Nathan Wallenstein Weinstein) (1903–1940) US writer who depicted the dark side of the American Dream, as in *The Day of the Locust*

West Rebecca (pen name of Cicily Isabel Fairfield Andrews) (1892–1983) English journalist and feminist novelist whose books include *The Fountain Overflows*

Wharton Edith (Newbold) (born Jones) (1862–1937) US novelist whose novels include the Pulitzer prizewinning *The Age of Innocence*

Wheatley Dennis (Yates) (1897–1977) English thriller and adventure novelist whose books include *Murder off Miami* and *The Devil Rides Out*

White Patrick (Victor Martindale) (1912–1990) Australian Nobel prizewinning writer of partly allegorical novels exploring early Australian settlement, such as *Voss*

Wilde Oscar (Fingal O'Flahertie Wills) (1854–1900) flamboyant Irish playwright and short story writer whose only novel is *The Picture of Dorian Gray*

Wilder Thornton (Niven) (1897–1975) US dramatist and novelist whose novels include *The Bridge of San Luis Rey*

Wilson Angus (Frank Johnstone) (1913–1991) acidly humorous English novelist, short story writer, and biographer whose novels include *Anglo-Saxon Attitudes*

Wodehouse P(ercival) G(renville) (1881–1975) English novelist whose humorous stories feature the socialite Bertie Wooster and his manservant Jeeves

Wolfe Thomas (Clayton) (1900–1938) US writer of mostly autobiographical novels, such as *Of Time and the River* and *You Can't Go Home Again*

Wolfe Tom (Thomas Kennerly Jr) (1931–) US journalist and novelist, founder of 'New Journalism', who wrote *The Bonfire of the Vanities*

Woolf (Adeline) Virginia (born Stephen) (1882–1941) English 'stream of consciousness' novelist and critic who explored feminist principles in *To the Lighthouse*

Wright Richard (1908–1960) US novelist who depicted the condition of African-Americans in US society in *Native Son* and *Black Boy*

Wyndham John (pen name of John Wyndham Parkes Lucas Beynon Harris) (1903–1969) English science-fiction writer whose work concentrated on people's response to disaster, as in *The Day of the Triffids*

Yourcenar Marguerite (pen name of Marguerite de Crayencour) (1903–1987) Belgian writer whose novels include *The New Eurydice* and *The Memoirs of Hadrian*

Zola Émile (Édouard Charles Antoine) (1840–1902) French novelist and social reformer whose books include *Thérèse Raquin*

Noteworthy Dramatists

Abbott George (1887–1995) US playwright, theatre director, and producer, author of *Fiorello!* and *Damn Yankees*

Achard Marcel (1899–1974) French dramatist, author of *Patate* and *La Vie est belle/Life is Beautiful*

Adamov Arthur (1908–1970) Russian-born French surrealist poet and dramatist, author of *Paolo Paoli* and *Le Printemps '71/Spring '71*

Aeschylus (c. 524–c. 456 BC) Greek tragic dramatist whose powerful plays include *Seven against Thebes* and the *Oresteia* trilogy

Albee Edward Franklin (1928–   ) US playwright, author of *Who's Afraid of Virginia Woolf?* and Pulitzer prizewinners *A Delicate Balance*, *Seascape*, and *Three Tall Women*

Anderson Maxwell (1888–1959) US dramatist, author of *What Price Glory?* and Pulitzer prizewinner *Both Your Houses*

Anouilh Jean (1910–1987) French dramatist, author of *Antigone* and *Becket*

Aristophanes (c. 450–c. 380 BC) Greek comic dramatist considered without equal whose works include *The Frogs* and *Lysistrata*

Ayckbourn Alan (1939–   ) English playwright, author of *Relatively Speaking* and *The Norman Conquests* trilogy

Barrie J(ames) M(atthew) (1860–1937) Scottish dramatist and novelist, author of the plays *The Admirable Crichton* and *Peter Pan*

Beaumarchais Pierre Augustin Caron de (1732–1799) French comic dramatist, author of *Le Barbier de Séville/The Barber of Séville* and *Le Mariage de Figaro/The Marriage of Figaro*

Beaumont Francis (1584–1616) English dramatist who collaborated with John Fletcher on *The Maid's Tragedy* and other plays

Beckett Samuel (Barclay) (1906–1989) Irish dramatist and novelist, author of the plays *Waiting for Godot* and *Endgame*

Behan Brendan (1923–1964) Irish dramatist, author of *The Quare Fellow* and *The Hostage*

Belasco David (1859–1931) US dramatist and producer, author of *Madame Butterfly* and *The Girl of the Golden West*

Bolt Robert Oxton (1924–1995) English historical dramatist and screenwriter, author of *A Man for All Seasons*

Bond Edward (1934–   ) English dramatist who wrote *Lear* and *Bingo*

Brecht Bertolt (Eugen Berthold Friedrich) (1898–1956) German dramatist and poet, author of many political dramas, including *Mutter Courage und ihre Kinder/Mother Courage and Her Children* and *Der kaukasische Kreiderkreis/The Caucasian Chalk Circle*

Čapek Karel (1890–1938) Czech writer, author of *RUR*, in which he coined the word 'robot'

Chapman George (c. 1559–1634) English dramatist who wrote *Bussy D'Ambois*

Chekhov Anton Pavlovich (1860–1904) Russian dramatist and writer of short stories whose plays include *Uncle Vanya*, *The Three Sisters*, and *The Cherry Orchard*

Churchill Caryl (1938–   ) English dramatist, author of *Cloud Nine* and *Mad Forest*

Congreve William (1670–1729) English dramatist who wrote *The Way of the World*

Corneille Pierre (1606–1684) French classical dramatist, author of *Cinna*, *Mélite*, and *Le Cid*

Coward Noël Peirce (1899–1973) English dramatist, actor, and composer, author of *Fallen Angels*, *Private Lives*, and *Blithe Spirit*

Dekker Thomas (c. 1570–1632) English dramatist who wrote *The Shoemaker's Holiday*

Dryden John (1631–1700) English poet and dramatist, author of *Marriage A-La-Mode*

Echegaray y Eizaguirre José (1832–1916) Spanish dramatist, author of *Madman or Saint* and *The World and his Wife*

Edgar David (1948–   ) English dramatist, author of *Destiny* and *The Shape of the Table*

Eliot T(homas) S(tearns) (1888–1965) US-born English poet and dramatist whose plays include *Murder in the Cathedral*

Euripides (c. 480–c. 406 BC) Greek tragic dramatist, ranked with Aeschylus and Sophocles, whose plays prefigured the later development of drama in dealing with ordinary people, and include *Andromache* and *The Trojan Women*

Feydeau Georges (1862–1921) French comic dramatist, author of *Le Dame de Chez Maxim/The Lady from Maxim's* and *Occupe-toi d'Amélie/Look after Lulu*

Fletcher John (1579–1625) English dramatist of broad range, co-author of *Philaster* and *The Maid's Tragedy*

Fo Dario (1926–   ) Italian Nobel prizewinning dramatist of political satire and author of *Morte accidentale di un anarchico/Accidental Death of an Anarchist* and *Non si paya, no si paya/Can't Pay? Won't Pay!*

Ford John (1586–c.1640) English dramatist who wrote *'Tis Pity She's a Whore*

Friel Brian (1929–   ) Northern Irish dramatist, author of *Philadelphia, Here I Come!* and *Dancing at Lughnasa*

Fry Christopher (Harris) (1907–   ) English dramatist, author of *The Lady's Not for Burning* and *Venus Observed*

Fugard Athol (Harold Lanigan) (1932–   ) South African dramatist, author of *The Blood Knot* and *Hello and Goodbye*

Galsworthy John (1867–1933) English novelist and dramatist whose plays include *Strife* and *Justice*

Gelber Jack (1932–   ) US playwright and novelist, author of *The Connection*

Genet Jean (1910–1986) French dramatist, novelist, and poet, author of *The Maids* and *The Balcony*

Giraudoux Jean (1882–1944) French dramatist and novelist whose plays include *La Guerre du Troie n'aura pas lieu/Tiger at the Gates*

Goethe Johann Wolfgang von (1749–1832) German Romantic poet, novelist, dramatist, and scholar, founder of modern German literature whose masterpiece is *Faust*, a poetic play

Gogol Nikolai (Vasilevich) (1809–1852) Russian novelist and dramatist whose best-known play is *The Inspector General*

Goldsmith Oliver (1728–1774) Irish dramatist who wrote *She Stoops to Conquer*

Gombrowicz Witold (1904–1969) Polish allegorical dramatist and novelist, author of *Ilona, Princess of Burgundy*

Gorky or **Gorki** Maksim (adopted name of Aleksei Maksimovich Peshkov) (1868–1936) Russian writer whose plays include *The Lower Depths*

Hansberry Lorraine (1930–1965) US playwright, author of *A Raisin in the Sun*

Hare David (1947–   ) British satirical dramatist and screenwriter, author of *Slag* and *Pravda*

Hart Moss (1904–1961) US dramatist, author of *The Man Who Came to Dinner*

Hauptmann Gerhart Johann Robert (1862–1946) German Nobel prizewinning dramatist, author of *Die Weben/The Weavers*

Havel Václav (1936–   ) Czech dramatist and politician, author of *Zahradní slavnost/The Garden Party* and *Vyrozumění/The Memorandum*

Hellman Lillian (Florence) (1907–1984) US political and social dramatist, author of *The Children's Hour* and *Toys in the Attic*

Heywood Thomas (c. 1574–1641) English dramatist who wrote *A Woman Killed with Kindness*

Hochhuth Rolf (1931–   ) Swiss dramatist, author of *Soldaten/Soldiers* and *Der Stellvertreter/The Representative*

Ibsen Henrik Johan (1828–1906) Norwegian dramatist and poet, author of *Et dukkehjem/A Doll's House* and *Gengangere/Ghosts*

Ionesco Eugène (1912–1994) Romanian-born French dramatist, author of *La Cantatrice chauve/The Bald Prima Donna* and *Le Roi se meurt/Exit the King*

(continued)

Noteworthy Dramatists (*continued*)

Jarry Alfred (1873–1907) French satiric dramatist whose play *King Ubu* foreshadowed the Theatre of the Absurd

Jonson Ben(jamin) (1572–1637) English dramatist, poet, and critic, author of *Every Man in his Humour* and *Volpone*

Klinger Friedrich Maximilian von (1752–1831) German playwright and poet, author of *Sturm und Drang/Storm and Stress*

Kyd Thomas (1558–1594) English dramatist who wrote *The Spanish Tragedy*

Lessing Gotthold Ephraim (1729–1781) German dramatist and critic, author of *Miss Sara Sampson* and *Emilia Galotti*

Lorca Federico Garcia (1899–1936) Spanish poet and dramatist whose plays include *Bodas de sangre/Blood Wedding* and *La casa de Bernarda Alba/The House of Bernarda Alba*

Maeterlinck Maurice (1862–1949) Belgian writer and dramatist whose plays included *L'Oiseau bleu/The Blue Bird*

Mamet David Alan (1947–) US dramatist, screenwriter, and director whose plays feature vivid language and urban settings, such as *Glengarry Glen Ross*

Marlowe Christopher (1564–1593) English poet and dramatist, author of *Tamburlaine the Great* and *Dr Faustus*

Miller Arthur (1915–) US dramatist, author of *Death of a Salesman* and *The Crucible*

Molière (Jean-Baptiste Poquelin) (1622–1673) French satirical dramatist and actor, author of *Le Tartuffe/The Impostor* and *L'Ecole des femmes/The School for Wives*

Nichols Peter Richard (1927–) English dramatist, author of *A Day in the Death of Joe Egg* and *Passion Play*

O'Casey Sean (adopted name of John Casey) (1884–1964) Irish dramatist, author of *Juno and the Paycock* and *The Plough and the Stars*

© Penguin Books Ltd.

Arthur Miller

Odets Clifford (1906–1963) US social-protest dramatist, author of *Waiting for Lefty* and *Awake and Sing*

O'Neill Eugene Gladstone (1888–1953) US playwright, author of Pulitzer prizewinners *Beyond the Horizon* and *A Long Day's Journey into Night*

Orton Joe (John Kingsley) (1933–1967) English dramatist, author of *Loot* and *What the Butler Saw*

Osborne John (James) (1929–1994) English dramatist, author of *Look Back in Anger* and *The Entertainer*

Ostrovsky Aleksander Nikolaevich (1823–1886) Russian dramatist, author of *The Storm* and *The Snow Maiden*

Pinero Arthur Wing (1855–1934) English dramatist, author of *The Magistrate* and *The Second Mrs Tanqueray*

Pinter Harold (1930–) English dramatist and actor, author of *The Birthday Party* and *The Caretaker*

Pirandello Luigi (1867–1936) Italian Nobel prizewinning dramatist, novelist, and short story writer, author of *Sei personaggi in cerca d'autore/Six Characters in Search of an Author*

Plautus Maccius (c. 254–c. 184 BC) Roman comic dramatist who took plots from Greek comedy to produce works, such as *Miles Gloriosus/The Boastful Soldier* and *Amphitryon*

Priestley J(ohn) B(oynton) (1894–1984) English dramatist and novelist, author of *An Inspector Calls* and *Dangerous Corner*

Racine Jean Baptiste (1639–1699) French dramatist, author of *Andromaque/Andromache* and *Phèdre/Phaedra*

Rattigan Terence Mervyn (1911–1977) English dramatist, author of *Separate Tables* and *The Winslow Boy*

Rice Elmer Leopold (1892–1967) US dramatist, author of *The Adding Machine* and Pulitzer prizewinner *Street Scene*

Rostand Edmond (1868–1918) French poetic dramatist, author of *Cyrano de Bergerac* and *L'Aiglon*

Sartre Jean-Paul (1905–1980) French philosopher, novelist, and dramatist whose plays include *Huit Clos/No Exit*

Schiller Johann Christoph Friedrich von (1759–1805) German poet and dramatist whose plays include *Maria Stuart* and *Wallenstein*

Schnitzler Arthur (1862–1931) Viennese dramatist, author of *Reigen/Merry-Go-Round*

Seneca (Lucius Annaeus) (c. 4 BC–AD 65) Roman orator, statesman, and dramatist who wrote *Medea* and other tragedies

Seymour Alan (1927–) Australian dramatist, author of *The One Day of the Year*

Shaffer Peter (1926–) English dramatist, author of *Equus* and *Amadeus*

Shakespeare William (1564–1616) English dramatist and poet, author of *Romeo and Juliet*, *As You Like It*, *Henry IV*, and *Hamlet*

Shaw George Bernard (1856–1950) Irish dramatist, critic, and novelist, author of *Man and Superman*, *Pygmalion*, and *St Joan*

Shepard Sam (adopted name of Samuel Shepard Rogers) (1943–) US dramatist and actor, author of Pulitzer prizewinner *Buried Child*

Sheridan Richard Brinsley (1751–1816) Irish dramatist and politician whose social comedies include *The Rivals* and *School for Scandal*

Sherwood Robert Emmet (1896–1955) US dramatist, author of Pulitzer prizewinners *Idiot's Delight* and *Abe Lincoln in Illinois*

Simon (Marvin) Neil (1927–) US dramatist and screenwriter, author of *The Odd Couple* and Pulitzer prizewinner *Lost in Yonkers*

Sophocles (c. 496–406 BC) Greek tragic dramatist whose plays include *Oedipus Rex/Oedipus the King* and *Antigone*

Soyinka Wole (Akinwande Oluwole Soyinka) (1934–) Nigerian novelist, poet, and dramatist whose plays include *Death and the King's Horsemen*

Stoppard Tom (adopted name of Tomas Straussler) (1937–) Czech-born British dramatist, author of *Rosencrantz and Guildenstern are Dead* and *Arcadia*

Storey David Malcolm (1933–) English dramatist and novelist, author of *In Celebration* and *The Contractor*

Strindberg (Johan) August (1849–1912) Swedish dramatist and novelist, author of *Dödsdansen/The Dance of Death* and *Fadren/The Father*

Synge J(ohn) M(illington) (1871–1909) Irish dramatist, author of *Riders to the Sea* and *The Playboy of the Western World*

Terence (Publius Terentius Afer) (c. 190–c. 159 BC) Roman comic dramatist whose stylish plays, based on Greek dramas, include *Eunuchus* and *Adelphi/The Brothers*

Tourneur Cyril (1575–1626) English dramatist, author of *The Atheist's Tragedy* and *The Revenger's Tragedy*

Vega Lope Félix de (Carpio) (1562–1635) Spanish poet and founder of modern Spanish drama whose plays include *Fuenteovejuna/The Sheep-Well*

Webster John (c. 1580–c. 1625) English dramatist, author of *The White Devil* and *The Duchess of Malfi*

Wedekind Frank (1864–1918) German dramatist, author of *Frühlings Erwachen/The Awakening of Spring* and *Büchse der Pandora/Pandora's Box*

Weiss Peter (Ulrich) (1916–1982) German-born Swedish dramatist, novelist, and film producer, author of *Marat/Sade* and *Die Ermittlung/The Investigation*

Wilde Oscar (Fingal O'Flahertie Wills) (1854–1900) Irish writer and dramatist, famous for a series of sharp comedies, including *The Importance of Being Earnest*

Wilder Thornton (Niven) (1897–1975) US dramatist and novelist, author of Pulitzer prizewinners *Our Town* and *The Skin of Our Teeth*

Williams (George) Emlyn (1905–1987) Welsh actor and dramatist, author of *Night Must Fall* and *The Corn Is Green*

Noteworthy Dramatists (*continued*)

Williams Tennessee (adopted name of Thomas Lanier Williams) (1911–1983) US dramatist, author of Pulitzer prizewinners *A Streetcar Named Desire* and *Cat on a Hot Tin Roof*

Wilson August (1945–) US playwright, author of Pulitzer prizewinners *Fences* and *The Piano Lesson*

Wycherley William (1640–1716) English dramatist who wrote *The Country-Wife*

Zuckmayer Carl (1896–1977) German dramatist and writer, author of *The Devil's General* and *The Cold Light*

Noteworthy Poets

Akhmatova Anna (adopted name of Anna Andreyevna Gorenko) (1889–1966) Russian poet and member of the Acmeist movement; her works include 'Requiem'

Apollinaire Guillaume (adopted name of Wilhelm Apollinaris de Kostrowitsky) (1880–1918) French avant-garde poet of Polish descent who wrote experimental poems in such volumes as *Alcools/Alcohol* and *Calligrammes/Word Pictures*

Aragon Louis (1897–1982) French poet, novelist, and leading Surrealist whose work includes *Le Crève-coeur/Heartbreak* and *Les Yeux d'Elsa/Elsa's Eyes*

Ariosto Ludovico (1474–1533) Italian poet and author of the epic poem *Orlando Furioso/Orlando Enraged*

Arnold Matthew (1822–1888) English poet and critic whose poem 'Dover Beach' expressed the spiritual anxieties of Victorian England

Auden W(ystan) H(ugh) (1907–1973) English-born US poet and dramatist whose work includes the volume *Look, Stranger!*

Barbour John (c. 1320–1395) Scottish poet whose epic poem *The Bruce* chronicled the war for Scottish independence

Bashō (adopted name of Matsuo Munefusa) (1644–1694) Japanese poet and haiku master; his work *The Narrow Road to the Deep North* combines haiku and prose

Baudelaire Charles (Pierre) (1821–1867) influential French poet who combined rhythmical and musical perfection with morbid romanticism and eroticism, as in *Les Fleurs du Mal/Flowers of Evil*

Berryman John (1914–1972) US poet whose collections include *Homage to Mistress Bradstreet*

Betjeman John (1906–1984) English poet laureate and essayist who wrote romantic and nostalgic light verse, such as the collection *New Bats in Old Belfries*

Binyon (Robert) Laurence (1869–1943) English poet of the war memorial ode 'For the Fallen'

Blake William (1757–1827) English Romantic poet, artist, engraver, and spiritual visionary whose works include *Songs of Innocence*

Blunden Edmund (Charles) (1896–1974) English poet and critic who wrote about rural life and war, for example in *Undertones of War*

Boileau-Despréaux Nicolas (1636–1711) French poet and critic whose works include *L'Art poétique/The Art of Poetry*

Brodsky Joseph (Alexandrovich) (1940–1996) Russian Nobel prizewinning poet and US poet laureate, known for his wit and under-statement, as in *A Part of Speech*

© Penguin Books Ltd.

Joseph Brodsky

Brooke Rupert (Chawner) (1887–1915) English poet and symbol of the 'lost generation' whose war sonnets include 'The Soldier'

Browning Elizabeth (Moulton) Barrett (born Barrett) (1806–1861) English poet whose work includes the poetic novel *Aurora Leigh*

Browning Robert (1812–1889) English poet who specialized in dramatic monologue, as in *Bishop Blougram's Apology*

Burns Robert (1759–1796) Scottish poet who wrote in Scots dialect, as in *Poems, Chiefly in the Scottish Dialect* and *Tam O'Shanter*

Byron (George Gordon Noel) Lord (1788–1824) English Romantic poet and political liberal who wrote the satirical epic *Don Juan*

Caedmon (lived c. 660) earliest known English Christian poet

Camoëns or Camoes Luis Vaz de (1524–1580) Portuguese poet and soldier whose *Os Lusiades/The Lusiadas* is Portugal's national epic

Carew Thomas (c. 1595–c. 1640) English Cavalier poet and author of *Coelum Britannicum*

Catullus Caius Valerius (c. 84–c. 54 BC) Roman lyric poet who wrote in a variety of metres, forms, and styles

Chatterton Thomas (1752–1770) English poet whose medieval style inspired English Romanticism

Chaucer Geoffrey (c. 1343–1400) the most influential English poet of the Middle Ages; his *The Canterbury Tales* shows his genius for metre and characterization

Chrétien de Troyes (died c. 1183) French poet whose epics introduced the Holy Grail concept, as in *Lancelot, ou le chavalier de la charrette/Lancelot, or the Knight of the Cart*

Clampitt Amy (1920–) US poets whose collections include *The Kingfisher*

Clare John (1793–1864) English poet whose work includes *Poems Descriptive of Rural Life and Scenery*

Coleridge Samuel Taylor (1772–1834) English Romantic poet whose poems include 'The Rime of the Ancient Mariner' and 'Kubla Khan'

Cowper William (1731–1800) English poet who wrote the ballad 'The Journey of John Gilpin'

Crabbe George (1754–1823) English poet who wrote the long poem on rural life *The Village*

cummings e(dward) e(stlin) (1894–1962) US poet whose work incorporates idiosyncratic punctuation and typography, as in *Tulips and Chimneys*

Dafydd ap Gwilym (c. 1340–c. 1400) Welsh poet concerned with nature whose work contains references to Classical and Italian poetry

Dante Alighieri (1265–1321) Italian poet who wrote *La divina commedia/The Divine Comedy*, an epic journey through Hell, Purgatory, and Paradise

Day-Lewis C(ecil) (1904–1972) influential left-wing Irish poet of the 1930s and British poet laureate (1968–72)

de la Mare Walter (John) (1873–1956) English poet and writer whose work includes verse for children, such as *Peacock Pie*

de Pisan Christine (1364–c. 1430) French poet and historian who created portraits of women in *Cité des dames/The City of Ladies*

Dickinson Emily (Elizabeth) (1830–1886) US poet whose poetry is characterized by wit and boldness, as in 'I Could Not Stop for Death'

Donne John (1572–1631) English metaphysical poet and preacher who wrote powerful poems about sexual love and his relationship with God

(continued)

Noteworthy Poets (*continued*)

Dryden John (1631–1700) English poet laureate and dramatist of satiric verse in the form of the heroic couplet whose work includes 'A Song for St Cecilia's Day' and *Absalom and Achitophel*

Dunbar William (*c.* 1460–*c.* 1520) Scottish poet who wrote *The Thissill and the Rois*

Eliot T(homas) S(tearns) (1888–1965) US-born English Nobel prizewinning poet, playwright, and critic whose poem *The Waste Land* is experimental in form and rhythm

Eluard Paul (adopted name of Eugène Grindel) (1895–1952) surrealist French poet who wrote about love and war, as in his collection *Poésie et vérité/Poetry and Truth*

Emerson Ralph Waldo (1803–1882) US philosopher, essayist, and poet whose *Nature* set principles of transcendentalism

Esenin or **Yesenin** Sergey Aleksandrovich (1895–1925) Soviet poet involved in the Symbolist and Imaginist movements

Firdausi (adopted name of Abdul Qasim Mansur) (*c.* 935–*c.* 1020) Persian epic poet; his *The Book of Kings* is a history of Persia

Frost Robert (Lee) (1874–1963) US poet whose verse is flavoured with New England speech patterns and penetrating vision, as in 'The Road Not Taken'

Gautier Théophile (1811–1872) French Romantic poet who emphasized perfect form, beautiful language, and imagery, as in *Emaux et camés/Enamels and Cameos*

Gay John (1685–1732) English poet and dramatist whose *Trivia* depicts London in verse

Ginsberg Allen (1926–1997) US poet whose poetry is informed by politics and Oriental philosophies, and whose 'Howl' shaped the spirit of the Beat Generation

Graves Robert (Ranke) (1895–1985) English poet and writer who first achieved notice for his war poetry, but who later wrote some of the finest of modern love poems

Goethe Johann Wolfgang von (1749–1832) German Romantic poet, dramatist and novelist whose poetry collections include *Roman Elegies*

Gray Thomas (1716–1771) English poet whose poetry was a precursor of Romanticism, and whose *Elegy Written in a Country Churchyard* is a dignified contemplation of death

Hâfiz Shams ud-Din Muhammed (*c.* 1325–*c.* 1389) Persian lyric poet whose *Divan* extols life's pleasures

Heaney Seamus (Justin) (1939–) Irish Nobel prizewinning poet and critic who writes about Northern Ireland and Ireland's cultural heritage, and whose works include *Field Work*

Heine Heinrich (1797–1856) German Romantic poet, journalist, and satirist whose work includes *Das Buch der Lieder/Book of Songs*

Herbert George (1593–1633) English poet whose poems embody religious struggles, as in 'The Temple'

Herrick Robert (1591–1674) English poet and cleric who wrote lyric poems such as 'Gather Ye Rosebuds While Ye May'

Hesiod (8th century BC) Greek poet, the 'father of Greek didactic poetry', whose surviving known works are the epics *Theogony* and *Works and Days*

Homer (9th or 8th century BC) Greek poet, reputed author of the great epic poems *Iliad* and *Odyssey*, probably originally composed orally, and notable for their vivid imagery and powerful depiction of emotion

Hopkins Gerard Manley (1844–1889) English Jesuit priest and profoundly religious poet whose innovative poems include 'The Wreck of the Deutschland'

Horace (Quintus Horatius Flaccus) (65–8 BC) Roman lyric and satirical poet whose work includes *Odes* and *Epistles*

Housman A(lfred) E(dward) (1859–1936) English poet and classical scholar; his *A Shropshire Lad* is a series of simple ballad-like poems

Hughes Ted (Edward James) (1930–) English poet and poet laureate from 1984 whose poetry reflects on nature's harshness and power, as in *Crow*

Iqbal Muhammad (1873–1938) Islamic poet whose poetry urged Muslims to take their place in the modern world

Juvenal (Decimus Junius Juvenalis) (*c.* 60–*c.* 130) Roman satirical poet whose vitriolic and politically provocative *Satires* lament the passing of traditional moral and social values

Keats John (1795–1821) English Romantic poet whose works include 'Ode to a Nightingale' and 'La Belle Dame sans Merci'

Kipling (Joseph) Rudyard (1865–1936) Nobel prizewinning, Indian-born English poet and writer who emphasized moral viewpoints, as in 'Gunga Din'

Klopstock Friedrich Gottlieb (1724–1803) German poet whose religious epic *The Messiah* anticipated Romanticism

La Fontaine Jean de (1621–1695) French poet of witty and bawdy tales in verse, such as *Contes et nouvelles en vers/Stories and Tales in Verse*

Laforgue Jules (1860–1887) French poet and pioneer of free verse, often lyrically ironic, as in *Les Complaintes*

Lamartine Alphonse Marie Louis de (1790–1869) French poet whose work is characterized by personal romantic poems, such as *Méditations poétiques/Poetical Meditations*

Langland William (*c.* 1332–*c.* 1400) English poet whose alliterative poem *The Vision of William Concerning Piers the Plowman* condemns social and moral evils

Larkin Philip (Arthur) (1922–1985) English poet who wrote perfectionist, pessimistic verse, such as *The Less Deceived*

Leconte de Lisle Charles Marie René (1818–1894) French poet inspired by the ancient world and leader of Les Parnassiens; his works include *Poèmes antiques/Antique Poems*

Lermontov Mikhail Yurevich (1814–1841) Russian Romantic poet and novelist whose poems include *Demon*

Li Po (*c.* 705–762) Chinese poet whose poems are characterized by exuberance, bold imagination, and intense feeling

Longfellow Henry Wadsworth (1807–1882) US poet who is known for ballads, such as 'Excelsior', and mythic narrative epics

Lorca Federico García (1898–1936) Spanish poet and playwright whose poetry includes *Romancero Gitano/Gypsy Ballads*

Lovelace Richard (1618–1658) English poet who wrote 'To Althea, from Prison'

Lowell Amy (Lawrence) (1874–1925) US Imagist poet whose work in free verse includes *Sword Blades and Poppy Seed*

Lowell Robert (Traill Spence Jr) (1917–1977) US Pulitzer prizewinning poet who stressed individualism, as in *Lit Studies*

MacNeice (Frederick) Louis (1907–1963) British poet of social but unpolitical verse, such as *Autumn Journal*

Mallarmé Stéphane (1842–1898) French Symbolist poet of condensed, hermetic verse and unorthodox syntax, as in *L'Après-midi d'un faune/The Afternoon of a Faun*

Malouf David George Joseph (1934–) Australian poet, novelist, and short story writer whose poetry collections include *Neighbours in a Thicket*

Mandelstam Osip Emilievich (1891–1938) Russian poet and literary critic whose poetry includes the collection *Tistia*

Marlowe Christopher (1564–1593) English poet and dramatist whose verse includes *Hero and Leander*

Marvell Andrew (1621–1678) English metaphysical poet and satirist whose poems include 'The Garden' and 'An Horatian Ode upon Cromwell's Return from Ireland'

Masefield John (1878–1967) English poet, novelist, and poet laureate; his poetry collections include *Salt Water Ballads*

Mickiewicz Adam Bernard (1798–1855) Polish revolutionary poet whose *Pan Tadeusz/Master Thadeus* is Poland's national epic

Noteworthy Poets (*continued*)

Milton John (1608–1674) English poet and writer who wrote the epic *Paradise Lost*

Moore Marianne (Craig) (1887–1972) US poet whose volumes included *Observations*

Muir Ewin (1887–1959) Scottish poet who explores dreams, myths, and menaces, as in *Autobiography*

Nash (Frederic) Ogden (1902–1971) US poet and wit who wrote humorous, quietly satirical verse with unorthodox rhymes and puns, as in *I'm a Stranger Here Myself*

Neruda Pablo (adopted name of Neftali Ricardo Reyes y Basoatto) (1904–1973) Chilean Nobel prizewinning poet and diplomat who wrote epic poems about the American continent, including *Canto General de Chile*

Novalis (Friedrich Leopold, Freiherr von Hardenberg) (1772–1801) pioneer of German Romantic poetry whose work includes *Hymnen an die Nacht/Hymns to the Night*

Ovid (Publius Ovidius Naso) (43 BC–AD 17) Roman poet whose works, such as *Ars Amatoria/The Art of Love* and *Tristia/Sorrows*, are distinguished by technical skill and an ironic, sophisticated style

Owen Wilfred (Edward Salter) (1893–1918) English poet who wrote moving war poetry such as 'Anthem for Doomed Youth'

Parker Dorothy (Rothschild) (1893–1967) US writer of ironic verses including *Enough Rope*

Pasternak Boris (Leonidovich) (1890–1960) Russian poet and novelist whose poetry collections include *My Sister, Life*

Paz Octavio (1914–1998) Mexican poet and essayist, influenced by Marxism, Surrealism, and Aztec mythology, whose poetry includes *Piedra del sol/Sun Stone*

Pearse Patrick (Henry) (1879–1916) Irish poet prominent in Irish nationalism

Petrarch or **Petrarca** Francesco (1304–1374) Italian poet and humanist whose influential love poetry was inspired by his beloved Laura

Plath Sylvia (1932–1963) US poet and novelist who wrote highly personal and intense poems expressing desolation; her *Collected Poems* won a Pulitzer prize

Pope Alexander (1688–1744) English poet and satirist whose works include the mock epic *The Rape of the Lock*

Pound Ezra (Loomis) (1885–1972) US poet and cultural critic who revolutionized modern poetry and promoted Imagism, as in *Cantos*

Pushkin Aleksandr (Sergeyevich) (1799–1837) Russian romantic poet and writer; *Eugene Onegin* is his novel in verse

Rilke Rainer Maria (1875–1926) Austrian writer of verse characterized by mystic pantheism, notably *Duino Elegies*

Rimbaud (Jean Nicolas) Arthur (1854–1891) French Symbolist poet who wrote most of his verse before the age of 20; *Les Illuminations* is an example

Roethke Theodore (1908–63) US poet whose collections include *Words for the Wind*

Ronsard Pierre de (1524–1585) French poet with a lightly sensitive style, as in *Amours de Marie/Loves of Marie*

Rossetti Christina (Georgina) (1830–1894) English poet whose work includes *Goblin Market and Other Poems*

Sandburg Carl (August) (1878–1967) US poet whose poems celebrate ordinary American life, as in *Chicago Poems*

Sappho (*c.* 620–*c.* 580 BC) Greek lyric poet, much admired by her contemporaries, whose metrically innovative work, of which only fragments remain, includes poems of love and on natural themes

Sassoon Siegfried (Lorraine) (1886–1967) English writer whose *War Poems* express his generation's disillusionment

Senghor Léopold Sédar (1906–) Senegalese politician and poet who founded *négritude*, a black literary and philosophical movement, and whose work includes *Chants d'ombre/Shadow Songs*

Shelley Percy Bysshe (1792–1822) English Romantic lyric poet who fought against religion and for political freedom; his works include 'Ode to the West Wind' and 'The Skylark'

Sidney Philip (1554–1586) English poet and soldier whose poetry includes *Arcadia*

Spender Stephen (Harold) (1909–1995) English poet and critic whose early poetry had a left-wing political content

Spenser Edmund (*c.* 1552–1599) English poet whose poem *The Faerie Queene* is a moral allegory

Stevens Wallace (1879–1955) US poet whose work includes *Harmonium* and *The Blue Guitar*

Surrey Henry Howard, Earl of Surrey (*c.* 1517–1547) English courtier, poet, and pioneer of blank verse

Swinburne Algernon Charles (1837–1909) English poet whose works include *Atalanta in Calydon*

Tagore Rabindranath (1861–1941) Nobel prizewinning Indian writer whose poetry collections include *Gitanjali*

Tasso Torquato (1544–1595) Italian poet who wrote the romantic epic poem of the First Crusade, *Gerusalemm liberata/Jerusalem Delivered*

Tate Nahum (1652–1715) Irish poet and British poet laureate whose poetry includes *While Shepherds Watched*

Tennyson Alfred (1809–1892) English poet laureate of majestic musical verse typified by the poem 'The Lady of Shalott'

Thomas Dylan (Marlais) (1914–1952) Welsh poet of complex imagery and musicality, as in *Poem in October*

Thomas R(onald) S(tuart) (1913–) Welsh poet and clergyman whose collections include *Frequencies*

Thomson James (1700–1748) Scottish poet whose long poem *The Seasons* anticipates Romanticism

Verlaine Paul Marie (1844–1896) French Symbolic lyric poet influenced by Charles Baudelaire and Arthur Rimbaud, as in *Poèmes saturniens/Saturnine Poems*

Villon François (1431–*c.* 1465) French poet of satiric humour, pathos, and lyric power, as in *Petit Testament*

Virgil (Publius Vergilius Maro) (70–19 BC) Roman poet who wrote the great heroic epic poem of Roman history, the *Aeneid*

Walcott Derek (Walton) (1930–) St Lucian Nobel prizewinning poet and playwright whose poetry includes *Omeros*

Walther von der Vogelweide (*c.* 1170–1230) German poet who wrote songs about courtly love

Warren Robert Penn (1905–1989) first US poet laureate; he was also a novelist and the only author to win Pulitzer prizes for prose and poetry; his poetry includes *Promises*

Whitman Walt(er) (1819–1892) US poet who used unconventional free verse, as in *Song of Myself*

Williams William Carlos (1883–1963) US poet, essayist, and theoretician associated with Imagism and Objectivism whose *Pictures from Brueghel* won a Pulitzer prize

Wordsworth William (1770–1850) English Romantic poet laureate whose work includes *Lyrical Ballads* and *The Prelude*

Yeats W(illiam) B(utler) (1865–1939) Nobel prizewinning Irish poet and leader of the Celtic revival whose works include the collections *The Wild Swans at Coole* and *The Winding Stair*

Yevtushenko Yevgeny Aleksandrovich (1933–) Soviet poet who wrote *Zima Junction* and *Babi Yar*

Thinkers and Reformers

Noteworthy Economists

Arrow Kenneth Joseph (1921–) US economist who helped develop mathematical models for the study of economic equilibrium

Bagehot Walter (1826–1877) British economist who wrote an analysis of the British political system

Bastiat Frédéric (1801–1850) French economist whose 'classical' approach put forward the idea of the natural harmony of economic interests; he advocated the nonintervention of government

Bentham Jeremy (1748–1832) British economist and social reformer who is best known today for putting forward the theory of utilitarianism

Beveridge William Henry (1879–1963) English economist whose Beveridge Report formed the basis of the British welfare state

Bowley Arthur Lyon (1869–1957) British economist and mathematician who pioneered the early statistical treatment of prices and wages in Britain

Burns Terence (1944–) British economist who was director of the London Business School for Economic Forecasting (1976–79)

Carey Henry (1793–1879) US economist who set about reforming classical economics in an American context and developed a reproduction theory of labour value

Cassel Carl Gustov (1866–1945) Swedish economist who simplified general equilibrium theory and formulated purchasing-power parity theory

Coombs Herbert Cole 'Nugget' (1906–) Australian economist who was governor of the Commonwealth Reserve Bank and chair of its board

Copland Douglas Berry (1894–1971) New Zealand-born Australian economist who was financial advisor to the Australian government during World War II

Cournot Antoine Augustin (1801–1877) French mathematician, philosopher, and economist who pioneered the use of the calculator to solve maximisation problems in economics and introduced the demand curve

Debreu Gerard (1921–) French-born US economist who developed an integrated economic equilibrium theory

Douglas Clifford Hugh (known as Major Douglas) (1879–1952) British economic theorist who formulated the economic theory of social credit

Ely Richard Theodore (1854–1943) US economist who was an early advocate of government economic planning

Fisher Irving (1867–1947) US economist who developed the quantity theory of money

Friedman Milton (1912–) US economist who was a pioneer of monetarism

Frisch Ragnar Anton Kittil (1895–1973) Norwegian economist who pioneered the field of econometrics and shared the first Nobel Prize for Economics with Jan Tinbergen in 1969

Galbraith J(ohn) K(enneth) (1908–) Canadian-born US economist whose theories on an 'affluent society' helped shape US government economic policy

George Henry (1839–1897) US economist whose land-tax theory influenced taxation policies in various countries

Greenspan Alan (1926–) US economist and chairman of the US Federal Reserve System from 1987

Hayek Friedrich August von (1899–1992) Austrian economist who wrote a critical study of socialist trends in Great Britain

Hicks John Richard (1904–1989) British Keynesian economist who developed a framework for the analysis of expenditure and money supply

Hilferding Rudolf (1877–1941) German economist whose *Finance Capital* sought to bring Marxist theory up to date

Hobson John Atkinson (1858–1940) British economist who opposed the Boer War for economic reasons

Hume David (1711–1776) British historian and philosopher who published a number of economic essays in *Political Discourses* (1752), which had a profound influence on Adam Smith

Jevons William Stanley (1835–1882) British economist who introduced the concept of marginal utility

Juglar Clément (1819–1905) French economist who identified the phenomenon of the periodic business cycle

Kaldor Nicholas (1908–1986) Hungarian-born British economist who was a critic of monetarism

Kalecki Michal (1899–1970) Polish economist who analysed the effects of uncertainty on economic activity

Kantorovich Leonid Vitalievich (1912–1986) Soviet economist who theorized that a rational price system is necessary in the decentralization of an economy

Keynes John Maynard (1883–1946) British economist who advocated government control of credit and currency to prevent financial crises

Kondratieff Nikolai Dmitrierich (1892–1931) Russian economist and statistician who wrote extensively on the problems of the economics of central planning and agriculture

Kuznets Simon Smith (1901–1985) Russian-born US economist who developed theories of national income and economic forecasting

Launhardt Carl Friedrick Wilhelm (1832–1918) German economist who was a pioneer of mathematical economics, principally researching into welfare economics and location theory

Law John (1671–1729) British economist who undertook an early study of money, trade, and the concept of value

Leontief Wassily (1906–) Soviet-born US economist who contributed to the development of input–output economic analysis

Lewis (William) Arthur (1915–1991) West Indies-born British economist who developed a model for trade between developed and less developed nations

List Friedrich (1789–1846) German economist who was one of the earliest critics of classical economics and Adam Smith; he advocated a system of protectionist measures

Locke John (1632–1704) British philosopher who expounded the labour theory of property, which influenced Adam Smith

Lucas Robert (1937–) US economist and leader of the University of Chicago school of 'new classical macroeconomics'

Malthus Thomas Robert (1766–1834) British economist who argued for population control and influenced Charles Darwin's thinking on natural selection

Marshall Alfred (1842–1924) British economist who was a pioneer of Neo-Classical economics

Martineau Harriet (1802–1876) British economist and writer who popularized economic theories

Meade James Edward (1907–1995) British Keynesian economist who published a four-volume *Principles of Economy*

Menger Carl (1840–1921) Austrian economist who developed the principle of diminishing marginal utility

Mitchell Wesley Clair (1874–1948) US economist who helped found the National Bureau of Economic Research

Monnet Jean (1888–1979) French economist who helped establish the European Common Market

Moore Henry Ludwell (1869–1958) US economist who pioneered the use of statistical techniques in the estimation of demand and supply curves, determinants of wage rates, and the causes of business cycles

Noteworthy Economists (*continued*)

Myrdal (Karl) Gunnar (1898–1987) Swedish economist who helped advance the field of development economics

Pareto Vilfredo (1848–1923) Italian economist who opposed socialism and liberalism for economic reasons

Proudhon Pierre-Joseph (1809–1865) French journalist, political theorist, and economist who was a pioneering advocate of socialist economic theory

Quesnay François (1694–1774) French economic theorist who headed the Physiocratic School (the first school of political economy)

Ricardo David (1772–1823) British economist who formulated the principle of comparative advantage and the law of diminishing returns

Robbins Lionel Charles (1898–1984) British economist who stressed the role of scarcity and constraints in economic decision-making

Robinson Joan Violet (born Maurice) (1903–1983) British economist who introduced Marxism to Keynesian economic theory

Rostow Walt Whitman (1916–) US economist and presidential adviser, best known for his theory of five stages of economic growth

Samuelson Paul Anthony (1915–) US economist who has applied scientific analysis to economic theory

Schultz Theodore William (1902–1998) US economist who is a specialist in agricultural economics

Schumacher Fritz Ernst Friedrich (1911–1977) German economist who established the Intermediate Technology Development Group

Schumpeter Joseph A(lois) (1883–1950) Austrian-born US economist who theorized that Western capitalism would evolve into a form of socialism

Smith Adam (1723–1790) Scottish economist whose major work was *Wealth of Nations*

Sraffa Piero (1898–) Italian-born economist who has suggested that prices are not wholly determined by supply and demand

Stone (John) Richard Nicholas (1913–1991) British economist who developed a system for 'national income accounting'

Thornton Henry (1760–1815) British economist who pioneered the early study of monetary theory

Thunen Johann Heinrich von (1783–1850) German economist who pioneered the study of land use, location theory, and marginal productivity theory of distribution

Tinbergen Jan (1903–) Dutch economist who helped develop the field of econometrics and shared the first Nobel Prize for Economics with Ragnar Friech in 1969

Tobin James (1918–) US Keynesian economist who formulated a 'general equilibrium theory' related to consumption and investment

Veblen Thorstein Bunde (1857–1929) US economist and social critic whose major work was *The Theory of the Leisure Class* (1899)

Volcker Paul Adolph (1927–) US economist who was chair of the US Federal Reserve System (1979–87)

Walras (Marie Espirit) Léon (1834–1910) French economist who originated the theory of diminishing marginal utility of a good (the increased value to a person of consuming more of a product)

Ward Barbara (1914–1981) British economist who was president of the Institute for Environment and Development

Noteworthy Historians

Africanus Leo (Al-Hassan ibn Muhammad al-Wazzan Al-Zayati Al-Fasi) (*c.* 1494–1552) Moroccan travel historian, the leading authority for contemporary European research into the history of Africa

An Chŏng-bok (*c.* 1712–*c.* 1791) Korean historian of great ability

Arai Hakuseki (1657–1725) Japanese historian who concentrated mainly on the military class of society

Armin Enci' (17th century) Indonesian historical writer whose works form a main reference point for Western researchers

Ashikpashazade Sheykh Ahmed Ashiki (*c.* 1400–post 1494) Ottoman chronicler, dervish, and warrior whose *Gestes of the House of Osman* is a major historical source as well as an important literary document

Bagrationi Vakhushti (1696–1757) Georgian historian who was an early exponent of systematic historiography

Bancroft George (1800–1891) US historian and author of a ten-volume study of the origins of the USA, who is regarded as the 'father of American history'

Beard Charles Austin (1874–1948) US historian and a leader of the Progressive movement who wrote *A Basic History of the United States*

Bede the Venerable (*c.* 672–735) Anglo-Saxon historian and theologian who devised the BC/AD system of dating, and who is the most influential historian of the early Middle Ages

Biondo Flavio (1392–1463) Italian Renaissance historian whose works display the author's critical historical sensibility

Bloch Marc Léopold Benjamin (1886–1944) French mediaevalist and Resistance hero whose interdisciplinary Annales school revolutionized modern historiography

Bolland Jean (1596–1665) Jesuit founder of the Bollandists whose huge compilation of the definitive lives of the Christian saints set new standards in historical criticism

Boorstin Daniel Joseph (1914–) US social historian whose three-volume *The Americans* is the most important modern study of American civilization

Braudel (Paul Achille) Fernand (1902–1985) French historian whose perception of long-term trends in global, social, and economic history transformed the study of the early modern world

Burckhardt Jacob Christopher (1818–1897) Swiss historian of art and culture whose *Die Kultur der Renaissance in Italien/The Civilization of the Renaissance in Italy* influenced all subsequent cultural historians

Camden William (1551–1623) English historian whose methods and scope make him the father of critical historical scholarship in the country

Cantemir Dimitrie (1673–1723) Romanian prince and historian, author of works whose scope earned him a place in world historiography

Carlyle Thomas (1795–1881) British historian whose studies of the hero in history brought new depth to the concept of history as a record of the deeds of great individuals

Childe V(ere) Gordon (1892–1957) Australian-born historian and pioneer of a global approach to the study of prehistory

Clarendon Edward Hyde (1609–1674) English chronicler and historian, famous for his *History of the Rebellion in England* (1704–07)

Clark Alan Kenneth McKenzie (1928–) English historian and Conservative politician, specializing in military history

Clavijero Francisco Javier (1731–1787) Mexican Jesuit priest and historian whose pioneering approach to the history of indigenous peoples of South America strives to be balanced and objective

Commynes Philippe de (*c.* 1447–*c.* 1511) chronicler and statesman whose detailed account of events in his own times make him one of the greatest historians of the later Middle Ages

Comnena Anna (1083–1153) Byzantine historian whose work combined historiography, politics, and the author's own dynastic ambitions

Denina Gerolamo (1731–1813) Italian historian whose works display the ideas and trends of the Enlightenment

(*continued*)

Noteworthy Historians (*continued*)

Diodorus Siculus (*c.* 104 BC–20 BC) Sicilian historian and compiler whose *Historical Library* is largely preserved

Dionysius of Halicarnassus (*c.* 75 BC–*c.* 7 BC) influential Greek historian, author of the earliest history of Rome

Długosz Jan (1415–1480) Polish historian and humanist, one of the greatest historians in Europe at the time, whose works demonstrate the author's careful methodology

Eusebius of Caesarea (*c.* 264–340) bishop and historian whose study of the early history of Christianity underpinned most historical writing of the Middle Ages

Froissart Jean (*c.* 1333–*c.* 1405) French historian and poet whose *Chronicles* provides the most detailed and accurate account of chivalric society

Froude James Anthony (1818–1894) English historian whose 12-volume work on Tudor England revolutionized the study of the period

Fustel de Coulanges Numa Denis (1830–1889) French historian and pioneer of the application of scientific principles to historical study

Garcilaso de la Vega (1539–1616) Peruvian historian who described, partly from his own memory, the history of Incas before the Spanish conquest and thereby laid foundations for early Peruvian history

Gibbon Edward (1737–1794) English Enlightenment historian and author of *The History of the Decline and Fall of the Roman Empire*, one of the world's greatest historiographical works

Gregory of Tours (Georgius Florentinus Gregorius, 'French Herodotus', 'father of French history') (*c.* 538–594) author of one of the first systematic approaches to the history of Gaul, *Historia Francorum*

Halévy Elie (1870–1937) French historian and author of the outstanding study of 19th-century British political, religious, and economic history

Herodotus (*c.* 484–*c.* 425 BC) Greek historian and traveller who wrote the first great narrative history, dealing with the Greco-Persian Wars

Hilendarski Paissi (*c.* 1722–*c.* 1773) the founder of Bulgarian historiography whose works were popular with his European contemporaries

Horathibodi Phra (18th century) Thai chronicler, whose work preceded the country's regal chronicles

Huang Zong-xi (Yu-yao of Zhejiang) (*c.* 1610–1695) Chinese historian and philosopher whose works illustrate close links between historiography and politics

Ibn Khaldun (1332–1406) author of the *Muqaddimah/Introduction to History*, which incorporates one of the world's most sophisticated secular philosophies of history

Isidore of Seville (*c.* 560–636) Spanish historian and encyclopaedist who associated the flow of history with the moral progress of humanity

Istvánffy Miklós (1538–1615) eminent historian of Hungary, a humanist well-known in the Renaissance Europe

Josephus Flavius (*c.* 38–100) Jewish historian, the leading authority on the history of the Jewish nation in the 1st century

Kala U (*c.* 1678–1730) Burmese historian whose writings are indispensable for any researcher of the region's early history

Khorenatsi Movses (**Moses of Khoren**) (5th century AD) Armenian historian whose works were invaluable for researchers of the history of Armenia and the region as well as for Armenian national identity

Kitabatake Chikafusa (*c.* 1293–1354) Japanese historian whose writings formed a landmark in the philosophy of history in Japan at the time

Klyuchevsky Vasily Osipovich (1841–1911) one of the most important Russian historians and an early exponent of the sociological approach to historical writing

Las Casas Bartolomé de (1474–1566) Spanish missionary and historian who first exposed colonial policy; his extensive knowledge of, and open attitude towards, indigenous peoples of South America made him a pioneer of cultural anthropology in the region

Le Quy Don (*c.* 1726–*c.* 1784) Vietnamese philosopher and historian who formulated, within his own culture, principles of social change and historical evolution

Livy (Titus Livius) (*c.* 60 BC–AD 17) Roman historian whose work influenced almost all subsequent historians until the 19th century

Lomonosov Mikhail Vasil'evich (1711–1765) Russian scholar who, in his historical writings, denounced serfdom and displayed an idealistic approach to social and historical phenomena

Lopes Fernão (*c.* 1380–*c.* 1460) Portuguese chronicler and the first mediaeval exponent of the use of documentary evidence as a guide to historical truth

Mabillon Jean (1632–1707) French monk and historian who was the founder of the Maurist school and the inventor of palaeography, the scientific study of ancient writing

Macaulay Thomas Babington, 1st Baron (1800–1859) English writer and historian whose five-volume *History of England* helped found the so-called 'Whig' school of history

McNeill William Hardy (1917–) Canadian historian whose monumental *The Rise of the West* greatly influenced modern historical theory

Ma Duanlin (fl. 13th century) Chinese author of perhaps the greatest institutional history of China up to or since his own time, and a major influence on all later Chinese historians

Mas'udi, or **Masodi**, Abu al-Hassan Ali al- (died 957) the first Arab historian to make extensive use of precise geographical information in a world history

Meinecke Friedrich (1862–1954) the greatest German historian of his time; he had a major influence on modern intellectual history

Muratori Ludovico Antonio (1672–1750) Italian archivist and historian whose work combines original documents and historical narrative

Niebuhr Barthold Georg (1776–1831) German pioneer of the rigorous criticism of sources now considered essential to all historical study

Olans Magnus (1490–1557) Swedish historian and cartographer whose 'Carta Marina' (1539) brought him international recognition

Piccolomini Enea Silvio (1405–1464) Italian humanist whose historical writings present diverse and reliable information in an attractive and involving manner

Plutarch (*c.* 46–*c.* 120) Greek historian and biographer

Porthan Henrik Gabriel (1739–1804) pioneer of Finnish historiography who used his knowledge of the country's folklore, tradition, and language to establish Finnish national identity

Prapañca (14th century) early Javanese historian

Rajić Jovan (1726–1801) historian of Serbs and south Slavs, one of the pioneers of Enlightened pan-Slavism

Ranke Leopold von (1795–1886) the greatest German historian of the 19th century; he was a key figure in the effort to develop a scientific methodology for history

Rostovtzeff Michael Ivanovich (1870–1952) Russian-born historian and archaeologist who was the most important authority of his time on Greek and Roman social and economic history

Sallustius (Gaius Sallustius Crispus) (86–*c.* 35 BC) Roman historian whose work combines historical competence, a moral sense, and artistic language

Sarkar Jadunath (1870–1958) the greatest modern Indian historian and the leading authority of his time on Mughal India

Noteworthy Historians (continued)

Schlesinger Arthur Meier (1888–1965) US historian whose focus on urbanization and social history has influenced almost all subsequent historians of the United States

Sharaf-han ibn Shamsaddin Bidlisi (c. 1543–c. 1604) Kurdish tribal leader and historian

Sima Guang (1019–1086) Chinese compiler of the *Zizhi Tongjian/Complete Mirror of Government*, an outstanding chronicle of Chinese history from 403 BC

Snorri Sturluson (c. 1178–1241) Icelandic historian and biographer who critically edited the early sagas

Strabo (c. 64 BC–c. AD 26) Greek historiographer and geographer whose works, in addition to factual information, contain references to numerous other authors

Suetonius (Gaius Suetonius Tranquillus) (c. 69–130) Roman historian and biographer, creator of 'Suetonius's biographical model', whose work complements that of Tacitus

Tabari, at- (c. 839–923) Arabic author of the *History of Prophets and Kings* and developer of a philosophy of history that influenced all later Islamic historians

Tacitus Publius (Gaius) Cornelius (c. 56–c. 120) perhaps the greatest of all Roman historians; he wrote works on the history of Rome from AD 14 to 96

Tatishchev Vasiliy Nikitich (1686–1750) Russian historian, a rationalist, who searched for laws of historical and social development, and who is also the author of the first periodization of the history of Russia

Tawney Richard Henry (1880–1962) English economic historian, social critic, and reformer who influenced the policy of the British Labour Party

Taylor A(lan) J(ohn) P(ercivale) (1906–1990) English historian who was an authority on modern British and European history

Thucydides (c. 460–c. 404 BC) the greatest Greek historian whose *History of the Peloponnesian War* includes a perceptive analysis of Athenian politics and strategy

Trevelyan George Macaulay (1876–1962) British historian, a pioneer of modern social history

Trevor-Roper Hugh Redwald (Baron Dacre of Glanton) (1914–) English historian whose work, often controversial and always vivid, encompasses a wide range of modern history topics

Turner Frederick Jackson (1861–1932) US historian whose theory of the influence of the frontier over a period of 300 years revolutionized US historical thinking

Vasari Giorgio (1511–1574) Italian artist and famous biographer of painters, sculptors, and architects; he saw the history of art as a steady progress of aesthetic achievements

Vico Gianbattista (Giovanni Battista) (1668–1744) Italian philosopher who is considered the founder of modern theories of history

Winckelmann Johann Joachim (1717–1768) German historian, founder of classical archaeology and the historiography of art

Xenophon (c. 430–c. 354 BC) Greek philosopher and historian

Yaqut Ibn 'Abd Allah (1179–1228) Muslim historian, biographer, genealogist, and lexicographer

Zheng Qiao (1108–1166) the greatest historian of Sung-period China whose style and approach influenced almost all subsequent Chinese historians

Noteworthy Philosophers

Aquinas Thomas, St (1225–1274) Italian philosopher and theologian, the greatest figure of the school of scholasticism

Archytas of Tarentum (c. 428–347 BC) Greek philosopher of the Pythagorean school who founded scientific mechanics

Aristippus (c. 410–c. 356 BC) Greek philosopher who founded the Cyrenaic or hedonist school

Aristotle (384–322 BC) Greek philosopher whose 22 surviving treatises cover a wide range of topics from logic to biology

Ayer A(lfred) J(ules) (1910–1989) English philosopher who developed logical positivism in his book *Language, Truth and Logic*

Bachelard Gaston (1884–1962) French philosopher who argued for a creative interplay between reason and experience

Bacon Francis (1561–1626) English philosopher who laid the foundations of modern scientific research

Bayle Pierre (1647–1706) French philosopher who published *Dictionnaire historique et critique/Historical and Critical Dictionary* (1697), which attacked contemporary views

Beattie James (1735–1803) Scottish philosopher who attempted to disprove the empiricism of David Hume

Beauvoir Simone de (1908–1986) French socialist, feminist, and writer regarded as one of the founders of modern feminist philosophy

Bentham Jeremy (1748–1832) British philosopher who was the founder of utilitarianism

Berdiaev Nikolai Aleksandrovich (1874–1948) Russian philosopher who was exiled from Russia in 1922 for defending the Orthodox Christian religion

Bergson Henri Louis (1859–1941) French philosopher who believed that time, change, and development were the essence of reality

Berkeley George (1685–1753) Irish philosopher who believed that nothing exists apart from perception

Berlin Isaiah (1909–1997) Latvian-born British philosopher and historian of ideas who attacked historical determinism in *Four Essays on Liberty*

Boethius Anicius Manlius Severinus (c. 475–524) Roman philosopher who wrote *De Consolatione Philosophiae/The Consolation of Philosophy*, which was highly regarded during the Middle Ages, and which formalized a classification of knowledge that was consequential for mediaeval scholarship

Bradley Francis Herbert (1846–1924) Welsh philosopher who promoted absolute idealism as a philosophy

Braithwaite Richard Bevan (1900–1990) British philosopher who applied the mathematical theory of games to the resolution of moral conflict

Carnap Rudolf (1891–1970) German-born US philosopher who was a member of the Vienna Circle and an exponent of logical positivism

Cassirer Ernst (1874–1945) German neo-Kantian philosopher who believed there are forms of thought that condition mythical, historical, and practical thinking

Chomsky Noam (1928–) US linguistic philosopher, educator, and political activist whose theories of generative grammar revolutionized linguistics

Collingwood Robin George (1889–1943) English philosopher who argued that the historical context of any position holds the key to its interpretation; he was also a prominent aesthetician

Croce Benedetto (1866–1952) Italian philosopher who wrote a classic work on idealism, *Filosofia dello spirito/The Philosophy of the Spirit*

Derrida Jacques (1930–) French philosopher who introduced the deconstruction theory into literary criticism

Descartes René (1596–1650) French rationalist philosopher who argued that **cogito ergo sum**/'I think therefore I am' is the foundation for human knowledge

(continued)

Noteworthy Philosophers (*continued*)

Diderot Denis (1713–1784) French Enlightenment philosopher and editor of the influential *Encylopédie/Encyclopedia*

Dilthey Wilhelm (1833–1911) German philosopher who argued that hermeneutics should be applied to culture and history, not simply to texts

Foucault Michel Paul (1926–1984) French philosopher who argued that human knowledge and subjectivity are dependent on specific institutions and practices

Gadamer Hans-Georg (1900–) German philosopher who theorized that in hermeneutics a dialogue takes place between text and interpreter

Hegel Georg Wilhelm Friedrich (1770–1831) German idealist philosopher who developed dialectic thinking and conceived of mind and nature as one indivisible whole

Heidegger Martin (1889–1976) German existentialist philosopher who taught the meaning of 'being' as the essential philosophical question

Hume David (1711–1776) Scottish philosopher whose *Treatise of Human Nature* is a central text of British empiricism

Husserl Edmund Gustav Albrecht (1859–1938) German philosopher who was the founder of phenomenology

Jaspers Karl Theodor (1883–1969) German existentialist philosopher who argued that philosophy is concerned with the analysis of one's own existence

Kant Immanuel (1724–1804) German philosopher who believed knowledge is dependent on the conceptual apparatus of the human understanding

Kierkegaard Søren Aabye (1813–1855) Danish philosopher and theologian often considered to be the founder of existentialism

Locke John (1632–1704) English empiricist philosopher whose work helped shape contemporary ideas of liberal democracy

Nietzsche Friedrich Wilhelm (1844–1900) German philosopher who argued against the existence of absolute moral values

Ortega y Gasset José (1883–1955) Spanish philosopher and critic who considered communism and fascism the causes of the downfall of Western civilization

Parmenides of Elea (*c.* 510–450 BC) Greek pre-Socratic philosopher who believed motion and change are illusory and logically impossible

Peirce Charles Sanders (1839–1914) US philosopher who pioneered pragmatism

Plato (*c.* 428–*c.* 348 BC) Greek philosopher whose teachings about the existence of absolute forms have had a major influence on Western philosophy

Popper Karl Raimund (1902–1994) Austrian-born British philosopher of science who argued that science is not certain knowledge but a series of 'conjectures and refutations'

Quine Willard Van Orman (1908–) US philosopher and logician with a highly scientific view of the world

Rawls John (1921–) US philosopher who revived the idea of the social contract in *A Theory of Justice* (1962)

Rousseau Jean-Jacques (1712–1778) French social philosopher whose work *Du Contrat social/Social Contract* (1762) was a significant influence on the French Revolution, and whose theories were paramount to ideologies of the Enlightenment era

Russell Bertrand Arthur William (1872–1970) English philosopher and mathematician who was a major exponent of logical positivism

Sartre Jean-Paul (1905–1980) French existentialist philosopher who tried to combine existentialism and Marxism

Schopenhauer Arthur (1788–1860) German philosopher who considered will as the inner principle of the world, and who strongly influenced Nietzsche and Sigmund Freud

Socrates (*c.* 469–399 BC) Athenian political and moral philosopher who was immortalized in the writings of Plato

Spinoza Benedict (or Baruch) (1632–1677) Dutch philosopher who believed in a rationalistic pantheism

Wittgenstein Ludwig Josef Johann (1889–1951) Austrian-born British philosopher who proposed that words represent things according to usage, not social agreement

Wolff Christian (1679–1754) German philosopher who coined the terms cosmology and teleology

Noteworthy Political Thinkers

Althusser Louis (1918–1990) Algerian-born French Marxist philosopher who argued that ruling class ideology is a crucial form of class control

Arendt Hannah (1906–1975) German-born US political theorist and philosopher who considered the moral implications of 20th-century political history

Aron Raymond (1905–1983) French political and social theorist who was critical of Marxism and emphasized pluralism as essential in any society

Bakunin Mikhail Aleksandrovich (1814–1876) Russian anarchist and revolutionary who supported communism as part of his 'withering away of the state' doctrine

Bodin Jean (1530–1596) French political philosopher whose six-volume *De la République/Of the Commonwealth* is considered the first work on political economy

Burke Edmund (1729–1797) Irish political theorist who supported the American colonists and denounced the French Revolution

Debray Régis (1941–) French Marxist theorist who was involved with Che Guevara in the 1960s revolutionary movement in Latin America

Engels Friedrich (1820–1895) German political philosopher who, with Karl Marx, founded the communist movement

Gentile Giovanni (1875–1944) Italian political philosopher whose writings formed the basis for Mussolini's fascist state in Italy

Godwin William (1756–1836) English political philosopher whose *Enquiry Concerning Political Justice* advocated an anarchic society

Gramsci Antonio (1891–1937) Italian Marxist who attempted to unify social theory and political practice

Hobbes Thomas (1588–1679) English political philosopher whose *Leviathan* advocated absolutist government as the only means of ensuring order

John of Salisbury (*c.* 1115–1180) English political thinker whose *Policraticus* portrayed the church as the guarantee of liberty against a secular authority

Korsch Karl (1886–1961) German Marxist philosopher who argued against the theory of dialectical materialism and attempted a reinterpretation of Marxism

Kropotkin Petr Alekseevich (1842–1921) Russian anarchist who wrote extensively on anarchism, history, and political and social justice

Lukács Geyorgy Szegedy (1885–1971) Hungarian political philosopher who was one of the founders of Western or Hegelian Marxism

Lyotard Jean François (1924–) French political philosopher who was one of the leading theorists of postmodernism

Machiavelli Niccolò (1469–1527) Italian political theorist whose works *Il principe/The Prince* and *Discorsi/Discourses* advocated amoral political manipulation of people

Noteworthy Political Thinkers (*continued*)

Marcuse Herbert (1898–1979) German-born US political philosopher who combined Marxism and Freudianism, and whose teaching influenced radical thought in the 1960s

Marx Karl Heinrich (1818–1883) German political philosopher whose *Das Kapital/Capital* is the fundamental text of Marxist economics and politics

Michels Robert (1876–1936) German social and political theorist whose *Political Parties* argued that an 'iron law of oligarchy' governs any organization or society

Mill John Stuart (1806–1873) English social and political theorist who wrote *On Liberty*, the classic philosophical defence of liberalism

Montesquieu Charles Louis de Secondat Baron de la Bréde et de (1689–1755) French political theorist whose *De L'Esprit des lois/The Spirit of Laws* advocated the separation of powers within government

Nozick Robert (1938–   ) US political philosopher who believes the state exists only to protect the rights of individuals

Ortega y Gasset José (1883–1955) Spanish political philosopher who argued that communism and fascism caused the downfall of Western civilization

Pareto Vilfredo (1848–1923) Italian political philosopher who opposed socialism and liberalism

Scruton Roger Vernon (1944–   ) British social and political theorist whose *The Meaning of Conservatism* influenced the free-market movements in Eastern Europe

Spengler Oswald (1880–1936) German political thinker who argued in *Der Untergang des Abendlandes/Decline of the West* that civilizations go through cycles of growth and decay

Stirner Max (pseudonym of Johannes Kaspar Schmidt) (1806–1856) German anarchist thinker who argued that the state, class, and humanity are meaningless abstractions

Smith Adam (1723–1790) Scottish economist and creator of the discipline of political economy that greatly influenced political theory in later years

Tocqueville Alexis Charles Henri Maurice Clérel de (1805–1859) French political and social theorist who authored the first analytical study of US society: *De la Démocratie en Amérique/Democracy in America*

Trotsky Leon (adopted name of Lev Davidovitch Bronstein) (1879–1940) Russian political theorist who believed in permanent world revolution, and who was assassinated by Ramon del Rio, an agent of Stalin

Noteworthy Religious Thinkers and Leaders

Abduh Muhammad (1849–1905) Egyptian religious thinker who was the founder of Islamic modernism

Abelard Peter (English form of Pierre Abailard) (1079–1142) French scholastic theologian who worked on logic and perception and whose romantic liaison with his pupil Héloïse created a mediaeval scandal

Albertus Magnus, St Graf von Bollstädt (1206–1280) German theologian who was known as 'doctor universalis' because of the breadth of his knowledge

Anandamurti Shrii Shrii (Prabhat Rainjan Sarkar; Baba) (1923–1990) Indian religious thinker who founded the Ananda Marga (Path of Bliss) organization

Anselm of Canterbury (1033–1109) French-born British archbishop whose *Cur Deus Homo* is a classic mediaeval text on the theology of the Atonement

Aquinas Thomas, St (1225–1274) Italian scholastic theologian whose writings form the basis for Roman Catholic theology

Augustine of Hippo (Aurelius Augustinus) (354–430) North African bishop whose teachings on sin and predestination influenced both Roman Catholic and Protestant traditions

Averröes or **Averrhoës** (Full Arabic name: Abū al-Walīd Muhammad ibn Ahmad ibn Muhammad ibn Rushd) (1126–1198) Spanish Islamic philosopher who attempted to reconcile Islamic teaching with Greek thought

Baader Benedict Franz von (1765–1841) German Roman Catholic theologian who opposed the claims of ecclesiastic authority in the field of speculation

Barth Karl (1886–1968) Swiss theologian whose *Kirchliche Dogmatik/Church Dogmatics* had a major impact on 20th-century Protestant theology

Bernard of Clairvaux ('the Mellifluous Doctor') (1090–1153) French Cistercian monk whose devotional works encouraged reform in the mediaeval church and monastic movement

Beza Theodorus (properly Théodore de Bèsze) (1519–1605) French-born Swiss theologian and translator who discovered the oldest Greek manuscript of the New Testament (*Codex Bezae*)

Blavatsky Helena Petrovna (born Hahn) (1831–1891) Russian spiritualist and mystic who co-founded the Theosophical Society in 1875 and later became a Buddhist

Boehme Jakob (1575–1624) German mystic who claimed to have found a way to reconcile good and evil

Booth William (1829–1912) British church leader who founded the Salvation Army

Bruno Giordano (born Filippo Bruno) (1548–1600) Italian Dominican monk who was burned at the stake for his opposition to Roman Catholic doctrines

Brunner (Heinrich) Emil (1889–1966) Swiss Protestant theologian whose *Das Gebot und die Ordnungen/The Divine Imperative* influenced the field of Christian ethics

Bryan William Jennings (1860–1925) US Protestant leader and politician who opposed Clarence Darrow in the Scopes monkey trial in Dayton, Tennessee, in 1923

Buber Martin (1878–1965) Austrian-born Jewish philosopher whose *Ich und Du/I and Thou* had a significant impact on Jewish and Christian theology

Bucer or **Butzer** Martin (1491–1551) German Protestant reformer who sought to reconcile the Eucharist views of Martin Luther and Ulrich Zwingli

Buddha, the 'enlightened one' (title of Prince Gautama Siddartha) (*c.* 563–483 BC) Indian religious leader and founder of Buddhism

Calvin John (1509–1564) French-born Swiss theologian whose works formed the basis for Calvinism and Presbyterianism

Camara (Dom) Helder Pessoa (1909–   ) Brazilian Catholic archbishop who has campaigned for social reform and the establishment of 'base ecclesial communities'

Cartwright Thomas (1535–1603) British Protestant theologian who, in 1603, drew up the Millenary Petition, which initiated reform in the Church of England

Chang Lu (*c.* 184–220) Chinese Taoist thinker who established the first theocratic state to follow Taoist teachings

Chateaubriand François Auguste René (1768–1848) French writer who was a leading exponent of Romanticism, and whose *Le Génie du Christianisme/Genius of Christianity* was a defence of the Christian faith

Chu Hsi (1130–1200) Chinese religious thinker who significantly influenced the development of the Confucian tradition in East Asia

(*continued*)

Noteworthy Religious Thinkers and Leaders (*continued*)

Cohen Hermann (1842–1912) German Jewish philosopher who thought Judaism was primarily a religion of ethical reason

Colet John (*c.* 1467–1519) English humanist who founded modern biblical exegesis

Confucius (Latinized form of Kongfuzi or K'ung Fu tzu, 'Kong the Master') (551–479 BC) Chinese thinker who emphasized moral order and obedience to patriarchal authority

Cordovero Moses (1522–1570) Palestinian Jewish mystic whose encyclopedic work on kabbalistic teachings, *Pardes Rimmonium/Pomegranate Orchard*, greatly influenced Jewish mysticism

Cyril of Alexandria (*c.* 376–444) patriarch of Alexandria who condemned Nestorius (d. *c.* 457, patriarch of Constantinople 428–31) for his refusal to call Mary the *Theotokos* ('God-bearer')

Dayananda Sarasvati (originally Mula Sankara) (1824–1883) Indian religious thinker who founded the Arya Samaj to promote neo-orthodox Hinduism

Dharmakirti (600–660) Indian Buddhist philosopher whose philosophical writings formed the basis for later Buddhist thought in India and Tibet

Duns Scotus John (*c.* 1265–1308) Scottish Franciscan monk who was a leading figure in mediaeval scholasticism

Eddy Mary Morse (born Baker) (1821–1910) US religious thinker who founded the Christian Science movement

Edwards Jonathan (1703–1758) US theologian whose writings on predestination and revivalist preaching greatly influenced early US Protestant theology

Emerson Ralph Waldo (1803–1882) US religious thinker who was a major figure in New England transcendentalism

Erasmus Desiderius (*c.* 1466–1536) Dutch humanist who pioneered the use of the Greek text of the New Testament in biblical exegesis

Erigena Johannes Scotus (also called Scotus Eriugena, or John the Scot) (*c.* 810–*c.* 877) Irish religious thinker who attempted to combine Christian thought with neo-Platonism

Francis of Assisi, St (originally Francesco di Pietro di Bernardone) (1181–1226) founder of the Franciscan order; he advocated poverty and chastity, and believed in the unity of creation

Feuerbach Ludwig Andreas (1804–1872) German religious philosopher who argued that religion is the elevation of human qualities into an object of worship

Foucauld Charles Eugene de (known as Brother Charles of Jesus) (1858–1916) French-born Trappist monk who formed the orders of the Little Brothers of Jesus and the Little Sisters of Jesus

Fox George (1624–1691) British religious thinker who founded the Society of Friends ('Quakers')

Gandhi Mahatma (originally Mohandas Karamchand Gandhi) (1869–1948) Indian religious thinker whose teaching on nonviolence greatly influenced the Indian independence movement

Geiger Abraham (1810–1874) German Jewish philosopher who was a leading figure in the formation of Reform Judaism

Gershom ben Judah (Rabbeau Gershom) (*c.* 960–1028) German Rabbinic thinker whose writings influenced the development of Jewish law

Geulincx Arnold (also known as Philaretus) (1624–1669) Belgian religious thinker who formed the theory of occasionalism

Ghazali Abu Hamid Muhammad al- (1058–1111) Iranian Islamic theologian whose writings served as an authoritative reference for later Islamic belief and practice

Gilson Etienne Henry (1884–1978) French philosopher whose work *L'Espirit de la philosophie médiéval/The Spirit of Mediaeval Philosophy* contributed to the development of neo-Thomism

Graham Billy (William Franklin) (1918–) US cleric who revolutionized revivalist techniques in the 20th century with his mass evangelistic crusades

Grotius Hugo (also called Huig de Groot) (1583–1645) Dutch Protestant jurist whose *De Veritate Religionis Christianae/On the Truth of the Christian Religion* sought to promote Protestant unity

Gutiérrez Gustavo (1928–) Peruvian theologian who was one of the founders of liberation theology in Latin America

Hasan al-Banna (1904–1949) Egyptian Islamic thinker who founded the Muslim Brotherhood in 1928

Herbert Edward (1583–1648) English philosopher who developed deism

Heschel Abraham Joshua (1907–1972) Polish-born US Jewish theologian who sought to combine traditional Hasidic piety with existentialist philosophy

Hooker Richard (1554–1600) British theologian whose *Of the Laws of Ecclesiastical Polity* significantly influenced later Anglican thought

Hubbard L(afayette) Ron(ald) (1911–1986) US religious thinker and writer who founded scientology

Hügel Friedrich von (1852–1925) Italian-born British philosopher who was a leading figure in Roman Catholic mysticism

Huss John (Czech Jan) (*c.* 1369–1415) Bohemian theologian whose *De ecclesia/The Church* helped initiate the Protestant Reformation in Europe

Ibiam Francis Akanu (1906–) Nigerian church leader who was a leading figure in the creation of the All Africa Conference of Churches in 1958

Ibn Daud Abraham (*c.* 1110–1180) Spanish Jewish philosopher who attempted to harmonize Judaism with Aristotelianism

Ibn Khaldun (1332–1406) Tunisian-born Islamic thinker who was a pioneer in the study of history and religion

Ignatius Loyola (Iñigo López de Recalde) (1491–1556) Spanish theologian who founded the Society of Jesus (Jesuits)

Jacob ben Asher (*c.* 1270–1340) German-born Spanish Jewish philosopher whose *Sefer ha-Turim/Book of Rows* is a major text in Rabbinic thought

Jerome, St (Eusebius Hieronymus) (*c.* 342–420) Christian scholar whose Latin translation of the Bible, *The Vulgate*, became the authoritative text for the mediaeval church

Jesus (Christ) (*c.* 5 BC–AD 29/30) Hebrew preacher on whose teachings Christianity was founded

al-Jilani Abd al-Qadir (1077–1166) Iranian-born Islamic thinker who founded the Qadiri Sufi order

John of Damascus, St (*c.* 676–754) Syrian-born Greek theologian whose *De fide orthodoxa/On the Orthodox Faith* was an influential text in the development of Greek Orthodox theology

John of Kronstadt (1829–1908) Russian church leader who promoted liturgical reform in the Russian Orthodox church

John of the Cross, St (Juan de Yepes y Álvarez) (1542–1591) Spanish Carmelite monk whose *Noche obscura del alma/The Dark Night of the Soul* is a major text in Catholic mysticism

John Paul II (Karol Wojtyła) (1920–) Roman Catholic Pope since 1978 who has emphasized traditional Catholic values in his leadership

Jones Eli Stanley (1884–1973) US missionary whose *Christ of the Indian Road* encouraged an ecumenical approach to other religions

Khomeini Ruhollah (originally Ruholla Hendi) (1900–1989) Islamic scholar and Iranian ayatollah who, on his return to Iran from exile in 1979, launched the Islamic revolution against Western influences

Noteworthy Religious Thinkers and Leaders (*continued*)

Knox John (*c.* 1513–1572) Scottish Protestant theologian and church reformer who founded the Church of Scotland

Krishnamurti Jiddu (1895–1986) Indian religious thinker who taught that an unconditioned state of mind is the goal of religious experience

Lao Zi or **Lao Tzu** (*c.* 604–531 BC) Chinese philosopher whose *Tao Te Ching/Classic of the Way and its Virtue* is the foundation for Taoist thought

Latimer Hugh (*c.* 1485–1555) English churchman who was burned at the stake in Oxford during the reign of Queen Mary for advocating Protestant views

Luther Martin (1483–1546) German Protestant reformer who founded Lutheranism

Maharishi Mahesh Yogi (Mahesh Prasad Varma) (1911–) Indian religious thinker who founded the transcendental meditation movement

Maimonides Moses (Moses ben Maimon or Rambam) (1135–1204) Spanish-born Jewish jurist and philosopher who attempted to reconcile Aristotelianism with Jewish tradition

More Henry (1614–1687) English theologian who opposed Cartesian dualism and was a member of the Cambridge Platonists

Muhammad or **Mohammed** (*c.* 570–*c.* 632) founder of Islam who believed that the words of the Koran were revealed to him by God

Muhammad Elijah (originally Elijah Poole) (1897–1975) US religious thinker who helped found the Nation of Islam

Nanak (1469–1539) Indian guru and founder of Sikhism

Nicholas of Cusa or **Nicolaus Cusanus** (1401–1464) German-born Roman Catholic cardinal whose *De docta ignorantia/Of Learned Ignorance* offered an alternative to scholastic thought

Occam or **Ockham** William of (*c.* 1285–1349) British Franciscan monk who revived the fundamentals of nominalism in the mediaeval church

Philo Judaeus (*c.* 20 BC–AD 50) Egyptian Jewish philosopher who sought to reconcile Judaism and Platonism

Ram Mohun Roy (or Rájá Rám Mohan Ráj) (1774–1833) Indian religious thinker and mystic who founded the Brahmo Samaj ('Theistic Society') in 1828

Russell Charles Taze (1852–1916) US founder of the Jehovah's Witness sect

Sánusi Sidi Muhammad ibn Ali as- (*c.* 1787–1859) Algerian-born Islamic philosopher who preached a return to the puritanism of early Islam

Savonarola Girolamo (1452–1498) Italian Dominican friar whose crusade against corruption overthrew the ruling Medici family in Florence in 1494

Schweitzer Albert (1875–1965) German theologian whose 'reverence for life' philosophy provided a rationale for humanitarianism

Segundo Juan Luis (1925–) Uruguayan-born theologian who was a pioneer in the liberation movement in Latin America

Smith Joseph (1805–1844) US founder of the Mormon sect (Church of Jesus Christ of Latter-day Saints)

Steiner Rudolf (1861–1925) Austrian religious thinker who founded Anthroposophy

Strauss David Friedrich (1808–1874) German Protestant theologian whose *Das Leben Jesu/Life of Jesus* attempted to dismiss all supernatural elements in the gospel accounts

Tagore Rabindranath (1817–1905) Indian Hindu thinker who attempted a reform of Hinduism and regarded traditional Hindu rituals as idolatrous

Tillich Paul Johannes (1886–1965) German-born US theologian whose *Systematic Theology* greatly influenced 20th-century Protestant theology

Tutu Desmond Mpilo (1931–) South African archbishop who was the primary church spokesperson in the struggle against apartheid in South Africa

Visser `t Hooft Willem Adolph (1900–1985) Dutch Protestant church leader who was a pioneer in the creation of the World Council of Churches

Vivekananda Swami (originally Narendranath Dutt or Datta) (1863–1902) Hindu religious leader who founded the Ramakrishna Order

Watts Alan Wilson (1915–1973) British-born US religious philosopher who popularized Zen teaching for Western audiences

Wesley John (1703–1791) British theologian who founded the Methodist movement

White Ellen Gould (1827–1915) US religious thinker who co-founded the Seventh-Day Adventist Church

Wycliffe John (*c.* 1329–1384) English theologian whose produced the first translation of the Bible into English

Yamazaki Ansai (1618–1682) Japanese thinker who was the founder of Suiga (or Suika) Shinto, which is a mixture of neo-Confucianism and Shinto thought

Yung-ming Yen-shou (Yomyo Enju) (904–975) Chinese thinker who advocated a synthesis of the Ch'an and Pure Land schools of Buddhist thought

Zwingli Ulrich (Latin: Ulricus Zuinglius) (1484–1531) Swiss theologian who was a leader in the Swiss Protestant Reformation

Noteworthy Social Reformers and Educators

Addams Jane (1860–1935) US social reformer who founded one of the earliest community welfare centres, Hull House in Chicago, Illinois, in 1899

Adler Cyrus (1863–1940) US educator who was president of Dropsie College in Philadelphia, Pennsylvania, USA

Altgeld John Peter (1847–1902) Prussian-born US politician and social reformer who, as governor of Illinois (1893–97), supported workers' rights

Arnold Matthew (1822–1888) English critic and son of Thomas Arnold; he recommended a national system of education encompassing all social classes and groups

Arnold Thomas (1795–1842) English educator who, as headmaster of Rugby School (1828–42), influenced public school education by modernizing the curriculum

Bacon Francis (1561–1626) English philosopher who promoted education, knowledge, and inquisitiveness as tools for gaining control over one's circumstances

Barzun Jacques Martin (1907–) French-born US historian and educator whose speciality was 19th-century European intellectual life

Beale Dorothea (1831–1906) British educator who was a pioneer in women's education

Bello Andrés (1781–1865) Venezuelan educator who influenced educational and legal reform in Chile

Binet Alfred (1857–1911) French psychologist who specialized in intelligence testing (Stanford-Binet scale) that influenced educational assessments

(*continued*)

Noteworthy Social Reformers and Educators (*continued*)

Bowlby (Edward) John (Mostyn) (1907–1990) English psychologist whose research into the mental health and emotional development of children and adolescents influenced modern educational approaches

Brougham Henry (1778–1868) British lawyer and politician who advocated elementary education for all in society

Burt Cyril (1883–1971) British psychologist who specialised in child and mental development

Buss Frances Mary (1827–1894) British educator who helped raise educational standards for women

Butler Josephine Elizabeth (born Gray) (1828–1906) English social reformer who promoted women's education and supported the Married Women's Property Act

Chadwick Edwin (1800–1890) English social reformer who was the author of the Poor Law Report in 1834

Colet John (1467–1515) English humanist who recommended an individual approach and understanding instead of inflexible and uniform teaching methods

Comenius Johann Amos (1592–1670) Moravian-born Polish educator and bishop whose ideas on curriculum and teaching were much ahead of his time

Cooper Whina Josephine (1895–1994) New Zealand reformer who campaigned for the political and economic rights of the Maori people

Cousin Victor (1792–1867) French educational reformer who reorganized the elementary education system in France in 1840

Dalgarno George (c. 1626–1687) Scottish educator who invented the first sign-language alphabet in 1680

Dewey John (1859–1952) US educator who developed new educational techniques that became widely used in US schools

Dix Dorothea Lynde (1802–1887) US educator and medical reformer who helped improve conditions and treatment for the mentally ill

Dunant Jean Henri (1828–1910) Swiss reformer who founded the International Red Cross in 1864

Eliot Charles William (1834–1926) US educator who established standards for graduate education in the USA

Erasmus Desiderius (originally Gerrit Gerritszoon) (1466–1536) Dutch Renaissance scholar and philosopher who stressed the importance of education in the development of the human spirit and described the duties of parents and teachers in the process of education

Forster William Edward (1819–1886) British reformer and politician who, in 1870, secured the passing of the Education Act in Great Britain

Freud Anna (1895–1982) Austrian-born British daughter of Sigmund Freud who developed research into applying ideas of psychoanalysis to education

Froebel Friedrich Wilhelm August (1782–1852) German educator who devised a new system of pre-school education using instructive play

Fuller (Sarah) Margaret, Marchioness Ossoli (1810–1850) US reformer who wrote extensively about women's rights

Galton Francis (1822–1911) UK statistician and medical scientist who developed psychometrics

Garrison William Lloyd (1805–1879) US abolitionist who was a leader in the American Anti-Slavery Society

Hahn Kurt Matthias Robert Martin (1886–1974) German educationalist who founded the Salem School in Germany and the Gordonstoun School in Scotland

Harris William T (1835–1909) one of the most distinguished US educators of the late 19th century

Herbart Johann Friedrich (1776–1841) German philosopher who promoted the idea of systematic teaching, comprizing stages of preparation, presentation, association, generalization, and application

Hill Octavia (1838–1912) English philanthropist and social reformer who campaigned for better housing for the poor, and, in 1895, was one of the founders of the National Trust

Hoggart (Herbert) Richard (1918–) English educator who wrote a number of influential books on the teaching of literature

Howe Samuel Gridley (1801–1876) US educational reformer who campaigned for expanded public education and better mental health facilities

Jaques-Dalcroze Emile (1865–1950) Swiss composer and promoter of artistic education who developed eurythmics, a method of movement to music, which has since been widely applied in schools

Jowett Benjamin (1817–1893) English scholar and educator who promoted university reform in the UK

Kant Immanuel (1724–1804) German philosopher who saw education as a decisive factor in an individual's realization of personal autonomy

Kay-Shuttleworth James (1804–1877) English physician who promoted education as the main weapon against poverty and disease

Kilpatrick William H (1871–1965) US educator who emphasized the value of real-life experiences in education and equated learning with living

Laban Rudolf (1879–1958) Slovakian-born dancer, dance theoretician, and choreographer who promoted the role of dance, as the expression of human personality, in education

Lancaster Joseph (1778–1833) English educator who promoted the 'monitorial system' in elementary education, whereby older pupils teach the younger ones

Lane Homer (1875–1925) US educator who pioneered modern treatment of delinquent and disturbed children

Las Casas Bartolomé de (known as 'the Apostle of the Indians') (1474–1566) Spanish missionary who called for the abolition of Indian slavery in Latin America

Livingstone Richard Winn (1880–1960) British educational reformer who emphasized the teaching of the classics in schools

Low Juliette Gordon (1860–1927) US social reformer who founded the Girl Scouts of America in 1912

McGuffey William Holmes (1800–1873) US educator who produced the *Eclectic Readers*, which became standard reading textbooks in the USA

Mann Horace (1796–1859) US education reformer who helped raise the level of public-education funding and instruction in Massachusetts

Mason Charlotte (1842–1923) British educator whose work improved the quality of home teaching

Mill John Stuart (1806–1873) English philosopher and social reformer who advocated the equality of women in education, liberal rather than vocational studies, and the development of emotions as well as the intellect

Montessori Maria (1870–1952) Italian educator who developed an educational system for children incorporating instructive play and self-paced learning

Moody Dwight Lyman (1837–1899) US evangelist who founded the Northfield School for girls (1879) and the Mount Hermon School for boys (1881), both in Massachusetts

Morris Henry (1889–1961) British educator who oversaw the introduction of the 'village college' and community school education

Mulcaster Richard (1530–1611) English educator whose ideas of teachers' training and good education for all children were ahead of his time

Nation Carrie Amelia Moore (1846–1911) US Temperance movement crusader who protested against disregard for the prohibition law, and who marched into illegal saloons with a hatchet

Noteworthy Social Reformers and Educators (*continued*)

Norton Caroline Elizabeth Sarah (born Sheridan) (1808–1877) British writer who produced 'social-problems novels' in the 1840s to raise public awareness

Oastler Richard (1789–1861) English social reformer who opposed child labour and secured the Factory Act in 1833

Orff Carl (1895–1982) German composer who greatly influenced musical education

Pankhurst Emeline (1858–1928) English suffragette who launched the militant suffragist campaign in 1905

Payne William H (1836–1907) first US professor of education

Pestalozzi Johann Heinrich (1746–1827) Swiss educator who stressed the value of individual experience in education and promoted the development of mind and spirit in line with the ideas of the Enlightenment

Phillips Wendell (1811–1884) US reformer who opposed slavery and sought improved conditions for Native Americans

Piaget Jean (1896–1980) Swiss psychologist who specialized in the development of children, and whose concept of developmental stages of intellect greatly influenced the theory of education

Plimsoll Samuel (1824–1898) British social reformer who helped secure passage of the Merchant Shipping Act in 1876

Rousseau Jean-Jacques (1712–1778) French philosopher and social reformer, and one of the leading figures of the Enlightenment era, who believed that children are naturally good, and that education must strive to preserve them from corruption

Russell Bertrand (1872–1970) British philosopher who opposed church and state involvement in education and advocated ideas of freedom and individuality instead

Ryder Sue (1923–) English philanthropist who set up the Sue Ryder Foundation to aid the sick and disabled worldwide

Sanger Margaret Louise (born Higgins) (1883–1966) US health reformer and crusader for birth control who founded the Planned Parenthood Federation

Scarman Leslie George (1911–) English jurist and legal reformer who called for the liberalization of British divorce laws and a bill of rights

Schonell Fred (1900–1968) Australian educational psychologist who pioneered the testing and teaching of mentally disabled children

Scott Rose (1847–1925) Australian social reformer who helped advance the suffragist movement in Australia

Search Preston W (1853–1932) US educator whose concept of individualized instruction, based on allowing pupils to work at their own pace, was to be commended in 20th-century educational theory

Shaftesbury Anthony Ashley Cooper, 1st Earl of Shaftesbury (1801–1885) English social reformer and philanthropist who fought for statutory working hours for women and children; he was notable for his campaign on behalf of child chimney sweeps

Simon John (1816–1904) English public health reformer who helped clean up the city of London in the 19th century

Skinner Burrhus Frederic (1904–1990) US psychologist and a leading behaviourist who devised the technique of 'programmed learning', and using feedback and adapting teaching to the individual's needs

Socrates (469–399 BC) Greek philosopher and teacher whose method of asking leading questions that showed the need for a deeper analysis of the debated issue became popular in educational and philosophical writings as the 'Socratic method' or 'dialogue'

Steiner Rudolf (1861–1925) US philosopher advocating, within his system of anthroposophy, coeducational schools, the intellectual and moral development of pupils, and mixed ability teaching

Stopes Marie Charlotte Carmichael (1880–1958) Scottish birth-control campaigner who, in 1921, founded the UK's first birth-control clinic in London

Street Jessie Mary (born Grey) (1889–1970) Australian leader in the suffragist movement in England and Australia

Terman Lewis Madison (1877–1956) US psychologist who devised the intelligence quotient (IQ), a measure widely used in educational assessments

Thring Edward (1821–1887) English teacher (headmaster of Uppingham) and an energetic innovator who broadened the curriculum and was involved in the development of new teaching methods

Varah (Edward) Chad (1911–) British cleric who founded the Samaritans organization

Wagner Robert F(erdinand) (1877–1953) US politician who helped draft US welfare reform legislation in the 1930s

Wald Lillian D (1867–1940) US public health reformer who founded the National Organization for Public Health Nursing in 1912

Wilberforce William (1759–1833) English evangelist and philanthropist who was a leading antislavery campaigner

Wilderspin Samuel (1792–1866) English pioneer of infant and pre-school education

Willard Emma (born Hart) (1787–1870) US educator and a pioneer of higher and equal education for women, whose work prepared the ground for coeducation

Willard Frances Elizabeth Caroline (1839–1898) US campaigner for the prohibition of alcohol and president of the Women's Christian Temperance Union (1879–98)

Noteworthy Social Scientists and Anthropologists

Adorno Theodor Wiesengrund (1903–1969) German social theorist, philosopher, critic of culture, and member of the Frankfurt School who was the main contributor to *The Authoritarian Personality*

Barthés Roland (1915–1980) influential French writer and critic who combined Marxist and structuralist elements in his critique of bourgeois thinking

Bateson Gregory (1861–1926) US anthropologist involved in the culture-and-personality movement, which was influenced by cybernetics and medical science

Baudrillard Jean (1929–) French cultural theorist who offered a critique of the consumer society and the impact of informational images on it

Bell Daniel (1919–) US sociologist whose *The End of Ideology* proposed that ideological thinking had ended in the West

Benedict Ruth (born Fulton) (1887–1948) US anthropologist who was a leading figure in the culture-and-personality movement and a pioneer of the 'configurational' method of social inquiry

Bentham Jeremy (1748–1832) English philosopher and social reformer who was a pioneer of utilitarianism

Bernstein Basil Bernard (1924–) British sociologist whose studies show how social origins affect the ability to communicate

Blau Peter Michael (1918–) US sociologist who argues that a system of reciprocation and obligation creates social bonding

Boas Franz (1858–1942) US anthropologist who broadened the scope of anthropology and social sciences by bringing together ethnology, linguistics, sociology, anthropology, and archaeology

Booth Charles (1840–1916) English sociologist who was a pioneer in the development of an old-age pension scheme

(*continued*)

Noteworthy Social Scientists and Anthropologists (*continued*)

Comte (Isidore) Auguste (Marie François Xavier) (1798–1857) French philosopher who coined the term 'sociology' and sought to establish it as an intellectual discipline

Dahrendorf Ralf Gustav (1929–) German-born British sociologist who argues that the aim of society is to improve the range of opportunities for individuals

Durkheim Emile (1858–1917) French sociologist who was one of the founders of modern sociology

Etzioni Amitai (1929–) German-born US sociologist who founded the Communitarian Movement in 1993

Evans-Pritchard Edward Ewan (1902–1973) English anthropologist who emphasized the need for historical and interpretational aspects in sociological and anthropological scholarship

Eysenck Hans Jurgen (1916–1997) German-born British psychologist whose research into race and intelligence has major sociological implications

Frazer James George (1854–1941) Scottish social anthropologist and ethnologist whose major work, *The Golden Bough: A Study in Comparative Religion* (1890; 12 vol-edition 1911–15) became a modern classic

Goffman Erving (1922–1982) Canadian social scientist whose studies show the ways self-image is defined and defended within social structures

Habermas Jurgen (1929–) German social theorist whose studies focus on the possibility of a rational political commitment to socialism within a scientific society

Horkheimer Max (1895–1973) German social theorist who believed that technology posed a threat to culture and civilization

Johnson Alvin Saunders (1874–1971) US social scientist who was a founder of the New School for Social Research in New York

LePlay (Pierre Guillaume) Frédéric (1806–1882) French social scientist whose studies provided the basis for empirical sociology

Lévi-Strauss Claude Gustave (1908–) French social anthropologist who helped formulate the principles of structuralism by stressing the interdependence of cultural systems

Malinowski Bronisław Kasper (1884–1942) Polish-born British anthropologist who set standards for modern social anthropology and was a pioneer of functionalism in the discipline

Mannheim Karl (1893–1947) Hungarian-born British sociologist who proposed that all knowledge is ideological in nature

Mauss Marcel (1872–1950) French sociologist who argued that the exchange of gifts creates a system of reciprocity fundamental for society

Mead George Herbert (1863–1931) US sociologist who helped found the philosophy of pragmatism

Mead Margaret (1901–1978) influential and popular US anthropologist who questioned the social values of the Western world and focused on the relativity of such values in various non-Western societies

Merton Robert King (1910–) US sociologist whose studies dealt with deviance, anomie, and role theory in sociological thought

Mills C(harles) Wright (1916–1962) US sociologist who criticized the US establishment over issues related to individual freedom

Park Robert Ezra (1864–1944) US sociologist and creator of urban sociology who also researched extensively into the issue of inter-racial relations

Parsons Talcott (1902–1979) US sociologist who attempted to integrate all the social sciences into a science of human action

Polanyi Michael (1891–1976) Hungarian social theorist whose work focused on the conflicts between personal freedom and central planning

Radcliffe-Brown Alfred Reginald (1881–1955) English social anthropologist who was the architect of the methodological foundations of the discipline

Riesman David (1909–) US sociologist who developed the distinctions of 'inner-directed', 'tradition-directed', and 'other-directed' societies

Rousseau Jean-Jacques (1712–1778) French social theorist whose book *Du Contrat social/The Social Contract* emphasized the rights of people over the rights of government

Saint-Simon Claude Henri de Rouvroy (1760–1825) pioneer of French socialism who advocated a total reorganization of social structures

Simmel Georg (1858–1918) German sociologist who made significant contributions to the methodology of the discipline and was a leading figure in German sociological formalism

Sorel Georges (1847–1922) French social philosopher who focused on violence as a means for political and social opposition

Sorokin Pitirim Aleksandrovich (1889–1968) Russian-born US sociologist who analysed macrosocial change

Spencer Herbert (1820–1903) British social philosopher whose *Social Statics* expounded laissez-faire views on social and political problems

Tönnies Ferdinand Julius (1855–1936) German social theorist who was a founder of the sociological tradition of community studies and urban studies

Tylor Edward Burnett (1832–1917) English anthropologist and a pioneer of systematic cultural studies who also developed the subsequently rejected idea of the evolutionary development of cultures

Veblen Thorstein Bunde (1857–1929) US social theorist who was a founder of the New School for Social Research in New York in 1919

Weber Max (1864–1920) German sociologist who was one of the founders of modern sociology

Scientists

Noteworthy Astronomers

Aristarchus of Samos (*c.* 320–*c.* 250 BC) Greek astronomer who was the first to argue that the Earth orbits the Sun

Bessel Friedrich Wilhelm (1784–1846) German astronomer and mathematician who was the first person to calculate the distance of a star other than the Sun

Boksenberg Alexander (1936–) English astronomer and physicist who developed a light-detecting system for telescopes, thereby greatly enhancing their optical power

Bradley James (1693–1762) English astronomer who calculated the speed of light in 1728

Brahe Tycho (1546–1601) Danish astronomer whose accurate calculation of the motion of the Sun led to the reform of the calendar in 1582, with the adoption of the Gregorian Calendar; he discovered and reported a supernova explosion in 1572

Cannon Annie Jump (1863–1941) US astronomer who first classified stars by their spectra

Celsius Anders (1701–1744) Swedish astronomer, physicist, and mathematician who introduced the Celsius scale of temperature in 1742

Copernicus Nicolaus (Latinized form of Mikołaj Kopernik) (1473–1543) Polish astronomer who argued that the Sun is the centre of the Solar System

Flamsteed John (1646–1719) English astronomer who became the first Astronomer Royal at Greenwich and pioneered work on the cataloguing of stars

Fowler William Alfred (1911–1995) US astrophysicist who worked on the life cycle of stars and the origin of chemical elements

Galileo (properly Galileo Galilei) (1564–1642) Italian mathematician, astronomer, and physicist who developed the astronomical telescope and confirmed that planets orbit the Sun

Gill David (1843–1914) Scottish astronomer who pioneered the use of photographic techniques in the cataloguing of stars

Greenstein Jesse Leonard (1909–) US astronomer who helped discover the interstellar magnetic field and quasars

Halley Edmond (or Edmund) (1656–1742) English astronomer who, in 1705, identified the comet now named after him; he also compiled a catalogue of stars and researched stellar motion

Heraklides of Pontus (388–315 BC) Greek astronomer and philosopher who was one of the first to recognize the 24-hour rotation of the Earth from west to east on its axis

Herschel (Frederick) William (1738–1822) German-born English astronomer who discovered the planet Uranus in 1781 and outlined the basic form of the Milky Way

Herschel John Frederick William (1792–1871) English astronomer who carried out a survey of the stars in the southern hemisphere and measured the brightness of stars

Hertzsprung Ejnar (1873–1967) Danish astronomer and physicist who introduced the concept of the absolute magnitude (brightness) of a star

Hipparchus (*c.* 190–*c.* 120 BC) Greek astronomer and mathematician who calculated the lengths of the solar year and lunar month

Hubble Edwin (1889–1953) US astronomer who discovered the existence of other galaxies and found evidence for the expansion of the universe

Huygens Christiaan (1629–1695) Dutch mathematical physicist and astronomer who observed Saturn's rings; he was also famous for his work in the field of optics

Jeans James Hopwood (1877–1946) English scientist and astronomer who did much to popularize astronomy through books and television broadcasts

Kepler Johannes (1571–1630) German mathematician and astronomer who described how planets orbit the Sun; he is particularly remembered for what are now termed Kepler's laws of motion

Laplace Pierre Simon (1749–1827) French astronomer and mathematician who formulated the nebular hypothesis of the origin of the solar system and developed the field of celestial mechanics

Lemaître Georges Edouard (1894–1966) Belgian cosmologist who proposed the Big Bang theory of the origin of the universe

Lowell Percival (1855–1916) US astronomer who predicted the existence of Pluto

Messier Charles (1730–1817) French astronomer who produced a catalogue of the locations of nebulae and star clusters

Minkowski Rudolph Leo (1895–1976) German-born US astrophysicist who compiled the National Geographic Society Palomar Observatory Sky Survey and was a pioneer in the field of radio-astronomy

Moore Patrick Alfred Calderwell (1923–) English astronomer, author, and broadcaster who has promoted the public understanding of astronomy through his popular television series *The Sky at Night* and more than 60 books

Newcomb Simon (1835–1909) Canadian-born US mathematician and astronomer who standardized the system of astronomical constants

Newton Isaac (1642–1727) English physicist, mathematician, and astronomer whose work is fundamental to the development of science; his theories on the nature of space and the action of force at a distance contributed greatly to the modern understanding of the universe

Ptolemy (Claudius Ptolemaeus) (*c.* 100–*c.* 170) Egyptian astronomer and geographer who developed the geocentric view of the Solar System

Schiaparelli Giovanni Virginio (1835–1910) Italian astronomer who drew attention to 'canals', or linear markings, on Mars

Shapley Harlow (1885–1972) US astronomer who established that our galaxy is much larger than was previously thought

Van Allen James Alfred (1914–) US physicist who discovered two zones of intense radiation around the Earth

Noteworthy Biologists

Avery Oswald Theodore (1877–1955) Canadian-born US bacteriologist who established that DNA is responsible for the transmission of heritable characteristics

Bateson William (1861–1926) English geneticist who introduced the term 'genetics' and translated the work of Gregor Mendel into English

Beadle George Wells (1903–1989) US biologist who formed the 'one gene–one enzyme' hypothesis (that a single gene codes for a single kind of enzyme)

Berg Paul (1926–) US molecular biologist who pioneered research on recombinant DNA

Bishop (John) Michael (1936–) US virologist and molecular biologist who helped discover cancer-causing genes known as oncogenes

Brenner Sidney (1927–) South African biologist who was one of the pioneers of genetic engineering and discovered messenger RNA

Brown Michael Stuart (1941–) US geneticist who helped discover how the human body metabolizes cholesterol

Brown Robert (1773–1858) Scottish botanist who investigated the impregnation of plants and noted that living cells contain a nucleus

Carson Rachel Louise (1907–1964) US biologist who inspired the modern environmental movement

Chargaff Erwin (1905–) Czech-born US biochemist who pioneered research on the base composition of DNA

Cohn Ferdinand Julius (1828–1898) German botanist and bacteriologist who developed a classification system for bacteria

Crick Francis Harry Compton (1916–) English biochemist and physicist who pioneered research on DNA

Darwin Charles Robert (1809–1882) English naturalist who developed the modern theory of evolution

Delbrück Max (1906–1981) German-born US biologist who pioneered techniques in molecular biology, studying genetic changes occurring when viruses invade bacteria

De Vries Hugo Marie (1848–1935) Dutch botanist who was a pioneer in the study of plant evolution

Dobzhansky Theodosius (originally Feodosy Grigorevich Dobrzhansky) (1900–1975) Ukrainian-born US geneticist who established evolutionary genetics as an independent discipline

Funk Casimir (1884–1967) Polish-born US biochemist who worked on vitamins and a cure for the disease beriberi

Galton Francis (1822–1911) English scientist who studied evolution and eugenics; he is credited with devising the system of fingerprint identification

Gilbert Walter (1932–) US molecular biologist who identified the lac repressor molecule in gene control

Goldstein Joseph Leonard (1940–) US geneticist who helped discover the gene involved in the removal of cholesterol

Golgi Camillo (1843–1926) Italian cell biologist who produced the first detailed knowledge of the fine structure of the nervous system

Gould Stephen Jay (1941–) US palaeontologist who proposed the evolutionary theory of punctuated equilibrium

Haeckel Ernst Heinrich Philipp August (1834–1919) German zoologist and philosopher who supported Charles Darwin's theory of evolution

Haldane J(ohn) B(urdon) S(anderson) (1892–1964) British physiologist, geneticist, and author of popular science books

Hershey Alfred Day (1908–1997) US biologist who pioneered research on DNA

Hill Archibald Vivian (1886–1977) English physiologist who investigated the physiology of muscle and nerve tissue

Hill Robert (1899–1991) British biochemist who demonstrated that during photosynthesis oxygen is produced from water

Holly Robert William (1922–) US biochemist who established the existence of transfer RNA

Hooke Robert (1635–1703) British scientist who pioneered the early use of the microscope

Hooker Joseph Dalton (1817–1911) English botanist who developed the classification of plants and began the compilation of *Index Kewensis*, still the standard reference work today

Hopkins Frederick Gowland (1861–1947) English biochemist who pioneered research on vitamins

Huxley Thomas Henry (1825–1895) English biologist who supported Darwin's theory of evolution vehemently, most notably in the 1860 debate with Bishop Samuel Wilberforce

Jeffreys Alec John (1950–) British geneticist who discovered the DNA probes necessary for genetic fingerprinting

Johanssen Wilhelm Ludwig (1857–1927) Danish botanist and geneticist who introduced the term 'gene' as a unit of heredity

Kendrew John Cowdery (1917–) English molecular biologist who determined the crystallographic structure of the muscle protein myoglobin using X-rays

Lamarck Jean Baptiste Pierre Antoine de Monet, Chevalier de (1744–1829) French naturalist who coined the word 'biology' and proposed a theory of evolution

Lederberg Joshua (1925–) US geneticist who showed that bacteria can reproduce sexually, combining genetic material so that offspring possess characteristics of both parent organisms

Leeuwenhoek Anton van (1632–1723) Dutch pioneer of microscopic research

Linnaeus Carolus (Latinized form of Carl von Linné) (1707–1778) Swedish naturalist and physician who developed the modern system of naming and classifying plants and animals

Lorenz Konrad Zacharias (1903–1989) Austrian ethologist who studied the relationship between instinct and behaviour, particularly in birds, and described the phenomenon of imprinting

Maynard Smith John (1920–) British geneticist and evolutionary biologist who applied game theory to animal behaviour

McCollum Elmer Verner (1879–1967) US biochemist who pioneered research into vitamins and discovered that vitamin D could be used in the prevention of rickets

Mendel Gregor Johann (1822–1884) Austrian biologist who pioneered the study of modern genetics

Monod Jacques (1910–1976) French biochemist who won the Nobel Prize, together with François Jacob, for work on genetic control mechanisms

Montagnier Luc (1932–) French molecular biologist who first identified the HIV virus and AIDS in 1983

Morgan Thomas Hunt (1866–1945) US geneticist who developed the chromosome theory of inheritance

Muller Hermann Joseph (1890–1967) US geneticist who was awarded a Nobel prize in 1946 for his work on the use of X-rays to cause genetic mutations

Perutz Max Ferdinand (1914–) Austrian-born biochemist who determined the structure of haemoglobin and myoglobin

Ray John (1627–1705) English naturalist who developed the basic principles of the classification of plants and animals

Sanger Frederick (1918–) English biochemist who determined the structure of insulin

Sharp Phillip Allen (1944–) US molecular biologist who discovered that genes are split into several sections, separated by stretches of DNA known as 'introns'

Schleiden Matthias Jacob (1804–1881) German botanist who developed cell theory by explaining the role of the nucleus in cell formation

Schwann Theodor (1810–1882) German physiologist who is credited with formulating cell theory

Noteworthy Biologists (*continued*)

Sherrington Charles Scott (1857–1952) English physiologist who worked on the structure and function of the nervous system and introduced the term 'synapse'

Spallanzani Lazzaro (1729–1799) Italian biologist who disproved the theory that microbes spontaneously generate out of rotten food

Sturtevant Alfred Henry (1891–1970) US geneticist who first mapped the position of genes on a chromosome

Tatum Edward Lawrie (1909–1975) US microbiologist who pioneered work in molecular genetics

Waksman Selman Abraham (1888–1973) Ukrainian-born US biochemist who coined the word 'antibiotic' and won a Nobel prize for his work on antibiotics

Wallace Alfred Russel (1823–1913) Welsh naturalist who collected animal and plant specimens in South America and Southeast Asia, and independently arrived at a theory of evolution by natural selection similar to that proposed by Charles Darwin

Watson James Dewey (1928–) US biologist who pioneered research on DNA

Weismann August Friedrich Leopold (1834–1914) German biologist who was one of the founders of genetics

Whipple George Hoyt (1878–1976) US pathologist who helped explain the formation of haemoglobin in the blood

Noteworthy Chemists

Arrhenius Svante August (1859–1927) Swedish scientist who was one of the founders of physical chemistry

Baekeland Leo Hendrik (1863–1944) Belgian-born US chemist who pioneered the development of plastics and invented Bakelite, the first commercial plastic

Berthollet Claude Lewis (1749–1822) French chemist who determined the composition of ammonia and worked with Lavoisier on a system of nomenclature

Berzelius Jons Jakob (1779–1848) Swedish chemist who devised the system of chemical symbols and formulae

Black Joseph (1728–1799) Scottish chemist who discovered carbon dioxide

Bunsen Robert Wilhelm (1811–1899) German chemist credited with the invention of the Bunsen burner

Butenandt Adolf Friedrich Johann (1903–1995) German biochemist who isolated the first sex hormones

Cannizzaro Stanislaus (1826–1910) Italian organic chemist who established atomic and molecular weights as the basis of chemical calculations

Carothers Wallace Hume (1896–1937) US industrial chemist who developed the synthetic products neoprene and nylon

Chain Ernst Boris (1906–1979) German-born British biochemist who isolated and purified penicillin

Coulson Charles Alfred (1910–1974) English theoretical chemist who developed a molecular orbital theory and studied the concept of partial valency

Curie Marie (born Maria Skłodowska) (1867–1934) Polish scientist, active in France, who, with her husband Pierre Curie (1859–1906) discovered two radioactive elements, polonium and radium

Dalton John (1766–1844) English chemist who first formulated atomic theory

Davy Humphry (1778–1829) English chemist who isolated the elements sodium, potassium, calcium, boron, magnesium, strontium, and barium, and discovered the anaesthetic effect of nitrous oxide (laughing gas)

Faraday Michael (1791–1867) English chemist and physicist who was a pioneer in electromagnetic research

Gay-Lussac Joseph Luis (1778–1850) French chemist and physicist who formulated a law of gas volumes and investigated sodium, potassium, boron, and silicon

Graham Thomas (1805–1869) Scottish chemist who pioneered work on diffusion of gases

Hess Germain Henri (1802–1850) Swiss-born Russian chemist who was a pioneer in thermochemistry and established the law of constant heat summation

Hodgkin Dorothy Mary Crowfoot (1910–1994) English biochemist who analysed the structure of penicillin, insulin, and vitamin B_{12}e

Hyatt John Wesley (1837–1920) US inventor who produced the first artificial plastic

Kekulé von Stradonitz Friedrich August (1829–1896) German chemist whose work on the structure of benzene and the tetrahedral carbon atom was fundamental to the development of organic chemistry

Kipping Frederic Stanley (1863–1949) English chemist who pioneered the study of silicon

Kornberg Arthur (1918–) US biochemist whose research led to the discovery of DNA polymerase, the enzyme that synthesizes new DNA

Langmuir Irving (1881–1957) US scientist who won a Nobel prize for his work on surface chemistry

Lavoisier Antoine Laurent (1743–1794) French chemist who described the chemistry of many compounds and who is considered the founder of modern chemistry

Libby Willard Frank (1908–1980) US chemist who developed radiocarbon dating

Liebig Justus von (1803–1873) German organic chemist who introduced the theory of compound radicals

Mendeleyev Dmitri Ivanovich (1834–1907) Russian chemist who framed the periodic law in chemistry

Meyer Julius Lothar von (1830–1895) German chemist who recognized the combination of oxygen with haemoglobin in respiration and discovered the ring structure of benzene

Meyer Viktor (1848–1897) German chemist who invented a method of measuring vapour densities and introduced the term 'stereochemistry'

Mullis Kary Banks (1944–) US molecular biologist who developed the PCR technique in DNA research

Nernst (Walther) Hermann (1864–1941) German physical chemist who formulated the third law of thermodynamics

Newlands John Alexander Reina (1837–1898) English chemist who, in 1865, drew up an early version of the periodic table based on his 'law of octaves'

Nobel Alfred Bernhard (1833–1896) Swedish chemist and engineer who invented dynamite

Ostwald (Friedrich) Wilhelm (1853–1932) Latvian-born German chemist who is regarded as one of the founders of physical chemistry

Pauling Linus Carl (1901–1994) US theoretical chemist and biologist whose ideas on chemical bonding are fundamental to modern theories of molecular structure

Perkin William Henry (1838–1907) English chemist who first extracted the dye mauve, and founded the modern dye industry

Prelog Vladimir (1906–1998) Bosnian-born Swiss organic chemist who developed a comprehensive molecular topology for stereochemistry

(continued)

Noteworthy Chemists (continued)

Priestley Joseph (1733–1804) English chemist who identified oxygen and several other gases

Ramsay William (1852–1916) Scottish chemist who discovered argon, neon, krypton, and xenon

Regnault Henri Victor (1810–1878) French chemist and physicist who discovered vinyl chloride and refined techniques for determining the specific heats of solids, liquids, and gases

Seaborg Glenn Theodore (1912–   ) US nuclear chemist who helped discover plutonium

Scheele Karl Wilhelm (1742–1786) Swedish chemist and pharmacist who pioneered research on oxygen and respiration

Tiselius Arne Wilhelm Kaurin (1902–1971) Swedish chemist who worked on the analysis of proteins and developed the technique of electrophoresis

Tswett Mikhail Semyonovich (1872–1919) Russian organic chemist who first developed the analytical technique known as chromatography

Willstätter Richard (1872–1942) German organic chemist who researched into alkaloids and their derivations and won a Nobel prize for his work on plant pigments

Windaus Adolf Otto Reinhold (1876–1959) German chemist who identified the structure of cholesterol

Wöler Friedrich (1800–1882) German chemist who prepared specimens of urea and aluminium for the first time

Noteworthy Earth Scientists

Agassiz (Jean) Louis (Rodolphe) (1807–1873) Swiss-born US palaeontologist and geologist who developed the idea of the ice age

Beaufort Francis (1774–1857) British naval officer and hydrographer who devised the Beaufort Scale of wind force

Bjerknes Vilhelm Firman Koren (1862–1951) Norwegian scientist who was a pioneer in weather forecasting

Bowen Norman Levi (1887–1956) Canadian-born US geologist who pioneered the study of petrology, particularly silicates and igneous rocks

Brongniart Alexandre (1770–1847) French naturalist and geologist who first used fossils to date the strata of rock

Crutzen Paul (1933–   ) Dutch meteorologist who helped explain the formation and decomposition of ozone

Cuvier Georges Léopold Chrétien Frédéric Dagobert (1769–1832) French comparative anatomist who was the founder of palaeontology

Davis William Morris (1850–1934) US geomorphologist who studied the role of rain in the process of erosion; he also studied the development of rivers

Edinger Tilly (Johanna Gabrielle Ottilie) (1897–1967) German-born US palaeontologist who pioneered research in vertebrate palaeontology

Elsasser Walter Maurice (1904–1991) German-born US geophysicist who pioneered analysis of the Earth's magnetic fields

Ewing (William) Morris (1906–1974) US marine geologist who studied mid-ocean ridges and the theory of plate tectonics

Hall James (1761–1832) Scottish geologist who was one of the founders of experimental geology

Hess Harry Hammond (1906–1969) US geologist who proposed the theory of sea-floor spreading

Holmes Arthur (1890–1965) English geologist who pioneered geochronology and dating techniques; he also studied the mechanism of continental plate movement

Humboldt (Friedrich Wilhelm Heinrich) Alexander (1769–1859) German geophysicist, botanist, and geologist who is considered a founder of ecology

Hutton James (1726–1797) Scottish geologist who was the founder of geology as an academic discipline

Lyell Charles (1797–1875) Scottish geologist who contributed to the acceptance of Charles Darwin's views on evolution

Maury Matthew Fontaine (1806–1873) US hydrographer and naval officer who was the founder of the US Naval Oceanographic Office

Mercator Gerardus (Latinized form of Gerhard Kremer) (1512–1594) Flemish map-maker who devised the first modern atlas

Murchison Roderick Impey (1792–1873) Scottish geologist who named the Silurian period and worked with Sedgwick on the identification of the Devonian system in southwest England

Powell John Wesley (1834–1902) US geologist who pioneered work on erosion and mountain formation

Richter Charles Francis (1900–1985) US seismologist who devised the Richter scale to measure earthquakes

Sedgwick Adam (1785–1873) English geologist who studied the stratiography of the British Isles and identified the Devonian system in southwest England

Smith William (1769–1839) English geologist who was the founder of stratigraphical geology

Vine Frederick J(ohn) (1939–1988) English geophysicist who worked on the hypothesis of sea-floor spreading

Wegener Alfred Lothar (1880–1930) German meteorologist who originally proposed the theory of continental drift

Werner Abraham Gottlob (1749–1817) German geologist who was the first to develop a classification of rocks and worked on a theory of deposition

Wilson John Tuzo (1908–1993) Canadian geologist and geophysicist who developed the concept of plate tectonics

Noteworthy Mathematicians

Abel Niels Henrik (1802–1829) Norwegian mathematician who developed the concept of elliptic functions, which was influential in the development of complex analysis

Agnesi Maria Gaetana (1718–1799) Italian mathematician who was the first recognized woman mathematician

Aleksandrov Pavel Sergeevich (1896–1982) Russian mathematician who introduced many of the basic concepts of topology

Alembert Jean le Rond d' (1717–1783) French mathematician, encyclopedist, and theoretical physicist who devised the theory of partial differential equations

Archimedes (c. 287–212 BC) Greek mathematician who made major discoveries in geometry, hydrostatics, and mechanics

Argand Jean-Robert (1768–1822) Swiss mathematician who developed the Argand diagram, in which complex numbers are represented by points in the plane

Noteworthy Mathematicians (*continued*)

Artin Emil (1898–1962) Austrian mathematician who was one of the founders of modern algebra

Babbage Charles (1792–1871) English mathematician who developed calculating machines; he is regarded as a pioneer of the electronic computer

Bernoulli Daniel (1700–1782) Swiss mathematical physicist who made important contributions to trigonometry, differential equations, and the field of hydrodynamics

Bernoulli Jakob (1654–1705) and his brother Johann (1667–1748) Swiss mathematicians who laid the foundations of the calculus of variations

Bolyai János (1802–1860) Hungarian mathematician who helped develop non-Euclidean geometry

Boole George (1815–1864) English mathematician who established the basis of modern mathematical logic

Briggs Henry (1561–1630) English mathematician who was one of the founders of calculation by logarithms

Cantor Georg Ferdinand Ludwig Philipp (1845–1918) German mathematician who worked on set theory

Cauchy Augustin Louis (1789–1857) French mathematician who founded the theory of functions of a complex variable

Cayley Arthur (1821–1895) English mathematician who developed matrix algebra and the theory of algebraic invariants

Chebyshev Pafnuti Lvovich (1821–1894) Russian mathematician who studied number theory and probability; he is best known for his theory of approximation to functions by polynomials

Church Alonzo (1903–) US mathematician who published the first precise definition of a calculable function

Cramer Gabriel (1704–1752) Swiss mathematician who introduced a method for the solution of linear equations

Dedekind Julius Wilhelm Richard (1831–1916) German mathematician who pioneered set theory and lattice theory

Descartes René (1596–1650) French philosopher, mathematician, and scientist who founded coordinate geometry and developed the science of optics

Diophantus (fl. 250) Greek mathematician who pioneered algebra

Dirichlet (Peter Gustav) Lejeune (1805–1859) German mathematician who worked on number theory, Fournier series, and boundary-value problems

Eratosthenes (*c.* 276–194 BC) Greek geographer and mathematician whose world map was the first to contain lines of latitude and longitude

Euclid (*c.* 330–260 BC) Greek mathematician who systematized solid geometry and number theory

Euler Leonhard (1707–1783) Swiss mathematician who developed the theory of differential equations and created the calculus of variations

Fermat Pierre de (1601–1665) French mathematician who co-founded the theory of probability and contributed to the modern theory of numbers

Fredholm Erik Ivar (1866–1927) Swedish mathematician who devised the modern theory of integral equations

Galois Évoriste (1811–1832) French mathematician who developed the theory of algebraic equations and introduced the concept of the group

Gauss (Johann) Carl Friedrich (1777–1855) German mathematician who worked on the theory of numbers, non-Euclidean geometry, and the mathematical development of electric and magnetic theory

Gödel Kurt (1906–1978) Austrian-born US mathematician and logician whose theorem demonstrated the existence of formally undecidable elements within any formal system of arithmetic

Hamilton William Rowan (1805–1865) Irish mathematician who developed the theory of dynamics, and whose 'quaternion' theory was a forerunner of the branch of mathematics known as vector analysis

Hilbert David (1862–1943) German mathematician, philosopher, and physicist whose work was fundamental to 20th-century mathematics

Hipparchus (*c.* 180–*c.* 125 BC) Greek astronomer and mathematician who invented trigonometry

Hopf Heine (1894–1971) German mathematician who researched into combinational topology, including homotopy theory and vector fields

Huygens Christiaan (1629–1695) Dutch mathematical physicist and astronomer who made important advances in the fields of wave theory and mechanics

Jacobi Carl Gustav Jacob (1804–1851) German mathematician who developed the theory of elliptic functions and studied differential equations, number theory, and determinants

Laplace Pierre Simon, marquis de Laplace (1749–1827) French mathematician and astronomer who developed probability theory and worked on celestial mechanics

Legendre Adrien-Marie (1752–1833) French mathematician who developed number theory and proposed the method of least squares

Leibniz Gottfried Wilhelm (1646–1716) German mathematician, philosopher, and diplomat who helped develop calculus as a discipline

Lie Marius Sophus (1842–1899) Norwegian mathematician who developed a theory of continuous groups of transformations now termed Lie groups

Lobachevsky Nikolai Ivanovich (1792–1856) Russian mathematician who developed a theory of non-Euclidean geometry

Mandelbrot Benoit B (1924–) Polish-born French mathematician who coined the term 'fractal' in chaos theory

Mersenne Marin (1588–1648) French mathematician who experimented with the pendulum, and, in his study of acoustics, measured the speed of sound

Minkowski Hermann (1864–1909) Russian-born German mathematician who introduced the concept of space–time

Moivre Abraham de (1667–1754) French mathematician who pioneered the development of analytical trigonometry, developing a theorem regarding complex numbers

Napier John (1550–1617) Scottish mathematician who invented logarithms

Pascal Blaise (1623–1662) French philosopher and mathematician who helped develop the theory of probability

Peano Giuseppe (1853–1932) Italian mathematician who pioneered the study of symbolic logic

Pearson Karl (1857–1936) British statistician who introduced the term 'standard deviation' into statistics

Penrose Roger (1931–) English mathematician who formulated some of the fundamental theorems describing black holes

Poincaré Jules Henri (1854–1912) French mathematician who developed the theory of differential equations and was a pioneer in relativity theory

Pythagoras (*c.* 580–500 BC) Greek mathematician who formulated the Pythagorean theorem

Quetelet Lambert Adolphe Jacques (1796–1874) Belgian statistician who developed the concept of the 'average person' in statistics

Riemann Georg Friedrich Bernhard (1826–1866) German mathematician whose system of non-Euclidian geometry was used by Albert Einstein in the formulation of his theory of general relativity

(*continued*)

Noteworthy Mathematicians (*continued*)

Russell Bertrand Arthur William (1872–1970) British philosopher and mathematician who contributed to the development of modern mathematical logic

Shannon Claude Elwood (1916–) US mathematician who founded the science of information theory

Turing Alan Mathison (1912–1954) English mathematician and logician who pioneered computer theory

Venn John (1834–1923) English mathematician and logician who further developed Boole's symbolic logic; he is best known for the 'Venn diagram', which is used for pictorially representing relationships between sets

Viète François (1540–1603) French mathematician who developed algebra and its notation, and introduced the term 'coefficient'

Weierstrass Karl Theodor Wilhelm (1815–1897) German mathematician who deepened understanding of functions

Weyl Hermann (1885–1955) German mathematician who studied Riemann geometry and number theory; he originated the gauge theory of particle interactions, which is fundamental to quantum mechanics

Wiener Norbert (1894–1964) US mathematician who was a pioneer in the development of computer logic

Noteworthy Medical Pioneers

Alzheimer Alois (1864–1915) German psychiatrist and neuropathologist who studied presenile dementia, now known as Alzheimer's disease

Anderson Elizabeth Garrett (1836–1917) English physician and the first English woman to qualify in medicine

Avicenna (Arabic name Ibn Sina) (979–1037) Arabian philosopher and physician whose *Canon Medicinae* was a standard work for many centuries

Banting Frederick Grant (1891–1941) Canadian physician whose research resulted in a treatment for diabetes

Barnard Christiaan Neethling (1922–) South African surgeon who performed the first successful human heart transplant

Beaumont William (1785–1853) US surgeon who conducted pioneering experiments on the digestive system

Behring Emil von (1854–1917) German physician who discovered that the body produces antitoxins, substances able to counteract poisons released by bacteria, and developed new treatments for such diseases as diphtheria

Bell Charles (1774–1842) Scottish anatomist who pioneered research on the human nervous system

Bichat Marie Francois Xavier (1771–1802) French physician and founder of histology

Black James Whyte (1924–) Scottish pharmacologist who developed the first beta-blocker drugs as well as anti-ulcer drugs

Blackwell Elizabeth (1821–1910) English-born US physician who was the first woman to qualify in medicine in the USA

Bright Richard (1789–1858) British physician who described many conditions and linked oedema to kidney disease

Burnet (Frank) Macfarlane (1899–1985) Australian physician who was an authority on immunology and viral diseases, such as influenza, poliomyelitis, and cholera

Cairns Hugh William Bell (1896–1952) Australian surgeon who pioneered work on head injuries and was a campaigner for the motorcycle crash helmet

Cardozo William Warrick (1905–1962) US physician who pioneered work on sickle-cell anaemia

Carrel Alexis (1873–1944) French-born US surgeon who contributed to the development of organ transplants

Chain Ernst Boris (1906–1979) German-born British biochemist who worked with Florey and Fleming on the purification of penicillin

Cushing Harvey Williams (1869–1939) US neurologist who pioneered neurosurgery

Doll (William) Richard Shaboe (1912–) British physician who helped provide the first statistical proof of the link between smoking and cancer

Domagk Gerhard Johannes Paul (1895–1964) German biochemist who discovered the antibacterial sulphonamide drugs

Edelman Gerald Maurice (1929–) US biochemist who established the sequence of amino acids in human immunoglobulin

Ehrlich Paul (1854–1915) German bacteriologist who produced the first cure for syphilis

Eijkman Christiaan (1858–1930) Dutch bacteriologist who pioneered the recognition of vitamins as essential to health and identified vitamin B_1 deficiency as the cause of the disease beriberi

Enders John Franklin (1897–1985) US microbiologist who contributed to the development of vaccines against polio and measles

Fleming Alexander (1881–1955) Scottish bacteriologist who discovered the first antibiotic drug, penicillin

Florey Howard Walter (1898–1968) Australian pathologist who purified and developed the antibiotic penicillin

Freud Sigmund (1856–1939) Austrian physician who pioneered psychoanalysis

Galen (*c.* 130–*c.* 200) Greek physician and anatomist whose thinking dominated Western medicine for almost 1,500 years

Gallo Robert Charles (1937–) US scientist credited with identifying the human immunodeficiency virus (HIV), the virus responsible for AIDS

Gray Henry (*c.* 1827–1861) British anatomist who wrote the definitive work on anatomy

Haller (Viktor) Albrecht von (1708–1777) Swiss physician and scientist who was the founder of neurology

Harvey William (1578–1657) English physician who discovered the circulation of the blood

Hippocrates (*c.* 460–377 BC) Greek physician called the founder of medicine and associated with the 'Hippocratic oath' of the medical profession

Hunter John (1728–1793) Scottish physiologist and surgeon who pioneered research in the fields of comparative anatomy and pathology

Issacs Alick (1921–1967) Scottish virologist who helped discover interferon

Jenner Edward (1749–1823) English physician who pioneered vaccination

Jung Carl Gustav (1875–1961) Swiss psychiatrist who pioneered analytical psychology

Kitasato Shibasaburō (1852–1931) Japanese bacteriologist who discovered the plague bacillus and was the first to grow the tetanus bacillus in pure culture

Koch (Heinrich Hermann) Robert (1843–1910) German bacteriologist who devised techniques for culturing bacteria outside the body and formulated the rules for showing whether or not a bacterium is the cause of a disease

Noteworthy Medical Pioneers (*continued*)

Laênnec René Théophile Hyacinthe (1781–1826) French physician who invented the stethoscope

Landsteiner Karl (1868–1943) US pathologist who discovered the four major human blood groups

Lister Joseph (1827–1912) English surgeon and founder of antiseptic surgery

Malpighi Marcello (1628–1694) Italian physiologist who discovered blood capillaries

Manson Patrick (1844–1922) Scottish physician who showed that insects are responsible for the spread of diseases like elephantiasis and malaria

Mechnikov Ilia Ilich (1845–1916) Russian-born French zoologist who discovered the function of white blood cells and phagocytes

Medawar Peter Brian (1915–1987) British zoologist and immunologist who studied skin grafting for burn victims

Menninger Karl Augustus (1893–1990) US psychiatrist who was instrumental in reforming public mental health facilities

Paget James (1814–1899) English surgeon who was one of the founders of pathology

Paracelsus (adopted name of Philippus Aureolus Theophrastus Bombastus von Hohenheim) (1493–1541) Swiss physician, alchemist, and scientist who developed the idea that minerals and chemicals might have medical uses and introduced the use of laudanum for pain relief

Paré Ambroise (*c.* 1509–1590) French military surgeon who introduced modern principles to the treatment of wounds

Pasteur Louis (1822–1895) French chemist and microbiologist who developed the germ theory of disease

Reed Aedes Walter (1851–1902) US physician and medical researcher who identified the mosquito as the carrier of yellow fever

Ross Ronald (1857–1932) British physician and bacteriologist who identified mosquitoes of the genus *Anopheles* as being responsible for the spread of malaria

Sabin Albert Bruce (1906–1993) Russian-born US microbiologist who developed a highly effective live vaccine against polio

Salk Jonas Edward (1914–1995) US physician and microbiologist who developed the original vaccine for polio

Sanger Margaret Louise (born Higgins) (1883–1966) US health reformer and crusader for birth control

Sharpey-Schafer Edward Albert (born Schäfer) (1850–1935) English physiologist, one of the founders of endocrinology

Vesalius Andreas (1514–1564) Belgian physician who revolutionized anatomy by performing postmortem dissections

Virchow Rudolf Carl (1821–1902) German pathologist who founded cellular pathology

Noteworthy Physicists

Alpher Ralph Asher (1921–   ) US physicist who worked with George Gamow and others on an account of the origin and nature of the elements based on a theory of nucleosynthesis

Alvarez Luis Walter (1911–1988) US physicist who led the research team that discovered the subatomic particle

Ampère André Marie (1775–1836) French physicist who pioneered work in electromagnetism and electrodynamics

Anderson Carl David (1905–1991) US physicist who discovered the positive electron (positron)

Avogadro (Lorenzo Romano) Amedeo Carlo (1776–1856) Italian physicist who was one of the founders of physical chemistry

Bardeen John (1908–1991) US physicist who helped develop the transistor

Becquerel (Antoine) Henri (1852–1908) French physicist who discovered penetrating radiation coming from uranium salts, the first indication of radioactivity

Bohr Niels Henrik David (1885–1962) Danish physicist who developed a new model of atomic structure

Boltzmann Ludwig Eduard (1844–1906) Austrian physicist who studied the kinetic theory of gases

Born Max (1882–1970) German-born British physicist who pioneered quantum theory

Bose Jagadis Chandra (1858–1937) Indian physicist and plant physiologist

Boyle Robert (1627–1691) Irish chemist and physicist who was a pioneer in the use of experiment and scientific method

Bragg William Henry (1862–1942) English physicist who shared with his son Lawrence (1890–1971) the Nobel Prize for Physics for their research work determining the atomic structure of crystals from their X-ray diffraction patterns

Brewster David (1781–1868) Scottish physicist who made discoveries about the diffraction and polarization of light

Niels Bohr

© AEA Technology

Broglie Louis Victor Pierre Raymond de (1892–1987) French theoretical physicist who laid the foundations of wave mechanics

Carnot (Nicolas Léonard) Sadi (1796–1832) French scientist and military engineer who founded the science of thermodynamics

Cavendish Henry (1731–1810) English physicist and chemist who discovered hydrogen

Chadwick James (1891–1974) English physicist who discovered the neutron in the atom

Charles Jacques Alexandre César (1746–1823) French physicist who made the first ascent in a hot air balloon (1783)

Clausius Rudolf Julius Emanuel (1822–1888) German physicist who was one of the founders of the science of thermodynamics

Cockcroft John Douglas (1897–1967) English physicist who, with Irish physicist Ernest Walton (1903–1995), succeeded in splitting the atom for the first time

Cooper Leon Niels (1930–   ) US physicist who worked on superconductivity and proposed that at low temperatures electrons would be bound in pairs (since known as Cooper pairs)

Coulomb Charles Augustin de (1736–1806) French physicist who invented the torsion balance for measuring the force of electric and magnetic attraction

Curie Marie (born Maria Skłodowska) (1867–1934) Polish scientist who, with her husband Pierre Curie (1859–1906), discovered two new radioactive elements, polonium and radium

Dirac Paul Adrien Maurice (1902–1984) English physicist who worked out a version of quantum mechanics consistent with special relativity

Doppler Christian Johann (1803–1853) Austrian physicist who enunciated the so-called 'Doppler effect', which explains the frequency variation observed when a vibrating source of waves and the observer approach or recede from one another

Einstein Albert (1879–1955) German-born US physicist who formulated theories of relativity

Fahrenheit Gabriel Daniel (1686–1736) Polish-born Dutch physicist who invented the first accurate thermometer

Faraday Michael (1791–1867) English chemist and physicist who discovered the induction of electric currents and made the first dynamo, the first electric motor, and the first transformer

(*continued*)

Noteworthy Physicists (*continued*)

Fermi Enrico (1901–1954) Italian-born US physicist who proved the existence of new radioactive elements produced by bombardment with neutrons, and discovered nuclear reactions produced by low-energy neutrons

Feynman Richard P(hillips) (1918–1988) US physicist whose work laid the foundations of quantum electrodynamics

Foucault Jean Bernard Léon (1819–1868) French physicist who used a pendulum to demonstrate the rotation of the Earth on its axis, and invented the gyroscope

Franklin Benjamin (1706–1790) US scientist, statesman, and writer who proved that lightning is a form of electricity

Fraunhofer Joseph von (1787–1826) German physicist who studied optics; he developed the prism spectrometer, discovering the dark lines in the Sun's spectrum

Fresnel Augustin Jean (1788–1827) French physicist who refined the theory of polarized light

Gay-Lussac Joseph Luis (1778–1850) French physicist and chemist who investigated the physical properties of gases

Geiger Hans Wilhelm (1882–1945) German physicist who produced the Geiger counter, which is used for detecting radioactive particles

Gibbs Josiah Willard (1839–1903) US theoretical physicist and chemist who developed a mathematical approach to thermodynamics

Gilbert William (1544–1603) English physicist who established the magnetic nature of the Earth and coined the terms 'electricity', 'electric force', and 'electric attraction'

Glashow Sheldon Lee (1932–) US physicist who developed the theory of the electroweak force first postulated by Weinberg and Abdus Salam

Grimaldi Francesco Maria (1618–1663) Italian physicist who discovered the diffraction of light and postulated a wave theory of light

Guericke Otto von (1602–1686) German engineer and physicist who developed a primitive version of the vacuum pump

Hahn Otto (1879–1968) German radiochemist who won a Nobel prize for his discovery of nuclear fission

Hawking Stephen William (1942–) English physicist whose work has advanced research on a quantum theory of gravity

Heisenberg Werner Karl (1901–1976) German physicist who developed quantum theory

Hertz Heinrich Rudolf (1857–1894) German physicist who studied electromagnetic waves, showing that their behaviour resembles that of light and heat waves

Hooke Robert (1635–1703) English scientist and inventor whose inventions include the telegraph system, marine barometer, and sea gauge; he also pioneered the early use of the microscope

Joule James Prescott (1818–1889) English physicist whose work on the relations between electrical, mechanical, and chemical effects led to the discovery of the first law of thermodynamics

Kelvin William Thomson, 1st Baron Kelvin (1824–1907) Scottish physicist who introduced the Kelvin scale of temperature

Kirchoff Gustav Robert (1824–1887) German physicist whose work on spectrum analysis led to the discovery of caesium and rubidium; he formulated a law of radiation and a magnetic theory of diffraction

Landau Lev Davidovich (1908–1968) Russian theoretical physicist who was awarded a Nobel prize for his work on condensed matter, particularly liquid helium

Laue Max Theodor Felix von (1879–1960) German physicist who pioneered work on X-ray diffraction in crystals

Lawrence Ernest O(rlando) (1901–1958) US physicist who invented the cyclotron

Lodge Oliver Joseph (1851–1940) British physicist who was a pioneer in the development of radio receivers

Lorentz Hendrik Antoon (1853–1928) Dutch physicist who won a Nobel prize for his work on the Zeeman effect

Mach Ernst (1838–1916) Austrian philosopher and physicist who contributed to the understanding of scientific method; he carried out important experimental work on supersonic projectiles and on the flow of gases

Malus Étienne Louis (1775–1812) French physicist who researched into optics, discovering the polarization of light by reflection

Maxwell James Clerk (1831–1879) Scottish physicist who was a pioneer in research on electromagnetic waves

Meitner Lise (1878–1968) Austrian-born Swedish physicist who worked with German radiochemist Otto Hahn and was the first to realize that they had inadvertently achieved the fission of uranium

Michelson Albert Abraham (1852–1931) German-born US physicist who established the speed of light as a fundamental constant, and who was the first American to be awarded a Nobel prize

Millikan Robert Andrews (1868–1953) US physicist who determined Planck's constant (a fundamental unit of quantum theory)

Newton Isaac (1642–1727) English physicist and mathematician who founded physics as a modern discipline

Oersted Hans Christian (1777–1851) Dutch physicist who founded the science of electromagnetism

Ohm Georg Simon (1789–1854) German physicist and pioneer in the study of electricity

Oppenheimer J(ulius) Robert (1904–1967) US physicist in charge of the Manhattan Project, which developed the first atom bomb

Pauli Wolfgang (1900–1958) Austrian-born Swiss physicist who originated the 'exclusion principle'

Planck Max Karl Ernst (1858–1947) German physicist who developed quantum theory

Richter Burton (1930–) US particle physicist who designed the Stanford Positron–Electron Accelerating Ring

Röntgen Wilhelm Konrad von (1845–1923) German physicist who discovered X-rays

Rutherford Ernest (1871–1937) New Zealand-born British physicist who was a pioneer of modern atomic science and discovered alpha, beta, and gamma rays

Salam Abdus (1926–1996) Pakistani physicist who proposed a theory linking the electromagnetic and weak interactions of atomic particles

Schrödinger Erwin (1887–1961) Austrian physicist who advanced the study of wave mechanics to describe the behaviour of electrons in atoms

Schwinger Julian (1918–1994) US physicist who pioneered the study of quantum electrodynamics

Stokes George Gabriel (1819–1903) Irish physicist who studied the viscosity of fluids and developed an explanation for the phenomenon of fluorescence

Szilard Leo (1898–1964) Hungarian-born US physicist who was one of the first scientists to realize the importance of nuclear fission

Teller Edward (1908–) Hungarian-born US physicist who helped develop the first hydrogen bomb

Tesla Nikola (1856–1943) Croatian-born US physicist and electrical engineer who invented fluorescent lighting and the Tesla induction motor; he also patented the alternating current electrical supply system

Thomson J(oseph) J(ohn) (1856–1940) English physicist who discovered the electron in 1897

Torricelli Evangelista (1608–1647) Italian physicist who established the existence of atmospheric pressure and devised the mercury barometer

Noteworthy Physicists (*continued*)

Townsend John Sealy Edward (1868–1957) Irish physicist who researched into the kinetics of ions and electrons in gases and studied the properties of electron clouds

Volta Alessandro Giuseppe Antonio Anastasio (1745–1827) Italian physicist who developed the first electric cell

Walton E(rnest) T(homas) S(inton) (1903–1995) Irish physicist who, with Sir John Cockcroft, produced the first disintegration of a nucleus in the first successful use of a particle accelerator

Waterson John James (1811–1883) Scottish natural philosopher and engineer who postulated the basic kinetic theory of gases

Weinberg Steven (1933–) US physicist who developed the theory of the electroweak force first postulated by Weinberg and Abdus Salam

Young Thomas (1773–1829) British physicist who revived the wave theory of light and identified the phenomenon of interference

Noteworthy Zoologists

Andrews Roy Chapman (1884–1960) US zoologist who was the first to find fossilized dinosaur eggs

Audubon John James (1785–1851) US ornithologist and bird artist best known for his publication *Birds of America*

Carter Herbert James (1858–1940) English-born Australian entomologist who described over 1,000 new species of beetle

Dawkins (Clinton) Richard (1941–) British scientist and zoologist who popularized the theories of sociobiology and evolution

De Beer Gavin Rylands (1899–1972) British zoologist who disproved the germ-layer theory and developed the concept of paedomorphism

Ehrenberg Christian Gottfried (1795–1876) German naturalist who was the first scientist to study the fossils of microorganisms

Eisner Thomas (1929–) German-born US entomologist and conservation activist who is an authority on the role of chemicals in insect behaviour

Fabre Jean Henri Casimir (1823–1915) French entomologist whose studies of wasps, bees, and other insects have become classics

Fabricus Johann Christian (1745–1808) Danish entomologist who developed a classification system for insects based on the mouth structure; he named and described over 10,000 insects

Fossey Dian (1938–1985) US zoologist who did pioneer studies on mountain gorillas

Frisch Karl von (1886–1982) Austrian zoologist who co-founded ethology with Niko Tinbergen and Konrad Lorenz

Geoffroy Saint-Hilaire Etienne (1772–1844) French zoologist who developed a classification system for the study of apes

Goodall Jane (1934–) English primatologist and conservationist who is a world authority on wild chimpanzees

Gosse Philip Henry (1810–1888) English naturalist who built the first aquarium ever used to house marine animals long-term and wrote influential works on marine zoology

Gray James (1891–1975) British zoologist who helped establish cytology (cell structure) as a distinct branch of zoology

Griffin Donald Redfield (1915–) US zoologist who discovered that bats use echolocation to navigate when flying

Hertwig Oscar Wilhelm August (1849–1922) German zoologist who discovered that fertilization involves the fusion of the nuclei of an egg and one sperm

Hyman Libbie Henrietta (1888–1969) US zoologist whose six-volume *The Invertebrates* provided an encyclopedic account of most invertebrate phyla

Kinsey Alfred Charles (1894–1956) US zoologist and pioneering sexologist who founded the Institute of Sex Research in 1942

Lankester Edwin Ray (1847–1929) English zoologist who demonstrated clear morphological distinctions between the different orders of invertebrates

Leuckart Karl Georg Friedrich Rudolf (1822–1898) German zoologist who developed the taxonomic divisions of jellyfish; he was a pioneer of parasitology

Lorenz Konrad Zacharias (1903–1989) Austrian zoologist who co-founded the study of ethology with Karl von Frisch and Niko Tinbergen

Manton Sidnie Milana (married name Harding) (1902–1979) English embryologist who specialized in the arthropods

Mayr Ernst Walter (1904–) German-born US zoologist who was influential in the development of modern evolutionary theories

Mechnikov Ilia Ilich (1845–1916) Russian-born French zoologist who discovered the function of white blood cells and phagocytes

Morgan Ann Haven (1882–1966) US zoologist who promoted the study of ecology and conservation

Morris Desmond John (1928–) British zoologist who popularized research on animal and human behaviour

Pennycuick Colin James (1933–) British zoologist who pioneered research on bird migration

Schaudinn Fritz Richard (1871–1906) German zoologist who determined the life cycle of the coccidiae (scale insects)

Schultze Max Johann Sigismund (1825–1874) German zoologist who adopted the term protoplasm in reference to the contents of cells

Sutton-Pringle John William (1912–) British zoologist who established much of our knowledge of the anatomical mechanisms involved in insect flight

Swammerdam Jan (1637–1680) Dutch naturalist who is considered a founder of both comparative anatomy and entomology

Tinbergen Niko(laas) (1907–1988) Dutch-born British zoologist who co-founded the study of ethology with Konrad Lorenz and Karl von Frisch

Wilson Edmund Beecher (1856–1939) US zoologist who was one of the founders of modern genetics

Wilson E(dward) O(sborne) (1929–) US zoologist who helped develop the fields of biogeography and sociobiology; he is a world authority on ants

Wynne-Edwards Vero Copner (1906–1997) English zoologist who argued that animal behaviour is often altruistic, and that animals will behave for the good of the group, even if this entails individual sacrifice

Young J(ohn) Z(achary) (1907–1997) British zoologist who discovered the giant nerve fibres in squid

Zuckerman Solly (1904–1993) South African-born British zoologist who did pioneer research on primates

Explorers and Pioneers

Noteworthy Explorers and Pioneers

Amundsen Roald Engelbregt Gravning (1872–1928) Norwegian explorer who was the first person to navigate the Northwest Passage and reach the South Pole

Armstrong Neil Alden (1930–) US astronaut who was the first person to walk on the moon during the *Apollo 11* mission in July 1969

Baffin William (c. 1584–1622) British navigator who reached Baffin Bay, northeast Canada, in 1616, which was the northernmost point explored by Europeans at that time

Balboa Vasco Núñez de (1475–1519) Spanish explorer and first European to see the Pacific Ocean (1513)

Bering Vitus Jonassen (1681–1741) Danish explorer who was the first European to sight Alaska

Burke Wills Robert O'Hara (1820–1861) and William (John) (1834–1861), the first white men to make the south-north crossing of Australia, dying from starvation on the return journey

Burton Richard Francis (1821–1890) British explorer and translator who made two attempts to find the source of the Nile

Byrd Richard Evelyn (1888–1957) US aviator who was the first person to fly over the North Pole (1926)

Caboto Giovanni (or Cabot, John) (1425–c. 1500) Italian navigator who was the first European to reach the North American mainland

Cartier Jacques (1491–1557) French navigator who was the first European to sail up the St Lawrence River in Canada (1534)

Champlain Samuel de (1567–1635) French explorer of Canada who founded Quebec in 1608

Clark William (1770–1838) US military officer who commanded the expedition that explored the northwest USA (1804–06)

Columbus Christopher (Spanish Cristóbal Colón) (1451–1506) Italian navigator and explorer who made four voyages to the New World, landing in the Bahamas and Cuba in 1492

Cook James (1728–1779) British naval explorer who surveyed the St Lawrence River in 1759 and charted the Siberian coast (1776–79), but is most famous for his voyages in the Pacific and Southern Oceans

Cousteau Jacques-Yves (1910–1997) French naval officer and underwater explorer who is best known for developing underwater filming techniques

Díaz Bartolomeu (c. 1450–1500) Portuguese explorer who was the first European to reach the Cape of Good Hope

Ericsson or **Ericksson** Leif (c. 970–1020) Norse explorer who sailed to Baffin Island and Newfoundland (Vinland)

Eric the Red (c. 950–1010) Norwegian explorer who founded the Norse colonies on Greenland

Fiennes Ranulph (1944–) British explorer who with Michael Stroud undertook the first unassisted crossing of the Antarctic continent

Gagarin Yuri Alexeyevich (1934–1968) Soviet cosmonaut who became the first man in space (1961)

Gama Vasco da (c. 1469–1525) Portuguese navigator who navigated the route to India around the Cape of Good Hope

Glenn John Herschel Jr (1921–) US astronaut who was the first American to orbit the Earth in 1962

Henry the Navigator (1394–1460) Prince of Portugal who set up a school for navigators in 1419

Hillary Edmund Percival (1919–) New Zealand mountaineer who, with Sherpa mountaineer Tenzing Norgay, was the first person to climb Mount Everest (1952)

Hudson Henry (c. 1565–1611) English explorer, seeker of the Northwest Passage and the first European to reach the Hudson River

Lewis Meriwether (1774–1809) US explorer of the northwest USA (1804–06)

Lindbergh Charles A(ugustus) (1902–1974) US aviator and plane designer who flew the first solo non-stop flight across the Atlantic Ocean in 1927

Livingstone David (1813–1873) Scottish missionary who explored East and Central Africa (1849–71), dying in his attempt to find the source of the Nile

Magellan Ferdinand (c. 1480–1521) Portuguese navigator, first to circumnavigate the globe, which he did via the South American strait bearing his name

Montgolfier Joseph Michel (1740–1810) and Jacques Etienne (1745–1799) French brothers who pioneered balloon flight

Nansen Fridtjof (1861–1930) Norwegian explorer and scientist who sailed to the Arctic in 1893 and reached the highest latitude for that time

Park Mungo (1771–1806) Scottish explorer who traced the course of the Niger river (1795–97)

Peary Robert Edwin (1856–1920) US Navy commander and the first person to reach the North Pole (1909)

Pizarro Francisco (c. 1475–1541) Spanish conquistador who explored the northwest coast of South America

Polo Marco (1254–1324) Venetian merchant, traveller, and writer who opened up the trade route from Venice to China

Ponce Leon Juan de (c. 1460–1521) Spanish soldier and explorer who was the first European to reach Florida

Post Wiley (1900–1935) US aviator who was the first person to fly solo around the world

Raleigh Walter (1552–1618) English explorer who organized expeditions to colonize North America (1584–87)

Rhodes Cecil John (1853–1902) British pioneer who became an influential statesman in southern Africa

Ross James Clark (1800–1862) British explorer who located the magnetic North Pole in 1831

Scott Robert Falcon (known as Scott of the Antarctic) (1868–1912) British explorer who commanded two Antarctic expeditions (1901–04 and 1910–12)

Shackleton Ernest Henry (1874–1922) Irish explorer who led the expedition that located the magnetic South Pole (1907–09)

Shepard Alan Bartlett (1923–) US astronaut who in 1961 was the first American in space

Smith John (1580–1631) British colonist who helped colonize Virginia and explore the northeast USA

Stanley Henry Morton (adopted name of John Rowlands) (1841–1904) Welsh-born US journalist who explored Africa and established the Congo Free State (1879–84)

Tasman Abel Janszoon (1603–1659) Dutch explorer and navigator who was the first European to see Tasmania in 1642

Tereshkova Valentina Vladimirovna (1937–) Soviet cosmonaut who in 1963 became the first woman in space

Wright Orville (1871–1948) and Wilbur (1867–1912) US inventors and brothers who were the first to make a successful powered flight

Yeager Chuck (Charles Elwood) (1923–) US test pilot who became the first man to 'break the sound barrier' in 1947

Leaders

Noteworthy Civil Rights Leaders

Abernathy Ralph David (1926–1990) US civil rights activist who helped organize the Southern Christian Leadership Conference (SCLC)

Azbug Bella Savitsky (1920–) US Congresswoman (1970–76) who promoted legislation for women's rights and civil rights

Baez Joan (1941–) US folk singer and pacifist activist who founded the Institute for the Study of Non-Violence in 1965

Baker Ella Josephine (1903–1986) US civil rights activist for over 40 years with several national and international civil rights organizations

Balch Emily Greene (1867–1961) US peace activist who was a leader in the Women's International League for Peace and Freedom

Baldwin James Arthur (1924–1987) US writer and civil rights activist whose novels depict the effects of racism in the USA

Barry Marion Jr (1936–) US mayor of Washington, DC (1978–90, 1995–) and co-founder of the Student Nonviolent Coordinating Committee (SNCC) in 1967

Bates Daisy Lee Gatson (1920–) US civil rights activist who helped integrate public schools in Little Rock, Arkansas in 1957

Bethune Mary McLeod (1875–1955) US educator who organized schools for black children and campaigned for community services for blacks

Biko Steve (Stephen) (1946–1977) South African civil rights leader who became a symbol of the anti-apartheid movement after dying in police custody

Chavis Benjamin Franklin Jr (1948–) US civil rights activist who was executive director of the National Association for the Advancement of Colored People (NAACP) (1993–95)

Douglass Frederick (born Frederick Augustus Washington Bailey) (1817–1895) US abolitionist and diplomat who campaigned for full civil rights for blacks and women

Du Bois W(illiam) E(dward) B(urghardt) (1868–1963) US social scientist whose book *The Souls of Black Folk* offered a new image of racial pride for African-Americans

Dworkin Andrea (1946–) US feminist writer who has been active in promoting legislation to outlaw pornography

Evers Medgar Wiley (1925–1963) US civil rights activist whose assassination in 1963 encouraged passage of the US Civil Rights bill

Farmer James (1920–) US civil rights activist who co-founded the Congress of Racial Equality (CORE) in 1942

Gandhi Mahatma 'Great Soul' (original name Mohandas Karamchand Gandhi) (1869–1948) Indian nationalist leader who led the struggle for Indian independence from the UK by advocating nonviolent noncooperation

Garvey Marcus (Mozian Manasseth) (1887–1940) Jamaican-born nationalist who organized the first black mass movement in the USA

Hamer Fannie Lou (1917–1977) US civil rights activist who founded the Freedom Farms Corporation in 1969 to provide social services for the poor

Hooks Benjamin Lawson (1925–) US civil rights leader who was executive director of the National Association for the Advancement of Colored People (NAACP) (1977–93)

Huddleston (Ernest Urban) Trevor (1913–) British Anglican missionary and campaigner for civil rights in South Africa who became the chairman of the Anti-Apartheid Movement in 1983

Innis Roy (1934–) Virgin Island-born US civil rights activist who was a leader in the Congress of Racial Equality from 1968

Jackson Jesse Louis (1941–) US cleric and campaigner for minority rights who ran for the US presidency in 1984 and 1988

Johnson James Weldon (1871–1938) US novelist, poet, and diplomat who was secretary of the National Association for the Advancement of Colored People (NAACP) (1916–30)

Jordan Vernon Eulion Jr (1935–) US civil rights leader and president of the National Urban League (1972–81)

King Coretta Scott (1927–) US civil rights activist who established the Martin Luther King Jr, Memorial in Atlanta, Georgia in 1980, and campaigned successfully for a national holiday on the day of her husband's assassination

King Martin Luther Jr (1929–1968) US minister who was awarded the Nobel Peace Prize in 1964 for his civil rights leadership

Kuhn Margaret (1905–1995) US social justice activist who founded the Gray Panthers in 1971 to support the rights of the elderly

Ling Chai (1966–) Chinese human rights activist who was a leader in the Tiananmen Square protest in 1989

Makeba Miriam (1932–) South African singer and international spokesperson for the anti-apartheid movement

Malcolm X (adopted name of Malcolm Little, Muslim name el-Hajj Malik el-Shabazz) (1925–1965) US black nationalist who espoused Muslim doctrines and advocated self-help and self-defence for blacks

Mandela Nelson (Rolihlahla) (1918–) South African politician, lawyer, and president from 1994 who became a symbol of unity for the worldwide anti-apartheid movement during his imprisonment (1964–90)

Mandela (Nomzamo) Winnie (Winifred) (Xhosa surname Madikizela) (1934–) South African anti-apartheid spokesperson for the African National Congress (ANC) during Nelson Mandela's imprisonment (1964–90)

Menchu Rigoberta Tum (1959–) Guatemalan-Indian rights activist who, in 1992, founded the Vincente Menchu Foundation to support human rights in Guatemala

Pankhurst Christabel Harriette (1880–1958) British campaigner for women's suffrage who with her mother Emmeline Pankhurst founded the Women's Social and Political Union

Pankhurst Emmeline (1857–1928) British campaigner for women's suffrage who founded the Women's Franchise League and the Women's Social and Political Union

Parks Rosa Lee McCauley (1913–) US civil rights activist who initiated the Montgomery bus boycott (1955–56) which started the US civil rights movement

Powell Adam Clayton Jr (1908–1972) US politician who was the first black US congressman from the eastern USA (1945–70)

Randolph Asa Philip (1889–1979) US businessman who founded the Brotherhood of Sleeping Car Porters in 1925 to aid black workers

Rankin Jeannette (1880–1973) US civil rights activist who was a leader in the US women's suffrage movement

Romero (y Galdames) Oscar (Anulfo) (1917–1980) El Salvadorean Roman Catholic archbishop who was assassinated in 1980 for his human rights activities

Roosevelt (Anna) Eleanor (1884–1962) US representative to the UN and chair of the UN Commission of Human Rights (1947–51)

Rustin Baynard (1910–1987) US civil rights leader who was a founder of the Southern Christian Leadership Conference

Sakharov Andrei Dimitriyevich (1921–1989) Russian physicist who was awarded the Nobel Peace Prize in 1975 for his human rights work

Sisulu Walter Max Ulyate (1912–) South African civil rights activist and a leading member of the African National Congress who was imprisoned with Nelson Mandela

(continued)

Noteworthy Civil Rights Leaders (*continued*)

Stewart Potter (1915–1985) US jurist who, as associate justice of the US Supreme Court (1958–81), supported civil rights for minorities

Still William (1821–1902) US abolitionist whose book *The Underground Railroad* is a record of his work with this organization

Sullivan Leon Howard (1922–) US cleric who founded the Opportunities Industrialization Center in 1964 to train inner-city youths

Tambo Oliver (1917–1993) South African politician and civil rights leader who was president of the African National Congress (1977–91)

Touré Kwame (formerly Carmichael, Stokely) (1941–) Trinidad-born US civil rights activist who was a leader in the Black Panthers (1967–69) and the Pan-African movement in Guinea in 1969

Trotter Monroe (1872–1934) US civil rights activist who founded the National Equal Rights League in 1908

Tubman Harriet Ross (1820–1913) US abolitionist who helped slaves escape from the South through the 'underground railroad'

Tutu Desmond Mpilo (1931–) South African prelate and civil rights leader who won the Nobel Peace Prize in 1984

Villard Oswald Garrison (1872–1949) US editor and civil rights leader who helped found the National Association for the Advancement of Colored People (NAACP)

Walker Alice Malsenior (1944–) US novelist whose book *The Color Purple* raised awareness of the oppression of black women by black men

Wilkins Roy (1901–1981) US civil rights leader who dedicated his working life to the National Association for the Advancement of Colored People (NAACP)

Wu Harry (1937–) Chinese-born US human rights activist who founded the Laogai Research Foundation in 1985 to report human rights abuses in China

Yasui Minoru (1916–1986) US civil rights lawyer who helped Japanese Americans receive reparations from the US government for World War II abuses

Young Andrew Jackson Jr (1932–) US clergyman, politician, and civil rights leader who served as executive director of the Southern Christian Leadership Conference (1964–70) and became US ambassador to the United Nations (1977–79)

Young Whitney Moore Jr (1921–1971) US civil rights activist who served as national director of the National Urban League

Noteworthy Business and Industrial Leaders

Al-Fayed Mohamed (1933–) Egyptian-born businessman who has been chairman of Harrods since 1985 and owner of the Ritz Hotel, Paris, since 1979

Alliance David (1932–) British industrialist who has been chairman of Coats Viyella since 1989

Arden Elizabeth (born Florence Nightingale Graham) (1884–1966) Canadian-born US beauty expert who moved to New York in 1908

Armour Philip Danforth (1832–1901) US merchant and philanthropist who built Armour & Co into the world's largest meatpacker

Astor John Jacob (1763–1848) German-born US fur trader, banker, and real estate magnate who was the richest man in the USA at his death

Bell Alexander Graham (1847–1922) Scottish-born US inventor who made the first telephonic transmission in 1876 and founded the Bell Telephone Company (modern AT&T) in 1877

Benz Karl Friedrich (1844–1929) German engineer and automotive pioneer

Birdseye Clarence (1886–1956) US businessman and inventor who developed improved methods of preserving foods, especially quick-frozen and dehydrated foods

Black Conrad Moffat (1944–) Canadian financier and publisher of more than 250 newspapers

Boeing William Edward (1881–1956) US pioneer of commercial and military aircraft

Bond Alan (1938–) English-born Australian entrepreneur and sponsor of the 1983 America's Cup winner

Brandenberger Jacques (1874–1954) French chemist who invented and manufactured cellophane

Branson Richard (1950–) English entrepreneur who founded the Virgin record company and whose empire now includes the Virgin Atlantic airline

Broackes Nigel (1934–) British businessman who has served as chairman of the construction giant Trafalgar House (1969–92) and has been its honorary president since 1992

Brown Cedric Harold (1935–) British businessman who has worked as an engineer and director for British Gas since 1953; he has been chief executive since 1992

Burnham James (1905–1987) US philosopher and author of *The Managerial Revolution*

Busch Adolphus (1839–1913) German-born US industrialist, beer magnate, and manufacturer of diesel engines

Candler Asa (1851–1929) US founder of the Coca-Cola Co

Carnegie Andrew (1835–1919) Scottish-born US industrialist and philanthropist who made Pittsburgh the steel capital of the world

Colt Samuel (1814–1862) US manufacturer of mass-produced revolvers

Conran Terence Orby (1931–) English designer/retailer of furnishings, fashion, and household goods whose Storehouse group includes Habitat and Conran Design in the UK and USA

Cook Thomas (1808–1892) British pioneer of the travel agency and creator of the traveller's cheque

Corness Colin (Ross) (1931–) British executive who served as a director of the Bank of England (1987–95) and has been chairman of Glaxo since 1995

Daimler Gottlieb Wilhelm (1834–1900) German-born mechanic and engineer whose company developed early internal combustion engines and the Mercedes automobile

Disney Walt(er) Elias (1901–1966) US animation pioneer and creator of Mickey Mouse and the Disney theme parks

Drucker Peter Ferdinand (1909–) Austrian-born US management expert

Dunlop John Boyd (1840–1921) Scottish inventor who is generally credited with the invention of the pneumatic tyre in 1887, and who founded the Dunlop Rubber Company

DuPont Pierre Samuel (1870–1954) US chemist and industrialist who expanded DuPont's product lines and is credited with its modern success

Eastman George (1854–1932) US inventor of dry photographic film and cameras sold under the Kodak brand

Edison Thomas Alva (1847–1931) US inventor of the phonograph record and electric light, and successful developer of the motion picture

Firestone Harvey Samuel (1868–1938) US founder in Ohio of Firestone Tire and Rubber Co in 1900

Noteworthy Business and Industrial Leaders (*continued*)

Forbes Malcom (1919–1990) US publisher and business executive who spectacularly revived the fortunes of the family-owned business magazine, *Forbes*, when he took it over in 1957

Ford Henry (1863–1947) US industrialist and automotive pioneer who perfected the moving assembly line

Fraze Ermal Cleon (1913–1989) US inventor of the ring-pull on cans

Gates Bill (William) Henry III (1955–) US business executive and chairman and chief executive of the Microsoft Corporation, which he co-founded with Paul Allen in 1975

Getty Jean Paul (1892–1976) US oil billionaire and founder of Getty Museum in Malibu, California

Giannini Amadeo Peter (1870–1949) US founder of the Bank of America

Girolami Paul (1926–) British business executive who has been chief executive (1980–86) and chairman (1985–94) of Glaxo

Graham Katherine Meyer (1917–) US publisher of the *Washington Post*

Hammer Armand (1899–1990) US entrepreneur and pioneer in trading with the former Soviet Union

Hanson James Edward (1922–) British industrialist who has been chairman of Hanson plc since 1965

Hartnett Laurence John (1898–1986) British-born engineer who created the first mass-produced all-Australian car, the Holden

Harvey-Jones John (1924–) British business executive who was chairman of Imperial Chemical Industries (ICI), and who is well known for his BBC television series *Troubleshooter*

Hefner Hugh Marston (1926–) US publisher of *Playboy* magazine

Heinz Henry John (1844–1919) US creator of Pittsburgh's H J Heinz Co who was an innovator of prepared foods and condiments

Henderson Denys (Hartley) (1932–) British business executive who has worked for ICI since 1957, serving as chairman (1987–95); he became chairman of the Rank Organization in 1995

Herreshoff Nathanael G (1848–1938) pre-eminent US yacht designer, naval architect, and founder of the Herreshoff Manufacturing Co

Hershey Milton (1857–1945) US philanthropist whose fortune was based first on caramels and then on the Hershey Bar

Hilton Conrad Nicholson (1887–1979) US founder of the luxury hotel chain

Holmes á Court (Michael) Robert (Hamilton) (1937–1990) Australian entrepreneur who was once the country's richest individual

Hoover William Henry (1849–1932) US industrialist who developed the vacuum cleaner and founded the Hoover Co

Hughes Howard Robard (1905–1976) US tycoon, aircraft-builder, filmmaker, and renowned recluse

Jobs Steven (1955–) US computer inventor and entrepreneur who co-founded Apple Computer Inc with Stephen Wozniak in 1976

Kalms Stanley (1931–) British businessman who founded the Dixons Group, of which he has been chairman since 1972

King John Leonard (1917–) British industrialist who has been chairman of British Airways (1981–93) and president from 1993

Kroc Raymond (1902–1984) US founder of McDonald's fast food chain

Krupp Alfred (1812–1887) German tycoon who reorganized the steelmaking company Krupp, expanded production, and founded an industrial empire

Land Edwin Herbert (1909–1991) US physicist and inventor who created instant photography

Leitz Ernst II (1871–1956) German industrialist who introduced the world's first 35 mm camera, the Leica, designed by Oskar Barnack

MacLaurin Ian (Charter) (1937–) British businessman who has transformed the performance of the giant retailer Tesco, of which he has been chairman since 1985

Marconi Guglielmo Marchese (1874–1937) Italian inventor and celebrity businessman who sent the first transatlantic wireless message and founded the Marconi Wireless Telegraph Company

Maxwell Robert Ian (originally Jan Ludwig Hoch) (1923–1991) Czech-born British publisher and newspaper magnate who founded the scientific publishing house Pergamon Press in 1951 and became chairman of Mirror Group Newspapers in 1984

Mellon Andrew W(illiam) (1855–1937) Pittsburgh industrialist and banker who loaned Carnegie money, served as secretary of the treasury, and bequeathed his enormous art collection to the National Gallery, Washington, USA

Morgan J(ohn) P(ierpont) Jr (1867–1943) multimillionaire US investment banker, financier, and 'wizard of Wall Street' who was also a philanthropist

Mort Thomas Sutcliffe (1816–1878) British-born Australian merchant who pioneered refrigeration of meat for export

Murdoch (Keith) Rupert (1931–) Australian-born US media mogul

Nobel Alfred Bernhard (1833–1896) Swedish-born chemist and industrialist who earned a fortune from dynamite and later founded the Nobel prize trust

Nuffield William Richard Morris (1877–1963) British manufacturer and philanthropist who created Morris Motors

Ochs Adolph (1858–1935) US publishing giant who borrowed money from J P Morgan to purchase the *New York Times*

Onassis Aristotle Socrates (1906–1975) Turkish-born Greek shipowner who constructed early supertankers

Peabody George (1795–1869) US entrepreneur, investment banker, and philanthropist

Peter Laurence J (1910–1990) Canadian writer, teacher, and author (with Raymond Hull) of *The Peter Principle*

Pinkham Lydia Estes (1819–1883) US creator of patent medicine for women who built a seaside estate in Marblehead, Massachusetts

Porter Michael (1947–) US management theorist

Reuter (Paul) Julius de, Baron Reuter (adopted name of Israel Beer Josaphat) (1816–1899) German founder of the telegraphic news agency, Reuters

Rockefeller John D(avison) (1839–1937) US founder of Standard Oil and the philanthropic Rockefeller Foundation

Roddick Anita Lucia (1943–) British entrepreneur who created The Body Shop

Rothschild Mayer Amschel (1744–1812) German who began as a money lender in Frankfurt-am-Main and whose children established business houses throughout Europe

Rubinstein Helena (1870–1965) Polish-born US cosmetics tycoon

Sainsbury John Davan (1927–) chairman of the retailing giant set up by the family (1969–92)

Sainsbury David John (1940–) chairman and chief executive of Sainsbury's since 1992

Sarnoff David (1891–1971) Russian-born US visionary of radio and TV who overcame anti-semitism to head RCA and found NBC

Saunders Clarence (1881–1953) US retailer who opened the first self-service supermarket, Piggly-Wiggly, in Memphis in 1919

Scholey Robert (1921–) British industrialist who served as an executive with British Steel (1968–1992)

Selfridge Harry Gordon (1858–1947) US entrepreneur who founded Britain's first large department store

Sheehy Patrick (1930–) British industrialist who has served as chairman of BAT Industries (1982–95)

Sheppard Allen John George (1932–) British business executive and chairman of leisure company Grand Metropolitan (1987–96)

Sholes Christopher Latham (1819–1890) US printer who with Carlos Glidden and Samuel Soule invented the typewriter and sold the patents to Remington & Sons

(continued)

Noteworthy Business and Industrial Leaders (*continued*)

Sloan Alfred Pritchard Jr (1875–1966) US executive who became president of General Motors in 1923 and made it the world's biggest car company

Stephen George, Baron Mount Stephen (1829–1921) Scottish-born Canadian financier who was instrumental in the construction of the Canadian Pacific Railway

Sterling Jeffrey Maurice (1934–) British industrialist who has been chairman of P&O since 1983

Sundback Gideon (1880–1954) Swedish-born US inventor who perfected and manufactured the slide fastener known as the zip

Thyssen Fritz (1873–1951) German iron and steel industrialist

Toyoda Sakichi (1894–1952) Japanese automobile manufacturer who founded the Toyota Motor Company in 1937

Trump Donald John (1946–) US real estate developer and financier

Turner (Jonathan) Adair (1955–) British business executive who has been director general of the Confederation of British Industry since 1995

Vallance Iain David (1943–) British businessman who has been chairman of British Telecommunications since 1987 and vice-chairman of the Royal Bank of Scotland since 1994

Vanderbilt Cornelius (1794–1877) US steamship magnate, railroad financier, and founder of Vanderbilt University

Wenner-Gren Axel Leonard (1881–1961) Swedish industrialist who founded the Electrolux Company in 1921

Westinghouse George (1846–1914) US inventor, manufacturer, developer of air brakes for railroad cars, and founder of the Westinghouse Electric Co

Whitney Eli (1765–1825) US inventor of the cotton gin that revolutionized southern agriculture and commerce

Wolfson Isaac (1897–1991) British store magnate and philanthropist who established the Wolfson Foundation and Colleges

Woolworth Frank Winfield (1852–1919) US entrepreneur who created the 'five and dime' store

Zeiss Carl (1816–1888) German optician and producer of cameras, microscopes, and binoculars

Noteworthy Military and Naval Commanders

Abd el-Krim Mahommed ibn (1882–1963) Moroccan guerrilla leader who fought against the French and the Spanish

Akbar (1542–1605) Mogul emperor of India

Alexander Harold Rupert Leofric, 1st Viscount Alexander (1891–1969) British field marshal who commanded British forces in Middle East and Italy during World War II

Alexander the Great (356–323 BC) king of Macedonia; military genius who defeated the Persian Empire

Allen Ethan (1739–1789) US soldier and politician in the American Revolution

Allenby Edmund Henry Hynman, 1st Viscount Allenby (1861–1936) British field marshal in World War I who fought a victorious Middle East campaign

Alvarez de Toledo Fernando, Duke of Alva (1507–1582) Spanish general who fought campaigns in Hungary, Germany, North Africa, Italy, and the Netherlands

Anders Władysław (1892–1970) Polish general who commanded the 2nd Polish Corps in the Italian campaign during World War II

Arnold Benedict (1741–1801) US turncoat soldier in the American Revolution

Arnold Henry ('Hap') (1861–1950) US aviator and general in World War II; head of the Army Air Corps

Attila the Hun (c. 406–453) king of the Huns; defeated the Romans at Chalons in AD 451, invaded Italy in AD 452

Auchinleck Sir Claude (1884–1891) British field marshal in World War II who commanded British forces in the Middle East

Babur (1483–1530) founder Mogul emperor who conquered northern India

Badoglio Pietro (1871–1956) Italian general during World War II who deposed Mussolini in July 1943

Belisarius (c. 505–565) Byzantine general; fought campaigns against the Vandals, Ostrogoths, Persians, and Kotrigur Huns

Billiere Peter de la (1935–) British general who commanded British forces during the Gulf War (1990–91)

Blücher Gebhard Leberecht von (1742–1819) Prussian general who fought against Napoleon at Waterloo

Bolivar Simon (1783–1830) Venezuelan soldier and political leader who eventually liberated Colombia in 1819

Bouillon Godfrey de (c. 1060–1100) leader of the first Crusade

Bradley Omar Nelson (1893–1981) US army general in World War II who fought in North Africa and commanded the 12th Army Group in Europe

Brian Boru (941–1014) high king of Ireland

Brusilov Aleksei Alekseevich (1853–1926) Russian general in World War I

Bülow Karl von (1846–1921) German general in World War I

Burgoyne John (1722–1792) British general in the American Revolution who was defeated at Saratoga in 1777

Cadorna Count Luigi (1850–1928) Italian general in World War I

Caesar Caius Julius (c. 100–44 BC) Roman emperor who conquered Gaul and defeated Pompey at Pharsalus in 48 BC

Charlemagne (Charles the Great) (742–814) king of the Franks and founder of the Holy Roman Empire

Charles XII (1682–1718) king of Sweden who led his country to defeat in the Great Northern War 1700–21

Chiang Kai-shek (1887–1975) nationalist Chinese general and leader who took part in the revolution of 1911

Chi'in Shih-huang ti (259–210 BC) Chinese emperor who united the seven rival kingdoms of China by military conquest (230–221 BC)

Churchill John, 1st Duke of Marlborough (1650–1722) English general in the War of Spanish Succession; victor at the battle of Blenheim in 1704

Chu Teh (1886–1976) commander of Chinese Communist forces during the anti-Japanese War (1937–45), and Chinese Civil War (1945–49)

Clark Mark Wayne (1896–1984) US general who served in Italy during World War II and fought in the Korean War

Clausewitz Karl Maria von (1780–1831) Prussian general and military theorist

Clive Robert, Baron (1725–1774) British general who was victor at Plassey in 1757

Noteworthy Military and Naval Commanders (*continued*)

Cordoba Gonzales de (1453–1515) Spanish general who defeated the French to secure Naples for Spain in 1503

Cornwallis Charles, 1st Marquess (1738–1805) British general in the American Revolution who was defeated at Yorktown in 1781

Cortés Hernan (1485–1547) Spanish general who conquered the Aztecs in 1521

Cromwell Oliver (1599–1658) English soldier and Lord Protector; he set up the New Model Army in 1645

Cumberland William Augustus, Duke of (1721–1765) British soldier and victor at Culloden in 1746

Cunningham Andrew Browne, 1st Viscount (1883–1963) British admiral in World War II

Custer George Armstrong (1839–1876) US army general who was killed at Little Big Horn

Cyrus the Great (559–530 BC) great king of Persia who captured Babylon in 539 BC

Darius (I) the Great (548–486 BC) king of Persia

Dayan Moshe (1915–1981) Israeli general and politician who was largely responsible for his country's victory in the 1967 Six Day War

Dearborn Henry (1751–1829) US army general in the American Revolution

Dönitz Karl (1891–1980) German admiral in World War II who developed the U-Boat 'Wolf Pack' strategy

Doolittle James ('Jimmy') Harold (1896–1993) US Air Force Commander in World War II

Drake Sir Francis (1540–1596) English sailor and victor against the Spanish Armada in 1588

Dudley Robert, Earl of Leicester (c. 1532–1588) English soldier and favourite of Queen Elizabeth I

Edward III (1312–1377) king of England and victor at Crécy, France, in 1346

Edward Plantagenet 'the Black Prince' (1330–1376) Prince of Wales and victor at Tours in 1356

Eisenhower Dwight David ('Ike') (1890–1969) US general who became Supreme Allied Commander in World War II and president of the USA (1952–60)

El Cid Rodrigo Diaz de Vivar (c. 1043–1099) Spanish general who defeated the Moors at Valencia in 1094

Eugen Prince of Savoy-Carignon (1663–1736) French-born soldier and diplomat in the War of Spanish Succession

Fabius Maximus Verrucosus Quintus ('Cunctator', The Delayer) (d. 203 BC) Roman general who fought against Hannibal

Falkenhayn Erich von (1861–1922) German general during World War I who ordered the bloody assault on Verdun in 1916

Farnese Alessandro, Duke of Parma (1545–1592) Spanish general in the Netherlands

Farragut David Glasgow (1801–1870) US (Union) admiral in the American Civil War who won victory at Mobile Bay in 1864

Foch Ferdinand (1851–1929) French general in World War I, he became Supreme Allied Commander in 1918

Frederick I ('Barbarossa') (c. 1123–1190) emperor of the Holy Roman Empire

Frederick (II) the Great (1713–1786) Prussian king who fought the Seven Years' War

French John Denton Pinkstone, 1st Earl (1852–1925) British field marshal in World War I who commanded the British Expeditionary Force (1914–15)

Gallieni Joseph-Simon (1849–1916) Marshal of France who dispatched troops in Paris taxis to the Battle of the Marne

Gamelin Maurice (1872–1958) French military commander, and Chief of Staff (1935–40)

Garibaldi Giuseppe (1807–1882) Italian general and patriot who fought to unify Italy

Gaulle Charles André Joseph Marie de (1890–1970) commander of Free French Forces during World War II, who later became President of France

Genghis Khan (Temujin) (1162–1227) fearsome soldier and founder of the Mongol Empire

Geronimo (c. 1829–1909) Native American (Apache) warband leader

Ghormley Robert Lee (1883–1953) US admiral in World War II

Giap Vo Nguyen (1910–   ) Vietnamese Communist military leader who fought against the French and the Americans

Glyn Dwr Owain (c. 1354–c. 1416) Welsh patriot ('Prince of Wales') and soldier

Gordon Charles George ('Gordon of Khartoum') (1833–1885) British general killed at Khartoum in the Sudan in 1885

Gort John (1886–1946) British field marshal in World War II who commanded the British Expeditionary Force (1939–40)

Grant Ulysses Simpson (born Hiram Ulysses Grant) (1822–1885) US (Union) general in the American Civil War who later became president of the USA

Greene Nathanael (1742–1786) US general in the American Revolution

Guderian Heinz (1888–1956) German general during World War II who developed use of armoured forces

Guesclin Bertrand de (c. 1320–1380) French general in the Hundred Years' War

Guevara Ernesto ('Che') (1928–1967) Argentinian-born revolutionary who fought in Cuba (1956–59) and was killed in Bolivia

Gustavus II Adolphus (1594–1632) king of Sweden who fought in the Thirty Years' War

Haig Douglas, 1st Earl (1861–1928) British field marshal, Commander in Chief of the British Expeditionary Force in World War I

Halsey William Frederick (1882–1959) US admiral in World War II who fought in the South Pacific

Hannibal (247–182 BC) Carthaginian soldier and victor at Cannae in 216 BC

Harris Arthur ('Bomber Harris') (1892–1984) British Air Commander during World War II who advocated strategic bombing of Germany

Henry V (1387–1422) king of England and victor at Agincourt, France, in 1415

Hildeyoshi Toyotomi (1536–1598) Japanese general

Hindenburg Paul Ludwig von Beneckendorf von (1847–1934) German general in World War I, he was elected President of the Weimar Republic in 1925

Hitler Adolf (1889–1945) German military and political leader during World War II

Hodges Courtney Hicks (1887–1966) US general who commanded the First Army in Europe during World War II

Homma Masaharu (1888–1946) Japanese general during World War II who invaded the Philippines

Horrocks Sir Brian (1895–1984) British general and corps commander in Africa and Europe during World War II

Hoth Hermann (1885–1971) German general who fought in Russia (1941–43) during World War II

Houston Sam(uel) (1793–1863) US general in the Mexican War of 1836 that gained independence for Texas

Howe Richard, 1st Earl (1726–1799) British admiral in the American Revolution

Jackson Thomas Jonathan ('Stonewall') (1824–1863) US Confederate general in the American Civil War

(continued)

Noteworthy Military and Naval Commanders (*continued*)

Jeanne d'Arc ('La Pucelle') (1412–1431) French peasant-girl patriot in the Hundred Years' War

Jellicoe John Rushworth, 1st Earl (1859–1935) British admiral in World War I who commanded British naval forces at the Battle of Jutland in 1916

Jervis John, 1st Earl of St Vincent (1735–1823) British admiral during the Napoleonic Wars

Joffre Joseph Jacques Cesaire (1852–1931) Marshal of France, and Commander in Chief of French Forces (1914–16)

Jones John Paul (1747–1792) US sailor in the American Revolution

Kemal Mustafa (known as Atatürk, 'Father of Turks') (1881–1938) Turkish general and statesman who fought in World War I and against the Greeks

Kesselring Albert (1885–1960) German field marshal, commander of German forces in Africa and Italy during World War II

King Ernest Joseph (1878–1956) US admiral and Commander in Chief and Chief of Naval Operations during World War II

Kinkaid Thomas Cassin (1888–1972) US admiral who fought at Coral Sea, Midway, Guadalcanal, Leyte, and Luzon during World War II

Kitchener Horatio Herbert, 1st Earl (1850–1916) British field marshal who fought in the Sudan and the Boer War; he raised a volunteer army in World War I

Kleist Paul Ewald von (1881–1954) German field marshal best known for campaigns in France and Russia during World War II

Koga Mineichi (1885–1944) Japanese admiral in World War II who became Commander in Chief on the death of Yamamoto

Konev Ivan Stepanovich (1897–1973) marshal of the USSR during World War II

Kościuszko Tadeusz Andrzej Bonawentura (1746–1817) Polish general who fought for Poland's independence and later in the American Revolution

Kutuzov Mikhail Larionovich Golenishchev (1745–1813) Russian general in the Napoleonic Wars who was defeated at Austerlitz but successfully countered Napoleon's invasion of Russia in 1812

Lafayette Joseph Paul Roch Yves Gilbert Motier (1757–1834) French general in the American Revolution

Lattre de Tassigny Jean Marie Gabriel de (1889–1952) French general in World War II and Indochina

Lawrence T(homas) E(dward) ('Lawrence of Arabia') (1888–1935) British military leader, soldier, and writer, best known for victories at Aqaba (1917) and Damascus (1918) during World War I

Lee Robert Edward (1807–1870) US Confederate general in the American Civil War

Leigh-Mallory Trafford (1892–1944) British air commander during World War II, he commanded Allied air forces during the Normandy invasion

LeMay Curtis Emerson (1906-1990) US Air Force general in World War II

Ludendorff Erich (1865–1937) German general in World War I, victor at Tannenberg (1914); his 1918 offensive ended in failure

MacArthur Douglas (1880–1964) US general in the Pacific during World War II, and in the Korean War

Mannerheim Carl Gustaf Emil, Baron von (1867–1951) Finnish general in World War II

Manstein Fritz Erich von (1887–1973) German field marshal during World War II, brilliant strategist who devised the plan to defeat France

Manteuffel Hasso-Eccard von (1897–1978) German general who fought campaigns in Africa, Russia, and the Ardennes during World War II

Mao Tse-tung (1893–1976) Chinese Communist war leader who fought against the Japanese (1937–45)

Marshall George Catlett (1880–1959) US general, Chief of Staff of US Armed Forces throughout World War II

Martel Charles (*c.* 689–741) Carolingian general who fought against the Muslims

Maurice of Nassau Prince of Orange (1567–1625) Dutch general who successfully defended the United Netherlands against Spain following the Dutch Revolt

Milch Erhard (1892–1972) German field marshal who was largely responsible for the setting up of the Luftwaffe

Mitscher Marc Andrew (1887–1947) US admiral in World War II who commanded carrier forces in the Pacific

Model Otto Moritz Walter (1891–1945) German field marshal during World War II who became known as the 'Führer's Fireman'

Moltke Helmuth Karl Bernhard von ('the Elder', 1800–1891) German general who designed the General Staff System and defeated France in the Franco-Prussian War

Moltke Helmut von ('the Younger', 1848–1916) German general during World War I whose flawed execution of Schlieffen's Plan caused Germany's defeat

Montcalm Louis Joseph (1712–1759) French general defeated at Québec in 1759

Montgomery Bernard Law, 1st Viscount of Al 'Alamayn (1887–1976) British general in World War II and victor at Al 'Alamayn, Egypt, in 1942

Moore (John) Jeremy (1928–) British general who commanded British land forces during the Falklands War in 1982

Mountbatten Louis Francis Albert Nicholas, Earl (1900–1979) British admiral and pioneer of combined operations during World War II who also fought the Japanese in Burma

Nagumo Chuichi (1886–1944) Japanese admiral during World War II who commanded carrier forces during Pearl Harbor and Midway

Napoleon I (Bonaparte) (1769–1821) emperor of France and military genius

Nelson Horatio, 1st Viscount (1758–1805) British admiral in the Napoleonic Wars and victor at Trafalgar in 1805

Ney Michel, Prince of Moscow (1769–1815) French general in the Napoleonic Wars

Nimitz Chester William (1885–1966) US admiral and Commander in Chief of the Pacific Fleet and Pacific Areas during World War II

Nivelle Robert-Georges (1856–1924) French general during World War I whose 1917 offensive was a costly failure

O'Connor Richard (1889–1981) British general during World War II who defeated Italian forces in the Western desert in 1940

Patton George Smith Jr (1885–1945) US general during World War II, famous for his breakout from the Normandy bridgehead

Perry Matthew Calbraith (1794–1858) US admiral who opened up Japan to trade

Pershing John Joseph ('Black Jack') (1860–1948) US general who commanded the American Expeditionary Force in France during World War I

Pétain Henri Philippe Omer (1856–1951) French general in World War I and leader of Vichy France in World War II

Peter (I) the Great (1672–1725) Russian tsar who successfully fought the Great Northern War against Sweden (1700–21)

Phillip II (*c.* 382–336 BC) king of the Macedonians who defeated the Greeks at Chaeronea in 338 BC

Pontiac (*c.* 1720–1769) Native American war-chief (Ottawa tribe) who allied with the French during the French–Indian War

Richard (I) the Lionheart (1157–1199) king of England and crusader

Rickover Hyman G (1900–1986) US admiral who pioneered the use of nuclear technology to power warships

Ridgway Matthew Bunker (1895–1993) US general in World War II and the Korean War

Noteworthy Military and Naval Commanders (*continued*)

Robert (I) the Bruce (1274–1329) king of Scotland and victor at Bannockburn in 1314

Roberts Frederick Sleigh, 1st Earl (1832–1914) British general in India

Rokossovski Konstantin Konstantinovich (1896)–1968) Soviet general in World War II

Rommel Erwin Johannes Eugen (1891–1944) German field marshal during World War II, best known for his North African campaign

Rundstedt Karl Rudolf Gerd von (1875–1953) German field marshal during World War II who fought successful campaigns in Poland and France

Ruyter Michiel Adriaanzoon de (1607–1676) Dutch admiral

Saladin (or Salah-al-din) (1138–1193) Muslim military leader who defeated the Crusaders at Hatlin and took Jerusalem in 1187

San Martin José de (1778–1850) Argentinian-born Latin American general

Saxe Herman Maurice (1696–1750) German-born French general in the War of Austrian Succession

Seeckt Hans von (1866–1936) German general who reformed the army between the wars and developed the Blitzkrieg tactics

Sherman William Tecumseh (1820–1891) Union general during the American Civil War

Schwarzkopf H(erbert) Norman ('Stormin Norman') (1934–) US general who commanded the multinational coalition forces to victory in the Gulf War

Scipio Africanus Publius Cornelius (237–183 BC) Roman general who defeated Hannibal at Zama in 202 BC and conquered Carthage

Scott Winfield (1786–1866) US general who modernized the army along European lines and fought in the Mexican War

Shaka (1787–1828) founder of the Zulu Empire in southern Africa

Sharon Ariel ('Arik') (1928–) Israeli general and politician

Sheridan Philip Henry (1831–1888) US Union general in the American Civil War

Sikorski Władysław (1881–1943) Polish general and commander of Free Polish forces during World War II

Sims William Sowden (1858–1936) US admiral in World War I

Skorzeny Otto (1908–1975) German commander whose unit successfully rescued Mussolini and fought during the Battle of the Bulge

Slim William Joseph, 1st Viscount (1891–1970) British general who commanded the 14th Army in the successful Burma campaign during World War II

Smith Holland McTyeire ('Howlin Mad') (1882–1967) tough US marine general who fought throughout the Pacific during World War II

Smuts Jan Christiaan (1870–1950) South African military commander who fought with the British during both World Wars

Somerset Fitzroy James Henry, 1st Baron Raglan (1788–1855) British general in the Crimean War

Spaatz Carl ('Tooey') (1891–1974) US Air Force general in World War II

Spruance Raymond Amos (1886–1969) US admiral who fought in the Pacific during World War II

Stilwell Joseph Warren (1883–1946) US general who fought in South East Asia during World War II

Stirling David (1915–1990) British soldier who created the Special Air Service (SAS) during World War II

Stuart James Ewell Brown ('Jeb') (1833–1864) US Confederate general in the American Civil War

Student Kurt (1890–1978) German general who pioneered the use of airborne forces during World War II

Suleiman (I) the Magnificent (1494–1566) Ottoman sultan who was victorious at Mohács in 1526 and besieged Vienna in 1529

Sun Tzu (dates unknown, *c.* 400 BC) ancient Chinese military theorist who wrote *The Art of War*

Suvorov Aleksandr Vasil'evich (1730–1800) Russian general in the Seven Years' War and French Revolutionary War who defeated the French at Adda (1799)

Terauchi Hisaichi (1879–1945) Japanese general who directed the invasions of Indochina, Siam, Malaya, and Java during World War II

Tilly Johann Tserclaes, Graf von (1559–1632) Flemish general in the Thirty Years' War

Timur-I-Leng (Tamerlane) (1336–1405) Mongol warrior who conquered Central Asia and founded the Timurid dynasty

Tito (Josip Broz) (1892–1980) Yugoslav guerrilla leader in World War II

Togo Count Heihachiro (1849–1934) Japanese admiral and victor at Tsushima in 1905

Tojo Hideki (1884–1948) Japanese general and politician in World War II

Turenne Henri de la Tur d'Auvergne, vicomte de (1611–1675) French general in the Thirty Years' War

Turner Richmond Kelly (1885–1961) US admiral who served in the Pacific in World War II

Vandegrift Alexander Archer (1887–1973) US marine general in World War II

Vasilevsky Aleksander Mikhailovich (1895–1977) Soviet general during World War II, best known for victories at Stalingrad and Kursk

Vatutin Nikolai (1901–1944) Soviet general who fought successfully at Stalingrad and Kursk, and retook Kiev during World War II

Vauban Sébastien le Prestre de (1633–1707) French military engineer and designer of fortifications

Villa Francisco ('Pancho') (1877–1923) Mexican revolutionary general

Villeneuve Pierre Charles Jean Baptiste de (1763–1806) French admiral defeated at Trafalgar in 1805

Wallenstein Albrecht Eusebius Wenzel von (1583–1634) Czech-born general in the Thirty Years' War

Washington George (1732–1799) US general during the American Revolution and first President of the USA

Wellesley Arthur, 1st Duke of Wellington (1769–1852) British general in the Napoleonic Wars and victor at Waterloo in 1815

Westmoreland William Childs (1914–) US general in the Vietnam War

Wingate Orde Charles (1903–1944) British general who pioneered the use of deep penetration 'Chindit' units in Burma

Wolfe James (1727–1759) British general and victor at Québec in 1759

Woodward John (Sandy) (1931–) British admiral who commanded the British Task Force during the Falklands War in 1982

Xenophon (*c.* 435–*c.* 354 BC) Greek soldier and writer

Xerxes I (*c.* 520–465 BC) king of Persia who was defeated at Thermopylae by Leonidas in 480 BC and in the naval battle at Salamis in 480 BC

Yamamoto Isoroku (1883–1943) Japanese admiral who was the architect of the Pearl Harbor battle in 1941

Yamashita Tomoyuki (1888–1946) Japanese general during World War II who defeated British forces in Malaya and Singapore

Zhukov Georgi Konstantinovich (1896–1974) Marshal of the USSR during World War II, he defended Moscow and captured Berlin

See Also **Sports Personalities (Sport)**

Original Names of Famous Personalities

Original Names of Famous Personalities

Adopted/professional name	Original name
Abdul-Jabbar, Kareem	Ferdinand Lewis Alcindor
Adams, Maude	Maude Kiskadden
Alain-Fournier	Henri-Alban Fournier
Aleichem, Sholem	Sholem Yakov Rabinowitz
Ali, Muhammad	Cassius Marcellus Clay Jr
Allen, Woody	Allen Stewart Konigsberg
Allyson, June	Ella Geisman
Andrews, Julie	Julia Elizabeth Wells
Angelico, Fra	Guidodi Pietro
Ann-Margret	Ann Margret Olsson
Apollinaire, Guillame	Wilhelm Apollinaris de Kostrowitzki
Arnaz, Desi	Desidero Albert Arnaz de Acha III
Astaire, Fred	Frederick Austerlitz
Bacall, Lauren	Betty Joan Perske
Bakst, Leon Nikolaevich	Lev Samoylovich Rosenberg
Balanchine, George	Georgi Melitonovich Balanchivadze
Bancroft, Anne	Anna Maria Luisa Italiano
Banky, Vilma	Vilma Lonchit
Bara, Theda	Theodosia Goodman
Baraka, Amiri	Everett LeRoi Jones
Bardot, Brigitte	Camille Javal
Basho	Matsuo Munefusa
Beiderbecke, Bix	Leon Bismarck
Ben-Gurion, David	David Gruen
Benatar, Pat	Patricia Andrzejewski
Bennett, Tony	Antonio Dominic Benedetto
Benny, Jack	Benjamin Kubelsky
Berkeley, Busby	William Berkeley Enos
Berlin, Irving	Israel Baline
Bernhardt, Sarah	Henriette-Rosine Bernard
Big Bopper	Jiles Perry Richardson
Billy the Kid	William H Bonney
Black, Cilla	Priscilla Maria Veronica White
Blondin, Charles	Jean François Gravelet
Bly, Nellie	Elizabeth Cochrane Seaman
Bogarde, Dirk	Derek Niven van den Bogaerde
Borge, Victor	Borge Rosenbaum
Botticelli, Sandro	Alessandro di Mariano Filipepi
Bowie, David	David Robert Jones
Boy George	George Alan O'Dowd
Brandt, Willy	Herbert Ernest Karl Frahm
Bronson, Charles	Charles Buchinsky
Bell, Acton (original nom de plume)	Anne Brontê
Bell, Currer (original nom de plume)	Charlotte Brontê
Bell, Ellis (original nom de plume)	Emily Brontê
Brooks, Mel	Melvin Kaminsky
Buffalo Bill	William F Cody
Burgess, Anthony	John Anthony Burgess Wilson
Burns, George	Nathan Birnbaum
Burton, Richard	Richard Walter Jenkins
Caesar	Gaius Julius Caesar
Cage, Nicolas	Nicholas Coppola
Caine, Michael	Maurice Joseph Micklewhite
Calamity Jane	Martha Jane Canary (Burke)
Callas, Maria	Maria Anna Sofia Cecilia Kalogeropoulos
Canaletto, Antonio	Giovanni Antonio Canal
Capote, Truman	Truman Streckfus Persons
Caravaggio	Michelangelo Merisi
Carr, Vikki	Florencia Bisenta de Carillas Martinez Cardona

Adopted/professional name	Original name
Carroll, Lewis	Charles Lutwidge Dodgson
Castagno, Andrea del	Andrea di Bartolo de Bargilla
Charles, Ray	Ray Charles Robinson
Checker, Chubby	Ernest Evans
Cher	Cherilyn Sarkisian La Pier
Christo	Christo Javacheff
Clair, René	Rene-Lucien Chomette
Cliburn, Van	Harvey Lavan Cliburn Jr
Cline, Patsy	Virginia Patterson Hensley
Conrad, Joseph	Józef Teodor Konrad Nalecz Korzeniowski
Cooper, Alice	Vincent Furnier
Copperfield, David	David Kotkin
Correggio	Antonio Allegri
Costello, Elvis	Declan Patrick MacManus
Crawford, Joan	Lucille Fay Le Sueur
Crawford, Michael	Michael Dumble-Smith
Crosby, Bing	Harry Lillis Crosby
Cruise, Tom	Thomas Mapother IV
Curtis, Tony	Bernard Schwartz
Damone, Vic	Vito Rocco Farinola
Dangerfield, Rodney	Jacob Cohen
Danza, Tony	Anthony Iadanza
Darin, Bobby	Walden Robert Cassotto
Davis, Bette	Ruth Elizabeth Davis
Day, Doris	Doris Mary Anne von Kappelhoff
de Valois, Ninette	Edris Stannus
Dean, James	James Byron
Denver, John	John Henry Deutschendorf
De Vito, Danny	Daniel Michaeli
Diddley, Bo	Ellas Bates
Dinesen, Isak	Karen Christence Blixen-Finecke
Dolin, Anton	Patrick Healey-Kay
Domenichino	Domenico Zampieri
Dors, Diana	Diana Fluck
Douglas, Kirk	Issur Danielovitch, later Isidore Demsky
Douglas, Melvyn	Melvyn Edouard Hesselberg
Duras, Marguerite (nom de plume)	Marguerite Donnadieu
Dylan, Bob	Robert Allen Zimmerman
Edwards, Blake	William Blake McEdwards
Eliot, George (nom de plume)	Mary Ann Evans
Éluard, Paul	Eugène Grindel
Emin Pasha, Mehmed	Eduard Schnitzer
Erté	Romain de Tirtoff
Fairbanks, Douglas Sr	Douglas Elton Ulman
Field, Sally	Sally Mahoney
Fields, W C	William Claude Dukenfield
Flynn, Errol	Errol Leslie Thomson Flynn
Fontaine, Joan	Joan de Beauvoir de Havilland
Fonteyn, Margot	Margaret Hookham
Ford, Gerald R	Leslie Lynch King Jr
Ford, John	Sean Aloysius O'Feeney
Foster, Jodie	Alicia Christian Foster
France, Anatole	Jacques Anatole François Thibault
Gabin, Jean	Jean-Alexis Moncorgé
Gabo, Naum	Naum Neemia Pevsner
Garbo, Greta	Greta Lovisa Gustafsson
Gardenia, Vincent	Vincent Scognamiglio
Gardner, Ava	Lucy Johnson
Garfield, John	Julius Garfinkle
Garland, Judy	Frances Ethel Gumm
Garner, James	James Scott Baumgarner
Gayle, Crystal	Brenda Gayle Webb

Original Names of Famous Personalities (*continued*)

Adopted/professional name	Original name	Adopted/professional name	Original name
Gaynor, Mitzi	Francesca Mitzi Marlene de Czanyi von Gerber	Lenya, Lotte	Karoline Wilhelmine Blamauer
		Lewis, Jerry	Joseph Levitch
Ghirlandaio, Domenico	Domenico di Tommaso Bigordi	Liberace	Wladziu Valentino Liberace
Giorgione *or* Giorgio Barbarelli	Giorgio da Castelfranco	Little Richard	Richard Wayne Penniman
Gish, Lillian	Lillian de Guiche	Lombard, Carole	Jane Alice Peters
Goddard, Paulette	Marion Goddard Levy	Loren, Sophia	Sofia Scicolone
Goldberg, Whoopi	Caryn Johnson	Lorre, Peter	Laszlo Loewenstein
Goldwyn, Samuel	Shmuel Gelbfisz	Louis, Joe	Joseph Louis Barrow
Gorky, Arshile	Vosdanig Manoug Adoian	Lugosi, Bela	Bela Ferenc Denzso Blasko
Gorky, Maksim	Aleksei Maksimovich Peshkov	Lully, Jean-Baptiste	Giovanni Battista Lulli
Granger, Stewart	James Lablache Stewart	Lulu	Marie McDonald McLaughlin
Grant, Cary	Archibald Alexander Leach	Lu Xun	Chon Shu-jeu
Grayson, Kathryn	Zelma Kathryn Hedrick	Mabuse, Jan	Jan Gossaert
Gris, Juan	José Vittoriano González	McBain, Ed	Evan Hunter
Hall, Radclyffe	Marguerite Radclyffe-Hall	Mackenzie, Compton	Edward Montague Compton Mackenzie
Harlow, Jean	Harlean Carpenter		
Harrison, Rex	Reginald Carey Harrison	MacLaine, Shirley	Shirley McLean Beaty
Harvey, Laurence	Larushka Mischa Skikne	Mack, Connie	Cornelius Alexander McGillicuddy
Hayworth, Rita	Margarita Carmen Cansino	MacPherson, Elle	Eleanor Gow
Henry, O	William Henry Porter	Madonna	Madonna Louise Veronica Ciccone
Hepburn, Audrey	Edda van Heemstra Hepburn-Ruston	Malcolm X	Malcolm Little
Herod Agrippa I	Marcus Julius Agrippa	Malden, Karl	Mladen Sekulovich
Herzog, Werner	Werner Stipetic	Manilow, Barry	Barry Alan Pinkus
Heston, Charlton	John Charles Carter	Mansfield, Jayne	Vera Jayne Palmer
Ho Chi Minh	Nguyen Tat Thanh	Mansfield, Katherine	Kathleen Beauchamp
Holden, William	William Franklin Beedle Jr	March, Fredric	Fredric Ernest McIntyre Bickel
Holiday, Billie	Eleanora Fagan	Marcus Aurelius Antoninus	Marcus Annius Verus
Holliday, Judy	Judith Tuvim	Marguerite of Navarre	Marguerite D'Angoulême
Hope, Bob	Leslie Townes Hope	Markova, Alicia	Lilian Alicia Marks
Houdini, Harry	Erich Weiss	Marshall, Penny	Penny Marscharelli
Howard, Moe, Curly, and Shemp (The Three Stooges)	Moses, Jerome, and Samuel Horowitz	Martin, Dean	Dino Paul Crocetti
		Marx, Chico, Groucho, Harpo, and Zeppo	Leonard, Julius Henry, Adolph Arthur, and Herbert Marx
Howlin' Wolf	Chester Arthur Burnett	Massine, Léonide	Leonid Fiodorovich Miassin
Hudson, Rock	Roy Harold Scherer Jr	Mata Hari	Margaretha Geertruida Zelle
Humperdinck, Engelbert	Arnold George Dorsey	Matthau, Walter	Walter Matuschanskavasky
Irving, Henry	John Henry Brodribb Irving	Maurois, André	Emile Salomon Wilhelm Herzog
Jillian, Ann	Ann Jura Nauseda	Mayer, Louis B(urt)	Eliezer Mayer
John, Elton	Reginald Kenneth Dwight	Meat Loaf	Marvin Lee Adair
Jolson, Al	Asa Yoelson	Melba, Nellie	Helen Porter Mitchell
Jones, Jennifer	Phylis Isley	Meyerbeer, Giacomo	Jakob Liebmann Meyer Beer
Jones, Tom	Thomas Jones Woodward	Mfume, Kweisi	Frizzell Gray
Karloff, Boris	William Henry Pratt	Michael, George	Georgios Kyriacos Panayiotou
Kaye, Danny	David Daniel Kominski	Milland, Ray	Reginald Alfred Truscott-Jones
Kazan, Elia	Elia Kazanjoglou	Miranda, Carmen	Maria de Carmo Miranda da Cunha
Keaton, Diane	Diane Hall	Mishima, Yukio	Kimitake Hiraoka
Keaton, Michael	Michael Douglas	Mistinguett	Jeanne Marie Bourgeois
Kenyatta, Jomo	Kamau wa Ngengi	Mitchell, Joni	Roberta Joan Anderson
King, Stephen (nom de plume)	Bachman, Richard	Molière	Jean-Baptiste Poquelin
Kingsley, Ben	Krishna Bhanji	Molotov, Viacheslav Mikhailovich	Viacheslav Mikhailovich Skriabin
Kinski, Nastassja	Nastassja Nakszybski	Monroe, Marilyn	Norma Jean Mortenson
Lamour, Dorothy	Mary Leta Dorothy Kaumeyer	Montand, Yves	Ivo Livi
Landon, Michael	Eugene Orowitz	Montez, Lola	Marie Dolores Eliza Rosanna Gilbert
Langtry, Lillie	Emilie Charlotte le Breton	Moore, Demi	Demetria Guynes
Lanza, Mario	Alfred Arnold Coccozza	Moravia, Alberto	Alberto Pincherle
Laurel and Hardy	Arthur Stanley Jefferson and Oliver Norvell Hardy	Morton, Jelly Roll	Ferdinand Joseph La Menthe
		Moses, Grandma	Anna Mary Robertson Moses
Lauren, Ralph	Ralph Lipschitz	Mr T	Lawrence Tureaud
Leadbelly	Huddie William Ledbetter	Muddy Waters	McKinley Morganfield
Le Carré, John	David John Moore Cornwell	Muni, Paul	Muni Weisenfreund
Le Corbusier	Charles-Édouard Jeanneret	Murnau, F W	Friedrich Wilhelm Plumpe
Lee, Bruce	Lee Yuen Kam	Muybridge, Eadweard	Edward James Muggeridge
Lee, Gypsy Rose	Rose Louise Hovick	Nero	Lucius Domitius Ahenobarbus
Lee, Peggy	Norma Deloris Engstrom	Neruda, Pablo	Neftalí Ricardo Reyes y Basoalto
Leigh, Janet	Jeanette Helen Morrison	Nerval, Gérard de	Gérard Labrunie
Leigh, Vivien	Vivian Mary Hartley	Ne Win	Maung Shu Maung
Lely, Peter	Pieter van der Faes	Nichols, Mike	Michael Igor Peschkowsky
Lemmon, Jack	John Uhler Lemmon III	Nilsson, Harry	Harry Edward Nelson III
Lenin, Vladimir Ilich	Vladimir Ilich Ulyanov		

(continued)

Original Names of Famous Personalities (*continued*)

Adopted/professional name	Original name	Adopted/professional name	Original name
Nolde, Emil	Emil Hansen	Stanwyck, Barbara	Ruby Stevens
Novalis	Friedrich Leopold von Hardenberg	Starr, Belle	Myra Belle Shirley
Novello, Ivor	David Ivor Davies	Starr, Ringo	Richard Starkey
O'Casey, Sean	John Casey	Stendhal	Marie-Henri Beyle
Ophüls, Max	Max Oppenheimer	Sting	Gordon Sumner
Ormandy, Eugene	Jenö Ormandy Blau	Stroheim, Erich von	Erich Oswald Stroheim
Orwell, George	Eric Arthur Blair	Swanson, Gloria	Gloria Josephine Mae Svensson
Ouida (nom de plume)	Marie Louise de la Ramée	Tati, Jacques	Jacques Tatischeff
Palance, Jack *or*		Terry-Thomas	Thomas Terry Hoar Stevens
Walter Jack Palahniuk	Vladimir Palanuik	Thomas, Danny	Muzyad Yakhoop, later Amos Jacobs
Paracelsus	Philippus Aureolus Theophrastus Bombastus von Hohenheim	Tintoretto	Jacopo Robusti
		Tiny Tim	Herbert Buckingham Khaury
Paul, Les	Lester William Polfus	Titian	Tiziano Vecellio
Pelé	Edson Arantes do Nascimento	Tito	Josip Broz
Piaf, Edith	Edith Giovanna Gassion	Tokyo Rose	Iva Ikiko Toguri D'Aquino
Pickford, Mary	Gladys Mary Smith	Toto	Antonio de Curtis Gagliardi Ducas Commeno di Bisanzio
Pol Pot	Saloth Sar		
Pressburger, Emeric	Imre Jozef Pressburger	Touré, Kwame	Ahmed Sékou Touré
Prince	Prince Rogers Nelson	Trotsky, Leon	Lev Davidovich Bronstein
Ramakrishna	Gadadhar Chatterji	Truth, Sojourner	Isabella Baumfree
Rambert, Marie	Miriam Rambach	Turner, Lana	Julia Jean Mildred Frances Turner
Rand, Ayn	Alice Rosenbaum	Turner, Tina	Annie Mae Bullock
Raphael *or* Rafaello Sanzio	Santi	Twain, Mark (nom de plume)	Samuel Langhorne Clemens
Ray, Man	Emmanuel Rabinovich Rudnitsky	Twiggy	Lesley Hornby
Ray, Nicholas	Raymond Nicholas Kienzle	Uccello	Paolo di Dono
Reuter, (Paul) Julius de, Baron Reuter	Israel Beer Josaphat	Valentino, Rudolph	Rodolfo Alphonso Guglielmi di Valentina d'Antonguolla *or* Rodolfo Pietro Filiberto Rafaello Guglielmi
Rhys, Jean (nom de plume)	Ella Gwendolen Rees Williams		
Rice, Elmer	Elmer Reizenstein		
Richard, Cliff	Harry Roger Webb	Van Damme, Jean-Claude	Jean-Claude Van Varenberg
Rivers, Joan	Joan Sandra Molinsky	Voltaire	François-Marie Arouet
Robinson, Edward G	Emmanuel Goldenberg	Walcott, Jersey Joe	Arnold Raymond Cream
Robinson, Sugar Ray	Walker Smith	Wall, Max	Maxwell George Lorimer
Rogers, Ginger	Virginia Katherine McMath	Ward, Artemus	Charles Farrar Browne
Rogers, Roy	Leonard Slye	Warhol, Andy	Andrew Warhola
Rohmer, Eric	Jean-Marie Maurice Scherer	Wayne, John	Marion Michael Morrison
Rooney, Mickey	Joe Yule Jr	Weaver, Sigourney	Susan Weaver
Rothko, Mark	Marcus Rothkovich	Webb, Clifton	Webb Parmallee Hollenbeck
Sand, George	Amandine Aurore Lucile (Lucie) Dupin	Welch, Raquel	Raquel Tejada
		Werner, Oskar	Oskar Josef Bschliessmayer
Sargon II	Sarru-Kinu	Wertmuller, Lina	Arcangela Felice Assunta Wertmuller von Elgg
Savile, Jimmy	James Wilson Vincent		
Schneider, Romy	Rosemarie Albach-Retty	West, Nathanael	Nathan Wallenstein Weinstein
Sennett, Mack *or* Mikall	Michell Sinnott	West, Rebecca	Cicily Isabel Fairfield Andrews
Seymour, Jane	Joyce Penelope Wilhelmina Frankenberg	Wilder, Gene	Jerry Silberman
		Williams, Tennessee	Thomas Lanier Williams
Sharif, Omar	Michael Chalhoub	Winters, Shelley	Shirley Schrift
Shaw, Artie	Arthur Arshawsky	Wonder, Stevie	Steveland Judkins Morris
Sheen, Charlie	Carlos Irwin Estevez	Wood, Natalie	Natasha Gurdin
Sheen, Martin	Ramon Estevez	Wyman, Jane	Sarah Jane Fulks
Sills, Beverly	Belle Miriam Silverman	Wyndham, John	John Wyndham Parkes Lucas Beynon Harris
Stalin, Joseph	Josif Vissarionovich Dzhugashvili		
Stanley, Henry Morton	John Rowlands	York, Susannah	Susannah Yolande Fletcher
		Yourcenar, Marguerite	Marguerite de Crayencour

Longest Serving Rulers and Political Leaders

Longest Serving Political Leaders

As of 1998

Rank	Name	Position	Country	Term(s)	Years
1	Chiang Kai-shek	general and president	China and Taiwan	1928–75	47[1]
2	Kim Il Sung	Communist leader	North Korea	1948–94	46
3	Ibrahim Didi	prime minister	Maldives	1883–1925	42
4	Enver Hoxha	Communist leader	Albania	1954–85	40
5	Fidel Castro Ruz	Communist leader	Cuba	1959–	39
6	Francisco Franco Bahamonde	dictator	Spain	1939–75	36
6=	Antonio de Oliveira Salazar	dictator	Portugal	1932–68	36
6=	Marshal Tito	Communist leader	Yugoslavia	1943–80	36
9	Todor Zhivkov	Communist leader	Bulgaria	1954–89	35
9=	Alfredo Stroessner	dictator	Paraguay	1954–89	35
11	Omar Bongo	president	Gabon	1964–	34
12	Felix Houphouet-Boigny	president	Côte d'Ivoire	1960–93	33
13	Mobuto Sese Seko	president	Zaire	1965–97	32
14	Suharto	president	Indonesia	1967–98	32
14=	Habib Bourguiba	president	Tunisia	1956–87	31
14=	Lee Kuan Yew	prime minister	Singapore	1959–90	31
14=	Josef Stalin	Communist leader	Soviet Union (Russia)	1922–53	31
18	John Compton	prime minister	St Lucia	1964–79 and 1982–	30
19	Vere Bird	prime minister	Antigua and Barbuda	1960–71 and 1976–94	29
19=	Moamer al Khaddhafi	revolutionary leader	Libya	1969–	29
21	Sheikh Khalifa bin-Sulman al-Khalifa	prime minister	Bahrain	1970–	28
22	William Tubman	president	Liberia	1944–71	27
22=	Kenneth Kaunda	president	Zambia	1964–91	27
22=	Mao Zedong	Communist leader	China	1949–76	27
22=	Klemens von Metternich	chancellor	Austria	1821–48	27

[1] During the late 1930s and 1940s, Chiang was leader in only a small nationalist stronghold portion of China.

Longest Reigning Monarchs

As of 1998

Rank	Name	Country	Reign	Years
1	King Mihti	Arakan (Myanmar)	c. 1279–1374	95[1]
2	Pharaoh Phiops (Pepi) II	Egypt (Neferkare)	c. 2269–2175 BC	94[1]
3	King Louis XIV	France	1643–1715	72
4	Prince Johannes II	Liechtenstein	1858–1929	71
5	King Harald I	Norway	c. 870–940	70
6	Emperor Franz-Josef	Austria	1848–1916	68
7	Queen Victoria	Great Britain	1837–1901	63
8	Emperor Hirohito (Showa)	Japan	1926–89	62
9	Emperor Kangxi	China	1661–1722	61
10	Emperor Qianlong	China	1735–96	60
11	King George III	Great Britain	1760–1820	59
11=	King Louis XV	France	1715–74	59
11=	King Christian IV	Denmark	1588–1648	59
11=	Prince Honore III	Monaco	1733–93	59
15	Emperor Pedro II	Brazil	1831–89	58
15=	Queen Wilhelmina	Netherlands	1890–1948	58
17	King Henry III	England	1216–72	56
18	King Sisavang Vong	Laos (Luang Prabang)	1904–59	55
19	Sultan Shaikh Isa bin Ali al-Khalifa	Bahrain	1869–1923	54
20	King Eric III	Norway	1389–1442	53
21	King Boleslaw V	Poland	1227–79	52
21=	Shah Tahmasp I	Iran (Persia)	1524–76	52
21=	King Bhumibol Adulyadej (Rama IX)	Thailand	1946–	52
24	Shogun Ienari Tokugawa	Japan	1787–1838	51
25	King Georgios I	Greece	1863–1913	50
25=	Sultan Said bin Sultan	Oman	1806–56	50

[1] The historical evidence to authenticate the length of these reigns is fragmented.

The World's Royal Families

Living Members of the World's Royal Families

Name	Date of birth	Relationship to monarch	Name	Date of birth	Relationship to monarch
Belgium			*Netherlands*		
Albert II	1934	king	Beatrix	1938	queen
Paola Ruffo de Calabria	1937	wife	Juliana	1909	mother
Philippe*	1960	son	Claus von Amsberg	1926	husband
Astrid	1962	daughter	Willem-Alexander*	1967	son
Laurent	1963	son	Johan Friso	1968	son
			Constantine	1969	son
Denmark			Irene	1939	sister
Margrethe II	1940	queen	Margriet	1943	sister
Henry de Laborde de Montpezat	1934	husband	Christina	1947	sister
Frederik*	1968	son			
Joachim	1969	son	*Norway*		
			Harald V	1937	king
Japan			Sonja Haraldsen	1937	wife
Akihito	1933	emperor	Marthan Louise	1971	daughter
Michiko	1934	wife	Haakon Magnus*	1973	son
Hiro (Naruhito)*	1960	son	Ragnhild	1930	sister
Aya (Fumihito)	1965	son	Astrid	1932	sister
Nori (Sayako)	1969	daughter			
			Spain		
Jordan			Juan Carlos I	1938	king
Hussein	1935	king	Sofia of Greece	1938	wife
Hassan*	1935	brother	Elena	1963	daughter
Alia	1956	daughter	Christina	1965	daughter
Abdullah	1962	son	Felipe*	1968	son
Faisal	1963	son			
Zein	1968	daughter	*Sweden*		
Aisha	1968	daughter	Carl XVI Gustaf	1946	king
Haya	1974	daughter	Silvia Sommerlath	1944	wife
Ali	1975	son	Victoria*	1977	daughter
Hamzah	1980	son	Carl Philip	1979	son
Hashem	1981	son	Madeleine	1982	daughter
Iman	1983	daughter	Margaretha	1934	sister
Raiya	1986	daughter	Birgitta	1937	sister
			Désirée	1938	sister
Liechtenstein			Christina	1953	sister
Johann Adam	1945	prince			
Marie Aglae Kinsky	1940	wife	*Thailand*		
Alois Philippe*	1968	son	Bhumibol Adulyadej (Rama IX)	1927	king
Maximillian	1969	son	Mom Rajwong Sirikit Kitayakorn	1932	wife
Constantine	1972	son	Ubol Ratana	1951	daughter
Tatiana	1973	daughter	Vajiralongkorn*	1952	son
Philipp	1946	brother	Sirimdhorn	1955	daughter
Nikolaus	1947	brother	Chulabhorn	1957	daughter
Nora	1950	sister			
			Tonga		
Luxembourg			Taufa'ahau Tupou IV	1918	king
Jean	1921	grand duke	Ma'Ataha	1926	wife
Josephine of Belgium	1927	wife	Tupouto'A*	1948	son
Marie-Astrid	1954	daughter	Pilolevu	1951	daughter
Henri*	1955	son	Fatafehi	1954	son
Jean	1957	son	Aho'Eitu	1959	son
Margaretha	1957	daughter			
Guillaume	1963	son	*United Kingdom*		
William John	1981	grandson	Elizabeth II	1926	queen
Mary Christine	1983	granddaughter	Elizabeth Bowes-Lyon	1900	mother
Felix	1984	grandson	Philip of Greece	1921	husband
Louis	1986	grandson	Charles*	1948	son
			Anne	1950	daughter
Monaco			Andrew	1960	son
Rainier III	1923	prince	Edward	1964	son
Caroline	1957	daughter	Peter	1977	grandson
Albert*	1958	son	Zara	1981	granddaughter
Stephanie	1965	daughter	William	1982	grandson
			Harry	1984	grandson
			Beatrice	1988	granddaughter
			Eugenie	1990	granddaughter
			Margaret Rose	1930	sister

* This member of each family is the heir to the throne.

CAN THE BRITISH MONARCHY CHANGE WITH THE TIMES?

BY HAYDN MIDDLETON

In the immediate aftermath of the death of Diana, Princess of Wales, commentators declared that Britain had become a more compassionate and demonstrative society. Did the country any longer want what was seen as an unfeeling and remote monarchy?

On 17 October 1997, the *Times* newspaper reported that: 'The Queen has accepted that the Royal Family must change its image after the death of Diana, Princess of Wales. A source close to the Queen spoke yesterday of the need to demonstrate "softer, gentler touches" in the wake of what he described as the first royal tragedy to occur in the mass media culture.'

An Acrimonious Debate

Six weeks earlier, in the immediate aftermath of Diana's fatal accident, far more significant changes had seemed to be afoot. The 'People's Princess' had not been universally popular, but her many fans had found her emotional, informal style a welcome change from the more remote image presented by other members of the Windsor clan. Her death was then followed by an often acrimonious public debate over how the royal family might survive with credibility into the 21st century. There were even suggestions that Prince Charles was so 'out of touch' with the British people that the crown should 'skip a generation' on the death of the present Queen and pass instead to Prince William, Charles's elder son by Diana.

For a short while, amid the tears and flowers of those extraordinary summer days, almost anything seemed possible. Since Britain has a highly flexible, unwritten constitution, a major revision of the royal family's role – or indeed its abolition – would not have been impossible.

However, the British monarchy has deep roots, and it has proved to be a tough old plant, ready and able to adapt itself to changes in its social and political environment. Kings and queens have been ruling in Britain since the first millennium AD and for centuries they were seen as superhuman: as late as 1712 Queen Anne was still practising the 'royal touch', a laying-on of hands that was believed to cure diseased skin. By that time, the monarchy had lost much of its real power to Parliament, and it has continued since then to make a slow constitutional retreat, its role becoming ever more symbolic.

But while most monarchies elsewhere were swept away entirely, the British royal family has managed to attune itself to democracy. The current queen has reigned since 1952 and is generally thought to have done a difficult job well. Although she lacks the charisma of a Diana, she is perceived to be conscientious and hard-working, and has attracted less criticism over the years than other members of her family such as Princess Michael of Kent, Princess Margaret, and the Duchess of York. A reduction in the number of such 'lesser royals' would, in the eyes of many, make for a leaner, fitter, and more acceptable monarchy.

But even a pared down royal family will now almost certainly be expected to display those 'softer, gentler touches' that were the trademark of Diana. There are 60 million people in Britain and they do not speak with a single voice, but the most vocal part of the nation seems to want a less formal, more 'hands-on' kind of monarchy than exists at present. This may not mean that the Windsors will have to travel around on bicycles, in the modest style of certain royal families in mainland Europe. The British public still expects some pomp and ceremony – an expectation that was lavishly met by the highly dignified funeral of Princess Diana. But it also now expects more informal touches too – such as the inclusion of a song performed by pop star Elton John at the same funeral.

Reforming the Constitution

The new Labour Government is keen to end inequalities in Britain, and it is no friend to privilege. With the future of the House of Lords under serious threat, the monarchy's future could appear to be in jeopardy too. Yet Prime Minister Tony Blair is not a republican and his relationship with Buckingham Palace is reported to be good. There is also no consensus on who might replace the queen as head of state, if the monarchy was to be abolished.

Just as the Labour Party put itself back in tune with the British electorate, so now – as the public mood mellows after the sometimes hysterical outbursts straight after Diana's tragic death – the monarchy could conceivably get in touch with more of its subjects by presenting itself in a less traditional fashion. Some would say that, in Britain, a 'modernized monarchy' is a contradiction in terms. However, all institutions have to make concessions to changing circumstances. In its way, the monarchy in Britain has been doing this for 1,500 years – so the Queen and her family know where their responsibilities lie.

European Rulers and Political Leaders

Belgian Monarchs from 1831

Reign	Name
1831–65	Leopold I
1865–1909	Leopold II
1909–14	Albert I
1914–18	German occupation
1918–34	Albert I
1934–40	Leopold III
1940–44	German occupation
1944–50	Prince Charles (regent)
1950–51	Leopold III
1951–93	Baudouin
1993–	Albert II

Belgian Prime Ministers from 1944

Term	Name	Party
1944–45	Hubert Pierlot	Catholic Party
1945–46	Achille van Acker	Socialist Party
1946	Paul-Henri Spaak	Socialist Party
1946	Achille van Acker	Socialist Party
1946–47	Camille Huysmans	Socialist Party
1947–49	Paul-Henri Spaak	Socialist Party
1949–50	Gaston Eyskens	Christian Social Party
1950	Jean Duvieusart	Christian Social Party
1950–52	Joseph Pholien	Christian Social Party
1952–54	Jean van Houtte	Christian Social Party
1954–58	Achille van Acker	Socialist Party
1958–61	Gaston Eyskens	Christian Social Party
1961–65	Théodore Lefèvre	Christian Social Party
1965–66	Pierre Harmel	Christian Social Party
1966–68	Paul van den Boeynants	Christian Social Party
1968–72	Gaston Eyskens	Christian Social Party
1972–74	Edmond Leburton	Socialist Party
1974–78	Léo Tindemans	Christian Social Party
1978–79	Paul van den Boeynants	Christian Social Party
1979–81	Wilfried Martens	Christian People's Party
1981	Mark Eyskens	Christian People's Party
1981–92	Wilfried Martens	Christian People's Party
1992–	Jean-Luc Dehaene	Christian People's Party

Danish Monarchs from 1848

	Reign	Name
House of Oldenburg	1848–63	Frederick VII
Line of Glücksburg	1863–1906	Christian IX
	1906–12	Frederick VIII
	1912–47	Christian X
	1947–72	Frederick IX
	1972–	Margrethe II

Danish Prime Ministers from 1945

Term	Name	Party
1945	Vilhelm Buhl	Social Democratic Party
1945–47	Knud Kristensen	Agrarian Party
1947–50	Hans Hedtoft	Social Democratic Party
1950–53	Erik Eriksen	Agrarian Party
1953–55	Hans Hedtoft	Social Democratic Party
1955–60	Hans Hansen	Social Democratic Party
1960–62	Viggo Kampmann	Social Democratic Party
1962–68	Jens-Otto Krag	Social Democratic Party
1968–71	Hilmar Baunsgaard	Radical Party
1971–72	Jens-Otto Krag	Social Democratic Party
1972–73	Anker Jørgensen	Social Democratic Party
1973–75	Poul Hartling	Liberal Party
1975–82	Anker Jørgensen	Social Democratic Party
1982–93	Poul Schlüter	Conservative Party
1993–	Poul Nyrup Rasmussen	Social Democratic Party

Dutch Monarchs from 1806

Reign	Name
1806–10	Lodewijk I
1810	Lodewijk II
1810–13	French annexation
1813–15	Provisional government
1815–40	Willem I
1840–49	Willem II
1849–90	Willem III
1890–1940	Wilhelmina
1940–45	German occupation
1945–48	Wilhelmina
1948–80	Juliana
1980–	Beatrix

Dutch Prime Ministers from 1945

Term	Name	Party
1945	Pieter Gerbrandy	Anti-Revolutionary Party
1945–46	Willem Schermerhorn	Socialist Party
1946–48	Louis Beel	Catholic Party
1948–58	Willem Drees	Socialist Party
1958–59	Louis Beel	Catholic Party
1959–63	Jan de Quay	Catholic Party
1963–65	Victor Marijnen	Catholic Party
1965–66	Joseph Cals	Catholic Party
1966–67	Jelle Zijlstra	Anti-Revolutionary Party
1967–71	Petrus de Jong	Catholic Party
1971–73	Barend Biesheuvel	Anti-Revolutionary Party
1973–77	Johannes (Joop) den Uyl	Labour Party
1977–82	Andreas van Agt	Christian Democratic Appeal Party
1982–94	Rudolphus (Ruud) Lubbers	Christian Democratic Appeal Party
1994–	Wim Kok	Labour Party

English Sovereigns from 899

Reign	Name	Relationship
West Saxon Kings		
899–924	Edward the Elder	son of Alfred the Great
924–39	Athelstan	son of Edward the Elder
939–46	Edmund	half-brother of Athelstan
946–55	Edred	brother of Edmund
955–59	Edwy	son of Edmund
959–75	Edgar	brother of Edwy
975–78	Edward the Martyr	son of Edgar
978–1016	Ethelred (II) the Unready	son of Edgar
1016	Edmund Ironside	son of Ethelred (II) the Unready
Danish Kings		
1016–35	Canute	son of Sweyn I of Denmark who conquered England in 1013
1035–40	Harold I	son of Canute
1040–42	Hardicanute	son of Canute
West Saxon Kings (restored)		
1042–66	Edward the Confessor	son of Ethelred (II) the Unready
1066	Harold II	son of Godwin
Norman Kings		
1066–87	William I	illegitimate son of Duke Robert the Devil
1087–1100	William II	son of William I
1100–35	Henry I	son of William I
1135–54	Stephen	grandson of William II
House of Plantagenet		
1154–89	Henry II	son of Matilda (daughter of Henry I)
1189–99	Richard I	son of Henry II
1199–1216	John	son of Henry II
1216–72	Henry III	son of John
1272–1307	Edward I	son of Henry III
1307–27	Edward II	son of Edward I
1327–77	Edward III	son of Edward II
1377–99	Richard II	son of the Black Prince
House of Lancaster		
1399–1413	Henry IV	son of John of Gaunt
1413–22	Henry V	son of Henry IV
1422–61, 1470–71	Henry VI	son of Henry V
House of York		
1461–70, 1471–83	Edward IV	son of Richard, Duke of York
1483	Edward V	son of Edward IV
1483–85	Richard III	brother of Edward IV
House of Tudor		
1485–1509	Henry VII	son of Edmund Tudor, Earl of Richmond
1509–47	Henry VIII	son of Henry VII
1547–53	Edward VI	son of Henry VIII
1553–58	Mary I	daughter of Henry VIII
1558–1603	Elizabeth I	daughter of Henry VIII
House of Stuart		
1603–25	James I	great-grandson of Margaret (daughter of Henry VII)
1625–49	Charles I	son of James I
1649–60	the Commonwealth	
House of Stuart (restored)		
1660–85	Charles II	son of Charles I
1685–88	James II	son of Charles I
1688–1702	William III and Mary	son of Mary (daughter of Charles I); daughter of James II
1702–14	Anne	daughter of James II
House of Hanover		
1714–27	George I	son of Sophia (granddaughter of James I)
1727–60	George II	son of George I
1760–1820	George III	son of Frederick (son of George II)
1820–30	George IV (regent 1811–20)	son of George III
1830–37	William IV	son of George III
1837–1901	Victoria	daughter of Edward (son of George III)
House of Saxe-Coburg		
1901–10	Edward VII	son of Victoria
House of Windsor		
1910–36	George V	son of Edward VII
1936	Edward VIII	son of George V
1936–52	George VI	son of George V
1952–	Elizabeth II	daughter of George VI

French Presidents and Prime Ministers from 1959 (the Fifth Republic)

Term	Name	Party
Presidents		
1959–69	General Charles de Gaulle	Gaullist
1969–74	Georges Pompidou	Gaullist
1974–81	Valéry Giscard d'Estaing	Republican/Union of French Democracy
1981–95	François Mitterand	Socialist
1995–	Jacques Chirac	Neo-Gaullist RPR
Prime Ministers		
1959–62	Michel Debré	Gaullist
1962–68	Georges Pompidou	Gaullist
1968–69	Maurice Couve de Murville	Gaullist
1969–72	Jacques Chaban-Delmas	Gaullist
Prime Ministers (continued)		
1972–74	Pierre Messmer	Gaullist
1974–76	Jacques Chirac	Gaullist
1976–81	Raymond Barre	Union of French Democracy
1981–84	Pierre Mauroy	Socialist
1984–86	Laurent Fabius	Socialist
1986–88	Jacques Chirac	Neo-Gaullist RPR
1988–91	Michel Rocard	Socialist
1991–92	Edith Cresson	Socialist
1992–93	Pierre Bérégovoy	Socialist
1993–95	Edouard Balladur	Neo-Gaullist RPR
1995–97	Alain Juppé	Neo-Gaullist RPR
1997–	Lionel Jospin	Socialist

French Rulers 751–1958

Date of accession	Title of ruler	Name	Date of accession	Title of ruler	Name
751	King	Pepin III/Childerich III	1560		Charles IX
752		Pepin III	1574		Henri III
768		Charlemagne/Carloman	1574		Henri IV
814		Louis I	1610		Louis XIII
840		Lothair I	1643		Louis XIV
843		Charles (II) the Bald	1715		Louis XV
877		Louis II	1774		Louis XVI
879		Louis III	1792	National Convention	
884		Charles (III) the Fat	1795	Directory (five members)	
888		Odo	1799	First Consul	Napoléon Bonaparte
893		Charles (III) the Simple	1804	Emperor	Napoléon I
922		Robert I	1814	King	Louis XVIII
923		Rudolf	1815	Emperor	Napoléon I
936		Louis IV	1815	King	Louis XVIII
954		Lothair II	1824		Charles X
986		Louis V	1830		Louis XIX
987		Hugues Capet	1830		Henri V
996		Robert II	1830		Louis-Philippe
1031		Henri I	1848	President of the National Assembly	Philippe Buchez
1060		Philippe I	1848	Minister of War	Louis Cavaignac
1108		Louis VI	1848	President	Louis Napoléon Bonaparte
1137		Louis VII	1852	Emperor	Napoléon III
1180		Philippe II	1871	President	Adolphe Thiers
1223		Louis VIII	1873		Patrice MacMahon
1226		Louis IX	1879		Jules Grevy
1270		Philippe III	1887		François Sadui-Carnot
1285		Philippe IV	1894		Jean Casimir-Périer
1314		Louis X	1895		François Faure
1316		Jean I	1899		Emile Loubet
1328		Philippe V	1913		Armand Fallières
1322		Charles IV	1913		Raymond Poincaré
1328		Philippe VI	1920		Paul Deschanel
1350		Jean II	1920		Alexandre Millerand
1356		Charles V	1924		Gaston Doumergue
1380		Charles VI	1931		Paul Doumer
1422		Charles VII	1932		Albert Le Brun
1461		Louis XI	1940	Vichy government	Philippe Pétain
1483		Charles VIII	1944	provisional government	
1498		Louis XII	1947	President	Vincent Auriol
1515		François I	1954		René Coty
1547		Henri II			
1559		François II			

(See also French Presidents and Prime Ministers from 1959)

German Political Leaders from 1949

Term	Name	Party	Term	Name
Federal Republic			**Democratic Republic**	
Chancellors			*Communist Party leaders*	
1949–63	Konrad Adenauer	Christian Democrat	1949–50	Wilhelm Pieck
1963–66	Ludwig Erhard	Christian Democrat	1950–71	Walter Ulbricht
1966–69	Kurt Kiesinger	Christian Democrat	1971–89	Erich Honecker
1969–74	Willy Brandt	Social Democrat	1989	Egon Krenz
1974–82	Helmut Schmidt	Social Democrat		
1982– [1]	Helmut Kohl	Christian Democrat	*Prime Ministers*	
			1989–90	Hans Modrow
			1990–91	Lothar de Maizière

[1] The official reunification of the two countries, with Kohl as chancellor, took place in 1990.

Holy Roman Emperors

Reign	Name
Carolingian Kings and Emperors	
800–14	Charlemagne (Charles the Great)
814–40	Louis the Pious
840–55	Lothair I
855–75	Louis II
875–77	Charles (II) the Bald
881–87	Charles (III) the Fat
891–94	Guido of Spoleto
892–98	Lambert of Spoleto (co-emperor)
896–901	Arnulf (rival)
901–05	Louis III of Provence
905–24	Berengar
911–18	Conrad (I) of Franconia (rival)
Saxon Kings and Emperors	
918–36	Henry I the Fowler
936–73	Otto (I) the Great
973–83	Otto II
983–1002	Otto III
1002–24	Henry (II) the Saint
Franconian (Salian) Emperors	
1024–39	Conrad II
1039–56	Henry (III) the Black
1056–1106	Henry IV
1077–80	Rudolf of Swabia (rival)
1081–93	Hermann of Luxembourg (rival)

Reign	Name
1093–1101	Conrad of Franconia (rival)
1106–25	Henry V
1126–37	Lothair II
Hohenstaufen Kings and Emperors	
1138–52	Conrad III
1152–90	Frederick Barbarossa
1190–97	Henry VI
1198–1215	Otto IV
1198–1208	Philip of Swabia (rival)
1215–50	Frederick II
1246–47	Henry Raspe of Thuringia (rival)
1247–56	William of Holland (rival)
1250–54	Conrad IV
1254–73	no ruler (the Great Interregnum)
Rulers from Various Noble Families	
1257–72	Richard of Cornwall (rival)
1257–73	Alfonso X of Castile (rival)
1273–91	Rudolf I, Habsburg
1292–98	Adolf I of Nassau
1298–1308	Albert I, Habsburg
1308–13	Henry VII, Luxembourg
1314–47	Louis IV of Bavaria
1314–25	Frederick of Habsburg (co-regent)

Reign	Name
1347–78	Charles IV, Luxembourg

Reign	Name
1378–1400	Wenceslas of Bohemia
1400	Frederick III of Brunswick
1400–10	Rupert of the Palatinate
1411–37	Sigismund, Luxembourg
Habsburg Emperors	
1438–39	Albert II
1440–93	Frederick III
1493–1519	Maximilian I
1519–56	Charles V
1556–64	Ferdinand I
1564–76	Maximilian II
1576–1612	Rudolf II
1612–19	Matthias
1619–37	Ferdinand II
1637–57	Ferdinand III
1658–1705	Leopold I
1705–11	Joseph I
1711–40	Charles VI
1742–45	Charles VII of Bavaria
Habsburg-Lorraine Emperors	
1745–65	Francis I of Lorraine
1765–90	Joseph II
1790–92	Leopold II

House of Habsburg 1804–1916

Reign	Name
Emperors of Austria	
1804–35	Francis (Franz) I (of Austria) and II (as Holy Roman emperor until 1806)
1835–48	Ferdinand
Emperors of Austria–Hungary	
1816–1818	Charles (Karl; abdicated)
1848–1916	Franz Josef

Italian Kings from 1861

Reign	Name
1861–78	Victor Emmanuel II
1878–1900	Umberto I
1900–46	Victor Emmanuel III
1946	Umberto II (abdicated)

Irish Prime Ministers from 1922

Term	Name	Party
1922	Michael Collins	Sinn Féin
1922–32	William T Cosgrave	Fine Gael
1932–48	Eamon de Valera	Fianna Fáil
1948–51	John A Costello	Fine Gael
1951–54	Eamon de Valera	Fianna Fáil
1954–57	John A Costello	Fine Gael
1957–59	Eamon de Valera	Fianna Fáil
1959–66	Sean Lemass	Fianna Fáil
1966–73	Jack Lynch	Fianna Fáil
1973–77	Liam Cosgrave	Fine Gael
1977–79	Jack Lynch	Fianna Fáil
1979–81	Charles Haughey	Fianna Fáil
1981–82	Garrett Fitzgerald	Fine Gael
1982	Charles Haughey	Fianna Fáil
1982–87	Garrett Fitzgerald	Fine Gael
1987–92	Charles Haughey	Fianna Fáil
1992–94	Albert Reynolds	Fianna Fáil
1994–96	John Bruton	Fine Gael
1996–	Bertie Ahern	Fianna Fáil

Italian Prime Ministers from 1945

Term	Name	Party	Term	Name	Party
1945–53	Alcide de Gasperi	Christian Democratic Party	1974–76	Aldo Moro	Christian Democratic Party
1953–54	Giuseppe Pella	Christian Democratic Party	1976–79	Giulio Andreotti	Christian Democratic Party
1954	Amintore Fanfani	Christian Democratic Party	1979–80	Francesco Cossiga	Christian Democratic Party
1954–55	Mario Scelba	Christian Democratic Party	1980–81	Arnaldo Forlani	Christian Democratic Party
1955–57	Antonio Segni	Christian Democratic Party	1981–82	Giovanni Spadolini	Republican Party
1957–58	Adone Zoli	Christian Democratic Party	1982–83	Amintore Fanfani	Christian Democratic Party
1958–59	Amintore Fanfani	Christian Democratic Party	1983–87	Benedetto (Bettino) Craxi	Socialist Party
1959–60	Antonio Segni	Christian Democratic Party	1987	Amintore Fanfani	Christian Democratic Party
1960	Fernando Tambroni	Christian Democratic Party	1987–88	Giovanni Goria	Christian Democratic Party
1960–63	Amintore Fanfani	Christian Democratic Party	1988–89	Ciriaco de Mita	Christian Democratic Party
1963	Giovanni Leone	Christian Democratic Party	1989–92	Giulio Andreotti	Christian Democratic Party
1963–68	Aldo Moro	Christian Democratic Party	1992–93	Giuliano Amato	Socialist Party
1968	Giovanni Leone	Christian Democratic Party	1993–94	Carlo Azeglio Ciampi	Christian Democratic Party
1968–70	Mariano Rumor	Christian Democratic Party	1994–95	Silvio Berlusconi	Freedom Alliance
1970–72	Emilio Colombo	Christian Democratic Party	1995–96	Lamberto Dini	independent
1972–73	Giulio Andreotti	Christian Democratic Party	1996–	Romano Prodi	Olive Tree Alliance
1973–74	Mariano Rumor	Christian Democratic Party			

Norwegian Prime Ministers from 1945

Term	Name	Party
1945–51	Einar Gerhardsen	Labour Party
1951–55	Oscar Torp	Labour Party
1955–63	Einar Gerhardsen	Labour Party
1963	John Lyng	Conservative Party
1963–65	Einar Gerhardsen	Labour Party
1965–71	Per Borten	Centre Party
1971–72	Trygve Bratteli	Labour Party
1972–73	Lars Korvald	Christian People's Party
1973–76	Trygve Bratteli	Labour Party
1976–81	Odvar Nordli	Labour Party
1981	Gro Harlem Brundtland	Labour Party
1981–86	Kaare Willoch	Conservative Party
1986–89	Gro Harlem Brundtland	Labour Party
1989–90	Jan Syse	Conservative Party
1990–96	Gro Harlem Brundtland	Labour Party
1996–97	Thorbjoern Jagland	Labour Party
1997–	Kjell Magne Bondevik	Christian People's Party

Norwegian Monarchs from 1905

Reign	Name
1905–40	Haakon VII (exiled)
1940–45	German occupation
1945–57	Haakon VII (restored)
1957–91	Olaf V
1991–	Harald V

Polish Political Leaders from 1945

Term	Name	Party
Communist Party Leaders[1]		
1945–48	Władysław Gomułka	
1948–56	Boleslaw Bierut	
1956	Edward Ochab	
1956–70	Władysław Gomułka	
1970–80	Edward Gierek	
1980–81	Stanisław Kania	
1981–89	Wojciech Jaruzelski	
Presidents		
1990–95	Lech Wałesa	Solidarity/independent
1995–	Aleksander Kwaśniewski	Democratic Left Alliance

[1] From 1945–90 the political leaders were the Communist Party leaders.

Roman Emperors 27 BC–337 AD

Reign	Name	Reign	Name	Reign	Name
Julio-Claudian Emperors		*Despotic Emperors*		238	Pupienus
27 BC–14 AD	Augustus	161–80	Marcus Aurelius	238–44	Gordian III
14–37	Tiberius I	180–92	Commodus[2]	244–49	Philip (I) the Arab
37–41	Caligula (Gaius Caesar)	193	Pertinax	249–51	Trajan Decius
41–54	Claudius I	193	Didius Julianus	251–53	Trebonianus Gallus
54–68	Nero			251–53	Volusianus
		The Severi		253–60	Valerian
Civil Wars		193–211	Septimus Severus	253–68	Gallienus
68–69	Galba	193–97	Clodius Albinus	268–70	Claudius II
69	Otho	193–94	Pescennius Niger	270	Quintillus
69	Vitellius	211–217	Caracalla	270–75	Aurelian
		209–12	Geta	275–76	Tacitus
Flavian Emperors		217–18	Macrinus	276	Florianus
69–79	Vespasian	218	Diadumenianus	276–82	Probus
79–81	Titus	218–22	Elagabalus	282–83	Carus
81–96	Domitian	222–35	Alexander Severus	283–85	Carinus
96–98	Nerva			283–84	Numerianus
98–117	Trajan	*The Soldier Emperors*		284–305	Diocletian[3]
117–38	Hadrian	235–38	Maximinus	286–305	Maximianus
		238	Gordian I	293–306	Constantius I
Antonine Emperors		238	Gordian II	293–311	Galerius
138–61[1]	Antoninus Pius	238	Balbinus	305–337	Constantine I
161–69[1]	Lucius Verus				

[1] Divided voluntarily between two brothers.
[2] Between 180 and 284 there was a succession of emperors placed on the throne by their respective armies or factions. Therefore, dates of emperors' reigns in this period often overlap.
[3] The end of Diocletian's reign marked the split of the Roman empire. Whereas Diocletian retained supreme power, Maximianus ruled Italy and Africa, Constantius I ruled Gaul and Spain, and Galerius ruled Thrace.

Russian Tsars from 1547

Reign	Name
House of Rurik	
1547–84	Ivan the Terrible
1584–98	Theodore (Fyodor) I
1598	Irina
House of Godunov	
1598–1605	Boris Godunov
1605	Theodore (Fyodor) II
Usurpers	
1605–06	Dimitri III
1606–10	Basil IV
1610–13 Interregnum	
House of Romanov	
1613–45	Michael Romanov
1645–76	Alexis
1676–82	Theodore III
1682–96	Peter (I) the Great and Ivan V (brothers)
1689–1721	Peter I, as tsar
1721–25	Peter I, as emperor
1725–27	Catherine I
1727–30	Peter II
1730–40	Anna Ivanovna
1740–41	Ivan VI
1741–62	Elizabeth
1762	Peter III
1762–96	Catherine (II) the Great
1796–1801	Paul
1801–25	Alexander I
1825–55	Nicholas I
1855–81	Alexander II
1881–94	Alexander III
1894–1917	Nicholas II

Scottish Monarchs 1005–1603

This table covers the period from the unification of Scotland to the union of the crowns of Scotland and England.

Reign	Name	Reign	Name
Celtic Kings		*English Domination*	
1005–34	Malcolm II	1292–96	John Baliol
1034–40	Duncan I	1296–1306	annexed to England
1040–57	Macbeth	*House of Bruce*	
1057–93	Malcolm III Canmore	1306–29	Robert I the Bruce
1093–94	Donald III Donalbane	1329–71	David II
1094	Duncan II		
1094–97	Donald III (restored)	*House of Stuart*	
1097–1107	Edgar	1371–90	Robert II
1107–24	Alexander I	1390–1406	Robert III
1124–53	David I	1406–37	James I
1153–65	Malcolm IV	1437–60	James II
1165–1214	William the Lion	1460–88	James III
1214–49	Alexander II	1488–1513	James IV
1249–86	Alexander III	1513–42	James V
1286–90	Margaret of Norway	1542–67	Mary
		1567–1625	James VI[1]

[1]After the union of crowns in 1603, he became James I of England.

Soviet and Russian Presidents and Communist Party Leaders

Term	Name	Term	Name
USSR		1960–64	Leonid Brezhnev
Communist Party Leaders		1964–65	Anastas Mikoyan
1917–22	Vladimir Ilich Lenin	1965–77	Nikolai Podgorny
1922–53	Joseph Stalin	1977–82	Leonid Brezhnev
1953–64	Nikita Khrushchev	1982–83	Valery Kuznetsov (acting)
1964–82	Leonid Brezhnev	1983–84	Yuri Andropov
1982–84	Yuri Andropov	1984	Valery Kuznetsov (acting)
1984–85	Konstantin Chernenko	1984–85	Konstantin Chernenko
1985–91	Mikhail Gorbachev	1985	Valery Kuznetsov (acting)
		1985–88	Andrei Gromyko
Presidents		1988–91	Mikhail Gorbachev
1917–22	Vladimir Ilich Lenin[1]		
1919–46	Mikhail Kalinin[2]	**Russia**	
1946–53	Nikolai Shvernik	*Presidents*	
1953–60	Marshal Kliment Voroshilov	1991–	Boris Yeltsin

© United Nations

Mikhail Gorbachev

[1] In 1917 Lenin was elected chairman of the Council of People's Commisars, that is, head of government. He held that post until 1922.
[2] In 1919, Kalinin became head of state (president of the Central Executive Committee of the Soviet government until 1937; president of the Presidium of the Supreme Soviet until 1946.)

Spanish Rulers 1516–1931

Reign	Name
House of Habsburg	
1516–56	Charles I
1556–98	Philip II
1598–1621	Philip III
1621–65	Philip IV
1665–1700	Charles II
House of Bourbon	
1700–46	Philip V
1746–59	Ferdinand VI
1759–88	Charles III
1788–1808	Charles IV
1808	Ferdinand VII (deposed)
1808–13	Joseph Napoleon[1]
1813–33	Ferdinand VII (restored)
1833–68	Isabel II
1868–70	provisional government
1870–73	Amadeus I[2] (abdicated)
1873–74	first republic
1874–86	Alfonso XII
1886–1931	Alfonso XIII (deposed)

[1] House of Bonaparte.
[2] House of Savoy.

Spanish Presidents, Chiefs of State, and Prime Ministers from 1931

Term	Name	Party
Presidents		
1931–36	Niceto Alcala Zamora	Liberal Republicans
1936	Diego Martínez y Barro	Radical Party
1936–39	Manuel Azaña y Diéz	Left Republican Party
Chiefs of State		
1939–75	Francisco Franco y Bahamonde	National Movement/Falange
Prime Ministers		
1931–33	Manuel Azaña y Diéz	Left Republican Party
1933	Alejandro Lerroux y García	Radical Republican Party
1933	Diego Martínez y Barro	Radical Republican Party
1933–34	Alejandro Lerroux y García	Radical Republican Party
1934	Ricardo Samper Ibañez	Radical Republican Party–Valencian branch
1934–35	Alejandro Lerroux y García	Radical Republican Party
1935	Joaquín Chapaprieta y Terragosa	independent
1935–36	Manuel Portela Valladares	Radical Republican Party
1936	Manuel Azaña y Diéz	Left Republican Party
1936	Santiago Cásares Quiroga	Left Republican Party
1936	José Giral y Pereira	Left Republican Party
1936–37	Francisco Largo Caballero	Socialist Party
1937–39	Juan Negrin	Socialist Party
1939–73	Francisco Franco Bahamonde	National Movement
1973	Luis Carrero Blanco	National Movement
1973–74	Torcuato Fernández Miranda	National Movement
1974–76	Carlos Arias Navarro	National Movement
1976–81	Adolfo Suárez González	Union of the Democratic Centre
1981–82	Leopoldo Calvo-Sotelo y Bustelo	Union of the Democratic Centre
1982–96	Felipe González Márquez	Socialist Workers' Party
1996–	José María Aznar	Popular Party

Swedish Prime Ministers from 1946

Term	Name	Party
1946–69	Tage Erlander	Social Democratic Labour Party
1969–76	Olof Palme	Social Democratic Labour Party
1976–78	Thorbjörn Fälldin	Centre Party
1978–79	Ola Ullsten	Liberal Party
1979–82	Thorbjörn Fälldin	Centre Party
1982–86	Olof Palme	Social Democratic Labour Party
1986–91	Ingvar Carlsson	Social Democratic Labour Party
1991–94	Carl Bildt	Moderate Party
1994–96	Ingvar Carlsson	Social Democratic Labour Party
1996–	Göran Persson	Social Democratic Labour Party

Swedish Monarchs from 950

Period	Name	Period	Name	Period	Name
950–95	Erik VIII	1356–59	Magnus II Eriksson/Eric XII	1560–68	Erik XIV
995–1022	Olof	1359–62	Magnus II Eriksson	1568–92	Johan III
1022–50	Anund Jakob	1362–63	Magnus II Eriksson/Haakon	1592–99	Sigismund
1050–60	Edmund	1364–89	Albrekt	1604–1611	Carl IX
1060–80	Stenkil	1389–97	Margrethe	1611–32	Gustaf II Adolf
1080–1110	Inge I/Halsten	1397–1434	Erik XIII	1632–54	Christina
1110–18	Filip	1434–36	Regent: Engelbrekt Engelbrektsson	1654–60	Carl X Gustaf
1118–22	Inge II			1660–97	Carl XI
1130–56	Sverker I	1436–40	Regent: Carl Knutsson	1697–1718	Carl XII
1150–60	Erik IX Jerdvardsson	1441–48	Christoffer	1718–20	Ulrica Eleonora
1161–67	Carl VII Sverkersson	1448–57	Carl VIII Knutsson	1720–51	Fredrik
1167–96	Knut I Eriksson	1457–64	Christian I	1751–71	Adolf Fredrik
1196–1208	Sverker II Carlsson	1464–65	Carl VIII Knutsson	1771–92	Gustaf III
1208–16	Erik X Eriksson	1465–67	Interregnum	1792–1809	Gustaf IV Adolf
1216–22	Johan I Sverkersson	1467–70	Carl VIII Knutsson	1809–18	Carl XIII
1222–29	Erik XI Eriksson	1470–97	Sten Sture the Elder (regent)	1818–44	Carl XIV Johan
1229–34	Knut II	1497–1501	Johan II	1844–59	Oscar I
1234–50	Erik XI Eriksson	1501–03	Sten Sture the Elder (regent)	1859–72	Carl XV
1250–75	Valdemar	1503–12	Svante Sture (regent)	1872–1907	Oscar II
1275–90	Magnus I Laduläs	1512–20	Sten Sture the Younger (regent)	1907–50	Gustaf V
1290–1318	Birgir Magnusson	1520–23	Christian II	1950–73	Gustaf VI Adolf
1319–56	Magnus II Eriksson	1523–60	Gustaf I	1973–	Carl XVI Gustaf

United Kingdom Prime Ministers from 1721

Term	Name	Party	Term	Name	Party
1721–42	Sir Robert Walpole	Whig	1886	W E Gladstone	Liberal
1742–43	Earl of Wilmington	Whig	1886–92	Marquess of Salisbury	Conservative
1743–54	Henry Pelham	Whig	1892–94	W E Gladstone	Liberal
1754–56	Duke of Newcastle	Whig	1894–95	Earl of Rosebery	Liberal
1756–57	Duke of Devonshire	Whig	1895–1902	Marquess of Salisbury	Conservative
1757–62	Duke of Newcastle	Whig	1902–05	Arthur James Balfour	Conservative
1762–63	Earl of Bute	Tory	1905–08	Sir H Campbell-Bannerman	Liberal
1763–65	George Grenville	Whig	1908–15	H H Asquith	Liberal
1765–66	Marquess of Rockingham	Whig	1915–16	H H Asquith	coalition
1767–70	Duke of Grafton	Whig	1916–22	David Lloyd George	coalition
1770–82	Lord North	Tory	1922–23	Andrew Bonar Law	Conservative
1782	Marquess of Rockingham	Whig	1923–24	Stanley Baldwin	Conservative
1782–83	Earl of Shelburne	Whig	1924	Ramsay MacDonald	Labour
1783	Duke of Portland	coalition	1924–29	Stanley Baldwin	Conservative
1783–1801	William Pitt the Younger	Tory	1929–31	Ramsay MacDonald	Labour
1801–04	Henry Addington	Tory	1931–35	Ramsay MacDonald	national coalition
1804–06	William Pitt the Younger	Tory	1935–37	Stanley Baldwin	national coalition
1806–07	Lord Grenville	coalition	1937–40	Neville Chamberlain	national coalition
1807–09	Duke of Portland	Tory	1940–45	Sir Winston Churchill	coalition
1809–12	Spencer Perceval	Tory	1945–51	Clement Attlee	Labour
1812–27	Earl of Liverpool	Tory	1951–55	Sir Winston Churchill	Conservative
1827	George Canning	coalition	1955–57	Sir Anthony Eden	Conservative
1827–28	Viscount Goderich	Tory	1957–63	Harold Macmillan	Conservative
1828–30	Duke of Wellington	Tory	1963–64	Sir Alec Douglas-Home	Conservative
1830–34	Earl Grey	Tory	1964–70	Harold Wilson	Labour
1834	Viscount Melbourne	Whig	1970–74	Edward Heath	Conservative
1834–35	Sir Robert Peel	Whig	1974–76	Harold Wilson	Labour
1835–41	Viscount Melbourne	Whig	1976–79	James Callaghan	Labour
1841–46	Sir Robert Peel	Conservative	1979–90	Margaret Thatcher	Conservative
1846–52	Lord Russell	Liberal	1990–97	John Major	Conservative
1852	Earl of Derby	Conservative	1997–	Tony Blair	Labour
1852–55	Lord Aberdeen	Peelite			
1855–58	Viscount Palmerston	Liberal			
1858–59	Earl of Derby	Conservative			
1859–65	Viscount Palmerston	Liberal			
1865–66	Lord Russell	Liberal			
1866–68	Earl of Derby	Conservative			
1868	Benjamin Disraeli	Conservative			
1868–74	W E Gladstone	Liberal			
1874–80	Benjamin Disraeli	Conservative			
1880–85	W E Gladstone	Liberal			
1885–86	Marquess of Salisbury	Conservative			

© United Nations

Margaret Thatcher

Rulers and Political Leaders of the Americas

Argentine Presidents from 1944

Term	Name	Party
1944–46	Edelmiro Farrell	military
1946–55	Juan Perón	Justice Front of Liberation
1955	Eduardo Lonardi	military
1955–58	Pedro Aramburu	military
1958–62	Arturo Frondizi	Civic Radical Union-Intransigent
1962–63	José Guido	acting: independent
1963–66	Arturo Illía	Civic Radical Union of the People
1966–70	Juan Onganía	military
1970–71	Roberto Levingston	military
1971–73	Alejandro Lanusse	military
1973	Héctor Cámpora	Justice Front of Liberation
1973	Raúl Lastiri	acting: independent
1973–74	Juan Perón	Justice Front of Liberation
1974–76	Maria Estela de Perón	Justice Front of Liberation
1976–81	Jorge Videla	military
1981	Roberto Viola	military
1981–82	Leopoldo Galtieri	military
1982	Alfredo Saint-Jean	acting: military
1982–83	Reynaldo Bignone	military
1983–89	Raúl Alfonsín	Civic Radical Union
1989–	Carlos Saúl Menem	Justice Party

Brazilian Presidents from 1945

Term	Name	Party
1945–46	José Linhares	independent
1946–51	Eurico Dutra	Social Democratic Party
1951–54	Getúlio Vargas	Brazil Labour Party
1954–55	João Café	Social Progressive Party
1955	Carlos da Luz	independent
1955–56	Nereu Ramos	independent
1956–61	Juscelino Kubitschek	Social Democratic Party
1961	Jânio Quadros	Christian Democratic Party/Democratic National Union
1961–64	João Goulart	Brazil Labour Party
1964	Ranieri Mazzili	independent
1964–67	Humberto Branco	military
1967–69	Arthur da Costa e Silva	military
1969–74	Emilio Medici	military
1974–79	Ernesto Geisel	military
1979–85	João Figueiredo	military
1985–89	José Sarney	Social Democratic Party
1989–92	Fernando Collor de Mello	National Reconstruction Party
1992–94	Itamar Franco	National Reconstruction Party
1995–	Fernando Henrique Cardoso	Social Democratic Party

Mexican Prime Ministers from 1946

Term	Name	Party
1946–52	Miguel Alemán Valdés	Institutional Revolutionary Party
1952–58	Adolfo Ruiz Cortines	Institutional Revolutionary Party
1958–64	Adolfo López Mateos	Institutional Revolutionary Party
1964–70	Gustavo Díaz Ordaz	Institutional Revolutionary Party
1970–76	Luís Echeverría Alvarez	Institutional Revolutionary Party
1976–82	José López Portillo y Pacheco	Institutional Revolutionary Party
1982–88	Miguel de la Madrid Hurtado	Institutional Revolutionary Party
1988–94	Carlos Salinas de Gortari	Institutional Revolutionary Party
1994–	Ernesto Zedillo Ponce de Léon	Institutional Revolutionary Party

Aztec Emperors c. 1372–1521

Reign[1]	Name
c. 1372–c. 91	Acamapichtli (chieftain at Tenochtitlán; traditional founder of Aztec royal house)
c. 1391–c. 1416	Huitzilihuitl (son)
c. 1416–c. 27	Chimalpopoca (son)
c. 1427–c. 40	Itzcoatl (son of Acamapichtli)
c. 1440–c. 68	(Huehue) Motecuhzoma
c. 1468–81	Axayacatl (grandson of Itzcoatl)
1481–86	Tizoc (brother)
1486–1502	Ahuitzotl (brother)
1502–20	Motecuhzoma Xocoyotl (son of Axayacatl); known as Montezuma II
1520	Cuitlahuac (brother)
1520–21	Cuauhtemoc (son of Ahuitzotl)

[1] Dates before 1468 are approximate

Inca Emperors c. 1200–1572

Reign	Name
The Kingdom of Cuzco	
c. 1200–1400	Manco Capac[1]
	Sinchi Roca[1]
	Lloque Yupanqui[1]
	Mayta Capac[1]
	Capac Yupanqui[2]
	Inca Roca[2]
	Yahuar Huacadc[2]
until 1438	Viracocha Inca
The Empire	
1438–71	Pachacuti
1471–93	Topa Inca
1493–1528	Huayna Capac
1528–32	Huascar
1532–33	Atahualpa
The Vilcabamba State	
1533	Topa Hualpa
1533–45	Manco Inca
1545–60	Sayri Tupac
1560–71	Titu Cusi Yupanqui
1571–72	Tupac Amaru

[1] This is a mythical figure.
[2] The dates of his reign are unknown.

Canadian Prime Ministers from 1867

Term	Name	Party	Term	Name	Party
1867–73	John A Macdonald	Conservative	1930–35	Richard B Bennett	Conservative
1873–78	Alexander Mackenzie	Liberal	1935–48	William L M King	Liberal
1878–91	John A Macdonald	Conservative	1948–57	Louis S St Laurent	Liberal
1891–92	John J Abbott	Conservative	1957–63	John G Diefenbaker	Conservative
1892–94	John S D Thompson	Conservative	1963–68	Lester B Pearson	Liberal
1894–96	Mackenzie Bowell	Conservative	1968–79	Pierre E Trudeau	Liberal
1896	Charles Tupper	Conservative	1979–80	Joseph Clark	Progressive Conservative
1896–1911	Wilfred Laurier	Liberal	1980–84	Pierre E Trudeau	Liberal
1911–20	Robert L Borden	Conservative	1984	John Turner	Liberal
1920–21	Arthur Meighen	Conservative	1984–93	Brian Mulroney	Progressive Conservative
1921–26	William L M King	Liberal	1993	Kim Campbell	Progressive Conservative
1926	Arthur Meighen	Conservative	1993–	Jean Chretien	Liberal
1926–30	William L M King	Liberal			

Leaders of South American Wars of Liberation

Leader	Lifespan	Details
Artigas, José Gervasio	1764–1850	Uruguayan independence leader from 1811 and national hero
Bolívar, Simón	1783–1830	born in Caracas, Venezuela, into a wealthy Creole[1] landowning family; he became president of Venezuela in 1817 and of Colombia in 1819; known as 'the Liberator'
Boyer, Jean-Pierre	1776–1850	Haitian mulatto[2] leader who left the regular army to join the revolutionary forces and became president (1818–43)
Christophe, Henry	1767–1820	Grenada-born Haitian revolutionary leader, from 1793, who became president of the black-led north in 1807 and ruled from 1811 as King Henry I
Dessalines, Jean-Jacques	1758–1806	Haitian revolutionary leader of African slave descent who took over the liberation struggle against the French after the arrest of Toussaint L'Ouverture in 1802, securing independence in 1804
Flores, Juan José	1800–1864	Ecuadoran freedom fighter and first president; the illegitimate son of a Spanish merchant, he fought in the royalist army until 1817, when, on being taken prisoner, he joined Bolívar's patriot forces
Lavalleja, Juan Antonio	1784–1853	Uruguayan soldier and independence leader from 1811 and loyal follower of Artigas
Miranda, Francisca de	1750–1816	born in Caracas, Venezuela, of Creole parents, he lived in exile in London, before leading a revolt against the Spanish in Venezuela in 1810; he capitulated to the royalists in 1812 and was disowned by fellow freedom fighters, including Bolívar, and died in a prison in Cadiz, Spain
O'Higgins, Bernardo	1778–1842	illegitimate son of an Irish-born viceroy of Chile and Peru, with San Martin he played a key role in the liberation of Chile between 1810 and 1818 and became head of the new government
Páez, José Antonio	1790–1873	Venezuelan military leader of the llaneros (plains people) who joined Bolívar's forces in 1818; he became president in 1831 and remained dominant until 1848
Rivera, José Fructuoso	1784–1854	Uruguayan independence leader, a follower of Artigas and the country's first president
San Martín, General José de	1778–1850	Argentinian-born leader of the Army of the Andes, which secured the independence of Chile in 1818 and Peru in 1821
Santander, Francisco de Paula	1792–1840	Colombian general and political leader who was left by Bolívar to organize newly liberated New Granada from 1819
Sucre, General Antonio José de	1795–1830	Venezuelan-born general in Bolívar's army who liberated Quito in 1822 and secured Bolivia's independence in 1824
Toussaint L'Ouverture, Dominique	1743–1803	Haitian revolutionary leader of African slave descent who led the revolt against French rule in 1800, but was captured and died in prison in France

[1] Creole = Spaniard born in America.
[2] Mulatto = of mixed European and African blood.

US Presidents

Year elected/ took office	President	Party	Losing candidate(s)	Party
1789	1. George Washington	Federalist	No opponent	
1792	Re-elected		No opponent	
1796	2. John Adams	Federalist	Thomas Jefferson	Democrat-Republican
1800	3. Thomas Jefferson	Democrat-Republican	Aaron Burr	Democrat-Republican
1804	Re-elected		Charles Pinckney	Federalist
1808	4. James Madison	Democrat-Republican	Charles Pinckney	Federalist
1812	Re-elected		DeWitt Clinton	Federalist
1816	5. James Monroe	Democrat-Republican	Rufus King	Federalist
1820	Re-elected		John Quincy Adams	Democrat-Republican
1824	6. John Quincy Adams	Democrat-Republican	Andrew Jackson	Democrat-Republican

(continued)

US Presidents (continued)

Year elected/ took office	President	Party	Losing candidate(s)	Party
			Henry Clay	Democrat-Republican
			William H Crawford	Democrat-Republican
1828	7. Andrew Jackson	Democrat	John Quincy Adams	National Republican
1832	Re-elected		Henry Clay	National Republican
1836	8. Martin Van Buren	Democrat	William Henry Harrusib	Whig
1840	9. William Henry Harrison	Whig	Martin Van Buren	Democrat
1841	10. John Tyler[1]	Whig		
1844	11. James Knox Polk	Democrat	Henry Clay	Whig
1848	12. Zachary Taylor	Whig	Lewis Cass	Democrat
1850	13. Millard Fillmore[2]	Whig		
1852	14. Franklin Pierce	Democrat	Winfield Scott	Whig
1856	15. James Buchanan	Democrat	John C Fremont	Republican
1860	16. Abraham Lincoln	Republican	Stephen Douglas	Democrat
			John Breckinridge	Democrat
			John Bell	Constitutional Union
1864	Re-elected		George McClellan	Democrat
1865	17. Andrew Johnson[3]	Democrat		
1868	18. Ulysses S Grant	Republican	Horatio Seymour	Democrat
1872	Re-elected		Horace Greeley	Democrat-Liberal Republican
1876	19. Rutherford B Hayes	Republican	Samuel Tilden	Democrat
1880	20. James A Garfield	Republican	Winfield Hancock	Democrat
1881	21. Chester Alun Arthur[4]	Republican		
1884	22. Grover Cleveland	Democrat	James Blaine	Republican
1888	23. Benjamin Harrison	Republican	Grover Cleveland	Democrat
1892	24. Grover Cleveland	Democrat	Benjamin Harrison	Republican
		James Weaver	People's	
1896	25. William McKinley	Republican	William J Bryan	Democrat-People's
1900	Re-elected		William J Bryan	Democrat
1901	26. Theodore Roosevelt[5]	Republican		
1904	Re-elected		Alton B Parker	Democrat
1908	27. William Howard Taft	Republican	William J Bryan	Democrat
1912	28. Woodrow Wilson	Democrat	Theodore Roosevelt	Progressive
			William Howard Taft	Republican
1916	Re-elected		Charles E Hughes	Republican
1920	29. Warren Gamaliel Harding	Republican	James M Cox	Democrat
1923	30. Calvin Coolidge[6]	Republican		
1924	Re-elected		John W Davis	Democrat
		Robert M LeFollette	Progressive	
1928	31. Herbert C Hoover	Republican	Alfred E Smith	Democrat
1932	32. Franklin Delano Roosevelt	Democrat	Herbert C Hoover	Republican
			Norman Thomas	Socialist
1936	Re-elected		Alfred Landon	Republican
1940	Re-elected		Wendell Wilkie	Republican
1944	Re-elected		Thomas E Dewey	Republican
1945	33. Harry S Truman[7]	Democrat		
1948	Re-elected		Thomas E Dewey	Republican
			J Strom Thurmond	States' Rights
			Henry A Wallace	Progressive
1952	34. Dwight D Eisenhower	Republican	Adlai E Stevenson	Democrat
1956	Re-elected		Adlai E Stevenson	Democrat
1960	35. John F Kennedy	Democrat	Richard M Nixon	Republican
1963	36. Lyndon B Johnson[8]	Democrat		
1964	Re-elected		Barry M Goldwater	Republican
1968	37. Richard M Nixon	Republican	Hubert H Humphrey	Democrat
		George C Wallace	American Independent	
1972	Re-elected		George S McGovern	Democrat
1974	38. Gerald R Ford[9]	Republican		
1976	39. James Earl Carter	Democrat	Gerald R Ford	Republican
1980	40. Ronald Reagan	Republican	James Earl Carter	Democrat
			John B Anderson	Independent
1984	Re-elected		Walter Mondale	Democrat
1988	41. George Bush	Republican	Michael Dukakis	Democrat
			Ross Perot	Independent
1992	42. Bill Clinton	Democrat	George Bush	Republican
1996	Re-elected		Bob Dole	Republican
			Ross Perot	Reform

[1] Became president on death of Harrison.
[2] Became president on death of Taylor.
[3] Became president on assassination of Lincoln.
[4] Became president on assassination of Garfield.
[5] Became president on assassination of McKinley.

[6] Became president on death of Harding.
[7] Became president on assassination of F D Roosevelt.
[8] Became president on assassination of Kennedy.
[9] Became president on resignation of Nixon.

Middle Eastern Rulers and Political Leaders

Egyptian Dynasties

Period	Name	Description	Period	Name	Description
Early Dynastic Period			*Third Intermediate Period*		
c. 3100–c. 2905 BC	First Dynastic Period	Thinite	c. 1070–c. 946 BC	Twenty-first Dynasty	Theban
c. 2905–c. 2755 BC	Second Dynasty	Thinite	c. 946–c. 712 BC	Twenty-second Dynasty	Bubastite
			c. 828–c. 720 BC	Twenty-third Dynasty	Tanite
Old Kingdom			c. 740–c. 712 BC	Twenty-fourth Dynasty	Saite
c. 2755–c. 2680 BC	Third Dynasty	Memphite	c. 767–c. 656 BC	Twenty-fifth Dynasty	Nubian
c. 2680–c. 2544 BC	Fourth Dynasty	Memphite			
c. 2544–c. 2407 BC	Fifth Dynasty	Memphite	*Saite Period*		
c. 2407–c. 2255 BC	Sixth Dynasty	Memphite	c. 664–c. 525 BC	Twenty-sixth Dynasty	Nubian
First Intermediate Period			*Later Dynastic Period*		
c. 2255–c. 2235 BC	Seventh–Eighth Dynasties	Memphite	c. 525–c. 405 BC	Twenty-seventh Dynasty	Persian Kings
c. 2235–c. 2035 BC	Ninth–Tenth Dynasties	Heracleopolitan	c. 405–c. 399 BC	Twenty-eighth Dynasty	Saite
			c. 399–c. 380 BC	Twenty-ninth Dynasty	Mendesian
Middle Kingdom			c. 380–c. 343 BC	Thirtieth Dynasty	Sebennytic
c. 2134–c. 1991 BC	Eleventh Dynasty	Theban	c. 343–332 BC	Thirty-first Dynasty	Persian Kings
c. 1991–c. 1786 BC	Twelfth Dynasty	Theban			
			Conquest of Egypt by Alexander the Great		
Second Intermediate Period			332–323 BC	Alexander the Great	
c. 1786–c. 1668 BC	Thirteenth Dynasty	Theban			
c. 1720–c. 1665 BC	Fourteenth Dynasty	Xoite	*Ptolemaic Period*		
c. 1668–c. 1560 BC	Fifteenth Dynasty	Hyksos	323–30 BC	Ptolemaic Dynasty	Ptolemies
c. 1665–c. 1565 BC	Sixteenth Dynasty	Hyksos			
c. 1668–c. 1570 BC	Seventeenth Dynasty	Theban	*Conquest of Egypt by Octavian (Augustus) in 30 BC*		
New Kingdom					
c. 1570–c. 1293 BC	Eighteenth Dynasty	Theban			
c. 1293–c. 1185 BC	Nineteenth Dynasty	Theban			
c. 1185–c. 1070 BC	Twentieth Dynasty	Theban			

Israeli Prime Ministers from 1948

Term	Name	Party	Term	Name	Party
1948–53	David Ben-Gurion	Mapai	1977–83	Menachem Begin	Likud
1953–55	M Sharett	Mapai	1983–84	Yitzhak Shamir	Likud
1955–63	David Ben-Gurion	Mapai	1984–86	Shimon Peres	Labour
1963–69	Levi Eshkol	Mapai/ Labour	1986–92	Yitzhak Shamir	Likud
			1992–95	Yitzhak Rabin	Labour
1969–74	Golda Meir	Labour	1995–96	Shimon Peres	Labour
1974–77	Yitzhak Rabin	Labour	1996–	Binjamin Netanyahu	Likud

Ottoman Emperors 1280–1922

Reign	Name	Reign	Name	Reign	Name
1280–c. 1326	Osman I	1520–66	Suleiman (I) the Magnificent	1703–30	Ahmed III
1324–62	Orhan	1566–74	Selim (II) the Sot	1730–54	Mahmud I
1362–89	Murad I	1574–95	Murad III	1754–57	Osman III
1389–1402	Bayezid(I) the Thunderbolt	1595–1603	Mehmed III	1757–74	Mustafa III
1402–03	Isa	1603–17	Ahmed I	1774–89	Abdulhamid I
1402–11	Suleiman	1617–18	Mustafa I	1789–1807	Selim III
1409–13	Mesa	1618–22	Osman II	1807–08	Mustafa IV
1413–21	Mehmed I	1622–23	Mustafa I	1808–39	Mahmud II
1421–44	Murad II	1623–40	Murad IV	1839–61	Abdulmecid I
1444–46	Mehmed (II) the Conqueror	1640–48	Ibrahim	1861–76	Abdulaziz
1446–51	Murad II	1648–87	Mehmed IV	1876	Murad V
1451–81	Mehmed (II) the Conqueror	1687–91	Suleiman II	1876–1909	Abdulhamid II
1481–1512	Bayezid II	1691–95	Ahmed II	1909–18	Mehmed V
1512–20	Selim (I) the Grim	1695–1703	Mustafa II	1918–22	Mehmed VI

African Rulers and Political Leaders

Kenyan Presidents from 1963

Term	Name	Party
1963–78	Jomo Kenyatta	Kenya African National Union (KANU)
1978–	Daniel arap Moi	KANU

South African Prime Ministers and Presidents from 1910

Term	Name
Prime Ministers	
1910–19	L Botha
1919–24	Jan Smuts
1924–39	James Hertzog
1939–48	Jan Smuts
1948–54	Daniel Malan
1954–58	J Strijdon
1958–66	Hendrik Verwoerd
1966–78	Balthazar Johannes Vorster
1978–84	Pieter Botha
Presidents[1]	
1984–89	Pieter Botha
1989–94	F W de Klerk
1994–	Nelson Mandela

[1] The post of prime minister was abolished in 1984 and combined with that of president.

Nigerian Leaders from 1960

Term	Name	Party
Governor-Generals		
1960	James Robertson	independent
1960–63	Nnamdi Azikiwe	Nigerian National Democratic Party
Presidents[1]		
1963–66	Nnamdi Azikiwe	Nigerian National Democratic Party
1966	Johnson Aguiyi-Ironsi	military
1966–75	Colonel Yakubu Gowon	military
1975–76	Murtala Mohammed	military
1976–79	General Olusegun Obasanjo	military
1979–83	Shehu Shagari	National Party of Nigeria
1983–85	Major General Mohammed Buhari	military
1985–93	Major General Ibrahim Babangida	military
1993	Ernest Shonekan	independent
1993–98	General Sani Abacha	military
1998–	General Abdusalam Abubakar	military

[1] Heads of state from January 1966 until October 1979 and from December 1983 did not officially use the title of president.

Asian Rulers and Political Leaders

Chinese Dynasties

Period	Dynasty	Major events
c. 2205–c. 1776 BC	Hsia[1]	agriculture; use of bronze, first writing
c. 1776–c. 1027 BC	Shang or Yin	first major dynasty; first Chinese calendar
c. 1027–c. 256 BC	Zhou	developed society using money, iron, and written laws; age of Confucius
221–206 BC	Qin	unification after period of Warring States; building of Great Wall begun; roads built
206 BC–AD 220	Han	first centralized and effectively administered empire; introduction of Buddhism
220–265	Wei, Shu, Wu (Three Kingdoms)	division into three parts; prolonged fighting (Three Kingdoms) and eventual victory of Wei over Shu and Wu; Confucianism superseded by Buddhism and Taoism
265–317	Tsin	beginning of Hun invasions in the north
581–618	Sui	reunification; barbarian invasions stopped; Great Wall refortified
618–907	T'ang	centralized government; empire greatly extended; period of excellence in sculpture, painting, and poetry
907–960	Wu Tai (Five Dynasties)	economic depression and loss of territory in northern China, central Asia, and Korea; first use of paper money
960–1279	Song	period of calm and creativity; printing developed (movable type); central government restored; northern and western frontiers neglected and Mongol incursions begun
1279–1368	Yüan	beginning of Mongol rule in China, under Kublai Khan; Marco Polo visited China; dynasty brought to an end by widespread revolts, centred in Mongolia
1368–1644	Ming	Mongols driven out by native Chinese, Mongolia captured by 2nd Ming emperor; period of architectural development; Beijing flourished as new capital
1644–1912	Qing (Manchu)	China once again under non-Chinese rule, the Qing conquered by nomads from Manchuria; trade with the West; culture flourished, but conservatism eventually led to the dynasty's overthrow by nationalistic revolutionaries led by Sun Yatsen

[1] This dynasty is also known as Xia. It was a legendary and historically doubtful dynasty.

Chinese Prime Ministers and Communist Party Leaders

Term	Name
Prime Ministers	
1949–76	Zhou Enlai
1976–80	Hua Guofeng
1980–88	Zhao Ziyang
1988–	Li Peng
Communist Party Leaders	
1935–76	Mao Zedong
1976–81	Hua Guofeng
1981–87	Hu Yaobang
1987–89	Zhao Ziyang
1989–	Jiang Zemin

Indian Prime Ministers

Term	Name	Party
1947–64	Jawaharlal Nehru	Congress
1964–66	Lal Bahadur Shastri	Congress
1966–77	Indira Gandhi	Congress (I)
1977–79	Morarji Desai	Janata
1979–80	Charan Singh	Janata/Lok Dal
1980–84	Indira Gandhi	Congress (I)
1984–89	Rajiv Gandhi	Congress (I)
1989–90	Viswanath Pratap Singh	Janata Dal
1990–91	Chandra Shekhar	Janata Dal (Socialist)
1991–96	P V Narasimha Rao	Congress (I)
1996	Atal Behari Vaj Payee	Bharatiya Janata Party
1996–97	H D Deve Gowda	Janata Dal
1997–	Inder Kumar Gujral	Janata Dal

Indian Dynasties and Rulers

Only major dynasties and the most important rulers are included. The dates given for dynasties and rulers cover periods of their importance. Dynasty names are in italic.

Reign	Name
Saisunaga Dynasty (Magadhan ascendancy, northern India) 7th–4th centuries BC	
c. 543–c. 491 BC	Bimbisara (Srenika)
c. 491–c. 461 BC	Ajashatru (Kunika)
Nandas[1] 4th century BC	
c. 362–c. 334 BC	Mahapadma and eight sons
Mauryan Empire (India, except the area south of Karnataka) 4th–2nd centuries BC	
c. 321–c. 298 BC	Chandragupta Maurya
c. 298–c. 272 BC	Bindusara Amitraghata
c. 272–c. 232 BC	Asoka (-vardhana)
c. 232–c. 185 BC	later Mauryas
Shungas (Ganges Valley and part of central India) 2nd–1st centuries BC	
c. 185–c. 173 BC	Pushyamitra (Pushpamitra)
Indo-Greeks (northwest India) 2nd–1st Centuries BC	
c. 180–c. 165 BC	Demetrius II
c. 155–c. 130 BC	Menander (Milinda)
Kanvas (northern India) c. 73–28 BC	
Satavahanas (north Deccan) 1st century BC–3rd cntury AD	
c. AD 120	Gautamiputra Satakarni
c. 130	Vashishthiputra Satakarni
c. 170–c. 200	Yajna Sri
Shakas (western India) 1st century BC–3rd century AD	
Kushanas (northern India and Central Asia) 1st century BC–3rd century AD	
c. 48–c. 78	Kadphises I
c. 78–c. 100	Kadphises II
c. 120–c. 162	Kanishka
c. 162–c. 182	Huvishka
c. 182–c. 220	Vasudeva
Guptas (northern India) 4th–6th centuries	
320–30	Chandragupta I
330–75	Samadragupta

Reign	Name
375–415	Chandragupta II Vikramaditya
415–54	Kumaragupta I
454–67	Skandagupta
467–99	Buddhagupta
Hunas (northwest India and Central Asia) 5th–6th centuries	
Maukharis 6th–7th centuries	
Later Guptas of Magadha 6th–7th centuries	
Harsha 7th century	
606–47	Harshavardana
Pallavas (Tamil Nadu) c. 300–888	
630–68	Narasimhavaraman
730–96	Nandivarman II
Chalukyas of Vatapi (west and central Deccan) c. 556–757	
610–43	Pukaleshin II
Pandyas of Madurai (Tamil Nadu) 7th–10th centuries	
768–815	Varuguna I
815–62	Shrimara Shrivallabha
862–67	Varuguna II
Eastern Chalukyas of Vengi (Andhra Pradesh) c. 630–970	
Palas (Bengal and Bihar) c. 750–1100	
c. 750	Gopala
770–813	Dharmapala
813–55	Devapala
1005–55	Mahipala
Rashtrakutas (west and central Deccan) c. 753–973	
780–93	Dhruva
793–833	Govinda III
814–78	Amoghavarsha
878–914	Krishna II
914–72	Indra II
972–86	Krishna III

Reign	Name
Pratiharas (west India and upper Ganges Valley) c. 773–1019	
773–93	Vatsaraja
793–833	Nagabhata
836–85	Bhoja
c. 908–42	Mahipala
Cholas of Thanjavur (Tamil Nadu) c. 850–1278	
984–1014	Rajaraja I
1014–44	Rajendra
1070–1118	Kulottunga I
Chandellas (Bundelkhand) c. 900–1203	
Kalachuris of Tripuri (Madhya Pradesh) c. 950–1195	
Chahamanis (east Rajasthan) c. 973–1192	
Chalukyas of Kalyani (west and central Deccan) 973–1189	
992–1008	Satyashraya
1043–68	Someshvara I
1076–1126	Vikramaditya VI
1181–89	Someshvara IV
Chaulukyas (Gujarat) c. 974–1238	
Gahadavalas (Qanauj) c. 974–1060	
Hoysalas of Dvarasamudra (central and south Deccan) c. 1110–1327	
Senas (Bengal) c. 1118–1199	
1158–69	Vallala Sena
Yadavas of Devagiri (north Deccan) c. 1190–1294	
Kakatiyas of Warangal (Andhra Pradesh) c. 1197–1323	
Sultans of Delhi 1206–1526	
1206–90	Slave Kings
1290–1320	Khaljis
1320–1413	Tughluqids
1414–51	Sayyids
1451–1526	Lodis

(continued)

Indian Dynasties and Rulers (continued)

Only major dynasties and the most important rulers are included. The dates given for dynasties and rulers cover periods of their importance.

Reign	Name
Sultans of Bengal 1336–1576	
1345–1414	line of Ilyas Shah
1414–36	line of Raja Ganesha
1437–87	line of Ilyas Shah (restored)
1487–94	line of Habashis
1494–1532	line of Sayyid Husain Shah
Sultans of Kashmir 1346–1589	
1346–1526	line of Shah Mirza Swati
Sultans of Gujarat 1391–1583	
1391–1411	Zafar Khan Muzaffar I
1411–42	Ahmad I
1458–1511	Mahmud I Begra
1511–26	Muzaffar II
Sharqi Sultans of Jaunpur 1394–1479	
Sultans of Malva 1401–1531	
Bahmanid Sultans of the Deccan and their successors 1347–1527	
Imadshahis of Berar 1484–1572	
Nizamshahis of Ahmadnagar 1490–1595	
Baridishahis of Bidar 1492–c. 1609	
Adilshahis of Bijapur 1489–1686	
Qutbshahis of Golconda 1512–1687	
Faruqi Sultans of Khandesh 1370–1601	
Pandyas of Madurai (Tamil Nadu) 1216–1327	

Reign	Name
Rulers of Vijayanagar Empire 1336–1646	
1336–54	Harihara I
1354–77	Bukka I
1377–c. 1404	Harihara II
c. 1404–06	Bukka I
1406–22	Devaraya I
1422–25	Vira Vijaya
1425–47	Devaraya II
1447–65	Mallikarjuna
1465–85	Virupaksa
1485–86	Praudhadevaraya
c. 1486–92	Saluva Narasimha
c. 1492–1503	Immadi Narasimha
1503–09	Vira Narasimha
1509–30	Krishnadevaraya
c. 1530–42	Achyuta
1542–c. 70	Sadashiva
c. 1570–73	Tirumala
c. 1573–85	Rauga I
1585	Venkata I
1642–46	Ranga II
Chatrapati Bhonsles 1674–1707	
1674–80	Shivaji I
1680–89	Sambhaji
1689–1700	Rajaram
1700–07	Tara Bai
Mogul Emperors 1526–1858	
Great Moguls 1526–1707	
1526–30	Babur (Zahiruddin Muhammad)

Reign	Name
1530–56	Humayun (Nasiruddin Muhammad)[2]
1556–1605	Akbar (Jalaluddin Muhammad)
1605–27	Jahangir (Nuruddin)
1627–28	Dewar Baksh
1628–58	Shah Jahan (Shihabuddin; dethroned)
1658–1707	Aurangzeb (Muhiyuddin)
Lesser Moguls 1707–1858	
1707–07	Azam Shah
1707–12	Shah Alam I (Muhammad Mu'azzam)
1712–12	Azim-ush Shan
1712–13	Jahandar Shah (Muhammad Muizzuddin)
1713–19	Farrukh Siyar (Jalaluddin Muhammad)
1719	Rafi ud-Darayat (Shamsuddin)
1719	Rafi ud-Daula Shah Jahan II
1719	Nikusiyar
1719–48	Muhammad Shah (Nasiruddin)
1748–54	Ahmad Shah Bahadur (Abu al-Nasir Muhammad)
1754–60	Alamgir II (Muhammad Azizuddin)
1760	Shah Jahan III
1760–1806	Shah Alam II (Jalaluddin Ali Jauhar; deposed briefly in 1788)
1806–37	Akbar Shah II (Muhiyuddin)
1837–58	Bahadur Shah II (Abul al-Zafar Muhammad Sirajuddin; banished)

[1] Low-caste Hindus, hostile to Brahmans and Kashatniyas; they were destroyed by Chandragupta Maurya.
[2] Humayun was defeated in 1540 and expelled from India until 1555, leaving northern India under the control of Sher Shah Suri (died 1545), Islam Shah, and Sikander Shah.

Japanese Emperors

Japanese chronology does not always match the emperor's reign dates. Rather, it is marked by occurrences, such as significant political events, military gains, and natural disasters.
(Date in parentheses = date of enthronement, when later than date of accession.)

| Reign dates[1] | | Name | Reign dates[1] | | Name |
Probable	Traditional		Probable	Traditional	
Legendary and Yamato Period 40 BC–592 AD			438–55	412–53	Ingyō
40–10 BC	660–585 BC	Jimmu	455–57	454–56	Ankō
10 BC–AD 20	581–49 BC	Suizei	457–90	457–79	Yūryaku
20–50	549–11 BC	Annei	490–95	480–84	Seinei
50–80	510–477 BC	Itoku	495–98	485–87	Kenzō
80–110	475–393 BC	Kōshō	498–504	488–98	Ninken
110–40	392–291 BC	Kōan	504–10	499–506	Buretsu
140–70	290–15 BC	Kōrei	510–34	507–31	Keitai
170–200	214–158 BC	Kōgen	534–36	531–35	Ankan
200–30	157–98 BC	Kaika	536–39	535–39	Senka
230–58	97–30 BC	Sujin	539–71		Kimmei
259–90	29 BC–70 AD	Suinin	572–85		Bidatsu
291–323	71–130	Keikō	585–87		Yomei
323–56	131–90	Seimu	587–92		Sushun
356–62	192–200	Chūai			
363–80	201–269	Jingū Kōgō (regent)	**Asuka Period 592–710**		
380–95	270–310	Ōjin	593–628		Suiko (empress)
395–428	313–99	Nintoku	629–41		Jomei
428–33	400–05	Richū	642–45		Kōgyoku (empress)
433–38	406–10	Hanzei	645–54		Kōtoku
			655–61		Saimei (empress)

Japanese Emperors (*continued*)

Japanese chronology does not always match the emperor's reign dates. Rather, it is marked by occurrences, such as significant political events, military gains, and natural disasters.
(Date in parentheses = date of enthronement, when later than date of accession.)

Reign dates[1]		Name	Reign dates[1]		Name
Probable	**Traditional**		**Probable**	**Traditional**	
661–72	(668)	Tenji	1246–60		Go-Fukakusa
672		Kōbun	1260–74		Kameyama
672–86	(673)	Temmu	1274–87		Go-Uda
686–97	(690)	Jitō (empress)	1287–98		Fushimi
697–707		Mommu	1298–1301		Go-Fushimi
			1301–08		Go-Nijo
Nara Period 710–794			1308–18		Hanazono
707–15		Gemmei (empress)			
715–24		Genshō (empress)	*Namboku Period 1334–92* [2]		
724–49		Shōmu	*The Southern Court*		
749–58		Kōken (empress)	1318–39		Go-Daigo
806–09		Heizei	1339–68		Go-Murakami
758–64		Junnin	1368–83		Chōkei
764–70		Shōtoku (empress)	1383–92		Go-Kameyama
770–81		Kōnin			
			The Northern Court		
Heian Period 794–1192			1331–33	(1332)	Kōgon
781–806		Kammu	1336–48	(1338)	Kōmyō
809–23		Saga	1348–51	(1350)	Sukō
823–33		Junna	1351–71	(1354)	Go-Kōgon
833–50		Nimmyō	1371–82	(1375)	Go-En'yū
850–58		Montoku			
858–76		Seiwa	*Muromachi Period 1392–1573* [3]		
876–84		Yōzei	1382–1412	(1392)	Go-Komatsu
884–87		Kōkō	1412–28	(1415)	Shōkō
887–97		Uda	1428–64	(1430)	Go-Hanazono
897–930		Daigo	1464–1500	(1466)	Go-Tsuchimikado
930–46		Suzaku	1500–26	(1521)	Go-Kashiwabara
946–67		Murakami	1526–57	(1536)	Go-Nara
967–69		Reizei			
969–84		En'yū	*Momoyama Period 1573–1603*		
984–86		Kazan	1557–86	(1560)	Ōgimachi
986–1011		Ichijō			
1011–16		Sanjō	*Edo Period 1603–1867*		
1016–36		Go-Ichijō	1586–1611	(1587)	Go-Yōzei
1036–45		Go-Suzaku	1611–29		Go-Mizunoo
1045–68		Go-Reizei	1629–43	(1630)	Meishō (empress)
1068–73		Go-Sanjō	1643–54		Go-Kōmyō
1073–87		Shirakawa (1086–1129 cloistered rule)	1655–63	(1656)	Gosai
1087–1107		Horikawa	1663–87		Reigen
1107–23	(1108)	Toba (1129–56 cloistered rule)	1687–1709		Higashiyama
1123–42		Sutoku	1709–35	(1710)	Nakamikado
1142–55		Konoe	1735–47		Sakuramachi
1155–58		Go-Shirakawa (1158–92 cloistered rule)	1747–62		Momozono
1158–65	(1159)	Nijō	1762–71	(1763)	Go-Sakuramachi (empress)
1165–68		Rokujō	1771–79		Go-Momozono
1168–80		Takakura	1780–1817		Kōkaku
1180–85		Antoku	1817–46		Ninkō
			1846–67	(1847)	Kōmei
Kamakura Period 1192–1333					
1183–98	(1184)	Go-Toba	*Meiji Period 1868–1912*		
1198–1210		Tsuchimikado	1867–1912	(1868)	Meiji (Mutsuhito)
1210–21	(1211)	Juntoku			
1221		Chūkyō	*Taisho Period 1912–26*		
1221–32	(1222)	Go-Horikawa	1912–26	(1915)	Taisho (Yoshihito)
1232–42	(1233)	Shijō			
1242–46		Go-Saga	*Showa Period 1926–89*		
			1926–89	(1928)	Showa (Hirohito)
			1989–		Heisei Akihito

[1] Reign dates for the first 28 emperors are the subject of some doubt and speculation. The traditional view, upon which the National Calendar is based, places the accession of Jimmu at 660 BC. Modern research approximates the date to be much later at *c.* 40 BC. Both probable and traditional dates are given until 539.
[2] Although the Southern Court was set up in exile, it retained the imperial regalia and is considered to be the legitimate line.
[3] The Muromachi Period begins with the unification of the Southern and Northern Courts in 1392.

Japanese Prime Ministers from 1945

Term	Name	Party	Term	Name	Party
1945–46	Kijurō Shidehara	coalition	1976–78	Takeo Fukuda	LDP
1946–47	Shigeru Yoshida	Liberal	1978–80	Masayoshi Ohira	LDP
1947–48	Tetsu Katayama	coalition	1980–82	Zenkō Suzuki	LDP
1948	Hitoshi Ashida	Democratic	1982–87	Yasuhiro Nakasone	LDP
1948–54	Shigeru Yoshida	Liberal	1987–89	Noboru Takeshita	LDP
1954–56	Ichirō Hatoyama	Liberal[1]	1989	Sōsuke Uno	LDP
1956–57	Tanzan Ishibashi	LDP	1989–91	Toshiki Kaifu	LDP
1957–60	Nobusuke Kishi	LDP	1991–93	Kiichi Miyazawa	LDP
1960–64	Hayato Ikeda	LDP	1993–94	Morohiro Hosokawa	JNP-led coalition
1964–72	Eisaku Satō	LDP	1994	Tsutoma Hata	Shinseito-led coalition
1972–74	Kakuei Tanaka	LDP	1994–96	Tomiichi Murayama	SDPJ-led coalition
1974–76	Takeo Miki	LDP	1996–	Ryutaro Hashimoto	LDP

[1] The conservative parties merged in 1955 to form the Liberal Democratic Party (LDP, Jiyū-Minshūtō).

Australasian Rulers and Political Leaders

Australian Prime Ministers from 1901

Term	Name	Party
1901–03	Edmund Barton	Protectionist
1903–04	Alfred Deakin	Protectionist
1904	John Watson	Labor
1904–05	George Reid	Free Trade–Protectionist coalition
1905–08	Alfred Deakin	Protectionist
1908–09	Andrew Fisher	Labor
1909–10	Alfred Deakin	Fusion
1910–13	Andrew Fisher	Labor
1913–14	Joseph Cook	Liberal
1914–15	Andrew Fisher	Labor
1915–23	William Hughes	Labor (National Labor from 1917)
1923–29	Stanley Bruce	National–Country Coalition
1929–32	James Scullin	Labor
1932–39	Joseph Lyons	United Australia–Country coalition
1939	Earle Page	United Australia–Country coalition
1939–41	Robert Menzies	United Australia
1941	Arthur Fadden	Country–United Australia coalition
1941–45	John Curtin	Labor
1945	Francis Forde	Labor
1945–49	Joseph Chifley	Labor
1949–66	Robert Menzies	Liberal–Country coalition
1966–67	Harold Holt	Liberal–Country coalition
1967–68	John McEwen	Liberal–Country coalition
1968–71	John Gorton	Liberal–Country coalition
1971–72	William McMahon	Liberal–Country coalition
1972–75	Gough Whitlam	Labor
1975–83	Malcolm Fraser	Liberal–National coalition
1983–91	Robert Hawke	Labor
1991–96	Paul Keating	Labor
1996–	John Howard	Liberal–National coalition

New Zealand Prime Ministers from 1891

Term	Name	Party
1891–93	John Ballance	Liberal
1893–1906	Richard Seddon	Liberal
1906	William Hall-Jones	Liberal
1906–12	Joseph Ward	Liberal
1912	Thomas MacKenzie	Liberal
1912–25	William Massey	Reform
1925–28	Joseph Coates	Reform
1928–30	Joseph Ward	United
1930–35	George Forbes	United
1935–40	Michael Savage	Labour
1940–49	Peter Fraser	Labour
1949–57	Sidney Holland	National
1957	Keith Holyoake	National
1957–60	Walter Nash	Labour
1960–72	Keith Holyoake	National
1972	John Marshall	National
1972–74	Norman Kirk	Labour
1974–75	Wallace Rowling	Labour
1975–84	Robert Muldoon	National
1984–89	David Lange	Labour
1989–90	Geoffrey Palmer	Labour
1990–97	Jim Bolger	National
1997–	Jenny Shipley	National

Other Political Leaders

Other Noteworthy Political Leaders

See individual country listings for leaders not included here.

Albright Madeleine (1937–) US secretary of state from 1997

Alia Ramiz (1925–) Albanian communist politician who was head of state (1982–92)

Allende (Gossens) Salvador (1908–1973) president of Chile who was overthrown in 1973 by an army coup backed by the CIA

Amin (Dada) Idi (1925–) Ugandan president (1971–79) who exercised a reign of terror over his people

Annan Kofi (1938–) Ghanaian secretary-general of the United Nations from 1997

Antall Jozef (1932–1993) Hungary's first post-communist prime minister (1990–93)

Aquino (Maria) Corazon (born Cojuangco) (1933–) president of the Philippines (1986–92) following ousting of Ferdinand Marcos

Arafat Yassir (born Mohammed Abed Ar'ouf Arafat) (1929–) chairman of Palestine Liberation Organization from 1969 and Palestine Authority from 1996

Aristide Jean-Bertrand (1953–) president of Haiti (December 1990–October 1991 and October 1994–December 1995)

Arzu Alvaro Irigoyen (1947–) president of Guatemala from 1996

Assad Hafez al (1928–) president of Syria from 1971

Atatürk Mustafa Kemal (adopted name of Mustafa Kemal Pasha) (1881–1938) first president of Turkey from 1923

Aung San (1916–1947) Burmese (Myanman) politician who helped lead Burma's fight for independence from the UK

Banda Hastings Kamuzu (1906–1997) president of Malawi (1966–94)

Bandaranaike Sirimavo (born Ratwatte) (1916–) Sri Lankan politician who was the world's first female prime minister (1960–65 and 1970–77)

Banzer Suarez Hugo (1926–) president of Bolivia (1971–80 and from 1997)

Barrios de Chamorro Violeta (c. 1939–) president of Nicaragua from 1990 whose election ended Sandinista rule

Batista Fulgencio (1901–1973) Cuban dictator who was overthrown by Fidel Castro in 1959

Ben Ali Zine el Abidine (1936–) president of Tunisia from 1987

Ben Bella Mohammed Ahmed (1919–) first prime minister of independent Algeria (1962–63) and president (1963–65)

Beneš Eduard (1884–1948) president of Czechoslovakia (1935–48)

Berisha Sali (1944–) president of Albania (1992–97)

Berlusconi Silvio (1936–) prime minister of Italy (1994–95)

Bhumibol Adulyadej (1927–) king of Thailand from 1946 who helped overthrow the military government in 1973

Bhutto Benazir (1953–) prime minister of Pakistan (1988–90 and 1993–96)

Bhutto Zulfikar Ali (1928–1979) prime minister of Pakistan overthrown in 1977 during an army coup led by General Zia ul-Haq

Birendra Bir Bikram Shah Dev (1945–) king of Nepal from 1972

Bismarck Otto Eduard Leopold von (1815–1898) chancellor of the German Empire (1871–90)

Biya Paul (1933–) president of Cameroon from 1982

Bokassa Jean-Bedel (1921–) self-proclaimed emperor of the Central African Republic (1977–79)

Bolkiah Hassanal (1946–) Sultan of Brunei from 1967

Bondevik Kjell Magne (1947–) prime minister of Norway from 1997

Bourguiba Habib ben Ali (1903–) first president of Tunisia (1957–87)

Boutros-Ghali Boutros (1922–) Egyptian diplomat who was United Nations secretary general (1992–96)

Brown Gordon (1951–) chancellor of the exchequer of the UK from 1997

Burnham (Linden) Forbes Sampson (1923–1985) prime minister of Guyana (1964–80)

Buthelezi Mangosuthu Gatsha, Chief (1928–) South African Zulu leader and politician

Castro Fidel (1927–) prime minister of Cuba (1959–76) and president from 1976

Cavaco Silva Anibal (1939–) prime minister of Portugal (1985–95) who led Portugal into the European Community in 1985

Ceausescu Nicolae (1918–1989) president of Romania (1967–89) who was overthrown in a bloody coup in December 1989

Charles (Mary) Eugenia (1919–) prime minister of Dominica (1980–95) who was the first female minister in the Caribbean

Chernomyrdin Viktor (1938–) prime minister of Russia from 1992

Chiang Kai-shek or **Jiang Jie Shi** (1887–1975) president of China (1928–31 and 1943–49) and president of Taiwan from 1949

Chiluba Frederick (1943–) president of Zambia from 1991

Chissano Joaquim (1939–) Mozambique nationalist who won the first free presidential elections in 1994

Clerides Glafkos John (1919–) president of Cyprus from 1993

Constantinescu Emil (1940–) president of Romania from 1996

Cook Robin (1946–) foreign secretary of the UK from 1997

Cosgrave William Thomas (1880–1965) Irish head of state (1922–33)

Craig James, 1st Viscount Craigavon (1871–1940) first prime minister of Northern Ireland (1921–40)

Craxi Bettino (Benedetto) (1934–) prime minister of Italy (1983–87)

Delors Jacques Lucien Jean (1925–) French politician and president of the European Commission (1984–94)

Deng Xiaoping or **Teng Hsiaoping** (1904–1997) Chinese political leader who introduced an economic modernization programme in the 1970s

Denktas Rauf R (1924–) Turkish-Cypriot politician and president of Northern Cyprus from 1983

Diem Ngo Dinh (1901–1963) prime minister of South Vietnam (1954–55) and president (1955–63)

Dini Lamberto (1931–) prime minister of Italy (1995–96)

Diouf Abdou (1935–) president of Senegal from 1980

Dos Santos Jose Eduardo (1942–) president of Angola from 1979 who negotiated the withdrawal of South African and Cuban forces from Angola

Duan Le (1908–1986) North Vietnamese leader who succeeded Ho Chi Minh

Duarte José Napoleon (1925–1990) president of El Salvador (1980–82 and 1984–88)

Dubček Alexander (1921–1992) Czechoslovak leader whose liberalization policies led to the Soviet invasion of Czechoslovakia in 1968

Duvalier François (1907–1971) president of Haiti (1957–71)

Fahd (Ibn Abdul Aziz) (1923–) king of Saudi Arabia from 1982

Faisal Ibn Abd al-Aziz (1905–1975) king of Saudi Arabia from 1964 who undertook modernization of his country

(continued)

Other Noteworthy Political Leaders (*continued*)

See individual country listings for leaders not included here.

Flores Carlos (1950–) president of Honduras from 1997

Franz Ferdinand or **Francis Ferdinand** (1863–1914) Archduke of Austria whose assassination precipitated World War I

Franz Josef or **Francis Joseph** (1830–1916) emperor of Austria–Hungary from 1848 whose attack on Serbia hastened World War I

Fujimori Alberto (1939–) president of Peru from 1990

Fulbright J William (1905–1995) US senator (1945–75) who opposed US involvement in the Vietnam war

Gaviria (Trujillo) Cesar (1947–) president of Colombia (1990–94)

Geingob Hage Gottfried (1941–) first prime minister of an independent Namibia from 1990

Gingrich Newt(on) Leroy (1943–) US politician and speaker of the US House of Representatives from 1995

Goebbels (Paul) Josef (1897–1945) German Nazi minister of propaganda from 1933

Goh Chok Tong (1941–) prime minister of Singapore from 1990

Gore Al(bert) (1948–) US vice president from 1993

Gramsci Antonio (1891–1937) Italian Marxist who helped to found the Italian Communist Party in 1921

Haig Alexander M (1924–) US secretary of state (1981–82)

Haile Selassie (Ras Tafari Makonnen) (1892–1975) emperor of Ethiopia (1930–74)

Hamilton Alexander (1757–1804) US politician who influenced the adoption of a US constitution with a strong central government

Hammarskjöld Dag (Hjalmar Agne Carl) (1905–1961) Swedish secretary general of the United Nations (1953–61)

Hasina Wazed Sheika (1947–) prime minister of Bangladesh from 1996

Hassan II (1929–) king of Morocco from 1961

Havel Václav (1936–) president of Czechoslovakia (1989–92) and president of Czech Republic from 1993

Hekmatyar Gulbuddin (1949–) prime minister of Afghanistan (1993–94 and 1996)

Hess (Walter Richard) Rudolf (1894–1987) German deputy Führer to Adolf Hitler (1933–39)

Hindenburg Paul Ludwig Hans Anton von Beneckendorf und (1847–1934) president of Germany (1925–33)

Hitler Adolf (1889–1945) Austrian-born German dictator (1933–45)

Ho Chi Minh (adopted name of Nguyen Tat Thanh) (1890–1969) North Vietnamese communist politician, premier, and president (1954–69)

Horn Gyula (1932–) prime minister of Hungary from 1994

Hoxha Enver (1908–1985) prime minister of Albania (1944–54) who was the founder of the Albanian Communist Party in 1941

Hull Cordell (1871–1955) US secretary of state (1933–44) who helped to lay the foundation for the United Nations

Hun Sen (1950–) prime minister of Cambodia (1985–93)

Hussein Saddam (1937–) leader of Iraq from 1968

Hussein ibn Talal (1935–) king of Jordan from 1952

Ibn Saud Abdul Aziz (c. 1880–1953) first king of Saudi Arabia from 1932

Iliescu Ion (1930–) president of Romania (1990–96)

Itagaki Taisuke (1837–1919) Japanese political leader who founded Japan's first political party

Itō Hirobumi Prince (1841–1909) Japanese politician who helped draft the Meiji constitution of 1889

Izetbegović Alija (1925–) president of Bosnia-Herzegovina from 1990

Jagan Janet (1920–) president of Guyana from 1997

Jayawardene Junius Richard (1906–) first president of Sri Lanka (1978–88)

Jiang Qing or **Chiang Ching** (1914–1991) Chinese minister for culture who played a key role in the 1966–76 Cultural Revolution

Jinnah Muhammad Ali (1876–1948) first governor general of Pakistan from 1947

Kabbah Ahmad Tejan (1932–) president of Sierra Leone from 1997

Kabila Laurent-Desiré (1939–) president of Democratic Republic of the Congo from 1997

Karadzic Radovan (1945–) leader of the unofficial government of the Bosnian Serbs (1992–98)

Karamanlis Konstantinos (1907–98) Greek prime minister (1955–58, 1961–63) and president (1980–85)

Kaunda Kenneth David (1924–) first president of independent Zambia (1964–91)

Kelly Petra (1947–1992) German politician who founded the German Green Party in 1972

Kerekou Mathieu Ahmed (1933–) president of Benin (1972–91 and from 1996)

Khaddhafi or **Gaddafi** or **Qaddafi** Moamer al (1942–) Libyan leader since 1969

Khama Seretse (1921–1980) first president of Botswana (1966–80)

Khatami Seyyed Mohammad (1943–) president of Iran from 1997

Khomeini Ayatollah Ruhollah (1900–1989) Iranian Shi'ite leader who established a fundamentalist Islamic republic

Kim Jong Il (1942–) North Korean national leader from 1994

Kim Dae Jung (1924–) president of South Korea from 1997

Kim Il Sung (1912–1994) prime minister of North Korea (1948–72) and president (1972–94)

Kim Young Sam (1927–) president of South Korea (1993–97)

Kissinger Henry Alfred (1923–) German-born US diplomat who negotiated US withdrawal from Vietnam in 1973

Klaus Vaclav (1941–) prime minister of Czechoslovakia from 1993

Konare Alpha Omar (1946–) president of Mali from 1992

Kravchuk Leonid (1934–) president of the Ukraine (1990–94)

Kruger (Stephanus Johannes) Paul(us) (1825–1904) president of the Transvaal (1883–1900) whose policies precipitated the Boer War

Kuchma Leonid (1938–) president of the Ukraine from 1994

Kwasniewski Alexander (1954–) president of Poland since 1995

Kyprianou Spyros (1932–) Cypriot president (1977–88)

Landsbergis Vytautas (1932–) president of Lithuania (1990–93) who drafted the Republic's declaration of independence from the USSR

Lee Kuan Yew (1923–) first prime minister of Singapore (1959–90)

Lee Teng Hui (1923–) president of Taiwan since 1988

Lodge Henry Cabot (1902–1985) US ambassador to South Vietnam (1963–64 and 1965–67)

McAleese Mary (1951–) president of Republic of Ireland from 1997

McCarthy Joe (Joseph) Raymond (1908–1957) US senator (1946–57) who conducted congressional search for suspected communist infiltration in the USA

McNamara Robert Strange (1916–) US secretary of defense (1961–68) who supported US military involvement in South Vietnam

Mahothis bin Mohamed (1925–) prime minister of Malaysia since 1981

Mandela Nelson Rolihlahla (1918–) president of South Africa from 1994

Other Noteworthy Political Leaders (continued)

See individual country listings for leaders not included here.

Manley Michael Norman (1924–) prime minister of Jamaica (1972–80 and 1989–92)

Marcos Ferdinand Edralin (1917–1989) president of the Philippines (1965–86)

Marcos Imelda Romualdez (1929–) Filipino politician and wife of Ferdinand Marcos

Masaryk Tomaš Garrigue (1850–1937) first president of the Czechoslovak Republic (1918–35)

Masire Quett Ketumile Joni (1925–) president of Botswana from 1980

Mbeki Thabo (1942–) South African president of the African National Congress from 1997

Meciar Vladimir (1942–) prime minister of Slovakia (January 1993–March 1994 and from October 1994)

Milošević Slobodan (1941–) president of Serbia from 1986 who supported the Dayton peace accord for Bosnia-Herzegovina

Mitsotakis Constantine (1918–) prime minister of Greece (1990–93)

Mkapa Benjamin William (1938–) president of Tanzania since 1995

Mobutu Sese Seko (1930–) president of Zaire (1965–97)

Molotov Vyacheslav Mikhailovich (assumed name of Vyacheslav Mikhailovich Skriabin) (1890–1986) Soviet foreign minister (1939–49 and 1953–56) who negotiated non-aggression treaty with Germany in 1939

Mubarak Hosni (1928–) president of Egypt from 1981

Mugabe Robert Gabriel (1924–) prime minister of Zimbabwe from 1980 and president from 1987

Muluzi Bakili (1943–) president of Malawi since 1994

Museveni Yoweri Kaguta (1945–) president of Uganda from 1986

Mussolini Benito Amilcare Andrea (1883–1945) Italian dictator (1925–43)

Muzorewa Abel Tendekayi (1925–) prime minister of Rhodesia/Zimbabwe (1979–80)

Mwinyi Ali Hassan (1925–) president of Tanzania (1985–95)

Nahayan Sheik Sultan bin Zayed al- (1918–) emir of Abu Dhabi from 1969

Nasser Gamal Abdel (1918–1970) president of Egypt (1956–70) who was an early leader of the non-aligned movement

Nazarbayev Nursultan (1940–) president of Kazakhstan from 1990

Nguyen Van Thieu (1923–) South Vietnamese president (1967–75)

Nkomo Joshua (1917–) vice president of Zimbabwe from 1988

Nkrumah Kwame (1909–1972) first president of Ghana (1960–66)

Noriega Manuel Antonio Morena (1940–) Panamanian military ruler (1982–89)

Nu U (Thakin) (1907–1995) prime minister of Burma (1947–62)

Nujoma Sam (1929–) first president of Namibia from 1990

Nyerere Julius Kambarage (1922–) first president of Tanzania (1964–85)

© United Nations

Kwame Nkrumah

Obote (Apollo) Milton (1924–) president of Uganda (1966–71 and 1980–85)

Ortega Saavedra Daniel (1945–) Nicaraguan head of state (1984–90)

Pahlavi Muhammad Reza Shah (1918–1980) shah of Iran (1941–79)

Papandreou Andreas (1919–1996) prime minister of Greece (1981–89 and 1993–96)

Park Chung Hee (1917–1979) president of South Korea (1963–79) whose policies generated swift economic growth

Paz (Estenssoro) Victor (1907–) president of Bolivia (1952–56, 1960–64, and 1985–89) and founder of the Movimiento Nacionalista Revolucionario

Perez de Cuellar Javier (1920–) Peruvian diplomat who was secretary general of the United Nations (1982–91)

Persson Goran (1949–) prime minister of Sweden from 1996

Pindling Lynden Oscar (1930–) first black prime minister of the Bahamas (1967–92)

Pinochet (Ugarte) Augusto (1915–) military ruler of Chile (1973–89)

Pol Pot (also known as Saloth Sar) (c. 1928–98) leader of Khmer Rouge government in Cambodia (1975–79)

Prasad Rajendra (1884–1963) India's first president after independence (1950–62)

Preval Rene (1943–) president of Haiti from 1996

Qaboos bin Said (1940–) sultan of Oman from 1970

Rabuka Sitiveni (1948–) prime minister of Fiji from 1992

Rafsanjani Ali Akbar Hashemi (1934–) president of Iran from 1989

Rahman Tunku (Prince) Abdul (1903–1990) first prime minister of independent Malaya (1957–63) and of Malaysia (1963–70)

Ramos Fidel (Eddie) (1928–) president of the Philippines from 1992

Rawlings Jerry (1947–) president of Ghana from 1981

Rene France-Albert (1935–) first prime minister of independent Seychelles

Rhee Syngman (1871–1965) president of South Korea (1948–60)

Robinson Mary (1944–) president of Republic of Ireland (1990–97)

Roh Tae-woo (1932–) South Korean president (1988–93)

Rusk Dean (1909–1994) US secretary of state (1961–69) who favoured US military involvement in South Vietnam

Sabah Sheik Jabir al-Ahmad ad-Jabir al- (1928–) emir of Kuwait from 1977

Sadat (Muhammad) Anwar (1918–1981) president of Egypt from 1970 who signed the Camp David Agreements

Santer Jacques (1937–) president of the European Commission from 1995

Sassau-Nguesso Denis (1943–) president of the Republic of the Congo (1979–92 and from 1997)

Savimbi Jonas Malheiro (1934–) Angolan revolutionary and founder of UNITA (National Union for the Total Independence of Angola)

Senghor Leopold Sedar (1906–) first president of independent Senegal (1960–80)

Shevardnadze Edvard Amvrosievich (1928–) Soviet foreign minister (1985–91) and president of Georgia from 1992

Sihanouk Norodom (1922–) king of Cambodia (1941–55 and from 1993)

Simitis Costas (1936–) prime minister of Greece from 1996

Smith Ian (Douglas) (1919–) founder of the Rhodesian Front in 1962 and prime minister of Rhodesia (1964–79)

Soares Mario Alberto Nobre Lopes (1924–) president of Portugal (1986–96)

Somoza Garci Anastasio (1896–1956) president of Nicaragua (1937–47 and 1950–56)

Suharto (1921–) president of Indonesia from 1967

Sukarno Achmed (1901–1970) first president of Indonesia (1945–67)

(continued)

Other Noteworthy Political Leaders (*continued*)

See individual country listings for leaders not included here.

Suu Kyi Aung San (1945–) Myanman (Burmese) opposition leader

Tito Marshal (adopted name of Josip Broz) (1892–1980) prime minister of Yugoslavia (1945–53) and president (1953–80)

Tudjman Franjo (1922–) president of Croatia from 1990

Vieira João Bernardo (1939–) president of Guinea-Bissau from 1980

Weizmann Chaim Azriel (1874–1952) first president of Israel (1948–52)

Weizsäcker Richard Baron von (1920–) president of Germany (1984–94)

Yilmaz Mesut (1947–) prime minister of Turkey from 1996

Zahir Shah Muhammad (1914–) king of Afghanistan (1933–73)

Zeroual Lamine (1941–) president of Algeria from 1994

Zhelev Zhelyu (1935–) president of Bulgaria (1990–96)

Assassinations and Suicides

Actual and Attempted Assassinations

Year	Victim	Details of attempted and actual assassination
681 BC	Sennacherib of Assyria	murdered by his two sons
514 BC	Hipparchus, tyrant of Athens	killed by Harmodius and Aristogeiton, two Athenians
336 BC	Philip II of Macedon	killed by Pausanias, a Spartan regent and general
44 BC	Julius Caesar, Roman dictator	stabbed to death by Brutus, Cassius, and others in the Senate
AD 41	Caligula, Roman emperor	murdered by Cassius Chaerea, an officer of his guard
54	Claudius I, Roman emperor	poisoned and killed by his wife Agrippina
96	Domitian, Roman dictator	stabbed in his bedroom by Stephanus, a freed slave
797	Constantine VI, Eastern Roman emperor	murdered on the orders of his mother
897	Pope Stephen VI	strangled to death in prison
946	Edmund I, king of England	stabbed to death
978	Edward the Martyr, king of England	murdered by an agent of his stepmother
1086	Canute IV, king of Denmark	murdered by a mob
1100	William II, king of England	assassinated while on a hunting trip by Walter Tirel; he was killed by an arrow in the back
1170	Thomas à Becket	killed in Canterbury Cathedral, England, by four knights, Fitzurse, Tracy, Morville, and Briton (from the court of King Henry II of England)
1250	Eric IV, king of Denmark	murdered by his brother
1369	Pedro the Cruel, king of Castile and Leon	murdered by his brother
1437	James I, king of Scotland	murdered in his court residence, a Dominican monastery, by assassins led by Walter, Earl of Atholl
1483	Edward V, 14-year-old king of England	smothered to death along with his brother Richard Plantagenet, the Duke of York, by order of King Richard III
1488	James III, king of Scotland	murdered by an unknown person following the defeat of the royal army at Sauchieburn
1536	Atahualpa, last king of Peru's Inca empire	strangled to death under the orders of the Spanish conquistador, Francisco Pizarro
	Ibrahim Pasha, the grand vizier of Turkey	strangled and killed by order of the Sultan
1541	Francisco Pizarro, Spanish conquistador of South America	assassinated by followers of his former partner and later rival, Diego de Almagro
1545	Manco Inca, heir to Atahualpa who led the resistance to Spanish rule	killed by fugitive supporters of Diego de Almagro
1566	David Rizzio, private foreign secretary to Mary Queen of Scots	stabbed to death at the Palace of Holyrood House in Edinburgh by allies of Lord Darnley
1567	Lord Darnley, second husband of Mary Queen of Scots	blown up and killed near Edinburgh while suffering from smallpox; the Earl of Bothwell was the suspected assassin
1584	William the Silent, Prince of Orange	shot dead at Delft by Balthasar Gérard, a religious zealot
1586	Elizabeth I, queen of England	a plot to murder the queen, arranged by Mary Queen of Scots and others, known as the Babington plot, was uncovered

Actual and Attempted Assassinations (*continued*)

Year	Victim	Details of attempted and actual assassination
1589	Henry III, king of France	stabbed to death by Jacques Clément, a fanatical Dominican monk
1605	James I, king of England	a 'gunpowder plot', by Guy Fawkes aimed to murder the king and members of Parliament, was uncovered
1610	Henry IV, king of France	murdered by François Ravaillac, a Catholic fanatic
1628	George Vilkes, 1st Duke of Buckingham	stabbed to death at Portsmouth, England, en route for La Rochelle, by John Felton, a discontented subaltern
1634	Prince Wallenstein, German general	killed in private train by Devereux
1762	Peter III, deposed Russian tsar	strangled and killed by Aleksey Grigoryevich Orlov on the orders of Catherine the Great
1792	Gustavus III, king of Sweden	shot dead during an aristocratic plot
1793	Jean Paul Marat, French revolutionary	stabbed to death in the bath by Charlotte Corday, a Girondist sympathizer
1801	Paul I, king of Russia	strangled and killed by army officers who had conspired to force his abdication
1806	Jean-Jacques Dessalines, emperor of Haiti	killed by Henri Christophe, who succeeded him as ruler of Haiti, while trying to repress a revolt
1812	Spencer Perceval, British prime minister	shot dead while entering the lobby of the House of Commons by John Bellingham, a bankrupt Liverpool broker
1865	Abraham Lincoln, US president	shot and killed by actor John Wilkes Booth in a theatre in Washington DC
1881	James A Garfield, US president	shot dead at a station by Charles Guiteau, a disappointed office-seeker
	Alexander II, king of Russia	died from injuries after a bomb was thrown into his carriage by the revolutionary group, the People's Will
1882	Lord Frederick Cavendish, chief secretary for Ireland	murdered by 'Irish Invincibles' in Phoenix Park, Dublin
1890	Sitting Bull, chief of the Sioux Native American-Indian tribe	killed while under arrest by American soldiers during a rescue attempt by his followers
1894	Marie François Carnot, French president	stabbed to death by Santo Caserio, an Italian anarchist, in Lyon
1897	Antonio Cánovas del Castillo, Spanish premier	shot dead by Italian anarchist Angiolillo at the bath of Santa Agueda, Vitoria
1900	Umberto I, king of Italy	murdered by anarchist Gaetano Bresci in Monza
1901	William McKinley, US president	shot dead by an anarchist, Leon Czolgosz, in Buffalo (NY)
1903	Alexander Obrenovich, king of Serbia, and his wife Draga	murdered by military conspirators
1908	Carlos I and Luis Philippe, king and crown prince of Portugal	ambushed and assassinated by anti-royalists
1909	Prince Hirobumi Ito, Japan's first prime minister	assassinated in Harbin, Manchuria, by a Korean nationalist named An Chung-gun
1911	Petr Arkadevich Stolypin, Russian prime minister	shot dead in a Kiev theatre by Dmitri Bogrov while in the company of the tsar
1912	Theodore Roosevelt, US president	shot and wounded by John Schrank while on his way to address a rally at Milwaukee (WI) during the presidential campaign for Roosevelt's Progressive Party
1913	George I, king of Greece	murdered by a Greek revolutionary in Salonika
1914	Archduke Francis Ferdinand	shot dead in a car with his wife by Gavrilo Princip in Sarajevo (resulted in World War I); an alleged Serbian plot
	Jean Jaurès, French socialist	shot dead by a nationalist, Raoul Villain, in a Paris café
1916	Grigori E Rasputin, Russian monk and advisor to the Court of Tsar Nicholas III	shot dead and dumped in the Moika Canal by a group of nobles led by Prince Feliks Yusupov
1919	Emiliano Zapata, Mexican revolutionary leader	ambushed and killed by Jesus Guajardo, acting under the orders of General Pablo Gonzalez, an ally of President Venustiano Carranza
	Rosa Luxemburg and Karl Liebknecht, German revolutionary leaders	beaten and shot dead by the military authorities
1921	Takashi Hara, Japanese prime minister	stabbed to death by a young assassin near Tokyo railway station
1922	Michael Collins, Irish Sinn Féin leader, head of state for ten days	killed in an ambush at Bealnamblath in the Irish Republic
1923	Francisco 'Pancho' Villa, Mexican former bandit and revolutionary leader	shot dead in Parral, Chihuahua, by a group of gunmen led by Mexican congressman, Jesus Salas Barrazas
1928	Chang Tso-Lin, Chinese warlord of Manchuria	killed by a bomb planted on a train by Japanese extremists who aimed to provoke the Japanese occupation of Manchuria

(*continued*)

Actual and Attempted Assassinations (*continued*)

Year	Victim	Details of attempted and actual assassination
1931	Prince Yuko Hamaguchi, Japanese prime minister	died from the wounds inflicted by a right-wing assassin
1933	Franklin D Roosevelt, US president	Guiseppe Zangara, an anti-capitalist, fired at the presidential motorcade in Miami (FL) missing, but killing Anton Cermak, mayor of Chicago
	Nadir Khan, king of Afghanistan	assassinated while distributing prizes at a school
1934	Dr Engelbert Dollfuss, Austrian chancellor	shot dead by Nazis in the Chancellery
	Alexander I, king of Yugoslavia	shot dead in Marseilles by Vlada Chernozamsky, an assassin sent by the Croat nationalist leader Ante Pavelic with the secret support of Mussolini
	Cesar Augusto Sandino, Nicaraguan rebel leader	assassinated in Managua by members of the National Guard to Stalin
	Sergei M Kirov, leading Soviet politician and former aide to Stalin	shot dead in Leningrad (St Petersburg) by Leonid Nikolayev, under orders from Stalin, to provide the pretext for the launching of show trials to purge Stalin's rivals
	Ernst Röhm, German soldier and leader of the Nazi Sturmabteilung (SA)	murdered on Hitler's orders during the 'night of the long knives'
1935	Huey Long, US politician	murdered by Dr Carl Austin Weiss, the son-in-law of a political opponent
1939	Adolf Hitler, German dictator	Johann Georg Elser, a Swabian who opposed Hitler's war policy, placed a bomb at a meeting attended by Hitler in Munich; the bomb exploded shortly after Hitler had left, killing seven people
1940	Leon Trotsky, exiled Russian communist leader	killed with an ice pick in Mexico by Ramon Mercador
1942	Reinhard Heydrich, second in command of the Nazi secret police	killed in a grenade attack by Jan Kubis and Josef Gabeik of the Free Czechoslovak army
1944	Adolf Hitler, German dictator	Lieutenant Colonel Klaus Schrenk von Stauffenberg placed a bomb in a briefcase at a staff conference at Hitler's headquarters in Rastenburg; Hitler was only slightly injured
1946	Ananda Mahidol, King Rama VIII of Thailand	shot dead in the royal palace in a conspiracy involving his private secretary
1947	U Aung San, Burmese (Myanman) head of government	assassinated by political opponents
1948	Mahatma Gandhi, Indian nationalist leader	shot dead by a Hindu fanatic, Nathuram Godse
	Count Folke Bernadotte, Swedish diplomat	murdered by Jewish extremists in an ambush in Jerusalem
1950	Harry Truman, US president	two Puerto Ricans were killed in Washington DC, by secret service agents during an exchange of gunfire directed at Truman
1951	Abdullah I, king of Jordan	murdered by a member of the Jehad faction named Mustafa Ashu
	Liaquat Ali Khan, first prime minister of Pakistan	murdered in Rawalpindi by a Muslim fanatic named Syed Azbar Khan
1956	Anastasio Somoza Garcia, ruler of Nicaragua	died eight days after a gunshot attack by Rigoberto Lopez Perez
1958	Faisal II, king of Iraq	murdered with his entire household during a military coup
1959	Solomon Bandaranaike, Ceylonese premier	murdered by a Buddhist monk, Talduwa Somarans Thero
1961	Rafael Trujillo Molina, Dominican Republic dictator	machine-gunned dead in a car by assassins, including General J T Díaz
	Patrice Lumumba, first prime minister of the Republic of the Congo	murdered by soldiers loyal to Joseph Mobutu
1962	General Charles de Gaulle, French president	the Organisation de l'Armée Secrète (OAS), a rebel military organization that blamed de Gaulle for France's loss of Algeria, launched an unsuccessful gunfire attack on the president's car near Petit Clamart; a year earlier, they had tried to assassinate the president with a bomb
1963	John F Kennedy, US president	shot dead in a car by rifle fire in Dallas (TX); alleged assassin, Lee Harvey Oswald, was himself shot two days later while under heavy police escort
	Ngo Dinh Diem, former president of South Vietnam	assassinated following his overthrow by a military coup
1965	Malcolm X (Little), US leading representative of the Black Muslims	shot dead at a political rally in New York by followers of rival Black Muslim leader Elijah Muhammad
1966	Alahaji Abubakar Tafawa Balewa, Nigeria's first prime minister	murdered during an army uprising
	Hendrik Verwoerd, South African premier	stabbed to death by a parliamentary messenger (who was later ruled mentally disordered)

Actual and Attempted Assassinations (*continued*)

Year	Victim	Details of attempted and actual assassination
1967	Ernesto 'Che' Guevara, Argentine-born Cuban revolutionary leader	killed by government troops in Bolivia
1968	Martin Luther King, US black civil rights leader	shot dead on a hotel balcony by James Earl Ray in Memphis (TN)
	Robert F Kennedy, US senator and Democrat presidential nomination candidate	shot dead by Arab immigrant Sirhan Sirhan in the Ambassador Hotel, Los Angeles (CA)
1972	George Wallace, governor of Alabama, USA	shot and seriously wounded by Arthur Bremer during a speech in Laurel (MD) when Wallace was campaigning for the Democratic Party's presidential nomination; Wallace was partially paralysed and confined to a wheelchair
1975	Gerald Ford, US president	in Sacramento (CA), a young woman, Lynette Fromme, brandished a pistol but was wrestled away by secret service agents before a shot could be fired
	Faisal, king of Saudi Arabia	murdered by his nephew during an audience with the oil minister of Kuwait
	Jimmy Hoffa, US labour leader	disappeared in 1975 and believed to have been murdered
	Ross McWhirter, co-editor of The Guinness Book of Records and political activist	shot dead at his Enfield home by IRA gunmen
	Sheikh Mujibur Rahman, founder and president of Bangladesh	murdered, along with family members, during an army coup
1976	Christopher Ewart Biggs, British ambassador to Republic of Ireland	killed when his car was blown up by an IRA landmine
1977	Marien Ngouabi, president of Congo	shot and killed in Brazzaville during an attempted coup
	Steve Biko, South African black student leader	died of head wounds while in police custody
1978	Georgi Markov, Bulgarian writer who had defected to the west in 1969	killed in London from poison injected into his leg by an umbrella, the work of a Bulgarian secret service agent
	Aldo Moro, president of Italy's Christian Democrats and twice prime minister	kidnapped by Red Brigade guerrillas and later found dead in a car; he had been shot
1979	Airey Neave, British Conservative MP and Northern Ireland spokesperson	killed by an IRA bomb while driving out of the House of Commons' car park
	Lord Mountbatten, uncle of the duke of Edinburgh	killed by an IRA bomb in sailing boat off coast of Ireland
	Nur Mohammad Taraki, Afghanistan's head of state and founder of leftist Khalq ('masses') party	killed in a coup organized by his rival Hafizullah Amin
	Park Chung Hee, president of South Korea	shot dead in a restaurant by the chief of the Korean Central Intelligence Agency
1980	Anastasio Somoza Debayle, deposed autocratic ruler of Nicaragua	killed by bazooka and machine-gun fire while in exile in Asunción, Paraguay
	John Lennon, singer and songwriter	shot dead outside his apartment block in New York
1981	Anwar al-Sadat, president of Egypt	shot dead by rebel soldiers while reviewing a military parade
	Ronald Reagan, US president	shot in the chest and seriously wounded outside the Washington Hilton hotel by John Hinckley; the president's press secretary, James Brady, was critically injured
	Pope John Paul II	shot and seriously wounded in St Peter's Square, Rome, by Mehmet Ali Agca, a Turk; the Bulgarian secret service were suspected of involvement in a wider conspiracy
	Zia ur-Rahman, president of Bangladesh	murdered while sleeping in a rest-house in Chittagong, along with aides and bodyguards, during a coup attempt
1982	Bashir Gemayel, president elect of Lebanon	killed in a bomb blast in the Beirut headquarters of his Christian Phalangist party
1983	Benigno Simeon Aquino, leader of the opposition to the autocratic regime of the Philippines' president Ferdinand Marcos	shot and killed while getting off a plane at Manila airport; his murder by security forces inspired a 'people power' movement, led by his widow Corazon, which toppled Marcos in 1986
1984	Indira Gandhi, Indian prime minister	murdered by members of her Sikh bodyguard
	Jerzy Popieluszco, Polish anti-communist Catholic priest and supporter of the Solidarity free trades-union movement	beaten to death by secret service officers
	Margaret Thatcher, UK prime minister	escaped unscathed when the Grand Hotel in Brighton, where the cabinet was staying, was bombed by the IRA, claiming five lives
1986	Olof Palme, Swedish prime minister	shot dead in Stockholm as he walked home with his wife

(continued)

Actual and Attempted Assassinations (*continued*)

Year	Victim	Details of attempted and actual assassination
1990	Ian Gow, English Conservative politician	long-time political confidant of Margaret Thatcher who fiercely condemned the activities of the IRA; he was murdered by the IRA in a car bomb attack
1991	John Major, UK prime minister	mortar bomb attack by the IRA on the prime minister's residence, 10 Downing Street, London; there were no serious injuries
	Rajiv Gandhi, former Indian prime minister	killed by a bomb during an election campaign
1992	Muhammad Boudiaf, president of Algeria's ruling High State Council	murdered during a speech in Annaba by machine-gun fire
	Paolo Borsellino, chief prosecutor in anti-Mafia investigations	killed by a car bomb
	Giovanni Lizzio, senior police official involved in anti-Mafia investigations	shot dead by gunmen on motorcycles
	Sadegh Sharafkandi, Iranian Kurdish opposition leader	shot dead by masked gunmen
	Pedro Huillca, leader of the General Federation of Peruvian Workers	shot and killed by eight people with submachine guns
1993	Chris Hani, secretary general of the South African Communist Party	shot dead outside his home in a Johannesburg suburb
	Ranasinghe Premadasa, Sri Lankan president	killed by a suicide bomber in Colombo during the May Day parade
	Lalith Athulathmudali, leader of Sri Lanka's opposition party	shot and killed at a campaign rally
	Melchior Ndadaye, president of Burundi	killed in a military coup
	Mouin Shabaytah, Lebanese PLO military leader	shot dead by gunmen in Sidon, Lebanon
1994	Luis Donaldo Colosio Murrieta, Mexican presidential candidate for the PRI	shot and killed following a campaign speech in Tijuana
	Cyprien Ntaryamira, president of Burundi	killed in a plane crash caused by gunfire, along with the president of Rwanda
	Juvenal Habyarimana, president of Rwanda	killed in a plane crash caused by gunfire, along with the president of Burundi
1995	Yitzhak Rabin, Israeli prime minister	shot dead following speech at a pro-peace rally in Tel Aviv
	Maurizio Gucci, former fashion designer	shot dead in Milan
1996	Yahya Ayyash, operative of the Islamic fundamentalist organization Hamas	killed by a booby-trapped cellular telephone
1997	Gianni Versace, Italian fashion designer	shot dead on the steps of his Miami Beach mansion

Famous Suicides

Name	Year	Circumstances
Aristodemus	724 BC	king of Messenia who killed himself on the tomb of his daughter, whom he had put to death
Richard Brautigan	1984	US novelist who never cared for critics but shot himself when he lost his readership
Wallace Carothers	1937	US industrial chemist and inventor who developed nylon
Cassius	42 BC	Roman soldier and politician who ordered a servant to stab him under the misapprehension that the Battle of Philippi had been lost
Lord Castlereagh	1822	British politician whose excessive workload and severe gout led him to cut his throat with a penknife
Cato	46 BC	Roman politician who made himself a martyr rather than accept Caesar's pardon
Thomas Chatterton	1770	English poet whose dire poverty drove him to rip up all his manuscripts and poison himself with arsenic
Cleopatra	30 BC	queen of Egypt who killed herself by the bite of an asp to avoid appearing before the triumphant Romans
Robert Clive	1774	British soldier and administrator who became an opium addict and shot himself
Kurt Cobain	1994	US rock singer who killed himself with a shotgun
Hart (Harold) Crane	1932	US poet who despaired of his work and drowned himself off the Florida coast
Emily Davison	1913	English suffragette who threw herself under the king's horse in the 1913 Derby as a political statement
George Eastman	1932	US inventor, entrepreneur, photographic innovator, and philanthropist who shot himself
Empedocles	433 BC	Greek philosopher and scientist who threw himself into the crater of Mount Etna

Famous Suicides (*continued*)

Name	Year	Circumstances
Brian Epstein	1967	British manager of the Beatles who took a drug overdose
Judy Garland	1969	US film star who took a drug overdose
Josef Goebbels	1945	German Nazi propagandist who, the day after Hitler's suicide, poisoned his children and then had his wife and himself shot by an orderly
Hermann Goering	1946	German Nazi leader who, having been sentenced to death at the Nuremberg trials, escaped execution by taking cyanide from a phial that he had somehow managed to conceal or that had been smuggled in to him
Tony Hancock	1968	English comedian who killed himself as his popularity waned
Hannibal	c. 182 BC	Carthaginian general who took poison to avoid being handed over to the Romans
Benjamin Robert Haydon	1846	English painter who shot himself after the failure of an exhibition
Ernest Hemingway	1961	US novelist who shot himself after failing to complete literary projects
Heinrich Himmler	1945	German Nazi leader and chief of police who was captured while trying to escape in disguise after the surrender of Germany, and then killed himself with poison
Adolf Hitler	1945	German dictator who killed himself as the final Soviet offensive across the Oder river closed in on the centre of Berlin
Abbie (Abbot) Hoffman	1989	US left-wing activist who shot himself after a long depression
Reverend Jim Jones	1978	leader of the People's Temple who, along with almost all the residents of Jonestown, Guyana, killed themselves or were killed with cyanide
Arthur Koestler	1983	British writer who committed suicide with his wife Cynthia after suffering for a long time with Parkinson's disease
Mariano José de Larra	1837	Spanish poet whose pessimism about Spanish society and an unhappy love affair led him to take his own life
Jack London	1916	US novelist who was dependent on pain killers and an alcoholic, and who killed himself with a morphine overdose
Lucretia	6th century BC	Roman woman who set an example of dedication to female chastity by suicide after rape
Aimee Semple McPherson	1944	US evangelist who took an overdose after being accused of improprieties
Mark Antony	30 BC	Roman politician and soldier who committed suicide in the wrongful belief that Cleopatra was dead
Vladimir Mayakovsky	1930	Russian writer whose unstable personal life and persecution by the Soviet authorities caused him to shoot himself
Yukio Mishima	1970	Japanese novelist who committed hari-kiri after the failure of a right-wing coup
Marilyn Monroe	1962	US film actress who died after an overdose of barbiturates; conspiracy theorists believe she was murdered
Nero	68	Roman emperor who stabbed himself with help from his secretary and is reported to have exclaimed, 'What an artist dies with me!'
Captain Laurence Oates	1912	British Antarctic explorer who walked out to his death in a blizzard, fearing that his condition would delay his companions
Jan Palach	1969	Czechoslovakian student who set fire to himself as a protest against the Russian invasion of his country
Cesare Pavese	1950	Italian novelist who killed himself, disillusioned with politics and upset by sex
Sylvia Plath	1963	US poet and novelist who died due to inhalation of toxic gas fumes
Erwin Rommel	1944	German field marshal who took his own life to protect his family after being implicated in a plot against Hitler
Mark Rothko	1970	US painter who slashed his wrists
Sardanapalus	640 BC	Assyrian king who burned himself along with his treasure, eunuchs, and women to stop anyone else enjoying them
Seneca	c. 65	Roman playwright and philosopher who had trouble obeying Nero's orders to die; he opened his veins, took poison, and suffocated himself
Anne Sexton	1974	US poet whose work focused on her role as a woman, and who committed suicide
Solar Temple cult	1994–95	contemporary religious cult, some of whose members committed mass suicide in Canada and Switzerland
Wolfe Tone	1798	Irish nationalist who was captured by the English and condemned to death, but cut his own throat in prison
Alan Turing	1954	British mathematician who pioneered the early development of the computer and worked on cryptography at Bletchley Park during World War II; he committed suicide after being prosecuted for homosexuality
Vincent Van Gogh	1890	Dutch painter who shot himself at the site of his last painting *Cornfields with Flight of Crows*
Harriet Westbrook	1816	English poet Shelley's estranged wife who drowned in the Serpentine leaving Shelley 'a prey to the reproaches of memory'
Virginia Woolf	1941	British novelist who drowned herself after a nervous collapse
Stefan Zweig	1942	Austrian writer who was exiled with his wife by the Nazis in 1934 and despaired at what they saw as the end of culture and civilization; both committed suicide

Obituaries

Deaths: July–December 1997

Acker Kathy (born Lehman), c. 53, US author, 29 November

Agnelli Giovanni, 33, Italian Fiat heir apparent; 13 December

Agosti Orlando, 72, Argentine Air Force commander who helped overthrow the government of Isabel Peron in 1976 and institute a military regime in Argentina; 6 October

Albert Harold (born Harold Kemp), 88, British biographer who wrote about 20 books on the British royal family, under the pseudonym of Helen Cathcart; 20 October

Al-Jawahri Mohammed, 98, Iraqi poet, writer, and scholar; 27 July

Allison Luther, 57, US blues singer and guitarist; 12 August

Anderson Stikkan ('Stig'), 66, Swedish lyric writer, music publisher, and manager, famous for his work with Abba; 12 September

Arcaro George Edward (Eddie), 81, US jockey who was the only rider to win thoroughbred racing's Triple Crown twice, in 1941 and 1948; 14 November

Ashburn Richie ('Don Richard'), 70, US baseball player and broadcaster; 9 September

Banda Hastings Kamuzu, c. 91, first president of Malawi 1966–94, who was instrumental in bringing about the withdrawal of British colonial government, and became known as a ruthless leader; 25 November

Barnard Lance Herbert, 78, Australian politician; 6 August

Barnes Mae, 89, US singer and dancer; 13 December

Bell Bob, 75, US actor of Bozo the Clown; 8 December

Berlin Isaiah, 88, Russian-born British philosopher and historian of ideas; 5 November

Bernard Jeffrey, 65, British journalist; 4 September

Bing Rudolf Franz Joseph, 95, Austrian opera administrator; 2 September

Boban Mate, 57, Croatian nationalist; 7 July

Bosch Jaime Milans del, 82, Spanish general who served under Franco and took part in a failed military coup in 1980; 26 July

Bradbury Norris Edwin, 88, US physicist who was instrumental in the development of mass-produced nuclear weapons; 20 August

Bremner Billy, 54, football player and manager; 7 December

Brennan William Joseph, 91, US judge and Associate Justice of the Supreme Court of the US; 24 July

Bristol Horace, 88, US photojournalist known for his depiction of war and poverty; 4 August

Brock Edwin, 69, British poet; 7 September

Bruner Wallace C (Wally), 66, US television host of the game show *What's My Line?* and the home-improvement programme *Wally's Workshop*; 3 November

Buckley Christopher, 81, US inventor and pioneer in the use of aluminium; 5 July

Burnett Murray, 86, US playwright; 23 September

Burnum Burnum (born Henry Penrith), 61, Australian aboriginal rights activist; 17 August

Burroughs William Seward, 83, US writer; 2 August

Buxton Glen, 50, US guitarist with Alice Cooper; 18 October

Calment Jeanne Louise, 122, French, oldest recorded person; 4 August

Çarçani Adil, 75, Albanian politician, prime minister of Albania 1982–91; 13 October

Canosa Jorge Mas, 58, Cuban-born US businessman and campaigner; 23 November

Capps Walter Holden, 63, US Democratic member of Congress from California; when he won the seat in 1996, he became the first Democrat to hold it since World War II; 28 October

Carcani Adil, 75, premier of Albania 1982–1991, the last of Albania's communist-era premiers; 13 October

Chambers George Michael, 69, prime minister of Trinidad and Tobago 1981–86; 4 November

Chandler Dorothy Buffum, 96, US philanthropist; 6 July

Chaplin Saul, 85, US composer, arranger, and producer; 15 November

Chapman Eddie (Arnold Edward), 83, British double agent during World War II who fed the Nazis misinformation so that bombs intended for Central London would miss their target; 11 December

Chisholm George, 82, British trombonist, pianist, and arranger; 6 December

Christian Gerda, 83, German, personal secretary of Adolf Hitler; 15 July

Clarke Shirley, 72, US filmmaker; 23 September

Coles Johnny, 71, US jazz trumpeter whose recordings include *Out of the Cool* (1960) with the Gil Evans orchestra; 21 December

Coombs Herbert Cole (Nugget), 91, Australian head of the central bank of Australia 1949–68, who also campaigned for rights for aboriginal peoples; 29 October

Cordell Alexander (born George Alexander Graber), 82, British novelist; c. 9 July

Crockett Jr, George William, 88, US Democratic congressman, judge, and attorney; 7 September

Dai Bao (born Nguyen Vinh Thuy), 83, Emperor of Annam 1925–45; 31 July

Dainton Fred(erick Sydney), 83, British chemist; 5 December

Daniel Eliot, 89, US composer who is said to have written the theme music for *I Love Lucy* in 20 minutes; 6 December

Danilova Alexandra Dionysievna, 92, Russian ballet dancer and teacher; 13 July

Dean Isabel, 79, British stage, screen, and television actress; 27 July

De Menil Dominique, 89, art collector and philanthropist who with her husband set up a foundation to support art scholarship, and with former US president Jimmy Carter set up the Carter-Menil Foundation; 31 December

Denver John (born Henry John Deutschendorf Jr), 53, US singer, guitarist, and songwriter; 12 October

Diana Princess of Wales (born Diana Frances Spencer), 36; 31 August

Dickerson Nancy Hanschmann, 70, US television news reporter and producer who was the first female correspondent for the CBS television network; 18 October

Disney Lillian B (born Lillian Bounds), 98, US widow of cartoonist Walt Disney and a philanthropist who came up with the name Mickey Mouse and was a leading patron of the arts; 16 December

Dolci Danilo, 73, Italian educationalist, writer, and poet, who campaigned for social change in Sicily and wrote books including *Outlaws* (1961) and *Sicilian Lives* (1981); 30 December

Dolmetsch Carl Frederick, 85, French-born British musician; 11 July

Dove Billie (born Lillian Bohny) 94, US actress who starred in numerous Hollywood silent films; 31 December

Duvalier Simone, 83 or 84, Haitian widow of François (Papa Doc) Duvalier who ruled Haiti 1957–71, and mother of Jean-Claude (Baby Doc) Duvalier who ruled 1971–86; 26 December

Eckersley Thomas, 82, British graphic designer; 4 August

Edel Leon ('Joseph'), 89, US literary critic and biographer; 5 September

Egeberg Roger Olaf, 93, US senior health official; 12 September

Erikson Joan Mowat, 95, Canadian-born occupational therapist who collaborated with her husband, psychoanalyst Erik Erikson, on projects including the theory of human development outlined in Erik's book *Childhood and Society* (1950); 3 August

Essen Louis, 88, British physicist, developer of atomic clocks; 24 August

Eysenck Hans Jurgen, 81, German-born British psychologist; 4 September

Farley Chris, 33, US comedian and actor who was a regular of *Saturday Night Live* and star of films including *Beverley Hills Ninja* (1997); 18 December

Frankl Viktor Emil, 92, Austrian psychiatrist and psychotherapist; 2 September

Fratellini Annie, 64, French clown and founder of the National Circus School in France; 1 July

Frey Roger, 84, French politician; 13 September

Fuller Samuel Michael, 86, US film director; 30 October

Gairy Eric Matthew, 75, Grenadan politician, first prime minister of Grenada; 23 August

Gallagher James Wesley (Wes), 86, US chief executive of the Associated Press (AP) 1962–76; 11 October

Geneen Harold S, 87, US president and chief executive of International Telephone and Telegraph Corporation (ITT) 1959–77; 21 November

Gill Brendan, 83, US author who was interested in urban preservation and who contributed to the *New Yorker* magazine from 1936; 27 December

Gill David Ian, 69, British filmmaker and film restorer; 28 September

Glover Brian, 63, British actor; 24 July

Goizueta Roberto Crispulo, 65, US chairman and chief executive of the Coca-Cola Company who was credited with raising the company's stock value from $4.3 billion in 1981 to $152 billion in 1997; 18 October

Gold Mary Jane, 88, US heiress who helped Jewish and anti-Nazi intellectuals escape from Europe during World War II; 5 October

Goldberg Bertrand, 84, US architect who designed Chicago's Marina City, Astor Towers Hotel, and River City apartments; 8 October

Goldsmith James Michael, 64, British-French businessman, publisher, and politician; 18 July

Grappelli Stéphane, 89, French violinist known for his jazz improvisations whose records included *Jazz Summit* (1966) and *The Reunion* (1976); 1 December

Guetary Georges (born Lambros Woriou), 82, Greek actor; 13 September

Hassan Joshua Abraham, 81, British-Gibraltarian lawyer and politician, first Chief Minister of Gibraltar; 1 July

Hauser Joseph John, 98, US baseball player; 11 July

Hines John E, 86, US presiding bishop of the Episcopalian Church 1965–74; 19 July

Hiratsuka Un'ichi, 102, Japanese woodblock artist; 18 November

Hogan Benjamin W, 84, US golfer; 25 July

Hornberger H Richard, 73, US novelist; 4 November

Hutchence Michael, 37, Australian lead singer of the rock group INXS, whose albums included *Welcome to Wherever You Are* (1993) and *Elegantly Wasted* (1997); 22 November

Ibuka Masaru, 89, Japanese electronics engineer and industrialist, founder of Sony; 19 December

Ingrams Doreen Constance (born Shortt), 91, British writer and broadcaster; 25 July

Itami Juzo (Yoshihiro Ikeuchi), 64, Japanese actor, film director, and writer whose films included *Tampopo* ('Dandelion' 1986) and *Daibyoin* ('The Great Patient' 1995); 20 December

Jackson Raymond Allen ('Jak'), 70, British cartoonist; 27 July

Jacobi Carl Richard, 89, US journalist, short story writer, and electronics inspector; 25 August

Jaffé Andrew Michael, 74, British art historian and curator; 13 July

Jaffe Leo, 88, US film executive; 20 August

Jarrico Paul, 82, US screenwriter who in 1951 was blacklisted as an alleged communist sympathizer, and whose films included *Salt of the Earth* (1953) about a Mexican labour strike; 28 October

Jepson Helen, 92, US opera singer; 16 September

Jewell Stuart, 84, US cinematographer; 13 July

Jones R(eginald) V(ictor), 86, British physicist who devised ways to thwart Nazi military technology during World War II; 17 December

Josephs Wilfred, 70, English composer who wrote for film and television as well as the concert hall; 17 November

Kaplan Edgar, 72, US champion bridge player; 7 September

Kaye Stubby, 79, US actor who sang 'Sit Down, You're Rockin' the Boat' in the musical *Guys and Dolls* (1950); 14 December

Keir Andrew, 71, British actor; 5 October

Kelley Clarence Marion, 85, US police officer, Director of the FBI 1973–78; 5 August

Kelly Edna F, 91, US Democratic member of Congress 1949–69, and the first woman to be elected to Congress from the borough of Brooklyn, New York City; 14 December

Kendrew John Cowdray, 80, British biochemist; 23 August

Kennedy Michael LeMoyne, 39, US, sixth of the 11 children of the late Senator Robert F Kennedy; he was campaign manager for his uncle Senator Edward M Kennedy and his brother Representative Joseph P Kennedy; 31 December

Khaldei Yevgeny, 80, Russian photographer, famous for his pictures of the fall of Berlin in 1945; 7 October

Khan Nusrat Fateh Ali, c. 49, Pakistani singer; 16 August

Kirk Grayson Louis, 94, US president of Columbia University, New York City, 1953–68; 21 November

Kirkbride-Helbaek Diana, 81, British archaeologist; 13 August

Knie Rodolphe, 75, Swiss elephant trainer and circus director; 18 August

Kuczynski Jürgen, 92, German historian; 6 August

Kulle Jarl, 70, Swedish actor; 3 October

Kuralt Charles Bishop, 62, US journalist and writer; 4 July

Kuti Fela (born Fela Ransome-Kuti), 58, Nigerian musician; 2 August

Lampell Millard, 78, US songwriter, screenwriter, and novelist who campaigned for social causes such as organized labour and racial equality; 3 October

Larson Nicolette , 45, US soul and country singer who had a top-10 hit with 'Lotta Love' in 1979; 16 December

Latsis Mary Jane, c. 70, US writer and one half of the detective novelist 'Emma Lathen'; 3 November

Laughlin James, 83, US publisher and poet who published early works by writers including Wallace Stevens, Ezra Pound, Gertrude Stein, and Henry Miller; his own books of poetry included *In Another Country* (1978); 12 November

Lees-Milne James, 89, English architectural historian and writer who exerted considerable influence on the development of the National Trust; 28 December

Leggett Robert Louis, 71, US congressman, targeted in the 1976 'Koreagate' investigation; 13 August

Lemelson Jerome, 74, US inventor; 1 October

Leonard Walter Fenner (Buck), 90, US baseball player, the third Negro League player to be voted to the Major League Baseball Hall of Fame; 27 November

Levertov Denise, 74, British-born US poet, essayist, and political activist whose campaigning work for civil rights and against the Vietnam war found expression in her writing; 20 December

Lewis Robert, 88, US actor, theatre director, and acting coach, who directed hits including *Brigadoon* and coached Marlon Brando and Meryl Streep; 23 November

Lichtenstein Roy, 73, US artist; 29 September

Liman Arthur L, 64, US attorney known for his contributions to the investigations of the 1971 Attica prison uprising, and the Iran-contra arms scandal in the 1980s; 17 July

Lipset Harold 'Hal', 78, US private detective and founder of World Association of Detectives; 8 December

Lorant Stefan (born István Lóránt), 96, Hungarian-born US filmmaker, editor, writer, and creator of *Picture Post*; 14 November

Loss Louis, 83, US professor of law; 13 December

Lutsko Alexander, 56, Belarusian nuclear physicist; 4 September

Maar Dora (born Henriette Theodora Markovitch), 89, French painter and artist's model for Pablo Picasso; 16 July

McGregor Oliver Ross, 76, British social scientist; 10 November

Manzo Luis Aguilar, 79, Mexican actor who starred in the film *The Wild Rooster* (1948); 24 October

Marchais Georges René Louis, 77, French, secretary general of the French Communist Party (PCF) 1972–1994; 16 November

Marr David Francis, 63, US professional golfer and sportscaster who became golf commentator for the ABC television network after a successful playing career; 5 October

Mas Canosa Jorge, 58, Cuban exile, founder and chairman of the Cuban-American National Foundation (CANF), which was influential in shaping US policy towards Cuba; 23 November

Mason Richard Lakin, 78, British writer; 13 October

Matthews Ted, 101, Australian survivor of unsuccessful Gallipoli landing in World War I; 9 December

Mehrtens Warren, 77, US jockey who in 1946 won thoroughbred racing's Kentucky Derby, Preakness Stakes, and Belmont Stakes triple crown, a feat accomplished by only ten jockeys; 30 December

Meredith George Burgess, 88, US actor, director, writer, and producer; 9 September

Merril Judith, 74, US science fiction writer; 12 September

Michener James Albert, 90, US writer; 17 October

Mifune Toshiro, 77, Japanese actor and film and television producer, best known as the star of several Akira Kurosawa films including *Rashomon* (1950) and *Seven Samurai* (1954); 24 December

Milburn Jr, Rod(ney), 47, US athlete who won a gold medal at the 1972 Olympic Games and matched or set several world records for hurdles; 11 November

Mills Victor, c. 100, US chemical engineer, developer of the disposable nappy; 1 November

Mitchum Robert Charles Duran, 79, US actor; 1 July

Mobutu Sese Seko Kuku Ngbendu wa za Banga (formerly Joseph Desire Mobutu), 66, Congolese politician and president of Zaire 1965–97; 7 September

Mohammed Gul, 40, Indian, at 57 cm/22.5 in tall the shortest living adult and the shortest man ever, according to the *Guinness Book of Records*; 1 October

Moss John Emerson, 82, US Democratic member of Congress who secured the passage of the 1966 Freedom of Information Act; 5 December

Nabrit Jr, James M, 97, US lawyer and educator who was involved in numerous major civil rights cases and who was president of Howard University 1960–69; 27 December

Najdorf Miguel (born Moishe Najdorf), 87, Polish-born Argentine chess grandmaster; 4 July

Nancarrow Conlon, 84, US composer; 10 August

Newby Percy Howard, 79, British broadcasting administrator and novelist; 6 September

Nikulin Yuri Vladimirovich, 75, Russian clown and actor; 21 August

Noble Peter, 80, British actor, producer, songwriter, journalist, writer, and broadcaster; 17 August

Oatis William N, 83, Associated Press (AP) reporter who was imprisoned in Czechoslovakia during the Cold War; 16 September

O'Brien Robert Hector, 93, US president of Metro-Goldwyn-Mayer Picture Corporation (MGM) 1963–69; 6 October

Oku Mumeo, 101, Japanese activist who founded consumer rights group the Housewives' Association during World War II; 7 July

Orr Buxton, 73, Scottish composer whose works include *Sinfonia Ricercante* (1987) and *Carmen Fantasy* (1987); 27 December

Parks Lillian Adele Rogers, 100, US White House seamstress and maid who wrote the bestselling memoir *My Thirty Years Backstairs at the White House* (1961); 6 November

Pastrana Borrero Misael, 73, president of Colombia 1970–74; 21 August

Pastrano Willie, 62, US light-heavyweight boxer, holder of the world light-heavyweight title 1963–65; 6 December

Peabody Endicott ('Chubb'), 77, US liberal Democrat who was governor of Massachussetts 1963–65 and in 1972 ran unsuccessfully for the Democratic nomination for vice president of the USA; 2 December

Peladeau Pierre, 72, Canadian newspaper publisher, head of Quebecor Incorporated, which published *Le Journal de Montréal*, Canada's largest French-language newspaper; 24 December

Peterson Esther, 91, US labour movement and women's rights lobbyist who was the first White House special assistant for consumer affairs; 20 December

Phelan James R, 85, US investigative journalist and author; 8 September

Pinget Robert, 78, Swiss-born novelist and playwright; 25 August

Pinkerton John (Maurice McClean), 78, English computer engineer who was responsible for building the pioneer computing machine Leo, which began operating in 1951; 22 December

Poliakov Léon, 87, Russian-born French historian; 8 December

Polunin Nicholas, 88, British botanist and environmentalist; 8 December

Pramoj Seni, 92, Thai premier (1945, 1975, and 1976) and diplomat; 28 July

Pyle Denver, 77, US actor, director, and writer who appeared in numerous Westerns, and played Uncle Jesse in the television series *The Dukes of Hazzard*; 25 December

Rapotec Stanislaus, 84, Italian-born Australian painter; 18 November

Remer Otto Ernst, c. 85, German soldier and political activist, whose loyalty to Hitler was crucial to the overthrow of a plot against the Nazi leader in 1944; 5 October

Rey Luise King, 83, US big band singer and television entertainer; 4 August

Reynolds William Henry, 87, US film editor; 16 July

Ricard Paul, 88, French liquor manufacturer who created and sold Ricard pastis; 6 November

Richter Sviatoslav Teofilovich, 81, Russian pianist; 1 August

Robbins Harold (born Francis Kane), 81, US writer; 14 October

Rodriguez Carlos Rafael, 84, Cuban communist intellectual who held several top posts in the Cuban government; 8 December

Rogers Ralph Burton, 87, US founder of the Public Broadcasting Service (PBS) and philanthropist who funded medical research; 4 November

Rosario Edwin (Chapo), 34, US lightweight boxer who won three world championships; 1 December

Rossi Aldo, 65, Italian architect; 4 September

de Rothschild Baron Edmond Adolphe Maurice Jules Jacques, c. 71, French banker; 2 November

Rowse Alfred Leslie, 93, British historian; 3 October

Rudolph Paul, 78, US architect and chairman of the School for Architecture at Yale University 1957–65; 8 August

Rugumbwa Cardinal Laurean, 85, Tanzanian Roman Catholic churchman who in 1960 became Africa's first cardinal; 8 December

Saw Maung, 68, Burmese general who organized a coup in 1988 and became leader of the military junta; 24 July

Schaefer George Louis, 76, US television director and producer; 10 September

Sejna Jan, 70, Czech general who defected to the West in 1968 and became a CIA informant; 23 August

Shoemaker Eugene Merle, 69, US geologist and astronomer; 18 July

Silkin Jon, 66, British poet and critic; 25 November

Simpson Robert Wilfred Levick, 76, British composer best known for his string quartets and symphonies; 21 November

Singh Ganesh Man, 81, Nepalese politician, leader of Nepal's 1990 pro-democracy movement; 18 September

Skelton Richard Bennett ('Red'), 87, US actor and comedian; 17 September

Smith Mary Louise, 82, US Republican Party official, first woman to serve as Republican National Committee chairperson (1974–77); 22 August

Soetens Robert, 100, French violinist; 22 October

Solti George (born György Stern), 84, Hungarian-born British conductor; 5 September

Sopinka John, 64, Canadian justice of the Supreme Court of Canada, who championed the rights of accused persons; 24 November

Spong William Beiser, 77, US Democratic senator from Virginia 1967–73; 8 October

Stanley Timothy Wadsworth, 69, US expert on defence and arms control who held several key defence posts from the 1950s to the 1970s; 21 September

Steel Dawn, 51, US film producer whose films included *Flashdance* (1983) and *The Accused* (1988); 20 December

Sterniuk Volodymyr, 90, Hungarian priest, leader of the Ukrainian Catholic Church, which was banned under the Soviets; 29 September

Stewart James Maitland, 89, US actor; 2 July

Strehler Giorgio, 76, Italian theatre director, who founded the Piccolo Teatro in Milan in 1947 and developed it into one of the world's leading theatres; 25 December

Stroud Dorothy (Nancy), 87, English museum curator at Sir John Soane's Museum and author of several books on the history of landscape gardening; 27 December

Swift Duncan, 54, British pianist; 8 August

al-Tariki Abdullah Ibn Hamound, 80, Saudi Arabian Oil Minister and founder of the Organization of Petroleum Exporting Countries; 7 September

Tartikoff Brandon, 48, US president of NBC television network's entertainment division 1980–91; 27 August

Taylor Dereck Wyn, 65, British publicist for rock groups, including the Beatles and the Beach Boys; 7 September

Tedesco Tommy, c. 67, US session guitarist who worked with artists such as Frank Sinatra, the Beach Boys, and Elvis Presley; 10 November

Teresa Mother (adopted name of Agnes Gonxha Bojaxhiu), 87, Indian nun and founder of the Missionaries of Charity; 5 September

Tonypandy Viscount (born Thomas George Thomas), 88, British parliamentarian, speaker of the House of Commons 1976–83; 22 September

Topping Norman H, 89, US viral researcher and president of the University of Southern California (USC), who helped develop a vaccine against typhus; 18 November

Ueno Jun-ichi, 87, Japanese co-owner of Japan's second largest newspaper, *Asahi Shimbun*; 19 October

Ulasewicz Anthony T, 79, US key witness at the US Senate's Watergate hearings, which led to the resignation of President Richard Nixon; he had been used by the Nixon administration to funnel 'hush' money to some of the eventual Watergate defendants; 17 December

Urban George, 76, Hungarian-born scholar who published studies of communist systems of government and was known for his belief in the possibility of a united Europe; 3 October

Vander Meer John Samuel (Johnny), 82, US Major League Baseball player, the only pitcher ever to throw consecutive no-hit games; 6 October

Versace Gianni, 50, Italian fashion designer; 15 July

Vestine Henry, 52, US guitarist with Canned Heat; 20 October

Villoresi Luigi ('Gigi'), 88, Italian racing driver; 24 August

Warbeck David (David Mitchell), 55, British actor and model; 23 July

Wayne Chuck (born Charles Jagelka), 74, US jazz guitarist; 29 July

Weaver Robert C, 89, US public servant and civil rights advocate, the first ever black US cabinet member; 17 July

Westwood Jean, 73, US Democratic Party activist, the first woman ever to head a major US political party; 18 August

Wethered Joyce, 96, British golfer who won numerous competitions and in 1950 was ranked by the Associated Press as the best woman golfer and the seventh best golfer overall since 1900; 18 November

Whitehead Nancy Dickerson, 70, US reporter; c. 27 October

Williams Stanley, 72, Danish ballet dancer and teacher; 21 October

Wilvers Bob, 65, US writer of the Alka Seltzer jingle, 'plop, plop, fizz, fizz, oh, what a relief it is'; 10 December

Winpisinger William W, 73, US labour leader and Democratic Party official who was president of the International Association of Machinists and Aerospace Workers 1977–89; 11 December

Witherspoon Jimmy (James), 74, US blues singer; 18 September

Wood Kenneth Maynard, 81, British electrical manufacturer, inventor of the Kenwood Chef; 19 October

Woodcock Bruce, 76, English boxer, British and Empire heavyweight champion 1945–50, European heavyweight champion 1946–49; 21 December

Wyatt Woodrow (Lord Wyatt of Weeford), 79, British political figure, newspaper columnist, and television personality, who moved from Labour to the Conservatives and was an interviewer for *Panorama*; 7 December

Yamashina Naoharu, 79, Japanese founder of Bandai Company, Japan's largest toy manufacturer, which produced Mighty Morphin Power Rangers and Tamagotchi virtual pets; 28 October

Yar'Adua Shehu Musa, 54, Nigerian Vice President 1976–79; 8 December

Yokoi Gumpei, 56, Japanese inventor of video games; 4 October

Yokoi Shoichi, 82, Japanese soldier who refused to surrender at the end of World War II and spent 27 years in the jungles of Guam; 22 September

Young Coleman Alexander, 79, US civil rights campaigner and the first black mayor of Detroit (1974–93), the longest-serving mayor in the city's history; 29 November

Young John Zachary, 90, British zoologist; 4 July

Zeibert Duke (David George), 86, restaurateur whose restaurant in Washington, DC was frequented by numerous celebrities; 15 August

Deaths: January–June 1998

Aaronovitch Samuel, 78, UK economist, academic, and author particularly involved in the relationship between economics and politics, as in *The Road from Thatcherism* 1981; 30 May

Abacha Sani, 54, Nigerian soldier, general, and president of Nigeria and commander-in-chief of its Armed Forces 1993–98; 8 June

Abd al-Rahman bin Yahya al-Iryani, 88, politician, jurist, and literary scholar, president of the Yemen Arab Republic 1967–74; 14 March

Abzug Bella (born Savitsky), 77, US politician and feminist, member of the House of Representatives 1970–76 and founder of the International Women's Environment and Development Association; 31 March

Algar James, 85, US producer and director for Walt Disney who shared nine Academy awards; 26 February

Alioto Joseph, 81, US mayor of San Francisco, California, 1968–76; 29 January

Allin John Maury, 76, US presiding bishop of the Episcopal Church from 1973 to 1986 who led the church during an era of doctrinal and social unrest; 6 March

Aury Dominique (Anne Desclos), 90, French author of erotic novels and translator of British and American fiction; 30 April

Ayraud Pierre, 89, French writer and dramatist, known as Thomas Narcejac, famous for his artistic partnership with Pierre Boileau; 10 June

Barton Derek, 79, English chemist, joint winner of the 1969 Nobel Prize, for his work on unusual reactions of steroids; 16 March

Bassey Hogan (Okon Bassey Asuquo) 55, Nigerian boxer, a great ambassador for African sport; 26 January

Beningfield Gordon George, 61, English artist, advocate for the protection of the countryside, especially interested in portraying wildlife; 4 May

Bermant Chaim Icyk, 68, Polish-born British writer who for two decades wrote a weekly column entitled 'On the Other Hand' for the UK *Jewish Chronicle*; 20 January

Bing Ilse, 98, German photographer known for her mastery of the 35 mm camera; 10 March

Bishop Jr, Walter, 70, US jazz pianist who played with Miles Davis and Charlie Parker; 24 January

Bold Alan, 54, Scottish poet, writer, critic, and anthologist, whose work included studies of his mentor Hugh MacDiarmid; 19 March

Bono Sonny (born Salvatore Phillip Bono), 62, US singer, songwriter, and politician who sang 'I Got You Babe' (1965) with Cher; 5 January

Bosse-Griffiths Kate (Käthe Bosse), German-born Egyptologist particularly active in Wales (Swansea), and writer in Welsh; 4 April

Bradley Owen, 82, US country music record producer who produced 'Crazy' by Patsy Cline and 'Coal Miner's Daughter' by Loretta Lynn; 7 January

Brenner F Cecil, 79, US fibre scientist who, in the 1970s, developed the government standard that rates the safety and performance of car tyres; 19 March

Bridges Lloyd (Lloyd Vernet Bridges Jr), 85, US TV and film actor who appeared in numerous movies, including *High Noon* and *Airplane!*, and the television series *Sea Hunt*; 10 March

Bubley Esther, 76, US photographer who is perhaps best known for documenting the workers in Washington as the USA mobilized for World War II; 16 March

Bunting-Smith Mary, 87, US visionary president of Radcliffe College when it was an all-girls college, who started Radcliffe's Institute for Independent Study, now called the Bunting Institute; 21 January

Bush Geoffrey, 77, English composer and teacher, whose works include *Christmas Cantata* (1947), *Summer Serenade* (1948), and *The Equation* (1967); 24 February

Calder); Alberto Pedro (born Mendoza), 77, Argentinian mathematician active in Argentina and the USA who transformed the study of partial differential equations by applying to it the theory of singular integrals; 16 April

Caliendi Stanley Charles Joseph, 78, English aerospace systems engineer and probably the first person to use the 'black box' to establish the cause of an aircraft accident; 1 March

Campbell Alan Keith, 74, US reformer of the US civil service and first director of the Office of Personnel Management 1979–80; 4 February

Capehart Jerry Neil, 69, US songwriter and manager, best known for *Summertime Blues* and *C'mon Everybody* written with Eddie Cochran; 7 June

Caray Harry (adopted name of Harry Christopher Carabina), c. 75–85, US baseball announcer and member of the Baseball Hall of Fame in Cooperstown, New York; 18 February

Cartwright Mary Lucy, 97, English mathematician, one of the first female fellows of the Royal Society, who in her later years worked on the study of dynamical systems; 3 April

Casaroli Agostino, 83, Italian priest, Vatican's top diplomat and Secretary of State (1979–90) who developed Vatican's links with countries of Eastern Europe; 9 June

Chatichai Choonhavan, 76, Thai soldier, diplomat, and politician, prime minister 1988–91; 6 May

Clark Roger, 58, English rally driver who won 27 major international rallies, including Britain's RAC International Rally in 1972 and 1976; 12 January

Cleaver Leroy Eldridge, 62, US political activist, environmentalist, and consultant on ethnic diversity; 1 May

Commager Henry Steele, 95, eminent US author and professor of US history; 2 March

Conedera Juan José Gerardi, 75, Guatemalan priest, Bishop of El Quiche 1973–84 and Auxiliary Bishop of Guatemala City 1984–98, died a victim of political violence; 26 April

Conrad Clyde Lee, 50, former US Army sergeant convicted of treason; 8 January

Cookson Catherine Ann McMullen, 91, English prolific writer of best-selling romantic and historical novels situated mainly in the northeast of England; 11 June

Copland Donald Frank, 67, English businessman and spiritual healer, author, and teacher, member of the National Federation of Spiritual Healers and initiator of its Healer Training programme; 24 April

Costa Lucio, 96, French architect and town planner, designer of Brasilia, the new capital city of Brazil (1957); 14 June

Cox Morris George, 94, English poet, writer, and printer, who appreciated intellectual qualities of 'ordinary people'; 31 March

Cudlipp Hugh, 84, English journalist, editor, and businessman; 17 May

Davis Fred, 84, English snooker player, World Professional Snooker Champion 1948, 1949, 1951–56, and World Billiards Champion 1980; 15 April

Diemer Walter E, 93, US inventor of bubble gum; 8 January

Dread Judge (born Alex Hughes), c. 53, English singer and songwriter whose ribald reggae songs appeared on albums including *Dreadmania* and *Working Class 'Ero*; 13 March

Duma Dervish, 89, Albanian diplomat, broadcaster, businessman, and community leader, from 1939 in the UK where, in 1940, he inaugurated the BBC Albanian service; 6 May

Duncan Todd, 95, US creator of the role of Porgy in George Gershwin's *Porgy and Bess* who was an important force in the desegregation of US opera; 28 February

Durbridge Francis Henry, 85, English crime writer; 11 April

Edwards Monica, 85, English writer who wrote children's books including *Wish for a Pony* (1947) and *Storm Ahead* (1953), as well as autobiographical books; 18 January

English David, 67, UK journalist, editor of the *Daily Mail* 1971–92, editor-in-chief for Associated Newspapers 1989–98, chairman of ITN 1997–98; 10 June

Epelbaum Renée, 77, Argentinian campaigner, founding member of the Mothers of the Plaza de Mayo, which campaigns for those whose children were killed during Argentine military rule; 7 February

Epstein Melvin (Mel Powell), 75, US pianist, composer, and arranger, Pulitzer prize winner in 1990 for his concerto for two pianos, and a successful jazz musician; 24 April

Evans Eugene Barton (Gene), 75, US actor best known for his roles in war films; 1 April

Fashanu Justinus Soni (Justin), 37, English footballer whose sexual orientation caused much controversy in the world of sport; 2 May

Faye Alice Jeanne (Lepert), 83, US actress, a popular musical star in the 'golden era' of Hollywood; 9 May

Ford Boris, 80, English educationist and writer who championed the role of media in education and was committed to developing a broad range of creative and intellectual interests through education; 19 May

Fowler Gene, Jn, 81, US film editor and director, best remembered for directing *I Was a Teenage Werewolf* 1957; 11 May

Fowley Daniel Vincent (Douglas), 87, US actor who appeared in over 100 films including *Singin' in the Rain* 1952; 21 May

Frank Frederick Charles, 87, English physicist born in South Africa, educated and active in the UK, major contributor to the dislocation theory, understanding of cold fusion, liquid crystals, alloy structures, polymers, earthquakes, and continental drift; 5 April

Freeman Joan, 80, Australian physicist who was the joint winner of the Rutherford Prize for work on beta-radioactivity of complex nuclei; 18 March

Friendly Fred W (born Frederick Friendly Wachenheimer), 82, US president of CBS News and Columbia University professor whose early documentaries with Edward R Murrow set the standard for television news; 3 March

Frist Sr, Thomas F, 87, US founder of the for-profit system of hospital administration, co-founding Hospital Corporation of America (HCA); 4 January

Fukui Kenichi, 79, Japanese chemist who was joint winner of the 1981 Nobel Prize for chemistry, for his research into chemical reactions; 9 January

Gellhorn Martha Ellis, 89, US journalist who reported on the Spanish Civil War, World War II, and the Vietnam War; 15 February

Gerrard Alfred Horace, 99, English sculptor and teacher at the Slade School of Art, who used stone, wood, and iron from bomb sites in his work; 13 June

Glyn Anthony (adopted name of Geoffrey Leo Simon Davson), 75, British biographer and novelist whose best-known work was *Elinor Glyn* (1955), a biography of his maternal grandmother; 20 January

Goacher Denis John, 72, English poet, translator, actor, and broadcaster, author of *Logbook* 1972; 23 April

Goldwater Barry Morris, 89, US politician, Republican senator 1952–64 and 1969–87, who contested the US presidency in 1964 elections; 29 May

Gray A(lexander) Stuart, 92, English architect known for his work for the UK National Health Service; 20 February

Grayson Cecil, 78, English Italianist who specialized in the cultural history of the Italian Renaissance; 28 April

Green Bernard (Benny), 70, English saxophonist and broadcaster, writer on jazz and literary critic to the *Spectator*; 22 June

Gruson Sydney, 81, Canadian-born prizewinning foreign correspondent for the *New York Times*; 8 March

Guion Raymond (Gene Raymond), 89, US actor, husband of Jeanette MacDonald, star of *Flying Down to Rio* 1933 and *Zoo in Budapest* 1933; 3 May

Haq Barbara (born Barbara McKay Green), 79, English campaigner and a key organizer for the Movement for Colonial Freedom (MCF), now known as Liberation; 2 March

Harris Derek (John Derek), 71, US actor and film director, husband of Bo Derek (Mary Cathleen Collins); 22 May

Harsch Joseph Close, 93, US writer and broadcaster specializing in foreign affairs; 3 June

Hartmann Philip Edward (also known as **Hartman**), 49, Canadian actor, comedian, scriptwriter, and impersonator, who contributed to *The Simpsons*, *Saturday Night Live*, and other programmes; 28 May

Hawkes John, 72, US writer and academic teacher, champion of postmodernism and formal experimentation in fiction; 15 May

Hayes Peter Lind (Joseph Conrad Lind), 82, US actor, composer, and writer; 22 April

Hicks David Nightingale, 69, English interior decorator and garden designer, author of books on decoration; 29 March

Hitchings George H, 92, US pharmaceutical company research chemist who was a co-winner of the 1988 Nobel Prize for Medicine or Physiology for his development of drugs to fight against leukemia, malaria, and viral infections such as herpes and AIDS; 27 February

Hollis (James) Martin, 59, English philosopher whose rationalism was based on the idea that humans can be seen as united by 'universal' beliefs; 27 February

Howell Denis Herbert, 74, English politician; 19 April

Huddie David Patrick, 82, Irish-born engineer active in the UK who, as managing director of the Aero Engine Division at Rolls-Royce, implemented a new type of fan-jet engine, the RB211, to power the L1011 TriStar 'jumbo jet' wide-body aircraft; 14 May

Huddleston Ernest Urban Trevor, 84, English priest, internationally involved in peace initiatives and anti-apartheid movement, member of National Peace Council 1983–98; 20 April

Hutchinson Josephine, 99, US cinema, theatre, and television actress, and a dramatic coach; 4 June

Hymes James L, 84, US originator of the Head Start early childhood education programme; 6 March

Innes Ralph Hammond, 84, English writer, author of best-selling, thoroughly researched thrillers; 10 June

James Robbie (Robert Mark James), 40, Welsh footballer who was a member of the Swansea team that won promotion from the Fourth Division to the First within four consecutive seasons. He was capped 47 times by Wales; 18 February

Jeannerot Aline ('Jandeline'), 87, French actress, wife of Jean Mercure; 24 June

Jewell Peter Arundel, 72, English biologist who specialized in ecology and animal conservation; 23 May

Johnson Ronald, 62, US poet and cookery writer whose works include *Ark* (1996), *The Book of the Green Man* (1967), and *The American Table* (1984); 4 March

Johnstone Anne Grahame, 70, English illustrator who worked with her twin sister Janet (1928–79) and then alone; 25 May

Jones Grandpa (Louis Marshall Jones), 84, US banjo player and comic who was a regular on *Hee Haww* from 1968 to 1993; 19 February

Jünger Ernst, 102, German writer whose works include *Auf den Marmorklippen/On the Marble Cliffs* (1939) and *Heliopolis* (1949); 17 February

Kahn Franz Daniel, 71, German astrophysicist who made theoretical studies of the dynamics and physics of space; 8 February

Karamanlis Constantine George, 91, Greek lawyer and politician, prime minister 1955–63 and 1974–80 and president of Greece 1980–85 and 1990–95; 23 April

Karff Mona May, 86, Russian-born US winner of seven US women's chess championships in 1938–1974; 10 January

Kazin Alfred, 82, US writer and literary critic, associated with distinguished universities, author of *On Native Grounds* 1942, *Bright Book of Life* 1973, and *God and the American writer* 1997; 4 June

Keating John R, 63, US Catholic bishop of Arlington, Vancouver; 22 March

Kelly William Russell, 92, businessman credited with founding the temporary work or 'temp' profession; 3 January

Kendall (Kykendall) Royce, 63, US country singer who formed a successful team with his daughter Jeannie; 22 May

Kenton Godfrey William, 96, English actor famous in particular for his appearances in Shakespearean plays; 27 April

Kestelman Morris, 92, English artist, known for his abstract paintings as well as landscapes and portraits; 15 June

Lawrence Sydney (Syd), 74, English cornet player and band leader, creator of the Syd Lawrence Orchestra and follower of the music of Glenn Miller; 5 May

Laxness Halldór (Halldór Gudjonsson), 95, Icelandic writer whose novels included *The Great Weaver from Kashmir* (1927) and *Paradise Reclaimed* (1957); winner of the 1955 Nobel Prize for Literature; 8 February

Leet Gerald Mackenzie, 85, English painter, teacher, and book collector; painted mainly neo-Romantic portraits; 18 June

Lestor Joan, 66, Canadian-born UK nursery teacher and politician, Labour MP for Eccles 1987–97, chairperson of the International Committee of the Labour Party 1978–97; 27 March

Limann Hilla, 63, Ghanian diplomat and politician, President of Ghana 1979–81, whose government was a civilian interlude in a series of military regimes; 23 January

Lingh Nguyen Van (Nguyen Van Cuc), 82, Vietnamese politician, general secretary of the Communist Party of Vietnam 1986–91; 27 April

Lippert Albert, 72, US co-founder of the Weight Watchers diet plan; 28 February

Lord Jack (born John Joseph Patrick Ryan), 77, US actor who played detective Steve McGarret in the television series *Hawaii Five-O*; 21 January

Lyotard Jean-François, 73, French philosopher, exponent of post-modernism (together with Michel Foucault, Gillez Deleuze, and Jacques Derrida); 21 April

McCartney Linda Louise, 56, musician and environmental campaigner, wife of Paul McCartney; 17 April

McCook Thomas (Tommy), 71, Jamaican tenor saxophonist, flautist, composer, and arranger, founder member of the Skatalites; 5 May

McGlew Derrick John, 69, South African cricketer, captain of Natal; 8 June

MacGregor Ian Kinloch, 85, Scottish businessman, former chairman of the National Coal Board; 13 April

McIntosh Patrick James, 91, Scottish artist, one of the most notable Scottish landscape painters; 7 April

Mahmood Talat, 74, Indian singer famous for his love songs; 9 May

Mairants Ivor, 89, Polish guitarist, composer, writer, and teacher who played in numerous dance bands and whose books included a flamenco guitar tutor and *The Great Jazz Guitarists* (1995); 20 February

Male George, 87, English footballer who won four League Championship titles and the FA Cup with Arsenal and was capped 19 times by England; 19 February

Mankowitz Cyril Wolf, 73, English author of reference books on antique porcelain as well as fiction – novels, plays, musicals, and film scripts; 20 May

Marx Enid Crystal Dorothy, 95, English designer and painter fascinated by abstract and geometric patterns which she used in stamps, fabrics, books, logos, wrapping paper designs, packaging labels, and other items; 18 May

Mastroianni Umberto, 87, Italian sculptor known for his municipal monuments to the Italian Resistance; 25 February

Maynard Vera Joan, 76, English trade unionist and politician, MP and member of the National Executive Committee of the Labour Party 1972–82, 1983–87; 27 March

Mellish Robert Joseph, 85, English trade union official and politician, Minister of Public Buildings and Works 1967–69, Parliamentary Secretary to Treasury and Government Chief Whip 1969–70 and 1974–76, Opposition Chief Whip 1970–74, Deputy Chairman of London Docklands Development Corporation 1981–85; 9 May

Mercure Jean (real name Pierre Libermann), 89, French theatre producer and director, who revived the Théatre National Populaire and Théatre de la Ville in Paris; 24 June

Merrill Bob, 76, US composer and lyricist who composed for Broadway musicals; his songs included 'How Much is That Doggie in the Window?'; 17 February

Millar, Ronald Graeme, 78, English playwright, screenwriter, and speechwriter; 16 April

Milne Alan John Mitchell, 76, English social and political philosopher, follower of post-Hegelian Idealism, author of *Freedom and Rights* 1968, who developed a successful academic career despite being blinded in military action in 1945; 24 May

Monahan Jay, 42, US NBC News legal advisor and husband of *Today Show* host Katie Couric; 24 January

Morgan Dermot, 45, Irish actor best known for his role as Father Ted Crilly in the Channel 4 comedy *Father Ted*; 1 March

Morrison Alistair Ardoch, 86, Australian writer, artist, and industrial designer; 15 March

Muir Frank, 77, English writer and broadcaster who, with Denis Norden, wrote numerous scripts for radio and television and appeared in programmes including *Call My Bluff* and *My Word!*; 2 January

Nadal Carlos, 81, Catalan painter, one of the last representatives of expressionism in Spain; 6 June

Narcejac Thomas: see **Ayraud** Pierre

Newland Rupert William, 79, New Zealand, potter and teacher, creator of deeply humanistic and accessible works; 30 April

Newton Keith Robert, 56, English footballer who played for Blackburn Rovers, Everton, and Burnley; 16 June

Nitschke Ray, 61, US defensive American football player for the Green Bay Packers when they won five National Football League championships in seven seasons; 8 March

Nolan Jeanette, 76, US actress famous for her radio performances; 5 June

O'Connor Philip Marie Constant Bancroft, 81, English writer, poet, and broadcaster, whose introspective work tends to be centred around the author's sense of being an outsider; 29 May

Olson Mancur Lloyd, 66, US economist whose work on political lobbies popularized the term a 'free-ride'; 19 February

Ortese Anna Maria, 83, Italian writer whose novels include *Il cardillo addolorato/The Lament of the Linnet* (1993) and *La Porta di Toledo/The Gate of Toledo* (1975); 9 March

O'Sullivan Maureen Paul, Irish-born US actress, best remembered for her performances in *Tarzan* films, mother of Mia Farrow; 22 June

Pabst von Ohain Hans-Joachim, 86, German engineer who implemented the first jet engine to be used successfully to fly an aircraft; 13 March

Parsons Claudia, 97, English writer and traveller, one of England's first female engineers; 5 June

Pasmore (Edwin John) Victor, 89, English artist who in 1948 made a dramatic transition from naturalism to abstract art and became a leading figure in the international abstract movement; 23 January

Pérez Martínez Manuel, 62, Spanish-born Colombian priest and guerrilla, known as 'El Cura', leader of Colombia's second-largest insurgent groups; 14 February

Perkins Carl Lee, 65, US musician and songwriter who wrote 'Blue Suede Shoes' and 'Everybody's Trying to be my Baby'; 19 January

Pilatus Robert, 32, US model and pop singer, member of Milli Vanilli; 2 April

Pol Pot (Saloth Sar), 73, Cambodian guerrilla and politician, leader of Khmer Rouge and prime minister of Cambodia 1976–79; 15 April

Porsche Ferdinand Anton Ernst, 88, Austrian engineer and businessman involved in car design and production; 27 March

Powell Colin (Cozy), 50, English drummer and composer; 5 April

Powell Enoch, 85, English Conservative politician and classical scholar, chiefly remembered for his 1968 speech on UK immigration; 8 February

Prelog Vladimir, 91, Swiss chemist who was joint winner of the 1975 Nobel Prize for chemistry, for research into the designs of complex molecules; 7 January

Premru Raymond Eugene, 63, US trombonist and composer, active in London 1956–88; 8 May

Prohias Antonio, 77, Cuban-born cartoonist of 'Spy vs. Spy' in *Mad* magazine; 24 February

Questal Mae, 89, US actress who gave voice to cartoon characters Betty Boop and Olive Oyl; 4 January

Rabbit Edward (Eddie) Thomas, 53, US country singer and songwriter; 7 May

Raphael Ralph Alexander, 77, English chemist and lecturer in organic chemistry who achieved the synthesis of carbohydrates and histamine from acetylenic precursors; 27 April

Rawley Donald Paul, 40, US writer of poetry and short stories published in the *New Yorker* and *Harper*; 3 May

Reiche Grosse-Neumann Maria, 95, German-born mathematician active in Peru where she investigated the lines and shapes of the Nazca desert; 8 June

Reid William Ronald (Bill), 78, Canadian sculptor, considered one of the country's greatest contemporary artists; 13 March

Ribicoff Abraham, 87, US former senator, governor of Connecticut, and member of President Kennedy's cabinet; 22 February

Richards Charles Coleridge ('Red'), 85, US jazz pianist and vocalist; 12 March

Rickards Maurice (Maurice George Mansbridge), 78, English designer, photographer, writer, and ephemerist who promoted the study of ephemera – 'the minor transient documents of everyday life' – as an academic discipline and in 1977 began work on an *Encyclopedia of Ephemera*; 11 February

Roberts Frank Kenyon, 90, British diplomat whose lengthy career is recalled in his memoirs *Dealing with Dictators* (1991); 7 January

Rochefort Christiane Renée, 80, French novelist who tackled controversial subjects of homosexuality and incest; 24 April

Rose-Innes Iona Jasmine (born Gordon-Forbes), 82, English designer, painter, photographer, writer, and teacher, author of *Writing in the Dust* 1968; 15 June

Rycroft Charles Frederick, 83, English psychoanalyst, author of the influential *Critical Dictionary of Psychoanalysis* 1968 and *The Innocence of Dreams* 1968; 24 May

Rysanek Leonie, 71, Austrian opera singer whose career spanned four and a half decades and numerous roles; 7 March

Sartoris Alberto, 97, Italian architect, draughtsman, critic, and journalist, representative of modernist architecture; 8 March

Saunders Nicholas (Carr-), 60, English writer and businessman who was the creative force behind the development of Neal's Yard in Covent Garden, and who wrote books, including *E for Ecstasy* about the 1990s drug culture; 3 February

Sauvage Catherine (Jeannine Saunier), 69, French singer and actress known for her sensitive and powerful interpretations of song lyrics; 20 March

Schifano Mario, 63, Italian painter whose work included the series *Oxygen Oxygen* (1967) and *TV Landscapes* (1969); 26 January

Schooling Elisabeth, 83, English dancer, producer, and teacher, associated with Ballet Rambert (later Rambert Dance Company); 22 June

Schultz Theodore W, 95, leading US agricultural economist and Nobel prizewinner who helped develop and popularize the concept of treating education spending as an investment in 'human capital'; 26 February

Scott Schomberg (born Walter Schomberg Hepburn Scott), 87, Scottish historic buildings architect, consultant to the National Trust for Scotland; 11 February

Scoular James (Jimmy), 73, Scottish footballer and manager who led Newcastle United to FA Cup victory in 1955 and was capped nine times by Scotland; 19 March

Shaukat Osman (Sheikh Azizur Rahman), 81, Bangladeshi writer, one of the most eminent cultural and literary figures of his country; 14 May

Shevchenko Arkady Nikolayevich, 67, high-ranking Soviet diplomat and top UN official who defected to the USA in 1978; 28 February

Shuman Eleanor I, 87, US survivor of the *Titanic*, which sank when she was 2 years old; 7 March

Sillett (Richard) Peter, 65, English footballer who won the English League Championship with Chelsea in 1954–55 and was capped three times by England; 12 March

Sinatra Francis Albert, 82, US singer and actor whose artistic gifts and colourful life made him into a 20th-century icon; 14 May

Skidmore James Richard (Jimmy), 83, English tenor saxophonist, and dedicated jazz-player; 23 April

Skinner (Russell Thomas) Francis, 89, British architect who was a founding member of the architectural practice Tecton, which was a major influence on the Modern Movement in Britain; 6 January

Smith John, 71, English architect, editor, and teacher, president of the Architectural Association (AA; 1971–73) and editorial chairman of the *AA Journal* until 1982; 28 April

Smith Reginald (Reg Smythe), 81, English cartoonist, creator of the Andy Capp character; 13 June

Spock Benjamin McLane, 94, US paediatrician whose liberal views on child-rearing were outlined in his book *The Common Sense Book of Baby and Child Care* (1946); 15 March 1998

Squires (Edna May) Dorothy, 83, Welsh singer; 14 April

Stevens Leslie, 74, US film and television scriptwriter, producer, and director, creator of the cult television series *Outer Limits*; 24 April

Stevens Roger L(acey), 87, US founding chairman of the Kennedy Center in Washington, DC, and producer of *West Side Story* and *Bus Stop on Broadway*; 2 February

Stickney Dorothy, 97, US actress and co-author of the Pulitzer prize-winning *State of the Union* and *Life with Father* (with Russel Crouse), which became the longest-running non-musical play in Broadway history; 2 June

Stoneman Marjory Douglas, 108, US environmentalist and author who devoted her life to environmental issues, particularly to the protection of Florida's Everglades; 14 May

Suzuki Shinichi, 99, Japanese violinist who developed the internationally used 'Suzuki Method'; 26 January

Tabarly Eric, 66, French navy captain and yachtsman, lost at sea; 12 June

Tanner Henry, 79, Swiss-born journalist and foreign correspondent for *The New York Times* and numerous other newspapers and magazines; 15 May

Taylor Telford, 90, US lawyer, writer, and teacher, prosecutor at the Nuremberg trials; 23 May

Tennstedt Klaus, 71, German conductor who achieved fame late in his career and was best known for his performances of romantic music; 11 January

Thomas, Rover, 72, Australian artist; 11 April

Tippett Michael (Kemp), 93, English composer whose work included *The Midsummer Marriage* (1952) and *The Vision of St Augustine* (1965); 8 January

Torok Maria, 72, Hungarian-born American psychoanalyst, famous for her critique of Freud and work on trauma; 25 March

Townsend Robert, 77, US business executive and best-selling author, who wrote *Up the Organization* 1970; 12 January

Trease Geoffrey, 88, English writer best known for his historical children's novels, such as *Bows Against Barons* (1934) and *Cue for Treason* (1940); 27 January

Ulanova Galina Sergeyevna, 88, Russian ballet dancer, who danced with the Kirov and Bolshoi before becoming a coach for the latter; 21 March

Uno Sosuke, 75, Japanese politician, prime minister 1989; 19 May

von Franz Marie-Louise, 83, German analytical psychologist who was the closest colleague of C G Jung, and wrote extensively on fairy tales; 16 February

Walsh J T, 54, US character actor who appeared in nearly 60 films, including *A Few Good Men*, *Sling Blade*, and *Good Morning Vietnam*; 27 February

Ward Helen, 81, US singer artistically associated with the clarinettist Benny Goodman; 21 April

Wells John (Campbell), 61, English writer, actor, and director, best known for his contributions to *Private Eye*; 11 January

Wells Junior (adopted name of Amos Blakemore), 63, US influential blues singer and harmonica player; 15 January

Whitney Betsey Maria (born Cushing), 89, US philanthropist, member of US society establishment, founder of the Greentree Foundation helping community groups and supporter of medical schools and US museums; 25 March

Wilkie Douglas Robert, 75, English physiologist, specialist in muscle mechanics and its relation to human performance; 21 May

Williams Wendy Orlean, 49, US singer, musician, songwriter, and actress; 6 April

Wills Moody Helen, 92, US tennis player who won numerous titles in the USA and Europe during the 1920s and 1930s; 1 January

Wilson Carl (Dean), 51, US singer, guitarist, and songwriter with the Beach Boys who had hits with 'Surfin' USA' (1963), 'I Get Around' (1964), and 'Good Vibrations' (1966); 6 February

Wood Beatrice, 105, famous US ceramist whose liaisons with artist Marcel Duchamp, writer Henri-Pierre Roche, and others in the Dada movement earned her the title 'Mama of Dada'; 12 March

Wynette Tammy (Virginia Wynette Pugh), 55, US country music singer, one of the most successful female vocalists in the field; 6 April

Youngman Henny (Henry), 91, English-born US comic dubbed the 'King of One-Liners'; 24 February

Full Obituaries

Abacha, Sani

(1943–1998)

Nigerian soldier, politician, and president 1993–98. Born in Kano, northern Nigeria, after school he enlisted in the army and underwent military training in Nigeria and England. Fighting with federalist forces in the Biafran civil war, 1967–69, he was commended for his bravery. Although he did not overtly seize power until 1993, Abacha was a leading activist in a series of coups from 1966 onwards. Rewarded for his support by the soldiers he helped to install, Abacha rose from the rank of lieutenant in 1966 to brigadier in 1980, and three years later emerged from the political shadows to become head of state in his own right.

Immediately after assuming the presidency, Abacha promised a return to constitutional rule and announced that his own tenure of the office would be brief. He broke both promises and embarked on a repressive policy that brought widespread international condemnation. His opponents and critics were either imprisoned or killed: the act causing most concern being the execution, in November 1995, of the writer Ken Saro-Wiwa and eight other associates.

Abacha died on 8 June 1998, reportedly of a heart attack. The news of his demise was greeted with few tears and much relief by the majority of his countrymen.

Acker, Kathy

(1944–1997)

US post-modern, punk feminist author whose explicit and pornographic writing assaults the reader with its alarming but inventive content and imagery. One of the new wave of avant garde writers influenced by cult figures such as William Burroughs, Jean Genet, Jorge Luis Borges, and Georges Bataille, Acker's eclectic style attracted notoriety when she published *Blood and Guts in High School* in 1978. In this seminal novel, her jarring juxtaposition of elements of autobiography, plagiarism, and pornography sought to challenge the reader's concept of fiction and push back the boundaries of writing.

Acker's first confrontational act was to escape her conventional Jewish home in New York at 18 to work in the sex industry as a stripper and show girl. Meanwhile she wrote journalistic pieces on the porn industry, inspired by the work of Burroughs. Her first two novels reflect his influence on her work: *I Dreamt I Was a Nymphomaniac: Imagining* (1974) and *The Childlike Life of the Black Tarantula* (1975). However, with these books Acker also established her own style, characterized by a refusal to develop plot, and provocative description of the sexual, the brutal, and the ugly.

The US feminist movement embraced Acker as a major voice of the new counterculture, but in the mid-1980s her love–hate relationship with her home country led her to move to England, where she became the darling of the avant garde following the 1984 UK publication of *Blood and Guts in High School*. Acker also turned to performance art; her spiky punk hair, leather gear, body piercings, and tattoos added to her notoriety, and she soon became a well-known figure. Her status as a 'serious' writer was lent considerable gravitas when she was featured in the British television arts programme *The South Bank Show*. Acker's later works such as *Don Quixote* (1986), *Empire of the Senseless* (1988), and *In Memoriam to Identity* (1990), caused many critics, unable to stomach the visceral quality of her writing, to question the validity of her continuing subversion of language and meaning. Yet in the USA, the esteem in which she was held led to an invitation in 1990 to set up a department of writing at the San Francisco Art Institute. Here she revealed a disciplined approach to her craft and a love of the classics which belied the 'wild child' image she had hitherto projected.

When Acker fell victim to breast cancer, her desire to retain control over her own body, which she had exploited as a canvas for her exploration of sexuality, led her to insist on fighting the disease in her own way after conventional medicine had failed her. She announced: 'I will make myself well or at least I will die in control of my own body.' She wrote obsessively about her illness and to the end sought to arrive at her own answers to her predicament, so that her untimely death should not be a meaningless one. She died in London on 29 November 1997.

Banda, Hastings Kamuzu

(1906–1997)

Malawi politician, physician, and president. He was born in Kasungu, which was then in the British protectorate of Nyasaland, at a date that is still uncertain. The official year of birth is 1906, but there is speculation that it might have been 1902 or even 1898. His mother was a servant for a Scottish missionary and it was the Presbyterians at the mission who gave him his early education and the name Hastings. He acquired the African name, Kamuzu, meaning herbal root, following his mother's resort to tribal medicine to cure her infertility. Information about his father is virtually non-existent.

At an early age he left Nyasaland for neighbouring Rhodesia, and then South Africa, where he worked in the gold mines. By 1925 he had saved enough money to buy a ticket to the USA to take up a scholarship at the Wilberforce Institute, Ohio. From there he went to Chicago University and then a medical college in Nashville, Tennessee, where he qualified as a doctor in 1937. To fulfil his ambition to practise in the UK he needed more qualifications, which he acquired in Edinburgh. He then went into general practice in the north of England and London.

Meanwhile Nyasaland had become, with Rhodesia, part of a white-dominated Central African Federation, a development which stimulated Banda to give up his lucrative practice in London, in 1953, and return to Africa, establishing a practice on the Gold Coast, now Ghana.

In 1958 he returned to his native country and in the following year founded the Malawi Congress Party (MCP), to lead the fight for independence. The MCP was to become his personal political machine. He was arrested in Rhodesia for subversion and imprisoned for nearly a year before being deported to Nyasaland. The 'wind of change' that the British prime minister, Harold Macmillan, had identified in his 1960 speech in Cape Town, was now blowing strongly throughout the African continent and in July 1964 Nyasaland achieved full independence, as Malawi. Banda, who had been prime minister since 1963, became its first president, and president-for-life in 1971.

He proceeded to govern in a highly personalized, idiosyncratic way. He established a one-party state, brooking no opposition, and astonished his African neighbours by officially recognizing the whites-only republic of South Africa, paying an official visit in 1971. At the same time he gave recognition to the socialist government in Angola. Meanwhile pressure was mounting on him to liberalize his regime and in 1977 he embarked on a cautious policy of reform. The pace of change was not sufficient for his opponents and in 1992 he promised a referendum on a new, democratic constitution, including the repeal of Banda's life presidency. The result was a clear mandate for change and in the multi-party elections held in 1994 he and his party were defeated. He then faced a murder trial for killings which had taken place during his presidency, but was eventually exonerated.

He died on November 25 1997, leaving behind a mixed legacy of success and failure. During two-thirds of his long life his achievements had been remarkable but in his later years he had degenerated into the kind of despot characterized by other African figures such as Mobutu and Amin. It will be the task of historians to balance the uneven quality of his life.

Berlin, Isaiah

(1909–1997)

Latvian-born UK philosopher and historian of ideas. A stubbornly modest man, who once remarked 'I have been overestimated all my life', Isaiah Berlin lived and worked for most of his life in Oxford, latterly (1966–75) as president of Wolfson College, Oxford University. Yet despite inhabiting the enclosed world of academia, he remained to the end a cosmopolitan man – a lover of life forever curious about the many and varied manifestations of human experience and philosophical thought. During his career he was the recipient of many academic prizes and honours, including the Order of Merit (OM) awarded in 1971. A man of great energy, Berlin's prodigious gifts – as philosopher, polymath, broadcaster, lecturer, and witty raconteur – were employed across the whole spectrum of intellectual life. Indeed it was only his irrepressible energy and versatility that allowed him to embrace so many wide-ranging interests, remaining intellectually astute until the very end, forever intrigued by the great moral questions of his times.

A witness to the Russian revolutions of 1905 and 1917, much of Berlin's later defence of pluralism was coloured by his experience of the reality of revolutionary change. Having settled with his family in England in 1921, Berlin's rise to eminence as a lecturer in philosophy at New College, Oxford, between 1932 and 1938, and later as a fellow of both New College and later All Souls College, established his reputation in the inter-war years. His highly idiosyncratic style of public speaking – at top speed he could lecture at 400 words per minute, rarely referring to notes, in a verbal cascade 'like a melting Russian river in spring' – made his lectures an experience that a wider audience of radio listeners also enjoyed in his frequent broadcasts on the Third Programme in the 1950s. By the end of the war, having served for a period at the UK Foreign Office in Moscow and at the UK Embassy in Washington, Berlin had decided to give up philosophy for a study of the history of ideas, which he had begun with his biographical study *Karl Marx* (1939). Disliking the domination of philosophy by the discipline of logic, he had come to the conclusion that philosophy 'can only be done by very clever people. I didn't think I'd ever be good enough. In the end, I thought it wasn't for me because I didn't lie awake in bed at night thinking of solutions to agonising philosophical problems.'

Not long after being elected to the chair of Social and Political Theory at All Souls in 1957, he published one of his seminal works, *Two Concepts of Liberty*. In it he defended the right to freedom of choice, and the book served as the cornerstone for his various and considerable essays on the great moral and philosophical question of how people should live – a problem which always preoccupied him. The pluralist thesis that he developed in this and other works such as *The Hedgehog and the Fox* (1953) and *Four Essays on Liberty* (1969) – that no single political or philosophical system can embrace the various and contradictory answers to the problem of how men should live without massive compromise – underlines his profound revulsion for totalitarian regimes, which have set out to establish political utopias at great human sacrifice. Some of Berlin's finest essays were collected not long before his death in *The Proper Study of Mankind* (1997); they provide a fitting retrospective of the work of an important thinker who never lost sight of the human predicament at the root of the wider philosophical and historical questions of his time. He died in Oxford on 5 November 1997.

Bremner, Billy (William John)

(1942–1997)

Scottish footballer who captained the Leeds United side, winning two league championships and four other domestic and European trophies between 1968 and 1974. A tenacious midfield player, just 5' 5" tall with fiery red hair and a temperament to match, he made 771 first team appearances for Leeds between 1959 and 1976, and scored 115 goals, many of them in crucial games. He was a fierce tackler and an excellent passer of the ball with the speed and the vision to turn defence into attack in an instant. Above all, however, it was passion and total commitment that made him such an influential member of the Leeds team. Sometimes he was over-competitive, but as you would expect from someone who called their autobiography *You Get Nowt for Being Second*, winning was everything to him.

Billy Bremner was born in Stirling, Scotland, on 9 December 1942. He signed for Leeds United as a teenager, making his league debut in December 1960 as a right-winger. At that time Leeds were struggling in the Second Division. By the time the team was promoted three seasons later, Bremner, now converted to a midfield position by the new manager Don Revie, had become a key member of what was a youthful and highly promising team. In 1965, the year he made his international debut for Scotland, Leeds were runners-up in the league and reached the FA Cup final. Bremner would suffer the bitter disappointment of finishing second in the league on four more occasions, and losing in the final of four important domestic and European cup finals. However, from 1968 to 1974 he led Leeds to the most fruitful period of its history, winning the league championship in 1969 and 1974, the European Fairs Cup in 1968 and 1971, the FA Cup in 1972, and the League Cup in 1968.

Bremner played 54 times for Scotland caps (scoring three goals) between 1965 and 1975, and captained them in the 1974 World Cup finals when they were unlucky to go out unbeaten at the group stage. Bremner, in particular, was outstanding in a 0–0 draw with the holders, Brazil. However, his international career ended in disgrace a year later when he was banned from playing for Scotland after being involved in an incident in a Copenhagen nightclub.

He left Leeds for Hull City in September 1976, moving to Doncaster Rovers two years later as player/manager, and won promotion for the club from the old Fourth Division. In 1985 he returned as manager to Leeds, who were now languishing in the Second Division, but was unable to revive the glory years he had enjoyed as a player and was sacked after three years. He spent a second spell at Doncaster (1989–92) after which he made a living as an after-dinner speaker and media pundit. He died on 7 December 1997 in Doncaster, shortly after suffering a heart attack.

Burroughs, William S(eward)

(1914–1997)

US cult author and leading light of the Beat Generation of writers. The product of a conventional, wealthy Southern family, Burroughs subsequently rejected his background; his personal journey through the hell of heroin addiction was to provide the basis for much of his writing. The controversial, if not repellent, character of his work – obsessed as it is with sex, drugs, human bodily functions, and the homo-erotic – at its best constitutes a vivid satire on the absurdities and profanities of a contemporary world fixated on greed and money. Since the publication of his first novel *Junkie: Confessions of an Unredeemed Drug Addict* (1953), debate has raged over the validity of Burroughs's work as true 'literature'. Although in the 1990s he has acquired a huge cult following, partly as a result of his endorsement of marijuana smoking, in many respects the jury is still out on the extent of his contribution to 20th-century literature.

Having studied at Harvard in the 1930s, Burroughs tried his hand at a succession of disparate professions, from private detective to newspaper reporter. After a brief marriage in the late 1940s, which ended with his wife's death in a shooting accident, Burroughs, by now already addicted to heroin, headed off for the life of an itinerant junkie in Peru and later Morocco. After his family had funded his treatment for drug addiction in 1958 he moved to Paris, where he wrote his seminal work *The Naked Lunch*, first published in 1959. But it was not until the shifts in social attitudes of the early 1960s that Burroughs gained international attention, and indeed notoriety, as the debate over his work took off. Having been adopted as one of the voices of the Beat Generation of writers of the 1950s – along with Allen Ginsberg and Jack Kerouac – Burroughs pioneered a random style of writing that involved a technique he described as 'cut up and fold in'; he would literally cut up, reposition and paste in pieces of narrative from various sources, in order to see what kind of creative results these generated. The novels that followed *The Naked Lunch* such as *The*

Soft Machine (1961) and *The Ticket that Exploded* (1962) developed the fantastical and sci-fi elements of Burroughs's work, with their bleak, nightmarish landscapes. Although his later work was more disciplined in terms of chronology and content, Burroughs never ceased experimenting, as works like *Cities of the Red Night* (1981), *The Place of Dead Roads* (1983), *Queer* (1986), and *Interzone* (1989) testify. Yet for all the outrageous and disturbing elements of Burroughs's work, there is a side to his writing that is inherently moralistic (in keeping with the contradictory image he cultivated in life, with his preference for sober, conventional suits and ties). This could be seen as a perceptive commentary on the aberrations of modern-day life, and will ensure Burroughs's place as an innovative chronicler of the seamier side of his times. He died in Lawrence, Kansas, on 2 August 1997.

Cookson, Catherine (born Kate McMullen)

(1906–1998)

Through a writing career spanning 50 years, Catherine Cookson stuck to doing what she knew best – writing period novels, mainly set in and around her own roots in northeast England, in particular Newcastle-upon-Tyne. In so doing, she plugged into a vast and hungry market that has kept her novels at the top of the best-seller lists.

Cookson's own early life reads like one of her own novels and she certainly drew on her background in and around the docks and shipyards of Tyneside, where she was born, the illegitimate daughter of an alcoholic mother. As an underprivileged, working-class girl, the only avenue open to her after leaving school at 13 was a life of drudgery. Cookson worked as a cushion maker and in a laundry, moving to Hastings on the south coast in 1929, where she took a post as head laundress at a workhouse. By now she had climbed a rung or two up the social ladder through self-education and elocution lessons, and, in 1940, achieved the respectability of marriage to a schoolmaster, Tom Cookson. However, she suffered recurring breakdowns in her health, the result of a rare blood disease, and, after suffering three miscarriages, her mental health collapsed completely and for some time she became a virtual recluse. It was then that she turned her hand to writing, publishing her first novel *Kate Hannigan* in 1950. Among her subsequent prolific output, her dynastic saga *The Mallens* was particularly popular, as was the series of eight *Mary Ann* novels. She researched all her novels scrupulously and her natural talent gravitated towards describing the gritty and often tragic lives of working-class people who suffer but stick together – through lust, grief, violence, love, and hate – a far cry from the heroines of her contemporary, Barbara Cartland.

Cookson's modesty and the low public profile she adopted mean that few people are aware of her considerable acts of philanthropy. Her 80 novels, which have been translated into 17 languages in around 100 million copies worldwide, enabled her to make considerable donations to hospitals and charities, including £1 million for research into haematology, as well as the establishment of the Catherine Cookson Foundation at Newcastle University, and a grant of £100,000 to fund science studies at St Hilda's College, Oxford.

Cookson's books have also generated a local tourist industry – 'Catherine Cookson Country' – and revived pride and interest in a formerly depressed and neglected area of industrial Britain, bolstered by the successful dramatization of her work through radio, television, and film. Whilst many literary critics unfairly dismiss her novels as formulaic, and lump them together with far less distinguished romantic fiction, Cookson's writing is defined by sincerity and compassion, backed up by detailed historical and social background research and a grasp of dialect and local colour. Throughout her long and difficult life, Cookson retained a strong sense of identity, returning to the northeast in later life. She remarked with characteristic humility: 'I am still a child of the Tyne whose far horizons reached only to Palmer's Shipyard in Jarrow and the sands at South Shields.' Cookson died on 11 June 1998.

Diana, Princess of Wales (born Diana Frances Spencer)

(1961–1997)

For the week between 31 August – the day of her death – and 6 September 1997 – the day of her funeral – many people around the world found themselves in an eerie limbo as they came to terms with the death of a princess who will undoubtedly be seen as one of the most pervasive icons of the 20th century. How was it that individuals of every colour and creed across the world could mourn on such a universal and unrestrained scale the death of a 36-year-old British princess, whom sixteen years earlier, as a chubby-faced teenager, they had witnessed walk up the aisle in the largest televised wedding in history? It was not simply her beauty, her fashion sense, her disarming charm and warmth, nor even her palpable compassion and many humanitarian works that provoked such an outpouring of grief, but rather something much more simple: the ability of ordinary people to identify on an everyday level with a woman whose very public life was marred by the emotional dislocations of marital breakdown.

Lady Diana Frances Spencer was born into one of England's great aristocratic families, but her privileged background was no guarantee of stability: her childhood was far from happy, scarred as it was by her parents' messy divorce. The wistful opening lines of her own account of that time, published in Andrew Morton's *Diana: Her True Story in Her Own Words*, reveal an element of the 'little girl lost' that was always to accompany her: 'My first memory is really the smell of the inside of my pram. It was plastic and the smell of the hood. Vivid memory. I was born at home not in hospital. The biggest disruption was when Mummy decided to leg it.'

Her upbringing of private education and Swiss finishing school left Diana ill-qualified for anything other than the life of an upper class socialite on the hunting, shooting, fishing, and skiing circuit, but her natural affection for children led her to take a job as a kindergarten assistant in the uppercrust end of London, where she appeared to be genuinely happy. However, her developing relationship with the heir to the throne, whom she had met at Sandringham earlier in her teens, suddenly propelled the shy 19-year-old into the limelight: she was the perfect, unsullied candidate for a future queen, and Prince Charles, under pressure to settle down and produce an heir, soon acquiesced to the demands of duty. As for Diana, despite her obviously deep love for the prince, such a dramatic change in her life inevitably had its consquences: 'I was a nobody, the next minute I was Princess of Wales, mother, media toy, member of this family and it was just too much for one person to handle.'

For a while the whole nation revelled in the euphoria of a fairy-tale state wedding and the rapid arrival of two male heirs to the throne, as well as having a princess whose beauty and fashion-sense captured the front pages wherever she went. But as early as 1985 the cracks had begun to show, with rumours of rows between the couple, of Diana's problems with post-natal depression, anorexia, and bulimia, and of Charles's renewed interest in an old flame, Camilla Parker Bowles. As the gulf between the couple widened, each built up their own rival camps of supporters, who made frequent, anonymous, and contradictory statements to the press about the state of the marriage. Eventually, the princess went public in 1992 with her own account of events, written through the intermediary of Andrew Morton; an ensuing tide of revelation, rumour, and leaks piled up, until the British prime minister, John Major, confirmed that the couple were separating. The ultimate act of public breast-beating was carried out by both partners in television interviews; but while Prince Charles's awkward and stilted admission of adultery only served to diminish his waning popularity, Diana's wide-eyed and unflinching straight-to-camera admission of adultery, and her palpable sense of rejection and betrayal, seemed only to raise her status as martyr and victim.

The media spotlight on Diana did not fade with her very public television confession, however, but became even more obsessive. She was pursued wherever she went in a relentless game of cat and mouse, towards which she always had an ambivalent attitude; she was able to project abject, tearful outpourings of despair at such intrusions into her privacy, while also having a knack for engineering the right photo opportunities when the occasion suited her.

The one salvation of Diana's fractured life, particularly in her last years, seemed to be her work for the causes she espoused with such undeniable dedication: the homeless, the victims of landmines, and sufferers from AIDS. As she said herself a couple of months before her death: 'Nothing brings me more happiness than trying to help the most vulnerable people in society. It is a goal and an essential part of my life, a kind of destiny. Whoever is in distress can call on me. I will come running, wherever they are.' Such simple expressions of her almost naive sense of altruism, with its unconscious religious overtones, guaranteed her elevation to sainthood in the popular consciousness.

Despite paring down her charity work to a few preferred causes after her separation from Prince Charles, it seemed clear that in the last year of her life, after her divorce, Diana had really found a sense of purpose and vocation. Resolute that she would never sit on the throne as Queen – albeit as a divorced one – she had nevertheless by now ensured a place in popular mythology for herself, as 'a queen in people's hearts', to use her own words. While the republican-spirited might dismiss the attribution of such emotional power and influence to a fundamentally quite ordinary and not-very-bright (by her own admission) former 'Sloane Ranger', Princess Diana's death has ensured, for good or bad, that the British monarchy will never be the same again. But as the public memory fades, just as the avalanche of flowers outside Kensington Palace did, the inevitable ring of cash registers is taking over as the princess is immortalized by a multimillion-dollar industry, where even her face is being registered as a trademark. A more fitting tribute, which she certainly would have wished for, is that three months after her death, 125 countries signed an international treaty in Ottawa to ban the use of landmines. She died in a car crash, along with her companion, Dodi Fayed, in Paris on 31 August 1997.

Eysenck, Hans Jurgen

(1916–1997)

German-born UK psychologist who worked on personality theory and testing by developing behaviour therapy. He was one of the most influential UK psychologists in the latter half of this century. Eysenck was an outspoken critic of psychoanalysis as a therapeutic method, claiming that it was unscientific. His theory that intelligence is almost entirely inherited and can be only slightly modified by education aroused enormous controversy, as did some of his other work, for example his support of the

idea that planet positions at birth affect personality, and his belief that smoking does not cause lung cancer. Despite his strong views he retained a sense of humour, claiming that he would not take seriously any scientific discipline that would have him as a dominant figure.

Eysenck was educated at various schools in Germany, France, and the UK. With the rise to power of Adolf Hitler in the 1930s he left Germany to pursue his career in psychology in the UK and the USA, where he held numerous university posts.

Eysenck investigated many areas of psychology, often producing highly controversial theories. However, it was his theory that intelligence is almost entirely inherited and can be only slightly modified by education that aroused the greatest opposition. The concept of intelligence is very difficult to define and measure – the commonly used intelligence tests, for example, are often criticized for being culturally biased, favouring well-educated white people and penalizing poorly educated black people. Eysenck attempted to devise a culture-free method for assessing intelligence. It involves neither problem-solving nor even conscious thought, and therefore, Eysenck argued, it cannot be criticized for being culturally biased. It involves subjecting a person to stroboscopic light flashes and buzzing sounds while recording the electrical activity of the brain with an elect-roencephalograph. It has been known since the early 1970s that the pattern of brain waves is related to intelligence (as measured by conventional intelligence tests) but the correlation has been too approximate to be of practical use. Eysenck, however, claimed to be able to measure the brain waves accurately enough to give a very high correlation with conventional tests. Using his method, Eysenck then did a cross-cultural comparison of intelligence and found that, on average, black people obtained significantly lower intelligence quotients than whites. Combining this result with his theory that intelligence is predominantly inherited, he claimed that black people are inherently less intelligent than are whites. This highly controversial claim met with great, and sometimes violent, opposition, with some critics concluding that the correlation between Eysenck's method and conventional intelligence tests meant that the two methods must contain the same biases.

Eysenck also studied personality traits, anxiety, neurosis, the influence of television violence on behaviour, and the psychology of smoking. He is probably best known for his four popular books, *Uses and Abuses of Psychology* (1953), *Sense and Nonsense in Psychology* (1957), *Know Your Own IQ* (1962), and *Fact and Fiction in Psychology* (1965), which sold millions of copies and were translated into many languages. He died in London on 4 September 1997.

Fuller, Samuel (Michael)

(1911–1997)

Maverick US screenwriter and film director, whose low-budget, visually-striking, sensational pulp culture films established him as one of the USA's first great independent filmmakers. Fueled by his experiences as a newspaper crime reporter, a pulp novelist, and a World War II veteran, Fuller's oeuvre is characterized by emotive and violent explorations of the darker side of the collective US psyche. Announced by tabloid-style titles, his films, from *Park Row* (1952) to *Shock Corridor* (1963) to *White Dog* (1982), constantly return to the motifs of the individual's struggle for personal freedom; his concern with the concepts of psychological, racial, and national identity; and mankind's never-ending propensity for violence.

Sam Fuller was born in Worcester, Massachusetts, on 12 August 1911. At the age of 12 he was hired by the *New York Journal* as a copy boy, and by the age of 17 was working as a crime reporter for the paper. The 'tabloid instinct' would inform much of his subsequent work as a filmmaker, and his experiences as a newspaperman were reflected in one of his first key films, *Park Row*. Equally influential on his worldview were his experiences with the First Infantry Division during World War II. These would form the backdrop of one of his last films as a director, *The Big Red One* (1980), but would also underpin such early works as the Korean War films *The Steel Helmet* (1951) and *Fixed Bayonets* (1951).

Fuller first entered the film industry in the late 1930s as a writer, drawing from his background both as a crime reporter and pulp novelist. He made his directorial debut in 1949 with the Western *I Shot Jesse James*, a genre he would return to in *Forty Guns* (1957) and *Run of the Arrow* (1957), among others. It was, however, in the genre of the hard-hitting *noirish* thriller that he would produce some of his most accomplished work: *Pickup on South Street* (1953), *The Crimson Kimono* (1959), *Underworld USA* (1961), and *The Naked Kiss* (1964) all saw him holding a mirror to the darker side of US society.

His powers both as a compelling storyteller and bold visual stylist, not to mention his own hard-boiled, cigar-chomping persona, endeared Fuller to an array of subsequent filmmakers, among them Godard, Wenders, Hopper, Scorsese, Tarantino, and Jarmusch. In his later years, having settled in Paris, and struggling to find financial backing for his own projects, Fuller would put in the occasional cameo appearance in such films as Godard's *Pierrot le fou/Pierrot the Madman* (1965) and Wenders's *Der amerikanische Freund/The American Friend* (1977).

Fuller died in Los Angeles, California, on 30 October 1997.

Gellhorn, Martha (Ellis)

(1908–1998)

Feisty US journalist and writer who equalled many of her male colleagues in her reporting from some of the world's most dangerous war zones, and who found the observation of war to be an 'emotional-mental necessity'. It led her to live a life constantly on the move, covering wars, revolutions, and coups wherever they might take her. Throughout this life, she always made a point of underlining the sufferings of the ordinary people caught up in conflicts through no fault of their own.

From a radical-liberal background in Missouri, Gellhorn attended the elite Bryn Mawr College in Pennsylvania, but dropped out to pursue a career in journalism. Her first experiences of raw human suffering were as a witness to the effects of the Depression, and she later turned these into a collection of stories, *TheTrouble I've Seen*, published in 1936.

Like many war correspondents of her generation, Gellhorn served her apprenticeship in the Spanish Civil War, writing for *Collier's Weekly*. Here she covered the war alongside the writer Ernest Hemingway, whom she later married in 1940. Theirs was an uneasy, competitive relationship, troubled by his jealousy of her talent as a war reporter; but her life with Hemingway was a subject on which Gellhorn refused to be drawn, despite numerous requests to tell her side of things. Together with Hemingway (who dedicated his novel *For Whom the Bell Tolls* to her), Gellhorn went on to report on World War II, when she was one of the first to witness the horrors of Dachau concentration camp after it was liberated. Her outrage at US military involvement in Vietnam during the 1960s led to a series of passionate reports so critical that in 1967 the US authorities refused her a visa to return there. Gellhorn stopped writing and publishing for several years, partly out of sheer fury, as she later observed: 'After all this time I still cannot think calmly about that war. It was the only war I reported on the wrong side.' But nothing would stop her from continuing to travel and observe – something she continued well into old age – and she later covered the 1980s conflict in Central America.

With three failed marriages behind her, Gellhorn spent the last 35 years of her life living a simple, pared-down existence. However, nothing ever dimmed her fiery commitment to the cause of justice, which she had espoused as a young woman, and which had been the motivating force behind so much of her work. Gellhorn's best reportage was collected in *The Face of War* (1959) and *The View from the Ground* (1988), and she also published several novels and collections of short stories. Martha Gellhorn died on 15 February 1998 in London.

Goldsmith, James Michael

(1933–1997)

Franco-British industrialist, publisher, and politician. Having amassed a vast personal fortune through his business interests, he entered the world of publishing – with more success in France than the UK – and then politics.

His political activities resulted in his securing a seat in the European Parliament in 1991, representing a French constituency, and the formation in Britain of the Referendum Party in 1995. The Referendum Party resulted partly from his experience in the European Parliament, partly from his dislike of what he saw as the EU's elitist decision-making process, and partly from his belief that the British electorate should be directly consulted before becoming more closely involved in European unification. He poured an estimated £20 million into the Referendum Party, which he hoped would harm, or even destroy, the prospects of pro-European candidates in the 1997 general election. In the event, it had little impact on the outcome.

A larger-than-life figure, in both physique and personality, Goldsmith was a highly successful businessman, willing to take risks when others showed more caution. He was co-founder in the UK of Mothercare and Cavenham Foods, which included several household brands such as Bovril and Procea bread; in France, of the holding company Generale Occidentale; and later, in the USA, of a major chain of supermarkets, Grand Union. His success in business was thought to stem from an instinctive ability to anticipate difficulties before they became calamities and from a ruthless pursuit of whatever goal he set himself. These attributes earned him a knighthood in 1976, from the British prime minister Harold Wilson, who was known for his admiration of flamboyant industrial adventurers.

The child of a distinguished Jewish banking family who fled from Germany in the face of growing anti-Semitism, he was born in Paris and moved to the UK with his parents to enjoy a privileged education, first at preparatory school and then at Eton. He soon established a reputation for rebelliousness and unorthodoxy, which was to be the pattern of his later life. Outside the worlds of business and politics he developed a colourful reputation as an unconventional character with three marriages and a number of barely disguised affairs.

He died in Benahavis, Spain, on 18 July 1997, at the end of a period of suffering from cancer of the pancreas, a condition which, characteristically, he had concealed from the outside world.

Grappelli, Stéphane

(1908–1997)

French jazz violinist who enjoyed two periods of fame. From 1934 until the outbreak of war Grappelli led the Quintette du Hot Club de France with the Belgian gypsy guitarist Django Reinhardt – an ensemble which at last gave the European jazz world credibility. Then from 1971, starting with an improvised duet with Yehudi Menuhin on a British television chat show, Grappelli was rediscovered, making five records with Menuhin, and working once again with some of the leading figures in jazz, all over the world.

After a miserable early childhood in orphanages, Grappelli learned piano and violin with his father, a poverty-stricken philosophy professor. He busked enough money to take a course at the Paris Conservatoire and got a job in a cinema pit band at the age of 14. He played piano in a French band for two seasons, then another two with Grégor and his Grégoriens, before Grégor persuaded him in to return to the fiddle. Meanwhile he had learned alto saxophone in a bohemian café in the south of France, where the Prince of Wales occasionally the drummer. Even when the famous Quintette was formed (violin, three guitars, and bass) Grappelli would play piano to accompany the singer Mabel Mercer in their intervals. The tune 'Mabel' became one of the Quintette's greatest hits.

Grappelli worked in Britain during World War II, and formed a notable partnership with pianist George Shearing. He retained a lifelong affection for London, and kept his watch set to London time. After the war he was reluctant to team up again with the unreliable Reinhardt, who frequently went missing before concerts. However, after Reinhardt's death in 1954, Grappelli often kept an empty seat on stage 'for Django'.

Grappelli's 1742 Gagliano violin was made to sound like a speaking voice, with all its nuance, according to the British violinist Nigel Kennedy, who struck up a musical friendship with Grappelli in the 1980s. His playing style was strongly influenced by Louis Armstrong's singing, Bix Beiderbecke's piano playing, and Gershwin. He had an irresistible swing and a remarkable gift for improvisation, fuelled by one stiff whisky, 'to liberate me', just before performances. His powers never waned, and he was active as a fine player up to his death.

Grappelli died in Paris on 1 December 1997.

Lichtenstein, Roy

(1923–1997)

US artist who was one of the leading figures of Pop Art in the 1960s. He used popular culture to create a style that was instantly recognizable – that of the comic strip. His work caught the new mood of affluence in 1960s America, a period when life seemed increasingly dominated by advertising, consumerism, popular culture, and mass entertainment.

Roy Lichtenstein was born in New York City in 1923. He studied at the Art Students' League and then at the School of Fine Arts at Ohio State University. During World War II he served as a soldier in Europe, and then returned to Ohio State, where he taught for several years. In the 1950s he experimented with a variety of styles: assemblages fashioned out of found objects, Geometric Abstraction, and Abstract Expressionism. Even at this stage, however, he had an interest in popular American imagery, in particular that of the Wild West and Disney.

The turning point came in 1960 when he moved to Rutgers University and came into contact with artists such as Allan Kaprow, Jim Dine, and Claes Oldenburg, who would soon become the leading figures of Pop Art. Like many young artists of the period, Lichtenstein felt the need to escape the influence of Abstract Expressionism. The Abstract Expressionists – artists like Jackson Pollock, Willem de Kooning, and Mark Rothko – had become internationally famous and their domination of American art seemed inescapable. For many of these younger artists the Abstract Expressionists seemed to be the last in the long line of Romantic 'struggling artists' – passionate, profound, and tormented. However, there had been a significant change of mood. To Lichtenstein and many others the Abstract Expressionists seemed increasingly irrelevant.

Lichtenstein's response to this new mood – a mood that would characterize American art for the rest of the century – was to make him one of the first 'cool' artists. Art was no longer a matter of intense feeling, but of critical intelligence: art should be playful, knowing, ironic, and self-consciously aware of its artifice, limitations, and pretensions.

Rejecting the many forms of abstraction then practised, Lichtenstein turned to a source of some of the boldest and most exuberant contemporary images – the comic. Parody was to be his theme. His famous *Whaam!* (1963; Tate Gallery, London) is typical: bold, black outlines and a few vivid colours, the subject taken from a war comic. Lichtenstein did not merely take the style and motifs: he took specific images and painted them enormously enlarged, even painstakingly reproducing the printing technique of using small uniform dots of colour. He contributed to the movement to display popular art in art galleries.

From his first one-man show at Leo Castelli's gallery in New York in 1962, Lichtenstein's career, both critical and commercial, was assured. His style – an immediately recognizable trademark – hardly changed. Only his subjects changed: he turned to advertising and landscapes, and also, with a final irony, to pastiches of the heroes of modern art, including Cézanne, Picasso, Matisse, and Mondrian. High art had become popular imagery.

Roy Lichtenstein died in New York on 27 October 1997.

Mitchum, Robert (Charles Duran)

(1917–1997)

US film actor, whose career spanned more than 50 years of filmmaking, and embraced more than 100 film and television roles. As one of Hollywood's most enduring stars, Mitchum's celebrity relied as much on his off-screen antics as on his lackadaisical, sleepy-eyed screen persona. He enjoyed a reputation as a heavy drinker and womanizer, and his film career was interrupted by a brief hiatus in 1948, when he was arrested and imprisoned for possession of marijuana. The 'bad boy' reputation lent itself well, however, to a series of hard-boiled, 'tough guy' roles that Mitchum played in a string of war films, melodramas, *films noirs*, and Westerns in the 1940s and early 1950s that served to establish him firmly in the pantheon of Hollywood's leading male performers.

Together with Kirk Douglas, Burt Lancaster, and William Holden, he was one of a new breed of actors to emerge in the cinema of the 1940s, announcing himself with assured performances in such films as *When Strangers Marry/Betrayed* (1944), *The Story of G I Joe* (1945), for which he won his only Academy Award nomination, *The Locket* (1946), *Pursued* (1947), *Crossfire* (1947), and *Out of the Past/Build My Gallows High* (1947).

Robert Mitchum was born in Bridgeport, Connecticut, on 6 August 1917. His father died when Mitchum was aged only 16, and he soon left home and worked his way through a series of mainly manual jobs (including, he would later mischievously claim, a stint on a Georgia chain gang, from which he escaped) before he arrived in Hollywood, after having been discovered by a talent scout at the Long Beach Theater Guild in southern California. His film career began in 1942 with *Leather Burners*, but initially was a relatively low-key affair, confined primarily to B-movies, including eight roles in Hopalong Cassidy Westerns. This was all to change, however, with his acclaimed performance in *The Story of G I Joe*, which thrust him into the limelight and brought him to the attention of a wider audience.

Mitchum's subsequent career was prolific if not exactly littered with a string of cinema classics. While there were many highpoints, foremost among them is his turn as Jeff Bailey, the definitive *noir* protagonist, in *Out of the Past* (1947) and his gleefully evil psychopaths in *The Night of the Hunter* (1955) and the original *Cape Fear* (1961). His lengthy filmography was generally characterized by run-of-the-mill fare in which his undoubted qualities as an actor invariably shone through. Among his other films are *The Lusty Men* (1952), *Angel Face* (1952), and the nostalgic neo-noir *Farewell, My Lovely* (1975), in which he played Raymond Chandler's world-weary private investigator, Philip Marlowe.

In his later years, Mitchum alternated film work and television work, including the mini serials *The Winds of War* (1983) and *War and Remembrance* (1988). Although he put in a few film appearances in the mid-1990s, most notably Jim Jarmusch's quirky Western *Dead Man* (1995), Mitchum began to suffer from the effects of emphysema. Shortly before his death, he was also diagnosed as suffering from lung cancer. His last film work was featured in the Italian movie *Calipso* (1996).

Mitchum married Dorothy Spence, his wife of 57 years, in 1940. They had two sons, Jim and Christopher, both of them actors (as is Mitchum's grandson Bentley), and a daughter, Petrine.

Mitchum died in Montecito, California, on 1 July 1997.

Mobutu, Sese Seko Kuku Ngbendu wa za Banga (formerly Joseph Desire Mobutu)

(1930–1997)

Zairian soldier, politician, and president in the years 1965–97. Born in Lisala, Belgian Congo, in relatively humble surroundings, his father being a cook and his mother a hotel maid, he rose to become black Africa's longest ruling head of state, bringing a measure of stability to what at one time seemed to be an ungovernable country.

After being expelled from a missionary school for lack of discipline, he was conscripted into the Congolese army in 1949, achieving the rank of sergeant-major in the accounts department. He left the army at the age of 25 for Belgium, where he enrolled at the Institute of Social Studies, Brussels, to equip himself for a career in journalism. Returning to Zaire, he edited newspapers founded by the then prime minister, Patrice Lumumba. As a protégé of the prime minister, he re-entered the army and, at the age of 29, was made Chief of Staff. There followed five years of anarchy, as rival factions fought over the country's natural wealth, particularly the rich mining province of Katanga. Mobutu seized the opportunity to take temporary control of the country. Lumumba was subsequently murdered but Mobutu survived. After the restoration of constitutional government there was a period of relative stability but, as the secessionist struggle over Katanga returned, Mobutu and the army stepped in again to establish what he called a 'second republic' in 1965. A new constitution was adopted in 1967 and in 1970 Mobutu was elected president.

He established a one-party state and developed a personality cult, changing his name from Joseph Desire Mobutu to Mobutu Sese Seko Koko Ngbendu wa za Banga, roughly translated as 'the all-powerful warrior who, because of endurance and an inflexible will to win, will go from conquest to conquest leaving fire in his wake'. Internally, he maintained his position by rewarding his supporters and dealing harshly with his opponents. Externally, he cultivated the leaders of the Western powers, particularly the USA, who saw him as a bulwark against the spread of communism in Africa, and were prepared to ignore his excesses because of his apparent value to them. Meanwhile, he delved into his country's rich resources and accumulated a personal fortune estimated in billions of US dollars.

Zaire's economy deteriorated rapidly and, as democracy began to spread through Africa in the late 1980s and early 1990s, Mobutu's future looked increasingly uncertain. Additionally he had been diagnosed as having prostate cancer, for which he was receiving treatment in Switzerland. While he was there, in 1996, the Hutu-Tutsi holocaust in neighbouring Rwanda spilled over into Zaire, providing an opportunity for an old enemy of Mobutu, Laurent Kabila, to occupy large parts of the country. In May 1997 Mobutu acknowledged defeat by Kabila's forces and was given asylum in Morocco, where he died at Rabat on 7 September 1997.

Muir, Frank

(1920–1998)

British humorist, scriptwriter, and broad-caster who was one of the pioneers of post-war radio comedy, but is probably best remembered for his distinctive, lisping voice and his dapper bow-ties. His gentlemanly charm and disarming wit, as demonstrated in his many television appearances, ensured his continuing popularity with audiences across all age ranges.

Before TV audiences got to know the face, they had for years enjoyed the voice of Frank Muir as one of the doyens of BBC Radio after World War II. Together with his friend and colleague Denis Norden, Muir wrote some classic radio comedy series, such as *Take It From Here* – which gave birth to the archetypal British comic family, the Glums – before moving into TV comedy, creating *Whack-O!* for Jimmy Edwards. Muir also proved himself an able programme maker, producing light entertainment programmes at the BBC and later at London Weekend Television, where he took charge of hit series such as *Please Sir* and *On the Buses*.

Most television audiences, however, will remember Muir for his long run, from the mid-sixties, as team captain on the TV quiz show *Call My Bluff*, where he demonstrated his inimitable gift for punning – a talent which he had turned into an art form during his years on the hit radio quiz *My Word!*. Muir also wrote a series of children's books, as well as publishing several collections of humorous prose and anecdotes, notably *The Oxford Book of Humorous Prose* (1990). Frank Muir died on 2 January 1998.

Pol Pot (also known as Saloth Sar, Tol Saut, and Pol Porth)

(1925–1998)

Cambodian guerrilla leader, politician, and prime minister 1976–79. Born in Kompong Thorn province in a family with royal connections, Pol Pot had radical ambitions and in the 1940s he joined the anti-French resistance movement, led by Ho Chi Minh. Then, in 1946, he entered the Cambodian Communist Party, becoming its leader in 1962. As an instrument for securing control of the country, he founded the guerrilla

movement Khmer Rouge and in 1975 succeeded in overthrowing the government led by General Lon Nol. With Chinese backing, he established the Democratic Republic of Kampuchea, with himself as prime minister.

His policies were to evacuate cities and put people to work in the countryside. The Khmer Rouge carried out a systematic and widespread extermination of Western influences; the Buddhist religion and culture was destroyed; families were split up; and peasants were forced to accept unpaid, collective labour. His enemies died in their millions on what became known as the 'killing fields' of Cambodia.

His regime was eventually overthrown by the Vietnamese in January 1979 and Pol Pot returned to his former role as guerrilla leader. However, splits began to appear in the Khmer Rouge ranks and in 1997 Pol Pot himself came under attack. He was put through a jungle show trial by his former colleagues and sentenced to house arrest in a Khmer Rouge village. During a 40-year political career there were several announcements of his demise but when his body was displayed for public view his death seemed certain. He was reported as having died on 15 April 1998.

Powell, (John) Enoch

(1912–1998)

British politician. An unusually talented man who enjoyed three distinct careers, in any one of which he could have established a lifetime ascendancy: as a brilliant classical scholar, as a soldier, or as a politician. He chose politics and, perversely, it was in this, the last of his possible careers, that he enjoyed least success.

Born in Stechford, Birmingham, he studied at King Edward School in that city and later went on to Trinity College, Cambridge, where he was an outstanding scholar, winning the first Chancellor's Classical Medal. He was made a Fellow in 1934 and, in 1937, at an incredibly early age, was appointed Professor of Greek in the University of Sydney, Australia.

On the outbreak of war in Europe in 1939, he returned to Britain and enlisted as a private in the Royal Warwickshire Regiment. His talents were soon recognized, and he rose quickly through the ranks, becoming a Brigadier-General in 1944. After the war, instead of returning to an academic career, he entered politics.

He joined the Conservative Party in 1946 and worked in the research department before winning a House of Commons seat in 1950, representing Wolverhampton. Five years later he was made a Housing and Local Government junior minister, and two years after that was promoted to the post of Treasury Financial Secretary. Within a year he had resigned, protesting against the government's refusal to curtail public spending, thus identifying himself as a 'Thatcherite' before Margaret Thatcher had

made her mark on the political scene. In 1960 he returned to the government as Minister of Health in Harold Macmillan's cabinet. However, when Macmillan retired because of ill health, three years later, Powell again resigned, protesting against the choice of Lord Home as Macmillan's successor. In 1965 he unsuccessfully entered the Conservative Party leadership contest, winning only 15 votes, but agreed to serve in the shadow cabinet of the successful candidate, Edward Heath. Then in 1968, after the publication of the Labour government's planned legislation on race relations, he made a speech in Birmingham, condemning what he regarded as the government's over-lax policies on immigration, emotively declaring 'I seem to see the River Tiber foaming with much blood'. This sentence had an explosive effect, critics seeing it as overtly racist, although Powell himself was merely using his classical background to illustrate his objections to increased immigration. Heath immediately dropped him from the shadow cabinet.

After Britain's entry into the European Community (EC) in 1970, Powell became increasingly critical of what he saw as the country's loss of sovereignty, and in the 1974 general election he declined to stand as a Conservative candidate. Instead, he chose to join the Ulster Unionists (UU), and in October 1974 returned to parliament, representing South Down for the UU. However, his days of protest were not yet over. After being re-elected in 1983 he resigned his seat, objecting to the Anglo-Irish Agreement. Within a month he returned to the Commons but lost his seat in the 1987 general election.

Because he tended to see things in absolute terms, Powell was a much misunderstood man and, although he continued to express his views on current political topics, he declined the offer of a life peerage. He turned again to research and writing, his translation of and commentary on the Gospel of St John (1994) being well received. He died in London on 8 February 1998.

Richter, Sviatoslav Teofilovich

(1915–1997)

Ukrainian-born Russian pianist who was possibly the most dedicated pianist of the 20th century. While his statement 'the task of the true performer is to submit entirely to the composer, his style, character, and outlook' is subscribed to by hundreds of artists, few, if any of them, fulfil it as did Richter himself. He played an extraordinary range of different composers as if he were a different pianist for each, and all with unsurpassed technical authority.

Born in the Ukrainian town of Zhitomir, Richter was brought up in the intensely musical city of Odessa, a Black Sea port with a strong tradition of visits from European performers. Richter learned the basics from his organist father, but from the age of nine seems to have been largely self-taught. He learned a lot of music by playing from orchestral scores, and throughout his life was known as a phenomenal sight-reader. This stood him in good stead when he became a *répètiteur* at the Odessa opera, playing accompaniments for singers in rehearsal. He was aged just 15.

Like his remarkable Odessa contemporary, Emil Gilels, he studied with Neuhaus at the Moscow Conservatory from the age of 19. Neuhaus later maintained that 'I didn't teach Richter, I learnt from him'. Richter's ability to shape a piece with clear outlines as well as immensely telling detail was spotted at his first public performances. However, the Soviet authorities would not let him travel to the West until 1960. Richter's eventual US debut, in Chicago, was encored 12 times amid audience hysteria.

Prokofiev immediately pronounced Richter his best interpreter on first hearing, and Richter gave the first performance of Prokofiev's enormously difficult Sixth, Seventh, and Ninth piano sonatas (the latter dedicated to him). Richter's recording of the great Eighth sonata remains unsurpassed. He was also a supremely dedicated pioneer of Schubert's sonatas. Besides these composers, Richter's enormous range covered a great deal of the classical period, especially Bach and Haydn (such music, he said, should form a third of the pianist's repertoire), Beethoven, Chopin, Brahms, and virtually every Russian composer of any note through to Shostakovich. He had few peers in his interpretations of Schumann and Liszt, and he also played a great deal of chamber music. The one curious gap was Beethoven's *Emperor Concerto*: he said that after hearing his teacher Neuhaus play it, he would not touch the work.

Richter became a great friend of Benjamin Britten, and a frequent visitor to Britten's Aldeburgh Festival in Suffolk. He was also the artistic inspiration of the *Fêtes Musicales of Grange de Meslay,* near Tours in France. Especially in later life, he was famous for cancelling performances at short notice, citing ill-health; his endorsement of Yamaha pianos was controversial (many critics thought the tone metallic); and he would play in a darkened hall with only a table lamp to illuminate the printed music.

Richter died in Moscow on 1 August 1997.

Robbins, Harold

(1916–1997)

US writer of glossy, pulp fiction whose life in many ways imitated his own art, and whose prolific output has reached a vast audience through world book sales of 750 million, as well as numerous film and television adaptations. Robbins never had any pretensions about his work: although his early novels achieved some critical acclaim, in particular *Never Love a Stranger,* he quickly recognized that literary kudos does not make money. Taking a ruthlessly pragmatic line, he subsequently developed a

winning formula by catering to a reading market that enjoyed the escapist fantasy of reading about the fictitious lives of the rich, powerful, famous, and sexy.

As a young man, the product of a Catholic foundling home, and a Jewish foster family who named him Harry Rubin, and in a close parallel to his fellow US writer James Michener, Robbins had a tough early life which left him streetwise and hard-working. Having survived a succession of dead-end jobs on New York's Lower East Side, his drive and the business acumen he had acquired from working in a grocery store led to the kind of beginner's luck found in his own stories: by the age of 20 he had made a fortune speculating on the stock exchange. But like all good rags-to-riches narratives, Robbins lost his new found wealth soon afterwards, at the outbreak of World War II, when he miscalculated in a speculation on the sugar market. Undaunted, he took a job as a clerk at Universal Pictures, and worked his way up to executive status. He fell into writing as the result of a $100 bet – that he could turn in a better script than the material Universal were paying screenwriters $300,000 a time for. His first three novels – *Never Love a Stranger* (1948), *The Dream Merchants* (1949), and *A Stone for Danny Fisher* (1951) – were immediate hits and the film rights were quickly snapped up. Robbins was soon earning a fortune with which he maintained a lavish lifestyle, with all the trappings of parties, beautiful women, yachts, Rolls Royces, gambling, and luxury homes that feature in his own stories.

Such a hedonistic lifestyle soon turned into a habit that Robbins was hard-pressed to sustain, despite his enormous earnings. However, such was his ability to churn out stories that he prided himself on being able to write a novel in eight weeks, holed up in a hotel somewhere, sometimes working for 30 hours at one sitting. And so the blockbusters continued to pour forth: *The Carpetbaggers* (1961), *The Adventurers* (1966), *Stiletto* (1969), *The Betsy* (1971), and *Dreams Die First* (1977) – to name but a few of the 23 best-selling novels he produced in his lifetime. However, the bubble did eventually burst: a stroke and a fall in the mid-1980s left him crippled and in constant pain; an expensive divorce from his second wife in 1992 and the continuing haemorrhage of huge medical bills drained his vast wealth. But he carried on turning out the books and had just finished *Wishing Well* at the time of his death. He died in Palm Springs, Florida, on 14 October 1997.

Rossi, Aldo

(1931–1997)

Italian architect who was one of the most influential and widely respected figures in contemporary architecture, despite never being as well known as contemporaries such as Richard Rogers, I M Pei, and Robert Venturi.

Born in Milan in 1931, he studied at the Milan Politecnico and from 1959 until 1964 he was closely associated with the architectural journal *Casabella-Continuità*: ideas about architecture were central to his approach. He taught at Milan, until expelled in 1972 for his left-wing sympathies, and later in Venice, Zurich, Yale, and New York.

By the late 1960s he had become a leading figure in a movement known as Neo-Rationalism. His aim, broadly, was to challenge the Functionalism that dominated so much modern architecture by stressing formal values – he wanted to restore a sculptural sense of mass and volume to architecture. Rossi's expression of this aim was the bold use of simple geometrical forms: cubes, cylinders, pyramids, and cones. An example is one of his best-known projects, the San Cataldo Cemetery in Modena (1971–84), where one of the central buildings is a large stark cube punctuated by austere rows of large square openings.

But his concern was not simply with formal values. He described the Cataldo Cemetery in these terms: 'I thought of fashioning the cemetery on a Rationalist concept of death, as a disruption of life. I tried therefore to represent it as a deserted house with empty windows and as a factory with a smokestack where work had been disrupted.' Here Rossi touches on a central theme: a building is not a self-contained machine (as Functionalism assumes), but a part of a specific physical, cultural, and historical setting. He believed that a building enters into a complex dialogue with its environment. He developed this idea in his most important book, *The Architecture of the City* (1966), in which he argues that buildings should be seen as elements of a living and interdependent whole: the city. In this book he develops a range of shared concepts by which both cities and buildings can be understood, drawing parallels, for example, between streets and a building's corridors, between city squares and apartment courtyards.

These themes allowed him to introduce the concepts of memory and history into architecture. His own works often include references to the arcades and galleries familiar in Italian architecture – concepts that make him an important figure in the radical changes in architecture taking place at the end of the 20th century.

His ability to work with great originality within a specific historical setting was illustrated by his contribution to the 1979 Venice Biennale: his Tearto del Mondo, a Renaissance-inspired theatre that was built on a barge so that it could be floated along Venice's canals. His later international standing is indicated by the range of his commissions, which include an apartment block in Berlin (1984–87), the Lighthouse Theater in Toronto (1987–88), a family house in Mount Pocono in Pennsylvania (1988), and the Il Palazzo Hotel in Fukuoka, Japan (1988–90).

Aldo Rossi died in Milan on 4 September 1997.

Sinatra, Frank (Francis Albert)

(1915–1998)

Bing Crosby once bemoaned the fact that Frank Sinatra's voice was the voice of the century, adding, 'unfortunately, it's my century'. Indeed, for most of his first 30 years in the business, Sinatra dominated the genre of the popular romantic ballad, becoming known as 'The Voice'. It was a voice that could make an indifferent song great through his unique talent for phrasing and personalizing a lyric.

The son of Italian immigrants, Sinatra was born in Hoboken, New Jersey, and set his sights on a singing career in his early teens. He had already cut a few records and achieved a small following when his first big break came – as singer with the Tommy Dorsey Band in 1940. He became hugely popular on radio and one of his first big hits, which perfectly fitted the wartime nostalgia of separated sweethearts, was 'I'll be Seeing You'. Shrewdly gauging his niche as the archetypal crooner, Sinatra left Dorsey to pursue a solo career, which quickly spilled over into acting in a series of lightweight films: it was hard for producers to find the right roles for a great voice attached to a rather scrawny and undernourished figure.

By the early 1950s, however, Sinatra's career seemed over: his contract with MGM had ended and heavy drinking and the failure of his first marriage – followed by his hasty remarriage to Ava Gardner – had alienated many of his fans. But after a few years in the doldrums he was back, surprising everyone with an accomplished performance in the 1953 film *From Here to Eternity*, which won him an Academy Award. Shortly afterwards, Sinatra's return to recording was equally emphatic with a contract with Capitol that marked the heyday of his recording career. The hits poured forth, many of them orchestrated by Nelson Riddle. It was a musical partnership that would pioneer the LP album and produce classics such as 'Come Fly With Me', 'In the Wee Small Hours', and 'Songs for Swingin' Lovers'. In the cinema, Sinatra also had several hit musical films such as *Guys and Dolls* (1955), *High Society* (1956), and *Pal Joey* (1957).

By the 1960s Sinatra had gathered around himself a coterie of friends and fellow-performers, who became known as the 'rat pack' and included Dean Martin, Sammy Davis Jr, and Peter Lawford. Together they made several less than memorable films, including *Oceans 11*, *Sergeants 3*, and *Robin and the Seven Hoods*. Many of the 40 films that Sinatra made after the 1950s were unsatisfying potboilers in which he was often miscast. A rare exception was the 1963 thriller *The Manchurian Candidate* and the Tony Rome detective films. By 1971, after his third failed marriage (to Mia Farrow), Sinatra once again seemed a spent force. He made a big show of announcing his retirement from the business in 1971, but was back again after an absence of only two years, relaunching himself with the catchphrase 'Ol' Blue Eyes is Back'. Despite diminishing vocal powers and recurrent press reports about his links with the Mafia, Sinatra was still able to fill massive venues around the world with devoted fans. He defied repeated criticism that his voice was now 'past it' right into the 1990s, until failing health (probably the onset of Alzheimer's disease) led to his final withdrawal from public performance.

Sinatra died on 15 May 1998.

Solti, Georg born György Stern

(1912–1997)

Hungarian-born British conductor who is renowned for his prolific touring and recording achievements. Although he worked with many international orchestras, he is perhaps best known for the 22 years of what he, and many critics, called 'happy marriage' with the Chicago Symphony Orchestra.

Encouraged to play the piano by his mother, he earned a place at the famous Budapest Liszt Academy at the age of 12. He then worked as an unpaid apprentice *répétiteur* at the State Opera House in Budapest, and aided Toscanini in the 1936 and 1937 Salzburg music festivals. As Jews were barred from holding posts at the Budapest Opera, he left for Switzerland in 1939 and remained there throughout the war. At this stage, he was still doing more piano playing than conducting – he won the 1942 Geneva International Piano Competition.

However, his determination to conduct eventually paid off and he was given the music directorship at the Bavarian State Opera, Germany (which he held 1946–52), after he had been heard conducting in Munich. Work followed in Frankfurt 1952–60 and then a pivotal period at the Covent Garden Opera House, London, 1961–71, which is regarded by many as the greatest moment in this particular opera house's history.

During his decade as music director at Covent Garden, Solti also began to produce some of the outstanding recordings for which he is remembered – most notably, perhaps, the first ever, and best-selling, complete Wagnerian Ring cycle of operas. As well as making an increasing number of guest appearances with international orchestras, he worked concurrently with the Chicago Symphony from 1969 and the Paris Orchestra and Opera 1971–75.

He was a fanatical, driven conductor, but also one who was able to communicate much of his enthusiasm to the orchestra and its audience. Solti, himself, said: 'I have one specific talent: I can make an orchestra play to the limit of its capacity, but only if the players are willing to make an effort.' This almost obsessive dedication to the task of conducting led some critics, however, to criticize certain performances, particularly of Mozart, for not having the required lightness of touch.

It is for his unrelenting devotion to conducting over the last 40 years that Solti will be remembered. A dynamic figure on the podium, who had concert dates booked right up to his death, he also left a testament to his enduring ability on CD, most notably, perhaps, in his recordings of Mahler and his fellow countryman, Bartók.

Solti died in Antibes, France, on 5 September, 1997.

Spock, Benjamin (McLane)

(1903–1998)

US paediatrician. As the post-war guru of childcare, Benjamin Spock succeeded in finally burying an outmoded and rigid ethos of child-rearing, where children were to be 'seen and not heard', in favour of a compassionate and humanizing approach that embraced all aspects of the child's growth and development as an individual.

Having studied at New Haven and Yale, Spock set up practice in New York in 1933, specializing in paediatrics and psychology. In 1946 he published his ground-breaking *The Common Sense Book of Baby and Child Care*, a work that challenged the traditional, disciplinarian approach to childcare. It went on to sell 50 million copies worldwide in over 30 different languages, rivalling the Bible as one of the most widely read books of all time.

The book arrived on the market during the post-war baby boom and quickly became an inspiration, with Spock encouraging mothers to trust their instincts more in dealing with their children and emphasizing the importance of physical contact – hugs, cuddles, and kisses – and all the other manifestations of the thing most needed by children – love.

Spock's liberal attitude towards childcare and his emphasis on respect for the individual child eschewed physical discipline and coercion of all kinds. It was an attitude that spilled over into an active political life, and in particular the position he took on the compulsory drafting of young US men to Vietnam. He became a violent critic of the war there, and in 1968 made the bold statement that 'To win in Vietnam, we will have to exterminate a whole nation'. His convictions were such that he was later prosecuted for advising young men to dodge the draft, and had to go to the appeal court to get his two-year conviction overturned. Inevitably, during the 1960s many laid responsibility at Spock's door for creating a new permissive society, where the younger generation sought only instant gratification. He was blamed for nurturing a generation of dropouts, who preferred to 'make love, not war'; even Spock himself later admitted that he had perhaps underemphasized the importance of discipline in the upbringing of children. In the 1970s, he responded to pressure from the women's movement to address feminist issues and the problems of the single parent, publishing *Bringing Up Children in Difficult Times* in 1974.

In general however, Spock remained unrepentant, and after his retirement maintained his commitment to political causes. It was a commitment that would cost him dear: the millions he made from *Baby and Child Care* disappeared in legal fees and donations to civil rights and pacifist groups. By the time of his death in San Diego, California, on 15 March 1998, he was penniless.

Stewart, James (Maitland)

(1908–1997)

US film actor, noted for his awkward, almost bemused screen presence, his hesitant, drawling delivery, and, in many of his film roles, his embodiment of traditional American values and ideals. Stewart was one of the most loved screen performers of his or any other generation. He first rose to popularity during the Depression, the height of Hollywood's 'Golden Era' of studio filmmaking, and sustained his appeal for film audiences well beyond the decline of the studio system that had made him a star. A life-long, and, in his later years, high-profile Republican, Stewart was also a decorated war veteran. Aged 33, he joined the US Army Air Corps during World War II, winning the Air Medal and the Distinguished Flying Cross, and rising from the rank of private to colonel. Following the war, he joined the Air Force Reserve, and eventually attained the rank of brigadier-general before retiring from the force in 1968.

Stewart was born in Indiana, Pennsylvania, on 20 May 1908. He studied architecture at Princeton University, where he befriended future film director Joshua Logan, who persuaded him to try his hand at acting. On graduating he joined Logan's theatre company, University Players, teaming up with actors Henry Fonda and Margaret Sullavan. Spotted by Hedda Hopper on the New York stage, Stewart was given a screen test by MGM, earning a long-term contract with the studio in 1935. His first feature film was *The Murder Man* (1935), but it was his performance in *Born to Dance* (1936), opposite Eleanor Powell, which secured his leading man status. A string of popular successes and fruitful collaborations followed. In *Shopworn Angel* (1938), *The Shop Around the Corner* (1939), and *The Mortal Storm* (1940), for example, he was reunited with his former theatre company colleague Margaret Sullavan. In *You Can't Take It With You* (1938), *Mr Smith Goes to Washington* (1939), and the post-war classic *It's a Wonderful Life* (1946), he teamed up with director Frank Capra. Other successes included *Destry Rides Again* (1939), the first of many Western roles, in which he starred opposite Marlene Dietrich, and the comedy *Philadelphia Story* (1940), for which his performance as a cynical journalist won him an Academy Award.

Following the war, after a small number of commercial failures (among them *It's a Wonderful Life*, when first released), Stewart got his career back on track with his role as a hard-bitten investigative reporter in *Call Northside 777* (1948). Moving away from the sentimental roles of the late 1930s, Stewart found himself presented with the opportunity to explore the darker side of human nature in his collaborations with directors Alfred Hitchcock and Anthony Mann, producing some of his most memorable work in such films as *Winchester 73* (1950), *The Naked Spur* (1953), *The Far Country* (1954), *Rear Window* (1954), and *Vertigo* (1958).

Stewart had one of the longest careers in the sound era of Hollywood filmmaking, spanning numerous genres and several fruitful collaborations with such celebrated directors as Capra, Hitchcock, Mann, and John Ford. Among his many other films were *Harvey* (1950), *The Glenn Miller Story* (1953), *Anatomy of a Murder* (1959), *The Man Who Shot Liberty Valance* (1961), and *The Shootist* (1976).

When his wife Gloria McLean died from lung cancer in 1994, Stewart, mourning her loss, effectively became a recluse. He died of a cardiac arrest at his home in Beverley Hills on 2 July 1997.

Teresa, Mother (born Agnes Gonxha Bojaxhiu)

(1910–1997)

Albanian-born Indian nun who devoted her life to working among the sick and poor of Calcutta, building up a worldwide order of over 3,000 Misssionaries of Charity. A diminutive, stooped figure, whose frailty belied a resilience that enabled her to spend a long life in some of the world's worst slums, Mother Teresa always made a point of underlining her total and willing subservience to a greater will: 'By blood and origin I am all Albanian. My citizenship is Indian. I am a Catholic nun. As to my calling, I belong to the whole world. As to my heart, I belong entirely to the heart of Jesus.'

Despite such heartfelt dedication Mother Teresa was not without her critics during and after her lifetime; many were suspicious that beneath the humility lay the makings of a personality cult. She has also been criticized over her fervent condemnation of abortion and artificial contraception, given that she witnessed the problems caused by overpopulation and overcrowding on a daily basis in Calcutta.

However, her deep sense of vocation was never in doubt, and was engendered at an early age. By the time she was 12, Teresa, the daughter of an ethnic Albanian merchant resident in Skopje, had already decided she wanted to serve the church. At 18 she joined an Irish order, the Sisters of Loretto, and went to Calcutta where she taught at a convent school for the daughters of the Bengali elite.

In 1946, divine revelation changed the course of Mother Teresa's life, when, as she has described, the voice of God called her to work with the poor and the dying as the obedient channel for his will: 'I don't claim anything of the work. It is his work. I am like a little pencil in his hand. That is all.' Together with a group of acolytes, she submitted herself to a rigorous life of self-denial, establishing her own order, The Missionaries of Charity, in 1950. Two years later, she and her sisters set up a hospice for the dying. Her work might have continued in relative obscurity had it not been for her discovery by the media in 1970, when the British broadcaster Malcolm Muggeridge made a documentary about her work entitled *Something Beautiful for God*.

Despite her propulsion into media stardom, Mother Teresa resisted the opportunity of making political capital out of her status as a guru on the plight of the underprivileged, and opened missions in countries of all political persuasions. She was showered with awards, including the Pope John XXIII Peace Prize in 1971 and the Nobel Peace Prize in 1979. Latterly, she extended her work to help the victims of the Bhopal disaster and AIDS. Tough and uncompromising, she finally succumbed to heart disease at the age of 87. Since her death, the Missionaries of Charity in Calcutta have been criticized for putting limits on their previously unconditional charity, by turning some people away from their doors. Without the firm leadership of its charismatic founder, the Home for the Destitute and Dying already seems to be losing its impetus, as its effectiveness in mitigating poverty and disease is questioned. Despite this, many feel that Mother Teresa herself will inevitably achieve the sainthood wished upon her by her many admirers around the world. She died in Calcutta on 5 September 1997.

Tippett, Michael (Kemp)

(1905–1998)

British composer who ranks with Benjamin Britten as one of the two great English composers of the post-war era. The talent and integrity of Michael Tippett was recognized as long ago as 1941 with his oratorio about Nazism and the Holocaust, *A Child of Our Time*. However, formal recognition for his contribution to 20th-century music did not begin to find its way to him until the 1960s.

Some of this long delay can be accounted for by Tippett's own non-conformist stance, both musically and socially. As a humanitarian and committed pacifist (for which beliefs he went to prison during the war), his primary concerns throughout his musical career were the social as well as spiritual issues of his time. After studying at the Royal College of Music, where his teachers Malcolm Sargent and Adrian Boult failed to recognize his talent as a musical maverick, Tippett became conductor of the Morley College Orchestra for unemployed musicians during the Depression of the 1930s. After teaching there for several years, he devoted himself entirely to composition from the early 1950s.

Tippett's musical roots were eclectic: from the simplicity of Elizabethan madrigals, to the Baroque of Bach, Handel, and Purcell, to the modernist style of Stravinsky; in later life he even incorporated elements of contemporary, popular music, such as blues, jazz, and even rap into his work. His early, more formal style produced fine chamber works, such as the Concerto for Double String Orchestra (1939) but subsequent work – on a more ambitious scale – was often protracted, only to be criticized for its complexity, if not downright unplayability (in the case of the Piano Concerto and 2nd Symphony) when it finally reached the public. Tippett's contribution to opera was highly innovative; as observations of the human condition, his operas were accompanied by Tippett's own quirky librettos, which, inviting criticism for their use of the vernacular, broke the mould of traditional libretto-writing. The major works *The Midsummer Marriage* (first performed in 1955), *King Priam* (1962), *The Knot Garden* (1970), and *The Ice Break* (1977) all challenged musical convention and attracted a following among younger audiences. In time, orchestral pieces, such as the ravishing *Fantasia Concertante on a Theme of Corelli* (1953) or the spiritually elevating oratorio *The Vision of St Augustine* (1965), became hugely popular, and Tippett was recognized by the establishment with a knighthood in 1966. However, he achieved his greatest musical recognition in the USA, and his work was only belatedly embraced by Europe.

To the end of his long and active life (he continued touring into his eighties), Tippett remained modest about his achievements and true to his own profound sense of justice, seeing his music as a vehicle for the humane values that were so important to him, and as a means of providing an element of spirituality lacking in so many people's lives: 'If, in the music I write, I can create a world of sound wherein some of my generation can find refreshment for the inner life, then I am doing my work properly. I have to sing songs for those who can't sing for themselves.' Sir Michael Tippett died in London on 8 January 1998.

Versace, Gianni

(1916–1997)

Italian fashion designer, one of the new school of Milan-based Italian designers who have dominated the fashion world since the 1980s. Whilst Versace's patronage by the glitterati of the pop and film world would seem to have more than endorsed his status as a leading contemporary designer, his work was frequently criticized by fashion pundits for its gaudy vulgarity and its predilection for elements of sado-masochist bondage and leather.

The son of a coal merchant and a dressmaker, he came from a poor district of Calabria and began by working as a buyer

for his mother's dress shop. He made his first tentative designs in 1970 and moved to Milan, where he found himself a financial backer and launched his first ready-to-wear collection in 1978. He soon began experimenting with aluminium mesh, rubber, and leather to create a raunchy style of clothing that attracted a clientele among the self-promoting stars of the pop world and cinema.

Soon the thriving business of Gianni Versace SpA was also employing his brother Santo and his sister Donatella, and by the early 1990s he had outlets all round the world, including a lavishly outfitted, palazzo-style shop in Old Bond Street, London. Before long Versace himself had luxurious homes around the world, crammed with works of art, and bought with the proceeds from a multi-million dollar business organization; Versace once admitted that he could spend $3 million in two hours in a single shopping spree. Although his wildly expensive designs may have hung only in the wardrobes of the rich and famous few, in 1994 suddenly the whole world knew what a Versace design meant, when actress Elizabeth Hurley wore one of his dresses to the English premiere of the film *Four Weddings and Funeral*. The dress in question – a fairly simple structure in black, held together with numerous, strategically placed gold safety pins – propelled his name onto the front pages the next day. Now everyone who could afford to wanted over-the-top designs from the man who dressed the likes of Elton John, Madonna, Courtney Love, Princess Diana, and the supermodel Naomi Campbell.

Versace was shot on 15 July 1997, on the steps of his Miami Beach mansion, in what appears to be an anti-homosexual killing. His memorial service in Milan cathedral, attended by a congregation of 2,000, was a grand affair in keeping with his status in the fashion world.

Wills Moody, Helen (Newington)

(1905–1998)

US tennis player and winner of eight Wimbledon singles titles. One of the game's all-time greats, Helen Wills Moody won 31 Grand Slam championships between 1922 and 1938, including 19 singles titles. Only Martina Navratilova has won more Wimbledon singles titles, while only Molla Mallory has bettered her seven US singles wins. Such was her dominance of the women's game, she was unbeaten in singles play from the autumn of 1926 until August 1933.

A hard-hitting baseline player, regarded as the first exponent of the power game, she hit the ball with both pace and unerring accuracy, relentlessly exposing her opponents' weaknesses. Imperturbable and unemotional, she was nicknamed 'Little Miss Poker Face'. However, this was rarely used in a derisory sense because, although

she lacked the crowd-pleasing style and film star-like presence of the great Suzanne Lenglen (whom she succeeded as the world's leading women's player), fans much admired her single-minded determination and unwavering concentration. They were perhaps intrigued too by her sheer inscrutability. Off court she was a very private person, introverted, intelligent, and placid. Much of her time away from tennis was devoted to art. In 1928 she graduated in fine art from the University of California and learnt to draw with considerable skill.

Helen Newington Wills was born at Centerville (now part of Fremont, California) on 6 October 1905. Encouraged by her surgeon father, she took up tennis at the age of eight. In 1922, aged just 16, she won the doubles title at the US Championships, and the following year she won the singles, defeating Molla Mallory, who had won in six of the previous seven years, in the final. After winning the title again in 1924 and 1925, a match was arranged at Cannes in February 1926 against Suzanne Lenglen, billed as a sort of unofficial world-title-decider between the queen of tennis and the young pretender. Wills, who had done little to prepare for the match, was beaten 6–3, 8–6, but it would be wrong to use this one-off, non-tournament match to compare her ability with Lenglen, especially as she had not reached her peak.

Illness held up her progress in 1926, but in 1927 she began a period of domination of women's tennis that has perhaps never been equalled. In singles play she won the Wimbledon championship six times in seven years (1927–33), the French Championships four times in a row, and the US Championships, from 1927 to 1929 and again in 1931. A back injury sustained in 1934 curtailed this run, but she won the Wimbledon singles in 1935 and again in 1938, before announcing her retirement.

In 1929 she married Frederick Moody, a US stockbroker, whom she had first met during her match against Lenglen in Cannes. They divorced in 1937, and two years later she married Aidan Roark, an American film writer and polo player. This marriage was dissolved in the early 1970s, after which she lived alone. She died at Carmel, California, on 1 January 1998.

Witherspoon, Jimmy

(1923–1997)

US blues singer who adapted to changing musical trends by moving into jazz when the onrush of rock and roll swamped rhythm and blues in the 1950s.

Like most of the greats of his musical genre, Witherspoon's grounding was in gospel music, singing with the First Baptist Church choir as a child in his home town of Gurdon, Arkansas. He ran away from home as a teenager, to seek his musical fortune in Los Angeles in the 1930s, but his struggle for recognition was interrupted by the onset of war. After serving in the Merchant Marines, Witherspoon returned to California in 1944 and joined Jay McShann's band, with which he remained for the next four years, touring the clubs, ballrooms, and dance halls of the USA. In the late 1940s Witherspoon recorded the blues standard forever associated with his name: 'Ain't Nobody's Business'. Going solo in the early 1950s, he worked one-nighters and made numerous other recordings before his career flagged during the rock and roll era. He was rescued from the doldrums when he changed tack and developed a jazz style, which he displayed to good effect at the Monterey Jazz Festival in 1959. In the 1960s he toured with Buck Clayton and Count Basie's bands, and kept going on the jazz club and festival circuit both in the USA and in the UK, until he developed cancer of the throat in the mid-1980s.

Illness did not prevent Witherspoon's eventual return to the stage, although his voice was now somewhat impaired. A revered master of the blues, renowned for his commanding presence, Witherspoon has guested at the concerts and on the albums of many other rock and blues performers who have been inspired by him, such as Van Morrison and Eric Clapton. He died in Los Angeles, California, on 18 September 1997.

Young, John Zachary

(1907–1997)

UK zoologist who discovered and studied the giant nerve fibres in squid, contributing greatly to knowledge of nerve structure and function. He also researched the central nervous system of octopuses, demonstrating that memory stores are located in the brain. He is probably most widely known for his zoological textbooks, *The Life of Vertebrates* (1950) and *The Life of Mammals* (1957). He received many honorary university degrees, and in 1967 was awarded the Royal Medal of the Royal Society of London.

Young was born in Bristol and studied at Magdalen College, Oxford University. In 1928 he went to Naples as a biological scholar and became interested in cephalopod biology. In all, he was to write more than 150 papers on cephalopods during his 65-year research career. In 1945 he became professor of anatomy at University College, London – the first non-medical scientist in the UK to hold a professorship in anatomy. He remained at University College until he retired in 1974.

Young began his work on the nerves of squid before World War II. He discovered that certain of their nerve fibres are exceptionally thick – up to 1 mm/0.04 in in diameter (about a hundred times the diameter of mammalian neurons) – and are covered with a relatively thin myelin sheath (unlike mammalian nerve fibres, which have thick sheaths), properties that make them easy to experiment on. For example, almost all the intracellular contents can be extracted without destroying the fibre's ability to conduct nerve impulses, and electrodes can easily be inserted into the fibres because of their large diameter. Moreover, extracting the contents of the giant fibres is still the only way of obtaining intracellular nerve material uncontaminated by the myelin sheath or other cells. Young's work on the giant nerve fibres in squid has been invaluable, not only because of his own findings, but also because these fibres are extremely useful for experimentation and have been used by many other researchers.

During the war, Young set up a unit at Oxford to study nerve regeneration in mammals and, with UK immunologist Peter Medawar and others, devised a method of rejoining small severed nerves by using intracellular plasma as a 'glue'. Young also researched the rates of neuron growth and the factors that determine neuron size.

After the war Young turned his attention to the central nervous system, using octopuses as research animals. Working with Brian Boycott, he showed that octopuses can learn to discriminate between different orientations of the same object – when presented with horizontal and vertical rectangles, for example, the octopuses attacked one but avoided the other. He also demonstrated (this time with M J Wells) that octopuses can learn to recognize objects by touch. In addition, Young proved that the memory stores are located in the brain and proposed a model to explain the processes involved in memory. He died in Oxford, on 4 July 1997.

Web Sites

Abraham Lincoln – Sixteenth President 1861–1865

URL: "http://www.whitehouse.gov/WH/glimpse/presidents/html/al16.html"

Biography and presidential record of the sixteenth president of the USA.

Alan Turing Home Page

URL: "http://www.turing.org.uk/turing/"

Authoritative illustrated biography of the computer pioneer, plus links to related sites. This site contains information on his origins and his code-breaking work during World War II.

Andy Warhol Museum Home Page

URL: "http://www.usaor.net/warhol/"

Samples of Warhol's art from the museum devoted to preserving his work. The online exhibition available here includes most of his famous works.

Angelico, Fra

URL: "http://www.oir.ucf.edu/wm/paint/auth/angelico/"

Site at the WebMuseum, Paris, devoted to Fra Angelico, providing biographical details, hyperlinks to related artists and movements, photographs, and critical discussion of his work.

Anna Akhmatova Page

URL: "http://funnelweb.utcc.utk.edu/~jtdybka/akh.htm"

Site featuring a biography of Anna Akhmatova and a bibliography, along with a number of paintings of the poet. It also contains links to other sites about the poet.

Armstrong, Neil

URL: "http://www.3d-interact.com/SpaceMuseum/armstrong.html"

Biography of the first man on the moon from the Neil A Armstrong Museum.

Auden, W H

URL: "http://www.lit.kobe-u.ac.jp/~hishika/auden.htm"

Appreciation of the work and life of W H Auden. There are also links to some of his poems.

Bacon, Francis (poet)

URL: "http://www.luminarium.org/sevenlit/bacon/index.html"

Biographical details, famous quotes, essays, and links to many works by this philosopher, politician, and essayist.

Bacon, Francis (artist)

URL: "http://www.oir.ucf.edu/wm/paint/auth/bacon/"

Site at the WebMuseum, Paris, devoted to Francis Bacon, providing biographical details and photographs of his work, including *Head VI* and *Man with Dog*.

Bartók, Béla

URL: "http://www.ultranet.com/%7Ecwholl/bartok/bartok.html"

Biography of the Hungarian composer. It describes his musical upbringing, the influence of Liszt, Brahms, and Richard Strauss, his interest in folk music, his career, and financial problems in old age.

Beaton, Cecil

URL: "http://www.harrowschool.org.uk/harrow/beaton.htm"

Lengthy profile of the life and career of the English photographer.

Beethoven, Ludwig

URL: "http://magic.hofstra.edu:7003/immortal/index.html"

Extensive site on Beethoven's work. As well as detailed information about his life, this site also contains a complete listing of his works, and an extensive selection of extracts to listen to.

Benjamin Franklin: His Autobiography

URL: `"http://odur.let.rug.nl/~usa/B/bfranklin/frankxx.htm"`

Part of a larger site on historical documents, this page is devoted to the full text of Benjamin Franklin's autobiography.

Bernstein, Leonard

URL: `"http://www.leonardbernstein.com/splash/index.html"`

Celebration of Bernstein's legacy. This is a very comprehensive guide to the US composer and conductor that includes images, audio and video clips and full scores of some of his works.

Bertolt Brecht Home Page

URL: `"http://www.geocities.com/Broadway/Stage/1052/brecht1.htm"`

Intimate profile of the German playwright.

Bertrand Russell Society

URL: `"http://daniel.drew.edu/~jlenz/brs.html"`

Links to biographies, images, and discussion of the philosopher Bertrand Russell. There are links to several essays about his philosophy, as well as to the text of a number of his writings.

Big Otis

URL: `"http://ourworld.compuserve.com/homepages/luke_the_gr8/otis_redding_main.html"`

Site for Otis Redding fans, welcomed by the voice of the man himself. There is a biography, details of albums (together with lyrics), sound clips, and links to other related sites.

Blake, William

URL: `"http://www.oir.ucf.edu/wm/paint/auth/blake/"`

Site at the WebMuseum, Paris devoted to William Blake.

Bob Dylan Music Lounge

URL: `"http://www.geocities.com/SunsetStrip/Alley/8361/index.html"`

Comprehensive tribute to Dylan. Contents include a full biography.

Bosch, Hieronymus

URL: `"http://www.oir.ucf.edu/wm/paint/auth/bosch/"`

Site at the WebMuseum, Paris devoted to Hieronymus Bosch.

Brahe, Tycho

URL: `"http://es.rice.edu/ES/humsoc/Galileo/People/tycho_brahe.html"`

Full account of the life and work of the Danish astronomer. There are pictures of Brahe, instruments he used, and the observatory he founded.

Brezhnev, Leonid Ilyich

URL: `"http://artnet.net/~upstart/brezhnev.html"`

Timeline that follows the major events in the life of Leonid Brezhnev, from his birth in the Ukraine through his years as leader of the USSR.

Britten, Benjamin

URL: `"http://www.geocities.com/Vienna/Strasse/1523/britten.htm"`

Comprehensive source of information on the British composer. In addition to a biography there is a huge bibliography of books, articles, and dissertations about Britten and a complete discography.

Brontë Sisters

URL: `"http://www2.sbbs.se/hp/cfalk/bronteng.htm"`

Extensive collection of information on each of the Brontë sisters, including online novels and poems, literary criticism and interpretation, biographies, bibliographies, and mailing lists.

Brueghel, Pieter the Elder

URL: `"http://mexplaza.udg.mx/wm/paint/auth/bruegel/"`

Profile of the 16th-century Flemish artist. There is a biography, notes on his paintings, and high resolution images of his best known works.

Burne-Jones, Sir Edward Coley

URL: `"http://sunsite.unc.edu/wm/paint/auth/burne-jones/"`

Profile of the English Pre-Raphaelite painter, designer, and illustrator. It traces his friendship with William Morris and their shared interest in the revival of medieval applied arts.

Canaletto

URL: `"http://www.oir.ucf.edu/wm/paint/auth/canaletto/"`

Site at the WebMuseum, Paris devoted to Canaletto, providing biographical details, photographs, and critical discussion of his work.

Cézanne, Paul

URL: `"http://www.oir.ucf.edu/wm/paint/auth/cezanne/"`

Contains an extensive biography and gallery dedicated to the French painter. This site contains writings on his paintings and his relationship with Impressionism, Classicism, and Cubism.

Christie, Agatha

URL: `"http://members.aol.com/mg4273/chris1.htm"`

Detailed biographical information on Agatha Christie's writing career, including a full list of her novels, details of her short stories, and the film adaptations of her novels.

Cole Porter Wide Web

URL: `"http://www.doitall.com/cole/index.html"`

Homage that includes biographical articles, recommended albums, quotations, lyrics, and a catalogue of all Porter's songs, sorted by title, musical, and year.

Columbus, Christopher

URL: `"http://sunsite.unc.edu/expo/1492.exhibit/c- Columbus/columbus.html"`

Historical background to Columbus's voyages of discovery, including the origins of his *Book of Privileges* and coat of arms.

Connery, Sean

URL: `"http://www.mcs.net/~klast/www/connery.html"`

In addition to a full biography and filmography there is a large selection of articles and interviews.

Constable, John

URL: `"http://www.oir.ucf.edu/wm/paint/auth/constable/"`

Site at the WebMuseum, Paris devoted to John Constable.

Constructing Franz Kafka

URL: `"http://info.pitt.edu/~kafka/intro.html"`

Very large Web site at the University of Pittsburgh's German department. A biography and a bibliography feature prominently here.

D Anthony Storm's Web Site on Kierkegaard

URL: `"http://www.2xtreme.net/dstorm/sk/"`

Devoted to the writings of existentialist philosopher Soren Aabye Kierkegaard, including a biography, bibliography, and gallery.

Darwin, Charles

URL: `"http://www.literature.org/Works/Charles-Darwin"`

Complete text of Darwin's works *On the Origin of Species* and *Voyage of the Beagle*.

David Bowie: Teenage Wildlife

URL: `"http://www.etete.com/Bowie/"`

Offers an extensive library of information about Bowie and his work. Includes details of songs and lyrics, films and videos, a large collection of images, and current news.

David Lynch

URL: `"http://us.imdb.com/cache/person-all/a104240"`

Combined biography and filmography of the American director. All the director's films are listed including his cameo, musical, and editing credits.

Degas, Edgar

URL: `"http://www.oir.ucf.edu/wm/paint/auth/degas/"`

Site at the WebMuseum, Paris devoted to Edgar Degas.

Descartes, René

URL: `"http://www.knight.org/advent/cathen/04744b.htm"`

Extensive treatment of the life and philosophical, scientific, and mathematical achievements of Renatus Cartesius.

Dickens, Charles

URL: `http://www.stg.brown.edu/projects/hypertext/landow/victorian/dickens/dickbioov.html`

Biographical page from the Victorian Web – including a chronology of Dickens's life; features on his working methods and his affair with Ellen Ternan; and overviews of *Little Dorrit* and *Great Expectations*.

Donne, John

URL: `http://www.luminarium.org/sevenlit/donne/index.html`

Biographical details, essays, and links to many works by Donne.

Dostoevsky

URL: `http://stange.simplenet.com/dostoevsky/index.htm`

Contents of this site are divided into three sections: a bibliography of Dostoevsky's published works, which includes books about Dostoevsky; a timeline of his tumultuous life and times; and Dostoevsky in the words of others.

Drabble, Margaret

URL: `http://tile.net/drabble/`

Comprehensive source of information on the English writer. The contents include interviews and articles about Drabble. There are full details of her books and summaries of their plots and themes.

Drake, Sir Francis

URL: `http://www.mcn.org/2/oseeler/drake.htm`

Network of pages on Drake, focusing mainly on his circumnavigation of the globe.

Dustin Hoffman – A Man of Many Faces

URL: `http://home.earthlink.net/~joepez/hoffman/`

Fan's tribute to the US actor. The contents include a biography, detailed filmography, listing of Academy Award nominations, and a large gallery of photographs.

Edison, Thomas

URL: `http://hfm.umd.umich.edu/histories/edison/tae.html`

Short, illustrated biography.

Edmund Spenser Home Page

URL: `http://darkwing.uoregon.edu/~rbear/`

Site devoted to the life and works of the 16th-century English poet Edmund Spenser. The numerous works include *The Faerie Queene*, which comes with its own search engine.

Elgar Society and Elgar Foundation

URL: `http://www.elgar.org/`

Includes a biography and chronology of Elgar's life, complete with pen portraits, photographs, and manuscript scans.

Eliot, T S

URL: `http://www.cc.columbia.edu/acis/bartleby/eliot/`

Online edition of selected poetry and prose by T S Eliot, including *The Wasteland* and *Prufrock and Other Observations*.

Elizabeth Barrett Browning: An Overview

URL: `http://www.stg.brown.edu/projects/hypertext/landow/victorian/ebb/browning2ov.html`

Part of the Victorian Web, this extensive site features a number of articles about the poet's life, relationships, and self-portrayal in her work.

Elizabeth I

URL: `http://www.luminarium.org/renlit/eliza.htm`

Biography which includes text of some of her poems and speeches, letters, and essays about her life.

Ella Fitzgerald Memorial Page

URL: `http://jazzcentralstation.com/jcs/station/musicexp/artists/ella/index.html`

Tribute to Ella Fitzgerald in the form of a number of essays about her life and music, an interview with her biographer, fans' reminiscences, a discography, and a number of sound files of her voice.

Elvis Presley Home Page

URL: `http://sunsite.unc.edu/elvis/elvishom.html`

Unofficial page that mixes factual information – a pictorial tour of Graceland, for example – and conjecture about continued sightings of Elvis. There are also links to related literature and a list of lyrics.

Emily Dickinson Page

URL: `http://www.planet.net/pkrisxle/emily/dickinson.html`

Life and works of US poet Emily Dickinson. Resources include an illustrated biography, several hundred of her poems online, links to discussion groups and the Emily Dickinson International Society, and further links to numerous related sites.

Fermat, Pierre de

URL: `http://www-history.mcs.st-and.ac.uk/~history/Mathematicians/Fermat.html`

Extensive biography of the French mathematical genius Pierre de Fermat.

Francis Ford Coppola Profile

URL: `http://www.achievement.org/autodoc/page/cop0pro-1`

Description the life and work of the US director, producer, and screen writer Francis Ford Coppola.

Francis of Assisi, St

URL: `http://www.knight.org/advent/cathen/06221a.htm`

Detailed biography of the founder of the Franciscan order.

Franklin, Aretha

URL: `http://imusic.com/showcase/urban/arethafranklin.html`

Profile of the career of the 'queen of soul'. Contents include a biography, discography, audio samples, latest news, and a bulletin board for Franklin fans.

Freud, Lucian

URL: `http://www.oir.ucf.edu/wm/paint/auth/freud/`

Site at the WebMuseum, Paris devoted to Lucian Freud, providing biographical details, photographs, and critical discussion of his work.

F Scott Fitzgerald Home Page

URL: `http://www.csd.scarolina.edu/fitzgerald/index.html`

Extensive introduction to F Scott Fitzgerald from the University of South Carolina, USA.

Gagarin, Yuri

URL: `http://www.allstar.fiu.edu/aerojava/gagarin.htm`

Biography of the peasant's son who became 'the Columbus of the cosmos'.

Gainsborough, Thomas

URL: `http://www.oir.ucf.edu/wm/paint/auth/gainsborough/`

Site at the WebMuseum, Paris devoted to Thomas Gainsborough, providing biographical details, hyperlinks to related artists, photographs, and critical discussion of his work.

Gaudi Central

URL: `http://futures.wharton.upenn.edu/~jonath22/gaudi.html`

Short biography of the renowned Catalonian architect together with a wide selection of photographs and information on his most celebrated buildings.

George Frideric Handel Home Page

URL: `http://www.intr.net/bleissa/handel/home.html`

Comprehensive site dedicated to the baroque composer Handel. This site features a chronology of his life, a detailed list of his compositions, plus links to related Web sites.

George Washington – First President 1789–1797

URL: `http://www.whitehouse.gov/WH/glimpse/presidents/html/gw1.html`

Biography and presidential record of the first president of the USA.

George and Ira Gershwin Archive

URL: `http://www.sju.edu/~bs065903/gershwin/homepage.htm`

Celebration of the talents of George and Ira Gershwin.

Gogh, Vincent van

URL: `http://www.oir.ucf.edu/wm/paint/auth/gogh/`

Site at the WebMuseum, Paris, devoted to Vincent van Gogh.

Gordimer, Nadine

URL: `http://nobel.sdsc.edu/laureates/literature-1991-1-bio.html`

Traces Gordimer's literary career, her commitment to free speech, and the background to the award of the Nobel Prize for Literature.

Goya, Francisco de

URL: `http://www.oir.ucf.edu/wm/paint/auth/goya/`

Site at the WebMuseum, Paris, devoted to Francisco de Goya.

Gustav Holst Site

URL: `http://wso.williams.edu/~ktaylor/gholst`

Illustrated chronology and biography of the composer Gustav Holst. There is a detailed list of Holst's compositions which features brief descriptions and audio clips.

Gustav Mahler WWW Pages

URL: `http://www.netaxs.com/~jgreshes/mahler/`

Pages devoted to an appreciation of the life and works of Gustav Mahler. The site includes a lengthy account of the Mahlerfest XI in Colorado, USA, as well as information on scores and newly released CD recordings.

Hawking, Stephen

URL: `http://www.damtp.cam.ac.uk/DAMTP/user/hawking/home.html`

Stephen Hawking's own home page, with a brief biography, disability advice, and a selection of his lectures, including 'the beginning of time' and a series debating the nature of space and time.

Hendrix, Jimi

URL: `http://gold.spectra.net/jimi/`

Wealth of information about Jimi Hendrix, with guitar tabulatures and chords, lyrics, photos, sound clips, newspaper and other articles, and links to related sites.

Hitchcock Page

URL: `http://www.primenet.com/~mwc/`

Fan page for Alfred Hitchcock. It includes a filmography, life story, film sequences (mainly stills), and links to other related sites.

Hockney, David

URL: `http://www.oir.ucf.edu/wm/paint/auth/hockney/`

Site at the WebMuseum, Paris, devoted to David Hockney, providing biographical details, hyperlinks to related movements, photographs, and critical discussion of his work.

Holiday, Billie

URL: `http://www.gibbs-smith.com/books/billie.html`

Biography of the legendary singer who asked in vain not to be talked about after she was gone.

Hume, David

URL: `http://swift.eng.ox.ac.uk/jdr/hume.html`

Hume's philosophy is briefly discussed, and there are links to the text and reviews of a number of his essays, including *An Enquiry Concerning Human Understanding*.

James Joyce Web Site

URL: `http://www.2street.com/joyce`

The site includes articles, e-texts, maps, links to both online and offline Joycean resources, a timeline, multimedia, and the online journal *Hypermedia Joyce Studies*.

Jane Austen Information Page

URL: `http://uts.cc.utexas.edu/~churchh/janeinfo.html`

Provides biographical details of Austen and her family, background information on the society of the time, the full text of many of her works, including a hypertext version of *Pride and Prejudice*, and some pieces of literary criticism.

John Paul II

URL: `http://www.vatican.va/holy_father/phf_en.htm`

Official Vatican account of the life, times, and achievements of Karol Wojtyla.

Jonson, Ben

URL: `http://www.luminarium.org/sevenlit/jonson/index.html`

Site includes famous quotes, essays, and links to many works by this famous playwright and poet.

JS Bach Archive and Bibliography

URL: `http://www.let.rug.nl/Linguistics/diversen/bach/intro.html`

Dedicated to the life and works of the composer, this page offers an illustrated biography, an extensive bibliography, portraits, and a guide for the 'Bach tourist'.

Kandinsky, Wassily

URL: `http://www.oir.ucf.edu/wm/paint/auth/kandinsky/`

Site at the WebMuseum, Paris, devoted to Wassily Kandinsky.

Kant, Immanuel

URL: `http://www.friesian.com/space.htm#kant`

Extensive discussion and explanation of Kant's philosophy.

Keats, John

URL: `http://www.cc.columbia.edu/acis/bartleby/keats/`

Online edition of the poetical works of John Keats, indexed by title and by first line.

Kennedy, John F

URL: `http://www.geocities.com/~newgeneration/`

Tribute to John F Kennedy, in which the user can – amongst other things – browse transcripts of his speeches, take a tour of the White House with Mrs Kennedy, see and hear photos and sound clips from memorial services, and take part in a virtual press conference with the president.

King of the Blues

URL: `http://prairie.lakes.com/~jkerekes/`

Detailed biography of the blues guitarist B B King, plus photos, and sound files. This site includes sections such as 'young bluesman', 'rise to stardom', and a complete discography.

Klee, Paul

URL: `http://www.oir.ucf.edu/wm/paint/auth/klee/`

Site at the WebMuseum, Paris, devoted to Paul Klee.

Klimt, Gustav

URL: `http://www.oir.ucf.edu/wm/paint/auth/klimt/`

Site at the WebMuseum, Paris devoted to Gustav Klimt, providing biographical details, hyperlinks to related artists, photographs (including *Love* and *Danae*), and critical discussion of his work.

Kubrick Multimedia Film Guide

URL: `http://www.lehigh.edu/~pjl2/kubrick.html`

In-depth site on the US film director. This site includes a wealth of images and commentary on many of his works, as well as some audio clips and rarely seen pictures.

Lawrence, D H

URL: `http://home.clara.net/rananim/lawrence/`

Substantial amount of biographical information and photographs, from Lawrence's early years in Nottingham to his unhappy expulsion from Cornwall and death in France.

Lenin, V I

URL: `http://www.idbsu.edu/surveyrc/Staff/jaynes/marxism/lenin.htm`

Leninism pages of the Marxism Leninism Project offering a short biography, a chronology of his life, photographs, and translations of his key writings.

Leonard, Elmore

URL: `http://www.bdd.com/bin/show_story.cgi?story_id=235`

Biography of the US author. This Web site contains a biography of Leonard, excerpts from his book *Out of Sight* plus review and publication information on six of his other works.

Leonardo da Vinci

URL: `http://www.oir.ucf.edu/wm/paint/auth/vinci/`

Site at the WebMuseum, Paris, devoted to Leonardo da Vinci.

Lewis Carroll Home Page

URL: `http://www.lewiscarroll.org/carroll.html`

Large site dedicated to Lewis Carroll as a writer, photographer, and mathematician. There is a large amount of information about studies of Carroll, together with information of his place in popular culture.

Life of Henry Ford

URL: `http://www.hfmgv.org/histories/hf/henry.html`

Biography of the car manufacturer from the Henry Ford Museum in Detroit.

Lou Reed and the Velvet Underground

URL: `http://www.poiHQ.com/loureed/`

Interviews with the band members, plus a gallery of album covers and photos, archives of fan material, and discographies.

Love Supreme

URL: `http://jazz.route66.net/aLoveSupreme/index.html`

Web site on John Coltrane, pioneer of modern jazz, including a year-by-year chronology, recommendations for new listeners, recent releases, discography, bibliography, a sound clip directory, and links to many other related sites.

Machiavelli, Nicolo

URL: `http://www.utm.edu/research/iep/m/machiave.htm`

Profile of the life and legacy of the first great political philosopher of the Renaissance. There is also a summary of his most famous work, *The Prince*.

Mahatma Gandhi Ashram

URL: `http://www.nuvs.com/ashram/`

Extensive information about Gandhi's life and philosophy.

Malcolm X – An Islamic Perspective

URL: `http://www.colostate.edu/Orgs/MSA/docs/m_x.html`

Concise biography, adapted from the pamphlet 'Malcolm X: Why I Embraced Islam' by Yusuf Siddiqui.

Mandela, Nelson

URL: `http://www.anc.org.za/people/mandela.html`

Detailed profile of South African president Nelson Mandela. Includes information on many aspects of his personal as well as political life.

Margaret Atwood Information Web Site

URL: `http://www.web.net/owtoad/frame.htm`

Comprehensive Web site on the Canadian author.

Marilyn Pages

URL: `http://www.ionet.net/~jellenc/marilyn.html`

Online adulation of the Hollywood screen actress Marilyn Monroe that includes a biography, filmography, library of images, and a list of memorabilia.

Mark Twain in His Times

URL: `http://etext.virginia.edu/railton/index2.html`

In-depth look at the life and work of Mark Twain. This site contains many photographs and illustrations from his most popular works.

Martin Amis Web

URL: `http://www.albion.edu/fac/engl/diedrick/amispge.htm`

Site devoted to the British contemporary novelist, with links to biographical information, interviews, criticisms, bibliographies, and postmodernism.

Marx/Engels Archive

URL: `http://csf.colorado.edu/psn/marx`

Several biographies, a large photo gallery, and a number of resources on these two philosophers. There is also an extensive library containing the texts of much of their work, including, amongst others, *The Communist Manifesto*.

Matisse, Henri

URL: `http://www.oir.ucf.edu/wm/paint/auth/matisse/`

Site at the WebMuseum, Paris devoted to Henri Matisse.

Meir, Golda

URL: `http://www.israel-mfa.gov.il/facts/state/gmeir.html`

Official biography of the Israeli foreign minister and prime minister.

Michael Jackson Internet Fan Club

URL: `http://www.fred.net/mjj/`

Site that claims to be the largest Michael Jackson information site on the Internet.

Michelangelo

URL: `http://www.oir.ucf.edu/wm/paint/auth/michelangelo/`

Site at the WebMuseum, Paris devoted to Michelangelo, providing biographical details, hyperlinks to related artists and movements, photographs, and critical discussion of his work.

Milestones: A Miles Davis World Wide Web Site

URL: `http://miles.rtvf.nwu.edu/miles/milestones.html`

Tribute to Miles Davis prepared by a fan. This frequently updated site contains a biography of Davis, a complete discography, latest news of bootleg albums and official re-releases, audio and video clips, and album covers.

Miller, Arthur

URL: `http://kennedy-center.org/honors/1984/miller.html`

Profile of the renowned US playwright.

Milton, John

URL: `http://www.luminarium.org/sevenlit/milton/index.html`

Biographical details, famous quotes, essays, and links to many works.

Mondrian, Piet

URL: `http://www.oir.ucf.edu/wm/paint/auth/mondrian/`

Site at the WebMuseum, Paris devoted to Piet Mondrian.

Monet, Claude

URL: `http://www.oir.ucf.edu/wm/paint/auth/monet/`

Site at the WebMuseum, Paris devoted to Claude Monet.

Mother Teresa

URL: `http://www.latimes.com/teresa/`

Contents include a comprehensive biography, pictures and audio clips, news of the campaign to hasten her canonization, and reports of the ongoing work of the Missionaries of Charity.

Napoleon Series – Life and Times of Napoleon Bonaparte

URL: `http://www.ping.be/~ping5895/`

The site offers a virtual visit to Napoleonic battlefields, details about Napoleon's marshals, an overview of his (in)famous last 100 days as emperor, a full calendar of Napoleonic events, and a series of articles by visitors on the Napoleonic period.

Nietzsche, Friedrick

URL: `http://www.usc.edu/dept/annenberg/thomas/nietzsche.html`

Site on Nietzsche run by the University of Southern California. It includes a list of works and detailed biographical information.

Noam Chomsky Archive

URL: `http://www.worldmedia.com/archive/`

Substantial collection of the political work and thought of the American academic and philosopher Noam Chomsky.

Picasso Official Web Site

URL: `http://www.clubinternet.com/picasso/`

Introduced by Pablo Picasso's son Claude, this site is dedicated to the Picasso exhibition at the Museum of Modern Art in New York City. Not only does it contain a number of reproductions of paintings from the exhibition itself, but it also provides information about Picasso events around the world.

Piero della Francesca

URL: `http://www.oir.ucf.edu/wm/paint/auth/piero/`

Site at the WebMuseum, Paris devoted to Piero della Francesca.

Pissarro, Camille

URL: `http://www.oir.ucf.edu/wm/paint/auth/pissarro/`

Site at the WebMuseum, Paris devoted to Camille Pissarro.

Plath, Sylvia

URL: `http://www.informatik.uni-leipzig.de/privat2/beckmann/public_html/plath.html`

Comprehensive information on the life, poetic output, and legacy of the US poet.

Pollock, Jackson

URL: `http://www.oir.ucf.edu/wm/paint/auth/pollock/`

Site at the WebMuseum, Paris, devoted to Jackson Pollock.

Pound, Ezra

URL: `http://www.lit.kobe-u.ac.jp/~hishika/pound.htm`

Central source of information on the life, works, and legacy of the influential US poet.

Prince

URL: `http://www.geocities.com/Sunset-Strip/Underground/7575/prince.htm`

Site for fans of the artist formerly known as Prince. Contents include a biography, sound clips, discography, photos, interviews, and articles.

Prince of Wales

URL: `http://www.royal.gov.uk/family/wales.htm`

Official biography of the heir to the British throne presented by the British monarchy Web site. There are full details of the Prince's education, military career, interests and overseas visits.

Prokofiev

URL: `http://www.siue.edu/~aho/musov/sergei.html`

Part of a larger site concerning composers of the Soviet Union, this page explores the relationship of composer Sergey Prokofiev to the Soviet state.

Queen of Hearts

URL: `http://www.royalnetwork.com/rnn/dibio.html`

Memorial site to the Princess of Wales in the form of an illustrated biography. This site also contains remembrance prayers for a wide variety of faiths and many personal tributes from people across the world.

Raleigh, Sir Walter

URL: `http://www.luminarium.org/renlit/ralegh.htm`

Devoted to the life and works of Sir Walter Raleigh. Click links to read about his life and access his works.

Ralph Vaughan Williams Web Page

URL: `http://www.cs.qub.ac.uk/~J.Collis/RVW.html`

Chronology of Ralph Vaughan Williams's life, analyses of his major works, anecdotes, and a listening guide for the uninitiated.

Raphael

URL: `http://www.oir.ucf.edu/wm/paint/auth/raphael/`

Site at the WebMuseum, Paris devoted to Raphael.

Raymond Chandler Web Page

URL: `http://www.geocities.com/Athens/Parthenon/3224`

Features a chronology of the life of novelist Raymond Chandler, together with essays and criticism, a gallery, and a bibliography.

Richard Wagner Archive

URL: `http://www.utu.fi/~hansalmi/wagner.spml`

Collection of all kinds of material relating to Wagner, prepared by a scholar of his life and work.

Roosevelt, Franklin D

URL: `http://www.whitehouse.gov/WH/glimpse/presidents/html/fr32.html`

Biographical guide to F D Roosevelt, the 32nd US president.

Rushdie, Salman

URL: `http://www.crl.com/~subir/rushdie.html`

General source of information about Salman Rushdie's published works, with quotations, interviews, and articles about him.

Salvador Dali Art Gallery

URL: `http://members.xoom.com/daliweb/main.htm`

Impressive Dali resource that includes many images as well as biographical information, analyses of his works and a collection of essays about Dali's influences and the Surrealist movement.

Samuel Beckett Home Page

URL: `http://www-personal.umich.edu/~kadaca/beckett.html`

Features a biography, chronology, and bibliography of the Irish writer. Also included are a list of Beckett's contemporaries and general information on the Absurdist movement.

Sargent, John Singer

URL: `http://www.oir.ucf.edu/wm/paint/auth/sargent/`

Site at the WebMuseum, Paris devoted to John Singer Sargent.

Sartre, Jean-Paul

URL: `http://members.aol.com/KatharenaE/private/Philo/Sartre/sartre.html`

Substantial source of information on the life, work, and legacy of the French existentialist.

Sassoon, Siegfried

URL: `http://www.geocities.com/CapitolHill/8103/index.html`

Short biography of the poet with links to some well known contemporaries. There is also a virtual exhibition of many of his poems, illustrated with images depicting the themes he covers.

Schubert Institute (UK)

URL: `http://dialspace.dial.pipex.com/ramorris/`

Information about the life and works of composer Franz Schubert. There is a bibliography, a number of articles, and details of Schubert-related events.

Scott Joplin Home Page

URL: `http://www.geocities.com/BourbonStreet/2783/`

Short biography of the 'King of Ragtime' and a near-complete sound library of his compositions.

Scruffle's Steven Spielberg Directory

URL: `http://www.geocities.com/~scruffles/main.html`

Tribute to the world's foremost popular film director. There is a biography and detailed filmography with details of his best known films.

Seamus Heaney Page

URL: `http://sunsite.unc.edu/dykki/poetry/heaney/heaney-cov.html`

Nobel prizewinning poet Seamus Heaney has this site dedicated to his life and works. It includes a biography, bibliography, and many quotations taken from his works.

Mary Shelley Resource Page

URL: `http://www.netaxs.com/~kwbridge/maryshel.html`

Resource on this English writer, most famed for her creation of *Frankenstein*. There is illustrated hypertext on her life, the literary sources of *Frankenstein*, and the events of the pivotal summer of 1816.

Shrine

URL: `http://web.syr.edu/~abjornho/shrine.html`

Informative site about the director Quentin Tarantino and his films.

Sidney, Sir Philip

URL: `http://www.luminarium.org/renlit/sidney.htm`

Brief biography of the poet, plus a number of his works, some of his famous quotes, essays, articles, and some contemporary music.

Sigmund Freud: The Father of Psychoanalysis

URL: `http://austria-info.at/personen/freud/index.html`

Maintained in English by the Austrian National Tourist Office, the page provides a timeline of biographical information about Freud, plus analyses of his ideas and the impact of his theories on his most notable followers.

Sinatra, Frank

URL: `http://www.celebsite.com/indexstar.html`

Profile of the legendary US entertainer. There are full cast, plot, and production details of his films and listings of his television appearances and music recordings. This site also includes links to a large number of Sinatra appreciation sites.

Sir Edmund Hillary Profile

URL: `http://www.achievement.org/autodoc/page/hil0pro-1`

Description of the life and achievements of Sir Edmund Hillary, the first person to climb Mount Everest.

Solzhenitsyn, Alexander

URL: "http://members.aol.com/
KatharenaE/private/Alsolz/alsolz.html"

Huge source of information on the Russian epic novelist.

Stalin Archive

URL: "http://acs2.bu.edu:8001/
~sbern/stalin.htm"

Biographical information on Joseph Stalin that includes an extensive biography, details about the Red Army (including statistics compiled by Stalin), a selection of quotes, and links to related resources.

Stein, Gertrude

URL: "http://dept.english.upenn.edu:80/
~afilreis/88/stein-bio.html"

Biography that traces Stein's passion for Cubism, the role of her Paris salon in shaping the careers of the 'lost generation' of writers and artists, and her long relationship with Alice B Toklas.

Tennyson, Alfred Lord

URL: "http://www.stg.brown.edu/
projects/hypertext/landow/victorian/te
nnyson/tennyov.html"

Introduction to Lord Alfred Tennyson from the Victorian Web. The site presents his work, with separate essays on its themes, symbolism, and structure.

Thelonious Monk Web Site

URL: "http://www.achilles.net/
~howardm/tsmonk.html"

Short biography, quotations by and about the man and his music, concert reviews, and links to related sites.

Thomas Carlyle: An Overview

URL: "http://www.stg.brown.edu/
projects/hypertext/landow/victorian/ca
rlyle/carlyleov.html"

Excellent access point to the Victorian writer and critic, with links to political and social context, works, science, visual arts, literary relations, themes, symbolism, religion, and philosophy.

Thomas, Dylan

URL: "http://pcug.org.au/~wwhatman/
dylan_thomas.html"

Run by the Dylan Thomas Society of Australia, this site includes a brief biography, some poems, pictures, a list of short stories, and a page on his wife, Caitlin. It also includes links to some audio recordings of Thomas's work.

Titian

URL: "http://www.oir.ucf.edu/wm/paint/
auth/titian/"

Site at the WebMuseum, Paris devoted to Titian.

Tony Hancock Home Page

URL: "http://www.achilles.net/
~howardm/tony.html"

Review of the life of the famous comedian. In addition to biographical details, you can listen to some of Hancock's most famous sketches.

Toulouse-Lautrec, Henri de

URL: "http://sunsite.unc.edu/wm/paint/
auth/toulouse-lautrec/"

Images of his work and information about the 19th-century French painter Henri de Toulouse-Lautrec.

Tribute to William Golding

URL: "http://www.geocities.com/Athens/
Forum/6249/index.html"

Dedicated to the life and works of English novelist William Golding.

Turner, Joseph Mallord William

URL: "http://www.oir.ucf.edu/wm/
paint/auth/turner/"

Site at the WebMuseum, Paris devoted to Joseph Mallord William Turner.

Updike, John Hoyer

URL: "http://www.users.fast.net/
~joyerkes/"

Information and forum for discussion about Updike's life and works. The site includes a biography, bibliography, and selections from his writings.

Van Morrison Home Page

URL: "http://www.harbour.sfu.ca/
~hayward/van/"

Information about Van Morrison and his music. There's even a glossary of terms and references, from barmbrack to Wagon Wheel biscuits, found in his lyrics.

Welcome to the Johannes Brahms Web-Source

URL: "http://www.mjq.net/brahms/"

Including a good biography, a list of compositions, a guide to Brahms festivals, and details of Brahms societies and scholars around the world.

William Blake Archive

URL: "http://jefferson.village.
virginia.edu/blake/"

Sample images from a project engaged in compiling a digital archive of Blake's illuminated books, paintings, and drawings.

Wright Brothers

URL: "http://hfm.umd.umich.edu/
histories/wright/wrights.html"

Brief illustrated biography of the brothers, plus a chronology and bibliography of related works.

Yeats, W B

URL: "http://www.lit.kobe-
u.ac.jp/~hishika/yeats.htm"

Appreciation of the life and work of the Irish poet as well as links to more than 300 poems, class notes for teaching on the poet, news letters, and Yeats fan clubs.

Yeltsin, Boris

URL: "http://www.cs.indiana.edu/hyplan/
dmiguse/Russian/bybio.html"

Biographical material about Boris Yeltsin, including sections on his family background, early education, engineering career, and gradual political involvement.

SPORT

The Year in Review

5 July 1997–6 July 1997 Martina Hingis of Switzerland, aged 16 years 279 days, becomes the youngest winner of the women's singles at the Wimbledon tennis championships since 1887 when Lottie Dod of England won at the age of 15 years 285 days. Pete Sampras of the USA wins his fourth men's singles title in five years, while Australia's Mark Woodforde and Todd Woodbridge win a record fifth consecutive men's doubles title.

9 July 1997 The Nevada State Athletic Commission revokes the licence of US boxer Mike Tyson and fines him $3 million for biting off the ear of US boxer Evander Holyfield in the 28 June World Boxing Association (WBA) heavyweight title fight in Las Vegas, Nevada.

13 July 1997 English golfer Alison Nicholas becomes only the second Briton, after Laura Davies, to win the US Women's Open, at North Plains, Oregon.

13 July 1997 Surrey beat Kent at Lord's to win the Benson and Hedges one day cricket cup final.

20 July 1997 The English cricketer Alistair Brown of Surrey scores 203 against Hampshire at Guildford, Surrey, the first ever double century in the 28-year history of the 40-over Sunday League competition.

20 July 1997 US golfer and former US amateur champion Justin Leonard wins the British Open at Royal Troon, Scotland.

27 July 1997 Jan Ullrich becomes the first German cyclist to win the Tour de France.

28 July 1997 English cricketer Graham Gooch, a former England captain, retires from Essex County Cricket Club after a career spanning 25 years with more than 45,000 runs.

3 August 1997 US sprinter Maurice Greene wins the men's 100-metres event at the International Amateur Athletics Federation (IAAF) World Championships in Athens, Greece. Marion Jones, also of the USA, wins the women's event.

3 August 1997–6 August 1997 Sri Lanka's cricketers score 952 for 6 declared in the first Test against India in Colombo, Sri Lanka, to break the record for the highest innings total in a Test match (previously held by England who scored 903 for 7 against Australia in 1938). It includes a record Test match partnership of 576 between opener Sanath Jayasuriya, who scores 340, and number three Roshan Mahanama, who scores 225.

4 August 1997 Cathy Freeman of Australia wins the women's 400-metres final at the International Amateur Athletics Federation (IAAF) World Championships in Athens, Greece, becoming the first Aboriginal to win a world title.

10 August 1997 Sergey Bubka of the Ukraine wins an unprecedented sixth successive pole vault title at the International Amateur Athletics Federation (IAAF) World Championships in Athens, Greece.

11 August 1997 At Trent Bridge, Australia beat England to retain the Ashes cricket trophy for the fifth consecutive time.

14 August 1997 Denmark's Kenyan-born runner Wilson Kipketer breaks the English athlete Sebastian Coe's 16-year-old 800-metres world record of 1 min 41.73 sec when he runs a time of 1 min 41.24 sec in Zürich, Switzerland. Ten days later in Brussels, Belgium, he reduces the record to 1 min 41.11 sec.

16 August 1997 The Bradford Bulls achieve their 19th successive victory since the beginning of the season to clinch Rugby League's Stones Super League.

17 August 1997 Australian golfer Karrie Webb wins her second British Women's Open Championship in three years, at Sunningdale.

17 August 1997 Michael Doohan of Australia, riding a Honda, wins the British Grand Prix at Donington Park, Castle Donington, Leicestershire, to capture his fourth successive 500-cc world motorcycle racing championship.

17 August 1997 US golfer Davis Love III wins the US Professional Golfers Association (PGA) Championship at Winged Foot Golf Club, Mamaroneck, New York, to record his first victory in a major tournament.

26 August 1997 US runner Carl Lewis runs in what he announces is the last race of his 15-year, nine Olympic gold medal career, at the Istaf Grand Prix in Berlin, Germany.

6 September 1997 Martina Hingis of Switzerland wins the women's singles tournament at the US Open tennis championships, her third Grand Slam singles title of the year after winning the Australian Open and Wimbledon.

7 September 1997 Patrick Rafter of Australia defeats Britain's Greg Rusedski in the final of the men's singles tournament at the US Open tennis championships. Rafter is the first Australian to win the title since John Newcombe in 1973, and Rusedski is the first Briton to reach a Grand Slam final since 1936.

8 September 1997 In the NatWest final, which had been delayed due to the funeral of Diana, Princess of Wales, Essex beat Warwickshire at Lord's.

21 September 1997 Patrice Martin of France wins an unprecedented fifth successive men's overall world water skiing title at the Water Skiing World Championships in Colombia.

25 September 1997 British driver Andy Green in the jet-powered *Thrust SSC* sets a new landspeed world record of 1,149.272 km/h/714.144 mph at Black Rock Desert, Nevada. The previous record of 1,019.467 km/h/633.468 mph had been set in 1983 by the Thrust SSC's project leader, British driver Richard Noble.

28 September 1997 Europe's golfers retain the Ryder Cup, defeating the USA $14\frac{1}{2}$–$13\frac{1}{2}$ at Valderrama, in southern Spain. It is the first time that Europe has hosted the competition at a non-British venue.

4 October 1997 British boxer Lennox Lewis retains his World Boxing Council (WBC) heavyweight title when he defeats Polish boxer Andrew Golota with a first round knockout in Atlantic City, New Jersey. The fight lasts for only 1 min 35 sec.

15 October 1997 Andy Green, driving *Thrust SSC*, sets a new land speed record and breaks the sound barrier with two runs of 1214.933 kph/759.333 mph (Mach 1.015) and 1226.574 kph/766.609 mph (Mach 1.020) at Black Rock Desert, Nevada. Similar speeds set two days earlier were unofficial because the second run occurred over an hour later.

26 October 1997 Jacques Villeneuve, driving a Williams–Renault, becomes the first Canadian to win the Formula 1 World Drivers' Championship.

2 November 1997 Kenyan runner John Kagwe wins the New York City Marathon with a time of 2 hr, 8 min, 12 sec, the second-fastest time ever on the course.

3 November 1997 Australian and US swimming officials protest against the results of the Chinese national swimming championships held in Shanghai in October in which two low-ranked Chinese female swimmers broke world records in the 200 and 400 metre relays. The officials allege that the Chinese swimmers were using performance-enhancing drugs.

8 November 1997 Skip Away, ridden by US jockey Mike Smith, wins the one and a quarter mile long Breeders' Cup Classic horse race at Hollywood Park, California, in a record time of 1 min 59 sec.

8 November 1997 US boxer Evander Holyfield defeats compatriot and International Boxing Federation (IBF) champion Michael Moorer with a technical knockout in the eighth round of the IBF heavyweight championship in Las Vegas, Nevada, making Holyfield both the World Boxing Association (WBA) and the IBF champion.

15 November 1997 England draw 15–15 with Australia in a Rugby Union International match at Twickenham, London, before a crowd of 74,000.

22 November 1997 In the first Rugby Union International in Manchester for 100 years, New Zealand All Blacks beat England 25–8 at Old Trafford football ground.

22 November 1997 New Zealand rowers Robert Hamill and Phil Stubbs break the record for crossing the Atlantic when they win a trans-Atlantic rowing race of 2,757 nautical miles from the Canary Islands to Barbados in a time of 41 days, 1 hr, 55 min. The previous record, set in 1986 by British rowers Sean Crowley and Mike Nestor, was 73 days.

29 November 1997 South Africa beat England 29–11 in a Rugby Union International at Twickenham.

30 November 1997 Sweden win the Davis Cup in tennis, defeating the USA 5–0 in Gothenburg, Sweden.

November 1997 US golfer Tiger Woods is the first player to win over $2 million in prize money in a season on the US PGA Tour. At the age of 22 he is also the youngest player ever to finish top of the money list.

6 December 1997 England draw against the New Zealand All Blacks 26–26 in a Rugby Union International at Twickenham, before a crowd of 74,000.

9 December 1997 British entrepreneur and balloonist Richard Branson is forced to abandon his effort to become the first person to travel around the world in a balloon when his balloon was blown away before the planned launch in Marrakesh, Morocco.

19 December 1997 The England cricket team, led by Adam Hollioake, secure the Champion's Trophy by beating the West Indies by three wickets, at Sharjah, United Arab Emirates.

23 December 1997 Talks between promoters for US boxer Evander Holyfield, British boxer Lennox Lewis, and Time Warner sports, which televises boxing on its cable stations, break down when Holyfield's promoter, Don King, demands a fee of around $8 million to arrange a bout between the two heavyweight champions.

12 January 1998 Chinese swimmer Yuan Yuan and her coach Zhou Zhewen are sent home from the World Swimming Championships in Perth, Australia, a week after being caught in possession of phials of the human growth hormone somatotrophin, a banned performance-enhancing substance used to build muscle bulk. Four other Chinese swimmers failed precompetition drug tests.

14 January 1998 Russian swimmer Alexander Popov sets a new world record for the 100 m freestyle of 48.93 seconds.

25 January 1998 Ethiopian runner Haile Gebrselassie reduces his own 3,000 m world record of 7 min 30.72 sec set in Stuttgart on 4 February 1996 by over four and a half seconds with a new time of 7min 26.14 sec, in Karlsruhe, Germany.

25 January 1998 The Denver Broncos defeat the Green Bag Packers 31–24 in the Super Bowl in San Diego. It is their first National Football League (NFL) championship in 38 years.

29 January 1998 In the first of a six match test series between England and the West Indies at Sabina Park, Kingston, Jamaica, the umpires take the unprecedented step of abandoning the match, after 56 minutes, because the pitch is judged to be dangerous. The pitch, which had recently been relaid, is producing such unpredictable bounce that the English physiotherapist has to treat six injuries to English batsmen before the umpires halt the match.

31 January 1998 Bath defeat the French side Brive 19–18 to win rugby union's European Cup, in Bordeaux, France.

31 January 1998 Martina Hingis of Switzerland beats Conchita Martinez of Spain 6–3, 6–3 to win the women's title at the Australian Open in Melbourne for the second straight year.

1 February 1998 Petr Korda of the Czech Republic defeats Marcelo Rios of Chile 6–2, 6–2, 6–2 in the men's final of the Australian Open in Melbourne.

7 February 1998 France defeat England 24–17 in a rugby union international at the Stade de France, Paris, France.

7 February 1998–22 February 1998 The 18th Winter Olympic Games are held at Nagano, Japan. They are the largest to date, with over 2,400 athletes from a 72 countries taking part. Snowboarding, curling, and women's ice hockey are included as medal sports for the first time. Tara Lipinski of the USA, aged 15 years 255 days, wins the women's figure skating title to become the youngest ever individual Winter Olympic gold medallist.

9 February 1998 The West Indies cricket team beat England by three wickets in Port of Spain, Trinidad and Tobago, to take a 1–0 lead in a six test series.

17 February 1998 In the third test the England cricket team beat the West Indies in Port of Spain, Trinidad and Tobago, to level the series 1–1.

21 February 1998 England record the highest ever score in the history of the International Championship in rugby union when they defeat Wales 60–26 at Twickenham.

2 March 1998 In the fourth test, the West Indies cricket team beat England by 242 runs, in Georgetown, Guyana, to take a 2–1 lead.

5 March 1998 US boxer Mike Tyson sues his former promoter Don King for more than $100 million for embezzling at least half of his $127 million in purse money.

10 March 1998 In the third and final cricket test between South Africa and Pakistan at Port Elizabeth, South Africa, South Africa gain the victory they need to level the series 1–1.

12 March 1998 Australian businessman Rupert Murdoch buys the Los Angeles Dodgers baseball team for a record $350 million. The sale includes Dodger Stadium.

16 March 1998 In the fifth test, the West Indies cricket team beat England in Barbados, to take an unassailable 3–1 lead.

19 March 1998 Cool Dawn, ridden by British jockey Tony McCoy, wins the Tote Cheltenham Gold Cup horse race.

22 March 1998–23 March 1998 At the World Cross Country Championships in Marrakesh, Morocco, Paul Tergat of Kenya wins the men's 12 km event for the fourth year in succession. Sonia O'Sullivan of Ireland wins both the women's 4 km and 8 km races.

23 March 1998 English footballer Paul Gascoigne announces that he is leaving Glasgow Rangers football club to join Middlesborough for £3.4 million.

24 March 1998 In the last of the six match test series, the West Indies cricket team draw against England, in Bridgetown, Barbados, to secure a 3–1 victory.

25 March 1998 British jockey Tony McCoy rides Petite Risk to victory in the Bundy Juvenile Novice Hurdle at Ludlow, Shropshire, to break British jockey Peter Scudamore's nine-year-old record of riding 221 winners in a British national hunt racing season.

25 March 1998–28 March 1998 Playing for Australia in the 3rd cricket test against India at Bangalore, Shane Warne passes the West Indian off spinner Lance Gibbs's career total of 309 test wickets, to become the most prolific spin bowler in Test history.

28 March 1998 Cambridge beat Oxford by three lengths in the University Boat Race on the river Thames.

30 March 1998 The University of Kentucky Wildcats defeat the University of Utah Runnin' Utes 78–69 to win the National Collegiate Athletic Association (NCAA) championship in San Antonio, Texas.

4 April 1998 British jockey Carl Llewellyn riding Earth Summit wins the Grand National at Aintree.

4 April 1998 The England Rugby Union team defeat Ireland 35–17 in front of a crowd 74,000 at Twickenham.

5 April 1998 France defeats Wales 51–0 at Wembley Stadium, to complete its second Five Nations rugby union championship grand slam in a row.

5 April 1998 Scottish squash player Peter Nicol wins the British Open.

12 April 1998 Mark O'Meara of the USA, aged 41, wins the US Masters golf tournament at Augusta, Georgia. Fellow US golfer Jack Nicklaus, aged 58 and competing in the event for the 40th consecutive year, finishes in sixth place.

20 April 1998 The Boston Marathon takes place in Boston, Massachusetts. Kenyan runner Moses Tanui is the fastest man with a time of 2 hr 7 min 44 sec, and Ethiopian runner Fatuma Roba is the fastest woman with a time of 2 hr 23 min 21 sec.

26 April 1998 The London Marathon takes place. Abel Anton is the fastest man with a time of 2 hr 7 min 57 sec, and Irish runner Catherina McKiernan, in her first marathon, is the fastest woman with a time of 2 hr 26 min 26 sec.

29 April 1998 Chelsea defeat Middlesborough 2–0 in front of 77,698 people in the FA Coca Cola Cup Final at Wembley.

3 May 1998 British footballer Justin Fashanu is found dead in a parking garage in London after hanging himself. He left the USA in April after Maryland police charged him with sexually abusing a 17-year-old boy.

4 May 1998 John Higgins of Scotland beats Ken Doherty of Ireland 18–12 in the world snooker championship final in Sheffield, England.

7 May 1998 The International Amateur Athletic Federation (IAAF) launches its Year of the Woman Athlete by staging the first ever mixed athletics meeting in the Gulf State of Qatar, where strict adherence to Muslim doctrine has hitherto prevented women from taking part in sport except in segregated, closed arenas.

13 May 1998 Chelsea defeat Stuttgart 1–0 to win the European Cup Winners' Cup Final in front of 30,216 people in Stockholm, Sweden.

13 May 1998 Inter Milan defeat Lazio 3–0 to win football's UEFA Cup, in Stockholm, Sweden.

16 May 1998 A fortnight after becoming the first foreign manager to win the English league championship, Frenchman Arsène Wenger leads his Arsenal side to a 2–0 victory over Newcastle United at Wembley Stadium in the FA Cup final. Arsenal become only the second club after Manchester United to win two league and cup 'doubles', having previously performed the double in 1971.

17 May 1998 Newcastle secure the Rugby Union Premiership Title in the first season they are members of the top division by defeating Harlequins 44–20 at the Stoop Memorial ground, London.

20 May 1998 Real Madrid of Spain defeat Juventus of Italy 1–0 in Amsterdam, to win the European Cup for a record seventh time.

24 May 1998 The Swedish-registered *EF Language* wins the Whitbread round-the-world yacht race.

24 May 1998 US driver Eddie Cheever wins the Indianapolis 500 at the Indianapolis Motor Speedway in Indiana.

25 May 1998 In the Nationwide Football League first division playoffs final at Wembley, Charlton beat Sunderland to gain promotion to the Premier League. The match was won 7–6 on penalties, after a 4–4 draw.

31 May 1998 Zimbabwean-born British cricketer Graeme Hick scores his hundredth first class century for Worcestershire against Sussex, at Worcester. Only 23 other cricketers have achieved this feat.

1 June 1998 Holland beat Spain 3–2 in the hockey World Cup final in Utrecht, the Netherlands.

5 June 1998 England football coach Glenn Hoddle causes a stir when he leaves Paul Gascoigne out of his World Cup squad. Hoddle judged that Gascoigne was not fit enough for the competition.

6 June 1998 High-Rise, ridden by French jockey Olivier Peslier, wins the Derby at Epsom.

6 June 1998 Victory Gallop, ridden by US jockey Gary Stevens, wins the 130th Belmont Stakes horse race.

8 June 1998 In the first of a five match cricket test series, England draw with South Africa at Edgbaston, Birmingham.

10 June 1998 In the opening game of football's World Cup finals, Brazil beat Scotland 2–1 in front of 80,000 people, at St Denis stadium, Paris, France.

14 June 1998 English football supporters in Marseille, for their World Cup game against Tunisia, clash with French supporters of North African descent, sparking concern over security for future matches.

14 June 1998 The Chicago Bulls, led by US basketball player Michael Jordan, defeat

the Utah Jazz for the second year in a row to win their sixth National Basketball Association (NBA) championship. The score was 87–86.

15 June 1998 England play Tunisia in the first game of their football World Cup bid. England win 2–0 in front of 54,587 people in Marseille.

16 June 1998 In the football World Cup finals, Scotland draw 1–1 with Norway in Bordeaux, in front of 30,236 people.

18 June 1998 Having at first declared their joint disapproval of many refereeing decisions, Sepp Blatter, the Swedish chairman-elect of FIFA, and Michel Platini, the French chairman of the World Cup organizing committee, now appear to disagree over the performance of referees in various World Cup games. Blatter believes that the referees are handing out an appropriate amount of red cards, while Platini believes that there are too many.

21 June 1998 Following Germany's football World Cup match against Yugoslavia, in Lens, German fans riot, targeting the French police. In one incident, a French policeman is beaten with a metal bar and suffers brain damage. German politicians suggest that their team should withdraw from the tournament, but the French and football authorities reject the offer.

21 June 1998 In the second cricket test, South Africa beat England at Lord's by 10 wickets.

21 June 1998 US golfer Lee Janzen wins the US Open by one stroke over US golfer Payne Stewart, in San Francisco, California.

22 June 1998 England lose 2–1 to Romania in their football World Cup qualifying group, at Toulouse, in front of 37,500 people.

22 June 1998 The Wimbledon tennis championships open.

23 June 1998 In the last of their group games in the football World Cup finals, Scotland lose unexpectedly 3–0 to Morocco. This match, at St Etienne, France, in front of 35,000 people, knocks Scotland out of the World Cup.

25 June 1998 German tennis player Tommy Haas defeats Andre Agassi of the US 4-6, 6-1, 7-6, 6-4 in the Wimbledon championships.

26 June 1998 England defeat Colombia 2–0 in Lens, to secure their place in the second round of the World Cup. This victory sets up a match between England and Argentina.

June 1998 The Detroit Red Wings defeat the Washington Capitals by 4 games to 0 to win the National Hockey League (NHL) Stanley Cup for the second successive year.

Sports Personalities

Aaron Henry 'Hank' (1934–) US baseball player; Milwaukee/Atlanta Braves outfielder, all-time leader in home runs (755) and RBIs (2,297), 3,771 career hits, four times NL leader in homers and RBIs, NL MVP in 1957

Abdul-Jabbar Kareem (1947–) US basketball player for Milwaukee and Los Angeles Lakers, 1971–89; six times NBA MVP; all-time NBA leading scorer with 38,387 points

Agassi Andre (1970–) US tennis player; Wimbledon singles champion, 1992; US Open, 1994; Australian Open, 1995

Agostini Giacomo (1942–) Italian motor cyclist; won 8,500 cc and 7,350 cc world titles, 1966–75

Akram Wasim (1966–) Pakistani cricketer; left-arm fast bowler who is the only person to have taken 300 wickets in both Test and One-Day International cricket

Ali Muhammad (1942–) US boxer; three times world heavyweight champion, undisputed 1964–67, 1974–78, WBA 1978–79; 1960 Olympic light heavyweight champion

Ambrose Curtly (1963–) West Indian cricketer; fast bowler who has taken more than 330 Test wickets since his debut in 1988

Andrew Rob (1963–) English rugby union fly half; England's record points scorer with 396 points from 71 appearances, 1985–97

Aouita Saïd (1959–) Moroccan runner; winner of the 1984 Olympic and 1987 World Championship 5,000 m titles; broke world records at 1,500, 2,000, 3,000, and 5,000 m

Archer Fred (1857–1886) English jockey; he rode 2,748 winners in 8,084 races, including 21 classic winners

Ashe Arthur (1943–1993) US tennis player; US singles champion, 1968; Australian Open, 1970; Wimbledon, 1975

Atherton Mike (1968–) English cricketer; an opening batsman who has captained England in a record number of Tests (52)

Bailey Donovan (1967–) Canadian sprinter; won the 1996 Olympic 100 m title in world record time (9.84 sec)

Ballesteros Severiano (1957–) Spanish golfer; three times British Open champion, 1979, 1984, 1988; twice Masters champion, 1980, 1983

Banks Gordon (1937–) English footballer; England's goalkeeper in the 1966 World Cup; won 73 caps in goal for England, 1963–72

Bannister Roger (1929–) English runner; achieved the first sub-four-minute mile at Oxford on 6 May 1954

Barnes John (1963–) Jamaican-born English footballer; English Football Writers' Association Footballer of the Year in 1988 and 1990

Barrington Jonah (1941–) English squash player; six times winner of the British Open, 1967–73

Beckenbauer Franz (1945–) German footballer and manager; winner of the World Cup as captain in 1974, and as coach in 1990; European Footballer of the Year in 1972 and 1976

Becker Boris (1967–) German tennis player; won six Grand Slam singles tournaments, 1985–96, including three Wimbledon titles

Bedser Alec (1918–) English cricketer; seam bowler who took 236 wickets for England in 51 Tests, 1946–55

Benaud Ritchie (1930–) Australian cricketer and cricket broadcaster; scored 2,201 runs and took 248 wickets in 63 Tests, 1952–64

Best George (1946–) Northern Irish footballer; 1968 English and European Footballer of the Year

Bevan Brian (1924–1991) Australian-born rugby league player who scored an all-time record 796 tries in English rugby league, 1945–64

Biondi Matt (1965–) US swimmer; won seven medals, including five golds, at the 1988 Olympics, and a gold and a silver at the 1992 Games

Bird Larry (1956–) US basketball forward; led Boston to three NBA titles in 1981, 1984, and 1986; regular season MVP, 1984–86; playoff MVP, 1984, 1986

Blanchflower Danny (1926–1993) Northern Irish footballer; captained Tottenham to the League and Cup double in 1960–61; won 56 Northern Ireland caps, 1949–62

Blanco Serge (1958–) French rugby union full back; scored 38 tries in 93 internationals, 1980–91

Blankers-Koen Fanny (1918–) Dutch athlete; won golds in 100 m, 200 m, 80 m hurdles, and sprint relay at 1948 Olympics

Boardman Chris (1968–) English cyclist; 1992 Olympic individual pursuit gold medallist; world One Hour Record holder since 1996 with a distance of 56.38 km

Border Allan (1955–) Australian cricketer; scored a record 11,174 runs in 156 Tests at an average of 50.56, 1978–94

Borg Bjorn (1956–) Swedish tennis player; won a record five successive Wimbledon singles titles, 1976–80; also won six French Open singles titles, 1974–75, 1978–81

Boston Billy (1934–) Welsh rugby league player; second in the all-time British rugby league scoring list with 571 tries from 574 appearances, 1953–70

Botham Ian (1955–) English cricketer; scored 5,200 runs and took 383 wickets in 102 Tests, 1977–1992

Boycott Geoff (1940–) English cricketer; scored 43,423 First Class runs, 1960–87, including 8,114 runs in 108 Tests, 1964–82

Brabham Jack (1926–) Australian motor racing driver; Formula One World Drivers' Champion in 1959, 1960, and 1966, when he won in a car of his own design

Bradman Don (1908–) Australian cricketer; scored 6,996 runs in 52 Tests at a record average of 99.94, 1928–48

Bristow Eric (1957–) English darts player; five times world champion between 1980 and 1986

Broome David (1940–) British show jumper; World Champion in 1970, and European Champion in 1961, 1967, and 1968

Brown Jim (1936–) US American Football player; Cleveland Browns fullback MVP 1958, 1965; led NFL rushers eight years; career marks: 12,312 yards rushing, 262 receptions, 15,459 combined net yards, 756 points scored

Bruno Frank (1961–) English boxer; WBA world heavyweight champion, 1995–96

Bubka Sergei (1963–) Ukrainian pole vaulter; set 17 outdoor world records, 1985–94; won six consecutive world titles, 1983–97

Budge Don (1915–) US tennis player; the first person to achieve the Grand Slam of winning the Australian, French, Wimbledon, and US singles titles in the same year (1938)

Bueno Maria (1939–) Brazilian tennis player; four times US women's singles champion, 1959, 1963–64, 1966, and three times Wimbledon champion, 1959–60, 1964

Busby Matt (1909–1994) Scottish football manager; as Manchester United manager, 1945–69, won the European Cup, five league titles, and two FA Cups

Campese David (1962–) Australian rugby union player; scored a world record 64 international tries in 101 appearances for Australia, 1982–96

Cantona Eric (1966–) French footballer; helped Leeds United to the league title in 1992, then won four further league titles (and two FA Cups) in five seasons with Manchester United, 1992–97

Carling Will (1965–) English rugby union centre; won 72 England caps, 1988–97, including a record 59 as captain

Carson Willie (1942–) Scottish jockey; rode four Derby winners and 13 other English Classic winners; five times Champion jockey

Cecil Henry (1943–) Scottish-born trainer; ten times leading trainer in British flat racing, 1973–93

Chamberlain Wilt (1936–) US basketball centre; scored 31,419 NBA points, 1960–73, leading the NBA in scoring seven times and rebounding 11 times; four times regular season MVP

Chapman Herbert (1878–1934) English football manager; led Huddersfield Town to the English league title in 1924 and 1925, and Arsenal in 1930, 1933, and 1934

Chappell Greg (1948–) Australian cricketer; scored 7,110 runs in 87 Tests at an average of 53.86, 1970–87

Charles John (1931–) Welsh footballer; scored 93 goals in 155 appearances for Juventus, 1957–1962, winning three Italian league championships

Charlton Bobby (1937–) English footballer; scored a record 49 goals for England in 106 appearances, 1958–70. English and European Footballer of the Year, 1966

Charlton Jack (1935–) English footballer and manager; won 35 England caps, 1965–1970; as a manager he led the Republic of Ireland to the 1990 and 1994 World Cup finals

Christie Linford (1960–) English sprinter; Olympic 100 m champion in 1992, and World champion in 1993

Clark Jim (1935–1948) Scottish motor racing driver; Formula 1 World Drivers' Champion in 1963 and 1965; won 25 Grand Prix, 1960–68

Clough Brian (1935–) English footballer and manager; led Nottingham Forest to the European Cup in 1979 and 1980

Coe Sebastian (1956–) English runner; won 1980 and 1984 Olympic 1,500 m titles; held the world 800 m record, 1981–97

Comaneci Nadia (1961–) Romanian gymnast who recorded seven perfect scores in winning three gold medals at the 1976 Olympics

Compton Denis (1918–1997) English cricketer and footballer; scored 5,807 runs in 78 Tests at an average of 50.06, 1937–57; helped Arsenal to the league title in 1948 and the FA Cup in 1950

Connolly Maureen (1934–1969) US tennis player; the first woman to achieve the Grand Slam, 1953; won nine Grand Slam championships in four years before her career was ended in 1954 by a riding accident

Connors Jimmy (1952–) US tennis player; won eight Grand Slam singles tournaments, 1974–83, including five US Open titles

Cooper Henry (1934–) English boxer; British and Commonwealth heavyweight champion, 1959–1970

Cotton Henry (1907–1987) English golfer; British Open champion in 1934, 1937, and 1948

Court Margaret Smith (1942–) Australian tennis player; won 62 Grand Slam tournaments, 1960–75, including 24 singles titles

Cousins Robin (1957–) English figure skater; 1980 Olympic champion

Cowdrey Colin (1932–) English cricketer; scored 42,719 first class runs, 1950–76, including 7,624 in Tests, 1954–75

Cram Steve (1960–) English runner; 1,500 m world champion in 1983; in 1985 he set world records in the mile, 1,500 m, and 2,000 m

Cruyff Johan (1947–) Dutch footballer; European Footballer of the Year in 1971, 1973, and 1974

Curry John (1949–) English figure skater; winner of the Olympic, world, and European individual titles in 1976

Dalglish Kenny (1951–) Scottish footballer and manager; scored 30 goals in 102 appearances for Scotland, 1971–86; led Liverpool and Blackburn to the league championship; now manager of Newcastle United

Davies Laura (1963–) English golfer; winner of four US women's golf majors, including the US Women's Open in 1987

Davies Lynn (1942–) Welsh long jumper; winner of the 1964 Olympic title

Davis Joe (1901–1978) English billiards and snooker player; world snooker champion, 1927–46, and world billiards champion, 1928–32

Davis Steve (1957–) English snooker player; six times world snooker champion between 1981 and 1989

Dean Christopher (1958–) English ice dancer who with Jayne Torvill won the 1984 Olympic title and four successive world titles, 1981–84

Dempsey Jack (1895–1983) US boxer; world heavyweight champion, 1919–26

Dettori Frankie (1970–) Italian jockey; champion flat race jockey in Britain in 1994 with 233 winners and in 1995 with 211

DiMaggio Joe (1914–) US baseball player; New York Yankees outfielder, hit safely in record 56 consecutive games in 1941

di Stéfano Alfredo (1926–) Argentinian-born footballer; scored a record 49 goals in 58 European Cup games for Real Madrid, 1955–64

Donoghue Steve (1884–1945) English jockey; rode six Derby winners including a record three-in-a-row, 1921–23; champion jockey for ten successive years, 1914–23

Douglas Desmond (1955–) English table tennis player; winner of a record 26 titles at the English Closed Championships; English Open champion in 1980 and 1984

Edberg Stefan (1966–) Swedish tennis player; US Open singles champion, 1991–92; Wimbledon, 1988, 1990; Australian Open, 1985, 1987

Eddery Pat (1952–) Irish jockey; winner of 13 English classic races, including the

Derby in 1975, 1982, and 1990; 11 times British champion jockey

Edwards Gareth (1947–) Welsh rugby union scrum half; scored 20 tries in 53 appearances for Wales, 1967–1978

Edwards Jonathan (1966–) English athlete; in 1995 won the world triple jump title and made the first ever 18 m jump

Edwards Shaun (1966–) English rugby league player; won 32 winners' medals with Wigan including a record nine in the Challenge Cup

Eusébio Ferreira da Silva (1942–) Portuguese footballer; led Benfica to the European Cup in 1961 and 1962; European Footballer of the Year in 1965

Evert Chris (1954–) US tennis player; won 18 Grand Slam singles tournaments, 1974–86, including six US Open, and a record seven French Open titles

Faldo Nick (1957–) English golfer; three times winner of both the Masters in 1989–90 and 1996, and the British Open in 1987, 1990, and 1992

Fangio Juan Manuel (1911–1995) Argentinian motor racing driver; five times Formula 1 World Champion, 1951 and 1954–57

Ferguson Alex (1941–) Scottish football manager; led Manchester United to four English League titles in five years, 1993–97, including the double in 1994 and 1996; at Aberdeen, 1978–86, won the Scottish league three times and the Scottish Cup four times

Finney Tom (1922–) English footballer; scored 30 goals in 76 appearances for England, 1946–58

Fischer Bobby (1943–) US chess player; the only US player to win the world chess championship, 1972–75

Foreman George (1949–) US boxer; world heavyweight champion, 1973–74 (undisputed) and 1994–95 (WBA, IBF), when he became the oldest ever world champion, aged 45

Fox Grant (1962–) New Zealand rugby union fly half; scored 645 points in 46 internationals, 1985–93

Francome John (1952–) English National Hunt jockey; seven times champion jockey, 1976–85

Fraser Dawn (1937–) Australian swimmer; won three successive Olympic 100 m freestyle gold medals, 1956–64

Frazier Joe (1944–) US boxer; undisputed world heavyweight champion, 1970–73; 1964 Olympic heavyweight champion

Gascoigne Paul (1967–) English footballer; voted 1990 BBC Sports Personality of the Year after his performances in the 1990 World Cup; 1996 Footballer of the Year in Scotland

Gavaskar Sunil (1949–) Indian cricketer; scored 10,122 runs in 125 Tests at an average of 51.12, 1971–87

Gebrselassie Haile (1973–) Ethiopian long-distance runner; winner of the 1996 Olympic 10,000 m title and three consecutive World titles, 1993–97

Gibson Althea (1927–) US tennis player; broke the colour barrier in tennis in the 1950s, and won five Grand Slam singles tournaments, including two US and two Wimbledon singles titles, 1956–58

Gooch Graham (1953–) English cricketer; scored 8,900 runs in 118 Tests, 1975–95, at an average of 42.58

Gower David (1957–) English cricketer; scored 8,231 runs in 117 Tests, at an average of 44.25, 1978–92

Grace William Gilbert (WG) (1848–1915) English cricketer; scored 54,896 first class runs and took 2,876 first class wickets, 1865–1908

Graf Steffi (1969–) German tennis player. Winner of 21 Grand Slam singles tournaments including seven Wimbledon and five US titles, 1988–96

Greaves Jimmy (1940–) English footballer; scored 22 goals in 57 England internationals, 1959–67, and 357 English First Division goals in 517 games, 1957–71

Green Lucinda (1953–) English three-day eventer; winner of the Badminton horse trials a record six times, 1973–1984; world champion in 1982

Gretzky Wayne (1961–) Canadian ice hockey player; all-time NHL leader in points, goals and assists; regular season MVP nine times 1979–87, 1989

Gullit Ruud (1962–) Dutch footballer and manager; won European Championship with Holland in 1988, and the European Cup with Milan in 1989 and 1990; as Chelsea player/coach, 1996–98, became the first foreign manager to win the FA Cup

Gunnell Sally (1966–) English runner; winner of the 400 m hurdles at the 1992 Olympics and 1993 World Championships

Guscott Jeremy (1965–) English rugby union centre for Bath, England, and the British Lions

Hadlee Richard (1951–) New Zealand cricketer; took 431 Test wickets in 86 Tests at an average of 22.30

Hagen Walter (1892–1969) US golfer; won five PGA Championships, four British Opens and two US Opens, 1914–29

Hagler Marvin (1954–) US boxer; world middleweight champion, 1980–87

Hailwood Mike (1940–1981) English motor cyclist and motor racing driver; winner of ten motor cycle racing world titles, 1961–78

Hamed 'Prince' Naseem (1974–) English boxer; WBO world featherweight champion since 1995

Hammond Wally (1903–1965) English cricketer; scored 7,249 runs in 85 Tests at an average of 58.45 runs, 1927–47

Hanley Ellery (1961–) English rugby league player; scored 20 tries in 35 internationals

Harris Reg (1920–1992) English cyclist; winner of four world professional sprint titles between 1949 and 1954; set two outdoor and three indoor world 1 km records

Hastings Gavin (1962–) Scottish rugby union full back; scored 755 points in 68 internationals for Scotland and the British Lions, 1986–95

Hemery David (1944–) English runner; winner of the 1968 Olympic 400 m hurdles title in a world record time of 48.12 sec

Hendry Stephen (1969–) Scottish snooker player; six times world champion since 1990

Henie Sonja (1912–1969) Norwegian figure skater; ten times world champion, 1927–36; three times Olympic champion, 1928–36

Henman Tim (1974–) English tennis player who in 1998 became the first Briton for 25 years to reach the semi-finals of the men's singles at Wimbledon

Herman George 'Babe' Ruth (1895–1948) US baseball player; New York Yankees outfielder, 12 times home run leader, six times RBI leader; 60 homers in 1927; 714 career homers; 2,213 career RBIs; scored record 177 runs in 1921; .342 career batting average, AL MVP in 1923

Hick Graeme (1966–) Rhodesian-born English cricketer who has scored over 29,000 first class runs since 1983

Hill Damon (1960–) English motor racing driver; 1996 Formula 1 World Drivers' Champion

Hill Graham (1929–1975) English motor racing driver; Formula 1 World Drivers' Champion, 1962 and 1968; five times Monaco Grand Prix winner, 1963–69

Hinault Bernard (1954–) French cyclist; winner of the Tour de France in 1978, 1979, 1981, 1982, and 1985

Hingis Martina (1980–) Swiss tennis player; won Australian Open in 1997 aged 16 years 92 days; became youngest winner of a Grand Slam singles title since 1887; also won 1997 US and Wimbledon and 1998 Australian titles

Hobbs Jack (1882–1963) English cricketer; scored a record 61,237 first class runs, including 197 centuries, 1905–34

Hoddle Glen (1957–) English footballer and manager; won 53 England caps, 1979–88; England coach since 1996

Hogan Ben (1912–1997) US golfer; won nine majors, 1946–53, including four US Opens

Holyfield Evander (1962–) US boxer; three times world heavyweight champion, 1990–92 (WBC, WBA, IBF), 1993–94 (WBA, IBF), 1996– (WBA), and 1997– (IBF)

Howe Gordie (1928–) Canadian ice hockey forward; second in all-time NHL scoring with 801 goals and 1,850 points

Hunt Geoff (1947–) Australian squash player; four times World Open champion, 1976–80; eight times British Open champion, 1969–81

Hunt James (1947–1993) English motor racing driver; Formula 1 World Drivers' Champion in 1976

Hurst Geoff (1941–) English footballer who scored a hat-trick in England's 4–2 victory over West Germany in the 1966 World Cup final

Hutton Len (1916–1990) English cricketer; scored 6,971 runs in 79 Tests at an average of 56.67

Induráin Miguel (1964–) Spanish cyclist; first cyclist to win the Tour de France five times in a row, 1991–95

Irvine Andy (1951–) Scottish rugby union full back; scored 301 points in 60 internationals for Scotland and the British Lions

Jacklin Tony (1944–) English golfer; winner of the British Open in 1969 and the US Open in 1970; Europe Ryder Cup Captain, 1983–89

Jackson Colin (1967–) Welsh athlete; winner of the 1993 World 110 m hurdles title in a world record time of 12.91 sec

Jennings Pat (1945–) Northern Irish footballer; made 119 appearances in goal for Northern Ireland, 1964–86

Johnson Earvin 'Magic' (1959–) US basketball guard; led Los Angeles Lakers to five NBA titles, 1980–87; regular season MVP, 1987, 1989–90; playoff MVP, 1980, 1982, 1987

Johnson Michael (1967–) US runner; three times world champion at both 200 and 400 m, 1991–97; 1996, became first man to win the 200 m and 400 m Olympic titles at the same games

Jones Ann (1938–) English tennis player; 1969 Wimbledon singles champion; also won the French singles title in 1961 and 1966

Jones Bobby (1902–1971) US golfer; achieved a unique 'grand slam' of the US and British amateur and Open titles in 1930; won four US and three British Opens, 1922–30

Kasparov Garry (1963–) Azerbaijani chess player; aged 22, he became the youngest ever world champion in 1985 and remains unbeaten in world championship play

Keegan Kevin (1951–) English footballer and manager; European Footballer of the Year in 1978 and 1979; Newcastle United manager, 1992–97, and now manager of Fulham

Kelly Sean (1956–) Irish cyclist; winner of the first World Cup series in 1989; record four times points leader in the Tour de France

Khan Imran (1952–) Pakistani cricketer; scored 3,807 runs and took 362 wickets in 88 Tests, 1971–92

Khan Jahangir (1963–) Pakistani squash player; six times winner of the World Open and ten times winner of the British Open between 1981 and 1991

Khan Jansher (1969–) Pakistani squash player; eight times winner of the World Open between 1987 and 1996

King Billie Jean (1943–) US tennis player; won 39 Grand Slam tournaments, 1961–80, including six Wimbledon and four US singles titles

Korbut Olga (1955–) Soviet gymnast; won three gold medals at 1972 Olympics

Laker Jim (1922–) English cricketer; off-spinner who returned record Test and first class figures of 19–90 against Australia at Manchester in 1956

Lara Brian (1969–) West Indian cricketer who, in 1994, set new records for the most runs in a Test innings and a First Class innings with scores of 375 and 501 not-out, respectively

Latynina Larissa (1934–) Soviet gymnast; won 18 Olympic medals including nine golds, 1956–64

Laver Rod (1938–) Australian tennis player; only player to win the singles Grand Slam twice, 1962, 1969; four times Wimbledon singles champion

Lemieux Mario (1965–) Canadian ice hockey player; six times NHL leading scorer, 1988–97

LeMond Greg (1961–) US cyclist; only US or non-European cyclist to win the Tour de France, winning in 1986 and 1989–90

Lendl Ivan (1960–) Czechoslovakian tennis player; won eight Grand Slam singles tournaments, 1984–90, including three US Opens

Lenglen Suzanne (1899–1938) French tennis player; won both French and Wimbledon singles and doubles titles six times, 1919–26

Leonard Sugar Ray (1956–) US boxer; won world titles in five different weight divisions, 1979–88; 1976 Olympic light welterweight champion

Lewis Carl (1961–) US athlete; won nine Olympic sprint and long jump golds, 1984–96, including four at the 1984 Games

Lewis Lennox (1965–) British boxer; WBC world heavyweight champion, 1992–94, regaining the title in 1997; 1988 Olympic super-heavyweight champion

Lillee Dennis (1949–) Australian cricketer; fast bowler who took 355 wickets in 70 Tests at an average 23.92, 1971–84

Lineker Gary (1960–) English footballer; scored 48 goals in 80 internationals, 1984–92

Lloyd Clive (1944–) West Indian cricketer; scorer of 7,515 runs in 110 Tests at an average of 46.67, 1966–85

Lombardi Vince (1913–1970) US American football coach of the Green Bay Packers; had 89–29–4 record, five NFL titles, and two Super Bowl victories

Louis Joe (1914–1981) US boxer; world heavyweight boxing champion for record 11 years and eight months, 1937–49, with 25 successful title defences

Lyle Sandy (1958–) British golfer; winner of the 1985 British Open and the 1988 US Masters

Lynagh Michael (1963–) Australian rugby union player; scored a world-record 911 points in 72 internationals, 1984–95

McBride Willie John (1940–) Irish rugby union player; won 80 international caps, including a record 17 for the British Lions, 1962–75

McEnroe John (1959–) US tennis player; won four US Open and three Wimbledon singles titles, 1979–84, and eight Grand Slam men's doubles titles, 1979–92

McKay Heather (1941–) Australian squash player; winner of the British Open a record 16 times, 1962–80

McRae Colin (1968–) Scottish rally driver; world champion, 1995; won RAC Rally in 1994, 1995, and 1997

Mansell Nigel (1953–) English motor racing driver; Formula 1 World Champion, 1992; won IndyCar series at first attempt, 1993

Maradona Diego (1960–) Argentinian soccer player; led Argentina to 1986 World Cup victory; sent home in disgrace from 1994 World Cup for drug abuse

Marciano Rocky (1923–1969) US boxer; world heavyweight champion, 1952–56; won all his 49 professional fights

Marshall Malcolm (1958–) West Indian cricketer; fast bowler who took 376 wickets in 81 Tests at an average of 20.94

Matthews Stanley (1915–) English footballer; his league career spanned a record 33 years, 1932–65; the first European Footballer of the Year in 1956

Mercyx Eddy (1945–) Belgian cyclist; five times winner of both the Tour de France and the Giro d'Italia, 1968–74

Montana Joe (1956–) US American football player; quarterback for San Francisco 49ers and Kansas City; won four Super Bowl championships; Super Bowl MVP in 1981, 1984, and 1989

Montgomerie Colin (1963–) Scottish golfer; winner of the European Order of Merit a record five times in a row, 1993–97

Moody Helen Wills (1905–1998) US tennis player; won eight Wimbledon, seven US, and four French singles titles, 1923–38

Moore Bobby (1941–1992) English footballer; captained England to victory in the 1966 World Cup final; won 108 international caps, including 90 as captain

Moses Ed (1955–) US hurdler; won record 122 consecutive 400 m hurdles races, 1977–87; Olympic 400 m hurdles champion, 1976, 1984

Navratilova Martina (1956–) Czechoslovakian-born US tennis player; won 18 Grand Slam singles tournaments, 1978–90, including a record nine Wimbledon titles

Newcombe John (1943–) Australian tennis player; won seven Grand Slam singles tournaments, 1967–75, including three Wimbledon and Australian titles

Nicklaus Jack (1940–) US golfer; won all-time record 20 majors, 1962–86, including six Masters and five PGA titles

Norman Greg (1955–) Australian golfer; all-time PGA Tour money winner; British Open champion, 1986, 1993

Nurmi Paavo (1897–1973) Finnish runner; won nine Olympic gold medals, 1920, 1924, 1928; set 22 world records at distances between 1,500 m and 20,000 m, 1923–31

Oerter Al (1936–) US discus thrower; first athlete to win four successive Olympic titles, 1956–68

Offiah Martin (1966–) English rugby player; scorer of over 540 tries in rugby league since 1987

Ovett Steve (1955–) English runner; winner of the 1980 Olympic 800 m title

Owens Jesse (1913–1980) US athlete; won four golds at 1936 Olympics for 100 m, 200 m, long jump, and sprint relay; set five world records in one day, 1935, one of which, for the long jump (26′ 8 1/4″), stood for 25 years

Paisley Bob (1919–1996) English football manager; led Liverpool to 13 trophies, including six league championships and three European Cups, 1974–83

Palmer Arnold (1929–) US golfer; won seven majors, 1958–64, including four Masters titles

Patterson Floyd (1935–) US boxer; world heavyweight champion, 1956–59, 1960–62; 1952 Olympic middleweight champion

Payton Walter (1954–) US American Football running back for Chicago Bears; NFL all-time leader in yards rushing

Pelé (Edson Arantes do Nascimento) (1940–) Brazilian soccer player; scored 1,281 goals in 1,363 games 1956–1977

Perec Marie-José (1968–) French runner; won 400 m gold at 1992 Olympics, and both 200 m and 400 m golds at 1996 Games

Perry Fred (1909–1995) English tennis player; winner of eight Grand Slam singles championships, 1933–36

Piggott Lester (1935–) English jockey; rode a record nine Derby winners and 21 other English classic races, 1954–92; 11 times champion jockey, 1960–82

Platini Michel (1955–) French footballer; European Footballer of the Year in 1983, 1984, and 1985

Player Gary (1936–) South African golfer; won nine majors, 1959–78, including the Masters and British Open three times each

Price Nick (1957–) Zimbabwean golfer; won PGA championship, 1992, 1994, and British Open, 1994

Prost Alain (1955–) French motor racing driver; Formula 1 World Champion, 1985–86, 1989, 1993; won an all-time record 51 Grand Prix

Puskás Ferenc (1927–) Hungarian footballer; scorer of 83 goals in 87 internationals, 1945–62

Ramsey Alf (1920–) English footballer and manager; England manager, 1963–74; led England to victory in the 1966 World Cup

Redgrave Steve (1962–) English rower; winner of four successive Olympic gold medals, 1984–96

Richards Gordon (1904–1986) English jockey; rode a record 4,870 British winners, 1921–54, and was champion jockey a record 26 times

Richards Vivian (1952–) West Indian cricketer; scored 8,540 runs in 121 Tests at an average of 50.23

Ripken Cal Jr (1960–) US baseball player; Baltimore Orioles shortstop and third-baseman; holder major league record of 2,478 consecutive games played (as of 1997 season's end)

Robinson Sugar Ray (1921–1989) US boxer; world welterweight champion, 1946–51; five times world middleweight champion, 1951–60

Roche Stephen (1959–) Irish cyclist; in 1987 became only the second cyclist to win the Tour de France, Giro d'Italia, and the world professional road race in the same year

Ronaldo (1976–) Brazilian footballer; voted FIFA World Footballer of the Year in 1996 and 1997

Rush Ian (1961–) Welsh footballer; scored a record 43 FA Cup goals; won 73 Welsh caps, 1980–96

Russell Bill (1934–) US basketball player; led Boston Celtics to 11 NBA titles, 1957–69; player coach, 1968–69 (the NBA's first black head coach); five times MVP, 1958–65

Sampras Pete (1971–) US tennis player; has won 12 Grand Slam singles tournaments since 1990, including five US and five Wimbledon titles

Sarazen Gene (1902–) US golfer; won seven majors, 1922–35, including three US Opens; pioneer of the sand wedge

Scudamore Peter (1958–) English National Hunt jockey; a record eight times champion jockey, 1979–1993

Seles Monica (1973–) Yugoslav-born tennis player; has won nine Grand Slam singles tournaments since 1990, including four Australian Opens

Sella Phillipe (1962–) French rugby union centre; winner of a world record 111 international caps for France, 1982–95

Senna Ayrton (1960–1994) Brazilian motor racing driver; three times Formula 1 world champion, 1988, 1990–91

Shankly Bill (1913–1981) Scottish football manager; led Liverpool to six trophies, including three league titles, 1959–74

Shearer Alan (1970–) English footballer whose £15 million transfer to Newcastle United from Blackburn Rovers in 1996 set a world record

Sheene Barry (1950–) English motor cyclist; 500 cc world champion in 1976 and 1977

Shilton Peter (1949–) English footballer; made a record 125 appearances in goal for England, 1970–90; in 1996 he made his 1,000th league appearance

Simpson O J (1947–) US American football player; Buffalo Bills running back; professional career record: 11,236 yards rushing, 203 receptions, 990 yards kickoff returns, 14,368 combined net yards

Sobers Gary (1936–) West Indian cricketer; in 93 Tests, 1954–74, scored 8,032 runs at an average of 57.78 and took 235 wickets at an average of 34.03

Spitz Mark (1950–) US swimmer; won seven gold medals at the 1972 Olympics

Stein Jock (1922–1985) Scottish football manager; led Celtic to the 1967 European Cup and to 24 domestic titles, including ten league championships, 1966–78

Stewart Jackie (1939–) Scottish motor racing driver; Formula 1 world champion, 1969, 1971, 1973

Surtees John (1934–) English motor cyclist and motor racing driver; four times 500 cc world champion between 1956 and 1960; Formula 1 World Drivers' Champion in 1964

Thompson Daley (1958–) English athlete; olympic decathlon champion in 1980 and 1984, and world champion in 1983; broke the world record four times

Thorpe Jim (1888–1953) US all-round athlete; won pentathlon and decathlon golds at 1912 Olympics; college and pro football star; major league baseball player, 1913–19

Tilden Bill (1893–1953) US tennis player; won seven US and three Wimbledon singles titles, 1920–30; led USA to seven successive Davis Cup titles, 1920–27

Torvill Jayne (1957–) English ice dancer who with Christopher Dean won the 1984 Olympic title and four successive world titles, 1981–84

Trevino Lee (1939–) US golfer; won US Open, PGA and British Open twice each, 1968–84

Trueman Fred (1931–) English cricketer; fast bowler who took 307 wickets in 67 Tests at an average of 21.57, 1952–65

Tyson Mike (1966–) US boxer; world heavyweight champion 1986–90 (undisputed 1987–90), WBA champion, 1996

Underwood Rory (1963–) English rugby union wing three-quarter; scored a British record 49 tries in 85 appearances for England,

land,1984–96

Van Basten Marco (1964–) Dutch footballer; European Footballer of the Year in 1988, 1989, and 1992

Vardon Harry (1870–1937) Jersey-born golfer; won the British Open a record six times, 1896–1914; also won the US Open in 1900

Venables Terry (1943–) English footballer and manager; coached England to the semi-finals of the 1996 European Championship; won the FA Cup with Spurs as a player in 1967, and as a manager in 1991

Villeneuve Jacques (1971–) Canadian motor racing driver; 1995 IndyCar and Indy 500 champion; 1997 Formula 1 World Champion

Viren Lasse (1949–) Finnish runner; won the 5,000 m and 10,000 m at both the 1972 and 1976 Olympics

Wade Virginia (1945–) English tennis player; winner of three Grand Slam singles titles, including Wimbledon in 1977

Warne Shane (1969–) Australian cricketer; wrist spinner who has taken over 300 Test wickets since making his debut in 1992

Watson Tom (1949–) US golfer; won eight majors, 1975–83, including five British Opens

Wells Allan (1952–) Scottish sprinter; winner of the 1980 Olympic 100 metres title

Whitbread Fatima (1961–) English javelin thrower; winner of the 1987 World Championships Javelin title

Wilkie David (1954–) Scottish swimmer; won the 1976 Olympic 200 m breast-stroke title in world-record time

Williams JPR (1949–) Welsh rugby union full back; won 55 caps for Wales and eight for the British Lions, 1969–1981

Woods Eldrick 'Tiger' (1975–) US golfer; in 1997 he became the youngest winner (aged 21) of the Masters, and the first to win over $2 million in a season on the PGA Tour; won a record three consecutive US amateur titles, 1994–96

Woosnam Ian (1958–) Welsh golfer; winner of the US Masters in 1981 and the World Matchplay championship in 1987 and 1990

Wright Billy (1924–1994) English footballer; winner of 105 England caps, 1946–59

Zatopek Emile (1922–) Czechoslovakian distance runner; won 5,000 m, 10,000 m, and marathon at 1952 Olympics

Sports Organizations

English County Cricket Clubs: Directory

Derbyshire County Cricket Club County Cricket Ground, Nottingham Road, Derby DE2 6DA; phone: (01332) 383211

Durham County Cricket Club County Ground, Riverside, Chester-le-Street, County Durham DH3 3QR; phone: (0191) 387 1717

Essex County Cricket Club County Ground, New Writtle Street, Chelmsford CM2 0PG; phone: (01245) 252420

Glamorgan County Cricket Club Sofia Gardens, Cardiff CF1 9XR; phone: (01222) 343478

Gloucestershire County Cricket Club Phoenix County Ground, Nevil Road, Bristol BS7 9EJ; phone: (0117) 924 5216

Hampshire County Cricket Club County Ground, Northlands Road, Southampton SO15 2UE; phone: (01703) 333788

Kent County Cricket Club St Lawrence Ground, Old Dover Road, Canterbury CT1 3NZ; phone: (01227) 456886

Lancashire County Cricket Club Old Trafford, Manchester M16 0PX; phone: (0161) 282 4000

Leicestershire County Cricket Club County Ground, Grace Road, Leicester LE2 8AD; phone: (0116) 283 2128

Middlesex County Cricket Club Lord's Cricket Ground, London NW8 8QN; phone: (0171) 289 1300

Northamptonshire County Cricket Club County Ground, Wantage Road, Northampton NN1 4TJ; phone: (01604) 32917

Nottinghamshire County Cricket Club Trent Bridge, Nottingham NG2 6AG; phone: (0115) 982 1525

Somerset County Cricket Club County Ground, St James's Street, Taunton TA1 1JT; phone: (01823) 272946

Surrey County Cricket Club Kennington Oval, London SE11 5SS; phone: (0171) 582 6660

Sussex County Cricket Club County Ground, Eaton Road, Hove BN3 3AN; phone: (01273) 732161

Warwickshire County Cricket Club County Ground, Edgbaston, Birmingham B5 7QU; phone: (0121) 446 4422

Worcestershire County Cricket Club County Ground, New Road, Worcester WR2 4QQ; phone: (01905) 748474

Yorkshire County Cricket Club Headingley Cricket Ground, Leeds LS6 3BU; phone: (0113) 278 7394

English and Scottish Football Clubs: Directory

FA Premiership Clubs

Arsenal Arsenal Stadium, Avenell Road, Highbury, London N5 1BU; phone: (0171) 704 4000

Aston Villa Villa Park, Trinity Road, Birmingham B6 6HE; phone: (0121) 327 2299

Blackburn Rovers Ewood Park, Blackburn BB2 4JF; phone: (01254) 698888

Charlton Athletic The Valley, Floyd Road, Charlton, London SE7 8BL; phone: (0181) 333 4000

Chelsea Stamford Bridge, Fulham Road, London SW6 1HS; phone: (0171) 385 5545

Coventry City Highfield Road Stadium, King Richard Street, Coventry CV2 4FW; phone: (01203) 234000

Derby County Pride Park Stadium, Derby DE24 8XL; phone: (01332) 340105

Everton Goodison Park, Liverpool L4 4EL; phone: (0151) 330 2200

Leeds United Elland Road, Leeds LS11 0ES; phone: (0113) 226 6000

Leicester City City Stadium, Filbert Street, Leicester LE2 7FL; phone: (0116) 291 5000

Liverpool Anfield Road, Liverpool L4 0TH; phone: (0151) 263 2361

Manchester United Sir Matt Busby Way, Old Trafford, Manchester M16 0RA; phone: (0161) 872 1661

Middlesborough Cellnet Riverside Stadium, Middlesborough, Cleveland TS3 6RS; phone: (01642) 877700

Newcastle United St James's Park, Newcastle-upon-Tyne NE1 4ST; phone: (0191) 201 8400

Nottingham Forest City Ground, Nottingham NG2 5FJ; phone: (0115) 952 6000

Sheffield Wednesday Hillsborough, Sheffield S6 1SW; phone: (0114) 221 2121

Southampton The Dell, Milton Road, Southampton SO15 2XH; phone: (01703) 220505

Tottenham Hotspur 748 High Road, Tottenham, London N17 0AP; phone: (0181) 365 5000

West Ham United Boleyn Ground, Green Street, Upton Park, London E13 9AZ; phone: (0181) 548 2748

Wimbledon Selhurst Park, South Norwood, London SE25 6PY; phone: (0181) 771 2233

Nationwide Football League Division One Clubs

Barnsley Oakwell Ground, Grove Street, Barnsley, South Yorkshire S71 1ET; phone: (01226) 211211

Birmingham City St Andrews, Birmingham B9 4NH; phone: (0121) 772 0101

Bolton Wanderers The Reebok Stadium, Mansell Way, Horwich; phone: (01204) 698800

Bradford City The Pulse Stadium at Valley Parade, Bradford BD8 7DY; phone: (01274) 773355

Bristol City Ashton Gate, Bristol BS3 2EJ; phone: 0117 963 0630

Bury Gigg Lane, Bury BL9 9HR; phone: (0161) 764 4881

Crewe Alexandra Gresty Road, Crewe CW2 6EB; phone: (01270) 213014

Crystal Palace Selhurst Park, South Norwood, London SE25 6PU; phone: (0181) 768 6000

Grimsby Town Blundell Park, Cleethorpes DN35 7PY; phone: (01472) 697111

Huddersfield Town The Alfred McAlpine Stadium, Leeds Road, Huddersfield HD1 6PX; phone: (01484) 424444

Ipswich Town Portman Road, Ipswich IP1 2DA; phone: (01473) 400500

Norwich City Carrow Road, Norwich NR1 1JE; phone: (01603) 760760

Oxford United Manor Ground, Headington, Oxford OX3 7RS; phone: (01865) 761503

Portsmouth Fratton Park, Portsmouth PO4 8RA; phone: (01705) 731204

Port Vale Vale Park, Burslem, Stoke-on-Trent ST6 1AW; phone: (01782) 814134

Queen's Park Rangers Loftus Road, South Africa Road, London W12 7PA; phone: (0181) 743 0262

Sheffield United Bramall Lane Ground, Sheffield S2 4SU; phone: (0114) 221 5757

Stockport County Edgeley Park, Hardcastle Road, Stockport, Cheshire SK3 9DD; phone: (0161) 286 8888

Sunderland Stadium of Light, Sunderland, Tyne-and-Wear SR2 1SU phone: (0191) 551 5000

Swindon Town County Ground, Swindon, Wiltshire SN1 2ED; phone: (01793) 430430

Tranmere Rovers Prenton Park, Prenton Road West, Birkenhead L42 9PN; phone: (0151) 608 4194

Watford Vicarage Road Stadium, Watford WD1 8ER; phone: (01923) 496000

West Bromwich Albion The Hawthorns, West Bromwich B71 4LF; phone: (0121) 525 8888

Wolverhampton Wanderers Molineaux Grounds, Wolverhampton WV1 4QR; phone: (01902) 655000

Bell's Scottish Premier Division Clubs
Aberdeen Pittodrie Stadium, Pittodrie Street, Aberdeen AB2 1QH; phone: (01224) 632328

Dundee United Tannadice Park, Tannadice Street, Dundee DD3 7JW; phone: (01382) 833166

Dunfermline Athletic East End Park, Halbeath Road, Dunfermline KY 7RB; phone: (01383) 724295

Glasgow Celtic Celtic Park, 95 Kerrydale Street, Glasgow G40 3RE; phone: (0141) 556 2611

Glasgow Rangers Ibrox Stadium, Edminston Drive, Glasgow G51 2XD; phone: (0141) 427 8500

Heart of Midlothian Tynecastle Park, Gorgie Road, Edinburgh EH11 2NL; phone: (0131) 337 6132

Hibernian Easter Road Stadium, Albion Road, Edinburgh EH7 5QG; phone: (0131) 661 2159

Kilmarnock Football Park, Kilmarnock KA1 2DP; phone: (01563) 525184

Motherwell Fir Park, Motherwell ML1 2QN; phone: (01698) 333333

St Johnstone McDiarmid Park, Crieff Road, Perth PH1 2SJ; phone: (01738) 626961

Rugby Super League Clubs: Directory

Bradford Bulls Odsal Stadium, Bradford BD6 1BS; phone: (01274) 733899; fax: 01274 724730

Castleford Tigers Wheldon Road, Castleford WF10 2SD; phone: (01977) 552674; fax: (01977) 518007

Halifax Blue Sox The Pavilion, Thrum Hall HX1 4TL; phone: (01422) 250600; fax: (01422) 251666

Huddersfield Giants Alfred McAlpine Stadium, Kirklees Way, Huddersfield HD1 6PZ; phone: (01484) 530710; fax: (01484) 531712

Hull Sharks The Boulevard, Airlie Street, Hull phone: (01482) 327200; fax: (01482) 320338

Leeds Rhinos Headingley, St Michael's Lane, Leeds LS6 3BR; phone: (0113) 278 6181; fax: (0113) 275 4284

London Broncos The Stoop Memorial Ground, Twickenham, Middlesex TW8 7SX; phone: (0181) 410 5000; fax: (0181) 410 5001

St Helens Knowsley Road, St Helens, Merseyside, WA10 4AD; phone: (01744) 23697; fax: (01744) 451302

Salford Reds The Willows, Willows Road, Weaste, Salford M5 2ST; phone: (0161) 737 6363; fax: (0161) 745 8072

Sheffield Eagles 824 Attercliffe Road, Sheffield S9 3RS; phone: (0114) 261 0326; fax: (0114) 261 0303

Warrington Wolves Wilderspool Stadium, Wilderspool Causeway, Warrington, WA4 6PY; phone: (01925) 635338; fax: (01925) 571744

Wigan Warriors The Pavilion, Central Park, Wigan WN1 1XF; phone: (01942) 231321; fax: (01942) 820111

English Rugby Union Clubs: Directory

Allied Dunbar Premiership Division One Clubs (1997–98)
Bath The Recreation Ground, Bath BA2 6PW; phone: (01225) 325200

Bristol Memorial Ground, Filton Avenue, Horfield, Bristol BS7 0AQ; phone: (0117) 908500

Gloucester Kingsholm, Kingsholm Road, Gloucester GL1 3AX; phone: (01452) 381087

Leicester Welford Road Ground, Aylestone Road, Leicester LE2 7LF; phone: (0116) 254 1607

London Irish The Avenue, Sunbury-on-Thames, Middlesex TW16 5EQ; phone: (01932) 783034

NEC Harlequins of London The Stoop Memorial Ground, Twickenham TW2 7SQ; phone: (0181) 410 6000

Newcastle Falcons Kingston Park, Brunton Road, Kenton Bank Foot, Newcastle NE13 8AF; phone: (0191) 214 0422

Northampton Franklins' Gardens, Weedon Road, Northampton NN5 5BG; phone: (01604) 751543

Richmond The Athletic Ground, Kew Foot Road, Richmond, Surrey TW9 2SS; phone: (0181) 332 7112

Sale Heywood Road, Brooklands, Sale, Cheshire M33 3WB; phone: (0161) 973 6348

Saracens Vicarage Road Stadium, Watford WD1 8ER; phone: (01923) 496200

Wasps Loftus Road Stadium, South Africa Road, London W12 7PA; phone: (0181) 743 0262

Scottish Rugby Union Clubs: Directory

Boroughmuir Meggetland, Colinton Road, Edinburgh EH14 1AS; phone: (0131) 443 7571

Currie Malleny Park, Balerno, Edinburgh EH14 5HA; phone: (0131) 449 2432

Edinburgh Academicals Raeburn Place, Stockbridge, Edinburgh EH4 1HQ; phone: (0131) 332 1070

Hawick Mansfield Park, Mansfield, Hawick; phone: (01450) 370687

Heriot's FP Goldenacre, Bangholm Terrace, Edinburgh EH3 5QN; phone: (0131) 552 5925

Jed-Forest Riverside Park, Jedburgh TD8 6UE; phone: (01835) 862855

Melrose The Greenyards, Melrose, Roxburghshire TD6 9SA; phone: (01896) 822993

Stirling County Bridgehaugh, Causewayhead Road, Stirling SK9 5EG; phone: (01786) 478866

Watsonians Myreside, Myreside Road, Edinburgh EH10 5DB; phone: (0131) 447 5200

West of Scotland Burnbrae, Glasgow Road, Milngavie, Glasgow G62 6HX; phone: (0141) 956 3116/2891

Sports Organizations in the United Kingdom: Directory

Sports Councils
Central Council of Physical Recreation Francis House, Francis Street, London SW1P 1DE; phone: (0171) 828 3163

The English Sports Council 16 Upper Woburn Place, London WC1H 0QP; phone: (0171) 273 1500

Scottish Sports Council Caledonia House, South Gyle, Edinburgh EH12 9DQ; phone: (0131) 317 7200

Sports Council for Northern Ireland House of Sport, Upper Malone Road, Belfast BT9 5LA; phone: (01232) 381222

Sports Council for Wales Sophia Gardens, Cardiff CF1 9SW; phone: (01222) 300500

UK Sports Council Walkden House, 3–10 Melton Street, London NW1 2EB; phone: (0171) 380 8000

American Football
World League of American Football 26A Albemarle Street, London W1X 3FA; phone: (0171) 355 1995

Angling
National Federation of Anglers Halliday House, Eggington Junction, Near Hitton, Derbyshire DE65 6GU; phone: (01283) 734735

Archery
Grand National Archery Society National Agricultural Centre, Seventh Street, Stoneleigh, Kenilworth, Warwickshire CV8 2LG; phone: (01203) 696631

Association Football
The Football Association 16 Lancaster Gate, London W2 3LW; phone: (0171) 262 4542

Football Association of Ireland 80 Merrion Square South, Dublin 2; phone: (00535) 1 676 6864

Football Association of Wales Plymouth Chambers, 3 Westgate Street, Cardiff CF1 1DD; phone: (01222) 372325

The Football League Ltd 319 Clifton Drive South, Lytham St Annes, Lancashire FY8 1JG; phone: (01253) 729421

The Football Supporters' Association PO Box 11, Liverpool L26 1XP; phone: (0151) 709 2594

Irish Football Association 20 Windsor Avenue, Belfast BT9 6EE; phone: (01232) 669458

Irish Football League 96 University Street, Belfast BT7 1HE; phone: (01232) 242888

Scottish Football Association 6 Park Gardens, Glasgow G3 7YF; phone: (0141) 332 6372

Scottish Football League 188 West Regent Street, Glasgow G2 4RY; phone: (0141) 248 3844

Women's Football Association 16 Lancaster Gate, London W2 3LW; phone: (0171) 262 4542

Athletics
British Athletic Federation 225A Bristol Road, Edgbaston, Birmingham B5 7UB; phone: (0121) 440 5000

Badminton
Badminton Association of England Ltd National Badminton Centre, Bradwell Road, Loughton Lodge, Milton Keynes MK8 9LA; phone: (01908) 568822

Scottish Badminton Union Cockburn Centre, 40 Bogmoor Place, Glasgow G51 4TQ; phone: (0141) 445 1218

Welsh Badminton Union Fourth Floor, 3 Westgate Street, Cardiff CF1 1ND; phone: (01222) 222082

Baseball
British Baseball Federation PO Box 45, Hessle, East Yorks, HU13 0YQ; phone: (01482) 643551

Basketball
Basketball Association of Wales Connies House, Rhymney River Bridge Road, Cardiff CF3 7YZ; phone: (01222) 454395

English Basketball Association 48 Bradford Road, Stanningley, Leeds LS28 6DF; phone: (0113) 236 1166

Scottish Basketball Association Caledonia House, South Gyle, Edinburgh EH12 9DQ; phone: (0131) 317 7260

Billiards and Snooker
World Professional Billiards and Snooker Association 27 Oakfield Road, Clifton, Bristol BS28 2AT; phone: (0117) 974 4491

Bobsleigh
British Bobsleigh Association The Chestnuts, 85 High Street, Codford, Warminster, Wilts BA12 0ND; phone: (01985) 850064

Bowls
British Isles Bowling Council 28 Woodford Park, Lurgan, County Armargh BT66 7HA; phone: (01762) 322036

British Isles Indoor Bowls Council 9 Highlight Lane, Barry CF62 8AA; phone: (01446) 733978

British Isles Women's Bowling Council 2 Case Gardens, Seaton, Devon EX12 2AP; phone: (01297) 21317

British Isles Women's Indoor Bowls Council 3 Scirocco Close, Moulton Park, Northampton NN3 6AP; phone: (01604) 494163

English Bowling Association Lyndhurst Road, Worthing, West Sussex BN11 2AZ; phone: (01903) 820222

English Indoor Bowling Association David Cornwell House, Bowling Green, Leicester Road, Melton Mowbray, Leicestershire LE13 0DA; phone: (01664) 481900

English Women's Bowling Association 2 Case Gardens, Seaton, Devon EX12 2AP; phone: (01297) 21317

English Women's Indoor Bowling Association 3 Scirocco Close, Moulton Park, Northampton NN3 6AP; phone: (01604) 494163

Boxing
Amateur Boxing Association of England Ltd Crystal Palace National Sports Centre, London SE19 2BB; phone: (0181) 778 0251

British Amateur Boxing Association High Street, Lochee, Dundee DD2 2AY; phone: (01382) 611412

British Boxing Board of Control Ltd Jack Petersen House, 52A Borough High Street, London SE1 1XY; phone: (0171) 403 5879

Canoeing
British Canoe Union John Dudderidge House, Adbolton Lane, West Bridgford, Nottingham NG2 5AS; phone: (0115) 982 1100

Chess
British Chess Federation 9A Grand Parade, St Leonards-on-Sea, East Sussex TN38 0DD; phone: (01424) 442500

Cricket
England and Wales Cricket Board Lord's, London NW8 8QN; phone: (0171) 432 1200

MCC Lord's, London NW8 8QN; phone: (0171) 289 1611

Women's Cricket Association c/o Warwickshire CCC, Edgbaston, Birmingham B5 7QX; phone: (0121) 440 0567

Croquet
Croquet Association c/o The Hurlingham Club, Ranelagh Gardens, London SW6 3PR; phone: (0171) 736 3148

Cycling
British Cycling Federation National Cycling Centre, Stuart Street, Manchester M11 4DQ; phone: (0161) 230 2301

Darts
Britsh Darts Organisation 2 Pages Lane, Muswell Hill, London N10 1PS; phone: (0181) 833 5544

Diving
Great Britain Diving Federation PO Box 222, Batley, West Yorkshire WT17 8XD; phone: (01924) 422322

Equestrianism
British Equestrian Federation British Equestrian Centre, Stoneleigh Park, Kenilworth, Warwickshire CV8 2LR; phone: (01203) 696697

British Horse Trials Association British Equestrian Centre, Stoneleigh Park, Kenilworth, Warwickshire CV8 2LR; phone: (01203) 696697

Fencing
British Fencing Association 1 Baron's Gate, 33–35 Rothschild Road, London W4 5HT; phone: (0181) 742 3032

General
British Olympic Association No. 1 Wandsworth Plain, London SW18 1EH; phone: (0181) 871 2677

British Paralympic Association Delta Point Room 13A, 35 Wellesley Road, Croydon CR9 2YZ; phone: (0181) 666 4556

Commonwealth Games Federation Walkden House, 3–10 Melton Street, London NW1 2EB; phone: (0171) 383 5596

Gliding
British Gliding Association Kimberley House, 47 Vaughan Way, Leicester LE1 4SE; phone: (0116) 253 1051

Golf
Royal and Ancient Golf Club of St Andrews Golf Place, St Andrews, Fife KY16 9JD; phone: (01334) 472112

European Golf Tour Wentworth Drive, Virginia Water, Surrey GU25 4LX; phone: (01344) 842881

Women's European Tour The Tytherington Club, Dorchester Way, Tytherington, Macclesfield, Cheshire SK10 2JP; phone: (01625) 611444

Greyhound Racing
National Greyhound Racing Club Ltd Twyman House, 16 Bonny Street, London NW1 9QD; phone: (0171) 267 9256

Gymnastics
British Amateur Gymnastics Association Registered Office, Ford Hall, Lilleshall National Sports Centre Newport, Shropshire TF10 9NB; phone: (01952) 820330

Hockey
The Hockey Association The Stadium, Silbury Boulevard, Milton Keynes MK9 1NR; phone: (01908) 689290

Horse Racing
British Horse Racing Board 42 Portman Square, London W1H 0EN; phone: (0171) 396 0011

The Jockey Club 42 Portman Square, London W1H 0EN; phone: (0171) 486 4921

Ice Hockey
British Ice Hockey Association 2nd Floor Suite, 517 Christchurch Road, Boscombe, Bournemouth BH1 4AG; phone: (01202) 303946

Ice Skating
National Ice Skating Association of the UK Ltd 15–27 Gee Street, London EC1V 3RE; phone: (0171) 273 3824

Judo
British Judo Association 7A Rutland Street, Leicester LE1 1RB; phone: (0116) 255 9669

Lacrosse
English Lacrosse Association 4 Western Court, Bromley Street, Digbeth, Birmingham B9 4AN; phone: (0121) 773 4422

Martial Arts
Martial Arts Development Commission PO Box 381, Erith, Kent DA8 1TF; phone: (01322) 430441

English Karate Governing Body 12 Princes Avenue, Woodford Green, Essex IG8 0LN; phone: (0181) 599 0711

Modern Pentathlon
Modern Pentathlon Association of Great Britain 8 The Commons, Shaftsbury, Dorset SP7 8JU; phone: (01747) 855833

Motor Sports
Auto-Cycle Union ACU House, Wood Street, Rugby, Warwickshire CV21 2YX; phone: (01788) 540519

RAC Motor Sports Association Ltd Motorsports House, Riverside Park, Colnbrook, Slough SL3 0HG; phone: (01753) 681736

Mountaineering
British Mountaineering Council 177–179 Burton Road, West Didsbury, Manchester M20 2BB; phone: (0161) 445 4747

Netball
All England Netball Association Ltd Netball House, 9 Paynes Park, Hitchin, Hertfordshire SG5 1EH; phone: (01462) 442344

Northern Ireland Netball Association House of Sport, Upper Malone Road, Belfast BT9 5LA; phone: (01232) 381222

Scottish Netball Association 24 Ainslie Road, Hillington Business Park, Hillington, Glasgow G5S 4RC; phone: (0141) 570 4016

Welsh Netball Association 50 Cathedral Road, Cardiff CF1 9LE; phone: (01222) 237048

Orienteering
British Orienteering Federation Riversdale, Dale Road North, Darley Dale, Matlock, Derbyshire DE4 2HX; phone: (01629) 734042

Polo
The Hurlingham Polo Association Winterlake, Kirtlington, Kidlington, Oxfordshire OX5 3HG; phone: (01869) 350044

Rackets and Real Tennis
Tennis and Rackets Association c/o The Queen's Club, Palliser Road, London W14 9EQ; phone: (0171) 386 3447/8

Rifle Shooting
National Rifle Association Bisley Camp, Brookwood, Woking, Surrey GU24 0PR; phone: (01483) 797777

Rowing
Amateur Rowing Association Ltd The Priory, 6 Lower Mall, London W6 9DJ; phone: (0181) 748 3632

Henley Royal Regatta Regatta Headquarters, Henley-on-Thames, Oxfordshire RG9 2LY; phone: (01491) 572153

Scottish Amateur Rowing Association 18 Daniel McLauchlin Place, Kirkintilloch, Glasgow G66 2LH; phone: (0141) 775 0522

Welsh Amateur Rowing Association Monmouth School, Monmouth NP5 3NP; phone: (01600) 713143

Rugby League
The Rugby Football League Red Hall, Red Hall Lane, Leeds LS17 8NB; phone: (0113) 232 9111

Rugby Union
Irish Rugby Football Union 62 Lansdowne Road, Ballsbridge, Dublin 4, Republic of Ireland; phone: (00 353)1 668 4601

Rugby Football Union Twickenham TW1 1DZ; phone: (0181) 892 2000

Scottish Rugby Union Murrayfield, Edinburgh EH12 5PJ; phone: (0131) 346 5000

Welsh Rugby Union PO Box 22, Hodge House, St Mary Street, Cardiff CF1 1DY; phone: (01222) 390111

Skiing
British Ski Federation 258 Main Street, East Calder, Livingstone, West Lothian EH53 0EE; phone: (01506) 884343

Speedway
Speedway Control Board Ltd ACU Headquarters, Wood Street, Rugby, Warwickshire CV21 2YX; phone: (01788) 540096

Squash Rackets
Squash Rackets Association PO Box 1106, London W3 0ZD; phone: (0181) 746 1616

Swimming
Amateur Swimming Association of Great Britain Harold Fern House, Derby Square, Loughborough, Leicestershire LE11 0AL; phone: (01509) 618700

Table Tennis
English Table Tennis Association Queens-bury House, Havelock Road, Hastings, East Sussex TN34 1HF; phone: (01424) 722525

Tennis
All England Lawn Tennis and Croquet Club Church Road, Wimbledon, London SW19 5AE; phone: (0181) 944 1066

Lawn Tennis Association The Queen's Club, London W14 9EG; phone: (0171) 381 7000

Trampolining
British Trampoline Federation Ltd 146 College Road, Harrow HA1 1BH; phone: (0181) 863 7278

Volleyball
British Volleyball Federation 27 South Road, West Bridgford, Nottingham NG2 7AG; phone: (0115) 945 6324

Water Skiing
British Water Ski Federation 390 City Road, London EC1V 2QA; phone: (0171) 833 2855

Weight Lifting
British Amateur Weightlifters Association Iffley Turn, Oxford OX4 4DU; phone: (01865) 200339

Wrestling
British Amateur Wrestling Association 41 Great Clowes Street, Salford, Manchester M7 9RQ; phone: (0161) 832 9209

Yachting
Royal Yachting Association RYA House, Romsey Road, Eastleigh, Hampshire SO50 9YA; phone: (01703) 627400

Major International Sports Organizations: Directory

International dialling codes are given for organizations not based in the UK or USA

Motor Racing
Federation Internationale de Sport Automobile (FISA – Formula One) 8 Bis rue Boissy d'Anglais, 75008 Paris, France; phone: (331) 4312 4455

Boxing
International Boxing Federation (IBF) 134 Evergreen Place, 9th Floor, East Orange, NJ 07018, USA; phone: (201) 414-0300

World Boxing Association (WBA) Centro Comercial Cuidad Turmero, Local no. 21, Piso no. 2, Calle Petion Cruce Con Urdaneta, Turmero, 2115 Estado Aragua, Venezuela; phone: (58) 44 63 1584

World Boxing Council (WBC) Genova 33-503, Col. Juarez, Delegacion Cuauhternac, Mexico 06600, DF Mexico; phone: (52)5 533 6546

World Boxing Organization (WBO) Borinquen St no. 57, Santa Rita, San Juan, Puerto Rico 00925; phone: (809) 765-7542

Golf
Royal and Ancient Golf Club of St Andrews St Andrews, Fife KY16 9JD; phone: (01334) 472112

Olympics
International Olympic Committee (IOC) Chateau de Vidy, CH-1007 Lausanne, Switzerland; phone: (41) 21 621 6111

Skiing
Federation Internationale de Ski (FIS) (International Ski Federation), Oberhofen 3653, Switzerland; phone: (41) 33 44 6161

Association Football
Federation Internationale de Football Associations (FIFA) PO Box 85, Hitzigweg 11, Zurich 8030, Switzerland; phone: (41) 1 384 9595

Union of European Football Associations (UEFA) Chemin de la Redoute 54, Case Postale 303 CH-1260, Nyon, Switzerland; phone: (41) 22 994 4444

Swimming
Federation Internationale de Natation Amateur (FINA) (International Amateur Swimming Federation), Avenue de Beaumont 9, 1012 Lausanne, Switzerland; phone: (41) 21 312 6602

Tennis
International Tennis Federation Pallisert Road, Barons Court, London W14 9EN; phone: (0171) 381 8060

Athletics
International Amateur Athletic Federation (IAAF) 17 Rue Princesse Florestine, BP 359, MC 9800, Monaco; phone: (33) 93 30 70 70

Summer Olympic Games

Final Summer Olympic Medal Standings

1996

Position	Country	Gold	Silver	Bronze	Total	Position	Country	Gold	Silver	Bronze	Total
1	USA	44	32	25	101	41=	Yugoslavia	1	1	2	4
2	Russia	26	21	16	63	43=	Iran	1	1	1	3
3	Germany	20	18	27	65	43=	Slovakia	1	1	1	3
4	China	16	22	12	50	45=	Armenia	1	1	0	2
5	France	15	7	15	37	45=	Croatia	1	1	0	2
6	Italy	13	10	12	35	47=	Portugal	1	0	1	2
7	Australia	9	9	23	41	47=	Thailand	1	0	1	2
8	Cuba	9	8	8	25	49=	Burundi	1	0	0	1
9	Ukraine	9	2	12	23	49=	Costa Rica	1	0	0	1
10	Korea, South	7	15	5	27	49=	Ecuador	1	0	0	1
11	Poland	7	5	5	17	49=	Hong Kong	1	0	0	1
12	Hungary	7	4	10	21	49=	Syria	1	0	0	1
13	Spain	5	6	6	17	54	Argentina	0	2	1	3
14	Romania	4	7	9	20	55=	Namibia	0	2	0	2
15	Netherlands	4	5	10	19	55=	Slovenia	0	2	0	2
16	Greece	4	4	0	8	57	Austria	0	1	2	3
17	Czech Republic	4	3	4	11	58=	Malaysia	0	1	1	2
18	Switzerland	4	3	0	7	58=	Moldova	0	1	1	2
19	Denmark	4	1	1	6	58=	Uzbekistan	0	1	1	2
20	Turkey	4	1	1	6	61=	Azerbaijan	0	1	0	1
21	Canada	3	11	8	22	61=	Bahamas	0	1	0	1
22	Bulgaria	3	7	5	15	61=	Latvia	0	1	0	1
23	Japan	3	6	5	14	61=	Philippines	0	1	0	1
24	Kazakhstan	3	4	4	11	61=	Taiwan	0	1	0	1
25	Brazil	3	3	9	15	61=	Tonga	0	1	0	1
26	New Zealand	3	2	1	6	61=	Zambia	0	1	0	1
27	South Africa	3	1	1	5	68=	Georgia	0	0	2	2
28	Ireland, Republic of	3	0	1	4	68=	Morocco	0	0	2	2
29	Sweden	2	4	2	8	68=	Trinidad and Tobago	0	0	2	2
30	Norway	2	2	3	7	71=	India	0	0	1	1
31	Belgium	2	2	2	6	71=	Israel	0	0	1	1
32	Nigeria	2	1	3	6	71=	Lithuania	0	0	1	1
33	Korea, North	2	1	2	5	71=	Mexico	0	0	1	1
34=	Algeria	2	0	1	3	71=	Mongolia	0	0	1	1
34=	Ethiopia	2	0	1	3	71=	Mozambique	0	0	1	1
36	Great Britain	1	8	6	15	71=	Puerto Rico	0	0	1	1
37	Belarus	1	6	8	15	71=	Tunisia	0	0	1	1
38	Kenya	1	4	3	8	71=	Uganda	0	0	1	1
39	Jamaica	1	3	2	6						
40	Finland	1	2	1	4		**Total**	**271**	**273**	**298**	**842**
41=	Indonesia	1	1	2	4						

Summer Olympic Games Venues

(– = not applicable.)

Year	Olympiad	Venue	Year	Olympiad	Venue	Year	Olympiad	Venue
1896	I	Athens, Greece	1932	X	Los Angeles, USA	1972	XX	Munich, West Germany
1900	II	Paris, France	1936	XI	Berlin, Germany	1976	XXI	Montreal, Canada
1904	III	St Louis, USA	1940	XII	Tokyo, Japan[3]	1980	XXII	Moscow, USSR
1906	–	Athens, Greece[1]	1944	XIII	London, Great Britain[3]	1984	XXIII	Los Angeles, USA
1908	IV	London, Great Britain	1948	XIV	London, Great Britain	1988	XXIV	Seoul, South Korea
1912	V	Stockholm, Sweden	1952	XV	Helsinki, Finland	1992	XXV	Barcelona, Spain
1916	VI	Berlin, Germany[2]	1956	XVI	Melbourne, Australia[4]	1996	XXVI	Atlanta, USA
1920	VII	Antwerp, Belgium	1960	XVII	Rome, Italy	2000	XXVII	Sydney, Australia
1924	VIII	Paris, France	1964	XVIII	Tokyo, Japan	2004	XXVIII	Athens, Greece
1928	IX	Amsterdam, Netherlands	1968	XIX	Mexico City, Mexico			

[1] The 1906 Intercalated (or Interim) Games at Athens are not regarded as official by the International Olympic Committee but the results are included in most Olympic record books.
[2] Cancelled because of World War I.
[3] Cancelled because of World War II.
[4] Equestrian events held in Stockholm, Sweden.

Archery: Olympic Gold Medallists

1996

Category	Archer	Country
Men		
Individual	Justin Huish	USA
Team		USA
Women		
Individual	Kim Kyung-Wook	South Korea
Team		South Korea

Men's Athletics: Olympic Gold Medallists since 1960

Year	Name	Country	Result	Year	Name	Country	Result
100 m				1968	Lee Evans	USA	43.86
1960	Armin Hary	Germany	10.20	1972	Vince Matthews	USA	44.66
1964	Bob Hayes	USA	10.00	1976	Alberto Juantorena	Cuba	44.26
1968	Jim Hines	USA	9.95	1980	Viktor Markin	USSR	44.60
1972	Valery Borzov	USSR	10.14	1984	Alonzo Babers	USA	44.27
1976	Hasely Crawford	Trinidad and Tobago	10.06	1988	Steve Lewis	USA	43.87
1980	Allan Wells	Great Britain	10.25	1992	Quincy Watts	USA	43.50
1984	Carl Lewis	USA	9.99	1996	Michael Johnson	USA	43.49
1988	Carl Lewis	USA	9.92				
1992	Linford Christie	Great Britain	9.96	**800 m**			
1996	Donovan Bailey	Canada	9.84	1960	Peter Snell	New Zealand	1:46.30
				1964	Peter Snell	New Zealand	1:45.10
200 m				1968	Ralph Doubell	Australia	1:44.30
1960	Livio Berruti	Italy	20.50	1972	Dave Wottle	USA	1:45.90
1964	Henry Carr	USA	20.30	1976	Alberto Juantorena	Cuba	1:43.50
1968	Tommie Smith	USA	19.83	1980	Steve Ovett	Great Britain	1:45.40
1972	Valery Borzov	USSR	20.00	1984	Joaquim Cruz	Brazil	1:43.00
1976	Don Quarrie	Jamaica	20.23	1988	Paul Ereng	Kenya	1:43.45
1980	Pietro Mennea	Italy	20.19	1992	William Tanui	Kenya	1:43.66
1984	Carl Lewis	USA	19.80	1996	Vebjörn Rodal	Norway	1:42.58
1988	Joe DeLoach	USA	19.75				
1992	Mike Marsh	USA	20.01	**1,500 m**			
1996	Michael Johnson	USA	19.32	1960	Herb Elliott	Australia	3:35.60
				1964	Peter Snell	New Zealand	3:38.10
400 m				1968	Kip Keino	Kenya	3:34.90
1960	Otis Davis	USA	44.90	1972	Pekka Vasala	Finland	3:36.30
1964	Mike Larrabee	USA	45.10	1976	John Walker	New Zealand	3:39.17

(continued)

Men's Athletics: Olympic Gold Medallists since 1960 (continued)

Year	Name	Country	Result
1980	Sebastian Coe	Great Britain	3:38.40
1984	Sebastian Coe	Great Britain	3:32.53
1988	Peter Rono	Kenya	3:35.96
1992	Fermin Cacho	Spain	3:40.12
1996	Noureddine Morceli	Algeria	3:35.78

5,000 m

Year	Name	Country	Result
1960	Murray Halberg	New Zealand	13:43.40
1964	Bob Schul	USA	13:48.80
1968	Mohammed Gammoudi	Tunisia	14:05.00
1972	Lasse Viren	Finland	13:26.40
1976	Lasse Viren	Finland	13:21.76
1980	Miruts Yitfer	Ethiopia	13:21.00
1984	Saïd Aoutia	Morocco	13:05.59
1988	John Ngugi	Kenya	13:11.70
1992	Dieter Baumann	Germany	13:12.52
1996	Venuste Niyongabo	Burundi	13:07.96

10,000 m

Year	Name	Country	Result
1960	Pyotr Bolotnikov	USSR	28:32.20
1964	Billy Mills	USA	28:24.40
1968	Naftali Temu	Kenya	29:27.40
1972	Lasse Viren	Finland	27:38.40
1976	Lasse Viren	Finland	27:40.38
1980	Miruts Yitfer	Ethiopia	27:42.70
1984	Alberto Cova	Italy	27:47.54
1988	Brahim Boutayeb	Morocco	27:21.46
1992	Khalid Skah	Morocco	27:46.70
1996	Haile Gebrselassie	Ethiopia	27:07.34

Marathon

Year	Name	Country	Result
1960	Abebe Bikila	Ethiopia	2h 15:16.20
1964	Abebe Bikila	Ethiopia	2h 12:11.20
1968	Mamo Wolde	Ethiopia	2h 20:26.40
1972	Frank Shorter	USA	2h 12:19.80
1976	Waldemar Cierpinski	East Germany	2h 09:55.00
1980	Waldemar Cierpinski	East Germany	2h 11:03.00
1984	Carlos Lopes	Portugal	2h 09:21.00
1988	Gelindo Bordin	Italy	2h 10:32.00
1992	Hwang Young-cho	South Korea	2h 13:23.00
1996	Josia Thugwane	South Africa	2h 12:36.00

110 m hurdles

Year	Name	Country	Result
1960	Lee Calhoun	USA	13.8
1964	Hayes Jones	USA	13.6
1968	Willie Davenport	USA	13.3
1972	Rod Milburn	USA	13.24
1976	Guy Drut	France	13.30
1980	Thomas Munkelt	East Germany	13.39
1984	Roger Kingdom	USA	13.20
1988	Roger Kingdom	USA	12.98
1992	Mark McCoy	Canada	13.12
1996	Allen Johnson	USA	12.95

400 m hurdles

Year	Name	Country	Result
1960	Glenn Davis	USA	49.3
1964	Rex Cawley	USA	49.6
1968	David Hemery	Great Britain	48.12
1972	John Akii-Bua	Uganda	47.82
1976	Edwin Moses	USA	47.64
1980	Volker Beck	East Germany	48.70
1984	Edwin Moses	USA	47.75
1988	Andre Phillips	USA	47.19
1992	Kevin Young	USA	46.78
1996	Derrick Adkins	USA	47.54

20 km Walk

Year	Name	Country	Result
1960	Vladimir Golubnichy	USSR	1h 34:07.20
1964	Ken Matthews	Great Britain	1h 29:34.00
1968	Vladimir Golubnichy	USSR	1h 33:58.40
1972	Peter Frenkel	East Germany	1h 26:42.40
1976	Daniel Bautista	Mexico	1h 24:40.60
1980	Maurizio Damilano	Italy	1h 23:35.50
1984	Ernesto Canto	Mexico	1h 23:13.00
1988	Josef Pribilinec	Czechoslovakia	1h 19:57.00
1992	Daniel Plaza	Spain	1h 21:45.00
1996	Jefferson Perez	Ecuador	1h 20.07.00

50 km Walk

Year	Name	Country	Result
1960	Don Thompson	Great Britain	4h 25:30.00
1964	Abdon Pamich	Italy	4h 11:12.40
1968	Christoph Höhne	East Germany	4h 20:13.60
1972	Bernd Kannenberg	West Germany	3h 56:11.60
1980	Hartwig Gauder	East Germany	3h 49:24.00
1984	Raul Gonzalez	Mexico	3h 47:26.00
1988	Vyacheslav Ivanenko	USSR	3h 38:29.00
1992	Andrei Perlov	USSR	3h 50:13.00
1996	Robert Korzeniowski	Poland	3h 43:30.00

3,000 m Steeplechase

Year	Name	Country	Result
1960	Zdzisław Krzyszkowiak	Poland	8:34.20
1964	Gaston Roelants	Belgium	8:30.80
1968	Amos Biwott	Kenya	8:51.00
1972	Kip Keino	Kenya	8:23.60
1976	Anders Gärderud	Sweden	8:08.20
1980	Bronisław Malinowski	Poland	8:09.70
1984	Julius Korir	Kenya	8:11.80
1988	Julius Kariuki	Kenya	8:05.51
1992	Matthew Birir	Kenya	8:08.84
1996	Joseph Keter	Kenya	8:07.12

High Jump

Year	Name	Country	Result
1960	Robert Shavlakadze	USSR	2.16 m/7 ft 1 in
1964	Valery Brumel	USSR	2.18 m/7 ft $1\frac{3}{4}$ in
1968	Dick Fosbury	USA	2.24 m/7 ft $4\frac{1}{4}$ in
1972	Yuri Tarmak	USSR	2.23 m/7 ft $3\frac{3}{4}$ in
1976	Jacek Wszoła	Poland	2.25 m/7 ft $4\frac{1}{2}$ in
1980	Gerd Wessig	East Germany	2.36 m/7 ft $8\frac{3}{4}$ in
1984	Dietmeir Mögenburg	West Germany	2.35 m/7 ft $8\frac{1}{2}$ in
1988	Gennady Avdeyenko	USSR	2.38 m/7 ft $9\frac{1}{2}$ in
1992	Javier Sotormayor	Cuba	2.34 m/7 ft 8 in
1996	Charles Austin	USA	2.39 m/7 ft 10 in

Pole Vault

Year	Name	Country	Result
1960	Donald Bragg	USA	4.70 m/15 ft 5 in
1964	Fred Hansen	USA	5.10 m/16 ft $8\frac{3}{4}$ in
1968	Bob Seagren	USA	5.40 m/17 ft $8\frac{1}{2}$ in
1972	Wolfgang Nordwig	East Germany	5.50 m/18 ft $\frac{1}{2}$ in
1976	Tadeusz Slusarski	Poland	5.50 m/18 ft $\frac{1}{2}$ in
1980	Władisław Kozakiewicz	Poland	5.78 m/18 ft $11\frac{1}{2}$ in
1984	Pierre Quinon	France	5.75 m/18 ft $10\frac{1}{4}$ in

Men's Athletics: Olympic Gold Medallists since 1960 (continued)

Year	Name	Country	Result
1988	Sergei Bubka	USSR	5.90 m/19 ft $4\frac{1}{4}$ in
1992	Maksim Tarassov	Unified Team[1]	5.80 m/19 ft $\frac{1}{4}$ in
1996	Jean Galfione	France	5.92 m/19 ft 5 in

Long Jump

Year	Name	Country	Result
1960	Ralph Boston	USA	8.12 m/26 ft $7\frac{3}{4}$ in
1964	Lynn Davies	Great Britain	8.07 m/26 ft $5\frac{3}{4}$ in
1968	Bob Beamon	USA	8.90 m/29 ft $2\frac{1}{2}$ in
1972	Randy Williams	USA	8.24 m/27 ft $\frac{1}{2}$ in
1976	Arnie Robinson	USA	8.35 m/27 ft $4\frac{1}{2}$ in
1980	Lutz Dombrowski	East Germany	8.54 m/28 ft $\frac{1}{4}$ in
1984	Carl Lewis	USA	8.54 m/28 ft $\frac{1}{4}$ in
1988	Carl Lewis	USA	8.72 m/28 ft $7\frac{1}{4}$ in
1992	Carl Lewis	USA	8.67 m/28 ft $5\frac{1}{2}$ in
1996	Carl Lewis	USA	8.50m/27 ft $10\frac{3}{4}$ in

Triple Jump

Year	Name	Country	Result
1960	Józef Schmidt	Poland	16.81 m/55 ft 2 in
1964	Józef Schmidt	Poland	16.85 m/55 ft $3\frac{1}{2}$ in
1968	Viktor Saneyev	USSR	17.39 m/57 ft $\frac{3}{4}$ in
1972	Viktor Saneyev	USSR	17.35 m/56 ft 11 in
1976	Viktor Saneyev	USSR	17.29 m/56 ft $8\frac{3}{4}$ in
1980	Jaak Udmäe	USSR	17.35 m/56 ft $11\frac{1}{4}$ in
1984	Al Joyner	USA	17.26 m/56 ft $7\frac{1}{2}$ in
1988	Khristo Markov	Bulgaria	17.61 m/57 ft $9\frac{1}{4}$ in
1992	Mike Conley	USA	18.17 m/57 ft $10\frac{1}{4}$ in
1996	Kenny Harrison	USA	18.09 m/59 ft $4\frac{1}{4}$ in

Shot Put

Year	Name	Country	Result
1960	Bill Neider	USA	19.68 m/64 ft $6\frac{3}{4}$ in
1964	Dallas Long	USA	20.33 m/66 ft $8\frac{1}{2}$ in
1968	Randy Matson	USA	20.54 m/67 ft $4\frac{3}{4}$ in
1972	Władysław Komar	Poland	21.18 m/69 ft 6 in
1976	Udo Beyer	East Germany	21.05 m/69 ft $\frac{3}{4}$ in
1980	Vladimir Kiselyev	USSR	21.35 m/70 ft $\frac{1}{2}$ in
1984	Alessandro Andrei	Italy	21.26 m/69 ft 9 in
1988	Ulf Timmermann	East Germany	22.47 m/73 ft $8\frac{3}{4}$ in
1992	Mike Stulce	USA	21.70 m/71 ft $2\frac{1}{4}$ in
1996	Randy Barnes	USA	21.62 m/70 ft $11\frac{1}{4}$ in

Discus

Year	Name	Country	Result
1960	Al Oerter	USA	59.18 m/194 ft 2 in
1964	Al Oerter	USA	61.00 m/200 ft $1\frac{1}{2}$ in
1968	Al Oerter	USA	64.78 m/212 ft $6\frac{1}{2}$ in
1972	Ludvik Daněk	Czechoslovakia	64.40 m/211 ft 3 in
1976	Mac Wilkins	USA	67.50 m/221 ft 5.4 in
1980	Viktor Rashchupkin	USSR	66.64 m/218 ft 8 in
1984	Rolf Danneburg	West Germany	66.60 m/218 ft 6 in
1988	Jürgen Schult	East Germany	68.82 m/225 ft $9\frac{1}{4}$ in
1992	Romas Ubartas	Lithuania	65.12 m/213 ft $7\frac{3}{4}$ in
1996	Lars Reidel	Germany	69.40 m/227 ft 8 in

Hammer

Year	Name	Country	Result
1960	Vasily Rudenkov	USSR	67.10 m/220 ft $1\frac{5}{8}$ in
1964	Romuald Klim	USSR	69.74 m/228 ft $9\frac{1}{2}$ in
1968	Gyula Zsivótzky	Hungary	73.36 m/240 ft 8 in
1972	Anatoly Bondarchuk	USSR	75.50 m/247 ft 8 in
1976	Yuri Sedykh	USSR	77.52 m/254 ft 4 in
1980	Yuri Sedykh	USSR	81.80 m/268 ft $4\frac{1}{2}$ in
1984	Juha Tiainen	Finland	78.08 m/256 ft 2 in
1988	Sergei Litvinov	USSR	84.80 m/278 ft $2\frac{1}{2}$ in
1992	Andrei Abduvaliyev	Unified Team[1]	82.54 m/270 ft $9\frac{1}{2}$ in
1996	Balazs Kiss	Hungary	81.24 m/266 ft 6 in

Javelin

Year	Name	Country	Result
1960	Viktor Tsibulenko	USSR	84.64 m/277 ft $8\frac{3}{8}$ in
1964	Pauli Nevala	Finland	82.66 m/271 ft $2\frac{1}{2}$ in
1968	Yanis Lusis	USSR	90.10 m/295 ft $7\frac{1}{4}$ in
1972	Klaus Wolfermann	West Germany	90.48 m/296 ft 10 in
1976	Miklos Németh	Hungary	94.58 m/310 ft 4 in
1980	Dainis Kula	USSR	91.20 m/299 ft $2\frac{3}{8}$ in
1984	Arto Härkonen	Finland	86.76 m/284 ft 8 in
1988	Tapio Korjus	Finland	84.28 m/276 ft 6 in
1992	Jan Zelezny	Czechoslovakia	89.66 m/294 ft 2 in
1996	Jan Zelezny	Czech Republic	88.16 m/289 ft 3 in

Decathlon

Year	Name	Country	Result
1960	Rafer Johnson	USA	8392 points
1964	Willi Holdorf	Germany	7887[2] points
1968	Bill Toomey	USA	8193 points
1972	Nikolai Avilov	USSR	8454 points
1976	Bruce Jenner	USA	8617 points
1980	Daley Thompson	Great Britain	8495 points
1984	Daley Thompson	Great Britain	8798 points
1988	Christan Schenk	East Germany	8488[1] points
1992	Robert Zmelic	Czechoslovakia	8611 points
1996	Dan O'Brien	USA	8824 points

4 × 100 m Relay

Year	Country	Result
1960	Germany	39.50
1964	USA	39.00
1968	USA	38.23
1972	USA	38.19
1976	USA	38.33
1980	USSR	38.26
1984	USA	37.83
1988	USSR	38.19
1992	USA	37.40
1996	Canada	37.69

(continued)

Men's Athletics: Olympic Gold Medallists since 1960 (continued)

Year	Country	Time	Year	Country	Time
4 × 400 m Relay					
1960	USA	3:02.20	1980	USSR	3:01.10
1964	USA	3:00.70	1984	USA	2:57.91
1968	USA	3:56.16	1988	USA	2:56.16
1972	Kenya	2:59.80	1992	USA	2:55.74
1976	USA	2:58.65	1996	USA	2:55.99

[1] Commonwealth of Independent States plus Georgia.
[1] New points systems were introduced before the 1964 and 1988 Games.

Women's Athletics: Olympic Gold Medallists since 1960

Year	Name	Country	Result	Year	Name	Country	Result
100 m				**1,500 m**			
1960	Wilma Rudolph	USA	11.00	1972	Lyudmila Bragina	USSR	4:01.40
1964	Wyomia Tyus	USA	11.40	1976	Tatyana Kazankina	USSR	4:05.48
1968	Wyomia Tyus	USA	11.08	1980	Tatyana Kazankina	USSR	3:56.60
1972	Renate Stecher	East Germany	11.07	1984	Gabriella Dorio	Italy	4:03.25
1976	Annegret Richter	West Germany	11.08	1988	Paula Ivan	Romania	3:53.96
1980	Lyudmila Kondratyeva	USSR	11.06	1992	Hassiba Boulmerka	Algeria	3:55.30
1984	Evelyn Ashford	USA	10.97	1996	Svetlana Masterkova	Russia	4:00.83
1988	Florence Griffith-Joyner	USA	10.54				
1992	Gail Devers	USA	10.82	**3,000 m**[1]			
1996	Gail Devers	USA	10.94	1984	Maricica Puica	Romania	8:35.96
				1988	Tatyana Samolenko	USSR	8:26.53
200 m				1992	Yelena Romanova	Unified Team[2]	8:46.04
1960	Wilma Rudolph	USA	24.00				
1964	Edith Maguire	USA	23.00	**5,000 m**			
1968	Irena Szewińska	Poland	22.58	1996	Wang Junxia	China	14:59.88
1972	Renate Stecher	East Germany	22.40				
1976	Bärbel Eckert	East Germany	22.37	**10,000 m**			
1980	Bärbel Wöckel	East Germany	22.03	1988	Olga Bondarenko	USSR	31:05.21
1984	Valerie Brisco-Hooks	USA	21.81	1992	Derartu Tulu	Ethiopia	31:06.02
1988	Florence Griffith-Joyner	USA	21.34	1996	Fernanda Ribeiro	Portugal	31:01.63
1992	Gwen Torrence	USA	21.81				
1996	Marie-José Pérec	France	22.12	**Marathon**			
				1984	Joan Benoit	USA	2h 24.52
400 m				1988	Rosa Mota	Portugal	2h 25.40
1964	Betty Cuthbert	Australia	52.00	1992	Valentina Yegorova	Unified Team[2]	2h 32.41
1968	Colette Besson	France	52.03	1996	Fatuma Roba	Ethiopia	2h 26:05
1972	Monika Zehrt	East Germany	51.08				
1976	Irena Szewińska	Poland	49.29	**100 m Hurdles**			
1980	Marita Koch	East Germany	48.88	1960	Irina Press	USSR	10.80
1984	Valerie Brisco-Hooks	USA	48.83	1964	Karin Balzer	Germany	10.50
1988	Olga Brzygina	USSR	48.65	1968	Maureen Caird	Australia	10.30
1992	Marie-José Pérec	France	48.83	1972	Annelie Ehrhardt	East Germany	12.59
1996	Marie-José Pérec	France	48.25	1976	Johanna Schaller	East Germany	12.77
				1980	Vera Komisova	USSR	12.56
800 m				1984	Benita Fitzgerald-Brown	USA	12.84
1960	Lyudmila Shevtsova	USSR	2:04.30	1988	Yordanka Donkova	Bulgaria	12.38
1964	Ann Packer	Great Britain	2:01.10	1992	Paraskevi Patoulidou	Greece	12.64
1968	Madeline Manning	USA	2:00.90	1996	Lyudmila Engquist	Sweden	12.58
1972	Hildegard Falck	West Germany	1:58.55				
1976	Tatyana Kazankina	USSR	1:54.94	**400 m Hurdles**			
1980	Nadyezda Olizarenko	USSR	1:53.42	1984	Nawal El Moutawakel	Morocco	54.61
1984	Doina Melinte	Romania	1:57.60	1988	Debra Flintoff-King	Australia	53.17
1988	Sigrun Wodars	East Germany	1:56.10	1992	Sally Gunnell	Great Britain	53.23
1992	Ellen van Langen	Netherlands	1:55.54	1996	Deon Hemmings	Jamaica	52.82
1996	Svetlana Masterkova	Russia	1:57.73				

Women's Athletics: Olympic Gold Medallists since 1960 (*continued*)

Year	Name	Country	Result
10 km Walk			
1992	Chen Yueling	China	44:32
1996	Yelena Nikolayeva	Russia	41:49
Triple Jump			
1996	Inessa Kravets	Ukraine	15.33 m/50 ft $3\frac{1}{2}$ in
High Jump			
1960	Iolanda Balas	Romania	1.85 m/6 ft $\frac{3}{4}$ in
1964	Iolanda Balas	Romania	1.90 m/6 ft $2\frac{3}{4}$ in
1968	Miloslava Režková	Czechoslovakia	1.82 m/5 ft $11\frac{1}{2}$ in
1972	Ulrike Meyfarth	West Germany	1.92 m/6 ft 4 in
1976	Rosemarie Ackermann	East Germany	1.93 m/6 ft $3\frac{3}{4}$ in
1980	Sara Simeoni	Italy	1.97 m/6 ft $5\frac{1}{2}$ in
1984	Ulrike Meyfarth	West Germany	2.02 m/6 ft $7\frac{1}{2}$ in
1988	Louise Ritter	USA	2.03 m/6 ft 8 in
1992	Heike Henkel	Germany	2.02 m/6 ft $7\frac{1}{2}$ in
1996	Stefka Kostadinova	Bulgaria	2.05 m/6 ft $8\frac{3}{4}$ in
Long Jump			
1960	Vera Krepkina	USSR	6.37 m/20 ft $10\frac{3}{4}$ in
1964	Mary Rand	Great Britain	6.76 m/22 ft $2\frac{1}{4}$ in
1968	Viorica Viscopoleanu	Romania	6.82 m/22 ft $4\frac{1}{2}$ in
1972	Heidemarie Rosendahl	West Germany	6.78 m/22 ft 3 in
1976	Angela Voigt	East Germany	6.72 m/22 ft $\frac{3}{4}$ in
1980	Tatyana Kolpakova	USSR	7.06 m/23 ft 2 in
1984	Anisoara Stanciu	Romania	6.96 m/22 ft 10 in
1988	Jackie Joyner-Kersee	USA	7.40 m/24 ft $3\frac{1}{2}$ in
1992	Heike Dreschler	Germany	7.14 m/23 ft $5\frac{1}{4}$ in
1996	Chioma Ajunwa	Nigeria	7.12 m/23 ft $4\frac{1}{2}$ in
Shot Put			
1960	Tamara Press	USSR	17.32 m/56 ft 10 in
1964	Tamara Press	USSR	18.14 m/59 ft $6\frac{1}{4}$ in
1968	Margitta Gummel	East Germany	19.61 m/64 ft 4 in
1972	Nadyezda Chizhova	USSR	21.03 m/69 ft 0 in
1976	Ivanka Christova	Bulgaria	21.16 m/69 ft $5\frac{1}{4}$ in
1980	Ilona Slupianek	East Germany	22.41 m/73 ft $6\frac{1}{4}$ in
1984	Claudia Losch	West Germany	20.48 m/67 ft $2\frac{1}{4}$ in
1988	Natalya Lisovskaya	USSR	22.24 m/72 ft $11\frac{1}{2}$ in
1992	Svetlana Krivelyova	Unified Team[2]	21.06 m/69 ft $1\frac{1}{2}$ in
1996	Astrid Kumbernuss	Germany	20.56 m/67 ft $5\frac{1}{2}$ in

Year	Name	Country	Result
Discus			
1960	Nina Ponomaryeva (Romashkova)	USSR	55.10 m/180 ft $8\frac{1}{4}$ in
1964	Tamara Press	USSR	57.25 m/187 ft 10 in
1968	Lia Manoliu	Romania	58.28 m/191 ft 2 in
1972	Faina Melnik	USSR	66.62 m/218 ft 7 in
1976	Evelin Schlaak	East Germany	69.00 m/226 ft 4 in
1980	Evelin Jahl	East Germany	69.96 m/229 ft 6 in
1984	Ria Stalman	Netherlands	65.36 m/214 ft 5 in
1988	Martina Hellmann	East Germany	72.30 m/237 ft $2\frac{1}{4}$ in
1992	Martiza Marten	Cuba	70.06 m/222 ft 10 in
1996	Ilke Wyludda	Germany	69.66 m/228 ft 6 in
Javelin			
1960	Elvira Ozolina	USSR	55.98 m/183 ft 8 in
1964	Mihaela Penes	Romania	60.54 m/198 ft $7\frac{1}{2}$ in
1968	Angéla Németh	Hungary	60.36 m/198 ft $\frac{1}{2}$ in
1972	Ruth Fuchs	East Germany	63.88 m/209 ft 7 in
1976	Ruth Fuchs	East Germany	65.94 m/216 ft 4 in
1980	Maria Colon	Cuba	68.40 m/224 ft 5 in
1984	Tessa Sanderson	Great Britain	69.56 m/228 ft 2 in
1988	Petra Felke	East Germany	74.68 m/245 ft 0 in
1992	Silke Renk	Germany	68.34 m/224 ft $2\frac{1}{2}$ in
1996	Heli Ratanen	Finland	67.94 m/222 ft 11 in
Pentathlon[3]			
1964	Irina Press	USSR	5246 points
1968	Ingrid Becker	West Germany	5098 points
1972	Mary Peters	Great Britain	4801 points
1976	Siegrun Siegl	East Germany	4745 points
1980	Nadyezda Tkachenko	USSR	5083 points
Heptathlon			
1984	Glynis Nunn	Australia	6390 points
1988	Jackie Joyner-Kersee	USA	7291 points
1992	Jackie Joyner-Kersee	USA	7044 points
1996	Ghada Shouaa	Syria	6780 points
4 × 100 m Relay			
1960		USA	44.50
1964		Poland	43.60
1968		USA	42.87
1972		West Germany	42.81
1976		East Germany	42.55
1980		East Germany	41.60
1984		USA	41.65
1988		USA	41.98
1992		USA	42.11
1996		USA	41.95
4 × 400 m Relay			
1972		East Germany	3:23.00
1976		East Germany	3:19.23
1980		USSR	3:20.20
1984		USA	3:18.29
1988		USSR	2:15.18
1992		Unified Team[2]	3:20.20
1996		USA	3:20.91

[1] Replaced by 5,000 metres in 1996.
[2] Commonweath of Independent States plus Georgia.
[3] Replaced by Heptathlon in 1984.

Badminton: Olympic Gold Medallists

1996

Category	Name	Country
Men's singles	Poul-Erik Hoyer-Larsen	Denmark
Men's doubles	Rexy Mainaky and Ricky Subagja	Indonesia
Women's singles	Bang Soo-hyun	South Korea
Women's doubles	Ge Fei and Gu Jun	China
Mixed doubles	Kim Dong-moon and Gil Young-ah	South Korea

Baseball: Olympic Medallists

Baseball was introduced as a medal sport in 1992.

Year	Gold	Silver	Bronze
1992	Cuba	Taiwan	Japan
1996	Cuba	Japan	USA

Basketball: Olympic Medallists since 1980

Year	Gold	Silver	Bronze	Year	Gold	Silver	Bronze
Men				**Women**			
1980	Yugoslavia	Italy	USSR	1980	USSR	Bulgaria	Yugoslavia
1984	USA	Spain	Yugoslavia	1984	USA	South Korea	China
1988	USSR	Yugoslavia	USA	1988	USA	Yugoslavia	USSR
1992	USA	Croatia	Lithuania	1992	Unified Team[1]	China	USA
1996	USA	Yugoslavia	Lithuania	1996	USA	Brazil	Australia

[1] Commonwealth of Independent States plus Georgia

Beach Volleyball: Olympic Medallists

Beach volleyball was introduced to the Olympics in 1996.

Year	Gold		Silver		Bronze	
	Name	Country	Name	Country	Name	Country
Men						
1996	Karch Kiraly and Kent Steffes	USA	Mike Dodd and Mike Whitmarsh	USA	John Child and Mark Heese	Canada
Women						
1996	Sandra Pires and Jackie Silva	Brazil	Monica Rodrigues and Adriana Samuel	Brazil	Natalie Cook and Kerri Ann Pottharst	Australia

Boxing: Olympic Gold Medallists

1996

Year	Name	Country	Year	Name	Country
Super Heavyweight (Over 91 kg/201 lb)			***Light Welterweight (Up to 63.5 kg/140 lb)***		
1996	Vladimir Klichko	Ukraine	1996	Hector Vinent	Cuba
Heavyweight (Since 1984 up to 91 kg/200.5 lb)			***Lightweight (Since 1952 up to 60 kg/132 lb)***		
1996	Felix Savon	Cuba	1996	Hocine Soltani	Algeria
Light Heavyweight (Since 1952 up to 81 kg/178.5 lb)			***Featherweight (Since 1952 up to 57 kg/126 lb)***		
1996	Vasili Jirov	Kyrgyzstan	1996	Somluck Kamsing	Thailand
Middleweight (Since 1952 up to 75 kg/165 lb)			***Bantamweight (Since 1948 up to 54 kg/119 lb)***		
1996	Ariel Hernández	Cuba	1996	István Kovacs	Hungary
Light Middleweight (Up to 71 kg/157 lb)			***Flyweight (Since 1948 up to 51 kg/112 lb)***		
1996	David Reid	USA	1996	Maikro Romero	Cuba
Welterweight (Since 1948 up to 67 kg/148 lb)			***Light Flyweight (Up to 48 kg/105.8 lb)***		
1996	Oleg Saitov	Russia	1996	Daniel Bojilov	Bulgaria

Kayak/Canoe: Olympic Gold Medallists

1996

Category	Name	Country	Category	Name	Country
Men			Canoe sprint 1,000 m pairs	Andreas Dittmer and Gunar Kirchbach	Germany
Kayak sprint 500 m singles	Antonio Rossi	Italy	Canoe slalom singles	Michal Martikan	Slovakia
Kayak sprint 1,000 m singles	Knut Holmann	Norway	Canoe slalom pairs	Frank Adisson and Wilfrid Forgues	France
Kayak sprint 500 m pairs	Kay Bluhm and Torsten Gutsche	Germany			
Kayak sprint 1,000 m pairs	Antonio Rossi and Daniele Scarpa	Italy	**Women**		
Kayak sprint 1,000 m fours		Germany	Kayak sprint 500 m singles	Rita Koban	Hungary
Kayak slalom singles	Oliver Fix	Germany	Kayak sprint 1,000 m pairs	Angneta Andersson and Susanne Gunnarsson	Sweden
Canoe sprint 500 m singles	Martin Doktor	Czech Republic	Kayak sprint 1,000 m fours		Germany
Canoe sprint 1,000 m singles	Martin Doktor	Czech Republic	Kayak slalom singles	Stepanka Hilgertová	Czech Republic
Canoe sprint 500 m pairs	Csaba Horvath and György Kolonics	Hungary			

Cycling: Olympic Gold Medallists

1996

Category	Name	Country	Category	Name	Country
Men			**Women**		
Road			*Road*		
Individual road race (225 km)	Pascal Richard	Switzerland	Individual road race (106 km)	Jeannie Longo-Ciprelli	France
Individual time trial (52 km)	Miguel Indurain	Spain	Individual time trial (26 km)	Zulfia Zabirova	Russia
Track			*Track*		
1 km time trial	Florian Rousseau	France	Individual match sprint	Felicia Ballanger	France
Individual match sprint	Jens Fiedler	Germany	3,000 m individual pursuit	Antonella Belluti	Italy
4,000 m individual pursuit	Andrea Collinelli	Italy	Individual points race (25 km)	Nathalie Even-Lancien	France
4,000 m team pursuit		France			
Individual points race (40 km)	Silvio Martinello	Italy	*Cross-Country*		
			Mountain bike (32 km)	Paola Pezzo	Italy
Cross-Country					
Mountain bike (47.7 km)	Bart Jan Brentjens	Netherlands			

Diving: Olympic Gold Medallists since 1980

Year	Name	Country	Year	Name	Country
Men			**Women**		
Springboard Diving			*Springboard Diving*		
1980	Alexsandr Portnov	USSR	1980	Irina Kalinina	USSR
1984	Greg Louganis	USA	1984	Sylvie Bernier	Canada
1988	Greg Louganis	USA	1988	Gao Min	China
1992	Mark Lenzi	USA	1992	Gao Min	China
1996	Ni Xiong	China	1996	Fu Mingxia	China
Platform Diving			*Platform Diving*		
1980	Falk Hoffmann	East Germany	1980	Martina Jäschke	East Germany
1984	Greg Louganis	USA	1984	Zhou Jihong	China
1988	Greg Louganis	USA	1988	Xu Yanmei	China
1992	Sun Shuwei	China	1992	Fu Mingxia	China
1996	Dimitri Sautin	Russia	1996	Fu Mingxia	China

Fencing: Olympic Gold Medallists

Olympic gold medallists automatically become world champions.

1996

Category	Name	Country	Category	Name	Country
Men			*Women*		
Foil	Alessandro Puccini	Italy	Foil	Laura Badea	Romania
Epée	Aleksandr Beketov	Russia	Epée	Laura Flessel	France
Sabre	Stanislav Pozdniakov	Russia	Team foil		Italy
Team foil		Russia	Team epée		France
Team epée		Italy			
Team sabre		Russia			

Football: Olympic Medallists since 1960

The USA won the inaugural women's Olympic soccer title, defeating China 2–1 in the final before a crowd of 76,481 at Sanford Stadium, Athens, Georgia.

Year	Gold	Silver	Bronze	Year	Gold	Silver	Bronze
Men				1988	USSR	Brazil	West Germany
				1992	Spain	Poland	Ghana
1960	Yugoslavia	Denmark	Hungary	1996	Nigeria	Argentina	Brazil
1964	Hungary	Czechoslovakia	Germany				
1968	Hungary	Bulgaria	Japan	*Women*			
1972	Poland	Hungary	East Germany/USSR[1]				
1976	East Germany	Poland	USSR	1996	USA	China	Norway
1980	Czechoslovakia	East Germany	USSR				
1984	France	Brazil	Yugoslavia	[1] Tie after overtime played.			

Gymnastics: Olympic Gold Medallists

1996

Category	Name	Country	Category	Name	Country
Men			*Women*		
Team		Russia	Floor	Lilia Podkopayeva	Ukraine
Individual combined exercises	Li Xiaoshuang	China	Team		USA
Floor	Ionnis Melissanidis	Greece	Individual combined exercises	Lilia Podkopayeva	Ukraine
Pommel	Li Donghua	Switzerland	Vault	Simona Amanar	Romania
Rings	Yuri Chechi	Italy	Asymmetric bars	Svetlana Chorkina	Russia
Vault	Alexei Nemov	Russia	Beam	Shannon Miller	USA
Parallel bars	Rustam Sharipov	Ukraine	Rhythmic Gymnastics		
High bar	Andreas Wecker	Germany	Group		Spain
			Individual	Ekaterina Serebranskaya	Ukraine

Gymnastics: Men's Individual Olympic Gold Medallists since 1960

Year	Name	Country	Year	Name	Country
1960	Boris Shakhlin	USSR	1980	Aleksandr Ditiatin	USSR
1964	Yukio Endo	Japan	1984	Koji Gushiken	Japan
1968	Sawao Kato	Japan	1988	Vladimir Artemov	USSR
1972	Sawao Kato	Japan	1992	Vitali Shcherbo	Unified Team[1]
1976	Nikolai Andrianov	USSR	1996	Li Xiaoshuang	China

[1] Commonwealth of Independent States plus Georgia.

Gymnastics: Men's Team Olympic Gold Medallists since 1960

Year	Country	Year	Country
1960	Japan	1980	USSR
1964	Japan	1984	USA
1968	Japan	1988	USSR
1972	Japan	1992	Unified Team[1]
1976	Japan	1996	Russia

[1] Commonwealth of Independent States plus Georgia.

Gymnastics: Women's Individual Olympic Gold Medallists since 1960

Year	Name	Country	Year	Name	Country
1960	Larissa Latynina	USSR	1980	Elena Davidova	USSR
1964	Vera Caslavska	Czechoslovakia	1984	Mary Lou Retton	USA
1968	Vera Caslavska	Czechoslovakia	1988	Elena Chouchounova	USSR
1972	Liudmila Tourischeva	USSR	1992	Tatiana Gutsu	Unified Team[1]
1976	Nadia Comaneci	Romania	1996	Lilia Podkopaieva	Ukraine

[1] Commonwealth of Independent States plus Georgia.

Gymnastics: Women's Team Olympic Gold Medallists since 1960

Year	Country	Year	Country
1960	USSR	1980	USSR
1964	USSR	1984	Romania
1968	USSR	1988	USSR
1972	USSR	1992	Unified Team[1]
1976	USSR	1996	USA

[1] Commonwealth of Independent States plus Georgia.

Handball: Olympic Gold Medallists

Handball was introduced in 1936 as an 11-a-side outdoor game. It was reintroduced in 1972 as a 7-a-side indoor game.

Year	Country	Year	Country
Men		**Women**	
1936	Germany	1976	USSR
1972	Yugoslavia	1980	USSR
1976	USSR	1984	Yugoslavia
1980	East Germany	1988	South Korea
1984	Yugoslavia	1992	South Korea
1988	USSR	1996	Denmark
1992	Unified Team[1]		
1996	Croatia		

[1] Commonwealth of Independent States plus Georgia.

Hockey: Olympic Medallists since 1980

Year	Gold	Silver	Bronze
Men			
1980	India	Spain	USSR
1984	Pakistan	West Germany	Great Britain
1988	Great Britain	West Germany	Netherlands
1992	Germany	Australia	Pakistan
1996	Netherlands	Spain	Australia
Women			
1980	Zimbabwe	Czechoslovakia	USSR
1984	Netherlands	West Germany	USA
1988	Australia	South Korea	Netherlands
1992	Spain	Germany	Great Britain
1996	Australia	South Korea	Netherlands

Judo: Olympic Gold Medallists

1996

Category	Name	Country	Category	Name	Country
Men			*Women*		
60 kg/132 lb	Tadahiro Nomura	Japan	48 kg/106 lb	Kye Sun-hi	North Korea
65 kg/143 lb	Udo Quellmalz	Germany	52 kg/115 lb	Marie-Claire Restoux	France
71 kg/157 lb	Kenzo Nakamura	Japan	56 kg/123 lb	Driulis Gonzalez	Cuba
78 kg/172 lb	Djamel Bouras	France	61 kg/134 lb	Yuko Emoto	Japan
86 kg/190 lb	Jeon Ki-young	South Korea	66 kg/146 lb	Cho Min-sun	South Korea
95 kg/209 lb	Pawél Nastula	Poland	72 kg/159 lb	Ulla Werbrouck	Belgium
>95 kg/>209 lb	David Douillet	France	>72 kg/>159 lb	Sun Fuming	China

Modern Pentathlon: Olympic Gold Medallists since 1980

(– = not applicable.)

Year	Country
1980	USSR
1984	Italy
1988	Hungary
1992	Poland
1996[1]	–

[1] Event not held in 1996.

Rowing: Olympic Gold Medallists

1996

Category	Name	Country
Men		
Single sculls	Xeno Müller	Switzerland
Double sculls	Davide Tizzano and Agostino Abbagnale	Italy
Lightweight double sculls	Markus Gier and Michael Gier	Switzerland
Quad sculls		Germany
Coxless pairs	Steve Redgrave and Matthew Pinsent	Great Britain
Coxless fours		Australia
Lightweight coxless fours		Denmark
Eights		Netherlands
Women		
Single sculls	Yekaterina Khodotovich	Belarus
Double sculls	Marnie McBean and Kathleen Heddle	Canada
Lightweight double sculls	Constanta Burcica and Camelia Macoviciuc	Romania
Quad sculls		Germany
Coxless pairs	Megan Still and Kathy Slatter	Australia
Eights		Romania

Shooting: Olympic Gold Medallists

1996

Category	Name	Country
Men		
25 m rapid pistol	Ralf Schumann	Germany
50 m free pistol	Boris Kokorev	Russia
10 m air pistol	Roberto di Donna	Italy
10 m air rifle	Artem Khadzhibekov	Russia
50 m free rifle three positions	Jean-Pierre Amat	France
50 m free rifle prone	Christian Klees	Germany
10 m running target	Yang Ling	China
Skeet	Ennio Falco	Italy
Trap	Michael Diamond	Australia
Double trap	Russell Mark	Australia
Women		
25 m sport pistol	Li Duihon	China
10 m air pistol	Olga Klochneva	Russia
10 m air rifle	Renata Mauer	Poland
50 m rifle three positions	Aleksandra Ivosev	Yugoslavia
Double trap	Kim Rhode	USA

Softball: Olympic Medallists

Softball was introduced as a medal sport for women in 1996.

Year	Gold	Silver	Bronze
1996	USA	China	Australia

Men's Swimming: Olympic Gold Medallists since 1980

Year	Name	Country	Time
50 m Freestyle			
1988	Matt Biondi	USA	22.14
1992	Aleksandr Popov	Unified Team[1]	21.91
1996	Aleksandr Popov	Russia	22.13
100 m Freestyle			
1980	Jörg Woithe	East Germany	50.40
1984	Ambrose Gaines	USA	49.80
1988	Matt Biondi	USA	48.63
1992	Aleksandr Popov	Unified Team[1]	49.02
1996	Aleksandr Popov	Russia	48.74
200 m Freestyle			
1980	Sergey Kopliakov	USSR	1:49.81
1984	Michael Gross	West Germany	1:47.44
1988	Duncan Armstrong	Australia	1:47.25
1992	Yevgeni Sadovyi	Unified Team[1]	1:46.70
1996	Danyon Loader	New Zealand	1:47.63
400 m Freestyle			
1980	Vladimir Salnikov	USSR	3:51.31
1984	George DiCarlo	USA	3:51.23
1988	Uwe Dassler	East Germany	3:46.95
1992	Yevgeni Sadovyi	Unified Team[1]	3:45.00
1996	Danyon Loader	New Zealand	3:47.97
1,500 m Freestyle			
1980	Vladimir Salnikov	USSR	14:58.27
1984	Michael O'Brien	USA	15:05.20
1988	Vladimir Salnikov	USSR	15:00.40
1992	Kieren Perkins	Australia	14:43.48
1996	Kieren Perkins	Australia	14:56.40
100 m Breaststroke			
1980	Duncan Goodhew	Great Britain	1:03.34
1984	Steve Lundquist	USA	1:01.65
1988	Adrian Moorhouse	Great Britain	1:02.04
1992	Nelson Diebel	USA	1:01.50
1996	Fred Deburghgraeve	Belgium	1:00.65
200 m Breaststroke			
1980	Robertas Zhulpa	USSR	2:15.85
1984	Victor Davis	Canada	2:13.34
1988	József Szabó	Hungary	2:13.52
1992	Mike Barrowman	USA	2:10.16
1996	Norbert Rozsa	Hungary	2:12.57
100 m Backstroke			
1980	Bengt Baron	Sweden	56.53
1984	Richard Carey	USA	55.79
1988	Daichi Suzuki	Japan	55.05
1992	Mark Tewksbury	Canada	53.98
1996	Jeff Rouse	USA	54.10

Year	Name	Country	Time
200 m Backstroke			
1980	Sándor Wladár	Hungary	2:01.93
1984	Richard Carey	USA	2:00.23
1988	Igor Polianski	USSR	1:59.37
1992	Martin Lopez-Zubero	Spain	1:58.47
1996	Brad Bridgewater	USA	1:58.54
100 m Butterfly			
1980	Pär Arvidsson	Sweden	54.92
1984	Michael Gross	West Germany	53.08
1988	Anthony Nesty	Suriname	53.00
1992	Pablo Morales	USA	53.32
1996	Denis Pankratov	Russia	52.27
200 m Butterfly			
1980	Sergey Fesenko	USSR	1:59.76
1984	Jon Sieben	Australia	1:57.04
1988	Michael Gross	West Germany	1:56.94
1992	Mel Stewart	USA	1:56.26
1996	Denis Pankratov	Russia	1:56.51
200 m Individual Medley			
1984	Alex Baumann	Canada	2:01.42
1988	Tamás Darnyi	Hungary	2:00.17
1992	Tamás Darnyi	Hungary	2:00.76
1996	Attila Czene	Hungary	1:59.91
400 m Individual Medley			
1980	Alexsandr Sidorenko	USSR	4:22.89
1984	Alex Baumann	Canada	4:17.41
1988	Tamás Darnyi	Hungary	4:14.75
1992	Tamás Darnyi	Hungary	4:14.23
1996	Tom Dolan	USA	4:14.90

4 × 100 m Freestyle Relay		
Year	Country	Time
1980	East Germany	3:42.71
1984	USA	3:43.43
1988	East Germany	3:40.63
1992	USA	3:39.46
1996	USA	3:39.29

4 × 200 m Freestyle Relay		
1996[2]	USA	7:59.87

4 × 100 m Medley Relay		
1980	East Germany	4:06.67
1984	USA	4:08.34
1988	East Germany	4:03.74
1992	USA	4:02.54
1996	USA	4:02.88

[1] Commonwealth of Independent States plus Georgia.
[2] Event first held in 1996.

Women's Swimming: Olympic Gold Medallists since 1980

Year	Name	Country	Time
50 m Freestyle			
1988	Kristin Otto	East Germany	25.49
1992	Yang Wenyi	China	24.79
1996	Amy Van Dyken	USA	24.87
100 m Freestyle			
1980	Barbara Krause	East Germany	54.79
1984	Carrie Steinseifer/ Nancy Hogshead (tie)	USA	55.92
1988	Kristin Otto	East Germany	54.93
1992	Zhuang Yong	China	54.64
1996	Le Jingyi	China	54.50
200 m Freestyle			
1980	Barbara Krause	East Germany	1:58.33
1984	Mary Wayte	USA	1:59.23
1988	Heike Friedrich	East Germany	1:57.65
1992	Nicole Haislett	USA	1:57.90
1996	Claudia Poll	Costa Rica	1:58.16
400 m Freestyle			
1980	Ines Diers	East Germany	4:08.76
1984	Tiffany Cohen	USA	4:07.10
1988	Janet Evans	USA	4:03.85
1992	Dagmar Hase	Germany	4:07.18
1996	Michelle Smith	Ireland, Republic of	4:07.25
800 m Freestyle			
1980	Michelle Ford	Australia	8:28.90
1984	Tiffany Cohen	USA	8:24.95
1988	Janet Evans	USA	8:20.20
1992	Janet Evans	USA	8:25.52
1996	Brooke Bennett	USA	8:27.89
100 m Breaststroke			
1980	Ute Geweniger	East Germany	1:10.22
1984	Petra Van Staveren	Netherlands	1:09.88
1988	Tania Dangalakova	Bulgaria	1:07.95
1992	Elena Rudkovskaia	Unified Team[1]	1:08.00
1996	Penny Heyns	South Africa	1:07.73
200 m Breaststroke			
1980	Lina Kachushite	USSR	2:29.54
1984	Anne Ottenbrite	Canada	2:30.38
1988	Silke Hörner	East Germany	2:26.71
1992	Kyoko Iwasaki	Japan	2:26.65
1996	Penny Heyns	South Africa	2:25.41
100 m Backstroke			
1980	Rica Reinisch	East Germany	1:00.86
1984	Theresa Andrews	USA	1:02.55
1988	Kristin Otto	East Germany	1:00.89
1992	Krisztina Egerszegi	Hungary	1:00.68
1996	Beth Botsford	USA	1:01.19

Year	Name	Country	Time
200 m Backstroke			
1980	Rica Reinisch	East Germany	2:11.77
1984	Jolanda De Rover	Netherlands	2:12.38
1988	Krisztina Egerszegi	Hungary	2:09.29
1992	Krisztina Egerszegi	Hungary	2:07.06
1996	Krisztina Egerszegi	Hungary	2:07.83
100 m Butterfly			
1980	Caren Metschuck	East Germany	1:00.42
1984	Mary Meagher	USA	59.26
1988	Kristin Otto	East Germany	59.00
1992	Qian Hong	China	58.62
1996	Amy Van Dyken	USA	59.13
200 m Butterfly			
1980	Ines Geissler	East Germany	2:10.44
1984	Mary Meagher	USA	2:06.90
1988	Kathleen Nord	East Germany	2:09.51
1992	Summer Sanders	USA	2:08.67
1996	Susan O'Neill	Australia	2:07.76
200 m Individual Medley			
1984	Tracy Caulkins	USA	2:12.64
1988	Daniela Hunger	East Germany	2:12.59
1992	Li Chin	China	2:11.65
1996	Michelle Smith	Ireland, Republic of	2:13.93
400 m Individual Medley			
1980	Petra Schneider	East Germany	4:36.29
1984	Tracy Caulkins	USA	4:39.24
1988	Janet Evans	USA	4:37.76
1992	Krisztina Egerszegi	Hungary	4:36.54
1996	Michelle Smith	Ireland, Republic of	4:39.29

4 × 100 m Freestyle Relay

Year	Country	Time
1984	USA	3:19.03
1988	USA	3:16.53
1992	USA	3:16.74
1996	USA	3:15.41

4 × 200 m Freestyle Relay

Year	Country	Time
1976	USSR	7:23.22
1980	USA	7:23.50
1984	USA	7:15.69
1988	USA	7:12.51
1992	USA	7:11.95
1996	USA	7:14.84

4 × 100 m Medley Relay

Year	Country	Time
1976	USA	3:42.22
1980	Australia	3:45.70
1984	USA	3:39.30
1988	USA	3:36.93
1992	USA	3:36.93
1996	USA	3:34.84

[1] Commonwealth of Independent States plus Georgia.

Table Tennis: Olympic Gold Medallists since 1992

Year	Name	Country
Men		
Singles		
1992	Jan-Ove Waldner	Sweden
1996	Liu Guoliang	China
Doubles		
1992	Lu Lin and Wang Tao	China
1996	Kong Linghui and Liu Guoliang	China
Women		
Singles		
1992	Deng Yaping	China
1996	Deng Yaping	China
Doubles		
1992	Deng Yaping and Qiao Hong	China
1996	Deng Yaping and Qiao Hong	China

Volleyball: Olympic Medallists since 1980

Year	Gold	Silver	Bronze
Men			
1980	USSR	Bulgaria	Romania
1984	USA	Brazil	Italy
1988	USA	USSR	Argentina
1992	Brazil	Netherlands	USA
1996	Netherlands	Italy	Yugoslavia
Women			
1980	USSR	East Gemany	Bulgaria
1984	China	USA	Japan
1988	USSR	Peru	China
1992	Cuba	Unified Team[1]	USA

[1] Commonwealth of Independent States plus Georgia.

Weightlifting: Olympic Gold Medallists

1996

Category	Name	Country	Weight
54 kg/119 lb	Halil Mutlu	Turkey	287.5 kg/632.5 lb
59 kg/130 lb	Tang Ningsheng	China	307.5 kg/677.75 lb
64 kg/141 lb	Naim Suleymanoglu	Turkey	335.0 kg/738.50 lb
70 kg/154 lb	Zhan Xugang	China	357.5 kg/786.5 lb
76 kg/168 lb	Pablo Lara	Cuba	367.5 kg/807.5 lb
83 kg/183 lb	Pyrros Dimas	Greece	392.5 kg/863.5 lb
91 kg/201 lb	Aleksei Petrov	Russia	402.5 kg/885.5 lb
99 kg/201 lb	Kakhi Kakhiashvili	Greece	420.0 kg/925.75 lb
108 kg/238 lb	Timor Taimazov	Ukraine	430.0 kg/946 lb
>108 kg/>238 lb	Andrei Chermerkin	Russia	457.5 kg/1008 lb

Tennis: Olympic Gold Medallists since 1988

Tennis was reintroduced as a medal sport in 1988 after an absence of 64 years.

Year	Name	Country
Men		
Singles		
1988	Miloslav Mecir	Czechoslovakia
1992	Marc Rosset	Switzerland
1996	Andre Agassi	USA
Doubles		
1988	Ken Flack and Robert Seguso	USA
1992	Boris Becker and Michael Stich	Germany
1996	Todd Woodbridge and Mark Woodforde	Australia
Women		
Singles		
1988	Steffi Graf	West Germany
1992	Jennifer Capriati	USA
1996	Lindsay Davenport	USA
Doubles		
1988	Pam Shriver and Zina Garrison	USA
1992	Gigi Fernandez and Mary Joe Fernandez	USA
1996	Gigi Fernandez and Mary Joe Fernandez	USA

Water Polo: Olympic Gold Medallists since 1980

Year	Country
1980	USSR
1984	Yugoslavia
1988	Yugoslavia
1992	Italy
1996	Spain

Yachting: Olympic Gold Medallists

1996

Category	Name	Country
Open		
Laser	Robert Scheidt	Brazil
Tornado	Jose Luis Ballester and Fernando Leon	Spain
Star	Torben Grael and Marcelo Ferreira	Brazil
Soling		Germany
Men		
Finn	Mateusz Kusznierewicz	Poland
Mistral	Nikolaos Kaklamanakis	Greece
470	Yevhen Braslavets and Iho Matviyenko	Ukraine
Women		
Europe	Kristine Roug	Denmark
Mistral	Lee Lai-Shan	Hong Kong
470	Begona Via Dufresne and Theresa Zabell	Spain

Wrestling: Olympic Gold Medallists

1996

Category	Name	Country	Category	Name	Country
Greco-Roman			*Freestyle*		
Light flyweight 48 kg/105.8 lb	Sim Kwon Ho	South Korea	Light flyweight 48 kg/105.8 lb	Kim Il	North Korea
Flyweight 52 kg/114.5 lb	Armen Nazarian	Armenia	Flyweight 52 kg/114.5 lb	Valentin Jordanov	Bulgaria
Bantamweight 57 kg/125.5 lb	Iuri Melnichenko	Kazakhstan	Bantamweight 57 kg/125.5 lb	Kendall Cross	USA
Featherweight 62 kg/136.5 lb	Włodzimierz Zawadzki	Poland	Featherweight 62 kg/136.5 lb	Tom Brands	USA
Lightweight 68 kg/149.5 lb	Ryszard Wolny	Poland	Lightweight 68 kg/149.5 lb	Vadim Bogiev	Russia
Welterweight 74 kg/163 lb	Feliberto Ascuy Aguilera	Cuba	Welterweight 74 kg/163 lb	Buvaisa Saitiev	Russia
Middleweight 82 kg/180.5 lb	Hamza Yerlikiya	Turkey	Middleweight 82 kg/180.5 lb	Khadzhimurad Magomedov	Russia
Light heavyweight 90 kg/198 lb	Viacheslav Oleinik	Ukraine	Light heavyweight 90 kg/198 lb	Rasull Khadem Azghadi	Iran
Heavyweight 100 kg/220 lb	Andrzej Wroński	Poland	Heavyweight 100 kg/220 lb	Kurt Angle	USA
Super heavyweight 130 kg/286 lb	Aleksandr Karelin	Russia	Super heavyweight 130 kg/286 lb	Mahmut Demir	Turkey

Winter Olympic Games

Winter Olympic Games Venues

Year	Venue
1924	Chamonix, France
1928	St Moritz, Switzerland
1932	Lake Placid, New York, USA
1936	Garmisch-Partenkirchen, Germany
1948	St Moritz, Switzerland
1952	Oslo, Norway
1956	Cortina d'Ampezzo, Italy
1960	Squaw Valley, Colorado, USA
1964	Innsbruck, Austria
1968	Grenoble, France
1972	Sapporo, Japan
1976	Innsbruck, Austria
1980	Lake Placid, New York, USA
1984	Sarajevo, Yugoslavia
1988	Calgary, Alberta, Canada
1992	Albertville, France
1994	Lillehammer, Norway
1998	Nagano, Japan
2002	Salt Lake City, Utah, USA

Final Winter Olympic Medal Standings

Standings are determined by the number of gold medals then by the number of silver medals rather than the total medals won.

1998

Position	Country	Gold	Silver	Bronze	Total
1	Germany	12	9	8	29
2	Norway	10	10	5	25
3	Russia	9	6	3	18
4	Canada	6	5	4	15
5	USA	6	3	4	13
6	Netherlands	5	4	2	11
7	Japan	5	1	4	10
8	Austria	3	5	9	17
9	South Korea	3	1	2	6
10	Italy	2	6	2	10
11	Finland	2	4	6	12
12	Switzerland	2	2	3	7
13	France	2	1	5	8
14	Czech Republic	1	1	1	3
15	Bulgaria	1	0	0	1
16	China	0	6	2	8
17	Sweden	0	2	1	3
18=	Denmark	0	1	0	1
18=	Ukraine	0	1	0	1
20=	Belarus	0	0	2	2
20=	Kazakhstan	0	0	2	2
22=	Australia	0	0	1	1
22=	Belgium	0	0	1	1
22=	Great Britain	0	0	1	1

Bobsleigh: Olympic Gold Medallists since 1980

Year	Country	Year	Country
Two-Man Bob		**Four-Man Bob**	
1980	Switzerland II	1980	East Germany I
1984	East Germany II	1984	East Germany I
1988	Soviet Union I	1988	Switzerland I
1992	Switzerland I	1992	Austria I
1994	Switzerland I	1994	Germany II
1998	Canada/Italy	1998	Canada

Curling: Olympic Gold Medallists

The curling event was introduced to the Olympic games in the XVIII winter Olympiad at Nagano, Japan in 1998.

Year	Country
Men	
1998	Switzerland
Women	
1998	Canada

Ice Hockey: Olympic Medallists since 1980

This event was first held at the 1920 Summer Games.

Year	Gold	Silver	Bronze
Men			
1980	USA	USSR	Sweden
1984	USSR	Czechoslovakia	Sweden
1988	USSR	Finland	Sweden
1992	Unified Team[1]	Canada	Czechoslovakia
1994	Sweden	Canada	Finland
1998	Czech Republic	Russia	Finland
Women			
1998	USA	Canada	Finland

[1] Commonwealth of Independent States plus Georgia.

Luge Tobogganing: Olympic Gold Medallists since 1980

Year	Name	Country
Men		
1980	Bernhard Glass	East Germany
1984	Paul Hildgartner	Italy
1988	Jens Müller	East Germany
1992	Georg Hackl	Germany
1994	Georg Hackl	Germany
1998	Georg Hackl	Germany
Two-Man		
1980		East Germany
1984		East Germany
1988		East Germany
1992		Germany
1994		Italy
1998		Germany
Women		
1980	Vera Sosulia	USSR
1984	Steffi Martin	East Germany
1988	Steffi Martin-Walter	East Germany
1992	Doris Neuner	Austria
1994	Silke Kraushaar	Germany
1998	Gerda Weissensteiner	Italy

Figure Skating: Olympic Gold Medallists since 1980

Year	Name	Country
Men's Individual		
1980	Robin Cousins	Great Britain
1984	Scot Hamilton	USA
1988	Brian Boitano	USA
1992	Viktor Petrenko	Unified Team[1]
1994	Aleksei Urmanov	Russia
1998	Ilia Kulik	Russia
Women's Individual		
1980	Anett Pötzsch	East Germany
1984	Katarina Witt	East Germany
1988	Katarina Witt	East Germany
1992	Kristi Yamaguchi	USA
1994	Oksana Baiul	Ukraine
1998	Tara Lipinski	USA
Pairs		
1980	Irina Rodnina/Aleksandr Zaitsev	USSR
1984	Elena Valova/Oleg Vasiliev	USSR
1988	Ekaterina Gordeieva/Sergei Grinkov	USSR
1992	Natalia Mishkutienok/Artur Dmitriev	Unified Team[1]
1994	Ekaterina Gordeieva/Sergei Grinkov	Russia
1998	Oksana Kazakova/Artur Dmitriev	Russia
Ice Dance		
1980	Natalia Linichuk/Gennadii Karponosov	USSR
1984	Jayne Torvill/Christopher Dean	Great Britain
1988	Natalia Bestemianova/Andrei Bukin	USSR
1992	Marina Klimova/Sergei Ponomarenko	Unified Team[1]
1994	Oksana Gritschuk/Evgenii Platov	Russia
1998	Oksana Grishuk/Evgenii Platov	Russia

[1] Commonwealth of Independent States plus Georgia.

Speed Skating: Olympic Gold Medallists since 1994

Year	Category	Name	Country
Men			
1994	500 m	Aleksandr Golubiev	Russia
	1,000 m	Dan Jansen	USA
	1,500 m	Johann-Olav Koss	Norway
	5,000 m	Johann-Olav Koss	Norway
	10,000 m	Johann-Olav Koss	Norway
1998	500 m	Hiroyasu Shimizu	Japan
	1,000 m	Ids Postma	Netherlands
	1,500 m	Aadne Sondral	Norway
	5,000 m	Gianni Romme	Netherlands
	10,000 m	Gianni Romme	Netherlands
Women			
1994	500 m	Bonnie Blair	USA
	1,000 m	Bonnie Blair	USA
	1,500 m	Emese Hunyady	Austria
	3,000 m	Svetlana Bazhanova	Russia
	5,000 m	Claudia Pechstein	Germany
1998	500 m	Catriona Lemay-Doan	Canada
	1,000 m	Marianne Timmer	Netherlands
	1,500 m	Marianne Timmer	Netherlands
	3,000 m	Gunda Niemann-Stirnemann	Germany
	5,000 m	Claudia Pechstein	Germany

Freestyle Skiing: Olympic Gold Medallists

Mogul events were introduced in 1992. Aerial events were introduced in 1994.

Year	Name	Country
Men		
Moguls		
1992	Edgar Grospiron	France
1994	Jean-Luc Brassard	Canada
1998	Jonny Moseley	USA
Aerials		
1994	Andreas Schonbachler	Switzerland
1998	Eric Bergoust	USA
Women		
Moguls		
1992	Donna Weinbrecht	USA
1994	Stine Lise Hattestad	Norway
1998	Tae Satoya	Japan
Aerials		
1994	Lina Cherjasova	Uzbekistan
1998	Nikki Stone	USA

Men's Alpine Skiing: Olympic Gold Medallists since 1980

Alpine skiing was introduced to the Olympic Games in 1936.

Year	Name	Country	Year	Name	Country
Alpine Combination (Downhill and Slalom)			1988	Alberto Tomba	Italy
1988	Hubert Strolz	Austria	1992	Alberto Tomba	Italy
1992	Josef Polig	Italy	1994	Markus Wasmeier	Germany
1994	Lasse Kjus	Norway	1998	Hermann Maier	Austria
1998	Mario Reiter	Norway			
			Slalom		
Downhill			1980	Ingemar Stenmark	Sweden
1980	Leonhard Stock	Austria	1984	Phil Mahre	USA
1984	William Johnson	USA	1988	Alberto Tomba	Italy
1988	Pirmin Zurbriggen	Switzerland	1992	Finn-Christian Jagge	Norway
1992	Patrick Ortlieb	Austria	1994	Thomas Stangassinger	Austria
1994	Tommy Moe	USA	1998	Hans-Petter Buraas	Norway
1998	Jean-Luc Crétier	France			
			Super Giant Slalom		
Giant Slalom			1988	Franck Riccad	France
1980	Ingemar Stenmark	Sweden	1992	Kjetil Andre Aamodt	Norway
1984	Max Julen	Switzerland	1994	Markus Wasmeier	Germany
			1998	Hermann Maier	Austria

Women's Alpine Skiing: Olympic Gold Medallists since 1980

Alpine skiing was introduced to the Olympic Games in 1936.

Year	Name	Country
Alpine Combination (Downhill and Slalom)		
1988	Anita Wachter	Austria
1992	Petra Kronberger	Austria
1994	Pernilla Wiberg	Sweden
1998	Katja Seizinger	Germany
Downhill		
1980	Annemarie Moser-Pröll	Austria
1984	Michela Figini	Switzerland
1988	Marina Kiehl	West Germany
1992	Kerrin Lee-Gartner	Canada
1994	Katja Seizinger	Germany
1998	Katja Seizinger	Germany
Giant Slalom		
1980	Hanni Wenzel	Liechtenstein
1984	Debbie Armstrong	USA

Year	Name	Country
1988	Vreni Schneider	Switzerland
1992	Pernilla Wiberg	Sweden
1994	Deborah Compagnoni	Italy
1998	Deborah Compagnoni	Italy
Slalom		
1980	Hanni Wenzel	Liechtenstein
1984	Paoletta Magoni	Italy
1988	Vreni Schneider	Switzerland
1992	Petra Kronberger	Austria
1994	Vreni Schneider	Switzerland
1998	Hilde Gerg	Germany
Super Giant Slalom		
1988	Sigrid Wolf	Austria
1992	Deborah Compagnoni	Italy
1994	Diann Roffe-Steinrotter	USA
1998	Picabo Street	USA

Nordic Skiing: Olympic Gold Medallists

1998

Event	Name	Country
Men		
10 km classical	Björn Dählie	Norway
15 km free/pursuit	Thomas Alsgaard	Norway
30 km classical	Mika Myllyllae	Finland
50 km free	Björn Dählie	Norway
4 × 10 km relay		Norway
Women		
5 km classical	Larissa Lazutina	Russia
10 km free/pursuit	Larissa Lazutina	Russia
15 km classical	Olga Danilova	Russia
30 km[1] free	Julija Tchepalova	Russia
4 × 5 km relay		Russia
Combined		
Individual	Bjarte Vik	Norway
Team		Norway

[1] 20 km prior to the XVIII winter Olympiad at Nagano, Japan, in 1998.

Ski Jumping: Olympic Gold Medallists since 1980

Year	Name	Country
Normal Hill (K90)		
1980	Toni Innauer	Austria
1984	Jens Weissflog	East Germany
1988	Matti Nykänen	Finland
1992	Ernst Vettori	Austria
1994	Espen Bredesen	Norway
1998	Jani Soininen	Finland
Large Hill (K120)		
1980	Jouko Törmänen	Finland
1984	Matti Nykänen	Finland
1988	Matti Nykänen	Finland
1992	Toni Nieminen	Finland
1994	Jens Weissflog	Germany
1998	Kazuynoshi Funaki	Japan
Large Hill – Team (K120)		
1988	Finland	
1992	Finland	
1994	Germany	
1998	Japan	

Snowboarding: Olympic Gold Medallists

The following snowboard events were introduced to the Olympic games in the XVIII winter Olympiad at Nagano, Japan, in 1998.

Year	Category	Name	Country
Men			
1998	Giant slalom	Ross Rebagliati	Canada
	Halfpipe	Gian Simmen	Switzerland
Women			
1998	Giant slalom	Katrine Ruby	France
	Halfpipe	Nicola Thost	Germany

American Football

The World Bowl

Year	Winning team	Score	Losing team	Score
1991	London Monarchs	21	Barcelona Dragons	0
1995	Frankfurt Galaxy	26	Amsterdam Admirals	22
1996	Scottish Claymores	32	Frankfurt Galaxy	27
1997	Barcelona Dragons	38	Rhein Fire	24

The Super Bowl

Super Bowl	Year	Result	Venue	Attendance
I	1967	Green Bay Packers 35, Kansas City Raiders 10	Los Angeles	61,946
II	1968	Green Bay Packers 33, Oakland Raiders 14	Miami	75,546
III	1969	New York Jets 16, Baltimore Colts 7	Miami	75,389
IV	1970	Kansas City Raiders 23, Minnesota Vikings 7	New Orleans	80,562
V	1971	Baltimore Colts 16, Dallas Cowboys 13	Miami	79,204
VI	1972	Dallas Cowboys 24, Miami Dolphins 3	New Orleans	80,591
VII	1973	Miami Dolphins 14, Washington Redskins 7	Los Angeles	90,182
VIII	1974	Miami Dolphins 24, Minnesota Vikings 7	Houston	71,882
IX	1975	Pittsburgh Steelers 16, Minnesota Vikings 6	New Orleans	80,997
X	1976	Pittsburgh Steelers 21, Dallas Cowboys 17	Miami	80,187
XI	1977	Oakland Raiders 32, Minnesota Vikings 14	Pasadena	103,424
XII	1978	Dallas Cowboys 27, Denver Broncos 10	New Orleans	75,583
XIII	1979	Pittsburgh Steelers 35, Dallas Cowboys 31	Miami	79,484
XIV	1980	Pittsburgh Steelers 31, Los Angeles Rams 19	Pasadena	103,985
XV	1981	Oakland Raiders 27, Philadelphia Eagles 10	New Orleans	76,135
XVI	1982	San Francisco 49ers 26, Cincinnati Bengals 21	Pontiac	81,270
XVII	1983	Washington Redskins 27, Miami Dolphins 17	Pasadena	103,667
XVIII	1984	Los Angeles Raiders 38, Washington Redskins 9	Tampa	72,920
XIX	1985	San Francisco 49ers 38, Miami Dolphins 16	Stanford	84,059
XX	1986	Chicago Bears 46, New England Patriots 10	New Orleans	73,818
XXI	1987	New York Giants 39, Denver Broncos 20	Pasadena	101,063
XXII	1988	Washington Redskins 42, Denver Broncos 10	San Diego	73,302
XXIII	1989	San Francisco 49ers 20, Cincinnati Bengals 16	Miami	75,179
XXIV	1990	San Francisco 49ers 55, Denver Broncos 10	New Orleans	72,919
XXV	1991	New York Giants 20, Buffalo Bills 19	Tampa	73,813
XXVI	1992	Washington Redskins 37, Buffalo Bills 24	Minneapolis	63,130
XXVII	1993	Dallas Cowboys 52, Buffalo Bills 17	Pasadena	102,000
XXVIII	1994	Dallas Cowboys 30, Buffalo Bills 13	Atlanta	72,817
XXIX	1995	San Francisco 49ers 49, San Diego Chargers 26	Miami	74,107
XXX	1996	Dallas Cowboys 27, Pittsburgh Steelers 17	Tempe (AZ)	76,347
XXXI	1997	Green Bay Packers 35, New England Patriots 21	New Orleans	72,301
XXXII	1998	Denver Broncos 31, Green Bay Packers 24	San Diego	68,912

Angling

World Individual Freshwater Champions since 1988

Year	Name	Country
1988	Jean-Pierre Fouquet	France
1989	Tom Pickering	England
1990	Bob Nudd	England
1991	Bob Nudd	England
1992	David Wesson	Australia
1993	Mario Barros	Portugal
1994	Bob Nudd	England
1995	Paul Jean	France
1996	Alan Scotthorne	England
1997	Alan Scotthorne	England

World Team Freshwater Champions since 1988

Year	Country
1988	England
1989	Wales
1990	France
1991	England
1992	Italy
1993	Italy
1994	England
1995	France
1996	Italy
1997	Italy

Archery

World Target Archery Championships (Olympic Bow) since 1981

This competition was first held in 1931.

Year	Name	Country	Year	Name	Country
Men – Individual			**Women – Individual**		
1981	Kyösti Laasonen	Finland	1981	Natalia Butuzova	USSR
1983	Richard McKinney	USA	1983	Jin-Ho Kim	South Korea
1985	Richard McKinney	USA	1985	Irina Soldatova	USSR
1987	Vladimir Yesheyev	USSR	1987	Ma Xiagjuan	China
1989	Stanislav Zabrodsky	USSR	1989	Soo Nyung-Kim	South Korea
1991	Simon Fairweather	Australia	1991	Soo Nyung-Kim	South Korea
1993	Kyung-Mo Park	South Korea	1993	Hyo-Jung Kim	South Korea
1995	Kyung-Chul Lee	South Korea	1995	Natalya Valeeva	Moldova
1997	Kyung-Ho Kim	South Korea	1997	Du-Ri Kim	South Korea
Men – Team			**Women – Team**		
1981		USA	1981		USSR
1983		USA	1983		South Korea
1985		South Korea	1985		USSR
1987		West Germany	1987		USSR
1989		USSR	1989		South Korea
1991		South Korea	1991		South Korea
1993		France	1993		South Korea
1995		South Korea	1995		South Korea
1997		South Korea	1997		South Korea

Athletics

International Amateur Athletic Federation World Championships: Gold Medallists (Men)

The competition was first held in 1983 in Helsinki, Finland. The following years were: 1987: Rome, Italy; 1991: Tokyo, Japan; 1993: Stuttgart, Germany; 1995: Gothenburg, Sweden; 1997: Athens, Greece.

Year	Name	Country	Result	Year	Name	Country	Result
100 m				**800 m**			
1983	Carl Lewis	USA	10.07	1983	Willi Wülbeck	West Germany	1:43.65
1987	Carl Lewis	USA	9.93	1987	Billy Konchellah	Kenya	1:43.06
1991	Carl Lewis	USA	9.86	1991	Billy Konchellah	Kenya	1:43.99
1993	Linford Christie	Great Britain	9.87	1993	Paul Ruto	Kenya	1:44.71
1995	Donovan Bailey	Canada	9.97	1995	Wilson Kipketer	Denmark	1:45.08
1997	Maurice Greene	USA	9.86	1997	Wilson Kipketer	Denmark	1:43.38
200 m				**1,500 m**			
1983	Calvin Smith	USA	20.14	1983	Steve Cram	Great Britain	3:41.59
1987	Calvin Smith	USA	20.16	1987	Abdi Bile	Somalia	3:36.80
1991	Michael Johnson	USA	20.01	1991	Noureddine Morceli	Algeria	3:32.84
1993	Frank Fredericks	Namibia	19.85	1993	Noureddine Morceli	Algeria	3:34.24
1995	Michael Johnson	USA	19.79	1995	Noureddine Morceli	Algeria	3:33.73
1997	Ato Boldon	Trinidad	20.04	1997	Hicham El Guerrouj	Morocco	3:35.83
400 m				**5,000 m**			
1983	Bert Cameron	Jamaica	45.05	1983	Eamonn Coghlan	Ireland, Republic of	13:28.53
1987	Thomas Schönlebe	East Germany	44.33	1987	Saïd Aouita	Morocco	13:26.44
1991	Antonio Pettigrew	USA	44.57	1991	Yobes Ondieki	Kenya	13:14.45
1993	Michael Johnson	USA	43.65	1993	Ismael Kirui	Kenya	13:02.75
1995	Michael Johnson	USA	43.39	1995	Ismael Kirui	Kenya	13:16.77
1997	Michael Johnson	USA	44.12	1997	Daniel Komen	Kenya	13:07.38

(continued)

International Amateur Athletic Federation World Championships: Gold Medallists (Men) *(continued)*

Year	Name	Country	Result	Year	Name	Country	Result
10,000 m				**50 km Walk**			
1983	Alberto Cova	Italy	28:01.04	1983	Ronald Weigel	East Germany	3h 43:08
1987	Paul Kipkoech	Kenya	27:38.63	1987	Hartwig Gauder	East Germany	3h 40:53
1991	Moses Tanui	Kenya	27:38.74	1991	Aleksandr Potashov	USSR	3h 53:09
1993	Haile Gebrselassie	Ethiopia	27:46.02	1993	Jesús Angel Garcia	Spain	3h 41:41
1995	Haile Gebrselassie	Ethiopia	27:12.95	1995	Valentin Kononen	Finland	3h 43:42
1997	Haile Gebrselassie	Ethiopia	27:24.58	1997	Robert Korzeniowski	Poland	3h 44:46
Marathon				**High Jump**			
1983	Rob de Castella	Australia	2h 10:03	1983	Gennadiy Avdeyenko	USSR	2.32 m
1987	Douglas Wakiihuri	Kenya	2h 11:48	1987	Patrik Sjöberg	Sweden	2.38 m
1991	Hiromi Taniguchi	Japan	2h 14:57	1991	Charles Austin	USA	2.38 m
1993	Mark Plaatjes	USA	2h 13:57	1993	Javier Sotomayor	Cuba	2.40 m
1995	Martin Fiz	Spain	2h 11:41	1995	Troy Kemp	Bahamas	2.37 m
1997	Abel Anton	Spain	2h 13:16	1997	Javier Sotomayor	Cuba	2.37 m
3,000 m Steeplechase				**Pole Vault**			
1983	Patriz Ilg	West Germany	8:15.06	1983	Sergei Bubka	USSR	5.70 m
1987	Francesco Panetta	Italy	8:08.57	1987	Sergei Bubka	USSR	5.85 m
1991	Moses Kiptanui	Kenya	8:12.59	1991	Sergei Bubka	USSR	5.95 m
1993	Moses Kiptanui	Kenya	8:06.36	1993	Sergei Bubka	Ukraine	6.00 m
1995	Moses Kiptanui	Kenya	8:04.16	1995	Sergei Bubka	Ukraine	5.92 m
1997	Wilson Boit Kipketer	Kenya	8:05.84	1997	Sergei Bubka	Ukraine	6.01 m
110 m Hurdles				**Long Jump**			
1983	Greg Foster	USA	13.42	1983	Carl Lewis	USA	8.55 m
1987	Greg Foster	USA	13.21	1987	Carl Lewis	USA	8.67 m
1991	Greg Foster	USA	13.06	1991	Mike Powell	USA	8.95 m
1993	Colin Jackson	Great Britian	12.91	1993	Mike Powell	USA	8.59 m
1995	Allen Johnson	USA	13.00	1995	Iván Pedroso	Cuba	8.70 m
1997	Allen Johnson	USA	12.93	1997	Iván Pedroso	Cuba	8.42 m
400 m Hurdles				**Triple Jump**			
1983	Ed Moses	USA	47.50	1983	Zdzislaw Hoffmann	Poland	17.42 m
1987	Ed Moses	USA	47.46	1987	Khristo Markov	Bulgaria	17.92 m
1991	Samuel Matete	Zambia	47.64	1991	Kenny Harrison	USA	17.78 m
1993	Kevin Young	USA	47.18	1993	Mike Conley	USA	17.86 m
1995	Derrick Adkins	USA	47.98	1995	Jonathan Edwards	Great Britain	18.29 m
1997	Stephane Diagana	France	47.70	1997	Yoelvis Quesada	Cuba	17.85 m
4 × 100 m Relay				**Shot**			
1983		USA	37.86	1983	Edward Sarul	Poland	21.39 m
1987		USA	37.90	1987	Werner Günthör	Switzerland	22.23 m
1991		USA	37.50	1991	Werner Günthör	Switzerland	21.67 m
1993		USA	37.48	1993	Werner Günthör	Switzerland	21.97 m
1995		Canada	38.31	1995	John Godina	USA	21.47 m
1997		Canada	37.86	1997	John Godina	USA	21.44 m
4 × 400 m Relay				**Discus**			
1983		USSR	3:00.79	1983	Imrich Bugár	Czechoslovakia	67.72 m
1987		USA	2:57.29	1987	Jürgen Schult	East Germany	68.74 m
1991		Great Britain	2:57.53	1991	Lars Riedel	Germany	66.20 m
1993		USA	2:54.29	1993	Lars Riedel	Germany	67.72 m
1995		USA	2:57.32	1995	Lars Riedel	Germany	68.76 m
1997		USA	2:56.47	1997	Lars Riedel	Germany	68.54 m
20 km Walk				**Hammer**			
1983	Ernesto Canto	Mexico	1h 20:49	1983	Sergei Litvinov	USSR	82.68 m
1987	Maurizio Damilano	Italy	1h 20:45	1987	Sergei Litvinov	USSR	83.06 m
1991	Maurizio Damilano	Italy	1h 19:37	1991	Yuriy Sedykh	USSR	81.70 m
1993	Valentin Massana	Spain	1h 22:31	1993	Andrey Abduvaliyev	Tajikistan	81.64 m
1995	Michele Didoni	Italy	1h 19:59	1995	Andrey Abduvaliyev	Tajikistan	81.56 m
1997	Daniel Garcia	Mexico	1h 21:43	1997	Heinz Weiss	Germany	81.78 m

International Amateur Athletic Federation World Championships: Gold Medallists (Men) *(continued)*

Year	Name	Country	Result	Year	Name	Country	Result
Javelin				**Decathlon**			
1983	Detlef Michel	East Germany	89.48 m[1]	1983	Daley Thompson	Great Britain	8,714 pts
1987	Seppo Räty	Finland	83.54 m	1987	Torsten Voss	East Germany	8,680 pts
1991	Kimmo Kinnunen	Finland	90.82 m	1991	Dan O'Brien	USA	8,812 pts
1993	Jan Zelezny	Czech Republic	85.98 m	1993	Dan O'Brien	USA	8,817 pts
1995	Jan Zelezny	Czech Republic	89.58 m	1995	Dan O'Brien	USA	8,695 pts
1997	Marius Corbett	South Africa	88.40 m	1997	Tomas Dvorak	Czech Republic	8,837 pts

[1] Old specification.

International Amateur Athletic Federation World Championships: Gold Medallists (Women)

Year	Name	Country	Result	Year	Name	Country	Result
100 m				**5,000 m**			
1983	Marlies Göhr	East Germany	10.97	1995	Sonia O'Sullivan	Ireland	14:46.47
1987	Silke Gladisch	East Germany	10.90	1997	Gabriela Szabo	Romania	14:57.68
1991	Katrin Krabbe	Germany	10.99				
1993	Gail Devers	USA	10.82	**10,000 m[3]**			
1995	Gwen Torrence	USA	10.85	1987	Ingrid Kristiansen	Norway	31:05.85
1997	Marion Jones	USA	10.83	1991	Liz McColgan	Great Britain	31:14.31
				1993	Wang Junxia	China	30:49.30
200 m				1995	Fernanda Ribeiro	Portugal	31:04.99
1983	Marita Koch	East Germany	22.13	1997	Sally Barsisio	Kenya	31:32.92
1987	Silke Gladisch	East Germany	21.74				
1991	Katrin Krabbe	Germany	22.09	**Marathon**			
1993	Merlene Ottey	Jamaica	21.98	1983	Grete Waitz	Norway	2h 28:09
1995	Merlene Ottey	Jamaica	22.12	1987	Rosa Mota	Portugal	2h 25:17
1997	Zhanna Pintussevich	Ukraine	22.32	1991	Wanda Panfil	Poland	2h 29:53
				1993	Junko Asari	Japan	2h 30:03
400 m				1995	Manuela Machado	Portugal	2h 25:39
1983	Jarmila Kratochvilová	Czechoslovakia	47.99	1997	Hiromi Suzuki	Japan	2h 29:48
1987	Olga Bryzgina	USSR	49.38				
1991	Marie-José Pérec	France	49.13	**100 m Hurdles**			
1993	Jearl Miles	USA	49.82	1983	Bettine Jahn	East Germany	12.35
1995	Marie-José Pérec	France	49.28	1987	Ginka Zagorcheva	Bulgaria	12.34
1997	Cathy Freeman	Australia	49.77	1991	Lyudmila Narozhilenko	USSR	12.59
				1993	Gail Devers	USA	12.46
800 m				1995	Gail Devers	USA	12.68
1983	Jarmila Kratochvilová	Czechoslovakia	1:54.68	1997	Lyudmila Engquist	Sweden	12.50
1987	Sigrun Wodars	East Germany	1:55.26				
1991	Lilia Nurutdinova	USSR	1:57.50	**400 m Hurdles**			
1993	Maria Mutola	Mozambique	1:55.43	1983	Yekaterina Fesenko	USSR	54.14
1995	Ana Quirot	Cuba	1:56.11	1987	Sabine Busch	East Germany	53.62
1997	Ana Quirot	Cuba	1:57.14	1991	Tatyana Ledovskaya	USSR	53.11
				1993	Sally Gunnell	Great Britain	52.74
1,500 m				1995	Kim Batten	USA	52.61
1983	Mary Decker	USA	4:00.90	1997	Nezha Bidouane	Morocco	52.97
1987	Tatyana Samolenko	USSR	3:58.56				
1991	Hassiba Boulmerka	Algeria	4:02.21	**4 × 100 m Relay**			
1993	Liu Dong	China	4:00:50	1983		East Germany	41.76
1995	Hassiba Boulmerka	Algeria	4:02.42	1987		USA	41.58
1997	Carla Sacramento	Portugal	4:04.24	1991		Jamaica	41.94
				1993		Russia	41.49
3,000 m[1]				1995		USA	42.11
1983	Mary Decker	USA	8:34.62	1997		USA	41.47
1987	Tatyana Samolenko	USSR	8:38.73				
1991	Tatyana Dorovskikh[2]	USSR	8:35.82				
1993	Qu Yunxia	China	8:28:71				

(continued)

International Amateur Athletic Federation World Championships: Gold Medallists (Women) (*continued*)

Year	Name	Country	Result	Year	Name	Country	Result
4 × 400 m Relay				**Shot**			
1983		East Germany	3:19.73	1983	Helena Fibingerová	Czechoslovakia	21.05 m
1987		East Germany	3:18.63	1987	Natalya Lisovskaya	USSR	21.24 m
1991		USSR	3:18.43	1991	Huang Zhihong	China	20.83 m
1993		USA	3:16.79	1993	Huang Zhihong	China	20.57 m
1995		USA	3:22.39	1995	Astrid Kumbernuss	Germany	21.22 m
1997		Germany	3:20.92	1997	Astrid Kumbernuss	Germany	20.71 m
10 km Walk[3]				**Discus**			
1987	Irina Strakhova	USSR	44:12	1983	Martina Opitz	East Germany	68.94 m
1991	Alina Ivanova	USSR	42:57	1987	Martina Hellmann[6]	East Germany	71.62 m
1993	Sari Essayah	Finland	42:59	1991	Tsvetanka Khristova	Bulgaria	71.02 m
1995	Irina Stankina	Russia	42:13	1993	Olga Burova	Russia	67.40 m
1997	Annarita Sidoti	Italy	42:55.59	1995	Ellina Zveryova	Belarus	68.64 m
				1997	Beatrice Faumuina	New Zealand	66.82 m
High Jump				**Javelin**			
1983	Tamara Bykova	USSR	2.01 m	1983	Tiina Lillak	Finland	70.82 m
1987	Stefka Kostadinova	Bulgaria	2.09 m	1987	Fatima Whitbread	Great Britain	76.64 m
1991	Heike Henkel	Germany	2.05 m	1991	Xu Demei	China	68.78 m
1993	Ioamnet Quintero	Cuba	1.99 m	1993	Trine Hattestad	Norway	69.18 m
1995	Stefka Kostadinova	Bulgaria	2.01 m	1995	Natalya Shikolenko	Belarus	67.56 m
				1997	Trine Hattestad	Norway	68.78 m
Long Jump				**Heptathlon**			
1983	Heike Daute	East Germany	7.27 m	1983	Ramona Neubert	East Germany	6,770 pts
1987	Jackie Joyner-Kersee	USA	7.36 m	1987	Jackie Joyner-Kersee	USA	7,128 pts
1991	Jackie Joyner-Kersee	USA	7.32 m	1991	Sabine Braun	Germany	6,672 pts
1993	Heike Drechsler[4]	Germany	7.11 m	1993	Jackie Joyner-Kersee	USA	6,837 pts
1995	Fiona May	Italy	6.98 m	1995	Ghada Shouaa	Syria	6,651 pts
1997	Lyudmila Galkina	Russia	7.05 m	1997	Sabine Braun	Germany	6,739 pts
Triple Jump[5]							
1993	Ana Biryukova	Russia	15.09 m				
1995	Inessa Kravets	Ukraine	15.50 m				
1997	Sarka Kasparkova	Czech Republic	15.20 m				

[1] Replaced by 5,000 Metres in 1995.
[2] Born Samolenko.
[3] First held in 1987.
[4] Born Daute.
[5] First held in 1993.
[6] Born Opitz.

World Cross-Country Championship since 1988

This championship is run over 12 km. In 1998 a new short course race run over 4 km was introduced.

Year	Name	Country	Year	Name	Country
Men's Individual			1993	Albertina Dias	Portugal
			1994	Helen Chepngeno	Kenya
1988	John Ngugi	Kenya	1995	Derartu Tulu	Ethiopia
1989	John Ngugi	Kenya	1996	Gete Wami	Ethiopia
1990	Khaled Skah	Morocco	1997	Derartu Tulu	Ethiopia
1991	Khaled Skah	Morocco	1998[1]	Sonia O'Sullivan	Ireland, Republic of
1992	John Ngugi	Kenya	1998[2]	Sonia O'Sullivan	Ireland, Republic of
1993	William Sigei	Kenya			
1994	William Sigei	Kenya	**Men's Team**		
1995	Paul Tergat	Kenya	1988		Kenya
1996	Paul Tergat	Kenya	1989		Kenya
1997	Paul Tergat	Kenya	1990		Kenya
1998[1]	Paul Tergat	Kenya	1991		Kenya
1998[2]	John Kibowen	Kenya	1992		Kenya
			1993		Kenya
Women's Individual			1994		Kenya
1988	Ingrid Kristiansen	Norway	1995		Kenya
1989	Annette Sergant	France	1996		Kenya
1990	Lynn Jennings	USA	1997		Kenya
1991	Lynn Jennings	USA	1998[1]		Kenya
1992	Lynn Jennings	USA	1998[2]		Kenya

World Cross-Country Championship since 1988 (*continued*)

Year	Name	Country	Year	Name	Country
Women's Team			1995		Kenya
			1996		Kenya
1988		USSR	1997		Kenya
1989		USSR	1998[1]		Kenya
1990		USSR	1998[2]		Morocco
1991		Kenya/Ethiopia			
1992		Kenya			
1993		Kenya	[1] Long course.		
1994		Portugal	[2] Short course.		

World Indoor Athletics Championships

The following are gold medallists from the Track and Field 1997 World Indoor Championships, Paris, France.

1997

Category	Name	Country	Result	Category	Name	Country	Result
Men				*Women*			
60 m	Haralambros Papadias	Greece	6.50	60 m	Gail Devers	USA	7.06
200 m	Kevin Little	USA	20.40	200 m	Ekaterini Koffa	Greece	22.76
400 m	Sunday Bada	Nigeria	45.51	400 m	Jearl Miles-Clark	USA	50.96
800 m	Wilson Kipketer	Denmark	1:42.67	800 m	Maria Mutola	Mozambique	1:58.96
1,500 m	Hicham El Guerrouj	Morocco	3:35.31	1,500 m	Yekaterina Podkopayeva	Russia	4:05.19
3,000 m	Haile Gebrselassie	Ethiopia	7:34.71	3,000 m	Gabriela Szabo	Romania	8:45.75
60 m hurdles	Anier Garcia	Cuba	7.48	60 m hurdles	Michelle Freeman	Jamaica	7.82
4 × 400 m relay		USA	3:04.93	4 × 400 m relay		Russia	3:26.84
High jump	Charles Austin	USA	2.35 m	High jump	Stefka Konstadinova	Bulgaria	2.02 m
Long jump	Ivan Pedroso	Cuba	8.51 m	Long jump	Fiona May	Italy	6.86 m
Triple jump	Yoelvis Garcia	Cuba	17.30 m	Triple jump	Inna Lasovskaya	Russia	15.01 m
Pole vault	Igor Potapovitch	Kazakhstan	5.90 m	Pole vault	Stacy Dragila	USA	4.40 m
Shot	Yuriy Bilonah	Ukraine	21.02 m	Shot	Vita Pavlysh	Ukraine	20.00 m
Heptathlon	Robert Zmelík	Czech Republic	6,228 pts	Pentathlon	Sabine Braun	Germany	4,780 pts

Men's Athletics World Records

(As of 14 July 1998.)

Category	Record	Name(s)	Country	Date	Location
100 m	9.84	Donovan Bailey	Canada	27 July 1996	Atlanta (GA), USA
200 m	19.32	Michael Johnson	USA	1 August 1996	Atlanta (GA), USA
400 m	43.29	Butch Reynolds	USA	17 August 1988	Zurich, Switzerland
800 m	1:41.11	Wilson Kipketer	Denmark	24 August 1997	Cologne, Germany
1,000 m	2:12.18	Sebastian Coe	Great Britain	11 July 1981	Oslo, Norway
1,500 m	3:26.00	Hicham El Guerrouj	Morocco	14 July 1998	Nice, France
Mile	3:44.39	Noureddine Morceli	Algeria	5 September 1993	Rieti, Italy
2,000 m	4:47.88	Noureddine Morceli	Algeria	3 July 1995	Paris, France
3,000 m	7:20.67	Daniel Komen	Kenya	1 September 1996	Rieti, Italy
5,000 m	12:39.36	Haile Gebrselassie	Ethiopia	13 June 1998	Helsinki, Finland
10,000 m	26:22.75[1]	Haile Gebrselassie	Ethiopia	1 June 1998	Hengelo, Netherlands
20,000 m	56:55.60	Arturo Barrios	Mexico	30 March 1991	La Flèche, France
25,000 m	1h 13:55.80	Toshihiko Seko	Japan	22 March 1981	Christchurch, New Zealand
3,000 m steeplechase	7:55.72	Bernard Barmasai	Kenya	24 August 1997	Cologne, Germany
Marathon	2h 6:50[2]	Belayneh Dinsamo	Ethiopia	17 April 1988	Rotterdam, Netherlands
110 m hurdles	12.91	Colin Jackson	Great Britain	20 August 1993	Stuttgart, Germany
400 m hurdles	46.78	Kevin Young	USA	6 August 1992	Barcelona, Spain
400 m relay	37.40	Marsh, Burrell, Mitchell, Lewis	USA	8 August 1992	Barcelona, Spain
		Drummond, Cason, Mitchell, Burrell	USA	21 August 1993	Stuttgart, Germany
4 × 200 m relay	1:18.68	Marsh, Burrell, Heard, Lewis	USA	17 April 1994	Walnut (CA), USA
4 × 400 m relay	2:54.29	Valmon, Watts, Reynolds, Johnson	USA	22 August 1993	Stuttgart, Germany
4 × 800 m relay	7:03.89	Elliott, Cook, Cram, Coe	Great Britain	30 August 1982	London, UK

(continued)

Men's Athletics World Records (*continued*)

Category	Record	Name(s)	Country	Date	Location
High jump	2.45 m/8 ft $\frac{1}{2}$ in	Javier Sotomayor	Cuba	27 July 1993	Salamanca, Spain
Long jump	8.95 m/29 ft 4$\frac{1}{2}$ in	Mike Powell	USA	30 August 1991	Tokyo, Japan
Triple jump	18.29 m/60 ft $\frac{1}{4}$ in	Jonathan Edwards	Great Britain	7 August 1995	Gothenburg, Sweden
Pole vault	6.14 m/20 ft 1$\frac{3}{4}$ in	Sergei Bubka	Ukraine	31 July 1994	Sestriere, Italy
Shot put	23.12 m/75 ft 10 $\frac{1}{4}$ in	Randy Barnes	USA	20 May 1990	Los Angeles (CA), USA
Discus	74.08 m/243 ft	Jürgen Schult	East Germany	6 June 1986	Neubrandenburg, Germany
Javelin	98.48 m/323 ft 1 in	Ján Zelezny	Czech Republic	25 May 1996	Jena, Germany
Hammer	86.74 m/284 ft 7 in	Yuriy Sedykh	USSR	30 August 1986	Stuttgart, Germany
Decathlon	8,891 pts	Dan O'Brien	USA	4–5 September 1992	Talence, France
20 km walk	1h 17:25.6	Bernardo Segura	Mexico	7 May 1994	Bergen, Norway
30 km walk	2h 01:44.1	Maurizio Damilano	Italy	3 October 1992	Cuneo, Italy
50 km walk	3h 40:57.9	Thierry Toutain	France	29 September 1996	Héricourt, France

[1] Awaiting ratification.
[2] World best performance.

Women's Athletics World Records

(As of 1 July 1998.)

Category	Record	Name(s)	Country	Date	Location
100 m	10.49	Florence Griffith-Joyner	USA	16 July 1988	Indianapolis (IN), USA
200 m	21.34	Florence Griffith-Joyner	USA	29 September 1988	Seoul, South Korea
400 m	47.60	Marita Koch	East Germany	6 October 1985	Canberra, Australia
800 m	1:53.28	Jarmila Kratochvílová	Czechoslovakia	26 July 1983	Munich, West Germany
1,000 m	2:28.98	Svetlana Masterkova	Russia	23 August 1996	Brussels, Belgium
1,500 m	3:50.46	Qu Yunxia	China	11 September 1993	Beijing, China
Mile	4:12.56	Svetlana Masterkova	Russia	14 August 1996	Zurich, Switzerland
2,000 m	5:25.36	Sonia O'Sullivan	Ireland, Republic of	9 July 1994	Edinburgh, UK
3,000 m	8:06.11	Wang Junxia	China	13 September 1993	Beijing, China
5,000 m	14:28.09	Jiang Bo	China	23 October 1997	Shanghai, China
10,000 m	29:31.78	Wang Junxia	China	8 September 1993	Beijing, China
Marathon	2h 20:47.00[1]	Tegla Loroupe	Kenya	19 April 1998	Rotterdam, Netherlands
100 m hurdles	12.21	Yordanka Donkova	Bulgaria	21 August 1988	Bulgaria
400 m hurdles	52.61	Kim Batten	USA	11 August 1995	Gothenburg, Sweden
4 × 100 m relay	41.37	Gladisch, Rieger, Auerswald, Göhr	East Germany	6 October 1985	Canberra, Australia
4 × 200 m relay	1:28.15	Göhr, Müller, Wöckel, Koch	East Germany	9 August 1980	Jena, East Germany
4 × 400 m relay	3:15.17	Ledovskaya, Nazarova, Pinigina, Bryzgina	USSR	1 October 1988	Seoul, South Korea
4 × 800 m relay	7:50.17	Olizarenko, Gurina, Borisova, Podyalovskaya	USSR	5 August 1984	Moscow, Russia
High jump	2.09 m/6 ft 10$\frac{1}{4}$ in	Stefka Kostadinova	Bulgaria	30 August 1987	Rome, Italy
Long jump	7.52 m/24 ft 8$\frac{1}{4}$ in	Galina Chistyakova	USSR	11 June 1988	Leningrad, Russia
Triple jump	15.50 m/50 ft 10$\frac{1}{4}$ in	Inessa Kravets	Ukraine	10 August 1995	Gothenburg, Sweden
Pole vault	4.59 m/14 ft 11 in	Emma George[2]	Australia	21 March 1998	Brisbane, Australia
Shot put	22.64 m/74 ft 3 in	Natalya Lisovskaya	USSR	7 June 1987	Moscow, Russia
Discus	76.80 m/252 ft	Gabriele Reinsch	East Germany	9 July 1988	Neubrandenburg, East Germany
Hammer	73.10 m/239 ft 10in	Olga Kuzenkova	Russia	22 June 1997	Munich, Germany
Javelin	80.00 m/262 ft 5 in	Petra Felke	East Germany	9 September 1988	Potsdam, Germany
Heptathlon	7,291 pts	Jackie Joyner-Kersee	USA	23–24 September 1988	Seoul, South Korea
5 km walk	20:13.26	Kerry Saxby-Junna	Australia	25 February 1996	Hobart, Australia
10 km walk	41:56.23	Nadezhda Ryashkina	USSR	24 July 1990	Seattle (WA), USA

[1] World best performance.
[2] Awaiting ratification.

London Marathon Winners

This event was first held in 1981, it is now sponsored by Flora.

Year	Name	Country	Time	Year	Name	Country	Time
Men				*Women*			
1981	Dick Beardsley/			1981	Joyce Smith	Great Britain	2h 29:57
	Inge Simonsen	USA/Norway	2h 11:48	1982	Joyce Smith	Great Britain	2h 29:43
1982	Hugh Jones	Great Britain	2h 9:24	1983	Grete Waitz	Norway	2h 25:29
1983	Mike Gratton	Great Britain	2h 9:43	1984	Ingrid Kristiansen	Norway	2h 24:26
1984	Charlie Spedding	Great Britain	2h 9:57	1985	Ingrid Kristiansen	Norway	2h 21:06
1985	Steve Jones	Great Britain	2h 8:16	1986	Grete Waitz	Norway	2h 24:54
1986	Toshihiko Seko	Japan	2h 10:02	1987	Ingrid Kristiansen	Norway	2h 22:48
1987	Hiromi Taniguchi	Japan	2h 9:50	1988	Ingrid Kristiansen	Norway	2h 25:41
1988	Henrik Jorgensen	Denmark	2h 10:20	1989	Véronique Marot	Great Britain	2h 25:56
1989	Douglas Wakihuri	Kenya	2h 10:20	1990	Wanda Panfil	Poland	2h 26:31
1990	Allister Hutton	Great Britain	2h 10:10	1991	Rosa Mota	Portugal	2h 26:41
1991	Yakov Tolstikov	USSR	2h 9:17	1992	Katrin Dörre	Germany	2h 29:39
1992	Antonio Pinto	Portugal	2h 10:02	1993	Katrin Dörre	Germany	2h 27:09
1993	Eamonn Martin	Great Britain	2h 10:50	1994	Katrin Dörre	Germany	2h 32:34
1994	Dionicio Ceron	Mexico	2h 8:53	1995	Malgorzata Sobanska	Poland	2h 27:43
1995	Dionicio Ceron	Mexico	2h 8:30	1996	Liz McColgan	Great Britain	2h 27:54
1996	Dionicio Ceron	Mexico	2h 10:00	1997	Joyce Chepchumba	Kenya	2h 25:51
1997	Antonio Pinto	Portugal	2h 7:55	1998	Catherina McKiernan	Ireland, Republic of	2h 26:26
1998	Abel Anton	Spain	2h 7:57				

Australian Rules Football

Australian Football League since 1988

Year	Team	Year	Team	Year	Team
1988	Hawthorn	1992	West Coast	1996	North Melbourne
1989	Hawthorn	1993	Essendon	1997	Adelaide
1990	Collingwood	1994	West Coast		
1991	Hawthorn	1995	Carlton Blues		

Badminton

All-England Badminton Championships

These championships were first held in 1899.

1998

Event	Name	Country
Mixed doubles	Kim Dong-moon/Ra Kyung-min	South Korea
Men		
Singles	Sun Jun	China
Doubles	Lee Dong-soo/Yoo Yong-sung	South Korea
Women		
Singles	Ye Zhaoying	China
Doubles	Ge Fei/Gu Yun	China

World Badminton Champions

The Thomas and Uber Cups were last held in 1998 (even years). The other events were last held in 1997 (odd years).

Event	Name	Country
1997 World Championships		
Men's singles	Peter Rasmussen	Denmark
Women's singles	Ye Zhaoying	China
Men's doubles	Budiarto Sigit and Candra Wijaya	Indonesia
Women's doubles	Ge Fei/Gu Yun	China
Sudirman trophy	(mixed team)	China
1998 Team Championships		
Thomas Cup (men's)		Indonesia
Uber Cup (women's)		China

Baseball

World Series Results since 1988

(AL = American League. NL = National League.)

Year	Winner	Loser	Score
1988	Los Angeles Dodgers, NL	Oakland Athletics, AL	4–1
1989	Oakland Athletics, AL	San Francisco Giants, NL	4–0
1990	Cincinnati Reds, NL	Oakland Athletics, AL	4–0
1991	Minnesota Twins, AL	Atlanta Braves, NL	4–3
1992	Toronto Blue Jays, AL	Atlanta Braves, NL	4–2
1993	Toronto Blue Jays, AL	Philadelphia Phillies, NL	4–2
1994	no World Series[1]		
1995	Atlanta Braves, NL	Cleveland Indians, AL	4–2
1996	New York Yankees, AL	Atlanta Braves, NL	4–2
1997	Florida Marlins, NL	Cleveland Indians, AL	4–3

[1] Due to a players' strike.

Basketball

English Basketball: The Budweiser League

1997–98

Final Standings

Position	Team	Played	Won	Lost	Points
1	Greater London Leopards[1] [2] [3]	36	29	7	58
2	Birmingham Bullets[1]	36	29	7	58
3	Newcastle Eagles[1]	36	25	11	50
4	Sheffield Sharks[1]	36	25	11	50
5	Thames Valley Tigers[1]	36	24	12	48
6	London Towers[1]	36	23	13	46
7	Derby Storm[1]	36	16	20	32
8	Manchester Giants[1]	36	15	21	30
9	Leicester Riders	36	15	21	30
10	Chester Jets	36	15	21	28
11	Crystal Palace	36	8	28	16
12	Worthing Bears	36	7	29	14
13	Watford Royals	36	3	33	6

[1] Qualified for play-offs.
[2] League champions.
[3] The Greater London Leopards finish above the Birmingham Bullets because they won the head-to-head tie back.

Play-Off Results

Quarter Finals First Legs
Derby Storm 79 Birmingham Bullets 111 (0–1); Thames Valley Tigers 84 Sheffield Sharks 83 (1–0); Manchester Giants 86 Greater London Leopards 93 (0–1); London Towers 68 Newcastle Eagles 63 (1–0)

Quarter Finals Second Legs
Birmingham Bullets 84 Derby Storm 86 (over time) (1–1); Newcastle Eagles 73 London Towers 50 (1–1); Sheffield Sharks 75 Thames Valley Tigers 97 (0–2); Greater London Leopards 98 Manchester Giants 107 (1–1)

Quarter Finals Third Legs
Birmingham Bullets 96 Derby Storm 81 (2–1); Greater London Leopards 81 Manchester Giants 90 (1–2); Newcastle Eagles 85 London Towers 87 (1-2)

Championship Play-Offs, Wembley Arena

Semi-Finals
Birmingham Bullets 90 Manchester Giants 80; London Towers 71 Thames Valley Tigers 78

Third Place Play-Off
Manchester Giants 87 London Towers 82

Final
Birmingham Bullets 78 Thames Valley Tigers 75

English Men's Club Basketball Champions

1998

Event	Name
Budweiser League	Greater London Leopards
Championship play-off winners	Birmingham Bullets
National Basketball League Division One	Richmond Jaguars
Division One National Basketball League play-off winners	Richmond Jaguars
National Basketball League Division Two	Solent Stars
Division Two National Basketball League play-off winners	Solent Stars
EBBA	Thames Valley Tigers
Uniball Trophy	Sheffield Sharks
National Trophy	Richmond Jaguars
Scottish League	Midlothian Bulls
Scottish Cup	Midlothian Bulls
European Cup	BC Zalgiris (Lithuania)
European Korac Cup	Riello Basket Verona (Italy)
European Ronchetti Cup	Gysev-Ringa (Hungary)
Euro League Final Four Champions	Kinder Bologna (Italy)

English Women's Club Basketball Champions

1998

Event	Name
National Basketball League Division One	Sheffield Hatters
National Basketball League Division One play-off winners	Sheffield Hatters
EBBA National Cup	Thames Valley Lady Tigers
National Trophy	Spelthorne Acers
Scottish League	Polonia Phoenix
Scottish Cup	Dalkeith Saints
Euro League Final Four Champions	CJM Bourges Basket (France)

National Basketball Association Champions (USA) since 1980

Year	Winner	Coach	Runner Up	Series
1980	Los Angeles	Paul Westhead	Philadelphia	4–2
1981	Boston	Bill Fitch	Houston	4–2
1982	Los Angeles	Pat Riley	Philadelphia	4–2
1983	Philadelphia	Billy Cunningham	Los Angeles	4–0
1984	Boston	K C Jones	Los Angeles	4–3
1985	Los Angeles	Pat Riley	Boston	4–2
1986	Boston	K C Jones	Houston	4–2
1987	Los Angeles	Pat Riley	Boston	4–2
1988	Los Angeles	Pat Riley	Detroit	4–3
1989	Detroit	Chuck Daly	Los Angeles	4–0
1990	Detroit	Chuck Daly	Portland	4–1
1991	Chicago	Phil Jackson	Los Angeles	4–1
1992	Chicago	Phil Jackson	Portland	4–2
1993	Chicago	Phil Jackson	Phoenix	4–2
1994	Houston	Rudy Tomjanovich	New York Knicks	4–3
1995	Houston	Rudy Tomjanovich	Orlando	4–0
1996	Chicago	Phil Jackson	Seattle	4–2
1997	Chicago	Phil Jackson	Utah	4–2
1998	Chicago	Phil Jackson	Utah	4–2

Basketball: World Champions

The world championship was first held in 1950 for men and 1953 for women. It is contested every four years.

Year	Country
Men	
1950	Argentina
1954	USA
1959	Brazil
1963	Brazil
1967	USSR
1970	Yugoslavia
1974	USSR
1978	Yugoslavia
1982	USSR
1986	USA
1990	Yugoslavia
1994	USA
1998	Yugoslavia
Women	
1953	USA
1957	USA
1959	USSR
1964	USSR
1967	USSR
1971	USSR
1975	USSR
1979	USA
1983	USSR
1986	USA
1990	USA
1994	Brazil
1998	USA

Billiards

World Professional Billiards Championship since 1988

The championship was instituted in 1870 on a challenge basis and restored as an annual tournament in 1980.

Year	Name	Country	Year	Name	Country
1988	Norman Dagley	England	1993	Geet Sethi	India
1989	Mike Russell	England	1994	Peter Gilchrist	England
1990	not held		1995	Geet Sethi	India
1991	Mike Russell	England	1996	Mike Russell	England
1992	Geet Sethi	India	1997	not held	

Bobsleighing

Bobsleighing World Champions since 1988

The four-person championship was introduced in 1924 and the two-person championship in 1931. In Olympic years, Olympic winners automatically become world champions.

Year	Two-person	Four-person	Year	Two-person	Four-person
1988	USSR[1]	Switzerland[1]	1994	Switzerland[1]	Germany[1]
1989	East Germany	Switzerland	1995	Germany	Germany
1990	Switzerland	Switzerland	1996	Germany	Germany
1991	Germany	Germany	1997	Switzerland	Germany
1992	Switzerland[1]	Austria[1]	1998	Canada/Italy[1]	Germany[1]
1993	Germany	Switzerland			

[1] Olympic year.

Bowls

World Indoor Bowls Championship since 1988

The championship was first held in 1979 for men and in 1988 for women.

Year	Name	Country	Year	Name	Country
Men			**Women**		
1988	Hugh Duff	Scotland	1988	Margaret Johnston	Ireland, Republic of
1989	Richard Corsie	Scotland	1989	Margaret Johnston	Ireland, Republic of
1990	John Price	Wales	1990	Fleur Bougourd	England
1991	Richard Corsie	Scotland	1991	Mary Price	England
1992	Ian Schuback	Australia	1992	Sarah Gourley	Scotland
1993	Richard Corsie	Scotland	1993	Kate Adams	Scotland
1994	Andy Thomson	England	1994	Jan Woodley	Scotland
1995	Andy Thomson	England	1995	Joyce Lindores	Scotland
1996	David Gourlay Jr	Scotland	1996	Sandy Hazell	England
1997	Hugh Duff	Scotland	1997	Norma Shaw	England
1998	Andrew Foster	Scotland	1998	Caroline McAllister	Scotland

World Outdoor Bowls Championship

The championship was first held in 1966 for men and in 1969 for women.

Year	Name	Country	Year	Name	Country
Men			*Women*		
1966	David Bryant	England	1969	Gladys Doyle	Papua New Guinea
1972	Maldwyn Evans	Wales	1973	Elsie Wilke	New Zealand
1976	Doug Watson	South Africa	1977	Elsie Wilke	New Zealand
1980	David Bryant	England	1981	Norma Shaw	England
1984	Peter Bellis	New Zealand	1985	Merle Richardson	Australia
1988	David Bryant	England	1988	Janet Ackland	Wales
1992	Tony Allcock	England	1992	Margaret Johnston	Ireland, Republic of
1996	Tony Allcock	England	1996	Carmelita Anderson	Norfolk Island

Boxing

Sanctioning Bodies in World Boxing

The major sanctioning bodies in world boxing are:

World Boxing Association (WBA) formed as the National Boxing Association (NBA) in the USA in 1920; it changed its name to WBA in 1962

New York State Athletic Commission a rival sanctioning body to the NBA for world title fights from the 1920s

World Boxing Council (WBC) formed in Mexico City in 1963

International Boxing Federation (IBF) formed as a breakaway from the WBA

There are several other sanctioning bodies. The main ones include: The World Boxing Organization (WBO); Intercontinental Boxing Council; World Boxing Union; and the International Boxing Organization

Current British Professional Boxing Champions

(As of 7 May 1998.)

Weight	Name
Heavyweight (over 86.2 kg/190 lb)	Julius Francis
Cruiserweight (limit 86.2 kg/190 lb)	Johnny Nelson
Light heavyweight (limit 79.4 kg/175 lb)	Crawford Ashley
Super middleweight (limit 76.2 kg/168 lb)	Dean Francis
Middleweight (limit 72.6 kg/160 lb)	Glen Catley
Light middleweight (limit 69.9 kg/154 lb)	Ensley Bingham
Welterweight (limit 66.7 kg/147 lb)	Geoff McCreesh
Light welterweight (limit 63.5 kg/140 lb)	Mark Winters
Lightweight (limit 61.2 kg/135 lb)	Wayne Rigby
Super featherweight (limit 59 kg/130 lb)	Charles Shepherd
Featherweight (limit 57.2 kg/126 lb)	vacant
Super bantamweight (limit 55.3 kg/122 lb)	Michael Brodie
Bantamweight (limit 53.5 kg/118 lb)	Paul Lloyd
Flyweight (limit 50.8 kg/112 lb)	Adi Lewis

The British-based World Boxing Organization (WBO), formed in 1988, has grown in stature in recent years and is beginning to earn respect in the USA. The current WBO champions are listed over page, but previous WBO champions are not. This listing reflects the growing credibility of the WBO.

Current World Professional Boxing Champions

Weights given are weight limit. (As of 1 May 1998.)

Weight	WBA	WBC	IBF	WBO
Heavyweight (>86.2 kg/ >190 lb)	Evander Holyfield (USA)	Lennox Lewis (UK)	Evander Holyfield (USA)	Herbie Hide (UK)
Cruiserweight (86.2 kg/190 lb)	Fabrice Tiozzo (France)	Juan Carlos Gomez (Cuba)	Imamu Mayfield (USA)	Carl Thompson (UK)
Light Heavyweight (79.4 kg/175 lb)	Lou del Valle(USA)	Roy Jones Jr (USA)	Reggie Johnson (USA)	Darius Michalczewski (Germany)
Super Middleweight (76.2 kg/168 lb)	Frank Liles (USA)	Richie Woodhall (UK)	Charles Brewer (USA)	Joe Calzaghe (UK)
Middleweight (72.6 kg/160 lb)	William Joppy (USA)	Hassine Cherifi (France)	Bernard Hopkins (USA)	Otis Grant (Canada)
Super Welterweight (69.9 kg/154 lb)	Laurent Boudouani (France)	Keith Mullings (USA)	Yory Boy Campas (Mexico)	Ronald Wright (USA)
Welterweight (66.7 kg/147 lb)	Ike Quartey (Ghana)	Oscar de la Hoya (USA)	Felix Trinidad (Puerto Rico)	Ahmed Katejev (Uzbekistan)
Junior Welterweight (63.5 kg/140 lb)	Khalid Rahilou (France)	vacant	Vince Phillips (USA)	Giovanni Parisi (Italy)
Lightweight (61.2 kg/135 lb)	Orzubek Nazarov (Russia)	Steve Johnston (USA)	Shane Mosley (USA)	Artur Grigorian (Germany)
Junior Lightweight (59 kg/130 lb)	Yong Soo Choi (South Korea)	Genaro Hernandez (USA)	Roberto Garcia (USA)	Barry Jones (UK)
Featherweight (57.2 kg/126 lb)	Freddie Norwood (USA)	Luisito Espinoza (Philippines)	Hector Lizarraga (USA)	Naseem Hamed (UK)
Junior Featherweight (55.3 kg/122 lb)	Enrique Sanchez (Mexico)	Erik Morales (Mexico)	Vuyani Bungu (South Africa)	Kennedy McKinney (USA)
Bantamweight (53.5 kg/118 lb)	Nana Konadu (Ghana)	Joichiro Tatsuyoshi (Japan)	Tim Austin (USA)	Eliecer Julio (Colombia)
Junior Bantamweight (52.2 kg/115 lb)	Satoshi Iida (Japan)	Gerry Penalosa (Philippines)	Johnny Tapia (USA)	Johnny Tapia (USA)
Flyweight (50.8 kg/112 lb)	José Bonilla (Venezuela)	Chatchai Sasakul (Thailand)	Mark Johnson (USA)	Carlos Salazar (Argentina)
Junior Flyweight (49 kg/108 lb)	Pichitnoi C Siriwat (Thailand)	Saman Sorjaturong (Thailand)	Mauricio Pastrana (Colombia)	Juan Cordoba (Argentina)
Strawweight (47.6 kg/105 lb)	Rosendo Alvarez (Nicaragua)	Ricardo Lopez (Mexico)	Zolani Petelo (South Africa)	Eric Jamili (Philippines)

Heavyweight Boxing Championship Bouts in which the Championship has Changed Hands

(Fighters are US nationals unless otherwise stated.) Key to abbreviations: KO = knockout; TKO = technical knockout; PTS = won on points; WBA = World Boxing Association; WBC = World Boxing Council; IBF = International Boxing Federation

Date	Winner	Loser	Result	Rounds	Venue
7 September 1892	James J Corbett	John L Sullivan[1]	KO	21	New Orleans (LA)
17 March 1897	Bob Fitzsimmons (UK)	James J Corbett	KO	14	Carson City (NV)
9 June 1899	James J Jeffries[2]	Bob Fitzsimmons (UK)	KO	11	Coney Island (NY)
3 July 1905	Marvin Hart	Jack Root	KO	12	Reno (NV) (for vacant world title)
23 February 1906	Tommy Burns (Canada)	Marvin Hart	PTS	20	Los Angeles (CA)
26 December 1908	Jack Johnson	Tommy Burns (Canada)	TKO	14	Sydney, Australia
5 April 1915	Jess Willard	Jack Johnson	KO	26	Havana, Cuba
4 July 1919	Jack Dempsey	Jess Willard	TKO	4	Toledo (OH)
23 September 1926	Gene Tunney[3]	Jack Dempsey	PTS	10	Philadelphia (PA)
12 June 1930	Max Schmeling (Germany)	Jack Sharkey	TKO	4	New York City (for vacant world title)
21 June 1932	Jack Sharkey	Max Schmeling (Germany)	PTS	15	Long Island City (NY)
29 June 1933	Primo Carnera (Italy)	Jack Sharkey	KO	6	Long Island City (NY)
14 June 1934	Max Baer	Primo Carnera (Italy)	TKO	11	Long Island City (NY)
13 June 1935	James J Braddock	Max Baer	PTS	15	Long Island City (NY)
22 June 1937	Joe Louis[4]	James J Braddock	KO	6	Chicago (IL)
22 June 1949	Ezzard Charles	Jersey Joe Walcott	PTS	15	Chicago (IL) (for vacant world title)
18 July 1951	Jersey Joe Walcott	Ezzard Charles	KO	7	Pittsburgh (PA)
23 September 1952	Rocky Marciano[5]	Jersey Joe Walcott	KO	13	Philadelphia (PA)
30 November 1956	Floyd Patterson	Archie Moore	KO	5	Chicago (IL) (for vacant world title)
26 June 1959	Ingemar Johansson (Sweden)	Floyd Patterson	TKO	3	New York City (NY)
20 June 1960	Floyd Patterson	Ingemar Johansson (Sweden)	KO	5	New York City (NY)
25 September 1962	Sonny Liston	Floyd Patterson	KO	1	Chicago (IL)

Heavyweight Boxing Championship Bouts in which the Championship has Changed Hands (*continued*)

Date	Winner	Loser	Result	Rounds	Venue
25 February 1964	Cassius Clay[6]	Sonny Liston	TKO	6	Miami (FL)
16 February 1970	Joe Frazier[7]	Jimmy Ellis	TKO	4	New York City (NY)
22 January 1973	George Foreman	Joe Frazier	TKO	2	Kingston, Jamaica
30 September 1974	Muhammad Ali	George Foreman	KO	8	Kinshasha, Zaire
15 February 1978	Leon Spinks[8]	Muhammad Ali	PTS	15	Las Vegas (NV)
9 June 1978	Larry Holmes[9]	Ken Norton	PTS	15	Las Vegas (NV) (for WBC title)
15 September 1978	Muhammad Ali	Leon Spinks	PTS	15	New Orleans (LA) (for WBA title)
20 October 1979	John Tate	Gerrie Coetzee (South Africa)	PTS	15	Pretoria, South Africa (for WBA title)
31 March 1980	Mike Weaver	John Tate	KO	15	Knoxville (TN) (for WBA title)
10 December 1982	Mike Dokes	Mike Weaver	TKO	1	Las Vegas (NV) (for WBA title)
23 September 1983	Gerrie Coetzee (South Africa)	Mike Dokes	KO	10	Richfield (OH) (for WBA title)
9 March 1984	Tim Witherspoon	Greg Page	PTS	12	Las Vegas (for vacant WBC title)
31 August 1984	Pinklon Thomas	Tim Witherspoon	PTS	12	Las Vegas (NV) (for WBC title)
1 December 1984	Greg Page	Gerrie Coetzee (South Africa)	KO	8	Sun City, Bophuthatswana (for WBA title)
29 April 1985	Tony Tubbs	Greg Page	PTS	15	Buffalo (NY) (for WBA title)
21 September 1985	Michael Spinks[10]	Larry Holmes	PTS	15	Las Vegas (NV) (for IBF title)
17 January 1986	Tim Witherspoon	Tony Tubbs	PTS	15	Atlanta (GA) (for WBA title)
23 March 1986	Trevor Berbick (Canada)	Pinklon Thomas	PTS	12	Las Vegas (NV) (for WBC title)
22 November 1986	Mike Tyson	Trevor Berbick (Canada)	TKO	2	Las Vegas (NV) (for WBC title)
12 December 1986	James 'Bonecrusher' Smith	Tim Witherspoon	TKO	1	New York City (NY) (for WBA title)
30 May 1987	Tony Tucker	James 'Buster' Douglas	TKO	10	Las Vegas (NV) (for vacant IBF title)
7 March 1987	Mike Tyson	James 'Bonecrusher' Smith	PTS	12	Las Vegas (NV) (for WBA title)
12 August 1987	Mike Tyson	Tony Tucker	PTS	12	Las Vegas (NV) (for WBA, WBC, IBF titles)
11 February 1990	James 'Buster' Douglas	Mike Tyson	KO	10	Tokyo, Japan (for WBA, WBC, IBF titles)
25 October 1990	Evander Holyfield	James 'Buster' Douglas	KO	3	Las Vegas (NV) (for WBA, WBC, IBF titles)
14 November 1992	Riddick Bowe[11]	Evander Holyfield	PTS	12	Las Vegas (NV) (for WBA, WBC, IBF titles)
6 November 1993	Evander Holyfield	Riddick Bowe	PTS	12	Las Vegas (NV) (for WBA, IBF titles)
22 April 1994	Michael Moorer	Evander Holyfield	PTS	12	Las Vegas (NV) (for WBA, IBF titles)
24 September 1994	Oliver McCall	Lennox Lewis (UK)	TKO	2	London, UK (for WBC title)
5 November 1994	George Foreman[12]	Michael Moorer	KO	10	Las Vegas (NV) (for WBA, IBF titles)
8 April 1995	Bruce Seldon	Tony Tucker	TKO	7	Las Vegas (NV) (for vacant WBA title)
2 September 1995	Frank Bruno (UK)	Oliver McCall	PTS	12	London, UK (for WBC title)
16 March 1996	Mike Tyson	Frank Bruno (UK)	TKO	3	Las Vegas (NV) (for WBC title)
22 June 1996	Michael Moorer	Axel Schulz (Germany)	PTS	12	Dortmund, Germany (for vacant IBF title)
7 September 1996	Mike Tyson[13]	Bruce Seldon	KO	1	Las Vegas (NV) (for WBA title)
10 November 1996	Evander Holyfield	Mike Tyson	TKO	11	Las Vegas (NV) (for WBA title)
9 February 1997	Lennox Lewis (UK)	Oliver McCall	TKO	5	Las Vegas (NV) (for vacant WBC title)
11 August 1997	Evander Holyfield	Michael Moorer	TKO	8	Las Vegas (NV) (for IBF title)

[1] Sullivan lost in this first world championship bout to take place under Marquis of Queensbury rules. He had been bareknuckle world champion since 1882.

[2] Jeffries retired as champion in 1905. He came out of retirement in 1910 to fight Jack Johnson.

[3] Tunney retired as champion in 1928.

[4] Louis retired as champion in 1949. He made an unsuccessful comeback in 1950, losing to Ezzard Charles on points.

[5] Marciano retired as champion in April 1956.

[6] Clay changed his name to Muhammad Ali after winning the title. In 1967 he was stripped of his heavyweight crown for refusing to be drafted into the US army.

[7] This fight was a unification bout for the undisputed world heavyweight championship. Since 1968 Frazier had held the New York version of the title, and Ellis the WBA version.

[8] Spinks was stripped of his WBC belt after he chose to fight Ali again rather than make a mandatory defence against the WBC's number one challenger Ken Norton. Norton was then recognized as the WBC's new champion.

[9] Holmes relinquished his WBC title to become the newly-formed IBF champion.

[10] Spinks was stripped of his IBF belt in 1987 for refusing to meet Tony Tucker in a mandatory defence.

[11] Bowe relinquished his WBC belt rather than make a mandatory defence against the WBC's number one contender, UK's Lennox Lewis. Lewis was then named as the WBC's new champion.

[12] Foreman was stripped of his WBA title in March 1995 for refusing to make a mandatory challenge against Tony Tucker, and relinquished his IBF title in July 1995 for refusing to meet Axel Schulz.

[13] After winning the WBA title from Seldon, Tyson gave up his WBC belt instead of making a mandatory defence against Lennox Lewis.

World Heavyweight Champions

(Present weight limit: over 86.2 kg/190 lb. Fighters are US nationals unless otherwise stated.)

Year	Name
Champions 1882–1978	
1882–92	John L Sullivan[1]
1892–97	James J Corbett
1897–99	Bob Fitzsimmons (UK)
1899–1904	James J Jeffries[2]
1905–06	Marvin Hart
1906–08	Tommy Burns (Canada)
1908–15	Jack Johnson
1915–19	Jess Willard
1919–26	Jack Dempsey
1926–28	Gene Tunney[2]
1928–30	vacant
1930–32	Max Schmeling (Germany)
1932–33	Jack Sharkey
1933–34	Primo Carnera (Italy)
1934–35	Max Baer
1935–37	James J Braddock
1937–49	Joe Louis[2]
1949–51	Ezzard Charles
1951–52	Jersey Joe Walcott
1952–56	Rocky Marciano[2]
1956–59	Floyd Patterson
1959–60	Ingemar Johansson (Sweden)
1960–62	Floyd Patterson
1962–64	Sonny Liston
1964–67	Cassius Clay (Muhammad Ali)[2,3]
1965–67	Ernie Terrell (WBA title)[4]
1968–70	Joe Frazier (New York title)
1968–70	Jimmy Ellis (WBA title)
1970–73	Joe Frazier
1973–74	George Foreman
1974–78	Muhammad Ali
1978	Leon Spinks[5]
WBA Champions (Since 1978)	
1978	Leon Spinks
1978–79	Muhammad Ali[2]
1979–80	John Tate
1980–82	Mike Weaver
1982–83	Michael Dokes
1983–84	Gerrie Coetzee (South Africa)
1984–85	Greg Page
1985–86	Tony Tubbs
1986	Tim Witherspoon

Year	Name
1986–87	James 'Bonecrusher' Smith
1987–90	Mike Tyson (& WBC, IBF)
1990	James 'Buster' Douglas (& WBC, IBF)
1990–92	Evander Holyfield (& WBC, IBF)
1992–93	Riddick Bowe (& IBF, WBC)[6]
1993–94	Evander Holyfield (& IBF)
1994	Michael Moorer (& IBF)
1994–95	George Foreman (& IBF)[2]
1995–96	Bruce Seldon
1996	Mike Tyson
1996–	Evander Holyfield (& IBF)
WBC Champions (Since 1978)	
1978	Ken Norton
1978–83	Larry Holmes[7]
1984	Tim Witherspoon
1984–86	Pinklon Thomas
1986	Trevor Berbick (Canada)
1986–90	Mike Tyson (& WBA, IBF 1987–90)
1990	James 'Buster' Douglas (& WBA, IBF)
1990–92	Evander Holyfield (& WBA, IBF)
1992	Riddick Bowe (& IBF, WBC)[6]
1992–94	Lennox Lewis (UK)
1994–95	Oliver McCall
1995–96	Frank Bruno (UK)
1996	Mike Tyson[2]
1997	Lennox Lewis (UK)
IBF Champions (Since 1983)	
1983–85	Larry Holmes
1985–87	Michael Spinks[2]
1987	Tony Tucker
1987–90	Mike Tyson (& WBA, WBC)
1990	James 'Buster' Douglas (& WBA, WBC)
1990–92	Evander Holyfield (& WBA, WBC)
1992–93	Riddick Bowe (& IBF, WBC)[6]
1993–94	Evander Holyfield (& WBA)
1994	Michael Moorer (& WBA)
1994–95	George Foreman (& WBA)[2]
1996	Michael Moorer
1997–	Evander Holyfield (& WBA)

[1] Sullivan was the last of the bareknuckle world champions.
[2] Relinquished or stripped of title, or retired as champion.
[3] Clay changed his name to Muhammad Ali after becoming world champion.
[4] The WBA withdrew recognition of Ali after he signed for a return match with Liston in 1964. Ernie Terrell won the vacant WBA title in 1965. However, Ali remained the widely accepted champion and two years later defeated Terrell to regain the undisputed title.
[5] Spinks was stripped of his WBC title in March 1978 and remained WBA champion until losing to Ali in September 1978.
[6] Bowe relinquished his WBC title in December 1992.
[7] Holmes relinquished his WBC title in December 1983 to become the newly formed IBF's first champion.

Chess

World Chess Champions

The first recognized world chess championship-title match took place in 1886 between Wilhelm Steinitz and Johannes Zuckertort. However, the winner of that match, Steinitz, had been widely regarded as the world champion since 1866. The Fédération Internationale de Échecs (FIDE) took over control of the world championship in 1948 and remained the sole governing body until 1993, when the breakaway Professional Chess Association (PCA), led by the world champion Garry Kasparov, organized a rival championship, which Kasparov himself won. Since then there have been two world champions, Kasparov and Anatoly Karpov, who, after Kasparov had been stripped of his title, won a playoff for the FIDE title. However, it is Kasparov who is widely regarded as the true world champion. The current Woman's World Chess Champion is Harriet Hunt of the UK.

Dates	Name	Country	Dates	Name	Country
1866–94	Wilhelm Steinitz	Austria	1960–61	Mikhail Tal	USSR
1894–21	Emanuel Lasker	Germany	1961–63	Mikhail Botvinnik	USSR
1921–27	José Raul Capablanca	Cuba	1963–69	Tigran Petrosian	USSR
1927–35	Alexander Alekhine	Russia[1]	1969–72	Boris Spassky	USSR
1935–37	Max Euwe	Netherlands	1972–75	Bobby Fischer	USA
1937–46	Alexander Alekhine	Russia[1]	1975–85	Anatoly Karpov	USSR
1948–56	Mikhail Botvinnik[2]	USSR	1985–	Garry Kasparov	USSR/Azerbaijan[3][4]
1957–58	Vassily Smyslov	USSR	1993–	Anatoly Karpov	Russia[5]
1958–60	Mikhail Botvinnik	USSR			

[1] Alekhine became a French citizen in 1927.
[2] Botvinnik won a five-man tournament organized by FIDE to determine a successor to Alekhine, who had died in 1946.
[3] Kasparov is an Azerbaijani but has represented Russia internationally at chess.
[4] FIDE world champion 1985–93; PCA world champion since 1993.
[5] FIDE world champion.

Cricket

England versus West Indies: 1998 Test Series: Results

West Indies won the series 3–1 to retain the Wisden Trophy.

First Test
Sabina Park, Kingston, Jamaica (29 January)
Match abandoned as a draw with England at 17 for 3 after 10.1 overs in their first innings, after it was deemed that the pitch was too dangerous to continue play.

Second Test
Port of Spain, Trinidad (5–9 February) (An extra test was added after the first test in Jamaica was abandoned.)
West Indies won by 3 wickets; England 214 and 258 (Ambrose 5–52), West Indies 191 (Fraser 8–53) and 282 for 7 (Hooper 94 not out).

Third Test
Port of Spain, Trinidad (6–9 February)
England won by 3 wickets; West Indies 159 (Caddick 5–67, Fraser 5–40) and 210 (Fraser 4–40, Headley 4–77), England 145 (Ambrose 5–25) and 225 for 7 (Stewart 83).

Fourth Test
Georgetown, Guyana (27 February–3 March)
West Indies won by 242 runs; West Indies 325 (Chanderpaul, 118) and 197, England 170 and 137 (Ambrose 4–38).

Fifth Test
Bridgetown, Barbados (12–16 March)
Match drawn; England 403 (Ramprakash 154, Thorpe 103, Hooper 5–80) and 233 for 3 declared, West Indies 262 and 112 for 3.

Sixth Test
St John's, Antigua (20–24 March)
West Indies won by an innings and 52 runs; England 127 (Ramnarine 4–29) and 321 (Hussain 106, Thorpe 84 not out, Walsh 4–80), West Indies 500 for 7 declared (Hooper 108 not out, Lambert 104, Lara 89).

England versus South Africa: 1998 Test Series

England won the series 2–1, their first 5-match series victory for 12 years.

First Test: Edgbaston, Birmingham (4-8 June) match drawn. *Second Test*: Lord's, London (18-21 June) South Africa won by 10 wickets. *Third Test*: Old Trafford, Manchester (2-6 July) match drawn. *Fourth Test*: Trent Bridge, Nottingham (23-27 July) England won by 8 wickets. *Fifth Test*: Headingley, Leeds (6-10 August) England won by 23 runs.

English County Cricket Championship Winners

The championship was sponsored by Schweppes, 1977–83. Since 1984 it has been sponsored by Britannic Assurance. Counties winning most championships: Yorkshire, 30 (including one shared); Surrey, 16 (including one shared); Middlesex, 12 (including two shared); Lancashire, 8 (including one shared).

Year	Team	Year	Team	Year	Team
1890	Surrey	1927	Lancashire	1966	Yorkshire
1891	Surrey	1928	Lancashire	1967	Yorkshire
1892	Surrey	1929	Nottinghamshire	1968	Yorkshire
1893	Yorkshire	1930	Lancashire	1969	Glamorgan
1894	Surrey	1931	Yorkshire	1970	Kent
1895	Surrey	1932	Yorkshire	1971	Surrey
1896	Yorkshire	1933	Yorkshire	1972	Warwickshire
1897	Lancashire	1934	Lancashire	1973	Hampshire
1898	Yorkshire	1935	Yorkshire	1974	Worcestershire
1899	Surrey	1936	Derbyshire	1975	Leicestershire
1900	Yorkshire	1937	Yorkshire	1976	Middlesex
1901	Yorkshire	1938	Yorkshire	1977	Kent/Middlesex (shared)
1902	Yorkshire	1939	Yorkshire	1978	Kent
1903	Middlesex	1940–45	not held	1979	Essex
1904	Lancashire	1946	Yorkshire	1980	Middlesex
1905	Yorkshire	1947	Middlesex	1981	Nottinghamshire
1906	Kent	1948	Glamorgan	1982	Middlesex
1907	Nottinghamshire	1949	Middlesex/Yorkshire (shared)	1983	Essex
1908	Yorkshire	1950	Lancashire/Surrey (shared)	1984	Essex
1909	Kent	1951	Warwickshire	1985	Middlesex
1910	Kent	1952	Surrey	1986	Essex
1911	Warwickshire	1953	Surrey	1987	Nottinghamshire
1912	Yorkshire	1954	Surrey	1988	Worcestershire
1913	Kent	1955	Surrey	1989	Worcestershire
1914	Surrey	1956	Surrey	1990	Middlesex
1915–18	not held	1957	Surrey	1991	Essex
1919	Yorkshire	1958	Surrey	1992	Essex
1920	Middlesex	1959	Yorkshire	1993	Middlesex
1921	Middlesex	1960	Yorkshire	1994	Warwickshire
1922	Yorkshire	1961	Hampshire	1995	Warwickshire
1923	Yorkshire	1962	Yorkshire	1996	Leicestershire
1924	Yorkshire	1963	Yorkshire	1997	Glamorgan
1925	Yorkshire	1964	Worcestershire		
1926	Lancashire	1965	Worcestershire		

County Cricket: Nat West Trophy Winners

This trophy competition was the first one-day county cricket tournament and was first held in 1963 as a 65-over (60 overs from 1964) -a-side knockout competition. It has been sponsored by Gillette, 1963–80, and National Westminster Bank (since 1981). All finals are played at Lords'. Most wins: Lancashire, 6; Warwickshire, 5; Sussex, Middlesex, 4.

Year	Team	Year	Team	Year	Team
1963	Sussex	1975	Lancashire	1987	Nottinghamshire
1964	Sussex	1976	Northamptonshire	1988	Middlesex
1965	Yorkshire	1977	Middlesex	1989	Warwickshire
1966	Warwickshire	1978	Sussex	1990	Lancashire
1967	Kent	1979	Somerset	1991	Hampshire
1968	Warwickshire	1980	Middlesex	1992	Northamptonshire
1969	Yorkshire	1981	Derbyshire	1993	Warwickshire
1970	Lancashire	1982	Surrey	1994	Worcestershire
1971	Lancashire	1983	Somerset	1995	Warwickshire
1972	Lancashire	1984	Middlesex	1996	Lancashire
1973	Gloucestershire	1985	Essex	1997	Essex
1974	Kent	1986	Sussex		

County Cricket: Benson and Hedges Cup Winners

This one-day 55-overs-a-side competition was first held in 1972. All finals are played at Lord's.

Year	Team	Year	Team	Year	Team	Year	Team
1972	Leicestershire	1979	Essex	1986	Middlesex	1993	Derbyshire
1973	Kent	1980	Northamptonshire	1987	Yorkshire	1994	Warwickshire
1974	Surrey	1981	Somerset	1988	Hampshire	1995	Lancashire
1975	Leicestershire	1982	Somerset	1989	Nottinghamshire	1996	Lancashire
1976	Kent	1983	Middlesex	1990	Lancashire	1997	Surrey
1977	Gloucestershire	1984	Lancashire	1991	Worcestershire	1998	Essex
1978	Kent	1985	Leicestershire	1992	Hampshire		

County Cricket: AXA Equity and Law League Winners

This 40-over-a-side Sunday league tournament was first held in 1969. It has been sponsored by John Player, 1969–86, Refuge Assurance, 1987–91, and AXA Equity and Law from 1992.

Year	Team	Year	Team	Year	Team	Year	Team
1969	Lancashire	1977	Leicestershire	1984	Essex	1991	Nottinghamshire
1970	Lancashire	1978	Hampshire	1985	Essex	1992	Middlesex
1971	Worcestershire	1979	Somerset	1986	Hampshire	1993	Glamorgan
1972	Kent	1980	Warwickshire	1987	Worcestershire	1994	Warwickshire
1973	Kent	1981	Essex	1988	Worcestershire	1995	Kent
1974	Leicestershire	1982	Sussex	1989	Lancashire	1996	Surrey
1975	Hampshire	1983	Yorkshire	1990	Derbyshire	1997	Warwickshire
1976	Kent						

English Minor Counties Cricket Championship since 1970

This competion was first contested in 1895.

Year	Team	Year	Team	Year	Team	Year	Team
1970	Bedfordshire	1977	Suffolk	1984	Durham	1991	Staffordshire
1971	Yorkshire II	1978	Devon	1985	Cheshire	1992	Staffordshire
1972	Bedfordshire	1979	Suffolk	1986	Cumberland	1993	Staffordshire
1973	Shropshire	1980	Durham	1987	Buckinghamshire	1994	Devon
1974	Oxfordshire	1981	Durham	1988	Cheshire	1995	Devon
1975	Hertfordshire	1982	Oxfordshire	1989	Oxfordshire	1996	Devon
1976	Durham	1983	Hertfordshire	1990	Hertfordshire	1997	Devon

Cricket: Britannic Assurance County Championship (Final Table)

The previous year's positions are shown in brackets.

1997

Position	Team	Played	Won	Lost	Drawn	Bonus points[1]		Points
						Batting[2]	Bowling[3]	
1	Glamorgan (10)	17	8	2	7	50	57	256
2	Kent (4)	17	8	4	5	44	60	252
3	Worcestershire (7)	17	6	3	8	49	54	228
4	Middlesex (9)	17	7	4	6	33	56	219
5	Warwickshire (8)	17	7	2	8	32	51	219
6	Yorkshire (6)	17	6	3	8	41	54	215
7	Gloucestershire (13)	17	6	6	5	35	60	206
8	Surrey (3)	17	5	5	7	39	52	192
9	Essex (5)	17	5	6	6	39	55	192
10	Leicestershire (1)	17	4	1	12	37	54	191
11	Lancashire (15)	17	5	6	6	34	54	186
12	Somerset (11)	17	3	3	11	38	64	183
13	Nottinghamshire (17)	17	4	3	10	26	55	175
14	Hampshire (14)	17	3	5	9	42	41	158
15	Northamptonshire (16)	17	3	5	9	33	48	156
16	Derbyshire (2)	17	2	9	6	32	59	141
17	Durham (18)	17	2	8	7	22	56	131
18	Sussex (12)	17	1	10	6	24	57	115

[1] Accrued in the first 100 overs of the first 2 innings.
[2] 1 point for every 50 runs above 150 (maximum 4 points).
[3] 1 point for every 2 wickets above and including 3 wickets fallen.

County Cricket: AXA Equity and Law League Final Table

The league's matches are played on Sundays and each innings consists of a maximum of 40 overs. The previous year's positions are shown in brackets.

1997

Position	Team	Games played	Wins	Losses	Ties	No result	Net run rate[1]	Points
1	Warwickshire (4)	17	13	4	0	0	14.14	52
2	Kent (10)	17	12	4	0	1	7.70	50
3	Lancashire (9)	17	10	4	1	2	1.89	46
4	Leicestershire (12)	17	9	5	1	2	7.11	42
5	Surrey (1)	17	9	5	0	3	1.06	42
6	Somerset (5)	17	9	6	0	2	4.31	40
7	Essex (17)	17	9	6	1	1	−2.38	40
8	Worcestershire (8)	17	8	6	1	2	6.87	38
9	Northamptonshire (6)	17	8	6	0	3	2.78	38
10	Yorkshire (3)	17	8	7	1	1	5.24	36
11	Gloucestershire (16)	17	7	6	0	4	1.01	36
12	Nottinghamshire (2)	17	7	7	0	3	−0.19	34
13	Glamorgan (13)	17	5	9	0	3	−4.01	26
14	Derbyshire (11)	17	4	9	0	4	−3.04	24
15	Hampshire (15)	17	5	11	0	1	−4.73	22
16	Middlesex (7)	17	3	10	1	3	−8.28	20
17	Durham (18)	17	3	13	0	1	−12.27	14
18	Sussex (14)	17	2	13	0	2	−16.72	12

[1] Total runs scored times 100 divided by balls received, minus the run rate of the opponent.

Final First Class Batting Averages

To qualify for inclusion, a player must participate in a minimum of eight matches.

1997

Name	Team	Matches	Innings	Not outs	Runs	Highest score	Average	100s	50s
Graeme Hick	Worcester	18	28	6	1,524	303[1]	69.27	6	4
Steve James	Glamorgan	18	30	4	1,775	162	68.26	7	8
Matthew Maynard	Glamorgan	18	25	7	1,170	161[1]	65.00	3	7
Rick Ponting	Australia	8	12	3	571	127	63.44	2	2
Darren Lehmann	Yorkshire	17	27	2	1,575	182	63.00	4	10
Neil Johnson	Leicestershire	12	18	5	819	150	63.00	2	5
Graham Thorpe	Surrey	14	23	4	1,160	222	61.05	3	6
Matthew Elliott	Australia	12	19	0	1,091	199	57.42	4	5
Stuart Law	Essex	17	28	2	1,482	175	57.00	5	8
Mark Ramprakash	Middlesex	19	30	4	1,453	190	55.88	6	7
Steve Waugh	Australia	13	17	0	924	154	54.35	4	4
Matthew Hayden	Hampshire	17	30	3	1,446	235[1]	53.55	4	7
Mark Ealham	Kent	18	30	10	1,055	139	52.75	3	6
Hugh Morris	Glamorgan	17	28	4	1,262	233[1]	52.58	4	3
David Leatherdale	Worcester	17	25	8	886	129	52.11	2	5
Robert Turner	Somerset	17	28	7	1,069	144	50.90	1	7
Kim Barnett	Derbyshire	15	24	3	1,055	210[1]	50.23	3	5
Graham Rose	Somerset	18	26	9	852	191	50.11	2	3
John Crawley	Lancashire	16	25	2	1,141	133	49.60	3	7
Philip Weston	Worcestershire	17	29	5	1,190	205	49.58	4	3
Nick Knight	Warwickshire	11	17	3	689	119[1]	49.21	2	3
Graham Lloyd	Lancashire	16	24	2	1,073	225	48.77	4	5
Tom Moody	Worcestershire	14	21	1	973	180[1]	48.65	3	4
Salim Elahi	Pakistan	8	13	0	625	229	48.07	1	3
Paul Prichard	Essex	17	27	2	1,184	224	47.36	3	9

[1] Not out.

Final First Class Bowling Averages

To qualify for inclusion, a player must take a minimum of 20 wickets.

1997

Name	Team	Overs	Maidens	Runs	Wickets	Average	Best bowling figures
Allan Donald	Warwickshire	387.5	123	938	60	15.63	6–55
Mike Smith	Gloucestershire	512.2	125	1,464	83	17.63	6–45
Paul Reiffel	Australia	188.4	49	520	28	18.57	5–49
Kevin James	Hampshire	161.1	37	504	27	18.66	8–49
Dougie Brown	Warwickshire	521.3	135	1,560	81	19.25	8–89
Saqlain Mushtaq	Surrey	254.5	75	617	32	19.28	5–17
Ben Phillips	Kent	282.1	73	877	44	19.23	5–47
Paul Hutchison	Yorkshire	233.1	56	741	37	20.02	7–38
Shane Warne	Australia	433.4	112	1,154	57	20.24	7–103
Jacques Kallis	Middlesex	234.3	61	655	32	20.46	5–54
Glen McGrath	Australia	363.4	104	1,012	49	20.65	8–38
Azhar Mahmoud	Pakistan	290.5	66	829	40	20.72	5–66
Phil Tufnell	Middlesex	560.5	174	1,205	55	21.90	7–66
Mark Ilott	Essex	332.0	91	946	43	22.00	7–59
Melvyn Betts	Durham	329.0	77	1,085	49	22.14	9–64
Waqar Younis	Glamorgan	441.4	83	1,551	68	22.80	8–17
Steve Watkins	Glamorgan	508.2	143	1,393	61	22.83	7–41
Peter Hartley	Yorkshire	170.0	39	532	23	23.13	5–34
Peter Martin	Lancashire	474.2	136	1,342	58	23.13	8–32
James Hewitt	Middlesex	439.0	97	1,393	60	23.21	6–14
Martin McCague	Kent	312.4	55	1,125	48	23.43	7–50
Devon Malcolm	Derbyshire	526.1	81	1,761	75	23.48	6–23
Jason Gillespie	Australia	198.4	43	692	29	23.86	7–37
Nathan Astle	Nottinghamshire	209.0	44	525	22	23.86	5–46
Graham Rose	Somerset	488.5	124	1,563	63	24.80	5–53

England Cricket Team: Test Record

(Results are as of 31 March 1998.)

Opponent	Tests	Won	Drawn	Lost
Australia	291	92	85	114
India	84	32	38	14
New Zealand	78	36	38	4
Pakistan	55	14	32	9
South Africa	110	47	43	20
Sri Lanka	5	3	1	1
West Indies	120	28	42	50
Zimbabwe	2	0	2	0
Total	745	252	281	212

Test Cricket: Other Teams – Summary of Results

(Results are as of 31 March 1998.)

Team	Tests	Won	Lost	Drawn	Tied
Australia	581	243	165	171	2
South Africa	220	57	88	75	0
West Indies	343	132	84	126	1
New Zealand	259	38	106	115	0
India	318	60	102	155	1
Pakistan	248	71	56	121	0
Sri Lanka	83	11	36	36	0
Zimbabwe	30	1	14	13	0

Cricket World Cup Winners

This competition was first held in 1975.

Year	Winner	Runner-up	Location
1975	West Indies	Australia	England
1979	West Indies	England	England
1983	India	West Indies	England
1987	Australia	England	India
1992	Pakistan	England	Australia
1996	Sri Lanka	Australia	India, Pakistan, and Sri Lanka

One Day Cricket International Top 10 Leading Career Run Makers

(As of 8 March 1998.)

Name	Runs	Matches	Innings	Not outs	Highest Score	Average
Desmond Haynes	8,648	238	237	28	152	41.37
Mohammad Azharuddin	7,719	273	252	48	111	37.83
Javed Miandad	7,381	233	218	41	119	41.70
Aravinda De Silva	7,113	227	220	24	145	36.29
Salim Malik	6,882	268	242	37	102	33.57
Viv Richards	6,721	187	167	24	189	47.00
Allan Border	6,524	273	252	39	127	30.62
A Ranatunga	6,341	230	216	43	131	36.65
Richie Richardson	6,248	224	217	30	122	33.41
Sachin Tendulkar	6,092	178	172	16	137	39.05

Curling

Curling World Champions since 1988

This championship was first held in 1959 for men and in 1979 for women.

Year	Country	Year	Country
Men		**Women**	
1988	Norway	1988	West Germany
1989	Canada	1989	Canada
1990	Canada	1990	Norway
1991	Scotland	1991	Norway
1992	Switzerland	1992	Sweden
1993	Canada	1993	Canada
1994	Canada	1994	Canada
1995	Canada	1995	Sweden
1996	Canada	1996	Canada
1997	Sweden	1997	Canada
1998	Canada	1998	Sweden

Cycling

Tour de France since 1980

Year	Name	Country
1980	Joop Zoetemelk	Netherlands
1981	Bernard Hinault	France
1982	Bernard Hinault	France
1983	Laurent Fignon	France
1984	Laurent Fignon	France
1985	Bernard Hinault	France
1986	Greg LeMond	USA
1987	Stephen Roche	Ireland, Republic of
1988	Pedro Delgado	Spain
1989	Greg LeMond	USA
1990	Greg LeMond	USA
1991	Miguel Induráin	Spain
1992	Miguel Induráin	Spain
1993	Miguel Induráin	Spain
1994	Miguel Induráin	Spain
1995	Miguel Induráin	Spain
1996	Bjarne Riis	Denmark
1997	Jan Ullrich	Germany
1998	Marco Pantani	Italy

Tour of Britain since 1988

The Tour of Britain, formerly the Milk Race, was first held in 1951. Following an absence of three years, it was revived in 1998 as the PruTour of Britain.

Year	Name	Country
1988	Vasily Zhdanov	USSR
1989	Brian Walton	Canada
1990	Shane Sutton	Australia
1991	Chris Walker	UK
1992	Conor Henry	UK
1993	Chris Lillywhite	UK
1994	Maurizio Fondriest	Italy
1995	no race	
1996	no race	
1997	no race	
1998	Stuart O'Grady	Australia

Cycling World Champions and Major Tour Winners

1997

Category	Name	Country	Category	Name	Country
Men			Sprint	Florian Rousseau	France
Road			Points race	Silvio Martinello	Italy
Tour de France	Jan Ullrich	Germany	Team pursuit		Italy
Giro d'Italia	Marco Pantani	Italy			
Vuelta a Espana	Alex Zülle	Switzerland	*Women*		
World Cup	Michele Bartoli	Italy	*Road*		
World Road Race Championship	Laurent Brochard	France	Tour de France	Fabiana Luperini	Italy
Time trial	Laurent Jalabert	France	World Road Race Championship	Allesandra Cappellotto	Italy
			Time trial	Jeannie Longo	France
Cyclo-cross					
Cyclo-cross	Daniele Pontoni	Italy	*Cyclo-cross*		
Mountain biking: cross country	Hubert Pallhuber	Italy	Mountain biking: cross country	Paola Pezzo	Italy
Mountain biking: downhill	Nicolas Vouillez	France	Mountain biking: downhill	Anne-Caroline Chausson	France
Track			*Track*		
1 km time trial	Shane Kelly	Australia	Points race	Natalia Karimova	Russia
Keirin	Frederic Magne	France	Sprint	Felicia Ballanger	France
Madison		Spain	500 m time trial	Felicia Ballanger	France
Olympic sprint		France	Individual pursuit	Judith Arndt	Germany
Individual pursuit	Phillipe Ermenault	France			

Darts

World Professional Darts Champions since 1988

Year	Name	Country
1988	Bob Anderson	England
1989	Jocky Wilson	Scotland
1990	Phil Taylor	England
1991	Dennis Priestley	England
1992	Phil Taylor	England
1993	John Lowe	England
1994	John Part	Canada
1995	Richie Burnett	Wales
1996	Steve Beaton	England
1997	Les Wallace	Scotland
1998	Raymond Barneveld	Netherlands

World Darts Council Champions

The World Darts Council Championships were first held in 1994.

Year	Name	Country
1994	Dennis Priestley	England
1995	Phil Taylor	England
1996	Phil Taylor	England
1997	Phil Taylor	England
1998	Phil Taylor	England

Equestrianism

British Show Jumping Championship since 1988

This championship first took place in 1961. It is held at Hickstead, Sussex, as part of the British Show Jumping Derby, and is now sponsored by Peugeot.

Year	Name	Country	Year	Name	Country
1988	Nick Skelton	Great Britain	1993	Michael Whitaker	Great Britain
1989	Nick Skelton	Great Britain	1994	Captain John Ledingham	Ireland, Republic of
1990	Joe Turi	Great Britain	1995	Captain John Ledingham	Ireland, Republic of
1991	Michael Whitaker	Great Britain	1996	Nelson Pessoa	Brazil
1992	Michael Whitaker	Great Britain	1997	John Popely	Great Britain

European Show Jumping Champions: Individual, since 1979

This championship was first held in 1957 with men and women competing separately; since 1975 they have competed together.

Year	Name	Country
1979	Gerd Wiltfang	West Germany
1981	Paul Schockemöle	West Germany
1983	Paul Schockemöle	West Germany
1985	Paul Schockemöle	West Germany
1987	Pierre Durand	France
1989	John Whitaker	Great Britain
1991	Eric Navet	France
1993	Willi Melliger	Switzerland
1995	Peter Charles	Ireland, Republic of
1997	Ludger Beerbaum	Germany

Volvo World Show Jumping Cup Champions since 1988

This championship was established by the Fédération Equestre Internationale (FEI) in 1979. Riders compete in a series of mostly indoor events, beginning in October and culminating in a final in April of the following year.

Year	Name	Country
1988	Ian Miller	Canada
1989	Ian Miller	Canada
1990	John Whitaker	Great Britain
1991	John Whitaker	Great Britain
1992	Thomas Fruhmann	Austria
1993	Ludger Beerbaum	Germany
1994	Jos Lansink	Netherlands
1995	Nick Skelton	Great Britain
1996	Hugo Simon	Austria
1997	Hugo Simon	Austria
1998	Rodrigo Pessoa	Brazil

European Show Jumping Champions: Team, since 1989

Year	Country	Year	Country
1989	Great Britain	1995	Switzerland
1991	Netherlands	1997	Germany
1993	Switzerland		

Three-Day Eventing: Badminton Horse Trials since 1988

This competition first took place in 1949. It is held at Badminton House, Gloucestershire, and is now sponsored by Mitsubishi Motors.

Year	Name	Country
1988	Ian Stark	Great Britain
1989	Virginia Leng[1]	Great Britain
1990	Nicola McIrvine	Great Britain
1991	Rodney Powell	Great Britain
1992	Mary Thomson	Great Britain
1993	Virginia Leng[1]	Great Britain
1994	Mark Todd	New Zealand
1995	Bruce Davidson	USA
1996	Mark Todd	New Zealand
1997	David O'Connor	USA
1998	Chris Bartle	Great Britain

[1] Born Holgate.

Three-Day Eventing: World Champions

This championship was first held in 1966.

Year	Name	Country
1966	Carlos Moratorio	Argentina
1970	Mary Gordon-Watson	Great Britain
1974	Bruce Davidson	USA
1978	Bruce Davidson	USA
1982	Lucinda Green[1]	Great Britain
1986	Virginia Leng[2]	Great Britain
1990	Blyth Tait	New Zealand
1994	Vaughan Jefferis	New Zealand

[1] Born Prior-Palmer.
[2] Born Holgate.

Fencing

World Fencing Champions

1997

Category	Name	Country	Category	Name	Country
Men			*Women*		
Épée	Eric Srecki	France	Épée	Miraide Garcia-Soto	Cuba
Foil	Sergei Golubitsky	Ukraine	Foil	Giovanna Trillini	Italy
Sabre	Stanislaw Pozdniakov	Russia	Team épée		Hungary
Team épée		Cuba	Team foil		Italy
Team foil		France			
Team sabre		France			

Football

WORLD CUP 1998

BY PHILIP EVANS

All night long they danced joyously along the Champs Elysées after France won the 16th FIFA World Cup. France '98 saw the first finals to feature 32 participants, and the final was an all-time record 64th match.

Group Stage: Few Upsets in the Phoney War

There were few suprises in Groups A and B. Brazil beat Scotland narrowly, but Morocco more convincingly. On the final day Morocco outplayed Scotland, and assumed they had qualified for the next stage. 83 minutes into the Brazil–Norway game however, Tore Andre Flo's masterly performance produced an equalizing goal, and in the 88th minute a penalty brought Norway victory. So Norway went through, after drawing with both Morocco and Scotland.

In Group B two goals by Marcelo Salas helped Chile against an Italian side who were fortunate to gain a draw. Italy regained face by beating a youthful Cameroon and then Austria, whose last-minute equalizers had previously gained them two draws. Chile, by far the classiest of the other three, also went through.

In Group C France, whom the experts said couldn't score, netted nine goals and qualified with maximum points. Denmark finished second, above South Africa and Saudi Arabia.

The First Major Surprise

Group D provided the first bombshell when Nigeria stunned Spain in an enthralling game, twice coming from behind to win 3-2. Defeating Bulgaria allowed Nigeria to rest some players for the game against Paraguay, who took full advantage of the situation to gain second place – their win included the fastest goal of the tournament, by Celso Ayala in 53 seconds. Spain's 6-1 trouncing of Bulgaria made them bitterly rue their earlier inability to beat Paraguay.

In Group E two goals from Luis Hernandez helped Mexico beat South Korea, who were also overwhelmed by Holland. When it came to their turn, Belgium, having gained two draws, were unable to add to an early goal, and allowed South Korea to equalize. There were no major surprises in Groups F, G, and H from which Germany, Yugoslavia, Romania, England, Argentina, and Croatia qualified.

In the early stages the refereeing did not reflect the strict implementation of the rules that had been threatened before the tournament began. While many commentators felt that the referees should be applauded for not interrupting the flow of games unnecessarily, others, including tournament director Michel Platini, complained that they were too lax. The result of this criticism was that referees began handing out cards with greater frequency; the previous record of 15 dismissals in a tournament was beaten on the 15th day, and on 18 June a record five players were sent off. The eventual red card total reached 22, with 250 yellow cards being shown. Some dismissals proved highly controversial, and there was also concern that some players were being deliberately theatrical in their reaction to challenges, so that their opponents would be penalized.

The 'Super Eagles' Crash to Earth

In the first knockout stage Italy scraped through against a negative Norway. Brazil finally showed some form against Chile, although an inventive Salas and Zamorano kept the Brazilian defence alert. Laurent Blanc's Golden Goal (the first in World Cup history) rescued an insipid France in the 114th minute

(continued)

against Paraguay. The star-studded Nigeria, 1996 Olympic champions and the only remaining African country, were also knocked out; hampered by internal division, they never recovered after Denmark scored two goals in the first 12 minutes. Germany, who had previously recovered from being two goals down against Yugoslavia, did it again against a stylish Mexico – who relaxed after taking a one-goal lead. Holland beat Yugoslavia, the winning goal coming from the tenacious Edgar Davids in the final minute.

Croatia beat the other survivors from Eastern Europe, Romania, with a penalty. That same evening came the most dramatic contest of the tournament, when Argentina met England. Two dubious penalties were followed by a spectacular goal from 18-year-old Michael Owen after a quicksilver sprint through the Argentine defence. Argentina scored a crucial equalizer a minute before half time. England's cause was soon damaged further by the dismissal of David Beckham for reacting to a spiteful tackle by Diego Simeone; England played the final 75 minutes a man short, had a goal harshly disallowed, and were beaten in the tournament's first penalty shoot-out.

Three Former Winners Removed

The first quarter final was also won on penalties, when a highly tactical game between France and Italy finished goalless. France, boosted by the return of Zinedine Zidane after a two-match suspension, spurned five chances, but a negative Italy never really suggested they could win. For the third consecutive World Cup Italy went out from a penalty shoot-out. In the evening Brazil overcame Denmark in a skilful game – showing how defensive inadequacies could be offset by splendid attack.

Holland's defeat of Argentina was one of the finest games of the tournament, with the deciding goal a classic. It was 1-1 at half time, while on the hour a shot from Batistuta bruised the crossbar. Two players were then dismissed – Arthur Numan for two bad tackles, and in the 87th minute Ariel Ortega for butting the goalkeeper. Punishment came swiftly – in the 90th minute Dennis Bergkamp collected a 50-metre pass and struck the ball high into the corner of Argentina's goal.

In the last quarter final the dismissal of Germany's Christian Worns proved crucial. Coming in the 40th minute, it made life impossible for the 10 ageing Germans who, after a sprightly Croatia took the lead just before half time, collapsed dispiritedly.

Glory for France at Last

In the first semi final Brazil, four times victors in the competition, and Holland, who had reached their second consecutive final in 1978, drew after 120 thrilling minutes. Brazil's goal, from the pacy Ronaldo, came in the first minute of the second half, and was answered in the 87th minute by a header from Kluivert – who narrowly failed to score again in extra time. The referee refused Holland a penalty soon afterwards, and Brazil won after a penalty shoot-out, in which Taffarel made two crucial saves.

The second semi saw France, who had never reached a final, meet Croatia, who were in the competition for the first time. The game was goalless at half time; but within seconds of the restart Davor Suker collected a superb pass to drill home a goal for Croatia. An instant later France equalized, when right-back Lilian Thuram took advantage of a Croatian mistake. He scored again in the 69th minute with a left-foot drive. Croatia failed to take advantage of the unkind expulsion of Blanc five minutes later, though the inspired French goalkeeper Barthez made a superb save during injury time.

Croatia, however, did beat the luckless Holland in an entertaining third place game. Although the side included players (Boban, Prosinecki, Suker) who had been with Yugoslavia in 1990, it was a triumph for the new, small country, who provided the leading scorer of the competition in Davor Suker.

The final, held in the newly built Stade de France St-Denis, was the first-ever between a host country and the holders. An inventive France, with Marcel Desailly outstanding in defence, overwhelmed an increasingly dispirited Brazil. Despite having earlier suffered a fit, the Brazilian star Ronaldo unwisely chose to play – and was hardly in the game. In the first half, an unmarked Zidane headed in two crosses from corners, while in the last minute Emmanuel Petit collected a pass from Patrick Viera and slotted home the tournament's 171st goal. France's dream had come home.

The World Cup Final

Held on Sunday 12th July at Paris St-Denis, 8.00 pm.

1998

Result	France 3	Brazil 0
Goal scorers	Zidane (2), Petit	–
Captain	Deschamps	Dunga
Manager	Jacquet	Zagallo
Attendance	75,000	

The World Cup Third and Fourth Place Play-Off

Held on Saturday 11th July at Paris St-Denis, 8.00 pm.

1998

Result	Croatia 2	Holland 1
Goal scorers	Prosinecki, Suker	Zenden
Captain	Boban	F de Boer
Manager	Blazevic	Hiddink
Attendance	45,500	

The World Cup First Round Results

1998

Date	Venue	Team	Score	Scorers	Winner
Group A					
10 June	Paris St-Denis	Brazil	2	Cesar Sampaio, Boyd[1]	Brazil
		Scotland	1	Collins[2]	
10 June	Montpellier	Morocco	2	Hadji, Hadda	Draw
		Norway	2	Chippo[1], Eggen	
16 June	Bordeaux	Scotland	1	Burley	Draw
		Norway	1	H Flo	
16 June	Nantes	Brazil	3	Ronaldo, Rivaldo, Bebeto	Brazil
		Morocco	0	–	
23 June	Marseille	Brazil	1	Bebeto	Norway
		Norway	2	T A Flo, Rekdal[2]	
23 June	St Etienne	Scotland	0	–	Morocco
		Morocco	3	Bassir (2), Hadda	
Group B					
11 June	Bordeaux	Italy	2	Vieri, R Baggio[2]	Draw
		Chile	2	Salas (2)	
11 June	Toulouse	Cameroon	1	Njanka	Draw
		Austria	1	Polster	
17 June	St Etienne	Chile	1	Salas	Draw
		Austria	1	Vastic	
17 June	Montpellier	Italy	3	Di Biagio, Vieri (2)	Italy
		Cameroon	0	–	
23 June	Paris St-Denis	Italy	2	Vieri, R Baggio	Italy
		Austria	1	Herzog[2]	
23 June	Nantes	Chile	1	Sierra	Draw
		Cameroon	1	Mboma	
Group C					
12 June	Lens	Saudi Arabia	0	–	Denmark
		Denmark	1	Rieper	
12 June	Marseille	France	3	Dugarry, Issa[1], Henry	France
		South Africa	0		
18 June	Toulouse	South Africa	1	McCarthy	Draw
		Denmark	1	Nielsen	
18 June	Paris St-Denis	France	4	Henry (2), Trezeguet, Lizarazu	France
		Saudia Arabia	0		
24 June	Lyon	France	2	Djorkaeff[2], Petit	France
		Denmark	1	M Laudrup[2]	
24 June	Bordeaux	South Africa	2	Bartlett (2)[3]	Draw
		Saudi Arabia	2	Al-Jaber[2], Al-Thyniyan[2]	
Group D					
12 June	Montpellier	Paraguay	0	–	Draw
		Bulgaria	0	–	
13 June	Nantes	Spain	2	Hierro, Raul	Nigeria
		Nigeria	3	Adepoju, Lawal, Oliseh	
19 June	Paris Parc des Princes	Nigeria	1	Ikpeba	Nigeria
		Bulgaria	0		
19 June	St Etienne	Spain	0	–	Draw
		Paraguay	0		
24 June	Lens	Spain	6	Hierro[2], Luis Enrique, Morientes (2), Kiko (2)	Spain
		Bulgaria	1	Kostadinov	
24 June	Toulouse	Nigeria	1	Oruma	Paraguay
		Paraguay	3	Ayala, Benitez, Cardoso	

(continued)

The World Cup First Round Results (*continued*)

Date	Venue	Team	Score	Scorers	Winner
Group E					
13 June	Lyon	South Korea	1	Ha Seok-Ju	Mexico
		Mexico	3	Pelaez, Hernandez (2)	
13 June	Paris St-Denis	Holland	0	–	Draw
		Belgium	0	–	
20 June	Marseille	Belgium	2	Wilmots (2)	Draw
		Mexico	2	Garcia Aspe, Blanco	
20 June	Bordeaux	Holland	5	Cocu, Overmars, Bergkamp, Van Hooijdonk, R de Boer	Holland
		South Korea	0	–	
25 June	St Etienne	Holland	2	Cocu, R de Boer	Draw
		Mexico	2	Pelaez, Hernandez	
25 June	Paris Parc des Princes	Belgium	1	Nilis	Draw
		South Korea	1	Yoo	
Group F					
14 June	St Etienne	Yugoslavia	1	Mihajlovic	Yugoslavia
		Iran	0	–	
15 June	Paris Parc des Princes	Germany	2	Möller, Klinsmann	Germany
		USA	0	–	
21 June	Lens	Germany	2	Tarnat, Bierhoff	Draw
		Yugoslavia	2	Stankovic, Stojkovic	
21 June	Lyon	USA	1	McBride	Iran
		Iran	2	Estili, Mahdavikia	
25 June	Montpellier	Germany	2	Bierhoff, Klinsmann	Germany
		Iran	0	–	
25 June	Nantes	USA	0	–	Yugoslavia
		Yugoslavia	1	Komljenovic	
Group G					
15 June	Marseille	England	2	Shearer, Scholes	England
		Tunisia	0	–	
15 June	Lyon	Romania	1	Ilie	Romania
		Colombia	0	–	
22 June	Montpellier	Colombia	1	Preciado	Colombia
		Tunisia	0	–	
22 June	Toulouse	England	1	Owen	Romania
		Romania	2	Moldovan, Petrescu	
26 June	Paris St-Denis	Romania	1	Moldovan	Draw
		Tunisia	1	Souayah[2]	
26 June	Lens	Colombia	0	–	England
		England	2	Anderton, Beckham	
Group H					
14 June	Toulouse	Argentina	1	Batistuta	Argentina
		Japan	0	–	
14 June	Lens	Jamaica	1	Earle	Croatia
		Croatia	3	Stanic, Prosinecki, Suker	
20 June	Nantes	Japan	0	–	Croatia
		Croatia	1	Suker	
21 June	Paris Parc des Princes	Argentina	5	Ortega (2), Batistuta (3)[3]	Argentina
		Jamaica	0	–	
26 June	Bordeaux	Argentina	1	Pineda	Argentina
		Croatia	0	–	
26 June	Lyon	Japan	1	Nakayama	Jamaica
		Jamaica	2	Whitmore (2)	

[1] Own goal.
[2] Penalty.
[3] Including a penalty.

The World Cup First Round Group tables

1998

Team	Played	Won	Drawn	Lost	Goals for	Goals against	Goal difference	Points
Group A								
Brazil	3	2	0	1	6	3	+3	6
Norway	3	1	2	0	5	4	+1	5
Morocco	3	1	1	1	5	5	0	4
Scotland	3	0	1	2	2	6	−4	1
Group B								
Italy	3	2	1	0	7	3	+4	7
Chile	3	0	3	0	4	4	0	3
Austria	3	0	2	1	3	4	−1	2
Cameroon	3	0	2	1	2	5	−3	2
Group C								
France	3	3	0	0	9	1	+8	9
Denmark	3	1	1	1	3	3	0	4
South Africa	3	0	2	1	3	6	−3	2
Saudi Arabia	3	0	1	2	2	7	−5	1
Group D								
Nigeria	3	2	0	1	5	5	0	6
Paraguay	3	1	2	0	3	1	+2	5
Spain	3	1	1	1	8	4	+4	4
Bulgaria	3	0	1	2	1	7	−6	1
Group E								
Holland	3	1	2	0	7	2	+5	5
Mexico	3	1	2	0	7	5	+2	5
Belgium	3	0	3	0	3	3	0	3
South Korea	3	0	1	2	2	9	−7	1
Group F								
Germany	3	2	1	0	6	2	+4	7
Yugoslavia	3	2	1	0	4	2	+2	7
Iran	3	1	0	2	2	4	−2	3
USA	3	0	0	3	1	5	−4	0
Group G								
Romania	3	2	1	0	4	2	+2	7
England	3	2	0	1	5	2	+3	6
Colombia	3	1	0	2	1	3	−2	3
Tunisia	3	0	1	2	1	4	−3	1
Group H								
Argentina	3	3	0	0	7	0	+7	9
Croatia	3	2	0	1	4	1	+2	6
Jamaica	3	1	0	2	3	9	−6	3
Japan	3	0	0	3	1	4	−3	0

The World Cup Second Round Results

1998

Date	Venue	Team	Score	Scorers	Winner
27 June	Paris Parc des Princes	Brazil	4	Cesar Sampaio (2), Ronaldo (2)[1]	Brazil
		Chile	1	Salas	
27 June	Marseille	Italy	1	Vieri	Italy
		Norway	0	–	
28 June	Lens	France	1	Blanc	France[2]
		Paraguay	0	–	
28 June	Paris St-Denis	Nigeria	1	Babangida	Denmark
		Denmark	4	Moller, B Laudrup, Sand, Helveg	
29 June	Toulouse	Holland	2	Bergkamp, Davids	Holland
		Yugoslavia	1	Komljenovic	
29 June	Montpellier	Germany	2	Klinsmann, Bierhoff	Germany
		Mexico	1	Hernandez	

(continued)

The World Cup Second Round Results (*continued*)

Date	Venue	Team	Score	Scorers	Winner
30 June	Bordeaux	Romania	0	–	Croatia
		Croatia	1	Suker[3]	
30 June	St Etienne	Argentina	2	Batistuta[3], Zanetti	Argentina[4]
		England	2	Shearer[3], Owen	

[1] Includes a penalty.
[2] Score after 90 minutes was 0-0. France scored a 'golden goal' in extra time.
[3] Penalty.
[4] Argentina won 4-3 on penalties after extra time.

The World Cup Quarter Final Results

1998

Date	Venue	Team	Score	Scorers	Winner
3 July	Nantes	Brazil	3	Bebeto, Rivaldo (2)	Brazil
		Denmark	2	Jorgensen, B Laudrup	
3 July	Paris St-Denis	Italy	0	–	France[1]
		France	0	–	
4 July	Marseille	Holland	2	Kluivert, Bergkamp	Holland
		Argentina	1	Lopez	
4 July	Lyon	Germany	0	–	Croatia
		Croatia	3	Jarni, Vlaovic, Suker	

[1] France won 4-3 on penalties after extra time.

The World Cup Semi Final Results

1998

Date	Venue	Team	Score	Scorers	Winner
7 July	Marseille	Brazil	1	Ronaldo	Brazil[1]
		Holland	1	Kluivert	
8 July	Paris St-Denis	France	2	Thuram (2)	France
		Croatia	1	Suker	

The World Cup Leading Goalscorers

The leading goalscorer for the world cup wins the 'Golden Boot award'. Suker's 6 goals is the same number scored as for Golden Boot winners in 1994 and 1990.

1998

Rank	Player	Team	Goals scored
1	Suker	Croatia	6[1]
2=	Vieri	Italy	5
2=	Batistuta	Argentina	5[2]
4=	Salas	Chile	4
4=	Hernandez	Mexico	4
4=	Ronaldo	Brazil	4[1]

[1] Includes 1 penalty
[2] Includes 2 penalties

English Football: FA Carling Premiership: Final Standings

(Key: P = played; W = won; D = drawn; L = lost; F = goals for; A = goals against; Pt = points; GD = goal difference.)

1997–98

Position	Team	P	Home					Away					Pt	GD
			W	D	L	F	A	W	D	L	F	A		
1	Arsenal	38	15	2	2	43	10	8	7	4	25	23	78	+35
2	Manchester United	38	13	4	2	42	9	10	4	5	31	17	77	+47
3	Liverpool	38	13	2	4	42	16	5	9	5	26	26	65	+26
4	Chelsea	38	13	2	4	37	14	7	1	11	34	29	63	+28
5	Leeds United	38	9	5	5	31	21	8	3	8	26	25	59	+11
6	Blackburn Rovers	38	11	4	4	40	26	5	6	8	17	26	58	+5
7	Aston Villa	38	9	7	7	26	24	8	3	8	23	24	57	+1
8	West Ham United	38	13	2	2	40	18	3	4	12	16	39	56	−1
9	Derby County	38	12	4	4	33	18	4	4	11	19	31	55	+3
10	Leicester City	38	6	3	3	21	15	7	4	8	30	26	53	+10
11	Coventry City	38	8	2	2	26	17	4	7	8	20	27	52	+2
12	Southampton	38	10	8	8	28	23	4	5	10	22	32	48	−5
13	Newcastle United	38	8	6	6	22	20	3	6	10	13	24	44	−9
14	Tottenham Hotspur	38	7	4	4	23	22	4	3	12	21	34	44	−12
15	Wimbledon	38	5	8	8	18	25	5	8	6	16	21	44	−12
16	Sheffield Wednesday	38	9	5	5	30	26	3	3	13	22	41	44	−15
17	Everton	38	7	7	7	25	27	2	8	9	16	29	40	−15
18	Bolton Wanderers[1]	38	7	4	4	25	22	2	5	12	16	39	40	−20
19	Barnsley[1]	38	7	8	8	25	35	3	1	15	12	47	35	−45
20	Crystal Palace[1]	38	2	12	12	15	39	6	4	9	22	32	33	−34

[1] Relegated

English Football: FA Carling Premiership: Leading Scorers

1997–98

Name	Team	Goals scored			
		League	Domestic cup competitions	European competitions	Total
Andy Cole	Manchester United	15	5	5	25
John Hartson	West Ham United	15	9	0	24
Dion Dublin	Coventry	18	5	0	23
Michael Owen	Liverpool	18	5	0	23
Dennis Bergkamp	Arsenal	16	5	1	22
Jimmy Floyd Hasselbaink	Leeds United	16	6	0	22
Chris Sutton	Blackburn Rovers	18	3	0	21
Kevin Gallacher	Blackburn Rovers	16	4	0	20
Gianluca Vialli	Chelsea	11	2	6	19
Paulo Wanchope	Derby County	13	4	0	17

English Football: League Champions

The championship was organized by the Football League from its inception in 1888 until 1992, when the 22 First Division clubs formed the Premier League under the auspices of the Football Association. Most titles: Liverpool, 18; Arsenal, Manchester United, 11; Everton, 9; Aston Villa, 7.

Year	Winners	Runners-up	Year	Winners	Runners-up
1888–89	Preston North End	Aston Villa	1948–49	Portsmouth	Manchester United
1889–90	Preston North End	Everton	1949–50	Portsmouth	Wolverhampton Wanderers
1890–91	Everton	Preston North End	1950–51	Tottenham Hotspur	Manchester United
1891–92	Sunderland	Preston North End	1951–52	Manchester United	Tottenham Hotspur
1892–93	Sunderland	Preston North End	1952–53	Arsenal	Preston North End
1893–94	Aston Villa	Sunderland	1953–54	Wolverhampton Wanderers	West Bromwich Albion
1894–95	Sunderland	Everton	1954–55	Chelsea	Wolverhampton Wanderers
1895–96	Aston Villa	Derby County	1955–56	Manchester United	Blackpool
1896–97	Aston Villa	Sheffield United	1956–57	Manchester United	Tottenham Hotspur
1897–98	Sheffield United	Sunderland	1957–58	Wolverhampton Wanderers	Preston North End
1898–99	Aston Villa	Liverpool	1958–59	Wolverhampton Wanderers	Manchester United
1899–1900	Aston Villa	Sheffield United	1959–60	Burnley	Wolverhampton Wanderers
1900–01	Liverpool	Sunderland	1960–61	Tottenham Hotspur	Sheffield Wednesday
1901–02	Sunderland	Everton	1961–62	Ipswich Town	Burnley
1902–03	Sheffield Wednesday	Aston Villa	1962–63	Everton	Tottenham Hotspur
1903–04	Sheffield Wednesday	Manchester City	1963–64	Liverpool	Manchester United
1904–05	Newcastle United	Everton	1964–65	Manchester United	Leeds United
1905–06	Liverpool	Preston North End	1965–66	Liverpool	Leeds United
1906–07	Newcastle United	Bristol City	1966–67	Manchester United	Nottingham Forest
1907–08	Manchester United	Aston Villa	1967–68	Manchester City	Manchester United
1908–09	Newcastle United	Everton	1968–69	Leeds United	Liverpool
1909–10	Aston Villa	Liverpool	1969–70	Everton	Leeds United
1910–11	Manchester United	Aston Villa	1970–71	Arsenal	Leeds United
1911–12	Blackburn Rovers	Everton	1971–72	Derby County	Leeds United
1912–13	Sunderland	Aston Villa	1972–73	Liverpool	Arsenal
1913–14	Blackburn Rovers	Aston Villa	1973–74	Leeds United	Liverpool
1914–15	Everton	Oldham Athletic	1974–75	Derby County	Liverpool
1916–18	not held		1975–76	Liverpool	Queens Park Rangers
1919–20	West Bromwich Albion	Burnley	1976–77	Liverpool	Manchester City
1920–21	Burnley	Manchester City	1977–78	Nottingham Forest	Liverpool
1921–22	Liverpool	Tottenham Hotspur	1978–79	Liverpool	Nottingham Forest
1922–23	Liverpool	Sunderland	1979–80	Liverpool	Manchester United
1923–24	Huddersfield Town	Cardiff City	1980–81	Aston Villa	Ipswich Town
1924–25	Huddersfield Town	West Bromwich Albion	1981–82	Liverpool	Ipswich Town
1925–26	Huddersfield Town	Arsenal	1982–83	Liverpool	Watford
1926–27	Newcastle United	Huddersfield Town	1983–84	Liverpool	Southampton
1927–28	Everton	Huddersfield Town	1984–85	Everton	Liverpool
1928–29	Sheffield Wednesday	Leicester City	1985–86	Liverpool	Everton
1929–30	Sheffield Wednesday	Derby County	1986–87	Everton	Liverpool
1930–31	Arsenal	Aston Villa	1987–88	Liverpool	Manchester United
1931–32	Everton	Arsenal	1988–89	Arsenal	Liverpool
1932–33	Arsenal	Aston Villa	1989–90	Liverpool	Aston Villa
1933–34	Arsenal	Huddersfield Town	1990–91	Arsenal	Liverpool
1934–35	Arsenal	Sunderland	1991–92	Leeds United	Manchester United
1935–36	Sunderland	Derby County	1992–93	Manchester United	Aston Villa
1936–37	Manchester City	Charlton Athletic	1993–94	Manchester United	Blackburn Rovers
1937–38	Arsenal	Wolverhampton Wanderers	1994–95	Blackburn Rovers	Manchester United
1938–39	Everton	Wolverhampton Wanderers	1995–96	Manchester United	Newcastle United
1940–45	not held		1996–97	Manchester United	Newcastle United
1946–47	Liverpool	Manchester United	1997–98	Arsenal	Manchester United
1947–48	Arsenal	Manchester United			

English Football: Nationwide Division One: Final Standings

(Key: P = played; W = won; D = drawn; L = lost; F = goals for; A = goals against; Pt = points; Gls = goals scored.)

1997–98

Position	Team	P	Home					Away					Pt	Gls
			W	D	L	F	A	W	D	L	F	A		
1	Nottingham Forest[1]	46	18	2	3	52	20	10	8	5	30	22	94	82
2	Middlesbrough[2]	46	17	4	2	51	12	10	6	7	26	29	91	77
3	Sunderland	46	14	7	2	49	22	12	5	6	37	28	90	86
4	Charlton Athletic[3]	46	17	5	1	48	17	9	5	9	32	32	88	80
5	Ipswich Town	46	14	5	4	47	20	9	9	5	30	23	83	77
6	Sheffield United	46	16	5	2	44	20	3	12	8	25	34	74	69
7	Birmingham City	46	10	8	5	27	15	9	9	5	33	20	74	60
8	Stockport County	46	14	6	3	46	21	5	2	16	25	48	65	71
9	Wolverhampton Wanderers	46	13	6	4	42	25	5	5	13	15	28	65	57
10	West Bromwich Albion	46	9	8	6	27	26	7	5	11	23	30	61	50
11	Crewe Alexandra	46	10	2	11	30	34	8	3	12	28	31	59	58
12	Oxford United	46	12	6	5	36	20	4	4	15	24	44	58	60
13	Bradford City	46	10	9	4	26	23	4	6	13	20	36	57	46
14	Tranmere Rovers	46	9	8	6	34	26	5	6	12	20	31	56	54
15	Norwich City	46	9	8	6	32	27	5	5	13	20	42	55	52
16	Huddersfield Town	46	9	5	9	28	28	5	6	12	22	44	53	50
17	Bury	46	7	10	6	22	22	4	9	10	20	36	52	42
18	Swindon Town	46	9	6	8	28	25	5	4	14	14	48	52	42
19	Port Vale	46	7	6	10	25	24	6	4	13	31	42	49	56
20	Portsmouth	46	8	6	9	28	30	5	4	14	23	33	49	51
21	Queens Park Rangers	46	8	9	6	28	21	2	10	11	23	42	49	51
22	Manchester City[4]	46	6	6	11	28	26	6	6	11	28	31	48	56
23	Stoke City[4]	46	8	5	10	30	40	3	8	12	14	34	46	44
24	Reading[4]	46	8	4	11	27	31	3	5	15	12	47	42	39

[1] Promoted as champions.
[2] Promoted.
[3] Promoted after play-offs.
[4] Relegated.

English Football: Nationwide League: Leading Scorers

1997–98

Position	Name	Team	Division	Goals
1	Kevin Phillips	Sunderland	1	35
2	Pierre Van Hooijdonk	Nottingham Forest	1	34
3	David Johnson	Ipswich Town	1	30[1]
4	Gary Jones	Notts County	3	28
4=	Clive Mendonca	Charlton Athletic	1	28
6	Barry Hayles	Bristol Rovers	2	26
6=	Steve Whitehall	Mansfield Town	3	26

[1] Includes 8 goals for Bury.

English Football: Nationwide Division Two: Final Standings

Play-offs Semi-finals over two legs played home and away Fulham 1 Grimsby Town 1; Grimsby Town 1 Fulham 0; Grimsby Town wins 1-0 on aggregate. Bristol Rovers 3 Northampton Town 1; Northampton Town 3 Bristol Rovers 0; Northampton Town wins 3-0 on aggregate. Final (Wembley Stadium 24 May) Grimsby Town 1 Northampton Town 0. Grimsby Town wins promotion to the First Division. (Key: P = played; W = won; D = drawn; L = lost; F = goals for; A = goals against; Pt = points; Gls = goals scored.)

1997–98

Position	Team	P	Home					Away					Pt	Gls
			W	D	L	F	A	W	D	L	F	A		
1	Watford[1]	46	13	7	3	36	22	11	9	3	31	19	88	67
2	Bristol City[2]	46	16	5	2	41	17	9	5	9	28	22	85	69
3	Grimsby Town[3]	46	11	7	5	30	14	8	8	7	25	23	72	55
4	Northampton Town	46	14	5	4	33	17	4	12	7	19	20	71	52
5	Bristol Rovers	46	13	2	8	43	33	7	8	8	27	31	70	70
6	Fulham	46	12	7	4	31	14	8	3	12	29	29	70	60
7	Wrexham	46	10	10	3	31	23	8	6	9	24	28	70	55
8	Gillingham	46	13	7	3	30	18	6	6	11	22	29	70	52
9	Bournemouth	46	11	8	4	28	15	7	4	12	29	37	66	57
10	Chesterfield	46	13	7	3	31	19	3	10	10	15	25	65	46
11	Wigan	46	12	5	6	41	31	5	6	12	23	35	62	64
12	Blackpool	46	13	6	4	35	24	4	5	14	24	43	62	59
13	Oldham Athletic	46	13	7	3	43	23	2	9	12	19	31	61	62
14	Wycombe Wanderers	46	10	10	3	32	20	4	8	11	19	33	60	51
15	Preston North End	46	10	6	7	29	26	5	8	10	27	30	59	56
16	York City	46	9	7	7	26	21	5	10	8	26	37	59	52
17	Luton Town	46	7	7	9	35	38	7	8	8	25	26	57	60
18	Millwall	46	7	8	8	23	23	7	5	11	20	31	55	43
19	Walsall	46	10	8	5	26	16	4	4	15	17	36	54	43
20	Burnley	46	10	9	4	34	23	3	4	16	21	42	52	55
21	Brentford[4]	46	9	7	7	33	29	2	10	11	17	42	50	50
22	Plymouth Argyle[4]	46	10	5	8	36	30	2	8	13	19	40	49	55
23	Carlisle United[4]	46	8	5	10	27	28	4	3	16	30	45	44	57
24	Southend United[4]	46	8	7	8	29	30	3	3	17	18	49	43	47

[1] Promoted as champions.
[2] Promoted.
[3] Promoted after play-offs
[4] Relegated.

English Football: Nationwide Division Three: Final Standings

(Key: P = played; W = won; D = drawn; L = lost; F = goals for; A = goals against; Pt = points; Gls = goals scored.)

1997–98

Position	Team	P	Home					Away					Pt	Gls
			W	D	L	F	A	W	D	L	F	A		
1	Notts County[1]	46	14	7	2	41	20	15	5	3	41	23	99	82
2	Macclesfield[2]	46	19	4	0	40	11	4	9	10	23	33	82	63
3	Lincoln City[2]	46	11	7	5	32	24	9	8	6	28	27	75	60
4	Colchester United[3]	46	14	5	4	41	24	7	6	10	31	36	74	72
5	Torquay United	46	14	4	5	39	22	7	7	9	29	37	74	68
6	Scarborough	46	14	6	3	44	23	5	9	9	23	35	72	67
7	Barnet	46	10	8	5	35	22	9	5	9	26	29	70	61
8	Scunthorpe United	46	11	7	5	30	24	8	5	10	26	28	69	56
9	Rotherham	46	10	9	4	41	30	6	10	7	26	31	67	67
10	Peterborough	46	13	6	4	37	16	5	7	11	26	35	67	63
11	Leyton Orient[4]	46	14	5	4	40	20	5	7	11	22	27	66	62
12	Mansfield Town	46	11	9	3	42	26	5	8	10	22	29	65	64
13	Shrewsbury Town	46	12	3	8	35	28	4	10	9	26	34	61	61
14	Chester	46	12	7	4	34	15	5	3	15	26	46	61	60
15	Exeter City	46	10	8	5	39	25	5	7	11	29	38	60	68
16	Cambridge United	46	11	8	4	39	27	3	10	10	24	30	60	63
17	Hartlepool	46	10	12	1	40	22	2	11	10	21	31	59	61
18	Rochdale	46	15	3	5	43	15	2	4	17	13	40	58	56
19	Darlington	46	13	6	4	43	28	1	6	16	13	44	54	56
20	Swansea Town	46	8	8	7	24	16	5	3	15	25	46	50	49

English Football: Nationwide Division Three: Final Standings (continued)

Position	Team	P	Home					Away					Pt	Gls
			W	D	L	F	A	W	D	L	F	A		
21	Cardiff City	46	5	13	5	27	22	4	10	9	21	30	50	48
22	Hull City	46	10	6	7	36	32	1	2	20	20	51	41	56
23	Brighton & Hove Albion	46	3	10	10	21	34	3	7	13	17	32	35	38
24	Doncaster Rovers[5]	46	3	3	17	14	48	1	5	17	16	65	20	30

[1] Promoted as champions.
[2] Promoted.
[3] Promoted after play-offs
[4] Leyton Orient deducted three points for fielding players under suspension.
[5] Relegated.

English Football: GM Vauxhall Conference: Final Standings

(Key: P = played; W = won; D = drawn; L = lost; F = goals for; A = goals against; Pt = points; GD = goal difference.)

1997–98

Position	Team	P	Home					Away					Pt	GD
			W	D	L	F	A	W	D	L	F	A		
1	Halifax Town[1]	42	17	4	0	51	15	8	8	5	23	28	87	31
2	Cheltenham Town	42	15	4	2	39	15	8	5	8	24	28	78	20
3	Woking	42	14	3	4	47	22	8	5	8	25	24	74	26
4	Rushden & Diamonds	42	12	4	5	44	26	11	1	9	35	31	74	22
5	Morecambe	42	11	4	6	35	30	10	6	5	42	34	73	13
6	Hereford United	42	11	7	3	30	19	7	6	8	26	30	67	7
7	Hednesford Town	42	14	4	3	28	12	4	8	9	31	38	66	9
8	Slough Town	42	10	6	5	34	21	8	4	9	24	28	64	9
9	Northwich Victoria	42	8	9	4	34	24	7	6	8	29	35	60	4
10	Welling United	42	11	5	5	39	27	6	4	11	25	35	60	2
11	Yeovil	42	14	4	3	45	24	3	5	13	28	39	59	10
12	Hayes	42	10	4	7	36	25	6	6	9	26	27	58	10
13	Dover Athletic	42	10	4	7	34	29	5	6	10	26	41	55	−10
14	Kettering Town	42	8	6	7	29	29	5	7	9	24	31	52	−7
15	Stevenage Borough	42	8	4	9	35	27	5	4	12	24	36	51	−4
16	Southport	42	9	5	7	32	26	4	6	11	24	32	50	−2
17	Kidderminster Harriers	42	6	8	7	32	31	5	6	10	24	32	47	−7
18	Farnborough Town	42	10	3	8	37	27	2	5	14	19	43	44	−14
19	Leek Town	42	8	8	5	34	26	2	6	13	18	41	44	−15
20	Telford United[2]	42	6	7	8	25	31	4	5	12	28	45	42	−23
21	Gateshead[2]	42	7	6	8	32	35	1	5	15	19	52	35	−36
22	Stalybridge Celtic[2]	42	6	5	10	33	38	1	3	17	15	55	29	−45

[1] Promoted.
[2] Relegated.

English Football: The FA Cup

Final: 16 May, Wembley Stadium. Score: Arsenal 2, Newcastle United 0. Scorers: Overmars (23 minutes), Anelka (69 minutes). Man of the match: Ray Parlour (Arsenal). Attendance: 79,183

1998

Round	Opponents	Venue	Score	Winning scorers
Arsenal				
3rd	Port Vale	Highbury	0–0	
Replay	Port Vale	Vale Park	1–1	Bergkamp[1]
				(Arsenal won on penalties)
4th	Middlesborough	Riverside Stadium	2–1	Overmars, Parlour
5th	Crystal Palace	Highbury	0–0	
Replay	Crystal Palace	Selhurst Park	2–1	Anelka, Bergkamp
6th	West Ham United	Highbury	1–1	Bergkamp[1]
Replay	West Ham United	Upton Park	1–1	Anelka[1]
				(Arsenal won on penalties)
Semi-final	Wolves	Villa Park	1–0	Wreh

(continued)

English Football: The FA Cup (*continued*)

Round	Opponents	Venue	Score	Winning scorers
Newcastle United				
3rd	Everton	Goodison Park	1–0	Rush
4th	Stevenage Borough	Stevenage	1–1	Shearer
Replay	Stevenage Borough	St James's Park	2–1	Shearer (2)
5th	Tranmere Rovers	St James's Park	1–0	Shearer
6th	Barnsley	St James's Park	3–1	Ketsbaia, Speed, Batty
Semi-final	Sheffield United	Old Trafford	1–0	Shearer

[1] Penalty.

English Football: FA Challenge Cup Winners

All finals have been played at Wembley Stadium since 1923, except for the 1970 Chelsea v Leeds replay, which was played at Old Trafford. Most wins: Manchester United, 9; Tottenham Hotspur, 8; Aston Villa, Arsenal, 7; Blackburn Rovers, Newcastle United, 6.

Year	Winners	Runners-up	Score	Year	Winners	Runners-up	Score
1872	Wanderers	Royal Engineers	1–0	replay	Bradford City	Newcastle United	1–0
1873	Wanderers	Oxford University	2–0	1912	Barnsley	West Bromwich Albion	0–0
1874	Oxford University	Royal Engineers	2–0	replay	Barnsley	West Bromwich Albion	1–0[*]
1875	Royal Engineers	Old Etonians	1–1[*]	1913	Aston Villa	Sunderland	1–0
replay	Royal Engineers	Old Etonians	2–0	1914	Burnley	Liverpool	1–0
1876	Wanderers	Old Etonians	1–1	1915	Sheffield United	Chelsea	3–0
replay	Wanderers	Old Etonians	3–0	1916–19	not held		
1877	Wanderers	Oxford University	2–1[*]	1920	Aston Villa	Huddersfield Town	1–0[*]
1878	Wanderers	Royal Engineers	3–1	1921	Tottenham Hotspur	Wolverhampton Wanderers	1–0
1879	Old Etonians	Clapham Rovers	1–0				
1880	Clapham Rovers	Oxford University	1–0	1922	Huddersfield Town	Preston North End	1–0
1881	Old Carthusians	Old Etonians	3–0	1923	Bolton Wanderers	West Ham United	2–0
1882	Old Etonians	Blackburn Rovers	1–0	1924	Newcastle United	Aston Villa	2–0
1883	Blackburn Olympic	Old Etonians	2–1	1925	Sheffield United	Cardiff City	1–0
1884	Blackburn Rovers	Queen's Park	2–1	1926	Bolton Wanderers	Manchester City	1–0
1885	Blackburn Rovers	Queen's Park	2–0	1927	Cardiff City	Arsenal	1–0
1886	Blackburn Rovers	West Bromwich Albion	0–0	1928	Blackburn Rovers	Huddersfield Town	3–1
replay	Blackburn Rovers	West Bromwich Albion	2–0	1929	Bolton Wanderers	Portsmouth	2–0
1887	Aston Villa	West Bromwich Albion	2–0	1930	Arsenal	Huddersfield Town	2–0
1888	West Bromwich Albion	Preston North End	2–1	1931	West Bromwich Albion	Birmingham City	2–1
1889	Preston North End	Wolverhampton Wanderers	3–0	1932	Newcastle United	Arsenal	2–1
				1933	Everton	Manchester City	3–0
1890	Blackburn Rovers	Sheffield Wednesday	6–1	1934	Manchester City	Portsmouth	2–1
1891	Blackburn Rovers	Notts County	3–1	1935	Sheffield Wednesday	West Bromwich Albion	4–2
1892	West Bromwich Albion	Aston Villa	3–0	1936	Arsenal	Sheffield United	1–0
1893	Wolverhampton Wanderers	Everton	1–0	1937	Sunderland	Preston North End	3–1
1894	Notts County	Bolton Wanderers	4–1	1938	Preston North End	Huddersfield Town	1–0[*]
1895	Aston Villa	West Bromwich Albion	1–0	1939	Portsmouth	Wolverhampton Wanderers	4–2
1896	Sheffield Wednesday	Wolverhampton Wanderers	2–1				
1897	Aston Villa	Everton	3–2	1940–45	not held		
1898	Nottingham Forest	Derby County	3–1	1946	Derby County	Charlton Athletic	4–1[*]
1899	Sheffield United	Derby County	4–1	1947	Charlton Athletic	Burnley	1–0[*]
1900	Bury	Southampton	4–0	1948	Manchester United	Blackpool	4–2
1901	Tottenham Hotspur	Sheffield United	2–2	1949	Wolverhampton Wanderers	Leicester City	3–1
replay	Tottenham Hotspur	Sheffield United	3–1	1950	Arsenal	Liverpool	2–0
1902	Sheffield United	Southampton	1–1	1951	Newcastle United	Blackpool	2–0
replay	Sheffield United	Southampton	2–1	1952	Newcastle United	Arsenal	1–0
1903	Bury	Derby County	6–0	1953	Blackpool	Bolton Wanderers	4–3
1904	Manchester City	Bolton Wanderers	1–0	1954	West Bromwich Albion	Preston North End	3–2
1905	Aston Villa	Newcastle United	2–0	1955	Newcastle United	Manchester City	3–1
1906	Everton	Newcastle United	1–0	1956	Manchester City	Birmingham City	3–1
1907	Sheffield Wednesday	Everton	2–1	1957	Aston Villa	Manchester United	2–1
1908	Wolverhampton Wanderers	Newcastle United	3–1	1958	Bolton Wanderers	Manchester United	2–0
1909	Manchester United	Bristol City	1–0	1959	Nottingham Forest	Luton Town	2–1
1910	Newcastle United	Barnsley	1–1	1960	Wolverhampton Wanderers	Blackburn Rovers	3–0
replay	Newcastle United	Barnsley	2–0	1961	Tottenham Hotspur	Leicester City	2–0
1911	Bradford City	Newcastle United	0–0	1962	Tottenham Hotspur	Burnley	3–1
				1963	Manchester United	Leicester City	3–1

English Football: FA Challenge Cup Winners (continued)

Year	Winners	Runners-up	Score	Year	Winners	Runners-up	Score
1964	West Ham United	Preston North End	3–2	1983	Manchester United	Brighton & Hove Albion	2–2*
1965	Liverpool	Leeds United	2–1*	replay	Manchester United	Brighton & Hove Albion	4–0
1966	Everton	Sheffield Wednesday	3–2	1984	Everton	Watford	2–0
1967	Tottenham Hotspur	Chelsea	2–1	1985	Manchester United	Everton	1–0
1968	West Bromwich Albion	Everton	1–0*	1986	Liverpool	Everton	3–1
1969	Manchester City	Leicester City	1–0	1987	Coventry City	Tottenham Hotspur	3–2
1970	Chelsea	Leeds United	2–2*	1988	Wimbledon	Liverpool	1–0
replay	Chelsea	Leeds United	2–1*	1989	Liverpool	Everton	3–2
1971	Arsenal	Liverpool	2–1*	1990	Manchester United	Crystal Palace	3–3*
1972	Leeds United	Arsenal	1–0	replay	Manchester United	Crystal Palace	1–0
1973	Sunderland	Leeds United	1–0	1991	Tottenham Hotspur	Nottingham Forest	2–1*
1974	Liverpool	Newcastle United	3–0	1992	Liverpool	Sunderland	2–0
1975	West Ham United	Fulham	2–0	1993	Arsenal	Sheffield Wednesday	1–1*
1976	Southampton	Manchester United	1–0	replay	Arsenal	Sheffield Wednesday	2–1*
1977	Manchester United	Liverpool	2–1	1994	Manchester United	Chelsea	4–0
1978	Ipswich Town	Arsenal	1–0	1995	Everton	Manchester United	1–0
1979	Arsenal	Manchester United	3–2	1996	Manchester United	Liverpool	1–0
1980	West Ham United	Arsenal	1–0	1997	Chelsea	Middlesborough	2–0
1981	Tottenham Hotspur	Manchester City	1–1*	1998	Arsenal	Newcastle United	2–0
replay	Tottenham Hotspur	Manchester City	3–2				
1982	Tottenham Hotspur	Queen's Park Rangers	1–1*				
replay	Tottenham Hotspur	Queen's Park Rangers	1–0	* After extra time.			

English Football: Coca-Cola Cup Winners

This competition was first held in 1960–61. It has been known as the Milk Cup, 1982–86, the Littlewoods Cup, 1987–90, the Rumbelows Cup, 1991–92, and from 1993 as the Coca-Cola Cup. Most wins: Aston Villa, Liverpool, 5; Nottingham Forest, 4.

Year	Team	Year	Team	Year	Team
1977	Aston Villa	1985	Norwich City	1993	Arsenal
1978	Nottingham Forest	1986	Oxford United	1994	Aston Villa
1979	Nottingham Forest	1987	Arsenal	1995	Liverpool
1980	Wolverhampton Wanderers	1988	Luton Town	1996	Aston Villa
1981	Liverpool	1989	Nottingham Forest	1997	Leicester City
1982	Liverpool	1990	Nottingham Forest	1998	Chelsea
1983	Liverpool	1991	Sheffield Wednesday		
1984	Liverpool	1992	Manchester United		

Bell's Scottish Premier Division: Final Standings

The team finishing bottom is automatically relegated. (Key: P = played; W = won; D = drawn; L = lost; F = goals for; A = goals against; Pt = points; GD = goal difference.)

1997–98

Position	Team	P	Home					Away					Pt	GD
			W	D	L	F	A	W	D	L	F	A		
1	Celtic	36	12	4	2	41	9	10	4	4	23	15	74	+40
2	Rangers	36	13	4	1	46	16	8	5	5	30	22	72	+38
3	Hearts	36	10	5	3	36	24	9	5	4	34	22	67	+24
4	Kilmarnock	36	9	4	5	24	21	4	7	7	16	31	50	–12
5	St Johnstone	36	7	5	6	20	21	6	4	8	18	21	48	–4
6	Aberdeen	36	6	6	6	20	18	3	6	9	19	35	39	–14
7	Dundee United	36	5	7	6	23	18	3	6	9	20	33	37	–8
8	Dunfermline Athletic	36	4	9	5	26	30	4	4	10	17	38	37	–25
9	Motherwell	36	6	4	8	26	28	3	3	12	20	36	34	–18
10	Hibernian	36	6	4	8	26	24	0	8	10	12	35	30	–21

Bell's Scottish Premier Division: Leading Scorers

1997–98

Name	Team	Goals scored			
		League	Domestic cup competitions	European competitions	Total
Marco Negri	Rangers	32	1	3	36
Andy Smith	Dunfermline	16	10	0	26
Kjell Olofsson	Dundee United	18	4	1	23
Henrik Larsson	Celtic	16	3	0	19
Robbie Winters	Dundee United	8	3	6	17
Gary McSwegan	Dundee United	5	6	6	17
Owen Coyle	Motherwell	14	1	0	15
Simon Donnelly	Celtic	10	3	3	16
Ally McCoist	Rangers	5	8	3	16
Tommy Coyne	Motherwell	14	1	0	15
Jim Hamilton	Hearts	14	1	0	15
Craig Burley	Celtic	10	3	2	15
Jorg Albertz	Rangers	10	3	2	15

Scottish League Champions

Year	Team	Year	Team	Year	Team
1890–91	Dumbarton and Rangers (shared)	1924–25	Rangers	1964–65	Kilmarnock
1891–92	Dumbarton	1925–26	Celtic	1965–66	Celtic
1892–93	Celtic	1926–27	Rangers	1966–67	Celtic
1893–94	Celtic	1927–28	Rangers	1967–68	Celtic
1894–95	Hearts	1928–29	Rangers	1968–69	Celtic
1895–96	Celtic	1929–30	Rangers	1969–70	Celtic
1896–97	Hearts	1930–31	Rangers	1970–71	Celtic
1897–98	Celtic	1931–32	Motherwell	1971–72	Celtic
1898–99	Rangers	1932–33	Rangers	1972–73	Celtic
1899–1900	Rangers	1933–34	Rangers	1973–74	Celtic
1900–01	Rangers	1934–35	Rangers	1974–75	Rangers
1901–02	Rangers	1935–36	Celtic	1975–76	Rangers
1902–03	Hibernian	1936–37	Rangers	1976–77	Celtic
1903–04	Third Lanark	1937–38	Celtic	1977–78	Rangers
1904–05	Celtic	1938–39	Rangers	1978–79	Celtic
1905–06	Celtic	1940–45	not held	1979–80	Aberdeen
1906–07	Celtic	1946–47	Rangers	1980–81	Celtic
1907–08	Celtic	1947–48	Hibernian	1981–82	Celtic
1908–09	Celtic	1948–49	Rangers	1982–83	Dundee United
1909–10	Celtic	1949–50	Rangers	1983–84	Aberdeen
1910–11	Rangers	1950–51	Hibernian	1984–85	Aberdeen
1911–12	Rangers	1951–52	Hibernian	1985–86	Celtic
1912–13	Rangers	1952–53	Rangers	1986–87	Rangers
1913–14	Celtic	1953–54	Celtic	1987–88	Celtic
1914–15	Celtic	1954–55	Aberdeen	1988–89	Rangers
1915–16	Celtic	1955–56	Rangers	1989–90	Rangers
1916–17	Celtic	1956–57	Rangers	1990–91	Rangers
1917–18	Rangers	1957–58	Hearts	1991–92	Rangers
1918–19	Celtic	1958–59	Rangers	1992–93	Rangers
1919–20	Rangers	1959–60	Hearts	1993–94	Rangers
1920–21	Rangers	1960–61	Rangers	1994–95	Rangers
1921–22	Celtic	1961–62	Dundee	1995–96	Rangers
1922–23	Rangers	1962–63	Rangers	1996–97	Rangers
1923–24	Rangers	1963–64	Rangers	1997–98	Celtic

Scottish First Division: Final Standings

(Key: P = played; W = won; D = drawn; L = lost; F = goals for; A = goals against; Pt = points; GD = goal difference.)

1997–98

Position	Team	P	Home					Away					Pt	GD
			W	D	L	F	A	W	D	L	F	A		
1	Dundee	36	8	6	4	20	12	12	4	2	32	12	70	+28
2	Falkirk	36	9	4	5	26	19	10	4	4	30	22	65	+15
3	Raith Rovers	36	9	5	4	25	12	8	4	6	26	21	60	+18
4	Airdrie	36	9	6	3	24	17	7	6	5	18	18	60	+7
5	Greenock Morton	36	7	4	7	21	22	5	6	7	26	26	46	−1
6	St Mirren	36	7	3	8	22	24	4	5	9	29	29	41	−12
7	Ayr United	36	6	4	8	27	29	4	6	8	13	27	40	−16
8	Hamilton Academicals	36	4	6	8	17	28	5	5	8	26	28	38	−13
9	Partick Thistle	36	3	5	10	26	35	5	7	6	19	20	36	−10
10	Stirling Albion	36	3	7	8	20	31	5	3	10	20	25	34	−16

Scottish Second Division: Final Standings

The teams finishing first and second are automatically promoted. The bottom two teams are automatically relegated to the Third Division. (Key: P = played; W = won; D = drawn; L = lost; F = goals for; A = goals against; Pt = points; GD = goal difference.)

1997–98

Position	Team	P	Home					Away					Pt	GD
			W	D	L	F	A	W	D	L	F	A		
1	Stranraer	36	10	3	5	38	22	8	4	6	24	22	61	+18
2	Clydebank	36	7	6	5	21	17	9	6	3	27	14	60	+17
3	Livingston	36	9	5	4	32	21	7	6	5	24	19	59	+16
4	Queen of the South	36	9	5	4	25	19	6	4	8	33	32	54	+7
5	Inverness	36	7	7	4	31	22	6	3	9	34	30	49	+13
6	East Fife	36	7	2	9	27	34	7	4	7	24	25	48	−8
7	Forfar Athletic	36	6	4	8	28	30	6	6	6	23	31	46	−10
8	Clyde	36	6	5	7	21	23	4	7	7	19	30	42	−13
9	Stenhousemuir	36	6	6	6	26	26	4	4	10	18	27	40	−9
10	Brechin City	36	5	6	7	22	32	2	5	11	20	41	32	−31

Scottish Third Division: Final Standings

The teams finishing first and second are automatically promoted. (Key: P = played; W = won; D = drawn; L = lost; F = goals for; A = goals against; Pt = points; GD = goal difference.)

1997–98

Position	Team	P	Home					Away					Pt	GD
			W	D	L	F	A	W	D	L	F	A		
1	Alloa Athletic	36	13	1	4	42	19	11	3	4	36	20	76	+39
2	Arbroath	36	11	5	2	41	20	9	3	6	26	19	68	+28
3	Ross County	36	10	4	4	41	20	9	6	3	30	16	67	+35
4	East Stirling	36	11	3	4	30	16	6	3	9	20	32	57	+2
5	Albion Rovers	36	9	3	6	35	25	4	2	12	25	48	44	−13
6	Berwick Rangers	36	5	8	5	28	27	5	4	9	19	28	42	−8
7	Queen's Park	36	5	3	10	20	33	5	8	5	22	22	41	−13
8	Cowdenbeath	36	6	2	10	15	26	6	0	12	18	31	38	−24
9	Montrose	36	5	4	9	25	35	5	4	9	28	45	38	−27
10	Dumbarton	36	2	5	11	16	29	5	5	8	26	32	31	−19

Bell's Scottish Divisions One, Two, and Three: Leading Scorers

1997–98

Rank	Name	Team	Division	Goals
1	Willie Irvine	Alloa	3	22
2=	Colin McGlashan	Montrose	3	21
2=	Derek Adams	Ross County	3	21
4=	Iain Stewart	Inverness	2	20
4=	Brian Thomson	Inverness	2	20

Scottish FA Cup Winners since 1980

(First final held in 1874.)

Year	Team	Year	Team
1980	Celtic	1990	Aberdeen
1981	Rangers	1991	Motherwell
1982	Aberdeen	1992	Rangers
1983	Aberdeen	1993	Rangers
1984	Aberdeen	1994	Dundee United
1985	Celtic	1995	Celtic
1986	Aberdeen	1996	Rangers
1987	St Mirren	1997	Kilmarnock
1988	Celtic	1998	Hearts
1989	Celtic		

English Football: Top 10 Transfers Involving British Clubs

August 1997–March 1998

Rank	Name	From	To	Fee (£ millions)
1	Faustino Asprilla	Newcastle United	Parma	6.1
2	Gary Speed	Everton	Newcastle United	5.5
3	Fabrizio Ravanelli	Middlesbrough	Marseille	5.3
4=	Henning Berg	Blackburn Rovers	Manchester United	5.0
4=	Graeme Le Saux	Blackburn Rovers	Chelsea	5.0
6	Alessandro Pistone	Inter Milan	Newcastle United	4.3
7	Emerson	Middlesbrough	Tenerife	4.2
8	Andreas Andersson	AC Milan	Newcastle United	3.6
9	Dean Holdsworth	Wimbledon	Bolton Wanderers	3.5
10	Paul Gascoigne	Glasgow Rangers	Middlesbrough	3.45

English Football Writers' Player of the Year

Year	Player	Team	Year	Player	Team
1948	Stanley Matthews	Blackpool	1973	Pat Jennings	Tottenham Hotspur
1949	Johnny Carey	Manchester United	1974	Ian Callaghan	Liverpool
1950	Joe Mercer	Arsenal	1975	Alan Mullery	Tottenham Hotspur
1951	Harry Johnston	Blackpool	1976	Kevin Keegan	Liverpool
1952	Billy Wright	Wolverhampton Wanderers	1977	Emlyn Hughes	Liverpool
1953	Nat Lofthouse	Bolton Wanderers	1978	Kenny Burns	Nottingham Forest
1954	Tom Finney	Preston North End	1979	Kenny Dalglish	Liverpool
1955	Don Revie	Manchester City	1980	Terry McDermott	Liverpool
1956	Bert Trautmann	Manchester City	1981	Frans Thijssen	Ipswich Town
1957	Tom Finney	Preston North End	1982	Steve Perryman	Tottenham Hotspur
1958	Danny Blanchflower	Tottenham Hotspur	1983	Kenny Dalglish	Liverpool
1959	Syd Owen	Luton Town	1984	Ian Rush	Liverpool
1960	Bill Slater	Wolverhampton Wanderers	1985	Neville Southall	Everton
1961	Danny Blanchflower	Tottenham Hotspur	1986	Gary Lineker	Everton
1962	Jimmy Adamson	Burnley	1987	Clive Allen	Tottenham Hotspur
1963	Stanley Matthews	Stoke City	1988	John Barnes	Liverpool
1964	Bobby Moore	West Ham United	1989	Steve Nicol	Liverpool
1965	Bobby Collins	Leeds United	1990	John Barnes	Liverpool
1966	Bobby Charlton	Manchester United	1991	Gordon Strachan	Leeds United
1967	Jackie Charlton	Leeds United	1992	Gary Lineker	Tottenham Hotspur
1968	George Best	Manchester United	1993	Chris Waddle	Sheffield Wednesday
1969	Tony Book	Manchester City	1994	Alan Shearer	Blackburn Rovers
	Dave Mackay	Derby County	1995	Jürgen Klinsmann	Tottenham Hotspur
1970	Billy Bremner	Leeds United	1996	Eric Cantona	Manchester United
1971	Frank McLintock	Arsenal	1997	Gianfranco Zola	Chelsea
1972	Gordon Banks	Stoke City	1998	Dennis Bergkamp	Arsenal

European Champions' Cup Winners

This championship was played entirely on a knock-out basis until 1992, when a Champions' League of two divisions replaced the quarter- and semi-final stages. In 1995 the League was increased to four groups of four teams who compete for places in the quarter-finals, which are played on a knock-out format. In 1996 the runners-up as well as the champion clubs of the leading European leagues were allowed to take part in the competition. Most wins: Real Madrid, 7; AC Milan, 5; Ajax Amsterdam, Bayern Munich, Liverpool, 4.

Year	Winners	Runners-up	Score	Year	Winners	Runners-up	Score
1956	Real Madrid	Stade de Reims	4–3	1978	Liverpool	Club Brugge	1–0
1957	Real Madrid	Fiorentina	2–0	1979	Nottingham Forest	Malmö	1–0
1958	Real Madrid	AC Milan	3–2[1]	1980	Nottingham Forest	Hamburg	1–0
1959	Real Madrid	Stade de Reims	2–0	1981	Liverpool	Real Madrid	1–0
1960	Real Madrid	Eintracht Frankfurt	7–3	1982	Aston Villa	Bayern Munich	1–0
1961	Benfica	Barcelona	3–2	1983	Hamburg	Juventus	1–0
1962	Benfica	Real Madrid	5–3	1984	Liverpool	Roma	1–1[2]
1963	AC Milan	Benfica	2–1	1985	Juventus	Liverpool	1–0
1964	Internazionale	Real Madrid	3–1	1986	Steaua Bucharest	Barcelona	0–0[3]
1965	Internazionale	Benfica	1–0	1987	Porto	Bayern Munich	2–1
1966	Real Madrid	Partizan Belgrade	2–1	1988	PSV Eindhoven	Benfica	0–0[4]
1967	Glasgow Celtic	Internazionale	2–1	1989	AC Milan	Steaua Bucharest	4–0
1968	Manchester United	Benfica	4–1[1]	1990	AC Milan	Benfica	1–0
1969	AC Milan	Ajax Amsterdam	4–1	1991	Red Star Belgrade	Olympique Marseille	0–0[5]
1970	Feyenoord	Glasgow Celtic	2–1[1]	1992	Barcelona	Sampdoria	1–0
1971	Ajax Amsterdam	Panathinaikos	2–0	1993	Olympique Marseille	AC Milan	1–0[7]
1972	Ajax Amsterdam	Inter Milan	2–0	1994	AC Milan	Barcelona	4–0
1973	Ajax Amsterdam	Juventus	1–0	1995	Ajax Amsterdam	AC Milan	1–0
1974	Bayern Munich	Atletico Madrid	1–1	1996	Juventus	Ajax Amsterdam	1–1[6]
Replay	Bayern Munich	Atletico Madrid	4–0	1997	Borussia Dortmund	Juventus	3–1
1975	Bayern Munich	Leeds United	2–0	1998	Real Madrid	Juventus	1–0
1976	Bayern Munich	St Etienne	1–0				
1977	Liverpool	Borussia Mönchengladbach	3–1				

[1] After extra time.
[2] Liverpool won 4–2 on penalties.
[3] Steaua won 2–0 on penalties.
[4] PSV won 6–5 on penalties.
[5] Red Star Belgrade won 5–3 on penalties.
[6] Juventus won 4–2 on penalties.

European Cup Winners' Cup

This cup is awarded to the winners of a competition between winners of the domestic knock-out cup competitions of each European country. The competition was first held in 1961.

Year	Team	Country	Year	Team	Country
1961	Fiorentina	Italy	1980	Valencia	Spain
1962	Athletico Madrid	Spain	1981	Dinamo Tbilisi	USSR
1963	Tottenham Hotspur	England	1982	Barcelona	Spain
1964	Sporting Lisbon	Portugal	1983	Aberdeen	Scotland
1965	West Ham United	England	1984	Juventus	Italy
1966	Borussia Dortmund	Germany	1985	Everton	England
1967	Bayern Munich	Germany	1986	Dinamo Kiev	USSR
1968	AC Milan	Italy	1987	Ajax	Holland
1969	Slovan Bratislava	Czechoslovakia	1988	Mechelen	Belgium
1970	Manchester City	England	1989	Barcelona	Spain
1971	Chelsea	England	1990	Sampdoria	Italy
1972	Glasgow Rangers	Scotland	1991	Manchester United	England
1973	AC Milan	Italy	1992	Werder Bremen	Germany
1974	Magdeburg	East Germany	1993	Parma	Italy
1975	Dinamo Kiev	USSR	1994	Arsenal	England
1976	Anderlecht	Belgium	1995	Real Zaragoza	Spain
1977	SV Hamburg	West Germany	1996	Paris St Germain	France
1978	Anderlecht	Belgium	1997	Barcelona	Spain
1979	Barcelona	Spain	1998	Chelsea	England

Union of European Football Associations (UEFA) Cup

Year	Team	Country	Year	Team	Country
1958	Barcelona	Spain	1979	Borussia Mönchengladbach	West Germany
1960	Barcelona	Spain	1980	Eintracht Frankfurt	West Germany
1961	Roma	Italy	1981	Ipswich Town	England
1962	Valencia	Spain	1982	IFK Gothenburg	Sweden
1963	Valencia	Spain	1983	Anderlecht	Belgium
1964	Zaragoza	Spain	1984	Tottenham Hotspur	England
1965	Ferencvaros	Hungary	1985	Real Madrid	Spain
1966	Barcelona	Spain	1986	Real Madrid	Spain
1967	Dinamo Zagreb	Yugoslavia	1987	IFK Gothenburg	Sweden
1968	Leeds United	England	1988	Bayer Leverkusen	West Germany
1969	Newcastle United	England	1989	Napoli	Italy
1970	Arsenal	England	1990	Juventus	Italy
1971	Leeds United	England	1991	Inter Milan	Italy
1972	Tottenham Hotspur	England	1992	Ajax	Holland
1973	Liverpool	England	1993	Juventus	Italy
1974	Feyenoord	Netherlands	1994	Inter Milan	Italy
1975	Borussia Mönchengladbach	West Germany	1995	Parma	Italy
1976	Liverpool	England	1996	Bayern Munich	Germany
1977	Juventus	Italy	1997	Schalke	Germany
1978	PSV Eindhoven	Holland	1998	Inter Milan	Italy

European Footballer of the Year

Year	Player	Club	Country of Origin	Year	Player	Club	Country of Origin
1980	Karl-Heinz Rummenigge	Bayern Munich	West Germany	1989	Marco Van Basten	AC Milan	Netherlands
1981	Karl-Heinz Rummenigge	Bayern Munich	West Germany	1990	Lothar Matthäus	Inter Milan	Germany
1982	Paolo Rossi	Juventus	Italy	1991	Jean-Pierre Papin	Marseille	France
1983	Michel Platini	Juventus	France	1992	Marco Van Basten	AC Milan	Netherlands
1984	Michel Platini	Juventus	France	1993	Roberto Baggio	Juventus	Italy
1985	Michel Platini	Juventus	France	1994	Hristo Stoichkov	Barcelona	Bulgaria
1986	Igor Belanov	Dynamo Kiev	Soviet Union	1995	George Weah	AC Milan	Liberia
1987	Ruud Gullit	AC Milan	Netherlands	1996	Matthias Sammer	Borussia Dortmund	Germany
1988	Marco Van Basten	AC Milan	Netherlands	1997	Ronaldo	Inter Milan	Brazil

FIFA World Player of the Year

This award was first presented in 1991. It is sponsored by FIFA, the European Sports Management Association, and Adidas, and is selected by national team coaches.

Year	Player	Team	Country of Origin	Year	Player	Team	Country of Origin
1991	Lothar Matthäus	Inter Milan	Germany	1995	George Weah	AC Milan	Liberia
1992	Marco Van Basten	AC Milan	Netherlands	1996	Ronaldo	Barcelona	Brazil
1993	Roberto Baggio	Juventus	Italy	1997	Ronaldo	Inter Milan	Brazil
1994	Romario	Barcelona	Brazil				

World Cup Finals

This tournament was not heldi n 1942 or 1946.

Year	Winner	Runner-up	Score	Venue	Year	Winner	Runner-up	Score	Venue
1930	Uruguay	Argentina	4–2	Uruguay	1970	Brazil	Italy	4–1	Mexico
1934	Italy	Czechoslovakia	2–1	Italy	1974	West Germany	Holland	2–1	West Germany
1938	Italy	Hungary	4–2	France	1978	Argentina	Holland	3–1	Argentina
1950	Uruguay	Brazil	2–1	Brazil	1982	Italy	West Germany	3–1	Spain
1954	West Germany	Hungary	3–2	Switzerland	1986	Argentina	West Germany	3–2	Mexico
1958	Brazil	Sweden	5–2	Sweden	1990	West Germany	Argentina	1–0	Italy
1962	Brazil	Czechoslovakia	3–1	Chile	1994	Brazil[1]	Italy	0–0	USA
1966	England	West Germany	4–2	England	1998	France	Brazil	3–0	France

[1] Brazil won 3–2 on penalties.

Federation Internationale de Football Association (FIFA) Women's World Cup

This cup was inaugurated in 1991.

Year	Winner	Runner-up	Score	Venue
1991	USA	Norway	2–1	China
1995	Norway	Germany	2–0	Sweden

Winners of Major International Competitions

(As of July 1998.)

Competition	Country	Year	Venue
Olympic Games (men)	Nigeria	1996	USA
Olympic Games (women)	USA	1996	USA
Copa America	Brazil	1997	Bolivia
European Championship	Germany	1996	England
African Nations' Cup	Egypt	1998	Burkina Faso
CONCACAF Gold Cup	Mexico	1998	USA

Association Football: Copa America Champions

The world's oldest existing international tournament, it was known as the South American Championship until 1975. It was expanded to include the USA and Mexico in 1993.

Year	Team	Year	Team	Year	Team	Year	Team
1910	Argentina[1]	1926	Uruguay	1947	Argentina	1975	Peru
1916	Uruguay[1]	1927	Argentina	1949	Brazil	1979	Paraguay
1917	Uruguay	1929	Argentina	1953	Paraguay	1983	Uruguay
1919	Brazil	1935	Uruguay	1955	Argentina	1987	Uruguay
1920	Uruguay	1937	Argentina	1956	Uruguay	1989	Brazil
1921	Argentina	1939	Peru	1957	Argentina	1991	Argentina
1922	Brazil	1941	Argentina	1959	Argentina	1993	Argentina
1923	Uruguay	1942	Uruguay	1961	Uruguay	1995	Uruguay
1924	Uruguay	1945	Argentina	1963	Bolivia	1997	Brazil
1925	Argentina	1946	Argentina	1967	Uruguay		

[1] Unofficial tournament.

Gaelic Football

The All-Ireland Gaelic Football Championship since 1988

Year	Team	Year	Team	Year	Team
1988	Meath	1991	Down	1995	Dublin
1989	Cork	1992	Donegal	1996	Meath
1990	Cork	1993	Derry	1997	Kerry
		1994	Down		

Golf

British Open Golf Championship Winners

The competition was played over 36 holes between 1860 and 1891; since 1892 it has been played over 72 holes.

Year	Name	Country	Location	Score	Year	Name	Country	Location	Score
1860	Willie Park, Sr	UK	Prestwick	174	1871	No competition			
1861	Tom Morris, Sr	UK	Prestwick	163	1872	Tom Morris, Jr	UK	Prestwick	166
1862	Tom Morris, Sr	UK	Prestwick	163	1873	Tom Kidd	UK	St Andrews	179
1863	Willie Park, Sr	UK	Prestwick	168	1874	Mungo Park	UK	Musselburgh	159
1864	Tom Morris, Sr	UK	Prestwick	167	1875	Willie Park, Sr	UK	Prestwick	166
1865	Andrew Strath	UK	Prestwick	162	1876	Bob Martin	UK	St Andrews	176
1866	Willie Park, Sr	UK	Prestwick	169	1877	Jamie Anderson	UK	Musselburgh	160
1867	Tom Morris, Sr	UK	Prestwick	170	1878	Jamie Anderson	UK	Prestwick	157
1868	Tom Morris, Jr	UK	Prestwick	157	1879	Jamie Anderson	UK	St Andrews	169
1869	Tom Morris, Jr	UK	Prestwick	154	1880	Robert Ferguson	UK	Musselburgh	162
1870	Tom Morris, Jr	UK	Prestwick	149	1881	Robert Ferguson	UK	Prestwick	170

(continued)

British Open Golf Championship Winners (*continued*)

Year	Name	Country	Location	Score	Year	Name	Country	Location	Score
1882	Robert Ferguson	UK	St Andrews	171	1946	Sam Snead	USA	St Andrews	290
1883	Willie Fernie	UK	Musselburgh	158	1947	Fred Daly	UK	Hoylake	293
1884	Jack Simpson	UK	Prestwick	160	1948	Henry Cotton	UK	Muirfield	284
1885	Bob Martin	UK	St Andrews	171	1949	Bobby Locke	South Africa	Sandwich	283
1886	David Brown	UK	Musselburgh	157	1950	Bobby Locke	South Africa	Troon	279
1887	Willie Park, Jr	UK	Prestwick	161	1951	Max Faulkner	UK	Portrush	285
1888	Jack Burns	UK	St Andrews	171	1952	Bobby Locke	South Africa	Royal Lytham	287
1889	Willie Park, Jr	UK	Musselburgh	155	1953	Ben Hogan	USA	Carnoustie	282
1890	John Ball[1]	UK	Prestwick	164	1954	Peter Thomson	Australia	Royal Birkdale	283
1891	Hugh Kirkaldy	UK	St Andrews	166	1955	Peter Thomson	Australia	St Andrews	281
1892	Harold Hilton[1]	UK	Muirfield	305	1956	Peter Thomson	Australia	Hoylake	286
1893	William Auchterlonie	UK	Prestwick	322	1957	Bobby Locke	South Africa	St Andrews	279
1894	John H Taylor	UK	Sandwich	326	1958	Peter Thomson	Australia	Royal Lytham	278
1895	John H Taylor	UK	St Andrews	322	1959	Gary Player	South Africa	Muirfield	284
1896	Harry Vardon	UK	Muirfield	316	1960	Kel Nagle	Australia	St Andrews	278
1897	Harold Hilton[1]	UK	Hoylake	314	1961	Arnold Palmer	USA	Royal Birkdale	284
1898	Harry Vardon	UK	Prestwick	307	1962	Arnold Palmer	USA	Troon	276
1899	Harry Vardon	UK	Sandwich	310	1963	Bob Charles	New Zealand	Royal Lytham	277
1900	John H Taylor	UK	St Andrews	309	1964	Tony Lema	USA	St Andrews	279
1901	James Braid	UK	Muirfield	309	1965	Peter Thomson	Australia	Royal Birkdale	285
1902	Sandy Herd	UK	Hoylake	307	1966	Jack Nicklaus	USA	Muirfield	282
1903	Harry Vardon	UK	Prestwick	300	1967	Roberto de Vincenzo	Argentina	Hoylake	278
1904	Jack White	UK	Sandwich	296	1968	Gary Player	South Africa	Carnoustie	289
1905	James Braid	UK	St Andrews	318	1969	Tony Jacklin	UK	Royal Lytham	280
1906	James Braid	UK	Muirfield	300	1970	Jack Nicklaus	USA	St Andrews	283
1907	Arnaud Massy	France	Hoylake	312	1971	Lee Trevino	USA	Royal Birkdale	278
1908	James Braid	UK	Prestwick	291	1972	Lee Trevino	USA	Muirfield	278
1909	John H Taylor	UK	Deal	295	1973	Tom Weiskopf	USA	Troon	276
1910	James Braid	UK	St Andrews	299	1974	Gary Player	South Africa	Royal Lytham	282
1911	Harry Vardon	UK	Sandwich	303	1975	Tom Watson	USA	Carnoustie	279
1912	Edward Ray	UK	Muirfield	295	1976	Johnny Miller	USA	Royal Birkdale	279
1913	John H Taylor	UK	Hoylake	304	1977	Tom Watson	USA	Turnberry	268
1914	Harry Vardon	UK	Prestwick	306	1978	Jack Nicklaus	USA	St Andrews	281
1915–19	No competition				1979	Seve Ballesteros	Spain	Royal Lytham	283
1920	George Duncan	UK	Deal	303	1980	Tom Watson	USA	Muirfield	271
1921	Jock Hutchison	USA	St Andrews	296	1981	Bill Rogers	USA	Sandwich	276
1922	Walter Hagen	USA	Sandwich	300	1982	Tom Watson	USA	Troon	284
1923	Arthur Havers	UK	Troon	295	1983	Tom Watson	USA	Royal Birkdale	275
1924	Walter Hagen	USA	Hoylake	301	1984	Seve Ballesteros	Spain	St Andrews	276
1925	Jim Barnes	USA	Prestwick	300	1985	Sandy Lyle	UK	Sandwich	282
1926	Bobby Jones[1]	USA	Royal Lytham	291	1986	Greg Norman	Australia	Turnberry	280
1927	Bobby Jones[1]	USA	St Andrews	285	1987	Nick Faldo	UK	Muirfield	279
1928	Walter Hagen	USA	Sandwich	292	1988	Seve Ballesteros	Spain	Royal Lytham	273
1929	Walter Hagen	USA	Muirfield	292	1989	Mark Calcavecchia	USA	Troon	275
1930	Bobby Jones[1]	USA	Hoylake	291	1990	Nick Faldo	UK	St Andrews	270
1931	Tommy Armour	USA	Carnoustie	296	1991	Ian Baker-Finch	Australia	Royal Birkdale	272
1932	Gene Sarazen	USA	Prince's	283	1992	Nick Faldo	UK	Muirfield	272
1933	Densmore Shute	USA	St Andrews	292	1993	Greg Norman	Australia	Sandwich	267
1934	Henry Cotton	UK	Sandwich	283	1994	Nick Price	Zimbabwe	Turnberry	268
1935	Alfred Perry	UK	Muirfield	283	1995	John Daly	USA	St Andrews	282
1936	Alfred Padgham	UK	Hoylake	287	1996	Tom Lehman	USA	Royal Lytham	271
1937	Henry Cotton	UK	Carnoustie	290	1997	Justin Leonard	USA	Troon	272
1938	Reg Whitcombe	UK	Sandwich	295	1998	Mark O'Meara	USA	Royal Birkdale	280[2]
1939	Dick Burton	UK	St Andrews	290					
1940–45	No competition								

[1] Amateur player.
[2] Won after a play-off.

British Amateur Golf Championship since 1988

This championship was first held in 1885. Winners are from UK or Republic of Ireland unless otherwise stated.

Year	Name	Year	Name	Year	Name
1988	Christian Hardin (Sweden)	1992	Stephen Dundas	1996	Warren Bladon
1989	Stephen Dodd	1993	Iain Pyman	1997	Craig Watson
1990	Rolf Muntz (Netherlands)	1994	Lee James	1998	Sergio Garcia (Spain)
1991	Gary Wolstenholme	1995	Gordon Sherry		

British Open Women's Golf Championship Winners since 1980

This championship has been held as a strokeplay event since 1976. It is now sponsored by Weetabix.

Year	Name	Country	Year	Name	Country
1980	Debbie Massey	USA	1989	Jane Geddes	USA
1981	Debbie Massey	USA	1990	Helen Alfredsson	Sweden
1982	Marta Figueras-Dotti[1]	Spain	1991	Penny Grice-Whittaker	UK
1983	not held		1992	Patty Sheehan	USA
1984	Ayako Okamoto	Japan	1993	Karen Lunn	Australia
1985	Betsy King	USA	1994	Liselotte Neumann	Sweden
1986	Laura Davies	UK	1995	Karrie Webb	Australia
1987	Alison Nicholas	UK	1996	Emilee Klein	USA
1988	Corinne Dibnah	Australia	1997	Karrie Webb	Australia

[1] Amateur player.

Men's US Open Golf Championship Winners since 1980

Year	Name	Country	Location	Score	Year	Name	Country	Location	Score
1980	Jack Nicklaus	USA	Baltusrol (NJ)	272	1991	Payne Stewart	USA	Hazeltine (MN)	282[1]
1981	David Graham	Australia	Merion (PA)	273	1992	Tom Kite	USA	Monterey (CA)	285
1982	Tom Watson	USA	Pebble Beach (CA)	282	1993	Lee Janzen	USA	Baltusrol (NJ)	272
1983	Larry Nelson	USA	Oakmont (PA)	280	1994	Ernie Els	South Africa	Oakmont (PA)	279
1984	Fuzzy Zoeller	USA	Winged Foot (NY)	276[1]					
1985	Andy North	USA	Oakland Hills (MI)	279	1995	Corey Pavin	USA	Shinnecock Hills (NY)	280
1986	Raymond Floyd	USA	Shinnecock Hills (NY)	279	1996	Steve Jones	USA	Oakland Hills (MI)	278
1987	Scott Simpson	USA	Olympic Club (CA)	277	1997	Ernie Els	South Africa	Congressional (MI)	276
1988	Curtis Strange	USA	Brookline (NY)	278					
1989	Curtis Strange	USA	Oak Hill (NY)	278	1998	Lee Janzen	USA	Olympic Club (CA)	280
1990	Hale Irwin	USA	Medinah (IL)	280[1]					

[1] Score after play-off.

US Professional Golf Association Championship Winners since 1988

This competition was first held in 1916. It was contested as a matchplay between 1916 and 1957, and has been contested as strokeplay since 1958. Players are of US nationality unless otherwise stated.

Year	Name	Score	Year	Name	Score	Year	Name	Score
1988	Jeff Sluman	272	1992	Nick Price (Zimbabwe)	278	1996	Mark Brooks	277[1]
1989	Payne Stewart	276	1993	Paul Azinger	272[1]	1997	Davis Love III	269
1990	Wayne Grady (Australia)	282	1994	Nick Price (Zimbabwe)	269			
1991	John Daly	276	1995	Steve Elkington (Australia)	267			

[1] Score after play-off.

US Masters Golf Winners since 1988

This competition has been held annually at the Augusta National course, Georgia, USA, since 1934.

Year	Name	Country	Score	Year	Name	Country	Score
1988	Sandy Lyle	UK	281	1995	Ben Crenshaw	USA	274
1989	Nick Faldo	UK	283[1]	1996	Nick Faldo	UK	276
1990	Nick Faldo	UK	278[1]	1997	Tiger Woods	USA	270
1991	Ian Woosnam	UK	277	1998	Mark O'Meara	USA	279
1992	Fred Couples	USA	275				
1993	Bernhard Langer	Germany	277				
1994	José-Maria Olazábal	Spain	279				

[1] Score after play-off.

World Golf Matchplay Champions since 1988

This competition has been held annually at Wentworth, Surrey, England, since 1964. Since 1992, it has been sponsored by Toyota.

Year	Name	Country	Year	Name	Country
1988	Sandy Lyle	UK	1993	Corey Pavin	USA
1989	Nick Faldo	UK	1994	Ernie Els	South Africa
1990	Ian Woosnam	UK	1995	Ernie Els	South Africa
1991	Seve Ballesteros	Spain	1996	Ernie Els	South Africa
1992	Nick Faldo	UK	1997	Vijay Singh	Fiji

Ryder Cup Winners

This competition is a biennial team event, inaugurated in 1927 between professional golfers of the USA and the UK. From 1973 to 1977, the event was between the USA and a combined UK and Republic of Ireland team. Since 1979, it has been between the USA and Europe. Locations are in the USA unless otherwise stated.

Year	Winner	Score	Location	Year	Winner	Score	Location
1927	USA	9.5–2.5	Worcester CC (MA)	1967	USA	23.5–8.5	Champions GC (TX)
1929	UK	7–5	Moortown, Yorkshire, UK	1969	tie	16–16	Royal Birkdale, Lancashire, UK
1931	USA	9–3	Scioto CC (OH)	1971	USA	18.5–13.5	Old Warson CC (MO)
1933	UK	6.5–5.5	Southport, Lancashire, UK	1973	USA	19–13	Muirfield, Scotland
1935	USA	9–3	Ridgewood CC (NJ)	1975	USA	21–11	Laurel Valley GC (PA)
1937	USA	8–4	Southport, Lancashire, UK	1977	USA	12.5–7.5	Royal Lytham, Lancashire, UK
1939–45	No competition			1979	USA	17–11	Greenbrier (WV)
1947	USA	11–1	Portland CC (OR)	1981	USA	18.5–9.5	Walton Heath, Surrey, UK
1949	USA	7–5	Ganton GC, Yorkshire, UK	1983	USA	14.5–13.5	PGA National GC (FL)
1951	USA	9.5–2.5	Pinehurst CC (NC)	1985	Europe	16.5–11.5	The Belfry, Sutton Coldfield, UK
1953	USA	6.5–5.5	Wentworth, Surrey, UK	1987	Europe	15–13	Muirfield Village GC (OH)
1955	USA	8–4	Thunderbird Ranch and CC (CA)	1989	tie	14–14	The Belfry, Sutton Coldfield, UK
1957	UK	7.5–4.5	Lindrick GC, Yorkshire, UK	1991	USA	14.5–13.5	Ocean Course (SC)
1959	USA	8.5–3.5	Eldorado CC (CA)	1993	USA	15–13	The Belfry, Sutton Coldfield, UK
1961	USA	14.5–9.5	Royal Lytham, Lancashire, UK	1995	Europe	14.5–13.5	Oak Hill CC (NY)
1963	USA	23–9	East Lake CC (GA)	1997	Europe	14.5–13.5	Valderrama, Andalucia, Spain
1965	USA	19.5–12.5	Royal Birkdale, Lancashire, UK				

Solheim Cup Winners

This is a biennial team competition between the women professional golfers of the USA and Europe. It was first held in 1990.

Year	Winner	Score	Location
1990	USA	11.5–4.5	Orlando (FL), USA
1992	Europe	11.5–6.5	Dalmahoy, Scotland, UK
1994	USA	13–7	Greenbrier (WV), USA
1996	USA	17–11	Chepstow, Wales, UK

Walker Cup Winners since 1979

This team competition has been held every two years since 1922 (except 1940–45) between the amateur golfers of the USA and those of the UK and Republic of Ireland.

Year	Winner	Score
1979	USA	15.5–8.5
1981	USA	15–9
1983	USA	13.5–10.5
1985	USA	13–11
1987	USA	16.5–7.5
1989	UK and Ireland, Republic of	12.5–11.5
1991	USA	14–10
1993	USA	19–5
1995	UK and Ireland, Republic of	14–10
1997	USA	18–6

Professional Golf Association Tour Annual Leading Money Winners since 1988

Players are of US nationality unless otherwise stated.

Year	Name	Winnings ($)	Year	Name	Winnings ($)
1988	Curtis Strange	1,147,644	1993	Nick Price (Zimbabwe)	1,478,557
1989	Tom Kite	1,395,278	1994	Nick Price (Zimbabwe)	1,499,927
1990	Greg Norman (Australia)	1,165,477	1995	Greg Norman (Australia)	1,654,959
1991	Corey Pavin	979,430	1996	Tom Lehman	1,780,159
1992	Fred Couples	1,344,188	1997	Tiger Woods	2,066,833

Ladies Professional Golf Association Tour Annual Leading Money Winners since 1988

Players are of US nationality unless otherwise stated.

Year	Name	Winnings ($)
1988	Sherri Turner	350,851
1989	Betsy King	654,132
1990	Beth Daniel	863,578
1991	Pat Bradley	763,118
1992	Dottie Mochrie	693,335
1993	Betsy King	595,992
1994	Laura Davies (UK)	687,201
1995	Annika Sorenstam (Sweden)	666,533
1996	Karrie Webb (Australia)	1,002,000
1997	Annika Sorenstam (Sweden)	1,200,000

European Professional Golfers' Association: Harry Vardon Trophy Winners since 1988

This trophy has been awarded since 1937 to the leader of the European PGA Order of Merit. Most wins: Severiano Ballesteros, 6; Colin Montgomerie, 5; Peter Oosterhuis, 4.

Year	Name	Country
1988	Severiano Ballesteros	Spain
1989	Ronan Rafferty	Ireland, Republic of
1990	Ian Woosnam	UK
1991	Severiano Ballesteros	Spain
1992	Nick Faldo	UK
1993	Colin Montgomerie	UK
1994	Colin Montgomerie	UK
1995	Colin Montgomerie	UK
1996	Colin Montgomerie	UK
1997	Colin Montgomerie	UK

Greyhound Racing

Greyhound Derby since 1988

This race was first held in 1927 at the White City. Since 1985 it has been held at Wimbledon. Current distance is 480 m. Most wins: Mick the Miller (1929, 1930), Patricia's Hope (1972, 1973), 2.

Year	Name	Year	Name	Year	Name
1988	Hit the Lid	1992	Farloe Melody	1996	Shanless Slippy
1989	Lartigue Note	1993	Ringa Hustle	1997	Some Picture
1990	Slippy Blue	1994	Moral Standards	1998	Toms The Best
1991	Ballinderry Ash	1995	Moaning Lad		

Gymnastics

Gymnastics World Champions

1997

Category	Name	Country
Men		
Individual all-round	Ivan Ivankov	Belarus
Floor	Alexei Nemov	Russia
Pommel horse	Valeri Belenki	Germany
Rings	Yuri Chechi	Italy
Vault	Sergei Fedorchenko	Kazakhstan
Parallel bars	Zhang Jinjing	China
Horizontal bar	Jani Tanskanen	Finland
Team		China
Women		
Individual all-round	Svetlana Khorkina	Russia
Beam	Gina Gogean	Romania
Vault	Simona Amanar	Romania
Asymmetric bars	Svetlana Khorkina	Russia
Floor	Gina Gogean	Romania
Team		Romania

Gymnastics World Championships: Overall Individual since 1991

These championships were first held in 1903 for men and in 1934 for women. It is contested every two years.

Category	Name	Country
Men		
1991	Gregori Misutin	USSR
1993	Vitaly Scherbo	Belarus
1995	Li Xiaoshuang	China
1997	Ivan Ivankov	Belarus
Women		
1991	Kim Zmeskal	USA
1993	Shannon Miller	USA
1995	Lilia Pôdkopaeva	Ukraine
1997	Svetlana Khorkina	Russia

Gymnastics World Championships: Team, since 1979

This championship was first held in 1903 for men and in 1934 for women. It is contested every two years.

Year	Country	Year	Country
Men		Women	
1979	USSR	1979	Romania
1981	USSR	1981	USSR
1983	China	1983	USSR
1985	USSR	1985	USSR
1987	USSR	1987	Romania
1989	USSR	1989	USSR
1991	USSR	1991	USSR
1993	Belarus	1993	USA
1995	China	1995	Romania
1997	China	1997	Romania

Hockey

English National Hockey League: Premier Division: Final Table

Men

1997–98

Position	Team	Played	Won	Drawn	Lost	Goals for	Goals against	Points
1	Cannock	22	18	2	2	89	36	56
2	Canterbury	22	15	2	4	99	55	48
3	Reading	22	14	2	6	77	57	44
4	Southgate	22	12	3	7	71	56	39
5	Old Loughtonians	22	10	5	7	62	52	35
6	Teddington	22	10	3	9	65	65	33
7	East Grinstead	22	9	3	10	51	59	30
8	Guildford	22	8	1	13	53	63	25
9	Hounslow	22	5	5	12	43	63	20
10	Beeston	22	5	3	14	40	74	18
11	Barford Tigers[1]	22	4	5	13	40	79	17
12	Doncaster[1]	22	2	5	15	55	86	11

[1] Barford Tigers and Doncaster were relegated.

English Hockey Association National League: Premier Division: Final Table

Women

1997–98

Position	Team	Played	Won	Drawn	Lost	Goals for	Goals against	Points
1	Slough	14	13	1	0	73	22	40
2	Clifton	14	8	2	4	27	21	26
3	Ipswich	14	8	1	5	32	20	25
4	Olton	14	6	2	6	24	29	20
5	Hightown	14	5	3	6	18	24	18
6	Sutton Coldfield	14	4	2	8	23	38	14
7	Doncaster	14	2	4	8	19	40	10
8	Trojans[1]	14	1	3	10	20	42	6

[1] Trojans were relegated.

Men's Hockey World Cup

This championship was inaugurated in 1971 by the Fédération Internationale de Hockey (FIH).

Year	Country
1971	Pakistan
1973	Netherlands
1975	India
1978	Pakistan
1982	Pakistan
1986	Australia
1990	Netherlands
1994	Pakistan
1998	Holland

Women's Hockey World Cup

This championship was inaugurated in 1974 by the Fédération Internationale de Hockey (FIH).

Year	Country
1974	Netherlands
1976	West Germany
1978	Netherlands
1981	West Germany
1983	Netherlands
1986	Netherlands
1990	Netherlands
1994	Australia
1998	Australia

Horse Racing

Flat Racing: The Epsom Derby since 1945

This race was first held in 1780 and is held at Epsom over 1 mile and 4 furlongs. Since 1984 it has been sponsored by Ever Ready. Colts carry 9 stone; fillies 8 stone 9 lb. Wins for a jockey: Lester Piggott, 9; Jem Robinson, Steve Donoghue, 6.

Year	Horse	Jockey	Year	Horse	Jockey
1945	Dante	Billy Nevett	1972	Roberto	Lester Piggott
1946	Airborne	Tommy Lowrey	1973	Morston	Eddie Hide
1947	Pearl Driver	George Bridgland	1974	Snow Knight	Brian Taylor
1948	My Love	Rae Johnstone	1975	Grundy	Pat Eddery
1949	Nimbus	Charlie Elliot	1976	Empery	Lester Piggott
1950	Galcador	Rae Johnstone	1977	The Minstrel	Lester Piggott
1951	Arctic Prince	Charlie Spares	1978	Shirley Heights	Greville Starkey
1952	Tulyar	Charlie Smirke	1979	Troy	Willie Carson
1953	Pinza	Gordon Richards	1980	Henbit	Willie Carson
1954	Never Say Die	Lester Piggott	1981	Shergar	Walter Swinburn
1955	Phil Drake	Freddie Palmer	1982	Golden Fleece	Pat Eddery
1956	Lavandin	Rae Johnstone	1983	Teenoso	Lester Piggott
1957	Crepello	Lester Piggott	1984	Secreto	Christy Roche
1958	Hard Ridden	Charlie Smirke	1985	Slip Anchor	Steve Cauthen
1959	Parthia	Harry Carr	1986	Shahrastani	Walter Swinburn
1960	St Paddy	Lester Piggott	1987	Reference Point	Steve Cauthen
1961	Psidium	Roger Poincelet	1988	Kahyashi	Ray Cochrane
1962	Larkspur	Neville Sellwood	1989	Nashwan	Willie Carson
1963	Relko	Yves Saint-Martin	1990	Quest For Fame	Pat Eddery
1964	Santa Claus	Scobie Breasley	1991	Generous	Alan Munro
1965	Sea Bird II	Pat Glennon	1992	Dr Devious	John Reid
1966	Charlottown	Scobie Breasley	1993	Commander in Chief	Michael Kinane
1967	Royal Palace	George Moore	1994	Erhaab	Willie Carson
1968	Sir Ivor	Lester Piggott	1995	Lammtarra	Walter Swinburn
1969	Blakeney	Ernie Johnson	1996	Shaamit	Michael Hills
1970	Nijinsky	Lester Piggott	1997	Benny The Dip	Willie Ryan
1971	Mill Reef	Geoff Lewis	1998	High-Rise	Olivier Peslier

Flat Racing: 2,000 Guineas since 1988

This race was first held in 1809 and is run over 1 mile at Newmarket. It is for three-year-olds only; colts carry 9 stone, fillies 8 stone 9 lb.

Year	Horse	Jockey	Year	Horse	Jockey
1988	Doyoun	Walter Swinburn	1994	Mister Baileys	Jason Weaver
1989	Nashwan	Willie Carson	1995	Pennekamp	Thierry Jarnet
1990	Tirol	Michael Kinane	1996	Mark of Esteem	Frankie Dettori
1991	Mystiko	Michael Roberts	1997	Entrepreneur	Michael Kinane
1992	Rodrigo de Triano	Lester Piggott	1998	King of Kings	Michael Kinane
1993	Zafonic	Pat Eddery			

Flat Racing: 1,000 Guineas since 1988

This race was first held in 1814 and is run over 1 mile at Newmarket. The race is for three-year-old fillies only, who each carry nine stone.

Year	Horse	Jockey	Year	Horse	Jockey
1988	Ravinella	Gary Moore	1994	Las Meninas	John Reid
1989	Musical Bliss	Walter Swinburn	1995	Harayir	Richard Hills
1990	Salsabil	Willie Carson	1996	Bosra Sham	Pat Eddery
1991	Shadayid	Willie Carson	1997	Sleepytime	Kieren Fallon
1992	Hatoof	Walter Swinburn	1998	Cape Verdi	Frankie Dettori
1993	Sayyedati	Walter Swinburn			

Flat Racing: The Oaks since 1988

This race was first held in 1779 and is run over 1 mile 4 furlongs at Epsom in Surrey. The Oaks is for three-year-old fillies only, who each carry 9 stone.

Year	Horse	Jockey	Year	Horse	Jockey
1988	Diminuendo	Steve Cauthen	1994	Balanchine	Frankie Dettori
1989	Snow Bride[1]	Steve Cauthen	1995	Moonshell	Frankie Dettori
1990	Salsabil	Willie Carson	1996	Lady Carla	Pat Eddery
1991	Jet Ski Lady	Christy Roche	1997	Reams of Verse	Kieren Fallon
1992	User Friendly	George Duffield	1998	Shahtoush	Michael Kinane
1993	Intrepidity	Michael Roberts			

[1] Aliysa, ridden by Walter Swinburn, won, but was disqualified after a post-race drug test.

Flat Racing: St Leger since 1988

This is the oldest English classic race and was first held in 1776. It is run over 1 mile 6 furlongs 132 yards at Doncaster. It is for three-year-olds; colts carry 9 stone, fillies 8 stone 9 lbs.

Year	Horse	Jockey	Year	Horse	Jockey
1988	Minster Son	Willie Carson	1993	Bob's Return	Philip Robinson
1989	Michelozza	Steve Cauthen	1994	Moonax	Pat Eddery
1990	Snurge	Richard Quinn	1995	Classic Cliché	Frankie Dettori
1991	Toulon	Pat Eddery	1996	Shantou	Frankie Dettori
1992	User Friendly[1]	George Duffield	1997	Silver Patriarch	Pat Eddery

[1] Filly.

Flat Racing: Prix de l'Arc de Triomphe since 1988

This race was first held in 1920 and is run over 2,400 m at Longchamp in Paris, France.

Year	Horse	Jockey	Year	Horse	Jockey
1988	Tony Bin	John Reid	1993	Urban Sea	Eric St Martin
1989	Caroll House	Michael Kinane	1994	Carnegie	Thierry Jarnet
1990	Saumarez	Gerald Mosse	1995	Lammtarra	Frankie Dettori
1991	Suave Dancer	Cash Asmussen	1996	Helissio	Olivier Peslier
1992	Subotica	Thierry Jarnet	1997	Peintre Celebre	Olivier Peslier

Flat Racing: Champion Jockeys since 1988

Year	Jockey	Number of winners	Year	Jockey	Number of winners
1988	Pat Eddery	183	1993	Pat Eddery	169
1989	Pat Eddery	171	1994	Frankie Dettori	233
1990	Pat Eddery	209	1995	Frankie Dettori	211
1991	Pat Eddery	165	1996	Pat Eddery	186
1992	Michael Roberts	206	1997	Kieren Fallon	196

National Hunt Racing: Tote Cheltenham Gold Cup Chase since 1988

This race was first run in 1924; it is held annually at Prestbury Park, Cheltenham, during the Cheltenham Spring Festival. Current distance is 3 miles, 2 furlongs and about 110 yards. Most wins for a horse: Golden Miller, 4; Cottage Rake, Arkle, 3. Most wins for a jockey: Pat Taafe, 4.

Year	Horse	Jockey	Year	Horse	Jockey
1988	Charter Party	Richard Dunwoody	1994	The Fellow	Adam Kondrat
1989	Desert Orchid	Simon Sherwood	1995	Master Oats	Norman Williamson
1990	Norton's Coin	Graham McCourt	1996	Imperial Call	Connor O'Dwyer
1991	Garrison Savannah	Mark Pitman	1997	Mr Mulligan	Tony McCoy
1992	Cool Ground	Adrian Maguire	1998	Cool Dawn	Richard Thornton
1993	Jodami	Mark Dwyer			

National Hunt Racing: The Grand National since 1946

This race has been run at Aintree, Liverpool since 1839 with the exception of the war years (1916–18) when it was held at Gatwick, Surrey. The race is a handicap steeplechase and the current course takes in 30 fences and is run over 4 miles 4 furlongs. Most wins for a horse: Red Rum, 3. Most wins for a jockey: George Stevens, 5; Tom Oliver, 4.

Year	Horse	Jockey	Year	Horse	Jockey
1946	Lovely Cottage	Bobby Petre	1974	Red Rum	Brian Fletcher
1947	Caughoo	Eddie Dempsey	1975	L'Escargot	Tommy Carberry
1948	Sheila's Cottage	Arthur Thompson	1976	Rag Trade	John Burke
1949	Russian Hero	Leo McMorrow	1977	Red Rum	Tommy Stack
1950	Freebooter	Jimmy Power	1978	Lucius	Bob Davies
1951	Nickel Coin	Johnny Bullock	1979	Rubstic	Maurice Barnes
1952	Teal	Arthur Thompson	1980	Ben Nevis	Charlie Fenwick
1953	Early Mist	Bryan Marshall	1981	Aldaniti	Bob Champion
1954	Royal Tan	Bryan Marshall	1982	Grittar	Dick Saunders
1955	Quare Times	Pat Taaffe	1983	Corbiére	Ben de Haan
1956	E.S.B	Dave Dick	1984	Hallo Dandy	Neale Doughty
1957	Sundew	Fred Winter	1985	Last Suspect	Hywel Davies
1958	Mr What	Arthur Freeman	1986	West Tip	Richard Dunwoody
1959	Oxo	Michael Scudamore	1987	Maori Venture	Steve Knight
1960	Merryman II	Gerry Scott	1988	Rhyme N' Reason	Brendan Powell
1961	Nicolaus Silver	Bobby Beasley	1989	Little Polvier	Jimmy Frost
1962	Kilmore	Fred Winter	1990	Mr Frisk	Marcus Armytage
1963	Ayala	Pat Buckley	1991	Seagram	Nigel Hawke
1964	Team Spirit	Willie Robinson	1992	Party Politics	Carl Lewellyn
1965	Jay Trump	Tommy Smith	1993[1]	—	
1966	Anglo	Tim Norman	1994	Miinnehoma	Richard Dunwoody
1967	Foinavon	John Buckingham	1995	Royal Athlete	Jason Tittley
1968	Red Alligator	Brian Fletcher	1996	Rough Quest	Mick Fitzgerald
1969	Highland Wedding	Eddie Harty	1997[2]	Lord Gyllene	Tony Dobbin
1970	Gay Trip	Pat Taaffe	1998	Earth Summit	Carl Lewellyn
1971	Specify	John Cook			
1972	Well To Do	Graham Thorner			
1973	Red Rum	Brian Fletcher			

[1] Race void after a false start.
[2] Held on the Monday following a bomb scare at the Saturday meeting.

National Hunt Racing: The Smurfit Champion Hurdle Challenge Trophy since 1988

This race was first run in 1927, and is held annually at Prestbury Park, Cheltenham, during the Cheltenham Spring Festival; current distance 2 miles 110 yards.

Year	Horse	Jockey	Year	Horse	Jockey
1988	Celtic Shot	Peter Scudamore	1994	Flakey Dove	Mark Dwyer
1989	Beech Road	Richard Guest	1995	Alderbrook	Norman Williamson
1990	Kribensis	Richard Dunwoody	1996	Collier Bay	Graham Bradley
1991	Morley Street	Jimmy Frost	1997	Make A Stand	Tony McCoy
1992	Royal Gait	Graham McCourt	1998	Istabraq	Charlie Swan
1993	Granville Again	Peter Scudamore			

National Hunt Racing: Other Selected Winners

Race	Date	Racecourse	Horse	Jockey
Murphy's Gold Cup	15 November 1997	Cheltenham	Senor El Betrutti	Jamie Osborne
Hennessy Gold Cup	29 November 1997	Newbury	Suny Bay	Graham Bradley
Tripleprint Gold Cup	13 December 1997	Cheltenham	Senor El Betrutti	Graham Bradley
King George VI Chase	26 December 1997	Kempton Park	More Business	Andrew Thornton
Queen Mother Champion Chase	18 March 1998	Cheltenham	One Man	Brian Harding
Irish Grand National	13 April 1998	Fairyhouse	Bobbyjo	Paul Carberry
Scottish Grand National	18 April 1998	Ayr	Baronet	Adrian Maguire
Whitbread Gold Cup	25 April 1998	Sandown	Call It A Day	Adrian Maguire

National Hunt Racing: Champion Jockeys since 1988–89

Year	Jockey	Number of winners	Year	Jockey	Number of winners
1988–89	Peter Scudamore	221	1993–94	Richard Dunwoody	198
1989–90	Peter Scudamore	170	1994–95	Richard Dunwoody	160
1990–91	Peter Scudamore	141	1995–96	Tony McCoy	175
1991–92	Peter Scudamore	175	1996–97	Tony McCoy	190
1992–93	Richard Dunwoody	173	1997–98	Tony McCoy	253

Hurling

All-Ireland Champions since 1988

This championship was first held in 1887.

Year	Team	Year	Team	Year	Team
1988	Galway	1992	Limerick	1995	Clare
1989	Tipperary	1993	Kilkenny	1996	Wexford
1990	Cork	1994	Offaly	1997	Clare
1991	Tipperary				

Ice Hockey

British Ice Hockey Superleague Final Standings

1997–98

Position	Team	Played	Won	Tied	Lost	Overtime losses	Goals for	Goals against	Points
1	Ayr Scottish Eagles	28	20	1	5	2	117	69	43
2	Manchester Storm	28	18	3	6	1	123	80	40
3	Cardiff Devils	28	15	2	9	2	99	79	34
4	Nottingham Panthers	28	14	3	11	0	95	99	31
5	Bracknell Bees	28	14	1	12	1	95	115	30
6	Sheffield Steelers	28	11	2	13	2	103	101	27
7	Basingstoke Bison	28	5	4	13	6	80	116	20
8	Newcastle Cobras	28	6	2	19	1	66	119	15

British Ice Hockey Superleague Play-Offs

1997–98

Position	Team	Played	Wins	Ties	Losses	Overtime losses	Goals for	Goals againts	Points
Group A Final Standings									
1	Ayr Scottish Eagles	6	4	1	1	0	19	12	9
2	Sheffield Steelers	6	2	2	1	1	16	14	7
3	Nottingham Panthers	6	2	1	1	2	16	19	7
4	Newcastle Cobras	6	1	0	5	0	15	21	4
Group B Final Standings									
1	Cardiff Devils	6	5	1	0	0	31	10	11
2	Manchester Storm	6	3	1	2	0	21	20	7
3	Bracknell Bees	6	3	0	3	0	22	30	6
4	Basingstoke Bisons	6	0	0	5	1	17	31	1

British Superleague Finals

(OT = overtime.)

Semi-Finals (Best of Three)

First leg Ayr Scottish Eagles 5, Manchester Storm 3

Second leg Manchester Storm 2, Ayr Scottish Eagles 7

Ayr Scottish Eagles win series 2–0

First leg Cardiff Devils 5, Sheffield Steelers 4 (OT)

Second leg Sheffield Steelers 2, Cardiff Devils 6

Cardiff Devils win series 2–0

3rd/4th Place Playoff
Sheffield Steelers 5, Manchester Storm 2

Final
Ayr Scottish Eagles 3, Cardiff Devils 2 (OT)

American National Hockey League (NHL): Stanley Cup Finals

1997–98

Game	Dates	Home team	Away team
Game 1	9 June	Detroit 2	Washington 1
Game 2	11 June	Detroit 5	Washington 4 (OT)
Game 3	13 June	Washington 1	Detroit 2
Game 4	16 June	Washington 1	Detroit 4

Detroit wins the series 4–0. (OT) = overtime.

American National Hockey League: Stanley Cup Winners since 1988

This tournament was inaugurated in 1927.

Year	Team
1988	Edmonton Oilers
1989	Calgary Flames
1990	Edmonton Oilers
1991	Pittsburgh Penguins
1992	Pittsburgh Penguins
1993	Montreal Canadiens
1994	New York Rangers
1995	New Jersey Devils
1996	Colorado Avalanche
1997	Detroit Red Wings
1998	Detroit Red Wings

Ice Hockey World Championship since 1989

Year	Country
1989	USSR
1990	USSR
1991	Sweden
1992	Sweden
1993	Russia
1994	Canada
1995	Finland
1996	Czech Republic
1997	Canada
1998	Sweden

Judo

World Judo Champions (Women)

The first world championship for women took place in 1980. The competition is held every two years and was last held 9–12 October 1997 in Paris.

1997

Category	Name	Country
Open	Daina Beltran	Cuba
>72 kg	Christine Cicot	France
<72 kg	Noriko Anno	Japan
<66 kg	Kate Howey	UK
<61 kg	Severine Vandenhende	France
<56 kg	Isabel Fernandez	Spain
<52 kg	Marie-Claire Restoux	France
<48 kg	Tamura Ryoko	Japan

World Judo Champions (Men)

The first world championship for men took place in 1956. The competition is held every two years and was last held 9–12 October 1997 in Paris.

1997

Category	Name	Country
Open	Rafal Kubacki	Poland
>95 kg	David Douillet	France
<95 kg	Pawel Nastula	Poland
<86 kg	Jeon Ki-Young	South Korea
<78 kg	Cho In-Chul	South Korea
<71 kg	Kenzo Nakamura	Japan
<65 kg	Kim Hyuk	South Korea
<60 kg	Tadahiro Nomura	Japan

Lacrosse

Lacrosse World Cup

This competition was first held in 1967. It was renamed as the World Championships in 1969, and since 1982 it has been called the World Cup.

Year	Country	Year	Country	Year	Country
Men		1990	USA	1978	Canada
		1994	USA	1982	USA
1967	USA			1986	Australia
1974	USA	*Women*		1989	USA
1978	Canada	1969	UK	1993	USA
1982	USA	1974	USA	1997	USA
1986	USA				

Motorcycling

Motorcycle Racing World Champions

(N/A = not applicable.)

1997

Category	Name	Country	Manufacturer	Category	Name	Country	Manufacturer
Road Racing				*Motocross*			
125cc	Valentino Rossi	Italy	Aprilia	125cc	Alessio Chiodi	Italy	Yamaha
250cc	Max Biaggi	Italy	Honda	250cc	Stefan Everts	Belgium	Honda
500cc	Michael Doohan	Australia	Honda	500cc	Joël Smets	Belgium	KTM
Superbike	John Kocinski	USA	Honda	Sidecar	Sergis Kristers and Artis Rasmanis	Latvia	BSU
Endurance	Peter Goddard and Doug Polen	Australia and USA	Suzuki	Trials	Doug Lampkin	UK	Beta
Sidecar (World Cup)	Steve Webster and David James	UK	LCR ADM R4	*Speedway*			
				Individual	Greg Hancock	USA	N/A
				Team		Denmark	N/A
				Long track	Tommy Dunker	Germany	N/A

World Superbike Champions

This event was first held in 1988.

Year	Name	Country	Manufacturer
1988	Fred Merkel	USA	Honda
1989	Fred Merkel	USA	Honda
1990	Raymond Roche	France	Ducati
1991	Doug Polen	USA	Ducati
1992	Doug Polen	USA	Ducati
1993	Scott Russell	USA	Kawasaki
1994	Carl Fogarty	UK	Ducati
1995	Carl Fogarty	UK	Ducati
1996	Troy Corser	Australia	Ducati
1997	John Kocinski	USA	Honda

500cc World Road Racing Champions since 1988

The championship was inaugurated in 1949.

Year	Name	Country	Manufacturer
1988	Eddie Lawson	USA	Yamaha
1989	Eddie Lawson	USA	Honda
1990	Wayne Rainey	USA	Yamaha
1991	Wayne Rainey	USA	Yamaha
1992	Wayne Rainey	USA	Yamaha
1993	Kevin Schwantz	USA	Suzuki
1994	Michael Doohan	Australia	Honda
1995	Michael Doohan	Australia	Honda
1996	Michael Doohan	Australia	Honda
1997	Michael Doohan	Australia	Honda

Isle of Man Tourist Trophy: Senior TT since 1988

This road race was first held in 1907.

Year	Name	Country	Manufacturer	Year	Name	Country	Manufacturer
1988	Joey Dunlop	UK	Honda	1994	Steve Hislop	UK	Honda
1989	Steve Hislop	UK	Honda	1995	Joey Dunlop	UK	Honda
1990	Carl Fogarty	UK	Honda	1996	Phillip McCallen	UK	Honda
1991	Steve Hislop	UK	Honda	1997	Phillip McCallen	UK	Honda
1992	Steve Hislop	UK	Norton	1998	Ian Simpson	UK	Honda
1993	Joey Dunlop	UK	Honda				

Motor Racing

Formula 1 Grand Prix Winners

Final standings 1st: Jacques Villeneuve (Canada), 81 points; 2nd: Michael Schumacher (Germany), 78 points; 3rd: Heinz-Harald Frentzen (Germany), 42 points.

1997

Date	Grand Prix	Venue	Name	Country	Car
9 March	Australian	Melbourne	David Coulthard	Great Britain	McLaren-Mercedes
30 March	Brazilian	Interlagos	Jacques Villeneuve	Canada	Williams-Renault
13 April	Argentinian	Buenos Aires	Jacques Villeneuve	Canada	Williams-Renault
27 April	San Marino	Imola	Heinz-Harald Frentzen	Germany	Williams-Renault
11 May	Monaco	Monte Carlo	Michael Schumacher	Germany	Ferrari
25 May	Spanish	Barcelona	Jacques Villeneuve	Canada	Williams-Renault
15 June	Canadian	Montreal	Michael Schumacher	Germany	Ferrari
29 June	French	Magny-Cours	Michael Schumacher	Germany	Ferrari
13 July	British	Silverstone	Jacques Villeneuve	Canada	Williams-Renault
27 July	German	Hockenheim	Gerhard Berger	Austria	Benetton-Renault
10 August	Hungarian	Budapest	Jacques Villeneuve	Canada	Williams-Renault
24 August	Belgian	Spa	Michael Schumacher	Germany	Ferrari
7 September	Italian	Monza	David Coulthard	Great Britain	McLaren-Mercedes
21 September	Austrian	Zeltwig	Jacques Villeneuve	Canada	Williams-Renault
28 September	Luxembourg	Nurburgring	Jacques Villeneuve	Canada	Williams-Renault
19 October	Japanese	Suzuka	Michael Schumacher	Germany	Ferrari
26 October	European	Jerez, Spain	Mika Hakkinen	Finland	McLaren-Mercedes

Formula 1 World Drivers' Championship Winners

This championship was inaugurated in 1950.

Year	Name	Country	Car	Year	Name	Country	Car
1950	Giuseppe Farina	Italy	Alfa Romeo	1974	Emerson Fittipaldi	Brazil	McLaren-Ford
1951	Juan Manuel Fangio	Argentina	Alfa Romeo	1975	Niki Lauda	Austria	Ferrari
1952	Alberto Ascari	Italy	Ferrari	1976	James Hunt	Great Britain	McLaren-Ford
1953	Alberto Ascari	Italy	Ferrari	1977	Niki Lauda	Austria	Ferrari
1954	Juan Manuel Fangio	Argentina	Maserati-Mercedes	1978	Mario Andretti	USA	Lotus-Ford
1955	Juan Manuel Fangio	Argentina	Mercedes-Benz	1979	Jody Scheckter	South Africa	Ferrari
1956	Juan Manuel Fangio	Argentina	Lancia-Ferrari	1980	Alan Jones	Australia	Williams-Ford
1957	Juan Manuel Fangio	Argentina	Maserati	1981	Nelson Piquet	Brazil	Brabham-Ford
1958	Mike Hawthorn	Great Britain	Ferrari	1982	Keke Rosberg	Finland	Williams-Ford
1959	Jack Brabham	Australia	Cooper-Climax	1983	Nelson Piquet	Brazil	Brabham-BMW
1960	Jack Brabham	Australia	Cooper-Climax	1984	Niki Lauda	Austria	McLaren-TAG
1961	Phil Hill	USA	Ferrari	1985	Alain Prost	France	McLaren-TAG
1962	Graham Hill	Great Britain	BRM	1986	Alain Prost	France	McLaren-TAG
1963	Jim Clark	Great Britain	Lotus-Climax	1987	Nelson Piquet	Brazil	Williams-Honda
1964	John Surtees	Great Britain	Ferrari	1988	Ayrton Senna	Brazil	McLaren-Honda
1965	Jim Clark	Great Britain	Lotus-Climax	1989	Alain Prost	France	McLaren-Honda
1966	Jack Brabham	Australia	Brabham-Repco	1990	Ayrton Senna	Brazil	McLaren-Honda
1967	Denny Hulme	New Zealand	Brabham-Repco	1991	Ayrton Senna	Brazil	McLaren-Honda
1968	Graham Hill	Great Britain	Lotus-Ford	1992	Nigel Mansell	Great Britain	Williams-Renault
1969	Jackie Stewart	Great Britain	Matra-Ford	1993	Alain Prost	France	Williams-Renault
1970	Jochen Rindt	Austria	Lotus-Ford	1994	Michael Schumacher	Germany	Benetton-Ford
1971	Jackie Stewart	Great Britain	Tyrrell-Ford	1995	Michael Schumacher	Germany	Benetton-Renault
1972	Emerson Fittipaldi	Brazil	Lotus-Ford	1996	Damon Hill	Great Britain	Williams-Renault
1973	Jackie Stewart	Great Britain	Tyrrell-Ford	1997	Jacques Villeneuve	France	Williams-Renault

Formula 1 World Constructors' Championship Winners

This championship was inaugurated in 1958.

Year	Constructor	Year	Constructor	Year	Constructor	Year	Constructor
1958	Vanwall	1968	Lotus-Ford	1978	Lotus-Ford	1988	McLaren-Honda
1959	Cooper-Climax	1969	Matra-Ford	1979	Ferrari	1989	McLaren-Honda
1960	Cooper-Climax	1970	Lotus-Ford	1980	Williams-Ford	1990	McLaren-Honda
1961	Ferrari	1971	Tyrrell-Ford	1981	Williams-Ford	1991	McLaren-Honda
1962	BRM	1972	Lotus-Ford	1982	Ferrari	1992	Williams-Renault
1963	Lotus-Climax	1973	Lotus-Ford	1983	Ferrari	1993	Williams-Renault
1964	Ferrari	1974	McLaren-Ford	1984	McLaren-TAG	1994	Williams-Renault
1965	Lotus-Climax	1975	Ferrari	1985	McLaren-TAG	1995	Williams-Renault
1966	Brabham-Repco	1976	Ferrari	1986	Williams-Honda	1996	Williams-Renault
1967	Brabham-Repco	1977	Ferrari	1987	Williams-Honda	1997	Williams-Renault

British Grand Prix Winners

The 1950 British Grand Prix was the first race of the inaugural World Drivers' Championship. Previous Grand Prix had taken place in the UK in 1926–27 at Brooklands, 1935–38 at Donnington, and 1948–49 at Silverstone. Most wins: Jim Clark, Alain Prost, 5; Nigel Mansell, 5.

Year	Name	Country	Car	Venue
1950	Giuseppe Farina	Italy	Alfa-Romeo	Silverstone
1951	José Froilan Gonzalez	Argentina	Ferrari	Silverstone
1952	Alberto Ascari	Italy	Ferrari	Silverstone
1953	Alberto Ascari	Italy	Ferrari	Silverstone
1954	José Froilan Gonzalez	Argentina	Ferrari	Silverstone
1955	Stirling Moss	UK	Mercedes-Benz	Aintree
1956	Juan Manuel Fangio	Argentina	Lancia-Ferrari	Silverstone
1957	Stirling Moss & Tony Brooks	UK	Vanwall	Aintree
1958	Peter Collins	UK	Ferrari	Silverstone
1959	Jack Brabham	Australia	Cooper-Climax	Aintree
1960	Jack Brabham	Australia	Cooper-Climax	Silverstone
1961	Wolfgang von Trips	West Germany	Ferrari	Aintree
1962	Jim Clark	UK	Lotus-Climax	Aintree
1963	Jim Clark	UK	Lotus-Climax	Silverstone

British Grand Prix Winners (*continued*)

Year	Name	Country	Car	Venue
1964	Jim Clark	UK	Lotus-Climax	Brands Hatch
1965	Jim Clark	UK	Lotus-Climax	Silverstone
1966	Jack Brabham	Australia	Brabham-Repco	Brands Hatch
1967	Jim Clark	UK	Lotus-Ford	Silverstone
1968	Jo Siffert	Switzerland	Lotus-Ford	Brands Hatch
1969	Jackie Stewart	UK	Matra-Ford	Silverstone
1970	Jochen Rindt	Austria	Lotus-Ford	Brands Hatch
1971	Jackie Stewart	UK	Tyrell-Ford	Silverstone
1972	Emerson Fittipaldi	Brazil	Lotus-Ford	Brands Hatch
1973	Peter Revson	USA	McLaren-Ford	Silverstone
1974	Jody Scheckter	South Africa	Tyrell-Ford	Brands Hatch
1975	Emerson Fittipaldi	Brazil	McLaren-Ford	Silverstone
1976	Niki Lauda	Austria	Ferrari	Brands Hatch
1977	James Hunt	UK	McLaren-Ford	Silverstone
1978	Carlos Reutemann	Argentina	Ferrari	Brands Hatch
1979	Clay Regazzoni	Switzerland	Williams-Ford	Silverstone
1980	Alan Jones	Australia	Williams-Ford	Brands Hatch
1981	John Watson	UK	McLaren-Ford	Silverstone
1982	Niki Lauda	Austria	McLaren-Ford	Brands Hatch
1983	Alain Prost	France	Renault	Silverstone
1984	Niki Lauda	Austria	McLaren-TAG	Brands Hatch
1985	Alain Prost	France	McLaren-TAG	Silverstone
1986	Nigel Mansell	UK	Williams-Honda	Brands Hatch
1987	Nigel Mansell	UK	Williams-Honda	Silverstone
1988	Ayrton Senna	Brazil	McLaren-Honda	Silverstone
1989	Alain Prost	France	McLaren-Honda	Silverstone
1990	Alain Prost	France	Ferrari	Silverstone
1991	Nigel Mansell	UK	Williams-Renault	Silverstone
1992	Nigel Mansell	UK	Williams-Renault	Silverstone
1993	Alain Prost	France	Williams-Renault	Silverstone
1994	Damon Hill	UK	Williams-Renault	Silverstone
1995	Johnny Herbert	UK	Benetton-Renault	Silverstone
1996	Jacques Villeneuve	Canada	Williams-Renault	Silverstone
1997	Jacques Villeneuve	Canada	Williams-Renault	Silverstone
1998	Michael Schumacher	Germany	Ferrari	Silverstone

Le Mans 24-Hour Race since 1988

This race was first held in 1923.

Year	Names	Car	Year	Names	Car
1988	Jan Lammers, Johnny Dumfries, Andy Wallace	Jaguar	1994	Yannick Dalmas, Hurley Haywood, Mauro Baldi	Porsche
1989	Jochen Mass, Manuel Reuter, Stanley Dickens	Mercedes	1995	Yannick Dalmas, J J Lehto, Masanori Sekiya	McLaren
1990	John Neilsen, Martin Brundle, Price Cobb	Jaguar	1996	Davy Jones, Manuel Reuter, Alexander Wurz	Porsche
1991	Johnny Herbert, Bertrand Gachot, Volker Wendler	Mazda	1997	Michele Alboreto, Stefan Johansson, Tom Kristensen	Porsche
1992	Derek Warwick, Mark Blundell, Yannick Dalmas	Peugeot	1998	Allan McNish, Stephane Ortelli, Laurent Aiello	Porsche
1993	Geoff Brabham, Cristophe Bouchut, Éric Hélary	Peugeot			

Indianapolis 500 Champions since 1988

This race was first held in 1911.

Year	Name	Car	Average speed		Year	Name	Car	Average speed	
			kph	mph				kph	mph
1988	Rick Mears	Penske-Chevrolet	233.041	144.809	1994	Al Unser Jr	Penske-Mercedes	258.891	160.872
1989	Emerson Fittipaldi	Penske-Chevrolet	269.688	167.581	1995	Jacques Villeneuve	Reynard-Ford	247.214	153.616
1990	Arie Luyendyk	Lola-Chevrolet	299.229	185.981	1996	Buddy Lazier	Reynard-Ford	238.106	147.956
1991	Rick Mears	Penske-Chevrolet	283.972	176.457	1997	Arie Luyendyk	G-Force-Aurora	234.679	145.827
1992	Al Unser Jr	Galmer-Chevrolet	216.414	134.477	1998	Eddie Cheever Jr	Dallara-Aurora	233.598	145.155
1993	Emerson Fittipaldi	Penske-Chevrolet	252.993	157.207					

World Rally Champions: Drivers

A manufacturers' world championship was established in 1968. The FIA Cup for Drivers, a championship for drivers, was inaugurated in 1977 and two years later became the official world drivers' championship.

Year	Name	Country	Car
1977	Sandro Munari	Italy[1]	Lancia Stratos
1978	Markku Alén	Finland[1]	Fiat Abarth
1979	Björn Waldegård	Sweden	Ford Escort
1980	Walter Röhrl	West Germany	Fiat Abarth
1981	Ari Vatanen	Finland	Ford Escort
1982	Walter Röhrl	West Germany	Opel Ascona
1983	Hannu Mikkola	Finland	Audi Quattro
1984	Stig Blomquist	Sweden	Audi Quattro
1985	Timu Salonen	Finland	Peugeot 205
1986	Juha Kankkunen	Finland	Peugeot 205
1987	Juha Kankkunen	Finland	Lancia Delta
1988	Mikki Biasion	Italy	Lancia Delta
1989	Mikki Biasion	Italy	Lancia Delta
1990	Carlos Sainz	Spain	Toyota Celica
1991	Juha Kankkunen	Finland	Lancia Delta
1992	Carlos Sainz	Spain	Toyota Celica
1993	Juha Kankkunen	Finland	Toyota Celica
1994	Didier Auriol	France	Toyota Celica
1995	Colin McRae	UK	Subaru Impreza
1996	Tommi Mäkinen	Finland	Mitsubishi Lancer
1997	Tommi Mäkinen	Finland	Mitsubishi Lancer

[1] FIA Cup for Drivers champions.

RAC Rally since 1980

This race was formerly known as the RAC International Rally of Great Britain. It was first held in 1927, though not recognised as an international event by the Fédération Internationale de l'Automobile (FIA) until 1951. Sponsored by Network Q since 1993.

Year	Name	Country	Car
1980	Henri Toivonen	Finland	Talbot Sunbeam
1981	Hannu Mikkola	Finland	Audi Quattro
1982	Hannu Mikkola	Finland	Audi Quattro
1983	Stig Blomquist	Sweden	Audi Quattro
1984	Ari Vatanen	Finland	Peugeot 205
1985	Henri Toivonen	Finland	Lancia Delta
1986	Timo Salonen	Finland	Peugeot 205
1987	Juha Kankkunen	Finland	Lancia Delta
1988	Markku Alén	Finland	Lancia Delta
1989	Pentti Arikkala	Finland	Mitsubishi Galant
1990	Carlos Sainz	Spain	Toyota Celica
1991	Juha Kankkunen	Finland	Lancia Delta
1992	Carlos Sainz	Spain	Toyota Celica
1993	Juha Kankkunen	Finland	Lancia Delta
1994	Colin McRae	UK	Subaru Impreza
1995	Colin McRae	UK	Subaru Impreza
1996	Armin Schwarz	Germany	Toyota Celica
1997	Colin McRae	UK	Subaru Impreza

Monte Carlo Rally since 1988

This race was first held in 1911.

Year	Name	Country	Year	Name	Country
1988	Bruno Saby	France	1994	François Delecour	France
1989	Mikki Biasion	Italy	1995	Carlos Sainz	Spain
1990	Didier Auriol	France	1996	Patrick Bernardini	France
1991	Carlos Sainz	Spain	1997	Piero Liatti	Italy
1992	Didier Auriol	France	1998	Carlos Sainz	Spain
1993	Didier Auriol	France			

Notable Land Speed World Records

All cars have petrol-driven internal-combustion engines unless marked (E) for electric, (S) for steam, (T) for turbine, (J) for jet, or (R) for rocket.

Date	Speed mph	Speed kph	Name	Country	Car	Location
18 December 1898	39.24	63.15	Gaston Chasseloup-Labat	France	Jeantaud (E)	Achères, France
4 March 1899	57.60	92.70	Gaston Chasseloup-Labat	France	Jeantaud (E)	Achères, France
13 April 1902	75.06	120.80	Leon Serpollet	France	Serpollet (E)	Nice, France
5 August 1902	76.08	122.44	William K Vanderbilt	USA	Mors	Ablis, France
17 July 1903	83.47	134.33	Arthur Duray	UK	Gobron-Brillé	Ostend, Belgium
12 January 1904[1]	91.37	147.05	Henry Ford	USA	Ford	Lake St Clair, Detroit (MI), USA
21 July 1904[1]	103.58	166.70	Louis Rigolly	France	Gobron-Brillé	Ostend, Belgium
13 November 1904	104.52	168.21	Paul Baras	France	Darracq	Ostend, Belgium
23 January 1906	121.57	195.65	Fred Marriott	USA	Stanley (S)	Daytona Beach (FL), USA
16 March 1910[1]	131.27	211.26	Barney Oldfield	USA	Benz	Daytona Beach (FL), USA
23 April 1911[1]	141.73	228.09	Bob Burman	USA	Benz	Daytona Beach (FL), USA
17 February 1919[1]	149.87	241.19	Ralph DePalma	USA	Packard	Daytona Beach (FL), USA
27 April 1920[1]	156.03	251.11	Tommy Milton	USA	Duesenberg	Daytona Beach (FL), USA
28 April 1926	171.02	275.23	Parry Thomas	UK	Babs	Pendine Sands, UK
29 March 1927	203.79	327.97	Henry Segrave	UK	Sunbeam	Daytona Beach (FL), USA
22 April 1928	207.55	334.02	Ray Keech	USA	White Triplex	Daytona Beach (FL), USA

Notable Land Speed World Records (*continued*)

Date	Speed		Name	Country	Car	Location
	mph	kph				
11 March 1929	231.45	372.48	Henry Seagrave	UK	Golden Arrow	Daytona Beach (FL), USA
5 February 1931	246.09	396.04	Malcolm Campbell	UK	Bluebird	Daytona Beach (FL), USA
24 February 1932	253.97	408.73	Malcolm Campbell	UK	Bluebird	Daytona Beach (FL), USA
22 February 1933	272.47	438.48	Malcolm Campbell	UK	Bluebird	Daytona Beach (FL), USA
3 September 1935	301.13	484.62	Malcolm Campbell	UK	Bluebird	Bonneville Salt Flats (UT), USA
19 November 1937	312.00	502.12	George Eyston	UK	Thunderbolt 1	Bonneville Salt Flats (UT), USA
15 September 1938	350.20	563.59	John Cobb	UK	Railton	Bonneville Salt Flats (UT), USA
16 September 1938	357.50	575.34	George Eyston	UK	Thunderbolt 1	Bonneville Salt Flats (UT), USA
23 August 1939	369.70	594.97	John Cobb	UK	Railton	Bonneville Salt Flats (UT), USA
16 September 1947	394.20	634.40	John Cobb	UK	Railton-Mobil	Bonneville Salt Flats (UT), USA
5 August 1963	407.45	655.73[1]	Craig Breedlove	USA	Spirit of America (J)	Bonneville Salt Flats (UT), USA
17 July 1964	403.10	648.73	Donald Campbell	UK	Bluebird (T)	Lake Eyre, Australia
5 October 1964	434.02	698.49	Art Arfons	USA	Green Monster (J)	Bonneville Salt Flats (UT), USA
15 October 1964	526.28	846.97	Craig Breedlove	USA	Spirit of America (J)	Bonneville Salt Flats (UT), USA
2 November 1965	555.127	893.39	Craig Breedlove	USA	Spirit of America Sonic 1 (J)	Bonneville Salt Flats (UT), USA
13 November 1965	409.277	658.67[2]	Bob Summers	USA	Goldenrod	Bonneville Salt Flats (UT), USA
15 November 1965	600.601	966.58	Craig Breedlove	USA	Spirit of America Sonic 1 (J)	Bonneville Salt Flats (UT), USA
23 October 1970	622.407	1,001.67	Gary Gabelich	USA	Blue Flame (R)	Bonneville Salt Flats (UT), USA
4 October 1983	633.468	1,019.47	Richard Noble	UK	Thrust 2 (J)	Black Rock Desert (NV), USA
25 September 1997	714.144	1,149.30	Andy Green	UK	Thrust SSC (J)	Black Rock Desert (NV), USA

[1] Unofficial record. Since 1911, the official record has been the average of two observed runs over a mile or kilometre made within one hour. All cars must be four-wheeled and remain on the ground throughout the run. Since 1964, when a requirement that the car must be driven by its wheels was dropped, records attempts in jet or rocket propelled cars have been permitted.
[2] Current record for internal combustion engine.

Netball

Netball World Championship

This championship was first held in 1963 and is held every four years.

Year	Country	Year	Country
1963	Australia	1983	Australia
1967	New Zealand	1987	New Zealand
1971	Australia	1991	Australia
1975	Australia	1995	Australia
1979	Australia, New Zealand, and Trinidad and Tobago		

Orienteering

Orienteering World Classic Race Champions: Individual, since 1981

Year	Name	Country	Year	Name	Country
Men			**Women**		
1981	Oyvin Thon	Norway	1981	Annichen Kringstad	Norway
1983	Morten Berglia	Norway	1983	Annichen Kringstad	Norway
1985	Kari Sallinen	Finland	1985	Annichen Kringstad	Norway
1987	Kent Olsson	Sweden	1987	Arja Hannus	Sweden
1989	Petter Thoresen	Norway	1989	Marita Skogum	Sweden
1991	Jörgen Mårtensson	Sweden	1991	Katarina Olch	Hungary
1994	Alan Morgensen	Denmark	1994	Marita Skogun	Sweden
1995	Jörgen Mårtensson	Sweden	1995	Katalin Oláh	Hungary
1997	Petter Thoresen	Norway	1997	Hanne Staff	Norway

Polo

Cowdray Park Gold Cup since 1988

This is the British Open Championship and it was first held in 1956.

Year	Team	Year	Team	Year	Team
1988	Tramontana	1992	Black Bears	1995	Ellerston White
1989	Tramontana	1993	Alcatel	1996	C S Brooks
1990	Hildon	1994	Ellerston Black	1997	Labegorce
1991	Tramontana				

Rowing

Henley Royal Regatta since 1988

Year	Name	Country	Year	Name	Country
Diamond Challenge Sculls[1]			*Grand Challenge Cup*[2]		
1988	Hamish McGlashen	Australia	1988	Leander/University of London	UK
1989	Vaclav Chalpa	Czechoslovakia	1989	RC Hansa Dortmund	West Germany
1990	Eric Verdonk	New Zealand	1990	RC Hansa Dortmund	Germany
1991	Wim van Belleghem	Belgium	1991	Leander/Star	UK
1992	Rosie Henderson	UK	1992	University of London	UK
1993	Thomas Lange	Germany	1993	Dortmund	Germany
1994	Xeno Müller	Switzerland	1994	Charles River/San Diego	USA
1995	Juri Jaanson	Estonia	1995	San Diego	USA
1996	Merlin Vervoorn	Netherlands	1996	Imperial College and Queen's Tower	UK
1997	Greg Searle	UK	1997	Australian Institute of Sport and NSW Institute of Sport	Australia
1998	Jamie Koven	USA	1998	RC Hansa Dortmund and Berliner RC	Germany

[1] First held in 1884.
[2] For eights; first held in 1839.

The Boat Race since 1988

This race was first held in 1829. It is rowed annually by crews from Oxford and Cambridge Universities, between Putney and Mortlake on the river Thames. Cambridge currently lead Oxford by 75 wins to 68. The 1877 race ended in a dead heat.

Year	Team	Year	Team	Year	Team
1988	Oxford	1992	Oxford	1996	Cambridge
1989	Oxford	1993	Cambridge	1997	Cambridge
1990	Oxford	1994	Cambridge	1998	Cambridge
1991	Oxford	1995	Cambridge		

World Rowing Championships

These championships were held at Lac d'Aiguebelette, France.

1997

Category	Name	Country
Men		
Single sculls	Jamie Koven	USA
Double sculls	Stephan Volkert and Andreas Hajek	Germany
Quad sculls		Italy
Lightweight single sculls	Karsten Neilsen	Denmark
Lightweight double sculls	Tomasz Kucharski and Robert Sycz	Poland
Lightweight quad sculls		Italy
Coxless pairs	Michel Andrieux and Jean-Chris Rolland	France
Coxed pairs	Scott Fentress, Jordan Irving, and Nicholas Anderson	USA
Coxless fours		UK
Coxed fours		France
Eights		USA
Lightweight coxless pairs	Mathias Binder and Benedict Schmidt	Switzerland
Lightweight coxless fours		Denmark
Lightweight eights		Australia
Women		
Single sculls	Yekaterina Khodotovich	Belarus
Double sculls	Evers Meike and Kathrin Boron	Germany
Quad sculls		Germany
Lightweight single sculls	Sarah Garner	USA
Lightweight double sculls	Michelle Darvill and Angelika Brand	Germany
Lightweight quad sculls		Germany
Coxless pairs	Emma Robinson and Alison Korn	Canada
Coxless fours		UK
Eights		Romania
Lightweight coxless pairs	Eliza Blair and Justine Joyce	Australia

Rugby League

Rugby League Challenge Cup since 1980

Year	Team	Year	Team	Year	Team
1980	Hull Kingston Rovers	1987	Halifax	1994	Wigan
1981	Widnes	1988	Wigan	1995	Wigan
1982	Hull	1989	Wigan	1996	St Helens
1983	Featherstone Rovers	1990	Wigan	1997	St Helens
1984	Widnes	1991	Wigan	1998	Sheffield Eagles
1985	Wigan	1992	Wigan		
1986	Castleford	1993	Wigan		

Rugby League Premiership Trophy since 1988

End of season knockout competition involving the top eight clubs in the JJB Sports Super League; inaugurated in 1975.

Year	Team	Year	Team	Year	Team
1988	Widnes	1992	Wigan	1995	Wigan
1989	Widnes	1993	St Helens	1996	Wigan
1990	Widnes	1994	Wigan	1997	Wigan
1991	Hull				

Rugby Union

English rugby: Allied Dunbar Premiership (Final Standings)

1997–98

Position	Team	Played	Won	Drawn	Lost	Points for	Points against	League points
Division 1								
1	Newcastle	22	19	0	3	645	387	38
2	Saracens	22	18	1	3	584	396	37
3	Bath	22	13	0	9	575	455	26
4	Leicester	22	12	2	8	569	449	26
5	Richmond	22	12	0	10	607	499	24
6	Gloucester	22	11	1	10	512	528	23
7	Sale	22	10	2	10	605	558	22
8	Northampton	22	9	1	12	493	472	19
9	Wasps	22	8	1	13	490	609	17
10	Harlequins	22	8	0	14	516	645	16
11	London Irish	22	6	0	16	457	673	12
12	Bristol[1]	22	2	0	20	351	733	4
Division 2								
1	Bedford[2]	22	20	0	2	791	365	40
2	West Hartlepool[2]	22	15	1	6	617	431	31
3	London Scottish	22	14	1	7	517	404	29
4	Rotherham	22	14	0	8	566	386	28
5	Orrell	22	12	0	10	533	400	24
6	Moseley	22	11	1	10	478	421	23
7	Coventry	22	11	1	10	444	532	23
8	Waterloo	22	11	0	11	510	525	22
9	Blackheath	22	8	0	14	474	621	16
10	Wakefield	22	6	0	16	382	556	12
11	Exeter[3]	22	6	0	16	334	553	12
12	Fylde[3]	22	2	0	20	258	710	4

[1] Relegated to Allied Dunbar Premiership Division 2.
[2] Promoted to Allied Dunbar Premiership Division 1.
[3] Relegated to Jewson National League Division 1.

English rugby: Allied Dunbar Premiership Champions (Division 1)

This championship was first held 1987–88; it was formerly known as the Courage Club Championship, Division 1.

Year	Team	Year	Team
1988	Leicester	1994	Bath
1989	Bath	1995	Leicester
1990	Wasps	1996	Bath
1991	Bath	1997	Wasps
1992	Bath	1998	Newcastle
1993	Bath		

English County Championship since 1988

This championship was first held in 1888.

Year	Team	Year	Team
1988	Lancashire	1994	Yorkshire
1989	Durham	1995	Warwickshire
1990	Lancashire	1996	Gloucestershire
1991	Cornwall	1997	Cumbria
1992	Lancashire	1998	Cheshire
1993	Lancashire		

International (Five Nations) Championship

This championship was instituted in 1884 and is now a tournament between England, France, Ireland, Scotland, and Wales. The Grand Slam is achieved by teams winning all four games. The Triple Crown does not apply to France. Italy will join the championship in 2000. Most outright championship wins: Wales, England, 22; Most Grand Slams: England, 11. Most Triple Crowns: England, 21.

Year	Team	Year	Team
1970	France and Wales	1986	France and Scotland
1971	Wales[1][2]	1987	France[1]
1972	(not completed)	1988	France and Wales[4]
1973	five way tie	1989	France
1974	Ireland	1990	Scotland[1][2]
1975	Wales	1991	England[1][2]
1976	Wales[1][2]	1992	England[1][2]
1977	France[3]	1993	France
1978	Wales[1][2]	1994	Wales
1979	Wales[2]	1995	England[1][2]
1980	England[1][2]	1996	England[2]
1981	France	1997	France[1][4]
1982	Ireland[2]	1998	France[1][4]
1983	France and Ireland		
1984	Scotland[1][2]		
1985	Ireland[2]		

[1] Grand Slam winners.
[2] Also won the Triple Crown.
[3] Wales won the Triple Crown.
[4] England won the Triple Crown.

International (Five Nations) Championship: Results

1998

Date	Home team	Away team	Result	Location
7 February	France	England	24–17	Paris
7 February	Ireland	Scotland	16–17	Landsdowne Road
21 February	England	Wales	60–26	Twickenham
21 February	Scotland	France	16–51	Murrayfield
7 March	France	Ireland	19–16	Paris
7 March	Wales	Scotland	19–13	Wembley Stadium
21 March	Ireland	Wales	21–30	Landsdowne Road
22 March	Scotland	England	20–34	Murrayfield
4 April	England	Ireland	35–17	Twickenham
5 April	Wales	France	0–51	Wembley Stadium

International (Five Nations) Championship: Final Table

1998

Position	Team	Played	Won	Drawn	Lost	Points for	Points against	Team points
1	France[1]	4	4	0	0	144	49	8
2	England[2]	4	3	0	1	146	87	6
3	Wales	4	2	0	2	75	145	4
4	Scotland	4	1	0	3	66	120	2
5	Ireland	4	0	0	4	70	100	0

[1] Grand Slam winner.
[2] Triple Crown winner.

English rugby: Tetley Bitter Cup since 1980

This English club knockout tournament has been sponsored by John Player and Pilkingtons, and is now sponsored by Tetley Bitter. It was first held in 1971–72.

Year	Team	Year	Team	Year	Team	Year	Team
1980	Leicester	1985	Bath	1990	Bath	1995	Bath
1981	Leicester	1986	Bath	1991	Harlequins	1996	Bath
1982	Gloucester and Moseley	1987	Bath	1992	Bath	1997	Leicester
1983	Bristol	1988	Harlequins	1993	Leicester	1998	Saracens
1984	Bath	1989	Bath	1994	Bath		

Heineken European Cup

This European club competition was first held in 1995–96.

Year	Winner	Runner-up	Score	Location
1996	Toulouse (France)	Cardiff (Wales)	21–18	Cardiff
1997	Brive (France)	Leicester (England)	28–9	Cardiff
1998	Bath (England)	Brive (France)	19–18	Bordeaux

Super 12

This tournament for club teams from Australia, New Zealand, and South Africa was first held in 1996.

Year	Team
1996	Auckland Blues
1997	Auckland Blues
1998	Canterbury Crusaders

Irish Rugby: All-Ireland Championship

This championship was first held in 990–91.

Year	Team
1991	Cork Constitution
1992	Garryowen
1993	Young Munster
1994	Garryowen
1995	Shannon
1996	Shannon
1997	Shannon
1998	Shannon

World Cup

This competition, for the William Webb Ellis Trophy, was first held in 1987.

Year	Country
1987	New Zealand
1991	Australia
1995	South Africa

Allied Irish Bank League Division One: Final Standings

Shannon defeated Garryowen 15–9 in the inaugural championship final at Landsdowne Road on 25 April 1998.

1997–98

Position	Team	Played	Won	Drawn	Lost	Points for	Points against	League points
1	Shannon[1]	13	12	0	1	367	142	24
2	Garryowen[2]	13	9	1	3	361	224	19
3	Young Munster[2]	13	9	1	3	244	176	19
4	St Mary's College[2]	13	9	0	4	409	274	18
5	Constitution	13	8	0	5	289	217	16
6	Ballymena	13	7	0	6	344	287	14
7	Clontarf	13	7	0	6	276	266	14
8	Terenure College	13	5	1	7	241	263	11
9	Lansdowne	13	4	2	7	264	328	10
10	Blackrock College	13	4	1	8	249	326	9
11	Dungannon[3]	13	4	0	9	239	309	8
12	Dolphin[3]	13	3	2	8	227	345	8
13	Old Crescent[3]	13	4	0	9	168	298	8
14	Old Belvedere[3]	13	2	0	11	208	431	4

[1] Champions.
[2] Gained a league play-off place to decide the championship.
[3] Relegated.

Scottish Rugby: Tennent's Premiership (Division 1) since 1988

This championship was first held in 1974; it was formerly known as the McEwan's League Division 1.

Year	Team
1988	Kelso
1989	Kelso
1990	Melrose
1991	Boroughmuir
1992	Melrose
1993	Melrose
1994	Melrose
1995	Stirling County
1996	Melrose
1997	Melrose
1998	Watsonians

Scottish Rugby Union Tennent's Velvet Cup

This Scottish knockout tournament was first held in 1996.

Year	Team
1996	Hawick
1997	Melrose
1998	Glasgow Hawks

Scottish Rugby Union Tennent's Premiership: Final Standings

1997–98

Position	Team	Played	Won	Drawn	Lost	Points for	Points against	League points
Division 1								
1	Watsonians	9	6	0	3	245	131	30
2	Melrose	9	6	0	3	212	130	29
3	Currie	9	6	0	3	182	177	27
4	Hawick	9	6	0	3	183	141	25
5	West of Scotland	9	5	0	4	191	151	24
6	Stirling County	9	5	0	4	163	129	23
7	Boroughmuir	9	5	0	4	129	140	22
8	Jed-Forest	9	3	0	6	144	253	13
9	Heriots F P	9	2	0	7	136	236	8
10	Edinburgh Academicals[1]	9	1	0	8	127	224	7

[1] Relegated to Division 2.

SWALEC Welsh Cup since 1988

This club knockout tournament was formerly known as the Schweppes Welsh Cup. It was first held in 1971–72.

Year	Team	Year	Team
1988	Llanelli	1994	Cardiff
1989	Neath	1995	Swansea
1990	Neath	1996	Pontypridd
1991	Llanelli	1997	Cardiff
1992	Llanelli	1998	Llanelli
1993	Llanelli		

Rugby Union: Welsh League (Premier Division)

This championship was first held in 1990–91.

Year	Team
1991	Neath
1992	Swansea
1993	Llanelli
1994	Swansea
1995	Cardiff
1996	Neath
1997	Pontypridd
1998	Swansea

Welsh National League Premier Division: Final Standings

1997–98

Position	Team	Played	Won	Drawn	Lost	Points for	Points against	Tries	Bonus points	League points
Premier Division										
1	Swansea	14	11	2	1	569	263	68	11	46
2	Cardiff	14	10	1	3	469	297	59	9	40
3	Pontypridd	14	8	2	4	441	299	55	9	35
4	Ebbw Vale	14	8	0	6	302	375	33	3	27
5	Neath	14	6	1	7	351	439	41	4	23
6	Llanelli	14	5	2	7	370	331	44	5	22
7	Bridgend	14	3	2	9	276	523	33	1	12
8	Newport[1]	14	0	0	14	224	484	23	2	2

[1] Relegated to Division 1. Caerphilly promoted.

Shinty

Camanachd Cup since 1988

Year	Team	Year	Team
		1993	Kingussie
1988	Kingussie	1994	Kyles Athletic
1989	Kingussie	1995	Kingussie
1990	Skye	1996	Oban Camanachd
1991	Kingussie	1997	Kingussie
1992	Fort William	1998	Kingussie

Skating

Figure Skating World Champions since 1988

Year	Name	Country	Year	Name	Country
Men			*Pairs*		
1988	Brian Boitano	USA	1988	Yelena Valova and Oleg Vasilyev	USSR
1989	Kurt Browning	Canada	1989	Yekaterina Gordeyeva and Sergei Grinkov	USSR
1990	Kurt Browning	Canada	1990	Yekaterina Gordeyeva and Sergei Grinkov	USSR
1991	Kurt Browning	Canada	1991	Natalya Mishkutienok and Artur Dmitriev	USSR
1992	Viktor Petrenko	USSR	1992	Natalya Mishkutienok and Artur Dmitriev	USSR
1993	Kurt Browning	Canada	1993	Lloyd Eisler and Isabelle Brasseur	Canada
1994	Elvis Stojko	Canada	1994	Vadim Naumov and Ergenia Shishkova	Russia
1995	Elvis Stojko	Canada	1995	Rene Novotny and Radka Kovarikova	Czech Republic
1996	Todd Eldredge	USA	1996	Andrei Bushkov and Marina Eltsova	Russia
1997	Elvis Stojko	Canada	1997	Yevgeny Platov and Mandy Wotzel	Russia
1998	Alexei Yagudin	Russia	1998	Anton Sikharudlidze and Elena Berezhnaya	Russia
Women			*Ice Dance*		
1988	Katarina Witt	East Germany	1988	Natalia Bestemianova and Andrei Bukin	USSR
1989	Midori Ito	Japan	1989	Marina Klimova and Sergei Ponomarenko	USSR
1990	Jill Trenary	USA	1990	Marina Klimova and Sergei Ponomarenko	USSR
1991	Kristi Yamaguchi	USA	1991	Isabelle Duchesnay and Paul Duchesnay	France
1992	Kristi Yamaguchi	USA	1992	Marina Klimova and Sergei Ponomarenko	USSR
1993	Oksana Baiul	Ukraine	1993	Maia Usova and Alexandr Zhulin	Russia
1994	Yuka Sato	Japan	1994	Yevgeny Platov and Oksana Gritschuk	Russia
1995	Lu Chen	China	1995	Yevgeny Platov and Oksana Gritschuk	Russia
1996	Michelle Kwan	USA	1996	Yevgeny Platov and Oksana Gritschuk	Russia
1997	Tara Lipinski	USA	1997	Yevgeny Platov and Oksana Gritschuk	Russia
1998	Michelle Kwan	USA	1998	Angelika Krylova and Oleg Ovsyannikov	Russia

Speed Skating World Championship: Overall Winners since 1988

This championship was first held in 1889 and is competed over four distances: 500 m, 1,000 m, 5,000 m, 10,000 m (men); 500 m, 1,000 m, 1,500 m, 3,000 m (women).

Year	Name	Country	Year	Name	Country
Men			*Women*		
1988	Eric Flaim	USA	1988	Karin Enke-Kania[1]	East Germany
1989	Leo Visser	Netherlands	1989	Constanze Moser	East Germany
1990	Johann Olav Koss	Norway	1990	Jacqueline Börner	East Germany
1991	Johann Olav Koss	Norway	1991	Gunda Kleemann	Germany
1992	Roberto Sighel	Italy	1992	Gunda Neimann[2]	Germany
1993	Falko Zandstra	Netherlands	1993	Gunda Neimann[2]	Germany
1994	Johann Olav Koss	Norway	1994	Emese Hunyady	Austria
1995	Rintje Ritsma	Netherlands	1995	Gunda Neimann[2]	Germany
1996	Rintje Ritsma	Netherlands	1996	Gunda Neimann[2]	Germany
1997	Ids Postma	Netherlands	1997	Gunda Neimann[2]	Germany

[1] Born Enke.
[2] Born Kleeman.

Skiing

World Alpine Skiing Championships

These championships were held at Sestriere, Italy, 2–16 February.

1998

Category	Name	Country	Category	Name	Country
Men			**Women**		
Downhill	Andreas Schifferer	Austria	Downhill	Katja Seizinger	Germany
Slalom	Thomas Sykora	Austria	Slalom	Ylva Nowen	Sweden
Giant slalom	Hermann Maier	Austria	Giant slalom	Martina Ertl	Germany
Super giant slalom	Hermann Maier	Austria	Super giant slalom	Katja Seizinger	Germany
Combination	Hermann Maier	Austria	Combination	Katja Seizinger	Germany

World Cup Alpine Skiing Champions since 1988

Year	Name	Country	Year	Name	Country
Men			**Women**		
1988	Pirmin Zurbriggen	Switzerland	1988	Michela Figini	Switzerland
1989	Marc Girardelli	Luxembourg	1989	Vreni Schneider	Switzerland
1990	Pirmin Zurbriggen	Switzerland	1990	Petra Kronberger	Austria
1991	Marc Girardelli	Luxembourg	1991	Petra Kronberger	Austria
1992	Paul Accola	Switzerland	1992	Petra Kronberger	Austria
1993	Marc Girardelli	Luxembourg	1993	Anita Wachter	Austria
1994	Kjetil Andre Aamodt	Norway	1994	Vreni Schneider	Switzerland
1995	Alberto Tomba	Italy	1995	Vreni Schneider	Switzerland
1996	Lasse Kjus	Norway	1996	Katja Seizinger	Germany
1997	Luc Alphand	France	1997	Pernilla Wiberg	Sweden
1998	Hermann Maier	Austria	1998	Katja Seizinger	Germany

Snooker

World Professional Snooker Championship since 1970

This championship was first held in 1926–27. Between 1952 and 1957, the professional players staged a match-play championship for the world title following a disagreement with the game's governing body at that time, the Billiards Association and Control Club. Between 1964 and 1968 the championship was organized on a challenge basis before becoming a knockout tournament in 1969. Since 1977 all finals have been held at the Crucible Theatre, Sheffield. It has been sponsored by Embassy since 1976.

Year	Name	Country	Year	Name	Country
1970	John Spencer	England	1985	Dennis Taylor	Northern Ireland
1971	Ray Reardon	Wales	1986	Joe Johnson	England
1972	John Spencer	England	1987	Steve Davis	England
1973	Ray Reardon	Wales	1988	Steve Davis	England
1974	Ray Reardon	Wales	1989	Steve Davis	England
1975	Ray Reardon	Wales	1990	Stephen Hendry	Scotland
1976	Ray Reardon	Wales	1991	John Parrott	England
1977	John Spencer	England	1992	Stephen Hendry	Scotland
1978	Ray Reardon	Wales	1993	Stephen Hendry	Scotland
1979	Terry Griffiths	Wales	1994	Stephen Hendry	Scotland
1980	Cliff Thorburn	Canada	1995	Stephen Hendry	Scotland
1981	Steve Davis	England	1996	Stephen Hendry	Scotland
1982	Alex Higgins	Northern Ireland	1997	Ken Doherty	Ireland, Republic of
1983	Steve Davis	England	1998	John Higgins	Scotland
1984	Steve Davis	England			

World Amateur Snooker Championship since 1988

This championship was first held in 1963.

Year	Name	Country	Year	Name	Country
1988	James Wattana	Thailand	1993	Chuchat Triratanapradit	Thailand
1989	Ken Doherty	Ireland, Republic of	1994	Mohammed Yusuf	Pakistan
1990	Stephen O'Connor	Ireland, Republic of	1995	Mohammed Yusuf	Pakistan
1991	Noppadon Noppachom	Thailand	1996	Stuart Bingham	England
1992	Neil Mosley	England	1997	Marco Fu	Hong Kong

Speedway

World Speedway Champions since 1980

Year	Name	Country	Year	Name	Country
1980	Mike Lee	England	1989	Hans Nielsen	Denmark
1981	Bruce Penhall	USA	1990	Per Jonsson	Sweden
1982	Bruce Penhall	USA	1991	Jan Pedersen	Denmark
1983	Egon Müller	West Germany	1992	Gary Havelock	England
1984	Erik Gundersen	Denmark	1993	Sam Ermolenko	USA
1985	Erik Gundersen	Denmark	1994	Tony Rickardsson	Sweden
1986	Hans Nielsen	Denmark	1995	Hans Nielsen	Denmark
1987	Hans Nielsen	Denmark	1996	Billy Hamill	USA
1988	Erik Gundersen	Denmark	1997	Greg Hancock	USA

Squash

British Open Squash Champions since 1988

The men's championship was first held in 1930, and the women's championship was first held in 1922. The Open is now sponsored by Leekes. Most wins men: 10 – Jahingir Khan; 8 – Geoff Hunt; 7 – Hashim Khan (Pakistan); 6 – Jonah Barrington (England), Amr Bey (Egypt), and Jansher Khan (Pakistan). Most wins women: 16 – Heather McKay (born Blundell) (Australia); 10 – Janet Morgan (England); 8 – Susan Devoy (New Zealand).

Year	Name	Country	Year	Name	Country
Men			**Women**		
1988	Jahangir Khan	Pakistan	1988	Susan Devoy	New Zealand
1989	Jahangir Khan	Pakistan	1989	Susan Devoy	New Zealand
1990	Jahangir Khan	Pakistan	1990	Susan Devoy	New Zealand
1991	Jahangir Khan	Pakistan	1991	Lisa Opie	England
1992	Jansher Khan	Pakistan	1992	Susan Devoy	New Zealand
1993	Jansher Khan	Pakistan	1993	Michelle Martin	Australia
1994	Jansher Khan	Pakistan	1994	Michelle Martin	Australia
1995	Jansher Khan	Pakistan	1995	Michelle Martin	Australia
1996	Jansher Khan	Pakistan	1996	Michelle Martin	Australia
1997	Jansher Khan	Pakistan	1997	Michelle Martin	Australia
1998	Peter Nicol	Scotland	1998	Michelle Martin	Australia

World Open Squash Champions since 1988

This competition was first held in 1976.

Year	Name	Country	Year	Name	Country
Men			*Women*		
1988	Jahangir Khan	Pakistan	1988	Not held	
1989	Jansher Khan	Pakistan	1989	Martine Le Moignan	UK
1990	Jansher Khan	Pakistan	1990	Susan Devoy	New Zealand
1991	Rodney Martin	Australia	1991	Susan Devoy	New Zealand
1992	Jansher Khan	Pakistan	1992	Susan Devoy	New Zealand
1993	Jansher Khan	Pakistan	1993	Michelle Martin	Australia
1994	Jansher Khan	Pakistan	1994	Michelle Martin	Australia
1995	Jansher Khan	Pakistan	1995	Michelle Martin	Australia
1996	Jansher Khan	Pakistan	1996	Sarah Fitz-Gerald	Australia
1997	Rodney Eyles	Australia	1997	Sarah Fitz-Gerald	Australia

Surfing

World Amateur Surfing Champions since 1988

This championship was first held in 1964.

Year	Name	Country	Year	Name	Country
Men			*Women*		
1988	Fabio Gouveia	Brazil	1988	Pauline Menczer	Australia
1990	Heifara Tahutini	Tahiti	1990	Kathy Newman	Australia
1992	Grant Foster	Australia	1992	Lyn MacKenzie	Australia
1994	Sasha Stocker	Australia	1994	Alessandra Vieira	Brazil
1996	Taylor Knox	USA	1996	Neridah Falconer	Australia

World Professional Surfing Champions since 1988

This championship was first held in 1970. It is now organized by the Association of Surfing Professionals and the ASP/World Championship Tour (WCT).

Year	Name	Country	Year	Name	Country
Men			*Women*		
1988	Barton Lynch	Australia	1988	Frieda Zamba	USA
1989	Martin Potter	UK	1989	Wendy Botha	South Africa
1990	Tommy Curren	USA	1990	Pam Burridge	Australia
1991	Damien Hardman	Australia	1991	Wendy Botha	South Africa
1992	Kelly Slater	USA	1992	Wendy Botha	Australia (ex-South Africa)
1993	Derek Ho	USA	1993	Pauline Menczer	Australia
1994	Kelly Slater	USA	1994	Lisa Andersen	USA
1995	Kelly Slater	USA	1995	Lisa Andersen	USA
1996	Kelly Slater	USA	1996	Lisa Andersen	USA
1997	Kelly Slater	USA	1997	Lisa Andersen	USA

Swimming

Fédération Internationale de Natation Amateur VIIIth World Swimming Championships: Winners

These championships were held at Perth, Australia, in January 1998.

Category	Name	Country	Time
Men			
50 m freestyle	Bill Pilczuk	USA	22.29
100 m freestyle	Alexander Popov	Russia	48.93
200 m freestyle	Michael Klim	Australia	1:47.41
400 m freestyle	Ian Thorpe	Australia	3:46.29
1,500 m freestyle	Grant Hackett	Australia	14:51.70
100 m backstroke	Lenny Krayzelburg	USA	55.00
200 m backstroke	Lenny Krayzelburg	USA	1:58.84
100 m breaststroke	Fred deBurghgraeve	Belgium	1:01.34
200 m breaststroke	Kurt Grote	USA	2:13.40
100 m butterfly	Michael Klim	Australia	52.25
200 m butterfly	Denys Sylantyev	Ukraine	1:56.61
200 m individual medley	Marcel Wouda	Netherlands	2:01.18
400 m individual medley	Tom Dolan	USA	4:14.95
4 × 100 m freestyle relay		USA	3:16.69
4 × 200 m freestyle relay		Australia	7:12.48
4 × 100 m medley relay		Australia	3:37.98
5 km individual open water	Alexei Akatiev	Russia	55:18.60
25 km individual open water	Alexei Akatiev	Russia	5h 05:42.1
5 km team open water		USA	2h 52:12.2
25 km team open water		Italy	16h 10:18.2
Women			
50 m freestyle	Amy Van Dyken	USA	25.15
100 m freestyle	Jenny Thompson	USA	54.95
200 m freestyle	Claudia Poll	Costa Rica	1:58.90
400 m freestyle	Yan Chen	China	4:06.72
800 m freestyle	Brooke Bennett	USA	8:28.71
100 m backstroke	Lea Loveless-Maurer	USA	1:01.16
200 m backstroke	Roxana Maracineanu	France	2:11.26
100 m breaststroke	Kristy Kowal	USA	1:08.42
200 m breaststroke	Agnes Kovacs	Hungary	2:25.45
100 m butterfly	Jenny Thompson	USA	58.46
200 m butterfly	Susie O'Neill	Australia	2:07.93
200 m individual medley	Yanyan Wu	China	2:10.88
400 m individual medley	Yan Chen	China	4:36.66
4 × 100 m freestyle relay		USA	3:42.11
4 × 200 m freestyle relay		Germany	8:01.46
4 × 100 m medley relay		USA	4:01.93
5 km open water	Erica Rose	USA	59:23.50
25 km open water	Tobie Smith	USA	5h 31:20.1

Fédération Internationale de Natation Amateur VIIIth World Swimming Championships: Diving

These championships were held at Perth, Australia, in January 1998.

Category	Name	Country	Category	Name	Country
Men			**Women**		
10 m platform	Dmitri Sautin	Russia	10 m platform	Olena Zhupyna	Ukraine
1 m springboard	Zhuocheng Yu	China	1 m springboard	Irina Lashko	Russia
3 m springboard	Dmitri Sautin	Russia	3 m springboard	Yulia Pakhalina	Russia
3 m springboard synchronized	Hao Xu and Zhuocheng Yu	China	3 m springboard synchronized	Irina Lashko and Yulia Pakhalina	Russia
Platform synchronized	Shuwei Sun and Liang Tian	China			

Swimming: Long Course World Records

(As of 31 October 1997.)

Category	Time	Name	Country	Date	Location
Men					
50 m freestyle	0:21.81	Tom Jager	USA	24 March 1990	Nashville (TN), USA
100 m freestyle	0:48.21	Alexander Popov	Russia	18 June 1994	Monte Carlo
200 m freestyle	1:46.69	Giorgio Lamberti	Italy	15 August 1989	Bonn, Germany
400 m freestyle	3:43.80	Kieren Perkins	Australia	9 September 1994	Rome, Italy
800 m freestyle	7:46.00	Kieren Perkins	Australia	24 August 1994	Victoria, Canada
1,500 m freestyle	14:41.66	Kieren Perkins	Australia	24 August 1994	Victoria, Canada
100 m backstroke	0:53.86	Jeff Rouse	USA	31 July 1992	Barcelona, Spain
200 m backstroke	1:56.57	M Lopez-Zubero	Spain	23 November 1991	Tuscaloosa (AL), USA
100 m breaststroke	1:00.60	Fred Deburghgraeve	Belgium	20 July 1996	Atlanta (GA), USA
200 m breaststroke	2:10.16	Mike Barrowman	USA	29 July 1992	Barcelona, Spain
100 m butterfly	0:52.27	Denis Pankratov	Russia	24 July 1996	Atlanta (GA), USA
200 m butterfly	1:55.22	Denis Pankratov	Russia	14 June 1995	Canet de Rousillon, France
200 m individual medley	1:58.16	Jani Sievinen	Finland	11 September 1994	Rome, Italy
400 m individual medley	4:12.30	Tom Dolan	USA	6 September 1994	Rome, Italy
4 × 100 m freestyle relay	3:15.11		USA	12 August 1995	Atlanta (GA), USA
4 × 200 m freestyle relay	7:11.95		CIS	27 July 1992	Barcelona, Spain
4 × 100 m medley relay	3:34.84		USA	26 July 1996	Atlanta (GA), USA
Women					
50 m freestyle	0:24.51	Jingyi Le	China	11 September 1994	Rome, Italy
100 m freestyle	0:54.01	Jingyi Le	China	5 September 1994	Rome, Italy
200 m freestyle	1:56.78	Franziska Van Almsick	Germany	6 September 1994	Rome, Italy
400 m freestyle	4:03.85	Janet Evans	USA	22 September 1988	Seoul, South Korea
800 m freestyle	8:16.22	Janet Evans	USA	20 August 1989	Tokyo, Japan
1,500 m freestyle	15:52.10	Janet Evans	USA	26 March 1988	Orlando (FL), USA
100 m backstroke	1:00.16	Cihong He	China	10 September 1994	Rome, Italy
200 m backstroke	2:06.62	Kristina Egerszegi	Hungary	25 August 1991	Athens, Greece
100 m breaststroke	1:07.02	Penelope Heyns	South Africa	21 July 1996	Atlanta (GA), USA
200 m breaststroke	2:24.76	Rebecca Brown	Australia	16 March 1994	Indianapolis (IN), USA
100 m butterfly	0:57.93	Mary T Meagher	USA	16 August 1981	Brown Deer (WI), USA
200 m butterfly	2:05.96	Mary T Meagher	USA	13 August 1981	Brown Deer (WI), USA
200 m individual medley	2:11.65	Li Lin	China	30 July 1992	Barcelona, Spain
400 m individual medley	4:36.10	Petra Schneider	East Germany	1 August 1982	Guayaquil, Ecuador
4 × 100 m freestyle relay	3:37.91		China	7 September 1994	Rome, Italy
4 × 200 m freestyle relay	7:55.47		East Germany	18 August 1987	Strasbourg, France
4 × 100 m medley relay	4:01.67		China	10 September 1994	Rome, Italy

Source: Fédération Internationale de Natation Amateur (FINA)

Table Tennis

World Table Tennis Champions: Teams, since 1989

Year	Team	Year	Team
Men (Swaythling Cup)		**Women (Corbillon Cup)**	
1989	Sweden	1989	China
1991	Sweden	1991	Korea
1993	Sweden	1993	China
1995	China	1995	China
1997	China	1997	China

Tennis

Wimbledon Tennis Championship: Singles Champions (Men)

The championship was not held during the years 1915–1918 due to World War I, or during the years 1939–1945 due to World War II. Wimbledon became an open championship in 1968.

Year	Name	Country	Year	Name	Country
1877	Spencer Gore	UK	1937	Donald Budge	USA
1878	Frank Hadow	UK	1938	Donald Budge	USA
1879	Reverend John Hartley	UK	1946	Yvon Petra	France
1880	Reverend John Hartley	UK	1947	Jack Kramer	USA
1881	William Renshaw	UK	1948	Bob Falkenburg	USA
1882	William Renshaw	UK	1949	Ted Schroeder	USA
1883	William Renshaw	UK	1950	Budge Patty	USA
1884	William Renshaw	UK	1951	Dick Savitt	USA
1885	William Renshaw	UK	1952	Frank Sedgman	Australia
1886	William Renshaw	UK	1953	Vic Seixas	USA
1887	Herbert Lawford	UK	1954	Jaroslav Drobny	Egypt
1888	Ernest Renshaw	UK	1955	Tony Trabert	USA
1889	William Renshaw	UK	1956	Lew Hoad	Australia
1890	Willoughby Hamilton	UK	1957	Lew Hoad	Australia
1891	Wilfred Baddeley	UK	1958	Ashley Cooper	Australia
1892	Wilfred Baddeley	UK	1959	Alex Olmedo	USA
1893	Joshua Pim	UK	1960	Neale Fraser	Australia
1894	Joshua Pim	UK	1961	Rod Laver	Australia
1895	Wilfred Baddeley	UK	1962	Rod Laver	Australia
1896	Harold Mahoney	UK	1963	Chuck McKinley	USA
1897	Reginald Doherty	UK	1964	Roy Emerson	Australia
1898	Reginald Doherty	UK	1965	Roy Emerson	Australia
1899	Reginald Doherty	UK	1966	Manuel Santana	Spain
1900	Reginald Doherty	UK	1967	John Newcombe	Australia
1901	Arthur Gore	UK	1968	Rod Laver	Australia
1902	Laurence Doherty	UK	1969	Rod Laver	Australia
1903	Laurence Doherty	UK	1970	John Newcombe	Australia
1904	Laurence Doherty	UK	1971	John Newcombe	Australia
1905	Laurence Doherty	UK	1972	Stan Smith	USA
1906	Laurence Doherty	UK	1973	Jan Kodes	Czechoslovakia
1907	Norman Brookes	Australia	1974	Jimmy Connors	USA
1908	Arthur Gore	UK	1975	Arthur Ashe	USA
1909	Arthur Gore	UK	1976	Bjorn Borg	Sweden
1910	Tony Wilding	New Zealand	1977	Bjorn Borg	Sweden
1911	Tony Wilding	New Zealand	1978	Bjorn Borg	Sweden
1912	Tony Wilding	New Zealand	1979	Bjorn Borg	Sweden
1913	Tony Wilding	New Zealand	1980	Bjorn Borg	Sweden
1914	Norman Brookes	Australia	1981	John McEnroe	USA
1919	Gerald Patterson	Australia	1982	Jimmy Connors	USA
1920	Bill Tilden	USA	1983	John McEnroe	USA
1921	Bill Tilden	USA	1984	John McEnroe	USA
1922	Gerald Patterson	Australia	1985	Boris Becker	West Germany
1923	William Johnston	USA	1986	Boris Becker	West Germany
1924	Jean Borotra	France	1987	Pat Cash	Australia
1925	René Lacoste	France	1988	Stefan Edberg	Sweden
1926	Jean Borotra	France	1989	Boris Becker	West Germany
1927	Henri Cochet	France	1990	Stefan Edberg	Sweden
1928	René Lacoste	France	1991	Michael Stich	Germany
1929	Henri Cochet	France	1992	Andre Agassi	USA
1930	Bill Tilden	USA	1993	Pete Sampras	USA
1931	Sidney Wood	USA	1994	Pete Sampras	USA
1932	Ellsworth Vines	USA	1995	Pete Sampras	USA
1933	Jack Crawford	USA	1996	Richard Krajicek	Netherlands
1934	Fred Perry	UK	1997	Pete Sampras	USA
1935	Fred Perry	UK	1998	Pete Sampras	USA
1936	Fred Perry	UK			

Wimbledon Tennis Championship: Singles Champions (Women)

The championship was not held during the years 1915–1918 due to World War I, or during the years 1939–1945 due to World War II. Wimbledon became an open championship in 1968.

Year	Name	Country	Year	Name	Country
1884	Maud Watson	UK	1950	Louise Brough	USA
1885	Maud Watson	UK	1951	Doris Hart	USA
1886	Blanche Bingley	UK	1952	Maureen Connolly	USA
1887	Lottie Dod	UK	1953	Maureen Connolly	USA
1888	Lottie Dod	UK	1954	Maureen Connolly	USA
1889	Blanche Hillyard[1]	UK	1955	Louise Brough	USA
1890	Helena Rice	UK	1956	Shirley Fry	USA
1891	Lottie Dod	UK	1957	Althea Gibson	USA
1892	Lottie Dod	UK	1958	Althea Gibson	USA
1893	Lottie Dod	UK	1959	Maria Bueno	Brazil
1894	Blanche Hillyard[1]	UK	1960	Maria Bueno	Brazil
1895	Charlotte Cooper	UK	1961	Angela Mortimer	UK
1896	Charlotte Cooper	UK	1962	Karen Susman	USA
1897	Blanche Hillyard[1]	UK	1963	Margaret Smith	Australia
1898	Charlotte Cooper	UK	1964	Maria Bueno	Brazil
1899	Blanche Hillyard[1]	UK	1965	Margaret Smith	Australia
1900	Blanche Hillyard[1]	UK	1966	Billie Jean King	USA
1901	Charlotte Sterry[2]	UK	1967	Billie Jean King	USA
1902	Muriel Robb	UK	1968	Billie Jean King	USA
1903	Dorothea Douglass	UK	1969	Ann Jones	UK
1904	Dorothea Douglass	UK	1970	Margaret Court[6]	Australia
1905	May Sutton	USA	1971	Evonne Goolagong	Australia
1906	Dorothea Douglass	UK	1972	Billie Jean King	USA
1907	May Sutton	USA	1973	Billie Jean King	USA
1908	Charlotte Sterry[2]	UK	1974	Chris Evert	USA
1909	Dora Boothby	UK	1975	Billie Jean King	USA
1910	Dorothea Lambert-Chambers[3]	UK	1976	Chris Evert	USA
1911	Dorothea Lambert-Chambers[3]	UK	1977	Virginia Wade	UK
1912	Ethel Larcombe	UK	1978	Martina Navratilova	Czechoslovakia
1913	Dorothea Lambert-Chambers[3]	UK	1979	Martina Navratilova	Czechoslovakia
1914	Dorothea Lambert-Chambers[3]	UK	1980	Evonne Cawley[7]	Australia
1919	Suzanne Lenglen	France	1981	Chris Evert Lloyd[8]	USA
1920	Suzanne Lenglen	France	1982	Martina Navratilova	USA
1921	Suzanne Lenglen	France	1983	Martina Navratilova	USA
1922	Suzanne Lenglen	France	1984	Martina Navratilova	USA
1923	Suzanne Lenglen	France	1985	Martina Navratilova	USA
1924	Kathleen McKane	UK	1986	Martina Navratilova	USA
1925	Suzanne Lenglen	France	1987	Martina Navratilova	USA
1926	Kathleen Godfree[4]	UK	1988	Steffi Graf	West Germany
1927	Helen Wills	USA	1989	Steffi Graf	West Germany
1928	Helen Wills	USA	1990	Martina Navratilova	USA
1929	Helen Wills	USA	1991	Steffi Graf	Germany
1930	Helen Wills Moody[5]	USA	1992	Steffi Graf	Germany
1931	Cilly Aussem	Germany	1993	Steffi Graf	Germany
1932	Helen Wills Moody[5]	USA	1994	Conchita Martinez	Spain
1933	Helen Wills Moody[5]	USA	1995	Steffi Graf	Germany
1934	Dorothy Round	UK	1996	Steffi Graf	Germany
1935	Helen Wills Moody[5]	USA	1997	Martina Hingis	Switzerland
1936	Helen Jacobs	USA	1998	Jana Novotna	Czech Republic
1937	Dorothy Round	UK			
1938	Helen Wills Moody[5]	USA			
1939	Alice Marble	USA			
1946	Pauline Betz	USA			
1947	Margaret Osborne	USA			
1948	Louise Brough	USA			
1949	Louise Brough	USA			

[1] Born Bingley.
[2] Born Cooper.
[3] Born Douglass.
[4] Born McKane.
[5] Born Wills.
[6] Born Smith.
[7] Born Goolagong.
[8] Born Evert.

French Tennis Championship: Singles Champions since 1988

This competition became an open championship in 1968.

Year	Name	Country	Year	Name	Country
Men			**Women**		
1988	Mats Wilander	Sweden	1988	Steffi Graf	West Germany
1989	Michael Chang	USA	1989	Arantxa Sanchez Vicario	Spain
1990	Andrés Gómez	Ecuador	1990	Monica Seles	Yugoslavia
1991	Jim Courier	USA	1991	Monica Seles	Yugoslavia
1992	Jim Courier	USA	1992	Monica Seles	Yugoslavia
1993	Sergi Bruguera	Spain	1993	Steffi Graf	Germany
1994	Sergi Bruguera	Spain	1994	Arantxa Sanchez Vicario	Spain
1995	Thomas Muster	Austria	1995	Steffi Graf	Germany
1996	Yevgeny Kafelnikov	Russia	1996	Steffi Graf	Germany
1997	Gustavo Kuerten	Brazil	1997	Iva Majoli	Croatia
1998	Carlos Moya	Spain	1998	Arantxa Sanchez Vicario	Spain

US Tennis Championship: Singles Champions since 1988

Winners are from the USA unless otherwise stated. The championship was first held in 1881. In 1968 and 1969, there was a separate Open Champion of professional players. In 1970, the championship became the US Open.

Year	Name	Year	Name
Men		**Women**	
1988	Mats Wilander (Sweden)	1988	Steffi Graf (West Germany)
1989	Boris Becker (West Germany)	1989	Steffi Graf (West Germany)
1990	Pete Sampras	1990	Gabriela Sabatini (Argentina)
1991	Stefan Edberg (Sweden)	1991	Monica Seles (Yugoslavia)
1992	Stefan Edberg (Sweden)	1992	Monica Seles (Yugoslavia)
1993	Pete Sampras	1993	Steffi Graf (Germany)
1994	Andre Agassi	1994	Arantxa Sanchez Vicario (Spain)
1995	Pete Sampras	1995	Steffi Graf (Germany)
1996	Pete Sampras	1996	Steffi Graf (Germany)
1997	Patrick Rafter (Australia)	1997	Martina Hingis (Switzerland)

Australian Tennis Championship: Singles Champions since 1988

This competition became an open championship in 1969.

Year	Name	Country	Year	Name	Country
Men			**Women**		
1988	Mats Wilander	Sweden	1988	Steffi Graf	West Germany
1989	Ivan Lendl	Czech Republic	1989	Steffi Graf	West Germany
1990	Ivan Lendl	Czech Republic	1990	Steffi Graf	West Germany
1991	Boris Becker	Germany	1991	Monica Seles	Yugoslavia
1992	Jim Courier	USA	1992	Monica Seles	Yugoslavia
1993	Jim Courier	USA	1993	Monica Seles	Yugoslavia
1994	Pete Sampras	USA	1994	Steffi Graf	Germany
1995	Andre Agassi	USA	1995	Mary Pierce	France
1996	Boris Becker	Germany	1996	Monica Seles	USA
1997	Pete Sampras	USA	1997	Martina Hingis	Switzerland
1998	Petr Korda	Czech Republic	1998	Martina Hingis	Switzerland

Davis Cup Winners since 1988

This international men's team competition was first held in 1900. Until 1972 the winner was decided in a Challenge Round in which the holders of the trophy met the winners of a knockout competition. Since then, the competition has been played entirely on a knockout basis.

Year	Winner	Runner-up	Score	Year	Winner	Runner-up	Score
1988	West Germany	Sweden	4–1	1993	Germany	Australia	4–1
1989	West Germany	Sweden	3–2	1994	Sweden	Russia	4–1
1990	USA	Australia	3–2	1995	USA	Russia	3–2
1991	France	USA	3–1	1996	France	Sweden	3–2
1992	USA	Switzerland	3–1	1997	Sweden	USA	5–0

Trampolining

Trampolining World Champions since 1988

Year	Name	Country	Year	Name	Country
Men			*Women*		
1988	Vadim Krasonchapka	USSR	1988	Khoperla Rusudum	USSR
1990	Alexandr Moskalenko	USSR	1990	Elena Merkulova	USSR
1992	Alexandr Moskalenko	USSR	1992	Elena Merkulova	USSR
1994	Alexandr Moskalenko	Russia	1994	Irina Karavaeva	Russia
1996	Dmitri Poliarouch	Belarus	1996	Tatiana Kovaleva	Russia

Triathlon

Hawaii Ironman Triathlon: Winners, since 1988

This ultradistance event consists of a 3.9 km/2.4 mile swim followed by a 180 km/122 mile cycle ride, and then a full marathon of 42.195 km/26 miles 385 yards. It was first held in 1978 at Waikiki Beach, Oahu, Hawaii. Since 1981 it has been held at Kailua-Kona, Hawaii. Winners are US nationals unless otherwise stated.

Year	Name	Time	Year	Name	Time
Men			*Women*		
1988	Scott Molina	8h 31:00	1988	Paula Newby-Fraser (Zimbabwe)	9h 01:01
1989	Mark Allen	8h 09:15	1989	Paula Newby-Fraser (Zimbabwe)	9h 00:56
1990	Mark Allen	8h 28:17	1990	Erin Baker (New Zealand)	9h 13:42
1991	Mark Allen	8h 18:32	1991	Paula Newby-Fraser (Zimbabwe)	9h 07:52
1992	Mark Allen	8h 09:08	1992	Paula Newby-Fraser (Zimbabwe)	8h 55:28
1993	Mark Allen	8h 07:45	1993	Paula Newby-Fraser (Zimbabwe)	8h 58:23
1994	Greg Welch (Australia)	8h 20:27	1994	Paula Newby-Fraser (Zimbabwe)	9h 20:14
1995	Mark Allen	8h 20:34	1995	Karen Smyers	9h 16:46
1996	Luc van Lierde (Belgium)	8h 04:08	1996	Paula Newby-Fraser (Zimbabwe)	9h 06:49
1997	Thomas Hellreigel (Germany)	8h 00:00	1997	Heather Fuhr (Canada)	9h 16:46

Volleyball

Volleyball World Champions since 1982

The men's championship was first held in 1949; the women's championship first held in 1952.

Year	Country	Year	Country	Year	Country	Year	Country
Men				*Women*			
1982	USSR	1990	Italy	1982	China	1990	USSR
1986	USA	1994	Italy	1986	China	1994	Cuba

Water Polo

Fédération Internationale de Natation Amateur VIIIth World Swimming Champions: Water Polo

This championship was held at Perth, Australia, in January 1998.

Gold	Silver	Bronze
Spain	Hungary	Yugoslavia

Water Skiing

Water Skiing World Championship since 1989

This championship was first held in 1949.

Year	Name	Country	Year	Name	Country
Men			**Women**		
1989	Patrice Martin	France	1989	Deena Maple[1]	USA
1991	Patrice Martin	France	1991	Karen Neville	USA
1993	Patrice Martin	France	1993	Natalya Rumyantseva	Russia
1995	Patrice Martin	France	1995	Judy Messer	Canada
1997	Patrice Martin	France	1997	Elena Milakova	Russia

[1] Born Brush.

Yachting

Yachting: Admiral's Cup since 1969

Year	Country	Year	Country	Year	Country
1969	USA	1979	Australia	1989	UK
1971	UK	1981	UK	1991	France
1973	West Germany	1983	West Germany	1993	Germany
1975	UK	1985	West Germany	1995	Italy
1977	UK	1987	New Zealand	1997	USA

America's Cup

In 1851 the US schooner *America* of the New York Yacht Club received a 'hundred guinea cup' from the Royal Yacht Squadron for winning a race around the Isle of Wight, England, against 15 British yachts. Renamed The America's Cup it was offered as a challenge trophy by the New York Yacht Club, with the first challenge taking place in 1870. The yachts are from the USA unless otherwise stated.

Year	Winning yacht	Winning skipper	Series	Challenger
1870	*Magic*	Andrew Comstock	1–0	*Cambria* (England)
1871	*Columbia/Sappho*[1]	Nelson Comstock and Sam Greenwood	4–1	*Livonia* (England)
1876	*Madeleine*	Josephus Williams	2–0	*Countess of Dufferin* (Canada)
1881	*Mischief*	Nathaniel Clock	2–0	*Atalanta* (Canada)
1885	*Puritan*	Aubrey Crocker	2–0	*Genesta* (England)
1886	*Mayflower*	Martin Stone	2–0	*Galatea* (England)
1887	*Volunteer*	Henry Haff	2–0	*Thistle* (Scotland)
1893	*Vigilant*	William Hansen	3–0	*Valkyrie II* (England)
1895	*Defender*	Henry Haff	3–0	*Valkyrie III* (England)
1899	*Columbia*	James Barr	3–0	*Shamrock* (England)
1901	*Columbia*	James Barr	3–0	*Shamrock II* (England)
1903	*Reliance*	James Barr	3–0	*Shamrock III* (England)
1920	*Resolute*	Charles Adams	3–2	*Shamrock IV* (England)
1930	*Enterprise*	Harold Vanderbilt	4–0	*Shamrock V* (England)
1934	*Rainbow*	Harold Vanderbilt	4–2	*Endeavour* (England)
1937	*Ranger*	Harold Vanderbilt	4–0	*Endeavour II* (England)
1958	*Columbia*	Briggs Cunningham	4–0	*Sceptre* (England)
1962	*Weatherly*	Emil Mosbacher Jr	4–1	*Gretel* (Australia)
1964	*Constellation*	Bob Bavier Jr	4–0	*Sovereign* (England)
1967	*Intrepid*	Emil Mosbacher Jr	4–0	*Dame Pattie* (Australia)
1970	*Intrepid*	Bill Ficker	4–1	*Gretel II* (Australia)
1974	*Courageous*	Ted Hood	4–0	*Southern Cross* (Australia)
1977	*Courageous*	Ted Turner	4–0	*Australia* (Australia)
1980	*Freedom*	Dennis Conner	4–1	*Australia* (Australia)
1983	*Australia II* (Australia)	John Bertrand	4–3	*Liberty*
1987	*Stars & Stripes*	Dennis Conner	4–0	*Kookaburra III* (Australia)
1988	*Stars & Stripes*	Dennis Conner	2–0	*New Zealand* (New Zealand)
1992	*America*	Bill Koch	4–1	*Il Moro di Venezia* (Italy)
1995	*Black Magic* (New Zealand)	Russell Coutts	5–0	*Young America*

[1] *Columbia* won two out of three races. *Sappho* won both its races.

Yacht Racing: International Sailing Federation (ISAF) World Championship: Gold Medallists

These races are held in Dubai in March of each year. (N/A - not applicable.)

1998

Class	Skipper	Country	Class	Skipper	Country
Open			*Women*		
Keelboats	François Brenac	France	Keelboats	Dorte Jensen	Denmark
Double-handed	Petri Leskinen/Kristian Heinila	Finland	Double-handed	Ruslana Taran/Olena Pakholchik	Ukraine
Multihulls	Shaun Ferry/Alison Lewis	South Africa	Multihulls	Inge Schabort/Gillian Anley	South Africa
Single-handed	Ben Ainslie	UK	Single-handed	Kristine Roug	Denmark
King's Cup	N/A	Italy	Match race	Betsy Alison	USA

Web Sites

Archery Index

URL:
'http://www.rmplc.co.uk/eduweb/sites/
splomas/myarch/archy1.html#British'

Home page maintained by a British archery enthusiast, with links to many related topics, events, and statistics.

Badminton Home Page

URL: 'http://mid1.external.hp.com/
stanb/badminton.html'

Laws of badminton, strategies for playing, and ways of organizing tournaments, plus information on current tournaments, links to other badminton pages, organizations promoting the sport, and where to play across the world.

British Water Skiing In Cyberspace

URL: 'http://www.u- net.com/waterski/'

British water skiing's home page, run by the British Water Skiing Association. All branches of the sport are covered here including kneeboarding, wakeboarding, and slalom.

Canoeing

URL: 'http://outwardbound.org/
obcanoe.htm'

These extracts from the *Outward Bound Canoeing Handbook* cover the basics of canoeing, from packing and waterproofing to canoeing with children.

Climbing Archive

URL: 'http://www.dtek.chalmers.se/
Climbing/index.html'

Climbing dictionary, a guide to rating systems, trip reports, climbing songs and poems, techniques and training, and a trivia quiz.

CricInfo: The Home of Cricket on the Internet

URL: 'http://www-uk.cricket.org/'

Online coverage of Cricket. The site includes reports on recent and live test matches, an interactive magazine, details of the domestic seasons throughout the cricket-playing world, an explanation of the laws of cricket, archival information, and statistics.

cyclingNet

URL: 'http://www.futurenet.com/
cyclingnet'

Latest cycle racing news and also information and feature articles for both the competitive and the recreational cyclist. This site also has regular sections on cycle routes, bike maintenance, and a discussion forum.

Fencing FAQ

URL: 'http://www.ii.uib.no/~arild/
fencing/faq/Top-view.html'

Answers to frequently asked questions about fencing, such as 'How did fencing originate?' and – more importantly perhaps – 'Does it hurt?'

Figure Skating Page

URL: 'http://frog.simplenet.com/
skateweb/'

Latest news stories, information on individual clubs and rinks, regional directories, training camps, and other links for participant skaters.

GearHead Mountain Bike Cyberzine

URL: 'http://www.gearhead.com/'

Regularly updated product reviews, articles, interviews, stories, trail information, race results, and shop guides for the mountain-bike enthusiast.

General Rules of Olympic Weightlifting

URL: 'http://www.usaw.org/information/
rules.htm'

Not only the rules, but also information on the different types of lifts, the way lifts are judged, and common errors to avoid in competition.

GolfWeb

URL: 'http://www.golfweb.com/'

Golf site which includes news, a library section, an interactive search facility of over 14,000 courses worldwide, and an online 'pro shop'.

History of the Olympic Games

URL: 'http://devlab.dartmouth.edu/
olympic/history/'

The site describes the birth, development, and significance of the institution in ancient times. It also explores the ancient myths surrounding the games, the prehistory of the games, and other similar events in Greece and as far away as China.

International Amateur Athletics Federation

URL: 'http://www.iaaf.org/'

Authoritative information about athletics, with news and press releases, and extracts from *New Studies in Athletics*, the IAAF's quarterly magazine.

Internet Squash Federation

URL: 'http://www.squash.org/'

Information about clubs, training, companies, doping policy, hardware, history, management, newsletters, player profiles, rules, and more.

Jockey Club

URL: "http://www.jockeyclub.com/"

Official site of the governing body of English thoroughbred horse racing. The contents include the rules and structure of the Jockey Club, a complete list of English thoroughbreds, handicapping rules, and the American Stud Book. There are links to other racing bodies around the world.

Judo Information Site

URL: "http://www.rain.org/~ssa/judo.htm"

A guide to the sport for beginners, an illustrated tour of the techniques of judo, history, tournament information, profiles and quotes from judo masters, a humour section, and a short 'Black Belt' quiz.

Karate CyberDojo

URL: "http://www.ryu.com/CyberDojo/"

Covering many styles of karate, the Cyber-Dojo aims to develop people's understanding of karate. Readers can post their queries and concerns and there is a searchable terminology database that translates many of the Japanese terms into English.

Major League Baseball

URL: "http://www.majorleaguebaseball.com/"

Official site of the US major league baseball organization. Every aspect of the USA's favourite pastime is covered here, including fan forums, league schedules, game reviews, team gossip, and live scoreboards in the season.

National Hockey League

URL: "http://www.nhl.com/"

Official site of the National Hockey League. You will find sections concerning NHL news, statistics, video highlights, scores and recaps, live radio clips, and schedules, plus links to team sites.

Official Site of the Championships – Wimbledon

URL: "http://www.wimbledon.org/"

Includes a comprehensive history of the championships, explanation of the seeding system, and technical details of how results and images are brought swiftly online. During Wimbledon fortnight there is a constantly updated news service.

Official Site of the National Basketball Association

URL: "http://www.nba.com"

Basketball Web site run by the sports governing body in the USA. Daily updated video clips, a fantasy league, and live commentary are just some of this site's features.

Orienteering

URL: "http://www.williams.edu:803/Biology/orienteering/o-index.html"

Introduction to this outdoor sport, with pages on the use of maps and compasses, and on the layout of a typical orienteering course.

Rules, Skills, and Objectives of Rugby League Explained

URL: "http://www.senet.com.au/~emjay/rules.htm#"

Full description of the rules of rugby league. The scoring system is fully explained, together with the names of the various positions, and the tactical aspects of this contact sport.

Scottish Highland Games

URL: "http://users.deltanet.com/~hilander/games.html"

Basic descriptions and rules for the individual events, such as tossing the caber, plus photographs and historical articles.

Soccernet

URL: "http://soccernet.com/"

Sections on English and Scottish football – bringing you news stories and comment, results, and profiles of the Premier League and national teams – and on European and global news and tournaments.

Sport of Gymnastics

URL: "http://www.usa-gymnastics.org/gymnastics/"

Basic guide to gymnastics from USA Gymnastics Online, with pages on its history, apparatus, scoring, and a glossary of terms.

Swimmers Guide Online

URL: "http://lornet.com/sgol/"

Database of over 4,000 full-size, year-round pools available in 47 countries.

Team NFL

URL: "http://www.nfl.com/index.html"

Official site of the National Football League, with up-to-the-minute news and locker-room gossip.

Tennis

URL: "http://www.cse.unsw.edu.au/~s2213093/tennis.html"

Regularly updated site for tennis fans. You can check current world ratings of the top male and female pros and see a complete list of winners of the four major Grand Slam events since 1980. There are links to official sites of Wimbledon and the US, French, and Australian championships.

Tenpin World

URL: "http://www.shef.ac.uk/~sutbc/"

Complete set of reference material including rules, news, events, and results from all over the world. A good starting point for investigation into the sport.

Triathlete's Web

URL: "http://w3.one.net/~triweb/triweb.html"

Answers to frequently asked questions, and articles on such topics as safe cycling, the triathlete's lifestyle the Triathlon Doctor, and links to related sites around the world.

Water Polo

URL: "http://www.ausport.gov.au/wpolo/wposp.html"

Australian Sports Commission's description of the game's history, rules, and tactics.

WebChess

URL: "http://www.delorie.com/game-room/chess/"

This site enables you to play online against a powerful chess computer. There are a series of game options, including who goes first, the type of pieces (from text to 3-D), and limits to the computer's thinking time.

Welcome to Cyber Darts

URL: "http://www.infohwy.com/darts/index.htm"

Details of championships around the world, campaigns to raise the status of the sport, and rules and regulations of the game.

INDEX